Presented
to

_____

From

_____

_____

_____

Date

Possibility Thinkers Bible

The New King James Version
Positive Verses for Possibility Thinking
Highlighted in Blue

Executive Editor—Robert H. Schuller

Commentaries by Paul David Dunn

THOMAS NELSON PUBLISHERS
Nashville • Camden • New York

When faced
with a mountain
I WILL NOT QUIT!
I will keep on striving
until I climb over,
find a pass through,
tunnel underneath—
or simply stay
and turn the mountain
into a gold mine,
with God's help!

Introduction

This *is* the day *which* the Lord has made;
We will rejoice and be glad in it (Ps. 118:24).

This is the day to be happy. For you hold in your hand today, God's special message to you! What could make the day happier than a message from your best friend? What greater gift could come to you today than a personal word from the God who created you and put you into this world? This is what you are holding in your hand—the Holy Bible! God's message to you.

How do you introduce the president of the United States to American citizens? How would you introduce the pope to Roman Catholic believers? How would you introduce the North Star to a group of astronomers?

If that would be difficult, then imagine how difficult it is to introduce the Holy Bible to Christian believers. I can only share my personal testimony.

I am immensely pleased and proud to present to you this copy of my favorite Book! It has been my guiding star, my central source of divine inspiration, since I was a little boy. Some children are blessed by being born into a privileged household. Such was my heritage. For no inheritance can match the value and the worth of the heritage of a godly faith in the Holy Book communicated through the life of a father and mother, who believe it and live by it. Every noon and every evening our family would gather around the humble kitchen table on our Iowa farm for a ritual that never varied. We would always pray with bowed heads before we ate the food. This was a prayer for God's blessing. After the food was enjoyed, my father would reach his hand underneath the table where a secret ledge held the family Bible. Then after an entire chapter from the Scriptures was read, he would offer a closing prayer of thanksgiving to God, "for the food we have now received for the soul as well as the body." Without fail, this happened every noon and every night, seven days a week, throughout my entire childhood!

Through my many years I have heard what critics have said about the Sacred Scriptures. I am reminded, however, of the anvil on my father's farm. Dad would often take pieces of iron, making them red hot, and then he would lift them with tongs to the anvil, hammering and beating the red-hot pieces of steel until they were shaped to form the tool that he had in mind. The hammers wore out in time. The handles broke. The chunks of molten iron changed shape and moved on to find their proper place. But the anvil survived all the blows and all the years. Now as I reach the mature years of my life, I can testify that this Book, like a great old anvil, has survived thousands of years, and has served me better than I could ever have expected from any printed matter.

Yes, it is my favorite Book. I am convinced, beyond a shadow of a doubt, that it is God's Book. That alone can explain why it never fails to nourish my faith. I believe in God because I have chosen this faith. I cannot prove that He is alive. If proof is possible, then faith is impossible. That is the way God wants it. He wants our relationship to be built on trust, not on scientific documentation. This is the only kind of interpersonal arrangement that allows for unalloyed affection. Yet, God is obligated to give us a solid basis for our faith. He is morally obligated to let us know that He is alive, what He expects from us, and what we can expect from Him. For conflict within interpersonal relationships is always a result of confused expectations, usually on the nonverbalized level. To clarify expectations in our relationship,

God has written this Book. It is a witness to Him—His life, His work, His hopes, and His dreams! Yes, God is the supernatural possibility thinker! He has plans; He has dreams; He has hopes.

In this Book, we read the story of His dreams of creating a place of beauty called the universe, unlimited as far as we know! Here we encounter His dreams of creating persons who could have a mind capable of believing in a God that is invisible to the eye! Here we have the marvelous story of God creating a creature called the human being, who would share the divine qualities of creativity, imagination, and the ability to think of possibilities! We see in this Book, God's dream coming to its grand and glorious opening in the Garden of Eden. We read how the dream fell and was broken. We see how God never gives up! Through prophets and through the centuries He keeps reaching to redeem a dream! Finally, the Father sends His Son into this world in human flesh and gives Him the name Jesus. Here God fulfills His Holy obligation to draw the draperies, lift the curtains, put the lights on Himself, and expose His true self for all of us to behold. We look at Jesus—His life, His work, His death, His Easter resurrection. We know that indeed God is alive. Therefore, the Holy Bible is called the Sacred Scriptures; it is God's Word about Himself. And Christ is the Word incarnate!

The divine inspirational nature of the Bible becomes convincing when we remember that it is a collection of sixty-six books, written by as many as forty authors over a period of approximately sixteen hundred years. I have often been asked, "But how reliable is the text if it is such an ancient writing? It must have been copied and recopied so often through the centuries. Have not many errors crept in?" The most exciting report I can bring is the news that when the latest manuscripts are matched with the oldest manuscripts few discrepancies are reflected, and those are of an extremely minor nature that in no way affect the substance of religious belief. Therefore, the latest findings are a convincing and final justification of trusting the reliability and integrity of the printed message. We can say without risk of error that what is written in the Sacred Scriptures, that you hold in your hand right now, is without a doubt the authentic message that the authors intended to convey.

The enormous span of centuries gives us a beautiful illustration of how God has operated with the human family. Nothing in the Sacred Scripture would lead us to believe that God is impatient. On the contrary, His patience is profound. Slowly, gradually, with a patient progressiveness, He reveals Himself in this Holy Book.

First in the opening chapters, He reveals that He is the creative source of all life. The revelation of Himself is progressive as we move through the story of Abraham where God revealed Himself as an ethical being and a single God. We call this "ethical monotheism." A very remarkable and indistinctive religious concept in the history of religion. But with the founding of the Hebrew faith and its concept that God was one God and a good God, a religion was established that has set faith apart from the practicing of primitive religion that employed a variety of abominations (e.g. human sacrifice and temple prostitution) under the name and authority of religion. Now through Abraham and later through the Ten Commandments, that were given to Moses, God revealed to the human race on planet earth that He expected a high level of human morality. Glimpses into the nature of God, that were perceived by Abraham, Moses, and later by the prophets, revealed Him to be a just and merciful Father in heaven. The psalmists came to understand this, and in poetry the beauty of the Lord reaches crystal- and gem-like insights of flashing glory! Yet even the Old Testament prophets at their best and the psalmists in their most positive writings lack the true knowledge of what the true God is like. It remained for Christ to take on the human form through the Incarnation, walking among the human family.

"If there is a God, then He is morally

obligated to reveal Himself in flesh and bones," was the challenging thought that came to me early in my ministry. The answer to that is Christ. He was and is the living appearance of the eternal God to the human flesh. In the Gospel of John He is called the Word. In Him we have the final revelation of what God is really like. Progressive revelation culminated in the character of the incarnated Jesus Christ! An understanding of how people responded to Him and found redemption in Him brings us into the New Testament Epistles. Finally, the Bible closes with the hope that one day life on planet earth will come to an end—and not when the sun runs out of gas, turning this planet earth into a frozen black ball, nor by some human catastrophic thermonuclear war which would destroy all human life. Instead this same God, who gave life to the creatures of the sea, the animals, the birds of the air, and finally His crowning glory—human being, will have His dream come true at last! In that final day, we shall all stand before Christ, the King of Kings and Lord of Lords.

So the Bible becomes a living Book! Not just a Book of dead history, but a Book alive with inspiring faith of the greatest heroes of the human family. For a start, you might want to read Hebrews chapter 11 which highlights faith, hope, and love, the central themes of Scripture. Approach the Sacred Scriptures to look for these coordinating themes—hope, faith, and love! See how God deals with human beings at their best and at their worst, at their sin and at their glory, and how God never gives up on the human race! The principles of possibility thinking are seen so clearly in how God deals with the human family. God simply does not accept ultimate defeat. He will not surrender to those negative emotions that human beings call depression and despair. After the flood, there came the rainbow. One can see a rainbow almost every day throughout the Holy Scriptures.

When you approach a well-decorated room, you will notice a single coordinated color that ties the entire decoration together. Observe the well-dressed man or woman and you will see that there is a central color that forms the unifying theme. Color the Bible with emotional colors of faith, hope, and love. Look for these themes recurring continually. They are the redemptive emotions. Avoid being trapped by the letter of the law. Be under the captured control of the compassionate, living Holy Spirit; breathe from the true stories found in these sacred pages. "The letter kills, but the Spirit gives life" (2 Cor. 3:6). Read it and you will find that God is at the opening of the Book; God is at the middle of it; and God will be at the end of it. God has the first word in Creation, and God will have the last word after human history has been fulfilled under the lordship of Christ.

So let this Book—my favorite Book, God's Book, the Living Book—become your Book! Find in it a picture of yourself. Here you will see a mirror of yourself, at your best, and you will praise God for creating you and for creating me. Here you will see a picture of yourself, at your worst, and you will not be depressed for you know that God loves you, even at your worst. You and I at our worst are still of a greater worth to the Lord than a mountain, a waterfall, or any bird. None of us are ever without some possibilities that can be developed under the miraculous touch of Jesus Christ our Savior!

So approach this Book and do not turn it into a textbook on science. Scientists can tell us much more about geology, genetics, or astronomy, than the Scriptures do. Do not make the mistake of trying to turn it into a chronological account of humanity on planet earth. Look for the deeper truths that transcend such shallow presumptions. The deeper truths are that God loves you—and we should love each other too! To help this living Book become your redeeming guide through life and into heaven, you will find in this special Possibility Thinkers Edition key verses highlighted for your inspiration. Commentary by my companion editor, Paul David Dunn, will help you to look for the positive thinking power that is contained in this—God's very special Book!

In the closing pages of this special edition, you will find some inspirational writings and special prayers that we trust will help you to become the great possibility thinker that God wants you to be. For what is possibility thinking? It is believing in God, then believing in ourselves, then believing in our fellow human beings, to the end that we might create God's kingdom on earth through the power of the Holy Spirit. What is God's kingdom? It is a collection of human beings, who can be redeemed from their sin, insecurity, and shame into a self-esteem instilled with the Holy Spirit. Result? We treat each other as a human family—a redeemed brotherhood and sisterhood!

Draw now from the power of the greatest Book ever written. You will come, through your own experience, to share my testimony that it is the Word of God given to us for our illumination and spiritual truth, showing us the path of salvation! Let your life become a living Bible!

Oh yes, we have retained the most classic of all English translations—the King James Version, with limited new revisions to carry the title the New King James Version. To all the women who read the Sacred Scriptures: We have left the male gender where the original text called for it. Please give yourself a special spiritual treat, substitute the word *woman* for *man* when you read these pages. Together we will feel that the Book was written just for ourselves.

Read the Scriptures the way you would solve a difficult problem. Work one part of it at a time. If there is a part of the problem that defies solution, leave it and come back to it later. The same way with the Sacred Scriptures. If there is a part of it that you find difficult to comprehend, grasp, understand, or accept, have the humility to assume that the truth is there, even if you cannot embrace it, keep reading, and let God continue to speak to you.

With that humble, faithful, believing, positive attitude, God's peace will surely fall upon you from these Holy pages.

Now, may the Lord bless you and keep you; the Lord make His face shine upon you, and be gracious to you; may God grant unto you His peace in your going out and in your coming in, in your lying down and in your rising up, in your labor and in your leisure, in your laughter and in your tears, until you come to stand before Jesus, in that day in which there is no sunset and no dawning. Amen.

God loves you and so do I,
Robert H. Schuller

Possibility Thinkers Bible

Table of Contents

Books of the Bible

Commentaries for Possibility Thinking

COMMENTARIES FOR POSSIBILITY THINKING

Preface

Purpose

In the Preface to the 1611 edition, the translators of the Authorized Version, known popularly as the King James Bible, state that it was not their purpose "to make a new translation . . . but to make a good one better." Indebted to the earlier work of William Tyndale and others, they saw their best contribution to consist in revising and enhancing the excellence of the English versions which had sprung from the Reformation of the sixteenth century. In harmony with the purpose of the King James scholars, the translators and editors of the present work have not pursued a goal of innovation. They have perceived the Holy Bible, New King James Version, as a continuation of the labors of the earlier translators, thus unlocking for today's readers the spiritual treasures found especially in the Authorized Version of the Holy Scriptures.

A Living Legacy

For nearly four hundred years, and throughout several revisions of its English form, the King James Bible has been deeply revered among the English-speaking peoples of the world. The precision of translation for which it is historically renowned, and its majesty of style, have enabled that monumental version of the Word of God to become the mainspring of the religion, language, and legal foundations of our civilization.

Although the Elizabethan period and our own era share in zeal for technical advance, the former period was more aggressively devoted to classical learning. Along with this awakened concern for the classics came a flourishing companion interest in the Scriptures, an interest that was enlivened by the conviction that the manuscripts were providentially handed down and were a trustworthy record of the inspired Word of God. The King James translators were committed to producing an English Bible that would be a precise translation, and by no means a paraphrase or a broadly approximate rendering. On the one hand, the scholars were almost as familiar with the original languages of the Bible as with their native English. On the other hand, their reverence for the divine Author and His Word assured a translation of the Scriptures in which only a principle of utmost accuracy could be accepted.

In 1786 the Catholic scholar, Alexander Geddes, said of the King James Bible, "If accuracy and strictest attention to the letter of the text be supposed to constitute an excellent version, this is of all versions the most excellent." George Bernard Shaw became a literary legend in our century because of his severe and often humorous criticisms of our most cherished values. Surprisingly, however, Shaw pays the following tribute to the scholars commissioned by King James: "The translation was extraordinarily well done because to the translators what they were translating was not merely a curious collection of ancient books written by different authors in different stages of culture, but the Word of God divinely revealed through His chosen and expressly inspired scribes. In this conviction they carried out their work with boundless reverence and care and achieved a beautifully artistic result." History agrees with these estimates. Therefore, while seeking to unveil the excellent *form* of the traditional English Bible, special care has also been taken in the present edition to preserve the work of *precision* which is the legacy of the 1611 translators.

Complete Equivalence in Translation

Where new translation has been necessary in the New King James Version, the most complete representation of the original has been rendered by considering the history of usage and etymology of words in their contexts. This principle of complete equivalence seeks to preserve *all* of the information in the text, while presenting it in good literary form. Dynamic equivalence, a recent procedure in Bible translation, commonly results in paraphrasing where a more literal rendering is needed to reflect a specific and vital sense. For example, references to Christ in some versions of John 3:16 as "only Son" or "one and only Son" are doubtless dynamic equivalents of sorts. However, they are not actual equivalents of the precisely literal "only begotten Son," especially in consideration of the historic Nicene statement concerning the person of Christ, "begotten, not made," which is a crucial Christian doctrine.

In keeping with the principle of complete equivalence, it is the policy to translate interjections which are commonly omitted in modern language renderings of the Bible. As an example, the interjection *behold,* in the older King James editions, continues to have a place in English usage, especially in dramatically calling attention to a spectacular scene, or an event of profound importance such as the Immanuel prophecy of Isaiah 7:14. Consequently, *behold* is retained for these occasions in the present edition. However, the Hebrew and Greek originals for this word can be translated variously, depending on the circumstances in the passage. Therefore, in addition to *behold,* words such as *indeed, look, see,* and *surely* are also rendered to convey the appropriate sense suggested by the context in each case.

In faithfulness to our readers, it has seemed consistent with our task to cooperate with competent scholars who are governed by the biblical principle of divine authorship of the Holy Scriptures. Therefore, all participating scholars have signed a document of subscription to the plenary and verbal inspiration of the original autographs of the Bible.

Devotional Quality

The King James scholars readily appreciated the intrinsic beauty of divine revelation. They accordingly disciplined their talents to render well-chosen English words of their time, as well as a graceful, often musical arrangement of language which has stirred the hearts of Bible readers through the years. The translators, the committees, and the editors of the present edition, while sensitive to the late twentieth-century English idiom, and while adhering faithfully to the Hebrew, Aramaic, and Greek texts, have sought to maintain that lyrical quality which is so highly regarded in the Authorized Version. This devotional quality is especially apparent in the poetic and prophetic books, although even the relatively plain style of the gospels and epistles cannot strictly be likened, as sometimes suggested, to modern newspaper style. The Koine Greek of the New Testament is influenced by the Hebrew background of the writers, for whom even the Gospel narratives were not merely flat utterance, but often song in various degrees of rhythm.

The Style

Students of the Bible applaud the timeless devotional character of our historic Bible. Yet it is also universally understood that our language, like all living languages, has undergone profound change since 1611. Subsequent revisions of the King James Bible have sought to keep abreast of changes in English speech. The present work is a further step toward this objective. Where obsolescence and other reading difficulties exist, present-day vocabulary, punctuation, and grammar have been carefully integrated. Words representing ancient objects, such as *chariot* and *phylactery*, have no modern substitutes and are therefore retained.

A special feature of the New King James Version is its conformity to the thought flow of the 1611 Bible. The reader discovers that the sequence and identity of words, phrases, and clauses of the new edition, while much clearer, are so close to the traditional that there is remarkable ease in listening to the reading of either edition while following with the other.

In the discipline of translating biblical and other ancient languages, a standard method of transliteration, that is, the English spelling of untranslated words, such as names of persons and places, has never been commonly adopted. In keeping with the design of the present work, the King James spelling of untranslated words is retained.

King James doctrinal and theological terms, for example, *propitiation, justification,* and *sanctification,* are generally familiar to English-speaking peoples. Such terms have been retained except where the original language indicates need for a more precise translation.

Readers of the Authorized Version will immediately be struck by the absence of several pronouns: *thee, thou,* and *ye* are replaced by the simple *you,* while *your* and *yours* are substituted for *thy* and *thine* as applicable. *Thee, thou, thy,* and *thine* were once forms of address to express a special relationship to human as well as divine persons. These pronouns are no longer part of our language. However, reverence for God in the present work is preserved by capitalizing pronouns, including *You, Your,* and *Yours,* which refer to Him. Additionally, capitalization of these pronouns benefits the reader by clearly distinguishing divine and human persons referred to in a passage. With-

out such capitalization the distinction is often obscure, because the antecedent of a pronoun is not always clear in the English translation.

In addition to the pronoun usages of the seventeenth century, the *-eth* and *-est* verb endings so familiar in the earlier King James editions are now obsolete. Unless a speaker is schooled in these verb endings, there is common difficulty in selecting the correct form to be used with a given subject of the verb in vocal prayer. That is, should we use *love, loveth,* or *lovest? do, doeth, doest,* or *dost? have, hath,* or *hast?* Because these forms are obsolete, contemporary English usage has been substituted for the previous verb endings.

The real character of the Authorized Version does not reside in its archaic pronouns or verbs or other grammatical forms of the seventeenth century, but rather in the care taken by its scholars to impart the letter and spirit of the original text in a majestic and reverent style.

The Format

The format of the New King James Version is designed to enhance the vividness and devotional quality of the Holy Scriptures:

— Subject headings assist the reader to identify topics and transitions in the biblical content.

— Words or phrases in *italics* indicate expressions in the original language which require clarification by additional English words, as also done throughout the history of the King James Bible.

— Verse numbers in bold type indicate the beginning of a paragraph.

— *Oblique type* in the New Testament indicates a quotation from the Old Testament.

— Poetry is structured as contemporary verse to reflect the poetic form and beauty of the passage in the original language.

— The covenant name of God was

xv

usually translated from the Hebrew as "LORD" (using capital letters as shown) in the King James Old Testament. This tradition is maintained. In the present edition the name is so capitalized whenever the covenant name is quoted in the New Testament from a passage in the Old Testament.

The Old Testament Text

The Hebrew Bible has come down to us through the scrupulous care of ancient scribes who copied the original text in successive generations. By the sixth century A.D. the scribes were succeeded by a group known as the Masoretes, who continued to preserve the sacred Scriptures for another five hundred years in a form known as the Masoretic Text. Babylonia, Palestine, and Tiberias were the main centers of Masoretic activity; but by the tenth century A.D. the Tiberian Masoretes, led by the family of ben Asher, gained the ascendancy. Through subsequent editions, the ben Asher text became in the twelfth century the only recognized form of the Hebrew Scriptures.

Daniel Bomberg printed the first Rabbinic Bible in 1516–17; that work was followed in 1524–25 by a second edition prepared by Jacob ben Chayyim and also published by Bomberg. The text of ben Chayyim was adopted in most subsequent Hebrew Bibles, including those used by the King James translators. The ben Chayyim text was also used for the first two editions of Rudolph Kittel's *Biblia Hebraica* of 1906 and 1912. In 1937 Paul Kahle published a third edition of *Biblia Hebraica*. This edition was based on the oldest dated manuscript of the ben Asher text, the Leningrad Manuscript B19a (A.D. 1008), which Kahle regarded as superior to that used by ben Chayyim.

For the New King James Version the text used was the 1967/1977 Stuttgart edition of *Biblia Hebraica*, with frequent comparisons being made with the Bomberg edition of 1524–25. The Septuagint (Greek) Version of the Old Testament and the Latin Vulgate were consulted. In addition to referring to a variety of ancient versions of the Hebrew Scriptures, the New King James Version also draws on the resources of relevant manuscripts from the Dead Sea Caves. In the few places where the Hebrew is so obscure that the King James followed one of the versions, but where information is now available to resolve the problems, the New King James Version follows the Hebrew text. Significant variations are recorded in footnotes.

The New Testament Text

There is more manuscript support for the New Testament than for any other body of ancient literature. Over five thousand Greek, eight thousand Latin, and many more manuscripts in other languages attest the integrity of the New Testament. There is only one basic New Testament used by Protestants, Roman Catholics, and Orthodox, by conservatives and liberals. Minor variations in hand copying have appeared through the centuries, before mechanical printing began in A.D. 1450.

Some variations exist in the spelling of Greek words, in word order, and in similar details. These ordinarily do not show up in translation and do not affect the sense of the text in any way.

Other manuscript differences, regarding the omission or inclusion of a word or a clause, and two paragraphs in the gospels, should not overshadow the overwhelming degree of *agreement* which exists among the ancient records. Bible readers may be assured that the most important differences in the English New Testament of today are due, not to manuscript divergence, but to the way in which translators view the task of translation: How literally should the text be rendered? How does the translator view the matter of biblical inspiration? Does the translator adopt a paraphrase when a literal rendering would be quite clear and more to the point? The New King James Version follows the historic precedent of the Authorized Version in maintaining a literal approach to translation, except where the idiom of the original language occasionally cannot be translated directly into our tongue.

The manuscript preferences cited in many contemporary translations of the New Testament are due to recent reliance on a relatively few manuscripts discovered in the late nineteenth and early twentieth centuries. Dependence on these manuscripts, especially two, the Sinaitic and Vatican manuscripts, is due to the greater age of these documents. However, in spite of their age, some scholars have reason to doubt their faithfulness to the autographs, since they often disagree with one another and show other signs of unreliability. The Greek text obtained by using these sources and related papyri is known as the Alexandrian Text.

On the other hand, the great majority of existing manuscripts are in substantial agreement. Even though many are late, and none are earlier than the fifth century, most of their readings are verified by ancient papyri, ancient versions, and quotations in the writings of the early church fathers. This large body of manuscripts is the source of the Greek text underlying the King James Bible. It is the Greek text used by Greek-speaking churches for many centuries, presently known as the *Textus Receptus,* or Received Text, of the New Testament.

Since the latter nineteenth century the theory has been held by some scholars that this traditional text of the New Testament had been officially edited by the fourth-century church. Recent studies have caused significant changes in this view, and a growing number of scholars now regard the Received Text as far more reliable than previously thought. In light of these developments, and with the knowledge that most textual variants have no practical effect on translation, the New King James New Testament has been based on this Received Text, thus perpetuating the tradition begun by William Tyndale in 1525 and continued by the 1611 translators in rendering the Authorized Version. Important textual variants are recorded in footnotes.

A newer group of New Testament scholars are persuaded that the best guide to a precise Greek text is the close consensus of the majority of Greek manuscripts. The Greek text obtained by using this rule is called the Majority Text, which is similar to the Received Text. At important places where the Majority Text or the Alexandrian Text differs from the Received Text, the variants are recorded in footnotes.

Footnotes

Significant explanatory notes, alternate translations, and cross-references, as well as New Testament citations of Old Testament passages, are supplied in footnotes.

Important textual variants in the Old Testament are footnoted in a standard form.

The textual information in the New Testament footnotes is a unique provision in the history of the English Bible. Terms in the footnotes such as "better manuscripts" are avoided. The footnotes in the present edition make no evaluation of readings, but do clearly indicate the manuscript sources of readings which diverge from the traditional text. Thus a clearly defined presentation of the variants is provided for the benefit of interested readers representing all textual persuasions.

Where significant variations occur in the New Testament Greek manuscripts, footnotes are classified as follows:

1. NU-Text
   These variations from the traditional text generally represent the Alexandrian or Egyptian type of

text described previously in "The New Testament Text." This text is published in the Twenty-Sixth Edition of the Nestle-Aland Greek New Testament (N) and in the United Bible Societies' Third Edition (U), hence the acronym, "NU-Text."

2. M-Text
This symbol indicates points of variation in the Majority Text

from the traditional text, as also previously discussed in "The New Testament Text."

With the assistance of these footnotes, which show lines of textual divergence more fully than commonly provided with English language versions of the Bible, it is trusted that readers will be enabled to better appreciate the substance and degree of variation in the manuscript sources of the New Testament.

The

OLD TESTAMENT

Introduction to Genesis

Genesis is the book of new beginnings, of creation, and of an ideal man walking with God in a positive life-giving relationship and environment. Out of nothing God created the heavens and the earth. As a Master Sculptor, He formed the land, carved out the mountains, filled the oceans, cast the first rays of light out of the darkness, planted trees, launched the birds in flight, placed the clouds above, and lit the night sky with stars. Then as a crowning triumph, God formed man from the dust of the earth and breathed into him His life-giving spirit, making man in His own image. God gave man a woman to be his helpmate to share their lives together in His creation. God looked around at all He had done—and He pronounced it good!

And it was good—until man failed to trust God and did what was wrong in the eyes of the Lord. Man's position and relationship with God were changed. Man was no longer allowed in the garden. The image of God in man was marred, but not destroyed. You can bomb a cathedral, but it still remains a cathedral. Man can turn from God and sin, but he intrinsically still has within him the image of God to create, bear life, and do good.

Immediately, Genesis records a promise of restoration initiated by God toward man, the promise of a Savior to bring man back to his proper relationship with God. The all-powerful God who created the universe was not to abandon His crowning glory. He was there with them when they fell and He promised to lift them up and to restore them to their original position, and even higher. This promise is continued throughout the lives of the patriarchs as recorded in Genesis. Abraham is assured that his generations will be blessed and will be a blessing. Out of this heritage will come the Son of God to redeem all peoples and to restore them to what God intended them to be.

The Book of Genesis tells us that we have intrinsic value and worth to God. We are created in His image. God has given us the creative powers, knowledge, and wisdom to do His will. Genesis reveals that the love of God is with us even in our failures. He has not abandoned us. We are God's project and God never fails! When we place our faith in God all things are possible!

The First Book of Moses Called
Genesis

The History of Creation

IN the beginning God created the heavens and the earth.
2 The earth was without form, and void; and darkness *was* on the face of the deep. And the Spirit of God was hovering over the face of the waters.
3 Then God said, "Let there be light"; and there was light.
4 And God saw the light, that *it was* good; and God divided the light from the darkness.
5 God called the light Day, and the darkness He called Night. So the evening and the morning were the first day.
6 Then God said, "Let there be a firmament in the midst of the waters, and let it divide the waters from the waters."
7 Thus God made the firmament, and divided the waters which *were* under the firmament from the waters which *were* above the firmament; and it was so.
8 And God called the firmament Heaven. So the evening and the morning were the second day.
9 Then God said, "Let the waters under the heavens be gathered together into one place, and let the dry *land* appear"; and it was so.
10 And God called the dry *land* Earth, and the gathering together of the waters He called Seas. And God saw that *it was* good.
11 Then God said, "Let the earth bring forth grass, the herb *that* yields seed, *and* the fruit tree *that* yields fruit according to its kind, whose seed *is* in itself, on the earth"; and it was so.
12 And the earth brought forth grass, the herb *that* yields seed according to its kind, and the tree *that* yields fruit, whose seed *is* in itself according to its kind. And God saw that *it was* good.
13 So the evening and the morning were the third day.
14 Then God said, "Let there be lights in the firmament of the heavens to divide the day from the night; and let them be for signs and seasons, and for days and years;
15 "and let them be for lights in the firmament of the heavens to give light on the earth"; and it was so.
16 Then God made two great lights: the greater light to rule the day, and the lesser light to rule the night. *He made* the stars also.
17 God set them in the firmament of the heavens to give light on the earth,
18 and to rule over the day and over the night, and to divide the light from the darkness. And God saw that *it was* good.
19 So the evening and the morning were the fourth day.
20 Then God said, "Let the waters abound with an abundance of living creatures, and let birds fly above the earth across the face of the firmament of the heavens."
21 So God created great sea creatures and every living thing that moves, with which the waters abounded, according to their kind, and every winged bird according to its kind. And God saw that *it was* good.
22 And God blessed them, saying, "Be fruitful and multiply, and fill the waters in the seas, and let birds multiply on the earth."
23 So the evening and the morning were the fifth day.
24 Then God said, "Let the earth bring forth the living creature according to its kind: cattle and creeping thing and beast of the earth, *each* according to its kind"; and it was so.
25 And God made the beast of the earth according to its kind, cattle according to its kind, and everything that creeps on the earth according to its kind. And God saw that *it was* good.
26 Then God said, "Let Us make man in Our image, according to Our likeness; let them have dominion over the fish of the sea, over the birds of the air, and over the cattle, over all[1] the earth and over every creeping thing that creeps on the earth."
27 So God created man in His *own*

1 Syriac reads *all the wild animals of.*

image; in the image of God He created him; male and female He created them.

28 Then God blessed them, and God said to them, "Be fruitful and multiply; fill the earth and subdue it; have dominion over the fish of the sea, over the birds of the air, and over every living thing that moves on the earth."

29 And God said, "See, I have given you every herb *that* yields seed which *is* on the face of all the earth, and every tree whose fruit yields seed; to you it shall be for food.

30 "Also, to every beast of the earth, to every bird of the air, and to everything that creeps on the earth, in which *there is* life, *I have given* every green herb for food"; and it was so.

31 Then God saw everything that He had made, and indeed *it was* very good. So the evening and the morning were the sixth day.

2 Thus the heavens and the earth, and all the host of them, were finished.

2 And on the seventh day God ended His work which He had done, and He rested on the seventh day from all His work which He had done.

3 Then God blessed the seventh day and sanctified it, because in it He rested from all His work which God had created and made.

4 This *is* the history[2] of the heavens and the earth when they were created, in the day that the LORD God made the earth and the heavens,

5 before any plant of the field was in the earth and before any herb of the field had grown. For the LORD God had not caused it to rain on the earth, and *there was* no man to till the ground;

6 but a mist went up from the earth and watered the whole face of the ground.

7 And the LORD God formed man *of* the dust of the ground, and breathed into his nostrils the breath of life; and man became a living being.

Life in God's Garden

8 The LORD God planted a garden eastward in Eden, and there He put the man whom He had formed.

9 And out of the ground the LORD God made every tree grow that is pleasant to the sight and good for food. The tree of life *was* also in the midst of the garden,

and the tree of the knowledge of good and evil.

10 Now a river went out of Eden to water the garden, and from there it parted and became four riverheads.

11 The name of the first *is* Pishon; it *is* the one which encompasses the whole land of Havilah, where *there is* gold.

12 And the gold of that land *is* good. Bdellium and the onyx stone *are* there.

13 The name of the second river *is* Gihon; it *is* the one which encompasses the whole land of Cush.

14 The name of the third river *is* Hiddekel;[3] it *is* the one which goes toward the east of Assyria. The fourth river *is* the Euphrates.

15 Then the LORD God took the man and put him in the garden of Eden to tend and keep it.

16 And the LORD God commanded the man, saying, "Of every tree of the garden you may freely eat;

17 "but of the tree of the knowledge of good and evil you shall not eat, for in the day that you eat of it you shall surely die."

18 And the LORD God said, "*It is* not good that man should be alone; I will make him a helper comparable to him."

19 Out of the ground the LORD God formed every beast of the field and every bird of the air, and brought *them* to Adam to see what he would call them. And whatever Adam called each living creature, that *was* its name.

20 So Adam gave names to all cattle, to the birds of the air, and to every beast of the field. But for Adam there was not found a helper comparable to him.

21 And the LORD God caused a deep sleep to fall on Adam, and he slept; and He took one of his ribs, and closed up the flesh in its place.

22 Then the rib which the LORD God had taken from man He made into a woman, and He brought her to the man.

23 And Adam said:

"This *is* now bone of my bones
And flesh of my flesh;
She shall be called Woman,
Because she was taken out of Man."

24 Therefore a man shall leave his father and mother and be joined to his wife, and they shall become one flesh.

2 Hebrew *toledoth*, literally *genealogy*   3 Or *Tigris*

25 And they were both naked, the man and his wife, and were not ashamed.

The Temptation and Fall of Man

3 Now the serpent was more cunning than any beast of the field which the LORD God had made. And he said to the woman, "Has God indeed said, 'You shall not eat of every tree of the garden'?" 2 And the woman said to the serpent, "We may eat the fruit of the trees of the garden; 3 "but of the fruit of the tree which *is* in the midst of the garden, God has said, 'You shall not eat it, nor shall you touch it, lest you die.'" 4 And the serpent said to the woman, "You will not surely die. 5 "For God knows that in the day you eat of it your eyes will be opened, and you will be like God, knowing good and evil." 6 So when the woman saw that the tree *was* good for food, that it *was* pleasant to the eyes, and a tree desirable to make *one* wise, she took of its fruit and ate. She also gave to her husband with her, and he ate. 7 Then the eyes of both of them were opened, and they knew that they *were* naked; and they sewed fig leaves together and made themselves coverings. 8 And they heard the sound of the LORD God walking in the garden in the cool of the day, and Adam and his wife hid themselves from the presence of the LORD God among the trees of the garden. 9 Then the LORD God called to Adam and said to him, "Where *are* you?" 10 So he said, "I heard Your voice in the garden, and I was afraid because I was naked; and I hid myself." 11 And He said, "Who told you that you *were* naked? Have you eaten from the tree of which I commanded you that you should not eat?" 12 Then the man said, "The woman whom You gave *to be* with me, she gave me of the tree, and I ate." 13 And the LORD God said to the woman, "What *is* this you have done?" And the woman said, "The serpent deceived me, and I ate." 14 So the LORD God said to the serpent:

"Because you have done this,
You *are* cursed more than all cattle,

And more than every beast of the field;
On your belly you shall go,
And you shall eat dust
All the days of your life.
15 And I will put enmity
Between you and the woman,
And between your seed and her Seed;
He shall bruise your head,
And you shall bruise His heel."

16 To the woman He said:

"I will greatly multiply
    your sorrow and your conception;
In pain you shall bring forth children;
Your desire *shall be* for your husband,
And he shall rule over you."

17 Then to Adam He said, "Because you have heeded the voice of your wife, and have eaten from the tree of which I commanded you, saying, 'You shall not eat of it':

"Cursed *is* the ground for your sake;
In toil you shall eat *of* it
All the days of your life.
18 Both thorns and thistles
    it shall bring forth for you,
And you shall eat the herb of the field.
19 In the sweat of your face
    you shall eat bread
Till you return to the ground,
For out of it you were taken;
For dust you *are*,
And to dust you shall return."

20 And Adam called his wife's name Eve, because she was the mother of all living. 21 Also for Adam and his wife the LORD God made tunics of skin, and clothed them. 22 Then the LORD God said, "Behold, the man has become like one of Us, to know good and evil. And now, lest he put out his hand and take also of the tree of life, and eat, and live forever"— 23 therefore the LORD God sent him out of the garden of Eden to till the ground from which he was taken. 24 So He drove out the man; and He placed cherubim at the east of the garden of Eden, and a flaming sword which turned every way, to guard the way to the tree of life.

Cain Murders Abel

4 Now Adam knew Eve his wife, and she conceived and bore Cain, and said, "I have gotten a man from the LORD."

2 Then she bore again, this time his brother Abel. Now Abel was a keeper of sheep, but Cain was a tiller of the ground.
3 And in the process of time it came to pass that Cain brought an offering of the fruit of the ground to the LORD.
4 Abel also brought of the firstlings of his flock and of their fat. And the LORD respected Abel and his offering,
5 but He did not respect Cain and his offering. And Cain was very angry, and his countenance fell.
6 So the LORD said to Cain, "Why are you angry? And why has your countenance fallen?
7 "If you do well, will you not be accepted? And if you do not do well, sin lies at the door. And its desire is for you, but you should rule over it."
8 Now Cain talked with Abel his brother;[4] and it came to pass, when they were in the field, that Cain rose against Abel his brother and killed him.
9 Then the LORD said to Cain, "Where is Abel your brother?" And he said, "I do not know. Am I my brother's keeper?"
10 And He said, "What have you done? The voice of your brother's blood cries out to Me from the ground.
11 "So now you are cursed from the earth, which has opened its mouth to receive your brother's blood from your hand.
12 "When you till the ground, it shall no longer yield its strength to you. A fugitive and a vagabond you shall be on the earth."
13 And Cain said to the LORD, "My punishment is greater than I can bear!
14 "Surely You have driven me out this day from the face of the ground; I shall be hidden from Your face; I shall be a fugitive and a vagabond on the earth, and it will happen that anyone who finds me will kill me."
15 And the LORD said to him, "Therefore,[5] whoever kills Cain, vengeance shall be taken on him sevenfold." And the LORD set a mark on Cain, lest anyone finding him should kill him.

The Family of Cain

16 Then Cain went out from the presence of the LORD and dwelt in the land of Nod on the east of Eden.

17 And Cain knew his wife, and she conceived and bore Enoch. And he built a city, and called the name of the city after the name of his son—Enoch.
18 To Enoch was born Irad; and Irad begot Mehujael, and Mehujael begot Methushael, and Methushael begot Lamech.
19 Then Lamech took for himself two wives: the name of one was Adah, and the name of the second was Zillah.
20 And Adah bore Jabal. He was the father of those who dwell in tents and have livestock.
21 His brother's name was Jubal. He was the father of all those who play the harp and flute.
22 And as for Zillah, she also bore Tubal-Cain, an instructor of every craftsman in bronze and iron. And the sister of Tubal-Cain was Naamah.
23 Then Lamech said to his wives:

"Adah and Zillah, hear my voice;
   O wives of Lamech,
      listen to my speech!
For I have killed a man
      for wounding me,
   Even a young man for hurting me.
24 If Cain shall be avenged sevenfold,
   Then Lamech seventy-sevenfold."

A New Son

25 And Adam knew his wife again, and she bore a son and named him Seth, "For God has appointed another seed for me instead of Abel, whom Cain killed."
26 And as for Seth, to him also a son was born; and he named him Enosh.[6] Then men began to call on the name of the LORD.

The Family of Adam

5 This is the book of the genealogy of Adam. In the day that God created man, He made him in the likeness of God.
2 He created them male and female, and blessed them and called them Mankind in the day they were created.
3 And Adam lived one hundred and thirty years, and begot a son in his own likeness, after his image, and named him Seth.
4 After he begot Seth, the days of Adam were eight hundred years; and he begot sons and daughters.
5 So all the days that Adam lived were

---

4 Samaritan Pentateuch, Septuagint, Syriac, and Vulgate add "Let us go out to the field."
5 Septuagint, Syriac, and Vulgate read not so.   6 Greek Enos

nine hundred and thirty years; and he died.

6 Seth lived one hundred and five years, and begot Enosh.

7 After he begot Enosh, Seth lived eight hundred and seven years, and begot sons and daughters.

8 So all the days of Seth were nine hundred and twelve years; and he died.

9 Enosh lived ninety years, and begot Cainan.[7]

10 After he begot Cainan, Enosh lived eight hundred and fifteen years, and begot sons and daughters.

11 So all the days of Enosh were nine hundred and five years; and he died.

12 Cainan lived seventy years, and begot Mahalaleel.[8]

13 After he begot Mahalaleel, Cainan lived eight hundred and forty years, and begot sons and daughters.

14 So all the days of Cainan were nine hundred and ten years; and he died.

15 Mahalaleel lived sixty-five years, and begot Jared.

16 After he begot Jared, Mahalaleel lived eight hundred and thirty years, and begot sons and daughters.

17 So all the days of Mahalaleel were eight hundred and ninety-five years; and he died.

18 Jared lived one hundred and sixty-two years, and begot Enoch.

19 After he begot Enoch, Jared lived eight hundred years, and begot sons and daughters.

20 So all the days of Jared were nine hundred and sixty-two years; and he died.

21 Enoch lived sixty-five years, and begot Methuselah.

22 After he begot Methuselah, Enoch walked with God three hundred years, and begot sons and daughters.

23 So all the days of Enoch were three hundred and sixty-five years.

24 And Enoch walked with God; and he was not, for God took him.

25 Methuselah lived one hundred and eighty-seven years, and begot Lamech.

26 After he begot Lamech, Methuselah lived seven hundred and eighty-two years, and begot sons and daughters.

27 So all the days of Methuselah were nine hundred and sixty-nine years; and he died.

28 Lamech lived one hundred and eighty-two years, and begot a son.

29 And he called his name Noah, saying, "This one will comfort us concerning our work and the toil of our hands, because of the ground which the LORD has cursed."

30 After he begot Noah, Lamech lived five hundred and ninety-five years, and begot sons and daughters.

31 So all the days of Lamech were seven hundred and seventy-seven years; and he died.

32 And Noah was five hundred years old, and Noah begot Shem, Ham, and Japheth.

The Wickedness and Judgment of Man

6 Now it came to pass, when men began to multiply on the face of the earth, and daughters were born to them,

2 that the sons of God saw the daughters of men, that they were beautiful; and they took wives for themselves of all whom they chose.

3 And the LORD said, "My Spirit shall not strive[9] with man forever, for he is indeed flesh; yet his days shall be one hundred and twenty years."

4 There were giants on the earth in those days, and also afterward, when the sons of God came in to the daughters of men and they bore children to them. Those were the mighty men who were of old, men of renown.

5 Then the LORD[10] saw that the wickedness of man was great in the earth, and that every intent of the thoughts of his heart was only evil continually.

6 And the LORD was sorry that He had made man on the earth, and He was grieved in His heart.

7 So the LORD said, "I will destroy man whom I have created from the face of the earth, both man and beast, creeping thing and birds of the air, for I am sorry that I have made them."

8 But Noah found grace in the eyes of the LORD.

Noah Pleases God

9 This is the genealogy of Noah. Noah was a just man, perfect in his generations. Noah walked with God.

10 And Noah begot three sons: Shem, Ham, and Japheth.

---

7 Hebrew Qenan   8 Spelled Mahalalel in Luke 3:37
9 Septuagint and Vulgate read abide.   10 Vulgate reads God.

11 The earth also was corrupt before God, and the earth was filled with violence.

12 So God looked upon the earth, and indeed it was corrupt; for all flesh had corrupted their way on the earth.

13 And God said to Noah, "The end of all flesh has come before Me, for the earth is filled with violence through them; and behold, I will destroy them with the earth.

The Ark Prepared

14 "Make yourself an ark of gopherwood; make rooms in the ark, and cover it inside and outside with pitch.

15 "And this is how you shall make it: The length of the ark *shall be* three hundred cubits, its width fifty cubits, and its height thirty cubits.

16 "You shall make a window for the ark, and you shall finish it to a cubit from above; and set the door of the ark in its side. You shall make it *with* lower, second, and third *decks.*

17 "And behold, I Myself am bringing the flood of waters on the earth, to destroy from under heaven all flesh in which *is* the breath of life; *and* everything that *is* on the earth shall die.

18 "But I will establish My covenant with you; and you shall go into the ark— you, your sons, your wife, and your sons' wives with you.

19 "And of every living thing of all flesh you shall bring two of every *sort* into the ark, to keep *them* alive with you; they shall be male and female.

20 "Of the birds after their kind, of animals after their kind, and of every creeping thing of the earth after its kind, two of every *kind* will come to you to keep *them* alive.

21 "And you shall take for yourself of all food that is eaten, and you shall gather *it* to yourself; and it shall be food for you and for them."

22 Thus Noah did; according to all that God commanded him, so he did.

The Great Flood

7 Then the LORD said to Noah, "Come into the ark, you and all your household, because I have seen *that* you *are* righteous before Me in this generation.

2 "You shall take with you seven each of every clean animal, a male and his female; two each of animals that *are* unclean, a male and his female;

3 "also seven each of birds of the air, male and female, to keep the species alive on the face of all the earth.

4 "For after seven more days I will cause it to rain on the earth forty days and forty nights, and I will destroy from the face of the earth all living things that I have made."

5 And Noah did according to all that the LORD commanded him.

6 Noah *was* six hundred years old when the flood of waters was on the earth.

7 So Noah, with his sons, his wife, and his sons' wives, went into the ark because of the waters of the flood.

8 Of clean beasts, of beasts that *are* unclean, of birds, and of everything that creeps on the earth,

9 two by two they went into the ark to Noah, male and female, as God had commanded Noah.

10 And it came to pass after seven days that the waters of the flood were on the earth.

11 In the six hundredth year of Noah's life, in the second month, the seventeenth day of the month, on that day all the fountains of the great deep were broken up, and the windows of heaven were opened.

12 And the rain was on the earth forty days and forty nights.

13 On the very same day Noah and Noah's sons, Shem, Ham, and Japheth, and Noah's wife and the three wives of his sons with them, entered the ark—

14 they and every beast after its kind, all cattle after their kind, every creeping thing that creeps on the earth after its kind, and every bird after its kind, every bird of every sort.

15 And they went into the ark to Noah, two by two, of all flesh in which *is* the breath of life.

16 So those that entered, male and female of all flesh, went in as God had commanded him; and the LORD shut him in.

17 Now the flood was on the earth forty days. The waters increased and lifted up the ark, and it rose high above the earth.

18 The waters prevailed and greatly increased on the earth, and the ark moved about on the surface of the waters.

19 And the waters prevailed exceedingly on the earth, and all the high hills under the whole heaven were covered.
20 The waters prevailed fifteen cubits upward, and the mountains were covered.
21 And all flesh died that moved on the earth: birds and cattle and beasts and every creeping thing that creeps on the earth, and every man.
22 All in whose nostrils *was* the breath of the spirit[11] of life, all that *was* on the dry *land*, died.
23 So He destroyed all living things which were on the face of the ground: both man and cattle, creeping thing and bird of the air. They were destroyed from the earth. Only Noah and those who *were* with him in the ark remained *alive.*
24 And the waters prevailed on the earth one hundred and fifty days.

Noah's Deliverance

8 Then God remembered Noah, and every living thing, and all the animals that *were* with him in the ark. And God made a wind to pass over the earth, and the waters subsided.
2 The fountains of the deep and the windows of heaven were also stopped, and the rain from heaven was restrained.
3 And the waters receded continually from the earth. At the end of the hundred and fifty days the waters decreased.
4 Then the ark rested in the seventh month, the seventeenth day of the month, on the mountains of Ararat.
5 And the waters decreased continually until the tenth month. In the tenth *month,* on the first *day* of the month, the tops of the mountains were seen.
6 So it came to pass, at the end of forty days, that Noah opened the window of the ark which he had made.
7 Then he sent out a raven, which kept going to and fro until the waters had dried up from the earth.
8 He also sent out from himself a dove, to see if the waters had abated from the face of the ground.
9 But the dove found no resting place for the sole of her foot, and she returned into the ark to him, for the waters *were* on the face of the whole earth. So he put out his hand and took her, and drew her into the ark to himself.
10 And he waited yet another seven days,

and again he sent the dove out from the ark.
11 Then the dove came to him in the evening, and behold, a freshly plucked olive leaf *was* in her mouth; and Noah knew that the waters had abated from the earth.
12 So he waited yet another seven days and sent out the dove, which did not return again to him anymore.
13 And it came to pass in the six hundred and first year, in the first *month,* the first *day* of the month, that the waters were dried up from the earth; and Noah removed the covering of the ark and looked, and indeed the surface of the ground was dry.
14 And in the second month, on the twenty-seventh day of the month, the earth was dried.
15 Then God spoke to Noah, saying,
16 "Go out of the ark, you and your wife, and your sons and your sons' wives with you.
17 "Bring out with you every living thing of all flesh that *is* with you: birds and cattle and every creeping thing that creeps on the earth, so that they may abound on the earth, and be fruitful and multiply on the earth."
18 So Noah went out, and his sons and his wife and his sons' wives with him.
19 Every beast, every creeping thing, every bird, *and* whatever creeps on the earth, according to their families, went out of the ark.

God's Covenant with Creation

20 Then Noah built an altar to the LORD, and took of every clean animal and of every clean bird, and offered burnt offerings on the altar.
21 And the LORD smelled a soothing aroma. Then the LORD said in His heart, "I will never again curse the ground for man's sake, although the imagination of man's heart *is* evil from his youth; nor will I again destroy every living thing as I have done.

22 "While the earth remains,
Seedtime and harvest,
And cold and heat,
And winter and summer,
And day and night
Shall not cease."

11 Septuagint and Vulgate omit *of the spirit.*

9 So God blessed Noah and his sons, and said to them: "Be fruitful and multiply, and fill the earth.[12]
2 "And the fear of you and the dread of you shall be on every beast of the earth, on every bird of the air, on all that move on the earth, and on all the fish of the sea. They are given into your hand.
3 "Every moving thing that lives shall be food for you. I have given you all things, even as the green herbs.
4 "But you shall not eat flesh with its life, *that is*, its blood.
5 "Surely for your lifeblood I will demand *a reckoning*; from the hand of every beast I will require it, and from the hand of man. From the hand of every man's brother I will require the life of man.

6 "Whoever sheds man's blood,
By man his blood shall be shed;
For in the image of God
He made man.
7 And as for you,
be fruitful and multiply;
Bring forth abundantly in the earth
And multiply in it."

8 Then God spoke to Noah and to his sons with him, saying:
9 "And as for Me, behold, I establish My covenant with you and with your descendants[13] after you,
10 "and with every living creature that *is* with you: the birds, the cattle, and every beast of the earth with you, of all that go out of the ark, every beast of the earth.
11 "Thus I establish My covenant with you: Never again shall all flesh be cut off by the waters of the flood; never again shall there be a flood to destroy the earth."
12 And God said: "This *is* the sign of the covenant which I make between Me and you, and every living creature that *is* with you, for perpetual generations:
13 "I set My rainbow in the cloud, and it shall be for the sign of the covenant between Me and the earth.
14 "It shall be, when I bring a cloud over the earth, that the rainbow shall be seen in the cloud;
15 "and I will remember My covenant which *is* between Me and you and every living creature of all flesh; the waters shall never again become a flood to destroy all flesh.
16 "The rainbow shall be in the cloud, and I will look on it to remember the everlasting covenant between God and every living creature of all flesh that *is* on the earth."
17 And God said to Noah, "This *is* the sign of the covenant which I have established between Me and all flesh that *is* on the earth."

Noah and His Sons

18 Now the sons of Noah who went out of the ark were Shem, Ham, and Japheth. And Ham *was* the father of Canaan.
19 These three *were* the sons of Noah, and from these the whole earth was populated.
20 And Noah began *to be* a farmer, and he planted a vineyard.
21 Then he drank of the wine and was drunk, and became uncovered in his tent.
22 And Ham, the father of Canaan, saw the nakedness of his father, and told his two brothers outside.
23 But Shem and Japheth took a garment, laid *it* on both their shoulders, and went backward and covered the nakedness of their father. Their faces *were* turned away, and they did not see their father's nakedness.
24 So Noah awoke from his wine, and knew what his younger son had done to him.
25 Then he said:

"Cursed *be* Canaan;
A servant of servants
He shall be to his brethren."

26 And he said:

"Blessed *be* the LORD,
The God of Shem,
And may Canaan be his servant.
27 May God enlarge Japheth,
And may he dwell
in the tents of Shem;
And may Canaan be his servant."

28 And Noah lived after the flood three hundred and fifty years.
29 So all the days of Noah were nine hundred and fifty years; and he died.

Nations Descended from Noah

10 Now this *is* the genealogy of the sons of Noah: Shem, Ham, and

12 Compare Genesis 1:28   13 Literally *seed*

Japheth. And sons were born to them after the flood.

2 The sons of Japheth *were* Gomer, Magog, Madai, Javan, Tubal, Meshech, and Tiras.

3 The sons of Gomer *were* Ashkenaz, Riphath,[14] and Togarmah.

4 The sons of Javan *were* Elishah, Tarshish, Kittim, and Dodanim.[15]

5 From these the coastland *peoples* of the Gentiles were separated into their lands, everyone according to his *own* language, according to their families, into their nations.

6 The sons of Ham *were* Cush, Mizraim, Put,[16] and Canaan.

7 The sons of Cush *were* Seba, Havilah, Sabtah, Raamah, and Sabtechah; and the sons of Raamah *were* Sheba and Dedan.

8 Cush begot Nimrod; he began to be a mighty one on the earth.

9 He was a mighty hunter before the LORD; therefore it is said, "Like Nimrod the mighty hunter before the LORD."

10 And the beginning of his kingdom was Babel, Erech, Accad, and Calneh, in the land of Shinar.

11 From that land he went to Assyria and built Nineveh, Rehoboth Ir, Calah,

12 and Resen between Nineveh and Calah (that *is* the principal city).

13 Mizraim begot Ludim, Anamim, Lehabim, Naphtuhim,

14 Pathrusim, and Casluhim (from whom came the Philistines and Caphtorim).

15 Canaan begot Sidon his firstborn, and Heth;

16 the Jebusite, the Amorite, and the Girgashite;

17 the Hivite, the Arkite, and the Sinite;

18 the Arvadite, the Zemarite, and the Hamathite. Afterward the families of the Canaanites were dispersed.

19 And the border of the Canaanites was from Sidon as you go toward Gerar, as far as Gaza; then as you go toward Sodom, Gomorrah, Admah, and Zeboim, as far as Lasha.

20 These *were* the sons of Ham, according to their families, according to their languages, in their lands *and* in their nations.

21 And *children* were born also to Shem, the father of all the children of Eber, the brother of Japheth the elder.

22 The sons of Shem *were* Elam, Asshur, Arphaxad, Lud, and Aram.

23 The sons of Aram *were* Uz, Hul, Gether, and Mash.[17]

24 Arphaxad begot Salah, and Salah begot Eber.

25 To Eber were born two sons: the name of one *was* Peleg, for in his days the earth was divided; and his brother's name *was* Joktan.

26 Joktan begot Almodad, Sheleph, Hazarmaveth, Jerah,

27 Hadoram, Uzal, Diklah,

28 Obal,[18] Abimael, Sheba,

29 Ophir, Havilah, and Jobab. All these *were* the sons of Joktan.

30 And their dwelling place was from Mesha as you go toward Sephar, the mountain of the east.

31 These *were* the sons of Shem, according to their families, according to their languages, in their lands, according to their nations.

32 These *were* the families of the sons of Noah, according to their generations, in their nations; and from these the nations were divided on the earth after the flood.

The Tower of Babel

11 Now the whole earth had one language and one speech.

2 And it came to pass, as they journeyed from the east, that they found a plain in the land of Shinar, and they dwelt there.

3 Then they said to one another, "Come, let us make bricks and bake *them* thoroughly." They had brick for stone, and they had asphalt for mortar.

4 And they said, "Come, let us build ourselves a city, and a tower whose top *is* in the heavens; let us make a name for ourselves, lest we be scattered abroad over the face of the whole earth."

5 But the LORD came down to see the city and the tower which the sons of men had built.

6 And the LORD said, "Indeed the people *are* one and they all have one language, and this is what they begin to do; now nothing that they propose to do will be withheld from them.

7 "Come, let Us go down and there confuse their language, that they may not understand one another's speech."

8 So the LORD scattered them abroad

---

14 Spelled *Diphath* in 1 Chronicles 1:6   15 Spelled *Rodanim* in 1 Chronicles 1:7 and Samaritan Pentateuch
16 Or *Phut*   17 Called *Meshech* in 1 Chronicles 1:17 and Septuagint   18 Spelled *Ebal* in 1 Chronicles 1:22

from there over the face of all the earth, and they ceased building the city.
9 Therefore its name is called Babel, because there the LORD confused the language of all the earth; and from there the LORD scattered them abroad over the face of all the earth.

Shem's Descendants

10 This *is* the genealogy of Shem: Shem *was* one hundred years old, and begot Arphaxad two years after the flood.
11 After he begot Arphaxad, Shem lived five hundred years, and begot sons and daughters.
12 Arphaxad lived thirty-five years, and begot Salah.
13 After he begot Salah, Arphaxad lived four hundred and three years, and begot sons and daughters.
14 Salah lived thirty years, and begot Eber.
15 After he begot Eber, Salah lived four hundred and three years, and begot sons and daughters.
16 Eber lived thirty-four years, and begot Peleg.
17 After he begot Peleg, Eber lived four hundred and thirty years, and begot sons and daughters.
18 Peleg lived thirty years, and begot Reu.
19 After he begot Reu, Peleg lived two hundred and nine years, and begot sons and daughters.
20 Reu lived thirty-two years, and begot Serug.
21 After he begot Serug, Reu lived two hundred and seven years, and begot sons and daughters.
22 Serug lived thirty years, and begot Nahor.
23 After he begot Nahor, Serug lived two hundred years, and begot sons and daughters.
24 Nahor lived twenty-nine years, and begot Terah.
25 After he begot Terah, Nahor lived one hundred and nineteen years, and begot sons and daughters.
26 Now Terah lived seventy years, and begot Abram, Nahor, and Haran.

Terah's Descendants

27 This *is* the genealogy of Terah: Terah begot Abram, Nahor, and Haran. Haran begot Lot.

28 And Haran died before his father Terah in his native land, in Ur of the Chaldeans.
29 Then Abram and Nahor took wives: the name of Abram's wife *was* Sarai, and the name of Nahor's wife, Milcah, the daughter of Haran the father of Milcah and the father of Iscah.
30 But Sarai was barren; she had no child.
31 And Terah took his son Abram and his grandson Lot, the son of Haran, and his daughter-in-law Sarai, his son Abram's wife, and they went out with them from Ur of the Chaldeans to go to the land of Canaan; and they came to Haran and dwelt there.
32 So the days of Terah were two hundred and five years, and Terah died in Haran.

Promises to Abram

12 Now the LORD had said to Abram:

"Get out of your country,
From your kindred
And from your father's house,
To a land that I will show you.
2 I will make you a great nation;
I will bless you
And make your name great;
And you shall be a blessing.
3 I will bless those who bless you,
And I will curse him who curses you;
And in you all the families
of the earth shall be blessed."

4 So Abram departed as the LORD had spoken to him, and Lot went with him. And Abram *was* seventy-five years old when he departed from Haran.
5 Then Abram took Sarai his wife and Lot his brother's son, and all their possessions that they had gathered, and the people whom they had acquired in Haran, and they departed to go to the land of Canaan. So they came to the land of Canaan.
6 Abram passed through the land to the place of Shechem, as far as the terebinth tree of Moreh.[19] And the Canaanites *were* then in the land.
7 Then the LORD appeared to Abram and said, "To your descendants I will give this land." And there he built an altar to the LORD, who had appeared to him.

19 Hebrew *Alon Moreh*

The Faith of Abraham

Abraham is a great example of possibility thinking faith. Few men have been called by God to attempt such a great task as to begin a nation for Him.

Following God's call was not an easy task for Abraham. He was a well-to-do citizen of the thriving cosmopolitan city, Ur of the Chaldees, in ancient Mesopotamia. Abraham was then called, "Abram"—exalted father. The city was a major urban center whose religious worship focused on the moon god, Nannar. Temple prostitution and human sacrifice were acceptable and well-established religious practices. From this city, Abraham was called to begin God's nation.

With a step of faith, Abraham and his family journeyed to the new land to begin the nation that God had promised. What awaited him was a great famine, pestilence, war, and strife among his family. Had God forsaken him? This hardly seemed like the "promised land." Even at age one hundred, Abraham and his ninety-year-old wife, Sarah, were without children. How could he be the "father of many nations"? But Abraham kept believing and as a sign of His covenant, God changed his name from "Abram" to "Abraham" meaning "father of many nations."

Shortly after the birth of his son, Isaac, Abraham faced the greatest challenge to his faith. God tested Abraham, saying, "Take now your son, your only *son* Isaac, whom you love, and go to the land of Moriah, and offer him there as a burnt offering on one of the mountains of which I shall tell you" (Gen. 22:2). Was God's covenant to no avail? Was He the same as the blood-thirsty false gods Abraham had left behind in Ur? Or could God raise Isaac from the dead? Torn between his love for God and for his son, Isaac, Abraham tied his son on the altar and raised the knife to complete the sacrifice. But God had a different plan. Seizing the hand of Abraham, an angel of the Lord said to him, "Do not lay your hand on the lad, or do anything to him; for now I know that you fear God, seeing you have not withheld your son, your only *son* from Me" (Gen. 22:12). And God provided a ram, caught in a thicket, for the sacrifice.

Abraham's faith was not to go unrewarded. For his descendants became as the stars of heaven in number and innumerable as the sands of the seashore.

Your life may not be as dramatic as Abraham's, but no matter who you are, God can use you to step out in faith and attempt something great for Him. When God gives you a dream, it may seem impossible. But if you have the faith of Abraham—nothing will be impossible for you!

8 And he moved from there to the mountain east of Bethel, and he pitched his tent *with* Bethel on the west and Ai on the east; there he built an altar to the LORD and called on the name of the LORD.
9 So Abram journeyed, going on still toward the South.[20]

Abram in Egypt

10 Now there was a famine in the land, and Abram went down to Egypt to sojourn there, for the famine *was* severe in the land.
11 And it came to pass, when he was close to entering Egypt, that he said to Sarai his wife, "Indeed I know that you *are* a woman of beautiful countenance.
12 "Therefore it will happen, when the Egyptians see you, that they will say, 'This *is* his wife'; and they will kill me, but they will let you live.
13 "Please say you *are* my sister, that it may be well with me for your sake, and that I[21] may live because of you."
14 So it was, when Abram came into Egypt, that the Egyptians saw the woman, that she *was* very beautiful.
15 The princes of Pharaoh also saw her and commended her to Pharaoh. And the woman was taken to Pharaoh's house.
16 He treated Abram well for her sake. He had sheep, oxen, male donkeys, male and female servants, female donkeys, and camels.
17 But the LORD plagued Pharaoh and his house with great plagues because of Sarai, Abram's wife.
18 And Pharaoh called Abram and said, "What *is* this you have done to me? Why did you not tell me that she *was* your wife?
19 "Why did you say, 'She *is* my sister'? I might have taken her as my wife. Now therefore, here is your wife; take *her* and go your way."
20 So Pharaoh commanded *his* men concerning him; and they sent him away, with his wife and all that he had.

Abram Inherits Canaan

13 Then Abram went up from Egypt, he and his wife and all that he had, and Lot with him, to the South.[22]
2 Abram *was* very rich in livestock, in silver, and in gold.

3 And he went on his journey from the South as far as Bethel, to the place where his tent had been at the beginning, between Bethel and Ai,
4 to the place of the altar which he had made there at first. And there Abram called on the name of the LORD.
5 Lot also, who went with Abram, had flocks and herds and tents.
6 Now the land was not able to support them, that they might dwell together, for their possessions were so great that they could not dwell together.
7 And there was strife between the herdsmen of Abram's livestock and the herdsmen of Lot's livestock. The Canaanites and the Perizzites then dwelt in the land.
8 So Abram said to Lot, "Please let there be no strife between you and me, and between my herdsmen and your herdsmen; for we *are* brethren.
9 "*Is* not the whole land before you? Please separate from me. If *you take* the left, then I will go to the right; or, if *you* go to the right, then I will go to the left."
10 And Lot lifted his eyes and saw all the plain of Jordan, that it *was* well watered everywhere (before the LORD destroyed Sodom and Gomorrah) like the garden of the LORD, like the land of Egypt as you go toward Zoar.
11 Then Lot chose for himself all the plain of Jordan, and Lot journeyed east. And they separated from each other.
12 Abram dwelt in the land of Canaan, and Lot dwelt in the cities of the plain and pitched *his* tent even as far as Sodom.
13 But the men of Sodom *were* exceedingly wicked and sinful against the LORD.
14 And the LORD said to Abram, after Lot had separated from him: "Lift your eyes now and look from the place where you are—northward, southward, eastward, and westward;
15 "for all the land which you see I give to you and your descendants[23] forever.
16 "And I will make your descendants as the dust of the earth; so that if a man could number the dust of the earth, *then* your descendants also could be numbered.
17 "Arise, walk in the land through its length and its width, for I give it to you."
18 Then Abram moved *his* tent, and went and dwelt by the terebinth trees of

20 Hebrew *Negev*   21 Literally *my soul*   22 Hebrew *Negev*   23 Literally *seed,* and so throughout the book

Mamre,[24] which *are* in Hebron, and built an altar there to the LORD.

Lot's Captivity and Rescue

14 And it came to pass in the days of Amraphel king of Shinar, Arioch king of Ellasar, Chedorlaomer king of Elam, and Tidal king of nations,[25]
2 *that* they made war with Bera king of Sodom, Birsha king of Gomorrah, Shinab king of Admah, Shemeber king of Zeboiim, and the king of Bela (that is, Zoar).
3 All these joined together in the Valley of Siddim (that is, the Salt Sea).
4 Twelve years they served Chedorlaomer, and in the thirteenth year they rebelled.
5 In the fourteenth year Chedorlaomer and the kings that *were* with him came and attacked the Rephaim in Ashteroth Karnaim, the Zuzim in Ham, the Emim in Shaveh Kiriathaim,
6 and the Horites in their mountain of Seir, as far as El Paran, which *is* by the wilderness.
7 Then they turned back and came to En Mishpat (that *is*, Kadesh), and attacked all the country of the Amalekites, and also the Amorites who dwelt in Hazezon Tamar.
8 And the king of Sodom, the king of Gomorrah, the king of Admah, the king of Zeboiim, and the king of Bela (that *is*, Zoar) went out and joined together in battle in the Valley of Siddim
9 against Chedorlaomer king of Elam, Tidal king of nations,[26] Amraphel king of Shinar, and Arioch king of Ellasar—four kings against five.
10 Now the Valley of Siddim *was full of* asphalt pits; and the kings of Sodom and Gomorrah fled; *some* fell there, and the remainder fled to the mountains.
11 Then they took all the goods of Sodom and Gomorrah, and all their provisions, and went their way.
12 They also took Lot, Abram's brother's son who dwelt in Sodom, and his goods, and departed.
13 Then one who had escaped came and told Abram the Hebrew, for he dwelt by the terebinth trees of Mamre[27] the Amorite, brother of Eshcol and brother of Aner; and they *were* allies with Abram.
14 Now when Abram heard that his brother was taken captive, he armed his three hundred and eighteen trained *servants* who were born in his own house, and went in pursuit as far as Dan.
15 He divided his forces against them by night, and he and his servants attacked them and pursued them as far as Hobah, which *is* north of Damascus.
16 So he brought back all the goods, and also brought back his brother Lot and his goods, as well as the women and the people.
17 And the king of Sodom went out to meet him at the Valley of Shaveh (that *is*, the King's Valley), after his return from the defeat of Chedorlaomer and the kings who *were* with him.

Abram and Melchizedek

18 Then Melchizedek king of Salem brought out bread and wine; he *was* the priest of God Most High.
19 And he blessed him and said:

"Blessed be Abram of God Most High,
    Possessor of heaven and earth;
20 And blessed be God Most High,
    Who has delivered your enemies
        into your hand."

And he gave him a tithe of all.
21 Now the king of Sodom said to Abram, "Give me the persons, and take the goods for yourself."
22 But Abram said to the king of Sodom, "I have lifted my hand to the LORD, God Most High, the Possessor of heaven and earth,
23 "that I *will take* nothing, from a thread to a sandal strap, and that I will not take anything that *is* yours, lest you should say, 'I have made Abram rich'—
24 "except only what the young men have eaten, and the portion of the men who went with me: Aner, Eshcol, and Mamre; let them take their portion."

God's Covenant with Abram

15 After these things the word of the LORD came to Abram in a vision, saying, "Do not be afraid, Abram. I *am* your shield, your exceedingly great reward."
2 But Abram said, "Lord GOD, what will You give me, seeing I go childless, and the heir of my house *is* Eliezer of Damascus?"
3 Then Abram said, "Look, You have

24 Hebrew *Alon Mamre* 25 Hebrew *goyim* 26 Hebrew *goyim* 27 Hebrew *Alon Mamre*

given me no offspring; indeed one born in my house is my heir!"

4 And behold, the word of the LORD *came* to him, saying, "This one shall not be your heir, but one who will come from your own body shall be your heir."

5 Then He brought him outside and said, "Look now toward heaven, and count the stars if you are able to number them." And He said to him, "So shall your descendants be."

6 And he believed in the LORD, and He accounted it to him for righteousness.

7 Then He said to him, "I *am* the LORD, who brought you out of Ur of the Chaldeans, to give you this land to inherit it."

8 And he said, "Lord GOD, how shall I know that I will inherit it?"

9 So He said to him, "Bring Me a three-year-old heifer, a three-year-old female goat, a three-year-old ram, a turtledove, and a young pigeon."

10 Then he brought all these to Him and cut them in two, down the middle, and placed each piece opposite the other; but he did not cut the birds in two.

11 And when the vultures came down on the carcasses, Abram drove them away.

12 Now when the sun was going down, a deep sleep fell upon Abram; and behold, horror *and* great darkness fell upon him.

13 Then He said to Abram: "Know certainly that your descendants will be strangers in a land *that is* not theirs, and will serve them, and they will afflict them four hundred years.

14 "And also the nation whom they serve I will judge; afterward they shall come out with great possessions.

15 "Now as for you, you shall go to your fathers in peace; you shall be buried at a good old age.

16 "But in the fourth generation they shall return here, for the iniquity of the Amorites *is* not yet complete."

17 And it came to pass, when the sun went down and it was dark, that behold, *there was* a smoking oven and a burning torch that passed between those pieces.

18 On the same day the LORD made a covenant with Abram, saying:

"To your descendants I have given this land, from the river of Egypt to the great river, the River Euphrates—

19 "the Kenites, the Kenezzites, and the Kadmonites;

20 "the Hittites, the Perizzites, and the Rephaim;

21 "the Amorites, the Canaanites, the Girgashites, and the Jebusites."

Hagar and Ishmael

16 Now Sarai, Abram's wife, had borne him no *children*. And she had an Egyptian maidservant whose name was Hagar.

2 So Sarai said to Abram, "See now, the LORD has restrained me from bearing *children*. Please, go in to my maid; perhaps I shall obtain children by her." And Abram heeded the voice of Sarai.

3 Then Sarai, Abram's wife, took Hagar her maid, the Egyptian, and gave her to her husband Abram to be his wife, after Abram had dwelt ten years in the land of Canaan.

4 So he went in to Hagar, and she conceived. And when she saw that she had conceived, her mistress became despised in her eyes.

5 Then Sarai said to Abram, "My wrong *be* upon you! I gave my maid into your embrace; and when she saw that she had conceived, I became despised in her eyes. The LORD judge between you and me."

6 So Abram said to Sarai, "Indeed your maid *is* in your hand; do to her as you please." And when Sarai dealt harshly with her, she fled from her presence.

7 Now the Angel of the LORD found her by a spring of water in the wilderness, by the spring on the way to Shur.

8 And He said, "Hagar, Sarai's maid, where have you come from, and where are you going?" And she said, "I am fleeing from the presence of my mistress Sarai."

9 So the Angel of the LORD said to her, "Return to your mistress, and submit yourself under her hand."

10 Then the Angel of the LORD said to her, "I will multiply your descendants exceedingly, so that they shall not be counted for multitude."

11 And the Angel of the LORD said to her:

"Behold, you *are* with child,
And you shall bear a son.
You shall call his name Ishmael,
Because the LORD has heard
    your affliction.

12 He shall be a wild man;
   His hand *shall be* against every man,
   And every man's hand against him.
   And he shall dwell in the presence
      of all his brethren."

13 Then she called the name of the LORD who spoke to her, You-Are-the-God-Who-Sees; for she said, "Have I also here seen Him who sees me?"
14 Therefore the well was called Beer Lahai Roi;[28] observe, *it is* between Kadesh and Bered.
15 So Hagar bore Abram a son; and Abram named his son, whom Hagar bore, Ishmael.
16 Abram *was* eighty-six years old when Hagar bore Ishmael to Abram.

The Sign of the Covenant

17 When Abram was ninety-nine years old, the LORD appeared to Abram and said to him, "I *am* Almighty God; walk before Me and be blameless.
2 "And I will make My covenant between Me and you, and will multiply you exceedingly."
3 Then Abram fell on his face, and God talked with him, saying:
4 "As for Me, behold, My covenant is with you, and you shall be a father of many nations.
5 "No longer shall your name be called Abram, but your name shall be Abraham; for I have made you a father of many nations.
6 "I will make you exceedingly fruitful; and I will make nations of you, and kings shall come from you.
7 "And I will establish My covenant between Me and you and your descendants after you in their generations, for an everlasting covenant, to be God to you and your descendants after you.
8 "Also I give to you and your descendants after you the land in which you are a stranger, all the land of Canaan, as an everlasting possession; and I will be their God."
9 And God said to Abraham: "As for you, you shall keep My covenant, you and your descendants after you throughout their generations.
10 "This *is* My covenant which you shall keep, between Me and you and your descendants after you: Every male child among you shall be circumcised;

11 "and you shall be circumcised in the flesh of your foreskins, and it shall be a sign of the covenant between Me and you.
12 "He who is eight days old among you shall be circumcised, every male child in your generations, he who is born in your house or bought with money from any stranger who is not your descendant.
13 "He who is born in your house and he who is bought with your money must be circumcised, and My covenant shall be in your flesh for an everlasting covenant.
14 "And the uncircumcised male child, who is not circumcised in the flesh of his foreskin, that person shall be cut off from his people; he has broken My covenant."
15 Then God said to Abraham, "As for Sarai your wife, you shall not call her name Sarai, but Sarah *shall be* her name.
16 "And I will bless her and also give you a son by her; then I will bless her, and she shall be *a mother of* nations; kings of peoples shall be from her."
17 Then Abraham fell on his face and laughed, and said in his heart, "Shall *a child* be born to a man who is one hundred years old? And shall Sarah, who is ninety years old, bear *a child*?"
18 And Abraham said to God, "Oh, that Ishmael might live before You!"
19 Then God said: "No, Sarah your wife shall bear you a son, and you shall call his name Isaac; I will establish My covenant with him for an everlasting covenant, *and* with his descendants after him.
20 "And as for Ishmael, I have heard you. Behold, I have blessed him, and will make him fruitful, and will multiply him exceedingly. He shall beget twelve princes, and I will make him a great nation.
21 "But My covenant I will establish with Isaac, whom Sarah shall bear to you at this set time next year."
22 Then He finished talking with him, and God went up from Abraham.
23 So Abraham took Ishmael his son, all who were born in his house and all who were bought with his money, every male among the men of Abraham's house, and circumcised the flesh of their foreskins that very same day, as God had said to him.
24 Abraham *was* ninety-nine years old

28 Literally *Well of the One Who Lives and Sees Me*

when he was circumcised in the flesh of his foreskin.

25 And Ishmael his son *was* thirteen years old when he was circumcised in the flesh of his foreskin.

26 That very same day Abraham was circumcised, and his son Ishmael;

27 and all the men of his house, born in the house or bought with money from a stranger, were circumcised with him.

The Son of Promise

18 Then the LORD appeared to him by the terebinth trees of Mamre,29 as he was sitting in the tent door in the heat of the day.

2 So he lifted his eyes and looked, and behold, three men were standing by him; and when he saw *them*, he ran from the tent door to meet them, and bowed himself to the ground,

3 and said, "My Lord, if I have now found favor in Your sight, do not pass on by Your servant.

4 "Please let a little water be brought, and wash your feet, and rest yourselves under the tree.

5 "And I will bring a morsel of bread, that you may refresh your hearts. After that you may pass by, inasmuch as you have come to your servant." And they said, "Do as you have said."

6 So Abraham hastened into the tent to Sarah and said, "Quickly, make ready three measures of fine meal; knead *it* and make cakes."

7 And Abraham ran to the herd, took a tender and good calf, gave *it* to a young man, and he hastened to prepare it.

8 So he took butter and milk and the calf which he had prepared, and set *it* before them; and he stood by them under the tree as they ate.

9 Then they said to him, "Where *is* Sarah your wife?" And he said, "Here, in the tent."

10 And He said, "I will certainly return to you according to the time of life, and behold, Sarah your wife shall have a son." And Sarah was listening in the tent door which *was* behind him.

11 Now Abraham and Sarah were old, well advanced in age; *and* Sarah had passed the age of childbearing.30

12 Therefore Sarah laughed within herself, saying, "After I have grown old, shall I have pleasure, my lord being old also?"

13 And the LORD said to Abraham, "Why did Sarah laugh, saying, 'Shall I surely bear *a child*, since I am old?'

14 "Is anything too hard for the LORD? At the appointed time I will return to you, according to the time of life, and Sarah shall have a son."

15 But Sarah denied *it*, saying, "I did not laugh," for she was afraid. And He said, "No, but you did laugh!"

Abraham Intercedes for Sodom

16 Then the men rose from there and looked toward Sodom, and Abraham went with them to send them on the way.

17 And the LORD said, "Shall I hide from Abraham what I am doing,

18 "since Abraham shall surely become a great and mighty nation, and all the nations of the earth shall be blessed in him?

19 "For I have known him, in order that he may command his children and his household after him, that they keep the way of the LORD, to do righteousness and justice, that the LORD may bring to Abraham what He has spoken to him."

20 And the LORD said, "Because the outcry against Sodom and Gomorrah is great, and because their sin is very grievous,

21 "I will go down now and see whether they have done altogether according to the outcry against it that has come to Me; and if not, I will know."

22 Then the men turned away from there and went toward Sodom, but Abraham still stood before the LORD.

23 And Abraham came near and said, "Would You also destroy the righteous with the wicked?

24 "Suppose there were fifty righteous within the city; would You also destroy the place and not spare *it* for the fifty righteous that were in it?

25 "Far be it from You to do such a thing as this, to slay the righteous with the wicked, so that the righteous should be as the wicked; far be it from You! Shall not the Judge of all the earth do right?"

26 And the LORD said, "If I find in Sodom fifty righteous within the city, then I will spare all the place for their sakes."

29 Hebrew *Alon Mamre*   30 Literally *the manner of women had ceased to be with Sarah*

²⁷ Then Abraham answered and said, "Indeed now, I who *am but* dust and ashes have taken it upon myself to speak to the Lord:
²⁸ "Suppose there were five less than the fifty righteous; would You destroy all of the city for *lack of* five?" And He said, "If I find there forty-five, I will not destroy *it*."
²⁹ Then he spoke to Him yet again and said, "Suppose there should be forty found there?" And He said, "I will not do *it* for the sake of forty."
³⁰ And he said, "Let not the Lord be angry, and I will speak: Suppose thirty should be found there?" And He said, "I will not do *it* if I find thirty there."
³¹ Then he said, "Indeed now, I have taken it upon myself to speak to the Lord: Suppose twenty should be found there?" And He said, "I will not destroy *it* for the sake of twenty."
³² And he said, "Let not the Lord be angry, and I will speak but once more: Suppose ten should be found there?" And He said, "I will not destroy *it* for the sake of ten."
³³ So the LORD went His way as soon as He had finished speaking with Abraham; and Abraham returned to his place.

Sodom's Depravity

19 Now the two angels came to Sodom in the evening, and Lot was sitting in the gate of Sodom. When Lot saw *them*, he rose to meet them, and he bowed himself with his face toward the ground.
² And he said, "Here now, my lords, please turn in to your servant's house and spend the night, and wash your feet; then you may rise early and go on your way." And they said, "No, but we will spend the night in the open square."
³ But he insisted strongly; so they turned in to him and entered his house. Then he made them a feast, and baked unleavened bread, and they ate.
⁴ Now before they lay down, the men of the city, the men of Sodom, both old and young, all the people from every quarter, surrounded the house.
⁵ And they called to Lot and said to him, "Where are the men who came to you tonight? Bring them out to us that we may know them *carnally*."

⁶ So Lot went out to them through the doorway, shut the door behind him,
⁷ and said, "Please, my brethren, do not do so wickedly!
⁸ "See now, I have two daughters who have not known a man; please, let me bring them out to you, and you may do to them as you wish; only do nothing to these men, since this is the reason they have come under the shadow of my roof."
⁹ And they said, "Stand back!" Then they said, "This one came in to sojourn, and he keeps acting as a judge; now we will deal worse with you than with them." So they pressed hard against the man Lot, and came near to break down the door.
¹⁰ But the men reached out their hands and pulled Lot into the house with them, and shut the door.
¹¹ And they struck the men who *were* at the doorway of the house with blindness, both small and great, so that they became weary *trying* to find the door.

Sodom and Gomorrah Destroyed

12 Then the men said to Lot, "Have you anyone else here? Son-in-law, your sons, your daughters, and whomever you have in the city—take *them* out of this place!
13 "For we will destroy this place, because the outcry against them has grown great before the face of the LORD, and the LORD has sent us to destroy it."
14 So Lot went out and spoke to his sons-in-law, who had married his daughters, and said, "Get up, get out of this place; for the LORD will destroy this city!" But to his sons-in-law he seemed to be joking.
15 When the morning dawned, the angels urged Lot to hurry, saying, "Arise, take your wife and your two daughters who are here, lest you be consumed in the punishment of the city."
16 And while he lingered, the men took hold of his hand, his wife's hand, and the hands of his two daughters, the LORD being merciful to him, and they brought him out and set him outside the city.
17 So it came to pass, when they had brought them outside, that he³¹ said, "Escape for your life! Do not look behind you nor stay anywhere in the plain. Escape to the mountains, lest you be destroyed."

---

31 Septuagint, Syriac, and Vulgate read *they*.

18 Then Lot said to them, "Please, no, my lords!
19 "Indeed now, your servant has found favor in your sight, and you have increased your mercy which you have shown me by saving my life; but I cannot escape to the mountains, lest some evil overtake me and I die.
20 "See now, this city is near enough to flee to, and it is a little one; please let me escape there (is it not a little one?) and my soul shall live."
21 And he said to him, "See, I have favored you concerning this thing also, in that I will not overthrow this city for which you have spoken.
22 "Hurry, escape there. For I cannot do anything until you arrive there." Therefore the name of the city was called Zoar.
23 The sun had risen upon the earth when Lot entered Zoar.
24 Then the LORD rained brimstone and fire on Sodom and Gomorrah, from the LORD out of the heavens.
25 So He overthrew those cities, all the plain, all the inhabitants of the cities, and what grew on the ground.
26 But his wife looked back behind him, and she became a pillar of salt.
27 And Abraham went early in the morning to the place where he had stood before the LORD.
28 Then he looked toward Sodom and Gomorrah, and toward all the land of the plain; and he saw, and behold, the smoke of the land which went up like the smoke of a furnace.
29 And it came to pass, when God destroyed the cities of the plain, that God remembered Abraham, and sent Lot out of the midst of the overthrow, when He overthrew the cities in which Lot had dwelt.

The Descendants of Lot

30 Then Lot went up out of Zoar and dwelt in the mountains, and his two daughters were with him; for he was afraid to dwell in Zoar. And he and his two daughters dwelt in a cave.
31 Now the firstborn said to the younger, "Our father is old, and there is no man on the earth to come in to us as is the custom of all the earth.
32 "Come, let us make our father drink wine, and we will lie with him, that we may preserve the lineage of our father."

33 So they made their father drink wine that night. And the firstborn went in and lay with her father, and he did not know when she lay down or when she arose.
34 It happened on the next day that the firstborn said to the younger, "Indeed I lay with my father last night; let us make him drink wine tonight also, and you go in and lie with him, that we may preserve the lineage of our father."
35 Then they made their father drink wine that night also. And the younger arose and lay with him, and he did not know when she lay down or when she arose.
36 Thus both the daughters of Lot were with child by their father.
37 The firstborn bore a son and called his name Moab; he is the father of the Moabites to this day.
38 And the younger, she also bore a son and called his name Ben-Ammi; he is the father of the people of Ammon to this day.

Abraham and Abimelech

20 And Abraham journeyed from there to the South, and dwelt between Kadesh and Shur, and sojourned in Gerar.
2 Now Abraham said of Sarah his wife, "She is my sister." And Abimelech king of Gerar sent and took Sarah.
3 But God came to Abimelech in a dream by night, and said to him, "Indeed you are a dead man because of the woman whom you have taken, for she is a man's wife."
4 But Abimelech had not come near her; and he said, "Lord, will You slay a righteous nation also?
5 "Did he not say to me, 'She is my sister'? And she, even she herself said, 'He is my brother.' In the integrity of my heart and innocence of my hands I have done this."
6 And God said to him in a dream, "Yes, I know that you did this in the integrity of your heart. For I also withheld you from sinning against Me; therefore I did not let you touch her.
7 "Now therefore, restore the man's wife; for he is a prophet, and he will pray for you and you shall live. But if you do not restore her, know that you shall surely die, you and all who are yours."
8 So Abimelech rose early in the morn-

ing, called all his servants, and told all these things in their hearing; and the men were very afraid.

9 And Abimelech called Abraham and said to him, "What have you done to us? How have I offended you, that you have brought on me and on my kingdom a great sin? You have done deeds to me that ought not to be done."

10 Then Abimelech said to Abraham, "What did you have in view, that you have done this thing?"

11 And Abraham said, "Because I thought, surely the fear of God is not in this place; and they will kill me on account of my wife.

12 "But indeed she is truly my sister. She is the daughter of my father, but not the daughter of my mother; and she became my wife.

13 "And it came to pass, when God caused me to wander from my father's house, that I said to her, 'This is your kindness that you should do for me: in every place, wherever we go, say of me, "He is my brother." ' "

14 Then Abimelech took sheep, oxen, and male and female servants, and gave them to Abraham; and he restored Sarah his wife to him.

15 And Abimelech said, "See, my land is before you; dwell where it pleases you."

16 Then to Sarah he said, "Behold, I have given your brother a thousand pieces of silver; indeed this vindicates you[32] before all who are with you and before all others." Thus she was reproved.

17 So Abraham prayed to God; and God healed Abimelech, his wife, and his maidservants. Then they bore children;

18 for the LORD had closed up all the wombs of the house of Abimelech because of Sarah, Abraham's wife.

Isaac Is Born

21 And the LORD visited Sarah as He had said, and the LORD did for Sarah as He had spoken.

2 For Sarah conceived and bore Abraham a son in his old age, at the set time of which God had spoken to him.

3 And Abraham called the name of his son who was born to him—whom Sarah bore to him—Isaac.

4 Then Abraham circumcised his son Isaac when he was eight days old, as God had commanded him.

5 Now Abraham was one hundred years old when his son Isaac was born to him.

6 And Sarah said, "God has made me laugh, so that all who hear will laugh with me."

7 She also said, "Who would have said to Abraham that Sarah would nurse children? For I have borne him a son in his old age."

Hagar and Ishmael Depart

8 So the child grew and was weaned. And Abraham made a great feast on the same day that Isaac was weaned.

9 And Sarah saw the son of Hagar the Egyptian, whom she had borne to Abraham, scoffing.

10 Therefore she said to Abraham, "Cast out this bondwoman and her son; for the son of this bondwoman shall not be heir with my son, namely with Isaac."

11 And the matter was very displeasing in Abraham's sight because of his son.

12 But God said to Abraham, "Do not let it be displeasing in your sight because of the lad or because of your bondwoman. Whatever Sarah has said to you, listen to her voice; for in Isaac your seed shall be called.

13 "Yet I will also make a nation of the son of the bondwoman, because he is your seed."

14 So Abraham rose early in the morning; and took bread and a skin of water; and putting it on her shoulder, he gave it and the boy to Hagar, and sent her away. Then she departed and wandered in the Wilderness of Beersheba.

15 And the water in the skin was used up, and she placed the boy under one of the shrubs.

16 Then she went and sat down across from him at a distance of about a bowshot; for she said to herself, "Let me not see the death of the boy." So she sat opposite him, and lifted her voice and wept.

17 And God heard the voice of the lad. Then the angel of God called to Hagar out of heaven, and said to her, "What ails you, Hagar? Fear not, for God has heard the voice of the lad where he is.

18 "Arise, lift up the lad and hold him with your hand, for I will make him a great nation."

19 And God opened her eyes, and she saw a well of water. Then she went and

32 Literally it is a covering of the eyes for you

filled the skin with water, and gave the lad a drink.

20 So God was with the lad; and he grew and dwelt in the wilderness, and became an archer.

21 He dwelt in the Wilderness of Paran; and his mother took a wife for him from the land of Egypt.

A Covenant with Abimelech

22 And it came to pass at that time that Abimelech and Phichol, the commander of his army, spoke to Abraham, saying, "God *is* with you in all that you do.

23 "Now therefore, swear to me by God that you will not deal falsely with me, with my offspring, or with my posterity; but that according to the kindness that I have done to you, you will do to me and to the land in which you have sojourned."

24 And Abraham said, "I will swear."

25 Then Abraham reproved Abimelech because of a well of water which Abimelech's servants had seized.

26 And Abimelech said, "I do not know who has done this thing; you did not tell me, nor had I heard *of it* until today."

27 So Abraham took sheep and oxen and gave them to Abimelech, and the two of them made a covenant.

28 And Abraham set seven ewe lambs of the flock by themselves.

29 Then Abimelech asked Abraham, "What *is the meaning of* these seven ewe lambs which you have set by themselves?"

30 And he said, "You will take *these* seven ewe lambs from my hand, that they may be my witness that I have dug this well."

31 Therefore he called that place Beersheba,[33] because the two of them swore an oath there.

32 Thus they made a covenant at Beersheba. So Abimelech rose with Phichol, the commander of his army, and they returned to the land of the Philistines.

33 Then *Abraham* planted a tamarisk tree in Beersheba, and there called on the name of the LORD, the Everlasting God.

34 And Abraham sojourned in the land of the Philistines many days.

Abraham's Faith Confirmed

22 Now it came to pass after these things that God tested Abraham,

and said to him, "Abraham!" And he said, "Here I am."

2 And He said, "Take now your son, your only *son* Isaac, whom you love, and go to the land of Moriah, and offer him there as a burnt offering on one of the mountains of which I shall tell you."

3 So Abraham rose early in the morning and saddled his donkey, and took two of his young men with him, and Isaac his son; and he split the wood for the burnt offering, and arose and went to the place of which God had told him.

4 Then on the third day Abraham lifted his eyes and saw the place afar off.

5 And Abraham said to his young men, "Stay here with the donkey; the lad[34] and I will go yonder and worship, and we will come back to you."

6 So Abraham took the wood of the burnt offering and laid *it* on Isaac his son; and he took the fire in his hand, and a knife, and the two of them went together.

7 But Isaac spoke to Abraham his father and said, "My father!" And he said, "Here I am, my son." And he said, "Look, the fire and the wood, but where *is* the lamb for a burnt offering?"

8 And Abraham said, "My son, God will provide for Himself the lamb for a burnt offering." And the two of them went together.

9 Then they came to the place of which God had told him. And Abraham built an altar there and placed the wood in order; and he bound Isaac his son and laid him on the altar, upon the wood.

10 And Abraham stretched out his hand and took the knife to slay his son.

11 But the Angel of the LORD called to him from heaven and said, "Abraham, Abraham!" And he said, "Here I am."

12 And He said, "Do not lay your hand on the lad, or do anything to him; for now I know that you fear God, seeing you have not withheld your son, your only *son*, from Me."

13 Then Abraham lifted his eyes and looked, and there behind *him was* a ram caught in a thicket by its horns. So Abraham went and took the ram, and offered it up for a burnt offering instead of his son.

14 And Abraham called the name of the place, The-LORD-Will-Provide;[35] as it is

---

33 Literally *Well of the Oath* or *Well of the Seven*   34 Literally *young man*   35 Hebrew *YHWH Jireh*

said *to* this day, "In the Mount of The
LORD it shall be provided."

15 Then the Angel of the LORD called to
Abraham a second time out of heaven,
16 and said: "By Myself I have sworn,
says the LORD, because you have done
this thing, and have not withheld your
son, your only *son*,
17 "in blessing I will bless you, and in
multiplying I will multiply your descendants as the stars of the heaven and as the
sand which *is* on the seashore; and your
descendants shall possess the gate of their
enemies.
18 "In your seed all the nations of the
earth shall be blessed, because you have
obeyed My voice."
19 So Abraham returned to his young
men, and they rose and went together to
Beersheba; and Abraham dwelt at Beersheba.

The Family of Nahor

20 Now it came to pass after these things
that it was told Abraham, saying, "Indeed Milcah also has borne children to
your brother Nahor:
21 "Huz his firstborn, Buz his brother,
Kemuel the father of Aram,
22 "Chesed, Hazo, Pildash, Jidlaph, and
Bethuel."
23 And Bethuel begot Rebekah.[36] These
eight Milcah bore to Nahor, Abraham's
brother.
24 His concubine, whose name was Reu-
mah, also bore Tebah, Gaham, Thahash,
and Maachah.

Sarah's Death and Burial

23 Sarah lived one hundred and
twenty-seven years; *these were* the
years of the life of Sarah.
2 So Sarah died in Kirjath Arba (that *is*,
Hebron) in the land of Canaan, and
Abraham came to mourn for Sarah and
to weep for her.
3 Then Abraham stood up from before
his dead, and spoke to the sons of Heth,
saying,
4 "I *am* a foreigner and a sojourner
among you. Give me property for a
burial place among you, that I may bury
my dead out of my sight."
5 And the sons of Heth answered Abraham, saying to him,
6 "Hear us, my lord: You *are* a mighty
prince among us; bury your dead in the

choicest of our burial places. None of us
will withhold from you his burial place,
that you may bury your dead."
7 Then Abraham stood up and bowed
himself to the people of the land, the sons
of Heth.
8 And he spoke with them, saying, "If it
is your wish that I bury my dead out of
my sight, hear me, and meet with Ephron
the son of Zohar for me,
9 "that he may give me the cave of
Machpelah which he has, which *is* at the
end of his field. Let him give it to me at
the full price, as property for a burial
place among you."
10 Now Ephron dwelt among the sons of
Heth; and Ephron the Hittite answered
Abraham in the presence of the sons of
Heth, all who entered at the gate of his
city, saying,
11 "No, my lord, hear me: I give you the
field and the cave that *is* in it; I give it to
you in the presence of the sons of my
people. I give it to you. Bury your
dead!"
12 Then Abraham bowed himself down
before the people of the land;
13 and he spoke to Ephron in the hearing
of the people of the land, saying, "If you
will give it, please hear me. I will give you
money for the field; take *it* from me and I
will bury my dead there."
14 And Ephron answered Abraham, saying to him,
15 "My lord, listen to me; the land *is*
worth four hundred shekels of silver.
What *is* that between you and me? So
bury your dead."
16 And Abraham listened to Ephron;
and Abraham weighed out the silver for
Ephron which he had named in the hearing of the sons of Heth, four hundred
shekels of silver, currency of the merchants.
17 So the field of Ephron which *was* in
Machpelah, which *was* before Mamre, the
field and the cave which *was* in it, and all
the trees that *were* in the field, which *were*
within all the surrounding borders, were
deeded
18 to Abraham as a possession in the
presence of the sons of Heth, before all
who went in at the gate of his city.
19 And after this, Abraham buried Sarah
his wife in the cave of the field of Machpelah, before Mamre (that *is*, Hebron) in
the land of Canaan.

36 Spelled *Rebecca* in Romans 9:10

20 So the field and the cave that *is* in it were deeded to Abraham by the sons of Heth as property for a burial place.

A Bride for Isaac

24 Now Abraham was old, well advanced in age; and the LORD had blessed Abraham in all things.
2 So Abraham said to the oldest servant of his house, who ruled over all that he had, "Please, put your hand under my thigh,
3 "and I will make you swear by the LORD, the God of heaven and the God of the earth, that you will not take a wife for my son from the daughters of the Canaanites, among whom I dwell;
4 "but you shall go to my country and to my kindred, and take a wife for my son Isaac."
5 And the servant said to him, "Perhaps the woman will not be willing to follow me to this land. Must I take your son back to the land from which you came?"
6 But Abraham said to him, "Beware that you do not take my son back there.
7 "The LORD God of heaven, who took me from my father's house and from the land of my kindred, and who spoke to me and swore to me, saying, 'To your descendants I give this land,' He will send His angel before you, and you shall take a wife for my son from there.
8 "And if the woman is not willing to follow you, then you will be released from this oath; only do not take my son back there."
9 So the servant put his hand under the thigh of Abraham his master, and swore to him concerning this matter.
10 Then the servant took ten of his master's camels and departed, for all his master's goods *were in* his hand. And he arose and went to Mesopotamia, to the city of Nahor.
11 And he made his camels kneel down outside the city by a well of water at evening time, the time when women go out to draw *water.*
12 Then he said, "O LORD God of my master Abraham, please give me success this day, and show kindness to my master Abraham.
13 "Behold, I stand *here* by the well of water, and the daughters of the men of the city are coming out to draw water.
14 "Now let it be that the young woman

to whom I say, 'Please let down your pitcher that I may drink,' and she says, 'Drink, and I will also give your camels a drink'—*let* her *be the one* whom You have appointed for Your servant Isaac. And by this I will know that You have shown kindness to my master."
15 And it happened, before he had finished speaking, that behold, Rebekah, who was born to Bethuel, son of Milcah, the wife of Nahor, Abraham's brother, came out with her pitcher on her shoulder.
16 Now the young woman *was* very beautiful to behold, a virgin; no man had known her. And she went down to the well, filled her pitcher, and came up.
17 And the servant ran to meet her and said, "Please let me drink a little water from your pitcher."
18 So she said, "Drink, my lord." Then she hastened and let her pitcher down to her hand, and gave him a drink.
19 And when she had finished giving him a drink, she said, "I will draw *water* for your camels also, until they have finished drinking."
20 Then she hastened and emptied her pitcher into the trough, ran back to the well to draw *water,* and drew for all his camels.
21 And the man, wondering at her, remained silent so as to know whether the LORD had made his journey prosperous or not.
22 So it was, when the camels had finished drinking, that the man took a golden nose ring weighing half a shekel, and two bracelets for her wrists weighing ten *shekels* of gold,
23 and said, "Whose daughter *are* you? Tell me, please, is there room *in* your father's house for us to lodge?"
24 So she said to him, "I *am* the daughter of Bethuel, Milcah's son, whom she bore to Nahor."
25 Moreover she said to him, "We have both straw and feed enough, and room to lodge."
26 Then the man bowed down his head and worshiped the LORD.
27 And he said, "Blessed *be* the LORD God of my master Abraham, who has not forsaken His mercy and His truth toward my master. As for me, being on the way, the LORD led me to the house of my master's brethren."

28 So the young woman ran and told *those of* her mother's house these things. 29 Now Rebekah had a brother whose name *was* Laban, and Laban ran out to the man by the well. 30 So it came to pass, when he saw the nose ring, and the bracelets on his sister's wrists, and when he heard the words of his sister Rebekah, saying, "Thus the man spoke to me," that he went to the man. And there he stood by the camels at the well. 31 And he said, "Come in, O blessed of the LORD! Why do you stand outside? For I have prepared the house, and a place for the camels." 32 Then the man came to the house. And he unloaded the camels, and provided straw and feed for the camels, and water to wash his feet and the feet of the men who *were* with him. 33 And *food* was set before him to eat, but he said, "I will not eat until I have told about my errand." And he said, "Speak on."

34 So he said, "I *am* Abraham's servant. 35 "The LORD has blessed my master greatly, and he has become great; and He has given him flocks and herds, silver and gold, male and female servants, and camels and donkeys. 36 "And Sarah my master's wife bore a son to my master when she was old; and to him he has given all that he has. 37 "Now my master made me swear, saying, 'You shall not take a wife for my son from the daughters of the Canaanites, in whose land I dwell; 38 'but you shall go to my father's house and to my kindred, and take a wife for my son.' 39 "And I said to my master, 'Perhaps the woman will not follow me.' 40 "But he said to me, 'The LORD, before whom I walk, will send His angel with you and prosper your way; and you shall take a wife for my son from my kindred and from my father's house. 41 'You will be clear from this oath when you arrive among my kindred; for if they will not give *her* to you, then you will be released from my oath.' 42 "And this day I came to the well and said, 'O LORD God of my master Abraham, if You will now prosper the way in which I go, 43 'behold, I stand by the well of water;

and it shall come to pass that when the virgin comes out to draw *water*, and I say to her, "Please give me a little water from your pitcher to drink," 44 'and she says to me, "Drink, and I will draw for your camels also,"—*let* her *be* the woman whom the LORD has appointed for my master's son.' 45 "But before I had finished speaking in my heart, there was Rebekah, coming out with her pitcher on her shoulder; and she went down to the well and drew *water*. And I said to her, 'Please let me drink.' 46 "And she made haste and let her pitcher down from her *shoulder*, and said, 'Drink, and I will give your camels a drink also.' So I drank, and she gave the camels a drink also. 47 "Then I asked her, and said, 'Whose daughter *are* you?' And she said, 'The daughter of Bethuel, Nahor's son, whom Milcah bore to him.' So I put the nose ring on her nose and the bracelets on her wrists. 48 "And I bowed my head and worshiped the LORD, and blessed the LORD God of my master Abraham, who had led me in the way of truth to take the daughter of my master's brother for his son. 49 "Now if you will deal kindly and truly with my master, tell me. And if not, tell me, that I may turn to the right hand or to the left."

50 Then Laban and Bethuel answered and said, "The thing comes from the LORD; we cannot speak to you either bad or good. 51 "Here *is* Rebekah before you; take *her* and go, and let her be your master's son's wife, as the LORD has spoken." 52 And it came to pass, when Abraham's servant heard their words, that he worshiped the LORD, *bowing himself* to the earth. 53 Then the servant brought out jewelry of silver, jewelry of gold, and clothing, and gave *them* to Rebekah. He also gave precious things to her brother and to her mother. 54 And he and the men who *were* with him ate and drank and stayed all night. Then they arose in the morning, and he said, "Send me away to my master." 55 But her brother and her mother said, "Let the young woman stay with us *a few* days, at least ten; after that she may go."

56 And he said to them, "Do not hinder me, since the LORD has prospered my way; send me away so that I may go to my master."
57 So they said, "We will call the young woman and ask her personally."
58 Then they called Rebekah and said to her, "Will you go with this man?" And she said, "I will go."
59 So they sent away Rebekah their sister and her nurse, and Abraham's servant and his men.
60 And they blessed Rebekah and said to her:

"Our sister, *may* you *become*
    The mother of thousands
        of ten thousands;
And may your descendants possess
    The gates of those who hate them."

61 Then Rebekah and her maids arose, and they rode on the camels and followed the man. So the servant took Rebekah and departed.
62 Now Isaac came from the way of Beer Lahai Roi, for he dwelt in the South.
63 And Isaac went out to meditate in the field in the evening; and he lifted his eyes and looked, and there, the camels *were* coming.
64 Then Rebekah lifted her eyes, and when she saw Isaac she dismounted from her camel;
65 for she had said to the servant, "Who *is* this man walking in the field to meet us?" And the servant said, "It *is* my master." So she took a veil and covered herself.
66 And the servant told Isaac all the things that he had done.
67 Then Isaac brought her into his mother Sarah's tent; and he took Rebekah and she became his wife, and he loved her. So Isaac was comforted after his mother's *death*.

Abraham and Keturah

25 Abraham again took a wife, and her name *was* Keturah.
2 And she bore him Zimran, Jokshan, Medan, Midian, Ishbak, and Shuah.
3 Jokshan begot Sheba and Dedan. And the sons of Dedan were Asshurim, Letushim, and Leummim.
4 And the sons of Midian *were* Ephah, Epher, Hanoch, Abidah, and Eldaah. All these *were* the children of Keturah.

5 And Abraham gave all that he had to Isaac.
6 But Abraham gave gifts to the sons of the concubines which Abraham had; and while he was still living he sent them eastward, away from Isaac his son, to the country of the east.

Abraham's Death and Burial

7 This *is* the sum of the years of Abraham's life which he lived: one hundred and seventy-five years.
8 Then Abraham breathed his last and died in a good old age, an old man and full *of years*, and was gathered to his people.
9 And his sons Isaac and Ishmael buried him in the cave of Machpelah, which *is* before Mamre, in the field of Ephron the son of Zohar the Hittite,
10 the field which Abraham purchased from the sons of Heth. There Abraham was buried, and Sarah his wife.
11 And it came to pass, after the death of Abraham, that God blessed his son Isaac. And Isaac dwelt at Beer Lahai Roi.

The Families of Ishmael and Isaac

12 Now this *is* the genealogy of Ishmael, Abraham's son, whom Hagar the Egyptian, Sarah's maidservant, bore to Abraham.
13 And these *were* the names of the sons of Ishmael, by their names, according to their generations: The firstborn of Ishmael, Nebajoth; then Kedar, Adbeel, Mibsam,
14 Mishma, Dumah, Massa,
15 Hadar,[37] Tema, Jetur, Naphish, and Kedemah.
16 These *were* the sons of Ishmael and these *were* their names, by their towns and their settlements, twelve princes according to their nations.
17 These *were* the years of the life of Ishmael: one hundred and thirty-seven years; and he breathed his last and died, and was gathered to his people.
18 (They dwelt from Havilah as far as Shur, which *is* east of Egypt as you go toward Assyria.) *And* he died in the presence of all his brethren.
19 This *is* the genealogy of Isaac, Abraham's son. Abraham begot Isaac.
20 Isaac was forty years old when he took Rebekah as wife, the daughter of

37 Masoretic Text reads *Hadad.*

Bethuel the Syrian of Padan Aram, the sister of Laban the Syrian.

21 Now Isaac pleaded with the LORD for his wife, because she *was* barren; and the LORD granted his plea, and Rebekah his wife conceived.

22 But the children struggled together within her; and she said, "If *all is* well, why *am I* this *way?*" So she went to inquire of the LORD.

23 And the LORD said to her:

"Two nations *are* in your womb,
Two peoples shall be separated
    from your body;
One people shall be stronger
    than the other,
And the older shall serve the younger."

24 So when her days were fulfilled *for her* to give birth, indeed *there were* twins in her womb.

25 And the first came out red. *He was* like a hairy garment all over; so they called his name Esau.[38]

26 Afterward his brother came out, and his hand took hold of Esau's heel; so his name was called Jacob.[39] Isaac *was* sixty years old when she bore them.

27 So the boys grew. And Esau was a skillful hunter, a man of the field; but Jacob was a mild man, dwelling in tents.

28 And Isaac loved Esau because he ate *of his* game, but Rebekah loved Jacob.

Esau Sells His Birthright

29 Now Jacob cooked a stew; and Esau came in from the field, and he *was* weary.

30 And Esau said to Jacob, "Please feed me with that same red *stew*, for I *am* weary." Therefore his name was called Edom.[40]

31 But Jacob said, "Sell me your birthright as of this day."

32 And Esau said, "Look, I *am* about to die; so what *profit* shall this birthright be to me?"

33 Then Jacob said, "Swear to me as of this day." So he swore to him, and sold his birthright to Jacob.

34 And Jacob gave Esau bread and stew of lentils; then he ate and drank, arose, and went his way. Thus Esau despised *his* birthright.

Isaac and Abimelech

26 There was a famine in the land, besides the first famine that was in the days of Abraham. And Isaac went to Abimelech king of the Philistines, in Gerar.

2 Then the LORD appeared to him and said: "Do not go down to Egypt; dwell in the land of which I shall tell you.

3 "Sojourn in this land, and I will be with you and bless you; for to you and your descendants I give all these lands, and I will perform the oath which I swore to Abraham your father.

4 "And I will make your descendants multiply as the stars of heaven; I will give to your descendants all these lands; and in your seed all the nations of the earth shall be blessed;

5 "because Abraham obeyed My voice and kept My charge, My commandments, My statutes, and My laws."

6 So Isaac dwelt in Gerar.

7 And the men of the place asked *him* about his wife. And he said, "She *is* my sister"; for he was afraid to say, "*She is* my wife," *because he thought,* "lest the men of the place should kill me for Rebekah, because she *is* beautiful to behold."

8 Now it came to pass, when he had been there a long time, that Abimelech king of the Philistines looked through a window, and saw, and there was Isaac, showing endearment to Rebekah his wife.

9 Then Abimelech called Isaac and said, "Quite obviously she *is* your wife; so how could you say, 'She *is* my sister'?" And Isaac said to him, "Because I said, 'Lest I die on account of her.'"

10 And Abimelech said, "What *is* this you have done to us? One of the people might soon have lain with your wife, and you would have brought guilt on us."

11 So Abimelech charged all *his* people, saying, "He who touches this man or his wife shall surely be put to death."

12 Then Isaac sowed in that land, and reaped in the same year a hundredfold; and the LORD blessed him.

13 The man began to prosper, and continued prospering until he became very prosperous;

14 for he had possessions of flocks and possessions of herds and a great number of servants. So the Philistines envied him.

15 Now the Philistines had stopped up all the wells which his father's servants

38 Literally *Hairy*   39 Literally *Supplanter*   40 Literally *Red*

Streams of Living Water

In the hot, parched summer months when temperatures rise upwards to and above one hundred degrees from Galilee to Jericho, water is a precious commodity for the people of Israel. Even in the winter months, many areas of the land get little or no rainfall.

This element was so vital that the Bible records neighboring tribes disputing over water—sometimes to the point of war. In Genesis 26, Isaac fought with the herdsmen of Gerar over the wells dug by Abraham.

There are three methods of obtaining water as recorded in the Bible: by collecting rainfall runoff in a cistern; by digging a well; and by locating a running stream or river. Both digging a well and hewing out a cistern are efforts which symbolize man's work. A stream, however, was considered a gift of grace, freely given by God.

Spring water is the most sought after type of water. Among ancient peoples this was considered to be "living water." In the Hebrew language, the words "running water" and "living water" are one and the same.

Beyond providing a perennial source of water, living water had a unique purpose for the early Israelites. The Jewish law required one to ritually purify himself before entering the holy temple. The only acceptable source of water for this purpose was "running water" or "living water" from a stream. In the first century however, there were no streams at the elevated height of the temple.

To accommodate the desires of the people under his rule, Herod the Great performed an engineering feat still visible today. To provide running water for the required purification baths at the temple, he built an aqueduct carrying water eighteen miles from the pools of Solomon, to the temple stairs in Jerusalem. Herod ingeniously accomplished the task of keeping water running downstream while dropping the aqueduct only ninety feet over eighteen miles.

In front of these famous purification baths adjacent to the stairway entrance of the temple, Jesus stood on the final day of the Feast of Dedication and cried out: "He who believes in Me . . . out of his heart will flow rivers of living water" (John 7:38).

In one bold statement, Jesus offered living water that could purify and satisfy the heart, mind, and soul. If we have faith in Him, this living water has the power to purify our lives from negative emotions, thoughts, and deeds. Even in the most scorched, dry days of our lives, there is an unending spring of love, joy, and peace.

How do we find this living water? Jesus told the Samaritan woman at the well, "Whoever drinks of this water will thirst again, but whoever drinks of the water that I shall give him will never thirst. . . a fountain of water springing up into everlasting life" (John 4:13, 14).

We find this living water in Jesus Himself and in the life that we experience through our faith in Him.

had dug in the days of Abraham his father, and they had filled them with earth.
16 And Abimelech said to Isaac, "Go away from us, for you are much mightier than we."
17 Then Isaac departed from there and pitched his tent in the Valley of Gerar, and dwelt there.
18 And Isaac dug again the wells of water which they had dug in the days of Abraham his father, for the Philistines had stopped them up after the death of Abraham. He called them by the names which his father had called them.
19 Also Isaac's servants dug in the valley, and found a well of running water there.
20 But the herdsmen of Gerar quarreled with Isaac's herdsmen, saying, "The water is ours." So he called the name of the well Esek,41 because they quarreled with him.
21 Then they dug another well, and they quarreled over that one also. So he called its name Sitnah.42
22 And he moved from there and dug another well, and they did not quarrel over it. So he called its name Rehoboth,43 because he said, "For now the LORD has made room for us, and we shall be fruitful in the land."
23 Then he went up from there to Beersheba.
24 And the LORD appeared to him the same night and said, "I am the God of your father Abraham; do not fear, for I am with you. I will bless you and multiply your descendants for My servant Abraham's sake."
25 So he built an altar there and called on the name of the LORD, and he pitched his tent there; and there Isaac's servants dug a well.
26 Then Abimelech came to him from Gerar with Ahuzzath, one of his friends, and Phichol the commander of his army.
27 And Isaac said to them, "Why have you come to me, since you hate me and have sent me away from you?"
28 But they said, "We have certainly seen that the LORD is with you. So we said, 'Let there now be an oath between us, between you and us; and let us make a covenant with you,
29 'that you will do us no harm, since we have not touched you, and since we have done nothing to you but good and have

sent you away in peace. You are now the blessed of the LORD.' "
30 So he made them a feast, and they ate and drank.
31 Then they arose early in the morning and swore an oath with one another; and Isaac sent them away, and they departed from him in peace.
32 It came to pass the same day that Isaac's servants came and told him about the well which they had dug, and said to him, "We have found water."
33 So he called it Shebah.44 Therefore the name of the city is Beersheba45 to this day.
34 When Esau was forty years old, he took as wives Judith the daughter of Beeri the Hittite, and Basemath the daughter of Elon the Hittite.
35 And they were a grief of mind to Isaac and Rebekah.

Isaac Blesses Jacob

27 Now it came to pass, when Isaac was old and his eyes were so dim that he could not see, that he called Esau his older son and said to him, "My son." And he answered him, "Here I am."
2 And he said, "Behold now, I am old. I do not know the day of my death.
3 "Now therefore, please take your weapons, your quiver and your bow, and go out to the field and hunt game for me.
4 "And make me savory food, such as I love, and bring it to me that I may eat, that my soul may bless you before I die."
5 Now Rebekah was listening when Isaac spoke to Esau his son. And Esau went to the field to hunt game and to bring it.
6 So Rebekah spoke to Jacob her son, saying, "Indeed I heard your father speak to Esau your brother, saying,
7 'Bring me game and make savory food for me, that I may eat it and bless you in the presence of the LORD before my death.'
8 "Now therefore, my son, obey my voice according to what I command you.
9 "Go now to the flock and bring me from there two choice kids of the goats, and I will make savory food from them for your father, such as he loves.
10 "Then you shall take it to your father, that he may eat it, and that he may bless you before his death."

---

41 Literally *Quarrel*   42 Literally *Enmity*   43 Literally *Spaciousness*
44 Literally *Oath* or *Seven*   45 Literally *Well of the Oath* or *Well of the Seven*

11 And Jacob said to Rebekah his mother, "Look, Esau my brother *is* a hairy man, and I *am* a smooth-*skinned* man.
12 "Perhaps my father will feel me, and I shall seem to be a deceiver to him; and I shall bring a curse on myself and not a blessing."
13 But his mother said to him, "*Let* your curse *be* on me, my son; only obey my voice, and go, get *them* for me."
14 And he went and got *them* and brought *them* to his mother, and his mother made savory food, such as his father loved.
15 Then Rebekah took the choice clothes of her elder son Esau, which *were* with her in the house, and put them on Jacob her younger son.
16 And she put the skins of the kids of the goats on his hands and on the smooth part of his neck.
17 Then she gave the savory food and the bread, which she had prepared, into the hand of her son Jacob.
18 So he went to his father and said, "My father"; and he said, "Here I am. Who *are* you, my son?"
19 And Jacob said to his father, "I *am* Esau your firstborn; I have done just as you told me; please arise, sit and eat of my game, that your soul may bless me."
20 But Isaac said to his son, "How *is it* that you have found *it* so quickly, my son?" And he said, "Because the LORD your God brought *it* to me."
21 Then Isaac said to Jacob, "Please come near, that I may feel you, my son, whether you *are* really my son Esau or not."
22 So Jacob went near to Isaac his father, and he felt him and said, "The voice *is* Jacob's voice, but the hands *are* the hands of Esau."
23 And he did not recognize him, because his hands were hairy like his brother Esau's hands; so he blessed him.
24 Then he said, "*Are* you really my son Esau?" And he said, "I *am*."
25 And he said, "Bring *it* near to me, and I will eat of my son's game, so that my soul may bless you." So he brought *it* near to him, and he ate; and he brought him wine, and he drank.
26 Then his father Isaac said to him, "Come near now and kiss me, my son."
27 And he came near and kissed him; and he smelled the smell of his clothing, and blessed him and said:

"Surely, the smell of my son
Is like the smell of a field
Which the LORD has blessed.
28 Therefore may God give you
Of the dew of heaven,
Of the fatness of the earth,
And plenty of grain and wine.
29 Let peoples serve you,
And nations bow down to you.
Be master over your brethren,
And let your mother's sons
bow down to you.
Cursed *be* everyone who curses you,
And blessed *be* those who bless you!"

Esau's Lost Hope

30 Then it happened, as soon as Isaac had finished blessing Jacob, and Jacob had scarcely gone out from the presence of Isaac his father, that Esau his brother came in from his hunting.
31 He also had made savory food, and brought it to his father, and said to his father, "Let my father arise and eat of his son's game, that your soul may bless me."
32 And his father Isaac said to him, "Who *are* you?" And he said, "I *am* your son, your firstborn, Esau."
33 Then Isaac trembled exceedingly, and said, "Who? Where *is* the one who hunted game and brought *it* to me? I ate all *of it* before you came, and I have blessed him—*and* indeed he shall be blessed."
34 When Esau heard the words of his father, he cried with an exceedingly great and bitter cry, and said to his father, "Bless me, *even* me also, O my father!"
35 But he said, "Your brother came with deceit and has taken away your blessing."
36 And Esau[46] said, "Is he not rightly named Jacob? For he has supplanted me these two times. He took away my birthright, and now look, he has taken away my blessing!" And he said, "Have you not reserved a blessing for me?"
37 Then Isaac answered and said to Esau, "Indeed I have made him your master, and all his brethren I have given to him as servants; with grain and wine I have sustained him. What shall I do now for you, my son?"
38 And Esau said to his father, "Have you only one blessing, my father? Bless

46 Literally *he*

me, *even* me also, O my father!" And
Esau lifted up his voice and wept.
39 Then Isaac his father answered and
said to him:

"Behold, your dwelling shall be
　of the fatness of the earth,
And of the dew of heaven from above.
40 By your sword you shall live,
And you shall serve your brother;
And it shall come to pass,
　when you become restless,
That you shall break his yoke
　from your neck."　.

Jacob Escapes from Esau

41 So Esau hated Jacob because of the
blessing with which his father blessed
him, and Esau said in his heart, "The
days of mourning for my father are at
hand; then I will kill my brother Jacob."
42 And the words of Esau her older son
were told to Rebekah. So she sent and
called Jacob her younger son, and said to
him, "Surely your brother Esau comforts
himself concerning you *by intending* to
kill you.
43 "Now therefore, my son, obey my
voice: arise, flee to my brother Laban in
Haran.
44 "And stay with him a few days, until
your brother's fury turns away,
45 "until your brother's anger turns away
from you, and he forgets what you have
done to him; then I will send and bring
you from there. Why should I be bereaved also of you both in one day?"
46 And Rebekah said to Isaac, "I am
weary of my life because of the daughters
of Heth; if Jacob takes a wife of the
daughters of Heth, like these *who are* the
daughters of the land, what good will my
life be to me?"

28 Then Isaac called Jacob and
blessed him, and charged him, and
said to him: "You shall not take a wife
from the daughters of Canaan.
2 "Arise, go to Padan Aram, to the
house of Bethuel your mother's father;
and take yourself a wife from there of the
daughters of Laban your mother's
brother.
3 "May God Almighty bless you,
And make you fruitful
　and multiply you,

That you may be an assembly
　of peoples;
4 And give you the blessing of Abraham,
To you and your descendants with you,
That you may inherit the land
In which you are a stranger,
Which God gave to Abraham."

5 So Isaac sent Jacob away, and he
went to Padan Aram, to Laban the son of
Bethuel the Syrian, the brother of Rebekah, the mother of Jacob and Esau.

Esau Marries Mahalath

6 Esau saw that Isaac had blessed Jacob
and sent him away to Padan Aram to
take himself a wife from there, *and that* as
he blessed him he gave him a charge, saying, "You shall not take a wife from the
daughters of Canaan,"
7 and that Jacob had obeyed his father
and his mother and had gone to Padan
Aram.
8 Also Esau saw that the daughters of
Canaan did not please his father Isaac.
9 So Esau went to Ishmael and took
Mahalath the daughter of Ishmael, Abraham's son, the sister of Nebajoth, to be
his wife in addition to the wives he had.

Jacob's Vow at Bethel

10 Now Jacob went out from Beersheba
and went toward Haran.
11 So he came to a certain place and
stayed there all night, because the sun
had set. And he took one of the stones of
that place and put it at his head, and he
lay down in that place to sleep.
12 Then he dreamed, and behold, a ladder *was* set up on the earth, and its top
reached to heaven; and there the angels
of God were ascending and descending
on it.
13 And behold, the LORD stood above it
and said: "I *am* the LORD God of Abraham your father and the God of Isaac;
the land on which you lie I will give to
you and your descendants.
14 "Also your descendants shall be as the
dust of the earth; you shall spread abroad
to the west and the east, to the north and
the south; and in you and in your seed all
the families of the earth shall be blessed.
15 "Behold, I *am* with you and will keep
you wherever you go, and will bring you
back to this land; for I will not leave you
until I have done what I have spoken to
you."

16 Then Jacob awoke from his sleep and said, "Surely the LORD is in this place, and I did not know *it*."
17 And he was afraid and said, "How awesome *is* this place! This *is* none other than the house of God, and this *is* the gate of heaven!"
18 Then Jacob rose early in the morning, and took the stone that he had put at his head, set it up as a pillar, and poured oil on top of it.
19 And he called the name of that place Bethel;[47] but the name of that city had been Luz previously.
20 Then Jacob made a vow, saying, "If God will be with me, and keep me in this way that I am going, and give me bread to eat and clothing to put on,
21 "so that I come back to my father's house in peace, then the LORD shall be my God.
22 "And this stone which I have set as a pillar shall be God's house, and of all that You give me I will surely give a tenth to You."

Jacob Meets Rachel

29 So Jacob went on his journey and came to the land of the people of the east.
2 And he looked, and saw a well in the field; and behold, there *were* three flocks of sheep lying by it; for out of that well they watered the flocks. A large stone *was* on the well's mouth.
3 Now all the flocks would be gathered there; and they would roll the stone from the well's mouth, water the sheep, and put the stone back in its place on the well's mouth.
4 And Jacob said to them, "My brethren, where *are* you from?" And they said, "We *are* from Haran."
5 Then he said to them, "Do you know Laban the son of Nahor?" And they said, "We know him."
6 So he said to them, "Is he well?" And they said, "*He is* well. And look, his daughter Rachel is coming with the sheep."
7 Then he said, "Look, *it is* still high day; *it is* not time for the cattle to be gathered together. Water the sheep, and go and feed *them*."
8 But they said, "We cannot until all the flocks are gathered together, and they

have rolled the stone from the well's mouth; then we water the sheep."
9 Now while he was still speaking with them, Rachel came with her father's sheep, for she was a shepherdess.
10 And it came to pass, when Jacob saw Rachel the daughter of Laban his mother's brother, and the sheep of Laban his mother's brother, that Jacob went near and rolled the stone from the well's mouth, and watered the flock of Laban his mother's brother.
11 Then Jacob kissed Rachel, and lifted up his voice and wept.
12 And Jacob told Rachel that he *was* her father's relative and that he *was* Rebekah's son. So she ran and told her father.
13 Then it came to pass, when Laban heard the report about Jacob his sister's son, that he ran to meet him, and embraced him and kissed him, and brought him to his house. So he told Laban all these things.
14 And Laban said to him, "Surely you *are* my bone and my flesh." And he stayed with him for a month.

Jacob Marries Leah and Rachel

15 Then Laban said to Jacob, "Because you *are* my relative, should you therefore serve me for nothing? Tell me, what *should* your wages *be*?"
16 Now Laban had two daughters: the name of the elder *was* Leah, and the name of the younger *was* Rachel.
17 Leah's eyes *were* delicate, but Rachel was beautiful of form and appearance.
18 Now Jacob loved Rachel; and he said, "I will serve you seven years for Rachel your younger daughter."
19 And Laban said, "*It is* better that I give her to you than that I should give her to another man. Stay with me."
20 So Jacob served seven years for Rachel, and they seemed *but* a few days to him because of the love he had for her.
21 Then Jacob said to Laban, "Give *me* my wife, for my days are fulfilled, that I may go in to her."
22 And Laban gathered together all the men of the place and made a feast.
23 Now it came to pass in the evening, that he took Leah his daughter and brought her to Jacob; and he went in to her.

47 Literally *House of God*

24 And Laban gave his maid Zilpah to his daughter Leah *as* a maid.
25 So it came to pass in the morning, that behold, it *was* Leah. And he said to Laban, "What is this you have done to me? Was it not for Rachel that I served you? Why then have you deceived me?"
26 And Laban said, "It must not be done so in our country, to give the younger before the firstborn.
27 "Fulfill her week, and we will give you this one also for the service which you will serve with me still another seven years."
28 Then Jacob did so and fulfilled her week. So he gave him his daughter Rachel as wife also.
29 And Laban gave his maid Bilhah to his daughter Rachel as a maid.
30 Then Jacob[48] also went in to Rachel, and he also loved Rachel more than Leah. And he served with Laban still another seven years.

The Children of Jacob

31 When the LORD saw that Leah *was* unloved, He opened her womb; but Rachel *was* barren.
32 So Leah conceived and bore a son, and she called his name Reuben;[49] for she said, "The LORD has surely looked on my affliction. Now therefore, my husband will love me."
33 Then she conceived again and bore a son, and said, "Because the LORD has heard that I *am* unloved, He has therefore given me this *son* also." And she called his name Simeon.[50]
34 She conceived again and bore a son, and said, "Now this time my husband will become attached to me, because I have borne him three sons." Therefore his name was called Levi.[51]
35 And she conceived again and bore a son, and said, "Now I will praise the LORD." Therefore she called his name Judah.[52] Then she stopped bearing.

30 Now when Rachel saw that she bore Jacob no children, Rachel envied her sister, and said to Jacob, "Give me children, or else I die!"
2 And Jacob's anger was aroused against Rachel, and he said, "*Am* I in the place of God, who has withheld from you the fruit of the womb?"

3 So she said, "Here is my maid Bilhah; go in to her, and she will bear *a child* on my knees, that I also may have children by her."
4 Then she gave him Bilhah her maid as wife, and Jacob went in to her.
5 And Bilhah conceived and bore Jacob a son.
6 Then Rachel said, "God has judged my case; and He has also heard my voice and given me a son." Therefore she called his name Dan.[53]
7 And Rachel's maid Bilhah conceived again and bore Jacob a second son.
8 Then Rachel said, "With great wrestlings I have wrestled with my sister, *and* indeed I have prevailed." So she called his name Naphtali.[54]
9 When Leah saw that she had stopped bearing, she took Zilpah her maid and gave her to Jacob as wife.
10 And Leah's maid Zilpah bore Jacob a son.
11 Then Leah said, "A troop[55] comes!" So she called his name Gad.[56]
12 And Leah's maid Zilpah bore Jacob a second son.
13 Then Leah said, "I am happy, for the daughters will call me blessed." So she called his name Asher.[57]
14 Now Reuben went in the days of wheat harvest and found mandrakes in the field, and brought them to his mother Leah. Then Rachel said to Leah, "Please give me *some* of your son's mandrakes."
15 But she said to her, "*Is it* a small matter that you have taken away my husband? Would you take away my son's mandrakes also?" And Rachel said, "Therefore he will lie with you tonight for your son's mandrakes."
16 When Jacob came out of the field in the evening, Leah went out to meet him and said, "You must come in to me, for I have surely hired you with my son's mandrakes." And he lay with her that night.
17 And God listened to Leah, and she conceived and bore Jacob a fifth son.
18 Leah said, "God has given me my hire, because I have given my maid to my husband." So she called his name Issachar.[58]
19 Then Leah conceived again and bore Jacob a sixth son.
20 And Leah said, "God has endowed

48 Literally *he*　49 Literally *See, a Son*　50 Literally *Heard*　51 Literally *Attached*　52 Literally *Praise*
53 Literally *Judge*　54 Literally *My Wrestling*　55 Or *fortune*　56 Literally *Troop* or *Fortune*　57 Literally *Happy*
58 Literally *Hire*

me *with* a good endowment; now my husband will dwell with me, because I have borne him six sons." So she called his name Zebulun.[59]

21 Afterward she bore a daughter, and called her name Dinah.

22 Then God remembered Rachel, and God listened to her and opened her womb.

23 And she conceived and bore a son, and said, "God has taken away my reproach."

24 So she called his name Joseph,[60] and said, "The LORD shall add to me another son."

Jacob's Agreement with Laban

25 And it came to pass, when Rachel had borne Joseph, that Jacob said to Laban, "Send me away, that I may go to my own place and to my country.

26 "Give *me* my wives and my children for whom I have served you, and let me go; for you know my service which I have done for you."

27 And Laban said to him, "Please *stay*, if I have found favor in your eyes, *for* I have learned by experience that the LORD has blessed me for your sake."

28 Then he said, "Name me your wages, and I will give *it*."

29 And Jacob[61] said to him, "You know how I have served you and how your livestock has been with me.

30 "For what you had before I *came was* little, and it is *now* increased to a great amount; the LORD has blessed you since my coming. And now, when shall I also provide for my own house?"

31 So he said, "What shall I give you?" And Jacob said, "You shall not give me anything. If you will do this thing for me, I will again feed and keep your flocks:

32 "Let me pass through all your flock today, removing from there all the speckled and spotted sheep, and all the brown ones among the lambs, and the spotted and speckled among the goats; and *these* shall be my wages.

33 "So my righteousness will answer for me in time to come, when the subject of my wages comes before you: every one that *is* not speckled and spotted among the goats, and brown among the lambs, will be considered stolen, if *it is* with me."

34 And Laban said, "Oh, that it were according to your word!"

35 So he removed that day the male goats that were speckled and spotted, all the female goats that were speckled and spotted, every one that had *some* white in it, and all the brown ones among the lambs, and gave *them* into the hand of his sons.

36 Then he put three days' journey between himself and Jacob, and Jacob fed the rest of Laban's flocks.

37 Now Jacob took for himself rods of green poplar and of the almond and chestnut trees, peeled white strips in them, and exposed the white which *was* in the rods.

38 And the rods which he had peeled, he set before the flocks in the gutters, in the watering troughs where the flocks came to drink, so that they should conceive when they came to drink.

39 So the flocks conceived before the rods, and the flocks brought forth streaked, speckled, and spotted.

40 Then Jacob separated the lambs, and made the flocks face toward the streaked and all the brown in the flock of Laban; but he put his own flocks by themselves and did not put them with Laban's flock.

41 And it came to pass, whenever the stronger livestock conceived, that Jacob placed the rods before the eyes of the livestock in the gutters, that they might conceive among the rods.

42 But when the flocks were feeble, he did not put *them* in; so the feebler were Laban's and the stronger Jacob's.

43 Thus the man became exceedingly prosperous, and had large flocks, female and male servants, and camels and donkeys.

Jacob Flees from Laban

31 Now Jacob[62] heard the words of Laban's sons, saying, "Jacob has taken away all that was our father's, and from what was our father's he has acquired all this wealth."

2 And Jacob saw the countenance of Laban, and indeed it *was* not *favorable* toward him as before.

3 Then the LORD said to Jacob, "Return to the land of your fathers and to your kindred, and I will be with you."

4 So Jacob sent and called Rachel and Leah to the field, to his flock,

5 and said to them, "I see your father's countenance, that it *is* not *favorable*

---

59 Literally *Dwelling* 60 Literally *He Will Add* 61 Literally *he* 62 Literally *he*

toward me as before; but the God of my father has been with me.

6 "And you know that with all my might I have served your father.

7 "Yet your father has deceived me and changed my wages ten times, but God did not allow him to hurt me.

8 "If he said thus: 'The speckled shall be your wages,' then all the flocks bore speckled. And if he said thus: 'The streaked shall be your wages,' then all the flocks bore streaked.

9 "So God has taken away the livestock of your father and given *them* to me.

10 "And it happened, at the time when the flocks conceived, that I lifted my eyes and saw in a dream, and behold, the rams which leaped upon the flocks *were* streaked, speckled, and gray-spotted.

11 "Then the Angel of God spoke to me in a dream, saying, 'Jacob.' And I said, 'Here I am.'

12 "And He said, 'Lift your eyes now and see, all the rams which leap on the flocks *are* streaked, speckled, and gray-spotted; for I have seen all that Laban is doing to you.

13 'I *am* the God of Bethel, where you anointed the pillar *and* where you made a vow to Me. Now arise, get out of this land, and return to the land of your kindred.' "

14 Then Rachel and Leah answered and said to him, "Is there still any portion or inheritance for us in our father's house?

15 "Are we not considered strangers by him? For he has sold us, and also completely consumed our money.

16 "For all these riches which God has taken from our father *are really* ours and our children's; now then, whatever God has said to you, do it."

17 Then Jacob rose and set his sons and his wives on camels.

18 And he carried away all his livestock and all his possessions which he had gained, his acquired livestock which he had gained in Padan Aram, to go to his father Isaac in the land of Canaan.

19 Now Laban had gone to shear his sheep, and Rachel had stolen the household idols that were her father's.

20 And Jacob stole away, unknown to Laban the Syrian, in that he did not tell him that he intended to flee.

21 So he fled with all that he had. He arose and crossed the river, and headed toward the mountains of Gilead.

Laban Pursues Jacob

22 And Laban was told on the third day that Jacob had fled.

23 Then he took his brethren with him and pursued him for seven days' journey, and he overtook him in the mountains of Gilead.

24 But God had come to Laban the Syrian in a dream by night, and said to him, "Be careful that you speak to Jacob neither good nor bad."

25 So Laban overtook Jacob. Now Jacob had pitched his tent in the mountains, and Laban with his brethren pitched in the mountains of Gilead.

26 And Laban said to Jacob: "What have you done, that you have stolen away unknown to me, and carried away my daughters like captives *taken* with the sword?

27 "Why did you flee away secretly, and steal away from me, and not tell me; for I might have sent you away with joy and songs, with timbrel and harp?

28 "And you did not allow me to kiss my sons and my daughters. Now you have done foolishly in *so* doing.

29 "It is in my power to do you harm, but the God of your father spoke to me last night, saying, 'Be careful that you speak to Jacob neither good nor bad.'

30 "And now you have surely gone because you greatly long for your father's house, *but* why did you steal my gods?"

31 Then Jacob answered and said to Laban, "Because I was afraid, for I said, 'Perhaps you would take your daughters from me by force.'

32 "With whomever you find your gods, do not let him live. In the presence of our brethren, identify what I have of yours and take *it* with you." For Jacob did not know that Rachel had stolen them.

33 And Laban went into Jacob's tent, into Leah's tent, and into the two maids' tents, but he did not find *them*. Then he went out of Leah's tent and entered Rachel's tent.

34 Now Rachel had taken the household idols, put them in the camel's saddle, and sat on them. And Laban searched all about the tent but did not find *them*.

35 And she said to her father, "Let it not

displease my lord that I cannot rise before you, for the manner of women *is* with me." And he searched but did not find the household idols.
36 Then Jacob was angry and rebuked Laban, and Jacob answered and said to Laban: "What *is* my trespass? What *is* my sin, that you have so hotly pursued me?
37 "Although you have searched all my things, what part of your household things have you found? Set *it* here before my brethren and your brethren, that they may judge between us both!
38 "These twenty years I *have been* with you; your ewes and your female goats have not miscarried their young, and I have not eaten the rams of your flock.
39 "That which was torn *by beasts* I did not bring to you; I bore the loss of it. You required it from my hand, *whether* stolen by day or stolen by night.
40 *"There* I was! In the day the drought consumed me, and the frost by night, and my sleep departed from my eyes.
41 "Thus I have been in your house twenty years; I served you fourteen years for your two daughters, and six years for your flock, and you have changed my wages ten times.
42 "Unless the God of my father, the God of Abraham and the Fear of Isaac, had been with me, surely now you would have sent me away empty-handed. God has seen my affliction and the labor of my hands, and rebuked *you* last night."

Laban's Covenant with Jacob

43 And Laban answered and said to Jacob, *"These* daughters *are* my daughters, and *these* children *are* my children, and *this* flock *is* my flock; all that you see *is* mine. But what can I do this day to these my daughters or to their children whom they have borne?
44 "Now therefore, come, let us make a covenant, you and I, and let it be a witness between you and me."
45 So Jacob took a stone and set it up *as* a pillar.
46 Then Jacob said to his brethren, "Gather stones." And they took stones and made a heap, and they ate there on the heap.
47 Laban called it Jegar Sahadutha,[63] but Jacob called it Galeed.[64]

48 And Laban said, "This heap *is* a witness between you and me this day." Therefore its name was called Galeed,
49 also Mizpah,[65] because he said, "May the LORD watch between you and me when we are absent one from another.
50 "If you afflict my daughters, or if you take *other* wives besides my daughters, *although* no man *is* with us—see, God *is* witness between you and me!"
51 Then Laban said to Jacob, "Here is this heap and here is *this* pillar, which I have placed between you and me.
52 "This heap *is* a witness, and *this* pillar *is* a witness, that I will not pass beyond this heap to you, and you will not pass beyond this heap and this pillar to me, for harm.
53 "The God of Abraham, the God of Nahor, and the God of their father judge between us." And Jacob swore by the Fear of his father Isaac.
54 Then Jacob offered a sacrifice on the mountain, and called his brethren to eat bread. And they ate bread and stayed all night on the mountain.
55 And early in the morning Laban arose, and kissed his sons and daughters and blessed them. Then Laban departed and returned to his place.

Esau Comes to Meet Jacob

32 So Jacob went on his way, and the angels of God met him.
2 When Jacob saw them, he said, "This *is* God's camp." And he called the name of that place Mahanaim.[66]
3 Then Jacob sent messengers before him to Esau his brother in the land of Seir, the country of Edom.
4 And he commanded them, saying, "Speak thus to my lord Esau, 'Thus your servant Jacob says: "I have sojourned with Laban and stayed there until now.
5 "I have oxen, donkeys, flocks, and male and female servants; and I have sent to tell my lord, that I may find favor in your sight." ' "
6 Then the messengers returned to Jacob, saying, "We came to your brother Esau, and he also is coming to meet you, and four hundred men *are* with him."
7 So Jacob was greatly afraid and distressed; and he divided the people that *were* with him, and the flocks and herds and camels, into two companies.

---

63 Literally, in Aramaic, *Heap of Witness*   64 Literally, in Hebrew, *Heap of Witness*   65 Literally *Watch*
66 Literally *Double Camp*

8 And he said, "If Esau comes to the one company and attacks it, then the other company which is left will escape."
9 Then Jacob said, "O God of my father Abraham and God of my father Isaac, the LORD who said to me, 'Return to your country and to your kindred, and I will deal well with you':
10 "I am not worthy of the least of all the mercies and of all the truth which You have shown Your servant; for I crossed over this Jordan with my staff, and now I have become two companies.
11 "Deliver me, I pray, from the hand of my brother, from the hand of Esau; for I fear him, lest he come and attack me *and* the mother with the children.
12 "For You said, 'I will surely treat you well, and make your descendants as the sand of the sea, which cannot be numbered for multitude.' "
13 So he lodged there that same night, and took what came to his hand as a present for Esau his brother:
14 two hundred female goats and twenty male goats, two hundred ewes and twenty rams,
15 thirty milk camels with their colts, forty cows and ten bulls, twenty female donkeys and ten foals.
16 Then he delivered *them* to the hand of his servants, every drove by itself, and said to his servants, "Pass over before me, and put some distance between successive droves."
17 And he commanded the first one, saying, "When Esau my brother meets you and asks you, saying, 'To whom do you belong, and where are you going? Whose *are* these in front of you?'
18 "then you shall say, 'They *are* your servant Jacob's. It *is* a present sent to my lord Esau; and behold, he also *is* behind us.' "
19 So he commanded the second, the third, and all who followed the droves, saying, "In this manner you shall speak to Esau when you find him;
20 "and also say, 'Behold, your servant Jacob *is* behind us.' " For he said, "I will appease him with the present that goes before me, and afterward I will see his face; perhaps he will accept me."
21 So the present went on over before him, but he himself lodged that night in the camp.

Wrestling with God

22 And he arose that night and took his two wives, his two maidservants, and his eleven sons, and crossed over the ford of Jabbok.
23 He took them, sent them over the brook, and sent over what he had.
24 Then Jacob was left alone; and a Man wrestled with him until the breaking of day.
25 Now when He saw that He did not prevail against him, He touched the socket of his hip; and the socket of Jacob's hip was out of joint as He wrestled with him.
26 And He said, "Let Me go, for the day breaks." But he said, "I will not let You go unless You bless me!"
27 So He said to him, "What *is* your name?" And he said, "Jacob."
28 And He said, "Your name shall no longer be called Jacob, but Israel;[67] for you have struggled with God and with men, and have prevailed."
29 Then Jacob asked *Him*, saying, "Tell *me* Your name, I pray." And He said, "Why *is* it *that* you ask about My name?" And He blessed him there.
30 And Jacob called the name of the place Peniel:[68] "For I have seen God face to face, and my life is preserved."
31 Just as he crossed over Penuel[69] the sun rose on him, and he limped on his hip.
32 Therefore to this day the children of Israel do not eat the muscle that shrank, which *is* on the hip socket, because He touched the socket of Jacob's hip in the muscle that shrank.

Jacob and Esau Meet

33 Now Jacob lifted his eyes and looked, and there, Esau was coming, and with him were four hundred men. So he divided the children among Leah, Rachel, and the two maidservants.
2 And he put the maidservants and their children in front, Leah and her children behind, and Rachel and Joseph last.
3 Then he crossed over before them and bowed himself to the ground seven times, until he came near to his brother.
4 But Esau ran to meet him, and embraced him, and fell on his neck and kissed him, and they wept.
5 And he lifted his eyes and saw the

67 Literally *Prince with God*   68 Literally *Face of God*   69 Same as *Peniel,* verse 30

women and children, and said, "Who *are* these with you?" And he said, "The children whom God has graciously given your servant."
6 Then the maidservants came near, they and their children, and bowed down.
7 And Leah also came near with her children, and they bowed down. Afterward Joseph and Rachel came near, and they bowed down.
8 Then Esau said, "What *do* you *mean by* all this company which I met?" And he said, "*These are* to find favor in the sight of my lord."
9 But Esau said, "I have enough, my brother; keep what you have for yourself."
10 And Jacob said, "No, please, if I have now found favor in your sight, then receive my present from my hand, inasmuch as I have seen your face as though I had seen the face of God, and you were pleased with me.
11 "Please, take my blessing that is brought to you, because God has dealt graciously with me, and because I have enough." And he urged him, and he took *it.*
12 Then Esau said, "Let us take our journey; let us go, and I will go before you."
13 But Jacob said to him, "My lord knows that the children *are* weak, and the flocks and herds which are nursing *are* with me. And if the men should drive them hard one day, all the flock will die.
14 "Please let my lord go on ahead before his servant. I will lead on slowly at a pace which the livestock that go before me, and the children, are able to endure, until I come to my lord in Seir."
15 And Esau said, "Now let me leave with you *some* of the people who *are* with me." But he said, "What need is there? Let me find favor in the sight of my lord."
16 So Esau returned that day on his way to Seir.
17 And Jacob journeyed to Succoth, built himself a house, and made booths for his livestock. Therefore the name of the place is called Succoth.[70]

Jacob Comes to Canaan

18 Then Jacob came safely to the city of Shechem, which *is* in the land of Canaan, when he came from Padan Aram; and he pitched his tent before the city.
19 And he bought the parcel of land,

where he had pitched his tent, from the children of Hamor, Shechem's father, for one hundred pieces of money.
20 Then he erected an altar there and called it El Elohe Israel.[71]

The Dinah Incident

34 Now Dinah the daughter of Leah, whom she had borne to Jacob, went out to see the daughters of the land.
2 And when Shechem the son of Hamor the Hivite, prince of the country, saw her, he took her and lay with her, and violated her.
3 His soul was strongly attracted to Dinah the daughter of Jacob, and he loved the young woman and spoke kindly to the young woman.
4 So Shechem spoke to his father Hamor, saying, "Get me this young woman as a wife."
5 And Jacob heard that he had defiled Dinah his daughter. Now his sons were with his livestock in the field; so Jacob held his peace until they came.
6 Then Hamor the father of Shechem went out to Jacob to speak with him.
7 And the sons of Jacob came in from the field when they heard *it;* and the men were grieved and very angry, because he had done a disgraceful thing in Israel by lying with Jacob's daughter, a thing which ought not to be done.
8 But Hamor spoke with them, saying, "The soul of my son Shechem longs for your daughter. Please give her to him as a wife.
9 "And make marriages with us; give your daughters to us, and take our daughters to yourselves.
10 "So you shall dwell with us, and the land shall be before you. Dwell and trade in it, and acquire possessions for yourselves in it."
11 Then Shechem said to her father and her brothers, "Let me find favor in your eyes, and whatever you say to me I will give.
12 "Ask me ever so much dowry and gift, and I will give according to what you say to me; but give me the young woman as a wife."
13 But the sons of Jacob answered Shechem and Hamor his father, and spoke deceitfully, because he had defiled Dinah their sister.
14 And they said to them, "We cannot

70 Literally *Booths*   71 Literally *God, the God of Israel*

do this thing, to give our sister to one who is uncircumcised, for that *would be* a reproach to us.

15 "But on this *condition* we will consent to you: If you will become as we *are*, if every male of you is circumcised,

16 "then we will give our daughters to you, and we will take your daughters to us; and we will dwell with you, and we will become one people.

17 "But if you will not heed us and be circumcised, then we will take our daughter and be gone."

18 And their words pleased Hamor and Shechem, Hamor's son.

19 So the young man did not delay to do the thing, because he delighted in Jacob's daughter. He *was* more honorable than all the household of his father.

20 And Hamor and Shechem his son came to the gate of their city, and spoke with the men of their city, saying:

21 "These men *are* at peace with us. Therefore let them dwell in the land and trade in it. For indeed the land *is* large enough for them. Let us take their daughters to us as wives, and let us give them our daughters.

22 "Only on this *condition* will the men consent to dwell with us, to be one people: if every male among us is circumcised as they *are* circumcised.

23 "*Will* not their livestock, their property, and every animal of theirs *be* ours? Only let us consent to them, and they will dwell with us."

24 And all who went out of the gate of his city heeded Hamor and Shechem his son; every male was circumcised, all who went out of the gate of his city.

25 Now it came to pass on the third day, when they were in pain, that two of the sons of Jacob, Simeon and Levi, Dinah's brothers, each took his sword and came boldly upon the city and killed all the males.

26 And they killed Hamor and Shechem his son with the edge of the sword, and took Dinah from Shechem's house, and went out.

27 The sons of Jacob came upon the slain, and plundered the city, because their sister had been defiled.

28 They took their sheep, their oxen, and their donkeys, what *was* in the city and what *was* in the field,

29 and all their wealth. All their little ones and their wives they took captive; and they plundered even all that *was* in the houses.

30 Then Jacob said to Simeon and Levi, "You have troubled me by making me obnoxious among the inhabitants of the land, among the Canaanites and the Perizzites; and since I *am* few in number, they will gather themselves together against me and kill me. I shall be destroyed, my household and I."

31 But they said, "Should he treat our sister like a harlot?"

Jacob's Return to Bethel

35 Then God said to Jacob, "Arise, go up to Bethel and dwell there; and make an altar there to God, who appeared to you when you fled from the face of Esau your brother."

2 And Jacob said to his household and to all who *were* with him, "Put away the foreign gods that *are* among you, purify yourselves, and change your garments.

3 "Then let us arise and go up to Bethel; and I will make an altar there to God, who answered me in the day of my distress and has been with me in the way which I have gone."

4 So they gave Jacob all the foreign gods which *were* in their hands, and *all their* earrings which *were* in their ears; and Jacob hid them under the terebinth tree which *was* by Shechem.

5 And they journeyed, and the terror of God was upon the cities that *were* all around them, and they did not pursue the sons of Jacob.

6 So Jacob came to Luz (that *is*, Bethel), which *is* in the land of Canaan, he and all the people who *were* with him.

7 And he built an altar there and called the place El Bethel,[72] because there God appeared to him when he fled from the face of his brother.

8 Now Deborah, Rebekah's nurse, died, and she was buried below Bethel under the terebinth tree. So the name of it was called Allon Bachuth.[73]

9 Then God appeared to Jacob again, when he came from Padan Aram, and blessed him.

10 And God said to him, "Your name *is* Jacob; your name shall not be called Jacob anymore, but Israel shall be your name." So He called his name Israel.

---

72 Literally *God of the House of God*   73 Literally *Terebinth of Weeping*

11 Also God said to him: "I *am* God Almighty. Be fruitful and multiply; a nation and a company of nations shall proceed from you, and kings shall come from your body.
12 "The land which I gave Abraham and Isaac I give to you; and to your descendants after you I give this land."
13 Then God went up from him in the place where He talked with him.
14 So Jacob set up a pillar in the place where He talked with him, a pillar of stone; and he poured a drink offering on it, and he poured oil on it.
15 And Jacob called the name of the place where God spoke with him, Bethel.

Death of Rachel

16 Then they journeyed from Bethel. And when there was but a little distance to go to Ephrath, Rachel travailed *in* *childbirth*, and she had hard labor.
17 Now it came to pass, when she was in hard labor, that the midwife said to her, "Do not fear; you will have this son also."
18 And so it was, as her soul was departing (for she died), that she called his name Ben-Oni;[74] but his father called him Benjamin.[75]
19 So Rachel died and was buried on the way to Ephrath (that *is*, Bethlehem).
20 And Jacob set a pillar on her grave, which *is* the pillar of Rachel's grave to this day.
21 Then Israel journeyed and pitched his tent beyond the tower of Eder.
22 And it happened, when Israel dwelt in that land, that Reuben went and lay with Bilhah his father's concubine; and Israel heard *about it.*

Jacob's Twelve Sons

Now the sons of Jacob were twelve:
23 the sons of Leah *were* Reuben, Jacob's firstborn, and Simeon, Levi, Judah, Issachar, and Zebulun;
24 the sons of Rachel *were* Joseph and Benjamin;
25 the sons of Bilhah, Rachel's maidservant, *were* Dan and Naphtali;
26 and the sons of Zilpah, Leah's maidservant, *were* Gad and Asher. These *were* the sons of Jacob who were born to him in Padan Aram.

Death of Isaac

27 Then Jacob came to his father Isaac at Mamre, or Kirjath Arba[76] (that *is*, Hebron), where Abraham and Isaac had sojourned.
28 Now the days of Isaac were one hundred and eighty years.
29 So Isaac breathed his last and died, and was gathered to his people, *being* old and full of days. And his sons Esau and Jacob buried him.

The Family of Esau

36 Now this *is* the genealogy of Esau, who is Edom.
2 Esau took his wives from the daughters of Canaan: Adah the daughter of Elon the Hittite; Aholibamah the daughter of Anah, the daughter of Zibeon the Hivite;
3 and Basemath, Ishmael's daughter, sister of Nebajoth.
4 Now Adah bore Eliphaz to Esau, and Basemath bore Reuel.
5 And Aholibamah bore Jeush, Jaalam, and Korah. These *were* the sons of Esau who were born to him in the land of Canaan.
6 Then Esau took his wives, his sons, his daughters, and all the persons of his household, his cattle and all his animals, and all his goods which he had gained in the land of Canaan, and went to a country away from the presence of his brother Jacob.
7 For their possessions were too great for them to dwell together, and the land where they were strangers could not support them because of their livestock.
8 So Esau dwelt in Mount Seir. Esau *is* Edom.
9 And this *is* the genealogy of Esau the father of the Edomites in Mount Seir.
10 These *were* the names of Esau's sons: Eliphaz the son of Adah the wife of Esau, and Reuel the son of Basemath the wife of Esau.
11 And the sons of Eliphaz were Teman, Omar, Zepho,[77] Gatam, and Kenaz.
12 Now Timna was the concubine of Eliphaz, Esau's son, and she bore Amalek to Eliphaz. These *were* the sons of Adah, Esau's wife.
13 These *were* the sons of Reuel: Nahath, Zerah, Shammah, and Mizzah. These were the sons of Basemath, Esau's wife.

74 Literally *Son of My Sorrow*   75 Literally *Son of the Right Hand*
76 Literally *Town of Arbah*   77 Spelled *Zephi* in 1 Chronicles 1:36

14 These were the sons of Aholibamah, Esau's wife, the daughter of Anah, the daughter of Zibeon. And she bore to Esau: Jeush, Jaalam, and Korah.

The Chiefs of Edom

15 These were the chiefs of the sons of Esau. The sons of Eliphaz, the firstborn son of Esau, were Chief Teman, Chief Omar, Chief Zepho, Chief Kenaz, 16 Chief Korah, Chief Gatam, and Chief Amalek. These were the chiefs of Eliphaz in the land of Edom. They were the sons of Adah. 17 These were the sons of Reuel, Esau's son: Chief Nahath, Chief Zerah, Chief Shammah, and Chief Mizzah. These were the chiefs of Reuel in the land of Edom. These were the sons of Basemath, Esau's wife. 18 And these were the sons of Aholibamah, Esau's wife: Chief Jeush, Chief Jaalam, and Chief Korah. These were the chiefs who descended from Aholibamah, Esau's wife, the daughter of Anah. 19 These were the sons of Esau, who is Edom, and these were their chiefs.

The Sons of Seir

20 These were the sons of Seir the Horite who inhabited the land: Lotan, Shobal, Zibeon, Anah, 21 Dishon, Ezer, and Dishan. These were the chiefs of the Horites, the sons of Seir, in the land of Edom. 22 And the sons of Lotan were Hori and Hemam.[78] Lotan's sister was Timna. 23 These were the sons of Shobal: Alvan,[79] Manahath, Ebal, Shepho,[80] and Onam. 24 These were the sons of Zibeon: both Ajah and Anah. This was the Anah who found the water in the wilderness as he pastured the donkeys of his father Zibeon. 25 These were the children of Anah: Dishon and Aholibamah the daughter of Anah. 26 These were the sons of Dishon:[81] Hemdan,[82] Eshban, Ithran, and Cheran. 27 These were the sons of Ezer: Bilhan, Zaavan, and Akan.[83] 28 These were the sons of Dishan: Uz and Aran. 29 These were the chiefs of the Horites:

Chief Lotan, Chief Shobal, Chief Zibeon, Chief Anah, 30 Chief Dishon, Chief Ezer, and Chief Dishan. These were the chiefs of the Horites, according to their chiefs in the land of Seir.

The Kings of Edom

31 Now these were the kings who reigned in the land of Edom before any king reigned over the children of Israel: 32 Bela the son of Beor reigned in Edom, and the name of his city was Dinhabah. 33 And when Bela died, Jobab the son of Zerah of Bozrah reigned in his place. 34 When Jobab died, Husham of the land of the Temanites reigned in his place. 35 And when Husham died, Hadad son of Bedad, who attacked Midian in the field of Moab, reigned in his place. And the name of his city was Avith. 36 When Hadad died, Samlah of Masrekah reigned in his place. 37 And when Samlah died, Saul of Rehoboth-by-the-River reigned in his place. 38 When Saul died, Baal-Hanan the son of Achbor reigned in his place. 39 And when Baal-Hanan the son of Achbor died, Hadar[84] reigned in his place; and the name of his city was Pau.[85] His wife's name was Mehetabel, the daughter of Matred, the daughter of Mezahab.

The Chiefs of Esau

40 And these were the names of the chiefs of Esau, according to their families and their places, by their names: Chief Timnah, Chief Alvah,[86] Chief Jetheth, 41 Chief Aholibamah, Chief Elah, Chief Pinon, 42 Chief Kenaz, Chief Teman, Chief Mibzar, 43 Chief Magdiel, and Chief Iram. These were the chiefs of Edom, according to their habitations in the land of their possession. Esau was the father of the Edomites.

Joseph Dreams of Greatness

37 Now Jacob dwelt in the land where his father was a stranger, in the land of Canaan. 2 This is the genealogy of Jacob.

---

78 Spelled *Homam* in 1 Chronicles 1:39   79 Spelled *Alian* in 1 Chronicles 1:40
80 Spelled *Shephi* in 1 Chronicles 1:40   81 Hebrew *Dishan*   82 Spelled *Hamran* in 1 Chronicles 1:41
83 Spelled *Jaakan* in 1 Chronicles 1:42   84 Spelled *Hadad* in 1 Chronicles 1:50, Samaritan Pentateuch and Syriac
85 Spelled *Pai* in 1 Chronicles 1:50   86 Spelled *Aliah* in 1 Chronicles 1:51

Joseph, *being* seventeen years old, was feeding the flock with his brothers. And the lad *was* with the sons of Bilhah and the sons of Zilpah, his father's wives; and Joseph brought a bad report of them to his father.

3 Now Israel loved Joseph more than all his children, because he *was* the son of his old age. Also he made him a tunic of *many* colors.

4 But when his brothers saw that their father loved him more than all his brothers, they hated him and could not speak peaceably to him.

5 Now Joseph dreamed a dream, and he told *it* to his brothers; and they hated him even more.

6 So he said to them, "Please hear this dream which I have dreamed:

7 "There we were, binding sheaves in the field. Then behold, my sheaf arose and also stood upright; and indeed your sheaves stood all around and bowed down to my sheaf."

8 And his brothers said to him, "Shall you indeed reign over us? Or shall you indeed have dominion over us?" So they hated him even more for his dreams and for his words.

9 Then he dreamed still another dream and told it to his brothers, and said, "Look, I have dreamed another dream. And this time, the sun, the moon, and the eleven stars bowed down to me."

10 So he told *it* to his father and his brothers; and his father rebuked him and said to him, "What *is* this dream that you have dreamed? Shall your mother and I and your brothers indeed come to bow down to the earth before you?"

11 And his brothers envied him, but his father kept the matter *in mind*.

Joseph Sold by His Brothers

12 Then his brothers went to feed their father's flock in Shechem.

13 And Israel said to Joseph, "Are not your brothers feeding *the flock* in Shechem? Come, I will send you to them." So he said to him, "Here I am."

14 Then he said to him, "Please go and see if it is well with your brothers and well with the flocks, and bring back word to me." So he sent him out of the Valley of Hebron, and he went to Shechem.

15 Now a certain man found him, and there he was, wandering in the field. And the man asked him, saying, "What are you seeking?"

16 So he said, "I am seeking my brothers. Please tell me where they are feeding *their flocks.*"

17 And the man said, "They have departed from here, for I heard them say, 'Let us go to Dothan.' " So Joseph went after his brothers and found them in Dothan.

18 Now when they saw him afar off, even before he came near them, they conspired against him to kill him.

19 Then they said to one another, "Look, this dreamer is coming!

20 "Come therefore, let us now kill him and cast him into some pit; and we shall say, 'Some wild beast has devoured him.' We shall see what will become of his dreams!"

21 But Reuben heard *it*, and he delivered him out of their hands, and said, "Let us not kill him."

22 And Reuben said to them, "Shed no blood, *but* cast him into this pit which *is* in the wilderness, and do not lay a hand on him"—that he might deliver him out of their hands, and bring him back to his father.

23 So it came to pass, when Joseph had come to his brothers, that they stripped Joseph of *his* tunic, the tunic of *many* colors that *was* on him.

24 Then they took him and cast him into a pit. And the pit *was* empty; *there was* no water in it.

25 And they sat down to eat a meal. Then they lifted their eyes and looked, and there was a company of Ishmaelites, coming from Gilead with their camels, bearing spices, balm, and myrrh, on their way to carry *them* down to Egypt.

26 So Judah said to his brothers, "What profit *is there* if we kill our brother and conceal his blood?

27 "Come and let us sell him to the Ishmaelites, and let not our hand be upon him, for he *is* our brother *and* our flesh." And his brothers listened.

28 Then Midianite traders passed by; so *the brothers* pulled Joseph up and lifted him out of the pit, and sold him to the Ishmaelites for twenty *shekels* of silver. And they took Joseph to Egypt.

29 Then Reuben returned to the pit, and indeed Joseph *was* not in the pit; and he tore his clothes.

30 And he returned to his brothers and said, "The lad *is* no *more*; and I, where shall I go?"
31 So they took Joseph's tunic, killed a kid of the goats, and dipped the tunic in the blood.
32 Then they sent the tunic of *many* colors, and they brought *it* to their father and said, "We have found this. Do you know whether it *is* your son's tunic or not?"
33 And he recognized it and said, "*It is* my son's tunic. A wild beast has devoured him. Without doubt Joseph is torn to pieces."
34 Then Jacob tore his clothes, put sackcloth on his waist, and mourned for his son many days.
35 And all his sons and all his daughters arose to comfort him; but he refused to be comforted, and he said, "For I shall go down into the grave to my son in mourning." Thus his father wept for him.
36 Now the Midianites had sold him in Egypt to Potiphar, an officer of Pharaoh *and* captain of the guard.

Judah and Tamar

38 It came to pass at that time that Judah departed from his brothers, and visited a certain Adullamite whose name *was* Hirah.
2 And Judah saw there a daughter of a certain Canaanite whose name *was* Shua, and he married her and went in to her.
3 So she conceived and bore a son, and he called his name Er.
4 She conceived again and bore a son, and she called his name Onan.
5 And she conceived yet again and bore a son, and called his name Shelah. He was at Chezib when she bore him.
6 Then Judah took a wife for Er his firstborn, and her name *was* Tamar.
7 But Er, Judah's firstborn, was wicked in the sight of the LORD, and the LORD killed him.
8 And Judah said to Onan, "Go in to your brother's wife and marry her, and raise up an heir to your brother."
9 But Onan knew that the heir would not be his; and it came to pass, when he went in to his brother's wife, that he emitted on the ground, lest he should give an heir to his brother.
10 And the thing which he did displeased the LORD; therefore He killed him also.

11 Then Judah said to Tamar his daughter-in-law, "Remain a widow in your father's house till my son Shelah is grown." For he said, "Lest he also die as his brothers *did*." And Tamar went and dwelt in her father's house.
12 Now in the process of time the daughter of Shua, Judah's wife, died; and Judah was comforted, and went up to his sheepshearers at Timnah, he and his friend Hirah the Adullamite.
13 And it was told Tamar, saying, "Look, your father-in-law is going up to Timnah to shear his sheep."
14 So she took off her widow's garments, covered *herself* with a veil and wrapped herself, and sat in an open place which *was* on the way to Timnah; for she saw that Shelah was grown, and she was not given to him as a wife.
15 When Judah saw her, he thought she *was* a harlot, because she had covered her face.
16 Then he turned to her by the way, and said, "Please let me come in to you"; for he did not know that she *was* his daughter-in-law. So she said, "What will you give me, that you may come in to me?"
17 And he said, "I will send *you* a young goat from the flock." And she said, "Will you give *me* a pledge till you send *it*?"
18 Then he said, "What pledge shall I give you?" So she said, "Your signet and cord, and your staff that *is* in your hand." Then he gave *them* to her, and went in to her, and she conceived by him.
19 So she arose and went away, and laid aside her veil and put on the garments of her widowhood.
20 And Judah sent the young goat by the hand of his friend the Adullamite, to receive *his* pledge from the woman's hand, but he did not find her.
21 Then he asked the men of that place, saying, "Where is the harlot who *was* openly by the roadside?" And they said, "There was no harlot in this *place*."
22 And he returned to Judah and said, "I cannot find her. Also, the men of the place said there was no harlot in this *place*."
23 Then Judah said, "Let her take *them* for herself, lest we be shamed; for I sent this young goat and you have not found her."
24 And it came to pass, about three months after, that Judah was told, saying,

"Tamar your daughter-in-law has played the harlot; furthermore she *is* with child by harlotry." So Judah said, "Bring her out and let her be burned!"

25 When she *was* brought out, she sent to her father-in-law, saying, "By the man to whom these belong, I *am* with child." And she said, "Please determine whose these *are*—the signet and cord, and staff."

26 So Judah acknowledged *them* and said, "She has been more righteous than I, because I did not give her to Shelah my son." And he never knew her again.

27 Now it came to pass, at the time for giving birth, that behold, twins *were* in her womb.

28 And so it was, when she was giving birth, that *the one* put out *his* hand; and the midwife took a scarlet *thread* and bound it on his hand, saying, "This one came out first."

29 Then it happened, as he drew back his hand, that his brother came out unexpectedly; and she said, "How did you break through? *This* breach *be* upon you!" Therefore his name was called Perez.[87]

30 Afterward his brother came out who had the scarlet *thread* on his hand. And his name was called Zerah.

Joseph a Slave in Egypt

39 Now Joseph had been taken down to Egypt. And Potiphar, an officer of Pharaoh, captain of the guard, an Egyptian, bought him from the Ishmaelites who had taken him down there.

2 The LORD was with Joseph, and he was a successful man; and he was in the house of his master the Egyptian.

3 And his master saw that the LORD *was* with him and that the LORD made all he did to prosper in his hand.

4 So Joseph found favor in his sight, and served him. Then he made him overseer of his house, and all *that* he had he put in his hand.

5 So it was, from the time *that* he had made him overseer of his house and all that he had, that the LORD blessed the Egyptian's house for Joseph's sake; and the blessing of the LORD was on all that he had in the house and in the field.

6 So he left all that he had in Joseph's hand, and he did not know what he had except for the bread which he ate. And

Joseph was handsome in form and appearance.

7 Now it came to pass after these things that his master's wife cast longing eyes on Joseph, and she said, "Lie with me."

8 But he refused and said to his master's wife, "Look, my master does not know what *is* with me in the house, and he has committed all that he has to my hand.

9 "*There is* no one greater in this house than I, nor has he kept back anything from me but you, because you *are* his wife. How then can I do this great wickedness, and sin against God?"

10 And so it was, as she spoke to Joseph day by day, that he did not heed her, to lie with her *or* to be with her.

11 But it happened about this time, when Joseph went into the house to do his work, and none of the men of the house *was* inside,

12 that she caught him by his garment, saying, "Lie with me." But he left his garment in her hand, and fled and ran outside.

13 And so it was, when she saw that he had left his garment in her hand and fled outside,

14 that she called to the men of her house and spoke to them, saying, "See, he has brought in to us a Hebrew to mock us. He came in to me to lie with me, and I cried out with a loud voice.

15 "And it happened, when he heard that I lifted my voice and cried out, that he left his garment with me, and fled and went outside."

16 So she kept his garment with her until his master came home.

17 Then she spoke to him with words like these, saying, "The Hebrew servant whom you brought to us came in to me to mock me;

18 "so it happened, as I lifted my voice and cried out, that he left his garment with me and fled outside."

19 So it was, when his master heard the words which his wife spoke to him, saying, "Your servant did to me after this manner," that his anger was aroused.

20 Then Joseph's master took him and put him into the prison, a place where the king's prisoners *were* confined. And he was there in the prison.

21 But the LORD was with Joseph and showed him mercy, and He gave him

87 Literally *Breach* or *Breakthrough*

favor in the sight of the keeper of the prison.
22 And the keeper of the prison committed to Joseph's hand all the prisoners who *were* in the prison; whatever they did there, it was his doing.
23 The keeper of the prison did not look into anything *that was* under Joseph's hand, because the LORD was with him; and whatever he did, the LORD made *it* prosper.

The Prisoners' Dreams

40 It came to pass after these things *that* the butler and the baker of the king of Egypt offended their lord, the king of Egypt.
2 And Pharaoh was angry with his two officers, the chief butler and the chief baker.
3 So he put them in custody in the house of the captain of the guard, in the prison, the place where Joseph *was* confined.
4 And the captain of the guard charged Joseph with them, and he served them; so they were in custody for a while.
5 Then the butler and the baker of the king of Egypt, who *were* confined in the prison, dreamed a dream, both of them, each man's dream in one night *and* each man's dream with its *own* interpretation.
6 And Joseph came in to them in the morning and looked at them, and saw that they *were* sad.
7 So he asked Pharaoh's officers who *were* with him in the custody of his lord's house, saying, "Why do you look *so* sad today?"
8 And they said to him, "We each have dreamed a dream, and *there is* no interpreter of it." And Joseph said to them, "Do not interpretations belong to God? Tell *them* to me, please."
9 Then the chief butler told his dream to Joseph, and said to him, "Behold, in my dream a vine *was* before me,
10 "and in the vine *were* three branches; it *was* as though it budded, its blossoms shot forth, and its clusters brought forth ripe grapes.
11 "Then Pharaoh's cup *was* in my hand; and I took the grapes and pressed them into Pharaoh's cup, and placed the cup in Pharaoh's hand."
12 And Joseph said to him, "This *is* the

interpretation of it: The three branches *are* three days.
13 "Now within three days Pharaoh will lift up your head and restore you to your place, and you will put Pharaoh's cup in his hand according to the former manner, when you were his butler.
14 "But remember me when it is well with you, and please show kindness to me; make mention of me to Pharaoh, and get me out of this house.
15 "For indeed I was stolen away from the land of the Hebrews; and also I have done nothing here that they should put me into the dungeon."
16 When the chief baker saw that the interpretation was good, he said to Joseph, "I also *was* in my dream, and there *I had* three white baskets on my head.
17 "In the uppermost basket *there were* all kinds of baked goods for Pharaoh, and the birds ate them out of the basket on my head."
18 So Joseph answered and said, "This *is* the interpretation of it: The three baskets *are* three days.
19 "Within three days Pharaoh will lift off your head from you and hang you on a tree; and the birds will eat your flesh from you."
20 Now it came to pass on the third day, *which was* Pharaoh's birthday, that he made a feast for all his servants; and he lifted up the head of the chief butler and of the chief baker among his servants.
21 Then he restored the chief butler to his butlership again, and he placed the cup in Pharaoh's hand.
22 But he hanged the chief baker, as Joseph had interpreted to them.
23 Yet the chief butler did not remember Joseph, but forgot him.

Pharaoh's Dreams

41 Then it came to pass, at the end of two full years, that Pharaoh had a dream; and behold, he stood by the river.
2 Suddenly there came up out of the river seven cows, fine looking and fat; and they fed in the meadow.
3 Then behold, seven other cows came up after them out of the river, ugly and gaunt, and stood by the *other* cows on the bank of the river.
4 And the ugly and gaunt cows ate up the seven fine looking and fat cows. So Pharaoh awoke.

5 He slept and dreamed a second time; and suddenly seven heads of grain came up on one stalk, plump and good.
6 Then behold, seven thin heads, blighted by the east wind, sprang up after them.
7 And the seven thin heads devoured the seven plump and full heads. So Pharaoh awoke, and indeed, it was a dream.
8 Now it came to pass in the morning that his spirit was troubled, and he sent and called for all the magicians of Egypt and all its wise men. And Pharaoh told them his dreams, but there was no one who could interpret them for Pharaoh.
9 Then the chief butler spoke to Pharaoh, saying: "I remember my faults this day.
10 "When Pharaoh was angry with his servants, and put me in custody in the house of the captain of the guard, both me and the chief baker,
11 "we each dreamed a dream in one night, he and I. Each of us dreamed according to the interpretation of his own dream.
12 "Now there was a young Hebrew man with us there, a servant of the captain of the guard. And we told him, and he interpreted our dreams for us; to each man he interpreted according to his own dream.
13 "And it came to pass just as he interpreted for us; so it happened. He restored me to my office, and he hanged him."
14 Then Pharaoh sent and called Joseph, and they brought him hastily out of the dungeon; and he shaved, changed his clothing, and came to Pharaoh.
15 And Pharaoh said to Joseph, "I have dreamed a dream, and there is no one who can interpret it. But I have heard it said of you that you can understand a dream, to interpret it."
16 So Joseph answered Pharaoh, saying, "It is not in me; God will give Pharaoh an answer of peace."
17 Then Pharaoh said to Joseph: "Behold, in my dream I stood on the bank of the river.
18 "Suddenly seven cows came up out of the river, fine looking and fat; and they fed in the meadow.
19 "Then behold, seven other cows came up after them, poor and very ugly and gaunt, such ugliness as I have never seen in all the land of Egypt.
20 "And the gaunt and ugly cows ate up the first seven, the fat cows.
21 "When they had eaten them up, no one would have known that they had eaten them, for they were just as ugly as at the beginning. So I awoke.
22 "Also I saw in my dream, and suddenly seven heads came up on one stalk, full and good.
23 "Then behold, seven heads, withered, thin, and blighted by the east wind, sprang up after them.
24 "And the thin heads devoured the seven good heads. So I told this to the magicians, but there was no one who could explain it to me."
25 Then Joseph said to Pharaoh, "The dreams of Pharaoh are one; God has shown Pharaoh what He is about to do:
26 "The seven good cows are seven years, and the seven good heads are seven years; the dreams are one.
27 "And the seven thin and ugly cows which came up after them are seven years, and the seven empty heads blighted by the east wind are seven years of famine.
28 "This is the thing which I have spoken to Pharaoh. God has shown Pharaoh what He is about to do.
29 "Indeed seven years of great plenty will come throughout all the land of Egypt;
30 "but after them seven years of famine will arise, and all the plenty will be forgotten in the land of Egypt; and the famine will deplete the land.
31 "So the plenty will not be known in the land because of the famine following, for it will be very severe.
32 "And the dream was repeated to Pharaoh twice because the thing is established by God, and God will shortly bring it to pass.
33 "Now therefore, let Pharaoh select a discerning and wise man, and set him over the land of Egypt.
34 "Let Pharaoh do this, and let him appoint officers over the land, to collect one-fifth of the produce of the land of Egypt in the seven plentiful years.
35 "And let them gather all the food of those good years that are coming, and store up grain under the authority of

Pharaoh, and let them keep food in the cities.

36 "Then that food shall be as a reserve for the land for the seven years of famine which shall be in the land of Egypt, that the land may not perish during the famine."

Joseph's Rise to Power

37 So the advice was good in the eyes of Pharaoh and in the eyes of all his servants.

38 And Pharaoh said to his servants, "Can we find *such a one* as this, a man in whom *is* the Spirit of God?"

39 Then Pharaoh said to Joseph, "Inasmuch as God has shown you all this, *there is* no one as discerning and wise as you.

40 "You shall be over my house, and all my people shall be ruled according to your word; only in regard to the throne will I be greater than you."

41 And Pharaoh said to Joseph, "See, I have set you over all the land of Egypt."

42 Then Pharaoh took his signet ring off his hand and put it on Joseph's hand; and he clothed him in garments of fine linen and put a gold chain around his neck.

43 And he had him ride in the second chariot which he had; and they cried out before him, "Bow the knee!" So he set him over all the land of Egypt.

44 Pharaoh also said to Joseph, "I *am* Pharaoh, and without your consent no man may lift his hand or foot in all the land of Egypt."

45 And Pharaoh called Joseph's name Zaphnath-Paaneah. And he gave him as a wife Asenath, the daughter of Poti-Pherah priest of On. So Joseph went out over *all* the land of Egypt.

46 Joseph was thirty years old when he stood before Pharaoh king of Egypt. And Joseph went out from the presence of Pharaoh, and went throughout all the land of Egypt.

47 Now in the seven plentiful years the ground brought forth abundantly.

48 So he gathered up all the food of the seven years which were in the land of Egypt, and laid up the food in the cities; he laid up in every city the food of the fields which surrounded them.

49 Joseph gathered very much grain, as the sand of the sea, until he stopped counting, for *it was* without number.

50 And to Joseph were born two sons before the years of famine came, whom Asenath, the daughter of Poti-Pherah priest of On, bore to him.

51 Joseph called the name of the first-born Manasseh:[88] "For God has made me forget all my toil and all my father's house."

52 And the name of the second he called Ephraim:[89] "For God has caused me to be fruitful in the land of my affliction."

53 Then the seven years of plenty which were in the land of Egypt ended,

54 and the seven years of famine began to come, as Joseph had said. The famine was in all lands, but in all the land of Egypt there was bread.

55 So when all the land of Egypt was famished, the people cried to Pharaoh for bread. Then Pharaoh said to all the Egyptians, "Go to Joseph; whatever he says to you, do."

56 The famine was over all the face of the earth, and Joseph opened all the storehouses[90] and sold to the Egyptians. And the famine became severe in the land of Egypt.

57 So all countries came to Joseph in Egypt to buy *grain*, because the famine was severe in all lands.

Joseph's Brothers Go to Egypt

42 When Jacob saw that there was grain in Egypt, Jacob said to his sons, "Why do you look at one another?"

2 And he said, "Indeed I have heard that there is grain in Egypt; go down to that place and buy for us there, that we may live and not die."

3 So Joseph's ten brothers went down to buy grain in Egypt.

4 But Jacob did not send Joseph's brother Benjamin with his brothers, for he said, "Lest some calamity befall him."

5 And the sons of Israel went to buy *grain* among those who journeyed, for the famine was in the land of Canaan.

6 Now Joseph *was* governor over the land; and it was he who sold to all the people of the land. And Joseph's brothers came and bowed down before him with *their* faces to the earth.

7 Joseph saw his brothers and recognized them, but he acted as a stranger to them and spoke roughly to them. Then

88 Literally *Making Forgetful* 89 Literally *Fruitfulness* 90 Literally *all that was in them*

he said to them, "Where do you come from?" And they said, "From the land of Canaan to buy food."

8 So Joseph recognized his brothers, but they did not recognize him.

9 Then Joseph remembered the dreams which he had dreamed about them, and said to them, "You *are* spies! You have come to see the nakedness of the land!"

10 And they said to him, "No, my lord, but your servants have come to buy food.

11 "We *are* all one man's sons; we *are* honest *men*; your servants are not spies."

12 But he said to them, "No, but you have come to see the nakedness of the land."

13 And they said, "Your servants *are* twelve brothers, the sons of one man in the land of Canaan; and in fact, the youngest *is* with our father today, and one *is* no more."

14 But Joseph said to them, "It *is* as I spoke to you, saying, 'You *are* spies!'

15 "In this *manner* you shall be tested: By the life of Pharaoh, you shall not leave this place unless your youngest brother comes here.

16 "Send one of you, and let him bring your brother; and you shall be kept in prison, that your words may be tested to see whether *there is* any truth in you; or else, by the life of Pharaoh, surely you *are* spies!"

17 So he put them all together in prison three days.

18 Then Joseph said to them the third day, "Do this and live, *for* I fear God:

19 "If you *are* honest *men*, let one of your brothers be confined to your prison house; but you, go and carry grain for the famine of your houses.

20 "And bring your youngest brother to me; so your words will be verified, and you shall not die." And they did so.

21 Then they said to one another, "We *are* truly guilty concerning our brother, for we saw the anguish of his soul when he pleaded with us, and we would not hear; therefore this distress has come upon us."

22 And Reuben answered them, saying, "Did I not speak to you, saying, 'Do not sin against the boy'; and you would not listen? Therefore behold, his blood is now required of us."

23 But they did not know that Joseph understood *them*, for he spoke to them through an interpreter.

24 And he turned himself away from them and wept. Then he returned to them again, and talked with them. And he took Simeon from them and bound him before their eyes.

The Brothers Return to Canaan

25 Then Joseph gave a command to fill their sacks with grain, to restore every man's money to his sack, and to give them provisions for the journey. Thus he did for them.

26 So they loaded their donkeys with the grain and departed from there.

27 But as one *of them* opened his sack to give his donkey feed at the encampment, he saw his money; and there it was, in the mouth of his sack.

28 So he said to his brothers, "My money has been restored, and there it is, in my sack!" Then their hearts failed *them* and they were afraid, saying to one another, "What *is* this *that* God has done to us?"

29 Then they went to Jacob their father in the land of Canaan and told him all that had happened to them, saying:

30 "The man *who is* lord of the land spoke roughly to us, and took us for spies of the country.

31 "But we said to him, 'We *are* honest *men*; we are not spies.

32 'We *are* twelve brothers, sons of our father; one *is* no *more*, and the youngest *is* with our father this day in the land of Canaan.'

33 "Then the man, the lord of the country, said to us, 'By this I will know that you *are* honest *men*: Leave one of your brothers *here* with me, take *food for* the famine of your households, and be gone.

34 'And bring your youngest brother to me; so I shall know that you *are* not spies, but *that* you *are* honest *men*. And I will deliver your brother to you, and you may trade in the land.' "

35 Then it happened as they emptied their sacks, that surprisingly each man's bundle of money *was* in his sack; and when *both* they and their father saw the bundles of money, they were afraid.

36 And Jacob their father said to them, "You have bereaved me *of my children*: Joseph is no *more*, Simeon is no *more*, and you want to take Benjamin *away*. All these things are against me."

37 Then Reuben spoke to his father, saying, "Kill my two sons if I do not bring him *back* to you; put him in my hands, and I will bring him back to you."
38 But he said, "My son shall not go down with you, for his brother is dead, and he is left alone. If any calamity should befall him along the way in which you go, then you would bring down my gray hair with sorrow to the grave."

The Return to Egypt with Benjamin

43 Now the famine *was* severe in the land.
2 And it came to pass, when they had eaten up the grain which they had brought from Egypt, that their father said to them, "Go back, buy us a little food."
3 But Judah spoke to him, saying, "The man solemnly warned us, saying, 'You shall not see my face unless your brother *is* with you.'"
4 "If you send our brother with us, we will go down and buy you food.
5 "But if you will not send *him*, we will not go down; for the man said to us, 'You shall not see my face unless your brother *is* with you.'"
6 And Israel said, "Why did you deal *so* wrongfully with me *as* to tell the man whether you had still *another* brother?"
7 But they said, "The man asked us pointedly about ourselves and our kindred, saying, '*Is* your father still alive? Have you *another* brother?' And we told him according to these words. Could we possibly have known that he would say, 'Bring your brother down'?"
8 Then Judah said to Israel his father, "Send the lad with me, and we will arise and go, that we may live and not die, both we and you *and* also our little ones.
9 "I myself will be surety for him; from my hand you shall require him. If I do not bring him *back* to you and set him before you, then let me bear the blame forever.
10 "For if we had not lingered, surely by now we would have returned this second time."
11 And their father Israel said to them, "If *it must be* so, then do this: Take some of the best fruits of the land in your vessels and carry down a present for the man—a little balm and a little honey,

spices and myrrh, pistachio nuts and almonds.
12 "Take double money in your hand, and take back in your hand the money that was returned in the mouth of your sacks; perhaps it was an oversight.
13 "Take your brother also, and arise, go back to the man.
14 "And may God Almighty give you mercy before the man, that he may release your other brother and Benjamin. If I am bereaved, I am bereaved!"
15 So the men took that present and Benjamin, and they took double money in their hand, and they arose and went down to Egypt; and they stood before Joseph.
16 When Joseph saw Benjamin with them, he said to the steward of his house, "Take *these* men to my home, and slaughter *an animal* and make ready; for *these* men will dine with me at noon."
17 Then the man did as Joseph ordered, and the man brought the men into Joseph's house.
18 Now the men were afraid because they were brought into Joseph's house; and they said, "*It is* because of the money, which was returned in our sacks the first time, that we are brought in, so that he may seek an occasion against us and fall upon us, to take us as slaves with our donkeys."
19 When they drew near to the steward of Joseph's house, they talked with him at the door of the house,
20 and said, "O sir, we indeed came down the first time to buy food;
21 "but it happened, when we came to the encampment, that we opened our sacks, and there, *each* man's money *was* in the mouth of his sack, our money in full weight; so we have brought it back in our hand.
22 "And we have brought down other money in our hands to buy food. We do not know who put our money in our sacks."
23 But he said, "Peace *be* with you, do not be afraid. Your God and the God of your father has given you treasure in your sacks; I had your money." Then he brought Simeon out to them.
24 So the man brought the men into Joseph's house and gave *them* water, and they washed their feet; and he gave their donkeys feed.
25 Then they made the present ready for

Joseph's coming at noon, for they heard that they would eat bread there.

26 And when Joseph came home, they brought him the present which *was* in their hand into the house, and bowed down before him to the earth.

27 Then he asked them about *their* well-being, and said, "*Is* your father well, the old man of whom you spoke? *Is* he still alive?"

28 And they answered, "Your servant our father *is* in good health; he *is* still alive." And they bowed their heads down and prostrated themselves.

29 Then he lifted his eyes and saw his brother Benjamin, his mother's son, and said, "*Is* this your younger brother of whom you spoke to me?" And he said, "God be gracious to you, my son."

30 Now his heart yearned for his brother; so Joseph made haste and sought *somewhere* to weep. And he went into *his* chamber and wept there.

31 Then he washed his face and came out; and he restrained himself, and said, "Serve the bread."

32 So they set him a place by himself, and them by themselves, and the Egyptians who ate with him by themselves; because the Egyptians could not eat food with the Hebrews, for that *is* an abomination to the Egyptians.

33 And they sat before him, the firstborn according to his birthright and the youngest according to his youth; and the men looked in astonishment at one another.

34 Then he took servings to them from before him, but Benjamin's serving was five times as much as any of theirs. So they drank and were merry with him.

Joseph's Cup

44 And he commanded the steward of his house, saying, "Fill the men's sacks with food, as much as they can carry, and put each man's money in the mouth of his sack.

2 "Also put my cup, the silver cup, in the mouth of the sack of the youngest, and his grain money." So he did according to the word that Joseph had spoken.

3 As soon as the morning dawned, the men were sent away, they and their donkeys.

4 *And* when they had gone out of the city, *and* were not *yet* far off, Joseph said to his steward, "Get up, follow the men; and when you overtake them, say to them, 'Why have you repaid evil for good?

5 '*Is* not this *the one* from which my lord drinks, and with which he indeed practices divination? You have done evil in so doing.' "

6 So he overtook them, and he spoke to them these same words.

7 And they said to him, "Why does my lord say these words? Far be it from us that your servants should do such a thing.

8 "Look, we brought back to you from the land of Canaan the money which we found in the mouth of our sacks. How then could we steal silver or gold from your lord's house?

9 "With whomever of your servants it is found, let him die, and we also will be my lord's slaves."

10 And he said, "Now also *let* it *be* according to your words; he with whom it is found shall be my slave, and you shall be blameless."

11 Then each man speedily let down his sack to the ground, and each opened his sack.

12 So he searched, *and* he began with the oldest and left off with the youngest; and the cup was found in Benjamin's sack.

13 Then they tore their clothes, and each man loaded his donkey and returned to the city.

14 So Judah and his brothers came to Joseph's house, and he *was* still there; and they fell before him on the ground.

15 And Joseph said to them, "What deed *is* this you have done? Did you not know that such a man as I can certainly practice divination?"

16 Then Judah said, "What shall we say to my lord? What shall we speak? Or how shall we clear ourselves? God has found out the iniquity of your servants; here we are, my lord's slaves, both we and *he* also with whom the cup was found."

17 But he said, "Far be it from me that I should do so; *but* the man in whose hand the cup was found, he shall be my slave. And as for you, go up in peace to your father."

Judah Intercedes for Benjamin

18 Then Judah came near to him and said: "O my lord, please let your servant speak a word in my lord's hearing, and do not let your anger burn against your

servant; for you *are* even like Pharaoh.
19 "My lord asked his servants, saying,
'Have you a father or a brother?'
20 "And we said to my lord, 'We have a
father, an old man, and a child of *his* old
age, *who is* young; his brother is dead,
and he alone is left of his mother's children, and his father loves him.'
21 "Then you said to your servants,
'Bring him down to me, that I may set my
eyes on him.'
22 "And we said to my lord, 'The lad
cannot leave his father, for *if* he should
leave his father, *his father* would die.'
23 "But you said to your servants, 'Unless your youngest brother comes down
with you, you shall see my face no more.'
24 "So it was, when we went up to your
servant my father, that we told him the
words of my lord.
25 "And our father said, 'Go back *and*
buy us a little food.'
26 "But we said, 'We cannot go down; if
our youngest brother is with us, then we
will go down; for we may not see the
man's face unless our youngest brother *is*
with us.'
27 "Then your servant my father said to
us, 'You know that my wife bore me two
sons;
28 'and the one went out from me, and I
said, "Surely he is torn to pieces"; and I
have not seen him since.
29 'But if you take this one also from me,
and calamity befalls him, you shall bring
down my gray hair with sorrow to the
grave.'
30 "Now therefore, when I come to your
servant my father, and the lad *is* not with
us, since his life is bound up in the lad's
life,
31 "it will happen, when he sees that the
lad *is* not *with us*, that he will die. So
your servants will bring down the gray
hair of your servant our father with sorrow to the grave.
32 "For your servant became surety for
the lad to my father, saying, 'If I do not
bring him *back* to you, then I shall bear
the blame before my father forever.'
33 "Now therefore, please let your servant remain instead of the lad as a slave
to my lord, and let the lad go up with his
brothers.
34 "For how shall I go up to my father if
the lad *is* not with me, lest perhaps I

see the evil that would come upon my
father?"

Joseph Revealed to His Brothers

45 Then Joseph could not restrain
himself before all those who stood
by him, and he cried out, "Make everyone go out from me!" So no one stood
with him while Joseph made himself
known to his brothers.
2   And he wept aloud, and the Egyptians
and the house of Pharaoh heard *it*.
3   Then Joseph said to his brothers, "I
am Joseph; does my father still live?"
But his brothers could not answer him,
for they were dismayed in his presence.
4   And Joseph said to his brothers,
"Please come near to me." And they
came near. And he said: "I *am* Joseph
your brother, whom you sold into Egypt.
5   "But now, do not therefore be grieved
nor angry with yourselves because you
sold me here; for God sent me before you
to preserve life.
6   "For these two years the famine *has
been* in the land, and *there are* still five
years in which *there will be* neither plowing nor harvesting.
7   "And God sent me before you to preserve a posterity for you in the earth, and
to save your lives by a great deliverance.
8   "So now *it was* not you *who* sent me
here, but God; and He has made me a
father to Pharaoh, and lord of all his
house, and a ruler throughout all the land
of Egypt.
9   "Hasten and go up to my father, and
say to him, 'Thus says your son Joseph:
"God has made me lord of all Egypt;
come down to me, do not tarry.
10 "You shall dwell in the land of Goshen, and you shall be near to me, you
and your children, your children's children, your flocks and your herds, and all
that you have.
11 "There I will provide for you, lest you
and your household, and all that you
have, come to poverty; for *there are* still
five years of famine."'
12 "And behold, your eyes and the eyes
of my brother Benjamin see that *it is* my
mouth that speaks to you.
13 "So you shall tell my father of all my
glory in Egypt, and of all that you have
seen; and you shall hasten and bring my
father down here."

14 Then he fell on his brother Benjamin's neck and wept, and Benjamin wept on his neck.
15 Moreover he kissed all his brothers and wept over them, and after that his brothers talked with him.
16 Now the report of it was heard in Pharaoh's house, saying, "Joseph's brothers have come." So it pleased Pharaoh and his servants well.
17 And Pharaoh said to Joseph, "Say to your brothers, 'Do this: Load your beasts and depart; go to the land of Canaan.
18 'Bring your father and your households and come to me; I will give you the best of the land of Egypt, and you will eat the fat of the land.
19 'Now you are commanded—do this: Take carts out of the land of Egypt for your little ones and your wives; bring your father and come.
20 'Also do not be concerned about your goods, for the best of all the land of Egypt is yours.'"
21 Then the sons of Israel did so; and Joseph gave them carts, according to the command of Pharaoh, and he gave them provisions for the journey.
22 He gave to all of them, to each man, changes of garments; but to Benjamin he gave three hundred *pieces* of silver and five changes of garments.
23 And he sent to his father these *things*: ten donkeys loaded with the good things of Egypt, and ten female donkeys loaded with grain, bread, and food for his father for the journey.
24 So he sent his brothers away, and they departed; and he said to them, "See that you do not become troubled along the way."
25 Then they went up out of Egypt, and came to the land of Canaan to Jacob their father.
26 And they told him, saying, "Joseph is still alive, and he is governor over all the land of Egypt." And Jacob's heart stood still, because he did not believe them.
27 But when they told him all the words which Joseph had said to them, and when he saw the carts which Joseph had sent to carry him, the spirit of Jacob their father revived.
28 Then Israel said, "*It is* enough.

Joseph my son *is* still alive. I will go and see him before I die."

Jacob's Journey to Egypt

46 So Israel took his journey with all that he had, and came to Beersheba, and offered sacrifices to the God of his father Isaac.
2 Then God spoke to Israel in the visions of the night, and said, "Jacob, Jacob!" And he said, "Here I am."
3 And He said, "I *am* God, the God of your father; do not fear to go down to Egypt, for I will make of you a great nation there.
4 "I will go down with you to Egypt, and I will also surely bring you up *again*; and Joseph will put his hand on your eyes."
5 Then Jacob arose from Beersheba; and the sons of Israel carried their father Jacob, their little ones, and their wives, in the carts which Pharaoh had sent to carry him.
6 So they took their livestock and their goods, which they had acquired in the land of Canaan, and went to Egypt, Jacob and all his descendants with him.
7 His sons and his sons' sons, his daughters and his sons' daughters, and all his descendants he brought with him to Egypt.
8 Now these *were* the names of the children of Israel, Jacob and his sons, who went to Egypt: Reuben *was* Jacob's firstborn.
9 The sons of Reuben *were* Hanoch, Pallu, Hezron, and Carmi.
10 The sons of Simeon *were* Jemuel,[91] Jamin, Ohad, Jachin,[92] Zohar,[93] and Shaul, the son of a Canaanite woman.
11 The sons of Levi *were* Gershon, Kohath, and Merari.
12 The sons of Judah *were* Er, Onan, Shelah, Perez, and Zerah (but Er and Onan died in the land of Canaan). The sons of Perez were Hezron and Hamul.
13 The sons of Issachar *were* Tola, Puvah,[94] Job,[95] and Shimron.
14 The sons of Zebulun *were* Sered, Elon, and Jahleel.
15 These *were* the sons of Leah, whom she bore to Jacob in Padan Aram, with his daughter Dinah. All the persons, his sons and his daughters, *were* thirty-three.

91 Spelled *Nemuel* in 1 Chronicles 4:24   92 Called *Jarib* in 1 Chronicles 4:24
93 Called *Zerah* in 1 Chronicles 4:24   94 Spelled *Puah* in 1 Chronicles 7:1
95 Same as *Jashub* in Numbers 26:24 and 1 Chronicles 7:1

16 The sons of Gad *were* Ziphion,[96] Haggi, Shuni, Ezbon,[97] Eri, Arodi,[98] and Areli.

17 The sons of Asher *were* Jimnah, Ishuah, Isui, Beriah, and Serah, their sister. And the sons of Beriah *were* Heber and Malchiel.

18 These *were* the sons of Zilpah, whom Laban gave to Leah his daughter; and these she bore to Jacob: sixteen persons.

19 The sons of Rachel, Jacob's wife, *were* Joseph and Benjamin.

20 And to Joseph in the land of Egypt were born Manasseh and Ephraim, whom Asenath, the daughter of Poti-Pherah priest of On, bore to him.

21 The sons of Benjamin *were* Belah, Becher, Ashbel, Gera, Naaman, Ehi, Rosh, Muppim, Huppim,[99] and Ard.

22 These *were* the sons of Rachel, who were born to Jacob: fourteen persons in all.

23 The son of Dan *was* Hushim.[100]

24 The sons of Naphtali *were* Jahzeel,[101] Guni, Jezer, and Shillem.[102]

25 These *were* the sons of Bilhah, whom Laban gave to Rachel his daughter, and she bore these to Jacob: seven persons in all.

26 All the persons who went with Jacob to Egypt, who came from his body, besides Jacob's sons' wives, *were* sixty-six persons in all.

27 And the sons of Joseph who were born to him in Egypt *were* two persons. All the persons of the house of Jacob who went to Egypt were seventy.

Jacob Settles in Goshen

28 Then he sent Judah before him to Joseph, to point out before him *the way* to Goshen. And they came to the land of Goshen.

29 So Joseph made ready his chariot and went up to Goshen to meet his father Israel; and he presented himself to him, and fell on his neck and wept on his neck a good while.

30 And Israel said to Joseph, "Now let me die, since I have seen your face, because you *are* still alive."

31 Then Joseph said to his brothers and to his father's household, "I will go up and tell Pharaoh, and say to him, 'My brothers and those of my father's house, who *were* in the land of Canaan, have come to me.

32 'And the men *are* shepherds, for their occupation has been to feed livestock; and they have brought their flocks, their herds, and all that they have.'

33 "So it shall be, when Pharaoh calls you and says, 'What is your occupation?'

34 "that you shall say, 'Your servants' occupation has been with livestock from our youth even till now, both we *and* also our fathers,' that you may dwell in the land of Goshen; for every shepherd *is* an abomination to the Egyptians."

47 Then Joseph went and told Pharaoh, and said, "My father and my brothers, their flocks and their herds and all that they possess, have come from the land of Canaan; and indeed they *are* in the land of Goshen."

2 And he took five men from among his brothers and presented them to Pharaoh.

3 Then Pharaoh said to his brothers, "What *is* your occupation?" And they said to Pharaoh, "Your servants *are* shepherds, both we *and* also our fathers."

4 And they said to Pharaoh, "We have come to sojourn in the land, because your servants have no pasture for their flocks, for the famine *is* severe in the land of Canaan. Now therefore, please let your servants dwell in the land of Goshen."

5 Then Pharaoh spoke to Joseph, saying, "Your father and your brothers have come to you.

6 "The land of Egypt *is* before you. Have your father and brothers dwell in the best of the land; let them dwell in the land of Goshen. And if you know *any* competent men among them, then make them chief herdsmen over my livestock."

7 Then Joseph brought in his father Jacob and set him before Pharaoh; and Jacob blessed Pharaoh.

8 Pharaoh said to Jacob, "How old *are* you?"

9 And Jacob said to Pharaoh, "The days of the years of my pilgrimage *are* one hundred and thirty years; few and evil have been the days of the years of my life, and they have not attained to the days of the years of the life of my fathers in the days of their pilgrimage."

---

96 Spelled *Zephon* in Numbers 26:15, Samaritan Pentateuch, and Septuagint   97 Called *Ozni* in Numbers 26:16
98 Spelled *Arod* in Numbers 26:17   99 Called *Hupham* in Numbers 26:39
100 Called *Shuham* in Numbers 26:42   101 Spelled *Jahziel* in 1 Chronicles 7:13
102 Spelled *Shallum* in 1 Chronicles 7:13

10 So Jacob blessed Pharaoh, and went out from before Pharaoh.
11 And Joseph situated his father and his brothers, and gave them a possession in the land of Egypt, in the best of the land, in the land of Rameses, as Pharaoh had commanded.
12 Then Joseph provided his father, his brothers, and all his father's household with bread, according to the number in *their* families.

Joseph Deals with the Famine

13 Now *there was* no bread in all the land; for the famine *was* very severe, so that the land of Egypt and *all* the land of Canaan languished because of the famine.
14 And Joseph gathered up all the money that was found in the land of Egypt and in the land of Canaan, for the grain which they bought; and Joseph brought the money into Pharaoh's house.
15 So when the money failed in the land of Egypt and in the land of Canaan, all the Egyptians came to Joseph and said, "Give us bread, for why should we die in your presence? For the money has failed."
16 Then Joseph said, "Give your livestock, and I will give you *bread* for your livestock, if the money is gone."
17 So they brought their livestock to Joseph, and Joseph gave them bread *in exchange* for the horses, the flocks, the cattle of the herds, and for the donkeys. Thus he fed them with bread *in exchange* for all their livestock that year.
18 When that year had ended, they came to him the next year and said to him, "We will not hide from my lord that our money is gone; my lord also has our herds of livestock. There is nothing left in the sight of my lord but our bodies and our lands.
19 "Why should we die before your eyes, both we and our land? Buy us and our land for bread, and we and our land will be servants of Pharaoh; give *us* seed, that we may live and not die, that the land may not be desolate."
20 Then Joseph bought all the land of Egypt for Pharaoh; for every man of the Egyptians sold his field, because the famine was severe upon them. So the land became Pharaoh's.
21 And as for the people, he moved them into the cities, from *one* end of the borders of Egypt to the *other* end.
22 Only the land of the priests he did not buy; for the priests had rations *allotted to them* by Pharaoh, and they ate their rations which Pharaoh gave them; therefore they did not sell their lands.
23 Then Joseph said to the people, "Indeed I have bought you and your land this day for Pharaoh. Look, *here is* seed for you, and you shall sow the land.
24 "And it shall come to pass in the harvest that you shall give one-fifth to Pharaoh. Four-fifths shall be your own, as seed for the field and for your food, for those of your households and as food for your little ones."
25 So they said, "You have saved our lives; let us find favor in the sight of my lord, and we will be Pharaoh's servants."
26 And Joseph made it a law over the land of Egypt to this day, *that* Pharaoh should have one-fifth, except for the land of the priests only, *which* did not become Pharaoh's.

Joseph's Vow to Jacob

27 So Israel dwelt in the land of Egypt, in the country of Goshen; and they had possessions there and grew and multiplied exceedingly.
28 And Jacob lived in the land of Egypt seventeen years. So the length of Jacob's life was one hundred and forty-seven years.
29 When the time drew near that Israel must die, he called his son Joseph and said to him, "Now if I have found favor in your sight, please put your hand under my thigh, and deal kindly and truly with me. Please do not bury me in Egypt,
30 "but let me lie with my fathers; you shall carry me out of Egypt and bury me in their burial place." And he said, "I will do as you have said."
31 Then he said, "Swear to me." And he swore to him. So Israel bowed himself on the head of the bed.

Jacob Blesses Joseph's Sons

48 Now it came to pass after these things that Joseph was told, "Indeed your father *is* sick"; and he took with him his two sons, Manasseh and Ephraim.
2 And Jacob was told, "Look, your son Joseph is coming to you"; and Israel

strengthened himself and sat up on the bed.

3 Then Jacob said to Joseph: "God Almighty appeared to me at Luz in the land of Canaan and blessed me,

4 "and said to me, 'Behold, I will make you fruitful and multiply you, and I will make of you a multitude of people, and give this land to your descendants after you *as* an everlasting possession.'

5 "And now your two sons, Ephraim and Manasseh, who were born to you in the land of Egypt before I came to you in Egypt, *are* mine; as Reuben and Simeon, they shall be mine.

6 "Your offspring whom you beget after them shall be yours, *and* will be called by the name of their brothers in their inheritance.

7 "But as for me, when I came from Padan, Rachel died beside me in the land of Canaan on the way, when *there was* but a little distance to go to Ephrath; and I buried her there on the way to Ephrath (that is, Bethlehem)."

8 Then Israel saw Joseph's sons, and said, "Who *are* these?"

9 And Joseph said to his father, "They *are* my sons, whom God has given me in this *place*." And he said, "Please bring them to me, and I will bless them."

10 Now the eyes of Israel were dim with age, *so that* he could not see. Then Joseph brought them near him, and he kissed them and embraced them.

11 And Israel said to Joseph, "I had not thought to see your face; but in fact, God has also shown me your offspring!"

12 So Joseph brought them from beside his knees, and he bowed down with his face to the earth.

13 And Joseph took them both, Ephraim with his right hand toward Israel's left hand, and Manasseh with his left hand toward Israel's right hand, and brought *them* near him.

14 Then Israel stretched out his right hand and laid *it* on Ephraim's head, who *was* the younger, and his left hand on Manasseh's head, guiding his hands knowingly, for Manasseh *was* the firstborn.

15 And he blessed Joseph, and said:

"God, before whom my fathers
    Abraham and Isaac walked,
The God who has fed me
    all my life long to this day,
16 The Angel who has redeemed me
    from all evil,
Bless the lads;
Let my name be named upon them,
And the name of my fathers
    Abraham and Isaac;
And let them grow into a multitude
    in the midst of the earth."

17 Now when Joseph saw that his father laid his right hand on the head of Ephraim, it displeased him; so he took hold of his father's hand to remove it from Ephraim's head to Manasseh's head.

18 And Joseph said to his father, "Not so, my father, for this *one is* the firstborn; put your right hand on his head."

19 But his father refused and said, "I know, my son, I know. He also shall become a people, and he also shall be great; but truly his younger brother shall be greater than he, and his descendants shall become a multitude of nations."

20 So he blessed them that day, saying, "By you Israel will bless, saying, 'May God make you as Ephraim and as Manasseh!' " And thus he set Ephraim before Manasseh.

21 Then Israel said to Joseph, "Behold, I am dying, but God will be with you and bring you back to the land of your fathers.

22 "Moreover I have given to you one portion above your brothers, which I took from the hand of the Amorite with my sword and my bow."

Jacob's Last Words to His Sons

49 And Jacob called his sons and said, "Gather together, that I may tell you what shall befall you in the last days:

2 "Gather together and hear,
    you sons of Jacob,
And listen to Israel your father.

3 "Reuben, you are my firstborn,
    My might and the beginning
        of my strength,
The excellency of dignity
    and the excellency of power.
4 Unstable as water, you shall not excel,
    Because you went up
        to your father's bed;

Then you defiled *it*—
He went up to my couch.

5 "Simeon and Levi *are* brothers;
Instruments of cruelty
are in their habitation.
6 Let not my soul enter their council;
Let not my honor be united
to their assembly;
For in their anger they slew a man,
And in their self-will
they hamstrung an ox.
7 Cursed *be* their anger, for *it is* fierce;
And their wrath, for it is cruel!
I will divide them in Jacob
And scatter them in Israel.

8 "Judah, you *are he* whom
your brothers shall praise;
Your hand *shall be* on the neck
of your enemies;
Your father's children
shall bow down before you.
9 Judah *is* a lion's whelp;
From the prey, my son,
you have gone up.
He bows down, he lies down as a lion;
And as a lion, who shall rouse him?
10 The scepter shall not depart
from Judah,
Nor a lawgiver from between his feet,
Until Shiloh comes;
And to Him *shall be*
the obedience of the people.
11 Binding his donkey to the vine,
And his donkey's colt
to the choice vine,
He washed his garments in wine,
And his clothes in the blood of grapes.
12 His eyes *are* darker than wine,
And his teeth whiter than milk.

13 "Zebulun shall dwell by
the haven of the sea;
He *shall become* a haven for ships,
And his border shall adjoin Sidon.

14 "Issachar is a strong donkey,
Lying down between two burdens;
15 He saw that rest *was* good,
And that the land *was* pleasant;
He bowed his shoulder
to bear *a burden,*
And became a band of slaves.

16 "Dan shall judge his people
As one of the tribes of Israel.
17 Dan shall be a serpent by the way,
A viper by the path,
That bites the horse's heels
So that its rider shall fall backward.

18 I have waited for your salvation,
O LORD!

19 "Gad, a troop shall tramp upon him,
But he shall triumph at last.

20 "Bread from Asher *shall be* rich,
And he shall yield royal dainties.

21 "Naphtali *is* a deer let loose;
He gives goodly words.

22 "Joseph *is* a fruitful bough,
A fruitful bough by a well;
His branches run over the wall.
23 The archers have bitterly grieved him,
Shot *at him* and hated him.
24 But his bow remained in strength,
And the arms of his hands
were made strong
By the hands of the Mighty *God*
of Jacob
(From there *is* the Shepherd,
the Stone of Israel),
25 By the God of your father
who will help you,
And by the Almighty who
will bless you
With blessings of heaven above,
Blessings of the deep that lies beneath,
Blessings of the breasts and
of the womb.
26 The blessings of your father
Have excelled the blessings
of my ancestors,
Up to the utmost bound of the
everlasting hills.
They shall be on the head of Joseph,
And on the crown of the head of him
who was separate from his brothers.

27 "Benjamin is a ravenous wolf;
In the morning he shall devour
the prey,
And at night he shall divide the spoil."

28 All these *are* the twelve tribes of Israel, and this *is* what their father spoke to them. And he blessed them; he blessed each one according to his own blessing.

Jacob's Death and Burial

29 Then he charged them and said to them: "I am to be gathered to my people; bury me with my fathers in the cave that *is* in the field of Ephron the Hittite,
30 "in the cave that *is* in the field of Machpelah, which *is* before Mamre in the

land of Canaan, which Abraham bought with the field of Ephron the Hittite as a possession for a burial place.

31 "There they buried Abraham and Sarah his wife, there they buried Isaac and Rebekah his wife, and there I buried Leah.

32 "The field and the cave that *is* there *were* purchased from the sons of Heth."

33 And when Jacob had finished commanding his sons, he drew his feet up into the bed and breathed his last, and was gathered to his people.

50 Then Joseph fell on his father's face, and wept over him, and kissed him.

2 And Joseph commanded his servants the physicians to embalm his father. So the physicians embalmed Israel.

3 Forty days were required for him, for such are the days required for those who are embalmed; and the Egyptians mourned for him seventy days.

4 And when the days of his mourning were past, Joseph spoke to the household of Pharaoh saying, "If now I have found favor in your eyes, please speak in the hearing of Pharaoh, saying,

5 'My father made me swear, saying, "Behold, I am dying; in my grave which I dug for myself in the land of Canaan, there you shall bury me." Now therefore, please let me go up and bury my father, and I will come back.' "

6 And Pharaoh said, "Go up and bury your father, as he made you swear."

7 So Joseph went up to bury his father; and with him went up all the servants of Pharaoh, the elders of his house, and all the elders of the land of Egypt,

8 as well as all the house of Joseph, his brothers, and his father's house. Only their little ones, their flocks, and their herds they left in the land of Goshen.

9 And there went up with him both chariots and horsemen, and it was a very great gathering.

10 Then they came to the threshing floor of Atad, which *is* beyond the Jordan, and they mourned there with a great and very solemn lamentation. He observed seven days of mourning for his father.

11 And when the inhabitants of the land, the Canaanites, saw the mourning at the threshing floor of Atad, they said, "This

is a grievous mourning of the Egyptians." Therefore its name was called Abel Mizraim,[103] which *is* beyond the Jordan.

12 So his sons did for him just as he had commanded them.

13 For his sons carried him to the land of Canaan, and buried him in the cave of the field of Machpelah, before Mamre, which Abraham bought with the field from Ephron the Hittite as property for a burial place.

14 And after he had buried his father, Joseph returned to Egypt, he and his brothers and all who went up with him to bury his father.

Joseph Reassures His Brothers

15 When Joseph's brothers saw that their father was dead, they said, "Perhaps Joseph will hate us, and may actually repay us for all the evil which we did to him."

16 So they sent *messengers* to Joseph, saying, "Before your father died he commanded, saying,

17 'Thus you shall say to Joseph: "I beg you, please forgive the trespass of your brothers and their sin; for they did evil to you." ' Now, please, forgive the trespass of the servants of the God of your father." And Joseph wept when they spoke to him.

18 Then his brothers also went and fell down before his face, and they said, "Behold, we *are* your servants."

19 Joseph said to them, "Do not be afraid, for *am* I in the place of God?

20 "But as for you, you meant evil against me; *but* God meant it for good, in order to bring it about as *it is* this day, to save many people alive.

21 "Now therefore, do not be afraid; I will provide for you and your little ones." And he comforted them and spoke kindly to them.

Death of Joseph

22 So Joseph dwelt in Egypt, he and his father's household. And Joseph lived one hundred and ten years.

23 Joseph saw Ephraim's children to the third *generation.* The children of Machir, the son of Manasseh, were also brought up on Joseph's knees.

24 And Joseph said to his brethren, "I am dying; but God will surely visit you,

103 Literally *Mourning of Egypt*

and bring you out of this land to the land of which He swore to Abraham, to Isaac, and to Jacob."

25 Then Joseph took an oath from the children of Israel, saying, "God will surely visit you, and you shall carry up my bones from here."

26 So Joseph died, *being* one hundred and ten years old; and they embalmed him, and he was put in a coffin in Egypt.

Introduction to Exodus

Moses was the right person at the right place at the right time! In the Book of Exodus, we learn how God used this possibility thinker to lead His people.

Written by Moses about 1400 B.C., Exodus opens with the story of the Israelites in exile in Egypt. Moses, an Israelite taken into Pharaoh's court as a baby, was the God-appointed leader to save God's people from their severe sufferings. Moses had God's backing and assurance that "I AM WHO I AM"—the name of the self-existent, all-powerful God would be with him.

In a series of plagues, Moses courageously challenged Pharaoh and the false gods of Egypt to let God's people go. The Egyptians worshiped the Nile River, cattle, locusts, frogs, insects, various animals, the fly-god (Beelzebub), and the sun. The plagues were directed at these false deities to show God's supreme power. Finally, Pharaoh relinquished his grip on the Israelites and let them go.

Moses faced his second greatest challenge outside of Egypt in the wilderness wanderings through Sinai. For forty years the people lived in the wilderness, completely dependent on God and Moses for all their needs. God appeared to Moses, giving him the Ten Commandments to help guide and direct His people. The Israelites often complained about their nomadic life-style. Moses had to keep the dream of the Promised Land alive, helping them to eliminate the negative and focus on the positive. Moses believed that if the people believed God's promise, their faith would build them up!

Despite all the negative-thinking "experts," those people who quickly offered their advice for the Israelites to quit their needless wanderings, Moses held true to the God-given dream. He never let his problems stop him from making the right decision. He made a decision and then solved his problems. Because of Moses' positive, unyielding faith, the Israelites acquired their goal. The Promised Land was theirs!

The Second Book of Moses Called
Exodus

Israel's Suffering in Egypt

NOW these *are* the names of the children of Israel who came to Egypt; each man and his household came with Jacob:
2 Reuben, Simeon, Levi, and Judah;
3 Issachar, Zebulun, and Benjamin;
4 Dan, Naphtali, Gad, and Asher.
5 All those who were descendants[1] of Jacob were seventy[2] persons (for Joseph was in Egypt *already*).
6 And Joseph died, all his brothers, and all that generation.
7 But the children of Israel were fruitful and increased abundantly, multiplied and grew exceedingly mighty; and the land was filled with them.
8 Now there arose a new king over Egypt, who did not know Joseph.
9 And he said to his people, "Look, the people of the children of Israel *are* more and mightier than we;
10 "come, let us deal wisely with them, lest they multiply, and it happen, in the event of war, that they also join our enemies and fight against us, and *so* go up out of the land."
11 Therefore they set taskmasters over them to afflict them with their burdens. And they built for Pharaoh supply cities, Pithom and Raamses.
12 But the more they afflicted them, the more they multiplied and grew. And they were in dread of the children of Israel.
13 So the Egyptians made the children of Israel serve with rigor.
14 And they made their lives bitter with hard bondage—in mortar, in brick, and in all manner of service in the field. All their service in which they made them serve *was* with rigor.
15 Then the king of Egypt spoke to the Hebrew midwives, of whom the name of one *was* Shiphrah and the name of the other Puah;
16 and he said, "When you do the duties of a midwife for the Hebrew women, and see *them* on the birthstools, if it *is* a son, then you shall kill him; but if it *is* a daughter, then she shall live."
17 But the midwives feared God, and did not do as the king of Egypt commanded them, but saved the male children alive.
18 So the king of Egypt called for the midwives and said to them, "Why have you done this thing, and saved the male children alive?"
19 And the midwives said to Pharaoh, "Because the Hebrew women *are* not like the Egyptian women; for they *are* lively and give birth before the midwives come to them."
20 Therefore God dealt well with the midwives, and the people multiplied and grew very mighty.
21 And so it was, because the midwives feared God, that He provided households for them.
22 So Pharaoh commanded all his people, saying, "Every son who is born[3] you shall cast into the river, and every daughter you shall save alive."

Moses Is Born

2 And a man of the house of Levi went and took *as wife* a daughter of Levi.
2 So the woman conceived and bore a son. And when she saw that he *was* a beautiful *child*, she hid him three months.
3 But when she could no longer hide him, she took an ark of bulrushes for him, daubed it with asphalt and pitch, put the child in it, and laid *it* in the reeds by the river's bank.
4 And his sister stood afar off, to know what would be done to him.
5 Then the daughter of Pharaoh came down to wash *herself* at the river. And her maidens walked along the river's side; and when she saw the ark among the reeds, she sent her maid to get it.
6 And when she had opened *it*, she saw the child, and behold, the baby wept. So she had compassion on him, and said, "This is one of the Hebrews' children."
7 Then his sister said to Pharaoh's daughter, "Shall I go and call a nurse for

---

1 Literally *who came from the loins of*   2 Dead Sea Scrolls and Septuagint read *seventy-five.*
3 Samaritan Pentateuch, Septuagint, and Targum add *to the Hebrews.*

you from the Hebrew women, that she
may nurse the child for you?"
8 And Pharaoh's daughter said to her,
"Go." So the maiden went and called the
child's mother.
9 Then Pharaoh's daughter said to her,
"Take this child away and nurse him for
me, and I will give *you* your wages." So
the woman took the child and nursed
him.
10 And the child grew, and she brought
him to Pharaoh's daughter, and he became her son. So she called his name
Moses,⁴ saying, "Because I drew him out
of the water."

Moses Flees to Midian

11 Now it came to pass in those days,
when Moses was grown, that he went out
to his brethren and looked at their burdens. And he saw an Egyptian beating a
Hebrew, one of his brethren.
12 So he looked this way and that way,
and when he saw no one, he killed the
Egyptian and hid him in the sand.
13 And when he went out the second
day, behold, two Hebrew men were fighting, and he said to the one who did the
wrong, "Why are you striking your companion?"
14 Then he said, "Who made you a
prince and a judge over us? Do you intend to kill me as you killed the Egyptian?" So Moses feared and said, "Surely
this thing is known!"
15 When Pharaoh heard of this matter,
he sought to kill Moses. But Moses fled
from the face of Pharaoh and dwelt in the
land of Midian; and he sat down by a
well.
16 Now the priest of Midian had seven
daughters. And they came and drew water, and they filled the troughs to water
their father's flock.
17 Then the shepherds came and drove
them away; but Moses stood up and
helped them, and watered their flock.
18 When they came to Reuel their father,
he said, "How *is it that* you have come so
soon today?"
19 And they said, "An Egyptian delivered us from the hand of the shepherds,
and he also drew enough water for us and
watered the flock."
20 So he said to his daughters, "And
where *is* he? Why *is it that* you have left

the man? Call him, that he may eat
bread."
21 Then Moses was content to live with
the man, and he gave Zipporah his
daughter to Moses.
22 And she bore *him* a son, and he called
his name Gershom;⁵ for he said, "I have
been a stranger in a foreign land."
23 Now it happened in the process of
time that the king of Egypt died. Then
the children of Israel groaned because of
the bondage, and they cried out; and
their cry came up to God because of the
bondage.
24 So God heard their groaning, and
God remembered His covenant with
Abraham, with Isaac, and with Jacob.
25 And God looked upon the children of
Israel, and God acknowledged *them*.

Moses at the Burning Bush

3 Now Moses kept the flock of Jethro
his father-in-law, the priest of Midian. And he led the flock to the back of
the desert, and came to Horeb, the mountain of God.
2 And the Angel of the LORD appeared
to him in a flame of fire from the midst of
a bush. So he looked, and behold, the
bush burned with fire, but the bush *was*
not consumed.
3 Then Moses said, "I will now turn
aside and see this great sight, why the
bush does not burn."
4 So when the LORD saw that he turned
aside to look, God called to him from the
midst of the bush and said, "Moses, Moses!" And he said, "Here I am."
5 Then He said, "Do not draw near this
place. Take your sandals off your feet,
for the place where you stand *is* holy
ground."
6 Moreover He said, "I *am* the God of
your father—the God of Abraham, the
God of Isaac, and the God of Jacob."
And Moses hid his face, for he was afraid
to look upon God.
7 And the LORD said: "I have surely
seen the oppression of My people who
are in Egypt, and have heard their cry
because of their taskmasters, for I know
their sorrows.
8 "So I have come down to deliver them
out of the hand of the Egyptians, and to
bring them up from that land to a good
and large land, to a land flowing with
milk and honey, to the place of the Ca-

4 Literally *Drawn Out* 5 Literally *Stranger There*

naanites and the Hittites and the Amorites and the Perizzites and the Hivites and the Jebusites.

9 "Now therefore, behold, the cry of the children of Israel has come to Me, and I have also seen the oppression with which the Egyptians oppress them.

10 "Come now, therefore, and I will send you to Pharaoh that you may bring My people, the children of Israel, out of Egypt."

11 But Moses said to God, "Who *am* I that I should go to Pharaoh, and that I should bring the children of Israel out of Egypt?"

12 So He said, "I will certainly be with you. And this *shall be* a sign to you that I have sent you: When you have brought the people out of Egypt, you shall serve God on this mountain."

13 Then Moses said to God, "Indeed, *when* I come to the children of Israel and say to them, 'The God of your fathers has sent me to you,' and they say to me, 'What *is* His name?' what shall I say to them?"

14 And God said to Moses, "I AM WHO I AM." And He said, "Thus you shall say to the children of Israel, 'I AM has sent me to you.' "

15 Moreover God said to Moses, "Thus you shall say to the children of Israel: 'The LORD God of your fathers, the God of Abraham, the God of Isaac, and the God of Jacob, has sent me to you. This *is* My name forever, and this *is* My memorial to all generations.'

16 "Go and gather the elders of Israel together, and say to them, 'The LORD God of your fathers, the God of Abraham, of Isaac, and of Jacob, appeared to me, saying, "I have surely visited you and *seen* what is done to you in Egypt;

17 "and I have said I will bring you up out of the affliction of Egypt to the land of the Canaanites and the Hittites and the Amorites and the Perizzites and the Hivites and the Jebusites, to a land flowing with milk and honey." '

18 "Then they will heed your voice; and you shall come, you and the elders of Israel, to the king of Egypt; and you shall say to him, 'The LORD God of the Hebrews has met with us; and now, please, let us go three days' journey into the wilderness, that we may sacrifice to the LORD our God.'

19 "But I am sure that the king of Egypt will not let you go, no, not even by a mighty hand.

20 "So I will stretch out My hand and strike Egypt with all My wonders which I will do in its midst; and after that he will let you go.

21 "And I will give this people favor in the sight of the Egyptians; and it shall be, when you go, that you shall not go empty-handed.

22 "But every woman shall ask of her neighbor, namely, of her who dwells near her house, articles of silver, articles of gold, and clothing; and you shall put *them* on your sons and on your daughters. So you shall plunder the Egyptians."

Miraculous Signs for Pharaoh

4 Then Moses answered and said, "But suppose they will not believe me or listen to my voice; suppose they say, 'The LORD has not appeared to you.' "

2 So the LORD said to him, "What *is* that in your hand?" And he said, "A rod."

3 And He said, "Cast it on the ground." So he cast it on the ground, and it became a serpent; and Moses fled from it.

4 Then the LORD said to Moses, "Reach out your hand and take *it* by the tail" (and he reached out his hand and caught it, and it became a rod in his hand),

5 "that they may believe that the LORD God of their fathers, the God of Abraham, the God of Isaac, and the God of Jacob, has appeared to you."

6 Furthermore the LORD said to him, "Now put your hand in your bosom." And he put his hand in his bosom, and when he took it out, behold, his hand *was* leprous, like snow.

7 And He said, "Put your hand in your bosom again." So he put his hand in his bosom again, and drew it out of his bosom, and behold, it was restored like his *other* flesh.

8 "Then it will be, if they do not believe you, nor heed the message of the first sign, that they may believe the message of the latter sign.

9 "And it shall be, if they do not believe even these two signs, or listen to your voice, that you shall take water from the river[6] and pour *it* on the dry *land*. And

6 That is, the Nile

the water which you take from the river will become blood on the dry *land*."

10 Then Moses said to the LORD, "O my Lord, I *am* not eloquent, neither before nor since You have spoken to Your servant; but I *am* slow of speech and slow of tongue."

11 So the LORD said to him, "Who has made man's mouth? Or who makes the mute, the deaf, the seeing, or the blind? *Have* not I, the LORD?

12 "Now therefore, go, and I will be with your mouth and teach you what you shall say."

13 But he said, "O my Lord, please send by the hand of whomever *else* You may send."

14 So the anger of the LORD was kindled against Moses, and He said: "Is not Aaron the Levite your brother? I know that he can speak well. And look, he is also coming out to meet you. When he sees you, he will be glad in his heart.

15 "Now you shall speak to him and put the words in his mouth. And I will be with your mouth and with his mouth, and I will teach you what you shall do.

16 "So he shall be your spokesman to the people. And he himself shall be as a mouth for you, and you shall be to him as God.

17 "And you shall take this rod in your hand, with which you shall do the signs."

Moses Goes to Egypt

18 So Moses went and returned to Jethro his father-in-law, and said to him, "Please let me go and return to my brethren who *are* in Egypt, and see whether they are still alive." And Jethro said to Moses, "Go in peace."

19 And the LORD said to Moses in Midian, "Go, return to Egypt; for all the men are dead who sought your life."

20 Then Moses took his wife and his sons and set them on a donkey, and he returned to the land of Egypt. And Moses took the rod of God in his hand.

21 And the LORD said to Moses, "When you go back to Egypt, see that you do all those wonders before Pharaoh which I have put in your hand. But I will harden his heart, so that he will not let the people go.

22 "Then you shall say to Pharaoh, 'Thus says the LORD: "Israel *is* My son, My firstborn.

23 "So I say to you, let My son go that he may serve Me. But if you refuse to let him go, indeed I will kill your son, your firstborn." '"

24 And it came to pass on the way, at the encampment, that the LORD met him and sought to kill him.

25 Then Zipporah took a sharp stone and cut off the foreskin of her son and cast *it* at Moses'[7] feet, and said, "Surely you *are* a husband of blood to me!"

26 So He let him go. Then she said, "*You are* a husband of blood!"—because of the circumcision.

27 And the LORD said to Aaron, "Go into the wilderness to meet Moses." So he went and met him on the mountain of God, and kissed him.

28 So Moses told Aaron all the words of the LORD who had sent him, and all the signs which He had commanded him.

29 Then Moses and Aaron went and gathered together all the elders of the children of Israel.

30 And Aaron spoke all the words which the LORD had spoken to Moses. Then he did the signs in the sight of the people.

31 So the people believed; and when they heard that the LORD had visited the children of Israel and that He had looked on their affliction, then they bowed their heads and worshiped.

First Encounter with Pharaoh

5 Afterward Moses and Aaron went in and told Pharaoh, "Thus says the LORD God of Israel: 'Let My people go, that they may hold a feast to Me in the wilderness.'"

2 And Pharaoh said, "Who *is* the LORD, that I should obey His voice to let Israel go? I do not know the LORD, nor will I let Israel go."

3 So they said, "The God of the Hebrews has met with us. Please, let us go three days' journey into the desert and sacrifice to the LORD our God, lest He fall upon us with pestilence or with the sword."

4 Then the king of Egypt said to them, "Moses and Aaron, why do you take the people from their work? Get *back* to your labor."

5 And Pharaoh said, "Look, the people of the land *are* many now, and you make them rest from their labor!"

6 So the same day Pharaoh commanded

7 Literally *his*

the taskmasters of the people and their officers, saying,

7 "You shall no longer give the people straw to make brick as before. Let them go and gather straw for themselves.

8 "And you shall lay on them the quota of bricks which they made before. You shall not diminish it. For they are idle; therefore they cry out, saying, 'Let us go and sacrifice to our God.'

9 "Let more work be laid on the men, that they may labor in it, and let them not regard false words."

10 And the taskmasters of the people and their officers went out and spoke to the people, saying, "Thus says Pharaoh: 'I will not give you straw.

11 'Go, get yourselves straw where you can find it; yet none of your work will be diminished.'"

12 So the people were scattered abroad throughout all the land of Egypt to gather stubble instead of straw.

13 And the taskmasters forced *them* to hurry, saying, "Fulfill your work, *your* daily quota, as when there was straw."

14 Also the officers of the children of Israel, whom Pharaoh's taskmasters had set over them, were beaten *and* were asked, "Why have you not fulfilled your task in making brick both yesterday and today, as before?"

15 Then the officers of the children of Israel came and cried out to Pharaoh, saying, "Why are you dealing thus with your servants?

16 "There is no straw given to your servants, and they say to us, 'Make brick!' And indeed your servants *are* beaten, but the fault *is* in your *own* people."

17 But he said, "You *are* idle! *You are* idle! Therefore you say, 'Let us go and sacrifice to the LORD.'

18 "Therefore go now *and* work; for no straw shall be given you, yet you shall deliver the quota of bricks."

19 And the officers of the children of Israel saw *that* they *were* in trouble after it was said, "You shall not diminish *any* bricks from your daily quota."

20 Then, as they came out from Pharaoh, they met Moses and Aaron who stood there to meet them.

21 And they said to them, "Let the LORD look on you and judge, because you have made us abhorrent in the sight of Pha-

raoh and in the sight of his servants, to put a sword in their hand to kill us."

Israel's Deliverance Assured

22 So Moses returned to the LORD and said, "Lord, why have You brought trouble on this people? Why *is* it You have sent me?

23 "For since I came to Pharaoh to speak in Your name, he has done evil to this people; neither have You delivered Your people at all."

6 Then the LORD said to Moses, "Now you shall see what I will do to Pharaoh. For with a strong hand he will let them go, and with a strong hand he will drive them out of his land."

2 And God spoke to Moses and said to him: "I *am* the LORD.

3 "I appeared to Abraham, to Isaac, and to Jacob, as God Almighty, but *by* My name, LORD,[8] I was not known to them.

4 "I have also established My covenant with them, to give them the land of Canaan, the land of their pilgrimage, in which they were strangers.

5 "And I have also heard the groaning of the children of Israel whom the Egyptians keep in bondage, and I have remembered My covenant.

6 "Therefore say to the children of Israel: 'I *am* the LORD; I will bring you out from under the burdens of the Egyptians, I will rescue you from their bondage, and I will redeem you with an outstretched arm and with great judgments.

7 'I will take you as My people, and I will be your God. Then you shall know that I *am* the LORD your God who brings you out from under the burdens of the Egyptians.

8 'And I will bring you into the land which I swore to give to Abraham, Isaac, and Jacob; and I will give it to you *as* a heritage: I *am* the LORD.'"

9 So Moses spoke thus to the children of Israel; but they would not heed Moses, because of anguish of spirit and cruel bondage.

10 And the LORD spoke to Moses, saying,

11 "Go in, speak to Pharaoh king of Egypt, that he must let the children of Israel go out of his land."

12 And Moses spoke before the LORD,

8 Hebrew *YHWH*, traditionally *Jehovah*

saying, "The children of Israel have not heeded me. How then shall Pharaoh heed me, for I *am* of uncircumcised lips?" ¹³ Then the LORD spoke to Moses and Aaron, and gave them a command for the children of Israel and for Pharaoh king of Egypt, to bring the children of Israel out of the land of Egypt.

The Family of Moses and Aaron

14 These *are* the heads of their fathers' houses: The sons of Reuben, the firstborn of Israel, *were* Hanoch, Pallu, Hezron, and Carmi. These are the families of Reuben.

¹⁵ And the sons of Simeon *were* Jemuel,⁹ Jamin, Ohad, Jachin, Zohar, and Shaul the son of a Canaanite woman. These *are* the families of Simeon.

¹⁶ These *are* the names of the sons of Levi according to their generations: Gershon, Kohath, and Merari. And the years of the life of Levi *were* one hundred and thirty-seven.

¹⁷ The sons of Gershon *were* Libni and Shimi according to their families.

¹⁸ And the sons of Kohath *were* Amram, Izhar, Hebron, and Uzziel. And the years of the life of Kohath *were* one hundred and thirty-three.

¹⁹ The sons of Merari *were* Mahali and Mushi. These *are* the families of Levi according to their generations.

20 Now Amram took for himself Jochebed, his father's sister, as wife; and she bore him Aaron and Moses. And the years of the life of Amram *were* one hundred and thirty-seven.

²¹ The sons of Izhar *were* Korah, Nepheg, and Zichri.

²² And the sons of Uzziel *were* Mishael, Elzaphan, and Zithri.

²³ Aaron took to himself Elisheba, daughter of Amminadab, sister of Nahshon, as wife; and she bore him Nadab, Abihu, Eleazar, and Ithamar.

²⁴ And the sons of Korah *were* Assir, Elkanah, and Abiasaph. These are the families of the Korahites.

²⁵ Eleazar, Aaron's son, took for himself one of the daughters of Putiel as wife; and she bore him Phinehas. These *are* the heads of the fathers of the Levites according to their families.

26 These *are the same* Aaron and Moses to whom the LORD said, "Bring out the

children of Israel from the land of Egypt according to their armies."

²⁷ These *are* the ones who spoke to Pharaoh king of Egypt, to bring out the children of Israel from Egypt. These *are the same* Moses and Aaron.

Aaron Is Moses' Spokesman

28 And it came to pass, on the day *when* the LORD spoke to Moses in the land of Egypt,

²⁹ that the LORD spoke to Moses, saying, "I *am* the LORD. Speak to Pharaoh king of Egypt all that I say to you."

³⁰ But Moses said before the LORD, "Behold, I *am* of uncircumcised lips, and how shall Pharaoh heed me?"

7 So the LORD said to Moses: "See, I have made you *as* God to Pharaoh, and Aaron your brother shall be your prophet.

² "You shall speak all that I command you. And Aaron your brother shall speak to Pharaoh, that he must send the children of Israel out of his land.

³ "And I will harden Pharaoh's heart, and multiply My signs and My wonders in the land of Egypt.

⁴ "But Pharaoh will not heed you, so that I may lay My hand on Egypt and bring My armies *and* My people, the children of Israel, out of the land of Egypt by great judgments.

⁵ "And the Egyptians shall know that I *am* the LORD, when I stretch out My hand on Egypt and bring out the children of Israel from among them."

⁶ Then Moses and Aaron did *so*; just as the LORD commanded them, so they did.

⁷ And Moses *was* eighty years old and Aaron eighty-three years old when they spoke to Pharaoh.

Aaron's Miraculous Rod

8 Then the LORD spoke to Moses and Aaron, saying,

⁹ "When Pharaoh speaks to you, saying, 'Show a miracle for yourselves,' then you shall say to Aaron, 'Take your rod and cast *it* before Pharaoh, *and* let it become a serpent.' "

¹⁰ So Moses and Aaron went in to Pharaoh, and they did so, just as the LORD commanded. And Aaron cast down his rod before Pharaoh and before his servants, and it became a serpent.

¹¹ But Pharaoh also called the wise men

9 Spelled *Nemuel* in Numbers 26:12

and the sorcerers; so the magicians of Egypt, they also did in like manner with their enchantments. 12 For every man threw down his rod, and they became serpents. But Aaron's rod swallowed up their rods. 13 And Pharaoh's heart grew hard, and he did not heed them, as the LORD had said.

The First Plague: Waters Become Blood

14 So the LORD said to Moses: "Pharaoh's heart *is* hard; he refuses to let the people go. 15 "Go to Pharaoh in the morning, when he goes out to the water, and you shall stand by the river's bank to meet him; and the rod which was turned to a serpent you shall take in your hand. 16 "And you shall say to him, 'The LORD God of the Hebrews has sent me to you, saying, "Let My people go, that they may serve Me in the wilderness"; but indeed, until now you would not hear! 17 'Thus says the LORD: "By this you shall know that I *am* the LORD. Behold, I will strike the waters which *are* in the river with the rod that *is* in my hand, and they shall be turned to blood. 18 "And the fish that *are* in the river shall die, the river shall stink, and the Egyptians will loathe to drink the water of the river." ' " *19* Then the LORD spoke to Moses, "Say to Aaron, 'Take your rod and stretch out your hand over the waters of Egypt, over their streams, over their rivers, over their ponds, and over all their pools of water, that they may become blood. And there shall be blood throughout all the land of Egypt, both in *vessels of* wood and *vessels of* stone.' " 20 And Moses and Aaron did so, just as the LORD commanded. So he lifted up the rod and struck the waters that *were* in the river, in the sight of Pharaoh and in the sight of his servants. And all the waters that *were* in the river were turned to blood. 21 The fish that *were* in the river died, the river stank, and the Egyptians could not drink the water of the river. So there was blood throughout all the land of Egypt. 22 Then the magicians of Egypt did so with their enchantments; and Pharaoh's heart grew hard, and he did not heed them, as the LORD had said.

23 And Pharaoh turned and went into his house. Neither was his heart moved by this. 24 So all the Egyptians dug all around the river for water to drink, because they could not drink the water of the river. 25 And seven days passed after the LORD had struck the river.

The Second Plague: Frogs

8 And the LORD spoke to Moses, "Go to Pharaoh and say to him, 'Thus says the LORD: "Let My people go, that they may serve Me. 2 "But if you refuse to let *them* go, behold, I will smite all your territory with frogs. 3 "So the river shall bring forth frogs abundantly, which shall go up and come into your house, into your bedchamber, on your bed, into the houses of your servants, on your people, into your ovens, and into your kneading bowls. 4 "And the frogs shall come up on you, on your people, and on all your servants." ' " 5 Then the LORD spoke to Moses, "Say to Aaron, 'Stretch out your hand with your rod over the streams, over the rivers, and over the ponds, and cause frogs to come up on the land of Egypt.' " 6 So Aaron stretched out his hand over the waters of Egypt, and the frogs came up and covered the land of Egypt. 7 And the magicians did so with their enchantments, and brought up frogs on the land of Egypt. 8 Then Pharaoh called for Moses and Aaron, and said, "Entreat the LORD that He may take away the frogs from me and from my people; and I will let the people go, that they may sacrifice to the LORD." 9 And Moses said to Pharaoh, "Accept the honor of saying when I shall intercede for you, for your servants, and for your people, to destroy the frogs from you and your houses, *that* they may remain in the river only." 10 So he said, "Tomorrow." And he said, "*Let it be* according to your word, that you may know that *there is* no one like the LORD our God. 11 "And the frogs shall depart from you, from your houses, from your servants, and from your people. They shall remain in the river only." 12 Then Moses and Aaron went out from

Let My People Go

The ancient Israelites had an appreciation for seeing God at work in the everyday events of life. They understood God's use of His creation and natural phenomenon to reveal Himself.

This attitude is often lost in modern society when we test God to reveal Himself in a "supernatural" way. There are times when God does perform extraordinary miracles, such as raising Lazarus from the dead, Jesus walking on the water, or the resurrection of Christ. But we also need to recognize God in the common events of life, such as bringing the right people into our lives when we need help and encouragement.

One example of this faith is found when Moses challenged the Egyptian Pharaoh to free the Israelites from slavery. Ten plagues fell upon the land of Egypt. These were not magical, but rather demonstrative of God's power. Each plague was also a natural phenomenon that periodically took place in Egypt. These included plagues of frogs, lice, flies, diseased cattle, boils, locusts, and more. Each time a plague fell on the land, the Egyptians invoked worship to a god-like image of whatever the plague was.

When God sent the plagues on the Egyptians, He showed His power over the false gods. The intensity, severity and timing of the plagues revealed the greatness of the God of the Israelites. Using a natural phenomenon, God worked miracles for His people.

Later when Moses died and Joshua commanded the Israelites, God used other natural events to reveal His greatness. Upon crossing the Jordan River, God miraculously parted the waters near the towns of Gilgal and Adamah. In our century many times the Jordan River has been dammed from mud slides which occur near these ancient towns. Whether God parted the waters for the Israelites supernaturally or through a beautiful illustration of natural phenomena such as the mud slides, timed perfectly, we do not know. But regardless, the Israelites saw God revealed in the miracle.

We must also develop an appreciation for God's lordship throughout His creation. His ability to use natural circumstances to aid us is as prominent as it was for the ancient Israelites. All we need to do is look around at the everyday events in our lives. God is revealing Himself to us in many ways.

Pharaoh. And Moses cried out to the LORD concerning the frogs which He had brought against Pharaoh. 13 So the LORD did according to the word of Moses. And the frogs died out of the houses, out of the courtyards, and out of the fields. 14 They gathered them together in heaps, and the land stank. 15 But when Pharaoh saw that there was relief, he hardened his heart and did not heed them, as the LORD had said.

The Third Plague: Lice

16 So the LORD said to Moses, "Say to Aaron, 'Stretch out your rod, and strike the dust of the land, so that it may become lice throughout all the land of Egypt.'" 17 And they did so. For Aaron stretched out his hand with his rod and struck the dust of the earth, and it became lice on man and beast. All the dust of the land became lice throughout all the land of Egypt. 18 Now the magicians so worked with their enchantments to bring forth lice, but they could not. So there were lice on man and beast. 19 Then the magicians said to Pharaoh, "This is the finger of God." But Pharaoh's heart grew hard, and he did not heed them, just as the LORD had said.

The Fourth Plague: Flies

20 And the LORD said to Moses, "Rise early in the morning and stand before Pharaoh as he comes out to the water. Then say to him, 'Thus says the LORD: "Let My people go, that they may serve Me. 21 Or else, if you will not let My people go, behold, I will send swarms of flies on you and your servants, on your people and into your houses. The houses of the Egyptians shall be full of swarms of flies, and also the ground on which they stand. 22 And in that day I will set apart the land of Goshen, in which My people dwell, that no swarms of flies shall be there, in order that you may know that I am the LORD in the midst of the land. 23 I will make a difference[10] between My people and your people. Tomorrow this sign shall be."'" 24 And the LORD did so. Thick swarms of flies came into the house of Pharaoh,

into his servants' houses, and into all the land of Egypt. The land was corrupted because of the swarms of flies. 25 Then Pharaoh called for Moses and Aaron, and said, "Go, sacrifice to your God in the land." 26 And Moses said, "It is not right to do so, for we would be sacrificing the abomination of the Egyptians to the LORD our God. If we sacrifice the abomination of the Egyptians before their eyes, then will they not stone us? 27 We will go three days' journey into the wilderness and sacrifice to the LORD our God as He will command us." 28 And Pharaoh said, "I will let you go, that you may sacrifice to the LORD your God in the wilderness; only you shall not go very far away. Intercede for me." 29 Then Moses said, "Indeed I am going out from you, and I will entreat the LORD, that the swarms of flies may depart tomorrow from Pharaoh, from his servants, and from his people. But let Pharaoh not deal deceitfully anymore in not letting the people go to sacrifice to the LORD." 30 So Moses went out from Pharaoh and entreated the LORD. 31 And the LORD did according to the word of Moses; He removed the swarms of flies from Pharaoh, from his servants, and from his people. Not one remained. 32 But Pharaoh hardened his heart at this time also; neither would he let the people go.

The Fifth Plague: Livestock Diseased

9 Then the LORD said to Moses, "Go in to Pharaoh and tell him, 'Thus says the LORD God of the Hebrews: "Let My people go, that they may serve Me. 2 For if you refuse to let them go, and still hold them, 3 behold, the hand of the LORD will be on your cattle in the field, on the horses, on the donkeys, on the camels, on the oxen, and on the sheep. There will be a very severe pestilence. 4 And the LORD will make a difference between the livestock of Israel and the livestock of Egypt. So nothing shall die of all that belongs to the children of Israel."'" 5 Then the LORD appointed a set time, saying, "Tomorrow the LORD will do this thing in the land."

10 Literally ransom (compare Exodus 9:4 and 11:7)

6 So the LORD did this thing on the next day, and all the livestock of Egypt died; but of the livestock of the children of Israel, not one died.
7 Then Pharaoh sent, and indeed, not even one of the livestock of the Israelites was dead. But the heart of Pharaoh became hard, and he did not let the people go.

The Sixth Plague: Boils

8 So the LORD said to Moses and Aaron, "Take for yourselves handfuls of ashes from a furnace, and let Moses scatter it toward the heavens in the sight of Pharaoh.
9 "And it will become fine dust in all the land of Egypt, and it will cause boils that break out in sores on man and beast throughout all the land of Egypt."
10 Then they took ashes from the furnace and stood before Pharaoh, and Moses scattered *them* toward heaven. And *they* caused boils that break out in sores on man and beast.
11 And the magicians could not stand before Moses because of the boils, for the boils were on the magicians and on all the Egyptians.
12 But the LORD hardened the heart of Pharaoh; and he did not heed them, just as the LORD had spoken to Moses.

The Seventh Plague: Hail

13 Then the LORD said to Moses, "Rise early in the morning and stand before Pharaoh, and say to him, 'Thus says the LORD God of the Hebrews: "Let My people go, that they may serve Me,
14 "for at this time I will send all My plagues to your very heart, and on your servants and on your people, that you may know that *there is* none like Me in all the earth.
15 "Now if I had stretched out My hand and struck you and your people with pestilence, then you would have been cut off from the earth.
16 "But indeed for this *purpose* I have raised you up, that I may show My power *in* you, and that My name may be declared in all the earth.
17 "As yet you exalt yourself against My people in that you will not let them go.
18 "Behold, tomorrow about this time I will cause very heavy hail to rain down,

such as has not been in Egypt since its founding until now.
19 "Therefore send now *and* gather your livestock and all that you have in the field, for the hail shall come down on every man and every beast which is found in the field and is not brought home; and they shall die." ' "
20 He who feared the word of the LORD among the servants of Pharaoh made his servants and his livestock flee to the houses.
21 But he who did not regard the word of the LORD left his servants and his livestock in the field.
22 Then the LORD said to Moses, "Stretch out your hand toward heaven, that there may be hail in all the land of Egypt—on man, on beast, and on every herb of the field, throughout the land of Egypt."
23 And Moses stretched out his rod toward heaven; and the LORD sent thunder and hail, and fire darted to the ground. And the LORD rained hail on the land of Egypt.
24 So there was hail, and fire mingled with the hail, so very heavy that there was none like it in all the land of Egypt since it became a nation.
25 And the hail struck throughout the whole land of Egypt, all that *was* in the field, both man and beast; and the hail struck every herb of the field and broke every tree of the field.
26 Only in the land of Goshen, where the children of Israel *were*, there was no hail.
27 And Pharaoh sent and called for Moses and Aaron, and said to them, "I have sinned this time. The LORD *is* righteous, and my people and I *are* wicked.
28 "Entreat the LORD, that there may be no *more* mighty thundering and hail, for *it is* enough. I will let you go, and you shall stay no longer."
29 And Moses said to him, "As soon as I have gone out of the city, I will spread out my hands to the LORD; the thunder will cease, and there will be no more hail, that you may know that the earth *is* the LORD'S.
30 "But as for you and your servants, I know that you will not yet fear the LORD God."
31 Now the flax and the barley were struck, for the barley *was* in the head and the flax *was* in bud.

32 But the wheat and the spelt were not struck, for they *are* late crops.

33 So Moses went out of the city from Pharaoh and spread out his hands to the LORD; then the thunder and the hail ceased, and the rain was not poured on the earth.

34 And when Pharaoh saw that the rain, the hail, and the thunder had ceased, he sinned yet more; and he hardened his heart, he and his servants.

35 So the heart of Pharaoh was hard; neither would he let the children of Israel go, as the LORD had spoken by Moses.

The Eighth Plague: Locusts

10 Now the LORD said to Moses, "Go in to Pharaoh; for I have hardened his heart and the hearts of his servants, that I may show these signs of Mine before him,

2 "and that you may tell in the hearing of your son and your son's son the mighty things I have done in Egypt, and My signs which I have done among them, that you may know that I *am* the LORD."

3 So Moses and Aaron came in to Pharaoh and said to him, "Thus says the LORD God of the Hebrews: 'How long will you refuse to humble yourself before Me? Let My people go, that they may serve Me.

4 'Or else, if you refuse to let My people go, behold, tomorrow I will bring locusts into your territory.

5 'And they shall cover the face of the earth, so that no one will be able to see the earth; and they shall eat the residue of what is left, which remains to you from the hail, and they shall eat every tree which grows up for you out of the field.

6 'They shall fill your houses, the houses of all your servants, and the houses of all the Egyptians—which neither your fathers nor your fathers' fathers have seen, since the day that they were on the earth to this day.' " And he turned and went out from Pharaoh.

7 Then Pharaoh's servants said to him, "How long shall this man be a snare to us? Let the men go, that they may serve the LORD their God. Do you not yet know that Egypt is destroyed?"

8 So Moses and Aaron were brought again to Pharaoh, and he said to them, "Go, serve the LORD your God. *But* who *are* the ones that are going?"

9 And Moses said, "We will go with our young and our old; with our sons and our daughters, with our flocks and our herds we will go, for we must hold a feast to the LORD."

10 Then he said to them, "The LORD had better be with you when I let you and your little ones go! Beware, for evil is ahead of you.

11 "Not so! Go now, you *who are* men, and serve the LORD, for that is what you desired." And they were driven out from Pharaoh's presence.

12 Then the LORD said to Moses, "Stretch out your hand over the land of Egypt for the locusts, that they may come upon the land of Egypt, and eat every herb of the land—all that the hail has left."

13 So Moses stretched out his rod over the land of Egypt, and the LORD brought an east wind on the land all that day and all *that* night. *And* when it was morning, the east wind brought the locusts.

14 And the locusts went up over all the land of Egypt and rested on all the territory of Egypt. *They were* very severe; previously there had been no such locusts as they, nor shall there be such after them.

15 For they covered the face of the whole earth, so that the land was darkened; and they ate every herb of the land and all the fruit of the trees which the hail had left. So there remained nothing green on the trees or on the plants of the field throughout all the land of Egypt.

16 Then Pharaoh called for Moses and Aaron in haste, and said, "I have sinned against the LORD your God and against you.

17 "Now therefore, please forgive my sin only this once, and entreat the LORD your God, that He may take away from me this death only."

18 So he went out from Pharaoh and entreated the LORD.

19 And the LORD turned a very strong west wind, which took the locusts away and blew them into the Red Sea. There remained not one locust in all the territory of Egypt.

20 But the LORD hardened Pharaoh's heart, and he did not let the children of Israel go.

The Ninth Plague: Darkness

21 Then the LORD said to Moses, "Stretch out your hand toward heaven, that there may be darkness over the land of Egypt, darkness *which* may even be felt."
22 So Moses stretched out his hand toward heaven, and there was thick darkness in all the land of Egypt three days.
23 They did not see one another; nor did anyone rise from his place for three days. But all the children of Israel had light in their dwellings.
24 Then Pharaoh called to Moses and said, "Go, serve the LORD; only let your flocks and your herds be kept back. Let your little ones also go with you."
25 But Moses said, "You must also give us sacrifices and burnt offerings, that we may sacrifice to the LORD our God.
26 "Our livestock also shall go with us; not a hoof shall be left behind. For we must take some of them to serve the LORD our God, and even we do not know with what we must serve the LORD until we arrive there."
27 But the LORD hardened Pharaoh's heart, and he would not let them go.
28 Then Pharaoh said to him, "Get away from me! Take heed to yourself and see my face no more! For in the day you see my face you shall die!"
29 And Moses said, "You have spoken well. I will never see your face again."

Death of the Firstborn Announced

11 And the LORD said to Moses, "I will bring yet one *more* plague on Pharaoh and on Egypt. Afterward he will let you go from here. When he lets *you* go, he will surely drive you out of here altogether.
2 "Speak now in the hearing of the people, and let every man ask from his neighbor and every woman from her neighbor, articles of silver and articles of gold."
3 And the LORD gave the people favor in the sight of the Egyptians. Moreover the man Moses *was* very great in the land of Egypt, in the sight of Pharaoh's servants and in the sight of the people.
4 Then Moses said, "Thus says the LORD: 'About midnight I will go out into the midst of Egypt;
5 'and all the firstborn in the land of Egypt shall die, from the firstborn of Pharaoh who sits on his throne, even to

the firstborn of the maidservant who *is* behind the handmill, and all the firstborn of the beasts.
6 'Then there shall be a great cry throughout all the land of Egypt, such as was not like it *before*, nor shall be like it again.
7 'But against none of the children of Israel shall a dog move its tongue, against man or beast, that you may know that the LORD does make a difference between the Egyptians and Israel.'
8 "And all these your servants shall come down to me and bow down to me, saying, 'Get out, and all the people who follow you!' After that I will go out." Then he went out from Pharaoh in great anger.
9 But the LORD said to Moses, "Pharaoh will not heed you, so that My wonders may be multiplied in the land of Egypt."
10 So Moses and Aaron did all these wonders before Pharaoh; and the LORD hardened Pharaoh's heart, and he did not let the children of Israel go out of his land.

The Passover Instituted

12 Now the LORD spoke to Moses and Aaron in the land of Egypt, saying,
2 "This month *shall be* your beginning of months; it *shall be* the first month of the year to you.
3 "Speak to all the congregation of Israel, saying: 'On the tenth *day* of this month every man shall take for himself a lamb, according to the house of *his* father, a lamb for a household.
4 'And if the household is too small for the lamb, let him and his neighbor next to his house take *it* according to the number of the persons; according to each man's need you shall make your count for the lamb.
5 'Your lamb shall be without blemish, a male of the first year. You may take *it* from the sheep or from the goats.
6 'Now you shall keep it until the fourteenth day of the same month. Then the whole assembly of the congregation of Israel shall kill it at twilight.
7 'And they shall take *some* of the blood and put *it* on the two doorposts and on the lintel of the houses where they eat it.
8 'Then they shall eat the flesh on that

God's Covenant—Forgiveness

In the Bible there are three ways of establishing and of sealing a covenant. The first and most common covenant is the word covenant. The second method is the salt covenant. This has been commonly used between enemies in establishing peace. Even today it is still practiced. President Anwar Sadat of Egypt and Prime Minister Menachem Begin of Israel signed a 1978 Camp David Peace Accord by taking a pinch of salt and tasting it together. The third, and perhaps the most interesting method of establishing a covenant in the Bible, is to eat a meal together. This is not only a sign of peace, but a sign of forgiveness. In the story of the Prodigal Son, the father ordered a feast to assure the boy of his forgiveness when he returned. The elder son did not participate in the meal because he was unable to forgive his younger brother.

During the Passover meal, Jesus instituted the Lord's Supper as a reminder of God's forgiveness. When Jesus was arrested and crucified, the disciples fled and abandoned Him. After His resurrection Jesus assured and comforted His disciples that they were forgiven by asking them if they had anything to eat. He broke bread with them and shared a complete meal with them by the shores of the Sea of Galilee.

Jesus offers us the same comfort and assurance that our sins are forgiven when He says, "Behold, I stand at the door and knock. If anyone hears My voice and opens the door, I will come in to him and dine with him, and he with Me" (Rev. 3:20).

night; roasted in fire, with unleavened bread *and* with bitter *herbs* they shall eat it.
9 'Do not eat it raw, nor boiled at all with water, but roasted in fire—its head with its legs and its entrails.
10 'You shall let none of it remain until morning, and what remains of it until morning you shall burn with fire.
11 'And thus you shall eat it: *with* a belt on your waist, your sandals on your feet, and your staff in your hand. So you shall eat it in haste. It *is* the LORD's Passover.
12 'For I will pass through the land of Egypt on that night, and will strike all the firstborn in the land of Egypt, both man and beast; and against all the gods of Egypt I will execute judgment: I *am* the LORD.
13 'Now the blood shall be a sign for you on the houses where you *are*. And when I see the blood, I will pass over you; and the plague shall not be on you to destroy *you* when I strike the land of Egypt.
14 'So this day shall be to you a memorial; and you shall keep it as a feast to the LORD throughout your generations. You shall keep it as a feast by an everlasting ordinance.
15 'Seven days you shall eat unleavened bread. On the first day you shall remove leaven from your houses. For whoever eats leavened bread from the first day until the seventh day, that person shall be cut off from Israel.
16 'On the first day *there shall be* a holy convocation, and on the seventh day there shall be a holy convocation for you. No manner of work shall be done on them; but *that* which everyone must eat—that only may be prepared by you.
17 'So you shall observe *the Feast of* Unleavened Bread, for on this same day I will have brought your armies out of the land of Egypt. Therefore you shall observe this day throughout your generations as an everlasting ordinance.
18 'In the first *month*, on the fourteenth day of the month at evening, you shall eat unleavened bread, until the twenty-first day of the month at evening.
19 'For seven days no leaven shall be found in your houses, since whoever eats what is leavened, that same person shall be cut off from the congregation of Israel, whether *he is* a stranger or a native of the land.

20 'You shall eat nothing leavened; in all your habitations you shall eat unleavened bread.' "
21 Then Moses called for all the elders of Israel and said to them, "Pick out and take lambs for yourselves according to your families, and kill the Passover *lamb*.
22 "And you shall take a bunch of hyssop, dip *it* in the blood that *is* in the basin, and strike the lintel and the two doorposts with the blood that *is* in the basin. And none of you shall go out of the door of his house until morning.
23 "For the LORD will pass through to strike the Egyptians; and when He sees the blood on the lintel and on the two doorposts, the LORD will pass over the door and not allow the destroyer to come into your houses to strike *you*.
24 "And you shall observe this thing as an ordinance for you and your sons forever.
25 "It will come to pass when you come to the land which the LORD will give you, just as He promised, that you shall keep this service.
26 "And it shall be, when your children say to you, 'What do you mean by this service?'
27 "that you shall say, 'It *is* the Passover sacrifice of the LORD, who passed over the houses of the children of Israel in Egypt when He struck the Egyptians and delivered our households.' " So the people bowed their heads and worshiped.
28 Then the children of Israel went away and did *so*; just as the LORD had commanded Moses and Aaron, so they did.

The Tenth Plague: Death of the Firstborn

29 And it came to pass at midnight that the LORD struck all the firstborn in the land of Egypt, from the firstborn of Pharaoh who sat on his throne to the firstborn of the captive who *was* in the dungeon, and all the firstborn of livestock.
30 So Pharaoh rose in the night, he, all his servants, and all the Egyptians; and there was a great cry in Egypt, for *there was* not a house where *there was* not one dead.

The Exodus

31 Then he called for Moses and Aaron by night, and said, "Rise *and* go out from among my people, both you and the chil-

dren of Israel. And go, serve the LORD as you have said.

32 "Also take your flocks and your herds, as you have said, and be gone; and bless me also."

33 And the Egyptians urged the people, that they might send them out of the land in haste. For they said, "We *shall* all *be* dead."

34 So the people took their dough before it was leavened, having their kneading bowls bound up in their clothes on their shoulders.

35 Now the children of Israel had done according to the word of Moses, and they had asked from the Egyptians articles of silver, articles of gold, and clothing.

36 And the LORD had given the people favor in the sight of the Egyptians, so that they granted them *what they requested.* Thus they plundered the Egyptians.

37 Then the children of Israel journeyed from Rameses to Succoth, about six hundred thousand men on foot, besides children.

38 A mixed multitude went up with them also, and flocks and herds—a great deal of livestock.

39 And they baked unleavened cakes of the dough which they had brought out of Egypt; for it was not leavened, because they were driven out of Egypt and could not wait, nor had they prepared provisions for themselves.

40 Now the sojourn of the children of Israel who lived in Egypt[11] *was* four hundred and thirty years.

41 And it came to pass at the end of the four hundred and thirty years—on that very same day—it came to pass that all the armies of the LORD went out from the land of Egypt.

42 It *is* a night of solemn observance to the LORD for bringing them out of the land of Egypt. This *is* that night of the LORD, a solemn observance for all the children of Israel throughout their generations.

Passover Regulations

43 And the LORD said to Moses and Aaron, "This *is* the ordinance of the Passover: No outsider shall eat it.

44 "But every man's servant who is bought for money, when you have circumcised him, then he may eat it.

45 "A sojourner and a hired servant shall not eat it.

46 "In one house it shall be eaten; you shall not carry any of the flesh outside the house, nor shall you break one of its bones.

47 "All the congregation of Israel shall keep it.

48 "And when a stranger sojourns with you *and wants* to keep the Passover to the LORD, let all his males be circumcised, and then let him come near and keep it; and he shall be as a native of the land. For no uncircumcised person shall eat it.

49 "One law shall be for the native-born and for the stranger who sojourns among you."

50 Thus all the children of Israel did; as the LORD commanded Moses and Aaron, so they did.

51 So it came to pass, on that very same day, that the LORD brought the children of Israel out of the land of Egypt according to their armies.

The Firstborn Consecrated

13 Then the LORD spoke to Moses, saying,

2 "Sanctify to Me all the firstborn, whatever opens the womb among the children of Israel, *both* of man and animal; it is Mine."

The Feast of Unleavened Bread

3 And Moses said to the people: "Remember this day in which you went out of Egypt, out of the house of bondage; for by strength of hand the LORD brought you out of this *place.* No leavened bread shall be eaten.

4 "On this day you are going out, in the month Abib.

5 "And it shall be, when the LORD brings you into the land of the Canaanites and the Hittites and the Amorites and the Hivites and the Jebusites, which He swore to your fathers to give you, a land flowing with milk and honey, that you shall keep this service in this month.

6 "Seven days you shall eat unleavened bread, and on the seventh day *there shall be* a feast to the LORD.

7 "Unleavened bread shall be eaten seven days. And no leavened bread shall be seen among you, nor shall leaven be seen among you in all your quarters.

11 Samaritan Pentateuch and Septuagint read *Egypt and Canaan.*

8 "And you shall tell your son in that day, saying, 'This is done because of what the LORD did for me when I came up from Egypt.'

9 "It shall be as a sign to you on your hand and as a memorial between your eyes, that the LORD's law may be in your mouth; for with a strong hand the LORD has brought you out of Egypt.

10 "You shall therefore keep this ordinance in its season from year to year.

The Law of the Firstborn

11 "And it shall be, when the LORD brings you into the land of the Canaanites, as He swore to you and your fathers, and gives it to you,

12 "that you shall set apart to the LORD all that open the womb, that is, every firstling that comes from an animal which you have; the males shall be the LORD's.

13 "But every firstling of a donkey you shall redeem with a lamb; and if you will not redeem it, then you shall break its neck. And all the firstborn of man among your sons you shall redeem.

14 "So it shall be, when your son asks you in time to come, saying, 'What is this?' that you shall say to him, 'By strength of hand the LORD brought us out of Egypt, out of the house of bondage.

15 'And it came to pass, when Pharaoh was stubborn about letting us go, that the LORD killed all the firstborn in the land of Egypt, both the firstborn of man and the firstborn of animal. Therefore I sacrifice to the LORD all males that open the womb, but all the firstborn of my sons I redeem.'

16 "It shall be as a sign on your hand and as frontlets between your eyes, for by strength of hand the LORD brought us out of Egypt."

The Wilderness Way

17 Then it came to pass, when Pharaoh had let the people go, that God did not lead them by way of the land of the Philistines, although that was near; for God said, "Lest perhaps the people change their minds when they see war, and return to Egypt."

18 So God led the people around by way of the wilderness of the Red Sea. And the children of Israel went up in orderly ranks out of the land of Egypt.

19 And Moses took the bones of Joseph with him, for he had placed the children of Israel under solemn oath, saying, "God will surely visit you, and you shall carry up my bones from here with you."[12]

20 So they took their journey from Succoth and camped in Etham at the edge of the wilderness.

21 And the LORD went before them by day in a pillar of cloud to lead the way, and by night in a pillar of fire to give them light, so as to go by day and night.

22 He did not take away the pillar of cloud by day or the pillar of fire by night from before the people.

The Red Sea Crossing

14 Now the LORD spoke to Moses, saying:

2 "Speak to the children of Israel, that they turn and camp before Pi Hahiroth, between Migdol and the sea, opposite Baal Zephon; you shall camp before it by the sea.

3 "For Pharaoh will say of the children of Israel, 'They are bewildered by the land; the wilderness has closed them in.'

4 "Then I will harden Pharaoh's heart, so that he will pursue them; and I will gain honor over Pharaoh and over all his army, that the Egyptians may know that I am the LORD." And they did so.

5 Now it was told the king of Egypt that the people had fled, and the heart of Pharaoh and his servants was turned against the people; and they said, "Why have we done this, that we have let Israel go from serving us?"

6 So he made ready his chariot and took his people with him.

7 Also, he took six hundred choice chariots, and all the chariots of Egypt with captains over every one of them.

8 And the LORD hardened the heart of Pharaoh king of Egypt, and he pursued the children of Israel; and the children of Israel went out with boldness.

9 So the Egyptians pursued them, all the horses and chariots of Pharaoh, his horsemen and his army, and overtook them camping by the sea beside Pi Hahiroth, before Baal Zephon.

10 And when Pharaoh drew near, the children of Israel lifted their eyes, and behold, the Egyptians marched after them. So they were very afraid, and the children of Israel cried out to the LORD.

11 Then they said to Moses, "Because

12 Compare Genesis 50:25

there were no graves in Egypt, have you taken us away to die in the wilderness? Why have you so dealt with us, to bring us up out of Egypt? 12 "*Is* this not the word that we told you in Egypt, saying, 'Let us alone that we may serve the Egyptians?' For *it would have been* better for us to serve the Egyptians than that we should die in the wilderness." 13 And Moses said to the people, "Do not be afraid. Stand still, and see the salvation of the LORD, which He will accomplish for you today. For the Egyptians whom you see today, you shall see again no more forever. 14 "The LORD will fight for you, and you shall hold your peace." 15 And the LORD said to Moses, "Why do you cry to Me? Tell the children of Israel to go forward. 16 "But lift up your rod, and stretch out your hand over the sea and divide it. And the children of Israel shall go on dry *ground* through the midst of the sea. 17 "And I indeed will harden the hearts of the Egyptians, and they shall follow them. So I will gain honor over Pharaoh and over all his army, his chariots, and his horsemen. 18 "Then the Egyptians shall know that I *am* the LORD, when I have gained honor for Myself over Pharaoh, his chariots, and his horsemen." 19 And the Angel of God, who went before the camp of Israel, moved and went behind them; and the pillar of cloud went from before them and stood behind them. 20 So it came between the camp of the Egyptians and the camp of Israel. Thus it was a cloud and darkness *to the one,* and it gave light by night *to the other,* so that the one did not come near the other all that night. 21 Then Moses stretched out his hand over the sea; and the LORD caused the sea to go *back* by a strong east wind all that night, and made the sea into dry *land,* and the waters were divided. 22 So the children of Israel went into the midst of the sea on the dry *ground,* and the waters *were* a wall to them on their right hand and on their left. 23 And the Egyptians pursued and went after them into the midst of the sea, all Pharaoh's horses, his chariots, and his horsemen.

24 Now it came to pass, in the morning watch, that the LORD looked down upon the army of the Egyptians through the pillar of fire and cloud, and He troubled the army of the Egyptians. 25 And He took off their chariot wheels, so that they drove them with difficulty; and the Egyptians said, "Let us flee from the face of Israel, for the LORD fights for them against the Egyptians." 26 Then the LORD said to Moses, "Stretch out your hand over the sea, that the waters may come back upon the Egyptians, on their chariots, and on their horsemen." 27 And Moses stretched out his hand over the sea; and when the morning appeared, the sea returned to its full depth, while the Egyptians were fleeing into it. So the LORD overthrew the Egyptians in the midst of the sea. 28 Then the waters returned and covered the chariots, the horsemen, *and* all the army of Pharaoh that came into the sea after them. Not so much as one of them remained. 29 But the children of Israel had walked on dry *land* in the midst of the sea, and the waters *were* a wall to them on their right hand and on their left. 30 So the LORD saved Israel that day out of the hand of the Egyptians, and Israel saw the Egyptians dead on the seashore. 31 Thus Israel saw the great work which the LORD had done in Egypt; so the people feared the LORD, and believed the LORD and His servant Moses.

The Song of Moses

15 Then Moses and the children of Israel sang this song to the LORD, and spoke, saying:

"I will sing to the LORD,
For He has triumphed gloriously!
The horse and its rider
He has thrown into the sea!
2 The LORD *is* my strength and song,
And He has become my salvation;
He *is* my God, and I will praise Him;
My father's God, and I will exalt Him.
3 The LORD *is* a man of war;
The LORD *is* His name.
4 Pharaoh's chariots and his army
He has cast into the sea;
His chosen captains also
are drowned in the Red Sea.

5 The depths have covered them;
   They sank to the bottom like a stone.

6 "Your right hand, O LORD,
   has become glorious in power;
   Your right hand, O LORD,
   has dashed the enemy in pieces.
7 And in the greatness
   of Your excellence
   You have overthrown those
   who rose against You;
   You sent forth Your wrath
   which consumed them like stubble.
8 And with the blast of Your nostrils
   The waters were gathered together;
   The floods stood upright like a heap;
   And the depths congealed
   in the heart of the sea.
9 The enemy said, 'I will pursue,
   I will overtake,
   I will divide the spoil;
   My desire shall be satisfied on them.
   I will draw my sword,
   My hand shall destroy them.'
10 You blew with Your wind,
   The sea covered them;
   They sank like lead
   in the mighty waters.

11 "Who is like You, O LORD,
   among the gods?
   Who is like You, glorious in holiness,
   Fearful in praises, doing wonders?
12 You stretched out Your right hand;
   The earth swallowed them.
13 You in Your mercy have led forth
   The people whom You have redeemed;
   You have guided them in Your strength
   To Your holy habitation.

14 "The people will hear and be afraid;
   Sorrow will take hold of the
   inhabitants of Palestina.
15 Then the chiefs of Edom
   will be dismayed;
   The mighty men of Moab,
   Trembling will take hold of them;
   All the inhabitants of Canaan
   will melt away.
16 Fear and dread will fall on them;
   By the greatness of Your arm
   They will be as still as a stone,
   Till Your people pass over, O LORD,
   Till the people pass over
   Whom You have purchased.
17 You will bring them in and plant them
   In the mountain of Your inheritance,
   In the place, O LORD,
   which You have made
   For Your own dwelling,

   The sanctuary, O LORD,
   which Your hands have established.
18 "The LORD shall reign
   forever and ever."

19 For the horses of Pharaoh went with
his chariots and his horsemen into the
sea, and the LORD brought back the waters of the sea upon them. But the children of Israel went on dry land in the
midst of the sea.

The Song of Miriam

20 Then Miriam the prophetess, the sister of Aaron, took the timbrel in her
hand; and all the women went out after
her with timbrels and with dances.
21 And Miriam answered them:

   "Sing to the LORD,
   For He has triumphed gloriously!
   The horse and its rider
   He has thrown into the sea!"

Bitter Waters Made Sweet

22 So Moses brought Israel from the Red
Sea; then they went out into the Wilderness of Shur. And they went three days
in the wilderness and found no water.
23 Now when they came to Marah, they
could not drink the waters of Marah, for
they were bitter. Therefore the name of it
was called Marah.[13]
24 And the people murmured against
Moses, saying, "What shall we drink?"
25 So he cried out to the LORD, and the
LORD showed him a tree; and when he
cast it into the waters, the waters were
made sweet. There He made a statute
and an ordinance for them. And there
He tested them,
26 and said, "If you diligently heed the
voice of the LORD your God and do what
is right in His sight, give ear to His commandments and keep all His statutes, I
will put none of the diseases on you
which I have brought on the Egyptians.
For I am the LORD who heals you."
27 Then they came to Elim, where there
were twelve wells of water and seventy
palm trees; so they camped there by the
waters.

Bread from Heaven

16 And they journeyed from Elim,
and all the congregation of the

13 Literally Bitter

children of Israel came to the Wilderness of Sin, which is between Elim and Sinai, on the fifteenth day of the second month after they departed from the land of Egypt.
2 Then the whole congregation of the children of Israel murmured against Moses and Aaron in the wilderness.
3 And the children of Israel said to them, "Oh, that we had died by the hand of the LORD in the land of Egypt, when we sat by the pots of meat *and* when we ate bread to the full! For you have brought us out into this wilderness to kill this whole assembly with hunger."
4 Then the LORD said to Moses, "Behold, I will rain bread from heaven for you. And the people shall go out and gather a certain quota every day, that I may test them, whether they will walk in My law or not.
5 "And it shall be on the sixth day that they shall prepare what they bring in, and it shall be twice as much as they gather daily."
6 Then Moses and Aaron said to all the children of Israel, "At evening you shall know that the LORD has brought you out of the land of Egypt.
7 "And in the morning you shall see the glory of the LORD; for He hears your murmurings against the LORD. But what *are* we, that you murmur against us?"
8 Also Moses said, "*This shall be seen* when the LORD gives you meat to eat in the evening, and in the morning bread to the full; for the LORD hears your murmurings which you make against Him. And what *are* we? Your murmurings *are* not against us but against the LORD."
9 Then Moses spoke to Aaron, "Say to all the congregation of the children of Israel, 'Come near before the LORD, for He has heard your murmurings.' "
10 Now it came to pass, as Aaron spoke to the whole congregation of the children of Israel, that they looked toward the wilderness, and behold, the glory of the LORD appeared in the cloud.
11 And the LORD spoke to Moses, saying,
12 "I have heard the murmurings of the children of Israel. Speak to them, saying, 'At twilight you shall eat meat, and in the morning you shall be filled with bread. And you shall know that I *am* the LORD your God.' "

13 So it was that quails came up at evening and covered the camp, and in the morning the dew lay all around the camp.
14 And when the layer of dew lifted, there, on the surface of the wilderness, was a small round substance, *as* fine as frost on the ground.
15 So when the children of Israel saw *it*, they said to one another, "What is it?" For they did not know what it *was*. And Moses said to them, "This *is* the bread which the LORD has given you to eat.
16 "This is the thing which the LORD has commanded: 'Let every man gather it according to each one's need, one omer for each person, *according to the* number of persons; let every man take for *those* who *are* in his tent.' "
17 And the children of Israel did so and gathered, some more, some less.
18 So when they measured *it* by omers, he who gathered much had nothing over, and he who gathered little had no lack. Every man had gathered according to each one's need.
19 And Moses said, "Let no one leave any of it till morning."
20 Notwithstanding they did not heed Moses. But some of them left part of it until morning, and it bred worms and stank. And Moses was angry with them.
21 So they gathered it every morning, every man according to his need. And when the sun became hot, it melted.
22 And so it was, on the sixth day, *that* they gathered twice as much bread, two omers for each one. And all the rulers of the congregation came and told Moses.
23 Then he said to them, "This *is what* the LORD has said: 'Tomorrow *is* a Sabbath rest, a holy Sabbath to the LORD. Bake what you will bake *today*, and boil what you will boil; and lay up for yourselves all that remains, to be kept until morning.' "
24 So they laid it up till morning, as Moses commanded; and it did not stink, nor were there any worms in it.
25 Then Moses said, "Eat that today, for today *is* a Sabbath to the LORD; today you will not find it in the field.
26 "Six days you shall gather it, but on the seventh day, *which is* the Sabbath, there will be none."
27 Now it happened *that some* of the

people went out on the seventh day to gather, but they found none.
28 And the LORD said to Moses, "How long do you refuse to keep My commandments and My laws?
29 "See! For the LORD has given you the Sabbath; therefore He gives you on the sixth day bread for two days. Let every man remain in his place; let no man go out of his place on the seventh day."
30 So the people rested on the seventh day.
31 And the house of Israel called its name Manna.[14] And it was like white coriander seed, and the taste of it was like wafers made with honey.
32 Then Moses said, "This is the thing which the LORD has commanded: 'Fill an omer with it, to be kept for your generations, that they may see the bread with which I fed you in the wilderness, when I brought you out of the land of Egypt.' "
33 And Moses said to Aaron, "Take a pot and put an omer of manna in it, and lay it up before the LORD, to be kept for your generations."
34 As the LORD commanded Moses, so Aaron laid it up before the Testimony, to be kept.
35 And the children of Israel ate manna forty years, until they came to an inhabited land; they ate manna until they came to the border of the land of Canaan.
36 Now an omer is one-tenth of an ephah.

Water from the Rock

17 Then all the congregation of the children of Israel set out on their journey from the Wilderness of Sin, according to the commandment of the LORD, and camped in Rephidim; but there was no water for the people to drink.
2 Therefore the people contended with Moses, and said, "Give us water, that we may drink." And Moses said to them, "Why do you contend with me? Why do you tempt the LORD?"
3 And the people thirsted there for water, and the people murmured against Moses, and said, "Why is it you have brought us up out of Egypt, to kill us and our children and our livestock with thirst?"
4 So Moses cried out to the LORD, say-ing, "What shall I do with this people? They are almost ready to stone me!"
5 And the LORD said to Moses, "Go on before the people, and take with you some of the elders of Israel. Also take in your hand your rod with which you struck the river, and go.
6 "Behold, I will stand before you there on the rock in Horeb; and you shall strike the rock, and water will come out of it, that the people may drink." And Moses did so in the sight of the elders of Israel.
7 So he called the name of the place Massah[15] and Meribah,[16] because of the contention of the children of Israel, and because they tempted the LORD, saying, "Is the LORD among us or not?"

Victory over the Amalekites

8 Now Amalek came and fought with Israel in Rephidim.
9 And Moses said to Joshua, "Choose us some men and go out, fight with Amalek. Tomorrow I will stand on the top of the hill with the rod of God in my hand."
10 So Joshua did as Moses said to him, and fought with Amalek. And Moses, Aaron, and Hur went up to the top of the hill.
11 And so it was, when Moses held up his hand, that Israel prevailed; and when he let down his hand, Amalek prevailed.
12 But Moses' hands became heavy; so they took a stone and put it under him, and he sat on it. And Aaron and Hur supported his hands, one on one side, and the other on the other side; and his hands were steady until the going down of the sun.
13 So Joshua defeated Amalek and his people with the edge of the sword.
14 Then the LORD said to Moses, "Write this for a memorial in the book and recount it in the hearing of Joshua, that I will utterly blot out the remembrance of Amalek from under heaven."
15 And Moses built an altar and called its name, The-LORD-Is-My-Banner;[17]
16 for he said, "Because the LORD has sworn: the LORD will have war with Amalek from generation to generation."

Jethro's Advice

18 And Jethro, the priest of Midian, Moses' father-in-law, heard of all

14 Literally What? (compare Exodus 16:15) 15 Literally Tempted
16 Literally Contention 17 Hebrew YHWH Nissi

that God had done for Moses and for Israel His people—that the LORD had brought Israel out of Egypt.

2 Then Jethro, Moses' father-in-law, took Zipporah, Moses' wife, after he had sent her back,

3 with her two sons, of whom the name of one was Gershom (for he said, "I have been a stranger in a foreign land")[18]

4 and the name of the other was Eliezer[19] (for he said, "The God of my father was my help, and delivered me from the sword of Pharaoh");

5 and Jethro, Moses' father-in-law, came with his sons and his wife to Moses in the wilderness, where he was encamped at the mountain of God.

6 Now he had said to Moses, "I, your father-in-law Jethro, am coming to you with your wife and her two sons with her."

7 So Moses went out to meet his father-in-law, bowed down, and kissed him. And they asked each other about their well-being, and they went into the tent.

8 And Moses told his father-in-law all that the LORD had done to Pharaoh and to the Egyptians for Israel's sake, all the hardship that had come upon them on the way, and how the LORD had delivered them.

9 Then Jethro rejoiced for all the good which the LORD had done for Israel, whom He had delivered out of the hand of the Egyptians.

10 And Jethro said, "Blessed be the LORD, who has delivered you out of the hand of the Egyptians and out of the hand of Pharaoh, and who has delivered the people from under the hand of the Egyptians.

11 "Now I know that the LORD is greater than all the gods; for in the very thing in which they behaved proudly, He was above them."

12 Then Jethro, Moses' father-in-law, took a burnt offering and sacrifices to God. And Aaron came with all the elders of Israel to eat bread with Moses' father-in-law before God.

13 And so it was, on the next day, that Moses sat to judge the people; and the people stood before Moses from morning until evening.

14 So when Moses' father-in-law saw all that he did for the people, he said, "What is this thing that you are doing for the people? Why do you alone sit, and all the people stand before you from morning until evening?"

15 And Moses said to his father-in-law, "Because the people come to me to inquire of God.

16 "When they have a difficulty, they come to me, and I judge between one and another; and I make known the statutes of God and His laws."

17 So Moses' father-in-law said to him, "The thing that you do is not good.

18 "Both you and these people who are with you will surely wear yourselves out. For this thing is too much for you; you are not able to perform it by yourself.

19 "Listen now to my voice; I will give you counsel, and God will be with you: Stand before God for the people, so that you may bring the difficulties to God.

20 "And you shall teach them the statutes and the laws, and show them the way in which they must walk and the work they must do.

21 "Moreover you shall select from all the people able men, such as fear God, men of truth, hating covetousness; and place such over them to be rulers of thousands, rulers of hundreds, rulers of fifties, and rulers of tens.

22 "And let them judge the people at all times. Then it will be that every great matter they shall bring to you, but every small matter they themselves shall judge. So it will be easier for you, for they will bear the burden with you.

23 "If you do this thing, and God so commands you, then you will be able to endure, and all this people will also go to their place in peace."

24 So Moses heeded the voice of his father-in-law and did all that he had said.

25 And Moses chose able men out of all Israel, and made them heads over the people: rulers of thousands, rulers of hundreds, rulers of fifties, and rulers of tens.

26 So they judged the people at all times; the hard cases they brought to Moses, but they judged every small case themselves.

27 Then Moses let his father-in-law depart, and he went his way to his own land.

Israel at Mount Sinai

19 In the third month after the children of Israel had gone out of the

18 Compare Exodus 2:22   19 Literally *My God Is Help*

land of Egypt, on the same day, they came *to* the Wilderness of Sinai.
2 For they had departed from Rephidim, had come *to* the Desert of Sinai, and camped in the wilderness. So Israel camped there before the mountain.
3 And Moses went up to God, and the LORD called to him from the mountain, saying, "Thus you shall say to the house of Jacob, and tell the children of Israel:
4 'You have seen what I did to the Egyptians, and *how* I bore you on eagles' wings and brought you to Myself.
5 'Now therefore, if you will indeed obey My voice and keep My covenant, then you shall be a special treasure to Me above all people; for all the earth *is* Mine.
6 'And you shall be to Me a kingdom of priests and a holy nation.' These *are* the words which you shall speak to the children of Israel."
7 So Moses came and called for the elders of the people, and laid before them all these words which the LORD commanded him.
8 Then all the people answered together and said, "All that the LORD has spoken we will do." So Moses brought back the words of the people to the LORD.
9 And the LORD said to Moses, "Behold, I come to you in the thick cloud, that the people may hear when I speak with you, and believe you forever." So Moses told the words of the people to the LORD.
10 Then the LORD said to Moses, "Go to the people and sanctify them today and tomorrow, and let them wash their clothes.
11 "And let them be ready for the third day. For on the third day the LORD will come down upon Mount Sinai in the sight of all the people.
12 "You shall set bounds for the people all around, saying, 'Take heed to yourselves *that* you do *not* go up to the mountain or touch its base. Whoever touches the mountain shall surely be put to death.
13 'Not a hand shall touch him, but he shall surely be stoned or shot *with an arrow;* whether man or beast, he shall not live.' When the trumpet sounds long, they shall come near the mountain."
14 Then Moses went down from the mountain to the people and sanctified the people, and they washed their clothes.
15 And he said to the people, "Be ready

for the third day; do not come near *your* wives."
16 Then it came to pass on the third day, in the morning, that there were thunderings and lightnings, and a thick cloud on the mountain; and the sound of the trumpet was very loud, so that all the people who *were* in the camp trembled.
17 And Moses brought the people out of the camp to meet with God, and they stood at the foot of the mountain.
18 Now Mount Sinai *was* completely in smoke, because the LORD descended upon it in fire. Its smoke ascended like the smoke of a furnace, and the whole mountain[20] quaked greatly.
19 And when the blast of the trumpet sounded long and became louder and louder, Moses spoke, and God answered him by voice.
20 Then the LORD came down upon Mount Sinai, on the top of the mountain. And the LORD called Moses to the top of the mountain, and Moses went up.
21 And the LORD said to Moses, "Go down and warn the people, lest they break through to gaze at the LORD, and many of them perish.
22 "Also let the priests who come near the LORD sanctify themselves, lest the LORD break out against them."
23 And Moses said to the LORD, "The people cannot come up to Mount Sinai; for You warned us, saying, 'Set bounds around the mountain and sanctify it.'"
24 Then the LORD said to him, "Away! Get down and then come up, you and Aaron with you. But do not let the priests and the people break through to come up to the LORD, lest He break out against them."
25 So Moses went down to the people and spoke to them.

The Ten Commandments

20 And God spoke all these words, saying:
2 "I *am* the LORD your God, who brought you out of the land of Egypt, out of the house of bondage.
3 "You shall have no other gods before Me.
4 "You shall not make for yourself any carved image, or any likeness *of anything* that *is* in heaven above, or that *is* in the earth beneath, or

20 Septuagint reads *all the people.*

that *is* in the water under the earth;

5 you shall not bow down to them nor serve them. For I, the LORD your God, *am* a jealous God, visiting the iniquity of the fathers on the children to the third and fourth *generations* of those who hate Me,

6 but showing mercy to thousands, to those who love Me and keep My commandments.

7 "You shall not take the name of the LORD your God in vain, for the LORD will not hold him guiltless who takes His name in vain.

8 "Remember the Sabbath day, to keep it holy.

9 Six days you shall labor and do all your work,

10 but the seventh day *is* the Sabbath of the LORD your God. *In it* you shall do no work: you, nor your son, nor your daughter, nor your manservant, nor your maidservant, nor your cattle, nor your stranger who *is* within your gates.

11 For *in* six days the LORD made the heavens and the earth, the sea, and all that *is* in them, and rested the seventh day. Therefore the LORD blessed the Sabbath day and hallowed it.

12 "Honor your father and your mother, that your days may be long upon the land which the LORD your God is giving you.

13 "You shall not murder.

14 "You shall not commit adultery.

15 "You shall not steal.

16 "You shall not bear false witness against your neighbor.

17 "You shall not covet your neighbor's house; you shall not covet your neighbor's wife, nor his manservant, nor his maidservant, nor his ox, nor his donkey, nor anything that *is* your neighbor's."

The People Afraid of God's Presence

18 Now all the people witnessed the thunderings, the lightning flashes, the sound of the trumpet, and the mountain smoking; and when the people saw *it*, they trembled and stood afar off.

19 Then they said to Moses, "You speak with us, and we will hear; but let not God speak with us, lest we die."

20 And Moses said to the people, "Do not fear; for God has come to test you, and that His fear may be before you, so that you may not sin."

21 So the people stood afar off, but Moses drew near the thick darkness where God *was*.

The Law of the Altar

22 Then the LORD said to Moses, "Thus you shall say to the children of Israel: 'You have seen that I have talked with you from heaven.

23 'You shall not make *anything to be* with Me—gods of silver or gods of gold you shall not make for yourselves.

24 'An altar of earth you shall make for Me, and you shall sacrifice on it your burnt offerings and your peace offerings, your sheep and your oxen. In every place where I record My name I will come to you, and I will bless you.

25 'And if you make Me an altar of stone, you shall not build it of hewn stone; for if you use your tool on it, you have profaned it.

26 'Nor shall you go up by steps to My altar, that your nakedness may not be exposed on it.'

The Law Concerning Servants

21 "Now these *are* the judgments which you shall set before them:

2 "If you buy a Hebrew servant, he shall serve six years; and in the seventh he shall go out free and pay nothing.

3 "If he comes in by himself, he shall go out by himself; if he *comes in* married, then his wife shall go out with him.

4 "If his master has given him a wife, and she has borne him sons or daughters, the wife and her children shall be her master's, and he shall go out by himself.

5 "But if the servant plainly says, 'I love my master, my wife, and my children; I will not go out free,'

6 "then his master shall bring him to the judges. He shall also bring him to the door, or to the doorpost, and his master shall pierce his ear with an awl; and he shall serve him forever.

7 "And if a man sells his daughter to be a maidservant, she shall not go out as the menservants do.

8 "If she does not please her master,

who has betrothed her to himself, then he shall let her be redeemed. He shall have no right to sell her to a foreign people, since he has dealt deceitfully with her.

9 "And if he has betrothed her to his son, he shall deal with her according to the custom of daughters.

10 "If he takes another *wife*, he shall not diminish her food, her clothing, and her marriage rights.

11 "And if he does not do these three for her, then she shall go out free, without *paying* money.

The Law Concerning Violence

12 "He who strikes a man so that he dies shall surely be put to death.

13 "But if he did not lie in wait, but God delivered *him* into his hand, then I will appoint for you a place where he may flee.

14 "But if a man acts with premeditation against his neighbor, to kill him with guile, you shall take him from My altar, that he may die.

15 "And he who strikes his father or his mother shall surely be put to death.

16 "He who kidnaps a man and sells him, or if he is found in his hand, shall surely be put to death.

17 "And he who curses his father or his mother shall surely be put to death.

18 "If men contend with each other, and one strikes the other with a stone or with *his* fist, and he does not die but is confined to *his* bed,

19 "if he rises again and walks about outside with his staff, then he who struck *him* shall be acquitted. He shall only pay *for* the loss of his time, and shall provide *for him* to be thoroughly healed.

20 "And if a man beats his servant or his maidservant with a rod, so that he dies under his hand, he shall surely be punished.

21 "Notwithstanding, if he remains alive a day or two, he shall not be punished; for he *is* his property.

22 "If men fight, and hurt a woman with child, so that she gives birth prematurely, yet no *lasting* harm follows, he shall surely be punished accordingly as the woman's husband imposes on him; and he shall pay as the judges *determine*.

23 "But if *any lasting* harm follows, then you shall give life for life,

24 "eye for eye, tooth for tooth, hand for hand, foot for foot,

25 "burn for burn, wound for wound, stripe for stripe.

26 "And if a man strikes the eye of his servant, or the eye of his maidservant, and destroys it, he shall let him go free for the sake of his eye.

27 "And if he knocks out his servant's tooth, or his maidservant's tooth, he shall let him go free for the sake of his tooth.

Animal Control Laws

28 "If an ox gores a man or a woman to death, then the ox shall surely be stoned, and its flesh shall not be eaten; but the owner of the ox *shall be* acquitted.

29 "But if the ox tended to thrust with its horn in times past, and it has been made known to his owner, and he has not kept it confined, so that it has killed a man or a woman, the ox shall be stoned and its owner also shall be put to death.

30 "If there is imposed on him a sum of money, then he shall pay to redeem his life, whatever is imposed on him.

31 "Whether it has gored a son or gored a daughter, according to this judgment it shall be done to him.

32 "If the ox gores a manservant or a maidservant, he shall give to their master thirty shekels of silver, and the ox shall be stoned.

33 "And if a man opens a pit, or if a man digs a pit and does not cover it, and an ox or a donkey falls in it,

34 "the owner of the pit shall make *it* good; he shall give money to their owner, but the dead *beast* shall be his.

35 "And if one man's ox hurts another's, so that it dies, then they shall sell the live ox and divide the money from it; and the dead *ox* they shall also divide.

36 "Or if it was known that the ox tended to thrust in time past, and its owner has not kept it confined, he shall surely pay ox for ox, and the dead beast shall be his own.

Responsibility for Property

22 "If a man steals an ox or a sheep, and slaughters it or sells it, he shall restore five oxen for an ox and four sheep for a sheep.

2 "If the thief is found breaking in, and he is struck so that he dies, *there shall be* no guilt for his bloodshed.

3 "If the sun has risen on him, *there shall be* guilt for his bloodshed. He should make full restitution; if he has nothing, then he shall be sold for his theft.

4 "If the theft is certainly found alive in his hand, whether it is an ox or donkey or sheep, he shall restore double.

5 "If a man causes a field or vineyard to be grazed, and lets loose his animal, and it feeds in another man's field, he shall make restitution from the best of his own field and the best of his own vineyard.

6 "If fire breaks out and catches in thorns, so that stacked grain, standing grain, or the field is consumed, he who kindled the fire shall surely make restitution.

7 "If a man delivers to his neighbor money or articles to keep, and it is stolen out of the man's house, if the thief is found, he shall pay double.

8 "If the thief is not found, then the master of the house shall be brought to the judges *to see* whether he has put his hand into his neighbor's goods.

9 "For any kind of trespass, *whether it concerns* an ox, a donkey, a sheep, or clothing, *or* for any kind of lost thing which *another* claims to be his, the cause of both parties shall come before the judges; *and* whomever the judges condemn shall pay double to his neighbor.

10 "If a man delivers to his neighbor a donkey, an ox, a sheep, or any beast to keep, and it dies, is hurt, or driven away, no one seeing *it*,

11 "*then* an oath of the LORD shall be between them both, that he has not put his hand into his neighbor's goods; and the owner of it shall accept *that*, and he shall not make *it* good.

12 "But if, in fact, it is stolen from him, he shall make restitution to the owner of it.

13 "If it is torn to pieces *by an animal*, *then* he shall bring it as evidence, *and* he shall not make good what was torn.

14 "And if a man borrows *anything* from his neighbor, and it becomes injured or dies, the owner of it not *being* with it, he shall surely make *it* good.

15 "*But* if its owner *was* with it, he shall not make *it* good; if it *was* hired, it came for its hire.

Moral and Ceremonial Principles

16 "And if a man entices a virgin who is not betrothed, and lies with her, he shall surely pay the bride-price for her *to be* his wife.

17 "If her father utterly refuses to give her to him, he shall pay money according to the bride-price of virgins.

18 "You shall not permit a sorceress to live.

19 "Whoever lies with a beast shall surely be put to death.

20 "He who sacrifices to *any* god, except to the LORD only, he shall be utterly destroyed.

21 "You shall neither mistreat a stranger nor oppress him, for you were strangers in the land of Egypt.

22 "You shall not afflict any widow or fatherless child.

23 "If you afflict them in any way, *and* they cry at all to Me, I will surely hear their cry;

24 "and My wrath will become hot, and I will kill you with the sword; your wives shall be widows, and your children fatherless.

25 "If you lend money to *any of* My people *who are* poor among you, you shall not be like a moneylender to him; you shall not charge him interest.

26 "If you ever take your neighbor's garment as a pledge, you shall return it to him before the sun goes down.

27 "For that *is* his only covering, it *is* his garment for his skin. What will he sleep in? And it will be that when he cries to Me, I will hear, for I *am* gracious.

28 "You shall not revile God, nor curse a ruler of your people.

29 "You shall not delay *to offer* the first of your ripe produce and your juices. The firstborn of your sons you shall give to Me.

30 "Likewise you shall do with your oxen *and* your sheep. It shall be with its mother seven days; on the eighth day you shall give it to Me.

31 "And you shall be holy men to Me: you shall not eat *any* meat *which is* torn *by beasts* in the field; you shall throw it to the dogs.

Justice for All

23 "You shall not circulate a false report. Do not put your hand with the wicked to be an unrighteous witness.

2 "You shall not follow a crowd to do evil; nor shall you testify in a dispute so as to turn aside after many to pervert *justice.*
3 "You shall not show partiality to a poor man in his dispute.
4 "If you meet your enemy's ox or his donkey going astray, you shall surely bring it back to him again.
5 "If you see the donkey of one who hates you lying under its burden, and you would refrain from helping it, you shall surely help him with it.
6 "You shall not pervert the judgment of your poor in his dispute.
7 "Keep yourself far from a false matter; do not kill the innocent and righteous. For I will not justify the wicked.
8 "And you shall take no bribe, for a bribe blinds the discerning and perverts the words of the righteous.
9 "Also you shall not oppress a stranger, for you know the heart of a stranger, because you were strangers in the land of Egypt.

The Law of Sabbaths

10 "Six years you shall sow your land and gather in its produce,
11 "but the seventh *year* you shall let it rest and lie fallow, that the poor of your people may eat; and what they leave, the beasts of the field may eat. In like manner you shall do with your vineyard *and* your olive grove.
12 "Six days you shall do your work, and on the seventh day you shall rest, that your ox and your donkey may rest, and the son of your maidservant and the stranger may be refreshed.
13 "And in all that I have said to you, be circumspect and make no mention of the name of other gods, nor let it be heard from your mouth.

Three Annual Feasts

14 "Three times you shall keep a feast to Me in the year:
15 "You shall keep the Feast of Unleavened Bread (you shall eat unleavened bread seven days, as I commanded you, at the time appointed in the month of Abib, for in it you came out of Egypt; none shall appear before Me empty);
16 "and the Feast of Harvest, the firstfruits of your labors which you have sown in the field; and the Feast of Ingathering,

which *is* at the end of the year, when you have gathered in *the fruit of* your labors from the field.
17 "Three times in the year all your males shall appear before the Lord GOD.[21]
18 "You shall not offer the blood of My sacrifice with leavened bread; nor shall the fat of My sacrifice remain until morning.
19 "The first of the firstfruits of your land you shall bring into the house of the LORD your God. You shall not boil a young goat in its mother's milk.

The Angel and the Promises

20 "Behold, I send an Angel before you to keep you in the way and to bring you into the place which I have prepared.
21 "Beware of Him and obey His voice; do not provoke Him, for He will not pardon your transgressions; for My name *is* in Him.
22 "But if you indeed obey His voice and do all that I speak, then I will be an enemy to your enemies and an adversary to your adversaries.
23 "For My Angel will go before you and bring you in to the Amorites and the Hittites and the Perizzites and the Canaanites and the Hivites and the Jebusites; and I will cut them off.
24 "You shall not bow down to their gods, nor serve them, nor do according to their works; but you shall utterly overthrow them and completely break down their *sacred* pillars.
25 "So you shall serve the LORD your God, and He will bless your bread and your water. And I will take sickness away from the midst of you.
26 "No one shall suffer miscarriage or be barren in your land; I will fulfill the number of your days.
27 "I will send My fear before you, I will cause confusion among all the people to whom you come, and will make all your enemies turn *their* backs to you.
28 "And I will send hornets before you, which shall drive out the Hivite, the Canaanite, and the Hittite from before you.
29 "I will not drive them out from before you in one year, lest the land become desolate and the beast of the field become too numerous for you.
30 "Little by little I will drive them out

21 Hebrew *YHWH*, usually translated LORD

from before you, until you have increased, and you inherit the land.
31 "And I will set your bounds from the Red Sea to the Sea of the Philistines, and from the desert to the River.[22] For I will deliver the inhabitants of the land into your hand, and you shall drive them out before you.
32 "You shall make no covenant with them, nor with their gods.
33 "They shall not dwell in your land, lest they make you sin against Me. For *if* you serve their gods, it will surely be a snare to you."

Israel Affirms the Covenant

24 Now He said to Moses, "Come up to the LORD, you and Aaron, Nadab and Abihu, and seventy of the elders of Israel, and worship from afar.
2 "And Moses alone shall come near the LORD, but they shall not come near; nor shall the people go up with him."
3 So Moses came and told the people all the words of the LORD and all the judgments. And all the people answered with one voice and said, "All the words which the LORD has said we will do."
4 And Moses wrote all the words of the LORD. And he rose early in the morning, and built an altar at the foot of the mountain, and twelve pillars according to the twelve tribes of Israel.
5 Then he sent young men of the children of Israel, who offered burnt offerings and sacrificed peace offerings of oxen to the LORD.
6 And Moses took half the blood and put *it* in basins, and half the blood he sprinkled on the altar.
7 Then he took the Book of the Covenant and read in the hearing of the people. And they said, "All that the LORD has said we will do, and be obedient."
8 And Moses took the blood, sprinkled *it* on the people, and said, "Behold, the blood of the covenant which the LORD has made with you according to all these words."

On the Mountain with God

9 Then Moses went up, also Aaron, Nadab, and Abihu, and seventy of the elders of Israel,
10 and they saw the God of Israel. And *there was* under His feet as it were a paved work of sapphire stone, and it was like the very heavens in *its* clarity.
11 But on the nobles of the children of Israel He did not lay His hand. So they saw God, and they ate and drank.
12 Then the LORD said to Moses, "Come up to Me on the mountain and be there; and I will give you tablets of stone, and the law and commandments which I have written, that you may teach them."
13 So Moses arose with his assistant Joshua, and Moses went up to the mountain of God.
14 And he said to the elders, "Wait here for us until we come back to you. Indeed Aaron and Hur *are* with you. If any man has a difficulty, let him go to them."
15 Then Moses went up into the mountain, and a cloud covered the mountain.
16 Now the glory of the LORD rested on Mount Sinai, and the cloud covered it six days. And on the seventh day He called to Moses out of the midst of the cloud.
17 The sight of the glory of the LORD *was* like a consuming fire on the top of the mountain in the eyes of the children of Israel.
18 So Moses went into the midst of the cloud and went up into the mountain. And Moses was on the mountain forty days and forty nights.

Offerings for the Sanctuary

25 Then the LORD spoke to Moses, saying:
2 "Speak to the children of Israel, that they bring Me an offering. From everyone who gives it willingly with his heart you shall take My offering.
3 "And this *is* the offering which you shall take from them: gold, silver, and bronze;
4 "blue and purple and scarlet *yarn*, fine linen *thread*, and goats' *hair*;
5 "rams' skins dyed red, badger skins, and acacia wood;
6 "oil for the light, and spices for the anointing oil and for the sweet incense;
7 "onyx stones, and stones to be set in the ephod and in the breastplate.
8 "And let them make Me a sanctuary, that I may dwell among them.
9 "According to all that I show you, *that is*, the pattern of the tabernacle and the pattern of all its furnishings, just so you shall make *it*.

22 Hebrew *Nahar*, the Euphrates

The Ark of the Testimony

10 "And they shall make an ark of acacia wood; two and a half cubits *shall be* its length, a cubit and a half its width, and a cubit and a half its height.
11 "And you shall overlay it with pure gold, inside and out you shall overlay it, and shall make on it a molding of gold all around.
12 "You shall cast four rings of gold for it, and put *them* in its four corners; two rings *shall be* on one side, and two rings on the other side.
13 "And you shall make poles *of* acacia wood, and overlay them with gold.
14 "You shall put the poles into the rings on the sides of the ark, that the ark may be carried by them.
15 "The poles shall be in the rings of the ark; they shall not be taken from it.
16 "And you shall put into the ark the Testimony which I will give you.
17 "You shall make a mercy seat of pure gold; two and a half cubits *shall be* its length and a cubit and a half its width.
18 "And you shall make two cherubim of gold; of hammered work you shall make them at the two ends of the mercy seat.
19 "Make one cherub at one end, and the other cherub at the other end; you shall make the cherubim at the two ends of it *of one piece* with the mercy seat.
20 "And the cherubim shall stretch out *their* wings above, covering the mercy seat with their wings, and they shall face one another; the faces of the cherubim *shall be* toward the mercy seat.
21 "You shall put the mercy seat on top of the ark, and in the ark you shall put the Testimony that I will give you.
22 "And there I will meet with you, and I will speak with you from above the mercy seat, from between the two cherubim which *are* on the ark of the Testimony, of all *things* which I will give you in commandment to the children of Israel.

The Table for the Showbread

23 "You shall also make a table of acacia wood; two cubits *shall be* its length, a cubit its width, and a cubit and a half its height.
24 "And you shall overlay it with pure gold, and make a molding of gold all around.
25 "You shall make for it a frame of a handbreadth all around, and you shall make a gold molding for the frame all around.
26 "And you shall make for it four rings of gold, and put the rings on the four corners that *are* at its four legs.
27 "The rings shall be close to the frame, as holders for the poles to bear the table.
28 "And you shall make the poles of acacia wood, and overlay them with gold, that the table may be carried with them.
29 "You shall make its dishes, its pans, its pitchers, and its bowls for pouring. You shall make them of pure gold.
30 "And you shall set the showbread on the table before Me always.

The Gold Lampstand

31 "You shall also make a lampstand of pure gold; the lampstand shall be of hammered work. Its shaft, its branches, its bowls, its ornamental knobs, and flowers shall be *of one piece.*
32 "And six branches shall come out of its sides: three branches of the lampstand out of one side, and three branches of the lampstand out of the other side.
33 "Three bowls *shall be* made like almond *blossoms* on one branch, *with* an *ornamental* knob and a flower, and three bowls made like almond *blossoms* on the other branch, *with* an *ornamental* knob and a flower—and so for the six branches that come out of the lampstand.
34 "On the lampstand itself four bowls *shall be* made like almond *blossoms, each with* its *ornamental* knob and flower.
35 "And *there shall be* a knob under the *first* two branches of the same, a knob under the *second* two branches of the same, and a knob under the *third* two branches of the same, according to the six branches that extend from the lampstand.
36 "Their knobs and their branches *shall be of one piece*; all of it *shall be* one hammered piece of pure gold.
37 "You shall make seven lamps for it, and they shall arrange its lamps so that they give light in front of it.
38 "And its wick-trimmers and their trays *shall be* of pure gold.
39 "It shall be made of a talent of pure gold, with all these utensils.
40 "And see to it that you make *them* according to the pattern which was shown you on the mountain.

The Tabernacle

26 "Moreover you shall make the tabernacle *with* ten curtains *woven of* fine linen thread, and blue and purple and scarlet *yarn*; with artistic designs of cherubim you shall weave them.
2 "The length of each curtain *shall be* twenty-eight cubits, and the width of each curtain four cubits. And every one of the curtains shall have the same measurements.
3 "Five curtains shall be coupled to one another, and *the other* five curtains *shall be* coupled to one another.
4 "And you shall make loops of blue *yarn* on the edge of the curtain on the selvedge of *one* set, and likewise you shall do on the outer edge of *the other* curtain of the second set.
5 "Fifty loops you shall make in the one curtain, and fifty loops you shall make on the edge of the curtain that *is* on the end of the second set, that the loops may be clasped to one another.
6 "And you shall make fifty clasps of gold, and couple the curtains together with the clasps, so that it may be one tabernacle.
7 "You shall also make curtains of goats' *hair*, to be a tent over the tabernacle. You shall make eleven curtains.
8 "The length of each curtain *shall be* thirty cubits, and the width of each curtain four cubits; and the eleven curtains shall all have the same measurements.
9 "And you shall couple five curtains by themselves and six curtains by themselves, and you shall double over the sixth curtain at the forefront of the tent.
10 "You shall make fifty loops on the edge of the curtain that is outermost in *one* set, and fifty loops on the edge of the curtain of the second set.
11 "And you shall make fifty bronze clasps, put the clasps into the loops, and couple the tent together, that it may be one.
12 "The remnant that remains of the curtains of the tent, the half curtain that remains, shall hang over the back of the tabernacle.
13 "And a cubit on one side and a cubit on the other side, of what remains of the length of the curtains of the tent, shall hang over the sides of the tabernacle, on this side and on that side, to cover it.
14 "You shall also make a covering of rams' skins dyed red for the tent, and a covering of badger skins above that.
15 "And for the tabernacle you shall make the boards of acacia wood, standing upright.
16 "Ten cubits *shall be* the length of a board, and a cubit and a half *shall be* the width of each board.
17 "Two tenons *shall be* in each board for binding one to another. Thus you shall make for all the boards of the tabernacle.
18 "And you shall make the boards for the tabernacle, twenty boards for the south side.
19 "You shall make forty sockets of silver under the twenty boards: two sockets under one board for its two tenons, and two sockets under another board for its two tenons.
20 "And for the second side of the tabernacle, the north side, *there shall be* twenty boards
21 "and their forty sockets of silver: two sockets under one board, and two sockets under another board.
22 "For the far side of the tabernacle, westward, you shall make six boards.
23 "And you shall also make two boards for the two back corners of the tabernacle.
24 "They shall be coupled together at the bottom and they shall be coupled together at the top by one ring. Thus it shall be for both of them. They shall be for the two corners.
25 "So there shall be eight boards with their sockets of silver—sixteen sockets— two sockets under one board, and two sockets under another board.
26 "And you shall make bars of acacia wood: five for the boards on one side of the tabernacle,
27 "five bars for the boards on the other side of the tabernacle, and five bars for the boards of the side of the tabernacle, for the far side westward.
28 "The middle bar shall pass through the midst of the boards from end to end.
29 "You shall overlay the boards with gold, make their rings of gold *as* holders for the bars, and overlay the bars with gold.
30 "And you shall raise up the tabernacle according to its pattern which you were shown on the mountain.
31 "You shall make a veil woven of blue

and purple and scarlet *yarn*, and fine linen thread. It shall be woven with an artistic design of cherubim.
32 "You shall hang it upon the four pillars of acacia *wood* overlaid with gold. Their hooks *shall be of* gold, upon four sockets of silver.
33 "And you shall hang the veil from the clasps. Then you shall bring the ark of the Testimony in there, behind the veil. The veil shall be a divider for you between the holy *place* and the Most Holy.
34 "You shall put the mercy seat upon the ark of the Testimony in the Most Holy.
35 "You shall set the table outside the veil, and the lampstand across from the table on the side of the tabernacle toward the south; and you shall put the table on the north side.
36 "You shall make a screen for the door of the tabernacle, *woven of* blue and purple and scarlet *yarn*, and fine linen thread, made by a weaver.
37 "And you shall make for the screen five pillars of acacia *wood*, and overlay them with gold; their hooks *shall be of* gold, and you shall cast five sockets of bronze for them.

The Altar of Burnt Offering

27 "You shall make an altar of acacia wood, five cubits long and five cubits broad—the altar shall be square—and its height *shall be* three cubits.
2 "You shall make its horns on its four corners; its horns shall be of one piece with it. And you shall overlay it with bronze.
3 "Also you shall make its pans to receive its ashes, and its shovels and its basins and its forks and its firepans; you shall make all its utensils of bronze.
4 "You shall make a grate for it, a network of bronze; and on the network you shall make four bronze rings at its four corners.
5 "You shall put it under the rim of the altar beneath, that the network may be midway up the altar.
6 "And you shall make poles for the altar, poles of acacia wood, and overlay them with bronze.
7 "The poles shall be put in the rings, and the poles shall be on the two sides of the altar to bear it.
8 "You shall make it hollow with

boards; as it was shown you on the mountain, so shall they make *it*.

The Court of the Tabernacle

9 "You shall also make the court of the tabernacle. For the south side *there shall be* hangings for the court *woven of* fine linen thread, one hundred cubits long for one side.
10 "And its twenty pillars and their twenty sockets *shall be* of bronze. The hooks of the pillars and their bands *shall be* of silver.
11 "Likewise along the length of the north side *there shall be* hangings one hundred *cubits* long, with its twenty pillars and their twenty sockets of bronze, and the hooks of the pillars and their bands of silver.
12 "And along the width of the court on the west side *shall be* hangings of fifty cubits, with their ten pillars and their ten sockets.
13 "The width of the court on the east side *shall be* fifty cubits.
14 "The hangings on *one* side *of the gate shall be* fifteen cubits, *with* their three pillars and their three sockets.
15 "And on the other side *shall be* hangings of fifteen *cubits, with* their three pillars and their three sockets.
16 "For the gate of the court *there shall be* a screen twenty cubits long, *woven of* blue and purple and scarlet *yarn*, and fine linen thread, made by a weaver. It *shall have* four pillars and four sockets.
17 "All the pillars around the court shall have bands of silver; their hooks *shall be* of silver and their sockets of bronze.
18 "The length of the court *shall be* one hundred cubits, the width fifty throughout, and the height five cubits, *woven of* fine linen thread, and its sockets of bronze.
19 "All the utensils of the tabernacle for all its service, all its pegs, and all the pegs of the court, *shall be* of bronze.

The Care of the Lampstand

20 "And you shall command the children of Israel that they bring you pure oil of pressed olives for the light, to cause the lamp to burn continually.
21 "In the tabernacle of meeting, outside the veil which *is* before the Testimony, Aaron and his sons shall tend it from evening until morning before the LORD. *It*

shall be a statute forever to their generations on behalf of the children of Israel.

Garments for the Priesthood

28 "Now take Aaron your brother, and his sons with him, from among the children of Israel, that he may minister to Me as priest, Aaron *and* Aaron's sons: Nadab, Abihu, Eleazar, and Ithamar.
2 "And you shall make holy garments for Aaron your brother, for glory and for beauty.
3 "So you shall speak to all *who are* gifted artisans, whom I have filled with the spirit of wisdom, that they may make Aaron's garments, to sanctify him, that he may minister to Me as priest.
4 "And these *are* the garments which they shall make: a breastplate, an ephod,[23] a robe, a skillfully woven tunic, a turban, and a sash. So they shall make holy garments for Aaron your brother and his sons, that he may minister to Me as priest.

The Ephod

5 "They shall take the gold and blue and purple and scarlet *thread*, and fine linen,
6 "and they shall make the ephod of gold and blue and purple *and* scarlet *thread*, and fine linen thread, artistically woven.
7 "It shall have two shoulder straps joined at its two edges, and *so* it shall be joined together.
8 "And the intricately woven band of the ephod, which *is* on it, shall be of the same workmanship, *woven of* gold and blue and purple and scarlet *thread*, and fine linen thread.
9 "Then you shall take two onyx stones and engrave on them the names of the sons of Israel:
10 "six of their names on one stone, and *the remaining* six names on the other stone, according to their birth.
11 "With the work of an engraver in stone, *like* the engravings of a signet, you shall engrave the two stones with the names of the sons of Israel. You shall set them in settings of gold.
12 "And you shall put the two stones on the shoulders of the ephod *as* memorial stones for the sons of Israel. So Aaron

shall bear their names before the LORD on his two shoulders as a memorial.
13 "You shall also make settings of gold,
14 "and you shall make two chains of pure gold like braided cords, and fasten the braided chains to the settings.

The Breastplate

15 "You shall make the breastplate of judgment. Artistically woven according to the workmanship of the ephod you shall make it: of gold and blue and purple and scarlet *thread*, and of fine linen thread, you shall make it.
16 "It shall be doubled into a square: a span *shall be* its length, and a span *shall be* its width.
17 "And you shall put settings of stones in it, four rows of stones: *The first* row *shall be* a sardius, a topaz, and an emerald; *this shall be* the first row;
18 "the second row *shall be* a turquoise, a sapphire, and a diamond;
19 "the third row, a jacinth, an agate, and an amethyst;
20 "and the fourth row, a beryl, an onyx, and a jasper. They shall be set in gold settings.
21 "And the stones shall have the names of the sons of Israel, twelve according to their names, *like* the engravings of a signet, each one with its own name; they shall be according to the twelve tribes.
22 "You shall make chains for the breastplate at the end, like braided cords of pure gold.
23 "And you shall make two rings of gold for the breastplate, and put the two rings on the two ends of the breastplate.
24 "Then you shall put the two braided *chains* of gold in the two rings which are on the ends of the breastplate;
25 "and the *other* two ends of the two braided chains you shall fasten to the two settings, and put *them* on the shoulder straps of the ephod in the front.
26 "You shall make two rings of gold, and put them on the two ends of the breastplate, on the edge of it, which is on the inner side of the ephod.
27 "And two *other* rings of gold you shall make, and put them on the two shoulder straps, underneath the ephod toward its front, right at the seam above the intricately woven band of the ephod.
28 "They shall bind the breastplate by means of its rings to the rings of the

23 That is, an ornamented vest

ephod, using a blue cord, so that it is above the intricately woven band of the ephod, and so that the breastplate does not come loose from the ephod.
29 "So Aaron shall bear the names of the sons of Israel on the breastplate of judgment over his heart, when he goes into the holy *place*, as a memorial before the LORD continually.
30 "And you shall put in the breastplate of judgment the Urim and the Thummim,[24] and they shall be over Aaron's heart when he goes in before the LORD. So Aaron shall bear the judgment of the children of Israel over his heart before the LORD continually.

Other Priestly Garments

31 "You shall make the robe of the ephod all of blue.
32 "There shall be an opening for his head in the middle of it; it shall have a woven binding all around its opening, like the opening in a coat of mail, so that it does not tear.
33 "And upon its hem you shall make pomegranates of blue and purple and scarlet *yarn*, all around its hem, and bells of gold between them all around:
34 "a golden bell and a pomegranate, a golden bell and a pomegranate, upon the hem of the robe all around.
35 "And it shall be upon Aaron when he ministers, and its sound will be heard when he goes into the holy *place* before the LORD and when he comes out, that he may not die.
36 "You shall also make a plate of pure gold and engrave on it, *like* the engraving of a signet:

HOLINESS TO THE LORD.

37 "And you shall put it on a blue cord, that it may be on the turban; it shall be on the front of the turban.
38 "So it shall be on Aaron's forehead, that Aaron may bear the iniquity of the holy things which the children of Israel hallow in all their holy gifts; and it shall always be on his forehead, that they may be accepted before the LORD.
39 "You shall skillfully weave the tunic of fine linen *thread*, you shall make the turban of fine linen, and you shall make the sash of woven work.
40 "For Aaron's sons you shall make tu-nics, and you shall make sashes for them. And you shall make hats for them, for glory and beauty.
41 "So you shall put them on Aaron your brother and on his sons with him. You shall anoint them, consecrate them, and sanctify them, that they may minister to Me as priests.
42 "And you shall make for them linen trousers to cover their nakedness; they shall reach from the waist to the thighs.
43 "They shall be on Aaron and on his sons when they come into the tabernacle of meeting, or when they come near the altar to minister in the holy *place*, that they do not incur iniquity and die. *It shall be* a statute forever to him and his descendants after him.

Aaron and His Sons Consecrated

29 "And this is what you shall do to them to hallow them for ministering to Me as priests: Take one young bull and two rams without blemish,
2 "and unleavened bread, unleavened cakes mixed with oil, and unleavened wafers anointed with oil (you shall make them of wheat flour).
3 "You shall put them in one basket and bring them in the basket, with the bull and the two rams.
4 "And Aaron and his sons you shall bring to the door of the tabernacle of meeting, and you shall wash them with water.
5 "Then you shall take the garments, put the tunic on Aaron, and the robe of the ephod, the ephod, and the breastplate, and gird him with the intricately woven band of the ephod.
6 "You shall put the turban on his head, and put the holy crown on the turban.
7 "And you shall take the anointing oil, pour *it* on his head, and anoint him.
8 "Then you shall bring his sons and put tunics on them.
9 "And you shall gird them with sashes, Aaron and his sons, and put the hats on them. The priesthood shall be theirs for a perpetual statute. So you shall conse-crate Aaron and his sons.
10 "You shall also have the bull brought before the tabernacle of meeting, and Aaron and his sons shall put their hands on the head of the bull.
11 "Then you shall kill the bull before

24 Literally *Lights and Perfections*

the LORD, *by* the door of the tabernacle of meeting.

12 "You shall take *some* of the blood of the bull and put *it* on the horns of the altar with your finger, and pour all the blood beside the base of the altar.

13 "And you shall take all the fat that covers the entrails, the fatty lobe attached to the liver, and the two kidneys and the fat that *is* on them, and burn *them* on the altar.

14 "But the flesh of the bull, with its skin and its offal, you shall burn with fire outside the camp. It *is* a sin offering.

15 "You shall also take one ram, and Aaron and his sons shall put their hands on the head of the ram;

16 "and you shall kill the ram, and you shall take its blood and sprinkle *it* all around on the altar.

17 "Then you shall cut the ram in pieces, wash its entrails and its legs, and put *them* with its pieces and with its head.

18 "And you shall burn the whole ram on the altar. It *is* a burnt offering to the LORD; it *is* a sweet aroma, an offering made by fire to the LORD.

19 "You shall also take the other ram, and Aaron and his sons shall put their hands on the head of the ram.

20 "Then you shall kill the ram, and take some of its blood and put *it* on the tip of the right ear of Aaron and on the tip of the right ear of his sons, on the thumb of their right hand and on the big toe of their right foot, and sprinkle the blood all around on the altar.

21 "And you shall take some of the blood that is on the altar, and some of the anointing oil, and sprinkle *it* on Aaron and on his garments, on his sons and on the garments of his sons with him; and he and his garments shall be hallowed, and his sons and his sons' garments with him.

22 "Also you shall take the fat of the ram, the fat tail, the fat that covers the entrails, the fatty lobe attached to the liver, the two kidneys and the fat on them, the right thigh (for it *is* a ram of consecration),

23 "one loaf of bread, one cake *made with* oil, and one wafer from the basket of the unleavened bread that *is* before the LORD;

24 "and you shall put all these in the hands of Aaron and in the hands of his sons, and you shall wave them *as* a wave offering before the LORD.

25 "You shall receive them back from their hands and burn *them* on the altar as a burnt offering, as a sweet aroma before the LORD. It *is* an offering made by fire to the LORD.

26 "Then you shall take the breast of the ram of Aaron's consecration and wave it *as* a wave offering before the LORD; and it shall be your portion.

27 "And from the ram of the consecration you shall sanctify the breast of the wave offering which is waved, and the thigh of the heave offering which is raised, of *that* which *is* for Aaron and of *that* which is for his sons.

28 "It shall be from the children of Israel *for* Aaron and his sons by a statute forever. For it is a heave offering; it shall be a heave offering from the children of Israel from the sacrifices of their peace offerings, *that is*, their heave offering to the LORD.

29 "And the holy garments of Aaron shall be his sons' after him, to be anointed in them and to be consecrated in them.

30 "That son who becomes priest in his place shall put them on for seven days, when he enters the tabernacle of meeting to minister in the holy *place*.

31 "And you shall take the ram of the consecration and boil its flesh in the holy place.

32 "Then Aaron and his sons shall eat the flesh of the ram, and the bread that *is* in the basket, *by* the door of the tabernacle of meeting.

33 "They shall eat those things with which the atonement was made, to consecrate *and* to sanctify them; but a stranger shall not eat *them*, because they *are* holy.

34 "And if any of the flesh of the consecration offerings, or of the bread, remains until the morning, then you shall burn the remainder with fire. It shall not be eaten, because it *is* holy.

35 "Thus you shall do to Aaron and his sons, according to all that I have commanded you. Seven days you shall consecrate them.

36 "And you shall offer a bull every day *as* a sin offering for atonement. You shall cleanse the altar when you make atonement for it, and you shall anoint it to sanctify it.

37 "Seven days you shall make atonement for the altar and sanctify it. And the altar shall be most holy. Whatever touches the altar must be holy.

The Daily Offerings

38 "Now this *is* what you shall offer on the altar: two lambs of the first year, day by day continually.
39 "One lamb you shall offer in the morning, and the other lamb you shall offer at twilight.
40 "With the one lamb *shall be* one-tenth *of an ephah* of flour mixed with one-fourth of a hin of pressed oil, and one-fourth of a hin of wine *as* a drink offering.
41 "And the other lamb you shall offer at twilight; and you shall offer with it the grain offering and the drink offering, as in the morning, for a sweet aroma, an offering made by fire to the LORD.
42 "*This shall be* a continual burnt offering throughout your generations *at the* door of the tabernacle of meeting before the LORD, where I will meet you to speak with you.
43 "And there I will meet with the children of Israel, and *the tabernacle* shall be sanctified by My glory.
44 "So I will sanctify the tabernacle of meeting and the altar. I will also sanctify both Aaron and his sons to minister to Me as priests.
45 "I will dwell among the children of Israel and will be their God.
46 "And they shall know that I *am* the LORD their God, who brought them up out of the land of Egypt, that I may dwell among them. I *am* the LORD their God.

The Altar of Incense

30 "You shall make an altar to burn incense on; you shall make it of acacia wood.
2 "A cubit *shall be* its length and a cubit its width—it shall be square—and two cubits *shall be* its height. Its horns *shall be* of one piece with it.
3 "And you shall overlay its top, its sides all around, and its horns with pure gold; and you shall make for it a molding of gold all around.
4 "Two gold rings you shall make for it, under the molding on both its sides. You shall place *them* on its two sides, and they will be holders for the poles with which to bear it.

5 "You shall make the poles of acacia wood, and overlay them with gold.
6 "And you shall put it before the veil that *is* before the ark of the Testimony, before the mercy seat that *is* over the Testimony, where I will meet with you.
7 "Aaron shall burn on it sweet incense every morning; when he tends the lamps, he shall burn incense on it.
8 "And when Aaron lights the lamps at twilight, he shall burn incense on it, a perpetual incense before the LORD throughout your generations.
9 "You shall not offer strange incense on it, or a burnt offering, or a meal offering; nor shall you pour a drink offering on it.
10 "And Aaron shall make atonement upon its horns once a year with the blood of the sin offering of atonement; once a year he shall make atonement upon it throughout your generations. It *is* most holy to the LORD."

The Ransom Money

11 Then the LORD spoke to Moses, saying:
12 "When you take the census of the children of Israel for their number, then every man shall give a ransom for himself to the LORD, when you number them, that there may be no plague among them when *you* number them.
13 "This is what everyone among those who are numbered shall give: half a shekel according to the shekel of the sanctuary (a shekel *is* twenty gerahs). The half-shekel *shall be* an offering to the LORD.
14 "Everyone included among those who are numbered, from twenty years old and above, shall give an offering to the LORD.
15 "The rich shall not give more and the poor shall not give less than half a shekel, when *you* give an offering to the LORD, to make atonement for yourselves.
16 "And you shall take the atonement money of the children of Israel, and shall appoint it for the service of the tabernacle of meeting, that it may be a memorial for the children of Israel before the LORD, to make atonement for yourselves."

The Bronze Laver

17 Then the LORD spoke to Moses, saying:
18 "You shall also make a laver of

bronze, with its base also of bronze, for washing. You shall put it between the tabernacle of meeting and the altar. And you shall put water in it,

19 "for Aaron and his sons shall wash their hands and their feet in water from it.

20 "When they go into the tabernacle of meeting, or when they come near the altar to minister, to burn an offering made by fire to the LORD, they shall wash with water, lest they die.

21 "So they shall wash their hands and their feet, lest they die. And it shall be a statute forever to them—to him and his descendants throughout their generations."

The Holy Anointing Oil

22 Moreover the LORD spoke to Moses, saying:

23 "Also take for yourself quality spices—five hundred *shekels* of liquid myrrh, half as much sweet-smelling cinnamon (two hundred and fifty *shekels*), two hundred and fifty *shekels* of sweet-smelling cane,

24 "five hundred *shekels* of cassia, according to the shekel of the sanctuary, and a hin of olive oil.

25 "And you shall make from these a holy anointing oil, an ointment compounded according to the art of the perfumer. It shall be a holy anointing oil.

26 "With it you shall anoint the tabernacle of meeting and the ark of the Testimony;

27 "the table and all its utensils, the lampstand and its utensils, and the altar of incense;

28 "the altar of burnt offering with all its utensils, and the laver and its base.

29 "You shall sanctify them, that they may be most holy; whatever touches them must be holy.

30 "And you shall anoint Aaron and his sons, and sanctify them, that *they* may minister to Me as priests.

31 "And you shall speak to the children of Israel, saying: 'This shall be a holy anointing oil to Me throughout your generations.

32 'It shall not be poured on man's flesh; nor shall you make *any other* like it, according to its composition. It *is* holy, *and* it shall be holy to you.

33 'Whoever compounds *any* like it, or

whoever puts *any* of it on an outsider, shall be cut off from his people.' "

The Incense

34 And the LORD said to Moses: "Take sweet spices, stacte and onycha and galbanum, and pure frankincense with *these* sweet spices; there shall be equal amounts of each.

35 "You shall make of these an incense, a compound according to the art of the perfumer, salted, pure, *and* holy.

36 "And you shall beat *some* of it very fine, and put some of it before the Testimony in the tabernacle of meeting where I will meet with you. It shall be most holy to you.

37 "But *as for* the incense which you shall make, you shall not make any for yourselves, according to its composition. It shall be to you holy for the LORD.

38 "Whoever makes *any* like it, to smell it, he shall be cut off from his people."

Artisans for Building the Tabernacle

31 Then the LORD spoke to Moses, saying:

2 "See, I have called by name Bezaleel the son of Uri, the son of Hur, of the tribe of Judah.

3 "And I have filled him with the Spirit of God, in wisdom, in understanding, in knowledge, and in all *manner of* workmanship,

4 "to design artistic works, to work in gold, in silver, in bronze,

5 "in cutting jewels for setting, in carving wood, and to work in all *manner of* workmanship.

6 "And I, indeed I, have appointed with him Aholiab the son of Ahisamach, of the tribe of Dan; and I have put wisdom in the hearts of all who are gifted artisans, that they may make all that I have commanded you:

7 "the tabernacle of meeting, the ark of the Testimony and the mercy seat that *is* on it, and all the furniture of the tabernacle—

8 "the table and its utensils, the pure lampstand with all its utensils, the altar of incense,

9 "the altar of burnt offering with all its utensils, and the laver and its base—

10 "the garments of ministry,[25] the holy garments for Aaron the priest and the

25 Or *woven garments*

garments of his sons, to minister as priests,

11 "and the anointing oil and sweet incense for the holy *place*. According to all that I have commanded you they shall do."

The Sabbath Law

12 And the LORD spoke to Moses, saying,

13 "Speak also to the children of Israel, saying: 'Surely My Sabbaths you shall keep, for it *is* a sign between Me and you throughout your generations, that *you* may know that I *am* the LORD who sanctifies you.

14 'You shall keep the Sabbath, therefore, for *it is* holy to you. Everyone who profanes it shall surely be put to death; for whoever does *any* work on it, that person shall be cut off from among his people.

15 'Work shall be done for six days, but the seventh *is* the Sabbath of rest, holy to the LORD. Whoever does *any* work on the Sabbath day, he shall surely be put to death.

16 'Therefore the children of Israel shall keep the Sabbath, to observe the Sabbath throughout their generations *as* a perpetual covenant.

17 'It *is* a sign between Me and the children of Israel forever; for *in* six days the LORD made the heavens and the earth, and on the seventh day He rested and was refreshed.' "

18 And when He had made an end of speaking with him on Mount Sinai, He gave Moses two tablets of the Testimony, tablets of stone, written with the finger of God.

The Gold Calf

32 Now when the people saw that Moses delayed coming down from the mountain, the people gathered together to Aaron, and said to him, "Come, make us gods that shall go before us; for *as for* this Moses, the man who brought us up out of the land of Egypt, we do not know what has become of him."

2 And Aaron said to them, "Break off the golden earrings which *are* in the ears of your wives, your sons, and your daughters, and bring *them* to me."

3 "So all the people broke off the golden earrings which *were* in their ears, and brought *them* to Aaron.

4 And he received *the gold* from their hand, and he fashioned it with an engraving tool, and made a molded calf. Then they said, "This *is* your god, O Israel, that brought you out of the land of Egypt!"

5 So when Aaron saw *it*, he built an altar before it. And Aaron made a proclamation and said, "Tomorrow *is* a feast to the LORD."

6 Then they rose early on the next day, offered burnt offerings, and brought peace offerings; and the people sat down to eat and drink, and rose up to play.

7 And the LORD said to Moses, "Go, get down! For your people whom you brought out of the land of Egypt have corrupted *themselves*.

8 "They have turned aside quickly out of the way which I commanded them. They have made themselves a molded calf, and worshiped it and sacrificed to it, and said, 'This *is* your god, O Israel, that brought you out of the land of Egypt!' "

9 And the LORD said to Moses, "I have seen this people, and indeed it *is* a stiff-necked people!

10 "Now therefore, let Me alone, that My wrath may burn hot against them and I may consume them. And I will make of you a great nation."

11 Then Moses pleaded with the LORD his God, and said: "LORD, why does Your wrath burn hot against Your people whom You have brought out of the land of Egypt with great power and with a mighty hand?

12 "Why should the Egyptians speak, and say, 'He brought them out to harm them, to kill them in the mountains, and to consume them from the face of the earth'? Turn from Your fierce wrath, and relent from this harm to Your people.

13 "Remember Abraham, Isaac, and Israel, Your servants, to whom You swore by Your own self, and said to them, 'I will multiply your descendants as the stars of heaven; and all this land that I have spoken of I give to your descendants, and they shall inherit *it* forever.' "[26]

14 So the LORD relented from the harm which He said He would do to His people.

15 And Moses turned and went down from the mountain, and the two tablets of

the Testimony *were* in his hand. The tablets *were* written on both sides; on the one *side* and on the other they were written.
16 Now the tablets *were* the work of God, and the writing *was* the writing of God engraved on the tablets.
17 And when Joshua heard the noise of the people as they shouted, he said to Moses, "*There is* a noise of war in the camp."
18 But he said:

"*It is* not the voice of *those*
  who shout in victory,
Nor *is it* the voice of *those*
  who cry out in defeat,
But the voice of *those*
  who sing that I hear."

19 So it was, as soon as he came near the camp, that he saw the calf *and* the dancing. So Moses' anger became hot, and he cast the tablets out of his hands and broke them at the foot of the mountain.
20 Then he took the calf which they had made, burned *it* in the fire, and ground *it* to powder; and he scattered *it* on the water and made the children of Israel drink *it*.
21 And Moses said to Aaron, "What did this people do to you that you have brought *so* great a sin upon them?"
22 So Aaron said, "Do not let the anger of my lord become hot. You know the people, that they *are set* on evil.
23 "For they said to me, 'Make us gods that shall go before us; *as for* this Moses, the man who brought us out of the land of Egypt, we do not know what has become of him.'
24 "And I said to them, 'Whoever has any gold, let them break *it* off.' So they gave *it* to me, and I cast it into the fire, and this calf came out."
25 Now when Moses saw that the people *were* unrestrained (for Aaron had not restrained them, to *their* shame among their enemies),
26 then Moses stood in the entrance of the camp, and said, "Whoever *is* on the LORD's side, *let him come* to me." And all the sons of Levi gathered themselves together to him.
27 And he said to them, "Thus says the LORD God of Israel: 'Let every man put his sword on his side, and go in and out from entrance to entrance throughout the camp, and let every man kill his brother, every man his companion, and every man his neighbor.'"
28 So the sons of Levi did according to the word of Moses. And about three thousand men of the people fell that day.
29 Then Moses said, "Consecrate yourselves today to the LORD, that He may bestow on you a blessing this day, for every man has opposed his son and his brother."
30 And it came to pass on the next day that Moses said to the people, "You have sinned a great sin. So now I will go up to the LORD; perhaps I can make atonement for your sin."
31 Then Moses returned to the LORD and said, "Oh, these people have sinned a great sin, and have made for themselves a god of gold!
32 "Yet now, if You will forgive their sin—but if not, I pray, blot me out of Your book which You have written."
33 And the LORD said to Moses, "Whoever has sinned against Me, I will blot him out of My book.
34 "Now therefore, go, lead the people to *the place* of which I have spoken to you. Behold, My Angel shall go before you. Nevertheless, in the day when I visit for punishment, I will visit punishment upon them for their sin."
35 So the LORD plagued the people because of what they did with the calf which Aaron made.

The Command to Leave Sinai

33 Then the LORD said to Moses, "Depart *and* go up from here, you and the people whom you have brought out of the land of Egypt, to the land of which I swore to Abraham, Isaac, and Jacob, saying, 'To your descendants I will give it.'
2 "And I will send *My* Angel before you, and I will drive out the Canaanite and the Amorite and the Hittite and the Perizzite and the Hivite and the Jebusite.
3 "*Go up* to a land flowing with milk and honey; for I will not go up in your midst, lest I consume you on the way for you *are* a stiff-necked people."
4 And when the people heard these grave tidings, they mourned, and no one put on his ornaments.
5 For the LORD had said to Moses, "Say

to the children of Israel, 'You *are* a stiff-necked people. I could come up into your midst in one moment and consume you. Now therefore, take off your ornaments, that I may know what to do to you.' "

6 So the children of Israel stripped themselves of their ornaments by Mount Horeb.

Moses Meets with the LORD

7 Moses took his tent and pitched it outside the camp, far from the camp, and called it the tabernacle of meeting. And it came to pass *that* everyone who sought the LORD went out to the tabernacle of meeting which *was* outside the camp.

8 So it was, whenever Moses went out to the tabernacle, *that* all the people rose, and each man stood *at* his tent door and watched Moses until he had gone into the tabernacle.

9 And it came to pass, when Moses entered the tabernacle, that the pillar of cloud descended and stood *at* the door of the tabernacle, and the LORD[27] talked with Moses.

10 All the people saw the pillar of cloud standing *at* the tabernacle door, and all the people rose and worshiped, each man *in* his tent door.

11 So the LORD spoke to Moses face to face, as a man speaks to his friend. And he would return to the camp, but his servant Joshua the son of Nun, a young man, did not depart from the tabernacle.

The Promise of God's Presence

12 Then Moses said to the LORD, "See, You say to me, 'Bring up this people.' But You have not let me know whom You will send with me. Yet You have said, 'I know you by name, and you have also found grace in My sight.'

13 "Now therefore, I pray, if I have found grace in Your sight, show me now Your way, that I may know You and that I may find grace in Your sight. And consider that this nation *is* Your people."

14 And He said, "My Presence will go *with you*, and I will give you rest."

15 Then he said to Him, "If Your Presence does not go *with us*, do not bring us up from here.

16 "For how then will it be known that Your people and I have found grace in Your sight, except You go with us? So

we shall be separate, Your people and I, from all the people who *are* upon the face of the earth."

17 Then the LORD said to Moses, "I will also do this thing that you have spoken; for you have found grace in My sight, and I know you by name."

18 And he said, "Please, show me Your glory."

19 Then He said, "I will make all My goodness pass before you, and I will proclaim the name of the LORD before you. I will be gracious to whom I will be gracious, and I will have compassion on whom I will have compassion."

20 But He said, "You cannot see My face; for no man shall see Me, and live."

21 And the LORD said, "Here is a place by Me, and you shall stand on the rock.

22 "So it shall be, while My glory passes by, that I will put you in the cleft of the rock, and will cover you with My hand while I pass by.

23 "Then I will take away My hand, and you shall see My back; but My face shall not be seen."

Moses Makes New Tablets

34 And the LORD said to Moses, "Cut two tablets of stone like the first *ones*, and I will write on *these* tablets the words that were on the first tablets which you broke.

2 "So be ready in the morning, and come up in the morning to Mount Sinai, and present yourself to Me there on the top of the mountain.

3 "And no man shall come up with you, and let no man be seen throughout all the mountain; let neither flocks nor herds feed before that mountain."

4 So he cut two tablets of stone like the first *ones*. Then Moses rose early in the morning and went up Mount Sinai, as the LORD had commanded him; and he took in his hand the two tablets of stone.

5 Then the LORD descended in the cloud and stood with him there, and proclaimed the name of the LORD.

6 And the LORD passed before him and proclaimed, "The LORD, the LORD God, merciful and gracious, long-suffering, and abounding in goodness and truth,

7 "keeping mercy for thousands, forgiving iniquity and transgression and sin, by no means clearing *the guilty*, visiting the iniquity of the fathers upon the children

27 Literally *He*

and the children's children to the third
and the fourth generation."
8 So Moses made haste and bowed his
head toward the earth, and worshiped.
9 Then he said, "If now I have found
grace in Your sight, O Lord, let my Lord,
I pray, go among us, even though we *are*
a stiff-necked people; and pardon our iniquity and our sin, and take us as Your
inheritance."

The Covenant Renewed

10 And He said: "Behold, I make a covenant. Before all your people I will do
marvels such as have not been done in all
the earth, nor in any nation; and all the
people among whom you *are* shall see the
work of the LORD. For it *is* an awesome
thing that I will do with you.
11 "Observe what I command you this
day. Behold, I am driving out from before you the Amorite and the Canaanite
and the Hittite and the Perizzite and the
Hivite and the Jebusite.
12 "Take heed to yourself, lest you make
a covenant with the inhabitants of the
land where you are going, lest it be a
snare in your midst.
13 "But you shall destroy their altars,
break their *sacred* pillars, and cut down
their *wooden* images
14 "(for you shall worship no other god,
for the LORD, whose name *is* Jealous, *is* a
jealous God),
15 "lest you make a covenant with the
inhabitants of the land, and they play the
harlot with their gods and make sacrifice
to their gods, and *one of them* invites you
and you eat of his sacrifice,
16 "and you take of his daughters for
your sons, and his daughters play the harlot with their gods and make your sons
play the harlot with their gods.
17 "You shall make no molded gods for
yourselves.
18 "The Feast of Unleavened Bread you
shall keep. Seven days you shall eat unleavened bread, as I commanded you, in
the appointed time of the month of Abib;
for in the month of Abib you came out
from Egypt.
19 "All that open the womb *are* Mine,
and every male firstling among your livestock, *whether* ox or sheep.
20 "But the firstling of a donkey you
shall redeem with a lamb. And if you will
not redeem *him*, then you shall break his

neck. All the firstborn of your sons you
shall redeem. And none shall appear before Me empty-handed.
21 "Six days you shall work, but on the
seventh day you shall rest; in plowing
time and in harvest you shall rest.
22 "And you shall observe the Feast of
Weeks, of the firstfruits of wheat harvest,
and the Feast of Ingathering at the year's
end.
23 "Three times in the year all your men
shall appear before the Lord, the LORD
God of Israel.
24 "For I will cast out the nations before
you and enlarge your borders; neither
will any man covet your land when you
go up to appear before the LORD your
God three times in the year.
25 "You shall not offer the blood of My
sacrifice with leaven, nor shall the sacrifice of the Feast of the Passover be left
until morning.
26 "The first of the firstfruits of your
land you shall bring to the house of the
LORD your God. You shall not boil a
young goat in its mother's milk."
27 Then the LORD said to Moses, "Write
these words, for according to the tenor of
these words I have made a covenant with
you and with Israel."
28 So he was there with the LORD forty
days and forty nights; he neither ate
bread nor drank water. And He wrote on
the tablets the words of the covenant, the
Ten Commandments.[28]

The Shining Face of Moses

29 Now it was so, when Moses came
down from Mount Sinai (and the two
tablets of the Testimony *were* in Moses'
hand when he came down from the
mountain), that Moses did not know that
the skin of his face shone while he talked
with Him.
30 So when Aaron and all the children of
Israel saw Moses, behold, the skin of his
face shone, and they were afraid to come
near him.
31 Then Moses called to them, and
Aaron and all the rulers of the congregation returned to him; and Moses talked
with them.
32 Afterward all the children of Israel
came near, and he gave them as commandments all that the LORD had spoken
with him on Mount Sinai.

28 Literally *Ten Words*

33 And when Moses had finished speaking with them, he put a veil on his face. 34 But whenever Moses went in before the LORD to speak with Him, he would take the veil off until he came out; and he would come out and speak to the children of Israel whatever he had been commanded. 35 And whenever the children of Israel saw the face of Moses, that the skin of Moses' face shone, then Moses would put the veil on his face again, until he went in to speak with Him.

Sabbath Regulations

35 Then Moses gathered all the congregation of the children of Israel together, and said to them, "These *are* the words which the LORD has commanded *you* to do:
2 "Work shall be done for six days, but the seventh day shall be a holy day for you, a Sabbath of rest to the LORD. Whoever does any work on it shall be put to death.
3 "You shall kindle no fire throughout your habitations on the Sabbath day."

Offerings for the Tabernacle

4 And Moses spoke to all the congregation of the children of Israel, saying, "This *is* the thing which the LORD commanded, saying:
5 'Take from among you an offering to the LORD. Whoever *is* of a willing heart, let him bring it as an offering to the LORD: gold, silver, and bronze;
6 'blue and purple and scarlet *yarn*, fine linen *thread*, and goats' *hair*;
7 'rams' skins dyed red, badger skins, and acacia wood;
8 'oil for the light, and spices for the anointing oil and for the sweet incense;
9 'onyx stones, and stones to be set in the ephod and in the breastplate.

Articles of the Tabernacle

10 'All who *are* skillful among you shall come and make all that the LORD has commanded:
11 'the tabernacle, its tent, its covering, its clasps, its boards, its bars, its pillars, and its sockets;
12 'the ark and its poles, *with* the mercy seat, and the veil of the covering;
13 'the table and its poles, all its utensils, and the showbread;

14 'also the lampstand for the light, its utensils, its lamps, and the oil for the light;
15 'the incense altar, its poles, the anointing oil, the sweet incense, and the screen for the door at the entrance of the tabernacle;
16 'the altar of burnt offering with its bronze grating, its poles, all its utensils, *and* the laver and its base;
17 'the hangings of the court, its pillars, their sockets, and the screen for the gate of the court;
18 'the pegs of the tabernacle, the pegs of the court, and their cords;
19 'the garments of ministry,[29] for ministering in the holy *place*—the holy garments for Aaron the priest and the garments of his sons, to minister as priests.' "

The Tabernacle Offerings Presented

20 And all the congregation of the children of Israel departed from the presence of Moses.
21 Then everyone came whose heart was stirred, and everyone whose spirit was willing, *and* they brought the LORD's offering for the work of the tabernacle of meeting, for all its service, and for the holy garments.
22 They came, both men and women, as many as had a willing heart, *and* brought earrings and nose rings, rings and necklaces, all jewelry of gold, that is, every man who *offered* an offering of gold to the LORD.
23 And every man, with whom was found blue and purple and scarlet, fine linen, goats' *hair*, red skins of rams, and badger skins, brought *them*.
24 Everyone who offered an offering of silver or bronze brought the LORD's offering. And everyone with whom was found acacia wood for any work of the service, brought *it*.
25 All the women who were gifted artisans spun yarn with their hands, and brought what they had spun, of blue and purple *and* scarlet, and fine linen.
26 And all the women whose hearts stirred with wisdom spun yarn of goats' *hair*.
27 The rulers brought onyx stones, and the stones to be set in the ephod and in the breastplate,

29 Or *woven garments*

28 and spices and oil for the light, for the anointing oil, and for the sweet incense.
29 The children of Israel brought a freewill offering to the LORD, all the men and women whose hearts were willing to bring *material* for all kinds of work which the LORD, by the hand of Moses, had commanded to be done.

The Artisans Called by God

30 And Moses said to the children of Israel, "See, the LORD has called by name Bezaleel the son of Uri, the son of Hur, of the tribe of Judah;
31 "and He has filled him with the Spirit of God, in wisdom and understanding, in knowledge and all manner of workmanship,
32 "to design artistic works, to work in gold and silver and bronze,
33 "in cutting jewels for setting, in carving wood, and to work in all manner of artistic workmanship.
34 "And He has put in his heart the ability to teach, *in* him and Aholiab the son of Ahisamach, of the tribe of Dan.
35 "He has filled them with skill to do all manner of work of the engraver and the designer and the tapestry maker, in blue and purple and scarlet and fine linen, and of the weaver—those who do every work and those who design artistic works.

36 "And Bezaleel and Aholiab, and every gifted artisan in whom the LORD has put wisdom and understanding, to know how to do all manner of work for the service of the sanctuary, shall do according to all that the LORD has commanded."

The People Give More than Enough

2 Then Moses called Bezaleel and Aholiab, and every gifted artisan in whose heart the LORD had put wisdom, everyone whose heart was stirred, to come and do the work.
3 And they received from Moses all the offering which the children of Israel had brought for the work of the service of making the sanctuary. So they continued bringing to him freewill offerings every morning.
4 Then all the craftsmen who were doing all the work of the sanctuary came, each from the work he was doing,
5 and they spoke to Moses, saying, "The people bring much more than

enough for the service of the work which the LORD commanded *us* to do."
6 So Moses gave a commandment, and they caused it to be proclaimed throughout the camp, saying, "Let neither man nor woman do any more work for the offering of the sanctuary." And the people were restrained from bringing,
7 for the material they had was sufficient for all the work to be done—indeed too much.

Building the Tabernacle

8 Then all the gifted artisans among them who worked on the tabernacle made ten curtains woven of fine linen thread, and blue and purple and scarlet *yarn;* *with* artistic designs of cherubim they made them.
9 The length of each curtain *was* twenty-eight cubits, and the width of each curtain four cubits; the curtains *were* all the same size.
10 And he coupled five curtains to one another, and *the other* five curtains he coupled to one another.
11 He made loops of blue yarn on the edge of the curtain on the selvedge of one set; likewise he did on the outer edge of *the other* curtain of the second set.
12 Fifty loops he made on one curtain, and fifty loops he made on the edge of the curtain on the end of the second set; the loops held one *curtain* to another.
13 And he made fifty clasps of gold, and coupled the curtains to one another with the clasps, that it might be one tabernacle.
14 He made curtains of goats' *hair* for the tent over the tabernacle; he made eleven curtains.
15 The length of each curtain *was* thirty cubits, and the width of each curtain four cubits; the eleven curtains *were* the same size.
16 He coupled five curtains by themselves and six curtains by themselves.
17 And he made fifty loops on the edge of the curtain that is outermost in one set, and fifty loops he made on the edge of the curtain of the second set.
18 He also made fifty bronze clasps to couple the tent together, that it might be one.
19 Then he made a covering for the tent of rams' skins dyed red, and a covering of badger skins above *that.*

20 For the tabernacle he made boards of acacia wood, standing upright.
21 The length of each board *was* ten cubits, and the width of each board a cubit and a half.
22 Each board had two tenons for binding one to another. Thus he made for all the boards of the tabernacle.
23 And he made boards for the tabernacle, twenty boards for the south side.
24 Forty sockets of silver he made to go under the twenty boards: two sockets under one board for its two tenons, and two sockets under another board for its two tenons.
25 And for the other side of the tabernacle, the north side, he made twenty boards
26 and their forty sockets of silver: two sockets under one board and two sockets under another board.
27 For the west side of the tabernacle he made six boards.
28 He also made two boards for the two back corners of the tabernacle.
29 And they were coupled at the bottom and coupled together at the top by one ring. Thus he made both of them for the two corners.
30 So there were eight boards and their sockets—sixteen sockets of silver—two sockets under every board.
31 And he made bars of acacia wood: five for the boards on one side of the tabernacle,
32 five bars for the boards on the other side of the tabernacle, and five bars for the boards of the tabernacle on the far side westward.
33 And he made the middle bar to pass through the boards from one end to the other.
34 He overlaid the boards with gold, made their rings of gold *to be* holders for the bars, and overlaid the bars with gold.
35 And he made a veil woven of blue and purple and scarlet *yarn*, and fine linen thread; it was woven *with* an artistic design of cherubim.
36 He made for it four pillars of acacia *wood*, and overlaid them with gold, with their hooks of gold; and he cast four sockets of silver for them.
37 He also made a screen for the tabernacle door, woven of blue and purple and scarlet *yarn*, and fine linen thread, made by a weaver,
38 and its five pillars with their hooks. And he overlaid their capitals and their rings with gold, but their five sockets *were* of bronze.

Making the Ark of the Testimony

37 Then Bezaleel made the ark of acacia wood; two and a half cubits *was* its length, a cubit and a half its width, and a cubit and a half its height.
2 He overlaid it with pure gold inside and outside, and made a molding of gold all around it.
3 And he cast for it four rings of gold *to be set* in its four corners: two rings on one side, and two rings on the other side of it.
4 He made poles of acacia wood, and overlaid them with gold.
5 And he put the poles into the rings at the sides of the ark, to bear the ark.
6 He also made the mercy seat of pure gold; two and a half cubits *was* its length and a cubit and a half its width.
7 He made two cherubim of beaten gold; he made them of one piece at the two ends of the mercy seat:
8 one cherub at one end on this side, and the other cherub at the *other* end on that side. He made the cherubim at the two ends *of one piece* with the mercy seat.
9 The cherubim spread out *their* wings above, *and* covered the mercy seat with their wings. They faced one another; the faces of the cherubim were toward the mercy seat.

Making the Table for the Showbread

10 He made the table of acacia wood; two cubits *was* its length, a cubit its width, and a cubit and a half its height.
11 And he overlaid it with pure gold, and made a molding of gold all around it.
12 Also he made a frame of a handbreadth all around it, and made a molding of gold for the frame all around it.
13 And he cast for it four rings of gold, and put the rings on the four corners that *were* at its four legs.
14 The rings were close to the frame, as holders for the poles to bear the table.
15 And he made the poles of acacia wood to bear the table, and overlaid them with gold.
16 He made of pure gold the utensils which were on the table: its dishes, its cups, its bowls, and its pitchers for pouring.

Making the Gold Lampstand

17 He also made the lampstand of pure gold; of hammered work he made the lampstand. Its shaft, its branches, its bowls, its ornamental knobs, and its flowers were of the same piece.
18 And six branches came out of its sides: three branches of the lampstand out of one side, and three branches of the lampstand out of the other side.
19 There were three bowls made like almond *blossoms* on one branch, with an *ornamental* knob and a flower, and three bowls made like almond *blossoms* on the other branch, with an *ornamental* knob and a flower—and so for the six branches coming out of the lampstand.
20 And on the lampstand itself *were* four bowls made like almond *blossoms, each with* its *ornamental* knob and flower.
21 *There was* a knob under the *first* two branches of the same, a knob under the *second* two branches of the same, and a knob under the *third* two branches of the same, according to the six branches extending from it.
22 Their knobs and their branches were of one piece; all of it *was* one hammered piece of pure gold.
23 And he made its seven lamps, its wick-trimmers, and its trays of pure gold.
24 Of a talent of pure gold he made it, with all its utensils.

Making the Altar of Incense

25 He made the incense altar of acacia wood. Its length *was* a cubit and its width a cubit—*it was* square—and two cubits *was* its height. Its horns were *of* one piece with it.
26 And he overlaid it with pure gold: its top, its sides all around, and its horns. He also made for it a molding of gold all around it.
27 He made two rings of gold for it under its molding, by its two corners on both sides, as holders for the poles with which to bear it.
28 And he made the poles of acacia wood, and overlaid them with gold.

Making the Anointing Oil and the Incense

29 He also made the holy anointing oil and the pure incense of sweet spices, according to the work of the perfumer.

Making the Altar of Burnt Offering

38 He made the altar of burnt offering of acacia wood; five cubits *was* its length and five cubits its width—*it was* square—and its height *was* three cubits.
2 He made its horns on its four corners; the horns were *of one piece* with it. And he overlaid it with bronze.
3 He made all the utensils for the altar: the pans, the shovels, the basins, the forks, and the firepans; all its utensils he made of bronze.
4 And he made a grate of bronze network for the altar, under its rim, midway from the bottom.
5 He cast four rings for the four corners of the bronze grating, *as* holders for the poles.
6 And he made the poles of acacia wood, and overlaid them with bronze.
7 Then he put the poles into the rings on the sides of the altar, with which to bear it. He made the altar hollow with boards.

Making the Bronze Laver

8 He made the laver of bronze and its base of bronze, from the bronze mirrors of the serving women who assembled at the door of the tabernacle of meeting.

Making the Court of the Tabernacle

9 Then he made the court on the south side; the hangings of the court *were woven of* fine linen, one hundred cubits long.
10 There *were* twenty pillars for them, with twenty bronze sockets. The hooks of the pillars and their bands *were of* silver.
11 On the north side *the hangings were* one hundred cubits *long*, with twenty pillars and their twenty bronze sockets. The hooks of the pillars and their bands *were of* silver.
12 And on the west side *there were* hangings of fifty cubits, with ten pillars and their ten sockets. The hooks of the pillars and their bands *were of* silver.
13 For the east side *the hangings were* fifty cubits.
14 The hangings of one side *of the gate were* fifteen cubits *long, with* their three pillars and their three sockets,
15 and the same for the other side of the court gate; on this side and that *were* hangings of fifteen cubits, *with* their three pillars and their three sockets.

16 All the hangings of the court all around *were woven of* fine linen.
17 The sockets for the pillars *were of* bronze, the hooks of the pillars and their bands *were of* silver, and the overlay of their capitals *was of* silver; and all the pillars of the court had bands of silver.
18 The screen for the gate of the court *was* woven of blue and purple and scarlet *yarn*, and fine linen thread. The length *was* twenty cubits, and the height along its width *was* five cubits, corresponding to the hangings of the court.
19 And *there were* four pillars *with* their four sockets of bronze; their hooks *were* of silver, and the overlay of their capitals and their bands *was of* silver.
20 All the pegs of the tabernacle, and of the court all around, *were of* bronze.

Materials of the Tabernacle

21 This is the inventory of the tabernacle, the tabernacle of the Testimony, which was counted according to the commandment of Moses, for the service of the Levites, by the hand of Ithamar, son of Aaron the priest.
22 Bezaleel the son of Uri, the son of Hur, of the tribe of Judah, made all that the LORD had commanded Moses.
23 And with him *was* Aholiab the son of Ahisamach, of the tribe of Dan, an engraver and designer, a weaver in blue and purple and scarlet *yarn*, and fine linen *thread*.
24 All the gold that was used in all the work of the holy *place*, that is, the gold of the offering, was twenty-nine talents and seven hundred and thirty shekels, according to the shekel of the sanctuary.
25 And the silver from those who were numbered of the congregation *was* one hundred talents and one thousand seven hundred and seventy-five shekels, according to the shekel of the sanctuary:
26 a bekah for each man (*that is*, half a shekel, according to the shekel of the sanctuary), for everyone included in the numbering from twenty years old and above, for six hundred and three thousand, five hundred and fifty *men*.
27 And from the hundred talents of silver were cast the sockets of the sanctuary and the bases of the veil: one hundred sockets from the hundred talents, one talent for each socket.
28 Then from the one thousand seven

hundred and seventy-five *shekels* he made hooks for the pillars, overlaid their capitals, and made bands for them.
29 The offering of bronze *was* seventy talents and two thousand four hundred shekels.
30 And with it he made the sockets for the door of the tabernacle of meeting, the bronze altar, the bronze grating for it, and all the utensils for the altar,
31 the sockets for the court all around, the bases for the court gate, all the pegs for the tabernacle, and all the pegs for the court all around.

Making the Garments of the Priesthood

39 Of the blue and purple and scarlet *thread* they made garments of ministry,[30] for ministering in the holy *place*, and made the holy garments for Aaron, as the LORD had commanded Moses.

Making the Ephod

2 He made the ephod of gold and blue and purple and scarlet *thread*, and of fine linen thread.
3 And they beat the gold into thin sheets and cut *it into* threads, to work *it* in with the blue and purple and scarlet and fine linen *thread, into* artistic designs.
4 They made shoulder straps for it to couple *it* together; it was coupled together at its two edges.
5 And the intricately woven band of his ephod that *was* on it *was* of the same workmanship, *woven of* gold and blue and purple and scarlet *thread*, and fine linen thread, as the LORD had commanded Moses.
6 And they set onyx stones, enclosed in settings of gold; they were engraved, as signets are engraved, with the names of the sons of Israel.
7 He put them on the shoulders of the ephod, *that they should be* stones for a memorial for the sons of Israel, as the LORD had commanded Moses.

Making the Breastplate

8 And he made the breastplate, artistically woven like the workmanship of the ephod, of gold and blue and purple and scarlet *thread*, and fine linen thread.
9 They made the breastplate square by doubling it; a span *was* its length and a span its width when doubled.

30 Or *woven garments*

10 And they set in it four rows of stones: a row with a sardius, a topaz, and an emerald was the first row;
11 the second row, a turquoise, a sapphire, and a diamond;
12 the third row, a jacinth, an agate, and an amethyst;
13 the fourth row, a beryl, an onyx, and a jasper. *They were* enclosed in settings of gold in their mountings.
14 *There were* twelve stones according to the names of the sons of Israel: according to their names, *engraved like* a signet, each one with its own name according to the twelve tribes.
15 And they made chains for the breastplate at the ends, like braided cords of pure gold.
16 They also made two settings of gold and two gold rings, and put the two rings on the two ends of the breastplate.
17 And they put the two braided chains of gold in the two rings on the ends of the breastplate.
18 The two ends of the two braided chains they fastened in the two settings, and put them on the shoulder straps of the ephod in the front.
19 And they made two rings of gold and put *them* on the two ends of the breastplate, on the edge of it, which *was* on the inward side of the ephod.
20 They made two *other* gold rings and put them on the two shoulder straps, underneath the ephod toward its front, right at the seam above the intricately woven band of the ephod.
21 And they bound the breastplate by means of its rings to the rings of the ephod with a blue cord, so that it would be above the intricately woven band of the ephod, and that the breastplate would not come loose from the ephod, as the LORD had commanded Moses.

Making the Other Priestly Garments

22 He made the robe of the ephod of woven work, all of blue.
23 And *there was* an opening in the middle of the robe, like the opening in a coat of mail, *with* a woven binding all around the opening, so that it would not tear.
24 They made on the hem of the robe pomegranates of blue and purple and scarlet and fine *linen* thread.
25 And they made bells of pure gold, and put the bells between the pomegranates

on the hem of the robe all around between the pomegranates:
26 a bell and a pomegranate, a bell and a pomegranate, all around the hem of the robe to minister in, as the LORD had commanded Moses.
27 They made tunics, artistically woven of fine linen, for Aaron and his sons,
28 a turban of fine linen, exquisite hats of fine linen, short trousers of fine linen,
29 and a sash of fine linen and blue and purple and scarlet thread, woven as the LORD had commanded Moses.
30 Then they made the plate of the holy crown of pure gold, and wrote on it an inscription *like* the engraving of a signet:

HOLINESS TO THE LORD.

31 And they tied to it a blue cord, to fasten *it* above on the turban, as the LORD had commanded Moses.

The Work Completed

32 Thus all the work of the tabernacle of the tent of meeting was finished. And the children of Israel did according to all that the LORD had commanded Moses; so they did.
33 And they brought the tabernacle to Moses, the tent and all its furnishings: its clasps, its boards, its bars, its pillars, and its sockets;
34 the covering of rams' skins dyed red, the covering of badger skins, and the veil of the covering;
35 the ark of the Testimony with its poles, and the mercy seat;
36 the table, all its utensils, and the showbread;
37 the pure lampstand with its lamps (the lamps set in order), all its utensils, and the oil for light;
38 the gold altar, the anointing oil, and the sweet incense; the screen for the tabernacle door;
39 the bronze altar, its grate of bronze, its poles, and all its utensils; the laver with its base;
40 the hangings of the court, its pillars and its sockets, the screen for the court gate, its cords, and its pegs; all the utensils for the service of the tabernacle, for the tent of meeting;
41 and the garments of ministry,[31] to minister in the holy *place*: the holy gar-

31 Or *woven garments*

ments for Aaron the priest, and his sons' garments, to minister as priests.
42 According to all that the LORD had commanded Moses, so the children of Israel did all the work.
43 Then Moses looked over all the work, and indeed they had done it; as the LORD had commanded, just so they had done it. And Moses blessed them.

The Tabernacle Erected and Arranged

40 Then the LORD spoke to Moses, saying:
2 "On the first day of the first month you shall set up the tabernacle of the tent of meeting.
3 "You shall put in it the ark of the Testimony, and partition off the ark with the veil.
4 "You shall bring in the table and arrange the things that are to be set in order on it; and you shall bring in the lampstand and light its lamps.
5 "You shall also set the altar of gold for the incense before the ark of the Testimony, and put up the screen for the door of the tabernacle.
6 "Then you shall set the altar of the burnt offering before the door of the tabernacle of the tent of meeting.
7 "And you shall set the laver between the tabernacle of meeting and the altar, and put water in it.
8 "You shall set up the court all around, and hang up the screen at the court gate.
9 "And you shall take the anointing oil, and anoint the tabernacle and all that is in it; and you shall hallow it and all its utensils, and it shall be holy.
10 "You shall anoint the altar of the burnt offering and all its utensils, and sanctify the altar. The altar shall be most holy.
11 "And you shall anoint the laver and its base, and sanctify it.
12 "Then you shall bring Aaron and his sons to the door of the tabernacle of meeting and wash them with water.
13 "You shall put the holy garments on Aaron, and anoint him and sanctify him, that he may minister to Me as priest.
14 "And you shall bring his sons and clothe them with tunics.
15 "You shall anoint them, as you anointed their father, that they may minister to Me as priests; for their anointing

shall surely be an everlasting priesthood throughout their generations."
16 Thus Moses did; according to all that the LORD had commanded him, so he did.
17 And it came to pass in the first month of the second year, on the first day of the month, that the tabernacle was raised up.
18 So Moses raised up the tabernacle, fastened its sockets, set up its boards, put in its bars, and raised up its pillars.
19 And he spread out the tent over the tabernacle and put the covering of the tent on top of it, as the LORD had commanded Moses.
20 He took the Testimony and put it into the ark, inserted the poles through the rings of the ark, and put the mercy seat on top of the ark.
21 And he brought the ark into the tabernacle, hung up the veil of the covering, and partitioned off the ark of the Testimony, as the LORD had commanded Moses.
22 He put the table in the tabernacle of meeting, on the north side of the tabernacle, outside the veil;
23 and he set the bread in order upon it before the LORD, as the LORD had commanded Moses.
24 He put the lampstand in the tabernacle of meeting, across from the table, on the south side of the tabernacle;
25 and he lit the lamps before the LORD, as the LORD had commanded Moses.
26 He put the gold altar in the tabernacle of meeting in front of the veil;
27 and he burned sweet incense on it, as the LORD had commanded Moses.
28 He hung up the screen at the door of the tabernacle.
29 And he put the altar of burnt offering before the door of the tabernacle of the tent of meeting, and offered upon it the burnt offering and the grain offering, as the LORD had commanded Moses.
30 He set the laver between the tabernacle of meeting and the altar, and put water there for washing;
31 and Moses, Aaron, and his sons washed their hands and their feet with water from it.
32 When they went into the tabernacle of meeting, and when they came near the altar, they washed, as the LORD had commanded Moses.

33 And he raised up the court all around the tabernacle and the altar, and hung up the screen of the court gate. So Moses finished the work.

The Cloud and the Glory

34 Then the cloud covered the tabernacle of meeting, and the glory of the LORD filled the tabernacle.
35 And Moses was not able to enter the tabernacle of meeting, because the cloud rested above it, and the glory of the LORD filled the tabernacle.
36 When the cloud was taken up from above the tabernacle, the children of Israel went onward in all their journeys.
37 But if the cloud was not taken up, then they did not journey till the day that it was taken up.
38 For the cloud of the LORD was above the tabernacle by day, and fire was over it by night, in the sight of all the house of Israel, throughout all their journeys.

Introduction to Leviticus

Leviticus is the third book of the Pentateuch—the first five books of the Bible written by Moses about 1400 B.C. Leviticus falls between the end of Exodus and the beginning of Numbers, a period of one month. The book picks up the story of Israel after the completion of the tabernacle and takes place entirely at the base of Mount Sinai.

Leviticus is the record of God's presence in the midst of His people during their wanderings. It contains laws by which the people could properly worship and serve God and live positively in their community.

God promised to dwell with the people in the tabernacle, assuring them that He would be there during difficult times and arduous wanderings. He would not leave them alone. Elsewhere in Moses' recounting of their life in the wilderness, we know that God led the children of Israel with a "pillar of cloud by day and in a pillar of fire by night" (Num. 14:14).

The laws that God gave them were to give positive direction to their lives and aspirations. The instruction would enable them to live healthy, positive lives, coupled with pledges that they would inherit the land promised to them.

Leviticus was God's way to the good life for the Israelites! The psalmist David surely was reflecting on these words when he wrote Psalm 19.

> The law of the LORD *is* perfect, converting the soul;
> The testimony of the LORD *is* sure, making wise the simple;
> The statutes of the LORD *are* right, rejoicing the heart;
> The commandment of the LORD *is* pure, enlightening the eyes;
> The fear of the LORD *is* clean, enduring forever;
> The judgments of the LORD *are* true *and* righteous altogether.
> More to be desired *are they* than gold,
> Yea, than much fine gold;
> Sweeter also than honey and the honeycomb.
> Moreover by them Your servant is warned,
> *And* in keeping them *there is* great reward.

(Ps. 19:7–11)

The Third Book of Moses Called

Leviticus

The Burnt Offering

NOW the LORD called to Moses, and spoke to him from the tabernacle of meeting, saying,
2 "Speak to the children of Israel, and say to them: 'When any one of you brings an offering to the LORD, you shall bring your offering of the livestock—of the herd and of the flock.
3 'If his offering *is* a burnt sacrifice of the herd, let him offer a male without blemish; he shall offer it of his own free will at the door of the tabernacle of meeting before the LORD.
4 'Then he shall put his hand on the head of the burnt offering, and it will be accepted on his behalf to make atonement for him.
5 'He shall kill the bull before the LORD; and the priests, Aaron's sons, shall bring the blood and sprinkle the blood all around on the altar that *is by* the door of the tabernacle of meeting.
6 'And he shall skin the burnt offering and cut it into its pieces.
7 'The sons of Aaron the priest shall put fire on the altar, and lay the wood in order on the fire.
8 'Then the priests, Aaron's sons, shall lay the parts, the head, and the fat in order on the wood that *is* on the fire upon the altar;
9 'but he shall wash its entrails and its legs with water. And the priest shall burn all on the altar as a burnt sacrifice, an offering made by fire, a sweet aroma to the LORD.
10 'And if his offering *is* of the flocks—of the sheep or of the goats—as a burnt sacrifice, he shall bring a male without blemish.
11 'He shall kill it on the north side of the altar before the LORD; and the priests, Aaron's sons, shall sprinkle its blood all around on the altar.
12 'And he shall cut it into its pieces, with its head and its fat; and the priest shall lay them in order on the wood that *is* on the fire upon the altar;

13 'but he shall wash the entrails and the legs with water. And the priest shall bring *it* all and burn *it* on the altar; it *is* a burnt sacrifice, an offering made by fire, a sweet aroma to the LORD.
14 'And if the burnt sacrifice of his offering to the LORD *is* of birds, then he shall bring his offering of turtledoves or young pigeons.
15 'The priest shall bring it to the altar, wring off its head, and burn *it* on the altar; its blood shall be drained out at the side of the altar.
16 'And he shall remove its crop with its feathers and cast it beside the altar on the east side, into the place for ashes.
17 'Then he shall split it at its wings, *but* shall not divide *it* completely; and the priest shall burn it on the altar, on the wood that *is* on the fire. It *is* a burnt sacrifice, an offering made by fire, a sweet aroma to the LORD.

The Grain Offering

2 'When anyone offers a grain offering to the LORD, his offering shall be *of* fine flour. And he shall pour oil on it, and put frankincense on it.
2 'He shall bring it to Aaron's sons, the priests, one of whom shall take from it his handful of fine flour and oil with all the frankincense. And the priest shall burn *it* as a memorial on the altar, an offering made by fire, a sweet aroma to the LORD.
3 'The rest of the grain offering *shall be* Aaron's and his sons'. *It is* a most holy *offering* of the offerings to the LORD made by fire.
4 'And if you bring as an offering a grain offering baked in the oven, *it shall be* unleavened cakes of fine flour mixed with oil, or unleavened wafers anointed with oil.
5 'But if your offering *is* a grain offering *baked* in a pan, *it shall be of* fine flour, unleavened, mixed with oil.
6 'You shall break it in pieces and pour oil on it; it *is* a grain offering.
7 'And if your offering *is* a grain offer-

ing *baked* in a covered pan, it shall be made *of* fine flour with oil.

8 'You shall bring the grain offering that is made of these things to the LORD. And when it is presented to the priest, he shall bring it to the altar.

9 'Then the priest shall take from the grain offering a memorial portion, and burn *it* on the altar. It *is* an offering made by fire, a sweet aroma to the LORD.

10 'And what is left of the grain offering *shall be* Aaron's and his sons'. It *is* a most holy *offering* of the offerings to the LORD made by fire.

11 'No grain offering which you bring to the LORD shall be made with leaven, for you shall burn no leaven nor any honey in any offering to the LORD made by fire.

12 'As for the offering of the firstfruits, you shall offer them to the LORD, but they shall not be burned on the altar for a sweet aroma.

13 'And every offering of your grain offering you shall season with salt; you shall not allow the salt of the covenant of your God to be lacking from your grain offering. With all your offerings you shall offer salt.

14 'If you offer a grain offering of your firstfruits to the LORD, you shall offer for the grain offering of your firstfruits green heads of grain roasted on the fire, grain beaten from full heads.

15 'And you shall put oil on it, and lay frankincense on it. It *is* a grain offering.

16 'Then the priest shall burn the memorial portion: *part* of its beaten grain and *part* of its oil, with all the frankincense, as an offering made by fire to the LORD.

The Peace Offering

3 'When his offering *is* a sacrifice of peace offering, if he offers *it* of the herd, whether male or female, he shall offer it without blemish before the LORD.

2 'And he shall lay his hand on the head of his offering, and kill it *at* the door of the tabernacle of meeting; and Aaron's sons, the priests, shall sprinkle the blood all around on the altar.

3 'Then he shall offer from the sacrifice of the peace offering an offering made by fire to the LORD. The fat that covers the entrails and all the fat that *is* on the entrails,

4 'the two kidneys and the fat that *is* on them by the flanks, and the fatty lobe *at-*

tached to the liver above the kidneys, he shall remove;

5 'and Aaron's sons shall burn it on the altar upon the burnt sacrifice, which *is* on the wood that *is* on the fire, *as* an offering made by fire, a sweet aroma to the LORD.

6 'If his offering as a sacrifice of peace offering to the LORD *is* of the flock, *whether* male or female, he shall offer it without blemish.

7 'If he offers a lamb as his offering, then he shall offer it before the LORD.

8 'And he shall lay his hand on the head of his offering, and kill it before the tabernacle of meeting; and Aaron's sons shall sprinkle its blood all around on the altar.

9 'Then he shall offer from the sacrifice of the peace offering, as an offering made by fire to the LORD, its fat *and* the whole fat tail which he shall remove close to the backbone. And the fat that covers the entrails and all the fat that *is* on the entrails,

10 'the two kidneys and the fat that *is* on them by the flanks, and the fatty lobe attached to the liver above the kidneys, he shall remove;

11 'and the priest shall burn *them* on the altar *as* food, an offering made by fire to the LORD.

12 'And if his offering *is* a goat, then he shall offer it before the LORD.

13 'He shall lay his hand on its head and kill it before the tabernacle of meeting; and the sons of Aaron shall sprinkle its blood all around on the altar.

14 'Then he shall offer from it his offering, as an offering made by fire to the LORD. The fat that covers the entrails and all the fat that *is* on the entrails,

15 'the two kidneys and the fat that *is* on them by the flanks, and the fatty lobe *attached to* the liver above the kidneys, he shall remove;

16 'and the priest shall burn them on the altar *as* food, an offering made by fire for a sweet aroma; all the fat *is* the LORD's.

17 *'This shall be* a perpetual statute throughout your generations in all your dwellings: you shall eat neither fat nor blood.' "

The Sin Offering

4 Now the LORD spoke to Moses, saying,

2 "Speak to the children of Israel, say-

ing: 'If a person sins unintentionally against any of the commandments of the LORD *in anything* which ought not to be done, and does any of them,

3 'if the anointed priest sins, bringing guilt on the people, then let him offer to the LORD for his sin which he has sinned a young bull without blemish as a sin offering.

4 'He shall bring the bull to the door of the tabernacle of meeting before the LORD, lay his hand on the bull's head, and kill the bull before the LORD.

5 'Then the anointed priest shall take some of the bull's blood and bring it to the tabernacle of meeting.

6 'The priest shall dip his finger in the blood and sprinkle some of the blood seven times before the LORD, in front of the veil of the sanctuary.

7 'And the priest shall put some of the blood on the horns of the altar of sweet incense before the LORD, which is in the tabernacle of meeting; and he shall pour the remaining blood of the bull at the base of the altar of the burnt offering, which is at the door of the tabernacle of meeting.

8 'He shall take from it all the fat of the bull as the sin offering. The fat that covers the entrails and all the fat which *is* on the entrails,

9 'the two kidneys and the fat that *is* on them by the flanks, and the fatty lobe *attached to* the liver above the kidneys, he shall remove,

10 'as it was taken from the bull of the sacrifice of the peace offering; and the priest shall burn them on the altar of the burnt offering.

11 'But the bull's hide and all its flesh, with its head and legs, its entrails and offal—

12 'the whole bull he shall carry outside the camp to a clean place, where the ashes are poured out, and burn it on wood with fire; where the ashes are poured out it shall be burned.

13 'Now if the whole congregation of Israel sins unintentionally, and the thing is hidden from the eyes of the assembly, and they have done *something against* any of the commandments of the LORD *in anything* which should not be done, and are guilty;

14 'when the sin which they have sinned becomes known, then the assembly shall

offer a young bull for the sin, and bring it before the tabernacle of meeting.

15 'And the elders of the congregation shall lay their hands on the head of the bull before the LORD. Then the bull shall be killed before the LORD.

16 'The anointed priest shall bring some of the bull's blood to the tabernacle of meeting.

17 'Then the priest shall dip his finger in the blood and sprinkle *it* seven times before the LORD, in front of the veil.

18 'And he shall put *some* of the blood on the horns of the altar which *is* before the LORD, which *is* in the tabernacle of meeting; and he shall pour the remaining blood at the base of the altar of burnt offering, which is at the door of the tabernacle of meeting.

19 'He shall take all the fat from it and burn *it* on the altar.

20 'And he shall do with the bull as he did with the bull as a sin offering; thus he shall do with it. So the priest shall make atonement for them, and it shall be forgiven them.

21 'Then he shall carry the bull outside the camp, and burn it as he burned the first bull. It *is* a sin offering for the assembly.

22 'When a ruler has sinned, and done *something* unintentionally *against* any of the commandments of the LORD his God *in anything* which should not be done, and is guilty,

23 'or if his sin which he has sinned comes to his knowledge, he shall bring as his offering a kid of the goats, a male without blemish.

24 'And he shall lay his hand on the head of the goat, and kill it at the place where they kill the burnt offering before the LORD. It *is* a sin offering.

25 'The priest shall take some of the blood of the sin offering with his finger, put *it* on the horns of the altar of burnt offering, and pour its blood at the base of the altar of burnt offering.

26 'And he shall burn all its fat on the altar, like the fat of the sacrifice of peace offering. So the priest shall make atonement for him concerning his sin, and it shall be forgiven him.

27 'If anyone of the common people sins unintentionally by doing *something against* any of the commandments of the

LORD *in anything* which ought not to be done, and is guilty,

28 'or if his sin which he has sinned comes to his knowledge, then he shall bring as his offering a kid of the goats, a female without blemish, for his sin which he has sinned.

29 'And he shall lay his hand on the head of the sin offering, and kill the sin offering in the place of the burnt offering.

30 'Then the priest shall take *some* of its blood with his finger, put *it* on the horns of the altar of burnt offering, and pour its remaining blood at the base of the altar.

31 'He shall remove all its fat, as fat is removed from the sacrifice of peace offering; and the priest shall burn *it* on the altar for a sweet aroma to the LORD. So the priest shall make atonement for him, and it shall be forgiven him.

32 'If he brings a lamb as his sin offering, he shall bring a female without blemish.

33 'Then he shall lay his hand on the head of the sin offering, and slay it as a sin offering at the place where they kill the burnt offering.

34 'The priest shall take *some* of the blood of the sin offering with his finger, put *it* on the horns of the altar of burnt offering, and pour its remaining blood at the base of the altar.

35 'He shall remove all its fat, as the fat of the lamb is removed from the sacrifice of the peace offering. Then the priest shall burn it on the altar, according to the offerings made by fire to the LORD. So the priest shall make atonement for his sin that he has committed, and it shall be forgiven him.

The Trespass Offering

5 'If a person sins in hearing the utterance of an oath, and *is* a witness, whether he has seen or known *of the matter*—if he does not tell *it*, he bears guilt.

2 'Or if a person touches any unclean thing, whether *it is* the carcass of an unclean beast, or the carcass of unclean livestock, or the carcass of unclean creeping things, and it is hidden from him, he also shall be unclean and guilty.

3 'Or if he touches human uncleanness, whatever *sort of* uncleanness *it is* with which a man may be defiled, and it is hidden from him—when he realizes *it*, then he shall be guilty.

4 'Or if a person swears, speaking thoughtlessly with *his* lips to do evil or to do good, whatever *it is* that a man may pronounce by an oath, and it is hidden from him—when he realizes *it*, then he shall be guilty in any of these *matters*.

5 'And it shall be, when he is guilty in any of these *matters*, that he shall confess that he has sinned in that *thing*;

6 'and he shall bring his trespass offering to the LORD for his sin which he has sinned, a female from the flock, a lamb or a kid of the goats as a sin offering. So the priest shall make atonement for him concerning his sin.

7 'If he is not able to bring a lamb, then he shall bring to the LORD, for his trespass which he has committed, two turtledoves or two young pigeons: one as a sin offering and the other as a burnt offering.

8 'And he shall bring them to the priest, who shall offer *that* which *is* for the sin offering first, and wring off its head from its neck, but shall not divide *it* completely.

9 'Then he shall sprinkle *some* of the blood of the sin offering on the side of the altar, and the rest of the blood shall be drained out at the base of the altar. It *is* a sin offering.

10 'And he shall offer the second *as* a burnt offering according to the prescribed manner. So the priest shall make atonement on his behalf for his sin which he has sinned, and it shall be forgiven him.

11 'But if he is not able to bring two turtledoves or two young pigeons, then he who sinned shall bring for his offering one-tenth of an ephah of fine flour as a sin offering. He shall put no oil on it, nor shall he put *any* frankincense on it, for it *is* a sin offering.

12 'Then he shall bring it to the priest, and the priest shall take his handful of it as a memorial portion, and burn *it* on the altar according to the offerings made by fire to the LORD. It *is* a sin offering.

13 'The priest shall make atonement for him, for his sin that he has sinned in any of these matters; and it shall be forgiven him. *The rest* shall be the priest's as a grain offering.' "

Offerings with Restitution

14 Then the LORD spoke to Moses, saying:

15 "If a person commits a trespass, and sins unintentionally in regard to the holy

things of the LORD, then he shall bring to the LORD as his trespass offering a ram without blemish from the flocks, with your valuation in shekels of silver according to the shekel of the sanctuary, as a trespass offering.

16 "And he shall make restitution for the harm that he has done in regard to the holy thing, and shall add one-fifth to it and give it to the priest. So the priest shall make atonement for him with the ram of the trespass offering, and it shall be forgiven him.

17 "If a person sins, and commits any of these things which are forbidden to be done by the commandments of the LORD, though he does not know it, yet he is guilty and shall bear his iniquity.

18 "And he shall bring to the priest a ram without blemish from the flock, with your valuation, as a trespass offering. So the priest shall make atonement for him regarding his ignorance in which he erred and did not know it, and it shall be forgiven him.

19 "It is a trespass offering; he has certainly trespassed against the LORD."

6 And the LORD spoke to Moses, saying:

2 "If a person sins and commits a trespass against the LORD by lying to his neighbor about what was delivered to him for safekeeping, or about a pledge, or about a robbery, or if he has extorted from his neighbor,

3 "or if he has found what was lost and lies concerning it, and swears falsely—in any one of these things that a man may do in which he sins:

4 "then it shall be, because he has sinned and is guilty, that he shall restore what he has stolen, or the thing which he has deceitfully obtained, or what was delivered to him for safekeeping, or the lost thing which he found,

5 "or all that about which he has sworn falsely. He shall restore its full value, add one-fifth more to it, and give it to whomever it belongs, on the day of his trespass offering.

6 "And he shall bring his trespass offering to the LORD, a ram without blemish from the flock, with your valuation, as a trespass offering, to the priest.

7 "So the priest shall make atonement for him before the LORD, and he shall be

forgiven for any one of these things that he may have done in which he trespasses."

The Law of the Burnt Offering

8 Then the LORD spoke to Moses, saying,

9 "Command Aaron and his sons, saying, 'This is the law of the burnt offering: The burnt offering shall be on the hearth upon the altar all night until morning, and the fire of the altar shall be kept burning on it.

10 'And the priest shall put on his linen garment, and his linen trousers he shall put on his body, and take up the ashes of the burnt offering which the fire has consumed on the altar, and he shall put them beside the altar.

11 'Then he shall take off his garments, put on other garments, and carry the ashes outside the camp to a clean place.

12 'And the fire on the altar shall be kept burning on it; it shall not be put out. And the priest shall burn wood on it every morning, and lay the burnt offering in order on it; and he shall burn on it the fat of the peace offerings.

13 'A perpetual fire shall burn on the altar; it shall never go out.

The Law of the Grain Offering

14 'This is the law of the grain offering: The sons of Aaron shall offer it on the altar before the LORD.

15 'He shall take from it his handful of the fine flour of the grain offering, with its oil, and all the frankincense which is on the grain offering, and shall burn it on the altar for a sweet aroma, as a memorial to the LORD.

16 'And the remainder of it Aaron and his sons shall eat; with unleavened bread it shall be eaten in a holy place; in the court of the tabernacle of meeting they shall eat it.

17 'It shall not be baked with leaven. I have given it to them as their portion of My offerings made by fire; it is most holy, like the sin offering and the trespass offering.

18 'All the males among the children of Aaron may eat it. It shall be a statute forever in your generations concerning the offerings made by fire to the LORD. Everyone who touches them must be holy.'"

19 And the LORD spoke to Moses, saying,
20 "This *is* the offering of Aaron and his sons, which they shall offer to the LORD, beginning on the day when he is anointed: one-tenth of an *ephah* of fine flour as a daily grain offering, half of it in the morning and half of it at night.
21 "It shall be made in a pan with oil. *When it is well* mixed, you shall bring it in. *And* the baked pieces of the grain offering you shall offer *for* a sweet aroma to the LORD.
22 "The priest from among his sons, who is anointed in his place, shall offer it. *It is* a statute forever to the LORD. It shall be wholly burned.
23 "For every grain offering for the priest shall be wholly burned. It shall not be eaten."

The Law of the Sin Offering

24 And the LORD spoke to Moses, saying,
25 "Speak to Aaron and to his sons, saying, 'This *is* the law of the sin offering: In the place where the burnt offering is killed, the sin offering shall be killed before the LORD. It *is* most holy.
26 'The priest who offers it for sin shall eat it. In a holy place it shall be eaten, in the court of the tabernacle of meeting.
27 'Everyone who touches its flesh must be holy. And when its blood is sprinkled on any garment, you shall wash that on which it was sprinkled, in a holy place.
28 'But the earthen vessel in which it is boiled shall be broken. And if it is boiled in a bronze pot, it shall be both scoured and rinsed in water.
29 'All the males among the priests may eat it. It *is* most holy.
30 'But no sin offering from which *any* of the blood is brought into the tabernacle of meeting, to make atonement in the holy *place*,[1] shall be eaten. It shall be burned in the fire.

The Law of the Trespass Offering

7 'Likewise this *is* the law of the trespass offering (it *is* most holy):
2 'In the place where they killed the burnt offering they shall kill the trespass offering. And its blood he shall sprinkle all around on the altar.
3 'And he shall offer from it all its fat.

The fat tail and the fat that covers the entrails,
4 'the two kidneys and the fat that *is* on them by the flanks, and the fatty lobe *attached to* the liver above the kidneys, he shall remove;
5 'and the priest shall burn them on the altar *as* an offering made by fire to the LORD. It *is* a trespass offering.
6 'Every male among the priests may eat it. It shall be eaten in a holy place. It *is* most holy.
7 'The trespass offering *is* like the sin offering; *there is* one law for them both: the priest who makes atonement with it shall have *it.*
8 'And the priest who offers anyone's burnt offering, that priest shall have for himself the skin of the burnt offering which he has offered.
9 'Also every grain offering that is baked in the oven and all that is prepared in the covered pan, or in a pan, shall be the priest's who offers it.
10 'Every grain offering mixed with oil, or dry, shall belong to all the sons of Aaron, to one *as much* as the other.

The Law of Peace Offerings

11 'This *is* the law of the sacrifice of peace offerings which he shall offer to the LORD:
12 'If he offers it for a thanksgiving, then he shall offer, with the sacrifice of thanksgiving, unleavened cakes mixed with oil, unleavened wafers anointed with oil, or cakes of *finely* blended flour mixed with oil.
13 'Besides the cakes, *as* his offering he shall offer leavened bread with the sacrifice of thanksgiving of his peace offering.
14 'And from it he shall offer one cake from each offering *as* a heave offering to the LORD. It shall belong to the priest who sprinkles the blood of the peace offering.
15 'The flesh of the sacrifice of his peace offering for thanksgiving shall be eaten the same day it is offered. He shall not leave any of it until morning.
16 'But if the sacrifice of his offering *is* a vow or a voluntary offering, it shall be eaten the same day that he offers his sacrifice; but on the next day the remainder of it also may be eaten;
17 'the remainder of the flesh of the sac-

1 *The Most Holy Place* when capitalized

rifice on the third day must be burned with fire.

18 'And if *any* of the flesh of the sacrifice of his peace offering is eaten at all on the third day, it shall not be accepted, nor shall it be imputed to him; whoever offers it shall be an abomination, and the person who eats of it shall bear guilt.

19 'The flesh that touches any unclean thing shall not be eaten. It shall be burned with fire. And as for the *clean* flesh, all who are clean may eat of it.

20 'But the person who eats the flesh of the sacrifice of the peace offering that *belongs* to the LORD, while he is unclean, that person shall be cut off from his people.

21 'Moreover the person who touches any unclean thing, *such as* human uncleanness, *any* unclean beast, or any abominable unclean thing, and who eats the flesh of the sacrifice of the peace offering that *belongs* to the LORD, that person shall be cut off from his people.' "

Fat and Blood May Not Be Eaten

22 And the LORD spoke to Moses, saying,

23 "Speak to the children of Israel, saying: 'You shall not eat any fat, of ox or sheep or goat.

24 'And the fat of a beast that dies *naturally*, and the fat of what is torn by wild animals, may be used in any other way; but you shall by no means eat it.

25 'For whoever eats the fat of the beast of which men offer an offering made by fire to the LORD, the person who eats *it* shall be cut off from his people.

26 'Moreover you shall not eat any blood in any of your dwellings, *whether* of bird or beast.

27 'Whoever eats any blood, that person shall be cut off from his people.' "

The Portion of Aaron and His Sons

28 Then the LORD spoke to Moses, saying,

29 "Speak to the children of Israel, saying: 'He who offers the sacrifice of his peace offering to the LORD shall bring his offering to the LORD from the sacrifice of his peace offering.

30 'His own hands shall bring the offerings made by fire to the LORD. The fat with the breast he shall bring, that the breast may be waved *as* a wave offering before the LORD.

31 'And the priest shall burn the fat on the altar, but the breast shall be Aaron's and his sons'.

32 'Also the right thigh you shall give to the priest *as* a heave offering from the sacrifices of your peace offerings.

33 'He among the sons of Aaron, who offers the blood of the peace offering, and the fat, shall have the right thigh for *his* part.

34 'For the breast of the wave offering and the thigh of the heave offering I have taken from the children of Israel, from the sacrifices of their peace offerings, and I have given them to Aaron the priest and to his sons from the children of Israel by a statute forever.' "

35 This *is* the consecrated portion for Aaron and his sons, from the offerings made by fire to the LORD, on the day when Moses presented them to minister to the LORD as priests.

36 The LORD commanded this to be given to them by the children of Israel, on the day that He anointed them, *by* a statute forever throughout their generations.

37 This *is* the law of the burnt offering, the grain offering, the sin offering, the trespass offering, the consecrations, and the sacrifice of the peace offering,

38 which the LORD commanded Moses on Mount Sinai, on the day when He commanded the children of Israel to offer their offerings to the LORD in the Wilderness of Sinai.

Aaron and His Sons Consecrated

8 And the LORD spoke to Moses, saying:

2 "Take Aaron and his sons with him, and the garments, the anointing oil, a bull as the sin offering, two rams, and a basket of unleavened bread;

3 "and gather all the congregation together at the door of the tabernacle of meeting."

4 So Moses did as the LORD commanded him. And the assembly was gathered together at the door of the tabernacle of meeting.

5 And Moses said to the congregation, "This *is* what the LORD commanded to be done."

6 Then Moses brought Aaron and his sons and washed them with water.

7 And he put the tunic on him, girded him with the sash, clothed him with the robe, and put the ephod on him; and he girded him with the intricately woven band of the ephod, and with it tied *the ephod* on him.

8 Then he put the breastplate on him, and he put the Urim and the Thummim[2] in the breastplate.

9 And he put the turban on his head. Also on the turban, on its front, he put the golden plate, the holy crown, as the LORD had commanded Moses.

10 Then Moses took the anointing oil, and anointed the tabernacle and all that *was* in it, and sanctified them.

11 He sprinkled some of it on the altar seven times, anointed the altar and all its utensils, and the laver and its base, to sanctify them.

12 And he poured some of the anointing oil on Aaron's head and anointed him, to sanctify him.

13 Then Moses brought Aaron's sons and put tunics on them, girded them with sashes, and put hats on them, as the LORD had commanded Moses.

14 And he brought the bull for the sin offering. Then Aaron and his sons laid their hands on the head of the bull for the sin offering,

15 and Moses killed *it.* Then he took the blood, and put *some* on the horns of the altar all around with his finger, and purified the altar; and he poured the blood at the base of the altar, and sanctified it, to make atonement for it.

16 Then he took all the fat that *was* on the entrails, the fatty lobe *attached to* the liver, and the two kidneys with their fat, and Moses burned *them* on the altar.

17 But the bull, its hide, its flesh, and its offal, he burned with fire outside the camp, as the LORD had commanded Moses.

18 Then he brought the ram as the burnt offering. And Aaron and his sons laid their hands on the head of the ram,

19 and Moses killed *it.* Then he sprinkled the blood all around on the altar.

20 And he cut the ram into pieces; and Moses burned the head, the pieces, and the fat.

21 Then he washed the entrails and the legs in water. And Moses burned the whole ram on the altar. It *was* a burnt sacrifice for a sweet aroma, *and* an offer-

ing made by fire to the LORD, as the LORD had commanded Moses.

22 And he brought the second ram, the ram of consecration. Then Aaron and his sons laid their hands on the head of the ram,

23 and Moses killed *it.* And he took *some* of its blood and put it on the tip of Aaron's right ear, on the thumb of his right hand, and on the big toe of his right foot.

24 Then he brought Aaron's sons. And Moses put *some* of the blood on the tips of their right ears, on the thumbs of their right hands, and on the big toes of their right feet. And Moses sprinkled the blood all around on the altar.

25 Then he took the fat and the fat tail, all the fat that *was* on the entrails, the fatty lobe *attached to* the liver, the two kidneys and their fat, and the right thigh;

26 and from the basket of unleavened bread that was before the LORD he took one unleavened cake, a cake of bread *anointed with* oil, and one wafer, and put *them* on the fat and on the right thigh;

27 and he put all *these* in Aaron's hands and in his sons' hands, and waved them *as* a wave offering before the LORD.

28 Then Moses took them from their hands and burned *them* on the altar, on the burnt offering. They *were* consecration offerings for a sweet aroma. That *was* an offering made by fire to the LORD.

29 And Moses took the breast and waved it *as* a wave offering before the LORD. It was Moses' part of the ram of consecration, as the LORD had commanded Moses.

30 Then Moses took some of the anointing oil and some of the blood which *was* on the altar, and sprinkled *it* on Aaron, on his garments, on his sons, and on the garments of his sons with him; and he sanctified Aaron, his garments, his sons, and the garments of his sons with him.

31 And Moses said to Aaron and his sons, "Boil the flesh *at* the door of the tabernacle of meeting, and eat it there with the bread that *is* in the basket of consecration offerings, as I commanded, saying, 'Aaron and his sons shall eat it.'

32 "What remains of the flesh and of the bread you shall burn with fire.

33 "And you shall not go outside the door of the tabernacle of meeting *for* seven days, until the days of your conse-

2 Literally *Lights and Perfections* (compare Exodus 28:30)

cration are ended. For seven days he shall consecrate you.

34 "As he has done this day, *so* the LORD has commanded to do, to make atonement for you.

35 "Therefore you shall abide *at* the door of the tabernacle of meeting day and night for seven days, and keep the charge of the LORD, so that you may not die; for so I have been commanded."

36 So Aaron and his sons did all the things that the LORD had commanded by the hand of Moses.

The Priestly Ministry Begins

9 It came to pass on the eighth day that Moses called Aaron and his sons and the elders of Israel.

2 And he said to Aaron, "Take for yourself a young bull as a sin offering and a ram as a burnt offering, without blemish, and offer *them* before the LORD.

3 "And to the children of Israel you shall speak, saying, 'Take a kid of the goats as a sin offering, and a calf and a lamb, *both* of the first year, without blemish, as a burnt offering,

4 'also a bull and a ram as peace offerings, to sacrifice before the LORD, and a grain offering mixed with oil; for today the LORD will appear to you.' "

5 So they brought what Moses commanded before the tabernacle of meeting. And all the congregation drew near and stood before the LORD.

6 Then Moses said, "This *is* the thing which the LORD commanded you to do, and the glory of the LORD will appear to you."

7 And Moses said to Aaron, "Go to the altar, offer your sin offering and your burnt offering, and make atonement for yourself and for the people. Offer the offering of the people, and make atonement for them, as the LORD commanded."

8 Aaron therefore went to the altar and killed the calf of the sin offering, which *was* for himself.

9 Then the sons of Aaron brought the blood to him. And he dipped his finger in the blood, put *it* on the horns of the altar, and poured the blood at the base of the altar.

10 But the fat, the kidneys, and the fatty lobe from the liver of the sin offering he burned on the altar, as the LORD had commanded Moses.

11 The flesh and the hide he burned with fire outside the camp.

12 And he killed the burnt offering; and Aaron's sons presented to him the blood, which he sprinkled all around on the altar.

13 Then they presented the burnt offering to him, with its pieces and head, and he burned *them* on the altar.

14 And he washed the entrails and the legs, and burned *them* with the burnt offering on the altar.

15 Then he brought the people's offering, and took the goat, which *was* the sin offering for the people, and killed it and offered it for sin, like the first one.

16 And he brought the burnt offering and offered it according to the prescribed manner.

17 Then he brought the grain offering, took a handful of it, and burned *it* on the altar, besides the burnt sacrifice of the morning.

18 He also killed the bull and the ram *as* sacrifices of peace offerings, which *were* for the people. And Aaron's sons presented to him the blood, which he sprinkled all around on the altar,

19 and the fat from the bull and the ram—the fatty tail, what covers *the entrails* and the kidneys, and the fatty lobe *attached to* the liver;

20 and they put the fat on the breasts. Then he burned the fat on the altar;

21 but the breasts and the right thigh Aaron waved *as* a wave offering before the LORD, as Moses had commanded.

22 Then Aaron lifted his hand toward the people, blessed them, and came down from offering the sin offering, the burnt offering, and peace offerings.

23 And Moses and Aaron went into the tabernacle of meeting, and came out and blessed the people. Then the glory of the LORD appeared to all the people,

24 and fire came out from before the LORD and consumed the burnt offering and the fat on the altar. When all the people saw *it*, they shouted and fell on their faces.

The Profane Fire of Nadab and Abihu

10 Then Nadab and Abihu, the sons of Aaron, each took his censer and put fire in it, put incense on it, and offered profane fire before the LORD, which He had not commanded them.

2 So fire went out from the LORD and devoured them, and they died before the LORD.

3 Then Moses said to Aaron, "This is what the LORD spoke, saying:

'By those who come near Me
I must be regarded as holy;
And before all the people
I must be glorified.' "

So Aaron held his peace.

4 And Moses called Mishael and Elzaphan, the sons of Uzziel the uncle of Aaron, and said to them, "Come near, carry your brethren from before the sanctuary out of the camp."

5 So they went near and carried them by their tunics out of the camp, as Moses had said.

6 And Moses said to Aaron, and to Eleazar and Ithamar, his sons, "Do not uncover your heads nor tear your clothes, lest you die, and wrath come upon all the people. But let your brethren, the whole house of Israel, bewail the burning which the LORD has kindled.

7 "You shall not go out from the door of the tabernacle of meeting, lest you die, for the anointing oil of the LORD is upon you." And they did according to the word of Moses.

Conduct Prescribed for Priests

8 Then the LORD spoke to Aaron, saying:

9 "Do not drink wine or intoxicating drink, you, nor your sons with you, when you go into the tabernacle of meeting, lest you die. It shall be a statute forever throughout your generations,

10 "that you may distinguish between holy and unholy, and between unclean and clean,

11 "and that you may teach the children of Israel all the statutes which the LORD has spoken to them by the hand of Moses."

12 Then Moses spoke to Aaron, and to Eleazar and Ithamar, his sons who were left: "Take the grain offering that remains of the offerings made by fire to the LORD, and eat it without leaven beside the altar; for it is most holy.

13 "And you shall eat it in a holy place, because it is your due and your sons' due,

of the sacrifices made by fire to the LORD; for so I have been commanded.

14 "The breast of the wave offering and the thigh of the heave offering you shall eat in a clean place, you, your sons, and your daughters with you; for they are your due and your sons' due, which are given from the sacrifices of peace offerings of the children of Israel.

15 "The thigh of the heave offering and the breast of the wave offering they shall bring with the offerings of fat made by fire, to offer as a wave offering before the LORD. And it shall be yours and your sons' with you, by a statute forever, as the LORD has commanded."

16 Then Moses diligently made inquiry about the goat of the sin offering, and there it was, burned up. And he was angry with Eleazar and Ithamar, the sons of Aaron who were left, saying,

17 "Why have you not eaten the sin offering in a holy place, since it is most holy, and God has given it to you to bear the guilt of the congregation, to make atonement for them before the LORD?

18 "See! Its blood was not brought inside the holy place;[3] indeed you should have eaten it in a holy place, as I commanded."

19 And Aaron said to Moses, "Look, this day they have offered their sin offering and their burnt offering before the LORD, and such things have befallen me! If I had eaten the sin offering today, would it have been accepted in the sight of the LORD?"

20 So when Moses heard that, he was content.

Foods Permitted and Forbidden

11 And the LORD spoke to Moses and Aaron, saying to them,

2 "Speak to the children of Israel, saying, 'These are the animals which you may eat among all the beasts that are on the earth:

3 'Among the beasts, whatever divides the hoof, having cloven hooves and chewing the cud—that you may eat.

4 'Nevertheless these you shall not eat among those that chew the cud or those that have cloven hooves: the camel, because it chews the cud but does not have cloven hooves, is unclean to you;

5 'the rock hyrax, because it chews the

3 *The Most Holy Place* when capitalized

cud but does not have cloven hooves, *is* unclean to you;

6 'the hare, because it chews the cud but does not have cloven hooves, *is* unclean to you;

7 'and the swine, though it divides the hoof, having cloven hooves, yet does not chew the cud, *is* unclean to you.

8 'Their flesh you shall not eat, and their carcasses you shall not touch. They *are* unclean to you.

9 'These you may eat of all that *are* in the water: whatever in the water has fins and scales, whether in the seas or in the rivers—that you may eat.

10 'But all in the seas or in the rivers that do not have fins and scales, all that move in the water or any living thing which *is* in the water, they *are* an abomination to you.

11 'They shall be an abomination to you; you shall not eat their flesh, but you shall regard their carcasses as an abomination.

12 'Whatever in the water does not have fins or scales—that *shall be* an abomination to you.

13 'And these you shall regard as an abomination among the birds; they shall not be eaten, they *are* an abomination: the eagle, the vulture, the buzzard,

14 'the kite, and the falcon after its kind;

15 'every raven after its kind,

16 'the ostrich, the short-eared owl, the seagull, and the hawk after its kind;

17 'the little owl, the fisher owl, and the screech owl;

18 'the white owl, the jackdaw, and the carrion vulture;

19 'the stork, the heron after its kind, the hoopoe, and the bat.

20 'All flying insects that creep on *all* fours *shall be* an abomination to you.

21 'Yet these you may eat of every flying insect that creeps on *all* fours: those which have jointed legs above their feet with which to leap on the earth.

22 'These you may eat: the locust after its kind, the destroying locust after its kind, the cricket after its kind, and the grasshopper after its kind.

23 'But all *other* flying insects which have four feet *shall be* an abomination to you.

Unclean Animals

24 'By these you shall become unclean;

whoever touches the carcass of any of them shall be unclean until evening;

25 'whoever carries part of the carcass of any of them shall wash his clothes and be unclean until evening:

26 'The carcass of any beast which divides the foot, but is not cloven-hoofed or does not chew the cud, *is* unclean to you. Everyone who touches it shall be unclean.

27 'And whatever goes on its paws, among all kinds of animals that go on *all* fours, those *are* unclean to you. Whoever touches any such carcass shall be unclean until evening.

28 'Whoever carries *any such* carcass shall wash his clothes and be unclean until evening. It *is* unclean to you.

29 'These also *shall be* unclean to you among the creeping things that creep on the earth: the mole, the mouse, and the large lizard after its kind;

30 'the gecko, the monitor lizard, the sand reptile, the sand lizard, and the chameleon.

31 'These *are* unclean to you among all that creep. Whoever touches them when they are dead shall be unclean until evening.

32 'Anything on which *any* of them falls, when they are dead shall be unclean, whether *it is* any item of wood or clothing or skin or sack, whatever item *it is*, in which *any* work is done, it must be put in water. And it shall be unclean until evening; then it shall be clean.

33 'Any earthen vessel into which *any* of them falls you shall break; and whatever *is* in it shall be unclean:

34 'in such a vessel, any edible food upon which water falls becomes unclean, and any drink that may be drunk from it becomes unclean.

35 'And everything on which *a part* of *any such* carcass falls shall be unclean; *whether it is* an oven or cooking stove, it shall be broken down; *for* they *are* unclean, and shall be unclean to you.

36 'Nevertheless a spring or a cistern, *in which there is* plenty of water, shall be clean, but whatever touches any such carcass becomes unclean.

37 'And if a part of *any such* carcass falls on any planting seed which is to be sown, it *remains* clean.

38 'But if *any* water is put on the seed, and if *a part* of *any such* carcass falls on it, it *becomes* unclean to you.

39 'And if any beast which you may eat dies, he who touches its carcass shall be unclean until evening.

40 'He who eats of its carcass shall wash his clothes and be unclean until evening. He also who carries its carcass shall wash his clothes and be unclean until evening.

41 'And every creeping thing that creeps on the earth *shall be* an abomination. It shall not be eaten.

42 'Whatever crawls on its belly, whatever goes on *all* fours, or whatever has many feet among all creeping things that creep on the earth—these you shall not eat, for they *are* an abomination.

43 'You shall not make yourselves abominable with any creeping thing that creeps; nor shall you make yourselves unclean with them, lest you be defiled by them.

44 'For I *am* the LORD your God. You shall therefore sanctify yourselves, and you shall be holy; for I *am* holy. Neither shall you defile yourselves with any creeping thing that creeps on the earth.

45 'For I *am* the LORD who brings you up out of the land of Egypt, to be your God. You shall therefore be holy, for I *am* holy.

46 'This *is* the law of the beasts and the birds and every living creature that moves in the waters, and of every creature that creeps on the earth,

47 'to distinguish between the unclean and the clean, and between the animal that may be eaten and the animal that may not be eaten.' "

The Ritual After Childbirth

12 Then the LORD spoke to Moses, saying,

2 "Speak to the children of Israel, saying: 'If a woman has conceived, and borne a male child, then she shall be unclean seven days; as in the days of her customary impurity she shall be unclean.

3 'And on the eighth day the flesh of his foreskin shall be circumcised.

4 'She shall then continue in the blood of *her* purification thirty-three days. She shall not touch any hallowed thing, nor come into the sanctuary until the days of her purification are fulfilled.

5 'But if she bears a female child, then she shall be unclean two weeks, as in her customary impurity, and she shall continue in the blood of *her* purification sixty-six days.

6 'When the days of her purification are fulfilled, whether for a son or a daughter, she shall bring to the priest a lamb of the first year as a burnt offering, and a young pigeon or a turtledove as a sin offering, to the door of the tabernacle of meeting.

7 'Then he shall offer it before the LORD, and make atonement for her. And she shall be clean from the flow of her blood. This *is* the law for her who has borne a male or a female.

8 'And if she is not able to bring a lamb, then she may bring two turtledoves or two young pigeons—one as a burnt offering and the other as a sin offering. So the priest shall make atonement for her, and she will be clean.' "

The Law Concerning Leprosy

13 And the LORD spoke to Moses and Aaron, saying:

2 "When a man has on the skin of his body a swelling, a scab, or a bright spot, and it becomes on the skin of his body *like* a leprous[4] sore, then he shall be brought to Aaron the priest or to one of his sons the priests.

3 "The priest shall look at the sore on the skin of the body; and if the hair on the sore has turned white, and the sore appears *to be* deeper than the skin of his body, it *is* a leprous sore. Then the priest shall look at him, and pronounce him unclean.

4 "But if the bright spot *is* white on the skin of his body, and does not appear *to be* deeper than the skin, and its hair has not turned white, then the priest shall isolate *the one who has* the sore seven days.

5 "And the priest shall look at him on the seventh day; and indeed *if* the sore appears to be as it was, *and* the sore has not spread on the skin, then the priest shall isolate him another seven days.

6 "Then the priest shall look at him again on the seventh day; and indeed *if* the sore has darkened, *and* the sore has not spread on the skin, then the priest shall pronounce him clean; it *is only* a scab, and he shall wash his clothes and be clean.

7 "But if the scab should at all spread over the skin, after he has been seen by

4 Hebrew *saraath,* disfiguring skin diseases, including leprosy, and so in verses 2–46 and 14:1–32

the priest for his cleansing, he shall be seen by the priest again.

8 "And if the priest sees that the scab has indeed spread on the skin, then the priest shall pronounce him unclean. It is leprosy.

9 "When the leprous sore is on a person, then he shall be brought to the priest.

10 "And the priest shall look at him; and indeed if the swelling on the skin is white, and it has turned the hair white, and there is a spot of raw flesh in the swelling,

11 "it is an old leprosy on the skin of his body. The priest shall pronounce him unclean, and shall not isolate him, for he is unclean.

12 "And if leprosy breaks out all over the skin, and the leprosy covers all the skin of the one who has the sore, from his head to his foot, wherever the priest looks,

13 "then the priest shall consider; and indeed if the leprosy has covered all his body, he shall pronounce him clean who has the sore. It has all turned white. He is clean.

14 "But when raw flesh appears on him, he shall be unclean.

15 "And the priest shall look at the raw flesh and pronounce him to be unclean; for the raw flesh is unclean. It is leprosy.

16 "Or if the raw flesh changes and turns white again, he shall come to the priest.

17 "And the priest shall look at him; and indeed if the sore has turned white, then the priest shall pronounce him clean who has the sore. He is clean.

18 "If the body develops a boil in the skin, and it is healed,

19 "and in the place of the boil there comes a white swelling or a bright spot, reddish-white, then it shall be shown to the priest;

20 "and if, when the priest sees it, it indeed appears deeper than the skin, and its hair has turned white, the priest shall pronounce him unclean. It is a leprous sore which has broken out of the boil.

21 "But if the priest looks at it, and indeed there are no white hairs in it, and if it is not deeper than the skin, but has faded, then the priest shall isolate him seven days;

22 "and if it should at all spread over the skin, then the priest shall pronounce him unclean. It is a leprous sore.

23 "But if the bright spot stays in one place, and has not spread, it is the scar of the boil; and the priest shall pronounce him clean.

24 "Or if the body receives a burn on its skin by fire, and the raw flesh of the burn becomes a bright spot, reddish-white or white,

25 "then the priest shall look at it; and indeed if the hair of the bright spot has turned white, and it appears deeper than the skin, it is leprosy broken out in the burn. Therefore the priest shall pronounce him unclean. It is a leprous sore.

26 "But if the priest looks at it, and indeed there are no white hairs in the bright spot, and it is not deeper than the skin, but has faded, then the priest shall isolate him seven days.

27 "And the priest shall look at him on the seventh day. If it has at all spread over the skin, then the priest shall pronounce him unclean. It is a leprous sore.

28 "But if the bright spot stays in one place, and has not spread on the skin, but has faded, it is a swelling from the burn. The priest shall pronounce him clean, for it is the scar from the burn.

29 "If a man or woman has a sore on the head or the beard,

30 "then the priest shall look at the sore; and indeed if it appears deeper than the skin, and there is in it thin yellow hair, then the priest shall pronounce him unclean. It is a scall, a leprosy of the head or beard.

31 "But if the priest looks at the sore of the scall, and indeed it does not appear deeper than the skin, and there is no black hair in it, then the priest shall isolate the one who has the sore of the scall seven days.

32 "And on the seventh day the priest shall look at the sore; and indeed if the scall has not spread, and there is no yellow hair in it, and the scall does not appear deeper than the skin,

33 "he shall shave himself, but the scall he shall not shave. And the priest shall isolate the one who has the scall another seven days.

34 "On the seventh day the priest shall look at the scall; and indeed if the scall has not spread over the skin, and does not appear deeper than the skin, then the priest shall pronounce him clean. He shall wash his clothes and be clean.

35 "But if the scall should at all spread over the skin after his cleansing,
36 "then the priest shall look at him; and indeed if the scall has spread over the skin, the priest need not seek for yellow hair. He *is* unclean.
37 "But if the scall appears to be at a standstill, and there is black hair grown up in it, the scall has healed. He *is* clean, and the priest shall pronounce him clean.
38 "If a man or a woman has bright spots on the skin of the body, *specifically* white bright spots,
39 "then the priest shall look; and indeed *if* the bright spots on the skin of the body *are* dull white, it *is* a white spot *that* grows on the skin. He *is* clean.
40 "As for the man whose hair has fallen from his head, he *is* bald, *but* he *is* clean.
41 "He whose hair has fallen from his forehead, he *is* bald on the forehead, *but* he *is* clean.
42 "And if there is on the bald head or bald forehead a reddish-white sore, it *is* leprosy breaking out on his bald head or his bald forehead.
43 "Then the priest shall look at it; and indeed *if* the swelling of the sore *is* reddish-white on his bald head or on his bald forehead, as the appearance of leprosy on the skin of the body,
44 "he is a leprous man. He *is* unclean. The priest shall surely pronounce him unclean; his sore *is* on his head.
45 "Now the leper on whom the sore *is,* his clothes shall be torn and his head bare; and he shall cover his mustache, and cry, 'Unclean! Unclean!'
46 "He shall be unclean. All the days he has the sore he shall be unclean. He *is* unclean, and he shall dwell alone; his habitation *shall be* outside the camp.

The Law Concerning Leprous Garments

47 "Also, if a garment has a leprous plague[5] in it, *whether it is* a woolen garment or a linen garment,
48 "whether *it is* in the warp or woof of linen or wool, whether in leather or in anything made of leather,
49 "and if the plague is greenish or reddish in the garment or in the leather, whether in the warp or in the woof, or in anything made of leather, it *is* a leprous plague and shall be shown to the priest.
50 "The priest shall look at the plague and isolate *that which has* the plague seven days.
51 "And he shall look at the plague on the seventh day. If the plague has spread in the garment, either in the warp or in the woof, in the leather *or* in anything made of leather, the plague *is* an active leprosy. It *is* unclean.
52 "He shall therefore burn that garment in which is the plague, whether warp or woof, in wool or in linen, or anything of leather, for it *is* an active leprosy; it shall be burned in the fire.
53 "But if the priest looks, and indeed the plague has not spread in the garment, either in the warp or in the woof, or in anything made of leather,
54 "then the priest shall command that they wash *the thing* in which *is* the plague; and he shall isolate it another seven days.
55 "Then the priest shall look at the plague after it has been washed; and indeed *if* the plague has not changed its color, though the plague has not spread, it *is* unclean, and you shall burn it in the fire; it continues eating away, *whether* the damage *is* outside or inside.
56 "If the priest looks, and indeed the plague has faded after washing it, then he shall tear it out of the garment, whether out of the warp or out of the woof, or out of the leather.
57 "But if it appears again in the garment, either in the warp or in the woof, or in anything made of leather, it *is* a spreading *plague*; you shall burn with fire that in which *is* the plague.
58 "And if you wash the garment, either warp or woof, or whatever is made of leather, if the plague has disappeared from it, then it shall be washed a second time, and shall be clean.
59 "This *is* the law of the leprous plague in a garment of wool or linen, either in the warp or woof, or in anything made of leather, to pronounce it clean or to pronounce it unclean."

The Ritual for Cleansing Healed Lepers

14 Then the LORD spoke to Moses, saying,
2 "This shall be the law of the leper for the day of his cleansing: He shall be brought to the priest.
3 "And the priest shall go out of the

5 A mold, fungus, or similar infestation, and so in verses 47–59

camp, and the priest shall look; and indeed, *if* the leprosy is healed in the leper, 4 "then the priest shall command to take for him who is to be cleansed two living *and* clean birds, cedar wood, scarlet, and hyssop.

5 "And the priest shall command that one of the birds be killed in an earthen vessel over running water.

6 "As for the living bird, he shall take it, the cedar wood and the scarlet and the hyssop, and dip them and the living bird in the blood of the bird *that was* killed over the running water.

7 "And he shall sprinkle it seven times on him who is to be cleansed from the leprosy, and shall pronounce him clean, and shall let the living bird loose in the open field.

8 "He who is to be cleansed shall wash his clothes, shave off all his hair, and wash himself in water, that he may be clean. After that he shall come into the camp, and shall stay outside his tent seven days.

9 "But on the seventh day he shall shave all the hair off his head and his beard and his eyebrows—all his hair he shall shave off. He shall wash his clothes and wash his body in water, and he shall be clean.

10 "And on the eighth day he shall take two male lambs without blemish, one ewe lamb of the first year without blemish, three-tenths *of an ephah* of fine flour mixed with oil as a grain offering, and one log of oil.

11 "Then the priest who makes *him* clean shall present the man who is to be made clean, and those things, before the LORD, *at* the door of the tabernacle of meeting.

12 "And the priest shall take one male lamb and offer it as a trespass offering, and the log of oil, and wave them *as* a wave offering before the LORD.

13 "Then he shall kill the lamb in the place where he kills the sin offering and the burnt offering, in a holy place; for as the sin offering *is* the priest's, so *is* the trespass offering. It *is* most holy.

14 "The priest shall take *some* of the blood of the trespass offering, and the priest shall put *it* on the tip of the right ear of him who is to be cleansed, on the thumb of his right hand, and on the big toe of his right foot.

15 "And the priest shall take *some* of the log of oil, and pour *it* into the palm of his own left hand.

16 "Then the priest shall dip his right finger in the oil that *is* in his left hand, and shall sprinkle some of the oil with his finger seven times before the LORD.

17 "And of the rest of the oil in his hand, the priest shall put *some* on the tip of the right ear of him who is to be cleansed, on the thumb of his right hand, and on the big toe of his right foot, on the blood of the trespass offering.

18 "The rest of the oil that *is* in the priest's hand he shall put on the head of him who is to be cleansed. So the priest shall make atonement for him before the LORD.

19 "Then the priest shall offer the sin offering, and make atonement for him who is to be cleansed from his uncleanness. Afterward he shall kill the burnt offering.

20 "And the priest shall offer the burnt offering and the grain offering on the altar. So the priest shall make atonement for him, and he shall be clean.

21 "But if he *is* poor and cannot afford it, then he shall take one male lamb *as* a trespass offering to be waved, to make atonement for him, one-tenth *of an ephah* of fine flour mixed with oil as a grain offering, a log of oil,

22 "and two turtledoves or two young pigeons, such as he is able to afford: one shall be a sin offering and the other a burnt offering.

23 "He shall bring them to the priest on the eighth day for his cleansing, to the door of the tabernacle of meeting, before the LORD.

24 "And the priest shall take the lamb of the trespass offering and the log of oil, and the priest shall wave them *as* a wave offering before the LORD.

25 "Then he shall kill the lamb of the trespass offering, and the priest shall take *some* of the blood of the trespass offering and put *it* on the tip of the right ear of him who is to be cleansed, on the thumb of his right hand, and on the big toe of his right foot.

26 "And the priest shall pour some of the oil into the palm of his own left hand.

27 "Then the priest shall sprinkle with his right finger *some* of the oil that *is* in his left hand seven times before the LORD.

28 "And the priest shall put *some* of the

oil that *is* in his hand on the tip of the right ear of him who is to be cleansed, on the thumb of the right hand, and on the big toe of his right foot, on the place of the blood of the trespass offering.

29 "The rest of the oil that *is* in the priest's hand he shall put on the head of him who is to be cleansed, to make atonement for him before the LORD.

30 "And he shall offer one of the turtledoves or young pigeons, such as he can afford—

31 "such as he is able to afford, the one *as* a sin offering and the other *as* a burnt offering, with the grain offering. So the priest shall make atonement for him who is to be cleansed before the LORD.

32 "This *is* the law *for one* who had a leprous sore, who cannot afford the usual cleansing."

The Law Concerning Leprous Houses

33 And the LORD spoke to Moses and Aaron, saying:

34 "When you have come into the land of Canaan, which I give you as a possession, and I put the leprous plague[6] in a house in the land of your possession,

35 "and he who owns the house comes and tells the priest, saying, 'It seems to me that *there is* some plague in the house,'

36 "then the priest shall command that they empty the house, before the priest goes *into it* to look at the plague, that all that *is* in the house may not be made unclean; and afterward the priest shall go in to look at the house.

37 "And he shall look at the plague; and indeed *if* the plague *is* on the walls of the house with ingrained streaks, greenish or reddish, which appear to be deep in the wall,

38 "then the priest shall go out of the house, to the door of the house, and shut up the house seven days.

39 "And the priest shall come again on the seventh day and look; and indeed *if* the plague has spread on the walls of the house,

40 "then the priest shall command that they take away the stones in which *is* the plague, and they shall cast them into an unclean place outside the city.

41 "And he shall cause the house to be scraped inside, all around, and the dust

that they scrape off they shall pour out in an unclean place outside the city.

42 "Then they shall take other stones and put *them* in the place of *those* stones, and he shall take other mortar and plaster the house.

43 "And if the plague comes back and breaks out in the house, after he has taken away the stones, after he has scraped the house, and after it is plastered,

44 "then the priest shall come and look; and indeed *if* the plague has spread in the house, it *is* an active leprosy in the house. It *is* unclean.

45 "And he shall break down the house, its stones, its timber, and all the plaster of the house, and he shall carry *them* outside the city to an unclean place.

46 "Moreover he who goes into the house at all while it is shut up shall be unclean until evening.

47 "And he who lies down in the house shall wash his clothes, and he who eats in the house shall wash his clothes.

48 "But if the priest comes in and looks *at it*, and indeed the plague has not spread in the house after the house was plastered, then the priest shall pronounce the house clean, because the plague is healed.

49 "And he shall take, to cleanse the house, two birds, cedar wood, scarlet, and hyssop.

50 "Then he shall kill one of the birds in an earthen vessel over running water;

51 "and he shall take the cedar wood, the hyssop, the scarlet, and the living bird, and dip them in the blood of the slain bird and in the running water, and sprinkle the house seven times.

52 "And he shall cleanse the house with the blood of the bird and the running water and the living bird, with the cedar wood, the hyssop, and the scarlet.

53 "Then he shall let the living bird loose outside the city in the open field, and make atonement for the house, and it shall be clean.

54 "This *is* the law for any leprous sore and scall,

55 "for the leprosy of a garment and of a house,

56 "for a swelling and a scab and a bright spot,

57 "to teach when *it is* unclean and when *it is* clean. This *is* the law of leprosy."

6 Decomposition by mildew, mold, dry rot, etc., and so in verses 34–53

The Law Concerning Bodily Discharges

15 And the LORD spoke to Moses and Aaron, saying,
2 "Speak to the children of Israel, and say to them: 'When any man has a discharge from his body, his discharge *is* unclean.
3 'And this shall be his uncleanness in regard to his discharge—whether his body runs with his discharge, or his body is stopped up by his discharge, it *is* his uncleanness.
4 'Every bed is unclean on which he who has the discharge lies, and everything on which he sits shall be unclean.
5 'And whoever touches his bed shall wash his clothes and bathe in water, and be unclean until evening.
6 'He who sits on anything on which he who has the discharge sat shall wash his clothes and bathe in water, and be unclean until evening.
7 'And he who touches the body of him who has the discharge shall wash his clothes and bathe in water, and be unclean until evening.
8 'If he who has the discharge spits on him who is clean, then he shall wash his clothes and bathe in water, and be unclean until evening.
9 'Any saddle on which he who has the discharge rides shall be unclean.
10 'Whoever touches anything that was under him shall be unclean until evening. He who carries *any of* those things shall wash his clothes and bathe in water, and be unclean until evening.
11 'And whomever he who has the discharge touches, and has not rinsed his hands in water, he shall wash his clothes and bathe in water, and be unclean until evening.
12 'The vessel of earth that he who has the discharge touches shall be broken, and every vessel of wood shall be rinsed in water.
13 'And when he who has a discharge is cleansed of his discharge, then he shall count for himself seven days for his cleansing, wash his clothes, and bathe his body in running water; then he shall be clean.
14 'On the eighth day he shall take for himself two turtledoves or two young pigeons, and come before the LORD, to the door of the tabernacle of meeting, and give them to the priest.
15 'Then the priest shall offer them, the one *as* a sin offering and the other *as* a burnt offering. So the priest shall make atonement for him before the LORD because of his discharge.
16 'If any man has an emission of semen, then he shall wash all his body in water, and be unclean until evening.
17 'And any garment and any leather on which there is semen, it shall be washed with water, and be unclean until evening.
18 'Also, when a woman lies with a man, and *there is* an emission of semen, they *both* shall bathe in water, and be unclean until evening.
19 'If a woman has a discharge, *and* the discharge from her body is blood, she shall be set apart seven days; and whoever touches her shall be unclean until evening.
20 'Everything that she lies on during her impurity shall be unclean; also everything that she sits on shall be unclean.
21 'Whoever touches her bed shall wash his clothes and bathe in water, and be unclean until evening.
22 'And whoever touches anything that she sat on shall wash his clothes and bathe in water, and be unclean until evening.
23 'If *anything* is on *her* bed or on anything on which she sits, when he touches it, he shall be unclean until evening.
24 'And if any man lies with her at all, so that her impurity is on him, he shall be unclean seven days; and every bed on which he lies shall be unclean.
25 'If a woman has a discharge of blood for many days, other than at the time of her *customary* impurity, or if it runs beyond her *usual* time of impurity, all the days of her unclean discharge shall be as the days of her customary impurity. She *shall be* unclean.
26 'Every bed on which she lies all the days of her discharge shall be to her as the bed of her impurity; and whatever she sits on shall be unclean, as the uncleanness of her impurity.
27 'Whoever touches those things shall be unclean; he shall wash his clothes and bathe in water, and be unclean until evening.

28 'But if she is cleansed of her discharge, then she shall count for herself seven days, and after that she shall be clean.

29 'And on the eighth day she shall take for herself two turtledoves or two young pigeons, and bring them to the priest, to the door of the tabernacle of meeting.

30 'Then the priest shall offer the one *as* a sin offering and the other *as* a burnt offering, and the priest shall make atonement for her before the LORD for the discharge of her uncleanness.

31 'Thus you shall separate the children of Israel from their uncleanness, lest they die in their uncleanness when they defile My tabernacle that *is* among them.

32 'This *is* the law for one who has a discharge, and *for him* who emits semen and is unclean thereby,

33 'and for her who is indisposed because of her customary impurity, and for one who has a discharge, either man or woman, and for him who lies with her who is unclean.' "

The Day of Atonement

16 Now the LORD spoke to Moses after the death of the two sons of Aaron, when they offered profane fire before the LORD, and died;

2 and the LORD said to Moses: "Tell Aaron your brother not to come at *simply* any time into the Holy *Place* inside the veil, before the mercy seat which *is* on the ark, lest he die; for I will appear in the cloud above the mercy seat.

3 "Thus Aaron shall come into the Holy *Place:* with *the blood of* a young bull as a sin offering, and *of* a ram as a burnt offering.

4 "He shall put the holy linen tunic and the linen trousers on his body; he shall be girded with a linen sash, and with the linen turban he shall be attired. These *are* holy garments. Therefore he shall wash his body in water, and put them on.

5 "And he shall take from the congregation of the children of Israel two kids of the goats as a sin offering, and one ram as a burnt offering.

6 "Aaron shall offer the bull as a sin offering, which *is* for himself, and make atonement for himself and for his house.

7 "He shall take the two goats and present them before the LORD *at* the door of the tabernacle of meeting.

8 "Then Aaron shall cast lots for the two goats: one lot for the LORD and the other lot for the scapegoat.

9 "And Aaron shall bring the goat on which the LORD's lot fell, and offer it *as* a sin offering.

10 "But the goat on which the lot fell to be the scapegoat shall be presented alive before the LORD, to make atonement upon it, *and* to let it go as the scapegoat into the wilderness.

11 "And Aaron shall bring the bull of the sin offering, which is for himself, and make atonement for himself and for his house, and shall kill the bull as the sin offering which *is* for himself.

12 "Then he shall take a censer full of burning coals of fire from the altar before the LORD, with his hands full of sweet incense beaten fine, and bring *it* inside the veil.

13 "And he shall put the incense on the fire before the LORD, that the cloud of incense may cover the mercy seat that *is* on the Testimony, lest he die.

14 "He shall take some of the blood of the bull and sprinkle *it* with his finger on the mercy seat on the east *side*; and before the mercy seat he shall sprinkle some of the blood with his finger seven times.

15 "Then he shall kill the goat of the sin offering, which *is* for the people, bring its blood inside the veil, do with that blood as he did with the blood of the bull, and sprinkle it on the mercy seat and before the mercy seat.

16 "So he shall make atonement for the Holy *Place*, because of the uncleanness of the children of Israel, and because of their transgressions, for all their sins; and so he shall do for the tabernacle of meeting which remains among them in the midst of their uncleanness.

17 "There shall be no man in the tabernacle of meeting when he goes in to make atonement in the Holy *Place*, until he comes out, that he may make atonement for himself, for his household, and for all the congregation of Israel.

18 "And he shall go out to the altar that *is* before the LORD, and make atonement for it, and shall take some of the blood of the bull and some of the blood of the goat, and put it on the horns of the altar all around.

19 "Then he shall sprinkle some of the

blood on it with his finger seven times, cleanse it, and sanctify it from the uncleanness of the children of Israel.

20 "And when he has made an end of atoning for the Holy *Place*, the tabernacle of meeting, and the altar, he shall bring the live goat;

21 "and Aaron shall lay both his hands on the head of the live goat, confess over it all the iniquities of the children of Israel, and all their transgressions, concerning all their sins, putting them on the head of the goat, and shall send *it* away into the wilderness by the hand of a suitable man.

22 "The goat shall bear on itself all their iniquities to an uninhabited land; and he shall release the goat in the wilderness.

23 "Then Aaron shall come into the tabernacle of meeting, shall take off the linen garments which he put on when he went into the Holy *Place*, and shall leave them there.

24 "And he shall wash his body with water in a holy place, put on his garments, come out and offer his burnt offering and the burnt offering of the people, and make atonement for himself and for the people.

25 "The fat of the sin offering he shall burn on the altar.

26 "And he who released the goat as the scapegoat shall wash his clothes and bathe his body in water, and afterward he may come into the camp.

27 "The bull *for* the sin offering and the goat *for* the sin offering, whose blood was brought in to make atonement in the Holy *Place*, shall be carried outside the camp. And they shall burn in the fire their skins, their flesh, and their offal.

28 "Then he who burns them shall wash his clothes and bathe his body in water, and afterward he may come into the camp.

29 "*This* shall be a statute forever for you: In the seventh month, on the tenth *day* of the month, you shall afflict your souls, and do no work at all, *whether* a native of your own country or a stranger who sojourns among you.

30 "For on that day *the priest* shall make atonement for you, to cleanse you, *that* you may be clean from all your sins before the LORD.

31 "It *is* a sabbath of solemn rest for you,

and you shall afflict your souls. *It is* a statute forever.

32 "And the priest, who is anointed and consecrated to minister as priest in his father's place, shall make atonement, and put on the linen clothes, the holy garments;

33 "then he shall make atonement for the Holy Sanctuary,[7] and he shall make atonement for the tabernacle of meeting and for the altar, and he shall make atonement for the priests and for all the people of the congregation.

34 "This shall be an everlasting statute for you, to make atonement for the children of Israel, for all their sins, once a year." And he did as the LORD commanded Moses.

The Sanctity of Blood

17 And the LORD spoke to Moses, saying,

2 "Speak to Aaron, to his sons, and to all the children of Israel, and say to them, 'This *is* the thing which the LORD has commanded, saying:

3 "Whatever man of the house of Israel, kills an ox or lamb or goat in the camp, or who kills *it* outside the camp,

4 "and does not bring it to the door of the tabernacle of meeting, to offer an offering to the LORD before the tabernacle of the LORD, bloodguilt shall be imputed to that man. He has shed blood; and that man shall be cut off from among his people,

5 "to the end that the children of Israel may bring their sacrifices which they offer in the open field, that they may bring them to the LORD at the door of the tabernacle of meeting, to the priest, and offer them *as* peace offerings to the LORD.

6 "And the priest shall sprinkle the blood on the altar of the LORD *at* the door of the tabernacle of meeting, and burn the fat for a sweet aroma to the LORD.

7 "They shall no more offer their sacrifices to demons, after whom they have played the harlot. This shall be a statute forever for them throughout their generations." '

8 "And you shall say to them: 'Whatever man of the house of Israel, or of the strangers who sojourn among you, who offers a burnt offering or sacrifice,

9 'and does not bring it to the door of

7 That is, the Most Holy Place

the tabernacle of meeting, to offer it to the LORD, that man shall be cut off from among his people.
10 'And whatever man of the house of Israel, or of the strangers who sojourn among you, who eats any blood, I will set My face against that person who eats blood, and will cut him off from among his people.
11 'For the life of the flesh *is* in the blood, and I have given it to you upon the altar to make atonement for your souls; for it *is* the blood *that* makes atonement for the soul.'
12 "Therefore I said to the children of Israel, 'No one among you shall eat blood, nor shall any stranger who sojourns among you eat blood.'
13 "And whatever man of the children of Israel, or of the strangers who sojourn among you, who hunts and catches any animal or bird that may be eaten, he shall pour out its blood and cover it with dust;
14 "for *it is* the life of all flesh. Its blood sustains its life. Therefore I said to the children of Israel, 'You shall not eat the blood of any flesh, for the life of all flesh is its blood. Whoever eats it shall be cut off.'
15 "And every person who eats what died *naturally* or what was torn *by beasts,* whether he is a native of your own country or a stranger, he shall both wash his clothes and bathe in water, and be unclean until evening. Then he shall be clean.
16 "But if he does not wash or bathe his body, then he shall bear his guilt."

Laws of Sexual Morality

18 Then the LORD spoke to Moses, saying,
2 "Speak to the children of Israel, and say to them: 'I am the LORD your God.
3 'According to the doings of the land of Egypt, where you dwelt, you shall not do; and according to the doings of the land of Canaan, where I am bringing you, you shall not do; nor shall you walk in their ordinances.
4 'You shall observe My judgments and keep My ordinances, to walk in them: I *am* the LORD your God.
5 'You shall therefore keep My statutes and My judgments, which if a man does, he shall live by them: I *am* the LORD.
6 'None of you shall approach anyone who is near of kin to him, to uncover his nakedness: I *am* the LORD.
7 'The nakedness of your father or the nakedness of your mother you shall not uncover. She *is* your mother; you shall not uncover her nakedness.
8 'The nakedness of your father's wife you shall not uncover; it *is* your father's nakedness.
9 'The nakedness of your sister, the daughter of your father, or the daughter of your mother, *whether* born at home or elsewhere, their nakedness you shall not uncover.
10 'The nakedness of your son's daughter or your daughter's daughter, their nakedness you shall not uncover; for theirs *is* your own nakedness.
11 'The nakedness of your father's wife's daughter, begotten by your father—she *is* your sister—you shall not uncover her nakedness.
12 'You shall not uncover the nakedness of your father's sister; she *is* near of kin to your father.
13 'You shall not uncover the nakedness of your mother's sister, for she *is* near of kin to your mother.
14 'You shall not uncover the nakedness of your father's brother. You shall not approach his wife; she *is* your aunt.
15 'You shall not uncover the nakedness of your daughter-in-law—she *is* your son's wife—you shall not uncover her nakedness.
16 'You shall not uncover the nakedness of your brother's wife; it *is* your brother's nakedness.
17 'You shall not uncover the nakedness of a woman and her daughter, nor shall you take her son's daughter or her daughter's daughter, to uncover her nakedness. They *are* near of kin to her. It *is* wickedness.
18 'Nor shall you take a woman as a rival to her sister, to uncover her nakedness while the other is alive.
19 'Also you shall not approach a woman to uncover her nakedness as long as she is in her *customary* impurity.
20 'Moreover you shall not lie carnally with your neighbor's wife, to defile yourself with her.
21 'And you shall not let any of your descendants pass through *the fire* to Molech, nor shall you profane the name of your God: I *am* the LORD.

22 'You shall not lie with a male as with a woman. It *is* an abomination.
23 'Nor shall you mate with any beast, to defile yourself with it. Nor shall any woman stand before a beast to mate with it. It *is* perversion.
24 'Do not defile yourselves with any of these things; for by all these the nations are defiled, which I am casting out before you.
25 'For the land is defiled; therefore I visit the punishment of its iniquity upon it, and the land vomits out its inhabitants.
26 'You shall therefore keep My statutes and My judgments, and shall not commit *any* of these abominations, *either* any of your own nation or any stranger who sojourns among you
27 '(for all these abominations the men of the land have done, who *were* before you, and thus the land is defiled),
28 'lest the land vomit you out also when you defile it, as it vomited out the nations that *were* before you.
29 'For whoever commits any of these abominations, the persons who commit *them* shall be cut off from among their people.
30 'Therefore you shall keep My ordinance, so that *you* do not commit *any* of these abominable customs which were committed before you, and that you do not defile yourselves by them: I *am* the LORD your God.' "

Moral and Ceremonial Laws

19 And the LORD spoke to Moses, saying,
2 "Speak to all the congregation of the children of Israel, and say to them: 'You shall be holy, for I the LORD your God *am* holy.
3 'Every one of you shall revere his mother and his father, and keep My Sabbaths: I *am* the LORD your God.
4 'Do not turn to idols, nor make for yourselves molded gods: I *am* the LORD your God.
5 'And if you offer a sacrifice of peace offering to the LORD, you shall offer it of your own free will.
6 'It shall be eaten the same day you offer *it*, and on the next day. And if any remains until the third day, it shall be burned in the fire.
7 'And if it is eaten at all on the third

day, it *is* an abomination. It shall not be accepted.
8 'Therefore *everyone* who eats it shall bear his iniquity, because he has profaned the hallowed *offering* of the LORD; and that person shall be cut off from his people.
9 'When you reap the harvest of your land, you shall not wholly reap the corners of your field, nor shall you gather the gleanings of your harvest.
10 'And you shall not glean your vineyard, nor shall you gather *every* grape of your vineyard; you shall leave them for the poor and the stranger: I *am* the LORD your God.
11 'You shall not steal, nor deal falsely, nor lie to one another.
12 'And you shall not swear by My name falsely, nor shall you profane the name of your God: I *am* the LORD.
13 'You shall not defraud your neighbor, nor rob *him*. The wages of him who is hired shall not remain with you all night until morning.
14 'You shall not curse the deaf, nor put a stumblingblock before the blind, but shall fear your God: I *am* the LORD.
15 'You shall do no injustice in judgment. You shall not be partial to the poor, nor honor the person of the mighty. *But* in righteousness you shall judge your neighbor.
16 'You shall not go about *as* a talebearer among your people; nor shall you take a stand against the life of your neighbor: I *am* the LORD.
17 'You shall not hate your brother in your heart. You shall surely rebuke your neighbor, and not bear sin because of him.
18 'You shall not take vengeance, nor bear any grudge against the children of your people, but you shall love your neighbor as yourself: I *am* the LORD.
19 'You shall keep My statutes. You shall not let your livestock breed with another kind. You shall not sow your field with mixed seed. Nor shall a garment of mixed linen and wool come upon you.
20 'Whoever lies carnally with a woman who *is* betrothed as a concubine to *another* man, and who has not at all been redeemed nor given her freedom, for this there shall be scourging; *but* they shall not be put to death, because she was not free.

21 'And he shall bring his trespass offering to the LORD, to the door of the tabernacle of meeting, a ram as a trespass offering.

22 'The priest shall make atonement for him with the ram of the trespass offering before the LORD for his sin which he has done. And the sin which he has done shall be forgiven him.

23 'When you come into the land, and have planted all kinds of trees for food, then you shall count their fruit as uncircumcised. Three years it shall be as uncircumcised to you. *It* shall not be eaten.

24 'But in the fourth year all its fruit shall be holy, a praise to the LORD.

25 'And in the fifth year you may eat its fruit, that it may yield to you its increase: I *am* the LORD your God.

26 'You shall not eat *anything* with the blood, nor shall you practice divination or soothsaying.

27 'You shall not shave around the sides of your head, nor shall you disfigure the edges of your beard.

28 'You shall not make any cuttings in your flesh for the dead, nor tattoo any marks on you: I *am* the LORD.

29 'Do not prostitute your daughter, to cause her to be a harlot, lest the land fall into harlotry, and the land become full of wickedness.

30 'You shall keep My Sabbaths and reverence My sanctuary: I *am* the LORD.

31 'Give no regard to mediums and familiar spirits; do not seek after them, to be defiled by them: I *am* the LORD your God.

32 'You shall rise before the gray headed and honor the presence of an old man, and fear your God: I *am* the LORD.

33 'And if a stranger sojourns with you in your land, you shall not mistreat him.

34 'But the stranger who dwells among you shall be to you as one born among you, and you shall love him as yourself; for you were strangers in the land of Egypt: I *am* the LORD your God.

35 'You shall do no injustice in judgment, in measurement of length, weight, or volume.

36 'You shall have just balances, just weights, a just ephah, and a just hin: I *am* the LORD your God, who brought you out of the land of Egypt.

37 'Therefore you shall observe all My statutes and all My judgments, and perform them: I *am* the LORD.' "

Penalties for Breaking the Law

20 Then the LORD spoke to Moses, saying,

2 "Again, you shall say to the children of Israel: 'Whoever of the children of Israel, or of the strangers who sojourn in Israel, who gives *any* of his descendants to Molech, he shall surely be put to death. The people of the land shall stone him with stones.

3 'I will set My face against that man, and will cut him off from his people, because he has given *some* of his descendants to Molech, to defile My sanctuary and profane My holy name.

4 'And if the people of the land should in any way hide their eyes from the man, when he gives *some* of his descendants to Molech, and they do not kill him,

5 'then I will set My face against that man and against his family; and I will cut him off from his people, and all who prostitute themselves with him to commit harlotry with Molech.

6 'And the person who turns after mediums and familiar spirits, to prostitute himself with them, I will set My face against that person and cut him off from his people.

7 'Sanctify yourselves therefore, and be holy, for I *am* the LORD your God.

8 'And you shall keep My statutes, and perform them: I *am* the LORD who sanctifies you.

9 'For everyone who curses his father or his mother shall surely be put to death. He has cursed his father or his mother. His blood *shall be* upon him.

10 'The man who commits adultery with *another* man's wife, *he* who commits adultery with his neighbor's wife, the adulterer and the adulteress, shall surely be put to death.

11 'The man who lies with his father's wife has uncovered his father's nakedness; both of them shall surely be put to death. Their blood *shall be* upon them.

12 'If a man lies with his daughter-in-law, both of them shall surely be put to death. They have committed perversion. Their blood *shall be* upon them.

13 'If a man lies with a male as he lies with a woman, both of them have committed an abomination. They shall surely

be put to death. Their blood *shall be* upon them.

14 'If a man marries a woman and her mother, it *is* wickedness. They shall be burned with fire, both he and they, that there may be no wickedness among you.

15 'If a man mates with a beast, he shall surely be put to death, and you shall kill the beast.

16 'If a woman approaches any beast and mates with it, you shall kill the woman and the beast. They shall surely be put to death. Their blood *is* upon them.

17 'If a man takes his sister, his father's daughter or his mother's daughter, and sees her nakedness and she sees his nakedness, it *is* a wicked thing. And they shall be cut off in the sight of their people. He has uncovered his sister's nakedness. He shall bear his guilt.

18 'If a man lies with a woman during her sickness and uncovers her nakedness, he has discovered her flow, and she has uncovered the flow of her blood. Both of them shall be cut off from their people.

19 'You shall not uncover the nakedness of your mother's sister nor of your father's sister, for that would uncover his near of kin. They shall bear their guilt.

20 'If a man lies with his uncle's wife, he has uncovered his uncle's nakedness. They shall bear their sin; they shall die childless.

21 'If a man takes his brother's wife, it *is* an unclean thing. He has uncovered his brother's nakedness. They shall be childless.

22 'You shall therefore keep all My statutes and all My judgments, and perform them, that the land where I am bringing you to dwell may not vomit you out.

23 'And you shall not walk in the statutes of the nation which I am casting out before you; for they commit all these things, and therefore I abhor them.

24 'But I have said to you, "You shall inherit their land, and I will give it to you to possess, a land flowing with milk and honey." I *am* the LORD your God, who has separated you from the peoples.

25 'You shall therefore distinguish between clean beasts and unclean, between unclean birds and clean, and you shall not make yourselves abominable by beast or by bird, or by any kind of living thing that creeps on the ground, which I have separated from you as unclean.

26 'And you shall be holy to Me, for I the LORD *am* holy, and have separated you from the peoples, that you should be Mine.

27 'A man or a woman who is a medium, or who has familiar spirits, shall surely be put to death; they shall stone them with stones. Their blood *shall be* upon them.' "

Regulations for Conduct of Priests

21 And the LORD said to Moses, "Speak to the priests, the sons of Aaron, and say to them: 'None shall defile himself for the dead among his people,

2 'except for his relatives who are nearest to him: his mother, his father, his son, his daughter, and his brother;

3 'also his virgin sister who is near to him, who has had no husband, for her he may defile himself.

4 '*Otherwise* he shall not defile himself, *being* a chief man among his people, to profane himself.

5 'They shall not make any bald *place* on their heads, nor shall they shave the edges of their beards nor make any cuttings in their flesh.

6 'They shall be holy to their God and not profane the name of their God, for they offer the offerings of the LORD made by fire, *and* the bread of their God; therefore they shall be holy.

7 'They shall not take a wife *who is* a harlot or a defiled woman, nor shall they take a woman divorced from her husband; for the priest[8] is holy to his God.

8 'Therefore you shall sanctify him, for he offers the bread of your God. He shall be holy to you, for I the LORD, who sanctify you, *am* holy.

9 'The daughter of any priest, if she profanes herself by playing the harlot, she profanes her father. She shall be burned with fire.

10 'And *he who is* the high priest among his brethren, on whose head the anointing oil was poured and who is consecrated to wear the garments, shall not uncover his head nor tear his clothes;

11 'nor shall he go near any dead body, nor defile himself for his father or his mother;

12 'nor shall he go out of the sanctuary, nor profane the sanctuary of his God; for

---

8 Literally *he*

the consecration of the anointing oil of his God *is* upon him: I *am* the LORD.
13 'And he shall take a wife in her virginity.
14 'A widow or a divorced woman or a defiled woman *or* a harlot—these he shall not marry; but he shall take a virgin of his own people as wife.
15 'Nor shall he profane his posterity among his people, for I the LORD sanctify him.' "
16 And the LORD spoke to Moses, saying,
17 "Speak to Aaron, saying: 'No man of your descendants in *succeeding* generations, who has *any* defect, may approach to offer the bread of his God.
18 'For any man who has a defect shall not approach: a man blind or lame, who has a marred *face* or any *limb* too long,
19 'a man who has a broken foot or broken hand,
20 'or is a hunchback or a dwarf, or *a man* who has a defect in his eye, or eczema or scab, or is a eunuch.
21 'No man of the descendants of Aaron the priest, who has a defect, shall come near to offer the offerings made by fire to the LORD. He has a defect; he shall not come near to offer the bread of his God.
22 'He may eat the bread of his God, *both* the most holy and the holy;
23 'only he shall not go near the veil or approach the altar, because he has a defect, lest he profane My sanctuaries; for I the LORD sanctify them.' "
24 And Moses told *it* to Aaron and his sons, and to all the children of Israel.

22 Then the LORD spoke to Moses, saying,
2 "Speak to Aaron and his sons, that they separate themselves from the holy things of the children of Israel, and that they do not profane My holy name *in those things* which they sanctify to Me: I *am* the LORD.
3 "Say to them: 'Whoever of all your descendants throughout your generations, who goes near the holy things which the children of Israel sanctify to the LORD, while he has uncleanness upon him, that person shall be cut off from My presence: I *am* the LORD.
4 'Whatever man of the descendants of Aaron, who *is* a leper or has a discharge, shall not eat the holy offerings until he is

clean. And whoever touches anything made unclean *by* a corpse, or a man who has had an emission of semen,
5 'or whoever touches any creeping thing by which he would be made unclean, or any person by whom he would become unclean, whatever his uncleanness may be—
6 'the person who has touched any such thing shall be unclean until evening, and shall not eat the holy *offerings* unless he washes his body with water.
7 'And when the sun goes down he shall be clean; and afterward he may eat the holy *offerings*, because it *is* his food.
8 'Whatever dies *naturally* or is torn *by beasts* he shall not eat, to defile himself with it: I *am* the LORD.
9 'They shall therefore keep My ordinance, lest they bear sin for it and die thereby, if they profane it: I the LORD sanctify them.
10 'No outsider shall eat the holy *offering*; one who sojourns with the priest, or a hired servant, shall not eat the holy thing.
11 'But if the priest buys a person with his money, he may eat it; and one who is born in his house may eat his food.
12 'If the priest's daughter is married to an outsider, she may not eat of the holy offerings.
13 'But if the priest's daughter is a widow or divorced, and has no child, and has returned to her father's house as in her youth, she may eat her father's food; but no outsider shall eat it.
14 'And if a man eats the holy *offering* unintentionally, then he shall restore a holy *offering* to the priest, and add one-fifth to it.
15 'They shall not profane the holy *offerings* of the children of Israel, which they offer to the LORD,
16 'or allow them to bear the guilt of trespass when they eat their holy *offerings*; for I the LORD sanctify them.' "

Offerings Accepted and Not Accepted

17 And the LORD spoke to Moses, saying,
18 "Speak to Aaron and his sons, and to all the children of Israel, and say to them: 'Whatever man of the house of Israel, or of the strangers in Israel, who offers his sacrifice for any of his vows or for any of

his freewill offerings, which they offer to the LORD as a burnt offering—

19 '*you shall offer* of your own free will a male without blemish from the cattle, from the sheep, or from the goats.

20 '*But* whatever has a defect, you shall not offer, for it shall not be acceptable on your behalf.

21 'And whoever offers a sacrifice of peace offering to the LORD, to fulfill *his* vow, or a freewill offering from the cattle or the sheep, it must be perfect to be accepted; there shall be no defect in it.

22 'Those *that are* blind or broken or maimed, or have an ulcer or eczema or scabs, you shall not offer to the LORD, nor make an offering by fire of them on the altar to the LORD.

23 'Either a bull or a lamb that has any limb too long or too short you may offer *as* a freewill offering, but for a vow it shall not be accepted.

24 'You shall not offer to the LORD what is bruised or crushed, or torn or cut; nor shall you make *any offering of them* in your land.

25 'Nor from a foreigner's hand shall you offer any of these as the bread of your God, because their corruption *is* in them, *and* defects *are* in them. They shall not be accepted on your behalf.' ''

26 And the LORD spoke to Moses, saying:

27 "When a bull or a sheep or a goat is born, it shall be seven days with its mother; and from the eighth day and thereafter it shall be accepted as an offering made by fire to the LORD.

28 "*Whether it is* a cow or ewe, do not kill both her and her young on the same day.

29 "And when you offer a sacrifice of thanksgiving to the LORD, offer *it* of your own free will.

30 "On the same day it shall be eaten; you shall leave none of it until morning: I *am* the LORD.

31 "Therefore you shall keep My commandments, and perform them: I *am* the LORD.

32 "You shall not profane My holy name, but I will be hallowed among the children of Israel. I *am* the LORD who sanctifies you,

33 "who brought you out of the land of Egypt, to be your God: I *am* the LORD."

Feasts of the LORD

23 And the LORD spoke to Moses, saying,

2 "Speak to the children of Israel, and say to them: 'The feasts of the LORD, which you shall proclaim *to be* holy convocations, these *are* My feasts.

The Sabbath

3 'Six days shall work be done, but the seventh day *is* a Sabbath of solemn rest, a holy convocation. You shall do no work *on it*; it *is* the Sabbath of the LORD in all your dwellings.

The Passover and Unleavened Bread

4 'These *are* the feasts of the LORD, holy convocations which you shall proclaim at their appointed times.

5 'On the fourteenth *day* of the first month at twilight *is* the LORD's Passover.

6 'And on the fifteenth day of the same month *is* the Feast of Unleavened Bread to the LORD; seven days you must eat unleavened bread.

7 'On the first day you shall have a holy convocation; you shall do no customary work on it.

8 'But you shall offer an offering made by fire to the LORD for seven days. The seventh day *shall be* a holy convocation; you shall do no customary work *on it*.' ''

The Feast of Firstfruits

9 And the LORD spoke to Moses, saying,

10 "Speak to the children of Israel, and say to them: 'When you come into the land which I give to you, and reap its harvest, then you shall bring a sheaf of the firstfruits of your harvest to the priest.

11 'He shall wave the sheaf before the LORD, to be accepted on your behalf; on the day after the Sabbath the priest shall wave it.

12 'And you shall offer on that day, when you wave the sheaf, a male lamb of the first year, without blemish, as a burnt offering to the LORD.

13 'Its grain offering *shall be* two-tenths *of an ephah* of fine flour mixed with oil, an offering made by fire to the LORD, for a sweet aroma; and its drink offering *shall be* of wine, one-fourth of a hin.

14 'You shall eat neither bread nor parched grain nor fresh grain until the same day that you have brought an offer-

ing to your God; *it shall be* a statute forever throughout your generations in all your dwellings.

The Feast of Weeks

15 'And you shall count for yourselves from the day after the Sabbath, from the day that you brought the sheaf of the wave offering: seven Sabbaths shall be completed.

16 'Count fifty days to the day after the seventh Sabbath; then you shall offer a new grain offering to the LORD.

17 'You shall bring from your habitations two wave *loaves* of two-tenths *of an ephah*. They shall be of fine flour; they shall be baked with leaven. *They are* the firstfruits to the LORD.

18 'And you shall offer with the bread seven lambs of the first year, without blemish, one young bull, and two rams. They shall be *as* a burnt offering to the LORD, with their grain offering and their drink offerings, an offering made by fire for a sweet aroma to the LORD.

19 'Then you shall sacrifice one kid of the goats as a sin offering, and two male lambs of the first year as a sacrifice of peace offering.

20 'The priest shall wave them with the bread of the firstfruits *as* a wave offering before the LORD, with the two lambs. They shall be holy to the LORD for the priest.

21 'And you shall proclaim on the same day *that* it is a holy convocation to you. You shall do no customary work *on it. It shall be* a statute forever in all your dwellings throughout your generations.

22 'When you reap the harvest of your land, you shall not wholly reap the corners of your field when you reap, nor shall you gather any gleaning from your harvest. You shall leave them for the poor and for the stranger: I *am* the LORD your God.'"

The Feast of Trumpets

23 Then the LORD spoke to Moses, saying,

24 "Speak to the children of Israel, saying: 'In the seventh month, on the first *day* of the month, you shall have a sabbath-*rest*, a memorial of blowing of trumpets, a holy convocation.

25 'You shall do no customary work *on*

it; and you shall offer an offering made by fire to the LORD.'"

The Day of Atonement

26 And the LORD spoke to Moses, saying:

27 "Also the tenth *day* of this seventh month *shall be* the Day of Atonement. It shall be a holy convocation for you; you shall afflict your souls, and offer an offering made by fire to the LORD.

28 "And you shall do no work on that same day, for it *is* the Day of Atonement, to make atonement for you before the LORD your God.

29 "For any person who is not afflicted *of soul* on that same day, he shall be cut off from his people.

30 "And any person who does any work on that same day, that person I will destroy from among his people.

31 "You shall do no manner of work; *it shall be* a statute forever throughout your generations in all your dwellings.

32 'It *shall be* to you a sabbath of *solemn* rest, and you shall afflict your souls; on the ninth *day* of the month at evening, from evening to evening, you shall celebrate your sabbath."

The Feast of Tabernacles

33 Then the LORD spoke to Moses, saying,

34 "Speak to the children of Israel, saying: 'The fifteenth day of this seventh month *shall be* the Feast of Tabernacles *for* seven days to the LORD.

35 'On the first day *there shall be* a holy convocation. You shall do no customary work *on it*.

36 'For seven days you shall offer an offering made by fire to the LORD. On the eighth day you shall have a holy convocation, and you shall offer an offering made by fire to the LORD. It *is* a sacred assembly, *and* you shall do no customary work *on it*.

37 'These *are* the feasts of the LORD which you shall proclaim *to be* holy convocations, to offer an offering made by fire to the LORD, a burnt offering and a grain offering, a sacrifice and drink offerings, everything on its day—

38 'besides the Sabbaths of the LORD, besides your gifts, besides all your vows, and besides all your freewill offerings which you give to the LORD.

39 'Also on the fifteenth day of the seventh month, when you have gathered in the fruit of the land, you shall keep the feast of the LORD *for* seven days; on the first day *there shall be* a sabbath-*rest*, and on the eighth day a sabbath-*rest*.

40 'And you shall take for yourselves on the first day the fruit of beautiful trees, branches of palm trees, the boughs of leafy trees, and willows of the brook; and you shall rejoice before the LORD your God for seven days.

41 'You shall keep it as a feast to the LORD for seven days in the year. *It shall be* a statute forever in your generations. You shall celebrate it in the seventh month.

42 'You shall dwell in booths for seven days. All who are native Israelites shall dwell in booths,

43 'that your generations may know that I made the children of Israel dwell in booths when I brought them out of the land of Egypt: I *am* the LORD your God.' "

44 So Moses declared to the children of Israel the feasts of the LORD.

Care of the Tabernacle Lamps

24 Then the LORD spoke to Moses, saying:

2 "Command the children of Israel that they bring to you pure oil of pressed olives for the light, to make the lamps burn continually.

3 "Outside the veil of the Testimony, in the tabernacle of meeting, Aaron shall be in charge of it from evening until morning before the LORD continually; *it shall be* a statute forever in your generations.

4 "He shall be in charge of the lamps on the pure *gold* lampstand before the LORD continually.

The Bread of the Tabernacle

5 "And you shall take fine flour and bake twelve cakes with it. Two-tenths *of an ephah* shall be in each cake.

6 "You shall set them in two rows, six in a row, on the pure table before the LORD.

7 "And you shall put pure frankincense on *each* row, that it may be on the bread for a memorial, an offering made by fire to the LORD.

8 "Every Sabbath he shall set it in order before the LORD continually, *being taken* from the children of Israel by an everlasting covenant.

9 "And it shall be for Aaron and his sons, and they shall eat it in a holy place; for it *is* most holy to him from the offerings of the LORD made by fire, by a perpetual statute."

The Penalty for Blasphemy

10 Now the son of an Israelite woman, whose father *was* an Egyptian, went out among the children of Israel; and this Israelite *woman's* son and a man of Israel fought each other in the camp.

11 And the Israelite woman's son blasphemed the name *of the* LORD and cursed; and so they brought him to Moses. (His mother's name *was* Shelomith the daughter of Dibri, of the tribe of Dan.)

12 Then they put him in custody, that the mind of the LORD might be shown to them.

13 And the LORD spoke to Moses, saying,

14 "Take outside the camp him who has cursed; then let all who heard *him* lay their hands on his head, and let all the congregation stone him.

15 "Then you shall speak to the children of Israel, saying: 'Whoever curses his God shall bear his sin.

16 'And whoever blasphemes the name of the LORD shall surely be put to death, *and* all the congregation shall certainly stone him, the stranger as well as him who is born in the land. When he blasphemes the name *of the* LORD, he shall be put to death.

17 'Whoever kills any man shall surely be put to death.

18 'Whoever kills an animal shall make it good, animal for animal.

19 'If a man causes disfigurement of his neighbor, as he has done, so shall it be done to him—

20 'fracture for fracture, eye for eye, tooth for tooth; as he has caused disfigurement of a man, so shall it be done to him.

21 'And whoever kills an animal shall restore it; but whoever kills a man shall be put to death.

22 'You shall have the same law for the stranger and for one from your own country; for I *am* the LORD your God.' "

23 Then Moses spoke to the children of

Israel; and they took outside the camp him who had cursed, and stoned him with stones. So the children of Israel did as the LORD commanded Moses.

The Sabbath of the Seventh Year

25 And the LORD spoke to Moses on Mount Sinai, saying,

2 "Speak to the children of Israel, and say to them: 'When you come into the land which I give you, then the land shall keep a sabbath to the LORD.

3 'Six years you shall sow your field, and six years you shall prune your vineyard, and gather in its fruit;

4 'but in the seventh year there shall be a sabbath of solemn rest for the land, a sabbath to the LORD. You shall neither sow your field nor prune your vineyard.

5 'What grows of its own accord of your harvest you shall not reap, nor gather the grapes of your untended vine, *for* it is a year of rest for the land.

6 'And the sabbath *produce* of the land shall be food for you: for you and your servant, for your maidservant and your hired servant, for the stranger who sojourns with you,

7 'for your livestock and the animals that *are* in your land—all its produce shall be for food.

The Year of Jubilee

8 'And you shall count seven sabbaths of years for yourself, seven times seven years; and the time of the seven sabbaths of years shall be to you forty-nine years.

9 'Then you shall cause the trumpet of the Jubilee to sound on the tenth *day* of the seventh month; on the Day of Atonement you shall make the trumpet to sound throughout all your land.

10 'And you shall consecrate the fiftieth year, and proclaim liberty throughout *all* the land to all its inhabitants. It shall be a Jubilee for you; and each of you shall return to his possession, and each of you shall return to his family.

11 'That fiftieth year shall be a Jubilee to you; in it you shall neither sow nor reap what grows of its own accord, nor gather *the grapes* of your untended vine.

12 'For it *is* the Jubilee; it shall be holy to you; you shall eat its produce from the field.

13 'In this Year of Jubilee, each of you shall return to his possession.

14 'And if you sell anything to your neighbor or buy from your neighbor's hand, you shall not oppress one another.

15 'According to the number of years after the Jubilee you shall buy from your neighbor, and according to the number of years of crops he shall sell to you.

16 'According to the multitude of years you shall increase its price, and according to the fewer number of years you shall diminish its price; for he sells to you *according* to the number *of the years* of the crops.

17 'Therefore you shall not oppress one another, but you shall fear your God; for I *am* the LORD your God.

Provisions for the Seventh Year

18 'So you shall observe My statutes and keep My judgments, and perform them; and you will dwell in the land in safety.

19 'Then the land will yield its fruit, and you will eat your fill, and dwell there in safety.

20 'And if you say, "What shall we eat in the seventh year, since we shall not sow nor gather in our produce?"

21 'Then I will command My blessing on you in the sixth year, and it will bring forth produce enough for three years.

22 'And you shall sow in the eighth year, and eat old produce until the ninth year; until its produce comes in, you shall eat *of* the old *harvest.*

Redemption of Property

23 'The land shall not be sold permanently, for the land *is* Mine; for you *are* strangers and sojourners with Me.

24 'And in all the land of your possession you shall grant redemption of the land.

25 'If one of your brethren becomes poor, and has sold *some* of his possession, and if his kinsman-redeemer comes to redeem it, then he may redeem what his brother sold.

26 'Or if the man has no one to redeem it, but he himself becomes able to redeem it,

27 'then let him count the years since its sale, and restore the balance to the man to whom he sold it, that he may return to his possession.

28 'But if he is not able to have *it* restored to himself, then what was sold shall remain in the hand of him who

bought it until the Year of Jubilee; and in the Jubilee it shall be released, and he shall return to his possession.

29 'And if a man sells a house in a walled city, then he may redeem it within a whole year after it is sold; *within* a full year he may redeem it.

30 'But if it is not redeemed within the space of a full year, then the house in the walled city shall belong permanently to him who bought it, throughout his generations. It shall not be released in the Jubilee.

31 'However the houses of villages which have no wall around them shall be counted as the fields of the country. They may be redeemed, and they shall be released in the Jubilee.

32 'Nevertheless the cities of the Levites, *and* the houses in the cities of their possession, the Levites may redeem at any time.

33 'And if a man purchases a house from the Levites, then the house that was sold in the city of his possession shall be released in *the Year of* Jubilee; for the houses in the cities of the Levites *are* their possession among the children of Israel.

34 'But the field of the common-land of their cities may not be sold, for it *is* their perpetual possession.

Lending to the Poor

35 'And if one of your brethren becomes poor, and falls into poverty among you, then you shall help him, like a stranger or a sojourner, that he may live with you.

36 'Take no usury or interest from him; but fear your God, that your brother may live with you.

37 'You shall not lend him your money for usury, nor lend him your food at a profit.

38 'I *am* the LORD your God, who brought you out of the land of Egypt, to give you the land of Canaan *and* to be your God.

The Law Concerning Slavery

39 'And if *one of* your brethren *who dwells* by you becomes poor, and sells himself to you, you shall not compel him to serve as a slave.

40 '*But* as a hired servant *and* a sojourner he shall be with you, *and* shall serve you until the Year of Jubilee.

41 'And *then* he shall depart from you, both he and his children with him, and shall return to his own family; he shall return to the possession of his fathers.

42 'For they *are* My servants, whom I brought out of the land of Egypt; they shall not be sold as slaves.

43 'You shall not rule over him with rigor, but you shall fear your God.

44 'And as for your male and female slaves whom you may have—from the nations that are around you, from them you may buy male and female slaves.

45 'Moreover you may buy the children of the strangers who sojourn among you, and their families who are with you, which they beget in your land; and they shall become your property.

46 'And you may take them as an inheritance for your children after you, to inherit *them as* a possession; they shall be your permanent slaves. But regarding your brethren, the children of Israel, you shall not rule over one another with rigor.

47 'Now if a sojourner or stranger close to you becomes rich, and *one of* your brethren *who dwells* by him becomes poor, and sells himself to the stranger *or* sojourner close to you, or to a member of the stranger's family,

48 'after he is sold he may be redeemed again. One of his brothers may redeem him;

49 'or his uncle or his uncle's son may redeem him; or *anyone* who is near of kin to him in his family may redeem him; or if he is able he may redeem himself.

50 'Thus he shall reckon with him who bought him: The price of his release shall be according to the number of years, from the year that he was sold to him until the Year of Jubilee; *it shall be* according to the time of a hired servant for him.

51 'If *there are* still many years *remaining*, according to them he shall repay the price of his redemption from the money with which he was bought.

52 'And if there remain but a few years until the Year of Jubilee, then he shall reckon with him, *and* according to his years he shall repay him the price of his redemption.

53 'He shall be with him as a yearly hired servant, and he shall not rule with rigor over him in your sight.

54 'And if he is not redeemed in these *years*, then he shall be released in the

Year of Jubilee, *both* he and his children with him.

55 'For the children of Israel *are* servants to Me; they *are* My servants whom I brought out of the land of Egypt: I *am* the LORD your God.

Promise of Blessing and Retribution

26 'You shall not make idols for yourselves;
neither a carved image nor a *sacred* pillar shall you rear up for yourselves;
nor shall you set up an engraved stone in your land, to bow down to it;
for I *am* the LORD your God.

2 You shall keep My Sabbaths and reverence My sanctuary: I *am* the LORD.

3 'If you walk in My statutes and keep My commandments, and perform them,
4 then I will give you rain in its season, the land shall yield its produce, and the trees of the field shall yield their fruit.
5 Your threshing shall last till the time of vintage, and the vintage shall last till the time of sowing; you shall eat your bread to the full, and dwell in your land safely.
6 I will give peace in the land, and you shall lie down, and none will make *you* afraid;
I will rid the land of evil beasts, and the sword will not go through your land.
7 You will chase your enemies, and they shall fall by the sword before you.
8 Five of you shall chase a hundred, and a hundred of you shall put ten thousand to flight; your enemies shall fall by the sword before you.
9 For I will look on you favorably and make you fruitful, multiply you and confirm My covenant with you.
10 You shall eat the old harvest, and clear out the old because of the new.
11 I will set My tabernacle among you, and My soul shall not abhor you.
12 I will walk among you and be your

God, and you shall be My people.
13 I *am* the LORD your God, who brought you out of the land of Egypt, that *you* should not be their slaves;
I have broken the bands of your yoke and made you walk upright.

14 'But if you do not obey Me, and do not observe all these commandments,
15 and if you despise My statutes, or if your soul abhors My judgments, so that you do not perform all My commandments, *but* break My covenant,
16 I also will do this to you:
I will even appoint terror over you, wasting disease and fever which shall consume the eyes and cause sorrow of heart.
And you shall sow your seed in vain, for your enemies shall eat it.
17 I will set My face against you, and you shall be defeated by your enemies.
Those who hate you shall reign over you, and you shall flee when no one pursues you.

18 'And after all this, if you do not obey Me, then I will punish you seven times more for your sins.
19 I will break the pride of your power;
I will make your heavens like iron and your earth like bronze.
20 And your strength shall be spent in vain;
for your land shall not yield its produce, nor shall the trees of the land yield their fruit.

21 'Then, if you walk contrary to Me, and are not willing to obey Me, I will bring on you seven times more plagues, according to your sins.
22 I will also send wild beasts among you, which shall rob you of your children, destroy your livestock, and make you few in number; and your highways shall be desolate.

23 'And if by these things you are not reformed by Me, but walk contrary to Me,

24 then I also will walk contrary to you, and I will punish you yet seven times for your sins.
25 And I will bring a sword against you that will execute the vengeance of *My* covenant;
when you are gathered together within your cities I will send pestilence among you;
and you shall be delivered into the hand of the enemy.
26 When I have cut off your supply of bread, ten women shall bake your bread in one oven, and they shall bring back *to you* your bread by weight, and you shall eat and not be satisfied.

27 'And after all this, if you do not obey Me, but walk contrary to Me,
28 then I also will walk contrary to you in fury;
and I, even I, will chastise you seven times for your sins.
29 You shall eat the flesh of your sons, and you shall eat the flesh of your daughters.
30 I will destroy your high places, cut down your incense altars, and cast your carcasses on the lifeless forms of your idols;
and My soul shall abhor you.
31 I will lay your cities waste and bring your sanctuaries to desolation, and I will not smell the fragrance of your sweet aromas.
32 I will bring the land to desolation, and your enemies who dwell in it shall be astonished at it.
33 I will scatter you among the nations and draw out a sword after you;
your land shall be desolate and your cities waste.
34 Then the land shall enjoy its sabbaths as long as it lies desolate and you *are* in your enemies' land;
then the land shall rest and enjoy its sabbaths.
35 As long as *it* lies desolate it shall rest—
for the time it did not rest on your sabbaths when you dwelt in it.

36 'And as for those of you who are left, I will send faintness into their hearts in the lands of their enemies;
the sound of a shaken leaf shall cause them to flee;
they shall flee as though fleeing from a sword, and they shall fall when no one pursues.
37 They shall stumble over one another, as it were before a sword, when no one pursues;
and you shall have no *power* to stand before your enemies.
38 You shall perish among the nations, and the land of your enemies shall eat you up.
39 And those of you who are left shall waste away in their iniquity in your enemies' lands;
also in their fathers' iniquities, which are with them, they shall waste away.

40 'But if they confess their iniquity and the iniquity of their fathers, with their unfaithfulness in which they were unfaithful to Me, and that they also have walked contrary to Me,
41 and *that* I also have walked contrary to them and have brought them into the land of their enemies;
if their uncircumcised hearts are humbled, and they accept their guilt—
42 then I will remember My covenant with Jacob, and My covenant with Isaac and My covenant with Abraham I will remember;
I will remember the land.
43 The land also shall be left empty by them, and will enjoy its sabbaths while it lies desolate without them;
they will accept their guilt, because they despised My judgments and because their soul abhorred My statutes.
44 Yet for all that, when they are in the land of their enemies, I will not cast them away, nor shall I abhor them, to utterly destroy them and break My covenant with them;
for I *am* the LORD their God.
45 But for their sake I will remember the covenant of their ancestors,

whom I brought out of the land of Egypt in the sight of the nations, that I might be their God: I *am* the LORD.' "

46 These *are* the statutes and judgments and laws which the LORD made between Himself and the children of Israel on Mount Sinai by the hand of Moses.

Redeeming Persons and Property Dedicated to God

27 Now the LORD spoke to Moses, saying,
2 "Speak to the children of Israel, and say to them: 'When a man consecrates by a vow certain persons to the LORD, according to your valuation,
3 'if your valuation is of a male from twenty years old up to sixty years old, then your valuation shall be fifty shekels of silver, according to the shekel of the sanctuary.
4 'If it *is* a female, then your valuation shall be thirty shekels;
5 'and if from five years old up to twenty years old, then your valuation for a male shall be twenty shekels, and for a female ten shekels;
6 'and if from a month old up to five years old, then your valuation for a male shall be five shekels of silver, and for a female your valuation shall be three shekels of silver;
7 'and if from sixty years old and above, if *it is* a male, then your valuation shall be fifteen shekels, and for a female ten shekels.
8 'But if he is too poor to pay your valuation, then he shall present himself before the priest, and the priest shall set a value for him; according to the ability of him who vowed, the priest shall value him.
9 'And if *it is* a beast such as men may bring as an offering to the LORD, all such that *any man* gives to the LORD shall be holy.
10 'He shall not substitute it or exchange it, good for bad or bad for good; and if he at all exchanges beast for beast, then both it and the one exchanged for it shall be holy.
11 'If *it is* an unclean beast which they do not offer as a sacrifice to the LORD, then he shall present the beast before the priest;
12 'and the priest shall set a value for it,

whether it is good or bad; as you, the priest, value it, so it shall be.
13 'But if he *wants* at all *to* redeem it, then he must add one-fifth to your valuation.
14 'And when a man sanctifies his house *to be* holy to the LORD, then the priest shall set a value for it, whether it is good or bad; as the priest values it, so it shall stand.
15 'If he who sanctified it *wants to* redeem his house, then he shall add one-fifth of the money of your valuation to it, and it shall be his.
16 'And if a man sanctifies to the LORD *some part* of a field of his possession, then your valuation shall be according to the seed for it. A homer of barley seed *shall be valued* at fifty shekels of silver.
17 'If he sanctifies his field from the Year of Jubilee, according to your valuation it shall stand.
18 'But if he sanctifies his field after the Jubilee, then the priest shall reckon to him the money due according to the years that remain till the Year of Jubilee, and it shall be deducted from your valuation.
19 'And if he who sanctifies the field ever wishes to redeem it, then he must add one-fifth of the money of your valuation to it, and it shall belong to him.
20 'But if he does not want to redeem the field, or if he has sold the field to another man, it shall not be redeemed anymore;
21 'but the field, when it is released in the Jubilee, shall be holy to the LORD, as a devoted field; it shall be the possession of the priest.
22 'And if a man sanctifies to the LORD a field which he has bought, which is not the field of his possession,
23 'then the priest shall reckon to him the worth of your valuation, up to the Year of Jubilee, and he shall give your valuation on that day *as* a holy *offering* to the LORD.
24 'In the Year of Jubilee the field shall return to him from whom it was bought, to the one who *owned* the land as a possession.
25 'And all your valuations shall be according to the shekel of the sanctuary: twenty gerahs to the shekel.
26 'But the firstling of the beasts, which should be the LORD's firstling, no man shall sanctify; whether *it is* an ox or sheep, it *is* the LORD's.

27 'And if *it is* an unclean beast, then he shall redeem *it* according to your valuation, and shall add one-fifth to it; or if it is not redeemed, then it shall be sold according to your valuation.

28 'Nevertheless no devoted *offering* that a man may devote to the LORD of all that he has, *both* man and beast, or the field of his possession, shall be sold or redeemed; every devoted *offering is* most holy to the LORD.

29 'No person under the ban, who may become doomed to destruction among men, shall be redeemed, *but* shall surely be put to death.

30 'And all the tithe of the land, *whether* of the seed of the land *or* of the fruit of the tree, *is* the LORD's. It *is* holy to the LORD.

31 'If a man wants at all to redeem *any* of his tithes, he shall add one-fifth to it.

32 'And concerning the tithe of the herd or the flock, of whatever passes under the rod, the tenth one shall be holy to the LORD.

33 'He shall not inquire whether it is good or bad, nor shall he exchange it; and if he exchanges it at all, then both it and the one exchanged for it shall be holy; it shall not be redeemed.' "

34 These *are* the commandments which the LORD commanded Moses for the children of Israel on Mount Sinai.

Introduction to Numbers

Only God can count the apples in a seed! Seeds of faith were sown among the ancient Israelites as they wandered in the desert wilderness.

Numbers is Moses' fourth book about these journeys. Written around 1400 B.C., this book concerns events just prior to the people's entrance into the Promised Land. It records the service and worship of the people before God. Two "numberings" are listed which outline specific functions of worship and service of the people. The first numbering took place during the second year of the Israelites' wanderings in the wilderness. The second was thirty-eight years later just prior to their conquest of Canaan.

Numbers also records the successful conquest of Transjordan. From the lofty heights of their newly conquered territory, Moses and the people looked down over the land of Canaan. They had a "peak" experience that enabled them to have a "peek" into their future homeland. With their dream within reach, the people took the time to number themselves and rededicate their lives to God. They also organized and planned their life in the new land, allotting territories and assigning leaders to each tribe. They planned their future, for they knew they had to live there!

They believed their dream was already a reality! In their minds, they believed it before they achieved it! Faith is adventuring into new territories. The Israelites looked out over the land with anticipation, unafraid with God as their guide. They knew God would always be with them. They could not travel beyond His care and keeping.

Numbers is a great example of what a "peak" to "peek" experience can do in your life. When God gives you a beautiful success, then you can go out with confidence to do even more for Him!

The Fourth Book of Moses Called

Numbers

The First Census of Israel

NOW the LORD spoke to Moses in the Wilderness of Sinai, in the tabernacle of meeting, on the first *day* of the second month, in the second year after they had come out of the land of Egypt, saying:

2 "Take a census of all the congregation of the children of Israel, by their families, by their fathers' houses, according to the number of names, every male individually,

3 "from twenty years old and above— all who *are able to* go to war in Israel. You and Aaron shall number them by their armies.

4 "And with you there shall be a man from every tribe, each one the head of his father's house.

5 "These are the names of the men who shall stand with you: from Reuben, Elizur the son of Shedeur;

6 "from Simeon, Shelumiel the son of Zurishaddai;

7 "from Judah, Nahshon the son of Amminadab;

8 "from Issachar, Nethaneel the son of Zuar;

9 "from Zebulun, Eliab the son of Helon;

10 "from the sons of Joseph: from Ephraim, Elishama the son of Ammihud; from Manasseh, Gamaliel the son of Pedahzur;

11 "from Benjamin, Abidan the son of Gideoni;

12 "from Dan, Ahiezer the son of Ammishaddai;

13 "from Asher, Pagiel the son of Ocran;

14 "from Gad, Eliasaph the son of Deuel;[1]

15 "from Naphtali, Ahira the son of Enan."

16 These *were* chosen from the congregation, leaders of their fathers' tribes, heads of the divisions in Israel.

17 Then Moses and Aaron took these men who had been mentioned by name,

18 and they assembled all the congregation together on the first *day* of the second month; and they recited their ancestry by families, by their fathers' houses, according to the number of names, from twenty years old and above, each one individually.

19 As the LORD commanded Moses, so he numbered them in the Wilderness of Sinai.

20 Now the children of Reuben, Israel's oldest son, their genealogies by their families, by their fathers' house, according to the number of names, every male individually, from twenty years old and above, all who *were able to* go to war:

21 those who were numbered of the tribe of Reuben *were* forty-six thousand five hundred.

22 From the children of Simeon, their genealogies by their families, by their fathers' house, of those who were numbered, according to the number of names, every male individually, from twenty years old and above, all who *were able to* go to war:

23 those who were numbered of the tribe of Simeon *were* fifty-nine thousand three hundred.

24 From the children of Gad, their genealogies by their families, by their fathers' house, according to the number of names, from twenty years old and above, all who *were able to* go to war:

25 those who were numbered of the tribe of Gad *were* forty-five thousand six hundred and fifty.

26 From the children of Judah, their genealogies by their families, by their fathers' house, according to the number of names, from twenty years old and above, all who *were able to* go to war:

27 those who were numbered of the tribe of Judah *were* seventy-four thousand six hundred.

28 From the children of Issachar, their genealogies by their families, by their fathers' house, according to the number of names, from twenty years old and above, all who *were able to* go to war:

29 those who were numbered of the tribe of Issachar *were* fifty-four thousand four hundred.

30 From the children of Zebulun, their genealogies by their families, by their fathers' house, according to the number of names, from twenty years old and above, all who *were able to* go to war:

31 those who were numbered of the tribe of Zebulun *were* fifty-seven thousand four hundred.

32 From the sons of Joseph, the children of Ephraim, their genealogies by their families, by their fathers' house, according to the number of names, from twenty years old and above, all who *were able to* go to war:

33 those who were numbered of the tribe of Ephraim *were* forty thousand five hundred.

34 From the children of Manasseh, their genealogies by their families, by their fathers' house, according to the number of names, from twenty years old and above, all who *were able to* go to war:

35 those who were numbered of the tribe of Manasseh *were* thirty-two thousand two hundred.

36 From the children of Benjamin, their genealogies by their families, by their fathers' house, according to the number of names, from twenty years old and above, all who *were able to* go to war:

37 those who were numbered of the tribe of Benjamin *were* thirty-five thousand four hundred.

38 From the children of Dan, their genealogies by their families, by their fathers' house, according to the number of names, from twenty years old and above, all who *were able to* go to war:

39 those who were numbered of the tribe of Dan *were* sixty-two thousand seven hundred.

40 From the children of Asher, their genealogies by their families, by their fathers' house, according to the number of names, from twenty years old and above, all who *were able to* go to war:

41 those who were numbered of the tribe of Asher *were* forty-one thousand five hundred.

42 From the children of Naphtali, their genealogies by their families, by their fathers' house, according to the number of names, from twenty years old and above, all who *were able to* go to war:

43 those who were numbered of the tribe of Naphtali *were* fifty-three thousand four hundred.

44 These are the ones who were numbered, whom Moses and Aaron numbered, with the leaders of Israel, twelve men, each one representing his father's house.

45 So all who were numbered of the children of Israel, by their fathers' houses, from twenty years old and above, all who *were able to* go to war in Israel—

46 all who were numbered were six hundred and three thousand five hundred and fifty.

47 But the Levites were not numbered among them by their fathers' tribe;

48 for the LORD had spoken to Moses, saying:

49 "Only the tribe of Levi you shall not number, nor take a census of them among the children of Israel;

50 "but you shall appoint the Levites over the tabernacle of the Testimony, over all its furnishings, and over all things that belong to it; they shall carry the tabernacle and all its furnishings; they shall attend to it and camp around the tabernacle.

51 "And when the tabernacle is to go forward, the Levites shall take it down; and when the tabernacle is to be set up, the Levites shall set it up. The outsider who comes near shall be put to death.

52 "The children of Israel shall pitch their tents, everyone by his own camp, everyone by his own standard, according to their armies;

53 "but the Levites shall camp around the tabernacle of the Testimony, that there may be no wrath on the congregation of the children of Israel; and the Levites shall keep charge of the tabernacle of the Testimony."

54 Thus the children of Israel did; according to all that the LORD commanded Moses, so they did.

The Tribes and Leaders by Armies

2 And the LORD spoke to Moses and Aaron, saying:

2 "Everyone of the children of Israel shall camp by his own standard, beside the emblems of his father's house; they shall camp some distance from the tabernacle of meeting.

3 "On the east side, toward the rising of

the sun, those of the standard of the forces with Judah shall camp according to their armies; and Nahshon the son of Amminadab *shall be* the leader of the children of Judah."

4 And his army was numbered at seventy-four thousand six hundred.

5 "Those who camp next to him *shall be* the tribe of Issachar, and Nethaneel the son of Zuar *shall be* the leader of the children of Issachar."

6 And his army was numbered at fifty-four thousand four hundred.

7 "Then *shall come* the tribe of Zebulun, and Eliab the son of Helon *shall be* the leader of the children of Zebulun."

8 And his army was numbered at fifty-seven thousand four hundred.

9 "All who were numbered according to their armies of the forces with Judah, one hundred and eighty-six thousand four hundred—these shall break camp first.

10 "On the south side *shall be* the standard of the forces with Reuben according to their armies, and the leader of the children of Reuben *shall be* Elizur the son of Shedeur."

11 And his army was numbered at forty-six thousand five hundred.

12 "Those who camp next to him *shall be* the tribe of Simeon, and the leader of the children of Simeon *shall be* Shelumiel the son of Zurishaddai."

13 And his army was numbered at fifty-nine thousand three hundred.

14 "Then *shall come* the tribe of Gad, and the leader of the children of Gad *shall be* Eliasaph the son of Reuel."[2]

15 And his army was numbered at forty-five thousand six hundred and fifty.

16 "All who were numbered according to their armies of the forces with Reuben, one hundred and fifty-one thousand four hundred and fifty—they shall be the second to break camp.

17 "Then the tabernacle of meeting shall move out with the camp of the Levites in the middle of the camps; as they camp, so they shall move out, everyone in his place, by their standards.

18 "On the west side *shall be* the standard of the forces with Ephraim according to their armies, and the leader of the children of Ephraim *shall be* Elishama the son of Ammihud."

19 And his army was numbered at forty thousand five hundred.

20 "Next to him *shall be* the tribe of Manasseh, and the leader of the children of Manasseh *shall be* Gamaliel the son of Pedahzur."

21 And his army was numbered at thirty-two thousand two hundred.

22 "Then *shall come* the tribe of Benjamin, and the leader of the children of Benjamin *shall be* Abidan the son of Gideoni."

23 And his army was numbered at thirty-five thousand four hundred.

24 "All who were numbered according to their armies of the forces with Ephraim, one hundred and eight thousand one hundred—they shall be the third to break camp.

25 "The standard of the forces with Dan *shall be* on the north side according to their armies, and the leader of the children of Dan *shall be* Ahiezer the son of Ammishaddai."

26 And his army was numbered at sixty-two thousand seven hundred.

27 "Those who camp next to him *shall be* the tribe of Asher, and the leader of the children of Asher *shall be* Pagiel the son of Ocran."

28 And his army was numbered at forty-one thousand five hundred.

29 "Then *shall come* the tribe of Naphtali, and the leader of the children of Naphtali *shall be* Ahira the son of Enan."

30 And his army was numbered at fifty-three thousand four hundred.

31 "All who were numbered of the forces with Dan, one hundred and fifty-seven thousand six hundred—they shall break camp last, with their standards."

32 These *are* the ones who were numbered of the children of Israel by their fathers' houses. All who were numbered according to their armies of the forces *were* six hundred and three thousand five hundred and fifty.

33 But the Levites were not numbered among the children of Israel, just as the LORD commanded Moses.

34 Thus the children of Israel did according to all that the LORD commanded Moses; so they camped by their standards and so they broke camp, each one by his family, according to their fathers' houses.

The Sons of Aaron

3 Now these *are* the records of Aaron and Moses when the LORD spoke with Moses on Mount Sinai.

2 Or *Deuel* in 1:14 and 7:42

2 And these *are* the names of the sons of Aaron: Nadab, the firstborn, and Abihu, Eleazar, and Ithamar.
3 These *are* the names of the sons of Aaron, the anointed priests, whom he consecrated to minister as priests.
4 Nadab and Abihu had died before the LORD when they offered profane fire before the LORD in the Wilderness of Sinai; and they had no children. So Eleazar and Ithamar ministered as priests under the oversight of Aaron their father.

The Levites Serve in the Tabernacle

5 And the LORD spoke to Moses, saying:
6 "Bring the tribe of Levi near, and present them before Aaron the priest, that they may serve him.
7 "And they shall attend to his needs and the needs of the whole congregation before the tabernacle of meeting, to do the work of the tabernacle.
8 "Also they shall attend to all the furnishings of the tabernacle of meeting, and to the needs of the children of Israel, to do the work of the tabernacle.
9 "And you shall give the Levites to Aaron and his sons; they *are* given entirely to him[3] from among the children of Israel.
10 "So you shall appoint Aaron and his sons, and they shall attend to their priesthood; but the outsider who comes near shall be put to death."
11 Then the LORD spoke to Moses, saying:
12 "Now behold, I Myself have taken the Levites from among the children of Israel instead of every firstborn who opens the womb among the children of Israel. Therefore the Levites shall be Mine,
13 "because all the firstborn *are* Mine. On the day that I struck all the firstborn in the land of Egypt, I sanctified to Myself all the firstborn in Israel, both man and beast. They shall be Mine: I *am* the LORD."

Census of the Levites Commanded

14 Then the LORD spoke to Moses in the Wilderness of Sinai, saying:
15 "Number the children of Levi by their fathers' houses, by their families; you shall number every male from a month old and above."
16 So Moses numbered them according to the word of the LORD, as he was commanded.
17 These were the sons of Levi by their names: Gershon, Kohath, and Merari.
18 And these *are* the names of the sons of Gershon by their families: Libni and Shimei.
19 And the sons of Kohath by their families: Amram, Izehar, Hebron, and Uzziel.
20 And the sons of Merari by their families: Mahli and Mushi. These *are* the families of the Levites by their fathers' houses.
21 From Gershon *came* the family of the Libnites and the family of the Shimites; these *were* the families of the Gershonites.
22 Those who were numbered, according to the number of all the males from a month old and above—of those who were numbered *there were* seven thousand five hundred.
23 The families of the Gershonites were to camp behind the tabernacle westward.
24 And the leader of the fathers' house of the Gershonites *was* Eliasaph the son of Lael.
25 The duties of the children of Gershon in the tabernacle of meeting *included* the tabernacle, the tent with its covering, the screen for the door of the tabernacle of meeting,
26 the screen for the door of the court, the hangings of the court which *are* around the tabernacle and the altar, and their cords, according to all the work relating to them.
27 From Kohath *came* the family of the Amramites, the family of the Izharites, the family of the Hebronites, and the family of the Uzzielites; these *were* the families of the Kohathites.
28 According to the number of all the males, from a month old and above, *there were* eight thousand six[4] hundred keeping charge of the sanctuary.
29 The families of the children of Kohath were to camp on the south side of the tabernacle.
30 And the leader of the fathers' house of the families of the Kohathites *was* Elizaphan the son of Uzziel.
31 Their duty *included* the ark, the table, the lampstand, the altars, the utensils of the sanctuary with which they minis-

---

3 Samaritan Pentateuch and Septuagint read *Me.*   4 Some manuscripts of the Septuagint read *three.*

tered, the screen, and all the work relating to them.

32 And Eleazar the son of Aaron the priest *was to be* chief over the leaders of the Levites, *with* oversight of those who kept charge of the sanctuary.

33 From Merari *came* the family of the Mahlites and the family of the Mushites; these *were* the families of Merari.

34 And those who were numbered, according to the number of all the males from a month old and above, *were* six thousand two hundred.

35 The leader of the fathers' house of the families of Merari *was* Zuriel the son of Abihail. These *were* to camp on the north side of the tabernacle.

36 And the appointed duty of the children of Merari *included* the boards of the tabernacle, its bars, its pillars, its sockets, its utensils, all the work relating to them,

37 and the pillars of the court all around, with their sockets, their pegs, and their cords.

38 Moreover those who were to camp before the tabernacle on the east, before the tabernacle of meeting, *were* Moses, Aaron, and his sons, keeping charge of the sanctuary, to meet the needs of the children of Israel; but the outsider who came near was to be put to death.

39 All who were numbered of the Levites, whom Moses and Aaron numbered at the commandment of the LORD, by their families, all the males from a month old and above, *were* twenty-two thousand.

Levites Dedicated Instead of the Firstborn

40 Then the LORD said to Moses: "Number all the firstborn males of the children of Israel from a month old and above, and take the number of their names.

41 "And you shall take the Levites for Me—I *am* the LORD—instead of all the firstborn among the children of Israel, and the livestock of the Levites instead of all the firstborn among the livestock of the children of Israel."

42 So Moses numbered all the firstborn among the children of Israel, as the LORD commanded him.

43 And all the firstborn males, according to the number of names from a month old and above, of those who were numbered of them, were twenty-two thousand two hundred and seventy-three.

44 Then the LORD spoke to Moses, saying:

45 "Take the Levites instead of all the firstborn among the children of Israel, and the livestock of the Levites instead of their livestock. The Levites shall be Mine: I *am* the LORD.

46 "And for the redemption of the two hundred and seventy-three of the firstborn of the children of Israel, who are more than the number of the Levites,

47 "you shall take five shekels for each one individually; you shall take *them* in the currency of the shekel of the sanctuary, the shekel of twenty gerahs.

48 "And you shall give the money, with which the excess number of them is redeemed, to Aaron and his sons."

49 So Moses took the redemption money from those who were over and above those who were redeemed by the Levites.

50 From the firstborn of the children of Israel he took the money, one thousand three hundred and sixty-five *shekels*, according to the shekel of the sanctuary.

51 And Moses gave their redemption money to Aaron and his sons, according to the word of the LORD, as the LORD commanded Moses.

Duties of the Sons of Kohath

4 Then the LORD spoke to Moses and Aaron, saying:

2 "Take a census of the sons of Kohath from among the children of Levi, by their families, by their fathers' house,

3 "from thirty years old and above, even to fifty years old, all who enter the service to do the work in the tabernacle of meeting.

4 "This *is* the service of the sons of Kohath in the tabernacle of meeting, *relating to* the most holy things:

5 "When the camp prepares to journey, Aaron and his sons shall come, and they shall take down the covering veil and cover the ark of the Testimony with it.

6 "Then they shall put on it a covering of badger skins, and spread over *that* a cloth entirely of blue; and they shall insert its poles.

7 "On the table of showbread they shall spread a blue cloth, and put on it the dishes, the pans, the bowls, and the pitchers for pouring; and the showbread[5] shall be on it.

8 "They shall spread over them a scarlet

5 Literally *the continual bread*

cloth, and cover the same with a covering of badger skins; and they shall insert its poles.

9 "And they shall take a blue cloth and cover the lampstand of the light, with its lamps, its wick-trimmers, its trays, and all its oil vessels, with which they service it.

10 "Then they shall put it with all its utensils in a covering of badger skins, and put it on a carrying beam.

11 "Over the golden altar they shall spread a blue cloth, and cover it with a covering of badger skins; and they shall insert its poles.

12 "Then they shall take all the utensils of service with which they minister in the sanctuary, put them in a blue cloth, cover them with a covering of badger skins, and put them on a carrying beam.

13 "Also they shall take away the ashes from the altar, and spread a purple cloth over it.

14 "They shall put on it all its implements with which they minister there—the firepans, the forks, the shovels, the basins, and all the utensils of the altar—and they shall spread on it a covering of badger skins, and insert its poles.

15 "And when Aaron and his sons have finished covering the sanctuary and all the furnishings of the sanctuary, when the camp is set to go, then the sons of Kohath shall come to carry them; but they shall not touch any holy thing, lest they die. These are the things in the tabernacle of meeting which the sons of Kohath are to carry.

16 "The appointed duty of Eleazar the son of Aaron the priest is the oil for the light, the sweet incense, the daily grain offering, the anointing oil, the oversight of all the tabernacle, of all that is in it, with the sanctuary and its furnishings."

17 Then the LORD spoke to Moses and Aaron, saying:

18 "Do not cut off the tribe of the families of the Kohathites from among the Levites;

19 "but do this in regard to them, that they may live and not die when they approach the most holy things: Aaron and his sons shall go in and appoint each of them to his service and his task.

20 "But they shall not go in to watch while the holy things are being covered, lest they die."

Duties of the Sons of Gershon

21 Then the LORD spoke to Moses, saying:

22 "Also take a census of the sons of Gershon, by their fathers' house, by their families.

23 "From thirty years old and above, even to fifty years old, you shall number them, all who enter to perform the service, to do the work in the tabernacle of meeting.

24 "This is the service of the families of the Gershonites, in serving and carrying:

25 "They shall carry the curtains of the tabernacle and the tabernacle of meeting with its covering, the covering of badger skins that is on it, the screen for the door of the tabernacle of meeting,

26 "the screen for the door of the gate of the court, the hangings of the court which are around the tabernacle and altar, and their cords, all the furnishings for their service and all that is made for these things: so shall they serve.

27 "Aaron and his sons shall assign all the service of the sons of the Gershonites, all their tasks and all their service. And you shall appoint to them all their tasks as their duty.

28 "This is the service of the families of the sons of Gershon in the tabernacle of meeting. And their duties shall be under the hand of Ithamar the son of Aaron the priest.

Duties of the Sons of Merari

29 "As for the sons of Merari, you shall number them by their families and by their fathers' house.

30 "From thirty years old and above, even to fifty years old, you shall number them, everyone who enters the service to do the work of the tabernacle of meeting.

31 "And this is what they must carry as all their service for the tabernacle of meeting: the boards of the tabernacle, its bars, its pillars, its sockets,

32 "and the pillars around the court with their sockets, pegs, and cords, with all their furnishings and all their service; and you shall assign to each man by name the items he must carry.

33 "This is the service of the families of the sons of Merari, as all their service for the tabernacle of meeting, under the hand of Ithamar the son of Aaron the priest."

Census of the Levites

34 And Moses, Aaron, and the leaders of the congregation numbered the sons of the Kohathites by their families and by their fathers' house,

35 from thirty years old and above, even to fifty years old, everyone who entered the service for work in the tabernacle of meeting;

36 and those who were numbered by their families were two thousand seven hundred and fifty.

37 These *were* the ones who were numbered of the families of the Kohathites, all who might serve in the tabernacle of meeting, whom Moses and Aaron numbered according to the commandment of the LORD by the hand of Moses.

38 And those who were numbered of the sons of Gershon, by their families and by their fathers' house,

39 from thirty years old and above, even to fifty years old, everyone who entered the service for work in the tabernacle of meeting—

40 those who were numbered by their families, by their fathers' house, were two thousand six hundred and thirty.

41 These *are* the ones who were numbered of the families of the sons of Gershon, of all who might serve in the tabernacle of meeting, whom Moses and Aaron numbered according to the commandment of the LORD.

42 Those of the families of the sons of Merari who were numbered, by their families, by their fathers' house,

43 from thirty years old and above, even to fifty years old, everyone who entered the service for work in the tabernacle of meeting—

44 those who were numbered by their families were three thousand two hundred.

45 These *are* the ones who were numbered of the families of the sons of Merari, whom Moses and Aaron numbered according to the word of the LORD by the hand of Moses.

46 All who were numbered of the Levites, whom Moses, Aaron, and the leaders of Israel numbered, by their families and by their fathers' houses,

47 from thirty years old and above, even to fifty years old, everyone who came to do the work of service and the work

of bearing burdens in the tabernacle of meeting—

48 those who were numbered were eight thousand five hundred and eighty.

49 According to the commandment of the LORD they were numbered by the hand of Moses, each according to his service and according to his task; thus were they numbered by him, as the LORD commanded Moses.

Ceremonially Unclean Persons Isolated

5 And the LORD spoke to Moses, saying:

2 "Command the children of Israel that they put out of the camp every leper, everyone who has a discharge, and whoever becomes defiled by a *dead* body.

3 "You shall put out both male and female; you shall put them outside the camp, that they may not defile their camps in the midst of which I dwell."

4 And the children of Israel did so, and put them outside the camp; as the LORD spoke to Moses, so the children of Israel did.

Confession and Restitution

5 Then the LORD spoke to Moses, saying,

6 "Speak to the children of Israel: 'When a man or woman commits any sin that men commit in unfaithfulness against the LORD, and that person is guilty,

7 'then he shall confess the sin which he has done. He shall make restitution for his trespass in full *value* plus one-fifth of it, and give *it* to the one he has wronged.

8 'But if the man has no kinsman to whom restitution may be made for the wrong, the restitution for the wrong *must* go to the LORD for the priest, in addition to the ram of the atonement with which atonement is made for him.

9 'Every offering of all the holy things of the children of Israel, which they bring to the priest, shall be his.

10 'And every man's holy things shall be his; whatever any man gives the priest shall be his.'"

Concerning Unfaithful Wives

11 And the LORD spoke to Moses, saying,

12 "Speak to the children of Israel, and

say to them: 'If any man's wife goes
astray and behaves unfaithfully toward
him,
13 'and a man lies with her carnally, and
it is hidden from the eyes of her husband,
and it is concealed that she has defiled
herself, and *there was* no witness against
her, nor was she caught—
14 'if the spirit of jealousy comes upon
him and he becomes jealous of his wife,
who has defiled herself; or if the spirit of
jealousy comes upon him and he becomes
jealous of his wife, although she has not
defiled herself—
15 'then the man shall bring his wife to
the priest. He shall bring the offering required for her, one-tenth of an ephah of
barley meal; he shall pour no oil on it
and put no frankincense on it, because it
is a grain offering of jealousy, an offering
for remembering, for bringing iniquity to
remembrance.
16 'And the priest shall bring her near,
and set her before the LORD.
17 'The priest shall take holy water in an
earthen vessel, and take some of the dust
that is on the floor of the tabernacle and
put *it* into the water.
18 'Then the priest shall stand the
woman before the LORD, uncover the woman's head, and put the offering for remembering in her hands, which *is* the
grain offering of jealousy. And the priest
shall have in his hand the bitter water
that brings a curse.
19 'And the priest shall put her under
oath, and say to the woman, "If no man
has lain with you, and if you have not
gone astray to uncleanness *while* under
your husband's *authority*, be free from
this bitter water that brings a curse.
20 "But if you have gone astray *while* under your husband's *authority*, and if you
have defiled yourself and some man other
than your husband has lain with you"—
21 'then the priest shall put the woman
under the oath of the curse, and he shall
say to the woman—"the LORD make you
a curse and an oath among your people,
when the LORD makes your thigh rot and
your belly swell;
22 "and may this water that causes the
curse go into your stomach, and make
your belly swell and *your* thigh rot."
Then the woman shall say, "Amen, so be
it."
23 'Then the priest shall write these

curses in a book, and he shall scrape *them*
off into the bitter water.
24 'And he shall make the woman drink
the bitter water that brings a curse, and
the water that brings the curse shall enter
her *to become* bitter.
25 'Then the priest shall take the grain
offering of jealousy from the woman's
hand, shall wave the offering before the
LORD, and bring it to the altar;
26 'and the priest shall take a handful of
the offering, as its memorial portion,
burn *it* on the altar, and afterward make
the woman drink the water.
27 'When he has made her drink the water, then it shall be, if she has defiled herself and behaved unfaithfully toward her
husband, that the water that brings a
curse will enter her *and become* bitter,
and her belly will swell, her thigh will rot,
and the woman will become a curse
among her people.
28 'But if the woman has not defiled herself, and is clean, then she shall be free
and may conceive children.
29 'This *is* the law of jealousy, when a
wife, *while* under her husband's *authority*,
goes astray and defiles herself,
30 'or when the spirit of jealousy comes
upon a man, and he becomes jealous of
his wife; then he shall stand the woman
before the LORD, and the priest shall execute all this law upon her.
31 'Then the man shall be free from iniquity, but that woman shall bear her
guilt.' "

The Law of the Nazirite

6 Then the LORD spoke to Moses,
saying,
2 "Speak to the children of Israel, and
say to them: 'When either a man or
woman consecrates an offering to take
the vow of a Nazirite, to separate himself
to the LORD,
3 'he shall separate himself from wine
and *similar* drink; he shall drink neither
vinegar made from wine nor vinegar
made from *similar* drink; neither shall he
drink any grape juice, nor eat fresh
grapes or raisins.
4 'All the days of his separation he shall
eat nothing that is produced by the
grapevine, from seed to skin.
5 'All the days of the vow of his separation no razor shall come upon his head;
until the days are fulfilled for which he

separated himself to the LORD, he shall
be holy. *Then* he shall let the locks of the
hair of his head grow.
6 'All the days that he separates himself
to the LORD he shall not go near a dead
body.
7 'He shall not make himself unclean
even for his father or his mother, for his
brother or his sister, when they die, because his separation to God *is* on his
head.
8 'All the days of his separation he shall
be holy to the LORD.
9 'And if anyone dies very suddenly beside him, and he defiles his consecrated
head, then he shall shave his head on the
day of his cleansing; on the seventh day
he shall shave it.
10 'Then on the eighth day he shall bring
two turtledoves or two young pigeons to
the priest, to the door of the tabernacle of
meeting;
11 'and the priest shall offer one as a sin
offering and *the* other as a burnt offering,
and make atonement for him, because he
sinned by reason of the *dead* body; and
he shall sanctify his head that same day.
12 'He shall consecrate to the LORD the
days of his separation, and bring a male
lamb in its first year as a trespass offering; but the former days shall be lost, because his separation was defiled.
13 'Now this *is* the law of the Nazirite:
When the days of his separation are fulfilled, he shall be brought to the door of
the tabernacle of meeting.
14 'And he shall present his offering to
the LORD: one male lamb in its first year
without blemish as a burnt offering, one
ewe lamb in its first year without blemish as a sin offering, one ram without
blemish as a peace offering,
15 'a basket of unleavened bread, cakes
of fine flour mixed with oil, unleavened
wafers anointed with oil, and their grain
offering with their drink offerings.
16 'Then the priest shall bring *them* before the LORD and offer his sin offering
and his burnt offering;
17 'and he shall offer the ram as a sacrifice of peace offering to the LORD, with
the basket of unleavened bread; the priest
shall also offer its grain offering and its
drink offering.
18 'Then the Nazirite shall shave his consecrated head *at* the door of the tabernacle of meeting, and shall take the hair

from his consecrated head and put *it* on
the fire which is under the sacrifice of the
peace offering.
19 'And the priest shall take the boiled
shoulder of the ram, one unleavened cake
from the basket, and one unleavened wafer, and put *them* upon the hands of the
Nazirite after he has shaved his consecrated *hair,*
20 'and the priest shall wave them as a
wave offering before the LORD; they *are*
holy for the priest, together with the
breast of the wave offering and the thigh
of the heave offering. After that the
Nazirite may drink wine.'
21 "This is the law of the Nazirite who
vows to the LORD the offering for his
separation, and besides that, whatever
else his hand is able to provide; according
to the vow which he takes, so he must do
according to the law of his separation."

The Priestly Blessing

22 And the LORD spoke to Moses,
saying:
23 "Speak to Aaron and his sons, saying,
'This is the way you shall bless the children of Israel. Say to them:

24 "The LORD bless you and keep you;
25 The LORD make His face shine
          upon you,
     And be gracious to you;
26 The LORD lift up His countenance
          upon you,
     And give you peace." '

27 "So they shall put My name on the
children of Israel, and I will bless them."

Offerings of the Leaders

7 Now it came to pass, when Moses
  had finished setting up the tabernacle, that he anointed it and sanctified it
and all its furnishings, and the altar and
all its utensils; so he anointed them and
sanctified them.
2 Then the leaders of Israel, the heads
of their fathers' houses, who *were* the
leaders of the tribes and over those who
were numbered, made an offering.
3 And they brought their offering before
the LORD, six covered carts and twelve
oxen, a cart for *every* two of the leaders,
and for each one an ox; and they presented them before the tabernacle.
4 Then the LORD spoke to Moses,
saying,

5 "Accept *these* from them, that they may be used in doing the work of the tabernacle of meeting; and you shall give them to the Levites, *to* every man according to his service."

6 So Moses took the carts and the oxen, and gave them to the Levites.

7 Two carts and four oxen he gave to the sons of Gershon, according to their service;

8 and four carts and eight oxen he gave to the sons of Merari, according to their service, under the hand of Ithamar the son of Aaron the priest.

9 But to the sons of Kohath he gave none, because theirs *was* the service of the holy things, *which* they carried on their shoulders.

10 Now the leaders offered the dedication *offering* for the altar when it was anointed; so the leaders offered their offering before the altar.

11 For the LORD said to Moses, "They shall offer their offering, one leader each day, for the dedication of the altar."

12 And the one who offered his offering on the first day *was* Nahshon the son of Amminadab, from the tribe of Judah.

13 His offering *was* one silver platter, the weight of which *was* one hundred and thirty *shekels*, and one silver bowl of seventy shekels, according to the shekel of the sanctuary, both of them full of fine flour mixed with oil as a grain offering;

14 one gold pan of ten *shekels*, full of incense;

15 one young bull, one ram, and one male lamb in its first year, as a burnt offering;

16 one kid of the goats as a sin offering;

17 and for the sacrifice of peace offerings: two oxen, five rams, five male goats, and five male lambs in their first year. This *was* the offering of Nahshon the son of Amminadab.

18 On the second day Nethaneel the son of Zuar, leader of Issachar, presented *an offering*.

19 *For* his offering he offered one silver platter, the weight of which *was* one hundred and thirty *shekels*, and one silver bowl of seventy shekels, according to the shekel of the sanctuary, both of them full of fine flour mixed with oil as a grain offering;

20 one gold pan of ten *shekels*, full of incense;

21 one young bull, one ram, and one male lamb in its first year, as a burnt offering;

22 one kid of the goats as a sin offering;

23 and as the sacrifice of peace offerings: two oxen, five rams, five male goats, and five male lambs in their first year. This *was* the offering of Nethaneel the son of Zuar.

24 On the third day Eliab the son of Helon, leader of the children of Zebulun, *presented an offering.*

25 His offering *was* one silver platter, the weight of which *was* one hundred and thirty *shekels*, and one silver bowl of seventy shekels, according to the shekel of the sanctuary, both of them full of fine flour mixed with oil as a grain offering;

26 one gold pan of ten *shekels*, full of incense;

27 one young bull, one ram, and one male lamb in its first year, as a burnt offering;

28 one kid of the goats as a sin offering;

29 and for the sacrifice of peace offerings: two oxen, five rams, five male goats, and five male lambs in their first year. This *was* the offering of Eliab the son of Helon.

30 On the fourth day Elizur the son of Shedeur, leader of the children of Reuben, *presented an offering.*

31 His offering *was* one silver platter, the weight of which *was* one hundred and thirty *shekels*, and one silver bowl of seventy shekels, according to the shekel of the sanctuary, both of them full of fine flour mixed with oil as a grain offering;

32 one gold pan of ten *shekels*, full of incense;

33 one young bull, one ram, and one male lamb in its first year, as a burnt offering;

34 one kid of the goats as a sin offering;

35 and as the sacrifice of peace offerings: two oxen, five rams, five male goats, and five male lambs in their first year. This *was* the offering of Elizur the son of Shedeur.

36 On the fifth day Shelumiel the son of Zurishaddai, leader of the children of Simeon, *presented an offering.*

37 His offering *was* one silver platter, the weight of which *was* one hundred and thirty *shekels*, and one silver bowl of seventy shekels, according to the shekel of the sanctuary, both of them full of fine

flour mixed with oil as a grain offering;
38 one gold pan of ten *shekels*, full of incense;
39 one young bull, one ram, and one male lamb in its first year, as a burnt offering;
40 one kid of the goats as a sin offering;
41 and as the sacrifice of peace offerings: two oxen, five rams, five male goats, and five male lambs in their first year. This *was* the offering of Shelumiel the son of Zurishaddai.
42 On the sixth day Eliasaph the son of Deuel,[6] leader of the children of Gad, *presented an offering.*
43 His offering *was* one silver platter, the weight of which *was* one hundred and thirty *shekels*, and one silver bowl of seventy shekels, according to the shekel of the sanctuary, both of them full of fine flour mixed with oil as a grain offering;
44 one gold pan of ten *shekels*, full of incense;
45 one young bull, one ram, and one male lamb in its first year, as a burnt offering;
46 one kid of the goats as a sin offering;
47 and as the sacrifice of peace offerings: two oxen, five rams, five male goats, and five male lambs in their first year. This *was* the offering of Eliasaph the son of Deuel.
48 On the seventh day Elishama the son of Ammihud, leader of the children of Ephraim, *presented an offering.*
49 His offering *was* one silver platter, the weight of which *was* one hundred and thirty *shekels*, and one silver bowl of seventy shekels, according to the shekel of the sanctuary, both of them full of fine flour mixed with oil as a grain offering;
50 one gold pan of ten *shekels*, full of incense;
51 one young bull, one ram, and one male lamb in its first year, as a burnt offering;
52 one kid of the goats as a sin offering;
53 and as the sacrifice of peace offerings: two oxen, five rams, five male goats, and five male lambs in their first year. This *was* the offering of Elishama the son of Ammihud.
54 On the eighth day Gamaliel the son of Pedahzur, leader of the children of Manasseh, *presented an offering.*
55 His offering *was* one silver platter, the weight of which *was* one hundred and

thirty *shekels*, and one silver bowl of seventy shekels, according to the shekel of the sanctuary, both of them full of fine flour mixed with oil as a grain offering;
56 one gold pan of ten *shekels*, full of incense;
57 one young bull, one ram, and one male lamb in its first year, as a burnt offering;
58 one kid of the goats as a sin offering;
59 and as the sacrifice of peace offerings: two oxen, five rams, five male goats, and five male lambs in their first year. This *was* the offering of Gamaliel the son of Pedahzur.
60 On the ninth day Abidan the son of Gideoni, leader of the children of Benjamin, *presented an offering.*
61 His offering *was* one silver platter, the weight of which *was* one hundred and thirty *shekels*, and one silver bowl of seventy shekels, according to the shekel of the sanctuary, both of them full of fine flour mixed with oil as a grain offering;
62 one gold pan of ten *shekels*, full of incense;
63 one young bull, one ram, and one male lamb in its first year, as a burnt offering;
64 one kid of the goats as a sin offering;
65 and as the sacrifice of peace offerings: two oxen, five rams, five male goats, and five male lambs in their first year. This *was* the offering of Abidan the son of Gideoni.
66 On the tenth day Ahiezer the son of Ammishaddai, leader of the children of Dan, *presented an offering.*
67 His offering *was* one silver platter, the weight of which *was* one hundred and thirty *shekels*, and one silver bowl of seventy shekels, according to the shekel of the sanctuary, both of them full of fine flour mixed with oil as a grain offering;
68 one gold pan of ten *shekels*, full of incense;
69 one young bull, one ram, and one male lamb in its first year, as a burnt offering;
70 one kid of the goats as a sin offering;
71 and as the sacrifice of peace offerings: two oxen, five rams, five male goats, and five male lambs in their first year. This *was* the offering of Ahiezer the son of Ammishaddai.
72 On the eleventh day Pagiel the son of

6 Or *Reuel* in 2:14

Ocran, leader of the children of Asher, *presented an offering.*
73 His offering *was* one silver platter, the weight of which *was* one hundred and thirty *shekels*, and one silver bowl of seventy shekels, according to the shekel of the sanctuary, both of them full of fine flour mixed with oil as a grain offering;
74 one gold pan of ten *shekels*, full of incense;
75 one young bull, one ram, and one male lamb in its first year, as a burnt offering;
76 one kid of the goats as a sin offering;
77 and as the sacrifice of peace offerings: two oxen, five rams, five male goats, and five male lambs in their first year. This *was* the offering of Pagiel the son of Ocran.
78 On the twelfth day Ahira the son of Enan, leader of the children of Naphtali, *presented an offering.*
79 His offering *was* one silver platter, the weight of which *was* one hundred and thirty *shekels*, and one silver bowl of seventy shekels, according to the shekel of the sanctuary, both of them full of fine flour mixed with oil as a grain offering;
80 one gold pan of ten *shekels*, full of incense;
81 one young bull, one ram, and one male lamb in its first year, as a burnt offering;
82 one kid of the goats as a sin offering;
83 and as the sacrifice of peace offerings: two oxen, five rams, five male goats, and five male lambs in their first year. This *was* the offering of Ahira the son of Enan.
84 This *was* the dedication *offering* for the altar from the leaders of Israel, when it was anointed: twelve silver platters, twelve silver bowls, and twelve gold pans.
85 Each silver platter *weighed* one hundred and thirty *shekels* and each bowl seventy *shekels.* All the silver of the vessels *weighed* two thousand four hundred *shekels,* according to the shekel of the sanctuary.
86 The twelve gold pans full of incense *weighed* ten *shekels* apiece, according to the shekel of the sanctuary; all the gold of the pans *weighed* one hundred and twenty *shekels.*
87 All the oxen for the burnt offering *were* twelve young bulls, the rams twelve, the male lambs in their first year twelve,

with their grain offering, and the kids of the goats as a sin offering twelve.
88 And all the oxen for the sacrifice of peace offerings were twenty-four bulls, the rams sixty, the male goats sixty, and the lambs in their first year sixty. This *was* the dedication *offering* for the altar after it was anointed.
89 Now when Moses went into the tabernacle of meeting to speak with Him, he heard the voice of One speaking to him from above the mercy seat that *was* on the ark of the Testimony, from between the two cherubim; thus He spoke to him.

Arrangement of the Lamps

8 And the Lord spoke to Moses, saying:
2 "Speak to Aaron, and say to him, 'When you arrange the lamps, the seven lamps shall give light in front of the lampstand.' "
3 And Aaron did so; he arranged the lamps to face toward the front of the lampstand, as the Lord commanded Moses.
4 Now this workmanship of the lampstand *was of* hammered gold; from its shaft to its flowers it *was* hammered work. According to the pattern which the Lord had shown Moses, so he made the lampstand.

Cleansing and Dedication of the Levites

5 Then the Lord spoke to Moses, saying:
6 "Take the Levites from among the children of Israel and cleanse them *ceremonially.*
7 "Thus you shall do to them to cleanse them: Sprinkle water of purification on them, and let them shave all their body, and let them wash their clothes, and *so* make themselves clean.
8 "Then let them take a young bull with its grain offering of fine flour mixed with oil, and you shall take another young bull as a sin offering.
9 "And you shall bring the Levites before the tabernacle of meeting, and you shall gather together the whole assembly of the children of Israel.
10 "So you shall bring the Levites before the Lord, and the children of Israel shall lay their hands on the Levites;
11 "and Aaron shall offer the Levites before the Lord, *as though* a wave offering

from the children of Israel, that they may
perform the work of the LORD.
12 "Then the Levites shall lay their
hands on the heads of the young bulls,
and you shall offer one as a sin offering
and the other as a burnt offering to the
LORD, to make atonement for the Levites.
13 "And you shall stand the Levites before Aaron and his sons, and then offer
them *as though* a wave offering to the
LORD.
14 "Thus you shall separate the Levites
from among the children of Israel, and
the Levites shall be Mine.
15 "After that the Levites shall go in to
service the tabernacle of meeting. So you
shall cleanse them and offer them, *as
though* a wave offering.
16 "For they *are* wholly given to Me
from among the children of Israel; I have
taken them for Myself instead of all who
open the womb, the firstborn of all the
children of Israel.
17 "For all the firstborn among the children of Israel *are* Mine, *both* man and
beast; on the day that I struck all the
firstborn in the land of Egypt I sanctified
them to Myself.
18 "I have taken the Levites instead of
all the firstborn of the children of Israel.
19 "And I have given the Levites as a gift
to Aaron and his sons from among the
children of Israel, to do the work for
the children of Israel in the tabernacle of
meeting, and to make atonement for the
children of Israel, that there be no plague
among the children of Israel when the
children of Israel come near the sanctuary."
20 Thus Moses and Aaron and all the
congregation of the children of Israel did
to the Levites; according to all that the
LORD commanded Moses concerning the
Levites, so the children of Israel did to
them.
21 And the Levites purified themselves
and washed their clothes; then Aaron
presented them, *as though* a wave offering
before the LORD, and Aaron made atonement for them to cleanse them.
22 After that the Levites went in to do
their work in the tabernacle of meeting
before Aaron and his sons; as the LORD
commanded Moses concerning the Levites, so they did to them.
23 Then the LORD spoke to Moses,
saying,

24 "This *is* what *pertains* to the Levites:
From twenty-five years old and above
one may enter to perform service in the
work of the tabernacle of meeting;
25 "and at the age of fifty years they
must cease performing this work, and
shall work no more.
26 "They may minister with their brethren in the tabernacle of meeting, to attend to needs, but they *themselves* shall
do no work. Thus you shall do to the
Levites regarding their duties."

The Second Passover

9 Now the LORD spoke to Moses in the
Wilderness of Sinai, in the first
month of the second year after they had
come out of the land of Egypt, saying:
2 "Let the children of Israel keep the
Passover at its appointed time.
3 "On the fourteenth day of this month,
at twilight, you shall keep it at its appointed time. According to all its rites
and ceremonies you shall keep it."
4 So Moses told the children of Israel
that they should keep the Passover.
5 And they kept the Passover on the
fourteenth day of the first month, at twilight, in the Wilderness of Sinai; according to all that the LORD commanded
Moses, so the children of Israel did.
6 Now there were *certain* men who were
defiled by *the dead* body of a man, so that
they could not keep the Passover on that
day; and they came before Moses and
Aaron that day.
7 And those men said to him, "We *became* defiled by *the dead* body of a man.
Why are we kept from presenting the offering of the LORD at its appointed time
among the children of Israel?"
8 And Moses said to them, "Stand still,
that I may hear what the LORD will command concerning you."
9 Then the LORD spoke to Moses,
saying,
10 "Speak to the children of Israel, saying: 'If anyone of you or your posterity is
unclean because of a *dead* body, or *is* far
away on a journey, he may still keep the
LORD's Passover.
11 'On the fourteenth day of the second
month, at twilight, they may keep it.
They shall eat it with unleavened bread
and bitter herbs.
12 'They shall leave none of it until
morning, nor break one of its bones. Ac-

cording to all the ordinances of the Passover they shall keep it.

13 'But the man who *is* clean and is not on a journey, and ceases to keep the Passover, that same person shall be cut off from among his people, because he did not bring the offering of the LORD at its appointed time; that man shall bear his sin.

14 'And if a stranger sojourns among you, and would keep the LORD's Passover, he must do so according to the rite of the Passover and according to its ceremony; you shall have one ordinance, both for the stranger and the native of the land.' "

The Cloud and the Fire

15 And on the day that the tabernacle was raised up, the cloud covered the tabernacle, the tent of the Testimony; from evening until morning it was above the tabernacle like the appearance of fire.

16 So it was always: the cloud covered it *by day*, and the appearance of fire by night.

17 Whenever the cloud was taken up from above the tabernacle, after that the children of Israel would journey; and in the place where the cloud settled, there the children of Israel would pitch their tents.

18 At the command of the LORD the children of Israel would journey, and at the command of the LORD they would camp; as long as the cloud stayed above the tabernacle they remained encamped.

19 Even when the cloud continued long, many days above the tabernacle, the children of Israel kept the charge of the LORD and did not journey.

20 So it was, when the cloud was above the tabernacle a few days: according to the command of the LORD they would remain encamped, and according to the command of the LORD they would journey.

21 So it was, when the cloud remained only from evening until morning: when the cloud was taken up in the morning, then they would journey; whether by day or by night, whenever the cloud was taken up, they would journey.

22 *Whether it was* two days, a month, or a year that the cloud remained above the tabernacle, the children of Israel would remain encamped and not journey; but when it was taken up, they would journey.

23 At the command of the LORD they remained encamped, and at the command of the LORD they journeyed; they kept the charge of the LORD, at the command of the LORD by the hand of Moses.

Two Silver Trumpets

10 And the LORD spoke to Moses, saying:

2 "Make two silver trumpets for yourself; you shall make them of hammered work; you shall use them for calling the assembly and for directing the movement of the camps.

3 "When they blow both of them, all the assembly shall gather before you at the door of the tabernacle of meeting.

4 "But if they blow *only* one, then the leaders, the heads of the divisions of Israel, shall gather to you.

5 "When you sound the advance, the camps that lie on the east side shall then begin their journey.

6 "When you sound the advance the second time, then the camps that lie on the south side shall begin their journey; they shall sound the call for them to begin their journeys.

7 "And when the congregation is to be gathered together, you shall blow, but not sound the advance.

8 "The sons of Aaron, the priests, shall blow the trumpets; and these shall be to you as an ordinance forever throughout your generations.

9 "When you go to war in your land against the enemy who oppresses you, then you shall sound an alarm with the trumpets, and you will be remembered before the LORD your God, and you will be saved from your enemies.

10 "Also in the day of your gladness, in your appointed feasts, and at the beginning of your months, you shall blow the trumpets over your burnt offerings and over the sacrifices of your peace offerings; and they shall be a memorial for you before your God: I *am* the LORD your God."

Departure from Sinai

11 Now it came to pass on the twentieth *day* of the second month, in the second year, that the cloud was taken up from above the tabernacle of the Testimony.

12 And the children of Israel set out from the Wilderness of Sinai on their journeys; then the cloud settled down in the Wilderness of Paran.

13 So they started out for the first time according to the command of the LORD by the hand of Moses.

14 The standard of the camp of the children of Judah set out first according to their armies; over their army was Nahshon the son of Amminadab.

15 Over the army of the tribe of the children of Issachar *was* Nethaneel the son of Zuar.

16 And over the army of the tribe of the children of Zebulun *was* Eliab the son of Helon.

17 Then the tabernacle was taken down; and the sons of Gershon and the sons of Merari set out, carrying the tabernacle.

18 And the standard of the camp of Reuben set out according to their armies; over their army *was* Elizur the son of Shedeur.

19 Over the army of the tribe of the children of Simeon *was* Shelumiel the son of Zurishaddai.

20 And over the army of the tribe of the children of Gad *was* Eliasaph the son of Deuel.

21 Then the Kohathites set out, carrying the holy things. (The tabernacle would be prepared for their arrival.)

22 And the standard of the camp of the children of Ephraim set out according to their armies; over their army *was* Elishama the son of Ammihud.

23 Over the army of the tribe of the children of Manasseh *was* Gamaliel the son of Pedahzur.

24 And over the army of the tribe of the children of Benjamin *was* Abidan the son of Gideoni.

25 Then the standard of the camp of the children of Dan, *which formed* the rear guard of all the camps, set out according to their armies; over their army *was* Ahiezer the son of Ammishaddai.

26 Over the army of the tribe of the children of Asher *was* Pagiel the son of Ocran.

27 And over the army of the tribe of the children of Naphtali *was* Ahira the son of Enan.

28 Thus *was* the order of march of the children of Israel, according to their armies, when they began their journey.

29 Now Moses said to Hobab the son of Reuel[7] the Midianite, Moses' father-in-law, "We are setting out for the place of which the LORD said, 'I will give it to you.' Come with us, and we will treat you well; for the LORD has promised good things to Israel."

30 And he said to him, "I will not go, but I will depart to my *own* land and to my kinsmen."

31 So Moses[8] said, "Please do not leave, inasmuch as you know how we are to camp in the wilderness, and you can be our eyes.

32 "And it shall be, if you go with us—indeed it shall be—that whatever good the LORD will do to us, the same we will do to you."

33 So they departed from the mountain of the LORD on a journey of three days; and the ark of the covenant of the LORD went before them for the three days' journey, to search out a resting place for them.

34 And the cloud of the LORD *was* above them by day when they went out from the camp.

35 So it was, whenever the ark set out, that Moses said:

"Rise up, O LORD!
Let Your enemies be scattered,
And let those who hate You
    flee before You."

36 And when it rested, he said:

"Return, O LORD, *to* the many
    thousands of Israel."

The People Complain

11 Now *when* the people complained, it displeased the LORD; for the LORD heard *it*, and His anger was aroused. So the fire of the LORD burned among them, and consumed *some* in the outskirts of the camp.

2 Then the people cried out to Moses, and when Moses prayed to the LORD, the fire was quenched.

3 So he called the name of the place Taberah,[9] because the fire of the LORD had burned among them.

4 Now the mixed multitude who were among them yielded to intense craving; so the children of Israel also wept again and said: "Who will give us meat to eat?

7 Septuagint reads *Raguel* (compare Exodus 2:18).   8 Literally *he*   9 Literally *Burning*

5 "We remember the fish which we ate freely in Egypt, the cucumbers, the melons, the leeks, the onions, and the garlic; 6 "but now our whole being *is* dried up; *there is* nothing at all except this manna *before* our eyes!"

7 Now the manna *was* like coriander seed, and its color like the color of bdellium. 8 The people went about and gathered *it*, ground *it* on millstones or beat *it* in the mortar, cooked *it* in pans, and made cakes of it; and its taste was like the taste of pastry prepared with oil. 9 And when the dew fell on the camp in the night, the manna fell on it.

10 Now Moses heard the people weeping throughout their families, everyone at the door of his tent; and the anger of the LORD was greatly aroused; Moses also was displeased. 11 So Moses said to the LORD, "Why have You afflicted Your servant? And why have I not found favor in Your sight, that You have laid the burden of all these people on me? 12 "Did I conceive all these people? Did I beget them, that You should say to me, 'Carry them in your bosom, as a guardian carries a nursing child,' to the land which You swore to their fathers? 13 "Where am I to get meat to give to all these people? For they weep all over me, saying, 'Give us meat, that we may eat.' 14 "I am not able to bear all these people alone, because the burden *is* too heavy for me. 15 "If You treat me like this, please kill me here and now—if I have found favor in Your sight—and do not let me see my wretchedness!"

The Seventy Elders

16 So the LORD said to Moses: "Gather to Me seventy men of the elders of Israel, whom you know to be the elders of the people and officers over them; bring them to the tabernacle of meeting, that they may stand there with you. 17 "Then I will come down and talk with you there. I will take of the Spirit that *is* upon you and will put *the same* upon them; and they shall bear the burden of the people with you, that you may not bear *it* yourself alone. 18 "Then you shall say to the people, 'Sanctify yourselves for tomorrow, and

you shall eat meat; for you have wept in the hearing of the LORD, saying, "Who will give us meat to eat? For *it was* well with us in Egypt." Therefore the LORD will give you meat, and you shall eat. 19 'You shall eat, not one day, nor two days, nor five days, nor ten days, nor twenty days, 20 'but *for* a whole month, until it comes out of your nostrils and becomes loathsome to you, because you have despised the LORD who is among you, and have wept before Him, saying, "Why did we ever come up out of Egypt?" ' "

21 And Moses said, "The people whom I *am* among *are* six hundred thousand men on foot; yet You have said, 'I will give them meat, that they may eat *for* a whole month.' 22 "Shall flocks and herds be slaughtered for them, to provide enough for them? Or shall all the fish of the sea be gathered together for them, to provide enough for them?"

23 And the LORD said to Moses, "Has the LORD's arm been shortened? Now you shall see whether My word will befall you or not."

24 So Moses went out and told the people the words of the LORD, and he gathered the seventy men of the elders of the people and placed them around the tabernacle. 25 Then the LORD came down in the cloud, and spoke to him, and took of the Spirit that *was* upon him, and placed *the same* upon the seventy elders; and it happened, when the Spirit rested upon them, that they prophesied, although they never did *so* again.[10]

26 But two men had remained in the camp: the name of one *was* Eldad, and the name of the other Medad. And the Spirit rested upon them. Now they *were* among those listed, but who had not gone out to the tabernacle; yet they prophesied in the camp. 27 And a young man ran and told Moses, and said, "Eldad and Medad are prophesying in the camp." 28 So Joshua the son of Nun, Moses' assistant, *one* of his choice men, answered and said, "Moses my lord, forbid them!" 29 Then Moses said to him, "Are you zealous for my sake? Oh, that all the LORD's people were prophets *and* that the LORD would put His Spirit upon them!"

10 Targum and Vulgate read *did not cease.*

30 And Moses returned to the camp, *both* he and the elders of Israel.

The LORD Sends Quail

31 Now a wind went out from the LORD, and it brought quail from the sea and left *them* fluttering near the camp, about a day's journey on this side and about a day's journey on the other side, all around the camp, and about two cubits above the surface of the ground.

32 And the people stayed up all that day, all *that* night, and all the next day, and gathered the quail (he who gathered least gathered ten homers); and they spread *them* out for themselves all around the camp.

33 But while the meat *was* still between their teeth, before it was chewed, the wrath of the LORD was aroused against the people, and the LORD struck the people with a very great plague.

34 So he called the name of that place Kibroth Hattaavah,[11] because there they buried the people who had yielded to craving.

35 From Kibroth Hattaavah the people moved to Hazeroth, and camped at Hazeroth.

Dissension of Aaron and Miriam

12 Then Miriam and Aaron spoke against Moses because of the Ethiopian woman whom he had married; for he had married an Ethiopian woman.

2 And they said, "Has the LORD indeed spoken only through Moses? Has He not spoken through us also?" And the LORD heard *it*.

3 (Now the man Moses *was* very humble, more than all men who *were* on the face of the earth.)

4 Suddenly the LORD said to Moses, Aaron, and Miriam, "Come out, you three, to the tabernacle of meeting!" So the three came out.

5 Then the LORD came down in the pillar of cloud and stood *in* the door of the tabernacle, and called Aaron and Miriam. And they both went forward.

6 Then He said, "Hear now My words:

If there is a prophet among you,
I, the LORD, make Myself known
   to him in a vision,
And I speak to him in a dream.

7 Not so with My servant Moses;
   He *is* faithful in all My house.
8 I speak with him face to face,
   Even plainly, and not in dark sayings;
   And he sees the form of the LORD.
   Why then were you not afraid
   To speak against My servant Moses?"

9 So the anger of the LORD was aroused against them, and He departed.

10 And when the cloud departed from above the tabernacle, suddenly Miriam *became* leprous, as *white as* snow. Then Aaron turned toward Miriam, and there she was, a leper.

11 So Aaron said to Moses, "Oh, my lord! Please do not lay *this* sin on us, in which we have done foolishly and in which we have sinned.

12 "Please do not let her be as one dead, whose flesh is half consumed when he comes out of his mother's womb!"

13 So Moses cried out to the LORD, saying, "Please heal her, O God, I pray!"

14 Then the LORD said to Moses, "If her father had but spit in her face, would she not be shamed seven days? Let her be shut out of the camp seven days, and after that she may be received *again.*"

15 So Miriam was shut out of the camp seven days, and the people did not journey on till Miriam was brought in *again.*

16 And afterward the people moved from Hazeroth and camped in the Wilderness of Paran.

Spies Sent into Canaan

13 And the LORD spoke to Moses, saying,

2 "Send men to spy out the land of Canaan, which I am giving to the children of Israel; from each tribe of their fathers you shall send a man, every one a leader among them."

3 So Moses sent them from the Wilderness of Paran according to the command of the LORD, all of them men who *were* heads of the children of Israel.

4 Now these *were* their names: from the tribe of Reuben, Shammua the son of Zaccur;

5 from the tribe of Simeon, Shaphat the son of Hori;

6 from the tribe of Judah, Caleb the son of Jephunneh;

7 from the tribe of Issachar, Igal the son of Joseph;

11 Literally *Graves of Craving*

8 from the tribe of Ephraim, Hoshea[12] the son of Nun;

9 from the tribe of Benjamin, Palti the son of Raphu;

10 from the tribe of Zebulun, Gaddiel the son of Sodi;

11 from the tribe of Joseph, *that is*, from the tribe of Manasseh, Gaddi the son of Susi;

12 from the tribe of Dan, Ammiel the son of Gemalli;

13 from the tribe of Asher, Sethur the son of Michael;

14 from the tribe of Naphtali, Nahbi the son of Vophsi;

15 from the tribe of Gad, Geuel the son of Machi.

16 These *are* the names of the men whom Moses sent to spy out the land. And Moses called Hoshea[13] the son of Nun, Joshua.

17 So Moses sent them to spy out the land of Canaan, and said to them, "Go up this *way* into the South, and go up to the mountains,

18 "and see what the land is like: whether the people who dwell in it *are* strong or weak, few or many;

19 "whether the land they dwell in *is* good or bad; whether the cities they inhabit *are* like camps or strongholds;

20 "whether the land *is* rich or poor; and whether there are forests there or not. Be of good courage. And bring some of the fruit of the land." Now the time *was* the season of the first ripe grapes.

21 So they went up and spied out the land from the Wilderness of Zin as far as Rehob, near the entrance of Hamath.

22 And they went up through the South and came to Hebron; Ahiman, Sheshai, and Talmai, the descendants of Anak, *were* there. (Now Hebron was built seven years before Zoan in Egypt.)

23 Then they came to the Valley of Eshcol, and there cut down a branch with one cluster of grapes; they carried it between two of them on a pole. *They* also *brought* some of the pomegranates and figs.

24 The place was called the Valley of Eshcol,[14] because of the cluster which the men of Israel cut down there.

25 And they returned from spying out the land after forty days.

26 So they departed and came back to Moses and Aaron and all the congregation of the children of Israel in the Wilderness of Paran, at Kadesh; they brought back word to them and to all the congregation, and showed them the fruit of the land.

27 Then they told him, and said: "We went to the land where you sent us. It truly flows with milk and honey, and this *is* its fruit.

28 "Nevertheless the people who dwell in the land *are* strong; the cities *are* fortified *and* very large; moreover we saw the descendants of Anak there.

29 "The Amalekites dwell in the land of the South; the Hittites, the Jebusites, and the Amorites dwell in the mountains; and the Canaanites dwell by the sea and along the banks of the Jordan."

30 Then Caleb quieted the people before Moses, and said, "Let us go up at once and take possession, for we are well able to overcome it."

31 But the men who had gone up with him said, "We are not able to go up against the people, for they *are* stronger than we."

32 And they gave the children of Israel a bad report of the land which they had spied out, saying, "The land through which we have gone as spies *is* a land that devours its inhabitants, and all the people whom we saw in it *are* men of *great* stature.

33 "There we saw the giants[15] (the descendants of Anak came from the giants); and we were like grasshoppers in our own sight, and so we were in their sight."

Israel Refuses to Enter Canaan

14 Then all the congregation lifted up their voices and cried, and the people wept that night.

2 And all the children of Israel murmured against Moses and Aaron, and the whole congregation said to them, "If only we had died in the land of Egypt! Or if only we had died in this wilderness!

3 "Why has the LORD brought us to this land to fall by the sword, that our wives and children should become victims? Would it not be better for us to return to Egypt?"

4 So they said to one another, "Let us select a leader and return to Egypt."

5 Then Moses and Aaron fell on their

---

12 Septuagint and Vulgate read *Oshea*. 13 Septuagint and Vulgate read *Oshea*.
14 Literally *Cluster* 15 Hebrew *nephilim*

Two Spies

Moses and the Israelites arrived at the borders of the long-awaited Promised Land, Canaan. Unsure of what lay before them, Moses sent twelve spies into the country to spy out its condition and bring back their report to the Israelites.

Of the twelve spies, ten returned with a gloomy, despondent picture. The country was dominated by giants who were unconquerable and unwilling to give up their land. The advice of the ten spies was to remain in the desert.

Two spies, however, returned with a completely different picture. Joshua and Caleb reported seeing a land filled with milk and honey. Compared to the desert, the land was beautiful. It was filled with green rolling hills, freshwater springs, and lush fruit trees. Their advice was to move ahead.

These two possibility thinkers looked at the opportunities, not the obstacles. Their only mention of the existing people and armies that needed to be conquered was "they *are* our bread; their protection has departed from them" (Num. 14:9). Their vision of the new land was greater than any problem that needed to be solved. In contrast, the other ten spies never mentioned the bounty of the country. They were too blinded by fear to see the good things.

After forty years of wandering in the inhospitable wilderness because of their unbelief, the Israelites advanced with Joshua and Caleb in command to conquer the land with a superb military strategy. Once they were aware of their problems they were able to overcome them. Their reward was worth the effort.

In our lives, we must guard against missing the beautiful opportunities because of seemingly impossible setbacks. We need to take on the attitude of the two spies and realize the possibilities around us. Once our eyes are set on the goal, the problems become minuscule and easily solved. Then we truly can move ahead with possibility thinking!

faces before all the assembly of the congregation of the children of Israel.
6 And Joshua the son of Nun and Caleb the son of Jephunneh, *who were* among those who had spied out the land, tore their clothes;
7 and they spoke to all the congregation of the children of Israel, saying: "The land we passed through to spy out *is* an exceedingly good land.
8 "If the LORD delights in us, then He will bring us into this land and give it to us, 'a land which flows with milk and honey.'[16]
9 "Only do not rebel against the LORD, nor fear the people of the land, for they *are* our bread; their protection has departed from them, and the LORD *is* with us. Do not fear them."
10 And all the congregation said to stone them with stones. Now the glory of the LORD appeared in the tabernacle of meeting before all the children of Israel.

Moses Intercedes for the People

11 And the LORD said to Moses: "How long will these people reject Me? And how long will they not believe Me, with all the signs which I have performed among them?
12 "I will strike them with the pestilence and disinherit them, and I will make of you a nation greater and mightier than they."
13 And Moses said to the LORD: "Then the Egyptians will hear *it*, for by Your might You brought these people up from among them,
14 "and they will tell *it* to the inhabitants of this land. They have heard that You, LORD, *are* among these people; that You, LORD, are seen face to face and *that* Your cloud stands above them; and You go before them in a pillar of cloud by day and in a pillar of fire by night.
15 "Now *if* You kill these people as one man, then the nations which have heard of Your fame will speak, saying,
16 'Because the LORD was not able to bring this people to the land which He swore to give them, therefore He killed them in the wilderness.'
17 "And now, I pray, let the power of my LORD be great, just as You have spoken, saying,
18 'The LORD is longsuffering and abundant in mercy, forgiving iniquity and

transgression; but He by no means clears *the guilty*, visiting the iniquity of the fathers on the children to the third and fourth *generation*.'[17]
19 "Pardon the iniquity of this people, I pray, according to the greatness of Your mercy, just as You have forgiven this people, from Egypt even until now."
20 Then the LORD said: "I have pardoned, according to your word;
21 "but truly, as I live, all the earth shall be filled with the glory of the LORD—
22 "because all these men who have seen My glory and the signs which I did in Egypt and in the wilderness, and have put Me to the test now these ten times, and have not heeded My voice,
23 "they certainly shall not see the land of which I swore to their fathers, nor shall any of those who rejected Me see it.
24 "But My servant Caleb, because he has a different spirit in him and has followed Me fully, I will bring into the land where he went, and his descendants shall inherit it.
25 "Now the Amalekites and the Canaanites dwell in the valley; tomorrow turn and move out into the wilderness by the Way of the Red Sea."

Death Sentence on the Rebels

26 Then the LORD spoke to Moses and Aaron, saying,
27 "How long *shall I bear with* this evil congregation who murmur against Me? I have heard the murmurings which the children of Israel murmur against Me.
28 "Say to them, 'As I live,' says the LORD, 'just as you have spoken in My hearing, so I will do to you:
29 'The carcasses of you who have murmured against Me shall fall in this wilderness, all of you who were numbered, according to your entire number, from twenty years old and above.
30 'Except for Caleb the son of Jephunneh and Joshua the son of Nun, you shall by no means enter the land which I swore I would make you dwell in.
31 'But your little ones, whom you said would be victims, I will bring in, and they shall know the land which you have despised.
32 'But *as for* you, your carcasses shall fall in this wilderness.
33 'And your sons shall be shepherds in the wilderness forty years, and bear the

16 Compare Exodus 3:8   17 Compare Exodus 34:6, 7

brunt of your infidelity, until your carcasses are consumed in the wilderness.

34 'According to the number of the days in which you spied out the land, forty days, for each day you shall bear your guilt one year, *namely* forty years, and you shall know My rejection.

35 'I the LORD have spoken this; I will surely do so to all this evil congregation who are gathered together against Me. In this wilderness they shall be consumed, and there they shall die.' "

36 And the men whom Moses sent to spy out the land, who returned and made all the congregation murmur against him by bringing a bad report of the land,

37 those very men who brought the evil report about the land, died by the plague before the LORD.

38 But Joshua the son of Nun and Caleb the son of Jephunneh remained alive, of the men who went to spy out the land.

A Futile Invasion Attempt

39 Then Moses told these words to all the children of Israel, and the people mourned greatly.

40 And they rose early in the morning and went up to the top of the mountain, saying, "Here we are, and we will go up to the place which the LORD has promised, for we have sinned!"

41 Then Moses said, "Now why do you transgress the command of the LORD? For this will not succeed.

42 "Do not go up, lest you be defeated by your enemies, for the LORD *is* not among you.

43 "For the Amalekites and the Canaanites *are* there before you, and you shall fall by the sword; because you have turned away from the LORD, the LORD will not be with you."

44 But they presumed to go up to the mountaintop; nevertheless, neither the ark of the covenant of the LORD nor Moses departed from the camp.

45 Then the Amalekites and the Canaanites who dwelt in that mountain came down and attacked them, and drove them back as far as Hormah.

Laws of Grain and Drink Offerings

15 And the LORD spoke to Moses, saying,

2 "Speak to the children of Israel, and say to them: 'When you have come into the land you are to inhabit, which I am giving to you,

3 'and you make an offering by fire to the LORD, a burnt offering or a sacrifice, to fulfill a vow or as a freewill offering or in your appointed feasts, to make a sweet aroma to the LORD, from the herd or the flock,

4 'then he who presents his offering to the LORD shall bring a grain offering of one-tenth *of an ephah* of fine flour mixed with one-fourth of a hin of oil;

5 'and one-fourth of a hin of wine as a drink offering you shall prepare with the burnt offering or the sacrifice, for each lamb.

6 'Or for a ram you shall prepare as a grain offering two-tenths *of an ephah* of fine flour mixed with one-third of a hin of oil;

7 'and as a drink offering you shall offer one-third of a hin of wine as a sweet aroma to the LORD.

8 'And when you prepare a young bull as a burnt offering, or as a sacrifice to fulfill a vow, or as a peace offering to the LORD,

9 'then shall be offered with the young bull a grain offering of three-tenths *of an ephah* of fine flour mixed with half a hin of oil;

10 'and you shall bring as the drink offering half a hin of wine as an offering made by fire, a sweet aroma to the LORD.

11 'Thus it shall be done for each young bull, for each ram, or for each lamb or young goat.

12 'According to the number that you prepare, so you shall do with everyone according to their number.

13 'All who are native-born shall do these things in this manner, in presenting an offering made by fire, a sweet aroma to the LORD.

14 'And if a stranger sojourns with you, or whoever *is* among you throughout your generations, and would present an offering made by fire, a sweet aroma to the LORD, just as you do, so shall he do.

15 'One ordinance *shall be* for you of the congregation and for the stranger who sojourns *with you*, an ordinance forever throughout your generations; as you are, so shall the stranger be before the LORD.

16 'One law and one custom shall be for you and for the stranger who sojourns with you.' "[18]

18 Compare Exodus 12:49

17 Again the LORD spoke to Moses, saying,
18 "Speak to the children of Israel, and say to them: 'When you come into the land to which I bring you,
19 'then it will be, when you eat of the bread of the land, that you shall offer up a heave offering to the LORD.
20 'You shall offer up a cake of the first of your ground meal *as* a heave offering; as a heave offering of the threshing floor, so shall you offer it up.
21 'Of the first of your ground meal you shall give to the LORD a heave offering throughout your generations.

Laws Concerning Unintentional Sin

22 'And if you sin unintentionally, and do not observe all these commandments which the LORD has spoken to Moses—
23 'all that the LORD has commanded you by the hand of Moses, from the day the LORD gave commandment and onward throughout your generations—
24 'then it will be, if it is unintentionally committed, without the knowledge of the congregation, that the whole congregation shall offer one young bull as a burnt offering, as a sweet aroma to the LORD, with its grain offering and its drink offering, according to the ordinance, and one kid of the goats as a sin offering.
25 'So the priest shall make atonement for the whole congregation of the children of Israel, and it shall be forgiven them, for it was unintentional; they shall bring their offering, an offering made by fire to the LORD, and their sin offering before the LORD, for their unintended sin.
26 'It shall be forgiven the whole congregation of the children of Israel and the stranger who sojourns among them, because all the people *did it* unintentionally.
27 'And if a person sins unintentionally, then he shall bring a female goat in its first year as a sin offering.
28 'So the priest shall make atonement for the person who sins unintentionally, when he sins unintentionally before the LORD, to make atonement for him; and it shall be forgiven him.
29 'You shall have one law for him who sins unintentionally, *both for* him who is native-born among the children of Israel and for the stranger who sojourns among them.

Laws Concerning Presumptuous Sin

30 'But the person who does *anything* presumptuously, *whether he is* native-born or a stranger, that one brings reproach on the LORD, and he shall be cut off from among his people.
31 'Because he has despised the word of the LORD, and has broken His commandment, that person shall be completely cut off; his guilt *shall be* upon him.' "

Penalty for Violating the Sabbath

32 Now while the children of Israel were in the wilderness, they found a man gathering sticks on the Sabbath day.
33 And those who found him gathering sticks brought him to Moses and Aaron, and to all the congregation.
34 They put him under guard, because it had not been explained what should be done to him.
35 Then the LORD said to Moses, "The man must surely be put to death; all the congregation shall stone him with stones outside the camp."
36 So, as the LORD commanded Moses, all the congregation brought him outside the camp and stoned him with stones, and he died.

Tassels on Garments

37 Again the LORD spoke to Moses, saying,
38 "Speak to the children of Israel: Tell them to make tassels on the corners of their garments throughout their generations, and to put a blue thread in the tassels of the corners.
39 "And you shall have the tassel, that you may look upon it and remember all the commandments of the LORD and do them, and that you *may* not follow the harlotry to which your own heart and your own eyes are inclined,
40 "and that you may remember and do all My commandments, and be holy for your God.
41 "I *am* the LORD your God, who brought you out of the land of Egypt, to be your God: I *am* the LORD your God."

Rebellion Against Moses and Aaron

16 Now Korah the son of Izhar, the son of Kohath, the son of Levi, with Dathan and Abiram the sons of Eliab, and On the son of Peleth, sons of Reuben, took *men*;
2 and they rose up before Moses with

some of the children of Israel, two hundred and fifty leaders of the congregation, representatives of the congregation, men of renown.

3 They gathered together against Moses and Aaron, and said to them, "*You take too much upon yourselves, for all the congregation is holy, every one of them, and the* LORD *is among them. Why then do you exalt yourselves above the congregation of the* LORD?"

4 So when Moses heard *it*, he fell on his face;

5 and he spoke to Korah and all his company, saying, "Tomorrow morning the LORD will show who *is* His and *who is* holy, and will cause *him* to come near to Him; that one whom He chooses He will cause to come near to Him.

6 "Do this: Take censers, Korah and all your company;

7 "put fire in them and put incense in them before the LORD tomorrow, and it shall be *that* the man whom the LORD chooses *shall be* the holy one. *You take too much upon yourselves, you sons of Levi!*"

8 Then Moses said to Korah, "Hear now, you sons of Levi:

9 "*Is it* a small thing to you that the God of Israel has separated you from the congregation of Israel, to bring you near to Himself, to do the work of the tabernacle of the LORD, and to stand before the congregation to serve them;

10 "and that He has brought you near *to Himself*, you and all your brethren, the sons of Levi, with you? And are you seeking the priesthood also?

11 "Therefore you and all your company *are* gathered together against the LORD. And what *is* Aaron that you murmur against him?"

12 And Moses sent to call Dathan and Abiram the sons of Eliab, but they said, "We will not come up!

13 "*Is it* a small thing that you have brought us up out of a land flowing with milk and honey, to kill us in the wilderness, that you should keep acting like a prince over us?

14 "Moreover you have not brought us into a land flowing with milk and honey, nor given us inheritance of fields and vineyards. Will you put out the eyes of these men? We will not come up!"

15 Then Moses was very angry, and said

to the LORD, "Do not respect their offering. I have not taken one donkey from them, nor have I hurt one of them."

16 And Moses said to Korah, "Tomorrow, you and all your company be present before the LORD—you and they, as well as Aaron.

17 "Each of you take his censer and put incense in it, and each of you bring his censer before the LORD, two hundred and fifty censers; you also, and Aaron, each *of you* with his censer."

18 So every man took his censer, put fire in it, laid incense on it, and stood at the door of the tabernacle of meeting with Moses and Aaron.

19 And Korah gathered all the congregation against them at the door of the tabernacle of meeting. Then the glory of the LORD appeared to all the congregation.

20 And the LORD spoke to Moses and Aaron, saying,

21 "Separate yourselves from among this congregation, that I may consume them in a moment."

22 Then they fell on their faces, and said, "O God, the God of the spirits of all flesh, shall one man sin, and You be angry with all the congregation?"

23 So the LORD spoke to Moses, saying,

24 "Speak to the congregation, saying, 'Get away from the tents of Korah, Dathan, and Abiram.' "

25 Then Moses rose and went to Dathan and Abiram, and the elders of Israel followed him.

26 And he spoke to the congregation, saying, "Depart now from the tents of these wicked men! Touch nothing of theirs, lest you be consumed in all their sins."

27 So they got away from around the tents of Korah, Dathan, and Abiram; and Dathan and Abiram came out and stood at the door of their tents, with their wives, their sons, and their little children.

28 Then Moses said: "By this you shall know that the LORD has sent me to do all these works, for *I have* not *done them* of my own will.

29 "If these men die naturally like all men, or if they are visited by the common fate of all men, *then* the LORD has not sent me.

30 "But if the LORD creates a new thing, and the earth opens its mouth and swallows them up with all that belongs to

them, and they go down alive into the pit, then you will understand that these men have rejected the LORD."

31 Then it came to pass, as he finished speaking all these words, that the ground split apart under them,

32 and the earth opened its mouth and swallowed them up, with their households and all the men with Korah, with all *their* goods.

33 So they and all those with them went down alive into the pit; the earth closed over them, and they perished from among the congregation.

34 Then all Israel who *were* around them fled at their cry, for they said, "Lest the earth swallow us up *also!*"

35 And a fire came out from the LORD and consumed the two hundred and fifty men who were offering incense.

36 Then the LORD spoke to Moses, saying:

37 "Tell Eleazar, the son of Aaron the priest, to pick up the censers out of the blaze, for they are holy, and scatter the fire some distance away.

38 "The censers of these men who sinned against their own souls, let them be made into hammered plates as a covering for the altar. Because they presented them before the LORD, therefore they are holy; and they shall be a sign to the children of Israel."

39 So Eleazar the priest took the bronze censers, which those who were burned up had presented, and they were hammered out as a covering on the altar,

40 *to be* a memorial to the children of Israel that no outsider, who *is* not a descendant of Aaron, should come near to offer incense before the LORD, that he might not become like Korah and his companions, just as the LORD had said to him through Moses.

Murmuring of the People

41 On the next day all the congregation of the children of Israel murmured against Moses and Aaron, saying, "You have killed the people of the LORD."

42 Now it happened, when the congregation had gathered against Moses and Aaron, that they turned toward the tabernacle of meeting; and suddenly the cloud covered it, and the glory of the LORD appeared.

43 Then Moses and Aaron came before the tabernacle of meeting.

44 And the LORD spoke to Moses, saying,

45 "Get away from among this congregation, that I may consume them in a moment." And they fell on their faces.

46 So Moses said to Aaron, "Take a censer and put fire in it from the altar, put incense *on it*, and take it quickly to the congregation and make atonement for them; for wrath has gone out from the LORD. The plague has begun."

47 Then Aaron took *it* as Moses commanded, and ran into the midst of the congregation; and already the plague had begun among the people. So he put in the incense and made atonement for the people.

48 And he stood between the dead and the living; so the plague was stopped.

49 Now those who died in the plague were fourteen thousand seven hundred, besides those who died in the Korah incident.

50 So Aaron returned to Moses at the door of the tabernacle of meeting, for the plague had stopped.

The Budding of Aaron's Rod

17 And the LORD spoke to Moses, saying:

2 "Speak to the children of Israel, and get from them a rod from each father's house, all their leaders according to their fathers' houses—twelve rods. Write each man's name on his rod.

3 "And you shall write Aaron's name on the rod of Levi. For there shall be one rod for the head of *each* father's house.

4 "Then you shall place them in the tabernacle of meeting before the Testimony, where I meet with you.

5 "And it shall be *that* the rod of the man whom I choose will blossom; thus I will rid Myself of the murmurings of the children of Israel, which they murmur against you."

6 So Moses spoke to the children of Israel, and each of their leaders gave him a rod apiece, for each leader according to their fathers' houses, twelve rods; and the rod of Aaron *was* among their rods.

7 And Moses placed the rods before the LORD in the tabernacle of witness.

8 Now it came to pass on the next day that Moses went into the tabernacle of witness, and behold, the rod of Aaron, of the house of Levi, had sprouted and put forth buds, had produced blossoms and yielded ripe almonds.

9 Then Moses brought out all the rods from before the LORD to all the children of Israel; and they looked, and each man took his rod.

10 And the LORD said to Moses, "Bring Aaron's rod back before the Testimony, to be kept as a sign against the rebels, that you may put their murmurings away from Me, lest they die."

11 Thus did Moses; just as the LORD had commanded him, so he did.

12 And the children of Israel spoke to Moses, saying, "Surely we die, we perish, we all perish!

13 "Whoever even comes near the tabernacle of the LORD must die. Shall we all utterly die?"

Duties of Priests and Levites

18 Then the LORD said to Aaron: "You and your sons and your father's house with you shall bear the iniquity *related to* the sanctuary, and you and your sons with you shall bear the iniquity *associated with* your priesthood.

2 "Also bring with you your brethren of the tribe of Levi, the tribe of your father, that they may be joined with you and serve you while you and your sons *are* with you before the tabernacle of witness.

3 "They shall attend to your needs and all the needs of the tabernacle; but they shall not come near the articles of the sanctuary and the altar, lest they die—they and you also.

4 "They shall be joined with you and attend to the needs of the tabernacle of meeting, for all the work of the tabernacle; but an outsider shall not come near you.

5 "And you shall attend to the duties of the sanctuary and the duties of the altar, that there *may* be no more wrath on the children of Israel.

6 "Behold, I Myself have taken your brethren the Levites from among the children of Israel; *they are* a gift to you, given by the LORD, to do the work of the tabernacle of meeting.

7 "Therefore you and your sons with you shall attend to your priesthood for everything at the altar and behind the veil; and you shall serve. I give your

priesthood *to you* as a gift for service, but the outsider who comes near shall be put to death."

Offerings for Support of the Priests

8 And the LORD spoke to Aaron: "Here, I Myself have also given you charge of My heave offerings, all the holy gifts of the children of Israel; I have given them as a portion to you and your sons, as an ordinance forever.

9 "This shall be yours of the most holy things *reserved* from the fire: every offering of theirs, every grain offering and every sin offering and every trespass offering which they render to Me, *shall be* most holy for you and your sons.

10 "In a most holy *place* you shall eat it; every male shall eat it. It shall be holy to you.

11 "This also *is* yours: the heave offering of their gift, with all the wave offerings of the children of Israel; I have given them to you, and your sons and daughters with you, as an ordinance forever. Everyone who is clean in your house may eat it.

12 "All the best of the oil, all the best of the new wine and the grain, their firstfruits which they offer to the LORD, I have given them to you.

13 "Whatever first ripe fruit is in their land, which they bring to the LORD, shall be yours. Everyone who is clean in your house may eat it.

14 "Every devoted thing in Israel shall be yours.

15 "Everything that first opens the womb of all flesh, which they bring to the LORD, whether man or beast, shall be yours; nevertheless the firstborn of man you shall surely redeem, and the firstborn of unclean animals you shall redeem.

16 "And those redeemed of the devoted things you shall redeem when one month old, according to your valuation, for five shekels of silver, according to the shekel of the sanctuary, which *is* twenty gerahs.

17 "But the firstborn of a cow, the firstborn of a sheep, or the firstborn of a goat you shall not redeem; they *are* holy. You shall sprinkle their blood on the altar, and burn their fat *as* an offering made by fire for a sweet aroma to the LORD.

18 "And their flesh shall be yours, just as the wave breast and the right thigh are yours.

19 "All the heave offerings of the holy

things, which the children of Israel offer to the LORD, I have given to you and your sons and daughters with you as an ordinance forever; it *is* a covenant of salt forever before the LORD with you and your descendants with you."
20 Then the LORD said to Aaron: "You shall have no inheritance in their land, nor shall you have any portion among them; I *am* your portion and your inheritance among the children of Israel.

Tithes for Support of the Levites

21 "Behold, I have given the children of Levi all the tithes in Israel as an inheritance in return for the work which they perform, the work of the tabernacle of meeting.
22 "Hereafter the children of Israel shall not come near the tabernacle of meeting, lest they bear sin and die.
23 "But the Levites shall perform the work of the tabernacle of meeting, and they shall bear their iniquity; *it shall be* a statute forever, throughout your generations, that among the children of Israel they shall have no inheritance.
24 "For the tithes of the children of Israel, which they offer up *as* a heave offering to the LORD, I have given to the Levites as an inheritance; therefore I have said to them, 'Among the children of Israel they shall have no inheritance.' "

The Tithe of the Levites

25 Then the LORD spoke to Moses, saying,
26 "Speak thus to the Levites, and say to them: 'When you take from the children of Israel the tithes which I have given you from them as your inheritance, then you shall offer up a heave offering of it to the LORD, a tenth of the tithe.
27 'And your heave offering shall be reckoned to you as though *it were* the grain of the threshing floor and as the fullness of the winepress.
28 'Thus you shall also offer a heave offering to the LORD from all your tithes which you receive from the children of Israel, and you shall give the LORD's heave offering from it to Aaron the priest.
29 'Of all your gifts you shall offer up every heave offering due to the LORD, from all the best of them, the sanctified part of them.'
30 "Therefore you shall say to them:

'When you have lifted up the best of it, then *the rest* shall be accounted to the Levites as the produce of the threshing floor and as the produce of the winepress.
31 'You may eat it in any place, you and your households, for it *is* your reward for your work in the tabernacle of meeting.
32 'And you shall bear no sin because of it, when you have lifted up the best of it. But you shall not profane the holy gifts of the children of Israel, lest you die.' "

Laws of Purification

19 Now the LORD spoke to Moses and Aaron, saying,
2 "This *is* the ordinance of the law which the LORD has commanded, saying: 'Speak to the children of Israel, that they bring you a red heifer without blemish, in which there *is* no defect *and* on which a yoke has never come.
3 'You shall give it to Eleazar the priest, that he may take it outside the camp, and it shall be slaughtered before him;
4 'and Eleazar the priest shall take some of its blood with his finger, and sprinkle some of its blood seven times directly in front of the tabernacle of meeting.
5 'Then the heifer shall be burned in his sight: its hide, its flesh, its blood, and its offal shall be burned.
6 'And the priest shall take cedar wood and hyssop and scarlet, and cast *them* into the midst of the fire burning the heifer.
7 'Then the priest shall wash his clothes, he shall bathe in water, and afterward he shall come into the camp; the priest shall be unclean until evening.
8 'And the one who burns it shall wash his clothes in water, bathe in water, and shall be unclean until evening.
9 'Then a man *who is* clean shall gather up the ashes of the heifer, and store *them* outside the camp in a clean place; and they shall be kept for the congregation of the children of Israel for the water of purification;[19] it *is* for purifying from sin.
10 'And the one who gathers the ashes of the heifer shall wash his clothes, and be unclean until evening. It shall be a statute forever to the children of Israel and to the stranger who sojourns among them.
11 'He who touches the dead body of anyone shall be unclean seven days.
12 'He shall purify himself with the water on the third day and on the seventh day;

19 Literally *impurity*

then he will be clean. But if he does not purify himself on the third day and on the seventh day, he will not be clean.

13 'Whoever touches the body of anyone who has died, and does not purify himself, defiles the tabernacle of the LORD. That person shall be cut off from Israel. He shall be unclean, because the water of purification was not sprinkled on him; his uncleanness *is* still on him.

14 'This *is* the law when a man dies in a tent: All who come into the tent and all who *are* in the tent shall be unclean seven days;

15 'and every open vessel, which has no cover fastened on it, *is* unclean.

16 'Whoever in the open field touches one who is slain by a sword or who has died, or a bone of a man, or a grave, shall be unclean seven days.

17 'And for an unclean *person* they shall take some of the ashes of the heifer burnt for purification from sin, and running water shall be put on them in a vessel.

18 'A clean person shall take hyssop and dip *it* in the water, sprinkle *it* on the tent, on all the vessels, on the persons who were there, or on the one who touched a bone, the slain, the dead, or a grave.

19 'The clean *person* shall sprinkle the unclean on the third day and on the seventh day; and on the seventh day he shall purify himself, wash his clothes, and bathe in water; and at evening he shall be clean.

20 'But the man who is unclean and does not purify himself, that person shall be cut off from among the congregation, because he has defiled the sanctuary of the LORD. The water of purification has not been sprinkled on him; he *is* unclean.

21 'It shall be a perpetual statute for them. He who sprinkles the water of purification shall wash his clothes; and he who touches the water of purification shall be unclean until evening.

22 'Whatever the unclean *person* touches shall be unclean; and the person who touches *it* shall be unclean until evening.' "

Moses' Error at Kadesh

20 Then the children of Israel, the whole congregation, came into the Wilderness of Zin in the first month, and the people stayed in Kadesh; and Miriam died there and was buried there.

2 Now there was no water for the congregation; so they gathered together against Moses and Aaron.

3 And the people contended with Moses and spoke, saying: "If only we had died when our brethren died before the LORD!

4 "Why have you brought up the congregation of the LORD into this wilderness, that we and our animals should die here?

5 "And why have you made us come up out of Egypt, to bring us to this evil place? It *is* not a place of grain or figs or vines or pomegranates; nor *is* there any water to drink."

6 So Moses and Aaron went from the presence of the assembly to the door of the tabernacle of meeting, and they fell on their faces. And the glory of the LORD appeared to them.

7 Then the LORD spoke to Moses, saying,

8 "Take the rod; you and your brother Aaron gather the assembly together. Speak to the rock before their eyes, and it will yield its water; thus you shall bring water for them out of the rock, and give drink to the congregation and their animals."

9 So Moses took the rod from before the LORD as He commanded him.

10 And Moses and Aaron gathered the congregation together before the rock; and he said to them, "Hear now, you rebels! Must we bring water for you out of this rock?"

11 Then Moses lifted his hand and struck the rock twice with his rod; and water came out abundantly, and the congregation and their animals drank.

12 Then the LORD spoke to Moses and Aaron, "Because you did not believe Me, to hallow Me in the eyes of the children of Israel, therefore you shall not bring this congregation into the land which I have given them."

13 This *was* the water of Meribah,[20] because the children of Israel contended with the LORD, and He was hallowed among them.

Passage Through Edom Refused

14 Now Moses sent messengers from Kadesh to the king of Edom. "Thus says your brother Israel: 'You know all the hardship that has befallen us,

15 'how our fathers went down to Egypt,

20 Literally *Contention*

Water from a Rock

There is no hopeless situation until you become a hopeless person. From Moses, we learn a powerful lesson to believe in God's unlimited ability!

With God's help, Moses faced the mighty Pharaoh to lead the children of Israel out of Egypt. Even through forty years in the desert of Sinai, he stood fast in his faithfulness. In the vast, harsh wilderness, Moses looked to God to provide the needs of his people. He learned the ancient survival secrets held and still practiced by the nomadic Bedouin shepherds who live in the Sinai desert today. A constant problem for Moses and the Bedouins today is the scarcity of food and water. But to those who know its secrets, the desert holds many life-giving resources.

Every year thousands of quail migrate south from modern-day Turkey across the Mediterranean to the coast of Sinai and North Africa. Exhausted from their trans-Mediterranean flight, the quail fall to the desert sand of the Sinai coast. It was a simple task for Moses and the children of Israel to gather the quail, but the timing and large number of quail demonstrates God's supernatural power as "the Provider." "Now a wind went out from the LORD, and it brought quail from the sea and left *them* fluttering near the camp" (Num. 11:31). Today, as a variation of this practice the Bedouin set up nets to entrap the tired quail for their meals.

The desert also provides water for the experienced traveler. The large, black granite mountains, rising sharply from the desert floor, hide reservoirs of water within their walls. Rainfall seeps into the mountain crevices and is trapped in the porous limestone veins woven throughout the granite cliffs. One sharp blow of a staff to the limestone, brings forth a gushing stream of water.

Moses knew of this common practice. Yet God asked Moses to perform the uncommon. He told Moses to go and speak to the rock. Moses, accustomed to hitting the rock, failed to recognize God's unlimited abilities. Moses was so skilled in the ordinary that he did not see God's power at work. He expected God to provide the water for that vast number of people in the ordinary way. God wanted to do the extraordinary.

God's plan for our lives may include extraordinary opportunities. Be open to the possibility of God doing the impossible in your life. Believe in God's unlimited ability!

and we dwelt in Egypt a long time, and the Egyptians afflicted us and our fathers.
16 'When we cried out to the LORD, He heard our voice and sent the Angel and brought us up out of Egypt; now here we are in Kadesh, a city on the edge of your border.
17 'Please let us pass through your country. We will not pass through fields or vineyards, nor will we drink water from wells; we will go along the King's Highway; we will not turn aside to the right hand or to the left until we have passed through your territory.' "
18 Then Edom said to him, "You shall not pass through my *land*, lest I come out against you with the sword."
19 So the children of Israel said to him, "We will go by the Highway, and if I or my livestock drink any of your water, then I will pay for it; let me only pass through on foot, nothing *more*."
20 Then he said, "You shall not pass through." So Edom came out against them with many men and with a strong hand.
21 Thus Edom refused to give Israel passage through his territory; so Israel turned away from him.

Death of Aaron

22 Then the children of Israel, the whole congregation, journeyed from Kadesh and came to Mount Hor.
23 And the LORD spoke to Moses and Aaron in Mount Hor by the border of the land of Edom, saying:
24 "Aaron shall be gathered to his people, for he shall not enter the land which I have given to the children of Israel, because you rebelled against My word at the water of Meribah.
25 "Take Aaron and Eleazar his son, and bring them up to Mount Hor;
26 "and strip Aaron of his garments and put them on Eleazar his son; for Aaron shall be gathered *to his people* and die there."
27 So Moses did just as the LORD commanded, and they went up to Mount Hor in the sight of all the congregation.
28 Moses stripped Aaron of his garments and put them on Eleazar his son; and Aaron died there on the top of the mountain. Then Moses and Eleazar came down from the mountain.
29 Now when all the congregation saw

that Aaron was dead, all the house of Israel mourned for Aaron thirty days.

Canaanites Defeated at Hormah

21 When the king of Arad, the Canaanite, who dwelt in the South, heard that Israel was coming on the road to Atharim, then he fought against Israel and took *some* of them prisoners.
2 So Israel made a vow to the LORD, and said, "If You will indeed deliver this people into my hand, then I will utterly destroy their cities."
3 And the LORD listened to the voice of Israel and delivered up the Canaanites, and they utterly destroyed them and their cities. So the name of that place was called Hormah.²¹

The Bronze Serpent

4 Then they journeyed from Mount Hor by the Way of the Red Sea, to go around the land of Edom; and the soul of the people became very discouraged on the way.
5 And the people spoke against God and against Moses: "Why have you brought us up out of Egypt to die in the wilderness? For *there is* no food and no water, and our soul loathes this worthless bread."
6 So the LORD sent fiery serpents among the people, and they bit the people; and many of the people of Israel died.
7 Therefore the people came to Moses, and said, "We have sinned, for we have spoken against the LORD and against you; pray to the LORD that He take away the serpents from us." So Moses prayed for the people.
8 Then the LORD said to Moses, "Make a fiery *serpent*, and set it on a pole; and it shall be that everyone who is bitten, when he looks at it, shall live."
9 So Moses made a bronze serpent, and put it on a pole; and so it was, if a serpent had bitten anyone, when he looked at the bronze serpent, he lived.

From Mount Hor to Moab

10 Now the children of Israel moved on and camped in Oboth.
11 And they journeyed from Oboth and camped at Ije Abarim, in the wilderness which *is* east of Moab, toward the sunrise.

21 Literally *Utter Destruction*

Allow God

A little-understood Scripture is Jesus' statement, "As Moses lifted up the serpent in the wilderness, even so must the Son of Man be lifted up" (John 3:14).

During the Israelite wanderings in Sinai, the people were inflicted with snake bites. God asked Moses to make an image of a bronze serpent and lift it up for all the people of Israel to see. Then when they were bitten by snakes, they needed only look at the bronze serpent to be healed.

We know from the Book of Exodus, that Moses' father-in-law was a priest in the land of Midian. Moses spent many years tending flocks in this country. Undoubtedly, he was exposed to the Midianite practice of worshiping snakes.

A recent archaeological discovery in Sinai verifies that Midianites worshiped snakes. A Midianite temple, with various cultic vessels, was discovered with a bronze serpent lying across the central altar.

When the Israelites were bitten by snakes, God used something that was thought by Moses to be negative in his past to produce a life-giving healing result for the people of Israel. Jesus' reference to this event, in association with His coming death and resurrection is quite clear now. God can use any negative event in the history of His people or in the life of His only Son to reinterpret it and turn it into a positive life-giving result. The cross of Jesus Christ is perhaps the most cruel, vicious act imposed on any innocent person in history. But God turned it around as the most positive life-giving event, the resurrection of Jesus Christ.

Do not limit God. Allow Him to take anything He wants from your life and turn it into a blessing for you and others. Modern educational disciplines, such as psychology and philosophy, can be used when they make room for God in a positive way. Allow God to take an old negative event in your life, and put it into a positive light. Remember, let go and let God!

12 From there they moved and camped in the Valley of Zered.

13 From there they moved and camped on the other side of the Arnon, which *is* in the wilderness that extends from the border of the Amorites; for the Arnon *is* the border of Moab, between Moab and the Amorites.

14 Therefore it is said in the Book of the Wars of the LORD:

"Waheb in Suphah,[22]
The brooks of the Arnon,
15 And the slope of the brooks
That reaches to the dwelling of Ar,
And lies on the border of Moab."

16 And from there *they* went to Beer, which *is* the well where the LORD said to Moses, "Gather the people together, and I will give them water."

17 Then Israel sang this song:

"Spring up, O well!
All of you sing to it—
18 The well the leaders sank,
Dug by the nation's nobles,
By the lawgiver, with their staves."

And from the wilderness *they* went to Mattanah,
19 from Mattanah to Nahaliel, from Nahaliel to Bamoth,
20 and from Bamoth, *in* the valley that *is* in the country of Moab, to the top of Pisgah which looks down on the wasteland.[23]

King Sihon Defeated

21 Then Israel sent messengers to Sihon king of the Amorites, saying,

22 "Let me pass through your land. We will not turn aside into fields or vineyards; we will not drink water from wells; *but* we will go by the King's Highway until we have passed through your territory."

23 But Sihon would not allow Israel to pass through his territory. So Sihon gathered all his people together and went out against Israel in the wilderness, and he came to Jahaz and fought against Israel.

24 Then Israel defeated him with the edge of the sword, and took possession of his land from the Arnon to the Jabbok, as far as the people of Ammon; for the border of the people of Ammon *was* fortified.

25 So Israel took all these cities, and Israel dwelt in all the cities of the Amorites, in Heshbon and in all its villages.

26 For Heshbon *was* the city of Sihon king of the Amorites, who had fought against the former king of Moab, and had taken all his land from his hand as far as the Arnon.

27 Therefore those who speak in proverbs say:

"Come to Heshbon, let it be built;
Let the city of Sihon be repaired.

28 "For fire went out from Heshbon,
A flame from the city of Sihon;
It consumed Ar of Moab,
The lords of the heights of the Arnon.

29 Woe to you, Moab!
You have perished,
O people of Chemosh!
He has given his sons as fugitives,
And his daughters into captivity,
To Sihon king of the Amorites.

30 "But we have shot at them;
Heshbon has perished as far as Dibon.
Then we laid waste as far as Nophah,
Which *reaches* to Medeba."

31 Thus Israel dwelt in the land of the Amorites.

32 Then Moses sent to spy out Jazer; and they took its villages and drove out the Amorites who *were* there.

King Og Defeated

33 And they turned and went up by the way to Bashan. So Og king of Bashan went out against them, he and all his people, to battle at Edrei.

34 Then the LORD said to Moses, "Do not fear him, for I have delivered him into your hand, with all his people and his land; and you shall do to him as you did to Sihon king of the Amorites, who dwelt at Heshbon."

35 So they defeated him, his sons, and all his people, until there was no survivor left him; and they took possession of his land.

Balak Sends for Balaam

22 Then the children of Israel moved, and camped in the plains of Moab on the side of the Jordan *across from* Jericho.

2 Now Balak the son of Zippor saw all that Israel had done to the Amorites.

22 Ancient unknown places; Vulgate reads *what He did in the Red Sea.*   23 Hebrew *Jeshimon*

3 And Moab was exceedingly afraid of the people because they *were* many, and Moab was sick with dread because of the children of Israel.

4 So Moab said to the elders of Midian, "Now this company will lick up all *that is* around us, as an ox licks up the grass of the field." And Balak the son of Zippor *was* king of the Moabites at that time.

5 Then he sent messengers to Balaam the son of Beor at Pethor, which *is* near the River[24] in the land of the sons of his people,[25] to call him, saying: "Look, a people has come from Egypt. See, they cover the face of the earth, and are settling next to me!

6 "Therefore please come at once, curse this people for me, for they *are* too mighty for me. Perhaps I shall be able to defeat them and drive them out of the land, for I know that he whom you bless *is* blessed, and he whom you curse is cursed."

7 So the elders of Moab and the elders of Midian departed with the diviner's fee in their hand, and they came to Balaam and spoke to him the words of Balak.

8 And he said to them, "Lodge here tonight, and I will bring back word to you, as the LORD speaks to me." So the princes of Moab stayed with Balaam.

9 Then God came to Balaam and said, "Who *are* these men with you?"

10 And Balaam said to God, "Balak the son of Zippor, king of Moab, has sent to me, *saying,*

11 'Look, a people has come out of Egypt, and they cover the face of the earth. Come now, curse them for me; perhaps I shall be able to overpower them and drive them out.' "

12 And God said to Balaam, "You shall not go with them; you shall not curse the people, for they *are* blessed."

13 So Balaam rose in the morning and said to the princes of Balak, "Go back to your land, for the LORD has refused to give me permission to go with you."

14 And the princes of Moab rose and went to Balak, and said, "Balaam refuses to come with us."

15 Then Balak again sent princes, more numerous and more honorable than they.

16 And they came to Balaam and said to him. "Thus says Balak the son of Zippor: 'Please let nothing hinder you from coming to me;

17 'for I will certainly honor you greatly, and I will do whatever you say to me. Therefore please come, curse this people for me.' "

18 Then Balaam answered and said to the servants of Balak, "Though Balak were to give me his house full of silver and gold, I could not go beyond the word of the LORD my God, to do less or more.

19 "Now therefore, please, you also stay here tonight, that I may know what more the LORD will say to me."

20 And God came to Balaam at night and said to him, "If the men come to call you, rise *and* go with them; but only the word which I speak to you—that you shall do."

21 So Balaam rose in the morning, saddled his donkey, and went with the princes of Moab.

Balaam, the Donkey, and the Angel

22 Then God's anger was aroused because he went, and the Angel of the LORD took His stand in the way as an adversary against him. And he was riding on his donkey, and his two servants *were* with him.

23 Now the donkey saw the Angel of the LORD standing in the way with His drawn sword in His hand, and the donkey turned aside out of the way and went into the field. So Balaam struck the donkey to turn her back onto the road.

24 Then the Angel of the LORD stood in a narrow path between the vineyards, *with* a wall on this side and a wall on that side.

25 And when the donkey saw the Angel of the LORD, she pushed herself against the wall and crushed Balaam's foot against the wall; so he struck her again.

26 Then the Angel of the LORD went further, and stood in a narrow place where there *was* no way to turn either to the right hand or to the left.

27 And when the donkey saw the Angel of the LORD, she lay down under Balaam; so Balaam's anger was aroused, and he struck the donkey with his staff.

28 Then the LORD opened the mouth of the donkey, and she said to Balaam, "What have I done to you, that you have struck me these three times?"

29 And Balaam said to the donkey, "Because you have abused me. I wish there

24 That is, the Euphrates 25 Or *the people of Amau*

were a sword in my hand, for now I would kill you!"

30 So the donkey said to Balaam, "*Am* I not your donkey on which you have ridden, ever since *I* became yours, to this day? Was I ever disposed to do this to you?" And he said, "No."

31 Then the LORD opened Balaam's eyes, and he saw the Angel of the LORD standing in the way with His drawn sword in His hand; and he bowed his head and fell flat on his face.

32 And the Angel of the LORD said to him, "Why have you struck your donkey these three times? Behold, I have come out to stand against you, because *your* way is perverse before Me.

33 "The donkey saw Me and turned aside from Me these three times. If she had not turned aside from Me, surely I would also have killed you by now, and let her live."

34 And Balaam said to the Angel of the LORD, "I have sinned, for I did not know You stood in the way against me. Now therefore, if it displeases You, I will turn back."

35 Then the Angel of the LORD said to Balaam, "Go with the men, but only the word that I speak to you, that you shall speak." So Balaam went with the princes of Balak.

36 Now when Balak heard that Balaam was coming, he went out to meet him at the city of Moab, which *is* on the border at the Arnon, the boundary of the territory.

37 Then Balak said to Balaam, "Did I not earnestly send to you, calling for you? Why did you not come to me? Am I not able to honor you?"

38 And Balaam said to Balak, "Look, I have come to you! Now, have I any power at all to say anything? The word that God puts in my mouth, that I must speak."

39 So Balaam went with Balak, and they came to Kirjath Huzoth.

40 Then Balak offered oxen and sheep, and he sent *some* to Balaam and to the princes who *were* with him.

Balaam's First Prophecy

41 So it was the next day, that Balak took Balaam and brought him up to the high places of Baal, that from there he might observe the extent of the people.

23 Then Balaam said to Balak, "Build seven altars for me here, and prepare for me here seven bulls and seven rams."

2 And Balak did just as Balaam had spoken, and Balak and Balaam offered a bull and a ram on *each* altar.

3 Then Balaam said to Balak, "Stand by your burnt offering, and I will go; perhaps the LORD will come to meet me, and whatever He shows me I will tell you." So he went to a desolate height.

4 And God met Balaam, and he said to Him, "I have prepared the seven altars, and I have offered on *each* altar a bull and a ram."

5 Then the LORD put a word in Balaam's mouth, and said, "Return to Balak, and thus you shall speak."

6 So he returned to him, and there he was, standing by his burnt offering, he and all the princes of Moab.

7 And he took up his oracle and said:

"Balak the king of Moab
　　has brought me from Aram,
From the mountains of the east.
'Come, curse Jacob for me,
And come, denounce Israel!'

8 "How shall I curse
　　whom God has not cursed?
And how shall I denounce
　　whom the LORD has not denounced?
9 For from the top of the rocks
　　I see him,
And from the hills I behold him;
There! A people dwelling alone,
Not reckoning itself among the nations.

10 "Who can count the dust of Jacob,
Or number one-fourth[26] of Israel?
Let me die the death of the righteous,
And let my end be like his!"

11 Then Balak said to Balaam, "What have you done to me? I took you to curse my enemies, and look, you have blessed *them* bountifully!"

12 So he answered and said, "Must I not take heed to speak what the LORD has put in my mouth?"

Balaam's Second Prophecy

13 Then Balak said to him, "Please come with me to another place from which you may see them; you shall see only the

---

26 Or *dust cloud*

outer part of them, and shall not see them all; curse them for me from there."
14 So he brought him to the field of Zophim, to the top of Pisgah, and built seven altars, and offered a bull and a ram on *each* altar.
15 And he said to Balak, "Stand here by your burnt offering while I meet *the* LORD over there."
16 Then the LORD met Balaam, and put a word in his mouth, and said, "Go back to Balak, and thus you shall speak."
17 So he came to him, and there he was, standing by his burnt offering, and the princes of Moab were with him. And Balak said to him, "What has the LORD spoken?"
18 Then he took up his oracle and said:

"Rise up, Balak, and hear!
Listen to me, son of Zippor!

19 "God *is* not a man, that He should lie,
Nor a son of man,
that He should repent.
Has He said, and will He not do *it?*
Or has He spoken,
and will He not make it good?
20 Behold, I have received
a command to bless;
He has blessed, and I cannot reverse it.

21 "He has not observed iniquity in Jacob,
Nor has He seen wickedness in Israel.
The LORD his God *is* with him,
And the shout of a King
is among them.
22 God brings them out of Egypt;
He has strength like a wild ox.

23 "For *there is* no sorcery against Jacob,
Nor *is there* any divination
against Israel.
It now must be said of Jacob
And of Israel,
'Oh, what God has done!'
24 Look, a people rises like a lioness,
And lifts itself up like a lion;
It shall not lie down
until it devours the prey,
And drinks the blood of the slain."

25 Then Balak said to Balaam, "Neither curse them at all, nor bless them at all!"
26 So Balaam answered and said to Balak, "Did I not tell you, saying, 'All that the LORD speaks, that I must do'?"

Balaam's Third Prophecy

27 Then Balak said to Balaam, "Please come, I will take you to another place; perhaps it will please God that you may curse them for me from there."
28 So Balak took Balaam to the top of Peor, that overlooks the wasteland.[27]
29 Then Balaam said to Balak, "Build for me here seven altars, and prepare for me here seven bulls and seven rams."
30 And Balak did as Balaam had said, and offered a bull and a ram on *every* altar.

24 Now when Balaam saw that it pleased the LORD to bless Israel, he did not go as at other times, to seek to use sorcery, but he set his face toward the wilderness.
2 And Balaam raised his eyes, and saw Israel encamped according to their tribes; and the Spirit of God came upon him.
3 Then he took up his oracle and said:

"The utterance of Balaam
the son of Beor,
The utterance of the man
whose eyes are opened,
4 The utterance of him
who hears the words of God,
Who sees the vision of the Almighty,
Who falls down,
with eyes opened wide:

5 "How lovely are your tents, O Jacob!
Your dwellings, O Israel!
6 Like valleys that stretch out,
Like gardens by the riverside,
Like aloes planted by the LORD,
Like cedars beside the waters.
7 He shall pour water from his buckets,
And his seed *shall be* in many waters.

"His king shall be higher than Agag,
And his kingdom shall be exalted.

8 "God brings him out of Egypt;
He has strength like a wild ox;
He shall consume the nations,
his enemies;
He shall break their bones
And pierce *them* with his arrows.
9 'He bows down, he lies down as a lion;
And as a lion, who will rouse him?'[28]

"Blessed *is* he who blesses you,
And cursed *is* he who curses you."

27 Hebrew *Jeshimon* 28 Compare Genesis 49:9

10 Then Balak's anger was aroused against Balaam, and he struck his hands together; and Balak said to Balaam, "I called you to curse my enemies, and look, you have bountifully blessed *them* these three times!
11 "Now therefore, flee to your place. I said I would greatly honor you, but in fact, the Lord has kept you back from honor."
12 So Balaam said to Balak, "Did I not also speak to your messengers whom you sent to me, saying,
13 'Though Balak were to give me his house full of silver and gold, I could not go beyond the word of the Lord, to do *either* good or bad of my own will; *but* what the Lord says, that I must speak'?
14 "And now, indeed, I am going to my people. Come, I will advise you what this people will do to your people in the latter days."

Balaam's Fourth Prophecy

15 Then he took up his oracle and said:

"The utterance of Balaam
   the son of Beor,
And the utterance of the man
   whose eyes are opened;
16 The utterance of him
   who hears the words of God,
And knows the knowledge
   of the Most High,
Who sees the vision of the Almighty,
Who falls down,
   with eyes opened wide:

17 "I see Him, but not now;
I behold Him, but not near;
A Star shall come out of Jacob;
A Scepter shall rise out of Israel,
And batter the brow of Moab,
And destroy all the sons of tumult.[29]

18 "And Edom shall be a possession;
Seir also, his enemies,
   shall be a possession,
While Israel does valiantly.
19 Out of Jacob One shall have dominion,
And destroy the remains of the city."

20 Then he looked on Amalek, and he took up his oracle and said:

"Amalek *was* first among the nations,
But *shall be* last until he perishes."

21 Then he looked on the Kenites, and he took up his oracle and said:

"Firm is your dwelling place,
And your nest is set in the rock;
22 Nevertheless Kain shall be burned.
How long until Asshur
   carries you away captive?"

23 Then he took up his oracle and said:

"Alas! Who shall live
   when God does this?
24 But ships *shall come*
   from the coasts of Cyprus,[30]
And they shall afflict Asshur
   and afflict Eber,
And so shall Amalek,[31]
   until he perishes."

25 Then Balaam rose and departed and returned to his place; Balak also went his way.

Israel's Harlotry in Moab

25 Then Israel remained in Acacia Grove,[32] and the people began to commit harlotry with the women of Moab.
2 They invited the people to the sacrifices of their gods, and the people ate and bowed down to their gods.
3 So Israel was joined to Baal of Peor, and the anger of the Lord was aroused against Israel.
4 Then the Lord said to Moses, "Take all the leaders of the people and hang the offenders before the Lord, out in the sun, that the fierce anger of the Lord may turn away from Israel."
5 So Moses said to the judges of Israel, "Every one of you kill his men who were joined to Baal of Peor."
6 And indeed, one of the children of Israel came and presented to his brethren a Midianite woman in the sight of Moses and in the sight of all the congregation of the children of Israel, who *were* weeping at the door of the tabernacle of meeting.
7 Now when Phinehas the son of Eleazar, the son of Aaron the priest, saw *it*, he rose from among the congregation and took a javelin in his hand;
8 and he went after the man of Israel into the tent and thrust both of them through, the man of Israel, and the woman through her body. So the plague was stopped among the children of Israel.
9 And those who died in the plague were twenty-four thousand.
10 Then the Lord spoke to Moses, saying:

11 "Phinehas the son of Eleazar, the son of Aaron the priest, has turned back My wrath from the children of Israel, because he was zealous with My zeal among them, so that I did not consume the children of Israel in My zeal.

12 "Therefore say, 'Behold, I give to him My covenant of peace;

13 'and it shall be to him and his descendants after him a covenant of an everlasting priesthood, because he was zealous for his God, and made atonement for the children of Israel.' "

14 Now the name of the Israelite who was killed, who was killed with the Midianite woman, *was* Zimri the son of Salu, a leader of a father's house among the Simeonites.

15 And the name of the Midianite woman who was killed *was* Cozbi the daughter of Zur; he *was* head of the people of a father's house in Midian.

16 Then the LORD spoke to Moses, saying:

17 "Harass the Midianites, and attack them;

18 "for they harassed you with their schemes by which they seduced you in the matter of Peor and in the matter of Cozbi, the daughter of a leader of Midian, their sister, who was killed in the day of the plague because of Peor."

The Second Census of Israel

26 And it came to pass, after the plague, that the LORD spoke to Moses and Eleazar the son of Aaron the priest, saying:

2 "Take a census of all the congregation of the children of Israel from twenty years old and above, by their fathers' houses, all who are able to go to war in Israel."

3 So Moses and Eleazar the priest spoke with them in the plains of Moab by the Jordan, *across from* Jericho, saying:

4 "*Take a census of the people* from twenty years old and above, just as the LORD commanded Moses and the children of Israel who came out of the land of Egypt."

5 Reuben *was* the firstborn of Israel. The children of Reuben *were: of* Hanoch, the family of the Hanochites; *of* Pallu, the family of the Palluites;

6 *of* Hezron, the family of the Hezronites; *of* Carmi, the family of the Carmites.

7 These *are* the families of the Reubenites: those who were numbered of them were forty-three thousand seven hundred and thirty.

8 And the son of Pallu *was* Eliab.

9 The sons of Eliab *were* Nemuel, Dathan, and Abiram. These *are* the Dathan and Abiram, representatives of the congregation, who contended against Moses and Aaron in the company of Korah, when they contended against the LORD;

10 and the earth opened its mouth and swallowed them up together with Korah when that company died, when the fire devoured two hundred and fifty men; and they became a sign.

11 Nevertheless the children of Korah did not die.

12 The sons of Simeon according to their families *were: of* Nemuel,[33] the family of the Nemuelites; *of* Jamin, the family of the Jaminites; *of* Jachin,[34] the family of the Jachinites;

13 *of* Zerah,[35] the family of the Zarhites; *of* Shaul, the family of the Shaulites.

14 These *are* the families of the Simeonites: twenty-two thousand two hundred.

15 The sons of Gad according to their families *were: of* Zephon,[36] the family of the Zephonites; *of* Haggi, the family of the Haggites; *of* Shuni, the family of the Shunites;

16 *of* Ozni,[37] the family of the Oznites; *of* Eri, the family of the Erites;

17 *of* Arod,[38] the family of the Arodites; *of* Areli the family of the Arelites.

18 These *are* the families of the sons of Gad according to those who were numbered of them: forty thousand five hundred.

19 The sons of Judah *were* Er and Onan; and Er and Onan died in the land of Canaan.

20 And the sons of Judah according to their families were: *of* Shelah, the family of the Shelanites; *of* Perez, the family of the Parzites; *of* Zerah, the family of the Zarhites.

21 And the sons of Perez were: *of* Hezron, the family of the Hezronites; *of* Hamul, the family of the Hamulites.

22 These *are* the families of Judah ac-

33 Spelled *Jemuel* in Genesis 46:10 and Exodus 6:15   34 Called *Jarib* in 1 Chronicles 4:24
35 Called *Zohar* in Genesis 46:10   36 Called *Ziphion* in Genesis 46:16   37 Called *Ezbon* in Genesis 46:16
38 Spelled *Arodi* in Genesis 46:16, Samaritan Pentateuch, and Syriac

cording to those who were numbered of them: seventy-six thousand five hundred.
23 The sons of Issachar according to their families *were: of* Tola, the family of the Tolaites; *of* Puah,[39] the family of the Punites;[40]
24 of Jashub, the family of the Jashubites; of Shimron, the family of the Shimronites.
25 These *are* the families of Issachar according to those who were numbered of them: sixty-four thousand three hundred.
26 The sons of Zebulun according to their families *were:* of Sered, the family of the Sardites; of Elon, the family of the Elonites; of Jahleel, the family of the Jahleelites.
27 These *are* the families of the Zebulunites according to those who were numbered of them: sixty thousand five hundred.
28 The sons of Joseph according to their families, by Manasseh and Ephraim, *were*:
29 The sons of Manasseh: of Machir, the family of the Machirites; and Machir begot Gilead; of Gilead, the family of the Gileadites.
30 These *are* the sons of Gilead: *of* Jeezer,[41] the family of the Jeezerites; of Helek, the family of the Helekites;
31 *of* Asriel, the family of the Asrielites; *of* Shechem, the family of the Shechemites;
32 *of* Shemida, the family of the Shemidaites; *of* Hepher, the family of the Hepherites.
33 Now Zelophehad the son of Hepher had no sons, but daughters; and the names of the daughters of Zelophehad *were* Mahlah, Noah, Hoglah, Milcah, and Tirzah.
34 These *are* the families of Manasseh; and those who were numbered of them *were* fifty-two thousand seven hundred.
35 These *are* the sons of Ephraim according to their families: of Shuthelah, the family of the Shuthalhites; of Becher,[42] the family of the Bachrites; of Tahan, the family of the Tahanites.
36 And these *are* the sons of Shuthelah: of Eran, the family of the Eranites.
37 These *are* the families of the sons of Ephraim according to those who were

numbered of them: thirty-two thousand five hundred. These *are* the sons of Joseph according to their families.
38 The sons of Benjamin according to their families were: of Bela, the family of the Belaites; of Ashbel, the family of the Ashbelites; of Ahiram, the family of the Ahiramites;
39 of Shupham,[43] the family of the Shuphamites; of Hupham,[44] the family of the Huphamites.
40 And the sons of Bela were Ard[45] and Naaman: *of Ard,* the family of the Ardites; of Naaman, the family of the Naamites.
41 These *are* the sons of Benjamin according to their families; and those who were numbered of them *were* forty-five thousand six hundred.
42 These *are* the sons of Dan according to their families: of Shuham,[46] the family of the Shuhamites. These *are* the families of Dan according to their families.
43 All the families of the Shuhamites, according to those who were numbered of them, *were* sixty-four thousand four hundred.
44 The sons of Asher according to their families *were:* of Jimna, the family of the Jimnites; of Jesui, the family of the Jesuites; of Beriah, the family of the Beriites.
45 Of the sons of Beriah: of Heber, the family of the Heberites; of Malchiel, the family of the Malchielites.
46 And the name of the daughter of Asher *was* Serah.
47 These *are* the families of the sons of Asher according to those who were numbered of them: fifty-three thousand four hundred.
48 The sons of Naphtali according to their families *were:* of Jahzeel, the family of the Jahzeelites; of Guni, the family of the Gunites;
49 of Jezer, the family of the Jezerites; of Shillem, the family of the Shillemites.
50 These *are* the families of Naphtali according to their families; and those who were numbered of them *were* forty-five thousand four hundred.
51 These *are* those who were numbered of the children of Israel: six hundred and one thousand seven hundred and thirty.

39 Hebrew *Puvah,* compare Genesis 46:13 and 1 Chronicles 7:1; Samaritan Pentateuch, Septuagint, Syriac, and Vulgate read *Puah.*   40 Samaritan Pentateuch, Septuagint, Syriac, and Vulgate read *Puaites.*
41 Called *Abiezer* in Joshua 17:2   42 Called *Bered* in 1 Chronicles 7:20
43 Masoretic Text reads *Shephupham,* spelled *Shephuphan* in 1 Chronicles 8:5.
44 Called *Huppim* in Genesis 46:21   45 Called *Addar* in 1 Chronicles 8:3   46 Called *Hushim* in Genesis 46:23

52 Then the LORD spoke to Moses, saying:
53 "To these the land shall be divided as an inheritance, according to the number of names.
54 "To a large *tribe* you shall give a larger inheritance, and to a small *tribe* you shall give a smaller inheritance. Each shall be given its inheritance according to those who were numbered of them.
55 "But the land shall be divided by lot; they shall inherit according to the names of the tribes of their fathers.
56 "According to the lot their inheritance shall be divided between the larger and the smaller."
57 And these *are* those who were numbered of the Levites according to their families: of Gershon, the family of the Gershonites; of Kohath, the family of the Kohathites; of Merari, the family of the Merarites.
58 These *are* the families of the Levites: the family of the Libnites, the family of the Hebronites, the family of the Mahlites, the family of the Mushites, and the family of the Korathites. And Kohath begot Amram.
59 The name of Amram's wife *was* Jochebed the daughter of Levi, who was born to Levi in Egypt; and to Amram she bore Aaron and Moses and their sister Miriam.
60 To Aaron were born Nadab and Abihu, Eleazar and Ithamar.
61 And Nadab and Abihu died when they offered profane fire before the LORD.
62 Now those who were numbered of them were twenty-three thousand, every male from a month old and above; for they were not numbered among the other children of Israel, because there was no inheritance given to them among the children of Israel.
63 These *are* those who were numbered by Moses and Eleazar the priest, who numbered the children of Israel in the plains of Moab by the Jordan, *across from* Jericho.
64 But among these there was not a man of those who were numbered by Moses and Aaron the priest when they numbered the children of Israel in the Wilderness of Sinai.
65 For the LORD had said of them, "They shall surely die in the wilderness." So there was not left a man of them, except Caleb the son of Jephunneh and Joshua the son of Nun.

Inheritance Laws

27 Then came the daughters of Zelophehad the son of Hepher, the son of Gilead, the son of Machir, the son of Manasseh, from the families of Manasseh the son of Joseph; and these *were* the names of his daughters: Mahlah, Noah, Hoglah, Milcah, and Tirzah.
2 And they stood before Moses, before Eleazar the priest, and before the leaders and all the congregation, *by* the doorway of the tabernacle of meeting, saying:
3 "Our father died in the wilderness; but he was not in the company of those who gathered together against the LORD, in company with Korah, but he died in his own sin; and he had no sons.
4 "Why should the name of our father be removed from among his family because he had no son? *Therefore* give us a possession among the brothers of our father."
5 So Moses brought their case before the LORD.
6 And the LORD spoke to Moses, saying:
7 "The daughters of Zelophehad speak *what is* right; you shall surely give them a possession of inheritance among their father's brothers, and cause the inheritance of their father to pass to them.
8 "And you shall speak to the children of Israel, saying: 'If a man dies and has no son, then you shall cause his inheritance to pass to his daughter.
9 'If he has no daughter, then you shall give his inheritance to his brothers.
10 'If he has no brothers, then you shall give his inheritance to his father's brothers.
11 'And if his father has no brothers, then you shall give his inheritance to the kinsman nearest him in his family, and he shall possess it.' " And it shall be to the children of Israel a statute of judgment, just as the LORD commanded Moses.

Joshua the Next Leader of Israel

12 Now the LORD said to Moses: "Go up into this Mount Abarim, and see the land which I have given to the children of Israel.
13 "And when you have seen it, you also

shall be gathered to your people, as Aaron your brother was gathered.

14 "For in the Wilderness of Zin, during the strife of the congregation, you rebelled against My command to hallow Me at the waters before their eyes." (These *are* the waters of Meribah, at Kadesh in the Wilderness of Zin.)

15 Then Moses spoke to the LORD, saying:

16 "Let the LORD, the God of the spirits of all flesh, set a man over the congregation,

17 "who may go out before them and go in before them, who may lead them out and bring them in, that the congregation of the LORD may not be like sheep which have no shepherd."

18 And the LORD said to Moses: "Take Joshua the son of Nun with you, a man in whom *is* the Spirit, and lay your hand on him;

19 "set him before Eleazar the priest and before all the congregation, and inaugurate him in their sight.

20 "And you shall give *some* of your authority to him, that all the congregation of the children of Israel may be obedient.

21 "He shall stand before Eleazar the priest, who shall inquire before the LORD for him by the judgment of the Urim; at his word they shall go out, and at his word they shall come in, *both* he and all the children of Israel with him, all the congregation."

22 So Moses did as the LORD commanded him. He took Joshua and set him before Eleazar the priest and before all the congregation.

23 And he laid his hands on him and inaugurated him, just as the LORD commanded by the hand of Moses.

Daily Offerings

28 Now the LORD spoke to Moses, saying,

2 "Command the children of Israel, and say to them, 'My offering, My food for My offerings made by fire as a sweet aroma to Me, you shall be careful to offer to Me at their appointed time.'

3 "And you shall say to them, 'This *is* the offering made by fire which you shall offer to the LORD: two male lambs in their first year without blemish, day by day, as a regular burnt offering.

4 'The one lamb you shall offer in the morning, the other lamb you shall offer in the evening,

5 'and one-tenth of an ephah of fine flour as a grain offering mixed with one-fourth of a hin of pressed oil.

6 '*It is* a regular burnt offering which was ordained at Mount Sinai for a sweet aroma, an offering made by fire to the LORD.

7 'And its drink offering *shall be* one-fourth of a hin for each lamb; in a holy *place* you shall pour out the drink to the LORD as an offering.

8 'The other lamb you shall offer in the evening; as the morning grain offering and its drink offering, you shall offer *it* as an offering made by fire, a sweet aroma to the LORD.

Sabbath Offerings

9 'And on the Sabbath day two lambs in their first year, without blemish, and two-tenths *of an ephah* of fine flour as a grain offering, mixed with oil, with its drink offering—

10 '*this is* the burnt offering for every Sabbath, besides the regular burnt offering with its drink offering.

Monthly Offerings

11 'At the beginnings of your months you shall present a burnt offering to the LORD: two young bulls, one ram, and seven lambs in their first year, without blemish;

12 'three-tenths *of an ephah* of fine flour as a grain offering, mixed with oil, for each bull; two-tenths *of an ephah* of fine flour as a grain offering, mixed with oil, for the one ram;

13 'and one-tenth *of an ephah* of fine flour, mixed with oil, as a grain offering for each lamb, as a burnt offering of sweet aroma, an offering made by fire to the LORD.

14 'Their drink offering shall be half a hin of wine for a bull, one-third of a hin for a ram, and one-fourth of a hin for a lamb; this *is* the burnt offering for each month throughout the months of the year.

15 'Also one kid of the goats as a sin offering to the LORD shall be offered, besides the regular burnt offering and its drink offering.

Offerings at Passover

16 'On the fourteenth day of the first month *is* the Passover of the LORD.
17 'And on the fifteenth day of this month *is* the feast; unleavened bread shall be eaten for seven days.
18 'On the first day *you shall have* a holy convocation. You shall do no customary work.
19 'And you shall present an offering made by fire as a burnt offering to the LORD: two young bulls, one ram, and seven lambs in their first year. Be sure they are without blemish.
20 'Their grain offering shall be of fine flour mixed with oil: three-tenths *of an ephah* you shall offer for a bull, and two-tenths for a ram;
21 'you shall offer one-tenth *of an ephah* for each of the seven lambs;
22 'also one goat *as* a sin offering, to make atonement for you.
23 'You shall offer these besides the burnt offering of the morning, which *is* for a regular burnt offering.
24 'In this manner you shall offer the food of the offering made by fire daily for seven days, as a sweet aroma to the LORD; it shall be offered besides the regular burnt offering and its drink offering.
25 'And on the seventh day you shall have a holy convocation. You shall do no customary work.

Offerings at the Feast of Weeks

26 'Also on the day of the firstfruits, when you bring a new grain offering to the LORD at your *Feast of* Weeks, you shall have a holy convocation. You shall do no customary work.
27 'You shall present a burnt offering as a sweet aroma to the LORD: two young bulls, one ram, and seven lambs in their first year,
28 'with their grain offering of fine flour mixed with oil: three-tenths *of an ephah* for each bull, two-tenths for the one ram,
29 'and one-tenth for each of the seven lambs;
30 '*also* one kid of the goats, to make atonement for you.
31 'Be sure they are without blemish. You shall present *them* with their drink offerings, besides the regular burnt offering with its grain offering.

Offerings at the Feast of Trumpets

29 'And in the seventh month, on the first *day* of the month, you shall have a holy convocation. You shall do no customary work. For you it is a day of blowing the trumpets.
2 'You shall offer a burnt offering as a sweet aroma to the LORD: one young bull, one ram, *and* seven lambs in their first year, without blemish.
3 'Their grain offering *shall be* fine flour mixed with oil: three-tenths *of an ephah* for the bull, two-tenths for the ram,
4 'and one-tenth for each of the seven lambs;
5 'also one kid of the goats *as* a sin offering, to make atonement for you;
6 'besides the burnt offering with its grain offering for the New Moon, the regular burnt offering with its grain offering, and their drink offerings, according to their ordinance, as a sweet aroma, an offering made by fire to the LORD.

Offerings on the Day of Atonement

7 'On the tenth *day* of this seventh month you shall have a holy convocation. You shall afflict your souls; you shall not do any work.
8 'You shall present a burnt offering to the LORD *as* a sweet aroma: one young bull, one ram, *and* seven lambs in their first year. Be sure they are without blemish.
9 'Their grain offering *shall be of* fine flour mixed with oil: three-tenths *of an ephah* for the bull, two-tenths for the one ram,
10 'and one-tenth for each of the seven lambs;
11 'also one kid of the goats *as* a sin offering, besides the sin offering for atonement, the regular burnt offering with its grain offering, and their drink offerings.

Offerings at the Feast of Tabernacles

12 'On the fifteenth day of the seventh month you shall have a holy convocation. You shall do no customary work, and you shall keep a feast to the LORD seven days.
13 'You shall present a burnt offering, an offering made by fire as a sweet aroma to the LORD: thirteen young bulls, two rams, *and* fourteen lambs in their first year. They shall be without blemish.

14 'Their grain offering *shall be of* fine
flour mixed with oil: three-tenths *of an
ephah* for each of the thirteen bulls, two-
tenths for each of the two rams,
15 'and one-tenth for each of the fourteen lambs;
16 'also one kid of the goats *as* a sin offering, besides the regular burnt offering,
its grain offering, and its drink offering.
17 'On the second day *present* twelve
young bulls, two rams, fourteen lambs in
their first year without blemish,
18 'and their grain offering and their
drink offerings for the bulls, for the rams,
and for the lambs, by their number, according to the ordinance;
19 'also one kid of the goats *as* a sin offering, besides the regular burnt offering
with its grain offering, and their drink offerings.
20 'On the third day *present* eleven bulls,
two rams, fourteen lambs in their first
year without blemish,
21 'and their grain offering and their
drink offerings for the bulls, for the rams,
and for the lambs, by their number, according to the ordinance;
22 'also one goat *as* a sin offering, besides
the regular burnt offering, its grain offering, and its drink offering.
23 'On the fourth day *present* ten bulls,
two rams, *and* fourteen lambs in their
first year, without blemish,
24 'and their grain offering and their
drink offerings for the bulls, for the rams,
and for the lambs, by their number, according to the ordinance;
25 'also one kid of the goats *as* a sin offering, besides the regular burnt offering,
its grain offering, and its drink offering.
26 'On the fifth day *present* nine bulls,
two rams, *and* fourteen lambs in their
first year without blemish,
27 'and their grain offering and their
drink offerings for the bulls, for the rams,
and for the lambs, by their number, according to the ordinance;
28 'also one goat *as* a sin offering, besides
the regular burnt offering, its grain offering, and its drink offering.
29 'On the sixth day *present* eight bulls,
two rams, *and* fourteen lambs in their
first year without blemish,
30 'and their grain offering and their
drink offerings for the bulls, for the rams,
and for the lambs, by their number, according to the ordinance;

31 'also one goat *as* a sin offering, besides
the regular burnt offering, its grain offering, and its drink offering.
32 'On the seventh day *present* seven
bulls, two rams, *and* fourteen lambs in
their first year without blemish,
33 'and their grain offering and their
drink offerings for the bulls, for the rams,
and for the lambs, by their number, according to the ordinance;
34 'also one goat *as* a sin offering, besides
the regular burnt offering, its grain offering, and its drink offering.
35 'On the eighth day you shall have a
sacred assembly. You shall do no customary work.
36 'You shall present a burnt offering, an
offering made by fire as a sweet aroma to
the LORD: one bull, one ram, seven lambs
in their first year without blemish,
37 'and their grain offering and their
drink offerings for the bull, for the ram,
and for the lambs, by their number, according to the ordinance;
38 'also one goat *as* a sin offering, besides
the regular burnt offering, its grain offering, and its drink offering.
39 'These *things* you shall present to the
LORD at your appointed feasts (besides
your vowed offerings and your freewill
offerings) as your burnt offerings and
your grain offerings, as your drink offerings and your peace offerings.' "
40 So Moses told the children of Israel
everything, just as the LORD commanded
Moses.

The Law Concerning Vows

30 Then Moses spoke to the heads of
the tribes concerning the children
of Israel, saying, "This *is* the thing which
the LORD has commanded:
2 "If a man vows a vow to the LORD, or
swears an oath to bind himself by some
agreement, he shall not break his word;
he shall do according to all that proceeds
out of his mouth.
3 "Or if a woman vows a vow to the
LORD, and binds *herself* by some agreement while in her father's house in her
youth,
4 "and her father hears her vow and the
agreement by which she has bound herself, and her father holds his peace, then
all her vows shall stand, and every agreement with which she has bound herself
shall stand.

5 "But if her father overrules her on the day that he hears, then none of her vows nor her agreements by which she has bound herself shall stand; and the LORD will forgive her, because her father overruled her.

6 "But if indeed she takes a husband, while bound by her vows or by a rash utterance from her lips by which she bound herself,

7 "and her husband hears it, and makes no response to her on the day that he hears, then her vows shall stand, and her agreements by which she bound herself shall stand.

8 "But if her husband overrules her on the day that he hears it, he shall make void her vow which she vowed and what she uttered with her lips, by which she bound herself, and the LORD will forgive her.

9 "But any vow of a widow or a divorced woman, by which she has bound herself, shall stand against her.

10 "If she vowed in her husband's house, or bound herself by an agreement with an oath,

11 "and her husband heard it, and made no response to her and did not overrule her, then all her vows shall stand, and every agreement by which she bound herself shall stand.

12 "But if her husband truly made them void on the day he heard them, then whatever proceeded from her lips concerning her vows or concerning the agreement binding her, it shall not stand; her husband has made them void, and the LORD will forgive her.

13 "Every vow and every binding oath to afflict her soul, her husband may confirm it, or her husband may make it void.

14 "But if her husband makes no response whatever to her from day to day, then he confirms all her vows or all the agreements that bind her; he confirms them, because he made no response to her on the day that he heard them.

15 "But if he does make them void after he has heard them, then he shall bear her guilt."

16 These are the statutes which the LORD commanded Moses, between a man and his wife, and between a father and his daughter in her youth in her father's house.

Vengeance on the Midianites

31 And the LORD spoke to Moses, saying:

2 "Take vengeance for the children of Israel on the Midianites. Afterward you shall be gathered to your people."

3 So Moses spoke to the people, saying, "Arm some of yourselves for the war, and let them go against the Midianites to take vengeance for the LORD on Midian.

4 "A thousand from each tribe of all the tribes of Israel you shall send to the war."

5 So there were recruited from the divisions of Israel one thousand from each tribe, twelve thousand armed for war.

6 Then Moses sent them to the war, one thousand from each tribe; he sent them to the war with Phinehas the son of Eleazar the priest, with the holy articles and the signal trumpets in his hand.

7 And they warred against the Midianites, just as the LORD commanded Moses, and they killed all the males.

8 They killed the kings of Midian with the rest of those who were killed, namely: Evi, Rekem, Zur, Hur, and Reba, the five kings of Midian. Balaam the son of Beor they also killed with the sword.

9 And the children of Israel took all the women of Midian captive, with their little ones, and took as spoil all their cattle, all their flocks, and all their goods.

10 They also burned with fire all the cities where they dwelt, and all their forts.

11 And they took all the spoil and all the booty, both of man and beast.

Return from the War

12 Then they brought the captives, the booty, and the spoil to Moses, to Eleazar the priest, and to the congregation of the children of Israel, to the camp in the plains of Moab by the Jordan, across from Jericho.

13 And Moses, Eleazar the priest, and all the leaders of the congregation, went to meet them outside the camp.

14 But Moses was angry with the officers of the army, with the captains over thousands and captains over hundreds, who had come from the battle.

15 And Moses said to them: "Have you kept all the women alive?

16 "Look, these women caused the children of Israel, through the counsel of Balaam, to trespass against the LORD in the

incident of Peor, and there was a plague among the congregation of the LORD.

17 "Now therefore, kill every male among the little ones, and kill every woman who has known a man intimately.

18 "But keep alive for yourselves all the young girls who have not known a man intimately.

19 "And as for you, remain outside the camp seven days; whoever has killed any person, and whoever has touched any slain, purify yourselves and your captives on the third day and on the seventh day.

20 "Purify every garment, everything made of leather, everything woven of goats' *hair*, and everything made of wood."

21 Then Eleazar the priest said to the men of war who had gone to the battle, "This *is* the ordinance of the law which the LORD commanded Moses:

22 "Only the gold, the silver, the bronze, the iron, the tin, and the lead,

23 "everything that can endure fire, you shall put through the fire, and it shall be clean; and it shall be purified with the water of purification. But all that cannot endure fire you shall put through water.

24 "And you shall wash your clothes on the seventh day and be clean, and afterward you may come into the camp."

Division of the Plunder

25 And the LORD spoke to Moses, saying:

26 "Count up the plunder that was taken, *both* of man and beast, you and Eleazar the priest and the chief fathers of the congregation;

27 "and divide the plunder into two parts, between those who took part in the war, who went out to battle, and all the congregation.

28 "And levy a tribute for the LORD on the men of war who went out to battle: one of every five hundred of the persons, the cattle, the donkeys, and the sheep;

29 "take *it* from their half, and give *it* to Eleazar the priest as a heave offering to the LORD.

30 "And from the children of Israel's half you shall take one of every fifty, drawn from the persons, the cattle, the donkeys, and the sheep, from all the livestock, and give them to the Levites who keep charge of the tabernacle of the LORD."

31 So Moses and Eleazar the priest did as the LORD commanded Moses.

32 And the booty remaining from the plunder, which the men of war had taken, was six hundred and seventy-five thousand sheep,

33 seventy-two thousand cattle,

34 sixty-one thousand donkeys,

35 and thirty-two thousand persons in all, of women who had not known a man intimately.

36 And the half, the portion for those who had gone out to war, was in number three hundred and thirty-seven thousand five hundred sheep;

37 and the LORD'S tribute of the sheep was six hundred and seventy-five.

38 The cattle *were* thirty-six thousand, of which the LORD'S tribute *was* seventy-two.

39 The donkeys *were* thirty thousand five hundred, of which the LORD's tribute *was* sixty-one.

40 The persons *were* sixteen thousand, of which the LORD's tribute *was* thirty-two persons.

41 So Moses gave the tribute *which was* the LORD's heave offering to Eleazar the priest, as the LORD commanded Moses.

42 And from the children of Israel's half, which Moses separated from the men who fought—

43 now the half belonging to the congregation was three hundred and thirty-seven thousand five hundred sheep,

44 thirty-six thousand cattle,

45 thirty thousand five hundred donkeys,

46 and sixteen thousand persons—

47 and from the children of Israel's half Moses took one of every fifty, drawn from man and beast, and gave them to the Levites, who kept charge of the tabernacle of the LORD, as the LORD commanded Moses.

48 Then the officers who *were* over thousands of the army, the captains of thousands and captains of hundreds, came near to Moses;

49 and they said to Moses, "Your servants have taken a count of the men of war who *are* under our command, and not a man of us is missing.

50 "Therefore we have brought an offering for the LORD, what every man found of ornaments of gold: armlets and bracelets and signet rings and earrings and

necklaces, to make atonement for ourselves before the LORD."

51 So Moses and Eleazar the priest received the gold from them, all the fashioned ornaments.

52 And all the gold of the offering that they offered to the LORD, from the captains of thousands and captains of hundreds, was sixteen thousand seven hundred and fifty shekels.

53 (The men of war had taken spoil, every man for himself.)

54 And Moses and Eleazar the priest received the gold from the captains of thousands and of hundreds, and brought it into the tabernacle of meeting as a memorial for the children of Israel before the LORD.

The Tribes Settling East of the Jordan

32 Now the children of Reuben and the children of Gad had a very great multitude of livestock; and when they saw the land of Jazer and the land of Gilead, that indeed the region was a place for livestock,

2 the children of Gad and the children of Reuben came and spoke to Moses, to Eleazar the priest, and to the leaders of the congregation, saying,

3 "Ataroth, Dibon, Jazer, Nimrah, Heshbon, Elealeh, Shebam, Nebo, and Beon,

4 "the country which the LORD defeated before the congregation of Israel, is a land for livestock, and your servants have livestock."

5 Therefore they said, "If we have found favor in your sight, let this land be given to your servants as a possession, and do not take us over the Jordan."

6 And Moses said to the children of Gad and to the children of Reuben: "Shall your brethren go to war while you sit here?

7 "Now why will you discourage the heart of the children of Israel from going over into the land which the LORD has given them?

8 "Thus your fathers did when I sent them away from Kadesh Barnea to see the land.

9 "For when they went up to the Valley of Eshcol and saw the land, they discouraged the heart of the children of Israel, so that they did not go into the land which the LORD had given them.

10 "So the LORD's anger was aroused on that day, and He swore an oath, saying,

11 'Surely none of the men who came up from Egypt, from twenty years old and above, shall see the land of which I swore to Abraham, Isaac, and Jacob, because they have not wholly followed Me,

12 'except Caleb the son of Jephunneh, the Kenizzite, and Joshua the son of Nun, for they have wholly followed the LORD.'

13 "So the LORD's anger was aroused against Israel, and He made them wander in the wilderness forty years, until all the generation that had done evil in the sight of the LORD was gone.

14 "And look! You have risen in your father's place, a brood of sinful men, to increase still more the fierce anger of the LORD against Israel.

15 "For if you turn away from following Him, He will once again leave them in the wilderness, and you will destroy all these people."

16 Then they came near to him and said: "We will build sheepfolds here for our livestock, and cities for our little ones,

17 "but we ourselves will be armed, ready to go before the children of Israel until we have brought them to their place; and our little ones will dwell in the fortified cities because of the inhabitants of the land.

18 "We will not return to our homes until every one of the children of Israel has received his inheritance.

19 "For we will not inherit with them on the other side of the Jordan and beyond, because our inheritance has fallen to us on this eastern side of the Jordan."

20 Then Moses said to them: "If you do this thing, if you arm yourselves before the LORD for the war,

21 "and all your armed men cross over the Jordan before the LORD until He has driven out His enemies from before Him,

22 "and the land is subdued before the LORD, then afterward you may return and be blameless before the LORD and before Israel; and this land shall be your possession before the LORD.

23 "But if you do not do so, then take note, you have sinned against the LORD; and be sure your sin will find you out.

24 "Build cities for your little ones and folds for your sheep, and do what has proceeded out of your mouth."

25 And the children of Gad and the chil-

dren of Reuben spoke to Moses, saying:
"Your servants will do as my lord commands.
26 "Our little ones, our wives, our flocks,
and all our livestock will be there in the
cities of Gilead;
27 "but your servants will cross over, every man armed for war, before the LORD
to battle, just as my lord says."
28 So Moses gave command concerning
them to Eleazar the priest, to Joshua the
son of Nun, and to the chief fathers of the
tribes of the children of Israel.
29 And Moses said to them: "If the children of Gad and the children of Reuben
cross over the Jordan with you, every
man armed for battle before the LORD,
and the land is subdued before you, then
you shall give them the land of Gilead as
a possession.
30 "But if they do not cross over armed
with you, they shall have possessions
among you in the land of Canaan."
31 Then the children of Gad and the
children of Reuben answered, saying:
"As the LORD has said to your servants,
so we will do.
32 "We will cross over armed before the
LORD into the land of Canaan, but the
possession of our inheritance *shall remain*
with us on this side of the Jordan."
33 So Moses gave to the children of Gad,
to the children of Reuben, and to half the
tribe of Manasseh the son of Joseph, the
kingdom of Sihon king of the Amorites
and the kingdom of Og king of Bashan,
the land with its cities within the borders,
the cities of the surrounding country.
34 And the children of Gad built Dibon
and Ataroth and Aroer,
35 Atroth and Shophan and Jazer and
Jogbehah,
36 Beth Nimrah and Beth Haran, fortified cities, and folds for sheep.
37 And the children of Reuben built
Heshbon and Elealeh and Kirjathaim,
38 Nebo and Baal Meon (*their* names being changed) and Shibmah; and they
gave *other* names to the cities which they
built.
39 And the children of Machir the son of
Manasseh went to Gilead and took it,
and dispossessed the Amorites who *were*
in it.
40 So Moses gave Gilead to Machir the

son of Manasseh, and he dwelt in it.
41 Also Jair the son of Manasseh went
and took its small towns, and called them
Havoth Jair.[47]
42 Then Nobah went and took Kenath
and its villages, and he called it Nobah,
after his own name.

Israel's Journey from Egypt Reviewed

33 These *are* the journeys of the children of Israel, who went out of the
land of Egypt by their armies under the
hand of Moses and Aaron.
2 Now Moses wrote down the starting
points of their journeys at the command
of the LORD. And these *are* their journeys according to their starting points:
3 They departed from Rameses in the
first month, on the fifteenth day of the
first month; on the day after the Passover
the children of Israel went out with boldness in the sight of all the Egyptians.
4 For the Egyptians were burying all
their firstborn, whom the LORD had killed
among them. Also on their gods the
LORD had executed judgments.
5 Then the children of Israel moved
from Rameses and camped at Succoth.
6 They departed from Succoth and
camped at Etham, which *is* on the edge of
the wilderness.
7 They moved from Etham and turned
back to Pi Hahiroth, which *is* east of Baal
Zephon; and they camped near Migdol.
8 They departed from before Hahiroth[48]
and passed through the midst of the sea
into the wilderness, went three days' journey in the Wilderness of Etham, and
camped at Marah.
9 They moved from Marah and came to
Elim. At Elim *were* twelve springs of
water and seventy palm trees; so they
camped there.
10 They moved from Elim and camped
by the Red Sea.
11 They moved from the Red Sea and
camped in the Wilderness of Sin.
12 They journeyed from the Wilderness
of Sin and camped at Dophkah.
13 They departed from Dophkah and
camped at Alush.
14 They moved from Alush and camped
at Rephidim, where there was no water
for the people to drink.

---

47 Literally *Towns of Jair*   48 Some Hebrew manuscripts, Samaritan Pentateuch, Syriac, Targum, and Vulgate
read *from Pi Hahiroth* (compare verse 7).

15 They departed from Rephidim and camped in the Wilderness of Sinai.
16 They moved from the Wilderness of Sinai and camped at Kibroth Hattaavah.
17 They departed from Kibroth Hattaavah and camped at Hazeroth.
18 They departed from Hazeroth and camped at Rithmah.
19 They departed from Rithmah and camped at Rimmon Perez.
20 They departed from Rimmon Perez and camped at Libnah.
21 They moved from Libnah and camped at Rissah.
22 They journeyed from Rissah and camped at Kehelathah.
23 They went from Kehelathah and camped at Mount Shepher.
24 They moved from Mount Shepher and camped at Haradah.
25 They moved from Haradah and camped at Makheloth.
26 They moved from Makheloth and camped at Tahath.
27 They departed from Tahath and camped at Terah.
28 They moved from Terah and camped at Mithkah.
29 They went from Mithkah and camped at Hashmonah.
30 They departed from Hashmonah and camped at Moseroth.
31 They departed from Moseroth and camped at Bene Jaakan.
32 They moved from Bene Jaakan and camped at Hor Hagidgad.
33 They went from Hor Hagidgad and camped at Jotbathah.
34 They moved from Jotbathah and camped at Abronah.
35 They departed from Abronah and camped at Ezion Geber.
36 They moved from Ezion Geber and camped in the Wilderness of Zin, which *is* Kadesh.
37 They moved from Kadesh and camped at Mount Hor, on the boundary of the land of Edom.
38 Then Aaron the priest went up to Mount Hor at the command of the LORD, and died there in the fortieth year after the children of Israel had come out of the land of Egypt, on the first *day* of the fifth month.
39 Aaron *was* one hundred and twenty-three years old when he died on Mount Hor.

40 Now the king of Arad, the Canaanite, who dwelt in the South in the land of Canaan, heard of the coming of the children of Israel.
41 So they departed from Mount Hor and camped at Zalmonah.
42 They departed from Zalmonah and camped at Punon.
43 They departed from Punon and camped at Oboth.
44 They departed from Oboth and camped at Ije Abarim, at the border of Moab.
45 They departed from Ijim[49] and camped at Dibon Gad.
46 They moved from Dibon Gad and camped at Almon Diblathaim.
47 They moved from Almon Diblathaim and camped in the mountains of Abarim, before Nebo.
48 They departed from the mountains of Abarim and camped in the plains of Moab by the Jordan, *across from* Jericho.
49 They camped by the Jordan, from Beth Jesimoth as far as the Abel Acacia Grove[50] in the plains of Moab.

Instructions for the Conquest of Canaan

50 Now the LORD spoke to Moses in the plains of Moab by the Jordan, *across from* Jericho, saying,
51 "Speak to the children of Israel, and say to them: 'When you have crossed the Jordan into the land of Canaan,
52 'then you shall drive out all the inhabitants of the land from before you, destroy all their engraved stones, destroy all their molded images, and demolish all their high places;
53 'you shall dispossess *the inhabitants of* the land and dwell in it, for I have given you the land to possess.
54 'And you shall divide the land by lot as an inheritance among your families; to the larger you shall give a larger inheritance, and to the smaller you shall give a smaller inheritance; there everyone's *inheritance* shall be whatever falls to him by lot. You shall inherit according to the tribes of your fathers.
55 'But if you do not drive out the inhabitants of the land from before you, then it shall be that those whom you let remain *shall be* irritants in your eyes and thorns in your sides, and they shall harass you in the land where you dwell.

49 Same as *Ije Abarim* (compare verse 44)   50 Hebrew *Abel Shittim*

56 'Moreover it shall be *that* I will do to you as I thought to do to them.' "

The Appointed Boundaries of Canaan

34 Then the LORD spoke to Moses, saying,

2 "Command the children of Israel, and say to them: 'When you come into the land of Canaan, this *is* the land that shall fall to you as an inheritance—the land of Canaan to its boundaries.

3 'Your southern border shall be from the Wilderness of Zin along the border of Edom; then your southern border shall extend eastward to the end of the Salt Sea;

4 'your border shall turn from the southern side of the Ascent of Akrabbim, continue to Zin, and be on the south of Kadesh Barnea; then it shall go on to Hazar Addar, and continue to Azmon;

5 'the border shall turn from Azmon to the Brook of Egypt, and it shall end at the Sea.

6 'As for the western border, you shall have the Great Sea for a border; this shall be your western border.

7 'And this shall be your northern border: From the Great Sea you shall mark out your *border* line to Mount Hor;

8 'from Mount Hor you shall mark out *your border* to the entrance of Hamath; then the direction of the border shall be toward Zedad;

9 'the border shall proceed to Ziphron, and it shall end at Hazar Enan. This shall be your northern border.

10 'You shall mark out your eastern border from Hazar Enan to Shepham;

11 'the border shall go down from Shepham to Riblah on the east side of Ain; the border shall go down and reach to the eastern side of the Sea of Chinnereth;

12 'the border shall go down along the Jordan, and it shall end at the Salt Sea. This shall be your land with its surrounding boundaries.' "

13 Then Moses commanded the children of Israel, saying: "This *is* the land which you shall inherit by lot, which the LORD has commanded to give to the nine tribes and to the half-tribe.

14 "For the tribe of the children of Reuben according to the house of their fathers, and the tribe of the children of Gad according to the house of their fathers, have received *their inheritance*; and the half-tribe of Manasseh has received its inheritance.

15 "The two tribes and the half-tribe have received their inheritance on this side of the Jordan, *across from* Jericho eastward, toward the sunrise."

The Leaders Appointed to Divide the Land

16 And the LORD spoke to Moses, saying,

17 "These *are* the names of the men who shall divide the land among you as an inheritance: Eleazar the priest and Joshua the son of Nun.

18 "And you shall take one leader of every tribe to divide the land for the inheritance.

19 "These *are* the names of the men: from the tribe of Judah, Caleb the son of Jephunneh;

20 "from the tribe of the children of Simeon, Shemuel the son of Ammihud;

21 "from the tribe of Benjamin, Elidad the son of Chislon;

22 "a leader from the tribe of the children of Dan, Bukki the son of Jogli;

23 "from the sons of Joseph: a leader from the tribe of the children of Manasseh, Hanniel the son of Ephod,

24 "and a leader from the tribe of the children of Ephraim, Kemuel the son of Shiphtan;

25 "a leader from the tribe of the children of Zebulun, Elizaphan the son of Parnach;

26 "a leader from the tribe of the children of Issachar, Paltiel the son of Azzan;

27 "a leader from the tribe of the children of Asher, Ahihud the son of Shelomi;

28 "and a leader from the tribe of the children of Naphtali, Pedahel the son of Ammihud."

29 These *are* the ones the LORD commanded to divide the inheritance among the children of Israel in the land of Canaan.

Cities for the Levites

35 And the LORD spoke to Moses in the plains of Moab by the Jordan *across from* Jericho, saying:

2 "Command the children of Israel that they give the Levites cities to dwell in from the inheritance of their posses-

sion, and you shall *also* give the Levites common-land around the cities.

3 "They shall have the cities to dwell in; and their common-land shall be for their cattle, for their herds, and for all their animals.

4 "The common-land of the cities which you shall give the Levites *shall extend* from the wall of the city outward a thousand cubits all around.

5 "And you shall measure outside the city on the east side two thousand cubits, on the south side two thousand cubits, on the west side two thousand cubits, and on the north side two thousand cubits. The city *shall be* in the middle. This shall belong to them as common-land for the cities.

6 "Now among the cities which you will give to the Levites *you shall appoint* six cities of refuge, to which a manslayer may flee. And to these you shall add forty-two cities.

7 "So all the cities you will give to the Levites *shall be* forty-eight; these *you shall give* with their common-land.

8 "And the cities which you will give *shall be* from the possession of the children of Israel; from the larger *tribe* you shall give many, from the smaller you shall give few; each shall give some of its cities to the Levites, in proportion to the inheritance that each inherits."

Cities of Refuge

9 Then the LORD spoke to Moses, saying,

10 "Speak to the children of Israel, and say to them: 'When you cross the Jordan into the land of Canaan,

11 'then you shall appoint cities to be cities of refuge for you, that the manslayer who kills any person accidentally may flee there.

12 'They shall be cities of refuge for you from the avenger, that the manslayer may not die until he stands before the congregation in judgment.

13 'And of the cities which you give, you shall have six cities of refuge.

14 'You shall appoint three cities on this side of the Jordan, and three cities you shall appoint in the land of Canaan, *which* will be cities of refuge.

15 'These six cities shall be for refuge for the children of Israel, for the stranger, and for the sojourner among them, that anyone who kills a person accidentally may flee there.

16 'But if he strikes him with an iron implement, so that he dies, he *is* a murderer; the murderer shall surely be put to death.

17 'And if he strikes him with a stone in the hand, by which one could die, and he does die, he *is* a murderer; the murderer shall surely be put to death.

18 'Or *if* he strikes him with a wooden hand weapon, by which one could die, and he does die, he *is* a murderer; the murderer shall surely be put to death.

19 'The avenger of blood himself shall put the murderer to death; when he meets him, he shall put him to death.

20 'If he pushes him out of hatred or, while lying in wait, hurls something at him so that he dies,

21 'or in enmity he strikes him with his hand so that he dies, the one who struck *him* shall surely be put to death, *for* he *is* a murderer; the avenger of blood shall put the murderer to death when he meets him.

22 'But if he pushes him suddenly without enmity, or throws anything at him without lying in wait,

23 'or uses a stone, by which a man could die, throwing *it* at him without seeing *him*, so that he dies, while he was not his enemy or seeking his harm,

24 'then the congregation shall judge between the manslayer and the avenger of blood according to these judgments.

25 'So the congregation shall deliver the manslayer from the hand of the avenger of blood, and the congregation shall return him to the city of refuge where he had fled, and he shall remain there until the death of the high priest who was anointed with the holy oil.

26 'But if the manslayer at any time goes outside the limits of the city of refuge where he fled,

27 'and the avenger of blood finds him outside the limits of his city of refuge, and the avenger of blood kills the manslayer, he shall not be guilty of blood,

28 'because he should have remained in his city of refuge until the death of the high priest. But after the death of the high priest the manslayer may return to the land of his possession.

29 'Now these *things* shall be a statute of judgment to you throughout your generations in all your dwellings.

30 'Whoever kills a person, the murderer shall be put to death on the testimony of witnesses; but one witness is not *sufficient* testimony against a person for the death *penalty*.
31 'Moreover you shall take no ransom for the life of a murderer who *is* guilty of death, but he shall surely be put to death.
32 'And you shall take no ransom for him who has fled to his city of refuge, that he may return to dwell in the land before the death of the priest.
33 'So you shall not pollute the land where you *are*; for blood defiles the land, and no atonement can be made for the land, for the blood that is shed on it, except by the blood of him who shed it.
34 'Therefore do not defile the land which you inhabit, in the midst of which I dwell; for I the LORD dwell among the children of Israel.' "

Marriage of Female Heirs

36 Now the chief fathers of the families of the children of Gilead the son of Machir, the son of Manasseh, of the families of the sons of Joseph, came near and spoke before Moses and before the leaders, the chief fathers of the children of Israel;
2 and they said: "The LORD commanded my lord *Moses* to give the land as an inheritance by lot to the children of Israel, and my lord was commanded by the LORD to give the inheritance of our brother Zelophehad to his daughters.
3 "Now if they are married to any of the sons of the *other* tribes of the children of Israel, then their inheritance will be taken from the inheritance of our fathers, and it will be added to the inheritance of the tribe into which they marry; so it will be taken from the lot of our inheritance.
4 "And when the Jubilee of the children of Israel comes, then their inheritance will be added to the inheritance of the tribe into which they marry; so their inheritance will be taken away from the inheritance of the tribe of our fathers."
5 Then Moses commanded the children of Israel according to the word of the LORD, saying: "What the tribe of the sons of Joseph speaks is right.
6 "This *is* what the LORD commands concerning the daughters of Zelophehad, saying, 'Let them marry whom they think best, but they may marry only within the family of their father's tribe.'
7 "So the inheritance of the children of Israel shall not change hands from tribe to tribe, for every one of the children of Israel shall keep the inheritance of the tribe of his fathers.
8 "And every daughter who possesses an inheritance in any tribe of the children of Israel shall be the wife of one of the family of her father's tribe, so that the children of Israel each may possess the inheritance of his fathers.
9 "Thus no inheritance shall change hands from *one* tribe to another, but every tribe of the children of Israel shall keep its own inheritance."
10 Just as the LORD commanded Moses, so did the daughters of Zelophehad;
11 for Mahlah, Tirzah, Hoglah, Milcah, and Noah, the daughters of Zelophehad, were married to the sons of their father's brothers.
12 They were married into the families of the children of Manasseh the son of Joseph, and their inheritance remained in the tribe of their father's family.
13 These *are* the commandments and the judgments which the LORD commanded the children of Israel by the hand of Moses in the plains of Moab by the Jordan, *across from* Jericho.

Introduction to Deuteronomy

Deuteronomy is an inspiring account of the children of Israel's preparation to enter the Promised Land. Their dream was about to become a reality!

Written by Moses about 1400 B.C., Deuteronomy summarizes the forty years of hard wilderness wandering and God's faithfulness throughout their time of need. Moses reiterates the Ten Commandments to the people as God's way to the good life. He also gives them new laws to help guard their minds and thoughts upon entering the new land with its foreign customs, cultures, and false gods.

Although Moses was not to participate himself in entering the land which he had led the people to, he was not bitter or negative. Rather, he presented a long dissertation on the blessings of God, His care and comfort of His people, their blessings upon reaching the Promised Land, special blessings for each tribe, and prayers for their continued success.

Moses also appointed Joshua as the new leader of the people and encouraged him with the promise, "Be strong and of good courage, for you must go with this people to this land which the LORD has sworn to their fathers to give them, and you shall cause them to inherit it. And the LORD, He *is* the one who goes before you. He will be with you, He will not leave you nor forsake you; do not fear nor be dismayed" (Deut. 31:7, 8).

When they were on the threshold of realizing their dream, Moses reminded them to "love the LORD your God with all your heart, with all your soul, and with all your might" (Deut. 6:5). Moses wanted to ensure that the Israelites would make a careful assessment of their lives. They needed to map out not only their future plans, but their personal relationships with God as well. Their dream would come true when they tapped into God's power!

The Fifth Book of Moses Called
Deuteronomy

The Previous Command to Enter Canaan

THESE *are* the words which Moses spoke to all Israel on this side of the Jordan in the wilderness, in the plain[1] opposite Suph,[2] between Paran, Tophel, Laban, Hazeroth, and Dizahab.
2 *It is* eleven days' *journey* from Horeb by way of Mount Seir to Kadesh Barnea.
3 Now it came to pass in the fortieth year, in the eleventh month, on the first *day* of the month, *that* Moses spoke to the children of Israel according to all that the LORD had given him as commandments to them,
4 after he had killed Sihon king of the Amorites, who dwelt in Heshbon, and Og king of Bashan, who dwelt at Ashtaroth in[3] Edrei.
5 On this side of the Jordan in the land of Moab, Moses began to explain this law, saying,
6 "The LORD our God spoke to us in Horeb, saying: 'You have dwelt long enough at this mountain.
7 'Turn and take your journey, and go to the mountains of the Amorites, to all the neighboring *places* in the plain,[4] in the mountains and in the lowland, in the South and on the seacoast, to the land of the Canaanites and to Lebanon, as far as the great river, the River Euphrates.
8 'See, I have set the land before you; go in and possess the land which the LORD swore to your fathers—to Abraham, Isaac, and Jacob—to give to them and their descendants after them.'

Tribal Leaders Appointed

9 "And I spoke to you at that time, saying: 'I alone am not able to bear you.
10 'The LORD your God has multiplied you, and here you *are* today, as the stars of heaven in multitude.
11 'May the LORD God of your fathers make you a thousand times more numerous than you are, and bless you as He has promised you!
12 'How can I alone bear your problems and your burdens and your complaints?

13 'Choose wise, understanding, and knowledgeable men from among your tribes, and I will make them heads over you.'
14 "And you answered me and said, 'The thing which you have told *us* to do *is* good.'
15 "So I took the heads of your tribes, wise and knowledgeable men, and made them heads over you, leaders of thousands, leaders of hundreds, leaders of fifties, leaders of tens, and officers for your tribes.
16 "Then I commanded your judges at that time, saying, 'Hear *the cases* between your brethren, and judge righteously between a man and his brother or the stranger who is with him.
17 'You shall not show partiality in judgment; you shall hear the small as well as the great; you shall not be afraid in any man's presence, for the judgment *is* God's. The case that is too hard for you, bring *it* to me, and I will hear it.'
18 "And I commanded you at that time all the things which you should do.

Israel's Refusal to Enter the Land

19 "So we departed from Horeb, and went through all that great and terrible wilderness which you saw on the way to the mountains of the Amorites, as the LORD our God had commanded us. Then we came to Kadesh Barnea.
20 "And I said to you, 'You have come to the mountains of the Amorites, which the LORD our God is giving us.
21 'Look, the LORD your God has set the land before you; go up *and* possess *it*, as the LORD God of your fathers has spoken to you; do not fear or be discouraged.'
22 "And everyone of you came near to me and said, 'Let us send men before us, and let them search out the land for us, and bring back word to us of the way by which we should go up, and of the cities into which we shall come.'
23 "And the plan pleased me well; so I

---

1 Hebrew *arabah*   2 One manuscript of the Septuagint, also Targum and Vulgate, read *Red Sea.*
3 Septuagint, Syriac, and Vulgate read *and* (compare Joshua 12:4).   4 Hebrew *arabah*

took twelve of your men, one man from *each* tribe.

24 "And they departed and went up into the mountains, and came to the Valley of Eshcol, and spied it out.

25 "They also took *some* of the fruit of the land in their hands and brought *it* down to us; and they brought back word to us, saying, '*It is* a good land which the LORD our God is giving us.'

26 "Nevertheless you would not go up, but rebelled against the command of the LORD your God;

27 "and you murmured in your tents, and said, 'Because the LORD hates us, He has brought us out of the land of Egypt to deliver us into the hand of the Amorites, to destroy us.

28 'Where can we go up? Our brethren have discouraged our hearts, saying, "The people *are* greater and taller than we; the cities *are* great and fortified up to heaven; moreover we have seen the sons of the Anakim there."'

29 "Then I said to you, 'Do not be terrified, or be afraid of them.

30 'The LORD your God, who goes before you, He will fight for you, according to all He did for you in Egypt before your eyes,

31 'and in the wilderness where you saw how the LORD your God carried you, as a man carries his son, in all the way that you went until you came to this place.'

32 "Yet, for all that, you did not believe the LORD your God,

33 "who went in the way before you to search out a place for you to pitch your tents, to show you the way you should go, in the fire by night and in the cloud by day.

The Penalty for Israel's Rebellion

34 "And the LORD heard the sound of your words, and was angry, and took an oath, saying,

35 'Surely not one of these men of this evil generation shall see that good land of which I swore to give to your fathers,

36 'except Caleb the son of Jephunneh; he shall see it, and to him and his children I am giving the land on which he walked, because he wholly followed the LORD.'

37 "The LORD was also angry with me for your sakes, saying, 'Even you shall not go in there;

38 '*but* Joshua the son of Nun, who stands before you, he shall go in there. Encourage him, for he shall cause Israel to inherit it.

39 'Moreover your little ones and your children, who you say will be victims, who today have no knowledge of good and evil, they shall go in there; to them I will give it, and they shall possess it.

40 'But *as for* you, turn and take your journey into the wilderness by the Way of the Red Sea.'

41 "Then you answered and said to me, 'We have sinned against the LORD; we will go up and fight, just as the LORD our God commanded us.' And when everyone of you had girded on his weapons of war, you were ready to go up into the mountain.

42 "And the LORD said to me, 'Tell them, "Do not go up nor fight, for I *am* not among you; lest you be defeated before your enemies."'

43 "So I spoke to you; yet you would not listen, but rebelled against the command of the LORD, and presumptuously went up into the mountain.

44 "And the Amorites who dwelt in that mountain came out against you and chased you as bees do, and drove you back from Seir to Hormah.

45 "Then you returned and wept before the LORD, but the LORD would not listen to your voice nor give ear to you.

46 "So you remained in Kadesh many days, according to the days that you spent *there.*

The Desert Years

2 "Then we turned and journeyed into the wilderness of the Way of the Red Sea, as the LORD spoke to me, and we skirted Mount Seir for many days.

2 "And the LORD spoke to me, saying:

3 'You have skirted this mountain long enough; turn northward.

4 'And command the people, saying, "You *are about to* pass through the territory of your brethren, the descendants of Esau, who live in Seir; and they will be afraid of you. Therefore watch yourselves carefully.

5 "Do not meddle with them, for I will not give you *any* of their land, no, not so much as one footstep, because I have given Mount Seir to Esau *as* a possession.

6 "You shall buy food from them with money, that you may eat; and you shall

also buy water from them with money, that you may drink.

7 "For the LORD your God has blessed you in all the work of your hand. He knows your trudging through this great wilderness. These forty years the LORD your God *has been* with you; you have lacked nothing." '

8 "And when we passed beyond our brethren, the descendants of Esau who dwell in Seir, away from the road of the plain, away from Elath and Ezion Geber, we turned and passed by way of the Wilderness of Moab.

9 "Then the LORD said to me, 'Do not harass Moab, nor contend with them in battle, for I will not give you *any* of their land *as* a possession, because I have given Ar to the descendants of Lot *as* a possession.' "

10 (The Emim had dwelt there in times past, a people as great and numerous and tall as the Anakim.

11 They were also regarded as giants,[5] like the Anakim, but the Moabites call them Emim.

12 The Horites formerly dwelt in Seir, but the descendants of Esau dispossessed them and destroyed them from before them, and dwelt in their place, just as Israel did to the land of their possession which the LORD gave them.)

13 " 'Now rise and cross over the Valley of the Zered.' So we crossed over the Valley of the Zered.

14 "And the time we took to come from Kadesh Barnea until we crossed over the Valley of the Zered *was* thirty-eight years, until all the generation of the men of war was consumed from the midst of the camp, just as the LORD had sworn to them.

15 "For indeed the hand of the LORD was against them, to destroy them from the midst of the camp until they were consumed.

16 "So it was, when all the men of war had finally perished from among the people,

17 "that the LORD spoke to me, saying:

18 'This day you are to cross over at Ar, the boundary of Moab.

19 'And *when* you come near the people of Ammon, do not harass them or meddle with them, for I will not give you *any* of the land of the people of Ammon *as* a

possession, because I have given it to the descendants of Lot *as* a possession.' "

20 (That was also regarded as a land of giants;[6] giants formerly dwelt there. But the Ammonites call them Zamzummim,

21 a people as great and numerous and tall as the Anakim. But the LORD destroyed them before them, and they dispossessed them and dwelt in their place,

22 just as He had done for the descendants of Esau, who dwelt in Seir, when He destroyed the Horites from before them. They dispossessed them and dwelt in their place, even to this day.

23 And the Avim, who dwelt in villages as far as Gaza—the Caphtorim, who came from Caphtor, destroyed them and dwelt in their place.)

24 " 'Rise, take your journey, and cross over the River Arnon. Look, I have given into your hand Sihon the Amorite, king of Heshbon, and his land. Begin to possess *it*, and engage him in battle.

25 'This day I will begin to put the dread and fear of you upon the nations under the whole heaven, who shall hear the report of you, and shall tremble and be in anguish because of you.'

King Sihon Defeated

26 "And I sent messengers from the Wilderness of Kedemoth to Sihon king of Heshbon, with words of peace, saying,

27 'Let me pass through your land; I will keep strictly to the road, and I will turn neither to the right nor to the left.

28 'You shall sell me food for money, that I may eat, and give me water for money, that I may drink; only let me pass through on foot,

29 'just as the descendants of Esau who dwell in Seir and the Moabites who dwell in Ar did for me, until I cross the Jordan to the land which the LORD our God is giving us.'

30 "But Sihon king of Heshbon would not let us pass through, for the LORD your God hardened his spirit and made his heart obstinate, that He might deliver him into your hand, as *it is* this day.

31 "And the LORD said to me, 'See, I have begun to give Sihon and his land over to you. Begin to possess *it*, that you may inherit his land.'

32 "Then Sihon and all his people came out against us to fight at Jahaz.

33 "And the LORD our God delivered

him over to us; so we defeated him, his sons, and all his people.
34 "We took all his cities at that time, and we utterly destroyed the men, women, and little ones of every city; we left none remaining.
35 "We took only the livestock as plunder for ourselves, with the spoil of the cities which we took.
36 "From Aroer, which *is* on the bank of the River Arnon, and *from* the city that *is* in the ravine, as far as Gilead, there was not one city too strong for us; the LORD our God delivered all to us.
37 "Only you did not go near the land of the people of Ammon, *or* anywhere along the River Jabbok, or to the cities of the mountains, or wherever the LORD our God had forbidden us.

King Og Defeated

3 "Then we turned and went up the road to Bashan; and Og king of Bashan came out against us, he and all his people, to battle at Edrei.
2 "And the LORD said to me, 'Do not fear him, for I have delivered him and all his people and his land into your hand; you shall do to him as you did to Sihon king of the Amorites, who dwelt at Heshbon.'
3 "So the LORD our God also delivered into our hands Og king of Bashan, with all his people, and we attacked him until he had no survivors remaining.
4 "And we took all his cities at that time; there was not a city which we did not take from them: sixty cities, all the region of Argob, the kingdom of Og in Bashan.
5 "All these cities *were* fortified with high walls, gates, and bars, besides a great many rural towns.
6 "And we utterly destroyed them, as we did to Sihon king of Heshbon, utterly destroying the men, women, and children of every city.
7 "But all the livestock and the spoil of the cities we took as booty for ourselves.
8 "And at that time we took the land from the hand of the two kings of the Amorites who *were* on this side of the Jordan, from the River Arnon to Mount Hermon
9 "(the Sidonians call Hermon Sirion, and the Amorites call it Senir),
10 "all the cities of the plain, all Gilead,

and all Bashan, as far as Salcah and Edrei, cities of the kingdom of Og in Bashan.
11 "For only Og king of Bashan remained of the remnant of the giants.[7] Indeed his bedstead *was* an iron bedstead. (*Is* it not in Rabbah of the people of Ammon?) Nine cubits *is* its length and four cubits its width, according to the standard cubit.

The Land East of the Jordan Divided

12 "And this land, *which* we possessed at that time, from Aroer, which *is* by the River Arnon, and half the mountains of Gilead and its cities, I gave to the Reubenites and the Gadites.
13 "The rest of Gilead, and all Bashan, the kingdom of Og, I gave to half the tribe of Manasseh. (All the region of Argob, with all Bashan, was called the land of the giants.[8]
14 "Jair the son of Manasseh took all the region of Argob, as far as the border of the Geshurites and the Maacathites, and called Bashan after his own name, Havoth Jair,[9] to this day.)
15 "And I gave Gilead to Machir.
16 "And to the Reubenites and the Gadites I gave from Gilead as far as the River Arnon, the middle of the river as *the* border, as far as the River Jabbok, the border of the people of Ammon;
17 "the plain also, with the Jordan as *the* border, from Chinnereth as far as the east side of the Sea of the Arabah (the Salt Sea), below the slopes of Pisgah.
18 "And I commanded you at that time, saying: 'The LORD your God has given you this land to possess. All you men of valor shall cross over armed before your brethren, the children of Israel.
19 'But your wives, your little ones, and your livestock (I know that you have much livestock) shall stay in your cities which I have given you,
20 'until the LORD has given rest to your brethren as to you, and they also possess the land which the LORD your God is giving them beyond the Jordan. Then each of you may return to his possession which I have given you.'
21 "And I commanded Joshua at that time, saying, 'Your eyes have seen all that the LORD your God has done to these two kings; so will the LORD do to all the kingdoms through which you pass.

---

7 Hebrew *rephaim*   8 Hebrew *rephaim*   9 Literally *Towns of Jair*

Alive and Flowing

The Jordan Rift Valley is one of the most interesting geological structures in the world, stretching from Lake Homs in Syria, all the way down to Lake Victoria in Africa.

This 1,500-mile-long earthquake fault passes through a variety of terrains, ranging from the snow-capped panoramic mountains of northern Syria to the barren desert landscape of Sinai. The Rift Valley encompasses two landlocked bodies of water: the Sea of Galilee, located 700 feet below sea level, and the Dead Sea, located 1,300 feet below sea level.

Both seas are located in the same valley, fed by the same Jordan River. Yet, they are completely different in nature. The Sea of Galilee is a freshwater lake teeming with fish, while the Dead Sea is thirty-three percent salt in which no living thing can exist.

The difference between the two lakes is that the northern Sea of Galilee has a southern exit in which it can give out the water it takes in. The Dead Sea does not. The water that enters the Dead Sea is not allowed to circulate. It has no exit, so it stagnates, dries up, and crystalizes, until it forms large blocks of salt around the shores of the sea.

We must be like the northern Sea of Galilee and allow imaginative dreams and creative ideas to flow into us, then circulate with our time, talents, abilities, energies, and education, and share them with others. They must be allowed to exit and enrich the lives of others.

If we can be of service to others, then we can be useful to God and to those around us!

22 'You must not fear them, for the LORD your God Himself fights for you.'

Moses Forbidden to Enter the Land

23 "Then I pleaded with the LORD at that time, saying:
24 'O Lord GOD, You have begun to show Your servant Your greatness and Your mighty hand, for what god *is there* in heaven or on earth who can do *anything* like Your works and Your mighty *deeds*?
25 'I pray, let me cross over and see the good land beyond the Jordan, those pleasant mountains, and Lebanon.'
26 "But the LORD was angry with me on your account, and would not listen to me. So the LORD said to me: 'Enough of that! Speak no more to Me of this matter.
27 'Go up to the top of Pisgah, and lift your eyes toward the west, the north, the south, and the east; behold *it* with your eyes, for you shall not cross over this Jordan.
28 'But command Joshua, and encourage him and strengthen him; for he shall go over before this people, and he shall cause them to inherit the land which you will see.'
29 "So we stayed in the valley opposite Beth Peor.

Moses Commands Obedience

4 "Now, O Israel, listen to the statutes and the judgments which I teach you to observe, that you may live, and go in and possess the land which the LORD God of your fathers is giving you.
2 "You shall not add to the word which I command you, nor take *anything* from it, that you may keep the commandments of the LORD your God which I command you.
3 "Your eyes have seen what the LORD did at Baal Peor; for the LORD your God has destroyed from among you all the men who followed Baal of Peor.
4 "But you who held fast to the LORD your God *are* alive today, every one of you.
5 "Surely I have taught you statutes and judgments, just as the LORD my God commanded me, that you should act according *to them* in the land which you go to possess.
6 "Therefore be careful to observe *them*; for this *is* your wisdom and your

understanding in the sight of the peoples who will hear all these statutes, and say, 'Surely this great nation *is* a wise and understanding people.'
7 "For what great nation *is there* that has God *so* near to it, as the LORD our God *is* to us, for whatever *reason* we may call upon Him?
8 "And what great nation *is there* that has *such* statutes and righteous judgments as are in all this law which I set before you this day?
9 "Only take heed to yourself, and diligently keep yourself, lest you forget the things your eyes have seen, and lest they depart from your heart all the days of your life. And teach them to your children and your grandchildren,
10 "*especially concerning* the day you stood before the LORD your God in Horeb, when the LORD said to me, 'Gather the people to Me, and I will let them hear My words, that they may learn to fear Me all the days they live on the earth, and *that* they may teach their children.'
11 "Then you came near and stood at the foot of the mountain, and the mountain burned with fire to the midst of heaven, with darkness, cloud, and thick darkness.
12 "And the LORD spoke to you out of the midst of the fire. You heard the sound of the words, but saw no form; *you* only *heard* a voice.
13 "So He declared to you His covenant which He commanded you to perform, *that is*, the Ten Commandments; and He wrote them on two tablets of stone.
14 "And the LORD commanded me at that time to teach you statutes and judgments, that you might observe them in the land which you cross over to possess.

Beware of Idolatry

15 "Take careful heed to yourselves, for you saw no form when the LORD spoke to you at Horeb out of the midst of the fire,
16 "lest you act corruptly and make for yourselves a carved image in the form of any figure: the likeness of male or female,
17 "the likeness of any beast that *is* on the earth or the likeness of any winged bird that flies in the air,
18 "the likeness of anything that creeps on the ground or the likeness of any fish that *is* in the water beneath the earth.
19 "And *take heed*, lest you lift your eyes

to heaven, and *when* you see the sun, the moon, and the stars, all the host of heaven, you feel driven to worship them and serve them, which the LORD your God has given to all the peoples under the whole heaven as a heritage.

20 "But the LORD has taken you and brought you out of the iron furnace, out of Egypt, to be His people, *His* inheritance, as you are this day.

21 "Furthermore the LORD was angry with me for your sakes, and swore that I would not cross over the Jordan, and that I would not enter the good land which the LORD your God is giving you as an inheritance.

22 "But I must die in this land, I must not cross over the Jordan; but you shall cross over and possess that good land.

23 "Take heed to yourselves, lest you forget the covenant of the LORD your God which He made with you, and make for yourselves a carved image in the form of anything which the LORD your God has forbidden you.

24 "For the LORD your God *is* a consuming fire, a jealous God.

25 "When you beget children and grandchildren and have grown old in the land, act corruptly and make a carved image in the form of anything, and do evil in the sight of the LORD your God to provoke Him to anger,

26 "I call heaven and earth to witness against you this day, that you will soon utterly perish from the land which you cross over the Jordan to possess; you will not prolong *your* days in it, but will be utterly destroyed.

27 "And the LORD will scatter you among the peoples, and you will be left few in number among the nations where the LORD will drive you.

28 "And there you will serve gods, the work of men's hands, wood and stone, which neither see nor hear nor eat nor smell.

29 "But from there you will seek the LORD your God, and you will find *Him* if you seek Him with all your heart and with all your soul.

30 "When you are in distress, and all these things come upon you in the latter days, when you turn to the LORD your God and obey His voice

31 "(for the LORD your God *is* a merciful God), He will not forsake you nor destroy you, nor forget the covenant of your fathers which He swore to them.

32 "For ask now concerning the days that are past, which were before you, since the day that God created man on the earth, and *ask* from one end of heaven to the other, whether *any* great *thing* like this has happened, or *anything* like it has been heard.

33 "Did *any* people *ever* hear the voice of God speaking out of the midst of the fire, as you have heard, and live?

34 "Or did God *ever* try to go *and* take for Himself a nation from the midst of *another* nation, by trials, by signs, by wonders, by war, by a mighty hand and an outstretched arm, and by great terrors, according to all that the LORD your God did for you in Egypt before your eyes?

35 "To you it was shown, that you might know that the LORD Himself *is* God; *there is* none other besides Him.

36 "Out of heaven He let you hear His voice, that He might instruct you; on earth He showed you His great fire, and you heard His words out of the midst of the fire.

37 "And because He loved your fathers, therefore He chose their descendants after them; and He brought you out of Egypt with His Presence, with His mighty power,

38 "driving out from before you nations greater and mightier than you, to bring you in, to give you their land *as* an inheritance, as *it is* this day.

39 "Therefore know this day, and consider *it* in your heart, that the LORD Himself *is* God in heaven above and on the earth beneath; *there is* no other.

40 "You shall therefore keep His statutes and His commandments which I command you today, that it may go well with you and with your children after you, and that you may prolong *your* days in the land which the LORD your God is giving you for all time."

Cities of Refuge East of the Jordan

41 Then Moses set apart three cities on this side of the Jordan, toward the rising of the sun,

42 that the manslayer might flee there, who kills his neighbor unintentionally, without having hated him in time past, and that by fleeing to one of these cities he might live:

43 Bezer in the wilderness on the plateau for the Reubenites, Ramoth in Gilead for the Gadites, and Golan in Bashan for the Manassites.

Introduction to God's Law

44 And this *is* the law which Moses set before the children of Israel.
45 These *are* the testimonies, the statutes, and the judgments which Moses spoke to the children of Israel after they came out of Egypt,
46 on this side of the Jordan, in the valley opposite Beth Peor, in the land of Sihon king of the Amorites, who dwelt at Heshbon, whom Moses and the children of Israel defeated after they came out of Egypt.
47 And they took possession of his land and the land of Og king of Bashan, two kings of the Amorites, who *were* on this side of the Jordan, toward the rising of the sun,
48 from Aroer, which *is* on the bank of the River Arnon, even to Mount Sion[10] (that is, Hermon),
49 and all the plain on the east side of the Jordan as far as the Sea of the Arabah, below the slopes of Pisgah.

The Ten Commandments Reviewed

5 And Moses called all Israel, and said to them: "Hear, O Israel, the statutes and judgments which I speak in your hearing today, that you may learn them and be careful to observe them.
2 "The LORD our God made a covenant with us in Horeb.
3 "The LORD did not make this covenant with our fathers, but with us, those who *are* here today, all of us who *are* alive.
4 "The LORD talked with you face to face on the mountain from the midst of the fire.
5 "I stood between the LORD and you at that time, to declare to you the word of the LORD; for you were afraid because of the fire, and you did not go up the mountain. *He* said:
6 'I *am* the LORD your God who brought you out of the land of Egypt, out of the house of bondage.
7 'You shall have no other gods before Me.
8 'You shall not make for yourself *any*

carved image, *or* any likeness *of anything* that *is* in heaven above, or that *is* in the earth beneath, or that *is* in the water under the earth;
9 you shall not bow down to them nor serve them. For I, the LORD your God, *am* a jealous God, visiting the iniquity of the fathers upon the children to the third and fourth *generations* of those who hate Me,
10 but showing mercy to thousands, to those who love Me and keep My commandments.
11 'You shall not take the name of the LORD your God in vain, for the LORD will not hold *him* guiltless who takes His name in vain.
12 'Observe the Sabbath day, to keep it holy, as the LORD your God commanded you.
13 Six days you shall labor and do all your work,
14 but the seventh day *is* the Sabbath of the LORD your God. *In it* you shall not do any work: you, nor your son, nor your daughter, nor your manservant, nor your maidservant, nor your ox, nor your donkey, nor any of your cattle, nor your stranger who *is* within your gates, that your manservant and your maidservant may rest as well as you.
15 And remember that you were a slave in the land of Egypt, and *that* the LORD your God brought you out from there by a mighty hand and by an outstretched arm; therefore the LORD your God commanded you to keep the Sabbath day.
16 'Honor your father and your mother, as the LORD your God has commanded you, that your days may be long, and that it may be well with you in the land which the LORD your God is giving you.
17 'You shall not murder.
18 'You shall not commit adultery.
19 'You shall not steal.
20 'You shall not bear false witness against your neighbor.
21 'You shall not covet your neighbor's wife; and you shall not desire your neighbor's house, his field, his

10 Syriac reads *Sirion* (compare 3:9).

manservant, his maidservant, his ox, his donkey, or anything that *is* your neighbor's.'

22 "These words the LORD spoke to all your assembly, in the mountain from the midst of the fire, the cloud, and the thick darkness, with a loud voice; and He added no more. And He wrote them on two tablets of stone and gave them to me.

The People Afraid of God's Presence

23 "So it was, when you heard the voice from the midst of the darkness, while the mountain was burning with fire, that you came near to me, all the heads of your tribes and your elders.
24 "And you said: 'Surely the LORD our God has shown us His glory and His greatness, and we have heard His voice from the midst of the fire. We have seen this day that God speaks with man; yet he *still* lives.
25 'Now therefore, why should we die? For this great fire will consume us; if we hear the voice of the LORD our God anymore, then we shall die.
26 'For who *is there* of all flesh who has heard the voice of the living God speaking from the midst of the fire, as we *have*, and lived?
27 'You go near and hear all that the LORD our God may say, and tell us all that the LORD our God says to you, and we will hear and do *it.*'
28 "Then the LORD heard the voice of your words when you spoke to me, and the LORD said to me: 'I have heard the voice of the words of this people which they have spoken to you. They are right *in* all that they have spoken.
29 'Oh, that they had such a heart in them that they would fear Me and always keep all My commandments, that it might be well with them and with their children forever!
30 'Go and say to them, "Return to your tents."
31 'But as for you, stand here by Me, and I will speak to you all the commandments, the statutes, and the judgments which you shall teach them, that they may observe *them* in the land which I am giving them to possess.'
32 "Therefore you shall be careful to do as the LORD your God has commanded you; you shall not turn aside to the right hand or to the left.

33 "You shall walk in all the ways which the LORD your God has commanded you, that you may live and *that it may be* well with you, and *that* you may prolong *your* days in the land which you shall possess.

The Greatest Commandment

6 "Now this *is* the commandment, *and these are* the statutes and judgments which the LORD your God has commanded to teach you, that you may observe *them* in the land which you are crossing over to possess,
2 "that you may fear the LORD your God, to keep all His statutes and His commandments which I command you, you and your son and your grandson, all the days of your life, and that your days may be prolonged.
3 "Therefore hear, O Israel, and be careful to observe *it,* that it may be well with you, and that you may multiply greatly as the LORD God of your fathers has promised you—'a land flowing with milk and honey.'[11]
4 "Hear, O Israel: The LORD our God, the LORD is one!
5 "You shall love the LORD your God with all your heart, with all your soul, and with all your might.
6 "And these words which I command you today shall be in your heart;
7 "you shall teach them diligently to your children, and shall talk of them when you sit in your house, when you walk by the way, when you lie down, and when you rise up.
8 "You shall bind them as a sign on your hand, and they shall be as frontlets between your eyes.
9 "You shall write them on the doorposts of your house and on your gates.

Caution Against Disobedience

10 "And it shall be, when the LORD your God brings you into the land of which He swore to your fathers, to Abraham, Isaac, and Jacob, to give you large and beautiful cities which you did not build,
11 "houses full of all good things, which you did not fill, hewn-out wells which you did not dig, vineyards and olive trees which you did not plant—when you have eaten and are full—
12 "*then* beware, lest you forget the LORD who brought you out of the land of Egypt, from the house of bondage.

11 Compare Exodus 3:8

13 "You shall fear the LORD your God and serve Him, and shall take oaths in His name.
14 "You shall not go after other gods, the gods of the peoples who *are* all around you
15 "(for the LORD your God *is* a jealous God among you), lest the anger of the LORD your God be aroused against you and destroy you from the face of the earth.
16 "You shall not tempt the LORD your God as you tempted *Him* in Massah.
17 "You shall diligently keep the commandments of the LORD your God, His testimonies, and His statutes which He has commanded you.
18 "And you shall do *what is* right and good in the sight of the LORD, that it may be well with you, and that you may go in and possess the good land of which the LORD swore to your fathers,
19 "to cast out all your enemies from before you, as the LORD has spoken.
20 "When your son asks you in time to come, saying, 'What *is the meaning of* the testimonies, the statutes, and the judgments which the LORD our God has commanded you?'
21 "then you shall say to your son: 'We were slaves of Pharaoh in Egypt, and the LORD brought us out of Egypt with a mighty hand;
22 'and the LORD showed signs and wonders before our eyes, great and severe, against Egypt, Pharaoh, and all his household.
23 'Then He brought us out from there, that He might bring us in, to give us the land of which He swore to our fathers.
24 'And the LORD commanded us to observe all these statutes, to fear the LORD our God, for our good always, that He might preserve us alive, as *it is* this day.
25 'Then it will be righteousness for us, if we are careful to observe all these commandments before the LORD our God, as He has commanded us.'

A Chosen People

7 "When the LORD your God brings you into the land which you go to possess, and has cast out many nations before you, the Hittites and the Girgashites and the Amorites and the Canaanites and the Perizzites and the Hivites and the Jebusites, seven nations greater and mightier than you,
2 "and when the LORD your God delivers them over to you, you shall conquer them *and* utterly destroy them. You shall make no covenant with them nor show mercy to them.
3 "Nor shall you make marriages with them. You shall not give your daughter to their son, nor take their daughter for your son.
4 "For they will turn your sons away from following Me, to serve other gods; so the anger of the LORD will be aroused against you and destroy you suddenly.
5 "But thus you shall deal with them: you shall destroy their altars, and break down their *sacred* pillars, and cut down their wooden images,[12] and burn their carved images with fire.
6 "For you *are* a holy people to the LORD your God; the LORD your God has chosen you to be a people for Himself, a special treasure above all the peoples on the face of the earth.
7 "The LORD did not set His love on you nor choose you because you were more in number than any other people, for you were the least of all peoples;
8 "but because the LORD loves you, and because He would keep the oath which He swore to your fathers, the LORD has brought you out with a mighty hand, and redeemed you from the house of bondage, from the hand of Pharaoh king of Egypt.
9 "Therefore know that the LORD your God, He *is* God, the faithful God who keeps covenant and mercy for a thousand generations with those who love Him and keep His commandments;
10 "and He repays those who hate Him to their face, to destroy them. He will not be slack with him who hates Him; He will repay him to his face.
11 "Therefore you shall keep the commandment, the statutes, and the judgments which I command you today, to observe them.

Blessings of Obedience

12 "Then it shall come to pass, because you listen to these judgments, and keep and do them, that the LORD your God will keep with you the covenant and the mercy which He swore to your fathers.

12 Hebrew *Asherim*, Canaanite deities

13 "And He will love you and bless you and multiply you; He will also bless the fruit of your womb and the fruit of your land, your grain and your new wine and your oil, the increase of your cattle and the offspring of your flock, in the land of which He swore to your fathers to give you.
14 "You shall be blessed above all peoples; there shall not be a male or female barren among you or among your livestock.
15 "And the LORD will take away from you all sickness, and will afflict you with none of the terrible diseases of Egypt which you have known, but will lay *them* on all those who hate you.
16 "And you shall destroy all the peoples whom the LORD your God delivers over to you; your eye shall have no pity on them; nor shall you serve their gods, for that *will be* a snare to you.
17 "If you should say in your heart, 'These nations are greater than I; how can I dispossess them?'—
18 "you shall not be afraid of them, *but* you shall remember well what the LORD your God did to Pharaoh and to all Egypt:
19 "the great trials which your eyes saw, the signs and the wonders, the mighty hand and the outstretched arm, by which the LORD your God brought you out. So shall the LORD your God do to all the peoples of whom you are afraid.
20 "Moreover the LORD your God will send the hornet among them until those who are left, who hide themselves from you, are destroyed.
21 "You shall not be terrified of them; for the LORD your God, the great and awesome God, *is* among you.
22 "And the LORD your God will drive out those nations before you little by little; you will be unable to destroy them at once, lest the beasts of the field become *too* numerous for you.
23 "But the LORD your God will deliver them over to you, and will inflict defeat upon them until they are destroyed.
24 "And He will deliver their kings into your hand, and you will destroy their name from under heaven; no one shall be able to stand against you until you have destroyed them.
25 "You shall burn the carved images of their gods with fire; you shall not covet

the silver or gold *that is* on them, nor take *it* for yourselves, lest you be snared by it; for it *is* an abomination to the LORD your God.
26 "Nor shall you bring an abomination into your house, lest you be doomed to destruction like it; *but* you shall utterly detest it and utterly abhor it, for it *is* an accursed thing.

Remember the LORD Your God

8 "Every commandment which I command you today you must be careful to observe, that you may live and multiply, and go in and possess the land of which the LORD swore to your fathers.
2 "And you shall remember that the LORD your God led you all the way these forty years in the wilderness, to humble you *and* test you, to know what *was* in your heart, whether you would keep His commandments or not.
3 "So He humbled you, allowed you to hunger, and fed you with manna which you did not know nor did your fathers know, that He might make you know that man shall not live by bread alone; but man lives by every *word* that proceeds from the mouth of the LORD.
4 "Your garments did not wear out on you, nor did your foot swell these forty years.
5 "So you should know in your heart that as a man chastens his son, *so* the LORD your God chastens you.
6 "Therefore you shall keep the commandments of the LORD your God, to walk in His ways and to fear Him.
7 "For the LORD your God is bringing you into a good land, a land of brooks of water, of fountains and springs, that flow out of valleys and hills;
8 "a land of wheat and barley, of vines and fig trees and pomegranates, a land of olive oil and honey;
9 "a land in which you will eat bread without scarcity, in which you will lack nothing; a land whose stones *are* iron and out of whose hills you can dig copper.
10 "When you have eaten and are full, then you shall bless the LORD your God for the good land which He has given you.
11 "Beware that you do not forget the LORD your God by not keeping His commandments, His judgments, and His statutes which I command you today,

12 "lest—*when* you have eaten and are full, and have built beautiful houses and dwell *in them*;
13 "and *when* your herds and your flocks multiply, and your silver and your gold are multiplied, and all that you have is multiplied;
14 "when your heart is lifted up, and you forget the LORD your God who brought you out of the land of Egypt, from the house of bondage;
15 "who led you through that great and terrible wilderness, *in which were* fiery serpents and scorpions and thirsty land where there was no water; who brought water for you out of the rock of flint;
16 "who fed you in the wilderness with manna, which your fathers did not know, that He might humble you and that He might test you, to do you good in the end—
17 "then you say in your heart, 'My power and the might of my hand have gained me this wealth.'
18 "And you shall remember the LORD your God, for *it is* He who gives you power to get wealth, that He may establish His covenant which He swore to your fathers, as *it is* this day.
19 "Then it shall be, if you by any means forget the LORD your God, and follow other gods, and serve them and worship them, I testify against you this day that you shall surely perish.
20 "As the nations which the LORD destroys before you, so you shall perish, because you would not be obedient to the voice of the LORD your God.

Israel's Rebellions Reviewed

9 "Hear, O Israel: You *are* to cross over the Jordan today, and go in to dispossess nations greater and mightier than yourself, cities great and fortified up to heaven,
2 "a people great and tall, the descendants of the Anakim, whom you know, and *of whom* you heard *it said,* 'Who can stand before the descendants of Anak?'
3 "Therefore understand today that the LORD your God *is* He who goes over before you *as* a consuming fire. He will destroy them and bring them down before you; so you shall drive them out and destroy them quickly, as the LORD has said to you.
4 "Do not think in your heart, after the LORD your God has cast them out before you, saying, 'Because of my righteousness the LORD has brought me in to possess this land'; but *it is* because of the wickedness of these nations *that* the LORD is driving them out from before you.
5 "*It is* not because of your righteousness or the uprightness of your heart *that* you go in to possess their land, but because of the wickedness of these nations *that* the LORD your God drives them out from before you, and that He may fulfill the word which the LORD swore to your fathers, to Abraham, Isaac, and Jacob.
6 "Therefore understand that the LORD your God is not giving you this good land to possess because of your righteousness, for you *are* a stiff-necked people.
7 "Remember *and* do not forget how you provoked the LORD your God to wrath in the wilderness; from the day that you departed from the land of Egypt until you came to this place, you have been rebellious against the LORD.
8 "Also in Horeb you provoked the LORD to wrath, so that the LORD was angry *enough* with you to have destroyed you.
9 "When I went up into the mountain to receive the tablets of stone, the tablets of the covenant which the LORD made with you, then I stayed on the mountain forty days and forty nights. I neither ate bread nor drank water.
10 "Then the LORD delivered to me two tablets of stone written with the finger of God, and on them *were* all the words which the LORD had spoken to you on the mountain from the midst of the fire in the day of the assembly.
11 "And it came to pass, at the end of forty days and forty nights, *that* the LORD gave me the two tablets of stone, the tablets of the covenant.
12 "Then the LORD said to me, 'Arise, go down quickly from here, for your people whom you brought out of Egypt have acted corruptly; they have quickly turned aside from the way which I commanded them; they have made themselves a molded image.'
13 "Furthermore the LORD spoke to me, saying, 'I have seen this people, and indeed they are a stiff-necked people.
14 'Let Me alone, that I may destroy them and blot out their name from under

heaven; and I will make of you a nation mightier and greater than they.'

15 "So I turned and came down from the mountain, and the mountain burned with fire; and the two tablets of the covenant *were* in my two hands.

16 "And I looked, and there, you had sinned against the LORD your God, *and* had made for yourselves a molded calf! You had turned aside quickly from the way which the LORD had commanded you.

17 "Then I took the two tablets and threw them out of my two hands and broke them before your eyes.

18 "And I fell down before the LORD, as at the first, forty days and forty nights; I neither ate bread nor drank water, because of all your sin which you committed in doing wickedly in the sight of the LORD, to provoke Him to anger.

19 "For I was afraid of the anger and hot displeasure with which the LORD was angry with you, to destroy you. But the LORD listened to me at that time also.

20 "And the LORD was very angry with Aaron *and* would have destroyed him; so I prayed for Aaron also at the same time.

21 "Then I took your sin, the calf which you had made, and burned it with fire and crushed it *and* ground *it* very small, until it was as fine as dust; and I threw its dust into the brook that descended from the mountain.

22 "Also at Taberah and Massah and Kibroth Hattaavah you provoked the LORD to wrath.

23 "Likewise, when the LORD sent you from Kadesh Barnea, saying, 'Go up and possess the land which I have given you,' then you rebelled against the commandment of the LORD your God, and you did not believe Him nor obey His voice.

24 "You have been rebellious against the LORD from the day that I knew you.

25 "Thus I prostrated myself before the LORD; forty days and forty nights I kept prostrating myself, because the LORD had said He would destroy you.

26 "Therefore I prayed to the LORD, and said: 'O Lord GOD, do not destroy Your people and Your inheritance whom You have redeemed through Your greatness, whom You have brought out of Egypt with a mighty hand.

27 'Remember Your servants, Abraham, Isaac, and Jacob; do not look on the stubbornness of this people, or on their wickedness or their sin,

28 'lest the land from which You brought us should say, "Because the LORD was not able to bring them to the land which He promised them, and because He hated them, He has brought them out to kill them in the wilderness."

29 'Yet they *are* Your people and Your inheritance, whom You brought out by Your mighty power and by Your outstretched arm.'

The Second Pair of Tablets

10 "At that time the LORD said to me, 'Hew for yourself two tablets of stone like the first, and come up to Me on the mountain and make yourself an ark of wood.

2 'And I will write on the tablets the words that were on the first tablets, which you broke; and you shall put them in the ark.'

3 "So I made an ark of acacia wood, hewed two tablets of stone like the first, and went up the mountain, having the two tablets in my hand.

4 "And He wrote on the tablets according to the first writing, the Ten Commandments, which the LORD had spoken to you in the mountain from the midst of the fire in the day of the assembly; and the LORD gave them to me.

5 "Then I turned and came down from the mountain, and put the tablets in the ark which I had made; and there they are, just as the LORD commanded me."

6 (Now the children of Israel journeyed from the wells of Bene Jaakan to Moserah. *That was the place* where Aaron died *later*, and where he was buried; and Eleazar his son ministered as priest in his stead.

7 From there they journeyed to Gudgodah, and from Gudgodah to Jotbathah, a land of rivers of water.

8 At that time the LORD separated the tribe of Levi to bear the ark of the covenant of the LORD, to stand before the LORD to minister to Him and to bless in His name, to this day.

9 Therefore Levi has no portion nor inheritance with his brethren; the LORD *is* his inheritance, just as the LORD your God promised him.)

10 "As at the first time, I stayed in the mountain forty days and forty nights;

the LORD also heard me at that time, *and* the LORD chose not to destroy you.

11 "Then the LORD said to me, 'Arise, begin *your* journey before the people, that they may go in and possess the land which I swore to their fathers to give them.'

The Essence of the Law

12 "And now, Israel, what does the LORD your God require of you, but to fear the LORD your God, to walk in all His ways and to love Him, to serve the LORD your God with all your heart and with all your soul,

13 "*and* to keep the commandments of the LORD and His statutes which I command you today for your good?

14 "Indeed heaven and the highest heavens belong to the LORD your God, *also* the earth with all that *is* in it.

15 "The LORD delighted only in your fathers, to love them; and He chose their descendants after them, you above all peoples, as *it is* this day.

16 "Therefore circumcise the foreskin of your heart, and be stiff-necked no longer.

17 "For the LORD your God *is* God of gods and Lord of lords, the great God, mighty and awesome, who shows no partiality nor takes a bribe.

18 "He administers justice for the fatherless and the widow, and loves the stranger, giving him food and clothing.

19 "Therefore love the stranger, for you were strangers in the land of Egypt.

20 "You shall fear the LORD your God; you shall serve Him, and to Him you shall hold fast, and take oaths in His name.

21 "He *is* your praise, and He *is* your God, who has done for you these great and awesome things which your eyes have seen.

22 "Your fathers went down to Egypt with seventy persons, and now the LORD your God has made you as the stars of heaven in multitude.

Love and Obedience Rewarded

11 "Therefore you shall love the LORD your God, and keep His charge, His statutes, His judgments, and His commandments always.

2 "Know today that *I do* not *speak* with your children, who have not known and who have not seen the chastening of the LORD your God, His greatness and His mighty hand and His outstretched arm—

3 "His signs and His acts which He did in the midst of Egypt, to Pharaoh king of Egypt, and to all his land;

4 "what He did to the army of Egypt, to their horses and their chariots: how He made the waters of the Red Sea overflow them as they pursued you, and *how* the LORD has destroyed them to this day;

5 "what He did for you in the wilderness until you came to this place;

6 "and what He did to Dathan and Abiram the sons of Eliab, the son of Reuben: how the earth opened its mouth and swallowed them up, their households, their tents, and all the substance that *was* in their possession, in the midst of all Israel—

7 "but your eyes have seen every great act of the LORD which He did.

8 "Therefore you shall keep every commandment which I command you today, that you may be strong, and go in and possess the land which you cross over to possess,

9 "and that you may prolong *your* days in the land which the LORD swore to give your fathers, to them and their descendants, 'a land flowing with milk and honey.'[13]

10 "For the land which you go to possess *is* not like the land of Egypt from which you have come, where you sowed your seed and watered *it* by foot, as a vegetable garden;

11 "but the land which you cross over to possess *is* a land of hills and valleys, which drinks water from the rain of heaven,

12 "a land for which the LORD your God cares; the eyes of the LORD your God *are* always on it, from the beginning of the year to the very end of the year.

13 'And it shall be that if you diligently obey My commandments which I command you today, to love the LORD your God and serve Him with all your heart and with all your soul,

14 'then I will give *you* the rain for your land in its season, the early rain and the latter rain, that you may gather in your grain, your new wine, and your oil.

15 'And I will send grass in your fields for your livestock, that you may eat and be filled.'

13 Compare Exodus 3:8

16 "Take heed to yourselves, lest your heart be deceived, and you turn aside and serve other gods and worship them,

17 "lest the LORD's anger be aroused against you, and He shut up the heavens so that there be no rain, and the land yield no produce, and you perish quickly from the good land which the LORD is giving you.

18 "Therefore you shall lay up these words of mine in your heart and in your soul, and bind them as a sign on your hand, and they shall be as frontlets between your eyes.

19 "You shall teach them to your children, speaking of them when you sit in your house, when you walk by the way, when you lie down, and when you rise up.

20 "And you shall write them on the doorposts of your house and on your gates,

21 "that your days and the days of your children may be multiplied in the land of which the LORD swore to your fathers to give them, like the days of the heavens above the earth.

22 "For if you carefully keep all these commandments which I command you to do—to love the LORD your God, to walk in all His ways, and to hold fast to Him—

23 "then the LORD will drive out all these nations from before you, and you will dispossess greater and mightier nations than yourselves.

24 "Every place on which the sole of your foot treads shall be yours: from the wilderness and Lebanon, from the river, the River Euphrates, even to the Western Sea,[14] shall be your territory.

25 "No man shall be able to stand against you; the LORD your God will put the dread of you and the fear of you upon all the land where you tread, just as He has said to you.

26 "Behold, I set before you today a blessing and a curse:

27 "the blessing, if you obey the commandments of the LORD your God which I command you today;

28 "and the curse, if you do not obey the commandments of the LORD your God, but turn aside from the way which I command you today, to go after other gods which you have not known.

29 "And it shall be, when the LORD your God has brought you into the land which you go to possess, that you shall put the blessing on Mount Gerizim and the curse on Mount Ebal.

30 "*Are* they not on the other side of the Jordan, toward the setting sun, in the land of the Canaanites who dwell in the plain opposite Gilgal, beside the terebinth trees of Moreh?

31 "For you will cross over the Jordan and go in to possess the land which the LORD your God is giving you, and you will possess it and dwell in it.

32 "And you shall be careful to observe all the statutes and judgments which I set before you today.

A Prescribed Place of Worship

12 "These *are* the statutes and judgments which you shall be careful to observe in the land which the LORD God of your fathers is giving you to possess, all the days that you live on the earth.

2 "You shall utterly destroy all the places where the nations which you shall dispossess served their gods, on the high mountains and on the hills and under every green tree.

3 "And you shall destroy their altars, break their *sacred* pillars, and burn their wooden images with fire; you shall cut down the carved images of their gods and destroy their names from that place.

4 "You shall not worship the LORD your God *with* such *things.*

5 "But you shall seek the place where the LORD your God chooses, out of all your tribes, to put His name for His habitation; and there you shall go.

6 "There you shall take your burnt offerings, your sacrifices, your tithes, the heave offerings of your hand, your vowed offerings, your freewill offerings, and the firstlings of your herds and flocks.

7 "And there you shall eat before the LORD your God, and you shall rejoice in all to which you have put your hand, you and your households, in which the LORD your God has blessed you.

8 "You shall not at all do as we are doing here today—every man doing whatever *is* right in his own eyes—

9 "for as yet you have not come to the rest and the inheritance which the LORD your God is giving you.

10 "But *when* you cross over the Jordan and dwell in the land which the LORD your God is giving you to inherit, and

14 That is, the Mediterranean

when He gives you rest from all your enemies round about, so that you dwell in safety,

11 "then there will be the place where the LORD your God chooses to make His name abide. There you shall bring all that I command you: your burnt offerings, your sacrifices, your tithes, the heave offerings of your hand, and all your choice offerings which you vow to the LORD.

12 "And you shall rejoice before the LORD your God, you and your sons and your daughters, your menservants and your maidservants, and the Levite who *is* within your gates, since he has no portion nor inheritance with you.

13 "Take heed to yourself that you do not offer your burnt offerings in every place that you see;

14 "but in the place which the LORD chooses, in one of your tribes, there you shall offer your burnt offerings, and there you shall do all that I command you.

15 "However, you may slaughter and eat meat within all your gates, whatever your heart desires, according to the blessing of the LORD your God which He has given you; the unclean and the clean may eat of it, of the gazelle and the deer alike.

16 "Only you shall not eat the blood; you shall pour it on the earth like water.

17 "You may not eat within your gates the tithe of your grain or your new wine or your oil, of the firstlings of your herd or your flock, of any of your offerings which you vow, of your freewill offerings, or of the heave offering of your hand.

18 "But you must eat them before the LORD your God in the place which the LORD your God chooses, you and your son and your daughter, your manservant and your maidservant, and the Levite who *is* within your gates; and you shall rejoice before the LORD your God in all to which you put your hands.

19 "Take heed to yourself that you do not forsake the Levite as long as you live in your land.

20 "When the LORD your God enlarges your border as He has promised you, and you say, 'Let me eat meat,' because you long to eat meat, you may eat as much meat as your heart desires.

21 "If the place where the LORD your God chooses to put His name is too far

from you, then you may slaughter from your herd and from your flock which the LORD has given you, just as I have commanded you, and you may eat within your gates as much as your heart desires.

22 "Just as the gazelle and the deer are eaten, so you may eat them; the unclean and the clean alike may eat them.

23 "Only be sure that you do not eat the blood, for the blood *is* the life; you may not eat the life with the meat.

24 "You shall not eat it; you shall pour it on the earth like water.

25 "You shall not eat it, that it may go well with you and your children after you, when you do *what is* right in the sight of the LORD.

26 "Only the holy things which you have, and your vowed offerings, you shall take and go to the place which the LORD chooses.

27 "And you shall offer your burnt offerings, the meat and the blood, on the altar of the LORD your God; and the blood of your sacrifices shall be poured out on the altar of the LORD your God, and you shall eat the meat.

28 "Observe and obey all these words which I command you, that it may go well with you and your children after you forever, when you do *what is* good and right in the sight of the LORD your God.

Beware of False Gods

29 "When the LORD your God cuts off from before you the nations which you go to dispossess, and you displace them and dwell in their land,

30 "take heed to yourself that you are not ensnared to follow them, after they are destroyed from before you, and that you do not inquire after their gods, saying, 'How did these nations serve their gods? I also will do likewise.'

31 "You shall not worship the LORD your God in that way; for every abomination to the LORD which He hates they have done to their gods; for they burn even their sons and daughters in the fire to their gods.

32 "Whatever I command you, be careful to observe it; you shall not add to it nor take away from it.

Punishment of Apostates

13 "If there arises among you a prophet or a dreamer of dreams, and he gives you a sign or a wonder,

2 "and the sign or the wonder of which he spoke to you comes to pass, saying, 'Let us go after other gods which you have not known, and let us serve them,'
3 "you shall not listen to the words of that prophet or that dreamer of dreams, for the LORD your God is testing you to know whether you love the LORD your God with all your heart and with all your soul.
4 "You shall walk after the LORD your God and fear Him, and keep His commandments and obey His voice, and you shall serve Him and hold fast to Him.
5 "But that prophet or that dreamer of dreams shall be put to death, because he has spoken in order to turn you away from the LORD your God, who brought you out of the land of Egypt and redeemed you from the house of bondage, to entice you from the way in which the LORD your God commanded you to walk. So you shall put away the evil from your midst.
6 "If your brother, the son of your mother, your son or your daughter, the wife of your bosom, or your friend who is as your own soul, secretly entices you, saying, 'Let us go and serve other gods,' which you have not known, neither you nor your fathers,
7 "of the gods of the people which are all around you, near to you or far off from you, from one end of the earth to the other end of the earth,
8 "you shall not consent to him or listen to him, nor shall your eye pity him, nor shall you spare him or conceal him;
9 "but you shall surely kill him; your hand shall be first against him to put him to death, and afterward the hand of all the people.
10 "And you shall stone him with stones until he dies, because he sought to entice you away from the LORD your God, who brought you out of the land of Egypt, from the house of bondage.
11 "So all Israel shall hear and fear, and not again do such wickedness as this among you.
12 "If you hear someone in one of your cities, which the LORD your God gives you to dwell in, saying,
13 'Certain corrupt men have gone out from among you and enticed the inhabitants of their city, saying, "Let us go and

serve other gods," gods whom you have not known,'
14 "then you shall inquire, search out, and ask diligently. And if it is indeed true and certain that such an abomination was committed among you,
15 "you shall surely strike the inhabitants of that city with the edge of the sword—utterly destroying it, all that is in it and its livestock, with the edge of the sword.
16 "And you shall gather all its plunder into the middle of the street, and completely burn with fire the city and all its plunder, for the LORD your God; and it shall be a heap forever. It shall not be built again.
17 "So none of the accursed things shall remain in your hand, that the LORD may turn from the fierceness of His anger and show you mercy, have compassion on you and multiply you, just as He swore to your fathers,
18 "because you have listened to the voice of the LORD your God, to keep all His commandments which I command you today, to do what is right in the eyes of the LORD your God.

Improper Mourning

14 "You are the children of the LORD your God; you shall not cut yourselves nor shave the front of your head for the dead.
2 "For you are a holy people to the LORD your God, and the LORD has chosen you to be a people for Himself, a special treasure above all the peoples who are on the face of the earth.

Clean and Unclean Meat

3 "You shall not eat any detestable thing.
4 "These are the animals which you may eat: the ox, the sheep, the goat,
5 "the deer, the gazelle, the roe deer, the wild goat, the mountain goat,[15] the antelope, and the mountain sheep.
6 "And you may eat every animal with cloven hooves, having the hoof split into two parts, and that chews the cud, among the animals.
7 "Nevertheless, of those that chew the cud or have cloven hooves, you shall not eat, such as these: the camel, the hare, and the rock hyrax; for they chew the cud

15 Or addax

but do not have cloven hooves; they *are* unclean for you.

8 "Also the swine is unclean for you, because it has cloven hooves, yet *does* not *chew* the cud; you shall not eat their flesh or touch their dead carcasses.

9 "These you may eat of all that *are* in the waters: you may eat all that have fins and scales.

10 "And whatever does not have fins and scales you shall not eat; it *is* unclean for you.

11 "All clean birds you may eat.

12 "But these you shall not eat: the eagle, the vulture, the buzzard,

13 "the red kite, the falcon, and the kite after their kinds;

14 "every raven after its kind;

15 "the ostrich, the short-eared owl, the seagull, and the hawk after their kinds;

16 "the little owl, the screech owl, the white owl,

17 "the jackdaw, the carrion vulture, the fisher owl,

18 "the stork, the heron after its kind, and the hoopoe and the bat.

19 "Also every creeping thing that flies is unclean for you; they shall not be eaten.

20 "You may eat all clean birds.

21 "You shall not eat anything that dies *of itself*; you may give it to the alien who *is* within your gates, that he may eat it, or you may sell it to a foreigner; for you *are* a holy people to the LORD your God. You shall not boil a young goat in its mother's milk.

Tithing Principles

22 "You shall truly tithe all the increase of your grain that the field produces year by year.

23 "And you shall eat before the LORD your God, in the place where He chooses to make His name abide, the tithe of your grain and your new wine and your oil, of the firstlings of your herds and your flocks, that you may learn to fear the LORD your God always.

24 "But if the journey is too long for you, so that you are not able to carry *the tithe, or* if the place where the LORD your God chooses to put His name is too far from you, when the LORD your God has blessed you,

25 "then you shall exchange *it* for money, take the money in your hand, and go to the place which the LORD your God chooses.

26 "And you shall spend that money for whatever your heart desires: for oxen or sheep, for wine or similar drink, for whatever your heart desires; you shall eat there before the LORD your God, and you shall rejoice, you and your household.

27 "You shall not forsake the Levite who *is* within your gates, for he has no part nor inheritance with you.

28 "At the end of *every* third year you shall bring out the tithe of your produce of that year and store *it* up within your gates.

29 "And the Levite, because he has no portion nor inheritance with you, and the stranger and the fatherless and the widow who *are* within your gates, may come and eat and be satisfied, that the LORD your God may bless you in all the work of your hand which you do.

Debts Canceled Every Seven Years

15 "At the end of *every* seven years you shall grant a release *of debts.*

2 "And this *is* the form of the release: Every creditor who has lent *anything* to his neighbor shall release *it*; he shall not require *it* of his neighbor or his brother, because it is called the LORD's release.

3 "Of a foreigner you may require *it*; but your hand shall release what is owed by your brother,

4 "except when there may be no poor among you; for the LORD will greatly bless you in the land which the LORD your God is giving you to possess *as* an inheritance—

5 "only if you carefully obey the voice of the LORD your God, to observe with care all these commandments which I command you today.

6 "For the LORD your God will bless you just as He promised you; you shall lend to many nations, but you shall not borrow; you shall reign over many nations, but they shall not reign over you.

Generosity to the Poor

7 "If there is among you a poor man of your brethren, within any of the gates in your land which the LORD your God is giving you, you shall not harden your heart nor shut your hand from your poor brother,

8 "but you shall open your hand wide

to him and willingly lend him sufficient for his need, whatever he needs.

9 "Beware lest there be a wicked thought in your heart, saying, 'The seventh year, the year of release, is at hand,' and your eye be evil against your poor brother and you give him nothing, and he cry out to the LORD against you, and it become sin among you.

10 "You shall surely give to him, and your heart should not be grieved when you give to him, because for this thing the LORD your God will bless you in all your works and in all to which you put your hand.

11 "For the poor will never cease from the land; therefore I command you, saying, 'You shall open your hand wide to your brother, to your poor and your needy, in your land.'

The Law Concerning Bond Servants

12 "If your brother, a Hebrew man, or a Hebrew woman, is sold to you and serves you six years, then in the seventh year you shall let him go free from you.

13 "And when you send him away free from you, you shall not let him go away empty-handed;.

14 "you shall supply him liberally from your flock, from your threshing floor, and from your winepress. *From what* the LORD has blessed you with, you shall give to him.

15 "You shall remember that you were a slave in the land of Egypt, and the LORD your God redeemed you; therefore I command you this thing today.

16 "And if it happens that he says to you, 'I will not go away from you,' because he loves you and your house, since he prospers with you,

17 "then you shall take an awl and thrust *it* through his ear to the door, and he shall be your servant forever. Also to your maidservant you shall do likewise.

18 "It shall not seem hard to you when you send him away free from you; for he has been worth a double hired servant in serving you six years. Then the LORD your God will bless you in all that you do.

The Law Concerning Firstborn Animals

19 "All the firstborn males that come from your herd and your flock you shall

sanctify to the LORD your God; you shall do no work with the firstborn of your herd, nor shear the firstborn of your flock.

20 "You and your household shall eat *it* before the LORD your God year by year in the place which the LORD chooses.

21 "But if there is *any* defect in it, *if it is* lame or blind *or has* any serious defect, you shall not sacrifice it to the LORD your God.

22 "You may eat it within your gates; the unclean and the clean *person* alike *may eat it,* as *if it were* a gazelle or a deer.

23 "Only you shall not eat its blood; you shall pour it on the ground like water.

The Passover Reviewed

16 "Observe the month of Abib, and keep the Passover to the LORD your God, for in the month of Abib the LORD your God brought you out of Egypt by night.

2 "Therefore you shall sacrifice the Passover to the LORD your God, from the flock and the herd, in the place where the LORD chooses to put His name.

3 "You shall eat no leavened bread with it; seven days you shall eat unleavened bread with it, *that is,* the bread of affliction (for you came out of the land of Egypt in haste), that you may remember the day in which you came out of the land of Egypt all the days of your life.

4 "And no leaven shall be seen among you in all your territory for seven days, nor shall *any* of the meat which you sacrifice the first day at twilight remain overnight until morning.

5 "You may not sacrifice the Passover within any of your gates which the LORD your God gives you;

6 "but at the place where the LORD your God chooses to make His name abide, there you shall sacrifice the Passover at twilight, at the going down of the sun, at the time you came out of Egypt.

7 "And you shall roast and eat *it* in the place which the LORD your God chooses, and in the morning you shall turn and go to your tents.

8 "Six days you shall eat unleavened bread, and on the seventh day there *shall be* a sacred assembly to the LORD your God. You shall do no work *on it.*

The Feast of Weeks Reviewed

9 "You shall count seven weeks for yourself; begin to count the seven weeks from *the time* you begin *to put* the sickle to the grain.

10 "Then you shall keep the Feast of Weeks to the LORD your God with the tribute of a freewill offering from your hand, which you shall give as the LORD your God blesses you.

11 "You shall rejoice before the LORD your God, you and your son and your daughter, your manservant and your maidservant, the Levite who *is* within your gates, the stranger and the fatherless and the widow who *are* among you, at the place where the LORD your God chooses to make His name abide.

12 "And you shall remember that you were a slave in Egypt, and you shall be careful to observe these statutes.

The Feast of Tabernacles Reviewed

13 "You shall observe the Feast of Tabernacles seven days, when you have gathered from your threshing floor and from your winepress;

14 "and you shall rejoice in your feast, you and your son and your daughter, your manservant and your maidservant and the Levite, the stranger and the fatherless and the widow, who *are* within your gates.

15 "Seven days you shall keep a sacred feast to the LORD your God in the place which the LORD chooses, because the LORD your God will bless you in all your produce and in all the work of your hands, so that you surely rejoice.

16 "Three times a year all your males shall appear before the LORD your God in the place which He chooses: at the Feast of Unleavened Bread, at the Feast of Weeks, and at the Feast of Tabernacles; and they shall not appear before the LORD empty-handed.

17 "Every man *shall give* as he is able, according to the blessing of the LORD your God which He has given you.

Justice Must Be Administered

18 "You shall appoint judges and officers in all your gates, which the LORD your God gives you, according to your tribes, and they shall judge the people with just judgment.

19 "You shall not pervert justice; you shall not show partiality, nor take a bribe, for a bribe blinds the eyes of the wise and twists the words of the righteous.

20 "You shall follow what is altogether just, that you may live and inherit the land which the LORD your God is giving you.

21 "You shall not plant for yourself any tree, as a wooden image, near the altar which you build for yourself to the LORD your God.

22 "You shall not set up a sacred pillar, which the LORD your God hates.

17 "You shall not sacrifice to the LORD your God a bull or sheep which has any blemish *or* defect, for that *is* an abomination to the LORD your God.

2 "If there is found among you, within any of your gates which the LORD your God gives you, a man or a woman who has been wicked in the sight of the LORD your God, in transgressing His covenant,

3 "who has gone and served other gods and worshiped them, either the sun or moon or any of the host of heaven, which I have not commanded,

4 "and it is told you, and you hear *of it*, then you shall inquire diligently. And if *it is* indeed true *and* certain that such an abomination has been committed in Israel,

5 "then you shall bring out to your gates that man or woman who has committed that wicked thing, and shall stone to death that man or woman with stones.

6 "Whoever is worthy of death shall be put to death on the testimony of two or three witnesses, *but* he shall not be put to death on the testimony of one witness.

7 "The hands of the witnesses shall be the first against him to put him to death, and afterward the hands of all the people. So you shall put away the evil *person* from among you.

8 "If a matter arises which is too hard for you to judge, between degrees of bloodguiltiness, between one judgment or another, or between one punishment or another, matters of controversy within your gates, then you shall arise and go up to the place which the LORD your God chooses,

9 "and you shall come to the priests, the Levites, and to the judge *there* in those

days, and inquire *of them*; they shall pronounce upon you the sentence of judgment.
10 "You shall do according to the sentence which they pronounce upon you in that place which the LORD chooses. And you shall be careful to do according to all that they order you.
11 "According to the sentence of the law in which they instruct you, according to the judgment which they tell you, you shall do; you shall not turn aside *to* the right hand or *to* the left from the sentence which they pronounce upon you.
12 "Now the man who acts presumptuously and will not heed the priest who stands to minister there before the LORD your God, or the judge, that man shall die. So you shall put away the evil *person* from Israel.
13 "And all the people shall hear and fear, and no longer act presumptuously.

Principles Governing Kings

14 "When you come to the land which the LORD your God is giving you, and possess it and dwell in it, and say, 'I will set a king over me like all the nations that *are* around me,'
15 "you shall surely set a king over you whom the LORD your God chooses; *one* from among your brethren you shall set as king over you; you may not set a foreigner over you, who *is* not your brother.
16 "But he shall not multiply horses for himself, nor cause the people to return to Egypt to multiply horses, for the LORD has said to you, 'You shall not return that way again.'
17 "Neither shall he multiply wives for himself, lest his heart turn away; nor shall he greatly multiply silver and gold for himself.
18 "Also it shall be, when he sits on the throne of his kingdom, that he shall write for himself a copy of this law in a book, from *the one* before the priests, the Levites.
19 "And it shall be with him, and he shall read it all the days of his life, that he may learn to fear the LORD his God and be careful to observe all the words of this law and these statutes,
20 "that his heart may not be lifted above his brethren, that he may not turn aside from the commandment *to* the right hand or *to* the left, and that he may pro-

long *his* days in his kingdom, he and his children in the midst of Israel.

The Portion of the Priests and Levites

18 "The priests, the Levites, *indeed* all the tribe of Levi, shall have no part nor inheritance with Israel; they shall eat the offerings of the LORD made by fire, and His portion.
2 "Therefore they shall have no inheritance among their brethren; the LORD is their inheritance, as He said to them.
3 "And this shall be the priest's due from the people, from those who offer a sacrifice, whether *it is* bull or sheep: they shall give to the priest the shoulder, the cheeks, and the stomach.
4 "The firstfruits of your grain and your new wine and your oil, and the first of the fleece of your sheep, you shall give him.
5 "For the LORD your God has chosen him out of all your tribes to stand to minister in the name of the LORD, him and his sons forever.
6 "And if a Levite comes from any of your gates, from where he sojourns among all Israel, and comes with all the desire of his mind to the place which the LORD chooses,
7 "then he may serve in the name of the LORD his God as all his brethren the Levites *do*, who stand there before the LORD.
8 "They shall have equal portions to eat, besides what comes from the sale of his inheritance.

Avoid Wicked Customs

9 "When you come into the land which the LORD your God is giving you, you shall not learn to follow the abominations of those nations.
10 "There shall not be found among you *anyone* who makes his son or his daughter pass through the fire, *or one* who practices witchcraft, *or* a soothsayer, or one who interprets omens, or a sorcerer,
11 "or one who conjures spells, or a medium, or a spiritist, or one who calls up the dead.
12 "For all who do these things *are* an abomination to the LORD, and because of these abominations the LORD your God drives them out from before you.
13 "You shall be blameless before the LORD your God.
14 "For these nations which you will dis-

possess listened to soothsayers and diviners; but as for you, the LORD your God has not appointed such for you.

A New Prophet Like Moses

15 "The LORD your God will raise up for you a Prophet like me from your midst, from your brethren. Him you shall hear,
16 "according to all you desired of the LORD your God in Horeb in the day of the assembly, saying, 'Let me not hear again the voice of the LORD my God, nor let me see this great fire anymore, lest I die.'
17 "And the LORD said to me: 'What they have spoken is good.
18 'I will raise up for them a Prophet like you from among their brethren, and will put My words in His mouth, and He shall speak to them all that I command Him.
19 'And it shall be *that* whoever will not hear My words, which He speaks in My name, I will require *it* of him.
20 'But the prophet who presumes to speak a word in My name, which I have not commanded him to speak, or who speaks in the name of other gods, that prophet shall die.'
21 "And if you say in your heart, 'How shall we know the word which the LORD has not spoken?'—
22 "when a prophet speaks in the name of the LORD, if the thing does not happen or come to pass, that *is* the thing which the LORD has not spoken; the prophet has spoken it presumptuously; you shall not be afraid of him.

Three Cities of Refuge

19 "When the LORD your God has cut off the nations whose land the LORD your God is giving you, and you dispossess them and dwell in their cities and in their houses,
2 "you shall separate three cities for yourself in the midst of your land which the LORD your God is giving you to possess.
3 "You shall prepare roads for yourself, and divide into three parts the territory of your land which the LORD your God is giving you to inherit, that any manslayer may flee there.
4 "And this *is* the case of the manslayer who flees there, that he may live: Who-

ever kills his neighbor unintentionally, not having hated him in time past—
5 "as when *a man* goes to the woods with his neighbor to cut timber, and his hand swings a stroke with the ax to cut down the tree, and the head slips from the handle and strikes his neighbor so that he dies—he shall flee to one of these cities and live;
6 "lest the avenger of blood, while his anger is hot, pursue the manslayer and overtake him, because the way is long, and kill him, though he *was* not worthy of death, since he had not hated the victim in time past.
7 "Therefore I command you, saying, 'You shall separate three cities for yourself.'
8 "Now if the LORD your God enlarges your territory, as He swore to your fathers, and gives you the land which He promised to give to your fathers,
9 "and if you keep all these commandments and do them, which I command you today, to love the LORD your God and to walk always in His ways, then you shall add three more cities for yourself besides these three,
10 "lest innocent blood be shed in the midst of your land which the LORD your God is giving you *as* an inheritance, and *thus* bloodguiltiness be upon you.
11 "But if anyone hates his neighbor, lies in wait for him, rises against him and strikes him mortally, so that he dies, and he flees to one of these cities,
12 "then the elders of his city shall send and bring him from there, and deliver him over to the hand of the avenger of blood, that he may die.
13 "Your eye shall not pity him, but you shall put away *the guilt of* innocent blood from Israel, that it may go well with you.

Property Boundaries

14 "You shall not remove your neighbor's landmark, which the men of old have set, in your inheritance which you will inherit in the land that the LORD your God is giving you to possess.

The Law Concerning Witnesses

15 "One witness shall not rise against a man concerning any iniquity or any sin that he commits; by the mouth of two or three witnesses the matter shall be established.

16 "If a false witness rises against any man to testify against him of wrongdoing, 17 "then both men in the controversy shall stand before the LORD, before the priests and the judges who serve in those days. 18 "And the judges shall make diligent inquiry, and indeed, *if* the witness *is* a false witness, who has testified falsely against his brother, 19 "then you shall do to him as he thought to have done to his brother; so you shall put away the evil *person* from among you. 20 "And those who remain shall hear and fear, and hereafter they shall not again commit such evil among you. 21 "Your eye shall not pity; *but* life *shall be* for life, eye for eye, tooth for tooth, hand for hand, foot for foot.

Principles Governing Warfare

20 "When you go out to battle against your enemies, and see horses and chariots *and* people more numerous than you, do not be afraid of them; for the LORD your God *is* with you, who brought you up from the land of Egypt. 2 "So it shall be, when you are on the verge of battle, that the priest shall approach and speak to the people. 3 "And he shall say to them, 'Hear, O Israel: Today you are on the verge of battle with your enemies; do not let your heart faint, do not be afraid, and do not tremble or be terrified because of them; 4 'for the LORD your God *is* He who goes with you, to fight for you against your enemies, to save you.' 5 "Then the officers shall speak to the people, saying: 'What man *is there* who has built a new house and has not dedicated it? Let him go and return to his house, lest he die in the battle and another man dedicate it. 6 'And what man *is there* who has planted a vineyard and has not *yet* eaten of it? Let him *also* go and return to his house, lest he die in the battle and another man eat of it. 7 'And what man *is there* who is betrothed to a woman and has not *yet* married her? Let him go and return to his house, lest he die in the battle and another man marry her.'

8 "Then the officers shall speak further to the people, and say, 'What man *is there who is* fearful and fainthearted? Let him go and return to his house, lest the heart of his brethren faint like his heart.' 9 "And so it shall be, when the officers have finished speaking to the people, that they shall make captains of the armies to lead the people. 10 "When you go near a city to fight against it, then proclaim an offer of peace to it. 11 "And it shall be that if they accept your offer of peace, and open to you, then all the people *who are* found in it shall be placed under tribute to you, and serve you. 12 "Now if the city will not make peace with you, but would make war against you, then you shall besiege it. 13 "And when the LORD your God delivers it into your hands, you shall strike every male in it with the edge of the sword. 14 "But the women, the little ones, the livestock, and all that is in the city, all its spoil, you shall plunder for yourself; and you shall eat the enemies' plunder which the LORD your God gives you. 15 "Thus you shall do to all the cities *which are* very far from you, which *are* not of the cities of these nations. 16 "But of the cities of these peoples which the LORD your God gives you *as* an inheritance, you shall let nothing that breathes remain alive, 17 "but you shall utterly destroy them: the Hittite and the Amorite and the Canaanite and the Perizzite and the Hivite and the Jebusite, just as the LORD your God has commanded you, 18 "lest they teach you to do according to all their abominations which they have done for their gods, and you sin against the LORD your God. 19 "When you besiege a city for a long time, while making war against it to take it, you shall not destroy its trees by wielding an ax against them; if you can eat of them, do not cut them down to use in the siege, for the tree of the field *is* man's *food*. 20 "Only the trees which you know *are* not trees for food you may destroy and cut down, to build siegeworks against the city that makes war with you, until it is subdued.

The Law Concerning Unsolved Murder

21 "If *anyone* is found slain, lying in the field in the land which the LORD your God is giving you to possess, *and* it is not known who killed him,

2 "then your elders and your judges shall go out, and they shall measure *the distance* from the slain man to the surrounding cities.

3 "And it shall be *that* the elders of the city nearest to the slain man will take a heifer which has not been worked *and* which has not pulled with a yoke;

4 "and the elders of that city shall bring the heifer down to a valley with flowing water, which is neither plowed nor sown, and they shall break the heifer's neck there in the valley.

5 "Then the priests, the sons of Levi, shall come near, for the LORD your God has chosen them to minister to Him and to bless in the name of the LORD; by their word every controversy and every assault shall be *settled.*

6 "And all the elders of that city nearest to the slain *man* shall wash their hands over the heifer whose neck was broken in the valley.

7 "Then they shall answer and say, 'Our hands have not shed this blood, nor have our eyes seen *it.*

8 'Provide atonement, O LORD, for Your people Israel, whom You have redeemed, and do not lay innocent blood to the charge of Your people Israel.' And atonement shall be provided on their behalf for the blood.

9 "So you shall put away the *guilt of* innocent blood from among you when you do *what is* right in the sight of the LORD.

Female War Prisoners

10 "When you go out to war against your enemies, and the LORD your God delivers them into your hand, and you take them captive,

11 "and you see among the captives a beautiful woman, and desire her and would take her for your wife,

12 "then you shall bring her home to your house, and she shall shave her head and trim her nails.

13 "She shall put off the clothes of her captivity, remain in your house, and mourn her father and her mother a full month; after that you may go in to her

and be her husband, and she shall be your wife.

14 "And it shall be, if you have no delight in her, then you shall set her free, but you certainly shall not sell her for money; you shall not treat her brutally, because you have humbled her.

Firstborn Inheritance Rights

15 "If a man has two wives, one loved and the other unloved, and they have borne him children, *both* the loved and the unloved, and *if* the firstborn son is of her who is unloved,

16 "then it shall be, on the day he bequeaths his possessions to his sons, *that* he must not bestow firstborn status on the son of the loved wife in preference to the son of the unloved, *who is truly* the firstborn.

17 "But he shall acknowledge the son of the unloved wife *as* the firstborn by giving him a double portion of all that he has, for he *is* the beginning of his strength; the right of the firstborn *is* his.

The Rebellious Son

18 "If a man has a stubborn and rebellious son who will not obey the voice of his father or the voice of his mother, and *who*, when they have chastened him, will not heed them,

19 "then his father and his mother shall take hold of him and bring him out to the elders of his city, to the gate of his city.

20 "And they shall say to the elders of his city, 'This son of ours is stubborn and rebellious; he will not obey our voice; he is a glutton and a drunkard.'

21 "Then all the men of his city shall stone him to death with stones; so you shall put away the evil *person* from among you, and all Israel shall hear and fear.

Miscellaneous Laws

22 "If a man has committed a sin worthy of death, and he is put to death, and you hang him on a tree,

23 "his body shall not remain overnight on the tree, but you shall surely bury him that day, so that you do not defile the land which the LORD your God is giving you *as* an inheritance; for he who is hanged *is* accursed of God.

22 "You shall not see your brother's
ox or his sheep going astray, and
hide yourself from them; you shall certainly bring them back to your brother.
2 "And if your brother *is* not near you,
or if you do not know him, then you shall
bring it to your own house, and it shall
remain with you until your brother seeks
it; then you shall restore it to him.
3 "You shall do the same with his
donkey, and so shall you do with his garment; with any lost thing of your brother's, which he has lost and you have
found, you shall do likewise; you must
not hide yourself.
4 "You shall not see your brother's donkey or his ox fall down along the road,
and hide yourself from them; you shall
surely help him lift *them* up again.
5 "A woman shall not wear anything
that pertains to a man, nor shall a man
put on a woman's garment, for all who do
so *are* an abomination to the LORD your
God.
6 "If a bird's nest happens to be before
you along the way, in any tree or on the
ground, with young ones or eggs, with
the mother sitting on the young or on the
eggs, you shall not take the mother with
the young;
7 "you shall surely let the mother go,
and take the young for yourself, that it
may be well with you and *that* you may
prolong *your* days.
8 "When you build a new house, then
you shall make a parapet for your roof,
that you may not bring bloodguiltiness
on your house if anyone falls from it.
9 "You shall not sow your vineyard
with different kinds of seed, lest the yield
of the seed which you have sown and the
fruit of your vineyard be defiled.
10 "You shall not plow with an ox and a
donkey together.
11 "You shall not wear a garment of different sorts, *such as* wool and linen mixed
together.
12 "You shall make tassels on the four
corners of the clothing with which you
cover *yourself*.

Laws of Sexual Morality

13 "If any man takes a wife, and goes in
to her, and detests her,
14 "and charges her with shameful conduct, and brings a bad name on her, and

says, 'I took this woman, and when I
came to her I found she *was* not a virgin,'
15 "then the father and mother of the
young woman shall take and bring out
the evidence of the young woman's virginity to the elders of the city at the gate.
16 "And the young woman's father shall
say to the elders, 'I gave my daughter to
this man as wife, and he detests her;
17 'now he has charged her with shameful conduct, saying, "I found your daughter *was* not a virgin," and yet these *are*
the evidences of my daughter's virginity.'
And they shall spread the cloth before the
elders of the city.
18 "Then the elders of that city shall take
that man and punish him;
19 "and they shall fine him one hundred
shekels of silver and give *them* to the father of the young woman, because he has
brought a bad name on a virgin of Israel.
And she shall be his wife; he cannot divorce her all his days.
20 "But if the thing is true, *and evidences*
of virginity are not found for the young
woman,
21 "then they shall bring out the young
woman to the door of her father's house,
and the men of her city shall stone her to
death with stones, because she has done a
disgraceful thing in Israel, to play the
harlot in her father's house; so you shall
put away the evil *person* from among you.
22 "If a man is found lying with a
woman married to a husband, then both
of them shall die, *both* the man that lay
with the woman, and the woman; so you
shall put away the evil *person* from Israel.
23 "If a young woman *who is* a virgin is
betrothed to a husband, and a man finds
her in the city and lies with her,
24 "then you shall bring them both out
to the gate of that city, and you shall
stone them to death with stones, the
young woman because she did not cry out
in the city, and the man because he humbled his neighbor's wife; so you shall put
away the evil *person* from among you.
25 "But if a man finds a betrothed young
woman in the countryside, and the man
forces her and lies with her, then only the
man who lay with her shall die.
26 "But you shall do nothing to the
young woman; *there is* in the young
woman no sin *worthy* of death, for just as
when a man rises against his neighbor
and kills him, even so *is* this matter;

27 "for he found her in the countryside, *and* the betrothed young woman cried out, but *there was* no one to save her.

28 "If a man finds a young woman *who is* a virgin, who is not betrothed, and he seizes her and lies with her, and they are found out,

29 "then the man who lay with her shall give to the young woman's father fifty *shekels* of silver, and she shall be his wife because he has humbled her; he shall not be permitted to divorce her all his days.

30 "A man shall not take his father's wife, nor uncover his father's bed.

Those Excluded from the Congregation

23 "He who is emasculated by crushing or mutilation shall not enter the congregation of the LORD.

2 "One of illegitimate birth shall not enter the congregation of the LORD; even to the tenth generation none of his *descendants* shall enter the congregation of the LORD.

3 "An Ammonite or Moabite shall not enter the congregation of the LORD; even to the tenth generation none of his *descendants* shall enter the congregation of the LORD forever,

4 "because they did not meet you with bread and water on the road when you came out of Egypt, and because they hired against you Balaam the son of Beor from Pethor of Mesopotamia,[16] to curse you.

5 "Nevertheless the LORD your God would not listen to Balaam, but the LORD your God turned the curse into a blessing for you, because the LORD your God loves you.

6 "You shall not seek their peace nor their prosperity all your days forever.

7 "You shall not abhor an Edomite, for he *is* your brother. You shall not abhor an Egyptian, because you were an alien in his land.

8 "The children of the third generation born to them may enter the congregation of the LORD.

Cleanliness of the Camp Site

9 "When the army goes out against your enemies, then keep yourself from every wicked thing.

10 "If there is any man among you who becomes unclean by some occurrence in the night, then he shall go outside the camp; he shall not come inside the camp.

11 "But it shall be, when evening comes, that he shall wash *himself* with water; and when the sun sets, he may come into the camp *again.*

12 "Also you shall have a place outside the camp, where you may go out;

13 "and you shall have an implement among your equipment, and when you sit down outside, you shall dig with it and turn and cover your refuse.

14 "For the LORD your God walks in the midst of your camp, to deliver you and give your enemies over to you; therefore your camp shall be holy, that He may see no unclean thing among you, and turn away from you.

Miscellaneous Laws

15 "You shall not give back to his master the slave who has escaped from his master to you.

16 "He may dwell with you in your midst, in the place which he chooses within one of your gates, where it seems best to him; you shall not oppress him.

17 "There shall be no *ritual* harlot[17] of the daughters of Israel, or a perverted[18] one of the sons of Israel.

18 "You shall not bring the hire of a harlot or the price of a dog to the house of the LORD your God for any vowed offering, for both of these *are* an abomination to the LORD your God.

19 "You shall not charge interest to your brother—interest on money *or* food *or* anything that is lent out at interest.

20 "To a foreigner you may charge interest, but to your brother you shall not charge interest, that the LORD your God may bless you in all to which you set your hand in the land which you are entering to possess.

21 "When you make a vow to the LORD your God, you shall not delay to pay it; for the LORD your God will surely require it of you, and it would be sin to you.

22 "But if you abstain from vowing, it shall not be sin to you.

23 "That which has gone from your lips you shall keep and perform, for you voluntarily vowed to the LORD your God what you have promised with your mouth.

24 "When you come into your neighbor's

---

16 Hebrew *Aram Naharaim*   17 Hebrew *qedeshah,* feminine of *qedesh* (see note 18)
18 Hebrew *qedesh,* one practicing sodomy and prostitution in religious rituals

vineyard, you may eat your fill of grapes at your pleasure, but you shall not put *any* in your container.
25 "When you come into your neighbor's standing grain, you may pluck the heads with your hand, but you shall not use a sickle on your neighbor's standing grain.

Laws Concerning Divorce

24 "When a man takes a wife and marries her, and it happens that she finds no favor in his eyes because he has found some uncleanness in her, and he writes her a certificate of divorce, puts *it* in her hand, and sends her out of his house,
2 "when she has departed from his house, and goes and becomes another man's *wife*,
3 "*if* the latter husband detests her and writes her a certificate of divorce, puts *it* in her hand, and sends her out of his house, or if the latter husband dies who took her *to be* his wife,
4 "*then* her former husband who divorced her must not take her back to be his wife after she has been defiled; for that *is* an abomination before the LORD, and you shall not bring sin on the land which the LORD your God is giving you *as* an inheritance.

Miscellaneous Laws

5 "When a man has taken a new wife, he shall not go out to war or be charged with any business; he shall be free at home one year, and bring happiness to his wife whom he has taken.
6 "No man shall take the lower or the upper millstone in pledge, for he takes *one's* living in pledge.
7 "If a man is found kidnapping any of his brethren of the children of Israel, and mistreats him or sells him, then that kidnapper shall die; and you shall put away the evil *person* from among you.
8 "Take heed in an outbreak of leprosy, that you diligently observe and do according to all that the priests, the Levites, shall teach you; just as I commanded them, *so* you shall be careful to do.
9 "Remember what the LORD your God did to Miriam on the way when you came out of Egypt.
10 "When you lend your brother anything, you shall not go into his house to get his pledge.

11 "You shall stand outside, and the man to whom you lend shall bring the pledge out to you.
12 "And if the man *is* poor, you shall not keep his pledge overnight.
13 "You shall in any case return the pledge to him again when the sun goes down, that he may sleep in his own garment and bless you; and it shall be righteousness to you before the LORD your God.
14 "You shall not oppress a hired servant *who is* poor and needy, *whether* one of your brethren or one of the aliens who *is* in your land within your gates.
15 "Each day you shall give *him* his wages, and not let the sun go down on it, for he *is* poor and has set his heart on it; lest he cry out against you to the LORD, and it be sin to you.
16 "The fathers shall not be put to death for *their* children, nor shall the children be put to death for *their* fathers; a person shall be put to death for his own sin.
17 "You shall not pervert justice due the stranger or the fatherless, nor take a widow's garment as a pledge.
18 "But you shall remember that you were a slave in Egypt, and the LORD your God redeemed you from there; therefore I command you to do this thing.
19 "When you reap your harvest in your field, and forget a sheaf in the field, you shall not go back to get it; it shall be for the stranger, the fatherless, and the widow, that the LORD your God may bless you in all the work of your hands.
20 "When you beat your olive trees, you shall not go over the boughs again; it shall be for the stranger, the fatherless, and the widow.
21 "When you gather the grapes of your vineyard, you shall not glean *it* afterward; it shall be for the stranger, the fatherless, and the widow.
22 "And you shall remember that you were a slave in the land of Egypt; therefore I command you to do this thing.

25 "If there is a dispute between men, and they come to court, that *the judges* may judge them, and they justify the righteous and condemn the wicked,
2 "then it shall be, if the wicked man deserves to be beaten, that the judge will cause him to lie down and be beaten in

his presence, according to his guilt, with a certain number of blows.

3 "Forty blows he may give him *and* no more, lest he should exceed this and beat him with many blows above these, and your brother be humiliated in your sight.

4 "You shall not muzzle an ox while it treads out *the grain.*

Marriage Duty of the Surviving Brother

5 "If brothers dwell together, and one of them dies and has no son, the widow of the dead man shall not be *married* to a stranger outside *the family*; her husband's brother shall go in to her, take her as his wife, and perform the duty of a husband's brother to her.

6 "And it shall be *that* the firstborn son which she bears will succeed to the name of his dead brother, that his name may not be blotted out of Israel.

7 "But if the man does not want to take his brother's wife, then let his brother's wife go up to the gate to the elders, and say, 'My husband's brother refuses to raise up a name to his brother in Israel; he will not perform the duty of my husband's brother.'

8 "Then the elders of his city shall call him and speak to him; and *if* he stands firm and says, 'I do not want to take her,'

9 "then his brother's wife shall come to him in the presence of the elders, remove his sandal from his foot, spit in his face, and answer and say, 'So shall it be done to the man who will not build up his brother's house.'

10 "And his name shall be called in Israel, 'The house of him who had his sandal removed.'

Miscellaneous Laws

11 "If *two* men fight together, and the wife of one draws near to rescue her husband from the hand of the one attacking him, and puts out her hand and seizes him by the genitals,

12 "then you shall cut off her hand; your eye shall not pity *her.*

13 "You shall not have in your bag differing weights, a heavy and a light.

14 "You shall not have in your house differing measures, a large and a small.

15 "You shall have a perfect and just weight, a perfect and just measure, that your days may be lengthened in the land which the LORD your God is giving you.

16 "For all who do such things, *and* all who behave unrighteously, *are* an abomination to the LORD your God.

Destroy the Amalekites

17 "Remember what Amalek did to you on the way as you were coming out of Egypt,

18 "how he met you on the way and attacked your rear ranks, all the stragglers at your rear, when you *were* tired and weary; and he did not fear God.

19 "Therefore it shall be, when the LORD your God has given you rest from your enemies all around, in the land which the LORD your God is giving you to possess *as* an inheritance, *that* you will blot out the remembrance of Amalek from under heaven. You shall not forget.

Offerings of Firstfruits and Tithes

26 "And it shall be, when you come into the land which the LORD your God is giving you *as* an inheritance, and you possess it and dwell in it,

2 "that you shall take some of the first of all the produce of the ground, which you shall bring from your land that the LORD your God is giving you, and put *it* in a basket and go to the place where the LORD your God chooses to make His name abide.

3 "And you shall go to the one who is priest in those days, and say to him, 'I declare today to the LORD your[19] God that I have come to the country which the LORD swore to our fathers to give us.'

4 "Then the priest shall take the basket out of your hand and set it down before the altar of the LORD your God.

5 "And you shall answer and say before the LORD your God: 'My father *was* a Syrian,[20] about to perish, and he went down to Egypt and sojourned there, few in number; and there he became a nation, great, mighty, and populous.

6 'But the Egyptians mistreated us, afflicted us, and laid hard bondage on us.

7 'Then we cried out to the LORD God of our fathers, and the LORD heard our voice and looked on our affliction and our labor and our oppression.

8 'So the LORD brought us out of Egypt with a mighty hand and with an outstretched arm, with great terror and with signs and wonders.

19 Septuagint reads *my.*   20 Or *Aramean*

9 'He has brought us to this place and has given us this land, "a land flowing with milk and honey";[21]
10 'and now, behold, I have brought the firstfruits of the land which you, O LORD, have given me.' Then you shall set it before the LORD your God, and worship before the LORD your God.
11 "So you shall rejoice in every good *thing* which the LORD your God has given to you and your house, you and the Levite and the stranger who *is* among you.
12 "When you have finished laying aside all the tithe of your increase in the third year, *which is* the year of tithing, and have given *it* to the Levite, the stranger, the fatherless, and the widow, so that they may eat within your gates and be filled,
13 "then you shall say before the LORD your God: 'I have removed the holy *tithe* from *my* house, and also have given them to the Levite, the stranger, the fatherless, and the widow, according to all Your commandments which You have commanded me; I have not transgressed Your commandments, nor have I forgotten *them*.
14 'I have not eaten any of it when in mourning, nor have I removed *any* of it for *any* unclean *use*, nor given *any* of it for the dead. I have obeyed the voice of the LORD my God, and have done according to all that You have commanded me.
15 'Look down from Your holy habitation, from heaven, and bless Your people Israel and the land which You have given us, just as You swore to our fathers, "a land flowing with milk and honey." '[22]

A Special People of God

16 "This day the LORD your God commands you to observe these statutes and judgments; therefore you shall be careful to observe them with all your heart and with all your soul.
17 "Today you have proclaimed the LORD to be your God, and that you will walk in His ways and keep His statutes, His commandments, and His judgments, and that you will obey His voice.
18 "Also today the LORD has proclaimed you to be His special people, just as He has promised you, that *you* should keep all His commandments,
19 "and that He will set you high above all nations which He has made, in praise,

in name, and in honor, and that you may be a holy people to the LORD your God, just as He has spoken."

The Law Inscribed on Stones

27 Then Moses, with the elders of Israel, commanded the people, saying: "Keep all the commandments which I command you today.
2 "And it shall be, on the day when you cross over the Jordan to the land which the LORD your God is giving you, that you shall set up for yourselves large stones, and whitewash them with lime.
3 "You shall write on them all the words of this law, when you have crossed over, that you may enter the land which the LORD your God is giving you, 'a land flowing with milk and honey,'[23] just as the LORD God of your fathers has promised you.
4 "Therefore it shall be, when you have crossed over the Jordan, *that* on Mount Ebal you shall set up these stones, which I command you today, and you shall whitewash them with lime.
5 "And there you shall build an altar to the LORD your God, an altar of stones; you shall not use *any* iron *tool* on them.
6 "You shall build with whole stones the altar of the LORD your God, and offer burnt offerings on it to the LORD your God.
7 "You shall offer peace offerings, and shall eat there, and rejoice before the LORD your God.
8 "And you shall write very plainly on the stones all the words of this law."
9 Then Moses and the priests, the Levites, spoke to all Israel, saying, "Take heed and listen, O Israel: This day you have become the people of the LORD your God.
10 "Therefore you shall obey the voice of the LORD your God, and observe His commandments and His statutes which I command you today."

Curses Pronounced from Mount Ebal

11 And Moses commanded the people on the same day, saying,
12 "These shall stand on Mount Gerizim to bless the people, when you have crossed over the Jordan: Simeon, Levi, Judah, Issachar, Joseph, and Benjamin;
13 "and these shall stand on Mount Ebal

21 Compare Exodus 3:8   22 Compare Exodus 3:8   23 Compare Exodus 3:8

to curse: Reuben, Gad, Asher, Zebulun, Dan, and Naphtali.

14 "And the Levites shall speak with a loud voice and say to all the men of Israel:

15 'Cursed *is* the one who makes *any* carved or molded image, an abomination to the LORD, the work of the hands of the craftsman, and sets *it* up in secret.' And all the people shall answer and say, 'Amen!'

16 'Cursed *is* the one who treats his father or his mother with contempt.' And all the people shall say, 'Amen!'

17 'Cursed *is* the one who moves his neighbor's landmark.' And all the people shall say, 'Amen!'

18 'Cursed *is* the one who makes the blind to wander off the road.' And all the people shall say, 'Amen!'

19 'Cursed *is* the one who perverts the justice due the stranger, the fatherless, and widow.' And all the people shall say, 'Amen!'

20 'Cursed *is* the one who lies with his father's wife, because he has uncovered his father's bed.' And all the people shall say, 'Amen!'

21 'Cursed *is* the one who lies with any kind of animal.' And all the people shall say, 'Amen!'

22 'Cursed *is* the one who lies with his sister, the daughter of his father or the daughter of his mother.' And all the people shall say, 'Amen!'

23 'Cursed *is* the one who lies with his mother-in-law.' And all the people shall say, 'Amen!'

24 'Cursed *is* the one who attacks his neighbor secretly.' And all the people shall say, 'Amen!'

25 'Cursed *is* the one who takes a bribe to slay an innocent person.' And all the people shall say, 'Amen!'

26 'Cursed *is* the one who does not confirm *all* the words of this law.' And all the people shall say, 'Amen!'

Blessings on Obedience

28 "Now it shall come to pass, if you diligently obey the voice of the LORD your God, to observe carefully all His commandments which I command you today, that the LORD your God will set you high above all nations of the earth.

2 "And all these blessings shall come upon you and overtake you, because you obey the voice of the LORD your God:

3 "Blessed *shall* you *be* in the city, and blessed *shall* you *be* in the country.

4 "Blessed *shall be* the fruit of your body, the produce of your ground and the increase of your herds, the increase of your cattle and the offspring of your flocks.

5 "Blessed *shall be* your basket and your kneading bowl.

6 "Blessed *shall* you *be* when you come in, and blessed *shall* you *be* when you go out.

7 "The LORD will cause your enemies who rise against you to be defeated before your face; they shall come out against you one way and flee before you seven ways.

8 "The LORD will command the blessing on you in your storehouses and in all to which you set your hand, and He will bless you in the land which the LORD your God is giving you.

9 "The LORD will establish you as a holy people to Himself, just as He has sworn to you, if you keep the commandments of the LORD your God and walk in His ways.

10 "Then all peoples of the earth shall see that you are called by the name of the LORD, and they shall be afraid of you.

11 "And the LORD will grant you plenty of goods, in the fruit of your body, in the increase of your livestock, and in the produce of your ground, in the land of which the LORD swore to your fathers to give you.

12 "The LORD will open to you His good treasure, the heavens, to give the rain to your land in its season, and to bless all the work of your hand. You shall lend to many nations, but you shall not borrow.

13 "And the LORD will make you the head and not the tail; you shall be above only, and not be beneath, if you heed the commandments of the LORD your God, which I command you today, and are careful to observe *them.*

14 "So you shall not turn aside from any of the words which I command you this day, *to* the right *hand* or *to* the left, to go after other gods to serve them.

Curses on Disobedience

15 "But it shall come to pass, if you do not obey the voice of the LORD your God,

to observe carefully all His commandments and His statutes which I command you today, that all these curses will come upon you and overtake you:

16 "Cursed *shall* you *be* in the city, and cursed *shall* you *be* in the country.

17 "Cursed *shall be* your basket and your kneading bowl.

18 "Cursed *shall be* the fruit of your body and the produce of your land, the increase of your cattle and the offspring of your flocks.

19 "Cursed *shall* you *be* when you come in, and cursed *shall* you *be* when you go out.

20 "The LORD will send on you cursing, confusion, and rebuke in all that you set your hand to do, until you are destroyed and until you perish quickly, because of the wickedness of your doings in which you have forsaken Me.

21 "The LORD will make the plague cling to you until He has consumed you from the land which you are going to possess.

22 "The LORD will strike you with consumption, with fever, with inflammation, with severe burning fever, with the sword, with scorching, and with mildew; they shall pursue you until you perish.

23 "And your heavens which *are* over your head shall be bronze, and the earth which is under you *shall be* iron.

24 "The LORD will change the rain of your land to powder and dust; from the heaven it shall come down on you until you are destroyed.

25 "The LORD will cause you to be defeated before your enemies; you shall go out one way against them and flee seven ways before them; and you shall become troublesome to all the kingdoms of the earth.

26 "Your carcasses shall be food for all the birds of the air and the beasts of the earth, and no one shall frighten *them* away.

27 "The LORD will strike you with the boils of Egypt, with tumors, with the scab, and with the itch, from which you cannot be healed.

28 "The LORD will strike you with madness and blindness and confusion of heart.

29 "And you shall grope at noonday, as a blind man gropes in darkness; you shall not prosper in your ways; you shall be

only oppressed and plundered continually, and no one shall save *you.*

30 "You shall betroth a wife, but another man shall lie with her; you shall build a house, but you shall not dwell in it; you shall plant a vineyard, but shall not gather its grapes.

31 "Your ox *shall be* slaughtered before your eyes, but you shall not eat of it; your donkey *shall be* violently taken away from before you, and shall not be restored to you; your sheep *shall be* given to your enemies, and you shall have no one to rescue *them.*

32 "Your sons and your daughters *shall be* given to another people, and your eyes shall look and fail *with longing* for them all day long; and *there shall be* no strength in your hand.

33 "A nation whom you have not known shall eat the fruit of your land and the produce of your labor, and you shall be only oppressed and crushed continually.

34 "So you shall be driven mad because of the sight which your eyes see.

35 "The LORD will strike you in the knees and on the legs with severe boils which cannot be healed, and from the sole of your foot to the top of your head.

36 "The LORD will bring you and the king whom you set over you to a nation which neither you nor your fathers have known, and there you shall serve other gods—wood and stone.

37 "And you shall become an astonishment, a proverb, and a byword among all nations where the LORD will lead you.

38 "You shall carry much seed out to the field and gather *but* little in, for the locust shall consume it.

39 "You shall plant vineyards and tend *them,* but you shall neither drink *of* the wine nor gather the *grapes;* for the worms shall eat them.

40 "You shall have olive trees throughout all your territory, but you shall not anoint *yourself* with the oil; for your olives shall drop off.

41 "You shall beget sons and daughters, but they shall not be yours; for they shall go into captivity.

42 "Locusts shall consume all your trees and the produce of your land.

43 "The alien who *is* among you shall rise higher and higher above you, and you shall come down lower and lower.

44 "He shall lend to you, but you shall

not lend to him; he shall be the head, and you shall be the tail.

45 "Moreover all these curses shall come upon you and pursue and overtake you, until you are destroyed, because you did not obey the voice of the LORD your God, to keep His commandments and His statutes which He commanded you.

46 "And they shall be upon you for a sign and a wonder, and on your descendants forever.

47 "Because you did not serve the LORD your God with joy and gladness of heart, for the abundance of all *things*,

48 "therefore you shall serve your enemies, whom the LORD will send against you, in hunger, in thirst, in nakedness, and in need of all *things*; and He will put a yoke of iron on your neck until He has destroyed you.

49 "The LORD will bring a nation against you from afar, from the end of the earth, *as swift* as the eagle flies, a nation whose language you will not understand,

50 "a nation of fierce countenance, which does not respect the elderly nor show favor to the young.

51 "And they shall eat the increase of your livestock and the produce of your land, until you are destroyed; they shall not leave you grain or new wine or oil, *or* the increase of your cattle or the offspring of your flocks, until they have destroyed you.

52 "They shall besiege you at all your gates until your high and fortified walls, in which you trust, come down throughout all your land; and they shall besiege you at all your gates throughout all your land which the LORD your God has given you.

53 "You shall eat the fruit of your own body, the flesh of your sons and your daughters whom the LORD your God has given you, in the siege and desperate straits in which your enemy shall distress you.

54 "The man among you *who is* sensitive and very refined will be hostile toward his brother, toward the wife of his bosom, and toward the rest of his children whom he leaves behind,

55 "so that he will not give any of them the flesh of his children whom he will eat, because he has nothing left in the siege and desperate straits in which your enemy shall distress you at all your gates.

56 "The tender and delicate woman among you, who would not venture to set the sole of her foot on the ground because of her delicateness and sensitivity, will refuse[24] to the husband of her bosom, and to her son and her daughter,

57 "her placenta which comes out from between her feet, and her children whom she bears; for she will eat them secretly for lack of all *things* in the siege and desperate straits in which your enemy shall distress you at all your gates.

58 "If you do not carefully observe all the words of this law that are written in this book, that you may fear this glorious and awesome name, THE LORD YOUR GOD,

59 "then the LORD will bring upon you and your descendants extraordinary plagues—great and prolonged plagues—and serious and prolonged sicknesses.

60 "Moreover He will bring back on you all the diseases of Egypt, of which you were afraid, and they shall cling to you.

61 "Also every sickness and every plague, which *is* not written in the book of this law, will the LORD bring upon you until you are destroyed.

62 "You shall be left few in number, whereas you were as the stars of heaven in multitude, because you would not obey the voice of the LORD your God.

63 "And it shall be, *that* just as the LORD rejoiced over you to do you good and multiply you, so the LORD will rejoice over you to destroy you and bring you to nothing; and you shall be plucked from off the land which you go to possess.

64 "Then the LORD will scatter you among all peoples, from one end of the earth to the other, and there you shall serve other gods, which neither you nor your fathers have known—wood and stone.

65 "And among those nations you shall find no rest, nor shall the sole of your foot have a resting place; but there the LORD will give you a trembling heart, failing eyes, and anguish of soul.

66 "Your life shall hang in doubt before you; you shall fear day and night, and have no assurance of life.

67 "In the morning you shall say, 'Oh, that it were evening!' And at evening you shall say, 'Oh, that it were morning!' because of the fear which terrifies your

24 Literally *her eye shall be evil toward*

heart, and because of the sight which
your eyes see.
68 "And the LORD will take you back to
Egypt in ships, by the way of which I said
to you, 'You shall never see it again.'
And there you shall be offered for sale to
your enemies as male and female slaves,
but no one will buy *you*."

The Covenant Renewed in Moab

29 These *are* the words of the covenant which the LORD com-
manded Moses to make with the children
of Israel in the land of Moab, besides the
covenant which He made with them in
Horeb.
2 Now Moses called all Israel and said
to them: "You have seen all that the
LORD did before your eyes in the land of
Egypt, to Pharaoh and to all his servants
and to all his land—
3 "the great trials which your eyes have
seen, the signs, and those great wonders.
4 "Yet the LORD has not given you a
heart to perceive and eyes to see and ears
to hear, to this *very* day.
5 "And I have led you forty years in the
wilderness. Your clothes have not worn
out on you, and your sandals have not
worn out on your feet;
6 "you have not eaten bread, nor have
you drunk wine or *similar* drink; that you
may know that I *am* the LORD your God.
7 "And when you came to this place,
Sihon king of Heshbon and Og king of
Bashan came out against us to battle, and
we conquered them.
8 "We took their land and gave it
as an inheritance to the Reubenites, to
the Gadites, and to half the tribe of
Manasseh.
9 "Therefore keep the words of this covenant, and do them, that you may prosper in all that you do.
10 "All of you stand today before the
LORD your God: your leaders and your
tribes and your elders and your officers,
all the men of Israel,
11 "your little ones and your wives—also
the stranger who *is* in your camp, from
the one who cuts your wood to the one
who draws your water—
12 "that you may enter into covenant
with the LORD your God, and into His
oath, which the LORD your God makes
with you today,
13 "that He may establish you today as a

people for Himself, and *that* He may be
God to you, just as He has spoken to you,
and just as He has sworn to your fathers,
to Abraham, Isaac, and Jacob.
14 "I make this covenant and this oath,
not with you alone,
15 "but also with *him* who stands here
with us today before the LORD our God,
as well as with *him* who *is* not here with
us today
16 (for you know that we dwelt in the
land of Egypt and that we came through
the nations which you passed by,
17 and you saw their abominations and
their idols which *were* among them—
wood and stone and silver and gold);
18 "so that there may not be among you
man or woman or family or tribe, whose
heart turns away today from the LORD
our God, to go *and* serve the gods of these
nations, and that there may not be among
you a root bearing bitterness or wormwood;
19 "and so it may not happen, when he
hears the words of this curse, that he
blesses himself in his heart, saying, 'I
shall have peace, even though I walk in
the imagination of my heart'—as though
the drunkard could be included with the
sober.
20 "The LORD would not spare him; for
then the anger of the LORD and His jealousy would burn against that man, and
every curse that is written in this book
would settle on him, and the LORD would
blot out his name from under heaven.
21 "And the LORD would separate him
from all the tribes of Israel for adversity,
according to all the curses of the covenant that are written in this Book of the
Law,
22 "so that the coming generation of
your children who rise up after you, and
the foreigner who comes from a far land,
would say, when they see the plagues of
that land and the sicknesses which the
LORD has laid on it:
23 'The whole land *is* brimstone, salt,
and burning; it is not sown, nor does it
bear, nor does any grass grow there, like
the overthrow of Sodom and Gomorrah,
Admah, and Zeboim, which the LORD
overthrew in His anger and His wrath.'
24 "All nations would say, 'Why has the
LORD done so to this land? What does
the heat of this great anger mean?'
25 "Then *men* would say: 'Because they

have forsaken the covenant of the LORD
God of their fathers, which He made with
them when He brought them out of the
land of Egypt;
26 'for they went and served other gods
and worshiped them, gods that they did
not know and that He had not given to
them.
27 'Then the anger of the LORD was
aroused against this land, to bring on it
every curse that is written in this book.
28 'And the LORD uprooted them from
their land in anger, in wrath, and in great
indignation, and cast them into another
land, as *it is* this day.'
29 "The secret *things belong* to the LORD
our God, but those *things which are* revealed *belong* to us and to our children
forever, that *we* may do all the words of
this law.

The Blessing of Returning to God

30 "Now it shall come to pass, when
all these things come upon you,
the blessing and the curse which I have
set before you, and you call *them* to mind
among all the nations where the LORD
your God drives you,
2 "and you return to the LORD your
God and obey His voice, according to all
that I command you today, you and your
children, with all your heart and with all
your soul,
3 "that the LORD your God will bring
you back from captivity, and have compassion on you, and gather you again
from all the nations where the LORD your
God has scattered you.
4 "If *any* of you are driven out to the
farthest *parts* under heaven, from there
the LORD your God will gather you, and
from there He will bring you.
5 "Then the LORD your God will bring
you to the land which your fathers possessed, and you shall possess it. He will
prosper you and multiply you more than
your fathers.
6 "And the LORD your God will circumcise your heart and the heart of your
descendants, to love the LORD your God
with all your heart and with all your soul,
that you may live.
7 "Also the LORD your God will put all
these curses on your enemies and on
those who hate you, who persecuted you.
8 "And you will again obey the voice of

the LORD and do all His commandments
which I command you today.
9 "The LORD your God will make you
abound in all the work of your hand, in
the fruit of your body, in the increase of
your livestock, and in the produce of your
land for good. For the LORD will again
rejoice over you for good as He rejoiced
over your fathers,
10 "if you obey the voice of the LORD
your God, to keep His commandments
and His statutes which are written in this
Book of the Law, *and* if you turn to the
LORD your God with all your heart and
with all your soul.

The Choice of Life or Death

11 "For this commandment which I
command you today, it *is* not *too* mysterious for you, nor *is* it far off.
12 "It *is* not in heaven, that you should
say, 'Who will ascend into heaven for us
and bring it to us, that we may hear it
and do it?'
13 "Nor *is* it beyond the sea, that you
should say, 'Who will go over the sea for
us and bring it to us, that we may hear it
and do it?'
14 "But the word *is* very near you, in
your mouth and in your heart, that you
may do it.
15 "See, I have set before you today life
and good, death and evil,
16 "in that I command you today to love
the LORD your God, to walk in His ways,
and to keep His commandments, His
statutes, and His judgments, that you
may live and multiply; and the LORD
your God will bless you in the land which
you go to possess.
17 "But if your heart turns away so that
you do not hear, and are drawn away,
and worship other gods and serve them,
18 "I announce to you today that you
shall surely perish; you shall not prolong
your days in the land which you cross
over the Jordan to go in and possess.
19 "I call heaven and earth as witnesses
today against you, *that* I have set before
you life and death, blessing and cursing;
therefore choose life, that both you and
your descendants may live;
20 "that you may love the LORD your
God, that you may obey His voice, and
that you may cling to Him, for He *is* your
life and the length of your days; and that
you may dwell in the land which the

LORD swore to your fathers, to Abraham, Isaac, and Jacob, to give them."

Joshua the New Leader of Israel

31 Then Moses went and spoke these words to all Israel.
2 And he said to them: "I *am* one hundred and twenty years old today. I can no longer go out and come in. Also the LORD has said to me, 'You shall not cross over this Jordan.'
3 "The LORD your God Himself crosses over before you; He will destroy these nations from before you, and you shall dispossess them. Joshua himself crosses over before you, just as the LORD has said.
4 "And the LORD will do to them as He did to Sihon and Og, the kings of the Amorites and their land, when He destroyed them.
5 "The LORD will give them over to you, that you may do to them according to every commandment which I have commanded you.
6 "Be strong and of good courage, do not fear nor be afraid of them; for the LORD your God, He *is* the One who goes with you. He will not leave you nor forsake you."
7 Then Moses called Joshua and said to him in the sight of all Israel, "Be strong and of good courage, for you must go with this people to the land which the LORD has sworn to their fathers to give them, and you shall cause them to inherit it.
8 "And the LORD, He *is* the one who goes before you. He will be with you, He will not leave you nor forsake you; do not fear nor be dismayed."

The Law to Be Read Every Seven Years

9 So Moses wrote this law and delivered it to the priests, the sons of Levi, who bore the ark of the covenant of the LORD, and to all the elders of Israel.
10 And Moses commanded them, saying: "At the end of *every* seven years, at the appointed time in the year of release, at the Feast of Tabernacles,
11 "when all Israel comes to appear before the LORD your God in the place which He chooses, you shall read this law before all Israel in their hearing.
12 "Gather the people together, men and women and little ones, and the stranger

who *is* within your gates, that they may hear and that they may learn to fear the LORD your God and carefully observe all the words of this law,
13 "and *that* their children, who have not known it, may hear and learn to fear the LORD your God as long as you live in the land which you cross the Jordan to possess."

Prediction of Israel's Rebellion

14 Then the LORD said to Moses, "Behold, the days approach when you must die; call Joshua, and present yourselves in the tabernacle of meeting, that I may inaugurate him." So Moses and Joshua went and presented themselves in the tabernacle of meeting.
15 Now the LORD appeared at the tabernacle in a pillar of cloud, and the pillar of cloud stood above the door of the tabernacle.
16 And the LORD said to Moses: "Behold, you will rest with your fathers; and this people will rise and play the harlot with the gods of the foreigners of the land, where they go *to be* among them, and they will forsake Me and break My covenant which I have made with them.
17 "Then My anger shall be aroused against them in that day, and I will forsake them, and I will hide My face from them, and they shall be devoured. And many evils and troubles shall befall them, so that they will say in that day, 'Have not these evils come upon us because our God *is* not among us?'
18 "And I will surely hide My face in that day because of all the evil which they have done, in that they have turned to other gods.
19 "Now therefore, write down this song for yourselves, and teach it to the children of Israel; put it in their mouths, that this song may be a witness for Me against the children of Israel.
20 "When I have brought them to the land flowing with milk and honey, of which I swore to their fathers, and they have eaten and filled themselves and grown fat, then they will turn to other gods and serve them; and they will provoke Me and break My covenant.
21 "Then it shall be, when many evils and troubles have come upon them, that this song will testify against them as a witness; for it will not be forgotten in the

mouths of their descendants, for I know the inclination of their behavior today, even before I have brought them to the land of which I swore *to give them.*"

22 Therefore Moses wrote this song the same day, and taught it to the children of Israel.

23 Then He inaugurated Joshua the son of Nun, and said, "Be strong and of good courage; for you shall bring the children of Israel into the land of which I swore to them, and I will be with you."

24 So it was, when Moses had completed writing the words of this law in a book, when they were finished,

25 that Moses commanded the Levites, who bore the ark of the covenant of the LORD, saying:

26 "Take this Book of the Law, and put it beside the ark of the covenant of the LORD your God, that it may be there as a witness against you;

27 "for I know your rebellion and your stiff neck. *If* today, while I am yet alive with you, you have been rebellious against the LORD, then how much more after my death?

28 "Gather to me all the elders of your tribes, and your officers, that I may speak these words in their hearing and call heaven and earth to witness against them.

29 "For I know that after my death you will become utterly corrupt, and turn aside from the way which I have commanded you; and evil will befall you in the latter days, because you will do evil in the sight of the LORD, to provoke Him to anger through the work of your hands."

The Song of Moses

30 Then Moses spoke in the hearing of all the congregation of Israel the words of this song until they were ended:

32 "Give ear, O heavens,
     and I will speak;
   And hear, O earth,
     the words of my mouth.
2   Let my teaching drop as the rain,
   My speech distill as the dew,
   As raindrops on the tender herb,
   And as showers on the grass.
3   For I proclaim the name of the LORD:
   Ascribe greatness to our God.
4   *He is* the Rock, His work *is* perfect;
   For all His ways *are* justice,
   A God of truth and without injustice;
   Righteous and upright *is* He.

5   "They have corrupted themselves;
   They are not His children,
   Because of their blemish:
   A perverse and crooked generation.
6   Do you thus deal with the LORD,
   O foolish and unwise people?
   Is He not your Father,
     who bought you?
   Has He not made you
     and established you?

7   "Remember the days of old,
   Consider the years
     of many generations.
   Ask your father, and he will show you;
   Your elders, and they will tell you:
8   When the Most High divided their
     inheritance to the nations,
   When He separated the sons of Adam,
   He set the boundaries of the peoples
   According to the number of the
     children of Israel.
9   For the LORD's portion *is* His people;
   Jacob *is* the place of His inheritance.

10 "He found him in a desert land
   And in the wasteland,
     a howling wilderness;
   He encircled him, He instructed him,
   He kept him as the apple of His eye.
11   As an eagle stirs up its nest,
   Hovers over its young,
   Spreading out its wings,
     taking them up,
   Carrying them on its wings,
12   *So* the LORD alone led him,
   And *there was* no foreign god with him.

13 "He made him ride in the heights
     of the earth,
   That he might eat
     the produce of the fields;
   He made him to draw honey
     from the rock,
   And oil from the flinty rock;
14   Curds from the cattle,
     and milk of the flock,
   With fat of lambs;
   And rams of the breed of Bashan,
     and goats,
   With the choicest wheat;
   And you drank wine,
     the blood of the grapes.

15 "But Jeshurun grew fat and kicked;
   You grew fat, you grew thick,
   You are covered *with fat*;
   Then he forsook God *who* made him,
   And scornfully esteemed
     the Rock of his salvation.

16 They provoked Him to jealousy
        with foreign *gods*;
    With abominations they provoked Him
        to anger.
17 They sacrificed to demons, not to God,
    To gods they did not know,
    To new *gods*, new arrivals
    That your fathers did not fear.
18 Of the Rock *who* begot you,
        you are unmindful,
    And have forgotten the God
        who fathered you.

19 "And when the LORD saw *it*,
        He spurned *them*,
    Because of the provocation of His sons
        and His daughters.
20 And He said: 'I will hide My face
        from them,
    I will see what their end *will be*,
    For they *are* a perverse generation,
    Children in whom *is* no faith.
21 They have provoked Me to jealousy
        by *what* is not God;
    They have moved Me to anger
        by their foolish idols.
    But I will provoke them to jealousy
        by *those who are* not a nation;
    I will move them to anger
        by a foolish nation.
22 For a fire is kindled in My anger,
    And shall burn to the lowest hell;
    It shall consume the earth
        with her increase,
    And set on fire
        the foundations of the mountains.

23 'I will heap disasters upon them;
    I will spend My arrows upon them.
24 *They shall be* wasted with hunger,
    Devoured by pestilence
        and bitter destruction;
    I will also send against them
        the teeth of beasts,
    With the poison
        of serpents of the dust.
25 The sword shall destroy outside;
    There shall be terror within
    For the young man and virgin,
    The nursing child
        with the man of gray hairs.
26 I would have said,
        "I will dash them in pieces,
    I will make the memory of them
        to cease from among men,"
27 Had I not feared
        the wrath of the enemy,
    Lest their adversaries should
        misunderstand,
    Lest they should say,
        "Our hand *is* high;

And it is not the LORD
    who has done all this." '

28 "For they *are* a nation void of counsel,
    Nor *is there any* understanding
        in them.
29 Oh, that they were wise,
        that they understood this,
    That they would consider
        their latter end!
30 How could one chase a thousand,
    And two put ten thousand to flight,
    Unless their Rock had sold them,
    And the LORD had surrendered them?
31 For their rock *is* not like our Rock,
    Even our enemies
        themselves *being* judges.
32 For their vine *is* of the vine of Sodom
    And of the fields of Gomorrah;
    Their grapes *are* grapes of gall,
    Their clusters *are* bitter.
33 Their wine *is* the poison of serpents,
    And the cruel venom of cobras.

34 '*Is* this not laid up in store with Me,
    Sealed up among My treasures?
35 Vengeance is Mine, and recompense;
    Their foot shall slip in *due* time;
    For the day of their calamity
        is at hand,
    And the things to come hasten
        upon them.'

36 "For the LORD will judge His people
    And have compassion on His servants,
    When He sees that *their* power is gone,
    And *there is* no one *remaining*,
        bond or free.
37 He will say: 'Where *are* their gods,
    The rock in which they sought refuge?
38 Who ate the fat of their sacrifices,
    And drank the wine
        of their drink offering?
    Let them rise and help you,
    And be your refuge.

39 'Now see that I, *even* I, *am* He,
    And *there is* no God besides Me;
    I kill and I make alive;
    I wound and I heal;
    Nor *is there any*
        who can deliver from My hand.
40 For I lift My hand to heaven,
    And say, "*As* I live forever,
41 If I whet My glittering sword,
    And My hand takes hold on judgment,
    I will render vengeance to My enemies,
    And repay those who hate Me.
42 I will make My arrows drunk
        with blood,

And My sword shall devour flesh,
With the blood of the slain
   and the captives,
From the heads
   of the leaders of the enemy." '

43 "Rejoice, O Gentiles, *with* His people;[25]
For He will avenge
   the blood of His servants,
And render vengeance
   to His adversaries;
He will provide atonement for His land
   and His people."

44 So Moses came with Joshua[26] the son of Nun and spoke all the words of this song in the hearing of the people.
45 Moses finished speaking all these words to all Israel,
46 and He said to them: "Set your hearts on all the words which I testify among you today, which you shall command your children to be careful to observe— all the words of this law.
47 "For it *is* not a futile thing for you, because it *is* your life, and by this word you shall prolong *your* days in the land which you cross over the Jordan to possess."

Moses to Die on Mount Nebo

48 Then the LORD spoke to Moses that very same day, saying:
49 "Go up this mountain of the Abarim, Mount Nebo, which *is* in the land of Moab, across from Jericho; view the land of Canaan, which I give to the children of Israel as a possession;
50 "and die on the mountain which you ascend, and be gathered to your people, just as Aaron your brother died on Mount Hor and was gathered to his people;
51 "because you trespassed against Me among the children of Israel at the waters of Meribah Kadesh, in the Wilderness of Zin, because you did not hallow Me in the midst of the children of Israel.
52 "Yet you shall see the land before *you,* though you shall not go there, into the land which I am giving to the children of Israel."

Moses' Final Blessing on Israel

33 Now this *is* the blessing with which Moses the man of God blessed the children of Israel before his death.

2 And he said:

"The LORD came from Sinai,
And dawned on them from Seir;
He shone forth from Mount Paran,
And He came with ten thousands
   of saints;
From His right hand
Came a fiery law for them.
3 Yes, He loves the people;
All His saints *are* in Your hand;
They sit down at Your feet;
Everyone receives Your words.
4 Moses commanded a law for us,
A heritage of the congregation
   of Jacob.
5 And He was King in Jeshurun,
When the leaders of the people
   were gathered,
All the tribes of Israel together.

6 "Let Reuben live, and not die,
Nor let his men be few."

7 And this he said of Judah:

"Hear, LORD, the voice of Judah,
And bring him to his people;
Let his hands be sufficient for him,
And may You be a help
   against his enemies."

8 And of Levi he said:

"*Let* Your Thummim and Your Urim
   be with Your holy one,
Whom You tested at Massah,
And with whom You contended
   at the waters of Meribah,
9 Who says of his father and mother,
'I have not seen them';
Nor did he acknowledge his brothers,
Or know his own children;
For they have observed Your word
And kept Your covenant.
10 They shall teach Jacob
   Your judgments,
And Israel Your law.
They shall put incense before You,
And a whole burnt sacrifice
   on Your altar.
11 Bless his substance, LORD,
And accept the work of his hands;
Strike the loins of those
   who rise against him,
And of those who hate him,
   that they rise not again."

25 Dead Sea Scrolls add *And let all the angels worship Him* (compare Septuagint and Hebrews 1:6).
26 Hebrew *Hoshea* (compare Numbers 13:8, 16)

12 Of Benjamin he said:

"The beloved of the LORD
    shall dwell in safety by Him,
Who shelters him all the day long;
And he shall dwell
    between His shoulders."

13 And of Joseph he said:

"Blessed of the LORD *is* his land,
With the precious things of heaven,
    with the dew,
And the deep lying beneath,
14 With the precious fruits of the sun,
With the precious produce
    of the months,
15 With the best things
    of the ancient mountains,
With the precious things
    of the everlasting hills,
16 With the precious things
    of the earth and its fullness,
And the favor of Him
    who dwelt in the bush.
Let *the blessing* come
    'on the head of Joseph,
And on the crown of the head of him
    who was separate from his
    brothers.'27
17 His glory *is like* a firstborn bull,
And his horns *are like* the horns
    of the wild ox;
Together with them
He shall push the peoples
To the ends of the earth;
They *are* the ten thousands
    of Ephraim,
And they *are* the thousands
    of Manasseh."

18 And of Zebulun he said:

"Rejoice, Zebulun, in your going out,
And Issachar in your tents!
19 They shall call the peoples
    to the mountain;
There they shall offer sacrifices
    of righteousness;
For they shall partake
    of the abundance of the seas
And *of* treasures hidden in the sand."

20 And of Gad he said:

"Blessed *is* he who enlarges Gad;
He dwells as a lion,
And tears the arm
    and the crown of his head.
21 He provided the first *part* for himself,

Because a lawgiver's portion
    was reserved there.
He came *with* the heads of the people;
He administered the justice
    of the LORD,
And His judgments with Israel."

22 And of Dan he said:

"Dan *is* a lion's whelp;
He shall leap from Bashan."

23 And of Naphtali he said:

"O Naphtali, satisfied with favor,
And full of the blessing of the LORD,
Possess the west and the south."

24 And of Asher he said:

"Asher *is* most blessed of sons;
Let him be favored by his brothers,
And let him dip his foot in oil.
25 Your sandals *shall be* iron and bronze;
As your days, *so shall* your strength *be.*

26 "*There is* no one
    like the God of Jeshurun,
Who rides the heavens to help you,
And in His excellency on the clouds.
27 The eternal God *is your* refuge,
And underneath *are*
    the everlasting arms;
He will thrust out the enemy
    from before you,
And will say, 'Destroy!'
28 Then Israel shall dwell in safety,
The fountain of Jacob alone,
In a land of grain and new wine;
His Heavens shall also drop dew.
29 Happy *are* you, O Israel!
Who *is* like you,
    a people saved by the LORD,
The shield of your help
And the sword of your majesty!
Your enemies shall submit to you,
And you shall tread down
    their high places."

Moses Dies on Mount Nebo

34 Then Moses went up from the plains of Moab to Mount Nebo, to the top of Pisgah, which is across from Jericho. And the LORD showed him all the land of Gilead as far as Dan,
2 all Naphtali and the land of Ephraim and Manasseh, all the land of Judah as far as the Western Sea,28
3 the South, and the plain of the Valley

27 Compare Genesis 49:26   28 That is, the Mediterranean

of Jericho, the city of palm trees, as far as Zoar.

4 Then the LORD said to him, "This is the land of which I swore to give Abraham, Isaac, and Jacob, saying, 'I will give it to your descendants.' I have caused you to see it with your eyes, but you shall not cross over there."

5 So Moses the servant of the LORD died there in the land of Moab, according to the word of the LORD.

6 And He buried him in a valley in the land of Moab, opposite Beth Peor; but no one knows his grave to this day.

7 Moses was one hundred and twenty years old when he died. His eyes were not dim nor his natural vigor abated.

8 And the children of Israel wept for Moses in the plains of Moab thirty days. So the days of weeping and mourning for Moses ended.

9 Now Joshua the son of Nun was full of the spirit of wisdom, for Moses had laid his hands on him; so the children of Israel heeded him, and did as the LORD had commanded Moses.

10 But since then there has not arisen in Israel a prophet like Moses, whom the LORD knew face to face,

11 in all the signs and wonders which the LORD sent him to do in the land of Egypt, before Pharaoh, before all his servants, and in all his land,

12 and by all that mighty power and all the great terror which Moses performed in the sight of all Israel.

Introduction to Joshua

Joshua dared to believe in conquest when others predicted catastrophe. He marched forth with faith and courage, dedicated to conquering the land God had promised the Israelites.

This fascinating account was written by Joshua sometime during the fourteenth or fifteenth century B.C. It vividly depicts brilliant military strategy and God's miraculous intervention in the conquest of Canaan.

Joshua ordered his division into a two-pronged attack. One initially at Jericho, the pantry of the wilderness, from which he could supply food and water to his troops and one north at Hazor, which controlled the major highway above the Sea of Galilee.

Joshua quickly secured the Judean ridge and high mountains of northern Galilee from which he launched guerilla-like warfare tactics into the surrounding areas.

Employing this battle plan, Joshua was able to cut his problem in half. He knew that his greatest asset was not in numerical superiority of military might, but in a deep-rooted faith in God's ability to conquer any problem. Joshua had an inspiring and committed faith. "Choose for yourselves this day whom you will serve . . . But as for me and my house, we will serve the LORD" (Josh. 24:15).

Life is a collection of decisions. Joshua knew the value of right ones. As a great possibility thinker, Joshua chose to look at his prospects, not his problems; his resources, not his reservations; and his opportunities, not his obstacles.

With this faith, Joshua's military campaign of the Promised Land resulted in conquest, not catastrophe. He knew they could inhabit the land if they were not inhibited. For with God all things are possible.

The Book of

Joshua

God's Commission to Joshua

AFTER the death of Moses the servant of the LORD, it came to pass that the LORD spoke to Joshua the son of Nun, Moses' assistant, saying: 2 "Moses My servant is dead. Now therefore, arise, go over this Jordan, you and all this people, to the land which I am giving to them—the children of Israel. 3 "Every place that the sole of your foot will tread upon I have given you, as I said to Moses. 4 "From the wilderness and this Lebanon as far as the great river, the River Euphrates, all the land of the Hittites, and to the Great Sea toward the going down of the sun, shall be your territory. 5 "No man shall *be able to* stand before you all the days of your life; as I was with Moses, *so* I will be with you. I will not leave you nor forsake you. 6 "Be strong and of good courage, for to this people you shall divide as an inheritance the land which I swore to their fathers to give them. 7 "Only be strong and very courageous, that you may observe to do according to all the law which Moses My servant commanded you; do not turn from it to the right hand or to the left, that you may prosper wherever you go. 8 "This Book of the Law shall not depart from your mouth, but you shall meditate in it day and night, that you may observe to do according to all that is written in it. For then you will make your way prosperous, and then you will have good success. 9 "Have I not commanded you? Be strong and of good courage; do not be afraid, nor be dismayed, for the LORD your God *is* with you wherever you go."

The Order to Cross the Jordan

10 Then Joshua commanded the officers of the people, saying, 11 "Pass through the camp and command the people, saying, 'Prepare provisions for yourselves, for within three days you will cross over this Jordan, to go in to possess the land which the LORD your God is giving you to possess.' " *12* And to the Reubenites, the Gadites, and half the tribe of Manasseh Joshua spoke, saying, 13 "Remember the word which Moses the servant of the LORD commanded you, saying, 'The LORD your God is giving you rest and is giving you this land.' 14 "Your wives, your little ones, and your livestock shall remain in the land which Moses gave you on this side of the Jordan. But you shall pass before your brethren armed, all your mighty men of valor, and help them, 15 "until the LORD has given your brethren rest, as He *has given* you, and they also have taken possession of the land which the LORD your God is giving them. Then you shall return to the land of your possession and enjoy it, which Moses the LORD's servant gave you on this side of the Jordan toward the sunrise." *16* And they answered Joshua, saying, "All that you command us we will do, and wherever you send us we will go. 17 "Just as we heeded Moses in all things, so we will heed you. Only the LORD your God be with you, as He was with Moses. 18 "Whoever rebels against your command and does not heed your words, in all that you command him, shall be put to death. Only be strong and of good courage."

Rahab Hides the Spies

2 Now Joshua the son of Nun sent out two men from Acacia Grove[1] to spy secretly, saying, "Go, view the land, especially Jericho." So they went, and came to the house of a harlot named Rahab, and lodged there. 2 And it was told the king of Jericho, saying, "Behold, men have come here tonight from the children of Israel to search out the country." 3 So the king of Jericho sent to Rahab, saying, "Bring out the men who have

---

1 Hebrew *Shittim*

No One Is Too Far
from God's Love

When Joshua and the Israelites conquered the city of Jericho, they were aided by a most unusual woman—a prostitute named Rahab. Hearing of the Israelites' faith in the one true God, Rahab took it upon herself to hide two of Joshua's top espionage agents who were scouting the land.

Jericho was the pantry of the wilderness. It was the only tree of the wilderness, the only city with supplies for the desert. The spring of Jericho pumped three thousand gallons of water a minute.

Joshua's strategy was to secure Jericho before moving into the hill country and continuing his conquest of Canaan. Perhaps one reason God commissioned the fall of Jericho was due to the city's Canaanite Baal worship, temple prostitution, ancestor worship, and other pagan religious rites. It was not uncommon for human sacrifice to be a dominant theme in this religion, as is evident from various literary sources and temple excavations in Megiddo, Hazor, and other sites of Canaanite worship. Rahab most likely welcomed the pure God-fearing worship of the Israelites.

In return for hiding the spies in her house, Rahab asked the Israelites to spare her and her family when they conquered Jericho. In exchange for her assistance, the Israelites welcomed her into their community. God acknowledged her faith by honoring her in history. Rahab became a respected citizen of the Israelite community and married the son of Caleb, one of the two spies. As a result of her faith, Rahab was included as an ancestor in the genealogy of Christ.

If God can use a prostitute like Rahab to accomplish His work, how much more can He use you? No one is too far from God's love. No one is too small for God's work. Like Rahab, recognize the one true God. Then do your part for the advancement of His kingdom. Believe in God—believe in His plan—and then believe in yourself!

come to you, who have entered your house, for they have come to search out all the country."

4 Then the woman took the two men and hid them; and she said, "Yes, the men came to me, but I did not know where they *were* from.

5 "And it happened as the gate was being shut, when it was dark, that the men went out. Where the men went I do not know; pursue them quickly, for you may overtake them."

6 (But she had brought them up to the roof and hidden them with the stalks of flax, which she had laid in order on the roof.)

7 Then the men pursued them by the road to the Jordan, to the fords. And as soon as those who pursued them had gone out, they shut the gate.

8 So before they lay down, she came up to them on the roof,

9 and said to the men: "I know that the LORD has given you the land, that the terror of you has fallen on us, and that all the inhabitants of the land are fainthearted because of you.

10 "For we have heard how the LORD dried up the water of the Red Sea for you when you came out of Egypt, and what you did to the two kings of the Amorites who *were* on the other side of the Jordan, Sihon and Og, whom you utterly destroyed.

11 "And as soon as we heard *these things*, our hearts melted; neither did there remain any more courage in anyone because of you, for the LORD your God, He *is* God in heaven above and on earth beneath.

12 "Now therefore, I beg you, swear to me by the LORD, since I have shown you kindness, that you also will show kindness to my father's house, and give me a true token,

13 "and spare my father, my mother, my brothers, my sisters, and all that they have, and deliver our lives from death."

14 So the men answered her, "Our lives for yours, if none of you tell this business of ours. And it shall be, when the LORD has given us the land, that we will deal kindly and truly with you."

15 Then she let them down by a rope through the window, for her house *was* on the city wall; she dwelt on the wall.

16 And she said to them, "Get to the mountain, lest the pursuers meet you. Hide there three days, until the pursuers have returned. Afterward you may go your way."

17 Then the men said to her: "We *will be* blameless of this oath of yours which you have made us swear,

18 "unless, *when* we come into the land, you bind this line of scarlet cord in the window through which you let us down, and unless you bring your father, your mother, your brothers, and all your father's household to your own home.

19 "So it shall be *that* whoever goes outside the doors of your house into the street, his blood *shall be* on his own head, and we *will be* guiltless. And whoever is with you in the house, his blood *shall be* on our head if a hand is laid on him.

20 "And if you tell this business of ours, then we will be free from your oath which you made us swear."

21 Then she said, "According to your words, so *be* it." And she sent them away, and they departed. And she bound the scarlet cord in the window.

22 Then they departed and went to the mountain, and stayed there three days until the pursuers returned. The pursuers sought *them* all along the way, but did not find *them*.

23 So the two men returned, descended from the mountain, and crossed over; and they came to Joshua the son of Nun, and told him all that had befallen them.

24 And they said to Joshua, "Truly the LORD has delivered all the land into our hands, for indeed all the inhabitants of the country are fainthearted because of us."

Israel Crosses the Jordan

3 Then Joshua rose early in the morning; and they set out from Acacia Grove[2] and came to the Jordan, he and all the children of Israel, and lodged there before they crossed over.

2 So it was, after three days, that the officers went through the camp;

3 and they commanded the people, saying, "When you see the ark of the covenant of the LORD your God, and the priests, the Levites, bearing it, then you shall set out from your place and go after it.

4 "Yet there shall be a space between you and it, about two thousand cubits by

2 Hebrew *Shittim*

measure. Do not come near it, that you may know the way by which you must go, for you have not passed *this* way before."

5 And Joshua said to the people, "Sanctify yourselves, for tomorrow the LORD will do wonders among you."

6 Then Joshua spoke to the priests, saying, "Take up the ark of the covenant and cross over before the people." So they took up the ark of the covenant and went before the people.

7 And the LORD said to Joshua, "This day I will begin to magnify you in the sight of all Israel, that they may know that, as I was with Moses, *so* I will be with you.

8 "You shall command the priests who bear the ark of the covenant, saying, 'When you have come to the edge of the water of the Jordan, you shall stand in the Jordan.' "

9 So Joshua said to the children of Israel, "Come here, and hear the words of the LORD your God."

10 And Joshua said, "By this you shall know that the living God *is* among you, and *that* He will without fail drive out from before you the Canaanites and the Hittites and the Hivites and the Perizzites and the Girgashites and the Amorites and the Jebusites:

11 "Behold, the ark of the covenant of the Lord of all the earth is crossing over before you into the Jordan.

12 "Now therefore, take for yourselves twelve men from the tribes of Israel, one man from every tribe.

13 "And it shall come to pass, as soon as the soles of the feet of the priests who bear the ark of the LORD, the Lord of all the earth, shall rest in the waters of the Jordan, *that* the waters of the Jordan shall be cut off, the waters that come down from upstream, and they shall stand as a heap."

14 So it was, when the people set out from their camp to cross over the Jordan, with the priests bearing the ark of the covenant before the people,

15 and as those who bore the ark came to the Jordan, and the feet of the priests who bore the ark dipped in the edge of the water (for the Jordan overflows all its banks during the whole time of harvest),

16 that the waters which came down from upstream stood *still, and* rose in a heap very far away at Adam, the city that

is beside Zaretan. So the waters that went down into the Sea of the Arabah, the Salt Sea, failed, *and* were cut off; and the people crossed over opposite Jericho.

17 Then the priests who bore the ark of the covenant of the LORD stood firm on dry ground in the midst of the Jordan; and all Israel crossed over on dry ground, until all the people had crossed completely over the Jordan.

The Memorial Stones

4 And it came to pass, when all the people had completely crossed over the Jordan, that the LORD spoke to Joshua, saying:

2 "Take for yourselves twelve men from the people, one man from every tribe,

3 "and command them, saying, 'Take for yourselves twelve stones from here, out of the midst of the Jordan, from the place where the priests' feet stood firm. You shall carry them over with you and leave them in the lodging place where you lodge tonight.' "

4 Then Joshua called the twelve men whom he had appointed from the children of Israel, one man from every tribe;

5 and Joshua said to them: "Cross over before the ark of the LORD your God into the midst of the Jordan, and each one of you take up a stone on his shoulder, according to the number of the tribes of the children of Israel,

6 "that this may be a sign among you when your children ask in time to come, saying, 'What do these stones *mean* to you?'

7 "Then you shall answer them that the waters of the Jordan were cut off before the ark of the covenant of the LORD; when it crossed over the Jordan, the waters of the Jordan were cut off. And these stones shall be for a memorial to the children of Israel forever."

8 And the children of Israel did so, just as Joshua commanded, and took up twelve stones from the midst of the Jordan, as the LORD had spoken to Joshua, according to the number of the tribes of the children of Israel, and carried them over with them to the place where they lodged, and laid them down there.

9 Then Joshua set up twelve stones in the midst of the Jordan, in the place where the feet of the priests who bore the

ark of the covenant stood; and they are there to this day.

10 So the priests who bore the ark stood in the midst of the Jordan until everything was finished that the LORD had commanded Joshua to speak to the people, according to all that Moses had commanded Joshua; and the people hastened and crossed over.

11 Then it came to pass, when all the people had completely crossed over, that the ark of the LORD and the priests crossed over in the presence of the people.

12 And the men of Reuben, the men of Gad, and half the tribe of Manasseh crossed over armed before the children of Israel, as Moses had spoken to them.

13 About forty thousand prepared for war crossed over before the LORD for battle, to the plains of Jericho.

14 On that day the LORD magnified Joshua in the sight of all Israel; and they feared him, as they had feared Moses, all the days of his life.

15 Then the LORD spoke to Joshua, saying,

16 "Command the priests who bear the ark of the Testimony to come up from the Jordan."

17 Joshua therefore commanded the priests, saying, "Come up from the Jordan."

18 And it came to pass, when the priests who bore the ark of the covenant of the LORD had come from the midst of the Jordan, and the soles of the priests' feet touched the dry land, that the waters of the Jordan returned to their place and flowed over all its banks as before.

19 Now the people came up from the Jordan on the tenth day of the first month, and they camped in Gilgal on the east border of Jericho.

20 And those twelve stones which they took out of the Jordan, Joshua set up in Gilgal.

21 Then he spoke to the children of Israel, saying: "When your children ask their fathers in time to come, saying, 'What are these stones?'

22 "then you shall let your children know, saying, 'Israel crossed over this Jordan on dry land';

23 "for the LORD your God dried up the waters of the Jordan before you until you had crossed over, as the LORD your God did to the Red Sea, which He dried up before us until we had crossed over,

24 "that all the peoples of the earth may know the hand of the LORD, that it is mighty, that you may fear the LORD your God forever."

The Second Generation Circumcised

5 So it was, when all the kings of the Amorites who were on the west side of the Jordan, and all the kings of the Canaanites who were by the sea, heard that the LORD had dried up the waters of the Jordan from before the children of Israel until we[3] had crossed over, that their heart melted; and there was no spirit in them any longer because of the children of Israel.

2 At that time the LORD said to Joshua, "Make flint knives for yourself, and circumcise the sons of Israel again the second time."

3 So Joshua made flint knives for himself, and circumcised the sons of Israel at the hill of the foreskins.[4]

4 And this is the reason why Joshua circumcised them: All the people who came out of Egypt who were males, all the men of war, had died in the wilderness on the way, after they had come out of Egypt.

5 For all the people who came out had been circumcised, but all the people who were born in the wilderness on the way as they came out of Egypt had not been circumcised.

6 For the children of Israel walked forty years in the wilderness, till all the people who were men of war, who came out of Egypt, were consumed, because they did not obey the voice of the LORD—to whom the LORD swore that He would not show them the land which the LORD had sworn to their fathers that He would give us, "a land flowing with milk and honey."[5]

7 So Joshua circumcised their sons whom He raised up in their place; for they were uncircumcised, because they had not been circumcised on the way.

8 So it was, when they had finished circumcising all the people, that they stayed in their places in the camp till they were healed.

9 Then the LORD said to Joshua, "This day I have rolled away the reproach of

---

3 Qere, some Hebrew manuscripts and editions, Septuagint, Syriac, Targum, and Vulgate read they.
4 Hebrew Gibeath Haaraloth   5 Compare Exodus 3:8

Egypt from you." Therefore the name of the place is called Gilgal[6] to this day.

10 So the children of Israel camped in Gilgal, and kept the Passover on the fourteenth day of the month at twilight on the plains of Jericho.

11 And they ate of the produce of the land on the day after the Passover, unleavened bread and parched grain on the very same day.

12 Now the manna ceased on the day after they had eaten the produce of the land; and the children of Israel no longer had manna, but they ate the food of the land of Canaan that year.

The Commander of the Army of the LORD

13 And it came to pass, when Joshua was by Jericho, that he lifted his eyes and looked, and behold, a Man stood opposite him with His sword drawn in His hand. And Joshua went to Him and said to Him, "*Are* You for us or for our adversaries?"

14 So He said, "No, but *as* Commander of the army of the LORD I have now come." And Joshua fell on his face to the earth and worshiped, and said to Him, "What does my Lord say to His servant?"

15 Then the Commander of the LORD's army said to Joshua, "Take your sandal off your foot, for the place where you stand *is* holy." And Joshua did so.

The Destruction of Jericho

6 Now Jericho was securely shut up because of the children of Israel; none went out, and none came in.

2 And the LORD said to Joshua: "See! I have given Jericho into your hand, its king, *and* the mighty men of valor.

3 "You shall march around the city, all *you* men of war; you shall go all around the city once. This you shall do six days.

4 "And seven priests shall bear seven trumpets of rams' horns before the ark. But the seventh day you shall march around the city seven times, and the priests shall blow the trumpets.

5 "Then it shall come to pass, when they make a long *blast* with the ram's horn, *and* when you hear the sound of the trumpet, that all the people shall shout with a great shout; then the wall of the city will fall down flat. And the people shall go up every man straight before him."

6 So Joshua the son of Nun called the priests and said to them, "Take up the ark of the covenant, and let seven priests bear seven trumpets of rams' horns before the ark of the LORD."

7 And he said to the people, "Proceed, and march around the city, and let him who is armed advance before the ark of the LORD."

8 So it was, when Joshua had spoken to the people, that the seven priests bearing the seven trumpets of rams' horns before the LORD advanced and blew the trumpets, and the ark of the covenant of the LORD followed them.

9 The armed men went before the priests who blew the trumpets, and the rear guard came after the ark, while *the priests* continued blowing the trumpets.

10 Now Joshua had commanded the people, saying, "You shall not shout or make any noise with your voice, nor shall *any* word proceed out of your mouth, until the day I say to you, 'Shout!' Then you shall shout."

11 So he had the ark of the LORD circle the city, going around *it* once. Then they came into the camp and lodged in the camp.

12 And Joshua rose early in the morning, and the priests took up the ark of the LORD.

13 Then seven priests bearing seven trumpets of rams' horns before the ark of the LORD went on continually and blew with the trumpets. And the armed men went before them. But the rear guard came after the ark of the LORD, while *the priests* continued blowing the trumpets.

14 And the second day they marched around the city once and returned to the camp. So they did six days.

15 But it came to pass on the seventh day that they rose early, about the dawning of the day, and marched around the city seven times in the same manner. On that day only they marched around the city seven times.

16 And the seventh time it was so, when the priests blew the trumpets, that Joshua said to the people: "Shout, for the LORD has given you the city!

17 "Now the city shall be doomed by the LORD to destruction, it and all who *are* in it. Only Rahab the harlot shall live, she and all who *are* with her in the house,

6 Literally *Rolling*

because she hid the messengers that we sent.

18 "And you, by all means keep *yourselves* from the accursed things, lest you become accursed when you take of the accursed things, and make the camp of Israel a curse, and trouble it.

19 "But all the silver and gold, and vessels of bronze and iron, *are* consecrated to the LORD; they shall come into the treasury of the LORD."

20 So the people shouted when *the priests* blew the trumpets. And it happened when the people heard the sound of the trumpet, and the people shouted with a great shout, that the wall fell down flat. Then the people went up into the city, every man straight before him, and they took the city.

21 And they utterly destroyed all that *was* in the city, both man and woman, young and old, ox and sheep and donkey, with the edge of the sword.

22 But Joshua had said to the two men who had spied out the country, "Go into the harlot's house, and from there bring out the woman and all that she has, as you swore to her."

23 And the young men who had been spies went in and brought out Rahab, her father, her mother, her brothers, and all that she had. So they brought out all her relatives and left them outside the camp of Israel.

24 But they burned the city and all that *was* in it with fire. Only the silver and gold, and the vessels of bronze and iron, they put into the treasury of the house of the LORD.

25 And Joshua spared Rahab the harlot, her father's household, and all that she had. So she dwells in Israel to this day, because she hid the messengers whom Joshua sent to spy out Jericho.

26 Then Joshua charged *them* at that time, saying, "Cursed *be* the man before the LORD who rises up and builds this city Jericho; he shall lay its foundation with his firstborn, and with his youngest he shall set up its gates."

27 So the LORD was with Joshua, and his fame spread throughout all the country.

Defeat at Ai

7 But the children of Israel committed a trespass regarding the accursed things, for Achan the son of Carmi, the son of Zabdi,[7] the son of Zerah, of the tribe of Judah, took of the accursed things; so the anger of the LORD burned against the children of Israel.

2 Now Joshua sent men from Jericho to Ai, which *is* beside Beth Aven, on the east side of Bethel, and spoke to them, saying, "Go up and spy out the country." So the men went up and spied out Ai.

3 And they returned to Joshua and said to him, "Do not let all the people go up, but let about two or three thousand men go up and attack Ai. Do not weary all the people there, for *the people of Ai are* few."

4 So about three thousand men went up there from the people, but they fled before the men of Ai.

5 And the men of Ai struck down about thirty-six men, for they chased them *from* before the gate as far as Shebarim, and struck them down on the descent; therefore the hearts of the people melted and became like water.

6 Then Joshua tore his clothes, and fell to the earth on his face before the ark of the LORD until evening, *both* he and the elders of Israel; and they put dust on their heads.

7 And Joshua said, "Alas, Lord GOD, why have You brought this people over the Jordan at all—to deliver us into the hand of the Amorites, to destroy us? Oh, that we had been content, and dwelt on the other side of the Jordan!

8 "O Lord, what shall I say when Israel turns its back before its enemies?

9 "For the Canaanites and all the inhabitants of the land will hear *of it*, and surround us, and cut off our name from the earth. Then what will You do for Your great name?"

The Sin of Achan

10 So the LORD said to Joshua: "Get up! Why do you lie thus on your face?

11 "Israel has sinned, and they have also transgressed My covenant which I commanded them. For they have even taken some of the accursed things, and have both stolen and deceived; and they have also put *it* among their own stuff.

12 "Therefore the children of Israel could not stand before their enemies, *but* turned *their* backs before their enemies, because they have become doomed to destruction. Neither will I be with you any-

7 Called *Zimri* in 1 Chronicles 2:6

more, unless you destroy the accursed from among you.

13 "Get up, sanctify the people, and say, 'Sanctify yourselves for tomorrow, because thus says the LORD God of Israel: *"There is* an accursed thing in your midst, O Israel; you cannot stand before your enemies until you take away the accursed thing from among you."

14 'In the morning therefore you shall be brought according to your tribes. And it shall be *that* the tribe which the LORD takes shall come according to families; and the family which the LORD takes shall come by households; and the household which the LORD takes shall come man by man.

15 'Then it shall be *that* he who is taken with the accursed thing shall be burned with fire, he and all that he has, because he has transgressed the covenant of the LORD, and because he has done a disgraceful thing in Israel.' "

16 So Joshua rose early in the morning and brought Israel by their tribes, and the tribe of Judah was taken;

17 and he brought the clan of Judah, and he took the family of the Zarhites; and he brought the family of the Zarhites man by man, and Zabdi was taken.

18 Then he brought his household man by man, and Achan the son of Carmi, the son of Zabdi, the son of Zerah, of the tribe of Judah, was taken.

19 So Joshua said to Achan, "My son, I beg you, give glory to the LORD God of Israel, and make confession to Him, and tell me now what you have done; do not hide *it* from me."

20 And Achan answered Joshua and said, "Indeed I have sinned against the LORD God of Israel, and this is what I have done:

21 "When I saw among the spoils a beautiful Babylonian garment, two hundred shekels of silver, and a wedge of gold weighing fifty shekels, I coveted them and took them. And there they are, hidden in the earth in the midst of my tent, with the silver under it."

22 So Joshua sent messengers, and they ran to the tent; and there it was, hidden in his tent, with the silver under it.

23 And they took them from the midst of the tent, brought them to Joshua and to all the children of Israel, and laid them out before the LORD.

24 Then Joshua, and all Israel with him, took Achan the son of Zerah, the silver, the garment, the wedge of gold, his sons, his daughters, his oxen, his donkeys, his sheep, his tent, and all that he had, and they brought them to the Valley of Achor.

25 And Joshua said, "Why have you troubled us? The LORD will trouble you this day." So all Israel stoned him with stones; and they burned them with fire after they had stoned them with stones.

26 Then they raised over him a great heap of stones, still there to this day. So the LORD turned from the fierceness of His anger. Therefore the name of that place has been called the Valley of Achor[8] to this day.

The Fall of Ai

8 Then the LORD said to Joshua: "Do not be afraid, nor be dismayed; take all the people of war with you, and arise, go up to Ai. See, I have given into your hand the king of Ai, his people, his city, and his land.

2 "And you shall do to Ai and its king as you did to Jericho and its king. Only its spoil and its cattle you shall take as booty for yourselves. Lay an ambush for the city behind it."

3 So Joshua arose, and all the people of war, to go up against Ai; and Joshua chose thirty thousand mighty men of valor and sent them away by night.

4 And he commanded them, saying: "Behold, you shall lie in ambush against the city, behind the city. Do not go very far from the city, but all of you be ready.

5 "Then I and all the people who *are* with me will approach the city; and it will come about, when they come out against us as at the first, that we shall flee before them.

6 "For they will come out after us till we have drawn them from the city, for they will say, 'They *are* fleeing before us as at the first.' Therefore we will flee before them.

7 "Then you shall rise from the ambush and seize the city, for the LORD your God will deliver it into your hand.

8 "And it will be, when you have taken the city, *that* you shall set the city on fire. According to the commandment of the

8 Literally *Trouble*

LORD you shall do. See, I have commanded you."

9 Joshua therefore sent them out; and they went to lie in ambush, and stayed between Bethel and Ai, on the west side of Ai; but Joshua lodged that night among the people.

10 Then Joshua rose up early in the morning and mustered the people, and went up, he and the elders of Israel, before the people to Ai.

11 And all the people of war who *were* with him went up and drew near; and they came before the city and camped on the north side of Ai. Now *there was* a valley between them and Ai.

12 So he took about five thousand men and set them in ambush between Bethel and Ai, on the west side of the city.

13 And when they had set the people, all the army that *was* on the north of the city, and its rear guard on the west of the city, Joshua went that night into the midst of the valley.

14 Now it happened, when the king of Ai saw *it*, that the men of the city hastened and rose early and went out against Israel to battle, he and all his people, at an appointed place before the plain. But he did not know that *there was* an ambush against him behind the city.

15 And Joshua and all Israel made as if they were beaten before them, and fled by the way of the wilderness.

16 So all the people who *were* in Ai were called together to pursue them. And they pursued Joshua and were drawn away from the city.

17 There was not a man left in Ai or Bethel who did not go out after Israel. So they left the city open and pursued Israel.

18 Then the LORD said to Joshua, "Stretch out the spear that *is* in your hand toward Ai, for I will give it into your hand." And Joshua stretched out the spear that *he had* in his hand toward the city.

19 So *those in* ambush arose quickly out of their place; they ran as soon as he had stretched out his hand, and they entered the city and took it, and hastened to set the city on fire.

20 And when the men of Ai looked behind them, they saw, and behold, the smoke of the city ascended to heaven. So they had no power to flee this way or that

way, and the people who had fled to the wilderness turned back on the pursuers.

21 Now when Joshua and all Israel saw that the ambush had taken the city and that the smoke of the city ascended, they turned back and struck down the men of Ai.

22 Then the others came out of the city against them; so they were *caught* in the midst of Israel, some on this side and some on that side. And they struck them down, so that they let none of them remain or escape.

23 But the king of Ai they took alive, and brought him to Joshua.

24 And it came to pass when Israel had made an end of slaying all the inhabitants of Ai in the field, in the wilderness where they pursued them, and when they all had fallen by the edge of the sword until they were consumed, that all the Israelites returned to Ai and struck it with the edge of the sword.

25 *So* it was *that* all who fell that day, both men and women, *were* twelve thousand—all the people of Ai.

26 For Joshua did not draw back his hand, with which he stretched out the spear, until he had utterly destroyed all the inhabitants of Ai.

27 Only the livestock and the spoil of that city Israel took as booty for themselves, according to the word of the LORD which He had commanded Joshua.

28 So Joshua burned Ai and made it a heap forever, a desolation to this day.

29 And the king of Ai he hanged on a tree until evening. And as soon as the sun was down, Joshua commanded that they should take his corpse down from the tree, cast it at the entrance of the gate of the city, and raise over it a great heap of stones *that remains* to this day.

Joshua Renews the Covenant

30 Now Joshua built an altar to the LORD God of Israel in Mount Ebal,

31 as Moses the servant of the LORD had commanded the children of Israel, as it is written in the Book of the Law of Moses: "an altar of whole stones over which no man has wielded *any* iron *tool*."9 And they offered on it burnt offerings to the LORD, and sacrificed peace offerings.

32 And there, in the presence of the children of Israel, he wrote on the stones a

---

9 Compare Deuteronomy 27:5, 6

copy of the law of Moses, which he had written.

33 Then all Israel, with their elders and officers and judges, stood on either side of the ark before the priests, the Levites, who bore the ark of the covenant of the LORD, the stranger as well as he who was born among them. Half of them *were* in front of Mount Gerizim and half of them in front of Mount Ebal, as Moses the servant of the LORD had commanded before, that they should bless the people of Israel.

34 And afterward he read all the words of the law, the blessings and the cursings, according to all that is written in the Book of the Law.

35 There was not a word of all that Moses had commanded which Joshua did not read before all the congregation of Israel, with the women, the little ones, and the strangers who were living among them.

The Treaty with the Gibeonites

9 And it came to pass when all the kings who *were* on this side of the Jordan, in the hills and in the lowland and in all the coasts of the Great Sea toward Lebanon—the Hittite, the Amorite, the Canaanite, the Perizzite, the Hivite, and the Jebusite—heard *of it*,

2 that they gathered together to fight with Joshua and Israel with one accord.

3 But when the inhabitants of Gibeon heard what Joshua had done to Jericho and Ai,

4 they worked craftily, and went and pretended to be ambassadors. And they took old sacks on their donkeys, old wineskins torn and mended,

5 old and patched sandals on their feet, and old garments on themselves; and all the bread of their provision was dry *and* moldy.

6 And they went to Joshua, to the camp at Gilgal, and said to him and to the men of Israel, "We have come from a far country; now therefore, make a covenant with us."

7 But the men of Israel said to the Hivites, "Perhaps you dwell among us; so how can we make a covenant with you?"

8 And they said to Joshua, "We *are* your servants." And Joshua said to them, "Who *are* you, and where do you come from?"

9 So they said to him: "From a very far country your servants have come, because of the name of the LORD your God; for we have heard of His fame, and all that He did in Egypt,

10 "and all that He did to the two kings of the Amorites who *were* beyond the Jordan—to Sihon king of Heshbon, and Og king of Bashan, who was at Ashtaroth.

11 "Therefore our elders and all the inhabitants of our country spoke to us, saying, 'Take provisions with you for the journey, and go to meet them, and say to them, "We *are* your servants; now therefore, make a covenant with us." '

12 "This bread of ours we took hot *for* our provision from our houses on the day we departed to come to you. But now look, it is dry and moldy.

13 "And these wineskins which we filled *were* new, and see, they are torn; and these our garments and our sandals have become old because of the very long journey."

14 Then the men of Israel took some of their provisions; but they did not ask counsel of the LORD.

15 So Joshua made peace with them, and made a covenant with them to let them live; and the rulers of the congregation swore to them.

16 And it happened at the end of three days, after they had made a covenant with them, that they heard that they *were* their neighbors who dwelt near them.

17 Then the children of Israel journeyed and came to their cities on the third day. Now their cities *were* Gibeon, Chephirah, Beeroth, and Kirjath Jearim.

18 But the children of Israel did not attack them, because the rulers of the congregation had sworn to them by the LORD God of Israel. And all the congregation murmured against the rulers.

19 Then all the rulers said to all the congregation, "We have sworn to them by the LORD God of Israel; now therefore, we may not touch them.

20 "This we will do to them: We will let them live, lest wrath be upon us because of the oath which we swore to them."

21 And the rulers said to them, "Let them live, but let them be woodcutters and water carriers for all the congregation, as the rulers had promised them."

22 Then Joshua called for them, and he

spoke to them, saying, "Why have you deceived us, saying, 'We *are* very far from you,' when you dwell near us?

23 "Now therefore, you *are* cursed, and none of you shall be freed from being slaves—woodcutters and water carriers for the house of my God."

24 So they answered Joshua and said, "Because it was certainly told your servants that the LORD your God commanded His servant Moses to give you all the land, and to destroy all the inhabitants of the land from before you; therefore we were very much afraid for our lives because of you, and have done this thing.

25 "And now, here we *are*, in your hands; do with us as it seems good and right to do to us."

26 So he did to them, and delivered them out of the hand of the children of Israel, so that they did not kill them.

27 And that day Joshua made them woodcutters and water carriers for the congregation and for the altar of the LORD, in the place which He would choose, even to this day.

The Sun Stands Still

10 Now it came to pass when Adoni-Zedek king of Jerusalem heard how Joshua had taken Ai and had utterly destroyed it—as he had done to Jericho and its king, so he had done to Ai and its king—and how the inhabitants of Gibeon had made peace with Israel and were among them,

2 that they feared greatly, because Gibeon *was* a great city, like one of the royal cities, and because it *was* greater than Ai, and all its men *were* mighty.

3 Therefore Adoni-Zedek king of Jerusalem sent to Hoham king of Hebron, Piram king of Jarmuth, Japhia king of Lachish, and Debir king of Eglon, saying,

4 "Come up to me and help me, that we may attack Gibeon, for it has made peace with Joshua and with the children of Israel."

5 Therefore the five kings of the Amorites, the king of Jerusalem, the king of Hebron, the king of Jarmuth, the king of Lachish, *and* the king of Eglon, gathered together and went up, they and all their armies, and camped before Gibeon and made war against it.

6 And the men of Gibeon sent to Joshua at the camp at Gilgal, saying, "Do not forsake your servants; come up to us quickly, save us and help us, for all the kings of the Amorites who dwell in the mountains have gathered together against us."

7 So Joshua ascended from Gilgal, he and all the people of war with him, and all the mighty men of valor.

8 And the LORD said to Joshua, "Do not fear them, for I have delivered them into your hand; not a man of them shall stand before you."

9 Joshua therefore came upon them suddenly, having marched all night from Gilgal.

10 So the LORD routed them before Israel, killed them with a great slaughter at Gibeon, chased them along the road that goes to Beth Horon, and struck them down as far as Azekah and Makkedah.

11 And it happened, as they fled before Israel *and* were on the descent of Beth Horon, that the LORD cast down large hailstones from heaven on them as far as Azekah, and they died. *There were* more who died from the hailstones than *those* whom the children of Israel killed with the sword.

12 Then Joshua spoke to the LORD in the day when the LORD delivered up the Amorites before the children of Israel, and he said in the sight of Israel:

"Sun, stand still over Gibeon;
And Moon, in the Valley of Aijalon."
13 So the sun stood still,
And the moon stopped,
Till the people had revenge
Upon their enemies.

Is this not written in the Book of Jasher? So the sun stood still in the midst of heaven, and did not hasten to go *down* for about a whole day.

14 And there has been no day like that, before it or after it, that the LORD heeded the voice of a man; for the LORD fought for Israel.

15 Then Joshua returned, and all Israel with him, to the camp at Gilgal.

The Amorite Kings Executed

16 But these five kings had fled and hidden themselves in a cave at Makkedah.

17 And it was told Joshua, saying, "The

A Peak to Peek Experience

When Joshua and the Israelites first conquered the land of Canaan they literally had a "peak to peek" experience. Following the conquest of Jericho, Joshua and his army led a campaign against the cities located on the Judean ridge. Joshua's strategy was to gain a foothold on these mountain peaks from which the Israelites could carry out lightning-like guerrilla raids into the surrounding country to broaden their base.

The Israelite army was tricked into an alliance with the local Gibeonites, who pretended to have traveled from a far-off land. When the Gibeonites were attacked by five armies from the south, Joshua kept his promise and came to their defense. Joshua saw this as an opportunity to gain control of the ridge. Marching from 1,300 feet below sea level to 3,000 feet above sea level, Joshua's men journeyed twenty-six miles under cover of darkness. When the sun was rising in the eyes of the five southerly kings and their armies, Joshua attacked and quickly gained victory.

The battle was hard but quick. Upon reaching the peak of the ridge, Joshua saw the five kings and their armies fleeing before him into the valley below. He got a glimpse, a peek, of a greater victory. This motivated him to push his men beyond their natural ability. The Israelite army continued their march another twenty miles to completely eliminate the enemy. Joshua prayed for strength and God's aid. God sent a hailstorm to assist the Israelites in their conquest. By nightfall they gained victory over the Canaanite kings.

Joshua's "peak to peek" experience was not unlike one you have probably had in your own life. A peak is a victory, a special accomplishment you have which enables you to get a "peek"—a look at an even greater possibility. Every success in your life does this for you. Success is never final. It is always transcended! Just when you think you have reached the peak of your efforts, the top of success, you realize and discover another opportunity.

Look back at the peak experiences of your life. You will know God was there to help you. And as you peek into the view of new mountains to climb, you know He will be there again!

five kings have been found hidden in the cave at Makkedah."

18 So Joshua said, "Roll large stones against the mouth of the cave, and set men by it to guard them.

19 "And do not stay *there* yourselves, *but* pursue your enemies, and attack their rear *ranks*; do not allow them to enter their cities, for the LORD your God has delivered them into your hand."

20 Then it happened, while Joshua and the children of Israel made an end of slaying them with a very great slaughter, till they had finished, that those who escaped entered fortified cities.

21 And all the people returned to the camp, to Joshua at Makkedah, in peace. No one moved his tongue against any of the children of Israel.

22 Then Joshua said, "Open the mouth of the cave, and bring out those five kings to me from the cave."

23 And they did so, and brought out those five kings to him from the cave: the king of Jerusalem, the king of Hebron, the king of Jarmuth, the king of Lachish, *and* the king of Eglon.

24 So it was, when they brought out those kings to Joshua, that Joshua called for all the men of Israel, and said to the captains of the men of war who went with him, "Come near, put your feet on the necks of these kings." And they drew near and put their feet on their necks.

25 Then Joshua said to them, "Do not be afraid, nor be dismayed; be strong and of good courage, for thus the LORD will do to all your enemies against whom you fight."

26 And afterward Joshua struck them and killed them, and hanged them on five trees; and they were hanging on the trees until evening.

27 So it was at the time of the going down of the sun *that* Joshua commanded, and they took them down from the trees, cast them into the cave where they had been hidden, and laid large stones against the cave's mouth, *which remain* until this very day.

Conquest of the Southland

28 On that day Joshua took Makkedah, and struck it and its king with the edge of the sword. He utterly destroyed them—10 all the people who *were* in it. He let none

remain. He also did to the king of Makkedah as he had done to the king of Jericho.

29 Then Joshua passed from Makkedah, and all Israel with him, to Libnah; and they fought against Libnah.

30 And the LORD also delivered it and its king into the hand of Israel; he struck it and all the people who *were* in it with the edge of the sword. He let none remain in it, but did to its king as he had done to the king of Jericho.

31 Then Joshua passed from Libnah, and all Israel with him, to Lachish; and they encamped against it and fought against it.

32 And the LORD delivered Lachish into the hand of Israel, who took it on the second day, and struck it and all the people who *were* in it with the edge of the sword, according to all that he had done to Libnah.

33 Then Horam king of Gezer came up to help Lachish; and Joshua struck him and his people, until he left him none remaining.

34 From Lachish Joshua passed to Eglon, and all Israel with him; and they encamped against it and fought against it.

35 They took it on that day and struck it with the edge of the sword; all the people who *were* in it he utterly destroyed that day, according to all that he had done to Lachish.

36 Then Joshua went up from Eglon, and all Israel with him, to Hebron; and they fought against it.

37 And they took it and struck it with the edge of the sword—its king, all its cities, and all the people who *were* in it; he left none remaining, according to all that he had done to Eglon, but utterly destroyed it and all the people who *were* in it.

38 Then Joshua returned, and all Israel with him, to Debir; and they fought against it.

39 And he took it and its king and all its cities; they struck them with the edge of the sword and utterly destroyed all the people who *were* in it. He left none remaining; as he had done to Hebron, so he did to Debir and its king, as he had done also to Libnah and its king.

40 So Joshua conquered all the land: the mountain country and the South[11] and the lowland and the wilderness slopes, and all their kings; he left none remaining, but utterly destroyed all that

---

10 Some ancient authorities read *it.*   11 Hebrew *Negev,* and so throughout the book

breathed, as the Lord God of Israel had commanded.

41 And Joshua conquered them from Kadesh Barnea as far as Gaza, and all the country of Goshen, even as far as Gibeon.

42 All these kings and their land Joshua took at one time, because the Lord God of Israel fought for Israel.

43 Then Joshua returned, and all Israel with him, to the camp at Gilgal.

The Northern Conquest

11 And it came to pass, when Jabin king of Hazor heard *these things*, that he sent to Jobab king of Madon, to the king of Shimron, to the king of Achshaph,

2 and to the kings who *were* from the north, in the mountains, in the plain south of Chinneroth, in the lowland, and in the heights of Dor on the west,

3 to the Canaanites in the east and in the west, the Amorite, the Hittite, the Perizzite, the Jebusite in the mountains, and the Hivite below Hermon in the land of Mizpah.

4 So they went out, they and all their armies with them, *as* many people *as* the sand that *is* on the seashore in multitude, with very many horses and chariots.

5 And when all these kings had met together, they came and camped together at the waters of Merom to fight against Israel.

6 But the Lord said to Joshua, "Do not be afraid because of them, for tomorrow about this time I will deliver all of them slain before Israel. You shall hamstring their horses and burn their chariots with fire."

7 So Joshua and all the people of war with him came against them suddenly by the waters of Merom, and they attacked them.

8 And the Lord delivered them into the hand of Israel, who defeated them and chased them to Greater Sidon, to the Brook Misrephoth,[12] and to the Valley of Mizpah eastward; they attacked them until they left none of them remaining.

9 So Joshua did to them as the Lord had told him: he hamstrung their horses and burned their chariots with fire.

10 Joshua turned back at that time and took Hazor, and struck its king with the sword; for Hazor was formerly the head of all those kingdoms.

11 And they struck all the people who *were* in it with the edge of the sword, utterly destroying *them*. There was none left breathing. Then he burned Hazor with fire.

12 So all the cities of those kings, and all their kings, Joshua took and struck with the edge of the sword. He utterly destroyed them, as Moses the servant of the Lord had commanded.

13 But *as for* the cities that stood on their mounds,[13] Israel burned none of them, except Hazor only, *which* Joshua burned.

14 And all the spoil of these cities and the livestock, the children of Israel took as booty for themselves; but they struck every man with the edge of the sword until they had destroyed them, and they left none breathing.

15 As the Lord had commanded Moses his servant, so Moses commanded Joshua, and so Joshua did. He left nothing undone of all that the Lord had commanded Moses.

Summary of Joshua's Conquests

16 So Joshua took all this land: the mountain country, all the South, all the land of Goshen, the lowland, and the Jordan plain[14]—the mountains of Israel and its lowlands,

17 from Mount Halak and the ascent to Seir, even as far as Baal Gad in the Valley of Lebanon below Mount Hermon. He captured all their kings, and struck them down and killed them.

18 Joshua made war a long time with all those kings.

19 There was not a city that made peace with the children of Israel, except the Hivites, the inhabitants of Gibeon. All *the others* they took in battle.

20 For it was of the Lord to harden their hearts, that they should come against Israel in battle, that He might utterly destroy them, *and* that they might receive no mercy, but that He might destroy them, as the Lord had commanded Moses.

21 And at that time Joshua came and cut off the Anakim from the mountains: from Hebron, from Debir, from Anab, from all the mountains of Judah, and from all the mountains of Israel; Joshua utterly destroyed them with their cities.

---

12 Hebrew *Misrephoth Maim*   13 Hebrew *tel*, a heap of successive city ruins   14 Hebrew *arabah*

22 None of the Anakim were left in the land of the children of Israel; they remained only in Gaza, in Gath, and in Ashdod.
23 So Joshua took the whole land, according to all that the LORD had said to Moses; and Joshua gave it as an inheritance to Israel according to their divisions by their tribes. Then the land rested from war.

The Kings Conquered by Moses

12 These *are* the kings of the land whom the children of Israel defeated, and whose land they possessed on the other side of the Jordan toward the rising of the sun, from the River Arnon to Mount Hermon, and all the eastern Jordan plain:
2 Sihon king of the Amorites, who dwelt in Heshbon *and* ruled half of Gilead, from Aroer, which is on the bank of the River Arnon, from the middle of that river, even as far as the River Jabbok, *which is* the border of the Ammonites,
3 and the eastern Jordan plain from the Sea of Chinneroth as far as the Sea of the Arabah (the Salt Sea), the road to Beth Jeshimoth, and southward below the slopes of Pisgah;
4 Og king of Bashan and his territory, *who was* of the remnant of the giants, who dwelt at Ashtaroth and at Edrei,
5 and reigned over Mount Hermon, over Salcah, over all Bashan, as far as the border of the Geshurites and the Maachathites, and over half of Gilead *as far as* the border of Sihon king of Heshbon.
6 These Moses the servant of the LORD and the children of Israel had conquered; and Moses the servant of the LORD had given it *as* a possession to the Reubenites, the Gadites, and half the tribe of Manasseh.

The Kings Conquered by Joshua

7 And these *are* the kings of the country which Joshua and the children of Israel conquered on this side of the Jordan, on the west, from Baal Gad in the Valley of Lebanon as far as Mount Halak and the ascent to Seir, which Joshua gave to the tribes of Israel *as* a possession according to their divisions,
8 in the mountain country, in the lowlands, in the *Jordan* plain, in the slopes, in the wilderness, and in the South—the

Hittites, the Amorites, the Canaanites, the Perizzites, the Hivites, and the Jebusites:
9 the king of Jericho, one; the king of Ai, which *is* beside Bethel, one;
10 the king of Jerusalem, one; the king of Hebron, one;
11 the king of Jarmuth, one; the king of Lachish, one;
12 the king of Eglon, one; the king of Gezer, one;
13 the king of Debir, one; the king of Geder, one;
14 the king of Hormah, one; the king of Arad, one;
15 the king of Libnah, one; the king of Adullam, one;
16 the king of Makkedah, one; the king of Bethel, one;
17 the king of Tappuah, one; the king of Hepher, one;
18 the king of Aphek, one; the king of Lasharon, one;
19 the king of Madon, one; the king of Hazor, one;
20 the king of Shimron Meron, one; the king of Achshaph, one;
21 the king of Taanach, one; the king of Megiddo, one;
22 the king of Kedesh, one; the king of Jokneam in Carmel, one;
23 the king of Dor in the heights of Dor, one; the king of the people of Gilgal, one;
24 the king of Tirzah, one—all the kings, thirty-one.

Remaining Land to Be Conquered

13 Now Joshua was old, advanced in years. And the LORD said to him: "You are old, advanced in years, and there remains very much land yet to be possessed.
2 "This is the land that yet remains: all the territory of the Philistines and all *that of* the Geshurites,
3 "from Sihor, which *is* east of Egypt, as far as the border of Ekron northward (*which* is counted as Canaanite); the five lords of the Philistines—the Gazites, the Ashdodites, the Ashkelonites, the Gittites, and the Ekronites; also the Avites;
4 "from the south, all the land of the Canaanites, and Mearah that belongs to the Sidonians as far as Aphek, to the border of the Amorites;
5 "the land of the Gebalites,[15] and all Lebanon, toward the sunrise, from Baal

15 Or *Giblites*

Gad below Mount Hermon as far as the entrance to Hamath;
6 "all the inhabitants of the mountains from Lebanon as far as the Brook Misrephoth,[16] *and* all the Sidonians—them I will drive out from before the children of Israel; only divide it by lot to Israel as an inheritance, as I have commanded you.
7 "Now therefore, divide this land as an inheritance to the nine tribes and half the tribe of Manasseh."

The Land Divided East of the Jordan

8 With the other half tribe the Reubenites and the Gadites received their inheritance, which Moses had given them, beyond the Jordan eastward, as Moses the servant of the LORD had given them:
9 from Aroer which *is* on the bank of the River Arnon, and the town that *is* in the midst of the ravine, and all the plain of Medeba as far as Dibon;
10 all the cities of Sihon king of the Amorites, who reigned in Heshbon, as far as the border of the children of Ammon;
11 Gilead, and the border of the Geshurites and Maachathites, all Mount Hermon, and all Bashan as far as Salcah;
12 all the kingdom of Og in Bashan, who reigned in Ashtaroth and Edrei, who remained of the remnant of the giants; for Moses had defeated and cast out these.
13 Nevertheless the children of Israel did not drive out the Geshurites or the Maachathites, but the Geshurites and the Maachathites dwell among the Israelites until this day.
14 Only to the tribe of Levi he had given no inheritance; the sacrifices of the LORD God of Israel made by fire *are* their inheritance, as He said to them.

The Land of Reuben

15 And Moses had given to the tribe of the children of Reuben *an inheritance* according to their families.
16 Their territory was from Aroer, which *is* on the bank of the River Arnon, and the city that *is* in the midst of the ravine, and all the plain by Medeba;
17 Heshbon and all its cities that *are* in the plain: Dibon, Bamoth Baal, Beth Baal Meon,
18 Jahaza, Kedemoth, Mephaath,
19 Kirjathaim, Sibmah, Zereth Shahar on the mountain of the valley,
20 Beth Peor, the slopes of Pisgah, and Beth Jeshimoth—

21 all the cities of the plain and all the kingdom of Sihon king of the Amorites, who reigned in Heshbon, whom Moses had struck with the princes of Midian: Evi, Rekem, Zur, Hur, and Reba, who *were* princes of Sihon dwelling in the country.
22 The children of Israel also killed with the sword Balaam the son of Beor, the soothsayer, among those who were killed by them.
23 And the border of the children of Reuben was the bank of the Jordan. This *was* the inheritance of the children of Reuben according to their families, the cities and their villages.

The Land of Gad

24 Moses also had given *an inheritance* to the tribe of Gad, to the children of Gad according to their families.
25 Their territory was Jazer, and all the cities of Gilead, and half the land of the Ammonites as far as Aroer, which *is* before Rabbah,
26 and from Heshbon to Ramath Mizpah and Betonim, and from Mahanaim to the border of Debir,
27 and in the valley Beth Haram, Beth Nimrah, Succoth, and Zaphon, the rest of the kingdom of Sihon king of Heshbon, with the Jordan as *its* border, as far as the edge of the Sea of Chinnereth, on the other side of the Jordan eastward.
28 This *is* the inheritance of the children of Gad according to their families, the cities and their villages.

Half the Tribe of Manasseh (East)

29 Moses also gave *an inheritance* to half the tribe of Manasseh; it was for half the tribe of the children of Manasseh according to their families:
30 Their territory was from Mahanaim, all Bashan, all the kingdom of Og king of Bashan, and all the towns of Jair which are in Bashan, sixty cities;
31 half of Gilead, and Ashtaroth and Edrei, cities of the kingdom of Og in Bashan, *were* for the children of Machir the son of Manasseh, for half of the children of Machir according to their families.
32 These *are the areas* which Moses had distributed as an inheritance in the plains of Moab on the other side of the Jordan, by Jericho eastward.

16 Hebrew *Misrephoth Maim*

33 But to the tribe of Levi Moses had given no inheritance; the LORD God of Israel *was* their inheritance, as He had said to them.

The Land Divided West of the Jordan

14 These *are the areas* which the children of Israel inherited in the land of Canaan, which Eleazar the priest, Joshua the son of Nun, and the heads of the fathers of the tribes of the children of Israel distributed as an inheritance to them.

2 Their inheritance *was* by lot, as the LORD had commanded by the hand of Moses, for the nine tribes and the half-tribe.

3 For Moses had given the inheritance of the two tribes and the half-tribe on the other side of the Jordan; but to the Levites he had given no inheritance among them.

4 For the children of Joseph were two tribes: Manasseh and Ephraim. And they gave no part to the Levites in the land, except cities to dwell *in*, with their common-lands for their livestock and their property.

5 As the LORD had commanded Moses, so the children of Israel did; and they divided the land.

Caleb Inherits Hebron

6 Then the children of Judah came to Joshua in Gilgal. And Caleb the son of Jephunneh the Kenizzite said to him: "You know the word which the LORD said to Moses the man of God concerning you and me in Kadesh Barnea.

7 "I *was* forty years old when Moses the servant of the LORD sent me from Kadesh Barnea to spy out the land, and I brought back word to him as *it was* in my heart.

8 "Nevertheless my brethren who went up with me made the heart of the people melt, but I wholly followed the LORD my God.

9 "So Moses swore on that day, saying, 'Surely the land where your foot has trodden shall be your inheritance and your children's forever, because you have wholly followed the LORD my God.'

10 "And now, behold, the LORD has kept me alive, as He said, these forty-five years, ever since the LORD spoke this word to Moses while Israel wandered in the wilderness; and now, here I am this day, eighty-five years old.

11 "As yet I *am as* strong this day as *I was* on the day that Moses sent me; just as my strength *was* then, so now *is* my strength for war, both for going out and for coming in.

12 "Now therefore, give me this mountain of which the LORD spoke in that day; for you heard in that day how the Anakim *were* there, and *that* the cities *were* great *and* fortified. It may be that the LORD *will be* with me, and I shall be able to drive them out as the LORD said."

13 And Joshua blessed him, and gave Hebron to Caleb the son of Jephunneh as an inheritance.

14 Hebron therefore became the inheritance of Caleb the son of Jephunneh the Kenizzite to this day, because he wholly followed the LORD God of Israel.

15 And the name of Hebron formerly was Kirjath Arba, *for Arba was* the greatest man among the Anakim. Then the land had rest from war.

The Land of Judah

15 *This* then was the lot of the tribe of the children of Judah according to their families: The border of Edom at the Wilderness of Zin southward *was* the extreme southern boundary.

2 And their southern border began at the shore of the Salt Sea, from the bay that faces southward.

3 Then it went out to the southern side of the Ascent of Akrabbim, passed along to Zin, ascended on the south side of Kadesh Barnea, passed along to Hezron, went up to Adar, and went around to Karkaa.

4 *From there* it passed toward Azmon and went out to the Brook of Egypt; and the border ended at the sea. This shall be your southern border.

5 The east border *was* the Salt Sea as far as the mouth of the Jordan. And the border on the northern quarter *began* at the bay of the sea at the mouth of the Jordan.

6 The border went up to Beth Hoglah and passed north of Beth Arabah; and the border went up to the stone of Bohan the son of Reuben.

7 Then the border went up toward Debir from the Valley of Achor, and it turned northward toward Gilgal, which *is* before the Ascent of Adummim, which *is*

on the south side of the valley. The border continued toward the waters of En Shemesh and ended at En Rogel.
8 And the border went up by the Valley of the Son of Hinnom to the southern slope of the Jebusite *city* (which *is* Jerusalem). The border went up to the top of the mountain that *lies* before the Valley of Hinnom westward, which *is* at the end of the Valley of Rephaim[17] northward.
9 Then the border went around from the top of the hill to the fountain of the water of Nephtoah, and extended to the cities of Mount Ephron. And the border went around to Baalah (which *is* Kirjath Jearim).
10 Then the border turned westward from Baalah to Mount Seir, passed along to the side of Mount Jearim on the north (which *is* Chesalon), went down to Beth Shemesh, and passed on to Timnah.
11 And the border went out to the side of Ekron northward. Then the border went around to Shicron, passed along to Mount Baalah, and extended to Jabneel; and the border ended at the sea.
12 The west border *was* the coastline of the Great Sea. This *is* the boundary of the children of Judah all around according to their families.

Caleb Occupies Hebron and Debir

13 Now to Caleb the son of Jephunneh he gave a portion among the children of Judah, according to the commandment of the LORD to Joshua, *namely*, Kirjath Arba, which *is* Hebron (*Arba was* the father of Anak).
14 Caleb drove out the three sons of Anak from there: Sheshai, Ahiman, and Talmai, the children of Anak.
15 Then he went up from there to the inhabitants of Debir (formerly the name of Debir *was* Kirjath Sepher).
16 And Caleb said, "He who attacks Kirjath Sepher and takes it, to him I will give Achsah my daughter as wife."
17 So Othniel the son of Kenaz, the brother of Caleb, took it; and he gave him Achsah his daughter as wife.
18 Now it came about, when she came *to him*, that she persuaded him to ask her father for a field. So she dismounted from *her* donkey, and Caleb said to her, "What do you wish?"
19 She answered, "Give me a blessing; since you have given me land in the South, give me also springs of water." So he gave her the upper springs and the lower springs.

The Cities of Judah

20 This *was* the inheritance of the tribe of the children of Judah according to their families:
21 The cities at the limits of the tribe of the children of Judah, toward the border of Edom in the South, were Kabzeel, Eder, Jagur,
22 Kinah, Dimonah, Adadah,
23 Kedesh, Hazor, Ithnan,
24 Ziph, Telem, Bealoth,
25 Hazor, Hadattah, Kerioth, Hezron (which *is* Hazor),
26 Amam, Shema, Moladah,
27 Hazar Gaddah, Heshmon, Beth Pelet,
28 Hazar Shual, Beersheba, Bizjothjah,
29 Baalah, Ijim, Ezem,
30 Eltolad, Chesil, Hormah,
31 Ziklag, Madmannah, Sansannah,
32 Lebaoth, Shilhim, Ain, and Rimmon: all the cities *are* twenty-nine, with their villages.
33 In the lowland: Eshtaol, Zorah, Ashnah,
34 Zanoah, En Gannim, Tappuah, Enam,
35 Jarmuth, Adullam, Socoh, Azekah,
36 Sharaim, Adithaim, Gederah, and Gederothaim: fourteen cities with their villages;
37 Zenan, Hadashah, Migdal Gad,
38 Dilean, Mizpah, Joktheel,
39 Lachish, Bozkath, Eglon,
40 Cabbon, Lahmas,[18] Kithlish,
41 Gederoth, Beth Dagon, Naamah, and Makkedah: sixteen cities with their villages;
42 Libnah, Ether, Ashan,
43 Jiphtah, Ashnah, Nezib,
44 Keilah, Achzib, and Mareshah: nine cities with their villages;
45 Ekron, with its towns and villages;
46 from Ekron to the sea, all that *lay* near Ashdod, with their villages;
47 Ashdod with its towns and villages, Gaza with its towns and villages—as far as the Brook of Egypt and the Great Sea with *its* coastline.
48 And in the mountain country: Shamir, Jattir, Sochoh,
49 Dannah, Kirjath Sannah (which *is* Debir),

17 Literally *Giants*   18 Or *Lahmam*

50 Anab, Eshtemoh, Anim,
51 Goshen, Holon, and Giloh: eleven cities with their villages;
52 Arab, Dumah, Eshean,
53 Janum, Beth Tappuah, Aphekah,
54 Humtah, Kirjath Arba (which *is* Hebron), and Zior: nine cities with their villages;
55 Maon, Carmel, Ziph, Juttah,
56 Jezreel, Jokdeam, Zanoah,
57 Kain, Gibeah, and Timnah: ten cities with their villages;
58 Halhul, Beth Zur, Gedor,
59 Maarath, Beth Anoth, and Eltekon: six cities with their villages;
60 Kirjath Baal (which *is* Kirjath Jearim) and Rabbah: two cities with their villages.
61 In the wilderness: Beth Arabah, Middin, Secacah,
62 Nibshan, the City of Salt, and En Gedi: six cities with their villages.
63 As for the Jebusites, the inhabitants of Jerusalem, the children of Judah could not drive them out; but the Jebusites dwell with the children of Judah at Jerusalem to this day.

Ephraim and West Manasseh

16 The lot fell to the children of Joseph from the Jordan, by Jericho, to the waters of Jericho on the east, to the wilderness that goes up from Jericho through the mountains to Bethel,
2 then went out from Bethel to Luz,[19] passed along to the border of the Archites at Ataroth,
3 and went down westward to the boundary of the Japhletites, as far as the boundary of Lower Beth Horon to Gezer; and it ended at the sea.
4 So the children of Joseph, Manasseh and Ephraim, took their inheritance.

The Land of Ephraim

5 The border of the children of Ephraim, according to their families, was *thus*: The border of their inheritance on the east side was Ataroth Addar as far as Upper Beth Horon.
6 And the border went out toward the sea on the north side of Michmethath; then the border went around eastward to Taanath Shiloh, and passed by it on the east of Janohah.
7 Then it went down from Janohah to Ataroth and Naarah,[20] reached to Jericho, and came out at the Jordan.
8 The border went out from Tappuah westward to the Brook Kanah, and it ended at the sea. This *was* the inheritance of the tribe of the children of Ephraim according to their families.
9 The separate cities for the children of Ephraim *were* among the inheritance of the children of Manasseh, all the cities with their villages.
10 And they did not drive out the Canaanites who dwelt in Gezer; but the Canaanites dwell among the Ephraimites to this day and have become forced laborers.

The Other Half-Tribe of Manasseh (West)

17 There was also a lot for the tribe of Manasseh, for he *was* the firstborn of Joseph: *namely* for Machir the firstborn of Manasseh, the father of Gilead, because he was a man of war; therefore he was given Gilead and Bashan.
2 And there was *a lot* for the rest of the children of Manasseh according to their families: for the children of Abiezer,[21] the children of Helek, the children of Asriel, the children of Shechem, the children of Hepher, and the children of Shemida; these *were* the male children of Manasseh the son of Joseph according to their families.
3 But Zelophehad the son of Hepher, the son of Gilead, the son of Machir, the son of Manasseh, had no sons, but only daughters. And these *are* the names of his daughters: Mahlah, Noah, Hoglah, Milcah, and Tirzah.
4 And they came near before Eleazar the priest, before Joshua the son of Nun, and before the rulers, saying, "The LORD commanded Moses to give us an inheritance among our brothers." Therefore, according to the commandment of the LORD, he gave them an inheritance among their father's brothers.
5 Ten portions fell to Manasseh, besides the land of Gilead and Bashan, which *were* on the other side of the Jordan,
6 because the daughters of Manasseh received an inheritance among his sons; and the rest of Manasseh's sons had the land of Gilead.
7 And the territory of Manasseh was from Asher to Michmethath, that *lies* east

19 Septuagint reads *Bethel* (that is, Luz).   20 Or *Naaran* (compare 1 Chronicles 7:28)
21 Called *Jeezer* in Numbers 26:30

of Shechem; and the border went along south to the inhabitants of En Tappuah.

8 Manasseh had the land of Tappuah, but Tappuah on the border of Manasseh *belonged* to the children of Ephraim.

9 And the border descended to the Brook Kanah, southward to the brook. These cities of Ephraim *are* among the cities of Manasseh. The border of Manasseh *was* on the north side of the brook; and it ended at the sea.

10 Southward *it was* Ephraim's, northward *it was* Manasseh's, and the sea was its border. Manasseh's territory was adjoining Asher on the north and Issachar on the east.

11 And in Issachar and in Asher, Manasseh had Beth Shean and its towns, Ibleam and its towns, the inhabitants of Dor and its towns, the inhabitants of En Dor and its towns, the inhabitants of Taanach and its towns, and the inhabitants of Megiddo and its towns—three hilly regions.

12 Yet the children of Manasseh could not drive out *the inhabitants of* those cities, but the Canaanites were determined to dwell in that land.

13 And it happened, when the children of Israel grew strong, that they put the Canaanites to forced labor, but did not utterly drive them out.

More Land for Ephraim and Manasseh

14 Then the children of Joseph spoke to Joshua, saying, "Why have you given us *but* one lot and one portion to inherit, since we *are* a great people, inasmuch as the LORD has blessed us until now?"

15 So Joshua answered them, "If you *are* a great people, *then* go up to the forest *country* and clear a place for yourself there in the land of the Perizzites and the giants, since the mountains of Ephraim are too confined for you."

16 But the children of Joseph said, "The mountain country is not enough for us; and all the Canaanites who dwell in the land of the valley have chariots of iron, *both those* who *are* of Beth Shean and its towns and *those* who *are* of the Valley of Jezreel."

17 And Joshua spoke to the house of Joseph—to Ephraim and Manasseh—saying, "You *are* a great people and have great power; you shall not have one lot *only,*

18 "but the mountain country shall be yours. Although it *is* wooded, you shall cut it down, and its farthest extent shall be yours; for you shall drive out the Canaanites, though they have iron chariots *and* are strong."

The Remainder of the Land Divided

18 Then the whole congregation of the children of Israel assembled together at Shiloh, and set up the tabernacle of meeting there. And the land was subdued before them.

2 But there remained among the children of Israel seven tribes which had not yet received their inheritance.

3 Then Joshua said to the children of Israel: "How long will you neglect to go and possess the land which the LORD God of your fathers has given you?

4 "Pick out from among you three men for *each* tribe, and I will send them; they shall rise and go through the land, survey it according to their inheritance, and come *back* to me.

5 "And they shall divide it into seven parts. Judah shall remain in their territory on the south, and the house of Joseph shall remain in their territory on the north.

6 "You shall therefore survey the land in seven parts and bring *the survey* here to me, that I may cast lots for you here before the LORD our God.

7 "But the Levites have no part among you, for the priesthood of the LORD *is* their inheritance. And Gad, Reuben, and half the tribe of Manasseh have received their inheritance beyond the Jordan on the east, which Moses the servant of the LORD gave them."

8 Then the men arose to go away; and Joshua charged those who went to survey the land, saying, "Go, walk through the land, survey it, and come back to me, that I may cast lots for you here before the LORD in Shiloh."

9 So the men went, passed through the land, and wrote the survey in a book in seven parts by cities; and they came to Joshua at the camp in Shiloh.

10 Then Joshua cast lots for them in Shiloh before the LORD, and there Joshua divided the land to the children of Israel according to their divisions.

The Land of Benjamin

11 Now the lot of the tribe of the children of Benjamin came up according to their families, and the territory of their lot came out between the children of Judah and the children of Joseph.
12 Their border on the north side began at the Jordan, and the border went up to the side of Jericho on the north, and went up through the mountains westward; it ended at the Wilderness of Beth Aven.
13 The border went over from there toward Luz, to the side of Luz (which *is* Bethel) southward; and the border descended to Ataroth Adar, near the hill that *lies* on the south side of Lower Beth Horon.
14 Then the border extended *from there* around the west side to the south, from the hill that *lies* before Beth Horon southward; and it ended at Kirjath Baal (which *is* Kirjath Jearim), a city of the children of Judah. This *was* the west side.
15 The south side *began* at the end of Kirjath Jearim, and the border extended on the west and went out to the spring of the waters of Nephtoah.
16 Then the border came down to the end of the mountain that *lies* before the Valley of the Son of Hinnom, which *is* in the Valley of the Rephaim[22] on the north, descended to the Valley of Hinnom, to the side of the Jebusite *city* on the south, and descended to En Rogel.
17 And it went around from the north, went out to En Shemesh, and extended toward Geliloth, which is before the Ascent of Adummim, and descended to the stone of Bohan the son of Reuben.
18 Then it passed along toward the north side of Arabah,[23] and went down to Arabah.
19 And the border passed along to the north side of Beth Hoglah; then the border ended at the north bay at the Salt Sea, at the south end of the Jordan. This *was* the southern boundary.
20 The Jordan was its border on the east side. This *was* the inheritance of the children of Benjamin, according to its boundaries all around, according to their families.
21 Now the cities of the tribe of the children of Benjamin, according to their families, were Jericho, Beth Hoglah, Emek Keziz,

22 Beth Arabah, Zemaraim, Bethel,
23 Avim, Parah, Ophrah,
24 Chephar Haammoni, Ophni, and Gaba: twelve cities with their villages;
25 Gibeon, Ramah, Beeroth,
26 Mizpah, Chephirah, Mozah,
27 Rekem, Irpeel, Taralah,
28 Zelah, Eleph, Jebus (which *is* Jerusalem), Gibeath, *and* Kirjath: fourteen cities with their villages. This was the inheritance of the children of Benjamin according to their families.

Simeon's Inheritance with Judah

19 The second lot came out for Simeon, for the tribe of the children of Simeon according to their families. And their inheritance was within the inheritance of the children of Judah.
2 They had in their inheritance Beersheba (Sheba), Moladah,
3 Hazar Shual, Balah, Ezem,
4 Eltolad, Bethul, Hormah,
5 Ziklag, Beth Marcaboth, Hazar Susah,
6 Beth Lebaoth, and Sharuhen: thirteen cities and their villages;
7 Ain, Rimmon, Ether, and Ashan: four cities and their villages;
8 and all the villages that *were* all around these cities as far as Baalath Beer, Ramah of the South. This *was* the inheritance of the tribe of the children of Simeon according to their families.
9 The inheritance of the children of Simeon *was included* in the portion of the children of Judah, for the portion of the children of Judah was too much for them. Therefore the children of Simeon had *their* inheritance within the inheritance of that people.

The Land of Zebulun

10 The third lot came out for the children of Zebulun according to their families, and the border of their inheritance was as far as Sarid.
11 Their border went toward the west and to Maralah, went to Dabbasheth, and extended along the brook that is east of Jokneam.
12 Then from Sarid it went eastward toward the sunrise along the border of Chisloth Tabor, and went out toward Daberath, bypassing Japhia.
13 And from there it passed along on the east of Gath Hepher, toward Eth Kazin,

22 Literally *Giants*   23 Or *Beth Arabah* (compare 15:6 and 18:22)

and extended to Rimmon, which borders on Neah.

14 Then the border went around it on the north side of Hannathon, and it ended in the Valley of Jiphthah El.

15 Included were Kattath, Nahallal, Shimron, Idalah, and Bethlehem: twelve cities with their villages.

16 This *was* the inheritance of the children of Zebulun according to their families, these cities with their villages.

The Land of Issachar

17 The fourth lot came out to Issachar, for the children of Issachar according to their families.

18 And their territory went to Jezreel, and *included* Chesulloth, Shunem,

19 Haphraim, Shion, Anaharath,

20 Rabbith, Kishion, Abez,

21 Remeth, En Gannim, En Haddah, and Beth Pazzez.

22 And the border reached to Tabor, Shahazimah, and Beth Shemesh; their border ended at the Jordan: sixteen cities with their villages.

23 This *was* the inheritance of the tribe of the children of Issachar according to their families, the cities and their villages.

The Land of Asher

24 The fifth lot came out for the tribe of the children of Asher according to their families.

25 And their territory included Helkath, Hali, Beten, Achshaph,

26 Alammelech, Amad, and Mishal; it reached to Mount Carmel westward, along *the Brook* Shihor Libnath.

27 It turned toward the sunrise to Beth Dagon; and it reached to Zebulun and to the Valley of Jiphthah El, then northward beyond Beth Emek and Neiel, bypassing Cabul *which was* on the left,

28 including Ebron, Rehob, Hammon, and Kanah, as far as Greater Sidon.

29 And the border turned to Ramah and to the fortified city of Tyre; then the border turned to Hosah, and ended at the sea by the region of Achzib.

30 Also Ummah, Aphek, and Rehob *were included*: twenty-two cities with their villages.

31 This *was* the inheritance of the tribe of the children of Asher according to their families, these cities with their villages.

The Land of Naphtali

32 The sixth lot came out to the children of Naphtali, for the children of Naphtali according to their families.

33 And their border began at Heleph, enclosing the territory from the terebinth tree in Zaanannim, Adami Nekeb, and Jabneel, as far as Lakkum; it ended at the Jordan.

34 From Heleph the border extended westward to Aznoth Tabor, and went out from there toward Hukkok; it adjoined Zebulun on the south side and Asher on the west side, and ended at Judah by the Jordan toward the sunrise.

35 And the fortified cities *are* Ziddim, Zer, Hammath, Rakkath, Chinnereth,

36 Adamah, Ramah, Hazor,

37 Kedesh, Edrei, En Hazor,

38 Iron, Migdal El, Horem, Beth Anath, and Beth Shemesh: nineteen cities with their villages.

39 This *was* the inheritance of the tribe of the children of Naphtali according to their families, the cities and their villages.

The Land of Dan

40 The seventh lot came out for the tribe of the children of Dan according to their families.

41 And the territory of their inheritance was Zorah, Eshtaol, Ir Shemesh,

42 Shaalabbin, Aijalon, Jethlah,

43 Elon, Timnah, Ekron,

44 Eltekeh, Gibbethon, Baalath,

45 Jehud, Bene Berak, Gath Rimmon,

46 Me Jarkon, and Rakkon, with the region near Joppa.

47 And the border of the children of Dan went beyond these, because the children of Dan went up to fight against Leshem and took it; and they struck it with the edge of the sword, took possession of it, and dwelt in it. They called Leshem, Dan, after the name of Dan their father.

48 This *is* the inheritance of the tribe of the children of Dan according to their families, these cities with their villages.

Joshua's Inheritance

49 When they had made an end of dividing the land as an inheritance according to their borders, the children of Israel gave an inheritance among them to Joshua the son of Nun.

50 According to the word of the LORD they gave him the city which he asked for,

Timnath Serah in the mountains of Ephraim; and he built the city and dwelt in it.

51 These *were* the inheritances which Eleazar the priest, Joshua the son of Nun, and the heads of the fathers of the tribes of the children of Israel divided as an inheritance by lot in Shiloh before the LORD, at the door of the tabernacle of meeting. So they made an end of dividing the country.

The Cities of Refuge

20 The LORD also spoke to Joshua, saying,

2 "Speak to the children of Israel, saying: 'Appoint for yourselves cities of refuge, of which I spoke to you through Moses,

3 'that the slayer who kills *any* person accidentally *or* unintentionally may flee there; and they shall be your refuge from the avenger of blood.

4 'And when he flees to one of those cities, and stands at the entrance of the gate of the city, and declares his case in the hearing of the elders of that city, they shall take him into the city as one of them, and give him a place, that he may dwell among them.

5 'Then if the avenger of blood pursues him, they shall not deliver the slayer into his hand, because he struck his neighbor unintentionally, but did not hate him beforehand.

6 'And he shall dwell in that city until he stands before the congregation for judgment, *and* until the death of the one who is high priest in those days. Then the slayer may return and come to his own city and his own house, to the city from which he fled.' "

7 So they appointed Kedesh in Galilee, in the mountains of Naphtali, Shechem in the mountains of Ephraim, and Kirjath Arba (which *is* Hebron) in the mountains of Judah.

8 And on the other side of the Jordan, by Jericho eastward, they assigned Bezer in the wilderness on the plain, from the tribe of Reuben, Ramoth in Gilead, from the tribe of Gad, and Golan in Bashan, from the tribe of Manasseh.

9 These were the cities appointed for all the children of Israel and for the stranger who sojourned among them, that whoever killed *any* person accidentally might flee there, and not die by the hand of the avenger of blood until he stood before the congregation.

Cities of the Levites

21 Now the heads of the fathers of the Levites came near to Eleazar the priest, to Joshua the son of Nun, and to the heads of the fathers of the tribes of the children of Israel.

2 And they spoke to them at Shiloh in the land of Canaan, saying, "The LORD commanded through Moses to give us cities to dwell in, with their common-lands for our livestock."

3 So the children of Israel gave to the Levites from their inheritance, at the commandment of the LORD, these cities and their common-lands:

4 Now the lot came out for the families of the Kohathites. And the children of Aaron the priest, *who were* of the Levites, had thirteen cities by lot from the tribe of Judah, from the tribe of Simeon, and from the tribe of Benjamin.

5 The rest of the children of Kohath had ten cities by lot from the families of the tribe of Ephraim, from the tribe of Dan, and from the half-tribe of Manasseh.

6 And the children of Gershon had thirteen cities by lot from the families of the tribe of Issachar, from the tribe of Asher, from the tribe of Naphtali, and from the half-tribe of Manasseh in Bashan.

7 The children of Merari according to their families had twelve cities from the tribe of Reuben, from the tribe of Gad, and from the tribe of Zebulun.

8 And the children of Israel gave these cities with their common-lands by lot to the Levites, as the LORD had commanded by the hand of Moses.

9 So they gave from the tribe of the children of Judah and from the tribe of the children of Simeon these cities which are mentioned *here* by name,

10 which were for the children of Aaron, one of the families of the Kohathites, *who were* of the children of Levi; for the lot was theirs first.

11 And they gave them Kirjath Arba (*Arba being* the father of Anak), which *is* Hebron, in the mountains of Judah, with the common-land surrounding it.

12 But the fields of the city and its vil-

lages they gave to Caleb the son of Jephunneh as his possession.
13 Thus to the children of Aaron the priest they gave Hebron with its common-land (a city of refuge for the slayer), Libnah with its common-land,
14 Jattir with its common-land, Eshtemoa with its common-land,
15 Holon with its common-land, Debir with its common-land,
16 Ain with its common-land, Juttah with its common-land, and Beth Shemesh with its common-land: nine cities from those two tribes;
17 and from the tribe of Benjamin, Gibeon with its common-land, Geba with its common-land,
18 Anathoth with its common-land, and Almon with its common-land: four cities.
19 All the cities of the children of Aaron, the priests, *were* thirteen cities with their common-lands.
20 And the families of the children of Kohath, the Levites, the rest of the children of Kohath, even they had the cities of their lot from the tribe of Ephraim.
21 For they gave them Shechem with its common-land in the mountains of Ephraim (a city of refuge for the slayer), Gezer with its common-land,
22 Kibzaim with its common-land, and Beth Horon with its common-land: four cities;
23 and from the tribe of Dan, Eltekeh with its common-land, Gibbethon with its common-land,
24 Aijalon with its common-land, *and* Gath Rimmon with its common-land: four cities;
25 and from the half-tribe of Manasseh, Tanach with its common-land and Gath Rimmon with its common-land: two cities.
26 All the ten cities with their common-lands were for the rest of the families of the children of Kohath.
27 And to the children of Gershon, of the families of the Levites, from the *other* half-tribe of Manasseh, *they gave* Golan in Bashan with its common-land (a city of refuge for the slayer), and Be Eshterah with its common-land: two cities;
28 and from the tribe of Issachar, Kishion with its common-land, Daberath with its common-land,
29 Jarmuth with its common-land, *and*

En Gannim with its common-land: four cities;
30 and from the tribe of Asher, Mishal with its common-land, Abdon with its common-land,
31 Helkath with its common-land, and Rehob with its common-land: four cities;
32 and from the tribe of Naphtali, Kedesh in Galilee with its common-land (a city of refuge for the slayer), Hammoth Dor with its common-land, and Kartan with its common-land: three cities.
33 All the cities of the Gershonites according to their families *were* thirteen cities with their common-lands.
34 And to the families of the children of Merari, the rest of the Levites, from the tribe of Zebulun, Jokneam with its common-land, Kartah with its common-land,
35 Dimnah with its common-land, *and* Nahalal with its common-land: four cities;
36 and from the tribe of Reuben, Bezer with its common-land, Jahaz with its common-land,
37 Kedemoth with its common-land, and Mephaath with its common-land: four cities;
38 and from the tribe of Gad, Ramoth in Gilead with its common-land (a city of refuge for the slayer), Mahanaim with its common-land,
39 Heshbon with its common-land, *and* Jazer with its common-land: four cities in all.
40 So all the cities for the children of Merari according to their families, the rest of the families of the Levites, were *by* their lot twelve cities.
41 All the cities of the Levites within the possession of the children of Israel *were* forty-eight cities with their common-lands.
42 Every one of these cities had its common-land surrounding it; thus *were* all these cities.

The Promise Fulfilled

43 So the LORD gave to Israel all the land of which He had sworn to give to their fathers, and they took possession of it and dwelt in it.
44 The LORD gave them rest all around, according to all that He had sworn to their fathers. And not a man of all their

enemies stood against them; the LORD delivered all their enemies into their hand.

45 Not a word failed of any good thing which the LORD had spoken to the house of Israel. All came to pass.

Eastern Tribes Return to Their Lands

22 Then Joshua called the Reubenites, the Gadites, and half the tribe of Manasseh,

2 and said to them: "You have kept all that Moses the servant of the LORD commanded you, and have obeyed my voice in all that I commanded you.

3 "You have not left your brethren these many days, up to this day, but have kept the charge of the commandment of the LORD your God.

4 "And now the LORD your God has given rest to your brethren, as He promised them; now therefore, return and go to your tents *and* to the land of your possession, which Moses the servant of the LORD gave you on the other side of the Jordan.

5 "But take diligent heed to do the commandment and the law which Moses the servant of the LORD commanded you, to love the LORD your God, to walk in all His ways, to keep His commandments, to hold fast to Him, and to serve Him with all your heart and with all your soul."

6 So Joshua blessed them and sent them away, and they went to their tents.

7 Now to half the tribe of Manasseh Moses had given a possession in Bashan, but to the *other* half of it Joshua gave *a possession* among their brethren on this side of the Jordan, westward. And indeed, when Joshua sent them away to their tents, he blessed them,

8 and spoke to them, saying, "Return with much riches to your tents, with very much livestock, with silver, with gold, with bronze, with iron, and with very much clothing. Divide the spoil of your enemies with your brethren."

9 So the children of Reuben, the children of Gad, and half the tribe of Manasseh returned, and departed from the children of Israel at Shiloh, which *is* in the land of Canaan, to go to the country of Gilead, to the land of their possession, which they possessed according to the word of the LORD by the hand of Moses.

An Altar by the Jordan

10 And when they came to the region of the Jordan which *is* in the land of Canaan, the children of Reuben, the children of Gad, and half the tribe of Manasseh built an altar there by the Jordan—a great, impressive altar.

11 Now the children of Israel heard *someone* say, "Behold, the children of Reuben, the children of Gad, and half the tribe of Manasseh have built an altar on the frontier of the land of Canaan, in the region of the Jordan, on the side *occupied by* the children of Israel."

12 And when the children of Israel heard *of it*, the whole congregation of the children of Israel gathered together at Shiloh to go to war against them.

13 Then the children of Israel sent Phinehas the son of Eleazar the priest to the children of Reuben, to the children of Gad, and to half the tribe of Manasseh, into the land of Gilead,

14 and with him ten rulers, one ruler each from the chief house of every tribe of Israel; and each one *was* the head of the house of his father among the divisions[24] of Israel.

15 Then they came to the children of Reuben, to the children of Gad, and to half the tribe of Manasseh, to the land of Gilead, and they spoke with them, saying,

16 "Thus says the whole congregation of the LORD: 'What treachery *is* this that you have committed against the God of Israel, to turn away this day from following the LORD, in that you have built for yourselves an altar, that you might rebel this day against the LORD?

17 '*Is* the iniquity of Peor not enough for us, from which we are not cleansed until this day, although there was a plague in the congregation of the LORD,

18 'but that you must turn away this day from following the LORD? And it shall be, if you rebel today against the LORD, that tomorrow He will be angry with the whole congregation of Israel.

19 'Nevertheless, if the land of your possession *is* unclean, *then* cross over to the land of the possession of the LORD, where the LORD'S tabernacle stands, and take possession among us; but do not rebel against the LORD, nor rebel against us, by building yourselves an altar besides the altar of the LORD our God.

24 Literally *thousands*

20 'Did not Achan the son of Zerah commit a trespass in the accursed thing, and wrath fell on all the congregation of Israel? And that man did not perish alone in his iniquity.' "

21 Then the children of Reuben, the children of Gad, and half the tribe of Manasseh answered and said to the heads of the divisions[25] of Israel:

22 "The LORD God of gods, the LORD God of gods, He knows, and let Israel itself know—if it is in rebellion, or if in treachery against the LORD, do not save us this day.

23 "If we have built ourselves an altar to turn from following the LORD, or if to offer on it burnt offerings or grain offerings, or if to offer peace offerings on it, let the LORD Himself require an account.

24 "But in fact we have done it for fear, for a reason, saying, 'In time to come your descendants may speak to our descendants, saying, "What have you to do with the LORD God of Israel?

25 "For the LORD has made the Jordan a border between you and us, you children of Reuben and children of Gad. You have no part in the LORD." So your descendants would make our descendants cease fearing the LORD.'

26 "Therefore we said, 'Let us now prepare to build ourselves an altar, not for burnt offering nor for sacrifice,

27 'but that it may be a witness between you and us and our generations after us, that we may perform the service of the LORD before Him with our burnt offerings, with our sacrifices, and with our peace offerings; that your descendants may not say to our descendants in time to come, "You have no part in the LORD." '

28 "Therefore we said that it will be, when they say this to us or to our generations in time to come, that we may say, 'Here is the replica of the altar of the LORD which our fathers made, though not for burnt offerings nor for sacrifices; but it is a witness between us and you.'

29 "Far be it from us that we should rebel against the LORD, and turn from following the LORD this day, to build an altar for burnt offerings, for grain offerings, or for sacrifices, besides the altar of the LORD our God which is before His tabernacle."

30 And when Phinehas the priest and the rulers of the congregation, the heads of the divisions[26] of Israel who were with him, heard the words that the children of Reuben, the children of Gad, and the children of Manasseh spoke, it pleased them.

31 Then Phinehas the son of Eleazar the priest said to the children of Reuben, the children of Gad, and the children of Manasseh, "This day we perceive that the LORD is among us, because you have not committed this treachery against the LORD. Now you have delivered the children of Israel out of the hand of the LORD."

32 And Phinehas the son of Eleazar the priest, and the rulers, returned from the children of Reuben and the children of Gad, from the land of Gilead to the land of Canaan, to the children of Israel, and brought back word to them.

33 So the thing pleased the children of Israel, and the children of Israel blessed God; they spoke no more of going against them in battle, to destroy the land where the children of Reuben and Gad dwelt.

34 And the children of Reuben and the children of Gad called the altar, Witness,[27] "For it is a witness between us that the LORD is God."

Joshua's Farewell Address

23 Now it came to pass, a long time after the LORD had given rest to Israel from all their enemies round about, that Joshua was old, advanced in age.

2 And Joshua called for all Israel, for their elders, for their heads, for their judges, and for their officers, and said to them: "I am old, advanced in age.

3 "You have seen all that the LORD your God has done to all these nations because of you, for the LORD your God is He who has fought for you.

4 "See, I have divided to you by lot these nations that remain, to be an inheritance for your tribes, from the Jordan, with all the nations that I have cut off, as far as the Great Sea westward.

5 "And the LORD your God will expel them from before you and drive them out of your sight. So you shall possess their land, as the LORD your God has promised you.

6 "Therefore be very courageous to keep and to do all that is written in the Book of the Law of Moses, lest you turn

25 Literally thousands 26 Literally thousands 27 Hebrew Ed

aside from it to the right hand or to the left,

7 *"and* lest you go among these nations, these who remain among you. You shall not make mention of the name of their gods, nor cause *anyone* to swear *by them*; you shall not serve them nor bow down to them,

8 "but you shall hold fast to the LORD your God, as you have done to this day.

9 "For the LORD has driven out from before you great and strong nations; but *as for* you, no one has been able to stand against you to this day.

10 "One man of you shall chase a thousand, for the LORD your God *is* He who fights for you, as He has promised you.

11 "Therefore take diligent heed to yourselves, that you love the LORD your God.

12 "Or else, if indeed you do go back, and cling to the remnant of these nations—these that remain among you—and make marriages with them, and go in to them and they to you,

13 "know for certain that the LORD your God will no longer drive out these nations from before you. But they shall be snares and traps to you, and scourges on your sides and thorns in your eyes, until you perish from this good land which the LORD your God has given you.

14 "Behold, this day I *am* going the way of all the earth. And you know in all your hearts and in all your souls that not one thing has failed of all the good things which the LORD your God spoke concerning you. All have come to pass for you, *and* not one word of them has failed.

15 "Therefore it shall come to pass, that as all the good things have come upon you which the LORD your God promised you, so the LORD will bring upon you all harmful things, until He has destroyed you from this good land which the LORD your God has given you.

16 "When you have transgressed the covenant of the LORD your God, which He commanded you, and have gone and served other gods, and bowed down to them, then the anger of the LORD will burn against you, and you shall perish quickly from the good land which He has given you."

The Covenant at Shechem

24 Then Joshua gathered all the tribes of Israel to Shechem and called for the elders of Israel, for their heads, for their judges, and for their officers; and they presented themselves before God.

2 And Joshua said to all the people, "Thus says the LORD God of Israel: 'Your fathers, *including* Terah, the father of Abraham and the father of Nahor, dwelt on the other side of the River[28] in old times; and they served other gods.

3 'Then I took your father Abraham from the other side of the River, led him throughout all the land of Canaan, and multiplied his descendants and gave him Isaac.

4 'To Isaac I gave Jacob and Esau. To Esau I gave the mountains of Seir to possess, but Jacob and his children went down to Egypt.

5 'Also I sent Moses and Aaron, and I plagued Egypt, according to what I did among them. Afterward I brought you out.

6 'Then I brought your fathers out of Egypt, and you came to the sea; and the Egyptians pursued your fathers with chariots and horsemen to the Red Sea.

7 'So they cried out to the LORD; and He put darkness between you and the Egyptians, brought the sea upon them, and covered them. And your eyes saw what I did in Egypt. Then you dwelt in the wilderness a long time.

8 'And I brought you into the land of the Amorites, who dwelt on the other side of the Jordan, and they fought with you. But I gave them into your hand, that you might possess their land, and I destroyed them from before you.

9 'Then Balak the son of Zippor, king of Moab, arose to make war against Israel, and sent and called Balaam the son of Beor to curse you.

10 'But I would not listen to Balaam; therefore he continued to bless you. So I delivered you out of his hand.

11 'Then you went over the Jordan and came to Jericho. And the men of Jericho fought against you—*also* the Amorites, the Perizzites, the Canaanites, the Hittites, the Girgashites, the Hivites, and the Jebusites. But I delivered them into your hand.

12 'I sent the hornet before you which drove them out from before you, *also* the two kings of the Amorites, *but* not with your sword or with your bow.

28 Hebrew *Nahar,* the Euphrates (so also verses 3, 14, and 15)

13 'I have given you a land for which you did not labor, and cities which you did not build, and you dwell in them; you eat of the vineyards and olive groves which you did not plant.'

14 "Now therefore, fear the LORD, serve Him in sincerity and in truth, and put away the gods which your fathers served on the other side of the River and in Egypt. Serve the LORD!

15 "And if it seems evil to you to serve the LORD, choose for yourselves this day whom you will serve, whether the gods which your fathers served that *were* on the other side of the River, or the gods of the Amorites, in whose land you dwell. But as for me and my house, we will serve the LORD."

16 So the people answered and said: "Far be it from us that we should forsake the LORD to serve other gods;

17 "for the LORD our God *is* He who brought us and our fathers up out of the land of Egypt, from the house of bondage, who did those great signs in our sight, and preserved us in all the way that we went and among all the people through whom we passed.

18 "And the LORD drove out from before us all the people, even the Amorites who dwelt in the land. We also will serve the LORD, for He *is* our God."

19 But Joshua said to the people, "You cannot serve the LORD, for He *is* a holy God. He *is* a jealous God; He will not forgive your transgressions nor your sins.

20 "If you forsake the LORD and serve foreign gods, then He will turn and do you harm and consume you, after He has done you good."

21 And the people said to Joshua, "No, but we will serve the LORD!"

22 So Joshua said to the people, "You *are* witnesses against yourselves that you have chosen the LORD for yourselves, to serve Him." And they said, "*We are* witnesses."

23 "Now therefore," *he said*, "put away the foreign gods which *are* among you, and incline your heart to the LORD God of Israel."

24 And the people said to Joshua, "The LORD our God we will serve, and His voice we will obey."

25 So Joshua made a covenant with the people that day, and made for them a statute and an ordinance in Shechem.

26 Then Joshua wrote these words in the Book of the Law of God. And he took a large stone, and set it up there under the oak that *was* by the sanctuary of the LORD.

27 And Joshua said to all the people, "Behold, this stone shall be a witness to us, for it has heard all the words of the LORD which He spoke to us. It shall therefore be a witness to you, lest you deny your God."

28 So Joshua let the people depart, each to his own inheritance.

Death of Joshua and Eleazar

29 Now it came to pass after these things that Joshua the son of Nun, the servant of the LORD, died, *being* one hundred and ten years old.

30 And they buried him within the border of his inheritance at Timnath Serah, which *is* in the mountains of Ephraim, on the north side of Mount Gaash.

31 Israel served the LORD all the days of Joshua, and all the days of the elders who outlived Joshua, who had known all the works of the LORD which He had done for Israel.

32 The bones of Joseph, which the children of Israel had brought up out of Egypt, they buried at Shechem, in the plot of ground which Jacob had bought from the sons of Hamor the father of Shechem for one hundred pieces of silver, and which had become an inheritance of the children of Joseph.

33 And Eleazar the son of Aaron died; and they buried him in a hill *that belonged to* Phinehas his son, which was given to him in the mountains of Ephraim.

Introduction to Judges

The Book of Judges shows God's faithfulness in raising up positive leaders for His people during times of adversity and trouble. The Israelites, faced with the negative influences of the Canaanite societies often adopted their neighbors' sinful ways. God gave them judges to lead the people out of this ungodly situation.

Judges was written between 1043 and 1004 B.C., probably by Samuel. The book records seven distinct instances when the people of Israel turned from God and needed His divine leadership through His appointed judges to bring them back to Him.

Judges includes some of the most fascinating possibility thinkers of the Bible. Each judge stood alone in the nation to present a positive message to return to God. When faced with insurmountable odds—they did not surrender leadership to their problems.

Deborah and Samson are two of the more familiar judges. Long before any women's movement, Deborah proved to be a successful leader of her people. Courageous, intelligent, and committed to her God, she defeated the warring Canaanite army. Deborah's famous song in chapter five suggests her leadership abilities.

> When leaders lead in Israel,
> When the people willingly offer themselves,
> Bless the LORD!
>
> Hear, O kings! Give ear, O princes!
> I, *even* I, will sing to the LORD;
> I will sing *praise* to the LORD God of Israel.

(Judg. 5:2, 3)

Samson is another example of one whose strength and leadership was used for God. The story of Samson reads like an ancient drama, depicting the strengths and weaknesses of a human being struggling to lead his people, yet torn by his human desire. Samson's dramatic defeat of the Philistines following his final prayer to God reveals his deepest loyalty.

The Book of Judges clearly indicates that everyone needs leadership. Without strong leaders in our life, we can easily be distracted by negative influences around us. This book demonstrates that the overall leadership in our work and deeds must be God, our Master, Lord, and Judge.

The Book of
Judges

The Continuing Conquest of Canaan

NOW after the death of Joshua it came to pass that the children of Israel asked the LORD, saying, "Who shall be first to go up for us against the Canaanites to fight against them?"

2 And the LORD said, "Judah shall go up. Indeed I have delivered the land into his hand."

3 So Judah said to Simeon his brother, "Come up with me to my allotted territory, that we may fight against the Canaanites; and I will likewise go with you to your allotted territory." And Simeon went with him.

4 Then Judah went up, and the LORD delivered the Canaanites and the Perizzites into their hand; and they killed ten thousand men at Bezek.

5 And they found Adoni-Bezek in Bezek, and fought against him; and they defeated the Canaanites and the Perizzites.

6 Then Adoni-Bezek fled, and they pursued him and caught him and cut off his thumbs and big toes.

7 And Adoni-Bezek said, "Seventy kings with their thumbs and big toes cut off used to gather *their food* under my table; as I have done, so God has repaid me." Then they brought him to Jerusalem, and there he died.

8 Now the children of Judah fought against Jerusalem and took it; they struck it with the edge of the sword and set the city on fire.

9 And afterward the children of Judah went down to fight against the Canaanites who dwelt in the mountains, in the South,[1] and in the lowland.

10 Then Judah went against the Canaanites who dwelt in Hebron. (Now the name of Hebron *was* formerly Kirjath Arba.) And they killed Sheshai, Ahiman, and Talmai.

11 From there they went against the inhabitants of Debir. (The name of Debir *was* formerly Kirjath Sepher.)

12 Then Caleb said, "He who attacks Kirjath Sepher and takes it, to him I will give my daughter Achsah as wife."

13 And Othniel the son of Kenaz, Caleb's younger brother, took it; so he gave him his daughter Achsah as wife.

14 Now it was so, when she came *to him*, that she urged him[2] to ask her father for a field. And she dismounted from *her* donkey, and Caleb said to her, "What do you wish?"

15 So she said to him, "Give me a blessing; since you have given me land in the South, give me also springs of water." Then Caleb gave her the upper springs and the lower springs.

16 Now the children of the Kenite, Moses' father-in-law, went up from the city of palms with the children of Judah into the Wilderness of Judah, which *lies* in the South *near* Arad; and they went and dwelt among the people.

17 And Judah went with his brother Simeon, and they attacked the Canaanites who inhabited Zephath, and utterly destroyed it. So the name of the city was called Hormah.

18 Also Judah took Gaza with its territory, Ashkelon with its territory, and Ekron with its territory.

19 So the LORD was with Judah. And they drove out *the inhabitants of* the mountains, but they could not drive out the inhabitants of the lowland, because they had chariots of iron.

20 And they gave Hebron to Caleb, as Moses had said. Then he expelled from there the three sons of Anak.

21 But the children of Benjamin did not drive out the Jebusites who inhabited Jerusalem; so the Jebusites dwell with the children of Benjamin in Jerusalem to this day.

22 And the house of Joseph also went up against Bethel, and the LORD *was* with them.

23 So the house of Joseph sent men to spy out Bethel. (The name of the city *was* formerly Luz.)

24 And when the spies saw a man coming out of the city, they said to him,

---

1 Hebrew *Negev*, and so throughout the book   2 Septuagint and Vulgate read *he urged her*.

"Please show us the entrance to the city, and we will show you mercy."

25 So he showed them the entrance to the city, and they struck the city with the edge of the sword; but they let the man and all his family go.

26 And the man went to the land of the Hittites, built a city, and called its name Luz, which *is* its name to this day.

Incomplete Conquest of the Land

27 However, Manasseh did not drive out *the inhabitants of* Beth Shean and its villages, or Taanach and its villages, or the inhabitants of Dor and its villages, or the inhabitants of Ibleam and its villages, or the inhabitants of Megiddo and its villages; for the Canaanites were determined to dwell in that land.

28 And it came to pass, when Israel was strong, that they put the Canaanites under tribute, but did not completely drive them out.

29 Nor did Ephraim drive out the Canaanites who dwelt in Gezer; so the Canaanites dwelt in Gezer among them.

30 Nor did Zebulun drive out the inhabitants of Kitron or the inhabitants of Nahalol; so the Canaanites dwelt among them, and were put under tribute.

31 Nor did Asher drive out the inhabitants of Acco or the inhabitants of Sidon, or of Ahlab, Achzib, Helbah, Aphik, or Rehob.

32 So the Asherites dwelt among the Canaanites, the inhabitants of the land; for they did not drive them out.

33 Nor did Naphtali drive out the inhabitants of Beth Shemesh or the inhabitants of Beth Anath; but they dwelt among the Canaanites, the inhabitants of the land. Nevertheless the inhabitants of Beth Shemesh and Beth Anath were put under tribute to them.

34 And the Amorites forced the children of Dan into the mountains, for they would not allow them to come down to the valley;

35 and the Amorites were determined to dwell in Mount Heres, in Aijalon, and in Shaalbim;³ yet when the hand of the house of Joseph became stronger, they were put under tribute.

36 Now the boundary of the Amorites *was* from the Ascent of Akrabbim, from Sela, and upward.

Israel's Disobedience

2 Then the Angel of the LORD came up from Gilgal to Bochim, and said: "I led you up from Egypt and brought you to the land of which I swore to your fathers; and I said, 'I will never break My covenant with you.

2 'And you shall make no covenant with the inhabitants of this land; you shall tear down their altars.' But you have not obeyed My voice. Why have you done this?

3 "Therefore I also said, 'I will not drive them out before you; but they shall be *thorns* in your side, and their gods shall be a snare to you.' "

4 And so it was, when the Angel of the LORD spoke these words to all the children of Israel, that the people lifted up their voice and wept.

5 Then they called the name of that place Bochim;⁴ and they sacrificed there to the LORD.

6 And when Joshua had dismissed the people, the children of Israel went each to his own inheritance to possess the land.

Death of Joshua

7 So the people served the LORD all the days of Joshua, and all the days of the elders who outlived Joshua, who had seen all the great works of the LORD which He had done for Israel.

8 Now Joshua the son of Nun, the servant of the LORD, died *when he was* one hundred and ten years old.

9 And they buried him within the border of his inheritance at Timnath Heres, in the mountains of Ephraim, on the north side of Mount Gaash.

10 When all that generation had been gathered to their fathers, another generation arose after them who did not know the LORD nor the work which He had done for Israel.

Israel's Unfaithfulness

11 Then the children of Israel did evil in the sight of the LORD, and served the Baals;

12 and they forsook the LORD God of their fathers, who had brought them out of the land of Egypt; and they followed other gods from *among* the gods of the people who *were* all around them, and

---

3 Spelled *Shaalabin* in Joshua 19:42   4 Literally *Weeping*

they bowed down to them; and they provoked the LORD to anger.
13 They forsook the LORD and served Baal and the Ashtoreths.[5]
14 And the anger of the LORD was hot against Israel. So He delivered them into the hands of plunderers who despoiled them; and He sold them into the hands of their enemies all around, so that they could no longer stand before their enemies.
15 Wherever they went out, the hand of the LORD was against them for calamity, as the LORD had said, and as the LORD had sworn to them. And they were greatly distressed.
16 Then the LORD raised up judges who delivered them out of the hand of those who plundered them.
17 Yet they would not listen to their judges, but they played the harlot with other gods, and bowed down to them. They turned quickly from the way in which their fathers walked, in obeying the commandments of the LORD; they did not do so.
18 And when the LORD raised up judges for them, the LORD was with the judge and delivered them out of the hand of their enemies all the days of the judge; for the LORD was moved to pity by their groaning because of those who oppressed them and harassed them.
19 And it came to pass, when the judge was dead, that they reverted and behaved more corruptly than their fathers, by following other gods, to serve them and bow down to them. They did not cease from their own doings nor from their stubborn way.
20 Then the anger of the LORD was hot against Israel; and He said, "Because this nation has transgressed My covenant which I commanded their fathers, and has not heeded My voice,
21 "I also will no longer drive out before them any of the nations which Joshua left when he died,
22 "so that through them I may test Israel, whether they will keep the ways of the LORD, to walk in them as their fathers kept them, or not."
23 Therefore the LORD left those nations, without driving them out immediately; nor did He deliver them into the hand of Joshua.

The Nations Remaining in the Land

3 Now these are the nations which the LORD left, that He might test Israel by them, that is, all who had not known any of the wars in Canaan
2 (this was only so that the generations of the children of Israel might be taught to know war, at least those who had not formerly known it),
3 namely, five lords of the Philistines, all the Canaanites, the Sidonians, and the Hivites who dwelt in Mount Lebanon, from Mount Baal Hermon to the entrance of Hamath.
4 And they were left, that He might test Israel by them, to know whether they would obey the commandments of the LORD, which He had commanded their fathers by the hand of Moses.
5 So the children of Israel dwelt among the Canaanites, the Hittites, the Amorites, the Perizzites, the Hivites, and the Jebusites.
6 And they took their daughters to be their wives, and gave their daughters to their sons; and they served their gods.

Othniel

7 So the children of Israel did evil in the sight of the LORD. They forgot the LORD their God, and served the Baals and Asherahs.[6]
8 Therefore the anger of the LORD was hot against Israel, and He sold them into the hand of Cushan-Rishathaim king of Mesopotamia; and the children of Israel served Cushan-Rishathaim eight years.
9 When the children of Israel cried out to the LORD, the LORD raised up a deliverer for the children of Israel, who delivered them: Othniel the son of Kenaz, Caleb's younger brother.
10 The Spirit of the LORD came upon him, and he judged Israel. He went out to war, and the LORD delivered Cushan-Rishathaim king of Mesopotamia into his hand; and his hand prevailed over Cushan-Rishathaim.
11 So the land had rest for forty years. Then Othniel the son of Kenaz died.

Ehud

12 And the children of Israel again did evil in the sight of the LORD. So the LORD strengthened Eglon king of Moab against Israel, because they had done evil in the sight of the LORD.

5 Canaanite goddesses   6 Name or symbol for Canaanite goddesses

13 Then he gathered to himself the people of Ammon and Amalek, went and defeated Israel, and took possession of the city of palms.
14 So the children of Israel served Eglon king of Moab eighteen years.
15 And when the children of Israel cried out to the LORD, the LORD raised up a deliverer for them: Ehud the son of Gera, the Benjamite, a left-handed man. By him the children of Israel sent tribute to Eglon king of Moab.
16 Now Ehud made himself a dagger (it was double-edged and a cubit in length) and fastened it under his clothes on his right thigh.
17 So he brought the tribute to Eglon king of Moab. (Now Eglon *was* a very fat man.)
18 And when he had finished presenting the tribute, he sent away the people who had carried the tribute.
19 But he himself turned back from the stone images that *were* at Gilgal, and said, "I have a secret message for you, O king." He said, "Keep silence!" And all who attended him went out from him.
20 And Ehud came to him (now he was sitting upstairs in his cool private chamber). Then Ehud said, "I have a message from God for you." So he arose from *his* seat.
21 Then Ehud reached with his left hand, took the dagger from his right thigh, and thrust it into his belly.
22 Even the hilt went in after the blade, and the fat closed over the blade, for he did not draw the dagger out of his belly; and his entrails came out.
23 Then Ehud went out through the porch and shut the doors of the upper room behind him and locked them.
24 When he had gone out, Eglon's[7] servants came to look, and *to their* surprise, the doors of the upper room were locked. So they said, "He is probably attending to his needs in the cool chamber."
25 So they waited till they were embarrassed, and still he had not opened the doors of the upper room. Therefore they took the key and opened *them*. And there was their master, fallen dead on the floor.
26 But Ehud escaped while they delayed, and passed beyond the stone images and escaped to Seirah.
27 And it happened, when he arrived, that he blew the trumpet in the mountains of Ephraim, and the children of Israel went down with him from the mountains; and he led them.
28 Then he said to them, "Follow *me*, for the LORD has delivered your enemies the Moabites into your hand." So they went down after him, seized the fords of the Jordan leading to Moab, and did not allow anyone to cross over.
29 And at that time they killed about ten thousand men of Moab, all stout men of valor; not a man escaped.
30 So Moab was subdued that day under the hand of Israel. And the land had rest for eighty years.

Shamgar

31 After him was Shamgar the son of Anath, who killed six hundred men of the Philistines with an ox goad; and he also delivered Israel.

Deborah

4 When Ehud was dead, the children of Israel again did evil in the sight of the LORD.
2 So the LORD sold them into the hand of Jabin king of Canaan, who reigned in Hazor. The commander of his army *was* Sisera, who dwelt in Harosheth Hagoyim.
3 And the children of Israel cried out to the LORD; for Jabin had nine hundred chariots of iron, and for twenty years he harshly oppressed the children of Israel.
4 Now Deborah, a prophetess, the wife of Lapidoth, was judging Israel at that time.
5 And she would sit under the palm tree of Deborah between Ramah and Bethel in the mountains of Ephraim. And the children of Israel came up to her for judgment.
6 Then she sent and called for Barak the son of Abinoam from Kedesh in Naphtali, and said to him, "Has not the LORD God of Israel commanded, *saying*, 'Go and deploy *troops* at Mount Tabor; take with you ten thousand men of the sons of Naphtali and of the sons of Zebulun;
7 'and against you I will deploy Sisera, the commander of Jabin's army, with his chariots and his multitude at the River Kishon; and I will deliver him into your hand'?"
8 And Barak said to her, "If you will go

7 Literally *his*

with me, then I will go; but if you will not go with me, I will not go."

9 So she said, "I will surely go with you; nevertheless there will be no glory for you in the journey you are taking, for the LORD will sell Sisera into the hand of a woman." Then Deborah arose and went with Barak to Kedesh.

10 And Barak called Zebulun and Naphtali to Kedesh; he went up with ten thousand men under his command,[8] and Deborah went up with him.

11 Now Heber the Kenite, of the children of Hobab the father-in-law of Moses, had separated himself from the Kenites and pitched his tent near the terebinth tree at Zaanaim, which is beside Kedesh.

12 And they reported to Sisera that Barak the son of Abinoam had gone up to Mount Tabor.

13 So Sisera gathered together all his chariots, nine hundred chariots of iron, and all the people who were with him, from Harosheth Hagoyim to the River Kishon.

14 Then Deborah said to Barak, "Up! For this is the day in which the LORD has delivered Sisera into your hand. Has not the LORD gone out before you?" So Barak went down from Mount Tabor with ten thousand men following him.

15 And the LORD routed Sisera and all his chariots and all his army with the edge of the sword before Barak; and Sisera alighted from his chariot and fled away on foot.

16 But Barak pursued the chariots and the army as far as Harosheth Hagoyim, and all the army of Sisera fell by the edge of the sword; not a man was left.

17 However, Sisera had fled away on foot to the tent of Jael, the wife of Heber the Kenite; for there was peace between Jabin king of Hazor and the house of Heber the Kenite.

18 And Jael went out to meet Sisera, and said to him, "Turn aside, my lord, turn aside to me; do not fear." And when he had turned aside with her into the tent, she covered him with a blanket.

19 Then he said to her, "Please give me a little water to drink, for I am thirsty." So she opened a jug of milk, gave him a drink, and covered him.

20 And he said to her, "Stand at the door of the tent, and if any man comes and inquires of you, and says, 'Is there any man here?' you shall say, 'No.'"

21 Then Jael, Heber's wife, took a tent peg and took a hammer in her hand, and went softly to him and drove the peg into his temple, and it went down into the ground; for he was fast asleep and weary. So he died.

22 And then, as Barak pursued Sisera, Jael came out to meet him, and said to him, "Come, I will show you the man whom you seek." And when he went into her tent, there lay Sisera, dead with the peg in his temple.

23 So on that day God subdued Jabin king of Canaan in the presence of the children of Israel.

24 And the hand of the children of Israel grew stronger and stronger against Jabin king of Canaan, until they had destroyed Jabin king of Canaan.

The Song of Deborah

5 Then Deborah and Barak the son of Abinoam sang on that day, saying:

2 "When leaders lead in Israel,
　　When the people willingly offer themselves,
　　Bless the LORD!

3 "Hear, O kings! Give ear, O princes!
　I, even I, will sing to the LORD;
　I will sing praise
　　to the LORD God of Israel.

4 "LORD, when You went out from Seir,
　When You marched
　　from the field of Edom,
　The earth trembled
　　and the heavens poured,
　The clouds also poured water;
5 The mountains gushed
　　before the LORD,
　This Sinai, before the LORD God
　　of Israel.

6 "In the days of Shamgar, son of Anath,
　In the days of Jael,
　The highways were deserted,
　And the travelers walked
　　along the byways.
7 Village life ceased, it ceased in Israel,
　Until I, Deborah, arose,
　Arose a mother in Israel.
8 They chose new gods;
　Then there was war in the gates;
　Not a shield or spear was seen among
　　forty thousand in Israel.

8 Literally at his feet

Women of Positive Faith

The Old Testament is filled with stories of women of positive faith. They were women much like the women of today—career women, mothers, wives, and friends. The passage of centuries has held fewer changes than might initially be expected. Long before any women's movement, the Old Testament women held roles of leadership and influence. Like all great people of faith, they had successes and failures which God used to help shape the course of their lives and their nation.

Sarah is the classic example of the wife of a prominent leader, who was respected and held in highest esteem by his people. With Abraham, Sarah left her comfortable surroundings to journey hundreds of miles into unknown territory. She was supportive and uncomplaining as they traveled over harsh countryside, and she willingly accepted the God of Israel. God promised a blessed generation to Abraham. Yet after years of believing, Sarah remained childless and barren. Her faith in God's promise waivered and she reacted much like any woman today might react. In offering Hagar to her husband, Sarah submitted to a surrogate-type solution, not unlike the modern medical techniques so popular in today's society. God had greater plans for Sarah. At age ninety, He proved that He could make even the most barren womb alive with new life. Sarah's lack of patience tripped her, but she did not fall. She praised God for her new son, Isaac, and raised him up for a life of service.

The judge, Deborah, was the successful career woman who was raised to a position of leading the entire nation of Israel. In a time of waivering faith, Deborah stood fast in her commitment to God. Because of her trust in God's ability, she was able to unite and lead the people of Israel in a major revolt against Sisera, a leader of the chariot-drawn Canaanites. Hardly weak-kneed, Deborah's campaign successfully defeated the militarily superior Canaanite nation. Like an ancient prime minister or president, Deborah was not afraid to assume the responsibilities thrust upon her. In her famous song Deborah's faith, determination, and courage as a woman of God are expressed.

Throughout the Old Testament women of positive faith speak out. Eve, Sarah, Rebekah, Deborah, Leah, Rachel, Miriam, Rahab, Ruth, and Hannah are all excellent examples of God's work in the lives of women. They were not all perfect saints who never lacked in belief, but they had a positive and a decisive faith. They faced the future unafraid. They adventured into new territories. They came back after defeat, and they stood up for their convictions.

The woman of faith in the Old Testament knew what the woman of positive faith today knows—that God can do great things through imperfect people!

9 My heart *is* with the rulers of Israel
    Who offered themselves willingly
        with the people.
    Bless the LORD!

10 "Speak, you who ride on white donkeys,
    Who sit in judges' attire,
    And who walk along the road.
11 Far from the noise of the archers,
        among the watering places,
    There they shall recount
        the righteous acts of the LORD,
    The righteous acts *for* His villagers
        in Israel;
    Then the people of the LORD
        shall go down to the gates.

12 "Awake, awake, Deborah!
    Awake, awake, sing a song!
    Arise, Barak,
        and lead your captives away,
    O son of Abinoam!

13 "Then the survivors came down,
        the people against the nobles;
    The LORD came down for me
        against the mighty.
14 From Ephraim *were* those
        whose roots were in Amalek.
    After you, Benjamin,
        with your peoples,
    From Machir rulers came down,
    And from Zebulun
        those who bear the recruiter's staff.
15 And the princes of Issachar[9]
        were with Deborah;
    As Issachar, so *was* Barak
    Sent into the valley
        under his command;[10]
    Among the divisions of Reuben
    There were great resolves of heart.
16 Why did you sit among the sheepfolds,
    To hear the pipings for the flocks?
    The divisions of Reuben
        have great searchings of heart.
17 Gilead stayed beyond the Jordan,
    And why did Dan remain on ships?
    Asher continued at the seashore,
    And stayed by his inlets.
18 Zebulun *is* a people *who* jeopardized
        their lives to the point of death,
    Naphtali also, on the heights
        of the battlefield.

19 "The kings came *and* fought,
    Then the kings of Canaan fought
    In Taanach, by the waters of Megiddo;
    They took no spoils of silver.
20 They fought from the heavens;
    The stars from their courses fought
        against Sisera.

21 The torrent of Kishon
        swept them away,
    That ancient torrent,
        the torrent of Kishon.
    O my soul, march on in strength!
22 Then the horses' hooves pounded,
    The galloping, galloping of his steeds.
23 'Curse Meroz,' said the angel[11]
        of the LORD,
    'Curse its inhabitants bitterly,
    Because they did not come
        to the help of the LORD,
    To the help of the LORD
        against the mighty.'

24 "Most blessed among women is Jael,
    The wife of Heber the Kenite;
    Blessed is she among women in tents.
25 He asked for water, she gave milk;
    She brought out cream
        in a lordly bowl.
26 She stretched her hand to the tent peg,
    Her right hand
        to the workmen's hammer;
    She pounded Sisera,
        she pierced his head,
    She split and struck
        through his temple.
27 At her feet he sank, he fell, he lay still;
    At her feet he sank, he fell;
    Where he sank, there he fell dead.

28 "The mother of Sisera looked
        through the window,
    And cried out through the lattice,
    'Why is his chariot *so* long in coming?
    Why tarries the clatter of his chariots?'
29 Her wisest ladies answered her,
    Yes, she answered herself,
30 'Are they not finding
        and dividing the spoil:
    To every man a girl *or* two;
    For Sisera, plunder of dyed garments,
    Plunder of garments
        embroidered and dyed,
    Two pieces of dyed embroidery
        for the neck of the looter?'

31 "Thus let all Your enemies perish,
        O LORD!
    But *let* those who love Him
        be like the sun
    When it comes out in full strength."

So the land had rest for forty years.

Midianites Oppress Israel

6 And the children of Israel did evil in the sight of the LORD. So the LORD

---

9 So with the ancient versions; Hebrew reads *And my princes in Issachar.*   10 Literally *at his feet*   11 Or *Angel*

delivered them into the hand of Midian for seven years,

2 and the hand of Midian prevailed against Israel. Because of the Midianites, the children of Israel made for themselves the dens, the caves, and the strongholds which *are* in the mountains.

3 So it was, whenever Israel had sown, Midianites would come up; also Amalekites and the people of the East would come up against them.

4 Then they would encamp against them and destroy the produce of the earth as far as Gaza, and leave no sustenance for Israel, neither sheep nor ox nor donkey.

5 For they would come up with their livestock and their tents, coming in as numerous as locusts; both they and their camels were without number; and they would enter the land to destroy it.

6 So Israel was greatly impoverished because of the Midianites, and the children of Israel cried out to the LORD.

7 And it came to pass, when the children of Israel cried out to the LORD because of the Midianites,

8 that the LORD sent a prophet to the children of Israel, who said to them, "Thus says the LORD God of Israel: 'I brought you up from Egypt and brought you out of the house of bondage;

9 'and I delivered you out of the hand of the Egyptians and out of the hand of all who oppressed you, and drove them out before you and gave you their land.

10 'Also I said to you, "I *am* the LORD your God; do not fear the gods of the Amorites, in whose land you dwell. But you have not obeyed My voice." ' "

Gideon

11 Now the Angel of the LORD came and sat under the terebinth tree which *was* in Ophrah, which *belonged* to Joash the Abiezrite, while his son Gideon threshed wheat in the winepress, in order to hide *it* from the Midianites.

12 And the Angel of the LORD appeared to him, and said to him, "The LORD *is* with you, you mighty man of valor!"

13 And Gideon said to Him, "O my lord,[12] if the LORD is with us, why then has all this happened to us? And where *are* all His miracles which our fathers told us about, saying, 'Did not the LORD bring us up from Egypt?' But now the LORD

has forsaken us and delivered us into the hands of the Midianites."

14 Then the LORD turned to him and said, "Go in this might of yours, and you shall save Israel from the hand of the Midianites. Have I not sent you?"

15 So he said to Him, "O my Lord,[13] how can I save Israel? Indeed my clan *is* the weakest in Manasseh, and I *am* the least in my father's house."

16 And the LORD said to him, "Surely I will be with you, and you shall defeat the Midianites as one man."

17 Then he said to Him, "If now I have found favor in Your sight, then show me a sign that it is You who talk with me.

18 "Do not depart from here, I pray, until I come to You and bring out my offering and set *it* before You." And He said, "I will wait until you come back."

19 Then Gideon went in and prepared a young goat, and unleavened bread from an ephah of flour. The meat he put in a basket, and he put the broth in a pot; and he brought *them* out to Him under the terebinth tree and presented *them*.

20 The Angel of God said to him, "Take the meat and the unleavened bread and lay *them* on this rock, and pour out the broth." And he did so.

21 Then the Angel of the LORD put out the end of the staff that *was* in His hand, and touched the meat and the unleavened bread; and fire rose out of the rock and consumed the meat and the unleavened bread. And the Angel of the LORD departed out of his sight.

22 Now Gideon perceived that He *was* the Angel of the LORD. So Gideon said, "Alas, O Lord GOD! For I have seen the Angel of the LORD face to face."

23 Then the LORD said to him, "Peace *be* with you; do not fear, you shall not die."

24 So Gideon built an altar there to the LORD, and called it The-LORD-Shalom.[14] To this day it *is* still in Ophrah of the Abiezrites.

25 Now it came to pass the same night that the LORD said to him, "Take your father's young bull, the second bull of seven years old, and tear down the altar of Baal that your father has, and cut down the wooden image[15] that *is* beside it;

26 "and build an altar to the LORD your God on top of this rock in the proper

---

12 Hebrew *adoni,* used of man   13 Hebrew *Adonai,* used of God
14 Literally *The LORD Is Peace*   15 Hebrew *Asherah,* a Canaanite goddess

arrangement, and take the second bull and offer a burnt sacrifice with the wood of the image which you shall cut down."

27 So Gideon took ten men from among his servants and did as the LORD had said to him. But because he feared his father's household and the men of the city too much to do *it* by day, he did *it* by night.

Gideon Destroys the Altar of Baal

28 And when the men of the city arose early in the morning, there was the altar of Baal, torn down; and the wooden image that *was* beside it was cut down, and the second bull was being offered on the altar *which had been* built.

29 So they said to one another, "Who has done this thing?" And when they had inquired and asked, they said, "Gideon the son of Joash has done this thing."

30 Then the men of the city said to Joash, "Bring out your son, that he may die, because he has torn down the altar of Baal, and because he has cut down the wooden image that *was* beside it."

31 And Joash said to all who stood against him, "Would you plead for Baal? Would you save him? Let the one who would plead for him be put to death by morning! If he *is* a god, let him plead for himself, because his altar has been torn down!"

32 Therefore on that day he called him Jerubbaal,[16] saying, "Let Baal plead against him, because he has torn down his altar."

33 Then all the Midianites and Amalekites, the people of the East, gathered together; and they crossed over and encamped in the Valley of Jezreel.

34 But the Spirit of the LORD came upon Gideon; then he blew the trumpet, and the Abiezrites gathered behind him.

35 And he sent messengers throughout all Manasseh, who also gathered behind him. He also sent messengers to Asher, Zebulun, and Naphtali; and they came up to meet them.

The Sign of the Fleece

36 Then Gideon said to God, "If You will save Israel by my hand as You have said—

37 "look, I shall put a fleece of wool on the threshing floor; if there is dew on the fleece only, and *it is* dry on all the ground, then I shall know that You will save Israel by my hand, as You have said."

38 And it was so. When he rose early the next morning and squeezed the fleece together, he wrung the dew out of the fleece, a bowl full of water.

39 Then Gideon said to God, "Do not be angry with me, and let me speak just once more: Let me test, I pray, just once more with the fleece; let it now be dry only on the fleece, but on all the ground let there be dew."

40 And God did so that night. It was dry on the fleece only, but there was dew on all the ground.

Gideon's Valiant Three Hundred

7 Then Jerubbaal (that *is*, Gideon) and all the people who *were* with him rose early and encamped beside the well of Harod, so that the camp of the Midianites was on the north side of them by the hill of Moreh in the valley.

2 And the LORD said to Gideon, "The people who *are* with you *are* too many for Me to give the Midianites into their hands, lest Israel claim glory for itself against Me, saying, 'My own hand has saved me.'

3 "Now therefore, proclaim in the hearing of the people, saying, 'Whoever *is* fearful and afraid, let him turn and depart at once from Mount Gilead.' " And twenty-two thousand of the people returned, and ten thousand remained.

4 And the LORD said to Gideon, "The people *are* still *too* many; bring them down to the water, and I will test them for you there. Then it will be, *that* of whom I say to you, 'This one shall go with you,' the same shall go with you; and of whomever I say to you, 'This one shall not go with you,' the same shall not go."

5 So he brought the people down to the water. And the LORD said to Gideon, "Everyone who laps from the water with his tongue, as a dog laps, you shall set apart by himself; likewise everyone who gets down on his knees to drink."

6 And the number of those who lapped, *putting* their hand to their mouth, was three hundred men; but all the rest of the people got down on their knees to drink water.

7 Then the LORD said to Gideon, "By the three hundred men who lapped I will

16 Literally *Let Baal Plead*

Gideon and the Midianites

When you think you have exhausted all the possibilities, remember, you have not.

During the period of the Judges, the Midianite army, aided by the Amalekites and the Ammonites, poured into Israel. They destroyed the countryside from Jezreel to the Gaza strip. The terrified Israelites fled their towns, homes, and villages, and they hid in mountain caves.

There was one man, however, who did not surrender to fear—Gideon. He believed that God would deliver his people. Gideon never lost faith or hope. He dared to believe that God would raise up a mighty army to smash the Midianites and return the people to their land. God asked Gideon to gather all of the able-bodied military men in the Valley of Jezreel at the hill of Moreh to organize an army to attack the Midianites. Gideon persuaded 32,000 men to join him at his camp.

However, God wanted Gideon to believe that anything was possible, so he asked Gideon to believe the impossible. He told him to multiply his resources by trimming down his forces. God ordered Gideon to get rid of 31,700 men. With only 300 men, Gideon was told he could defeat hundreds of thousands of Midianites.

Gideon dared to believe God. At nightfall, Gideon assembled his troops on the slopes of the hill of Moreh. On his command, they were to light torches, smash empty water pitchers, and shout at the top of their lungs while attacking the Midianite army. At night this looked like a tremendous swarm of soldiers coming down on the Midianite army. The Midianites turned and fled in fear. In the darkness of the evening, the Midianite soldiers began to attack each other. Hundreds of thousands of soldiers fell on the slopes of the hills around the Jordan and Jezreel valleys. Inspired by Gideon's great courage, the Israelites from all over the land came and aided in the battle. Finally, the Midianites were completely defeated.

Be like Gideon: when you think you have exhausted all the possibilities, remember—you have not. Pray, think, ask God for an idea and a solution. Be clever and bold. Go after your problem; trick your problem! Multiply your resources by stripping away unneeded excess. Gideon multiplied his resources by trimming down his forces. When the call came for Gideon to fight, he was not negative. Gideon was gathering wheat; he was not sitting around doing nothing. He was doing something! This was his strength—he was not a quitter! He was not defeated! The result was that Gideon was able to lead his people to victory!

What is holding you back? Are you waiting for conditions to be perfect? Move ahead with possibility thinking!

save you, and deliver the Midianites into your hand. Let all the *other* people go, every man to his place."

8 So the people took provisions and their trumpets in their hands. And he sent away all *the rest of* Israel, every man to his tent, and retained those three hundred men. Now the camp of Midian was below him in the valley.

9 And it happened on the same night that the LORD said to him, "Arise, go down against the camp, for I have delivered it into your hand.

10 "But if you are afraid to go down, go down to the camp with Purah your servant,

11 "and you shall hear what they say; and afterward your hands shall be strengthened to go down against the camp." Then he went down with Purah his servant to the outpost of the armed men who *were* in the camp.

12 Now the Midianites and Amalekites, all the people of the East, were lying in the valley as numerous as locusts; and their camels *were* without number, as the sand by the seashore in multitude.

13 And when Gideon had come, there was a man telling a dream to his companion. He said, "I have *just* had a dream: *To my* surprise, a loaf of barley bread tumbled into the camp of Midian; it came to a tent and struck it so that it fell and overturned, and the tent collapsed."

14 Then his companion answered and said, "This *is* nothing else but the sword of Gideon the son of Joash, a man of Israel; *for* into his hand God has delivered Midian and the whole camp."

15 And so it was, when Gideon heard the telling of the dream and its interpretation, that he worshiped. He returned to the camp of Israel, and said, "Arise, for the LORD has delivered the camp of Midian into your hand."

16 Then he divided the three hundred men *into* three companies, and he put a trumpet into every man's hand, with empty pitchers, and torches inside the pitchers.

17 And he said to them, "Look at me and do likewise; watch, and when I come to the edge of the camp you shall do *just* as I do:

18 "When I blow the trumpet, I and all who *are* with me, then you also blow the trumpets on every side of the whole camp, and say, '*The sword of* the LORD and of Gideon!' "

19 So Gideon and the hundred men who *were* with him came to the outpost of the camp at the beginning of the middle watch, just as they had posted the watch; and they blew the trumpets and broke the pitchers that *were* in their hands.

20 Then the three companies blew the trumpets and broke the pitchers—they held the torches in their left hands and the trumpets in their right hands for blowing—and they cried, "The sword of the LORD and of Gideon!"

21 And every man stood in his place all around the camp; and the whole army ran and cried out and fled.

22 When the three hundred blew the trumpets, the LORD set every man's sword against his companion throughout the whole camp; and the army fled to Beth Acacia,[17] toward Zererah, as far as the border of Abel Meholah, by Tabbath.

23 And the men of Israel gathered together from Naphtali, Asher, and all Manasseh, and pursued the Midianites.

24 Then Gideon sent messengers throughout all the mountains of Ephraim, saying, "Come down against the Midianites, and seize from them the watering places as far as Beth Barah and the Jordan." Then all the men of Ephraim gathered together and seized the watering places as far as Beth Barah and the Jordan.

25 And they captured two princes of the Midianites, Oreb and Zeeb. They killed Oreb at the rock of Oreb, and Zeeb they killed at the winepress of Zeeb. They pursued Midian and brought the heads of Oreb and Zeeb to Gideon on the other side of the Jordan.

Gideon Subdues the Midianites

8 Now the men of Ephraim said to him, "Why have you done this to us by not calling us when you went to fight with the Midianites?" And they reprimanded him sharply.

2 So he said to them, "What have I done now in comparison with you? *Is* not the gleaning *of the grapes* of Ephraim better than the vintage of Abiezer?

3 "God has delivered into your hands the princes of Midian, Oreb and Zeeb. And what was I able to do in comparison

17 Hebrew *Beth Shittah*

with you?" Then their anger toward him abated when he said that.

4 When Gideon came to the Jordan, he and the three hundred men who *were* with him crossed over, exhausted but still in pursuit.

5 Then he said to the men of Succoth, "Please give loaves of bread to the people who follow me, for they are exhausted, and I am pursuing Zebah and Zalmunna, kings of Midian."

6 And the leaders of Succoth said, "*Are* the hands of Zebah and Zalmunna now in your hand, that we should give bread to your army?"

7 So Gideon said, "For this cause, when the LORD has delivered Zebah and Zalmunna into my hand, then I will tear your flesh with the thorns of the wilderness and with briers!"

8 Then he went up from there to Penuel and spoke to them in the same way. And the men of Penuel answered him as the men of Succoth had answered *him*.

9 So he also spoke to the men of Penuel, saying, "When I come back in peace, I will tear down this tower!"

10 Now Zebah and Zalmunna *were* at Karkor, and their armies with them, about fifteen thousand *men*, all who were left of all the army of the people of the East; for one hundred and twenty thousand men who drew the sword had fallen.

11 Then Gideon went up by the road of those who dwell in tents on the east of Nobah and Jogbehah; and he attacked the army while the camp felt secure.

12 When Zebah and Zalmunna fled, he pursued them; and he took the two kings of Midian, Zebah and Zalmunna, and routed the whole army.

13 Then Gideon the son of Joash returned from battle, from the Ascent of Heres.

14 And he caught a young man of the men of Succoth and interrogated him; and he wrote down for him the leaders of Succoth and its elders, seventy-seven men.

15 Then he came to the men of Succoth and said, "Here are Zebah and Zalmunna, about whom you ridiculed me, saying, 'Are the hands of Zebah and Zalmunna now in your hand, that we should give bread to your weary men?' "

16 And he took the elders of the city, and thorns of the wilderness and briers, and with them he taught the men of Succoth.

17 Then he tore down the tower of Penuel and killed the men of the city.

18 And he said to Zebah and Zalmunna, "What kind of men *were they* whom you killed at Tabor?" So they answered, "As you *are*, so *were* they; each one resembled the son of a king."

19 Then he said, "They *were* my brothers, the sons of my mother. *As* the LORD lives, if you had let them live, I would not kill you."

20 And he said to Jether his firstborn, "Rise, kill them!" But the youth would not draw his sword; for he was afraid, because he *was* still a youth.

21 So Zebah and Zalmunna said, "Rise yourself, and kill us; for as a man *is, so is* his strength." So Gideon arose and killed Zebah and Zalmunna, and took the crescent ornaments that *were* on their camels' necks.

Gideon's Ephod

22 Then the men of Israel said to Gideon, "Rule over us, both you and your son, and your grandson also; for you have delivered us from the hand of Midian."

23 But Gideon said to them, "I will not rule over you, nor shall my son rule over you; the LORD shall rule over you."

24 Then Gideon said to them, "I would like to make a request of you, that each of you would give me the earrings from his plunder." For they had gold earrings, because they *were* Ishmaelites.

25 So they answered, "We will gladly give *them*." And they spread out a garment, and each man threw into it the earrings from his plunder.

26 Now the weight of the gold earrings that he requested was one thousand seven hundred *shekels* of gold, besides the crescent ornaments, pendants, and purple robes which *were* on the kings of Midian, and besides the chains that *were* around their camels' necks.

27 Then Gideon made it into an ephod and set it up in his city, Ophrah. And all Israel played the harlot with it there. It became a snare to Gideon and to his house.

28 Thus Midian was subdued before the children of Israel, so that they lifted their heads no more. And the country was

quiet for forty years in the days of Gideon.

Death of Gideon

29 Then Jerubbaal the son of Joash went and dwelt in his own house. **30** Gideon had seventy sons who were his own offspring, for he had many wives. **31** And his concubine who *was* in Shechem also bore him a son, whose name he called Abimelech. **32** Now Gideon the son of Joash died at a good old age, and was buried in the tomb of Joash his father, in Ophrah of the Abiezrites. **33** And it was so, as soon as Gideon was dead, that the children of Israel again played the harlot with the Baals, and made Baal-Berith their god. **34** Thus the children of Israel did not remember the LORD their God, who had delivered them from the hands of all their enemies on every side; **35** nor did they show kindness to the house of Jerubbaal (*that is*, Gideon) in accordance with the good he had done for Israel.

Abimelech's Conspiracy

9 And Abimelech the son of Jerubbaal went to Shechem, to his mother's brothers, and spoke with them and with all the family of the house of his mother's father, saying, **2** "Please speak in the hearing of all the men of Shechem: 'Which is better for you, that all seventy of the sons of Jerubbaal reign over you, or that one reign over you?' Remember that I *am* your own flesh and bone." **3** And his mother's brothers spoke all these words concerning him in the hearing of all the men of Shechem; and their heart was inclined to follow Abimelech, for they said, "He is our brother." **4** So they gave him seventy *shekels* of silver from the temple of Baal-Berith, with which Abimelech hired worthless and reckless men; and they followed him. **5** Then he went to his father's house at Ophrah and killed his brothers, the seventy sons of Jerubbaal, on one stone. But Jotham the youngest son of Jerubbaal was left, because he hid himself. **6** And all the men of Shechem gathered together, all of Beth Millo, and they went and made Abimelech king beside the terebinth tree at the pillar that *was* in Shechem.

The Parable of the Trees

7 Now when they told *it* to Jotham, he went and stood on top of Mount Gerizim, and lifted his voice and cried out, and said to them:

"Listen to me, you men of Shechem,
   That God may listen to you!

8 "The trees once went forth
      to anoint a king over them.
   And they said to the olive tree,
      'Reign over us!'
9   But the olive tree said to them,
      'Should I cease giving my oil,
      With which they honor God and men,
      And go to sway over trees?'

10 "Then the trees said to the fig tree,
      'You come *and* reign over us!'
11   But the fig tree said to them,
      'Should I cease my sweetness
         and my good fruit,
      And go to sway over trees?'

12 "Then the trees said to the vine,
      'You come *and* reign over us!'
13   But the vine said to them,
      'Should I cease my new wine,
      Which cheers *both* God and men,
      And go to sway over trees?'

14 "Then all the trees said to the bramble,
      'You come *and* reign over us!'
15   And the bramble said to the trees,
      'If in truth you anoint me
         as king over you,
      Then come *and* take shelter
         in my shade;
      But if not,
      let fire come out of the bramble
      And devour the cedars of Lebanon!'

16 "Now therefore, if you have acted in truth and sincerity in making Abimelech king, and if you have dealt well with Jerubbaal and his house, and have done to him as he deserves— **17** "for my father fought for you, risked his life, and delivered you out of the hand of Midian; **18** "but you have risen up against my father's house this day, and killed his seventy sons on one stone, and made Abimelech, the son of his maidservant, king over the men of Shechem, because he is your brother—

19 "if then you have acted in truth and sincerity with Jerubbaal and with his house this day, *then* rejoice in Abimelech, and let him also rejoice in you.

20 "But if not, let fire come from Abimelech and devour the men of Shechem and Beth Millo; and let fire come from the men of Shechem and from Beth Millo and devour Abimelech!"

21 And Jotham ran away and fled; and he went to Beer and dwelt there, for fear of Abimelech his brother.

Downfall of Abimelech

22 After Abimelech had reigned over Israel three years,

23 God sent a spirit of ill will between Abimelech and the men of Shechem; and the men of Shechem dealt treacherously with Abimelech,

24 that the crime *done* to the seventy sons of Jerubbaal might be settled and their blood be laid on Abimelech their brother, who killed them, and on the men of Shechem, who aided him in the killing of his brothers.

25 And the men of Shechem set men in ambush against him on the tops of the mountains, and they robbed all who passed by them along that way; and it was told Abimelech.

26 Now Gaal the son of Ebed came with his brothers and went over to Shechem; and the men of Shechem put their confidence in him.

27 So they went out into the fields, and gathered *grapes* from their vineyards and trod *them*, and made merry. And they went into the house of their god, and ate and drank, and cursed Abimelech.

28 Then Gaal the son of Ebed said, "Who *is* Abimelech, and who *is* Shechem, that we should serve him? *Is he* not the son of Jerubbaal, and *is not* Zebul his officer? Serve the men of Hamor the father of Shechem; but why should we serve him?

29 "If only this people were under my hand! Then I would remove Abimelech." So he said to Abimelech, "Increase your army and come out!"

30 When Zebul, the ruler of the city, heard the words of Gaal the son of Ebed, his anger was aroused.

31 And he sent messengers to Abimelech secretly, saying, "Take note! Gaal the son of Ebed and his brothers have come to Shechem; and here they are, fortifying the city against you.

32 "Now therefore, get up by night, you and the people who *are* with you, and lie in wait in the field.

33 "And it shall be, as soon as the sun is up in the morning, *that* you shall rise early and rush upon the city; and *as soon as* he and the people who are with him come out against you, you may then do to them as you find opportunity."

34 So Abimelech and all the people who *were* with him rose by night, and laid in wait against Shechem in four companies.

35 When Gaal the son of Ebed went out and stood in the entrance to the city gate, Abimelech and the people who *were* with him rose from lying in wait.

36 And when Gaal saw the people, he said to Zebul, "Look, people are coming down from the tops of the mountains!" But Zebul said to him, "You see the shadows of the mountains as *if they were* men."

37 So Gaal spoke again and said, "See, people are coming down from the center of the land, and another company is coming from the Diviners'[18] Terebinth Tree."

38 Then Zebul said to him, "Where indeed *is* your mouth now, with which you said, 'Who *is* Abimelech, that we should serve him?' *Are* not these the people whom you despised? Go out, if you will, and fight with them now."

39 So Gaal went out, leading the men of Shechem, and fought with Abimelech.

40 And Abimelech chased him, and he fled from him; and many fell wounded, *even* to the entrance of the gate.

41 Then Abimelech dwelt at Arumah, and Zebul drove out Gaal and his brothers, so that they would not dwell in Shechem.

42 And it came about on the next day that the people went out into the field, and they told Abimelech.

43 So he took his people, divided them into three companies, and laid in wait in the field. And he looked, and there were the people, coming out of the city; and he rose against them and attacked them.

44 Then Abimelech and the company that *was* with him rushed forward and stood at the entrance of the gate of the city; and the *other* two companies rushed

18 Hebrew *Meonenim*

upon all who *were* in the fields and killed them.

45 So Abimelech fought against the city all that day; he took the city and killed the people who *were* in it; and he demolished the city and sowed it with salt.

46 Now when all the men of the tower of Shechem had heard *that*, they entered the stronghold of the temple of the god Berith.

47 And it was told Abimelech that all the men of the tower of Shechem were gathered together.

48 Then Abimelech went up to Mount Zalmon, he and all the people who *were* with him. And Abimelech took an ax in his hand and cut down a bough from the trees, and took it and laid *it* on his shoulder; then he said to the people who were with him, "What you have seen me do, make haste *and* do as I *have done*."

49 So each of the people likewise cut down his own bough and followed Abimelech, put *them* against the stronghold, and set the stronghold on fire above them, so that all the people of the tower of Shechem died, about a thousand men and women.

50 Then Abimelech went to Thebez, and he encamped against Thebez and took it.

51 But there was a strong tower in the city, and all the men and women—all the people of the city—fled there and shut themselves in; then they went up to the top of the tower.

52 So Abimelech came as far as the tower and fought against it; and he drew near the door of the tower to burn it with fire.

53 But a certain woman dropped an upper millstone on Abimelech's head and crushed his skull.

54 Then he called quickly to the young man, his armorbearer, and said to him, "Draw your sword and kill me, lest men say of me, 'A woman killed him.' " So his young man thrust him through, and he died.

55 And when the men of Israel saw that Abimelech was dead, they departed, every man to his *own* place.

56 Thus God repaid the wickedness of Abimelech, which he had done to his father by killing his seventy brothers.

57 And all the evil of the men of Shechem God returned on their own heads,

and on them came the curse of Jotham the son of Jerubbaal.

Tola

10 After Abimelech there arose to save Israel Tola the son of Puah, the son of Dodo, a man of Issachar; and he dwelt in Shamir in the mountains of Ephraim.

2 He judged Israel twenty-three years; and he died and was buried in Shamir.

Jair

3 After him arose Jair, a Gileadite; and he judged Israel twenty-two years.

4 Now he had thirty sons who rode on thirty donkeys; they also had thirty towns, which are called "Havoth Jair"[19] to this day, which *are* in the land of Gilead.

5 And Jair died and was buried in Camon.

Israel Oppressed Again

6 Then the children of Israel again did evil in the sight of the LORD, and served the Baals and the Ashtoreths, the gods of Syria, the gods of Sidon, the gods of Moab, the gods of the people of Ammon, and the gods of the Philistines; and they forsook the LORD and did not serve Him.

7 So the anger of the LORD was hot against Israel; and He sold them into the hands of the Philistines and into the hands of the people of Ammon.

8 From that year they harassed and oppressed the children of Israel for eighteen years—all the children of Israel who *were* on the other side of the Jordan in the land of the Amorites, in Gilead.

9 Moreover the people of Ammon crossed over the Jordan to fight against Judah also, against Benjamin, and against the house of Ephraim, so that Israel was severely distressed.

10 And the children of Israel cried out to the LORD, saying, "We have sinned against You, because we have both forsaken our God and served the Baals!"

11 So the LORD said to the children of Israel, "*Did I* not *deliver you* from the Egyptians and from the Amorites and from the people of Ammon and from the Philistines?

12 "Also the Sidonians and Amalekites and Maonites[20] oppressed you; and you

19 Literally *Towns of Jair* (compare Numbers 32:41 and Deuteronomy 3:14)
20 Some Septuagint manuscripts read *Midianites.*

cried out to Me, and I delivered you from their hand.
13 "Yet you have forsaken Me and served other gods. Therefore I will deliver you no more.
14 "Go and cry out to the gods which you have chosen; let them deliver you in your time of distress."
15 Then the children of Israel said to the LORD, "We have sinned! Do to us whatever seems best to You; only deliver us this day, we pray."
16 So they put away the foreign gods from among them and served the LORD. And His soul could no longer endure the misery of Israel.
17 Then the people of Ammon gathered together and encamped in Gilead. And the children of Israel assembled together and encamped in Mizpah.
18 And the people, the leaders of Gilead, said to one another, "Who is the man who will begin the fight against the people of Ammon? He shall be head over all the inhabitants of Gilead."

Jephthah

11 Now Jephthah the Gileadite was a mighty man of valor, but he *was* the son of a harlot; and Gilead begot Jephthah.
2 Gilead's wife bore sons; and when his wife's sons grew up, they drove Jephthah out, and said to him, "You shall have no inheritance in our father's house, for you *are* the son of another woman."
3 Then Jephthah fled from his brothers and dwelt in the land of Tob; and worthless men banded together with Jephthah and went out *raiding* with him.
4 Now it came to pass after a time that the people of Ammon made war against Israel.
5 And so it was, when the people of Ammon made war against Israel, that the elders of Gilead went to get Jephthah from the land of Tob.
6 Then they said to Jephthah, "Come and be our commander, that we may fight against the people of Ammon."
7 So Jephthah said to the elders of Gilead, "Did you not hate me, and expel me from my father's house? Why have you come to me now when you are in distress?"
8 And the elders of Gilead said to Jephthah, "That is why we have turned again

to you now, that you may go with us and fight against the people of Ammon, and be our head over all the inhabitants of Gilead."
9 So Jephthah said to the elders of Gilead, "If you take me back home to fight against the people of Ammon, and the LORD delivers them to me, shall I be your head?"
10 And the elders of Gilead said to Jephthah, "The LORD will be a witness between us, if we do not do according to your words."
11 Then Jephthah went with the elders of Gilead, and the people made him head and commander over them; and Jephthah spoke all his words before the LORD in Mizpah.
12 Now Jephthah sent messengers to the king of the people of Ammon, saying, "What do you have against me, that you have come to fight against me in my land?"
13 And the king of the people of Ammon answered the messengers of Jephthah, "Because Israel took away my land when they came up out of Egypt, from the Arnon as far as the Jabbok, and to the Jordan. Now therefore, restore those *lands* peaceably."
14 So Jephthah again sent messengers to the king of the people of Ammon,
15 and said to him, "Thus says Jephthah: 'Israel did not take away the land of Moab, nor the land of the people of Ammon;
16 'for when Israel came up from Egypt, they walked through the wilderness as far as the Red Sea and came to Kadesh.
17 'Then Israel sent messengers to the king of Edom, saying, "Please let me pass through your land." But the king of Edom would not heed. And in like manner they sent to the king of Moab, but he would not *consent*. So Israel remained in Kadesh.
18 'And they went along through the wilderness and bypassed the land of Edom and the land of Moab, came to the east side of the land of Moab, and encamped on the other side of the Arnon. But they did not enter the border of Moab, for the Arnon *was* the border of Moab.
19 'Then Israel sent messengers to Sihon king of the Amorites, king of Heshbon; and Israel said to him, "Please let us pass through your land into our place."

20 'But Sihon did not trust Israel to pass through his territory. So Sihon gathered all his people together, encamped in Jahaz, and fought against Israel.

21 'And the LORD God of Israel delivered Sihon and all his people into the hand of Israel, and they defeated them. Thus Israel gained possession of all the land of the Amorites, who inhabited that country.

22 'They took possession of all the territory of the Amorites, from the Arnon to the Jabbok and from the wilderness to the Jordan.

23 'So now the LORD God of Israel has dispossessed the Amorites from before His people Israel; should you then possess it?

24 'Will you not possess whatever Chemosh your god gives you to possess? So whatever the LORD our God takes possession of before us, we will possess.

25 'And now, *are* you any better than Balak the son of Zippor, king of Moab? Did he ever strive against Israel? Did he ever fight against them?

26 'While Israel dwelt in Heshbon and its villages, in Aroer and its villages, and in all the cities along the banks of the Arnon, for three hundred years, why did you not recover *them* within that time?

27 'Therefore I have not sinned against you, but you wronged me by fighting against me. May the LORD, the Judge, render judgment this day between the children of Israel and the people of Ammon.' "

28 However, the king of the people of Ammon did not heed the words which Jephthah sent him.

Jephthah's Vow and Victory

29 Then the Spirit of the LORD came upon Jephthah, and he passed through Gilead and Manasseh, and passed through Mizpah of Gilead; and from Mizpah of Gilead he advanced *toward* the people of Ammon.

30 And Jephthah made a vow to the LORD, and said, "If You will indeed deliver the people of Ammon into my hands,

31 "then it will be that whatever comes out of the doors of my house to meet me, when I return in peace from the people of Ammon, shall surely be the LORD's, and I will offer it up as a burnt offering."

32 So Jephthah advanced toward the people of Ammon to fight against them, and the LORD delivered them into his hands.

33 And he defeated them from Aroer as far as Minnith—twenty cities—and to Abel Keramim,[21] with a very great slaughter. Thus the people of Ammon were subdued before the children of Israel.

The Daughter of Jephthah

34 When Jephthah came to his house at Mizpah, there was his daughter, coming out to meet him with timbrels and dancing; and she *was his* only child. Besides her he had neither son nor daughter.

35 And it came to pass, when he saw her, that he tore his clothes, and said, "Alas, my daughter! You have brought me very low! You are among those who trouble me! For I have given my word to the LORD, and I cannot go back on it."

36 So she said to him, "My father, *if* you have given your word to the LORD, do to me according to what has gone out of your mouth, because the LORD has avenged you of your enemies, the people of Ammon."

37 Then she said to her father, "Let this thing be done for me: let me alone for two months, that I may go and wander on the mountains and bewail my virginity, my friends and I."

38 So he said, "Go." And he sent her away *for* two months; and she went with her friends, and bewailed her virginity on the mountains.

39 And it was so at the end of two months that she returned to her father, and he carried out his vow with her which he had vowed. She knew no man. And it became a custom in Israel

40 *that* the daughters of Israel went four days each year to lament the daughter of Jephthah the Gileadite.

Jephthah's Conflict with Ephraim

12 Then the men of Ephraim gathered together, crossed over toward Zaphon, and said to Jephthah, "Why did you cross over to fight against the people of Ammon, and did not call us to go with you? We will burn your house down on you with fire!"

2 And Jephthah said to them, "My people and I were in a great struggle with the

---

21 Literally *Plain of Vineyards*

people of Ammon; and when I called you, you did not deliver me out of their hands.

3 "So when I saw that you would not deliver *me*, I took my life in my hands and crossed over against the people of Ammon; and the LORD delivered them into my hand. Why then have you come up to me this day to fight against me?"

4 Now Jephthah gathered together all the men of Gilead and fought against Ephraim. And the men of Gilead defeated Ephraim, because they said, "You Gileadites *are* fugitives of Ephraim among the Ephraimites *and* among the Manassites."

5 The Gileadites seized the fords of the Jordan before the Ephraimites *arrived.* And when *any* Ephraimite who escaped said, "Let me cross over," the men of Gilead would say to him, "*Are* you an Ephraimite?" If he said, "No,"

6 then they would say to him, "Then say, 'Shibboleth'!" And he would say, "Sibboleth," for he could not pronounce *it* right. Then they would take him and kill him at the fords of the Jordan. There fell at that time forty-two thousand Ephraimites.

7 And Jephthah judged Israel six years. Then Jephthah the Gileadite died and was buried in *one of* the cities of Gilead.

Ibzan, Elon, and Abdon

8 After him, Ibzan of Bethlehem judged Israel.

9 He had thirty sons. And he gave away thirty daughters in marriage, and brought in thirty daughters from elsewhere for his sons. He judged Israel seven years.

10 Then Ibzan died and was buried at Bethlehem.

11 After him, Elon the Zebulunite judged Israel. He judged Israel ten years.

12 And Elon the Zebulunite died and was buried at Aijalon in the country of Zebulun.

13 After him, Abdon the son of Hillel the Pirathonite judged Israel.

14 He had forty sons and thirty grandsons, who rode on seventy young donkeys. He judged Israel eight years.

15 Then Abdon the son of Hillel the Pirathonite died and was buried in Pirathon in the land of Ephraim, in the mountains of the Amalekites.

The Birth of Samson

13 Again the children of Israel did evil in the sight of the LORD, and the LORD delivered them into the hand of the Philistines for forty years.

2 Now there was a certain man from Zorah, of the family of the Danites, whose name *was* Manoah; and his wife *was* barren and had no children.

3 And the Angel of the LORD appeared to the woman and said to her, "Indeed now, you are barren and have borne no children, but you shall conceive and bear a son.

4 "Now therefore, please be careful not to drink wine or *similar* drink, and not to eat any unclean *thing.*

5 "For behold, you shall conceive and bear a son. And no razor shall come upon his head, for the child shall be a Nazirite to God from the womb; and he shall begin to deliver Israel out of the hand of the Philistines."

6 So the woman came and told her husband, saying, "A Man of God came to me, and His countenance *was* like the countenance of the Angel of God, very awesome; but I did not ask Him where He *was* from, and He did not tell me His name.

7 "And He said to me, 'Behold, you shall conceive and bear a son. Now drink no wine or *similar* drink, nor eat anything unclean, for the child shall be a Nazirite to God from the womb to the day of his death.'"

8 Then Manoah prayed to the LORD, and said, "O my Lord, please let the Man of God whom You sent come to us again and teach us what we shall do for the child who will be born."

9 And God listened to the voice of Manoah, and the Angel of God came to the woman again as she was sitting in the field; but Manoah her husband *was* not with her.

10 Then the woman ran in haste and told her husband, and said to him, "Look, the Man has just now appeared to me, *the One* who came to me the *other* day!"

11 So Manoah arose and followed his wife. When he came to the Man, he said to Him, "Are You the Man who spoke to this woman?" And He said, "I *am.*"

12 And Manoah said, "Now let Your

words come *to pass*! What will be the boy's rule of life, and his work?"
13 So the Angel of the LORD said to Manoah, "Of all that I said to the woman let her be careful.
14 "She may not eat anything that comes from the vine, nor may she drink wine or *similar* drink, nor eat anything unclean. All that I commanded her let her observe."
15 Then Manoah said to the Angel of the LORD, "Please let us detain You, and we will prepare a young goat for You."
16 And the Angel of the LORD said to Manoah, "Though you detain Me, I will not eat your food. But if you offer a burnt offering, you must offer it to the LORD." (For Manoah did not know He *was* the Angel of the LORD.)
17 Then Manoah said to the Angel of the LORD, "What *is* Your name, that when Your words come *to pass* we may honor You?"
18 And the Angel of the LORD said to him, "Why do you ask My name, seeing it *is* wonderful?"
19 So Manoah took the young goat with the grain offering, and offered it upon the rock to the LORD. And He did a wondrous thing while Manoah and his wife looked on:
20 as the flame went up toward heaven from the altar, it happened that the Angel of the LORD ascended in the flame of the altar. When Manoah and his wife saw *this*, they fell on their faces to the ground.
21 When the Angel of the LORD appeared no more to Manoah and his wife, then Manoah knew that He *was* the Angel of the LORD.
22 And Manoah said to his wife, "We shall surely die, because we have seen God!"
23 Then his wife said to him, "If the LORD had desired to kill us, He would not have accepted a burnt offering and a grain offering from our hands, nor would He have shown us all these *things*, nor would He have told us *such things* as these at this time."
24 So the woman bore a son and called his name Samson; and the child grew, and the LORD blessed him.
25 And the Spirit of the LORD began to move upon him at Mahaneh Dan[22] between Zorah and Eshtaol.

Samson's Philistine Wife

14 Now Samson went down to Timnah, and saw a woman in Timnah of the daughters of the Philistines.
2 So he went up and told his father and mother, saying, "I have seen a woman in Timnah of the daughters of the Philistines; now therefore, get her for me as a wife."
3 Then his father and mother said to him, "*Is there* no woman among the daughters of your brethren, or among all my people, that you must go and get a wife from the uncircumcised Philistines?" And Samson said to his father, "Get her for me, for she pleases me well."
4 But his father and mother did not know that it was of the LORD—that He was seeking an occasion to move against the Philistines. For at that time the Philistines had dominion over Israel.
5 So Samson went down to Timnah with his father and mother, and came to the vineyards of Timnah.
Now *to his* surprise, a young lion *came* roaring against him.
6 And the Spirit of the LORD came mightily upon him, and he tore the lion apart as one would have torn apart a young goat, though *he had* nothing in his hand. But he did not tell his father or his mother what he had done.
7 Then he went down and talked with the woman; and she pleased Samson well.
8 After some time, when he returned to get her, he turned aside to see the carcass of the lion. And behold, a swarm of bees and honey *were* in the carcass of the lion.
9 He took some of it in his hands and went along, eating. When he came to his father and mother, he gave *some* to them, and they also ate. But he did not tell them that he had taken the honey out of the carcass of the lion.
10 So his father went down to the woman. And Samson gave a feast there, for young men used to do so.
11 And it was so, when they saw him, that they brought thirty companions to be with him.
12 Then Samson said to them, "Let me pose a riddle to you. If you can correctly solve and explain it to me within the seven days of the feast, then I will give you thirty linen garments and thirty changes of clothing.

22 Literally *Camp of Dan* (compare 18:12)

13 "But if you cannot explain it to me, then you shall give me thirty linen garments and thirty changes of clothing." And they said to him, "Pose your riddle, that we may hear it."
14 So he said to them:

"Out of the eater
    came something to eat,
And out of the strong
    came something sweet."

Now for three days they could not explain the riddle.
15 So it came to pass on the seventh[23] day that they said to Samson's wife, "Entice your husband, that he may explain the riddle to us, or else we will burn you and your father's house with fire. Have you invited us in order to take what is ours? Is that not so?"
16 Then Samson's wife wept on him, and said, "You only hate me! You do not love me! You have posed a riddle to the sons of my people, but you have not explained it to me." And he said to her, "Look, I have not explained it to my father or my mother; so should I explain it to you?"
17 Now she had wept on him the seven days while their feast lasted. And it happened on the seventh day that he told her, because she pressed him so much. Then she explained the riddle to the sons of her people.
18 So the men of the city said to him on the seventh day before the sun went down:

"What is sweeter than honey?
And what is stronger than a lion?"

And he said to them:

"If you had not plowed with my heifer,
You would not have solved my riddle!"

19 Then the Spirit of the LORD came upon him mightily, and he went down to Ashkelon and killed thirty of their men, took their apparel, and gave the changes of clothing to those who had explained the riddle. So his anger was aroused, and he went back up to his father's house.
20 And Samson's wife was given to his companion, who had been his best man.

Samson Defeats the Philistines

15 And after a while, in the time of wheat harvest, it happened that Samson visited his wife with a young goat. And he said, "Let me go in to my wife, into her room." But her father would not permit him to go in.
2 Her father said, "I really thought that you thoroughly hated her; therefore I gave her to your companion. Is not her younger sister better than she? Please, take her instead."
3 And Samson said to them, "This time I shall be blameless regarding the Philistines if I harm them!"
4 Then Samson went and caught three hundred foxes; and he took torches, turned the foxes tail to tail, and put a torch between each pair of tails.
5 When he had set the torches on fire, he let the foxes go into the standing grain of the Philistines, and burned up both the shocks and the standing grain, as well as the vineyards and olive groves.
6 Then the Philistines said, "Who has done this?" And they answered, "Samson, the son-in-law of the Timnite, because he has taken his wife and given her to his companion." So the Philistines came up and burned her and her father with fire.
7 And Samson said to them, "Since you would do a thing like this, I will surely take revenge on you, and after that I will cease."
8 So he attacked them hip and thigh with a great slaughter; then he went down and dwelt in the cleft of the rock of Etam.
9 Now the Philistines went up, encamped in Judah, and deployed themselves against Lehi.
10 And the men of Judah said, "Why have you come up against us?" So they answered, "We have come up to arrest Samson, to do to him as he has done to us."
11 Then three thousand men of Judah went down to the cleft of the rock of Etam, and said to Samson, "Do you not know that the Philistines rule over us? What is this you have done to us?" And he said to them, "As they did to me, so I have done to them."
12 And they said to him, "We have come down to arrest you, that we may deliver

23 Some ancient authorities read fourth.

you into the hand of the Philistines."
Then Samson said to them, "Swear to me
that you will not kill me yourselves."
13 So they spoke to him, saying, "No,
but we will tie you securely and deliver
you into their hand; but we will surely
not kill you." And they bound him with
two new ropes and brought him up from
the rock.
14 When he came to Lehi, the Philistines
came shouting against him. Then the
Spirit of the LORD came mightily upon
him; and the ropes that *were* on his arms
became like flax that is burned with fire,
and his bonds broke loose from his
hands.
15 He found a fresh jawbone of a donkey, reached out his hand and took it,
and killed a thousand men with it.
16 Then Samson said:

"With the jawbone of a donkey,
  Heaps upon heaps,
With the jawbone of a donkey
  I have slain a thousand men!"

17 And so it was, when he had finished
speaking, that he threw the jawbone from
his hand, and called that place Ramath
Lehi.[24]
18 Then he became very thirsty; so he
cried out to the LORD and said, "You
have given this great deliverance by the
hand of Your servant; and now shall I die
of thirst and fall into the hand of the uncircumcised?"
19 So God split the hollow place that *is*
in Lehi,[25] and water came out, and he
drank; and his spirit returned, and he revived. Therefore he called its name En
Hakkore,[26] which is in Lehi to this day.
20 And he judged Israel twenty years in
the days of the Philistines.

Samson and Delilah

16 Then Samson went to Gaza and
saw a harlot there, and went in
to her.
2 *When* the Gazites *were told,* "Samson
has come here!" they surrounded *the
place* and lay in wait for him all night at
the gate of the city. They were quiet all
night, saying, "In the morning, when it is
daylight, we will kill him."
3 And Samson lay *low* till midnight;
then he arose at midnight, took hold of
the doors of the gate of the city and the
two gateposts, pulled them up, bar and
all, put *them* on his shoulders, and carried
them to the top of the hill that faces Hebron.
4 Now afterward it happened that he
loved a woman in the Valley of Sorek,
whose name *was* Delilah.
5 And the lords of the Philistines came
up to her and said to her, "Entice him,
and find out where his great strength *lies,*
and by what *means* we may overpower
him, that we may bind him to afflict him;
and every one of us will give you eleven
hundred *pieces* of silver."
6 So Delilah said to Samson, "Please
tell me where your great strength *lies,* and
with what you may be bound to afflict
you."
7 And Samson said to her, "If they bind
me with seven fresh bowstrings, not yet
dried, then I shall become weak, and be
like any *other* man."
8 So the lords of the Philistines brought
up to her seven fresh bowstrings, not yet
dried, and she bound him with them.
9 Now *there were men* lying in wait,
staying with her in the room. And she
said to him, "The Philistines *are* upon
you, Samson!" But he broke the bowstrings as a strand of yarn breaks when it
touches fire. So the secret of his strength
was not known.
10 Then Delilah said to Samson, "Look,
you have mocked me and told me lies.
Now, please tell me what you may be
bound with."
11 So he said to her, "If they bind me
securely with new ropes that have never
been used, then I shall become weak, and
be like any *other* man."
12 Therefore Delilah took new ropes and
bound him with them, and said to him,
"The Philistines *are* upon you, Samson!"
And *there were men* lying in wait, staying
in the room. But he broke them off his
arms like a thread.
13 Then Delilah said to Samson, "Until
now you have mocked me and told me
lies. Tell me what you may be bound
with." And he said to her, "If you weave
the seven locks of my head into the web
of the loom"—
14 So she wove *it* tightly with the batten
of the loom, and said to him, "The Philistines *are* upon you, Samson!" But he
awoke from his sleep, and pulled out the
batten and the web from the loom.

---

24 Literally *Jawbone Heights*   25 Literally *Jawbone* (compare verse 14)   26 Literally *Spring of the Caller*

15 Then she said to him, "How can you say, 'I love you,' when your heart *is* not with me? You have mocked me these three times, and have not told me where your great strength *lies*."

16 And it came to pass, when she pestered him daily with her words and pressed him, *so* that his soul was vexed to death,

17 that he told her all his heart, and said to her, "No razor has ever come upon my head, for I *have been* a Nazirite to God from my mother's womb. If I am shaven, then my strength will leave me, and I shall become weak, and be like any *other* man."

18 When Delilah saw that he had told her all his heart, she sent and called for the lords of the Philistines, saying, "Come up once more, for he has told me all his heart." So the lords of the Philistines came up to her and brought the money in their hand.

19 Then she lulled him to sleep on her knees, and called for a man and had him shave off the seven locks of his head. Then she began to torment him, and his strength left him.

20 And she said, "The Philistines *are* upon you, Samson!" So he awoke from his sleep, and said, "I will go out as before, at other times, and shake myself free!" But he did not know that the LORD had departed from him.

21 Then the Philistines took him and put out his eyes, and brought him down to Gaza. They bound him with bronze fetters, and he became a grinder in the prison.

22 However, the hair of his head began to grow again after it had been shaven.

Samson Dies with the Philistines

23 Now the lords of the Philistines gathered together to offer a great sacrifice to Dagon their god, and to rejoice. And they said:

"Our god has delivered into our hands Samson our enemy!"

24 When the people saw him, they praised their god; for they said:

"Our god has delivered into our hands our enemy,

The destroyer of our land, And the one who multiplied our dead."

25 So it happened, when their hearts were merry, that they said, "Call for Samson, that he may perform for us." So they called for Samson from the prison, and he performed for them. And they stationed him between the pillars.

26 Then Samson said to the lad who held him by the hand, "Let me feel the pillars which support the temple, so that I can lean on them."

27 Now the temple was full of men and women; all the lords of the Philistines *were* there. *In fact, there were* about three thousand men and women on the roof who watched while Samson performed.

28 Then Samson called to the LORD, saying, "O Lord GOD, remember me, I pray! Strengthen me, I pray, just this once, O God, that I may with one *blow* take vengeance on the Philistines for my two eyes!"

29 And Samson took hold of the two middle pillars which supported the temple, and he braced himself against them, one on his right and the other on his left.

30 Then Samson said, "Let me die with the Philistines!" And he pushed with *all* his might, and the temple fell on the lords and all the people who *were* in it. So the dead that he killed at his death were more than he had killed in his life.

31 And his brothers and all his father's household came down and took him, and brought *him* up and buried him between Zorah and Eshtaol in the tomb of his father Manoah. He had judged Israel twenty years.

Micah's Idolatry

17 Now there was a man from the mountains of Ephraim, whose name *was* Micah.

2 And he said to his mother, "The eleven hundred *shekels* of silver that were taken from you, and on which you put a curse, even saying it in my ears—here *is* the silver with me; I took it." And his mother said, "*May you be* blessed by the LORD, my son!"

3 So when he had returned the eleven hundred *shekels* of silver to his mother, his mother said, "I had wholly dedicated the silver from my hand to the LORD for my son, to make a carved image and a

molded image; now therefore, I will return it to you."

4 Thus he returned the silver to his mother. Then his mother took two hundred *shekels* of silver and gave them to the silversmith, and he made it into a carved image and a molded image; and they were in the house of Micah.

5 The man Micah had a shrine, and made an ephod and household idols;[27] and he consecrated one of his sons, who became his priest.

6 In those days *there was* no king in Israel; everyone did *what was* right in his own eyes.

7 Now there was a young man from Bethlehem in Judah, of the family of Judah; he *was* a Levite, and was sojourning there.

8 The man departed from the city of Bethlehem in Judah to sojourn wherever he could find *a place*. Then he came to the mountains of Ephraim, to the house of Micah, as he journeyed.

9 And Micah said to him, "Where do you come from?" So he said to him, "I *am* a Levite from Bethlehem in Judah, and I am on my way to find *a place* to sojourn."

10 Micah said to him, "Dwell with me, and be a father and a priest to me, and I will give you ten *shekels* of silver per year, a suit of clothes, and your sustenance." So the Levite went in.

11 Then the Levite was content to dwell with the man; and the young man became like one of his sons to him.

12 So Micah consecrated the Levite, and the young man became his priest, and lived in the house of Micah.

13 Then Micah said, "Now I know that the LORD will be good to me, since I have a Levite as priest!"

The Danites Adopt Micah's Idolatry

18 In those days *there was* no king in Israel. And in those days the tribe of the Danites was seeking an inheritance for itself to dwell in; for until that day *their whole* inheritance among the tribes of Israel had not *yet* fallen to them.

2 So the children of Dan sent five men of their family from their territory, men of valor from Zorah and Eshtaol, to spy out the land and search it. They said to them, "Go, search the land." So they went to the mountains of Ephraim, to the house of Micah, and lodged there.

3 While they *were* at the house of Micah, they recognized the voice of the young Levite. They turned aside and said to him, "Who brought you here? What are you doing in this *place*? What do you have here?"

4 He said to them, "Thus and so Micah did for me. He has hired me, and I have become his priest."

5 So they said to him, "Please inquire of God, that we may know whether the journey on which we go will be prosperous."

6 And the priest said to them, "Go in peace. *May* the presence of the LORD *be* with you on your way."

7 So the five men departed and went to Laish. They saw the people who *were* there, how they dwelt safely, in the manner of the Sidonians, quiet and secure. *There were* no rulers in the land who might put *them* to shame for anything. They *were* far from the Sidonians, and they had no ties with anyone.

8 Then the spies[28] came back to their brethren at Zorah and Eshtaol, and their brethren said to them, "What *is* your report?"

9 So they said, "Arise, let us go up against them. For we have seen the land, and indeed it *is* very good. *Would* you *do* nothing? Do not hesitate to go, *that you may* enter to possess the land.

10 "When you go, you will come to a secure people and a large land. For God has given it into your hands, a place where *there is* no lack of anything that *is* on the earth."

11 And six hundred men of the family of the Danites went from there, from Zorah and Eshtaol, armed with weapons of war.

12 Then they went up and encamped in Kirjath Jearim in Judah. (Therefore they call that place Mahaneh Dan[29] to this day. There *it is*, west of Kirjath Jearim.)

13 And they passed from there to the mountains of Ephraim, and came to the house of Micah.

14 Then the five men who had gone to spy out the country of Laish answered and said to their brethren, "Do you know that there are in these houses an ephod, household idols, a carved image, and a molded image? Now therefore, consider what you should do."

27 Hebrew *teraphim*   28 Literally *they*   29 Literally *Camp of Dan*

15 So they turned aside there, and came to the house of the young Levite man, *that is,* to the house of Micah, and greeted him.

16 The six hundred men armed with their weapons of war, who *were* of the children of Dan, stood by the entrance of the gate.

17 Then the five men who had gone to spy out the land went up, *and* entering there, they took the carved image, the ephod, the household idols, and the molded image. The priest stood at the entrance of the gate with the six hundred men *who were* armed with weapons of war.

18 When these went into Micah's house and took the graven image, the ephod, the household idols, and the molded image, the priest said to them, "What are you doing?"

19 And they said to him, "Be quiet, put your hand over your mouth, and come with us; be a father and a priest to us. *Is it* better for you to be a priest to the household of one man, or that you be a priest to a tribe and a family in Israel?"

20 So the priest's heart was glad; and he took the ephod, the household idols, and the carved image, and took his place among the people.

21 Then they turned and departed, and put the little ones, the livestock, and the goods in front of them.

22 When they were a good way from the house of Micah, the men who *were* in the houses near Micah's house gathered together and overtook the children of Dan.

23 And they called out to the children of Dan. So they turned around and said to Micah, "What ails you, that you have gathered such a company?"

24 So he said, "You have taken away my gods which I made, and the priest, and you have gone away. Now what more do I have? How can you say to me, 'What ails you?' "

25 And the children of Dan said to him, "Do not let your voice be heard among us, lest angry men fall upon you, and you lose your life, with the lives of your household!"

26 Then the children of Dan went their way. And when Micah saw that they *were* too strong for him, he turned and went back to his house.

Danites Settle in Laish

27 So they took *the things* Micah had made, and the priest who had belonged to him, and went to Laish, to a people *who were* quiet and secure; and they struck them with the edge of the sword and burned the city with fire.

28 *There was* no deliverer, because it *was* far from Sidon, and they had no ties with anyone. It was in the valley that belongs to Beth Rehob. So they rebuilt the city and dwelt there.

29 And they called the name of the city Dan, after the name of Dan their father, who was born to Israel. However, the name of the city formerly *was* Laish.

30 Then the children of Dan set up for themselves the carved image; and Jonathan the son of Gershom, the son of Manasseh,[30] and his sons were priests to the tribe of Dan until the day of the captivity of the land.

31 So they set up for themselves Micah's carved image which he made, all the time that the house of God was in Shiloh.

The Levite's Concubine

19 And it came to pass in those days, when *there was* no king in Israel, that there was a certain Levite sojourning in the remote mountains of Ephraim. He took for himself a concubine from Bethlehem in Judah.

2 But his concubine played the harlot against him, and went away from him to her father's house at Bethlehem in Judah, and was there four whole months.

3 Then her husband arose and went after her, to speak kindly to her *and* bring her back, having his servant and a couple of donkeys with him. So she brought him into her father's house; and when the father of the young woman saw him, he was glad to meet him.

4 Now his father-in-law, the young woman's father, detained him; and he stayed with him three days. So they ate and drank and lodged there.

5 Then it came to pass on the fourth day that they arose early in the morning, and he stood to depart; but the young woman's father said to his son-in-law, "Refresh your heart with a morsel of bread, and afterward go your way."

6 So they sat down, and the two of them ate and drank together. Then the young

30 Septuagint and Vulgate read *Moses.*

woman's father said to the man, "Please be content to stay all night, and let your heart be merry."

7 And when the man stood to depart, his father-in-law urged him; so he lodged there again.

8 Then he arose early in the morning on the fifth day to depart, but the young woman's father said, "Please refresh your heart." So they delayed until afternoon; and both of them ate.

9 And when the man stood to depart— he and his concubine and his servant— his father-in-law, the young woman's father, said to him, "Look, the day is now drawing toward evening; please spend the night. See, the day is coming to an end; lodge here, that your heart may be merry. Tomorrow go your way early, so that you may get home."

10 But the man was not willing to spend that night; so he rose and departed, and came to *a place* opposite Jebus (that *is*, Jerusalem). With him were the two saddled donkeys; his concubine *was* also with him.

11 They *were* near Jebus, and the day was far spent; and the servant said to his master, "Come, please, and let us turn aside into this city of the Jebusites and lodge in it."

12 But his master said to him, "We will not turn aside here into a city of foreigners, who *are* not of the children of Israel; we will go on to Gibeah."

13 So he said to his servant, "Come, let us draw near to one of these places, and spend the night in Gibeah or in Ramah."

14 And they passed by and went their way; and the sun went down on them near Gibeah, which belongs to Benjamin.

15 They turned aside there to go in to lodge in Gibeah. And when he went in, he sat down in the open square of the city, for no one would take them into *his* house to spend the night.

16 Just then an old man came in from his work in the field at evening, who also *was* from the mountains of Ephraim; he was sojourning in Gibeah, whereas the men of the place *were* Benjamites.

17 And when he raised his eyes, he saw the traveler in the open square of the city; and the old man said, "Where are you going, and where do you come from?"

18 So he said to him, "We *are* passing from Bethlehem in Judah toward the re-mote mountains of Ephraim; I *am* from there. I went to Bethlehem in Judah, *and now* I am going to the house of the LORD. But there *is* no one who will take me into his house,

19 "although we have both straw and fodder for our donkeys, and bread and wine for myself, for your maidservant, and for the young man *who is* with your servant; *there is* no lack of anything."

20 And the old man said, "Peace *be* with you! However, *let* all your needs *be* my responsibility; only do not spend the night in the open square."

21 So he brought him into his house, and gave fodder to the donkeys. And they washed their feet, and ate and drank.

Gibeah's Crime

22 *Now* as they were enjoying themselves, suddenly certain men of the city, perverted men,[31] surrounded the house *and* beat on the door. They spoke to the master of the house, the old man, saying, "Bring out the man who came to your house, that we may know him *carnally!*"

23 But the man, the master of the house, went out to them and said to them, "No, my brethren! I beg you, do not act *so* wickedly! Seeing this man has come into my house, do not commit this outrage.

24 "Look, *here is* my virgin daughter and the man's[32] concubine; let me bring them out now. Humble them, and do with them as you please; but to this man do not do such a vile thing!"

25 But the men would not heed him. So the man took his concubine and brought *her* out to them. And they knew her and abused her all night until morning; and when the day began to break, they let her go.

26 Then the woman came as the day was dawning, and fell down at the door of the man's house where her master *was*, till it was light.

27 When her master arose in the morning, and opened the doors of the house and went out to go his way, there was his concubine, fallen *at* the door of the house with her hands on the threshold.

28 And he said to her, "Get up and let us be going." But there was no answer. So the man lifted her onto the donkey; and the man got up and went to his place.

29 When he entered his house he took a knife, laid hold of his concubine, and dis-

---

31 Literally *sons of Belial* 32 Literally *his*

membered her into twelve pieces, limb by limb,[33] and sent her throughout all the territory of Israel.

30 And so it was that all who saw it said, "No such deed has been done or seen from the day that the children of Israel came up from the land of Egypt until this day. Consider it, take counsel, and speak up!"

Israel's War with the Benjamites

20 Then all the children of Israel came out, from Dan to Beersheba, as well as from the land of Gilead, and the congregation gathered together as one man before the LORD at Mizpah.

2 And the leaders of all the people, all the tribes of Israel, presented themselves in the assembly of the people of God, four hundred thousand foot soldiers who drew the sword.

3 (Now the children of Benjamin heard that the children of Israel had gone up to Mizpah.) Then the children of Israel said, "Tell us, how did this wicked deed happen?"

4 So the Levite, the husband of the woman who was murdered, answered and said, "My concubine and I went into Gibeah, which belongs to Benjamin, to spend the night.

5 "And the men of Gibeah rose against me, and surrounded the house at night because of me. They intended to kill me, but instead they ravished my concubine so that she died.

6 "So I took hold of my concubine, cut her in pieces, and sent her throughout all the territory of the inheritance of Israel, because they committed lewdness and outrage in Israel.

7 "Look! All of you are children of Israel; give your advice and counsel here and now!"

8 Then all the people arose as one man, saying, "None of us will go to his tent, nor will any of us turn back to his house;

9 "but now this is the thing which we will do to Gibeah: We will go up against it by lot.

10 "We will take ten men out of every hundred throughout all the tribes of Israel, a hundred out of every thousand, and a thousand out of every ten thousand, to make provisions for the people, that when they come to Gibeah in Benjamin,

they may repay all the vileness that they have done in Israel."

11 So all the men of Israel were gathered against the city, united together as one man.

12 Then the tribes of Israel sent men through all the tribe of Benjamin, saying, "What is this wickedness that has occurred among you?

13 "Now therefore, deliver up the men, the perverted men[34] who are in Gibeah, that we may put them to death and remove the evil from Israel!" But the children of Benjamin would not listen to the voice of their brethren, the children of Israel.

14 Instead, the children of Benjamin gathered together from their cities to Gibeah, to go to battle against the children of Israel.

15 And from their cities at that time the children of Benjamin numbered twenty-six thousand men who drew the sword, besides the inhabitants of Gibeah, who numbered seven hundred select men.

16 Among all this people there were seven hundred select men who were left-handed; every one could sling a stone at a hair's breadth and not miss.

17 Now besides Benjamin, the men of Israel numbered four hundred thousand men who drew the sword; all of these were men of war.

18 And the children of Israel arose and went up to the house of God[35] to ask counsel of God. They said, "Which of us shall go up first to battle against the children of Benjamin?" And the LORD said, "Judah shall go up first."

19 So the children of Israel rose in the morning and encamped against Gibeah.

20 And the men of Israel went out to battle against Benjamin, and the men of Israel put themselves in battle array to fight against them at Gibeah.

21 Then the children of Benjamin came out of Gibeah, and on that day cut down to the ground twenty-two thousand men of the Israelites.

22 And the people, that is, the men of Israel, encouraged themselves and again formed the battle line at the place where they had put themselves in array on the first day.

23 Then the children of Israel went up and wept before the LORD until evening, and asked counsel of the LORD, saying,

---

33 Literally with her bones   34 Literally sons of Belial   35 Hebrew Bethel

"Shall I again draw near for battle against the children of my brother Benjamin?" And the LORD said, "Go up against him."

24 So the children of Israel approached the children of Benjamin on the second day.

25 And Benjamin went out against them from Gibeah on the second day, and cut down to the ground eighteen thousand more of the children of Israel; all these drew the sword.

26 Then all the children of Israel, that is, all the people, went up and came to the house of God[36] and wept. They sat there before the LORD and fasted that day until evening; and they offered burnt offerings and peace offerings before the LORD.

27 So the children of Israel inquired of the LORD (the ark of the covenant of God *was* there in those days,

28 and Phinehas the son of Eleazar, the son of Aaron, stood before it in those days), saying, "Shall I yet again go out to battle against the children of my brother Benjamin, or shall I cease?" And the LORD said, "Go up, for tomorrow I will deliver them into your hand."

29 Then Israel set men in ambush all around Gibeah.

30 And the children of Israel went up against the children of Benjamin on the third day, and put themselves in battle array against Gibeah as at the other times.

31 So the children of Benjamin went out against the people, *and* were drawn away from the city. They began to strike down *and* kill some of the people, as at the other times, in the highways (one of which goes up to Bethel and the other to Gibeah) and in the field, about thirty men of Israel.

32 And the children of Benjamin said, "They *are* struck down before us, as at first." But the children of Israel said, "Let us flee and draw them away from the city to the highways."

33 So all the men of Israel rose from their place and put themselves in battle array at Baal Tamar. Then Israel's men in ambush burst forth from their position in the plain of Geba.

34 And ten thousand select men from all Israel came against Gibeah, and the battle was fierce. But the Benjamites[37] did not know that disaster *was* upon them.

35 The LORD defeated Benjamin before Israel. And the children of Israel destroyed that day twenty-five thousand one hundred Benjamites; all these drew the sword.

36 So the children of Benjamin saw that they were defeated. The men of Israel had given ground to the Benjamites, because they relied on the men in ambush whom they had set against Gibeah.

37 And the men in ambush quickly rushed upon Gibeah; the men in ambush spread out and struck the whole city with the edge of the sword.

38 Now the appointed signal between the men of Israel and the men in ambush was that they would make a great cloud of smoke rise up from the city,

39 whereupon the men of Israel would turn in battle. Now Benjamin had begun to strike *and* kill about thirty of the men of Israel. For they said, "Surely they are defeated before us, as *in* the first battle."

40 But when the cloud began to rise from the city in a column of smoke, the Benjamites looked behind them, and there was the whole city going up *in smoke* to heaven.

41 And when the men of Israel turned back, the men of Benjamin panicked, for they saw that disaster had come upon them.

42 Therefore they turned *their backs* before the men of Israel in the direction of the wilderness; but the battle overtook them, and whoever *had come* out of the cities they destroyed in their midst.

43 They surrounded the Benjamites *and* chased them, *and* easily trampled them down as far as the front of Gibeah toward the east.

44 And eighteen thousand men of Benjamin fell; all these *were* men of valor.

45 Then they[38] turned and fled toward the wilderness to the rock of Rimmon; and they cut down five thousand of them on the highways. Then they pursued them relentlessly up to Gidom, and killed two thousand of them.

46 So all who fell of Benjamin that day were twenty-five thousand men who drew the sword; all these *were* men of valor.

47 But six hundred men turned and fled toward the wilderness to the rock of Rimmon, and they stayed at the rock of Rimmon for four months.

48 And the men of Israel turned back

---

36 Hebrew *Bethel*   37 Literally *they*   38 Septuagint reads *the rest.*

against the children of Benjamin, and struck them down with the edge of the sword—from *every* city, men and beasts, all who were found. They also set fire to all the cities they came to.

Wives Provided for the Benjamites

21 Now the men of Israel had sworn an oath at Mizpah, saying, "None of us shall give his daughter to Benjamin as a wife."

2 Then the people came to the house of God,[39] and remained there before God till evening. They lifted up their voices and wept bitterly,

3 and said, "O LORD God of Israel, why has this come to pass in Israel, that today there should be one tribe *missing* in Israel?"

4 So it was, on the next morning, that the people rose early and built an altar there, and offered burnt offerings and peace offerings.

5 The children of Israel said, "Who *is there* among all the tribes of Israel who did not come up with the assembly to the LORD?" For they had made a great oath concerning anyone who had not come up to the LORD at Mizpah, saying, "He shall surely be put to death."

6 And the children of Israel grieved for Benjamin their brother, and said, "One tribe is cut off from Israel today.

7 "What shall we do for wives for those who remain, seeing we have sworn by the LORD that we will not give them our daughters as wives?"

8 And they said, "What one *is there* from the tribes of Israel who did not come up to Mizpah to the LORD?" And, in fact, no one had come to the camp from Jabesh Gilead to the assembly.

9 For when the people were counted, indeed, not one of the inhabitants of Jabesh Gilead *was* there.

10 So the congregation sent out there twelve thousand of their most valiant men, and commanded them, saying, "Go and strike the inhabitants of Jabesh Gilead with the edge of the sword, including the women and children.

11 "And this *is* the thing that you shall do: You shall utterly destroy every male, and every woman who has known a man intimately."

12 So they found among the inhabitants of Jabesh Gilead four hundred young virgins who had not known a man intimately; and they brought them to the camp at Shiloh, which is in the land of Canaan.

13 Then the whole congregation sent *word* to the children of Benjamin who *were* at the rock of Rimmon, and announced peace to them.

14 So Benjamin came back at that time, and they gave them the women whom they had saved alive of the women of Jabesh Gilead; and yet they had not found enough peace for them.

15 And the people grieved for Benjamin, because the LORD had made a void in the tribes of Israel.

16 Then the elders of the congregation said, "What shall we do for wives for those who remain, since the women of Benjamin have been destroyed?"

17 And they said, "*There must be* an inheritance for the survivors of Benjamin, that a tribe may not be destroyed from Israel.

18 "However, we cannot give them wives from our daughters, for the children of Israel have sworn an oath, saying, 'Cursed *be* the one who gives a wife to Benjamin.' "

19 Then they said, "In fact, *there is* a yearly feast of the LORD in Shiloh, which *is* north of Bethel, on the east side of the highway that goes up from Bethel to Shechem, and south of Lebonah."

20 Therefore they instructed the children of Benjamin, saying, "Go, lie in wait in the vineyards,

21 "and watch; and just when the daughters of Shiloh come out to perform their dances, then come out from the vineyards, and every man catch a wife for himself from the daughters of Shiloh; then go to the land of Benjamin.

22 "Then it shall be, when their fathers or their brothers come to us to complain, that we will say to them, 'Be kind to them for our sakes, because we did not take a wife for any of them in the war; for *it is* not *as though* you have given the *young women* to them at this time, making yourselves guilty of your oath.' "

23 And the children of Benjamin did so; they took *themselves* enough wives for their number from those who danced,

39 Hebrew *Bethel*

whom they caught. Then they went and returned to their inheritance, and they rebuilt the cities and dwelt in them.
24 So the children of Israel departed from there at that time, every man to his tribe and family; they went out from there, every man to his inheritance.
25 In those days *there was* no king in Israel; everyone did *what was* right in his own eyes.

Introduction to Ruth

Ruth is the story of an exceptionally positive woman committed to trusting in God. Ruth means "friend," and she was dedicated to a rare friendship with her mother-in-law, Naomi.

Robbed by the death of her husband of ten years, Ruth was left childless and in poverty. Yet nowhere in the book is there any record of self-pity. Rather, she exuded a positive, unselfish devotion to Naomi as she left her homeland of Moab and journeyed to the foreign land of Israel. Having become a worshiper of the true God of her Hebrew husband, Ruth avoided the temptation of yielding to her comfortable surroundings and returning to the worship of false gods. Knowing that God sees the end from the beginning, Ruth calmly submitted herself to God's will in a foreign setting.

Entreat me not to leave you
Or to turn back from following after you;
For wherever you go, I will go;
And wherever you lodge, I will lodge;
Your people *shall be* my people,
And your God, my God.
Where you die, I will die,
And there will I be buried.
The LORD do so to me, and more also,
If *anything but* death parts you and me.

(Ruth 1:16, 17)

The widowed, self-reliant Ruth took on the positive quality of doing what she could, where she was, and with what she had. Daily she gleaned in the fields of the wealthy landowner, Boaz. She stood out as a positive person who joyfully did her work unashamed.

Boaz noticed Ruth among all others and was impressed with her diligence and beauty. In a beautiful love story, Boaz married Ruth, lifting her out of obscurity, replacing her rags with riches, and elevating her from poverty to plenty.

Ruth, a woman who withstood hard times with faith, received the blessings she trusted God would provide. She even became the great-grandmother of King David and was in the lineage of the Messiah (Matt. 1:5).

The Book of
Ruth

Elimelech's Family Goes to Moab

NOW it came to pass, in the days when the judges ruled, that there was a famine in the land. And a certain man of Bethlehem, Judah, went to sojourn in the country of Moab, he and his wife and his two sons.
2 The name of the man *was* Elimelech, the name of his wife *was* Naomi, and the names of his two sons *were* Mahlon and Chilion—Ephrathites of Bethlehem, Judah. And they went to the country of Moab and remained there.
3 Then Elimelech, Naomi's husband, died; and she was left, and her two sons.
4 Now they took wives of the women of Moab: the name of the one *was* Orpah, and the name of the other Ruth. And they dwelt there about ten years.
5 Then both Mahlon and Chilion also died; so the woman survived her two sons and her husband.

Naomi Returns with Ruth

6 Then she arose with her daughters-in-law that she might return from the country of Moab, for she had heard in the country of Moab that the LORD had visited His people in giving them bread.
7 Therefore she went out from the place where she was, and her two daughters-in-law with her; and they went on the way to return to the land of Judah.
8 And Naomi said to her two daughters-in-law, "Go, return each to her mother's house. The LORD deal kindly with you, as you have dealt with the dead and with me.
9 "The LORD grant that you may find rest, each in the house of her husband." Then she kissed them, and they lifted up their voices and wept.
10 And they said to her, "Surely we will return with you to your people."
11 But Naomi said, "Turn back, my daughters; why will you go with me? *Are* there still sons in my womb, that they may be your husbands?
12 "Turn back, my daughters, go *your*
way; for I am too old to have a husband. If I should say I have hope, *even if* I should have a husband tonight and should also bear sons,
13 "would you wait for them till they were grown? Would you restrain yourselves from having husbands? No, my daughters; for it grieves me very much for your sakes that the hand of the LORD has gone out against me!"
14 Then they lifted up their voices and wept again; and Orpah kissed her mother-in-law, but Ruth clung to her.
15 And she said, "Look, your sister-in-law has gone back to her people and to her gods; return after your sister-in-law."
16 But Ruth said:

"Entreat me not to leave you,
  Or to turn back
    from following after you;
  For wherever you go, I will go;
  And wherever you lodge, I will lodge;
  Your people *shall be* my people,
  And your God, my God.
17 Where you die, I will die,
  And there will I be buried.
  The LORD do so to me, and more also,
  If *anything but* death
    parts you and me."

18 When she saw that she was determined to go with her, she stopped speaking to her.
19 Now the two of them went until they came to Bethlehem. And it happened, when they had come to Bethlehem, that all the city was excited because of them; and the women said, "*Is* this Naomi?"
20 So she said to them, "Do not call me Naomi;[1] call me Mara,[2] for the Almighty has dealt very bitterly with me.
21 "I went out full, and the LORD has brought me home again empty. Why do you call me Naomi, since the LORD has testified against me, and the Almighty has afflicted me?"
22 So Naomi returned, and Ruth the Moabitess her daughter-in-law with her, who returned from the country of Moab.

---

1 Literally *Pleasant* 2 Literally *Bitter*

Now they came to Bethlehem at the beginning of barley harvest.

Ruth Meets Boaz

2 And Naomi had a kinsman of her husband's, a man of great wealth, of the family of Elimelech; his name *was* Boaz.

2 So Ruth the Moabitess said to Naomi, "Please let me go to the field, and glean heads of grain after *him* in whose sight I may find favor." And she said to her, "Go, my daughter."

3 Then she left, and went and gleaned in the field after the reapers. And she happened to come to the part of the field *belonging* to Boaz, who *was* of the family of Elimelech.

4 Now behold, Boaz came from Bethlehem, and said to the reapers, "The LORD *be* with you!" And they answered him, "The LORD bless you!"

5 Then Boaz said to his servant who was in charge of the reapers, "Whose young woman *is* this?"

6 So the servant who was in charge of the reapers answered and said, "It *is* the young Moabite woman who came back with Naomi from the country of Moab.

7 "And she said, 'Please let me glean and gather after the reapers among the sheaves.' So she came and has continued from morning until now, though she rested a little in the house."

8 Then Boaz said to Ruth, "You will listen, my daughter, will you not? Do not go to glean in another field, nor go from here, but stay close by my young women.

9 "*Let* your eyes *be* on the field which they reap, and go after them. Have I not commanded the young men not to touch you? And when you are thirsty, go to the vessels and drink from what the young men have drawn."

10 Then she fell on her face, bowed down to the ground, and said to him, "Why have I found favor in your eyes, that you should take notice of me, since I *am* a foreigner?"

11 And Boaz answered and said to her, "It has been fully reported to me, all that you have done for your mother-in-law since the death of your husband, and *how* you have left your father and your mother and the land of your birth, and have come to a people whom you did not know before.

12 "The LORD repay your work, and a full reward be given you by the LORD God of Israel, under whose wings you have come for refuge."

13 Then she said, "Let me find favor in your sight, my lord; for you have comforted me, and have spoken kindly to your maidservant, though I am not like one of your maidservants."

14 Now Boaz said to her at mealtime, "Come here, and eat of the bread, and dip your piece of bread in the vinegar." So she sat beside the reapers, and he passed parched *grain* to her; and she ate and was satisfied, and kept some back.

15 And when she rose up to glean, Boaz commanded his young men, saying, "Let her glean even among the sheaves, and do not reproach her.

16 "Also let *some grain* from the bundles fall purposely for her; leave *it* that she may glean, and do not rebuke her."

17 So she gleaned in the field until evening, and beat out what she had gleaned, and it was about an ephah of barley.

18 Then she took *it* up and went into the city, and her mother-in-law saw what she had gleaned. So she brought out and gave to her what she had kept back after she had been satisfied.

19 And her mother-in-law said to her, "Where have you gleaned today? And where did you work? Blessed be the one who took notice of you." So she told her mother-in-law with whom she had worked, and said, "The man's name with whom I worked today *is* Boaz."

20 Then Naomi said to her daughter-in-law, "Blessed *be* he of the LORD, who has not forsaken His kindness to the living and the dead!" And Naomi said to her, "The man *is* a relative of ours, one of our near kinsmen."

21 Then Ruth the Moabitess said, "He also said to me, 'You shall stay close by my young men until they have finished all my harvest.'"

22 And Naomi said to Ruth her daughter-in-law, "*It is* good, my daughter, that you go out with his young women, and that people do not meet you in any other field."

23 So she stayed close by the young women of Boaz, to glean until the end of barley harvest and wheat harvest; and she dwelt with her mother-in-law.

Ruth's Redemption Assured

3 Then Naomi her mother-in-law said to her, "My daughter, shall I not seek security for you, that it may be well with you?
2 "Now Boaz, whose young women you were with, *is he* not our kinsman? In fact, he is winnowing barley tonight at the threshing floor.
3 "Therefore wash yourself and anoint yourself, put on your *best* garment and go down to the threshing floor; *but* do not make yourself known to the man until he has finished eating and drinking.
4 "Then it shall be, when he lies down, that you shall notice the place where he lies; and you shall go in, uncover his feet, and lie down; and he will tell you what you should do."
5 And she said to her, "All that you say to me I will do."
6 So she went down to the threshing floor and did according to all that her mother-in-law instructed her.
7 And after Boaz had eaten and drunk, and his heart was cheerful, he went to lie down at the end of the heap of grain; and she came softly, uncovered his feet, and lay down.
8 Now it happened at midnight that the man was startled, and turned himself; and there, a woman was lying at his feet.
9 And he said, "Who *are* you?" So she answered, "I *am* Ruth, your maidservant. Take your maidservant under your wing,[3] for you are a near kinsman."
10 Then he said, "Blessed *are* you of the LORD, my daughter! For you have shown more kindness at the end than at the beginning, in that you did not go after young men, whether poor or rich.
11 "And now, my daughter, do not fear. I will do for you all that you request, for all the people of my town know that you *are* a virtuous woman.
12 "Now it is true that I *am your* near kinsman; however, there is a kinsman nearer than I.
13 "Stay this night, and in the morning it shall be *that* if he will perform the duty of a near kinsman for you—good; let him do it. But if he does not want to perform the duty for you, then I will perform the duty for you, *as* the LORD lives! Lie down until morning."

14 So she lay at his feet until morning, and she arose before one could recognize another. Then he said, "Do not let it be known that the woman came to the threshing floor."
15 Also he said, "Bring the shawl that *is* on you and hold it." And when she held it, he measured six *ephahs* of barley, and laid *it* on her. Then she[4] went into the city.
16 So when she came to her mother-in-law, she said, "*Is* that you, my daughter?" Then she told her all that the man had done for her.
17 And she said, "These six *ephahs* of barley he gave me; for he said to me, 'Do not go empty-handed to your mother-in-law.' "
18 Then she said, "Sit still, my daughter, until you know how the matter will turn out; for the man will not rest until he has concluded the matter this day."

Boaz Redeems Ruth

4 Now Boaz went up to the gate and sat down there; and behold, the near kinsman of whom Boaz had spoken came by. So Boaz said, "Come aside, friend,[5] sit down here." So he came aside and sat down.
2 And he took ten men of the elders of the city, and said, "Sit down here." So they sat down.
3 Then he said to the near kinsman, "Naomi, who has come back from the country of Moab, sold the piece of land which *belonged* to our brother Elimelech.
4 "And I thought to inform you, saying, 'Buy *it* back in the presence of the inhabitants and the elders of my people. If you will redeem *it,* redeem *it;* but if you will not redeem *it, then* tell me, that I may know; for *there is* no one but you to redeem *it,* and I *am* next after you.' " And he said, "I will redeem *it.*"
5 Then Boaz said, "On the day you buy the field from the hand of Naomi, you must also buy *it* from Ruth the Moabitess, the wife of the dead, to raise up the name of the dead on his inheritance."
6 And the near kinsman said, "I cannot redeem *it* for myself, lest I ruin my own inheritance. You redeem my right of redemption for yourself, for I cannot redeem *it.*"

3 Or *spread the corner of your garment over your maidservant*
4 Masoretic Text reads *he;* some Hebrew manuscripts, Syriac, and Vulgate read *she.*
5 Hebrew *peloni almoni;* literally *so and so*

7 Now this *was the custom* in former times in Israel concerning redeeming and exchanging, to confirm anything: one man took off his sandal and gave *it* to the other, and this *was* an attestation in Israel.

8 Therefore the near kinsman said to Boaz, "Buy *it* for yourself." So he took off his sandal.

9 And Boaz said to the elders and *to* all the people, "You *are* witnesses this day that I have bought all that was Elimelech's, and all that *was* Chilion's and Mahlon's, from the hand of Naomi.

10 "Moreover, Ruth the Moabitess, the wife of Mahlon, I have acquired as my wife, to raise up the name of the dead on his inheritance, that the name of the dead may not be cut off from among his brethren and from the gate of his place. You *are* witnesses this day."

11 And all the people who *were* at the gate, and the elders, said, "*We are* witnesses. The LORD make the woman who is coming to your house like Rachel and Leah, the two who built the house of Israel; and may you prosper in Ephrathah and be famous in Bethlehem.

12 "May your house be like the house of Perez, whom Tamar bore to Judah, because of the offspring which the LORD will give you from this young woman."

6 Hebrew *Salmah*

Descendants of Boaz and Ruth

13 So Boaz took Ruth and she became his wife; and when he went in to her, the LORD gave her conception, and she bore a son.

14 Then the women said to Naomi, "Blessed *be* the LORD, who has not left you this day without a near kinsman; and may his name be famous in Israel!

15 "And may he be to you a restorer of life and a nourisher of your old age; for your daughter-in-law, who loves you, who is better to you than seven sons, has borne him."

16 Then Naomi took the child and laid him on her bosom, and became a nurse to him.

17 Also the neighbor women gave him a name, saying, "There is a son born to Naomi." And they called his name Obed. He *is* the father of Jesse, the father of David.

18 Now this *is* the genealogy of Perez: Perez begot Hezron;

19 Hezron begot Ram, and Ram begot Amminadab;

20 Amminadab begot Nahshon, and Nahshon begot Salmon;[6]

21 Salmon begot Boaz, and Boaz begot Obed;

22 Obed begot Jesse, and Jesse begot David.

Introduction to First Samuel

First Samuel records the reigns of the first two kings of Israel—Saul and David. This represented a major change in the leadership of the nation from a theocracy under Moses, Joshua, and the Judges, to a monarchy of God's appointed men. Written by Samuel, David, Nathan, and Gad between 1150 and 950 B.C., First Samuel may have been put in its final form at a later date.

Through the life of David we see the outstanding positive qualities that made him a great leader chosen by God to rule the people. David was a young boy tending his father's flocks near Bethlehem when the prophet Samuel announced boldly that this lad was God's anointed. Immediately David rose to the task and challenged the Philistine giant, Goliath. With faith, he knew that God was bigger than his problem. When Saul became jealous of David's great victory and tried to kill him, the young man believed God was in control, and so he would not fight King Saul.

David was committed to Saul's son, Jonathan, and won his allegiance. Refusing to strike back at Saul, David demonstrated great control over his emotions. After Saul's death, David was sorrowful at the loss of Israel's first king.

From David's reactions in times of crises, we gain great insight into his character. David was loving, forgiving, brave, bold, intelligent, godly, and sacrificing. He put his life on the line for others. But most of all, David was a possibility thinker. He took chances and took charge!

The source of David's strength and courage is probably best revealed in one of his many psalms:

> The LORD *is* my light and my salvation;
> Whom shall I fear?
> The LORD *is* the strength of my life;
> Of whom shall I be afraid?
> One *thing* I have desired of the LORD,
> That will I seek:
> That I may dwell in the house of the LORD
> All the days of my life.

(Ps. 27:1, 4)

The First Book of
Samuel

The Family of Elkanah

NOW there was a certain man of Ramathaim Zophim, of the mountains of Ephraim, and his name was Elkanah the son of Jeroham, the son of Elihu,[1] the son of Tohu,[2] the son of Zuph, an Ephraimite.

2 And he had two wives: the name of one was Hannah, and the name of the other Peninnah. Peninnah had children, but Hannah had no children.

3 This man went up from his city yearly to worship and sacrifice to the LORD of hosts in Shiloh. Also the two sons of Eli, Hophni and Phinehas, the priests of the LORD, were there.

4 And whenever the time came for Elkanah to make an offering, he would give portions to Peninnah his wife and to all her sons and daughters.

5 But to Hannah he would give a double portion, for he loved Hannah, although the LORD had closed her womb.

6 And her rival also provoked her severely, to make her miserable, because the LORD had closed her womb.

7 So it was, year by year, when she went up to the house of the LORD, that she provoked her; therefore she wept and did not eat.

Hannah's Vow

8 Then Elkanah her husband said to her, "Hannah, why do you weep? Why do you not eat? And why is your heart grieved? Am I not better to you than ten sons?"

9 So Hannah arose after they had finished eating and drinking in Shiloh. Now Eli the priest was sitting on the seat by the doorpost of the tabernacle[3] of the LORD.

10 And she was in bitterness of soul, and prayed to the LORD and wept in anguish.

11 Then she made a vow and said, "O LORD of hosts, if You will indeed look on the affliction of your maidservant and remember me, and not forget your maidservant, but will give your maidservant a male child, then I will give him to the LORD all the days of his life, and no razor shall come upon his head."

12 And it happened, as she continued praying before the LORD, that Eli watched her mouth.

13 Now Hannah spoke in her heart; only her lips moved, but her voice was not heard. Therefore Eli thought she was drunk.

14 So Eli said to her, "How long will you be drunk? Put your wine away from you!"

15 And Hannah answered and said, "No, my lord, I am a woman of sorrowful spirit. I have drunk neither wine nor intoxicating drink, but have poured out my soul before the LORD.

16 "Do not consider your maidservant a wicked woman,[4] for out of the abundance of my complaint and grief I have spoken until now."

17 Then Eli answered and said, "Go in peace, and the God of Israel grant your petition which you have asked of Him."

18 And she said, "Let your maidservant find favor in your sight." So the woman went her way and ate, and her face was no longer sad.

Samuel Is Born and Dedicated

19 Then they rose early in the morning and worshiped before the LORD, and returned and came to their house at Ramah. And Elkanah knew Hannah his wife, and the LORD remembered her.

20 So it came to pass in the process of time that Hannah conceived and bore a son, and called his name Samuel,[5] saying, "Because I have asked for him from the LORD."

21 And the man Elkanah and all his house went up to offer to the LORD the yearly sacrifice and his vow.

22 But Hannah did not go up, for she said to her husband, "I will not go up until the child is weaned; then I will take him, that he may appear before the LORD and remain there forever."

---

1 Spelled Eliel in 1 Chronicles 6:34   2 Spelled Toah in 1 Chronicles 6:34   3 Hebrew hekal, palace or temple
4 Literally daughter of Belial   5 Literally Heard by God

23 And Elkanah her husband said to her, "Do what seems best to you; wait until you have weaned him. Only let the LORD establish His word." So the woman stayed and nursed her son until she had weaned him.
24 Now when she had weaned him, she took him up with her, with three bulls,[6] one ephah of flour, and a skin of wine, and brought him to the house of the LORD in Shiloh. And the child was young.
25 Then they slaughtered a bull, and brought the child to Eli.
26 And she said, "O my lord! As your soul lives, my lord, I am the woman who stood by you here, praying to the LORD.
27 "For this child I prayed, and the LORD has granted me my petition which I asked of Him.
28 "Therefore I also have lent him to the LORD; as long as he lives he shall be lent to the LORD." So they worshiped the LORD there.

Hannah's Prayer

2 And Hannah prayed and said:

"My heart rejoices in the LORD;
My horn[7] is exalted in the LORD.
I smile at my enemies,
Because I rejoice in Your salvation.

2 "There is none holy like the LORD,
For there is none besides You,
Nor is there any rock like our God.

3 "Talk no more so very proudly;
Let no arrogance
come from your mouth,
For the LORD is
the God of knowledge;
And by Him actions are weighed.

4 "The bows of the mighty men
are broken,
And those who stumbled
are girded with strength.
5 Those who were full
have hired themselves out for bread,
And those who were hungry
have ceased to hunger.
Even the barren has borne seven,
And she who has many children has
become feeble.

6 "The LORD kills and makes alive;
He brings down to the grave
and brings up.

7 The LORD makes poor and makes rich;
He brings low and lifts up.
8 He raises the poor from the dust
And lifts the beggar
from the ash heap,
To set them among princes
And make them inherit
the throne of glory.

"For the pillars of the earth
are the LORD'S,
And He has set the world upon them.
9 He will guard the feet of His saints,
But the wicked shall be silent
in darkness.

"For by strength no man shall prevail.
10 The adversaries of the LORD
shall be broken in pieces;
From heaven He will thunder
against them.
The LORD will judge
the ends of the earth.

"He will give strength to His king,
And exalt the horn of His anointed."

11 Then Elkanah went to his house at Ramah. But the child ministered to the LORD before Eli the priest.

The Wicked Sons of Eli

12 Now the sons of Eli were corrupt;[8] they did not know the LORD.
13 And the priests' custom with the people was that when any man offered a sacrifice, the priest's servant would come with a three-pronged fleshhook in his hand while the meat was boiling.
14 Then he would thrust it into the pan, or kettle, or caldron, or pot; and the priest would take for himself all that the fleshhook brought up. So they did in Shiloh to all the Israelites who came there.
15 Also, before they burned the fat, the priest's servant would come and say to the man who sacrificed, "Give meat for roasting to the priest, for he will not take boiled meat from you, but raw."
16 And if the man said to him, "They should really burn the fat first; then you may take as much as your heart desires," he would then answer him, "No, but you must give it to me now; and if not, I will take it by force."
17 Therefore the sin of the young men was very great before the LORD, for men abhorred the offering of the LORD.

---

6 Dead Sea Scrolls, Septuagint, and Syriac read a three-year-old bull.
7 That is, strength   8 Literally sons of Belial

Samuel's Childhood Ministry

18 But Samuel ministered before the LORD, *even as* a child, wearing a linen ephod.

19 Moreover his mother used to make him a little robe, and bring *it* to him year by year when she came up with her husband to offer the yearly sacrifice.

20 And Eli would bless Elkanah and his wife, and say, "The LORD give you descendants from this woman for the loan that was lent to the LORD." Then they would go to their own home.

21 And the LORD visited Hannah, so that she conceived and bore three sons and two daughters. Meanwhile the child Samuel grew before the LORD.

Prophecy Against Eli's Household

22 Now Eli was very old; and he heard everything his sons did to all Israel, and how they lay with the women who assembled at the door of the tabernacle of meeting.

23 So he said to them, "Why do you do such things? For I hear of your evil dealings from all the people.

24 "No, my sons! For *it is* not a good report that I hear. You make the LORD's people transgress.

25 "If one man sins against another, God will judge him. But if a man sins against the LORD, who will intercede for him?" Nevertheless they did not heed the voice of their father, because the LORD desired to kill them.

26 And the child Samuel grew in stature, and in favor both with the LORD and men.

27 Then a man of God came to Eli and said to him, "Thus says the LORD: 'Did I not clearly reveal Myself to the house of your father when they were in Egypt in Pharaoh's house?

28 'Did I not choose him out of all the tribes of Israel *to be* My priest, to offer upon My altar, to burn incense, and to wear an ephod before Me? And did I not give to the house of your father all the offerings of the children of Israel made by fire?

29 'Why do you kick at My sacrifice and My offering which I have commanded *in My* habitation, and honor your sons more than Me, to make yourselves fat with the best of all the offerings of Israel My people?'

30 "Therefore the LORD God of Israel says: 'I said indeed *that* your house and the house of your father would walk before Me forever'; but now the LORD says: 'Far be it from Me; for those who honor Me I will honor, and those who despise Me shall be lightly esteemed.

31 'Behold, the days are coming that I will cut off your arm and the arm of your father's house, so that there will not be an old man in your house.

32 'And you will see an enemy *in My* habitation, *despite* all the good which God does for Israel. And there shall not be an old man in your house forever.

33 'But any of your men *whom* I do not cut off from My altar shall consume your eyes and grieve your heart. And all the descendants of your house shall die in the flower of their age.

34 'Now this *shall be* a sign to you that will come upon your two sons, on Hophni and Phinehas: in one day they shall die, both of them.

35 'Then I will raise up for Myself a faithful priest *who* shall do according to what *is* in My heart and in My mind. I will build him a sure house, and he shall walk before My anointed forever.

36 'And it shall come to pass that everyone who is left in your house will come *and* bow down to him for a piece of silver and a morsel of bread, and say, "Please, put me in one of the priestly positions, that I may eat a piece of bread." ' "

Samuel's First Prophecy

3 Then the boy Samuel ministered to the LORD before Eli. And the word of the LORD was rare in those days; *there was* no widespread revelation.

2 And it came to pass at that time, while Eli *was* lying down in his place, and when his eyes had begun to grow so dim that he could not see,

3 and before the lamp of God went out in the tabernacle[9] of the LORD where the ark of God *was*, and while Samuel was lying down *to sleep*,

4 that the LORD called Samuel. And he answered, "Here I am!"

5 So he ran to Eli and said, "Here I am, for you called me." And he said, "I did not call; lie down again." And he went and lay down.

6 And the LORD called yet again, "Samuel!" So Samuel arose and went to Eli,

9 Hebrew *hekal*, palace or temple

and said, "Here I am, for you called me."
And he answered, "I did not call, my son;
lie down again."
7 (Now Samuel did not yet know the
LORD, nor was the word of the LORD yet
revealed to him.)
8 And the LORD called Samuel again
the third time. Then he arose and went
to Eli, and said, "Here I am, for you did
call me." Then Eli perceived that the
LORD had called the boy.
9 Therefore Eli said to Samuel, "Go, lie
down; and it shall be, if He calls you, that
you must say, 'Speak, LORD, for Your
servant hears.' " So Samuel went and lay
down in his place.
10 Then the LORD came and stood and
called as at other times, "Samuel! Samuel!" And Samuel answered, "Speak, for
Your servant hears."
11 Then the LORD said to Samuel: "Behold, I will do something in Israel at
which both ears of everyone who hears it
will tingle.
12 "In that day I will perform against Eli
all that I have spoken concerning his
house, from beginning to end.
13 "For I have told him that I will judge
his house forever for the iniquity which
he knows, because his sons made themselves vile, and he did not restrain them.
14 "And therefore I have sworn to the
house of Eli that the iniquity of Eli's
house shall not be atoned for by sacrifice
or offering forever."
15 So Samuel lay down until morning,
and opened the doors of the house of the
LORD. And Samuel was afraid to tell Eli
the vision.
16 Then Eli called Samuel and said,
"Samuel, my son!" And he answered,
"Here I am."
17 And he said, "What *is* the thing that
the LORD has said to you? Please do not
hide *it* from me. God do so to you, and
more also, if you hide anything from me
of all the things that He said to you."
18 Then Samuel told him everything, and
hid nothing from him. And he said, "It *is*
the LORD. Let Him do what seems good
to Him."
19 So Samuel grew, and the LORD was
with him and let none of his words fall to
the ground.
20 And all Israel from Dan to Beersheba
knew that Samuel *had been* established as
a prophet of the LORD.

21 Then the LORD appeared again in Shi-
loh. For the LORD revealed Himself to
Samuel in Shiloh by the word of the
LORD.

4 And the word of Samuel came to all
Israel.

The Ark of God Captured

Now Israel went out to battle against
the Philistines, and encamped beside Ebenezer; and the Philistines encamped in
Aphek.
2 Then the Philistines put themselves in
battle array against Israel. And when
they joined battle, Israel was defeated by
the Philistines, who killed about four
thousand men of the army in the field.
3 And when the people had come into
the camp, the elders of Israel said, "Why
has the LORD defeated us today before
the Philistines? Let us bring the ark of
the covenant of the LORD from Shiloh to
us, that when it comes among us it may
save us from the hand of our enemies."
4 So the people sent to Shiloh, that they
might bring from there the ark of the covenant of the LORD of hosts, who dwells
between the cherubim. And the two sons
of Eli, Hophni and Phinehas, *were* there
with the ark of the covenant of God.
5 And when the ark of the covenant of
the LORD came into the camp, all Israel
shouted so loudly that the earth shook.
6 Now when the Philistines heard the
noise of the shout, they said, "What *does*
the sound of this great shout in the camp
of the Hebrews *mean*?" Then they understood that the ark of the LORD had come
into the camp.
7 So the Philistines were afraid, for they
said, "God has come into the camp!"
And they said, "Woe to us! For such a
thing has never happened before.
8 "Woe to us! Who will deliver us from
the hand of these mighty gods? These *are*
the gods who struck the Egyptians with
all the plagues in the wilderness.
9 "Be strong and conduct yourselves
like men, you Philistines, that you do not
become servants of the Hebrews, as they
have been to you. Conduct yourselves
like men, and fight!"
10 So the Philistines fought, and Israel
was defeated, and every man fled to his
tent. There was a very great slaughter,
and there fell of Israel thirty thousand
foot soldiers.

11 Also the ark of God was captured; and the two sons of Eli, Hophni and Phinehas, died.

Death of Eli

12 Then a man of Benjamin ran from the battle line the same day, and came to Shiloh with his clothes torn and dirt on his head.
13 Now when he came, there was Eli, sitting on a seat by the wayside watching, for his heart trembled for the ark of God. And when the man came into the city and told it, all the city cried out.
14 When Eli heard the noise of the outcry, he said, "What *does* the sound of this tumult *mean*?" And the man came hastily and told Eli.
15 Eli was ninety-eight years old, and his eyes were so dim that he could not see.
16 Then the man said to Eli, "I *am* he who came from the battle. And I fled today from the battle line." And he said, "What happened, my son?"
17 So the messenger answered and said, "Israel has fled before the Philistines, and there has been a great slaughter among the people. Also your two sons, Hophni and Phinehas, are dead; and the ark of God has been captured."
18 Then it happened, when he made mention of the ark of God, that Eli fell off the seat backward by the side of the gate; and his neck was broken and he died, for the man was old and heavy. And he had judged Israel forty years.

Ichabod

19 Now his daughter-in-law, Phinehas' wife, was with child, *due* to be delivered; and when she heard the news that the ark of God was captured, and that her father-in-law and her husband were dead, she bowed herself and gave birth, for her labor pains came upon her.
20 And about the time of her death the women who stood by her said to her, "Do not fear, for you have borne a son." But she did not answer, nor did she regard *it*.
21 Then she named the child Ichabod,10 saying, "The glory has departed from Israel!" because the ark of God had been captured and because of her father-in-law and her husband.
22 And she said, "The glory has departed from Israel, for the ark of God has been captured."

The Philistines and the Ark

5 Then the Philistines took the ark of God and brought it from Ebenezer to Ashdod.
2 When the Philistines took the ark of God, they brought it into the temple of Dagon11 and set it by Dagon.
3 And when the people of Ashdod arose early in the morning, there was Dagon, fallen on its face to the earth before the ark of the LORD. So they took Dagon and set it in its place again.
4 And when they arose early the next morning, there was Dagon, fallen on its face to the ground before the ark of the LORD. The head of Dagon and both the palms of its hands *were* broken off on the threshold; only *the torso of* Dagon was left of it.
5 Therefore neither the priests of Dagon nor any who come into Dagon's temple tread on the threshold of Dagon in Ashdod to this day.
6 But the hand of the LORD was heavy on the people of Ashdod, and He ravaged them and struck them with tumors,12 *both* Ashdod and its territory.
7 And when the men of Ashdod saw how *it was*, they said, "The ark of the God of Israel must not remain with us, for His hand is harsh toward us and Dagon our god."
8 Therefore they sent and gathered to themselves all the lords of the Philistines, and said, "What shall we do with the ark of the God of Israel?" And they answered, "Let the ark of the God of Israel be carried away to Gath." So they carried the ark of the God of Israel away.
9 And *so* it was, after they had carried it away, that the hand of the LORD was against the city with a very great destruction; and He struck the men of the city, both small and great, and tumors broke out on them.
10 Therefore they sent the ark of God to Ekron. So it was, as the ark of God came to Ekron, that the Ekronites cried out, saying, "They have brought the ark of the God of Israel to us, to kill us and our people!"
11 So they sent and gathered together all the lords of the Philistines, and said, "Send away the ark of the God of Israel, and let it go back to its own place, so that it does not kill us and our people." For

10 Literally *Inglorious*　11 A Philistine idol　12 Probably bubonic plague

there was a deadly destruction throughout all the city; the hand of God was very
heavy there.
12 And the men who did not die were
stricken with the tumors, and the cry of
the city went up to heaven.

The Ark Returned to Israel

6 Now the ark of the LORD was in the
country of the Philistines seven
months.
2 And the Philistines called for the
priests and the diviners, saying, "What
shall we do with the ark of the LORD?
Tell us how we should send it to its
place."
3 So they said, "If you send away the
ark of the God of Israel, do not send it
empty; but by all means return *it* to Him
with a trespass offering. Then you will be
healed, and it will be known to you why
His hand is not removed from you."
4 Then they said, "What *is* the trespass
offering which we shall return to Him?"
They answered, "Five golden tumors and
five golden rats, *according to* the number
of the lords of the Philistines. For the
same plague *was* on all of you and on
your lords.
5 "Therefore you shall make images of
your tumors and images of your rats that
ravage the land, and you shall give glory
to the God of Israel; perhaps He will
lighten His hand from you, from your
gods, and from your land.
6 "Why then do you harden your hearts
as the Egyptians and Pharaoh hardened
their hearts? When He did mighty things
among them, did they not let the people
go, that they might depart?
7 "Now therefore, make a new cart,
take two milk cows which have never
been yoked, and hitch the cows to the
cart; and take their calves home, away
from them.
8 "Then take the ark of the LORD and
set it on the cart; and put the articles of
gold which you are returning to Him *as* a
trespass offering in a chest by its side.
Then send it away, and let it go.
9 "And watch: if it goes up the road to
its own territory, to Beth Shemesh, *then*
He has done us this great evil. But if not,
then we shall know that *it is* not His hand
that struck us; it *was* by chance *that* it
happened to us."
10 Then the men did so; they took two

milk cows and hitched them to the cart,
and shut up their calves at home.
11 And they set the ark of the LORD on
the cart, and the chest with the gold rats
and the images of their tumors.
12 Then the cows headed straight for the
road to Beth Shemesh, *and* went along
the highway, lowing as they went, and did
not turn aside to the right hand or the
left. And the lords of the Philistines went
after them to the border of Beth Shemesh.
13 Now *the people of* Beth Shemesh *were*
reaping their wheat harvest in the valley;
and they lifted their eyes and saw the ark,
and rejoiced to see *it*.
14 Then the cart came into the field of
Joshua of Beth Shemesh, and stood there;
a large stone *was there*. So they split the
wood of the cart and offered the cows as
a burnt offering to the LORD.
15 The Levites took down the ark of the
LORD and the chest that *was* with it, in
which *were* the articles of gold, and put
them on the large stone. Then the men of
Beth Shemesh offered burnt offerings and
made sacrifices the same day to the
LORD.
16 So when the five lords of the Philistines had seen *it*, they returned to Ekron
the same day.
17 Now these *are* the gold tumors which
the Philistines returned *as* a trespass offering to the LORD: one for Ashdod, one
for Gaza, one for Ashkelon, one for
Gath, one for Ekron;
18 and the gold rats, *according to* the
number of all the cities of the Philistines
belonging to the five lords, *both* fortified
cities and country villages, even as far as
the large *stone of* Abel on which they set
the ark of the LORD, *which stone remains*
to this day in the field of Joshua of Beth
Shemesh.
19 Then He struck the men of Beth Shemesh, because they had looked into the
ark of the LORD. He struck fifty thousand and seventy men[13] of the people,
and the people lamented because the
LORD had struck the people with a great
slaughter.

The Ark at Kirjath Jearim

20 And the men of Beth Shemesh said,
"Who is able to stand before this holy
LORD God? And to whom shall it go up
from us?"

13 Or *He struck seventy men of the people and fifty oxen of a man*

21 So they sent messengers to the inhabitants of Kirjath Jearim, saying, "The Philistines have brought back the ark of the LORD; come down *and* take it up with you."

7 Then the men of Kirjath Jearim came and took the ark of the LORD, and brought it into the house of Abinadab on the hill, and consecrated Eleazar his son to keep the ark of the LORD.

Samuel Judges Israel

2 So it was that the ark remained in Kirjath Jearim a long time; it was there twenty years. And all the house of Israel lamented after the LORD.

3 Then Samuel spoke to all the house of Israel, saying, "If you return to the LORD with all your hearts, *then* put away the foreign gods and the Ashtoreths[14] from among you, and prepare your hearts for the LORD, and serve Him only; and He will deliver you from the hand of the Philistines."

4 So the children of Israel put away the Baals and the Ashtoreths,[15] and served the LORD only.

5 And Samuel said, "Gather all Israel to Mizpah, and I will pray to the LORD for you."

6 So they gathered together at Mizpah, drew water, and poured *it* out before the LORD. And they fasted that day, and said there, "We have sinned against the LORD." And Samuel judged the children of Israel at Mizpah.

7 Now when the Philistines heard that the children of Israel had gathered together at Mizpah, the lords of the Philistines went up against Israel. And when the children of Israel heard *of it*, they were afraid of the Philistines.

8 So the children of Israel said to Samuel, "Do not cease to cry out to the LORD our God for us, that He may save us from the hand of the Philistines."

9 And Samuel took a suckling lamb and offered *it as* a whole burnt offering to the LORD. Then Samuel cried out to the LORD for Israel, and the LORD answered him.

10 Now as Samuel was offering up the burnt offering, the Philistines drew near to battle against Israel. But the LORD thundered with a loud thunder upon the Philistines that day, and so confused them that they were overcome before Israel.

11 And the men of Israel went out of Mizpah and pursued the Philistines, and drove them back as far as below Beth Car.

12 Then Samuel took a stone and set *it* up between Mizpah and Shen, and called its name Ebenezer,[16] saying, "Thus far the LORD has helped us."

13 So the Philistines were subdued, and they did not come anymore into the territory of Israel. And the hand of the LORD was against the Philistines all the days of Samuel.

14 Then the cities which the Philistines had taken from Israel were restored to Israel, from Ekron to Gath; and Israel recovered its territory from the hands of the Philistines. Also there was peace between Israel and the Amorites.

15 So Samuel judged Israel all the days of his life.

16 He went from year to year on a circuit to Bethel, Gilgal, and Mizpah, and judged Israel in all those places.

17 But he always returned to Ramah, for his home *was* there. There he judged Israel, and there he built an altar to the LORD.

Israel Demands a King

8 Now it came to pass when Samuel was old that he made his sons judges over Israel.

2 The name of his firstborn was Joel, and the name of his second, Abijah; *they were* judges in Beersheba.

3 But his sons did not walk in his ways; they turned aside after dishonest gain, took bribes, and perverted justice.

4 Then all the elders of Israel gathered together and came to Samuel at Ramah,

5 and said to him, "Look, you are old, and your sons do not walk in your ways. Now make *for* us a king to judge us like all the nations."

6 But the thing displeased Samuel when they said, "Give us a king to judge us." So Samuel prayed to the LORD.

7 And the LORD said to Samuel, "Heed the voice of the people in all that they say to you; for they have not rejected you, but they have rejected Me, that I should not reign over them.

8 "According to all the works which they have done since the day that I

14 Canaanite goddesses   15 Canaanite goddesses   16 Literally *Stone of Help*

brought them up out of Egypt, even to this day—with which they have forsaken Me and served other gods—so they are doing to you also.

9 "Now therefore, heed their voice. However, you shall solemnly forewarn them, and show them the behavior of the king who will reign over them."

10 So Samuel told all the words of the LORD to the people who asked him for a king.

11 And he said, "This will be the behavior of the king who will reign over you: He will take your sons and appoint *them* for his own chariots and *to be* his horsemen, and *some* will run before his chariots.

12 "He will appoint captains over his thousands and captains over his fifties, *will set some* to plow his ground and reap his harvest, and *some* to make his weapons of war and equipment for his chariots.

13 "He will take your daughters *to be* perfumers, cooks, and bakers.

14 "And he will take the best of your fields, your vineyards, and your olive groves, and give *them* to his servants.

15 "He will take a tenth of your grain and your vintage, and give it to his officers and servants.

16 "And he will take your menservants and your maidservants and your finest young men and your donkeys, and put *them* to his work.

17 "He will take a tenth of your sheep. And you will be his servants.

18 "And you will cry out in that day because of your king whom you have chosen for yourselves, and the LORD will not hear you in that day."

19 Nevertheless the people refused to obey the voice of Samuel; and they said, "No, but we will have a king over us,

20 that we also may be like all the nations, and that our king may judge us and go out before us and fight our battles."

21 And Samuel heard all the words of the people, and he repeated them in the hearing of the LORD.

22 So the LORD said to Samuel, "Heed their voice, and make them a king." And Samuel said to the men of Israel, "Every man go to his city."

Saul Chosen to Be King

9 There was a man of Benjamin whose name *was* Kish the son of Abiel, the son of Zeror, the son of Bechorath, the son of Aphiah, a Benjamite, a mighty man of power.

2 And he had a son whose name *was* Saul, a choice and handsome *young man. There was* not a more handsome person than he among the children of Israel. From his shoulders upward *he was* taller than any of the people.

3 Now the donkeys of Kish, Saul's father, were lost. And Kish said to his son Saul, "Please, take one of the servants with you, and arise, go and look for the donkeys."

4 So he passed through the mountains of Ephraim and through the land of Shalisha, but they did not find *them*. Then they passed through the land of Shaalim, and *they were* not *there*. Then he passed through the land of the Benjamites, but they did not find *them*.

5 When they had come to the land of Zuph, Saul said to his servant who *was* with him, "Come, let us return, lest my father cease *caring* about the donkeys and become worried about us."

6 And he said to him, "Look now, *there is* in this city a man of God, and *he is* an honorable man; all that he says surely comes to pass. So let us go there; perhaps he can show us the way that we should go."

7 Then Saul said to his servant, "But look, *if* we go, what shall we bring the man? For the bread in our vessels is all gone, and *there is* no present to bring to the man of God. What do we have?"

8 And the servant answered Saul again and said, "Look, I have here at hand one fourth of a shekel of silver. I will give *that* to the man of God, to tell us our way."

9 (Formerly in Israel, when a man went to inquire of God, he spoke thus: "Come, let us go to the seer"; for *he who is* now *called* a prophet was formerly called a seer.)

10 Then Saul said to his servant, "Well said; come, let us go." So they went to the city where the man of God *was*.

11 As they went up the hill to the city, they met some young women going out to

draw water, and said to them, "Is the seer here?"

12 And they answered them and said, "Yes, there he is, just ahead of you. Hurry now; for today he came to this city, because there is a sacrifice of the people today on the high place.

13 "As soon as you come into the city, you will surely find him before he goes up to the high place to eat. For the people will not eat until he comes, because he must bless the sacrifice; afterward those who are invited will eat. Now therefore, go up, for about this time you will find him."

14 So they went up to the city. *And* as they were coming into the city, there was Samuel, coming out toward them on his way up to the high place.

15 Now the LORD had told Samuel in his ear the day before Saul came, saying,

16 "Tomorrow about this time I will send you a man from the land of Benjamin, and you shall anoint him commander over My people Israel, that he may save My people from the hand of the Philistines; for I have looked upon My people, because their cry has come to me."

17 And when Samuel saw Saul, the LORD said to him, "There he is, the man of whom I spoke to you. This one shall reign over My people."

18 Then Saul drew near to Samuel in the gate, and said, "Please tell me, where *is* the seer's house?"

19 And Samuel answered Saul and said, "I *am* the seer. Go up before me to the high place, for you shall eat with me today; and tomorrow I will let you go and will tell you all that *is* in your heart.

20 "But as for your donkeys that were lost three days ago, do not be anxious about them, for they have been found. And on whom *is* all the desire of Israel? *Is it* not on you and on all your father's house?"

21 And Saul answered and said, "*Am* I not a Benjamite, of the smallest of the tribes of Israel, and my family the least of all the families of the tribe of Benjamin? Why then do you speak like this to me?"

22 Then Samuel took Saul and his servant and brought them into the hall, and had them sit in the place of honor among those who were invited; there *were* about thirty persons.

23 And Samuel said to the cook, "Bring the portion which I gave you, of which I said to you, 'Set it apart.'"

24 So the cook took up the thigh with its upper part and set *it* before Saul. And Samuel said, "Here it is, what was kept back. *It* was set apart for you. Eat; for until this time it has been kept for you, since I said I invited the people." So Saul ate with Samuel that day.

25 When they had come down from the high place into the city, *Samuel* spoke with Saul on the top of the house.

26 They arose early; and it was about the dawning of the day that Samuel called to Saul on the top of the house, saying, "Get up, that I may send you on your way." And Saul arose, and both of them went outside, he and Samuel.

Saul Anointed King

27 *Now* as they were going down to the outskirts of the city, Samuel said to Saul, "Tell the servant to go on ahead of us." And he went on. "But you stand here awhile, that I may announce to you the word of God."

10 Then Samuel took a flask of oil and poured *it* on his head, and kissed him and said: "*Is it* not because the LORD has anointed you commander over His inheritance?

2 "When you have departed from me today, you will find two men by Rachel's tomb in the territory of Benjamin at Zelzah; and they will say to you, 'The donkeys which you went to look for have been found. And now your father has ceased caring about the donkeys and is worrying about you, saying, "What shall I do about my son?"'

3 "Then you shall go on forward from there and come to the terebinth tree of Tabor. There three men going up to God at Bethel will meet you, one carrying three young goats, another carrying three loaves of bread, and another carrying a skin of wine.

4 "And they will greet you and give you two *loaves* of bread, which you shall receive from their hands.

5 "After that you shall come to the hill of God where the Philistine garrison *is*. And it will happen, when you have come there to the city, that you will meet a group of prophets coming down from the

high place with a stringed instrument, a tambourine, a flute, and a harp before them; and they will be prophesying.
6 "Then the Spirit of the LORD will come upon you, and you will prophesy with them and be turned into another man.
7 "And let it be, when these signs come to you, *that* you do as the occasion demands; for God *is* with you.
8 "You shall go down before me to Gilgal; and surely I will come down to you to offer burnt offerings *and* make sacrifices of peace offerings. Seven days you shall wait, till I come to you and show you what you should do."
9 And *so* it was, when he had turned his back to go from Samuel, that God gave him another heart; and all those signs came to pass that day.
10 When they came there to the hill, there was a group of prophets to meet him; then the Spirit of God came upon him, and he prophesied among them.
11 And it happened, when all who knew him formerly saw that he indeed prophesied among the prophets, that the people said to one another, "What *is* this *that* has come upon the son of Kish? *Is* Saul also among the prophets?"
12 Then a man from there answered and said, "But who *is* their father?" Therefore it became a proverb: "*Is* Saul also among the prophets?"
13 And when he had finished prophesying, he went to the high place.
14 Then Saul's uncle said to him and his servant, "Where did you go?" And he said, "To look for the donkeys. When we saw that *they were* nowhere *to be found,* we went to Samuel."
15 And Saul's uncle said, "Tell me, please, what Samuel said to you."
16 So Saul said to his uncle, "He told us plainly that the donkeys had been found." But about the matter of the kingdom, he did not tell him what Samuel had said.

Saul Proclaimed King

17 Then Samuel called the people together to the LORD at Mizpah,
18 and said to the children of Israel, "Thus says the LORD God of Israel: 'I brought up Israel out of Egypt, and delivered you from the hand of the Egyptians *and* from the hand of all kingdoms and from those who oppressed you.'
19 "But you have today rejected your God, who Himself saved you out of all your adversities and your tribulations; and you have said to Him, '*No,* but set a king over us!' Now therefore, present yourselves before the LORD by your tribes and by your clans."17
20 And when Samuel had caused all the tribes of Israel to come near, the tribe of Benjamin was chosen.
21 When he had caused the tribe of Benjamin to come near by their families, the family of Matri was chosen. And Saul the son of Kish was chosen. But when they sought him, he could not be found.
22 Therefore they inquired of the LORD further, "Has the man come here yet?" And the LORD answered, "There he is, hidden among the equipment."
23 So they ran and brought him from there; and when he stood among the people, he was taller than any of the people from his shoulders upward.
24 And Samuel said to all the people, "Do you see him whom the LORD has chosen, that *there is* no one like him among all the people?" So all the people shouted and said, "Long live the king!"
25 Then Samuel explained to the people the behavior of royalty, and wrote *it* in a book and laid *it* up before the LORD. And Samuel sent all the people away, every man to his house.
26 And Saul also went home to Gibeah; and valiant *men* went with him, whose hearts God had touched.
27 But some rebels said, "How can this man save us?" So they despised him, and brought him no presents. But he held his peace.

Saul Saves Jabesh Gilead

11 Then Nahash the Ammonite came up and encamped against Jabesh Gilead; and all the men of Jabesh said to Nahash, "Make a covenant with us, and we will serve you."
2 And Nahash the Ammonite answered them, "On this *condition* I will make *a covenant* with you, that I may put out all your right eyes, and bring reproach on all Israel."
3 Then the elders of Jabesh said to him, "Hold off for seven days, that we may send messengers to all the territory of Is-

17 Literally *thousands*

rael. And then, if *there is* no one to save us, we will come out to you."

4 So the messengers came to Gibeah of Saul and told the news in the hearing of the people. And all the people lifted up their voices and wept.

5 Now there was Saul, coming behind the herd from the field; and Saul said, "What *troubles* the people, that they weep?" And they told him the words of the men of Jabesh.

6 Then the Spirit of God came upon Saul when he heard this news, and his anger was greatly aroused.

7 So he took a yoke of oxen and cut them in pieces, and sent *them* throughout all the territory of Israel by the hands of messengers, saying, "Whoever does not go out with Saul and Samuel to battle, so it shall be done to his oxen." And the fear of the LORD fell on the people, and they came out with one consent.

8 When he numbered them in Bezek, the children of Israel were three hundred thousand, and the men of Judah thirty thousand.

9 And they said to the messengers who came, "Thus you shall say to the men of Jabesh Gilead: 'Tomorrow, by *the time* the sun is hot, you shall have help.'" Then the messengers came and reported *it* to the men of Jabesh, and they were glad.

10 Therefore the men of Jabesh said, "Tomorrow we will come out to you, and you may do with us whatever seems good to you."

11 So it was, on the next day, that Saul put the people in three companies; and they came into the midst of the camp in the morning watch, and killed Ammonites until the heat of the day. And it happened that those who survived were scattered, so that no two of them were left together.

12 Then the people said to Samuel, "Who *is* he who said, 'Shall Saul reign over us?' Bring the men, that we may put them to death."

13 But Saul said, "Not a man shall be put to death this day, for today the LORD has accomplished salvation in Israel."

14 Then Samuel said to the people, "Come, let us go to Gilgal and renew the kingdom there."

15 So all the people went to Gilgal, and there they made Saul king before the LORD in Gilgal. There they made sacrifices of peace offerings before the LORD, and there Saul and all the men of Israel rejoiced greatly.

Samuel's Address at Saul's Coronation

12 Now Samuel said to all Israel: "Indeed I have heeded your voice in all that you said to me, and have made a king over you.

2 "And now here is the king, walking before you; and I am old and gray-headed, and look, my sons *are* with you. I have walked before you from my childhood to this day.

3 "Here I am. Witness against me before the LORD and before His anointed: Whose ox have I taken, or whose donkey have I taken, or whom have I defrauded? Whom have I oppressed, or from whose hand have I received *any* bribe with which to blind my eyes? I will restore *it* to you."

4 And they said, "You have not defrauded us or oppressed us, nor have you taken anything from any man's hand."

5 Then he said to them, "The LORD *is* witness against you, and His anointed *is* witness this day, that you have not found anything in my hand." And they answered, "*He is* witness."

6 And Samuel said to the people, "*It is* the LORD who raised up Moses and Aaron, and who brought your fathers up from the land of Egypt.

7 "Now therefore, stand still, that I may reason with you before the LORD concerning all the righteous acts of the LORD which He did to you and your fathers:

8 "When Jacob had gone into Egypt, and your fathers cried out to the LORD, then the LORD sent Moses and Aaron, who brought your fathers out of Egypt and made them dwell in this place.

9 "And when they forgot the LORD their God, He sold them into the hand of Sisera, commander of the army of Hazor, into the hand of the Philistines, and into the hand of the king of Moab; and they fought against them.

10 "Then they cried out to the LORD, and said, 'We have sinned, because we have forsaken the LORD and served the Baals and Ashtoreths;[18] but now deliver us from the hand of our enemies, and we will serve You.'

18 Canaanite goddesses

11 "And the LORD sent Jerubbaal, Bedan,[19] Jephthah, and Samuel, and delivered you out of the hand of your enemies on every side; and you dwelt in safety.
12 "And when you saw that Nahash king of the Ammonites came against you, you said to me, 'No, but a king shall reign over us,' when the LORD your God *was* your king.
13 "Now therefore, here is the king whom you have chosen *and* whom you have desired. And take note, the LORD has set a king over you.
14 "If you fear the LORD and serve Him and obey His voice, and do not rebel against the commandment of the LORD, then both you and the king who reigns over you will continue following the LORD your God.
15 "However, if you do not obey the voice of the LORD, but rebel against the commandment of the LORD, then the hand of the LORD will be against you, as *it was* against your fathers.
16 "Now therefore, stand and see this great thing which the LORD will do before your eyes:
17 "*Is* today not the wheat harvest? I will call to the LORD, and He will send thunder and rain, that you may perceive and see that your wickedness *is* great, which you have done in the sight of the LORD, in asking a king for yourselves."
18 So Samuel called to the LORD, and the LORD sent thunder and rain that day; and all the people greatly feared the LORD and Samuel.
19 And all the people said to Samuel, "Pray for your servants to the LORD your God, that we may not die; for we have added to all our sins the evil of asking a king for ourselves."
20 Then Samuel said to the people, "Do not fear. You have done all this wickedness; yet do not turn aside from following the LORD, but serve the LORD with all your heart.
21 "And do not turn aside; for *then you would go* after empty things which cannot profit or deliver, for they *are* nothing.
22 "For the LORD will not forsake His people, for His great name's sake, because it has pleased the LORD to make you His people.
23 "Moreover, as for me, far be it from me that I should sin against the LORD in ceasing to pray for you; but I will teach you the good and the right way.
24 "Only fear the LORD, and serve Him in truth with all your heart; for consider what great things He has done for you.
25 "But if you still do wickedly, you shall be swept away, both you and your king."

Saul's Unlawful Sacrifice

13 Saul reigned one year; and when he had reigned two years over Israel,[20]
2 Saul chose for himself three thousand *men* of Israel. Two thousand were with Saul in Michmash and in the mountains of Bethel, and a thousand were with Jonathan in Gibeah of Benjamin. The rest of the people he sent away, every man to his tent.
3 And Jonathan attacked the garrison of the Philistines that *was* in Geba, and the Philistines heard *of it*. Then Saul blew the trumpet throughout all the land, saying, "Let the Hebrews hear!"
4 Now all Israel heard it said *that* Saul had attacked a garrison of the Philistines, and *that* Israel had also become an abomination to the Philistines. And the people were called together to Saul at Gilgal.
5 Then the Philistines gathered together to fight with Israel, thirty thousand chariots and six thousand horsemen, and people as the sand which *is* on the seashore in multitude. And they came up and encamped in Michmash, to the east of Beth Aven.
6 When the men of Israel saw that they were in danger (for the people were distressed), then the people hid in caves, in thickets, in rocks, in holes, and in pits.
7 And *some of* the Hebrews crossed over the Jordan to the land of Gad and Gilead. As for Saul, he *was* still in Gilgal, and all the people followed him trembling.
8 Then he waited seven days, according to the time set by Samuel. But Samuel did not come to Gilgal; and the people were scattered from him.
9 So Saul said, "Bring a burnt offering and peace offerings here to me." And he offered the burnt offering.
10 Now it happened, as soon as he had finished offering the burnt offering, that

19 Septuagint and Syriac read *Barak.*
20 The Hebrew is difficult (compare 2 Samuel 5:4, 1 Kings 14:2; see also 2 Samuel 2:10, Acts 13:21).

Samuel came; and Saul went out to meet him, that he might greet him.

11 And Samuel said, "What have you done?" And Saul said, "When I saw that the people were scattered from me, and *that* you did not come within the days appointed, and *that* the Philistines gathered together at Michmash,

12 "then I said, 'The Philistines will now come down on me at Gilgal, and I have not made supplication to the LORD.' Therefore I felt compelled, and offered a burnt offering."

13 And Samuel said to Saul, "You have done foolishly. You have not kept the commandment of the LORD your God, which He commanded you. For now the LORD would have established your kingdom over Israel forever.

14 "But now your kingdom shall not continue. The LORD has sought for Himself a man after His own heart, and the LORD has commanded him *to be* commander over His people, because you have not kept what the LORD commanded you."

15 Then Samuel arose and went up from Gilgal to Gibeah of Benjamin. And Saul numbered the people *who were* present with him, about six hundred men.

No Weapons for the Army

16 Saul, Jonathan his son, and the people *who were* present with them remained in Gibeah of Benjamin. But the Philistines encamped in Michmash.

17 Then raiders came out of the camp of the Philistines in three companies. One company turned to the road *that leads* to Ophrah, to the land of Shual,

18 another company turned to the road *to* Beth Horon, and another company turned *to* the road of the border that overlooks the Valley of Zeboim toward the wilderness.

19 Now there was no blacksmith to be found throughout all the land of Israel, for the Philistines said, "Lest the Hebrews make swords or spears."

20 But all the Israelites would go down to the Philistines to sharpen each man's plowshare, his mattock, his ax, and his sickle;

21 and the charge for a sharpening was a pim[21] for the plowshares, the mattocks, the forks, and the axes, and to set the points of the goads.

22 So it came about, on the day of battle, that there was neither sword nor spear found in the hand of any of the people who *were* with Saul and Jonathan. But they were found with Saul and Jonathan his son.

23 And the garrison of the Philistines went out to the pass of Michmash.

Jonathan Defeats the Philistines

14 Now it happened one day that Jonathan the son of Saul said to the young man who bore his armor, "Come, let us go over to the Philistines' garrison that *is* on the other side." But he did not tell his father.

2 And Saul was sitting in the outskirts of Gibeah under a pomegranate tree which *is* in Migron. The people who *were* with him *were* about six hundred men.

3 Ahijah the son of Ahitub, Ichabod's brother, the son of Phinehas, the son of Eli, the LORD's priest in Shiloh, was wearing an ephod. But the people did not know that Jonathan had gone.

4 Now between the passes, by which Jonathan sought to go over to the Philistines' garrison, *there was* a sharp rock on one side and a sharp rock on the other side. And the name of one *was* Bozez, and the name of the other Seneh.

5 The front of one faced northward opposite Michmash, and the other southward opposite Gibeah.

6 Then Jonathan said to the young man who bore his armor, "Come, let us go over to the garrison of these uncircumcised; it may be that the LORD will work for us. For nothing restrains the LORD from saving by many or by few."

7 So his armorbearer said to him, "Do all that is in your heart. Go then; here I am with you, according to your heart."

8 Then Jonathan said, "Very well, let us cross over to *these* men, and we will show ourselves to them.

9 "If they say thus to us, 'Wait until we come to you,' then we will stand still in our place and not go up to them.

10 "But if they say thus, 'Come up to us,' then we will go up. For the LORD has delivered them into our hand, and this *will be* a sign to us."

11 So both of them showed themselves to the garrison of the Philistines. And the Philistines said, "Look, the Hebrews are

---

21 About two-thirds shekel weight

coming out of the holes where they have hidden."

12 Then the men of the garrison called to Jonathan and his armorbearer, and said, "Come up to us, and we will show you something." So Jonathan said to his armorbearer, "Come up after me, for the LORD has delivered them into the hand of Israel."

13 And Jonathan climbed up on his hands and knees with his armorbearer after him; and they fell before Jonathan. And as he came after him, his armorbearer killed them.

14 That first slaughter which Jonathan and his armorbearer made was about twenty men within about half an acre of land.[22]

15 And there was trembling in the camp, in the field, and among all the people. The garrison and the raiders also trembled; and the earth quaked, so that it was a very great trembling.

16 Now the watchmen of Saul in Gibeah of Benjamin looked, and there was the multitude, melting away; and they went here and there.

17 Then Saul said to the people who were with him, "Now call the roll and see who has gone from us." And when they had called the roll, surprisingly, Jonathan and his armorbearer were not there.

18 And Saul said to Ahijah, "Bring the ark of God here" (for at that time the ark of God was with the children of Israel).

19 Now it happened, while Saul talked to the priest, that the noise which was in the camp of the Philistines continued to increase; so Saul said to the priest, "Withdraw your hand."

20 Then Saul and all the people who were with him assembled, and they went to the battle; and indeed every man's sword was against his neighbor, and there was very great confusion.

21 Moreover the Hebrews who were with the Philistines before that time, who went up with them into the camp from the surrounding country, they also joined the Israelites who were with Saul and Jonathan.

22 Likewise all the men of Israel who had hidden in the mountains of Ephraim, when they heard that the Philistines fled, they also followed hard after them in the battle.

23 So the LORD saved Israel that day, and the battle shifted to Beth Aven.

Saul's Rash Oath

24 And the men of Israel were distressed that day, for Saul had placed the people under oath, saying, "Cursed is the man who eats any food until evening, before I have taken vengeance on my enemies." So none of the people tasted food.

25 Now all the people of the land came to a forest; and there was honey on the ground.

26 And when the people had come into the woods, there was the honey, dripping; but no one put his hand to his mouth, for the people feared the oath.

27 But Jonathan had not heard his father charge the people with the oath; therefore he stretched out the end of the rod that was in his hand and dipped it in a honeycomb, and put his hand to his mouth; and his countenance brightened.

28 Then one of the people said, "Your father strictly charged the people with an oath, saying, 'Cursed is the man who eats food this day.' " And the people were faint.

29 But Jonathan said, "My father has troubled the land. Look now, how my countenance has brightened because I tasted a little of this honey.

30 "How much better if the people had eaten freely today of the spoil of their enemies which they found! For now would there not have been a much greater slaughter among the Philistines?"

31 Now they had driven back the Philistines that day from Michmash to Aijalon. So the people were very faint.

32 And the people rushed on the spoil, and took sheep, oxen, and calves, and slaughtered them on the ground; and the people ate them with the blood.

33 Then they told Saul, saying, "Look, the people are sinning against the LORD by eating with the blood!" And he said, "You have dealt treacherously; roll a large stone to me this day."

34 And Saul said, "Disperse yourselves among the people, and say to them, 'Bring me here every man's ox and every man's sheep, slaughter them here, and eat; and do not sin against the LORD by eating with the blood.' " So every one of the people brought his ox with him that night, and slaughtered it there.

35 Then Saul built an altar to the LORD.

---

22 Literally half the area plowed by a yoke (of oxen in a day)

This was the first altar that he built to the LORD.

36 And Saul said, "Let us go down after the Philistines by night, and plunder them until the morning light; and let us not leave a man of them." And they said, "Do whatever seems good to you." Then the priest said, "Let us draw near to God here."

37 So Saul asked counsel of God, "Shall I go down after the Philistines? Will You deliver them into the hand of Israel?" But He did not answer him that day.

38 And Saul said, "Come over here, all you chiefs of the people, and know and see what this sin was today.

39 "For as the LORD lives, who saves Israel, though it be in Jonathan my son, he shall surely die." But not a man among all the people answered him.

40 Then he said to all Israel, "You be on one side, and my son Jonathan and I will be on the other side." And the people said to Saul, "Do what seems good to you."

41 Therefore Saul said to the LORD God of Israel, "Give a perfect lot." So Saul and Jonathan were taken, but the people escaped.

42 And Saul said, "Cast lots between my son Jonathan and me." So Jonathan was taken.

43 Then Saul said to Jonathan, "Tell me what you have done." And Jonathan told him, and said, "I only tasted a little honey with the end of the rod that was in my hand. So now I must die!"

44 And Saul answered, "God do so and more also; for you shall surely die, Jonathan."

45 But the people said to Saul, "Shall Jonathan die, who has accomplished this great salvation in Israel? Certainly not! As the LORD lives, not one hair of his head shall fall to the ground, for he has worked with God this day." So the people rescued Jonathan, and he did not die.

46 Then Saul returned from pursuing the Philistines, and the Philistines went to their own place.

Saul's Continuing Wars

47 So Saul established his sovereignty over Israel, and fought against all his enemies on every side, against Moab, against the people of Ammon, against Edom, against the kings of Zobah, and against the Philistines. Wherever he turned, he harassed *them*.

48 And he gathered an army and attacked the Amalekites, and delivered Israel from the hands of those who plundered them.

49 Now the sons of Saul were Jonathan and Jishui[23] and Malchishua. And the names of his two daughters *were these*: the name of the firstborn Merab, and the name of the younger Michal.

50 The name of Saul's wife *was* Ahinoam the daughter of Ahimaaz. And the name of the commander of his army *was* Abner the son of Ner, Saul's uncle.

51 Kish *was* the father of Saul, and Ner the father of Abner *was* the son of Abiel.

52 Now there was fierce war with the Philistines all the days of Saul. And when Saul saw any strong man or any valiant man, he took him for himself.

Saul Spares King Agag

15 Samuel also said to Saul, "The LORD sent me to anoint you king over His people, over Israel. Now therefore, heed the voice of the words of the LORD.

2 "Thus says the LORD of hosts: 'I will punish what Amalek did to Israel, how he laid *wait* for him on the way when he came up from Egypt.

3 'Now go and attack Amalek, and utterly destroy all that they have, and do not spare them. But kill both man and woman, infant and nursing child, ox and sheep, camel and donkey.' "

4 So Saul gathered the people together and numbered them in Telaim, two hundred thousand foot soldiers and ten thousand men of Judah.

5 And Saul came to a city of Amalek, and lay in wait in the valley.

6 Then Saul said to the Kenites, "Go, depart, get down from among the Amalekites, lest I destroy you with them. For you showed kindness to all the children of Israel when they came up out of Egypt." So the Kenites departed from among the Amalekites.

7 And Saul attacked the Amalekites, from Havilah all the way to Shur, which is east of Egypt.

8 He also took Agag king of the Amalekites alive, and utterly destroyed all the people with the edge of the sword.

9 But Saul and the people spared Agag

23 Called *Abinadab* in 1 Chronicles 8:33 and 9:39

and the best of the sheep, the oxen, the fatlings, the lambs, and all *that was* good, and were unwilling to utterly destroy them. But everything despised and worthless, that they utterly destroyed.

Saul Rejected as King

10 Now the word of the LORD came to Samuel, saying, 11 "I greatly regret that I have set up Saul *as* king, for he has turned back from following Me, and has not performed My commandments." And it grieved Samuel, and he cried out to the LORD all night. 12 So when Samuel rose early in the morning to meet Saul, it was told Samuel, saying, "Saul went to Carmel, and indeed, he set up a monument for himself; and he has gone on around, passed by, and gone down to Gilgal." 13 Then Samuel went to Saul, and Saul said to him, "Blessed *are* you of the LORD! I have performed the commandment of the LORD." 14 But Samuel said, "What then *is* this bleating of the sheep in my ears, and the lowing of the oxen which I hear?" 15 And Saul said, "They have brought them from the Amalekites; for the people spared the best of the sheep and the oxen, to sacrifice to the LORD your God; and the rest we have utterly destroyed." 16 Then Samuel said to Saul, "Be quiet! And I will tell you what the LORD said to me last night." And he said to him, "Speak on." 17 So Samuel said, "When you *were* little in your own eyes, *were* you not head of the tribes of Israel? And did not the LORD anoint you king over Israel? 18 "Now the LORD sent you on a mission, and said, 'Go, and utterly destroy the sinners, the Amalekites, and fight against them until they are consumed.' 19 "Why then did you not obey the voice of the LORD? Why did you swoop down on the spoil, and do evil in the sight of the LORD?" 20 And Saul said to Samuel, "But I have obeyed the voice of the LORD, and gone on the mission on which the LORD sent me, and brought back Agag king of Amalek; I have utterly destroyed the Amalekites.

21 "But the people took of the plunder, sheep and oxen, the best of the things which should have been utterly destroyed, to sacrifice to the LORD your God in Gilgal." 22 Then Samuel said:

"Has the LORD *as great* delight
      in burnt offerings and sacrifices,
   As in obeying the voice of the LORD?
   Behold, to obey is better than sacrifice,
   And to heed than the fat of rams.
23 For rebellion *is as* the sin of witchcraft,
   And stubbornness *is*
      as iniquity and idolatry.
   Because you have rejected
      the word of the LORD,
   He also has rejected you
      from *being* king."

24 Then Saul said to Samuel, "I have sinned, for I have transgressed the commandment of the LORD and your words, because I feared the people and obeyed their voice. 25 "Now therefore, please pardon my sin, and return with me, that I may worship the LORD." 26 But Samuel said to Saul, "I will not return with you, for you have rejected the word of the LORD, and the LORD has rejected you from being king over Israel." 27 And as Samuel turned around to go away, *Saul* seized the edge of his robe, and it tore. 28 So Samuel said to him, "The LORD has torn the kingdom of Israel from you today, and has given it to a neighbor of yours, *who is* better than you. 29 "And also the Strength of Israel will not lie nor relent. For He *is* not a man, that He should relent." 30 Then he said, "I have sinned; *yet* honor me now, please, before the elders of my people and before Israel, and return with me, that I may worship the LORD your God." 31 So Samuel turned back after Saul, and Saul worshiped the LORD. 32 Then Samuel said, "Bring Agag king of the Amalekites here to me." So Agag came to him cautiously. And Agag said, "Surely the bitterness of death is past." 33 But Samuel said, "As your sword has made women childless, so shall your mother be childless among women." And Samuel hacked Agag in pieces before the LORD in Gilgal.

34 Then Samuel went to Ramah, and Saul went up to his house at Gibeah of Saul.

35 And Samuel went no more to see Saul until the day of his death. Nevertheless Samuel mourned for Saul, and the LORD regretted that He had made Saul king over Israel.

David Anointed King

16 Then the LORD said to Samuel, "How long will you mourn for Saul, seeing I have rejected him from reigning over Israel? Fill your horn with oil, and go; I am sending you to Jesse the Bethlehemite. For I have provided Myself a king among his sons."

2 And Samuel said, "How can I go? If Saul hears it, he will kill me." And the LORD said, "Take a heifer with you, and say, 'I have come to sacrifice to the LORD.'

3 "Then invite Jesse to the sacrifice, and I will show you what you shall do; you shall anoint for Me the one I name to you."

4 So Samuel did what the LORD said, and went to Bethlehem. And the elders of the town trembled at his coming, and said, "Do you come peaceably?"

5 And he said, "Peaceably; I have come to sacrifice to the LORD. Sanctify yourselves, and come with me to the sacrifice." Then he sanctified Jesse and his sons, and invited them to the sacrifice.

6 So it was, when they came, that he looked at Eliab and said, "Surely the LORD's anointed is before Him."

7 But the LORD said to Samuel, "Do not look at his appearance or at the height of his stature, because I have refused him. For the LORD does not see as man sees; for man looks at the outward appearance, but the LORD looks at the heart."

8 So Jesse called Abinadab, and made him pass before Samuel. And he said, "Neither has the LORD chosen this one."

9 Then Jesse made Shammah pass by. And he said, "Neither has the LORD chosen this one."

10 Thus Jesse made seven of his sons pass before Samuel. And Samuel said to Jesse, "The LORD has not chosen these."

11 And Samuel said to Jesse, "Are all the young men here?" Then he said, "There remains yet the youngest, and there he is, keeping the sheep." And Samuel said to Jesse, "Send and bring him. For we will not sit down till he comes here."

12 So he sent and brought him in. Now he was ruddy, with bright eyes, and good-looking. And the LORD said, "Arise, anoint him; for this is the one!"

13 Then Samuel took the horn of oil and anointed him in the midst of his brothers; and the Spirit of the LORD came upon David from that day forward. So Samuel arose and went to Ramah.

A Distressing Spirit Troubles Saul

14 But the Spirit of the LORD departed from Saul, and a distressing spirit from the LORD troubled him.

15 And Saul's servants said to him, "Surely, a distressing spirit from God is troubling you.

16 "Let our master now command your servants, who are before you, to seek out a man who is a skillful player on the harp; and it shall be that he will play it with his hand when the distressing spirit from God is upon you, and you shall be well."

17 So Saul said to his servants, "Provide me now a man who can play well, and bring him to me."

18 Then one of the servants answered and said, "Look, I have seen a son of Jesse the Bethlehemite, who is skillful in playing, a mighty man of valor, a man of war, prudent in speech, and a handsome person; and the LORD is with him."

19 Therefore Saul sent messengers to Jesse, and said, "Send me your son David, who is with the sheep."

20 And Jesse took a donkey loaded with bread, a skin of wine, and a young goat, and sent them by his son David to Saul.

21 So David came to Saul and stood before him. And he loved him greatly, and he became his armorbearer.

22 Then Saul sent to Jesse, saying, "Please let David stand before me, for he has found favor in my sight."

23 And so it was, whenever the spirit from God was upon Saul, that David would take a harp and play it with his hand. Then Saul would become refreshed and well, and the distressing spirit would depart from him.

David and Goliath

17 Now the Philistines gathered their armies together to battle, and were gathered together at Sochoh, which

belongs to Judah; they encamped between Sochoh and Azekah, in Ephes Dammim.
2 And Saul and the men of Israel were gathered together, and they encamped in the Valley of Elah, and drew up in battle array against the Philistines.
3 The Philistines stood on a mountain on one side, and Israel stood on a mountain on the other side, with a valley between them.
4 And a champion went out from the camp of the Philistines, named Goliath, from Gath, whose height *was* six cubits and a span.
5 *He had* a bronze helmet on his head, and he *was* armed with a coat of mail, and the weight of the coat *was* five thousand shekels of bronze.
6 And *he had* bronze greaves on his legs and a bronze javelin between his shoulders.
7 Now the staff of his spear *was* like a weaver's beam, and his iron spearhead *weighed* six hundred shekels; and a shield-bearer went before him.
8 Then he stood and cried out to the armies of Israel, and said to them, "Why have you come out to line up for battle? *Am* I not a Philistine, and you the servants of Saul? Choose a man for yourselves, and let him come down to me.
9 "If he is able to fight with me and kill me, then we will be your servants. But if I prevail against him and kill him, then you shall be our servants and serve us."
10 And the Philistine said, "I defy the armies of Israel this day; give me a man, that we may fight together."
11 When Saul and all Israel heard these words of the Philistine, they were dismayed and greatly afraid.
12 Now David *was* the son of that Ephrathite of Bethlehem Judah, whose name *was* Jesse, and who had eight sons. And the man was old, advanced *in years*, in the days of Saul.
13 The three oldest sons of Jesse had gone to follow Saul to the battle. The names of his three sons who went to the battle *were* Eliab the firstborn, next to him Abinadab, and the third Shammah.
14 David *was* the youngest. And the three oldest followed Saul.
15 But David occasionally went and returned from Saul to feed his father's sheep at Bethlehem.
16 And the Philistine drew near and pre-sented himself forty days, morning and evening.
17 Then Jesse said to his son David, "Take now for your brothers an ephah of this dried *grain* and these ten loaves, and run to your brothers at the camp.
18 "And carry these ten cheeses to the captain of *their* thousand, and see how your brothers fare, and bring back news of them."
19 Now Saul and they and all the men of Israel *were* in the Valley of Elah, fighting with the Philistines.
20 So David rose early in the morning, left the sheep with a keeper, and took *the things* and went as Jesse had commanded him. And he came to the camp as the army was going out to the fight and shouting for the battle.
21 For Israel and the Philistines had drawn up in battle array, army against army.
22 And David left his supplies in the hand of the supply keeper, ran to the army, and came and greeted his brothers.
23 Then as he talked with them, there was the champion, the Philistine of Gath, Goliath by name, coming up from the armies of the Philistines; and he spoke according to the same words. So David heard *them*.
24 And all the men of Israel, when they saw the man, fled from him and were dreadfully afraid.
25 So the men of Israel said, "Have you seen this man who has come up? Surely he has come up to defy Israel; and it shall be *that* the man who kills him the king will enrich with great riches, will give him his daughter, and give his father's house exemption in Israel."
26 Then David spoke to the men who stood by him, saying, "What shall be done for the man who kills this Philistine and takes away the reproach from Israel? For who *is* this uncircumcised Philistine, that he should defy the armies of the living God?"
27 And the people answered him in this manner, saying, "So shall it be done for the man who kills him."
28 Now Eliab his oldest brother heard when he spoke to the men; and Eliab's anger was aroused against David, and he said, "Why did you come down here? And with whom have you left those few sheep in the wilderness? I know your

pride and the insolence of your heart, for you have come down to see the battle."
29 And David said, "What have I done now? *Is there* not a cause?"
30 Then he turned from him toward another and said the same thing; and these people answered him as the first ones *did*.
31 And when the words which David spoke were heard, they reported *them* to Saul; and he sent for him.
32 Then David said to Saul, "Let no man's heart fail because of him; your servant will go and fight with this Philistine."
33 And Saul said to David, "You are not able to go against this Philistine to fight with him; for you *are but* a youth, and he a man of war from his youth."
34 But David said to Saul, "Your servant used to keep his father's sheep, and when a lion or a bear came and took a lamb out of the flock,
35 I went out after it and struck it, and delivered *the lamb* from its mouth; and when it arose against me, I caught *it* by its beard, and struck and killed it.
36 "Your servant has killed both lion and bear; and this uncircumcised Philistine will be like one of them, seeing he has defied the armies of the living God."
37 Moreover David said, "The LORD, who delivered me from the paw of the lion and from the paw of the bear, He will deliver me from the hand of this Philistine." And Saul said to David, "Go, and the LORD be with you!"
38 So Saul clothed David with his armor, and he put a bronze helmet on his head; he also clothed him with a coat of mail.
39 And David fastened his sword to his armor, and he tried to walk, for he had not tested *them*. And David said to Saul, "I cannot walk with these, for I have not tested *them*." So David took them off.
40 Then he took his staff in his hand; and he chose for himself five smooth stones from the brook, and put them in a shepherd's bag, in a pouch which he had, and his sling was in his hand. And he drew near to the Philistine.
41 So the Philistine came, and began drawing near to David, and the man who bore the shield *went* before him.
42 And when the Philistine looked about and saw David, he disdained him; for he was *but* a youth, ruddy and good-looking.

43 So the Philistine said to David, "*Am* I a dog, that you come to me with sticks?" And the Philistine cursed David by his gods.
44 And the Philistine said to David, "Come to me, and I will give your flesh to the birds of the air and the beasts of the field!"
45 Then David said to the Philistine, "You come to me with a sword, with a spear, and with a javelin. But I come to you in the name of the LORD of hosts, the God of the armies of Israel, whom you have defied.
46 "This day the LORD will deliver you into my hand, and I will strike you and take your head from you. And this day I will give the carcasses of the camp of the Philistines to the birds of the air and the wild beasts of the earth, that all the earth may know that there is a God in Israel.
47 "Then all this assembly shall know that the LORD does not save with sword and spear; for the battle *is* the LORD's, and He will give you into our hands."
48 And it was so, when the Philistine arose and came and drew near to meet David, that David hastened and ran toward the army to meet the Philistine.
49 Then David put his hand in his bag and took out a stone; and he slung *it* and struck the Philistine in his forehead, so that the stone sank into his forehead, and he fell on his face to the earth.
50 So David prevailed over the Philistine with a sling and a stone, and struck the Philistine and killed him. But *there was* no sword in the hand of David.
51 Therefore David ran and stood over the Philistine, took his sword and drew it out of its sheath and killed him, and cut off his head with it. And when the Philistines saw that their champion was dead, they fled.
52 Now the men of Israel and Judah arose and shouted, and pursued the Philistines as far as the entrance of the valley and to the gates of Ekron. And the wounded of the Philistines fell along the road to Shaaraim, even as far as Gath and Ekron.
53 Then the children of Israel returned from chasing the Philistines, and they plundered their tents.
54 And David took the head of the Philistine and brought it to Jerusalem, but he put his armor in his tent.

David and Goliath

Often the Bible tells us that the Israelites were faced with insurmountable problems. Perhaps one of the most dramatic events occurred when King Saul reigned over the land. The Philistine army from the coast threatened to advance up the low-lying hilly passes to Jerusalem. Determined to defend their country, the Israelites boldly went forth to fight. But upon seeing the Philistine army, the Israelites shrank in fear, for the invading army was like giants. One soldier in particular was awesome—that was the mighty Goliath.

Recent archaeological excavations near the Valley of Elah, between the Israelite camp and the Philistine camp have revealed Philistine villages and burial sites. Many Philistine skeletons have been measured as large as six to seven feet tall. Although there is no way of knowing Goliath's exact size, estimates place him between seven and nine feet in height.

Every day the Israelites and Philistines lined up for battle, Goliath stepped forward. He issued a challenge to fight, one on one, with any Israelite brave enough to face him. No one, not even the king's mightest warriors, dared to step out.

No one, that is, until a small shepherd boy heard the giant's mockery. David, son of Jesse, was out in the hills of Bethlehem tending his father's flock when he was ordered to bring food to his fighting brothers in the army. Upon completing the twenty-mile hike to the Israelite camp, David was present for Goliath's daily challenge.

When David heard Goliath mock the army of God, his tremendous love and faith in his Creator, instilled a strong belief in himself. David knew that no problem was too big for God. And so in total faith, this armorless runt of a boy marched straight down to face the armor-clad giant. With only a tiny stone from the brook of Elah and his sling-shot, David defeated the invincible Goliath.

David's act of faith encouraged the entire Israelite army. Attacking the Philistines with full force, they drove back and destroyed the advancing army, all the way to the gates of their coastal cities. David was fearless for he knew God was on his side. He faced his problems with God's ability, not his own ability. David knew that God's ideas would only work if he did.

With God's ability, we too can conquer our seemingly impossible problems. Like giants that would mock and weaken us, these problems are not as insurmountable as we would think. For God is larger and stronger than our problems. With Him on our side, we can never lose!

55 Now when Saul saw David going out against the Philistine, he said to Abner, the commander of the army, "Abner, whose son *is* this youth?" And Abner said, "As your soul lives, O king, I do not know."
56 And the king said, "Inquire whose son this young man *is*."
57 Then, as David returned from the slaughter of the Philistine, Abner took him and brought him before Saul with the head of the Philistine in his hand.
58 And Saul said to him, "Whose son *are* you, young man?" And David answered, "*I am* the son of your servant Jesse the Bethlehemite."

Saul Resents David

18 And it was so, when he had finished speaking to Saul, that the soul of Jonathan was knit to the soul of David, and Jonathan loved him as his own soul.
2 Saul took him that day, and would not let him go home to his father's house anymore.
3 Then Jonathan and David made a covenant, because he loved him as his own soul.
4 And Jonathan took off the robe that *was* on him and gave it to David, with his armor, even to his sword and his bow and his belt.
5 So David went out wherever Saul sent him, *and* behaved wisely. And Saul set him over the men of war, and he was accepted in the sight of all the people and also in the sight of Saul's servants.
6 Now it had happened as they were coming *home*, when David was returning from the slaughter of the Philistine, that the women had come out of all the cities of Israel, singing and dancing, to meet King Saul, with tambourines, with joy, and with musical instruments.
7 So the women sang as they danced, and said:

"Saul has slain his thousands,
And David his ten thousands."

8 Then Saul was very angry, and the saying displeased him; and he said, "They have ascribed to David ten thousands, and to me they have ascribed *but* thousands. Now *what* more can he have but the kingdom?"

9 So Saul eyed David from that day forward.
10 And it happened on the next day that the distressing spirit from God came upon Saul, and he prophesied inside the house. So David played *music* with his hand, as at other times; but *there was* a spear in Saul's hand.
11 And Saul cast the spear, for he said, "I will pin David to the wall *with it*." But David escaped his presence twice.
12 Now Saul was afraid of David, because the LORD was with him, but had departed from Saul.
13 Therefore Saul removed him from his presence, and made him his captain over a thousand; and he went out and came in before the people.
14 And David behaved wisely in all his ways, and the LORD *was* with him.
15 Therefore, when Saul saw that he behaved very wisely, he was afraid of him.
16 But all Israel and Judah loved David, because he went out and came in before them.

David Marries Michal

17 Then Saul said to David, "Here is my older daughter Merab; I will give her to you as a wife. Only be valiant for me, and fight the LORD's battles." For Saul thought, "Let my hand not be against him, but let the hand of the Philistines be against him."
18 So David said to Saul, "Who *am* I, and what *is* my life *or* my father's family in Israel, that I should be son-in-law to the king?"
19 But it happened at the time when Merab, Saul's daughter, should have been given to David, that she was given to Adriel the Meholathite as a wife.
20 Now Michal, Saul's daughter, loved David. And they told Saul, and the thing pleased him.
21 So Saul said, "I will give her to him, that she may be a snare to him, and that the hand of the Philistines may be against him." Therefore Saul said to David a second time, "You shall be my son-in-law today."
22 And Saul commanded his servants, "Communicate with David secretly, and say, 'Look, the king has delight in you, and all his servants love you. Now therefore, become the king's son-in-law.' "
23 So Saul's servants spoke those words

in the hearing of David. And David said, "Does it seem to you *a* light *thing* to be a king's son-in-law, seeing I *am* a poor and lightly esteemed man?"

24 And the servants of Saul told him, saying, "In this manner David spoke."

25 Then Saul said, "Thus you shall say to David: 'The king does not desire any dowry but one hundred foreskins of the Philistines, to take vengeance on the king's enemies.' " But Saul thought to make David fall by the hand of the Philistines.

26 So when his servants told David these words, it pleased David well to become the king's son-in-law. Now the days had not expired;

27 therefore David arose and went, he and his men, and killed two hundred men of the Philistines. And David brought their foreskins, and they gave them in full count to the king, that he might become the king's son-in-law. Then Saul gave him Michal his daughter as a wife.

28 Thus Saul saw and knew that the LORD *was* with David, and *that* Michal, Saul's daughter, loved him;

29 and Saul was still more afraid of David. So Saul became David's enemy continually.

30 Then the princes of the Philistines went out *to war*. And so it was, whenever they went out, *that* David behaved more wisely than all the servants of Saul, so that his name became highly esteemed.

Saul Persecutes David

19 Now Saul spoke to Jonathan his son and to all his servants, that they should kill David; but Jonathan, Saul's son, delighted much in David.

2 So Jonathan told David, saying, "My father Saul seeks to kill you. Therefore please be on your guard until morning, and stay in a secret *place* and hide.

3 "And I will go out and stand beside my father in the field where you *are*, and I will speak with my father about you. Then what I observe, I will tell you."

4 Now Jonathan spoke well of David to Saul his father, and said to him, "Let not the king sin against his servant, against David, because he has not sinned against you, and because his works *have been* very good toward you.

5 "For he took his life in his hands and killed the Philistine, and the LORD brought about a great salvation for all Israel. You saw *it* and rejoiced. Why then will you sin against innocent blood, to kill David without a cause?"

6 So Saul heeded the voice of Jonathan, and Saul swore, "*As* the LORD lives, he shall not be killed."

7 Then Jonathan called David, and Jonathan told him all these things. So Jonathan brought David to Saul, and he was in his presence as in times past.

8 And there was war again; and David went out and fought with the Philistines, and struck them with a mighty blow, and they fled from him.

9 Now the distressing spirit from the LORD came upon Saul as he sat in his house with his spear in his hand. And David was playing *music* with *his* hand.

10 Then Saul sought to pin David to the wall with the spear, but he slipped away from Saul's presence; and he drove the spear into the wall. So David fled and escaped that night.

11 Saul also sent messengers to David's house to watch him and to kill him in the morning. And Michal, David's wife, told him, saying, "If you do not save your life tonight, tomorrow you will be killed."

12 So Michal let David down through a window. And he went and fled and escaped.

13 And Michal took an image and laid *it* in the bed, put a cover of goats' *hair* for his head, and covered *it* with clothes.

14 So when Saul sent messengers to take David, she said, "He *is* sick."

15 Then Saul sent the messengers *back* to see David, saying, "Bring him up to me in the bed, that I may kill him."

16 And when the messengers had come in, there was the image in the bed, with a cover of goats' *hair* for his head.

17 Then Saul said to Michal, "Why have you deceived me like this, and sent my enemy away, so that he has escaped?" And Michal answered Saul, "He said to me, 'Let me go! Why should I kill you?' "

18 So David fled and escaped, and went to Samuel at Ramah, and told him all that Saul had done to him. And he and Samuel went and stayed in Naioth.

19 Now it was told Saul, saying, "Take note, David *is* at Naioth in Ramah!"

20 Then Saul sent messengers to take David. And when they saw the group of prophets prophesying, and Samuel stand-

ing *as* leader over them, the Spirit of God came upon the messengers of Saul, and they also prophesied.
21 And when Saul was told, he sent other messengers, and they prophesied likewise. Then Saul sent messengers again the third time, and they prophesied also.
22 Then he also went to Ramah, and came to the great well that *is* at Sechu. So he asked, and said, "Where *are* Samuel and David?" And *someone* said, "Indeed *they are* at Naioth in Ramah."
23 So he went there to Naioth in Ramah. Then the Spirit of God was upon him also, and he went on and prophesied until he came to Naioth in Ramah.
24 And he also stripped off his clothes and prophesied before Samuel in like manner, and lay down naked all that day and all that night. Therefore they say, "*Is* Saul also among the prophets?"²⁴

Jonathan's Loyalty to David

20 Then David fled from Naioth in Ramah, and went and said to Jonathan, "What have I done? What *is* my iniquity, and what *is* my sin before your father, that he seeks my life?"
2 So Jonathan said to him, "By no means! You shall not die! Indeed, my father will do nothing either great or small without first telling me. And why should my father hide this thing from me? It *is* not *so!*"
3 Then David took an oath again, and said, "Your father certainly knows that I have found favor in your eyes, and he says, 'Do not let Jonathan know this, lest he be grieved.' But truly, *as* the LORD lives and *as* your soul lives, *there is* but a step between me and death."
4 So Jonathan said to David, "Whatever you yourself desire, I will do *it* for you."
5 And David said to Jonathan, "Indeed tomorrow *is* the New Moon, and I should not fail to sit with the king to eat. But let me go, that I may hide in the field until the third *day* at evening.
6 "If your father misses me at all, then say, 'David earnestly asked *permission* of me that he might run over to Bethlehem, his city, for *there is* a yearly sacrifice there for all the family.'
7 "If he says thus: '*It is* well,' your servant will be safe. But if he is very angry,

then be sure that evil is determined by him.
8 "Therefore you shall deal kindly with your servant, for you have brought your servant into a covenant of the LORD with you. Nevertheless, if there is iniquity in me, kill me yourself, for why should you bring me to your father?"
9 And Jonathan said, "Far be it from you! For if I knew certainly that evil was determined by my father to come upon you, then would I not tell you?"
10 Then David said to Jonathan, "Who will tell me, or what *if* your father answers you roughly?"
11 And Jonathan said to David, "Come, and let us go out into the field." So both of them went out into the field.
12 Then Jonathan said to David: "The LORD God of Israel *is witness*! When I have sounded out my father sometime tomorrow, *or* the third *day*, and indeed *there is* good toward David, and I do not send to you and tell you,
13 "may the LORD do so and much more to Jonathan. But if it pleases my father *to do* you evil, then I will report it to you and send you away, that you may go in safety. And the LORD be with you as He has been with my father.
14 "And you shall not only show me the kindness of the LORD while I still live, that I may not die;
15 "but you shall not cut off your kindness from my house forever, no, not when the LORD has cut off every one of the enemies of David from the face of the earth."
16 So Jonathan made *a covenant* with the house of David, *saying*, "Let the LORD require *it* at the hand of David's enemies."
17 And Jonathan again caused David to vow, because he loved him; for he loved him as he loved his own soul.
18 Then Jonathan said to David, "Tomorrow *is* the New Moon; and you will be missed, because your seat will be empty.
19 "And *when* you have stayed three days, go down quickly and come to the place where you hid on the day of the deed; and remain by the stone Ezel.
20 "Then I will shoot three arrows to the side *of it*, as though I shot at a target;
21 "and there I will send a lad, *saying*, 'Go, find the arrows.' If I expressly say to

24 Compare 1 Samuel 10:12

Peace: It's All in the Word

When God gives His word, we know He will keep it. His word is in fact a work already accomplished. It is known that in biblical times, the spoken word carried with it the same credibility as a legal written contract. Verbal oaths were binding agreements between two parties. In the speaking of the word, the work was literally accomplished.

This is still evident in the Middle East today. The common greeting, "Peace be with you," and "Peace be with you also," is exchanged primarily among friends. For the speaking of the word, peace actually establishes peace.

In fact, should a disagreement break out between friends, or even new acquaintances, it is not uncommon for either party to ask for his "peace" back. The other person must return the peace with the phrase, "I give your peace back to you."

Unlike the peace of men, God's promise is forever. He will never take His peace from us for He said, "My peace I give to you; not as the world gives" (John 14:27). "Let not your heart be troubled; you believe in God, believe also in Me" (John 14:1).

What is peace? Peace is the inner knowledge that your relationship with God is secure. It is the assurance that your sins are forgiven. Your life is clean and new.

Peace—it's all in the word. And the Living Word is the person and work of Jesus Christ. Look to Him for peace with God and peace with others. God's peace is eternal and will bring us into a loving, lasting relationship with Him forever.

him, 'Look, the arrows *are* on this side of you; get them and come'—then, as the LORD lives, *there is* safety for you and no harm.

22 "But if I say thus to the young man, 'Look, the arrows *are* beyond you'—go your way, for the LORD has sent you away.

23 "And as for the matter which you and I have spoken of, indeed the LORD *be* between you and me forever."

24 So David hid in the field. And when the New Moon had come, the king sat down to eat the feast.

25 Now the king sat on his seat, as at other times, on a seat by the wall. And Jonathan arose, and Abner sat by Saul's side, but David's place was empty.

26 Nevertheless Saul did not say anything that day, for he thought, "Something has happened to him; he *is* unclean, surely he *is* unclean."

27 And it happened the next day, the second *day* of the month, that David's place was empty. And Saul said to Jonathan his son, "Why has the son of Jesse not come to eat, either yesterday or today?"

28 So Jonathan answered Saul, "David earnestly asked *permission* of me *to go to* Bethlehem.

29 "And he said, 'Please let me go, for our family has a sacrifice in the city, and my brother has commanded me *to be there*. And now, if I have found favor in your eyes, please let me get away and see my brothers.' Therefore he has not come to the king's table."

30 Then Saul's anger was aroused against Jonathan, and he said to him, "You son of a perverse, rebellious *woman*! Do I not know that you have chosen the son of Jesse to your own shame and to the shame of your mother's nakedness?

31 "For as long as the son of Jesse lives on the earth, you shall not be established, nor your kingdom. Now therefore, send and bring him to me, for he shall surely die."

32 And Jonathan answered Saul his father, and said to him, "Why should he be killed? What has he done?"

33 Then Saul cast a spear at him to kill him, by which Jonathan knew that it was determined by his father to kill David.

34 So Jonathan arose from the table in fierce anger, and ate no food the second day of the month, for he was grieved for David, because his father had treated him shamefully.

35 And so it was, in the morning, that Jonathan went out into the field at the time appointed with David, and a little lad *was* with him.

36 Then he said to his lad, "Now run, find the arrows which I shoot." As the lad ran, he shot an arrow beyond him.

37 When the lad had come to the place where the arrow was which Jonathan had shot, Jonathan cried out after the lad and said, "*Is* not the arrow beyond you?"

38 And Jonathan cried out after the lad, "Make haste, hurry, do not delay!" So Jonathan's lad gathered up the arrows and came back to his master.

39 But the lad did not know anything. Only Jonathan and David knew of the matter.

40 Then Jonathan gave his weapons to his lad, and said to him, "Go, carry *them* to the city."

41 Now as soon as the lad had gone, David arose from *a place* toward the south, fell on his face to the ground, and bowed down three times. And they kissed one another; and they wept together, but David more so.

42 Then Jonathan said to David, "Go in peace, since we have both sworn in the name of the LORD, saying, 'May the LORD be between you and me, and between your descendants and my descendants, forever.' " So he arose and departed, and Jonathan went into the city.

David and the Holy Bread

21 Now David came to Nob, to Ahimelech the priest. And Ahimelech was afraid when he met David, and said to him, "Why *are* you alone, and no one is with you?"

2 So David said to Ahimelech the priest, "The king has ordered me on some business, and said to me, 'Do not let anyone know anything about the business on which I send you, or what I have commanded you.' And I have directed *my* young men to such and such a place.

3 "Now therefore, what have you on hand? Give *me* five *loaves of* bread in my hand, or whatever can be found."

4 And the priest answered David and said, "*There is* no common bread on hand; but there is holy bread, if the

young men have at least kept themselves from women."

5 Then David answered the priest, and said to him, "Truly, women *have been* kept from us about three days since I came out. And the vessels of the young men are holy, and *the bread is* in effect common, even though it was sanctified in the vessel this day."

6 So the priest gave him holy *bread*; for there was no bread there but the show-bread which had been taken from before the LORD, in order to put hot bread *in its place* on the day when it was taken away.

7 Now a certain man of the servants of Saul *was* there that day, detained before the LORD. And his name *was* Doeg, an Edomite, the chief of the herdsmen who *belonged* to Saul.

8 And David said to Ahimelech, "Is there not here on hand a spear or a sword? For I have brought neither my sword nor my weapons with me, because the king's business required haste."

9 So the priest said, "The sword of Goliath the Philistine, whom you killed in the Valley of Elah, there it is, wrapped in a cloth behind the ephod. If you will take that, take *it*. For *there is* no other except that one here." And David said, "*There is* none like it; give it to me."

David Flees to Gath

10 Then David arose and fled that day from before Saul, and went to Achish the king of Gath.

11 And the servants of Achish said to him, "*Is* this not David the king of the land? Did they not sing of him to one another in dances, saying:

'Saul has slain his thousands,
And David his ten thousands'?"[25]

12 Now David took these words to heart, and was very much afraid of Achish the king of Gath.

13 So he changed his behavior before them, feigned madness in their hands, scratched on the doors of the gate, and let his saliva fall down on his beard.

14 Then Achish said to his servants, "Look, you see the man is insane. Why have you brought him to me?

15 "Have I need of madmen, that you have brought this *fellow* to play the mad-

man in my presence? Shall this *fellow* come into my house?"

David's Four Hundred Men

22 David therefore departed from there and escaped to the cave of Adullam. And when his brothers and all his father's house heard *it*, they went down there to him.

2 And everyone *who was* in distress, everyone who *was* in debt, and everyone *who was* discontented gathered to him. So he became captain over them. And there were about four hundred men with him.

3 Then David went from there to Mizpah of Moab; and he said to the king of Moab, "Please let my father and mother come here with you, till I know what God will do for me."

4 So he brought them before the king of Moab, and they dwelt with him all the time that David was in the stronghold.

5 Then the prophet Gad said to David, "Do not stay in the stronghold; depart, and go to the land of Judah." So David departed and went into the forest of Hereth.

Saul Murders the Priests

6 When Saul heard that David and the men who *were* with him had been discovered—now Saul was staying in Gibeah under a tamarisk tree in Ramah, with his spear in his hand, and all his servants standing about him—

7 then Saul said to his servants who stood about him, "Hear now, you Benjamites! Will the son of Jesse give every one of you fields and vineyards, *and* make you all captains of thousands and captains of hundreds?

8 "All of you have conspired against me, and *there is* no one who reveals to me that my son has made a covenant with the son of Jesse; and *there is* not one of you who is sorry for me or reveals to me that my son has stirred up my servant against me, to lie in wait, as *it is* this day."

9 Then answered Doeg the Edomite, who was set over the servants of Saul, and said, "I saw the son of Jesse going to Nob, to Ahimelech the son of Ahitub.

10 "And he inquired of the LORD for him, gave him provisions, and gave him the sword of Goliath the Philistine."

25 Compare 1 Samuel 18:7

11 Then the king sent to call Ahimelech the priest, the son of Ahitub, and all his father's house, the priests who *were* in Nob. And they all came to the king.

12 And Saul said, "Hear now, son of Ahitub!" And he answered, "Here I am, my lord."

13 Then Saul said to him, "Why have you conspired against me, you and the son of Jesse, in that you have given him bread and a sword, and have inquired of God for him, that he should rise against me, to lie in wait, as it is this day?"

14 So Ahimelech answered the king and said, "And who among all your servants *is so* faithful as David, who is the king's son-in-law, who goes at your bidding, and is honorable in your house?

15 "Did I then begin to inquire of God for him? Far be it from me! Let not the king impute anything to his servant, *or* to any in the house of my father. For your servant knew nothing of all this, little or much."

16 And the king said, "You shall surely die, Ahimelech, you and all your father's house!"

17 Then the king said to the guards who stood about him, "Turn and kill the priests of the LORD, because their hand also *is* with David, and because they knew when he fled and did not tell it to me." But the servants of the king would not lift their hands to strike the priests of the LORD.

18 And the king said to Doeg, "You turn and kill the priests!" So Doeg the Edomite turned and struck the priests, and killed on that day eighty-five men who wore a linen ephod.

19 Also Nob, the city of the priests, he struck with the edge of the sword, both men and women, children and nursing infants, oxen and donkeys and sheep—with the edge of the sword.

20 Now one of the sons of Ahimelech the son of Ahitub, named Abiathar, escaped and fled after David.

21 And Abiathar told David that Saul had killed the LORD's priests.

22 So David said to Abiathar, "I knew that day, when Doeg the Edomite *was* there, that he would surely tell Saul. I have caused *the death* of all the persons of your father's house.

23 "Stay with me; do not fear. For he who seeks my life seeks your life, but with me you *shall be* safe."

David Saves the City of Keilah

23 Then they told David, saying, "Look, the Philistines are fighting against Keilah, and they are robbing the threshing floors."

2 Therefore David inquired of the LORD, saying, "Shall I go and attack these Philistines?" And the LORD said to David, "Go and attack the Philistines, and save Keilah."

3 And David's men said to him, "Look, we are afraid here in Judah. How much more then if we go to Keilah against the armies of the Philistines?"

4 Then David inquired of the LORD once again. And the LORD answered him and said, "Arise, go down to Keilah. For I will deliver the Philistines into your hand."

5 And David and his men went to Keilah and fought with the Philistines, struck them with a mighty blow, and took away their livestock. So David saved the inhabitants of Keilah.

6 Now it happened, when Abiathar the son of Ahimelech fled to David at Keilah, *that* he went down *with* an ephod in his hand.

7 And Saul was told that David had gone to Keilah. So Saul said, "God has delivered him into my hand, for he has shut himself in by entering a town that has gates and bars."

8 Then Saul called all the people together for war, to go down to Keilah to besiege David and his men.

9 When David knew that Saul plotted evil against him, he said to Abiathar the priest, "Bring the ephod here."

10 Then David said, "O LORD God of Israel, Your servant has certainly heard that Saul seeks to come to Keilah to destroy the city for my sake.

11 "Will the men of Keilah deliver me into his hand? Will Saul come down, as Your servant has heard? O LORD God of Israel, I pray, tell Your servant." And the LORD said, "He will come down."

12 Then David said, "Will the men of Keilah deliver me and my men into the hand of Saul?" And the LORD said, "They will deliver *you*."

13 So David and his men, about six hundred, arose and departed from Keilah and went wherever they could go. Then it was told Saul that David had escaped from Keilah; so he halted the expedition.

David in Wilderness Strongholds

14 And David stayed in strongholds in the wilderness, and remained in the mountains in the Wilderness of Ziph. Saul sought him every day, but God did not deliver him into his hand. *15* So David saw that Saul had come out to seek his life. And David *was* in the Wilderness of Ziph in a forest.[26] *16* Then Jonathan, Saul's son, arose and went to David in the woods and strengthened his hand in God. *17* And he said to him, "Do not fear, for the hand of Saul my father shall not find you. You shall be king over Israel, and I shall be next to you. Even my father Saul knows that." *18* So the two of them made a covenant before the LORD. And David stayed in the woods, and Jonathan went to his own house.

19 Then the Ziphites came up to Saul at Gibeah, saying, "Is David not hiding with us in strongholds in the woods, in the hill of Hachilah, which *is* on the south of Jeshimon? *20* "Now therefore, O king, come down according to all the desire of your soul to come down; and our part *shall be* to deliver him into the king's hand." *21* And Saul said, "Blessed *are* you of the LORD, for you have compassion on me. *22* "Please go and find out for sure, and see the place where his hideout is, *and* who has seen him there. For I am told *that* he is very crafty. *23* "See therefore, and take knowledge of all the lurking places where he hides; and come back to me with certainty, and I will go with you. And it shall be, if he is in the land, that I will search for him throughout all the clans[27] of Judah." *24* So they arose and went to Ziph before Saul. But David and his men *were* in the Wilderness of Maon, in the plain on the south of Jeshimon. *25* When Saul and his men went to seek *him*, they told David. Therefore he went down to the rock, and stayed in the Wilderness of Maon. And when Saul heard *that*, he pursued David in the Wilderness of Maon. *26* Then Saul went on one side of the mountain, and David and his men on the other side of the mountain. So David made haste to get away from Saul, for Saul and his men were encircling David and his men to take them. *27* But a messenger came to Saul, saying, "Hasten and come, for the Philistines have invaded the land!" *28* Therefore Saul returned from pursuing David, and went against the Philistines; so they called that place the Rock of Escaping.[28] *29* Then David went up from there and dwelt in strongholds at En Gedi.

David Spares Saul

24 Now it happened, when Saul had returned from following the Philistines, that it was told him, saying, "Take note! David *is* in the Wilderness of En Gedi." *2* Then Saul took three thousand chosen men from all Israel, and went to seek David and his men on the Rocks of the Wild Goats. *3* So he came to the sheepfolds by the road, where there *was* a cave; and Saul went in to attend to his needs. (David and his men were staying in the recesses of the cave.) *4* Then the men of David said to him, "This is the day of which the LORD said to you, 'Behold, I will deliver your enemy into your hand, that you may do to him as it seems good to you.'" And David arose and secretly cut off a corner of Saul's robe. *5* Now it happened afterward that David's heart troubled him because he had cut Saul's *robe*. *6* And he said to his men, "The LORD forbid that I should do this thing to my master, the LORD's anointed, to stretch out my hand against him, seeing he *is* the anointed of the LORD." *7* So David restrained his servants with *these* words, and did not allow them to rise against Saul. And Saul got up from the cave and went on *his* way. *8* David also arose afterward, went out of the cave, and called out to Saul, saying, "My lord the king!" And when Saul looked behind him, David stooped with his face to the earth, and bowed down. *9* And David said to Saul: "Why do you listen to the words of men who say, 'Indeed David seeks your harm'?

26 Or *in Horesh*   27 Literally *thousands*   28 Hebrew *Sela Hammahlekoth*

10 "Look, this day your eyes have seen that the LORD delivered you today into my hand in the cave, and *someone* urged *me* to kill you. But *my eye* spared you, and I said, 'I will not stretch out my hand against my lord, for he *is* the LORD's anointed.'

11 "Moreover, my father, see! Yes, see the corner of your robe in my hand! For in that I cut off the corner of your robe, and did not kill you, know and see that *there is* neither evil nor rebellion in my hand, and I have not sinned against you. Yet you hunt my life to take it.

12 "Let the LORD judge between you and me, and let the LORD avenge me on you. But my hand shall not be against you.

13 "As the proverb of the ancients says, 'Wickedness proceeds from the wicked.' But my hand shall not be against you.

14 "After whom has the king of Israel come out? Whom do you pursue? A dead dog? A flea?

15 "Therefore let the LORD be judge, and judge between you and me, and see and plead my case, and deliver me out of your hand."

16 So it was, when David had finished speaking these words to Saul, that Saul said, "*Is* this your voice, my son David?" And Saul lifted his voice and wept.

17 Then he said to David: "You *are* more righteous than I; for you have rewarded me with good, whereas I have rewarded you with evil.

18 "And you have shown this day how you have dealt well with me; for when the LORD delivered me into your hand, you did not kill me.

19 "For if a man finds his enemy, will he let him get away safely? Therefore may the LORD reward you with good for what you have done to me this day.

20 "And now I know indeed that you shall surely be king, and that the kingdom of Israel shall be established in your hand.

21 "Therefore swear now to me by the LORD that you will not cut off my descendants after me, and that you will not destroy my name from my father's house."

22 So David swore to Saul. And Saul went home, but David and his men went up to the stronghold.

Death of Samuel

25 Then Samuel died; and the Israelites gathered together and lamented for him, and buried him at his home in Ramah. And David arose and went down to the Wilderness of Paran.

David and the Wife of Nabal

2 Now *there was* a man in Maon whose business *was* in Carmel, and the man *was* very rich. He had three thousand sheep and a thousand goats. And he was shearing his sheep in Carmel.

3 The name of the man *was* Nabal, and the name of his wife Abigail. And *she was* a woman of good understanding and beautiful appearance; but the man *was* harsh and evil in *his* doings. And he *was of the house of* Caleb.

4 When David heard in the wilderness that Nabal was shearing his sheep,

5 David sent ten young men; and David said to the young men, "Go up to Carmel, go to Nabal, and greet him in my name.

6 "And thus you shall say to him who lives *in prosperity*: 'Peace *be* to you, peace to your house, and peace to all that you have!

7 'Now I have heard that you have shearers. Your shepherds were with us, and we did not hurt them, nor was there anything missing from them all the while they were in Carmel.

8 'Ask your young men, and they will tell you. Therefore let *my* young men find favor in your eyes, for we come on a feast day. Please give whatever comes to your hand to your servants and to your son David.' "

9 So when David's young men came, they spoke to Nabal according to all these words in the name of David, and waited.

10 Then Nabal answered David's servants, and said, "Who *is* David, and who *is* the son of Jesse? There are many servants nowadays who break away each one from his master.

11 "Shall I then take my bread and my water and my meat that I have killed for my shearers, and give *it* to men when I do not know where they *are* from?"

12 So David's young men turned on their heels and went back; and they came and told him all these words.

13 Then David said to his men, "Every man gird on his sword." So every man girded on his sword, and David also girded on his sword. And about four hundred men went with David, and two hundred stayed with the supplies.

14 Now one of the young men told Abigail, Nabal's wife, saying, "Look, David sent messengers from the wilderness to greet our master; and he reviled them.

15 "But the men *were* very good to us, and we were not hurt, nor did we miss anything as long as we accompanied them, when we were in the fields.

16 "They were a wall to us both by night and day, all the time we were with them keeping the sheep.

17 "Now therefore, know and consider what you will do, for harm is determined against our master and against all his household. For he *is such* a scoundrel[29] that *one* cannot speak to him."

18 Then Abigail made haste and took two hundred *loaves* of bread, two skins of wine, five sheep already dressed, five seahs of roasted *grain*, one hundred clusters of raisins, and two hundred cakes of figs, and loaded *them* on donkeys.

19 And she said to her servants, "Go on before me; see, I am coming after you." But she did not tell her husband Nabal.

20 So it was, *as* she rode on the donkey, that she went down under cover of the hill; and there were David and his men, coming down toward her, and she met them.

21 Now David had said, "Surely in vain I have protected all that this *fellow* has in the wilderness, so that nothing was missed of all that *belongs* to him. And he has repaid me evil for good.

22 "May God do so, and more also, to the enemies of David, if I leave one male of all who *belong* to him by morning light."

23 Now when Abigail saw David, she hastened to dismount from the donkey, fell on her face before David, and bowed down to the ground.

24 So she fell at his feet and said: "On me, my lord, *on* me *let* this iniquity *be*! And please let your maidservant speak in your ears, and hear the words of your maidservant.

25 "Please, let not my lord regard this scoundrel Nabal. For as his name *is*, so *is* he: Nabal[30] *is* his name, and folly *is* with

him. But I, your maidservant, did not see the young men of my lord whom you sent.

26 "Now therefore, my lord, *as* the LORD lives and *as* your soul lives, since the LORD has held you back from coming to bloodshed and from avenging yourself with your own hand, now then, let your enemies and those who seek harm for my lord be as Nabal.

27 "And now this present which your maidservant has brought to my lord, let it be given to the young men who follow my lord.

28 "Please forgive the trespass of your maidservant. For the LORD will certainly make for my lord an enduring house, because my lord fights the battles of the LORD, and evil is not found in you throughout your days.

29 "Yet a man has risen to pursue you and seek your life, but the life of my lord shall be bound in the bundle of the living with the LORD your God; and the lives of your enemies He shall sling out, *as from* the pocket of a sling.

30 "And it shall come to pass, when the LORD has done for my lord according to all the good that He has spoken concerning you, and has appointed you ruler over Israel,

31 "that this will be no grief to you, nor offense of heart to my lord, either that you have shed blood without cause, or that my lord has avenged himself. But when the LORD has dealt well with my lord, then remember your maidservant."

32 Then David said to Abigail: "Blessed *be* the LORD God of Israel, who sent you this day to meet me!

33 "And blessed *is* your advice and blessed *are* you, because you have kept me this day from coming to bloodshed and from avenging myself with my own hand.

34 "For indeed, *as* the LORD God of Israel lives, who has kept me back from hurting you, unless you had hastened and come to meet me, surely by morning light no males would have been left to Nabal."

35 So David received from her hand what she had brought him, and said to her, "Go up in peace to your house. See, I have heeded your voice and respected your person."

36 Then Abigail went to Nabal, and there he was, holding a feast in his house,

29 Literally *son of Belial*   30 Literally *Fool*

like the feast of a king. And Nabal's heart *was* merry within him, for he *was* very drunk; therefore she told him nothing, little or much, until morning light. 37 So it was, in the morning, when the wine had gone from Nabal, and his wife had told him these things, that his heart died within him, and he became *like* a stone. 38 Then it came about, *after* about ten days, that the LORD struck Nabal, and he died.

39 So when David heard that Nabal was dead, he said, "Blessed *be* the LORD, who has pleaded the cause of my reproach from the hand of Nabal, and has kept His servant from evil! For the LORD has returned the wickedness of Nabal on his own head." And David sent and proposed to Abigail, to take her as his wife. 40 And when the servants of David had come to Abigail at Carmel, they spoke to her saying, "David sent us to you, to ask you to become his wife." 41 Then she arose, bowed her face to the earth, and said, "Here is your maidservant, a servant to wash the feet of the servants of my lord." 42 So Abigail rose in haste and rode on a donkey, attended by five of her maidens; and she followed the messengers of David, and became his wife. 43 David also took Ahinoam of Jezreel, and so both of them were his wives. 44 But Saul had given Michal his daughter, David's wife, to Palti[31] the son of Laish, who *was* from Gallim.

David Spares Saul a Second Time

26 Now the Ziphites came to Saul at Gibeah, saying, "Is David not hiding in the hill of Hachilah, *which is* opposite Jeshimon?" 2 Then Saul arose and went down to the Wilderness of Ziph, having three thousand chosen men of Israel with him, to seek David in the Wilderness of Ziph. 3 And Saul encamped in the hill of Hachilah, which *is* opposite Jeshimon, by the road. But David stayed in the wilderness, and he saw that Saul came after him into the wilderness. 4 David therefore sent out spies, and understood that Saul had indeed come. 5 So David arose and came to the place where Saul had encamped. And David saw the place where Saul lay, and Abner

the son of Ner, the commander of his army. Now Saul lay within the camp, with the people encamped all around him.

6 Then David answered, and said to Ahimelech the Hittite and to Abishai the son of Zeruiah, brother of Joab, saying, "Who will go down with me to Saul in the camp?" And Abishai said, "I will go down with you." 7 So David and Abishai came to the people by night; and there Saul lay sleeping within the camp, with his spear stuck in the ground by his head. And Abner and the people lay all around him. 8 Then Abishai said to David, "God has delivered your enemy into your hand this day. Now therefore, please, let me strike him at once with the spear, right to the earth; and I will not *have to strike* him a second time!" 9 And David said to Abishai, "Do not destroy him; for who can stretch out his hand against the LORD'S anointed, and be guiltless?" 10 David said furthermore, "*As* the LORD lives, the LORD shall strike him, or his day shall come to die, or he shall go out to battle and perish. 11 "The LORD forbid that I should stretch out my hand against the LORD'S anointed. But please, take now the spear and the jug of water that *are* by his head, and let us go." 12 So David took the spear and the jug of water *by* Saul's head, and they got away; and no man saw *it* or knew *it* or awoke. For they *were* all asleep, because a deep sleep from the LORD had fallen on them. 13 Then David went over to the other side, and stood on the top of a hill afar off, a great distance *being* between them. 14 And David called out to the people and to Abner the son of Ner, saying, "Do you not answer, Abner?" Then Abner answered and said, "Who *are* you, calling out to the king?" 15 So David said to Abner, "*Are* you not a man? And who *is* like you in Israel? Why then have you not guarded your lord the king? For one of the people came in to destroy your lord the king. 16 "This thing that you have done *is* not good. *As* the LORD lives, you *are* worthy to die, because you have not guarded your master, the LORD'S anointed. And

31 Spelled *Paltiel* in 2 Samuel 3:15

now see where the king's spear *is*, and the jug of water that *was* by his head."
17 Then Saul knew David's voice, and said, "*Is* that your voice, my son David?" And David said, "*It is* my voice, my lord, O king."
18 And he said, "Why does my lord thus pursue his servant? For what have I done, or what evil *is* in my hand?
19 "Now therefore, please, let my lord the king hear the words of his servant: If the LORD has stirred you up against me, let Him accept an offering. But if *it is* the children of men, *may* they *be* cursed before the LORD, for they have driven me out this day from abiding in the inheritance of the LORD, saying, 'Go, serve other gods.'
20 "Now therefore, do not let my blood fall to the earth before the face of the LORD. For the king of Israel has come out to seek a flea, as when one hunts a partridge in the mountains."
21 Then Saul said, "I have sinned. Return, my son David. For I will harm you no more, because my life was precious in your eyes this day. Indeed I have played the fool and erred exceedingly."
22 And David answered and said, "Here is the king's spear. Let one of the young men come over and get it.
23 "May the LORD repay every man *for* his righteousness and his faithfulness; for the LORD delivered you into *my* hand today, but I would not stretch out my hand against the LORD's anointed.
24 "And indeed, as your life was valued much this day in my eyes, so let my life be valued much in the eyes of the LORD, and let Him deliver me out of all tribulation."
25 Then Saul said to David, "*May* you *be* blessed, my son David! You shall both do great things and also still prevail." So David went on his way, and Saul returned to his place.

David Allied with the Philistines

27 And David said in his heart, "Now I shall perish someday by the hand of Saul. *There is* nothing better for me than that I should speedily escape to the land of the Philistines; and Saul will despair of me, to seek me anymore in any part of Israel. So I shall escape out of his hand."
2 Then David arose and went over with the six hundred men who *were* with him to Achish the son of Maoch, king of Gath.
3 So David dwelt with Achish at Gath, he and his men, each man with his household, *and* David with his two wives, Ahinoam the Jezreelitess, and Abigail the Carmelitess, Nabal's widow.
4 And it was told Saul that David had fled to Gath; so he sought him no more.
5 Then David said to Achish, "If I have now found favor in your eyes, let them give me a place in some town in the country, that I may dwell there. For why should your servant dwell in the royal city with you?"
6 So Achish gave him Ziklag that day. Therefore Ziklag has belonged to the kings of Judah to this day.
7 Now the time that David dwelt in the country of the Philistines was one full year and four months.
8 And David and his men went up and raided the Geshurites, the Girzites,[32] and the Amalekites. For those nations were the inhabitants of the land from of old, as you go to Shur, even as far as the land of Egypt.
9 Whenever David attacked the land, he left neither man nor woman alive, but took away the sheep, the oxen, the donkeys, the camels, and the apparel, and returned and came to Achish.
10 Then Achish would say, "Where have you made a raid today?" And David would say, "Against the southern area of Judah, or against the southern area of the Jerahmeelites, or against the southern area of the Kenites."
11 David would save neither man nor woman alive, to bring *news* to Gath, saying, "Lest they should inform on us, saying, 'Thus David did.' " And so *was* his behavior all the time he dwelt in the country of the Philistines.
12 So Achish believed David, saying, "He has made his people Israel utterly abhor him; therefore he will be my servant forever."

28 Now it happened in those days that the Philistines gathered their armies together for war, to fight with Israel. And Achish said to David, "You assuredly know that you will go out with me to battle, you and your men."
2 And David said to Achish, "Surely

Making Peace
with Your Enemies

One of the qualities that made David a great leader was his ability to overcome any obstacle which lay in his path. When faced with a difficult situation he believed in exhausting all possibilities!

Following his victory over the Philistine giant, Goliath, the young man, David, spent years fleeing from the jealous King Saul. Many times David had the opportunity to strike back at Saul, but he refused to harm God's anointed king. David believed God could deliver him in any and all circumstances.

Perhaps one of the most difficult situations David encountered was during a narrow escape from King Saul in the lower hill country near the dangerous Philistine coastal territory. David continually fled from Saul in the eastern wilderness areas, only to be flushed out by the king's army. This left him with only one avenue of escape—directly through Philistine territory and the royal city of Gath. David knew that within the city was one of his most vengeful adversaries, Achish, king of Gath, a ruler who had every reason to kill him.

Achish ruled Gath, one of five royal Philistine cities which also included Ashdod, Ashkelon, Ekron, and Gaza. He was a member of the royal family and most likely a relative and possibly the brother of Goliath. Achish knew of David's wars against the Philistines and would have remembered David's slaying of not only Goliath but the giant's sons and brothers as well (1 Chr. 20:4-8). There seemed to be no reasonable way that King Achish would protect David from Saul, but David believed that with God all things are possible. With the same indomitable spirit which the youth David believed God would deliver him from the bear and the lion, the man David now approached Achish, king of Gath, and requested his protection.

God honored David's attempt to make peace with his enemy. Impressed by his bravery, Achish not only welcomed David but appointed him as ruler over the city of Ziklag, an important Philistine defense post. David knew that if he believed God, no situation was hopeless. Making peace with an enemy becomes a possibility with faith in God! "You prepare a table before me in the presence of my enemies" (Ps. 23:5).

you know what your servant can do."
And Achish said to David, "Therefore I
will make you one of my chief guardians
forever."

Saul Consults a Medium

3 Now Samuel had died, and all Israel
had lamented for him and buried him in
Ramah, in his own city. And Saul had
put the mediums and the spiritists out of
the land.
4 Then the Philistines gathered together, and came and encamped at Shunem. So Saul gathered all Israel together,
and they encamped at Gilboa.
5 When Saul saw the army of the Philistines, he was afraid, and his heart trembled greatly.
6 And when Saul inquired of the LORD,
the LORD did not answer him, either by
dreams or by Urim or by the prophets.
7 Then Saul said to his servants, "Find
me a woman who is a medium, that I may
go to her and inquire of her." And his
servants said to him, "In fact, there is a
woman who is a medium at En Dor."
8 So Saul disguised himself and put on
other clothes, and he went, and two men
with him; and they came to the woman
by night. And he said, "Please conduct a
séance for me, and bring up for me the
one I shall name to you."
9 Then the woman said to him, "Look,
you know what Saul has done, how he
has cut off the mediums and the spiritists
from the land. Why then do you lay a
snare for my life, to cause me to die?"
10 And Saul swore to her by the LORD,
saying, "As the LORD lives, no punishment shall come upon you for this thing."
11 Then the woman said, "Whom shall I
bring up for you?" And he said, "Bring
up Samuel for me."
12 When the woman saw Samuel, she
cried out with a loud voice. And the
woman spoke to Saul, saying, "Why have
you deceived me? For you are Saul!"
13 And the king said to her, "Do not be
afraid. What did you see?" And the
woman said to Saul, "I saw a spirit[33] ascending out of the earth."
14 So he said to her, "What is his form?"
And she said, "An old man is coming up,
and he is covered with a mantle." And
Saul perceived that it was Samuel, and he
stooped with his face to the ground and
bowed down.

15 Now Samuel said to Saul, "Why have
you disturbed me by bringing me up?"
And Saul answered, "I am deeply distressed; for the Philistines make war
against me, and God has departed from
me and does not answer me anymore,
neither by prophets nor by dreams.
Therefore I have called you, that you may
reveal to me what I should do."
16 Then Samuel said: "Why then do you
ask me, seeing the LORD has departed
from you and has become your enemy?
17 "And the LORD has done for Himself[34] as He spoke by me. For the LORD
has torn the kingdom out of your hand
and given it to your neighbor, namely,
David.
18 "Because you did not obey the voice
of the LORD nor execute His fierce wrath
upon Amalek, therefore the LORD has
done this thing to you this day.
19 "Moreover the LORD will also deliver
Israel with you into the hand of the Philistines. And tomorrow you and your
sons will be with me. The LORD will also
deliver the army of Israel into the hand of
the Philistines."
20 Then immediately Saul fell full length
on the ground, and was dreadfully afraid
because of the words of Samuel. And
there was no strength in him, for he had
eaten no food all day or all night.
21 And the woman came to Saul and saw
that he was severely troubled, and said to
him, "Look, your maidservant has
obeyed your voice, and I have put my life
in my hands and heeded the words which
you spoke to me.
22 "Now therefore, please, heed also the
voice of your maidservant, and let me set
a piece of bread before you; and eat, that
you may have strength when you go on
your way."
23 But he refused and said, "I will not
eat." But his servants, together with the
woman, urged him; and he heeded their
voice. So he arose from the ground and
sat on the bed.
24 Now the woman had a fatted calf in
the house, and she hastened to kill it.
And she took flour and kneaded it, and
baked unleavened bread from it.
25 So she brought it before Saul and his
servants, and they ate. Then they rose
and went away that night.

33 Hebrew elohim   34 Or him, that is, David

The Philistines Reject David

29 Then the Philistines gathered together all their armies at Aphek, and the Israelites encamped by a fountain which *is* in Jezreel.

2 And the lords of the Philistines passed in review by hundreds and by thousands, but David and his men passed in review at the rear with Achish.

3 Then the princes of the Philistines said, "What *are* these Hebrews *doing here*?" And Achish said to the princes of the Philistines, "*Is* this not David, the servant of Saul king of Israel, who has been with me these days, or these years? And to this day I have found no fault in him since he defected *to me.*"

4 But the princes of the Philistines were angry with him; so the princes of the Philistines said to him, "Make this fellow return, that he may go back to the place which you have appointed for him, and do not let him go down with us to battle, lest in the battle he become our adversary. For with what could he reconcile himself to his master, if not with the heads of these men?

5 "*Is* this not David, of whom they sang to one another in dances, saying:

'Saul has slain his thousands,
And David his ten thousands'?"[35]

6 Then Achish called David and said to him, "Surely, *as* the LORD lives, you have been upright, and your going out and your coming in with me in the army *is* good in my sight. For to this day I have not found evil in you since the day of your coming to me. Nevertheless the lords do not favor you.

7 "Therefore return now, and go in peace, that you may not displease the lords of the Philistines."

8 Then David said to Achish, "But what have I done? And to this day what have you found in your servant as long as I have been with you, that I may not go and fight against the enemies of my lord the king?"

9 But Achish answered and said to David, "I know that you *are* as good in my sight as an angel of God; nevertheless the princes of the Philistines have said, 'He shall not go up with us to the battle.'

10 "Now therefore, rise early in the morning with your master's servants who have come with you. And as soon as you are up early in the morning and have light, depart."

11 So David and his men rose early to depart in the morning, to return to the land of the Philistines. And the Philistines went up to Jezreel.

David's Conflict with the Amalekites

30 Now it happened, when David and his men came to Ziklag, on the third day, that the Amalekites had invaded the South and Ziklag, attacked Ziklag and burned it with fire,

2 and had taken captive the women and those who *were* there, from small to great; they did not kill anyone, but carried *them* away and went their way.

3 So David and his men came to the city, and there it was, burned with fire; and their wives, their sons, and their daughters had been taken captive.

4 Then David and the people who *were* with him lifted up their voices and wept, until they had no more power to weep.

5 And David's two wives, Ahinoam the Jezreelitess, and Abigail the widow of Nabal the Carmelite, had been taken captive.

6 Then David was greatly distressed, for the people spoke of stoning him, because the soul of all the people was grieved, every man for his sons and his daughters. But David strengthened himself in the LORD his God.

7 Then David said to Abiathar the priest, Ahimelech's son, "Please bring the ephod here to me." And Abiathar brought the ephod to David.

8 So David inquired of the LORD, saying, "Shall I pursue this troop? Shall I overtake them?" And He answered him, "Pursue, for you shall surely overtake *them* and without fail recover *all.*"

9 So David went, he and the six hundred men who *were* with him, and came to the Brook Besor, where those stayed who were left behind.

10 But David pursued, he and four hundred men; for two hundred stayed *behind*, who were so weary that they could not cross the Brook Besor.

11 Then they found an Egyptian in the field, and brought him to David; and they gave him bread and he ate, and they let him drink water.

12 And they gave him a piece of a cake

---

35 Compare 1 Samuel 18:7

of figs and two clusters of raisins. So when he had eaten, his strength came back to him; for he had eaten no bread nor drunk *any* water for three days and three nights.

13 Then David said to him, "To whom do you *belong*, and where *are* you from?" And he said, "I *am* a young man from Egypt, servant of an Amalekite; and my master left me behind, because three days ago I fell sick.

14 "We made an invasion of the southern *area* of the Cherethites, in the *territory* which *belongs* to Judah, and of the southern *area* of Caleb; and we burned Ziklag with fire."

15 And David said to him, "Can you take me down to this troop?" And he said, "Swear to me by God that you will neither kill me nor deliver me into the hands of my master, and I will take you down to this troop."

16 So when he had brought him down, there they were, spread out over all the land, eating and drinking and dancing, because of all the great spoil which they had taken from the land of the Philistines and from the land of Judah.

17 And David attacked them from twilight until the evening of the next day. Not a man of them escaped, except four hundred young men who rode on camels and fled.

18 So David recovered all that the Amalekites had carried away, and David rescued his two wives.

19 And nothing of theirs was lacking, either small or great, sons or daughters, spoil or anything which they had taken from them; David recovered all.

20 Then David took all the flocks and herds *which* they had driven before those *other* livestock, and said, "This *is* David's spoil."

21 Now David came to the two hundred men who had been so weary that they could not follow David, whom they also had made to stay at the Brook Besor. So they went out to meet David and to meet the people who *were* with him. And when David came near the people, he greeted them.

22 Then all the wicked and worthless men[36] of those who went with David answered and said, "Because they did not go with us, we will not give them *any* of the spoil that we have recovered, except

for every man's wife and children, that they may lead *them* away and depart."

23 But David said, "My brethren, you shall not do so with what the LORD has given us, who has preserved us and delivered into our hand the troop that came against us.

24 "For who will heed you in this matter? But as his part *is* who goes down to the battle, so *shall* his part *be* who stays by the supplies; they shall share alike."

25 And *so* it was, from that day forward; he made it a statute and an ordinance for Israel to this day.

26 Now when David came to Ziklag, he sent *some* of the spoil to the elders of Judah, to his friends, saying, "Here is a present for you from the spoil of the enemies of the LORD"—

27 to *those* who *were* in Bethel, *those* who *were* in Ramoth of the South, *those* who *were* in Jattir,

28 *those* who *were* in Aroer, *those* who *were* in Siphmoth, *those* who *were* in Eshtemoa,

29 *those* who *were* in Rachal, *those* who *were* in the cities of the Jerahmeelites, *those* who *were* in the cities of the Kenites,

30 *those* who *were* in Hormah, *those* who *were* in Chorashan,[37] *those* who *were* in Athach,

31 *those* who *were* in Hebron, and to all the places where David himself and his men were accustomed to rove.

The Tragic End of Saul and His Sons

31 So the Philistines fought against Israel; and the men of Israel fled from before the Philistines, and fell slain on Mount Gilboa.

2 Then the Philistines followed hard after Saul and his sons. And the Philistines killed Jonathan, Abinadab, and Malchishua, Saul's sons.

3 Now the battle became intense against Saul; and the archers hit him, and he was severely wounded by the archers.

4 Then Saul said to his armorbearer, "Draw your sword, and thrust me through with it, lest these uncircumcised men come and thrust me through and abuse me." But his armorbearer would not, for he was greatly afraid. Therefore Saul took a sword and fell on it.

36 Literally *men of Belial*   37 Or *Borashan*

5 And when his armorbearer saw that Saul was dead, he also fell on his sword, and died with him.

6 So Saul, his three sons, his armorbearer, and all his men died together that same day.

7 And when the men of Israel who *were* on the other side of the valley, and *those* who *were* on the other side of the Jordan, saw that the men of Israel had fled and that Saul and his sons were dead, they forsook the cities and fled; and the Philistines came and dwelt in them.

8 So it came to pass the next day, when the Philistines came to strip the slain, that they found Saul and his three sons fallen on Mount Gilboa.

9 And they cut off his head and stripped

38 Spelled *Beth Shean* in Joshua 17:11 and elsewhere

off his armor, and sent *word* throughout the land of the Philistines, to proclaim *it in* the temple of their idols and among the people.

10 Then they put his armor in the temple of the Ashtoreths, and they fastened his body to the wall of Beth Shan.[38]

11 And when the inhabitants of Jabesh Gilead heard what the Philistines had done to Saul,

12 all the valiant men arose and traveled all night, and took the body of Saul and the bodies of his sons from the wall of Beth Shan; and they came to Jabesh and burned them there.

13 Then they took their bones and buried *them* under the tamarisk tree at Jabesh, and fasted seven days.

Introduction to Second Samuel

Second Samuel was compiled from the writings of Samuel, David, Nathan, and Gad between 1150–950 B.C. It is the continuation of the life of King David.

The book opens with the ascension of King David to Israel's throne following the death of Saul. Second Samuel records David's strength as a leader in difficult times. There were ten wars in a period of forty years, and David's early years as king were filled with the task of suppressing civil war. Chapter five describes the heroic capture of Jerusalem by David and his commanding officers.

David's rule as king was not to be void of family and personal problems. Though a great leader in Israel's history, David faced failure and sin that could have ruined his life. In an incident with one of his commanding officer's wife, David committed adultery and then tried to cover up his sin by murder. He married Bathsheba, the widowed wife of the commander Uriah, who David had ordered into the front lines and certain death.

Rebuked for his sins by the prophet Nathan, David anguished over his failure, fearful that God could not forgive him. But God did forgive him, and later David and Bathsheba gave birth to Solomon, who was to become successor to the throne and was included in the genealogy of Jesus Christ. David and Bathsheba experienced firsthand God's ability to turn their scar into a star! This forgiveness is evident in many of David's psalms:

> Blessed *is he whose* transgression *is* forgiven,
> *Whose* sin *is* covered.
> Blessed *is* the man to whom the LORD does not impute iniquity,
> And in whose spirit *there is* no guile.

(Ps. 32:1,2)

David was a king who turned impossibilities into possibilities, problems into opportunities, and scars into stars—with God's help!

The Second Book of

Samuel

The Report of Saul's Death

NOW it came to pass after the death of Saul, when David had returned from the slaughter of the Amalekites, and David had stayed two days in Ziklag,
2 on the third day, behold, it happened that a man came from Saul's camp with his clothes torn and dust on his head. So it was, when he came to David, that he fell to the ground and prostrated himself.
3 And David said to him, "Where have you come from?" So he said to him, "I have escaped from the camp of Israel."
4 Then David said to him, "How did the matter go? Please tell me." And he answered, "The people have fled from the battle, many of the people are fallen and dead, and Saul and Jonathan his son are dead also."
5 So David said to the young man who told him, "How do you know that Saul and Jonathan his son are dead?"
6 And the young man who told him said, "As I happened by chance *to be* on Mount Gilboa, there was Saul, leaning on his spear; and indeed the chariots and horsemen followed hard after him.
7 "Now when he looked behind him, he saw me and called to me. And I answered, 'Here I am.'
8 "And he said to me, 'Who *are* you?' So I answered him, 'I *am* an Amalekite.'
9 "He said to me again, 'Please stand over me and kill me, for anguish has come upon me, but my life still *remains* in me.'
10 "So I stood over him and killed him, because I was sure that he could not live after he had fallen. And I took the crown that *was* on his head and the bracelet that *was* on his arm, and have brought them here to my lord."
11 Then David took hold of his own clothes and tore them, and *so did* all the men who *were* with him.
12 And they mourned and wept and fasted until evening for Saul and for Jonathan his son, for the people of the LORD and for the house of Israel, because they had fallen by the sword.
13 Then David said to the young man who told him, "Where *are* you from?" And he answered, "I *am* the son of an alien, an Amalekite."
14 And David said to him, "How was it you were not afraid to put forth your hand to destroy the LORD's anointed?"
15 Then David called one of the young men and said, "Go near, *and* execute him!" And he struck him so that he died.
16 So David said to him, "Your blood *is* on your own head, for your own mouth has testified against you, saying, 'I have killed the LORD's anointed.'"

The Song of the Bow

17 Then David lamented with this lamentation over Saul and over Jonathan his son,
18 and he told *them* to teach the children of Judah *the Song of* the Bow; indeed *it is* written in the Book of Jasher:

19 "The beauty of Israel is slain
　　on your high places!
　How the mighty have fallen!
20 Tell *it* not in Gath,
　Proclaim *it* not
　　in the streets of Ashkelon—
　Lest the daughters of the Philistines
　　rejoice,
　Lest the daughters of the
　　uncircumcised triumph.

21 "O mountains of Gilboa,
　Let there be no dew,
　　nor *let there be* rain upon you,
　Nor fields of offerings.
　For the shield of the mighty
　　is cast away there!
　The shield of Saul,
　　not anointed with oil.
22 From the blood of the slain,
　From the fat of the mighty,
　The bow of Jonathan
　　did not turn back,
　And the sword of Saul
　　did not return empty.

> 23 "Saul and Jonathan *were* beloved
>   and pleasant in their lives,
> And in their death
>   they were not divided;
> They were swifter than eagles,
> They were stronger than lions.

24 "O daughters of Israel, weep over Saul,
        Who clothed you in scarlet,
        with luxury;
Who put ornaments of gold
        on your apparel.

25 "How the mighty have fallen
        in the midst of the battle!
Jonathan *was* slain in your high places.
26 I am distressed for you,
        my brother Jonathan;
You have been very pleasant to me;
Your love to me was wonderful,
Surpassing the love of women.

27 "How the mighty have fallen,
        And the weapons of war perished!"

David Anointed King of Judah

2 It happened after this that David inquired of the LORD, saying, "Shall I go up to any of the cities of Judah?" And the LORD said to him, "Go up." David said, "Where shall I go up?" And He said, "To Hebron."
2 So David went up there, and his two wives also, Ahinoam the Jezreelitess, and Abigail the widow of Nabal the Carmelite.
3 And David brought up the men who *were* with him, every man with his household. So they dwelt in the cities of Hebron.
4 Then the men of Judah came, and there they anointed David king over the house of Judah. And they told David, saying, "The men of Jabesh Gilead *were* the ones who buried Saul."
5 So David sent messengers to the men of Jabesh Gilead, and said to them, "You *are* blessed of the LORD, for you have shown this kindness to your lord, to Saul, and have buried him.
6 "And now may the LORD show kindness and truth to you. I also will repay you this kindness, because you have done this thing.
7 "Now therefore, let your hands be strengthened, and be valiant; for your master Saul is dead, and also the house of Judah has anointed me king over them."

Ishbosheth Made King of Israel

8 But Abner the son of Ner, commander of Saul's army, took Ishbosheth[1] the son of Saul and brought him over to Mahanaim;
9 and he made him king over Gilead, over the Ashurites, over Jezreel, over Ephraim, over Benjamin, and over all Israel.
10 Ishbosheth, Saul's son, *was* forty years old when he began to reign over Israel, and he reigned two years. Only the house of Judah followed David.
11 And the time that David was king in Hebron over the house of Judah was seven years and six months.

Israel and Judah at War

12 Now Abner the son of Ner, and the servants of Ishbosheth the son of Saul, went out from Mahanaim to Gibeon.
13 And Joab the son of Zeruiah, and the servants of David, went out and met them by the pool of Gibeon. So they sat down, one on one side of the pool and the other on the other side of the pool.
14 Then Abner said to Joab, "Let the young men now arise and compete before us." And Joab said, "Let them arise."
15 So they arose and went over by number, twelve from Benjamin, *followers* of Ishbosheth the son of Saul, and twelve from the servants of David.
16 And each one grasped his opponent by the head and *thrust* his sword in his opponent's side; so they fell down together. Therefore that place was called the Field of Sharp Swords,[2] which *is* in Gibeon.
17 So there was a very fierce battle that day, and Abner and the men of Israel were beaten before the servants of David.
18 Now the three sons of Zeruiah were there: Joab and Abishai and Asahel. And Asahel *was as* fleet of foot as a wild gazelle.
19 So Asahel pursued Abner, and in going he did not turn to the right hand or to the left from following Abner.
20 Then Abner looked behind him and said, "*Are* you Asahel?" And he answered, "I *am.*"
21 And Abner said to him, "Turn aside to your right hand or to your left, and lay hold on one of the young men and take his armor for yourself." But Asahel

---

1 Called *Esh-Baal* in 1 Chronicles 8:33 and 9:39   2 Hebrew *Helkath Hazzurim*

would not turn aside from following him.
22 So Abner said again to Asahel, "Turn aside from following me. Why should I strike you to the ground? How then could I face your brother Joab?"
23 However, he refused to turn aside. Therefore Abner struck him in the stomach with the blunt end of the spear, so that the spear came out of his back; and he fell down there and died on the spot. So it was *that* as many as came to the place where Asahel fell down and died, stood still.
24 Joab and Abishai also pursued Abner. And the sun was going down when they came to the hill of Ammah, which *is* before Giah by the road to the Wilderness of Gibeon.
25 Now the children of Benjamin gathered together behind Abner and became a unit, and took their stand on top of a hill.
26 Then Abner called to Joab and said, "Shall the sword devour forever? Do you not know that it will be bitter in the latter end? How long will it be then until you tell the people to return from pursuing their brethren?"
27 And Joab said, "*As* God lives, unless you had spoken, surely then by morning all the people would have given up pursuing their brethren."
28 So Joab blew a trumpet; and all the people stood still and did not pursue Israel anymore, nor did they fight anymore.
29 Then Abner and his men went on all that night through the plain, crossed over the Jordan, and went through all Bithron; and they came to Mahanaim.
30 So Joab returned from pursuing Abner. And when he had gathered all the people together, there were missing of David's servants nineteen men and Asahel.
31 But the servants of David had struck down, of Benjamin and Abner's men, three hundred and sixty men who died.
32 Then they took up Asahel and buried him in his father's tomb, which *was in* Bethlehem. And Joab and his men went all night, and they came to Hebron at daybreak.

3 Now there was a long war between the house of Saul and the house of David. But David grew stronger and

stronger, and the house of Saul grew weaker and weaker.

Sons of David

2 Sons were born to David in Hebron: His firstborn was Amnon by Ahinoam the Jezreelitess;
3 his second, Chileab, by Abigail the widow of Nabal the Carmelite; the third, Absalom the son of Maacah, the daughter of Talmai, king of Geshur;
4 the fourth, Adonijah the son of Haggith; the fifth, Shephatiah the son of Abital;
5 and the sixth, Ithream, by David's wife Eglah. These were born to David in Hebron.

Abner Joins Forces with David

6 Now it was so, while there was war between the house of Saul and the house of David, that Abner was strengthening *his hold* on the house of Saul.
7 And Saul had a concubine, whose name *was* Rizpah, the daughter of Aiah. So Ishbosheth said to Abner, "Why have you gone in to my father's concubine?"
8 Then Abner became very angry at the words of Ishbosheth, and said, "*Am* I a dog's head that belongs to Judah? Today I show loyalty to the house of Saul your father, to his brothers, and to his friends, and have not delivered you into the hand of David; and you charge me today with a fault concerning this woman?
9 "May God do so to Abner, and more also, if I do not do for David as the LORD has sworn to him—
10 "to transfer the kingdom from the house of Saul, and set up the throne of David over Israel and over Judah, from Dan to Beersheba."
11 And he could not answer Abner another word, because he feared him.
12 Then Abner sent messengers on his behalf to David, saying, "Whose *is* the land?" saying *also*, "Make your covenant with me, and indeed my hand *shall be* with you to bring all Israel to you."
13 And David[3] said, "Good, I will make a covenant with you. But one thing I require of you: you shall not see my face unless you first bring Michal, Saul's daughter, when you come to see my face."
14 So David sent messengers to Ishbosheth, Saul's son, saying, "Give *me* my

3 Literally *he*

wife Michal, whom I betrothed to myself for a hundred foreskins of the Philistines."

15 And Ishbosheth sent and took her from *her* husband, from Paltiel[4] the son of Laish.

16 Then her husband went along with her to Bahurim, weeping behind her. So Abner said to him, "Go, return!" And he returned.

17 Now Abner had communicated with the elders of Israel, saying, "In time past you were seeking for David *to be* king over you.

18 "Now then, do *it*! For the LORD has spoken of David, saying, 'By the hand of My servant David, I[5] will save My people Israel from the hand of the Philistines and the hand of all their enemies.' "

19 And Abner also spoke in the hearing of Benjamin. Then Abner also went to speak in the hearing of David in Hebron all that seemed good to Israel and the whole house of Benjamin.

20 So Abner and twenty men with him came to David at Hebron. And David made a feast for Abner and the men who *were* with him.

21 Then Abner said to David, "I will arise and go, and gather all Israel to my lord the king, that they may make a covenant with you, and that you may reign over all that your heart desires." So David sent Abner away, and he went in peace.

Joab Murders Abner

22 At that moment the servants of David and Joab came from a raid and brought much spoil with them. But Abner *was* not with David in Hebron, for he had sent him away, and he had gone in peace.

23 When Joab and all the troops that *were* with him had come, they told Joab, saying, "Abner the son of Ner came to the king, and he sent him away, and he has gone in peace."

24 Then Joab came to the king and said, "What have you done? Look, Abner came to you; why *is* it *that* you sent him away, and he has already gone?

25 "Surely you realize that Abner the son of Ner came to deceive you, to know your going out and your coming in, and to know all that you are doing."

26 And when Joab had gone from David's presence, he sent messengers after Abner, who brought him back from the well of Sirah. But David did not know *it*.

27 Now when Abner had returned to Hebron, Joab took him aside in the gate to speak with him privately, and there stabbed him in the stomach, so that he died for the blood of Asahel his brother.

28 And afterward, when David heard *it*, he said, "My kingdom and I *are* guiltless before the LORD forever of the blood of Abner the son of Ner.

29 "Let it rest on the head of Joab and on all his father's house; and let there never fail to be in the house of Joab one who has a discharge or is a leper, who leans on a staff or falls by the sword, or who lacks bread."

30 So Joab and Abishai his brother killed Abner, because he had killed their brother Asahel at Gibeon in the battle.

David's Mourning for Abner

31 Then David said to Joab and to all the people who were with him, "Tear your clothes, gird yourselves with sackcloth, and mourn for Abner." And King David followed the coffin.

32 So they buried Abner in Hebron; and the king lifted up his voice and wept at the grave of Abner, and all the people wept.

33 And the king sang *a lament* over Abner and said:

"Should Abner die as a fool dies?
34   Your hands were not bound
     Nor your feet put into fetters;
     As a man falls before wicked men,
       so you fell."

Then all the people wept over him again.

35 And when all the people came to persuade David to eat food while it was still day, David took an oath, saying, "God do so to me, and more also, if I taste bread or anything else till the sun goes down!"

36 Now all the people took note *of it*, and it pleased them, since whatever the king did pleased all the people.

37 For all the people and all Israel understood that day that it had not been the king's *intent* to kill Abner the son of Ner.

38 Then the king said to his servants, "Do you not know that a prince and a great man has fallen this day in Israel?

4 Spelled *Palti* in 1 Samuel 25:44
5 Masoretic Text reads *he;* the ancient versions and many Hebrew manuscripts read *I.*

³⁹ "And I *am* weak today, though anointed king; and these men, the sons of Zeruiah, *are* too harsh for me. The LORD shall repay the evildoer according to his wickedness."

Ishbosheth Is Murdered

4 And when Saul's son⁶ heard that Abner had died in Hebron, he lost heart, and all Israel was troubled. ² Now Saul's son *had* two men *who were* captains of troops. The name of one *was* Baanah and the name of the other Rechab, the sons of Rimmon the Beerothite, of the children of Benjamin. (For Beeroth also was *part* of Benjamin, ³ because the Beerothites fled to Gittaim and have been sojourners there until this day.)

⁴ Jonathan, Saul's son, had a son *who was* lame in *his* feet. He was five years old when the news about Saul and Jonathan came from Jezreel; and his nurse took him up and fled. And it happened, as she made haste to flee, that he fell and became lame. So his name *was* Mephibosheth.⁷

⁵ Then the sons of Rimmon the Beerothite, Rechab and Baanah, set out and came at about the heat of the day to the house of Ishbosheth, who was lying on his bed at noon. ⁶ And they came there, all the way into the house, *as though* to get wheat, and they stabbed him in the stomach. Then Rechab and Baanah his brother escaped. ⁷ For when they came into the house, he was lying on his bed in his bedroom; then they struck him and killed him, beheaded him and took his head, and were all night escaping through the plain. ⁸ And they brought the head of Ishbosheth to David at Hebron, and said to the king, "Here is the head of Ishbosheth, the son of Saul your enemy, who sought your life; and the LORD has avenged my lord the king this day of Saul and his descendants."

⁹ Then David answered Rechab and Baanah his brother, the sons of Rimmon the Beerothite, and said to them, "*As the* LORD lives, who has redeemed my life from all adversity, ¹⁰ "when someone told me, saying, 'Look, Saul is dead,' thinking to have brought good news, I arrested him and had him executed in Ziklag—the one who thought I would give him a reward for *his* news. ¹¹ "How much more, when wicked men have killed a righteous person in his own house on his bed? Therefore, shall I not now require his blood at your hand and remove you from the earth?"

¹² So David commanded his young men, and they executed them, cut off their hands and feet, and hanged *them* by the pool in Hebron. But they took the head of Ishbosheth and buried *it* in the tomb of Abner in Hebron.

David Reigns over All Israel

5 Then all the tribes of Israel came to David at Hebron and spoke, saying, "Indeed we *are* your bone and your flesh. ² "Also, in time past, when Saul was king over us, you were the one who led Israel out and brought them in; and the LORD said to you, 'You shall shepherd My people Israel, and be ruler over Israel.' "

³ So all the elders of Israel came to the king at Hebron, and King David made a covenant with them at Hebron before the LORD. And they anointed David king over Israel. ⁴ David *was* thirty years old when he began to reign, *and* he reigned forty years. ⁵ In Hebron he reigned over Judah seven years and six months, and in Jerusalem he reigned thirty-three years over all Israel and Judah.

The Conquest of Jerusalem

⁶ And the king and his men went to Jerusalem against the Jebusites, the inhabitants of the land, who spoke to David, saying, "You shall not come in here; but the blind and the lame will repel you," thinking, "David cannot come in here." ⁷ Nevertheless David took the stronghold of Zion (that *is*, the City of David). ⁸ Now David said on that day, "Whoever climbs up by way of the water shaft and defeats the Jebusites (the lame and the blind, *who are* hated by David's soul), *he shall be chief and captain.*"⁸ Therefore they say, "The blind and the lame shall not come into the house."

⁹ So David dwelt in the stronghold, and called it the City of David. Then David built all around from the Millo and inward.

---

6 That is, Ishbosheth   7 Called *Meribbaal* in 1 Chronicles 8:34 and 9:40   8 Compare 1 Chronicles 11:6

Find a Pass Through

The city of Jerusalem did not always belong to the Israelites. For over two hundred years, the once powerful city-state (then called Jebus) was controlled by the Jebusites. God had promised the city to the Israelites, but how were they to get it?

David, the God-appointed leader, and his mighty, valiant Israelite warriors were no match for the large Jebusite army. Their city was impregnable with thirty-foot-wide fortress walls, punctuated by ninety-foot-high towers from which soldiers easily defended the city. The Bible records that the Jebusites were so confident in their ability to defend Jerusalem that they mocked David and his army saying, "the blind and lame will repel you" (2 Sam. 5:6).

Outraged, David was determined to capture the city God had promised to them. The mountainous task seemed impossible, yet David examined his alternatives. He couldn't climb over, for this would be too costly in lives. But perhaps one man could get inside the walls to open the city gates, thus allowing his troops to storm the city.

The Jebusite stronghold was built high on a mountain. The only water source was outside the city walls at the base of the hill. By analyzing where the Jebusites obtained their water to withstand the siege, David surmised that there must be a secret water source coming from outside the city. Perhaps a shaft or tunnel, sunk deep beneath the earth, brought water from an underground spring. God led David to the secret passage—a water shaft over forty feet high. David challenged his men. Whoever could climb the shaft and let their army into the city would be made chief over the troops. Responding to God's call, Joab, one of David's finest soldiers, undertook the dangerous mission of climbing the shaft, the pass through.

This water shaft is still visible in Jerusalem today and has been climbed by only a few skilled climbers. It has no footholds or handholds. Anyone attempting to climb the shaft must brace himself with his back against one wall and his feet extended to the opposite wall. Slowly, he must inch his way upwards.

Joab was successful in his climb, entered the city, and allowed David and his men to defeat the Jebusites. Their victory was dependent on David's belief that they could find a pass through. When faced with a mountain, they did not quit! They found a pass through!

When you face a mountainous problem, remember, do not quit. Climb over, tunnel underneath, find a pass through, or simply stay and turn your mountain into a gold mine with God's help!

10 So David went on and became great, and the LORD God of hosts *was* with him. 11 Then Hiram king of Tyre sent messengers to David, and cedar trees, and carpenters and masons. And they built David a house.
12 So David knew that the LORD had established him as king over Israel, and that He had exalted His kingdom for His people Israel's sake.
13 And David took more concubines and wives from Jerusalem, after he had come from Hebron. Also more sons and daughters were born to David.
14 Now these *are* the names of those who were born to him in Jerusalem: Shammua,[9] Shobab, Nathan, Solomon,
15 Ibhar, Elishua,[10] Nepheg, Japhia,
16 Elishama, Eliada, and Eliphelet.

The Philistines Defeated

17 Now when the Philistines heard that they had anointed David king over Israel, all the Philistines went up to search for David. And David heard *of it* and went down to the stronghold.
18 The Philistines also went and deployed themselves in the Valley of Rephaim.
19 And David inquired of the LORD, saying, "Shall I go up against the Philistines? Will You deliver them into my hand?" And the LORD said to David, "Go up, for I will doubtless deliver the Philistines into your hand."
20 So David went to Baal Perazim, and David defeated them there; and he said, "The LORD has broken through my enemies before me, like a breakthrough of water." Therefore he called the name of that place Baal Perazim.[11]
21 And they left their images there, and David and his men carried them away.
22 Then the Philistines went up once again and deployed themselves in the Valley of Rephaim.
23 And when David inquired of the LORD, He said, "You shall not go up; circle around behind them, and come upon them in front of the mulberry trees.
24 "So it shall be, when you hear the sound of marching in the tops of the mulberry trees, then you shall advance quickly. For then the LORD will go out

before you to strike the camp of the Philistines."
25 And David did so, as the LORD commanded him; and he drove back the Philistines from Geba as far as Gezer.

The Ark Brought to Jerusalem

6 Again David gathered all *the* choice men of Israel, thirty thousand.
2 And David arose and went with all the people who *were* with him from Baale Judah to bring up from there the ark of God, whose name is called by the Name, the LORD of Hosts, who dwells *between* the cherubim.
3 So they set the ark of God on a new cart, and brought it out of the house of Abinadab, which *was* on the hill; and Uzzah and Ahio, the sons of Abinadab, drove the new cart.
4 And they brought it out of the house of Abinadab, which *was* on the hill, accompanying the ark of God; and Ahio went before the ark.
5 Then David and all the house of Israel played *music* before the LORD on all kinds of *instruments made of* fir wood, on harps, on stringed instruments, on tambourines, on sistrums, and on cymbals.
6 And when they came to Nachon's threshingfloor, Uzzah put out *his hand* to the ark of God and took hold of it, for the oxen stumbled.
7 Then the anger of the LORD was aroused against Uzzah, and God struck him there for *his* error; and he died there by the ark of God.
8 And David became angry because of the LORD's outbreak against Uzzah; and he called the name of the place Perez Uzzah[12] to this day.
9 David was afraid of the LORD that day; and he said, "How can the ark of the LORD come to me?"
10 So David would not move the ark of the LORD with him into the City of David; but David took it aside into the house of Obed-Edom the Gittite.
11 The ark of the LORD remained in the house of Obed-Edom the Gittite three months. And the LORD blessed Obed-Edom and all his household.
12 And it was told King David, saying, "The LORD has blessed the house of Obed-Edom and all that *belongs* to him,

9 Spelled *Shimea* in 1 Chronicles 3:5   10 Spelled *Elishama* in 1 Chronicles 3:6
11 Literally *Baal Is Broken*   12 Literally *Outburst Against Uzzah*

because of the ark of God." So David went and brought up the ark of God from the house of Obed-Edom to the City of David with gladness.

13 And *so* it was, when those bearing the ark of the LORD had gone six paces, that he sacrificed oxen and fatted sheep.

14 Then David danced before the LORD with all *his* might; and David *was* wearing a linen ephod.

15 So David and all the house of Israel brought up the ark of the LORD with shouting and with the sound of the trumpet.

16 And as the ark of the LORD came into the City of David, Michal, Saul's daughter, looked through a window and saw King David leaping and whirling before the LORD; and she despised him in her heart.

17 So they brought the ark of the LORD, and set it in its place in the midst of the tabernacle that David had erected for it. Then David offered burnt offerings and peace offerings before the LORD.

18 And when David had finished offering burnt offerings and peace offerings, he blessed the people in the name of the LORD of hosts.

19 Then he distributed among all the people, among the whole multitude of Israel, both the women and the men, to everyone a loaf of bread, a piece *of meat*, and a cake of raisins. So all the people departed, everyone to his house.

20 Then David returned to bless his household. And Michal the daughter of Saul came out to meet David, and said, "How glorious was the king of Israel today, uncovering himself today in the eyes of the maids of his servants, as one of the base fellows shamelessly uncovers himself!"

21 So David said to Michal, "*It was* before the LORD, who chose me instead of your father and all his house, to appoint me ruler over the people of the LORD, over Israel. Therefore I will play *music* before the LORD.

22 "And I will be even more undignified than this, and will be humble in my own sight. But as for the maidservants of whom you have spoken, by them I will be held in honor."

23 Therefore Michal the daughter of Saul had no children to the day of her death.

God's Covenant with David

7 Now it came to pass when the king was dwelling in his house, and the LORD had given him rest from all his enemies all around,

2 that the king said to Nathan the prophet, "See now, I dwell in a house of cedar, but the ark of God dwells inside tent curtains."

3 Then Nathan said to the king, "Go, do all that *is* in your heart, for the LORD *is* with you."

4 But it happened that night that the word of the LORD came to Nathan, saying,

5 "Go and tell My servant David, 'Thus says the LORD: "Would you build a house for Me to dwell in?

6 "For I have not dwelt in a house since the time that I brought the children of Israel up from Egypt, even to this day, but have moved about in a tent and in a tabernacle.

7 "In all *the places* where I have walked with all the children of Israel, have I ever spoken a word to anyone from the tribes of Israel, whom I commanded to shepherd My people Israel, saying, 'Why have you not built Me a house of cedar?' " '

8 "Now therefore, thus shall you say to My servant David, 'Thus says the LORD of hosts: "I took you from the sheepfold, from following the sheep, to be ruler over My people, over Israel.

9 "And I have been with you wherever you have gone, and have cut off all your enemies from before you, and have made you a great name, like the name of the great *men* who *are* on the earth.

10 "Moreover I will appoint a place for My people Israel, and will plant them, that they may dwell in a place of their own and move no more; nor shall the sons of wickedness oppress them anymore, as previously,

11 "since the time that I commanded judges *to be* over My people Israel, and have caused you to rest from all your enemies. Also the LORD tells you that He will make you a house.

12 "When your days are fulfilled and you rest with your fathers, I will set up your seed after you, who will come from your body, and I will establish his kingdom.

13 "He shall build a house for My name,

and I will establish the throne of his kingdom forever.

14 "I will be his Father, and he shall be My son. If he commits iniquity, I will chasten him with the rod of men and with the blows of the sons of men.

15 "But My mercy shall not depart from him, as I took *it* from Saul, whom I removed from before you.

16 "And your house and your kingdom shall be established forever before you.[13] Your throne shall be established forever.' ' "

17 According to all these words and according to all this vision, so Nathan spoke to David.

David's Thanksgiving to God

18 Then King David went in and sat before the LORD; and he said: "Who *am* I, O Lord GOD? And what is my house, that You have brought me this far?

19 "And yet this was a small thing in Your sight, O Lord GOD; and You have also spoken of Your servant's house for a great while to come. *Is* this the manner of man, O Lord GOD?

20 "Now what more can David say to You? For You, Lord GOD, know Your servant.

21 "For Your word's sake, and according to Your own heart, You have done all these great things, to make Your servant know *them.*

22 "Therefore You are great, O Lord GOD.[14] For *there is* none like You, nor *is there any* God besides You, according to all that we have heard with our ears.

23 "And who *is* like Your people, like Israel, the one nation on the earth whom God went to redeem for Himself as a people, to make for Himself a name— and to do for You great and awesome deeds for Your land—before Your people whom You redeemed for Yourself from Egypt, *from* the nations and their gods?

24 "For You have made Your people Israel Your very own people forever; and You, LORD, have become their God.

25 "And now, O LORD God, the word which You have spoken concerning Your servant and concerning his house, establish *it* forever and do as You have said.

26 "So let Your name be magnified forever, saying, 'The LORD of hosts *is* the

God over Israel.' And let the house of Your servant David be established before You.

27 "For You, O LORD of hosts, God of Israel, have revealed *this* to Your servant, saying, 'I will build you a house.' Therefore Your servant found it in his heart to pray this prayer to You.

28 "And now, O Lord GOD, You *are* God, and Your words are true, and You have promised this goodness to Your servant.

29 "Now therefore, let it please You to bless the house of Your servant, that it may continue forever before You; for You, O Lord GOD, have spoken *it*, and with Your blessing let the house of Your servant be blessed forever."

David's Further Conquests

8 After this it came to pass that David attacked the Philistines and subdued them. And David took Metheg Ammah from the hand of the Philistines.

2 Then he defeated Moab. Forcing them down to the ground, he measured them off with a line. With two lines he measured off those to be put to death, and with one full line those to be kept alive. So the Moabites became David's servants, *and* brought tribute.

3 David also defeated Hadadezer the son of Rehob, king of Zobah, as he went to recover his territory at the River Euphrates.

4 David took from him one thousand *chariots*, seven hundred[15] horsemen, and twenty thousand foot soldiers. Also David hamstrung all the chariot horses, except that he spared *enough* of them for one hundred chariots.

5 When the Syrians of Damascus came to help Hadadezer king of Zobah, David killed twenty-two thousand of the Syrians.

6 Then David put garrisons in Syria of Damascus; and the Syrians became David's servants, *and* brought tribute. The LORD preserved David wherever he went.

7 And David took the shields of gold that had belonged to the servants of Hadadezer, and brought them to Jerusalem.

8 Also from Betah[16] and from Berothai, cities of Hadadezer, King David took a large amount of bronze.

9 When Toi[17] king of Hamath heard

---

13 Septuagint reads *Me.* 14 Targum and Syriac read *O LORD God.*
15 Or *seven thousand* (compare 1 Chronicles 18:4) 16 Spelled *Tibhah* in 1 Chronicles 18:8
17 Spelled *Tou* in 1 Chronicles 18:9

that David had defeated all the army of Hadadezer,

10 then Toi sent Joram[18] his son to King David, to greet him and bless him, because he had fought against Hadadezer and defeated him; for Hadadezer had wars with Toi. And *Joram* brought with him articles of silver, articles of gold, and articles of bronze.

11 King David dedicated these to the LORD, along with the silver and gold that he had dedicated from all the nations which he had subdued—

12 from Syria,[19] from Moab, from the people of Ammon, from the Philistines, from Amalek, and from the spoil of Hadadezer the son of Rehob, king of Zobah.

13 And David made *himself* a name when he returned from killing eighteen thousand Syrians[20] in the Valley of Salt.

14 He also put garrisons in Edom; throughout all Edom he put garrisons, and all the Edomites became David's servants. And the LORD preserved David wherever he went.

David's Administration

15 So David reigned over all Israel; and David administered judgment and justice to all his people.

16 Joab the son of Zeruiah *was* over the army; Jehoshaphat the son of Ahilud *was* recorder;

17 Zadok the son of Ahitub and Ahimelech the son of Abiathar *were* the priests; Seraiah[21] *was* the scribe;

18 Benaiah the son of Jehoiada *was* over both the Cherethites and the Pelethites; and David's sons were chief ministers.

David's Kindness to Mephibosheth

9 Now David said, "Is there still anyone who is left of the house of Saul, that I may show him kindness for Jonathan's sake?"

2 And *there was* a servant of the house of Saul whose name *was* Ziba. So when they had called him to David, the king said to him, "*Are* you Ziba?" And he said, "At your service!"

3 Then the king said, "*Is* there not still someone of the house of Saul, to whom I may show the kindness of God?" And Ziba said to the king, "There is still a son of Jonathan *who is* lame in *his* feet."

4 So the king said to him, "Where *is*

he?" And Ziba said to the king, "Indeed he *is* in the house of Machir the son of Ammiel, in Lo Debar."

5 Then King David sent and brought him out of the house of Machir the son of Ammiel, from Lo Debar.

6 Now when Mephibosheth the son of Jonathan, the son of Saul, had come to David, he fell on his face and prostrated himself. Then David said, "Mephibosheth?" And he answered, "Here is your servant!"

7 So David said to him, "Do not fear, for I will surely show you kindness for Jonathan your father's sake, and will restore to you all the land of Saul your grandfather; and you shall eat bread at my table continually."

8 Then he bowed himself, and said, "What *is* your servant, that you should look upon such a dead dog as I?"

9 And the king called to Ziba, Saul's servant, and said to him, "I have given to your master's son all that belonged to Saul and to all his house.

10 "You therefore, and your sons and your servants, shall work the land for him, and you shall bring in *the harvest*, that your master's son may have food to eat. But Mephibosheth your master's son shall eat bread at my table always." Now Ziba had fifteen sons and twenty servants.

11 Then Ziba said to the king, "According to all that my lord the king has commanded his servant, so will your servant do." "As for Mephibosheth," *said the king*, "he shall eat at my table like one of the king's sons."

12 Mephibosheth had a young son whose name *was* Micha. And all who dwelt in the house of Ziba *were* servants of Mephibosheth.

13 So Mephibosheth dwelt in Jerusalem, for he ate continually at the king's table. And he was lame in both his feet.

The Ammonites and Syrians Defeated

10 And it happened after this that the king of the people of Ammon died, and Hanun his son reigned in his place.

2 Then David said, "I will show kindness to Hanun the son of Nahash, as his father showed kindness to me." So David sent by the hand of his servants to

---

18 Spelled *Hadoram* in 1 Chronicles 18:10   19 Septuagint, Syriac, and some Hebrew manuscripts read *Edom.*
20 Septuagint, Syriac, and some Hebrew manuscripts read *Edomites* (compare 1 Chronicles 18:12).
21 Spelled *Shavsha* in 1 Chronicles 18:16

comfort him concerning his father. And David's servants came into the land of the people of Ammon.

3 Then the princes of the people of Ammon said to Hanun their lord, "Do you think that David really honors your father because he has sent comforters to you? Has David not *rather* sent his servants to you to search the city, to spy it out, and to overthrow it?"

4 Therefore Hanun took David's servants, shaved off half of their beards, cut off their garments in the middle, at their buttocks, and sent them away.

5 When they told David, he sent to meet them, because the men were greatly ashamed. And the king said, "Wait at Jericho until your beards have grown, and *then* return."

6 So when the people of Ammon saw that they had made themselves repulsive to David, the people of Ammon sent and hired the Syrians of Beth Rehob and the Syrians of Zoba, twenty thousand foot soldiers; and from King Maacah one thousand men, and from Ish-Tob twelve thousand men.

7 Now when David heard *of it*, he sent Joab and all the army of the mighty men.

8 Then the people of Ammon came out and put themselves in battle array at the entrance of the gate. And the Syrians of Zoba, Rehob, Ish-Tob, and Maacah *were* by themselves in the field.

9 When Joab saw that the battle line was against him before and behind, he chose some of the choice *men* of Israel and put *them* in battle array against the Syrians.

10 And the rest of the people he put under the command of Abishai his brother, that he might put *them* in battle array against the people of Ammon.

11 Then he said, "If the Syrians are too strong for me, then you shall help me. But if the people of Ammon are too strong for you, then I will come and help you.

12 "Be of good courage, and let us be strong for our people and for the cities of our God. And may the Lord do what seems good to Him."

13 So Joab and the people who *were* with him drew near for the battle against the Syrians, and they fled before him.

14 And when the people of Ammon saw that the Syrians were fleeing, they *also*

fled before Abishai, and entered the city. So Joab returned from the people of Ammon and went to Jerusalem.

15 Now when the Syrians saw that they had been defeated before Israel, they gathered together.

16 Then Hadadezer[22] sent and brought out the Syrians who *were* beyond the River,[23] and they came to Helam. And Shobach the commander of Hadadezer's army *went* before them.

17 When it was told David, he gathered all Israel, crossed over the Jordan, and came to Helam. And the Syrians set themselves in battle array against David and fought with him.

18 Then the Syrians fled before Israel; and David killed seven hundred charioteers and forty thousand horsemen of the Syrians, and struck Shobach the commander of their army, who died there.

19 And when all the kings *who were* servants to Hadadezer[24] saw that they were defeated by Israel, they made peace with Israel and served them. So the Syrians were afraid to help the people of Ammon anymore.

David, Bathsheba, and Uriah

11 Now it came to pass in the spring of the year, at the time when kings go out *to battle*, that David sent Joab and his servants with him, and all Israel; and they destroyed the people of Ammon and besieged Rabbah. But David remained at Jerusalem.

2 Then it happened one evening that David arose from his bed and walked on the roof of the king's house. And from the roof he saw a woman bathing, and the woman *was* very beautiful to behold.

3 So David sent and inquired about the woman. And *someone* said, "*Is* this not Bathsheba, the daughter of Eliam, the wife of Uriah the Hittite?"

4 Then David sent messengers, and took her; and she came to him, and he lay with her, for she was cleansed from her impurity; and she returned to her house.

5 And the woman conceived; so she sent and told David, and said, "I *am* with child."

6 Then David sent to Joab, *saying,* "Send me Uriah the Hittite." And Joab sent Uriah to David.

7 When Uriah had come to him, David

22 Hebrew *Hadarezer* 23 That is, the Euphrates 24 Hebrew *Hadarezer*

asked how Joab was doing, and how the people were doing, and how the war prospered.

8 And David said to Uriah, "Go down to your house and wash your feet." So Uriah departed from the king's house, and a gift *of food* from the king followed him.

9 But Uriah slept at the door of the king's house with all the servants of his lord, and did not go down to his house.

10 So when they told David, saying, "Uriah did not go down to his house," David said to Uriah, "Did you not come from a journey? Why did you not go down to your house?"

11 And Uriah said to David, "The ark and Israel and Judah are dwelling in tents, and my lord Joab and the servants of my lord are encamped in the open fields. Shall I then go to my house to eat and drink, and to lie with my wife? *As* you live, and *as* your soul lives, I will not do this thing."

12 Then David said to Uriah, "Wait here today also, and tomorrow I will let you depart." So Uriah remained in Jerusalem that day and the next.

13 Now when David called him, he ate and drank before him; and he made him drunk. And at evening he went out to lie on his bed with the servants of his lord, but he did not go down to his house.

14 Then in the morning it was so that David wrote a letter to Joab and sent *it* by the hand of Uriah.

15 And he wrote in the letter, saying, "Set Uriah in the forefront of the hottest battle, and retreat from him, that he may be struck down and die."

16 So it happened, while Joab besieged the city, that he assigned Uriah to a place where he knew there *were* valiant men.

17 Then the men of the city came out and fought with Joab. And *some* of the people of the servants of David fell; and Uriah the Hittite died also.

18 Then Joab sent and told David all the things concerning the war,

19 and charged the messenger, saying, "When you have finished telling the matters of the war to the king,

20 if it happens that the king's wrath rises, and he says to you: 'Why did you approach so near to the city when you fought? Did you not know that they would shoot from the wall?

21 'Who struck Abimelech the son of Jerubbesheth?[25] Was it not a woman who cast a piece of a millstone on him from the wall, so that he died in Thebez? Why did you go near the wall?'—then you shall say, 'Your servant Uriah the Hittite is dead also.' "

22 So the messenger went, and came and told David all that Joab had sent by him.

23 And the messenger said to David, "Surely the men prevailed against us and came out to us in the field; then we drove them back as far as the entrance of the gate.

24 "The archers shot from the wall at your servants; and *some* of the king's servants are dead, and your servant Uriah the Hittite is dead also."

25 Then David said to the messenger, "Thus you shall say to Joab: 'Do not let this thing displease you, for the sword devours one as well as another. Strengthen your attack against the city, and overthrow it.' So encourage him."

26 When the wife of Uriah heard that Uriah her husband was dead, she mourned for her husband.

27 And when her mourning was over, David sent and brought her to his house, and she became his wife and bore him a son. But the thing that David had done displeased the LORD.

Nathan's Parable and David's Confession

12 Then the LORD sent Nathan to David. And he came to him, and said to him: "There were two men in one city, one rich and the other poor.

2 "The rich *man* had exceedingly many flocks and herds.

3 "But the poor *man* had nothing, except one little ewe lamb which he had bought and nourished; and it grew up together with him and with his children. It ate of his own food and drank from his own cup and lay in his bosom; and it was like a daughter to him."

4 "And a traveler came to the rich man, who refused to take from his own flock and from his own herd to prepare one for the wayfaring man who had come to him; but he took the poor man's lamb and prepared it for the man who had come to him."

5 Then David's anger was greatly aroused against the man, and he said to

25 Same as *Jerubbaal*, that is, Gideon (Judges 6:32f)

Nathan, "*As* the LORD lives, the man who has done this shall surely die!
6 "And he shall restore fourfold for the lamb, because he did this thing and because he had no pity."
7 Then Nathan said to David, "You *are* the man! Thus says the LORD God of Israel: 'I anointed you king over Israel, and I delivered you from the hand of Saul.
8 'I gave you your master's house and your master's wives into your keeping, and gave you the house of Israel and Judah. And if *that had been* too little, I also would have given you much more!
9 'Why have you despised the commandment of the LORD, to do evil in His sight? You have killed Uriah the Hittite with the sword; you have taken his wife *to be* your wife, and have killed him with the sword of the people of Ammon.
10 'Now therefore, the sword shall never depart from your house, because you have despised Me, and have taken the wife of Uriah the Hittite to be your wife.'
11 "Thus says the LORD: 'Behold, I will raise up adversity against you from your own house; and I will take your wives before your eyes and give *them* to your neighbor, and he shall lie with your wives in the sight of this sun.
12 'For you did *it* secretly, but I will do this thing before all Israel, before the sun.' "
13 Then David said to Nathan, "I have sinned against the LORD." And Nathan said to David, "The LORD also has put away your sin; you shall not die.
14 "However, because by this deed you have given great occasion to the enemies of the LORD to blaspheme, the child also *who is* born to you shall surely die."
15 Then Nathan departed to his house.

The Death of David's Son

And the LORD struck the child that Uriah's wife bore to David, and it became *very* ill.
16 David therefore pleaded with God for the child, and David fasted and went in and lay all night on the ground.
17 So the elders of his house arose *and went* to him, to raise him up from the ground. But he would not, nor did he eat food with them.
18 Then on the seventh day it came to pass that the child died. And the servants of David were afraid to tell him that the child was dead. For they said, "Indeed, while the child was *still* alive, we spoke to him, and he would not heed our voice. How can we tell him that the child is dead? He may do some harm!"
19 When David saw that his servants were whispering, David perceived that the child was dead. Therefore David said to his servants, "Is the child dead?" And they said, "He is dead."
20 So David arose from the ground, washed and anointed himself, and changed his clothes; and he went into the house of the LORD and worshiped. Then he went to his own house; and when he requested, they set food before him, and he ate.
21 Then his servants said to him, "What *is* this that you have done? You fasted and wept for the child *while he was* alive, but when the child died, you arose and ate food."
22 So he said, "While the child was *still* alive, I fasted and wept; for I said, 'Who can tell *whether* the LORD[26] will be gracious to me, that the child may live?'
23 "But now he is dead; why should I fast? Can I bring him back again? I shall go to him, but he shall not return to me."

Solomon Is Born

24 Then David comforted Bathsheba his wife, and went in to her and lay with her. So she bore a son, and he called his name Solomon. And the LORD loved him.
25 And He sent *word* by the hand of Nathan the prophet; so he[27] called his name Jedidiah,[28] because of the LORD.

Rabbah Is Captured

26 Now Joab fought against Rabbah of the people of Ammon, and took the royal city.
27 And Joab sent messengers to David, and said, "I have fought against Rabbah, and I have taken the city's water *supply*.
28 "Now therefore, gather the rest of the people together and encamp against the city and take it, lest I take the city and it be called after my name."
29 So David gathered all the people together and went to Rabbah, fought against it, and took it.
30 Then he took their king's crown from

---

26 A few Hebrew manuscripts and Syriac read *God.*
27 Qere, Syriac, Targum, and some Hebrew manuscripts read *she.*   28 Literally *Beloved of the LORD*

his head. Its weight *was* a talent of gold, with precious stones. And it was *set* on David's head. Also he brought out the spoil of the city in great abundance.

31 And he brought out the people who *were* in it, and put *them to work* with saws and iron picks and iron axes, and made them cross over to the brick works. So he did with all the cities of the people of Ammon. Then David and all the people returned to Jerusalem.

Amnon and Tamar

13 Now after this it was so that Absalom the son of David had a lovely sister, whose name *was* Tamar; and Amnon the son of David loved her.

2 Amnon was so distressed over his sister Tamar that he became sick; for she *was* a virgin. And it was improper for Amnon to do anything to her.

3 But Amnon had a friend whose name *was* Jonadab the son of Shimeah, David's brother. Now Jonadab *was* a very crafty man.

4 And he said to him, "Why *are* you, the king's son, becoming thinner day after day? Will you not tell me?" And Amnon said to him, "I love Tamar, my brother Absalom's sister."

5 So Jonadab said to him, "Lie down on your bed and pretend to be ill. And when your father comes to see you, say to him, 'Please let my sister Tamar come and give me food, and prepare the food in my sight, that I may see *it* and eat it from her hand.'"

6 Then Amnon lay down and pretended to be ill; and when the king came to see him, Amnon said to the king, "Please let Tamar my sister come and make a couple of cakes for me in my sight, that I may eat from her hand."

7 And David sent home to Tamar, saying, "Now go to your brother Amnon's house, and prepare food for him."

8 So Tamar went to her brother Amnon's house; and he was lying down. Then she took flour and kneaded *it*, made cakes in his sight, and baked the cakes.

9 And she took the pan and placed *them* out before him, but he refused to eat. Then Amnon said, "Have everyone go out from me." And they all went out from him.

10 Then Amnon said to Tamar, "Bring the food into the bedroom, that I may eat from your hand." And Tamar took the cakes which she had made, and brought *them* to Amnon her brother in the bedroom.

11 Now when she had brought *them* to him to eat, he took hold of her and said to her, "Come, lie with me, my sister."

12 And she answered him, "No, my brother, do not force me, for no such thing should be done in Israel. Do not do this disgraceful thing!

13 "And I, where could I take my shame? And as for you, you would be like one of the fools in Israel. Now therefore, please speak to the king; for he will not withhold me from you."

14 However, he would not heed her voice; and being stronger than she, he forced her and lay with her.

15 Then Amnon hated her exceedingly, so that the hatred with which he hated her *was* greater than the love with which he had loved her. And Amnon said to her, "Arise, be gone!"

16 And she said to him, "No, indeed! This evil of sending me away *is* worse than the other that you did to me." But he would not listen to her.

17 Then he called his servant who attended him, and said, "Here! Put this *woman* out, away from me, and bolt the door behind her."

18 Now she had on a robe of many colors, for the king's virgin daughters wore such apparel. And his servant put her out and bolted the door behind her.

19 Then Tamar put ashes on her head, and tore her robe of many colors that *was* on her, and laid her hand on her head and went away crying bitterly.

20 And Absalom her brother said to her, "Has Amnon your brother been with you? But now hold your peace, my sister. He *is* your brother; do not take this thing to heart." So Tamar remained desolate in her brother Absalom's house.

21 But when King David heard of all these things, he was very angry.

22 And Absalom spoke to his brother Amnon neither good nor bad. For Absalom hated Amnon, because he had forced his sister Tamar.

Absalom Murders Amnon

23 And it came to pass, after two full years, that Absalom had sheepshearers in

Baal Hazor, which *is* near Ephraim; so Absalom invited all the king's sons.
24 Then Absalom came to the king and said, "Kindly note, your servant has sheepshearers; please, let the king and his servants go with your servant."
25 But the king said to Absalom, "No, my son, let us not all go now, lest we be a burden to you." Then he urged him, but he would not go; and he blessed him.
26 Then Absalom said, "If not, please let my brother Amnon go with us." And the king said to him, "Why should he go with you?"
27 But Absalom urged him; so he let Amnon and all the king's sons go with him.
28 Now Absalom had commanded his servants, saying, "Watch now, when Amnon's heart is merry with wine, and when I say to you, 'Strike Amnon!' then kill him. Do not be afraid. Have I not commanded you? Be courageous and valiant."
29 So the servants of Absalom did to Amnon as Absalom had commanded. Then all the king's sons arose, and each one got on his mule and fled.
30 And it came to pass, while they were on the way, that news came to David, saying, "Absalom has killed all the king's sons, and not one of them is left!"
31 So the king arose and tore his garments and lay on the ground, and all his servants stood by with their clothes torn.
32 Then Jonadab the son of Shimeah, David's brother, answered and said, "Let not my lord suppose *that* they have killed all the young men, the king's sons, for only Amnon is dead. For by the command of Absalom this has been determined from the day that he forced his sister Tamar.
33 "Now therefore, let not my lord the king take the thing to his heart, to think that all the king's sons are dead. For only Amnon is dead."

Absalom Flees to Geshur

34 Then Absalom fled. And the young man who was keeping watch lifted his eyes and looked, and there, many people were coming from the road on the hillside behind him.
35 And Jonadab said to the king, "Look, the king's sons are coming; as your servant said, so it is."
36 So it was, as soon as he had finished speaking, that the king's sons indeed came, and they lifted up their voice and wept. Also the king and all his servants wept very bitterly.
37 But Absalom fled and went to Talmai the son of Ammihud, king of Geshur. And *David* mourned for his son every day.
38 So Absalom fled and went to Geshur, and was there three years.
39 And King David longed to go to Absalom. For he had been comforted concerning Amnon, because he was dead.

Absalom Returns to Jerusalem

14 So Joab the son of Zeruiah perceived that the king's heart *was* concerned about Absalom.
2 And Joab sent to Tekoa and brought from there a wise woman, and said to her, "Please pretend to be a mourner, and put on mourning apparel; do not anoint yourself with oil, but act like a woman who has been mourning a long time for the dead.
3 "Go to the king and speak to him in this manner." So Joab put the words in her mouth.
4 And when the woman of Tekoa spoke[29] to the king, she fell on her face to the ground and prostrated herself, and said, "Help, O king!"
5 Then the king said to her, "What troubles you?" And she answered, "Indeed I *am* a widow, my husband is dead.
6 "Now your maidservant had two sons; and the two fought with each other in the field, and *there was* no one to part them, but the one struck the other and killed him.
7 "And now the whole family has risen up against your maidservant, and they said, 'Deliver him who struck his brother, that we may execute him for the life of his brother whom he killed; and we will destroy the heir also.' So they would extinguish my ember that is left, and leave to my husband *neither* name nor remnant on the earth."
8 Then the king said to the woman, "Go to your house, and I will give orders concerning you."
9 And the woman of Tekoa said to the king, "My lord, O king, *let* the iniquity *be* on me and on my father's house, and the king and his throne *be* guiltless."

---

29 Septuagint, Syriac, Vulgate, and many Hebrew manuscripts read *came.*

10 So the king said, "Whoever says *anything* to you, bring him to me, and he shall not touch you anymore."
11 Then she said, "Please let the king remember the LORD your God, and do not permit the avenger of blood to destroy anymore, lest they destroy my son." And he said, "*As* the LORD lives, not one hair of your son shall fall to the ground."
12 Then the woman said, "Please, let your maidservant speak *another* word to my lord the king." And he said, "Say on."
13 And the woman said: "Why then have you schemed such a thing against the people of God? For the king speaks this thing as one who is guilty, *in that* the king does not bring his banished one home again.
14 "For we will surely die and *become* like water spilled on the ground, which cannot be gathered up again. Yet God does not take away a life; but He devises means, so that His banished ones are not expelled from Him.
15 "Now therefore, I have come to speak of this thing to my lord the king because the people have made me afraid. And your maidservant said, 'I will now speak to the king; it may be that the king will perform the request of his maidservant.
16 'For the king will hear and deliver his maidservant from the hand of the man *who would* destroy me and my son together from the inheritance of God.'
17 "Your maidservant said, 'The word of my lord the king will now be comforting; for as the angel of God, so *is* my lord the king in discerning good and evil. And may the LORD your God be with you.'"
18 Then the king answered and said to the woman, "Please do not hide from me anything that I ask you." And the woman said, "Please, let my lord the king speak."
19 And the king said, "*Is* the hand of Joab with you in all this?" And the woman answered and said, "*As* you live, my lord the king, no one can turn to the right hand or to the left from anything that my lord the king has spoken. For your servant Joab commanded me, and he put all these words in the mouth of your maidservant.
20 "To bring about this change of affairs your servant Joab has done this thing; but my lord *is* wise, according to the wisdom of the angel of God, to know all *things* that *are* in the earth."
21 And the king said to Joab, "All right, I have granted this thing. Go therefore, bring back the young man Absalom."
22 Then Joab fell to the ground on his face and bowed himself, and thanked the king. And Joab said, "Today your servant knows that I have found favor in your sight, my lord, O king, in that the king has fulfilled the request of his servant."
23 So Joab arose and went to Geshur, and brought Absalom to Jerusalem.
24 And the king said, "Let him return to his own house, but do not let him see my face." So Absalom returned to his own house, but did not see the king's face.

David Forgives Absalom

25 Now in all Israel there was no one who was praised as much as Absalom for his good looks. From the sole of his foot to the crown of his head there was no blemish in him.
26 And when he cut the hair of his head—at the end of every year he cut *it* because it was heavy on him—when he cut it, he weighed the hair of his head at two hundred shekels according to the king's standard.
27 To Absalom were born three sons, and one daughter whose name *was* Tamar. She was a woman of beautiful appearance.
28 And Absalom dwelt two full years in Jerusalem, but did not see the king's face.
29 Therefore Absalom sent for Joab, to send him to the king, but he would not come to him. And when he sent again the second time, he would not come.
30 So he said to his servants, "See, Joab's field is near mine, and he has barley there; go and set it on fire." And Absalom's servants set the field on fire.
31 Then Joab arose and came to Absalom's house, and said to him, "Why have your servants set my field on fire?"
32 And Absalom answered Joab, "Look, I sent to you, saying, 'Come here, so that I may send you to the king, to say, "Why have I come from Geshur? *It would be* better for me *to be* there still."' Now therefore, let me see the king's face; but if there is *any* iniquity in me, let him execute me."
33 So Joab went to the king and told

him. And when he had called for Absalom, he came to the king and bowed himself on his face to the ground before the king. Then the king kissed Absalom.

Absalom's Treason

15 After this it happened that Absalom provided himself with chariots and horses, and fifty men to run before him. 2 Now Absalom would rise early and stand beside the way to the gate. So it was, whenever anyone who had a lawsuit came to the king for a decision, that Absalom would call to him and say, "What city *are* you from?" And he would say, "Your servant *is* from such and such a tribe of Israel." 3 Then Absalom would say to him, "Look, your case *is* good and right; but *there is* no deputy of the king to hear you." 4 Moreover Absalom would say, "Oh, that I were made judge in the land, and everyone who has any suit or cause would come to me; then I would give him justice." 5 And *so* it was, whenever anyone came near *him* to bow down to him, that he would put out his hand and take him and kiss him. 6 In this manner Absalom acted toward all Israel who came to the king for judgment. So Absalom stole the hearts of the men of Israel.

7 And it came to pass after forty[30] years that Absalom said to the king, "Please, let me go to Hebron and pay the vow which I vowed to the LORD. 8 "For your servant vowed a vow while I dwelt at Geshur in Syria, saying, 'If the LORD indeed brings me back to Jerusalem, then I will serve the LORD.'" 9 And the king said to him, "Go in peace." So he arose and went to Hebron. 10 Then Absalom sent spies throughout all the tribes of Israel, saying, "As soon as you hear the sound of the trumpet, then you shall say, 'Absalom reigns in Hebron!'" 11 And with Absalom went two hundred men from Jerusalem *who were* invited, and they went along innocently and did not know anything. 12 Then Absalom sent for Ahithophel the Gilonite, David's counselor, from his city, *namely* from Giloh, while he offered sacrifices. And the conspiracy grew strong, for the people with Absalom continually increased in number.

David Escapes from Jerusalem

13 And a messenger came to David, saying, "The hearts of the men of Israel are with Absalom." 14 So David said to all his servants who *were* with him at Jerusalem, "Arise, and let us flee; or *else* we shall not escape from Absalom. Make haste to depart, lest he overtake us suddenly and bring disaster upon us, and strike the city with the edge of the sword." 15 And the king's servants said to the king, "We *are* your servants, *ready to do* whatever my lord the king commands." 16 Then the king went out with all his household after him. But the king left ten women, concubines, to keep the house. 17 And the king went out with all the people after him, and stopped at the outskirts. 18 Then all his servants passed before him; and all the Cherethites, all the Pelethites, and all the Gittites, six hundred men who had followed him from Gath, passed before the king.

19 And the king said to Ittai the Gittite, "Why are you also going with us? Return and remain with the king. For you *are* a foreigner and also an exile from your own place. 20 "In fact, you came *only* yesterday. Should I make you wander up and down with us today, since I go I know not where? Return, and take your brethren back. Mercy and truth *be* with you." 21 And Ittai answered the king and said, "*As* the LORD lives, and *as* my lord the king lives, surely in whatever place my lord the king shall be, whether in death or life, even there also your servant will be." 22 So David said to Ittai, "Go, and cross over." Then Ittai the Gittite and all his men and all the little ones who *were* with him crossed over. 23 And all the country wept with a loud voice, and all the people crossed over. The king himself also crossed over the Brook Kidron, and all the people crossed over toward the way of the wilderness. 24 There was Zadok also, and all the Levites with him, bearing the ark of the covenant of God. And they set down the ark of God, and Abiathar went up until all

---

30 Septuagint manuscripts, Syriac, and Josephus read *four.*

the people had finished crossing over from the city.

25 Then the king said to Zadok, "Carry the ark of God back into the city. If I find favor in the eyes of the LORD, He will bring me back and show me *both* it and His habitation.

26 "But if He says thus: 'I have no delight in you,' here I am, let Him do to me as seems good to Him."

27 The king also said to Zadok the priest, "*Are* you *not* a seer? Return to the city in peace, and your two sons with you, Ahimaaz your son, and Jonathan the son of Abiathar.

28 "See, I will wait in the plains of the wilderness until word comes from you to inform me."

29 Therefore Zadok and Abiathar carried the ark of God back to Jerusalem. And they remained there.

30 So David went up by the ascent of the *Mount of* Olives, and wept as he went up; and he had his head covered and went barefoot. And all the people who *were* with him covered their heads and went up, weeping as they went up.

31 Then *someone* told David, saying, "Ahithophel *is* among the conspirators with Absalom." And David said, "O LORD, I pray, turn the counsel of Ahithophel into foolishness!"

32 Now it happened when David had come to the top *of the mountain*, where he worshiped God, that there was Hushai the Archite, coming to meet him with his robe torn and dust on his head.

33 David said to him, "If you go on with me, then you will become a burden to me.

34 "But if you return to the city, and say to Absalom, 'I will be your servant, O king; *just as* I *have been* your father's servant previously, so I *will* now also *be* your servant,' then you may defeat the counsel of Ahithophel for me.

35 "And *do* you not *have* Zadok and Abiathar the priests with you there? Therefore it will be *that* whatever you hear from the king's house, you shall tell to Zadok and Abiathar the priests.

36 "Indeed *they have* there with them their two sons, Ahimaaz, Zadok's *son*, and Jonathan, Abiathar's *son*; and by them you shall send me everything you hear."

37 So Hushai, David's friend, went into the city. And Absalom came into Jerusalem.

Mephibosheth's Servant

16 When David was a little past the top *of the mountain*, there was Ziba the servant of Mephibosheth, who met him with a couple of saddled donkeys, and on them two hundred *loaves* of bread, one hundred clusters of raisins, one hundred summer fruits, and a skin of wine.

2 And the king said to Ziba, "What do you mean to do with these?" So Ziba said, "The donkeys *are* for the king's household to ride on, the bread and summer fruit for the young men to eat, and the wine for those who are faint in the wilderness to drink."

3 Then the king said, "And where *is* your master's son?" And Ziba said to the king, "Indeed he is staying in Jerusalem, for he said, 'Today the house of Israel will restore the kingdom of my father to me.'"

4 So the king said to Ziba, "Here, all that *belongs* to Mephibosheth *is* yours." And Ziba said, "I humbly bow before you, *that* I may find favor in your sight, my lord, O king!"

Shimei Curses David

5 Now when King David came to Bahurim, there was a man from the family of the house of Saul, whose name *was* Shimei the son of Gera, coming from there. He came out, cursing continuously as he came.

6 And he threw stones at David and at all the servants of King David. And all the people and all the mighty men *were* on his right hand and on his left.

7 Also Shimei said thus when he cursed: "Come out! Come out! You bloodthirsty man, you rogue!

8 "The LORD has brought upon you all the blood of the house of Saul, in whose place you have reigned; and the LORD has delivered the kingdom into the hand of Absalom your son. So now you *are* caught in your own evil, because you are a bloodthirsty man!"

9 Then Abishai the son of Zeruiah said to the king, "Why should this dead dog curse my lord the king? Please, let me go over and take off his head!"

10 And the king said, "What have I to do

with you, you sons of Zeruiah? So let him curse, because the LORD has said to him, 'Curse David.' Who then shall say, 'Why have you done so?' "

11 And David said to Abishai and all his servants, "See how my son who came from my own body seeks my life. How much more now *may this* Benjamite? Let him alone, and let him curse; for so the LORD has ordered him.

12 "It may be that the LORD will look on my affliction, and that the LORD will repay me with good for his cursing this day."

13 And as David and his men went along the road, Shimei went along the hillside opposite him and cursed as he went, threw stones at him and kicked up dust.

14 Now the king and all the people who *were* with him became weary; so they refreshed themselves there.

The Counsel of Ahithophel

15 Meanwhile Absalom and all the people, the men of Israel, came to Jerusalem; and Ahithophel *was* with him.

16 And so it was, when Hushai the Archite, David's friend, came to Absalom, that Hushai said to Absalom, "*Long* live the king! *Long* live the king!"

17 So Absalom said to Hushai, "*Is* this your loyalty to your friend? Why did you not go with your friend?"

18 And Hushai said to Absalom, "No, but whom the LORD and this people and all the men of Israel choose, his I will be, and with him I will remain.

19 "Furthermore, whom should I serve? *Should I* not *serve* in the presence of his son? As I have served in your father's presence, so will I be in your presence."

20 Then Absalom said to Ahithophel, "Give counsel as to what we should do."

21 And Ahithophel said to Absalom, "Go in to your father's concubines, whom he has left to keep the house; and all Israel will hear that you are abhorred by your father. Then the hands of all who are with you will be strong."

22 So they pitched a tent for Absalom on the top of the house, and Absalom went in to his father's concubines in the sight of all Israel.

23 And the counsel of Ahithophel, which he gave in those days, *was* as if one had inquired at the oracle of God. So *was* all the counsel of Ahithophel both with David and with Absalom.

17 Moreover Ahithophel said to Absalom, "Now let me choose twelve thousand men, and I will arise and pursue David tonight.

2 "I will come upon him while he *is* weary and weak, and make him afraid. And all the people who *are* with him will flee, and I will strike only the king.

3 "Then I will bring back all the people to you. When all return except the man whom you seek, *then* all the people will be at peace."

4 And the saying pleased Absalom and all the elders of Israel.

The Counsel of Hushai

5 Then Absalom said, "Now call Hushai the Archite also, and let us hear what he says too."

6 And when Hushai came to Absalom, Absalom spoke to him, saying, "Ahithophel has spoken in this manner. Shall we do as he says? If not, speak up."

7 So Hushai said to Absalom: "The counsel that Ahithophel has given *is* not good at this time."

8 "For," said Hushai, "you know your father and his men, that they *are* mighty men, and they *are* enraged in their minds, like a bear robbed of her cubs in the field; and your father *is* a man of war, and will not camp with the people.

9 "Surely by now he is hidden in some pit, or in some *other* place. And it will be, when some of them are overthrown at the first, that whoever hears *it* will say, 'There is a slaughter among the people who follow Absalom.'

10 "And even he *who is* valiant, whose heart *is* like the heart of a lion, will melt completely. For all Israel knows that your father *is* a mighty man, and *those* who *are* with him *are* valiant men.

11 "Therefore I counsel that all Israel be fully gathered to you, from Dan to Beersheba, like the sand that *is* by the sea for multitude, and that you go to battle in person.

12 "So we will come upon him in some place where he may be found, and we will fall on him as the dew falls on the ground. And of him and all the men who *are* with him there shall not be left so much as one.

13 "Moreover, if he has withdrawn into a

city, then all Israel shall bring ropes to that city; and we will pull it into the river, until there is not one small stone found there."

14 So Absalom and all the men of Israel said, "The counsel of Hushai the Archite *is* better than the counsel of Ahithophel." For the LORD had purposed to defeat the good counsel of Ahithophel, to the intent that the LORD might bring disaster on Absalom.

Hushai Warns David to Escape

15 Then Hushai said to Zadok and Abiathar the priests, "Thus and so Ahithophel counseled Absalom and the elders of Israel, and thus and so I have counseled. 16 "Now therefore, send quickly and tell David, saying, 'Do not spend this night in the plains of the wilderness, but speedily cross over, lest the king and all the people who *are* with him be swallowed up.' "

17 Now Jonathan and Ahimaaz stayed at En Rogel, for they dared not be seen coming into the city; so a maidservant would come and tell them, and they would go and tell King David. 18 Nevertheless a lad saw them, and told Absalom. But both of them went away quickly and came to a man's house in Bahurim, who had a well in his court; and they went down into it. 19 Then the woman took and spread a covering over the well's mouth, and spread ground grain on it; and the thing was not known. 20 And when Absalom's servants came to the woman at the house, they said, "Where *are* Ahimaaz and Jonathan?" So the woman said to them, "They have gone over the water brook." And when they had searched and could not find *them,* they returned to Jerusalem. 21 Now it came to pass, after they had departed, that they came up out of the well and went and told King David, and said to David, "Arise and cross over the water quickly. For thus has Ahithophel counseled against you." 22 So David and all the people who *were* with him arose and crossed over the Jordan. By morning light not one of them was left who had not gone over the Jordan. 23 Now when Ahithophel saw that his counsel was not followed, he saddled *his* donkey, and arose and went home to

his house, to his city. Then he put his household in order, and hanged himself, and died; and he was buried in his father's tomb.

24 Then David went to Mahanaim. And Absalom crossed over the Jordan, he and all the men of Israel with him. 25 And Absalom made Amasa captain of the army instead of Joab. This Amasa *was* the son of a man whose name *was* Jithra,[31] an Israelite, who had gone in to Abigail the daughter of Nahash, sister of Zeruiah, Joab's mother. 26 So Israel and Absalom encamped in the land of Gilead.

27 Now it happened, when David had come to Mahanaim, that Shobi the son of Nahash from Rabbah of the people of Ammon, Machir the son of Ammiel from Lo Debar, and Barzillai the Gileadite from Rogelim, 28 brought beds and basins, earthen vessels and wheat, barley and flour, parched *grain* and beans, lentils and parched *seeds,* 29 honey and curds, sheep and cheese of the herd, for David and the people who *were* with him to eat. For they said, "The people are hungry and weary and thirsty in the wilderness."

Absalom's Defeat and Death

18 And David numbered the people who *were* with him, and set captains of thousands and captains of hundreds over them. 2 Then David sent out one third of the people under the hand of Joab, one third under the hand of Abishai the son of Zeruiah, Joab's brother, and one third under the hand of Ittai the Gittite. And the king said to the people, "I also will surely go out with you myself." 3 But the people answered, "You shall not go out. For if we flee away, they will not care about us; nor if half of us die, will they care about us. But *you are* worth ten thousand of us now. For you are now more help to us in the city." 4 So the king said to them, "Whatever seems best to you I will do." So the king stood beside the gate, and all the people went out by hundreds and by thousands. 5 Now the king had commanded Joab, Abishai, and Ittai, saying, "*Deal* gently for my sake with the young man Absalom." And all the people heard when the

31 Spelled *Jether* in 1 Chronicles 2:17 and elsewhere

king gave all the captains orders concerning Absalom.

6 So the people went out into the field of battle against Israel. And the battle was in the woods of Ephraim.

7 The people of Israel were overthrown there before the servants of David, and a great slaughter of twenty thousand *men* took place there that day.

8 For the battle there was scattered over the face of the whole countryside, and the woods devoured more people that day than the sword devoured.

9 Then Absalom met the servants of David. Absalom rode on a mule. The mule went under the thick boughs of a great terebinth tree, and his head caught in the terebinth; so he was left hanging between heaven and earth. And the mule which *was* under him went on.

10 Now a certain man saw *it* and told Joab, and said, "I just saw Absalom hanging in a terebinth tree!"

11 So Joab said to the man who told him, "You just saw *him*! And why did you not strike him there to the ground? I would have given you ten *shekels* of silver and a belt."

12 But the man said to Joab, "Though I were to receive a thousand *shekels* of silver in my hand, I would not raise my hand against the king's son. For in our hearing the king commanded you and Abishai and Ittai, saying, 'Beware lest anyone *touch* the young man Absalom!'32

13 "Otherwise I would have dealt falsely against my own life. For there is nothing hidden from the king, and you yourself would have set yourself against *me*."

14 Then Joab said, "I cannot linger with you." And he took three spears in his hand and thrust them through Absalom's heart, while he was *still* alive in the midst of the terebinth tree.

15 And ten young men who bore Joab's armor surrounded Absalom, and struck and killed him.

16 Then Joab blew the trumpet, and the people returned from pursuing Israel. For Joab held back the people.

17 And they took Absalom and cast him into a large pit in the woods, and laid a very large heap of stones over him. Then all Israel fled, everyone to his tent.

18 Now Absalom in his lifetime had taken and set up a pillar for himself, which *is* in the King's Valley. For he

said, "I have no son to keep my name in remembrance." He called the pillar after his own name. And to this day it is called Absalom's Monument.

David Hears of Absalom's Death

19 Then Ahimaaz the son of Zadok said, "Let me run now and take the news to the king, how the LORD has avenged him of his enemies."

20 And Joab said to him, "You shall not take the news this day, for you shall take the news another day. But today you shall take no news, because the king's son is dead."

21 Then Joab said to the Cushite, "Go, tell the king what you have seen." So the Cushite bowed himself to Joab and ran.

22 And Ahimaaz the son of Zadok said again to Joab, "But whatever happens, please let me also run after the Cushite." And Joab said, "Why will you run, my son, since you have no news ready?"

23 "But whatever happens," *he said,* "let me run." So he said to him, "Run." Then Ahimaaz ran by way of the plain, and outran the Cushite.

24 Now David was sitting between the two gates. And the watchman went up to the roof over the gate, to the wall, lifted his eyes and looked, and there was a man, running alone.

25 Then the watchman cried out and told the king. And the king said, "If he *is* alone, *there is* news in his mouth." And he came rapidly and drew near.

26 Then the watchman saw *another* man running, and the watchman called to the gatekeeper and said, "There is *another* man, running alone!" And the king said, "He also brings news."

27 So the watchman said, "I think the running of the first is like the running of Ahimaaz the son of Zadok." And the king said, "He *is* a good man, and comes with good news."

28 And Ahimaaz called out and said to the king, "All is well!" Then he bowed down with his face to the earth before the king, and said, "Blessed *be* the LORD your God, who has delivered up the men who raised their hand against my lord the king!"

29 The king said, "Is the young man Absalom safe?" And Ahimaaz answered, "When Joab sent the king's servant and

32 The ancient versions read '*Protect the young man Absalom for me!*'

me your servant, I saw a great tumult, but I did not know what *it was about.*"
30 And the king said, "Turn aside *and* stand here." So he turned aside and stood still.
31 Just then the Cushite came, and the Cushite said, "There is good news, my lord the king! For the LORD has avenged you this day of all those who rose against you."
32 And the king said to the Cushite, "Is the young man Absalom safe?" And the Cushite answered, "May the enemies of my lord the king, and all who rise against you to do *you* harm, be as *that* young man *is!*"

David's Mourning for Absalom

33 Then the king was deeply moved, and went up to the chamber over the gate, and wept. And as he went, he said thus: "O my son Absalom—my son, my son Absalom—if only I had died in your place! O Absalom my son, my son!"

19 And Joab was told, "Behold, the king is weeping and mourning for Absalom."
2 So the victory that day was *turned* into mourning for all the people. For the people heard it said that day, "The king is grieved for his son."
3 And the people stole back into the city that day, as people who are ashamed steal away when they flee in battle.
4 But the king covered his face, and the king cried out with a loud voice, "O my son Absalom! O Absalom, my son, my son!"
5 Then Joab came into the house to the king, and said, "Today you have disgraced all your servants who today have saved your life, the lives of your sons and daughters, the lives of your wives and the lives of your concubines,
6 "in that you love your enemies and hate your friends. For you have declared today that you regard neither princes nor servants; for today I perceive that if Absalom had lived and all of us had died today, then it would have pleased you well.
7 "Now therefore, arise, go out and speak comfort to your servants. For I swear by the LORD, if you do not go out, not one will stay with you this night.

And that will be worse for you than all the evil that has befallen you from your youth until now."
8 Then the king arose and sat in the gate. And they told all the people, saying, "There is the king, sitting in the gate." So all the people came before king. For everyone of Israel had fled to his tent.

David Returns to Jerusalem

9 Now all the people were in a dispute throughout all the tribes of Israel, saying, "The king saved us from the hand of our enemies, he delivered us from the hand of the Philistines, and now he has fled from the land because of Absalom.
10 "But Absalom, whom we anointed over us, has died in battle. Now therefore, why do you say nothing about bringing back the king?"
11 Then King David sent to Zadok and Abiathar the priests, saying, "Speak to the elders of Judah, saying, 'Why are you the last to bring the king back to his house, since the words of all Israel have come to the king, *even* to his house?
12 'You *are* my brethren, you *are* my bone and my flesh. Why then are you the last to bring back the king?'
13 "And say to Amasa, '*Are* you not my bone and my flesh? God do so to me, and more also, if you are not commander of the army before me continually in place of Joab.'"
14 So he swayed the hearts of all the men of Judah, just as *the heart of* one man, so that they sent *this word* to the king: "Return, you and all your servants!"
15 Then the king returned and came to the Jordan. And Judah came to Gilgal, to go to meet the king, to escort the king across the Jordan.
16 And Shimei the son of Gera, a Benjamite, who *was* from Bahurim, hastened and came down with the men of Judah to meet King David.
17 *There were* a thousand men of Benjamin with him, and Ziba the servant of the house of Saul, and his fifteen sons and his twenty servants with him; and they went over the Jordan before the king.
18 Then a ferryboat went across to carry over the king's household, and to do what he thought good.

David's Mercy to Shimei

Now Shimei the son of Gera fell down before the king when he had crossed the Jordan.
19 Then he said to the king, "Do not let my lord impute iniquity to me, or remember what wrong your servant did on the day that my lord the king left Jerusalem, that the king should take *it* to heart.
20 "For I, your servant, know that I have sinned. Therefore here I am, the first to come today of all the house of Joseph to go down to meet my lord the king."
21 But Abishai the son of Zeruiah answered and said, "Shall not Shimei be put to death for this, because he cursed the LORD's anointed?"
22 And David said, "What have I to do with you, you sons of Zeruiah, that you should be adversaries to me today? Shall any man be put to death today in Israel? For do I not know that today I *am* king over Israel?"
23 Therefore the king said to Shimei, "You shall not die." And the king swore to him.

David and Mephibosheth Meet

24 Now Mephibosheth the son of Saul came down to meet the king. And he had not cared for his feet, nor trimmed his mustache, nor washed his clothes, from the day the king departed until the day he came *back* in peace.
25 So it was, when he had come to Jerusalem to meet the king, that the king said to him, "Why did you not go with me, Mephibosheth?"
26 And he answered, "My lord, O king, my servant deceived me. For your servant said, 'I will saddle a donkey for myself, that I may ride on it and go to the king,' because your servant *is* lame.
27 "And he has slandered your servant to my lord the king, but my lord the king *is* like the angel of God. Therefore do *what is* good in your eyes.
28 "For all *of* my father's house were but dead men before my lord the king. Yet you set your servant among those who eat at your own table. Therefore what right have I still to cry out anymore to the king?"
29 So the king said to him, "Why do you speak anymore of your matters? I have said, 'You and Ziba divide the land.' "

30 Then Mephibosheth said to the king, "Rather, let him take it all, inasmuch as my lord the king has come back in peace to his own house."

David's Kindness to Barzillai

31 And Barzillai the Gileadite came down from Rogelim and went across the Jordan with the king, to escort him across the Jordan.
32 Now Barzillai was a very aged man, eighty years old. And he had provided the king with supplies while he stayed at Mahanaim, for he *was* a very rich man.
33 And the king said to Barzillai, "Come across with me, and I will provide for you while you are with me in Jerusalem."
34 But Barzillai said to the king, "How long have I to live, that I should go up with the king to Jerusalem?
35 "I *am* today eighty years old. Can I discern between the good and bad? Can your servant taste what I eat or what I drink? Can I hear any longer the voice of singing men and singing women? Why then should your servant be a further burden to my lord the king?
36 "Your servant will go a little way across the Jordan with the king. And why should the king repay me *with* such a reward?
37 "Please let your servant turn back again, that I may die in my own city, *and be buried* by the grave of my father and mother. But here is your servant Chimham; let him cross over with my lord the king, and do for him what seems good to you."
38 And the king answered, "Chimham shall cross over with me, and I will do for him what seems good to you. Now whatever you request of me, I will do for you."
39 Then all the people went over the Jordan. And when the king had crossed over, the king kissed Barzillai and blessed him, and he returned to his own place.

The Quarrel about the King

40 Now the king went on to Gilgal, and Chimham[33] went on with him. And all the people of Judah escorted the king, and also half the people of Israel.
41 Just then all the men of Israel came to the king, and said to the king, "Why have our brethren, the men of Judah, stolen you away and brought the king, his

33 Masoretic Text reads *Chimhan.*

household, and all David's men with him across the Jordan?"
42 So all the men of Judah answered the men of Israel, "Because the king is a close relative of ours. Why then are you angry over this matter? Have we ever eaten at the king's expense? Or has he given us any gift?"
43 And the men of Israel answered the men of Judah, and said, "We have ten shares in the king; therefore we also have more right to David than you. Why then do you despise us—were we not the first to advise bringing back our king?" Yet the words of the men of Judah were fiercer than the words of the men of Israel.

The Rebellion of Sheba

20 And there happened to be there a rebel,[34] whose name was Sheba the son of Bichri, a Benjamite. And he blew a trumpet, and said:

"We have no part in David,
    Nor do we have inheritance
        in the son of Jesse;
    Every man to his tents, O Israel!"

2 So every man of Israel deserted David, and followed Sheba the son of Bichri. But the men of Judah, from the Jordan as far as Jerusalem, remained loyal to their king.
3 Now David came to his house at Jerusalem. And the king took the ten women, his concubines whom he had left to keep the house, and put them in seclusion and supported them, but did not go in to them. So they were shut up to the day of their death, living in widowhood.
4 Then the king said to Amasa, "Assemble the men of Judah for me within three days, and be present here yourself."
5 So Amasa went to assemble the men of Judah. But he delayed longer than the set time which David had appointed him.
6 And David said to Abishai, "Now Sheba the son of Bichri will do us more harm than Absalom. Take your lord's servants and pursue him, lest he find for himself fortified cities, and escape us."
7 So Joab's men, with the Cherethites, the Pelethites, and all the mighty men, went out after him. And they went out of Jerusalem to pursue Sheba the son of Bichri.

8 When they were at the large stone which is in Gibeon, Amasa came before them. Now Joab was dressed in battle armor; on it was a belt with a sword fastened in its sheath at his hips; and as he was going forward, it fell out.
9 Then Joab said to Amasa, "Are you in health, my brother?" And Joab took Amasa by the beard with his right hand to kiss him.
10 But Amasa did not notice the sword that was in Joab's hand. And he struck him with it in the stomach, and his entrails poured out on the ground; and he did not strike him again. Thus he died. Then Joab and Abishai his brother pursued Sheba the son of Bichri.
11 Meanwhile one of Joab's men stood near Amasa, and said, "Whoever favors Joab and whoever is for David, let him follow Joab!"
12 But Amasa wallowed in his blood in the middle of the highway. And when the man saw that all the people stood still, he moved Amasa from the highway to the field and threw a garment over him, when he saw that everyone who came upon him halted.
13 When he was removed from the highway, all the people went on after Joab to pursue Sheba the son of Bichri.
14 And he went through all the tribes of Israel to Abel and Beth Maachah and all the Berites. So they were gathered together and also went after Sheba.
15 Then they came and besieged him in Abel of Beth Maachah; and they cast up a siege mound against the city, and it stood by the rampart. And all the people who were with Joab battered the wall to throw it down.
16 Then a wise woman cried out from the city, "Hear, Hear! Please say to Joab, 'Come nearby, that I may speak with you.' "
17 When he had come near to her, the woman said, "Are you Joab?" He answered, "I am." Then she said to him, "Hear the words of your maidservant." And he answered, "I am listening."
18 Then she spoke, saying, "They used to talk in former times, saying, 'They shall surely ask counsel at Abel,' and so they would end disputes.
19 "I am among the peaceable and faithful in Israel. You seek to destroy a city

34 Literally man of Belial

and a mother in Israel. Why would you swallow up the inheritance of the LORD?"
20 And Joab answered and said, "Far be it, far be it from me, that I should swallow up or destroy!
21 "That *is* not so. But a man from the mountains of Ephraim, Sheba the son of Bichri by name, has raised his hand against the king, against David. Deliver him only, and I will depart from the city." And the woman said to Joab, "Watch, his head will be thrown to you over the wall."
22 Then the woman in her wisdom went to all the people. And they cut off the head of Sheba the son of Bichri, and threw *it* out to Joab. Then he blew a trumpet, and they withdrew from the city, every man to his tent. So Joab returned to the king at Jerusalem.

David's Government Officers

23 And Joab *was* over all the army of Israel; Benaiah the son of Jehoiada *was* over the Cherethites and the Pelethites;
24 Adoram *was* in charge of revenue; Jehoshaphat the son of Ahilud *was* recorder;
25 Sheva *was* scribe; Zadok and Abiathar *were* the priests;
26 and Ira the Jairite was a chief minister under David.

David Avenges the Gibeonites

21 Now there was a famine in the days of David for three years, year after year; and David inquired of the LORD. And the LORD answered, "*It is* because of Saul and *his* bloodthirsty house, because he killed the Gibeonites."
2 So the king called the Gibeonites and spoke to them. Now the Gibeonites *were* not of the children of Israel, but of the remnant of the Amorites; the children of Israel had sworn protection to them, but Saul had sought to kill them in his zeal for the children of Israel and Judah.
3 Therefore David said to the Gibeonites, "What shall I do for you? And with what shall I make atonement, that you may bless the inheritance of the LORD?"
4 And the Gibeonites said to him, "We will have no silver or gold from Saul or from his house, nor shall you kill any man in Israel for us." And he said,

"Whatever you say, *that* will I do for you."
5 So they answered the king, "As for the man who consumed us and plotted against us, *that* we should be destroyed from remaining in any of the territories of Israel,
6 "let seven men of his descendants be delivered to us, and we will hang them before the LORD in Gibeah of Saul, *whom* the LORD chose." And the king said, "I will give *them*."
7 But the king spared Mephibosheth the son of Jonathan, the son of Saul, because of the LORD's oath that *was* between them, between David and Jonathan the son of Saul.
8 So the king took Armoni and Mephibosheth, the two sons of Rizpah the daughter of Aiah, whom she bore to Saul; and the five sons of Michal[35] the daughter of Saul, whom she brought up for Adriel the son of Barzillai the Meholathite;
9 and he delivered them into the hands of the Gibeonites, and they hanged them on the hill before the LORD. So they fell, *all* seven together, and were put to death in the days of harvest, in the first *days*, in the beginning of barley harvest.
10 Now Rizpah the daughter of Aiah took sackcloth and spread it for herself on the rock, from the beginning of harvest until the late rains poured on them from heaven. And she did not allow the birds of the air to rest on them by day nor the beasts of the field by night.
11 And David was told what Rizpah the daughter of Aiah, the concubine of Saul, had done.
12 Then David went and took the bones of Saul, and the bones of Jonathan his son, from the men of Jabesh Gilead who had stolen them from the street of Beth Shan,[36] where the Philistines had hung them up, after the Philistines had struck down Saul in Gilboa.
13 So he brought up the bones of Saul and the bones of Jonathan his son from there; and they gathered the bones of those who had been hanged.
14 They buried the bones of Saul and Jonathan his son in the country of Benjamin in Zelah, in the tomb of Kish his father. So they performed all that the king commanded. And after that God heeded the prayer for the land.

35 Or *Merab* (compare 1 Samuel 18:19 and 25:44; 2 Samuel 3:15 and 6:23)
36 Spelled *Beth Shean* in Joshua 17:11 and elsewhere

Philistine Giants Destroyed

15 When the Philistines were at war again with Israel, David and his servants with him went down and fought against the Philistines; and David grew faint. 16 Then Ishbi-Benob, who *was* one of the sons of the giant, the weight of whose bronze spear *was* three hundred *shekels*, who was bearing a new *sword*, thought he could kill David. 17 But Abishai the son of Zeruiah came to his aid, and struck the Philistine and killed him. Then the men of David swore to him, saying, "You shall go out no more with us to battle, lest you quench the lamp of Israel." 18 Now it happened afterward that there was again a battle with the Philistines at Gob. Then Sibbechai the Hushathite killed Saph,[37] who *was* one of the sons of the giant. 19 Again there was a battle in Gob with the Philistines, where Elhanan the son of Jaare-Oregim[38] the Bethlehemite killed *the brother of* Goliath the Gittite, the shaft of whose spear *was* like a weaver's beam. 20 Yet again there was a battle in Gath, where there was a man of *great* stature, who had six fingers on each hand and six toes on each foot, twenty-four in number; and he also was born to the giant. 21 So when he defied Israel, Jonathan the son of Shimeah,[39] the brother of David, killed him. 22 These four were born to the giant in Gath, and fell by the hand of David and by the hand of his servants.

Praise for God's Deliverance

22 Then David spoke to the LORD the words of this song, on the day when the LORD had delivered him from the hand of all his enemies, and from the hand of Saul. 2 And he said:[40]

"The LORD *is* my rock,
　my fortress and my deliverer;
3 The God of my strength,
　in Him I will trust,
My shield and the horn of my
　salvation,
My stronghold and my refuge;
My Savior, You save me from violence.

4 I will call upon the LORD,
　who is worthy to be praised;
So shall I be saved from my enemies.

5 "When the waves of death
　encompassed me,
The floods of ungodliness
　made me afraid;
6 The sorrows of Sheol surrounded me,
The snares of death confronted me.
7 In my distress I called upon the LORD,
And cried to my God.
He heard my voice from His temple,
And my cry *entered* His ears.

8 "Then the earth shook and trembled;
The foundations of heaven
　moved and shook,
Because He was angry.
9 Smoke went up from His nostrils,
And devouring fire from His mouth;
Coals were kindled by it.
10 He bowed the heavens also,
　and came down
With darkness under His feet.
11 He rode upon a cherub, and flew;
And He was seen upon the wings
　of the wind.
12 He made darkness canopies
　around Him,
Dark waters *and* thick clouds
　of the skies.
13 From the brightness before Him
Coals of fire were kindled.

14 "The LORD thundered from heaven,
And the Most High uttered His voice.
15 He sent out arrows and scattered them;
Lightning bolts,
　and He vanquished them.
16 Then the channels of the sea were seen,
The foundations of the world
　were uncovered,
At the rebuke of the LORD,
At the blast of the breath of His
　nostrils.

17 "He sent from above, He took me,
He drew me out of many waters.
18 He delivered me
　from my strong enemy,
From those who hated me;
For they were too strong for me.
19 They confronted me in the day
　of my calamity,
But the LORD was my support.
20 He also brought me out
　into a broad place;
He delivered me,
　because He delighted in me.

---

37 Spelled *Sippai* in 1 Chronicles 20:4　　38 Spelled *Jair* in 1 Chronicles 20:5
39 Spelled *Shammah* in 1 Samuel 16:9 and elsewhere　　40 Compare Psalm 18

21 "The LORD rewarded me
      according to my righteousness;
   According to the cleanness of my
      hands
   He has recompensed me.
22 For I have kept the ways of the LORD,
   And have not wickedly departed
      from my God.
23 For all His judgments *were* before me;
   And *as for* His statutes,
      I did not depart from them.
24 I was also blameless before Him,
   And I kept myself from my iniquity.
25 Therefore the LORD has recompensed
      me according to my righteousness,
   According to my cleanness in His eyes.

26 "With the merciful You will show
      Yourself merciful;
   With a blameless man You will show
      Yourself blameless;
27 With the pure You will show
      Yourself pure;
   And with the devious You will show
      Yourself shrewd.
28 You will save the humble people;
   But Your eyes *are* on the haughty,
      that You may bring *them* down.

29 "For You *are* my lamp, O LORD;
   The LORD shall enlighten my darkness.
30 For by You I can run against a troop;
   By my God I can leap over a wall.
31 *As for* God, His way *is* perfect;
   The word of the LORD *is* proven;
   He *is* a shield to all who trust in Him.

32 "For who *is* God, except the LORD?
   And who *is* a rock, except our God?
33 God *is* my strength *and* power,
   And He makes my way perfect.
34 He makes my feet like the *feet* of deer,
   And sets me on my high places.
35 He teaches my hands to make war,
   So that my arms
      can bend a bow of bronze.

36 "You have also given me
      the shield of Your salvation,
   And Your gentleness
      has made me great.
37 You enlarged my path under me;
   So my feet did not slip.

38 "I have pursued my enemies
      and destroyed them;
   Neither did I turn back again
      till they were destroyed.
39 And I have destroyed them
      and wounded them,
   So that they could not rise;
   They have fallen under my feet.

40 For You have armed me with strength
      for the battle;
   You have subdued under me those
      who rose against me.
41 You have also given me
      the necks of my enemies,
   So that I destroyed those
      who hated me.
42 They looked,
      but *there was* none to save;
   Even to the LORD,
      but He did not answer them.
43 Then I beat them
      as fine as the dust of the earth;
   I trod them like dirt in the streets,
   And I spread them out.

44 "You have also delivered me
      from the strivings of my people;
   You have kept me
      as the head of the nations.
   A people *whom* I have not known
      shall serve me.
45 The foreigners submit to me;
   As soon as they hear, they obey me.
46 The foreigners fade away,
   And come frightened
      from their hideouts.

47 "The LORD lives!
   Blessed *be* my Rock!
   Let God be exalted,
   The Rock of my salvation!
48 It *is* God who avenges me,
   Who subdues the people under me,
49 Who delivers me from my enemies.
   You also lift me
      above those who rise against me;
   You have delivered me
      from the violent man.
50 Therefore I will give thanks to You,
      O LORD, among the Gentiles,
   And sing praises to Your name.
51 *He is* the tower of salvation
      to His king,
   And shows mercy to His anointed,
   To David and his descendants
      forevermore."

David's Last Words

23 Now these *are* the last words of
      David.

   Thus says David the son of Jesse;
   Thus says the man raised up on high,
   The anointed of the God of Jacob,
   And the sweet psalmist of Israel:

2 "The Spirit of the LORD spoke by me,
   And His word *was* on my tongue.

On the High Places

The strong, determined ibex (wild goat) scales the steepest cliffs with rapid agility, nimbly leaping up the sheer face of the rocks. Found throughout the wilderness, the ibex has symbolized beauty to the people of ancient times.

It is not uncommon to see herds of ibex scale and descend more than twenty mountains a day. It is amazing how the ibex can use only a small crack in the sheerest cliff as a foothold to leap two or three yards. Usually traveling in herds of thirty or more, the ibex feed on the leaves of small bushes and trees scantily dotting the mountaintops. Upon the approach of an enemy or intruding predator, the ibex will leap quickly up the side of the cliff to higher ground.

The biblical writer draws from the agility of the ibex to describe the power of God in one's life. "He makes my feet like the *feet* of [ibex] and sets me on my high places" (2 Sam. 22:34).

God makes us like the ibex. When faced with a mountainous problem, we can climb over it. Straight up with grace and agility, we can leap over our problems even with the smallest footholds. Then we can stand on the high places.

When faced with a mountain, I will not quit! Like the ibex, I will climb over!

3 The God of Israel said,
   The Rock of Israel spoke to me:
   'He who rules over men *must be* just,
4 Ruling in the fear of God.
   And *he shall be* like the light
     of the morning *when* the sun rises,
   A morning without clouds,
   Like the tender grass
     springing out of the earth,
   By clear shining after rain.'

5 "Although my house *is* not so with God,
   Yet He has made with me
     an everlasting covenant,
   Ordered in all *things* and secure.
   For *this is* all my salvation
     and all *my* desire;
   Will He not make *it* increase?
6 But *the sons* of rebellion *shall* all *be*
     as thorns thrust away,
   Because they cannot be taken
     with hands.
7 But the man *who* touches them
   Must be armed with iron
     and the shaft of a spear,
   And they shall be utterly burned
     with fire in *their* place."

David's Mighty Men

8 These *are* the names of the mighty
men whom David had: Josheb-Basshe-
beth[41] the Tachmonite, chief among the
captains. He was called Adino the Ez-
nite, because he had killed eight hundred
men at one time.
9 And after him *was* Eleazar the son of
Dodo,[42] the Ahohite, *one* of the three
mighty men with David when they defied
the Philistines *who* were gathered there
for battle, and the men of Israel had re-
treated.
10 He arose and attacked the Philistines
until his hand was weary, and his hand
stuck to the sword. The LORD brought
about a great victory that day; and the
people returned after him only to
plunder.
11 And after him *was* Shammah the son
of Agee the Hararite. The Philistines had
gathered together into a troop where
there was a piece of ground full of lentils.
Then the people fled from the Philistines.
12 But he stationed himself in the middle
of the field, defended it, and killed the
Philistines. And the LORD brought about
a great victory.
13 Then three of the thirty chief men
went down at harvest time and came to

David at the cave of Adullam. And the
troop of Philistines encamped in the Valley of Rephaim.
14 David *was* then in the stronghold, and
the garrison of the Philistines *was* then *in*
Bethlehem.
15 And David said with longing, "Oh,
that someone would give me a drink of
the water from the well of Bethlehem,
which *is* by the gate!"
16 So the three mighty men broke
through the camp of the Philistines, drew
water from the well of Bethlehem that
was by the gate, and took it and brought
it to David. Nevertheless he would not
drink it, but poured it out to the LORD.
17 And he said, "Far be it from me, O
LORD, that I should do this! *Is this not*
the blood of the men who went in jeopardy of their lives?" Therefore he would
not drink it. These things were done by
the three mighty men.
18 Now Abishai the brother of Joab, the
son of Zeruiah, was chief of *another* three.
He lifted his spear against three hundred
men and killed *them*, and won a name
among *these* three.
19 Was he not the most honored of
three? Therefore he became their captain. However, he did not attain to the
first three.
20 Benaiah *was* the son of Jehoiada, the
son of a valiant man from Kabzeel, who
had done many deeds. He had killed two
lion-like heroes of Moab. He also went
down and killed a lion in the midst of a
pit on a snowy day.
21 And he killed an Egyptian, a spectacular man. The Egyptian *had* a spear in
his hand; so he went down to him with a
staff, wrested the spear out of the Egyptian's hand, and killed him with his own
spear.
22 These *things* Benaiah the son of Jehoiada did, and won a name among three
mighty men.
23 He was more honored than the thirty,
but he did not attain to the *first* three.
And David appointed him over his guard.
24 Asahel the brother of Joab *was* one of
the thirty; Elhanan the son of Dodo of
Bethlehem,
25 Shammah the Harodite, Elika the
Harodite,
26 Helez the Paltite, Ira the son of Ikkesh
the Tekoite,

---

41 Literally *One Who Sits in the Seat* (compare 1 Chronicles 11:11)   42 Spelled *Dodai* in 1 Chronicles 27:4

27 Abiezer the Anathothite, Mebunnai the Hushathite,
28 Zalmon the Ahohite, Maharai the Netophathite,
29 Heleb the son of Baanah (the Netophathite), Ittai the son of Ribai from Gibeah of the children of Benjamin,
30 Benaiah a Pirathonite, Hiddai from the brooks of Gaash,
31 Abi-Albon the Arbathite, Azmaveth the Barhumite,
32 Eliahba the Shaalbonite (of the sons of Jashen), Jonathan,
33 Shammah the Hararite, Ahiam the son of Sharar the Hararite,
34 Eliphelet the son of Ahasbai, the son of the Maacathite, Eliam the son of Ahithophel the Gilonite,
35 Hezrai[43] the Carmelite, Paarai the Arbite,
36 Igal the son of Nathan of Zobah, Bani the Gadite,
37 Zelek the Ammonite, Naharai the Beerothite (armorbearer of Joab the son of Zeruiah),
38 Ira the Ithrite, Gareb the Ithrite,
39 *and* Uriah the Hittite: thirty-seven in all.

David's Census of Israel and Judah

24 Again the anger of the LORD was aroused against Israel, and He moved David against them to say, "Go, number Israel and Judah."
2 So the king said to Joab the commander of the army who *was* with him, "Now go throughout all the tribes of Israel, from Dan to Beersheba, and count the people, that I may know the number of the people."
3 And Joab said to the king, "Now may the LORD your God add to the people a hundredfold more than there are, and may the eyes of my lord the king see *it.* But why does my lord the king desire this thing?"
4 Nevertheless the king's word prevailed against Joab and against the captains of the army. So Joab and the captains of the army went out from the presence of the king to count the people of Israel.
5 And they crossed over the Jordan and camped in Aroer, on the right side of the town which *is* in the midst of the ravine of Gad, and toward Jazer.
6 Then they came to Gilead and to the land of Tahtim Hodshi; they came to Dan Jaan and around to Sidon;
7 and they came to the stronghold of Tyre and to all the cities of the Hivites and the Canaanites. Then they went out to South Judah *as far as* Beersheba.
8 So when they had gone through all the land, they came to Jerusalem at the end of nine months and twenty days.
9 Then Joab gave the sum of the number of the people to the king. And there were in Israel eight hundred thousand valiant men who drew the sword, and the men of Judah were five hundred thousand men.

The Judgment on David's Sin

10 And David's heart condemned him after he had numbered the people. So David said to the LORD, "I have sinned greatly in what I have done; but now, I pray, O LORD, take away the iniquity of Your servant, for I have done very foolishly."
11 Now when David arose in the morning, the word of the LORD came to the prophet Gad, David's seer, saying,
12 "Go and tell David, 'Thus says the LORD: "I offer you three *things*; choose one of them for yourself, that I may do *it* to you." ' "
13 So Gad came to David and told him; and he said to him, "Shall seven[44] years of famine come to you in your land? Or shall you flee three months before your enemies, while they pursue you? Or shall there be three days' plague in your land? Now consider and see what answer I should take back to Him who sent me."
14 And David said to Gad, "I am in great distress. Please let us fall into the hand of the LORD, for His mercies *are* great; but do not let me fall into the hand of man."
15 So the LORD sent a plague upon Israel from the morning till the appointed time. From Dan to Beersheba seventy thousand men of the people died.
16 And when the angel[45] stretched out His hand over Jerusalem to destroy it, the LORD relented from the destruction, and said to the angel who was destroying the people, "It is enough; now restrain Your hand." And the angel of the LORD was by the threshing floor of Araunah[46] the Jebusite.

---

43 Spelled *Hezro* in 1 Chronicles 11:37   44 Or *three* in 1 Chronicles 21:12   45 Or *Angel*
46 Spelled *Ornan* in 1 Chronicles 21:15

17 Then David spoke to the LORD when he saw the angel who was striking the people, and said, "Surely I have sinned, and I have done wickedly; but these sheep, what have they done? Let Your hand, I pray, be against me and against my father's house."

The Altar on the Threshing Floor

18 And Gad came that day to David and said to him, "Go up, erect an altar to the LORD on the threshing floor of Araunah the Jebusite."
19 So David, according to the word of Gad, went up as the LORD commanded.
20 Now Araunah looked, and saw the king and his servants coming toward him. So Araunah went out and bowed before the king with his face to the ground.
21 Then Araunah said, "Why has my lord the king come to his servant?" And David said, "To buy the threshing floor from you, to build an altar to the LORD, that the plague may be withdrawn from the people."
22 Now Araunah said to David, "Let my lord the king take and offer up whatever *seems* good to him. Look, *here are* oxen for burnt sacrifice, and threshing implements and the yokes of the oxen for wood.
23 "All these, O king, Araunah has given to the king." And Araunah said to the king, "May the LORD your God accept you."
24 Then the king said to Araunah, "No, but I will surely buy *it* from you for a price; nor will I offer burnt offerings to the LORD my God with that which costs me nothing." So David bought the threshing floor and the oxen for fifty shekels of silver.
25 And David built there an altar to the LORD, and offered burnt offerings and peace offerings. So the LORD heeded the prayers for the land, and the plague was withdrawn from Israel.

Introduction to First Kings

First Kings dramatically illustrates the importance of positive leadership as it records the history of the kings of Israel and Judah from the time of King Solomon through King Ahaziah. This book was written by scribes and prophets whose duty it was to record the history of Israel between approximately 1000 and 600 B.C.

The rule of Solomon highlights the Book of First Kings. Crowned by David before the monarch's death, Solomon was one of the greatest kings in Israel's history. His dedication and faith led the people for over forty years. Upon his coronation, Solomon asked of God one gift to help him rule the people—wisdom and understanding. Solomon's goal was not riches or power, but the discerning wisdom to help other people with their problems. He knew that true leadership was willingness to make other people's problems his problems. God not only granted his request by making his wisdom known throughout many lands, but He granted him riches and power as well.

Solomon's writings, including his famous proverbs, are a living memorial to his divinely-given wisdom.

> Trust in the LORD with all your heart,
> And lean not on your own understanding;
> Do not withhold good from those to whom it is due,
> When it is in the power of your hand to do *so.*
> The fear of the LORD *is* the beginning of wisdom,
> And the knowledge of the Holy One *is* understanding.

(Prov. 3:5, 27; 9:10)

Solomon was also a great visionary who dreamed of building a great temple for God of which the people could be proud. He instilled this vision into the people who readily gave their time, talents, and energy to the completion of this project.

Solomon truly was one of the greatest positive leaders of Israel, teaching his people the main principles of possibility thinking: Attempt great things for God and expect great things from God!

The First Book of the

Kings

Adonijah Presumes to Be King

NOW King David was old, advanced in years; and they put covers on him, but he could not get warm.

2 Therefore his servants said to him, "Let a young woman, a virgin, be sought for our lord the king, and let her stand before the king, and let her care for him; and let her lie in your bosom, that our lord the king may be warm."

3 So they sought for a lovely young woman throughout all the territory of Israel, and found Abishag the Shunammite, and brought her to the king.

4 And the young woman *was* very lovely; and she cared for the king, and served him; but the king did not know her.

5 Now Adonijah the son of Haggith exalted himself, saying, "I will be king"; and he prepared for himself chariots and horsemen, and fifty men to run before him.

6 (And his father had not rebuked him at any time by saying, "Why have you done so?" He *was* also a very good-looking *man. His mother* had borne him after Absalom.)

7 Then he conferred with Joab the son of Zeruiah and with Abiathar the priest, and they followed and helped Adonijah.

8 But Zadok the priest, Benaiah the son of Jehoiada, Nathan the prophet, Shimei, Rei, and the mighty men who *belonged* to David were not with Adonijah.

9 And Adonijah sacrificed sheep and oxen and fattened cattle by the stone of Zoheleth, which *is* by En Rogel; he also invited all his brothers, the king's sons, and all the men of Judah, the king's servants.

10 But he did not invite Nathan the prophet, Benaiah, the mighty men, or Solomon his brother.

11 So Nathan spoke to Bathsheba the mother of Solomon, saying, "Have you not heard that Adonijah the son of Haggith has become king, and David our lord does not know *it*?

12 "Come, please, let me now give you counsel, that you may save your own life and the life of your son Solomon.

13 "Go immediately to King David and say to him, 'Did you not, my lord, O king, swear to your maidservant, saying, "Assuredly your son Solomon shall reign after me, and he shall sit on my throne"? Why then has Adonijah become king?'

14 "Then, while you are still talking there with the king, I also will come in after you and confirm your words."

15 So Bathsheba went into the chamber to the king. (Now the king was very old, and Abishag the Shunammite was serving the king.)

16 And Bathsheba bowed and did homage to the king. Then the king said, "What is your wish?"

17 Then she said to him, "My lord, you swore by the LORD your God to your maidservant, *saying,* 'Assuredly Solomon your son shall reign after me, and he shall sit on my throne.'

18 "So now, look! Adonijah has become king; and now, my lord the king, you do not know about *it*.

19 "He has sacrificed oxen and fattened cattle and sheep in abundance, and has invited all the sons of the king, Abiathar the priest, and Joab the commander of the army; but Solomon your servant he has not invited.

20 "And as for you, my lord, O king, the eyes of all Israel *are* on you, that you should tell them who will sit on the throne of my lord the king after him.

21 "Otherwise it will happen, when my lord the king rests with his fathers, that I and my son Solomon will be counted as offenders."

22 And just then, while she was still talking with the king, Nathan the prophet also came in.

23 So they told the king, saying, "Here is Nathan the prophet." And when he came in before the king, he bowed down before the king with his face to the ground.

24 And Nathan said, "My lord, O king, have you said, 'Adonijah shall reign after me, and he shall sit on my throne'?
25 "For he has gone down today, and has sacrificed oxen and fattened cattle and sheep in abundance, and has invited all the king's sons, and the commanders of the army, and Abiathar the priest; and look! They are eating and drinking before him; and they say, 'Long live King Adonijah!'
26 "But he has not invited me, *even* me your servant, nor Zadok the priest, nor Benaiah the son of Jehoiada, nor your servant Solomon.
27 "Has this thing been done by my lord the king, and you have not told your servant who should sit on the throne of my lord the king after him?"

David Proclaims Solomon King

28 Then King David answered and said, "Call Bathsheba to me." So she came into the king's presence and stood before the king.
29 And the king took an oath and said, "*As* the LORD lives, who has redeemed my life from every distress,
30 "just as I swore to you by the LORD God of Israel, saying, 'Assuredly Solomon your son shall be king after me, and he shall sit on my throne in my place,' so I certainly will do this day."
31 Then Bathsheba bowed with *her* face to the earth, and did homage to the king, and said, "Let my lord King David live forever!"
32 And King David said, "Call to me Zadok the priest, Nathan the prophet, and Benaiah the son of Jehoiada." So they came before the king.
33 The king also said to them, "Take with you the servants of your lord, and have Solomon my son ride on my own mule, and take him down to Gihon.
34 "There let Zadok the priest and Nathan the prophet anoint him king over Israel; and blow the horn, and say, 'Long live King Solomon!'
35 "Then you shall come up after him, and he shall come and sit on my throne, and he shall be king in my place. For I have appointed him to be ruler over Israel and Judah."
36 And Benaiah the son of Jehoiada answered the king and said, "Amen! May the LORD God of my lord the king say so *too*.
37 "As the LORD has been with my lord the king, even so may He be with Solomon, and make his throne greater than the throne of my lord King David."
38 So Zadok the priest, Nathan the prophet, Benaiah the son of Jehoiada, the Cherethites, and the Pelethites went down and had Solomon ride on King David's mule, and took him to Gihon.
39 Then Zadok the priest took a horn of oil from the tabernacle and anointed Solomon. And they blew the horn, and all the people said, "Long live King Solomon!"
40 And all the people went up after him; and the people played the flutes and rejoiced with great joy, so that the earth *seemed to* split with their sound.
41 So Adonijah and all the guests who *were* with him heard *it* as they finished eating. And when Joab heard the sound of the horn, he said, "Why *is* the city in such a noisy uproar?"
42 While he was still speaking, there came Jonathan, the son of Abiathar the priest. And Adonijah said to him, "Come in, for you *are* a prominent man, and bring good tidings."
43 Then Jonathan answered and said to Adonijah, "No! Our lord King David has made Solomon king.
44 "The king has sent with him Zadok the priest, Nathan the prophet, Benaiah the son of Jehoiada, the Cherethites, and the Pelethites; and they have made him ride on the king's mule.
45 "So Zadok the priest and Nathan the prophet have anointed him king at Gihon; and they have gone up from there rejoicing, so that the city is in an uproar. This *is* the noise that you have heard.
46 "Also Solomon sits on the throne of the kingdom.
47 "And moreover the king's servants have gone to bless our lord King David, saying, 'May God make the name of Solomon better than your name, and may He make his throne greater than your throne.' Then the king bowed himself on the bed.
48 "Also the king said thus, 'Blessed *be* the LORD God of Israel, who has given *one* to sit on my throne this day, while my eyes see *it*!' "
49 Then all the guests who were with

Adonijah were afraid, and arose, and each one went his way.

50 Now Adonijah was afraid of Solomon; so he arose, and went and took hold of the horns of the altar.

51 And it was told Solomon, saying, "Indeed Adonijah is afraid of King Solomon; for look, he has taken hold of the horns of the altar, saying, 'Let King Solomon swear to me today that he will not put his servant to death with the sword.' "

52 Then Solomon said, "If he proves himself a worthy man, not one hair of him shall fall to the earth; but if wickedness is found in him, he shall die."

53 So King Solomon sent them to bring him down from the altar. And he came and fell down before King Solomon; and Solomon said to him, "Go to your house."

David's Instructions to Solomon

2 Then the days of David drew near that he should die, and he charged Solomon his son, saying:

2 "I go the way of all the earth; be strong, therefore, and prove yourself a man.

3 "And keep the charge of the LORD your God: to walk in His ways, to keep His statutes, His commandments, His judgments, and His testimonies, as it is written in the Law of Moses, that you may prosper in all that you do and wherever you turn;

4 "that the LORD may fulfill His word which He spoke concerning me, saying, 'If your sons take heed to their way, to walk before Me in truth with all their heart and with all their soul,' He said, 'you shall not lack a man on the throne of Israel.'

5 "Moreover you know also what Joab the son of Zeruiah did to me, and what he did to the two commanders of the armies of Israel, to Abner the son of Ner and Amasa the son of Jether, whom he killed. And he shed the blood of war in peacetime, and put the blood of war on his belt that was around his waist, and on his sandals that were on his feet.

6 "Therefore do according to your wisdom, and do not let his gray hair go down to the grave in peace.

7 "But show kindness to the sons of Barzillai the Gileadite, and let them be among those who eat at your table, for so

they came to me when I fled from Absalom your brother.

8 "And see, you have with you Shimei the son of Gera, a Benjamite from Bahurim, who cursed me with a malicious curse in the day when I went to Mahanaim. But he came down to meet me at the Jordan, and I swore to him by the LORD, saying, 'I will not put you to death with the sword.'

9 "Now therefore, do not hold him guiltless, for you are a wise man and know what you ought to do to him; but bring his gray hair down to the grave with blood."

Death of David

10 So David rested with his fathers, and was buried in the City of David.

11 The period that David reigned over Israel was forty years; seven years he reigned in Hebron, and in Jerusalem he reigned thirty-three years.

12 Then Solomon sat on the throne of his father David; and his kingdom was firmly established.

Solomon Executes Adonijah

13 Now Adonijah the son of Haggith came to Bathsheba the mother of Solomon. And she said, "Do you come peaceably?" And he said, "Peaceably."

14 Moreover he said, "I have something to say to you." And she said, "Say it."

15 Then he said, "You know that the kingdom was mine, and all Israel had set their expectations on me, that I should reign. However, the kingdom has been turned over, and has become my brother's; for it was his from the LORD.

16 "Now I ask one petition of you; do not deny me." And she said to him, "Say it."

17 Then he said, "Please speak to King Solomon, for he will not refuse you, that he may give me Abishag the Shunammite as wife."

18 So Bathsheba said, "Very well, I will speak for you to the king."

19 Bathsheba therefore went to King Solomon, to speak to him for Adonijah. And the king rose up to meet her and bowed down to her, and sat down on his throne and had a throne set for the king's mother; so she sat at his right hand.

20 Then she said, "I desire one small petition of you; do not refuse me." And the

king said to her, "Ask it, my mother, for I will not refuse you."

21 So she said, "Let Abishag the Shunammite be given to Adonijah your brother as wife."

22 And King Solomon answered and said to his mother, "Now why do you ask Abishag the Shunammite for Adonijah? Ask for him the kingdom also—for he *is* my older brother—for him, and for Abiathar the priest, and for Joab the son of Zeruiah."

23 Then King Solomon swore by the LORD, saying, "May God do so to me, and more also, if Adonijah has not spoken this word against his own life!

24 "Now therefore, *as* the LORD lives, who has established me and set me on the throne of David my father, and who has made me a house, as He promised, Adonijah shall be put to death today!"

25 So King Solomon sent by the hand of Benaiah the son of Jehoiada; and he struck him down, and he died.

Abiathar Exiled, Joab Executed

26 And to Abiathar the priest the king said, "Go to Anathoth, to your own fields, for you *are* worthy of death; but I will not put you to death at this time, because you carried the ark of the Lord GOD before my father David, and because you were afflicted every time my father was afflicted."

27 So Solomon removed Abiathar from being priest to the LORD, that he might fulfill the word of the LORD which He spoke concerning the house of Eli at Shiloh.

28 Then news came to Joab, for Joab had defected to Adonijah, though he had not defected to Absalom. So Joab fled to the tabernacle of the LORD, and took hold of the horns of the altar.

29 And King Solomon was told, "Joab has fled to the tabernacle of the LORD; there *he is*, by the altar." Then Solomon sent Benaiah the son of Jehoiada, saying, "Go, strike him down."

30 So Benaiah went to the tabernacle of the LORD, and said to him, "Thus says the king, 'Come out!' " And he said, "No, but I will die here." And Benaiah brought back word to the king, saying, "Thus said Joab, and thus he answered me."

31 And the king said to him, "Do as he has said, and strike him down and bury him, that you may take away from me and from the house of my father the innocent blood which Joab shed.

32 "So the LORD will return his blood on his head, because he struck down two men more righteous and better than he, and killed them with the sword—Abner the son of Ner, the commander of the army of Israel, and Amasa the son of Jether, the commander of the army of Judah—though my father David did not know *it.*

33 "Their blood shall therefore return upon the head of Joab and upon the head of his descendants forever. But upon David and his descendants, upon his house and his throne, there shall be peace forever from the LORD."

34 So Benaiah the son of Jehoiada went up and struck and killed him; and he was buried in his own house in the wilderness.

35 The king put Benaiah the son of Jehoiada in his place over the army, and the king put Zadok the priest in the place of Abiathar.

Shimei Executed

36 Then the king sent and called for Shimei, and said to him, "Build yourself a house in Jerusalem and dwell there, and do not go out from there anywhere.

37 "For it shall be, on the day you go out and cross the Brook Kidron, know for certain you shall surely die; your blood shall be on your own head."

38 And Shimei said to the king, "The saying *is* good. As my lord the king has said, so your servant will do." So Shimei dwelt in Jerusalem many days.

39 Now it happened at the end of three years, that two slaves of Shimei ran away to Achish the son of Maachah, king of Gath. And they told Shimei, saying, "Look, your slaves *are* in Gath!"

40 So Shimei arose, saddled his donkey, and went to Achish at Gath to seek his slaves. And Shimei went and brought his slaves from Gath.

41 And Solomon was told that Shimei had gone from Jerusalem to Gath and had come back.

42 Then the king sent and called for Shimei, and said to him, "Did I not make you swear by the LORD, and warn you, saying, 'Know for certain that on the day you go out and travel anywhere, you shall

surely die'? And you said to me, 'The word I have heard *is* good.'

43 "Why then have you not kept the oath of the LORD and the commandment that I gave you?"

44 The king said moreover to Shimei, "You know, as your heart acknowledges, all the wickedness that you did to my father David; therefore the LORD will return your wickedness on your own head.

45 "But King Solomon *shall be* blessed, and the throne of David shall be established before the LORD forever."

46 So the king commanded Benaiah the son of Jehoiada; and he went out and struck him down, and he died. Thus the kingdom was established in the hand of Solomon.

Solomon Requests Wisdom

3 Now Solomon made a treaty with Pharaoh king of Egypt, and married Pharaoh's daughter; then he brought her to the City of David until he had finished building his own house, and the house of the LORD, and the wall all around Jerusalem.

2 Meanwhile the people sacrificed at the high places, because there was no house built for the name of the LORD until those days.

3 And Solomon loved the LORD, walking in the statutes of his father David, except that he sacrificed and burned incense at the high places.

4 Now the king went to Gibeon to sacrifice there, for that *was* the great high place: Solomon offered a thousand burnt offerings on that altar.

5 At Gibeon the LORD appeared to Solomon in a dream by night; and God said, "Ask! What shall I give you?"

6 And Solomon said: "You have shown great mercy to your servant David my father, because he walked before You in truth, in righteousness, and in uprightness of heart with You; You have continued this great kindness for him, and You have given him a son to sit on his throne, as *it is* this day.

7 "Now, O LORD my God, You have made Your servant king instead of my father David, but I *am* a little child; I do not know *how* to go out or come in.

8 "And Your servant *is* in the midst of Your people whom You have chosen, a great people, too numerous to be numbered or counted.

9 "Therefore give to Your servant an understanding heart to judge Your people, that I may discern between good and evil. For who is able to judge this great people of Yours?"

10 And the speech pleased the LORD, that Solomon had asked this thing.

11 Then God said to him: "Because you have asked this thing, and have not asked long life for yourself, nor have asked riches for yourself, nor have asked the life of your enemies, but have asked for yourself understanding to discern justice,

12 "behold, I have done according to your words; see, I have given you a wise and understanding heart, so that there has not been anyone like you before you, nor shall any like you arise after you.

13 "And I have also given you what you have not asked: both riches and honor, so that there shall not be anyone like you among the kings all your days.

14 "So if you walk in My ways, to keep My statutes and My commandments, as your father David walked, then I will lengthen your days."

15 Then Solomon awoke; and indeed it had been a dream. And he came to Jerusalem and stood before the ark of the covenant of the LORD, offered up burnt offerings, offered peace offerings, and made a feast for all his servants.

Solomon's Wise Judgment

16 Then two women *who were* harlots came to the king, and stood before him.

17 And one woman said, "O my lord, this woman and I dwell in the same house; and I gave birth while she *was* in the house.

18 "Then it happened, the third day after I had given birth, that this woman also gave birth. And we *were* together; *there was* no one with us in the house, except the two of us in the house.

19 "And this woman's son died in the night, because she lay on him.

20 "So she arose in the middle of the night and took my son from my side, while your maidservant slept, and laid him in her bosom, and laid her dead child in my bosom.

21 "And when I rose in the morning to nurse my son, there he was, dead. But when I had examined him in the morn-

ing, indeed, he was not my son whom I had borne."

22 Then the other woman said, "No! But the living one is my son, and the dead one is your son." And the first woman said, "No! But the dead one is your son, and the living one is my son." Thus they spoke before the king.

23 And the king said, "The one says, 'This is my son, who lives, and your son is the dead one'; and the other says, 'No! But your son is the dead one, and my son is the living one.'"

24 Then the king said, "Bring me a sword." So they brought a sword before the king.

25 And the king said, "Divide the living child in two, and give half to one, and half to the other."

26 Then the woman whose son was living spoke to the king, for she yearned with compassion for her son; and she said, "O my lord, give her the living child, and by no means kill him!" But the other said, "Let him be neither mine nor yours, but divide him."

27 So the king answered and said, "Give the first woman the living child, and by no means kill him; she is his mother."

28 And all Israel heard of the judgment which the king had rendered; and they feared the king, for they saw that the wisdom of God was in him to administer justice.

Solomon's Administration

4 So King Solomon was king over all Israel.

2 And these were his officials: Azariah the son of Zadok, the priest;

3 Elihoreph and Ahijah, the sons of Shisha, scribes; Jehoshaphat the son of Ahilud, the recorder;

4 Benaiah the son of Jehoiada, over the army; Zadok and Abiathar, the priests;

5 Azariah the son of Nathan, over the officers; Zabud the son of Nathan, a priest and the king's friend;

6 Ahishar, over the household; and Adoniram the son of Abda, over the labor force.

7 And Solomon had twelve governors over all Israel, who provided food for the king and his household; each one made provision for one month of the year.

8 These are their names: Ben-Hur,[1] in the mountains of Ephraim;

9 Ben-Deker,[2] in Makaz, Shaalbim, Beth Shemesh, and Elon Beth Hanan;

10 Ben-Hesed,[3] in Arubboth; to him belonged Sochoh and all the land of Hepher;

11 Ben-Abinadab,[4] in all the regions of Dor; he had Taphath the daughter of Solomon as wife;

12 Baana the son of Ahilud, in Taanach, Megiddo, and all Beth Shean, which is beside Zaretan below Jezreel, from Beth Shean to Abel Meholah, as far as the other side of Jokneam;

13 Ben-Geber,[5] in Ramoth Gilead; to him belonged the towns of Jair the son of Manasseh, in Gilead; to him also belonged the region of Argob in Bashan—sixty large cities with walls and bronze gate-bars;

14 Ahinadab the son of Iddo, in Mahanaim;

15 Ahimaaz, in Naphtali; he also took Basemath the daughter of Solomon as wife;

16 Baanah the son of Hushai, in Asher and Aloth;

17 Jehoshaphat the son of Paruah, in Issachar;

18 Shimei the son of Elah, in Benjamin;

19 Geber the son of Uri, in the land of Gilead, in the country of Sihon king of the Amorites and of Og king of Bashan; and he was the only governor who was in the land.

Prosperity and Wisdom of Solomon's Reign

20 Judah and Israel were as numerous as the sand by the sea in multitude, eating and drinking and rejoicing.

21 So Solomon reigned over all kingdoms from the River[6] to the land of the Philistines, as far as the border of Egypt. They brought tribute and served Solomon all the days of his life.

22 Now Solomon's provision for one day was thirty kors of fine flour, sixty kors of meal,

23 ten fatted oxen, twenty oxen from the pastures, and one hundred sheep, besides deer, gazelles, roebucks, and fatted fowl.

24 For he had dominion over all the region on this side of the River[7] from Tiphsah even to Gaza, namely over all the

1 Literally son of Hur   2 Literally son of Deker   3 Literally son of Hesed   4 Literally son of Abinadab
5 Literally son of Geber   6 That is, the Euphrates   7 That is, the Euphrates

kings on this side of the River; and he had peace on every side all around him. 25 And Judah and Israel dwelt safely, each man under his vine and his fig tree, from Dan as far as Beersheba, all the days of Solomon. 26 Solomon had forty thousand stalls of horses for his chariots, and twelve thousand horsemen. 27 And these governors, each man in his month, provided food for King Solomon and for all who came to King Solomon's table. There was no lack in their supply. 28 They also brought barley and straw to the proper place, for the horses and steeds, each man according to his charge. 29 And God gave Solomon wisdom and exceedingly great understanding, and largeness of heart like the sand on the seashore. 30 Thus Solomon's wisdom excelled the wisdom of all the men of the East and all the wisdom of Egypt. 31 For he was wiser than all men—than Ethan the Ezrahite, and Heman, Chalcol, and Darda, the sons of Mahol; and his fame was in all the surrounding nations. 32 He spoke three thousand proverbs, and his songs were one thousand and five. 33 Also he spoke of trees, from the cedar tree of Lebanon even to the hyssop that springs out of the wall; he spoke also of animals, of birds, of creeping things, and of fish. 34 And men of all nations, from all the kings of the earth who had heard of his wisdom, came to hear the wisdom of Solomon.

Solomon Prepares to Build the Temple

5 Now Hiram king of Tyre sent his servants to Solomon, because he heard that they had anointed him king in place of his father, for Hiram had always loved David. 2 Then Solomon sent to Hiram, saying: 3 "You know how my father David could not build a house for the name of the LORD his God because of the wars which were fought against him on every side, until the LORD put his foes[8] under the soles of his feet. 4 "But now the LORD my God has given me rest on every side, *so that there is* neither adversary nor evil occurrence. 5 "And behold, I propose to build a house for the name of the LORD my God,

as the LORD spoke to my father David, saying, 'Your son, whom I will set on your throne in your place, he shall build the house for My name.' 6 "Now therefore, command that they cut down cedars for me from Lebanon; and my servants will be with your servants, and I will pay you wages for your servants according to whatever you say. For you know *there is* none among us who has skill to cut timber like the Sidonians." 7 So it was, when Hiram heard the words of Solomon, that he rejoiced greatly and said, "Blessed *be* the LORD this day, for He has given David a wise son over this great people!" 8 Then Hiram sent to Solomon, saying: "I have considered *the message* which you sent me, *and* I will do all you desire concerning the cedar and cypress logs. 9 "My servants shall bring *them* down from Lebanon to the sea; I will float them in rafts by sea to the place you indicate to me, and will have them broken apart there; then you can take *them* away. And you shall fulfill my desire by giving food for my household." 10 So Hiram gave Solomon cedar and cypress logs *according to* all his desire. 11 And Solomon gave Hiram twenty thousand kors of wheat *as* food for his household, and twenty kors of pressed oil. Thus Solomon gave to Hiram year by year. 12 So the LORD gave Solomon wisdom, as He had promised him; and there was peace between Hiram and Solomon, and the two of them made a treaty together. 13 Then King Solomon raised up a labor force out of all Israel; and the labor force was thirty thousand men. 14 And he sent them to Lebanon, ten thousand a month in shifts: they were one month in Lebanon *and* two months at home; Adoniram *was* in charge of the labor force. 15 Solomon had seventy thousand who carried burdens, and eighty thousand who quarried *stone* in the mountains, 16 besides three thousand three hundred from the chiefs of Solomon's deputies, who supervised the people who labored in the work. 17 And the king commanded them to quarry large stones, costly stones, *and*

8 Literally *them*

hewn stones, to lay the foundation of the temple.[9]

18 So Solomon's builders, Hiram's builders, and the Gebalites quarried *them*; and they prepared timber and stones to build the temple.

Solomon Builds the Temple

6 And it came to pass in the four hundred and eightieth year after the children of Israel had come out of the land of Egypt, in the fourth year of Solomon's reign over Israel, in the month of Ziv, which *is* the second month, that he began to build the house of the LORD.

2 Now the house which King Solomon built for the LORD, its length *was* sixty cubits, its width twenty, and its height thirty cubits.

3 The vestibule in front of the sanctuary[10] of the house *was* twenty cubits long across the breadth of the house, *and* its width *extended* ten cubits from the front of the house.

4 And he made for the house windows with beveled frames.

5 Against the wall of the temple he built chambers all around, *against* the walls of the temple, all around *both* the sanctuary and the inner sanctuary.[11] Thus he made side chambers all around it.

6 The lowest chamber *was* five cubits wide, the middle *was* six cubits wide, and the third *was* seven cubits wide; for he made narrow ledges around the outside of the temple, so that *the support beams* would not be fastened into the walls of the temple.

7 And the temple, when it was being built, was built with stone finished at the quarry, so that no hammer or chisel *or* any iron tool was heard in the temple while it was being built.

8 The doorway for the middle story *was* on the right side of the temple. They went up by stairs to the middle *story*, and from the middle to the third.

9 So he built the temple and finished it, and he paneled the temple with beams and boards of cedar.

10 And he built side chambers against the entire temple, each five cubits high; they were attached to the temple with cedar beams.

11 Then the word of the LORD came to Solomon, saying:

12 "*Concerning* this temple which you are building, if you walk in My statutes, execute My judgments, keep all My commandments, and walk in them, then I will perform My word with you, which I spoke to your father David.

13 "And I will dwell among the children of Israel, and will not forsake My people Israel."

14 So Solomon built the temple and finished it.

15 And he built the inside walls of the temple with cedar boards; from the floor of the temple to the ceiling he paneled *them* on the inside with wood; and he covered the floor of the temple with planks of cypress.

16 Then he built the twenty-cubit room at the rear of the temple, from floor to ceiling, with cedar boards; he built *it* inside as the inner sanctuary, as the Most Holy *Place*.

17 And in front of it the temple sanctuary was forty cubits *long*.

18 The inside of the temple was cedar, carved with ornamental buds and open flowers. All *was* cedar; there was no stone *to be* seen.

19 And he prepared the inner sanctuary inside the temple, to set the ark of the covenant of the LORD there.

20 The inner sanctuary *was* twenty cubits long, twenty cubits wide, and twenty cubits high. He overlaid it with pure gold, and overlaid the altar of cedar.

21 So Solomon overlaid the inside of the temple with pure gold. He stretched gold chains across the front of the inner sanctuary; and he overlaid it with gold.

22 The whole temple he overlaid with gold, until he had finished all the temple; also he overlaid with gold the entire altar that *was* by the inner sanctuary.

23 Inside the inner sanctuary he made two cherubim *of* olive wood, *each* ten cubits high.

24 One wing of the cherub *was* five cubits, and the other wing of the cherub five cubits: ten cubits from the tip of one wing to the tip of the other.

25 And the other cherub *was* ten cubits;

9 Literally *house,* and so frequently throughout the book
10 Hebrew *heykal;* here the main room of the temple, elsewhere called the *holy place* (compare Exodus 26:33 and Ezekiel 41:1)
11 Hebrew *debir;* here the inner room of the temple, elsewhere called the *Most Holy Place* (compare verse 16)

both cherubim *were* of the same size and shape.

26 The height of one cherub *was* ten cubits, and so *was* the other cherub.

27 Then he set the cherubim inside the inner room;[12] and they stretched out the wings of the cherubim so that the wing of the one touched *one* wall, and the wing of the other cherub touched the other wall. And their wings touched each other in the middle of the room.

28 Also he overlaid the cherubim with gold.

29 Then he carved all the walls of the temple all around, both the inner and outer *sanctuaries*, with carved figures of cherubim, palm trees, and open flowers.

30 And the floor of the temple he overlaid with gold, both the inner and outer *sanctuaries*.

31 For the entrance of the inner sanctuary he made doors *of* olive wood; the lintel *and* doorposts *were* one-fifth *of the wall*.

32 The two doors *were of* olive wood; and he carved on them figures of cherubim, palm trees, and open flowers, and overlaid *them* with gold; and he spread gold on the cherubim and on the palm trees.

33 So for the door of the sanctuary he also made doorposts *of* olive wood, one-fourth *of the wall*.

34 And the two doors *were of* cypress wood; two panels *comprised* one folding door, and two panels *comprised* the other folding door.

35 Then he carved cherubim, palm trees, and open flowers *on them*, and overlaid *them* with gold applied evenly on the carved work.

36 And he built the inner court with three rows of hewn stone and a row of cedar beams.

37 In the fourth year the foundation of the house of the LORD was laid, in the month of Ziv.

38 And in the eleventh year, in the month of Bul, which is the eighth month, the house was finished in all its details and according to all its plans. So he was seven years in building it.

Solomon's Other Buildings

7 But Solomon took thirteen years to build his own house; so he finished all his house.

2 He also built the House of the Forest of Lebanon; its length *was* one hundred cubits, its width fifty cubits, and its height thirty cubits, with four rows of cedar pillars, and cedar beams on the pillars.

3 And *it was* paneled with cedar above the beams that *were* on forty-five pillars, fifteen *to* a row.

4 *There were* windows *with beveled frames in* three rows, and window *was* opposite window *in* three tiers.

5 And all the doorways and doorposts *had* rectangular frames; and window *was* opposite window *in* three tiers.

6 He also made the Hall of Pillars: its length *was* fifty cubits, and its width thirty cubits; and in front of them *was* a portico with pillars, and a canopy *was* in front of them.

7 Then he made a hall for the throne, the Hall of Judgment, where he might judge; and *it was* paneled with cedar from floor to ceiling.[13]

8 And the house where he dwelt *had* another court inside the hall, of like workmanship. Solomon also made a house like this hall for Pharaoh's daughter, whom he had taken *as wife*.

9 All these *were of* costly stones hewn to size, trimmed with saws, inside and out, from the foundation to the eaves, and also on the outside to the great court.

10 The foundation *was of* costly stones, large stones, some ten cubits and some eight cubits.

11 And above *were* costly stones, hewn to size, and cedar wood.

12 The great court *was* enclosed with three rows of hewn stones and a row of cedar beams. So were the inner court of the house of the LORD and the vestibule of the temple.

Hiram the Craftsman

13 Now King Solomon sent and brought Hiram[14] from Tyre.

14 He *was* the son of a widow from the tribe of Naphtali, and his father *was* a man of Tyre, a bronze worker; he was filled with wisdom and understanding and skill in working with all kinds of bronze work. So he came to King Solomon and did all his work.

The Bronze Pillars for the Temple

15 And he cast two pillars of bronze,

---

12 Literally *house*   13 Literally *floor,* that is, of the upper level   14 Spelled *Huram* in 2 Chronicles 2:13

each one eighteen cubits high, and a line of twelve cubits measured the circumference of each.

16 Then he made two capitals *of* cast bronze, to set on the tops of the pillars. The height of one capital *was* five cubits, and the height of the other capital *was* five cubits.

17 *He made* a lattice network, with wreaths of chainwork, for the capitals which *were* on top of the pillars: seven chains for one capital and seven for the other capital.

18 So he made the pillars, and two rows of pomegranates above the network all around to cover the capitals that *were* on top; and thus he did for the other capital.

19 And the capitals which *were* on top of the pillars in the hall *were* in the shape of lilies, four cubits.

20 The capitals on the two pillars also *had pomegranates* above, by the convex surface which *was* next to the network; and there *were* two hundred such pomegranates in rows on each of the capitals all around.

21 Then he set up the pillars by the vestibule of the temple; he set up the pillar on the right and called its name Jachin, and he set up the pillar on the left and called its name Boaz.

22 The tops of the pillars were in the shape of lilies. So the work of the pillars was finished.

The Sea and the Oxen

23 Then he made the Sea of cast bronze, ten cubits from one brim to the other; *it was* completely round. Its height *was* five cubits, and a line of thirty cubits measured its circumference.

24 And below its brim *were* ornamental buds encircling it all around, ten to a cubit, all the way around the Sea. The ornamental buds *were* cast in two rows when it was cast.

25 It stood on twelve oxen: three looking toward the north, three looking toward the west, three looking toward the south, and three looking toward the east; the Sea *was set* upon them, and all their back parts *pointed* inward.

26 It *was* a handbreadth thick; and its brim was shaped like the brim of a cup, *like* a lily blossom. It contained two thousand baths.

The Carts and the Lavers

27 He also made ten carts of bronze; four cubits *was* the length of each cart, four cubits its width, and three cubits its height.

28 And this *was* the design of the carts: They had panels, and the panels *were* between frames;

29 on the panels that *were* between the frames *were* lions, oxen, and cherubim. And on the frames *was* a pedestal on top. Below the lions and oxen *were* wreaths of plaited work.

30 Every cart had four bronze wheels and axles of bronze, and its four feet had supports. Under the laver *were* supports of cast *bronze* beside each wreath.

31 Its opening inside the crown at the top *was* one cubit in diameter; and the opening *was* round, shaped *like* a pedestal, one and a half cubits in outside diameter; and also on the opening *were* engravings, but the panels were square, not round.

32 Under the panels *were* the four wheels, and the axles of the wheels *were joined* to the cart. The height of a wheel *was* one and a half cubits.

33 The workmanship of the wheels *was* like the workmanship of a chariot wheel; their axle pins, their rims, their spokes, and their hubs *were* all of cast *bronze*.

34 And *there were* four supports at the four corners of each cart, *and* its supports *were* part of the cart itself.

35 On the top of the cart, at the height of half a cubit, *it was* perfectly round. And on the top of the cart, its flanges and its panels *were* of the same casting.

36 On the plates of its flanges and on its panels he engraved cherubim, lions, and palm trees, wherever there was a clear space on each, with wreaths all around.

37 After this *manner* he made the ten carts. All of them were of the same mold, one measure, *and* one shape.

38 Then he made ten lavers of bronze; each laver contained forty baths, *and* each laver *was* four cubits. On each of the ten carts *was* a laver.

39 And he put five carts on the right side of the house, and five on the left side of the house. He set the Sea on the right side of the house toward the southeast.

Furnishings of the Temple

40 Hiram made the lavers and the shovels and the bowls. So Hiram finished doing all the work that he was to do for King Solomon *on* the house of the LORD: **41** the two pillars, the *two* bowl-shaped capitals that *were* on top of the two pillars, and the two networks covering the two bowl-shaped capitals which *were* on top of the pillars; **42** four hundred pomegranates for the two networks (two rows of pomegranates for each network, to cover the two bowl-shaped capitals that *were* on top of the pillars); **43** the ten carts, and ten lavers on the carts; **44** one Sea, and twelve oxen under the Sea; **45** the pots, the shovels, and the bowls. All these articles which Hiram made for King Solomon *for* the house of the LORD *were of* burnished bronze. **46** In the plain of Jordan the king had them cast in clay molds, between Succoth and Zaretan. **47** And Solomon did not weigh all the articles, because *there were* so many; the weight of the bronze was not determined. **48** Solomon had all the furnishings made for the house of the LORD: the altar of gold, and the table of gold on which *was* the showbread; **49** the lampstands of pure gold, five on the right *side* and five on the left in front of the inner sanctuary, with the flowers and the lamps and the wick-trimmers *of* gold; **50** the basins, the trimmers, the bowls, the ladles, and the censers *of* pure gold; and the hinges *of* gold, *both* for the doors of the inner room (the Most Holy *Place*) *and* for the doors of the main hall of the temple.

51 Thus all the work that King Solomon had done *for* the house of the LORD was finished; and Solomon brought in the things which his father David had dedicated: the silver and the gold and the furnishings. *And* he put them in the treasuries of the house of the LORD.

The Ark Brought into the Temple

8 Now Solomon assembled the elders of Israel and all the heads of the tribes, the chief fathers of the children of Israel, to King Solomon in Jerusalem, that they might bring up the ark of the covenant of the LORD from the City of David, which *is* Zion. **2** And all the men of Israel assembled to King Solomon at the feast in the month of Ethanim, which *is* the seventh month. **3** Then all the elders of Israel came, and the priests took up the ark. **4** And they brought up the ark of the LORD, the tabernacle of meeting, and all the holy furnishings that *were* in the tabernacle. The priests and the Levites brought them up. **5** Also King Solomon, and all the congregation of Israel who were assembled to him, *were* with him before the ark, sacrificing sheep and oxen that could not be counted or numbered for multitude. **6** Then the priests brought in the ark of the covenant of the LORD to its place, into the inner sanctuary of the temple, to the Most Holy *Place*, under the wings of the cherubim. **7** For the cherubim spread *their* two wings over the place of the ark, and the cherubim overshadowed the ark and its poles. **8** And the poles extended so that the ends of the poles could be seen from holy *place*, in front of the inner sanctuary; but they could not be seen from outside. So they are there to this day. **9** *There was* nothing in the ark except the two tablets of stone which Moses put there at Horeb, when the LORD made *a* covenant with the children of Israel, when they came out of the land of Egypt. **10** And it came to pass, when the priests came out of the holy *place*, that the cloud filled the house of the LORD, **11** so that the priests could not continue ministering because of the cloud; for the glory of the LORD filled the house of the LORD.

12 Then Solomon spoke:

> "The LORD said He would dwell
> in the dark cloud.
> **13** I have surely built You
> an exalted house,
> And a place for You
> to dwell in forever."

Solomon's Speech at Completion of the Work

14 And the king turned around and blessed the whole congregation of Israel,

Jerusalem

There are infinite possibilities in little beginnings if God is in them. One beautiful example of this is the city of Jerusalem. Once a small village located by a tiny stream, Jerusalem had a population of less than five hundred people prior to the time of Abraham. Yet by the New Testament period, she would grow to a city of two million inhabitants during the Passover Feast.

Jerusalem had none of the conditions of a great city. No heavily traveled highway passed by her doors. She had no harbor from which to launch her ships for trade with her neighbors. Her back door was the wilderness of Judea, one of the most devastated and desolate areas in the region. There were no fertile fields to develop the city's agriculture. Security for the town's defenses were precarious. The city's water sources were barely large enough to supply the needs of a few thousand people. In New Testament times water was brought from eighteen miles away to meet the needs of the expanding city.

All the great cities of the ancient world were aided by natural resources in their growth. Athens had a seaport and an easy travel route connecting it with Asia Minor and Europe. Alexandria and Memphis in North Africa had the famous Egyptian Nile which provided food and water for the region. Babylon in Mesopotamia was near the great Euphrates River, and Rome sat on seven major hills around the Tiber River. All of these cities possessed tokens of civic promise.

What was the success behind Jerusalem? Perhaps it is found in her name, meaning, "Possession of Peace." The real character and strength of Jerusalem was not in her natural resources, but in her people's faith in God. Throughout Jerusalem's history the inhabitants' commitment to God, lifted her above the limiting conditions and resources. With faith, she became an influential power center of the world.

Like the city of Jerusalem, our lives are often limited by what we may consider to be important resources—talent, money, education, or contacts. We look at successful people and feel that they have had more of the important resources than we have. Yet as Christians, we have a greater resource. With a committed faith in God, we are assured that He will make up the difference between what we have and what we need.

Allow God to turn your little beginnings into infinite possibilities! Put your faith in Him. He is the unending resource for the accomplishment of your dreams.

while all the congregation of Israel was standing.

15 Then he said: "Blessed *be* the LORD God of Israel, who spoke with His mouth to my father David, and with His hand has fulfilled *it*, saying,

16 'Since the day that I brought My people Israel out of Egypt, I have chosen no city from any tribe of Israel *in which* to build a house, that My name might be there; but I chose David to be over My people Israel.'

17 "Now it was in the heart of my father David to build a house for the name of the LORD God of Israel.

18 "But the LORD said to my father David, 'Whereas it was in your heart to build a house for My name, you did well that it was in your heart.

19 'Nevertheless you shall not build the house, but your son, who shall come from your loins, he shall build the house for My name.'

20 "So the LORD has fulfilled His word which He spoke; and I have filled the position of my father David, and sit on the throne of Israel, as the LORD promised; and I have built a house for the name of the LORD God of Israel.

21 "And there I have made a place for the ark, in which *is* the covenant of the LORD which He made with our fathers, when He brought them out of the land of Egypt."

Solomon's Prayer of Dedication

22 Then Solomon stood before the altar of the LORD in the presence of all the congregation of Israel, and spread out his hands toward heaven;

23 and he said: "LORD God of Israel, *there is* no God in heaven above or on earth below like You, who keep Your covenant and mercy with Your servants who walk before You with all their heart.

24 "You have kept what You promised Your servant David my father; You have both spoken with Your mouth and fulfilled *it* with Your hand, as *it is* this day.

25 "Therefore, LORD God of Israel, now keep what You promised Your servant David my father, saying, 'You shall not fail to have a man sit before Me on the throne of Israel, only if your sons take heed to their way, that they walk before Me as you have walked before Me.'

26 "And now I pray, O God of Israel, let

Your word come true, which You have spoken to Your servant David my father.

27 "But will God indeed dwell on the earth? Behold, heaven and the heaven of heavens cannot contain You. How much less this temple which I have built!

28 "Yet regard the prayer of Your servant and his supplication, O LORD my God, and listen to the cry and the prayer which Your servant is praying before You today:

29 "that Your eyes may be open toward this temple night and day, toward the place of which You said, 'My name shall be there,' that You may hear the prayer which Your servant makes toward this place.

30 "And may You hear the supplication of Your servant and of Your people Israel. When they pray toward this place, then hear in heaven Your dwelling place; and when You hear, forgive.

31 "When anyone sins against his neighbor, and is forced to take an oath, and comes *and* takes an oath before Your altar in this temple,

32 "then hear in heaven, and act and judge Your servants, condemning the wicked, bringing his way on his head, and justifying the righteous by giving him according to his righteousness.

33 "When Your people Israel are defeated before an enemy because they have sinned against You, and when they turn back to You and confess Your name, and pray and make supplication to You in this temple,

34 "then hear in heaven, and forgive the sin of Your people Israel, and bring them back to the land which You gave to their fathers.

35 "When the heavens are shut up and there is no rain because they have sinned against You, when they pray toward this place and confess Your name, and turn from their sin because You afflict them,

36 "then hear in heaven, and forgive the sin of Your servants, Your people Israel, that You may teach them the good way in which they should walk; and give rain on Your land which You have given to Your people as an inheritance.

37 "When there is famine in the land, *or* pestilence, blight *or* mildew, locusts *or* grasshoppers; when their enemy besieges them in the land of their cities; whatever plague or whatever sickness *there is*;

38 "whatever prayer, whatever supplication is *made* by anyone, *or* by all Your people Israel, when each one knows the plague of his own heart, and spreads out his hands toward this temple:
39 "then hear in heaven Your dwelling place, and forgive, and act, and give to everyone according to all his ways, whose heart You know (for You, only You, know the hearts of all the sons of men),
40 "that they may fear You all the days that they live in the land which You gave to our fathers.
41 "Moreover, concerning a foreigner, who *is* not of Your people Israel, but has come from a far country for Your name's sake
42 "(for they will hear of Your great name and Your strong hand and Your outstretched arm), when he comes and prays toward this temple,
43 "hear in heaven Your dwelling place, and do according to all for which the foreigner calls to You, that all peoples of the earth may know Your name and fear You, as *do* Your people Israel, and that they may know that this temple which I have built is called by Your name.
44 "When Your people go out to battle against their enemy, wherever You send them, and when they pray to the LORD toward the city which You have chosen and *toward* the temple which I have built for Your name,
45 "then hear in heaven their prayer and their supplication, and maintain their cause.
46 "When they sin against You (for *there is* no one who does not sin), and You become angry with them and deliver them to the enemy, and they take them captive to the land of the enemy, far or near;
47 "*yet* when they come to themselves in the land where they were carried captive, and repent, and make supplication to You in the land of those who took them captive, saying, 'We have sinned and done wrong, we have committed wickedness';
48 "and *when* they return to You with all their heart and with all their soul in the land of their enemies who led them away captive, and pray to You toward their land which You gave to their fathers, the city which You have chosen and the temple which I have built for Your name:
49 "then hear in heaven Your dwelling

place their prayer and their supplication, and maintain their cause,
50 "and forgive Your people who have sinned against You, and all their transgressions which they have transgressed against You; and grant them compassion before those who took them captive, that they may have compassion on them
51 "(for they *are* Your people and Your inheritance, whom You brought out of Egypt, out of the iron furnace),
52 "that Your eyes may be open to the supplication of Your servant and the supplication of Your people Israel, to listen to them whenever they call to You.
53 "For You separated them from among all the peoples of the earth *to be* Your inheritance, as You spoke by the hand of Your servant Moses, when You brought our fathers out of Egypt, O Lord GOD."

Solomon Blesses the Congregation

54 And so it was, when Solomon had finished praying all this prayer and supplication to the LORD, that he arose from before the altar of the LORD, from kneeling on his knees with his hands spread up to heaven.
55 Then he stood and blessed all the congregation of Israel with a loud voice, saying:
56 "Blessed *be* the LORD, who has given rest to His people Israel, according to all that He promised. There has not failed one word of all His good promise, which He promised through His servant Moses.
57 "May the LORD our God be with us, as He was with our fathers. May He not leave us nor forsake us,
58 "that He may incline our hearts to Himself, to walk in all His ways, and to keep His commandments and His statutes and His judgments, which He commanded our fathers.
59 "And may these words of mine, with which I have made supplication before the LORD, be near the LORD our God day and night, that He may maintain the cause of His servant and the cause of His people Israel, as each day may require,
60 "that all the peoples of the earth may know that the LORD *is* God; *there is* no other.
61 "Let your heart therefore be loyal to the LORD our God, to walk in His stat-

utes and keep His commandments, as at this day."

Solomon Dedicates the Temple

62 Then the king and all Israel with him offered sacrifices before the LORD.
63 And Solomon offered a sacrifice of peace offerings, which he offered to the LORD, twenty-two thousand bulls and one hundred and twenty thousand sheep. So the king and all the children of Israel dedicated the house of the LORD.
64 On the same day the king consecrated the middle of the court that *was* in front of the house of the LORD; for there he offered burnt offerings, grain offerings, and the fat of the peace offerings, because the bronze altar that *was* before the LORD *was* too small to receive the burnt offerings, the grain offerings, and the fat of the peace offerings.
65 At that time Solomon held a feast, and all Israel with him, a great congregation from the entrance of Hamath to the Brook of Egypt, before the LORD our God, seven days and seven *more* days—fourteen days.
66 On the eighth day he sent the people away; and they blessed the king, and went to their tents joyful and glad of heart for all the goodness that the LORD had done for His servant David, and for Israel His people.

God's Second Appearance to Solomon

9 And it came to pass, when Solomon had finished building the house of the LORD and the king's house, and all Solomon's desire which he wanted to do,
2 that the LORD appeared to Solomon the second time, as He had appeared to him at Gibeon.
3 And the LORD said to him: "I have heard your prayer and your supplication that you have made before Me; I have sanctified this house which you have built to put My name there forever, and My eyes and My heart will be there perpetually.
4 "Now if you walk before Me as your father David walked, in integrity of heart and in uprightness, to do according to all that I have commanded you, *and* if you keep My statutes and My judgments,
5 "then I will establish the throne of your kingdom over Israel forever, as I promised David your father, saying, 'You shall not fail to have a man on the throne of Israel.'
6 "But if you or your sons at all turn from following Me, and do not keep My commandments *and* My statutes which I have set before you, but go and serve other gods and worship them,
7 "then I will cut off Israel from the land which I have given them; and this house which I have sanctified for My name I will cast out of My sight. Israel will be a proverb and a byword among all peoples.
8 "And this house will be exalted; yet everyone who passes by it will be astonished and will hiss, and say, 'Why has the LORD done thus to this land and to this house?'
9 "Then they will answer, 'Because they forsook the LORD their God, who brought their fathers out of the land of Egypt, and have embraced other gods, and worshiped them and served them; therefore the LORD has brought all this calamity on them.' "

Solomon and Hiram Exchange Gifts

10 Now it happened at the end of twenty years, when Solomon had built the two houses, the house of the LORD and the king's house
11 (Hiram the king of Tyre had supplied Solomon with cedar and cypress and gold, as much as he desired), *that* King Solomon then gave Hiram twenty cities in the land of Galilee.
12 Then Hiram went from Tyre to see the cities which Solomon had given him, but they did not please him.
13 So he said, "What *kind of* cities *are* these which you have given me, my brother?" And he called them the land of Cabul,15 as they are to this day.
14 Then Hiram sent the king one hundred and twenty talents of gold.

Solomon's Additional Achievements

15 And this *is* the reason for the labor force which King Solomon raised: to build the house of the LORD, his own house, the Millo, the wall of Jerusalem, Hazor, Megiddo, and Gezer.
16 (Pharaoh king of Egypt had gone up and taken Gezer and burned it with fire, had killed the Canaanites who dwelt in the city, and had given it *as* a dowry to his daughter, Solomon's wife.)

15 Literally *Good for Nothing*

17 And Solomon built Gezer, Lower Beth Horon,
18 Baalath, and Tadmor in the wilderness, in the land of Judah,
19 all the storage cities that Solomon had, cities for his chariots and cities for his cavalry, and whatever Solomon desired to build in Jerusalem, in Lebanon, and in all the land of his dominion.
20 All the people who were left of the Amorites, Hittites, Perizzites, Hivites, and Jebusites, who were not of the children of Israel—
21 that is, their descendants who were left in the land after them, whom the children of Israel had not been able to destroy completely—from these Solomon raised forced labor, as it is to this day.
22 But of the children of Israel Solomon made no forced laborers, because they were men of war and his servants: his officers, his captains, commanders of his chariots, and his cavalry.
23 Others were chiefs of the officials who were over Solomon's work: five hundred and fifty, who ruled over the people who did the work.
24 But Pharaoh's daughter came up from the City of David to her house which Solomon had built for her. Then he built the Millo.
25 Now three times a year Solomon offered burnt offerings and peace offerings on the altar which he had built for the LORD, and he burned incense with them on the altar that was before the LORD. So he finished the temple.
26 King Solomon also built a fleet of ships at Ezion Geber, which is near Elath[16] on the shore of the Red Sea, in the land of Edom.
27 Then Hiram sent his servants with the fleet, seamen who knew the sea, to work with the servants of Solomon.
28 And they went to Ophir, and acquired four hundred and twenty talents of gold from there, and brought it to King Solomon.

The Queen of Sheba's Praise of Solomon

10 Now when the queen of Sheba heard of the fame of Solomon concerning the name of the LORD, she came to test him with hard questions.
2 She came to Jerusalem with a very great retinue, with camels that bore spices, very much gold, and precious stones; and when she came to Solomon, she spoke with him about all that was in her heart.
3 So Solomon answered all her questions; there was nothing so difficult for the king that he could not explain it to her.
4 And when the queen of Sheba had seen all the wisdom of Solomon, the house that he had built,
5 the food on his table, the seating of his servants, the service of his waiters and their apparel, his cupbearers, and his entryway by which he went up to the house of the LORD, there was no more spirit in her.
6 Then she said to the king: "It was a true report which I heard in my own land about your words and your wisdom.
7 "However I did not believe the words until I came and saw it with my own eyes; and indeed the half was not told me. Your wisdom and prosperity exceed the fame of which I heard.
8 "Happy are your men and happy are these your servants, who stand continually before you and hear your wisdom!
9 "Blessed be the LORD your God, who delighted in you, setting you on the throne of Israel! Because the LORD has loved Israel forever, therefore He made you king, to do justice and righteousness."
10 Then she gave the king one hundred and twenty talents of gold, spices in great abundance, and precious stones. There never again came such abundance of spices as the queen of Sheba gave to King Solomon.
11 Also, the ships of Hiram, which brought gold from Ophir, brought great quantities of almug[17] wood and precious stones from Ophir.
12 And the king made steps of the almug wood for the house of the LORD and for the king's house, also harps and stringed instruments for singers. There never again came such almug wood, nor has the like been seen to this day.
13 And King Solomon gave the queen of Sheba all she desired, whatever she asked, besides what Solomon had given her according to the royal bounty. So she turned and went to her own country, she and her servants.

16 Hebrew Eloth (compare 2 Kings 14:22)   17 Or algum (compare 2 Chronicles 9:10, 11)

Solomon's Great Wealth

14 The weight of gold that came to Solomon yearly was six hundred and sixty-six talents of gold,
15 besides *that* from the traveling merchants, from the income of traders, from all the kings of Arabia, and from the governors of the country.
16 And King Solomon made two hundred large shields *of* hammered gold; six hundred *shekels* of gold went into each shield.
17 He also *made* three hundred shields *of* hammered gold; three minas of gold went into each shield. And the king put them in the House of the Forest of Lebanon.
18 Moreover the king made a great throne of ivory, and overlaid it with pure gold.
19 The throne had six steps, and the top of the throne *was* round at the back; *there were* armrests on either side of the place of the seat, and two lions stood beside the armrests.
20 Twelve lions stood there, one on each side of the six steps; nothing like *this* had been made for any other kingdom.
21 All King Solomon's drinking vessels *were of* gold, and all the vessels of the House of the Forest of Lebanon *were of* pure gold; not *one was of* silver, for this was accounted as nothing in the days of Solomon.
22 For the king had merchant ships[18] at sea with the fleet of Hiram. Once every three years the merchant ships came bringing gold, silver, ivory, apes, and monkeys.[19]
23 So King Solomon surpassed all the kings of the earth in riches and wisdom.
24 And all the earth sought the presence of Solomon to hear his wisdom, which God had put in his heart.
25 Each man brought his present: articles of silver and gold, garments, armor, spices, horses, and mules, at a set rate year by year.
26 And Solomon gathered chariots and horsemen; he had one thousand four hundred chariots and twelve thousand horsemen, whom he stationed in the chariot cities and with the king in Jerusalem.
27 The king made silver *as common* in Jerusalem as stones, and he made cedars as abundant as the sycamores which are in the lowland.
28 And Solomon had horses imported from Egypt and Keveh; the king's merchants bought them in Keveh at the *current* price.
29 Now a chariot that was imported from Egypt cost six hundred *shekels* of silver, and a horse one hundred and fifty; and thus, through their agents,[20] they exported *them* to all the kings of the Hittites and the kings of Syria.

Solomon's Heart Turns from the LORD

11 But King Solomon loved many foreign women, as well as the daughter of Pharaoh: women of the Moabites, Ammonites, Edomites, Sidonians, *and* Hittites—
2 from the nations of whom the LORD had said to the children of Israel, "You shall not intermarry with them, nor they with you. *For* surely they will turn away your hearts after their gods." Solomon clung to these in love.
3 And he had seven hundred wives, princesses, and three hundred concubines; and his wives turned away his heart.
4 For it was so, when Solomon was old, that his wives turned his heart after other gods; and his heart was not loyal to the LORD his God, as *was* the heart of his father David.
5 For Solomon went after Ashtoreth the goddess of the Sidonians, and after Milcom the abomination of the Ammonites.
6 Solomon did evil in the sight of the LORD, and did not fully follow the LORD, as *did* his father David.
7 Then Solomon built a high place for Chemosh the abomination of Moab, on the hill that *is* east of Jerusalem, and for Molech the abomination of the people of Ammon.
8 And he did likewise for all his foreign wives, who burned incense and sacrificed to their gods.
9 So the LORD became angry with Solomon, because his heart had turned from the LORD God of Israel, who had appeared to him twice,
10 and had commanded him concerning this thing, that he should not go after other gods; but he did not keep what the LORD had commanded.

18 Literally *ships of Tarshish* (deep-sea vessels)   **19** Or *peacocks*   **20** Literally *by their hands*

11 Therefore the LORD said to Solomon, "Because you have done this, and have not kept My covenant and My statutes, which I have commanded you, I will surely tear the kingdom away from you and give it to your servant.

12 "Nevertheless I will not do it in your days, for the sake of your father David; *but* I will tear it out of the hand of your son.

13 "However I will not tear away the whole kingdom, *but* I will give one tribe to your son for the sake of my servant David, and for the sake of Jerusalem which I have chosen."

Adversaries of Solomon

14 Now the LORD raised up an adversary against Solomon, Hadad the Edomite; he *was* a descendant of the king in Edom.

15 For it happened, when David was in Edom, and Joab the commander of the army had gone up to bury the slain, after he had killed every male in Edom

16 (because for six months Joab remained there with all Israel, until he had cut down every male in Edom),

17 that Hadad fled to go to Egypt, he and certain Edomites of his father's servants with him. Hadad *was* still a little child.

18 Then they arose from Midian and came to Paran; and they took men with them from Paran and came to Egypt, to Pharaoh king of Egypt, who gave him a house, apportioned food for him, and gave him land.

19 And Hadad found great favor in the sight of Pharaoh, so that he gave him as wife the sister of his own wife, that is, the sister of Queen Tahpenes.

20 Then the sister of Tahpenes bore him Genubath his son, whom Tahpenes weaned in Pharaoh's house. And Genubath was in Pharaoh's household among the sons of Pharaoh.

21 Now when Hadad heard in Egypt that David rested with his fathers, and that Joab the commander of the army was dead, Hadad said to Pharaoh, "Let me depart, that I may go to my own country."

22 Then Pharaoh said to him, "But what have you lacked with me, that suddenly you seek to go to your own country?" So he answered, "Nothing, but do let me go anyway."

23 And God raised up *another* adversary against him, Rezon the son of Eliadah, who had fled from his lord, Hadadezer king of Zobah.

24 So he gathered men to him and became captain over a band *of raiders*, when David killed those *of Zobah*. And they went to Damascus and dwelt there, and reigned in Damascus.

25 He was an adversary of Israel all the days of Solomon (besides the trouble that Hadad *caused*); and he abhorred Israel, and reigned over Syria.

Jeroboam's Rebellion

26 Then Solomon's servant, Jeroboam the son of Nebat, an Ephraimite from Zereda, whose mother's name *was* Zeruah, a widow, also rebelled against the king.

27 And this *is* what caused him to rebel against the king: Solomon had built the Millo *and* repaired the damages to the City of David his father.

28 The man Jeroboam *was* a mighty man of valor; and Solomon, seeing that the young man was industrious, made him the officer over all the labor force of the house of Joseph.

29 Now it happened at that time, when Jeroboam went out of Jerusalem, that the prophet Ahijah the Shilonite met him on the way; and he had clothed himself with a new garment, and the two *were* alone in the field.

30 Then Ahijah took hold of the new garment that *was* on him, and tore it *into* twelve pieces.

31 And he said to Jeroboam, "Take for yourself ten pieces, for thus says the LORD, the God of Israel: 'Behold, I will tear the kingdom out of the hand of Solomon and will give ten tribes to you

32 '(but he shall have one tribe for the sake of My servant David, and for the sake of Jerusalem, the city which I have chosen out of all the tribes of Israel),

33 'because they have forsaken Me, and worshiped Ashtoreth the goddess of the Sidonians, Chemosh the god of the Moabites, and Milcom the god of the people of Ammon, and have not walked in My ways to do *what is* right in My eyes and *keep* My statutes and My judgments, as *did* his father David.

34 'However I will not take the whole kingdom out of his hand, because I have made him ruler all the days of his life for the sake of My servant David, whom I chose because he kept My commandments and My statutes.

35 'But I will take the kingdom out of his son's hand and give it to you—ten tribes.

36 'And to his son I will give one tribe, that My servant David may always have a lamp before Me in Jerusalem, the city which I have chosen for Myself, to put My name there.

37 'So I will take you, and you shall reign over all your heart desires, and you shall be king over Israel.

38 'Then it shall be, if you heed all that I command you, walk in My ways, and do *what is* right in My sight, to keep My statutes and My commandments, as My servant David did, then I will be with you and build for you an enduring house, as I built for David, and will give Israel to you.

39 'And I will afflict the descendants of David because of this, but not forever.' "

40 Solomon therefore sought to kill Jeroboam. But Jeroboam arose and fled to Egypt, to Shishak king of Egypt, and was in Egypt until the death of Solomon.

Death of Solomon

41 Now the rest of the acts of Solomon, all that he did, and his wisdom, *are* they not written in the book of the acts of Solomon?

42 And the period that Solomon reigned in Jerusalem over all Israel *was* forty years.

43 Then Solomon rested with his fathers, and was buried in the City of David his father. And Rehoboam his son reigned in his place.

The Revolt Against Rehoboam

12 Now Rehoboam went to Shechem, for all Israel had gone to Shechem to make him king.

2 So it was, when Jeroboam the son of Nebat heard *it* (he was still in Egypt, for he had fled from the presence of King Solomon and had been dwelling in Egypt),

3 that they sent and called him. Then Jeroboam and the whole congregation of Israel came and spoke to Rehoboam, saying,

4 "Your father made our yoke heavy; now therefore, lighten the burdensome service of your father, and his heavy yoke which he put on us, and we will serve you."

5 So he said to them, "Depart *for* three days, then come back to me." And the people departed.

6 Then King Rehoboam consulted the elders who stood before his father Solomon while he still lived, and he said, "How do you advise me to answer these people?"

7 And they spoke to him, saying, "If you will be a servant to these people today, and serve them, and answer them, and speak good words to them, then they will be your servants forever."

8 But he rejected the counsel which the elders gave him, and consulted the young men who had grown up with him, who stood before him.

9 And he said to them, "What counsel do you give? How should we answer this people who have spoken to me, saying, 'Lighten the yoke which your father put on us'?"

10 Then the young men who had grown up with him spoke to him, saying, "Thus you should speak to this people who have spoken to you, saying, 'Your father made our yoke heavy, but you make *it* lighter on us'—thus you shall say to them: 'My little *finger* shall be thicker than my father's waist!

11 'And now, whereas my father laid a heavy yoke on you, I will add to your yoke; my father chastised you with whips, but I will chastise you with scourges!' "21

12 So Jeroboam and all the people came to Rehoboam the third day, as the king directed, saying, "Come back to me the third day."

13 Then the king answered the people roughly, and rejected the counsel which the elders had given him;

14 and he spoke to them according to the counsel of the young men, saying, "My father made your yoke heavy, but I will add to your yoke; my father chastised you with whips, but I will chastise you with scourges!"22

15 So the king did not listen to the people; for the turn *of affairs* was from the LORD, that He might fulfill His word, which the LORD had spoken by Ahijah

21 Literally *scorpions* 22 Literally *scorpions*

the Shilonite to Jeroboam the son of
Nebat.
16 Now when all Israel saw that the king
did not listen to them, the people answered the king, saying:

"What portion have we in David?
We have no inheritance
    in the son of Jesse.
To your tents, O Israel!
Now, see to your own house,
    O David!"

So Israel departed to their tents.
17 But Rehoboam reigned over the children of Israel who dwelt in the cities of
Judah.
18 Then King Rehoboam sent Adoram,
who *was* in charge of the revenue; but
all Israel stoned him with stones, and
he died. Therefore King Rehoboam
mounted his chariot in haste to flee to
Jerusalem.
19 So Israel has been in rebellion against
the house of David to this day.
20 Now it came to pass when all Israel
heard that Jeroboam had come back, they
sent for him and called him to the congregation, and made him king over all Israel.
There was none who followed the house
of David, but the tribe of Judah only.
21 And when Rehoboam came to Jerusalem, he assembled all the house of Judah
with the tribe of Benjamin, one hundred
and eighty thousand chosen men who
were warriors, to fight against the house
of Israel, that he might restore the kingdom to Rehoboam the son of Solomon.
22 But the word of God came to Shemaiah the man of God, saying,
23 "Speak to Rehoboam the son of Solomon, king of Judah, to all the house of
Judah and Benjamin, and to the rest of
the people, saying,
24 'Thus says the LORD: "You shall not
go up nor fight against your brethren the
children of Israel. Let every man return
to his house, for this thing is from
Me." ' " Therefore they obeyed the word
of the LORD, and turned back, according
to the word of the LORD.

Jeroboam's Gold Calves

25 Then Jeroboam built Shechem in the
mountains of Ephraim, and dwelt there.
Also he went out from there and built
Penuel.

26 And Jeroboam said in his heart,
"Now the kingdom may return to the
house of David:
27 "If these people go up to offer sacrifices in the house of the LORD at Jerusalem, then the heart of this people will
turn back to their lord, Rehoboam king
of Judah, and they will kill me and go
back to Rehoboam king of Judah."
28 Therefore the king took counsel and
made two calves *of* gold, and said to the
people, "It is too much for you to go up
to Jerusalem. Here are your gods, O Israel, which brought you up from the land
of Egypt!"
29 And he set up one in Bethel, and the
other he put in Dan.
30 Now this thing became a sin, for the
people went *to worship* before the one as
far as Dan.
31 He made shrines[23] on the high places,
and made priests from every class of people, who were not of the sons of Levi.
32 Jeroboam ordained a feast on the fifteenth day of the eighth month, like the
feast that *was* in Judah, and offered sacrifices on the altar. So he did at Bethel,
sacrificing to the calves that he had made.
And at Bethel he installed the priests of
the high places which he had made.
33 So he made offerings on the altar
which he had made at Bethel on the fifteenth day of the eighth month, in the
month which he had devised in his own
heart. And he ordained a feast for the
children of Israel, and offered sacrifices
on the altar and burned incense.

The Message of the Man of God

13 And behold, a man of God went
from Judah to Bethel by the word
of the LORD, and Jeroboam stood by the
altar to burn incense.
2 Then he cried out against the altar by
the word of the LORD, and said, "O altar,
altar! Thus says the LORD: 'Behold, a
child, Josiah by name, shall be born to
the house of David; and on you he shall
sacrifice the priests of the high places who
burn incense on you, and men's bones
shall be burned on you.' "
3 And he gave a sign the same day, saying, "This *is* the sign which the LORD has
spoken: Surely the altar shall split apart,
and the ashes on it shall be poured out."
4 So it came to pass when King Jeroboam heard the saying of the man of

23 Literally *houses*

God, who cried out against the altar in Bethel, that he stretched out his hand from the altar, saying, "Arrest him!" Then his hand, which he stretched out toward him, withered, so that he could not pull it back to himself.

5 The altar also was split apart, and the ashes poured out from the altar, according to the sign which the man of God had given by the word of the LORD.

6 Then the king answered and said to the man of God, "Please entreat the favor of the LORD your God, and pray for me, that my hand may be restored to me." So the man of God entreated the LORD, and the king's hand was restored to him, and became as it was before.

7 Then the king said to the man of God, "Come home with me and refresh yourself, and I will give you a reward."

8 But the man of God said to the king, "If you were to give me half your house, I would not go in with you; nor would I eat bread nor drink water in this place.

9 "For so it was commanded me by the word of the LORD, saying, 'You shall not eat bread, nor drink water, nor return by the same way you came.' "

10 So he went another way and did not return by the way he came to Bethel.

Death of the Man of God

11 Now an old prophet dwelt in Bethel, and his sons came and told him all the works that the man of God had done that day in Bethel; they also told their father the words which he had spoken to the king.

12 And their father said to them, "Which way did he go?" For his sons had seen which way the man of God went who came from Judah.

13 Then he said to his sons, "Saddle the donkey for me." So they saddled the donkey for him; and he rode on it,

14 and went after the man of God, and found him sitting under an oak. Then he said to him, "Are you the man of God who came from Judah?" And he said, "I am."

15 Then he said to him, "Come home with me and eat bread."

16 And he said, "I cannot return with you nor go in with you; neither can I eat bread nor drink water with you in this place.

17 "For I have been told by the word of the LORD, 'You shall not eat bread nor drink water there, nor return by going the way you came.' "

18 He said to him, "I too am a prophet as you are, and an angel spoke to me by the word of the LORD, saying, 'Bring him back with you to your house, that he may eat bread and drink water.' " But he lied to him.

19 So he went back with him, and ate bread in his house, and drank water.

20 Now it happened, as they sat at the table, that the word of the LORD came to the prophet who had brought him back;

21 and he cried out to the man of God who came from Judah, saying, "Thus says the LORD: 'Because you have disobeyed the word of the LORD, and have not kept the commandment which the LORD your God commanded you,

22 'but you came back, ate bread, and drank water in the place of which the LORD said to you, "Eat no bread and drink no water," your corpse shall not come to the tomb of your fathers.' "

23 So it was, after he had eaten bread and after he had drunk, that he saddled the donkey for him, the prophet whom he had brought back.

24 So when he was gone, a lion met him on the road and killed him. And his corpse was thrown on the road, and the donkey stood by it; the lion also stood by the corpse.

25 And there, men passed by and saw the corpse thrown on the road, and the lion standing by the corpse. Then they went and told it in the city where the old prophet dwelt.

26 So when the prophet who had brought him back from the way heard it, he said, "It is the man of God who was disobedient to the word of the LORD. Therefore the LORD has delivered him to the lion, which has torn him and killed him, according to the word of the LORD which He spoke to him."

27 And he spoke to his sons, saying, "Saddle the donkey for me." And they saddled it.

28 Then he went and found his corpse thrown on the road, and the donkey and the lion standing by the corpse. The lion had not eaten the corpse nor torn the donkey.

29 And the prophet took up the corpse of the man of God, laid it on the donkey,

and brought it back. So the old prophet came to the city to mourn, and to bury him.

30 Then he laid the corpse in his own tomb; and they mourned over him, *saying,* "Alas, my brother!"

31 So it was, after he had buried him, that he spoke to his sons, saying, "When I am dead, then bury me in the tomb where the man of God *is* buried; lay my bones beside his bones.

32 "For the saying which he cried out by the word of the LORD against the altar in Bethel, and against all the shrines[24] on the high places which *are* in the cities of Samaria, will surely come to pass."

33 After this event Jeroboam did not turn from his evil way, but again he made priests from every class of people for the high places; whoever wished, he consecrated him, and he became *one* of the priests of the high places. .

34 And this thing was the sin of the house of Jeroboam, so as to exterminate and destroy *it* from the face of the earth.

Judgment on the House of Jeroboam

14 At that time Abijah the son of Jeroboam became sick.

2 And Jeroboam said to his wife, "Please arise, and disguise yourself, that they may not recognize you as the wife of Jeroboam, and go to Shiloh. Indeed, Ahijah the prophet *is* there, who told me that *I would be* king over this people.

3 "Also take with you ten loaves, *some* cakes, and a jar of honey, and go to him; he will tell you what will become of the child."

4 And Jeroboam's wife did so; she arose and went to Shiloh, and came to the house of Ahijah. But Ahijah could not see, for his eyes were glazed by reason of his age.

5 Now the LORD had said to Ahijah, "Here is the wife of Jeroboam, coming to ask you something about her son, for he *is* sick. Thus and thus you shall say to her; for it will be, when she comes in, that she will pretend *to be* another *woman.*"

6 And so it was, when Ahijah heard the sound of her footsteps as she came through the door, he said, "Come in, wife of Jeroboam. Why do you pretend *to be* another *person?* For I *have been* sent to you *with* bad *news.*

7 "Go, tell Jeroboam, 'Thus says the LORD God of Israel: "Because I exalted you from among the people, and made you ruler over My people Israel,

8 "and tore the kingdom away from the house of David, and gave it to you; and *yet* you have not been as My servant David, who kept My commandments and who followed Me with all his heart, to do only *what was* right in My eyes;

9 "but you have done more evil than all who were before you, for you have gone and made for yourself other gods and molded images to provoke Me to anger, and have cast Me behind your back—

10 "therefore behold! I will bring disaster on the house of Jeroboam, and will cut off from Jeroboam every male in Israel, bond and free; *and* I will take away the remnant of the house of Jeroboam, as one takes away refuse until it is all gone.

11 "The dogs shall eat whoever belongs to Jeroboam and dies in the city, and the birds of the air shall eat whoever dies in the field; for the LORD has spoken *it!*" '

12 "Arise therefore, go to your own house. When your feet enter the city, the child shall die.

13 "And all Israel shall mourn for him and bury him, for he is the only one of Jeroboam who shall come to the grave, because in him there is found something good toward the LORD God of Israel in the house of Jeroboam.

14 "Moreover the LORD will raise up for Himself a king over Israel who shall cut off the house of Jeroboam; this is the day. What? Even now!

15 "For the LORD will strike Israel, as a reed is shaken in the water. He will uproot Israel from this good land which He gave to their fathers, and will scatter them beyond the River,[25] because they have made their wooden images,[26] provoking the LORD to anger.

16 "And He will give Israel up because of the sins of Jeroboam, who sinned and who made Israel sin."

17 Then Jeroboam's wife arose and departed, and came to Tirzah. When she came to the threshold of the house, the child died.

18 And they buried him; and all Israel mourned for him, according to the word of the LORD which He spoke through His servant Ahijah the prophet.

24 Literally *houses* 25 That is, the Euphrates 26 Hebrew *Asherah,* Canaanite goddess

Death of Jeroboam

19 Now the rest of the acts of Jeroboam, how he made war and how he reigned, indeed they *are* written in the book of the chronicles of the kings of Israel.
20 The period that Jeroboam reigned *was* twenty-two years. So he rested with his fathers. Then Nadab his son reigned in his place.

Rehoboam Reigns in Judah

21 And Rehoboam the son of Solomon reigned in Judah. Rehoboam *was* forty-one years old when he became king. He reigned seventeen years in Jerusalem, the city which the LORD had chosen out of all the tribes of Israel, to put His name there. His mother's name *was* Naamah, an Ammonitess.
22 Now Judah did evil in the sight of the LORD, and they provoked Him to jealousy with their sins which they committed, more than all that their fathers had done.
23 For they also built for themselves high places, *sacred* pillars, and wooden images on every high hill and under every green tree.
24 And there were also perverted persons[27] in the land. They did according to all the abominations of the nations which the LORD had cast out before the children of Israel.
25 Now it happened, in the fifth year of King Rehoboam, *that* Shishak king of Egypt came up against Jerusalem.
26 And he took away the treasures of the house of the LORD and the treasures of the king's house; he took away everything. He also took away all the gold shields which Solomon had made.
27 Then King Rehoboam made bronze shields in their place, and committed *them* to the hands of the captains of the guards, who guarded the doorway of the king's house.
28 And so it was, whenever the king went into the house of the LORD, *that* the guards carried them, then brought them back into the guard chamber.
29 Now the rest of the acts of Rehoboam, and all that he did, *are* they not written in the book of the chronicles of the kings of Judah?

30 And there was war between Rehoboam and Jeroboam all *their* days.
31 So Rehoboam rested with his fathers, and was buried with his fathers in the City of David. His mother's name *was* Naamah, an Ammonitess. Then Abijam[28] his son reigned in his place.

Abijam Reigns in Judah

15 Now in the eighteenth year of King Jeroboam the son of Nebat, Abijam became king over Judah.
2 He reigned three years in Jerusalem. His mother's name *was* Maachah the granddaughter of Abishalom.
3 And he walked in all the sins of his father, which he had done before him; his heart was not loyal to the LORD his God, as was the heart of his father David.
4 Nevertheless for David's sake the LORD his God gave him a lamp in Jerusalem, by setting up his son after him and by establishing Jerusalem;
5 because David did *what was* right in the eyes of the LORD, and had not turned aside from anything that He commanded him all the days of his life, except in the matter of Uriah the Hittite.
6 And there was war between Rehoboam and Jeroboam all the days of his life.
7 Now the rest of the acts of Abijam, and all that he did, *are* they not written in the book of the chronicles of the kings of Judah? And there was war between Abijam and Jeroboam.
8 So Abijam rested with his fathers, and they buried him in the City of David. Then Asa his son reigned in his place.

Asa Reigns in Judah

9 In the twentieth year of Jeroboam king of Israel, Asa became king over Judah.
10 And he reigned forty-one years in Jerusalem. His grandmother's name *was* Maachah the granddaughter of Abishalom.
11 Asa did *what was* right in the eyes of the LORD, as *did* his father David.
12 And he banished the perverted persons[29] from the land, and removed all the idols that his fathers had made.
13 Also he removed Maachah his grandmother from *being* queen mother, because she had made an obscene image of Ashe-

27 Hebrew *qedeshim*, that is, those practicing sodomy and prostitution in religious rituals
28 Spelled *Abijah* in 2 Chronicles 12:16ff   29 See note 27

rah.[30] And Asa cut down her obscene image and burned *it* by the Brook Kidron.

14 But the high places were not removed. Nevertheless Asa's heart was loyal to the LORD all his days.

15 He also brought into the house of the LORD the things which his father had dedicated, and the things which he himself had dedicated: silver and gold and utensils.

16 Now there was war between Asa and Baasha king of Israel all their days.

17 And Baasha king of Israel came up against Judah, and built Ramah, that he might let none go out or come in to Asa king of Judah.

18 Then Asa took all the silver and gold *that was* left in the treasuries of the house of the LORD and the treasuries of the king's house, and delivered them into the hand of his servants. And King Asa sent them to Ben-Hadad the son of Tabrimmon, the son of Hezion, king of Syria, who dwelt in Damascus, saying,

19 "*Let there be* a treaty between you and me, as there was between my father and your father. See, I have sent you a present of silver and gold. Come and break your treaty with Baasha king of Israel, so that he will withdraw from me."

20 So Ben-Hadad heeded King Asa, and sent the captains of his armies against the cities of Israel. He attacked Ijon, Dan, Abel Beth Maachah, and all Chinneroth, with all the land of Naphtali.

21 Now it happened, when Baasha heard *it*, that he stopped building Ramah, and remained in Tirzah.

22 Then King Asa made a proclamation throughout all Judah; none *was* exempted. And they took away the stones and timber of Ramah, which Baasha had used for building; and with them King Asa built Geba of Benjamin, and Mizpah.

23 The rest of all the acts of Asa, all his might, all that he did and the cities which he built, *are* they not written in the book of the chronicles of the kings of Judah? But in the time of his old age he was diseased in his feet.

24 So Asa rested with his fathers, and was buried with his fathers in the City of David his father. Then Jehoshaphat his son reigned in his place.

Nadab Reigns in Israel

25 Now Nadab the son of Jeroboam became king over Israel in the second year of Asa king of Judah, and he reigned over Israel two years.

26 And he did evil in the sight of the LORD, and walked in the way of his father, and in his sin by which he had made Israel sin.

27 Then Baasha the son of Ahijah, of the house of Issachar, conspired against him. And Baasha killed him at Gibbethon, which *belonged* to the Philistines, while Nadab and all Israel laid siege to Gibbethon.

28 Baasha killed him in the third year of Asa king of Judah, and reigned in his place.

29 And it was so, when he became king, *that* he killed all the house of Jeroboam. He did not leave to Jeroboam anyone that breathed, until he had destroyed him, according to the word of the LORD which He had spoken by His servant Ahijah the Shilonite,

30 because of the sins of Jeroboam, which he had sinned and by which he had made Israel sin, because of his provocation with which he had provoked the LORD God of Israel to anger.

31 Now the rest of the acts of Nadab, and all that he did, *are* they not written in the book of the chronicles of the kings of Israel?

32 And there was war between Asa and Baasha king of Israel all their days.

Baasha Reigns in Israel

33 In the third year of Asa king of Judah, Baasha the son of Ahijah became king over all Israel in Tirzah, and *reigned* twenty-four years.

34 He did evil in the sight of the LORD, and walked in the way of Jeroboam, and in his sin by which he had made Israel sin.

16 Then the word of the LORD came to Jehu the son of Hanani, against Baasha, saying:

2 "Inasmuch as I lifted you out of the dust and made you ruler over My people Israel, and you have walked in the way of Jeroboam, and have made My people Israel sin, to provoke Me to anger with their sins,

3 "surely I will take away the posterity of Baasha and the posterity of his house,

---

30 A Canaanite goddess

and I will make your house like the house of Jeroboam the son of Nebat.

4 "The dogs shall eat whoever belongs to Baasha and dies in the city, and the birds of the air shall eat whoever dies in the fields."

5 Now the rest of the acts of Baasha, what he did, and his might, *are* they not written in the book of the chronicles of the kings of Israel?

6 So Baasha rested with his fathers and was buried in Tirzah. Then Elah his son reigned in his place.

7 And also the word of the LORD came by the prophet Jehu the son of Hanani against Baasha and his house, because of all the evil that he did in the sight of the LORD in provoking Him to anger with the work of his hands, in being like the house of Jeroboam, and because he killed them.

Elah Reigns in Israel

8 In the twenty-sixth year of Asa king of Judah, Elah the son of Baasha became king over Israel, *and reigned* two years in Tirzah.

9 Now his servant Zimri, commander of half *his* chariots, conspired against him as he was in Tirzah drinking himself drunk in the house of Arza, steward of *his* house in Tirzah;

10 and Zimri went in and struck him and killed him in the twenty-seventh year of Asa king of Judah, and reigned in his place.

11 Then it came to pass, when he began to reign, as soon as he was seated on his throne, *that* he killed all the household of Baasha; he did not leave him one male, neither of his kinsmen nor of his friends.

12 Thus Zimri destroyed all the household of Baasha, according to the word of the LORD, which He spoke against Baasha by Jehu the prophet,

13 for all the sins of Baasha and the sins of Elah his son, by which they had sinned and by which they had made Israel sin, in provoking the LORD God of Israel to anger with their idols.

14 Now the rest of the acts of Elah, and all that he did, *are* they not written in the book of the chronicles of the kings of Israel?

Zimri Reigns in Israel

15 In the twenty-seventh year of Asa king of Judah, Zimri had reigned in Tirzah seven days. And the people *were* encamped against Gibbethon, which *belonged* to the Philistines.

16 Now the people *who were* encamped heard it said, "Zimri has conspired and also has killed the king." So all Israel made Omri, the commander of the army, king over Israel that day in the camp.

17 Then Omri and all Israel with him went up from Gibbethon, and they besieged Tirzah.

18 And it happened, when Zimri saw that the city was taken, that he went into the citadel of the king's house and burned the king's house down upon himself with fire, and died,

19 because of the sins which he had sinned in doing evil in the sight of the LORD, in walking in the way of Jeroboam, and in his sin which he had committed to make Israel sin.

20 Now the rest of the acts of Zimri, and the treason he committed, *are* they not written in the book of the chronicles of the kings of Israel?

Omri Reigns in Israel

21 Then the people of Israel were divided into two parts: half of the people followed Tibni the son of Ginath, to make him king, and half followed Omri.

22 But the people who followed Omri prevailed over the people who followed Tibni the son of Ginath. So Tibni died and Omri reigned.

23 In the thirty-first year of Asa king of Judah, Omri became king over Israel, *and reigned* twelve years. Six years he reigned in Tirzah.

24 And he bought the hill of Samaria from Shemer for two talents of silver; then he built on the hill, and called the name of the city which he built, Samaria, after the name of Shemer, owner of the hill.

25 Omri did evil in the eyes of the LORD, and did worse than all who *were* before him.

26 For he walked in all the ways of Jeroboam the son of Nebat, and in his sin by which he had made Israel sin, provoking the LORD God of Israel to anger with their idols.

27 Now the rest of the acts of Omri which he did, and the might that he showed, *are* they not written in the book of the chronicles of the kings of Israel?

28 So Omri rested with his fathers and

was buried in Samaria. Then Ahab his son reigned in his place.

Ahab Reigns in Israel

29 In the thirty-eighth year of Asa king of Judah, Ahab the son of Omri became king over Israel; and Ahab the son of Omri reigned over Israel in Samaria twenty-two years.
30 Now Ahab the son of Omri did evil in the sight of the LORD, more than all who *were* before him.
31 And it came to pass, as though it had been a trivial thing for him to walk in the sins of Jeroboam the son of Nebat, that he took as wife Jezebel the daughter of Ethbaal, king of the Sidonians; and he went and served Baal and worshiped him.
32 Then he set up an altar for Baal in the temple of Baal, which he had built in Samaria.
33 And Ahab made a wooden image.[31] Ahab did more to provoke the LORD God of Israel to anger than all the kings of Israel who were before him.
34 In his days Hiel of Bethel built Jericho. He laid its foundation with Abiram his firstborn, and with his youngest *son* Segub he set up its gates, according to the word of the LORD, which He had spoken through Joshua the son of Nun.[32]

Elijah Proclaims a Drought

17 And Elijah the Tishbite, of the inhabitants of Gilead, said to Ahab, "*As* the LORD God of Israel lives, before whom I stand, there shall not be dew nor rain these years, except at my word."
2 Then the word of the LORD came to him, saying,
3 "Get away from here and turn eastward, and hide by the Brook Cherith, which flows into the Jordan.
4 "And it will be *that* you shall drink from the brook, and I have commanded the ravens to feed you there."
5 So he went and did according to the word of the LORD, for he went and stayed by the Brook Cherith, which flows into the Jordan.
6 The ravens brought him bread and meat in the morning, and bread and meat in the evening; and he drank from the brook.
7 And it happened after a while that the brook dried up, because there had been no rain in the land.

Elijah and the Widow

8 Then the word of the LORD came to him, saying,
9 "Arise, go to Zarephath, which *belongs* to Sidon, and dwell there. See, I have commanded a widow there to provide for you."
10 So he arose and went to Zarephath. And when he came to the gate of the city, indeed a widow *was* there gathering sticks. And he called to her and said, "Please bring me a little water in a cup, that I may drink."
11 And as she was going to get *it*, he called to her and said, "Please bring me a morsel of bread in your hand."
12 Then she said, "As the LORD your God lives, I do not have bread, only a handful of flour in a bin, and a little oil in a jar; and see, I *am* gathering a couple of sticks that I may go in and prepare it for myself and my son, that we may eat it, and die."
13 And Elijah said to her, "Do not fear; go *and* do as you have said, but make me a small cake from it first, and bring *it* to me; and afterward make *some* for yourself and your son.
14 "For thus says the LORD God of Israel: 'The bin of flour shall not be used up, nor shall the jar of oil run dry, until the day the LORD sends rain on the earth.' "
15 So she went away and did according to the word of Elijah; and she and he and her household ate for *many* days.
16 The bin of flour was not used up, nor did the jar of oil run dry, according to the word of the LORD which He spoke by Elijah.

Elijah Revives the Widow's Son

17 Now it happened after these things *that* the son of the woman who owned the house became sick. And his sickness was so serious that there was no breath left in him.
18 So she said to Elijah, "What have I to do with you, O man of God? Have you come to me to bring my sin to remembrance, and to kill my son?"
19 And he said to her, "Give me your son." So he took him out of her arms and carried him to the upper room where he

was staying, and laid him on his own bed.
20 Then he cried out to the LORD and
said, "O LORD my God, have You also
brought tragedy on the widow with
whom I lodge, by killing her son?"
21 And he stretched himself out on the
child three times, and cried out to the
LORD and said, "O LORD my God, I
pray, let this child's soul come back to
him."
22 Then the LORD heard the voice of Elijah; and the soul of the child came back
to him, and he revived.
23 And Elijah took the child and brought
him down from the upper room into the
house, and gave him to his mother. And
Elijah said, "See, your son lives!"
24 Then the woman said to Elijah, "Now
by this I know that you *are* a man of
God, *and* that the word of the LORD in
your mouth *is* the truth."

Elijah's Message to Ahab

18 Now it came to pass *after* many
days that the word of the LORD
came to Elijah, in the third year, saying,
"Go, present yourself to Ahab, and I will
send rain on the earth."
2 So Elijah went to present himself to
Ahab; and *there was* a severe famine in
Samaria.
3 And Ahab had called Obadiah, who
was in charge of *his* house. (Now Obadiah feared the LORD greatly.
4 For so it was, while Jezebel massacred
the prophets of the LORD, that Obadiah
had taken one hundred prophets and hidden them, fifty to a cave, and had fed
them with bread and water.)
5 And Ahab had said to Obadiah, "Go
into the land to all the springs of water
and to all the brooks; perhaps we may
find grass to keep the horses and mules
alive, so that we will not have to kill any
livestock.
6 So they divided the land between
them to explore it; Ahab went one way
by himself, and Obadiah went another
way by himself.
7 Now as Obadiah was on his way, suddenly Elijah met him; and he recognized
him, and fell on his face, and said, "*Is*
that you, my lord Elijah?"
8 And he answered him, "*It is* I. Go,
tell your master, 'Elijah *is here*.' "
9 Then he said, "How have I sinned,

that you are delivering your servant into
the hand of Ahab, to kill me?
10 "*As* the LORD your God lives, there is
no nation or kingdom where my master
has not sent someone to hunt for you;
and when they said, '*He is* not *here*,' he
took an oath from the kingdom or nation
that they could not find you.
11 "And now you say, 'Go, tell your
master, "Elijah *is here*" '!
12 "And it shall come to pass, *as soon as*
I am gone from you, that the Spirit of the
LORD will carry you to a place I do not
know; so when I go and tell Ahab, and he
cannot find you, he will kill me. But I
your servant have feared the LORD from
my youth.
13 "Was it not reported to my lord what
I did when Jezebel killed the prophets of
the LORD, how I hid one hundred men
of the LORD's prophets, fifty to a cave,
and fed them with bread and water?
14 "And now you say, 'Go, tell your
master, "Elijah *is here*!" ' and he will kill
me."
15 Then Elijah said, "*As* the LORD of
hosts lives, before whom I stand, I will
surely present myself to him today."
16 So Obadiah went to meet Ahab, and
told him; and Ahab went to meet Elijah.
17 Then it happened, when Ahab saw
Elijah, that Ahab said to him, "*Is that*
you, O troubler of Israel?"
18 And he answered, "I have not troubled Israel, but you and your father's
house *have*, in that you have forsaken the
commandments of the LORD, and you
have followed the Baals.
19 "Now therefore, send *and* gather all
Israel to me on Mount Carmel, the four
hundred and fifty prophets of Baal, and
the four hundred prophets of Asherah,[33]
who eat at Jezebel's table."

Elijah's Mount Carmel Victory

20 So Ahab sent for all the children of
Israel, and gathered the prophets together
on Mount Carmel.
21 And Elijah came to all the people, and
said, "How long will you falter between
two opinions? If the LORD *is* God, follow
Him; but if Baal, *then* follow him." But
the people answered him not a word.
22 Then Elijah said to the people, "I
alone am left a prophet of the LORD; but
Baal's prophets *are* four hundred and
fifty men.

33 A Canaanite goddess

23 "Therefore let them give us two bulls; and let them choose one bull for themselves, cut it in pieces, and lay *it* on the wood, but put no fire *under it*; and I will prepare the other bull, and lay *it* on the wood, but put no fire *under it*.
24 "Then you call on the name of your gods, and I will call on the name of the LORD; and the God who answers by fire, He is God." So all the people answered and said, "It is well spoken."
25 Now Elijah said to the prophets of Baal, "Choose one bull for yourselves and prepare *it* first, for you *are* many; and call on the name of your god, but put no fire *under it*."
26 So they took the bull which was given them, and they prepared *it*, and called on the name of Baal from morning even till noon, saying, "O Baal, hear us!" But *there was* no voice; no one answered. And they leaped about the altar which they had made.
27 And so it was, at noon, that Elijah mocked them and said, "Cry aloud, for he *is* a god; either he is meditating, or he is busy, or he is on a journey, *or* perhaps he is sleeping and must be awakened."
28 So they cried aloud, and cut themselves, as was their custom, with knives and lances, until the blood gushed out on them.
29 And it was so, when midday was past, that they prophesied until the *time* of the offering of the *evening* sacrifice. But *there was* no voice; no one answered, no one paid attention.
30 Then Elijah said to all the people, "Come near to me." So all the people came near to him. And he repaired the altar of the LORD *that was* broken down.
31 And Elijah took twelve stones, according to the number of the tribes of the sons of Jacob, to whom the word of the LORD had come, saying, "Israel shall be your name."[34]
32 Then with the stones he built an altar in the name of the LORD; and he made a trench around the altar large enough to hold two seahs of seed.
33 And he put the wood in order, cut the bull in pieces, and laid *it* on the wood, and said, "Fill four waterpots with water, and pour *it* on the burnt sacrifice and on the wood."
34 Then he said, "Do *it* a second time,"

and they did *it* a second time; and he said, "Do *it* a third time," and they did *it* a third time.
35 So the water ran all around the altar; and he also filled the trench with water.
36 And it came to pass, at *the time of* the offering of the *evening* sacrifice, that Elijah the prophet came near and said, "LORD God of Abraham, Isaac, and Israel, let it be known this day that You *are* God in Israel, and *that* I *am* Your servant, and *that* I have done all these things at Your word.
37 "Hear me, O LORD, hear me, that this people may know that You *are* the LORD God, and *that* You have turned their hearts back *to You* again."
38 Then the fire of the LORD fell and consumed the burnt sacrifice, and the wood and the stones and the dust, and it licked up the water that *was* in the trench.
39 Now when all the people saw *it*, they fell on their faces; and they said, "The LORD, He *is* God! The LORD, He *is* God!"
40 And Elijah said to them, "Seize the prophets of Baal! Do not let one of them escape!" So they seized them; and Elijah brought them down to the Brook Kishon and executed them there.

The Drought Ends

41 Then Elijah said to Ahab, "Go up, eat and drink; for *there is* the sound of abundance of rain."
42 So Ahab went up to eat and drink. And Elijah went up to the top of Carmel; then he bowed down on the ground, and put his face between his knees,
43 and said to his servant, "Go up now, look toward the sea." So he went up and looked, and said, "There *is* nothing." And seven times he said, "Go again."
44 Then it came to pass the seventh *time*, that he said, "There is a cloud, as small as a man's hand, rising out of the sea!" So he said, "Go up, say to Ahab, 'Prepare *your chariot*, and go down before the rain stops you.'"
45 Now it happened in the meantime that the sky became black with clouds and wind, and there was a heavy rain. So Ahab rode away and went to Jezreel.
46 Then the hand of the LORD came upon Elijah; and he girded up his loins and ran ahead of Ahab to the entrance of Jezreel.

34 Compare Genesis 32:28

Elijah's Triumph

Have you ever known someone who, just when he seemed to succeed, fell flat on his face? Such a man was the Old Testament prophet, Elijah. But Elijah did not quit. He went on to have tremendous victories for God.

During the reign of King Ahab, the people of Israel turned to the pagan worship of Baal. Fashioned in the image of a calf, Baal was a nature god. It was thought that during a lightning storm, Baal was throwing his spear of fire from heaven. Thunder was caused by Baal clapping his hands to produce rain.

Following three years of famine, Elijah, who was called by God, directly challenged this false god, Baal. He called together the prophets of Baal in a contest to determine the one true God. A sacrifice was to be placed on an altar atop Mount Carmel. Then the true God would consume the sacrifice with fire. Despite the prophets' screaming, yelling, and cutting themselves for hours before their god, the altar and sacrifice remained untouched. However, Elijah, determined to reveal God's power, threw water over his sacrifice before sending up his prayers. Immediately God sent fire upon the altar consuming the sacrifice.

The contest of the sacrifice took place approximately from 3 to 6 p.m. After chasing the prophets some twenty miles, Elijah gained victory early in the morning. Undoubtedly, Elijah was emotionally, spiritually, and physically fatigued. News came to Elijah that Queen Jezebel (whose name means "princess of Baal") wanted to kill him. In this state, he made a rash decision and fled 167 miles to Beersheba. There, he wondered why God had failed him. Elijah's hopes for national repentance were gone. King Ahab and Jezebel's power seemed invincible. Elijah's self-respect was at its lowest point; he wanted to die.

Alone in the wilderness, God met Elijah's needs. First, God fed him, then inspired him by promising Elijah that He would be with him always. God strengthened him, turning Elijah's self-pity into power. God spoke to Elijah in a still, small voice at the opening of a cave. God asked him, "What are you doing here?" Elijah answered, "I alone am left; and they seek to take my life" (1 Kin. 19:13, 14). God assured him that he was not alone, for over seven thousand men in Israel had not bowed down to Baal. No matter what problem arose, Elijah and God were strong enough to overcome. Encouraged and strengthened by this time alone with God, Elijah returned to complete his ministry.

There are times in all our lives when, like Elijah, we are fatigued and exhausted that we make a decision that does not reflect our faith in God. Yet, like Elijah, we must retreat to find time alone with God to be strengthened and nourished. We must see God in famine and feast, in success and failure. Failure does not mean that God has abandoned us. It means He has a better idea.

It is possible for even God's greatest people to flee and doubt in times of stress and turmoil. When this happens, remember to be quiet before God. Listen to His still, small voice. His power will strengthen you to go out and, like Elijah, with God's help defeat any problem! Trying times are a time to triumph. That's try + umph!

Elijah Escapes from Jezebel

19 And Ahab told Jezebel all that Elijah had done, also how he had executed all the prophets with the sword.
2 Then Jezebel sent a messenger to Elijah, saying, "So let the gods do *to me*, and more also, if I do not make your life as the life of one of them by tomorrow about this time."
3 And when he saw *that*, he arose and ran for his life, and went to Beersheba, which *belongs* to Judah, and left his servant there.
4 But he himself went a day's journey into the wilderness, and came and sat down under a broom tree. And he prayed that he might die, and said, "It is enough! Now, LORD, take my life, for I *am* no better than my fathers!"
5 Then as he lay and slept under a broom tree, suddenly an angel[35] touched him, and said to him, "Arise *and* eat."
6 Then he looked, and *there* by his head *was* a cake baked on coals, and a jar of water. So he ate and drank, and lay down again.
7 And the angel[36] of the LORD came back the second time, and touched him, and said, "Arise *and* eat, because the journey *is* too great for you."
8 So he arose, and ate and drank; and he went in the strength of that food forty days and forty nights as far as Horeb, the mountain of God.
9 And there he went into a cave, and spent the night in that place; and behold, the word of the LORD *came* to him, and He said to him, "What are you doing here, Elijah?"
10 So he said, "I have been very zealous for the LORD God of hosts; for the children of Israel have forsaken Your covenant, torn down Your altars, and killed Your prophets with the sword. I alone am left; and they seek to take my life."

God's Revelation to Elijah

11 Then He said, "Go out, and stand on the mountain before the LORD." And behold, the LORD passed by, and a great and strong wind tore into the mountains and broke the rocks in pieces before the LORD, *but* the LORD *was* not in the wind; and after the wind an earthquake, *but* the LORD *was* not in the earthquake;
12 and after the earthquake a fire, *but* the LORD *was* not in the fire; and after the fire a still small voice.
13 So it was, when Elijah heard *it*, that he wrapped his face in his mantle and went out and stood in the entrance of the cave. And suddenly a voice *came* to him, and said, "What are you doing here, Elijah?"
14 So he said, "I have been very zealous for the LORD God of hosts; because the children of Israel have forsaken Your covenant, torn down Your altars, and killed Your prophets with the sword. I alone am left; and they seek to take my life."
15 Then the LORD said to him: "Go, return on your way to the Wilderness of Damascus; and when you arrive, anoint Hazael *as* king over Syria.
16 "Also you shall anoint Jehu the son of Nimshi *as* king over Israel. And Elisha the son of Shaphat of Abel Meholah you shall anoint *as* prophet in your place.
17 "It shall be *that* whoever escapes the sword of Hazael, Jehu will kill; and whoever escapes from the sword of Jehu, Elisha will kill.
18 "Yet I have reserved seven thousand in Israel, all whose knees have not bowed to Baal, and every mouth that has not kissed him."

Elisha Follows Elijah

19 So he departed from there, and found Elisha the son of Shaphat, who *was* plowing *with* twelve yoke *of oxen* before him, and he was with the twelfth. Then Elijah passed by him and threw his mantle on him.
20 And he left the oxen and ran after Elijah, and said, "Please let me kiss my father and my mother, and *then* I will follow you." And he said to him, "Go back again, for what have I done to you?"
21 So Elisha[37] turned back from him, and took a yoke of oxen and slaughtered them and boiled their flesh, using the oxen's equipment, and gave it to the people, and they ate. Then he arose and followed Elijah, and served him.

Ahab Defeats the Syrians

20 Now Ben-Hadad the king of Syria gathered all his forces together; *there were* thirty-two kings with him, with horses and chariots. And he went up and besieged Samaria, and made war against it.

35 Or *Angel*   36 Or *Angel*   37 Literally *he*

2 Then he sent messengers into the city to Ahab king of Israel, and said to him, "Thus says Ben-Hadad:
3 'Your silver and your gold *are* mine; your loveliest wives and children are mine.' "
4 And the king of Israel answered and said, "My lord, O king, just as you say, I and all that I have *are* yours."
5 Then the messengers came back and said, "Thus speaks Ben-Hadad, saying, 'Indeed I have sent to you, saying, "You shall deliver to me your silver and your gold, your wives and your children";
6 'but I will send my servants to you tomorrow about this time, and they shall search your house and the houses of your servants. And it shall be, *that* whatever is pleasant in your eyes, they shall put in their hands and take *it*.' "
7 Then the king of Israel called all the elders of the land, and said, "Notice, please, and see how this *man* seeks trouble, for he sent to me for my wives, my children, my silver, and my gold; and I did not deny him."
8 And all the elders and all the people said to him, "Do not listen or consent."
9 Therefore he said to the messengers of Ben-Hadad, "Tell my lord the king, 'All that you sent for to your servant the first time I will do, but this thing I cannot do.' " And the messengers departed and brought back word to him.
10 Then Ben-Hadad sent to him and said, "The gods do so to me, and more also, if enough dust is left of Samaria for a handful for each of the people who follow me."
11 So the king of Israel answered and said, "Tell *him*, 'Let not the one who puts on *his* armor boast like the one who takes *it off*.' "
12 And it happened when *Ben-Hadad* heard this message, as he and the kings *were* drinking at the command post, that he said to his servants, "Get ready." And they got ready to attack the city.
13 Suddenly a prophet approached Ahab king of Israel, saying, "Thus says the LORD: 'Have you seen all this great multitude? Behold, I will deliver it into your hand today, and you shall know that I *am* the LORD.' "
14 So Ahab said, "By whom?" And he said, "Thus says the LORD: 'By the young leaders of the provinces.' " Then he said,

"Who will set the battle in order?" And he answered, "You."
15 Then he mustered the young leaders of the provinces, and there were two hundred and thirty-two; and after them he mustered all the people, all the children of Israel—seven thousand.
16 So they went out at noon. Meanwhile Ben-Hadad and the thirty-two kings helping him were getting drunk at the command post.
17 The young leaders of the provinces went out first. And Ben-Hadad sent out *a patrol*, and they told him, saying, "Men are coming out of Samaria!"
18 So he said, "If they have come out for peace, take them alive; and if they have come out for war, take them alive."
19 Then these young leaders of the provinces went out of the city with the army which followed them.
20 And each one killed his man; so the Syrians fled, and Israel pursued them; and Ben-Hadad the king of Syria escaped on a horse with the cavalry.
21 Then the king of Israel went out and attacked the horses and chariots, and killed the Syrians with a great slaughter.
22 And the prophet came to the king of Israel and said to him, "Go, strengthen yourself; take note, and see what you should do, for in the spring of the year the king of Syria will come up against you."

The Syrians Again Defeated

23 Then the servants of the king of Syria said to him, "Their gods *are* gods of the hills. Therefore they were stronger than we; but if we fight against them in the plain, *then* surely we will be stronger than they.
24 "So do this thing: Dismiss the kings, each from his position, and put captains in their places;
25 "and you shall muster an army like the army that you have lost, horse for horse and chariot for chariot. Then we will fight against them in the plain; surely we will be stronger than they." And he listened to their voice and did so.
26 So it was, in the spring of the year, that Ben-Hadad mustered the Syrians and went up to Aphek to fight against Israel.
27 And the children of Israel were mustered and given provisions, and they went

against them. Now the children of Israel encamped before them like two little flocks of goats, while the Syrians filled the countryside.

28 Then a man of God came and spoke to the king of Israel, and said, "Thus says the LORD: 'Because the Syrians have said, "The LORD *is* God of the hills, but He *is* not God of the valleys," therefore I will deliver all this great multitude into your hand, and you shall know that I *am* the LORD.' "

29 And they encamped opposite each other for seven days. So it was that on the seventh day the battle was joined; and the children of Israel killed one hundred thousand foot soldiers *of* the Syrians in one day.

30 But the rest fled to Aphek, into the city; then a wall fell on twenty-seven thousand of the men *who were* left. And Ben-Hadad fled and went into the city, into an inner chamber.

Ahab's Treaty with Ben-Hadad

31 And his servants said to him, "Look now, we have heard that the kings of the house of Israel *are* merciful kings. Please, let us put sackcloth around our waists and ropes around our heads, and go out to the king of Israel; perhaps he will spare your life."

32 So they wore sackcloth around their waists and *put* ropes around their heads, and came to the king of Israel and said, "Your servant Ben-Hadad says, 'Please let me live.' " And he said, "*Is* he still alive? He *is* my brother."

33 Now the men were diligently watching to see whether *any sign of mercy would come* from him; and they quickly grasped *at this word* and said, "Your brother Ben-Hadad." So he said, "Go, bring him." Then Ben-Hadad came out to him; and he had him come up into the chariot.

34 Then *Ben-Hadad* said to him, "The cities which my father took from your father I will restore; and you may set up marketplaces for yourself in Damascus, as my father did in Samaria." Then *Ahab said*, "I will send you away with this treaty." So he made a treaty with him and sent him away.

Ahab Condemned

35 Now a certain man of the sons of the prophets said to his neighbor by the word of the LORD, "Strike me, please." And the man refused to strike him.

36 Then he said to him, "Because you have not obeyed the voice of the LORD, surely, as soon as you depart from me, a lion shall kill you." And as soon as he left him, a lion found him and killed him.

37 And he found another man, and said, "Strike me, please." So the man struck him, inflicting a wound.

38 Then the prophet departed and waited for the king by the road, and disguised himself with a bandage over his eyes.

39 Now as the king passed by, he cried out to the king and said, "Your servant went out into the midst of the battle; and there, a man came over and brought a man to me, and said, 'Guard this man; if by any means he is missing, your life shall be for his life, or else you shall pay a talent of silver.'

40 "And while your servant was busy here and there, he was gone." And the king of Israel said to him, "So *shall* your judgment *be*; you yourself have decided *it*."

41 Then he hastened to take the bandage away from his eyes; and the king of Israel recognized him as one of the prophets.

42 And he said to him, "Thus says the LORD: 'Because you have let slip out of *your* hand a man whom I appointed to utter destruction, therefore your life shall go for his life, and your people for his people.' "

43 So the king of Israel went to his house sullen and displeased, and came to Samaria.

Naboth Is Murdered for His Vineyard

21 And it came to pass after these things *that* Naboth the Jezreelite had a vineyard which *was* in Jezreel, next to the palace of Ahab king of Samaria.

2 So Ahab spoke to Naboth, saying, "Give me your vineyard, that I may have it for a vegetable garden, because it *is* near, next to my house; and for it I will give you a vineyard better than it. *Or*, if it seems good to you, I will give you its worth in money."

3 And Naboth said to Ahab, "The LORD forbid that I should give the inheritance of my fathers to you!"

4 So Ahab went into his house sullen and displeased because of the word which

Naboth the Jezreelite had spoken to him; for he had said, "I will not give you the inheritance of my fathers." And he lay down on his bed, and turned away his face, and would eat no food.

5 But Jezebel his wife came to him, and said to him, "Why is your spirit so sullen that you eat no food?"

6 So he said to her, "Because I spoke to Naboth the Jezreelite, and said to him, 'Give me your vineyard for money; or else, if it pleases you, I will give you *another* vineyard for it.' And he answered, 'I will not give you my vineyard.'"

7 Then Jezebel his wife said to him, "You now exercise authority over Israel! Arise *and* eat food, and let your heart be cheerful; I will give you the vineyard of Naboth the Jezreelite."

8 So she wrote letters in Ahab's name, sealed *them* with his seal, and sent the letters to the elders and the nobles who *were* dwelling in the city with Naboth.

9 And she wrote in the letters, saying, "Proclaim a fast, and seat Naboth with high honor among the people;

10 "and seat two men, scoundrels, before him to bear witness against him, saying, 'You have blasphemed God and the king.' *Then* take him out, and stone him, that he may die."

11 So the men of his city, the elders and nobles who were inhabitants of his city, did as Jezebel had sent to them, as it *was* written in the letters which she had sent to them.

12 They proclaimed a fast, and seated Naboth with high honor among the people.

13 And two men, scoundrels, came in and sat before him; and the scoundrels witnessed against him, against Naboth, in the presence of the people, saying, "Naboth has blasphemed God and the king!" Then they took him outside the city and stoned him with stones, so that he died.

14 Then they sent to Jezebel, saying, "Naboth has been stoned and is dead."

15 And it came to pass, when Jezebel heard that Naboth had been stoned and was dead, that Jezebel said to Ahab, "Arise, take possession of the vineyard of Naboth the Jezreelite, which he refused to give you for money; for Naboth is not alive, but dead."

16 So it was, when Ahab heard that Naboth was dead, that Ahab got up and went down to take possession of the vineyard of Naboth the Jezreelite.

The LORD Condemns Ahab

17 Then the word of the LORD came to Elijah the Tishbite, saying,

18 "Arise, go down to meet Ahab king of Israel, who *lives* in Samaria. There *he is*, in the vineyard of Naboth, where he has gone down to take possession of it.

19 "You shall speak to him, saying, 'Thus says the LORD: "Have you murdered and also taken possession?"' And you shall speak to him, saying, 'Thus says the LORD: "In the place where dogs licked the blood of Naboth, dogs shall lick your blood, even yours."'"

20 Then Ahab said to Elijah, "Have you found me, O my enemy?" And he answered, "I have found *you*, because you have sold yourself to do evil in the sight of the LORD:

21 'Behold, I will bring calamity on you. I will take away your posterity, and will cut off from Ahab every male in Israel, both bond and free.

22 'I will make your house like the house of Jeroboam the son of Nebat, and like the house of Baasha the son of Ahijah, because of the provocation with which you have provoked *Me* to anger, and made Israel sin.'

23 "And concerning Jezebel the LORD also spoke, saying, 'The dogs shall eat Jezebel by the wall of Jezreel.'

24 "The dogs shall eat whoever belongs to Ahab and dies in the city, and the birds of the air shall eat whoever dies in the field."

25 But there was no one like Ahab who sold himself to do wickedness in the sight of the LORD, because Jezebel his wife stirred him up.

26 And he behaved very abominably in following idols, according to all *that* the Amorites had done, whom the LORD had cast out before the children of Israel.

27 So it was, when Ahab heard those words, that he tore his clothes and put sackcloth on his body, and fasted and lay in sackcloth, and went about mourning.

28 And the word of the LORD came to Elijah the Tishbite, saying,

29 "See how Ahab has humbled himself before Me? Because he has humbled himself before Me, I will not bring the

calamity in his days; *but* in the days of his son I will bring the calamity on his house."

Micaiah Warns Ahab

22 Now three years passed without war between Syria and Israel.
2 Then it came to pass, in the third year, that Jehoshaphat the king of Judah went down to *visit* the king of Israel.
3 And the king of Israel said to his servants, "Do you know that Ramoth in Gilead *is* ours, but we hesitate to take it out of the hand of the king of Syria?"
4 So he said to Jehoshaphat, "Will you go with me to fight at Ramoth Gilead?" And Jehoshaphat said to the king of Israel, "I *am* as you *are*, my people as your people, my horses as your horses."
5 And Jehoshaphat said to the king of Israel, "Please inquire for the word of the LORD today."
6 Then the king of Israel gathered the prophets together, about four hundred men, and said to them, "Shall I go against Ramoth Gilead to fight, or shall I refrain?" So they said, "Go up, for the Lord will deliver *it* into the hand of the king."
7 And Jehoshaphat said, "*Is there* not still a prophet of the LORD here, that we may inquire of Him?"[38]
8 So the king of Israel said to Jehoshaphat, "*There is* still one man, Micaiah the son of Imlah, by whom we may inquire of the LORD; but I hate him, because he does not prophesy good concerning me, but evil." And Jehoshaphat said, "Let not the king say such things!"
9 Then the king of Israel called an officer and said, "Bring Micaiah the son of Imlah quickly!"
10 The king of Israel and Jehoshaphat the king of Judah, having put on *their* robes, sat each on his throne, at a threshing floor at the entrance of the gate of Samaria; and all the prophets prophesied before them.
11 Now Zedekiah the son of Chenaanah had made horns of iron for himself; and he said, "Thus says the LORD: 'With these you shall gore the Syrians until they are destroyed.' "
12 And all the prophets prophesied so, saying, "Go up to Ramoth Gilead and prosper, for the LORD will deliver *it* into the king's hand."

13 Then the messenger who had gone to call Micaiah spoke to him, saying, "Now listen, the words of the prophets with one accord *encourage* the king. Please, let your word be like *the word of* one of them, and speak encouragement."
14 And Micaiah said, "*As* the LORD lives, whatever the LORD says to me, that I will speak."
15 Then he came to the king; and the king said to him, "Micaiah, shall we go to war against Ramoth Gilead, or shall we refrain?" And he answered him, "Go and prosper, for the LORD will deliver *it* into the hand of the king!"
16 So the king said to him, "How many times shall I make you swear that you tell me nothing but the truth in the name of the LORD?"
17 Then he said, "I saw all Israel scattered on the mountains, as sheep that have no shepherd. And the LORD said, 'These have no master. Let each return to his house in peace.' "
18 And the king of Israel said to Jehoshaphat, "Did I not tell you that he would not prophesy good concerning me, but evil?"
19 Then Micaiah[39] said, "Therefore hear the word of the LORD: I saw the LORD sitting on His throne, and all the host of heaven standing by, on His right hand and on His left.
20 "And the LORD said, 'Who will persuade Ahab to go up, that he may fall at Ramoth Gilead?' So one spoke in this manner, and another spoke in that manner.
21 "Then a spirit came forward and stood before the LORD, and said, 'I will persuade him.'
22 "The LORD said to him, 'In what way?' So he said, 'I will go out and be a lying spirit in the mouth of all his prophets.' And He said, 'You shall persuade *him*, and also prevail. Go out and do so.'
23 "Now therefore, look! The LORD has put a lying spirit in the mouth of all these prophets of yours, and the LORD has declared disaster against you."
24 Then Zedekiah the son of Chenaanah went near and struck Micaiah on the cheek, and said, "Which way did the spirit from the LORD go from me to speak to you?"
25 And Micaiah said, "Indeed, you shall

see on that day when you go into an inner chamber to hide!"

26 Then the king of Israel said, "Take Micaiah, and return him to Amon the governor of the city and to Joash the king's son;

27 "and say, 'Thus says the king: "Put this *fellow* in prison, and feed him with bread of affliction and water of affliction, until I come in peace." ' "

28 Then Micaiah said, "If you ever return in peace, the LORD has not spoken by me." And he said, "Take heed, all you people!"

Ahab Dies in Battle

29 So the king of Israel and Jehoshaphat the king of Judah went up to Ramoth Gilead.

30 And the king of Israel said to Jehoshaphat, "I will disguise myself and go into battle; but you put on your robes." So the king of Israel disguised himself and went into battle.

31 Now the king of Syria had commanded the thirty-two captains of his chariots, saying, "Fight with no one small or great, but only with the king of Israel."

32 So it was, when the captains of the chariots saw Jehoshaphat, that they said, "Surely it *is* the king of Israel!" Therefore they turned aside to fight against him, and Jehoshaphat cried out.

33 And it happened, when the captains of the chariots saw that it *was* not the king of Israel, that they turned back from pursuing him.

34 Now a *certain* man drew a bow at random, and struck the king of Israel between the joints of his armor. So he said to the driver of his chariot, "Turn around and take me out of the battle, for I am wounded."

35 The battle increased that day; and the king was propped up in his chariot, facing the Syrians, and died at evening. The blood ran out from the wound onto the floor of the chariot.

36 Then, as the sun was going down, a shout went throughout the army, saying, "Every man to his city, and every man to his own country!"

37 So the king died, and was brought to Samaria. And they buried the king in Samaria.

38 Then *someone* washed the chariot at a pool in Samaria, and the dogs licked up his blood while the harlots bathed,[40] according to the word of the LORD which He had spoken.

39 Now the rest of the acts of Ahab and all that he did, the ivory house which he built and all the cities that he built, *are* they not written in the book of the chronicles of the kings of Israel?

40 So Ahab rested with his fathers. Then Ahaziah his son reigned in his place.

Jehoshaphat Reigns in Judah

41 Now Jehoshaphat the son of Asa had become king over Judah in the fourth year of Ahab king of Israel.

42 Jehoshaphat *was* thirty-five years old when he became king, and he reigned twenty-five years in Jerusalem. His mother's name *was* Azubah the daughter of Shilhi.

43 And he walked in all the ways of his father Asa. He did not turn aside from them, doing *what was* right in the eyes of the LORD. Nevertheless the high places were not taken away, *for* the people offered sacrifices and burned incense on the high places.

44 Also Jehoshaphat made peace with the king of Israel.

45 Now the rest of the acts of Jehoshaphat, the might that he showed, and how he made war, *are* they not written in the book of the chronicles of the kings of Judah?

46 And the rest of the perverted persons,[41] who remained in the days of his father Asa, he banished from the land.

47 *There was* then no king in Edom, only a deputy of the king.

48 Jehoshaphat made merchant ships to go to Ophir for gold; but they never sailed, for the ships were wrecked at Ezion Geber.

49 Then Ahaziah the son of Ahab said to Jehoshaphat, "Let my servants go with your servants in the ships." But Jehoshaphat would not.

50 And Jehoshaphat rested with his fathers, and was buried with his fathers in the City of David his father. Then Jehoram his son reigned in his place.

Ahaziah Reigns in Israel

51 Ahaziah the son of Ahab became king

---

40 Syriac and Targum read *they washed his armor.*

41 Hebrew *qedeshim,* that is, those practicing sodomy and prostitution in religious rituals

over Israel in Samaria in the seventeenth year of Jehoshaphat king of Judah, and reigned two years over Israel.
52 He did evil in the sight of the LORD, and walked in the way of his father and in the way of his mother and in the way of Jeroboam the son of Nebat, who had made Israel sin;
53 for he served Baal and worshiped him, and provoked the LORD God of Israel to anger, according to all that his father had done.

Introduction to Second Kings

In the time span of Second Kings, the people lived in a world of constant change. Uncertainty and insecurity dominated their lives. No sooner would one invading army pour over the land than another neighboring kingdom would ravage their cities. The divided monarchy, Judah and Israel, warred against each other and other foreign nations. One God-fearing ruler would shortly be followed with a godless king who would turn the hearts of the people to the worship of false gods, bringing upon them the negative results.

But God would not give up on His people. He provided many leaders to keep His light shining. Such prophets as Elijah and Elisha encouraged the people to remain committed to their faith in God and to turn from foreign, pagan influences.

Then the king stood by a pillar and made a covenant before the LORD, to follow the LORD and to keep His commandments and His testimonies and His statutes, with all *his* heart and all *his* soul, to perform the words of this covenant that were written in this book. And all the people took their stand for the covenant.

(2 Kin. 23:3)

Second Kings reveals that life is a record of choices. It is also the confidence that God is able to turn negatives into positives, rebellion into reform, and captivity into freedom! Even at the close of the book with the people in captivity in Babylon, God placed the ruler of Israel in a position of prominence, preparing the way for the people's freedom. Second Kings is a book of confidence that God will never leave or forsake His people.

The Second Book of the

Kings

God Judges Ahaziah

MOAB rebelled against Israel after the death of Ahab. 2 Now Ahaziah fell through the lattice of his upper room in Samaria, and was injured; so he sent messengers and said to them, "Go, inquire of Baal-Zebub, the god of Ekron, whether I shall recover from this injury."

3 But the angel[1] of the LORD said to Elijah the Tishbite, "Arise, go up to meet the messengers of the king of Samaria, and say to them, 'Is it because there is no God in Israel that you are going to inquire of Baal-Zebub, the god of Ekron?'

4 "Now therefore, thus says the LORD: 'You shall not come down from the bed to which you have gone up, but you shall surely die.' " So Elijah departed.

5 And when the messengers returned to him, he said to them, "Why have you come back?"

6 So they said to him, "A man came up to meet us, and said to us, 'Go, return to the king who sent you, and say to him, "Thus says the LORD: 'Is it because there is no God in Israel that you are sending to inquire of Baal-Zebub, the god of Ekron? Therefore you shall not come down from the bed to which you have gone up, but you shall surely die.' " ' "

7 Then he said to them, "What kind of man was it who came up to meet you and told you these words?"

8 So they answered him, "He was a hairy man, and wore a leather belt around his waist." And he said, "It is Elijah the Tishbite."

9 Then the king sent to him a captain of fifty with his fifty men. So he went up to him; and there he was, sitting on the top of a hill. And he spoke to him: "Man of God, the king has said, 'Come down!' "

10 So Elijah answered and said to the captain of fifty, "If I am a man of God, then let fire come down from heaven and consume you and your fifty men." And fire came down from heaven and consumed him and his fifty.

11 Then he sent to him another captain of fifty with his fifty men. And he answered and said to him: "Man of God, thus has the king said, 'Come down quickly!' "

12 So Elijah answered and said to them, "If I am a man of God, let fire come down from heaven and consume you and your fifty men." And the fire of God came down from heaven and consumed him and his fifty.

13 Again, he sent a third captain of fifty with his fifty men. And the third captain of fifty went up, and came and fell on his knees before Elijah, and pleaded with him, and said to him: "Man of God, please let my life and the life of these fifty servants of yours be precious in your sight.

14 "Look, fire has come down from heaven and burned up the first two captains of fifties with their fifties. But let my life now be precious in your sight."

15 And the angel[2] of the LORD said to Elijah, "Go down with him; do not be afraid of him." So he arose and went down with him to the king.

16 Then he said to him, "Thus says the LORD: 'Because you have sent messengers to inquire of Baal-Zebub, the god of Ekron, is it because there is no God in Israel to inquire of His word? Therefore you shall not come down from the bed to which you have gone up, but you shall surely die.' "

17 So Ahaziah[3] died according to the word of the LORD which Elijah had spoken. Because he had no son, Jehoram[4] became king in his place, in the second year of Jehoram the son of Jehoshaphat, king of Judah.

18 Now the rest of the acts of Ahaziah which he did, are they not written in the book of the chronicles of the kings of Israel?

Elijah Ascends to Heaven

2 And it came to pass, when the LORD was about to take up Elijah into

1 Or *Angel*   2 Or *Angel*   3 Literally *he*   4 The son of Ahab king of Israel (compare 3:1)

heaven by a whirlwind, that Elijah went with Elisha from Gilgal.
2 Then Elijah said to Elisha, "Stay here, please, for the LORD has sent me on to Bethel." And Elisha said, "*As* the LORD lives, and *as* your soul lives, I will not leave you!" So they went down to Bethel.
3 And the sons of the prophets who *were* at Bethel came out to Elisha, and said to him, "Do you know that the LORD will take away your master from over you today?" And he said, "Yes, I know; keep silent!"
4 Then Elijah said to him, "Elisha, stay here, please, for the LORD has sent me on to Jericho." And he said, "*As* the LORD lives, and *as* your soul lives, I will not leave you!" So they came to Jericho.
5 And the sons of the prophets who *were* at Jericho came to Elisha and said to him, "Do you know that the LORD will take away your master from over you today?" So he answered, "Yes, I know; keep silent!"
6 Then Elijah said to him, "Stay here, please, for the LORD has sent me on to the Jordan." And he said, "*As* the LORD lives, and *as* your soul lives, I will not leave you!" So the two of them went on.
7 And fifty men of the sons of the prophets went and stood facing *them* at a distance, while the two of them stood by the Jordan.
8 Now Elijah took his mantle, rolled *it* up, and struck the water; and it was divided this way and that, so that the two of them crossed over on dry ground.
9 And so it was, when they had crossed over, that Elijah said to Elisha, "Ask! What may I do for you, before I am taken away from you?" And Elisha said, "Please let a double portion of your spirit be upon me."
10 So he said, "You have asked a hard thing. *Nevertheless*, if you see me *when I am* taken from you, it shall be so for you; but if not, it shall not be *so*."
11 Then it happened, as they continued on and talked, that suddenly a chariot of fire *appeared* with horses of fire, and separated the two of them; and Elijah went up by a whirlwind into heaven.
12 Now Elisha saw *it*, and he cried out, "My father, my father, the chariot of Israel and its horsemen!" So he saw him

no more. And he took hold of his own clothes and tore them into two pieces.
13 He also took up the mantle of Elijah that had fallen from him, and went back and stood by the bank of the Jordan.
14 Then he took the mantle of Elijah that had fallen from him, and struck the water, and said, "Where *is* the LORD God of Elijah?" And when he also had struck the water, it was divided this way and that; and Elisha crossed over.
15 Now when the sons of the prophets who *were* from Jericho saw him, they said, "The spirit of Elijah rests on Elisha." And they came to meet him, and bowed to the ground before him.
16 Then they said to him, "Look now, there are fifty strong men with your servants. Please let them go and search for your master, lest perhaps the Spirit of the LORD has taken him up and cast him upon some mountain or into some valley." And he said, "You shall not send anyone."
17 But when they urged him till he was ashamed, he said, "Send *them* out." Therefore they sent fifty men, and they searched for three days but did not find him.
18 And when they came back to him, for he had stayed in Jericho, he said to them, "Did I not say to you, 'Do not go'?"

Elisha Performs Miracles

19 Then the men of the city said to Elisha, "Please notice, the situation of this city *is* pleasant, as my lord sees; but the water *is* bad, and the ground barren."
20 And he said, "Bring me a new bowl, and put salt in it." So they brought *it* to him.
21 Then he went out to the source of the water, and cast in the salt there, and said, "Thus says the LORD: 'I have healed this water; from it there shall be no more death or barrenness.' "
22 So the water remains healed to this day, according to the saying of Elisha which he spoke.
23 And he went up from there to Bethel; and as he was going up the road, some youths came from the city and mocked him, and said to him, "Go up, you baldhead! Go up, you baldhead!"
24 So he turned around and looked at them, and pronounced a curse on them in the name of the LORD. And two female

bears came out of the woods and mauled forty-two of the youths.

25 Then he went from there to Mount Carmel, and from there he returned to Samaria.

Moab Rebels Against Israel

3 Now Jehoram the son of Ahab became king over Israel at Samaria in the eighteenth year of Jehoshaphat king of Judah, and reigned twelve years.

2 And he did evil in the sight of the LORD, but not like his father and mother; for he put away the *sacred* pillar of Baal that his father had made.

3 Nevertheless he persisted in the sins of Jeroboam the son of Nebat, who had made Israel sin; he did not depart from them.

4 Now Mesha king of Moab was a sheepbreeder, and he regularly paid the king of Israel one hundred thousand lambs and the wool of one hundred thousand rams.

5 But it happened, when Ahab died, that the king of Moab rebelled against the king of Israel.

6 So King Jehoram went out of Samaria at that time and mustered all Israel.

7 Then he went and sent to Jehoshaphat king of Judah, saying, "The king of Moab has rebelled against me. Will you go with me to fight against Moab?" And he said, "I will go up; I *am* as you *are*, my people as your people, my horses as your horses."

8 And he said, "Which way shall we go up?" And he answered, "By way of the Wilderness of Edom."

9 So the king of Israel went with the king of Judah and the king of Edom, and they marched on that roundabout route seven days; and there was no water for the army, nor for the animals that followed them.

10 And the king of Israel said, "Alas! For the LORD has called these three kings together to deliver them into the hand of Moab."

11 But Jehoshaphat said, "*Is there* no prophet of the LORD here, that we may inquire of the LORD by him?" And one of the servants of the king of Israel answered and said, "Elisha the son of Shaphat *is* here, who poured water on the hands of Elijah."

12 And Jehoshaphat said, "The word of the LORD is with him." So the king of Israel and Jehoshaphat and the king of Edom went down to him.

13 Then Elisha said to the king of Israel, "What have I to do with you? Go to the prophets of your father and the prophets of your mother." And the king of Israel said to him, "No, for the LORD has called these three kings *together* to deliver them into the hand of Moab."

14 And Elisha said, "*As* the LORD of hosts lives, before whom I stand, surely were it not that I regard the presence of Jehoshaphat king of Judah, I would not look at you, nor see you.

15 "But now bring me a musician." And it happened, when the musician played, that the hand of the LORD came upon him.

16 And he said, "Thus says the LORD: 'Make this valley full of ditches.'

17 "For thus says the LORD: 'You shall not see wind, nor shall you see rain; yet that valley shall be filled with water, so that you, your cattle, and your animals may drink.'

18 "And this is *but* a trivial thing in the sight of the LORD; He will also deliver the Moabites into your hand.

19 "Also you shall attack every fortified city and every choice city, and shall cut down every good tree, and stop up every spring of water, and ruin every good piece of land with stones."

20 Now it happened in the morning, when the grain offering was offered, that suddenly water came by way of Edom, and the land was filled with water.

21 And when all the Moabites heard that the kings had come up to fight against them, all who were able to bear arms and older were gathered; and they stood at the border.

22 Then they rose up early in the morning, and the sun was shining on the water; and the Moabites saw the water on the other side *as* red as blood.

23 And they said, "This is blood; the kings have surely struck swords and have killed one another; now therefore, Moab, to the spoil!"

24 So when they came to the camp of Israel, Israel rose up and attacked the Moabites, so that they fled before them; and they entered *their* land, killing the Moabites.

25 Then they destroyed the cities, and

each man threw a stone on every good piece of land and filled it; and they stopped up all the springs of water and cut down all the good trees, except that they left *intact* the stones of Kir Haraseth. However the slingers surrounded and attacked it.

26 And when the king of Moab saw that the battle was too intense for him, he took with him seven hundred men who drew swords, to break through to the king of Edom, but they could not.

27 Then he took his eldest son who would have reigned in his place, and offered him *as* a burnt offering upon the wall; and there was great indignation against Israel. So they departed from him and returned to *their own* land.

Elisha and the Widow's Oil

4 A certain woman of the wives of the sons of the prophets cried out to Elisha, saying, "Your servant my husband is dead, and you know that your servant feared the LORD. And the creditor is coming to take my two sons to be his slaves."

2 So Elisha said to her, "What shall I do for you? Tell me, what do you have in the house?" And she said, "Your maidservant has nothing in the house but a jar of oil."

3 Then he said, "Go, borrow vessels from everywhere, from all your neighbors—empty vessels; do not gather just a few.

4 "And when you have come in, you shall shut the door behind you and your sons; then pour it into all those vessels, and set aside the full ones."

5 So she went from him and shut the door behind her and her sons, who brought *the vessels* to her; and she poured *it* out.

6 Now it came to pass, when the vessels were full, that she said to her son, "Bring me another vessel." And he said to her, "*There is* not another vessel." So the oil ceased.

7 Then she came and told the man of God. And he said, "Go, sell the oil and pay your debt; and you *and* your sons live on the rest."

Elisha Raises the Shunammite's Son

8 Now it happened one day that Elisha went to Shunem, where there *was* a nota-

ble woman, and she constrained him to eat some food. So it was, as often as he passed by, *that* he turned in there to eat some food.

9 And she said to her husband, "Look now, I know that this *is* a holy man of God, who passes by us regularly.

10 "Please, let us make a small upper room on the wall; and let us put a bed for him there, and a table and a chair and a lampstand; so it will be, whenever he comes to us, he can turn in there."

11 And it happened one day that he came there, and he turned in to the upper room and lay down there.

12 Then he said to Gehazi his servant, "Call this Shunammite woman." When he had called her, she stood before him.

13 And he said to him, "Say now to her, 'Look, you have been concerned for us with all this care. What *can I* do for you? Do you want me to speak on your behalf to the king or to the commander of the army?' " And she answered, "I dwell among my own people."

14 So he said, "What then *is* to be done for her?" And Gehazi answered, "Actually, she has no son, and her husband is old."

15 And he said, "Call her." When he had called her, she stood in the doorway.

16 Then he said, "About this time next year you shall embrace a son." And she said, "No, my lord. Man of God, do not lie to your maidservant!"

17 And the woman conceived, and bore a son when the appointed time had come, of which Elisha had told her.

18 So the child grew. Now it happened one day that he went out to his father, to the reapers.

19 And he said to his father, "My head, my head!" So he said to a servant, "Carry him to his mother."

20 When he had taken him and brought him to his mother, he sat on her knees till noon, and *then* died.

21 And she went up and laid him on the bed of the man of God, shut *the door* upon him, and went out.

22 Then she called to her husband, and said, "Please send me one of the young men and one of the donkeys, that I may run to the man of God and come back."

23 So he said, "Why are you going to him today? *It is* neither the New Moon

I Say to You "Arise"

At the base of Mount Moreh in the Jezreel Valley is the ancient city of Nain. Due to its location overlooking the fertile valley with springs, the city's name means "pleasant."

One day, as Jesus approached the city's gate, a large funeral procession was in progress. The burial was for the only son of a widow. Jesus moved through the mourning crowd toward the coffin and stopped the pallbearers. Turning to the widow, who had no chance for another son, Jesus comforted her, saying, "Do not weep." Then Jesus touched the coffin and said, "Young man, I say to you, arise" (Luke 7:14). Immediately, the son sat up and began to speak.

Astonished, the crowd ran throughout the countryside exclaiming that a prophet had raised the boy from the dead. Most certainly, the New Testament inhabitants of Nain recalled a similar event which took place hundreds of years earlier on the other side of Mount Moreh in the village of Shunem, only one mile from Nain. The great prophet Elisha had entered the house of the Shunammite woman whose son was also dead. Under God's command, Elisha breathed life back into her son, raising him from the dead. Perhaps, the amazed people considered Jesus to be the prophet Elisha.

What a beautiful parallel of God's power over death! Of course Jesus was much more than the prophet. He was the fulfillment of the prophet's messages. Even today, Jesus is fulfilling the promises He gave when He said, "Whoever lives and believes in Me shall never die" (John 11:26).

Jesus promises to raise us from the dead, not only physically but spiritually and emotionally. When we are depressed and have given up hope, Jesus brings new life to our dreams. In our most desperate time of need, Jesus says to us, "Do not weep."

His promise of eternal life is our assurance that we have been given the ultimate victory over death. Allow Jesus to do the impossible in your life. Heed His call when He says, "I say to you, arise!"

nor the Sabbath." And she said, "*It is* well."

24 Then she saddled a donkey, and said to her servant, "Drive, and go forward; do not slacken the pace for me unless I tell you."

25 So she departed, and went to the man of God at Mount Carmel.

And so it was, when the man of God saw her afar off, that he said to his servant Gehazi, "Look, *there is* the Shunammite woman.

26 "Please run now to meet her, and say to her, '*Is it* well with you? *Is it* well with your husband? *Is it* well with the child?' " And she answered, "*It is* well."

27 Now when she came to the man of God at the hill, she caught him by the feet, but Gehazi came near to push her away. But the man of God said, "Let her alone; for her soul *is* in deep distress, and the LORD has hidden *it* from me, and has not told me."

28 And she said, "Did I ask a son of my lord? Did I not say, 'Do not deceive me'?"

29 Then he said to Gehazi, "Get yourself ready, and take my staff in your hand, and be on your way. If you meet anyone, do not greet him; and if anyone greets you, do not answer him; but lay my staff on the face of the child."

30 And the mother of the child said, "*As* the LORD lives, and *as* your soul lives, I will not leave you." So he arose and followed her.

31 Now Gehazi went on ahead of them, and laid the staff on the face of the child; but *there was* neither voice nor hearing. Therefore he went back to meet him, and told him, saying, "The child has not awakened."

32 And when Elisha came into the house, there was the child, lying dead on his bed.

33 He went in therefore, shut the door behind the two of them, and prayed to the LORD.

34 And he went up and lay on the child, and put his mouth on his mouth, his eyes on his eyes, and his hands on his hands; and he stretched himself out on the child, and the flesh of the child became warm.

35 He returned and walked back and forth in the house, and again went up and stretched himself out on him; then the child sneezed seven times, and the child opened his eyes.

36 And he called Gehazi and said, "Call this Shunammite woman." So he called her. And when she came in to him, he said, "Pick up your son."

37 So she went in, fell at his feet, and bowed to the ground; then she picked up her son and went out.

Elisha Purifies the Pot of Stew

38 And Elisha returned to Gilgal, and *there was* a famine in the land. Now the sons of the prophets *were* sitting before him; and he said to his servant, "Put on the large pot, and boil stew for the sons of the prophets."

39 So one went out into the field to gather herbs, and found a wild vine, and gathered from it a lap full of wild gourds, and came and sliced *them* into the pot of stew, though they did not know *what they were.*

40 Then they served it to the men to eat. Now it happened, as they were eating the stew, that they cried out and said, "O man of God, *there is* death in the pot!" And they could not eat *it.*

41 So he said, "Then bring some flour." And he put *it* into the pot, and said, "Serve *it* to the people, that they may eat." And there was nothing harmful in the pot.

Elisha Feeds One Hundred Men

42 Then a man came from Baal Shalisha, and brought the man of God bread of the firstfruits, twenty loaves of barley bread, and newly ripened grain in his knapsack. And he said, "Give *it* to the people, that they may eat."

43 And his servant said, "What? Shall I set this before one hundred men?" He said again, "Give it to the people, that they may eat; for thus says the LORD: 'They shall eat and have *some* left over.' "

44 So he set *it* before them; and they ate and had *some* left over, according to the word of the LORD.

Naaman's Leprosy Healed

5 Now Naaman, commander of the army of the king of Syria, was a great and honorable man in the eyes of his master, because by him the LORD had given victory to Syria. He was also a mighty man of valor, *but he was* a leper.

2 And the Syrians had gone out on raids, and had brought back captive a

young girl from the land of Israel. She waited on Naaman's wife.

3 Then she said to her mistress, "If only my master *were* with the prophet who *is* in Samaria! For he would heal him of his leprosy."

4 And Naaman[5] went in and told his master, saying, "Thus and thus said the girl who *is* from the land of Israel."

5 So the king of Syria said, "Go now, and I will send a letter to the king of Israel." So he departed and took with him ten talents of silver, six thousand *shekels* of gold, and ten changes of clothing.

6 Then he brought the letter to the king of Israel, which said,

"Now be advised, when this letter comes to you, that I have sent Naaman my servant to you, that you may heal him of his leprosy."

7 And it happened, when the king of Israel read the letter, that he tore his clothes and said, "*Am* I God, to kill and make alive, that this man sends a man to me to heal him of his leprosy? Therefore please consider, and see how he seeks a quarrel with me."

8 So it was, when Elisha the man of God heard that the king of Israel had torn his clothes, that he sent to the king, saying, "Why have you torn your clothes? Please let him come to me, and he shall know that there is a prophet in Israel."

9 Then Naaman went with his horses and chariot, and he stood at the door of the house of Elisha.

10 And Elisha sent a messenger to him, saying, "Go and wash in the Jordan seven times, and your flesh shall be restored to you, and *you shall* be clean."

11 But Naaman became furious, and went away and said, "Indeed, I said to myself, 'He will surely come out to me, and stand and call on the name of the LORD his God, and wave his hand over the place, and heal the leprosy.'

12 "*Are* not the Abanah[6] and the Pharpar, the rivers of Damascus, better than all the waters of Israel? Could I not wash in them and be clean?" So he turned and went away in a rage.

13 And his servants came near and spoke to him, and said, "My father, *if* the prophet had told you *to do* something great, would you not have done *it?* How much more then, when he says to you, 'Wash, and be clean'?"

14 So he went down and dipped seven times in the Jordan, according to the saying of the man of God; and his flesh was restored like the flesh of a little child, and he was clean.

15 Then he returned to the man of God, he and all his aides, and came and stood before him; and he said, "Indeed, now I know that *there is* no God in all the earth, except in Israel; now therefore, please take a gift from your servant."

16 But he said, "*As* the LORD lives, before whom I stand, I will receive nothing." And he urged him to take *it,* but he refused.

17 So Naaman said, "Then, if not, please let your servant be given two mule-loads of earth; for your servant will no longer offer either burnt offering or sacrifice to other gods, but to the LORD.

18 "Yet in this thing may the LORD pardon your servant: when my master goes into the temple of Rimmon to worship there, and he leans on my hand, and I bow down in the temple of Rimmon— when I bow down in the temple of Rimmon, may the LORD please pardon your servant in this thing."

19 Then he said to him, "Go in peace." So he departed from him a short distance.

Gehazi's Greed

20 But Gehazi, the servant of Elisha the man of God, said, "Look, my master has spared Naaman this Syrian, while not receiving from his hands what he brought; but *as* the LORD lives, I will run after him and take something from him."

21 So Gehazi pursued Naaman. When Naaman saw *him* running after him, he got down from the chariot to meet him, and said, "*Is* all well?"

22 And he said, "All *is* well. My master has sent me, saying, 'Indeed, just now two young men of the sons of the prophets have come to me from the mountains of Ephraim. Please give them a talent of silver and two changes of garments.' "

23 So Naaman said, "Please, take two talents." And he urged him, and bound two talents of silver in two bags, with two changes of garments, and handed *them* to two of his servants; and they carried *them* on ahead of him.

24 When he came to the citadel, he took *them* from their hand, and stored *them* away in the house; then he let the men go, and they departed.

5 Literally *he*   6 Many manuscripts, Qere, Targum, and Syriac read *Amanah.*

25 Now he went in and stood before his master. And Elisha said to him, "Where *did you go*, Gehazi?" And he said, "Your servant did not go anywhere."
26 Then he said to him, "Did not my heart go *with you* when the man turned back from his chariot to meet you? *Is it* time to receive money and to receive clothing, olive groves and vineyards, sheep and oxen, male and female servants?
27 "Therefore the leprosy of Naaman shall cling to you and your descendants forever." And he went out from his presence leprous, *as white* as snow.

The Floating Ax Head

6 And the sons of the prophets said to Elisha, "See now, the place where we dwell with you is too small for us.
2 "Please, let us go to the Jordan, and let every man take a beam from there, and let us make there a place where we may dwell." And he answered, "Go."
3 Then one said, "Please consent to go with your servants." And he answered, "I will go."
4 So he went with them. And when they came to the Jordan, they cut down trees.
5 But as one was cutting down a tree, the iron *ax head* fell into the water; and he cried out and said, "Alas, master! For it was borrowed."
6 And the man of God said, "Where did it fall?" And he showed him the place. So he cut off a stick, and threw *it* in there; and he made the iron float.
7 Therefore he said, "Pick *it* up for yourself." So he reached out his hand and took it.

The Blinded Syrians Captured

8 Now the king of Syria was making war against Israel; and he took counsel with his servants, saying, "My camp *will be* in such and such a place."
9 And the man of God sent to the king of Israel, saying, "Beware that you do not pass this place, for the Syrians are coming down there."
10 Then the king of Israel sent *someone* to the place of which the man of God had told him. Thus he warned him, and he was watchful there, not just once or twice.
11 Therefore the heart of the king of Syria was greatly troubled by this thing; and he called his servants and said to them, "Will you not show me which of us *is* for the king of Israel?"
12 And one of his servants said, "None, my lord, O king; but Elisha, the prophet who *is* in Israel, tells the king of Israel the words that you speak in your bedroom."
13 So he said, "Go and see where he *is*, that I may send and get him." And it was told him, saying, "Surely *he is* in Dothan."
14 Therefore he sent horses and chariots and a great army there, and they came by night and surrounded the city.
15 And when the servant of the man of God arose early and went out, there was an army, surrounding the city with horses and chariots. And his servant said to him, "Alas, my master! What shall we do?"
16 So he answered, "Do not fear, for those who *are* with us *are* more than those who *are* with them."
17 And Elisha prayed, and said, "LORD, I pray, open his eyes that he may see." Then the LORD opened the eyes of the young man, and he saw. And behold, the mountain *was* full of horses and chariots of fire all around Elisha.
18 So when the Syrians[7] came down to him, Elisha prayed to the LORD, and said, "Strike this people, I pray, with blindness." And He struck them with blindness according to the word of Elisha.
19 Now Elisha said to them, "This *is* not the way, nor *is* this the city. Follow me, and I will bring you to the man whom you seek." But he led them to Samaria.
20 So it was, when they had come to Samaria, that Elisha said, "LORD, open the eyes of these *men*, that they may see." And the LORD opened their eyes, and they saw; and there *they were*, inside Samaria!
21 Now when the king of Israel saw them, he said to Elisha, "My father, shall I kill *them*? Shall I kill *them*?"
22 And he answered, "You shall not kill *them*. Would you kill those whom you have taken captive with your sword and your bow? Set food and water before them, that they may eat and drink and go to their master."
23 Then he prepared a great feast for them; and after they ate and drank, he

7 Literally *they*

sent them away and they went to their master. So the bands of Syrian *raiders* came no more into the land of Israel.

Syria Besieges Samaria in Famine

24 And it happened after this that Ben-Hadad king of Syria gathered all his army, and went up and besieged Samaria. **25** And there was a great famine in Samaria; and indeed they besieged it until a donkey's head was *sold* for eighty *shekels* of silver, and one-fourth of a kab of dove droppings for five *shekels* of silver. **26** Then, as the king of Israel was passing by on the wall, a woman cried out to him, saying, "Help, my lord, O king!" **27** And he said, "If the LORD does not help you, where can I find help for you? From the threshing floor or from the winepress?" **28** Then the king said to her, "What is troubling you?" And she answered, "This woman said to me, 'Give your son, that we may eat him today, and we will eat my son tomorrow.' **29** "So we boiled my son, and ate him. And I said to her on the next day, 'Give your son, that we may eat him'; but she has hidden her son." **30** Now it happened, when the king heard the words of the woman, that he tore his clothes; and as he passed by on the wall, the people looked, and there underneath *he had* sackcloth on his body. **31** Then he said, "God do so to me and more also, if the head of Elisha the son of Shaphat remains on him today." **32** But Elisha was sitting in his house, and the elders were sitting with him. And the king[8] sent a man ahead of him, but before the messenger came to him, he said to the elders, "Do you see how this son of a murderer has sent someone to take away my head? Look, when the messenger comes, shut the door, and hold him fast at the door. *Is* not the sound of his master's feet behind him?" **33** And while he was still talking with them, there was the messenger, coming down to him; and then he said, "Surely this calamity *is* from the LORD; why should I wait for the LORD any longer?"

7 Then Elisha said, "Hear the word of the LORD. Thus says the LORD: 'Tomorrow about this time a seah of fine flour *shall be sold* for a shekel, and two

8 Literally *he*

seahs of barley for a shekel, at the gate of Samaria.'" **2** So an officer on whose hand the king leaned answered the man of God and said, "Look, *if* the LORD would make windows in heaven, could this thing be?" And he said, "In fact, you shall see *it* with your eyes, but you shall not eat of it."

The Syrians Flee

3 Now there were four leprous men at the entrance of the gate; and they said to one another, "Why are we sitting here until we die? **4** "If we say, 'We will enter the city,' the famine *is* in the city, and we shall die there. And if we sit here, we die also. Now therefore, come, let us surrender to the army of the Syrians. If they keep us alive, we shall live; and if they kill us, we shall but die." **5** And they rose at twilight to go to the camp of the Syrians; and when they had come to the outskirts of the Syrian camp, to their surprise no one *was* there. **6** For the LORD had caused the army of the Syrians to hear the noise of chariots and the noise of horses—the noise of a great army; so they said to one another, "Look, the king of Israel has hired against us the kings of the Hittites and the kings of the Egyptians to attack us!" **7** Therefore they arose and fled at twilight, and left the camp intact—their tents, their horses, and their donkeys— and they fled for their lives. **8** And when these lepers came to the outskirts of the camp, they went into one tent and ate and drank, and carried from it silver and gold and clothing, and went and hid *them*; then they came back and entered another tent, and carried *some* from there *also*, and went and hid *it*. **9** Then they said to one another, "We are not doing what is right. This day *is* a day of good news, and we remain silent. If we wait until morning light, some punishment will come upon us. Now therefore, come, let us go and tell the king's household." **10** So they went and called to the gatekeepers of the city, and told them, saying, "We went to the Syrian camp, and surprisingly no one *was* there, not a human sound—only horses and donkeys tied, and the tents intact."

11 And the gatekeepers called out, and they told *it* to the king's household inside. 12 Then the king arose in the night and said to his servants, "Let me now tell you what the Syrians have done to us. They know that we *are* hungry; therefore they have gone out of the camp to hide themselves in the field, saying, 'When they come out of the city, we shall catch them alive, and get into the city.' "

13 And one of his servants answered and said, "Please, let several *men* take five of the remaining horses which are left in the city. Look, they *may either become* like all the multitude of Israel that are left in it; or indeed, *I say*, they *may become* like all the multitude of Israel left from those who are consumed; so let us send them and see."

14 Therefore they took two chariots with horses; and the king sent them in the direction of the Syrian army, saying, "Go and see."

15 And they went after them to the Jordan; and indeed all the road *was* full of garments and weapons which the Syrians had thrown away in their haste. So the messengers returned and told the king.

16 Then the people went out and plundered the tents of the Syrians. So a seah of fine flour was *sold* for a shekel, and two seahs of barley for a shekel, according to the word of the LORD.

17 Now the king had appointed the officer on whose hand he leaned to have charge of the gate. But the people trampled him in the gate, and he died, just as the man of God had said, who spoke when the king came down to him.

18 So it happened just as the man of God had spoken to the king, saying, "Two seahs of barley for a shekel, and a seah of fine flour for a shekel, shall be *sold* tomorrow about this time in the gate of Samaria."

19 Then that officer had answered the man of God, and said, "Now look, *if* the LORD would make windows in heaven, could such a thing be?" And he had said, "In fact, you shall see it with your eyes, but you shall not eat of it."

20 And so it happened to him, for the people trampled him in the gate, and he died.

The King Restores the Shunammite's Land

8 Then Elisha spoke to the woman whose son he had restored to life, saying, "Arise and go, you and your household, and sojourn wherever you can sojourn; for the LORD has called for a famine, and furthermore, it will come upon the land for seven years."

2 So the woman arose and did according to the saying of the man of God, and she went with her household and sojourned in the land of the Philistines seven years.

3 It came to pass, at the end of seven years, that the woman returned from the land of the Philistines; and she went to make an appeal to the king for her house and for her land.

4 Then the king talked with Gehazi, the servant of the man of God, saying, "Tell me, please, all the great things Elisha has done."

5 Now it happened, as he was telling the king how he had restored the dead to life, that there was the woman whose son he had restored to life, appealing to the king for her house and for her land. And Gehazi said, "My lord, O king, this *is* the woman, and this *is* her son whom Elisha restored to life."

6 And when the king asked the woman, she told him. So the king appointed a certain officer for her, saying, "Restore all that *was* hers, and all the proceeds of the field from the day that she left the land until now."

Death of Ben-Hadad

7 Then Elisha went to Damascus, and Ben-Hadad king of Syria was sick; and it was told him, saying, "The man of God has come here."

8 And the king said to Hazael, "Take a present in your hand, and go to meet the man of God, and inquire of the LORD by him, saying, 'Shall I recover from this disease?' "

9 So Hazael went to meet him and took a present with him, of every good thing of Damascus, forty camel-loads; and he came and stood before him, and said, "Your son Ben-Hadad king of Syria has sent me to you, saying, 'Shall I recover from this disease?' "

10 And Elisha said to him, "Go, say to him, 'You shall certainly recover.' How-

ever the LORD has shown me that he will really die."

11 Then he set his countenance in a stare until he was ashamed; and the man of God wept.

12 And Hazael said, "Why is my lord weeping?" And he answered, "Because I know the evil that you will do to the children of Israel: Their strongholds you will set on fire, and their young men you will kill with the sword; and you will dash their children, and rip open their women with child."

13 So Hazael said, "But what is your servant—a dog, that he should do this gross thing?" And Elisha answered, "The LORD has shown me that you will become king over Syria."

14 Then he departed from Elisha, and came to his master, who said to him, "What did Elisha say to you?" And he answered, "He told me that you would surely recover."

15 But it happened on the next day that he took a thick cloth and dipped it in water, and spread it over his face so that he died; and Hazael reigned in his place.

Jehoram Reigns in Judah

16 Now in the fifth year of Joram the son of Ahab, king of Israel, Jehoshaphat having been king of Judah, Jehoram the son of Jehoshaphat began to reign as king of Judah.

17 He was thirty-two years old when he became king, and he reigned eight years in Jerusalem.

18 And he walked in the way of the kings of Israel, just as the house of Ahab had done, for the daughter of Ahab was his wife; and he did evil in the sight of the LORD.

19 Yet the LORD would not destroy Judah, for the sake of his servant David, as He promised him to give a lamp to him and his sons forever.

20 In his days Edom revolted against Judah's authority, and made a king over themselves.

21 So Joram went to Zair, and all his chariots with him. And he rose by night and attacked the Edomites who had surrounded him and the captains of the chariots, but his people fled to their tents.

22 Thus Edom has been in revolt against Judah's authority to this day. And Libnah revolted at that time.

23 Now the rest of the acts of Joram,[9] and all that he did, are they not written in the book of the chronicles of the kings of Judah?

24 So Joram rested with his fathers, and was buried with his fathers in the City of David. Then Ahaziah his son reigned in his place.

Ahaziah Reigns in Judah

25 In the twelfth year of Joram the son of Ahab, king of Israel, Ahaziah the son of Jehoram, king of Judah, began to reign.

26 Ahaziah was twenty-two years old when he became king, and he reigned one year in Jerusalem. His mother's name was Athaliah the granddaughter of Omri, king of Israel.

27 And he walked in the way of the house of Ahab, and did evil in the sight of the LORD, as the house of Ahab had done, for he was the son-in-law of the house of Ahab.

28 Now he went with Joram the son of Ahab to war against Hazael king of Syria at Ramoth Gilead; and the Syrians wounded Joram.

29 Then King Joram went back to Jezreel to recover from the wounds which the Syrians had inflicted on him at Ramah, when he fought against Hazael king of Syria. And Ahaziah the son of Jehoram, king of Judah, went down to see Joram the son of Ahab in Jezreel, because he was sick.

Jehu Anointed King of Israel

9 And Elisha the prophet called one of the sons of the prophets, and said to him, "Get yourself ready, take this flask of oil in your hand, and go to Ramoth Gilead.

2 "Now when you arrive at that place, look there for Jehu the son of Jehoshaphat, the son of Nimshi, and go in and make him rise up from among his associates, and take him to an inner room.

3 "Then take the flask of oil, and pour it on his head, and say, 'Thus says the LORD: "I have anointed you king over Israel." ' Then open the door and flee, and do not delay."

4 So the young man, the servant of the prophet, went to Ramoth Gilead.

5 And when he arrived, there were the captains of the army sitting; and he said,

9 Spelled Jehoram in verse 16ff

"I have a message for you, O commander." And Jehu said, "For which one of us?" And he said, "For you, commander."
6 Then he arose and went into the house. And he poured the oil on his head, and said to him, "Thus says the LORD God of Israel: 'I have anointed you king over the people of the LORD, over Israel.
7 'You shall strike down the house of Ahab your master, that I may avenge the blood of My servants the prophets, and the blood of all the servants of the LORD, at the hand of Jezebel.
8 'For the whole house of Ahab shall perish; and I will cut off from Ahab all the males in Israel, both bond and free.
9 'So I will make the house of Ahab like the house of Jeroboam the son of Nebat, and like the house of Baasha the son of Ahijah.
10 'The dogs shall eat Jezebel in the vicinity of Jezreel, and *there shall be* none to bury *her.*'" And he opened the door and fled.
11 Then Jehu came out to the servants of his master, and *one* said to him, "*Is* all well? Why did this madman come to you?" And he said to them, "You know the man and his babble."
12 And they said, "A lie! Tell us now." So he said, "Thus and thus he spoke to me, saying, 'Thus says the LORD: "I have anointed you king over Israel." ' "
13 Then each man hastened to take his garment and put *it* under him on the top of the steps; and they blew trumpets, saying, "Jehu is king!"

Joram of Israel Killed

14 So Jehu the son of Jehoshaphat, the son of Nimshi, conspired against Joram. (Now Joram had been defending Ramoth Gilead, he and all Israel, against Hazael king of Syria.
15 But King Joram had returned to Jezreel to recover from the wounds which the Syrians had inflicted on him when he fought with Hazael king of Syria.) And Jehu said, "If you are so minded, let no one leave *or* escape from the city to go and tell *it* in Jezreel."
16 So Jehu rode in a chariot and went to Jezreel, for Joram was laid up there; and Ahaziah king of Judah had come down to see Joram.

17 Now a watchman stood on the tower in Jezreel, and he saw the company of Jehu as he came, and said, "I see a company of men." And Joram said, "Get a horseman and send him to meet them, and let him say, 'Is it peace?' "
18 So the horseman went to meet him, and said, "Thus says the king: '*Is it* peace?' " And Jehu said, "What have you to do with peace? Turn around and follow me." And the watchman reported, saying, "The messenger went to them, but is not coming back."
19 Then he sent out a second horseman who came to them, and said, "Thus says the king: '*Is it* peace?' " And Jehu answered, "What have you to do with peace? Turn around and follow me."
20 And the watchman reported, saying, "He went up to them and is not coming back; and the driving *is* like the driving of Jehu the son of Nimshi, for he drives furiously!"
21 So Joram said, "Make ready." And his chariot was made ready. Then Joram king of Israel and Ahaziah king of Judah went out, each in his chariot; and they went out to meet Jehu, and met him on the property of Naboth the Jezreelite.
22 Now it happened, when Joram saw Jehu, that he said, "*Is it* peace, Jehu?" So he answered, "What peace, as long as the harlotries of your mother Jezebel and her witchcraft *are so* many?"
23 Then Joram turned around and fled, and said to Ahaziah, "Treachery, Ahaziah!"
24 Now Jehu drew his bow with full strength and shot Jehoram between his arms; and the arrow came out at his heart, and he sank down in his chariot.
25 Then *Jehu* said to Bidkar his captain, "Pick *him* up, *and* throw him into the tract of the field of Naboth the Jezreelite; for remember, when you and I were riding together behind Ahab his father, that the LORD laid this burden upon him:
26 'Surely I saw yesterday the blood of Naboth and the blood of his sons,' says the LORD, 'and I will repay you in this plot,' says the LORD. Now therefore, take *and* throw him on the plot *of ground,* according to the word of the LORD."

Ahaziah of Judah Killed

27 But when Ahaziah king of Judah saw *this,* he fled by the road to Beth Haggan.[10]

10 That is, The Garden House

So Jehu pursued him, and said, "Shoot him also in the chariot." *And they did so* at the ascent to Gur, which is by Ibleam. Then he fled to Megiddo, and died there.
28 And his servants carried him in the chariot to Jerusalem, and buried him in his tomb with his fathers in the City of David.
29 In the eleventh year of Joram the son of Ahab, Ahaziah had become king over Judah.

Jezebel's Violent Death

30 And when Jehu had come to Jezreel, Jezebel heard *of it*; and she put paint on her eyes and adorned her head, and looked through a window.
31 Then, as Jehu entered at the gate, she said, "*Is it* peace, Zimri, murderer of your master?"
32 And he looked up at the window, and said, "Who *is* on my side? Who?" And two *or* three eunuchs looked out at him.
33 Then he said, "Throw her down." So they threw her down, and *some* of her blood spattered on the wall and on the horses; and he trampled her under foot.
34 And when he had gone in, he ate and drank. Then he said, "Go now, see to this accursed *woman*, and bury her, for she was a king's daughter."
35 So they went to bury her, but they found no more of her than the skull and the feet and the palms of *her* hands.
36 Therefore they came back and told him. And he said, "This *is* the word of the LORD, which He spoke by His servant Elijah the Tishbite, saying, 'On the plot *of ground* at Jezreel dogs shall eat the flesh of Jezebel;[11]
37 'and the corpse of Jezebel shall be as refuse on the surface of the field, in the plot at Jezreel, so that they shall not say, "Here *lies* Jezebel." ' "

Ahab's Seventy Sons Killed

10 Now Ahab had seventy sons in Samaria. And Jehu wrote letters and sent *them* to Samaria, to the rulers of Jezreel, to the elders, and to those who reared Ahab's *sons*, saying:
2 Now as soon as this letter comes to you, since your master's sons *are* with you, and you have chariots and horses, a fortified city also, and weapons,

3 choose the best qualified of your master's sons, set *him* on his father's throne, and fight for your master's house.
4 But they were exceedingly afraid, and said, "Look, two kings could not stand up to him; how then can we stand?"
5 And he who *was* in charge of the house, and he who *was* in charge of the city, the elders also, and those who reared *the sons*, sent to Jehu, saying, "We *are* your servants, we will do all you tell us; but we will not make anyone king. Do *what is* good in your sight."
6 Then he wrote a second letter to them, saying:
If you *are* for me, and *if* you will obey my voice, take the heads of the men, your master's sons, and come to me at Jezreel by this time tomorrow.
Now the king's sons, seventy persons, *were* with the great men of the city, *who* were rearing them.
7 So it was, when the letter came to them, that they took the king's sons and slaughtered seventy persons, put their heads in baskets and sent *them* to him at Jezreel.
8 Then a messenger came and told him, saying, "They have brought the heads of the king's sons." And he said, "Lay them in two heaps at the entrance of the gate until morning."
9 So it was, in the morning, that he went out and stood, and said to all the people, "You *are* righteous. Indeed I conspired against my master and killed him; but who killed all these?
10 "Know now that nothing shall fall to the earth of the word of the LORD which the LORD spoke concerning the house of Ahab; for the LORD has done what He spoke by His servant Elijah."
11 So Jehu killed all who remained of the house of Ahab in Jezreel, and all his great men and his close acquaintances and his priests, until he left him none remaining.

Ahaziah's Forty-Two Brothers Killed

12 And he arose and departed and went to Samaria. On the way, at Beth Eked of the Shepherds,[12]
13 Jehu met with the brothers of Ahaziah king of Judah, and said, "Who *are* you?" And they answered, "We *are* the brothers of Ahaziah; we have come down to greet

11 Compare 1 Kings 21:23   12 Or *the shearing house*

the sons of the king and the sons of the queen mother."

14 And he said, "Take them alive!" So they took them alive, and killed them at the well of Beth Eked, forty-two men; and he left none of them.

The Rest of Ahab's Family Killed

15 Now when he departed from there, he met Jehonadab the son of Rechab, *coming* to meet him; and he greeted him and said to him, "Is your heart right, as my heart *is* toward your heart?" And Jehonadab answered, "It is." *Jehu said,* "If it is, give *me* your hand." So he gave *him* his hand, and he took him up to him into the chariot.

16 Then he said, "Come with me, and see my zeal for the LORD." So they had him ride in his chariot.

17 And when he came to Samaria, he killed all who remained to Ahab in Samaria, till he had destroyed them, according to the word of the LORD which He spoke to Elijah.

Worshipers of Baal Killed

18 Then Jehu gathered all the people together, and said to them, "Ahab served Baal a little, *but* Jehu will serve him much.

19 "Now, therefore, call to me all the prophets of Baal, all his servants, and all his priests. Let no one be missing, for I have a great sacrifice *to make* to Baal. Whoever is missing shall not live." But Jehu acted deceptively, with the intent of destroying the worshipers of Baal.

20 And Jehu said, "Proclaim a solemn assembly for Baal." So they proclaimed *it*.

21 Then Jehu sent throughout all Israel; and all the worshipers of Baal came, so that there was not a man left who did not come. So they came into the temple[13] of Baal, and the temple of Baal was full from one end to the other.

22 And he said to the one in charge of the wardrobe, "Bring out vestments for all the worshipers of Baal." So he brought out vestments for them.

23 Then Jehu and Jehonadab the son of Rechab went into the temple of Baal, and said to the worshipers of Baal, "Search and see that no servants of the LORD are here with you, but only the worshipers of Baal."

24 So they went in to offer sacrifices and burnt offerings. Now Jehu had appointed for himself eighty men on the outside, and had said, "*If* any of the men whom I have brought into your hands escapes, *whoever lets him escape, it shall be* his life for the life of the other."

25 Now it was so, as soon as he had made an end of offering the burnt offering, that Jehu said to the guard and to the captains, "Go in *and* kill them; let no one come out!" And they killed them with the edge of the sword; then the guards and the officers threw *them* out, and went into the inner room of the temple of Baal.

26 And they brought the *sacred* pillars out of the temple of Baal and burned them.

27 Then they broke down the *sacred* pillar of Baal, and tore down the temple of Baal and made it a refuse dump to this day.

28 Thus Jehu destroyed Baal from Israel.

29 However Jehu did not turn away from the sins of Jeroboam the son of Nebat, who had made Israel sin, *that is,* from the golden calves that *were* at Bethel and Dan.

30 And the LORD said to Jehu, "Because you have done well in doing *what is* right in My sight, *and* have done to the house of Ahab all that *was* in My heart, your sons shall sit on the throne of Israel to the fourth *generation*."

31 But Jehu took no heed to walk in the law of the LORD God of Israel with all his heart; for he did not depart from the sins of Jeroboam, who had made Israel sin.

Death of Jehu

32 In those days the LORD began to cut off *parts* of Israel; and Hazael conquered them in all the territory of Israel

33 from the Jordan eastward: all the land of Gilead—Gad, Reuben, and Manasseh—from Aroer, which *is* by the River Arnon, including Gilead and Bashan.

34 Now the rest of the acts of Jehu, all that he did, and all his might, *are* they not written in the book of the chronicles of the kings of Israel?

35 So Jehu rested with his fathers, and they buried him in Samaria. Then Jehoahaz his son reigned in his place.

36 And the period that Jehu reigned over Israel in Samaria *was* twenty-eight years.

---

13 Literally *house,* and so elsewhere in this chapter

Athaliah Reigns in Judah

11 When Athaliah the mother of Ahaziah saw that her son was dead, she arose and destroyed all the royal heirs.

2 But Jehosheba, the daughter of King Joram, sister of Ahaziah, took Joash the son of Ahaziah, and stole him away from among the king's sons *who were* being murdered; and they hid him and his nurse in the bedroom, from Athaliah, so that he was not killed.

3 So he was hidden with her in the house of the LORD for six years, while Athaliah reigned over the land.

Joash Crowned King of Judah

4 In the seventh year Jehoiada sent and brought the captains of hundreds, of the bodyguards and the escorts, and brought them into the house of the LORD to him. And he made a covenant with them and took an oath from them in the house of the LORD, and showed them the king's son.

5 Then he commanded them, saying, "This *is* what you shall do: One-third of you who come on duty on the Sabbath shall be keeping watch over the king's house,

6 "one-third *shall be* at the gate of Sur, and one-third at the gate behind the escorts. You shall keep the watch of the house, lest it be broken down.

7 "The two contingents of you who go off duty on the Sabbath shall keep the watch of the house of the LORD for the king.

8 "But you shall surround the king on all sides, every man with his weapons in his hand; and whoever comes within range, let him be put to death. You are to be with the king as he goes out and as he comes in."

9 So the captains of the hundreds did according to all that Jehoiada the priest commanded. Each of them took his men who were to be on duty on the Sabbath, with those who were going off duty on the Sabbath, and came to Jehoiada the priest.

10 And the priest gave the captains of hundreds the spears and shields which *had belonged* to King David, that were in the temple of the LORD.

11 Then the escorts stood, every man with his weapons in his hand, all around the king, from the right side of the temple to the left side of the temple, by the altar and the temple.

12 And he brought out the king's son, put the crown on him, and *gave him* the Testimony;[14] they made him king and anointed him, and they clapped their hands and said, "Long live the king!"

Death of Athaliah

13 Now when Athaliah heard the noise of the escorts *and* the people, she came to the people, into the temple of the LORD.

14 When she looked, there was the king, standing by a pillar according to custom; and the leaders and the trumpeters were by the king. All the people of the land were rejoicing and blowing trumpets. And Athaliah tore her clothes and cried out, "Treason! Treason!"

15 Then Jehoiada the priest commanded the captains of the hundreds, the officers of the army, and said to them, "Take her outside under guard, and slay with the sword whoever follows her." For the priest had said, "Do not let her be killed in the house of the LORD."

16 So they seized her; and she went by way of the horses' entrance to the king's house, and there she was killed.

17 Then Jehoiada made a covenant between the LORD, the king, and the people, that they should be the LORD'S people, and *also* between the king and the people.

18 And all the people of the land went to the temple of Baal, and tore it down. They thoroughly broke in pieces its altars and images, and killed Mattan the priest of Baal before the altars. And the priest appointed officers over the house of the LORD.

19 Then he took the captains of hundreds, the bodyguards, the escorts, and all the people of the land; and they brought the king down from the house of the LORD, and went by way of the gate of the escorts to the king's house; and he sat on the throne of the kings.

20 So all the people of the land rejoiced; and the city was quiet, for they had slain Athaliah with the sword *in* the king's house.

21 Jehoash *was* seven years old when he became king.

---

14 That is, the Law (compare Exodus 25:16, 21 and Deuteronomy 31:9)

Jehoash Repairs the Temple

12 In the seventh year of Jehu, Jehoash[15] became king, and he reigned forty years in Jerusalem. His mother's name *was* Zibiah of Beersheba.
2 Jehoash did *what was* right in the sight of the LORD all the days in which Jehoiada the priest instructed him.
3 But the high places were not taken away; the people still sacrificed and burned incense on the high places.
4 And Jehoash said to the priests, "All the money of the dedicated gifts that are brought into the house of the LORD—each man's census money, each man's assessment money[16]—*and* all the money that a man purposes in his heart to bring into the house of the LORD,
5 "let the priests take *it* themselves, each from his constituency; and let them repair the damages of the temple, wherever any dilapidation is found."
6 Now it was so, by the twenty-third year of King Jehoash, *that* the priests had not repaired the damages of the temple.
7 So King Jehoash called Jehoiada the priest and the *other* priests, and said to them, "Why have you not repaired the damages of the temple? Now therefore, do not take *any more* money from your constituency, but deliver it for repairing the damages of the temple."
8 And the priests agreed that they would neither receive any *more* money from the people, nor repair the damages of the temple.
9 Then Jehoiada the priest took a chest, bored a hole in its lid, and set it beside the altar, on the right side as one comes into the house of the LORD; and the priests who kept the door put there all the money *that was* brought into the house of the LORD.
10 So it was, whenever they saw that *there was* much money in the chest, that the king's scribe and the high priest came up and put it in bags, and counted the money that was found in the house of the LORD.
11 Then they gave the money, which had been apportioned, into the hands of those who did the work, who had the oversight of the house of the LORD; and they paid it out to the carpenters and builders who worked on the house of the LORD,
12 and to masons and stonecutters, and for buying timber and hewn stone, to repair the damage of the house of the LORD, and for all that was paid out to repair the temple.
13 However there were not made for the house of the LORD basins of silver, trimmers, sprinkling-bowls, trumpets, any articles of gold, or articles of silver, from the money *that was* brought into the house of the LORD.
14 But they gave that to the workmen, and they repaired the house of the LORD with it.
15 Moreover they did not require an account from the men into whose hand they delivered the money to be paid to workmen, for they dealt faithfully.
16 The money from the trespass offerings and the money from the sin offerings was not brought into the house of the LORD. It belonged to the priests.

Hazael Threatens Jerusalem

17 Now Hazael king of Syria went up and fought against Gath, and took it; so Hazael set his face to go up to Jerusalem.
18 And Jehoash king of Judah took all the sacred things that his fathers, Jehoshaphat and Jehoram and Ahaziah, kings of Judah, had dedicated, and his own sacred things, and all the gold found in the treasuries of the house of the LORD and in the king's house, and sent *them* to Hazael king of Syria. Then he went away from Jerusalem.

Death of Joash

19 Now the rest of the acts of Joash,[17] and all that he did, *are* they not written in the book of the chronicles of the kings of Judah?
20 And his servants arose and made a conspiracy, and killed Joash in the house of the Millo, which goes down to Silla.
21 For Jozachar[18] the son of Shimeath and Jehozabad the son of Shomer,[19] his servants, struck him. So he died, and they buried him with his fathers in the City of David. Then Amaziah his son reigned in his place.

Jehoahaz Reigns in Israel

13 In the twenty-third year of Joash[20] the son of Ahaziah, king of Judah, Jehoahaz the son of Jehu became king

---

15 Spelled *Joash* in 11:2ff   16 Compare Leviticus 27:2f   17 Spelled *Jehoash* in 12:1–18
18 Called *Zabad* in 2 Chronicles 24:26   19 Called *Shimrith* in 2 Chronicles 24:26   20 Spelled *Jehoash* in 12:1–18

over Israel in Samaria, *and reigned* seventeen years.

2 And he did evil in the sight of the LORD, and followed the sins of Jeroboam the son of Nebat, who had made Israel sin. He did not depart from them.

3 Then the anger of the LORD was aroused against Israel, and He delivered them into the hand of Hazael king of Syria, and into the hand of Ben-Hadad the son of Hazael, all *their* days.

4 So Jehoahaz pleaded with the LORD, and the LORD listened to him; for He saw the oppression of Israel, because the king of Syria oppressed them.

5 Then the LORD gave Israel a deliverer, so that they escaped from under the hand of the Syrians; and the children of Israel dwelt in their tents as before.

6 Nevertheless they did not depart from the sins of the house of Jeroboam, who had made Israel sin, *but* walked in them; and the wooden images[21] also remained in Samaria.

7 For He left of the army of Jehoahaz only fifty horsemen, ten chariots, and ten thousand foot soldiers; for the king of Syria had destroyed them and made them like the dust at threshing.

8 Now the rest of the acts of Jehoahaz, all that he did, and his might, *are* they not written in the book of the chronicles of the kings of Israel?

9 So Jehoahaz rested with his fathers, and they buried him in Samaria. Then Joash his son reigned in his place.

Jehoash Reigns in Israel

10 In the thirty-seventh year of Joash king of Judah, Jehoash[22] the son of Jehoahaz became king over Israel in Samaria, *and reigned* sixteen years.

11 And he did evil in the sight of the LORD; he did not depart from all the sins of Jeroboam the son of Nebat, who had made Israel sin; *but* he walked in them.

12 Now the rest of the acts of Joash, all that he did, and his might with which he fought against Amaziah king of Judah, *are* they not written in the book of the chronicles of the kings of Israel?

13 So Joash rested with his fathers. Then Jeroboam sat on his throne. And Joash was buried in Samaria with the kings of Israel.

Death of Elisha

14 Elisha had become sick with the illness of which he would die. Then Joash the king of Israel came down to him, and wept over his face, and said, "O my father, my father, the chariots of Israel and their horsemen!"

15 And Elisha said to him, "Take a bow and some arrows." So he took himself a bow and some arrows.

16 Then he said to the king of Israel, "Put your hand on the bow." So he put his hand *on it*, and Elisha put his hands on the king's hands.

17 And he said, "Open the east window"; and he opened *it*. Then Elisha said, "Shoot"; and he shot. And he said, "The arrow of the LORD's deliverance and the arrow of deliverance from Syria; for you must strike the Syrians at Aphek till you have destroyed *them*."

18 Then he said, "Take the arrows"; so he took *them*. And he said to the king of Israel, "Strike the ground"; so he struck three times, and stopped.

19 And the man of God was angry with him, and said, "You should have struck five or six times; then you would have struck Syria till you had destroyed *it*. But now you will strike Syria *only* three times."

20 Then Elisha died, and they buried him. And the *raiding* bands from Moab invaded the land in the spring of the year.

21 So it was, as they were burying a man, that suddenly they spied a band *of raiders*; and they put the man in the tomb of Elisha; and when the man was let down and touched the bones of Elisha, he revived and stood on his feet.

Israel Recaptures Cities from Syria

22 And Hazael king of Syria oppressed Israel all the days of Jehoahaz.

23 But the LORD was gracious to them, had compassion on them, and regarded them, because of His covenant with Abraham, Isaac, and Jacob, and would not yet destroy them or cast them from His presence.

24 Now Hazael king of Syria died. Then Ben-Hadad his son reigned in his place.

25 And Jehoash[23] the son of Jehoahaz recaptured from the hand of Ben-Hadad, the son of Hazael, the cities which he had taken out of the hand of Jehoahaz his fa-

---

21 Hebrew *Asherah*, a Canaanite goddess   22 Spelled *Joash* in verse 9   23 Spelled *Joash* in verses 14–19, 25

ther by war. Three times Joash defeated him and recaptured the cities of Israel.

Amaziah Reigns in Judah

14 In the second year of Joash the son of Jehoahaz, king of Israel, Amaziah the son of Joash, king of Judah, became king.

2 He was twenty-five years old when he became king, and he reigned twenty-nine years in Jerusalem. His mother's name was Jehoaddan of Jerusalem.

3 And he did *what was* right in the sight of the LORD, yet not like his father David; he did everything as his father Joash had done.

4 However the high places were not taken away, and the people still sacrificed and burned incense on the high places.

5 Now it happened, as soon as the kingdom was established in his hand, that he executed his servants who had murdered his father the king.

6 But the children of the murderers he did not execute, according to what is written in the Book of the Law of Moses, in which the LORD commanded, saying, "The fathers shall not be put to death for the children, nor shall the children be put to death for the fathers; but a person shall be put to death for his own sin."24

7 He killed ten thousand Edomites in the Valley of Salt, and took Sela by war, and called its name Joktheel to this day.

8 Then Amaziah sent messengers to Jehoash25 the son of Jehoahaz, the son of Jehu, king of Israel, saying, "Come, let us face one another *in battle*."

9 And Jehoash king of Israel sent to Amaziah king of Judah, saying, "The thistle that *was* in Lebanon sent to the cedar that *was* in Lebanon, saying, 'Give your daughter to my son as wife'; and a wild beast that *was* in Lebanon passed by and trampled the thistle.

10 "You have indeed defeated Edom, and your heart has lifted you up. Glory *in your success*, and stay at home; for why should you meddle with trouble so that you fall—you and Judah with you?"

11 But Amaziah would not heed. Therefore Jehoash king of Israel went out; so he and Amaziah king of Judah faced one another at Beth Shemesh, which *belongs* to Judah.

12 And Judah was defeated by Israel, and every man fled to his tent.

13 Then Jehoash king of Israel captured Amaziah king of Judah, the son of Jehoash, the son of Ahaziah, at Beth Shemesh; and he went to Jerusalem, and broke down the wall of Jerusalem from the Gate of Ephraim to the Corner Gate—four hundred cubits.

14 And he took all the gold and silver, all the articles that were found in the house of the LORD and in the treasuries of the king's house, and hostages, and returned to Samaria.

15 Now the rest of the acts of Jehoash which he did—his might, and how he fought with Amaziah king of Judah—*are* they not written in the book of the chronicles of the kings of Israel?

16 So Jehoash rested with his fathers, and was buried in Samaria with the kings of Israel. Then Jeroboam his son reigned in his place.

17 Amaziah the son of Joash, king of Judah, lived fifteen years after the death of Jehoash the son of Jehoahaz, king of Israel.

18 Now the rest of the acts of Amaziah, *are* they not written in the book of the chronicles of the kings of Judah?

19 And they made a conspiracy against him in Jerusalem, and he fled to Lachish; but they sent after him to Lachish and killed him there.

20 Then they brought him on horses, and he was buried at Jerusalem with his fathers in the City of David.

21 And all the people of Judah took Azariah,26 who *was* sixteen years old, and made him king instead of his father Amaziah.

22 He built Elath and restored it to Judah, after the king rested with his fathers.

Jeroboam II Reigns in Israel

23 In the fifteenth year of Amaziah the son of Joash, king of Judah, Jeroboam the son of Joash, king of Israel, became king in Samaria, *and reigned* forty-one years.

24 And he did evil in the sight of the LORD; he did not depart from all the sins of Jeroboam the son of Nebat, who had made Israel sin.

25 He restored the territory of Israel from the entrance of Hamath to the Sea

---

24 Deuteronomy 24:16 25 Spelled *Joash* in 13:14–19ff and 2 Chronicles 25:17ff
26 Called *Uzziah* in 2 Chronicles 26:1ff, Isaiah 6:1, and elsewhere

of the Arabah, according to the word of the LORD God of Israel, which He had spoken through His servant Jonah the son of Amittai, the prophet who *was* from Gath Hepher.

26 For the LORD saw *that* the affliction of Israel *was* very bitter; and whether bond or free, there was no helper for Israel.

27 And the LORD did not say that He would blot out the name of Israel from under heaven; but He saved them by the hand of Jeroboam the son of Joash.

28 Now the rest of the acts of Jeroboam, and all that he did—his might, how he made war, and how he recaptured for Israel, from Damascus and Hamath, *what had belonged* to Judah—*are* they not written in the book of the chronicles of the kings of Israel?

29 So Jeroboam rested with his fathers, the kings of Israel. Then Zechariah his son reigned in his place.

Azariah Reigns in Judah

15 In the twenty-seventh year of Jeroboam king of Israel, Azariah the son of Amaziah, king of Judah, became king.

2 He was sixteen years old when he became king, and he reigned fifty-two years in Jerusalem. His mother's name *was* Jecholiah of Jerusalem.

3 And he did *what was* right in the sight of the LORD, according to all that his father Amaziah had done,

4 except that the high places were not removed; the people still sacrificed and burned incense on the high places.

5 Then the LORD struck the king, so that he was a leper until the day of his death; so he dwelt in an isolated house. And Jotham the king's son *was* over the *royal* house, judging the people of the land.

6 Now the rest of the acts of Azariah, and all that he did, *are* they not written in the book of the chronicles of the kings of Judah?

7 So Azariah rested with his fathers, and they buried him with his fathers in the City of David. Then Jotham his son reigned in his place.

Zechariah Reigns in Israel

8 In the thirty-eighth year of Azariah king of Judah, Zechariah the son of Jeroboam reigned over Israel in Samaria six months.

9 And he did evil in the sight of the LORD, as his fathers had done; he did not depart from the sins of Jeroboam the son of Nebat, who had made Israel sin.

10 Then Shallum the son of Jabesh conspired against him, and struck and killed him in front of the people; and he reigned in his place.

11 Now the rest of the acts of Zechariah, indeed they *are* written in the book of the chronicles of the kings of Israel.

12 This *was* the word of the LORD which He spoke to Jehu, saying, "Your sons shall sit on the throne of Israel to the fourth *generation*."27 And so it was.

Shallum Reigns in Israel

13 Shallum the son of Jabesh became king in the thirty-ninth year of Uzziah28 king of Judah; and he reigned a full month in Samaria.

14 For Menahem the son of Gadi went up from Tirzah, came to Samaria, and struck Shallum the son of Jabesh in Samaria and killed him; and he reigned in his place.

15 Now the rest of the acts of Shallum, and the conspiracy which he led, indeed they *are* written in the book of the chronicles of the kings of Israel.

16 Then from Tirzah, Menahem attacked Tiphsah, all who *were* there, and its territory; because they did not open *it to him*, therefore he attacked *it. And* all the women there who were with child he ripped open.

Menahem Reigns in Israel

17 In the thirty-ninth year of Azariah king of Judah, Menahem the son of Gadi became king over Israel, *and reigned* ten years in Samaria.

18 And he did evil in the sight of the LORD; he did not depart all his days from the sins of Jeroboam the son of Nebat, who had made Israel sin.

19 Pul29 king of Assyria came against the land; and Menahem gave Pul a thousand talents of silver, that his hand might be with him to strengthen the kingdom in his hand.

20 And Menahem exacted the money from Israel, from all the very wealthy, from each man fifty shekels of silver, to give to the king of Assyria. So the king of

---

27 2 Kings 10:30   28 Called *Azariah* in 14:21ff and 15:1ff   29 That is, Tiglath-Pileser III (compare verse 29)

Assyria turned back, and did not stay there in the land.
21 Now the rest of the acts of Menahem, and all that he did, *are* they not written in the book of the chronicles of the kings of Israel?
22 So Menahem rested with his fathers. Then Pekahiah his son reigned in his place.

Pekahiah Reigns in Israel

23 In the fiftieth year of Azariah king of Judah, Pekahiah the son of Menahem became king over Israel in Samaria, *and reigned* two years.
24 And he did evil in the sight of the LORD; he did not depart from the sins of Jeroboam the son of Nebat, who had made Israel sin.
25 Then Pekah the son of Remaliah, an officer of his, conspired against him and killed him in Samaria, in the citadel of the king's house, along with Argob and Arieh; and with him were fifty men of Gilead. He killed him and reigned in his place.
26 Now the rest of the acts of Pekahiah, and all that he did, indeed they *are* written in the book of the chronicles of the kings of Israel.

Pekah Reigns in Israel

27 In the fifty-second year of Azariah king of Judah, Pekah the son of Remaliah became king over Israel in Samaria, *and reigned* twenty years.
28 And he did evil in the sight of the LORD; he did not depart from the sins of Jeroboam the son of Nebat, who had made Israel sin.
29 In the days of Pekah king of Israel, Tiglath-Pileser king of Assyria came and took Ijon, Abel Beth Maachah, Janoah, Kedesh, Hazor, Gilead, and Galilee, all the land of Naphtali; and he carried them captive to Assyria.
30 Then Hoshea the son of Elah led a conspiracy against Pekah the son of Remaliah, and struck and killed him; so he reigned in his place in the twentieth year of Jotham the son of Uzziah.
31 Now the rest of the acts of Pekah, and all that he did, indeed they *are* written in the book of the chronicles of the kings of Israel.

Jotham Reigns in Judah

32 In the second year of Pekah the son of Remaliah, king of Israel, Jotham the son of Uzziah, king of Judah, began to reign.
33 He was twenty-five years old when he became king, and he reigned sixteen years in Jerusalem. His mother's name *was* Jerusha30 the daughter of Zadok.
34 And he did *what was* right in the sight of the LORD; he did according to all that his father Uzziah had done.
35 However the high places were not removed; the people still sacrificed and burned incense on the high places. He built the Upper Gate of the house of the LORD.
36 Now the rest of the acts of Jotham, and all that he did, *are* they not written in the book of the chronicles of the kings of Judah?
37 In those days the LORD began to send Rezin king of Syria and Pekah the son of Remaliah against Judah.
38 So Jotham rested with his fathers, and was buried with his fathers in the City of David his father. Then Ahaz his son reigned in his place.

Ahaz Reigns in Judah

16 In the seventeenth year of Pekah the son of Remaliah, Ahaz the son of Jotham, king of Judah, began to reign.
2 Ahaz *was* twenty years old when he became king, and he reigned sixteen years in Jerusalem; and he did not do *what was* right in the sight of the LORD his God, as his father David *had done.*
3 But he walked in the way of the kings of Israel; indeed he made his son pass through the fire, according to the abominations of the nations whom the LORD had cast out from before the children of Israel.
4 And he sacrificed and burned incense on the high places, on the hills, and under every green tree.
5 Then Rezin king of Syria and Pekah the son of Remaliah, king of Israel, came up to Jerusalem to *make* war; and they besieged Ahaz but could not overcome *him.*
6 At that time Rezin king of Syria captured Elath for Syria, and drove the men of Judah from Elath. Then the Edomites31 went to Elath, and dwell there to this day.

30 Spelled *Jerushah* in 2 Chronicles 27:1   31 Some ancient authorities read *Syrians.*

7 So Ahaz sent messengers to Tiglath-Pileser king of Assyria, saying, "I *am* your servant and your son. Come up and save me from the hand of the king of Syria and from the hand of the king of Israel, who rise up against me."
8 And Ahaz took the silver and gold that was found in the house of the LORD, and in the treasuries of the king's house, and sent *it as* a present to the king of Assyria.
9 So the king of Assyria heeded him; for the king of Assyria went up against Damascus and took it, carried *its people* captive to Kir, and killed Rezin.
10 Now King Ahaz went to Damascus to meet Tiglath-Pileser king of Assyria, and saw an altar that *was* at Damascus; and King Ahaz sent to Urijah the priest the design of the altar and its pattern, according to all its workmanship.
11 Then Urijah the priest built an altar according to all that King Ahaz had sent from Damascus. So Urijah the priest made *it* before King Ahaz came from Damascus.
12 And when the king came from Damascus, the king saw the altar; and the king approached the altar and made offerings on it.
13 So he burned his burnt offering and his grain offering; and he poured his drink offering and sprinkled the blood of his peace offerings on the altar.
14 He also brought the bronze altar which *was* before the LORD, from the front of the temple—from between the *new* altar and the house of the LORD—and put it on the north side of the *new* altar.
15 Then King Ahaz commanded Urijah the priest, saying, "On the great *new* altar burn the morning burnt offering, the evening grain offering, the king's burnt sacrifice, and his grain offering, with the burnt offering of all the people of the land, their grain offering, and their drink offerings; and sprinkle on it all the blood of the burnt offering and all the blood of the sacrifice. And the bronze altar shall be for me to inquire *by*."
16 Thus did Urijah the priest, according to all that King Ahaz commanded.
17 And King Ahaz cut off the panels of the carts, and removed the lavers from them; and he took down the Sea from the bronze oxen that *were* under it, and put it on a pavement of stones.
18 Also he removed the Sabbath pavilion which they had built in the temple, and he removed the king's outer entrance from the house of the LORD, on account of the king of Assyria.
19 Now the rest of the acts of Ahaz which he did, *are* they not written in the book of the chronicles of the kings of Judah?
20 So Ahaz rested with his fathers, and was buried with his fathers in the City of David. Then Hezekiah his son reigned in his place.

Hoshea Reigns in Israel

17 In the twelfth year of Ahaz king of Judah, Hoshea the son of Elah became king of Israel in Samaria, *and he reigned* nine years.
2 And he did evil in the sight of the LORD, but not as the kings of Israel who were before him.
3 Shalmaneser king of Assyria came up against him; and Hoshea became his vassal, and paid him tribute money.
4 And the king of Assyria uncovered a conspiracy by Hoshea; for he had sent messengers to So, king of Egypt, and brought no tribute to the king of Assyria, as *he had done* year by year. Therefore the king of Assyria shut him up, and bound him in prison.

Israel Carried Captive to Assyria

5 Now the king of Assyria went throughout all the land, and went up to Samaria and besieged it for three years.
6 In the ninth year of Hoshea, the king of Assyria took Samaria and carried Israel away to Assyria, and placed them in Halah and by the Habor, the River of Gozan, and in the cities of the Medes.
7 For so it was that the children of Israel had sinned against the LORD their God, who had brought them up out of the land of Egypt, from under the hand of Pharaoh king of Egypt; and they had feared other gods,
8 and had walked in the statutes of the nations whom the LORD had cast out from before the children of Israel, and of the kings of Israel, which they had made.
9 Also the children of Israel secretly did against the LORD their God things that

were not right, and they built for themselves high places in all their cities, from watchtower to fortified city.

10 They set up for themselves *sacred* pillars and wooden images[32] on every high hill and under every green tree;

11 and there they burned incense on all the high places, as the nations *had done* whom the LORD had carried away before them; and they did wicked things to provoke the LORD to anger,

12 for they served idols, of which the LORD had said to them, "You shall not do this thing."

13 Yet the LORD testified against Israel and against Judah, by all of His prophets, *namely* every seer, saying, "Turn from your evil ways, and keep My commandments *and* My statutes, according to all the law which I commanded your fathers, and which I sent to you by My servants the prophets."

14 Nevertheless they would not hear, but stiffened their necks, like the necks of their fathers, who did not believe in the LORD their God.

15 And they rejected His statutes and His covenant that He had made with their fathers, and His testimonies which He had testified against them; they followed idols, became idolaters, and *went* after the nations who *were* all around them, *concerning* whom the LORD had charged them that they should not do like them.

16 So they left all the commandments of the LORD their God, made for themselves a molded image *and* two calves, made a wooden image and worshiped all the host of heaven, and served Baal.

17 And they caused their sons and daughters to pass through the fire, practiced witchcraft and soothsaying, and sold themselves to do evil in the sight of the LORD, to provoke Him to anger.

18 Therefore the LORD was very angry with Israel, and removed them from His sight; there was none left but the tribe of Judah alone.

19 Also Judah did not keep the commandments of the LORD their God, but walked in the statutes of Israel which they made.

20 And the LORD rejected all the descendants of Israel, afflicted them, and delivered them into the hand of plunder-

ers, until He had cast them from His sight.

21 For He tore Israel from the house of David, and they made Jeroboam the son of Nebat king. Then Jeroboam drove Israel from following the LORD, and made them commit a great sin.

22 For the children of Israel walked in all the sins of Jeroboam which he did; they did not depart from them,

23 until the LORD removed Israel out of His sight, as He had said by all His servants the prophets. So Israel was carried away from their own land to Assyria, *as it is* to this day.

Assyria Resettles Samaria

24 Then the king of Assyria brought *people* from Babylon, Cuthah, Ava, Hamath, and from Sepharvaim, and placed *them* in the cities of Samaria instead of the children of Israel; and they took possession of Samaria and dwelt in its cities.

25 And it was so, at the beginning of their dwelling there, *that* they did not fear the LORD; therefore the LORD sent lions among them, which killed *some* of them.

26 So they spoke to the king of Assyria, saying, "The nations whom you have removed and placed in the cities of Samaria do not know the rituals of the God of the land; therefore He has sent lions among them, and indeed, they are killing them because they do not know the rituals of the God of the land."

27 Then the king of Assyria commanded, saying, "Send there one of the priests whom you brought from there; let him go and dwell there, and let him teach them the rituals of the God of the land."

28 Then one of the priests whom they had carried away from Samaria came and dwelt in Bethel, and taught them how they should fear the LORD.

29 However every nation continued to make gods of its own, and put *them* in the houses of the high places which the Samaritans had made, *every* nation in the cities where they dwelt.

30 The men of Babylon made Succoth Benoth, the men of Cuth made Nergal, the men of Hamath made Ashima,

31 and the Avites made Nibhaz and Tartak; and the Sepharvites burned their children in fire to Adrammelech and Anammelech, the gods of Sepharvaim.

32 Hebrew *Asherim,* Canaanite deities

32 So they feared the LORD, and from every class they appointed for themselves priests of the high places, who sacrificed for them in the shrines of the high places.
33 They feared the LORD, yet served their own gods—according to the rituals of the nations from among whom they were carried away.
34 To this day they continue practicing the former rituals; they do not fear the LORD, nor do they follow their statutes or their ordinances, or the law and commandment which the LORD had commanded the children of Jacob, whom He named Israel,
35 with whom the LORD had made a covenant and charged them, saying: "You shall not fear other gods, nor bow down to them nor serve them nor sacrifice to them;
36 "but the LORD, who brought you up from the land of Egypt with great power and an outstretched arm, Him you shall fear, Him you shall worship, and to Him you shall offer sacrifice.
37 "And the statutes, the ordinances, the law, and the commandment which He wrote for you, you shall be careful to observe forever; you shall not fear other gods.
38 "And the covenant that I have made with you, you shall not forget, nor shall you fear other gods.
39 "But the LORD your God you shall fear; and He will deliver you from the hand of all your enemies."
40 However they did not obey, but they followed their former rituals.
41 So these nations feared the LORD, yet served their carved images; also their children and their children's children have continued doing as their fathers did, even to this day.

Hezekiah Reigns in Judah

18 Now it came to pass in the third year of Hoshea the son of Elah, king of Israel, that Hezekiah the son of Ahaz, king of Judah, began to reign.
2 He was twenty-five years old when he became king, and he reigned twenty-nine years in Jerusalem. His mother's name was Abi[33] the daughter of Zechariah.
3 And he did what was right in the sight of the LORD, according to all that his father David had done.

4 He removed the high places and broke the sacred pillars, cut down the wooden images[34] and broke in pieces the bronze serpent that Moses had made; for until those days the children of Israel burned incense to it, and called it Nehushtan.[35]
5 He trusted in the LORD God of Israel, so that after him was none like him among all the kings of Judah, nor any who were before him.
6 For he held fast to the LORD; he did not depart from following Him, but kept His commandments, which the LORD had commanded Moses.
7 The LORD was with him; he prospered wherever he went. And he rebelled against the king of Assyria and did not serve him.
8 He subdued the Philistines, as far as Gaza and its territory, from watchtower to fortified city.
9 Now it came to pass in the fourth year of King Hezekiah, which was the seventh year of Hoshea the son of Elah, king of Israel, that Shalmaneser king of Assyria came up against Samaria and besieged it.
10 And at the end of three years they took it. In the sixth year of Hezekiah, that is, the ninth year of Hoshea king of Israel, Samaria was taken.
11 Then the king of Assyria carried Israel away captive to Assyria, and put them in Halah and by the Habor, the River of Gozan, and in the cities of the Medes,
12 because they did not obey the voice of the LORD their God, but transgressed His covenant and all that Moses the servant of the LORD had commanded; and they would neither hear nor do them.
13 And in the fourteenth year of King Hezekiah, Sennacherib king of Assyria came up against all the fortified cities of Judah and took them.
14 Then Hezekiah king of Judah sent to the king of Assyria at Lachish, saying, "I have done wrong; turn away from me; whatever you impose on me I will pay." And the king of Assyria assessed Hezekiah king of Judah three hundred talents of silver and thirty talents of gold.
15 So Hezekiah gave him all the silver that was found in the house of the LORD and in the treasuries of the king's house.
16 At that time Hezekiah stripped the gold from the doors of the temple of the

33 Called *Abijah* in 2 Chronicles 29:1ff   34 Hebrew *Asherah,* a Canaanite goddess   35 Literally *A Bronze Thing*

LORD, and *from* the pillars which Hezekiah king of Judah had overlaid, and gave it to the king of Assyria.

Sennacherib Boasts Against the LORD

17 Then the king of Assyria sent the Tartan,[36] the Rabsaris,[37] and the Rabshakeh[38] from Lachish, with a great army against Jerusalem, to King Hezekiah. And they went up and came to Jerusalem. When they had come up, they came and stood by the aqueduct from the upper pool, which *was* on the highway to the Fuller's Field.
18 And when they had called to the king, Eliakim the son of Hilkiah, who *was* over the household, Shebna the scribe, and Joah the son of Asaph, the recorder, came out to them.
19 Then the Rabshakeh said to them, "Say now to Hezekiah, 'Thus says the great king, the king of Assyria: "What confidence *is* this in which you trust?
20 "You speak of *having* counsel and strength for war; but *they are* vain words. And in whom do you trust, that you rebel against me?
21 "Now look! You are trusting in the staff of this broken reed, Egypt, on which if a man leans, it will go into his hand and pierce it. So *is* Pharaoh king of Egypt to all who trust in him.
22 "But if you say to me, 'We trust in the LORD our God,' *is* it not He whose high places and whose altars Hezekiah has taken away, and said to Judah and Jerusalem, 'You shall worship before this altar in Jerusalem'?'
23 "Now therefore, I urge you, give a pledge to my master the king of Assyria, and I will give you two thousand horses—if you are able on your part to put riders on them!
24 "How then will you repel one captain of the least of my master's servants, and put your trust in Egypt for chariots and horsemen?
25 "Have I now come up without the LORD against this place to destroy it? The LORD said to me, 'Go up against this land, and destroy it.'"
26 Then Eliakim the son of Hilkiah, Shebna, and Joah said to the Rabshakeh, "Please speak to your servants in the Aramaic language, for we understand *it*; and do not speak to us in Hebrew[39] in the hearing of the people who *are* on the wall."
27 But the Rabshakeh said to them, "Has my master sent me to your master and to you to speak these words, and not to the men who sit on the wall, who will eat and drink their own waste with you?"
28 Then the Rabshakeh stood and called out with a loud voice in Hebrew, and spoke, saying, "Hear the word of the great king, the king of Assyria!
29 "Thus says the king: 'Do not let Hezekiah deceive you, for he shall not be able to deliver you from his hand;
30 'nor let Hezekiah make you trust in the LORD, saying, "The LORD will surely deliver us; this city shall not be given into the hand of the king of Assyria."'
31 "Do not listen to Hezekiah; for thus says the king of Assyria: 'Make *peace* with me by a present and come out to me; and every one of you eat from his own vine and every one from his own fig tree, and every one of you drink the waters of his own cistern;
32 'until I come and take you away to a land like your own land, a land of grain and new wine, a land of bread and vineyards, a land of olive groves and honey, that you may live and not die. But do not listen to Hezekiah, lest he persuade you, saying, "The LORD will deliver us."
33 'Has any of the gods of the nations at all delivered its land from the hand of the king of Assyria?
34 'Where *are* the gods of Hamath and Arpad? Where *are* the gods of Sepharvaim and Hena and Ivah? Indeed, have they delivered Samaria from my hand?
35 'Who among all the gods of the lands have delivered their countries from my hand, that the LORD should deliver Jerusalem from my hand?'"
36 But the people held their peace and answered him not a word; for the king's commandment was, "Do not answer him."
37 Then Eliakim the son of Hilkiah, who *was* over the household, Shebna the scribe, and Joah the son of Asaph, the recorder, came to Hezekiah with *their* clothes torn, and told him the words of the Rabshakeh.

---

36 A title, probably *Commander in Chief*   37 A title, probably *Chief Officer*
38 A title, probably *Chief of Staff* or *Governor*   39 Literally *Judean*

Isaiah Assures Deliverance

19 And so it was, when King Hezekiah heard *it*, that he tore his clothes, covered himself with sackcloth, and went into the house of the LORD.
2 Then he sent Eliakim, who *was* over the household, Shebna the scribe, and the elders of the priests, covered with sackcloth, to Isaiah the prophet, the son of Amoz.
3 And they said to him, "Thus says Hezekiah: 'This day *is* a day of trouble, and rebuke, and blasphemy; for the children have come to birth, but *there is* no strength to bring them forth.
4 'It may be that the LORD your God will hear all the words of the Rabshakeh, whom his master the king of Assyria has sent to reproach the living God, and will reprove the words which the LORD your God has heard. Therefore lift up *your* prayer for the remnant that is left.' "
5 So the servants of King Hezekiah came to Isaiah.
6 And Isaiah said to them, "Thus you shall say to your master, 'Thus says the LORD: "Do not be afraid of the words which you have heard, with which the servants of the king of Assyria have blasphemed Me.
7 "Surely I will send a spirit upon him, and he shall hear a rumor and return to his own land; and I will cause him to fall by the sword in his own land." ' "

Sennacherib's Threat and Hezekiah's Prayer

8 So the Rabshakeh returned and found the king of Assyria warring against Libnah, for he heard that he had departed from Lachish.
9 And the king heard concerning Tirhakah king of Ethiopia, "Look, he has come out to make war with you." So he again sent messengers to Hezekiah, saying,
10 "Thus you shall speak to Hezekiah king of Judah, saying: 'Do not let your God in whom you trust deceive you, saying, "Jerusalem shall not be given into the hand of the king of Assyria."
11 'Look! You have heard what the kings of Assyria have done to all lands by utterly destroying them; and shall you be delivered?
12 'Have the gods of the nations delivered those whom my fathers have destroyed, Gozan and Haran and Re-

zeph, and the people of Eden who *were* in Telassar?
13 'Where *is* the king of Hamath, the king of Arpad, and the king of the city of Sepharvaim, Hena, and Ivah?' "
14 And Hezekiah received the letter from the hand of the messengers, and read it; and Hezekiah went up to the house of the LORD, and spread it before the LORD.
15 Then Hezekiah prayed before the LORD, and said: "O LORD God of Israel, *the One* who dwells *between* the cherubim, You are God, You alone, of all the kingdoms of the earth. You have made heaven and earth.
16 "Incline Your ear, O LORD, and hear; open Your eyes, O LORD, and see; and hear the words of Sennacherib, which he has sent to reproach the living God.
17 "Truly, LORD, the kings of Assyria have laid waste the nations and their lands,
18 "and have cast their gods into the fire; for they *were* not gods, but the work of men's hands—wood and stone. Therefore they have destroyed them.
19 "Now therefore, O LORD our God, I pray, save us from his hand, that all the kingdoms of the earth may know that You *are* the LORD God, You alone."

The Word of the LORD Concerning Sennacherib

20 Then Isaiah the son of Amoz sent to Hezekiah, saying, "Thus says the LORD God of Israel: '*That* which you have prayed to Me against Sennacherib king of Assyria I have heard.'
21 "This *is* the word which the LORD has spoken concerning him:

'The virgin, the daughter of Zion,
  Has despised you,
    laughed you to scorn;
  The daughter of Jerusalem
  Has shaken *her* head
    behind your back!
22 'Whom have you reproached
    and blasphemed?
  Against whom have you raised
    your voice,
  And lifted up your eyes on high?
  Against the Holy *One* of Israel.
23 By your messengers you have
    reproached the Lord,
  And said: "By the multitude
    of my chariots

I have come up
  to the height of the mountains,
To the limits of Lebanon;
I will cut down its tall cedars
And its choice cypress trees;
I will enter the extremity of its borders,
To its fruitful forest.
24 I have dug and drunk strange water,
And with the soles of my feet
  I have dried up
All the brooks of defense."

25 'Did you not hear long ago
How I made it,
From ancient times that I formed it?
Now I have brought it to pass,
That you should be
For crushing fortified cities
into heaps of ruins.
26 Therefore their inhabitants
  had little power;
They were dismayed and confounded;
They were *as* the grass of the field
And the green herb,
As the grass on the housetops
And *grain* blighted before it is grown.

27 'But I know your dwelling place,
Your going out and your coming in,
And your rage against Me.
28 Because your rage against Me
  and your tumult
Have come up to My ears,
Therefore I will put
  My hook in your nose
And My bridle in your lips,
And I will turn you back
By the way which you came.

29 'This *shall be* a sign to you:

You shall eat this year
  such as grows of itself,
And in the second year
  what springs from the same;
Also in the third year sow and reap,
Plant vineyards and eat
  the fruit of them.
30 And the remnant who have escaped
  of the house of Judah
Shall again take root downward,
And bear fruit upward.
31 For out of Jerusalem
  shall go a remnant,
And those who escape
  from Mount Zion.
The zeal of the LORD *of hosts*
  shall do this.'

32 "Therefore thus says the LORD concerning the king of Assyria:

'He shall not come into this city,
Nor shoot an arrow there,
Nor come before it with shield,
Nor build a siege mound against it.
33 By the way that he came,
By the same shall he return;
And he shall not come into this city,'
Says the LORD.
34 'For I will defend this city, to save it
For My own sake
  and for My servant David's sake.' "

Sennacherib's Defeat and Death

35 And it came to pass on a certain night that the angel[40] of the LORD went out, and killed in the camp of the Assyrians one hundred and eighty-five thousand; and when people[41] arose early in the morning, there *were* the corpses—all dead.
36 So Sennacherib king of Assyria departed and went away, returned *home*, and remained at Nineveh.
37 Now it came to pass, as he was worshiping in the temple of Nisroch his god, that his sons Adrammelech and Sharezer struck him down with the sword; and they escaped into the land of Ararat. Then Esarhaddon his son reigned in his place.

Hezekiah's Life Extended

20 In those days Hezekiah was sick and near death. And Isaiah the prophet, the son of Amoz, went to him and said to him, "Thus says the LORD: 'Set your house in order, for you shall die, and not live.' "
2 Then he turned his face toward the wall, and prayed to the LORD, saying,
3 "Remember now, O LORD, I pray, how I have walked before You in truth and with a loyal heart, and have done *what was* good in Your sight." And Hezekiah wept bitterly.
4 Then it happened, before Isaiah had gone out into the middle court, that the word of the LORD came to him, saying,
5 "Return and tell Hezekiah the leader of My people, 'Thus says the LORD, the God of David your father: "I have heard your prayer, I have seen your tears; surely I will heal you. On the third day you shall go up to the house of the LORD.

40 Or *Angel*   41 Literally *they*

When Faced with a Mountain—
Tunnel Underneath

In 721 B.C. the mighty Assyrian empire came marching down on the kingdom of Israel as "a wolf upon the fold." The Assyrian king, Sennacherib, led his soldiers on a lightning-quick campaign smashing towns and villages which lay in his path. His military strategy was to conquer Galilee and the coastal plains. Once these were controlled, Sennacherib could march on Jerusalem, knowing that all escape routes from the city would be cut off.

The monarch of Jerusalem, King Hezekiah, was terrified. Undoubtedly he had looked down from the heights of Judea and seen the columns of smoke rising from the destroyed villages which lay in the wake of the advancing Assyrian army. King Hezekiah knew Jerusalem was next. He was faced with an insurmountable problem—how to defend Jerusalem against this powerful foe.

The first thing King Hezekiah did was pray! God gave him the strength to believe and think clearly. Second, he fortified the city wall. Third, God gave him an "impossible" solution to his greatest problem of all—to protect Jerusalem's water source. The only spring providing water for Jerusalem was located outside the city wall at the bottom of a hill. If the Assyrian army cut off the water supply, Jerusalem would fall within a few days.

As the Assyrian army approached, King Hezekiah ordered a tunnel to be dug which would bring water from outside the wall, inside the city. One work crew would not have enough time to accomplish this before Sennacherib and his army arrived. To solve this, Hezekiah conceived the impossible: two work crews, one outside and one inside the city walls would tunnel toward each other. Day and night they worked, cutting through the mountain of solid rock. Winding and twisting, the tunnel became a 1,700-foot-long maze.

Finally, early one morning, just before the Assyrian army crested the hill overlooking Jerusalem, each of the work crews, deep in the bowels of the earth, heard the sounds of the other's pick axes. Miraculously, they had met less than one foot from each other. They had saved the city. Jerusalem withstood the siege and the Assyrian army returned home. No known mathematical or engineering formula could have accomplished this. The world's greatest archaeologists are still puzzled by this feat.

When faced with a mountain, King Hezekiah did not quit—he tunneled underneath. When you face your mountain, remember: do not quit! Climb over, find a pass through, tunnel underneath or simply stay and turn your mountain into a gold mine with God's help!

6 "And I will add to your days fifteen years. I will deliver you and this city from the hand of the king of Assyria; and I will defend this city for My own sake, and for the sake of My servant David." ' "

7 Then Isaiah said, "Take a lump of figs." So they took and laid it on the boil, and he recovered.

8 And Hezekiah said to Isaiah, "What is the sign that the LORD will heal me, and that I shall go up to the house of the LORD the third day?"

9 Then Isaiah said, "This is the sign to you from the LORD, that the LORD will do the thing which He has spoken: shall the shadow go forward ten degrees or go backward ten degrees?"

10 And Hezekiah answered, "It is an easy thing for the shadow to go down ten degrees; no, but let the shadow go backward ten degrees."

11 So Isaiah the prophet cried out to the LORD, and He brought the shadow ten degrees backward, by which it had gone down on the sundial of Ahaz.

The Babylonian Envoys

12 At that time Berodach-Baladan[42] the son of Baladan, king of Babylon, sent letters and a present to Hezekiah, for he heard that Hezekiah had been sick.

13 And Hezekiah was attentive to them, and showed them all the house of his treasures—the silver and gold, the spices and precious ointment, and all his armory—all that was found among his treasures. There was nothing in his house or in all his dominion that Hezekiah did not show them.

14 Then Isaiah the prophet went to King Hezekiah, and said to him, "What did these men say, and from where did they come to you?" And Hezekiah said, "They came from a far country, from Babylon."

15 And he said, "What have they seen in your house?" So Hezekiah answered, "They have seen all that is in my house; there is nothing among my treasures that I have not shown them."

16 Then Isaiah said to Hezekiah, "Hear the word of the LORD:

17 'Behold, the days are coming when all that is in your house, and what your fathers have accumulated until this day, shall be carried to Babylon; nothing shall be left,' says the LORD.

18 'And they shall take away some of your sons who will descend from you, whom you will beget; and they shall be eunuchs in the palace of the king of Babylon.' "

19 Then Hezekiah said to Isaiah, "The word of the LORD which you have spoken is good!" For he said, "Will there not be peace and truth at least in my days?"

Death of Hezekiah

20 Now the rest of the acts of Hezekiah—all his might, and how he made a pool and a tunnel and brought water into the city—are they not written in the book of the chronicles of the kings of Judah?

21 So Hezekiah rested with his fathers. Then Manasseh his son reigned in his place.

Manasseh Reigns in Judah

21 Manasseh was twelve years old when he became king, and he reigned fifty-five years in Jerusalem. His mother's name was Hephzibah.

2 And he did evil in the sight of the LORD, according to the abominations of the nations whom the LORD had cast out before the children of Israel.

3 For he rebuilt the high places which Hezekiah his father had destroyed; he raised up altars for Baal, and made a wooden image,[43] as Ahab king of Israel had done; and he worshiped all the host of heaven[44] and served them.

4 He also built altars in the house of the LORD, of which the LORD had said, "In Jerusalem I will put My name."

5 And he built altars for all the host of heaven in the two courts of the house of the LORD.

6 Also he made his son pass through the fire, practiced soothsaying, used witchcraft, and consulted spiritists and mediums. He did much evil in the sight of the LORD, to provoke Him to anger.

7 He even set a carved image of Asherah[45] that he had made, in the house of which the LORD had said to David and to Solomon his son, "In this house and in Jerusalem, which I have chosen out of all the tribes of Israel, I will put My name forever;

42 Spelled *Merodach-Baladan* in Isaiah 39:1   43 Hebrew *Asherah,* a Canaanite goddess
44 The gods of the Assyrians   45 A Canaanite goddess

8 "and I will not make the feet of Israel wander anymore from the land which I gave their fathers—only if they are careful to do according to all that I have commanded them, and according to all the law that My servant Moses commanded them."

9 But they paid no attention, and Manasseh seduced them to do more evil than the nations whom the LORD had destroyed before the children of Israel.

10 And the LORD spoke by His servants the prophets, saying,

11 "Because Manasseh king of Judah has done these abominations (he has acted more wickedly than all the Amorites who *were* before him, and has also made Judah sin with his idols),

12 "therefore thus says the LORD God of Israel: 'Behold, *I* am bringing *such* calamity upon Jerusalem and Judah, that whoever hears of it, both his ears will tingle.

13 'And I will stretch over Jerusalem the measuring line of Samaria and the plummet of the house of Ahab; I will wipe Jerusalem as *one* wipes a dish, wiping *it* and turning *it* upside down.

14 'So I will forsake the remnant of My inheritance and deliver them into the hand of their enemies; and they shall become victims of plunder to all their enemies,

15 'because they have done evil in My sight, and have provoked Me to anger since the day their fathers came out of Egypt, even to this day.' "

16 Moreover Manasseh shed very much innocent blood, till he had filled Jerusalem from one end to another, besides his sin with which he made Judah sin, in doing evil in the sight of the LORD.

17 Now the rest of the acts of Manasseh—all that he did, and the sin that he committed—*are* they not written in the book of the chronicles of the kings of Judah?

18 So Manasseh rested with his fathers, and was buried in the garden of his own house, in the garden of Uzza. Then his son Amon reigned in his place.

Amon's Reign and Death

19 Amon *was* twenty-two years old when he became king, and he reigned two years in Jerusalem. His mother's name *was* Meshullemeth the daughter of Haruz of Jotbah.

20 And he did evil in the sight of the LORD, as his father Manasseh had done.

21 So he walked in all the ways that his father had walked; and he served the idols that his father had served, and worshiped them.

22 He forsook the LORD God of his fathers, and did not walk in the way of the LORD.

23 Then the servants of Amon conspired against him, and killed the king in his own house.

24 But the people of the land executed all those who had conspired against King Amon. Then the people of the land made his son Josiah king in his place.

25 Now the rest of the acts of Amon which he did, *are* they not written in the book of the chronicles of the kings of Judah?

26 And he was buried in his tomb in the garden of Uzza. Then Josiah his son reigned in his place.

Josiah Reigns in Judah

22 Josiah *was* eight years old when he became king, and he reigned thirty-one years in Jerusalem. His mother's name *was* Jedidah the daughter of Adaiah of Bozkath.

2 And he did *what was* right in the sight of the LORD, and walked in all the ways of his father David; he did not turn aside to the right hand or to the left.

Hilkiah Finds the Book of the Law

3 Now it came to pass, in the eighteenth year of King Josiah, *that* the king sent Shaphan the scribe, the son of Azaliah, the son of Meshullam, to the house of the LORD, saying:

4 "Go up to Hilkiah the high priest, that he may count the money which has been brought into the house of the LORD, which the doorkeepers have gathered from the people.

5 "And let them deliver it into the hand of those doing the work, who are the overseers in the house of the LORD; let them give it to those who *are* in the house of the LORD doing the work, to repair the damages of the house—

6 "to carpenters and builders and masons—and to buy timber and hewn stone to repair the house.

7 "However there need be no accounting made with them of the money deliv-

ered into their hand, because they deal faithfully."

8 Then Hilkiah the high priest said to Shaphan the scribe, "I have found the Book of the Law in the house of the LORD." And Hilkiah gave the book to Shaphan, and he read it.

9 So Shaphan the scribe went to the king, bringing the king word, saying, "Your servants have gathered the money that was found in the house, and have delivered it into the hand of those who do the work, who oversee the house of the LORD."

10 Then Shaphan the scribe showed the king, saying, "Hilkiah the priest has given me a book." And Shaphan read it before the king.

11 Now it happened, when the king heard the words of the Book of the Law, that he tore his clothes.

12 Then the king commanded Hilkiah the priest, Ahikam the son of Shaphan, Achbor[46] the son of Michaiah, Shaphan the scribe, and Asaiah a servant of the king, saying,

13 "Go, inquire of the LORD for me, for the people and for all Judah, concerning the words of this book that has been found; for great *is* the wrath of the LORD that is aroused against us, because our fathers have not obeyed the words of this book, to do according to all that is written concerning us."

14 So Hilkiah the priest, Ahikam, Achbor, Shaphan, and Asaiah went to Huldah the prophetess, the wife of Shallum the son of Tikvah, the son of Harhas, keeper of the wardrobe. (She dwelt in Jerusalem in the Second Quarter.) And they spoke with her.

15 Then she said to them, "Thus says the LORD God of Israel, 'Tell the man who sent you to me,

16 "Thus says the LORD: 'Behold, I will bring calamity on this place and on its inhabitants—all the words of the book which the king of Judah has read—

17 'because they have forsaken Me and burned incense to other gods, that they might provoke Me to anger with all the works of their hands. Therefore My wrath shall be aroused against this place and shall not be quenched.' " '

18 "But to the king of Judah, who sent you to inquire of the LORD, in this man-

ner you shall speak to him, 'Thus says the LORD God of Israel: "*Concerning* the words which you have heard—

19 "because your heart was tender, and you humbled yourself before the LORD when you heard what I spoke against this place and against its inhabitants, that they would become a desolation and a curse, and you tore your clothes and wept before Me, I also have heard *you*," says the LORD.

20 "Surely, therefore, I will gather you to your fathers, and you shall be gathered to your grave in peace; and your eyes shall not see all the calamity which I will bring on this place." ' " So they brought word to the king.

Josiah Restores True Worship

23 Then the king sent them to gather all the elders of Judah and Jerusalem to him.

2 And the king went up to the house of the LORD with all the men of Judah, and with him all the inhabitants of Jerusalem—the priests and the prophets and all the people, both small and great; and he read in their hearing all the words of the Book of the Covenant which had been found in the house of the LORD.

3 Then the king stood by a pillar and made a covenant before the LORD, to follow the LORD and to keep His commandments and His testimonies and His statutes, with all *his* heart and all *his* soul, to perform the words of this covenant that were written in this book. And all the people took their stand for the covenant.

4 And the king commanded Hilkiah the high priest, the priests of the second order, and the doorkeepers, to bring out of the temple of the LORD all the articles that were made for Baal, for Asherah,[47] and for all the host of heaven;[48] and he burned them outside Jerusalem in the fields of Kidron, and carried their ashes to Bethel.

5 Then he removed the idolatrous priests whom the kings of Judah had ordained to burn incense on the high places in the cities of Judah and in the places all around Jerusalem, and those who burned incense to Baal, to the sun, to the moon, to the constellations, and to all the host of heaven.

---

46 *Abdon the son of Micah* in 2 Chronicles 34:20   47 A Canaanite goddess   48 The gods of the Assyrians

6 And he brought out the wooden image[49] from the house of the LORD, to the Brook Kidron outside Jerusalem, burned it at the Brook Kidron and ground it to ashes, and threw its ashes on the graves of the common people.
7 Then he tore down the ritual booths of the perverted persons[50] that were in the house of the LORD, where the women wove hangings for the wooden image.
8 And he brought all the priests from the cities of Judah, and defiled the high places where the priests had burned incense, from Geba to Beersheba; also he broke down the high places at the gates which were at the entrance of the Gate of Joshua the governor of the city, which were to the left of the city gate.
9 Nevertheless the priests of the high places did not come up to the altar of the LORD in Jerusalem, but they ate unleavened bread among their brethren.
10 And he defiled Topheth, which is in the Valley of the Son[51] of Hinnom, that no man might make his son or his daughter pass through the fire to Molech.
11 Then he removed the horses that the kings of Judah had dedicated to the sun, at the entrance to the house of the LORD, by the chamber of Nathan-Melech, the officer who was in the court; and he burned the chariots of the sun with fire.
12 The altars that were on the roof, the upper chamber of Ahaz, which the kings of Judah had made, and the altars which Manasseh had made in the two courts of the house of the LORD, the king broke down and pulverized there, and threw their dust into the Brook Kidron.
13 Then the king defiled the high places that were east of Jerusalem, which were on the south of the Mount of Corruption, which Solomon king of Israel had built for Ashtoreth the abomination of the Sidonians, for Chemosh the abomination of the Moabites, and for Milcom the abomination of the people of Ammon.
14 And he broke in pieces the sacred pillars and cut down the wooden images, and filled their places with the bones of men.
15 Moreover the altar that was at Bethel, and the high place which Jeroboam the son of Nebat, who made Israel sin, had made, both that altar and the high place

he broke down; and he burned the high place and crushed it to powder, and burned the wooden image.
16 As Josiah turned, he saw the tombs that were there on the mountain. And he sent and took the bones out of the tombs and burned them on the altar, and defiled it according to the word of the LORD which the man of God proclaimed, who proclaimed these words.
17 Then he said, "What gravestone is this that I see?" And the men of the city told him, "It is the tomb of the man of God who came from Judah and proclaimed these things which you have done against the altar of Bethel."
18 And he said, "Let him alone; let no one move his bones." So they let his bones alone, with the bones of the prophet who came from Samaria.
19 Then Josiah also took away all the shrines of the high places that were in the cities of Samaria, which the kings of Israel had made to provoke the LORD to anger; and he did to them according to all the deeds he had done in Bethel.
20 He executed all the priests of the high places who were there on the altars, and burned men's bones on them; and he returned to Jerusalem.
21 Then the king commanded all the people, saying, "Keep the Passover to the LORD your God, as it is written in this Book of the Covenant."
22 Surely such a Passover had never been held since the days of the judges who judged Israel, nor in all the days of the kings of Israel and the kings of Judah.
23 But in the eighteenth year of King Josiah this Passover was held before the LORD in Jerusalem.
24 Moreover Josiah put away those who consulted mediums and spiritists, the household gods and idols, all the abominations that were seen in the land of Judah and in Jerusalem, that he might perform the words of the law which were written in the book that Hilkiah the priest found in the house of the LORD.
25 Now before him there was no king like him, who turned to the LORD with all his heart, with all his soul, and with all his might, according to all the Law of Moses; nor after him did any arise like him.

49 Hebrew Asherah, a Canaanite goddess
50 Hebrew qedeshim, that is, those practicing sodomy and prostitution in religious rituals   51 Kethib reads sons.

Impending Judgment on Judah

26 Nevertheless the LORD did not turn from the fierceness of His great wrath, with which His anger was aroused against Judah, because of all the provocations with which Manasseh had provoked Him. **27** And the LORD said, "I will also remove Judah from My sight, as I have removed Israel, and will cast off this city Jerusalem which I have chosen, and the house of which I said, 'My name shall be there.' "⁵²

Josiah Dies in Battle

28 Now the rest of the acts of Josiah, and all that he did, *are* they not written in the book of the chronicles of the kings of Judah? **29** In his days Pharaoh Necho king of Egypt went to the aid of the king of Assyria, to the River Euphrates; and King Josiah went against him. And Pharaoh Necho⁵³ killed him at Megiddo when he confronted him. **30** Then his servants moved his body in a chariot from Megiddo, brought him to Jerusalem, and buried him in his own tomb. And the people of the land took Jehoahaz the son of Josiah, anointed him, and made him king in his father's place.

The Reign and Captivity of Jehoahaz

31 Jehoahaz *was* twenty-three years old when he became king, and he reigned three months in Jerusalem. His mother's name *was* Hamutal the daughter of Jeremiah of Libnah. **32** And he did evil in the sight of the LORD, according to all that his fathers had done. **33** Now Pharaoh Necho put him in prison at Riblah in the land of Hamath, that he might not reign in Jerusalem; and he imposed on the land a tribute of one hundred talents of silver and a talent of gold. **34** Then Pharaoh Necho made Eliakim the son of Josiah king in place of his father Josiah, and changed his name to Jehoiakim. And Pharaoh⁵⁴ took Jehoahaz and went to Egypt, and he⁵⁵ died there.

Jehoiakim Reigns in Judah

35 So Jehoiakim gave the silver and gold to Pharaoh; but he taxed the land to give money according to the commandment of Pharaoh; he exacted the silver and gold from the people of the land, from every one according to his assessment, to give *it* to Pharaoh Necho. **36** Jehoiakim *was* twenty-five years old when he became king, and he reigned eleven years in Jerusalem. His mother's name *was* Zebudah the daughter of Pedaiah of Rumah. **37** And he did evil in the sight of the LORD, according to all that his fathers had done.

Judah Overrun by Enemies

24 In his days Nebuchadnezzar king of Babylon came up, and Jehoiakim became his vassal *for* three years. Then he turned and rebelled against him. **2** And the LORD sent against him *raiding* bands of Chaldeans, bands of Syrians, bands of Moabites, and bands of the people of Ammon; He sent them against Judah to destroy it, according to the word of the LORD which He had spoken by His servants the prophets. **3** Surely at the commandment of the LORD *this* came upon Judah, to remove *them* from His sight because of the sins of Manasseh, according to all that he had done, **4** and also because of the innocent blood that he had shed; for he had filled Jerusalem with innocent blood, which the LORD would not pardon. **5** Now the rest of the acts of Jehoiakim, and all that he did, *are* they not written in the book of the chronicles of the kings of Judah? **6** So Jehoiakim rested with his fathers. Then Jehoiachin his son reigned in his place. **7** And the king of Egypt did not come out of his land anymore, for the king of Babylon had taken all that belonged to the king of Egypt from the Brook of Egypt to the River Euphrates.

The Reign and Captivity of Jehoiachin

8 Jehoiachin *was* eighteen years old when he became king, and he reigned in Jerusalem three months. His mother's name *was* Nehushta the daughter of Elnathan of Jerusalem. **9** And he did evil in the sight of the LORD, according to all that his father had done.

---

52 1 Kings 8:29   53 Literally *he*   54 Literally *he*   55 That is, Jehoahaz

10 At that time the servants of Nebuchadnezzar king of Babylon came up against Jerusalem, and the city was besieged.
11 And Nebuchadnezzar king of Babylon came against the city, as his servants were besieging it.
12 Then Jehoiachin king of Judah, his mother, his servants, his princes, and his officers went out to the king of Babylon; and the king of Babylon, in the eighth year of his reign, took him prisoner.

The Captivity of Jerusalem

13 And he carried out from there all the treasures of the house of the LORD and the treasures of the king's house, and he cut in pieces all the articles of gold which Solomon king of Israel had made in the temple of the LORD, as the LORD had said.
14 Also he carried into captivity all Jerusalem: all the captains and all the mighty men of valor, ten thousand captives, and all the craftsmen and smiths. None remained except the poorest people of the land.
15 And he carried Jehoiachin captive to Babylon. The king's mother, the king's wives, his officers, and the mighty of the land he carried into captivity from Jerusalem to Babylon.
16 All the valiant men, seven thousand, and craftsmen and smiths, one thousand, all who were strong and fit for war, these the king of Babylon brought captive to Babylon.

Zedekiah Reigns in Judah

17 Then the king of Babylon made Mattaniah, Jehoiachin's[56] uncle, king in his place, and changed his name to Zedekiah.
18 Zedekiah was twenty-one years old when he became king, and he reigned eleven years in Jerusalem. His mother's name was Hamutal the daughter of Jeremiah of Libnah.
19 He also did evil in the sight of the LORD, according to all that Jehoiakim had done.
20 For because of the anger of the LORD this happened in Jerusalem and Judah, that He finally cast them out from His presence. Then Zedekiah rebelled against the king of Babylon.

The Fall and Exile of Judah

25 Now it came to pass in the ninth year of his reign, in the tenth month, on the tenth day of the month, that Nebuchadnezzar king of Babylon and all his army came against Jerusalem and encamped against it; and they built a siege wall against it all around.
2 So the city was besieged until the eleventh year of King Zedekiah.
3 By the ninth day of the fourth month the famine had become so severe in the city that there was no food for the people of the land.
4 Then the city wall was broken through, and all the men of war fled at night by way of the gate between two walls, which was by the king's garden, even though the Chaldeans were still encamped all around against the city. And the king went by way of the plain.[57]
5 But the army of the Chaldeans pursued the king, and they overtook him in the plains of Jericho. All his army was scattered from him.
6 So they took the king and brought him up to the king of Babylon at Riblah, and they pronounced judgment on him.
7 Then they killed the sons of Zedekiah before his eyes, put out the eyes of Zedekiah, bound him with bronze fetters, and took him to Babylon.
8 Now in the fifth month, on the seventh day of the month (which was the nineteenth year of King Nebuchadnezzar king of Babylon), Nebuzaradan the captain of the guard, a servant of the king of Babylon, came to Jerusalem.
9 He burned the house of the LORD and the king's house; all the houses of Jerusalem, that is, all the houses of the great men, he burned with fire.
10 And all the army of the Chaldeans who were with the captain of the guard broke down the walls of Jerusalem all around.
11 Then Nebuzaradan the captain of the guard carried away captive the rest of the people who remained in the city and the defectors who had deserted to the king of Babylon, with the rest of the multitude.
12 But the captain of the guard left some of the poor of the land as vinedressers and farmers.
13 The bronze pillars that were in the

56 Literally his   57 Or arabah, that is, the Jordan Valley

house of the LORD, and the carts and the bronze Sea that *were* in the house of the LORD, the Chaldeans broke in pieces, and carried their bronze to Babylon.

14 They also took away the pots, the shovels, the trimmers, the spoons, and all the bronze utensils with which the priests ministered.

15 The firepans and the basins, the things *made* of solid gold and solid silver, the captain of the guard took away.

16 The two pillars, one Sea, and the carts, which Solomon had made for the house of the LORD, the bronze of all these articles was beyond measure.

17 The height of one pillar *was* eighteen cubits, and the capital on it *was* of bronze. The height of the capital was three cubits, and the network and pomegranates all around the capital were all of bronze. The second pillar was the same, with a network.

18 And the captain of the guard took Seraiah the chief priest, Zephaniah the second priest, and the three doorkeepers.

19 He also took out of the city an officer who had charge of the men of war, five men of the king's close associates who were found in the city, the principal scribe of the army who mustered the people of the land, and sixty men of the people of the land *who were* found in the city.

20 So Nebuzaradan, captain of the guard, took these and brought them to the king of Babylon at Riblah.

21 Then the king of Babylon struck them and put them to death at Riblah in the land of Hamath. Thus Judah was carried away captive from its own land.

Gedaliah Made Governor of Judah

22 Then he made Gedaliah the son of Ahikam, the son of Shaphan, governor over the people who remained in the land

of Judah, whom Nebuchadnezzar king of Babylon had left.

23 Now when all the captains of the armies, they and *their* men, heard that the king of Babylon had made Gedaliah governor, they came to Gedaliah at Mizpah—Ishmael the son of Nethaniah, Johanan the son of Careah, Seraiah the son of Tanhumeth the Netophathite, and Jaazaniah[58] the son of a Maachathite, they and their men.

24 And Gedaliah took an oath before them and their men, and said to them, "Do not be afraid of the servants of the Chaldeans. Dwell in the land and serve the king of Babylon, and it shall be well with you."

25 Now it happened in the seventh month that Ishmael the son of Nethaniah, the son of Elishama, of the royal family, came with ten men and struck and killed Gedaliah, the Jews, and the Chaldeans who were with him at Mizpah.

26 And all the people, small and great, and the captains of the armies, arose and went to Egypt; for they were afraid of the Chaldeans.

Jehoiachin Released from Prison

27 Now it came to pass in the thirty-seventh year of the captivity of Jehoiachin king of Judah, in the twelfth month, on the twenty-seventh *day* of the month, *that* Evil-Merodach[59] king of Babylon, in the year that he began to reign, released Jehoiachin king of Judah from prison.

28 He spoke kindly to him, and gave him a more prominent seat than those of the kings who *were* with him in Babylon.

29 So Jehoiachin changed from his prison garments, and he ate bread regularly before the king all the days of his life.

30 And as for his provisions, *there was* a regular ration given him by the king, a portion for each day, all the days of his life.

58 Spelled *Jezaniah* in Jeremiah 40:8   59 Literally *Man of Marduk*

Introduction to First Chronicles

The Book of First Chronicles is to be seen as a supplement and a companion volume to the Books of First and Second Samuel and First and Second Kings. It was most likely compiled by Ezra using public records of the scribes and prophets through the centuries between 1000 and 500 B.C.

Containing a multitude of genealogies, First Chronicles lists the family background of Israel's leaders. Focusing on Saul and David, Chronicles records their rule as Israel's first two kings.

Highlighting the Book of First Chronicles is the reign of King David who was a just and godly king who fought many wars, gaining victory over the Assyrians, Ammonites, and Philistines. David was a powerful personality who instilled courage in his men to fight against insurmountable odds. They were known as "the mighty men."

David understood the nature of worship. In praising God he said, "O LORD, *there is none like You, nor is there any* God besides You . . ." (1 Chr. 17:20). He brought the ark of the covenant which had been removed from its rightful place, back to the tabernacle in Jerusalem. David also organized a large choir and put his beautiful psalms to music.

O LORD, our Lord,
How excellent *is* Your name in all the earth,
You who set Your glory above the heavens!
When I consider Your heavens, the work of Your fingers,
The moon and the stars, which You have ordained,
What is man that You are mindful of him,
And the son of man that You visit him?
For You have made him a little lower than the angels,
And You have crowned him with glory and honor.
O LORD, our Lord,
How excellent *is* Your name in all the earth!

(Ps. 8:1, 3–5, 9)

Finally, although David was not to build the temple, he prepared the hearts of the people for the task. Having accomplished much, David was able to say at the end of his life that he had a dream. He instilled positive, motivational thoughts and desires in the people that would last beyond his lifetime! David shared a dream to build a future!

The First Book of the

Chronicles

The Family of Adam—Seth to Abraham

ADAM, Seth, Enosh,
2 Cainan,[1] Mahalaleel,[2] Jared,
3 Enoch, Methuselah, Lamech,
4 Noah, Shem, Ham, and Japheth.
5 The sons of Japheth were Gomer, Magog, Madai, Javan, Tubal, Meshech, and Tiras.
6 The sons of Gomer were Ashkenaz, Diphath,[3] and Togarmah.
7 The sons of Javan were Elishah, Tarshishah,[4] Kittim, and Rodanim.[5]
8 The sons of Ham were Cush, Mizraim, Put, and Canaan.
9 The sons of Cush were Seba, Havilah, Sabta,[6] Raama,[7] and Sabtecha. The sons of Raama were Sheba and Dedan.
10 Cush begot Nimrod; he began to be a mighty one on the earth.
11 Mizraim begot Ludim, Anamim, Lehabim, Naphtuhim,
12 Pathrusim, Casluhim (from whom came the Philistines and the Caphtorim).
13 Canaan begot Sidon, his firstborn, and Heth;
14 the Jebusite, the Amorite, and the Girgashite;
15 the Hivite, the Arkite, and the Sinite;
16 the Arvadite, the Zemarite, and the Hamathite.
17 The sons of Shem were Elam, Asshur, Arphaxad, Lud, Aram, Uz, Hul, Gether, and Meshech.[8]
18 Arphaxad begot Shelah, and Shelah begot Eber.
19 To Eber were born two sons: the name of one was Peleg,[9] for in his days the earth was divided; and his brother's name was Joktan.
20 Joktan begot Almodad, Sheleph, Hazarmaveth, Jerah,
21 Hadoram, Uzal, Diklah,
22 Ebal,[10] Abimael, Sheba,
23 Ophir, Havilah, and Jobab. All these were the sons of Joktan.

24 Shem, Arphaxad, Shelah,
25 Eber, Peleg, Reu,
26 Serug, Nahor, Terah,
27 and Abram, that is Abraham.
28 The sons of Abraham were Isaac and Ishmael.

The Family of Ishmael

29 These are their genealogies: The firstborn of Ishmael was Nabajoth; then Kedar, Adbeel, Mibsam,
30 Mishma, Dumah, Massa, Hadad,[11] Tema,
31 Jetur, Naphish, and Kedemah. These were the sons of Ishmael.

The Family of Keturah

32 Now the sons born to Keturah, Abraham's concubine, were Zimran, Jokshan, Medan, Midian, Ishbak, and Shuah. The sons of Jokshan were Sheba and Dedan.
33 The sons of Midian were Ephah, Epher, Hanoch, Abida, and Eldaah. All these were the children of Keturah.

The Family of Isaac

34 And Abraham begot Isaac. The sons of Isaac were Esau and Israel.
35 The sons of Esau were Eliphaz, Reuel, Jeush, Jaalam, and Korah.
36 And the sons of Eliphaz were Teman, Omar, Zephi,[12] Gatam, and Kenaz; and by Timna,[13] Amalek.
37 The sons of Reuel were Nahath, Zerah, Shammah, and Mizzah.

The Family of Seir

38 The sons of Seir were Lotan, Shobal, Zibeon, Anah, Dishon, Ezer, and Dishan.
39 And the sons of Lotan were Hori and Homam; Lotan's sister was Timna.
40 The sons of Shobal were Alian,[14] Manahath, Ebal, Shephi,[15] and Onam. The sons of Zibeon were Ajah and Anah.

---

1 Hebrew Qenan   2 Spelled Mehalalel in the New Testament (Luke 3:37)   3 Spelled Riphath in Genesis 10:3
4 Spelled Tarshish in Genesis 10:4   5 Spelled Dodanim in Genesis 10:4   6 Spelled Sabtah in Genesis 10:7
7 Spelled Raamah in Genesis 10:7   8 Spelled Mash in Genesis 10:23   9 Literally Division
10 Spelled Obal in Genesis 10:28   11 Spelled Hadar in Genesis 25:15   12 Spelled Zepho in Genesis 36:11
13 Compare Genesis 36:12   14 Spelled Alvan in Genesis 36:23   15 Spelled Shepho in Genesis 36:23

41 The son of Anah was Dishon. The sons of Dishon were Hamran,[16] Eshban, Ithran, and Cheran.

42 The sons of Ezer were Bilhan, Zaavan, and Jaakan.[17] The sons of Dishan were Uz and Aran.

The Kings of Edom

43 Now these were the kings who reigned in the land of Edom before any king reigned over the children of Israel: Bela the son of Beor, and the name of his city was Dinhabah.

44 And when Bela died, Jobab the son of Zerah of Bozrah reigned in his place.

45 When Jobab died, Husham of the land of the Temanites reigned in his place.

46 And when Husham died, Hadad the son of Bedad, who attacked Midian in the field of Moab, reigned in his place. The name of his city was Avith.

47 When Hadad died, Samlah of Masrekah reigned in his place.

48 And when Samlah died, Saul of Rehoboth-by-the-River reigned in his place.

49 When Saul died, Baal-Hanan the son of Achbor reigned in his place.

50 And when Baal-Hanan died, Hadad[18] reigned in his place; and the name of his city was Pai.[19] His wife's name was Mehetabel the daughter of Matred, the daughter of Mezahab.

51 Hadad died also. And the chiefs of Edom were Chief Timnah, Chief Aliah,[20] Chief Jetheth,

52 Chief Aholibamah, Chief Elah, Chief Pinon,

53 Chief Kenaz, Chief Teman, Chief Mibzar,

54 Chief Magdiel, and Chief Iram. These were the chiefs of Edom.

The Family of Israel

2 These were the sons of Israel: Reuben, Simeon, Levi, Judah, Issachar, Zebulun,

2 Dan, Joseph, Benjamin, Naphtali, Gad, and Asher.

From Judah to David

3 The sons of Judah were Er, Onan, and Shelah. These three were born to him by the daughter of Shua, the Canaanitess. Er, the firstborn of Judah, was wicked in the sight of the LORD; and He killed him.

4 And Tamar, his daughter-in-law, bore him Perez and Zerah. All the sons of Judah were five.

5 The sons of Perez were Hezron and Hamul.

6 The sons of Zerah were Zimri, Ethan, Heman, Calcol, and Dara—five of them in all.

7 The son of Carmi was Achar,[21] the troubler of Israel, who transgressed in the accursed thing.

8 The son of Ethan was Azariah.

9 Also the sons of Hezron who were born to him were Jerahmeel, Ram, and Chelubai.[22]

10 Ram begot Amminadab, and Amminadab begot Nahshon, leader of the children of Judah;

11 Nahshon begot Salma,[23] and Salma begot Boaz;

12 Boaz begot Obed, and Obed begot Jesse;

13 Jesse begot Eliab his firstborn, Abinadab the second, Shimea[24] the third,

14 Nethanel the fourth, Raddai the fifth,

15 Ozem the sixth, and David the seventh.

16 Now their sisters were Zeruiah and Abigail. And the sons of Zeruiah were Abishai, Joab, and Asahel—three.

17 Abigail bore Amasa; and the father of Amasa was Jether the Ishmaelite.[25]

The Family of Hezron

18 Caleb the son of Hezron begot children by Azubah, his wife, and by Jerioth. Now these were her sons: Jesher, Shobab, and Ardon.

19 When Azubah died, Caleb took Ephrath[26] as his wife, who bore him Hur.

20 And Hur begot Uri, and Uri begot Bezaleel.

21 Now afterward Hezron went in to the daughter of Machir the father of Gilead, whom he married when he was sixty years old; and she bore him Segub.

22 Segub begot Jair, who had twenty-three cities in the land of Gilead.

23 (Geshur and Syria took from them the towns of Jair, with Kenath and its towns—sixty towns.) All these belonged

---

16 Spelled Hemdan in Genesis 36:26   17 Spelled Akan in Genesis 36:27   18 Spelled Hadar in Genesis 36:39
19 Spelled Pau in Genesis 36:39   20 Spelled Alvah in Genesis 36:40
21 Spelled Achan in Joshua 7:1 and elsewhere   22 Spelled Caleb in 2:18, 42
23 Spelled Salmon in Ruth 4:21 and Luke 3:32   24 Spelled Shammah in 1 Samuel 16:9 and elsewhere
25 Compare 2 Samuel 17:25   26 Spelled Ephrathah elsewhere

to the sons of Machir the father of Gilead.

24 After Hezron died in Caleb Ephrathah, Hezron's wife Abijah bore him Ashhur the father of Tekoa.

The Family of Jerahmeel

25 The sons of Jerahmeel, the firstborn of Hezron, *were* Ram, the firstborn, and Bunah, Oren, Ozem, *and* Ahijah.
26 Jerahmeel had another wife, whose name was Atarah; she was the mother of Onam.
27 The sons of Ram, the firstborn of Jerahmeel, were Maaz, Jamin, and Eker.
28 The sons of Onam were Shammai and Jada. The sons of Shammai *were* Nadab and Abishur.
29 And the name of the wife of Abishur *was* Abihail, and she bore him Ahban and Molid.
30 The sons of Nadab *were* Seled and Appaim; Seled died without children.
31 The son of Appaim *was* Ishi, the son of Ishi *was* Sheshan, and Sheshan's child *was* Ahlai.
32 The sons of Jada, the brother of Shammai, *were* Jether and Jonathan; Jether died without children.
33 The sons of Jonathan *were* Peleth and Zaza. These were the sons of Jerahmeel.
34 Now Sheshan had no sons, only daughters. And Sheshan had an Egyptian servant whose name *was* Jarha.
35 Sheshan gave his daughter to Jarha his servant as wife, and she bore him Attai.
36 Attai begot Nathan, and Nathan begot Zabad;
37 Zabad begot Ephlal, and Ephlal begot Obed;
38 Obed begot Jehu, and Jehu begot Azariah;
39 Azariah begot Helez, and Helez begot Eleasah;
40 Eleasah begot Sismai, and Sismai begot Shallum;
41 Shallum begot Jekamiah, and Jekamiah begot Elishama.

The Family of Caleb

42 The descendants of Caleb the brother of Jerahmeel *were* Mesha, his firstborn, who was the father of Ziph, and the sons of Mareshah the father of Hebron.

43 The sons of Hebron *were* Korah, Tappuah, Rekem, and Shema.
44 Shema begot Raham the father of Jorkoam, and Rekem begot Shammai.
45 And the son of Shammai *was* Maon, and Maon *was* the father of Beth Zur.
46 Ephah, Caleb's concubine, bore Haran, Moza, and Gazez; and Haran begot Gazez.
47 And the sons of Jahdai *were* Regem, Jotham, Geshan, Pelet, Ephah, and Shaaph.
48 Maachah, Caleb's concubine, bore Sheber and Tirhanah.
49 She also bore Shaaph the father of Madmannah, Sheva the father of Machbenah and the father of Gibea; and the daughter of Caleb *was* Achsah.
50 These were the descendants of Caleb: The sons of Hur, the firstborn of Ephrathah, *were* Shobal the father of Kirjath Jearim,
51 Salma the father of Bethlehem, *and* Hareph the father of Beth Gader.
52 And Shobal the father of Kirjath Jearim had descendants: Haroeh, *and* half of the *families of* Manuhoth.27
53 The families of Kirjath Jearim *were* the Ithrites, the Puthites, the Shumathites, and the Mishraites. From these came the Zorathites and the Eshtaolites.
54 The sons of Salma *were* Bethlehem, the Netophathites, Atroth Beth Joab, half of the Manahethites, and the Zorites.
55 And the families of the scribes who dwelt at Jabez *were* the Tirathites, the Shimeathites, *and* the Suchathites. These *were* the Kenites who came from Hammath, the father of the house of Rechab.

The Family of David

3 Now these were the sons of David who were born to him in Hebron: The firstborn *was* Amnon, by Ahinoam the Jezreelitess; the second, Daniel,28 by Abigail the Carmelitess;
2 the third, Absalom the son of Maacah, the daughter of Talmai, king of Geshur; the fourth, Adonijah the son of Haggith;
3 the fifth, Shephatiah, by Abital; the sixth, Ithream, by his wife Eglah.
4 *These* six were born to him in Hebron. There he reigned seven years and six months, and in Jerusalem he reigned thirty-three years.

27 Same as *the Manahethites* in verse 54   28 Called *Chileab* in 2 Samuel 3:3

5   And these were born to him in Jerusalem: Shimea,[29] Shobab, Nathan, and Solomon—four by Bathshua[30] the daughter of Ammiel.[31]
6   Also *there* were Ibhar, Elishama,[32] Eliphelet,[33]
7   Nogah, Nepheg, Japhia,
8   Elishama, Eliada,[34] and Eliphelet—nine *in all.*
9   *These were* all the sons of David, besides the sons of the concubines, and Tamar their sister.

The Family of Solomon

10 Solomon's son *was* Rehoboam; Abijah[35] *was* his son, Asa his son, Jehoshaphat his son,
11 Joram[36] his son, Ahaziah his son, Joash[37] his son,
12 Amaziah his son, Azariah[38] his son, Jotham his son,
13 Ahaz his son, Hezekiah his son, Manasseh his son,
14 Amon his son, *and* Josiah his son.
15 The sons of Josiah *were* Johanan the firstborn, the second Jehoiakim, the third Zedekiah, and the fourth Shallum.[39]
16 The sons of Jehoiakim *were* Jeconiah his son *and* Zedekiah[40] his son.

The Family of Jeconiah

17 And the sons of Jeconiah[41] *were* Assir,[42] Shealtiel his son,
18 *and* Malchiram, Pedaiah, Shenazzar, Jecamiah, Hoshama, and Nedabiah.
19 The sons of Pedaiah *were* Zerubbabel and Shimei. The sons of Zerubbabel *were* Meshullam, Hananiah, Shelomith their sister,
20 and Hashubah, Ohel, Berechiah, Hasadiah, and Jushab-Hesed—five *in all.*
21 The sons of Hananiah *were* Pelatiah and Jeshaiah, the sons of Rephaiah, the sons of Arnan, the sons of Obadiah, and the sons of Shechaniah.
22 The son of Shechaniah was Shemaiah. The sons of Shemaiah *were* Hattush, Igal, Bariah, Neariah, and Shaphat—six *in all.*
23 The sons of Neariah *were* Elioenai, Hezekiah, and Azrikam—three *in all.*
24 The sons of Elioenai *were* Hodaviah, Eliashib, Pelaiah, Akkub, Johanan, Delaiah, and Anani—seven *in all.*

The Family of Judah

4 The sons of Judah *were* Perez, Hezron, Carmi, Hur, and Shobal.
2   And Reaiah the son of Shobal begot Jahath, and Jahath begot Ahumai and Lahad. These *were* the families of the Zorathites.
3   These *were* the sons *of the father* of Etam: Jezreel, Ishma, and Idbash; and the name of their sister *was* Hazelelponi;
4   and Penuel *was* the father of Gedor, and Ezer *was the* father of Hushah. These *were* the sons of Hur, the firstborn of Ephrathah 'the father of Bethlehem.
5   And Ashhur the father of Tekoa had two wives, Helah and Naarah.
6   Naarah bore him Ahuzzam, Hepher, Temeni, and Haahashtari. These *were* the sons of Naarah.
7   The sons of Helah *were* Zereth, Zohar, and Ethnan;
8   and Koz begot Anub, Zobebah, and the families of Aharhel the son of Harum.
9   Now Jabez was more honorable than his brothers, and his mother called his name Jabez,[43] saying, "Because I bore *him* in pain."
10 And Jabez called on the God of Israel saying, "Oh, that You would bless me indeed, and enlarge my territory, that Your hand would be with me, and that You would keep *me* from evil, that I may not *cause pain!*" So God granted him what he requested.
11 Chelub the brother of Shuhah begot Mehir, who *was* the father of Eshton.
12 And Eshton begot Beth-Rapha, Paseah, and Tehinnah the father of Ir-Nahash. These *were* the men of Rechah.
13 The sons of Kenaz *were* Othniel and Seraiah. The sons of Othniel *were* Hathath,
14 and Meonothai who begot Ophrah. Seraiah begot Joab the father of Ge-Harashim,[44] for they were craftsmen.
15 The sons of Caleb the son of Jephunneh *were* Iru, Elah, and Naam. The son of Elah *was* Kenaz.
16 The sons of Jahaleleel *were* Ziph, Ziphah, Tiria, and Asarel.
17 The sons of Ezrah *were* Jether, Mered, Epher, and Jalon. And Mered's wife[45]

29 Spelled *Shammua* in 14:4 and 2 Samuel 5:14   30 Spelled *Bathsheba* in 2 Samuel 11:3
31 Called *Eliam* in 2 Samuel 11:3   32 Spelled *Elishua* in 14:5 and 2 Samuel 5:15   33 Spelled *Elpelet* in 14:5
34 Spelled *Beeliada* in 14:7   35 Spelled *Abijam* in 1 Kings 15:1   36 Spelled *Jehoram* in 2 Kings 1:17 and 8:16
37 Spelled *Jehoash* in 2 Kings 12:1   38 Spelled *Uzziah* in Isaiah 6:1   39 Called *Jehoahaz* in 2 Kings 23:31
40 Compare 2 Kings 24:17   41 Also called *Coniah* in Jeremiah 22:24 and *Jehoiachin* in 2 Kings 24:8
42 Or *the captive*   43 Literally *He Will Cause Pain*   44 Literally *Valley of Craftsmen*   45 Literally *she*

bore Miriam, Shammai, and Ishbah the father of Eshtemoa.

18 (His wife Jehudijah[46] bore Jered the father of Gedor, Heber the father of Sochoh, and Jekuthiel the father of Zanoah.) And these were the sons of Bithiah the daughter of Pharaoh, whom Mered took.

19 The sons of Hodiah's wife, the sister of Naham, *were* the fathers of Keilah the Garmite and of Eshtemoa the Maachathite.

20 And the sons of Shimon *were* Amnon, Rinnah, Ben-Hanan, and Tilon. And the sons of Ishi *were* Zoheth and Ben-Zoheth.

21 The sons of Shelah the son of Judah *were* Er the father of Lecah, Laadah the father of Mareshah, and the families of the house of the linen workers of the house of Ashbea;

22 also Jokim, the men of Chozeba, and Joash; Saraph, who ruled in Moab, and Jashubi-Lehem. Now the records are ancient.

23 These *were* the potters and those who dwell at Netaim[47] and Gederah;[48] there they dwelt with the king for his work.

The Family of Simeon

24 The sons of Simeon *were* Nemuel, Jamin, Jarib,[49] Zerah,[50] *and* Shaul,
25 Shallum his son, Mibsam his son, and Mishma his son.
26 And the sons of Mishma *were* Hamuel his son, Zacchur his son, and Shimei his son.
27 Shimei had sixteen sons and six daughters; but his brothers did not have many children, nor did any of their families multiply as much as the children of Judah.
28 They dwelt at Beersheba, Moladah, Hazar Shual,
29 Bilhah, Ezem, Tolad,
30 Bethuel, Hormah, Ziklag,
31 Beth Marcaboth, Hazar Susim, Beth Biri, and at Shaaraim. These *were* their cities until the reign of David.
32 And their villages *were* Etam, Ain, Rimmon, Tochen, and Ashan—five cities—
33 and all the villages that *were* around these cities as far as Baal.[51] These *were* their habitations, and they maintained their genealogy:

34 Meshobab, Jamlech, and Joshah the son of Amaziah;
35 Joel, and Jehu the son of Joshibiah, the son of Seraiah, the son of Asiel;
36 Elioenai, Jaakobah, Jeshohaiah, Asaiah, Adiel, Jesimiel, and Benaiah;
37 Ziza the son of Shiphi, the son of Allon, the son of Jedaiah, the son of Shimri, the son of Shemaiah—
38 these mentioned by name *were* leaders in their families, and their father's house increased greatly.
39 So they went to the entrance of Gedor, as far as the east side of the valley, to seek pasture for their flocks.
40 And they found rich, good pasture, and the land *was* broad, quiet, and peaceful; for some Hamites formerly lived there.
41 These recorded by name came in the days of Hezekiah king of Judah; and they attacked their tents and the Meunites who were found there, and utterly destroyed them, as it is to this day. So they dwelt in their place, because *there was* pasture for their flocks there.
42 Now *some* of them, five hundred men of the sons of Simeon, went to Mount Seir, having as their captains Pelatiah, Neariah, Rephaiah, and Uzziel, the sons of Ishi.
43 And they defeated the rest of the Amalekites who had escaped. They have dwelt there to this day.

The Family of Reuben

5 Now the sons of Reuben the firstborn of Israel—he *was* indeed the firstborn, but because he defiled his father's bed, his birthright was given to the sons of Joseph, the son of Israel, so that the genealogy is not listed according to the birthright;
2 yet Judah prevailed over his brothers, and from him *came* a ruler, although the birthright was Joseph's—
3 the sons of Reuben the firstborn of Israel were Hanoch, Pallu, Hezron, and Carmi.
4 The sons of Joel *were* Shemaiah his son, Gog his son, Shimei his son,
5 Micah his son, Reaiah his son, Baal his son,
6 and Beerah his son, whom Tiglath-Pileser[52] king of Assyria carried into captivity. He *was* leader of the Reubenites.

---

46 Or *his Judean wife*   47 Literally *Plants*   48 Literally *Hedges*   49 Called *Jachin* in Genesis 46:10
50 Called *Zohar* in Genesis 46:10   51 Or *Baalath Beer* (compare Joshua 19:8)   52 Hebrew *Tilgath-Pileser*

7 And his brethren by their families, when the genealogy of their generations was registered: the chief, Jeiel, and Zechariah,

8 and Bela the son of Azaz, the son of Shema, the son of Joel, who dwelt in Aroer, as far as Nebo and Baal Meon.

9 Eastward they settled as far as the entrance of the wilderness this side of the River Euphrates, because their cattle had multiplied in the land of Gilead.

10 Now in the days of Saul they made war with the Hagrites, who fell by their hand; and they dwelt in their tents throughout the entire *area* east of Gilead.

The Family of Gad

11 And the children of Gad dwelt next to them in the land of Bashan as far as Salcah:

12 Joel *was* the chief, Shapham the next, then Jaanai and Shaphat in Bashan,

13 and their brethren of their father's house: Michael, Meshullam, Sheba, Jorai, Jachan, Zia, and Heber—seven *in all.*

14 These *were* the children of Abihail the son of Huri, the son of Jaroah, the son of Gilead, the son of Michael, the son of Jeshishai, the son of Jahdo, the son of Buz;

15 Ahi the son of Abdiel, the son of Guni, *was* chief of their father's house.

16 And the Gadites[53] dwelt in Gilead, in Bashan and in its villages, and in all the common-lands of Sharon within their borders.

17 All these were registered by genealogies in the days of Jotham king of Judah, and in the days of Jeroboam king of Israel.

18 The sons of Reuben, the Gadites, and half the tribe of Manasseh *had* forty-four thousand seven hundred and sixty valiant men, men able to bear shield and sword, to shoot with the bow, and skillful in war, who went to war.

19 They made war with the Hagrites, Jetur, Naphish, and Nodab.

20 And they were helped against them, and the Hagrites were delivered into their hand, and all who *were* with them, for they cried out to God in the battle. He heeded their prayer, because they put their trust in Him.

21 Then they took away their livestock—fifty thousand of their camels, two hundred and fifty thousand of their sheep,

and two thousand of their donkeys—also one hundred thousand of their men;

22 for many fell dead, because the war *was* God's. And they dwelt in their place until the captivity.

The Family of Manasseh (East)

23 So the children of the half-tribe of Manasseh dwelt in the land. Their *numbers* increased from Bashan to Baal Hermon, that is, to Senir, or Mount Hermon.

24 These *were* the heads of their fathers' houses: Epher, Ishi, Eliel, Azriel, Jeremiah, Hodaviah, and Jahdiel. They were mighty men of valor, famous men, *and* heads of their fathers' houses.

25 And they were unfaithful to the God of their fathers, and played the harlot after the gods of the peoples of the land, whom God had destroyed before them.

26 So the God of Israel stirred up the spirit of Pul king of Assyria, that is, Tiglath-Pileser[54] king of Assyria. He carried the Reubenites, the Gadites, and the half-tribe of Manasseh into captivity. He took them to Halah, Habor, Hara, and the river of Gozan to this day.

The Family of Levi

6 The sons of Levi *were* Gershon, Kohath, and Merari.

2 The sons of Kohath *were* Amram, Izhar, Hebron, and Uzziel.

3 The children of Amram *were* Aaron, Moses, and Miriam. And the sons of Aaron *were* Nadab, Abihu, Eleazar, and Ithamar.

4 Eleazar begot Phinehas, *and* Phinehas begot Abishua;

5 Abishua begot Bukki, and Bukki begot Uzzi;

6 Uzzi begot Zerahiah, and Zerahiah begot Meraioth;

7 Meraioth begot Amariah, and Amariah begot Ahitub;

8 Ahitub begot Zadok, and Zadok begot Ahimaaz;

9 Ahimaaz begot Azariah, and Azariah begot Johanan;

10 Johanan begot Azariah (it was he who ministered as priest in the temple that Solomon built in Jerusalem);

11 Azariah begot Amariah, and Amariah begot Ahitub;

12 Ahitub begot Zadok, and Zadok begot Shallum;

---

53 Literally *they*   54 Hebrew *Tilgath-Pilneser*

13 Shallum begot Hilkiah, and Hilkiah begot Azariah;
14 Azariah begot Seraiah, and Seraiah begot Jehozadak.
15 Jehozadak went *into captivity* when the LORD carried Judah and Jerusalem into captivity by the hand of Nebuchadnezzar.
16 The sons of Levi *were* Gershon,[55] Kohath, and Merari.
17 These are the names of the sons of Gershon: Libni and Shimei.
18 The sons of Kohath *were* Amram, Izhar, Hebron, and Uzziel.
19 The sons of Merari *were* Mahli and Mushi. Now these *are* the families of the Levites according to their fathers:
20 Of Gershon *were* Libni his son, Jahath his son, Zimmah his son,
21 Joah his son, Iddo his son, Zerah his son, *and* Jeatherai his son.
22 The sons of Kohath *were* Amminadab his son, Korah his son, Assir his son,
23 Elkanah his son, Ebiasaph his son, Assir his son,
24 Tahath his son, Uriel his son, Uzziah his son, and Shaul his son.
25 The sons of Elkanah *were* Amasai and Ahimoth.
26 *As for* Elkanah,[56] the sons of Elkanah *were* Zophai[57] his son, Nahath[58] his son,
27 Eliab[59] his son, Jeroham his son, *and* Elkanah his son.
28 The sons of Samuel *were Joel*[60] the firstborn, and Abijah the second.[61]
29 The sons of Merari *were* Mahli, Libni his son, Shimei his son, Uzzah his son,
30 Shimea his son, Haggiah his son, *and* Asaiah his son.

Musicians in the House of the LORD

31 Now these are the men whom David appointed over the service of song in the house of the LORD, after the ark came to rest.
32 They were ministering with music before the dwelling place of the tabernacle of meeting, until Solomon had built the house of the LORD in Jerusalem, and they served in their office according to their order.
33 And these *are* the ones who ministered with their sons: Of the sons of the Kohathites *were* Heman the singer, the son of Joel, the son of Samuel,

34 the son of Elkanah, the son of Jeroham, the son of Eliel,[62] the son of Toah,[63]
35 the son of Zuph, the son of Elkanah, the son of Mahath, the son of Amasai,
36 the son of Elkanah, the son of Joel, the son of Azariah, the son of Zephaniah,
37 the son of Tahath, the son of Assir, the son of Ebiasaph, the son of Korah,
38 the son of Izhar, the son of Kohath, the son of Levi, the son of Israel.
39 And his brother Asaph, who stood at his right hand, *was* Asaph the son of Berachiah, the son of Shimea,
40 the son of Michael, the son of Baaseiah, the son of Malchijah,
41 the son of Ethni, the son of Zerah, the son of Adaiah,
42 the son of Ethan, the son of Zimmah, the son of Shimei,
43 the son of Jahath, the son of Gershon, the son of Levi.
44 And their brethren, the sons of Merari, on the left hand, *were* Ethan the son of Kishi, the son of Abdi, the son of Malluch,
45 the son of Hashabiah, the son of Amaziah, the son of Hilkiah,
46 the son of Amzi, the son of Bani, the son of Shamer,
47 the son of Mahli, the son of Mushi, the son of Merari, the son of Levi.
48 And their brethren, the Levites, *were* appointed to every kind of service of the tabernacle of the house of God.

The Family of Aaron

49 But Aaron and his sons offered sacrifices on the altar of burnt offering and on the altar of incense, for all the work of the Most Holy *Place*, and to make atonement for Israel, according to all that Moses the servant of God had commanded.
50 Now these *are* the sons of Aaron: Eleazar his son, Phinehas his son, Abishua his son,
51 Bukki his son, Uzzi his son, Zerahiah his son,
52 Meraioth his son, Amariah his son, Ahitub his son,
53 Zadok his son, *and* Ahimaaz his son.

Dwelling Places of the Levites

54 Now these *are* their dwelling places throughout their settlements in their territory, for they were *assigned* by lot to the

---

55 Hebrew *Gershom* (alternate spelling of *Gershon*, as in verses 1, 17, 20, 43, 62, and 71)   56 Compare verse 35
57 Spelled *Zuph* in verse 35 and 1 Samuel 1:1   58 Compare verse 34   59 Compare verse 34
60 Following Septuagint, Syriac, and Arabic (compare verse 33 and 1 Samuel 8:2)   61 Hebrew *Vasheni*
62 Spelled *Elihu* in 1 Samuel 1:1   63 Spelled *Tohu* in 1 Samuel 1:1

sons of Aaron, of the family of the Kohathites:
55 They gave them Hebron in the land of Judah, with its surrounding commonlands.
56 But the fields of the city and its villages they gave to Caleb the son of Jephunneh.
57 And to the sons of Aaron they gave *one of* the cities of refuge, Hebron; also Libnah with its common-lands, Jattir, Eshtemoa with its common-lands,
58 Hilen[64] with its common-lands, Debir with its common-lands,
59 Ashan[65] with its common-lands, and Beth Shemesh with its common-lands.
60 And from the tribe of Benjamin: Geba with its common-lands, Alemeth[66] with its common-lands, and Anathoth with its common-lands. All their cities among their families *were* thirteen.
61 To the rest of the family of the tribe of the Kohathites *they gave* by lot ten cities from half the tribe of Manasseh.
62 And to the sons of Gershon, throughout their families, *they gave* thirteen cities from the tribe of Issachar, from the tribe of Asher, from the tribe of Naphtali, and from the tribe of Manasseh in Bashan.
63 To the sons of Merari, throughout their families, *they gave* twelve cities from the tribe of Reuben, from the tribe of Gad, and from the tribe of Zebulun.
64 So the children of Israel gave *these* cities with their common-lands to the Levites.
65 And they gave by lot from the tribe of the children of Judah, from the tribe of the children of Simeon, and from the tribe of the children of Benjamin these cities which are called by *their* names.
66 Now some of the families of the sons of Kohath *were given* cities as their territory from the tribe of Ephraim.
67 And they gave them *one of* the cities of refuge, Shechem with its common-lands, in the mountains of Ephraim, also Gezer with its common-lands,
68 Jokmeam with its common-lands, Beth Horon with its common-lands,
69 Aijalon with its common-lands, and Gath Rimmon with its common-lands.
70 And from the half-tribe of Manasseh: Aner with its common-lands and Bileam with its common-lands, for the rest of the family of the sons of Kohath.

71 From the family of the half-tribe of Manasseh the sons of Gershon *were given* Golan in Bashan with its common-lands and Ashtaroth with its common-lands.
72 And from the tribe of Issachar: Kedesh with its common-lands, Daberath with its common-lands,
73 Ramoth with its common-lands, and Anem with its common-lands.
74 And from the tribe of Asher: Mashal with its common-lands, Abdon with its common-lands,
75 Hukok with its common-lands, and Rehob with its common-lands.
76 And from the tribe of Naphtali: Kedesh in Galilee with its common-lands, Hammon with its common-lands, and Kirjathaim with its common-lands.
77 From the tribe of Zebulun the rest of the children of Merari *were given* Rimmon[67] with its common-lands and Tabor with its common-lands.
78 And on the other side of the Jordan, across from Jericho, on the east side of the Jordan, *they were given* from the tribe of Reuben: Bezer in the wilderness with its common-lands, Jahzah with its common-lands,
79 Kedemoth with its common-lands, and Mephaath with its common-lands.
80 And from the tribe of Gad: Ramoth in Gilead with its common-lands, Mahanaim with its common-lands,
81 Heshbon with its common-lands, and Jazer with its common-lands.

The Family of Issachar

7 The sons of Issachar *were* Tola, Puah,[68] Jashub, and Shimron—four *in all.*
2 The sons of Tola *were* Uzzi, Raphaiah, Jeriel, Jahmai, Jibsam, and Shemuel, heads of their father's house. *The sons of* Tola *were* mighty men of valor in their generations; their number in the days of David *was* twenty-two thousand six hundred.
3 The son of Uzzi *was* Izrahiah, and the sons of Izrahiah *were* Michael, Obadiah, Joel, and Ishiah. All five of them *were* chief men.
4 And with them, by their generations, according to their fathers' houses, *were* thirty-six thousand *troops* of the army ready for war; for they had many wives and sons.

---

64 Spelled *Holon* in Joshua 21:15   65 Spelled *Ain* in Joshua 21:16   66 Spelled *Almon* in Joshua 21:18
67 Hebrew *Rimmono,* alternate spelling of *Rimmon;* see 4:32   68 Spelled *Puvah* in Genesis 46:13

5 Now their brethren among all the families of Issachar *were* mighty men of valor, listed by their genealogies, eighty-seven thousand in all.

The Family of Benjamin

6 *The sons* of Benjamin *were* Bela, Becher, and Jediael—three *in all*.
7 The sons of Bela were Ezbon, Uzzi, Uzziel, Jerimoth, and Iri—five *in all*. They *were* heads of *their* fathers' houses, and they were listed by their genealogies, twenty-two thousand and thirty-four mighty men of valor.
8 The sons of Becher *were* Zemirah, Joash, Eliezer, Elioenai, Omri, Jerimoth, Abijah, Anathoth, and Alemeth. All these *are* the sons of Becher.
9 And they were recorded by genealogy according to their generations, heads of their fathers' houses, twenty thousand two hundred mighty men of valor.
10 The son of Jediael *was* Bilhan, and the sons of Bilhan *were* Jeush, Benjamin, Ehud, Chenaanah, Zethan, Tharshish, and Ahishahar.
11 All these sons of Jediael *were* heads of their fathers' houses; *there were* seventeen thousand two hundred mighty men of valor fit to go out for war *and* battle.
12 Shuppim and Huppim[69] *were* the sons of Ir, *and* Hushim *was* the son of Aher.

The Family of Naphtali

13 The sons of Naphtali *were* Jahziel,[70] Guni, Jezer, and Shallum,[71] the sons of Bilhah.

The Family of Manasseh (West)

14 The descendants of Manasseh: his Syrian concubine bore him Machir the father of Gilead, the father of Asriel.[72]
15 Machir took as his wife *the sister* of Huppim and Shuppim,[73] whose name *was* Maachah. The name of *Gilead's* grandson[74] *was* Zelophehad,[75] but Zelophehad begot only daughters.
16 (Maachah the wife of Machir bore a son, and she called his name Peresh. The name of his brother *was* Sheresh, and his sons *were* Ulam and Rakem.
17 The son of Ulam *was* Bedan.) These *were* the descendants of Gilead the son of Machir, the son of Manasseh.

18 His sister Hammoleketh bore Ishhod, Abiezer, and Mahlah.
19 And the sons of Shemida were Ahian, Shechem, Likhi, and Aniam.

The Family of Ephraim

20 The sons of Ephraim *were* Shuthelah, Bered his son, Tahath his son, Eladah his son, Tahath his son,
21 Zabad his son, Shuthelah his son, and Ezer and Elead. The men of Gath who were born in *that* land killed *them* because they came down to take away their cattle.
22 Then Ephraim their father mourned many days, and his brethren came to comfort him.
23 And when he went in to his wife, she conceived and bore a son; and he called his name Beriah,[76] because tragedy had come upon his house.
24 Now his daughter *was* Sheerah, who built Lower and Upper Beth Horon and Uzzen Sheerah;
25 and Rephah *was* his son, *as well* as Resheph, and Telah his son, Tahan his son,
26 Laadan his son, Ammihud his son, Elishama his son,
27 Nun[77] his son, and Joshua his son.
28 Now their possessions and habitations *were* Bethel and its towns: to the east Naaran, to the west Gezer and its towns, and Shechem and its towns, as far as Ayyah[78] and its towns;
29 and by the borders of the children of Manasseh *were* Beth Shean and its towns, Taanach and its towns, Megiddo and its towns, Dor and its towns. In these dwelt the children of Joseph, the son of Israel.

The Family of Asher

30 The sons of Asher *were* Imnah, Ishvah, Ishvi, Beriah, and their sister Serah.
31 The sons of Beriah *were* Heber and Malchiel, who was the father of Birzaith.[79]
32 And Heber begot Japhlet, Shomer,[80] Hotham,[81] and their sister Shua.
33 The sons of Japhlet *were* Pasach, Bimhal, and Ashvath. These *were* the children of Japhlet.
34 The sons of Shemer *were* Ahi, Rohgah, Jehubbah, and Aram.

---

69 Called *Hupham* in Numbers 26:39   70 Spelled *Jahzeel* in Genesis 46:24   71 Spelled *Shillam* in Genesis 46:24
72 The son of Gilead (compare Numbers 26:30, 31)   73 Compare verse 12   74 Literally *his other one*
75 Compare Numbers 26:30–33   76 Literally *In Tragedy*   77 Hebrew *Non*
78 Many Hebrew manuscripts, Bomberg, Septuagint, Targum, and Vulgate read *Gazza.*
79 Or *Birzavith* or *Birzoth*   80 Spelled *Shemer* in verse 34   81 Spelled *Helem* in verse 35

35 And the sons of his brother Helem *were* Zophah, Imna, Shelesh, and Amal.
36 The sons of Zophah *were* Suah, Harnepher, Shual, Beri, Imrah,
37 Bezer, Hod, Shamma, Shilshah, Jithran,[82] and Beera.
38 The sons of Jether *were* Jephunneh, Pispah, and Ara.
39 The sons of Ulla *were* Arah, Haniel, and Rizia.
40 All these *were* the children of Asher, heads of *their* fathers' houses, choice men, mighty men of valor, chief leaders. And they were recorded by genealogies among the army fit for battle; their number *was* twenty-six thousand.

The Family Tree of King Saul of Benjamin

8 Now Benjamin begot Bela his firstborn, Ashbel the second, Aharah[83] the third,
2 Nohah the fourth, and Rapha the fifth.
3 The sons of Bela *were* Addar,[84] Gera, Abihud,
4 Abishua, Naaman, Ahoah,
5 Gera, Shephuphan, and Huram.
6 And these *are* the sons of Ehud, who were the heads of the fathers' *houses* of the inhabitants of Geba, and who forced them to move to Manahath:
7 Naaman, Ahijah, and Gera who forced them to move. He begot Uzza and Ahihud.
8 And Shaharaim begot *children* in the country of Moab, after he had sent away Hushim and Baara his wives.
9 By Hodesh his wife he begot Jobab, Zibia, Mesha, Malcam,
10 Jeuz, Sachiah, and Mirmah. These *were* his sons, heads of their fathers' *houses*.
11 And by Hushim he begot Abitub and Elpaal.
12 The sons of Elpaal *were* Eber, Misham, and Shemed, who built Ono and Lod with its towns;
13 and Beriah and Shema, who *were* heads of their fathers' *houses* of the inhabitants of Aijalon, who drove out the inhabitants of Gath.
14 Ahio, Shashak, Jeremoth,
15 Zebadiah, Arad, Eder,
16 Michael, Ispah, and Joha *were* the sons of Beriah.

17 Zebadiah, Meshullam, Hizki, Heber,
18 Ishmerai, Jizliah, and Jobab *were* the sons of Elpaal.
19 Jakim, Zichri, Zabdi,
20 Elienai, Zillethai, Eliel,
21 Adaiah, Beraiah, and Shimrath *were* the sons of Shimei.
22 Ishpan, Eber, Eliel,
23 Abdon, Zichri, Hanan,
24 Hananiah, Elam, Antothijah,
25 Iphdeiah, and Penuel *were* the sons of Shashak.
26 Shamsherai, Shehariah, Athaliah,
27 Jaareshiah, Elijah, and Zichri *were* the sons of Jeroham.
28 These *were* heads of the fathers' *houses* by their generations, chief men. These dwelt in Jerusalem.
29 Now the father of Gibeon, whose wife's name *was* Maacah, dwelt at Gibeon.
30 And his firstborn son *was* Abdon, then Zur, Kish, Baal, Nadab,
31 Gedor, Ahio, Zecher.
32 and Mikloth, *who* begot Shimeah.[85] They also dwelt alongside their relatives in Jerusalem, with their brethren.
33 Ner[86] begot Kish, Kish begot Saul, and Saul begot Jonathan, Malchishua, Abinadab,[87] and Esh-Baal.[88]
34 The son of Jonathan *was* Merib-Baal,[89] and Merib-Baal begot Micah.
35 The sons of Micah *were* Pithon, Melech, Tarea, and Ahaz.
36 And Ahaz begot Jehoaddah;[90] Jehoaddah begot Alemeth, Azmaveth, and Zimri; and Zimri begot Moza.
37 Moza begot Binea, Raphah[91] his son, Eleasah his son, *and* Azel his son.
38 Azel had six sons whose names *were* these: Azrikam, Bocheru, Ishmael, Sheariah, Obadiah, and Hanan. All these *were* the sons of Azel.
39 And the sons of Eshek his brother *were* Ulam his firstborn, Jeush the second, and Eliphelet the third.
40 The sons of Ulam were mighty men of valor—archers. *They* had many sons and grandsons, one hundred and fifty *in all*. These *were* all sons of Benjamin.

9 So all Israel was recorded by genealogies, and indeed, they *were* inscribed in the book of the kings of Israel. But Judah was carried away captive to Babylon because of their unfaithfulness.

---

82 Spelled *Jether* in verse 38   83 Spelled *Ahiram* in Numbers 26:38   84 Called *Ard* in Numbers 26:40
85 Spelled *Shimeam* in 9:38   86 Also the son of Gibeon (compare 9:36, 39)   87 Called *Jishui* in 1 Samuel 14:49
88 Called *Ishbosheth* in 2 Samuel 2:8 and elsewhere   89 Called *Mephibosheth* in 2 Samuel 4:4
90 Spelled *Jarah* in 9:42   91 Spelled *Rephaiah* in 9:43

2 And the first inhabitants who *dwelt* in their possessions in their cities *were* Israelites, priests, Levites, and the Nethinim.

Dwellers in Jerusalem

3 Now in Jerusalem the children of Judah dwelt, and some of the children of Benjamin, and of the children of Ephraim and Manasseh:
4 Uthai the son of Ammihud, the son of Omri, the son of Imri, the son of Bani, of the descendants of Perez, the son of Judah.
5 Of the Shilonites: Asaiah the firstborn and his sons.
6 Of the sons of Zerah: Jeuel, and their brethren—six hundred and ninety.
7 Of the sons of Benjamin: Sallu the son of Meshullam, the son of Hodaviah, the son of Hassenuah;
8 Ibneiah the son of Jeroham; Elah the son of Uzzi, the son of Michri; Meshullam the son of Shephatiah, the son of Reuel, the son of Ibnijah;
9 and their brethren, according to their generations—nine hundred and fifty-six. All these men *were* heads of a father's *house* in their fathers' houses.

The Priests at Jerusalem

10 Of the priests: Jedaiah, Jehoiarib, and Jachin;
11 Azariah the son of Hilkiah, the son of Meshullam, the son of Zadok, the son of Meraioth, the son of Ahitub, the officer over the house of God;
12 Adaiah the son of Jeroham, the son of Pashur, the son of Malchijah; Maasai the son of Adiel, the son of Jahzerah, the son of Meshullam, the son of Meshillemith, the son of Immer;
13 and their brethren, heads of their fathers' *houses*—one thousand seven hundred and sixty. *They were* very able men for the work of the service of the house of God.

The Levites at Jerusalem

14 Of the Levites: Shemaiah the son of Hasshub, the son of Azrikam, the son of Hashabiah, of the sons of Merari;
15 Bakbakkar, Heresh, Galal, and Mattaniah the son of Micah, the son of Zichri, the son of Asaph;
16 Obadiah the son of Shemaiah, the son of Galal, the son of Jeduthun; and Berechiah the son of Asa, the son of Elkanah, who lived in the villages of the Netophathites.

The Levite Gatekeepers

17 And the gatekeepers *were* Shallum, Akkub, Talmon, Ahiman, and their brethren. Shallum *was* the chief.
18 Until then *they had been* gatekeepers for the camps of the children of Levi at the King's Gate on the east.
19 Shallum the son of Kore, the son of Ebiasaph, the son of Korah, and his brethren, from his father's house, the Korahites, *were* in charge of the work of the service, gatekeepers of the tabernacle. Their fathers had been keepers of the entrance to the camp of the LORD.
20 And Phinehas the son of Eleazar had been the officer over them in time past; the LORD *was* with him.
21 Zechariah the son of Meshelemiah *was* keeper of the door of the tabernacle of meeting.
22 All those chosen as gatekeepers *were* two hundred and twelve. They were recorded by their genealogy, in their villages. David and Samuel the seer had appointed them to their trusted office.
23 So they and their children *were* in charge of the gates of the house of the LORD, the house of the tabernacle, by assignment.
24 The gatekeepers were assigned to the four directions: the east, west, north, and south.
25 And their brethren in their villages *had* to come with them from time to time for seven days.
26 For in this trusted office *were* four chief gatekeepers; they were Levites. And they had charge over the chambers and treasuries of the house of God.
27 And they lodged *all* around the house of God because they *had* the responsibility, and they *were* in charge of opening *it* every morning.

Other Levite Responsibilities

28 Now *some* of them were in charge of the serving vessels, for they brought them in and took them out by count.
29 *Some* of them *were* appointed over the furnishings and over all the implements of the sanctuary, and over the fine flour and the wine and the oil and the incense and the spices.

30 And *some* of the sons of the priests made the ointment of the spices.
31 Mattithiah of the Levites, the first-born of Shallum the Korahite, had the trusted office over the things that were baked in the pans.
32 And some of their brethren of the sons of the Kohathites *were* in charge of preparing the showbread for every Sabbath.
33 These are the singers, heads of the fathers' *houses* of the Levites, *who lodged* in the chambers, *and were* free *from other duties*; for they were employed in *that* work day and night.
34 These heads of the fathers' *houses* of the Levites *were* heads throughout their generations. They dwelt at Jerusalem.

The Family of King Saul

35 Jeiel the father of Gibeon, whose wife's name *was* Maacah, dwelt at Gibeon.
36 His firstborn son *was* Abdon, then Zur, Kish, Baal, Ner, Nadab,
37 Gedor, Ahio, Zechariah,[92] and Mikloth.
38 And Mikloth begot Shimeam.[93] They also dwelt alongside their relatives in Jerusalem, with their brethren.
39 Ner begot Kish, Kish begot Saul, and Saul begot Jonathan, Malchishua, Abinadab, and Esh-Baal.
40 The son of Jonathan *was* Merib-Baal, and Merib-Baal begot Micah.
41 The sons of Micah *were* Pithon, Melech, Tahrea,[94] *and Ahaz.*
42 And Ahaz begot Jarah;[95] Jarah begot Alemeth, Azmaveth, and Zimri; and Zimri begot Moza;
43 Moza begot Binea, Rephaiah[96] his son, Eleasah his son, and Azel his son.
44 And Azel had six sons whose names *were* these: Azrikam, Bocheru, Ishmael, Sheariah, Obadiah, and Hanan; these *were* the sons of Azel.

Tragic End of Saul and His Sons

10 Now the Philistines fought against Israel; and the men of Israel fled from before the Philistines, and fell slain on Mount Gilboa.
2 Then the Philistines followed hard after Saul and his sons. And the Philistines killed Jonathan, Abinadab, and Malchishua, Saul's sons.

3 The battle became intense against Saul; and the archers hit him, and he was wounded by the archers.
4 Then Saul said to his armorbearer, "Draw your sword, and thrust me through with it, lest these uncircumcised *men* come and abuse me." But his armorbearer would not, for he was greatly afraid. Therefore Saul took a sword and fell on it.
5 And when his armorbearer saw that Saul was dead, he also fell on his sword and died.
6 So Saul and his three sons died, and all his house died together.
7 And when all the men of Israel who *were* in the valley saw that they had fled and that Saul and his sons were dead, they forsook their cities and fled; then the Philistines came and dwelt in them.
8 So it happened the next day, when the Philistines came to strip the slain, that they found Saul and his sons fallen on Mount Gilboa.
9 And they stripped him and took his head and his armor, and sent word *throughout* the land of the Philistines to proclaim the news *in the temple* of their idols and among the people.
10 Then they put his armor in the temple of their gods, and fastened his head in the temple of Dagon.
11 And when all Jabesh Gilead heard all that the Philistines had done to Saul,
12 all the valiant men arose and took the body of Saul and the bodies of his sons; and they brought them to Jabesh, and buried their bones under the tamarisk tree at Jabesh, and fasted seven days.
13 So Saul died for his unfaithfulness which he had committed against the LORD, because he did not keep the word of the LORD, and also because he consulted a medium for guidance.
14 But *he* did not inquire of the LORD; therefore He killed him, and turned the kingdom over to David the son of Jesse.

David Made King over All Israel

11 Then all Israel came together to David at Hebron, saying, "Indeed we *are* your bone and your flesh.
2 "Also, in time past, even when Saul was king, you *were* the one who led Israel out and brought them in; and the LORD your God said to you, 'You shall shep-

---

92 Called *Zecher* in 8:31   93 Spelled *Shimeah* in 8:32   94 Spelled *Tarea* in 8:35
95 Spelled *Jehoaddah* in 8:36   96 Spelled *Raphah* in 8:37

herd My people Israel, and be ruler over My people Israel.'"

3 Therefore all the elders of Israel came to the king at Hebron, and David made a covenant with them at Hebron before the LORD. Then they anointed David king over Israel, according to the word of the LORD by Samuel.

The City of David

4 And David and all Israel went to Jerusalem, which is Jebus, where the Jebusites were, the inhabitants of the land. 5 Then the inhabitants of Jebus said to David, "You shall not come in here." Nevertheless David took the stronghold of Zion (that is, the City of David). 6 Now David said, "Whoever attacks the Jebusites first shall be chief and captain." And Joab the son of Zeruiah went up first, and became chief. 7 Then David dwelt in the stronghold; therefore they called it the City of David. 8 And he built the city around it, from the Millo to the surrounding area. Joab repaired the rest of the city. 9 Then David went on and became great, and the LORD of hosts was with him.

The Mighty Men of David

10 Now these were the heads of the mighty men whom David had, who strengthened themselves with him in his kingdom, with all Israel, to make him king, according to the word of the LORD concerning Israel. 11 And this is the number of the mighty men whom David had: Jashobeam the son of a Hachmonite, chief of the captains; he had lifted up his spear against three hundred, killed by him at one time. 12 After him was Eleazar the son of Dodo, the Ahohite, who was one of the three mighty men. 13 He was with David at Pasdammim. Now there the Philistines were gathered for battle, and there was a piece of ground full of barley. And the people fled from the Philistines. 14 But they stationed themselves in the midst of that field, defended it, and killed the Philistines. And the LORD saved them by a great deliverance.

15 Now three of the thirty chief men went down to the rock to David, into the cave of Adullam; and the army of the Philistines encamped in the Valley of Rephaim. 16 David was then in the stronghold, and the garrison of the Philistines was then in Bethlehem. 17 And David said with longing, "Oh, that someone would give me a drink of water from the well of Bethlehem, which is by the gate!" 18 So the three broke through the camp of the Philistines, drew water from the well of Bethlehem that was by the gate, and took it and brought it to David. Nevertheless David would not drink it, but poured it out to the LORD. 19 And he said, "Far be it from me, O my God, that I should do this! Shall I drink the blood of these men who have put their lives in jeopardy? For at the risk of their lives they brought it." Therefore he would not drink it. These things were done by the three mighty men.

20 Now Abishai the brother of Joab was chief of another three. He had lifted up his spear against three hundred men and killed them, and won a name among these three. 21 Of the three he was more honored than the other two men. Therefore he became their captain. However he did not attain to the first three. 22 Benaiah was the son of Jehoiada, the son of a valiant man from Kabzeel, who had done many deeds. He had killed two lion-like heroes of Moab. He also had gone down and killed a lion in the midst of a pit on a snowy day. 23 And he killed an Egyptian, a man of great height, five cubits tall. In the Egyptian's hand there had been a spear like a weaver's beam; and he went down to him with a staff, wrested the spear out of the Egyptian's hand, and killed him with his own spear. 24 These things Benaiah the son of Jehoiada had done, and won a name among three mighty men. 25 Indeed he was more honored than the thirty, but he did not attain to the first three. And David appointed him over his guard. 26 Also the mighty warriors were Asahel the brother of Joab, Elhanan the son of Dodo of Bethlehem, 27 Shammoth the Harorite,[97] Helez the Pelonite,[98]

---

97 Spelled *Harodite* in 2 Samuel 23:25   98 Called *Paltite* in 2 Samuel 23:26

28 Ira the son of Ikkesh the Tekoite, Abiezer the Anathothite,
29 Sibbechai the Hushathite, Ilai the Ahohite,
30 Maharai the Netophathite, Heled[99] the son of Baanah the Netophathite,
31 Ithai[100] the son of Ribai of Gibeah, of the children of Benjamin, Benaiah the Pirathonite,
32 Hurai[101] of the brooks of Gaash, Abiel[102] the Arbathite,
33 Azmaveth the Baharumite,[103] Eliahba the Shaalbonite,
34 the sons of Hashem the Gizonite, Jonathan the son of Shageh the Hararite,
35 Ahiam the son of Sacar the Hararite, Eliphal the son of Ur,
36 Hepher the Mecherathite, Ahijah the Pelonite,
37 Hezro the Carmelite, Naarai the son of Ezbai,
38 Joel the brother of Nathan, Mibhar the son of Hagri,
39 Zelek the Ammonite, Naharai the Berothite[104] (the armorbearer of Joab the son of Zeruiah),
40 Ira the Ithrite, Gareb the Ithrite,
41 Uriah the Hittite, Zabad the son of Ahlai,
42 Adina the son of Shiza the Reubenite (a chief of the Reubenites) and thirty with him,
43 Hanan the son of Maachah, Joshaphat the Mithnite,
44 Uzzia the Ashterathite, Shama and Jeiel the sons of Hotham the Aroerite,
45 Jediael the son of Shimri, and Joha his brother, the Tizite,
46 Eliel the Mahavite, Jeribai and Joshaviah the sons of Elnaam, Ithmah the Moabite,
47 Eliel, Obed, and Jaasiel the Mezobaite.

The Growth of David's Army

12 Now these *were* the men who came to David at Ziklag while he was still a fugitive from Saul the son of Kish; and they *were* among the mighty men, helpers in the war,
2 armed with bows, using both the right hand and the left in *hurling* stones and *shooting* arrows with the bow. *They were* of Benjamin, Saul's brethren.

3 The chief *was* Ahiezer, then Joash, the sons of Shemaah the Gibeathite; Jeziel and Pelet the sons of Azmaveth; Berachah, and Jehu the Anathothite;
4 Ishmaiah the Gibeonite, a mighty man among the thirty, and over the thirty; Jeremiah, Jahaziel, Johanan, and Jozabad the Gederathite;
5 Eluzai, Jerimoth, Bealiah, Shemariah, and Shephatiah the Haruphite;
6 Elkanah, Jisshiah, Azareel, Joezer, and Jashobeam, the Korahites;
7 and Joelah and Zebadiah the sons of Jeroham of Gedor.
8 *Some* Gadites joined David at the stronghold in the wilderness, mighty men of valor, men trained for battle, who could handle shield and spear, whose faces *were like* the faces of lions, and *were* as swift as gazelles on the mountains:
9 Ezer the first, Obadiah the second, Eliab the third,
10 Mishmannah the fourth, Jeremiah the fifth,
11 Attai the sixth, Eliel the seventh,
12 Johanan the eighth, Elzabad the ninth,
13 Jeremiah the tenth, and Machbanai the eleventh.
14 These *were* from the sons of Gad, captains of the army; the least was over a hundred, and the greatest was over a thousand.
15 These *are* the ones who crossed the Jordan in the first month, when it had overflowed all its banks; and they put to flight all *those* in the valleys, to the east and to the west.
16 Then some of the children of Benjamin and Judah came to David at the stronghold.
17 And David went out to meet them, and answered and said to them, "If you have come peaceably to me to help me, my heart will be united with you; but if to betray me to my enemies, since *there is* no wrong in my hands, may the God of our fathers look and bring judgment."
18 Then the Spirit came upon Amasai, chief of the captains, *and he said*:

"*We are* yours, O David;
We *are* on your side, O son of Jesse!
Peace, peace to you,
And peace to your helpers!
For your God helps you."

---

99 Spelled *Heleb* in 2 Samuel 23:29 and *Heldai* in 1 Chronicles 27:15   100 Spelled *Ittai* in 2 Samuel 23:29
101 Spelled *Hiddai* in 2 Samuel 23:30   102 Spelled *Abialbon* in 2 Samuel 23:31
103 Spelled *Barhumite* in 2 Samuel 23:31   104 Spelled *Beerothite* in 2 Samuel 23:37

So David received them, and made them captains of the troop.

19 And *some* from Manasseh defected to David when he was going with the Philistines to battle against Saul; but they did not help them, for the lords of the Philistines sent him away by counsel, saying, "He may defect to his master Saul *and endanger* our heads."

20 When he went to Ziklag, those of Manasseh who defected to him were Adnah, Jozabad, Jediael, Michael, Jozabad, Elihu, and Zillethai, captains of the thousands who *were* from Manasseh.

21 And they helped David against the bands *of raiders*, for they *were* all mighty men of valor, and they were captains in the army.

22 For at *that* time they came to David day by day to help him, until *it was* a great army, like the army of God.

David's Army at Hebron

23 Now these *were* the numbers of the divisions *that were* equipped for the war, *and* came to David at Hebron to turn *over* the kingdom of Saul to him, according to the word of the LORD:

24 of the children of Judah bearing shield and spear, six thousand eight hundred armed for war;

25 of the children of Simeon, mighty men of valor fit for war, seven thousand one hundred;

26 of the children of Levi four thousand six hundred;

27 Jehoiada, the leader of the Aaronites, and with him three thousand seven hundred;

28 Zadok, a young man, a valiant warrior, and from his father's house twenty-two captains;

29 of the children of Benjamin, kinsmen of Saul, three thousand (until then the greatest part of them had remained loyal to the house of Saul);

30 of the children of Ephraim twenty thousand eight hundred, mighty men of valor, famous men throughout their father's house;

31 of the half-tribe of Manasseh eighteen thousand, who were designated by name to come and make David king;

32 of the children of Issachar who had understanding of the times, to know what Israel ought to do, their chiefs were two

hundred; and all their brethren were at their command;

33 of Zebulun there were fifty thousand who went out to battle, expert in war with all weapons of war, stouthearted men who could keep ranks;

34 of Naphtali one thousand captains, and with them thirty-seven thousand with shield and spear;

35 of the Danites who could keep battle formation, twenty-eight thousand six hundred;

36 of Asher, those who could go out to war, able to keep battle formation, forty thousand;

37 of the Reubenites and the Gadites and the half-tribe of Manasseh, from the other side of the Jordan, one hundred and twenty thousand armed for battle with every *kind* of weapon of war.

38 All these men of war, who could keep ranks, came to Hebron with a loyal heart, to make David king over all Israel; and all the rest of Israel *were* of one mind to make David king.

39 And they were there with David three days, eating and drinking, for their brethren had prepared for them.

40 Moreover those who were near to them, from as far away as Issachar and Zebulun and Naphtali, were bringing food on donkeys and camels, on mules and oxen—provisions of flour and cakes of figs and cakes of raisins, wine and oil and oxen and sheep abundantly, for *there was* joy in Israel.

The Ark Brought from Kirjath Jearim

13 Then David consulted with the captains of thousands and hundreds, *and* with every leader.

2 And David said to all the congregation of Israel, "If *it seems* good to you, and if it is of the LORD our God, let us send out to our brethren everywhere *who are* left in all the land of Israel, and with them to the priests and Levites *who are* in their cities *and* their common-lands, that they may gather together to us;

3 "and let us bring the ark of our God back to us, for we have not inquired at it since the days of Saul."

4 Then all the congregation said that they would do so, for the thing was right in the eyes of all the people.

5 So David gathered all Israel together,

from Shihor in Egypt to as far as the entrance of Hamath, to bring the ark of God from Kirjath Jearim.

6 And David and all Israel went up to Baalah,[105] to Kirjath Jearim, which belonged to Judah, to bring up from there the ark of God the LORD, who dwells *between* the cherubim, where *His* name is proclaimed.

7 So they carried the ark of God on a new cart from the house of Abinadab, and Uzza and Ahio drove the cart.

8 Then David and all Israel played *music* before God with all *their* might, with singing, on harps, on stringed instruments, on tambourines, on cymbals, and with trumpets.

9 And when they came to Chidon's[106] threshing floor, Uzza put out his hand to hold the ark, for the oxen stumbled.

10 Then the anger of the LORD was aroused against Uzza, and He struck him because he put his hand to the ark; and he died there before God.

11 And David became angry because of the LORD's outbreak against Uzza; therefore that place is called Perez Uzza[107] to this day.

12 David was afraid of God that day, saying, "How can I bring the ark of God to me?"

13 And David would not move the ark with him into the City of David, but took it aside into the house of Obed-Edom the Gittite.

14 The ark of God remained with the family of Obed-Edom in his house three months. And the LORD blessed the house of Obed-Edom and all that he had.

David Established at Jerusalem

14 Now Hiram king of Tyre sent messengers to David, and cedar trees, with masons and carpenters, to build him a house.

2 And David perceived that the LORD had established him as king over Israel, for his kingdom was highly exalted because of His people Israel.

3 Then David took more wives in Jerusalem, and David begot more sons and daughters.

4 And these are the names of his children whom he had in Jerusalem: Shammua,[108] Shobab, Nathan, Solomon,

5 Ibhar, Elishua,[109] Elpelet,[110]

6 Nogah, Nepheg, Japhia,

7 Elishama, Beeliada,[111] and Eliphelet.

The Philistines Defeated

8 Now when the Philistines heard that David had been anointed king over all Israel, all the Philistines went up to search for David. And David heard *of it* and went out against them.

9 Then the Philistines went and made a raid on the Valley of Rephaim.

10 And David inquired of God, saying, "Shall I go up against the Philistines? Will You deliver them into my hand?" And the LORD said to him, "Go up, for I will deliver them into your hand."

11 So they went up to Baal Perazim, and David defeated them there. Then David said, "God has broken through my enemies by my hand like a breakthrough of water." Therefore they called the name of that place Baal Perazim.[112]

12 And when they left their gods there, David gave a commandment, and they were burned with fire.

13 Then the Philistines once again made a raid on the valley.

14 Therefore David inquired again of God, and God said to him, "You shall not go up after them; circle around them, and come upon them in front of the mulberry trees.

15 "And it shall be, when you hear a sound of marching in the tops of the mulberry trees, then you shall go out to battle, for God has gone out before you to strike the camp of the Philistines."

16 So David did as God commanded him, and they drove back the army of the Philistines from Gibeon as far as Gezer.

17 Then the fame of David went out into all lands, and the LORD brought the fear of him upon all nations.

The Ark Brought to Jerusalem

15 David built houses for himself in the City of David; and he prepared a place for the ark of God, and pitched a tent for it.

2 Then David said, "No one may carry the ark of God but the Levites, for the LORD has chosen them to carry the ark of God and to minister before Him forever."

3 And David gathered all Israel together at Jerusalem, to bring up the ark

---

105 Called *Baale Judah* in 2 Samuel 6:2   106 Called *Nachon* in 2 Samuel 6:6   107 Literally *Outbreak of Uzza*
108 Spelled *Shimea* in 3:5   109 Spelled *Elishama* in 3:6   110 Spelled *Eliphelet* in 3:6
111 Spelled *Eliada* in 3:8   112 Literally *Master of Breakthroughs*

of the LORD to its place, which he had prepared for it.

4 Then David assembled the children of Aaron and the Levites:

5 of the sons of Kohath, Uriel the chief, and one hundred and twenty of his brethren;

6 of the sons of Merari, Asaiah the chief, and two hundred and twenty of his brethren;

7 of the sons of Gershom, Joel the chief, and one hundred and thirty of his brethren;

8 of the sons of Elizaphan, Shemaiah the chief, and two hundred of his brethren;

9 of the sons of Hebron, Eliel the chief, and eighty of his brethren;

10 of the sons of Uzziel, Amminadab the chief, and one hundred and twelve of his brethren.

11 And David called for Zadok and Abiathar the priests, and for the Levites: for Uriel, Asaiah, Joel, Shemaiah, Eliel, and Amminadab.

12 Then he said to them, "You are the heads of the fathers' houses of the Levites; sanctify yourselves, you and your brethren, that you may bring up the ark of the LORD God of Israel to the place I have prepared for it.

13 "For because you did not do it the first time, the LORD our God broke out against us, because we did not consult Him about the proper order."

14 So the priests and the Levites sanctified themselves to bring up the ark of the LORD God of Israel.

15 And the children of the Levites bore the ark of God on their shoulders, by its poles, as Moses had commanded according to the word of the LORD.

16 Then David spoke to the leaders of the Levites to appoint their brethren to be the singers accompanied by instruments of music, stringed instruments, harps, and cymbals, by raising the voice with resounding joy.

17 So the Levites appointed Heman the son of Joel; and of his brethren, Asaph the son of Berechiah; and of their brethren, the sons of Merari, Ethan the son of Kushaiah;

18 and with them their brethren of the second rank: Zechariah, Ben, Jaaziel, Shemiramoth, Jehiel, Unni, Eliab, Bena-

iah, Maaseiah, Mattithiah, Elipheleh, Mikneiah, Obed-Edom, and Jeiel, the gatekeepers;

19 the singers, Heman, Asaph, and Ethan, were to sound the cymbals of bronze;   .

20 Zechariah, Aziel, Shemiramoth, Jehiel, Unni, Eliab, Maaseiah, and Benaiah, with strings according to Alamoth;

21 Mattithiah, Elipheleh, Mikneiah, Obed-Edom, Jeiel, and Azaziah, to direct with harps on the Sheminith;

22 Chenaniah, leader of the Levites, was instructor in charge of the music, because he was skillful;

23 Berechiah and Elkanah were doorkeepers for the ark;

24 Shebaniah, Joshaphat, Nethaneel, Amasai, Zechariah, Benaiah, and Eliezer, the priests, were to blow the trumpets before the ark of God; and Obed-Edom and Jehiah, doorkeepers for the ark.

25 So David, the elders of Israel, and the captains over thousands went to bring up the ark of the covenant of the LORD from the house of Obed-Edom with joy.

26 And so it was, when God helped the Levites who bore the ark of the covenant of the LORD, that they offered seven bulls and seven rams.

27 David was clothed with a robe of fine linen, as were all the Levites who bore the ark, the singers, and Chenaniah the music master with the singers. David also wore a linen ephod.

28 Thus all Israel brought up the ark of the covenant of the LORD with shouting and with the sound of the horn, with trumpets and with cymbals, making music with stringed instruments and harps.

29 And it happened, as the ark of the covenant of the LORD came to the City of David, that Michal the daughter of Saul, looking through a window, saw King David whirling and playing music; and she despised him in her heart.

The Ark Placed in the Tabernacle

16 So they brought the ark of God, and set it in the midst of the tabernacle that David had erected for it. Then they offered burnt offerings and peace offerings before God.

2 And when David had finished offering the burnt offerings and the peace offerings, he blessed the people in the name of the LORD.

3 Then he distributed to everyone of Israel, both man and woman, to everyone a loaf of bread, a piece *of meat*, and a cake of raisins.

4 And he appointed some of the Levites to minister before the ark of the LORD, to commemorate, to thank, and to praise the LORD God of Israel:

5 Asaph the chief, and next to him Zechariah, *then* Jeiel, Shemiramoth, Jehiel, Mattithiah, Eliab, Benaiah, and Obed-Edom: Jeiel with stringed instruments and harps, but Asaph made music with cymbals;

6 Benaiah and Jahaziel the priests regularly *blew* the trumpets before the ark of the covenant of God.

David's Song of Thanksgiving

7 And on that day David first delivered *this psalm* into the hand of Asaph and his brethren, to thank the LORD:

8 Oh, give thanks to the LORD!
    Call upon His name;
    Make known His deeds
        among the peoples!
9 Sing to Him, sing psalms to Him;
    Talk of all His wondrous works!
10 Glory in His holy name;
    Let the hearts of those rejoice
        who seek the LORD!
11 Seek the LORD and His strength;
    Seek His face evermore!
12 Remember His marvelous works
        which He has done,
    His wonders and the judgments
        of His mouth,
13 O seed of Israel His servant,
    You children of Jacob,
        His chosen ones!

14 He *is* the LORD our God;
    His judgments *are* in all the earth.
15 Remember His covenant always,
    The word which He commanded,
        for a thousand generations,
16 *The covenant* which He made
        with Abraham,
    And His oath to Isaac,
17 And confirmed it to Jacob
        for a statute,
    To Israel *for* an everlasting covenant,
18 Saying, "To you I will give
        the land of Canaan
    As the allotment of your inheritance,"
19 When you were but few in number,
    Indeed very few, and strangers in it.

20 *When* they went from one nation
        to another,
    And from *one* kingdom
        to another people,
21 He permitted no man
        to do them wrong;
    Yes, He reproved kings for their sakes,
22 *Saying,* "Do not touch
        My anointed ones,
    And do My prophets no harm.'' [113]

23 Sing to the LORD, all the earth;
    Proclaim the good news of His
        salvation from day to day.
24 Declare His glory among the nations,
    His wonders among all peoples.

25 For the LORD *is* great
        and greatly to be praised;
    He *is* also to be feared above all gods.
26 For all the gods of the peoples
        are idols,
    But the LORD made the heavens.
27 Honor and majesty *are* before Him;
    Strength and gladness are in His place.

28 Give to the LORD,
        O kindreds of the peoples,
    Give to the LORD glory and strength.
29 Give to the LORD
        the glory *due* His name;
    Bring an offering,
        and come before Him.
    Oh, worship the LORD
        in the beauty of holiness!
30 Tremble before Him, all the earth.
    The world also is firmly established,
    It shall not be moved.

31 Let the heavens rejoice,
        and let the earth be glad;
    And let them say among the nations,
        "The LORD reigns."
32 Let the sea roar, and all its fullness;
    Let the field rejoice,
        and all that *is* in it.
33 Then the trees of the woods shall
        rejoice before the LORD,
    For He is coming to judge the earth. [114]

34 Oh, give thanks to the LORD,
        for *He is* good!
    For His mercy *endures* forever. [115]
35 And say, "Save us,
        O God of our salvation;
    Gather us together,
        and deliver us from the Gentiles,
    To give thanks to Your holy name,
    To triumph in Your praise."

113 Verses 8–22 (compare Psalm 105:1-15)   114 Verses 23–33 (compare Psalm 96:1-13)
115 Verse 34 (compare Psalm 106:1)

36 Blessed *be* the LORD God of Israel
From everlasting to everlasting![116]

And all the people said, "Amen!" and
praised the LORD.

Regular Worship Maintained

37 So he left Asaph and his brothers
there before the ark of the covenant of
the LORD to minister before the ark regularly, as every day's work required;
38 and Obed-Edom with his sixty-eight
brethren, including Obed-Edom the son
of Jeduthun, and Hosah, *to be* gatekeepers;
39 and Zadok the priest and his brethren
the priests, before the tabernacle of the
LORD at the high place that *was* at
Gibeon,
40 to offer burnt offerings to the LORD
on the altar of burnt offering regularly
morning and evening, and *to do* according to all that is written in the Law of the
LORD which He commanded Israel;
41 and with them Heman and Jeduthun
and the rest who were chosen, who were
designated by name, to give thanks to
the LORD, because His mercy *endures*
forever;
42 and with them Heman and Jeduthun,
to sound aloud with trumpets and cymbals and the musical instruments of God.
Now the sons of Jeduthun *were* gatekeepers.
43 Then all the people departed, every
man to his house; and David returned to
bless his house.

God's Covenant with David

17 Now it came to pass, when David
was dwelling in his house, that
David said to Nathan the prophet, "See
now, I dwell in a house of cedar, but the
ark of the covenant of the LORD *is* under
tent curtains."
2 Then Nathan said to David, "Do all
that *is* in your heart, for God *is* with
you."
3 But it happened that night that the
word of God came to Nathan, saying,
4 "Go and tell My servant David, 'Thus
says the LORD: "You shall not build Me a
house to dwell in.
5 "For I have not dwelt in a house since
the time that I brought up Israel, even to
this day, but have gone from tent to tent,
and from *one* tabernacle *to another*.

6 "Wherever I have moved about with
all Israel, have I ever spoken a word to
any of the judges of Israel, whom I commanded to shepherd My people, saying,
'Why have you not built Me a house of
cedar?' "'
7 "Now therefore, thus shall you say to
My servant David, 'Thus says the LORD
of hosts: "I took you from the sheepfold,
from following the sheep, that you should
be ruler over My people Israel.
8 "And I have been with you wherever
you have gone, and have cut off all your
enemies from before you, and have made
you a name like the name of the great
men who *are* on the earth.
9 "Moreover I will appoint a place for
My people Israel, and will plant them,
that they may dwell in a place of their
own and move no more; nor shall the
sons of wickedness oppress them anymore, as previously,
10 "since the time that I commanded
judges *to be* over My people Israel. Also
I will subdue all your enemies. Furthermore I tell you that the LORD will build
you a house.
11 "And it shall be, when your days are
fulfilled, when you must go *to be* with
your fathers, that I will set up your seed
after you, who will be of your sons; and I
will establish his kingdom.
12 "He shall build Me a house, and I will
establish his throne forever.
13 "I will be his Father, and he shall be
My son; and I will not take My mercy
away from him, as I took *it* from *him* who
was before you.
14 "And I will establish him in My house
and in My kingdom forever; and his
throne shall be established forever." ' "
15 According to all these words and according to all this vision, so did Nathan
speak to David.
16 Then King David went in and sat before the LORD; and he said: "Who *am* I,
O LORD God? And what is my house,
that You have brought me this far?
17 "And *yet* this was a small thing in
Your sight, O God; and You have *also*
spoken of Your servant's house for a
great while to come, and have regarded
me according to the estate of a man of
high degree, O LORD God.
18 "What more can David *say* to You for
the honor of Your servant? For You
know Your servant.

116 Verses 35, 36 (compare Psalm 106:47, 48)

19 "O LORD, for Your servant's sake, and according to Your own heart, You have done all this greatness, in making known all *these* great things.

20 "O LORD, *there is* none like You, nor *is there any* God besides You, according to all that we have heard with our ears.

21 "And who *is* like Your people Israel, the one nation on the earth whom God went to redeem for Himself *as* a people— to make for Yourself a name by great and awesome deeds, by driving out nations from before Your people whom You redeemed from Egypt?

22 "For You have made Your people Israel Your very own people forever; and You, LORD, have become their God.

23 "And now, O LORD, the word which You have spoken concerning Your servant and concerning his house, *let it* be established forever, and do as You have said.

24 "So let it be established, that Your name may be magnified forever, saying, 'The LORD of hosts, the God of Israel, is Israel's God; and *let* the house of Your servant David be established before You.'

25 "For You, O my God, have told Your servant that You will build him a house. Therefore Your servant has found it *in his heart* to pray before You.

26 "And now, LORD, You are God, and have promised this goodness to Your servant.

27 "Now You have been pleased to bless the house of Your servant, that it may continue before You forever; for You have blessed it, O LORD, and *it shall be* blessed forever."

David's Further Conquests

18 After this it came to pass that David attacked the Philistines, subdued them, and took Gath and its towns from the hand of the Philistines.

2 Then he defeated Moab, and the Moabites became David's servants, *and* brought tribute.

3 And David defeated Hadadezer[117] king of Zobah *as far as* Hamath, as he went to establish his power by the River Euphrates.

4 David took from him one thousand chariots, seven thousand[118] horsemen, and twenty thousand foot soldiers. And

David also hamstrung all the chariot *horses*, except that he spared enough of them for one hundred chariots.

5 When the Syrians of Damascus came to help Hadadezer king of Zobah, David killed twenty-two thousand of the Syrians.

6 Then David put *garrisons* in Syria of Damascus; and the Syrians became David's servants, *and* brought tribute. Thus the LORD preserved David wherever he went.

7 And David took the shields of gold that were on the servants of Hadadezer, and brought them to Jerusalem.

8 Also from Tibhath[119] and from Chun, cities of Hadadezer, David brought a large amount of bronze, with which Solomon made the bronze Sea, the pillars, and the articles of bronze.

9 When Tou[120] king of Hamath heard that David had defeated all the army of Hadadezer king of Zobah,

10 he sent Hadoram[121] his son to King David, to greet him and bless him, because he had fought against Hadadezer and defeated him (for Hadadezer had been at war with Tou); and *Hadoram brought with him* all kinds of articles of gold, silver, and bronze.

11 King David also dedicated these to the LORD, along with the silver and gold that he had brought from all *these* nations—from Edom, from Moab, from the people of Ammon, from the Philistines, and from Amalek.

12 Moreover Abishai the son of Zeruiah killed eighteen thousand Edomites[122] in the Valley of Salt.

13 He also put garrisons in Edom, and all the Edomites became David's servants. And the LORD preserved David wherever he went.

David's Administration

14 So David reigned over all Israel, and administered judgment and justice to all his people.

15 Joab the son of Zeruiah *was* over the army; Jehoshaphat the son of Ahilud *was* recorder;

16 Zadok the son of Ahitub and Abimelech the son of Abiathar *were* the priests; Shavsha[123] *was* the scribe;

---

117 Hebrew *Hadarezer,* and so throughout chapters 18 and 19   118 Or *seven hundred* (compare 2 Samuel 8:4)
119 Spelled *Betah* in 2 Samuel 8:8   120 Spelled *Toi* in 2 Samuel 8:9 and elsewhere
121 Spelled *Joram* in 2 Samuel 8:10   122 Or *Syrians* (compare 2 Samuel 8:13)
123 Spelled *Seraiah* in 2 Samuel 8:17

17 Benaiah the son of Jehoiada *was* over the Cherethites and the Pelethites; and David's sons *were* chief ministers at the king's side.

The Ammonites and Syrians Defeated

19 Now it happened after this that Nahash the king of the people of Ammon died, and his son reigned in his place.

2 Then David said, "I will show kindness to Hanun the son of Nahash, because his father showed kindness to me." So David sent messengers to comfort him concerning his father. And the servants of David came to Hanun in the land of the people of Ammon to comfort him.

3 And the princes of the people of Ammon said to Hanun, "Do you think that David really honors your father because he has sent comforters to you? Did his servants not come to you to search and to overthrow and to spy out the land?"

4 Therefore Hanun took David's servants, shaved them, and cut off their garments in the middle, at their buttocks, and sent them away.

5 Then *some* went and told David about the men; and he sent to meet them, because the men were greatly ashamed. And the king said, "Wait at Jericho until your beards have grown, and *then* return."

6 When the people of Ammon saw that they had made themselves repulsive to David, Hanun and the people of Ammon sent a thousand talents of silver to hire for themselves chariots and horsemen from Mesopotamia,[124] from Syrian Maachah, and from Zobah.[125]

7 So they hired for themselves thirty-two thousand chariots, with the king of Maachah and his people, who came and encamped before Medeba. Also the people of Ammon gathered together from their cities, and came to battle.

8 And when David heard *of it,* he sent Joab and all the army of the mighty men.

9 Then the people of Ammon came out and put themselves in battle array before the gate of the city, and the kings who had come *were* by themselves in the field.

10 When Joab saw that the battle line was set against him before and behind, he chose some of the choice men of Israel, and put *them* in battle array against the Syrians.

11 And the rest of the people he put under the command of Abishai his brother, and they set *themselves* in battle array against the people of Ammon.

12 Then he said, "If the Syrians are too strong for me, then you shall help me; but if the people of Ammon are too strong for you, then I will help you.

13 "Be of good courage, and let us be strong for our people and for the cities of our God. And may the LORD do *what is* good in His sight."

14 So Joab and the people who *were* with him drew near for the battle against the Syrians, and they fled before him.

15 When the people of Ammon saw that the Syrians were fleeing, they also fled before Abishai his brother, and entered the city. So Joab went to Jerusalem.

16 Now when the Syrians saw that they had been defeated by Israel, they sent messengers and brought the Syrians who were beyond the River,[126] and Shophach[127] the commander of Hadadezer's army *went* before them.

17 When it was told David, he gathered all Israel, crossed over the Jordan and came upon them, and set up in battle array against them. So when David had set up in *battle* array against the Syrians, they fought with him.

18 Then the Syrians fled before Israel; and David killed seven thousand[128] charioteers and forty thousand foot soldiers[129] of the Syrians, and killed Shophach commander of the army.

19 And when the servants of Hadadezer saw that they were defeated by Israel, they made peace with David and became his servants. So the Syrians were not willing to help the people of Ammon anymore.

Rabbah Is Conquered

20 And it happened, in the spring of the year, at the time kings go out *to battle,* that Joab led out the armed forces and ravaged the country of the people of Ammon, and came and besieged Rabbah. But David stayed at Jerusalem. And Joab defeated Rabbah and overthrew it.

2 Then David took their king's crown

---

124 Hebrew *Aram Naharaim*   125 Spelled *Zoba* in 2 Samuel 10:6   126 That is, the Euphrates
127 Spelled *Shobach* in 2 Samuel 10:16   128 Or *seven hundred* (compare 2 Samuel 10:18)
129 Or *horsemen* (compare 2 Samuel 10:18)

from his head, and found it to weigh a talent of gold, and *there were* precious stones in it. And it was set on David's head. Also he brought out the spoil of the city in great abundance.

3 And he brought out the people who *were* in it, and put *them* to work[130] with saws, with iron picks, and with axes. So David did to all the cities of the people of Ammon. Then David and all the people returned *to* Jerusalem.

Philistine Giants Destroyed

4 Now it happened afterward that war broke out at Gezer with the Philistines, at which time Sibbechai the Hushathite killed Sippai,[131] *who was one* of the sons of the giant. And they were subdued.

5 Again there was war with the Philistines, and Elhanan the son of Jair[132] killed Lahmi the brother of Goliath the Gittite, the shaft of whose spear *was* like a weaver's beam.

6 Yet again there was war at Gath, where there was a man of *great* stature, with twenty-four fingers and toes, six *on each hand* and six *on each foot*; and he also was born to the giant.

7 So when he defied Israel, Jonathan the son of Shimea,[133] David's brother, killed him.

8 These were born to the giant in Gath, and they fell by the hand of David and by the hand of his servants.

The Census of Israel and Judah

21 Now Satan stood up against Israel, and moved David to number Israel.

2 So David said to Joab and to the leaders of the people, "Go, number Israel from Beersheba to Dan, and bring the number of them to me that I may know *it*."

3 And Joab answered, "May the LORD make His people a hundred times more than they are. But, my lord the king, *are* they not all my lord's servants? Why then does my lord require this thing? Why should he be a cause of guilt in Israel?"

4 Nevertheless the king's word prevailed against Joab. Therefore Joab departed and went throughout all Israel and came to Jerusalem.

5 Then Joab gave the sum of the number of the people to David. All Israel *had* one million one hundred thousand men who drew the sword, and Judah *had* four hundred and seventy thousand men who drew the sword.

6 But he did not count Levi and Benjamin among them, for the king's word was abominable to Joab.

7 And God was displeased with this thing; therefore He struck Israel.

8 So David said to God, "I have sinned greatly, because I have done this thing; but now, I pray, take away the iniquity of Your servant, for I have done very foolishly."

9 And the LORD spoke to Gad, David's seer, saying,

10 "Go and tell David, saying, 'Thus says the LORD: "I offer you three *things*; choose one of them for yourself, that I may do *it* to you." ' "

11 So Gad came to David and said to him, "Thus says the LORD: 'Choose for yourself,

12 'either three[134] years of famine, or three months to be defeated by your foes with the sword of your enemies overtaking *you*, or else for three days the sword of the LORD—the plague in the land, with the angel[135] of the LORD destroying throughout all the territory of Israel.' Now consider what answer I should take back to Him who sent me."

13 And David said to Gad, "I am in great distress. Please let me fall into the hand of the LORD, for His mercies *are* very great; but do not let me fall into the hand of man."

14 So the LORD sent a plague upon Israel, and seventy thousand men of Israel fell.

15 And God sent an angel to Jerusalem to destroy it. As he[136] was destroying, the LORD looked and relented of the disaster, and said to the angel who was destroying, "It is enough; now restrain your[137] hand." And the angel of the LORD stood by the threshing floor of Ornan[138] the Jebusite.

16 Then David lifted his eyes and saw the angel of the LORD standing between earth and heaven, having in his hand a drawn sword stretched out over Jerusalem. So David and the elders, clothed in sackcloth, fell on their faces.

130 Septuagint reads *cut them.*   131 Spelled *Saph* in 2 Samuel 21:18   132 Spelled *Jaare-Oregim* in 2 Samuel 21:19
133 Spelled *Shimeah* in 2 Samuel 21:21 and *Shammah* in 1 Samuel 16:9   134 Or *seven* (compare 2 Samuel 24:13)
135 Or *Angel* and so elsewhere in this chapter   136 Or *He*   137 Or *Your*   138 Spelled *Araunah* in 2 Samuel 24:16

17 And David said to God, "Was it not I who commanded the people to be numbered? I am the one who has sinned and done evil indeed; but these sheep, what have they done? Let Your hand, I pray, O LORD my God, be against me and my father's house, but not against Your people that they should be plagued."

18 Then the angel of the LORD commanded Gad to say to David that David should go and erect an altar to the LORD on the threshing floor of Ornan the Jebusite.

19 So David went up at the word of Gad, which he had spoken in the name of the LORD.

20 Now Ornan turned and saw the angel; and his four sons *who were* with him hid themselves, but Ornan continued threshing wheat.

21 Then David came to Ornan, and Ornan looked and saw David. And he went out from the threshing floor, and bowed *down* to David with *his* face to the ground.

22 Then David said to Ornan, "Grant me the place of *this* threshing floor, that I may build an altar on it to the LORD. You shall grant it to me at the full price, that the plague may be withdrawn from the people."

23 And Ornan said to David, "Take *it* to yourself, and let my lord the king do *what is* good in his eyes. Look, I *also* give *you* the oxen for burnt offerings, the threshing implements for wood, and the wheat for the grain offering; I give *it* all."

24 Then King David said to Ornan, "No, but I will surely buy *it* for the full price, for I will not take what is yours for the LORD, nor offer burnt offerings with *that which* costs *me* nothing."

25 So David gave Ornan six hundred shekels of gold by weight for the place.

26 And David built there an altar to the LORD, and offered burnt offerings and peace offerings, and called on the LORD; and He answered him from heaven by fire on the altar of burnt offering.

27 Then the LORD commanded the angel, and he returned his sword to its sheath.

28 At that time, when David saw that the LORD had answered him on the threshing floor of Ornan the Jebusite, he sacrificed there.

29 For the tabernacle of the LORD and the altar of the burnt offering, which Moses had made in the wilderness, *were* at that time at the high place in Gibeon.

30 But David could not go before it to inquire of God, for he was afraid of the sword of the angel of the LORD.

David Prepares to Build the Temple

22 Then David said, "This *is* the house of the LORD God, and this *is* the altar of burnt offering for Israel."

2 So David commanded to gather the aliens who *were* in the land of Israel; and he appointed masons to cut hewn stones to build the house of God.

3 And David prepared iron in abundance for the nails of the doors of the gates and for the joints, and bronze in abundance beyond measure,

4 and cedar trees in abundance; for the Sidonians and those from Tyre brought much cedar wood to David.

5 Now David said, "Solomon my son *is* young and inexperienced, and the house *that is* to be built for the LORD *must be* exceedingly magnificent, famous and glorious throughout all countries. I will now make preparation for it." So David made abundant preparations before his death.

6 Then he called for his son Solomon, and charged him to build a house for the LORD God of Israel.

7 And David said to Solomon: "My son, as for me, it was in my mind to build a house to the name of the LORD my God;

8 "but the word of the LORD came to me, saying, 'You have shed much blood and have made great wars; you shall not build a house for My name, because you have shed much blood on the earth in My sight.

9 'Behold, a son shall be born to you, who shall be a man of rest; and I will give him rest from all his enemies all around. His name shall be Solomon,[139] for I will give peace and quietness to Israel in his days.

10 'He shall build a house for My name, and he shall be My son, and I *will be* his Father; and I will establish the throne of his kingdom over Israel forever.'

11 "Now, my son, may the LORD be with you; and may you prosper, and build the house of the LORD your God, as He has said to you.

139 Literally *Peaceful*

12 "Only may the LORD give you wisdom and understanding, and give you charge concerning Israel, that you may keep the law of the LORD your God. 13 "Then you will prosper, if you take care to fulfill the statutes and judgments with which the LORD charged Moses concerning Israel. Be strong and of good courage; do not fear nor be dismayed. 14 "Indeed I have taken much trouble to prepare for the house of the LORD one hundred thousand talents of gold and one million talents of silver, and bronze and iron beyond measure, for it is so abundant. I have prepared timber and stone also, and you may add to them. 15 "Moreover *there are* workmen with you in abundance: hewers and workers of stone and timber, and all types of skillful men for every kind of work. 16 "Of gold and silver and bronze and iron *there is* no limit. Arise and begin working, and the LORD be with you." 17 David also commanded all the leaders of Israel to help Solomon his son, *saying,* 18 "*Is* not the LORD your God with you? And has He *not* given you rest on every side? For He has given the inhabitants of the land into my hand, and the land is subdued before the LORD and before His people. 19 "Now set your heart and your soul to seek the LORD your God. Therefore arise and build the sanctuary of the LORD God, to bring the ark of the covenant of the LORD and the holy articles of God into the house that is to be built for the name of the LORD."

The Divisions of the Levites

23 So when David was old and full of days, he made his son Solomon king over Israel. 2 And he gathered together all the leaders of Israel, with the priests and the Levites. 3 Now the Levites were numbered from the age of thirty years and above; and the number of individual males was thirty-eight thousand. 4 Of these, twenty-four thousand *were* to look after the work of the house of the LORD, six thousand *were* officers and judges, 5 four thousand *were* gatekeepers, and four thousand praised the LORD with *musical* instruments, "which I made," *said David*, "for giving praise." 6 And David divided them into divisions among the sons of Levi: Gershon, Kohath, and Merari. 7 Of the Gershonites: Laadan[140] and Shimei. 8 The sons of Laadan: the first Jehiel, then Zetham and Joel—three *in all.* 9 The sons of Shimei: Shelomith, Haziel, and Haran—three *in all.* These were the heads of the fathers' *houses* of Laadan. 10 And the sons of Shimei: Jahath, Zina,[141] Jeush, and Beriah. These *were* the four sons of Shimei. 11 Jahath was the first and Zizah the second. But Jeush and Beriah did not have many sons; therefore they were assigned as one father's house. 12 The sons of Kohath: Amram, Izhar, Hebron, and Uzziel—four *in all.* 13 The sons of Amram: Aaron and Moses; and Aaron was set apart, he and his sons forever, that he should sanctify the most holy things, to burn incense before the LORD, to minister to Him, and to give the blessing in His name forever. 14 Now the sons of Moses the man of God were reckoned to the tribe of Levi. 15 The sons of Moses *were* Gershon[142] and Eliezer. 16 Of the sons of Gershon, Shebuel[143] *was* the first. 17 Of the descendants of Eliezer, Rehabiah was the first. And Eliezer had no other sons, but the sons of Rehabiah were very many. 18 Of the sons of Izhar, Shelomith *was* the first. 19 Of the sons of Hebron, Jeriah *was* the first, Amariah the second, Jahaziel the third, and Jekameam the fourth. 20 Of the sons of Uzziel, Michah *was* the first and Jesshiah the second. 21 The sons of Merari *were* Mahli and Mushi. The sons of Mahli *were* Eleazar and Kish. 22 And Eleazar died, and had no sons, but only daughters; and their brethren, the sons of Kish, took them *as wives.* 23 The sons of Mushi *were* Mahli, Eder, and Jeremoth—three *in all.* 24 These *were* the sons of Levi by their

---

140 Spelled *Libni* in Exodus 6:17   141 Septuagint and Vulgate read *Zizah* (compare verse 11).
142 Hebrew *Gershom* (compare 6:16)   143 Spelled *Shubael* in 24:20

fathers' houses—the heads of the fathers' houses as they were counted individually by the number of their names, who did the work for the service of the house of the LORD, from the age of twenty years and above.

25 For David said, "The LORD God of Israel has given rest to His people, that they may dwell in Jerusalem forever";

26 and also to the Levites, "They shall no longer carry the tabernacle, or any of the articles for its service."

27 For by the last words of David the Levites *were* numbered from twenty years old and above;

28 because their duty *was* to help the sons of Aaron in the service of the house of the LORD, in the courts and in the chambers, in the purifying of all holy things and the work of the service of the house of God,

29 both with the showbread and the fine flour for the grain offering, with the unleavened cakes and *what is baked in* the pan, with what is mixed and with all kinds of measures and sizes;

30 to stand every morning to thank and praise the LORD, and likewise at evening;

31 and at every presentation of a burnt offering to the LORD on the Sabbaths and on the New Moons and on the set feasts, by number according to the ordinance governing them, regularly before the LORD;

32 and that they should attend to the needs of the tabernacle of meeting, the needs of the holy *place*, and the needs of the sons of Aaron their brethren in the work of the house of the LORD.

The Divisions of the Priests

24 Now *these are* the divisions of the sons of Aaron. The sons of Aaron *were* Nadab, Abihu, Eleazar, and Ithamar.

2 And Nadab and Abihu died before their father, and had no children; therefore Eleazar and Ithamar ministered as priests.

3 Then David with Zadok of the sons of Eleazar, and Ahimelech of the sons of Ithamar, divided them according to the schedule of their service.

4 Now there were more leaders found of the sons of Eleazar than of the sons of Ithamar, and *thus* they were divided. Among the sons of Eleazar *there were* sixteen heads of *their* fathers' houses, and eight heads of their fathers' houses among the sons of Ithamar.

5 Thus they were divided by lot, one group as another, for there were officials of the sanctuary and officials *of the house* of God, from the sons of Eleazar and from the sons of Ithamar.

6 And the scribe, Shemaiah the son of Nethaneel, *one of* the Levites, wrote them down before the king, the leaders, Zadok the priest, Ahimelech the son of Abiathar, and the heads of the fathers' *houses* of the priests and Levites, one father's house taken for Eleazar and *one* for Ithamar.

7 Now the first lot fell to Jehoiarib, the second to Jedaiah,

8 the third to Harim, the fourth to Seorim,

9 the fifth to Malchijah, the sixth to Mijamin,

10 the seventh to Hakkoz, the eighth to Abijah,

11 the ninth to Jeshua, the tenth to Shecaniah,

12 the eleventh to Eliashib, the twelfth to Jakim,

13 the thirteenth to Huppah, the fourteenth to Jeshebeab,

14 the fifteenth to Bilgah, the sixteenth to Immer,

15 the seventeenth to Hezir, the eighteenth to Happizzez,[144]

16 the nineteenth to Pethahiah, the twentieth to Jehezekel,[145]

17 the twenty-first to Jachin, the twenty-second to Gamul,

18 the twenty-third to Delaiah, the twenty-fourth to Maaziah.

19 This *was* the schedule of their service for coming into the house of the LORD according to their ordinance by the hand of Aaron their father, as the LORD God of Israel had commanded him.

Other Levites

20 Now the rest of the sons of Levi: of the sons of Amram, Shubael;[146] of the sons of Shubael, Jehdeiah.

21 Concerning Rehabiah, of the sons of Rehabiah, the first *was* Isshiah.

22 Of the Izharites, Shelomoth;[147] of the sons of Shelomoth, Jahath.

23 Of the sons *of Hebron*, Jeriah *was the*

---

144 Septuagint and Vulgate read *Aphses.*   145 Masoretic Text reads *Jehezkel.*
146 Spelled *Shebuel* in 23:16   147 Spelled *Shelomith* in 23:18

first, Amariah the second, Jahaziel the third, *and* Jekameam the fourth.
24 Of the sons of Uzziel, Michah; of the sons of Michah, Shamir.
25 The brother of Michah, Isshiah; of the sons of Isshiah, Zechariah.
26 The sons of Merari *were* Mahli and Mushi; the son of Jaaziah, Beno.
27 The sons of Merari by Jaaziah *were* Beno, Shoham, Zaccur, and Ibri.
28 Of Mahli: Eleazar, who had no sons.
29 Of Kish: the son of Kish, Jerahmeel.
30 Also the sons of Mushi *were* Mahli, Eder, and Jerimoth. These *were* the sons of the Levites according to their fathers' houses.
31 These also cast lots just as their brothers the sons of Aaron did, in the presence of King David, Zadok, Ahimelech, and the heads of the fathers' *houses* of the priests and Levites. The chief fathers *did* just as their younger brethren.

The Musicians

25 Moreover David and the captains of the army separated for the service *some* of the sons of Asaph, of Heman, and of Jeduthun, who *should* prophesy with harps, stringed instruments, and cymbals. And the number of the workmen according to their service was:
2 Of the sons of Asaph: Zaccur, Joseph, Nethaniah, and Asharelah;[148] the sons of Asaph *were* under the direction of Asaph, who prophesied according to the order of the king.
3 Of Jeduthun, the sons of Jeduthun: Gedaliah, Zeri,[149] Jeshaiah, *Shimei*, Hashabiah, and Mattithiah, six,[150] under the direction of their father Jeduthun, who prophesied with a harp to give thanks and to praise the LORD.
4 Of Heman, the sons of Heman: Bukkiah, Mattaniah, Uzziel,[151] Shebuel,[152] Jerimoth,[153] Hananiah, Hanani, Eliathah, Giddalti, Romamti-Ezer, Joshbekashah, Mallothi, Hothir, *and* Mahazioth.
5 All these *were* the sons of Heman the king's seer in the words of God, to exalt his horn.[154] For God gave Heman fourteen sons and three daughters.
6 All these *were* under the direction of their father for the music *in* the house of the LORD, with cymbals, stringed instruments, and harps, for the service of the house of God. Asaph, Jeduthun, and Heman *were* under the authority of the king.
7 So the number of them, with their brethren who were instructed in the songs of the LORD, all who were skillful, *was* two hundred and eighty-eight.
8 And they cast lots for their duty, the small as well as the great, the teacher with the student.
9 Now the first lot for Asaph came out for Joseph; the second for Gedaliah, him with his brethren and sons, twelve;
10 the third for Zaccur, his sons and his brethren, twelve;
11 the fourth for Jizri,[155] his sons and his brethren, twelve;
12 the fifth for Nethaniah, his sons and his brethren, twelve;
13 the sixth for Bukkiah, his sons and his brethren, twelve;
14 the seventh for Jesharelah,[156] his sons and his brethren, twelve;
15 the eighth for Jeshaiah, his sons and his brethren, twelve;
16 the ninth for Mattaniah, his sons and his brethren, twelve;
17 the tenth for Shimei, his sons and his brethren, twelve;
18 the eleventh for Azarel,[157] his sons and his brethren, twelve;
19 the twelfth for Hashabiah, his sons and his brethren, twelve;
20 the thirteenth for Shubael,[158] his sons and his brethren, twelve;
21 the fourteenth for Mattithiah, his sons and his brethren, twelve;
22 the fifteenth for Jeremoth,[159] his sons and his brethren, twelve;
23 the sixteenth for Hananiah, his sons and his brethren, twelve;
24 the seventeenth for Joshbekashah, his sons and his brethren, twelve;
25 the eighteenth for Hanani, his sons and his brethren, twelve;
26 the nineteenth for Mallothi, his sons and his brethren, twelve;
27 the twentieth for Eliathah, his sons and his brethren, twelve;
28 the twenty-first for Hothir, his sons and his brethren, twelve;
29 the twenty-second for Giddalti, his sons and his brethren, twelve;

---

148 Spelled *Jesharelah* in verse 14   149 Spelled *Jizri* in verse 11
150 *Shimei*, appearing in one Hebrew and several Septuagint manuscripts, completes the total of six sons (compare verse 17).   151 Spelled *Azarel* in verse 18   152 Spelled *Shubael* in verse 20   153 Spelled *Jeremoth* in verse 22
154 That is, to increase his power or influence   155 Spelled *Zeri* in verse 3   156 Spelled *Asharelah* in verse 2
157 Spelled *Uzziel* in verse 4   158 Spelled *Shebuel* in verse 4   159 Spelled *Jerimoth* in verse 4

30 the twenty-third for Mahazioth, his sons and his brethren, twelve;
31 the twenty-fourth for Romamti-Ezer, his sons and his brethren, twelve.

The Gatekeepers

26 Concerning the divisions of the gatekeepers: of the Korahites, Meshelemiah the son of Kore, of the sons of Asaph.
2 And the sons of Meshelemiah were Zechariah the firstborn, Jediael the second, Zebadiah the third, Jathniel the fourth,
3 Elam the fifth, Jehohanan the sixth, Eljehoenai the seventh.
4 Moreover the sons of Obed-Edom were Shemaiah the firstborn, Jehozabad the second, Joah the third, Sacar the fourth, Nethanel the fifth,
5 Ammiel the sixth, Issachar the seventh, Peulthai the eighth; for God blessed him.
6 Also to Shemaiah his son were sons born who governed their fathers' houses, because they were men of great ability.
7 The sons of Shemaiah were Othni, Rephael, Obed, and Elzabad, whose brothers Elihu and Semachiah were able men.
8 All these were of the sons of Obed-Edom, they and their sons and their brethren, able men with strength for the work: sixty-two of Obed-Edom.
9 And Meshelemiah had sons and brethren, eighteen able men.
10 Also Hosah, of the children of Merari, had sons: Shimri the first (for though he was not the firstborn, his father made him the first),
11 Hilkiah the second, Tebaliah the third, Zechariah the fourth; all the sons and brethren of Hosah were thirteen.
12 Among these were the divisions of the gatekeepers, among the chief men, having duties just like their brethren, to serve in the house of the LORD.
13 And they cast lots for each gate, the small as well as the great, according to their father's house.
14 The lot for the East Gate fell to Shelemiah. Then they cast lots for his son Zechariah, a wise counselor, and his lot came out for the North Gate;
15 to Obed-Edom the South Gate, and to his sons the storehouse.[160]
16 To Shuppim and Hosah the lot came out for the West Gate, with the Shalle-

cheth Gate on the ascending highway—watchman opposite watchman.
17 On the east were six Levites, on the north four each day, on the south four each day, and for the storehouse[161] two by two.
18 As for the Parbar on the west, there were four on the highway and two at the Parbar.
19 These were the divisions of the gatekeepers among the sons of Korah and among the sons of Merari.

The Treasuries and Other Duties

20 Of the Levites, Ahijah was over the treasuries of the house of God and over the treasuries of the dedicated things.
21 The sons of Laadan, the descendants of the Gershonites of Laadan, heads of their fathers' houses, of Laadan the Gershonite: Jehieli.
22 The sons of Jehieli, Zetham and Joel his brother, were over the treasuries of the house of the LORD.
23 Of the Amramites, the Izharites, the Hebronites, and the Uzzielites:
24 Shebuel the son of Gershom, the son of Moses, was overseer of the treasuries.
25 And his brethren by Eliezer were Rehabiah his son, Jeshaiah his son, Joram his son, Zichri his son, and Shelomith his son.
26 This Shelomith and his brethren were over all the treasuries of the dedicated things which King David and the heads of fathers' houses, the captains over thousands and hundreds, and the captains of the army, had dedicated.
27 Some of the spoils won in battles they dedicated to maintain the house of the LORD.
28 And all that Samuel the seer, Saul the son of Kish, Abner the son of Ner, and Joab the son of Zeruiah had dedicated, every dedicated thing, was under the hand of Shelomith and his brethren.
29 Of the Izharites, Chenaniah and his sons performed duties as officials and judges over Israel outside Jerusalem.
30 Of the Hebronites, Hashabiah and his brethren, one thousand seven hundred able men, had the oversight of Israel on the west side of the Jordan for all the business of the LORD, and in the service of the king.
31 Among the Hebronites, Jerijah was head of the Hebronites according to his

---

160 Hebrew asuppim   161 Hebrew asuppim

genealogy of the fathers. In the fortieth year of the reign of David they were sought, and there were found among them capable men at Jazer of Gilead.

32 And his brethren *were* two thousand seven hundred able men, heads of fathers' *houses*, whom King David made officials over the' Reubenites, the Gadites, and the half-tribe of Manasseh, for every matter pertaining to God and the affairs of the king.

The Military Divisions

27 And the children of Israel, according to their number, the heads of fathers' *houses*, the captains of thousands and hundreds and their officers, served the king in every matter of the *military* divisions. *These divisions* came in and went out month by month throughout all the months of the year, each division *having* twenty-four thousand.

2 Over the first division for the first month *was* Jashobeam the son of Zabdiel, and in his division *were* twenty-four thousand;

3 *he was* of the children of Perez, and the chief of all the captains of the army for the first month.

4 Over the division of the second month *was* Dodai[162] an Ahohite, and of his division Mikloth also *was* the leader; in his division *were* twenty-four thousand.

5 The third captain of the army for the third month *was* Benaiah, the son of Jehoiada the priest, who *was* chief; in his division *were* twenty-four thousand.

6 This *was* the Benaiah *who was* mighty *among* the thirty, and was over the thirty; in his division *was* Ammizabad his son.

7 The fourth *captain* for the fourth month *was* Asahel the brother of Joab, and Zebadiah his son after him; in his division *were* twenty-four thousand.

8 The fifth *captain* for the fifth month *was* Shamhuth[163] the Izrahite; in his division *were* twenty-four thousand.

9 The sixth *captain* for the sixth month *was* Ira the son of Ikkesh the Tekoite; in his division *were* twenty-four thousand.

10 The seventh *captain* for the seventh month *was* Helez the Pelonite, of the children of Ephraim; in his division *were* twenty-four thousand.

11 The eighth *captain* for the eighth month *was* Sibbechai the Hushathite, of the Zarhites; in his division *were* twenty-four thousand.

12 The ninth *captain* for the ninth month *was* Abiezer the Anathothite, of the Benjamites; in his division *were* twenty-four thousand.

13 The tenth *captain* for the tenth month *was* Maharai the Netophathite, of the Zarhites; in his division *were* twenty-four thousand.

14 The eleventh *captain* for the eleventh month *was* Benaiah the Pirathonite, of the children of Ephraim; in his division *were* twenty-four thousand.

15 The twelfth *captain* for the twelfth month *was* Heldai[164] the Netophathite, of Othniel; in his division *were* twenty-four thousand.

Leaders of Tribes

16 Furthermore, over the tribes of Israel: the officer over the Reubenites *was* Eliezer the son of Zichri; over the Simeonites, Shephatiah the son of Maachah;

17 *over* the Levites, Hashabiah the son of Kemuel; over the Aaronites, Zadok;

18 *over* Judah, Elihu, *one* of David's brothers; *over* Issachar, Omri the son of Michael;

19 *over* Zebulun, Ishmaiah the son of Obadiah; *over* Naphtali, Jerimoth the son of Azriel;

20 *over* the children of Ephraim, Hoshea the son of Azaziah; *over* the half-tribe of Manasseh, Joel the son of Pedaiah;

21 *over* the half-*tribe* of Manasseh in Gilead, Iddo the son of Zechariah; *over* Benjamin, Jaasiel the son of Abner;

22 *over* Dan, Azarel the son of Jeroham. These *were* the leaders of the tribes of Israel.

23 But David did not take the number of those twenty years old and under, because the LORD had said He would multiply Israel like the stars of the heavens.

24 Joab the son of Zeruiah began a census, but he did not finish, for wrath came upon Israel because of this census; nor was the number recorded in the account of the chronicles of King David.

Other State Officials

25 And Azmaveth the son of Adiel *was* over the king's treasuries; and Jehona-

---

162 Hebrew *Dodai*, usually spelled Dodo (compare 2 Samuel 23:9)
163 Spelled *Shammoth* in 11:27 and *Shammah* in 2 Samuel 23:11
164 Spelled *Heled* in 11:30 and *Heleb* in 2 Samuel 23:29

than the son of Uzziah was over the storehouses in the field, in the cities, in the villages, and in the fortresses.

26 Ezri the son of Chelub was over those who did the work of the field for tilling the ground.

27 And Shimei the Ramathite was over the vineyards, and Zabdi the Shiphmite was over the produce of the vineyards for the supply of wine.

28 Baal-Hanan the Gederite was over the olive trees and the sycamore trees that were in the lowlands, and Joash was over the store of oil.

29 And Shitrai the Sharonite was over the herds that fed in Sharon, and Shaphat the son of Adlai was over the herds that were in the valleys.

30 Obil the Ishmaelite was over the camels, Jehdeiah the Meronothite was over the donkeys,

31 and Jaziz the Hagerite was over the flocks. All these were the officials over King David's property.

32 Also Jehonathan, David's uncle, was a counselor, a wise man, and a scribe; and Jehiel the son of Hachmoni was with the king's sons.

33 Ahithophel was the king's counselor, and Hushai the Archite was the king's companion.

34 After Ahithophel was Jehoiada the son of Benaiah, then Abiathar. And the general of the king's army was Joab.

Solomon Instructed to Build the Temple

28 Now David assembled at Jerusalem all the leaders of Israel: the officers of the tribes and the captains of the divisions who served the king, the captains over thousands and captains over hundreds, and the stewards over all the substance and possessions of the king and of his sons, with the officials, the valiant men, and all the mighty men of valor.

2 Then King David rose to his feet and said, "Hear me, my brethren and my people: I had it in my heart to build a house of rest for the ark of the covenant of the LORD, and for the footstool of our God, and had made preparations to build it.

3 "But God said to me, 'You shall not build a house for My name, because you have been a man of war and have shed blood.'

4 "However the LORD God of Israel chose me above all the house of my father to be king over Israel forever, for He has chosen Judah to be the ruler; and of the house of Judah, the house of my father, and among the sons of my father, He was pleased with me to make me king over all Israel.

5 "And of all my sons (for the LORD has given me many sons) He has chosen my son Solomon to sit on the throne of the kingdom of the LORD over Israel.

6 "Now He said to me, 'It is your son Solomon who shall build My house and My courts; for I have chosen him to be My son, and I will be his Father.

7 'Moreover I will establish his kingdom forever, if he is steadfast to observe My commandments and My judgments, as it is this day.'

8 "Now therefore, in the sight of all Israel, the congregation of the LORD, and in the hearing of our God, be careful to seek out all the commandments of the LORD your God, that you may possess this good land, and leave it as an inheritance for your children after you forever.

9 "As for you, my son Solomon, know the God of your father, and serve Him with a loyal heart and with a willing mind; for the LORD searches all hearts and understands all the intent of the thoughts. If you seek Him, He will be found by you; but if you forsake Him, He will cast you off forever.

10 "Consider now, for the LORD has chosen you to build a house for the sanctuary; be strong, and do it."

11 Then David gave his son Solomon the plans for the vestibule, its houses, its treasuries, its upper chambers, its inner chambers, and the place of the mercy seat;

12 and the plans for all that he had by the Spirit, of the courts of the house of the LORD, of all the chambers all around, of the treasuries of the house of God, and of the treasuries for the dedicated things;

13 also for the division of the priests and the Levites, for all the work of the service of the house of the LORD, and for all the articles of service in the house of the LORD.

14 *He gave* gold by weight for *things* of gold, for all articles used in every kind of service; also *silver* for all articles of silver by weight, for all articles used in every kind of service;
15 the weight for the lampstands of gold, and their lamps of gold, by weight for each lampstand and its lamps; for the lampstands of silver by weight, for the lampstand and its lamps, according to the use of each lampstand.
16 And by weight *he gave* gold for the tables of the showbread, for each table, and silver for the tables of silver;
17 also pure gold for the forks, the basins, the pitchers of pure gold, and the golden bowls—*he gave gold* by weight for every bowl; and for the silver bowls, *silver* by weight for every bowl;
18 and refined gold by weight for the altar of incense, and for the construction of the chariot, that is, the gold cherubim that spread *their wings* and overshadowed the ark of the covenant of the LORD.
19 "All *this,*" said David, "the LORD made me understand in writing, by *His* hand upon me, all the works of these plans."
20 And David said to his son Solomon, "Be strong and of good courage, and do *it*; do not fear nor be dismayed, for the LORD God—my God—*will be* with you. He will not leave you nor forsake you, until you have finished all the work for the service of the house of the LORD.
21 "*Here are* the divisions of the priests and the Levites for all the service of the house of God; and every willing craftsman *will be* with you for all manner of workmanship, for every kind of service; also the leaders and all the people *will be* completely at your command."

Offerings for Building the Temple

29 Furthermore King David said to all the congregation: "My son Solomon, whom alone God has chosen, *is* young and inexperienced; and the work *is* great, because the temple[165] *is* not for man but for the LORD God.
2 "Now for the house of my God I have prepared with all my might: gold for *things to be made of* gold, silver for *things of* silver, bronze for *things of* bronze, iron for *things of* iron, wood for *things of* wood, onyx stones, *stones* to be set, glistening stones of various colors, all kinds

of precious stones, and marble slabs in abundance.
3 "Moreover, because I have set my affection on the house of my God, I have given to the house of my God, over and above all that I have prepared for the holy house, my own special treasure of gold and silver:
4 "three thousand talents of gold, of the gold of Ophir, and seven thousand talents of refined silver, to overlay the walls of the houses;
5 "the gold for *things of* gold and the silver for *things of* silver, and for all kinds of work *to be done* by the hands of craftsmen. Who *then* is willing to consecrate himself this day to the LORD?"
6 Then the leaders of the fathers' *houses,* leaders of the tribes of Israel, the captains of thousands and of hundreds, with the officers over the king's work, offered willingly.
7 They gave for the work of the house of God five thousand talents and ten thousand darics of gold, ten thousand talents of silver, eighteen thousand talents of bronze, and one hundred thousand talents of iron.
8 And whoever had *precious* stones gave *them* to the treasury of the house of the LORD, into the hand of Jehiel[166] the Gershonite.
9 Then the people rejoiced, for they had offered willingly, because with a loyal heart they had offered willingly to the LORD; and King David also rejoiced greatly.

David's Praise to God

10 Therefore David blessed the LORD before all the congregation; and David said:

"Blessed are You, LORD God of Israel,
    our Father, forever and ever.
11 Yours, O LORD, *is* the greatness,
    The power and the glory,
    The victory and the majesty;
    For all *that is* in heaven
        and in earth *is Yours*;
    Yours *is* the kingdom, O LORD,
    And You are exalted as head over all.
12 Both riches and honor *come* from You,
    And You reign over all.
    In Your hand *is* power and might;
    In Your hand *it is* to make great
    And to give strength to all.

165 Literally *palace* 166 Possibly the same as *Jehieli* (compare 26:21, 22)

13 "Now therefore, our God,
We thank You
And praise Your glorious name.
14 But who *am* I, and who *are* my people,
That we should be able to offer
so willingly as this?
For all things *come* from You,
And of Your own we have given You.
15 For we *are* aliens and pilgrims
before You,
As *were* all our fathers;
Our days on earth *are* as a shadow,
And without hope.

16 "O LORD our God, all this abundance
that we have prepared to build You a
house for Your holy name is from Your
hand, and *is* all Your own.
17 "I know also, my God, that You test
the heart and have pleasure in uprightness. As for me, in the uprightness of my
heart I have willingly offered all these
things; and now with joy I have seen
Your people, who are present here to offer willingly to You.
18 "O LORD God of Abraham, Isaac,
and Israel, our fathers, keep this forever
in the intent of the thoughts of the heart
of Your people, and fix their heart toward
You.
19 "And give my son Solomon a loyal
heart to keep Your commandments and
Your testimonies and Your statutes, to
do all *these things*, and to build the tem-
ple167 for which I have made provision."
20 Then David said to all the congregation, "Now bless the LORD your God."
So all the congregation blessed the LORD
God of their fathers, and bowed their
heads and prostrated themselves before
the LORD and the king.

Solomon Anointed King
21 And they made sacrifices to the LORD

167 Literally *palace*

and offered burnt offerings to the LORD
on the next day: a thousand bulls, a thousand rams, a thousand lambs, with their
drink offerings, and sacrifices in abundance for all Israel.
22 So they ate and drank before the
LORD with great gladness on that day.
And they made Solomon the son of David king the second time, and anointed
him before the LORD *to be* the leader, and
Zadok *to be* priest.
23 Then Solomon sat on the throne of
the LORD as king instead of David his
father, and prospered; and all Israel
obeyed him.
24 All the leaders and the mighty men,
and also all the sons of King David, submitted themselves to King Solomon.
25 So the LORD exalted Solomon exceedingly in the sight of all Israel, and bestowed on him *such* royal majesty as had
not been on any king before him in Israel.

The Close of David's Reign
26 Thus David the son of Jesse reigned
over all Israel.
27 And the period that he reigned over
Israel *was* forty years; seven years he
reigned in Hebron, and thirty-three *years*
he reigned in Jerusalem.
28 So he died in a good old age, full of
days and riches and honor; and Solomon
his son reigned in his place.
29 Now the acts of King David, first and
last, indeed they *are* written in the book
of Samuel the seer, in the book of Nathan
the prophet, and in the book of Gad the
seer,
30 with all his reign and his might, and
the events that happened to him, to Israel, and to all the kingdoms of the lands.

Introduction to
Second Chronicles

Second Chronicles covers the period from the reign of Solomon through the Babylonian captivity and with First Chronicles should be read as a companion volume to First and Second Samuel and First and Second Kings. It was probably compiled by Ezra about 450 B.C.

The focal point of the book is a moving account of a completion of a vision. One of King David's dreams that outlived him was to build a beautiful temple to the glory of God. Solomon, David's son and successor to the throne, shared his father's dream and made it a reality. The people rallied around Solomon's leadership and committed themselves to the completion of this task. The building project took approximately twenty years and required the complete dedication of the nation. People from far-off lands participated by sending cedar and fir trees, silver, brass, iron, and gold. Solomon put together a core task force of 200,000 men to oversee the project. Solomon taught the nation that it takes two to complete a project—God and man. By giving them a vision, Solomon directed their hearts to God. God was to dwell in this temple, and they knew that they had to make their plans big enough for God to fit in.

Then Solomon said:

"The LORD said
He would dwell in the dark cloud.
But I have built You an exalted house,
And a place for You to dwell in forever"

"But will God indeed dwell with men on the earth? Behold, heaven and the heaven of heavens cannot contain You; how much less this temple which I have built! Yet regard the prayer of Your servant . . . that Your eyes may be open toward this temple day and night, toward the place where *You* said *You would* put Your name, that You may hear the prayer which Your servant prays toward this place."

Now when Solomon had finished praying, fire came down from heaven and consumed the burnt offering and the sacrifices; and the glory of the LORD filled the temple.

(2 Chr. 6:1, 2, 18–20; 7:1)

Solomon and the people believed that they would rather attempt something great for God than to do nothing and succeed. For if they could attempt great things for God, they could expect great things from God!

The Second Book of the

Chronicles

Solomon Requests Wisdom

NOW Solomon the son of David was strengthened in his kingdom, and the LORD his God *was* with him and exalted him exceedingly.
2 And Solomon spoke to all Israel, to the captains of thousands and of hundreds, to the judges, and to every leader in all Israel, the heads of the fathers' *houses.*
3 Then Solomon, and all the congregation with him, went to the high place that *was* at Gibeon; for the tabernacle of meeting with God was there, which Moses the servant of the LORD had made in the wilderness.
4 But David had brought up the ark of God from Kirjath Jearim to *the place* David had prepared for it, for he had pitched a tent for it at Jerusalem.
5 Now the bronze altar that Bezaleel the son of Uri, the son of Hur, had made, he put[1] before the tabernacle of the LORD; Solomon and the congregation sought Him *there.*
6 And Solomon went up there to the bronze altar before the LORD, which *was* at the tabernacle of meeting, and offered a thousand burnt offerings on it.
7 On that night God appeared to Solomon, and said to him, "Ask! What shall I give you?"
8 And Solomon said to God: "You have shown great mercy to David my father, and have made me king in his place.
9 "Now, O LORD God, let Your promise to David my father be established, for You have made me king over a people like the dust of the earth in multitude.
10 "Now give me wisdom and knowledge, that I may go out and come in before this people; for who can judge this great people of Yours?"
11 And God said to Solomon: "Because this was in your heart, and you have not asked riches or wealth or honor or the life of your enemies, nor have you asked long life—but have asked wisdom and knowledge for yourself, that you may judge My people over whom I have made you king—
12 "wisdom and knowledge *are* granted to you; and I will give you riches and wealth and honor, such as none of the kings have had who *have been* before you, nor shall any after you have the like."

Solomon's Military and Economic Power

13 So Solomon came to Jerusalem from the high place that *was* at Gibeon, from before the tabernacle of meeting, and reigned over Israel.
14 And Solomon gathered chariots and horsemen; he had one thousand four hundred chariots and twelve thousand horsemen, whom he stationed in the chariot cities and with the king in Jerusalem.
15 Also the king made silver and gold as common in Jerusalem as stones, and he made cedars as abundant as the sycamores which *are* in the lowland.
16 And Solomon had horses imported from Egypt and Keveh; the king's merchants bought them in Keveh at the *current* price.
17 They also acquired and imported from Egypt a chariot for six hundred *shekels* of silver, and a horse for one hundred and fifty; thus, through their agents,[2] they exported them to all the kings of the Hittites and the kings of Syria.

Solomon Prepares to Build the Temple

2 Then Solomon determined to build a temple for the name of the LORD, and a royal house for himself.
2 Solomon selected seventy thousand men to bear burdens, eighty thousand to quarry *stone* in the mountains, and three thousand six hundred to oversee them.
3 Then Solomon sent to Hiram[3] king of Tyre, saying:

As you have dealt with David my father, and sent him cedars to build himself a house to dwell in, *so deal with me.*

1 Some authorities read *it was there.* 2 Literally *by their hands* 3 Hebrew *Huram,* and so elsewhere

471   2 CHRONICLES 3

4 Behold, I am building a temple for the name of the LORD my God, to dedicate *it* to Him, to burn before Him sweet incense, for the continual showbread, for the burnt offerings morning and evening, on the Sabbaths, on the New Moons, and on the set feasts of the LORD our God. This *is an ordinance* forever to Israel.

5 And the temple which I build *will be* great, for our God is greater than all gods.

6 But who is able to build Him a temple, since heaven and the heaven of heavens cannot contain Him? Who *am* I then, that I should build Him a temple, except to burn sacrifice before Him?

7 Therefore send me at once a man skillful to work in gold and silver, in bronze and iron, in purple and crimson and blue, who has skill to engrave with the skillful men who are with me in Judah and Jerusalem, whom David my father provided.

8 Also send me cedar and cypress and algum logs from Lebanon, for I know that your servants have skill to cut timber in Lebanon; and indeed my servants *will be* with your servants,

9 to prepare timber *for* me in abundance, for the temple which I am about to build *shall be* great and wonderful.

10 And indeed I will give to your servants, the hewers who cut timber, twenty thousand kors of ground wheat, twenty thousand kors of barley, twenty thousand baths of wine, and twenty thousand baths of oil.

11 Then Hiram king of Tyre answered in writing, which he sent to Solomon: Because the LORD loves His people, He has made you king over them.

12 Hiram also said:

Blessed *be* the LORD God of Israel, who made heaven and earth, for He has given King David a wise son, endowed with prudence and understanding, who will build a temple for the LORD and a royal house for himself!

13 And now I have sent a skillful man, endowed with understanding, Huram[4] my master[5] *craftsman*

14 (the son of a woman of the daughters of Dan, and his father was a man of Tyre), skilled to work in gold and silver, bronze and iron, stone and wood, purple and blue, fine linen and crimson, and to make any engraving and to accomplish any plan which may be given to him, with your skillful men and with the skillful men of my lord David your father.

15 Now therefore, the wheat, the barley, the oil, and the wine which my lord has spoken of, let him send to his servants.

16 And we will cut wood from Lebanon, as much as you need; we will bring it to you in rafts by sea to Joppa, and you will carry it up to Jerusalem.

17 Then Solomon numbered all the aliens who *were* in the land of Israel, after the census in which David his father had numbered them; and there were found to be one hundred and fifty-three thousand six hundred.

18 And he made seventy thousand of them bearers of burdens, eighty thousand hewers of *stone* in the mountain, and three thousand six hundred overseers to make the people work.

Solomon Builds the Temple

3 Now Solomon began to build the house of the LORD at Jerusalem on Mount Moriah, where the LORD had appeared to his father David, at the place that David had prepared on the threshing floor of Ornan[6] the Jebusite.

2 And he began to build on the second *day* of the second month in the fourth year of his reign.

3 This is the foundation which Solomon laid for building the house of God: The length *was* sixty cubits (by cubits according to the former measure) and the width twenty cubits.

4 And the vestibule that *was* in front *of* the sanctuary[7] was twenty cubits long across the width of the house, and the height *was* one hundred and twenty. He overlaid the inside with pure gold.

---

4 Spelled *Hiram* in 1 Kings 7:13   5 Literally *father* (compare 1 Kings 7:13, 14)
6 Spelled *Araunah* in 2 Samuel 24:16ff
7 The main room of the temple; elsewhere called the *Holy Place* (compare 1 Kings 6:3)

5 The larger room[8] he paneled with cypress which he overlaid with fine gold, and he carved palm trees and chainwork on it.

6 And he decorated the house with precious stones for beauty, and the gold *was* gold from Parvaim.

7 He also overlaid the house—the beams and doorposts, its walls and doors—with gold; and he carved cherubim on the walls.

8 And he made the Most Holy Place. Its length was according to the width of the house, twenty cubits, and its width twenty cubits. He overlaid it with six hundred talents of fine gold.

9 The weight of the nails *was* fifty shekels of gold; and he overlaid the upper area with gold.

10 In the Most Holy Place he made two cherubim, fashioned by carving, and overlaid them with gold.

11 The wings of the cherubim *were* twenty cubits in *overall* length: one wing *of the one cherub was* five cubits, touching the wall of the room, and the other wing *was* five cubits, touching the wing of the other cherub;

12 *one* wing of the other cherub *was* five cubits, touching the wall of the room, and the other wing *also was* five cubits, touching the wing of the other cherub.

13 The wings of these cherubim spanned twenty cubits overall. They stood on their feet, and they faced inward.

14 And he made the veil of blue and purple and crimson and fine linen, and wove cherubim into it.

15 Also he made in front of the temple[9] two pillars thirty-five cubits high,[10] and the capital that *was* on the top of each of *them* was five cubits.

16 He made wreaths of chainwork, as in the inner sanctuary, and put *them* on top of the pillars; and he made one hundred pomegranates, and put *them* on the wreaths of chainwork.

17 Then he set up the pillars before the temple, one on the right hand and the other on the left; he called the name of the one on the right hand Jachin, and the name of the one on the left Boaz.

Furnishings of the Temple

4 Moreover he made a bronze altar: twenty cubits was its length, twenty cubits its width, and ten cubits its height.

2 Then he made the Sea of cast *bronze*, ten cubits from one brim to the other; it was completely round. Its height *was* five cubits, and a line of thirty cubits measured its circumference.

3 And under it *was* the likeness of oxen encircling it all around, ten to a cubit, all the way around the Sea. The oxen *were* cast in two rows, when it was cast.

4 It stood on twelve oxen: three looking toward the north, three looking toward the west, three looking toward the south, and three looking toward the east; the Sea *was set* upon them, and all their back parts pointed inward.

5 It *was* a handbreadth thick; and its brim was shaped like the brim of a cup, *like* a lily blossom. It contained three thousand baths.

6 He also made ten lavers, and put five on the right side and five on the left, to wash in them; such things as they offered for the burnt offering they would wash in them, but the Sea *was* for the priests to wash in.

7 And he made ten lampstands of gold according to their design, and set *them* in the temple, five on the right side and five on the left.

8 He also made ten tables, and placed *them* in the temple, five on the right side and five on the left. And he made one hundred bowls of gold.

9 Furthermore he made the court of the priests, and the great court and doors for the court; and he overlaid these doors with bronze.

10 He set the Sea on the right side, to the southeast.

11 Then Huram made the pots and the shovels and the bowls. So Huram finished doing the work that he was to do for King Solomon for the house of God:

12 the two pillars and the bowl-shaped capitals *that were* on top of the two pillars; the two networks covering the two bowl-shaped capitals which *were* on top of the pillars;

13 four hundred pomegranates for the two networks (two rows of pomegranates for each network, to cover the two bowl-shaped capitals that *were* on the pillars);

14 he also made carts and the lavers on the carts;

15 one Sea and twelve oxen under it;

16 also the pots, the shovels, the forks—

---

8 Literally *house* 9 Literally *house* 10 Or *eighteen* (compare 1 Kings 7:15; 2 Kings 25:17; and Jeremiah 52:51)

and all their articles Huram his master[11] *craftsman* made of burnished bronze for King Solomon for the house of the LORD.
17 In the plain of Jordan the king had them cast in clay molds, between Succoth and Zeredah.[12]
18 And Solomon had all these articles made in such great abundance that the weight of the bronze was not determined.
19 Thus Solomon had all the furnishings made for the house of God: the altar of gold and the tables on which *was* the showbread;
20 the lampstands with their lamps of pure gold, to burn in the prescribed manner in front of the inner sanctuary,
21 with the flowers and the lamps and the wick-trimmers of gold, of purest gold;
22 the trimmers, the bowls, the ladles, and the censers of pure gold. As for the entry of the sanctuary, its inner doors to the Most Holy *Place*, and the doors of the main hall of the temple, *were of* gold.

5 So all the work that Solomon had done for the house of the LORD was finished; and Solomon brought in *all* the things which his father David had dedicated: the silver and the gold and all the furnishings. And he put *them* in the treasuries of the house of God.

The Ark Brought into the Temple

2 Now Solomon assembled the elders of Israel and all the heads of the tribes, the chief fathers of the children of Israel, in Jerusalem, that they might bring the ark of the covenant of the LORD up from the City of David, which *is* Zion.
3 Therefore all the men of Israel assembled together with the king at the feast, which *was* in the seventh month.
4 So all the elders of Israel came, and the Levites took up the ark.
5 Then they brought up the ark, the tabernacle of meeting, and all the holy furnishings that *were* in the tabernacle. The priests and the Levites brought them up.
6 Also King Solomon, and all the congregation of Israel who were assembled with him before the ark, were sacrificing sheep and oxen that could not be counted or numbered for multitude.
7 Then the priests brought in the ark of the covenant of the LORD to its place, into the inner sanctuary of the temple,[13] to the Most Holy *Place*, under the wings of the cherubim.

8 For the cherubim spread *their* wings over the place of the ark, and the cherubim overshadowed the ark and its poles.
9 And the poles extended so that the ends of the poles of the ark could be seen from *the holy place*, in front of the inner sanctuary; but they could not be seen from outside. And they are there to this day.
10 *There was* nothing in the ark except the two tablets which Moses put *there* at Horeb, when the LORD made *a covenant* with the children of Israel, when they had come out of Egypt.
11 And it came to pass when the priests came out of the *Most* Holy *Place* (for all the priests who *were* present had sanctified themselves, without keeping to their divisions),
12 and the Levites *who were* the singers, all those of Asaph and Heman and Jeduthun, with their sons and their brethren, stood at the east end of the altar, clothed in white linen, having cymbals, stringed instruments and harps, and with them one hundred and twenty priests sounding with trumpets—
13 indeed it came to pass, when the trumpeters and singers *were* as one, to make one sound to be heard in praising and thanking the LORD, and when they lifted up their voice with the trumpets and cymbals and instruments of music, and praised the LORD, *saying*:

"*For He is* good,
    For His mercy *endures* forever,"[14]

that the house, the house of the LORD, was filled with a cloud,
14 so that the priests could not continue ministering because of the cloud; for the glory of the LORD filled the house of God.

6 Then Solomon said:

"The LORD said
    He would dwell in the dark cloud.
2 But I have built You an exalted house,
    And a place for You
        to dwell in forever."

Solomon's Speech upon Completion of the Work

3 Then the king turned around and blessed the whole congregation of Israel, while all the congregation of Israel stood.

11 Literally *father*   12 Spelled *Zaretan* in 1 Kings 7:46   13 Literally *house*   14 Compare Psalm 106:1

4 And he said: "Blessed *be* the LORD God of Israel, who has fulfilled with His hands *what* He spoke with His mouth to my father David, saying,
5 'Since the day that I brought My people out of the land of Egypt, I have chosen no city from any tribe of Israel *in which* to build a house, that My name might be there, nor did I choose any man to be a ruler over My people Israel;
6 'but I have chosen Jerusalem, that My name may be there; and I have chosen David to be over My people Israel.'
7 "Now it was in the heart of my father David to build a temple for the name of the LORD God of Israel.
8 "But the LORD said to my father David, 'Whereas it was in your heart to build a temple for My name, you did well in that it was in your heart.
9 'Nevertheless you shall not build the house, but your son who will come forth from your own loins, he shall build the temple for My name.'
10 "So the LORD has fulfilled His word which He spoke, and I have filled the position of my father David, and sit on the throne of Israel, as the LORD promised; and I have built the temple for the name of the LORD God of Israel.
11 "And there I have put the ark, in which *is* the covenant of the LORD which He made with the children of Israel."

Solomon's Prayer of Dedication

12 Then *Solomon*[15] stood before the altar of the LORD in the presence of all the congregation of Israel, and spread out his hands
13 (for Solomon had made a bronze platform five cubits long, five cubits broad, and three cubits high, and had set it in the midst of the court; and he stood on it, knelt down on his knees before all the congregation of Israel, and spread out his hands toward heaven),
14 and said: "LORD God of Israel, *there is* no God in heaven or on earth like You, who keep *Your* covenant and mercy with Your servants who walk before You with all their hearts.
15 "You have kept what You promised Your servant David my father; You have both spoken with Your mouth and fulfilled *it* with Your hand, as *it is* this day.
16 "Therefore, LORD God of Israel, now keep what You promised Your servant David my father, saying, 'You shall not fail to have a man sit before Me on the throne of Israel, only if your sons take heed to their way, to walk in My law as you have walked before Me.'
17 "Now then, O LORD God of Israel, let Your word come true, which You have spoken to Your servant David.
18 "But will God indeed dwell with men on the earth? Behold, heaven and the heaven of heavens cannot contain You; how much less this temple[16] which I have built!
19 "Yet regard the prayer of Your servant and his supplication, O LORD my God, and listen to the cry and to the prayer which Your servant is praying before You:
20 "that Your eyes may be open toward this temple day and night, toward the place where *You* said *You would* put Your name, that You may hear the prayer which Your servant prays toward this place.
21 "And may You hear the supplications of Your servant and of Your people Israel, when they pray toward this place; hear from Your dwelling place, in heaven; and when You hear, forgive.
22 "If anyone sins against his neighbor, and is forced to take an oath, and comes *and* takes an oath before Your altar in this temple,
23 "then hear from heaven, and act, and judge Your servants, bringing retribution on the wicked by bringing his way on his own head, and justifying the righteous by giving him according to his righteousness.
24 "Or if Your people Israel are defeated before an enemy because they have sinned against You, and return and confess Your name, and pray and make supplication before You in this temple,
25 "then hear from heaven and forgive the sin of Your people Israel, and bring them back to the land which You gave to them and their fathers.
26 "When heaven is shut up and there is no rain because they have sinned against You, when they pray toward this place and confess Your name, and turn from their sin because You afflict them,
27 "then hear *in* heaven, and forgive the sin of Your servants, Your people Israel, that You may teach them the good way in which they should walk; and send rain on

15 Literally *he* (compare 1 Kings 8:22) 16 Literally *house*

Your land which You have given to Your people as an inheritance.

28 "When there is famine in the land, pestilence or blight or mildew, locusts or grasshoppers; when their enemies besiege them in the land of their cities; whatever plague or whatever sickness *there is*;

29 "whatever prayer, whatever supplication is made by anyone, or by all Your people Israel, when each one knows his own burden and his own grief, and spreads out his hands to this house:

30 "then hear from heaven Your dwelling place, and forgive, and give to everyone according to all his ways, whose heart You know (for You alone know the hearts of the sons of men),

31 "that they may fear You, to walk in Your ways as long as they live in the land which You gave to our fathers.

32 "Moreover, concerning a foreigner, who is not of Your people Israel, but who comes from a far country for the sake of Your great name and Your mighty hand and Your outstretched arm, when they come and pray in this temple;

33 "then hear from heaven Your dwelling place, and do according to all for which the foreigner calls to You, that all people of the earth may know Your name and fear You, as *do* Your people Israel, and that they may know that this temple which I have built is called by Your name.

34 "When Your people go out to battle against their enemies, wherever You send them, and when they pray to You toward this city which You have chosen and toward the temple which I have built for Your name,

35 "then hear from heaven their prayer and their supplication, and maintain their cause.

36 "When they sin against You (for *there is* no one who does not sin), and You become angry with them and deliver them to the enemy, and they take them captive to a land far or near,

37 "yet when they come to themselves in the land where they were carried captive, and repent, and make supplication to You in the land of their captivity, saying, 'We have sinned, we have done wrong, and have acted wickedly';

38 "and when they return to You with all their heart and with all their soul in the land of their captivity, where they have

been carried captive, and pray toward their land which You gave to their fathers, *toward* the city which You have chosen, and toward the temple which I have built for Your name:

39 "then hear from heaven Your dwelling place their prayer and their supplications, and maintain their cause, and forgive Your people who have sinned against You.

40 "Now, my God, I pray, let Your eyes be open and *let* Your ears *be* attentive to the prayer *made* in this place.

41 "Now therefore,
Arise, O LORD God,
     to Your resting place,
You and the ark of Your strength.
Let Your priests, O LORD God,
     be clothed with salvation,
And let Your saints
     rejoice in goodness.

42 "O LORD God, do not turn away
     the face of Your anointed;
Remember the mercies
     of Your servant David."[17]

Solomon Dedicates the Temple

7 Now when Solomon had finished praying, fire came down from heaven and consumed the burnt offering and the sacrifices; and the glory of the LORD filled the temple.[18]

2 And the priests could not enter the house of the LORD, because the glory of the LORD had filled the LORD's house.

3 When all the children of Israel saw how the fire came down, and the glory of the LORD on the temple, they bowed their faces to the ground on the pavement, and worshiped and praised the LORD, *saying*:

"For *He is* good,
For His mercy *endures* forever."[19]

4 Then the king and all the people offered sacrifices before the LORD.

5 King Solomon offered a sacrifice of twenty-two thousand bulls and one hundred and twenty thousand sheep. So the king and all the people dedicated the house of God.

6 And the priests attended to their services; the Levites also with instruments of the music of the LORD, which King David had made to praise the LORD, saying, "For His mercy *endures* forever,"[20] when-

---

17 Compare Psalm 132:8–10   18 Literally *house*   19 Compare Psalm 106:1   20 Compare Psalm 106:1

ever David offered praise by their ministry. The priests sounded trumpets opposite them, while all Israel stood.

7 Furthermore Solomon consecrated the middle of the court that *was* in front of the house of the LORD; for there he offered burnt offerings and the fat of the peace offerings, because the bronze altar which Solomon had made was not able to receive the burnt offerings, the grain offerings, and the fat.

8 At that time Solomon kept the feast seven days, and all Israel with him, a very great congregation from the entrance of Hamath to the Brook of Egypt.[21]

9 And on the eighth day they held a sacred assembly, for they observed the dedication of the altar seven days, and the feast seven days.

10 On the twenty-third day of the seventh month he sent the people away to their tents, joyful and glad of heart for the goodness that the LORD had done for David, for Solomon, and for His people Israel.

11 Thus Solomon finished the house of the LORD and the king's house; and Solomon successfully accomplished all that came into his heart to make in the house of the LORD and in his own house.

God's Second Appearance to Solomon

12 Then the LORD appeared to Solomon by night, and said to him: "I have heard your prayer, and have chosen this place for Myself as a house of sacrifice.

13 "When I shut up heaven and there is no rain, or command the locusts to devour the land, or send pestilence among My people,

14 "if My people who are called by My name will humble themselves, and pray and seek My face, and turn from their wicked ways, then I will hear from heaven, and will forgive their sin and heal their land.

15 "Now My eyes will be open and My ears attentive to prayer *made* in this place.

16 "For now I have chosen and sanctified this house, that My name may be there forever; and My eyes and My heart will be there perpetually.

17 "As for you, if you walk before Me as your father David walked, and do according to all that I have commanded

you, and if you keep My statutes and My judgments,

18 "then I will establish the throne of your kingdom, as I covenanted with David your father, saying, 'You shall never fail *to have* a man as ruler in Israel.'

19 "But if you turn away and forsake My statutes and My commandments which I have set before you, and go and serve other gods, and worship them,

20 "then I will uproot them from My land which I have given them; and this house which I have sanctified for My name I will cast out of My sight, and will make it *to be* a proverb and a byword among all nations.

21 "And *as for* this house, which is exalted, everyone who passes by it will be astonished and say, 'Why has the LORD done thus to this land and this house?'

22 "Then they will answer, 'Because they forsook the LORD God of their fathers, who brought them out of the land of Egypt, and embraced other gods, and worshiped them and served them; therefore He has brought all this calamity on them.' "

Solomon's Additional Achievements

8 It came to pass at the end of twenty years, in which Solomon had built the house of the LORD and his own house,

2 that the cities which Hiram[22] had given to Solomon, Solomon built them; and he settled the children of Israel there.

3 And Solomon went to Hamath Zobah and seized it.

4 He also built Tadmor in the wilderness, and all the storage cities which he built in Hamath.

5 He built Upper Beth Horon and Lower Beth Horon, fortified cities *with* walls, gates, and bars,

6 also Baalath and all the storage cities that Solomon had, and all the chariot cities and the cities of the cavalry, and all that Solomon desired to build in Jerusalem, in Lebanon, and throughout all the land of his dominion.

7 All the people *who were* left of the Hittites, Amorites, Perizzites, Hivites, and Jebusites, who *were* not of Israel

8 (that is, their descendants who were left in the land after them, whom the children of Israel did not destroy), from these Solomon raised forced labor, as it is to this day.

21 That is, the Shihor (compare 1 Chronicles 13:5) 22 Hebrew *Huram* (compare 2 Chronicles 2:3)

9 But Solomon did not make the children of Israel servants for his work. Some *were* men of war, captains of his officers, captains of his chariots, and his cavalry.

10 And others *were* chiefs of the officials of King Solomon: two hundred and fifty, who ruled over the people.

11 Now Solomon brought the daughter of Pharaoh up from the City of David to the house he had built for her, for he said, "My wife shall not dwell in the house of David king of Israel, because *the places* to which the ark of the LORD has come are holy."

12 Then Solomon offered burnt offerings to the LORD on the altar of the LORD which he had built before the vestibule,

13 according to the daily rate, offering according to the commandment of Moses, for the Sabbaths, the New Moons, and the three appointed yearly feasts— the Feast of Unleavened Bread, the Feast of Weeks, and the Feast of Tabernacles.

14 And, according to the order of David his father, he appointed the divisions of the priests for their service, the Levites for their duties (to praise and serve before the priests) as the duty of each day required, and the gatekeepers by their divisions at each gate; for so David the man of God had commanded.

15 They did not depart from the command of the king to the priests and Levites concerning any matter or concerning the treasuries.

16 Now all the work of Solomon was well-ordered from the day of the foundation of the house of the LORD until it was finished. So the house of the LORD was completed.

17 Then Solomon went to Ezion Geber and Elath[23] on the seacoast, in the land of Edom.

18 And Hiram sent him ships by the hand of his servants, and servants who knew the sea. They went with the servants of Solomon to Ophir, and acquired four hundred and fifty talents of gold from there, and brought it to King Solomon.

The Queen of Sheba's Praise of Solomon

9 Now when the queen of Sheba heard of the fame of Solomon, she came to Jerusalem to test Solomon with hard questions, *having* a very great retinue, camels that bore spices, gold in abundance, and precious stones; and when she came to Solomon, she spoke with him about all that was in her heart.

2 So Solomon answered all her questions; there was nothing so difficult for Solomon that he could not explain it to her.

3 And when the queen of Sheba had seen the wisdom of Solomon, the house that he had built,

4 the food on his table, the seating of his servants, the service of his waiters and their apparel, his cupbearers and their apparel, and his entryway by which he went up to the house of the LORD, there was no more spirit in her.

5 Then she said to the king: "*It was* a true report which I heard in my own land about your words and your wisdom.

6 "However I did not believe their words until I came and saw with my own eyes; and indeed, the half of the greatness of your wisdom was not told me. You exceed the fame of which I heard.

7 "Happy *are* your men and happy *are* these your servants, who stand continually before you and hear your wisdom!

8 "Blessed be the LORD your God, who delighted in you, setting you on His throne *to be* king for the LORD your God! Because your God has loved Israel, to establish them forever, therefore He made you king over them, to do justice and righteousness."

9 Then she gave the king one hundred and twenty talents of gold, spices in great abundance, and precious stones; there never were any spices such as those the queen of Sheba gave to King Solomon.

10 Also, the servants of Hiram and the servants of Solomon, who brought gold from Ophir, brought algum[24] wood and precious stones.

11 And the king made walkways *of* the algum[25] wood for the house of the LORD and for the king's house, also harps and stringed instruments for singers; and there were none such *as these* seen before in the land of Judah.

12 Now King Solomon gave to the queen of Sheba all she desired, whatever she asked, *much more* than she had brought to the king. So she turned and went to her own country, she and her servants.

23 Hebrew *Eloth* (compare 2 Kings 14:22)   24 Or *almug* (compare 1 Kings 10:11, 12)
25 Or *almug* (compare 1 Kings 10:11, 12)

Solomon's Great Wealth

13 The weight of gold that came to Solomon yearly was six hundred and sixty-six talents of gold,

14 besides *what* the traveling merchants and traders brought. And all the kings of Arabia and governors of the country brought gold and silver to Solomon.

15 And King Solomon made two hundred large shields of hammered gold; six hundred *shekels* of hammered gold went into each shield.

16 *He* also *made* three hundred shields of hammered gold; three hundred *shekels*26 of gold went into each shield. The king put them in the House of the Forest of Lebanon.

17 Moreover the king made a great throne of ivory, and overlaid it with pure gold.

18 The throne *had* six steps, with a footstool of gold, *which were* fastened to the throne; there were armrests on either side of the place of the seat, and two lions stood beside the armrests.

19 Twelve lions stood there, one on each side of the six steps; nothing like *this* had been made for any *other* kingdom.

20 All King Solomon's drinking vessels *were of* gold, and all the vessels of the House of the Forest of Lebanon *were of* pure gold. Not one *was of* silver, for this was accounted as nothing in the days of Solomon.

21 For the king's ships went to Tarshish with the servants of Huram.27 Once every three years the merchant ships28 came, bringing gold, silver, ivory, apes, and monkeys.29

22 So King Solomon surpassed all the kings of the earth in riches and wisdom.

23 And all the kings of the earth sought the presence of Solomon to hear his wisdom, which God had put in his heart.

24 Each man brought his present: articles of silver and gold, garments, armor, spices, horses, and mules, at a set rate year by year.

25 Solomon had four thousand stalls for horses and chariots, and twelve thousand horsemen whom he stationed in the chariot cities and with the king at Jerusalem.

26 So he reigned over all the kings from the River30 to the land of the Philistines, as far as the border of Egypt.

27 The king made silver *as common* in Jerusalem as stones, and he made cedar trees as abundant as the sycamores which *are* in the lowland.

28 And they brought horses to Solomon from Egypt and from all lands.

Death of Solomon

29 Now the rest of the acts of Solomon, first and last, *are* they not written in the book of Nathan the prophet, in the prophecy of Ahijah the Shilonite, and in the visions of Iddo the seer concerning Jeroboam the son of Nebat?

30 Solomon reigned in Jerusalem over all Israel forty years.

31 Then Solomon rested with his fathers, and was buried in the City of David his father. And Rehoboam his son reigned in his place.

The Revolt Against Rehoboam

10 And Rehoboam went to Shechem, for all Israel had gone to Shechem to make him king.

2 So it happened when Jeroboam the son of Nebat heard *it* (he was in Egypt, where he had fled from the presence of Solomon the king), that Jeroboam returned from Egypt.

3 Then they sent for him and called him. And Jeroboam and all Israel came and spoke to Rehoboam, saying,

4 "Your father made our yoke heavy; now therefore, lighten the burdensome service of your father and his heavy yoke which he put on us, and we will serve you."

5 So he said to them, "Come back to me after three days." And the people departed.

6 Then King Rehoboam consulted the elders who stood before his father Solomon while he still lived, saying, "How do you advise *me* to answer these people?"

7 And they spoke to him, saying, "If you are kind to these people, and please them, and speak good words to them, they will be your servants forever."

8 But he rejected the counsel which the elders had given him, and consulted the young men who had grown up with him, who stood before him.

9 And he said to them, "What advice do you give? How should we answer this people who have spoken to me, saying,

---

26 Or *three minas* (compare 1 Kings 10:17)   27 Or *Hiram* (compare 1 Kings 10:22)
28 Literally *ships of Tarshish* (deep-sea vessels)   29 Or *peacocks*   30 That is, the Euphrates

'Lighten the yoke which your father put on us'?"

10 Then the young men who had grown up with him spoke to him, saying, "Thus you should speak to the people who have spoken to you, saying, 'Your father made our yoke heavy, but you make *it* lighter on us'—thus you shall say to them: 'My little *finger* shall be thicker than my father's waist!

11 'And now, whereas my father put a heavy yoke on you, I will add to your yoke; my father chastised you with whips, but I *will chastise you* with scourges!' "[31]

12 So Jeroboam and all the people came to Rehoboam on the third day, as the king had appointed, saying, "Come back to me the third day."

13 Then the king answered them roughly. King Rehoboam rejected the counsel of the elders,

14 and he spoke to them according to the counsel of the young men, saying, "My father made your yoke heavy, but I will add to it; my father chastised you with whips, but I *will chastise you* with scourges!"[32]

15 So the king did not listen to the people; for the turn *of affairs* was from God, that the LORD might fulfill His word, which He had spoken by the hand of Ahijah the Shilonite to Jeroboam the son of Nebat.

16 Now when all Israel *saw* that the king did not listen to them, the people answered the king, saying:

"What portion *have we* in David?
We have no inheritance
   in the son of Jesse.
Every man to your tents, O Israel!
Now see to your own house,
   O David!"

So all Israel departed to their tents.

17 But Rehoboam reigned over the children of Israel who dwelt in the cities of Judah.

18 Then King Rehoboam sent Hadoram, who *was* in charge of revenue; but the children of Israel stoned him with stones, and he died. Therefore King Rehoboam mounted *his* chariot in haste to flee to Jerusalem.

19 So Israel has been in rebellion against the house of David to this day.

11 Now when Rehoboam came to Jerusalem, he assembled from the house of Judah and Benjamin one hundred and eighty thousand chosen *men* who were warriors, to fight against Israel, that he might restore the kingdom to Rehoboam.

2 But the word of the LORD came to Shemaiah the man of God, saying,

3 "Speak to Rehoboam the son of Solomon, king of Judah, and to all Israel in Judah and Benjamin, saying,

4 'Thus says the LORD: "You shall not go up or fight against your brethren! Let every man return to his house, for this thing is from Me." ' " Therefore they obeyed the words of the LORD, and turned back from attacking Jeroboam.

Rehoboam Fortifies the Cities

5 So Rehoboam dwelt in Jerusalem, and built cities for defense in Judah.

6 And he built Bethlehem, Etam, Tekoa,

7 Beth Zur, Sochoh, Adullam,

8 Gath, Mareshah, Ziph,

9 Adoraim, Lachish, Azekah,

10 Zorah, Aijalon, and Hebron, which are in Judah and Benjamin, fortified cities.

11 And he fortified the strongholds, and put captains in them, and stores of food, oil, and wine.

12 Also in every city *he put* shields and spears, and made them very strong, having Judah and Benjamin on his side.

Priests and Levites Move to Judah

13 And from all their territories the priests and the Levites who *were* in all Israel took their stand with him.

14 For the Levites left their commonlands and their possessions and came to Judah and Jerusalem, for Jeroboam and his sons had rejected them from serving as priests to the LORD.

15 Then he appointed for himself priests for the high places, for the demons, and the calf idols which he had made.

16 And after the Levites[33] *left*, those from all the tribes of Israel, such as set their heart to seek the LORD God of Israel, came to Jerusalem to sacrifice to the LORD God of their fathers.

17 So they strengthened the kingdom of Judah, and made Rehoboam the son of Solomon strong for three years, because

---

31 Literally *scorpions* 32 Literally *scorpions* 33 Literally *they*

they walked in the way of David and Solomon for three years.

The Family of Rehoboam

18 Then Rehoboam took for himself as wife Mahalath the daughter of Jerimoth the son of David, *and* *of* Abihail the daughter of Eliah the son of Jesse.
19 And she bore him children: Jeush, Shamariah, and Zaham.
20 After her he took Maacah the grand-daughter[34] of Absalom; and she bore him Abijah, Attai, Ziza, and Shelomith.
21 Now Rehoboam loved Maacah the granddaughter of Absalom more than all his wives and his concubines; for he took eighteen wives and sixty concubines, and begot twenty-eight sons and sixty daughters.
22 And Rehoboam appointed Abijah the son of Maacah as chief, *to* *be* leader among his brothers; for he *intended* to make him king.
23 He dealt wisely, and dispersed some of his sons throughout all the territories of Judah and Benjamin, to every fortified city; and he gave them provisions in abundance. He also sought many wives *for* *them.*

Egypt Attacks Judah

12 Now it came to pass, when Rehoboam had established the kingdom and had strengthened himself, that he forsook the law of the LORD, and all Israel along with him.
2 And it happened, in the fifth year of King Rehoboam, that Shishak king of Egypt came up against Jerusalem, because they had transgressed against the LORD,
3 with twelve hundred chariots, sixty thousand horsemen, and people without number who came with him out of Egypt—the Lubim and the Sukkiim and the Ethiopians.
4 And he took the fortified cities of Judah and came to Jerusalem.
5 Then Shemaiah the prophet came to Rehoboam and the leaders of Judah, who were gathered together in Jerusalem because of Shishak, and said to them, "Thus says the LORD: 'You have forsaken Me, and therefore I also have left you in the hand of Shishak.' "
6 So the leaders of Israel and the king

humbled themselves; and they said, "The LORD *is* righteous."
7 Now when the LORD saw that they humbled themselves, the word of the LORD came to Shemaiah, saying, "They have humbled themselves; *therefore* I will not destroy them, but I will grant them some deliverance. My wrath shall not be poured out on Jerusalem by the hand of Shishak.
8 "Nevertheless they will be his servants, that they may distinguish My service from the service of the kingdoms of the nations."
9 So Shishak king of Egypt came up against Jerusalem, and took away the treasures of the house of the LORD and the treasures of the king's house; he took everything. He also carried away the gold shields which Solomon had made.
10 In their place King Rehoboam made bronze shields and committed *them* to the hands of the captains of the guard, who guarded the entrance of the king's house.
11 And whenever the king entered the house of the LORD, the guard would go and bring them out; *then* they would take them back into the guardroom.
12 When he humbled himself, the wrath of the LORD turned from him, so as not to destroy *him* completely; and things also went well in Judah.

The End of Rehoboam's Reign

13 So King Rehoboam strengthened himself in Jerusalem and reigned. Now Rehoboam *was* forty-one years old when he became king; and he reigned seventeen years in Jerusalem, the city which the LORD had chosen out of all the tribes of Israel, to put His name there. His mother's name *was* Naamah, an Ammonitess.
14 And he did evil, because he did not prepare his heart to seek the LORD.
15 The acts of Rehoboam, first and last, *are* they not written in the book of Shemaiah the prophet, and of Iddo the seer concerning genealogies? And *there* *were* wars between Rehoboam and Jeroboam all their days.
16 So Rehoboam rested with his fathers, and was buried in the City of David. Then Abijah[35] his son reigned in his place.

34 Literally *daughter,* but in the broader sense of granddaughter (compare 2 Chronicles 13:2)
35 Spelled *Abijam* in 1 Kings 14:31

Abijah Reigns in Judah

13 In the eighteenth year of King Jeroboam, Abijah became king over Judah.

2 He reigned three years in Jerusalem. His mother's name *was* Michaiah[36] the daughter of Uriel of Gibeah. And there was war between Abijah and Jeroboam.

3 Abijah set the battle in order with an army of valiant warriors, four hundred thousand choice men. Jeroboam also drew up in battle formation against him with eight hundred thousand choice men, mighty men of valor.

4 Then Abijah stood on Mount Zemaraim, which *is* in the mountains of Ephraim, and said, "Hear me, Jeroboam and all Israel:

5 "Should you not know that the LORD God of Israel gave the dominion over Israel to David forever, to him and his sons, by a covenant of salt?

6 "Yet Jeroboam the son of Nebat, the servant of Solomon the son of David, rose up and rebelled against his lord.

7 "Then worthless rogues gathered to him, and strengthened themselves against Rehoboam the son of Solomon, when Rehoboam was young and inexperienced and could not withstand them.

8 "And now you think to withstand the kingdom of the LORD, which is in the hand of the sons of David; and you *are* a great multitude, and with you are the gold calves which Jeroboam made for you as gods.

9 "Have you not cast out the priests of the LORD, the sons of Aaron, and the Levites, and made for yourselves priests, like the peoples of *other* lands, so that whoever comes to consecrate himself with a young bull and seven rams may be a priest of *things that are* not gods?

10 "But as for us, the LORD *is* our God, and we have not forsaken Him; and the priests who minister to the LORD *are* the sons of Aaron, and the Levites *attend* to *their* duties.

11 "And they burn to the LORD every morning and every evening burnt sacrifices and sweet incense; *they* also *set* the showbread *in order on* the pure table, and the lampstand of gold with its lamps to burn every evening; for we keep the command of the LORD our God, but you have forsaken Him.

12 "Now look, God Himself is with us as *our* head, and His priests with sounding trumpets to sound the alarm against you. O children of Israel, do not fight against the LORD God of your fathers, for you shall not prosper!"

13 But Jeroboam caused an ambush to go around behind them; so they were in front of Judah, and the ambush *was* behind them.

14 And when Judah looked around, to their surprise the battle line *was* at both front and rear; and they cried out to the LORD, and the priests sounded the trumpets.

15 Then the men of Judah gave a shout; and as the men of Judah shouted, it happened that God struck Jeroboam and all Israel before Abijah and Judah.

16 And the children of Israel fled before Judah, and God delivered them into their hand.

17 Then Abijah and his people struck them with a great slaughter; so five hundred thousand choice men of Israel fell slain.

18 Thus the children of Israel were subdued at that time; and the children of Judah prevailed, because they relied on the LORD God of their fathers.

19 And Abijah pursued Jeroboam and took cities from him: Bethel with its villages, Jeshanah with its villages, and Ephrain[37] with its villages.

20 So Jeroboam did not recover strength again in the days of Abijah; and the LORD struck him, and he died.

21 But Abijah grew mighty, married fourteen wives, and begot twenty-two sons and sixteen daughters.

22 Now the rest of the acts of Abijah, his ways, and his sayings *are* written in the annals of the prophet Iddo.

14 So Abijah rested with his fathers, and they buried him in the City of David. Then Asa his son reigned in his place. In his days the land was quiet for ten years.

Asa Reigns in Judah

2 Asa did *what was* good and right in the eyes of the LORD his God,

3 for he removed the altars of the foreign *gods* and the high places, and broke down the *sacred* pillars and cut down the wooden images.

---

36 Spelled *Maachah* in 11:20, 21 and 1 Kings 15:2   37 Or *Ephron*

4 He commanded Judah to seek the LORD God of their fathers, and to observe the law and the commandment.

5 He also removed the high places and the incense altars from all the cities of Judah, and the kingdom was quiet under him.

6 And he built fortified cities in Judah, for the land had rest; he had no war in those years, because the LORD had given him rest.

7 Therefore he said to Judah, "Let us build these cities and make walls around *them*, and towers, gates, and bars, *while* the land *is* yet before us, because we have sought the LORD our God; we have sought *Him*, and He has given us rest on every side." So they built and prospered.

8 And Asa had an army of three hundred thousand *men* from Judah who carried shields and spears, and from Benjamin two hundred and eighty thousand men who carried shields and drew bows; all these *were* mighty men of valor.

9 Then Zerah the Ethiopian came out against them with an army of a million men and three hundred chariots, and he came to Mareshah.

10 So Asa went out against him, and they set the troops in battle array in the Valley of Zephathah at Mareshah.

11 And Asa cried out to the LORD his God, and said, "LORD, *it is* nothing for You to help, whether with many or with those who have no power; help us, O LORD our God, for we rest on You, and in Your name we go against this multitude. O LORD, You *are* our God; do not let man prevail against You!"

12 So the LORD struck the Ethiopians before Asa and Judah, and the Ethiopians fled.

13 And Asa and the people who *were* with him pursued them to Gerar. So the Ethiopians were overthrown, and they could not recover, for they were broken before the LORD and His army. And they carried away very much spoil.

14 Then they defeated all the cities around Gerar, for the fear of the LORD came upon them; and they plundered all the cities, for there was exceedingly much spoil in them.

15 They also attacked the livestock enclosures, and carried off sheep and camels in abundance, and returned to Jerusalem.

The Reforms of Asa

15 Now the Spirit of God came upon Azariah the son of Oded.

2 And he went out to meet Asa, and said to him: "Hear me, Asa, and all Judah and Benjamin. The LORD *is* with you while you are with Him. If you seek Him, He will be found by you; but if you forsake Him, He will forsake you.

3 "For a long time Israel *has been* without the true God, without a teaching priest, and without law;

4 "but when in their trouble they turned to the LORD God of Israel, and sought Him, He was found by them.

5 "And in those times *there was* no peace to the one who went out, nor to the one who came in, but great turmoil *was* on all the inhabitants of the lands.

6 "So nation was destroyed by nation, and city by city, for God troubled them with every adversity.

7 "But you, be strong and do not let your hands be weak, for your work shall be rewarded!"

8 And when Asa heard these words and the prophecy of Oded the prophet, he took courage, and removed the abominable idols from all the land of Judah and Benjamin and from the cities which he had taken in the mountains of Ephraim; and he restored the altar of the LORD that *was* before the vestibule of the LORD.

9 Then he gathered all Judah and Benjamin, and those who sojourned with them from Ephraim, Manasseh, and Simeon, for they came over to him in great numbers from Israel when they saw that the LORD his God was with him.

10 So they gathered together at Jerusalem in the third month, in the fifteenth year of the reign of Asa.

11 And they offered to the LORD at that time seven hundred bulls and seven thousand sheep from the spoil *which* they had brought.

12 Then they entered into a covenant to seek the LORD God of their fathers with all their heart and with all their soul;

13 and whoever would not seek the LORD God of Israel was to be put to death, whether small or great, whether man or woman.

14 Then they took an oath before the LORD with a loud voice, with shouting and trumpets and rams' horns.

The Pinnacle of the Temple

Archaeologists have recently unearthed an interesting inscription in Jerusalem which sheds new light on one of the major events in Jesus' life. This inscription is at the base of the southern-most point of the temple mount. It reads, "to the place of the blowing of the shofar."

Every Sabbath in ancient Jerusalem, the new day was announced with the blowing of the shofar—a ram's horn. The ancient historian Josephus records that the ram's horn was always blown from the pinnacle of the temple.

During Jesus' temptation, He was taken to the pinnacle of the temple. There He was told that if He truly was the Son of God, He should throw Himself off and God would send angels to bear Him up, so that not even His foot should strike the stones.

For years, scholars thought that the pinnacle of the temple was an isolated area at the far-eastern corner of the temple mount. They interpreted Jesus' temptation as merely testing God's faithfulness to Him. But this recent archaeological discovery reveals that it meant much more than that. The pinnacle was in fact at the opposite side of the temple. It overlooked the marketplace of the nations. Here merchants and business-men from all corners of the Roman empire gathered to trade goods and exchange sto-ries of far-off lands. Jesus had a perfect opportunity to show representatives of the then-known world that He was the Son of God, simply by jumping off and letting God's angels protect Him. But He chose to keep to His divine calling. Rather than seek glory from men, Jesus honored God by fulfilling His purpose on earth.

There are many times when we are seduced to do the spectacular simply to receive recognition, honor, and praise from others. Sometimes this recognition is deserved and ordained by God. But when it comes in direct conflict with God's will for our lives, then we must follow Christ's example. We must stay single-minded in our purpose and accept God's divine calling for our lives. The reward for doing so cannot compare with any passing praise on earth.

15 And all Judah rejoiced at the oath, for they had sworn with all their heart and sought Him with all their soul; and He was found by them, and the LORD gave them rest all around.

16 Also he removed Maacah, the mother of Asa the king, from *being* queen mother, because she had made an obscene image of Asherah;[38] and Asa cut down her obscene image, crushed *it*, and burned *it* by the Brook Kidron.

17 But the high places were not removed from Israel. Nevertheless the heart of Asa was loyal all his days.

18 He also brought into the house of God the things that his father had dedicated and that he himself had dedicated: silver and gold and utensils.

19 And there was no *more* war until the thirty-fifth year of the reign of Asa.

Asa's Treaty with Syria

16 In the thirty-sixth year of the reign of Asa, Baasha king of Israel came up against Judah and built Ramah, that he might let none go out or come in to Asa king of Judah.

2 Then Asa brought silver and gold from the treasuries of the house of the LORD and of the king's house, and sent to Ben-Hadad king of Syria, who dwelt in Damascus, saying,

3 "*Let there be* a treaty between you and me, as there was between my father and your father. Here, I have sent you silver and gold; come, break your treaty with Baasha king of Israel, so that he will withdraw from me."

4 So Ben-Hadad heeded King Asa, and sent the captains of his armies against the cities of Israel. They attacked Ijon, Dan, Abel Maim, and all the storage cities of Naphtali.

5 Now it happened, when Baasha heard *it*, that he stopped building Ramah and ceased his work.

6 Then King Asa took all Judah, and they carried away the stones and timber of Ramah, which Baasha had used for building; and with them he built Geba and Mizpah.

Hanani's Message to Asa

7 And at that time Hanani the seer came to Asa king of Judah, and said to him: "Because you have relied on the king of Syria, and have not relied on the

LORD your God, therefore the army of the king of Syria has escaped from your hand.

8 "Were the Ethiopians and the Lubim not a huge army with very many chariots and horsemen? Yet, because you relied on the LORD, He delivered them into your hand.

9 "For the eyes of the LORD run to and fro throughout the whole earth, to show Himself strong on behalf of *those* whose heart *is* loyal to Him. In this you have done foolishly; therefore from now on you shall have wars."

10 Then Asa was angry with the seer, and put him in prison, for *he was* enraged at him because of this. And Asa oppressed *some* of the people at that time.

Illness and Death of Asa

11 Note that the acts of Asa, first and last, are indeed written in the book of the kings of Judah and Israel.

12 And in the thirty-ninth year of his reign, Asa became diseased in his feet, and his malady was *very* severe; yet in his disease he did not seek the LORD, but the physicians.

13 So Asa rested with his fathers; he died in the forty-first year of his reign.

14 They buried him in his own tomb, which he had made for himself in the City of David; and they laid him in the bed which was filled with spices and various ingredients prepared in a mixture of ointments. They made a very great burning for him.

Jehoshaphat Reigns in Judah

17 Then Jehoshaphat his son reigned in his place, and strengthened himself against Israel.

2 And he placed troops in all the fortified cities of Judah, and set garrisons in the land of Judah and in the cities of Ephraim which Asa his father had taken.

3 Now the LORD was with Jehoshaphat, because he walked in the former ways of his father David; he did not seek the Baals,

4 but sought the God[39] of his father, and walked in His commandments and not according to the acts of Israel.

5 Therefore the LORD established the kingdom in his hand; and all Judah gave presents to Jehoshaphat, and he had riches and honor in abundance.

38 A Canaanite deity   39 Septuagint reads LORD God.

6 And his heart took delight in the ways of the LORD; moreover he removed the high places and wooden images from Judah.

7 Also in the third year of his reign he sent his leaders, Ben-Hail, Obadiah, Zechariah, Nethaneel, and Michaiah, to teach in the cities of Judah.

8 And with them *he sent* Levites: Shemaiah, Nethaniah, Zebadiah, Asahel, Shemiramoth, Jehonathan, Adonijah, Tobijah, and Tobadonijah—the Levites; and with them Elishama and Jehoram, the priests.

9 So they taught in Judah, and *had* the Book of the Law of the LORD with them; they went throughout all the cities of Judah and taught the people.

10 And the fear of the LORD fell on all the kingdoms of the lands that *were* around Judah, so that they did not make war against Jehoshaphat.

11 Also *some* of the Philistines brought Jehoshaphat presents and silver as tribute; and the Arabians brought him flocks, seven thousand seven hundred rams and seven thousand seven hundred male goats.

12 So Jehoshaphat became increasingly powerful, and he built fortresses and storage cities in Judah.

13 He had much property in the cities of Judah; and the men of war, mighty men of valor, *were* in Jerusalem.

14 These *are* their numbers, according to their fathers' houses. Of Judah, the captains of thousands: Adnah the captain, and with him three hundred thousand mighty men of valor;

15 and next to him *was* Jehohanan the captain, and with him two hundred and eighty thousand;

16 and next to him *was* Amasiah the son of Zichri, who willingly offered himself to the LORD, and with him two hundred thousand mighty men of valor.

17 Of Benjamin: Eliada a mighty man of valor, and with him two hundred thousand men armed with bow and shield;

18 and next to him *was* Jehozabad, and with him one hundred and eighty thousand prepared for war.

19 These served the king, besides *those* whom the king put in the fortified cities throughout all Judah.

Micaiah Warns Ahab

18 Jehoshaphat had riches and honor in abundance; and by marriage he allied himself with Ahab.

2 After some years he went down to *visit* Ahab in Samaria; and Ahab killed sheep and oxen in abundance for him and the people who were with him, and persuaded him to go up *with him* to Ramoth Gilead.

3 So Ahab king of Israel said to Jehoshaphat king of Judah, "Will you go with me *against* Ramoth Gilead?" And he answered him, "I *am* as you *are*, and my people as your people; *we will be* with you in the war."

4 And Jehoshaphat said to the king of Israel, "Please inquire for the word of the LORD today."

5 Then the king of Israel gathered the prophets together, four hundred men, and said to them, "Shall we go to war against Ramoth Gilead, or shall I refrain?" And they said, "Go up, for God will deliver *it* into the king's hand."

6 But Jehoshaphat said, "*Is there* not still a prophet of the LORD here, that we may inquire of Him?"[40]

7 So the king of Israel said to Jehoshaphat, "*There is* still one man by whom we may inquire of the LORD; but I hate him, because he never prophesies good concerning me, but always evil. He *is* Micaiah the son of Imla." And Jehoshaphat said, "Let not the king say such things!"

8 Then the king of Israel called one *of* his officers and said, "Bring Micaiah the son of Imla quickly!"

9 And the king of Israel and Jehoshaphat king of Judah, clothed in *their* robes, sat each on his throne; and they sat at a threshing floor at the entrance of the gate of Samaria; and all the prophets prophesied before them.

10 Now Zedekiah the son of Chenaanah had made horns of iron for himself; and he said, "Thus says the LORD: 'With these you shall gore the Syrians until they are destroyed.'"

11 And all the prophets prophesied so, saying, "Go up to Ramoth Gilead and prosper, for the LORD will deliver *it* into the king's hand."

12 Then the messenger who had gone to call Micaiah spoke to him, saying, "Now listen, the words of the prophets with one

40 Or *him*

accord encourage the king. Therefore please let your word be like *the word of one of them, and speak encouragement.*"
13 And Micaiah said, "*As* the LORD lives, whatever my God says, that I will speak."
14 Then he came to the king; and the king said to him, "Micaiah, shall we go to war against Ramoth Gilead, or shall I refrain?" And he said, "Go and prosper, and they shall be delivered into your hand!"
15 So the king said to him, "How many times shall I make you swear that you tell me nothing but the truth in the name of the LORD?"
16 Then he said, "I saw all Israel scattered on the mountains, as sheep that have no shepherd. And the LORD said, 'These have no master. Let each return to his house in peace.'"
17 And the king of Israel said to Jehoshaphat, "Did I not tell you *that* he would not prophesy good concerning me, but evil?"
18 Then Micaiah[41] said, "Therefore hear the word of the LORD: I saw the LORD sitting on His throne, and all the host of heaven standing on His right hand and *on* His left.
19 "And the LORD said, 'Who will persuade Ahab king of Israel to go up, that he may fall at Ramoth Gilead?' And one spoke in this manner, and another spoke in that manner.
20 "Then a spirit came forward and stood before the LORD, and said, 'I will persuade him.' The LORD said to him, 'In what way?'
21 "So he said, 'I will go out and be a lying spirit in the mouth of all his prophets.' And *the* LORD said, 'You shall persuade *him* and also prevail; go out and do so.'
22 "Now therefore, look! The LORD has put a lying spirit in the mouth of these prophets of yours, and the LORD has declared disaster against you."
23 Then Zedekiah the son of Chenaanah went near and struck Micaiah on the cheek, and said, "Which way did the spirit from the LORD go from me to speak to you?"
24 And Micaiah said, "Indeed you shall see on that day when you go into an inner chamber to hide!"
25 Then the king of Israel said, "Take

Micaiah, and return him to Amon the governor of the city and to Joash the king's son;
26 "and say, 'Thus says the king: "Put this *fellow* in prison, and feed him with bread of affliction and water of affliction until I return in peace."'"
27 Then Micaiah said, "If you ever return in peace, the LORD has not spoken by me." And he said, "Take heed, all you people!"

Ahab Dies in Battle

28 So the king of Israel and Jehoshaphat the king of Judah went up to Ramoth Gilead.
29 And the king of Israel said to Jehoshaphat, "I will disguise myself and go into battle; but you put on your robes." So the king of Israel disguised himself, and they went into battle.
30 Now the king of Syria had commanded the captains of the chariots who *were* with him, saying, "Fight with no one small or great, but only with the king of Israel."
31 So it was, when the captains of the chariots saw Jehoshaphat, that they said, "It *is* the king of Israel!" Therefore they surrounded him to attack; but Jehoshaphat cried out, and the LORD helped him, and God moved them *to turn away* from him.
32 For so it was, when the captains of the chariots saw that it was not the king of Israel, that they turned back from pursuing him.
33 Now a certain man drew a bow at random, and struck the king of Israel between the joints of his armor. So he said to the driver of his chariot, "Turn around and take me out of the battle, for I am wounded."
34 The battle increased that day, and the king of Israel propped *himself* up in *his* chariot facing the Syrians until evening; and about the time of sunset he died.

19 Then Jehoshaphat the king of Judah returned safely to his house in Jerusalem.
2 And Jehu the son of Hanani the seer went out to meet him, and said to King Jehoshaphat, "Should you help the wicked and love those who hate the LORD? Therefore the wrath of the LORD *is* upon you.

41 Literally *he*

3 "Nevertheless good things are found in you, in that you have removed the wooden images from the land, and have prepared your heart to seek God."

The Reforms of Jehoshaphat

4 So Jehoshaphat dwelt at Jerusalem; and he went out again among the people from Beersheba to the mountains of Ephraim, and brought them back to the LORD God of their fathers.
5 Then he set judges in the land throughout all the fortified cities of Judah, city by city,
6 and said to the judges, "Take heed to what you are doing, for you do not judge for man but for the LORD, who *is* with you in the judgment.
7 "Now therefore, let the fear of the LORD be upon you; take care and do *it*, for *there is* no iniquity with the LORD our God, no partiality, nor taking of bribes."
8 Moreover in Jerusalem, for the judgment of the LORD and for controversies, Jehoshaphat appointed some of the Levites and priests, and some of the chief fathers of Israel, when they returned to Jerusalem.
9 And he commanded them, saying, "Thus you shall act in the fear of the LORD, faithfully and with a loyal heart:
10 "Whatever case comes to you from your brethren who dwell in their cities, whether of bloodshed or offences against law or commandment, against statutes or ordinances, you shall warn them, lest they trespass against the LORD and wrath come upon you and your brethren. Do this, and you will not be guilty.
11 "And take notice: Amariah the chief priest *is* over you in all matters of the LORD; and Zebadiah the son of Ishmael, the ruler of the house of Judah, for all the king's matters; also the Levites *will be* officials before you. Behave courageously, and the LORD will be with the good."

Ammon, Moab, and Mount Seir Defeated

20 It happened after this *that* the people of Moab with the people of Ammon, and *others* with them besides the Ammonites, came to battle against Jehoshaphat.
2 Then some came and told Jehoshaphat, saying, "A great multitude is coming against you from beyond the sea, from Syria; and they are in Hazazon Tamar" (which *is* En Gedi).
3 And Jehoshaphat feared, and set himself to seek the LORD, and proclaimed a fast throughout all Judah.
4 So Judah gathered together to ask *help* from the LORD; and from all the cities of Judah they came to seek the LORD.
5 Then Jehoshaphat stood in the congregation of Judah and Jerusalem, in the house of the LORD, before the new court,
6 and said: "O LORD God of our fathers, *are* You not God in heaven, and do You *not* rule over all the kingdoms of the nations, and in Your hand *is there not* power and might, so that no one is able to withstand You?
7 "*Are* You not our God, *who* drove out the inhabitants of this land before Your people Israel, and gave it to the descendants of Abraham Your friend forever?
8 "And they dwell in it, and have built You a sanctuary in it for Your name, saying,
9 'If disaster comes upon us, *such as* the sword, judgment, pestilence, or famine, we will stand before this temple and in Your presence (for Your name *is* in this temple), and cry out to You in our affliction, and You will hear and save.'
10 "And now, here are the people of Ammon, Moab, and Mount Seir—whom You would not let Israel invade when they came out of the land of Egypt, but they turned from them and did not destroy them—
11 "here they are, rewarding us by coming to throw us out of Your possession which You have given us to inherit.
12 "O our God, will You not judge them? For we have no power against this great multitude that is coming against us; nor do we know what to do, but our eyes *are* upon You."
13 Now all Judah, with their little ones, their wives, and their children, stood before the LORD.
14 Then the Spirit of the LORD came upon Jahaziel the son of Zechariah, the son of Benaiah, the son of Jeiel, the son of Mattaniah, a Levite of the sons of Asaph, in the midst of the congregation;
15 and he said, "Listen, all you of Judah and you inhabitants of Jerusalem, and you, King Jehoshaphat! Thus says the

LORD to you: 'Do not be afraid nor dismayed because of this great multitude, for the battle *is* not yours, but God's.
16 'Tomorrow go down against them. They will surely come up by the ascent of Ziz, and you will find them at the end of the brook before the Wilderness of Jeruel.
17 'You will not *need* to fight in this *battle*. Position yourselves, stand still and see the salvation of the LORD, who is with you, O Judah and Jerusalem!' Do not fear or be dismayed; tomorrow go out against them, for the LORD *is* with you.'"
18 And Jehoshaphat bowed his head with *his* face to the ground, and all Judah and the inhabitants of Jerusalem bowed before the LORD, worshiping the LORD.
19 Then the Levites of the children of the Kohathites and of the children of the Korahites stood up to praise the LORD God of Israel with voices loud and high.
20 And they rose early in the morning and went out into the Wilderness of Tekoa; and as they went out, Jehoshaphat stood and said, "Hear me, O Judah and you inhabitants of Jerusalem: Believe in the LORD your God, and you shall be established; believe His prophets, and you shall prosper."
21 And when he had consulted with the people, he appointed those who should sing to the LORD, and who should praise the beauty of holiness, as they went out before the army and were saying:

"Praise the LORD,
　For His mercy *endures* forever."42

22 Now when they began to sing and to praise, the LORD set ambushes against the people of Ammon, Moab, and Mount Seir, who had come against Judah; and they were defeated.
23 For the people of Ammon and Moab stood up against the inhabitants of Mount Seir to utterly kill and destroy *them*. And when they had made an end of the inhabitants of Seir, they helped to destroy one another.
24 So when Judah came to a place overlooking the wilderness, they looked toward the multitude; and there *were* their dead bodies, fallen on the earth. No one had escaped.
25 When Jehoshaphat and his people came to take away their spoil, they found

among them an abundance of valuables on the dead bodies,43 and precious jewelry, which they stripped off for themselves, more than they could carry away; and they were three days gathering the spoil because there was so much.
26 And on the fourth day they assembled in the Valley of Berachah, for there they blessed the LORD; therefore the name of that place was called The Valley of Berachah44 until this day.
27 Then they returned, every man of Judah and Jerusalem, with Jehoshaphat in front of them, to go back to Jerusalem with joy, for the LORD had made them rejoice over their enemies.
28 So they came to Jerusalem, with stringed instruments and harps and trumpets, to the house of the LORD.
29 And the fear of God was on all the kingdoms of *those* countries when they heard that the LORD had fought against the enemies of Israel.
30 Then the realm of Jehoshaphat was quiet, for his God gave him rest all around.

The End of Jehoshaphat's Reign

31 So Jehoshaphat was king over Judah. *He was* thirty-five years old when he became king, and he reigned twenty-five years in Jerusalem. His mother's name *was* Azubah the daughter of Shilhi.
32 And he walked in the way of his father Asa, and did not turn aside from it, doing *what was* right in the sight of the LORD.
33 Nevertheless the high places were not taken away, for as yet the people had not directed their hearts to the God of their fathers.
34 Now the rest of the acts of Jehoshaphat, first and last, indeed they *are* written in the book of Jehu the son of Hanani, which *is* mentioned in the book of the kings of Israel.
35 After this Jehoshaphat king of Judah allied himself with Ahaziah king of Israel, who acted very wickedly.
36 And he allied himself with him to make ships to go to Tarshish, and they made the ships in Ezion Geber.
37 But Eliezer the son of Dodavah of Mareshah prophesied against Jehoshaphat, saying, "Because you have allied

42 Compare Psalm 106:1
43 A few Hebrew manuscripts, Old Latin, and Vulgate read *garments;* Septuagint reads *armor.*
44 Literally *blessing*

yourself with Ahaziah, the LORD has destroyed your works." Then the ships were wrecked, so that they were not able to go to Tarshish.

Jehoram Reigns in Judah

21 And Jehoshaphat rested with his fathers, and was buried with his fathers in the City of David. Then Jehoram his son reigned in his place.
2 He had brothers, the sons of Jehoshaphat: Azariah, Jehiel, Zechariah, Azaryahu, Michael, and Shephatiah; all these *were* the sons of Jehoshaphat king of Israel.
3 Their father gave them great gifts of silver and gold and precious things, with fortified cities in Judah; but he gave the kingdom to Jehoram, because he *was* the firstborn.
4 Now when Jehoram was established over the kingdom of his father, he strengthened himself and killed all his brothers with the sword, and also *others* of the princes of Israel.
5 Jehoram *was* thirty-two years old when he became king, and he reigned eight years in Jerusalem.
6 And he walked in the way of the kings of Israel, just as the house of Ahab had done, for he had the daughter of Ahab as a wife; and he did evil in the sight of the LORD.
7 Yet the LORD would not destroy the house of David, because of the covenant that He had made with David, and since He had promised to give a lamp to him and to his sons forever.
8 In his days the Edomites revolted against Judah's authority, and made a king over themselves.
9 So Jehoram went out with his officers, and all his chariots with him. And he rose by night and attacked the Edomites who had surrounded him and the captains of the chariots.
10 Thus the Edomites have been in revolt against Judah's authority to this day. At that time Libnah revolted against his rule, because he had forsaken the LORD God of his fathers.
11 Moreover he made high places in the mountains of Judah, and caused the inhabitants of Jerusalem to commit harlotry, and led Judah astray.
12 And a letter came to him from Elijah the prophet, saying,

Thus says the LORD God of your father David:
"Because you have not walked in the ways of Jehoshaphat your father, or in the ways of Asa king of Judah,
13 "but have walked in the way of the kings of Israel, and have made Judah and the inhabitants of Jerusalem to play the harlot like the harlotry of the house of Ahab, and also have killed your brothers, those of your father's household, *who were* better than yourself,
14 "behold, the LORD will strike your people with a serious affliction—your children, your wives, and all your possessions;
15 "and you *will become* very sick with a disease of your intestines, until your intestines come out by reason of the sickness, day by day."
16 Moreover the LORD stirred up against Jehoram the spirit of the Philistines and the Arabians who *were* near the Ethiopians.
17 And they came up into Judah and invaded it, and carried away all the possessions that were found in the king's house, and also his sons and his wives, so that there was not a son left to him except Jehoahaz,[45] the youngest of his sons.
18 After all this the LORD struck him in his intestines with an incurable disease.
19 Then it happened in the course of time, after the end of two years, that his intestines came out because of his sickness; so he died in severe pain. And his people made no burning for him, like the burning for his fathers.
20 He was thirty-two years old when he became king. He reigned in Jerusalem eight years and, to no one's sorrow, departed. However they buried him in the City of David, but not in the tombs of the kings.

Ahaziah Reigns in Judah

22 Then the inhabitants of Jerusalem made Ahaziah his youngest son king in his place, for the raiders who came with the Arabians into the camp had killed all the older *sons*. So Ahaziah the son of Jehoram, king of Judah, reigned.
2 Ahaziah *was* forty-two[46] years old when he became king, and he reigned one

---

45 Elsewhere called *Ahaziah* (compare 2 Chronicles 22:1)　　46 Or *twenty-two* (compare 2 Kings 8:26)

year in Jerusalem. His mother's name *was* Athaliah the granddaughter of Omri.
3 He also walked in the ways of the house of Ahab, for his mother counseled him to do wickedly.
4 Therefore he did evil in the sight of the LORD, like the house of Ahab; for they were his counselors after the death of his father, to his destruction.
5 He also walked in their counsel, and went with Jehoram[47] the son of Ahab king of Israel to *make* war against Hazael king of Syria at Ramoth Gilead; and the Syrians wounded Joram.
6 Then he returned to Jezreel to recover from the wounds which he had received at Ramah, when he fought against Hazael king of Syria. And Azariah[48] the son of Jehoram, king of Judah, went down to see Jehoram the son of Ahab in Jezreel, because he was sick.
7 His going to Joram was God's occasion for Ahaziah's downfall; for when he arrived, he went out with Jehoram[49] against Jehu the son of Nimshi, whom the LORD had anointed to cut off the house of Ahab.
8 And it happened, when Jehu was executing judgment on the house of Ahab, and found the princes of Judah and the sons of Ahaziah's brothers who served Ahaziah, that he killed them.
9 Then he searched for Ahaziah; and they caught him (he was hiding in Samaria), and brought him to Jehu. When they had killed him, they buried him, "because," they said, "he is the son of Jehoshaphat, who sought the LORD with all his heart." So the house of Ahaziah had no one to assume power over the kingdom.

Athaliah Reigns in Judah

10 Now when Athaliah the mother of Ahaziah saw that her son was dead, she arose and destroyed all the royal heirs of the house of Judah.
11 But Jehoshabeath,[50] the daughter of the king, took Joash the son of Ahaziah, and stole him away from among the king's sons who were being murdered, and put him and his nurse in a bedroom. So Jehoshabeath, the daughter of King Jehoram, the wife of Jehoiada the priest (for she was the sister of Ahaziah), hid

him from Athaliah so that she did not kill him.
12 And he was hidden with them in the house of God for six years, while Athaliah reigned over the land.

Joash Crowned King of Judah

23 In the seventh year Jehoiada strengthened himself, *and made a* covenant with the captains of hundreds: Azariah the son of Jeroham, Ishmael the son of Jehohanan, Azariah the son of Obed, Maaseiah the son of Adaiah, and Elishaphat the son of Zichri.
2 And they went throughout Judah and gathered the Levites from all the cities of Judah, and the chief fathers of Israel, and they came to Jerusalem.
3 Then all the congregation made a covenant with the king in the house of God. And he said to them, "Behold, the king's son shall reign, as the LORD has said of the sons of David.
4 "This *is* what you shall do: One-third of you entering on the Sabbath, of the priests and the Levites, *shall be* keeping watch over the doors;
5 "one-third *shall be* at the king's house; and one-third at the Gate of the Foundation. All the people *shall be* in the courts of the house of the LORD.
6 "But let no one come into the house of the LORD except the priests and those of the Levites who serve. They may go in, for they *are* holy; but all the people shall keep the watch of the LORD.
7 "And the Levites shall surround the king on all sides, every man with his weapons in his hand; and whoever comes into the house, let him be put to death. You are to be with the king when he comes in and when he goes out."
8 So the Levites and all Judah did according to all that Jehoiada the priest commanded. And each man took his men who were to be on duty on the Sabbath, with those who were going *off duty* on the Sabbath; for Jehoiada the priest had not dismissed the divisions.
9 And Jehoiada the priest gave to the captains of hundreds the spears and the large and small shields which *had been* King David's, that *were* in the temple of God.
10 Then he set all the people, every man

47 Also spelled *Joram* (compare verses 5 and 7; 2 Kings 8:28; and elsewhere)
48 Some Hebrew manuscripts, Septuagint, Syriac, Vulgate, and 2 Kings 8:29 read *Ahaziah.*
49 See note 47.   50 Spelled *Jehosheba* in 2 Kings 11:2

with his weapon in his hand, from the right side of the temple to the left side of the temple, along by the altar and by the temple, all around the king.
11 And they brought out the king's son, put the crown on him, *gave him* the Testimony,[51] and made him king. Then Jehoiada and his sons anointed him, and said, "*Long* live the king!"

Death of Athaliah

12 Now when Athaliah heard the noise of the people running and praising the king, she came to the people in the temple of the LORD.
13 And *when* she looked, there was the king standing by his pillar at the entrance; and the leaders and the trumpeters *were* by the king. There were all the people of the land, rejoicing and blowing trumpets, also the singers with instruments of music, and those who led in praise. So Athaliah tore her clothes and said, "Treason! Treason!"
14 Then Jehoiada the priest brought out the captains of hundreds who were set over the army, and said to them, "Take her outside under guard, and slay with the sword whoever follows her." For the priest said, "Do not kill her in the house of the LORD."
15 So they seized her; and she went by way of the entrance of the Horse Gate into the king's house, and they killed her there.
16 Then Jehoiada made a covenant between himself, the people, and the king, that they should be the LORD's people.
17 And all the people went to the temple[52] of Baal, and tore it down. They broke in pieces its altars and images, and killed Mattan the priest of Baal before the altars.
18 Also Jehoiada appointed the oversight of the house of the LORD to the hand of the priests, the Levites, whom David had assigned in the house of the LORD, to offer the burnt offerings of the LORD, as *it is* written in the Law of Moses, with rejoicing and with singing, *as it was established* by David.
19 And he set the gatekeepers at the gates of the house of the LORD, so that no one *who was* in any way unclean should enter.
20 Then he took the captains of hundreds, the nobles, the governors of the people, and all the people of the land, and brought the king down from the house of the LORD; and they went through the Upper Gate to the king's house, and set the king on the throne of the kingdom.
21 So all the people of the land rejoiced; and the city was quiet, for they had slain Athaliah with the sword.

Joash Repairs the Temple

24 Joash *was* seven years old when he became king, and he reigned forty years in Jerusalem. His mother's name *was* Zibiah of Beersheba.
2 Joash did *what was* right in the sight of the LORD all the days of Jehoiada the priest.
3 And Jehoiada took for him two wives, and he had sons and daughters.
4 Now it happened after this *that* Joash set his heart on repairing the house of the LORD.
5 Then he gathered the priests and the Levites, and said to them, "Go out to the cities of Judah, and gather from all Israel money to repair the house of your God from year to year, and see that you do it quickly." However the Levites did not do it quickly.
6 So the king called Jehoiada the chief *priest*, and said to him, "Why have you not required the Levites to bring in from Judah and from Jerusalem the collection, *according to the commandment* of Moses the servant of the LORD and of the congregation of Israel, for the tabernacle of witness?"
7 For the sons of Athaliah, that wicked woman, had broken into the house of God, and had also presented all the dedicated things of the house of the LORD to the Baals.
8 Then at the king's commandment they made a chest, and set it outside at the gate of the house of the LORD.
9 And they made a proclamation throughout Judah and Jerusalem to bring to the LORD the collection *that* Moses the servant of God *had imposed* on Israel in the wilderness.
10 Then all the leaders and all the people rejoiced, brought their contributions, and put *them* into the chest until all had given.
11 So it was, at that time, when the chest was brought to the king's official by the

---

51 That is, the Law (compare Exodus 25:16, 21 and Deuteronomy 31:9)   52 Literally *house*

hand of the Levites, and when they saw that *there was* much money, that the king's scribe and the high priest's officer came and emptied the chest, and took it and returned it to its place. Thus they did day by day, and gathered money in abundance.

12 Then the king and Jehoiada gave it to those who did the work of the service of the house of the LORD; and they hired masons and carpenters to repair the house of the LORD, and also those who worked in iron and bronze to restore the house of the LORD.

13 So the workmen labored, and the work was completed by them; they restored the house of God to its original condition and reinforced it.

14 When they had finished, they brought the rest of the money before the king and Jehoiada; they made from it articles for the house of the LORD, articles for serving and offering, spoons and vessels of gold and silver. And they offered burnt offerings in the house of the LORD continually all the days of Jehoiada.

Apostasy of Joash

15 But Jehoiada grew old and was full of days, and he died; *he was* one hundred and thirty years old when he died.

16 And they buried him in the City of David among the kings, because he had done good in Israel, both toward God and His house.

17 Now after the death of Jehoiada the leaders of Judah came and bowed down to the king. And the king listened to them.

18 Therefore they left the house of the LORD God of their fathers, and served wooden images and idols; and wrath came upon Judah and Jerusalem because of their trespass.

19 Yet He sent prophets to them, to bring them back to the LORD; and they testified against them, but they would not listen.

20 Then the Spirit of God came upon Zechariah the son of Jehoiada the priest, who stood above the people, and said to them, "Thus says God: 'Why do you transgress the commandments of the LORD, so that you cannot prosper? Because you have forsaken the LORD, He also has forsaken you.'"

21 So they conspired against him, and at the commandment of the king they stoned him with stones in the court of the house of the LORD.

22 Thus Joash the king did not remember the kindness which Jehoiada his father had done to him, but killed his son; and as he died, he said, "The LORD look on *it*, and repay!"

Death of Joash

23 So it happened in the spring of the year *that* the army of Syria came up against him; and they came to Judah and Jerusalem, and destroyed all the leaders of the people from among the people, and sent all their spoil to the king of Damascus.

24 For the army of the Syrians came with a small company of men; but the LORD delivered a very great army into their hand, because they had forsaken the LORD God of their fathers. So they executed judgment against Joash.

25 And when they had withdrawn from him (for they left him severely wounded), his own servants conspired against him because of the blood of the sons[53] of Jehoiada the priest, and killed him on his bed. So he died. And they buried him in the City of David, but they did not bury him in the tombs of the kings.

26 These are the ones who conspired against him: Zabad[54] the son of Shimeath the Ammonitess, and Jehozabad the son of Shimrith[55] the Moabitess.

27 Now *concerning* his sons, and the many oracles about him, and the repairing of the house of God, indeed they *are* written in the annals of the book of the kings. Then Amaziah his son reigned in his place.

Amaziah Reigns in Judah

25 Amaziah *was* twenty-five years old *when* he became king, and he reigned twenty-nine years in Jerusalem. His mother's name *was* Jehoaddan of Jerusalem.

2 And he did *what was* right in the sight of the LORD, but not with a loyal heart.

3 Now it was so, when the kingdom was established for him, that he executed his servants who had murdered his father the king.

53 Septuagint and Vulgate read *son* (compare verses 20-22).
54 Or *Jozachar* (compare 2 Kings 12:21)   55 Or *Shomer* (compare 2 Kings 12:21)

4 However he did not execute their children, but *did* as *it is* written in the Law in the Book of Moses, where the LORD commanded, saying, "The fathers shall not be put to death for their children, nor shall the children be put to death for their fathers; but a person shall die for his own sin."[56]

The War Against Edom

5 Moreover Amaziah gathered Judah together and set over them captains of thousands and captains of hundreds, according to *their* fathers' houses, throughout all Judah and Benjamin; and he numbered them from twenty years old and above, and found them to be three hundred thousand choice *men, able* to go to war, who could handle spear and shield.
6 He also hired one hundred thousand mighty men of valor from Israel for one hundred talents of silver.
7 But a man of God came to him, saying, "O king, do not let the army of Israel go with you, for the LORD *is* not with Israel—*not with* any of the children of Ephraim.
8 "But if you go, be gone! Be strong in battle! *Even so,* God shall make you fall before the enemy; for God has power to help and to overthrow."
9 Then Amaziah said to the man of God, "But what *shall we* do about the hundred talents which I have given to the troops of Israel?" And the man of God answered, "The LORD is able to give you much more than this."
10 So Amaziah discharged the troops that had come to him from Ephraim, to go back home. Therefore their anger was greatly aroused against Judah, and they returned home in great anger.
11 Then Amaziah strengthened himself, and leading his people, he went to the Valley of Salt and killed ten thousand of the people of Seir.
12 And the children of Judah took captive *another* ten thousand alive, brought them to the top of the rock, and cast them down from the top of the rock, so that they all were dashed in pieces.
13 But as for the soldiers of the army which Amaziah had discharged, so that they would not go with him to battle, they raided the cities of Judah from Sa-

maria to Beth Horon, killed three thousand in them, and took much spoil.
14 Now it was so, after Amaziah came from the slaughter of the Edomites, that he brought the gods of the people of Seir, set them up *to be* his gods, and bowed down before them and burned incense to them.
15 Therefore the anger of the LORD was aroused against Amaziah, and He sent him a prophet who said to him, "Why have you sought the gods of the people, which could not rescue their own people from your hand?"
16 So it was, as he talked with him, that *the king* said to him, "Have we made you the king's counsel? Cease! Why should you be killed?" Then the prophet ceased, and said, "I know that God has determined to destroy you, because you have done this and have not heeded my counsel."

Israel Defeats Judah

17 Then Amaziah king of Judah took counsel and sent to Joash[57] the son of Jehoahaz, the son of Jehu, king of Israel, saying, "Come, let us face one another in battle."
18 And Joash king of Israel sent to Amaziah king of Judah, saying, "The thistle that *was* in Lebanon sent to the cedar that was in Lebanon, saying, 'Give your daughter to my son as wife'; and a wild beast that *was* in Lebanon passed by and trampled the thistle.
19 "Indeed you say that you have defeated the Edomites, and your heart is lifted up to boast. Stay at home now; why should you meddle with trouble, that you should fall—you and Judah with you?"
20 But Amaziah would not heed, for it *came* from God, that He might give them into the hand *of their enemies,* because they sought the gods of Edom.
21 So Joash king of Israel went out; and he and Amaziah king of Judah faced one another at Beth Shemesh, which *belongs* to Judah.
22 And Judah was defeated by Israel, and every man fled to his tent.
23 Then Joash the king of Israel captured Amaziah king of Judah, the son of Joash, the son of Jehoahaz, at Beth Shemesh; and he brought him to Jerusalem, and broke down the wall of Jerusalem from

---

56 Compare Deuteronomy 24:16   57 Spelled *Jehoash* in 2 Kings 14:8ff

the Gate of Ephraim to the Corner Gate—four hundred cubits.
24 And *he took* all the gold and silver, all the articles that were found in the house of God with Obed-Edom, the treasures of the king's house, and hostages, and returned to Samaria.

Death of Amaziah

25 Amaziah the son of Joash, king of Judah, lived fifteen years after the death of Joash the son of Jehoahaz, king of Israel.
26 Now the rest of the acts of Amaziah, from first to last, indeed *are* they not written in the book of the kings of Judah and Israel?
27 After the time that Amaziah turned away from following the LORD, they made a conspiracy against him in Jerusalem, and he fled to Lachish; but they sent after him to Lachish and killed him there.
28 Then they brought him on horses and buried him with his fathers in the City of Judah.

Uzziah Reigns in Judah

26 Now all the people of Judah took Uzziah,[58] who *was* sixteen years old, and made him king instead of his father Amaziah.
2 He built Elath[59] and restored it to Judah, after the king rested with his fathers.
3 Uzziah *was* sixteen years old when he became king, and he reigned fifty-two years in Jerusalem. His mother's name was Jecholiah of Jerusalem.
4 And he did *what was* right in the sight of the LORD, according to all that his father Amaziah had done.
5 He sought God in the days of Zechariah, who had understanding in the visions[60] of God; and as long as he sought the LORD, God made him prosper.
6 Now he went out and made war against the Philistines, and broke down the wall of Gath, the wall of Jabneh, and the wall of Ashdod; and he built cities *around* Ashdod and among the Philistines.
7 God helped him against the Philistines, against the Arabians who lived in Gur Baal, and against the Meunites.
8 Also the Ammonites brought tribute to Uzziah. His fame spread as far as the entrance of Egypt, for he strengthened *himself* exceedingly.

9 And Uzziah built towers in Jerusalem at the Corner Gate, at the Valley Gate, and at the corner buttress of the wall; then he fortified them.
10 Also he built towers in the desert. He dug many wells, for he had much livestock, both in the lowlands and in the plains; *he also had* farmers and vinedressers in the mountains and in Carmel, for he loved the soil.
11 Moreover Uzziah had an army of fighting men who went out to war by companies, according to the number on their roll as prepared by Jeiel the scribe and Maaseiah the officer, under the hand of Hananiah, *one* of the king's captains.
12 The total number of chief officers[61] of the mighty men of valor *was* two thousand six hundred.
13 And under their hand *was* an army of three hundred and seven thousand five hundred, that made war with mighty power, to help the king against the enemy.
14 Then Uzziah prepared for them, for the entire army, shields, spears, helmets, body armor, bows, and slings *to cast* stones.
15 And he made devices in Jerusalem, invented by skillful men, to be on the towers and the corners, to shoot arrows and large stones. So his fame spread far and wide, for he was marvelously helped till he *became* strong.

The Penalty for Uzziah's Pride

16 But when he was strong his heart was lifted up, to *his* destruction, for he transgressed against the LORD his God by entering the temple of the LORD to burn incense on the altar of incense.
17 So Azariah the priest went in after him, and with him were eighty priests of the LORD, *who were* valiant men.
18 And they withstood King Uzziah, and said to him, "*It is* not for you, Uzziah, to burn incense to the LORD, but for the priests, the sons of Aaron, who are consecrated to burn incense. Get out of the sanctuary, for you have trespassed! You *shall have* no honor from the LORD God."
19 Then Uzziah became furious; and he *had* a censer in his hand to burn incense. And while he was angry with the priests, leprosy broke out on his forehead, before

58 Called *Azariah* in 2 Kings 14:21ff   59 Hebrew *Eloth*
60 Several Hebrew manuscripts, Septuagint, Syriac, Targum, and Arabic read *fear.*   61 Literally *chief fathers*

the priests in the house of the LORD, beside the incense altar.

20 And Azariah the chief priest and all the priests looked at him, and there, on his forehead, he *was* leprous; so they thrust him out of that place. Indeed he also hurried to get out, because the LORD had struck him.

21 King Uzziah was a leper until the day of his death. He dwelt in an isolated house, because he was a leper; for he was cut off from the house of the LORD. Then Jotham his son *was* over the king's house, judging the people of the land.

22 Now the rest of the acts of Uzziah, from first to last, the prophet Isaiah the son of Amoz wrote.

23 So Uzziah rested with his fathers, and they buried him with his fathers in the field of burial which *belonged* to the kings, for they said, "He is a leper." Then Jotham his son reigned in his place.

Jotham Reigns in Judah

27 Jotham *was* twenty-five years old when he became king, and he reigned sixteen years in Jerusalem. His mother's name *was* Jerushah[62] the daughter of Zadok.

2 And he did *what was* right in the sight of the LORD, according to all that his father Uzziah had done (although he did not enter the temple of the LORD). But still the people acted corruptly.

3 He built the Upper Gate of the house of the LORD, and he built extensively on the wall of Ophel.

4 Moreover he built cities in the mountains of Judah, and in the forests he built fortresses and towers.

5 He also fought with the king of the Ammonites and defeated them. And the people of Ammon gave him in that year one hundred talents of silver, ten thousand kors of wheat, and ten thousand of barley. The people of Ammon paid him this *amount* in the second and third years also.

6 So Jotham became mighty, because he prepared his ways before the LORD his God.

7 Now the rest of the acts of Jotham, and all his wars and his ways, indeed they *are* written in the book of the kings of Israel and Judah.

8 He was twenty-five years old when he became king, and he reigned sixteen years in Jerusalem.

9 So Jotham rested with his fathers, and they buried him in the City of David. Then Ahaz his son reigned in his place.

Ahaz Reigns in Judah

28 Ahaz *was* twenty years old when he became king, and he reigned sixteen years in Jerusalem; and he did not do *what was* right in the sight of the LORD, as his father David *had done.*

2 For he walked in the ways of the kings of Israel, and made molded images for the Baals.

3 He burned incense in the Valley of the Son of Hinnom, and burned his children in the fire, according to the abominations of the nations whom the LORD had cast out before the children of Israel.

4 And he sacrificed and burned incense on the high places, on the hills, and under every green tree.

Syria and Israel Defeat Judah

5 Therefore the LORD his God delivered him into the hand of the king of Syria. They defeated him, and carried away a great multitude of them as captives, and brought *them* to Damascus. Then he was also delivered into the hand of the king of Israel, who defeated him with a great slaughter.

6 For Pekah the son of Remaliah killed one hundred and twenty thousand in Judah in one day, all valiant men, because they had forsaken the LORD God of their fathers.

7 Zichri, a mighty man of Ephraim, killed Maaseiah the king's son, Azrikam the officer over the house, and Elkanah *who was* second to the king.

8 And the children of Israel carried away captive of their brethren two hundred thousand women, sons, and daughters; and they also took away much spoil from them, and brought the spoil to Samaria.

Israel Returns the Captives

9 But a prophet of the LORD was there, whose name *was* Oded; and he went out before the army that came to Samaria, and said to them: "Look, because the LORD God of your fathers was angry with

62 Spelled *Jerusha* in 2 Kings 15:33

Judah, He has delivered them into your hand; but you have killed them in a rage *that* reaches up to heaven.

10 "And now you propose to force the children of Judah and Jerusalem to be your male and female slaves; *but are* you not also guilty before the LORD your God?

11 "Now hear me, therefore, and return the captives, whom you have taken captive from your brethren, for the fierce wrath of the LORD *is* upon you."

12 Then some of the heads of the children of Ephraim, Azariah the son of Johanan, Berechiah the son of Meshillemoth, Jehizkiah the son of Shallum, and Amasa the son of Hadlai, stood up against those who came from the war,

13 and said to them, "You shall not bring the captives here, for we *already* have offended the LORD. You intend to add to our sins and to our guilt; for our guilt is great, and *there is* fierce wrath against Israel."

14 So the armed men left the captives and the spoil before the leaders and all the congregation.

15 Then the men who were designated by name rose up and took the captives, and from the spoil they clothed all who were naked among them, dressed them and gave them sandals, gave them food and drink, and anointed them; and they let all the feeble ones ride on donkeys. So they brought them to their brethren at Jericho, the city of palm trees. Then they returned to Samaria.

Assyria Refuses to Help Judah

16 At the same time King Ahaz sent to the kings of Assyria to help him.

17 For again the Edomites had come, attacked Judah, and carried away captives.

18 The Philistines also had invaded the cities of the lowland and of the South of Judah, and had taken Beth Shemesh, Aijalon, Gederoth, Sochoh with its villages, Timnah with its villages, and Gimzo with its villages; and they dwelt there.

19 For the LORD brought Judah low because of Ahaz king of Israel, for he had encouraged moral decline in Judah and had been continually unfaithful to the LORD.

20 Also Tiglath-Pileser[63] king of Assyria came to him and distressed him, and did not assist him.

21 For Ahaz took part *of the treasures* from the house of the LORD, from the house of the king, and from the leaders, and he gave *it* to the king of Assyria; but he did not help him.

Apostasy and Death of Ahaz

22 Now in the time of his distress King Ahaz became increasingly unfaithful to the LORD. This *is that* King Ahaz.

23 For he sacrificed to the gods of Damascus which had defeated him, saying, "Because the gods of the kings of Syria help them, I will sacrifice to them that they may help me." But they were the ruin of him and of all Israel.

24 So Ahaz gathered the articles of the house of God, cut in pieces the articles of the house of God, shut up the doors of the house of the LORD, and made for himself altars in every corner of Jerusalem.

25 And in every single city of Judah he made high places to burn incense to other gods, and provoked to anger the LORD God of his fathers.

26 Now the rest of his acts and all his ways, from first to last, indeed they *are* written in the book of the kings of Judah and Israel.

27 So Ahaz rested with his fathers, and they buried him in the city, in Jerusalem; but they did not bring him into the tombs of the kings of Israel. Then Hezekiah his son reigned in his place.

Hezekiah Reigns in Judah

29 Hezekiah became king *when he was* twenty-five years old, and he reigned twenty-nine years in Jerusalem. His mother's name *was* Abijah[64] the daughter of Zechariah.

2 And he did *what was* right in the sight of the LORD, according to all that his father David had done.

Hezekiah Cleanses the Temple

3 In the first year of his reign, in the first month, he opened the doors of the house of the LORD and repaired them.

4 Then he brought in the priests and the Levites, and gathered them in the East Square,

5 and said to them: "Hear me, Levites! Now sanctify yourselves, sanctify the house of the LORD God of your fathers,

---

63 Hebrew *Tilgath-Pilneser* 64 Spelled *Abi* in 2 Kings 18:2

and carry out the rubbish from the holy *place.*

6 "For our fathers have trespassed and done evil in the eyes of the LORD our God; they have forsaken Him, have turned their faces away from the habitation of the LORD, and turned *their* backs *on Him.*

7 "They have also shut up the doors of the vestibule, put out the lamps, and have not burned incense or offered burnt offerings in the holy *place* to the God of Israel.

8 "Therefore the wrath of the LORD fell upon Judah and Jerusalem, and He has given them up to trouble, to astonishment, and to jeering, as you see with your eyes.

9 "For indeed, because of this our fathers have fallen by the sword; and our sons, our daughters, and our wives *are* in captivity.

10 "Now *it is* in my heart to make a covenant with the LORD God of Israel, that His fierce wrath may turn away from us.

11 "My sons, do not be negligent now, for the LORD has chosen you to stand before Him, to serve Him, and that you should minister to Him and burn incense."

12 Then these Levites arose: Mahath the son of Amasai and Joel the son of Azariah, of the sons of the Kohathites; of the sons of Merari, Kish the son of Abdi and Azariah the son of Jehalelel; of the Gershonites, Joah the son of Zimmah and Eden the son of Joah;

13 of the sons of Elizaphan, Shimri and Jeiel; of the sons of Asaph, Zechariah and Mattaniah;

14 of the sons of Heman, Jehiel and Shimei; and of the sons of Jeduthun, Shemaiah and Uzziel.

15 And they gathered their brethren, sanctified themselves, and went according to the commandment of the king, at the words of the LORD, to cleanse the house of the LORD.

16 Then the priests went into the inner part of the house of the LORD to cleanse *it,* and brought out all the debris that they found in the temple of the LORD to the court of the house of the LORD. And the Levites took *it* out and carried *it* to the Brook Kidron.

17 Now they began to sanctify on the first *day* of the first month, and on the eighth day of the month they came to the vestibule of the LORD. Then they sanctified the house of the LORD in eight days, and on the sixteenth day of the first month they finished.

18 Then they went in to King Hezekiah and said, "We have cleansed all the house of the LORD, the altar of burnt offerings with all its articles, and the table of the showbread with all its articles.

19 "Moreover all the articles which King Ahaz in his reign had cast aside in his transgression we have prepared and sanctified; and there they *are,* before the altar of the LORD."

Hezekiah Restores Temple Worship

20 Then King Hezekiah rose early, gathered the rulers of the city, and went up to the house of the LORD.

21 And they brought seven bulls, seven rams, seven lambs, and seven male goats for a sin offering for the kingdom, for the sanctuary, and for Judah. Then he commanded the priests, the sons of Aaron, to offer *them* on the altar of the LORD.

22 So they killed the bulls, and the priests received the blood and sprinkled *it* on the altar. Likewise they killed the rams and sprinkled the blood on the altar. They also killed the lambs and sprinkled the blood on the altar.

23 Then they brought out the male goats *for* the sin offering before the king and the congregation, and they laid their hands on them.

24 And the priests killed them; and they presented their blood on the altar as a sin offering to make an atonement for all Israel, for the king commanded *that* the burnt offering and the sin offering *be made* for all Israel.

25 Then he stationed the Levites in the house of the LORD with cymbals, with stringed instruments, and with harps, according to the commandment of David, of Gad the king's seer, and of Nathan the prophet; for thus *was* the commandment of the LORD by his prophets.

26 The Levites stood with the instruments of David, and the priests with the trumpets.

27 Then Hezekiah commanded *them* to offer the burnt offering on the altar. And when the burnt offering began, the song of the LORD *also* began, with the trumpets and with the instruments of David king of Israel.

28 So all the congregation worshiped, the singers sang, and the trumpeters sounded; all *this continued* until the burnt offering was finished.

29 And when they had finished offering, the king and all who were present with him bowed and worshiped.

30 Moreover King Hezekiah and the leaders commanded the Levites to sing praise to the LORD with the words of David and of Asaph the seer. So they sang praises with gladness, and they bowed their heads and worshiped.

31 Then Hezekiah answered and said, "Now *that* you have consecrated yourselves to the LORD, come near, and bring sacrifices and thank offerings into the house of the LORD." So the congregation brought in sacrifices and thank offerings, and as many as were of a willing heart *brought* burnt offerings.

32 And the number of the burnt offerings which the congregation brought was seventy bulls, one hundred rams, *and* two hundred lambs; all these *were* for a burnt offering to the LORD.

33 The consecrated things *were* six hundred bulls and three thousand sheep.

34 But the priests were too few, so that they could not skin all the burnt offerings; therefore their brethren the Levites helped them until the work was ended and until the *other* priests had sanctified themselves, for the Levites were more diligent in sanctifying themselves than the priests.

35 Also the burnt offerings *were* in abundance, with the fat of the peace offerings and *with* the drink offerings for *every* burnt offering. So the service of the house of the LORD was set in order.

36 Then Hezekiah and all the people rejoiced that God had prepared the people, since the events took place so suddenly.

Hezekiah Keeps the Passover

30 And Hezekiah sent to all Israel and Judah, and also wrote letters to Ephraim and Manasseh, that they should come to the house of the LORD at Jerusalem, to keep the Passover to the LORD God of Israel.

2 For the king and his leaders and all the congregation in Jerusalem had agreed to keep the Passover in the second month.

3 For they could not keep it at that time, because a sufficient number of priests had not sanctified themselves, nor had the people gathered together at Jerusalem.

4 And the matter pleased the king and all the congregation.

5 So they resolved to make a proclamation throughout all Israel, from Beersheba to Dan, that they should come to keep the Passover to the LORD God of Israel at Jerusalem, since they had not done *it* for a long *time* in the *prescribed* manner.

6 Then the runners went throughout all Israel and Judah with the letters from the king and his leaders, and spoke according to the commandment of the king: "Children of Israel, return to the LORD God of Abraham, Isaac, and Israel; then He will return to the remnant of you who have escaped from the hand of the kings of Assyria.

7 "And do not be like your fathers and your brethren, who trespassed against the LORD God of their fathers, so that He gave them up to astonishment, as you see.

8 "Now do not be stiffnecked, as your fathers *were,* but yield yourselves to the LORD; and enter His sanctuary, which He has sanctified forever, and serve the LORD your God, that the fierceness of His wrath may turn away from you.

9 "For if you return to the LORD, your brethren and your children *will be treated* with compassion by those who lead them captive, so that they may come back to this land; for the LORD your God *is* gracious and merciful, and will not turn *His* face from you if you return to Him."

10 So the runners passed from city to city through the country of Ephraim and Manasseh, as far as Zebulun; but they laughed them to scorn and mocked them.

11 Nevertheless some from Asher, Manasseh, and Zebulun humbled themselves and came to Jerusalem.

12 Also the hand of God was on Judah to give them singleness of heart to do the commandment of the king and the leaders, at the word of the LORD.

13 Now many people, a very great congregation, assembled at Jerusalem to keep the Feast of Unleavened Bread in the second month.

14 They arose and took away the altars that *were* in Jerusalem, and they took

away all the incense altars and cast *them* into the Brook Kidron.
15 Then they slaughtered the Passover *lambs* on the fourteenth *day* of the second month. The priests and the Levites were ashamed, and sanctified themselves, and brought the burnt offerings to the house of the LORD.
16 They stood in their place according to their custom, according to the Law of Moses the man of God; the priests sprinkled the blood *which they received* from the hand of the Levites.
17 For *there were* many in the congregation who had not sanctified themselves; therefore the Levites had charge of the slaughter of the Passover *lambs* for everyone *who was* not clean, to sanctify *them* to the LORD.
18 For a multitude of the people, many from Ephraim, Manasseh, Issachar, and Zebulun, had not cleansed themselves, yet they ate the Passover contrary to what was written. But Hezekiah prayed for them, saying, "May the good LORD provide atonement for everyone
19 *who* prepares his heart to seek God, the LORD God of his fathers, though *he is* not *cleansed* according to the purification of the sanctuary."
20 And the LORD listened to Hezekiah and healed the people.
21 So the children of Israel who were present at Jerusalem kept the Feast of Unleavened Bread seven days with great gladness; and the Levites and the priests praised the LORD day by day, *singing* to the LORD, accompanied by loud instruments.
22 And Hezekiah gave encouragement to all the Levites who taught the good knowledge of the LORD; and they ate throughout the feast seven days, offering peace offerings and making confession to the LORD God of their fathers.
23 Then the whole assembly agreed to keep *the feast* another seven days, and they kept it *another* seven days with gladness.
24 For Hezekiah king of Judah gave to the congregation a thousand bulls and seven thousand sheep, and the leaders gave to the congregation a thousand bulls and ten thousand sheep; and a great number of priests sanctified themselves.
25 The whole congregation of Judah rejoiced, also the priests and Levites, all the

congregation that came from Israel, the sojourners who came from the land of Israel, and those who dwelt in Judah.
26 So there was great joy in Jerusalem, for since the time of Solomon the son of David, king of Israel, *there had* been nothing like this in Jerusalem.
27 Then the priests, the Levites, arose and blessed the people, and their voice was heard; and their prayer came *up* to His holy dwelling place, to heaven.

The Reforms of Hezekiah

31 Now when all this was finished, all Israel who were present went out to the cities of Judah and broke the sacred pillars in pieces, cut down the wooden images, and threw down the high places and the altars—from all Judah, Benjamin, Ephraim, and Manasseh—until they had utterly destroyed them all. Then all the children of Israel returned to their own cities, every man to his possession.
2 And Hezekiah appointed the divisions of the priests and the Levites according to their divisions, each man according to his service, the priests and Levites for burnt offerings and peace offerings, to serve, to give thanks, and to praise in the gates of the camp[65] of the LORD.
3 The king also *appointed* a portion of his possessions for the burnt offerings: for the morning and evening burnt offerings, the burnt offerings for the Sabbaths and the New Moons and the set feasts, as *it is* written in the Law of the LORD.
4 Moreover he commanded the people who dwelt in Jerusalem to contribute support for the priests and the Levites, that they might devote themselves to the Law of the LORD.
5 As soon as the commandment was circulated, the children of Israel brought in abundance the firstfruits of grain and wine, oil and honey, and of all the produce of the field; and they brought in abundantly the tithe of everything.
6 And the children of Israel and Judah, who dwelt in the cities of Judah, brought the tithe of oxen and sheep; also the tithe of holy things which were consecrated to the LORD their God they laid in heaps.
7 In the third month they began laying them in heaps, and they finished in the seventh month.

65 That is, the temple

8 And when Hezekiah and the leaders came and saw the heaps, they blessed the LORD and His people Israel.

9 Then Hezekiah questioned the priests and the Levites concerning the heaps.

10 And Azariah the chief priest, from the house of Zadok, answered him and said, "Since *the people* began to bring the offerings into the house of the LORD, we have had enough to eat and have plenty left, for the LORD has blessed His people; and what is left *is* this great abundance."

11 Now Hezekiah commanded *them* to prepare rooms in the house of the LORD, and they prepared them.

12 Then they faithfully brought in the offerings, the tithes, and the dedicated things; Cononiah the Levite *was* ruler over them, and Shimei his brother *was* the next.

13 Jehiel, Azaziah, Nahath, Asahel, Jerimoth, Jozabad, Eliel, Ismachiah, Mahath, and Benaiah *were* overseers under the hand of Cononiah and Shimei his brother, at the commandment of Hezekiah the king and Azariah the ruler of the house of God.

14 Kore the son of Imnah the Levite, the keeper of the East Gate, *was* over the freewill offerings to God, to distribute the offerings of the LORD and the most holy things.

15 And under him *were* Eden, Miniamin, Jeshua, Shemaiah, Amariah, and Shecaniah, *his* faithful assistants in the cities of the priests, to distribute allotments to their brethren by divisions, to the great as well as the small.

16 Besides those males from three years old and up who were written in the genealogy, they distributed to everyone who entered the house of the LORD his daily portion for the work of his service, by his division,

17 and to the priests who were written in the genealogy according to their father's house, and to the Levites from twenty years old and up according to their work, by their divisions,

18 and to all who were written in the genealogy—their little ones and their wives, their sons and daughters, the whole company of them—for in their faithfulness they sanctified themselves in holiness.

19 Also for the sons of Aaron the priests, *who were* in the fields of the commonlands of their cities, in every single city,

there were men who were designated by name to distribute portions to all the males among the priests and to all who were listed by genealogies among the Levites.

20 Thus Hezekiah did throughout all Judah, and he did what *was* good and right and true before the LORD his God.

21 And in every work that he began in the service of the house of God, in the law and in the commandment, to seek his God, he did *it* with all his heart. So he prospered.

Sennacherib Boasts Against the LORD

32 After these deeds of faithfulness, Sennacherib king of Assyria came and entered Judah; he encamped against the fortified cities, thinking to win them over to himself.

2 And when Hezekiah saw that Sennacherib had come, and that his purpose was to make war against Jerusalem,

3 he took counsel with his leaders and commanders[66] to stop the water from the springs which *were* outside the city; and they helped him.

4 Thus many people gathered together who stopped all the springs and the brook that ran through the land, saying, "Why should the kings of Assyria come and find much water?"

5 And he strengthened himself, built up all the wall that was broken, raised *it* up to the towers, and *built* another wall outside; also he repaired the Millo *in* the City of David, and made weapons and shields in abundance.

6 Then he set military captains over the people, gathered them together to him in the open square of the city gate, and gave them encouragement, saying,

7 "Be strong and courageous; do not be afraid nor dismayed before the king of Assyria, nor before all the multitude that *is* with him; for *there are* more with us than with him.

8 "With him *is* an arm of flesh; but with us *is* the LORD our God, to help us and to fight our battles." And the people were strengthened by the words of Hezekiah king of Judah.

9 After this Sennacherib king of Assyria sent his servants to Jerusalem (but he *himself*, and all the forces with him, *laid siege* against Lachish), to Hezekiah king

---

66 Literally *mighty men*

of Judah, and to all Judah who *were* in Jerusalem, saying,

10 "Thus says Sennacherib king of Assyria: 'In what do you trust, that you remain under siege in Jerusalem?

11 'Does not Hezekiah persuade you to give yourselves over to die by famine and by thirst, saying, "The LORD our God will deliver us from the hand of the king of Assyria"?

12 'Has not the same Hezekiah taken away His high places and His altars, and commanded Judah and Jerusalem, saying, "You shall worship before one altar and burn incense on it"?

13 'Do you not know what I and my fathers have done to all the peoples of *other* lands? Were the gods of the nations of those lands in any way able to deliver their lands out of my hand?

14 'Who *was there* among all the gods of those nations that my fathers utterly destroyed that could deliver his people from my hand, that your God should be able to deliver you from my hand?

15 'Now therefore, do not let Hezekiah deceive you or persuade you like this, and do not believe him; for no god of any nation or kingdom was able to deliver his people from my hand or the hand of my fathers. How much less will your God deliver you from my hand?' "

16 And his servants spoke even *more* against the LORD God and against His servant Hezekiah.

17 He also wrote letters to revile the LORD God of Israel, and to speak against Him, saying, "As the gods of the nations of *other* lands have not delivered their people from my hand, so the God of Hezekiah will not deliver His people from my hand."

18 Then they called out with a loud voice in Hebrew[67] to the people of Jerusalem who *were* on the wall, to frighten them and trouble them, that they might take the city.

19 And they spoke against the God of Jerusalem, as against the gods of the people of the earth—the work of men's hands.

Sennacherib's Defeat and Death

20 Now for this *cause* King Hezekiah and the prophet Isaiah, the son of Amoz, prayed and cried out to heaven.

21 Then the LORD sent an angel who cut down every mighty man of valor, leader, and captain in the camp of the king of Assyria. So he returned shamefaced to his own land. And when he had gone into the temple of his god, some of his own offspring struck him down with the sword there.

22 Thus the LORD saved Hezekiah and the inhabitants of Jerusalem from the hand of Sennacherib the king of Assyria, and from the hand of all *others*, and guided them on every side.

23 And many brought gifts to the LORD at Jerusalem, and presents to Hezekiah king of Judah, so that he was exalted in the sight of all nations thereafter.

Hezekiah Humbles Himself

24 In those days Hezekiah was sick and near death, and he prayed to the LORD; and He spoke to him and gave him a sign.

25 But Hezekiah did not repay according to the favor *shown* him, for his heart was lifted up; therefore wrath was looming over him and over Judah and Jerusalem.

26 Then Hezekiah humbled himself for the pride of his heart, he and the inhabitants of Jerusalem, so that the wrath of the LORD did not come upon them in the days of Hezekiah.

Hezekiah's Wealth and Honor

27 Hezekiah had very great riches and honor. And he made himself treasuries for silver, for gold, for precious stones, for spices, for shields, and for all kinds of desirable items;

28 storehouses for the harvest of grain, wine, and oil; and stalls for all kinds of livestock, and folds for flocks.

29 Moreover he provided cities for himself, and possessions of flocks and herds in abundance; for God had given him very much property.

30 This same Hezekiah also stopped the water outlet of Upper Gihon, and brought the water by tunnel[68] to the west side of the City of David. Hezekiah prospered in all his works.

31 However, *regarding* the ambassadors of the princes of Babylon, whom they sent to him to inquire about the wonder that was *done* in the land, God withdrew from him, in order to test him, that He might know all *that was* in his heart.

---

67 Literally *Judean*   68 Literally *brought it straight* (compare 2 Kings 20:20)

Death of Hezekiah

32 Now the rest of the acts of Hezekiah, and his goodness, indeed they *are* written in the vision of Isaiah the prophet, the son of Amoz, *and* in the book of the kings of Judah and Israel.

33 So Hezekiah rested with his fathers, and they buried him in the upper tombs of the sons of David; and all Judah and the inhabitants of Jerusalem honored him at his death. Then Manasseh his son reigned in his place.

Manasseh Reigns in Judah

33 Manasseh *was* twelve years old when he became king, and he reigned fifty-five years in Jerusalem.

2 But he did evil in the sight of the LORD, according to the abominations of the nations whom the LORD had cast out before the children of Israel.

3 For he rebuilt the high places which Hezekiah his father had broken down; he raised up altars for the Baals, and made wooden images; and he worshiped all the host of heaven[69] and served them.

4 He also built altars in the house of the LORD, of which the LORD had said, "In Jerusalem shall My name be forever."

5 And he built altars for all the host of heaven in the two courts of the house of the LORD.

6 Also he caused his sons to pass through the fire in the Valley of the Son of Hinnom; he practiced soothsaying, used witchcraft and sorcery, and consulted mediums and spiritists. He did much evil in the sight of the LORD, to provoke Him *to anger.*

7 He even set a carved image, the idol which he had made, in the house of God, of which God had said to David and to Solomon his son, "In this house and in Jerusalem, which I have chosen out of all the tribes of Israel, I will put My name forever;

8 "and I will not again remove the foot of Israel from the land which I have appointed for your fathers—only if they are careful to do all that I have commanded them, according to the whole law and the statutes and the ordinances by the hand of Moses."

9 So Manasseh seduced Judah and the inhabitants of Jerusalem to do more evil than the nations whom the LORD had destroyed before the children of Israel.

Manasseh Restored after Repentance

10 And the LORD spoke to Manasseh and his people, but they would not listen.

11 Therefore the LORD brought upon them the captains of the army of the king of Assyria, who took Manasseh with hooks,[70] bound him with bronze *fetters,* and carried him off to Babylon.

12 Now when he was in affliction, he implored the LORD his God, and humbled himself greatly before the God of his fathers,

13 and prayed to Him; and He received his entreaty, heard his supplication, and brought him back to Jerusalem into his kingdom. Then Manasseh knew that the LORD *was* God.

14 After this he built a wall outside the City of David on the west side of Gihon, in the valley, as far as the entrance of the Fish Gate; and *it* enclosed Ophel, and he raised it to a very great height. Then he put military captains in all the fortified cities of Judah.

15 He took away the foreign gods and the idol from the house of the LORD, and all the altars that he had built in the mount of the house of the LORD and in Jerusalem; and he cast *them* out of the city.

16 He also repaired the altar of the LORD, sacrificed peace offerings and thank offerings on it, and commanded Judah to serve the LORD God of Israel.

17 Nevertheless the people still sacrificed on the high places, *but* only to the LORD their God.

Death of Manasseh

18 Now the rest of the acts of Manasseh, his prayer to his God, and the words of the seers who spoke to him in the name of the LORD God of Israel, indeed they *are written* in the book[71] of the kings of Israel.

19 Also his prayer and *how God* received his entreaty, and all his sin and trespass, and the sites where he built high places and set up wooden images and carved images, before he was humbled, indeed they *are* written among the sayings of Hozai.[72]

20 So Manasseh rested with his fathers, and they buried him in his own house. Then his son Amon reigned in his place.

69 The gods of the Assyrians   70 That is, nose hook (compare 2 Kings 19:28)
71 Literally *words*   72 Septuagint reads *the seers.*

Amon's Reign and Death

21 Amon *was* twenty-two years old when he became king, and he reigned two years in Jerusalem.
22 But he did evil in the sight of the LORD, as his father Manasseh had done; for Amon sacrificed to all the carved images which his father Manasseh had made, and served them.
23 And he did not humble himself before the LORD, as his father Manasseh had humbled himself; but Amon trespassed more and more.
24 Then his servants conspired against him, and killed him in his own house.
25 But the people of the land executed all those who had conspired against King Amon. Then the people of the land made his son Josiah king in his place.

Josiah Reigns in Judah

34 Josiah *was* eight years old when he became king, and he reigned thirty-one years in Jerusalem.
2 And he did *what was* right in the sight of the LORD, and walked in the ways of his father David; *he* did *not* turn aside to the right hand or to the left.
3 For in the eighth year of his reign, while he was still young, he began to seek the God of his father David; and in the twelfth year he began to purge Judah and Jerusalem of the high places, the wooden images, the carved images, and the molded images.
4 They broke down the altars of the Baals in his presence, and the incense altars which *were* above them he cut down; and the wooden images, the carved images, and the molded images he broke in pieces, and made dust of them and scattered *it* on the graves of those who had sacrificed to them.
5 He also burned the bones of the priests on their altars, and cleansed Judah and Jerusalem.
6 And *so he did* in the cities of Manasseh, Ephraim, and Simeon, as far as Naphtali and all around, with axes.[73]
7 When he had broken down the altars and the wooden images, had beaten the carved images into powder, and cut down all the incense altars throughout all the land of Israel, he returned to Jerusalem.

Hilkiah Finds the Book of the Law

8 Now in the eighteenth year of his reign, when he had purged the land and the temple,[74] he sent Shaphan the son of Azaliah, Maaseiah the governor of the city, and Joah the son of Joahaz the recorder, to repair the house of the LORD his God.
9 When they came to Hilkiah the high priest, they delivered the money that was brought into the house of God, which the Levites who kept the doors had gathered from the hand of Manasseh and Ephraim, from all the remnant of Israel, from all Judah and Benjamin, and *which* they had brought back to Jerusalem.
10 Then they put *it* in the hand of the workmen who had the oversight of the house of the LORD; and they gave it to the workmen who worked in the house of the LORD, to repair and restore the house.
11 They gave *it* to the craftsmen and builders to buy hewn stone and timber for beams, and to floor the houses which the kings of Judah had destroyed.
12 And the men did the work faithfully. Their overseers *were* Jahath and Obadiah the Levites, of the sons of Merari, and Zechariah and Meshullam, of the sons of the Kohathites, to supervise. *Others of* the Levites, all of whom were skillful with instruments of music,
13 *were* over the burden bearers and *were* overseers of all who did work in any kind of service. And *some* of the Levites *were* scribes, officers, and gatekeepers.
14 Now when they brought out the money that was brought into the house of the LORD, Hilkiah the priest found the Book of the Law of the LORD *given* by Moses.
15 Then Hilkiah answered and said to Shaphan the scribe, "I have found the Book of the Law in the house of the LORD." And Hilkiah gave the book to Shaphan.
16 So Shaphan carried the book to the king, bringing the king word, saying, "All that was committed to your servants they are doing.
17 "And they have gathered the money that was found in the house of the LORD, and have delivered it into the hand of the overseers and the workmen."
18 Then Shaphan the scribe told the king, saying, "Hilkiah the priest has given

73 Literally *swords* 74 Literally *house*

me a book." And Shaphan read it before the king.
19 Now it happened, when the king heard the words of the Law, that he tore his clothes.
20 Then the king commanded Hilkiah, Ahikam the son of Shaphan, Abdon[75] the son of Micah, Shaphan the scribe, and Asaiah a servant of the king, saying,
21 "Go, inquire of the LORD for me, and for those who are left in Israel and Judah, concerning the words of the book that is found; for great is the wrath of the LORD that is poured out on us, because our fathers have not kept the word of the LORD, to do according to all that is written in this book."
22 So Hilkiah and those whom the king had appointed went to Huldah the prophetess, the wife of Shallum the son of Tokhath,[76] the son of Hasrah,[77] keeper of the wardrobe. (She dwelt in Jerusalem in the Second Quarter.) And they spoke to her to that effect.
23 Then she answered them, "Thus says the LORD God of Israel, 'Tell the man who sent you to Me,
24 "Thus says the LORD: 'Behold, I will bring calamity on this place and on its inhabitants, all the curses that are written in the book which they have read before the king of Judah,
25 'because they have forsaken Me and burned incense to other gods, that they might provoke Me to anger with all the works of their hands. Therefore My wrath will be poured out on this place, and not be quenched.' " '
26 "And as for the king of Judah, who sent you to inquire of the LORD, in this manner you shall speak to him, 'Thus says the LORD God of Israel: "Concerning the words which you have heard—
27 "because your heart was tender, and you humbled yourself before God when you heard His words against this place and against its inhabitants, and you humbled yourself before Me, and you tore your clothes and wept before Me, I also have heard you," says the LORD.
28 "Surely I will gather you to your fathers, and you shall be gathered to your grave in peace; and your eyes shall not see all the calamity which I will bring on this place and its inhabitants." ' " So they brought back word to the king.

Josiah Restores True Worship

29 Then the king sent and gathered all the elders of Judah and Jerusalem.
30 And the king went up to the house of the LORD, with all the men of Judah and the inhabitants of Jerusalem: the priests and the Levites, and all the people, great and small; and he read in their hearing all the words of the book of the covenant which had been found in the house of the LORD.
31 Then the king stood in his place and made a covenant before the LORD, to follow the LORD, and to keep His commandments and His testimonies and His statutes with all his heart and all his soul, to perform the words of the covenant that were written in this book.
32 And he made all who were present in Jerusalem and Benjamin take their stand for it. So the inhabitants of Jerusalem did according to the covenant of God, the God of their fathers.
33 Thus Josiah removed all the abominations from all the country that belonged to the children of Israel, and made all who were present in Israel diligently serve the LORD their God. All his days they did not depart from following the LORD God of their fathers.

Josiah Keeps the Passover

35 Now Josiah kept a Passover to the LORD in Jerusalem, and they slaughtered the Passover lambs on the fourteenth day of the first month.
2 And he set the priests in their duties and encouraged them for the service of the house of the LORD.
3 Then he said to the Levites who taught all Israel, who were holy to the LORD: "Put the holy ark in the house which Solomon the son of David, king of Israel, built. It shall no longer be a burden on your shoulders. Now serve the LORD your God and His people Israel.
4 "Prepare yourselves according to your fathers' houses, according to your divisions, following the written instruction of David king of Israel and the written instruction of Solomon his son.
5 "And stand in the holy place according to the divisions of the fathers' houses of your brethren the lay people, and according to the division of the father's house of the Levites.

---

75 Achbor the son of Michaiah in 2 Kings 22:12   76 Spelled Tikvah in 2 Kings 22:14
77 Spelled Harhas in 2 Kings 22:14

Freedom to Stand Before God

As Christians, we experience great freedom in worship before God. In light of the ancient Jewish worship of God, we can gain a greater appreciation of our relationship with our Lord.

Recent archaeological excavations of the Jerusalem temple provide insight into the worship of the early Israelites. Two stone plaques bear the inscription, "Gentiles or nations prohibited beyond this point." Dated to the time of Christ, these inscriptions were affixed to the outer court area of the temple. It was forbidden for anyone of a different nation other than Jew to enter the temple's inner court. Paul was falsely accused of violating this law by bringing his gentile friends into this area.

The temple consisted of numerous inner sanctuaries, but none was as important as the "Holy of Holies." This court was separated from all others by a veil stretching ninety feet from top to bottom. Once a year the high priest entered the "Holy of Holies." This was done at Passover when the priest symbolically made an atonement for the sins of the nation by placing blood from a sacrificial lamb on the mercy seat of the altar.

The Book of Hebrews confirms that once and for all individuals can approach God directly. Because of the sacrificial death and resurrection of Jesus Christ, nations and Gentiles are no longer separated from God. Instead, they can enter the "Holy of Holies" and experience the presence of God.

The New Testament records that when Jesus was crucified and died, the temple veil covering the "Holy of Holies" was torn in two. Ancient Jewish literature also records an unusual occurrence at the temple one Passover. The "Holy of Holies" curtain was torn in two during the reign of Pontius Pilate, the governor under which Jesus was crucified. Could this be a reference to the same event as recorded in the Bible? It is quite possible.

Through Jesus' death and resurrection, we have the confidence to draw near to God in full assurance. We have the freedom to stand before God knowing He will meet our needs. We are not bound like those unable to enter the temple's inner courts. Nor are we like those who could not enter the "Holy of Holies." Rather, we have the blessings of a beautiful relationship with God, free to boldly walk into His presence.

6 "So slaughter the Passover *offerings*, sanctify yourselves, and prepare *them* for your brethren, that *they* may do according to the word of the LORD by the hand of Moses."

7 Then Josiah gave the *lay* people lambs and young goats from the flock, all for Passover *offerings* for all who were present, to the number of thirty thousand, as well as three thousand cattle; these *were* from the king's possessions.

8 And his leaders gave willingly to the people, to the priests, and to the Levites. Hilkiah, Zechariah, and Jehiel, rulers of the house of God, gave to the priests for the Passover *offerings* two thousand six hundred *from the flock*, and three hundred cattle;

9 also Conaniah, his brothers Shemaiah and Nethaneel, and Hashabiah and Jeiel and Jozabad, chief of the Levites, gave to the Levites for Passover *offerings* five thousand *from the flock* and five hundred cattle.

10 So the service was prepared, and the priests stood in their places, and the Levites in their divisions, according to the king's command.

11 And they slaughtered the Passover *offerings*; and the priests sprinkled *the blood* with their hands, while the Levites skinned *the animals*.

12 Then they removed the burnt offerings that *they* might give them to the divisions of the fathers' houses of the *lay* people, to offer to the LORD, as *it is* written in the Book of Moses. And so *they did* with the cattle.

13 Also they roasted the Passover *offerings* with fire according to the ordinance; but the *other* holy *offerings* they boiled in pots, in caldrons, and in pans, and divided *them* quickly among all the *lay* people.

14 Then afterward they prepared portions for themselves and for the priests, because the priests, the sons of Aaron, *were busy* in offering burnt offerings and fat until night; therefore the Levites prepared portions for themselves and for the priests, the sons of Aaron.

15 And the singers, the sons of Asaph, *were* in their places, according to the command of David, Asaph, Heman, and Jeduthun the king's seer. Also the gatekeepers were at each gate; they did not have to leave their position, because their brethren the Levites prepared portions for them.

16 So all the service of the LORD was prepared the same day, to keep the Passover and to offer burnt offerings on the altar of the LORD, according to the command of King Josiah.

17 And the children of Israel who were present kept the Passover at that time, and the Feast of Unleavened Bread for seven days.

18 There had been no Passover kept in Israel like that since the days of Samuel the prophet; and none of the kings of Israel had kept such a Passover as Josiah kept, with the priests and the Levites, all Judah and Israel who were present, and the inhabitants of Jerusalem.

19 In the eighteenth year of the reign of Josiah this Passover was kept.

Josiah Dies in Battle

20 After all this, when Josiah had prepared the temple, Necho king of Egypt came up to fight against Carchemish by the Euphrates; and Josiah went out against him.

21 But he sent messengers to him, saying, "What have I to do with you, king of Judah? *I have* not *come* against you this day, but against the house with which I have war; for God commanded me to make haste. Refrain *from meddling with* God, who *is* with me, lest He destroy you."

22 Nevertheless Josiah would not turn his face from him, but disguised himself so that he might fight with him, and did not heed the words of Necho from the mouth of God. So he came to fight in the Valley of Megiddo.

23 And the archers shot King Josiah; and the king said to his servants, "Take me away, for I am severely wounded."

24 His servants therefore took him out of that chariot and put him in the second chariot that he had, and they brought him to Jerusalem. So he died, and was buried in *one of* the tombs of his fathers. And all Judah and Jerusalem mourned for Josiah.

25 Jeremiah also lamented for Josiah. And to this day all the singing men and the singing women speak of Josiah in their lamentations. They made it a custom in Israel; and indeed they *are* written in the Laments.

26 Now the rest of the acts of Josiah and his goodness, according to *what was* written in the Law of the LORD,
27 and his deeds from first to last, indeed they *are* written in the book of the kings of Israel and Judah.

The Reign and Captivity of Jehoahaz

36 Then the people of the land took Jehoahaz the son of Josiah, and made him king in his father's place in Jerusalem.
2 Jehoahaz[78] *was* twenty-three years old when he became king, and he reigned three months in Jerusalem.
3 Now the king of Egypt deposed him at Jerusalem; and he imposed on the land a tribute of one hundred talents of silver and a talent of gold.
4 Then the king of Egypt made his brother Eliakim king over Judah and Jerusalem, and changed his name to Jehoiakim. And Necho took Jehoahaz[79] his brother and carried him off to Egypt.

The Reign and Captivity of Jehoiakim

5 Jehoiakim *was* twenty-five years old when he became king, and he reigned eleven years in Jerusalem. And he did evil in the sight of the LORD his God.
6 Nebuchadnezzar king of Babylon came up against him, and bound him in bronze *fetters* to carry him off to Babylon.
7 Nebuchadnezzar also carried off *some* of the articles from the house of the LORD to Babylon, and put them in his temple at Babylon.
8 Now the rest of the acts of Jehoiakim, the abominations which he did, and what was found against him, indeed they *are* written in the book of the kings of Israel and Judah. Then Jehoiachin his son reigned in his place.

The Reign and Captivity of Jehoiachin

9 Jehoiachin *was* eight[80] years old when he became king, and he reigned in Jerusalem three months and ten days. And he did evil in the sight of the LORD.
10 At the turn of the year King Nebuchadnezzar summoned *him* and took him to Babylon, with the costly articles from the house of the LORD, and made Zedekiah, Jehoiakim's[81] brother, king over Judah and Jerusalem.

Zedekiah Reigns in Judah

11 Zedekiah *was* twenty-one years old when he became king, and he reigned eleven years in Jerusalem.
12 He *also* did evil in the sight of the LORD his God, *and* did not humble himself before Jeremiah the prophet, *who spoke* from the mouth of the LORD.
13 And he also rebelled against King Nebuchadnezzar, who had made him swear *an oath* by God; but he stiffened his neck and hardened his heart against turning to the LORD God of Israel.
14 Moreover all the leaders of the priests and the people transgressed more and more, *according* to all the abominations of the nations, and defiled the house of the LORD which He had consecrated in Jerusalem.

The Fall of Jerusalem

15 And the LORD God of their fathers sent *warnings* to them by His messengers, rising up early and sending *them*, because He had compassion on His people and on His dwelling place.
16 But they mocked the messengers of God, despised His words, and scoffed at His prophets, until the wrath of the LORD arose against His people, till *there was* no remedy.
17 Therefore He brought against them the king of the Chaldeans, who killed their young men with the sword in the house of their sanctuary, and had no compassion on young man or virgin, on the aged or the weak; He gave *them* all into his hand.
18 And all the articles from the house of God, great and small, the treasures of the house of the LORD, and the treasures of the king and of his leaders, all *these* he took to Babylon.
19 Then they burned the house of God, broke down the wall of Jerusalem, burned all its palaces with fire, and destroyed all its precious possessions.
20 And those who escaped from the sword he carried away to Babylon, where they became servants to him and his sons until the reign of the kingdom of Persia,
21 to fulfill the word of the LORD by the mouth of Jeremiah, until the land had en-

---

78 Masoretic Text reads *Joahaz.*   79 Masoretic Text reads *Joahaz.*
80 Some Hebrew manuscripts, Septuagint, Syriac, and 2 Kings 24:8 read *eighteen.*
81 Literally *his* (compare 2 Kings 24:17)

joyed her Sabbaths. As long as she lay desolate she kept Sabbath, to fulfill seventy years.

The Proclamation of Cyrus

22 Now in the first year of Cyrus king of Persia, that the word of the LORD spoken by the mouth of Jeremiah might be fulfilled, the LORD stirred up the spirit of Cyrus king of Persia, so that he made a proclamation throughout all his kingdom, and also put it in writing, saying,

23 "Thus says Cyrus king of Persia: 'All the kingdoms of the earth the LORD God of heaven has given me. And He has commanded me to build Him a house at Jerusalem which is in Judah. Who is there among you of all His people? May the LORD his God be with him, and let him go up!' "

Introduction to Ezra

The Book of Ezra teaches that even if you have good reason to be sorrowful you can still be resourceful and ultimately successful!

Written by the scribe Ezra between 457 and 444 B.C., the book records two major exoduses of the Jewish people from Babylon.

Ezra chronicles the events concerning the rebuilding of the temple. Instilled with a dream, the people began the task of rebuilding the place of worship. Slowly they saw their dream rise from the rubble and ashes of the destruction wrought by Nebuchadnezzar on the ancient city of Jerusalem. Ezra told the people that now was the time to build a sanctuary of worship for their God.

Who *is there* among you of all His people? May his God be with him! Now let him go up to Jerusalem, which *is* in Judah, and build the house of the LORD God of Israel (He *is* God), which *is* in Jerusalem. And whoever remains in any place where he sojourns, let the man of his place help him with silver and gold, with goods and livestock, besides the freewill offerings for the house of God which *is* in Jerusalem.

(Ezra 1:3, 4)

He encouraged them not to look at the ruins but toward the results. They faced many obstacles—lack of finances, lack of manpower, and pressure from local military authorities who opposed the project. There were many reasons the temple should not have been built. But Ezra looked toward his goal. He made his decisions, and then he solved his problems. He never let his problems stop him from completing his God-ordained dream.

Ezra set out to find solutions to the obstacles in his way. Because of his faith and leadership, the dream of the temple became a reality!

The Book of

Ezra

End of the Babylonian Captivity

NOW in the first year of Cyrus king of Persia, that the word of the LORD *spoken* by the mouth of Jeremiah might be fulfilled, the LORD stirred up the spirit of Cyrus king of Persia, so that he made a proclamation throughout all his kingdom, and also *put it* in writing, saying,

2 Thus says Cyrus king of Persia: All the kingdoms of the earth the LORD God of heaven has given me. And He has commanded me to build Him a house at Jerusalem which *is* in Judah.

3 Who *is there* among you of all His people? May his God be with him! Now let him go up to Jerusalem, which *is* in Judah, and build the house of the LORD God of Israel (He *is* God), which *is* in Jerusalem.

4 And whoever remains in any place where he sojourns, let the men of his place help him with silver and gold, with goods and livestock, besides the freewill offerings for the house of God which *is* in Jerusalem.

5 Then the heads of the fathers' *houses* of Judah and Benjamin, and the priests and the Levites, with all *those* whose spirits God had moved, arose to go up and build the house of the LORD which *is* in Jerusalem.

6 And all those who *were* around them encouraged them with articles of silver and gold, with goods and livestock, and with precious things, besides all *that* was willingly offered.

7 King Cyrus also brought out the articles of the house of the LORD, which Nebuchadnezzar had taken from Jerusalem and put in the temple of his gods;

8 and Cyrus king of Persia brought them out by the hand of Mithredath the treasurer, and counted them out to Sheshbazzar the prince of Judah.

9 This *is* the number of them: thirty gold platters, one thousand silver platters, twenty-nine knives,

10 thirty gold basins, four hundred and ten silver basins of a similar *kind, and* one thousand other articles.

11 All the articles of gold and silver *were* five thousand four hundred. All *these* Sheshbazzar took with the captives who were brought from Babylon to Jerusalem.

The Captives Who Returned to Jerusalem

2 Now[1] these *are* the people of the province who came back from the captivity, of those who had been carried away, whom Nebuchadnezzar the king of Babylon had carried away to Babylon, and who returned to Jerusalem and Judah, everyone to his *own* city.

2 *Those* who came with Zerubbabel *were* Jeshua, Nehemiah, Seraiah, Reelaiah, Mordecai, Bilshan, Mispar,[2] Bigvai, Rehum,[3] *and* Baanah. The number of the men of the people of Israel:

3 the people of Parosh, two thousand one hundred and seventy-two;

4 the people of Shephatiah, three hundred and seventy-two;

5 the people of Arah, seven hundred and seventy-five;

6 the people of Pahath-Moab, of the people of Jeshua *and* Joab, two thousand eight hundred and twelve;

7 the people of Elam, one thousand two hundred and fifty-four;

8 the people of Zattu, nine hundred and forty-five;

9 the people of Zaccai, seven hundred and sixty;

10 the people of Bani,[4] six hundred and forty-two;

11 the people of Bebai, six hundred and twenty-three;

12 the people of Azgad, one thousand two hundred and twenty-two;

13 the people of Adonikam, six hundred and sixty-six;

14 the people of Bigvai, two thousand and fifty-six;

the people of Kirjath Arim,[8] Chephirah, and Beeroth, seven hundred and forty-three;

the people of the other Elam, one thousand two hundred and fifty-four;

the people of Lod, Hadid, and Ono, seven hundred and twenty-five;

The priests: the sons of Jedaiah, of the house of Jeshua, nine hundred and seventy-three;

The Levites: the sons of Jeshua and Kadmiel, of the sons of Hodaviah,[9] seventy-four.

The singers: the sons of Asaph, one hundred and twenty-eight.

The sons of the gatekeepers: the sons of Shallum, the sons of Ater, the sons of Talmon, the sons of Akkub, the sons of Hatita, and the sons of Shobai, one hundred and thirty-nine in all.

The Nethinim: the sons of Ziha, the sons of Hasupha, the sons of Tabbaoth,

the sons of Keros, the sons of Siaha,[10] the sons of Padon,

the sons of Lebanah, the sons of Hagabah, the sons of Akkub,

the sons of Hagab, the sons of Shalmai, the sons of Hanan,

the sons of Giddel, the sons of Gahar, the sons of Reaiah,

the sons of Rezin, the sons of Nekoda, the sons of Gazzam,

the sons of Uzza, the sons of Paseah, the sons of Besai,

the sons of Asnah, the sons of Meunim, the sons of Nephusim,[11]

the sons of Bakbuk, the sons of Hakupha, the sons of Harhur,

the sons of Bazluth,[12] the sons of Mehida, the sons of Harsha,

the sons of Barkos, the sons of Sisera, the sons of Tamah,

The sons of Solomon's servants: the sons of Sotai, the sons of Sophereth, the sons of Peruda,[13]

the sons of Jaala, the sons of Darkon, the sons of Giddel,

the sons of Shephatiah, the sons of Hattil, the sons of Pochereth of Zebaim, and the sons of Ami.[14]

All the Nethinim and the children of Solomon's servants were three hundred and ninety-two.

And these were the ones who came up from Tel Melah, Tel Harsha, Cherub, Addan,[15] and Immer; but they could not identify their father's house or their genealogy,[16] whether they were of Israel:

the sons of Delaiah, the sons of Tobiah, and the sons of Nekoda, six hundred and fifty-two;

and of the sons of the priests: the sons of Habaiah, the sons of Koz,[17] and the sons of Barzillai, who took a wife of the daughters of Barzillai the Gileadite, and was called by their name.

---

5 Called *Hariph* in Nehemiah 7:24   6 Called *Gibeon* in Nehemiah 7:25
7 Called *Beth Azmaveth* in Nehemiah 7:28   8 Called *Kirjath Jearim* in Nehemiah 7:29
9 Spelled *Hodevah* in Nehemiah 7:43   10 Spelled *Sia* in Nehemiah 7:47   11 Spelled *Nephishesim* in Nehemiah 7:52
12 Spelled *Bazlith* in Nehemiah 7:54   13 Spelled *Perida* in Nehemiah 7:57   14 Spelled *Amon* in Nehemiah 7:59
15 Spelled *Addon* in Nehemiah 7:61   16 Literally *seed*   17 Or *Hakkoz*

62 These sought their listing *among* those who were registered by genealogy, but they were not found; therefore they *were* excluded from the priesthood as defiled. 63 And the governor[18] said to them that they should not eat of the most holy things till a priest could consult with the Urim and Thummim.

64 The whole congregation together *was* forty-two thousand three hundred *and* sixty, 65 besides their male and female servants, of whom *there were* seven thousand three hundred and thirty-seven; and they had two hundred men and women singers. 66 Their horses *were* seven hundred and thirty-six, their mules two hundred and forty-five, 67 their camels four hundred and thirty-five, and *their* donkeys six thousand seven hundred and twenty.

68 *Some of the heads of the fathers' houses*, when they came to the house of the LORD which *is* in Jerusalem, offered freely for the house of God, to erect it in its place: 69 According to their ability, they gave to the treasury for the work sixty-one thousand gold drachmas, five thousand minas of silver, and one hundred priestly garments.

70 So the priests and the Levites, *some* of the people, the singers, the gatekeepers, and the Nethanim, dwelt in their cities, and all Israel in their cities.

Worship Restored at Jerusalem

3 And when the seventh month had come, and the children of Israel *were* in the cities, the people gathered together as one man to Jerusalem. 2 Then Jeshua the son of Jozadak[19] and his brethren the priests, and Zerubbabel the son of Shealtiel and his brethren, arose and built the altar of the God of Israel, to offer burnt offerings on it, as *it is* written in the Law of Moses the man of God. 3 Though fear *had come* upon them because of the people of those countries, they set the altar on its bases; and they offered burnt offerings on it to the LORD, *both* the morning and evening burnt offerings. 4 They also kept the Feast of Tabernacles, as *it is* written, and *offered* the

daily burnt offerings in the number required by ordinance for each day; 5 and afterward *they offered* the regular burnt offering, and *those* for New Moons and for all the appointed feasts of the LORD that were consecrated, and *those* of everyone who willingly offered a freewill offering to the LORD. 6 From the first day of the seventh month they began to offer burnt offerings to the LORD. But the foundation of the temple of the LORD had not *yet* been laid. 7 They also gave money to the masons and the carpenters, and food, drink, and oil to the people of Sidon and Tyre to bring cedar logs from Lebanon to the sea at Joppa, according to the permission which they had from Cyrus king of Persia.

Restoration of the Temple Begins

8 Now in the second month of the second year of their coming to the house of God at Jerusalem, Zerubbabel the son of Shealtiel, Jeshua the son of Jozadak,[20] and the rest of their brethren the priests and the Levites, and all those who had come out of the captivity to Jerusalem, began *work* and appointed the Levites from twenty years old and above to oversee the work of the house of the LORD. 9 Then Jeshua *with* his sons and brothers, Kadmiel *with* his sons, and the sons of Judah,[21] arose as one to oversee those working on the house of God: the sons of Henadad *with* their sons and their brethren the Levites. 10 When the builders laid the foundation of the temple of the LORD, the priests stood in their apparel with trumpets, and the Levites, the sons of Asaph, with cymbals, to praise the LORD, according to the ordinance of David king of Israel. 11 And they sang responsively, praising and giving thanks to the LORD:

"For *He is* good,
  For His mercy *endures* forever
    toward Israel."[22]

Then all the people shouted with a great shout, when they praised the LORD, because the foundation of the house of the LORD was laid. 12 But many of the priests and Levites and heads of the fathers' *houses, who were* old men, who had seen the first temple,

18 Hebrew *tirshatha*   19 Spelled *Jehozadak* in 1 Chronicles 6:14   20 Spelled *Jehozadak* in 1 Chronicles 6:14
21 Or *Hodaviah* (compare 2:40)   22 Compare Psalm 136:1

wept with a loud voice when the foundation of this temple was laid before their eyes; yet many shouted aloud for joy, 13 so that the people could not discern the noise of the shout of joy from the noise of the weeping of the people, for the people shouted with a loud shout, and the sound was heard afar off.

Resistance to Rebuilding the Temple

4 Now when the adversaries of Judah and Benjamin heard that the descendants of the captivity were building the temple of the LORD God of Israel, 2 they came to Zerubbabel and the heads of the fathers' *houses,* and said to them, "Let us build with you, for we seek your God as you *do;* and we have sacrificed to Him since the days of Esarhaddon king of Assyria, who brought us here."
3 But Zerubbabel and Jeshua and the rest of the heads of the fathers' *houses* of Israel said to them, "You may do nothing with us to build a house for our God; but we alone will build to the LORD God of Israel, as King Cyrus the king of Persia has commanded us."
4 Then the people of the land tried to discourage the people of Judah. They troubled them in building,
5 and hired counselors against them to frustrate their purpose all the days of Cyrus king of Persia, even until the reign of Darius king of Persia.

Rebuilding of Jerusalem Opposed

6 Now in the reign of Ahasuerus, in the beginning of his reign, they wrote an accusation against the inhabitants of Judah and Jerusalem.
7 In the days of Artaxerxes also, Bishlam, Mithredath, Tabeel, and the rest of their companions wrote to Artaxerxes king of Persia; and the letter *was* written in Aramaic script, and translated into the Aramaic language.
8 Rehum[23] the commander and Shimshai the scribe wrote a letter against Jerusalem to King Artaxerxes in this fashion:
9 From[24] Rehum the commander, Shimshai the scribe, and the rest of their companions—*representatives* of the Dinaites, the Apharsathchites, the Tarpelites, the people of Persia and Erech and Babylon and

Shushan,[25] the Dehavites, the Elamites,
10 and the rest of the nations whom the great and noble Osnapper took captive and settled in the cities of Samaria and the rest *of the region* beyond the River[26]—and so forth.[27]
11 This *is* a copy of the letter that they sent him—
To King Artaxerxes from your servants the men *of the region* beyond the River, and so forth:[28]
12 Let it be known to the king that the Jews who came up from you have come to us at Jerusalem, and are building the rebellious and evil city, and are finishing *its* walls and repairing the foundations.
13 Let it now be known to the king that, if this city is built and the walls completed, they will not pay tax, tribute, or custom, and the king's treasury will be diminished.
14 Now because we receive support from the palace, it was not proper for us to see the king's dishonor; therefore we have sent and informed the king,
15 that search may be made in the book of the records of your fathers. And you will find in the book of the records and know that this city *is* a rebellious city, harmful to kings and provinces, and that they have incited sedition within the city in former times, for which cause this city was destroyed.
16 We inform the king that if this city is rebuilt and its walls are completed, the result will be that you will have no dominion *over the region* beyond the River.

17 *Then* the king sent an answer:

To Rehum the commander, *to* Shimshai the scribe, *to* the rest of their companions who dwell in Samaria, and *to* the rest *in the region* beyond the River:
Peace, and so forth.[29]
18 The letter which you sent to us has been clearly read before me.
19 And I gave the command, and a search has been made, and it was found that this city in former times

---

23 The original language of Ezra 4:8 through 6:18 is Aramaic. 24 Literally *Then* 25 Or *Susa*
26 That is, the Euphrates 27 Literally *and now* 28 Literally *and now* 29 Literally *and now*

has made insurrection against kings,
and *that* rebellion and sedition have
been fostered in it.

20 There have also been mighty kings
over Jerusalem, who have ruled over
all *the provinces* beyond the River;
and tax, tribute, and custom were
paid to them.

21 Now give the command to make
these men cease, that this city may
not be built until the command is
given by me.

22 Take heed now that you do not fail
to do this. Why should damage
increase to the hurt of the kings?

23 Now when the copy of King Artaxerxes' letter *was* read before Rehum,
Shimshai the scribe, and their companions, they went up in haste to Jerusalem
against the Jews, and by force of arms
made them cease.

24 Thus the work of the house of God
which *is* at Jerusalem ceased, and it was
discontinued until the second year of the
reign of Darius king of Persia.

Restoration of the Temple Resumed

5 Then the prophet Haggai and Zechariah the son of Iddo, prophets,
prophesied to the Jews who *were* in Judah
and Jerusalem, in the name of the God of
Israel, *who was* over them.

2 So Zerubbabel the son of Shealtiel
and Jeshua the son of Jozadak[30] rose up
and began to build the house of God
which *is* in Jerusalem; and the prophets
of God *were* with them, helping them.

3 At the same time Tattenai the governor *of the region* beyond the River[31] and
Shethar-Bozenai and their companions
came to them and spoke thus to them:
"Who has commanded you to build this
temple and finish this wall?"

4 Then, accordingly, we told them the
names of the men who were constructing
this building.

5 But the eye of their God was upon the
elders of the Jews, so that they could not
make them cease till a report could go to
Darius. Then a written answer was returned concerning this *matter.*

6 This is a copy of the letter that Tattenai sent:

The governor of *the region* beyond
the River, and Shethar-Baznai, and
his companions, the Persians who

were in the region beyond the River,
to Darius the king.

7 They sent a letter to him, in which
was written thus—
To Darius the king:
All peace.

8 Let it be known to the king that we
went into the province of Judea, to
the temple of the great God, which is
being built with heavy stones, and
timber is being laid in the walls; and
this work goes on diligently and
prospers in their hands.

9 Then we asked those elders, *and*
spoke thus to them: "Who
commanded you to build this temple
and to finish these walls?"

10 We also asked them their names to
inform you, that we might write the
names of the men who *were* chief
among them.

11 And thus they returned us an
answer, saying: "We are the servants
of the God of heaven and earth, and
we are rebuilding the temple that
was built many years ago, which a
great king of Israel built and
completed.

12 "But because our fathers provoked the
God of heaven to wrath, He gave
them into the hand of
Nebuchadnezzar king of Babylon,
the Chaldean, *who* destroyed this
temple and carried the people away
to Babylon.

13 "However, in the first year of Cyrus
king of Babylon, King Cyrus issued
a decree to build this house of God.

14 "Also, the gold and silver articles of
the house of God, which
Nebuchadnezzar had taken from the
temple that *was* in Jerusalem and
carried into the temple of Babylon—
those King Cyrus took from the
temple of Babylon, and they were
given to one named Sheshbazzar,
whom he had made governor.

15 "And he said to him, 'Take these
articles; go, carry them to the temple
site that *is* in Jerusalem, and let the
house of God be rebuilt on its
former site.'

16 "Then the same Sheshbazzar came
and laid the foundation of the house
of God which *is* in Jerusalem; and
from that time even until now it has

---

30 Spelled *Jehozadak* in 1 Chronicles 6:14   31 That is, the Euphrates

been under construction, and it is not *yet* finished."

17 Now therefore, if *it seems* good to the king, let a search be made in the king's treasure house, which *is* there in Babylon, whether it is *so* that a decree was issued by King Cyrus to build this house of God at Jerusalem, and let the king send us his pleasure concerning this *matter*.

The Decree of Darius

6 Then King Darius issued a decree, and a search was made in the archives,[32] where the treasures were stored in Babylon.

2 And at Achmetha,[33] in the palace that *is* in the province of Media, a scroll was found, and in it a record *was* written thus:

3 In the first year of King Cyrus, King Cyrus issued a decree *concerning* the house of God at Jerusalem: "Let the house be rebuilt, the place where they offered sacrifices; and let the foundations of it be firmly laid, its height sixty cubits *and* its width sixty cubits,

4 *with* three rows of heavy stones and one row of new timber. Let the expenses be paid from the king's treasury.

5 Also let the gold and silver articles of the house of God, which Nebuchadnezzar took from the temple which *is* in Jerusalem and brought to Babylon, be restored and taken back to the temple which *is* in Jerusalem, *each* to its place; and deposit *them* in the house of God"—

6 Now *therefore*, Tattenai, governor *of the region* beyond the River, and Shethar-Boznai, and your companions the Persians who *are* beyond the River, keep yourselves far from there.

7 Let the work of this house of God alone; let the governor of the Jews and the elders of the Jews build this house of God on its site.

8 Moreover I issue a decree *as to* what you shall do for the elders of these Jews, for the building of this house of God: Let the cost be paid at the king's expense from taxes *on the region* beyond the River; this is to be given immediately to these men, so that they are not hindered.

9 And whatever they need—young bulls, rams, and lambs for the burnt offerings of the God of heaven, wheat, salt, wine, and oil, according to the request of the priests who *are* in Jerusalem—let it be given them day by day without fail,

10 that they may offer sacrifices of sweet aroma to the God of heaven, and pray for the life of the king and his sons.

11 Also I issue a decree that whoever alters this edict, let a timber be pulled from his house and erected, and let him be hanged on it; and let his house be made a refuse heap because of this.

12 And may the God who causes His name to dwell there destroy any king or people who put their hand to alter it, or to destroy this house of God which is in Jerusalem. I Darius issue *the* decree; let it be done diligently.

The Temple Completed and Dedicated

13 Then Tattenai, governor of *the region* beyond the River, Shethar-Boznai, and their companions diligently did according to what King Darius had sent.

14 So the elders of the Jews built, and they prospered through the prophesying of Haggai the prophet and Zechariah the son of Iddo. And they built and finished *it*, according to the commandment of the God of Israel, and according to the command of Cyrus, Darius, and Artaxerxes king of Persia.

15 Now the temple was finished on the third day of the month of Adar, which was in the sixth year of the reign of King Darius.

16 Then the children of Israel, the priests and the Levites and the rest of the descendants of the captivity, celebrated the dedication of this house of God with joy.

17 And they offered sacrifices at the dedication of this house of God, one hundred bulls, two hundred rams, four hundred lambs, and as a sin offering for all Israel twelve male goats, according to the number of the tribes of Israel.

18 They assigned the priests to their divisions and the Levites to their divisions, over the service of God in Jerusalem, as it is written in the Book of Moses.

---

32 Literally *house of the scrolls*   33 Probably *Ecbatana*, the ancient capital of Media

The Passover Celebrated

19 And the descendants of the captivity kept the Passover on the fourteenth *day* of the first month.

20 For the priests and the Levites had purified themselves; all of them *were ritually* clean. And they slaughtered the Passover *lambs* for all the descendants of the captivity, for their brethren the priests, and for themselves.

21 Then the children of Israel who had returned from the captivity ate together with all who had separated themselves from the filth of the nations of the land in order to seek the LORD God of Israel.

22 And they kept the Feast of Unleavened Bread seven days with joy; for the LORD made them joyful, and turned the heart of the king of Assyria toward them, to strengthen their hands in the work of the house of God, the God of Israel.

The Arrival of Ezra

7 Now after these things, in the reign of Artaxerxes king of Persia, Ezra the son of Seraiah, the son of Azariah, the son of Hilkiah,

2 the son of Shallum, the son of Zadok, the son of Ahitub,

3 the son of Amariah, the son of Azariah, the son of Meraioth,

4 the son of Zerahiah, the son of Uzzi, the son of Bukki,

5 the son of Abishua, the son of Phinehas, the son of Eleazar, the son of Aaron the chief priest—

6 this Ezra came up from Babylon; and he *was* a skilled scribe in the Law of Moses, which the LORD God of Israel had given. The king granted him all his request, according to the hand of the LORD his God upon him.

7 *Some* of the children of Israel, the priests, the Levites, the singers, the gatekeepers, and the Nethinim came up to Jerusalem in the seventh year of King Artaxerxes.

8 And Ezra came to Jerusalem in the fifth month, which *was* in the seventh year of the king.

9 On the first *day* of the first month he began *his* journey from Babylon, and on the first *day* of the fifth month he came to Jerusalem, according to the good hand of his God upon him.

10 For Ezra had prepared his heart to seek the Law of the LORD, and to do *it,* and to teach statutes and ordinances in Israel.

The Letter of Artaxerxes to Ezra

11 Now this *is* the copy of the letter that King Artaxerxes gave Ezra the priest, the scribe, expert in the words of the commandments of the LORD, and of His statutes to Israel:

12 Artaxerxes,[34] king of kings,
To Ezra the priest, a scribe of the Law of the God of heaven:
Perfect *peace,* and so forth.[35]

13 I issue a decree that all those of the people of Israel and the priests and Levites in my realm, who volunteer to go up to Jerusalem, may go with you.

14 And whereas you are being sent by the king and his seven counselors to inquire concerning Judah and Jerusalem, with regard to the Law of your God which *is* in your hand;

15 and *whereas you are* to carry the silver and gold which the king and his counselors have freely offered to the God of Israel, whose dwelling *is* in Jerusalem;

16 and *whereas* all the silver and gold that you may find in all the province of Babylon, along with the freewill offering of the people and the priests, *are to be* freely offered for the house of their God in Jerusalem—

17 now therefore, be careful to buy with this money bulls, rams, and lambs, with their grain offerings and their drink offerings, and offer them on the altar of the house of your God in Jerusalem.

18 And whatever seems good to you and your brethren to do with the rest of the silver and the gold, do it according to the will of your God.

19 Also the articles that are given to you for the service of the house of your God, deliver in full before the God of Jerusalem.

20 And whatever more may be needed for the house of your God, which you may have occasion to provide, pay *for it* from the king's treasury.

21 And I, *even* I, Artaxerxes the king, do issue a decree to all the treasurers who *are in the region* beyond the River, that whatever Ezra the priest, the scribe of the Law of the God of

---

34 The original language of Ezra 7:12–26 is Aramaic.   35 Literally *and now*

heaven, may require of you, let it be done diligently,

22 up to one hundred talents of silver, one hundred kors of wheat, one hundred baths of wine, one hundred baths of oil, and salt without prescribed limit.

23 Whatever is commanded by the God of heaven, let it diligently be done for the house of the God of heaven. For why should there be wrath against the realm of the king and his sons?

24 Also we inform you that it shall not be lawful to impose tax, tribute, or custom *on* any of the priests, Levites, singers, gatekeepers, Nethinim, or servants of this house of God.

25 And you, Ezra, according to your God-given wisdom, set magistrates and judges who may judge all the people who *are in the region* beyond the River, all such as know the laws of your God; and teach those who do not know *them.*

26 Whoever will not observe the law of your God and the law of the king, let judgment be executed speedily on him, whether *it be* death, or banishment, or confiscation of goods, or imprisonment.

27 Blessed *be* the LORD God of our fathers, who has put *such a thing* as this in the king's heart, to beautify the house of the LORD which *is* in Jerusalem,

28 and has extended mercy to me before the king and his counselors, and before all the king's mighty princes.

So I was encouraged, as the hand of the LORD my God *was* upon me; and I gathered chief men of Israel to go up with me.

Heads of Families Who Returned with Ezra

8 These *are* the heads of their fathers' houses, and *this is* the genealogy of those who went up with me from Babylon, in the reign of King Artaxerxes:

2 of the sons of Phinehas, Gershom; of the sons of Ithamar, Daniel; of the sons of David, Hattush;

3 of the sons of Shecaniah, of the sons of Parosh, Zechariah; and registered with him *were* one hundred and fifty males;

4 of the sons of Pahath-Moab, Elihoenai the son of Zerahiah, and with him two hundred males;

5 of the sons of Shechaniah, Ben-Jahaziel, and with him three hundred males;

6 of the sons of Adin, Ebed the son of Jonathan, and with him fifty males;

7 of the sons of Elam, Jeshaiah the son of Athaliah, and with him seventy males;

8 of the sons of Shephatiah, Zebadiah the son of Michael, and with him eighty males;

9 of the sons of Joab, Obadiah the son of Jehiel, and with him two hundred and eighteen males;

10 of the sons of Shelomith, Ben-Josiphiah, and with him one hundred and sixty males;

11 of the sons of Bebai, Zechariah the son of Bebai, and with him twenty-eight males;

12 of the sons of Azgad, Johanan the son of Hakkatan, and with him one hundred and ten males;

13 of the last sons of Adonikam, whose names *are* these—Eliphelet, Jeiel, and Shemaiah—and with them sixty males;

14 also of the sons of Bigvai, Uthai and Zabbud, and with them seventy males.

Servants for the Temple

15 Now I gathered them by the river that flows to Ahava, and we camped there three days. And I looked among the people and the priests, and found none of the sons of Levi there.

16 Then I sent for Eliezer, Ariel, Shemaiah, Elnathan, Jarib, Elnathan, Nathan, Zechariah, and Meshullam, leaders; also for Joiarib and Elnathan, men of understanding.

17 And I gave them a command for Iddo the chief man at the place Casiphia, and I told them what they should say to Iddo *and* his brethren the Nethinim at the place Casiphia—that they should bring us servants for the house of our God.

18 Then, by the good hand of our God upon us, they brought us a man of understanding, of the sons of Mahli the son of Levi, the son of Israel, namely Sherebiah, with his sons and brothers, eighteen men;

19 and Hashabiah, and with him Jeshaiah of the sons of Merari, his brothers and their sons, twenty men;

20 also of the Nethinim, whom David and the leaders had appointed for the service of the Levites, two hundred and

twenty Nethinim. All of them were designated by name.

Fasting and Prayer for Protection

21 Then I proclaimed a fast there at the river of Ahava, that we might humble ourselves before our God, to seek from Him the right way for us and our little ones and all our possessions.
22 For I was ashamed to request of the king an escort of soldiers and horsemen to help us against the enemy on the road, because we had spoken to the king, saying, "The hand of our God *is* upon all those for good who seek Him, but His power and His wrath *are* against all those who forsake Him."
23 So we fasted and entreated our God for this, and He answered our prayer.

Gifts for the Temple

24 Then I separated twelve of the leaders of the priests—Sherebiah, Hashabiah, and ten of their brethren with them—
25 and weighed out to them the silver, the gold, and the articles, the offering for the house of our God which the king and his counselors and his princes, and all Israel *who were* present, had offered.
26 I even weighed into their hand six hundred and fifty talents of silver, silver articles *weighing* one hundred talents, one hundred talents of gold,
27 twenty gold basins *worth* a thousand drachmas, and two vessels of fine polished bronze, precious as gold.
28 And I said to them, "You *are* holy to the LORD; the articles *are* holy also; and the silver and the gold *are* a freewill offering to the LORD God of your fathers.
29 "Watch and keep *them* until you weigh *them* before the leaders of the priests and the Levites and heads of the fathers' *houses* of Israel in Jerusalem, *in* the chambers of the house of the LORD."
30 So the priests and the Levites received the silver and the gold and the articles by weight, to bring *them* to Jerusalem to the house of our God.

The Return to Jerusalem

31 Then we departed from the river of Ahava on the twelfth *day* of the first month, to go to Jerusalem. And the hand of our God was upon us, and He delivered us from the hand of the enemy and from ambush along the road.

32 So we came to Jerusalem, and stayed there three days.
33 Now on the fourth day the silver and the gold and the articles were weighed in the house of our God by the hand of Meremoth the son of Uriah the priest, and with him *was* Eleazar the son of Phinehas; with them *were* the Levites, Jozabad the son of Jeshua and Noadiah the son of Binnui,
34 with the number *and* weight of everything. All the weight was written down at that time.
35 The children of those who had been carried away captive, who had come from the captivity, offered burnt offerings to the God of Israel: twelve bulls for all Israel, ninety-six rams, seventy-seven lambs, and twelve male goats *as* a sin offering. All *this was* a burnt offering to the LORD.
36 And they delivered the king's orders to the king's satraps and the governors *in the region* beyond the River. So they gave support to the people and the house of God.

Intermarriage with Pagans

9 When these things were done, the leaders came to me, saying, "The people of Israel and the priests and the Levites have not separated themselves from the peoples of the lands, with respect to the abominations of the Canaanites, the Hittites, the Perizzites, the Jebusites, the Ammonites, the Moabites, the Egyptians, and the Amorites.
2 "For they have taken some of their daughters *as wives* for themselves and their sons, so that the holy seed is intermingled with the peoples of *those* lands. Indeed, the hand of the leaders and rulers has been foremost in this trespass."
3 So when I heard this thing, I tore my garment and my robe, and plucked out some of the hair of my head and beard, and sat down astonished.
4 Then everyone who trembled at the words of the God of Israel assembled to me, because of the transgression of those who had been carried away captive, and I sat astonished until the evening sacrifice.
5 At the evening sacrifice I arose from my fasting; and having torn my garment and my robe, I fell on my knees and spread out my hands to the LORD my God,

6 and said, "O my God: I am too ashamed and humiliated to lift up my face to You, my God; for our iniquities have risen higher than *our* heads, and our guilt has grown up to the heavens.

7 "Since the days of our fathers to this day we *have been* very guilty, and for our iniquities we, our kings, *and* our priests have been delivered into the hand of the kings of the lands, to the sword, to captivity, to plunder, and to humiliation, as *it is* this day.

8 "And now for a little while grace has been *shown* from the LORD our God, to leave us a remnant to escape, and to give us a peg in His holy place, that our God may enlighten our eyes and give us a measure of revival in our bondage.

9 "For we *were* slaves. Yet our God did not forsake us in our bondage; but He extended mercy to us in the sight of the kings of Persia, to revive us, to repair the house of our God, to rebuild its ruins, and to give us a wall in Judah and Jerusalem.

10 "And now, O our God, what shall we say after this? For we have forsaken Your commandments,

11 "which You have commanded by Your servants the prophets, saying, 'The land which you are entering to possess is an unclean land, with the uncleanness of the peoples of the lands, with their abominations which have filled it from one end to another with their impurity.

12 'Now therefore, do not give your daughters as wives for their sons, nor take their daughters to your sons; and never seek their peace or prosperity, that you may be strong and eat the good of the land, and leave *it* as an inheritance to your children forever.'

13 "And after all that has come upon us for our evil deeds and for our great guilt, since You our God have punished us less than our iniquities *deserve*, and have given us *such* deliverance as this,

14 "should we again break Your commandments, and join in marriage with the people of these abominations? Would You not be angry with us until You had consumed *us*, so that *there would be* no remnant or survivor?

15 "O LORD God of Israel, You *are* righteous, for we are left as a remnant, as *it is* this day. Here we *are* before You, in

our guilt, though no one can stand before You because of this!"

Confession of Improper Marriages

10 Now while Ezra was praying, and while he was confessing, weeping, and bowing down before the house of God, a very large congregation of men, women, and children assembled to him from Israel; for the people wept very bitterly.

2 And Shechaniah the son of Jehiel, *one* of the sons of Elam, spoke up and said to Ezra, "We have trespassed against our God, and have taken pagan wives from the peoples of the land; yet now there is hope in Israel in spite of this.

3 "Now therefore, let us make a covenant with our God to put away all these wives and those who have been born to them, according to the counsel of my master and of those who tremble at the commandment of our God; and let it be done according to the law.

4 "Arise, for *this* matter *is* your *responsibility*. We also *will be* with you. Be of good courage, and do *it*."

5 Then Ezra arose, and made the leaders of the priests, the Levites, and all Israel swear an oath that they would do according to this word. So they swore an oath.

6 Then Ezra rose up from before the house of God, and went into the chamber of Jehohanan the son of Eliashib; and *when* he came there, he ate no bread and drank no water, for he mourned because of the guilt of those from the captivity.

7 And they issued a proclamation throughout Judah and Jerusalem to all the descendants of the captivity, that they must gather at Jerusalem,

8 and that whoever would not come within three days, according to the counsel of the leaders and elders, all his property would be confiscated, and he himself would be separated from the congregation of those from the captivity.

9 So all the men of Judah and Benjamin gathered at Jerusalem within three days. It *was* the ninth month, on the twentieth *day* of the month; and all the people sat in the open square of the house of God, trembling because of *this* matter and because of heavy rain.

10 Then Ezra the priest stood up and said to them, "You have transgressed and

have taken pagan wives, adding to the guilt of Israel.

11 "Now therefore, make confession to the LORD God of your fathers, and do His will; separate yourselves from the peoples of the land, and from the pagan wives."

12 Then all the congregation answered and said with a loud voice, "Yes! As you have said, so we must do.

13 "But *there are* many people; *it is* the season for heavy rain, and we are not able to stand outside. Nor *is this* the work of one or two days, for *there are* many of us who have transgressed in this matter.

14 "Please, let the leaders of our entire congregation stand; and let all those in our cities who have taken pagan wives come at appointed times, together with the elders and judges of their cities, until the fierce wrath of our God is turned away from us in this matter."

15 Only Jonathan the son of Asahel and Jahaziah the son of Tikvah opposed this, and Meshullam and Shabbethai the Levite gave them support.

16 Then the descendants of the captivity did so. And Ezra the priest, *with* certain heads of the fathers' *households*, were set apart by the fathers' *households*, each of them by name; and they sat down on the first day of the tenth month to examine the matter.

17 By the first day of the first month they finished *questioning* all the men who had taken pagan wives.

Pagan Wives Put Away

18 And among the sons of the priests who had taken pagan wives *the following* were found of the sons of Jeshua the son of Jozadak,[36] and his brothers: Maaseiah, Eliezer, Jarib, and Gedaliah.

19 And they gave their promise that they would put away their wives; and *being* guilty, *they presented* a ram of the flock as their trespass offering.

20 Also of the sons of Immer: Hanani and Zebadiah;

21 of the sons of Harim: Maaseiah, Elijah, Shemaiah, Jehiel, and Uzziah;

22 of the sons of Pashhur: Elioenai, Maaseiah, Ishmael, Nethaneel, Jozabad, and Elasah.

23 Also of the Levites: Jozabad, Shimei, Kelaiah (the same *is* Kelita), Pethahiah, Judah, and Eliezer.

24 Also of the singers: Eliashib; and of the gatekeepers: Shallum, Telem, and Uri.

25 And others of Israel: of the sons of Parosh: Ramiah, Jeziah, Malchiah, Mijamin, Eleazar, Malchijah, and Benaiah;

26 of the sons of Elam: Mattaniah, Zechariah, Jehiel, Abdi, Jeremoth, and Eliah;

27 of the sons of Zattu: Elioenai, Eliashib, Mattaniah, Jeremoth, Zabad, and Aziza;

28 of the sons of Bebai: Jehohanan, Hananiah, Zabbai, *and* Athlai;

29 of the sons of Bani: Meshullam, Malluch, Adaiah, Jashub, Sheal, *and* Ramoth;[37]

30 of the sons of Pahath-Moab: Adna, Chelal, Benaiah, Maaseiah, Mattaniah, Bezaleel, Binnui, and Manasseh;

31 *of* the sons of Harim: Eliezer, Ishijah, Malchijah, Shemaiah, Shimeon,

32 Benjamin, Malluch, *and* Shemariah;

33 of the sons of Hashum: Mattenai, Mattattah, Zabad, Eliphelet, Jeremai, Manasseh, *and* Shimei;

34 of the sons of Bani: Maadai, Amram, Uel,

35 Benaiah, Bedeiah, Cheluh,[38]

36 Vaniah, Meremoth, Eliashib,

37 Mattaniah, Mattenai, Jaasai,[39]

38 Bani, Binnui, Shimei,

39 Shelemiah, Nathan, Adaiah,

40 Machnadebai, Shashai, Sharai,

41 Azareel, Shelemiah, Shemariah,

42 Shallum, Amariah, *and* Joseph;

43 of the sons of Nebo: Jeiel, Mattithiah, Zabad, Zebina, Jaddai,[40] Joel, *and* Benaiah.

44 All these had taken pagan wives, and *some* of them had wives *by whom* they had children.

---

36 Spelled *Jehozadak* in 1 Chronicles 6:14   37 Or *Jeremoth*   38 Or *Cheluhi*, or *Cheluhu*
39 Or *Jaasu*   40 Or *Jaddu*

Introduction to Nehemiah

The Book of Nehemiah relates the story of common people committed to a great and uncommon goal—the rebuilding of God's temple!

The name Nehemiah means "the comfort of Yahweh." This book was written approximately 445 B.C., following the return of the Jewish people from exile in Babylon. Nehemiah faced the task of motivating the returning Jews to rebuild the temple and the walls of Jerusalem which had fallen into disrepair during the destruction wrought by Nebuchadnezzar in 587–586 B.C.

Nehemiah and the leaders asked the people of Jerusalem to tithe in the rebuilding of the temple and city walls. Elsewhere in Levitical law a tenth and sometimes a quarter of all one's possessions and income was the normal amount given back to God. This time, Nehemiah asked not for a percentage, but requested the people to give what they could and commit themselves to the rebuilding of the temple and city walls. Because of this approach, the people of Jerusalem became united in their efforts to complete the projects. As a result, they brought an overabundance of offerings. Nehemiah had to ask the people to cease bringing their gifts. They had more than they could use!

When people get together and believe in the completion of a dream, their giving will be endless and they can accomplish anything they choose!

Praise You the Lord, the Almighty, the King of Creation! Oh my soul praise Him, for He is your health and salvation! All you who hear, now to His temple draw near; join me in glad adoration!

The Book of

Nehemiah

Nehemiah Prays for His People

THE words of Nehemiah the son of Hachaliah.

It came to pass in the month of Chislev, *in* the twentieth year, as I was in Shushan[1] the citadel,

2 that Hanani one of my brethren came with men from Judah; and I asked them concerning the Jews who had escaped, who had survived the captivity, and concerning Jerusalem.

3 And they said to me, "The survivors who are left from the captivity in the province *are* there in great distress and reproach. The wall of Jerusalem *is* also broken down, and its gates *are* burned with fire."

4 So it was, when I heard these words, that I sat down and wept, and mourned *for many* days; I was fasting and praying before the God of heaven.

5 And I said: "I pray, Lord God of heaven, O great and awesome God, *You* who keep Your covenant and mercy with those who love You[2] and observe Your[3] commandments,

6 "please let Your ear be attentive and Your eyes open, that You may hear the prayer of Your servant which I pray before You now, day and night, for the children of Israel Your servants, and confess the sins of the children of Israel which we have sinned against You. Both my father's house and I have sinned.

7 "We have acted very corruptly against You, and have not kept the commandments, the statutes, nor the ordinances which You commanded Your servant Moses.

8 "Remember, I pray, the word that You commanded Your servant Moses, saying, '*If* you are unfaithful, I will scatter you among the nations,[4]

9 'but *if* you return to Me, and keep My commandments and do them, though some of you were cast out to the farthest part of the heavens, *yet* I will gather them

from there, and bring them to the place which I have chosen as a dwelling for My name.'[5]

10 "Now these *are* Your servants and Your people, whom You have redeemed by Your great power, and by Your strong hand.

11 "O Lord, I pray, please let Your ear be attentive to the prayer of Your servant, and to the prayer of Your servants who desire to fear Your name; and let Your servant prosper this day, I pray, and grant him mercy in the sight of this man." For I was the king's cupbearer.

Nehemiah Sent to Judah

2 And it came to pass in the month of Nisan, in the twentieth year of King Artaxerxes, *when* wine *was* before him, that I took the wine and gave it to the king. Now I had never been sad in his presence before.

2 Therefore the king said to me, "Why *is* your face sad, since you *are* not sick? This *is* nothing but sorrow of heart." Then I became dreadfully afraid,

3 and said to the king, "May the king live forever! Why should my face not be sad, when the city, the place of my fathers' tombs, *lies* waste, and its gates are burned with fire?"

4 Then the king said to me, "What do you request?" So I prayed to the God of heaven.

5 And I said to the king, "If it pleases the king, and if your servant has found favor in your sight, I ask that you send me to Judah, to the city of my fathers' tombs, that I may rebuild it."

6 So the king said to me (the queen also sitting beside him), "How long will your journey be? And when will you return?" So it pleased the king to send me; and I set him a time.

7 Furthermore I said to the king, "If it pleases the king, let letters be given to me for the governors *of the region* beyond the River,[6] that they must permit me to pass through till I come to Judah,

---

1 Or *Susa* 2 Or *Him* 3 Or *His* 4 Compare Leviticus 26:33
5 Compare Deuteronomy 30:2–5 6 That is, the Euphrates, and so elsewhere in this book

8 "and a letter to Asaph the keeper of the king's forest, that he must give me timber to make beams for the gates of the citadel which *pertains* to the temple,[7] for the city wall, and for the house that I will occupy." And the king granted *them* to me according to the good hand of my God upon me.

9 Then I went to the governors *in the region* beyond the River, and gave them the king's letters. Now the king had sent captains of the army and horsemen with me.

10 When Sanballat the Horonite and Tobiah the Ammonite official[8] heard *of it*, they were deeply disturbed that a man had come to seek the well-being of the children of Israel.

Nehemiah Views the Wall of Jerusalem

11 So I came to Jerusalem and was there three days.

12 Then I arose in the night, I and a few men with me; I told no one what my God had put in my heart to do at Jerusalem; nor was there any animal with me, except the one on which I rode.

13 And I went out by night through the Valley Gate to the Serpent Well and the Refuse Gate, and viewed the walls of Jerusalem which were broken down and its gates which were burned with fire.

14 Then I went on to the Fountain Gate and to the King's Pool, but *there was* no room for the animal *that was* under me to pass.

15 So I went up in the night by the valley, and viewed the wall; then I turned back and entered by the Valley Gate, and so returned.

16 And the officials did not know where I had gone or what I had done; I had not yet told the Jews, the priests, the nobles, the officials, or the others who did the work.

17 Then I said to them, "You see the distress that we *are* in, how Jerusalem *lies* waste, and its gates are burned with fire. Come and let us build the wall of Jerusalem, that we may no longer be a reproach."

18 And I told them of the hand of my God which had been good upon me, and also of the king's words that he had spoken to me. So they said, "Let us rise up

and build." Then they set their hands to *do this* good *work*.

19 But when Sanballat the Horonite, Tobiah the Ammonite official, and Geshem the Arab heard *of it*, they laughed us to scorn and despised us, and said, "What *is* this thing that you are doing? Will you rebel against the king?"

20 So I answered them, and said to them, "The God of heaven Himself will prosper us; therefore we His servants will arise and build, but you have no heritage or right or memorial in Jerusalem."

Rebuilding the Wall

3 Then Eliashib the high priest rose up with his brethren the priests and built the Sheep Gate; they consecrated it and hung its doors. They built as far as the Tower of the Hundred,[9] *and* consecrated it, then as far as the Tower of Hananeel.

2 Next to Eliashib[10] the men of Jericho built. And next to them Zaccur the son of Imri built.

3 Also the sons of Hassenaah built the Fish Gate; they laid its beams and hung its doors with its bolts and bars.

4 And next to them Meremoth the son of Urijah, the son of Koz,[11] made repairs. Next to them Meshullam the son of Berechiah, the son of Meshezabeel, made repairs. Next to them Zadok the son of Baana made repairs.

5 Next to them the Tekoites made repairs; but their nobles did not put their shoulders[12] to the work of their Lord.

6 Moreover Jehoiada the son of Paseah and Meshullam the son of Besodeiah repaired the Old Gate; they laid its beams and hung its doors, with its bolts and bars.

7 And next to them Melatiah the Gibeonite, Jadon the Meronothite, the men of Gibeon and Mizpah, repaired the residence[13] of the governor *of the region* beyond the River.

8 Next to him Uzziel the son of Harhaiah, one of the goldsmiths, made repairs. Also next to him Hananiah, one[14] of the perfumers, made repairs; and they fortified Jerusalem as far as the Broad Wall.

9 And next to them Rephaiah the son of Hur, leader of half the district of Jerusalem, made repairs.

---

7 Literally *house* 8 Literally *servant*, and so elsewhere in this book 9 Hebrew *Hammeah*, also at 12:39 10 Literally *him* 11 Or *Hakkoz* 12 Literally *necks* 13 Literally *throne* 14 Literally *the son*

10 Next to them Jedaiah the son of Harumaph made repairs in front of his house. And next to him Hattush the son of Hashabniah made repairs.
11 Malchijah the son of Harim and Hashub the son of Pahath-Moab repaired another section, as well as the Tower of the Ovens.
12 And next to him was Shallum the son of Hallohesh, leader of half the district of Jerusalem; he and his daughters made repairs.
13 Hanun and the inhabitants of Zanoah repaired the Valley Gate. They built it, hung its doors with its bolts and bars, and *repaired* a thousand cubits of the wall as far as the Refuse Gate.
14 Malchijah the son of Rechab, leader of the district of Beth Haccerem, repaired the Refuse Gate; he built it and hung its doors with its bolts and bars.
15 Shallun the son of Col-Hozeh, leader of the district of Mizpah, repaired the Fountain Gate; he built it, covered it, hung its doors with its bolts and bars, and repaired the wall of the Pool of Shelah by the King's Garden, as far as the stairs that go down from the City of David.
16 After him Nehemiah the son of Azbuk, leader of half the district of Beth Zur, made repairs as far as *the place* in front of the tombs of David, to the manmade pool, and as far as the House of the Mighty.
17 After him the Levites, *under* Rehum the son of Bani, made repairs. Next to him Hashabiah, leader of half the district of Keilah, made repairs for his district.
18 After him their brethren, *under* Bavai the son of Henadad, leader of the *other* half of the district of Keilah, made repairs.
19 And next to him Ezer the son of Jeshua, the leader of Mizpah, repaired another section in front of the Ascent to the Armory at the buttress.
20 After him Baruch the son of Zabbai[15] diligently repaired the other section, from the buttress to the door of the house of Eliashib the high priest.
21 After him Meremoth the son of Urijah, the son of Koz,[16] repaired another section, from the door of the house of Eliashib to the end of the house of Eliashib.

22 And after him the priests, the men of the plain, made repairs.
23 After him Benjamin and Hasshub made repairs opposite their house. After them Azariah the son of Maaseiah, the son of Ananiah, made repairs by his house.
24 After him Binnui the son of Henadad repaired another section, from the house of Azariah to the buttress, even as far as the corner.
25 Palal the son of Uzai *made repairs* opposite the buttress, and on the tower which projects from the king's upper house that *was* by the court of the prison. After him Pedaiah the son of Parosh *made repairs.*
26 Moreover the Nethinim who dwelt in Ophel *made repairs* as far as *the place* in front of the Water Gate toward the east, and on the projecting tower.
27 After them the Tekoites repaired another section, next to the great projecting tower, and as far as the wall of Ophel.
28 Beyond the Horse Gate the priests made repairs, each in front of his *own* house.
29 After them Zadok the son of Immer made repairs in front of his *own* house. After him Shemaiah the son of Shechaniah, the keeper of the East Gate, made repairs.
30 After him Hananiah the son of Shelemiah, and Hanun, the sixth son of Zalaph, repaired another section. After him Meshullam the son of Berechiah made repairs in front of his dwelling.
31 After him Malchijah, one of the goldsmiths, made repairs as far as the house of the Nethinim and of the merchants, in front of the Miphkad[17] Gate, and as far as the upper room at the corner.
32 And between the upper room at the corner, as far as the Sheep Gate, the goldsmiths and the merchants made repairs.

The Wall Defended Against Enemies

4 But it so happened, when Sanballat heard that we were rebuilding the wall, that he was furious and very indignant, and mocked the Jews.
2 And he spoke before his brethren and the army of Samaria, and said, "What are these feeble Jews doing? Will they fortify themselves? Will they offer sacrifices? Will they complete it in a day? Will they

---

15 A few Hebrew manuscripts, Syriac, and Vulgate read *Zaccai.* 16 Or *Hakkoz*
17 Literally *Inspection* or *Recruiting*

revive the stones from the heaps of rubbish—*stones* that are burned?"

3 Now Tobiah the Ammonite *was* beside him, and he said, "Whatever they build, if even a fox goes up *on it*, he will break down their stone wall."

4 Hear, O our God, for we are despised; turn their reproach on their own heads, and give them as plunder to a land of captivity!

5 Do not cover their iniquity, and do not let their sin be blotted out from before You; for they have provoked *You* to anger before the builders.

6 So we built the wall, and the entire wall was joined together up to half its *height*, for the people had a mind to work.

7 Now it happened, when Sanballat, Tobiah, the Arabs, the Ammonites, and the Ashdodites heard that the walls of Jerusalem were being restored and the gaps were beginning to be closed, that they became very angry,

8 and all of them conspired together to come *and* attack Jerusalem and create confusion.

9 Nevertheless we made our prayer to our God, and because of them we set a watch against them day and night.

10 Then Judah said, "The strength of the laborers is failing, and *there is* so much rubbish that we are not able to build the wall."

11 And our adversaries said, "They will neither know nor see anything, till we come into their midst and kill them and cause the work to cease."

12 So it was, when the Jews who dwelt near them came, that they told us ten times, "From whatever place you turn, *they will be* upon us."

13 Therefore I positioned *men* behind the lower parts of the wall, at the openings; and I set the people according to their families, with their swords, their spears, and their bows.

14 And I looked, and arose and said to the nobles, to the leaders, and to the rest of the people, "Do not be afraid of them. Remember the Lord, great and awesome, and fight for your brethren, your sons, your daughters, your wives, and your houses."

15 And it happened, when our enemies heard that it was known to us, and *that* God had brought their counsel to nothing, that all of us returned to the wall, everyone to his work.

16 So it was, from that time on, *that* half of my servants worked at construction, while the other half held the spears, the shields, the bows, and *wore* armor; and the leaders *were* behind all the house of Judah.

17 Those who built on the wall, and those who carried burdens, loaded themselves so that with one hand they worked at construction, and with the other held a weapon.

18 Every one of the builders had his sword girded at his side as he built. And the one who sounded the trumpet *was* beside me.

19 Then I said to the nobles, the rulers, and the rest of the people, "The work *is* great and extensive, and we are separated far from one another on the wall.

20 "*Therefore*, wherever you hear the sound of the trumpet, rally to us there. Our God will fight for us."

21 So we labored in the work, and half of the men[18] held the spears from daybreak until the stars appeared.

22 At the same time I also said to the people, "Let each man and his servant stay at night in Jerusalem, that they may be our guard by night and a working party by day."

23 So neither I, my brethren, my servants, nor the men of the guard who followed me took off our clothes, *except* that everyone took them off for washing.

Nehemiah Deals with Oppression

5 And there was a great outcry of the people and their wives against their Jewish brethren.

2 For there were those who said, "We, our sons, and our daughters *are* many; therefore let us get grain *for them*, that we may eat and live."

3 There were also *some* who said, "We have mortgaged our lands and vineyards and houses, that we might buy grain because of the famine."

4 There were also those who said, "We have borrowed money for the king's tax *on* our lands and vineyards.

5 "Yet now our flesh *is* as the flesh of our brethren, our children as their children; and indeed we are forcing our sons and our daughters to be slaves, and *some* of our daughters are brought into slavery

18 Literally *them*

already. It is not in our power *to redeem them,* for other men have our lands and vineyards."

6 And I became very angry when I heard their outcry and these words.

7 After serious thought, I rebuked the nobles and rulers, and said to them, "Each of you is exacting usury from his brother." So I called a great assembly against them.

8 And I said to them, "According to our ability we have redeemed our Jewish brethren who were sold to the nations. Now indeed, will you even sell your brethren? Or should they be sold to us?" Then they were silenced and found nothing *to say.*

9 Then I said, "What you are doing *is* not good. Should you not walk in the fear of our God because of the reproach of the nations, our enemies?"

10 "I also, *with* my brethren and my servants, am lending them money and grain. Please, let us stop this usury!

11 "Restore now to them, even this day, their lands, their vineyards, their olive groves, and their houses, also the hundredth *part* of the money and the grain, the new wine and the oil, that you have charged them."

12 So they said, "We will restore *it,* and will require nothing from them; we will do as you say." Then I called the priests, and required an oath from them that they would do according to this promise.

13 Then I shook out the fold of my garment[19] and said, "So may God shake out each man from his house, and from his property, who does not perform this promise. Even thus may he be shaken out and emptied." And all the congregation said, "Amen!" and praised the LORD. Then the people did according to this promise.

The Generosity of Nehemiah

14 Moreover, from the time that I was appointed to be their governor in the land of Judah, from the twentieth year until the thirty-second year of King Artaxerxes, twelve years, neither I nor my brothers ate the governor's provisions.

15 But the former governors who *had been* before me laid burdens on the people, and took from them bread and wine, besides forty shekels of silver; yes, even

their servants bore rule over the people, but I did not do so, because of the fear of God.

16 Indeed, I also continued the work on this wall, and we did not buy any land. All my servants *were* gathered there for the work.

17 Moreover *there were* at my table one hundred and fifty Jews and rulers, besides those who came to us from the nations around us.

18 Now *that* which was prepared *for me* daily *was* one ox *and* six choice sheep; also fowl were prepared for me, and once every ten days an abundance of all kinds of wine; yet in spite of this I did not demand the governor's provisions, because the bondage was heavy on this people.

19 Remember me, my God, for good, *according to* all that I have done for this people.

Conspiracy Against Nehemiah

6 Now it happened when Sanballat, Tobiah, Geshem the Arab, and the rest of our enemies heard that I had rebuilt the wall, and *that* there were no breaks left in it (though at that time I had not hung the doors in the gates),

2 that Sanballat and Geshem sent to me, saying, "Come, let us meet together in *one of* the villages in the plain of Ono." But they thought to do me harm.

3 So I sent messengers to them, saying, "I *am* doing a great work, so that I cannot come down. Why should the work cease while I leave it and go down to you?"

4 But they sent me this message four times, and I answered them in the same manner.

5 Then Sanballat sent his servant to me as before, the fifth time, with an open letter in his hand.

6 In it *was* written:

It is reported among the nations, and Geshem[20] says, *that* you and the Jews plan to rebel; therefore, according to these rumors, you are rebuilding the wall, that you may be their king.

7 And you have also appointed prophets to proclaim concerning you at Jerusalem, saying, '*There is* a king in Judah!' Now these matters will be reported to the king. So come, therefore, and let us take counsel together.

19 Literally *my lap*   20 Hebrew *Gashmu*

8 Then I sent to him, saying, "No such things as you say are being done, but you invent them in your own heart."

9 For they all *were trying to* make us afraid, saying, "Their hands will be weakened in the work, and it will not be done."

Now therefore, O God, strengthen my hands.

10 Afterward I came to the house of Shemaiah the son of Delaiah, the son of Mehetabeel, who *was* a secret informer; and he said, "Let us meet together in the house of God, within the temple, and let us close the doors of the temple, for they are coming to kill you; indeed, at night they will come to kill you."

11 And I said, "Should such a man as I flee? And who *is there* such as I who would go into the temple to save his life? I will not go in!"

12 Then I perceived that God had not sent him at all, but that he pronounced *this* prophecy against me because Tobiah and Sanballat had hired him.

13 For this reason he *was* hired, that I should be afraid and act that way and sin, so *that* they might have *occasion* for an evil report, that they might reproach me.

14 My God, remember Tobiah and Sanballat, according to these their works, and the prophetess Noadiah and the rest of the prophets who would have made me afraid.

The Wall Completed

15 So the wall was finished on the twenty-fifth *day* of *the month* of Elul, in fifty-two days.

16 And it happened, when all our enemies heard *of it,* and all the nations around us saw *these things,* that they were very disheartened in their own eyes; for they perceived that this work was done by our God.

17 Moreover in those days the nobles of Judah sent many letters to Tobiah, and *the letters of* Tobiah came to them.

18 For many in Judah were pledged to him, because he was the son-in-law of Shechaniah the son of Arah, and his son Jehohanan had married the daughter of Meshullam the son of Berechiah.

19 Also they reported his good deeds before me, and reported my words to him. *And* Tobiah sent letters to frighten me.

7 Then it was, when the wall was built and I had hung the doors, when the gatekeepers, the singers, and the Levites had been appointed,

2 that I gave the charge of Jerusalem to my brother Hanani, and Hananiah the leader of the citadel, for he *was* a faithful man and feared God more than many.

3 And I said to them, "Do not let the gates of Jerusalem be opened until the sun is hot; and while they stand *guard,* let them shut the doors and bar *them*; and appoint guards from among the inhabitants of Jerusalem, one at his watch station and another in front of his own house."

The Captives Who Returned to Jerusalem

4 Now the city *was* large and spacious, but the people in it *were* few, and the houses *were* not rebuilt.

5 Then my God put it into my heart to gather the nobles, the rulers, and the people, that they might be registered by genealogy. And I found a register of the genealogy of those who had come up in the first *return,* and found written in it:

6 These[21] *are* the people of the province who came back from the captivity, of those who had been carried away, whom Nebuchadnezzar the king of Babylon had carried away *captive,* and who returned to Jerusalem and Judah, everyone to his *own* city.

7 Those who came with Zerubbabel *were* Jeshua, Nehemiah, Azariah, Raamiah, Nahamani, Mordecai, Bilshan, Mispereth,[22] Bigvai, Nehum, and Baanah.

The number of the men of the people of Israel:

8 the children of Parosh, two thousand one hundred and seventy-two;

9 the children of Shephatiah, three hundred and seventy-two;

10 the children of Arah, six hundred and fifty-two;

11 the children of Pahath-Moab, of the children of Jeshua and Joab, two thousand eight hundred and eighteen;

12 the children of Elam, one thousand two hundred and fifty-four;

13 the children of Zattu, eight hundred and forty-five;

21 Verses 6–72 (compare Ezra 2:1–70)   22 Spelled *Mispar* in Ezra 2:2

14 the children of Zaccai, seven hundred and sixty;
15 the children of Binnui,[23] six hundred and forty-eight;
16 the children of Bebai, six hundred and twenty-eight;
17 the children of Azgad, two thousand three hundred and twenty-two;
18 the children of Adonikam, six hundred and sixty-seven;
19 the children of Bigvai, two thousand and sixty-seven;
20 the children of Adin, six hundred and fifty-five;
21 the children of Ater of Hezekiah, ninety-eight;
22 the children of Hashum, three hundred and twenty-eight;
23 the children of Bezai, three hundred and twenty-four;
24 the children of Hariph,[24] one hundred and twelve;
25 the children of Gibeon,[25] ninety-five;
26 the men of Bethlehem and Netophah, one hundred and eighty-eight;
27 the men of Anathoth, one hundred and twenty-eight;
28 the men of Beth Azmaveth,[26] forty-two;
29 the men of Kirjath Jearim, Chephirah, and Beeroth, seven hundred and forty-three;
30 the men of Ramah and Geba, six hundred and twenty-one;
31 the men of Michmas, one hundred and twenty-two;
32 the men of Bethel and Ai, one hundred and twenty-three;
33 the men of the other Nebo, fifty-two;
34 the children of the other Elam, one thousand two hundred and fifty-four;
35 the children of Harim, three hundred and twenty;
36 the children of Jericho, three hundred and forty-five;
37 the children of Lod, Hadid, and Ono, seven hundred and twenty-one;
38 the children of Senaah, three thousand nine hundred and thirty.
39 The priests: the children of Jedaiah, of the house of Jeshua, nine hundred and seventy-three;

40 the children of Immer, one thousand and fifty-two;
41 the children of Pashhur, one thousand two hundred and forty-seven;
42 the children of Harim, one thousand and seventeen.
43 The Levites: the children of Jeshua, of Kadmiel, *and* of the children of Hodevah,[27] seventy-four.
44 The singers: the children of Asaph, one hundred and forty-eight.
45 The gatekeepers: the children of Shallum, the children of Ater, the children of Talmon, the children of Akkub, the children of Hatita, the children of Shobai, one hundred and thirty-eight.
46 The Nethinim: the children of Ziha, the children of Hasupha, the children of Tabbaoth,
47 the children of Keros, the children of Sia,[28] the children of Padon,
48 the children of Lebana,[29] the children of Hagaba,[30] the children of Salmai,[31]
49 the children of Hanan, the children of Giddel, the children of Gahar,
50 the children of Reaiah, the children of Rezin, the children of Nekoda,
51 the children of Gazzam, the children of Uzza, the children of Paseah,
52 the children of Besai, the children of Meunim, the children of Nephishesim,[32]
53 the children of Bakbuk, the children of Hakupha, the children of Harhur,
54 the children of Bazlith,[33] the children of Mehida, the children of Harsha,
55 the children of Barkos, the children of Sisera, the children of Tamah,
56 the children of Neziah, and the children of Hatipha.
57 The children of Solomon's servants: the children of Sotai, the children of Sophereth, the children of Perida,[34]
58 the children of Jaala, the children of Darkon, the children of Giddel,
59 the children of Shephatiah, the children of Hattil, the children of Pochereth of Zebaim, and the children of Amon.[35]
60 All the Nethinim, and the children of

23 Spelled *Bani* in Ezra 2:10   24 Called *Jorah* in Ezra 2:18   25 Called *Gibbar* in Ezra 2:20
26 Called *Azmaveth* in Ezra 2:24   27 Spelled *Hodaviah* in Ezra 2:40   28 Spelled *Siaha* in Ezra 2:44
29 Masoretic Text reads *Lebanah*.   30 Masoretic Text reads *Hogabah*.   31 Or *Shalmai*, or *Shamlai*
32 Spelled *Nephusim* in Ezra 2:50   33 Spelled *Bazluth* in Ezra 2:52
34 Spelled *Peruda* in Ezra 2:55   35 Spelled *Ami* in Ezra 2:57

Solomon's servants, *were* three hundred and ninety-two.

61 And these *were* the ones who came up from Tel Melah, Tel Harsha, Cherub, Addon,[36] and Immer, but they could not identify their father's house nor their lineage, whether they *were* of Israel:

62 the children of Delaiah, the children of Tobiah, the children(of Nekoda, six hundred and forty-two;

63 and of the priests: the children of Habaiah, the children of Koz,[37] the children of Barzillai, who took a wife of the daughters of Barzillai the Gileadite, and was called by their name.

64 These sought their listing *among* those who were registered by genealogy, but it was not found; therefore they were excluded from the priesthood as defiled.

65 And the governor said to them that they should not eat of the most holy things till a priest could consult with the Urim and Thummim.

66 Altogether the whole congregation *was* forty-two thousand three hundred and sixty,

67 besides their male and female servants, of whom *there were* seven thousand three hundred and thirty-seven; and they had two hundred and forty-five men and women singers.

68 Their horses were seven hundred and thirty-six, their mules two hundred and forty-five,

69 *their* camels four hundred and thirty-five, *and* donkeys six thousand seven hundred and twenty.

70 And some of the heads of the fathers' houses gave to the work. The governor gave to the treasury one thousand gold drachmas, fifty basins, and five hundred and thirty priestly garments.

71 Some of the heads of the fathers' *houses* gave to the treasury of the work twenty thousand gold drachmas, and two thousand two hundred silver minas.

72 And *that* which the rest of the people gave *was* twenty thousand gold drachmas, two thousand silver minas, and sixty-seven priestly garments.

73 So the priests, the Levites, the gatekeepers, the singers, *some* of the people, the Nethinim, and all Israel dwelt in their cities.

Ezra Reads the Law

When the seventh month came, the children of Israel *were* in their cities.

8 Now all the people gathered together as one man in the open square that *was* in front of the Water Gate; and they told Ezra the scribe to bring the Book of the Law of Moses, which the LORD had commanded Israel.

2 So Ezra the priest brought the Law before the congregation, of men and women and all who *could* hear with understanding, on the first day of the seventh month.

3 Then he read from it in the open square that *was* in front of the Water Gate from morning until midday, before the men and women and those who could understand; and the ears of all the people *were attentive* to the Book of the Law.

4 So Ezra the scribe stood on a platform of wood which they had made for the purpose; and beside him, at his right hand, stood Mattithiah, Shema, Anaiah, Urijah, Hilkiah, and Maaseiah; and at his left hand Pedaiah, Mishael, Malchijah, Hashum, Hashbadana, Zechariah, *and* Meshullam.

5 And Ezra opened the book in the sight of all the people, for he was *standing* above all the people; and when he opened it, all the people stood up.

6 And Ezra blessed the LORD, the great God. Then all the people answered, "Amen, Amen!" while lifting up their hands. And they bowed their heads and worshiped the LORD with *their* faces to the ground.

7 Also Jeshua, Bani, Sherebiah, Jamin, Akkub, Shabbethai, Hodijah, Maaseiah, Kelita, Azariah, Jozabad, Hanan, Pelaiah, and the Levites, helped the people to understand the Law; and the people *stood* in their place.

8 So they read distinctly from the book, in the Law of God; and they gave the sense, and helped *them* to understand the reading.

9 And Nehemiah, who *was* the governor, Ezra the priest *and* scribe, and the Levites who taught the people said to all the people, "This day *is* holy to the LORD

---

36 Spelled *Addan* in Ezra 2:59   37 Or *Hakkoz*

your God; do not mourn nor weep." For all the people wept, when they heard the words of the Law.

10 Then he said to them, "Go your way, eat the fat, drink the sweet, and send portions to those for whom nothing is prepared; for *this* day *is* holy to our LORD. Do not sorrow, for the joy of the LORD is your strength."

11 So the Levites quieted all the people, saying, "Be still, for the day *is* holy; do not be grieved."

12 And all the people went their way to eat and drink, to send portions and rejoice greatly, because they understood the words that were declared to them.

The Feast of Tabernacles

13 Now on the second day the heads of the fathers' *houses* of all the people, with the priests and Levites, were gathered to Ezra the scribe, in order to understand the words of the Law.

14 And they found written in the Law, which the LORD had commanded by Moses, that the children of Israel should dwell in booths during the feast of the seventh month,

15 and that they should announce and proclaim in all their cities and in Jerusalem, saying, "Go out to the mountain, and bring olive branches, branches of oil trees, myrtle branches, palm branches, and branches of leafy trees, to make booths, as *it is* written."

16 Then the people went out and brought *them* and made themselves booths, each one on the roof of his house, or in their courtyards or the courts of the house of God, and in the open square of the Water Gate and in the open square of the Gate of Ephraim.

17 So the whole congregation of those who had returned from the captivity made booths and sat under the booths; for since the days of Joshua the son of Nun until that day the children of Israel had not done so. And there was very great gladness.

18 Also day by day, from the first day until the last day, he read from the Book of the Law of God. And they kept the feast seven days; and on the eighth day *there was* a sacred assembly, according to the *prescribed* manner.

The People Confess Their Sins

9 Now on the twenty-fourth day of this month the children of Israel were assembled with fasting, in sackcloth, and with dust on their heads.[38]

2 Then those of Israelite lineage separated themselves from all foreigners; and they stood and confessed their sins and the iniquities of their fathers.

3 And they stood up in their place and read from the Book of the Law of the LORD their God *for one*-fourth of the day; and *for another* fourth they confessed and worshiped the LORD their God.

4 Then Jeshua, Bani, Kadmiel, Shebaniah, Bunni, Sherebiah, Bani, *and* Chenani stood on the stairs of the Levites and cried out with a loud voice to the LORD their God.

5 Then the Levites, Jeshua, Kadmiel, Bani, Hashabniah, Sherebiah, Hodijah, Shebaniah, *and* Pethahiah, said:

"Stand up *and* bless the LORD your God
Forever and ever!

"Blessed be Your glorious name,
Which is exalted above all blessing
    and praise!
6 You alone *are* the LORD;
You have made heaven,
The heaven of heavens,
    with all their host,
The earth and all *things* on it,
The seas and all that is in them,
And You preserve them all.
The host of heaven worships You.

7 "You *are* the LORD God,
Who chose Abram,
And brought him out of Ur
    of the Chaldees,
And gave him the name Abraham;
8 You found his heart faithful
    before You,
And made a covenant with him
To give the land of the Canaanites,
The Hittites, the Amorites,
The Perizzites, the Jebusites,
And the Girgashites—
To give *it* to his descendants.
You have performed Your words,
For You *are* righteous.

9 "You saw the affliction
    of our fathers in Egypt,
And heard their cry by the Red Sea.

38 Literally *earth on them*

10 You showed signs and wonders
    against Pharaoh,
Against all his servants,
And against all the people of his land.
For You knew that they acted proudly
    against them.
So You made a name for Yourself,
    as *it is* this day.
11 And You divided the sea before them,
So that they went through the midst
    of the sea on the dry land;
And their persecutors You threw
    into the deep,
As a stone into the mighty waters.
12 Moreover You led them by day
    with a cloudy pillar,
And by night with a pillar of fire,
To give them light on the road
Which they should travel.

13 "You came down also on Mount Sinai,
And spoke with them from heaven,
And gave them just ordinances
    and true laws,
Good statutes and commandments.
14 You made known to them Your
    holy Sabbath,
And commanded them precepts,
    statutes and laws,
By the hand of Moses Your servant.
15 You gave them bread from heaven
    for their hunger,
And brought them water out of the
    rock for their thirst,
And told them to go in to possess
    the land
Which You had sworn to give them.

16 "But they and our fathers acted proudly,
Hardened their necks,
And did not heed Your
    commandments.
17 They refused to obey,
And they were not mindful
    of Your wonders
That You did among them.
But they hardened their necks,
And in their rebellion
They appointed a leader
To return to their bondage.
But You *are* God,
Ready to pardon,
Gracious and merciful,
Slow to anger,
Abundant in kindness,
And did not forsake them.

18 "Even when they made a molded calf
    for themselves,

And said, 'This *is* your god
That brought you up out of Egypt,'
And worked great provocations,
19 Yet in Your manifold mercies
You did not forsake them in the
    wilderness.
The pillar of the cloud did not depart
    from them by day,
To lead them on the road;
Nor the pillar of fire by night,
To show them light,
And the way they should go.
20 You also gave Your good Spirit
    to instruct them,
And did not withhold Your manna
    from their mouth,
And gave them water for their thirst.
21 Forty years You sustained them
    in the wilderness,
So that they lacked nothing;
Their clothes did not wear out[39]
And their feet did not swell.

22 "Moreover You gave them kingdoms
    and nations,
And divided them into districts.[40]
So they took possession of the land
    of Sihon,
The land of the king of Heshbon,
And the land of Og king of Bashan.
23 You also multiplied their children as
    the stars of heaven,
And brought them into the land
Which You had told their fathers
To go in and possess.
24 So the people went in
And possessed the land;
You subdued before them the
    inhabitants of the land,
The Canaanites,
And gave them into their hands,
With their kings
And the people of the land,
That they might do with them
    as they would.
25 And they took strong cities
    and a rich land,
And possessed houses full of all goods,
Cisterns *already* dug, vineyards,
    olive groves,
And fruit trees in abundance.
So they ate and were filled
    and grew fat,
And delighted themselves
    in Your great goodness.

26 "Nevertheless they were disobedient
And rebelled against You,
Cast Your law behind their backs

39 Compare Deuteronomy 29:5   40 Literally *corners*

And killed Your prophets,
who testified against them
To turn them to Yourself;
And they worked great provocations.
27 Therefore You delivered them into the
hand of their enemies,
Who oppressed them;
And in the time of their trouble,
When they cried to You,
You heard from heaven;
And according to Your
abundant mercies
You gave them deliverers
who saved them
From the hand of their enemies.

28 "But after they had rest,
They again did evil before You.
Therefore You left them in the hand
of their enemies,
So that they had dominion over them;
Yet when they returned
and cried out to You,
You heard from heaven;
And many times You delivered them
according to Your mercies,
29 And testified against them,
That You might bring them back
to Your law.
Yet they acted proudly,
And did not heed Your
commandments,
But sinned against Your judgments,
'Which if a man does,
he shall live by them.'[41]
And they shrugged their shoulders,
Stiffened their necks,
And would not hear.
30 Yet for many years
You had patience with them,
And testified against them by Your
Spirit in Your prophets.
Yet they would not listen;
Therefore You gave them into the hand
of the peoples of the lands.
31 Nevertheless in Your great mercy
You did not utterly consume them
nor forsake them;
For You are God,
gracious and merciful.

32 "Now therefore, our God,
The great, the mighty,
and awesome God,
Who keeps covenant and mercy:
Do not let all the trouble seem small
before You
That has come upon us,
Our kings and our princes,
Our priests and our prophets,

Our fathers and on all Your people,
From the days of the kings of Assyria
until this day.
33 However You are just in all
that has befallen us;
For You have dealt faithfully,
But we have done wickedly.
34 Neither our kings nor our princes,
Our priests nor our fathers,
Have kept Your law,
Nor heeded Your commandments
and Your testimonies,
With which You testified against them.
35 For they have not served You
in their kingdom,
Or in the many good things
that You gave them,
Or in the large and rich land
which You set before them;
Nor did they turn from their wicked
works.

36 "Here we are, servants today!
And the land that You gave
to our fathers,
To eat its fruit and its good things,
Here we are, servants in it!
37 And it yields much increase
to the kings
You have set over us,
Because of our sins;
Also they have dominion over our
bodies and our cattle
At their pleasure;
And we are in great distress.

38 "And because of all this,
We make a sure covenant, and write it;
And our leaders and our Levites
and our priests seal it."

The People Who Sealed the Covenant

10 Now those who placed their seal
on the document were:
Nehemiah the governor, the son of
Hacaliah, and Zedekiah,
2 Seraiah, Azariah, Jeremiah,
3 Pashhur, Amariah, Malchijah,
4 Hattush, Shebaniah, Malluch,
5 Harim, Meremoth, Obadiah,
6 Daniel, Ginnethon, Baruch,
7 Meshullam, Abijah, Mijamin,
8 Maaziah, Bilgai, and Shemaiah.
These were the priests.
9 The Levites: Jeshua the son of Aza-
niah, Binnui of the sons of Henadad, and
Kadmiel.
10 Their brethren: Shebaniah, Hodijah, Kelita, Pelaiah, Hanan,

41 Compare Leviticus 18:5

11 Micha, Rehob, Hashabiah,
12 Zaccur, Sherebiah, Shebaniah,
13 Hodijah, Bani, *and* Beninu.
14 The leaders of the people: Parosh, Pahath-Moab, Elam, Zattu, Bani,
15 Bunni, Azgad, Bebai,
16 Adonijah, Bigvai, Adin,
17 Ater, Hezekiah, Azzur,
18 Hodijah, Hashum, Bezai,
19 Hariph, Anathoth, Nebai,
20 Magpiash, Meshullam, Hezir,
21 Meshezabeel, Zadok, Jaddua,
22 Pelatiah, Hanan, Anaiah,
23 Hoshea, Hananiah, Hasshub,
24 Hallohesh, Pilha, Shobek,
25 Rehum, Hashabnah, Maaseiah,
26 Ahijah, Hanan, Anan,
27 Malluch, Harim, *and* Baanah.

The Covenant That Was Sealed

28 Now the rest of the people (the priests, the Levites, the gatekeepers, the singers, the Nethinim, and all those who had separated themselves from the peoples of the lands to the Law of God, their wives, their sons, and their daughters, everyone who had knowledge and understanding),
29 they joined with their brethren, their nobles, and entered into a curse and an oath to walk in God's Law, which was given by Moses the servant of God, and to observe and do all the commandments of the LORD our Lord, and His ordinances and His statutes—
30 that we would not give our daughters as wives to the peoples of the land, nor take their daughters for our sons;
31 *that if* the peoples of the land bring wares or any grain to sell on the Sabbath day, we would not buy it from them on the Sabbath, or on a holy day; and *that* we would forego the seventh year's *produce* and the exaction of every debt.
32 Also we made ordinances for ourselves, to exact from ourselves yearly one-third of a shekel for the service of the house of our God:
33 for the showbread, for the regular grain offering, for the regular burnt offering of the Sabbaths, the New Moons, and the set feasts; for the holy things, for the sin offerings to make atonement for Israel, and all the work of the house of our God.
34 We cast lots among the priests, the Levites, and the people, for *bringing* the wood offering into the house of our God, according to our fathers' houses, at the appointed times year by year, to burn on the altar of the LORD our God as *it is* written in the Law.
35 And *we made ordinances* to bring the firstfruits of our ground and the firstfruits of all fruit of all trees, year by year, to the house of the LORD;
36 to bring the firstborn of our sons and our cattle, as *it is* written in the Law, and the firstlings of our herds and our flocks, to the house of our God, to the priests who minister in the house of our God;
37 to bring the firstfruits of our dough, our offerings, the fruit from all kinds of trees, *the* new wine and oil, to the priests, to the storerooms of the house of our God; and to bring the tithes of our land to the Levites, for the Levites should receive the tithes in all our farming communities.
38 And the priest, the descendant of Aaron, shall be with the Levites when the Levites receive tithes; and the Levites shall bring up a tenth of the tithes to the house of our God, to the rooms of the storehouse.
39 For the children of Israel and the children of Levi shall bring the offering of the grain, of the new wine and the oil, to the storerooms where the articles of the sanctuary *are*, *where* the priests who minister and the gatekeepers and the singers *are*; and we will not neglect the house of our God.

The People Dwelling in Jerusalem

11 Now the leaders of the people dwelt at Jerusalem; the rest of the people cast lots to bring one out of ten to dwell in Jerusalem, the holy city, and nine-tenths *were to dwell* in *other* cities.
2 And the people blessed all the men who willingly offered themselves to dwell at Jerusalem.
3 Now these *are* the heads of the province who dwelt in Jerusalem. (But in the cities of Judah everyone dwelt in his own possession in their cities—Israelites, priests, Levites, Nethinim, and descendants of Solomon's servants.)
4 Also in Jerusalem dwelt *certain* of the children of Judah and of the children of Benjamin.

The children of Judah: Athaiah the son of Uzziah, the son of Zechariah, the son of Amariah, the son of Shephatiah, the son of Mahalaleel, of the children of Perez;

5 and Maaseiah the son of Baruch, the son of Col-Hozeh, the son of Hazaiah, the son of Adaiah, the son of Joiarib, the son of Zechariah, the son of Shiloni.

6 All the sons of Perez who dwelt at Jerusalem *were* four hundred and sixty-eight valiant men.

7 And these are the sons of Benjamin: Sallu the son of Meshullam, the son of Joed, the son of Pedaiah, the son of Kolaiah, the son of Maaseiah, the son of Ithiel, the son of Jeshaiah;

8 and after him Gabbai *and* Sallai, nine hundred and twenty-eight.

9 Joel the son of Zichri *was* their overseer, and Judah the son of Senuah[42] *was* second over the city.

10 Of the priests: Jedaiah the son of Joiarib, and Jachin;

11 Seraiah the son of Hilkiah, the son of Meshullam, the son of Zadok, the son of Meraioth, the son of Ahitub, *was* the leader of the house of God.

12 Their brethren who did the work of the house *were* eight hundred and twenty-two; and Adaiah the son of Jeroham, the son of Pelaliah, the son of Amzi, the son of Zechariah, the son of Pashhur, the son of Malchijah,

13 and his brethren, heads of the fathers' *houses, were* two hundred and forty-two; and Amashai the son of Azareel, the son of Ahzai, the son of Meshillemoth, the son of Immer,

14 and their brethren, mighty men of valor, *were* one hundred and twenty-eight. Their overseer *was* Zabdiel the son of *one of* the great men.[43]

15 Also of the Levites: Shemaiah the son of Hasshub, the son of Azrikam, the son of Hashabiah, the son of Bunni;

16 Shabbethai and Jozabad, of the heads of the Levites, *had* the oversight of the business outside of the house of God;

17 and Mattaniah the son of Micha,[44] the son of Zabdi, the son of Asaph, *who was* the leader *who* began the thanksgiving with prayer, and Bakbukiah the second among his brethren, and Abda the son of Shammua, the son of Galal, the son of Jeduthun.

18 All the Levites in the holy city *were* two hundred and eighty-four.

19 Moreover the gatekeepers, Akkub, Talmon, and their brethren who kept the gates, *were* one hundred and seventy-two.

20 And the rest of Israel, of the priests *and* Levites, *were* in all the cities of Judah, everyone in his *own* inheritance.

21 But the Nethinim dwelt in Ophel. And Ziha and Gishpa *were* over the Nethinim.

22 Also the overseer of the Levites at Jerusalem *was* Uzzi the son of Bani, the son of Hashabiah, the son of Mattaniah, the son of Micha, of the sons of Asaph, the singers in charge of the service of the house of God.

23 For *it was* the king's command concerning them that a certain portion should be for the singers, a quota day by day.

24 Pethahiah the son of Meshezabeel, of the children of Zerah the son of Judah, *was* the king's deputy[45] in all matters concerning the people.

The People Dwelling Outside Jerusalem

25 And as for the villages with their fields, *some* of the children of Judah dwelt in Kirjath Arba and its villages, Dibon and its villages, Jekabzeel and its villages;

26 in Jeshua, Moladah, Beth Pelet,

27 Hazar Shual, and Beersheba and its villages;

28 in Ziklag and Meconah and its villages;

29 in En Rimmon, Zorah, Jarmuth,

30 Zanoah, Adullam, and their villages; in Lachish and its fields; in Azekah and its villages. They dwelt from Beersheba to the Valley of Hinnom.

31 Also the children of Benjamin from Geba *dwelt* in Michmash, Aija, and Bethel, and their villages;

32 in Anathoth, Nob, Ananiah;

33 in Hazor, Ramah, Gittaim;

34 in Hadid, Zeboim, Neballat;

35 in Lod, Ono, *and* the Valley of Craftsmen.

36 Some of the Judean divisions of Levites *were* in Benjamin.

The Priests and Levites

12 Now these *are* the priests and the Levites who came up with Zerubbabel the son of Shealtiel, and Jeshua: Seraiah, Jeremiah, Ezra,

2 Amariah, Malluch, Hattush,

3 Shechaniah, Rehum, Meremoth,

---

42 Or *Hassenuah*   43 Or *the son of Haggedolim*   44 Or *Michah*   45 Literally *at the king's hand*

4 Iddo, Ginnethoi,[46] Abijah,
5 Mijamin, Maadiah, Bilgah,
6 Shemaiah, Joiarib, Jedaiah,
7 Sallu, Amok, Hilkiah, *and* Jedaiah.
These *were* the heads of the priests and their brethren in the days of Jeshua.
8 Moreover the Levites *were* Jeshua, Binnui, Kadmiel, Sherebiah, Judah, *and* Mattaniah *who led* the thanksgiving *psalms*, he and his brethren.
9 Also Bakbukiah and Unni, their brethren, *stood* across from them in *their* duties.
10 Jeshua begot Joiakim, Joiakim begot Eliashib, Eliashib begot Joiada,
11 Joiada begot Jonathan, and Jonathan begot Jaddua.
12 Now in the days of Joiakim, the priests, the heads of the fathers' *houses were*: of Seraiah, Meraiah; of Jeremiah, Hananiah;
13 of Ezra, Meshullam; of Amariah, Jehohanan;
14 of Melichu,[47] Jonathan; of Shebaniah,[48] Joseph;
15 of Harim,[49] Adna; of Meraioth,[50] Helkai;
16 of Iddo, Zechariah; of Ginnethon, Meshullam;
17 of Abijah, Zichri; *the son* of Minjamin;[51] of Moadiah,[52] Piltai;
18 of Bilgah, Shammua; of Shemaiah, Jehonathan;
19 of Joiarib, Mattenai; of Jedaiah, Uzzi;
20 of Sallai,[53] Kallai; of Amok, Eber;
21 of Hilkiah, Hashabiah; *and* of Jedaiah, Nethaneal.
22 During the reign of Darius the Persian, a record *was also kept* of the Levites and priests *who had been* heads of their fathers' *houses* in the days of Eliashib, Joiada, Johanan, and Jaddua.
23 The sons of Levi, the heads of the fathers' *houses* until the days of Johanan the son of Eliashib, *were* written in the book of the chronicles.
24 And the heads of the Levites *were* Hashabiah, Sherebiah, and Jeshua the son of Kadmiel, with their brothers across from them, to praise *and* give thanks, group alternating with group, according to the command of David the man of God.
25 Mattaniah, Bakbukiah, Obadiah, Meshullam, Talmon, and Akkub *were*

gatekeepers keeping the watch at the storerooms of the gates.
26 These *lived* in the days of Joiakim the son of Jeshua, the son of Jozadak,[54] and in the days of Nehemiah the governor, and of Ezra the priest, the scribe.

Nehemiah Dedicates the Wall

27 Now at the dedication of the wall of Jerusalem they sought out the Levites in all their places, to bring them to Jerusalem to celebrate the dedication with gladness, both with thanksgivings and singing, *with* cymbals and stringed instruments and harps.
28 And the sons of the singers gathered together from the countryside around Jerusalem, from the villages of the Netophathites,
29 from the house of Gilgal, and from the fields of Geba and Azmaveth; for the singers had built themselves villages all around Jerusalem.
30 Then the priests and Levites purified themselves, and purified the people, the gates, and the wall.
31 So I brought the leaders of Judah up on the wall, and appointed two large thanksgiving choirs, *one of which* went to the right hand on the wall toward the Refuse Gate;
32 after them went Hoshaiah and half of the leaders of Judah,
33 and Azariah, Ezra, Meshullam,
34 Judah, Benjamin, Shemaiah, Jeremiah,
35 and *certain* of the priests' sons with trumpets, *namely*, Zechariah the son of Jonathan, the son of Shemaiah, the son of Mattaniah, the son of Michaiah, the son of Zaccur, the son of Asaph,
36 and his brethren, Shemaiah, Azarel, Milalai, Gilalai, Maai, Nethaneal, Judah, *and* Hanani, with the musical instruments of David the man of God; and Ezra the scribe *went* before them.
37 By the Fountain Gate, in front of them, they went up the stairs of the City of David, on the stairway of the wall, beyond the house of David, as far as the Water Gate eastward.
38 The other thanksgiving choir went the opposite *way*, and I *was* behind them with half of the people on the wall, going past

---

46 Or *Ginnethon* (compare verse 16)   47 Or *Malluch* (compare verse 2)   48 Or *Shechaniah* (compare verse 7)
49 Or *Rehum* (compare verse 3)   50 Or *Meremoth* (compare verse 3)   51 Or *Mijamin* (compare verse 5)
52 Or *Maadiah* (compare verse 5)   53 Or *Sallu* (compare verse 7)   54 Spelled *Jehozadak* in 1 Chronicles 6:14

the Tower of the Ovens as far as the Broad Wall,

39 and above the Gate of Ephraim, above the Old Gate, above the Fish Gate, the Tower of Hananeal, the Tower of the Hundred, as far as the Sheep Gate; and they stopped by the Gate of the Prison.

40 So the two thanksgiving choirs stood in the house of God, likewise I and the half of the rulers with me;

41 and the priests, Eliakim, Maaseiah, Minjamin,[55] Michaiah, Elioenai, Zechariah, *and* Hananiah, with trumpets;

42 also Maaseiah, Shemaiah, Eleazar, Uzzi, Jehohanan, Malchijah, Elam, and Ezer. The singers sang loudly with Jezrahiah *as their* director.

43 Also that day they offered great sacrifices, and rejoiced, for God had made them rejoice with great joy; the women and the children also rejoiced, so that the joy of Jerusalem was heard afar off.

Temple Responsibilities

44 And at the same time some were appointed over the rooms of the storehouse for the offerings, the firstfruits, and the tithes, to gather into them from the fields of the cities the portions specified by the Law for the priests and Levites; for Judah rejoiced over the priests and Levites who ministered.

45 Both the singers and the gatekeepers kept the charge of their God and the charge of the purification, according to the command of David *and* Solomon his son.

46 For in the days of David and Asaph of old *there were* chiefs of the singers, and songs of praise and thanksgiving to God.

47 In the days of Zerubbabel and in the days of Nehemiah all Israel gave the portions for the singers and the gatekeepers, a portion for each day. They also consecrated *holy things* for the Levites, and the Levites consecrated *them* for the children of Aaron.

Principles of Separation

13 On that day they read from the Book of Moses in the hearing of the people, and in it was found written that no Ammonite or Moabite should ever come into the congregation of God,

2 because they had not met the children of Israel with bread and water, but hired Balaam against them to curse them.

However, our God turned the curse into a blessing.

3 So it was, when they had heard the Law, that they separated all the mixed multitude from Israel.

The Reforms of Nehemiah

4 Now before this, Eliashib the priest, having authority over the storerooms of the house of our God, *was* allied with Tobiah.

5 And he had prepared for him a large room, where previously they had stored the grain offerings, the frankincense, the articles, the tithes of grain, the new wine and oil, which were commanded *to be given* to the Levites and singers and gatekeepers, and the offerings for the priests.

6 But during all this I was not in Jerusalem, for in the thirty-second year of Artaxerxes king of Babylon I had returned to the king. Then after certain days I obtained leave from the king,

7 and I came to Jerusalem and discovered the evil that Eliashib had done for Tobiah, in preparing a room for him in the courts of the house of God.

8 And it grieved me bitterly; therefore I threw all the household goods of Tobiah out of the room.

9 Then I commanded them to cleanse the rooms; and I brought back into them the articles of the house of God, with the grain offering and the frankincense.

10 I also realized that the portions for the Levites had not been given *them*; for each of the Levites and the singers who did the work had gone back to his field.

11 So I contended with the rulers, and said, "Why is the house of God forsaken?" And I gathered them together and set them in their place.

12 Then all Judah brought the tithe of the grain and the new wine and the oil to the storehouse.

13 And I appointed as treasurers over the storehouse Shelemiah the priest and Zadok the scribe, and of the Levites, Pedaiah; and next to them *was* Hanan the son of Zaccur, the son of Mattaniah; for they were considered faithful, and their task *was* to distribute to their brethren.

14 Remember me, O my God, concerning this, and do not wipe out my good deeds that I have done for the house of my God, and for its services!

55 Or *Mijamin* (compare 12:5)

15 In those days I saw in Judah *some people* treading wine presses on the Sabbath, and bringing in sheaves, and loading donkeys with wine, grapes, figs, and all *kinds of* burdens, which they brought into Jerusalem on the Sabbath day. And I warned *them* about the day on which they were selling provisions.
16 Men of Tyre dwelt there also, who brought in fish and all kinds of goods, and sold *them* on the Sabbath to the children of Judah, and in Jerusalem.
17 Then I contended with the nobles of Judah, and said to them, "What evil thing *is* this that you do, by which you profane the Sabbath day?
18 "Did not your fathers do thus, and did not our God bring all this disaster on us and on this city? Yet you bring added wrath on Israel by profaning the Sabbath."
19 So it was, at the gates of Jerusalem, as it began to be dark before the Sabbath, that I commanded the gates to be shut, and charged that they must not be opened till after the Sabbath. Then I posted *some* of my servants at the gates, *so that* no burdens would be brought in on the Sabbath day.
20 Now the merchants and sellers of all kinds of wares lodged outside Jerusalem once or twice.
21 So I warned them, and said to them, "Why do you spend the night around the wall? If you do *so* again, I will lay hands on you!" From that time on they came no *more* on the Sabbath.
22 And I commanded the Levites that they should cleanse themselves, and that they should go and guard the gates, to sanctify the Sabbath day.

Remember me, O my God, *concerning* this also, and spare me according to the greatness of Your mercy!
23 In those days I also saw Jews *who* had married women of Ashdod, Ammon, *and* Moab.
24 And half of their children spoke the language of Ashdod, and could not speak the language of Judah, but spoke according to the language of one or the other people.
25 So I contended with them and cursed them, struck some of them and pulled out their hair, and made them swear by God, *saying*, "You shall not give your daughters as wives to their sons, nor take their daughters for your sons or yourselves.
26 "Did not Solomon king of Israel sin by these things? Yet among many nations there was no king like him, who was beloved of his God; and God made him king over all Israel. Nevertheless pagan women caused even him to sin.
27 "Should we then hear of your doing all this great evil, transgressing against our God by marrying pagan women?"
28 And *one* of the sons of Joiada, the son of Eliashib the high priest, *was* a son-in-law of Sanballat the Horonite; therefore I drove him from me.
29 Remember them, O my God, because they have defiled the priesthood and the covenant of the priesthood and the Levites.
30 Thus I cleansed them of everything pagan. I also assigned duties to the priests and the Levites, each to his service,
31 and *to bringing* the wood offering and the firstfruits at appointed times.

Remember me, O my God, for good!

Introduction to Esther

The Book of Esther is a fascinating account of God's ability to send the right person to the right place at the right time.

The exact date and author of this book are unknown. Most scholars, however, attribute it to a Jewish writer living in the Persian period (539–332 B.C.). The king of this book is generally accepted to be Xerxes (486–464 B.C.), king of Persia whose reign spanned from the Indus River in India, north to the Black Sea, west through Asia Minor and to the shores of North Africa.

The empire of Xerxes was not only powerful, but full of wealth, as is evident from the description of Xerxes' palace in the summer capital of Susa (Esth. 1:4–7). Into this power center walked Esther—a young Jewish virgin—called by God to a mighty position.

Her role as queen was not secure, for even she was subject to the emotional whims of the king. Yet her ascent to royalty held an incredible purpose—to save the Jewish people from destruction; she was the only person who could persuade the king to spare her people.

Esther was beautiful in person and character. But more importantly, she was courageous and wise. Haman, a great enemy of the Jews, had gained Xerxes' approval to put to death all the Jews of the land. Esther felt powerless to help her people. She faced her fear of the king through prayer and fasting. Then by exercising her charm and womanly gifts, she went before Xerxes. If he accepted her, she was spared, but if he rejected her presence before him, she would be put to death. "And so I will go to the king, which *is* against the law; and if I perish, I perish!" (Esth. 4:16).

Arrayed in all her beauty, she stood before the king and was accepted. Esther played up to his emotions by holding a banquet in his honor. When he was overwhelmed by her graciousness, Xerxes promised her anything. Esther's request was not for herself, but for her people, for their lives and their freedom. The Jewish people were saved!

Esther was the right person at the right time at the right place. And she proved that it takes two to work a miracle—you and God! You must have the faith and the courage, and God will work the miracle.

The Book of
Esther

The King Dethrones Queen Vashti

NOW it came to pass in the days of Ahasuerus[1] (this *was* the Ahasuerus who reigned from India to Ethiopia, *over* one hundred and twenty-seven provinces),
2 in those days when King Ahasuerus sat on the throne of his kingdom, which *was* in Shushan[2] the citadel,
3 *that* in the third year of his reign he made a feast for all his officials and servants—the powers of Persia and Media, the nobles, and the princes of the provinces *being* before him—
4 when he showed the riches of his glorious kingdom and the splendor of his excellent majesty for many days, one hundred and eighty days *in all.*
5 And when these days were completed, the king made a feast lasting seven days for all the people who were present in Shushan the citadel, from great to small, in the court of the garden of the king's palace.
6 *There were* white and blue linen *curtains* fastened with cords of fine linen and purple on silver rods and marble pillars; *and the* couches *were* of gold and silver on a *mosaic* pavement of alabaster, turquoise, and white and black marble.
7 And they served drinks in golden vessels, each vessel being different from the other, with royal wine in abundance, according to the generosity of the king.
8 In accordance with the law, the drinking was not compulsory; for so the king had ordered all the officers of his household, that they should do according to each man's pleasure.
9 Queen Vashti also made a feast for the women *in* the royal palace which *belonged* to King Ahasuerus.
10 On the seventh day, when the heart of the king was merry with wine, he commanded Mehuman, Biztha, Harbona, Bigtha, Abagtha, Zethar, and Carcas, seven eunuchs who served in the presence of King Ahasuerus,
11 to bring Queen Vashti before the king, *wearing* her royal crown, in order to show her beauty to the people and the officials, for she *was* beautiful to behold.
12 But Queen Vashti refused to come at the king's command *brought* by *his* eunuchs; therefore the king was furious, and his anger burned within him.
13 Then the king said to the wise men who understood the times (for this *was* the king's manner toward all who knew law and justice,
14 those closest to him *being* Carshena, Shethar, Admatha, Tarshish, Meres, Marsena, and Memucan, the seven princes of Persia and Media, who had access to the king's presence, *and* who ranked highest in the kingdom):
15 "What *shall* we do to Queen Vashti, according to law, because she did not obey the command of King Ahasuerus *brought to her* by the eunuchs?"
16 And Memucan answered before the king and the princes: "Queen Vashti has not only wronged the king, but also all the princes, and all the people who *are* in all the provinces of King Ahasuerus.
17 "For the queen's behavior will become known to all women, so that they will despise their husbands in their eyes, when they report, 'King Ahasuerus commanded Queen Vashti to be brought in before him, but she did not come.'
18 "This very day the *noble* ladies of Persia and Media will say to all the king's officials that they have heard of the behavior of the queen. Thus *there will be* excessive contempt and wrath.
19 "If it pleases the king, let a royal decree go out from him, and let it be recorded in the laws of the Persians and the Medes, so that it will not be altered, that Vashti shall come no more before King Ahasuerus; and let the king give her royal position to another who is better than she.
20 "When the king's decree which he will make is proclaimed throughout all his empire (for it is great), all wives will honor their husbands, both great and small."

---

1 Generally identified with Xerxes I (485–464 B.C.)   2 Or *Susa,* and so throughout this book

21 And the reply pleased the king and the princes, and the king did according to the word of Memucan.

22 Then he sent letters to all the king's provinces, to each province in its own script, and to every people in their own language, that each man should be master in his own house, and speak in the language of his own people.

Esther Becomes Queen

2 After these things, when the wrath of King Ahasuerus subsided, he remembered Vashti, what she had done, and what had been decreed against her.

2 Then the king's servants who attended him said: "Let beautiful young virgins be sought for the king;

3 "and let the king appoint officers in all the provinces of his kingdom, that they may gather all the beautiful young virgins to Shushan the citadel, into the women's quarters, under the custody of Hegai[3] the king's eunuch, custodian of the women. And let beauty preparations be given them.

4 "Then let the young woman who pleases the king be queen instead of Vashti." This thing pleased the king, and he did so.

5 Now in Shushan the citadel there was a certain Jew whose name was Mordecai the son of Jair, the son of Shimei, the son of Kish, a Benjamite.

6 Kish[4] had been carried away from Jerusalem with the captives who had been captured with Jeconiah[5] king of Judah, whom Nebuchadnezzar the king of Babylon had carried away.

7 And Mordecai[6] had brought up Hadassah, that is, Esther, his uncle's daughter, for she had neither father nor mother. The young woman was lovely and beautiful. When her father and mother died, Mordecai took her as his own daughter.

8 So it was, when the king's command and decree were heard, and when many young women were gathered at Shushan the citadel, under the custody of Hegai, that Esther also was taken to the king's palace, into the care of Hegai the custodian of the women.

9 Now the young woman pleased him, and she obtained his favor; so he readily gave beauty preparations to her, besides her allowance. Then seven choice maidservants were provided for her from the king's palace, and he moved her and her maidservants to the best place in the house of the women.

10 Esther had not revealed her people or kindred, for Mordecai had charged her not to reveal it.

11 And every day Mordecai paced in front of the court of the women's quarters, to learn of Esther's welfare and what was happening to her.

12 Each young woman's turn came to go in to King Ahasuerus after she had completed twelve months' preparation, according to the regulations for the women, for thus were the days of their preparation apportioned: six months with oil of myrrh, and six months with perfumes and preparations for beautifying women.

13 Thus prepared, each young woman went to the king, and she was given whatever she desired to take with her from the women's quarters to the king's palace.

14 In the evening she went, and in the morning she returned to the second house of the women, to the custody of Shaashgaz, the king's eunuch who kept the concubines. She would not go in to the king again unless the king delighted in her and called for her by name.

15 Now when the turn came for Esther the daughter of Abihail the uncle of Mordecai, who had taken her as his daughter, to go in to the king, she requested nothing but what Hegai the king's eunuch, the custodian of the women, advised. And Esther obtained favor in the sight of all who saw her.

16 So Esther was taken to King Ahasuerus, into his royal palace, in the tenth month, which is the month of Tebeth, in the seventh year of his reign.

17 The king loved Esther more than all the other women, and she obtained grace and favor in his sight more than all the virgins; so he set the royal crown upon her head and made her queen instead of Vashti.

18 Then the king made a great feast, the Feast of Esther, for all his officials and servants; and he proclaimed a holiday in the provinces and gave gifts according to the generosity of a king.

---

3 Hebrew Hege   4 Literally who   5 Same as Jehoiachin (compare 2 Kings 24:6 and elsewhere)   6 Literally he

Mordecai Discovers a Plot

19 When virgins were gathered together a second time, Mordecai sat within the king's gate.

20 Now Esther had not *yet* revealed her kindred and her people, just as Mordecai had charged her, for Esther obeyed the command of Mordecai as when she was brought up by him.

21 In those days, while Mordecai sat within the king's gate, two of the king's eunuchs, Bigthan and Teresh, doorkeepers, became furious and sought to lay hands on King Ahasuerus.

22 So the matter became known to Mordecai, who told Queen Esther, and Esther informed the king in Mordecai's name.

23 And when an inquiry was made into the matter, it was confirmed, and both were hanged on a gallows; and it was written in the book of the chronicles in the presence of the king.

Haman's Conspiracy Against the Jews

3 After these things King Ahasuerus promoted Haman, the son of Hammedatha the Agagite, and advanced him and set his seat above all the princes who *were* with him.

2 And all the king's servants who *were* within the king's gate bowed and paid homage to Haman, for so the king had commanded concerning him. But Mordecai would not bow or pay homage.

3 Then the king's servants who *were* within the king's gate said to Mordecai, "Why do you transgress the king's command?"

4 Now it happened, when they spoke to him daily and he would not listen to them, that they told *it* to Haman, to see whether Mordecai's words would stand; for Mordecai[7] had told them that he *was* a Jew.

5 When Haman saw that Mordecai did not bow or pay him homage, Haman was filled with wrath.

6 But he disdained to lay hands on Mordecai alone, for they had told him of the people of Mordecai. Instead, Haman sought to destroy all the Jews who *were* throughout the whole kingdom of Ahasuerus—the people of Mordecai.

7 In the first month, which is the month of Nisan, in the twelfth year of King Ahasuerus, they cast Pur (that *is*, the lot), before Haman to determine the day and the month, until *it fell on the* twelfth *month*, which *is* the month of Adar.

8 Then Haman said to King Ahasuerus, "There is a certain people scattered and dispersed among the people in all the provinces of your kingdom; their laws *are* different from all *other* people's, and they do not keep the king's laws. Therefore it *is* not fitting for the king to let them remain.

9 "If it pleases the king, let *a decree* be written that they be destroyed, and I will pay ten thousand talents of silver into the hands of those who do the work, to bring *it* into the king's treasuries."

10 So the king took his signet ring from his hand and gave it to Haman, the son of Hammedatha the Agagite, the enemy of the Jews.

11 And the king said to Haman, "The money and the people *are* given to you, to do with them as seems good to you."

12 Then the king's scribes were called on the thirteenth day of the first month, and *a decree* was written according to all that Haman commanded—to the king's satraps, to the governors who *were* over each province, to the officials of all people, to every province according to its script, and to every people in their language. In the name of King Ahasuerus it was written, and sealed with the king's signet ring.

13 And the letters were sent by couriers into all the king's provinces, to destroy, to kill, and to annihilate all the Jews, both young and old, little children and women, in one day, on the thirteenth *day* of the twelfth *month*, which *is* the month of Adar, and to plunder their possessions.

14 A copy of the document was to be issued as law in every province, being published for all people, that they should be ready for that day.

15 The couriers went out, hastened by the king's command; and the decree was proclaimed in Shushan the citadel. So the king and Haman sat down to drink, but the city of Shushan was perplexed.

Esther Agrees to Help the Jews

4 When Mordecai learned all that had happened, he tore his clothes and put on sackcloth and ashes, and went out into

---

7 Literally *he*

the midst of the city. He cried out with a loud and bitter cry.

2 He went as far as *the square* in front of the king's gate, for no one *might* enter the king's gate clothed with sackcloth.

3 And in every province where the king's command and decree arrived, *there was* great mourning among the Jews, with fasting, weeping, and wailing; and many lay in sackcloth and ashes.

4 So Esther's maids and eunuchs came and told her, and the queen was deeply distressed. Then she sent garments to clothe Mordecai and take his sackcloth away from him, but he would not accept *them.*

5 Then Esther called Hathach, *one* of the king's eunuchs whom he had appointed to attend her, and she gave him a command concerning Mordecai, to learn what and why this *was.*

6 So Hathach went out to Mordecai in the city square that *was* in front of the king's gate.

7 And Mordecai told him all that had happened to him, and the sum of money that Haman had promised to pay into the king's treasuries to destroy the Jews.

8 He also gave him a copy of the written decree for their destruction, which was given at Shushan, that he might show it to Esther and explain it to her, and that he might command her to go in to the king to make supplication to him and plead before him for her people.

9 So Hathach returned and told Esther the words of Mordecai.

10 Then Esther spoke to Hathach, and gave him a command for Mordecai:

11 "All the king's servants and the people of the king's provinces know that any man or woman who goes into the inner court to the king, who has not been called, *he has* but one law: put *all* to death, except the one to whom the king holds out the golden scepter, that he may live. Yet I myself have not been called to go in to the king these thirty days."

12 So they told Mordecai Esther's words.

13 Then Mordecai told *them* to answer Esther: "Do not think in your heart that you will escape in the king's palace any more than all the other Jews.

14 "For if you remain completely silent at this time, relief and deliverance will arise for the Jews from another place, but you and your father's house will perish. Yet who knows whether you have come to the kingdom for *such* a time as this?"

15 Then Esther told *them* to return *this answer* to Mordecai:

16 "Go, gather all the Jews who are present in Shushan, and fast for me; neither eat nor drink for three days, night or day. My maids and I will fast likewise. And so I will go to the king, which *is* against the law; and if I perish, I perish!"

17 Then Mordecai went his way and did according to all that Esther commanded him.

Esther's Banquet

5 Now it happened on the third day that Esther put on *her* royal *robes* and stood in the inner court of the king's palace, across from the king's house, while the king sat on his royal throne in the royal house, facing the entrance of the house.

2 So it was, when the king saw Queen Esther standing in the court, *that* she found favor in his sight, and the king held out to Esther the golden scepter that *was* in his hand. Then Esther went near and touched the top of the scepter.

3 And the king said to her, "What do you wish, Queen Esther? What *is* your request? It shall be given to you—up to half *my* kingdom!"

4 So Esther answered, "If it pleases the king, let the king and Haman come today to the banquet that I have prepared for him."

5 Then the king said, "Bring Haman quickly, that he may do as Esther has said." So the king and Haman went to the banquet that Esther had prepared.

6 At the banquet of wine the king said to Esther, "What *is* your petition? It shall be granted you. What *is* your request, up to half *my* kingdom? It shall be done!"

7 Then Esther answered and said, "My petition and request *is this:*

8 "If I have found favor in the sight of the king, and if it pleases the king to grant my petition and fulfill my request, then let the king and Haman come to the banquet which I will prepare for them, and tomorrow I will do as the king has said."

Haman's Plot Against Mordecai

9 So Haman went out that day joyful and with a glad heart; but when Haman saw Mordecai in the king's gate, and that he did not stand or tremble before him, he was filled with indignation against Mordecai.

10 Nevertheless Haman restrained himself and went home, and he sent and called for his friends and his wife Zeresh. 11 Then Haman told them of his great riches, the multitude of his children, all *the ways* in which the king had promoted him, and how he had advanced him above the officials and servants of the king. 12 Moreover Haman said, "Besides, Queen Esther invited no one but me to come in with the king to the banquet that she prepared; and tomorrow I am again invited by her, along with the king. 13 "Yet all this avails me nothing, so long as I see Mordecai the Jew sitting at the king's gate." 14 Then his wife Zeresh and all his friends said to him, "Let a gallows be made, fifty cubits high, and in the morning suggest to the king that Mordecai be hanged on it; then go merrily with the king to the banquet." And the thing pleased Haman; so he had the gallows made.

The King Honors Mordecai

6 That night the king could not sleep. So one was commanded to bring the book of the records of the chronicles; and they were read before the king. 2 And it was found written that Mordecai had told of Bigthana and Teresh, two of the king's eunuchs, the doorkeepers who had sought to lay hands on King Ahasuerus. 3 Then the king said, "What honor or dignity has been bestowed on Mordecai for this?" And the king's servants who attended him said, "Nothing has been done for him." 4 And the king said, "Who *is* in the court?" Now Haman had *just* entered the outer court of the king's palace to suggest that the king hang Mordecai on the gallows that he had prepared for him. 5 The king's servants said to him, "Haman is there, standing in the court." And the king said, "Let him come in."

6 So Haman came in, and the king asked him, "What shall be done for the man whom the king delights to honor?" Now Haman thought in his heart, "Whom would the king delight to honor more than me?" 7 And Haman answered the king, "*For* the man whom the king delights to honor, 8 "let a royal robe be brought which the king has worn, and a horse on which the king has ridden, which has a royal crest placed on its head. 9 "Then let this robe and horse be delivered to the hand of one of the king's most noble princes, that he may array the man whom the king delights to honor. Then parade him on horseback through the city square, and proclaim before him: 'Thus shall it be done to the man whom the king delights to honor!' " 10 Then the king said to Haman, "Hasten, take the robe and the horse, as you have suggested, and do so for Mordecai the Jew who sits within the king's gate. Leave nothing undone of all that you have spoken." 11 So Haman took the robe and the horse, arrayed Mordecai and led him on horseback through the city square, and proclaimed before him, "Thus shall it be done to the man the king delights to honor."

12 Afterward Mordecai went back to the king's gate. But Haman hastened to his house, mourning and with his head covered. 13 When Haman told his wife Zeresh and all his friends everything that had happened to him, his wise men and his wife Zeresh said to him, "If Mordecai, before whom you have begun to fall, is of Jewish descent, you will not prevail against him but will surely fall before him." 14 While they *were* still talking with him, the king's eunuchs came, and hastened to bring Haman to the banquet which Esther had prepared.

Haman Hanged Instead of Mordecai

7 So the king and Haman went to dine with Queen Esther. 2 And on the second day, at the banquet of wine, the king again said to Esther, "What *is* your petition, Queen Esther? It shall be granted you. And what

is your request, up to half *my* kingdom? It shall be done!"

3 Then Queen Esther answered and said, "If I have found favor in your sight, O king, and if it pleases the king, let my life be given me at my petition, and my people at my request.

4 "For we have been sold, my people and I, to be destroyed, to be killed, and to be annihilated. Had we been sold as male and female slaves, I would have held my tongue, although the enemy could never compensate for the king's loss."

5 Then King Ahasuerus answered and said to Queen Esther, "Who is he, and where is he, who would dare presume in his heart to do such a thing?"

6 And Esther said, "The adversary and enemy *is* this wicked Haman!" So Haman was terrified before the king and queen.

7 Then the king arose in his wrath from the banquet of wine *and went* into the palace garden; but Haman stood before Queen Esther, pleading for his life, for he saw that evil was determined against him by the king.

8 When the king returned from the palace garden to the place of the banquet of wine, Haman had fallen across the couch where Esther *was*. Then the king said, "Will he also assault the queen while I *am* in the house?" As the word left the king's mouth, they covered Haman's face.

9 Now Harbonah, one of the eunuchs, said to the king, "Look! The gallows, fifty cubits high, which Haman made for Mordecai, who spoke good on the king's behalf, is standing at the house of Haman." Then the king said, "Hang him on it!"

10 So they hanged Haman on the gallows that he had prepared for Mordecai. Then the king's wrath subsided.

Esther Saves the Jews

8 On that day King Ahasuerus gave Queen Esther the house of Haman, the enemy of the Jews. And Mordecai came before the king, for Esther had told how he *was related* to her.

2 So the king took off his signet ring, which he had taken from Haman, and gave it to Mordecai; and Esther appointed Mordecai over the house of Haman.

3 Now Esther spoke again to the king, fell down at his feet, and implored him with tears to counteract the evil *plot* of Haman the Agagite, and the scheme which he had devised against the Jews.

4 And the king held out the golden scepter toward Esther. So Esther arose and stood before the king,

5 and said, "If it pleases the king, and if I have found favor in his sight and the thing *seems* right to the king and I am pleasing in his eyes, let it be written to revoke the letters devised by Haman, the son of Hammedatha the Agagite, which he wrote to annihilate the Jews who *are* in all the king's provinces.

6 "For how can I endure to see the evil that will come to my people? Or how can I endure to see the destruction of my kindred?"

7 Then King Ahasuerus said to Queen Esther and Mordecai the Jew, "Indeed, I have given Esther the house of Haman, and they have hanged him on the gallows because he *tried to* lay his hand on the Jews.

8 "You yourselves write *a decree* for the Jews, as you please, in the king's name, and seal *it* with the king's signet ring; for a letter which is written in the king's name and sealed with the king's signet ring no one can revoke."

9 So the king's scribes were called at that time, in the third month, which *is* the month of Sivan, on the twenty-third *day*; and it was written, according to all that Mordecai commanded, to the Jews, the satraps, the governors, and the princes of the provinces from India to Ethiopia, one hundred and twenty-seven provinces *in all*, to every province in its own script, to every people in their own language, and to the Jews in their own script and language.

10 And he wrote in the name of King Ahasuerus, sealed *it* with the king's signet ring, and sent letters by couriers on horseback, riding on royal horses bred from swift steeds.[8]

11 By these letters the king permitted the Jews who *were* in every city to gather together and protect their lives—to destroy, kill, and annihilate all the forces of any people or province that would assault them, *both* little children and women, and to plunder their possessions,

---

8 Literally *sons of the swift horses*

12 on one day in all the provinces of King Ahasuerus, on the thirteenth *day* of the twelfth month, which *is* the month of Adar.

13 A copy of the document was to be issued as a decree in every province and published to all people, so that the Jews would be ready on that day to avenge themselves on their enemies.

14 *Then* the couriers who rode on royal horses went out, hastened and pressed on by the king's command. And the decree was issued in Shushan the citadel.

15 Now Mordecai went out from the presence of the king in royal apparel of blue and white, with a great crown of gold and a garment of fine linen and purple; and the city of Shushan rejoiced and was glad.

16 The Jews had light and gladness, joy and honor.

17 And in every province and city, wherever the king's command and decree came, the Jews had joy and gladness, a feast and a holiday. Then many of the people of the land became Jews, because fear of the Jews fell upon them.

The Jews Destroy Their Tormentors

9 Now in the twelfth month, that *is,* the month of Adar, on the thirteenth day, *the time* came for the king's command and his decree to be executed. On the day that the enemies of the Jews had hoped to overpower them, the opposite occurred, in that the Jews themselves overpowered those who hated them.

2 The Jews gathered together in their cities throughout all the provinces of King Ahasuerus to lay hands on those who sought their harm. And no one could withstand them, because fear of them fell upon all people.

3 And all the officials of the provinces, the satraps, the governors, and all those doing the king's work, helped the Jews, because the fear of Mordecai fell upon them.

4 For Mordecai *was* great in the king's palace, and his fame spread throughout all the provinces; for this man Mordecai became increasingly prominent.

5 Thus the Jews defeated all their enemies with the stroke of the sword, with slaughter and destruction, and did what they pleased with those who hated them.

6 And in Shushan the citadel the Jews killed and destroyed five hundred men.

7 Also Parshandatha, Dalphon, Aspatha,

8 Poratha, Adalia, Aridatha,

9 Parmashta, Arisai, Aridai, and Vajezatha—

10 the ten sons of Haman the son of Hammedatha, the enemy of the Jews—they killed; but they did not lay a hand on the plunder.

11 On that day the number of those who were killed in Shushan the citadel was brought to the king.

12 And the king said to Queen Esther, "The Jews have killed and destroyed five hundred men in Shushan the citadel, and the ten sons of Haman. What have they done in the rest of the king's provinces? Now what *is* your petition? It shall be granted to you. Or what *is* your further request? It shall be done."

13 Then Esther said, "If it pleases the king, let it be granted to the Jews who *are* in Shushan to do again tomorrow according to today's decree, and let Haman's ten sons be hanged on the gallows."

14 So the king commanded this to be done; the decree was issued in Shushan, and they hanged Haman's ten sons.

15 And the Jews who *were* in Shushan gathered together again on the fourteenth day of the month of Adar and killed three hundred men at Shushan; but they did not lay a hand on the plunder.

16 The remainder of the Jews in the king's provinces gathered together and protected their lives, had rest from their enemies, and killed seventy-five thousand of their enemies; but they did not lay a hand on the plunder.

17 *This was* on the thirteenth day of the month of Adar. And on the fourteenth day of the month[9] they rested and made it a day of feasting and gladness.

The Feast of Purim

18 But the Jews who *were* at Shushan assembled together on the thirteenth *day,* as well as on the fourteenth *day*; and on the fifteenth *day* of the month[10] they rested, and made it a day of feasting and gladness.

19 Therefore the Jews of the villages who dwelt in the unwalled towns celebrated the fourteenth day of the month of Adar *as a day of* gladness and feasting, as a

9 Literally *it* 10 Literally *it*

holiday, and for sending presents to one another.

20 And Mordecai wrote these things and sent letters to all the Jews who were in all the provinces of King Ahasuerus, both near and far,
21 to establish among them that they should celebrate yearly the fourteenth and fifteenth days of the month of Adar,
22 as the days on which the Jews had rest from their enemies, as the month which was turned from sorrow to joy for them, and from mourning to a holiday; that they should make them days of feasting and joy, of sending presents to one another and gifts to the poor.
23 So the Jews accepted the custom which they had begun, as Mordecai had written to them,
24 because Haman, the son of Hammedatha the Agagite, the enemy of all the Jews, had plotted against the Jews to annihilate them, and had cast Pur (that is, the lot), to consume them and destroy them;
25 but when Esther[11] came before the king, he commanded by letter that this wicked plot which Haman[12] had devised against the Jews should return on his own head, and that he and his sons should be hanged on the gallows.
26 So they called these days Purim, after the name Pur. Therefore, because of all the words of this letter, what they had seen concerning this matter, and what had happened to them,
27 the Jews established and imposed it upon themselves and their descendants and all who should join them, that without fail they should celebrate these two days every year, according to the written instructions and according to the prescribed time,

28 that these days should be remembered and kept throughout every generation, every family, every province, and every city, that these days of Purim should not fail to be observed among the Jews, and that the memory of them should not perish among their descendants.
29 Then Queen Esther, the daughter of Abihail, with Mordecai the Jew, wrote with full authority to confirm this second letter about Purim.
30 And Mordecai[13] sent letters to all the Jews, to the one hundred and twenty-seven provinces of the kingdom of Ahasuerus, with words of peace and truth,
31 to confirm these days of Purim at their appointed time, as Mordecai the Jew and Queen Esther had prescribed for them, and as they had decreed for themselves and their descendants concerning matters of their fasting and lamenting.
32 So the decree of Esther confirmed these matters of Purim, and it was written in the book.

Mordecai's Advancement

10 And King Ahasuerus imposed tribute on the land and on the islands of the sea.
2 Now all the acts of his power and his might, and the account of the greatness of Mordecai, to which the king advanced him, are they not written in the book of the chronicles of the kings of Media and Persia?
3 For Mordecai the Jew was second to King Ahasuerus, and was great among the Jews and well-received by the multitude of his brethren, seeking the good of his people and speaking peace to all his kindred.[14]

11 Literally she or it 12 Literally he 13 Literally he 14 Literally seed

Introduction to Job

"Though He slay me, yet will I trust Him." This theme dominates the Book of Job, presenting Job as both doubting and trusting God's ultimate providential blessings.

Often considered the oldest book of the Bible, Job may have been written between 2100 and 1900 B.C. It is the story of one of the world's wealthiest, most prosperous men who was tested for his faith in God. Everything was taken from him, including children, land, camels, oxen, donkeys, sheep, and money—all the possessions he had. Job was also afflicted with a severe and loathsome disease.

This ancient literary masterpiece presents insight into human suffering as found nowhere else. Job asks the tough questions concerning life's hardships. Throughout its pages are profound truths which can be revealed only by one such as Job, who experienced such terrible suffering.

Job's initial response was one of obvious grief, yet showing an unyielding faith in God's care. As even greater trouble beset him and he found himself criticized by friends, pressured from all sides, and abandoned on a garbage pit, Job's faith turned to doubt.

Job challenged God's love for him and asked, Why me? Why have you left me? and How could you do these things to me?

In a series of dialogues with Job, God revealed His ultimate power and deity, finally making it clear that, as God, He was worthy of Job's praise regardless of the situation. God wanted Job to quit focusing on the unfathomable, mysterious questions of life and to live in a positive joyful state of praise. Although it is difficult to praise God in tough times, God is to be praised.

Job finally responded with praise and was rewarded with twice as many possessions as he ever had.

"Though He slay me, yet will I trust Him" (Job 13:15).

The Book of

Job

Job and His Family in Uz

THERE was a man in the land of Uz, whose name *was* Job; and that man was blameless and upright, and one who feared God and shunned evil.

2 And seven sons and three daughters were born to him.

3 Also, his possessions were seven thousand sheep, three thousand camels, five hundred yoke of oxen, five hundred female donkeys, and a very large household, so that this man was the greatest of all the people of the East.

4 Now his sons would go and feast *in their* houses, each on his appointed day, and would send and invite their three sisters to eat and drink with them.

5 So it was, when the days of feasting had run their course, that Job would send and sanctify them, and he would rise early in the morning and offer burnt offerings *according to* the number of them all. For Job said, "It may be that my sons have sinned and cursed¹ God in their hearts." Thus Job did regularly.

Satan Attacks Job's Character

6 Now there was a day when the sons of God came to present themselves before the LORD, and Satan² also came among them.

7 And the LORD said to Satan, "From where do you come?" So Satan answered the LORD and said, "From going to and fro on the earth, and from walking back and forth on it."

8 Then the LORD said to Satan, "Have you considered My servant Job, that *there is* none like him on the earth, a blameless and upright man, one who fears God and shuns evil?"

9 So Satan answered the LORD and said, "Does Job fear God for nothing?

10 "Have You not made a hedge around him, around his household, and around all that he has on every side? You have blessed the work of his hands, and his possessions have increased in the land.

11 "But now, stretch out Your hand and touch all that he has, and he will surely curse You to Your face!"

12 So the LORD said to Satan, "Behold, all that he has *is* in your power; only do not lay a hand on his *person*." Then Satan went out from the presence of the LORD.

Job Loses His Property and Children

13 Now there was a day when his sons and daughters *were* eating and drinking wine in their oldest brother's house;

14 and a messenger came to Job and said, "The oxen were plowing and the donkeys feeding beside them,

15 "when the Sabeans³ raided *them* and took them away—indeed they have killed the servants with the edge of the sword; and I alone have escaped to tell you!"

16 While he *was* still speaking, another also came and said, "The fire of God fell from heaven and burned up the sheep and the servants, and consumed them; and I alone have escaped to tell you!"

17 While he *was* still speaking, another also came and said, "The Chaldeans formed three bands, raided the camels and took them away, yes, and killed the servants with the edge of the sword; and I alone have escaped to tell you!"

18 While he *was* still speaking, another also came and said, "Your sons and daughters *were* eating and drinking wine in their oldest brother's house,

19 "and suddenly a great wind came from across⁴ the wilderness and struck the four corners of the house, and it fell on the young men, and they are dead; and I alone have escaped to tell you!"

20 Then Job arose and tore his robe and shaved his head, and he fell to the ground and worshiped.

21 And he said:

---

1 Literally *blessed,* but used here in the evil sense, and so also in 1:11 and 2:5, 9
2 Literally *the Adversary,* and so throughout the book   3 Literally *Sheba* (compare 6:19)
4 Septuagint omits *across.*

"Naked I came from my mother's
      womb,
And naked shall I return there.
The LORD gave, and the LORD
      has taken away;
Blessed be the name of the LORD."

22 In all this Job did not sin nor charge
God with wrong.

Satan Attacks Job's Health

2 Again there was a day when the sons
of God came to present themselves
before the LORD, and Satan came also
among them to present himself before the
LORD.
2 And the LORD said to Satan, "From
where do you come?" So Satan answered
the LORD and said, "From going to and
fro on the earth, and from walking back
and forth on it."
3 Then the LORD said to Satan, "Have
you considered My servant Job, that *there
is* none like him on the earth, a blameless
and upright man, one who fears God and
shuns evil? And still he holds fast to his
integrity, although you incited Me
against him, to destroy him without
cause."
4 So Satan answered the LORD and
said, "Skin for skin! Yes, all that a man
has he will give for his life.
5 "But stretch out Your hand now, and
touch his bone and his flesh, and he will
surely curse You to Your face!"
6 So the LORD said to Satan, "Behold,
he *is* in your hand, but spare his life."
7 Then Satan went out from the presence of the LORD, and struck Job with
painful boils from the sole of his foot to
the crown of his head.
8 And he took for himself a potsherd
with which to scrape himself while he sat
in the midst of the ashes.
9 Then his wife said to him, "Do you
still hold to your integrity? Curse God
and die!"
10 But he said to her, "You speak as one
of the foolish women speaks. Shall we
indeed accept good from God, and shall
we not accept adversity?" In all this Job
did not sin with his lips.

Job's Three Friends

11 Now when Job's three friends heard
of all this adversity that had come upon

him, each one came from his own place—
Eliphaz the Temanite, Bildad the Shuhite,
and Zophar the Naamathite. For they
had made an appointment together to
come and mourn with him, and to comfort him.
12 And when they raised their eyes from
afar, and did not recognize him, they
lifted their voices and wept; and each one
tore his robe and sprinkled dust on his
head toward heaven.
13 So they sat down with him on the
ground seven days and seven nights, and
no one spoke a word to him, for they saw
that *his* grief was very great.

Job Deplores His Birth

3 After this Job opened his mouth and
cursed the day of his *birth*.
2 And Job spoke, and said:

3 "May the day perish on which
      I was born,
And the night *in which* it was said,
'A male child is conceived.'
4 May that day be darkness;
May God above not seek it,
Nor the light shine upon it.
5 May darkness and the shadow
      of death claim it;
May a cloud settle on it;
May the blackness of the day terrify it.
6 *As for* that night, may darkness seize
      it;
May it not be included among the days
      of the year,
May it not come into the number
      of the months.
7 Oh, may that night be barren!
May no joyful shout come into it!
8 May those curse it who curse the day,
Those who are ready to arouse
      Leviathan.
9 May the stars of its morning be dark;
May it look for light, but *have* none,
And not see the dawning of the day;
10 Because it did not shut up the doors
      of my *mother's* womb,
Nor hide sorrow from my eyes.

11 "Why did I not die at birth?
Why did I *not* perish
      when I came from the womb?
12 Why did the knees receive me?
Or why the breasts,
      that I should nurse?
13 For now I would have lain still
      and been quiet,
I would have been asleep;
Then I would have been at rest

14 With kings and counselors of the earth,
Who built ruins for themselves,
15 Or with princes who had gold,
Who filled their houses *with* silver;
16 Or *why* was I not hidden
like a stillborn child,
Like infants who never saw light?
17 There the wicked cease *from* troubling,
And there the weary are at rest.
18 *There* the prisoners rest together;
They do not hear the voice
of the oppressor.
19 The small and great are there,
And the servant *is* free from his
master.

20 "Why is light given to him
who is in misery,
And life to the bitter of soul,
21 Who long for death,
but it does not *come*,
And search for it more
than hidden treasures;
22 Who rejoice exceedingly,
And are glad when they can find the
grave?
23 *Why is light given* to a man
whose way is hidden,
And whom God has hedged in?
24 For my sighing comes before I eat,⁵
And my groanings pour out like water.
25 For the thing I greatly feared
has come upon me,
And what I dreaded
has happened to me.
26 I am not at ease, nor am I quiet;
I have no rest, for trouble comes."

Eliphaz: Job Has Sinned

4 Then Eliphaz the Temanite answered
and said:

2 "If one attempts a word with you,
will you become weary?
But who can withhold himself
from speaking?
3 Surely you have instructed many,
And you have strengthened weak
hands.
4 Your words have upheld him
who was stumbling,
And you have strengthened
the feeble knees;
5 But now it comes upon you,
and you are weary;
It touches you, and you are troubled.
6 *Is* not your reverence your confidence?
And the integrity of your ways your
hope?

7 "Remember now, who *ever* perished
being innocent?
Or where were the upright *ever* cut off?
8 Even as I have seen,
Those who plow iniquity
And sow trouble reap the same.
9 By the blast of God they perish,
And by the breath of His anger
they are consumed.
10 The roaring of the lion,
The voice of the fierce lion,
And the teeth of the young lions
are broken.
11 The old lion perishes for lack of prey,
And the cubs of the lioness are
scattered.

12 "Now a word was secretly brought
to me,
And my ear received a whisper of it.
13 In disquieting thoughts from the
visions of the night,
When deep sleep falls on men,
14 Fear came upon me, and trembling,
Which made all my bones shake.
15 Then a spirit passed before my face;
The hair on my body stood up.
16 It stood still,
But I could not discern its appearance.
A form *was* before my eyes;
There was silence;
Then I heard a voice *saying*:
17 'Can a mortal be more righteous
than God?
Can a man be more pure
than his Maker?
18 If He puts no trust in His servants,
If He charges His angels with error,
19 How much more those who dwell
in houses of clay,
Whose foundation is in the dust,
Who are crushed before a moth?
20 They are broken in pieces from
morning till evening;
They perish forever,
with no one regarding.
21 Does not their own excellence go
away?
They die, even without wisdom.'

Job Is Chastened by God

5 "Call out now;
Is there anyone who will answer you?
And to which of the holy ones
will you turn?
2 For wrath kills a foolish man,
And envy slays a simple one.
3 I have seen the foolish taking root,
But suddenly I cursed his habitation.
4 His sons are far from safety,
They are crushed in the gate,
And *there is* no deliverer.

5 Literally *my bread*

5 Because the hungry eat up his harvest,
   Taking it even from the thorns,
   And a snare snatches their substance.
6 For affliction does not come
      from the dust,
   Nor does trouble spring
      from the ground;
7 Yet man is born to trouble,
   As the sparks fly upward.

8 "But as for me, I would seek God,
   And to God I would commit my
      cause—
9 Who does great things,
      and unsearchable,
   Marvelous things without number.
10 He gives rain on the earth,
   And sends waters on the fields.
11 He sets on high those who are lowly,
   And those who mourn are lifted
      to safety.
12 He frustrates the devices of the crafty,
   So that their hands cannot carry out
      their plans.
13 He catches the wise in their own
      craftiness,
   And the counsel of the cunning
      comes quickly upon them.
14 They meet with darkness in the
      daytime,
   And grope at noontime as in the night.
15 But He saves the needy from the
      sword,
   From the mouth of the mighty,
   And from their hand.
16 So the poor have hope,
   And injustice shuts her mouth.

17 "Behold, happy is the man
      whom God corrects;
   Therefore do not despise the
      chastening of the Almighty.
18 For He bruises, but He binds up;
   He wounds, but His hands make
      whole.
19 He shall deliver you in six troubles,
   Yes, in seven no evil shall touch you.
20 In famine He shall redeem you
      from death,
   And in war from the power
      of the sword.
21 You shall be hidden from the scourge
      of the tongue,
   And you shall not be afraid of
      destruction when it comes.
22 You shall laugh at destruction and
      famine,
   And you shall not be afraid of the
      beasts of the earth.

23 For you shall have a covenant
      with the stones of the field,
   And the beasts of the field
      shall be at peace with you.
24 You shall know that your tent is in
      peace;
   You shall visit your habitation
      and find nothing amiss.
25 You shall also know that your
      descendants shall be many,
   And your offspring like the grass
      of the earth.
26 You shall come to the grave
      at a full age,
   As a sheaf of grain ripens in its season.
27 Behold, this we have searched out;
   It is true.
   Hear it, and know for yourself."

Job: My Complaint Is Just

6 Then Job answered and said:

2 "Oh, that my grief were fully weighed,
   And my calamity laid with it in the
      balances!
3 For then it would be heavier than the
      sand of the sea—
   Therefore my words have been rash.
4 For the arrows of the Almighty are
      within me;
   My spirit drinks in their poison;
   The terrors of God are arrayed
      against me.
5 Does the wild donkey bray
      when it has grass,
   Or does the ox low over its fodder?
6 Can flavorless food be eaten without
      salt?
   Or is there any taste in the white
      of an egg?
7 My soul refuses to touch them;
   They are as loathsome food to me.

8 "Oh, that I might have my request,
   That God would grant me the thing
      that I long for!
9 That it would please God to crush me,
   That He would loose his hand
      and cut me off!
10 Then I would still have comfort;
   Though in anguish, I would exult.
   Let Him not spare,
   For I have not concealed the words
      of the Holy One.

11 "What strength do I have,
      that I should hope?
   And what is my end,
      that I should prolong my life?

12 Is my strength the strength of stones?
  Or is my flesh bronze?
13 Is my help not within me?
  And is success driven from me?

14 "To him who is afflicted, kindness
    should be shown by his friend,
  Even though he forsakes the fear
    of the Almighty.
15 My brothers have dealt deceitfully like
    a brook,
  Like the streams of the brooks that
    pass away,
16 Which are dark because of the ice,
  And into which the snow vanishes.
17 When it is warm,
    they cease to flow;
  When it is hot,
    they vanish from their place.
18 The paths of their way turn aside,
  They go nowhere and perish.
19 The caravans of Tema look,
  The travelers of Sheba hope for them.
20 They are disappointed because they
    were confident;
  They come there and are confused.
21 For now you are nothing,
  You see terror and are afraid.
22 Did I ever say, 'Bring something to
    me'?
  Or, 'Offer a bribe for me from your
    wealth'?
23 Or, 'Deliver me from the enemy's
    hand'?
  Or, 'Redeem me from the hand of
    oppressors'?

24 "Teach me, and I will hold my tongue;
  Cause me to understand wherein I
    have erred.
25 How forceful are right words!
  But what does your arguing prove?
26 Do you intend to reprove my words,
  And the speeches of a desperate one,
    which are as wind?
27 Yes, you overwhelm the fatherless,
  And you undermine your friend.
28 Now therefore, be pleased
    to look at me;
  For I would never lie to your face.
29 Turn now, let there be no injustice;
  Yes, turn again, my righteousness still
    stands.
30 Is there injustice on my tongue?
  Cannot my taste discern the unsavory?

Job: My Suffering Is Comfortless

7 "Is there not a time of hard service for
    man on earth?
  Are not his days also like the days
    of a hired man?

2 Like a servant who earnestly desires
    the shade,
  And like a hired man who eagerly
    looks for his wages,
3 So I have been allotted months of
    futility,
  And wearisome nights have been
    appointed to me.
4 When I lie down, I say,
    'When shall I arise,
  And the night be ended?'
  For I have had my fill of tossing till
    dawn.
5 My flesh is caked with worms and
    dust,
  My skin is cracked
    and breaks out afresh.

6 "My days are swifter than a weaver's
    shuttle,
  And are spent without hope.
7 Oh, remember that my life is a breath!
  My eye will never again see good.
8 The eye of him who sees me will see
    me no more;
  While your eyes are upon me,
    I shall no longer be.
9 As the cloud disappears
    and vanishes away,
  So he who goes down to the grave
    does not come up.
10 He shall never return to his house,
  Nor shall his place know him anymore.

11 "Therefore I will not restrain my mouth;
  I will speak in the anguish of my spirit;
  I will complain in the bitterness of my
    soul.
12 Am I a sea, or a sea serpent,
  That You set a guard over me?
13 When I say, 'My bed will comfort me,
  My couch will ease my complaint,'
14 Then You scare me with dreams
  And terrify me with visions,
15 So that my soul chooses strangling
  And death rather than my body.6
16 I loathe my life;
  I would not live forever.
  Let me alone,
  For my days are but a breath.

17 "What is man,
    that You should magnify him,
  That You should set Your heart on
    him,
18 That You should visit him every
    morning,
  And test him every moment?
19 How long?
  Will You not look away from me,

6 Literally my bones

And let me alone till I swallow my
  saliva?
20 Have I sinned?
  What have I done to You,
  O watcher of men?
  Why have You set me as Your target,
  So that I am a burden to myself?
21 Why then do You not pardon my
    transgression,
  And take away my iniquity?
  For now I will lie down in the dust,
  And You will seek me diligently,
  But I *will* no longer *be*."

Bildad: Job Should Repent

8 Then Bildad the Shuhite answered
  and said:

2 "How long will you speak these *things*,
  And the words of your mouth
    be like a strong wind?
3 Does God subvert judgment?
  Or does the Almighty pervert justice?
4 If your sons have sinned against Him,
  He has cast them away for their
    transgression.
5 If you would earnestly seek God
  And make your supplication to the
    Almighty,
6 If you *were* pure and upright,
  Surely now He would awake for you,
  And prosper your rightful habitation.
7 Though your beginning was small,
  Yet your latter end would increase
    abundantly.

8 "For inquire, please, of the former age,
  And consider the things discovered
    by their fathers;
9 For we *are but of* yesterday,
    and know nothing,
  Because our days on earth *are* a
    shadow.
10 Will they not teach you and tell you,
  And utter words from their heart?

11 "Can the papyrus grow up
    without a marsh?
  Can the reeds flourish without water?
12 While it *is* yet green *and* not cut down,
  It withers before any *other* plant.
13 So *are* the paths of all who forget God;
  And the hope of the hypocrite shall
    perish,
14 Whose confidence shall be cut off,
  And whose trust *is* a spider's web.
15 He leans on his house,
    but it does not stand.
  He holds it fast, but it does not endure.
16 He grows green in the sun,

And his branches spread out in his
  garden.
17 His roots wrap around the rock heap,
  And look for a place in the stones.
18 If he is destroyed from his place,
  Then *it* will deny him, *saying,*
    'I have not seen you.'

19 "Behold, this is the joy of His way,
  And out of the earth others will grow.
20 Behold, God will not cast away the
    blameless,
  Nor will He uphold the evildoers.
21 He will yet fill your mouth with
    laughing,
  And your lips with rejoicing.
22 Those who hate you will be clothed
    with shame,
  And the dwelling place of the wicked
    will come to nothing."[7]

Job: There Is No Mediator

9 Then Job answered and said:

2 "Truly I know *it is* so,
  But how can a man be righteous
    before God?
3 If one wished to contend with Him,
  He could not answer Him
    one time out of a thousand.
4 God[8] *is* wise in heart
    and mighty in strength.
  Who has hardened *himself* against Him
    and prospered?
5 He removes the mountains,
    and they do not know
  When He overturns them in His anger;
6 He shakes the earth out of its place,
  And its pillars tremble;
7 He commands the sun,
    and it does not rise;
  He seals off the stars;
8 He alone spreads out the heavens,
  And treads on the waves of the sea;
9 He made the Bear, Orion,
    and the Pleiades,
  And the chambers of the south;
10 He does great things past finding out,
  Yes, wonders without number.
11 If He goes by me, I do not see *Him*;
  If He moves past, I do not perceive
    Him;
12 If He takes away, who can hinder
    Him?
  Who can say to Him, 'What are You
    doing?'
13 God will not withdraw His anger,
  The allies of the proud[9] lie prostrate
    beneath Him.

---

7 Literally *will not be*   8 Literally *He*   9 Hebrew *rahab*

14"How then can I answer Him,
   And choose my words *to reason* with
      Him?
15 For though I were righteous,
      I could not answer Him;
   I would beg mercy of my Judge.
16 If I called and He answered me,
   I would not believe that He was
      listening to my voice.
17 For He crushes me with a tempest,
   And multiplies my wounds without
      cause.
18 He will not allow me to catch my
      breath,
   But fills me with bitterness.
19 If *it is a matter* of strength,
      indeed *He is* strong;
   And if of justice,
      who will appoint my day *in court?*
20 Though I were righteous,
      my own mouth would condemn me;
   Though I *were* blameless,
      it would prove me perverse.

21 "I am blameless,
      yet I do not know myself;
   I despise my life.
22 It *is* all one *thing*;
   Therefore I say, 'He destroys the
      blameless and the wicked.'
23 If the scourge slays suddenly,
   He laughs at the plight of the innocent.
24 The earth is given into the hand
      of the wicked.
   He covers the faces of its judges.
   If it is not *He,* who else could it be?

25 "Now my days are swifter than a
      runner;
   They flee away, they see no good.
26 They pass by like swift ships,
   Like an eagle swooping on its prey.
27 If I say, 'I will forget my complaint,
   I will put off my sad face
      and wear a smile,'
28 I am afraid of all my sufferings;
   I know that You will not hold me
      innocent.
29 *If* I am condemned,
   Why then do I labor in vain?
30 If I wash myself with snow water,
   And cleanse my hands with soap,
31 Yet You will plunge me into the pit,
   And my own clothes will abhor me.

32 "For *He is* not a man, as I *am,*
   That I may answer Him,
   And *that* we should go to court
      together.
33 Nor is there any mediator between us,
   Who may lay his hand on us both.

34 Let Him take His rod away from me,
   And do not let dread of Him
      terrify me.
35 *Then* I would speak and not fear Him,
   But it is not so with me.

Job: I Would Plead with God

10 "My soul loathes my life;
   I will give free course to my
      complaint,
   I will speak in the bitterness
      of my soul.
2 I will say to God,
   'Do not condemn me;
   Show me why You contend with me.
3 *Does it* seem good to You that You
      should oppress,
   That You should despise the work
      of Your hands,
   And shine on the counsel of the
      wicked?
4 Do You have eyes of flesh?
   Or do You see as man sees?
5 *Are* Your days like the days of a
      mortal man?
   Are Your years like the days of a
      mighty man,
6 That You should seek for my iniquity
   And search out my sin,
7 Although You know that I am not
      wicked,
   And *there is* no one who can deliver
      from Your hand?

8 'Your hands have made me
      and fashioned me,
   An intricate unity;
   Yet You would destroy me.
9 Remember, I pray, that You have
      made me like clay.
   And will You turn me into dust again?
10 Did you not pour me out like milk,
   And curdle me like cheese,
11 Clothe me with skin and flesh,
   And knit me together with bones
      and sinews?
12 You have granted me life and favor,
   And Your care has preserved my spirit.

13 'And these *things* You have hidden
      in Your heart;
   I know that this *was* with You:
14 If I sin, then You mark me,
   And will not acquit me of my iniquity.
15 If I am wicked, woe to me;
   Even *if* I am righteous,
      I cannot lift up my head.
   I am full of disgrace;
   See my misery!

16 If my head[10] is exalted,
You hunt me like a fierce lion,
And again You show Yourself
awesome against me.
17 You renew Your witnesses against me,
And increase Your indignation
toward me;
Changes and war are *ever* with me.

18 'Why then have You brought me
out of the womb?
Oh, that I had perished
and no eye had seen me!
19 I would have been as though
I had not been.
I would have been carried from the
womb to the grave.
20 Are not my days few?
Cease! Leave me alone,
that I may take a little comfort,
21 Before I go *to the place from which*
I shall not return,
To the land of darkness
and the shadow of death,
22 A land as dark as darkness *itself*,
As the shadow of death,
without any order,
Where even the light *is* like darkness.' "

Zophar Urges Job to Repent

11 Then Zophar the Naamathite answered and said:

2 "Should not the multitude of words
be answered?
And should a man full of talk be
vindicated?
3 Should your empty talk make men
hold their peace?
And when you mock,
should no one rebuke you?
4 For you have said,
'My doctrine *is* pure,
And I am clean in your eyes.'
5 But oh, that God would speak,
And open His lips against you,
6 That He would show you the secrets
of wisdom!
For *they would* double *your* prudence.
Know therefore that God exacts from
you
Less than your iniquity *deserves*.

7 "Can you search out the deep things
of God?
Can you find out the limits of the
Almighty?
8 *They are* higher than heaven—
what can you do?

Deeper than Sheol—
what can you know?
9 Their measure *is* longer than the earth
And broader than the sea.

10 "If He passes by, imprisons,
and gathers *to judgment*,
Then who can hinder Him?
11 For He knows deceitful men;
He sees wickedness also.
Will He not then consider *it?*
12 For an empty-headed man will be wise,
When a wild donkey's colt is born a
man.

13 "If you would prepare your heart,
And stretch out your hands toward
Him;
14 If iniquity *were* in your hand,
and you put it far away,
And would not let wickedness dwell
in your tents;
15 Then surely you could lift up your face
without spot;
Yes, you could be steadfast,
and not fear;
16 Because you would forget *your* misery,
And remember *it* as waters *that have*
passed away,
17 And *your* life would be brighter than
noonday.
Though you were dark,
you would be like the morning.
18 And you would be secure,
because there is hope;
Yes, you would dig *about you,*
and take your rest in safety.
19 You would also lie down,
and no one would make *you* afraid;
Yes, many would court your favor.
20 But the eyes of the wicked will fail,
And they shall not escape,
And their hope—loss of life!"

Job Answers His Critics

12 Then Job answered and said:

2 "No doubt you *are* the people,
And wisdom will die with you!
3 But I have understanding
as well as you;
I *am* not inferior to you.
Indeed, who does not *know*
such things as these?

4 "I am one mocked by his friends,
Who called on God,
and He answered him,
The just and blameless *who is* laughed
to scorn.

10 Literally *it*

5 A lamp[11] is despised in the thought
   of one who is at ease;
   It is made ready for those
   whose feet slip.
6 The tents of robbers prosper,
   And those who provoke God are
   secure—
   In what God provides by His hand.

7 "But now ask the beasts,
   and they will teach you;
   And the birds of the air,
   and they will tell you;
8 Or speak to the earth,
   and it will teach you;
   And the fish of the sea
   will explain to you.
9 Who among all these does not know
   That the hand of the LORD has done
   this,
10 In whose hand *is* the life
   of every living thing,
   And the breath of all mankind?
11 Does not the ear test words
   And the mouth taste its food?
12 Wisdom *is* with aged men,
   And with length of days,
   understanding.

13 "With Him *are* wisdom and strength,
   He has counsel and understanding.
14 If He breaks *a thing* down,
   it cannot be rebuilt;
   If He imprisons a man,
   there can be no release.
15 If He withholds the waters,
   they dry up;
   If He sends them out,
   they overwhelm the earth.
16 With Him *are* strength and prudence.
   The deceived and the deceiver *are* His.
17 He leads counselors away plundered,
   And makes fools of the judges.
18 He loosens the bonds of kings,
   And binds their waist with a belt.
19 He leads princes[12] away plundered,
   And overthrows the mighty.
20 He deprives the trusted ones of speech,
   And takes away the discernment
   of the elders.
21 He pours contempt on princes,
   And disarms the mighty.
22 He uncovers deep things out of
   darkness,
   And brings the shadow of death
   to light.
23 He makes nations great,
   and destroys them;
   He enlarges nations, and guides them.

24 He takes away the understanding[13] of
   the chiefs of the people of the earth,
   And makes them wander in a pathless
   wilderness.
25 They grope in the dark without light,
   And He makes them stagger like a
   drunken *man.*

13

"Behold, my eye has seen all *this,*
My ear has heard and understood
it.
2 What you know, I also know;
   I *am* not inferior to you.
3 But I would speak to the Almighty,
   And I desire to reason with God.
4 But you forgers of lies,
   You *are* all worthless physicians.
5 Oh, that you would be silent,
   And it would be your wisdom!
6 Now hear my reasoning,
   And heed the pleadings of my lips.
7 Will you speak wickedly for God,
   And talk deceitfully for Him?
8 Will you show partiality for Him?
   Will you contend for God?
9 Will it be well
   when He searches you out?
   Or can you mock Him
   as one mocks a man?
10 He will surely reprove you
   If you secretly show partiality.
11 Will not His excellence make you
   afraid,
   And the dread of Him fall upon you?
12 Your platitudes *are* proverbs of ashes,
   Your defenses are defenses of clay.

13 "Hold your peace with me,
   and let me speak,
   Then let come on me what *may!*
14 Why do I take my flesh in my teeth,
   And put my life in my hands?
15 Though He slay me,
   yet will I trust Him.
   Even so, I will defend my own ways
   before Him.
16 He also *shall* be my salvation,
   For a hypocrite could not come
   before Him.
17 Listen diligently to my speech,
   And to my declaration with your ears.
18 See now, I have prepared *my* case,
   I know that I shall be vindicated.
19 Who *is* he *who* will contend with me?
   If now I hold my tongue, I perish.

Job's Despondent Prayer

20 "Only two *things* do not do to me,
   Then I will not hide myself from You:
21 Withdraw Your hand far from me,

11 Or *disaster* 12 Literally *priests*, but not in the technical sense 13 Literally *heart*

And let not the dread of You
 make me afraid.
22 Then call, and I will answer;
 Or let me speak,
 then You respond to me.
23 How many *are* my iniquities and sins?
 Make me know my transgression and
 my sin.
24 Why do You hide Your face,
 And regard me as Your enemy?
25 Will You frighten a leaf
 driven to and fro?
 And will You pursue dry stubble?
26 For You write bitter things against me,
 And make me inherit the iniquities
 of my youth.
27 You put my feet in the stocks,
 And watch closely all my paths.
 You set a limit[14] for the soles of my
 feet.

28 "Man[15] decays like a rotten thing,
 Like a garment that is moth-eaten.

14 "Man *who is* born of woman
 Is of few days and full of trouble.
2 He comes forth like a flower
 and fades away;
 He flees like a shadow and does not
 continue.
3 And do You open Your eyes
 on such a one,
 And bring me[16] to judgment with
 Yourself?
4 Who can bring a clean *thing*
 out of an unclean?
 No one!
5 Since his days *are* determined,
 The number of his months *is* with
 You;
 You have appointed his limits,
 so that he cannot pass.
6 Look away from him that he may rest,
 Till like a hired man he finishes his
 day.

7 "For there is hope for a tree,
 If it is cut down,
 that it will sprout again,
 And that its tender shoots will not
 cease.
8 Though its root may grow old
 in the earth,
 And its stump may die in the ground,
9 *Yet* at the scent of water it will bud
 And bring forth branches like a plant.
10 But man dies and is laid away;
 Indeed he breathes his last
 And where *is* he?

11 *As* water disappears from the sea,
 And a river becomes parched
 and dries up,
12 So man lies down and does not rise.
 Till the heavens *are* no more,
 They will not awake
 Nor be roused from their sleep.

13 "Oh, that You would hide me
 in the grave,
 That You would conceal me until Your
 wrath is past,
 That You would appoint me a set time,
 and remember me!
14 If a man dies, shall he live *again?*
 All the days of my hard service
 I will wait,
 Till my change comes.
15 You shall call, and I will answer You;
 You shall desire the work of Your
 hands.
16 For now You number my steps,
 But do not watch over my sin.
17 My transgression *is* sealed up in a bag,
 And You cover[17] my iniquity.

18 "But *as* a mountain falls
 and crumbles away,
 And *as* a rock is moved from its place;
19 *As* water wears away stones,
 And as torrents wash away the soil
 of the earth;
 So You destroy the hope of man.
20 You prevail forever against him,
 and he passes on;
 You change his countenance
 and send him away.
21 His sons come to honor,
 and he does not know *it;*
 They are brought low,
 and he does not perceive *it.*
22 But his flesh will be in pain over it,
 And his soul will mourn over it."

Eliphaz Accuses Job of Folly

15 Then Eliphaz the Temanite answered and said:

2 "Should a wise man answer
 with empty knowledge,
 And fill himself with the east wind?
3 Should he reason with unprofitable
 talk,
 Or by speeches with which he
 can do no good?
4 Yes, you cast off fear,
 And restrain prayer before God.
5 For your iniquity teaches your mouth,
 And you choose the tongue of the
 crafty.

14 Literally *inscribe a print* 15 Literally *He* 16 Septuagint, Syriac, and Vulgate read *him.*
17 Literally *plaster over*

6 Your own mouth condemns you,
     and not I;
   Yes, your own lips testify against you.

7 "Are you the first man who was born?
     Or were you made before the hills?
8 Have you heard the counsel of God?
     Do you limit wisdom to yourself?
9 What do you know
     that we do not know?
   What do you understand
     that is not in us?
10 Both the gray-haired and the aged
     are among us,
   Much older than your father.
11 Are the consolations of God
     too small for you,
   And the word spoken gently[18] with
     you?
12 Why does your heart carry you away,
     And what do your eyes wink at,
13 That you turn your spirit against God,
   And let such words go out of your
     mouth?

14 "What is man, that he could be pure?
     And he who is born of a woman,
       that he could be righteous?
15 If God[19] puts no trust in His saints,
     And the heavens are not pure
       in His sight,
16 How much less man,
     who is abominable and filthy,
   Who drinks iniquity like water!

17 "I will tell you, hear me;
     What I have seen I will declare,
18 What wise men have told,
     Not hiding anything received
       from their fathers,
19 To whom alone the land was given,
     And no alien passed among them:
20 The wicked man writhes with pain
     all his days,
   And the number of years is hidden
     from the oppressor.
21 Dreadful sounds are in his ears;
     In prosperity the destroyer comes
       upon him.
22 He does not believe that he
     will return from darkness,
   And he watches for the sword.
23 He wanders about for bread, saying,
     'Where is it?'
   He knows that a day of darkness is
     ready at his hand.
24 Trouble and anguish make him afraid;
     They overpower him,
       like a king ready for battle.
25 For he stretches out his hand
     against God,

And acts defiantly against
  the Almighty,
26 Running stubbornly against Him
   With his strong, embossed shield.

27 "Though he has covered his face
     with his fatness,
   And made his waist heavy with fat,
28 He dwells in desolate cities,
     In houses which no one inhabits,
   Which are destined to become ruins.
29 He will not be rich,
     Nor will his wealth continue,
   Nor will his possessions overspread
     the earth.
30 He will not depart from darkness;
     The flame will dry out his branches,
   And by the breath of His mouth he
     will go away.
31 Let him not trust in futile things,
     deceiving himself,
   For futility will be his reward.
32 It will be accomplished before his time,
     And his branch will not be green.
33 He will shake off his unripe grape
     like a vine,
   And cast off his blossom
     like an olive tree.
34 For the company of hypocrites
     will be barren,
   And fire will consume the tents
     of bribery.
35 They conceive trouble
     and bring forth futility;
   Their womb prepares deceit."

Job Reproaches His Pitiless Friends

16 Then Job answered and said:

2 "I have heard many such things;
     Miserable comforters are you all!
3 Shall words of wind have an end?
     Or what provokes you that you
       answer?
4 I also could speak as you do,
     If your soul were in my soul's place.
   I could heap up words against you,
     And shake my head at you;
5 But I would strengthen you
     with my mouth,
   And the comfort of my lips would
     relieve your grief.

6 "Though I speak,
     my grief is not relieved;
   And though I remain silent,
     how am I eased?

18 Septuagint reads a secret thing.   19 Literally He

7 But now He has worn me out;
   You have made desolate all my
     company.
8 You have shriveled me up,
   And it is a witness *against me*;
   My leanness rises up against me
   And bears witness to my face.
9 He tears *me* in His wrath,
     and hates me;
   He gnashes at me with His teeth;
   My adversary sharpens His gaze
     on me.
10 They gape at me with their mouth,
   They strike me reproachfully
     on the cheek,
   They gather together against me.
11 God has delivered me to the ungodly,
   And turned me over to the hands
     of the wicked.
12 I was at ease, but He has shattered me;
   He also has taken *me* by my neck,
     and shaken me to pieces;
   He has set me up for His target,
13 His archers surround me.
   He pierces my heart²⁰
     and does not pity;
   He pours out my gall on the ground.
14 He breaks me with wound upon
     wound;
   He runs at me like a warrior.²¹

15 "I have sewn sackcloth over my skin,
   And laid my head²² in the dust.
16 My face is flushed from weeping,
   And on my eyelids *is* the shadow
     of death;
17 Although no violence *is* in my hands,
   And my prayer *is* pure.

18 "O earth, do not cover my blood,
   And let my cry have no *resting* place!
19 Surely even now my witness *is* in
     heaven,
   And my evidence *is* on high.
20 My friends scorn me;
   My eyes pour out *tears* to God.
21 Oh, that one might plead for a man
     with God,
   As a man *pleads* for his neighbor!
22 For when a few years are finished,
   I shall go the way of no return.

Job Prays for Relief

17 "My spirit is broken,
       My days are extinguished,
     The grave *is ready* for me.
2 *Are* not mockers with me?
   And does not my eye dwell on their
     provocation?

3 "Now put down a pledge for me
     with Yourself.

Who *is* he *who* will shake hands
  with me?
4 For You have hidden their heart
     from understanding;
   Therefore You will not exalt *them*.
5 He who speaks flattery to *his* friends,
   Even the eyes of his children will fail.

6 "But He has made me a byword
     of the people,
   And I have become one in whose face
     men spit.
7 My eye has also grown dim because
     of sorrow,
   And all my members *are* like shadows.
8 Upright *men* are astonished at this,
   And the innocent stirs himself up
     against the hypocrite.
9 Yet the righteous will hold to his way,
   And he who has clean hands will be
     stronger and stronger.

10 "But please, come back again,
     all of you,
   For I shall not find *one* wise *man*
     among you.
11 My days are past,
   My purposes are broken off,
   Even the thoughts of my heart.
12 They change the night into day;
   'The light *is* near,' *they say*,
     in the face of darkness.
13 If I wait *for* the grave *as* my house,
   If I make my bed in the darkness,
14 If I say to corruption,
     'You *are* my father,'
   And to the worm,
     'You *are* my mother and my sister,'
15 Where then *is* my hope?
   As for my hope, who can see it?
16 *Will* they go down to the gates of
     Sheol?
   Shall *we have* rest together in the
     dust?"

Bildad: The Wicked Are Punished

18 Then Bildad the Shuhite answered
       and said:

2 "How long *till* you put an end to words?
   Gain understanding,
     and afterward we will speak.
3 Why are we counted as beasts,
   And regarded as stupid in your sight?
4 You who tear yourself in anger,
   Shall the earth be forsaken for you?
   Or shall the rock be removed from its
     place?

5 "The light of the wicked
     indeed goes out,

20 Literally *kidney*   21 Vulgate reads *giant*.   22 Literally *horn*

And the flame of his fire
does not shine.
6 The light is dark in his tent,
And his lamp beside him is put out.
7 The steps of his strength are shortened,
And his own counsel casts him down.
8 For he is cast into a net
by his own feet,
And he walks into a snare.
9 The net takes *him* by the heel,
And a snare lays hold of him.
10 A noose *is* hidden for him on the
ground,
And a trap for him in the road.
11 Terrors frighten him on every side,
And drive him to his feet.
12 His strength is starved,
And destruction *is* ready at his side.
13 It devours patches of his skin;
The firstborn of death devours his
limbs.
14 He is uprooted from the shelter
of his tent,
And they parade him before the king
of terrors.
15 They dwell in his tent *who are*
none of his;
Brimstone is scattered on his
habitation.
16 His roots are dried out below,
And his branch withers above.
17 The memory of him perishes
from the earth,
And he has no name among the
renowned.[23]
18 He is driven from light into darkness,
And chased out of the world.
19 He has neither son nor posterity
among his people,
Nor any remaining in his dwellings.
20 Those in the west are astonished
at his day,
As those in the east are frightened.
21 Surely such *are* the dwellings
of the wicked,
And this *is* the place *of him*
who does not know God."

Job Trusts in His Redeemer

19 Then Job answered and said:

2 "How long will you torment my soul,
And break me in pieces with words?
3 These ten times you have reproached
me;
You are not ashamed *that* you have
wronged[24] me.
4 And if indeed I have erred,
My error remains with me.

5 If indeed you magnify *yourselves*
against me,
And plead my disgrace against me,
6 Know then that God has wronged me,
And has surrounded me with His net.

7 "If I cry out concerning wrong,
I am not heard.
If I cry aloud, *there is* no justice.
8 He has fenced up my way,
so that I cannot pass;
And He has set darkness in my paths.
9 He has stripped me of my glory,
And taken the crown *from* my head.
10 He breaks me down on every side,
And I am gone;
My hope He has uprooted like a tree.
11 He has also kindled His wrath
against me,
And He counts me as *one*
of His enemies.
12 His troops come together
And build up their road against me;
They encamp all around my tent.

13 "He has removed my brothers
far from me,
And my acquaintances
are completely estranged from me.
14 My relatives have failed,
And my close friends
have forgotten me.
15 Those who dwell in my house,
and my maidservants,
Count me as a stranger;
I am an alien in their sight.
16 I call my servant,
but he gives no answer;
I beg him with my mouth.
17 My breath is offensive to my wife,
And I am repulsive to the children
of my own body.
18 Even young children despise me;
I arise, and they speak against me.
19 All my close friends abhor me,
And those whom I love have turned
against me.
20 My bone clings to my skin
and to my flesh,
And I have escaped by the skin
of my teeth.

21 "Have pity on me, have pity on me,
O you my friends,
For the hand of God has struck me!
22 Why do you persecute me as God *does*,
And are not satisfied with my flesh?

23 "Oh, that my words were written!
Oh, that they were inscribed in a book!

---

23 Literally *before the outside,* meaning distinguished, famous 24 A Jewish tradition reads *make yourselves strange.*

24 That they were engraved on a rock
  With an iron pen and lead, forever!
25 For I know *that* my Redeemer lives,
  And He shall stand at last on the
  earth;
26 And after my skin is destroyed,
  this *I know*,
  That in my flesh I shall see God,
27 Whom I shall see for myself,
  And my eyes shall behold,
  and not another.
  How my heart yearns within me!
28 If you should say, 'How shall we
  persecute him?'—'
  Since the root of the matter
  is found in me,
29 Be afraid of the sword for yourselves;
  For wrath *brings* the punishment
  of the sword,
  That you may know *there is* a
  judgment."

Zophar's Sermon on the Wicked Man

20 Then Zophar the Naamathite answered and said:

2 "Therefore my anxious thoughts make
  me answer,
  Because of the turmoil within me.
3 I have heard the reproof that
  reproaches me,
  And the spirit of my understanding
  causes me to answer.

4 "Do you *not* know this of old,
  Since man was placed on earth,
5 That the triumphing of the wicked
  is short,
  And the joy of the hypocrite is *but* for
  a moment?
6 Though his haughtiness mounts up to
  the heavens,
  And his head reaches to the clouds,
7 *Yet* he will perish forever like his own
  refuse;
  Those who have seen him will say,
  'Where is he?'
8 He will fly away like a dream,
  and not be found;
  Yes, he will be chased away like a
  vision of the night.
9 The eye *that* saw him will *see him*
  no more,
  Nor will his place behold him
  anymore.
10 His children will seek the favor
  of the poor,
  And his hands will restore his wealth.
11 His bones are full of his youthful vigor,

But it will lie down with him in the
  dust.

12 "Though evil is sweet in his mouth,
  And he hides it under his tongue,
13 *Though* he spares it
  and does not forsake it,
  But still keeps it in his mouth,
14 *Yet* his food in his stomach turns sour;
  It becomes cobra venom within him.
15 He swallows down riches
  And vomits them up again;
  God casts them out of his belly.
16 He will suck the poison of cobras;
  The viper's tongue will slay him.
17 He will not see the streams,
  The rivers flowing with honey
  and cream.
18 He will restore that
  for which he labored,
  And will not swallow *it* down;
  From the proceeds of *his* business
  He will get no enjoyment.
19 For he has oppressed
  and forsaken the poor,
  He has violently seized a house
  which he did not build.

20 "Because he knows no quietness
  in his heart,[25]
  He will not save anything he desires.
21 Nothing is left for him to eat;
  Therefore his well-being will not last.
22 In his self-sufficiency he will be
  in distress;
  Every hand of misery will come
  against him.
23 *When* he is about to fill his stomach,
  God will cast on him the fury
  of His wrath,
  And will rain *it* on him while
  he is eating.
24 He will flee from the iron weapon;
  A bronze bow will pierce him through.
25 It is drawn, and comes out of the
  body;
  Yes, the glittering *point comes*
  out of his gall.
  Terrors *come* upon him;
26 Total darkness *is* reserved for his
  treasures.
  An unfanned fire will consume him;
  It shall go ill with him who is left
  in his tent.
27 The heavens will reveal his iniquity,
  And the earth will rise up against him.
28 The increase of his house will depart,
  And his goods will flow away in
  the day of His wrath.
29 This *is* the portion from God
  for a wicked man,

25 Literally *belly*

The heritage appointed to him
by God."

Job's Discourse on the Wicked

21 Then Job answered and said:

2 "Listen carefully to my speech,
And let this be your consolation.
3 Bear with me that I may speak,
And after I have spoken,
keep mocking.

4 "As for me, *is* my complaint against
man?
And if *it were*, why should I not be
impatient?
5 Look at me and be astonished;
Put *your* hand over *your* mouth.
6 Even when I remember I am terrified,
And trembling takes hold of my flesh.
7 Why do the wicked live
and become old,
Yes, become mighty in power?
8 Their descendants are established
with them in their sight,
And their offspring before their eyes.
9 Their houses *are* safe from fear,
Neither *is* the rod of God upon them.
10 Their bull breeds without failure;
Their cow calves without miscarriage.
11 They send forth their little ones
like a flock,
And their children dance.
12 They sing to the tambourine and harp,
And rejoice to the sound of the flute.
13 They spend their days in wealth,
And in a moment go down
to the grave.[26]
14 Yet they say to God, 'Depart from us,
For we do not desire the knowledge
of Your ways.
15 Who *is* the Almighty,
that we should serve Him?
And what profit do we have
if we pray to Him?'
16 Indeed their prosperity
is not in their hand;
The counsel of the wicked
is far from me.

17 "How often is the lamp of the wicked
put out?
How often does their destruction come
upon them,
The sorrows God distributes in His
anger?
18 They are like straw before the wind,
And like chaff that a storm carries
away.

19 *They say*, 'God lays up one's[27] iniquity
for his children';
Let Him recompense him,
that he may know *it*.
20 Let his eyes see his destruction,
And let him drink of the wrath
of the Almighty.
21 For what does he care about his
household after him,
When the number of his months is cut
in half?

22 "Can *anyone* teach God knowledge,
Since He judges those *who are* on high?
23 One dies in his full strength,
Being wholly at ease and secure;
24 His pails are full of milk,
And the marrow of his bones is moist.
25 Another man dies in the bitterness of
his soul,
Never having eaten with pleasure.
26 They lie down alike in the dust,
And worms cover them.

27 "Look, I know your thoughts,
And the schemes *with which* you
would wrong me.
28 For you say,
'Where *is* the house of the prince?
And where *is* the tent,[28]
The dwelling place of the wicked?'
29 Have you not asked those who travel
the road?
And do you not know their signs?
30 For the wicked are reserved
for the day of doom;
They shall be brought out
on the day of wrath.
31 Who condemns his way to his face?
And who repays him *for what* he has
done?
32 Yet he shall be brought to the grave,
And a vigil kept over the tomb.
33 The clods of the valley shall be sweet
to him;
Everyone shall follow him,
As countless *have gone* before him.
34 How then can you comfort me with
empty words,
Since falsehood remains in your
answers?"

Eliphaz Accuses Job of Wickedness

22 Then Eliphaz the Temanite answered and said:

2 "Can a man be profitable to God,
Though he who is wise may be
profitable to himself?
3 *Is it* any pleasure to the Almighty
that you are righteous?

---

26 Hebrew *Sheol*   27 Literally *his*   28 Vulgate omits *the tent.*

Or *is it* gain *to Him* that you make
your ways blameless?

4 "Is it because of your fear of Him
that He reproves you,
And enters into judgment with you?
5 *Is* not your wickedness great,
And your iniquity without end?
6 For you have taken pledges from your
brother for no reason,
And stripped the naked of their
clothing.
7 You have not given the weary water
to drink,
And you have withheld bread from
the hungry.
8 But the mighty man possessed the
land,
And the honorable man dwelt in it.
9 You have sent widows away empty,
And the strength of the fatherless
was crushed.
10 Therefore snares *are* all around you,
And sudden fear troubles you,
11 Or darkness *so that* you cannot see;
And an abundance of water covers
you.

12 "Is not God in the height of heaven?
And see the highest stars,
how lofty they are!
13 And you say, 'What does God know?
Can He judge through the deep
darkness?
14 Thick clouds cover Him,
so that He cannot see,
And He walks above the circle of
heaven.'
15 Will you keep to the old way
Which wicked men have trod,
16 Who were cut down before their time,
Whose foundations were swept away
by a flood?
17 They said to God, 'Depart from us!
What can the Almighty do to them?'²⁹
18 Yet He filled their houses
with good *things;*
But the counsel of the wicked is far
from me.

19 "The righteous see *it* and are glad,
And the innocent laugh them to scorn:
20 'Surely our adversaries³⁰ are cut down,
And the fire consumes their remnant.'

21 "Now acquaint yourself with Him,
and be at peace;
Thereby good will come to you.

22 Receive, please, instruction from His
mouth,
And lay up His words in your heart.
23 If you return to the Almighty,
you will be built up;
You will remove iniquity far
from your tents.
24 Then you will lay your gold
in the dust,
And the *gold* of Ophir among the
stones of the brooks.
25 Yes, the Almighty will be your gold³¹
And your precious silver;
26 For then you will have your delight
in the Almighty,
And lift up your face to God.
27 You will make your prayer to Him,
He will hear you,
And you will pay your vows.
28 You will also declare a thing,
And it will be established for you;
So light will shine on your ways.
29 When they cast *you* down, and you say,
'Exaltation *will come!*'
Then He will save the humble *person.*
30 He will *even* deliver one who is not
innocent;
Yes, he will be delivered by the purity
of your hands."

Job Proclaims God's Righteous Judgments

23 Then Job answered and said:

2 "Even today my complaint is bitter;
My hand is listless because of my
groaning.
3 Oh, that I knew where I might find
Him,
That I might come to His seat!
4 I would present *my* case before Him,
And fill my mouth with arguments.
5 I would know the words *which* He
would answer me,
And understand what He would say
to me.
6 Would He contend with me in His
great power?
No! But He would take *note* of me.
7 There the upright could reason with
Him,
And I would be delivered forever
from my Judge.

8 "Look, I go forward,
but He is not *there,*
And backward,
but I cannot perceive Him;
9 When He works on the left hand,
I cannot behold *Him;*

---

29 Septuagint and Syriac read *us.*   30 Septuagint reads *substance.*
31 The ancient versions suggest *defense;* Hebrew reads *gold* as in verse 24.

When He turns to the right hand,
I cannot see *Him*.
10 But He knows the way that I take;
When He has tested me,
I shall come forth as gold.
11 My foot has held fast to His steps;
I have kept His way
and not turned aside.
12 I have not departed from the
commandment of His lips;
I have treasured the words
of His mouth
More than my necessary *food*.

13 "But He *is* unique,
and who can make Him change?
And *whatever* His soul desires,
that He does.
14 For He performs *what is* appointed
for me,
And many such *things are* with Him.
15 Therefore I am terrified at His
presence;
When I consider *this*,
I am afraid of Him.
16 For God made my heart weak,
And the Almighty terrifies me;
17 Because I was not cut off from the
presence of darkness,
And He did *not* hide deep darkness
from my face.

Job Complains of Violence on the Earth

24 "Since times are not hidden from
the Almighty,
Why do those who know Him see not
His days?

2 "*Some* remove landmarks;
They seize flocks violently
and feed *on them*;
3 They drive away the donkey
of the fatherless;
They take the widow's ox as a pledge.
4 They push the needy off the road,
So that the poor of the land
are forced to hide.
5 Indeed, *like* wild donkeys in the desert,
They go out to their work,
seeking diligently for food.
The wilderness *yields* food for them
and for *their* children.
6 They gather their fodder in the field
And glean in the vineyard of the
wicked.
7 They spend the night naked,
without clothing,
And have no covering in the cold.
8 They are wet with the showers
of the mountains,

And huddle around the rock
for want of shelter.

9 "*Some* snatch the fatherless
from the breast,
And take a pledge from the poor.
10 They cause *the poor* to go naked,
without clothing;
And they take away the sheaves
from the hungry.
11 They press out oil within their walls,
And tread winepresses, yet suffer thirst.
12 The dying groan in the city,
And the souls of the wounded cry out;
Yet God does not charge *them* with
wrong.

13 "There are those who rebel
against the light;
They do not know its ways
Nor abide in its paths.
14 The murderer rises with the light;
He kills the poor and needy;
And in the night he is like a thief.
15 The eye of the adulterer waits
for the twilight,
Saying, 'No eye will see me';
And he disguises *his* face.
16 In the dark they break into houses
Which they marked for themselves
in the daytime;
They do not know the light.
17 For the morning is the same to them
as the shadow of death;
If *someone* recognizes *them*,
They are in the terrors of the shadow
of death.

18 "They *should be* swift on the face
of the waters,
Their portion *should be* cursed in the
earth,
So that no *one would* turn into the way
of their vineyards.
19 As drought and heat consume
the snow waters,
So should the grave[32] *those who* have
sinned.
20 The womb should forget him,
The worm *should* feed sweetly on him;
He should be remembered no more,
And wickedness should be broken
like a tree.
21 For he preys on the barren
who do not bear,
And does no good for the widow.

22 "But God[33] draws the mighty away
with His power;
He rises up, but no *man* is sure of life.

32 Hebrew *Sheol*   33 Literally *He*

23 He gives them security,
  and they rely *on it*;
  Yet His eyes *are* on their ways.
24 They are exalted for a little while,
  Then they are gone.
  They are brought low;
  They are taken out of the way
    like all *others*;
  They dry out like the heads of grain.

25 "Now if *it is* not *so*,
  who will prove me a liar,
  And make my speech worth nothing?"

Bildad: How Can Man Be Righteous?

25 Then Bildad the Shuhite answered and said:

2 "Dominion and fear *belong* to Him;
  He makes peace in His high places.
3 Is there any number to His armies?
  Upon whom does His light not rise?
4 How then can man be righteous
    before God?
  Or how can he be pure *who is* born
    of a woman?
5 If even the moon does not shine,
  And the stars are not pure in His sight,
6 How much less man, *who is* a maggot,
  And a son of man, *who is* a worm?"

Job: Man's Frailty and God's Majesty

26 But Job answered and said:

2 "How have you helped *him who is*
    without power?
  How have you saved the arm
    that has no strength?
3 How have you counseled *one*
    who has no wisdom?
  And *how* have you declared sound
    advice to many?
4 To whom have you uttered words?
  And whose spirit came from you?

5 "The dead tremble,
  Those under the waters
    and those inhabiting them.
6 Sheol *is* naked before Him,
  And Destruction has no covering.
7 He stretches out the north
    over empty space;
  He hangs the earth on nothing.
8 He binds up the water in His thick
    clouds,
  Yet the clouds are not broken under it.
9 He covers the face of *His* throne,
  And spreads His cloud over it.
10 He drew a circular horizon on the face
    of the waters,

  At the boundary of light and darkness.
11 The pillars of heaven tremble,
  And are astonished at His reproof.
12 He stirs up the sea with His power,
  And by His understanding He breaks
    up the storm.
13 By His Spirit He adorned the heavens;
  His hand pierced the fleeing serpent.
14 Indeed these *are* the mere edges
    of His ways,
  And how small a whisper we hear
    of Him!
  But the thunder of His power
    who can understand?"

Job Maintains His Integrity

27 Moreover Job continued his discourse, and said:

2 "*As* God lives,
    who has taken away my justice,
  And the Almighty,
    who has made my soul bitter,
3 As long as my breath *is* in me,
  And the breath of God in my nostrils,
4 My lips will not speak wickedness,
  Nor my tongue utter deceit.
5 Far be it from me
  That I should say you are right;
  Till I die I will not put away my
    integrity from me.
6 My righteousness I hold fast,
    and will not let it go;
  My heart shall not reproach *me*
    as long as I live.

7 "May my enemy be like the wicked,
  And he who rises up against me like
    the unrighteous.
8 For what is the hope of the hypocrite,
  Though he may gain *much*,
  If God takes away his life?
9 Will God hear his cry
  When trouble comes upon him?
10 Will he delight himself in the
    Almighty?
  Will he always call on God?

11 "I will teach you about the hand
    of God;
  What *is* with the Almighty
    I will not conceal.
12 Surely all of you have seen *it*;
  Why then do you behave with
    complete nonsense?

13 "This is the portion of a wicked man
    with God,
  And the heritage of oppressors,
    received from the Almighty:
14 If his children are multiplied,
    it is for the sword;

And his offspring shall not be satisfied
  with bread.
15 Those who survive him shall be buried
    in death,
  And their[34] widows shall not weep,
16 Though he heaps up silver like dust,
  And piles up clothing like clay—
17 He may pile *it* up,
    but the just will wear *it*,
  And the innocent will divide the silver.
18 He builds his house like a moth,
  Like a booth *which* a watchman makes.
19 The rich man will lie down,
  But not be gathered *up*;
  He opens his eyes,
  And he *is* no more.
20 Terrors overtake him like a flood;
  A tempest steals him away in the night.
21 The east wind carries him away,
    and he is gone;
  It sweeps him out of his place.
22 It hurls against him
    and does not spare;
  He flees desperately from its power.
23 *Men* shall clap their hands at him,
  And shall hiss him out of his place.

Job's Discourse on Wisdom

28 "Surely there is a mine for silver,
  And a place *where* gold is refined.
2 Iron is taken from the earth,
  And copper *is* smelted *from* ore.
3 *Man* puts an end to darkness,
  And searches every recess
  For ore in the darkness and the
    shadow of death.
4 He breaks open a shaft away from
    people;
  In places forgotten by feet
  They hang far away from men;
  They swing to and fro.
5 *As for* the earth, from it comes bread,
  But underneath it is turned up
    as by fire;
6 Its stones *are* the source of sapphires,
  And it contains gold dust.
7 *That* path no bird knows,
  Nor has the falcon's eye seen it.
8 The proud lions[35] have not trodden it,
  Nor has the fierce lion passed over it.
9 He puts his hand on the flint;
  He overturns the mountains
    at the roots.
10 He cuts out channels in the rocks,
  And his eye sees every precious thing.
11 He dams up the streams from trickling;
  What is hidden he brings forth to light.

12 "But where can wisdom be found?
  And where *is* the place of
    understanding?
13 Man does not know its value,
  Nor is it found in the land
    of the living.
14 The deep says, '*It is* not in me';
  And the sea says, '*It is* not with me.'
15 It cannot be purchased for gold,
  Nor can silver be weighed *for* its price.
16 It cannot be valued in the gold
    of Ophir,
  In precious onyx or sapphire.
17 Neither gold nor crystal can equal it,
  Nor can it be exchanged for jewelry
    of fine gold.
18 No mention shall be made of coral
    or quartz,
  For the price of wisdom *is* above
    rubies.
19 The topaz of Ethiopia cannot equal it,
  Nor can it be valued in pure gold.

20 "From where then does wisdom come?
  And where *is* the place of
    understanding?
21 It is hidden from the eyes of all living,
  And concealed from the birds of the
    air.
22 Destruction and Death say,
  'We have heard a report about it
    with our ears.'
23 God understands its way,
  And He knows its place.
24 For He looks to the ends of the earth,
  And sees under the whole heavens,
25 To establish a weight for the wind,
  And mete out the waters by measure.
26 When He made a law for the rain,
  And a path for the thunderbolt,
27 Then He saw wisdom[36] and declared it;
  He prepared it,
    indeed, He searched it out.
28 And to man He said,
  'Behold, the fear of the Lord,
    that *is* wisdom,
  And to depart from evil *is*
    understanding.' "

Job's Summary Defense

29 Job further continued his discourse, and said:

2 "Oh, that I were as *in* months past,
  As *in* the days *when* God watched over
    me;
3 When His lamp shone upon my head,
  And when by His light I walked *through*
    darkness;

---

34 Literally *his*   35 Literally *sons of pride,* figurative of the great lions   36 Literally *it*

4 Just as I was in the days of my prime,
When the friendly counsel of God *was*
over my tent;
5 When the Almighty *was* yet with me,
When my children *were* around me;
6 When my steps were bathed with
cream,[37]
And the rock poured out rivers
of oil for me!

7 "When I went out to the gate
by the city,
When I took my seat in the open
square,
8 The young men saw me and hid,
And the aged arose *and* stood;
9 The princes refrained from talking,
And put *their* hand on their mouth;
10 The voice of nobles was hushed,
And their tongue stuck to the roof
of their mouth.
11 When the ear heard,
then it blessed me,
And when the eye saw,
then it approved me;
12 Because I delivered the poor
who cried out,
And the fatherless
and *he who had* no helper.
13 The blessing of a perishing *man*
came upon me,
And I caused the widow's heart
to sing for joy.
14 I put on righteousness,
and it clothed me;
My justice *was* like a robe
and a turban.
15 I *was* eyes to the blind,
And I *was* feet to the lame.
16 I *was* a father to the poor,
And I searched out the case
that I did not know.
17 I broke the fangs of the wicked,
And plucked the victim from his teeth.

18 "Then I said, 'I shall die in my nest,
And multiply *my* days as the sand.
19 My root *is* spread out to the waters,
And the dew lies all night on my
branch.
20 My glory *is* fresh within me,
And my bow is renewed in my hand.'

21 "Men listened to me and waited,
And kept silence for my counsel.
22 After my words they did not speak
again,
And my speech settled on them *as* dew.
23 They waited for me *as* for the rain,

And they opened their mouth wide
as for the spring rain.
24 *If* I mocked at them,
they did not believe *it*,
And the light of my countenance
they did not cast down.
25 I chose the way for them,
and sat as chief;
So I dwelt as a king in the army,
As one *who* comforts mourners.

30 "But now they mock at me,
men younger than I,
Whose fathers I disdained to put with
the dogs of my flock.
2 Indeed, what *profit is* the strength
of their hands to me?
Their vigor has perished.
3 *They are* gaunt from want and famine,
Fleeing late to the wilderness,
desolate and waste,
4 Who pluck mallow by the bushes,
And broom tree roots *for* their food.
5 They were driven out from among *men*,
They shouted at them as *at* a thief.
6 *They had* to live in the clefts
of the valleys,
In caves of the earth and the rocks.
7 Among the bushes they brayed,
Under the nettles they nestled.
8 *They were* sons of fools,
Yes, sons of vile men;
They were scourged from the land.

9 "And now I am their taunt-song;
Yes, I am their byword.
10 They abhor me, they keep far from me;
They do not hesitate to spit in my face.
11 Because He has loosed my bowstring
and afflicted me,
They have cast off restraint before me.
12 At *my* right *hand* the rabble arises;
They push away my feet,
And they raise against me their ways
of destruction.
13 They break up my path,
They promote my calamity;
They have no helper.
14 They come as broad breakers;
Under the ruinous storm
they roll along.
15 Terrors are turned upon me;
They pursue my honor as the wind,
And my prosperity has passed like a
cloud.

16 "And now my soul is poured out
because of my *plight*;
The days of affliction take hold of me.

37 Masoretic Text reads *wrath;* ancient versions and some Hebrew manuscripts read *cream* (compare 20:17).

17 My bones are pierced in me at night,
And my gnawing pains take no rest.
18 By great force my garment is
disfigured;
It binds me about as the collar
of my coat.
19 He has cast me into the mire,
And I have become like dust
and ashes.

20"I cry out to You,
but You do not answer me;
I stand up, and You regard me.
21 *But* You have become cruel to me;
With the strength of Your hand
You oppose me.
22 You lift me up to the wind
and cause me to ride *on it*;
You spoil my success.
23 For I know *that* You will bring
me *to* death,
And *to* the house appointed
for all living.

24"Surely He would not stretch out *His*
hand against a heap of ruins,
If they cry out when He destroys *it*.
25 Have I not wept for him who was
in trouble?
Has *not* my soul grieved for the poor?
26 But when I looked for good,
evil came *to me*;
And when I waited for light,
then came darkness.
27 My heart is in turmoil and cannot rest;
Days of affliction confront me.
28 I go about mourning,
but not in the sun;
I stand up in the congregation
and cry out for help.
29 I am a brother of jackals,
And a companion of ostriches.
30 My skin grows black
and falls from me;
My bones burn with fever.
31 My harp is *turned* to mourning,
And my flute to the voice of those
who weep.

31 "I have made a covenant
with my eyes;
Why then should I look upon a young
woman?
2 For what *is* the allotment of God
from above,
And the inheritance of the Almighty
from on high?
3 *Is* it not destruction for the wicked,
And disaster for the workers
of iniquity?
4 Does He not see my ways,

And count all my steps?

5 "If I have walked with falsehood,
Or if my foot has hastened to deceit,
6 Let me be weighed in a just balance,
That God may know my integrity.
7 If my step has turned from the way,
Or my heart walked after my eyes,
Or if any spot adheres to my hands,
8 *Then* let me sow, and another eat;
Yes, let my harvest be rooted out.

9 "If my heart has been enticed
by a woman,
Or *if* I have lurked
at my neighbor's door,
10 *Then* let my wife grind for another,
And let others bow down over her.
11 For that *would be* wickedness;
Yes, it *would be* iniquity *worthy of*
judgment.
12 For that *would be* a fire *that* consumes
to destruction,
And would root out all my increase.

13 "If I have despised the cause of my
manservant or my maidservant
When they complained against me,
14 What then shall I do when God
rises up?
When He punishes,
how shall I answer Him?
15 Did not He who made me in the womb
make them?
Did not the same One fashion us
in the womb?

16 "If I have kept the poor
from *their* desire,
Or caused the eyes of the widow
to fail,
17 Or eaten my morsel by myself,
So that the fatherless may not eat of it
18 (But from my youth I reared him
as a father,
And from my mother's womb
I guided the widow[38]);
19 If I have seen anyone perish for lack
of clothing,
Or any poor *man* without covering;
20 If his heart[39] has not blessed me,
And *if* he was *not* warmed with the
fleece of my sheep;
21 If I have raised my hand against
the fatherless,
When I saw I had help in the gate;
22 *Then* let my arm fall from my shoulder,
Let my arm be torn from the socket.
23 For destruction *from* God *is* a terror
to me,

38 Literally *her* (compare verse 16)   39 Literally *loins*

And because of His magnificence
I could not endure.

24 "If I have made gold my hope,
Or said to fine gold,
'*You are* my confidence';
25 If I have rejoiced because my wealth
was great,
And because my hand had gained
much;
26 If I have observed the sun[40] when it
shines,
Or the moon moving *in* brightness,
27 So that my heart has been secretly
enticed,
And my mouth has kissed my hand;
28 This also *would be* an iniquity *worthy*
of judgment,
For I would have denied God
who is above.

29 "If I have rejoiced at the destruction
of him who hated me,
Or lifted myself up when evil
found him
30 (Indeed I have not allowed
my mouth to sin
By asking for a curse on his soul);
31 If the men of my tent have not said,
'Who is there that has not been satisfied
with his meat?'
32 (*But* no sojourner had to lodge
in the street,
For I have opened my doors
to the traveler);
33 If I have covered my transgressions
as Adam,
By hiding my iniquity in my bosom,
34 Because I feared the great multitude,
And dreaded the contempt of families,
So that I kept silence
And did not go out of the door—
35 Oh, that I had one to hear me!
Here is my mark.
Oh, that the Almighty
would answer me,
That my Prosecutor had written a
book!
36 Surely I would carry it on my shoulder,
And bind it on me *like* a crown;
37 I would declare to Him the number
of my steps;
Like a prince I would approach Him.

38 "If my land cries out against me,
And its furrows weep together;
39 If I have eaten its fruit[41] without
money,
Or caused its owners to lose their lives;

40 *Then* let thistles grow instead of wheat,
And weeds instead of barley."

The words of Job are ended.

Elihu Contradicts Job's Friends

32 So these three men ceased answering Job, because he *was* righteous in his own eyes.
2 Then the wrath of Elihu, the son of Barachel the Buzite, of the family of Ram, was aroused against Job; his wrath was aroused because he justified himself rather than God.
3 Also against his three friends his wrath was aroused, because they had found no answer, and *yet* had condemned Job.
4 Now because they *were* years older than he, Elihu had waited to speak[42] to Job.
5 When Elihu saw that *there was* no answer in the mouth of these three men, his wrath was aroused.
6 So Elihu, the son of Barachel the Buzite, answered and said:

"I *am* young in years,
and you *are* very old;
Therefore I was afraid,
And dared not declare my opinion
to you.
7 I said, 'Age[43] should speak,
And multitude of years should teach
wisdom.'
8 But *there is* a spirit in man,
And the breath of the Almighty gives
him understanding.
9 Great men[44] are not *always* wise,
Nor do the aged *always* understand
justice.

10 "Therefore I say, 'Listen to me,
I also will declare my opinion.'
11 Indeed I waited for your words,
I listened to your reasonings,
while you searched out what to say.
12 I paid close attention to you;
And surely not one of you
convinced Job,
Or answered his words—
13 Lest you say,
'We have found wisdom';
God will vanquish him, not man.
14 Now he has not directed *his* words
against me;
So I will not answer him
with your words.

---

40 Literally *light*   41 Literally *its strength*   42 Vulgate reads *Elihu had waited till Job had spoken.*
43 Literally *days,* that is, years   44 Or *men of many years*

15 "They are dismayed
    and answer no more;
    Words escape them.
16 And I have waited,
    because they did not speak,
    Because they stood still
    and answered no more.
17 I also will answer my part,
    I too will declare my opinion.
18 For I am full of words;
    The spirit within me compels me.
19 Indeed my belly *is* like wine *that* has
    no vent;
    It is ready to burst like new wineskins.
20 I will speak, that I may find relief;
    I must open my lips and answer.
21 Let me not, I pray,
    show partiality to anyone;
    Nor let me flatter any man.
22 For I do not know how to flatter,
    Else my Maker would soon take me
    away.

Elihu Contradicts Job

33 "But please, Job, hear my speech,
      And listen to all my words.
2 Now, I open my mouth;
    My tongue speaks in my mouth.
3 My words *come* from my upright heart;
    My lips utter pure knowledge.
4 The Spirit of God has made me,
    And the breath of the Almighty
    gives me life.
5 If you can answer me,
    Set *your words* in order before me;
    Take your stand.
6 Truly I *am* as your spokesman[45] before
    God;
    I also have been formed out of clay.
7 Surely no fear of me will terrify you,
    Nor will my hand be heavy on you.

8 "Surely you have spoken in my hearing,
    And I have heard the sound of *your*
    words, *saying,*
9 'I *am* pure, without transgression;
    I *am* innocent,
    and *there is* no iniquity in me.
10 Yet He finds occasions against me,
    He counts me as His enemy;
11 He puts my feet in the stocks,
    He watches all my paths.'

12 "Look, *in* this you are not righteous.
    I will answer you,
    For God is greater than man.
13 Why do you contend with Him?
    For He does not give an accounting
    of any of His words.

14 For God may speak in one way,
    or in another,
    Yet man does not perceive it.
15 In a dream, in a vision of the night,
    When deep sleep falls upon men,
    While slumbering on their beds,
16 Then He opens the ears of men,
    And seals their instruction.
17 In order to turn man *from his* deed,
    And conceal pride from man,
18 He keeps back his soul from the Pit,
    And his life from perishing by the
    sword.

19 "Man[46] is also chastened with pain
    on his bed,
    And with strong *pain* in many
    of his bones,
20 So that his life abhors bread,
    And his soul succulent food.
21 His flesh wastes away from sight,
    And his bones stick out *which once*
    were not seen.
22 Yes, his soul draws near the Pit,
    And his life to the executioners.

23 "If there is a messenger for him,
    A mediator, one among a thousand,
    To show man His uprightness,
24 Then He is gracious to him, and says,
    'Deliver him from going down
    to the Pit,
    I have found a ransom';
25 His flesh shall be young like a child's,
    He shall return to the days of his
    youth.
26 He shall pray to God,
    and He will delight in him,
    He shall see His face with joy,
    For He restores to man His
    righteousness.
27 And he looks at men and says,
    'I have sinned,
    and perverted *what was* right,
    And it did not profit me.'
28 He will redeem his[47] soul from going
    down to the Pit,
    And his[47] life shall see the light.

29 "Behold, God works all these *things,*
    Twice, *in fact,* three *times* with a man,
30 To bring back his soul from the Pit,
    That he may be enlightened with the
    light of life.

31 "Give ear, Job, listen to me;
    Hold your peace, and I will speak.
32 If you have anything to say,
    answer me;

---

45 Literally *as your mouth*   46 Literally *He*   47 Or *my* (Kethib)

Speak, for I desire to justify you.
33 If not, listen to me;
Hold your peace,
and I will teach you wisdom."

Elihu Proclaims God's Justice

34 Elihu further answered and said:

2 "Hear my words, you wise *men*;
Give ear to me, you who have
knowledge.
3 For the ear tests words
As the palate tastes food.
4 Let us choose justice for ourselves;
Let us know among ourselves
what *is* good.

5 "For Job has said, 'I am righteous,
But God has taken away my justice;
6 Should I lie concerning my right?
My wound *is* incurable,
though I am without transgression.'
7 What man *is* like Job,
Who drinks scorn like water,
8 Who goes in company
with the workers of iniquity,
And walks with wicked men?
9 For he has said,
'It profits a man nothing
That he should delight in God.'

10 "Therefore listen to me,
you men of understanding:
Far be it from God *to do* wickedness,
And *from* the Almighty to *commit*
iniquity.
11 For He repays man *according to* his
work,
And makes man to find a reward
according to *his* way.
12 Surely God will never do wickedly,
Nor will the Almighty pervert justice.
13 Who gave Him charge over the earth?
Or who appointed *Him over* the whole
world?
14 If He should set His heart on it,
If He should gather to Himself His
Spirit and His breath,
15 All flesh would perish together,
And man would return to dust.

16 "If *you have* understanding, hear this;
Listen to the sound of my words:
17 Should one who hates justice govern?
Will you condemn *Him who is* most
just?
18 *Is it fitting* to say to a king,
'*You are* worthless,'
And to nobles, '*You are* wicked'?

19 Yet He is not partial to princes,
Nor does He regard the rich
more than the poor;
For they *are* all the work of His hands.
20 In a moment they die,
in the middle of the night;
The people are shaken and pass away;
The mighty are taken away without a
hand.

21 "For His eyes *are* on the ways of man,
And He sees all his steps.
22 There is no darkness nor shadow
of death
Where the workers of iniquity may
hide themselves.
23 For He need not further consider
a man,
That he should go before God in
judgment.
24 He breaks in pieces mighty men
without inquiry,
And sets others in their place.
25 Therefore he knows their works;
He overthrows *them* in the night,
And they are crushed.
26 He strikes them as wicked *men*
In the open sight of others,
27 Because they turned back from Him,
And would not consider any of His
ways,
28 So that they caused the cry
of the poor to come to Him;
For He hears the cry of the afflicted.
29 When He gives quietness,
who then can make trouble?
And when He hides *His* face,
who then can see Him,
Whether *it is* against a nation
or a man alone?—
30 That the hypocrite should not reign,
Lest the people be ensnared.

31 "For has *anyone* said to God,
'I have borne *chastening*;
I will offend no more;
32 Teach me *what* I do not see;
If I have done iniquity,
I will do no more'?
33 Should He repay *it* according
to your *terms*,
Just because you disavow it?
You must choose, and not I;
Therefore speak what you know.

34 "Men of understanding say to me,
Wise men who listen to me:
35 'Job speaks without knowledge,
His words *are* without wisdom.'

36 Oh, that Job were tried to the utmost,
Because *his* answers *are like* those of
wicked men!
37 For he adds rebellion to his sin;
He claps *his hands* among us,
And multiplies his words against God."

Elihu Condemns Self-Righteousness

35 Moreover Elihu answered and said:

2 "Do you think this is right?
Do you say,
'My righteousness is more than God's'?
3 For you say,
'What advantage will it be to You?
What profit shall I have,
more than *if* I had sinned?'

4 "I will answer you,
And your companions with you.
5 Look to the heavens, and see;
And behold the clouds
which are higher than you.
6 If you sin,
what do you accomplish against
Him?
Or, *if* your transgressions are
multiplied, what do you do to Him?
7 If you are righteous,
what do you give Him?
Or what does He receive from your
hand?
8 Your wickedness affects a man
such as you,
And your righteousness a son of man.

9 "Because of the multitude of
oppressions they cry out;
They cry out for help because of the
arm of the mighty.
10 But no one says,
'Where *is* God my Maker,
Who gives songs in the night,
11 Who teaches us more
than the beasts of the earth,
And makes us wiser
than the birds of heaven?'
12 There they cry out,
but He does not answer,
Because of the pride of evil men.
13 Surely God will not listen to empty
talk,
Nor will the Almighty regard it.
14 Although you say you do not see Him,
Yet justice *is* before Him,
and you must wait for Him.

15 And now, because He has not punished
in His anger,
Nor taken much notice of folly,
16 Therefore Job opens his mouth in vain;
He multiplies words without
knowledge."

Elihu Proclaims God's Goodness

36 Elihu also proceeded and said:

2 "Bear with me a little,
and I will show you
That *there are* yet words to speak
on God's behalf.
3 I will fetch my knowledge from afar;
I will ascribe righteousness to my
Maker.
4 For truly my words *are* not false;
One who is perfect in knowledge
is with you.

5 "Behold, God *is* mighty,
but despises *no one*;
He is mighty in strength of
understanding.
6 He does not preserve the life
of the wicked,
But gives justice to the oppressed.
7 He does not withdraw His eyes from
the righteous;
But *they are* on the throne with kings,
For He has seated them forever,
And they are exalted.
8 And if *they are* bound in fetters,
Held in the cords of affliction,
9 Then He tells them their work and
their transgressions—
That they have acted defiantly.
10 He also opens their ear to instruction,
And commands that they turn
from iniquity.
11 If they obey and serve *Him*,
They shall spend their days in
prosperity,
And their years in pleasures.
12 But if they do not obey,
They shall perish by the sword,
And they shall die without
knowledge.[48]

13"But the hypocrites in heart
store up wrath;
They do not cry for help
when He binds them.
14 They die in youth,
And their life *ends* among the
perverted persons.[49]
15 He delivers the poor in their affliction,
And opens their ears in oppression.

48 Masoretic Text reads *as one without knowledge.*
49 Hebrew *qedeshim,* that is, those practicing sodomy and prostitution in religious rituals

16 "Indeed He would have brought you
     out of dire distress,
   Into a broad place where *there
   is* no restraint;
   And what is set on your table
   would be full of richness.
17 But you are filled with the judgment
     due the wicked;
   Judgment and justice take hold *of you.*
18 Because *there is* wrath, *beware* lest He
     take you away with *one* blow;
   For a large ransom would not help
     you avoid *it.*
19 Will your riches,
   Or all the mighty forces,
   Keep you from distress?
20 Do not desire the night,
   When people are cut off in their place.
21 Take heed, do not turn to iniquity,
   For you have chosen this rather than
     affliction.

22 "Behold, God is exalted by His power;
   Who teaches like Him?
23 Who has assigned Him His way,
   Or who has said, 'You have done
     wrong'?

Elihu Proclaims God's Majesty

24 "Remember to magnify His work,
   Of which men have sung.
25 Everyone has seen it;
   Man looks on *it* from afar.

26 "Behold, God *is* great,
     and we do not know *Him;*
   Nor can the number of His years
     be discovered.
27 For He draws up drops of water,
   Which distill as rain from the mist,
28 Which the clouds drop down
   And pour abundantly on man.
29 Indeed, can *anyone* understand the
     spreading of clouds,
   The thunder from His canopy?
30 Look, He scatters his light upon it,
   And covers the depths of the sea.
31 For by these He judges the peoples;
   He gives food in abundance.
32 He covers *His* hands with lightning,
   And commands it to strike.
33 His thunder declares it,
   The cattle also, concerning the rising
     storm.

37

"At this also my heart trembles,
   And leaps from its place.
2 Hear attentively the thunder
   of His voice,

And the rumbling *that* comes
   from His mouth.
3 He sends it forth under the whole
     heaven,
   His lightning to the ends of the earth.
4 After it a voice roars;
   He thunders with His majestic voice,
   And He does not restrain them when
     His voice is heard.
5 God thunders marvelously with His
     voice;
   He does great things which we cannot
     comprehend.
6 For He says to the snow,
     'Be *on* the earth';
   Likewise to the gentle rain and the
     heavy rain of His strength.
7 He seals the hand of every man,
   That all men may know His work.
8 The animals enter dens,
   And remain in their lairs.
9 From the chamber *of the south*
     comes the whirlwind,
   And cold from the scattering winds
     of the north.
10 By the breath of God ice is given,
   And the broad waters are frozen.
11 Also with moisture He saturates the
     thick clouds;
   He scatters His bright clouds.
12 And they swirl about,
     being turned by His guidance,
   That they may do whatever He
     commands them
   On the face of the whole earth.[50]
13 He causes it to come,
   Whether for correction,
   Or for His land,
   Or for mercy.

14 "Listen to this, O Job;
   Stand still and consider the wondrous
     works of God.
15 Do you know when God dispatches
     them,
   And causes the light of His cloud
     to shine?
16 Do you know the balance of clouds,
   Those wondrous works of Him
     who is perfect in knowledge?
17 Why *are* your garments hot,
   When He quiets the earth
     by the south *wind?*
18 With Him, have you spread
     out the skies,
   Strong as a cast metal mirror?

19 "Teach us what we should say to Him,
   For we can prepare nothing because of
     the darkness.

50 Literally *the world of the earth*

20 Should He be told that I *wish to* speak?
　　If a man were to speak,
　　　surely he would be swallowed up.
21 Even now *men* cannot look at the light
　　　when it is bright in the skies,
　　When the wind has passed
　　　and cleared them.
22 He comes from the north *as* golden
　　　splendor;
　　With God *is* awesome majesty.
23 *As for* the Almighty,
　　　we cannot find Him;
　　He is excellent in power,
　　In judgment and abundant justice;
　　He does not oppress.
24 Therefore men fear Him;
　　He shows no partiality to any
　　　who are wise of heart."

The LORD Reveals His Omnipotence to Job

38 Then the LORD answered Job out
　　of the whirlwind, and said:

2 "Who *is* this who darkens counsel
　　By words without knowledge?
3 Now prepare yourself like a man;
　　I will question you,
　　　and you shall answer Me.

4 "Where were you when I laid the
　　　foundations of the earth?
　　Tell *Me*, if you have understanding.
5 Who determined its measurements?
　　Surely you know!
　　Or who stretched the line upon it?
6 To what were its foundations fastened?
　　Or who laid its cornerstone,
7 When the morning stars sang together,
　　And all the sons of God shouted for
　　　joy?

8 "Or *who* shut in the sea with doors,
　　When it burst forth
　　　and issued from the womb;
9 When I made the clouds its garment,
　　And thick darkness its swaddling band;
10 When I fixed My limit for it,
　　And set bars and doors;
11 When I said,
　　'This far you may come, but no farther,
　　And here your proud waves must stop!'

12 "Have you commanded the morning
　　　since your days *began*,
　　And caused the dawn to know its place,
13 That it might take hold of the ends
　　　of the earth,
　　And the wicked be shaken out of it?
14 It takes on form like clay *under* a seal,
　　And stands out like a garment.

15 From the wicked their light is withheld,
　　And the upraised arm is broken.
16 "Have you entered the springs
　　　of the sea?
　　Or have you walked in search
　　　of the depths?
17 Have the gates of death
　　　been revealed to you?
　　Or have you seen the doors
　　　of the shadow of death?
18 Have you comprehended the breadth
　　　of the earth?
　　Tell *Me*, if you know all this.

19 "Where *is* the way *to* the dwelling
　　　of light?
　　And darkness, where *is* its place,
20 That you may take it to its territory,
　　That you may know the paths *to* its
　　　home?
21 Do you know *it*,
　　　because you were born then,
　　Or *because* the number of your days
　　　is great?

22 "Have you entered the treasury of snow,
　　Or have you seen the treasury of hail,
23 Which I have reserved for the time
　　　of trouble,
　　For the day of battle and war?
24 By what way is light diffused,
　　Or the east wind scattered over the
　　　earth?

25 "Who has divided a channel
　　　for the overflowing *water*,
　　Or a path for the thunderbolt,
26 To cause it to rain on a land *where*
　　　there is no one,
　　A wilderness in which *there is* no man;
27 To satisfy the desolate waste,
　　And cause to spring forth the growth
　　　of tender grass?
28 Has the rain a father?
　　Or who has begotten the drops of dew?
29 From whose womb comes the ice?
　　And the frost of heaven,
　　　who gives it birth?
30 The waters harden like stone,
　　And the surface of the deep is frozen.

31 "Can you bind the cluster of the
　　　Pleiades,
　　Or loose the belt of Orion?
32 Can you bring out Mazzaroth[51]
　　　in its season?
　　Or can you guide the Great Bear
　　　with its cubs?
33 Do you know the ordinances
　　　of the heavens?

51 Literally *Constellations*

Can you set their dominion
over the earth?

34 "Can you lift up your voice
to the clouds,
That an abundance of water
may cover you?
35 Can you send out lightnings,
that they may go,
And say to you, 'Here we *are!*'?
36 Who has put wisdom in the mind?[52]
Or who has given understanding
to the heart?
37 Who can number the clouds by
wisdom?
Or who can pour out the bottles
of heaven,
38 When the dust hardens in clumps,
And the clods cling together?

39"Can you hunt the prey for the lion,
Or satisfy the appetite of the young
lions,
40 When they crouch in *their* dens,
Or lurk in their lairs to lie in wait?
41 Who provides food for the raven,
When its young ones cry to God,
And wander about for lack of food?

39
"Do you know the time when the
wild mountain goats bear young?
Or can you mark when the deer
gives birth?
2 Can you number the months
that they fulfill?
Or do you know the time
when they bear young?
3 They bow down,
They bring forth their young,
They deliver their offspring.[53]
4 Their young ones are healthy,
They grow strong with grain;
They depart and do not return to
them.

5 "Who set the wild donkey free?
Who loosed the bonds of the onager,
6 Whose home I have made the
wilderness,
And the barren land his dwelling?
7 He scorns the tumult of the city;
He does not heed the shouts of the
driver.
8 The range of the mountains *is* his
pasture,
And he searches after every green
thing.

9 "Will the wild ox be willing to serve
you?
Will he bed by your manger?

10 Can you bind the wild ox in the furrow
with ropes?
Or will he plow the valleys behind you?
11 Will you trust him because his strength
is great?
Or will you leave your labor to him?
12 Will you trust him to bring home your
grain,
And gather it to your threshing floor?

13 "The wings of the ostrich wave proudly,
But are her wings and pinions *like the*
kindly stork's?
14 For she leaves her eggs on the ground,
And warms them in the dust;
15 She forgets that a foot may crush them,
Or that a wild beast may break them.
16 She treats her young harshly,
as though *they were* not hers;
Her labor is in vain, without concern,
17 Because God deprived her of wisdom,
And did not endow her with
understanding.
18 When she lifts herself on high,
She scorns the horse and its rider.

19 "Have you given the horse strength?
Have you clothed his neck with
thunder?[54]
20 Can you frighten him like a locust?
His majestic snorting strikes terror.
21 He paws in the valley,
and rejoices in *his* strength;
He gallops into the clash of arms.
22 He mocks at fear,
and is not frightened;
Nor does he turn back from the sword.
23 The quiver rattles against him,
The glittering spear and javelin.
24 He devours the distance with fierceness
and rage;
Nor does he stand firm,
because the trumpet *has* sounded.
25 At the *blast of* the trumpet he says,
'Aha!'
He smells the battle from afar,
The thunder of captains and shouting.

26 "Does the hawk fly by your wisdom,
And spread its wings toward the south?
27 Does the eagle mount up at your
command,
And make its nest on high?
28 It dwells on the rock, and resides
On the crag of the rock and the
stronghold.
29 From there it spies out the prey;
Its eyes observe from afar.
30 Its young ones suck up blood;
And where the slain *are*, there it *is*."

---

52 Literally *inward parts* 53 Literally *pangs*, figurative of offspring 54 Or *a mane*

40 Moreover the LORD answered Job, and said:

2 "Shall the one who contends with the Almighty correct *Him?*
He who rebukes God,
let him answer it."

Job's Response to God

3 Then Job answered the LORD and said:

4 "Behold, I am vile;
What shall I answer You?
I lay my hand over my mouth.
5 Once I have spoken,
but I will not answer;
Yes, twice,
but I will proceed no further."

God's Challenge to Job

6 Then the LORD answered Job out of the whirlwind, and said:

7 "Now prepare yourself like a man;
I will question you,
and you shall answer Me:

8 "Would you indeed annul My judgment?
Would you condemn Me
that you may be justified?
9 Have you an arm like God?
Or can you thunder with a voice like His?
10 Then adorn yourself
with majesty and splendor,
And array yourself
with glory and beauty.
11 Disperse the rage of your wrath;
Look on everyone *who is* proud,
and humble him.
12 Look on everyone *who is* proud,
and bring him low;
Tread down the wicked in their place.
13 Hide them in the dust together,
Bind their faces in hidden *darkness.*
14 Then I will also confess to you
That your own right hand can save you.

15"Look now at the behemoth,[55]
which I made *along* with you;
He eats grass like an ox.
16 See now, his strength *is* in his hips,
And his power *is* in his stomach muscles.
17 He moves his tail like a cedar;
The sinews of his thighs are tightly knit.

18 His bones *are like* beams of bronze,
His ribs like bars of iron.
19 He *is* the first of the ways of God;
Only He who made him can bring near His sword.
20 Surely the mountains yield food for him,
And all the beasts of the field play there.
21 He lies under the lotus trees,
In a covert of reeds and marsh.
22 The lotus trees cover him *with* their shade;
The willows by the brook surround him.
23 Indeed the river may rage,
Yet he is not disturbed;
He is confident, though the Jordan gushes into his mouth,
24 *Though* he takes it in his eyes,
Or one pierces *his* nose with a snare.

41 "Can you draw out Leviathan[56] with a hook,
Or *snare* his tongue with a line *which* you lower?
2 Can you put a reed through his nose,
Or pierce his jaw with a hook?
3 Will he make many supplications to you?
Will he speak softly to you?
4 Will he make a covenant with you?
Will you take him as a servant forever?
5 Will you play with him as *with* a bird,
Or will you leash him for your maidens?
6 Will *your* companions make a banquet[57] of him?
Will they apportion him among the merchants?
7 Can you fill his skin with harpoons,
Or his head with fishing spears?
8 Lay your hand on him;
Remember the battle—
Never do it again!
9 Indeed, *any* hope of *overcoming* him is vain;[58]
Shall *one not* be overwhelmed at the sight of him?
10 No one *is so* fierce that he would dare stir him up.
Who then is able to stand against Me?
11 Who has preceded Me,
that I should pay *him?*
Everything under heaven is Mine.

12 "I will not conceal[59] his limbs,
His mighty power,
or his graceful proportions.

---

55 A large animal, exact identity unknown 56 A large sea creature, exact identity unknown
57 Or *bargain over him* 58 Literally *false* 59 Literally *keep silent about*

13 Who can remove his outer coat?
   Who can approach *him* with a double
      bridle?
14 Who can open the doors of his face,
   With his terrible teeth all around?
15 *His* rows of scales are *his* pride,
   Shut up tightly *as with* a seal;
16 One is so near another
   That no air can come between them;
17 They are joined one to another,
   They stick together
      and cannot be parted.
18 His sneezings flash forth light,
   And his eyes *are* like the eyelids
      of the morning.
19 Out of his mouth go burning lights;
   Sparks of fire shoot out.
20 Smoke goes out of his nostrils,
   As *from* a boiling pot and burning
      rushes.
21 His breath kindles coals,
   And a flame goes out of his mouth.
22 Strength dwells in his neck,
   And sorrow dances before him.
23 The folds of his flesh are joined
      together;
   They are firm on him
      and cannot be moved.
24 His heart is as hard as stone,
   Even as hard as the lower *millstone*.
25 When he raises himself up,
      the mighty are afraid;
   Because of his crashings they are
      beside [60] themselves.
26 *Though* the sword reaches him,
      it cannot avail;
   Nor does spear, dart, or javelin.
27 He regards iron as straw,
   And bronze as rotten wood.
28 The arrow cannot make him flee;
   Slingstones become like stubble to him.
29 Darts are regarded as straw;
   He laughs at the threat of javelins.
30 His undersides *are* like sharp
      potsherds;
   He spreads pointed *marks* in the mire.
31 He makes the deep boil like a pot;
   He makes the sea like a pot of
      ointment.
32 He leaves a shining wake behind him;
   One would think the deep had white
      hair.
33 On earth there is nothing like him,
   Which is made without fear.
34 He beholds every high *thing*;
   He *is* king over all the children of
      pride."

Job's Repentance and Restoration

42 Then Job answered the LORD and
said:

2 "I know that You can do everything,
   And that no purpose *of Yours* can be
      withheld from You.
3 *You asked,* 'Who *is* this who hides
      counsel without knowledge?'
   Therefore I have uttered
      what I did not understand,
   Things too wonderful for me,
      which I did not know.
4 Listen, please, and let me speak;
   You said, 'I will question you,
      and you shall answer Me.'

5 "I have heard of You by the hearing
      of the ear,
   But now my eye sees You.
6 Therefore I abhor *myself*,
   And repent in dust and ashes."

7 And so it was, after the LORD had
spoken these words to Job, that the LORD
said to Eliphaz the Temanite, "My wrath
is aroused against you and your two
friends, for you have not spoken of Me
what is right, as My servant Job *has*.
8 "Now therefore, take for yourselves
seven bulls and seven rams, go to My servant Job, and offer up for yourselves a
burnt offering; and My servant Job shall
pray for you. For I will accept him, lest I
deal with you *according to your* folly; because you have not spoken of Me *what is*
right, as My servant Job *has*."
9 So Eliphaz the Temanite and Bildad
the Shuhite *and* Zophar the Naamathite
went and did as the LORD commanded
them; for the LORD had accepted Job.
10 And the LORD restored Job's losses[61]
when he prayed for his friends. Indeed
the LORD gave Job twice as much as he
had before.
11 Then all his brothers, all his sisters,
and all those who had been his acquaintances before, came to him and ate food
with him in his house; and they consoled
him and comforted him for all the adversity that the LORD had brought upon
him. Each one gave him a piece of silver
and each a ring of gold.
12 Now the LORD blessed the latter *days*
of Job more than his beginning; for he
had fourteen thousand sheep, six thou-

---

60 Or *purify themselves*   61 Literally *Job's captivity*, that is, what was captured from Job

sand camels, one thousand yoke of oxen, and one thousand female donkeys.
13 He also had seven sons and three daughters.
14 And he called the name of the first Jemimah, the name of the second Keziah, and the name of the third Keren-Happuch.

15 In all the land were found no women *so* beautiful as the daughters of Job; and their father gave them an inheritance among their brothers.
16 After this Job lived one hundred and forty years, and saw his children and grandchildren *for* four generations.
17 So Job died, old and full of days.

Introduction to Psalms

Praise! The very nature of the word invokes worship and thanksgiving to God. This is the purpose and response of the psalms, for the Hebrew title of the book means "praise."

Most of the psalms of praise were written by David, Moses, and other Israelite leaders between 1450 and 400 B.C. They are the heartfelt prayers of the nation's most devoted and committed men. The psalms reflect all aspects of life, extolling God for His creation, praising Him for His blessings, and enlisting His help in times of turmoil and distress. Many of these psalms were originally to be accompanied by the trumpet, harp, or flute.

David and the other authors were able to look around them and find reasons to praise God despite their circumstances. They saw God at work during times of feasting in Israel, as well as the captivity in Babylon. Whether it was good or bad, the psalmist focused his eyes on God, not on his situation.

The psalms are alive with vivid descriptions of the ancient land of Israel and nature in general. Those attributed to David are particularly full of beautiful illustrations. It is believed that David wrote many of the psalms at a small spring in the wilderness adjacent to the Dead Sea known as En Gedi. Here, near the beautiful waterfalls and lush gardens, David compared God's care for His people to the life-giving spring in the wilderness.

When fleeing from his enemies, David wrote that God made his feet like those of an antelope-like deer, who scaled cliffs with ease.

> He makes my feet like the *feet of* deer,
> And sets me on my high places.

(Ps. 18:33)

God sheltered the psalmist from his problems by hiding him under the rocky overhangs. The Dead Sea, adjacent to En Gedi, is the lowest place on the face of the earth. David wrote:

> *If* I take the wings of the morning,
> *And* dwell in the uttermost parts of the sea,
> Even there Your hand shall lead me,
> And Your right hand shall hold me.

(Ps. 139:9, 10)

These words of praise can be our own as we worship and reflect on what God has done in our life. How appropriate it is that the final recorded psalm is one of continual praise. Let us look around us in our world and find ways to praise God. And when we face stress and tough times, praise God anyway!

The Book of
Psalms

BOOK ONE
Psalms 1–41

PSALM 1

The Way of the Righteous and the End of the Ungodly

BLESSED *is* the man
Who walks not in the counsel
of the ungodly,
Nor stands in the path of sinners,
Nor sits in the seat of the scornful;
2 But his delight *is* in the law of the
LORD,
And in His law he meditates day
and night.
3 He shall be like a tree
Planted by the rivers of water,
That brings forth its fruit in its
season,
Whose leaf also shall not wither;
And whatever he does shall prosper.

4 The ungodly *are* not so,
But *are* like the chaff which the wind
drives away.
5 Therefore the ungodly shall not stand
in the judgment,
Nor sinners in the congregation of the
righteous.

6 For the LORD knows the way of the
righteous,
But the way of the ungodly shall
perish.

PSALM 2

The Messiah's Triumph and Kingdom

WHY do the nations rage,
And the people plot a vain thing?
2 The kings of the earth set themselves,
And the rulers take counsel together,
Against the LORD and against His
Anointed, *saying,*
3 "Let us break Their bonds in pieces
And cast away Their cords from us."

4 He who sits in the heavens shall laugh;
The LORD shall hold them in derision.
5 Then He shall speak to them in His
wrath,
And distress them in His deep
displeasure:
6 "Yet I have set My King
On My holy hill of Zion."

7 "I will declare the decree:
The LORD has said to Me,
'You *are* My Son,
Today I have begotten You.
8 Ask of Me, and I will give *You*
The nations *for* Your inheritance,
And the ends of the earth *for* Your
possession.
9 You shall break them with a rod
of iron;
You shall dash them in pieces like a
potter's vessel.' "

10 Now therefore, be wise, O kings;
Be instructed, you judges of the earth.
11 Serve the LORD with fear,
And rejoice with trembling.
12 Kiss the Son, lest He be angry,
And you perish *in* the way,
When His wrath is kindled but a little.
Blessed *are* all those who put their
trust in Him.

PSALM 3

The LORD Helps His Troubled People

A Psalm of David when he fled from Absalom his
son.

LORD, how they have increased who
trouble me!
Many *are* they who rise up against me.
2 Many *are* they who say of me,
"*There is* no help for him in God."   Selah

3 But You, O LORD, *are* a shield for me,
My glory and the One who lifts up my
head.
4 I cried to the LORD with my voice,
And He heard me from His
holy hill.   Selah

5 I lay down and slept;
I awoke, for the LORD sustained me.
6 I will not be afraid of ten thousands
of people
Who have set *themselves* against me all
around.

7 Arise, O LORD;
   Save me, O my God!
   For You have struck all my enemies on
      the cheekbone;
   You have broken the teeth of the
      ungodly.
8 Salvation *belongs* to the LORD.
   Your blessing *is* upon Your people.
                                    Selah

PSALM 4

The Safety of the Faithful

To the Chief Musician. With stringed instruments.
A Psalm of David.

HEAR me when I call,
   O God of my righteousness!
You have relieved me *when I was*
   in distress;
Have mercy on me,
   and hear my prayer.

2 How long, O you sons of men,
   Will you turn my glory to shame?
   How long will you love worthlessness
   And seek falsehood?   Selah
3 But know that the LORD has set apart
   for Himself him who is godly;
   The LORD will hear when I call to
      Him.

4 Be angry, and do not sin.
   Meditate within your heart on your
      bed, and be still.   Selah
5 Offer the sacrifices of righteousness,
   And put your trust in the LORD.

6 *There are* many who say,
   "Who will show us *any* good?"
   LORD, lift up the light of Your
      countenance upon us.
7 You have put gladness in my heart,
   More than in the season that their
      grain and wine increased.
8 I will both lie down in peace,
      and sleep;
   For You alone, O LORD, make me
      dwell in safety.

PSALM 5

A Prayer for Guidance

To the Chief Musician. With flutes.[1] A Psalm of
David.

GIVE ear to my words, O LORD,
   Consider my meditation.
2 Give heed to the voice of my cry,
   My King and my God,
   For to You I will pray.
3 My voice You shall hear in the
      morning, O LORD;

In the morning I will direct *it* to You,
And I will look up.

4 For You *are* not a God who takes
      pleasure in wickedness,
   Nor shall evil dwell with You.
5 The boastful shall not stand in Your
      sight;
   You hate all workers of iniquity.
6 You shall destroy those who speak
      falsehood;
   The LORD abhors the bloodthirsty and
      deceitful man.

7 But as for me, I will come into Your
      house in the multitude of Your
      mercy;
   In fear of You I will worship toward
      Your holy temple.
8 Lead me, O LORD, in Your
      righteousness because of
      my enemies;
   Make Your way straight before
      my face.

9 For *there is* no faithfulness in their
      mouth;
   Their inward part *is* destruction;
   Their throat *is* an open tomb;
   They flatter with their tongue.
10 Pronounce them guilty, O God!
   Let them fall by their own counsels;
   Cast them out in the multitude of their
      transgressions,
   For they have rebelled against You.

11 But let all those rejoice who put their
      trust in You;
   Let them ever shout for joy,
      because You defend them;
   Let those also who love Your name
   Be joyful in You.
12 For You, O LORD, will bless the
      righteous;
   With favor You will surround him as
      with a shield.

PSALM 6

A Prayer of Faith in Time of Distress

To the Chief Musician. With stringed instruments.
On an eight-stringed harp.[2] A Psalm of David.

O LORD, do not rebuke me in Your
      anger,
   Nor chasten me in Your hot
      displeasure.
2 Have mercy on me, O LORD,
      for I *am* weak;
   O LORD, heal me,
      for my bones are troubled.
3 My soul also is greatly troubled;
   But You, O LORD—how long?

1 Hebrew *nehiloth* 2 Hebrew *sheminith*

4 Return, O LORD, deliver me!
   Oh, save me for Your mercies' sake!
5 For in death *there is* no remembrance
      of You;
   In the grave who will give You thanks?

6 I am weary with my groaning;
   All night I make my bed swim;
   I drench my couch with my tears.
7 My eye wastes away because of grief;
   It grows old because of all my enemies.

8 Depart from me,
      all you workers of iniquity;
   For the LORD has heard the voice of
      my weeping.
9 The LORD has heard my supplication;
   The LORD will receive my prayer.
10 Let all my enemies be ashamed
      and greatly troubled;
   Let them turn back
      and be ashamed suddenly.

PSALM 7

Prayer and Praise for Deliverance from Enemies

A Meditation of David, which he sang to the LORD
concerning the words of Cush, a Benjamite.

O LORD my God,
   in You I put my trust;
Save me from all those who
   persecute me;
And deliver me,
2 Lest they tear me like a lion,
   Rending *me* in pieces,
      while *there is* none to deliver.

3 O LORD my God, if I have done this:
   If there is iniquity in my hands,
4 If I have repaid evil to him who was at
      peace with me,
   Or have plundered my enemy without
      cause,
5 Let the enemy pursue me
      and overtake *me*;
   Yes, let him trample my life to the
      earth,
   And lay my honor in the dust.   Selah

6 Arise, O LORD, in Your anger;
   Lift Yourself up because of the rage of
      my enemies,
   And awake for me *to* the judgment
      You have commanded!
7 So the congregation of the peoples
      shall surround You;
   For their sakes, therefore,
      return on high.

8 The LORD shall judge the peoples;
   Judge me, O LORD, according to my
      righteousness,
   And according to my integrity
      within me.

9 Oh, let the wickedness of the wicked
      come to an end,
   But establish the just;
   For the righteous God tests the hearts
      and minds.
10 My defense *is* of God,
   Who saves the upright in heart.

11 God *is* a just judge,
   And God is angry *with the wicked*
      every day.
12 If he does not turn back,
   He will sharpen His sword;
   He bends His bow and makes it ready.
13 He also prepares for Himself
      instruments of death;
   He makes His arrows into fiery shafts.

14 Behold, *the wicked* travails with
      iniquity,
   Conceives trouble and brings forth
      falsehood.
15 He made a pit and dug it out,
   And has fallen into the ditch *which* he
      made.
16 His trouble shall return upon his own
      head,
   And his violent dealing shall come
      down on his own crown.

17 I will praise the LORD according to His
      righteousness,
   And will sing praise to the name of the
      LORD Most High.

PSALM 8

The Glory of the LORD in Creation

To the Chief Musician. On the instrument of
Gath.[3] A Psalm of David.

O LORD, our Lord,
   How excellent *is* Your name in all
      the earth,
   You who set Your glory above the
      heavens!

2 Out of the mouth of babes and infants
   You have ordained strength,
   Because of Your enemies,
   That You may silence the enemy and
      the avenger.

3 When I consider Your heavens,
      the work of Your fingers,

3 Hebrew *Al Gittith*

The moon and the stars,
which You have ordained,
4 What is man that You are mindful
of him,
And the son of man that You visit
him?
5 For You have made him a little lower
than the angels,[4]
And You have crowned him with glory
and honor.

6 You have made him to have dominion
over the works of Your hands;
You have put all *things* under his feet,
7 All sheep and oxen—
Even the beasts of the field,
8 The birds of the air,
And the fish of the sea
That pass through the paths of the
seas.

9 O LORD, our Lord,
How excellent *is* Your name ir all the
earth!

PSALM 9

Prayer and Thanksgiving for the LORD'S Righteous Judgments

To the Chief Musician. To *the tune of* "Death of
the Son."[5] A Psalm of David.

I WILL praise *You*, O LORD, with my
whole heart;
I will tell of all Your marvelous works.
2 I will be glad and rejoice in You;
I will sing praise to Your name,
O Most High.

3 When my enemies turn back,
They shall fall and perish at Your
presence.
4 For You have maintained my right and
my cause;
You sat on the throne judging in
righteousness.
5 You have rebuked the nations,
You have destroyed the wicked;
You have blotted out their name
forever and ever.

6 O enemy, destructions are finished
forever!
And you have destroyed cities;
Even their memory has perished.
7 But the LORD shall endure forever;
He has prepared His throne for
judgment.
8 He shall judge the world in
righteousness,
And He shall administer judgment for
the peoples in uprightness.

9 The LORD also will be a refuge for the
oppressed,
A refuge in times of trouble.
10 And those who know Your name will
put their trust in You;
For You, LORD, have not forsaken
those who seek You.

11 Sing praises to the LORD,
who dwells in Zion!
Declare His deeds among the people.
12 When He avenges blood,
He remembers them;
He does not forget the cry of the
humble.

13 Have mercy on me, O LORD!
Consider my trouble from those who
hate me,
You who lift me up from the gates of
death,
14 That I may tell of all Your praise
In the gates of the daughter of Zion.
I will rejoice in Your salvation.

15 The nations have sunk down in the pit
which they made;
In the net which they hid,
their own foot is caught.
16 The LORD is known *by* the judgment
He executes;
The wicked is snared in the work of his
own hands.
                    Meditation.[6]   Selah

17 The wicked shall be turned into hell,
And all the nations that forget God.
18 For the needy shall not always be
forgotten;
The expectation of the poor shall *not*
perish forever.

19 Arise, O LORD,
Do not let man prevail;
Let the nations be judged in Your
sight.
20 Put them in fear, O LORD,
That the nations may know themselves
to be but men.   Selah

PSALM 10

A Song of Confidence in God's Triumph over Evil

WHY do You stand afar off, O LORD?
Why do You hide *Yourself* in times
of trouble?
2 The wicked in *his* pride persecutes the
poor;
Let them be caught in the plots which
they have devised.

---

4 Hebrew *Elohim, God;* Septuagint, Syriac, Targum, and Jewish tradition translate as *angels.*
5 Hebrew *Muth Labben*   6 Hebrew *Higgaion*

3 For the wicked boasts of his heart's
   desire;
   He blesses the greedy
   and renounces the LORD.
4 The wicked in his proud countenance
   does not seek *God*;
   God *is* in none of his thoughts.

5 His ways are always prospering;
   Your judgments *are* far above,
   out of his sight;
   As for all his enemies,
   he sneers at them.
6 He has said in his heart,
   "I shall not be moved;
   I shall never be in adversity."
7 His mouth is full of cursing and deceit
   and oppression;
   Under his tongue *is* trouble and
   iniquity.

8 He sits in the lurking places of the
   villages;
   In the secret places he murders the
   innocent;
   His eyes are secretly fixed on the
   helpless.
9 He lies in wait secretly,
   as a lion in his den;
   He lies in wait to catch the poor;
   He catches the poor when he draws
   him into his net.
10 So he crouches, he lies low,
   That the helpless may fall by his
   strength.
11 He has said in his heart,
   "God has forgotten;
   He hides His face;
   He will never see *it.*"

12 Arise, O LORD!
   O God, lift up Your hand!
   Do not forget the humble.
13 Why do the wicked renounce God?
   He has said in his heart,
   "You will not require *an account.*"

14 But You have seen *it,*
   for You observe trouble and grief,
   To repay *it* by Your hand.
   The helpless commits himself to You;
   You are the helper of the fatherless.
15 Break the arm of the wicked
   and the evil *man;*
   Seek out his wickedness *until* You find
   none.

16 The LORD *is* King forever and ever;
   The nations have perished out of His
   land.

17 LORD, You have heard the desire of
   the humble;
   You will prepare their heart;
   You will cause Your ear to hear,
18 To do justice to the fatherless and the
   oppressed,
   That the man of the earth may oppress
   no more.

PSALM 11

Faith in the LORD'S Righteousness

To the Chief Musician. A Psalm of David.

IN the LORD I put my trust;
   How can you say to my soul,
   "Flee *as* a bird to your mountain"?
2 For look! The wicked bend *their* bow,
   They make ready their arrow on the
   string,
   That they may shoot secretly at the
   upright in heart.
3 If the foundations are destroyed,
   What can the righteous do?

4 The LORD *is* in His holy temple,
   The LORD'S throne *is* in heaven;
   His eyes behold,
   His eyelids test the sons of men.
5 The LORD tests the righteous,
   But the wicked and the one who loves
   violence His soul hates.
6 Upon the wicked He will rain coals,
   Fire and brimstone and a burning
   wind;
   This shall be the portion of their cup.

7 For the LORD *is* righteous,
   He loves righteousness;
   His countenance beholds the upright.⁷

PSALM 12

Man's Treachery and God's Constancy

To the Chief Musician. On an eight-stringed harp.⁸
A Psalm of David.

HELP, LORD, for the godly man ceases!
   For the faithful disappear from
   among the sons of men.
2 They speak idly everyone with his
   neighbor;
   With flattering lips *and* a double heart
   they speak.

3 May the LORD cut off all flattering lips,
   And the tongue that speaks proud
   things,
4 Who have said,
   "With our tongue we will prevail;
   Our lips *are* our own;
   Who *is* lord over us?"

7 Or *the upright beholds His countenance*   8 Hebrew *sheminith*

5 "For the oppression of the poor,
    for the sighing of the needy,
    Now I will arise," says the LORD;
    "I will set *him* in the safety for which he
    yearns."

6 The words of the LORD *are* pure words,
    Like silver tried in a furnace of earth,
    Purified seven times.
7 You shall keep them, O LORD,
    You shall preserve them from this
    generation forever.

8 The wicked prowl on every side,
    When vileness is exalted among the
    sons of men.

PSALM 13

Trust in the Salvation of the LORD

To the Chief Musician. A Psalm of David.

H OW long, O LORD?
    Will You forget me forever?
    How long will You hide Your face
    from me?
2 How long shall I take counsel in my
    soul,
    Having sorrow in my heart daily?
    How long will my enemy be exalted
    over me?

3 Consider *and* hear me,
    O LORD my God;
    Enlighten my eyes,
    Lest I sleep the *sleep of* death;
4 Lest my enemy say,
    "I have prevailed against him";
    Lest those who trouble me rejoice when
    I am moved.

5 But I have trusted in Your mercy;
    My heart shall rejoice in Your
    salvation.
6 I will sing to the LORD,
    Because He has dealt bountifully
    with me.

PSALM 14

Folly of the Godless, and God's Final Triumph

To the Chief Musician. A Psalm of David.

T HE fool has said in his heart,
    "*There is* no God."
    They are corrupt,
    They have done abominable works,
    There is none who does good.

2 The LORD looks down from heaven
    upon the children of men,
    To see if there are any who
    understand, who seek God.

3 They have all turned aside,
    They have together become corrupt;
    There is none who does good,
    No, not one.

4 Have all the workers of iniquity no
    knowledge,
    Who eat up my people *as* they eat
    bread,
    And do not call on the LORD?
5 There they are in great fear,
    For God *is* with the generation of the
    righteous.
6 You shame the counsel of the poor,
    But the LORD *is* his refuge.

7 Oh, that the salvation of Israel *would
    come* out of Zion!
    When the LORD brings back the
    captivity of His people,
    Let Jacob rejoice *and* Israel be glad.

PSALM 15

**The Character of Those Who May Dwell with
the LORD**

A Psalm of David.

L ORD, who may abide in Your
    tabernacle?
    Who may dwell in Your holy hill?

2 He who walks uprightly,
    And works righteousness,
    And speaks the truth in his heart;
3 He *who* does not backbite with his
    tongue,
    Nor does evil to his neighbor,
    Nor does he take up a reproach
    against his friend;
4 In whose eyes a vile person is despised,
    But he honors those who fear the
    LORD;
    He *who* swears to his own hurt and
    does not change;
5 He *who* does not put out his money at
    usury,
    Nor does he take a bribe against the
    innocent.

He who does these *things* shall never
    be moved.

PSALM 16

**The Hope of the Faithful, and the Messiah's
Victory**

A Michtam of David.

P RESERVE me, O God,
    for in You I put my trust.

2 *O my soul,* you have said to the LORD,
    "You *are* my Lord,

My goodness is nothing apart from
   You"—
3 *And* to the saints who *are* on the earth,
"They are the excellent ones,
   in whom is all my delight."

4 Their sorrows shall be multiplied who
   hasten *after* another *god;*
   Their drink offerings of blood I will
   not offer,
Nor take up their names on my lips.

5 *You,* O LORD, *are* the portion of my
   inheritance and my cup;
You maintain my lot.
6 The lines have fallen to me in pleasant
   places;
Yes, I have a good inheritance.

7 I will bless the LORD who has given me
   counsel;
My heart also instructs me in the night
   seasons.
8 I have set the LORD always before me;
Because *He is* at my right hand I shall
   not be moved.

9 Therefore my heart is glad,
   and my glory rejoices;
My flesh also will rest in hope.
10 For You will not leave my soul
   in Sheol,
Nor will You allow Your Holy One
   to see corruption.
11 You will show me the path of life;
In Your presence *is* fullness of joy;
At Your right hand *are* pleasures
   forevermore.

PSALM 17

Prayer with Confidence in Final Salvation

A Prayer of David.

H EAR a just cause, O LORD,
   Attend to my cry;
Give ear to my prayer *that is* not from
   deceitful lips.
2 Let my vindication come from Your
   presence;
Let Your eyes look on the things that
   are upright.

3 You have tested my heart;
You have visited *me* in the night;
You have tried me
   and have found nothing;
I have purposed that my mouth shall
   not transgress.
4 Concerning the works of men,
By the word of Your lips,

I have kept *myself* from the paths of
   the destroyer.
5 Uphold my steps in Your paths,
That my footsteps may not slip.

6 I have called upon You,
   for You will hear me, O God;
Incline Your ear to me,
   and hear my speech.
7 Show Your marvelous lovingkindness
   by Your right hand,
O You who save those who trust
   in You
From those who rise up *against them.*
8 Keep me as the apple of Your eye;
Hide me under the shadow of Your
   wings,
9 From the wicked who oppress me,
From my deadly enemies who
   surround me.

10 They have closed up their fat *hearts;*
With their mouths they speak proudly.
11 They have now surrounded us in our
   steps;
They have set their eyes,
   crouching down to the earth,
12 Like a lion *that* is eager to tear his
   prey,
And as a young lion lurking in secret
   places.

13 Arise, O LORD,
Confront him, cast him down;
Deliver my life from the wicked with
   Your sword,
14 With Your hand from men, O LORD,
From men of the world *who have* their
   portion in *this* life,
And whose belly You fill with Your
   hidden treasure.
They are satisfied with children,
And leave the rest of their *substance* for
   their babes.

15 As for me, I will see Your face in
   righteousness;
I shall be satisfied when I awake in
   Your likeness.

PSALM 18

God the Sovereign Savior

To the Chief Musician. A Psalm of David the
servant of the LORD, who spoke to the LORD the
words of this song on the day that the LORD
delivered him from the hand of all his enemies
and from the hand of Saul. And he said:

I WILL love You,
   O LORD, my strength.

2 The LORD is my rock and my fortress
  and my deliverer;
  My God, my strength,
  in whom I will trust;
  My shield and the horn of my
  salvation, my stronghold.
3 I will call upon the LORD,
  who is worthy to be praised;
  So shall I be saved from my enemies.

4 The pangs of death encompassed me,
  And the floods of ungodliness
  made me afraid.
5 The sorrows of Sheol surrounded me;
  The snares of death confronted me.
6 In my distress I called upon the LORD,
  And cried out to my God;
  He heard my voice from His temple,
  And my cry came before Him,
  even to His ears.

7 Then the earth shook and trembled;
  The foundations of the hills also
  quaked and were shaken,
  Because He was angry.
8 Smoke went up from His nostrils,
  And devouring fire from His mouth;
  Coals were kindled by it.
9 He bowed the heavens also,
  and came down
  With darkness under His feet.
10 And He rode upon a cherub, and flew;
  He flew upon the wings of the wind.
11 He made darkness His secret place;
  His canopy around Him *was*
  dark waters
  And thick clouds of the skies.
12 From the brightness before Him,
  His thick clouds passed with hailstones
  and coals of fire.

13 The LORD also thundered in the
  heavens,
  And the Most High uttered His voice,
  Hailstones and coals of fire.
14 He sent out His arrows
  and scattered the foe,
  Lightnings in abundance,
  and He vanquished them.
15 Then the channels of waters were seen,
  And the foundations of the world were
  uncovered
  At Your rebuke, O LORD,
  At the blast of the breath of Your
  nostrils.

16 He sent from above, He took me;
  He drew me out of many waters.
17 He delivered me from my strong
  enemy,
  From those who hated me,
  For they were too strong for me.
18 They confronted me in the day of my
  calamity,
  But the LORD was my support.
19 He also brought me out into a broad
  place;
  He delivered me because He delighted
  in me.

20 The LORD rewarded me according to
  my righteousness;
  According to the cleanness of my
  hands He has recompensed me.
21 For I have kept the ways of the LORD,
  And have not wickedly departed from
  my God.
22 For all His judgments *were* before me,
  And I did not put away His statutes
  from me.
23 I was also blameless before Him,
  And I kept myself from my iniquity.
24 Therefore the LORD has recompensed
  me according to my righteousness,
  According to the cleanness
  of my hands in His sight.

25 With the merciful
  You will show Yourself merciful;
  With a blameless man
  You will show Yourself blameless;
26 With the pure
  You will show Yourself pure;
  And with the devious
  You will show Yourself shrewd.
27 For You will save the humble people,
  But will bring down haughty looks.

28 For You will light my lamp;
  The LORD my God will enlighten my
  darkness.
29 For by You I can run against a troop,
  And by my God I can leap over a wall.
30 *As for* God, His way *is* perfect;
  The word of the LORD is proven;
  He *is* a shield to all who trust in Him.

31 For who *is* God, except the LORD?
  And who *is* a rock, except our God?
32 *It is* God who arms me with strength,
  And makes my way perfect.
33 He makes my feet like the *feet of* deer,
  And sets me on my high places.
34 He teaches my hands to make war,
  So that my arms can bend a bow of
  bronze.

35 You have also given me the shield of
  Your salvation;
  Your right hand has held me up,

Your gentleness has made me great.
36 You enlarged my path under me;
So that my feet did not slip.

37 I have pursued my enemies
and overtaken them;
Neither did I turn back again
till they were destroyed.
38 I have wounded them,
So that they were not able to rise;
They have fallen under my feet.
39 For You have armed me with strength
for the battle;
You have subdued under me those who
rose up against me.
40 You have also given me
the necks of my enemies,
So that I destroyed those who hated
me.
41 They cried out,
but *there was* none to save *them,*
Even to the LORD,
but He did not answer them.
42 Then I beat them as fine as the dust
before the wind;
I cast them out like dirt in the streets.

43 You have delivered me from the
strivings of the people,
You have made me the head of the
nations;
A people I have not known shall serve
me.
44 As soon as they hear of me
they obey me;
The foreigners submit to me.
45 The foreigners fade away,
And come frightened from their
hideouts.

46 The LORD lives!
Blessed *be* my Rock!
Let the God of my salvation be
exalted.
47 *It is* God who avenges me,
And subdues the peoples under me;
48 He delivers me from my enemies.
You also lift me up above those who
rise against me;
You have delivered me from the
violent man.
49 Therefore I will give thanks to You,
O LORD, among the Gentiles,
And sing praises to Your name.

50 Great deliverance He gives to His king,
And shows mercy to His anointed,
To David and his descendants
forevermore.

PSALM 19

The Perfect Revelation of the LORD

To the Chief Musician. A Psalm of David.

THE heavens declare the glory of God;
And the firmament shows His
handiwork.
2 Day unto day utters speech,
And night unto night reveals
knowledge.
3 *There is* no speech nor language
Where their voice is not heard.
4 Their line has gone out through all the
earth,
And their words to the end of the
world.

In them He has set a tabernacle for the
sun,
5 Which *is* like a bridegroom coming out
of his chamber,
And rejoices like a strong man to run
its race.
6 Its rising *is* from one end of heaven,
And its circuit to the other end;
And there is nothing hidden from its
heat.

7 The law of the LORD *is* perfect,
converting the soul;
The testimony of the LORD *is* sure,
making wise the simple;
8 The statutes of the LORD *are* right,
rejoicing the heart;
The commandment of the LORD *is*
pure, enlightening the eyes;
9 The fear of the LORD *is* clean,
enduring forever;
The judgments of the LORD *are* true
and righteous altogether.
10 More to be desired *are they* than gold,
Yea, than much fine gold;
Sweeter also than honey and the
honeycomb.
11 Moreover by them Your servant is
warned,
And in keeping them *there is* great
reward.

12 Who can understand *his* errors?
Cleanse me from secret *faults.*
13 Keep back Your servant also from
presumptuous *sins;*
Let them not have dominion over me.
Then I shall be blameless,
And I shall be innocent of great
transgression.

14 Let the words of my mouth
and the meditation of my heart

Be acceptable in Your sight,
O LORD, my strength and my
redeemer.

PSALM 20

The Assurance of God's Saving Work

To the Chief Musician. A Psalm of David.

MAY the LORD answer you in the day
of trouble;
May the name of the God of Jacob
defend you;
2 May He send you help from the
sanctuary,
And strengthen you out of Zion;
3 May He remember all your offerings,
And accept your burnt sacrifice.   Selah

4 May He grant you according to
your heart's *desire,*
And fulfill all your purpose.
5 We will rejoice in your salvation,
And in the name of our God we will
set up *our* banners!
May the LORD fulfill all your petitions.

6 Now I know that the LORD saves His
anointed;
He will answer him from His holy
heaven
With the saving strength of His right
hand.

7 Some *trust* in chariots,
and some in horses;
But we will remember the name of the
LORD our God.
8 They have bowed down and fallen;
But we have risen and stand upright.

9 Save, LORD!
May the King answer us when we call.

PSALM 21

Joy in the Salvation of the LORD

To the Chief Musician. A Psalm of David.

THE king shall have joy in Your
strength, O LORD;
And in Your salvation how greatly
shall he rejoice!
2 You have given him his heart's desire,
And have not withheld the request of
his lips.   Selah

3 For You meet him with the blessings
of goodness;
You set a crown of pure gold upon his
head.
4 He asked life from You,
and You gave *it* to him—
Length of days forever and ever.

5 His glory *is* great in Your salvation;
Honor and majesty You have placed
upon him.
6 For You have made him most blessed
forever;
You have made him exceedingly glad
with Your presence.
7 For the king trusts in the LORD,
And through the mercy of the Most
High he shall not be moved.

8 Your hand will find all Your enemies;
Your right hand will find those who
hate You.
9 You shall make them as a fiery oven
in the time of Your anger;
The LORD shall swallow them up
in His wrath,
And the fire shall devour them.
10 Their offspring You shall destroy from
the earth,
And their descendants from among the
sons of men.
11 For they intended evil against You;
They devised a plot *which* they are not
able *to perform.*
12 Therefore You will make them turn
their back;
You will make ready *Your arrows* on
Your string toward their faces.

13 Be exalted, O LORD, in Your own
strength!
We will sing and praise Your power.

PSALM 22

The Suffering, Praise, and Posterity of the Messiah

To the Chief Musician. Set to "The Deer of the
Dawn."[9] A Psalm of David.

MY God, My God,
why have You forsaken Me?
Why are You so far from helping Me,
And from the words of My groaning?
2 O My God, I cry in the daytime,
but You do not hear;
And in the night season,
and am not silent.

3 But You *are* holy,
Who inhabit the praises of Israel.
4 Our fathers trusted in You;
They trusted, and You delivered them.
5 They cried to You, and were delivered;
They trusted in You, and were not
ashamed.

6 But I *am* a worm, and no man;
A reproach of men, and despised of the
people.

9 Hebrew *Aijeleth Hashahar*

7 All those who see Me laugh Me to
    scorn;
  They shoot out the lip,
    they shake the head, *saying,*
8 "He trusted in the LORD,
    let Him rescue Him;
  Let Him deliver Him,
    since He delights in Him!"

9 But You *are* He who took Me out of
    the womb;
  You made Me trust *when I was* on My
    mother's breasts.
10 I was cast upon You from birth.
   From My mother's womb
   You *have been* My God.
11 Be not far from Me,
   For trouble *is* near;
   For *there is* none to help.

12 Many bulls have surrounded Me;
   Strong *bulls* of Bashan have encircled
     Me.
13 They gape at Me *with* their mouths,
   As a raging and roaring lion.

14 I am poured out like water,
   And all My bones are out of joint;
   My heart is like wax;
   It has melted within Me.
15 My strength is dried up like a
     potsherd,
   And My tongue clings to My jaws;
   You have brought Me to the dust of
     death.

16 For dogs have surrounded Me;
   The assembly of the wicked has
     enclosed Me.
   They pierced My hands and My feet;
17 I can count all My bones.
   They look *and* stare at Me.
18 They divide My garments among them,
   And for My clothing they cast lots.

19 But You, O LORD,
     do not be far from Me;
   O My Strength, hasten to help Me!
20 Deliver Me from the sword,
   My precious *life* from the power of the
     dog.
21 Save Me from the lion's mouth
   And from the horns of the wild oxen!

   You have answered Me.

22 I will declare Your name to My
     brethren;
   In the midst of the congregation I will
     praise You.

23 You who fear the LORD, praise Him!
   All you descendants of Jacob,
     glorify Him,
   And fear Him,
     all you offspring of Israel!
24 For He has not despised nor abhorred
     the affliction of the afflicted;
   Nor has He hidden His face from
     Him;
   But when He cried to Him, He heard.

25 My praise *shall be* of You in the great
     congregation;
   I will pay My vows before those who
     fear Him.
26 The poor shall eat and be satisfied;
   Those who seek Him will praise the
     LORD.
   Let your heart live forever!

27 All the ends of the world
   Shall remember and turn to the LORD,
   And all the families of the nations
   Shall worship before You.
28 For the kingdom *is* the LORD'S,
   And He rules over the nations.

29 All the prosperous of the earth
   Shall eat and worship;
   All those who go down to the dust
   Shall bow before Him,
   Even he who cannot keep himself alive.

30 A posterity shall serve Him.
   It will be recounted of the Lord
     to the *next* generation,
31 They will come and declare His
     righteousness to a people who will be
       born,
   That He has done *this.*

PSALM 23

The LORD the Shepherd of His People

A Psalm of David.

THE LORD *is* my shepherd;
   I shall not want.
2 He makes me to lie down in green
     pastures;
   He leads me beside the still waters.
3 He restores my soul;
   He leads me in the paths of
     righteousness
   For His name's sake.

4 Yea, though I walk through the valley
     of the shadow of death,
   I will fear no evil;
   For You *are* with me;
   Your rod and Your staff,
     they comfort me.

The Lord Is My Shepherd

Psalm 23 beautifully reflects David's early life as a shepherd boy in the hills surrounding Bethlehem as well as his adult reign as king of Israel.

The youngest child of Jesse, David, was responsible for caring for his father's sheep. He was a small lad, yet he was strong and skilled in his work. Daily he guided the flock through the desert wilderness of Judah.

"The LORD *is* my shepherd; I shall not want" (Ps. 23:1). David's knowledge of shepherding was unsurpassed. He was very familiar with the demands placed on a shepherd to locate food and water for his flock, both of which were scarce in the parched land.

"He makes me to lie down in green pastures; He leads me beside the still waters. He restores my soul; He leads me in the paths of righteousness for His name's sake" (Ps. 23:2, 3).

David the shepherd knew of the few underground springs hidden in the rocky crevices of the wilderness. There he would lead his sheep to the pools of fresh water where they could drink and be restored.

It was not uncommon to spend the night with the flock out in the hills. At dusk, just when the sun sat low in the afternoon sky, the chalky wilderness suddenly became a row of hills and valleys with long dark shadows crisscrossing the land. The high mountain cliffs totally blocked the sunlight, causing dark black ravines, where the shepherd and his flock would be found. David recalls these frightful moments when he and his flock were easy prey for wild leopards, lions, and bears.

"Yea, though I walk through the valley of the shadow of death, I will fear no evil; for You *are* with me; Your rod and Your staff, they comfort me" (Ps. 23:4). David's reference to a physical fear as a child adds an even greater spiritual meaning to his psalm of praise.

As king of Israel, David draws from his kingly experience to further illustrate God's goodness. "You prepare a table before me in the presence of my enemies; You anoint my head with oil; my cup runs over" (Ps. 23:5).

A noted practice of David's day was to break bread—or eat a meal together as a covenant of peace, security, and forgiveness. Here David acknowledges that God makes peace with His enemies. God anoints his head with oil as a sign of His blessing. And his cup running over signifies the success and prosperity God bestowed upon him.

The psalm reflects a beautiful relationship between David and his Lord. For David saw God at work in the ordinary daily activities of life. His psalm of praise can also be our own as we realize God's gifts of security, peace, and prosperity in our lives. Then we can also say with David, "Surely goodness and mercy shall follow me all the days of my life; and I will dwell in the house of the LORD forever" (Ps. 23:6).

5 You prepare a table before me in the
   presence of my enemies;
   You anoint my head with oil;
   My cup runs over.
6 Surely goodness and mercy shall
   follow me
   All the days of my life;
   And I will dwell in the house
      of the LORD
   Forever.

PSALM 24

The King of Glory and His Kingdom

A Psalm of David.

THE earth is the LORD'S,
   and all its fullness,
The world and those who dwell
   therein.
2 For He has founded it upon the seas,
   And established it upon the waters.

3 Who may ascend into the hill of the
      LORD?
   Or who may stand in His holy place?
4 He who has clean hands and a pure
      heart,
   Who has not lifted up his soul to an
      idol,
   Nor sworn deceitfully.
5 He shall receive blessing from the
      LORD,
   And righteousness from the God of his
      salvation.
6 This is Jacob, the generation of those
      who seek Him,
   Who seek Your face.   Selah

7 Lift up your heads, O you gates!
   And be lifted up, you everlasting
      doors!
   And the King of glory shall come in.
8 Who is this King of glory?
   The LORD strong and mighty,
   The LORD mighty in battle.
9 Lift up your heads, O you gates!
   And lift them up, you everlasting
      doors!
   And the King of glory shall come in.
10 Who is this King of glory?
   The LORD of hosts,
   He is the King of glory.   Selah

PSALM 25

A Plea for Deliverance and Forgiveness

A Psalm of David.

TO You, O LORD,
   I lift up my soul.
2 O my God, I trust in You;

Let me not be ashamed;
Let not my enemies triumph over me.
3 Indeed, let no one who waits on You
   be ashamed;
Let those be ashamed who deal
   treacherously without cause.

4 Show me Your ways, O LORD;
   Teach me Your paths.
5 Lead me in Your truth and teach me,
   For You are the God of my salvation;
   On You I wait all the day.

6 Remember, O LORD, Your tender
   mercies and Your lovingkindnesses,
   For they have been from of old.
7 Do not remember the sins of my
   youth, nor my transgressions;
   According to Your mercy
      remember me,
   For Your goodness' sake, O LORD.

8 Good and upright is the LORD;
   Therefore He teaches sinners in the
      way.
9 The humble He guides in justice,
   And the humble He teaches His way.
10 All the paths of the LORD are mercy
      and truth,
   To such as keep His covenant and His
      testimonies.
11 For Your name's sake, O LORD,
   Pardon my iniquity, for it is great.

12 Who is the man that fears the LORD?
   Him shall He[10] teach in the way He[10]
      chooses.
13 He himself shall dwell in prosperity,
   And his descendants shall inherit the
      earth.
14 The secret of the LORD is with those
   who fear Him,
   And He will show them His covenant.
15 My eyes are ever toward the LORD,
   For He shall pluck my feet out of the
      net.

16 Turn Yourself to me,
   and have mercy on me,
   For I am desolate and afflicted.
17 The troubles of my heart have
      enlarged;
   Oh, bring me out of my distresses!
18 Look on my affliction and my pain,
   And forgive all my sins.
19 Consider my enemies,
   for they are many;
   And they hate me with cruel hatred.
20 Oh, keep my soul, and deliver me;
   Let me not be ashamed,
   for I put my trust in You.

10 Or he

21 Let integrity and uprightness preserve
   me,
   For I wait for You.

22 Redeem Israel, O God,
   Out of all their troubles!

PSALM 26

A Prayer for Divine Scrutiny and Redemption

A Psalm of David.

VINDICATE me, O LORD,
   For I have walked in my integrity.
   I have also trusted in the LORD;
   I shall not slip.
2 Examine me, O LORD, and prove me;
   Try my mind and my heart.
3 For Your lovingkindness *is* before my
   eyes,
   And I have walked in Your truth.
4 I have not sat with idolatrous mortals,
   Nor will I go in with hypocrites.
5 I have hated the congregation of
   evildoers,
   And will not sit with the wicked.

6 I will wash my hands in innocence;
   So I will go about Your altar, O LORD,
7 That I may proclaim with the voice of
   thanksgiving,
   And tell of all Your wondrous works.
8 LORD, I have loved the habitation of
   Your house,
   And the place where Your glory dwells.

9 Do not gather my soul *together* with
   sinners,
   Nor my life with bloodthirsty men,
10 In whose hands *is* a sinister scheme,
   And whose right hand is full of bribes.

11 But as for me,
   I will walk in my integrity;
   Redeem me and be merciful to me.
12 My foot stands in an even place;
   In the congregations I will bless the
   LORD.

PSALM 27

An Exuberant Declaration of Faith

A Psalm of David.

THE LORD *is* my light and my
   salvation;
   Whom shall I fear?
   The LORD *is* the strength of my life;
   Of whom shall I be afraid?
2 When the wicked came against me
   To eat up my flesh,
   My enemies and foes,
   They stumbled and fell.

3 Though an army should encamp
   against me,
   My heart shall not fear;
   Though war should rise against me,
   In this I *will be* confident.

4 One *thing* I have desired of the LORD,
   That will I seek:
   That I may dwell in the house of the
   LORD
   All the days of my life,
   To behold the beauty of the LORD,
   And to inquire in His temple.
5 For in the time of trouble
   He shall hide me in His pavilion;
   In the secret place of His tabernacle
   He shall hide me;
   He shall set me high upon a rock.

6 And now my head shall be lifted up
   above my enemies all around me;
   Therefore I will offer sacrifices of joy
   in His tabernacle;
   I will sing, yes, I will sing praises to
   the LORD.

7 Hear, O LORD, *when* I cry with my
   voice!
   Have mercy also upon me,
   and answer me.
8 *When You said*, "Seek My face,"
   My heart said to You,
   "Your face, LORD, I will seek."
9 Do not hide Your face from me;
   Do not turn Your servant away in
   anger;
   You have been my help;
   Do not leave me nor forsake me,
   O God of my salvation.
10 When my father and my mother
   forsake me,
   Then the LORD will take care of me.

11 Teach me Your way, O LORD,
   And lead me in a smooth path,
   because of my enemies.
12 Do not deliver me to the will of my
   adversaries;
   For false witnesses have risen
   against me,
   And such as breathe out violence.
13 *I would have lost heart*, unless I had
   believed
   That I would see the goodness of the
   LORD
   In the land of the living.

14 Wait on the LORD;
   Be of good courage,
   And He shall strengthen your heart;
   Wait, I say, on the LORD!

PSALM 28

Rejoicing in Answered Prayer

A Psalm of David.

TO You I will cry, O LORD my Rock:
Do not be silent to me,
Lest, if You *are* silent to me,
I become like those who go down to
   the pit.
2 Hear the voice of my supplications
When I cry to You,
When I lift up my hands toward Your
   holy sanctuary.

3 Do not take me away with the wicked
And with the workers of iniquity,
Who speak peace to their neighbors,
But evil *is* in their hearts.
4 Give to them according to their deeds,
And according to the wickedness of
   their endeavors;
Give to them according to the work of
   their hands;
Render to them what they deserve.
5 Because they do not regard the works
   of the LORD,
Nor the operation of His hands,
He shall destroy them
And not build them up.

6 Blessed *be* the LORD,
Because He has heard the voice of my
   supplications!
7 The LORD *is* my strength
   and my shield;
My heart trusted in Him,
   and I am helped;
Therefore my heart greatly rejoices,
And with my song I will praise Him.

8 The LORD *is* their strength,
And He *is* the saving refuge of His
   anointed.
9 Save Your people,
And bless Your inheritance;
Shepherd them also,
And bear them up forever.

PSALM 29

Praise to God in His Holiness and Majesty

A Psalm of David.

GIVE unto the LORD,
O you mighty ones,
Give unto the LORD
   glory and strength.
2 Give unto the LORD
   the glory due to His name;
Worship the LORD
   in the beauty of holiness.

3 The voice of the LORD *is* over the
   waters;
The God of glory thunders;
The LORD *is* over many waters.
4 The voice of the LORD *is* powerful;
The voice of the LORD *is* full of
   majesty.

5 The voice of the LORD breaks the
   cedars,
Yes, the LORD splinters the cedars of
   Lebanon.
6 He makes them also skip like a calf,
Lebanon and Sirion like a young
   wild ox.
7 The voice of the LORD divides the
   flames of fire.

8 The voice of the LORD shakes the
   wilderness;
The LORD shakes the Wilderness of
   Kadesh.
9 The voice of the LORD makes the deer
   give birth,
And strips the forests bare;
And in His temple everyone says,
   "Glory!"

10 The LORD sat *enthroned* at the Flood,
And the LORD sits as King forever.
11 The LORD will give strength to His
   people;
The LORD will bless His people with
   peace.

PSALM 30

The Blessedness of Answered Prayer

A Psalm. A Song at the dedication of the house of
David.

I WILL extol You, O LORD,
for You have lifted me up,
And have not let my foes rejoice
   over me.
2 O LORD my God, I cried out to You,
And You have healed me.
3 O LORD, You have brought my soul up
   from the grave;
You have kept me alive, that I should
   not go down to the pit.

4 Sing praise to the LORD,
You saints of His,
And give thanks at the remembrance of
   His holy name.[11]
5 For His anger *is but for* a moment,
His favor *is for* life;
Weeping may endure for a night,
But joy *comes* in the morning.

11 Or *His holiness*

6 Now in my prosperity I said,
   "I shall never be moved."
7 LORD, by Your favor You have made
      my mountain stand strong;
   You hid Your face, *and* I was troubled.

8 I cried out to You, O LORD;
   And to the LORD I made supplication:
9 "What profit *is there* in my blood,
      When I go down to the pit?
   Will the dust praise You?
   Will it declare Your truth?
10 Hear, O LORD, and have mercy on me;
   LORD, be my helper!"

11 You have turned for me my mourning
      into dancing;
   You have put off my sackcloth and
      clothed me with gladness,
12 To the end that *my* glory may sing
      praise to You and not be silent.
   O LORD my God,
   I will give thanks to You forever.

PSALM 31

The LORD a Fortress in Adversity

To the Chief Musician. A Psalm of David.

IN You, O LORD, I put my trust;
   Let me never be ashamed;
   Deliver me in Your righteousness.
2 Bow down Your ear to me,
   Deliver me speedily;
   Be my rock of refuge,
   A fortress of defense to save me.

3 For You *are* my rock and my fortress;
   Therefore, for Your name's sake,
   Lead me and guide me.
4 Pull me out of the net which they have
      secretly laid for me,
   For You *are* my strength.
5 Into Your hand I commit my spirit;
   You have redeemed me,
   O LORD God of truth.

6 I have hated those who regard vain
      idols;
   But I trust in the LORD.
7 I will be glad
      and rejoice in Your mercy,
   For You have considered my trouble;
   You have known my soul in
      adversities,
8 And have not shut me up into the
      hand of the enemy;
   You have set my feet in a wide place.

9 Have mercy on me, O LORD,
      for I am in trouble;

My eye wastes away with grief,
   Yes, my soul and my body!
10 For my life is spent with grief,
   And my years with sighing;
   My strength fails because of my
      iniquity,
   And my bones waste away.
11 I am a reproach among all my enemies,
   But especially among my neighbors,
   And *am* repulsive to my acquaintances;
   Those who see me outside flee from
      me.
12 I am forgotten like a dead man,
      out of mind;
   I am like a broken vessel.
13 For I hear the slander of many;
   Fear *is* on every side;
   While they take counsel together
      against me,
   They scheme to take away my life.

14 But as for me, I trust in You, O LORD;
   I say, "You *are* my God."
15 My times *are* in Your hand;
   Deliver me from the hand of my
      enemies,
   And from those who persecute me.
16 Make Your face shine upon Your
      servant;
   Save me for Your mercies' sake.
17 Do not let me be ashamed, O LORD,
      for I have called upon You;
   Let the wicked be ashamed;
   Let them be silent in the grave.
18 Let the lying lips be put to silence,
   Which speak insolent things proudly
      and contemptuously against the
      righteous.

19 Oh, how great *is* Your goodness,
   Which You have laid up for those who
      fear You,
   Which You have prepared for those
      who trust in You
   In the presence of the sons of men!
20 You shall hide them in the secret place
      of Your presence
   From the plots of man;
   You shall keep them secretly in a
      pavilion
   From the strife of tongues.

21 Blessed *be* the LORD,
   For He has shown me His marvelous
      kindness in a strong city!
22 For I said in my haste,
   "I am cut off from before Your eyes";
   Nevertheless You heard the voice of
      my supplications
   When I cried out to You.

23 Oh, love the LORD, all you His saints!
   For the LORD preserves the faithful,
   And fully repays the proud person.
24 Be of good courage,
   And He shall strengthen your heart,
   All you who hope in the LORD.

PSALM 32

The Joy of Forgiveness

A Psalm of David. A Contemplation.¹²

BLESSED *is he whose* transgression *is*
     forgiven,
   Whose sin *is* covered.
2 Blessed *is* the man to whom
     the LORD does not impute iniquity,
   And in whose spirit *there is* no guile.

3 When I kept silent, my bones grew old
   Through my groaning all the day long.
4 For day and night Your hand was
     heavy upon me;
   My vitality was turned into the
     drought of summer.   Selah
5 I acknowledged my sin to You,
   And my iniquity I have not hidden.
   I said, "I will confess my transgressions
     to the LORD,"
   And You forgave the iniquity
     of my sin.   Selah

6 For this cause everyone who is godly
     shall pray to You
   In a time when You may be found;
   Surely in a flood of great waters
   They shall not come near him.
7 You *are* my hiding place;
   You shall preserve me from trouble;
   You shall surround me with songs of
     deliverance.   Selah

8 I will instruct you and teach you in the
     way you should go;
   I will guide you with My eye.
9 Do not be like the horse
     or like the mule,
   Which have no understanding,
   Which must be harnessed with bit and
     bridle,
   Else they will not come near you.

10 Many sorrows *shall be* to the wicked;
   But he who trusts in the LORD,
     mercy shall surround him.
11 Be glad in the LORD and rejoice,
     you righteous;
   And shout for joy,
     all *you* upright in heart!

12 Hebrew *Maschil*

PSALM 33

The Sovereignty of the LORD in Creation and History

REJOICE in the LORD,
     O you righteous!
   For praise from the upright is
     beautiful.
2 Praise the LORD with the harp;
   Make melody to Him with an
     instrument of ten strings.
3 Sing to Him a new song;
   Play skillfully with a shout of joy.

4 For the word of the LORD *is* right,
   And all His work *is done* in truth.
5 He loves righteousness and justice;
   The earth is full of the goodness of the
     LORD.

6 By the word of the LORD
     the heavens were made,
   And all the host of them
     by the breath of His mouth.
7 He gathers the waters of the sea
     together as a heap;
   He lays up the deep in storehouses.

8 Let all the earth fear the LORD;
   Let all the inhabitants of the world
     stand in awe of Him.
9 For He spoke, and it was *done;*
   He commanded, and it stood fast.

10 The LORD brings the counsel of the
     nations to nothing;
   He makes the plans of the peoples
     of no effect.
11 The counsel of the LORD stands
     forever,
   The plans of His heart to all
     generations.
12 Blessed *is* the nation whose God *is* the
     LORD,
   And the people *whom* He has chosen
     as His own inheritance.

13 The LORD looks from heaven;
   He sees all the sons of men.
14 From the place of His habitation He
     looks
   On all the inhabitants of the earth;
15 He fashions their hearts individually;
   He considers all their works.

16 No king *is* saved
     by the multitude of an army;
   A mighty man is not delivered
     by great strength.

17 A horse *is* a vain hope for safety;
   Neither shall it deliver *any*
      by its great strength.

18 Behold, the eye of the LORD *is* on
      those who fear Him,
   On those who hope in His mercy,
19 To deliver their soul from death,
   And to keep them alive in famine.

20 Our soul waits for the LORD;
   He *is* our help and our shield.
21 For our heart shall rejoice in Him,
   Because we have trusted in His holy
      name.
22 Let Your mercy, O LORD, be upon us,
   Just as we hope in You.

PSALM 34

The Happiness of Those Who Trust in God

A Psalm of David when he pretended madness
before Abimelech, who drove him away, and he
departed.

I WILL bless the LORD at all times;
   His praise *shall* continually *be* in my
   mouth.
2 My soul shall make its boast in the
      LORD;
   The humble shall hear *of it* and be
      glad.
3 Oh, magnify the LORD with me,
   And let us exalt His name together.

4 I sought the LORD, and He heard me,
   And delivered me from all my fears.
5 They looked to Him and were radiant,
   And their faces were not ashamed.
6 This poor man cried out,
      and the LORD heard *him,*
   And saved him out of all his troubles.
7 The angel[13] of the LORD encamps
      all around those who fear Him,
   And delivers them.

8 Oh, taste and see that the LORD *is*
      good;
   Blessed *is* the man *who* trusts in Him!
9 Oh, fear the LORD, you His saints!
   There is no want to those who fear
      Him.
10 The young lions lack
      and suffer hunger;
   But those who seek the LORD shall not
      lack any good *thing.*

11 Come, you children, listen to me;
   I will teach you the fear of the LORD.
12 Who *is* the man *who* desires life,
   And loves *many* days,
      that he may see good?

13 Keep your tongue from evil,
   And your lips from speaking guile.
14 Depart from evil, and do good;
   Seek peace, and pursue it.

15 The eyes of the LORD *are* on the
      righteous,
   And His ears *are open* to their cry.
16 The face of the LORD *is* against those
      who do evil,
   To cut off the remembrance of them
      from the earth.

17 *The righteous* cry out,
      and the LORD hears,
   And delivers them out of all their
      troubles.
18 The LORD *is* near to those who have a
      broken heart,
   And saves such as have a contrite
      spirit.

19 Many *are* the afflictions of the
      righteous,
   But the LORD delivers him
      out of them all.
20 He guards all his bones;
   Not one of them is broken.
21 Evil shall slay the wicked,
   And those who hate the righteous shall
      be condemned.
22 The LORD redeems the soul of His
      servants,
   And none of those who trust in Him
      shall be condemned.

PSALM 35

The LORD the Avenger of His People

A Psalm of David.

PLEAD *my cause,* O LORD, with those
   who strive with me;
   Fight against those who fight against
      me.
2 Take hold of shield and buckler,
   And stand up for my help.
3 Also draw out the spear,
   And stop those who pursue me.
   Say to my soul,
   "I *am* your salvation."

4 Let those be put to shame
      and brought to dishonor
   Who seek after my life;
   Let those be turned back
      and brought to confusion
   Who plot my hurt.
5 Let them be like chaff before the wind,
   And let the angel[14] of the LORD chase
      them.

13 Or *Angel*   14 Or *Angel*

6 Let their way be dark and slippery,
And let the angel of the LORD pursue
them.
7 For without cause they have hidden
their net for me *in* a pit,
Which they have dug without cause for
my life.
8 Let destruction come upon him
unexpectedly,
And let his net that he has hidden
catch himself;
Into that very destruction let him fall.

9 And my soul shall be joyful in the
LORD;
It shall rejoice in His salvation.
10 All my bones shall say,
"LORD, who *is* like You,
Delivering the poor from him who is
too strong for him,
Yes, the poor and the needy from him
who plunders him?"

11 Fierce witnesses rise up;
They ask me *things* that I do not know.
12 They reward me evil for good,
To the sorrow of my soul.
13 But as for me, when they were sick,
My clothing *was* sackcloth;
I humbled myself with fasting;
And my prayer would return to my
own heart.
14 I paced about as though *he were* my
friend *or* brother;
I bowed down heavily, as one who
mourns *for his* mother.

15 But in my adversity they rejoiced
And gathered together;
Attackers gathered against me,
And I did not know *it;*
They tore *at me* and did not cease;
16 With ungodly mockers at feasts
They gnashed at me with their teeth.

17 Lord, how long will You look on?
Rescue me from their destructions,
My precious *life* from the lions.
18 I will give You thanks in the great
congregation;
I will praise You among many people.

19 Let them not rejoice over me
who are wrongfully my enemies;
Nor let them wink with the eye
who hate me without a cause.
20 For they do not speak peace,
But they devise deceitful matters
Against *those who are* quiet in the land.
21 They also opened their mouth wide
against me,

And said, "Aha, aha!
Our eyes have seen *it.*"

22 *This* You have seen, O LORD;
Do not keep silence.
O Lord, do not be far from me.
23 Stir up Yourself,
and awake to my vindication,
To my cause, my God and my Lord.
24 Vindicate me, O LORD my God,
according to Your righteousness;
And let them not rejoice over me.
25 Let them not say in their hearts,
"Ah, so we would have it!"
Let them not say,
"We have swallowed him up."

26 Let them be ashamed
and brought to mutual confusion
Who rejoice at my hurt;
Let them be clothed with shame and
dishonor
Who magnify themselves against me.

27 Let them shout for joy and be glad,
Who favor my righteous cause;
And let them say continually,
"Let the LORD be magnified,
Who has pleasure in the prosperity of
His servant."
28 And my tongue shall speak of Your
righteousness
And of Your praise all the day long.

PSALM 36

Man's Wickedness and God's Perfections

To the Chief Musician. A Psalm of David the
servant of the LORD.

A N oracle within my heart concerning
the transgression of the wicked:
There is no fear of God before his eyes.
2 For he flatters himself in his own eyes,
When he finds out his iniquity *and*
when he hates.
3 The words of his mouth *are* wickedness
and deceit;
He has ceased to be wise *and* to do
good.
4 He devises wickedness on his bed;
He sets himself in a way *that is* not
good;
He does not abhor evil.

5 Your mercy, O LORD, *is* in the
heavens,
And Your faithfulness *reaches* to the
clouds.
6 Your righteousness *is* like the great
mountains;
Your judgments *are* a great deep;
O LORD, You preserve man and beast.

7 How precious *is* Your lovingkindness,
  O God!
  Therefore the children of men put their
  trust under the shadow of Your
  wings.
8 They are abundantly satisfied with the
  fullness of Your house,
  And You give them drink from the
  river of Your pleasures.
9 For with You *is* the fountain of life;
  In Your light we see light.

10 Oh, continue Your lovingkindness
   to those who know You,
   And Your righteousness
   to the upright in heart.
11 Let not the foot of pride come against
   me,
   And let not the hand of the wicked
   drive me away.
12 There the workers of iniquity have
   fallen;
   They have been cast down
   and are not able to rise.

PSALM 37

The Heritage of the Righteous and the Calamity of the Wicked

A Psalm of David.

D O not fret because of evildoers,
    Nor be envious of the workers of
    iniquity.
2 For they shall soon be cut down like
  the grass,
  And wither as the green herb.

3 Trust in the LORD, and do good;
  Dwell in the land, and feed on His
  faithfulness.
4 Delight yourself also in the LORD,
  And He shall give you the desires of
  your heart.

5 Commit your way to the LORD,
  Trust also in Him,
  And He shall bring *it* to pass.
6 He shall bring forth your righteousness
  as the light,
  And your justice as the noonday.

7 Rest in the LORD,
  and wait patiently for Him;
  Do not fret because of him who
  prospers in his way,
  Because of the man who brings wicked
  schemes to pass.
8 Cease from anger, and forsake wrath;
  Do not fret—*it* only *causes* harm.

9 For evildoers shall be cut off;
  But those who wait on the LORD,
  They shall inherit the earth.
10 For yet a little while
   and the wicked *shall be* no *more;*
   Indeed, you will look diligently for his
   place,
   But it *shall be* no *more.*
11 But the meek shall inherit the earth,
   And shall delight themselves
   in the abundance of peace.

12 The wicked plots against the just,
   And gnashes at him with his teeth.
13 The Lord laughs at him,
   For He sees that his day is coming.
14 The wicked have drawn the sword
   And have bent their bow,
   To cast down the poor and needy,
   To slay those who are of upright
   conduct.
15 Their sword shall enter their own heart,
   And their bows shall be broken.

16 A little that a righteous man has
   Is better than the riches of many
   wicked.
17 For the arms of the wicked shall be
   broken,
   But the LORD upholds the righteous.

18 The LORD knows the days of the
   upright,
   And their inheritance shall be forever.
19 They shall not be ashamed in the evil
   time,
   And in the days of famine they shall
   be satisfied.
20 But the wicked shall perish;
   And the enemies of the LORD,
   Like the splendor of the meadows,
   shall vanish.
   Into smoke they shall vanish away.

21 The wicked borrows
   and does not repay,
   But the righteous shows mercy
   and gives.
22 For *those who are* blessed by Him
   shall inherit the earth,
   But *those who are* cursed by Him
   shall be cut off.

23 The steps of a *good* man are ordered
   by the LORD,
   And He delights in his way.
24 Though he fall,
   he shall not be utterly cast down;
   For the LORD upholds *him with* His
   hand.

25 I have been young, and *now* am old;
Yet I have not seen the righteous
    forsaken,
Nor his descendants begging bread.
26 *He is* ever merciful, and lends;
And his descendants *are* blessed.

27 Depart from evil, and do good;
And dwell forevermore.
28 For the LORD loves justice,
And does not forsake His saints;
They are preserved forever,
But the descendants of the wicked shall
    be cut off.
29 The righteous shall inherit the land,
And dwell in it forever.

30 The mouth of the righteous speaks
    wisdom,
And his tongue talks of justice.
31 The law of his God *is* in his heart;
None of his steps shall slide.

32 The wicked watches the righteous,
And seeks to slay him.
33 The LORD will not leave him in his
    hand,
Nor condemn him when he is judged.

34 Wait on the LORD,
And keep His way,
And He shall exalt you to inherit the
    land;
When the wicked are cut off,
    you shall see *it.*
35 I have seen the wicked in great power,
And spreading himself like a native
    green tree.
36 Yet he passed away, and behold,
    he *was* no *more;*
Indeed I sought him,
    but he could not be found.

37 Mark the blameless *man,*
    and observe the upright;
For the future of *that* man *is* peace.
38 But the transgressors shall be destroyed
    together;
The future of the wicked shall be
    cut off.

39 But the salvation of the righteous *is*
    from the LORD;
He is their strength in the time of
    trouble.
40 And the LORD shall help them
    and deliver them;
He shall deliver them from the wicked,
And save them,
Because they trust in Him.

PSALM 38

Prayer in Time of Chastening

A Psalm of David. To bring to remembrance.

O LORD, do not rebuke me in Your
    wrath,
Nor chasten me in Your hot
    displeasure!
2 For Your arrows pierce me deeply,
And Your hand presses me down.

3 *There is* no soundness in my flesh
Because of Your anger,
Nor *is there any* health in my bones
Because of my sin.
4 For my iniquities have gone over my
    head;
Like a heavy burden they are too
    heavy for me.
5 My wounds are foul *and* festering
Because of my foolishness.

6 I am troubled,
    I am bowed down greatly;
I go mourning all the day long.
7 For my loins are full of inflammation,
And *there is* no soundness in my flesh.
8 I am feeble and severely broken;
I groan because of the turmoil of my
    heart.

9 Lord, all my desire *is* before You;
And my sighing is not hidden from
    You.
10 My heart pants, my strength fails me;
As for the light of my eyes,
    it also has gone from me.

11 My loved ones and my friends stand
    aloof from my plague,
And my kinsmen stand afar off.
12 Those also who seek my life lay snares
    for me;
Those who seek my hurt speak of
    destruction,
And plan deception all the day long.

13 But I, like a deaf *man,* do not hear;
And *I am* like a mute *who* does not
    open his mouth.
14 Thus I am like a man who does not
    hear,
And in whose mouth *is* no response.

15 For in You, O LORD, I hope;
You will hear, O Lord my God.
16 For I said, "*Hear me,*
    lest they rejoice over me,
Lest, when my foot slips,
    they magnify *themselves* against me."

17 For I *am* ready to fall,
And my sorrow *is* continually before
me.
18 For I will declare my iniquity;
I will be in anguish over my sin.
19 But my enemies *are* vigorous,
and they are strong;
And those who hate me wrongfully
have multiplied.
20 Those also who render evil for good,
They are my adversaries,
because I follow *what is* good.

21 Do not forsake me, O LORD;
O my God, be not far from me!
22 Make haste to help me,
O Lord, my salvation!

PSALM 39

Prayer for Wisdom and Forgiveness

To the Chief Musician. To Jeduthun. A Psalm of
David.

I SAID, "I will guard my ways,
Lest I sin with my tongue;
I will restrain my mouth with a muzzle,
While the wicked are before me."
2 I was mute with silence,
I held my peace *even* from good;
And my sorrow was stirred up.
3 My heart was hot within me;
While I was musing, the fire burned.
Then I spoke with my tongue:

4 "LORD, make me to know my end,
And what *is* the measure of my days,
That I may know how frail I *am.*
5 Indeed, You have made my days *as*
handbreadths,
And my age *is* as nothing before You;
Certainly every man at his best state *is*
but vapor.   Selah
6 Surely every man walks about like a
shadow;
Surely they busy themselves in vain;
He heaps up *riches,*
And does not know who will gather
them.

7 "And now, Lord, what do I wait for?
My hope *is* in You.
8 Deliver me from all my transgressions;
Do not make me the reproach of the
foolish.
9 I was mute, I did not open my mouth,
Because it was You who did *it.*
10 Remove Your plague from me;
I am consumed by the blow of Your
hand.

11 When with rebukes You correct man
for iniquity,
You make his beauty melt away like a
moth;
Surely every man *is* vapor.   Selah

12 "Hear my prayer, O LORD,
And give ear to my cry;
Do not be silent at my tears;
For I *am* a stranger with You,
A sojourner, as all my fathers *were.*
13 Remove Your gaze from me,
that I may regain strength,
Before I go away and am no more."

PSALM 40

Faith Persevering in Trial

To the Chief Musician. A Psalm of David.

I WAITED patiently for the LORD;
And He inclined to me,
And heard my cry.
2 He also brought me up out of a
horrible pit,
Out of the miry clay,
And set my feet upon a rock,
And established my steps.
3 He has put a new song in my mouth—
Praise to our God;
Many will see *it* and fear,
And will trust in the LORD.

4 Blessed *is* that man who makes the
LORD his trust,
And does not respect the proud,
nor such as turn aside to lies.
5 Many, O LORD my God,
are Your wonderful works
Which You have done;
And Your thoughts *which are*
toward us
Cannot be recounted to You in order;
If I would declare and speak *of them,*
They are more than can be numbered.

6 Sacrifice and offering
You did not desire;
My ears You have opened;
Burnt offering and sin offering
You did not require.
7 Then I said, "Behold, I come;
In the scroll of the Book *it is* written of
me.
8 I delight to do Your will, O my God,
And Your law *is* within my heart."

9 I have proclaimed the good news of
righteousness
In the great congregation;
Indeed, I do not restrain my lips,
O LORD, You Yourself know.

The Remote Places

Throughout Jesus' ministry, our Lord took time to be alone with His Father to pray. After long days of ministering to the people in Galilee, Jesus withdrew to deserted places around the sea.

In Christ's day, Galilee was one of the most fertile agricultural areas in all of Palestine. It bustled with life and was a major cosmopolitan center. The region's population was in the millions, with more than twenty-five cities surrounding the lake and another ninety cities within walking distance.

Somehow, Jesus found time and space to be alone with God. The desert places can actually be translated "the remote places" of Galilee. These remote places are the high mountain ranges with beautiful panoramic views of the lake and the surrounding Decapolis mountains. They are the still valleys and the quiet fields covered with beautiful red anemones.

Jesus realized the importance and value of withdrawing to beautiful serene places to commune with God before spending Himself in His ministry. We must do the same. We must draw our serenity and strength from quiet moments alone with God.

If you live in a bustling cosmopolitan center, seize the opportunity to share your faith with the people around you. But remember to make time to retreat to the remote places where you can commune with God. If you live near the ocean, take a moment to walk in the waves and let them lap around your feet. If you are near the mountains, walk with God through the quiet woods and tall majestic trees. If you are in the heart of the city, go to the top of your apartment building and catch the first rays of sunrise as it illuminates the sky above you.

No matter where you are, you can find a remote place to spend time with God. If you are in a hospital, close your eyes and remember the beautiful sunsets and sunrises that you have seen throughout your life. The remote places can become oases. There you commune with God so you can go into the cosmopolitan centers, renewed with strength and faith. Whatever you do, remember, do it with God!

10 I have not hidden Your righteousness
      within my heart;
    I have declared Your faithfulness and
      Your salvation;
    I have not concealed Your
      lovingkindness and Your truth
    From the great congregation.

11 Do not withhold Your tender mercies
      from me, O LORD;
    Let Your lovingkindness and Your
      truth continually preserve me.
12 For innumerable evils have surrounded
      me;
    My iniquities have overtaken me,
      so that I am not able to look up;
    They are more than the hairs of my
      head;
    Therefore my heart fails me.

13 Be pleased, O LORD, to deliver me;
    O LORD, make haste to help me!
14 Let them be ashamed
      and brought to mutual confusion
    Who seek to destroy my life;
    Let them be driven backward
      and brought to dishonor
    Who wish me evil.
15 Let them be appalled because of their
      shame,
    Who say to me, "Aha, aha!"

16 Let all those who seek You
      rejoice and be glad in You;
    Let such as love Your salvation
      say continually,
    "The LORD be magnified!"
17 But I am poor and needy;
    Yet the LORD thinks upon me.
    You are my help and my deliverer;
    Do not delay, O my God.

PSALM 41

The Blessing and Suffering of the Godly

To the Chief Musician. A Psalm of David.

BLESSED is he who considers the poor;
    The LORD will deliver him in time of
      trouble.
2 The LORD will preserve him
    and keep him alive,
    And he will be blessed on the earth;
    You will not deliver him to the will of
      his enemies.
3 The LORD will strengthen him on his
      bed of illness;
    You will sustain him on his sickbed.

4 I said, "LORD, be merciful to me;
    Heal my soul, for I have sinned against
    You."

5 My enemies speak evil of me:
    "When will he die,
      and his name perish?"
6 And if he comes to see me,
      he speaks vain words;
    His heart gathers iniquity to itself;
    When he goes out, he tells it.

7 All who hate me whisper together
      against me;
    Against me they devise my hurt.
8 "An evil disease," they say, "clings to
      him.
    And now that he lies down,
      he will rise up no more."
9 Even my own familiar friend in whom
      I trusted,
    Who ate my bread,
    Has lifted up his heel against me.

10 But You, O LORD, be merciful to me,
      and raise me up,
    That I may repay them.
11 By this I know that You are well
      pleased with me,
    Because my enemy does not triumph
      over me.
12 As for me, You uphold me in my
      integrity,
    And set me before Your face forever.

13 Blessed be the LORD God of Israel
    From everlasting to everlasting!
    Amen and Amen.

BOOK TWO

Psalms 42–72

PSALM 42

Yearning for God in the Midst of Distresses

To the Chief Musician. A Contemplation[15] of the
sons of Korah.

AS the deer pants for the water brooks,
    So pants my soul for You, O God.
2 My soul thirsts for God,
    for the living God.
    When shall I come and appear before
      God?
3 My tears have been my food day and
      night,
    While they continually say to me,
    "Where is your God?"

4 When I remember these things,
    I pour out my soul within me.
    For I used to go with the multitude;
    I went with them to the house of God,
    With the voice of joy and praise,

15 Hebrew Maschil

With a multitude that kept a pilgrim
feast.

5 Why are you cast down, O my soul?
And *why* are you disquieted within me?
Hope in God,
for I shall yet praise Him
For the help of His countenance.

6 O my God, my soul is cast down
within me;
Therefore I will remember You from
the land of the Jordan,
And from the heights of Hermon,
From the Hill Mizar.
7 Deep calls unto deep at the noise of
Your waterfalls;
All Your waves and billows have gone
over me.
8 The LORD will command His
lovingkindness in the daytime,
And in the night His song *shall be* with
me—
A prayer to the God of my life.

9 I will say to God my Rock,
"Why have You forgotten me?
Why do I go mourning because of
the oppression of the enemy?"
10 *As* with a breaking of my bones,
My enemies reproach me,
While they say to me all day long,
"Where *is* your God?"

11 Why are you cast down, O my soul?
And why are you disquieted within
me?
Hope in God;
For I shall yet praise Him,
The help of my countenance and my
God.

PSALM 43

Prayer to God in Time of Trouble

VINDICATE me, O God,
And plead my cause against an
ungodly nation;
Oh, deliver me from the deceitful and
unjust man!
2 For You *are* the God of my strength;
Why do You cast me off?
Why do I go mourning because of
the oppression of the enemy?

3 Oh, send out Your light and Your
truth!
Let them lead me;
Let them bring me to Your holy hill
And to Your tabernacle.

16 Hebrew *Maschil*

4 Then I will go to the altar of God,
To God my exceeding joy;
And on the harp I will praise You,
O God, my God.

5 Why are you cast down, O my soul?
And why are you disquieted within
me?
Hope in God;
For I shall yet praise Him,
The help of my countenance and my
God.

PSALM 44

Redemption Remembered in Present Dishonor

To the Chief Musician. A Contemplation[16] of the
sons of Korah.

WE have heard with our ears, O God,
Our fathers have told us,
What deeds You did in their days,
In days of old:
2 *How* You drove out the nations with
Your hand,
But them You planted;
How You afflicted the peoples,
and cast them out.
3 For they did not gain possession of the
land by their own sword,
Nor did their own arm save them;
But it was Your right hand, Your arm,
and the light of Your countenance,
Because You favored them.

4 You are my King, O God;
Command victories for Jacob.
5 Through You we will push down our
enemies;
Through Your name we will trample
those who rise up against us.
6 For I will not trust in my bow,
Nor shall my sword save me.
7 But You have saved us from our
enemies,
And have put to shame those who
hated us.
8 In God we boast all day long,
And praise Your name forever.   Selah

9 But You have cast *us* off
and put us to shame,
And You do not go out with our
armies.
10 You make us turn back from the
enemy,
And those who hate us have taken
spoil for themselves.
11 You have given us up like sheep
intended for food,
And have scattered us among the
nations.

12 You sell Your people for naught,
    And are not enriched by their price.
13 You make us a reproach
    to our neighbors,
    A scorn and a derision
    to those all around us.
14 You make us a byword
    among the nations,
    A shaking of the head
    among the peoples.
15 My dishonor *is* continually before me,
    And the shame of my face
    has covered me,
16 Because of the voice of him who
    reproaches and reviles,
    Because of the enemy and the avenger.
17 All this has come upon us;
    But we have not forgotten You,
    Nor have we dealt falsely with Your
    covenant.
18 Our heart has not turned back,
    Nor have our steps departed from
    Your way;
19 But You have severely broken us
    in the place of jackals,
    And covered us with the shadow of
    death.
20 If we had forgotten the name of our
    God,
    Or stretched out our hands to a foreign
    god,
21 Would not God search this out?
    For He knows the secrets of the heart.
22 Yet for Your sake we are killed all day
    long;
    We are accounted as sheep for the
    slaughter.

23 Awake! Why do You sleep, O Lord?
    Arise! Do not cast *us* off forever.
24 Why do You hide Your face,
    And forget our affliction and our
    oppression?
25 For our soul is bowed down to the
    dust;
    Our body clings to the ground.
26 Arise for our help,
    And redeem us for Your mercies' sake.

PSALM 45

The Glories of the Messiah and His Bride

To the Chief Musician. Set to "The Lilies."[17] A
Contemplation[18] of the sons of Korah. A Song of
Love.

MY heart is overflowing with a good
    theme;
    I recite my composition concerning
    the King;
    My tongue *is* the pen of a ready writer.

2 You are fairer than the sons of men;
    Grace is poured upon Your lips;
    Therefore God has blessed You
    forever.
3 Gird Your sword upon *Your* thigh,
    O Mighty One,
    With Your glory and Your majesty.
4 And in Your majesty ride prosperously
    because of truth, humility, *and*
    righteousness;
    And Your right hand shall teach You
    awesome things.
5 Your arrows *are* sharp in the heart of
    the King's enemies;
    The peoples fall under You.
6 Your throne, O God, *is* forever and
    ever;
    A scepter of righteousness *is* the
    scepter of Your kingdom.
7 You love righteousness
    and hate wickedness;
    Therefore God, Your God, has
    anointed You
    With the oil of gladness more than
    Your companions.
8 All Your garments are scented with
    myrrh and aloes *and* cassia,
    Out of the ivory palaces,
    by which they have made You glad.
9 Kings' daughters *are* among Your
    honorable women;
    At Your right hand stands the queen
    in gold from Ophir.

10 Listen, O daughter,
    Consider and incline your ear;
    Forget your own people also,
    and your father's house;
11 So the King will greatly desire your
    beauty;
    Because He *is* your Lord, worship Him.
12 And the daughter of Tyre *will be there*
    with a gift;
    The rich among the people will seek
    your favor.
13 The royal daughter *is* all glorious
    within *the palace;*
    Her clothing *is* woven with gold.
14 She shall be brought to the King
    in robes of many colors;
    The virgins, her companions who
    follow her, shall be brought to You.
15 With gladness and rejoicing they shall
    be brought;
    They shall enter the King's palace.
16 Instead of Your fathers shall be Your
    sons,

17 Hebrew *Shoshannim*   18 Hebrew *Maschil*

Whom You shall make princes in all
the earth.
17 I will make Your name to be
remembered in all generations;
Therefore the people shall praise You
forever and ever.

PSALM 46

God the Refuge of His People and Conqueror of the Nations

To the Chief Musician. A Psalm of the sons of
Korah. A Song for Alamoth.

GOD is our refuge and strength,
A very present help in trouble.
2 Therefore we will not fear,
Though the earth be removed,
And though the mountains be carried
into the midst of the sea;
3 Though its waters roar and be troubled,
Though the mountains shake with its
swelling.   Selah

4 There is a river whose streams shall
make glad the city of God,
The holy place of the tabernacle of the
Most High.
5 God is in the midst of her,
she shall not be moved;
God shall help her,
just at the break of dawn.
6 The nations raged, the kingdoms were
moved;
He uttered His voice, the earth melted.

7 The LORD of hosts is with us;
The God of Jacob is our refuge.   Selah

8 Come, behold the works of the LORD,
Who has made desolations in the earth.
9 He makes wars cease to the end of the
earth;
He breaks the bow
and cuts the spear in two;
He burns the chariot in the fire.

10 Be still, and know that I am God;
I will be exalted among the nations,
I will be exalted in the earth!

11 The LORD of hosts is with us;
The God of Jacob is our refuge.   Selah

PSALM 47

Praise to God, the Ruler of the Earth

To the Chief Musician. A Psalm of the sons of
Korah.

OH, clap your hands, all you peoples!
Shout to God with the voice of
triumph!

2 For the LORD Most High is awesome;
He is a great King over all the earth.
3 He will subdue the peoples under us,
And the nations under our feet.
4 He will choose our inheritance for us,
The excellence of Jacob whom He
loves.   Selah

5 God has gone up with a shout,
The LORD with the sound of a trumpet.
6 Sing praises to God, sing praises!
Sing praises to our King, sing praises!
7 For God is the King of all the earth;
Sing praises with understanding.

8 God reigns over the nations;
God sits on His holy throne.
9 The princes of the people have
gathered together,
The people of the God of Abraham.
For the shields of the earth belong to
God;
He is greatly exalted.

PSALM 48

The Glory of God in Zion

A Song. A Psalm of the sons of Korah.

GREAT is the LORD,
and greatly to be praised
In the city of our God,
In His holy mountain.
2 Beautiful in elevation,
The joy of the whole earth,
Is Mount Zion on the sides of the
north,
The city of the great King.
3 God is in her palaces;
He is known as her refuge.

4 For behold, the kings assembled,
They passed by together.
5 They saw it, and so they marveled;
They were troubled, they hastened
away.
6 Fear took hold of them there,
And pain, as of a woman in travail,
7 As when You break the ships of
Tarshish
With an east wind.

8 As we have heard,
So we have seen
In the city of the LORD of hosts,
In the city of our God:
God will establish it forever.   Selah

9 We have thought, O God, on Your
lovingkindness,
In the midst of Your temple.

Put God on Your North

Beautiful in elevation,
The joy of the whole earth,
Is Mount Zion *on* the sides
of the north,
The city of the great King.

(Ps. 48:2)

The city so foremost in the psalmist's mind is Jerusalem—the city of God's presence and peace. Jerusalem is set above the surrounding countryside of Judea on an opal-shaped hill. Steep valleys on three sides of the city magnify its impenetrable position. To the east is the Mount of Olives and the Kidron Valley, and to the south and west are the Hinnom and Tyropean Valleys. Only from the north is the city yielding and approachable.

In biblical times, this easy northern access was the main approach route to Jerusalem. Even today it remains a major travel route. However, it also posed a real threat to the people of the city. For only on the north could an enemy attack the city with success.

It was here at Jerusalem's vulnerable point, that the mighty temple was built with its high walls and impregnable fortress. The temple was all that stood between the people of the city and the approaching armies.

The psalmist may have often sat on the Mount of Olives overlooking Jerusalem with her temple, "Mount Zion," reflecting on her geographical position and observing the strong northern walls of God's temple which protected the city. He knew how dependent Jerusalem was on God's protection from her potential problems and enemies. His psalm of praise so appropriately reflects this prayer, "*Is* Mount Zion *on* the sides of the north, the city of the great King."

God's presence in His temple, both physically and spiritually, was able to fortify the city where it was vulnerable. Only He can strengthen you where you are weak. Let Him be the fortress between you and the negative influences which would destroy you. Let God be the "Mount Zion" in your life. Put God on your north!

10 According to Your name, O God,
  So *is* Your praise to the ends of the
    earth;
  Your right hand is full of
    righteousness.
11 Let Mount Zion rejoice,
  Let the daughters of Judah be glad,
  Because of Your judgments.

12 Walk about Zion,
  And go all around her.
  Count her towers;
13 Mark well her bulwarks;
  Consider her palaces;
  That you may tell *it*
    to the generation following.
14 For this *is* God,
  Our God forever and ever;
  He will be our guide
  Even to death.

PSALM 49

The Confidence of the Foolish

To the Chief Musician. A Psalm of the sons of Korah.

HEAR this, all *you* peoples;
  Give ear, all *you* inhabitants of the
    world,
2 Both low and high,
  Rich and poor together.
3 My mouth shall speak wisdom,
  And the meditation of my heart *shall*
    bring understanding.
4 I will incline my ear to a proverb;
  I will disclose my dark saying on the
    harp.

5 Why should I fear in the days of evil,
  When the iniquity at my heels
    surrounds me?
6 Those who trust in their wealth
  And boast in the multitude of their
    riches,
7 None *of them* can by any means
    redeem *his* brother,
  Nor give to God a ransom for him—
8 For the redemption of their souls *is*
    costly,
  And it shall cease forever—
9 That he should continue to live
    eternally,
  And not see the Pit.

10 For he sees *that* wise men die;
  Likewise the fool and the senseless
    person perish,
  And leave their wealth to others.
11 Their inner thought *is that* their houses
    will continue forever,

And their dwelling places to all
    generations;
  They call *their* lands after their own
    names.
12 Nevertheless man, *though* in honor,
    does not remain;
  He is like the beasts *that* perish.

13 This is the way of those who *are*
    foolish,
  And of their posterity who approve
    their sayings.   Selah
14 Like sheep they are laid in the grave;
  Death shall feed on them;
  The upright shall have dominion over
    them in the morning;
  And their beauty shall be consumed
    in the grave, far from their dwelling.
15 But God will redeem my soul
    from the power of the grave,
  For He shall receive me.   Selah

16 Do not be afraid when one becomes
    rich,
  When the glory of his house is
    increased;
17 For when he dies he shall carry
    nothing away;
  His glory shall not descend after him.
18 Though while he lives he blesses
    himself
  (For *men* will praise you when you do
    well for yourself),
19 He shall go to the generation of his
    fathers;
  They shall never see light.
20 Man *who is* in honor,
    yet does not understand,
  Is like the beasts *that* perish.

PSALM 50

God the Righteous Judge

A Psalm of Asaph.

THE Mighty One, God the LORD,
  Has spoken and called the earth
  From the rising of the sun to its going
    down.
2 Out of Zion, the perfection of beauty,
  God will shine forth.
3 Our God shall come,
    and shall not keep silent;
  A fire shall devour before Him,
  And it shall be very tempestuous
    all around Him.

4 He shall call to the heavens from
    above,
  And to the earth,
    that He may judge His people:

5 "Gather My saints together to Me,
　Those who have made a covenant with
　Me by sacrifice."
6 Let the heavens declare His
　righteousness,
　For God Himself *is* Judge.　　　Selah

7 "Hear, O My people, and I will speak,
　O Israel, and I will testify against you;
　I *am* God, your God!
8 I will not reprove you for your
　sacrifices
　Or your burnt offerings,
　Which are continually before Me.
9 I will not take a bull from your house,
　Nor goats out of your folds.
10 For every beast of the forest *is* Mine,
　And the cattle on a thousand hills.
11 I know all the birds of the mountains,
　And the wild beasts of the field *are*
　Mine.

12 "If I were hungry, I would not tell you;
　For the world *is* Mine,
　　and all its fullness.
13 Will I eat the flesh of bulls,
　Or drink the blood of goats?
14 Offer to God thanksgiving,
　And pay your vows to the Most High.
15 Call upon Me in the day of trouble;
　I will deliver you,
　　and you shall glorify Me."

16 But to the wicked God says:
　"What *right* have you to declare My
　statutes,
　Or take My covenant in your mouth,
17 Seeing you hate instruction
　And cast My words behind you?
18 When you saw a thief,
　　you consented with him,
　And have been a partaker with
　adulterers.
19 You give your mouth to evil,
　And your tongue frames deceit.
20 You sit *and* speak against your
　brother;
　You slander your own mother's son.
21 These *things* you have done,
　　and I kept silent;
　You thought that I was altogether like
　you;
　But I will reprove you,
　And set *them* in order before your eyes.

22 "Now consider this,
　　you who forget God,
　Lest I tear *you* in pieces,
　And *there be* none to deliver:

23 Whoever offers praise glorifies Me;
　And to him who orders *his* conduct
　aright
　I will show the salvation of God."

PSALM 51

A Prayer of Repentance

To the Chief Musician. A Psalm of David when
Nathan the prophet went to him, after he had gone
in to Bathsheba.

HAVE mercy upon me, O God,
　According to Your lovingkindness;
　According to the multitude of Your
　tender mercies,
　Blot out my transgressions.
2 Wash me thoroughly from my iniquity,
　And cleanse me from my sin.

3 For I acknowledge my transgressions,
　And my sin *is* ever before me.
4 Against You, You only, have I sinned,
　And done *this* evil in Your sight—
　That You may be found just when
　You speak,
　And blameless when You judge.

5 Behold, I was brought forth in iniquity,
　And in sin my mother conceived me.
6 Behold, You desire truth in the inward
　parts,
　And in the hidden *part* You will make
　me to know wisdom.

7 Purge me with hyssop,
　　and I shall be clean;
　Wash me,
　　and I shall be whiter than snow.
8 Make me to hear joy and gladness,
　That the bones *which* You have broken
　　may rejoice.
9 Hide Your face from my sins,
　And blot out all my iniquities.

10 Create in me a clean heart, O God,
　And renew a steadfast spirit within me.
11 Do not cast me away from Your
　presence,
　And do not take Your Holy Spirit
　from me.

12 Restore to me the joy of Your
　salvation,
　And uphold me *with Your* generous
　Spirit.
13 *Then* I will teach transgressors Your
　ways,
　And sinners shall be converted to You.

14 Deliver me from bloodguiltiness,
　O God,

The God of my salvation,
And my tongue shall sing aloud of
Your righteousness.
15 O Lord, open my lips,
And my mouth shall show forth Your
praise.
16 For You do not desire sacrifice,
or else I would give *it;*
You do not delight in burnt offering.
17 The sacrifices of God *are* a broken
spirit,
A broken and a contrite heart—
These, O God, You will not despise.

18 Do good in Your good pleasure to
Zion;
Build the walls of Jerusalem.
19 Then You shall be pleased with the
sacrifices of righteousness,
With burnt offering and whole burnt
offering;
Then they shall offer bulls on Your
altar.

PSALM 52

**The End of the Wicked and the Peace of the
Godly**

To the Chief Musician. A Contemplation[19] of
David when Doeg the Edomite went and told Saul,
and said to him, "David has gone to the house of
Ahimelech."

W HY do you boast in evil,
O mighty man?
The goodness of God *endures*
continually.
2 Your tongue devises destruction,
Like a sharp razor, working deceitfully.
3 You love evil more than good,
And lying rather than speaking
righteousness.   Selah
4 You love all devouring words,
You deceitful tongue.

5 God shall likewise destroy you forever;
He shall take you away, and pluck you
out of *your* dwelling place,
And uproot you from the land
of the living.   Selah
6 The righteous also shall see and fear,
And shall laugh at him, *saying,*
7 "Here is the man *who* did not make
God his strength,
But trusted in the abundance
of his riches,
And strengthened himself
in his wickedness."

8 But I *am* like a green olive tree in the
house of God;

I trust in the mercy of God
forever and ever.
9 I will praise You forever,
Because You have done *it;*
And in the presence of Your saints
I will wait on Your name,
for *it is* good.

PSALM 53

**Folly of the Godless, and the Restoration of
Israel**

To the Chief Musician. Set to "Mahalath." A
Contemplation[20] of David.

T HE fool has said in his heart,
"*There is* no God."
They are corrupt,
and have done abominable iniquity;
There is none who does good.

2 God looks down from heaven upon the
children of men,
To see if there are *any* who understand,
who seek God.
3 Every one of them has turned aside;
They have together become corrupt;
There is none who does good,
No, not one.

4 Have the workers of iniquity no
knowledge,
Who eat up my people *as* they eat
bread,
And do not call upon God?
5 There they are in great fear
Where no fear was,
For God has scattered the bones of
him who encamps against you;
You have put *them* to shame,
Because God has despised them.

6 Oh, that the salvation of Israel would
come out of Zion!
When God brings back the captivity of
His people,
Let Jacob rejoice *and* Israel be glad.

PSALM 54

**Answered Prayer for Deliverance from
Adversaries**

To the Chief Musician. With stringed instruments.[21]
A Contemplation[22] of David when the Ziphites went
and said to Saul, "Is David not hiding with us?"

S AVE me, O God, by Your name,
And vindicate me by Your strength.
2 Hear my prayer, O God;
Give ear to the words of my mouth.
3 For strangers have risen up against me,
And oppressors have sought after
my life;

19 Hebrew *Maschil*   20 Hebrew *Maschil*   21 Hebrew *neginoth*   22 Hebrew *Maschil*

They have not set God before them.
Selah

4 Behold, God *is* my helper;
The Lord *is* with those who uphold
my life.
5 He will repay my enemies for their evil.
Cut them off in Your truth.

6 I will freely sacrifice to You;
I will praise Your name, O LORD,
for *it is* good.
7 For He has delivered me out of all
trouble;
And my eye has seen *its desire* upon
my enemies.

PSALM 55

Trust in God Concerning the Treachery of Friends

To the Chief Musician. With stringed instruments.[23]
A Contemplation[24] of David.

GIVE ear to my prayer, O God,
And do not hide Yourself from my
supplication.
2 Attend to me, and hear me;
I am restless in my complaint,
and moan noisily,
3 Because of the voice of the enemy,
Because of the oppression of the
wicked;
For they bring down trouble upon me,
And in wrath they hate me.

4 My heart is severely pained within me,
And the terrors of death have fallen
upon me.
5 Fearfulness and trembling have come
upon me,
And horror has overwhelmed me.
6 And I said, "Oh, that I had wings like
a dove!
For then I would fly away
and be at rest.
7 Indeed, I would wander far off,
And remain in the wilderness. Selah
8 I would hasten my escape
From the windy storm *and* tempest."

9 Destroy, O Lord, *and* divide their
tongues,
For I have seen violence and strife
in the city.
10 Day and night they go around it on its
walls;
Iniquity and trouble *are* also in the
midst of it.
11 Destruction *is* in its midst;
Deceit and guile do not depart from its
streets.

12 For *it is* not an enemy *who* reproaches
me;
Then I could bear *it.*
Nor *is it* one *who* hates me who has
magnified *himself* against me;
Then I could hide from him.
13 But *it was* you, a man my equal,
My companion and my acquaintance.
14 We took sweet counsel together,
And walked to the house of God
in the throng.

15 Let death seize them;
Let them go down alive into hell,
For wickedness *is* in their dwellings
and among them.

16 As for me, I will call upon God,
And the LORD shall save me.
17 Evening and morning and at noon
I will pray, and cry aloud,
And He shall hear my voice.
18 He has redeemed my soul in peace
from the battle *which was*
against me,
For there were many against me.
19 God will hear, and afflict them,
Even He who abides from
of old.   Selah
Because they do not change,
Therefore they do not fear God.

20 He has put forth his hands against
those who were at peace with him;
He has broken his covenant.
21 *The words* of his mouth were smoother
than butter,
But war *was* in his heart;
His words were softer than oil,
Yet they *were* drawn swords.

22 Cast your burden on the LORD,
And He shall sustain you;
He shall never permit the righteous
to be moved.

23 But You, O God, shall bring them
down to the pit of destruction;
Bloodthirsty and deceitful men shall
not live out half their days;
But I will trust in You.

PSALM 56

Prayer for Relief from Tormentors

To the Chief Musician. Set to "The Silent Dove in
Distant Lands."[25] A Michtam of David when the
Philistines captured him in Gath.

BE merciful to me, O God,
for man would swallow me up;
Fighting all day he oppresses me.

---

23 Hebrew *neginoth*   24 Hebrew *Maschil*   25 Hebrew *Jonath Elem Rechokim*

2 My enemies would hound *me* all day,
For *there are* many who fight against
   me, O Most High.
3 Whenever I am afraid,
I will trust in You.
4 In God (I will praise His word),
In God I have put my trust;
I will not fear.
What can flesh do to me?

5 All day they twist my words;
All their thoughts *are* against me for
   evil.
6 They gather together,
They hide, they mark my steps,
When they lie in wait for my life.
7 Shall they escape by iniquity?
In anger cast down the peoples,
   O God!

8 You number my wanderings;
Put my tears into Your bottle;
Are they not in Your book?
9 When I cry out *to You,*
Then my enemies will turn back;
This I know, because God *is* for me.
10 In God (I will praise *His* word),
In the LORD (I will praise *His* word),
11 In God I have put my trust;
I will not be afraid.
What can man do to me?

12 Vows *made* to You *are binding* upon
   me, O God;
I will render praises to You,
13 For You have delivered my soul
   from death.
Have You not *delivered* my feet
   from falling,
That I may walk before God
In the light of the living?

PSALM 57

Prayer for Safety from Enemies

To the Chief Musician. Set to "Do Not Destroy."[26]
A Michtam of David when he fled from Saul into
the cave.

B E merciful to me, O God,
   be merciful to me!
For my soul trusts in You;
And in the shadow of Your wings
I will make my refuge,
Until *these* calamities have passed by.

2 I will cry out to God Most High,
To God who performs *all things* for
   me.
3 He shall send from heaven
   and save me;

He reproaches the one who would
   swallow me up.   Selah
God shall send forth His mercy and
   His truth.

4 My soul *is* among lions;
I lie *among* the sons of men
Who are set on fire,
Whose teeth *are* spears and arrows,
And their tongue a sharp sword.
5 Be exalted, O God, above the heavens;
Let Your glory *be* above all the earth.

6 They have prepared a net for my steps;
My soul is bowed down;
They have dug a pit before me;
Into the midst of it they *themselves*
   have fallen.   Selah

7 My heart is steadfast, O God,
   my heart is steadfast;
I will sing and give praise.
8 Awake, my glory!
Awake, lute and harp!
I will awaken the dawn.

9 I will praise You, O Lord,
   among the peoples;
I will sing to You among the nations.
10 For Your mercy reaches unto the
   heavens,
And Your truth unto the clouds.

11 Be exalted, O God, above the heavens;
Let Your glory *be* above all the earth.

PSALM 58

The Just Judgment of the Wicked

To the Chief Musician. Set to "Do Not Destroy."[27]
A Michtam of David.

D O you indeed speak righteousness,
   you silent ones?
Do you judge uprightly,
   you sons of men?
2 No, in heart you work wickedness;
You weigh out the violence of your
   hands in the earth.

3 The wicked are estranged from the
   womb;
They go astray as soon as they are
   born, speaking lies.
4 Their poison *is* like the poison of a
   serpent;
They are like the deaf cobra *that* stops
   its ear,
5 Which will not heed the voice of
   charmers,
Charming ever so skillfully.

26 Hebrew *Al Tashcheth*   27 Hebrew *Al Tashcheth*

6 Break their teeth in their mouth,
O God!
Break out the fangs of the young lions,
O LORD!
7 Let them flow away as waters *which*
run continually;
When he bends *his* bow,
Let his arrows be as if cut in pieces.
8 *Let them be* like a snail which melts
away as it goes,
Like a stillborn child of a woman,
that they may not see the sun.

9 Before your pots can feel *the burning*
thorns,
He shall take them away as with a
whirlwind,
As in His living and burning wrath.
10 The righteous shall rejoice when he
sees the vengeance;
He shall wash his feet in the blood of
the wicked,
11 So that men will say,
"Surely *there is* a reward for the
righteous;
Surely He is God who judges in the
earth."

PSALM 59

The Assured Judgment of the Wicked

To the Chief Musician. Set to "Do Not Destroy."[28]
A Michtam of David when Saul sent men, and they
watched the house in order to kill him.

D ELIVER me from my enemies,
O my God;
Defend me from those who rise up
against me.
2 Deliver me from the workers of
iniquity,
And save me from bloodthirsty men.

3 For look, they lie in wait for my life;
The mighty gather against me,
Not *for* my transgression nor *for* my
sin, O LORD.
4 They run and prepare themselves
through no fault of *mine.*

Awake to help me, and behold!
5 You therefore, O LORD God of hosts,
the God of Israel,
Awake to punish all the nations;
Do not be merciful to any wicked
transgressors.   Selah

6 At evening they return,
They growl like a dog,
And go all around the city.
7 Indeed, they belch out with their
mouth;

Swords *are* in their lips;
For *they say,* "Who hears?"

8 But You, O LORD, shall laugh at them;
You shall have all the nations in
derision.
9 *O You* his Strength,
I will wait for You.

For God *is* my defense;
10 My merciful God shall come to meet
me;
God shall let me see *my desire* on my
enemies.

11 Do not slay them,
lest my people forget;
Scatter them by Your power,
And bring them down,
O Lord our shield.
12 *For* the sin of their mouth *and* the
words of their lips,
Let them even be taken in their pride,
And for the cursing and lying *which*
they speak.
13 Consume *them* in wrath,
consume *them,*
That they *may* not *be;*
And let them know that God rules in
Jacob
To the ends of the earth.   Selah

14 And at evening they return,
They growl like a dog,
And go all around the city.
15 They wander up and down for food,
And howl if they are not satisfied.

16 But I will sing of Your power;
Yes, I will sing aloud of Your mercy in
the morning;
For You have been my defense
And refuge in the day of my trouble.
17 To You, O my Strength,
I will sing praises;
For God *is* my defense,
The God of my mercy.

PSALM 60

Urgent Prayer for the Restored Favor of God

To the Chief Musician. Set to "Lily of the
Testimony."[29] A Michtam of David. For teaching.
When he fought against Mesopotamia and Syria of
Zobah, and Joab returned and killed twelve
thousand Edomites in the Valley of Salt.

O GOD, You have cast us off;
You have broken us down;
You have been displeased;
Oh, restore us again!

28 Hebrew *Al Tashcheth*   29 Hebrew *Shushan Eduth*

2 You have made the earth tremble;
  You have broken it;
  Heal its breaches, for it is shaking.
3 You have shown Your people hard
    things;
  You have made us drink the wine of
    confusion.

4 You have given a banner to those who
    fear You,
  That it may be displayed because of
    the truth.   Selah
5 That Your beloved may be delivered,
  Save *with* Your right hand,
    and hear me.

6 God has spoken in His holiness:
  "I will rejoice;
  I will divide Shechem
  And measure out the Valley of
    Succoth.
7 Gilead *is* Mine, and Manasseh *is* Mine;
  Ephraim also *is* the helmet for My
    head;
  Judah *is* My lawgiver.
8 Moab *is* My washpot;
  Over Edom I will cast My shoe;
  Philistia, shout in triumph because of
    Me."

9 Who will bring me *into* the strong city?
  Who will lead me to Edom?
10 *Is it* not You, O God, *who* cast us off?
  And *You,* O God, *who* did not go out
    with our armies?
11 Give us help from trouble,
  For vain *is* the help of man.
12 Through God we will do valiantly,
  For *it is* He *who* shall tread down our
    enemies.30

PSALM 61

Assurance of God's Eternal Protection

To the Chief Musician. On a stringed instrument.31
A Psalm of David.

HEAR my cry, O God;
  Attend to my prayer.
2 From the end of the earth I will cry to
    You,
  When my heart is overwhelmed;
  Lead me to the rock that is higher
    than I.

3 For You have been a shelter for me,
  And a strong tower from the enemy.
4 I will abide in Your tabernacle forever;
  I will trust in the shelter of Your
    wings.   Selah

5 For You, O God, have heard my vows;
  You have given *me* the heritage of
    those who fear Your name.
6 You will prolong the king's life,
  His years as many generations.
7 He shall abide before God forever.
  Oh, prepare mercy and truth,
    which may preserve him!

8 So I will sing praise to Your name
    forever,
  That I may daily perform my vows.

PSALM 62

A Calm Resolve to Wait for the Salvation of God

To the Chief Musician. To Jeduthun. A Psalm of
David.

TRULY my soul silently *waits* for God;
  From Him *comes* my salvation.
2 He only *is* my rock and my salvation;
  He is my defense;
  I shall not be greatly moved.

3 How long will you attack a man?
  You shall be slain, all of you,
  Like a leaning wall and a tottering
    fence.
4 They only consult to cast *him* down
    from his high position;
  They delight in lies;
  They bless with their mouth,
  But they curse inwardly.   Selah

5 My soul, wait silently for God alone,
  For my expectation *is* from Him.
6 He only *is* my rock and my salvation;
  He is my defense;
  I shall not be moved.
7 In God *is* my salvation and my glory;
  The rock of my strength,
  And my refuge, *is* in God.

8 Trust in Him at all times, you people;
  Pour out your heart before Him;
  God *is* a refuge for us.   Selah

9 Surely men of low degree *are* a vapor,
  Men of high degree *are* a lie;
  If they are weighed in the balances,
  They *are* altogether *lighter* than vapor.
10 Do not trust in oppression,
  Nor vainly hope in robbery;
  If riches increase,
  Do not set *your* heart *on them.*

11 God has spoken once,
  Twice I have heard this:
  That power *belongs* to God.

30 Verses 5–12 (compare Psalm 108:6–13)   31 Hebrew *neginah*

12 Also to You, O Lord, *belongs* mercy;
For You render to each one according
to his work.

PSALM 63

Joy in the Fellowship of God

A Psalm of David when he was in the wilderness of
Judah.

O GOD, You *are* my God;
Early will I seek You;
My soul thirsts for You;
My flesh longs for You
In a dry and thirsty land
Where there is no water.
2 So I have looked for You
in the sanctuary,
To see Your power and Your glory.

3 Because Your lovingkindness *is* better
than life,
My lips shall praise You.
4 Thus I will bless You while I live;
I will lift up my hands in Your name.
5 My soul shall be satisfied as with
marrow and fatness,
And my mouth shall praise You with
joyful lips.

6 When I remember You on my bed,
I meditate on You in the *night* watches.
7 Because You have been my help,
Therefore in the shadow of Your wings
I will rejoice.
8 My soul follows close behind You;
Your right hand upholds me.

9 But those *who* seek my life,
to destroy *it,*
Shall go into the lower parts of the
earth.
10 They shall fall by the sword;
They shall be a portion for jackals.

11 But the king shall rejoice in God;
Everyone who swears by Him shall
glory;
But the mouth of those who speak lies
shall be stopped.

PSALM 64

Oppressed by the Wicked but Rejoicing in the LORD

To the Chief Musician. A Psalm of David.

H EAR my voice, O God, in my
meditation;
Preserve my life from fear of the
enemy.
2 Hide me from the secret counsel of the
wicked,

From the insurrection of the workers
of iniquity,
3 Who sharpen their tongue like a sword,
And bend *their bows to shoot* their
arrows—bitter words,
4 That they may shoot in secret at the
blameless;
Suddenly they shoot at him and do not
fear.

5 They encourage themselves *in* an evil
matter;
They talk of laying snares secretly;
They say, "Who will see them?"
6 They devise iniquities:
"We have perfected a shrewd scheme."
Both the inward thought and the heart
of man are deep.

7 But God shall shoot at them *with* an
arrow;
Suddenly they shall be wounded.
8 So He will make them stumble over
their own tongue;
All who see them shall flee away.
9 All men shall fear,
And shall declare the work of God;
For they shall wisely consider His
doing.

10 The righteous shall be glad in the
LORD, and trust in Him.
And all the upright in heart shall glory.

PSALM 65

Praise to God for His Salvation and Providence

To the Chief Musician. A Psalm of David. A Song.

P RAISE is awaiting You, O God, in
Zion;
And to You the vow shall be
performed.
2 O You who hear prayer,
To You all flesh will come.
3 Iniquities prevail against me;
As for our transgressions,
You will provide atonement for them.

4 Blessed *is the man whom* You choose,
And cause to approach *You,*
That he may dwell in Your courts.
We shall be satisfied with the goodness
of Your house,
Of Your holy temple.

5 *By* awesome deeds in righteousness
You will answer us,
O God of our salvation,
You who are the confidence of all the
ends of the earth,
And of the far-off seas;

6 Who established the mountains by His
strength,
Being clothed with power;
7 You who still the noise of the seas,
The noise of their waves,
And the tumult of the peoples.
8 They also who dwell in the farthest
parts are afraid of Your signs;
You make the outgoings of the
morning and evening rejoice.

9 You visit the earth and water it,
You greatly enrich it;
The river of God is full of water;
You provide their grain,
For so You have prepared it.
10 You water its ridges abundantly,
You settle its furrows;
You make it soft with showers,
You bless its growth.

11 You crown the year with Your
goodness,
And Your paths drip *with* abundance.
12 They drop *on* the pastures of the
wilderness,
And the little hills rejoice on every
side.
13 The pastures are clothed with flocks;
The valleys also are covered with grain;
They shout for joy, they also sing.

PSALM 66

Praise to God for His Awesome Works

To the Chief Musician. A Song. A Psalm.

MAKE a joyful shout to God,
all the earth!
2 Sing out the honor of His name;
Make His praise glorious.
3 Say to God,
"How awesome are Your works!
Through the greatness of Your power
Your enemies shall submit themselves
to You.
4 All the earth shall worship You
And sing praises to You;
They shall sing praises
to Your name."   Selah

5 Come and see the works of God;
He is awesome *in His* doing toward the
sons of men.
6 He turned the sea into dry *land;*
They went through the river on foot.
There we will rejoice in Him.
7 He rules by His power forever;
His eyes observe the nations;
Do not let the rebellious exalt
themselves.   Selah

8 Oh, bless our God, you peoples!
And make the voice of His praise to be
heard,
9 Who keeps our soul among the living,
And does not allow our feet to be
moved.
10 For You, O God, have proved us;
You have refined us as silver is refined.
11 You brought us into the net;
You laid affliction on our backs.
12 You have caused men to ride over our
heads;
We went through fire
and through water;
But You brought us out to rich
fulfillment.

13 I will go into Your house with burnt
offerings;
I will pay You my vows,
14 Which my lips have uttered
And my mouth has spoken when I was
in trouble.
15 I will offer You burnt sacrifices of fat
animals,
With the sweet aroma of rams;
I will offer bulls with goats.   Selah

16 Come *and* hear, all you who fear God,
And I will declare what He has done
for my soul.
17 I cried to Him with my mouth,
And He was extolled with my tongue.
18 If I regard iniquity in my heart,
The Lord will not hear.
19 *But* certainly God has heard *me;*
He has attended to the voice of my
prayer.

20 Blessed *be* God,   .
Who has not turned away my prayer,
Nor His mercy from me!

PSALM 67

An Invocation and a Doxology

To the Chief Musician. On stringed instruments.[32]
A Psalm. A Song.

GOD be merciful to us and bless us,
And cause His face to shine
upon us.   Selah
2 That Your way may be known on
earth,
Your salvation among all nations.

3 Let the peoples praise You, O God;
Let all the peoples praise You.
4 Oh, let the nations be glad
and sing for joy!

32 Hebrew *neginoth*

For You shall judge the people
   righteously,
And govern the nations on earth. Selah

5 Let the peoples praise You, O God;
   Let all the peoples praise You.
6 *Then* the earth shall yield her increase;
   God, our own God, shall bless us.
7 God shall bless us,
   And all the ends of the earth shall fear
   Him.

PSALM 68

The Glory of God in His Goodness to Israel

To the Chief Musician. A Psalm of David. A Song.

LET God arise,
   Let His enemies be scattered;
   Let those also who hate Him flee
     before Him.
2 As smoke is driven away,
   So drive *them* away;
   As wax melts before the fire,
   So let the wicked perish at the presence
     of God.
3 But let the righteous be glad;
   Let them rejoice before God;
   Yes, let them rejoice exceedingly.

4 Sing to God, sing praises to His name;
   Extol Him who rides on the clouds,[33]
   By His name YAH,
   And rejoice before Him.

5 A father of the fatherless,
     a defender of widows,
   Is God in His holy habitation.
6 God sets the solitary in families;
   He brings out those who are bound
     into prosperity;
   But the rebellious dwell in a dry *land.*

7 O God, when You went out before
     Your people,
   When You marched through the
     wilderness,   Selah
8 The earth shook;
   The heavens also dropped *rain* at the
     presence of God;
   Sinai itself *was moved* at the presence
     of God, the God of Israel.
9 You, O God, sent a plentiful rain,
   Whereby You confirmed Your
     inheritance,
   When it was weary.
10 Your congregation dwelt in it;
   You, O God, provided from Your
     goodness for the poor.

11 The Lord gave the word;
   Great *was* the company of those who
     proclaimed *it:*

12 "Kings of armies flee, they flee,
   And she who remains at home divides
     the spoil.
13 Though you lie down among the
     sheepfolds,
   Yet you will be like the wings of a dove
     covered with silver,
   And her feathers with yellow gold."
14 When the Almighty scattered kings
     in it,
   It was *white* as snow in Zalmon.

15 A mountain of God
     is the mountain of Bashan;
   A mountain *of many* peaks
     is the mountain of Bashan.
16 Why do you fume with envy,
     you mountains of *many* peaks?
   This is the mountain *which* God desires
     to dwell in;
   Yes, the LORD will dwell *in it* forever.

17 The chariots of God *are* twenty
     thousand,
   Even thousands of thousands;
   The Lord is among them *as in* Sinai,
     in the Holy *Place.*
18 You have ascended on high,
   You have led captivity captive;
   You have received gifts among men,
   Even *among* the rebellious,
   That the LORD God might dwell *there.*

19 Blessed *be* the Lord,
   Who daily loads us *with benefits,*
   The God of our salvation!   Selah
20 Our God *is* the God of salvation;
   And to GOD the Lord *belong* escapes
     from death.

21 But God will wound the head of His
     enemies,
   The hairy scalp of the one who still
     goes on in His trespasses.
22 The Lord said, "I will bring back from
     Bashan,
   I will bring *them* back from the depths
     of the sea,
23 That your foot may crush *them* in
     blood,
   And the tongues of your dogs *may have*
     their portion from *your* enemies."

24 They have seen Your procession,
     O God,
   The procession of my God, my King,
     into the sanctuary.
25 The singers went before, the players on
     instruments *followed* after;
   Among *them were* the maidens playing
     timbrels.

---

33 Masoretic Text reads *deserts;* Targum reads *heavens* (compare 68:34 and Isaiah 19:1).

26 Bless God in the congregations,
The Lord, from the fountain of Israel.
27 There *is* little Benjamin, their leader,
The princes of Judah *and* their
company,
The princes of Zebulun *and* the princes
of Naphtali.
28 Your God has commanded your
strength;
Strengthen, O God, what You have
done for us.
29 Because of Your temple at Jerusalem,
Kings will bring presents to You.
30 Rebuke the beasts of the reeds,
The herd of bulls with the calves of the
peoples,
Till everyone submits himself with
pieces of silver.
Scatter the peoples *who* delight in war.
31 Envoys will come out of Egypt;
Ethiopia will quickly stretch out her
hands to God.

32 Sing to God, you kingdoms of the
earth;
Oh, sing praises to the Lord,　　Selah
33 To Him who rides on the heaven of
heavens, *which were* of old!
Indeed, He sends out His voice,
a mighty voice.
34 Ascribe strength to God;
His excellence *is* over Israel,
And His strength *is* in the clouds.
35 O God, *You are* more awesome than
Your holy places.
The God of Israel *is* He who gives
strength and power to *His* people.

Blessed *be* God!

PSALM 69

An Urgent Plea for Help in Trouble

To the Chief Musician. Set to "The Lilies."[34] A
Psalm of David.

S AVE me, O God!
For the waters have come up
to *my* neck.
2 I sink in deep mire,
Where *there is* no standing;
I have come into deep waters,
Where the floods overflow me.
3 I am weary with my crying;
My throat is dry;
My eyes fail while I wait for my God.

4 Those who hate me without a cause
Are more than the hairs of my head;
They are mighty who would destroy
me,

Being my enemies wrongfully;
Though I have stolen nothing,
I *still* must restore *it.*

5 O God, You know my foolishness;
And my sins are not hidden from You.
6 Let not those who wait for You,
O Lord GOD of hosts, be ashamed
because of me;
Let not those who seek You be
confounded because of me,
O God of Israel.
7 Because for Your sake I have borne
reproach;
Shame has covered my face.
8 I have become a stranger to my
brothers,
And an alien to my mother's children;
9 Because zeal for Your house has eaten
me up,
And the reproaches of those who
reproach You have fallen on me.
10 When I wept *and chastened* my soul
with fasting,
That became my reproach.
11 I also made sackcloth my garment;
I became a byword to them.
12 Those who sit in the gate speak against
me,
And I *am* the song of the drunkards.

13 But as for me, my prayer *is* to You,
O LORD, *in* the acceptable time;
O God, in the multitude of Your
mercy,
Hear me in the truth of Your salvation.
14 Deliver me out of the mire,
And let me not sink;
Let me be delivered from those who
hate me,
And out of the deep waters.
15 Let not the floodwater overflow me,
Nor let the deep swallow me up;
And let not the pit shut its mouth on
me.

16 Hear me, O LORD,
for Your lovingkindness *is* good;
Turn to me according to the multitude
of Your tender mercies.
17 And do not hide Your face from Your
servant,
For I am in trouble;
Hear me speedily.
18 Draw near to my soul, *and* redeem it;
Deliver me because of my enemies.

19 You know my reproach, my shame,
and my dishonor;
My adversaries *are* all before You.

34 Hebrew *Shoshannim*

20 Reproach has broken my heart,
And I am full of heaviness;
I looked *for someone* to take pity,
but *there was* none;
And for comforters, but I found none.
21 They also gave me gall for my food,
And for my thirst they gave me vinegar
to drink.

22 Let their table become a snare before
them,
And their well-being a trap.
23 Let their eyes be darkened,
so that they do not see;
And make their loins shake
continually.
24 Pour out Your indignation upon them,
And let Your wrathful anger take hold
of them.
25 Let their habitation be desolate;
Let no one dwell in their tents.
26 For they persecute *him* whom You
have struck,
And talk of the grief of those You have
wounded.
27 Add iniquity to their iniquity,
And let them not come into Your
righteousness.
28 Let them be blotted out of the book of
the living,
And not be written with the righteous.

29 But I *am* poor and sorrowful;
Let Your salvation, O God, set me up
on high.
30 I will praise the name of God with a
song,
And will magnify Him with
thanksgiving.
31 *This* also shall please the LORD better
than an ox *or* bull,
Which has horns and hooves.
32 The humble shall see *this and* be glad;
And you who seek God,
your hearts shall live.
33 For the LORD hears the poor,
And does not despise His prisoners.

34 Let heaven and earth praise Him,
The seas and everything that moves in
them.
35 For God will save Zion
And build the cities of Judah,
That they may dwell there
and possess it.
36 Also, the descendants of His servants
shall inherit it,
And those who love His name shall
dwell in it.

PSALM 70

Prayer for Relief from Adversaries

To the Chief Musician. *A Psalm* of David. To
bring to remembrance.

MAKE *haste,* O God, to deliver me!
Make haste to help me, O LORD!

2 Let them be ashamed and confounded
Who seek my life;
Let them be turned back and confused
Who desire my hurt.
3 Let them be turned back because of
their shame,
Who say, "Aha, aha!"

4 Let all those who seek You
rejoice and be glad in You;
And let those who love Your salvation
say continually,
"Let God be magnified!"

5 But I *am* poor and needy;
Make haste to me, O God!
You *are* my help and my deliverer;
O LORD, do not delay.

PSALM 71

God the Rock of Salvation

IN You, O LORD, I put my trust;
Let me never be put to shame.
2 Deliver me in Your righteousness,
and cause me to escape;
Incline Your ear to me, and save me.
3 Be my strong habitation,
To which I may resort continually;
You have given the commandment to
save me,
For You *are* my rock and my fortress.

4 Deliver me, O my God, out of the
hand of the wicked,
Out of the hand of the unrighteous and
cruel man.
5 For You are my hope, O Lord GOD;
You are my trust from my youth.
6 By You I have been upheld from *my*
birth;
You are He who took me out of my
mother's womb.
My praise *shall be* continually of You.

7 I have become as a wonder to many,
But You *are* my strong refuge.
8 Let my mouth be filled *with* Your
praise
And with Your glory all the day.

9 Do not cast me off in the time of old
age;

Do not forsake me when my strength
fails.
10 For my enemies speak against me;
And those who lie in wait for my life
take counsel together,
11 Saying, "God has forsaken him;
Pursue and take him,
for *there is* none to deliver *him.*"

12 O God, do not be far from me;
O my God, make haste to help me!
13 Let them be confounded *and* consumed
Who are adversaries of my life;
Let them be covered *with* reproach and
dishonor
Who seek my hurt.

14 But I will hope continually,
And will praise You yet more and
more.
15 My mouth shall tell of Your
righteousness
And Your salvation all the day,
For I do not know *their* limits.
16 I will go in the strength of the Lord
GOD;
I will make mention of Your
righteousness, of Yours only.

17 O God, You have taught me from my
youth;
And to this *day* I declare Your
wondrous works.
18 Now also when *I am* old and gray-
headed,
O God, do not forsake me,
Until I declare Your strength to *this*
generation,
Your power to everyone *who* is to
come.

19 Also Your righteousness, O God,
is very high,
You who have done great things;
O God, who *is* like You?
20 *You*, who have shown me great and
severe troubles,
Shall revive me again,
And bring me up again from the
depths of the earth.
21 You shall increase my greatness,
And comfort me on every side.

22 Also with the lute I will praise you—
And Your faithfulness, O my God!
To You I will sing with the harp,
O Holy One of Israel.
23 My lips shall greatly rejoice when I
sing to You,

And my soul, which You have
redeemed.
24 My tongue also shall talk of Your
righteousness all the day long;
For they are confounded,
For they are brought to shame
Who seek my hurt.

PSALM 72

Glory and Universality of the Messiah's Reign

A Psalm of Solomon.

GIVE the king Your judgments, O God,
And Your righteousness to the king's
Son.
2 He will judge Your people with
righteousness,
And Your poor with justice.
3 The mountains will bring peace to the
people,
And the little hills, by righteousness.
4 He will bring justice to the poor of the
people;
He will save the children of the needy,
And will break in pieces the oppressor.

5 They shall fear You
As long as the sun and moon endure,
Throughout all generations.
6 He shall come down like rain upon the
mown grass,
Like showers *that* water the earth.
7 In His days the righteous shall flourish,
And abundance of peace,
Until the moon is no more.

8 He shall have dominion also from sea
to sea,
And from the River to the ends of the
earth.
9 Those who dwell in the wilderness will
bow before Him,
And His enemies will lick the dust.
10 The kings of Tarshish and of the isles
Will bring presents;
The kings of Sheba and Seba
Will offer gifts.
11 Yes, all kings shall fall down before
Him;
All nations shall serve Him.

12 For He will deliver the needy when he
cries,
The poor also, and *him* who has no
helper.
13 He will spare the poor and needy,
And will save the souls of the needy.
14 He will redeem their life from
oppression and violence;
And precious shall be their blood in
His sight.

15 And He shall live;
And the gold of Sheba will be given to
Him;
Prayer also will be made for Him
continually,
And daily He shall be praised.

16 There will be an abundance of grain in
the earth,
On the top of the mountains;
Its fruit shall wave like Lebanon;
And *those* of the city shall flourish like
grass of the earth.

17 His name shall endure forever;
His name shall continue as long as the
sun.
And *men* shall be blessed in Him;
All nations shall call Him blessed.

18 Blessed *be* the LORD God,
the God of Israel,
Who only does wondrous things!
19 And blessed *be* His glorious name
forever!
And let the whole earth be filled *with*
His glory.
Amen and Amen.

20 The prayers of David the son of Jesse
are ended.

BOOK THREE
Psalms 73–89

PSALM 73

**The Tragedy of the Wicked, and the
Blessedness of Trust in God**

A Psalm of Asaph.

TRULY God *is* good to Israel,
To such as are pure in heart.
2 But as for me,
my feet had almost stumbled;
My steps had nearly slipped.
3 For I *was* envious of the boastful,
When I saw the prosperity of the
wicked.

4 For *there are* no pangs in their death,
But their strength *is* firm.
5 They *are* not in trouble *as other* men,
Nor are they plagued like *other* men.
6 Therefore pride serves as their
necklace;
Violence covers them *like* a garment.
7 Their eyes bulge with abundance;
They have more than heart could wish.

8 They scoff and speak wickedly
concerning oppression;
They speak loftily.
9 They set their mouth
against the heavens,
And their tongue walks
through the earth.

10 Therefore his people return here,
And waters of a full *cup* are drained by
them.
11 And they say, "How does God know?
And is there knowledge in the Most
High?"

12 Behold, these *are* the ungodly,
Who are always at ease;
They increase *in* riches.
13 Surely I have cleansed my heart *in*
vain,
And washed my hands in innocence.
14 For all day long I have been plagued,
And chastened every morning.

15 If I had said, "I will speak thus,"
Behold, I would have been untrue to
the generation of Your children.
16 When I thought *how* to understand
this,
It *was* too painful for me—
17 Until I went into the sanctuary of
God;
Then I understood their end.

18 Surely You set them in slippery places;
You cast them down to destruction.
19 Oh, how they are *brought* to desolation,
as in a moment!
They are utterly consumed with terrors.
20 As a dream when *one* awakes,
So, Lord, when You awake,
You shall despise their image.

21 Thus my heart was grieved,
And I was vexed in my mind.
22 I *was* so foolish and ignorant;
I was *like* a beast before You.
23 Nevertheless I *am* continually with
You;
You hold *me* by my right hand.
24 You will guide me with Your counsel,
And afterward receive me *to* glory.

25 Whom have I in heaven *but You?*
And *there is* none upon earth *that* I
desire besides You.
26 My flesh and my heart fail;
But God *is* the strength of my heart
and my portion forever.

27 For indeed, those who are far from
You shall perish;

You have destroyed all those who
  desert You for harlotry.
28 But *it is* good for me to draw near to
  God;
I have put my trust in the Lord GOD,
That I may declare all Your works.

PSALM 74

A Plea for Relief from Oppressors

A Contemplation[35] of Asaph.

O GOD, why have You cast *us* off
  forever?
Why does Your anger smoke against
  the sheep of Your pasture?
2 Remember Your congregation,
  which You have purchased of old,
The tribe of Your inheritance,
  which You have redeemed—
This Mount Zion where You have
  dwelt.
3 Lift up Your feet to the perpetual
  desolations.
The enemy has damaged everything in
  the sanctuary.
4 Your enemies roar in the midst of
  Your meeting place;
They set up their banners *for* signs.
5 They seem like men who lift up
Axes among the thick trees.
6 And now they break down its carved
  work, all at once,
With axes and hammers.
7 They have set fire to Your sanctuary;
They have defiled the dwelling place of
  Your name to the ground.
8 They said in their hearts,
"Let us destroy them altogether."
They have burned up all the meeting
  places of God in the land.

9 We do not see our signs;
There is no longer any prophet;
Nor *is there* any among us who knows
  how long.
10 O God, how long will the adversary
  reproach?
Will the enemy blaspheme Your name
  forever?
11 Why do You withdraw Your hand,
  even Your right hand?
Take it out of Your bosom
  and destroy *them*.
12 For God *is* my King from of old,
Working salvation in the midst of the
  earth.
13 You divided the sea by Your strength;
You broke the heads of the sea
  serpents in the waters.
14 You broke the heads of Leviathan in
  pieces,

And gave him *as* food to the people
  inhabiting the wilderness.
15 You broke open the fountain and the
  flood;
You dried up mighty rivers.
16 The day *is* Yours,
  the night also *is* Yours;
You have prepared the light
  and the sun.
17 You have set all the borders of the
  earth;
You have made summer and winter.

18 Remember this, *that* the enemy has
  reproached, O LORD,
And *that* a foolish people has
  blasphemed Your name.
19 Oh, do not deliver the life of Your
  turtledove to the wild beast!
Do not forget the life of Your poor
  forever.
20 Have respect to the covenant;
For the dark places of the earth are
  full of the habitations of cruelty.
21 Oh, do not let the oppressed return
  ashamed!
Let the poor and needy praise Your
  name.

22 Arise, O God, plead Your own cause;
Remember how the foolish man
  reproaches You daily.
23 Do not forget the voice of Your
  enemies;
The tumult of those who rise up
  against You increases continually.

PSALM 75

Thanksgiving for God's Righteous Judgment

To the Chief Musician. Set to "Do Not Destroy."[36]
A Psalm of Asaph. A Song.

WE give thanks to You, O God,
  we give thanks!
For Your wondrous works declare *that*
  Your name is near.

2 "When I choose the proper time,
  I will judge uprightly.
3 The earth and all its inhabitants are
  dissolved;
I set up its pillars firmly.   Selah

4 "I said to the boastful,
  'Do not deal boastfully,'
And to the wicked,
  'Do not lift up the horn.
5 Do not lift up your horn on high;
Do *not* speak with a stiff neck.' "

35 Hebrew *Maschil*   36 Hebrew *Al Tashcheth*

6 For exaltation *comes* neither from the
  east
  Nor from the west nor from the south.
7 But God *is* the Judge:
  He puts down one,
  And exalts another.
8 For in the hand of the LORD *there is* a
  cup,
  And the wine is red;
  It is fully mixed, and He pours it out;
  Surely its dregs shall all the wicked of
  the earth
  Drain *and* drink down.

9 But I will declare forever,
  I will sing praises to the God of Jacob.

10 "All the horns of the wicked
  I will also cut off,
  But the horns of the righteous
  shall be exalted."

PSALM 76

The Majesty of God in Judgment

To the Chief Musician. On stringed instruments.[37]
A Psalm of Asaph. A Song.

IN Judah God *is* known;
  His name *is* great in Israel.
2 In Salem[38] also is His tabernacle,
  And His dwelling place in Zion.
3 There He broke the arrows of the bow,
  The shield and the sword and the
  battle-*ax.*   Selah

4 You *are* more glorious and excellent
  Than the mountains of prey.
5 The stouthearted were plundered;
  They have sunk into their sleep;
  And none of the mighty men have
  found the use of their hands.
6 At Your rebuke, O God of Jacob,
  Both the chariot and horse were cast
  into a dead sleep.

7 You, Yourself, *are* to be feared;
  And who may stand in Your presence
  When once You are angry?
8 You caused judgment to be heard from
  heaven;
  The earth feared and was still,
9 When God arose to judgment,
  To deliver all the oppressed of the
  earth.   Selah

10 Surely the wrath of man shall praise
  You;
  With the remainder of wrath You shall
  gird Yourself.

11 Make vows to the LORD your God,
  and pay *them;*
  Let all who are around Him bring
  presents to Him who ought to be
  feared.
12 He shall cut off the spirit of princes;
  He is awesome to the kings of the
  earth.

PSALM 77

The Consoling Memory of God's Redemptive Works

To the Chief Musician. To Jeduthun. A Psalm of
Asaph.

I CRIED out to God with my voice—
  To God with my voice;
  And He gave ear to me.
2 In the day of my trouble I sought the
  Lord;
  My hand was stretched out in the night
  without ceasing;
  My soul refused to be comforted.
3 I remembered God, and was troubled;
  I complained, and my spirit was
  overwhelmed.   Selah

4 You hold my eyelids *open;*
  I am so troubled that I cannot speak.
5 I have considered the days of old,
  The years of ancient times.
6 I call to remembrance my song in the
  night;
  I meditate within my heart,
  And my spirit makes diligent search.

7 Will the Lord cast off forever?
  And will He be favorable no more?
8 Has His mercy ceased forever?
  Has *His* promise failed forevermore?
9 Has God forgotten to be gracious?
  Has He in anger shut up His tender
  mercies?   Selah

10 And I said, "This *is* my anguish;
  But I will remember the years of the
  right hand of the Most High."
11 I will remember the works of the
  LORD;
  Surely I will remember Your wonders
  of old.
12 I will also meditate on all Your work,
  And talk of Your deeds.
13 Your way, O God, *is* in the sanctuary;
  Who *is* so great a God as *our* God?
14 You *are* the God who does wonders;
  You have declared Your strength
  among the peoples.
15 You have with *Your* arm redeemed
  Your people,
  The sons of Jacob and Joseph.   Selah

37 Hebrew *neginoth*   38 That is, Jerusalem

16 The waters saw You, O God;
The waters saw You, they were afraid;
The depths also trembled.
17 The clouds poured out water;
The skies sent out a sound;
Your arrows also flashed about.
18 The voice of Your thunder *was* in the
whirlwind;
The lightnings lit up the world;
The earth trembled and shook.
19 Your way *was* in the sea,
Your path in the great waters,
And Your footsteps were not known.
20 You led Your people like a flock
By the hand of Moses and Aaron.

PSALM 78

God's Kindness to Rebellious Israel

A Contemplation[39] of Asaph.

GIVE ear, O my people, *to* my law;
Incline your ears to the words of my
mouth.
2 I will open my mouth in a parable;
I will utter dark sayings of old,
3 Which we have heard and known,
And our fathers have told us.
4 We will not hide *them* from their
children,
Telling to the generation to come the
praises of the LORD,
And His strength and His wonderful
works that He has done.

5 For He established a testimony in
Jacob,
And appointed a law in Israel,
Which He commanded our fathers,
That they should make them known to
their children;
6 That the generation to come might
know *them,*
The children *who* would be born,
That they may arise and declare *them*
to their children,
7 That they may set their hope in God,
And not forget the works of God,
But keep His commandments;
8 And may not be like their fathers,
A stubborn and rebellious generation,
A generation *that* did not set its heart
aright,
And whose spirit was not faithful to
God.

9 The children of Ephraim,
being armed *and* carrying bows,
Turned back in the day of battle.
10 They did not keep the covenant of
God;
They refused to walk in His law,

11 And forgot His works
And His wonders that He had shown
them.
12 Marvelous things He did
in the sight of their fathers,
In the land of Egypt,
in the field of Zoan.
13 He divided the sea
and caused them to pass through;
And He made the waters stand up like
a heap.
14 In the daytime also He led them with
the cloud,
And all the night with a light of fire.
15 He split the rocks in the wilderness,
And gave *them* drink in abundance like
the depths.
16 He also brought streams out of the
rock,
And caused waters to run down like
rivers.

17 But they sinned even more against Him
By rebelling against the Most High in
the wilderness.
18 And they tested God in their heart
By asking for the food of their fancy.
19 Yes, they spoke against God:
They said, "Can God prepare a table
in the wilderness?
20 Behold, He struck the rock,
So that the waters gushed out,
And the streams overflowed.
Can He give bread also?
Can He provide meat for His people?"

21 Therefore the LORD heard *this*
and was furious;
So a fire was kindled against Jacob,
And anger also came up against Israel,
22 Because they did not believe in God,
And did not trust in His salvation.
23 Yet He had commanded the clouds
above,
And opened the doors of heaven,
24 Had rained down manna on them to
eat,
And given them of the bread of
heaven.
25 Men ate angels' food;
He sent them food to the full.
26 He caused an east wind to blow in the
heavens;
And by His power He brought in the
south wind.
27 He also rained meat on them like the
dust,
Feathered fowl like the sand of the
seas;

39 Hebrew *Maschil*

28 And He let *them* fall in the midst of
their camp,
All around their habitations.
29 So they ate and were well filled,
For He gave them their own desire.
30 They were not deprived of their
craving;
But while their food *was* still in their
mouths,
31 The wrath of God came against them,
And slew the stoutest of them,
And struck down the choice *men* of
Israel.

32 In spite of this they still sinned,
And did not believe in His wondrous
works.
33 Therefore their days He consumed in
futility,
And their years in fear.

34 When He slew them,
then they sought Him;
And they returned
and sought diligently for God.
35 Then they remembered that God *was*
their rock,
And the Most High God their
redeemer.
36 Nevertheless they flattered Him with
their mouth,
And they lied to Him with their
tongue;
37 For their heart was not steadfast with
Him,
Nor were they faithful in His covenant.
38 But He, *being* full of compassion,
forgave *their* iniquity,
And did not destroy *them.*
Yes, many a time He turned His anger
away,
And did not stir up all His wrath;
39 For He remembered that they *were but*
flesh,
A breath that passes away
and does not come again.

40 How often they provoked Him in the
wilderness,
And grieved Him in the desert!
41 Yes, again and again they tempted
God,
And limited the Holy One of Israel.
42 They did not remember His power:
The day when He redeemed them from
the enemy,
43 When He worked His signs in Egypt,
And His wonders in the field of Zoan;
44 Turned their rivers into blood,
And their streams,
that they could not drink.

45 He sent swarms of flies among them,
which devoured them,
And frogs, which destroyed them.
46 He also gave their crops to the
caterpillar,
And their labor to the locust.
47 He destroyed their vines with hail,
And their sycamore trees with frost.
48 He also gave up their cattle to the hail,
And their flocks to fiery lightning.
49 He cast on them the fierceness of His
anger,
Wrath, indignation, and trouble,
By sending angels of destruction *among
them.*
50 He made a path for His anger;
He did not spare their soul from death,
But gave their life over to the plague,
51 And destroyed all the firstborn in
Egypt,
The first of *their* strength in the tents
of Ham.
52 But He made His own people go forth
like sheep,
And guided them in the wilderness like
a flock;
53 And He led them on safely,
so that they did not fear;
But the sea overwhelmed their enemies.
54 And He brought them to His holy
border,
This mountain *which* His right hand
had acquired.
55 He also drove out the nations before
them,
Allotted them an inheritance by survey,
And made the tribes of Israel dwell in
their tents.

56 Yet they tested and provoked the Most
High God,
And did not keep His testimonies,
57 But turned back and acted unfaithfully
like their fathers;
They were turned aside like a deceitful
bow.
58 For they provoked Him to anger with
their high places,
And moved Him to jealousy with their
carved images.
59 When God heard *this,* He was furious,
And greatly abhorred Israel,
60 So that He forsook the tabernacle of
Shiloh,
The tent *which* He had placed among
men,
61 And delivered His strength into
captivity,
And His glory into the enemy's hand.

⁶² He also gave His people over to the
sword,
And was furious with His inheritance.
⁶³ The fire consumed their young men,
And their maidens were not given in
marriage.
⁶⁴ Their priests fell by the sword,
And their widows made no
lamentation.

⁶⁵ Then the Lord awoke as *one out of*
sleep,
And like a mighty man who shouts
because of wine.
⁶⁶ And He beat back His enemies;
He put them to a perpetual reproach.

⁶⁷ Moreover He rejected the tent of
Joseph,
And did not choose the tribe of
Ephraim,
⁶⁸ But chose the tribe of Judah,
Mount Zion which He loved.
⁶⁹ And He built His sanctuary like the
heights,
Like the earth which He has
established forever.
⁷⁰ He also chose David His servant,
And took him from the sheepfolds;
⁷¹ From following the ewes that had
young He brought him,
To shepherd Jacob His people,
And Israel His inheritance.
⁷² So he shepherded them according to
the integrity of his heart,
And guided them by the skillfulness of
his hands.

PSALM 79

**A Dirge and a Prayer for Israel, Destroyed by
Enemies**

A Psalm of Asaph.

O GOD, the nations have come into
Your inheritance;
Your holy temple they have defiled;
They have laid Jerusalem in heaps.
² The dead bodies of Your servants
They have given *as* food
for the birds of the heavens,
The flesh of Your saints
to the beasts of the earth.
³ Their blood they have shed like water
all around Jerusalem,
And *there was* no one to bury *them.*
⁴ We have become a reproach to our
neighbors,
A scorn and derision to those who are
around us.

⁵ How long, LORD?
Will You be angry forever?
Will Your jealousy burn like fire?
⁶ Pour out Your wrath on the nations
that do not know You,
And on the kingdoms that do not call
on Your name.
⁷ For they have devoured Jacob,
And laid waste his dwelling place.

⁸ Oh, do not remember former iniquities
against us!
Let Your tender mercies come speedily
to meet us,
For we have been brought very low.
⁹ Help us, O God of our salvation,
For the glory of Your name;
And deliver us,
and provide atonement for our sins,
For Your name's sake!
¹⁰ Why should the nations say,
"Where *is* their God?"
Let there be known among the nations
in our sight
The avenging of the blood of Your
servants *which has been* shed.

¹¹ Let the groaning of the prisoner come
before You;
According to the greatness of Your
power
Preserve those who are appointed to
die;
¹² And return to our neighbors sevenfold
into their bosom
Their reproach with which they have
reproached You, O Lord.

¹³ So we, Your people and sheep of Your
pasture,
Will give You thanks forever;
We will show forth Your praise to all
generations.

PSALM 80

Prayer for Israel's Restoration

To the Chief Musician. Set to "The Lilies."[40]
A Testimony[41] of Asaph. A Psalm.

G IVE ear, O Shepherd of Israel,
You who lead Joseph like a flock;
You who dwell *between* the cherubim,
shine forth!
² Before Ephraim, Benjamin, and
Manasseh,
Stir up Your strength,
And come *and* save us!

³ Restore us, O God;
Cause Your face to shine,
And we shall be saved!

40 Hebrew *El Shoshannim*   41 Hebrew *Eduth*

4 O LORD God of hosts,
How long will You be angry
Against the prayer of Your people?
5 You have fed them with the bread of
tears,
And given them tears to drink in great
measure.
6 You have made us a strife to our
neighbors,
And our enemies laugh among
themselves.

7 Restore us, O God of hosts;
Cause Your face to shine,
And we shall be saved!

8 You have brought a vine out of Egypt;
You have cast out the nations,
and planted it.
9 You prepared *room* for it,
And caused it to take deep root,
And it filled the land.
10 The hills were covered with its shadow,
And the mighty cedars with its boughs.
11 She sent out her boughs to the Sea,[42]
And her branches to the River.[43]

12 Why have You broken down her
hedges,
So that all who pass by the way pluck
her *fruit?*
13 The boar out of the woods uproots it,
And the wild beast of the field
devours it.

14 Return, we beseech You,
O God of hosts;
Look down from heaven and see,
And visit this vine
15 And the vineyard which Your right
hand has planted,
And the branch *that* You made strong
for Yourself.
16 *It is* burned with fire, *it is* cut down;
They perish at the rebuke of Your
countenance.
17 Let Your hand be upon the man of
Your right hand,
Upon the son of man *whom* You made
strong for Yourself.
18 Then we will not turn back from You;
Revive us, and we will call upon Your
name.

19 Restore us, O LORD God of hosts;
Cause Your face to shine,
And we shall be saved!

PSALM 81

An Appeal for Israel's Repentance

To the Chief Musician. On an instrument of
Gath.[44] A Psalm of Asaph.

SING aloud to God our strength;
Make a joyful shout to the God of
Jacob.
2 Raise a song and strike the timbrel,
The pleasant harp with the lute.

3 Blow the trumpet at the time of the
New Moon,
At the full moon,
on our solemn feast day.
4 For this *is* a statute for Israel,
And a law of the God of Jacob.
5 This He established in Joseph *for* a
testimony,
When He went throughout the land of
Egypt,
Where I heard a language *that* I did
not understand.

6 "I removed his shoulder from the
burden;
His hands were freed from the baskets.
7 You called in trouble,
and I delivered you;
I answered you in the secret place of
thunder;
I proved you at the waters of Meribah.
Selah

8 "Hear, O My people,
and I will admonish you!
O Israel, if you will listen to Me!
9 There shall be no foreign god among
you;
Nor shall you worship any foreign god.
10 I *am* the LORD your God,
Who brought you out of the land of
Egypt;
Open your mouth wide,
and I will fill it.

11 "But My people would not heed My
voice,
And Israel would *have* none of Me.
12 So I gave them over to their own
stubborn heart,
To walk in their own counsels.

13 "Oh, that My people would listen to
Me,
That Israel would walk in My ways!
14 I would soon subdue their enemies,
And turn My hand against their
adversaries.

42 That is, the Mediterranean   43 That is, the Euphrates   44 Hebrew *Al Gittith*

15 The haters of the LORD would pretend
    submission to Him,
    But their fate would endure forever.
16 He would have fed them also
    with the finest of wheat;
    And with honey from the rock
    I would have satisfied you."

PSALM 82

A Plea for Justice

A Psalm of Asaph.

G OD stands in the congregation of the
    mighty;
He judges among the gods.⁴⁵
2 How long will you judge unjustly,
    And show partiality to the
    wicked?   Selah
3 Defend the poor and fatherless;
    Do justice to the afflicted and needy.
4 Deliver the poor and needy;
    Free *them* from the hand of the wicked.

5 They do not know,
    nor do they understand;
    They walk about in darkness;
    All the foundations of the earth are
    unstable.

6 I said, "You *are* gods,⁴⁶
    And all of you *are* children of the Most
    High.
7 But you shall die like men,
    And fall like one of the princes."

8 Arise, O God, judge the earth;
    For You shall inherit all nations.

PSALM 83

Prayer to Frustrate Conspiracy Against Israel

A Song. A Psalm of Asaph.

D O not keep silent, O God!
    Do not hold Your peace,
    And do not be still, O God!
2 For behold, Your enemies make a
    tumult;
    And those who hate You have lifted up
    their head.
3 They have taken crafty counsel against
    Your people,
    And consulted together against Your
    sheltered ones.
4 They have said, "Come, and let us cut
    them off from *being* a nation,
    That the name of Israel may be
    remembered no more."

5 For they have consulted together with
    one *consent;*
    They form a confederacy against You:

6 The tents of Edom and the Ishmaelites;
    Moab and the Hagarites;
7 Gebal, Ammon, and Amalek;
    Philistia with the inhabitants of Tyre;
8 Assyria also has joined with them;
    They have helped the children of Lot.
                                    Selah

9 Deal with them as *with* Midian,
    As *with* Sisera,
    As *with* Jabin at the Brook Kishon,
10 Who perished at Endor,
    Who became *as* refuse on the earth.
11 Make their nobles like Oreb and like
    Zeeb,
    Yes, all their princes like Zebah and
    Zalmunna,
12 Who said, "Let us take for ourselves
    The pastures of God for a possession."

13 O my God, make them like the
    whirling dust,
    Like the chaff before the wind!
14 As the fire burns the woods,
    And as the flame sets the mountains on
    fire,
15 So pursue them with Your tempest,
    And frighten them with Your storm.
16 Fill their faces with shame,
    That they may seek Your name,
    O LORD.
17 Let them be confounded
    and dismayed forever;
    Yes, let them be put to shame
    and perish,
18 That *men* may know that You,
    whose name alone *is* the LORD,
    Are the Most High over all the earth.

PSALM 84

**The Blessedness of Dwelling in the House of
God**

To the Chief Musician. On an instrument of
Gath.⁴⁷ A Psalm of the sons of Korah.

H OW lovely *is* Your tabernacle,
    O LORD of hosts!
2 My soul longs, yes, even faints
    For the courts of the LORD;
    My heart and my flesh cry out for the
    living God.

3 Even the sparrow has found a home,
    And the swallow a nest for herself,
    Where she may lay her young—
    Even Your altars, O LORD of hosts,
    My King and my God.
4 Blessed *are* those who dwell in Your
    house;
    They will still be praising You.   Selah

45 Hebrew *elohim, mighty ones;* that is, the judges   46 Hebrew *elohim, mighty ones;* that is, the judges
47 Hebrew *Al Gittith*

5 Blessed *is* the man whose strength *is* in
  You,
  Whose heart *is* set on pilgrimage.
6 *As they* pass through the Valley of
  Baca,
  They make it a spring;
  The rain also covers it with pools.
7 They go from strength to strength;
  Every one of them appears before God
  in Zion.

8 O LORD God of hosts, hear my prayer;
  Give ear, O God of Jacob!   Selah
9 O God, behold our shield,
  And look upon the face of Your
  anointed.

10 For a day in Your courts *is* better than
  a thousand.
  I would rather be a doorkeeper in the
  house of my God
  Than dwell in the tents of wickedness.
11 For the LORD God *is* a sun and shield;
  The LORD will give grace and glory;
  No good *thing* will He withhold
  From those who walk uprightly.

12 O LORD of hosts,
  Blessed *is* the man who trusts in You!

PSALM 85

Prayer that the LORD Will Restore Favor to the Land

To the Chief Musician. A Psalm of the sons of Korah.

LORD, You have been favorable to Your
  land;
  You have brought back the captivity of
  Jacob.
2 You have forgiven the iniquity of Your
  people;
  You have covered all their sin.   Selah
3 You have taken away all Your wrath;
  You have turned from the fierceness of
  Your anger.

4 Restore us, O God of our salvation,
  And cause Your anger toward us to
  cease.
5 Will You be angry with us forever?
  Will You prolong Your anger to all
  generations?
6 Will You not revive us again,
  That Your people may rejoice in You?
7 Show us Your mercy, O LORD,
  And grant us Your salvation.

8 I will hear what God the LORD will
  speak,
  For He will speak peace

To His people and to His saints;
  But let them not turn back to folly.
9 Surely His salvation *is* near to those
  who fear Him,
  That glory may dwell in our land.

10 Mercy and truth have met together;
  Righteousness and peace have kissed
  each other.
11 Truth shall spring out of the earth,
  And righteousness shall look down
  from heaven.
12 Yes, the LORD will give *what is* good;
  And our land will yield its increase.
13 Righteousness will go before Him,
  And shall make His footsteps *our*
  pathway.

PSALM 86

Prayer for Mercy, with Meditation on the Excellencies of the LORD

A Prayer of David.

BOW down Your ear, O LORD,
  hear me;
  For I *am* poor and needy.
2 Preserve my life, for I *am* holy;
  You are my God;
  Save Your servant who trusts in You!
3 Be merciful to me, O Lord,
  For I cry to You all day long.
4 Rejoice the soul of Your servant,
  For to You, O Lord, I lift up my soul.
5 For You, Lord, *are* good,
  and ready to forgive,
  And abundant in mercy to all those
  who call upon You.

6 Give ear, O LORD, to my prayer;
  And attend to the voice of my
  supplications.
7 In the day of my trouble I will call
  upon You,
  For You will answer me.

8 Among the gods *there is* none like You,
  O Lord;
  Nor *are there any works* like Your
  works.
9 All nations whom You have made
  Shall come and worship before You,
  O Lord,
  And shall glorify Your name.
10 For You *are* great,
  and do wondrous things;
  You alone *are* God.

11 Teach me Your way, O LORD;
  I will walk in Your truth;
  Unite my heart to fear Your name.

12 I will praise You, O Lord my God,
   with all my heart,
   And I will glorify Your name
      forevermore.
13 For great *is* Your mercy toward me,
   And You have delivered my soul from
      the depths of Sheol.

14 O God, the proud have risen against
      me,
   And a mob of violent *men* have sought
      my life,
   And have not set You before them.
15 But You, O Lord, *are* a God full of
      compassion, and gracious,
   Longsuffering and abundant in mercy
      and truth.

16 Oh, turn to me,
      and have mercy on me!
   Give Your strength to Your servant,
   And save the son of Your maidservant.
17 Show me a sign for good,
   That those who hate me may see *it*
      and be ashamed,
   Because You, Lord, have helped me
      and comforted me.

PSALM 87

The Glories of the City of God

A Psalm of the sons of Korah. A Song.

HIS foundation *is* in the holy
      mountains.
2 The LORD loves the gates of Zion
   More than all the dwellings of Jacob.
3 Glorious things are spoken of you,
   O city of God!   Selah

4 "I will make mention of Rahab and
      Babylon to those who know Me;
   Behold, O Philistia and Tyre,
      with Ethiopia:
   'This *one* was born there.'"

5 And of Zion it will be said,
   "This *one* and that *one* were born in
      her;
   And the Most High Himself shall
      establish her."
6 The LORD will record,
   When He registers the peoples:
   "This *one* was born there."   Selah

7 Both the singers and the players on
      instruments *say,*
   "All my springs *are* in you."

48 Hebrew *Maschil*

PSALM 88

A Prayer for Help in Despondency

A Song. A Psalm of the sons of Korah. To the
Chief Musician. Set to "Mahalath Leannoth." A
Contemplation[48] of Heman the Ezrahite.

O LORD, God of my salvation,
   I have cried out day and night
      before You.
2 Let my prayer come before You;
   Incline Your ear to my cry.

3 For my soul is full of troubles,
   And my life draws near to the grave.
4 I am counted with those who go down
      to the pit;
   I am like a man *who has* no strength,
5 Adrift among the dead,
   Like the slain who lie in the grave,
   Whom You remember no more,
   And who are cut off from Your hand.
6 You have laid me in the lowest pit,
   In darkness, in the depths.
7 Your wrath lies heavy upon me,
   And You have afflicted *me* with all
      Your waves.   Selah
8 You have put away my acquaintances
      far from me;
   You have made me an abomination to
      them;
   I am shut up, and I cannot get out;
9 My eye wastes away because of
      affliction.

   LORD, I have called daily upon You;
   I have stretched out my hands to You.
10 Will You work wonders for the dead?
   Shall the dead arise *and*
      praise You?   Selah
11 Shall Your lovingkindness be declared
      in the grave?
   Or Your faithfulness
      in the place of destruction?
12 Shall Your wonders be known
      in the dark?
   And Your righteousness
      in the land of forgetfulness?

13 But to You I have cried out, O LORD,
   And in the morning my prayer comes
      before You.
14 LORD, why do You cast off my soul?
   Why do You hide Your face from me?
15 I *have been* afflicted and ready to die
      from *my* youth *up;*
   I suffer Your terrors;
   I am distraught.
16 Your fierce wrath has gone over me;
   Your terrors have cut me off.

17 They came around me all day long like
water;
They engulfed me altogether.
18 Loved one and friend You have put far
from me,
And my acquaintances into darkness.

PSALM 89

Remembering the Covenant with David, and Sorrow for Lost Blessings

A Contemplation[49] of Ethan the Ezrahite.

I WILL sing of the mercies of the LORD
forever;
With my mouth will I make known
Your faithfulness to all generations.
2 For I have said,
"Mercy shall be built up forever;
Your faithfulness You shall establish in
the very heavens."

3 "I have made a covenant with My
chosen,
I have sworn to My servant David:
4 'Your seed I will establish forever,
And build up your throne to all
generations.' "   Selah

5 And the heavens will praise Your
wonders, O LORD;
Your faithfulness also in the
congregation of the saints.
6 For who in the heavens can be
compared to the LORD?
Who among the sons of the mighty can
be likened to the LORD?
7 God is greatly to be feared in the
assembly of the saints,
And to be held in reverence by all
those who are around Him.
8 O LORD God of hosts,
Who *is* mighty like You, O LORD?
Your faithfulness also surrounds You.
9 You rule the raging of the sea;
When its waves rise, You still them.
10 You have broken Rahab in pieces,
as one who is slain;
You have scattered Your enemies with
Your mighty arm.

11 The heavens *are* Yours,
the earth also *is* Yours;
The world and all its fullness,
You have founded them.
12 The north and the south,
You have created them;
Tabor and Hermon rejoice in Your
name.
13 You have a mighty arm;
Strong is Your hand,
and high is Your right hand.

14 Righteousness and justice *are* the
foundation of Your throne;
Mercy and truth go before Your face.
15 Blessed *are* the people who know the
joyful sound!
They walk, O LORD, in the light of
Your countenance.
16 In Your name they rejoice all day long,
And in Your righteousness they are
exalted.
17 For You *are* the glory of their strength,
And in Your favor our horn is exalted.
18 For our shield *belongs* to the LORD,
And our king to the Holy One of
Israel.

19 Then You spoke in a vision to Your
holy one,[50]
And said: "I have given help to *one
who is* mighty;
I have exalted one chosen from the
people.
20 I have found My servant David;
With My holy oil I have anointed him,
21 With whom My hand shall be
established;
Also My arm shall strengthen him.
22 The enemy shall not outwit him,
Nor the son of wickedness afflict him.
23 I will beat down his foes before his
face,
And plague those who hate him.

24 "But My faithfulness and My mercy
shall be with him,
And in My name his horn shall be
exalted.
25 Also I will set his hand over the sea,
And his right hand over the rivers.
26 He shall cry to Me,
'You *are* my Father,
My God, and the rock of my
salvation.'
27 Also I will make him *My* firstborn,
The highest of the kings of the earth.
28 My mercy I will keep for him forever,
And My covenant shall stand firm with
him.
29 His seed also I will make *to endure*
forever,
And his throne as the days of heaven.

30 "If his sons forsake My law
And do not walk in My judgments,
31 If they break My statutes
And do not keep My commandments,
32 Then I will visit their transgression
with the rod,
And their iniquity with stripes.

---

49 Hebrew *Maschil*
50 Masoretic Text, Septuagint, and Vulgate read *holy ones;* many Hebrew manuscripts read *holy one.*

33 Nevertheless My lovingkindness I will
   not utterly take from him,
   Nor allow My faithfulness to fail.
34 My covenant I will not break,
   Nor alter the word that has gone out
   of My lips.
35 Once I have sworn by My holiness;
   I will not lie to David:
36 His seed shall endure forever,
   And his throne as the sun before Me;
37 It shall be established forever like the
   moon,
   Even *like* the faithful witness in the
   sky."   Selah

38 But You have cast off and abhorred,
   You have been furious with Your
   anointed.
39 You have renounced the covenant of
   Your servant;
   You have profaned his crown *by
   casting it* to the ground.
40 You have broken down all his hedges;
   You have brought his strongholds to
   ruin.
41 All who pass by the way plunder him;
   He is a reproach to his neighbors.
42 You have exalted the right hand of his
   adversaries;
   You have made all his enemies rejoice.
43 You have also turned back the edge of
   his sword,
   And have not sustained him in the
   battle.
44 You have made his glory cease,
   And cast his throne down to the
   ground.
45 The days of his youth You have
   shortened;
   You have covered him with shame.
                                      Selah

46 How long, LORD?
   Will You hide Yourself forever?
   Will Your wrath burn like fire?
47 Remember how short my time is;
   For what futility have You created all
   the children of men?
48 What man can live and not see death?
   Can he deliver his life from the power
   of the grave?   Selah

49 Lord, where *are* Your former
   lovingkindnesses,
   Which You swore to David in Your
   truth?
50 Remember, Lord, the reproach of Your
   servants—
   How I bear in my bosom *the reproach
   of* all the many peoples,

51 With which Your enemies have
   reproached, O LORD,
   With which they have reproached the
   footsteps of Your anointed.

52 Blessed *be* the LORD forevermore!
   Amen and Amen.

BOOK FOUR
Psalms 90–106

PSALM 90

The Eternity of God, and Man's Frailty

A Prayer of Moses the man of God.

LORD, You have been our dwelling place
    in all generations.
2 Before the mountains were brought
   forth,
   Or ever You had formed the earth and
   the world,
   Even from everlasting to everlasting,
   You *are* God.

3 You turn man to destruction,
   And say, "Return, O children of men."
4 For a thousand years in Your sight
   Are like yesterday when it is past,
   And *like* a watch in the night.
5 You carry them away *like* a flood;
   They are like a sleep.
   In the morning they are like grass
   which grows up:
6 In the morning it flourishes
   and grows up;
   In the evening it is cut down
   and withers.

7 For we have been consumed by Your
   anger,
   And by Your wrath we are terrified.
8 You have set our iniquities before You,
   Our secret *sins* in the light of Your
   countenance.
9 For all our days have passed away in
   Your wrath;
   We finish our years like a sigh.
10 The days of our lives *are* seventy years;
   And if by reason of strength *they are*
   eighty years,
   Yet their boast *is* only labor and
   sorrow;
   For it is soon cut off, and we fly away.
11 Who knows the power of Your anger?
   For as the fear of You,
   so is Your wrath.
12 So teach *us* to number our days,
   That we may gain a heart of wisdom.

13 Return, O LORD!
How long?
And have compassion on Your
servants.
14 Oh, satisfy us early with Your mercy,
That we may rejoice and be glad all
our days!
15 Make us glad according to the days *in
which* You have afflicted us,
And the years *in which* we have seen
evil.
16 Let Your work appear to Your
servants,
And Your glory to their children.
17 And let the beauty of the LORD our
God be upon us,
And establish the work of our hands
for us;
Yes, establish the work of our hands.

PSALM 91

Safety of Abiding in the Presence of God

HE who dwells in the secret place of
the Most High
Shall abide under the shadow of the
Almighty.
2 I will say of the LORD, "*He is* my
refuge and my fortress;
My God, in Him I will trust."

3 Surely He shall deliver you from the
snare of the fowler
And from the perilous pestilence.
4 He shall cover you with His feathers,
And under His wings you shall take
refuge;
His truth *shall be your* shield and
buckler.
5 You shall not be afraid of the terror by
night,
Nor of the arrow *that* flies by day,
6 *Nor* of the pestilence *that* walks
in darkness,
Nor of the destruction *that* lays waste
at noonday.

7 A thousand may fall at your side,
And ten thousand at your right hand;
But it shall not come near you.
8 Only with your eyes shall you look,
And see the reward of the wicked.

9 Because you have made the LORD,
who is my refuge,
Even the Most High, your habitation,
10 No evil shall befall you,
Nor shall any plague come near your
dwelling;

11 For He shall give His angels charge
over you,
To keep you in all your ways.
12 They shall bear you up in *their* hands,
Lest you dash your foot against a
stone.
13 You shall tread upon
the lion and the cobra,
The young lion and the serpent
you shall trample under foot.

14 Because he has set his love upon Me,
therefore I will deliver him;
I will set him on high,
because he has known My name.
15 He shall call upon Me,
and I will answer him;
I *will be* with him in trouble;
I will deliver him and honor him.
16 With long life I will satisfy him,
And show him My salvation.

PSALM 92

Praise to the LORD for His Love and Faithfulness

A Psalm. A Song for the Sabbath day.

IT *is* good to give thanks to the LORD,
And to sing praises to Your name,
O Most High;
2 To declare Your lovingkindness in the
morning,
And Your faithfulness every night,
3 On an instrument of ten strings,
On the lute,
And on the harp,
With harmonious sound.
4 For You, LORD, have made me glad
through Your work;
I will triumph in the works of Your
hands.

5 O LORD, how great are Your works!
Your thoughts are very deep.
6 A senseless man does not know,
Nor does a fool understand this.
7 When the wicked spring up like grass,
And when all the workers of iniquity
flourish,
It is that they may be destroyed
forever.

8 But You, LORD, *are* on high
forevermore.
9 For behold, Your enemies, O LORD,
For behold, Your enemies shall perish;
All the workers of iniquity shall be
scattered.

10 But my horn You have exalted like a
wild ox;
I have been anointed with fresh oil.

11 My eye also has seen *my desire* on my
   enemies;
   My ears hear *my desire* on the wicked
   Who rise up against me.

12 The righteous shall flourish like a palm
   tree,
   He shall grow like a cedar in Lebanon.
13 Those who are planted in the house of
   the LORD
   Shall flourish in the courts of our God.
14 They shall still bear fruit in old age;
   They shall be fresh and flourishing,
15 To declare that the LORD is upright;
   He is my rock, and *there is* no
   unrighteousness in Him.

PSALM 93

The Eternal Reign of the LORD

THE LORD reigns,
   He is clothed with majesty;
The LORD is clothed,
He has girded Himself with strength.
Surely the world is established,
   so that it cannot be moved.
2 Your throne *is* established from of old;
You *are* from everlasting.

3 The floods have lifted up, O LORD,
The floods have lifted up their voice;
The floods lift up their waves.
4 The LORD on high *is* mightier
Than the noise of many waters,
Than the mighty waves of the sea.

5 Your testimonies are very sure;
Holiness adorns Your house,
O LORD, forever.

PSALM 94

God the Refuge of the Righteous

O LORD God, to whom vengeance
   belongs—
   O God, to whom vengeance belongs,
   shine forth!
2 Rise up, O Judge of the earth;
Render punishment to the proud.
3 LORD, how long will the wicked,
How long will the wicked triumph?

4 They utter speech,
and speak insolent things;
All the workers of iniquity boast in
   themselves.
5 They break in pieces Your people,
   O LORD,
And afflict Your heritage.

6 They slay the widow and the stranger,
And murder the fatherless.
7 Yet they say, "The LORD does not see,
Nor does the God of Jacob
   understand."

8 Understand, you senseless among the
   people;
And *you* fools, when will you be wise?
9 He who planted the ear,
   shall He not hear?
He who formed the eye,
   shall He not see?
10 He who instructs the nations,
   shall He not correct,
He who teaches man knowledge?
11 The LORD knows the thoughts of man,
That they *are* futile.

12 Blessed *is* the man whom You instruct,
   O LORD,
And teach out of Your law,
13 That You may give him rest from the
   days of adversity,
Until the pit is dug for the wicked.
14 For the LORD will not cast off His
   people,
Nor will He forsake His inheritance.
15 But judgment will return to
   righteousness,
And all the upright in heart
   will follow it.

16 Who will rise up for me against the
   evildoers?
Who will stand up for me against the
   workers of iniquity?
17 Unless the LORD *had been* my help,
My soul would soon have settled in
   silence.
18 If I say, "My foot slips,"
Your mercy, O LORD, will hold me up.
19 In the multitude of my anxieties within
   me,
Your comforts delight my soul.

20 Shall the throne of iniquity,
   which devises evil by law,
Have fellowship with You?
21 They gather together against the life of
   the righteous,
And condemn innocent blood.
22 But the LORD has been my defense,
And my God the rock of my refuge.
23 He has brought on them their own
   iniquity,
And shall cut them off in their own
   wickedness;
The LORD our God shall cut them off.

PSALM 95

A Call to Worship and Obedience

OH come, let us sing to the LORD!
    Let us shout joyfully to the Rock of
    our salvation.
2 Let us come before His presence with
    thanksgiving;
    Let us shout joyfully to Him with
    psalms.
3 For the LORD *is* the great God,
    And the great King above all gods.
4 In His hand *are* the deep places of the
    earth;
    The heights of the hills *are* His also.
5 The sea *is* His, for He made it;
    And His hands formed the dry *land.*

6 Oh come, let us worship
    and bow down;
    Let us kneel before the LORD our
    Maker.
7 For He *is* our God,
    And we *are* the people of His pasture,
    And the sheep of His hand.

    Today, if you will hear His voice:
8 "Do not harden your hearts,
    as in the rebellion,[51]
    And as *in* the day of trial[52] in the
    wilderness,
9 When your fathers tested Me;
    They proved Me,
    though they saw My work.
10 For forty years I was grieved with *that*
    generation,
    And said, 'It *is* a people who go astray
    in their hearts,
    And they do not know My ways.'
11 So I swore in My wrath,
    'They shall not enter My rest.' "

PSALM 96

A Song of Praise to God Coming in Judgment

OH, sing to the LORD a new song!
    Sing to the LORD, all the earth.
2 Sing to the LORD, bless His name;
    Proclaim the good news of His
    salvation from day to day.
3 Declare His glory among the nations,
    His wonders among all peoples.

4 For the LORD *is* great
    and greatly to be praised;
    He *is* to be feared above all gods.
5 For *all* the gods of the peoples *are*
    idols,
    But the LORD made the heavens.

51 Hebrew *Meribah*   52 Hebrew *Massah*

6 Honor and majesty *are* before Him;
    Strength and beauty *are* in His
    sanctuary.

7 Give to the LORD,
    O kindreds of the peoples,
    Give to the LORD glory and strength.
8 Give to the LORD the glory *due* His
    name;
    Bring an offering,
    and come into His courts.
9 Oh, worship the LORD in the beauty of
    holiness!
    Tremble before Him, all the earth.

10 Say among the nations,
    "The LORD reigns;
    The world also is firmly established,
    It shall not be moved;
    He shall judge the peoples righteously."

11 Let the heavens rejoice,
    and let the earth be glad;
    Let the sea roar, and all its fullness;
12 Let the field be joyful,
    and all that *is* in it.
    Then all the trees of the woods will
    rejoice before the LORD.
13 For He is coming,
    for He is coming to judge the earth.
    He shall judge the world with
    righteousness,
    And the peoples with His truth.

PSALM 97

A Song of Praise to the Sovereign LORD

THE LORD reigns;
    Let the earth rejoice;
    Let the multitude of isles be glad!

2 Clouds and darkness surround Him;
    Righteousness and justice *are* the
    foundation of His throne.
3 A fire goes before Him,
    And burns up His enemies round
    about.
4 His lightnings light the world;
    The earth sees and trembles.
5 The mountains melt like wax at the
    presence of the LORD,
    At the presence of the Lord of the
    whole earth.
6 The heavens declare His righteousness,
    And all the peoples see His glory.

7 Let all be put to shame who serve
    carved images,
    Who boast of idols.
    Worship Him, all *you* gods.

8 Zion hears and is glad,
And the daughters of Judah rejoice
Because of Your judgments, O LORD.
9 For You, LORD, *are* most high above
all the earth;
You are exalted far above all gods.

10 You who love the LORD, hate evil!
He preserves the souls of His saints;
He delivers them out of the hand of
the wicked.
11 Light is sown for the righteous,
And gladness for the upright in heart.
12 Rejoice in the LORD, you righteous,
And give thanks at the remembrance of
His holy name.[53]

PSALM 98

A Song of Praise to the LORD for His Salvation and Judgment

A Psalm.

OH, sing to the LORD a new song!
For He has done marvelous things;
His right hand and His holy arm have
gained Him the victory.
2 The LORD has made known His
salvation;
His righteousness He has openly shown
in the sight of the nations.
3 He has remembered His mercy and His
faithfulness to the house of Israel;
All the ends of the earth have seen the
salvation of our God.

4 Shout joyfully to the LORD,
all the earth;
Break forth in song, rejoice,
and sing praises.
5 Sing to the LORD with the harp,
With the harp and the sound of a
psalm,
6 With trumpets and the sound of a
horn;
Shout joyfully before the LORD,
the King.

7 Let the sea roar, and all its fullness,
The world and those who dwell in it;
8 Let the rivers clap *their* hands;
Let the hills be joyful together
before the LORD,
9 For He is coming to judge the earth.
With righteousness He shall judge
the world,
And the peoples with equity.

PSALM 99

Praise to the LORD for His Holiness

THE LORD reigns;
Let the peoples tremble!

He dwells *between* the cherubim;
Let the earth be moved!
2 The LORD *is* great in Zion,
And He *is* high above all the peoples.
3 Let them praise Your great and
awesome name—
He *is* holy.

4 The King's strength also loves justice;
You have established equity;
You have executed justice and
righteousness in Jacob.
5 Exalt the LORD our God,
And worship at His footstool;
For He *is* holy.

6 Moses and Aaron were among His
priests,
And Samuel was among those who
called upon His name;
They called upon the LORD,
and He answered them.
7 He spoke to them in the cloudy pillar;
They kept His testimonies and the
ordinance *that* He gave them.

8 You answered them, O LORD our God;
You were to them God-Who-Forgives,
Though You took vengeance on their
deeds.
9 Exalt the LORD our God,
And worship at His holy hill;
For the LORD our God *is* holy.

PSALM 100

A Song of Praise for the LORD'S Faithfulness to His People

A Psalm of Thanksgiving.

MAKE a joyful shout to the LORD,
all you lands!
2 Serve the LORD with gladness;
Come before His presence with singing.
3 Know that the LORD, He *is* God;
It is He *who* has made us,
and not we ourselves;
We are His people
and the sheep of His pasture.

4 Enter into His gates with thanksgiving,
And into His courts with praise.
Be thankful to Him,
and bless His name.
5 For the LORD *is* good;
His mercy *is* everlasting,
And His truth *endures* to all
generations.

53 Or *His holiness*

God's Shepherds in the Wilderness

A shepherd's life in Palestine is much the same today as it was in biblical times; it is a constant vigil tending to his flock. He can be seen roaming the inhospitable countryside locating food and water for his sheep while guarding against wild animals and thieves.

His workplace is the Judean wilderness. In the Old Testament this area is called "Jeshimon," a Hebrew name meaning devastation. The wilderness of Judea, east of the Mount of Olives does not offer the pleasant green pastures often associated with shepherding. There are no fertile plains such as those located on the coast of Palestine. The chocolate brown soil, red poppies, and fragrant orange blossoms of Galilee are missing here. Instead, the wilderness is known for its scorching heat, chalky yellow sand, and deep limestone gorges. The prevailing life of the shepherd is silent, lonely, and exhausting.

In biblical days, the wilderness was the only place available for the shepherd and his flocks. The great nations of the Philistines and Phoenicians possessed the coastal plains. Galilee was overrun by other mighty kingdoms. Israel was never able to completely drive out these nations and was left with the difficult task of developing a country on the border of a vast wilderness.

From this countryside emerge many biblical images of the shepherd. His life, customs, and habits are used throughout the Bible to illustrate and communicate God's truths. Many of God's great leaders lived the hard life of leading the sheep, before being called to shepherd the people of Israel. The patriarchs Abraham, Isaac, Jacob, Joseph, Moses, and David were all shepherds. At the forefront of Israel's history was the common shepherd.

The psalmist David drew often from his shepherding experiences. In Psalms 23:1 and 100:3 God is referred to as "the shepherd" who cared for "His people and the sheep of His pasture."

In this harsh wilderness the shepherd cares for his flock even to the point of laying down his life for his sheep. In this wasteland Jesus Christ Himself declared, "I am the good shepherd. The good shepherd gives His life for the sheep" (John 10:11).

PSALM 101

Promised Faithfulness to the LORD

A Psalm of David.

I WILL sing of mercy and justice;
To You, O LORD, I will sing praises.

2 I will behave wisely in a perfect way.
Oh, when will You come to me?
I will walk within my house with a
perfect heart.

3 I will set nothing wicked before my
eyes;
I hate the work of those who fall away;
It shall not cling to me.

4 A perverse heart shall depart from me;
I will not know wickedness.

5 Whoever secretly slanders his neighbor,
Him I will destroy;
The one who has a haughty look and a
proud heart,
Him I will not endure.

6 My eyes *shall be* on the faithful of the
land,
That they may dwell with me;
He who walks in a perfect way,
He shall serve me.

7 He who works deceit shall not dwell
within my house;
He who tells lies shall not continue in
my presence.

8 Early I will destroy all the wicked of
the land,
That I may cut off all the evildoers
from the city of the LORD.

PSALM 102

The LORD'S Eternal Love

A Prayer of the afflicted, when he is overwhelmed
and pours out his complaint before the LORD.

HEAR my prayer, O LORD,
And let my cry come to You.

2 Do not hide Your face from me in the
day of my trouble;
Incline Your ear to me;
In the day that I call,
answer me speedily.

3 For my days are consumed like smoke,
And my bones are burned like a
hearth.

4 My heart is stricken and withered like
grass,
So that I forget to eat my bread.

5 Because of the sound of my groaning
My bones cling to my skin.

6 I am like a pelican of the wilderness;
I am like an owl of the desert.

7 I lie awake,
And am like a sparrow alone on the
housetop.

8 My enemies reproach me all day long,
And those who deride me swear an
oath against me.

9 For I have eaten ashes like bread,
And mingled my drink with weeping,

10 Because of Your indignation and Your
wrath;
For You have lifted me up
and cast me away.

11 My days *are* like a shadow that
lengthens,
And I wither away like grass.

12 But You, O LORD, shall endure forever,
And the remembrance of Your name to
all generations.

13 You will arise *and* have mercy on Zion;
For the time to favor her,
Yes, the set time, has come.

14 For Your servants take pleasure in her
stones,
And show favor to her dust.

15 So the nations shall fear
the name of the LORD,
And all the kings of the earth
Your glory.

16 For the LORD shall build up Zion;
He shall appear in His glory.

17 He shall regard the prayer of the
destitute,
And shall not despise their prayer.

18 This will be written for the generation
to come,
That a people yet to be created may
praise the LORD.

19 For He looked down from the height
of His sanctuary;
From heaven the LORD viewed the
earth,

20 To hear the groaning of the prisoner,
To loose those appointed to death,

21 To declare the name of the LORD in
Zion,
And His praise in Jerusalem,

22 When the peoples are gathered
together,
And the kingdoms, to serve the LORD.

23 He weakened my strength in the way;
He shortened my days.

24 I said, "O my God,
Do not take me away in the midst of
my days;
Your years *are* throughout all
generations.

25 Of old You laid the foundation of the
   earth,
   And the heavens *are* the work of Your
   hands.
26 They will perish, but You will endure;
   Yes, all of them will grow old like a
   garment;
   Like a cloak You will change them,
   And they will be changed.
27 But You *are* the same,
   And Your years will have no end.
28 The children of Your servants will
   continue,
   And their descendants will be
   established before You."

PSALM 103

Praise for the LORD's Mercies

A Psalm of David.

BLESS the LORD, O my soul;
   And all that is within me,
      bless His holy name!
2 Bless the LORD, O my soul,
   And forget not all His benefits:
3 Who forgives all your iniquities,
   Who heals all your diseases,
4 Who redeems your life from
   destruction,
   Who crowns you with lovingkindness
   and tender mercies,
5 Who satisfies your mouth with good
   things,
   So that your youth is renewed like the
   eagle's.

6 The LORD executes righteousness
   And justice for all who are oppressed.
7 He made known His ways to Moses,
   His acts to the children of Israel.
8 The LORD *is* merciful and gracious,
   Slow to anger,
   and abounding in mercy.
9 He will not always strive *with us,*
   Nor will He keep *His anger* forever.
10 He has not dealt with us according to
   our sins,
   Nor punished us according to our
   iniquities.

11 For as the heavens are high above the
   earth,
   So great is His mercy toward those
   who fear Him;
12 As far as the east is from the west,
   So far has He removed our
   transgressions from us.
13 As a father pities *his* children,
   So the LORD pities those who fear
   Him.

14 For He knows our frame;
   He remembers that we *are* dust.

15 *As for* man, his days *are* like grass;
   As a flower of the field,
      so he flourishes.
16 For the wind passes over it,
      and it is gone,
   And its place remembers it no more.[54]
17 But the mercy of the LORD *is* from
      everlasting to everlasting
   On those who fear Him,
   And His righteousness to children's
      children,
18 To such as keep His covenant,
   And to those who remember His
      commandments to do them.

19 The LORD has established His throne
      in heaven,
   And His kingdom rules over all.

20 Bless the LORD, you His angels,
   Who excel in strength,
      who do His word,
   Heeding the voice of His word.
21 Bless the LORD, all *you* His hosts,
   You ministers of His,
      who do His pleasure.
22 Bless the LORD, all His works,
   In all places of His dominion.

   Bless the LORD, O my soul!

PSALM 104

Praise to the Sovereign LORD for His Creation and Providence

BLESS the LORD, O my soul!

   O LORD my God, You are very great:
   You are clothed with honor and
      majesty,
2 Who cover *Yourself* with light as *with* a
      garment,
   Who stretch out the heavens like a
      curtain.

3 He lays the beams of His upper
      chambers in the waters,
   Who makes the clouds His chariot,
   Who walks on the wings of the wind,
4 Who makes His angels spirits,
   His ministers a flame of fire.

5 *You who* laid the foundations of the
      earth,
   So *that* it should not be moved forever,
6 You covered it with the deep as *with* a
      garment;
   The waters stood above the mountains.

54 Compare Job 7:10

7 At Your rebuke they fled;
   At the voice of Your thunder they
      hastened away.
8 They went up over the mountains;
   They went down into the valleys,
   To the place which You founded for
      them.
9 You have set a boundary that they
      may not pass over,
   That they may not return to cover the
      earth.

10 He sends the springs into the valleys,
   Which flow among the hills.
11 They give drink to every beast of the
      field;
   The wild donkeys quench their thirst.
12 By them the birds of the heavens have
      their habitation;
   They sing among the branches.
13 He waters the hills from His upper
      chambers;
   The earth is satisfied with the fruit of
      Your works.

14 He causes the grass to grow for the
      cattle,
   And vegetation for the service of man,
   That he may bring forth food from the
      earth,
15 And wine that makes glad the heart of
      man,
   Oil to make his face shine,
   And bread which strengthens man's
      heart.
16 The trees of the LORD are full of sap,
   The cedars of Lebanon which He
      planted,
17 Where the birds make their nests;
   The stork has her home in the fir trees.
18 The high hills are for the wild goats;
   The cliffs are a refuge for the rock
      badgers.[55]

19 He appointed the moon for seasons;
   The sun knows its going down.
20 You make darkness, and it is night,
   In which all the beasts of the forest
      creep about.
21 The young lions roar after their prey,
   And seek their food from God.
22 When the sun arises, they gather
      together
   And lie down in their dens.
23 Man goes out to his work
   And to his labor until the evening.

24 O LORD, how manifold are Your
      works!
   In wisdom You have made them all.
   The earth is full of Your possessions—

25 This great and wide sea,
   In which are innumerable teeming
      things,
   Living things both small and great.
26 There the ships sail about;
   And there is that Leviathan
   Which You have made to play there.

27 These all wait for You,
   That You may give them their food in
      due season.
28 What You give them they gather in;
   You open Your hand,
      they are filled with good.
29 You hide Your face, they are troubled;
   You take away their breath,
      they die and return to their dust.
30 You send forth Your Spirit,
      they are created;
   And You renew the face of the earth.

31 May the glory of the LORD endure
      forever;
   May the LORD rejoice in His works.
32 He looks on the earth, and it trembles;
   He touches the hills, and they smoke.

33 I will sing to the LORD as long as I
      live;
   I will sing praise to my God while I
      have my being.
34 May my meditation be sweet to Him;
   I will be glad in the LORD.
35 May sinners be consumed from the
      earth,
   And the wicked be no more.

   Bless the LORD, O my soul!
   Praise the LORD!

PSALM 105

The Eternal Faithfulness of the LORD

OH, give thanks to the LORD!
   Call upon His name;
   Make known His deeds among the
      peoples.
2 Sing to Him, sing psalms to Him;
   Talk of all His wondrous works.
3 Glory in His holy name;
   Let the hearts of those rejoice who seek
      the LORD.
4 Seek the LORD and His strength;
   Seek His face evermore.
5 Remember His marvelous works which
      He has done,
   His wonders, and the judgments of His
      mouth,
6 O seed of Abraham His servant,
   You children of Jacob,
      His chosen ones!

55 Or rock hyrax (compare Leviticus 11:5)

7 He *is* the LORD our God;
His judgments *are* in all the earth.
8 He has remembered His covenant
forever,
The word *which* He commanded,
for a thousand generations,
9 *The covenant* which He made with
Abraham,
And His oath to Isaac,
10 And confirmed it to Jacob for a
statute,
To Israel *for* an everlasting covenant,
11 Saying, "To you I will give the land of
Canaan
As the allotment of your inheritance,"
12 When they were *but* few in number,
Indeed very few, and strangers in it.

13 When they went from one nation to
another,
From *one* kingdom to another people,
14 He permitted no one to do them
wrong;
Yes, He reproved kings for their sakes,
15 *Saying*, "Do not touch My anointed
ones,
And do My prophets no harm."

16 Moreover He called for a famine in the
land;
He destroyed all the provision of
bread.
17 He sent a man before them—
Joseph—*who* was sold as a slave.
18 They hurt his feet with fetters,
He was laid in irons.
19 Until the time that his word came to
pass,
The word of the LORD tested him.
20 The king sent and released him,
The ruler of the people let him go free.
21 He made him lord of his house,
And ruler of all his possessions,
22 To bind his princes at his pleasure,
And teach his elders wisdom.

23 Israel also came into Egypt,
And Jacob sojourned in the land of
Ham.
24 And He increased His people greatly,
And made them stronger than their
enemies.
25 He turned their heart to hate His
people,
To deal craftily with His servants.

26 He sent Moses His servant,
And Aaron whom He had chosen.
27 They performed His signs among them,
And wonders in the land of Ham.
28 He sent darkness, and made *it* dark;

And they did not rebel against His
word.
29 He turned their waters into blood,
And killed their fish.
30 Their land abounded with frogs,
Even in the chambers of their kings.
31 He spoke, and there came swarms of
flies,
And lice in all their territory.
32 He gave them hail for rain,
And flaming fire in their land.
33 He struck their vines also,
and their fig trees,
And splintered the trees of their
territory.
34 He spoke, and locusts came,
Young locusts without number,
35 And ate up all the vegetation in their
land,
And devoured the fruit of their ground.
36 He also destroyed all the firstborn in
their land,
The first of all their strength.

37 He also brought them out with silver
and gold,
And *there was* none feeble among His
tribes.
38 Egypt was glad when they departed,
For the fear of them had fallen upon
them.
39 He spread a cloud for a covering,
And fire to give light in the night.
40 *The people* asked, and He brought
quail,
And satisfied them with the bread of
heaven.
41 He opened the rock,
and water gushed out;
It ran in the dry places *like* a river.

42 For He remembered His holy promise,
And Abraham His servant.
43 He brought out His people with joy,
His chosen ones with gladness.
44 He gave them the lands of the
Gentiles,
And they inherited the labor of the
nations,
45 That they might observe His statutes
And keep His laws.

Praise the LORD!

PSALM 106

Joy in Forgiveness of Israel's Sins

PRAISE the LORD!

Oh, give thanks to the LORD,
for *He is* good!
For His mercy *endures* forever.

2 Who can utter the mighty acts of the
    LORD?
    Or can declare all His praise?
3 Blessed *are* those who keep justice,
    And he who does righteousness at all
    times!

4 Remember me, O LORD, with the favor
    You have toward Your people;
    Oh, visit me with Your salvation,
5 That I may see the benefit of Your
    chosen ones,
    That I may rejoice in the gladness of
    Your nation,
    That I may glory with Your
    inheritance.

6 We have sinned with our fathers,
    We have committed iniquity,
    We have done wickedly.
7 Our fathers in Egypt did not
    understand Your wonders;
    They did not remember the multitude
    of Your mercies,
    But rebelled by the sea—the Red Sea.

8 Nevertheless He saved them for His
    name's sake,
    That He might make His mighty power
    known.
9 He rebuked the Red Sea also,
    and it dried up;
    So He led them through the depths,
    As through the wilderness.
10 He saved them from the hand of him
    who hated *them,*
    And redeemed them from the hand of
    the enemy.
11 The waters covered their enemies;
    There was not one of them left.
12 Then they believed His words;
    They sang His praise.

13 They soon forgot His works;
    They did not wait for His counsel,
14 But lusted exceedingly in the
    wilderness,
    And tested God in the desert.
15 And He gave them their request,
    But sent leanness into their soul.

16 When they envied Moses in the camp,
    And Aaron the saint of the LORD,
17 The earth opened up and swallowed
    Dathan,
    And covered the faction of Abiram.
18 A fire was kindled in their company;
    The flame burned up the wicked.

19 They made a calf in Horeb,
    And worshiped the molded image.
20 Thus they changed their glory
    Into the image of an ox that eats grass.
21 They forgot God their Savior,
    Who had done great things in Egypt,
22 Wondrous works in the land of Ham,
    Awesome things by the Red Sea.
23 Therefore He said that He would
    destroy them,
    Had not Moses His chosen one stood
    before Him in the breach,
    To turn away His wrath,
    lest He destroy *them.*

24 Then they despised the pleasant land;
    They did not believe His word,
25 But murmured in their tents,
    And did not heed the voice of the
    LORD.
26 Therefore He lifted up His hand *in an
    oath* against them,
    To overthrow them in the wilderness,
27 To overthrow their descendants among
    the nations,
    And to scatter them in the lands.

28 They joined themselves also to Baal of
    Peor,
    And ate sacrifices made to the dead.
29 Thus they provoked *Him* to anger with
    their deeds,
    And the plague broke out among them.
30 Then Phinehas stood up and
    intervened,
    And *so* the plague was stopped.
31 And that was accounted to him for
    righteousness
    To all generations forevermore.

32 They angered *Him* also at the waters
    of strife,[56]
    So that it went ill with Moses on
    account of them;
33 Because they rebelled against His
    Spirit,
    So that he spoke rashly with his lips.

34 They did not destroy the peoples,
    Concerning whom the LORD had
    commanded them,
35 But they mingled with the Gentiles
    And learned their works;
36 They served their idols,
    Which became a snare to them.
37 They even sacrificed their sons
    And their daughters to demons,
38 And shed innocent blood,
    Even the blood of their sons and
    daughters,

56 Hebrew *Meribah*

Whom they sacrificed to the idols of
  Canaan;
And the land was polluted with blood.
39 Thus they were defiled by their own
  works,
And played the harlot by their own
  deeds.

40 Therefore the wrath of the LORD was
  kindled against His people,
So that He abhorred His own
  inheritance.
41 And He gave them into the hand of the
  Gentiles,
And those who hated them ruled over
  them.
42 Their enemies also oppressed them,
And they were brought into subjection
  under their hand.
43 Many times He delivered them;
But they rebelled *against Him* by their
  counsel,
And were brought low for their
  iniquity.

44 Nevertheless He regarded their
  affliction,
When He heard their cry;
45 And for their sake He remembered His
  covenant,
And relented according to the
  multitude of His mercies.
46 He also made them to be pitied
By all those who carried them away
  captive.

47 Save us, O LORD our God,
And gather us from among the
  Gentiles,
To give thanks to Your holy name,
And to triumph in Your praise.

48 Blessed *be* the LORD God of Israel
From everlasting to everlasting!
And let all the people say, "Amen!"

Praise the LORD!

BOOK FIVE
Psalms 107–150

PSALM 107

Thanksgiving to the LORD for His Great Works of Deliverance

O H, give thanks to the LORD,
  for *He is* good!
For His mercy *endures* forever.

2 Let the redeemed of the LORD say *so,*
Whom He has redeemed from the hand
  of the enemy,
3 And gathered out of the lands,
From the east and from the west,
From the north and from the south.

4 They wandered in the wilderness in a
  desolate way;
They found no city to dwell in.
5 Hungry and thirsty,
Their soul fainted in them.
6 Then they cried out to the LORD in
  their trouble,
And He delivered them out of their
  distresses.
7 And He led them forth by the right
  way,
That they might go to a city for
  habitation.
8 Oh, that *men* would give thanks to the
  LORD *for* His goodness,
And *for* His wonderful works to the
  children of men!
9 For He satisfies the longing soul,
And fills the hungry soul with
  goodness.

10 Those who sat in darkness
  and in the shadow of death,
Bound in affliction and irons—
11 Because they rebelled against the words
  of God,
And despised the counsel of the Most
  High,
12 Therefore He brought down their heart
  with labor;
They fell down,
  and *there was* none to help.
13 Then they cried out to the LORD in
  their trouble,
And He saved them out of their
  distresses.
14 He brought them out of darkness and
  the shadow of death,
And broke their chains in pieces.
15 Oh, that *men* would give thanks to the
  LORD *for* His goodness,
And *for* His wonderful works to the
  children of men!
16 For He has broken the gates of bronze,
And cut the bars of iron in two.

17 Fools, because of their transgression,
And because of their iniquities,
  were afflicted.
18 Their soul abhorred all manner of
  food,
And they drew near to the gates of
  death.

19 Then they cried out to the LORD in
   their trouble,
   And He saved them out of their
   distresses.
20 He sent His word and healed them,
   And delivered *them* from their
   destructions.
21 Oh, that *men* would give thanks to the
   LORD *for* His goodness,
   And *for* His wonderful works to the
   children of men!
22 Let them sacrifice the sacrifices of
   thanksgiving,
   And declare His works with rejoicing.

23 Those who go down to the sea in ships,
   Who do business on great waters,
24 They see the works of the LORD,
   And His wonders in the deep.
25 For He commands and raises the
   stormy wind,
   Which lifts up the waves of the sea.
26 They mount up to the heavens,
   They go down again to the depths;
   Their soul melts because of trouble.
27 They reel to and fro,
   and stagger like a drunken man,
   And are at their wits' end.
28 Then they cry out to the LORD in their
   trouble,
   And He brings them out of their
   distresses.
29 He calms the storm,
   So that its waves are still.
30 Then they are glad because they are
   quiet;
   So He guides them to their desired
   haven.
31 Oh, that *men* would give thanks to the
   LORD *for* His goodness,
   And *for* His wonderful works to the
   children of men!
32 Let them exalt Him also in the
   congregation of the people,
   And praise Him in the assembly of the
   elders.

33 He turns rivers into a wilderness,
   And the watersprings into dry ground;
34 A fruitful land into barrenness,
   For the wickedness of those who dwell
   in it.
35 He turns a wilderness into pools of
   water,
   And dry land into watersprings.
36 There He makes the hungry dwell,
   That they may establish a city for
   habitation,
37 And sow fields and plant vineyards,
   That they may yield a fruitful harvest.

38 He also blesses them,
   and they multiply greatly;
   And He does not let their cattle
   decrease.

39 When they are diminished
   and brought low
   Through oppression, affliction and
   sorrow,
40 He pours contempt on princes,
   And causes them to wander in the
   wilderness *where there is* no way;
41 Yet He sets the poor on high,
   far from affliction,
   And makes *their* families like a flock.
42 The righteous see *it* and rejoice,
   And all iniquity stops its mouth.

43 Whoever *is* wise will observe these
   things,
   And they will understand the
   lovingkindness of the LORD.

PSALM 108

Assurance of God's Victory over Enemies

A Song. A Psalm of David.

O GOD, my heart is steadfast;
   I will sing and give praise,
      even with my glory.
2 Awake, lute and harp!
   I will awaken the dawn.
3 I will praise You, O LORD, among the
      peoples,
   And I will sing praises to You among
      the nations.
4 For Your mercy *is* great above the
      heavens,
   And Your truth *reaches* to the clouds.

5 Be exalted, O God, above the heavens,
   And Your glory above all the earth;
6 That Your beloved may be delivered,
   Save *with* Your right hand,
      and hear me.

7 God has spoken in His holiness:
   "I will rejoice;
   I will divide Shechem
   And measure out the Valley of
      Succoth.
8 Gilead *is* Mine;
   Manasseh *is* Mine;
   Ephraim also *is* the helmet for My
      head;
   Judah *is* My lawgiver.
9 Moab *is* My washpot;
   Over Edom I will cast My shoe;
   Over Philistia I will triumph."

10 Who will bring me into the strong city?
   Who will lead me to Edom?

11 *Is it* not You, O God, *who* cast us off?
   And You, O God, *who* did not go out
       with our armies?
12 Give us help from trouble,
   For vain *is* the help of man.
13 Through God we will do valiantly,
   For *it is* He *who* shall tread down our
       enemies.[57]

PSALM 109

Plea for Judgment of False Accusers

To the Chief Musician. A Psalm of David.

D O not keep silent,
   O God of my praise!
2 For the mouth of the wicked and the
       mouth of the deceitful
   Have opened against me;
   They have spoken against me with a
       lying tongue.
3 They have also surrounded me with
       words of hatred,
   And fought against me without a
       cause.
4 In return for my love they are my
       accusers,
   But I *give myself to* prayer.
5 Thus they have rewarded me evil for
       good,
   And hatred for my love.

6 Set a wicked man over him,
   And let an accuser[58] stand at his right
       hand.
7 When he is judged,
       let him be found guilty,
   And let his prayer become sin.
8 Let his days be few,
   And let another take his office.
9 Let his children be fatherless,
   And his wife a widow.
10 Let his children continually be
       vagabonds, and beg;
   Let them seek *their bread* also from
       their desolate places.
11 Let the creditor seize all that he has,
   And let strangers plunder his labor.
12 Let there be none to extend mercy to
       him,
   Nor let there be any to favor his
       fatherless children.
13 Let his posterity be cut off,
   And in the generation following let
       their name be blotted out.

14 Let the iniquity of his fathers be
       remembered before the LORD,
   And let not the sin of his mother be
       blotted out.

15 Let them be continually before the
       LORD,
   That He may cut off the memory of
       them from the earth;
16 Because he did not remember to show
       mercy,
   But persecuted the poor and needy
       man,
   That he might even slay the broken in
       heart.
17 As he loved cursing,
       so let it come to him;
   As he did not delight in blessing,
       so let it be far from him.
18 As he clothed himself with cursing as
       with his garment,
   So let it enter his body like water,
   And like oil into his bones.
19 Let it be to him like the garment which
       covers him,
   And for a belt with which he girds
       himself continually.
20 *Let* this *be* the LORD's reward to my
       accusers,
   And to those who speak evil against
       my person.

21 But You, O GOD the Lord,
   Deal with me for Your name's sake;
   Because Your mercy *is* good,
       deliver me.
22 For I *am* poor and needy,
   And my heart is wounded within me.
23 I am gone like a shadow when it
       lengthens;
   I am shaken off like a locust.
24 My knees are weak through fasting,
   And my flesh is feeble from lack of
       fatness.
25 I also have become a reproach to
       them;
   When they look at me,
       they shake their heads.

26 Help me, O LORD my God!
   Oh, save me according to Your mercy,
27 That they may know that this *is* Your
       hand—
   That You, LORD, have done it!
28 Let them curse, but You bless;
   When they arise, let them be ashamed,
   But let Your servant rejoice.
29 Let my accusers be clothed with
       shame,
   And let them cover themselves with
       their own disgrace as with a mantle.
30 I will greatly praise the LORD with my
       mouth;
   Yes, I will praise Him among the
       multitude.

57 Verses 6–13 (compare Psalm 60:5–12) 58 Hebrew *Satan*

31 For He shall stand at the right hand of
the poor,
To save *him* from those who condemn
him.

PSALM 110

Announcement of the Messiah's Reign

A Psalm of David.

THE LORD said to my Lord,
"Sit at My right hand,
Till I make Your enemies Your
footstool."
2 The LORD shall send the rod of Your
strength out of Zion.
Rule in the midst of Your enemies!

3 Your people *shall be* volunteers
In the day of Your power;
In the beauties of holiness,
from the womb of the morning,
You have the dew of Your youth.
4 The LORD has sworn
And will not relent,
"You *are* a priest forever
According to the order of
Melchizedek."

5 The Lord *is* at Your right hand;
He shall execute kings in the day of
His wrath.
6 He shall judge among the nations,
He shall fill *the places* with dead
bodies,
He shall execute the heads of many
countries.
7 He shall drink of the brook by the
wayside;
Therefore He shall lift up the head.

PSALM 111

Praise to God for His Faithfulness and Justice

PRAISE the LORD!

I will praise the LORD with *my* whole
heart,
In the assembly of the upright and *in*
the congregation.

2 The works of the LORD *are* great,
Studied by all who have pleasure in
them.
3 His work *is* honorable and glorious,
And His righteousness endures forever.
4 He has made His wonderful works to
be remembered;
The LORD *is* gracious
and full of compassion.

5 He has given food to those who fear
Him;
He will ever be mindful of His
covenant.
6 He has declared to His people the
power of His works,
In giving them the heritage of the
nations.

7 The works of His hands
are verity and justice;
All His precepts *are* sure.
8 They stand fast forever and ever,
And are done in truth and uprightness.
9 He has sent redemption to His people;
He has commanded His covenant
forever:
Holy and awesome *is* His name.

10 The fear of the LORD
is the beginning of wisdom;
A good understanding have all those
who do *His commandments.*
His praise endures forever.

PSALM 112

The Blessed State of the Righteous

PRAISE the LORD!

Blessed *is* the man *who* fears the LORD,
Who delights greatly in His
commandments.

2 His descendants will be
mighty on earth;
The generation of the upright will be
blessed.
3 Wealth and riches *will be* in his house,
And his righteousness endures forever.
4 Unto the upright there arises light in
the darkness;
He is gracious, and full of compassion,
and righteous.
5 A good man deals graciously and
lends;
He will guide his affairs with
discretion.
6 Surely he will never be shaken;
The righteous will be in everlasting
remembrance.
7 He will not be afraid of evil tidings;
His heart is steadfast,
trusting in the LORD.
8 His heart *is* established;
He will not be afraid,
Until he sees *his desire* upon his
enemies.

9 He has dispersed abroad,
He has given to the poor;

His righteousness endures forever;
His horn will be exalted with honor.
10 The wicked will see *it* and be grieved;
He will gnash his teeth and melt away;
The desire of the wicked shall perish.

PSALM 113
The Majesty and Condescension of God

PRAISE the LORD!

Praise, O servants of the LORD,
Praise the name of the LORD!
2 Blessed be the name of the LORD
From this time forth and forevermore!
3 From the rising of the sun to its going
down
The LORD'S name *is* to be praised.

4 The LORD *is* high above all nations,
And His glory above the heavens.
5 Who *is* like the LORD our God,
Who dwells on high,
6 Who humbles Himself to behold
The things that are in the heavens and
in the earth?

7 He raises the poor out of the dust,
And lifts the needy out of the ash heap,
8 That He may seat *him* with princes—
With the princes of His people.
9 He grants the barren woman a home,
Like a joyful mother of children.

Praise the LORD!

PSALM 114
The Power of God in His Deliverance of Israel

WHEN Israel went out of Egypt,
The house of Jacob from a people of
strange language,
2 Judah became His sanctuary,
And Israel His dominion.

3 The sea saw *it* and fled;
Jordan turned back.
4 The mountains skipped like rams,
The little hills like lambs.
5 What ails you, O sea, that you fled?
O Jordan, *that* you turned back?
6 O mountains, *that* you skipped like
rams?
O little hills, like lambs?

7 Tremble, O earth, at the presence of
the Lord,
At the presence of the God of Jacob,
8 Who turned the rock *into* a pool of
water,
The flint into a fountain of waters.

PSALM 115
The Futility of Idols and the Trustworthiness of God

NOT unto us, O LORD, not unto us,
But to Your name give glory,
Because of Your mercy,
And because of Your truth.
2 Why should the Gentiles say,
"Where now *is* their God?"

3 But our God *is* in heaven;
He does whatever He pleases.
4 Their idols *are* silver and gold,
The work of men's hands.
5 They have mouths,
but they do not speak;
Eyes they have, but they do not see;
6 They have ears, but they do not hear;
Noses they have,
but they do not smell;
7 They have hands,
but they do not handle;
Feet they have, but they do not walk;
Nor do they mutter through their
throat.
8 Those who make them are like them;
So is everyone who trusts in them.

9 O Israel, trust in the LORD;
He *is* their help and their shield.
10 O house of Aaron, trust in the LORD;
He *is* their help and their shield.
11 You who fear the LORD,
trust in the LORD;
He *is* their help and their shield

12 The LORD has been mindful of *us;*
He will bless us;
He will bless the house of Israel;
He will bless the house of Aaron.
13 He will bless those who fear the LORD,
Both small and great.

14 May the LORD give you increase more
and more,
You and your children.
15 *May* you *be* blessed by the LORD,
Who made heaven and earth.

16 The heaven, *even* the heavens,
are the LORD'S;
But the earth He has given to the
children of men.
17 The dead do not praise the LORD,
Nor any who go down into silence.
18 But we will bless the LORD
From this time forth and forevermore.

Praise the LORD!

PSALM 116

Thanksgiving for Deliverance from Death

I LOVE the LORD, because He has heard
My voice *and* my supplications.
2 Because He has inclined His ear to me,
Therefore I will call *upon Him* as long
as I live.

3 The pains of death encompassed me,
And the pangs of Sheol laid hold of
me;
I found trouble and sorrow.
4 Then I called upon the name of the
LORD:
"O LORD, I implore You,
deliver my soul!"

5 Gracious *is* the LORD, and righteous;
Yes, our God *is* merciful.
6 The LORD preserves the simple;
I was brought low, and He saved me.
7 Return to your rest, O my soul,
For the LORD has dealt bountifully
with you.

8 For You have delivered my soul
from death,
My eyes from tears,
And my feet from falling.
9 I will walk before the LORD
In the land of the living.
10 I believed, therefore I spoke,
"I am greatly afflicted."
11 I said in my haste,
"All men *are* liars."

12 What shall I render to the LORD
For all His benefits toward me?
13 I will take up the cup of salvation,
And call upon the name of the LORD.
14 I will pay my vows to the LORD
Now in the presence of all His people.

15 Precious in the sight of the LORD
Is the death of His saints.

16 O LORD, truly I *am* Your servant;
I *am* Your servant,
the son of Your maidservant;
You have loosed my bonds.
17 I will offer to You the sacrifice of
thanksgiving,
And will call upon the name of the
LORD.
18 I will pay my vows to the LORD
Now in the presence of all His people,

19 In the courts of the LORD's house,
In the midst of you, O Jerusalem.

Praise the LORD!

PSALM 117

Let All Peoples Praise the LORD

O H, praise the LORD, all you Gentiles!
Laud Him, all you peoples!
2 For His merciful kindness is great
toward us,
And the truth of the LORD *endures*
forever.

Praise the LORD!

PSALM 118

Praise to God for His Everlasting Mercy

O H, give thanks to the LORD,
for *He is* good!
Because His mercy *endures* forever.

2 Let Israel now say,
"His mercy *endures* forever."
3 Let the house of Aaron now say,
"His mercy *endures* forever."
4 Let those who fear the LORD now say,
"His mercy *endures* forever."

5 I called on the LORD in distress;
The LORD answered me
and set me in a broad place.
6 The LORD *is* on my side;
I will not fear.
What can man do to me?
7 The LORD is for me among those who
help me;
Therefore I shall see *my desire* on those
who hate me.
8 *It is* better to trust in the LORD
Than to put confidence in man.
9 *It is* better to trust in the LORD
Than to put confidence in princes.

10 All nations surrounded me,
But in the name of the LORD I will
destroy them.
11 They surrounded me,
Yes, they surrounded me;
But in the name of the LORD I will
destroy them.
12 They surrounded me like bees;
They were quenched like a fire of
thorns;
For in the name of the LORD I will
destroy them.
13 You pushed me violently,
that I might fall,
But the LORD helped me.

And They Went Out Singing

The first-century celebration of Passover ended with the singing of Psalms 116 and 118. These are known as the Hallel songs or the Egyptian Hallel.

The Gospel of Matthew records that when Jesus and the disciples finished the Passover meal they left the upper city of Jerusalem singing as they went to the Garden of Gethsemane. It is revealing to take a look at some of the verses that Jesus sang as He went to pray in the garden.

> I love the LORD, because He has heard
> My voice *and* my supplications (Ps. 116:1).
> Therefore I will call *upon Him* as long as I live (Ps. 116:2).
> For You have delivered my soul from death,
> My eyes from tears,
> *And* my feet from falling (Ps. 116:8).
> I will walk before the LORD
> In the land of the living (Ps. 116:9).
> Precious in the sight of the LORD
> *Is* the death of His saints (Ps. 116:15).
> The LORD *is* on my side; I will not fear.
> What can man do to me? (Ps. 118:6).
> The LORD is for me among those who help me (Ps. 118:7).
> You pushed me violently, that I might fall,
> But the LORD helped me (Ps. 118:13).
> The LORD *is* my strength and song,
> And He has become my salvation (Ps. 118:14).
> I shall not die, but live,
> And declare the works of the LORD (Ps. 118:17).
> The stone *which* the builders rejected
> Has become the chief cornerstone (Ps. 118:22).
> This was the LORD'S doing;
> It *is* marvelous in our eyes (Ps. 118:23).
> This *is* the day *which* the LORD has made;
> We will rejoice and be glad in it (Ps. 118:24).

The stress, turmoil, and pressure that Jesus experienced in the garden will never be fully understood by us. But perhaps by knowing the songs He sang, we can gain a deeper appreciation of God's love and forgiveness for us.

If Jesus was able to sing in His most difficult moment, "This is the day the LORD has made; we will rejoice and be glad in it," how much more can we look at our negative circumstances and trust God to turn them into a positive life-giving hope!

God turned death for Jesus Christ into life so that His words about our death could be more fully understood. Jesus said, "I am the resurrection and the life. He who believes in Me, though he may die, he shall live" (John 11:25).

14 The LORD *is* my strength and song,
    And He has become my salvation.[59]

15 The voice of rejoicing and salvation
    Is in the tents of the righteous;
    The right hand of the LORD does
    valiantly.
16 The right hand of the LORD is exalted;
    The right hand of the LORD does
    valiantly.
17 I shall not die, but live,
    And declare the works of the LORD.
18 The LORD has chastened me severely,
    But He has not given me over to death.

19 Open to me the gates of righteousness;
    I will go through them,
    And I will praise the LORD.
20 This is the gate of the LORD,
    Through which the righteous shall
    enter.

21 I will praise You,
    For You have answered me,
    And have become my salvation.

22 The stone *which* the builders rejected
    Has become the chief cornerstone.
23 This was the LORD's doing;
    It *is* marvelous in our eyes.
24 This *is* the day *which* the LORD has
    made;
    We will rejoice and be glad in it.

25 Save now, I pray, O LORD;
    O LORD, I pray, send now prosperity.
26 Blessed *is* he who comes in the name
    of the LORD!
    We have blessed you from the house of
    the LORD.
27 God *is* the LORD,
    And He has given us light;
    Bind the sacrifice with cords to the
    horns of the altar.
28 You *are* my God,
    and I will praise You;
    You are my God, I will exalt You.

29 Oh, give thanks to the LORD,
    for *He is* good!
    For His mercy *endures* forever.

PSALM 119

**Meditations on the Excellencies of the Word
of God**

א ALEPH

B LESSED *are* the undefiled in the way,
    Who walk in the law of the LORD!

59 Compare Exodus 15:2

2 Blessed *are* those who keep His
    testimonies,
    Who seek Him with the whole heart!
3 They also do no iniquity;
    They walk in His ways.
4 You have commanded *us*
    To keep Your precepts diligently.
5 Oh, that my ways were directed
    To keep Your statutes!
6 Then I would not be ashamed,
    When I look into all Your
    commandments.
7 I will praise You with uprightness
    of heart,
    When I learn Your righteous
    judgments.
8 I will keep Your statutes;
    Oh, do not forsake me utterly!

ב BETH

9 How can a young man cleanse his
    way?
    By taking heed according to Your
    word.
10 With my whole heart I have sought
    You;
    Oh, let me not wander from Your
    commandments!
11 Your word I have hidden in my heart,
    That I might not sin against You.
12 Blessed *are* You, O LORD!
    Teach me Your statutes.
13 With my lips I have declared
    All the judgments of Your mouth.
14 I have rejoiced in the way of Your
    testimonies,
    As *much as* in all riches.
15 I will meditate on Your precepts,
    And contemplate Your ways.
16 I will delight myself in Your statutes;
    I will not forget Your word.

ג GIMEL

17 Deal bountifully with Your servant,
    That I may live and keep Your word.
18 Open my eyes, that I may see
    Wondrous things from Your law.
19 I *am* a stranger in the earth;
    Do not hide Your commandments
    from me.
20 My soul breaks with longing
    For Your judgments at all times.
21 You rebuke the proud—the cursed,
    Who stray from Your commandments.
22 Remove from me reproach and
    contempt,
    For I have kept Your testimonies.

23 Princes also sit *and* speak against me,
   But Your servant meditates on Your
      statutes.
24 Your testimonies also *are* my delight
   And my counselors.

ד DALETH
25 My soul clings to the dust;
   Revive me according to Your word.
26 I have declared my ways,
      and You answered me;
   Teach me Your statutes.
27 Make me understand the way of Your
      precepts;
   So shall I meditate on Your wondrous
      works.
28 My soul melts from heaviness;
   Strengthen me according to Your word.
29 Remove from me the way of lying,
   And grant me Your law graciously.
30 I have chosen the way of truth;
   Your judgments I have laid *before me.*
31 I cling to Your testimonies;
   O LORD, do not put me to shame!
32 I will run in the way of Your
      commandments,
   For You shall enlarge my heart.

ה HE
33 Teach me, O LORD, the way of Your
      statutes,
   And I shall keep it *to* the end.
34 Give me understanding,
      and I shall keep Your law;
   Indeed, I shall observe it with *my*
      whole heart.
35 Make me walk in the path of Your
      commandments,
   For I delight in it.
36 Incline my heart to Your testimonies,
   And not to covetousness.
37 Turn away my eyes from looking at
      worthless things,
   And revive me in Your way.
38 Establish Your word to Your servant,
   Who *is devoted* to fearing You.
39 Turn away my reproach which I dread,
   For Your judgments *are* good.
40 Behold, I long for Your precepts;
   Revive me in Your righteousness.

ו WAW
41 Let Your mercies come also to me,
      O LORD—
   Your salvation according to Your
      word.

42 So shall I have an answer for him who
      reproaches me,
   For I trust in Your word.
43 And take not the word of truth utterly
      out of my mouth,
   For I have hoped in Your ordinances.
44 So shall I keep Your law continually,
   Forever and ever.
45 And I will walk at liberty,
   For I seek Your precepts.
46 I will speak of Your testimonies also
      before kings,
   And will not be ashamed.
47 And I will delight myself in Your
      commandments,
   Which I love.
48 My hands also I will lift up to Your
      commandments,
   Which I love,
   And I will meditate on Your statutes.

ז ZAYIN
49 Remember the word to Your servant,
   Upon which You have caused me to
      hope.
50 This *is* my comfort in my affliction,
   For Your word has given me life.
51 The proud have me in great derision,
   Yet I do not turn aside from Your law.
52 I remembered Your judgments of old,
      O LORD,
   And have comforted myself.
53 Indignation has taken hold of me
   Because of the wicked,
      who forsake Your law.
54 Your statutes have been my songs
   In the house of my pilgrimage.
55 I remember Your name in the night,
      O LORD,
   And I keep Your law.
56 This has become mine,
   Because I kept Your precepts.

ח HETH
57 *You are* my portion, O LORD;
   I have said that I would keep Your
      words.
58 I entreated Your favor with *my* whole
      heart;
   Be merciful to me according to Your
      word.
59 I thought about my ways,
   And turned my feet to Your
      testimonies.
60 I made haste, and did not delay
   To keep Your commandments.

61 The cords of the wicked have bound
me,
But I have not forgotten Your law.
62 At midnight I will rise to give thanks
to You,
Because of Your righteous judgments.
63 I *am* a companion of all *those* who fear
You,
And of those who keep Your precepts.
64 The earth, O LORD, is full of Your
mercy;
Teach me Your statutes.

ט TETH
65 You have dealt well with Your servant,
O LORD, according to Your word.
66 Teach me good judgment and
knowledge,
For I believe Your commandments.
67 Before I was afflicted I went astray,
But now I keep Your word.
68 You *are* good, and do good;
Teach me Your statutes.
69 The proud have forged a lie
against me,
But I will keep Your precepts with *my*
whole heart.
70 Their heart is as fat as grease,
But I delight in Your law.
71 *It is* good for me that I have been
afflicted,
That I may learn Your statutes.
72 The law of Your mouth *is* better to me
Than thousands of *shekels of* gold and
silver.

י YOD
73 Your hands have made me and
fashioned me;
Give me understanding, that I may
learn Your commandments.
74 Those who fear You will be glad when
they see me,
Because I have hoped in Your word.
75 I know, O LORD, that Your judgments
are right,
And *that* in faithfulness You have
afflicted me.
76 Let, I pray, Your merciful kindness be
for my comfort,
According to Your word to Your
servant.
77 Let Your tender mercies come to me,
that I may live;
For Your law *is* my delight.
78 Let the proud be ashamed,
For they treated me wrongfully with
falsehood;
But I will meditate on Your precepts.

79 Let those who fear You turn to me,
Those who know Your testimonies.
80 Let my heart be blameless regarding
Your statutes,
That I may not be ashamed.

כ KAPH
81 My soul faints for Your salvation,
But I hope in Your word.
82 My eyes fail *from seeking* Your word,
Saying, "When will You comfort me?"
83 For I have become like a wineskin in
smoke,
Yet I do not forget Your statutes.
84 How many *are* the days of Your
servant?
When will You execute judgment on
those who persecute me?
85 The proud have dug pits for me,
Which *is* not·according to Your law.
86 All Your commandments *are* faithful;
They persecute me wrongfully;
Help me!
87 They almost made an end of me on
earth,
But I did not forsake Your precepts.
88 Revive me according to Your
lovingkindness,
So that I may keep the testimony of
Your mouth.

ל LAMED
89 Forever, O LORD,
Your word is settled in heaven.
90 Your faithfulness *endures* to all
generations;
You established the earth,
and it abides.
91 They continue this day according to
Your ordinances,
For all *are* Your servants.
92 Unless Your law *had been* my delight,
I would then have perished in my
affliction.
93 I will never forget Your precepts,
For by them You have given me life.
94 I *am* Yours, save me;
For I have sought Your precepts.
95 The wicked wait for me to destroy me,
But I will consider Your testimonies.
96 I have seen the consummation of all
perfection,
But Your commandment *is* exceedingly
broad.

מ MEM
97 Oh, how I love Your law!
It *is* my meditation all the day.

98 You, through Your commandments,
make me wiser than my enemies;
For they *are* ever with me.
99 I have more understanding than all
my teachers,
For Your testimonies *are* my
meditation.
100 I understand more than the ancients,
Because I keep Your precepts.
101 I have restrained my feet from every
evil way,
That I may keep Your word.
102 I have not departed from Your
judgments,
For You Yourself have taught me.
103 How sweet are Your words to my
taste,
Sweeter than honey to my mouth!
104 Through Your precepts I get
understanding;
Therefore I hate every false way.

ב NUN

105 Your word *is* a lamp to my feet
And a light to my path.
106 I have sworn and confirmed
That I will keep Your righteous
judgments.
107 I am afflicted very much;
Revive me, O LORD, according to
Your word.
108 Accept, I pray, the freewill offerings
of my mouth, O LORD,
And teach me Your judgments.
109 My life *is* continually in my hand,
Yet I do not forget Your law.
110 The wicked have laid a snare for me,
Yet I have not strayed from Your
precepts.
111 Your testimonies I have taken as a
heritage forever,
For they *are* the rejoicing of my heart.
112 I have inclined my heart to perform
Your statutes
Forever, to the very end.

ם SAMEK

113 I hate the double-minded,
But I love Your law.
114 You *are* my hiding place and my
shield;
I hope in Your word.
115 Depart from me, you evildoers,
For I will keep the commandments of
my God!
116 Uphold me according to Your word,
that I may live;
And do not let me be ashamed of my
hope.

117 Hold me up, and I shall be safe,
And I shall observe Your statutes
continually.
118 You reject all those who stray from
Your statutes,
For their deceit *is* falsehood.
119 You put away all the wicked of the
earth *like* dross;
Therefore I love Your testimonies.
120 My flesh trembles for fear of You,
And I am afraid of Your judgments.

ע AYIN

121 I have done justice and righteousness;
Do not leave me to my oppressors.
122 Be surety for Your servant for good;
Do not let the proud oppress me.
123 My eyes fail *from seeking* Your
salvation
And Your righteous word.
124 Deal with Your servant according to
Your mercy,
And teach me Your statutes.
125 I *am* Your servant;
Give me understanding,
That I may know Your testimonies.
126 *It is* time for *You* to act, O LORD,
For they have regarded Your law as
void.
127 Therefore I love Your commandments
More than gold, yes, than fine gold!
128 Therefore all *Your* precepts *concerning*
all *things*
I consider *to be* right;
I hate every false way.

פ PE

129 Your testimonies are wonderful;
Therefore my soul keeps them.
130 The entrance of Your words gives
light;
It gives understanding to the simple.
131 I opened my mouth and panted,
For I longed for Your
commandments.
132 Look upon me and be merciful to me,
As Your custom *is* toward those who
love Your name.
133 Direct my steps by Your word,
And let no iniquity have dominion
over me.
134 Redeem me from the oppression of
man,
That I may keep Your precepts.
135 Make Your face shine upon Your
servant,
And teach me Your statutes.

136 Rivers of water run down from my
    eyes,
    Because *men* do not keep Your law.

 צ TSADDE

137 Righteous *are* You, O LORD,
    And upright *are* Your judgments.
138 Your testimonies, *which* You have
    commanded,
    Are righteous and very faithful.
139 My zeal has consumed me,
    Because my enemies have forgotten
    Your words.
140 Your word *is* very pure;
    Therefore Your servant loves it.
141 I *am* small and despised,
    Yet I do not forget Your precepts.
142 Your righteousness *is* an everlasting
    righteousness,
    And Your law *is* truth.
143 Trouble and anguish have overtaken
    me,
    Yet Your commandments *are* my
    delights.
144 The righteousness of Your testimonies
    is everlasting;
    Give me understanding,
    and I shall live.

ק QOPH

145 I cry out with *my* whole heart;
    Hear me, O LORD!
    I will keep Your statutes.
146 I cry out to You;
    Save me, and I will keep Your
    testimonies.
147 I rise before the dawning of the
    morning,
    And cry for help;
    I hope in Your word.
148 My eyes are awake through the *night*
    watches,
    That I may meditate on Your word.
149 Hear my voice according to Your
    lovingkindness;
    O LORD, revive me according to Your
    justice.
150 They draw near who follow after
    wickedness;
    They are far from Your law.
151 You *are* near, O LORD,
    And all Your commandments *are*
    truth.
152 Concerning Your testimonies,
    I have known of old that You have
    founded them forever.

ר RESH

153 Consider my affliction and deliver me,
    For I do not forget Your law.
154 Plead my cause and redeem me;
    Revive me according to Your word.
155 Salvation *is* far from the wicked,
    For they do not seek Your statutes.
156 Great *are* Your tender mercies,
    O LORD;
    Revive me according to Your
    judgments.
157 Many *are* my persecutors and my
    enemies,
    Yet I do not turn from Your
    testimonies.
158 I see the treacherous,
    and am disgusted,
    Because they do not keep Your word.
159 Consider how I love Your precepts;
    Revive me, O LORD, according to
    Your lovingkindness.
160 The entirety of Your word *is* truth,
    And every one of Your righteous
    judgments *endures* forever.

ש SHIN

161 Princes persecute me without a cause,
    But my heart stands in awe of Your
    word.
162 I rejoice at Your word
    As one who finds great treasure.
163 I hate and abhor lying,
    But I love Your law.
164 Seven times a day I praise You,
    Because of Your righteous judgments.
165 Great peace have those who love
    Your law,
    And nothing causes them to stumble.
166 LORD, I hope for Your salvation,
    And I do Your commandments.
167 My soul keeps Your testimonies,
    And I love them exceedingly.
168 I keep Your precepts and Your
    testimonies,
    For all my ways *are* before You.

ת TAU

169 Let my cry come before You,
    O LORD;
    Give me understanding according to
    Your word.
170 Let my supplication come before
    You;
    Deliver me according to Your word.
171 My lips shall utter praise,
    For You teach me Your statutes.

172 My tongue shall speak of Your word,
    For all Your commandments *are*
    righteousness.
173 Let Your hand become my help,
    For I have chosen Your precepts.
174 I long for Your salvation, O LORD,
    And Your law *is* my delight.
175 Let my soul live,
    and it shall praise You;
    And let Your judgments help me.
176 I have gone astray like a lost sheep;
    Seek Your servant,
    For I do not forget Your
    commandments.

PSALM 120

Plea for Relief from Bitter Foes

A Song of Ascents.

I N my distress I cried to the LORD,
  And He heard me.
2 Deliver my soul, O LORD, from lying
    lips
    And from a deceitful tongue.

3 What shall be given to you,
    Or what shall be done to you,
    You false tongue?
4 Sharp arrows of the warrior,
    With coals of the broom tree!

5 Woe is me, that I sojourn in Meshech,
    That I dwell among the tents of Kedar!
6 My soul has dwelt too long
    With one who hates peace.
7 I *am for* peace;
    But when I speak, they *are* for war.

PSALM 121

God the Help of Those Who Seek Him

A Song of Ascents.

I WILL lift up my eyes to the hills—
  From whence comes my help?
2 My help *comes* from the LORD,
    Who made heaven and earth.

3 He will not allow your foot to be
    moved;
    He who keeps you will not slumber.
4 Behold, He who keeps Israel
    Shall neither slumber nor sleep.

5 The LORD *is* your keeper;
    The LORD *is* your shade at your right
    hand.
6 The sun shall not strike you by day,
    Nor the moon by night.

7 The LORD shall preserve you from all
    evil;
    He shall preserve your soul.
8 The LORD shall preserve your going
    out and your coming in
    From this time forth,
    and even forevermore.

PSALM 122

The Joy of Going to the House of the LORD

A Song of Ascents. Of David.

I WAS glad when they said to me,
  "Let us go into the house of the
  LORD."
2 Our feet have been standing
    Within your gates, O Jerusalem!

3 Jerusalem is built
    As a city that is compact together,
4 Where the tribes go up,
    The tribes of the LORD,
    To the Testimony of Israel,
    To give thanks to the name of the
    LORD.
5 For thrones are set there for judgment,
    The thrones of the house of David.

6 Pray for the peace of Jerusalem:
    "May they prosper who love you.
7 Peace be within your walls,
    Prosperity within your palaces."
8 For the sake of my brethren and
    companions,
    I will now say, "Peace *be* within you."
9 Because of the house of the LORD our
    God
    I will seek your good.

PSALM 123

Prayer for Relief from Contempt

A Song of Ascents.

U NTO You I lift up my eyes,
  O You who dwell in the heavens.
2 Behold, as the eyes of servants *look* to
    the hand of their masters,
    As the eyes of a maid to the hand of
    her mistress,
    So our eyes *look* to the LORD our God,
    Until He has mercy on us.

3 Have mercy on us, O LORD,
    have mercy on us!
    For we are exceedingly filled with
    contempt.
4 Our soul is exceedingly filled
    With the scorn of those who are at
    ease,
    With the contempt of the proud.

PSALM 124

The LORD the Defense of His People

A Song of Ascents. Of David.

"IF it had not been the LORD who was
on our side,"
Let Israel now say—
2   "If it had not been the LORD who was
on our side,
When men rose up against us,
3   Then they would have swallowed us
alive,
When their wrath was kindled
against us;
4   Then the waters would have
overwhelmed us,
The stream would have gone over our
soul;
5   Then the swollen waters
Would have gone over our soul."

6   Blessed *be* the LORD,
Who has not given us *as* prey to their
teeth.
7   Our soul has escaped as a bird from
the snare of the fowlers;
The snare is broken,
and we have escaped.
8   Our help *is* in the name of the LORD,
Who made heaven and earth.

PSALM 125

The LORD the Strength of His People

A Song of Ascents.

THOSE who trust in the LORD
Are like Mount Zion,
Which cannot be moved,
but abides forever.
2   As the mountains surround Jerusalem,
So the LORD surrounds His people
From this time forth and forever.

3   For the scepter of wickedness
shall not rest
On the land allotted to the righteous,
Lest the righteous reach out their
hands to iniquity.

4   Do good, O LORD, to *those who are*
good,
And to *those who are* upright in their
hearts.

5   As for such as turn aside to their
crooked ways,
The LORD shall lead them away
With the workers of iniquity.

Peace *be* upon Israel!

PSALM 126

A Joyful Return to Zion

A Song of Ascents.

WHEN the LORD brought back the
captivity of Zion,
We were like those who dream.
2   Then our mouth was filled with
laughter,
And our tongue with singing.
Then they said among the nations,
"The LORD has done great things for
them."
3   The LORD has done great things for us,
Whereof we are glad.

4   Bring back our captivity, O LORD,
As the streams in the South.

5   Those who sow in tears
Shall reap in joy.
6   He who continually goes forth weeping,
Bearing seed for sowing,
Shall doubtless come again with
rejoicing,
Bringing his sheaves *with him.*

PSALM 127

Laboring and Prospering with the LORD

A Song of Ascents. Of Solomon.

UNLESS the LORD builds the house,
They labor in vain who build it;
Unless the LORD guards the city,
The watchman stays awake in vain.
2   *It is* vain for you to rise up early,
To sit up late,
To eat the bread of sorrows;
For so He gives His beloved sleep.

3   Behold, children *are* a heritage from
the LORD,
The fruit of the womb *is His* reward.
4   Like arrows in the hand of a warrior,
So *are* the children of one's youth.
5   Happy *is* the man who has his quiver
full of them;
They shall not be ashamed,
But shall speak with their enemies in
the gate.

PSALM 128

Blessings of Those Who Fear the LORD

A Song of Ascents.

BLESSED *is* every one who fears the
LORD,
Who walks in His ways.
2   When you eat the labor of your hands,
You *shall be* happy,
and *it shall be* well with you.

The Mountains
Surround Jerusalem

Those who trust in the LORD
Are like Mount Zion,
Which cannot be moved, *but* abides forever.
As the mountains surround Jerusalem,
So the LORD surrounds His people
From this time forth and forever.

(Ps. 125:1, 2)

The city of Jerusalem, located twenty-nine hundred feet above sea level on the crest of the Judean ridge is surrounded by hills and steep valleys. The psalmist uses the city's geographical location to paint a vivid picture of God's love toward His people. He compares the permanence of the rocky limestone mountains to the enduring quality of God's love toward us forever.

Certainly the quality of elevation was in the psalmist's mind as he looked north of Jerusalem to the high mountain which acted as sentinels protecting the city from its most vulnerable approach route. God's protection is like the steep mountains west of Jerusalem with their narrow passes easily defended by the city's inhabitants. South and east of Jerusalem lay the barren wilderness that was inhospitable to any advancing army with scorching hot summers and flash floods in the winter.

The ancient Israelites had a constant reminder that their security came from God. Their natural environment encouraged them in their faith. The mountains surrounding Jerusalem became to them a symbol of God's love, power, and care.

We too can realize the security of God's power in our lives as we trust in God and are assured that we will live forever. Problems which come into our life cannot move us. God's love is permanent. It elevates us and protects us from life's problems. His love surrounds us, as the psalmist assures, "from this time forth and forever."

3 Your wife *shall be* like a fruitful vine
   In the very heart of your house,
   Your children like olive plants
   All around your table.
4 Behold, thus shall the man be blessed
   Who fears the LORD.

5 The LORD bless you out of Zion,
   And may you see the good of
      Jerusalem
   All the days of your life.
6 Yes, may you see your children's
      children.

   Peace *be* upon Israel!

PSALM 129

Song of Victory over Zion's Enemies

A Song of Ascents.

"MANY a time they have afflicted
   me from my youth,"
   Let Israel now say—
2 "Many a time they have afflicted me
      from my youth;
   Yet they have not prevailed against me.
3 The plowers plowed on my back;
   They made their furrows long."
4 The LORD *is* righteous;
   He has cut in pieces the cords of the
      wicked.

5 Let all those who hate Zion
   Be put to shame and turned back.
6 Let them be as the grass *on* the
      housetops,
   Which withers before it grows up,
7 With which the reaper does not fill his
      hand,
   Nor he who binds sheaves, his arms.
8 Neither let those who pass by them
      say,
   "The blessing of the LORD *be* upon you;
   We bless you in the name of the
      LORD!"

PSALM 130

Waiting for the Redemption of the LORD

A Song of Ascents.

OUT of the depths I have cried to You,
   O LORD;
2 Lord, hear my voice!
   Let Your ears be attentive
   To the voice of my supplications.

3 If You, LORD, should mark iniquities,
   O Lord, who could stand?
4 But *there is* forgiveness with You,
   That You may be feared.

5 I wait for the LORD, my soul waits,
   And in His word I do hope.
6 My soul *waits* for the Lord
   More than those who watch for the
      morning—
   I say, more than those who watch for
      the morning.

7 O Israel, hope in the LORD;
   For with the LORD *there is* mercy,
   And with Him *is* abundant redemption.
8 And He shall redeem Israel
   From all his iniquities.

PSALM 131

Simple Trust in the LORD

A Song of Ascents. Of David.

LORD, my heart is not haughty,
   Nor my eyes lofty.
   Neither do I concern myself with great
      matters,
   Nor with things too profound for me.

2 Surely I have calmed and quieted my
      soul,
   Like a weaned child with his mother;
   Like a weaned child *is* my soul within
      me.

3 O Israel, hope in the LORD
   From this time forth and forever.

PSALM 132

The Eternal Dwelling of God in Zion

A Song of Ascents.

LORD, remember David
   And all his afflictions;
2 How he swore to the LORD,
   And vowed to the Mighty *God* of
      Jacob:
3 "Surely I will not go into the chamber
      of my house,
   Or go up to the comfort of my bed;
4 I will not give sleep to my eyes
   Or slumber to my eyelids,
5 Until I find a place for the LORD,
   A dwelling place for the Mighty *God* of
      Jacob."

6 Behold, we heard of it in Ephrathah;
   We found it in the fields of the
      woods.[60]
7 Let us go into His tabernacle;
   Let us worship at His footstool.
8 Arise, O LORD, to Your resting place,
   You and the ark of Your strength.

60 Hebrew *Jaar*

9 Let Your priests be clothed with
righteousness,
And let Your saints shout for joy.

10 For Your servant David's sake,
Do not turn away the face of Your
Anointed.

11 The LORD has sworn *in* truth to David;
He will not turn from it:
"I will set upon your throne the fruit of
your body.
12 If your sons will keep My covenant
And My testimony which I shall teach
them,
Their sons also shall sit upon your
throne forevermore."

13 For the LORD has chosen Zion;
He has desired *it* for His habitation:
14 "This *is* My resting place forever;
Here I will dwell, for I have desired it.
15 I will abundantly bless her provision;
I will satisfy her poor with bread.
16 I will also clothe her priests with
salvation,
And her saints shall shout aloud for
joy.
17 There I will make the horn of David
grow;
I will prepare a lamp for My Anointed.
18 His enemies I will clothe with shame,
But upon Himself His crown shall
flourish."

PSALM 133

Blessed Unity of the People of God

A Song of Ascents. Of David.

BEHOLD, how good and how pleasant
it is
For brethren to dwell together in unity!

2 *It is* like the precious oil upon the
head,
Running down on the beard,
The beard of Aaron,
Running down on the edge of his
garments.
3 *It is* like the dew of Hermon,
Descending upon the mountains of
Zion;
For there the LORD commanded the
blessing—
Life forevermore.

PSALM 134

Praising the LORD in His House at Night

A Song of Ascents.

BEHOLD, bless the LORD,
All *you* servants of the LORD,

Who by night stand in the house of the
LORD!
2 Lift up your hands *in* the sanctuary,
And bless the LORD.

3 The LORD who made heaven and earth
Bless you from Zion!

PSALM 135

Praise to God in Creation and Redemption

PRAISE the LORD!

Praise the name of the LORD;
Praise *Him*,
O you servants of the LORD!
2 You who stand in the house of the
LORD,
In the courts of the house of our God,
3 Praise the LORD, for the LORD *is* good;
Sing praises to His name,
for *it is* pleasant.
4 For the LORD has chosen Jacob for
Himself,
Israel for His special treasure.

5 For I know that the LORD *is* great,
And our Lord *is* above all gods.
6 Whatever the LORD pleases He does,
In heaven and in earth,
In the seas and in all deep places.
7 He causes the vapors to ascend from
the ends of the earth;
He makes lightning for the rain;
He brings the wind out of His
treasuries.

8 He destroyed the firstborn of Egypt,
Both of man and beast.
9 He sent signs and wonders into the
midst of you, O Egypt,
Upon Pharaoh and all his servants.
10 He defeated many nations
And slew mighty kings—
11 Sihon king of the Amorites,
Og king of Bashan,
And all the kingdoms of Canaan—
12 And gave their land *as* a heritage,
A heritage to Israel His people.

13 Your name, O LORD, *endures* forever,
Your fame, O LORD, throughout all
generations.
14 For the LORD will judge His people,
And He will have compassion on His
servants.

15 The idols of the nations *are* silver and
gold,
The work of men's hands.

16 They have mouths,
    but they do not speak;
  Eyes they have, but they do not see;
17 They have ears, but they do not hear;
  Nor is there *any* breath in their
    mouths.
18 Those who make them are like them;
  So is everyone who trusts in them.

19 Bless the LORD, O house of Israel!
  Bless the LORD, O house of Aaron!
20 Bless the LORD, O house of Levi!
  You who fear the LORD,
    bless the LORD!
21 Blessed be the LORD out of Zion,
  Who dwells in Jerusalem!

  Praise the LORD!

PSALM 136

Thanksgiving to God for His Enduring Mercy

O H, give thanks to the LORD,
   for *He is* good!
  For His mercy *endures* forever.
2 Oh, give thanks to the God of gods!
  For His mercy *endures* forever.
3 Oh, give thanks to the Lord of lords!
  For His mercy *endures* forever:

4 To Him who alone does great wonders,
  For His mercy *endures* forever;
5 To Him who by wisdom made the
   heavens,
  For His mercy *endures* forever;
6 To Him who laid out the earth above
   the waters,
  For His mercy *endures* forever;
7 To Him who made great lights,
  For His mercy *endures* forever—
8 The sun to rule by day,
  For His mercy *endures* forever;
9 The moon and stars to rule by night,
  For His mercy *endures* forever.

10 To Him who struck Egypt in their
   firstborn,
  For His mercy *endures* forever;
11 And brought out Israel from among
   them,
  For His mercy *endures* forever;
12 With a strong hand,
   and with an outstretched arm,
  For His mercy *endures* forever;
13 To Him who divided the Red Sea in
   two,
  For His mercy *endures* forever;
14 And made Israel pass through the
   midst of it,
  For His mercy *endures* forever;

15 But overthrew Pharaoh and his army in
   the Red Sea,
  For His mercy *endures* forever;
16 To Him who led His people through
   the wilderness,
  For His mercy *endures* forever;
17 To Him who struck down great kings,
  For His mercy *endures* forever;
18 And slew famous kings,
  For His mercy *endures* forever—
19 Sihon king of the Amorites,
  For His mercy *endures* forever;
20 And Og king of Bashan,
  For His mercy *endures* forever—
21 And gave their land as a heritage,
  For His mercy *endures* forever;
22 A heritage to Israel His servant,
  For His mercy *endures* forever.

23 Who remembered us in our lowly state,
  For His mercy *endures* forever;
24 And rescued us from our enemies,
  For His mercy *endures* forever;
25 Who gives food to all flesh,
  For His mercy *endures* forever.

26 Oh, give thanks to the God of heaven!
  For His mercy *endures* forever.

PSALM 137

Longing for Zion in a Foreign Land

B Y the rivers of Babylon,
  There we sat down, yea, we wept
  When we remembered Zion.
2 We hung our harps
  Upon the willows in the midst of it.
3 For there those who carried us away
   captive required of us a song,
  And those who plundered us *required*
   of us mirth,
  Saying, "Sing us *one* of the songs of
   Zion!"

4 How shall we sing the LORD's song
  In a foreign land?
5 If I forget you, O Jerusalem,
  Let my right hand forget *her skill!*
6 If I do not remember you,
  Let my tongue cling to the roof of my
   mouth—
  If I do not exalt Jerusalem
  Above my chief joy.

7 Remember, O LORD, against the sons
   of Edom
  The day of Jerusalem,
  Who said, "Raze *it*, raze *it*,
  To its very foundation!"

8 O daughter of Babylon,
    who are to be destroyed,
    Happy *shall he be* who repays you as
    you have served us!
9 Happy *shall he be* who takes and
    dashes
    Your little ones against the rock.

PSALM 138

The LORD'S Goodness to the Faithful

A Psalm of David.

I WILL praise You with my whole heart;
    Before the gods I will sing praises to
    You.
2 I will worship toward Your holy
    temple,
    And praise Your name
    For Your lovingkindness and Your
    truth;
    For You have magnified Your word
    above all Your name.
3 In the day when I cried out,
    You answered me,
    And made me bold *with* strength in my
    soul.

4 All the kings of the earth shall praise
    You, O LORD,
    When they hear the words of Your
    mouth.
5 Yes, they shall sing of the ways of the
    LORD,
    For great *is* the glory of the LORD.
6 Though the LORD *is* on high,
    Yet He regards the lowly;
    But the proud He knows from afar.

7 Though I walk in the midst of trouble,
    You will revive me;
    You will stretch out Your hand
    Against the wrath of my enemies,
    And Your right hand will save me.
8 The LORD will perfect *that which*
    concerns me;
    Your mercy, O LORD, *endures* forever;
    Do not forsake the works of Your
    hands.

PSALM 139

God's Perfect Knowledge of Man

For the Chief Musician. A Psalm of David.

O LORD, You have searched me
    and known *me.*
2 You know my sitting down
    and my rising up;
    You understand my thought afar off.
3 You comprehend my path
    and my lying down,
    And are acquainted with all my ways.

4 For *there is* not a word on my tongue,
    But behold, O LORD,
    You know it altogether.
5 You have hedged me behind
    and before,
    And laid Your hand upon me.
6 *Such* knowledge *is* too wonderful for
    me;
    It is high, I cannot *attain* it.

7 Where can I go from Your Spirit?
    Or where can I flee from Your
    presence?
8 If I ascend into heaven, You *are* there;
    If I make my bed in hell, behold,
    You *are there.*
9 *If* I take the wings of the morning,
    And dwell in the uttermost parts of the
    sea,
10 Even there Your hand shall lead me,
    And Your right hand shall hold me.
11 If I say, "Surely the darkness shall
    fall[61] on me,"
    Even the night shall be light about me;
12 Indeed, the darkness shall not hide
    from You,
    But the night shines as the day;
    The darkness and the light *are* both
    alike *to You.*

13 For You have formed my inward parts;
    You have covered me in my mother's
    womb.
14 I will praise You, for I am fearfully
    and wonderfully made;
    Marvelous are Your works,
    And *that* my soul knows very well.
15 My frame was not hidden from You,
    When I was made in secret,
    And skillfully wrought in the lowest
    parts of the earth.
16 Your eyes saw my substance,
    being yet unformed.
    And in Your book they all were
    written,
    The days fashioned for me,
    When *as yet there were* none of them.

17 How precious also are Your thoughts
    to me, O God!
    How great is the sum of them!
18 *If* I should count them, they would be
    more in number than the sand;
    When I awake, I am still with You.

19 Oh, that You would slay the wicked,
    O God!
    Depart from me, therefore, you
    bloodthirsty men.

61 Vulgate and Symmachus read *cover.*

20 For they speak against You wickedly;
Your enemies take *Your name* in vain.
21 Do I not hate them, O LORD, who hate
You?
And do I not loathe those who rise up
against You?
22 I hate them with perfect hatred;
I count them my enemies.

23 Search me, O God,
and know my heart;
Try me, and know my anxieties;
24 And see if *there is any* wicked way in
me,
And lead me in the way everlasting.

PSALM 140

Prayer for Deliverance from Evil Men

To the Chief Musician. A Psalm of David.

DELIVER me, O LORD, from evil men;
Preserve me from violent men,
2 Who plan evil things in *their* hearts;
They continually gather together *for*
war.
3 They sharpen their tongues like a
serpent;
The poison of asps *is* under their lips.
Selah

4 Keep me, O LORD, from the hands of
the wicked;
Preserve me from violent men,
Who have purposed to make my steps
stumble.
5 The proud have hidden a snare for me,
and cords;
They have spread a net by the wayside;
They have set traps for me. Selah

6 I said to the LORD: "You *are* my God;
Hear the voice of my supplications,
O LORD.
7 O GOD the Lord,
the strength of my salvation,
You have covered my head in the day
of battle.
8 Do not grant, O LORD, the desires of
the wicked;
Do not further his *wicked* scheme,
Lest they be exalted. Selah

9 "*As for* the head of those who surround
me,
Let the evil of their lips cover them;
10 Let burning coals fall upon them;
Let them be cast into the fire,
Into deep pits, that they rise not up
again.

11 Let not a slanderer be established in
the earth;
Let evil hunt the violent man to
overthrow *him.*"

12 I know that the LORD will maintain
The cause of the afflicted,
And justice for the poor.
13 Surely the righteous shall give thanks
to Your name;
The upright shall dwell in Your
presence.

PSALM 141

Prayer for Safekeeping from Wickedness

A Psalm of David.

LORD, I cry out to You;
Make haste to me!
Give ear to my voice when I cry out to
You.
2 Let my prayer be set before You *as*
incense,
The lifting up of my hands *as* the
evening sacrifice.

3 Set a guard, O LORD, over my mouth;
Keep watch over the door of my lips.
4 Do not incline my heart
to any evil thing,
To practice wicked works
With men who work iniquity;
And do not let me eat of their
delicacies.

5 Let the righteous strike me;
It shall be a kindness.
And let him reprove me;
It shall be as excellent oil;
Let my head not refuse it.

For still my prayer *is* against the deeds
of the wicked.
6 Their judges are overthrown by the
sides of the cliff,
And they hear my words,
for they are sweet.
7 Our bones are scattered at the mouth
of the grave,
As when one plows and breaks up the
earth.

8 But my eyes *are* upon You,
O GOD the Lord;
In You I take refuge;
Do not leave my soul destitute.
9 Keep me from the snares *which* they
have laid for me,
And from the traps of the workers of
iniquity.

10 Let the wicked fall into their own nets,
While I escape safely.

PSALM 142

A Plea for Relief from Persecutors

A Contemplation[62] of David. A Prayer when he
was in the cave.

I CRY out to the LORD with my voice;
With my voice to the LORD I make my
supplication.
2 I pour out my complaint before Him;
I declare before Him my trouble.

3 When my spirit was overwhelmed
within me,
Then You knew my path.
In the way in which I walk
They have secretly set a snare for me.
4 Look on *my* right hand and see,
For *there is* no one who acknowledges
me;
Refuge has failed me;
No one cares for my soul.

5 I cried out to You, O LORD:
I said, "You *are* my refuge,
My portion in the land of the living.
6 Attend to my cry,
For I am brought very low;
Deliver me from my persecutors,
For they are stronger than I.
7 Bring my soul out of prison,
That I may praise Your name;
The righteous shall surround me,
For You shall deal bountifully
with me."

PSALM 143

An Earnest Appeal for Guidance and Deliverance

A Psalm of David.

H EAR my prayer, O LORD,
Give ear to my supplications!
In Your faithfulness answer me,
And in Your righteousness.
2 Do not enter into judgment with Your
servant,
For in Your sight no one living is
righteous.

3 For the enemy has persecuted my soul;
He has crushed my life to the ground;
He has made me dwell in darkness,
Like those who have long been dead.
4 Therefore my spirit is overwhelmed
within me;
My heart within me is distressed.

5 I remember the days of old;
I meditate on all Your works;
I muse on the work of Your hands.
6 I spread out my hands to You;
My soul *longs* for You like a thirsty
land.   Selah

7 Answer me speedily, O LORD;
My spirit fails!
Do not hide Your face from me,
Lest I be like those who go down into
the pit.
8 Cause me to hear Your lovingkindness
in the morning,
For in You do I trust;
Cause me to know the way in which I
should walk,
For I lift up my soul to You.

9 Deliver me, O LORD, from my
enemies;
In You I take shelter.[63]
10 Teach me to do Your will,
For You *are* my God;
Your Spirit *is* good.
Lead me in the land of uprightness.

11 Revive me, O LORD, for Your name's
sake!
For Your righteousness' sake bring my
soul out of trouble.
12 In Your mercy cut off my enemies,
And destroy all those who afflict my
soul;
For I *am* Your servant.

PSALM 144

A Song to the LORD Who Preserves and Prospers His People

A Psalm of David.

B LESSED *be* the LORD my Rock,
Who trains my hands for war,
And my fingers for battle—
2 My lovingkindness and my fortress,
My high tower and my deliverer,
My shield and *the One* in whom I take
refuge,
Who subdues my people under me.

3 LORD, what *is* man,
that You take knowledge of him?
Or the son of man,
that You are mindful of him?
4 Man is like a breath;
His days *are* like a passing shadow.

5 Bow down Your heavens, O LORD,
and come down;
Touch the mountains,
and they shall smoke.

62 Hebrew *Maschil*   63 Septuagint and Vulgate read *to You I flee.*

6 Flash forth lightning and scatter them;
Shoot out Your arrows
and destroy them.
7 Stretch out Your hand from above;
Rescue me and deliver me out of great
waters,
From the hand of foreigners,
8 Whose mouth speaks vain words,
And whose right hand *is* a right hand
of falsehood.

9 I will sing a new song to You, O God;
On a harp of ten strings I will sing
praises to You,
10 *The One* who gives salvation to kings,
Who delivers David His servant
From the deadly sword.

11 Rescue me and deliver me from the
hand of foreigners,
Whose mouth speaks vain words,
And whose right hand *is* a right hand
of falsehood—
12 That our sons *may be* as plants grown
up in their youth;
That our daughters *may be* as pillars,
Sculptured in palace style;
13 *That* our barns *may be* full,
Supplying all kinds of produce;
That our sheep may bring forth
thousands
And ten thousands in our fields;
14 *That* our oxen *may be* well-laden;
That there be no breaking in
or going out;
That there be no outcry in our streets.
15 Happy *are* the people
who are in such a state;
Happy *are* the people
whose God *is* the LORD!

PSALM 145

A Song of God's Majesty and Love

A Praise of David.

I WILL extol You, my God, O King;
And I will bless Your name
forever and ever.
2 Every day I will bless You,
And I will praise Your name
forever and ever.
3 Great *is* the LORD,
and greatly to be praised;
And His greatness *is* unsearchable.

4 One generation shall praise Your works
to another,
And shall declare Your mighty acts.
5 I will meditate on the glorious splendor
of Your majesty,
And on Your wondrous works.

6 *Men* shall speak of the might of Your
awesome acts,
And I will declare Your greatness.
7 They shall utter the memory of Your
great goodness,
And shall sing of Your righteousness.

8 The LORD *is* gracious and full of
compassion,
Slow to anger and great in mercy.
9 The LORD *is* good to all,
And His tender mercies *are* over all
His works.

10 All Your works shall praise You,
O LORD,
And Your saints shall bless You.
11 They shall speak of the glory of Your
kingdom,
And talk of Your power,
12 To make known to the sons of men
His mighty acts,
And the glorious majesty of His
kingdom.
13 Your kingdom *is* an everlasting
kingdom,
And Your dominion *endures*
throughout all generations.

14 The LORD upholds all who fall,
And raises up all *those who are* bowed
down.
15 The eyes of all look expectantly to
You,
And You give them their food in due
season.
16 You open Your hand
And satisfy the desire of every living
thing.

17 The LORD *is* righteous in all His ways,
Gracious in all His works.
18 The LORD *is* near to all who call upon
Him,
To all who call upon Him in truth.
19 He will fulfill the desire of those who
fear Him;
He also will hear their cry and save
them.
20 The LORD preserves all who love Him,
But all the wicked He will destroy.
21 My mouth shall speak the praise of the
LORD,
And all flesh shall bless His holy name
Forever and ever.

PSALM 146

The Happiness of Those Whose Help Is the LORD

PRAISE the LORD!

Praise the LORD, O my soul!

2 While I live I will praise the LORD;
   I will sing praises to my God while I
      have my being.

3 Do not put your trust in princes,
   Nor in a son of man,
      in whom *there is* no help.
4 His spirit departs,
      he returns to his earth;
   In that very day his plans perish.

5 Happy *is he* who *has* the God of Jacob
      for his help,
   Whose hope *is* in the LORD his God,
6 Who made heaven and earth,
   The sea, and all that *is* in them;
   Who keeps truth forever,
7 Who executes justice for the oppressed,
   Who gives food to the hungry.
   The LORD gives freedom to the
      prisoners.

8 The LORD opens *the eyes of* the blind;
   The LORD raises those who are bowed
      down;
   The LORD loves the righteous.
9 The LORD watches over the strangers;
   He relieves the fatherless and widow;
   But the way of the wicked He turns
      upside down.

10 The LORD shall reign forever—
   Your God, O Zion, to all generations.

   Praise the LORD!

PSALM 147

Praise to God for His Word and Providence

PRAISE the LORD!
   For *it is* good to sing praises to our
      God;
   For *it is* pleasant, *and* praise is
      beautiful.

2 The LORD builds up Jerusalem;
   He gathers together the outcasts of
      Israel.
3 He heals the broken-hearted
   And binds up their wounds.
4 He counts the number of the stars;
   He calls them all by name.
5 Great *is* our Lord,
      and mighty in power;
   His understanding *is* infinite.
6 The LORD lifts up the humble;
   He casts the wicked down to the
      ground.

7 Sing to the LORD with thanksgiving;
   Sing praises on the harp to our God,

8 Who covers the heavens with clouds,
   Who prepares rain for the earth,
   Who makes grass to grow on the
      mountains.
9 He gives to the beast its food,
   And to the young ravens that cry.

10 He does not delight
      in the strength of the horse;
   He takes no pleasure
      in the legs of a man.
11 The LORD takes pleasure
      in those who fear Him,
   In those who hope in His mercy.

12 Praise the LORD, O Jerusalem!
   Praise your God, O Zion!
13 For He has strengthened the bars of
      your gates;
   He has blessed your children within
      you.
14 He makes peace *in* your borders,
   And fills you with the finest wheat.

15 He sends out His command *to the*
      earth;
   His word runs very swiftly.
16 He gives snow like wool;
   He scatters the frost like ashes;
17 He casts out His hail like morsels;
   Who can stand before His cold?
18 He sends out His word
      and melts them;
   He causes His wind to blow,
      and the waters flow.

19 He declares His word to Jacob,
   His statutes and His judgments to
      Israel.
20 He has not dealt thus with any nation;
   And *as for His* judgments,
      they have not known them.

   Praise the LORD!

PSALM 148

Praise to the LORD from Creation

PRAISE the LORD!

   Praise the LORD from the heavens;
   Praise Him in the heights!
2 Praise Him, all His angels;
   Praise Him, all His hosts!
3 Praise Him, sun and moon;
   Praise Him, all you stars of light!
4 Praise Him, you heavens of heavens,
   And you waters above the heavens!

5 Let them praise the name of the LORD,
For He commanded
and they were created.
6 He has also established them forever
and ever;
He has made a decree which shall not
pass away.

7 Praise the LORD from the earth,
You great sea creatures and all the
depths;
8 Fire and hail, snow and clouds;
Stormy wind, fulfilling His word;
9 Mountains and all hills;
Fruitful trees and all cedars;
10 Beasts and all cattle;
Creeping things and flying fowl;
11 Kings of the earth and all peoples;
Princes and all judges of the earth;
12 Both young men and maidens;
Old men and children.

13 Let them praise the name of the LORD,
For His name alone is exalted;
His glory *is* above the earth and
heaven.
14 And He has exalted the horn of His
people,
The praise of all His saints—
Of the children of Israel,
A people near to Him.

Praise the LORD!

PSALM 149

Praise to God for His Salvation and Judgment

PRAISE the LORD!

Sing to the LORD a new song,
And His praise in the congregation of
saints.
2 Let Israel rejoice in their Maker;
Let the children of Zion be joyful in
their King.
3 Let them praise His name with the
dance;
Let them sing praises to Him with the
timbrel and harp.

4 For the LORD takes pleasure in His
people;
He will beautify the humble with
salvation.

5 Let the saints be joyful in glory;
Let them sing aloud on their beds.
6 *Let* the high praises of God *be* in their
mouth,
And a two-edged sword in their hand,
7 To execute vengeance on the nations,
And punishments on the peoples;
8 To bind their kings with chains,
And their nobles with fetters of iron;
9 To execute on them the written
judgment—
This honor have all His saints.

Praise the LORD!

PSALM 150

Let All Things Praise the LORD

PRAISE the LORD!

Praise God in His sanctuary;
Praise Him in His mighty firmament!

2 Praise Him for His mighty acts;
Praise Him according to His excellent
greatness!

3 Praise Him with the sound of the
trumpet;
Praise Him with the lute and harp!
4 Praise Him with the timbrel and
dance;
Praise Him with stringed instruments
and flutes!
5 Praise Him with loud cymbals;
Praise Him with high sounding
cymbals!

6 Let everything that has breath praise
the LORD.

Praise the LORD!

Introduction to Proverbs

The Book of Proverbs is one of the most practical, positive, life-guiding sources ever written. Written largely by King Solomon, about 1000 B.C., these proverbs are treasures of wisdom commenting on life.

Solomon was known to be one of the wisest men of all time. This book records that he was renowned for over three thousand proverbs. Five hundred and sixty of those are recorded here. While Solomon is known to have written the first twenty-nine chapters, chapters 30 and 31 are attributed to Agur the son of Jakeh (Prov. 30:1) and King Lemuel (Prov. 31:1), neither are mentioned elsewhere in Scripture.

Each proverb is like a beautiful diamond, shining gloriously on its own. But put together with the other verses, the effect is dazzling, like a glorious shimmering necklace.

> Trust in the LORD with all your heart,
> And lean not on your own understanding;
> In all your ways acknowledge Him,
> And He shall direct your paths . . .
> Do not withhold good from those to whom it is due,
> When it is in the power of your hand to do *so* . . .
> Wisdom *is* the principal thing;
> *Therefore* get wisdom.
> And in all your getting, get understanding . . .
> Commit your works to the LORD,
> And your thoughts will be established . . .
> Train up a child in the way he should go,
> And when he is old he will not depart from it.

(Prov. 3:5, 6, 27; 4:7; 16:3; 22:6)

The proverbs are sensitively presented as if from a grandfather giving advice to his grandchildren. Rich in God's wisdom, they act as signs on a road, giving us a glimpse of what is around the next bend. They aim to keep us from detouring from our faith in God.

If you live by these words of faith, you will come to the end of your life with love around you, peace within you, and hope before you!

The Book of
Proverbs

The Beginning of Knowledge

THE proverbs of Solomon the son of
David, king of Israel:

2 To know wisdom and instruction,
To perceive the words of
understanding,
3 To receive the instruction of wisdom,
Justice, judgment, and equity;
4 To give prudence to the simple,
To the young man knowledge and
discretion—
5 A wise *man* will hear
and increase learning,
And a man of understanding
will attain wise counsel,
6 To understand a proverb
and an enigma,
The words of the wise
and their riddles.

7 The fear of the LORD *is* the beginning
of knowledge,
But fools despise wisdom and
instruction.

Shun Evil Counsel

8 My son, hear the instruction
of your father,
And do not forsake the law
of your mother;
9 For they *will be* graceful ornaments
on your head,
And chains about your neck.

10 My son, if sinners entice you,
Do not consent.
11 If they say, "Come with us,
Let us lie in wait to *shed* blood;
Let us lurk secretly for the innocent
without cause;
12 Let us swallow them alive like Sheol,[1]
And whole, like those who go down to
the Pit;
13 We shall find all *kinds* of precious
possessions,
We shall fill our houses with spoil;
14 Cast in your lot among us,
Let us all have one purse"—

15 My son, do not walk in the way with
them,
Keep your foot from their path;
16 For their feet run to evil,
And they make haste to shed blood.
17 Surely, in vain the net is spread
In the sight of any bird;
18 But they lie in wait for their *own*
blood,
They lurk secretly for their *own* lives.
19 So *are* the ways of everyone who is
greedy for gain;
It takes away the life of its owners.

The Call of Wisdom

20 Wisdom calls aloud outside;
She raises her voice in the open
squares.
21 She cries out in the chief concourses,
At the openings of the gates in the city
She speaks her words:
22 "How long, you simple ones,
will you love simplicity?
For scorners delight in their scorning,
And fools hate knowledge.
23 Turn at my reproof;
Surely I will pour out my spirit on
you;
I will make my words known to you.
24 Because I have called and you refused,
I have stretched out my hand
and no one regarded,
25 Because you disdained all my counsel,
And would have none of my reproof,
26 I also will laugh at your calamity;
I will mock when your terror comes,
27 When your terror comes like a storm,
And your destruction comes like a
whirlwind,
When distress and anguish come upon
you.

28 "Then they will call on me,
but I will not answer;
They will seek me diligently,
but they will not find me.
29 Because they hated knowledge
And did not choose the fear of the
LORD,
30 They would have none of my counsel
And despised all my reproof,

1 Or *the grave*

31 Therefore they shall eat the fruit of
     their own way,
   And be filled to the full with their own
     fancies.
32 For the turning away of the simple
     will slay them,
   And the complacency of fools
     will destroy them;
33 But whoever listens to me
     will dwell safely,
   And will be secure,
     without fear of evil."

The Value of Wisdom

2 My son, if you receive my words,
   And treasure my commands
     within you,
2 So that you incline your ear to wisdom,
   And apply your heart to understanding;
3 Yes, if you cry out for discernment,
   And lift up your voice for
     understanding,
4 If you seek her as silver,
   And search for her as *for* hidden
     treasures;
5 Then you will understand the fear
     of the LORD,
   And find the knowledge of God.
6 For the LORD gives wisdom;
   From His mouth *come* knowledge and
     understanding;
7 He stores up sound wisdom for the
     upright;
   He is a shield to those who walk
     uprightly;
8 He guards the paths of justice,
   And preserves the way of His saints.
9 Then you will understand righteousness
     and justice,
   Equity *and* every good path.

10 When wisdom enters your heart,
   And knowledge is pleasant to your
     soul,
11 Discretion will preserve you;
   Understanding will keep you,
12 To deliver you from the way of evil,
   From the man who speaks perverse
     things,
13 From those who leave the paths
     of uprightness
   To walk in the ways of darkness;
14 Who rejoice in doing evil,
   And delight in the perversity
     of the wicked;
15 Whose ways *are* crooked,
   And *who are* devious in their paths;
16 To deliver you from the immoral
     woman,

From the seductress *who* flatters with
     her words,
17 Who forsakes the companion of her
     youth,
   And forgets the covenant of her God.
18 For her house leads down to death,
   And her paths to the dead;
19 None who go to her return,
   Nor do they regain the paths of life—
20 So you may walk in the way of
     goodness,
   And keep *to* the paths of righteousness.
21 For the upright will dwell in the land,
   And the blameless will remain in it;
22 But the wicked will be cut off from the
     earth,
   And the unfaithful will be uprooted
     from it.

Guidance for the Young

3 My son, do not forget my law,
   But let your heart keep my
     commands;
2 For length of days and long life
   And peace they will add to you.

3 Let not mercy and truth forsake you;
   Bind them around your neck,
   Write them on the tablet of your heart,
4 *And* so find favor and high esteem
   In the sight of God and man.

5 Trust in the LORD with all your heart,
   And lean not on your own
     understanding;
6 In all your ways acknowledge Him,
   And He shall direct[2] your paths.

7 Do not be wise in your own eyes;
   Fear the LORD and depart from evil.
8 It will be health to your flesh,[3]
   And strength[4] to your bones.

9 Honor the LORD with your possessions,
   And with the firstfruits of all your
     increase;
10 So your barns will be filled with plenty,
   And your vats will overflow with new
     wine.

11 My son, do not despise the chastening
     of the LORD,
   Nor detest His correction;
12 For whom the LORD loves He corrects,
   Just as a father the son *in whom* he
     delights.

13 Happy *is* the man *who* finds wisdom,
   And the man *who* gains understanding;

---

2 Literally *make smooth* or *straight*   3 Literally *navel,* figurative of the body   4 Literally *drink* or *refreshment*

14 For her proceeds *are* better than the
profits of silver,
And her gain than fine gold.
15 She *is* more precious than rubies,
And all the things you may desire
cannot compare with her.
16 Length of days *is* in her right hand,
In her left hand riches and honor.
17 Her ways *are* ways of pleasantness,
And all her paths *are* peace.
18 She *is* a tree of life to those who take
hold of her,
And happy *are all* who retain her.

19 The LORD by wisdom
founded the earth;
By understanding
He established the heavens;
20 By His knowledge
the depths were broken up,
And clouds drop down the dew.

21 My son, let them not depart from your
eyes—
Keep sound wisdom and discretion;
22 So they will be life to your soul
And grace to your neck.
23 Then you will walk safely in your way,
And your foot will not stumble.
24 When you lie down,
you will not be afraid;
Yes, you will lie down
and your sleep will be sweet.
25 Do not be afraid of sudden terror,
Nor of trouble from the wicked when it
comes;
26 For the LORD will be your confidence,
And will keep your foot from being
caught.

27 Do not withhold good from those to
whom it is due,
When it is in the power of your hand
to do *so.*
28 Do not say to your neighbor,
"Go, and come back,
And tomorrow I will give *it,*"
When *you have* it with you.
29 Do not devise evil against your
neighbor,
For he dwells by you for safety's sake.
30 Do not strive with a man without
cause,
If he has done you no harm.

31 Do not envy the oppressor,
And choose none of his ways;
32 For the perverse *person*
is an abomination to the LORD,
But His secret *counsel*
is with the upright.

33 The curse of the LORD *is* on the house
of the wicked,
But He blesses the habitation of the
just.
34 Surely He scorns the scornful,
But gives grace to the humble.
35 The wise shall inherit glory,
But shame shall be the legacy of fools.

Security in Wisdom

4 Hear, *my* children,
the instruction of a father,
And give attention to know
understanding;
2 For I give you good doctrine:
Do not forsake my law.
3 When I was my father's son,
Tender and the only one in the sight
of my mother,
4 He also taught me, and said to me:
"Let your heart retain my words;
Keep my commands, and live.
5 Get wisdom! Get understanding!
Do not forget, nor turn away from the
words of my mouth.
6 Do not forsake her,
and she will preserve you;
Love her, and she will keep you.
7 Wisdom *is* the principal thing;
Therefore get wisdom.
And in all your getting,
get understanding.
8 Exalt her, and she will promote you;
She will bring you honor,
when you embrace her.
9 She will place on your head an
ornament of grace;
A crown of glory she will deliver
to you."

10 Hear, my son, and receive my sayings,
And the years of your life will be
many.
11 I have taught you in the way of
wisdom;
I have led you in right paths.
12 When you walk,
your steps will not be hindered,
And when you run,
you will not stumble.
13 Take firm hold of instruction,
do not let go;
Keep her, for she *is* your life.

14 Do not enter the path of the wicked,
And do not walk in the way of evil.
15 Avoid it, do not travel on it;
Turn away from it and pass on.
16 For they do not sleep
unless they have done evil;

And their sleep is taken away
    unless they make *someone* fall.
17 For they eat the bread of wickedness,
    And drink the wine of violence.

18 But the path of the just *is* like the
    shining sun,[5]
    That shines ever brighter unto the
    perfect day.
19 The way of the wicked *is* like darkness;
    They do not know what makes them
    stumble.

20 My son, give attention to my words;
    Incline your ear to my sayings.
21 Do not let them depart from your eyes;
    Keep them in the midst of your heart;
22 For they *are* life to those who find
    them,
    And health to all their flesh.
23 Keep your heart with all diligence,
    For out of it *spring* the issues of life.
24 Put away from you a deceitful mouth,
    And put perverse lips far from you.
25 Let your eyes look straight ahead,
    And your eyelids look right before you.
26 Ponder the path of your feet,
    And let all your ways be established.
27 Do not turn to the right or the left;
    Remove your foot from evil.

The Peril of Adultery

5 My son, pay attention to my wisdom;
    Lend your ear to my understanding,
2 That you may preserve discretion,
    And *that* your lips may keep
    knowledge.
3 For the lips of an immoral woman
    drip honey,
    And her mouth *is* smoother than oil;
4 But in the end she is bitter as
    wormwood,
    Sharp as a two-edged sword.
5 Her feet go down to death,
    Her steps lay hold of hell.[6]
6 Lest you ponder *her* path of life—
    Her ways are unstable;
    You do not know *them*.

7 Therefore hear me now, *my* children,
    And do not depart from the words of
    my mouth.
8 Remove your way far from her,
    And do not go near the door of her
    house,
9 Lest you give your honor to others,
    And your years to the cruel one;
10 Lest aliens be filled with your wealth,
    And your labors *go* to the house of a
    foreigner;

11 And you mourn at last,
    When your flesh and your body
    are consumed,
12 And say:
    "How I have hated instruction,
    And my heart despised reproof!
13 I have not obeyed the voice of my
    teachers,
    Nor inclined my ear to those who
    instructed me!
14 I was on the verge of total ruin,
    In the midst of the congregation and
    assembly."

15 Drink water from your own cistern,
    And running water from your own
    well.
16 Should your fountains be dispersed
    abroad,
    Streams of water in the streets?
17 Let them be only your own,
    And not for strangers with you.
18 Let your fountain be blessed,
    And rejoice with the wife of your
    youth.
19 *As a* loving deer and a graceful doe,
    Let her breasts satisfy you at all times;
    And always be enraptured with her
    love.
20 For why should you, my son,
    be enraptured by an immoral
    woman,
    And be embraced in the arms of a
    seductress?

21 For the ways of man *are* before the
    eyes of the LORD,
    And He ponders all his paths.
22 His own iniquities entrap the wicked
    man,
    And he is caught in the cords of his
    sin.
23 He shall die for lack of instruction,
    And in the greatness of his folly
    he shall go astray.

Dangerous Promises

6 My son, if you become surety
    for your friend,
    If you have shaken hands in pledge
    for a stranger,
2 You are snared by the words of your
    own mouth;
    You are taken by the words of your
    mouth.
3 So do this, my son,
    and deliver yourself;
    For you have come into the hand
    of your friend:

---

5 Literally *light*   6 Hebrew *sheol*

Go and humble yourself;
Plead with your friend.
4 Give no sleep to your eyes,
Nor slumber to your eyelids.
5 Deliver yourself like a gazelle from the
hand *of the hunter*,
And like a bird from the hand of the
fowler.

The Folly of Indolence

6 Go to the ant, you sluggard!
Consider her ways and be wise,
7 Which, having no captain,
Overseer or ruler,
8 Provides her supplies in the summer,
And gathers her food in the harvest.
9 How long will you slumber,
O sluggard?
When will you rise from your sleep?
10 A little sleep, a little slumber,
A little folding of the hands to sleep—
11 So shall your poverty come on you like
a robber,
And your need like an armed man.

The Wicked Man

12 A worthless person, a wicked man,
Walks with a perverse mouth;
13 He winks with his eyes,
He shuffles his feet,
He points with his fingers;
14 Perversity *is* in his heart,
He devises evil continually,
He sows discord.
15 Therefore his calamity shall come
suddenly;
Suddenly he shall be broken without
remedy.

16 These six *things* the LORD hates,
Yes, seven *are* an abomination to Him:
17 A proud look,
A lying tongue,
Hands that shed innocent blood,
18 A heart that devises wicked plans,
Feet that are swift in running to evil,
19 A false witness *who* speaks lies,
And one who sows discord among
brethren.

Beware of Adultery

20 My son, keep your father's command,
And do not forsake the law of your
mother.
21 Bind them continually upon your
heart;
Tie them around your neck.

22 When you roam, they[7] will lead you;
When you sleep, they will keep you;
And *when* you awake, they will speak
with you.
23 For the commandment *is* a lamp,
And the law *is* light;
Reproofs of instruction *are* the way
of life,
24 To keep you from the evil woman,
From the flattering tongue of a
seductress.
25 Do not lust after her beauty in your
heart,
Nor let her allure you with her eyelids.
26 For by means of a harlot
A man is reduced to a crust of bread;
And an adulteress[8] will prey upon his
precious life.
27 Can a man take fire to his bosom,
And his clothes not be burned?
28 Can one walk on hot coals,
And his feet not be seared?
29 So *is* he who goes in to his neighbor's
wife;
Whoever touches her shall not be
innocent.

30 *People* do not despise a thief
If he steals to satisfy himself when he
is starving.
31 Yet *when* he is found,
he must restore sevenfold;
He may have to give up all the
substance of his house.
32 Whoever commits adultery with a
woman lacks understanding;
He *who* does so destroys his own soul.
33 Wounds and dishonor he will get,
And his reproach will not be wiped
away.
34 For jealousy *is* a husband's fury;
Therefore he will not spare in the day
of vengeance.
35 He will accept no recompense,
Nor will he be appeased
though you give many gifts.

7 My son, keep my words,
And treasure my commands
within you.
2 Keep my commands and live,
And my law as the apple of your eye.
3 Bind them on your fingers;
Write them on the tablet of your heart.
4 Say to wisdom, "You *are* my sister,"
And call understanding *your* nearest
kin,
5 That they may keep you from the
immoral woman,

7 Literally *it*   8 Literally *a man's wife,* that is, of another

From the seductress
who flatters with her words.

The Crafty Harlot

6 For at the window of my house
I looked through my lattice,
7 And saw among the simple,
I perceived among the youths,
A young man devoid of understanding,
8 Passing along the street near her
corner;
And he took the path to her house
9 In the twilight, in the evening,
In the black and dark night.

10 And there a woman met him,
With the attire of a harlot,
and a crafty heart.
11 She *was* loud and rebellious,
Her feet would not stay at home.
12 At times *she was* outside,
at times in the open square,
Lurking at every corner.
13 So she caught him and kissed him;
With an impudent face
she said to him:
14 "*I have* peace offerings with me;
Today I have paid my vows.
15 So I came out to meet you,
Diligently to seek your face,
And I have found you.
16 I have spread my bed with tapestry,
Colored coverings of Egyptian linen.
17 I have perfumed my bed
With myrrh, aloes, and cinnamon.
18 Come, let us take our fill of love until
morning;
Let us delight ourselves with love.
19 For my husband *is* not at home;
He has gone on a long journey;
20 He has taken a bag of money with him,
And will come home on the appointed
day."

21 With her enticing speech
she caused him to yield,
With her flattering lips
she seduced him.
22 Immediately he went after her,
as an ox goes to the slaughter,
Or as a fool to the correction of the
stocks,[9]
23 Till an arrow struck his liver.
As a bird hastens to the snare,
He did not know it *would take* his life.

24 Now therefore, listen to me,
my children;

Pay attention to the words of my
mouth:
25 Do not let your heart turn aside to her
ways,
Do not stray into her paths;
26 For she has cast down many wounded,
And all who were slain by her were
strong *men*.
27 Her house *is* the way to hell,[10]
Descending to the chambers of death.

The Excellence of Wisdom

8 Does not wisdom cry out,
And understanding lift up her voice?
2 She takes her stand on the top of the
high hill,
Beside the way, where the paths meet.
3 She cries out by the gates,
at the entry of the city,
At the entrance of the doors:
4 "To you, O men, I call,
And my voice *is* to the sons of men.
5 O you simple ones,
understand prudence,
And you fools,
be of an understanding heart.
6 Listen, for I will speak of excellent
things,
And from the opening of my lips
will come right things;
7 For my mouth will speak truth;
Wickedness *is* an abomination
to my lips.
8 All the words of my mouth *are* with
righteousness;
Nothing crooked or perverse *is* in
them.
9 They *are* all plain to him
who understands,
And right to those
who find knowledge.
10 Receive my instruction, and not silver,
And knowledge
rather than choice gold;
11 For wisdom *is* better than rubies,
And all the things one may desire
cannot be compared with her.

12 "I, wisdom, dwell with prudence,
And find out knowledge *and* discretion.
13 The fear of the LORD *is* to hate evil;
Pride and arrogance and the evil way
And the perverse mouth I hate.
14 Counsel *is* mine, and sound wisdom;
I *am* understanding, I have strength.
15 By me kings reign,
And rulers decree justice.
16 By me princes rule, and nobles,
All the judges of the earth.[11]

9 Septuagint, Syriac, and Targum read *as a dog to bonds;* Vulgate reads *as a lamb . . . to bonds.*   10 Hebrew *sheol*
11 Masoretic Text, Syriac, Targum, and Vulgate read *righteousness;* Bomberg, Septuagint, and some manuscripts
and editions read *earth.*

¹⁷ I love those who love me,
And those who seek me diligently
will find me.
¹⁸ Riches and honor *are* with me,
Enduring riches and righteousness.
¹⁹ My fruit *is* better than gold,
yes, than fine gold,
And my revenue than choice silver.
²⁰ I traverse the way of righteousness,
In the midst of the paths of justice,
²¹ That I may cause those who love me
to inherit wealth,
That I may fill their treasuries.

²²"The LORD possessed me at the
beginning of His way,
Before His works of old.
²³ I have been established from
everlasting,
From the beginning,
before there was ever an earth.
²⁴ When *there were* no depths
I was brought forth,
When *there were* no fountains
abounding with water.
²⁵ Before the mountains were settled,
Before the hills, I was brought forth;
²⁶ While as yet He had not made the
earth or the fields,
Or the primeval dust of the world.
²⁷ When He prepared the heavens,
I *was* there,
When He drew a circle on the face
of the deep,
²⁸ When He established the clouds above,
When He strengthened the fountains of
the deep,
²⁹ When He assigned to the sea its limit,
So that the waters would not transgress
His command,
When He marked out the foundations
of the earth,
³⁰ Then I was beside Him,
as a master craftsman;¹²
And I was daily *His* delight,
Rejoicing always before Him,
³¹ Rejoicing in His inhabited world,
And my delight *was* with the sons
of men.

³²"Now therefore, listen to me,
my children,
For blessed *are those who* keep my
ways.
³³ Hear instruction and be wise,
And do not disdain *it*.
³⁴ Blessed is the man who listens to me,
Watching daily at my gates,
Waiting at the posts of my doors.

---

12 A Jewish tradition reads *one brought up*.

³⁵ For whoever finds me finds life,
And obtains favor from the LORD;
³⁶ But he who sins against me
wrongs his own soul;
All those who hate me love death."

The Way of Wisdom

9 Wisdom has built her house,
She has hewn out her seven pillars;
² She has slaughtered her meat,
She has mixed her wine,
She has also furnished her table.
³ She has sent out her maidens,
She cries out from the highest places
of the city,
⁴ "Whoever *is* simple,
let him turn in here!"
As for him who lacks understanding,
she says to him,
⁵ "Come, eat of my bread
And drink of the wine *which* I have
mixed.
⁶ Forsake foolishness and live,
And go in the way of understanding.

⁷ "He who reproves a scoffer
gets shame for himself,
And he who rebukes a wicked *man*
gets himself a blemish.
⁸ Do not reprove a scoffer,
lest he hate you;
Rebuke a wise man,
and he will love you.
⁹ Give *instruction* to a wise *man*,
and he will be still wiser;
Teach a just *man*,
and he will increase in learning.

¹⁰ "The fear of the LORD
is the beginning of wisdom,
And the knowledge of the Holy One
is understanding.
¹¹ For by me your days will be
multiplied,
And years of life will be added to you.
¹² If you are wise,
you are wise for yourself,
And *if* you scoff,
you alone will bear *it*."

The Way of Folly

¹³ A foolish woman is clamorous;
She is simple, and knows nothing.
¹⁴ For she sits at the door of her house,
On a seat *by* the highest places of the
city,
¹⁵ To call to those who pass by,
Who go straight on their way:
¹⁶ "Whoever *is* simple,
let him turn in here";

And *as for* him who lacks
understanding, she says to him,
17 "Stolen water is sweet,
And bread *eaten* in secret is pleasant."
18 But he does not know that the dead
are there,
That her guests *are* in the depths
of hell.[13]

Wise Sayings of Solomon

10 The Proverbs of Solomon:

A wise son makes a glad father,
But a foolish son *is* the grief of his
mother.

2 Treasures of wickedness profit nothing,
But righteousness delivers from death.
3 The LORD will not allow the righteous
soul to famish,
But He casts away the desire of the
wicked.

4 He who deals *with* a slack hand
becomes poor,
But the hand of the diligent
makes *one* rich.
5 He who gathers in summer
is a wise son,
But he who sleeps in harvest
is a son who causes shame.

6 Blessings *are* on the head of the
righteous,
But violence covers the mouth
of the wicked.
7 The memory of the righteous *is*
blessed,
But the name of the wicked will rot.

8 The wise in heart will receive
commands,
But a prating fool will fall.

9 He who walks with integrity
walks securely,
But he who perverts his ways
will become known.

10 He who winks with the eye causes
trouble,
But a prating fool will fall.

11 The mouth of the righteous *is* a well
of life,
But violence covers the mouth of the
wicked.

12 Hatred stirs up strife,
But love covers all sins.

13 Wisdom is found on the lips of him
who has understanding,
But a rod *is* for the back of him
who is devoid of understanding.

14 Wise *people* store up knowledge,
But the mouth of the foolish *is* near
destruction.

15 The rich man's wealth
is his strong city;
The destruction of the poor
is their poverty.

16 The labor of the righteous *leads* to life,
The wages of the wicked to sin.

17 He who keeps instruction *is in* the way
of life,
But he who refuses reproof goes astray.

18 Whoever hides hatred *has* lying lips,
And whoever spreads slander *is* a fool.

19 In the multitude of words
sin is not lacking,
But he who restrains his lips *is* wise.
20 The tongue of the righteous
is choice silver;
The heart of the wicked *is worth* little.
21 The lips of the righteous feed many,
But fools die for lack of wisdom.[14]

22 The blessing of the LORD makes *one*
rich,
And He adds no sorrow with it.

23 To do evil *is* like sport to a fool,
But a man of understanding has
wisdom.
24 The fear of the wicked
will come upon him,
And the desire of the righteous
will be granted.
25 When the whirlwind passes by,
the wicked *is* no *more*,
But the righteous
has an everlasting foundation.

26 As vinegar to the teeth
and smoke to the eyes,
So *is* the sluggard to those
who send him.

27 The fear of the LORD prolongs days,
But the years of the wicked
will be shortened.
28 The hope of the righteous
will be gladness,
But the expectation of the wicked
will perish.

13 Hebrew *sheol*   14 Literally *heart*

29 The way of the LORD *is* strength
for the upright,
But destruction *will come*
to the workers of iniquity.

30 The righteous will never be removed,
But the wicked will not inhabit the
earth.

31 The mouth of the righteous brings
forth wisdom,
But the perverse tongue will be cut out.

32 The lips of the righteous know
what is acceptable,
But the mouth of the wicked
what is perverse.

11 A false balance *is* an abomination
to the LORD,
But a just weight *is* His delight.

2 When pride comes, then comes shame;
But with the humble *is* wisdom.

3 The integrity of the upright
will guide them,
But the perversity of the unfaithful
will destroy them.

4 Riches do not profit in the day of
wrath,
But righteousness delivers from death.

5 The righteousness of the blameless
will direct his way aright,
But the wicked will fall
by his own wickedness.

6 The righteousness of the upright
will deliver them,
But the unfaithful will be taken
by *their own* lust.

7 When a wicked man dies,
his expectation will perish,
And the hope of the unjust perishes.

8 The righteous is delivered from trouble,
And it comes to the wicked instead.

9 The hypocrite with *his* mouth destroys
his neighbor,
But through knowledge the righteous
will be delivered.

10 When it goes well with the righteous,
the city rejoices;
And when the wicked perish,
there is shouting.

11 By the blessing of the upright
the city is exalted,
But it is overthrown
by the mouth of the wicked.

12 He who is devoid of wisdom despises
his neighbor,
But a man of understanding holds his
peace.

13 A talebearer reveals secrets,
But he who is of a faithful spirit
conceals a matter.

14 Where *there is* no counsel,
the people fall;
But in the multitude of counselors
there is safety.

15 He who is surety for a stranger will
suffer *for it*,
But one who hates being surety is
secure.

16 A gracious woman retains honor,
But ruthless *men* retain riches.

17 The merciful man
does good for his own soul,
But *he who is* cruel
troubles his own flesh.

18 The wicked man does deceptive work,
But to him who sows righteousness
will be a sure reward.

19 As righteousness *leads* to life,
So he who pursues evil *pursues it* to his
own death.

20 Those who are of a perverse heart
are an abomination to the LORD,
But *such as are* blameless in their ways
are His delight.

21 *Though they join* forces,[15]
the wicked will not go unpunished;
But the posterity of the righteous will
be delivered.

22 *As* a ring of gold in a swine's snout,
So is a lovely woman who lacks
discretion.

23 The desire of the righteous
is only good,
But the expectation of the wicked
is wrath.

24 There is *one* who scatters,
yet increases more;
And there is *one* who withholds more
than is right,
But it *leads* to poverty.

25 The generous soul will be made rich,
And he who waters will also be
watered himself.

26 The people will curse him who
withholds grain,
But blessing *will be* on the head
of him who sells *it*.

27 He who diligently seeks good
finds favor,
But trouble will come to him
who seeks *evil*.

15 Literally *hand in hand*

28 He who trusts in his riches will fall,
But the righteous will flourish like
foliage.

29 He who troubles his own house will
inherit the wind,
And the fool *will be* servant to the wise
of heart.

30 The fruit of the righteous *is a* tree
of life,
And he who wins souls *is* wise.

31 If the righteous will be recompensed
on the earth,
How much more the wicked and the
sinner.

12

Whoever loves instruction loves
knowledge,
But he who hates reproof *is* stupid.

2 A good *man* obtains favor from the
LORD,
But a man of wicked devices He will
condemn.

3 A man is not established
by wickedness,
But the root of the righteous
cannot be moved.

4 An excellent[16] wife *is* the crown of her
husband,
But she who causes shame *is* like
rottenness in his bones.

5 The thoughts of the righteous *are* right,
But the counsels of the wicked *are*
deceitful.

6 The words of the wicked *are*,
"Lie in wait for blood,"
But the mouth of the upright
will deliver them.

7 The wicked are overthrown
and *are* no more,
But the house of the righteous
will stand.

8 A man will be commended according
to his wisdom,
But he who is of a perverse heart will
be despised.

9 Better *is the* one who is slighted
but has a servant,
Than he who honors himself
but lacks bread.

10 A righteous *man* regards the life of his
animal,
But the tender mercies of the wicked
are cruel.

11 He who tills his land will be satisfied
with bread,
But he who follows frivolity *is* devoid
of understanding.[17]

12 The wicked covet the catch of evil *men*,
But the root of the righteous yields
fruit.

13 The wicked is ensnared by the
transgression of *his* lips,
But the righteous will come through
trouble.

14 A man will be satisifed with good by
the fruit of *his* mouth,
And the recompense of a man's hands
will be rendered to him.

15 The way of a fool *is* right in his own
eyes,
But he who heeds counsel *is* wise.

16 A fool's wrath is known at once,
But a prudent *man* covers shame.

17 He *who* speaks truth declares
righteousness,
But a false witness, deceit.

18 There is one who speaks like the
piercings of a sword,
But the tongue of the wise *promotes*
health.

19 The truthful lip shall be established
forever,
But a lying tongue *is* but for a
moment.

20 Deceit is in the heart of those who
devise evil,
But counselors of peace have joy.

21 No grave trouble will overtake the
righteous,
But the wicked shall be filled with evil.

22 Lying lips *are* an abomination to the
LORD,
But those who deal truthfully
are His delight.

23 A prudent man conceals knowledge,
But the heart of fools proclaims
foolishness.

24 The hand of the diligent will rule,
But the slothful will be put to forced
labor.

25 Anxiety in the heart of man causes
depression,
But a good word makes it glad.

16 Literally *a woman of valor*   17 Literally *heart*

26 The righteous should choose his friends
   carefully,
   For the way of the wicked leads them
   astray.

27 The slothful *man* does not roast
   what he took in hunting,
   But diligence *is* man's precious
   possession.

28 In the way of righteousness *is* life,
   And in *its* pathway *there is* no death.

13 A wise son *heeds* his father's
   instruction,
   But a scoffer does not listen to rebuke.

2 A man shall eat well
   by the fruit of *his* mouth,
   But the soul of the unfaithful
   feeds on violence.

3 He who guards his mouth
   preserves his life,
   But he who opens wide his lips
   shall have destruction.

4 The soul of a sluggard desires,
   and *has* nothing;
   But the soul of the diligent
   shall be made rich.

5 A righteous *man* hates lying,
   But a wicked *man* is loathsome
   and comes to shame.

6 Righteousness keeps *him whose* way is
   blameless,
   But wickedness overthrows the sinner.

7 There is one who makes himself rich,
   yet *has* nothing;
   And one who makes himself poor,
   yet *has* great riches.

8 The ransom of a man's life *is* his
   riches,
   But the poor does not hear rebuke.

9 The light of the righteous rejoices,
   But the lamp of the wicked will be
   put out.

10 By pride comes only contention,
   But with the well-advised *is* wisdom.

11 Wealth *gained by* dishonesty
   will be diminished,
   But he who gathers by labor
   will increase.

12 Hope deferred makes the heart sick,

But *when* the desire comes,
   it is a tree of life.

13 He who despises the word
   will be destroyed,
   But he who fears the commandment
   will be rewarded.

14 The law of the wise *is* a fountain
   of life,
   To turn *one* away from the snares
   of death.

15 Good understanding gains favor,
   But the way of the unfaithful *is* hard.

16 Every prudent *man* acts with
   knowledge,
   But a fool lays open *his* folly.

17 A wicked messenger falls into trouble,
   But a faithful ambassador *brings*
   health.

18 Poverty and shame *will come* to him
   who disdains correction,
   But he who regards reproof will be
   honored.

19 A desire accomplished is sweet
   to the soul,
   But *it is* an abomination to fools to
   depart from evil.

20 He who walks with wise *men*
   will be wise,
   But the companion of fools
   will be destroyed.

21 Evil pursues sinners,
   But to the righteous,
   good shall be repaid.

22 A good *man* leaves an inheritance to
   his children's children,
   But the wealth of the sinner is stored
   up for the righteous.

23 Much food *is in* the fallow *ground* of
   the poor,
   And for lack of justice there is waste.[18]

24 He who spares his rod hates his son,
   But he who loves him disciplines him
   promptly.

25 The righteous eats to the satisfying of
   his soul,
   But the stomach of the wicked shall be
   in want.

14 Every wise woman builds her
   house,

18 Literally *what is swept away*

But the foolish pulls it down with her
hands.

2 He who walks in his uprightness
     fears the LORD,
   But *he who is* perverse in his ways
     despises Him.

3 In the mouth of a fool *is* a rod of
     pride,
   But the lips of the wise will preserve
     them.

4 Where no oxen *are*, the trough *is* clean;
   But much increase *comes* by the
     strength of an ox.

5 A faithful witness does not lie,
   But a false witness will utter lies.

6 A scoffer seeks wisdom
     and does not *find it*,
   But knowledge
     is easy to him who understands.

7 Go from the presence of a foolish man,
   When you do not perceive *in him* the
     lips of knowledge.

8 The wisdom of the prudent
     is to understand his way,
   But the folly of fools *is* deceit.

9 Fools mock at sin,
   But among the upright *there is* favor.

10 The heart knows its own bitterness,
    And a stranger does not share its joy.

11 The house of the wicked will be
      overthrown,
    But the tent of the upright will flourish.

12 There is a way which seems right to a
      man,
    But its end *is* the way of death.

13 Even in laughter the heart may sorrow,
    And the end of mirth *may be* grief.

14 The backslider in heart will be filled
      with his own ways,
    But a good man *will be satisfied* from
      above.[19]

15 The simple believes every word,
    But the prudent *man* considers well his
      steps.

16 A wise *man* fears
      and departs from evil,
    But a fool rages and is self-confident.

17 *He who is* quick-tempered
      acts foolishly,
    And a man of wicked intentions
      is hated.

18 The simple inherit folly,
    But the prudent are crowned with
      knowledge.

19 The evil will bow before the good,
    And the wicked at the gates of the
      righteous.

20 The poor *man* is hated
      even by his own neighbor,
    But the rich *has* many friends.

21 He who despises his neighbor sins;
    But he who has mercy on the poor,
      happy *is* he.

22 Do they not go astray who devise evil?
    But mercy and truth *belong* to those
      who devise good.

23 In all labor there is profit,
    But idle chatter[20] *leads* only to poverty.

24 The crown of the wise is their riches,
    But the foolishness of fools *is* folly.

25 A true witness delivers souls,
    But a deceitful *witness* speaks lies.

26 In the fear of the LORD
      there is strong confidence,
    And His children will have a place of
      refuge.

27 The fear of the LORD
      is a fountain of life,
    To avoid the snares of death.

28 In a multitude of people
      is a king's honor,
    But in the lack of people
      is the downfall of a prince.

29 *He who is* slow to wrath
      has great understanding,
    But *he who is* impulsive[21] exalts folly.

30 A sound heart *is* life to the body,
    But envy *is* rottenness to the bones.

31 He who oppresses the poor
      reproaches his Maker,
    But he who honors Him
      has mercy on the needy.

32 The wicked is banished
      in his wickedness,
    But the righteous has a refuge
      in his death.

19 Literally *from above himself*   20 Literally *talk of the lips*   21 Literally *short of spirit*

33 Wisdom rests *quietly* in the heart of
    him who has understanding,
But *what is* in the heart of fools is
    made known.

34 Righteousness exalts a nation,
But sin *is* a reproach to *any* people.

35 The king's favor *is* toward a wise
    servant,
But his wrath *is against* him who
    causes shame.

15 A soft answer turns away wrath,
    But a harsh word stirs up anger.
2 The tongue of the wise uses knowledge
    rightly,
But the mouth of fools pours forth
    foolishness.

3 The eyes of the LORD *are* in every
    place,
Keeping watch on the evil and the
    good.

4 A wholesome tongue *is* a tree of life,
But perverseness in it breaks the spirit.

5 A fool despises his father's instruction,
But he who receives reproof is prudent.

6 *In* the house of the righteous
    there is much treasure,
But in the revenue of the wicked
    is trouble.

7 The lips of the wise disperse
    knowledge,
But the heart of the fool *does* not
    do so.

8 The sacrifice of the wicked
    is an abomination to the LORD,
But the prayer of the upright
    is His delight.

9 The way of the wicked
    is an abomination to the LORD,
But He loves him
    who follows righteousness.

10 Harsh correction *is* for him who
    forsakes the way,
And he who hates reproof will die.

11 Hell[22] and Destruction[23] *are* before the
    LORD;
So how much more the hearts of the
    sons of men.

12 A scoffer does not love one who
    reproves him,
Nor will he go to the wise.

13 A merry heart
    makes a cheerful countenance,
But by sorrow of the heart
    the spirit is broken.

14 The heart of him who has
    understanding seeks knowledge,
But the mouth of fools feeds on
    foolishness.

15 All the days of the afflicted *are* evil,
But he who is of a merry heart *has* a
    continual feast.

16 Better *is* a little with the fear of the
    LORD,
Than great treasure with trouble.

17 Better *is* a dinner of herbs[24]
    where love is,
Than a fatted calf with hatred.

18 A wrathful man stirs up strife,
But *he who is* slow to anger allays
    contention.

19 The way of the slothful *man*
    is like a hedge of thorns,
But the way of the upright
    is a highway.

20 A wise son makes a father glad,
But a foolish man despises his mother.

21 Folly *is* joy *to him who is* destitute of
    discernment,
But a man of understanding walks
    uprightly.

22 Without counsel, plans go awry,
But in the multitude of counselors
    they are established.

23 A man has joy by the answer of his
    mouth,
And a word *spoken* in due season,
    how good *it is!*

24 The way of life *winds* upward for the
    wise,
That he may turn away from hell[25]
    below.

25 The LORD will destroy the house of the
    proud,
But He will establish the boundary of
    the widow.

26 The thoughts of the wicked
    are an abomination to the LORD,
But *the words* of the pure *are* pleasant.

22 Hebrew *sheol*   23 Hebrew *Abaddon*   24 Or *vegetables*   25 Hebrew *Sheol*

27 He who is greedy for gain troubles his
    own house,
    But he who hates bribes will live.

28 The heart of the righteous
    studies how to answer,
    But the mouth of the wicked
    pours forth evil.

29 The LORD *is* far from the wicked,
    But He hears the prayer of the
    righteous.

30 The light of the eyes rejoices the heart,
    And a good report makes the bones
    healthy.[26]

31 The ear that hears the reproof of life
    Will abide among the wise.

32 He who disdains instruction
    despises his own soul,
    But he who heeds reproof
    gets understanding.

33 The fear of the LORD *is* the instruction
    of wisdom,
    And before honor *is* humility.

16 The preparations of the heart
    belong to man,
    But the answer of the tongue *is* from
    the LORD.

2   All the ways of a man *are* pure in his
    own eyes,
    But the LORD weighs the spirits.

3   Commit your works to the LORD,
    And your thoughts will be established.

4   The LORD has made all *things* for
    Himself,
    Yes, even the wicked for the day of
    doom.

5   Everyone *who is* proud in heart *is* an
    abomination to the LORD;
    Though they join forces,[27]
    none will go unpunished.

6   In mercy and truth
    Atonement is provided for iniquity;
    And by the fear of the LORD
    one departs from evil.

7   When a man's ways please the LORD,
    He makes even his enemies to be at
    peace with him.

8   Better *is* a little with righteousness,
    Than vast revenues without justice.

9   A man's heart plans his way,
    But the LORD directs his steps.

10 *Even though* divination *is* on the lips
    of the king,
    His mouth must not transgress in
    judgment.

11 A just weight and balance
    are the LORD'S;
    All the weights in the bag
    are His work.

12 *It is* an abomination for kings to
    commit wickedness,
    For a throne is established by
    righteousness.

13 Righteous lips *are* the delight of kings,
    And they love him who speaks *what is*
    right.

14 As messengers of death *is* the king's
    wrath,
    But a wise man will appease it.

15 In the light of the king's face *is* life,
    And his favor *is* like a cloud of the
    latter rain.

16 How much better *it is* to get wisdom
    than gold!
    And to get understanding is to be
    chosen rather than silver.

17 The highway of the upright *is* to depart
    from evil;
    He who keeps his way preserves his
    soul.

18 Pride *goes* before destruction,
    And a haughty spirit before a fall.

19 Better *to be* of a humble spirit
    with the lowly,
    Than to divide the spoil
    with the proud.

20 He who heeds the word wisely
    will find good,
    And whoever trusts in the LORD,
    happy *is* he.

21 The wise in heart will be called
    prudent,
    And sweetness of the lips increases
    learning.

22 Understanding *is* a wellspring of life
    to him who has it.
    But the correction of fools *is* folly.

23 The heart of the wise teaches his
    mouth,
    And adds learning to his lips.

26 Literally *fat*   27 Literally *hand in hand*

24 Pleasant words *are like* a honeycomb,
   Sweetness to the soul
   and health to the bones.

25 There is a way *that seems* right to a
   man,
   But its end *is* the way of death.

26 The person who labors,
   labors for himself,
   For his *hungry* mouth drives him *on.*

27 An ungodly man digs up evil,
   And *it is* on his lips like a burning fire.
28 A perverse man sows strife,
   And a whisperer separates the best of
   friends.
29 A violent man entices his neighbor,
   And leads him in a way *that is* not
   good.
30 He winks his eye to devise perverse
   things;
   He purses his lips
   and brings about evil.

31 The silver-haired head *is* a crown of
   glory,
   If it is found in the way of
   righteousness.

32 *He who is* slow to anger *is* better than
   the mighty,
   And he who rules his spirit than he
   who takes a city.

33 The lot is cast into the lap,
   But its every decision *is* from the
   LORD.

17 Better *is* a dry morsel
       with quietness,
Than a house full of feasting[28]
with strife.

2 A wise servant will rule over a son who
   causes shame,
   And will share an inheritance among
   the brothers.

3 The refining pot *is* for silver
   and the furnace for gold,
   But the LORD tests the hearts.

4 An evildoer gives heed to false lips;
   A liar listens eagerly to a spiteful
   tongue.

5 He who mocks the poor
   reproaches his Maker;

He who is glad at calamity
   will not go unpunished.

6 Children's children *are* the crown of
   old men,
   And the glory of children *is* their
   father.

7 Excellent speech is not becoming
   to a fool,
   Much less lying lips to a prince.

8 A present *is* a precious stone in the
   eyes of its possessor;
   Wherever he turns, he prospers.

9 He who covers a transgression
   seeks love,
   But he who repeats a matter
   separates *the best of* friends.

10 Reproof is more effective for a wise
   man
   Than a hundred blows on a fool.

11 An evil *man* seeks only rebellion;
   Therefore a cruel messenger will be
   sent against him.

12 Let a man meet a bear robbed of her
   cubs,
   Rather than a fool in his folly.

13 Whoever rewards evil for good,
   Evil will not depart from his house.

14 The beginning of strife *is like* releasing
   water;
   Therefore stop contention before a
   quarrel starts.

15 He who justifies the wicked,
   and he who condemns the just,
   Both of them alike *are* an abomination
   to the LORD.

16 Why *is there* in the hand of a fool the
   purchase price of wisdom,
   Since *he has* no heart *for it?*

17 A friend loves at all times,
   And a brother is born for adversity.

18 A man devoid of understanding shakes
   hands in a pledge,
   And becomes surety for his friend.

19 He who loves transgression loves strife,
   And he who exalts his gate seeks
   destruction.

28 Or *sacrificial meals*

20 He who has a deceitful heart
    finds no good,
  And he who has a perverse tongue
    falls into evil.

21 He who begets a scoffer *does so* to his
    sorrow,
  And the father of a fool has no joy.

22 A merry heart does good,
  like medicine,[29]
  But a broken spirit dries the bones.

23 A wicked *man* accepts a bribe behind
    the back[30]
  To pervert the ways of justice.

24 Wisdom *is* in the sight of him who has
    understanding,
  But the eyes of a fool *are* on the ends
    of the earth.

25 A foolish son *is* a grief to his father,
  And bitterness to her who bore him.

26 Also, to punish the righteous *is* not
    good,
  Nor to strike princes for *their*
    uprightness.

27 He who has knowledge
    spares his words,
  And a man of understanding
    is of a calm spirit.

28 Even a fool is counted wise
    when he holds his peace;
  When he shuts his lips,
    he is considered perceptive.

18 A man who isolates himself seeks
      his own desire;
  He rages against all wise judgment.

2 A fool has no delight in understanding,
  But in expressing his own heart.

3 When the wicked comes,
    contempt comes also;
  And with dishonor *comes* reproach.

4 The words of a man's mouth
    are deep waters;
  The wellspring of wisdom
    is a flowing brook.

5 *It is* not good to show partiality
    to the wicked,
  Or to overthrow the righteous in
    judgment.

6 A fool's lips enter into contention,
  And his mouth calls for blows.

7 A fool's mouth *is* his destruction,
  And his lips *are* the snare of his soul.

8 The words of a talebearer *are* like tasty
    trifles,[31]
  And they go down into the inmost
    body.

9 He who is slothful in his work
  Is a brother to him who is a great
    destroyer.

10 The name of the LORD
    is a strong tower;
  The righteous run to it and are safe.

11 The rich man's wealth
    is his strong city,
  And like a high wall in his own esteem.

12 Before destruction the heart of a man
    is haughty,
  And before honor *is* humility.

13 He who answers a matter before he
    hears *it*,
  It *is* folly and shame to him.

14 The spirit of a man will sustain him
    in sickness,
  But who can bear a broken spirit?

15 The heart of the prudent
    acquires knowledge,
  And the ear of the wise
    seeks knowledge.

16 A man's gift makes room for him,
  And brings him before great men.

17 The first *one* to plead his cause *seems*
    right,
  Until his neighbor comes and examines
    him.

18 Casting lots causes contentions to
    cease,
  And keeps the mighty apart.

19 A brother offended *is harder to win*
    than a strong city,
  And contentions *are* like the bars
    of a castle.

20 A man's stomach shall be satisfied
    from the fruit of his mouth,
  And from the produce of his lips
    he shall be filled.

29 Or *makes medicine even better*   30 Literally *from the bosom*   31 A Jewish tradition reads *wounds*.

21 Death and life *are* in the power of the
   tongue,
   And those who love it will eat its fruit.

22 *He who* finds a wife finds a good *thing*,
   And obtains favor from the LORD.

23 The poor *man* uses entreaties,
   But the rich answers roughly.

24 A man *who has* friends must himself be
   friendly,[32]
   But there is a friend *who* sticks closer
   than a brother.

19 Better *is* the poor
      who walks in his integrity
   Than *one who is* perverse in his lips,
   and is a fool.

2 Also it is not good *for* a soul *to be*
   without knowledge,
   And he sins who hastens with *his* feet.

3 The foolishness of a man twists his
   way,
   And his heart frets against the LORD.

4 Wealth makes many friends,
   But the poor is separated from his
   friend.

5 A false witness will not go unpunished,
   And *he who* speaks lies will not escape.

6 Many entreat the favor of the nobility,
   And every man *is* a friend to one who
   gives gifts.

7 All the brothers of the poor hate him;
   How much more do his friends go far
   from him!
   He may pursue *them with* words,
   yet they abandon *him*.

8 He who gets wisdom
   loves his own soul;
   He who keeps understanding
   will find good.

9 A false witness will not go unpunished,
   And *he who* speaks lies shall perish.

10 Luxury is not fitting for a fool,
   Much less for a servant to rule over
   princes.

11 The discretion of a man makes him
   slow to anger,

And *it is to* his glory to overlook a
transgression.

12 The king's wrath *is* like the roaring
   of a lion,
   But his favor *is* like dew on the grass.

13 A foolish son *is* the ruin of his father,
   And the contentions of a wife *are* a
   continual dripping.

14 Houses and riches *are* an inheritance
   from fathers,
   But a prudent wife *is* from the LORD.

15 Slothfulness casts *one* into a deep sleep,
   And an idle person will suffer hunger.

16 He who keeps the commandment keeps
   his soul,
   But he who is careless[33] of his ways will
   die.

17 He who has pity on the poor lends to
   the LORD,
   And He will pay back what he has
   given.

18 Chasten your son while there is hope,
   And do not set your heart on his
   destruction.[34]

19 *A man of* great wrath will suffer
   punishment;
   For if you deliver *him*,
   you will have to do it again.

20 Listen to counsel
   and receive instruction,
   That you may be wise in your latter
   days.

21 There are many plans in a man's heart,
   Nevertheless the LORD's counsel—
   that will stand.

22 What is desired in a man is kindness,
   And a poor man is better than a liar.

23 The fear of the LORD *leads* to life,
   And *he who has it* will abide in
   satisfaction;
   He will not be visited with evil.

24 A slothful *man* buries his hand in the
   bowl,[35]

32 Or *may come to ruin*   33 Literally *despises*, figurative of recklessness or carelessness
34 Literally *to put him to death;* a Jewish tradition reads *his crying.*
35 Septuagint and Syriac read *bosom;* Targum and Vulgate read *armpit.*

And will not so much as bring it to his
mouth again.

25 Strike a scoffer,
and the simple will become wary;
Reprove one who has understanding,
and he will discern knowledge.

26 He who mistreats *his* father
and chases away *his* mother
Is a son who causes shame
and brings reproach.

27 Cease listening to instruction, my son,
And you will stray from the words of
knowledge.

28 A disreputable witness scorns justice,
And the mouth of the wicked devours
iniquity.

29 Judgments are prepared for scoffers,
And beatings for the backs of fools.

20 Wine is a mocker,
Intoxicating drink arouses
brawling,
And whoever is led astray by it is not
wise.

2 The wrath[36] of a king *is* like the roaring
of a lion;
Whoever provokes him to anger sins
against his own life.

3 *It is* honorable for a man to stop
striving,
Since any fool can start a quarrel.

4 The sluggard will not plow because of
winter;
Therefore he will beg during the harvest
And *have* nothing.

5 Counsel in the heart of man *is like*
deep water,
But a man of understanding will draw
it out.

6 Most men will proclaim each his own
goodness,
But who can find a faithful man?

7 The righteous *man* walks in his
integrity;
His children *are* blessed after him.

8 A king who sits on the throne of
judgment
Scatters all evil with his eyes.

9 Who can say,
"I have made my heart clean,
I am pure from my sin"?

10 Diverse weights *and* diverse measures,
They *are* both alike,
an abomination to the LORD.

11 Even a child is known by his deeds,
By whether what he does *is* pure and
right.

12 The hearing ear and the seeing eye,
The LORD has made both of them.

13 Do not love sleep,
lest you come to poverty;
Open your eyes, *and* you will be
satisfied with bread.

14 "*It is* good for nothing,"[37]
cries the buyer;
But when he has gone his way,
then he boasts.

15 There is gold and a multitude of
rubies,
But the lips of knowledge *are* a
precious jewel.

16 Take the garment of one who is surety
for a stranger,
And hold it as a pledge *when it* is for a
seductress.

17 Bread gained by deceit *is* sweet to a
man,
But afterward his mouth will be filled
with gravel.

18 *Every* purpose is established by
counsel;
By wise counsel wage war.

19 He who goes about *as* a talebearer
reveals secrets;
Therefore do not associate with one
who flatters with his lips.

20 Whoever curses his father or his
mother,
His lamp will be put out in deep
darkness.

21 An inheritance gained hastily at the
beginning
Will not be blessed at the end.

22 Do not say, "I will recompense evil";
Wait for the LORD,
and He will save you.

36 Literally *fear* or *terror* which is produced by the king's wrath   37 Literally *evil, evil*

23 Diverse weights *are* an abomination
    to the LORD,
    And a false balance *is* not good.

24 A man's steps *are* of the LORD;
    How then can a man understand his
    own way?

25 *It is* a snare for a man to devote rashly
    something as holy,
    And afterward to reconsider *his* vows.

26 A wise king sifts out the wicked,
    And brings the threshing wheel over
    them.

27 The spirit of a man *is* the lamp
    of the LORD,
    Searching all the inner depths of
    his heart.[38]

28 Mercy and truth preserve the king,
    And by lovingkindness he upholds his
    throne.

29 The glory of young men
    is their strength,
    And the splendor of old men
    is their gray head.

30 Blows that hurt cleanse away evil,
    As *do* stripes the inner depths of the
    heart.[39]

21 The king's heart *is* in the hand of
    the LORD,
    Like the rivers of water;
    He turns it wherever He wishes.

2 Every way of a man *is* right
    in his own eyes,
    But the LORD weighs the hearts.

3 To do righteousness and justice
    Is more acceptable to the LORD than
    sacrifice.

4 A haughty look, a proud heart,
    And the plowing[40] of the wicked *are*
    sin.

5 The plans of the diligent *lead* surely to
    plenty,
    But *those of* everyone *who is* hasty,
    surely to poverty.

6 Getting treasures by a lying tongue
    Is the fleeting fantasy of those who
    seek death.

7 The violence of the wicked will destroy
    them,[41]
    Because they refuse to do justice.

8 The way of a guilty man *is* perverse;[42]
    But *as for* the pure, his work *is* right.

9 *It is* better to dwell in a corner of a
    housetop,
    Than in a house shared with a
    contentious woman.

10 The soul of the wicked desires evil;
    His neighbor finds no favor in his eyes.

11 When the scoffer is punished,
    the simple is made wise;
    But when the wise is instructed,
    he receives knowledge.

12 The righteous *God* wisely considers the
    house of the wicked,
    Overthrowing the wicked for *their*
    wickedness.

13 Whoever shuts his ears to the cry of
    the poor
    Will also cry himself and not be heard.

14 A gift in secret pacifies anger,
    And a bribe behind the back,[43]
    strong wrath.

15 *It is* a joy for the just to do justice,
    But destruction *will come* to the
    workers of iniquity.

16 A man who wanders from the way of
    understanding
    Will rest in the congregation of the
    dead.

17 He who loves pleasure
    will be a poor man;
    He who loves wine and oil
    will not be rich.

18 The wicked *shall be* a ransom for the
    righteous,
    And the unfaithful for the upright.

19 *It is* better to dwell in the wilderness,
    Than with a contentious and angry
    woman.

20 *There is* desirable treasure,
    And oil in the dwelling of the wise,
    But a foolish man squanders it.

---

38 Literally *the rooms of the belly*   39 Literally *the rooms of the belly*   40 Or *lamp*
41 Literally *drag them away*   42 Or *the way of a man is perverse and strange*   43 Literally *in the bosom*

21 He who follows righteousness
and mercy
Finds life, righteousness and honor.

22 A wise *man* scales the city of the
mighty,
And brings down the trusted
stronghold.

23 Whoever guards his mouth and tongue
Keeps his soul from troubles.

24 A proud *and* haughty *man*—
"Scoffer" *is* his name;
He acts with arrogant pride.

25 The desire of the slothful kills him,
For his hands refuse to labor.

26 He covets greedily all day long,
But the righteous gives
and does not spare.

27 The sacrifice of the wicked *is* an
abomination;
How much more *when* he brings it with
wicked intent!

28 A false witness shall perish,
But the man who hears *him* will speak
endlessly.

29 A wicked man hardens his face,
But *as for* the upright,
he establishes[44] his way.

30 *There is* no wisdom or understanding
Or counsel against the LORD.

31 The horse *is* prepared for the day of
battle,
But deliverance *is* of the LORD.

22 A *good* name is to be chosen rather
than great riches,
Loving favor rather than silver and
gold.

2 The rich and the poor have this in
common,
The LORD *is* the maker of them all.

3 A prudent *man* foresees evil
and hides himself,
But the simple pass on
and are punished.

4 By humility *and* the fear of the LORD
Are riches and honor and life.

5 Thorns *and* snares *are* in the way of
the perverse;

He who guards his soul will be far
from them.

6 Train up a child
in the way he should go,
And when he is old
he will not depart from it.

7 The rich rules over the poor,
And the borrower *is* servant to the
lender.

8 He who sows iniquity will reap sorrow,
And the rod of his anger will fail.

9 He who has a bountiful eye will be
blessed,
For he gives of his bread to the poor.

10 Cast out the scoffer,
and contention will leave;
Yes, strife and reproach will cease.

11 He who loves purity of heart
And has grace on his lips,
The king *will be* his friend.

12 The eyes of the LORD preserve
knowledge,
But He overthrows the words of the
faithless.

13 The slothful *man* says,
"*There is* a lion outside!
I shall be slain in the streets!"

14 The mouth of an immoral woman *is* a
deep pit;
He who is abhorred of the LORD will
fall there.

15 Foolishness *is* bound up in the heart of
a child,
But the rod of correction will drive it
far from him.

16 He who oppresses the poor to increase
his *riches*,
And he who gives to the rich,
will surely *come* to poverty.

Sayings of the Wise

17 Incline your ear
and hear the words of the wise,
And apply your heart to my
knowledge;

18 For *it is* a pleasant thing if you keep
them within you;
Let them all be fixed upon your lips,

44 Qere and Septuagint read *understands.*

19 So that your trust may be in the LORD;
   I have instructed you today, even you.
20 Have I not written to you excellent
      things
   Of counsels and knowledge,
21 That I may make you know
      the certainty of the words of truth,
   That you may answer words of truth
   To those who send to you?

22 Do not rob the poor because he *is*
      poor,
   Nor oppress the afflicted at the gate;
23 For the LORD will plead their cause,
   And plunder the soul of those who
      plunder them.

24 Make no friendship with an angry
      man,
   And with a furious man do not go,
25 Lest you learn his ways
   And set a snare for your soul.

26 Do not be one of those
      who shakes hands in a pledge,
   One of those
      who is surety for debts;
27 If you have nothing *with which* to pay,
   Why should he take away your bed
      from under you?

28 Do not remove the ancient landmark
   Which your fathers have set.

29 Do you see a man *who* excels in his
      work?
   He will stand before kings;
   He will not stand before unknown *men.*

23 When you sit down to eat with a
   ruler,
   Consider carefully what *is* before you;
2 And put a knife to your throat
   If you *are* a man given to appetite.
3 Do not desire his delicacies,
   For they *are* deceptive food.

4 Do not overwork to be rich;
   Because of your own understanding,
      cease!
5 Will you set your eyes on that
      which is not?
   For *riches* certainly make themselves
      wings;
   They fly away like an eagle *toward*
      heaven.

6 Do not eat the bread of a miser,[45]
   Nor desire his delicacies;
7 For as he thinks in his heart, so *is* he.

"Eat and drink!" he says to you,
   But his heart is not with you.
8 The morsel you have eaten,
      you will vomit up,
   And waste your pleasant words.

9 Do not speak in the hearing of a fool,
   For he will despise the wisdom of your
      words.

10 Do not remove the ancient landmark,
   Nor enter the fields of the fatherless;
11 For their Redeemer *is* mighty;
   He will plead their cause against you.

12 Apply your heart to instruction,
   And your ears to words of knowledge.

13 Do not withhold correction from a
      child,
   For *if* you beat him with a rod,
      he will not die.
14 You shall beat him with a rod,
   And deliver his soul from hell.[46]

15 My son, if your heart is wise,
   My heart will rejoice—indeed, I
      myself;
16 Yes, my inmost being will rejoice
   When your lips speak right things.

17 Do not let your heart envy sinners,
   But in the fear of the LORD
      continue all day *long*;
18 For surely there is a hereafter,
   And your hope will not be cut off.

19 Hear, my son, and be wise;
   And guide your heart in the way.
20 Do not mix with winebibbers,
   Or with gluttonous eaters of meat;
21 For the drunkard and the glutton
      will come to poverty,
   And drowsiness will clothe *a man* with
      rags.

22 Listen to your father who begot you,
   And do not despise your mother when
      she is old.

23 Buy the truth, and do not sell *it,*
   Also wisdom and instruction
      and understanding.

24 The father of the righteous
      will greatly rejoice,
   And he who begets a wise *child*
      will delight in him.
25 Let your father and your mother be
      glad,
   And let her who bore you rejoice.

45 Literally *one who has an evil eye*   46 Hebrew *sheol*

26 My son, give me your heart,
   And let your eyes observe my ways.
27 For a harlot *is* a deep pit,
   And a seductress *is* a narrow well.
28 She also lies in wait as *for* a victim,
   And increases the unfaithful among
      men.

29 Who has woe?
   Who has sorrow?
   Who has contentions?
   Who has complaints?
   Who has wounds without cause?
   Who has redness of eyes?
30 Those who linger long at the wine,
   Those who go in search of mixed wine.
31 Do not look on the wine when it is red,
   When it sparkles in the cup,
   When it swirls around smoothly;
32 At the last it bites like a serpent,
   And stings like a viper.
33 Your eyes will see strange things,
   And your heart will utter perverse
      things.
34 Yes, you will be like one who lies
      down in the midst of the sea,
   Or like one who lies at the top of the
      mast, *saying:*
35 "They have struck me,
      but I was not hurt;
   They have beaten me,
      but I did not feel *it.*
   When shall I awake,
      that I may seek another *drink?*"

24 Do not be envious of evil men,
   Nor desire to be with them;
2 For their heart devises violence,
   And their lips talk of troublemaking.

3 Through wisdom a house is built,
   And by understanding it is established;
4 By knowledge the rooms are filled
   With all precious and pleasant riches.

5 A wise man *is* strong,
   Yes, a man of knowledge increases
      strength;
6 For by wise counsel
      you will wage your own war,
   And in a multitude of counselors
      there is safety.

7 Wisdom *is* too lofty for a fool;
   He does not open his mouth in the
      gate.

8 He who plots to do evil
   Will be called a schemer.
9 The devising of foolishness *is* sin,

And the scoffer *is* an abomination to
   men.

10 *If* you faint in the day of adversity,
   Your strength *is* small.

11 Deliver *those who* are drawn toward
      death,
   And hold back *those* stumbling to the
      slaughter.
12 If you say,
      "Surely we did not know this,"
   Does not He who weighs the hearts
      consider *it?*
   He who keeps your soul,
      does He *not* know *it?*
   And will He *not* render to *each* man
      according to his deeds?

13 My son, eat honey because *it is* good,
   And the honeycomb *which is* sweet to
      your taste;
14 So *shall* the knowledge of wisdom
      be to your soul;
   If you have found *it,*
      there is a prospect,
   And your hope will not be cut off.

15 Do not lie in wait, O wicked *man,*
      against the dwelling of the righteous;
   Do not plunder his resting place;
16 For a righteous *man* may fall seven
      times
   And rise again,
   But the wicked shall fall by calamity.

17 Do not rejoice when your enemy falls,
   And do not let your heart be glad
      when he stumbles;
18 Lest the LORD see *it,*
      and it displease Him,
   And He turn away His wrath from
      him.

19 Do not fret because of evil *doers,*
   Nor be envious of the wicked;
20 For there will be no prospect
      for the evil *man;*
   The lamp of the wicked
      will be put out.

21 My son, fear the LORD and the king;
   Do not associate with those given to
      change;
22 For their calamity will rise suddenly,
   And who knows the ruin those two can
      bring?

Further Sayings of the Wise
23 These *things* also *belong* to the wise:

It is not good to show partiality in
judgment.
24 He who says to the wicked,
"You *are* righteous,"
Him the people will curse;
Nations will abhor him.
25 But those who rebuke *the wicked*
will have delight,
And a good blessing will come upon
them.

26 He who gives a right answer
kisses the lips.

27 Prepare your outside work,
Make it fit for yourself in the field;
And afterward build your house.

28 Do not be a witness against your
neighbor without cause,
For would you deceive[47] with your
lips?
29 Do not say, "I will do to him
just as he has done to me;
I will render to the man
according to his work."

30 I went by the field of the slothful,
And by the vineyard of the man devoid
of understanding;
31 And there it was,
all overgrown with thorns;
Its surface was covered with nettles;
Its stone wall was broken down.
32 When I saw *it*, I considered *it* well;
I looked on *it and* received instruction:
33 A little sleep, a little slumber,
A little folding of the hands to rest;
34 So your poverty will come *like* a
prowler,
And your want like an armed man.

Further Wise Sayings of Solomon

25 These also *are* proverbs of Solomon which the men of Hezekiah
king of Judah copied:

2 *It is* the glory of God
to conceal a matter,
But the glory of kings
is to search out a matter.

3 *As* the heavens for height
and the earth for depth,
So the heart of kings *is* unsearchable.

4 Take away the dross from silver,
And it will go to the silversmith *for*
jewelry.

5 Take away the wicked from before the
king,
And his throne will be established in
righteousness.

6 Do not exalt yourself in the presence
of the king,
And do not stand in the place of great
men;
7 For *it is* better that he say to you,
"Come up here,"
Than that you should be put lower in
the presence of the prince,
Whom your eyes have seen.

8 Do not go hastily to court;
For what will you do in the end,
When your neighbor has put you to
shame?
9 Debate your case with your neighbor
himself,
And do not disclose the secret to
another;
10 Lest he who hears *it* expose your
shame,
And your reputation be ruined.

11 A word fitly spoken
is like apples of gold
In settings of silver.
12 *Like* an earring of gold
and an ornament of fine gold
Is a wise reprover to an obedient ear.

13 Like the cold of snow in time of
harvest
Is a faithful messenger to those who
send him,
For he refreshes the soul of his
masters.

14 Whoever falsely boasts of giving
Is like clouds and wind without rain.

15 By long forbearance a ruler is
persuaded,
And a gentle tongue breaks a bone.

16 Have you found honey?
Eat only as much as you need,
Lest you be filled with it and vomit.

17 Seldom set foot in your neighbor's
house,
Lest he become weary of you
and hate you.

18 A man who bears false witness against
his neighbor
Is like a club, a sword,
and a sharp arrow.

47 Septuagint and Vulgate read *do not deceive.*

19 Confidence in an unfaithful man in
 time of trouble
 Is like a bad tooth
 and a foot out of joint.

20 *Like* one who takes away a garment
 in cold weather,
 And like vinegar on soda,
 Is one who sings songs to a heavy
 heart.

21 If your enemy is hungry,
 give him bread to eat;
 And if he is thirsty,
 give him water to drink;
22 For *so* you will heap coals of fire
 on his head,
 And the LORD will reward you.

23 The north wind brings forth rain,
 And a backbiting tongue an angry
 countenance.

24 *It is* better to dwell in a corner of a
 housetop,
 Than in a house shared with a
 contentious woman.

25 *As* cold water to a weary soul,
 So *is* good news from a far country.

26 A righteous man who falters before the
 wicked
 Is like a murky spring
 and a polluted well.

27 *It is* not good to eat much honey;
 So to seek one's own glory *is not* glory.

28 Whoever *has* no rule over his own
 spirit
 Is like a city broken down,
 without walls.

26 As snow in summer
 and rain in harvest,
 So honor is not fitting for a fool.

2 Like a flitting sparrow,
 like a flying swallow,
 So a curse without cause shall not
 alight.

3 A whip for the horse,
 A bridle for the donkey,
 And a rod for the fool's back.
4 Do not answer a fool according to his
 folly,
 Lest you also be like him.

5 Answer a fool according to his folly,
 Lest he be wise in his own eyes.
6 He who sends a message by the hand
 of a fool
 Cuts off *his own* feet
 and drinks violence.
7 *Like* the legs of the lame that hang
 limp
 Is a proverb in the mouth of fools.
8 Like one who binds a stone in a sling
 Is he who gives honor to a fool.
9 *Like* a thorn *that* goes into the hand
 of a drunkard
 Is a proverb in the mouth of fools.
10 The great *God* who formed all *things*
 Gives the fool *his* hire
 and the transgressor *his* wages.[48]
11 As a dog returns to his own vomit,
 So a fool repeats his folly.
12 Do you see a man wise in his own
 eyes?
 There is more hope for a fool
 than for him.

13 The slothful *man* says,
 "*There is* a lion in the road!
 A fierce lion *is* in the streets!"
14 *As* a door turns on its hinges,
 So *does* the slothful *turn* on his bed.
15 The slothful *man* buries his hand
 in the bowl;[49]
 It wearies him to bring it back to his
 mouth.
16 The sluggard *is* wiser in his own eyes
 Than seven men who can answer
 sensibly.

17 He who passes by *and* meddles in a
 quarrel not his own
 Is like one who takes a dog by the
 ears.

18 Like a madman who throws firebrands,
 arrows, and death,
19 *Is* the man *who* deceives his neighbor,
 And says, "I was only joking!"

20 Where *there is* no wood,
 the fire goes out;
 And where *there is* no talebearer,
 strife ceases.
21 *As* charcoal *is* to burning coals,
 and wood to fire,
 So *is* a contentious man
 to kindle strife.
22 The words of a talebearer *are* like tasty
 trifles,
 And they go down into the inmost
 body.

48 The Hebrew is difficult; ancient and modern translators differ greatly.   49 Compare 19:24

23 Fervent lips with a wicked heart
   Are like earthenware covered with
   silver dross.

24 He who hates, disguises *it* with his lips,
   And lays up deceit within himself;
25 When he speaks kindly,
   do not believe him,
   For *there are* seven abominations in his
   heart;
26 *Though his* hatred is covered by deceit,
   His wickedness will be revealed before
   the *whole* congregation.

27 Whoever digs a pit will fall into it,
   And he who rolls a stone
   will have it roll back on him

28 A lying tongue hates *those who are*
   crushed by it,
   And a flattering mouth works ruin.

27 Do not boast about tomorrow,
   For you do not know what a day
   may bring forth.

2 Let another man praise you,
   and not your own mouth;
   A stranger, and not your own lips.

3 A stone *is* heavy and sand *is* weighty,
   But a fool's wrath *is* heavier than both
   of them.

4 Wrath *is* cruel and anger a torrent,
   But who *is* able to stand before
   jealousy?

5 Open rebuke *is* better
   Than love carefully concealed.

6 Faithful *are* the wounds of a friend,
   But the kisses of an enemy *are*
   deceitful.

7 A satisfied soul loathes the honeycomb,
   But to a hungry soul every bitter thing
   is sweet.

8 Like a bird that wanders from its nest
   Is a man who wanders from his place.

9 Ointment and perfume
   delight the heart,
   And the sweetness of a man's friend
   does so by hearty counsel.

10 Do not forsake your own friend
   or your father's friend,
   Nor go to your brother's house in the
   day of your calamity;
   For better *is* a neighbor nearby than a
   brother far away.

11 My son, be wise,
   and make my heart glad,
   That I may answer him who reproaches
   me.

12 A prudent *man* foresees evil
   and hides himself;
   The simple pass on *and* are punished.

13 Take the garment of him who is surety
   for a stranger,
   And hold it in pledge *when* he is surety
   for a seductress.

14 He who blesses his friend with a loud
   voice, rising early in the morning,
   It will be counted a curse to him.

15 A continual dripping on a very rainy
   day
   And a contentious woman are alike;
16 Whoever restrains her
   restrains the wind,
   And grasps oil with his right hand.

17 *As* iron sharpens iron,
   So a man sharpens the countenance of
   his friend.

18 Whoever keeps the fig tree
   will eat its fruit;
   So he who waits on his master
   will be honored.

19 As in water face *reveals* face,
   So a man's heart *reveals* the man.

20 Hell[50] and Destruction[51] are never full;
   So the eyes of man are never satisfied.

21 The refining pot *is* for silver
   and the furnace for gold,
   And a man *is valued* by what others
   say of him.

22 Though you grind a fool in a mortar
   with a pestle along with crushed
   grain,
   Yet his foolishness will not depart from
   him.

23 Be diligent to know the state of your
   flocks,
   And attend to your herds;
24 For riches *are* not forever,

---

50 Hebrew *Sheol*   51 Hebrew *Abaddon*

Nor does a crown *endure* to all
generations.
25 *When* the hay is removed,
and the tender grass shows itself,
And the herbs of the mountains are
gathered in,
26 The lambs *will provide* your clothing,
And the goats the price of a field;
27 *You shall have* enough goats' milk for
your food,
For the food of your household,
And the nourishment of your
maidservants.

28 The wicked flee when no one
pursues,
But the righteous are bold as a lion.

2 Because of the transgression of a land,
many *are* its princes;
But by a man of understanding
and knowledge
Right will be prolonged.

3 A poor man who oppresses the poor
Is like a driving rain which leaves no
food.

4 Those who forsake the law praise the
wicked,
But such as keep the law contend with
them.

5 Evil men do not understand justice,
But those who seek the LORD
understand all.

6 Better *is* the poor who walks
in his integrity
Than one perverse *in his* ways,
though he *be* rich.

7 Whoever keeps the law
is a discerning son,
But a companion of gluttons
shames his father.

8 One who increases his possessions by
usury and extortion
Gathers it for him who will pity the
poor.

9 One who turns away his ear from
hearing the law,
Even his prayer *shall be* an
abomination.

10 Whoever causes the upright to go
astray in an evil way,
He himself will fall into his own pit;

But the blameless will inherit good
things.

11 The rich man *is* wise in his own eyes,
But the poor who has understanding
searches him out.

12 When the righteous rejoice,
there is great glory;
But when the wicked arise,
men hide themselves.

13 He who covers his sins will not
prosper,
But whoever confesses and forsakes
them will have mercy.

14 Happy *is* the man
who is always reverent,
But he who hardens his heart
will fall into calamity.

15 *Like* a roaring lion and a charging bear
Is a wicked ruler over poor people.

16 A ruler who lacks understanding
is a great oppressor,
But he who hates covetousness
will prolong *his* days.

17 A man burdened with bloodshed
will flee into a pit;
Let no one help him.

18 Whoever walks blamelessly
will be saved,
But *he who is* perverse *in his* ways
will fall at once.

19 He who tills his land
will have plenty of bread,
But he who follows frivolity
will have poverty enough!

20 A faithful man
will abound with blessings,
But he who hastens to be rich
will not go unpunished.

21 To show partiality *is* not good,
Because for a piece of bread a man will
transgress.

22 A man with an evil eye hastens after
riches,
And does not consider that poverty
will come upon him.

23 He who rebukes a man will find more
favor afterward
Than he who flatters with the tongue.

24 Whoever robs his father or his mother,
And says, "*It is* no transgression,"
The same *is* companion to a destroyer.

25 He who is of a proud heart
stirs up strife,
But he who trusts in the LORD
will be prospered.

26 He who trusts in his own heart
is a fool,
But whoever walks wisely
will be delivered.

27 He who gives to the poor will not lack,
But he who hides his eyes will have
many curses.

28 When the wicked arise,
men hide themselves;
But when they perish,
the righteous increase.

29 He who is often reproved,
and hardens *his* neck,
Will suddenly be destroyed,
and that without remedy.

2 When the righteous are in authority,
the people rejoice;
But when a wicked *man* rules,
the people groan.

3 Whoever loves wisdom makes his
father rejoice,
But a companion of harlots wastes *his*
wealth.

4 The king establishes the land by
justice,
But he who receives bribes
overthrows it.

5 A man who flatters his neighbor
Spreads a net for his feet.

6 By transgression an evil man is snared,
But the righteous sings and rejoices.

7 The righteous considers the cause of
the poor,
But the wicked does not understand
such knowledge.

8 Scoffers ensnare a city,
But wise *men* turn away wrath.

9 *If* a wise man contends with a foolish
man,

Whether the fool[52] rages or laughs,
there is no peace.

10 The bloodthirsty hate the blameless,
But the just seek his well-being.[53]

11 A fool vents all his feelings,[54]
But a wise *man* holds them back.

12 If a ruler pays attention to lies,
All his servants *become* wicked.

13 The poor *man* and the oppressor
have this in common:
The LORD gives light to the eyes of
both.

14 The king who judges the poor with
truth,
His throne will be established forever.

15 The rod and reproof give wisdom,
But a child left *to himself* brings shame
to his mother.

16 When the wicked are multiplied,
transgression increases;
But the righteous will see their fall.

17 Correct your son,
and he will give you rest;
Yes, he will give delight to your soul.

18 Where *there is* no revelation,[55]
the people cast off restraint;
But happy *is* he who keeps the law.

19 A servant will not be corrected by
mere words;
For though he understands,
he will not respond.

20 Do you see a man hasty in his words?
There is more hope for a fool than for
him.

21 He who pampers his servant from
childhood
Will have him as a son in the end.

22 An angry man stirs up strife,
And a furious man abounds in
transgression.

23 A man's pride will bring him low,
But the humble in spirit will retain
honor.

24 Whoever is a partner with a thief
hates his own life;

---

52 Literally *he*   53 Literally *soul*   54 Literally *spirit*   55 Or *prophetic vision*

He swears to tell the truth,[56]
but reveals nothing.

25 The fear of man brings a snare,
But whoever trusts in the LORD
shall be safe.

26 Many seek the ruler's favor,
But justice for man *comes* from the
LORD.

27 An unjust man *is* an abomination to
the righteous,
And *he who is* upright in the way *is* an
abomination to the wicked.

The Wisdom of Agur

30 The words of Agur the son of Jakeh, *his* utterance. This man declared to Ithiel—to Ithiel and Ucal:

2 Surely I *am* more stupid than *any* man,
And do not have the understanding of
a man.
3 I neither learned wisdom
Nor have knowledge of the Holy One.

4 Who has ascended into heaven,
or descended?
Who has gathered the wind in His
fists?
Who has bound the waters in a
garment?
Who has established all the ends of the
earth?
What *is* His name,
and what *is* His Son's name,
If you know?

5 Every word of God *is* pure;
He *is* a shield to those who put their
trust in Him.
6 Do not add to His words,
Lest He reprove you,
and you be found a liar.

7 Two *things* I request of You
(Deprive me not before I die):
8 Remove falsehood and lies far from
me;
Give me neither poverty nor riches—
Feed me with the food *You* prescribe
for me;
9 Lest I be full and deny *You,*
And say, "Who *is* the LORD?"
Or lest I be poor and steal,
And profane the name of my God.

10 Do not malign a servant to his master,

Lest he curse you,
and you be found guilty.

11 *There is* a generation
that curses its father,
And does not bless its mother.
12 *There is* a generation
that is pure in its own eyes,
Yet is not washed from its filthiness.
13 *There is* a generation—
oh, how lofty are their eyes!
And their eyelids are lifted up.
14 *There is* a generation whose teeth *are*
like swords,
And whose fangs *are like* knives,
To devour the poor from off the earth,
And the needy from *among* men.

15 The leech has two daughters,
Crying, "Give! Give!"

There are three *things that* are never
satisfied,
Four *things* never say, "*It is* enough":
16 The grave,[57]
The barren womb,
The earth *that* is not satisfied with
water,
And the fire *that* never says,
"*It is* enough."

17 The eye *that* mocks *his* father,
And scorns obedience to *his* mother,
The ravens of the valley will pick it
out,
And the young eagles will eat it.

18 There are three *things which* are too
wonderful for me,
Yes, four *which* I do not understand:
19 The way of an eagle in the air,
The way of a serpent on a rock,
The way of a ship in the midst of the
sea,
And the way of a man with a virgin.

20 This *is* the way of an adulterous
woman:
She eats and wipes her mouth,
And says,
"I have done no wickedness."

21 For three *things* the earth is perturbed,
Yes, for four it cannot bear up:
22 For a servant when he reigns,
A fool when he is filled with food,
23 A hateful *woman* when she is married,
And a maidservant who succeeds her
mistress.

56 Literally *hears the adjuration*   57 Hebrew *sheol*

24 There are four *things which* are little on
the earth,
But they *are* exceedingly wise:
25 The ants *are* a people not strong,
Yet they prepare their food in the
summer;
26 The rock badgers[58] are a feeble folk,
Yet they make their homes in the
crags;
27 The locusts have no king,
Yet they all advance in ranks;
28 The spider[59] skillfully grasps
with its hands,
And it is in kings' palaces.

29 There are three *things which* are
majestic in pace,
Yes, four *which* are stately in walk:
30 A lion, *which is* mighty among beasts
And does not turn away from any;
31 A greyhound,[60]
A male goat also,
And a king *whose* troops *are* with
him.[61]

32 If you have been foolish in exalting
yourself,
Or if you have devised evil,
put your hand on *your* mouth.
33 For *as* the churning of milk produces
butter,
And *as* wringing the nose produces
blood,
So the forcing of wrath produces strife.

The Words of King Lemuel's Mother

31 The words of King Lemuel, the
utterance which his mother taught
him;

2 What, my son?
And what, son of my womb?
And what, son of my vows?
3 Do not give your strength to women,
Nor your ways to that which destroys
kings.

4 *It is* not for kings, O Lemuel,
It is not for kings to drink wine,
Nor for princes intoxicating drink;
5 Lest they drink and forget the law,
And pervert the justice of all the
afflicted.
6 Give strong drink to him who is
perishing,
And wine to those who are bitter of
heart.

7 Let him drink and forget his poverty,
And remember his misery no more.

8 Open your mouth for the speechless,
In the cause of all *who are* appointed
to die.[62]
9 Open your mouth, judge righteously,
And plead the cause of the poor and
needy.

The Virtuous Wife

10 Who can find a virtuous[63] wife?
For her worth *is* far above rubies.
11 The heart of her husband safely trusts
her;
So he will have no lack of gain.
12 She does him good and not evil
All the days of her life.
13 She seeks wool and flax,
And willingly works with her hands.
14 She is like the merchant ships,
She brings her food from afar.
15 She also rises while it is yet night,
And provides food for her household,
And a portion for her maidservants.
16 She considers a field and buys it;
From her profits she plants a vineyard.
17 She girds herself with strength,
And strengthens her arms.
18 She perceives that her merchandise *is*
good,
And her lamp does not go out by
night.
19 She stretches out her hands to the
distaff,
And her hand holds the spindle.
20 She extends her hand to the poor,
Yes, she reaches out her hands to the
needy.
21 She is not afraid of snow for her
household,
For all her household *is* clothed with
scarlet.
22 She makes tapestry for herself;
Her clothing *is* fine linen and purple.
23 Her husband is known in the gates,
When he sits among the elders of the
land.
24 She makes linen garments
and sells *them*,
And supplies sashes for the merchants.
25 Strength and honor *are* her clothing;
She shall rejoice in time to come.
26 She opens her mouth with wisdom,
And on her tongue *is* the law of
kindness.
27 She watches over the ways of her
household,

---

58 Or *hyrax* 59 Or *lizard* 60 Exact identity unknown
61 A Jewish tradition reads *a king against whom there is no uprising.* 62 Literally *sons of passing away*
63 Literally *a wife of valor,* in the sense of all forms of excellence

And does not eat the bread of idleness.
28 Her children rise up
and call her blessed;
Her husband *also*, and he praises her:
29 "Many daughters have done well,
But you excel them all."

30 Charm *is* deceitful and beauty *is* vain,
But a woman *who* fears the LORD,
she shall be praised.
31 Give her of the fruit of her hands,
And let her own works praise her in
the gates.

Introduction to Ecclesiastes

When Solomon was anointed king over Israel he requested one special gift—the insight of wisdom. God granted his request as is evident from Solomon's literary contributions to the Bible—Proverbs, Song of Solomon, Ecclesiastes, and two of the Psalms. Written by King Solomon about 940 B.C., Ecclesiastes shares the mature wisdom of one who, near the end of his life, looks back to realize that only a life lived for God is a life fulfilled.

Ecclesiastes presents an exciting message of renewed joy and enthusiasm. Its words of wisdom are an excellent guide for a prosperous and abundant life. Ecclesiastes tackles life's tough questions. God answers throughout its pages that we can only know all things when we know the One who created us in His image. When we know God, then life's secrets are revealed.

Solomon begins by exploring a multitude of life's experiences, concluding that a person's relationship to God is the ultimate positive value. In Solomon's words, ''all is vanity''—all else falls short of the joy and beauty of knowing God. Solomon does appreciate life, but feels one must have a positive relationship with God to fully enjoy its blessings. Finally, Solomon relates to the need of God in all work and achievement.

> Cast your bread upon the waters,
> For you will find it after many days . . .
> He who observes the wind will not sow,
> And he who regards the clouds will not reap.
> As you do not know what is the way of the wind,
> *Or* how the bones *grow* in the womb of her who is with child,
> So you do not know the works of God who makes all *things*.
> In the morning sow your seed,
> And in the evening do not withhold your hand;
> For you do not know which will prosper,
> Either this or that,
> Or whether both alike *will be* good.

(Eccl. 11:1, 4–6)

Ecclesiastes truly is God's way to the good life.

The Book of
Ecclesiastes

The Vanity of Life

THE words of the Preacher, the son of David, king in Jerusalem.

2 "Vanity[1] of vanities," says the Preacher;
"Vanity of vanities, all *is* vanity."

3 What profit has a man
from all his labor
In which he toils under the sun?
4 *One* generation passes away,
and *another* generation comes;
But the earth abides forever.
5 The sun also rises,
and the sun goes down,
And hastens to the place
where it arose.
6 The wind goes toward the south,
And turns around to the north;
The wind whirls about continually,
And comes again on its circuit.
7 All the rivers run into the sea,
Yet the sea *is* not full;
To the place from which the rivers
come,
There they return again.
8 All things *are* full of labor;
Man cannot express *it.*
The eye is not satisfied with seeing,
Nor the ear filled with hearing.

9 That which has been *is* what will be,
That which *is* done
is what will be done,
And *there is* nothing new under the
sun.
10 Is there anything of which it may be
said,
"See, this *is* new"?
It has already been in ancient times
before us.
11 *There is* no remembrance of former
things,
Nor will there be any remembrance
of *things* that are to come
By *those* who will come after.

The Grief of Wisdom

12 I, the Preacher, was king over Israel in Jerusalem.
13 And I set my heart to seek and search out by wisdom concerning all that is done under heaven; this grievous task God has given to the sons of man, by which they may be exercised.
14 I have seen all the works that are done under the sun; and indeed, all *is* vanity and grasping for the wind.

15 *What is* crooked
cannot be made straight,
And what is lacking
cannot be numbered.

16 I communed with my heart, saying, "Look, I have attained greatness, and have gained more wisdom than all who were before me in Jerusalem. My heart has understood great wisdom and knowledge."
17 And I set my heart to know wisdom and to know madness and folly. I perceived that this also is grasping for the wind.

18 For in much wisdom *is* much grief,
And he who increases knowledge
increases sorrow.

The Vanity of Pleasure

2 I said in my heart, "Come now, I will test you with mirth; therefore enjoy pleasure"; but surely, this also *was* vanity.
2 I said of laughter, "*It is* madness"; and of mirth, "What does it accomplish?"
3 I searched in my heart *how* to gratify my flesh with wine, while guiding my heart with wisdom, and how to lay hold on folly, till I might see what *was* good for the sons of men to do under heaven all the days of their lives.
4 I made my works great, I built myself houses, and planted myself vineyards.
5 I made myself gardens and orchards, and I planted all *kinds* of fruit trees in them.
6 I made myself waterpools from which to water the growing trees of the grove.
7 I acquired male and female servants, and had servants born in my house. Yes, I had greater possessions of herds and

1 Or *absurdity, frustration, futility, nonsense;* and so throughout the book

flocks than all who were in Jerusalem before me.

8 I also gathered for myself silver and gold and the special treasures of kings and of the provinces. I acquired male and female singers, the delights of the sons of men, *and* musical instruments[2] of all kinds.

9 So I became great and excelled more than all who were before me in Jerusalem. Also my wisdom remained with me.

10 Whatever my eyes desired
    I did not keep from them.
I did not withhold my heart
    from any pleasure,
For my heart rejoiced in all my labor;
And this was my reward from all my
    labor.
11 Then I looked on all the works that my
    hands had done
And on the labor in which I had
    toiled;
And indeed all *was* vanity
    and grasping for the wind.
There was no profit under the sun.

The End of the Wise and the Fool

12 Then I turned myself to consider
    wisdom and madness and folly;
For what *can* the man *do* who succeeds
    the king?—
Only what he has already done.
13 Then I saw that wisdom excels folly
As light excels darkness.
14 The wise man's eyes *are* in his head,
But the fool walks in darkness.
Yet I myself perceived
That the same event happens to them
    all.

15 So I said in my heart,
"As it happens to the fool,
It also happens to me,
And why was I then more wise?"
Then I said in my heart,
"This also *is* vanity."
16 For *there is* no more remembrance of
    the wise than of the fool forever,
Since all that now *is* will be forgotten
    in the days to come.
And how does a wise *man* die?
As the fool!

17 Therefore I hated life because the work that was done under the sun *was* grievous to me, for all *is* vanity and grasping for the wind.

18 Then I hated all my labor in which I had toiled under the sun, because I must leave it to the man who will come after me.

19 And who knows whether he will be a wise *man* or a fool? Yet he will rule over all my labor in which I toiled and in which I have shown myself wise under the sun. This also *is* vanity.

20 Therefore I turned my heart and despaired of all the labor in which I had toiled under the sun.

21 For there is a man whose labor *is* with wisdom, knowledge, and skill; yet he must leave his heritage to a man who has not labored for it. This also *is* vanity and a great evil.

22 For what has man for all his labor, and for the striving of his heart with which he has toiled under the sun?

23 For all his days *are* sorrowful, and his work grievous; even in the night his heart takes no rest. This also is vanity.

24 *There is* nothing better for a man *than* that he should eat and drink, and *that* his soul should enjoy good in his labor. This also, I saw, was from the hand of God.

25 For who can eat, or who can have enjoyment more than I?[3]

26 For *God* gives wisdom and knowledge and joy to a man who *is* good in His sight; but to the sinner He gives the work of gathering and collecting, that he may give to *him who is* good before God. This also *is* vanity and grasping for the wind.

Everything Has Its Time

3 To everything *there is* a season,
    A time for every purpose under
      heaven:

2 A time to be born,
    And a time to die;
A time to plant,
    And a time to pluck
      what is planted;
3 A time to kill,
    And a time to heal;
A time to break down,
    And a time to build up;
4 A time to weep,
    And a time to laugh;
A time to mourn,
    And a time to dance;
5 A time to cast away stones,
    And a time to gather stones;

---

2 Exact meaning unknown   3 Some Hebrew manuscripts, Septuagint, Syriac, and Vulgate read *without Him.*

A time to embrace,
And a time to refrain from
embracing;
6 A time to gain,
And a time to lose;
A time to keep,
And a time to throw away;
7 A time to tear,
And a time to sew;
A time to keep silence,
And a time to speak;
8 A time to love,
And a time to hate;
A time of war,
And a time of peace.

The God-Given Task

9 What profit has the worker from that in which he labors? 10 I have seen the God-given task with which the sons of men are to be occupied. 11 He has made everything beautiful in its time. Also He has put eternity in their hearts, except that no one can find out the work that God does from beginning to end. 12 I know that *there is* nothing better for them than to rejoice, and to do good in their lives, 13 and also that every man should eat and drink and enjoy the good of all his labor—it *is* the gift of God.

14 I know that whatever God does,
It shall be forever.
Nothing can be added to it,
And nothing taken from it.
God does *it*, that men should fear
before Him.
15 That which is has already been,
And what is to be has already been;
And God requires an account of what
is past.

Injustice Seems to Prevail

16 Moreover I saw under the sun:

In the place of judgment,
Wickedness *was* there;
And *in* the place of righteousness,
Iniquity *was* there.

17 I said in my heart,

"God shall judge the righteous
and the wicked,

For *there shall be* a time there for
every purpose and for every work."

18 I said in my heart, "Concerning the estate of the sons of men, God tests them, that they may see that they themselves are *like* beasts." 19 For what happens to the sons of men also happens to beasts; one thing befalls them: as one dies, so dies the other. Surely, they all have one breath; man has no advantage over beasts, for all *is* vanity. 20 All go to one place: all are from the dust, and all return to dust. 21 Who knows the spirit of the sons of men, which goes upward, and the spirit of the beast, which goes down to the earth?⁴ 22 So I perceived that *there is* nothing better than that a man should rejoice in his own works, for that *is* his heritage. For who can bring him to see what will happen after him?

4 Then I returned and considered all the oppression that is done under the sun:

And look! The tears of the oppressed,
But they have no comforter—
On the side of their oppressors *there*
was power,
But they have no comforter.
2 Therefore I praised the dead who were
already dead,
More than the living who are still alive.
3 Yet, better than both *is he* who has
never existed,
Who has not seen the evil work that is
done under the sun.

The Vanity of Selfish Toil

4 Again, I saw that for all toil and every skillful work a man is envied by his neighbor. This also *is* vanity and grasping for the wind.

5 The fool folds his hands
And consumes his own flesh.
6 Better *is* a handful *with* quietness
Than both hands full, *together with* toil
and grasping for the wind.

7 Then I returned, and I saw vanity under the sun:

8 There is one alone,
without companion:
He has neither son nor brother.

4 Septuagint, Syriac, Targum, and Vulgate read *Who knows whether the spirit . . . goes upward, and whether . . . goes downward to the earth?*

Yet *there is* no end to all his labors,
Nor is his eye satisfied with riches.
But he never asks,
"For whom do I toil and deprive myself
    of good?"
This also *is* vanity
    and a grave misfortune.

The Value of a Friend

9 Two *are* better than one,
    Because they have a good reward for
    their labor.
10 For if they fall,
    one will lift up his companion.
    But woe to him *who is* alone when he
    falls,
    For *he has* no one to help him up.
11 Again, if two lie down together,
    they will keep warm;
    But how can one be warm *alone?*
12 Though one may be overpowered by
    another, two can withstand him.
    And a threefold cord is not quickly
    broken.

Popularity Passes Away

13 Better *is* a poor and wise youth
    Than an old and foolish king who will
    be admonished no more.
14 For he comes out of prison to be king,
    Although he was born poor in his
    kingdom.
15 I saw all the living who walk under the
    sun;
    They were with the second youth who
    stands in his place.
16 *There was* no end of all the people over
    whom he was made king;
    Yet those who come afterward will not
    rejoice in him.
    Surely this also *is* vanity
    and grasping for the wind.

Fear God, Keep Your Vows

5 Walk prudently when you go to the
    house of God; and draw near to hear
rather than to give the sacrifice of fools,
for they do not know that they do evil.

2 Do not be rash with your mouth,
    And let not your heart utter anything
    hastily before God.
    For God *is* in heaven,
    and you on earth;
    Therefore let your words be few.
3 For a dream comes through much
    activity,

And a fool's voice *is known* by *his*
    many words.

4 When you make a vow to God,
    do not delay to pay it;
    For *He has* no pleasure in fools.
    Pay what you have vowed.
5 *It is* better not to vow
    than to vow and not pay.

6 Do not let your mouth cause your
flesh to sin, nor say before the messenger
of God that it *was* an error. Why should
God be angry at your excuse[5] and destroy the work of your hands?
7 For in the multitude of dreams and
many words *there is* also vanity. But fear
God.

The Vanity of Gain and Honor

8 If you see the oppression of the poor,
and the violent perversion of justice and
righteousness in a province, do not marvel at the matter; for high official watches
over high official, and higher officials are
over them.
9 Moreover the profit of the land is for
all; the king *himself* is served from the
field.

10 He who loves silver will not be satisfied
    with silver;
    Nor he who loves abundance,
    with increase.
    This also *is* vanity.

11 When goods increase,
    They increase who eat them;
    So what profit have the owners
    Except to see *them* with their eyes?

12 The sleep of a laboring man *is* sweet,
    Whether he eats little or much;
    But the abundance of the rich
    will not permit him to sleep.

13 There is a severe evil *which* I have seen
    under the sun:
    Riches kept for their owner to his hurt.
14 But those riches perish through
    misfortune;
    When he begets a son,
    there is nothing in his hand.
15 As he came from his mother's womb,
    naked shall he return,
    To go as he came;
    And he shall take nothing from his
    labor
    Which he may carry away in his hand.

5 Literally *voice*

16 And this also *is* a severe evil,
  That just exactly as he came,
    so shall he go.
  And what profit has he
    who has labored for the wind?
17 All his days he also eats in darkness,
  And *he has* much sorrow and sickness
    and anger.

18 Here is what I have seen: *It is* good
and fitting *for one* to eat and drink, and
to enjoy the good of all his labor in which
he toils under the sun all the days of his
life which God gives him; for it *is* his
heritage.
19 As for every man to whom God has
given riches and wealth, and given him
power to eat of it, to receive his heritage
and rejoice in his labor—this *is* the gift of
God.
20 For he will not dwell unduly on the
days of his life, because God keeps *him*
busy with the joy of his heart.

6 There is an evil which I have seen
under the sun, and it *is* common
among men:
2 A man to whom God has given riches
and wealth and honor, so that he lacks
nothing for himself of all he desires; yet
God does not give him power to eat of it,
but a foreigner consumes it. This *is* vanity, and it *is* an evil affliction.
3 If a man begets a hundred *children*
and lives many years, so that the days of
his years are many, but his soul is not
satisfied with goodness, or indeed he has
no burial, I say *that* a stillborn child *is*
better than he—
4 for it comes in vanity and departs in
darkness, and its name is covered with
darkness.
5 Though it has not seen the sun or
known *anything*, this has more rest than
that man,
6 even if he lives a thousand years twice
over—but has not seen goodness. Do not
all go to one place?

7 All the labor of man *is* for his mouth,
  And yet the soul is not satisfied.
8 For what more has the wise *man* than
    the fool?
  What does the poor man have,
  Who knows *how* to walk before the
    living?
9 Better *is* the sight of the eyes than the
    wandering of desire.

This also *is* vanity
  and grasping for the wind.
10 Whatever one is,
  he has been named already,
  For it is known that he *is* man;
  And he cannot contend with Him
    who is mightier than he.
11 Since there are many things that
    increase vanity,
  How *is* man the better?

12 For who knows what *is* good for man
in life, all the days of his vain life which
he passes like a shadow? Who can tell a
man what will happen after him under
the sun?

The Value of Practical Wisdom

7 A good name *is* better than precious
  ointment,
  And the day of death than the day of
    one's birth.
2 *It is* better to go to the house of
    mourning
  Than to go to the house of feasting,
  For that *is* the end of all men;
  And the living will take *it* to heart.
3 Sorrow *is* better than laughter,
  For by a sad countenance the heart is
    made better.
4 The heart of the wise *is* in the house
    of mourning,
  But the heart of fools *is* in the house
    of mirth.

5 *It is* better to hear the rebuke
    of the wise
  Than for a man to hear the song
    of fools.
6 For like the crackling of thorns
    under a pot,
  So *is* the laughter of the fool.
  This also is vanity.
7 Surely oppression destroys a wise
    man's reason,
  And a bribe debases the heart.

8 The end of a thing *is* better
    than its beginning,
  And the patient in spirit *is* better
    than the proud in spirit.
9 Do not hasten in your spirit to be
    angry,
  For anger rests in the bosom of fools.
10 Do not say,
  "Why were the former days better than
    these?"
  For you do not inquire wisely
    concerning this.

11 Wisdom *is* good with an inheritance,
And profitable to those who see the
sun.
12 For wisdom *is* a defense *as* money *is* a
defense,
But the excellence of knowledge
is that wisdom gives life
to those who have it.

13 Consider the work of God;
For who can make straight what He
has made crooked?
14 In the day of prosperity be joyful,
But in the day of adversity consider:
Surely God has appointed the one as
well as the other,
So that man can find nothing *that will
happen* after him.

15 I have seen all *things* in my days of
vanity:

There is a just *man* who perishes
in his righteousness,
And there is a wicked *man* who
prolongs *his life* in his wickedness.

16 Do not be overly righteous,
Nor be overly wise:
Why should you destroy yourself?
17 Do not be overly wicked,
Nor be foolish:
Why should you die before your time?
18 *It is* good that you grasp this,
And also not remove your hand
from the other;
For he who fears God
will escape them all.

19 Wisdom strengthens the wise
More than ten rulers of the city.

20 For *there is* not a just man on earth
who does good
And does not sin.

21 Also do not take to heart everything
people say,
Lest you hear your servant cursing you.
22 For many times, also, your own heart
has known
That even you have cursed others.

23 All this I have proved by wisdom.
I said, "I will be wise";
But it *was* far from me.
24 As for that which is far off
and exceedingly deep,
Who can find it out?
25 I applied my heart to know,
To search and seek out wisdom
and the reason *of things*,

To know the wickedness of folly,
Even of foolishness *and* madness.
26 And I find more bitter than death
The woman whose heart *is* snares
and nets,
Whose hands *are* fetters.
He who pleases God shall escape from
her,
But the sinner shall be taken by her.

27 "Here is what I have found,"
says the Preacher,
"*Adding* one thing to the other to find
out the reason,
28 Which my soul still seeks
but I cannot find:
One man among a thousand
I have found,
But a woman among all these
I have not found.
29 Truly, this only I have found:
That God made man upright,
But they have sought out many
schemes."

8 Who *is* like a wise *man*?
And who knows the interpretation of
a thing?
A man's wisdom makes his face shine,
And the sternness of his face is
changed.

Obey Authorities for God's Sake

2 I *counsel you,* "Keep the king's commandment for the sake of your oath to
God.
3 "Do not be hasty to go from his presence. Do not take your stand for an evil
thing, for he does whatever pleases him."
4 Where the word of a king *is,*
there is power;
And who may say to him,
"What are you doing?"
5 He who keeps his command will
experience nothing harmful;
And a wise man's heart discerns both
time and judgment.
6 Because for every matter there is a
time and judgment,
Though the misery of man increases
greatly.
7 For he does not know what will
happen;
So who can tell him when it will occur?
8 No one has power over the spirit to
retain the spirit,
And no one has power in the day of
death.

There is no discharge in that war,
And wickedness will not deliver those
   who are given to it.

9 All this I have seen, and applied my heart to every work that is done under the sun: *There is* a time in which one man rules over another to his own hurt.

Death Comes to All

10 Then I saw the wicked buried, who had come and gone from the place of holiness, and they were forgotten in the city where they had so done. This also *is* vanity.
11 Because the sentence against an evil work is not executed speedily, therefore the heart of the sons of men is fully set in them to do evil.
12 Though a sinner does evil a hundred *times*, and his *days* are prolonged, yet I surely know that it will be well with those who fear God, who fear before Him.
13 But it will not be well with the wicked; nor will he prolong *his* days, *which are* as a shadow, because he does not fear before God.
14 There is a vanity which occurs on earth, that there are just *men* to whom it happens according to the work of the wicked; again, there are wicked *men* to whom it happens according to the work of the righteous. I said that this also *is* vanity.
15 So I commended enjoyment, because a man has nothing better under the sun than to eat, drink, and be merry; for this will remain with him in his labor *for* the days of his life which God gives him under the sun.
16 When I applied my heart to know wisdom and to see the business that is done on earth, even though one sees no sleep day or night,
17 then I saw all the work of God, that a man cannot find out the work that is done under the sun. For though a man labors to discover *it*, yet he will not find *it*; moreover, though a wise *man* attempts to know *it*, he will not be able to find *it*.

9 For I considered all this in my heart, so that I could declare it all: that the righteous and the wise and their works *are* in the hand of God. People know neither love nor hatred *by* anything *that is* before them.
2 Everything *occurs* alike to all:

One event *happens* to the righteous
   and the wicked;
To the good, the clean,
   and the unclean;
To him who sacrifices
   and him who does not sacrifice.
As is the good, so *is* the sinner;
And he who takes an oath
   as *he* who fears an oath.

3 This *is* an evil in all that is done under the sun: that one thing *happens* to all. Truly the hearts of the sons of men are full of evil; madness *is* in their hearts while they live, and after that *they go* to the dead.
4 But for him who is joined to all the living there is hope, for a living dog is better than a dead lion.

5 For the living know that they will die;
But the dead know nothing,
And they have no more reward,
For the memory of them is forgotten.
6 Also their love, their hatred,
   and their envy have now perished;
Nevermore will they have a share
In anything done under the sun.

7 Go, eat your bread with joy,
And drink your wine with a merry
   heart;
For God has already accepted your
   works.
8 Let your garments always be white,
And let your head lack no oil.

9 Live joyfully with the wife whom you love all the days of your vain life which He has given you under the sun, all your days of vanity; for that *is* your portion in life, and in the labor which you perform under the sun.
10 Whatever your hand finds to do, do *it* with your might; for *there is* no work or device or knowledge or wisdom in the grave where you are going.
11 I returned and saw under the sun that—

The race *is* not to the swift,
Nor the battle to the strong,
Nor bread to the wise,
Nor riches to men of understanding,
Nor favor to men of skill;
But time and chance
   happen to them all.
12 For man also does not know his time:
Like fish taken in a cruel net,
Like birds caught in a snare,

So the sons of men *are* snared in an
    evil time,
When it falls suddenly upon them.

Wisdom Superior to Folly

13 This wisdom I have also seen under
the sun, and it *seemed* great to me:
14 *There was* a little city with few men in
it; and a great king came against it,
besieged it, and built great snares[6]
around it.
15 Now there was found in it a poor wise
man, and he by his wisdom delivered the
city. Yet no one remembered that same
poor man.
16 Then I said:

"Wisdom *is* better than strength.
    Nevertheless the poor man's wisdom *is*
    despised,
    And his words are not heard.
17 Words of the wise, *spoken* quietly,
    should be heard
    Rather than the shout of a ruler of
    fools.
18 Wisdom *is* better than weapons of war;
    But one sinner destroys much good."

10 Dead flies putrefy[7] the perfumer's
    ointment,
    And cause it to give off a foul odor;
    So does a little folly to one respected
    for wisdom *and* honor.
2 A wise man's heart *is* at his right hand,
    But a fool's heart at his left.
3 Even when a fool walks along the way,
    He lacks wisdom,
    And he shows everyone *that* he *is* a
    fool.
4 If the spirit of the ruler rises against
    you,
    Do not leave your post;
    For conciliation pacifies great offenses.

5 There is an evil I have seen
    under the sun,
    As an error proceeding from the ruler:
6 Folly is set in great dignity,
    While the rich sit in a lowly place.
7 I have seen servants on horses,
    While princes walk on the ground like
    servants.

8 He who digs a pit will fall into it,
    And whoever breaks through a wall
    will be bitten by a serpent.
9 He who quarries stones
    may be hurt by them,

And he who splits wood
    may be endangered by it.
10 If the ax is dull,
    And one does not sharpen the edge,
    Then he must use more strength;
    But wisdom brings success.

11 A serpent may bite
    when *it is* not charmed;
    The babbler is no different.
12 The words of a wise man's mouth
    are gracious,
    But the lips of a fool
    shall swallow him up;
13 The words of his mouth
    begin with foolishness,
    And the end of his talk
    is raving madness.
14 A fool also multiplies words.
    No man knows what is to be;
    Who can tell him what will be after
    him?
15 The labor of fools wearies them,
    For they do not even know how to go
    to the city!

16 Woe to you, O land,
    when your king *is* a child,
    And your princes feast in the morning!
17 Blessed *are* you, O land,
    when your king *is* the son of nobles,
    And your princes feast at the proper
    time—
    For strength and not for drunkenness!
18 Because of laziness the building decays,
    And through idleness of hands the
    house leaks.
19 A feast is made for laughter,
    And wine makes merry;
    But money answers every thing.

20 Do not curse the king,
    even in your thought;
    Do not curse the rich,
    even in your bedroom;
    For a bird of the air
    may carry your voice,
    And a bird in flight
    may tell the matter.

The Value of Diligence

11 Cast your bread upon the waters,
    For you will find it after many
    days.
2 Give a serving to seven,
    and also to eight,
    For you do not know what evil
    will be on the earth.

3 If the clouds are full of rain,
    They empty *themselves* upon the earth;

6 Septuagint, Syriac, and Vulgate read *bulwarks.*   7 Targum and Vulgate omit *putrefy.*

And if a tree falls to the south
or the north,
In the place where the tree falls,
there it shall lie.
4 He who observes the wind
will not sow,
And he who regards the clouds
will not reap.

5 As you do not know what is the way
of the wind,[8]
Or how the bones *grow* in the womb
of her who is with child,
So you do not know the works of God
who makes all *things.*
6 In the morning sow your seed,
And in the evening do not withhold
your hand;
For you do not know which will
prosper,
Either this or that,
Or whether both alike *will be* good.

7 Truly the light is sweet,
And *it is* pleasant for the eyes
to behold the sun;
8 But if a man lives many years
And rejoices in them all,
Yet let him remember the days
of darkness,
For they will be many.
All that is coming *is* vanity.

Seek God in Early Life

9 Rejoice, O young man, in your youth,
And let your heart cheer you in the
days of your youth;
Walk in the ways of your heart,
And in the sight of your eyes;
But know that for all these
God will bring you into judgment.
10 Therefore remove sorrow from your
heart,
And put away evil from your flesh,
For childhood and youth *are* vanity.

12 Remember *now* your Creator
in the days of your youth,
Before the difficult days come,
And the years draw near when you say,
"I have no pleasure in them":
2 While the sun and the light,
The moon and the stars,
Are not darkened,
And the clouds do not return
after the rain;
3 In the day when the keepers of the
house tremble,

And the strong men bow down;
When the grinders cease because they
are few,
And those that look through the
windows grow dim;
4 When the doors are shut in the streets,
And the sound of grinding is low;
When one rises up at the sound
of a bird,
And all the daughters of music
are brought low;
5 Also *when* they are afraid of height,
And of terrors in the way;
When the almond tree blossoms,
The grasshopper is a burden,
And desire fails.
For man goes to his eternal home,
And the mourners go about the streets.

6 *Remember your Creator* before the
silver cord is loosed,
Or the golden bowl is broken,
Or the pitcher shattered at the
fountain,
Or the wheel broken at the well.
7 Then the dust will return to the earth
as it was,
And the spirit will return to God
who gave it.

8 "Vanity of vanities," says the Preacher,
"All *is* vanity."

The Whole Duty of Man

9 And moreover, because the Preacher
was wise, he still taught the people
knowledge; yes, he pondered and sought
out *and* set in order many proverbs.
10 The Preacher sought to find acceptable words; and *what was* written *was* upright—words of truth.
11 The words of the wise are like goads,
and the words of scholars[9] are like well-
driven nails, given by one Shepherd.
12 And further, my son, be admonished
by these. Of making many books *there is*
no end, and much study *is* wearisome to
the flesh.
13 Let us hear the conclusion of the
whole matter:

Fear God and keep His
commandments,
For this is the whole duty of man.
14 For God will bring every work into
judgment,
Including every secret thing,
Whether *it is* good or whether *it is* evil.

8 Or *spirit*   9 Literally *masters of the assemblies*

Introduction to Song of Solomon

The Song of Solomon is a glorious celebration of the love between a man and a woman. Written by King Solomon about 960 B.C., this is the correspondence between himself and a young shepherd girl.

In a beautiful courting dialogue, love's greatest attributes are highlighted. Although physical beauty is a powerful attractive force, love's deeper qualities are also extolled. There is no lack of words to describe their love. Their dialogue overflows with references to the land and all its glory in springtime. Like the spring, love is a new birth, a finding, a uniting, a bursting forth after the captivity of a cold lonely winter.

At first glance, it may seem awkward to compare a lover to vineyards, a watchtower, lamb's wool, and pomegranates. But on closer examination, these analogies reveal the mind-set of the ancient lovers. Love's value is measured in function as well as appearance. True love is giving, unselfish, supportive, honest, and unconditional. By calling his beloved the rose of Sharon, Solomon brings to mind the symbol of God's blessing which was represented by the blossoming of this flower.

In the Song of Solomon, love is depicted in all its beauty and glory:

> For lo, the winter is past,
> The rain is over *and* gone.
> The flowers appear on the earth;
> The time of singing has come,
> And the voice of the turtledove
> Is heard in our land.
>
> (Song 2:11, 12)

The
Song of Solomon

THE song of songs, which *is* Solomon's.

The Banquet

THE SHULAMITE[1]

2 Let him kiss me with the kisses of his
   mouth—
   For your[2] love *is* better than wine.
3 Because of the fragrance of your good
   ointments,
   Your name *is* ointment poured forth;
   Therefore the virgins love you.
4 Lead me away!

THE DAUGHTERS OF JERUSALEM

   We will run after you.[3]

THE SHULAMITE

   The king has brought me into his
   chambers.

THE DAUGHTERS OF JERUSALEM

   We will be glad and rejoice in you.[4]

   We will remember your[5] love
   more than wine.

THE SHULAMITE

   Rightly do they love you.[6]

5 I *am* dark, but lovely,
   O daughters of Jerusalem,
   Like the tents of Kedar,
   Like the curtains of Solomon.
6 Do not look upon me,
   because I *am* dark,
   Because the sun has tanned me.
   My mother's sons were angry with me;
   They made me the keeper of the
   vineyards,
   But my own vineyard I have not kept.

(TO HER BELOVED)

7 Tell me, O you whom I love,
   Where you feed *your flock*,

Where you make *it* rest at noon.
For why should I be as one
   who veils herself
By the flocks of your companions?

THE BELOVED

8 If you do not know,
   O fairest among women,
   Follow in the footsteps of the flock,
   And feed your little goats
   Beside the shepherds' tents.
9 I have compared you, my love,
   To my filly among Pharaoh's chariots.
10 Your cheeks are lovely with ornaments,
   Your neck with chains *of gold.*

THE DAUGHTERS OF JERUSALEM

11 We will make you[7] ornaments of gold
   With studs of silver.

THE SHULAMITE

12 While the king *is* at his table,
   My spikenard sends forth its fragrance.
13 A bundle of myrrh *is* my beloved
   to me,
   That lies all night between my breasts.
14 My beloved *is* to me
   a cluster of henna *blooms*
   In the vineyards of En Gedi.

THE BELOVED

15 Behold, you *are* fair, my love!
   Behold, you *are* fair!
   You *have* dove's eyes.

THE SHULAMITE

16 Behold, you *are* handsome, my
   beloved!
   Yes, pleasant!
   Also our bed *is* green.
17 The beams of our houses *are* cedar,
   And our rafters of fir.

2 I *am* the rose of Sharon,
   And the lily of the valleys.

---

1 A Palestinian young woman (compare 6:13). The speaker and audience are identified according to the number,
gender, and person of the Hebrew words. Occasionally the identity is not certain.
2 Masculine singular, that is, the Beloved   3 Masculine singular, that is, the Beloved
4 Feminine singular, that is, the Shulamite   5 Masculine singular, that is, the Beloved
6 Masculine singular, that is, the Beloved   7 Feminine singular, that is, the Shulamite

THE BELOVED

2 Like a lily among thorns,
So is my love among the daughters.

THE SHULAMITE

3 Like an apple tree among the trees
of the woods,
So *is* my beloved among the sons.
I sat down in his shade with great
delight,
And his fruit *was* sweet to my taste.

THE SHULAMITE TO THE DAUGHTERS OF
JERUSALEM

4 He brought me to the banqueting
house,
And his banner over me *was* love.
5 Sustain me with cakes of raisins,
Refresh me with apples,
For I *am* lovesick.

6 His left hand *is* under my head,
And his right hand embraces me.
7 I charge you,
O daughters of Jerusalem,
By the gazelles
or by the does of the field,
Do not stir up nor awaken love
Until it pleases.

The Beloved's Request

THE SHULAMITE

8 The voice of my beloved!
Behold, he comes
Leaping upon the mountains,
Skipping upon the hills.
9 My beloved is like a gazelle
or a young stag.
Behold, he stands behind our wall;
He is looking through the windows,
Gazing through the lattice.

10 My beloved spoke, and said to me:
"Rise up, my love, my fair one,
And come away.
11 For lo, the winter is past,
The rain is over *and* gone.
12 The flowers appear on the earth;
The time of singing has come,
And the voice of the turtledove
Is heard in our land.
13 The fig tree puts forth her green figs,
And the vines *with* the tender grapes
Give a good smell.

Rise up, my love, my fair one,
And come away!

14 "O my dove, in the clefts of the rock,
In the secret *places* of the cliff,
Let me see your countenance,
Let me hear your voice;
For your voice *is* sweet,
And your countenance *is* lovely."

HER BROTHERS

15 Catch us the foxes,
The little foxes that spoil the vines,
For our vines *have* tender grapes.

THE SHULAMITE

16 My beloved *is* mine, and I *am* his.
He feeds *his flock* among the lilies.

(TO HER BELOVED)

17 Until the day breaks
And the shadows flee away,
Turn, my beloved,
And be like a gazelle
Or a young stag
Upon the mountains of Bether.[8]

A Troubled Night

THE SHULAMITE

3 By night on my bed I sought
the one I love;
I sought him, but I did not find him.
2 "I will rise now," *I said,*
"And go about the city;
In the streets and in the squares
I will seek the one I love."
I sought him, but I did not find him.
3 The watchmen who go about the city
found me,
To whom I said,
"Have you seen the one I love?"

4 Scarcely had I passed by them,
When I found the one I love.
I held him and would not let him go,
Until I had brought him to the house
of my mother,
And into the chamber of her who
conceived me.

5 I charge you,
O daughters of Jerusalem,
By the gazelles
or by the does of the field,
Do not stir up nor awaken love
Until it pleases.

8 Literally *Separation*

The Coming of Solomon

THE SHULAMITE

6 Who *is* this coming out of the
    wilderness
    Like pillars of smoke,
    Perfumed with myrrh and frankincense,
    With all the merchant's fragrant
      powders?
7 Behold, it *is* Solomon's couch,
    With sixty valiant men around it,
    Of the valiant of Israel.
8 They all hold swords,
    Being expert in war.
    Every man *has* his sword on his thigh
    Because of fear in the night.

9 Of the wood of Lebanon
    Solomon the King
    Made himself a palanquin:[9]
10 He made its pillars *of* silver,
    Its support *of* gold,
    Its seat *of* purple,
    Its interior paved *with* love
    By the daughters of Jerusalem.
11 Go forth, O daughters of Zion,
    And see King Solomon with the crown
    With which his mother crowned him
    On the day of his espousals,
    The day of the gladness of his heart.

THE BELOVED

4   Behold, you *are* fair, my love!
    Behold, you *are* fair!
    You *have* dove's eyes behind your veil.
    Your hair *is* like a flock of goats,
    Going down from Mount Gilead.
2 Your teeth *are* like a flock of shorn
      sheep
    Which have come up from the washing,
    Every one of which bears twins,
    And none *is* barren among them.
3 Your lips *are* like a strand of scarlet,
    And your mouth is lovely.
    Your temples behind your veil
    Are like a piece of pomegranate.
4 Your neck *is* like the tower of David,
    Built for an armory,
    On which hang a thousand bucklers,
    All shields of mighty men.
5 Your two breasts *are* like two fawns,
    Twins of a gazelle,
    Which feed among the lilies.

6 Until the day breaks
    And the shadows flee away,
    I will go my way to the mountain
      of myrrh
    And to the hill of frankincense.

7 You *are* all fair, my love,
    And *there is* no spot in you.
8 Come with me from Lebanon,
    my spouse,
    With me from Lebanon.
    Look from the top of Amana,
    From the top of Senir and Hermon,
    From the lions' dens,
    From the mountains of the leopards.

9 You have ravished my heart,
    My sister, *my* spouse;
    You have ravished my heart
    With one *look* of your eyes,
    With one link of your necklace.
10 How fair is your love,
    My sister, *my* spouse!
    How much better than wine
      is your love,
    And the scent of your perfumes
    Than all spices!
11 Your lips, O *my* spouse,
    Drip as the honeycomb;
    Honey and milk *are* under your
      tongue;
    And the fragrance of your garments
    Is like the fragrance of Lebanon.

12 A garden enclosed
    Is my sister, *my* spouse,
    A spring shut up,
    A fountain sealed.
13 Your plants *are* an orchard of
      pomegranates
    With pleasant fruits,
    Fragrant henna with spikenard,
14 Spikenard and saffron,
    Calamus and cinnamon,
    With all trees of frankincense,
    Myrrh and aloes,
    With all the chief spices—
15 A fountain of gardens,
    A well of living waters,
    And streams from Lebanon.

THE SHULAMITE

16 Awake, O north *wind*,
    And come, O south!
    Blow upon my garden,
    That its spices may flow out.
    Let my beloved come to his garden
    And eat its pleasant fruits.

THE BELOVED

5   I have come to my garden,
    my sister, *my* spouse;
    I have gathered my myrrh
      with my spice;

9 A portable enclosed chair

I have eaten my honeycomb
with my honey;
I have drunk my wine with my milk.

(To his friends)

Eat, O friends!
Drink, yes, drink deeply,
O beloved ones!

The Shulamite's Troubled Evening

The Shulamite

2 I sleep, but my heart is awake;
It is the voice of my beloved!
He knocks, *saying,*
"Open for me, my sister, my love,
My dove, my perfect one;
For my head is covered with dew,
My locks with the drops of the night."

3 I have taken off my robe;
How can I put it on *again?*
I have washed my feet;
How can I defile them?
4 My beloved put his hand
By the latch *of the door,*
And my heart yearned for him.
5 I arose to open for my beloved,
And my hands dripped *with* myrrh,
My fingers with liquid myrrh,
On the handles of the lock.

6 I opened for my beloved,
But my beloved had turned away
and was gone.
My heart went out *to him* when he
spoke.
I sought him,
but I could not find him;
I called him,
but he gave me no answer.
7 The watchmen who went about the city
found me.
They struck me, they wounded me;
The keepers of the walls
Took my veil away from me.
8 I charge you,
O daughters of Jerusalem,
If you find my beloved,
That you tell him I *am* lovesick!

The Daughters of Jerusalem

9 What *is* your beloved
More than *another* beloved,
O fairest among women?
What *is* your beloved
More than *another* beloved,
That you so charge us?

The Shulamite

10 My beloved *is* white and ruddy,
Chief among ten thousand.
11 His head *is like* the finest gold;
His locks *are* wavy,
And black as a raven.
12 His eyes *are* like doves
By the rivers of waters,
Washed with milk,
And fitly set.
13 His cheeks *are* like a bed of spices,
Like banks of scented herbs.
His lips *are* lilies,
Dripping liquid myrrh.

14 His hands *are* rods of gold
Set with beryl.
His body *is* carved ivory
Inlaid *with* sapphires.
15 His legs *are* pillars of marble
Set on bases of fine gold.
His countenance *is* like Lebanon,
Excellent as the cedars.
16 His mouth *is* most sweet,
Yes, he *is* altogether lovely.
This *is* my beloved,
And this *is* my friend,
O daughters of Jerusalem!

The Daughters of Jerusalem

6 Where has your beloved gone,
O fairest among women?
Where has your beloved turned aside,
That we may seek him with you?

The Shulamite

2 My beloved has gone to his garden,
To the beds of spices,
To feed *his flock* in the gardens,
And to gather lilies.
3 I *am* my beloved's,
And my beloved *is* mine.
He feeds *his flock* among the lilies.

Praise of the Shulamite's Beauty

The Beloved

4 O my love, you *are as* beautiful
as Tirzah,
Lovely as Jerusalem,
Awesome as *an army* with banners!
5 Turn your eyes away from me,
For they have overcome me.
Your hair *is* like a flock of goats
Going down from Gilead.
6 Your teeth *are* like a flock of sheep
Which have come up from the washing;

Every one bears twins,
And none *is* barren among them.
7 Like a piece of pomegranate
Are your temples behind your veil.

8 There are sixty queens
And eighty concubines,
And virgins without number.
9 My dove, my perfect one,
Is the only one,
The only one of her mother,
The favorite of the one who bore her.
The daughters saw her
And called her blessed,
The queens and the concubines,
And they praised her.

10 Who is she *who* looks forth
    as the morning,
Fair as the moon,
Clear as the sun,
Awesome as *an army* with banners?

THE SHULAMITE

11 I went down to the garden of nuts
To see the verdure of the valley,
To see whether the vine had budded
And the pomegranates had bloomed.
12 Before I was even aware,
My soul had made me
As the chariots of my noble people.[10]

THE BELOVED AND HIS FRIENDS

13 Return, return, O Shulamite;
Return, return,
    that we may look upon you!

THE SHULAMITE

What would you see in the
    Shulamite—

As it were, the dance of the double
    camp?[11]

Expressions of Praise

THE BELOVED

7 How beautiful are your feet
    in sandals,
O prince's daughter!
The curves of your thighs
    are like jewels,
The work of the hands of a skillful
    workman.
2 Your navel *is* a rounded goblet
Which lacks no blended beverage.
Your waist *is* a heap of wheat
Set about with lilies.

3 Your two breasts *are* like two fawns,
Twins of a gazelle.
4 Your neck *is* like an ivory tower,
Your eyes *like* the pools in Heshbon
By the gate of Bath Rabbim.
Your nose *is* like the tower of Lebanon
Which looks toward Damascus.
5 Your head *crowns* you
    like *Mount* Carmel,
And the hair of your head
    is like purple;
The king *is* held captive by *its* tresses.

6 How fair and how pleasant you are,
O love, with your delights!
7 This stature of yours
    is like a palm tree,
And your breasts *like* its clusters.
8 I said, "I will go up to the palm tree,
I will take hold of its branches."
Let now your breasts be like clusters
    of the vine,
The fragrance of your breath
    like apples,
9 And the roof of your mouth
    like the best wine.

THE SHULAMITE

The wine[12] goes *down* smoothly for my
    beloved,
Moving gently the lips of sleepers.
10 I *am* my beloved's,
And his desire *is* toward me.

11 Come, my beloved,
Let us go forth to the field;
Let us lodge in the villages.
12 Let us get up early to the vineyards;
Let us see *if* the vine has budded,
Whether the grape blossoms are open,
And the pomegranates are in bloom.
There I will give you my love.
13 The mandrakes give off a fragrance,
And at our gates *are* pleasant *fruits*,
All manner, new and old,
Which I have laid up for you,
    my beloved.

8 Oh, that you *were* like my brother,
Who nursed at my mother's breasts!
If I should find you outside,
I would kiss you;
I would not be despised.
2 I would lead you *and* bring you
Into the house of my mother,
She *who* used to instruct me.
I would cause you to drink of spiced
    wine,
Of the juice of my pomegranate.

10 Hebrew *Ammi Nadab*   11 Hebrew *mahanaim*   12 Literally *it*

(To the Daughters of Jerusalem)

3 His left hand *is* under my head,
And his right hand embraces me.
4 I charge you,
O daughters of Jerusalem,
Do not stir up nor awaken love
Until it pleases.

Love Renewed in Lebanon

A Relative

5 Who *is* this coming up from the
wilderness,
Leaning upon her beloved?

I awakened you under the apple tree.
There your mother brought you forth;
There she *who* bore you brought *you*
forth.

The Shulamite to Her Beloved

6 Set me as a seal upon your heart,
As a seal upon your arm;
For love *is as* strong as death,
Jealousy *as* cruel as the grave;
Its flames *are* flames of fire,
A most vehement flame.

7 Many waters cannot quench love,
Nor can the floods drown it.
If a man would give for love
All the wealth of his house,
It would be utterly despised.

The Shulamite's Brothers

8 We have a little sister,
And she has no breasts.

What shall we do for our sister
In the day when she is spoken for?
9 If she *is* a wall,
We will build upon her
A battlement of silver;
And if she *is* a door,
We will enclose her
With boards of cedar.

The Shulamite

10 I *am* a wall,
And my breasts like towers;
Then I became in his eyes
As one who found peace.
11 Solomon had a vineyard at Baal
Hamon;
He leased the vineyard to keepers;
Everyone was to bring for its fruit
A thousand *pieces* of silver.

(To Solomon)

12 My own vineyard *is* before me.
You, O Solomon, *may have* a thousand,
And those who keep its fruit two
hundred.

The Beloved

13 You who dwell in the gardens,
The companions listen for your voice—
Let me hear it!

The Shulamite

14 Make haste, my beloved,
And be like a gazelle
Or a young stag
On the mountains of spices.

Introduction to Isaiah

The Book of Isaiah is a beautiful example of God's strength and the promises He gave to the people when they needed them most. In this instance, God sent the prophet Isaiah to forewarn and prepare the people of Israel for the problems that were to beset them. Like a novelist foretelling his readers of future tragedies and events, God sent the prophet to announce the coming captivity by warring nations and the destruction of Jerusalem. Throughout the historical narrative of these happenings is interwoven the thread of hope—the coming of the Messiah.

> Therefore the Lord Himself will give you a sign: Behold, the virgin shall conceive and bear a Son, and shall call His name Immanuel.

> (Is. 7:14)

> For unto us a Child is born,
> Unto us a Son is given;
> And the government will be upon His shoulder.
> And His name will be called
> Wonderful, Counselor, Mighty God,
> Everlasting Father, Prince of Peace.
> Of the increase of *His* government and peace
> *There will be* no end,

> (Is. 9:6, 7)

Isaiah promises the people that the coming Messiah will bring them into a loving relationship with God. (See Chapter 53.) If they look to God and cling to the hope of the Savior, they will be able to handle any circumstance that surrounds them. Despite the coming captivity, Isaiah encourages the people to look beyond their problems. "Those who wait on the LORD shall renew *their* strength; they shall mount up with wings like eagles, they shall run and not be weary, they shall walk and not faint" (Is. 40:31).

In comparing their lives to the desolate wilderness area, Isaiah promises that:

> Every valley shall be exalted,
> And every mountain and hill shall be made low;
> The crooked places shall be made straight,
> And the rough places smooth;

> (Is. 40:4)

God promises that even the most desolate and unfortunate life will become successful and productive with His power. When problems would hold us captive, we can hold on to the same hope Isaiah promised—that Jesus will come again. We can look to God for strength, for we know that the ultimate outcome is in His hands. Even the end of the world will be a new beginning. "Behold, I make all things new" (Rev. 21:5).

The Book of

Isaiah

THE vision of Isaiah the son of Amoz, which he saw concerning Judah and Jerusalem in the days of Uzziah, Jotham, Ahaz, *and* Hezekiah, kings of Judah.

The Wickedness of Judah

2 Hear, O heavens,
    and give ear, O earth!
For the LORD has spoken:
"I have nourished and brought up children,
And they have rebelled against Me;
3 The ox knows its owner
And the donkey its master's crib;
But Israel does not know,
My people do not consider."

4 Alas, sinful nation,
A people laden with iniquity,
A brood of evildoers,
Children who are corrupters!
They have forsaken the LORD,
They have provoked to anger
The Holy One of Israel,
They have turned away backward.

5 Why should you be stricken again?
You will revolt more and more.
The whole head is sick,
And the whole heart faints.
6 From the sole of the foot
    even to the head,
There is no soundness in it,
But wounds and bruises
    and putrefying sores;
They have not been closed
    or bound up,
Or soothed with ointment.

7 Your country *is* desolate,
Your cities *are* burned with fire;
Strangers devour your land in your presence;
And *it is* desolate,
    as overthrown by strangers.
8 So the daughter of Zion is left as a booth in a vineyard,
As a hut in a garden of cucumbers,
As a besieged city.

9 Unless the LORD of hosts
Had left to us a very small remnant,
We would have become like Sodom,
We would have been made like Gomorrah.

10 Hear the word of the LORD,
You rulers of Sodom;
Give ear to the law of our God,
You people of Gomorrah:
11 "To what purpose *is* the multitude of your sacrifices to Me?"
Says the LORD.
"I have had enough of burnt offerings of rams
And the fat of fed cattle.
I do not delight in the blood of bulls,
Or of lambs or goats.

12 "When you come to appear before Me,
Who has required this from your hand,
To trample My courts?
13 Bring no more futile sacrifices;
Incense is an abomination to Me.
The New Moons, the Sabbaths,
    and the calling of assemblies—
I cannot endure iniquity
    and the sacred meeting.
14 Your New Moons
    and your appointed feasts
My soul hates;
They are a trouble to Me,
I am weary of bearing *them.*
15 When you spread out your hands,
I will hide My eyes from you;
Even though you make many prayers,
I will not hear.
Your hands are full of blood.

16 "Wash yourselves,
    make yourselves clean;
Put away the evil of your doings
    from before My eyes.
Cease to do evil,
17 Learn to do good;
Seek justice,
Reprove the oppressor;[1]
Defend the fatherless,
Plead for the widow.

18 "Come now, and let us reason together,"
Says the LORD,
"Though your sins are like scarlet,
They shall be as white as snow;

1 Some ancient versions read *the oppressed.*

Though they are red like crimson,
They shall be as wool.
19 If you are willing and obedient,
You shall eat the good of the land;
20 But if you refuse and rebel,
You shall be devoured by the sword";
For the mouth of the LORD has
spoken.

The Degenerate City

21 How the faithful city
has become a harlot!
It was full of justice;
Righteousness lodged in it,
But now murderers.
22 Your silver has become dross,
Your wine mixed with water.
23 Your princes *are* rebellious,
And companions of thieves;
Everyone loves bribes,
And follows after rewards.
They do not defend the fatherless,
Nor does the cause of the widow
come before them.

24 Therefore the Lord says,
The LORD of hosts,
the Mighty One of Israel,
"Ah, I will rid Myself of My
adversaries,
And take vengeance on My enemies.
25 I will turn My hand against you,
And thoroughly purge away your
dross,
And take away all your alloy.
26 I will restore your judges as at the first,
And your counselors as at the
beginning.
Afterward you shall be called the city
of righteousness, the faithful city."

27 Zion shall be redeemed with justice,
And her penitents with righteousness.
28 The destruction of transgressors
and of sinners *shall be* together,
And those who forsake the LORD
shall be consumed.
29 For they shall be ashamed of the
terebinth trees
Which you have desired;
And you shall be embarrassed
because of the gardens
Which you have chosen.
30 For you shall be as a terebinth whose
leaf fades,
And as a garden that has no water.
31 The strong shall be as tinder,
And the work of it as a spark;
Both will burn together,
And no one shall quench *them.*

The Future House of God

2 The word that Isaiah the son of
Amoz saw concerning Judah and Jerusalem.

2 Now it shall come to pass
in the latter days
That the mountain of the LORD's house
Shall be established on the top of the
mountains,
And shall be exalted above the hills;
And all nations shall flow to it.
3 Many people shall come and say,
"Come, and let us go up to the
mountain of the LORD,
To the house of the God of Jacob;
He will teach us His ways,
And we shall walk in His paths."
For out of Zion shall go forth the law,
And the word of the LORD from
Jerusalem.
4 He shall judge between the nations,
And shall rebuke many people;
They shall beat their swords
into plowshares,
And their spears into pruning hooks;
Nation shall not lift up sword against
nation,
Neither shall they learn war anymore.

The Day of the LORD

5 O house of Jacob,
come and let us walk
In the light of the LORD.

6 For You have forsaken Your people,
the house of Jacob,
Because they are filled with eastern
ways;
They *are* soothsayers like the
Philistines,
And they are pleased with the children
of foreigners.
7 Their land is also full of silver and
gold,
And *there is no* end to their treasures;
Their land is also full of horses,
And *there is no* end to their chariots.
8 Their land is also full of idols;
They worship the work of their own
hands,
That which their own fingers have
made.
9 People bow down,
And each man humbles himself;
Therefore do not forgive them.

10 Enter into the rock,
and hide in the dust,

From the terror of the LORD
And the glory of His majesty.
11 The lofty looks of man shall be
    humbled,
The haughtiness of men
    shall be bowed down,
And the LORD alone
    shall be exalted in that day.

12 For the day of the LORD of hosts
Shall come upon everything proud and
    lofty,
Upon everything lifted up—
And it shall be brought low—
13 Upon all the cedars of Lebanon
    that are high and lifted up,
And upon all the oaks of Bashan;
14 Upon all the high mountains,
And upon all the hills
    that are lifted up;
15 Upon every high tower,
And upon every fortified wall;
16 Upon all the ships of Tarshish,
And upon all the beautiful sloops.
17 The loftiness of man
    shall be bowed down,
And the haughtiness of men
    shall be brought low;
The LORD alone will be exalted
    in that day,
18 But the idols He shall utterly abolish.

19 They shall go into the holes of the
    rocks,
And into the caves of the earth,
From the terror of the LORD
And the glory of His majesty,
When He arises to shake the earth
    mightily.

20 In that day a man will cast away
    his idols of silver
And his idols of gold,
Which they made,
    each for himself to worship,
To the moles and bats,
21 To go into the clefts of the rocks,
And into the crags of the rugged rocks,
From the terror of the LORD
And the glory of His majesty,
When He arises to shake the earth
    mightily.

22 Sever yourselves from such a man,
Whose breath *is* in his nostrils;
For of what account is he?

Judgment on Judah and Jerusalem

3 For behold, the Lord,
    the LORD of hosts,

Takes away from Jerusalem
    and from Judah
The stock and the store,
The whole supply of bread
    and the whole supply of water;
2 The mighty man and the man of war,
The judge and the prophet,
And the diviner and the elder;
3 The captain of fifty
    and the honorable man,
The counselor and the skillful artisan,
And the expert enchanter.

4 "I will give children *to be* their princes,
And babes shall rule over them.
5 The people will be oppressed,
Every one by another and every one
    by his neighbor;
The child will be insolent toward the
    elder,
And the base toward the honorable."

6 When a man takes hold of his brother
In the house of his father, *saying*,
"You have clothing;
You be our ruler,
And *let* these ruins *be* under your
    hand,"
7 In that day he will protest, saying,
"I cannot cure *your* ills,
For in my house *is* neither food
    nor clothing;
Do not make me a ruler of the
    people."

8 For Jerusalem stumbled,
And Judah is fallen,
Because their tongue and their doings
Are against the LORD,
To provoke the eyes of His glory.
9 The look on their countenance
    witnesses against them,
And they declare their sin as Sodom;
They do not hide *it*.
Woe to their soul!
For they have brought evil upon
    themselves.

10 "Say to the righteous
    that *it shall be* well *with them*,
For they shall eat the fruit of their
    doings.
11 Woe to the wicked!
    It shall be ill *with him*,
For the reward of his hands shall be
    given him.
12 *As for* My people,
    children *are* their oppressors,
And women rule over them.

O My people! Those who lead you
  cause *you* to err,
And destroy the way of your paths."

Oppression and Luxury Condemned

13 The LORD stands up to plead,
  And stands to judge the people.
14 The LORD will enter into judgment
  With the elders of His people
  And His princes:
  "For you have eaten up the vineyard;
  The plunder of the poor *is* in your
    houses.
15 What do you mean by crushing My
    people
  And grinding the faces of the poor?"
  Says the Lord GOD of hosts.

16 Moreover the LORD says:

"Because the daughters of Zion are
    haughty,
And walk with outstretched necks
And wanton eyes,
Walking and mincing *as* they go,
Making a jingling with their feet,
17 Therefore the Lord will strike
  with a scab
The crown of the head
  of the daughters of Zion,
And the LORD will uncover
  their secret parts."

18 In that day the Lord will take away the
  finery:
The jingling anklets,
  the scarves,
  and the crescents;
19 The pendants,
  the bracelets,
  and the veils;
20 The headdresses,
  the leg ornaments,
  and the headbands;
The perfume boxes,
  the charms,
21   and the rings;
The nose jewels,
22   the festal apparel,
  and the mantles;
The outer garments,
  the purses,
23   and the mirrors;
The fine linen,
  the turbans,
  and the robes.

24 And so it shall be:

Instead of a sweet smell
  there will be a stench;
Instead of a sash, a rope;
Instead of well-set hair, baldness;
Instead of a rich robe,
  a girding of sackcloth;
And branding instead of beauty.
25 Your men shall fall by the sword,
  And your mighty in the war.

26 Her gates shall lament and mourn,
  And she *being* desolate
  shall sit on the ground.

4 And in that day seven women shall
  take hold of one man, saying,
"We will eat our own food
  and wear our own apparel;
Only let us be called by your name,
To take away our reproach."

The Renewal of Zion

2 In that day the Branch of the LORD
  shall be beautiful and glorious;
And the fruit of the earth *shall be*
  excellent and appealing
For those of Israel who have escaped.

3 And it shall come to pass that *he who
is* left in Zion and *he who* remains in Jerusalem will be called holy—everyone who
is recorded among the living in Jerusalem.
4 When the Lord has washed away the
filth of the daughters of Zion, and purged
the blood of Jerusalem from her midst,
by the spirit of judgment and by the spirit
of burning,
5 then the LORD will create above every
dwelling place of Mount Zion, and above
her assemblies, a cloud and smoke by day
and the shining of a flaming fire by night.
For over all the glory there *will be* a covering.
6 And there will be a tabernacle for
shade in the daytime from the heat, for a
place of refuge, and for a shelter from
storm and rain.

God's Disappointing Vineyard

5 Now let me sing to my Well-beloved
  A song of my Beloved regarding His
    vineyard:

My Well-beloved has a vineyard
On a very fruitful hill.
2 He dug it up and cleared out its stones,
And planted it with the choicest vine.

He built a tower in its midst,
And also made a winepress in it;
So He expected *it* to bring forth *good*
grapes,
But it brought forth wild grapes.

3 "And now, O inhabitants of Jerusalem
and men of Judah,
Judge, please, between Me and My
vineyard.
4 What more could have been done to
My vineyard
That I have not done in it?
Why then, when I expected *it* to bring
forth *good* grapes,
Did it bring forth wild grapes?
5 And now, please let Me tell you
what I will do to My vineyard:
I will take away its hedge,
and it shall be burned;
And break down its wall,
and it shall be trampled down.
6 I will lay it waste;
It shall not be pruned or dug,
But there shall come up briers and
thorns.
I will also command the clouds
That they rain no rain on it."

7 For the vineyard of the LORD of hosts
is the house of Israel,
And the men of Judah
are His pleasant plant.
He looked for justice,
but behold, oppression;
For righteousness, but behold, weeping.

Impending Judgment on Excesses

8 Woe to those who join house to house,
Who add field to field,
Till *there is* no place
Where they may dwell alone
in the midst of the land!
9 In my hearing the LORD of hosts *said*,
"Truly, many houses shall be desolate,
Great and beautiful ones,
without inhabitant.
10 For ten acres of vineyard shall yield
one bath,
And a homer of seed shall yield one
ephah."

11 Woe to those who rise early in the
morning,
That they may follow intoxicating
drink;
Who continue until night,
till wine inflames them!

12 The harp and the strings,
The tambourine and flute,
And wine are in their feasts;
But they do not regard the work
of the LORD,
Nor consider the operation of His
hands.

13 Therefore my people have gone
into captivity,
Because *they have* no knowledge;
Their honorable men *are* famished,
And their multitude dried up with
thirst.
14 Therefore Sheol has enlarged itself
And opened its mouth beyond
measure;
Their glory and their multitude
and their pomp,
And he who is jubilant,
shall descend into it.
15 People shall be brought down,
Each man shall be humbled,
And the eyes of the lofty
shall be humbled.
16 But the LORD of hosts
shall be exalted in judgment,
And God who is holy shall be
hallowed in righteousness.
17 Then the lambs shall feed in their
pasture,
And in the waste places of the fat ones
strangers shall eat.

18 Woe to those who draw iniquity
with cords of vanity,
And sin as if with a cart rope;
19 That say, "Let Him make speed
and hasten His work,
That we may see *it*;
And let the counsel of the Holy One
of Israel draw near and come,
That we may know *it*."

20 Woe to those who call evil good,
and good evil;
Who put darkness for light,
and light for darkness;
Who put bitter for sweet,
and sweet for bitter!

21 Woe to *those who are* wise
in their own eyes,
And prudent in their own sight!

22 Woe to men mighty at drinking wine,
Woe to men valiant for mixing
intoxicating drink,
23 Who justify the wicked for a bribe,

And take away justice from the
righteous man!

24 Therefore, as the fire devours the
    stubble,
And the flame consumes the chaff,
So their root will be as rottenness,
And their blossom will ascend like
    dust;
Because they have rejected the law of
    the LORD of hosts,
And despised the word of the Holy
    One of Israel.
25 Therefore the anger of the LORD is
    aroused against His people;
He has stretched out His hand
    against them
And stricken them,
And the hills trembled.
Their carcasses *were* as refuse
    in the midst of the streets.

For all this His anger is not turned
    away,
But His hand *is* stretched out still.

26 He will lift up a banner to the nations
    from afar,
And will whistle to them from the end
    of the earth;
Surely they shall come with speed,
    swiftly.
27 No one will be weary or stumble
    among them,
No one will slumber or sleep;
Nor will the belt on their loins
    be loosed,
Nor the strap of their sandals
    be broken;
28 Whose arrows *are* sharp,
And all their bows bent;
Their horses' hooves will seem like
    flint,
And their wheels like a whirlwind.
29 Their roaring *will be* like a lion,
They will roar like young lions;
Yes, they will roar
And lay hold of the prey;
They will carry *it* away safely,
And no one will deliver.
30 In that day they will roar against them
Like the roaring of the sea.
And if *one* looks to the land,
Behold, darkness *and* sorrow;
And the light is darkened by the
    clouds.

Isaiah Called to Be a Prophet

6 In the year that King Uzziah died, I
saw the Lord sitting on a throne,

high and lifted up, and the train of His
robe filled the temple.
2 Above it stood seraphim; each one
had six wings: with two he covered his
face, with two he covered his feet, and
with two he flew.
3 And one cried to another and said:

    "Holy, holy, holy *is* the LORD of hosts;
    The whole earth *is* full of His glory!"

4 And the posts of the door were shaken
by the voice of him who cried out, and
the house was filled with smoke.

5 Then I said:

    "Woe *is* me, for I am undone!
    Because I *am* a man of unclean lips,
    And I dwell in the midst of a people
      of unclean lips;
    For my eyes have seen the King,
    The LORD of hosts."

6 Then one of the seraphim flew to me,
having in his hand a live coal *which* he
had taken with the tongs from the altar.
7 And he touched my mouth *with it,*
and said:

    "Behold, this has touched your lips;
    Your iniquity is taken away,
    And your sin purged."

8 Also I heard the voice of the Lord,
saying:

    "Whom shall I send,
    And who will go for Us?"

Then I said, "Here *am* I! Send me."

9 And He said, "Go, and tell this people:

    'Keep on hearing, but do not
      understand;
    Keep on seeing, but do not perceive.'

10 "Make the heart of this people dull,
    And their ears heavy,
    And shut their eyes;
    Lest they see with their eyes,
    And hear with their ears,
    And understand with their heart,
    And return and be healed."

11 Then I said, "Lord, how long?" And
He answered:

"Until the cities are laid waste
  and without inhabitant,
The houses are without a man,
The land is utterly desolate,
12 The LORD has removed men far away,
And the forsaken places *are* many in
  the midst of the land.
13 But yet a tenth *will be* in it,
And will return and be for consuming,
As a terebinth tree or as an oak,
Whose stump *remains* when it is cut
  down.
So the holy seed *shall be* its stump."

Isaiah Sent to King Ahaz

7 Now it came to pass in the days of
  Ahaz the son of Jotham, the son of
Uzziah, king of Judah, *that* Rezin king
of Syria and Pekah the son of Remaliah,
king of Israel, went up to Jerusalem to
make war against it, but could not prevail
against it. 2 And it was told to the house of David,
saying, "Syria's forces are deployed in
Ephraim." So his heart and the heart of
his people were moved as the trees of the
woods are moved with the wind. 3 Then the LORD said to Isaiah, "Go
out now to meet Ahaz, you and Shear-
Jashub² your son, at the end of the aqueduct from the upper pool, on the highway
to the Fuller's Field, 4 "and say to him: 'Take heed, and be
quiet; do not fear or be fainthearted for
these two stubs of smoking firebrands, for
the fierce anger of Rezin and Syria, and
the son of Remaliah. 5 'Because Syria, Ephraim, and the son
of Remaliah have taken evil counsel
against you, saying, 6 "Let us go up against Judah and trouble it, and let us make a gap in its wall for
ourselves, and set a king over them, the
son of Tabeel"— 7 'thus says the Lord GOD:

"It shall not stand,
  Nor shall it come to pass.
8 For the head of Syria *is* Damascus,
And the head of Damascus *is* Rezin.
Within sixty-five years
  Ephraim will be broken,
So that it will not *be* a people.
9 The head of Ephraim *is* Samaria,
And the head of Samaria
  is Remaliah's son.
If you will not believe,
Surely you shall not be established." ' "

The Immanuel Prophecy

10 Moreover the LORD spoke again to
Ahaz, saying, 11 "Ask a sign for yourself from the
LORD your God; ask it either in the depth
or in the height above." 12 But Ahaz said, "I will not ask, nor will
I test the LORD!" 13 Then he said, "Hear now, O house of
David! *Is it* a small thing for you to
weary men, but will you weary my God
also? 14 "Therefore the Lord Himself will give
you a sign: Behold, the virgin shall conceive and bear a Son, and shall call His
name Immanuel.³ 15 "Curds and honey He shall eat, that
He may know to refuse the evil and
choose the good. 16 "For before the Child shall know to
refuse the evil and choose the good, the
land that you dread will be forsaken by
both her kings. 17 "The LORD will bring the king of Assyria upon you and your people and your
father's house—days that have not come
since the day that Ephraim departed
from Judah."

18 And it shall come to pass in that day
That the LORD will whistle for the fly
That *is* in the farthest part of the rivers
  of Egypt,
And for the bee that *is* in the land of
  Assyria.
19 They will come,
  and all of them will rest
In the desolate valleys
  and in the clefts of the rocks,
And on all thorns and in all pastures.

20 In the same day the Lord will shave
  with a hired razor,
With those from beyond the River,⁴
  with the king of Assyria,
The head and the hair of the legs,
And will also remove the beard.

21 It shall be in that day
That a man will keep alive
  a young cow and two sheep;
22 So it shall be, from the abundance of
  milk they give,
That he will eat curds;
For curds and honey everyone will eat
  who is left in the land.

23 It shall happen in that day,

2 Literally *A Remnant Shall Return*   3 Literally *God-With-Us*   4 That is, the Euphrates

That wherever there could be a
  thousand vines
Worth a thousand *shekels* of silver,
It will be for briers and thorns.
24 With arrows and bows men will come
  there,
Because all the land will become briers
  and thorns.

25 And to any hill which could be dug
  with the hoe,
You will not go there for fear of briers
  and thorns;
But it will become a range for oxen
And a place for sheep to roam.

Assyria Will Invade the Land

8 Moreover the LORD said to me,
  "Take a large scroll, and write on it
with a man's pen concerning Maher-
Shalal-Hash-Baz.[5]
2 "And I will take for Myself faithful
witnesses to record, Uriah the priest and
Zechariah the son of Jeberechiah."
3 Then I went to the prophetess, and
she conceived and bore a son. Then the
LORD said to me, "Call his name Maher-
Shalal-Hash-Baz;
4 "for before the child shall have knowledge to cry 'My father' and 'My mother,'
the riches of Damascus and the spoil of
Samaria will be taken away before the
king of Assyria."
5 The LORD also spoke to me again,
saying:

6 "Inasmuch as these people refused
  The waters of Shiloah that flow softly,
  And rejoice in Rezin
    and in Remaliah's son;
7 Now therefore, behold,
    the Lord brings up over them
  The waters of the River,[6]
    strong and mighty—
  The king of Assyria and all his glory;
  He will go up over all his channels
  And go over all his banks.
8 He will pass through Judah,
  He will overflow and pass over,
  He will reach up to the neck;
  And the stretching out of his wings
  Will fill the breadth of Your land,
  O Immanuel.[7]

9 "Be shattered, O you peoples,
    and be broken in pieces!
  Give ear, all you from far countries.

Gird yourselves,
  but be broken in pieces;
Gird yourselves,
  but be broken in pieces.
10 Take counsel together,
  but it will come to nothing;
Speak the word, but it will not stand,
For God *is* with us."[8]

Fear God, Heed His Word

11 For the LORD spoke thus to me with a
strong hand, and instructed me that I
should not walk in the way of this people,
saying:

12 "Do not say, 'A conspiracy,'
  Concerning all that this people
    call a conspiracy,
  Nor be afraid of their threats,
    nor be troubled.
13 The LORD of hosts,
    Him you shall hallow;
  Let Him *be* your fear,
  And *let* Him *be* your dread.
14 He will be as a sanctuary,
  But a stone of stumbling
    and a rock of offense
  To both the houses of Israel,
  As a trap and a snare to the
    inhabitants of Jerusalem.
15 And many among them shall stumble;
  They shall fall and be broken,
  Be snared and taken."

16 Bind up the testimony,
  Seal the law among my disciples.
17 And I will wait on the LORD,
  Who hides His face from the house
    of Jacob;
  And I will hope in Him.
18 Here am I and the children whom the
    LORD has given me!
  We are for signs and wonders in Israel
  From the LORD of hosts,
  Who dwells in Mount Zion.

19 And when they say to you, "Seek
those who are mediums and wizards, who
whisper and mutter," should not a people
seek their God? *Should they seek* the
dead on behalf of the living?
20 To the law and to the testimony! If
they do not speak according to this word,
it is because *there is* no light in them.
21 And they will pass through it hard
pressed and hungry; and it shall happen,
when they are hungry, that they will be
enraged and curse their king and their
God, and look upward.

---

5 Literally *Speed the Spoil, Hasten the Booty*   6 That is, the Euphrates   7 Literally *God-With-Us*
8 Hebrew *Immanuel*

22 Then they will look to the earth, and see trouble and darkness, gloom of anguish; and *they will be* driven into darkness.

The Government of the Promised Son

9 Nevertheless the gloom *will* not *be*
　　upon her who *is* distressed,
As when at first He lightly esteemed
The land of Zebulun
　　and the land of Naphtali,
And afterward more heavily
　　oppressed *her,*
By the way of the sea,
　　beyond the Jordan,
In Galilee of the Gentiles.
2 The people who walked in darkness
　Have seen a great light;
　Those who dwelt in the land of the
　　shadow of death,
　Upon them a light has shined.

3 You have multiplied the nation
　And increased its joy;
　They rejoice before You
　According to the joy of harvest,
　As *men* rejoice when they divide the
　　spoil.
4 For You have broken the yoke
　　of his burden
　And the staff of his shoulder,
　The rod of his oppressor,
　As in the day of Midian.
5 For every warrior's sandal from the
　　noisy battle,
　And garments rolled in blood,
　Will be used for burning *and* fuel of
　　fire.

6 For unto us a Child is born,
　Unto us a Son is given;
　And the government will be upon His
　　shoulder.
　And His name will be called
　Wonderful, Counselor, Mighty God,
　Everlasting Father, Prince of Peace.
7 Of the increase of *His* government
　　and peace
　There will be no end,
　Upon the throne of David
　　and over His kingdom,
　To order it and establish it with
　　judgment and justice
　From that time forward, even forever.
　The zeal of the LORD of hosts will
　　perform this.

The Punishment of Samaria

8 The LORD sent a word against Jacob,
　And it has fallen on Israel.

9 All the people will know—
　Ephraim and the inhabitant of
　　Samaria—
　Who say in pride
　　and arrogance of heart:
10 "The bricks have fallen down,
　But we will rebuild with hewn stones;
　The sycamores are cut down,
　But we will replace *them* with cedars."
11 Therefore the LORD shall set up
　The adversaries of Rezin against him,
　And spur his enemies on,
12 The Syrians before
　　and the Philistines behind;
　And they shall devour Israel with an
　　open mouth.

For all this His anger is not turned
　away,
But His hand *is* stretched out still.

13 For the people do not turn to Him
　　who strikes them,
　Nor do they seek the LORD of hosts.
14 Therefore the LORD will cut off
　　head and tail from Israel,
　Palm branch and bulrush in one day.
15 The elder and honorable,
　　he *is* the head;
　The prophet who teaches lies,
　　he *is* the tail.
16 For the leaders of this people cause
　　them to err,
　And *those who are* led by them are
　　destroyed.
17 Therefore the LORD will have no joy in
　　their young men,
　Nor have mercy on their fatherless and
　　widows;
　For everyone *is* a hypocrite
　　and an evildoer,
　And every mouth speaks folly.

For all this His anger is not turned
　away,
But His hand *is* stretched out still.

18 For wickedness burns as the fire;
　It shall devour the briers and thorns,
　And kindle in the thickets of the
　　forest;
　They shall mount up *like* rising smoke.
19 Through the wrath of the LORD of
　　hosts
　The land is burned up,
　And the people shall be as fuel
　　for the fire;
　No man shall spare his brother.
20 And he shall snatch on the right hand
　And be hungry;

Light in a Land of Darkness

The land of Zebulun and the land of Naphtali . . .
Those who dwelt in the land of the shadow of death,
Upon them a light has shined.

(Is. 9:1, 2)

From the dawn of recorded history, the inhabitants of Zebulun and Naphtali on the northwest shores of the Sea of Galilee have been trampled beneath the heel of invading armies. Their home was located on the famous *Via Maris*—"the way of the sea," which connected the empires of the ancient world. Assyria, Babylon, Mesopotamia, Rome, and Greece—all sought to control this road to further expand their kingdom.

The *Via Maris* was the important land bridge linking the three continents of Europe, Africa, and Asia. Stretching from Egypt and North Africa, this strategic highway ran along the coast of Palestine. In the area of Mount Carmel the *Via Maris* turned inland through the famous town of Megiddo, across the Jezreel Valley. It continued north through a narrow pass along the Sea of Galilee, and onward to Damascus.

The people of Galilee benefited from the commerce and trade provided by the merchant caravans that traveled along this road. But they also suffered greatly under the constant wave of warring armies, who in their quest for power, destroyed villages, killed men, raped women, enslaved children, and pillaged the land.

Nation after nation mounted their campaigns along this thoroughfare. Pharaoh's Thutmose III, Amenhotep II, Ramses II, Seti I; Assyria's Sennacherib; Babylon's Nebuchadnezzar; Macedonia's Alexander the Great; Egypt's Cleopatra; and Rome's Mark Anthony, Vespasian, Titus, and many others marched on this highway.

Along the *Via Maris*, Jesus first began His ministry and it was here that Jesus appeared after His resurrection to declare the final victory over sin and death. To an area that was overrun by nations trying by force to build their kingdoms, Jesus brought the healing kingdom of God. Where empires had carried on campaigns of violence, destruction and death, Jesus carried His campaign of peace, hope, and life. To a region that had seen great darkness, Jesus brought light!

He shall devour on the left hand
And not be satisfied;
Every man shall eat the flesh of his
own arm.
21 Manasseh *shall devour* Ephraim,
and Ephraim Manasseh,
And they together *shall be* against
Judah.

For all this His anger is not turned
away,
But His hand *is* stretched out still.

10 "Woe to those who decree
unrighteous decrees,
Who write misfortune,
Which they have prescribed,
2 To rob the needy of justice,
And to take what is right from the
poor of My people,
That widows may be their prey,
And *that* they may rob the fatherless.
3 What will you do in the day of
punishment,
And in the desolation *which* will come
from afar?
To whom will you flee for help?
And where will you leave your glory?
4 Without Me they shall bow down
among the prisoners,
And they shall fall among the slain."

For all this His anger is not turned
away,
But His hand *is* stretched out still.

Arrogant Assyria Also Judged

5 "Woe to Assyria, the rod of My anger
And the staff in whose hand is My
indignation.
6 I will send him against an ungodly
nation,
And against the people of My wrath
I will give him charge,
To seize the spoil, to take the prey,
And to tread them down like the mire
of the streets.
7 Yet he does not mean so,
Nor does his heart think so;
But *it is* in his heart to destroy,
And cut off not a few nations.
8 For he says,
'*Are* not my princes altogether kings?
9 *Is* not Calno like Carchemish?
Is not Hamath like Arpad?
Is not Samaria like Damascus?
10 As my hand has found the kingdoms
of the idols,
Whose carved images excelled those
of Jerusalem and Samaria,

11 As I have done to Samaria and her
idols,
Shall I not do also to Jerusalem
and her idols?' "

12 Therefore it shall come to pass, when
the LORD has performed all His work on
Mount Zion and on Jerusalem, *that He
will say,* "I will punish the fruit of the
arrogant heart of the king of Assyria, and
the glory of his haughty looks."
13 For he says:

"By the strength of my hand
I have done *it*,
And by my wisdom, for I am prudent;
Also I have removed the boundaries
of the people,
And have robbed their treasuries;
So I have put down the inhabitants
like a valiant *man.*
14 My hand has found like a nest the
riches of the people,
And as one gathers eggs *that are* left,
I have gathered all the earth;
And there was no one
who moved *his* wing,
Nor opened *his* mouth
with even a peep."

15 Shall the ax boast itself against
him who chops with it?
Or shall the saw magnify itself against
him who saws with it?
As if a rod could wield *itself* against
those who lift it up,
Or as if a staff could lift up,
as if it were not wood!
16 Therefore the Lord,
the Lord[9] of hosts,
Will send leanness among his fat ones;
And under his glory
He will kindle a burning
Like the burning of a fire.
17 So the Light of Israel will be for a fire,
And his Holy One for a flame;
It will burn and devour
His thorns and his briers in one day.
18 And it will consume the glory of his
forest and of his fruitful field,
Both soul and body;
And they will be as when a sick man
wastes away.
19 Then the rest of the trees of his forest
Will be so few in number
That a child may write them.

The Returning Remnant of Israel

20 And it shall come to pass in that day
That the remnant of Israel,

9 Masoretic Text and Dead Sea Scrolls read *YHWH.*

And such as have escaped of the house
of Jacob,
Will never again depend on him who
defeated them,
But will depend on the LORD,
the Holy One of Israel, in truth.
21 The remnant will return,
the remnant of Jacob,
To the Mighty God.
22 For though your people, O Israel,
be as the sand of the sea,
Yet a remnant of them will return;
The destruction decreed shall overflow
with righteousness.
23 For the Lord GOD of hosts
Will make a determined end
In the midst of all the land.

24 Therefore thus says the Lord GOD of
hosts: "O My people, who dwell in Zion,
do not be afraid of the Assyrian. He shall
strike you with a rod and lift up his staff
against you, in the manner of Egypt.
25 "For yet a very little while and the
indignation will cease, as will My anger
in their destruction."
26 And the LORD of hosts will stir up a
scourge for him like the slaughter of Midian at the rock of Oreb; *as* His rod was on
the sea, so will He lift it up in the manner
of Egypt.

27 It shall come to pass in that day
That his burden will be taken away
from your shoulder,
And his yoke from your neck,
And the yoke will be destroyed because
of the anointing oil.

28 He has come to Aiath,
He has passed Migron;
At Michmash he has attended to his
equipment.
29 They have gone along the ridge,
They have taken up lodging at Geba.
Ramah is afraid,
Gibeah of Saul has fled.
30 Lift up your voice,
O daughter of Gallim!
Cause it to be heard as far as Laish—
O poor Anathoth!
31 Madmenah has fled,
The inhabitants of Gebim seek refuge.
32 As yet he will remain at Nob that day;
He will shake his fist at the mount of
the daughter of Zion,
The hill of Jerusalem.

33 Behold, the Lord,
The LORD of hosts,

Will lop off the bough with terror;
Those of high stature
will be hewn down,
And the haughty will be humbled.
34 He will cut down the thickets of the
forest with iron,
And Lebanon will fall by the Mighty
One.

The Reign of Jesse's Offspring

11 There shall come forth a Rod
from the stem of Jesse,
And a Branch shall grow
out of his roots.
2 The Spirit of the LORD
shall rest upon Him,
The Spirit of wisdom
and understanding,
The Spirit of counsel and might,
The Spirit of knowledge
and of the fear of the LORD.

3 His delight *is* in the fear of the LORD,
And He shall not judge by the sight of
His eyes,
Nor decide by the hearing of His ears;
4 But with righteousness He shall judge
the poor,
And decide with equity for the meek of
the earth;
He shall strike the earth with the rod
of His mouth,
And with the breath of His lips He
shall slay the wicked.
5 Righteousness shall be the belt of His
loins,
And faithfulness the belt of His waist.

6 "The wolf also shall dwell
with the lamb,
The leopard shall lie down
with the young goat,
The calf and the young lion
and the fatling together;
And a little child shall lead them.
7 The cow and the bear shall graze;
Their young ones shall lie down
together;
And the lion shall eat straw like the ox.
8 The nursing child shall play
by the cobra's hole,
And the weaned child shall put his
hand in the viper's den.
9 They shall not hurt nor destroy in all
My holy mountain,
For the earth shall be full of the
knowledge of the LORD
As the waters cover the sea.

10"And in that day there shall be a Root
of Jesse,

Who shall stand as a banner to the
people;
For the Gentiles shall seek Him,
And His resting place shall be
glorious."

11 It shall come to pass in that day
That the LORD shall set His hand again
the second time
To recover the remnant of His people
who are left,
From Assyria and Egypt,
From Pathros and Cush,
From Elam and Shinar,
From Hamath and the islands
of the sea.

12 He will set up a banner for the nations,
And will assemble the outcasts of
Israel,
And gather together the dispersed of
Judah
From the four corners of the earth.
13 Also the envy of Ephraim shall depart,
And the adversaries of Judah shall be
cut off;
Ephraim shall not envy Judah,
And Judah shall not harass Ephraim.
14 But they shall fly down upon the
shoulder of the Philistines toward the
west;
Together they shall plunder the people
of the east;
They shall lay their hand on Edom and
Moab;
And the people of Ammon shall obey
them.
15 The LORD will utterly destroy the
tongue of the Sea of Egypt;
With His mighty wind He will shake
His fist over the River,[10]
And strike it in the seven streams,
And make *men* cross over dryshod.
16 There will be a highway for the
remnant of His people
Who will be left from Assyria,
As it was for Israel
In the day that he came up
from the land of Egypt.

A Hymn of Praise

12 And in that day you will say:

"O LORD, I will praise You;
Though You were angry with me,
Your anger is turned away,
and You comfort me.
2 Behold, God *is* my salvation,
I will trust and not be afraid;

'For YAH, the LORD,
is my strength and *my* song;
He also has become my salvation.' "[11]

3 Therefore with joy you will draw water
From the wells of salvation.

4 And in that day you will say:

"Praise the LORD, call upon His name;
Declare His deeds among the peoples,
Make mention that His name is
exalted.
5 Sing to the LORD,
For He has done excellent things;
This *is* known in all the earth.
6 Cry out and shout,
O inhabitant of Zion,
For great *is* the Holy One of Israel
in your midst!"

Proclamation Against Babylon

13 The burden against Babylon
which Isaiah the son of Amoz saw.

2 "Lift up a banner on the high mountain,
Raise your voice to them;
Wave your hand, that they may enter
the gates of the nobles.
3 I have commanded My sanctified ones;
I have also called My mighty ones for
My anger—
Those who rejoice in My exaltation."

4 The noise of a multitude in the
mountains,
Like that of many people!
A tumultuous noise of the kingdoms
of nations gathered together!
The LORD of hosts musters
The army for battle.
5 They come from a far country,
From the end of heaven,
Even the LORD and His weapons
of indignation,
To destroy the whole land.

6 Wail, for the day of the LORD *is* at
hand!
It will come as destruction from the
Almighty.
7 Therefore all hands will be limp,
Every man's heart will melt,
8 And they will be afraid.
Pangs and sorrows
will take hold of *them*;
They will be in pain
as a woman in childbirth;
They will be amazed at one another;
Their faces *will be like* flames.

10 That is, the Euphrates   11 Compare Exodus 15:2

9 Behold, the day of the LORD comes,
  Cruel, with both wrath and fierce
      anger,
  To lay the land desolate;
  And He will destroy its sinners from it.
10 For the stars of heaven and their
      constellations
  Will not give their light;
  The sun will be darkened in its going
      forth,
  And the moon will not cause its light
      to shine.

11 "I will punish the world for *its* evil,
  And the wicked for their iniquity;
  I will halt the arrogance of the proud,
  And will lay low the haughtiness of the
      terrible.
12 I will make a mortal more rare than
      fine gold,
  A man more than the golden wedge of
      Ophir.
13 Therefore I will shake the heavens,
  And the earth will move out of her
      place,
  In the wrath of the LORD of hosts
  And in the day of His fierce anger.
14 It shall be as the hunted gazelle,
  And as a sheep that no man takes up;
  Every man will turn to his own people,
  And everyone will flee to his own land.
15 Everyone who is found
      will be thrust through,
  And everyone who is captured
      will fall by the sword.
16 Their children also will be dashed
      to pieces before their eyes;
  Their houses will be plundered
  And their wives ravished.

17 "Behold, I will stir up the Medes
      against them,
  Who will not regard silver;
  And *as for* gold,
      they will not delight in it.
18 Also *their* bows will dash
      the young men to pieces,
  And they will have no pity
      on the fruit of the womb;
  Their eye will not spare children.
19 And Babylon, the glory of kingdoms,
  The beauty of the Chaldeans' pride,
  Will be as when God overthrew Sodom
      and Gomorrah.
20 It will never be inhabited,
  Nor will it be settled
      from generation to generation;
  Nor will the Arabian pitch tents there,
  Nor will the shepherds make their
      sheepfolds there.

21 But wild beasts of the desert will lie
      there,
  And their houses will be full of owls;
  Ostriches will dwell there,
  And wild goats will caper there.
22 The hyenas will howl in their citadels,
  And jackals in their pleasant palaces.
  Her time *is* near to come,
  And her days will not be prolonged."

Mercy on Jacob

14 For the LORD will have mercy on
  Jacob, and will still choose Israel,
and settle them in their own land. The
strangers will be joined with them, and
they will cling to the house of Jacob.
2 Then people will take them and bring
them to their place, and the house of Israel will possess them for servants and
maids in the land of the LORD; they will
take them captive whose captives they
were, and rule over their oppressors.

Fall of the King of Babylon

3 It shall come to pass in the day the
LORD gives you rest from your sorrow,
and from your fear and the hard bondage
in which you were made to serve,
4 that you will take up this proverb
against the king of Babylon, and say:

  "How the oppressor has ceased,
  The golden[12] city ceased!
5 The LORD has broken the staff
      of the wicked,
  The scepter of the rulers;
6 He who struck the people in wrath
      with a continual stroke,
  He who ruled the nations in anger,
  Is persecuted *and* no one hinders.
7 The whole earth is at rest *and* quiet;
  They break forth into singing.
8 Indeed the cypress trees rejoice over
      you,
  And the cedars of Lebanon,
  Saying, 'Since you were cut down,
  No woodsman has come up against us.'

9 "Hell from beneath is excited about you,
  To meet *you* at your coming;
  It stirs up the dead for you,
  All the chief ones of the earth;
  It has raised up from their thrones
  All the kings of the nations.
10 They all shall speak and say to you:
  'Have you also become as weak as we?
  Have you become like us?
11 Your pomp is brought down to Sheol,

12 Or *insolent*

And the sound of your stringed
  instruments;
The maggot is spread under you,
And worms cover you.'

The Fall of Lucifer

12"How you are fallen from heaven,
  O Lucifer,[13] son of the morning!
How you are cut down to the ground,
  You who weakened the nations!
13 For you have said in your heart:
  'I will ascend into heaven,
  I will exalt my throne above the stars
    of God;
  I will also sit on the mount of the
    congregation
  On the farthest sides of the north;
14 I will ascend above the heights of the
    clouds,
  I will be like the Most High.'
15 Yet you shall be brought down to
    Sheol,
  To the lowest depths of the Pit.

16 "Those who see you will gaze at you,
  And consider you, *saying*:
  '*Is* this the man who made the earth
    tremble,
  Who shook kingdoms,
17 Who made the world as a wilderness
  And destroyed its cities,
  Who did not open the house of his
    prisoners?'

18 "All the kings of the nations,
  All of them, sleep in glory,
  Everyone in his own house;
19 But you are cast out of your grave
  Like an abominable branch,
  Like the garment of those who are
    slain,
  Thrust through with a sword,
  Who go down to the stones of the pit,
  Like a corpse trodden under foot.
20 You will not be joined with them in
    burial,
  Because you have destroyed your land
  And slain your people.
  The brood of evildoers shall never be
    named.
21 Prepare slaughter for his children
  Because of the iniquity of their fathers,
  Lest they rise up and possess the land,
  And fill the face of the world with
    cities."

Babylon Destroyed

22"For I will rise up against them,"
  says the LORD of hosts,

"And cut off from Babylon
  the name and remnant,
  And offspring and posterity,"
  says the LORD.
23 "I will also make it a possession
    for the porcupine,
  And marshes of muddy water;
  I will sweep it with the broom of
    destruction," says the LORD of hosts.

Assyria Destroyed

24 The LORD of hosts has sworn, saying,
  "Surely, as I have thought,
    so it shall come to pass,
  And as I have purposed,
  so it shall stand:
25 That I will break the Assyrian
    in My land,
  And on My mountains tread him
    under foot.
  Then his yoke shall be removed
    from them,
  And his burden removed from their
    shoulders.
26 This *is* the purpose that is purposed
    against the whole earth,
  And this *is* the hand that is stretched
    out over all the nations.
27 For the LORD of hosts has purposed,
  And who will annul *it*?
  His hand *is* stretched out,
  And who will turn it back?"

Philistia Destroyed

28 This is the burden which came in the
year that King Ahaz died.

29 "Do not rejoice, all you of Philistia,
  Because the rod that struck you is
    broken;
  For out of the serpent's roots
    will come forth a viper,
  And its offspring *will be*
    a fiery flying serpent.
30 The firstborn of the poor will feed,
  And the needy will lie down in safety;
  I will kill your roots with famine,
  And it will slay your remnant.
31 Wail, O gate! Cry, O city!
  All you of Philistia *are* dissolved;
  For smoke will come from the north,
  And no one *will be* alone in his
    appointed times."

32 What will *one* then answer the
    messengers of the nation?
  That the LORD has founded Zion,
  And the poor of His people shall take
    refuge in it.

13 Literally *Day Star*

Proclamation Against Moab

15
The burden against Moab.

Because in the night
   Ar of Moab is laid waste
And destroyed,
Because in the night
   Kir of Moab is laid waste
And destroyed,
2   He has gone up to the temple[14]
      and Dibon,
   To the high places to weep.
   Moab will wail over Nebo
      and over Medeba;
   On all their heads *will be* baldness,
   And every beard cut off.
3   In their streets they will clothe
      themselves with sackcloth;
   On the tops of their houses
   And in their streets
   Everyone will wail, weeping bitterly.
4   Heshbon and Elealeh will cry out,
   Their voice shall be heard as far as
      Jahaz;
   Therefore the armed soldiers of Moab
      will cry out;
   His life will be burdensome to him.

5   "My heart will cry out for Moab;
   His fugitives *shall flee* to Zoar,
   Like a three-year-old heifer.[15]
   For by the ascent of Luhith
   They will go up with weeping;
   For in the way of Horonaim
   They will raise up a cry of destruction,
6   For the waters of Nimrim
      will be desolate,
   For the green grass has withered away;
   The grass fails, there is nothing green.
7   Therefore the abundance they have
      gained,
   And what they have laid up,
   They will carry away to the Brook of
      the Willows.
8   For the cry has gone all around the
      borders of Moab,
   Its wailing to Eglaim
   And its wailing to Beer Elim.
9   For the waters of Dimon
      will be full of blood;
   Because I will bring more upon
      Dimon,
   Lions upon him who escapes from
      Moab,
   And on the remnant of the land."

Moab Destroyed

16
Send the lamb to the ruler of the
land,

From Sela to the wilderness,
To the mount of the daughter of Zion.
2   For it shall be as a wandering bird
      thrown out of the nest;
   So shall be the daughters of Moab at
      the fords of the Arnon.

3   "Take counsel, execute judgment;
   Make your shadow like the night
      in the middle of the day;
   Hide the outcasts,
   Do not betray him who escapes.
4   Let My outcasts dwell with you,
      O Moab;
   Be a shelter to them from the face
      of the spoiler.
   For the extortioner is at an end,
   Devastation ceases,
   The oppressors are consumed
      out of the land.
5   In mercy the throne will be
      established;
   And One will sit on it in truth,
      in the tabernacle of David,
   Judging and seeking justice
      and hastening righteousness."

6   We have heard of the pride of Moab—
   He is very proud—
   Of his haughtiness and his pride
      and his wrath;
   But his lies *shall* not *be* so.
7   Therefore Moab shall wail for Moab;
   Everyone shall wail.
   For the foundations of Kir Hareseth
      you shall mourn;
   Surely *they are* stricken.

8   For the fields of Heshbon languish,
   And the vine of Sibmah;
   The lords of the nations have broken
      down its choice plants,
   Which have reached to Jazer
   And wandered through the wilderness.
   Her branches are stretched out,
   They are gone over the sea.
9   Therefore I will bewail the vine
      of Sibmah,
   With the weeping of Jazer;
   I will drench you with my tears,
   O Heshbon and Elealeh;
   For battle cries have fallen
   Over your summer fruits
      and your harvest.

10   Gladness is taken away,
   And joy from the plentiful field;
   In the vineyards there will be no
      singing,
   Nor will there be shouting;

14 Hebrew *bayith* (house)   15 Or *The Third Eglath,* an unknown city (compare Jeremiah 48:34)

No treaders will tread out wine
  in *their* presses;
I have made their shouting cease.
11 Therefore my heart shall resound
  like a harp for Moab,
And my inner being for Kir Heres.

12 And it shall come to pass,
  When it is seen that Moab is weary
    on the high place,
That he will come to his sanctuary
    to pray;
But he will not prevail.

13 This *is* the word which the LORD has
spoken concerning Moab since that time.
14 But now the LORD has spoken, saying,
"Within three years, as the years of a
hired man, the glory of Moab will be despised with all that great multitude, and
the remnant *will be* very small *and* feeble."

Proclamation Against Syria and Israel

17 The burden against Damascus.

"Behold, Damascus will cease from
  being a city,
And it will be a ruinous heap.
2 The cities of Aroer *are* forsaken;
  They will be for flocks
Which lie down,
  and no one will make *them* afraid.
3 The fortress also will cease from
  Ephraim,
The kingdom from Damascus,
And the remnant of Syria;
  They will be as the glory of the
    children of Israel,"
Says the LORD of hosts.

4 "In that day it shall come to pass
  That the glory of Jacob will wane,
And the fatness of his flesh grow lean.
5 It shall be as when the harvester
  gathers the grain,
And reaps the heads with his arm;
It shall be as he who gathers heads
  of grain
In the Valley of Rephaim.
6 Yet gleaning grapes will be left in it,
  Like the shaking of an olive tree,
Two *or* three olives at the top of the
  uppermost bough,
Four *or* five in its most fruitful
  branches,"
Says the LORD God of Israel.

7 In that day a man will look to his
  Maker,

And his eyes will have respect
  for the Holy One of Israel.
8 He will not look to the altars,
  The work of his hands;
He will not respect what his fingers
  have made,
Nor the wooden images[16]
  nor the incense altars.

9 In that day his strong cities
  will be as a forsaken bough
And an uppermost branch,
  Which they left because of
    the children of Israel;
And there will be desolation.

10 Because you have forgotten
  the God of your salvation,
And have not been mindful of the
  Rock of your stronghold,
Therefore you will plant pleasant
  plants
And set out foreign seedlings;
11 In the day you will make
  your plant to grow,
And in the morning you will make
  your seed to flourish;
But the harvest *will be* a heap of ruins
In the day of grief and desperate
  sorrow.

12 Woe to the multitude of many people
  Who make a noise like the roar of the
    seas,
And to the rushing of nations
  That make a rushing like the rushing
    of mighty waters!
13 The nations will rush like the rushing
  of many waters;
But *God* will rebuke them
  and they will flee far away,
And be chased like the chaff of the
  mountains before the wind,
Like a rolling thing before the
  whirlwind.
14 Then behold, at eventide, trouble!
  And before the morning, he *is* no more.
This *is* the portion of those who
  plunder us,
And the lot of those who rob us.

Proclamation Against Ethiopia

18 Woe to the land shadowed with
  buzzing wings,
Which *is* beyond the rivers of Ethiopia,
2 Which sends ambassadors by sea,
  Even in vessels of reed on the waters,
    saying,
"Go, swift messengers,
  to a nation tall and smooth of skin,

16 Hebrew *Asherah,* a Canaanite goddess

To a people terrible
from their beginning onward,
A nation powerful and treading down,
Whose land the rivers divide."

3 All inhabitants of the world and
dwellers on the earth:
When he lifts up a banner on the
mountains, you see *it*;
And when he blows a trumpet,
you hear *it*.
4 For so the LORD said to me,
"I will take My rest,
And I will look from My dwelling
place
Like clear heat in sunshine,
Like a cloud of dew in the heat
of harvest."
5 For before the harvest,
when the bud is perfect
And the sour grape is ripening
in the flower,
He will both cut off the sprigs with
pruning hooks
And take away *and* cut down the
branches.
6 They will be left together for the
mountain birds of prey
And for the beasts of the earth;
The birds of prey will summer on
them,
And all the beasts of the earth will
winter on them.

7 In that time a present will be brought
to the LORD of hosts
From a people tall and smooth *of skin*,
And from a people terrible from their
beginning onward,
A nation powerful and treading down,
Whose land the rivers divide—
To the place of the name of the LORD
of hosts,
To Mount Zion.

Proclamation Against Egypt

19 The burden against Egypt.

Behold, the LORD rides
on a swift cloud,
And will come into Egypt;
The idols of Egypt will totter
at His presence,
And the heart of Egypt
will melt in its midst.

2 "I will set Egyptians against Egyptians;
Everyone will fight against his brother,
And everyone against his neighbor,

City against city,
kingdom against kingdom.
3 The spirit of Egypt will fail in its
midst;
I will destroy their counsel,
And they will consult the idols
and the charmers,
The mediums and the sorcerers.
4 And the Egyptians I will give
Into the hand of a cruel master,
And a fierce king will rule over them,"
Says the Lord, the LORD of hosts.

5 The waters will fail from the sea,
And the river will be wasted
and dried up.
6 The rivers will turn foul,
And the brooks of defense will be
emptied and dried up;
The reeds and rushes will wither.
7 The papyrus reeds by the River,[17]
by the mouth of the River,
And everything sown by the River,
Will wither, be driven away,
and be no more.
8 The fishermen also will mourn;
All those will lament who cast hooks
into the River,
And they will languish who spread nets
on the waters.
9 Moreover those who work in fine flax
And those who weave fine fabric will
be ashamed;
10 And its foundations will be broken.
All who make wages will be troubled
of soul.

11 Surely the princes of Zoan *are* fools;
Pharaoh's wise counselors give foolish
counsel.
How do you say to Pharaoh,
"I *am* the son of the wise,
The son of ancient kings?"
12 Where *are* they?
Where are your wise men?
Let them tell you now,
And let them know what the LORD of
hosts has purposed against Egypt.
13 The princes of Zoan have become
fools;
The princes of Noph[18] are deceived;
They have also deluded Egypt,
Those who are the mainstay of its
tribes.
14 The LORD has mingled
a perverse spirit in her midst;
And they have caused Egypt
to err in all her work,
As a drunken man staggers
in his vomit.

17 That is, the Nile   18 That is, ancient Memphis

15 Neither will there be *any* work
  for Egypt,
  Which the head or tail,
  Palm branch or bulrush, may do.[19]

16 In that day Egypt will be like women, and will be afraid and fear because of the waving of the hand of the LORD of hosts, which He waves over it.
17 And the land of Judah will be a terror to Egypt; everyone who makes mention of it will be afraid in himself, because of the counsel of the LORD of hosts which He has determined against it.

Egypt, Assyria, and Israel Blessed

18 In that day five cities in the land of Egypt will speak the language of Canaan and swear by the LORD of hosts; one will be called the City of Destruction.
19 In that day there will be an altar to the LORD in the midst of the land of Egypt, and a pillar to the LORD at its border.
20 And it will be for a sign and for a witness to the LORD of hosts in the land of Egypt; for they will cry to the LORD because of the oppressors, and He will send them a Savior and a Mighty One, and He will deliver them.
21 Then the LORD will be known to Egypt, and the Egyptians will know the LORD in that day, and will make sacrifice and offering; yes, they will make a vow to the LORD and perform *it*.
22 And the LORD will strike Egypt, He will strike and heal *it*; they will return to the LORD, and He will be entreated by them and heal them.
23 In that day there will be a highway from Egypt to Assyria, and the Assyrian will come into Egypt and the Egyptian into Assyria, and the Egyptians will serve with the Assyrians.
24 In that day Israel will be one of three with Egypt and Assyria, *even* a blessing in the midst of the land,
25 whom the LORD of hosts shall bless, saying, "Blessed *is* Egypt My people, and Assyria the work of My hands, and Israel My inheritance."

The Sign Against Egypt and Ethiopia

20 In the year that Tartan[20] came to Ashdod, when Sargon the king of Assyria sent him, and he fought against Ashdod and took it,

2 at the same time the LORD spoke by Isaiah the son of Amoz, saying, "Go, and remove the sackcloth from your body, and take your sandals off your feet." And he did so, walking naked and barefoot.
3 Then the LORD said, "Just as My servant Isaiah has walked naked and barefoot three years *for* a sign and a wonder against Egypt and Ethiopia,
4 "so shall the king of Assyria lead away the Egyptians as prisoners and the Ethiopians as captives, young and old, naked and barefoot, with their buttocks uncovered, to the shame of Egypt.
5 "Then they shall be afraid and ashamed of Ethiopia their expectation and Egypt their glory.
6 "And the inhabitant of this territory will say in that day, 'Surely such *is* our expectation, wherever we flee for help to be delivered from the king of Assyria; and how shall we escape?'"

The Fall of Babylon Proclaimed

21 The burden against the Wilderness of the Sea.

  As whirlwinds in the South pass
    through,
  So it comes from the desert,
    from a terrible land.
2 A distressing vision is declared to me;
  The treacherous dealer deals
    treacherously,
  And the plunderer plunders.
  Go up, O Elam!
  Besiege, O Media!
  All its sighing I have made to cease.

3 Therefore my loins are filled with pain;
  Pangs have taken hold of me,
    like the pangs of a woman in labor.
  I was distressed when *I* heard *it*;
  I was dismayed when *I* saw *it*.
4 My heart wavered,
    fearfulness frightened me;
  The night for which I longed
    He turned into fear for me.
5 Prepare the table,
  Set a watchman in the tower,
  Eat and drink.
  Arise, you princes,
  Anoint the shield!

6 For thus has the Lord said to me:
  "Go, set a watchman,
  Let him declare what he sees."

---

19 Compare Isaiah 9:14–16   20 Or *the Commander in Chief*

7 And he saw a chariot
  with a pair of horsemen,
  A chariot of donkeys,
  and a chariot of camels,
  And he listened diligently with great
     care.
8 Then he cried, "A lion,[21] my Lord!
  I stand continually on the watchtower
     in the daytime;
  I have sat at my post every night.
9 And look, here comes a chariot of men
  with a pair of horsemen!"
  And he answered and said,
  "Babylon is fallen, is fallen!
  And all the carved images of her gods
  He has broken to the ground."

10 Oh, my threshing
   and the grain of my floor!
   That which I have heard
   from the LORD of hosts,
   The God of Israel,
   I have declared to you.

Proclamation Against Edom

11 The burden against Dumah.

   He calls to me out of Seir,
   "Watchman, what of the night?
   Watchman, what of the night?"
12 The watchman said,
   "The morning comes, and also the night.
   If you will inquire, inquire;
   Return! Come back!"

Proclamation Against Arabia

13 The burden against Arabia.

   In the forest in Arabia you will lodge,
   O you traveling companies of
      Dedanites.
14 O inhabitants of the land of Tema,
   Bring water to him who is thirsty;
   With their bread they met him who
      fled.
15 For they fled from the swords,
      from the drawn sword,
   From the bent bow,
      and from the distress of war.

16 For thus the LORD has said to me:
"Within a year, according to the year of a
hired man, all the glory of Kedar will fail;
17 "and the remainder of the number of
archers, the mighty men of the people of
Kedar, will be diminished; for the LORD
God of Israel has spoken *it*."

21 Dead Sea Scrolls read *Then the observer cried.*

Proclamation Against Jerusalem

22 The burden against the Valley of
       Vision.

   What ails you now, that you have
      all gone up to the housetops,
2 You who are full of noise,
   A tumultuous city, a joyous city?
   Your slain *men are* not slain
      with the sword,
   Nor dead in battle.
3 All your rulers have fled together;
   They are captured by the archers.
   All who are found in you are bound
      together,
   Who have fled from afar.
4 Therefore I said, "Look away from me,
   I will weep bitterly;
   Do not labor to comfort me
   Because of the plundering of the
      daughter of my people."

5 For *it is* a day of trouble
      and treading down and perplexity
   By the Lord GOD of hosts
   In the Valley of Vision—
   Breaking down the walls
   And of crying to the mountain.
6 Elam bore the quiver
   With chariots of men *and* horsemen,
   And Kir uncovered the shield.
7 It shall come to pass *that* your choicest
      valleys
   Shall be full of chariots,
   And the horsemen shall set themselves
      in array at the gate.

8 He removed the protection of Judah.
   You looked in that day to the armor
      of the House of the Forest;
9 You also saw the damage to the city
      of David,
   That it was great;
   And you gathered together the waters
      of the lower pool.
10 You numbered the houses of
      Jerusalem,
   And the houses you broke down
   To fortify the wall.
11 You also made a reservoir
      between the two walls
   For the water of the old pool.
   But you did not look to its Maker,
   Nor did you have respect for Him who
      fashioned it long ago.

12 And in that day the Lord GOD of hosts
   Called for weeping and for mourning,
   For baldness and for girding with
      sackcloth.

13 But instead, joy and gladness,
Slaying oxen and killing sheep,
Eating meat and drinking wine:
"Let us eat and drink,
for tomorrow we die!"

14 Then it was revealed in my hearing
by the LORD of hosts,
"Surely for this iniquity there will be no
atonement for you,
Even to your death,"
says the Lord GOD of hosts.

The Judgment on Shebna

15 Thus says the Lord GOD of hosts:

"Go, proceed to this steward,
To Shebna, who *is* over the house,
and say:
16 'What have you here,
and whom have you here,
That you have hewn a sepulcher here,
As he who hews himself a sepulcher on
high,
Who carves a tomb for himself
in a rock?
17 Indeed, the LORD will throw you away
violently,
O mighty man,
And will surely seize you.
18 He will surely turn violently
and toss you like a ball
Into a large country;
There you shall die,
and there your glorious chariots
Shall be the shame of your master's
house.
19 So I will drive you out of your office,
And from your position he will pull
you down.

20 'Then it shall be in that day,
That I will call My servant Eliakim
the son of Hilkiah;
21 I will clothe him with your robe
And strengthen him with your belt;
I will commit your responsibility into
his hand.
He shall be a father to the inhabitants
of Jerusalem
And to the house of Judah.
22 The key of the house of David
I will lay on his shoulder;
So he shall open,
and no one shall shut;
And he shall shut,
and no one shall open.
23 I will fasten him *as* a peg in a secure
place,

And he will become a glorious throne
to his father's house.

24 'They will hang on him all the glory of
his father's house, the offspring and the
issue, all vessels of small quantity, from
the cups to all the pitchers.
25 'In that day,' says the LORD of hosts,
'the peg that is fastened in the secure
place will be removed and be cut down
and fall, and the burden that *was* on it
will be cut off; for the LORD has spoken.' "

Proclamation Against Tyre

23 The burden against Tyre.

Wail, you ships of Tarshish!
For it is laid waste,
So that there is no house, no harbor;
From the land of Cyprus[22] it is
revealed to them.

2 Be still, you inhabitants of the
coastland,
You merchants of Sidon,
Whom those who cross the sea have
filled.
3 And on great waters the grain of
Shihor,
The harvest of the River,[23]
is her revenue;
And she is a marketplace
for the nations.

4 Be ashamed, O Sidon;
For the sea has spoken,
The strength of the sea, saying,
"I do not labor, nor bring forth
children;
Neither do I rear young men,
Nor bring up virgins."
5 When the report *comes to* Egypt,
They also will be in agony at the report
of Tyre.

6 Cross over to Tarshish;
Wail, you inhabitants of the coastland!
7 *Is* this your joyous *city*,
Whose antiquity *is* from ancient days,
Whose feet carried her far off to
sojourn?
8 Who has taken this counsel against
Tyre, the crowning *city*,
Whose merchants *are* princes,
Whose traders *are* the honorable
of the earth?
9 The LORD of hosts has purposed it,
To bring to dishonor the pride
of all glory,

---

22 Hebrew *Kittim*, western lands, especially Cyprus   23 That is, the Nile

And to bring into contempt all the
honorable of the earth.

10 Overflow through your land like the
River,[24]
O daughter of Tarshish;
There is no more strength.
11 He stretched out His hand over the
sea,
He shook the kingdoms;
The LORD has given a commandment
against Canaan
To destroy its strongholds.
12 And He said,
"You will rejoice no more,
O you oppressed virgin daughter
of Sidon.
Arise, cross over to Cyprus;
There also you will have no rest."

13 Behold, the land of the Chaldeans,
This people *which* was not;
Assyria founded it for wild beasts
of the desert.
They set up its towers,
They raised up its palaces,
And brought it to ruin.

14 Wail, you ships of Tarshish!
For your strength is laid waste.

15 Now it shall come to pass in that day
that Tyre will be forgotten seventy years,
according to the days of one king. At the
end of seventy years it will happen to
Tyre as *in* the song of the harlot:

16 "Take a harp, go about the city,
You forgotten harlot;
Make sweet melody, sing many songs,
That you may be remembered."

17 And it shall be, at the end of seventy
years, that the LORD will visit Tyre. She
will return to her pay, and commit fornication with all the kingdoms of the world
on the face of the earth.
18 Her gain and her pay will be set apart
for the LORD; it will not be treasured nor
laid up, for her gain will be for those who
dwell before the LORD, to eat sufficiently,
and for fine clothing.

Impending Judgment on the Earth

24 Behold, the LORD makes the earth
empty and makes it waste,
Distorts its surface
And scatters abroad its inhabitants.

2 And it shall be:
As with the people,
so with the priest;
As with the servant,
so with his master;
As with the maid,
so with her mistress;
As with the buyer,
so with the seller;
As with the lender,
so with the borrower;
As with the creditor,
so with the debtor.
3 The land shall be entirely emptied
and utterly plundered,
For the LORD has spoken this word.

4 The earth mourns *and* fades away,
The world languishes *and* fades away;
The haughty people of the earth
languish.
5 The earth is also defiled under its
inhabitants,
Because they have transgressed the
laws,
Changed the ordinance,
Broken the everlasting covenant.
6 Therefore the curse has devoured the
earth,
And those who dwell in it are desolate.
Therefore the inhabitants of the earth
are burned,
And few men *are* left.

7 The new wine fails, the vine languishes,
All the merry-hearted sigh.
8 The mirth of the tambourine ceases,
The noise of the jubilant ends,
The joy of the harp ceases.
9 They shall not drink wine with a song;
Strong drink is bitter to those who
drink it.
10 The city of confusion is broken down;
Every house is shut up,
so that none may go in.
11 *There is* a crying for wine in the streets,
All joy is darkened,
The mirth of the land is gone.
12 In the city desolation is left,
And the gate is stricken with
destruction.
13 When it shall be thus in the midst
of the land among the people,
It shall be like the shaking of an olive
tree,
Like the gleaning of grapes when the
vintage is done.

14 They shall lift up their voice,
they shall sing;

24 That is, the Nile

For the majesty of the LORD
They shall cry aloud from the sea.
15 Therefore glorify the LORD in the
dawning light,
The name of the LORD God of Israel
in the coastlands of the sea.
16 From the ends of the earth we have
heard songs:
"Glory to the righteous!"
But I said, "I am ruined, ruined!
Woe to me!
The treacherous dealers have dealt
treacherously,
Indeed, the treacherous dealers have
dealt very treacherously."

17 Fear and the pit and the snare
Are upon you,
O inhabitant of the earth.
18 And it shall be
That he who flees from the noise
of the fear
Shall fall into the pit,
And he who comes up from the midst
of the pit
Shall be caught in the snare;
For the windows from on high
are open,
And the foundations of the earth
are shaken.

19 The earth is violently broken,
The earth is split open,
The earth is shaken exceedingly.
20 The earth shall reel to and fro
like a drunkard,
And shall totter like a hut;
Its transgression shall be heavy upon it,
And it will fall, and not rise again.

21 It shall come to pass in that day
That the LORD will punish on high
the host of exalted ones,
And on the earth
the kings of the earth.
22 They will be gathered together,
As prisoners are gathered in the pit,
And will be shut up in the prison;
After many days they will be punished.
23 Then the moon will be disgraced
And the sun ashamed;
For the LORD of hosts will reign
On Mount Zion and in Jerusalem
And before His elders, gloriously.

Praise to God

25 O LORD, You *are* my God.
I will exalt You,
I will praise Your name,
For You have done wonderful *things*;

Your counsels of old *are* faithfulness
and truth.
2 For You have made a city a ruin,
A fortified city a ruin,
A palace of foreigners to be a city no
more;
It will never be rebuilt.
3 Therefore the strong people
will glorify You;
The city of the terrible nations
will fear You.
4 For You have been a strength to the
poor,
A strength to the needy in his distress,
A refuge from the storm,
A shade from the heat;
For the blast of the terrible ones *is* as a
storm *against* the wall.
5 You will reduce the noise of aliens,
As heat in a dry place;
As heat in the shadow of a cloud,
The song of the terrible ones
will be diminished.

6 And in this mountain
The LORD of hosts will make
for all people
A feast of choice pieces,
A feast of wines on the lees,
Of fat things full of marrow,
Of well-refined wines on the lees.
7 And He will destroy on this mountain
The surface of the covering cast over
all people,
And the veil that is spread over all
nations.
8 He will swallow up death forever,
And the Lord GOD will wipe away
tears from all faces;
The rebuke of His people
He will take away from all the earth;
For the LORD has spoken.

9 And it will be said in that day:
"Behold, this *is* our God;
We have waited for Him,
and He will save us.
This *is* the LORD;
We have waited for Him;
We will be glad and rejoice
in His salvation."

10 For on this mountain the hand
of the LORD will rest,
And Moab shall be trampled down
under Him,
As straw is trampled down for the
refuse heap.
11 And He will spread out His hands
in their midst

As he who swims spreads out *his hands*
   to swim,
And He will bring down their pride
Together with the trickery of their
   hands.
12 The fortress of the high fort of your
   walls
He will bring down, lay low,
And bring to the ground,
   down to the dust.

A Song of Salvation

26 In that day this song will be sung
in the land of Judah:

"We have a strong city;
   God will appoint salvation *for* walls
   and bulwarks.
2 Open the gates,
   That the righteous nation which keeps
   the truth may enter in.
3 You will keep *him* in perfect peace,
   Whose mind *is* stayed *on You,*
   Because he trusts in You.
4 Trust in the LORD forever,
   For in YAH, the LORD,
   is everlasting strength.[25]
5 For He brings down those
   who dwell on high,
   The lofty city;
   He lays it low,
   He lays it low to the ground,
   He brings it down to the dust.
6 The foot shall tread it down—
   The feet of the poor
   And the steps of the needy."

7 The way of the just *is* uprightness;
   O Most Upright,
   You weigh the path of the just.
8 Yes, in the way of Your judgments,
   O LORD, we have waited for You;
   The desire of *our* soul *is* for Your name
   And for the remembrance of You.
9 With my soul I have desired You in
   the night,
   Yes, by my spirit within me
   I will seek You early;
   For when Your judgments
   are in the earth,
   The inhabitants of the world
   will learn righteousness.

10 Let grace be shown to the wicked,
   Yet he will not learn righteousness;
   In the land of uprightness
   he will deal unjustly,
   And will not behold the majesty
   of the LORD.

25 Or *Rock of Ages*

11 LORD, *when* Your hand is lifted up,
   they will not see.
But they will see and be ashamed
For *their* envy of people;
Yes, the fire of Your enemies
   shall devour them.

12 LORD, You will establish peace for us,
   For You have also done all our works
   in us.
13 O LORD our God,
   other masters besides You
   Have had dominion over us;
   But by You only we make mention
   of Your name.
14 *They are* dead, they will not live;
   They are deceased, they will not rise.
   Therefore You have punished
   and destroyed them,
   And made all their memory to perish.
15 You have increased the nation,
   O LORD,
   You have increased the nation;
   You are glorified;
   You have expanded all the borders
   of the land.

16 LORD, in trouble they have visited
   You,
   They poured out a prayer *when* Your
   chastening *was* upon them.
17 As a woman with child
   Is in pain and cries out in her pangs,
   When she draws near the time
   of her delivery,
   So have we been in Your sight,
   O LORD.
18 We have been with child,
   we have been in pain;
   We have, as it were,
   brought forth wind;
   We have not accomplished any
   deliverance in the earth,
   Nor have the inhabitants
   of the world fallen.

19 Your dead shall live;
   Together with my dead body
   they shall arise.
   Awake and sing,
   you who dwell in dust;
   For your dew *is like* the dew of herbs,
   And the earth shall cast out the dead.

Take Refuge from the Coming Judgment

20 Come, my people,
   enter your chambers,
   And shut your doors behind you;

Hide yourself, as it were,
for a little moment,
Until the indignation is past.
21 For behold, the LORD comes
out of His place
To punish the inhabitants of the earth
for their iniquity;
The earth will also disclose her blood,
And will no more cover her slain.

27 In that day the LORD with His
severe sword, great and strong,
Will punish Leviathan the fleeing
serpent,
Leviathan that twisted serpent;
And He will slay the reptile
that *is* in the sea.

The Restoration of Israel

2 In that day sing to her,
"A vineyard of red wine!
3 I, the LORD, keep it,
I water it every moment;
Lest any hurt it,
I keep it night and day.
4 Fury *is* not in Me.
Who would set briers *and* thorns
Against Me in battle?
I would go through them,
I would burn them together.
5 Or let him take hold of My strength,
That he may make peace with Me;
And he shall make peace with Me."

6 Those who come He shall cause
to take root in Jacob;
Israel shall blossom and bud,
And fill the face of the world with
fruit.

7 Has He struck Israel as He struck
those who struck him?
Or has He been slain according to the
slaughter of those who were slain by
Him?
8 In measure, by sending it away,
You contended with it.
He removes *it* by His rough wind
In the day of the east wind.
9 Therefore by this the iniquity of Jacob
will be covered;
And this *is* all the fruit of taking away
his sin:
When he makes all the stones of the
altar
Like chalkstones that are beaten to
dust,
When wooden images[26] and incense
altars do not stand up.

10 Yet the fortified city *will be* desolate,
The habitation forsaken
and left like a wilderness;
There the calf will feed,
and there it will lie down
And consume its branches.
11 When its boughs are withered,
they will be broken off;
The women come *and* set them on fire.
For it *is* a people of no understanding;
Therefore He who made them will not
have mercy on them,
And He who formed them will show
them no favor.

12 And it shall come to pass in that day
That the LORD will thresh,
From the channel of the River[27]
to the Brook of Egypt;
And you will be gathered one by one,
O you children of Israel.

13 So it shall be in that day.
That the great trumpet will be blown;
They will come, who are about to
perish in the land of Assyria,
And they who are outcasts in the land
of Egypt,
And shall worship the LORD in the
holy mount at Jerusalem.

Woe to Ephraim and Jerusalem

28 Woe to the crown of pride,
to the drunkards of Ephraim,
Whose glorious beauty *is* a fading
flower
Which *is* at the head of the verdant
valleys,
To those who are overcome with wine!
2 Behold, the Lord has a mighty and
strong one,
Like a tempest of hail
and a destroying storm,
Like a flood of mighty waters
overflowing,
Who will bring *them* down
to the earth with *His* hand.
3 The crown of pride, the drunkards
of Ephraim,
Will be trampled under foot;
4 And the glorious beauty is a fading
flower
Which *is* at the head of the verdant
valley,
Like the first fruit before the summer,
Which an observer sees;
He eats it up while it is still in his
hand.

5 In that day the LORD of hosts will be

---

26 Hebrew *Asherim*, Canaanite deities   27 That is, the Euphrates

For a crown of glory
and a diadem of beauty
To the remnant of His people,
6 For a spirit of justice to him
who sits in judgment,
And for strength to those who turn
back the battle at the gate.

7 But they also have erred through wine,
And through intoxicating drink are out
of the way;
The priest and the prophet have erred
through intoxicating drink,
They are swallowed up by wine,
They are out of the way through
intoxicating drink;
They err in vision,
they stumble *in* judgment.
8 For all tables are full of vomit
and filthiness,
So that no place *is clean.*

9 "Whom will he teach knowledge?
And whom will he make to understand
the message?
Those *just* weaned from milk?
Those *just* drawn from the breasts?
10 For precept *must be* upon precept,
precept upon precept,
Line upon line, line upon line,
Here a little, there a little."

11 For with stammering lips
and another tongue
He will speak to this people,
12 To whom He said,
"This *is* the rest *with which*
You may cause the weary to rest,"
And, "This *is* the refreshing";
Yet they would not hear.
13 But the word of the LORD was to them,
"Precept upon precept,
precept upon precept,
Line upon line, line upon line,
Here a little, there a little,"
That they might go and fall backward,
and be broken
And snared and caught.

14 Therefore hear the word of the LORD,
you scornful men,
Who rule this people who *are* in
Jerusalem,
15 Because you have said,
"We have made a covenant with
death,
And with Sheol we are in agreement.
When the overflowing scourge passes
through,
It will not come to us,

For we have made lies our refuge,
And under falsehood we have hidden
ourselves."

A Cornerstone in Zion

16 Therefore thus says the Lord GOD:

"Behold, I lay in Zion a stone for a
foundation,
A tried stone, a precious cornerstone,
a sure foundation;
Whoever believes will not act hastily.
17 Also I will make justice the measuring
line,
And righteousness the plummet;
The hail will sweep away
the refuge of lies,
And the waters will overflow
the hiding place.
18 Your covenant with death
will be annulled,
And your agreement with Sheol
will not stand;
When the overflowing scourge passes
through,
Then you will be trampled down by it.
19 As often as it goes out it will take you;
For morning by morning it will pass
over,
And by day and by night;
It will be a terror just to understand
the report."

20 For the bed is too short for *a man*
to stretch out *on,*
And the covering so narrow that he
cannot wrap himself *in it.*
21 For the LORD will rise up as *at* Mount
Perazim,
He will be angry as in the Valley of
Gibeon—
That He may do His work,
His awesome work,
And bring to pass His act,
His unusual act.
22 Now therefore, do not be mockers,
Lest your bonds be made strong;
For I have heard from the Lord GOD
of hosts,
A destruction determined even upon
the whole earth.

Listen to the Teaching of God

23 Give ear and hear my voice,
Listen and hear my speech.
24 Does the plowman keep plowing all
day to sow?
Does he keep turning his soil
and breaking the clods?

25 When he has leveled its surface,
Does he not sow the black cummin
And scatter the cummin,
Plant the wheat in rows,
The barley in the appointed place,
And the spelt in its place?
26 For He instructs him in right
judgment,
His God teaches him.

27 For the black cummin is not threshed
with a threshing sledge,
Nor is a cartwheel rolled over the
cummin;
But the black cummin is beaten out
with a stick,
And the cummin with a rod.
28 Bread *flour* must be ground;
Therefore he does not thresh it forever,
Break *it with* his cartwheel,
Or crush *it with* his horsemen.
29 This also comes from the LORD of
hosts,
Who is wonderful in counsel
and excellent in guidance.

Woe to Jerusalem

29 "Woe to Ariel,[28] to Ariel,
the city *where* David dwelt!
Add year to year;
Let feasts come around.
2 Yet I will distress Ariel;
There shall be heaviness and sorrow,
And it shall be to Me as Ariel.
3 I will encamp against you all around,
I will lay siege against you with a
mound,
And I will raise siegeworks against you.
4 You shall be brought down,
You shall speak out of the ground;
Your speech shall be low,
out of the dust;
Your voice shall be like a medium's,
out of the ground;
And your speech shall whisper
out of the dust.

5 "Moreover the multitude of your foes
Shall be like fine dust,
And the multitude of the terrible ones
Shall be as chaff that passes away;
Yes, it shall be in an instant, suddenly.
6 You will be punished by the LORD of
hosts
With thunder and earthquake
and great noise,
With storm and tempest
And the flame of devouring fire.
7 The multitude of all the nations
who fight against Ariel,

Even all who fight against her
and her fortress,
And distress her,
Shall be as a dream of a night vision.
8 It shall even be as when a hungry man
dreams,
And look—he eats;
But he awakes,
and his soul is still empty;
Or as when a thirsty man dreams,
And look—he drinks;
But he awakes, and indeed *he is* faint,
And his soul still craves:
So the multitude of all the nations
shall be,
Who fight against Mount Zion."

The Blindness of Disobedience

9 Pause and wonder!
Blind yourselves and be blind!
They are drunk, but not with wine;
They stagger, but not with
intoxicating drink.
10 For the LORD has poured out on you
The spirit of deep sleep,
And has closed your eyes,
namely, the prophets;
And He has covered your heads,
namely, the seers.

11 The whole vision has become to you
like the words of a book that is sealed,
which *men* deliver to one who is literate,
saying, "Read this, please"; and he says,
"I cannot, for it *is* sealed."
12 Then the book is delivered to one who
is illiterate, saying, "Read this, please";
and he says, "I am not literate."
13 Therefore the LORD said:

"Inasmuch as these people draw near *to*
Me with their mouths
And honor Me with their lips,
But have removed their hearts
far from Me,
And their fear toward Me is taught by
the commandment of men,
14 Therefore, behold, I will again do a
marvelous work
Among this people,
A marvelous work and a wonder;
For the wisdom of their wise men shall
perish,
And the understanding of their prudent
men shall be hidden."

15 Woe to those who seek deep to hide
their counsel far from the LORD,

28 That is, Jerusalem

And their works are in the dark;
They say, "Who sees us?"
and, "Who knows us?"
16 Surely you have things turned around!
Shall the potter be esteemed as the
clay;
For shall the thing made say of him
who made it,
"He did not make me"?
Or shall the thing formed say of him
who formed it,
"He has no understanding"?

Future Recovery of Wisdom

17 Is it not yet a very little while
Till Lebanon shall be turned into a
fruitful field,
And the fruitful field be esteemed
as a forest?
18 In that day the deaf shall hear the
words of the book,
And the eyes of the blind shall see out
of obscurity and out of darkness.
19 The humble also shall increase their joy
in the LORD,
And the poor among men shall rejoice
In the Holy One of Israel.
20 For the terrible one is brought to
nothing,
The scornful one is consumed,
And all who watch for iniquity
are cut off—
21 Who make a man an offender by a
word,
And lay a snare for him who reproves
in the gate,
And turn aside the just for a thing of
naught.

22 Therefore thus says the LORD, who redeemed Abraham, concerning the house
of Jacob:

"Jacob shall not now be ashamed,
Nor shall his face now grow pale;
23 But when he sees his children,
The work of My hands, in his midst,
They will hallow My name,
And hallow the Holy One of Jacob,
And fear the God of Israel.
24 These also who erred in spirit
will come to understanding,
And those who murmured
will learn doctrine."

Futile Confidence in Egypt

30 "Woe to the rebellious children,"
says the LORD,
"Who take counsel, but not of Me,

And who devise plans,
but not of My Spirit,
That they may add sin to sin;
2 Who walk to go down to Egypt,
And have not asked My advice,
To strengthen themselves in the
strength of Pharaoh,
And to trust in the shadow of Egypt!
3 Therefore the strength of Pharaoh
Shall be your shame,
And trust in the shadow of Egypt
Shall be your humiliation.
4 For his princes were at Zoan,
And his ambassadors came to Hanes.
5 They were all ashamed of a people who
could not benefit them,
Or be help or benefit,
But a shame and also a reproach."

6 The burden against the beasts of the
South.

Through a land of trouble and anguish,
From which came the lioness and lion,
The viper and fiery flying serpent,
They will carry their riches on the
backs of young donkeys,
And their treasures on the humps
of camels,
To a people who shall not benefit them;
7 For the Egyptians shall help in vain
and to no purpose.
Therefore I have called her
Rahab-Hem-Shebeth.[29]

A Rebellious People

8 Now go, write it before them
on a tablet,
And note it on a scroll,
That it may be for time to come,
Forever and ever:
9 That this is a rebellious people,
Lying children,
Children who will not hear the law
of the LORD;
10 Who say to the seers, "Do not see,"
And to the prophets,
"Do not prophesy to us right things;
Speak to us smooth things,
prophesy deceits.
11 Get out of the way,
Turn aside from the path,
Cause the Holy One of Israel
To cease from before us."

12 Therefore thus says the Holy One of
Israel:

"Because you despise this word,
And trust in oppression and perversity,
And rely on them,

29 Literally Rahab Sits Idle

13 Therefore this iniquity shall be to you
    Like a breach ready to fall,
    A bulge in a high wall,
    Whose breaking comes suddenly,
        in an instant.
14 And He shall break it like the breaking
        of the potter's vessel,
    Which is broken in pieces;
    He shall not spare.
    So there shall not be found among its
        fragments
    A shard to take fire from the hearth,
    Or to take water from the cistern."

15 For thus says the Lord GOD, the Holy
One of Israel:

    "In returning and rest
        you shall be saved;
    In quietness and confidence
        shall be your strength."
    But you would not,
16 And you said,
    "No, for we will flee on horses"—
    Therefore you shall flee!
    And, "We will ride on swift *horses*"—
    Therefore those who pursue you shall
        be swift!

17 One thousand *shall flee* at the threat
        of one,
    At the threat of five you shall flee,
    Till you are left as a pole on top
        of a mountain
    And as a banner on a hill.

God Will Be Gracious
18 Therefore the LORD will wait,
        that He may be gracious to you;
    And therefore He will be exalted,
        that He may have mercy on you.
    For the LORD *is* a God of justice;
    Blessed *are* all those who wait for Him.

19 For the people shall dwell in Zion at
        Jerusalem;
    You shall weep no more.
    He will be very gracious to you at the
        sound of your cry;
    When He hears it, He will answer you.
20 And *though* the Lord gives you
    The bread of adversity
        and the water of affliction,
    Yet your teachers will not be moved
        into a corner anymore,
    But your eyes shall see your teachers.
21 Your ears shall hear a word behind
        you, saying,
    "This *is* the way, walk in it,"

Whenever you turn to the right hand
    Or whenever you turn to the left.
22 You will also defile the covering of
        your graven images of silver,
    And the ornament of your molded
        images of gold.
    You will throw them away as an
        unclean thing;
    You will say to them, "Get away!"

23 Then He will give the rain for your
        seed
    With which you sow the ground,
    And bread of the increase of the earth;
    It will be fat and plenteous.
    In that day your cattle will feed
    In large pastures.
24 Likewise the oxen and the young
        donkeys that work the ground
    Will eat cured fodder,
    Which has been winnowed with the
        shovel and fan.
25 There will be on every high mountain
    And on every high hill
    Rivers *and* streams of waters,
    In the day of the great slaughter,
    When the towers fall.
26 Moreover the light of the moon
        will be as the light of the sun,
    And the light of the sun will be
        sevenfold,
    As the light of seven days,
    In the day that the LORD binds up the
        bruise of His people
    And heals the stroke of their wound.

Judgment on Assyria
27 Behold, the name of the LORD comes
        from afar,
    Burning *with* His anger,
    And *His* burden *is* heavy;
    His lips are full of indignation,
    And His tongue like a devouring fire;
28 His breath is like an overflowing
        stream,
    Which reaches up to the neck,
    To sift the nations with the sieve of
        futility;
    And *there shall be* a bridle in the jaws
        of the people,
    Causing *them* to err.

29 You shall have a song
    As in the night *when* a holy festival is
        kept,
    And gladness of heart as when one
        goes with a flute,
    To come into the mountain of the
        LORD,
    To the Mighty One of Israel.

30 The LORD will cause His glorious voice
      to be heard,
   And show the descent of His arm,
   With the indignation of *His* anger
   And the flame of a devouring fire,
   With scattering, tempest,
      and hailstones.
31 For through the voice of the LORD
   Assyria will be beaten down,
   Who struck with a rod.
32 And *in* every place where the staff of
      punishment passes,
   Which the LORD lays on him,
   It will be with tambourines and harps;
   And in battles of brandishing He will
      fight with it.
33 For Tophet *was* established of old,
   Yes, for the king it is prepared.
   He has made *it* deep and large;
   Its pyre *is* fire with much wood;
   The breath of the LORD,
      like a stream of brimstone,
   Kindles it.

The Folly of Not Trusting God

31 Woe to those who go down to
      Egypt for help,
   And rely on horses,
   Who trust in chariots
      because *they are* many,
   And in horsemen
      because they are very strong,
   But who do not look to the Holy One
      of Israel,
   Nor seek the LORD!
2 Yet He also *is* wise
      and will bring disaster,
   And will not call back His words,
   But will arise against the house of
      evildoers,
   And against the help of those who
      work iniquity.
3 Now the Egyptians *are* men,
      and not God;
   And their horses are flesh,
      and not spirit.
   When the LORD stretches out His
      hand,
   Both he who helps will fall,
   And he who is helped will fall down;
   They all will perish together.

God Will Deliver Jerusalem

4 For thus the LORD has spoken to me:

   "As a lion roars,
   And a young lion over his prey
   (When a multitude of shepherds is
      summoned against him,

He will not be afraid of their voice
   Nor be disturbed by their noise),
   So the LORD of hosts will come down
   To fight for Mount Zion
      and for its hill.
5 Like birds flying about,
   So will the LORD of hosts defend
      Jerusalem.
   Defending, He will also deliver *it*;
   Passing over, He will preserve *it*."

6 Return *to Him* against whom the children of Israel have deeply revolted.
7 For in that day every man shall throw
away his idols of silver and his idols of
gold—sin, which your own hands have
made for yourselves.

8 "Then Assyria shall fall
      by a sword not of man,
   And a sword not of mankind shall
      devour him.
   But he shall flee from the sword,
   And his young men shall become
      forced labor.
9 He shall cross over to his stronghold
      for fear,
   And his princes shall be afraid of the
      banner,"
   Says the LORD,
   Whose fire *is* in Zion
   And whose furnace *is* in Jerusalem.

A Reign of Righteousness

32 Behold, a king will reign in
      righteousness,
   And princes will rule with justice.
2 A man will be as a hiding place from
      the wind,
   And a cover from the tempest,
   As rivers of water in a dry place,
   As the shadow of a great rock in a
      weary land.
3 The eyes of those who see
      will not be dim,
   And the ears of those who hear
      will listen.
4 Also the heart of the rash
      will understand knowledge,
   And the tongue of the stammerers
      will be ready to speak plainly.
5 The foolish person will no longer
      be called generous,
   Nor the miser said *to be* bountiful;
6 For the foolish person will speak
      foolishness,
   And his heart will work iniquity:
   To practice ungodliness,
   To utter error against the LORD,

To keep the hungry unsatisfied,
And he will cause the drink of the
    thirsty to fail.
7 Also the schemes of the schemer *are*
    evil;
He devises wicked plans
To destroy the poor with lying words,
Even when the needy speaks justice.
8 But a generous man devises generous
    things,
And by generosity he shall stand.

Consequences of Complacency

9 Rise up, you women who are at ease,
    Hear my voice;
You complacent daughters,
    Give ear to my speech.
10 In a year and *some* days
    You will be troubled,
      you complacent women;
For the vintage will fail,
    The gathering will not come.
11 Tremble, you *women* who are at ease;
    Be troubled, you complacent ones;
Strip yourselves, make yourselves bare,
And gird *sackcloth* on *your* waists.

12 People shall mourn upon their breasts
    For the pleasant fields,
      for the fruitful vine.
13 On the land of my people will come up
    thorns *and* briers,
Yes, on all the happy homes *in* the
    joyous city;
14 Because the palaces will be forsaken,
    The bustling city will be deserted.
The forts and towers
    will become lairs forever,
A joy of wild donkeys,
    a pasture of flocks—
15 Until the Spirit is poured upon us
    from on high,
And the wilderness
    becomes a fruitful field,
And the fruitful field
    is counted as a forest.

The Peace of God's Reign

16 Then justice will dwell in the
    wilderness,
And righteousness remain in the
    fruitful field.
17 The work of righteousness will be
    peace,
And the effect of righteousness,
    quietness and assurance forever.
18 My people will dwell in a peaceful
    habitation,

In secure dwellings,
    and in quiet resting places,
19 Though hail comes down on the forest,
And the city is brought low in
    humiliation.

20 Blessed *are* you who sow beside all
    waters,
Who send out freely the feet of the ox
    and the donkey.

A Prayer in Deep Distress

33 Woe to you who plunder,
    though you *have* not *been*
    plundered;
And you who deal treacherously,
    though they have not dealt
    treacherously with you!
When you cease plundering,
    You will be plundered;
And when you make an end
    of dealing treacherously,
They will deal treacherously with you.

2 O LORD, be gracious to us;
    We have waited for You.
Be their arm every morning,
Our salvation also in the time of
    trouble.
3 At the noise of the tumult
    the people shall flee;
When You lift Yourself up,
    the nations shall be scattered;
4 And Your plunder shall be gathered
    Like the gathering of the caterpillar;
As the running to and fro of locusts,
    He shall run upon them.

5 The LORD is exalted,
    for He dwells on high;
He has filled Zion with justice
    and righteousness.
6 Wisdom and knowledge
    will be the stability of your times,
And the strength of salvation;
The fear of the LORD *is* His treasure.

7 Surely their valiant ones
    shall cry outside,
The ambassadors of peace
    shall weep bitterly.
8 The highways lie waste,
    The wayfaring man ceases.
He has broken the covenant,
He has despised the cities,
    He regards no man.
9 The earth mourns *and* languishes,
    Lebanon is shamed *and* shriveled;
Sharon is like a wilderness,

And Bashan and Carmel
  shake off *their fruits.*

Impending Judgment on Zion

10 "Now I will rise," says the LORD;
  "Now I will be exalted,
  Now I will lift Myself up.
11 You shall conceive chaff,
  You shall bring forth stubble;
  Your breath, *as* fire, shall devour you.
12 And the people shall be *like* the
    burnings of lime;
  Like thorns cut up they shall be
    burned in the fire.
13 Hear, you *who are* afar off,
    what I have done;
  And you *who are* near,
    acknowledge My might."

14 The sinners in Zion are afraid;
  Fearfulness has seized the hypocrites:
  "Who among us shall dwell with the
    devouring fire?
  Who among us shall dwell with
    everlasting burnings?"
15 He who walks righteously
    and speaks uprightly,
  He who despises the gain of
    oppressions,
  Who gestures with his hands,
    refusing bribes,
  Who stops his ears from hearing
    of bloodshed,
  And shuts his eyes from seeing evil:
16 He will dwell on high;
  His place of defense *will be* the fortress
    of rocks;
  Bread will be given him,
  His water *will be* sure.

The Land of the Majestic King

17 Your eyes will see the King in His
    beauty;
  They will see the land that is very far
    off.
18 Your heart will meditate on terror:
  "Where *is* the scribe?
  Where *is* he who weighs?
  Where *is* he who counts the towers?"
19 You will not see a fierce people,
  A people of obscure speech,
    beyond perception,
  Of a stammering tongue *that you*
    cannot understand.

20 Look upon Zion,
    the city of our appointed feasts;
  Your eyes will see Jerusalem,
    a quiet habitation,

A tabernacle *that* will not be taken
    down;
  Not one of its stakes will ever be
    removed,
  Nor will any of its cords be broken.
21 But there the majestic LORD
  will be for us
  A place of broad rivers *and* streams,
  In which no galley with oars will sail,
  Nor majestic ships pass by
22 (For the LORD *is* our Judge,
  The LORD *is* our Lawgiver,
  The LORD *is* our King;
  He will save us);
23 Your tackle is loosed,
  They could not strengthen their mast,
  They could not spread the sail.

Then the prey of great plunder is
    divided;
  The lame take the prey.
24 And the inhabitant will not say,
    "I am sick";
  The people who dwell in it *will be*
    forgiven *their* iniquity.

Judgment on the Nations

34 Come near, you nations, to hear;
    And heed, you people!
  Let the earth hear, and all that is in it,
  The world and all things that come
    forth from it.
2 For the indignation of the LORD
  is against all nations,
  And *His* fury against all their armies;
  He has utterly destroyed them,
  He has given them over to the
    slaughter.
3 Also their slain shall be thrown out;
  Their stench shall rise from their
    corpses,
  And the mountains shall be melted
    with their blood.
4 All the host of heaven shall be
    dissolved,
  And the heavens shall be rolled up
    like a scroll;
  All their host shall fall down
  As the leaf falls from the vine,
  And as *fruit* falling from a fig tree.

5 "For My sword shall be bathed in
    heaven;
  Indeed it shall come down on Edom,
  And on the people of My curse,
    for judgment.
6 The sword of the LORD is filled with
    blood,
  It is made overflowing with fatness,
  And with the blood of lambs and goats,

With the fat of the kidneys of rams.
For the LORD has a sacrifice in Bozrah,
And a great slaughter in the land of
   Edom.
7 The wild oxen shall come down with
   them,
And the young bulls with the mighty
   bulls;
Their land shall be soaked with blood,
And their dust saturated with fatness."

8 For *it is* the day of the LORD's
   vengeance,
The year of recompense for the cause
   of Zion.
9 Its streams shall be turned into pitch,
And its dust into brimstone;
Its land shall become burning pitch.
10 It shall not be quenched night or day;
Its smoke shall ascend forever.
From generation to generation
   it shall lie waste;
No one shall pass through it forever
   and ever.
11 But the pelican and the porcupine
   shall possess it,
Also the owl and the raven
   shall dwell in it.
And He shall stretch out over it
The line of confusion
   and the stones of emptiness.
12 They shall call its nobles to the
   kingdom,
But none *shall be* there,
   and all its princes shall be nothing.

13 And thorns shall come up in its
   palaces,
Nettles and brambles in its fortresses;
It shall be a habitation of jackals,
A courtyard for ostriches.
14 The wild beasts of the desert
   shall also meet with the jackals,
And the wild goat shall bleat
   to its companion;
Also the night creature shall rest there,
And find for herself a place of rest.
15 There the arrow snake shall make her
   nest and lay *eggs*
And hatch, and gather *them* under her
   shadow;
There also shall the hawks be gathered,
Every one with her mate.

16 "Search from the book of the LORD,
   and read:
Not one of these shall fail;
Not one shall lack her mate.
For My mouth has commanded it,
   and His Spirit has gathered them.

17 He has cast the lot for them,
And His hand has divided it among
   them with a measuring line.
They shall possess it forever;
From generation to generation they
   shall dwell in it."

The Future Glory of Zion

35 The wilderness and the wasteland
   shall be glad for them,
And the desert shall rejoice
   and blossom as the rose;
2 It shall blossom abundantly
   and rejoice,
Even with joy and singing.
The glory of Lebanon
   shall be given to it,
The excellence of Carmel and Sharon.
They shall see the glory of the LORD,
The excellency of our God.

3 Strengthen the weak hands,
And make firm the feeble knees.
4 Say to those *who are* fearful-hearted,
"Be strong, do not fear!
Behold, your God will come *with*
   vengeance,
With the recompense of God;
He will come and save you."

5 Then the eyes of the blind
   shall be opened,
And the ears of the deaf
   shall be unstopped.
6 Then the lame
   shall leap like a deer,
And the tongue of the dumb sing.
For waters shall burst forth in the
   wilderness,
And streams in the desert.
7 The parched ground
   shall become a pool,
And the thirsty land springs of water;
In the habitation of jackals,
   where each lay,
There shall be grass with reeds and
   rushes.

8 A highway shall be there, and a road,
And it shall be called
   the Highway of Holiness.
The unclean shall not pass over it,
But it *shall be* for others.
Whoever walks the road,
   although a fool,
Shall not go astray.
9 No lion shall be there,
Nor shall *any* ravenous beast
   go up on it;
It shall not be found there.
But the redeemed shall walk *there*,

The Desert—a Garden

The grass withers, the flower fades,
But the word of our God stands forever.

(Is. 40:8)

Springtime in Israel is adorned with bright red poppies, yellow mustard plants, and green rolling hills. Yet, within one week the land can be scorched into a dry, colorless dust bowl. The *hamsins*, desert winds from the east, come without warning in April. Like fire, they parch the land of its new growth. Throughout the Old Testament, the psalmist and the prophets note this sudden disaster. Yet it is always followed with a promise: God will make the desert bloom. He will turn the wasteland into glory.

Like the *hamsins*, problems and tragedies can come into out lives without warning. Just when a business begins to grow, a project starts to develop, or a relationship begins to flourish, an unforeseen circumstance can change the landscape of our life. This is when we must not lose hope. We must cling to the promises. God will make the deserts in our life bloom with new growth. Patience, perseverance, and understanding are all required to let God work. We must give God time to heal our hurts. We must offer Him the chance to reseed and restore our dreams.

Then the problem will become an opportunity! The scar—a star! The desert—a living garden! "The wilderness and the wasteland shall be glad for them, and the desert shall rejoice and blossom as the rose" (Is. 35:1).

10 And the ransomed of the LORD
  shall return,
And come to Zion with singing,
With everlasting joy on their heads.
They shall obtain joy and gladness,
And sorrow and sighing
  shall flee away.

Sennacherib Boasts Against the LORD

36 Now it came to pass in the fourteenth year of King Hezekiah *that* Sennacherib king of Assyria came up against all the fortified cities of Judah and took them.
2 Then the king of Assyria sent *the* Rabshakeh[30] with a great army from Lachish to King Hezekiah at Jerusalem. And he stood by the aqueduct from the upper pool, on the highway to the Fuller's Field.
3 And Eliakim the son of Hilkiah, who was over the household, Shebna the scribe, and Joah the son of Asaph, the recorder, came out to him.
4 Then *the* Rabshakeh said to them, "Say now to Hezekiah, 'Thus says the great king, the king of Assyria: "What confidence is this in which you trust?
5 "I say you speak of having counsel and strength for war; but *they are* vain words. Now in whom do you trust, that you rebel against me?
6 "Look! You are trusting in the staff of this broken reed, Egypt, on which if a man leans, it will go into his hand and pierce it. So *is* Pharaoh king of Egypt to all who trust in him.
7 "But if you say to me, 'We trust in the LORD our God,' *is it* not He whose high places and whose altars Hezekiah has taken away, and said to Judah and Jerusalem, 'You shall worship before this altar'?" '
8 "Now therefore, I urge you, give a pledge to my master the king of Assyria, and I will give you two thousand horses—if you are able on your part to put riders on them!
9 "How then will you repel one captain of the least of my master's servants, and put your trust in Egypt for chariots and horsemen?
10 "Have I now come up without the LORD against this land to destroy it? The LORD said to me, 'Go up against this land, and destroy it.' "
11 Then Eliakim, Shebna, and Joah said to *the* Rabshakeh, "Please speak to your servants in the Aramaic language, for we understand *it*; and do not speak to us in Hebrew[31] in the hearing of the people who *are* on the wall."
12 But *the* Rabshakeh said, "Has my master sent me to your master and to you to speak these words, and not to the men who sit on the wall, who will eat and drink their own waste with you?"
13 Then *the* Rabshakeh stood and called out with a loud voice in Hebrew, and said, "Hear the words of the great king, the king of Assyria!
14 "Thus says the king: 'Do not let Hezekiah deceive you, for he will not be able to deliver you;
15 'nor let Hezekiah make you trust in the LORD, saying, "The LORD will surely deliver us; this city will not be given into the hand of the king of Assyria." '
16 "Do not listen to Hezekiah; for thus says the king of Assyria: 'Make *peace* with me *by a* present and come out to me; and every one of you eat from his own vine and every one from his own fig tree, and every one of you drink the waters of his own cistern;
17 'until I come and take you away to a land like your own land, a land of grain and new wine, a land of bread and vineyards.
18 'Beware lest Hezekiah persuade you, saying, "The LORD will deliver us." Has any one of the gods of the nations delivered its land from the hand of the king of Assyria?
19 'Where *are* the gods of Hamath and Arpad? Where *are* the gods of Sepharvaim? Indeed, have they delivered Samaria from my hand?
20 'Who among all the gods of these lands have delivered their countries from my hand, that the LORD should deliver Jerusalem from my hand?' "
21 But they held their peace and answered him not a word; for the king's commandment was, "Do not answer him."
22 Then Eliakim the son of Hilkiah, who *was* over the household, Shebna the scribe, and Joah the son of Asaph, the recorder, came to Hezekiah with *their* clothes torn, and told him the words of *the* Rabshakeh.

30 A title, probably *Chief of Staff* or *Governor*   31 Literally *Judean*

Isaiah Assures Deliverance

37 And so it was, when King Hezekiah heard *it*, that he tore his clothes, covered himself with sackcloth, and went into the house of the LORD.
2 Then he sent Eliakim, who *was* over the household, Shebna the scribe, and the elders of the priests, covered with sackcloth, to Isaiah the prophet, the son of Amoz.
3 And they said to him, "Thus says Hezekiah: 'This day *is* a day of trouble and rebuke and blasphemy; for the children have come to birth, but *there is* no strength to bring them forth.
4 'It may be that the LORD your God will hear the words of *the* Rabshakeh, whom his master the king of Assyria has sent to reproach the living God, and will reprove the words which the LORD your God has heard. Therefore lift up *your* prayer for the remnant that is left.' "
5 So the servants of King Hezekiah came to Isaiah.
6 And Isaiah said to them, "Thus shall you say to your master, 'Thus says the LORD: "Do not be afraid of the words which you have heard, with which the servants of the king of Assyria have blasphemed Me.
7 "Surely I will send a spirit upon him, and he shall hear a rumor and return to his own land; and I will cause him to fall by the sword in his own land." ' "

Sennacherib's Threat and Hezekiah's Prayer

8 So *the* Rabshakeh returned, and found the king of Assyria warring against Libnah, for he had heard that he had departed from Lachish.
9 And the king heard concerning Tirhakah king of Ethiopia, "He has come out to make war with you." So when he heard *it*, he sent messengers to Hezekiah, saying,
10 "Thus you shall speak to Hezekiah king of Judah, saying: 'Do not let your God in whom you trust deceive you, saying, "Jerusalem will not be given into the hand of the king of Assyria."
11 'Look! You have heard what the kings of Assyria have done to all lands by utterly destroying them; and will you be delivered?
12 'Have the gods of the nations delivered those whom my fathers have destroyed, Gozan and Haran and Rezeph,

and the people of Eden who *were* in Telassar?
13 'Where *is* the king of Hamath, the king of Arpad, and the king of the city of Sepharvaim, Hena, and Ivah?' "
14 And Hezekiah received the letter from the hand of the messengers, and read it; and Hezekiah went up to the house of the LORD, and spread it before the LORD.
15 Then Hezekiah prayed to the LORD, saying:
16 "O LORD of hosts, God of Israel, *the One* who dwells *between* the cherubim, You *are* God, You alone, of all the kingdoms of the earth. You have made heaven and earth.
17 "Incline Your ear, O LORD, and hear; open Your eyes, O LORD, and see; and hear all the words of Sennacherib, who has sent to reproach the living God.
18 "Truly, LORD, the kings of Assyria have laid waste all the nations and their lands,
19 "and have cast their gods into the fire; for they *were* not gods, but the work of men's hands—wood and stone. Therefore they have destroyed them.
20 "Now therefore, O LORD our God, save us from his hand, that all the kingdoms of the earth may know that You *are* the LORD, You alone."

The Word of the LORD Concerning Sennacherib

21 Then Isaiah the son of Amoz sent to Hezekiah, saying, "Thus says the LORD God of Israel, 'Because you have prayed to Me against Sennacherib king of Assyria,
22 'this *is* the word which the LORD has spoken concerning him:

"The virgin, the daughter of Zion,
Has despised you,
    laughed you to scorn;
The daughter of Jerusalem has shaken
    her head behind your back!

23 "Whom have you reproached and
        blasphemed?
    Against whom have you raised *your*
        voice,
    And lifted up your eyes on high?
    Against the Holy One of Israel.
24 By your servants you have reproached
        the Lord,
    And said, 'By the multitude of my
        chariots

I have come up to the height of the
  mountains,
To the limits of Lebanon;
I will cut down its tall cedars
And its choice cypress trees;
I will enter its farthest height,
To its fruitful forest.
25 I have dug and drunk water,
  And with the soles of my feet
    I have dried up
  All the brooks of defense.'

26 "Did you not hear long ago
    How I made it,
  From ancient times that I formed it?
  Now I have brought it to pass,
  That you should be
  For crushing fortified cities into heaps
    of ruins.
27 Therefore their inhabitants *had* little
    power;
  They were dismayed and confounded;
  They were *as* the grass of the field
  And *as* the green herb,
  As the grass on the housetops
  And *as grain* blighted before it is
    grown.

28 "But I know your dwelling place,
  Your going out and your coming in,
  And your rage against Me.
29 Because your rage against Me
    and your tumult
  Have come up to My ears,
  Therefore I will put My hook
    in your nose
  And My bridle in your lips,
  And I will turn you back
  By the way which you came." '

30 "This *shall be* a sign to you:

  You shall eat *this* year such as grows
    of itself,
  And the second year what springs
    from the same;
  Also in the third year sow and reap,
  Plant vineyards,
    and eat the fruit of them.
31 And the remnant who have escaped
    of the house of Judah
  Shall again take root downward,
  And bear fruit upward.
32 For out of Jerusalem shall go a
    remnant,
  And those who escape from Mount
    Zion.
  The zeal of the LORD of hosts
    will do this.

33 "Therefore thus says the LORD
    concerning the king of Assyria:

  'He shall not come into this city,
    Nor shoot an arrow there,
    Nor come before it with shield,
    Nor build a siege mound against it.
34 By the way that he came,
    By the same shall he return;
    And he shall not come into this city,'
    Says the LORD.
35 'For I will defend this city, to save it
    For My own sake
    and for My servant David's sake.' "

Sennacherib's Defeat and Death

36 Then the angel[32] of the LORD went
out, and killed in the camp of the Assyrians one hundred and eighty-five thousand; and when people[33] arose early in
the morning, there were the corpses—all
dead.
37 So Sennacherib king of Assyria departed and went away, returned *home*,
and remained at Nineveh.
38 Now it came to pass, as he was worshiping in the house of Nisroch his god,
that Adrammelech and Sharezer his sons
struck him down with the sword; and
they escaped into the land of Ararat.
Then Esarhaddon his son reigned in his
place.

Hezekiah's Life Extended

38 In those days Hezekiah was sick
and near death. And Isaiah the
prophet, the son of Amoz, went to him
and said to him, "Thus says the LORD:
'Set your house in order, for you shall die
and not live.' "
2 Then Hezekiah turned his face toward
the wall, and prayed to the LORD,
3 and said, "Remember now, O LORD, I
pray, how I have walked before You in
truth and with a loyal heart, and have
done *what is* good in Your sight." And
Hezekiah wept bitterly.
4 Then the word of the LORD came to
Isaiah, saying,
5 "Go and say to Hezekiah, 'Thus says
the LORD, the God of David your father:
"I have heard your prayer, I have seen
your tears; and I will add to your days
fifteen years.
6 "I will deliver you and this city from
the hand of the king of Assyria, and I will
defend this city." '
7 "And this *is* the sign to you from the

32 Or *Angel*   33 Literally *they*

LORD, that the LORD will do this thing which He has spoken:

8 "Behold, I will bring the shadow on the sundial, which has gone down with the sun on the sundial of Ahaz, ten degrees backward." So the sun returned ten degrees on the dial by which it had gone down.

9 This is the writing of Hezekiah king of Judah, when he had been sick and had recovered from his sickness:

10 I said,
"In the prime of my life
I shall go to the gates of Sheol;
I am deprived of the remainder
of my years."
11 I said,
"I shall not see YAH,
The LORD[34] in the land of the living;
I shall observe man no more among
the inhabitants of the world.
12 My life span is gone,
Taken from me like a shepherd's tent;
I have cut off my life like a weaver.
He cuts me off from the loom;
From day until night
You make an end of me.
13 I have considered until morning—
Like a lion,
So He breaks all my bones;
From day until night
You make an end of me.
14 Like a crane or a swallow,
so I chattered;
I mourned like a dove;
My eyes fail from looking upward.
O LORD,[35] I am oppressed;
Undertake for me!

15 "What shall I say?
He has both spoken to me,
And He Himself has done it.
I shall walk carefully all my years
In the bitterness of my soul.
16 O LORD, by these things men live;
And in all these things is the life
of my spirit;
So You will restore me
and make me live.
17 Indeed it was for my own peace
That I had great bitterness;
But You have lovingly delivered my
soul from the pit of corruption,
For You have cast all my sins behind
Your back.
18 For Sheol cannot thank You,
Death cannot praise You;

Those who go down to the pit cannot
hope for Your truth.
19 The living, the living man,
he shall praise You,
As I do this day;
The father shall make known Your
truth to the children.

20 "The LORD was ready to save me;
Therefore we will sing my songs with
stringed instruments
All the days of our life,
in the house of the LORD."

21 Now Isaiah had said, "Let them take a lump of figs, and apply it as a poultice on the boil, and he shall recover."
22 And Hezekiah had said, "What is the sign that I shall go up to the house of the LORD?"

The Babylonian Envoys

39 At that time Merodach-Baladan[36] the son of Baladan, king of Babylon, sent letters and a present to Hezekiah, for he heard that he had been sick and had recovered.

2 And Hezekiah was pleased with them, and showed them the house of his treasures—the silver and gold, the spices and precious ointment, and all his armory— all that was found among his treasures. There was nothing in his house or in all his dominion that Hezekiah did not show them.

3 Then Isaiah the prophet went to King Hezekiah, and said to him, "What did these men say, and from where did they come to you?" And Hezekiah said, "They came to me from a far country, from Babylon."

4 And he said, "What have they seen in your house?" So Hezekiah answered, "They have seen all that is in my house; there is nothing among my treasures that I have not shown them."

5 Then Isaiah said to Hezekiah, "Hear the word of the LORD of hosts:

6 'Behold, the days are coming when all that is in your house, and what your fathers have accumulated until this day, shall be carried to Babylon; nothing shall be left,' says the LORD.

7 'And they shall take away some of your sons who will descend from you, whom you will beget; and they shall be

---

34 Hebrew YAH-YAH   35 Masoretic Text and Dead Sea Scrolls read Lord.
36 Spelled Berodach-Baladan in 2 Kings 20:12

eunuchs in the palace of the king of Babylon.'"

8 Then Hezekiah said to Isaiah, "The word of the LORD which you have spoken *is* good!" For he said, "At least there will be peace and truth in my days."

God's People Are Comforted

40 "Comfort, yes, comfort My people!" Says your God.
2 "Speak comfort to Jerusalem,
    and cry out to her,
That her warfare is ended,
That her iniquity is pardoned;
For she has received from the LORD's hand
Double for all her sins."

3 The voice of one crying in the wilderness:
"Prepare the way of the LORD;
Make straight in the desert
A highway for our God.
4 Every valley shall be exalted,
And every mountain and hill
    shall be made low;
The crooked places
    shall be made straight,
And the rough places smooth;
5 The glory of the LORD
    shall be revealed,
And all flesh shall see *it* together;
For the mouth of the LORD has
    spoken."

6 The voice said, "Cry out!"
And he said, "What shall I cry?"

"All flesh *is* grass,
And all its loveliness *is* like the flower
    of the field.
7 The grass withers, the flower fades,
Because the breath of the LORD blows
    upon it;
Surely the people *are* grass.
8 The grass withers, the flower fades,
But the word of our God stands
    forever."

9 O Zion,
You who bring good tidings,
Get up into the high mountain;
O Jerusalem,
You who bring good tidings,
Lift up your voice with strength,
Lift *it* up, be not afraid;
Say to the cities of Judah,
    "Behold your God!"

10 Behold, the Lord GOD shall come
    with a strong *hand*,
And His arm shall rule for Him;
Behold, His reward *is* with Him,
And His work before Him.
11 He will feed His flock like a shepherd;
He will gather the lambs with His arm,
And carry *them* in His bosom,
And gently lead those who are with
    young.

12 Who has measured the waters
    in the hollow of his hand,
Measured heaven with a span
And calculated the dust of the earth
    in a measure?
Weighed the mountains in scales
And the hills in a balance?
13 Who has directed the Spirit of the
    LORD,
Or *as* His counselor has taught Him?
14 With whom did He take counsel,
    and *who* instructed Him,
And taught Him in the path of justice?
Who taught Him knowledge,
And showed Him the way of
    understanding?

15 Behold, the nations *are* as a drop
    in a bucket,
And are counted as the small dust
    on the balance;
Look, He lifts up the isles as a very
    little thing.
16 And Lebanon *is* not sufficient to burn,
Nor its beasts sufficient for a burnt
    offering.
17 All nations before Him *are* as nothing,
And they are counted by Him less than
    nothing and worthless.

18 To whom then will you liken God?
Or what likeness will you compare to
    Him?
19 The workman molds a graven image,
The goldsmith overspreads it with gold,
And the silversmith casts silver chains.
20 Whoever *is* too impoverished for *such* a
    contribution
Chooses a tree *that* will not rot;
He seeks for himself a skillful workman
To prepare a carved image *that* will not
    totter.

21 Have you not known?
Have you not heard?
Has it not been told you
    from the beginning?
Have you not understood
    from the foundations of the earth?

The Crooked Made Straight

The Judean wilderness is a foreboding and desolate area. Due to its precarious location on one of the earth's greatest geological faults, it has suffered violent earthquakes since the dawn of time. The earth strata normally found deep beneath the surface have been pushed up here, forming twisted riverbeds and steep canyons. The wilderness itself plummets to the depths of 1,300 feet below sea level, rising again to 3,000 feet above sea level.

This wilderness was a symbol to Israel's prophets of the power of God to change people's lives. Isaiah foretold that "Every valley shall be exalted, and every mountain and hill shall be made low; the crooked places shall be made straight, and the rough places smooth; the glory of the LORD shall be revealed" (Is. 40:4, 5).

It was customary in ancient times for kings and princes to send out messengers before them. These scouts made sure the paths were clear to travel. They removed rocks, bushes and thorns, forded rivers and built bridges, widened narrow passes in the road, and sought out threatening thieves or robbers. John the Baptist was the "scout" for the Lord Jesus Christ. He prepared the hearts of listeners for the message of the Lord.

Jesus fulfilled the prophecy of Isaiah. In His ministry, He made the valleys high, the mountains low and the way straight in the lives of all who believed in Him. Today, Jesus Christ has the power to overcome the valleys of despair and depression in our lives. He makes our mountainous problems into plains. He takes the crooked, twisted, confused aspects of life and makes them a straight highway to move ahead. And He smoothes the rough spots along the way.

Nothing is too great for God's power! Let the glory of the Lord be revealed in your life today!

22 *It is* He who sits above the circle
  of the earth,
And its inhabitants *are* like
  grasshoppers,
Who stretches out the heavens
  like a curtain,
And spreads them out like a tent
  to dwell in.
23 He brings the princes to nothing;
He makes the judges of the earth
  useless.
24 Scarcely shall they be planted,
Scarcely shall they be sown,
Scarcely shall their stock take root
  in the earth,
When He will also blow on them,
And they will wither,
And the whirlwind will take them away
  like stubble.

25 "To whom then will you liken Me,
Or *to whom* shall I be equal?"
  says the Holy One.
26 Lift up your eyes on high,
And see who has created these *things*,
Who brings out their host by number;
He calls them all by name,
By the greatness of His might
And the strength of *His* power;
Not one is missing.

27 Why do you say, O Jacob,
And speak, O Israel:
"My way is hidden from the LORD,
And my just claim is passed over
  by my God"?
28 Have you not known?
Have you not heard?
The everlasting God, the LORD,
The Creator of the ends of the earth,
Neither faints nor is weary.
There is no searching of His
  understanding.
29 He gives power to the weak,
And to *those who have* no might
He increases strength.
30 Even the youths shall faint
  and be weary,
And the young men shall utterly fall,
31 But those who wait on the LORD
Shall renew *their* strength;
They shall mount up with wings like
  eagles,
They shall run and not be weary,
They shall walk and not faint.

Israel Assured of God's Help

41 "Keep silence before Me,
     O coastlands,

And let the people renew *their*
  strength!
Let them come near,
  then let them speak;
Let us come near together for
  judgment.

2 "Who raised up one from the east?
Who in righteousness called him
  to His feet?
Who gave the nations before him,
And made *him* rule over kings?
Who gave *them* as the dust *to* his
  sword,
As driven stubble to his bow?
3 Who pursued them, *and* passed safely
By the way *that* he had not gone with
  his feet?
4 Who has performed and done *it*,
Calling the generations from the
  beginning?
'I, the LORD, am the first;
And with the last I *am* He.' "

5 The coastlands saw *it* and feared,
The ends of the earth were afraid;
They drew near and came.
6 Everyone helped his neighbor,
And said to his brother,
"Be of good courage!"
7 So the craftsman encouraged the
  goldsmith,
And he who smooths *with* the hammer
  inspired him who strikes the anvil,
Saying, "It *is* ready for the soldering";
Then he fastened it with pegs,
That it might not totter.

8 "But you, Israel, *are* My servant,
Jacob, whom I have chosen,
The descendants of Abraham My
  friend.
9 *You* whom I have taken from the ends
  of the earth,
And called from its farthest regions,
And said to You,
'You *are* My servant,
I have chosen you
  and have not cast you away:
10 Fear not, for I *am* with you;
Be not dismayed, for I *am* your God.
I will strengthen you,
Yes, I will help you,
I will uphold you with My righteous
  right hand.'

11 "Behold, all those who were incensed
  against you
Shall be ashamed and disgraced;
They shall be as nothing,

On the Wings of Eagles

From the 9,000 foot-high snow-capped mountains of Lebanon to the jagged peaks of the Sinai wilderness, the majestic golden eagle can be seen floating effortlessly in the wind. He soars, circles, and dives down to the rocks below in search of his prey. The sole monarch of the sky, the eagle has long been a symbol to biblical writers.

After forty years of aimless wandering in the harsh wilderness of Sinai, the Israelites must have looked up into the sky to see these great birds soaring overhead. With uplifted spirits they believed that God would bear them "on eagles' wings" (Ex. 19:4). Swift in flight, eagles can reach a speed of eighty miles per hour. Likewise, the Israelites would be swift and mighty in the conquest of the Promised Land.

God's care and comfort for His people is often likened to the eagle's care for her young. Set on a high ledge, the eagle's nest is secure and virtually inaccessible to predators. Any mountain climber who has been near an eagle's nest knows all too well the fury of the mother eagle protecting her home. With wingspans from nine to ten feet, the bird encompasses her young to shelter them from harm. The psalmist compares God's care for His people to the eagle's wings. "Hide me under the shadow of Your wings" (Ps. 17:8).

Looking to the strong, muscular eagle, the biblical writer described his all-powerful God. "But those who wait on the LORD shall renew *their* strength; they shall mount up with wings like eagles, they shall run and not be weary, they shall walk and not faint" (Is. 40:31).

Like the ancient Israelites, look to God for an eagle-powered faith. Prepare yourself by waiting patiently for your dreams. And when the Almighty God gives them to you, let them soar to new heights of reality. Attempt to do something great for God, even though you might fail, rather than do nothing and succeed.

And those who strive with you shall
   perish.
12 You shall seek them
   and not find them—
Those who contended with you.
Those who war against you
Shall be as nothing,
As a nonexistent thing.
13 For I, the LORD your God,
   will hold your right hand,
Saying to you, 'Fear not,
   I will help you.'

14 "Fear not, you worm Jacob,
   You men of Israel!
I will help you," says the LORD
And your Redeemer,
   the Holy One of Israel.
15 "Behold, I will make you into a new
   threshing sledge with sharp teeth;
You shall thresh the mountains
   and beat *them* small,
And make the hills like chaff.
16 You shall winnow them,
   the wind shall carry them away,
And the whirlwind shall scatter them;
You shall rejoice in the LORD,
And glory in the Holy One of Israel.

17 "*When* the poor and needy seek water,
   and *there is* none,
And their tongues fail for thirst,
I, the LORD, will hear them;
I, the God of Israel,
   will not forsake them.
18 I will open rivers in desolate heights,
And fountains in the midst of the
   valleys;
I will make the wilderness a pool of
   water,
And the dry land springs of water.
19 I will plant in the wilderness the cedar
   and the acacia tree,
The myrtle and the oil tree;
I will set in the desert the cypress tree
   and the pine
And the box tree together,
20 That they may see and know,
And consider and understand together,
That the hand of the LORD has done
   this,
And the Holy One of Israel
   has created it.

The Futility of Idols

21 "Present your case," says the LORD.
   "Bring forth your strong *reasons*," says
   the King of Jacob.
22 "Let them bring forth and show us
   what will happen;

Let them show the former things,
   what they *were*,
That we may consider them,
And know the latter end of them;
Or declare to us things to come.
23 Show the things that are to come
   hereafter,
That we may know that you *are* gods;
Yes, do good or do evil,
That we may be dismayed
   and see *it* together.
24 Indeed you *are* nothing,
And your work *is* nothing;
He who chooses you *is* an abomination.

25 "I have raised up one from the north,
And he shall come;
From the rising of the sun he shall call
   on My name;
And he shall come against princes as
   though mortar,
As the potter treads clay.
26 Who has declared from the beginning,
   that we may know?
And former times, that we may say,
   '*He is* righteous'?
Surely *there is* no one who shows,
Surely *there is* no one who declares,
Surely *there is* no one who hears your
   words.
27 The first time *I said* to Zion,
   'Look, there they are!'
And I will give to Jerusalem one who
   brings good tidings.
28 For I looked, and *there was* no man;
I looked among them,
   but *there was* no counselor,
Who, when I asked of them,
   could answer a word.
29 Indeed they *are* all worthless;
Their works *are* nothing;
Their molded images *are* wind and
   confusion.

The Servant of the LORD

42 "Behold! My Servant whom I
   uphold,
My Elect One *in whom* My soul
   delights!
I have put My Spirit upon Him;
He will bring forth justice to the
   Gentiles.
2 He will not cry out, nor raise *His voice*,
Nor cause His voice to be heard in the
   street.
3 A bruised reed He will not break,
And smoking flax He will not quench;
He will bring forth justice for truth.
4 He will not fail nor be discouraged,

Till He has established justice in the
earth;
And the coastlands shall wait for His
law."

5 Thus says God the LORD,
Who created the heavens
and stretched them out,
Who spread forth the earth
and that which comes from it,
Who gives breath to the people on it,
And spirit to those who walk on it:
6 "I, the LORD, have called You in
righteousness,
And will hold Your hand;
I will keep You and give You as a
covenant to the people,
As a light to the Gentiles,
7 To open blind eyes,
To bring out prisoners from the prison,
Those who sit in darkness from the
prison house.
8 I am the LORD, that is My name;
And My glory I will not give to
another,
Nor My praise to graven images.
9 Behold, the former things have come
to pass,
And new things I declare;
Before they spring forth
I tell you of them."

Praise to the LORD
10 Sing to the LORD a new song,
And His praise from the ends
of the earth,
You who go down to the sea,
and all that is in it,
You coastlands and you inhabitants
of them!
11 Let the wilderness and its cities
lift up their voice,
The villages that Kedar inhabits.
Let the inhabitants of Sela sing,
Let them shout from the top of the
mountains.
12 Let them give glory to the LORD,
And declare His praise in the
coastlands.
13 The LORD shall go forth
like a mighty man;
He shall stir up His zeal
like a man of war.
He shall cry out, yes, shout aloud;
He shall prevail against His enemies.

Promise of the LORD'S Help
14 "I have held My peace a long time,
I have been still and restrained Myself.

Now I will cry like a woman in labor,
I will pant and gasp at once.
15 I will lay waste the mountains and
hills,
And dry up all their vegetation;
I will make the rivers coastlands,
And I will dry up the pools.
16 I will bring the blind by a way
they did not know;
I will lead them in paths
they have not known.
I will make darkness light before them,
And crooked places straight.
These things I will do for them,
And not forsake them.
17 They shall be turned back,
They shall be greatly ashamed,
Who trust in carved images,
Who say to the molded images,
'You are our gods.'

18 "Hear, you deaf;
And look, you blind, that you may see.
19 Who is blind but My servant,
Or deaf as My messenger whom I send?
Who is blind as he who is perfect,
And blind as the LORD'S servant?
20 Seeing many things,
but you do not observe;
Opening the ears,
but he does not hear."

Israel's Obstinate Disobedience
21 The LORD is well pleased for His
righteousness' sake;
He will magnify the law
and make it honorable.
22 But this is a people robbed
and plundered;
All of them are snared in holes,
And they are hidden in prison houses;
They are for prey, and no one delivers;
For plunder, and no one says,
"Restore!"
23 Who among you will give ear to this?
Who will listen and hear for the time
to come?
24 Who gave Jacob for plunder,
and Israel to the robbers?
Was it not the LORD,
He against whom we have sinned?
For they would not walk in His ways,
Nor were they obedient to His law.
25 Therefore He has poured on him the
fury of His anger
And the strength of battle;
It has set him on fire all around,
Yet he did not know;

And it burned him,
Yet he did not take *it* to heart.

The Redeemer of Israel

43 But now, thus says the LORD, who
created you, O Jacob,
And He who formed you, O Israel:
"Fear not, for I have redeemed you;
I have called *you* by your name;
You *are* Mine.
2 When you pass through the waters,
I *will be* with you;
And through the rivers,
they shall not overflow you.
When you walk through the fire,
you shall not be burned,
Nor shall the flame scorch you.
3 For I *am* the LORD your God,
The Holy One of Israel, your Savior;
I gave Egypt for your ransom,
Ethiopia and Seba in your place.
4 Since you were precious in My sight,
You have been honored,
And I have loved you;
Therefore I will give men for you,
And people for your life.
5 Fear not, for I *am* with you;
I will bring your descendants
from the east,
And gather you from the west;
6 I will say to the north, 'Give them up!'
And to the south,
'Do not keep them back!'
Bring My sons from afar,
And My daughters from the ends
of the earth—
7 Everyone who is called by My name,
Whom I have created for My glory;
I have formed him,
yes, I have made him."

8 Bring out the blind people
who have eyes,
And the deaf who have ears.
9 Let all the nations be gathered
together,
And let the people be assembled.
Who among them can declare this,
And show us former things?
Let them bring out their witnesses,
that they may be justified;
Or let them hear and say, "*It is* truth."
10 "You *are* My witnesses," says the LORD,
"And My servant whom I have chosen,
That you may know and believe Me,
And understand that I *am* He.
Before Me there was no God formed,
Nor shall there be after Me.

11 I, *even* I, *am* the LORD,
And besides Me *there is* no savior.
12 I have declared and saved,
I have proclaimed,
And *there was* no foreign *god* among
you;
Therefore you *are* My witnesses,"
Says the LORD, "that I *am* God.
13 Indeed before the day *was*, I *am* He;
And *there is* no one who can deliver
out of My hand;
I work, and who will reverse it?"

14 Thus says the LORD, your Redeemer,
The Holy One of Israel:
"For your sake I will send to Babylon,
And bring them all down as fugitives—
The Chaldeans, who rejoice in their
ships.
15 I *am* the LORD, your Holy One,
The Creator of Israel, your King."

16 Thus says the LORD,
who makes a way in the sea
And a path through the mighty waters,
17 Who brings forth the chariot and
horse,
The army and the power
(They shall lie down together,
they shall not rise;
They are extinguished,
they are quenched like a wick):
18 "Do not remember the former things,
Nor consider the things of old.
19 Behold, I will do a new thing,
Now it shall spring forth;
Shall you not know it?
I will even make a road in the
wilderness
And rivers in the desert.
20 The beast of the field will honor Me,
The jackals and the ostriches,
Because I give waters in the wilderness
And rivers in the desert,
To give drink to My people,
My chosen.
21 This people I have formed for Myself;
They shall declare My praise.

Pleading with Unfaithful Israel

22 "But you have not called upon Me,
O Jacob;
And you have been weary of Me,
O Israel.
23 You have not brought Me the sheep
for your burnt offerings,
Nor have you honored Me
with your sacrifices.
I have not caused you to serve
with grain offerings,

Nor wearied you with incense.
24 You have bought Me no sweet cane
　with money,
Nor have you satisfied Me
　with the fat of your sacrifices;
But you have burdened Me
　with your sins,
You have wearied Me
　with your iniquities.

25 "I, *even* I, *am* He who blots out your
　transgressions for My own sake;
And I will not remember your sins.
26 Put Me in remembrance;
Let us contend together;
State your *case*,
　that you may be acquitted.
27 Your first father sinned,
And your mediators have transgressed
　against Me.
28 Therefore I will profane the princes
　of the sanctuary;
I will give Jacob to the curse,
And Israel to reproaches.

God's Blessing on Israel

44 "Yet hear now, O Jacob My servant,
　And Israel whom I have chosen.
2 Thus says the LORD who made you
And formed you from the womb,
　who will help you:
'Fear not, O Jacob My servant;
And you, Jeshurun,
　whom I have chosen.
3 For I will pour water on him
　who is thirsty,
And floods on the dry ground;
I will pour My Spirit on your
　descendants,
And My blessing on your offspring;
4 They will spring up among the grass
Like willows by the watercourses.'
5 "One will say, 'I *am* the LORD's';
Another will call *himself*
　by the name of Jacob;
Another will write *with* his hand,
　'The LORD's,'
And name *himself*
　by the name of Israel.

There Is No Other God

6 "Thus says the LORD, the King of Israel,
And his Redeemer, the LORD of hosts:
'I *am* the First and I *am* the Last;
Besides Me *there is* no God.
7 And who can proclaim as I do?
Then let him declare it
　and set it in order for Me,
Since I appointed the ancient people.

And the things that are coming and
　shall come,
Let them show these to them.
8 Do not fear, nor be afraid;
Have I not told you from that time,
　and declared *it?*
You *are* My witnesses.
Is there a God besides Me?
Indeed *there is* no other Rock;
I know not *one.*' "

Idolatry Is Foolishness

9 Those who make a graven image,
　all of them *are* useless,
And their precious things shall not
　profit;
They *are* their own witnesses;
They neither see nor know,
　that they may be ashamed.
10 Who would form a god or cast a
　graven image
That profits him nothing?
11 Surely all his companions would be
　ashamed;
And the workmen, they *are* mere men.
Let them all be gathered together,
Let them stand up;
Yet they shall fear,
They shall be ashamed together.

12 The blacksmith with the tongs works
　one in the coals,
Fashions it with hammers,
And works it with the strength
　of his arms.
Even so, he is hungry,
　and his strength fails;
He drinks no water and is faint.

13 The craftsman stretches out *his* rule,
He marks one out with chalk;
He fashions it with a plane,
He marks it out with the compass,
And makes it like the figure of a man,
According to the beauty of a man,
　that it may remain in the house.
14 He hews down cedars for himself,
And takes the cypress and the oak;
He secures *it* for himself among the
　trees of the forest.
He plants a pine,
　and the rain nourishes *it.*

15 Then it shall be for a man to burn,
For he will take some of it
　and warm himself;
Yes, he kindles *it* and bakes bread;
Indeed he makes a god
　and worships *it;*

He makes it a carved image,
and falls down to it.
16 He burns half of it in the fire;
With this half he eats meat;
He roasts a roast, and is satisfied.
He even warms *himself* and says,
"Ah! I am warm,
I have seen the fire."
17 And the rest of it he makes into a god,
His carved image.
He falls down before it
and worships *it*,
Prays to it and says,
"Deliver me, for you *are* my god."

18 They do not know nor understand;
For He has shut their eyes,
so that they cannot see,
And their hearts,
so that they cannot understand.
19 And no one considers in his heart,
Nor *is there* knowledge
nor understanding to say,
"I have burned half of it in the fire,
Yes, I have also baked bread on its
coals;
I have roasted meat and eaten *it*;
And shall I make the rest of it an
abomination?
Shall I fall down before a block of
wood?"
20 He feeds on ashes;
A deceived heart has turned him aside;
And he cannot deliver his soul,
Nor say, "*Is there* not a lie in my right
hand?"

Israel Is Not Forgotten

21 "Remember these, O Jacob,
And Israel, for you *are* My servant;
I have formed you,
you *are* My servant;
O Israel, you will not be forgotten
by Me!
22 I have blotted out, like a thick cloud,
your transgressions,
And like a cloud, your sins.
Return to Me, for I have redeemed
you."

23 Sing, O heavens,
for the LORD has done *it!*
Shout, you lower parts of the earth;
Break forth into singing,
you mountains,
O forest, and every tree in it!
For the LORD has redeemed Jacob,
And glorified Himself in Israel.

Judah Will Be Restored

24 Thus says the LORD, your Redeemer,
And He who formed you from the
womb:
"I *am* the LORD, who makes all *things*,
Who stretches out the heavens all
alone,
Who spreads abroad the earth by
Myself;
25 Who frustrates the signs of the
babblers,
And drives diviners mad;
Who turns wise men backward,
And makes their knowledge
foolishness;
26 Who confirms the word of His servant,
And performs the counsel of His
messengers;
Who says to Jerusalem,
'You shall be inhabited,'
To the cities of Judah,
'You shall be built,'
And I will raise up her waste places;
27 Who says to the deep, 'Be dry!
And I will dry up your rivers';
28 Who says of Cyrus,
'*He is* My shepherd,
And he shall perform all My pleasure,
Even saying to Jerusalem,
"You shall be built,"
And to the temple,
"Your foundation shall be laid." '

Cyrus, God's Instrument

45 "Thus says the LORD to His
anointed,
To Cyrus, whose right hand I have
held—
To subdue nations before him
And loose the armor of kings,
To open before him the double doors,
So that the gates will not be shut:
2 'I will go before you
And make the crooked places straight;
I will break in pieces the gates of
bronze
And cut the bars of iron.
3 I will give you the treasures of
darkness
And hidden riches of secret places,
That you may know that I, the LORD,
Who call *you* by your name,
Am the God of Israel.
4 For Jacob My servant's sake,
And Israel My elect,
I have even called you by your name;
I have named you,
though you have not known Me.
5 I *am* the LORD, and *there is* no other;
There is no God besides Me.

I will gird you,
  though you have not known Me,
6 That they may know from the rising
  of the sun to its setting
  That *there is* none besides Me.
  I *am* the LORD, and *there is* no other;
7 I form the light and create darkness,
  I make peace and create calamity;
  I, the LORD, do all these *things*.'

8 "Rain down, you heavens, from above,
  And let the skies pour down
    righteousness;
  Let the earth open,
    let them bring forth salvation,
  And let righteousness spring up
    together.
  I, the LORD, have created it.

9 "Woe to him who strives
    with his Maker!
  Let the potsherd *strive*
    with the potsherds of the earth.
  Shall the clay say to him who forms it,
    'What are you making?'
  Or shall your handiwork *say*,
    'He has no hands'?
10 Woe to him who says to *his* father,
    'What are you begetting?'
  Or to the woman,
    'What have you brought forth?' "

11 Thus says the LORD,
  The Holy One of Israel,
    and his Maker:
  "Ask Me of things to come concerning
    My sons;
  And concerning the work of My hands,
    you command Me.
12 I have made the earth,
  And created man on it.
  It was I—
  My hands *that* stretched out the
    heavens,
  And all their host I have commanded.
13 I have raised him up in righteousness,
  And I will direct all his ways;
  He shall build My city
  And let My exiles go free,
  Not for price nor reward,"
  Says the LORD of hosts.

The LORD, the Only Savior
14 Thus says the LORD:

  "The labor of Egypt
    and merchandise of Cush
  And of the Sabeans, men of stature,

Shall come over to you,
  and they shall be yours;
They shall walk behind you,
They shall come over in chains;
And they shall bow down to you.
They will make supplication to you,
  saying, 'Surely God *is* in you,
And *there is* no other;
There is no other God.' "

15 Truly You *are* God, who hide Yourself,
  O God of Israel, the Savior!
16 They shall be ashamed
  And also disgraced, all of them;
  They shall go in confusion together,
  Who are makers of idols.
17 *But* Israel shall be saved by the LORD
  With an everlasting salvation;
  You shall not be ashamed or disgraced
  Forever and ever.

18 For thus says the LORD,
  Who created the heavens,
  Who is God,
  Who formed the earth and made it,
  Who has established it,
  Who did not create it in vain,
  Who formed it to be inhabited:
  "I *am* the LORD, and *there is* no other.
19 I have not spoken in secret,
  In a dark place of the earth;
  I did not say to the seed of Jacob,
    'Seek Me in vain';
  I, the LORD, speak righteousness,
  I declare things that are right.

20 "Assemble yourselves and come;
  Draw near together,
  You *who have* escaped from the
    nations.
  They have no knowledge,
  Who carry the wood of their carved
    image,
  And pray to a god *that* cannot save.
21 Tell and bring forth *your case*;
  Yes, let them take counsel together.
  Who has declared this from ancient
    time?
  Who has told it from that time?
  Have not I, the LORD?
  And *there is* no other God besides Me,
  A just God and a Savior;
  There is none besides Me.

22 "Look to Me, and be saved,
  All you ends of the earth!
  For I *am* God, and *there is* no other.
23 I have sworn by Myself;
  The word has gone out of My mouth
    in righteousness,

And shall not return,
That to Me every knee shall bow,
Every tongue shall take an oath.
24 He shall say,
'Surely in the LORD I have
righteousness and strength.
To Him *men* shall come,
And all shall be ashamed
Who are incensed against Him.
25 In the LORD all the descendants of
Israel
Shall be justified, and shall glory.' "

Dead Idols and the Living God

46 Bel bows down, Nebo stoops;
Their idols were on the beasts
and on the cattle.
Your carriages *were* heavily loaded,
A burden to the weary *beast*.
2 They stoop, they bow down together;
They could not deliver the burden,
But have themselves gone into
captivity.

3 "Listen to Me, O house of Jacob,
And all the remnant of the house of
Israel,
Who have been upheld *by Me*
from birth,
Who have been carried
from the womb:
4 Even to *your* old age, I *am* He,
And *even* to gray hairs I will carry *you!*
I have made, and I will bear;
Even I will carry, and will deliver *you*.

5 "To whom will you liken Me,
and make *Me* equal
And compare Me,
that we should be alike?
6 They lavish gold out of the bag,
And weigh silver in the balance;
They hire a goldsmith,
and he makes it a god;
They prostrate themselves,
yes, they worship.
7 They bear it on the shoulder,
they carry it
And set it in its place, and it stands;
From its place it shall not move.
Though *one* cries out to it,
yet it cannot answer
Nor save him out of his trouble.

8 "Remember this,
and show yourselves men;
Recall to mind, O you transgressors.
9 Remember the former things of old,
For I *am* God, and *there is* no other;
I am God, and *there is* none like Me,

10 Declaring the end from the beginning,
And from ancient times *things* that are
not *yet* done,
Saying, 'My counsel shall stand,
And I will do all My pleasure,'
11 Calling a bird of prey from the east,
The man who executes My counsel,
from a far country.
Indeed I have spoken *it*;
I will also bring it to pass.
I have purposed *it*;
I will also do it.

12 "Listen to Me, you stubborn-hearted,
Who *are* far from righteousness:
13 I bring My righteousness near,
it shall not be far off;
My salvation shall not linger.
And I will place salvation in Zion,
For Israel My glory.

The Humiliation of Babylon

47 "Come down and sit in the dust,
O virgin daughter of Babylon;
Sit on the ground without a throne,
O daughter of the Chaldeans!
For you shall no more be called
Tender and delicate.
2 Take the millstones and grind meal.
Remove your veil,
Take off the skirt,
Uncover the thigh,
Pass through the rivers.
3 Your nakedness shall be uncovered,
Yes, your shame will be seen;
I will take vengeance,
And I will not arbitrate with a man."

4 *As for* our Redeemer,
the LORD of hosts *is* His name,
The Holy One of Israel.

5 "Sit in silence, and go into darkness,
O daughter of the Chaldeans;
For you shall no longer be called
The Lady of Kingdoms.
6 I was angry with My people;
I have profaned My inheritance,
And given them into your hand.
You showed them no mercy;
On the elderly you laid your yoke very
heavily.
7 And you said, 'I shall be a lady
forever,'
So that you did not take these *things* to
heart,
Nor remember the latter end of them.

8 "Therefore hear this now,
you who are given to pleasures,

Who dwell securely,
Who say in your heart,
'I *am*, and *there is* no one else
     besides me;
I shall not sit *as* a widow,
Nor shall I know the loss of children';
9 But these two *things* shall come to you
   In a moment, in one day:
   The loss of children, and widowhood.
   They shall come upon you in their
        fullness
   Because of the multitude of your
        sorceries,
   For the great abundance of your
        enchantments.

10 "For you have trusted in your
        wickedness;
   You have said, 'No one sees me';
   Your wisdom and your knowledge have
        warped you;
   And you have said in your heart,
   'I *am*, and *there is* no one else
        besides me.'
11 Therefore evil shall come upon you;
   You shall not know from where it
        arises.
   And trouble shall fall upon you;
   You will not be able to put it off.
   And desolation shall come upon you
        suddenly,
   Which you shall not know.

12 "Stand now with your enchantments
   And the multitude of your sorceries,
   In which you have labored from your
        youth—
   Perhaps you will be able to profit,
   Perhaps you will prevail.
13 You are wearied in the multitude of
        your counsels;
   Let now the astrologers, the stargazers,
   And the monthly prognosticators
   Stand up and save you
   From *these things* that shall come upon
        you.
14 Behold, they shall be as stubble,
   The fire shall burn them;
   They shall not deliver themselves
   From the power of the flame;
   It shall not *be* a coal to be warmed by,
   Nor a fire to sit before!
15 Thus shall they be to you
   With whom you have labored,
   Your merchants from your youth;
   They shall wander each one to his
        quarter.
   No one shall save you.

Israel Refined for God's Glory

48 "Hear this, O house of Jacob,
       Who are called by the name
            of Israel,
   And have come forth from
        the wellsprings of Judah;
   Who swear by the name of the LORD,
   And make mention of the God
        of Israel,
   But not in truth or in righteousness;
2 For they call themselves after the holy
        city,
   And lean on the God of Israel;
   The LORD of hosts *is* His name:

3 "I have declared the former things
        from the beginning;
   They went forth from My mouth,
        and I caused them to hear it.
   Suddenly I did *them*,
        and they came to pass.
4 Because I knew that you *were*
        obstinate,
   And your neck *was* an iron sinew,
   And your brow bronze,
5 Even from the beginning
        I have declared *it* to you;
   Before it came to pass
        I proclaimed *it* to you,
   Lest you should say,
        'My idol has done them,
   And my carved image
        and my molded image
   Have commanded them.'

6 "You have heard;
   See all this.
   And will you not declare *it?*
   I have made you hear new things
        from this time,
   Even hidden things,
        and you did not know them.
7 They are created now
        and not from the beginning;
   And before this day you have not
        heard them,
   Lest you should say,
        'Of course I knew them.'
8 Surely you did not hear,
   Surely you did not know;
   Surely from long ago your ear was not
        opened.
   For I knew that you would deal very
        treacherously,
   And were called a transgressor from
        the womb.

9 "For My name's sake I will defer My
        anger,

And *for* My praise I will restrain it
from you,
So that I do not cut you off.
10 Behold, I have refined you,
but not as silver;
I have tested you in the furnace of
affliction.
11 For My own sake, for My own sake,
I will do *it*;
For how should *My name* be profaned?
And I will not give My glory to
another.

God's Ancient Plan to Redeem Israel

12 "Listen to Me, O Jacob,
And Israel, My called:
I *am* He, I *am* the First,
I *am* also the Last.
13 Indeed My hand has laid the
foundation of the earth,
And My right hand has stretched out
the heavens;
When I call to them,
They stand up together.

14 "All of you, assemble yourselves,
and hear!
Who among them has declared these
things?
The LORD loves him;
He shall do His pleasure on Babylon,
And His arm *shall be against* the
Chaldeans.
15 I, *even* I, have spoken;
Yes, I have called him,
I have brought him,
and his way will prosper.

16 "Come near to Me, hear this:
I have not spoken in secret from the
beginning;
From the time that it was, I *was* there.
And now the Lord GOD and His Spirit
Have[37] sent Me."

17 Thus says the LORD, your Redeemer,
The Holy One of Israel:
"I *am* the LORD your God,
Who teaches you to profit,
Who leads you by the way you
should go.
18 Oh, that you had heeded My
commandments!
Then your peace would have been
like a river,
And your righteousness like the waves
of the sea.

19 Your descendants also would have
been like the sand,
And the offspring of your body
like the grains of sand;
His name would not have been cut off
Nor destroyed from before Me."

20 Go forth from Babylon!
Flee from the Chaldees!
With a voice of singing,
Declare, proclaim this,
Utter it *even* to the end of the earth;
Say, "The LORD has redeemed
His servant Jacob!"
21 And they did not thirst
When He led them through the deserts;
He caused the waters to flow from the
rock for them;
He also split the rock,
and the waters gushed out.

22 "*There is* no peace," says the LORD,
"for the wicked."

The Servant, the Light to the Gentiles

49 "Listen, O coastlands, to Me,
And take heed,
you peoples from afar!
The LORD has called Me
from the womb;
From the matrix of My mother
He has made mention of My name.
2 And He has made My mouth like a
sharp sword;
In the shadow of His hand He has
hidden Me,
And made Me a polished shaft;
In His quiver He has hidden Me."

3 "And He said to me,
'You *are* My servant, O Israel,
In whom I will be glorified.'
4 Then I said, 'I have labored in vain,
I have spent my strength for nothing
and in vain;
Yet surely my just reward *is* with the
LORD,
And my work with my God.' "

5 "And now the LORD says,
Who formed Me from the womb
to be His Servant,
To bring Jacob back to Him,
So that Israel is gathered to Him[38]
(For I shall be glorious in the eyes of
the LORD,
And My God shall be My strength),
6 Indeed He says,

37 The Hebrew verb is singular.
38 Masoretic Text Qere, Dead Sea Scrolls, and Septuagint read *is gathered to Him;* Masoretic Text Kethiv reads *is not gathered.*

'It is too small a thing that You should
be My Servant
To raise up the tribes of Jacob,
And to restore the preserved ones
of Israel;
I will also give You as a light
to the Gentiles,
That You should be My salvation
to the ends of the earth.' "

7 Thus says the LORD,
The Redeemer of Israel,
their Holy One,
To Him whom man despises,
To Him whom the nation abhors,
To the Servant of rulers:
"Kings shall see and arise,
Princes also shall worship,
Because of the LORD who is faithful,
The Holy One of Israel;
And He has chosen You."

8 Thus says the LORD:

"In an acceptable time I have heard You,
And in the day of salvation
I have helped You;
I will preserve You and give You
As a covenant to the people,
To restore the earth,
To cause them to inherit
the desolate heritages;
9 That You may say to the prisoners,
'Go forth,'
To those who are in darkness,
'Show yourselves.'

"They shall feed along the roads,
And their pastures shall be on all
desolate heights.
10 They shall neither hunger nor thirst,
Neither heat nor sun shall strike them;
For He who has mercy on them will
lead them,
Even by the springs of water He will
guide them.
11 I will make each of My mountains a
road,
And My highways shall be elevated.
12 Surely these shall come from afar;
Look! Those from the north
and the west,
And these from the land of Sinim."

13 Sing, O heavens!
Be joyful, O earth!
And break out in singing,
O mountains!
For the LORD has comforted His
people,
And will have mercy on His afflicted.

God Will Remember Zion

14 But Zion said,
"The LORD has forsaken me,
And my Lord has forgotten me."

15 "Can a woman forget her nursing child,
And not have compassion on the son
of her womb?
Surely they may forget,
Yet I will not forget you.
16 See, I have inscribed you on the palms
of My hands;
Your walls are continually before Me.
17 Your sons shall make haste;
Your destroyers and those who laid
you waste
Shall go away from you.
18 Lift up your eyes, look around and see;
All these gather together
and come to you.
As I live," says the LORD,
"You shall surely clothe yourselves with
them all as an ornament,
And bind them on you as a bride does.

19 "For your waste and desolate places,
And the land of your destruction,
Will even now be too small for the
inhabitants;
And those who swallowed you up
will be far away.
20 The children you will have,
After you have lost the others,
Will say again in your ears,
'The place is too small for me;
Give me a place where I may dwell.'
21 Then you will say in your heart,
'Who has begotten these for me,
Since I have lost my children
and am desolate,
A captive, and wandering to and fro?
And who has brought these up?
There I was, left alone;
But these, where were they?' "

22 Thus says the Lord GOD:

"Behold, I will lift My hand
in an oath to the nations,
And set up My standard for the
peoples;
They shall bring your sons in their
arms,
And your daughters shall be carried
on their shoulders;
23 Kings shall be your foster fathers,
And their queens your nursing
mothers;
They shall bow down to you
with their faces to the earth,

And lick up the dust of your feet.
Then you will know that I *am* the
LORD,
For they shall not be ashamed
who wait for Me."

24 Shall the prey be taken from the
mighty,
Or the captives of the righteous
be delivered?

25 But thus says the LORD:

"Even the captives of the mighty
shall be taken away,
And the prey of the terrible be
delivered;
For I will contend with him who
contends with you,
And I will save your children.
26 I will feed those who oppress you
with their own flesh,
And they shall be drunk with their own
blood as with sweet wine.
All flesh shall know
That I, the LORD, *am* your Savior,
And your Redeemer,
the Mighty One of Jacob."

The Servant, Israel's Hope

50 Thus says the LORD:

"Where *is* the certificate of your
mother's divorce,
Whom I have put away?
Or which of My creditors *is it*
to whom I have sold you?
For your iniquities you have sold
yourselves,
And for your transgressions your
mother has been put away.
2 Why, when I came, *was there* no man?
Why, when I called,
was there none to answer?
Is My hand shortened at all that it
cannot redeem?
Or have I no power to deliver?
Indeed with My rebuke
I dry up the sea,
I make the rivers a wilderness;
Their fish stink because *there is* no
water,
And die of thirst.
3 I clothe the heavens with blackness,
And I make sackcloth their covering."

4 "The Lord GOD has given Me
The tongue of the learned,
That I should know how to speak
A word in season to *him who is* weary.

He awakens Me morning by morning,
He awakens My ear
To hear as the learned.
5 The Lord GOD has opened My ear;
And I was not rebellious,
Nor did I turn away.
6 I gave My back to those
who struck *Me,*
And My cheeks to those
who plucked out the beard;
I did not hide My face from shame
and spitting.

7 "For the Lord GOD will help Me;
Therefore I will not be disgraced;
Therefore I have set My face like a
flint,
And I know that I will not be
ashamed.
8 *He is* near who justifies Me;
Who will contend with Me?
Let us stand together.
Who *is* My adversary?
Let him come near Me.
9 Surely the Lord GOD will help Me;
Who *is he who* will condemn Me?
Indeed they will all grow old like a
garment;
The moth will eat them up.

10 "Who among you fears the LORD?
Who obeys the voice of His Servant?
Who walks in darkness
And has no light?
Let him trust in the name of the LORD
And rely upon his God.
11 Look, all you who kindle a fire,
Who encircle *yourselves* with sparks:
Walk in the light of your fire and in
the sparks you have kindled—
This you shall have from My hand:
You shall lie down in torment.

The LORD Comforts Zion

51 "Listen to Me, you who follow after
righteousness,
You who seek the LORD:
Look to the rock *from which* you
were hewn,
And to the hole of the pit
from which you were dug.
2 Look to Abraham your father,
And to Sarah *who* bore you;
For I called him alone,
And blessed him and increased him."

3 For the LORD will comfort Zion,
He will comfort all her waste places;
He will make her wilderness like Eden,

And her desert like the garden of the
LORD;
Joy and gladness will be found in it,
Thanksgiving and the voice of melody.

4 "Listen to Me, My people;
And give ear to Me, O My nation:
For law will proceed from Me,
And I will make My justice rest
As a light of the peoples.
5 My righteousness *is* near,
My salvation has gone forth,
And My arms will judge the peoples;
The coastlands will wait upon Me,
And on My arm they will trust.
6 Lift up your eyes to the heavens,
And look on the earth beneath.
For the heavens will vanish away like
smoke,
The earth will grow old like a garment,
And those who dwell in it will die in
like manner;
But My salvation will be forever,
And My righteousness will not be
abolished.

7 "Listen to Me,
you who know righteousness,
You people in whose heart *is* My law:
Do not fear the reproach of men,
Nor be afraid of their revilings.
8 For the moth will eat them up like a
garment,
And the worm will eat them like wool;
But My righteousness will be forever,
And My salvation from generation to
generation."

9 Awake, awake, put on strength,
O arm of the LORD!
Awake as in the ancient days,
In the generations of old.
Are you not *the arm* that cut Rahab
apart,
And wounded the serpent?
10 *Are* you not *the One*
who dried up the sea,
The waters of the great deep;
That made the depths of the sea a road
For the redeemed to cross over?
11 So the ransomed of the LORD shall
return,
And come to Zion with singing,
With everlasting joy on their heads;
They shall obtain joy and gladness,
And sorrow and sighing shall flee away.

12 "I, *even* I, *am* He who comforts you.
Who *are* you that you should be afraid

Of a man *who* will die,
And of the son of a man *who* will be
made like grass?
13 And you forget the LORD your Maker,
Who stretched out the heavens
And laid the foundations of the earth;
You have feared continually every day
Because of the fury of the oppressor,
When *he has* prepared to destroy.
And where *is* the fury of the oppressor?
14 The captive exile hastens,
that he may be loosed,
That he should not die in the pit,
And that his bread should not fail.
15 But I *am* the LORD your God,
Who divided the sea whose waves
roared—
The LORD of hosts *is* His name.
16 And I have put My words in your
mouth;
I have covered you with the shadow
of My hand,
That I may plant the heavens,
Lay the foundations of the earth,
And say to Zion,
'You *are* My people.' "

God's Fury Removed

17 Awake, awake!
Stand up, O Jerusalem,
You who have drunk at the hand
of the LORD
The cup of His fury;
You have drunk the dregs of the cup
of trembling,
And drained *it* out.
18 *There is* no one to guide her
Among all the sons she has brought
forth;
Nor *is there any* who takes her
by the hand
Among all the sons she has brought
up.
19 These two *things* have come to you;
Who will be sorry for you?—
Desolation and destruction,
famine and sword—
By whom will I comfort you?
20 Your sons have fainted,
They lie at the head of all the streets,
Like an antelope in a net;
They are full of the fury of the LORD,
The rebuke of your God.

21 Therefore please hear this,
you afflicted,
And drunk but not with wine.
22 Thus says your Lord,
The LORD and your God,

Who pleads the cause of His people:
"See, I have taken out of your hand
The cup of trembling,
The dregs of the cup of My fury;
You shall no longer drink it.
23 But I will put it into the hand
    of those who afflict you,
Who have said to you,[39]
'Lie down, that we may walk over you.'
And you have laid your body like the
    ground,
And as the street,
    for those who walk over."

God Redeems Jerusalem

52 Awake, awake!
    Put on your strength, O Zion;
Put on your beautiful garments,
O Jerusalem, the holy city!
For the uncircumcised and the unclean
Shall no longer come to you.
2 Shake yourself from the dust, arise,
And sit down, O Jerusalem;
Loose yourself from the bonds
    of your neck,
O captive daughter of Zion!

3 For thus says the LORD:

"You have sold yourselves for nothing,
And you shall be redeemed without
    money."

4 For thus says the Lord GOD:

"My people went down at first
Into Egypt to sojourn there;
Then the Assyrian oppressed them
    without cause.
5 Now therefore, what have I here,"
says the LORD,
"That My people are taken away
    for nothing?
Those who rule over them
Make them wail," says the LORD,
"And My name *is* blasphemed
    continually every day.
6 Therefore My people shall know My
    name;
Therefore *they shall know* in that day
That I *am* He who speaks:
'Behold, *it is* I.' "

7 How beautiful upon the mountains
Are the feet of him who brings good
    news,
Who proclaims peace,
Who brings glad tidings of good *things*,
Who proclaims salvation,

Who says to Zion,
"Your God reigns!"
8 Your watchmen shall lift up *their*
    voices,
With their voices they shall sing
    together;
For they shall see eye to eye
When the LORD brings back Zion.
9 Break forth into joy, sing together,
You waste places of Jerusalem!
For the LORD has comforted His
    people,
He has redeemed Jerusalem.
10 The LORD has made bare His holy arm
In the eyes of all the nations;
And all the ends of the earth shall see
The salvation of our God.

11 Depart! Depart! Go out from there,
Touch no unclean *thing*;
Go out from the midst of her,
Be clean,
You who bear the vessels of the LORD.
12 For you shall not go out with haste,
Nor go by flight;
For the LORD will go before you,
And the God of Israel *will be* your rear
    guard.

The Sin-Bearing Servant

13 Behold, My Servant shall deal
    prudently,
He shall be exalted and extolled
    and be very high.
14 Just as many were astonished at you,
So His visage was marred more than
    any man,
And His form more than the sons of
    men;
15 So shall He sprinkle[40] many nations.
Kings shall shut their mouths at Him;
For what had not been told them
    they shall see,
And what they had not heard
    they shall consider.

53 Who has believed our report?
    And to whom has the arm of the
    LORD been revealed?
2 For He shall grow up before Him
    as a tender plant,
And as a root out of dry ground.
He has no form or comeliness;
And when we see Him,
There is no beauty
    that we should desire Him.
3 He is despised and rejected by men,
A man of sorrows
    and acquainted with grief.

39 Literally *your soul*   40 Or *startle*

And we hid, as it were,
  our faces from Him;
He was despised,
  and we did not esteem Him.

4 Surely He has borne our griefs
   And carried our sorrows;
   Yet we esteemed Him stricken,
   Smitten by God, and afflicted.
5 But He *was* wounded for our
     transgressions,
   He was bruised for our iniquities;
   The chastisement for our peace *was*
     upon Him,
   And by His stripes we are healed.
6 All we like sheep have gone astray;
   We have turned, every one,
     to his own way;
   And the LORD has laid on Him the
     iniquity of us all.

7 He was oppressed and He was afflicted,
   Yet He opened not His mouth;
   He was led as a lamb to the slaughter,
   And as a sheep before its shearers is
     silent,
   So He opened not his mouth.
8 He was taken from prison
     and from judgment,
   And who will declare His generation?
   For He was cut off from the land of
     the living;
   For the transgressions of My people
   He was stricken.
9 And they[41] made His grave
     with the wicked—
   But with the rich at His death,
   Because He had done no violence,
   Nor *was any* deceit in His mouth.

10 Yet it pleased the LORD to bruise Him;
    He has put *Him* to grief.
    When You make His soul an offering
      for sin,
    He shall see *His* seed,
    He shall prolong *His* days,
    And the pleasure of the LORD shall
      prosper in His hand.
11 He shall see the travail of His soul,
    and be satisfied.
    By His knowledge My righteous
      Servant shall justify many,
    For He shall bear their iniquities.
12 Therefore I will divide Him a portion
      with the great,
    And He shall divide the spoil
      with the strong,
    Because He poured out His soul unto
      death,

41 Literally *he*

And He was numbered
  with the transgressors,
And He bore the sin of many,
And made intercession for the
  transgressors.

A Perpetual Covenant of Peace

54 "Sing, O barren,
     You *who* have not borne!
Break forth into singing,
  and cry aloud,
You *who* have not travailed with child!
For more *are* the children of the
  desolate
Than the children of the married
  woman," says the LORD.
2 "Enlarge the place of your tent,
   And let them stretch out the curtains
     of your habitations;
   Do not spare;
   Lengthen your cords,
   And strengthen your stakes.
3 For you shall expand to the right and
     to the left,
   And your descendants will inherit the
     nations,
   And make the desolate cities inhabited.

4 "Do not fear,
     for you will not be ashamed;
   Nor be disgraced,
     for you will not be put to shame;
   For you will forget the shame of your
     youth,
   And will not remember the reproach of
     your widowhood anymore.
5 For your Maker *is* your husband,
   The LORD of hosts *is* His name;
   And your Redeemer *is* the Holy One
     of Israel;
   He is called the God of the whole
     earth.
6 For the LORD has called you
   Like a woman forsaken
     and grieved in spirit,
   Like a youthful wife when you were
     refused,"
   Says your God.
7 "For a mere moment
     I have forsaken you,
   But with great mercies
     I will gather you.
8 With a little wrath I hid My face from
     you for a moment;
   But with everlasting kindness I will
     have mercy on you,"
   Says the LORD, your Redeemer.

9 "For this *is* like the waters of Noah
     to Me;

For as I have sworn
That the waters of Noah would
no longer cover the earth,
So have I sworn
That I would not be angry with you,
nor rebuke you.
10 For the mountains shall depart
And the hills be removed,
But My kindness shall not depart
from you,
Nor shall My covenant of peace be
removed,"
Says the LORD, who has mercy on you.

11 "O you afflicted one,
Tossed with tempest,
and not comforted,
Behold, I will lay your stones with
colorful gems,
And lay your foundations with
sapphires.
12 I will make your pinnacles of rubies,
Your gates of crystal,
And all your walls of precious stones.
13 All your children shall be taught by the
LORD,
And great shall be the peace of your
children.
14 In righteousness you shall be
established;
You shall be far from oppression,
for you shall not fear;
And from terror,
for it shall not come near you.
15 Indeed they shall surely assemble,
but not because of Me.
Whoever assembles against you
shall fall for your sake.

16 "Behold, I have created the blacksmith
Who blows the coals in the fire,
Who brings forth an instrument
for his work;
And I have created the spoiler to
destroy.
17 No weapon formed against you shall
prosper,
And every tongue which rises against
you in judgment
You shall condemn.
This is the heritage of the servants
of the LORD,
And their righteousness is from Me,"
Says the LORD.

An Invitation to Abundant Life

55 "Ho! Everyone who thirsts,
Come to the waters;
And you who have no money,
Come, buy and eat.
Yes, come, buy wine and milk
Without money and without price.
2 Why do you spend money
for what is not bread,
And your wages
for what does not satisfy?
Listen diligently to Me,
and eat what is good,
And let your soul delight itself in
abundance.
3 Incline your ear, and come to Me.
Hear, and your soul shall live;
And I will make an everlasting
covenant with you—
The sure mercies of David.
4 Indeed I have given him as a witness
to the people,
A leader and commander for the
people.
5 Surely you shall call a nation
you do not know,
And nations who do not know you
shall run to you,
Because of the LORD your God,
And the Holy One of Israel;
For He has glorified you."

6 Seek the LORD while He may be found,
Call upon Him while He is near.
7 Let the wicked forsake his way,
And the unrighteous man his thoughts;
Let him return to the LORD,
And He will have mercy on him;
And to our God,
For He will abundantly pardon.

8 "For My thoughts are not your
thoughts,
Nor are your ways My ways,"
says the LORD.
9 "For as the heavens are higher than the
earth,
So are My ways higher than your ways,
And My thoughts than your thoughts.

10 "For as the rain comes down,
and the snow from heaven,
And do not return there,
But water the earth,
And make it bring forth and bud,
That it may give seed to the sower
And bread to the eater,
11 So shall My word be that goes forth
from My mouth;
It shall not return to Me void,
But it shall accomplish what I please,
And it shall prosper in the thing for
which I sent it.

God's Word—
a Foundation for Faith

The accuracy and reliability of the Bible you hold in your hand is unsurpassed by any other literature from the ancient world. Recent archaeological discoveries further confirm and support this claim.

There are literally thousands of manuscripts from the Old and New Testament which, with the exception of minor textual variations, parallel each other perfectly.

Prior to the discovery of the Dead Sea Scrolls, the oldest complete manuscript of the Old Testament was from A.D. 1000. At that time there was reason to doubt whether or not the Bible had been transmitted accurately through the centuries. Or was there? The people who copied the Old Testament text were known as Masoretes. They lived a life of seclusion and discipline, committed to copying every single Old Testament manuscript they could find. Once they copied a manuscript, they destroyed the original, for they believed the new copy was more or equally accurate as the manuscript they had copied from.

The Masoretes recorded the words of every book of the Old Testament verbatim. Each line on a page had the same amount of letters, with an assigned numerical value to each letter. They added the number up and recorded it in the left-hand column. When they added the entire column from top to bottom, they had a cumulative number which had to match the number on the original manuscript.

Any reasonable doubt as to the accuracy of the Scriptures was removed by the discovery of the Dead Sea Scrolls. A complete manuscript of the entire Book of Isaiah was discovered in 1947. With the exception of seventeen letters, the Dead Sea Scroll was identical with Isaiah of the Masoretic text. Written no later than 150 B.C., the Dead Sea Scroll predated the Masoretic text by almost 1200 years.

During the middle of the nineteenth century a discovery shocked the world of archaeology. Professor Constantin von Tischendorf of the University of Liepzig was visiting the monastery of St. Catharine on Mount Sinai. One evening he noticed that the monks were about to use what looked like papyrus leaves as kindling for their fire. On closer examination Professor Tischendorf discovered the monks had been using ancient manuscripts of the Septuagint version of the Old Testament to light their fires. He quickly salvaged as many as possible, then brought them back to Europe where they were diciphered and compared with existing manuscripts. On a later trip to the same monastery Tischendorf discovered a copy of most of the Septuagint and the entire New Testament, dating back to the fourth century A.D.

Sources for some New Testament books were written within a few years of Christ's death, burial, and resurrection. The Bible you hold in your hand is a firm foundation for belief. As you read the Bible, you can be confident that God has preserved His truths to inspire, motivate, and enable you to serve Him, to reach your dreams, and to become the person He wants you to be. His Word truly is a rock solid foundation for your faith!

12 "For you shall go out with joy,
    And be led out with peace;
    The mountains and the hills
    Shall break forth into singing before
        you,
    And all the trees of the field shall clap
        their hands.
13 Instead of the thorn shall come up the
        cypress tree,
    And instead of the brier shall come up
        the myrtle tree;
    And it shall be to the LORD for a
        name,
    For an everlasting sign *that* shall not
        be cut off."

Salvation for the Gentiles

56 Thus says the LORD:

"Keep justice, and do righteousness,
For My salvation *is* about to come,
And My righteousness to be revealed.
2 Blessed *is* the man *who* does this,
    And the son of man
        who lays hold on it;
    Who keeps from defiling the Sabbath,
    And keeps his hand from doing any
        evil."

3 Do not let the son of the foreigner
    Who has joined himself to the LORD
    Speak, saying,
    "The LORD has utterly separated me
        from His people";
    Nor let the eunuch say,
    "Here I am, a dry tree."
4 For thus says the LORD:
    "To the eunuchs who keep My
        Sabbaths,
    And choose what pleases Me,
    And hold fast My covenant,
5 Even to them I will give in My house
    And within My walls a place and a
        name
    Better than that of sons and daughters;
    I will give them an everlasting name
    That shall not be cut off.

6 "Also the sons of the foreigner
    Who join themselves to the LORD,
        to serve Him,
    And to love the name of the LORD,
        to be His servants—
    Everyone who keeps from defiling the
        Sabbath,
    And holds fast My covenant—
7 Even them I will bring to My holy
        mountain,
    And make them joyful in My house
        of prayer.

Their burnt offerings and their
        sacrifices
    Will be accepted on My altar;
    For My house shall be called a house
        of prayer for all nations."
8 The Lord GOD, who gathers the
        outcasts of Israel, says,
    "Yet I will gather to him
    Others besides those who are gathered
        to him."

Israel's Irresponsible Leaders

9 All you beasts of the field,
        come to devour,
    All you beasts in the forest.
10 His watchmen *are* blind,
    They are all ignorant;
    They *are* all dumb dogs,
    They cannot bark;
    Sleeping, lying down,
        loving to slumber.
11 Yes, *they are* greedy dogs
    Which never have enough.
    And they *are* shepherds
    Who cannot understand;
    They all look to their own way,
    Every one for his own gain,
    From his *own* territory.
12 "Come," *one says,* "I will bring wine,
    And we will fill ourselves with
        intoxicating drink;
    Tomorrow will be as today,
    And much more abundant."

Israel's Futile Idolatry

57 The righteous perishes,
        And no man takes *it* to heart;
    Merciful men *are* taken away,
    While no one considers
    That the righteous is taken away
        from evil.
2 He shall enter into peace;
    They shall rest in their beds,
    Each one walking *in* his uprightness.

3 "But come here,
    You sons of the sorceress,
    You offspring of the adulterer
        and the harlot!
4 Whom do you ridicule?
    Against whom do you make a wide
        mouth
    And stick out the tongue?
    Are you not children of transgression,
    Offspring of falsehood,
5 Inflaming yourselves with gods under
        every green tree,
    Slaying the children in the valleys,
    Under the clefts of the rocks?

6   Among the smooth *stones* of the stream
    Is your portion;
    They, they, *are* your lot!
    Even to them you have poured a drink
      offering,
    You have offered a grain offering.
    Should I receive comfort in these?

7   "On a lofty and high mountain
    You have set your bed;
    Even there you went up
    To offer sacrifice.
8   Also behind the doors and their posts
    You have set up your remembrance;
    For you have uncovered yourself *to*
      those other than Me,
    And have gone up to them;
    You have enlarged your bed
    And made *a covenant* with them;
    You have loved their bed,
    Where you saw *their* hand.
9   You went to the king with ointment,
    And increased your perfumes;
    You sent your messengers far off,
    And debased *yourself even* to Sheol.
10 You are wearied in the length of your
      way;
    Yet you did not say, 'There is no hope.'
    You have found the life of your hand;
    Therefore you were not grieved.

11"And of whom have you been afraid,
      or feared,
    That you have lied
    And not remembered Me,
    Nor taken *it* to your heart?
    Is it not because I have held My peace
      from of old
    That you do not fear Me?
12 I will declare your righteousness
    And your works,
    For they will not profit you.
13 When you cry out,
    Let your collection *of idols* deliver you.
    But the wind will carry them all away,
    A breath will take *them.*
    But he who puts his trust in Me shall
      possess the land,
    And shall inherit My holy mountain."

Healing for the Backslider

14 And one shall say,
    "Heap it up! Heap it up!
    Prepare the way,
    Take the stumbling block
      out of the way of My people."

15 For thus says the High and Lofty One
    Who inhabits eternity,
      whose name *is* Holy:

"I dwell in the high and holy *place,*
    With him *who* has
      a contrite and humble spirit,
    To revive the spirit of the humble,
    And to revive the heart
      of the contrite ones.
16 For I will not contend forever,
    Nor will I always be angry;
    For the spirit would fail before Me,
    And the souls *which* I have made.
17 For the iniquity of his covetousness
    I was angry and struck him;
    I hid and was angry,
    And he went on backsliding
      in the way of his heart.
18 I have seen his ways,
      and will heal him;
    I will also lead him,
    And restore comforts to him
    And to his mourners.

19 "I create the fruit of the lips:
    Peace, peace to *him who is* far off
      and to *him who is* near,"
    Says the LORD,
    "And I will heal him."
20 But the wicked *are* like the troubled
      sea,
    When it cannot rest,
    Whose waters cast up mire and dirt.

21 "*There is* no peace,"
    Says my God, "for the wicked."

Fasting That Pleases God

58 "Cry aloud, spare not;
    Lift up your voice like a trumpet;
    Tell My people their transgression,
    And the house of Jacob their sins.
2   Yet they seek Me daily,
    And delight to know My ways,
    As a nation that did righteousness,
    And did not forsake the ordinance
      of their God.
    They ask of Me the ordinances of
      justice;
    They take delight in approaching God.
3   'Why have we fasted,' *they say,*
      'and You have not seen?
    Why have we afflicted our souls,
      and You take no notice?'

"In fact, in the day of your fast
      you find pleasure,
    And exploit all your laborers.
4   Indeed you fast for strife and debate,
    And to strike with the fist of
      wickedness.
    You will not fast as *you do* this day,
    To make your voice heard on high.

5 Is it a fast that I have chosen,
A day for a man to afflict his soul?
Is it to bow down his head like a
bulrush,
And to spread out sackcloth and ashes?
Would you call this a fast,
And an acceptable day to the LORD?

6 "*Is* this not the fast that I have chosen:
To loose the bonds of wickedness,
To undo the heavy burdens,
To let the oppressed go free,
And that you break every yoke?
7 *Is it* not to share your bread with the
hungry,
And that you bring to your house the
poor who are cast out;
When you see the naked,
that you cover him,
And not hide yourself from your own
flesh?
8 Then your light shall break forth like
the morning,
Your healing shall spring forth
speedily,
And your righteousness shall go before
you;
The glory of the LORD shall be your
rear guard.
9 Then you shall call,
and the LORD will answer;
You shall cry, and He will say,
'Here I *am.*'

"If you take away the yoke
from your midst,
The pointing of the finger,
and speaking wickedness,
10 *If* you extend your soul to the hungry
And satisfy the afflicted soul,
Then your light shall dawn in the
darkness,
And your darkness shall *be* as the
noonday.
11 The LORD will guide you continually,
And satisfy your soul in drought,
And strengthen your bones;
You shall be like a watered garden,
And like a spring of water,
whose waters do not fail.
12 Those from among you
Shall build the old waste places;
You shall raise up the foundations
of many generations;
And you shall be called
the Repairer of the Breach,
The Restorer of Streets to Dwell In.

13 "If you turn away your foot
from the Sabbath,

From doing your pleasure
on My holy day,
And call the Sabbath a delight,
The holy *day* of the LORD honorable,
And shall honor Him,
not doing your own ways,
Nor finding your own pleasure,
Nor speaking *your own* words,
14 Then you shall delight yourself
in the LORD;
And I will cause you to ride on the
high hills of the earth,
And feed you with the heritage of
Jacob your father.
The mouth of the LORD has spoken."

Separated from God

59 Behold, the LORD's hand is not
shortened,
That it cannot save;
Nor His ear heavy,
That it cannot hear.
2 But your iniquities have separated
you from your God;
And your sins have hidden
His face from you,
So that He will not hear.
3 For your hands are defiled with blood,
And your fingers with iniquity;
Your lips have spoken lies,
Your tongue has muttered perversity.

4 No one calls for justice,
Nor does *any* plead for truth.
They trust in empty words
and speak lies;
They conceive evil
and bring forth iniquity.
5 They hatch vipers' eggs
and weave the spider's web;
He who eats of their eggs dies,
And *from* that which is crushed
a viper breaks out.

6 Their webs will not become garments,
Nor will they cover themselves with
their works;
Their works *are* works of iniquity,
And the act of violence *is* in their
hands.
7 Their feet run to evil,
And they make haste to shed innocent
blood;
Their thoughts *are* thoughts of iniquity;
Wasting and destruction *are* in their
paths.
8 The way of peace they have not
known,
And *there is* no justice in their ways;

They have made themselves crooked
paths;
Whoever takes that way
shall not know peace.

Sin Confessed

9 Therefore justice is far from us,
Nor does righteousness overtake us;
We look for light,
but there is darkness!
For brightness,
but we walk in blackness!
10 We grope for the wall like the blind,
And we grope as if *we had* no eyes;
We stumble at noonday as at twilight;
We are as dead *men* in desolate places.
11 We all growl like bears,
And moan sadly like doves;
We look for justice, but *there is* none;
For salvation, *but* it is far from us.
12 For our transgressions are multiplied
before You,
And our sins testify against us;
For our transgressions *are* with us,
And *as for* our iniquities,
we know them:
13 In transgressing and lying
against the LORD,
And departing from our God,
Speaking oppression and revolt,
Conceiving and uttering from the heart
words of falsehood.
14 Justice is turned back,
And righteousness stands afar off;
For truth is fallen in the street,
And equity cannot enter.
15 So truth fails,
And he *who* departs from evil makes
himself a prey.

The Redeemer of Zion

Then the LORD saw *it,*
and it displeased Him
That *there was* no justice.
16 He saw that *there was* no man,
And wondered that *there was* no
intercessor;
Therefore His own arm brought
salvation for Him;
And His own righteousness,
it sustained Him.
17 For He put on righteousness as a
breastplate,
And a helmet of salvation on His head;
He put on the garments of vengeance
for clothing,
And was clad with zeal as a cloak.

18 According to *their* deeds,
accordingly He will repay,
Fury to His adversaries,
Recompense to His enemies;
The coastlands He will fully repay.
19 So shall they fear
The name of the LORD from the west,
And His glory from the rising of the
sun;
When the enemy comes in like a flood,
The Spirit of the LORD will lift up a
standard against him.

20"The Redeemer will come to Zion,
And to those who turn from
transgression in Jacob,"
Says the LORD.

21 "As for Me," says the LORD, "this *is*
My covenant with them: My Spirit who *is*
upon you, and My words which I have
put in your mouth, shall not depart from
your mouth, nor from the mouth of your
descendants, nor from the mouth of
your descendants' descendants," says the
LORD, "from this time and forevermore."

The Gentiles Bless Zion

60 Arise, shine;
For your light has come!
And the glory of the LORD
is risen upon you.
2 For behold, the darkness shall cover
the earth,
And deep darkness the people;
But the LORD will arise over you,
And His glory will be seen upon you.
3 The Gentiles shall come to your light,
And kings to the brightness of your
rising.

4 "Lift up your eyes all around, and see:
They all gather together,
they come to you;
Your sons shall come from afar,
And your daughters shall be nursed at
your side.
5 Then you shall see and become radiant,
And your heart shall swell with joy;
Because the abundance of the sea shall
be turned to you,
The wealth of the Gentiles shall come
to you.
6 The multitude of camels shall cover
your land,
The dromedaries of Midian
and Ephah;
All those from Sheba shall come;
They shall bring gold and incense,

And they shall proclaim the praises
of the LORD.
7 All the flocks of Kedar shall be
gathered together to you,
The rams of Nebaioth shall minister
to you;
They shall ascend with acceptance on
My altar,
And I will glorify the house of My
glory.

8 "Who *are* these *who* fly like a cloud,
And like doves to their roosts?
9 Surely the coastlands shall wait for
Me;
And the ships of Tarshish *will come*
first,
To bring your sons from afar,
Their silver and their gold with them,
To the name of the LORD your God,
And to the Holy One of Israel,
Because He has glorified you.

10"The sons of foreigners shall build up
your walls,
And their kings shall minister to you;
For in My wrath I struck you,
But in My favor I have had mercy
on you.
11 Therefore your gates shall be open
continually;
They shall not be shut day or night,
That *men* may bring to you the wealth
of the Gentiles,
And their kings in procession.
12 For the nation and kingdom
which will not serve you shall perish,
And *those* nations shall be utterly
ruined.

13 "The glory of Lebanon
shall come to you,
The cypress, the pine,
and the box tree together,
To beautify the place of My sanctuary;
And I will make the place of My feet
glorious.
14 Also the sons of those who afflicted
you
Shall come bowing to you,
And all those who despised you
shall fall prostrate at the soles of
your feet;
And they shall call you
The City of the LORD,
Zion of the Holy One of Israel.

15"Whereas you have been forsaken
and hated,
So that no one went through *you,*

I will make you an eternal excellence,
A joy of many generations.
16 You shall drink *dry* the milk of the
Gentiles,
And shall milk the breast of kings;
You shall know that I, the LORD,
am your Savior
And your Redeemer,
the Mighty One of Jacob.

17"Instead of bronze I will bring gold,
Instead of iron I will bring silver,
Instead of wood, bronze,
And instead of stones, iron.
I will also make your officers peace,
And your magistrates righteousness.
18 Violence shall no longer be heard
in your land,
Neither wasting nor destruction
within your borders;
But you shall call your walls Salvation,
And your gates Praise.

God the Glory of His People

19"The sun shall no longer be your light
by day,
Nor for brightness shall the moon
give light to you;
But the LORD will be to you an
everlasting light,
And your God your glory.
20 Your sun shall no longer go down,
Nor shall your moon withdraw itself;
For the LORD will be your everlasting
light,
And the days of your mourning shall
be ended.
21 Also your people *shall* all *be* righteous;
They shall inherit the land forever,
The branch of My planting,
The work of My hands,
That I may be glorified.
22 A little one shall become a thousand,
And a small one a strong nation.
I, the LORD, will hasten it in its time."

The Good News of Salvation

61 "The Spirit of the Lord GOD
is upon Me,
Because the LORD has anointed Me
To preach good tidings to the poor;
He has sent Me to heal the
brokenhearted,
To proclaim liberty to the captives,
And the opening of the prison to *those
who are* bound;
2 To proclaim the acceptable year
of the LORD,

And the day of vengeance of our God;
To comfort all who mourn,
3 To console those who mourn in Zion,
To give them beauty for ashes,
The oil of joy for mourning,
The garment of praise for the spirit
of heaviness;
That they may be called trees of
righteousness,
The planting of the LORD,
that He may be glorified."

4 And they shall rebuild the old ruins,
They shall raise up the former
desolations,
And they shall repair the ruined cities,
The desolations of many generations.
5 Strangers shall stand
and feed your flocks,
And the sons of the foreigner
Shall be your plowmen
and your vinedressers.
6 But you shall be named
the Priests of the LORD,
Men shall call you
the Servants of our God.
You shall eat the riches of the Gentiles,
And in their glory you shall boast.
7 Instead of your shame
you shall have double honor,
And instead of confusion
they shall rejoice in their portion.
Therefore in their land
they shall possess double;
Everlasting joy shall be theirs.

8 "For I, the LORD, love justice;
I hate robbery for burnt offering;
I will direct their work in truth,
And will make with them an
everlasting covenant.
9 Their descendants shall be known
among the Gentiles,
And their offspring among the people.
All who see them
shall acknowledge them,
That they are the posterity
whom the LORD has blessed."

10 I will greatly rejoice in the LORD,
My soul shall be joyful in my God;
For He has clothed me
with the garments of salvation,
He has covered me
with the robe of righteousness,
As a bridegroom decks himself
with ornaments,
And as a bride adorns herself
with her jewels.
11 For as the earth brings forth its bud,

As the garden causes the things that
are sown in it to spring forth,
So the Lord GOD will cause
righteousness and praise to spring
forth before all the nations.

Assurance of Zion's Salvation

62 For Zion's sake I will not hold My
peace,
And for Jerusalem's sake I will not
rest,
Until her righteousness goes forth
as brightness,
And her salvation as a lamp that burns.
2 The Gentiles shall see your
righteousness,
And all kings your glory.
You shall be called by a new name,
Which the mouth of the LORD will
name.
3 You shall also be a crown of glory
In the hand of the LORD,
And a royal diadem
In the hand of your God.
4 You shall no longer be termed
Forsaken,
Nor shall your land any more be
termed Desolate;
But you shall be called Hephzibah,[42]
and your land Beulah;[43]
For the LORD delights in you,
And your land shall be married.
5 For as a young man marries a virgin,
So shall your sons marry you;
And as the bridegroom rejoices over
the bride,
So shall your God rejoice over you.

6 I have set watchmen on your walls,
O Jerusalem,
Who shall never hold their peace
day or night.
You who make mention of the LORD,
do not keep silent,
7 And give Him no rest till He
establishes
And till He makes Jerusalem
a praise in the earth.

8 The LORD has sworn by His right hand
And by the arm of His strength:
"Surely I will no longer give your grain
To be food for your enemies;
And the sons of the foreigner
shall not drink your new wine,
For which you have labored.
9 But those who have gathered it
shall eat it,
And praise the LORD;

---

42 Literally My Delight in Her   43 Literally Married

Those who have brought it together
shall drink it in My holy courts."

10 Go through,
Go through the gates!
Prepare the way for the people;
Build up,
Build up the highway!
Take out the stones,
Lift up a banner for the peoples!

11 Indeed the LORD has proclaimed
To the end of the world:
"Say to the daughter of Zion,
'Surely your salvation is coming;
Behold, His reward *is* with Him,
And His work before Him.'"
12 And they shall call them
The Holy People,
The Redeemed of the LORD;
And you shall be called Sought Out,
A City Not Forsaken.

The LORD in Judgment and Salvation

63 Who *is* this who comes from
Edom,
With dyed garments from Bozrah,
This *One who is* glorious
in His apparel,
Traveling in the greatness
of His strength?—

"I who speak in righteousness,
mighty to save."

2 Why *is* Your apparel red,
And Your garments like one who
treads in the winepress?

3 "I have trodden the winepress alone,
And from the peoples no one *was* with
Me.
For I have trodden them in My anger,
And trampled them in My fury;
Their blood is sprinkled upon My
garments,
And I have stained all My robes.
4 For the day of vengeance *is* in My
heart,
And the year of My redeemed has
come.
5 I looked, but *there was* no one to help,
And I wondered
That *there was* no one to uphold;
Therefore My own arm brought
salvation for Me;
And My own fury, it sustained Me.
6 I have trodden down the peoples
in My anger,
Made them drunk in My fury,

And brought down their strength
to the earth."

God's Mercy Remembered

7 I will mention the lovingkindnesses
of the LORD
And the praises of the LORD,
According to all that the LORD has
bestowed on us,
And the great goodness toward the
house of Israel,
Which He has bestowed on them
according to His mercies,
According to the multitude of His
lovingkindnesses.
8 For He said,
"Surely they *are* My people,
Children *who* will not lie."
So He became their Savior.
9 In all their affliction He was afflicted,
And the Angel of His Presence
saved them;
In His love and in His pity
He redeemed them;
And He bore them and carried them
All the days of old.
10 But they rebelled and grieved
His Holy Spirit;
So He turned Himself against them
as an enemy,
And He fought against them.

11 Then he remembered the days of old,
Moses *and* his people, *saying*:
"Where *is* He who brought them up out
of the sea
With the shepherd of His flock?
Where *is* He who put His Holy Spirit
within them,
12 Who led *them* by the right hand
of Moses,
With His glorious arm,
Dividing the water before them
To make for Himself
an everlasting name,
13 Who led them through the deep,
As a horse in the wilderness,
That they might not stumble?"

14 As a beast goes down into the valley,
And the Spirit of the LORD causes him
to rest,
So You lead Your people,
To make Yourself a glorious name.

A Prayer of Penitence

15 Look down from heaven,
And see from Your habitation,
holy and glorious.

Where *are* Your zeal
  and Your strength,
The yearning of Your heart
  and Your mercies toward me?
Are they restrained?

16 Doubtless You *are* our Father,
  Though Abraham was ignorant of us,
  And Israel does not acknowledge us.
  You, O Lord, *are* our Father;
  Our Redeemer from Everlasting
    is Your name.

17 O Lord, why have You made us stray
    from Your ways,
  And hardened our heart from Your
    fear?
  Return for Your servants' sake,
  The tribes of Your inheritance.

18 Your holy people have possessed *it*
    but a little while;
  Our adversaries have trodden down
    Your sanctuary.

19 We have become *like* those of old,
    over whom You never ruled,
  Those who were never called
    by Your name.

64

Oh, that You would rend the
  heavens!
That You would come down!
That the mountains might shake
  at Your presence—

2 As fire burns brushwood,
  As fire causes water to boil—
  To make Your name known
    to Your adversaries,
  That the nations may tremble
    at Your presence!

3 When You did awesome things *for*
    which we did not look,
  You came down,
  The mountains shook at Your
    presence.

4 For since the beginning of the world
  Men have not heard
    nor perceived by the ear,
  Nor has the eye seen any God besides
    You,
  Who acts for the one who waits for
    Him.

5 You meet him who rejoices and does
    righteousness,
  Who remembers You in Your ways.
  You are indeed angry,
    for we have sinned—
  In these ways we continue;
  And we need to be saved.

6 But we are all like an unclean *thing*,
  And all our righteousnesses *are* like
    filthy rags;

We all fade as a leaf,
  And our iniquities, like the wind,
  Have taken us away.

7 And *there is* no one who calls
    on Your name,
  Who stirs himself up to take hold
    of You;
  For You have hidden Your face
    from us,
  And have consumed us
    because of our iniquities.

8 But now, O Lord,
  You *are* our Father;
  We *are* the clay, and You our potter;
  And all we *are* the work of Your hand.

9 Do not be furious, O Lord,
  Nor remember iniquity forever;
  Indeed, please look—we all *are* Your
    people!

10 Your holy cities are a wilderness,
  Zion is a wilderness,
  Jerusalem a desolation.

11 Our holy and beautiful temple,
  Where our fathers praised You,
  Is burned up with fire;
  And all our pleasant things are laid
    waste.

12 Will You restrain Yourself
    because of these *things*, O Lord?
  Will You hold Your peace,
    and afflict us very severely?

The Righteousness of God's Judgment

65

"I was sought by *those who* did not
  ask *for Me*;
I was found by *those who* did not seek
  Me.
I said, 'Here I am, here I am,'
  To a nation *that* was not called
    by My name.

2 I have stretched out My hands
    all day long to a rebellious people,
  Who walk in a way *that is* not good,
  According to their own thoughts;

3 A people who provoke Me to anger
    continually to My face;
  Who sacrifice in gardens,
  And burn incense on altars of brick;

4 Who sit among the graves,
  And spend the night in the tombs;
  Who eat swine's flesh,
  And the broth of abominable things
    is *in* their vessels;

5 Who say, 'Keep to yourself,
  Do not come near me,
  For I am holier than you!'
  These *are* smoke in My nostrils,
  A fire that burns all the day.

6 "Behold, *it is* written before Me:
I will not keep silence, but will repay—
Even repay into their bosom—
7 Your iniquities and the iniquities
of your fathers together,"
Says the LORD,
"Who have burned incense on the
mountains
And blasphemed Me on the hills;
Therefore I will measure their former
work into their bosom."

8 Thus says the LORD:

"As the new wine is found in the cluster,
And *one* says, 'Do not destroy it,
For a blessing *is* in it,'
So will I do for My servants' sake,
That I may not destroy them all.
9 I will bring forth descendants from
Jacob,
And from Judah an heir of My
mountains;
My elect shall inherit it,
And My servants shall dwell there.
10 Sharon shall be a fold of flocks,
And the Valley of Achor a place for
herds to lie down,
For My people who have sought Me.

11 "But you *are* those who forsake the
LORD,
Who forget My holy mountain,
Who prepare a table for Gad,[44]
And who furnish a drink offering for
Meni.[45]
12 Therefore I will number you for the
sword,
And you shall all bow down to the
slaughter;
Because, when I called,
you did not answer;
When I spoke, you did not hear,
But did evil before My eyes,
And chose *that* in which I do not
delight."

13 Therefore thus says the Lord GOD:

"Behold, My servants shall eat,
But you shall be hungry;
Behold, My servants shall drink,
But you shall be thirsty;
Behold, My servants shall rejoice,
But you shall be ashamed;
14 Behold, My servants shall sing
for joy of heart,
But you shall cry for sorrow of heart,
And wail for grief of spirit.

15 You shall leave your name as a curse
to My chosen;
For the Lord GOD will slay you,
And call His servants by another
name;
16 So that he who blesses himself
in the earth
Shall bless himself in the God of truth;
And he who swears in the earth
Shall swear by the God of truth;
Because the former troubles are
forgotten,
And because they are hidden
from My eyes.

The Glorious New Creation

17 "For behold, I create new heavens
and a new earth;
And the former shall not be
remembered or come to mind.
18 But be glad and rejoice forever in what
I create;
For behold, I create Jerusalem
as a rejoicing,
And her people a joy.
19 I will rejoice in Jerusalem,
And joy in My people;
The voice of weeping shall no longer
be heard in her,
Nor the voice of crying.

20 "No more shall an infant from there
live but a few days,
Nor an old man who has not fulfilled
his days;
For the child shall die one hundred
years old,
But the sinner *being* one hundred years
old shall be accursed.
21 They shall build houses
and inhabit *them*;
They shall plant vineyards
and eat their fruit.
22 They shall not build
and another inhabit;
They shall not plant and another eat;
For as the days of a tree,
so shall be the days of My people,
And My elect shall long enjoy the
work of their hands.
23 They shall not labor in vain,
Nor bring forth children for trouble;
For they *shall be* the descendants of
the blessed of the LORD,
And their offspring with them.
24 "It shall come to pass
That before they call, I will answer;

---

44 Literally *Troop* or *Fortune,* a pagan deity   45 Literally *Number* or *Destiny,* a pagan deity

And while they are still speaking,
I will hear.
25 The wolf and the lamb
shall feed together,
The lion shall eat straw like the ox,
And dust *shall be* the serpent's food.
They shall not hurt nor destroy in all
My holy mountain,"
Says the LORD.

True Worship and False

66 Thus says the LORD:
"Heaven *is* My throne,
And earth *is* My footstool.
Where *is* the house that you
will build Me?
And where *is* the place of My rest?
2 For all those *things* My hand has
made,
And all those *things* exist,"
Says the LORD.
"But on this *one* will I look:
On *him who is* poor
and of a contrite spirit,
And who trembles at My word.

3 "He who kills a bull *is as if* he slays a
man;
He who sacrifices a lamb,
as if he breaks a dog's neck;
He who offers a grain offering,
as if he offers swine's blood;
He who burns incense,
as if he blesses an idol.
Just as they have chosen
their own ways,
And their soul delights
in their abominations,
4 So will I choose their delusions,
And bring their fears on them;
Because, when I called,
no one answered,
When I spoke they did not hear;
But they did evil before My eyes,
And chose *that* in which I do not
delight."

The LORD Vindicates Zion

5 Hear the word of the LORD,
You who tremble at His word:
"Your brethren who hated you,
Who cast you out for My name's sake,
said,
'Let the LORD be glorified,
That we may see your joy.'
But they shall be ashamed."

6 The sound of noise from the city!
A voice from the temple!

The voice of the LORD,
Who fully repays His enemies!

7 "Before she travailed, she gave birth;
Before her pain came,
She delivered a male child.
8 Who has heard such a thing?
Who has seen such things?
Shall the earth be made to give birth
in one day?
Or shall a nation be born at once?
For as soon as Zion travailed,
She gave birth to her children.
9 Shall I bring to the time of birth, and
not cause delivery?" says the LORD.
"Shall I who cause delivery shut up *the
womb?*" says your God.
10 "Rejoice with Jerusalem,
And be glad with her,
all you who love her;
Rejoice for joy with her,
all you who mourn for her;
11 That you may feed and be satisfied
With the consolation of her bosom,
That you may drink deeply and be
delighted
With the abundance of her glory."

12 For thus says the LORD:

"Behold, I will extend peace to her
like a river,
And the glory of the Gentiles
like a flowing stream.
Then you shall feed;
On *her* sides shall you be carried,
And be dandled on *her* knees.
13 As one whom his mother comforts,
So I will comfort you;
And you shall be comforted in
Jerusalem."

The Reign and Indignation of God

14 When you see *this,*
your heart shall rejoice,
And your bones shall flourish like
grass;
The hand of the LORD shall be known
to His servants,
And *His* indignation to His enemies.
15 For behold, the LORD will come with
fire
And with His chariots,
like a whirlwind,
To render His anger with fury,
And His rebuke with flames of fire.
16 For by fire and by His sword
The LORD will judge all flesh;

And the slain of the LORD
   shall be many.

17 "Those who sanctify themselves
   and purify themselves,
To go to the gardens
After an *idol* in the midst,
Eating swine's flesh and the
   abomination and the mouse,
Shall be consumed together,"
   says the LORD.

18 "For I *know* their works and their thoughts. It shall be that I will gather all nations and tongues; and they shall come and see My glory.
19 "I will set a sign among them; and those among them who escape I will send to the nations: *to* Tarshish and Pul and Lud, who draw the bow, and Tubal and Javan, *to* the coastlands afar off who have not heard My fame nor seen My glory. And they shall declare My glory among the Gentiles.
20 "Then they shall bring all your brethren for an offering to the LORD out of all nations, on horses and in chariots and in litters, on mules and on camels, to My holy mountain Jerusalem," says the LORD, "as the children of Israel bring an offering in a clean vessel into the house of the LORD.
21 "And I will also take some of them for priests *and* Levites," says the LORD.

22 "For as the new heavens
   and the new earth
Which I will make shall remain before
   Me," says the LORD,
"So shall your descendants
   and your name remain.
23 And it shall come to pass
That from one New Moon to another,
And from one Sabbath to another,
All flesh shall come to worship before
   Me," says the LORD.

24 "And they shall go forth and look
Upon the corpses of the men
Who have transgressed against Me.
For their worm does not die,
And their fire is not quenched.
They shall be an abhorrence
   to all flesh."

Introduction to Jeremiah

The Book of Jeremiah is a dramatic adventure of the call of a young man by God to boldly proclaim His truth to a nation which had turned away from Him. The book was written by Jeremiah, aided by his scribe, Baruch, about 627–580 B.C.

Initially, the remarkable young man hesitated to follow God's call, citing his young age as an excuse. "Ah, Lord GOD! Behold, I cannot speak, for I *am* a youth" (Jer. 1:6). But God's reassurance that He would be with Jeremiah gave him hope and strength to carry out his appointed task.

Jeremiah's responsibility was to forewarn the people of Judah of the coming destruction should they fail to turn their hearts back to God. The people had adopted the pagan practices from the surrounding nations and thought to please false gods through such depraved acts as infant sacrifice. Temples and high places to false gods were built throughout the land, while the rightful temple of God was neglected.

Jeremiah's message was not a popular one, but with boldness and confidence he went out to proclaim it. He faced tremendous suffering, including imprisonment, excommunication from the temple, and beatings. Jeremiah was brave enough to accept the responsibility to take positive actions in negative times. It is hard to find someone willing to stand up against the crowd. But Jeremiah obeyed God in the face of obstacles.

Interwoven throughout Jeremiah's warnings to the people are beautiful promises of God. Despite destruction, God's ultimate commitment to His people guaranteed their success and future. "For I know the thoughts that I think toward you, says the LORD, thoughts of peace and not of evil, to give you a future and a hope" (Jer. 29:11).

The Book of
Jeremiah

THE words of Jeremiah the son of Hilkiah, of the priests who *were* in Anathoth in the land of Benjamin, 2 to whom the word of the LORD came in the days of Josiah the son of Amon, king of Judah, in the thirteenth year of his reign. 3 It came also in the days of Jehoiakim the son of Josiah, king of Judah, until the end of the eleventh year of Zedekiah the son of Josiah, king of Judah, until the carrying away of Jerusalem captive in the fifth month.

The Prophet Is Called

4 Then the word of the LORD came to me, saying:

5 "Before I formed you in the womb
    I knew you;
Before you were born I sanctified you;
And I ordained you a prophet to the
    nations."

6 Then said I:

"Ah, Lord GOD!
Behold, I cannot speak,
    for I *am* a youth."

7 But the LORD said to me:

"Do not say, 'I *am* a youth,'
For you shall go to all to whom
    I send you,
And whatever I command you,
    you shall speak.
8 Do not be afraid of their faces,
For I *am* with you to deliver you,"
    says the LORD.

9 Then the LORD put forth His hand and touched my mouth, and the LORD said to me:

"Behold, I have put My words in your
    mouth.
10 See, I have this day set you over the
    nations and over the kingdoms,
To root out and to pull down,
To destroy and to throw down,
To build and to plant."

11 Moreover the word of the LORD came to me, saying, "Jeremiah, what do you see?" And I said, "I see a branch of an almond tree." 12 Then the LORD said to me, "You have seen well, for I am ready to perform My word."

13 And the word of the LORD came to me the second time, saying, "What do you see?" And I said, "I see a boiling pot, and it is facing away from the north." 14 Then the LORD said to me:

"Out of the north calamity shall break
    forth
On all the inhabitants of the land.
15 For behold, I am calling
All the families of the kingdoms of the
    north," says the LORD;
"They shall come and each one
    set his throne
At the entrance of the gates of
    Jerusalem,
Against all its walls all around,
And against all the cities of Judah.
16 I will utter My judgments
Against them concerning all their
    wickedness,
Because they have forsaken Me,
Burned incense to other gods,
And worshiped the works of their
    own hands.
17 Therefore prepare yourself and arise,
And speak to them all that I command
    you.
Do not be dismayed before their faces,
Lest I dismay you before them.
18 For behold, I have made you this day
A fortified city and an iron pillar,
And bronze walls against the whole
    land—
Against the kings of Judah,
Against its princes,
Against its priests,
And against the people of the land.
19 They will fight against you,
But they shall not prevail against you.
For I *am* with you," says the LORD,
    "to deliver you."

God's Case Against Israel

2 Moreover the word of the LORD came to me, saying,
2 "Go and cry in the hearing of Jerusalem, saying, 'Thus says the LORD:

"I remember you,
The kindness of your youth,
The love of your betrothal,
When you went after Me in the
wilderness,
In a land *that was* not sown.
3 Israel *was* holiness to the LORD,
The firstfruits of His increase.
All that devour him will offend;
Disaster will come upon them,"
says the LORD.' "

4 Hear the word of the LORD, O house of Jacob and all the families of the house of Israel.
5 Thus says the LORD:

"What injustice have your fathers
found in Me,
That they have gone far from Me,
Have followed idols,
And have become idolaters?
6 Neither did they say,
'Where *is* the LORD,
Who brought us up out of the land
of Egypt,
Who led us through the wilderness,
Through a land of deserts and pits,
Through a land of drought
and the shadow of death,
Through a land that no one crossed
And where no one dwelt?'
7 I brought you into a bountiful country,
To eat its fruit and its goodness.
But when you entered,
you defiled My land
And made My heritage
an abomination.
8 The priests did not say,
'Where *is* the LORD?'
And those who handle the law
did not know Me;
The rulers also transgressed
against Me;
The prophets prophesied by Baal,
And walked after *things that* do not
profit.

9 "Therefore I will yet bring charges
against you," says the LORD,
"And against your children's children I
will bring charges.

10 For pass beyond the coasts of Cyprus[1]
and see,
Send to Kedar[2] and consider diligently,
And see if there has been such *a thing.*
11 Has a nation changed *its* gods,
Which *are* not gods?
But My people have changed
their Glory
For *what* does not profit.
12 Be astonished, O heavens, at this,
And be horribly afraid;
Be very desolate," says the LORD.
13 "For My people have committed two
evils:
They have forsaken Me,
the fountain of living waters,
And hewn themselves cisterns—broken
cisterns that can hold no water.

14 *Is* Israel a servant?
Is he a homeborn *slave?*
Why is he plundered?
15 The young lions roared at him,
and growled;
They made his land waste;
His cities are burned,
without inhabitant.
16 Also the people of Noph[3]
and Tahpanhes
Have broken the crown of your head.
17 Have you not brought this on yourself,
In that you have forsaken the LORD
your God
When He led you in the way?
18 And now why take the road to Egypt,
To drink the waters of Sihor?
Or why take the road to Assyria,
To drink the waters of the River?[4]
19 Your own wickedness will correct you,
And your backslidings will
reprove you.
Know therefore and see that *it is* an
evil and bitter *thing*
That you have forsaken the LORD
your God,
And the fear of Me *is* not in you,"
Says the Lord GOD of hosts.

20 "For of old I have broken your yoke
and burst your bonds;
And you said, 'I will not transgress,'
When on every high hill
and under every green tree
You lay down, playing the harlot.
21 Yet I had planted you a noble vine,
a seed of highest quality.
How then have you turned before Me
Into the degenerate plant of an alien
vine?

1 Hebrew *Kittim,* western lands, especially Cyprus
2 In the northern Arabian desert, representative of the eastern cultures   3 That is, Memphis in ancient Egypt
4 That is, the Euphrates

22 For though you wash yourself with lye,
and use much soap,
Yet your iniquity is marked before
Me,"says the Lord GOD.

23 "How can you say, 'I am not polluted,
I have not gone after the Baals'?
See your way in the valley;
Know what you have done:
You are a swift dromedary
breaking loose in her ways,
24 A wild donkey used to the wilderness,
That sniffs at the wind in her desire;
In her time of mating,
who can turn her away?
All those who seek her will not weary
themselves;
In her month they will find her.
25 Withhold your foot from being unshod,
and your throat from thirst.
But you said, 'There is no hope.
No! For I have loved aliens,
and after them I will go.'

26 "As the thief is ashamed
when he is found out,
So is the house of Israel ashamed;
They and their kings and their princes,
and their priests and their prophets,
27 Saying to a tree, 'You *are* my father,'
And to a stone, 'You gave birth to me.'
For they have turned *their* back to Me,
and not *their* face.
But in the time of their trouble
They will say, 'Arise and save us.'
28 But where *are* your gods
that you have made for yourselves?
Let them arise,
If they can save you in the time of
your trouble;
For *according to* the number of your
cities
Are your gods, O Judah.

29 "Why will you plead with Me?
You all have transgressed against Me,"
says the LORD.
30 "In vain I have chastened your children;
They received no correction.
Your sword has devoured your
prophets
Like a destroying lion.

31 "O generation,
see the word of the LORD!
Have I been a wilderness to Israel,
Or a land of darkness?
Why do My people say, 'We are lords;
We will come no more to You'?

32 Can a virgin forget her ornaments,
Or a bride her attire?
Yet My people have forgotten Me
days without number.

33 "Why do you beautify your way to seek
love?
Therefore you have also taught
The wicked women your ways.
34 Also on your skirts is found
The blood of the lives of the poor
innocents.
I have not found it by secret search,
But plainly on all these things.
35 Yet you say, 'Because I am innocent,
Surely His anger shall turn from me.'
Behold, I will plead My case against
you,
Because you say, 'I have not sinned.'
36 Why do you gad about so much
to change your way?
Also you shall be ashamed of Egypt
as you were ashamed of Assyria.
37 Indeed you will go forth from him
With your hands on your head;
For the LORD has rejected your trusted
allies,
And you will not prosper by them.

Israel Is Shameless

3 "They say, 'If a man divorces his wife,
And she goes from him
And becomes another man's,
May he return to her again?'
Would not that land be greatly
polluted?
But you have played the harlot with
many lovers;
Yet return to Me," says the LORD.

2 "Lift up your eyes to the desolate
heights and see:
Where have you not lain *with men?*
By the road you have sat for them
Like an Arabian in the wilderness;
And you have polluted the land
With your harlotries
and your wickedness.
3 Therefore the showers have been
withheld,
And there has been no latter rain.
You have had a harlot's forehead;
You refuse to be ashamed.
4 Will you not from this time cry to Me,
'My father, You *are* the guide
of my youth?
5 Will He remain angry forever?
Will He keep it to the end?'

Behold, you have spoken
and done evil things,
As you were able."

A Call to Repentance

6 The LORD said also to me in the days of Josiah the king: "Have you seen what backsliding Israel has done? She has gone up on every high mountain and under every green tree, and there played the harlot.
7 "And I said, after she had done all these *things*, 'Return to Me.' But she did not return. And her treacherous sister Judah saw it.
8 "Then I saw that for all the causes for which backsliding Israel had committed adultery, I had put her away and given her a certificate of divorce; yet her treacherous sister Judah did not fear, but went and played the harlot also.
9 "So it came to pass, through her casual harlotry, that she defiled the land and committed adultery with stones and trees.
10 "And yet for all this her treacherous sister Judah has not turned to Me with her whole heart, but in pretense," says the LORD.
11 Then the LORD said to me, "Backsliding Israel has shown herself more righteous than treacherous Judah.
12 "Go and proclaim these words toward the north, and say:

'Return, backsliding Israel,'
says the LORD,
'*And* I will not cause My anger
to fall on you;
For I *am* merciful,' says the LORD,
'*And* I will not remain angry forever.
13 Only acknowledge your iniquity,
That you have transgressed against the
LORD your God,
And have scattered your charms
To alien deities under every green tree,
And you have not obeyed My voice,'
says the LORD.

14 "Return, O backsliding children," says the LORD; "for I am married to you. I will take you, one from a city and two from a family, and I will bring you to Zion.
15 "And I will give you shepherds according to My heart, who will feed you with knowledge and understanding.
16 "Then it shall come to pass, when you

are multiplied and increased in the land in those days," says the LORD, "that they will say no more, 'The ark of the covenant of the LORD.' It shall not come to mind, nor shall they remember it, nor shall they visit *it*, nor shall it be made anymore.
17 "At that time Jerusalem shall be called The Throne of the LORD, and all the nations shall be gathered to it, to the name of the LORD, to Jerusalem; they shall walk no more after the stubbornness of their evil heart.
18 "In those days the house of Judah shall walk with the house of Israel, and they shall come together out of the land of the north to the land that I have given as an inheritance to your fathers.
19 "But I said:

'How can I put you among the children
And give you a pleasant land,
A beautiful heritage of the hosts of
nations?'

"And I said:

'You shall call Me, "My Father,"
And not turn away from Me.'
20 Surely, *as* a wife treacherously departs
from her husband,
So have you dealt treacherously
with Me,
O house of Israel," says the LORD.

21 A voice was heard on the desolate
heights,
Weeping *and* supplications of the
children of Israel;
For they have perverted their way,
And they have forgotten the LORD their
God.

22 "Return, you backsliding children,
And I will heal your backslidings."

"Indeed we do come to You,
For You are the LORD our God.
23 Truly, in vain *is salvation hoped for*
from the hills,
And from the multitude of mountains;
Truly, in the LORD our God
Is the salvation of Israel.
24 For shame has devoured
The labor of our fathers from our
youth—
Their flocks and their herds,
Their sons and their daughters.

25 We lie down in our shame,
And our reproach covers us.
For we have sinned against the LORD
    our God,
We and our fathers,
From our youth even to this day,
And have not obeyed the voice of the
    LORD our God."

4 "If you will return, O Israel,"
    says the LORD,
"Return to Me;
And if you will put away your
    abominations out of My sight,
Then you shall not be moved.
2 And you shall swear, 'The LORD lives,'
In truth, in judgment, and
    in righteousness;
The nations shall bless themselves in
    Him,
And in Him they shall glory."

3 For thus says the LORD to the men of
Judah and Jerusalem:

"Break up your fallow ground,
And do not sow among thorns.
4 Circumcise yourselves to the LORD,
And take away the foreskins of your
    hearts,
You men of Judah
    and inhabitants of Jerusalem,
Lest My fury come forth like fire,
And burn so that no one can quench it,
Because of the evil of your doings."

An Imminent Invasion

5 Declare in Judah and proclaim in Jerusalem, and say:

"Blow the trumpet in the land;
Cry, 'Gather together,'
And say, 'Assemble yourselves,
And let us go into the fortified cities.'
6 Set up the standard toward Zion.
Take refuge! Do not delay!
For I will bring disaster from the
    north,
And great destruction."

7 The lion has come up from his thicket,
And the destroyer of nations is on his
    way.
He has gone forth from his place
To make your land desolate.
Your cities will be laid waste,
Without inhabitant.
8 For this, clothe yourself with sackcloth,
Lament and wail.

For the fierce anger of the LORD
Has not turned back from us.

9 "And it shall come to pass in that day,"
    says the LORD,
"That the heart of the king shall perish,
And the heart of the princes;
The priests shall be astonished,
And the prophets shall wonder."

10 Then I said, "Ah, Lord GOD!
Surely You have greatly deceived
    this people and Jerusalem,
Saying, 'You shall have peace,'
Whereas the sword reaches to the
    heart."

11 At that time it will be said
To this people and to Jerusalem,
"A dry wind of the desolate heights
    blows in the wilderness
Toward the daughter of My people—
Not to fan or to cleanse—
12 A wind too strong for these will come
    for Me;
Now I will also speak judgment against
    them."

13 "Behold, he shall come up like clouds,
And his chariots like a whirlwind.
His horses are swifter than eagles.
Woe to us, for we are plundered!"

14 O Jerusalem, wash your heart from
    wickedness,
That you may be saved.
How long shall your evil thoughts
    lodge within you?
15 For a voice declares from Dan
And proclaims affliction
    from Mount Ephraim:
16 "Make mention to the nations,
Yes, proclaim against Jerusalem,
That watchers come from a far country
And raise their voice against the cities
    of Judah.
17 Like keepers of a field
    they are against her all around,
Because she has been rebellious against
    Me," says the LORD.
18 "Your ways and your doings
Have procured these things for you.
This is your wickedness,
Because it is bitter,
Because it reaches to your heart."

Sorrow for the Doomed Nation

19 O my soul, my soul!
I am pained in my very heart!

My heart makes a noise in me;
I cannot hold my peace,
Because you have heard, O my soul,
The sound of the trumpet,
The alarm of war.
20 Destruction upon destruction is cried,
For the whole land is plundered.
Suddenly my tents are plundered,
And my curtains in a moment.
21 How long will I see the standard,
And hear the sound of the trumpet?

22 "For My people *are* foolish,
They have not known Me.
They *are* silly children,
And they have no understanding.
They *are* wise to do evil,
But to do good
they have no knowledge."

23 I beheld the earth, and indeed
it was without form, and void;
And the heavens, they *had* no light.
24 I beheld the mountains,
and indeed they trembled,
And all the hills moved back and forth.
25 I beheld, and indeed *there was* no man,
And all the birds of the heavens had
fled.
26 I beheld, and indeed the fruitful land
was a wilderness,
And all its cities were broken down
At the presence of the LORD,
By His fierce anger.

27 For thus says the LORD:

"The whole land shall be desolate;
Yet I will not make a full end.
28 For this shall the earth mourn,
And the heavens above be black,
Because I have spoken.
I have purposed and will not relent,
Nor will I turn back from it.
29 The whole city shall flee from the noise
of the horsemen and bowmen.
They shall go into thickets
and climb up on the rocks.
Every city *shall be* forsaken,
And not a man shall dwell in it.

30 "And *when* you *are* plundered,
What will you do?
Though you clothe yourself
with crimson,
Though you adorn *yourself*
with ornaments of gold,
Though you enlarge your eyes
with paint,
In vain you will make yourself fair;

Your lovers will despise you;
They will seek your life.

31 "For I have heard a voice
as of a woman in labor,
The anguish as of her
who brings forth her first child,
The voice of the daughter of Zion
bewailing herself,
Who spreads her hands, *saying*,
'Woe *is* me now, for my soul is weary
Because of murderers!'

The Justice of God's Judgment

5 "Run to and fro through the streets
of Jerusalem;
See now and know;
And seek in her open places
If you can find a man,
If there is *anyone* who executes
judgment,
Who seeks the truth,
And I will pardon her.
2 Though they say, '*As* the LORD lives,'
Surely they swear falsely."

3 O LORD, *are* not Your eyes on the
truth?
You have stricken them,
But they have not grieved;
You have consumed them,
But they have refused to receive
correction.
They have made their faces harder
than rock;
They have refused to return.

4 Therefore I said,
"Surely these *are* poor.
They are foolish;
For they do not know the way
of the LORD,
The judgment of their God.
5 I will go to the great men
and speak to them,
For they have known the way
of the LORD,
The judgment of their God."
But these have altogether broken the
yoke
And burst the bonds.
6 Therefore a lion from the forest
shall slay them,
A wolf of the deserts
shall destroy them;
A leopard will watch over their cities.
Everyone who goes out from there
shall be torn in pieces,

Because their transgressions are many;
Their backslidings have increased.

7 "How shall I pardon you for this?
Your children have forsaken Me
And sworn by *those that are* not gods.
When I had fed them to the full,
Then they committed adultery
And assembled themselves by troops
in the harlots' houses.
8 They were *like* well-fed lusty stallions;
Every one neighed after his neighbor's
wife.
9 Shall I not punish *them* for these
things?" says the LORD.
"And shall I not avenge Myself
on such a nation as this?

10 "Go up on her walls and destroy,
But do not make a complete end.
Take away her branches,
For they *are* not the LORD's.
11 For the house of Israel
and the house of Judah
Have dealt very treacherously with
Me," says the LORD.

12 They have lied about the LORD,
And said, "*It is* not He.
Neither will evil come upon us,
Nor shall we see sword or famine.
13 And the prophets become wind,
For the word *is* not in them.
Thus shall it be done to them."

14 Therefore thus says the LORD God of
hosts:

"Because you speak this word,
Behold, I will make My words in your
mouth fire,
And this people wood,
And it shall devour them.
15 Behold, I will bring a nation against
you from afar,
O house of Israel," says the LORD.
"It *is* a mighty nation,
It *is* an ancient nation,
A nation whose language
you do not know,
Nor can you understand
what they say.
16 Their quiver *is* like an open tomb;
They *are* all mighty men.
17 And they shall eat up your harvest
and your bread,
Which your sons and daughters
should eat.
They shall eat up your flocks
and your herds;

They shall eat up your vines
and your fig trees;
They shall destroy your fortified cities,
In which you trust, with the sword.

18 "Nevertheless in those days," says the
LORD, "I will not make a complete end of
you.
19 "And it will be when you say, 'Why
does the LORD our God do all these
things to us?' then you shall answer
them, 'Just as you have forsaken Me and
served foreign gods in your land, so you
shall serve aliens in a land *that is* not
yours.'

20 "Declare this in the house of Jacob
And proclaim it in Judah, saying,
21 'Hear this now, O foolish people,
Without understanding,
Who have eyes and see not,
And who have ears and hear not:
22 Do you not fear Me?' says the LORD.
'Will you not tremble at My presence,
Who have placed the sand
as the bound of the sea,
By a perpetual decree,
that it cannot pass beyond it?
And though its waves toss
to and fro,
Yet they cannot prevail;
Though they roar,
yet they cannot pass over it.
23 But this people has a defiant and
rebellious heart;
They have revolted and departed.
24 They do not say in their heart,
"Let us now fear the LORD our God,
Who gives rain, both the former
and the latter, in its season.
He reserves for us the appointed weeks
of the harvest."
25 Your iniquities have turned these *things*
away,
And your sins have withheld good
things from you.

26 'For among My people are found
wicked *men*;
They lie in wait as one who sets snares;
They set a trap;
They catch men.
27 As a cage is full of birds,
So their houses *are* full of deceit.
Therefore they have become great
and grown rich.
28 They have grown fat, they are sleek;
Yes, they surpass the deeds of the
wicked;
They do not plead the cause,

The cause of the fatherless;
Yet they prosper,
And the right of the needy
they do not defend.
29 Shall I not punish *them* for these
things?' says the LORD.
'Shall I not avenge Myself
on such a nation as this?'

30"An astonishing and horrible thing
Has been committed in the land:
31 The prophets prophesy falsely,
And the priests rule by their *own*
power;
And My people love *to have it* so.
But what will you do in the end?

Impending Destruction from the North

6 "O you children of Benjamin,
Gather yourselves to flee from the
midst of Jerusalem!
Blow the trumpet in Tekoa,
And set up a signal-fire in Beth
Haccherem;
For disaster appears out of the north,
And great destruction.
2 I have likened the daughter of Zion
To a lovely and delicate woman.
3 The shepherds with their flocks shall
come to her.
They shall pitch *their* tents against her
all around.
Each one shall pasture in his own
place."

4 "Prepare war against her;
Arise, and let us go up at noon.
Woe to us, for the day goes away,
For the shadows of the evening
are lengthening.
5 Arise, and let us go by night,
And let us destroy her palaces."

6 For thus has the LORD of hosts said:

"Hew down trees,
And build a mound against Jerusalem.
This *is* the city to be punished.
She *is* full of oppression in her midst.
7 As a fountain wells up with water,
So she wells up with her wickedness.
Violence and plundering are heard
in her.
Before Me continually
are grief and wounds.
8 Be instructed, O Jerusalem,
Lest My soul depart from you;
Lest I make you desolate,
A land not inhabited."

9 Thus says the LORD of hosts:

"They shall thoroughly glean as a vine
the remnant of Israel;
As a grape-gatherer,
put your hand back into the
branches."

10 To whom shall I speak
and give warning,
That they may hear?
Indeed their ear *is* uncircumcised,
And they cannot give heed.
Behold, the word of the LORD is a
reproach to them;
They have no delight in it.
11 Therefore I am full of the fury of the
LORD.
I am weary of holding *it* in.
"I will pour it out on the children
outside,
And on the assembly of young men
together;
For even the husband shall be taken
with the wife,
The aged with *him who is* full of days.
12 And their houses shall be turned over
to others,
Fields and wives together;
For I will stretch out My hand
Against the inhabitants of the land,"
says the LORD.
13 "Because from the least of them
even to the greatest of them,
Everyone *is* given to covetousness;
And from the prophet
even to the priest,
Everyone deals falsely.
14 They have also healed the hurt
of My people slightly,
Saying, 'Peace, peace!'
When *there is* no peace.
15 Were they ashamed when they had
committed abomination?
No! They were not at all ashamed;
Nor did they know how to blush.
Therefore they shall fall among those
who fall;
At the time I punish them,
They shall be cast down,"
says the LORD.

16 Thus says the LORD:

"Stand in the ways and see,
And ask for the old paths,
where the good way *is*,
And walk in it;
Then you will find rest for your souls.
But they said, 'We will not walk *in it.*'

17 Also, I set watchmen over you, *saying*,
'Listen to the sound of the trumpet!'
But they said, 'We will not listen.'
18 Therefore hear, you nations,
And know, O congregation,
what *is* among them.
19 Hear, O earth!
Behold, I will certainly bring calamity
on this people,
Even the fruit of their thoughts,
Because they have not heeded My
words,
Nor My law, but rejected it.
20 For what purpose to Me
Comes frankincense from Sheba,
And sweet cane from a far country?
Your burnt offerings *are* not
acceptable,
Nor your sacrifices sweet to Me."

21 Therefore thus says the LORD:

"Behold, I will lay stumbling blocks
before this people,
And the fathers and the sons together
shall fall on them.
The neighbor and his friend
shall perish."

22 Thus says the LORD:

"Behold, a people comes from the north
country,
And a great nation will be raised from
the farthest parts of the earth.
23 They will lay hold on bow and spear;
They *are* cruel and have no mercy;
Their voice roars like the sea;
And they ride on horses,
As men of war set in array against you,
O daughter of Zion."

24 We have heard the report of it;
Our hands grow feeble.
Anguish has taken hold of us,
Pain as of a woman in labor.
25 Do not go out into the field,
Nor walk by the way.
Because of the sword of the enemy,
Fear *is* on every side.
26 O daughter of my people,
Clothe *yourself* with sackcloth,
And roll about in ashes!
Make mourning *as for* an only son,
most bitter lamentation;
For the plunderer will suddenly come
upon us.

27"I have set you *as* an assayer
and a fortress among My people,

That you may know and test their way.
28 They *are* all stubborn rebels,
walking as slanderers.
They are bronze and iron,
They *are* all corrupters;
29 The bellows blow fiercely,
The lead is consumed by the fire;
The smelter refines in vain,
For the wicked are not drawn off.
30 *People* will call them rejected silver,
Because the LORD has rejected them."

Trusting in Lying Words

7 The word that came to Jeremiah
from the LORD, saying,
2 "Stand in the gate of the LORD's
house, and proclaim there this word, and
say, 'Hear the word of the LORD, all *you
of* Judah who enter in at these gates to
worship the LORD!'"
3 Thus says the LORD of hosts, the God
of Israel: "Amend your ways and your
doings, and I will cause you to dwell in
this place.
4 "Do not trust in these lying words,
saying, 'The temple of the LORD, the temple of the LORD, the temple of the LORD
are these.'
5 "For if you thoroughly amend your
ways and your doings, if you thoroughly
execute judgment between a man and his
neighbor,
6 "*if* you do not oppress the stranger,
the fatherless, and the widow, and do not
shed innocent blood in this place, or walk
after other gods to your hurt,
7 "then I will cause you to dwell in this
place, in the land that I gave to your fathers forever and ever.
8 "Behold, you trust in lying words that
cannot profit.
9 "Will you steal, murder, commit adultery, swear falsely, burn incense to Baal,
and walk after other gods whom you do
not know,
10 "and *then* come and stand before Me
in this house which is called by My name,
and say, 'We are delivered to do all these
abominations'?
11 "Has this house, which is called by
My name, become a den of thieves in
your eyes? Behold, I, even I, have seen
it," says the LORD.
12 "But go now to My place which *was*
in Shiloh, where I set My name at the
first, and see what I did to it because of
the wickedness of My people Israel.

13 "And now, because you have done all these works," says the LORD, "and I spoke to you, rising up early and speaking, but you did not hear, and I called you, but you did not answer,

14 "therefore I will do to *this* house which is called by My name, in which you trust, and to this place which I gave to you and your fathers, as I have done to Shiloh.

15 "And I will cast you out of My sight, as I have cast out all your brethren—the whole posterity of Ephraim.

16 "Therefore do not pray for this people, nor lift up a cry or prayer for them, nor make intercession to Me; for I will not hear you.

17 "Do you not see what they do in the cities of Judah and in the streets of Jerusalem?

18 "The children gather wood, the fathers kindle the fire, and the women knead *their* dough, to make cakes for the queen of heaven; and *they* pour out drink offerings to other gods, that they may provoke Me to anger.

19 "Do they provoke Me to anger?" says the LORD. "*Do they* not *provoke* themselves, to the shame of their own faces?"

20 Therefore thus says the Lord GOD: "Behold, My anger and My fury will be poured out on this place—on man and on beast, on the trees of the field and on the fruit of the ground. And it will burn and not be quenched."

21 Thus says the LORD of hosts, the God of Israel: "Add your burnt offerings to your sacrifices and eat meat.

22 "For I did not speak to your fathers, or command them in the day that I brought them out of the land of Egypt, concerning burnt offerings or sacrifices.

23 "But this is what I commanded them, saying, 'Obey My voice, and I will be your God, and you shall be My people. And walk in all the ways that I have commanded you, that it may be well with you.'

24 "Yet they did not obey or incline their ear, but walked in the counsels *and* in the imagination of their evil heart, and went backward and not forward.

25 "Since the day that your fathers came out of the land of Egypt until this day, I have even sent to you all My servants the prophets, daily rising up early and sending *them*.

26 "Yet they did not obey Me or incline their ear, but stiffened their neck. They did worse than their fathers.

27 "Therefore you shall speak all these words to them, but they will not obey you. You shall also call to them, but they will not answer you.

Judgment on Obscene Religion

28 "So you shall say to them, 'This *is* a nation that does not obey the voice of the LORD their God nor receive correction. Truth has perished and has been cut off from their mouth.

29 'Cut off your hair and cast *it* away, and take up a lamentation on the desolate heights; for the LORD has rejected and forsaken the generation of His wrath.'

30 "For the children of Judah have done evil in My sight," says the LORD. "They have set their abominations in the house which is called by My name, to pollute it.

31 "And they have built the high places of Tophet, which *is* in the Valley of the Son of Hinnom, to burn their sons and their daughters in the fire, which I did not command, nor did it come into My heart.

32 "Therefore behold, the days are coming," says the LORD, "when it will no more be called Tophet, or the Valley of the Son of Hinnom, but the Valley of Slaughter; for they will bury in Tophet until there is no room.

33 "The corpses of this people will be food for the birds of the heaven and for the beasts of the earth. And no one will frighten *them away*.

34 "Then I will cause to cease from the cities of Judah and from the streets of Jerusalem the voice of mirth and the voice of gladness, the voice of the bridegroom and the voice of the bride. For the land shall be desolate.

8 "At that time," says the LORD, "they shall bring out the bones of the kings of Judah, and the bones of its princes, and the bones of the priests, and the bones of the prophets, and the bones of the inhabitants of Jerusalem, out of their graves.

2 "They shall spread them before the sun and the moon and all the host of heaven, which they have loved and which they have served and after which they have walked, which they have sought and which they have worshiped. They shall

not be gathered nor buried; they shall be like refuse on the face of the earth.

3 "Then death shall be chosen rather than life by all the residue of those who remain of this evil family, who remain in all the places where I have driven them," says the LORD of hosts.

The Peril of False Teaching

4 "Moreover you shall say to them, 'Thus says the LORD:

"Will they fall and not rise?
Will one turn away and not return?
5 Why then has this people slidden back,
Jerusalem, in a perpetual backsliding?
They hold fast to deceit,
They refuse to return.
6 I listened and heard,
But they do not speak aright.
No man repented of his wickedness,
Saying, 'What have I done?'
Everyone turned to his own course,
As the horse rushes into the battle.

7 "Even the stork in the heavens
Knows her appointed times;
And the turtledove, the swift,
and the swallow
Observe the time of their coming.
But My people do not know the
judgment of the LORD.

8 "How can you say, 'We are wise,
And the law of the LORD is with us'?
Look, the false pen of the scribe
certainly works falsehood.
9 The wise men are ashamed,
They are dismayed and taken.
Behold, they have rejected the word
of the LORD;
So what wisdom do they have?
10 Therefore I will give their wives to
others,
And their fields to those who will
inherit them;
Because from the least
even to the greatest
Everyone is given to covetousness;
From the prophet even to the priest
Everyone deals falsely.
11 For they have healed the hurt of the
daughter of My people slightly,
Saying, 'Peace, peace!'
When there is no peace.
12 Were they ashamed when they had
committed abomination?
No! They were not at all ashamed,
Nor did they know how to blush.

Therefore they shall fall among those
who fall;
In the time of their punishment
They shall be cast down,"
says the LORD.

13 "I will surely consume them,"
says the LORD.
"There shall be no grapes on the vine,
Nor figs on the fig tree,
And the leaf shall fade;
And the things I have given them
shall pass away from them." ' "

14 "Why do we sit still?
Assemble yourselves,
And let us enter the fortified cities,
And let us be silent there.
For the LORD our God has put us to
silence
And given us water of gall to drink,
Because we have sinned against the
LORD.

15 "We looked for peace,
but no good came;
And for a time of health,
and there was trouble!
16 The snorting of His horses
was heard from Dan.
The whole land trembled at the sound
of the neighing of His strong ones;
For they have come and devoured the
land and all that is in it,
The city and those who dwell in it."

17 "For behold, I will send serpents
among you,
Vipers which cannot be charmed,
And they shall bite you,"
says the LORD.

The Prophet Mourns for the People

18 I would comfort myself in sorrow;
My heart is faint in me.
19 Listen! The voice,
The cry of the daughter of my people
From a far country:
"Is not the LORD in Zion?
Is not her King in her?"

"Why have they provoked Me to anger
With their carved images,
And with foreign idols?"

20 "The harvest is past,
The summer is ended,
And we are not saved!"

21 For the hurt of the daughter of my
    people I am hurt.
  I am mourning;
  Astonishment has taken hold of me.
22 *Is there* no balm in Gilead,
  Is there no physician there?
  Why then is there no recovery
  For the health of the daughter of my
    people?

9 Oh, that my head were waters,
    And my eyes a fountain of tears,
  That I might weep day and night
  For the slain of the daughter
    of my people!
2 Oh, that I had in the wilderness
  A lodging place for wayfaring men;
  That I might leave my people,
  And go from them!
  For they *are* all adulterers,
  An assembly of treacherous men.

3 "And *like* their bow
    they have bent their tongues *for* lies.
  They are not valiant for the truth on
    the earth.
  For they proceed from evil to evil,
  And they do not know Me,"
    says the LORD.
4 "Everyone take heed to his neighbor,
  And do not trust any brother;
  For every brother will utterly supplant,
  And every neighbor will walk with
    slanderers.
5 Everyone will deceive his neighbor,
  And will not speak the truth;
  They have taught their tongue to speak
    lies,
  And weary themselves to commit
    iniquity.
6 Your habitation *is* in the midst of
    deceit;
  Through deceit they refuse to know
    Me," says the LORD.

7 Therefore thus says the LORD of
hosts:

  "Behold, I will refine them
    and try them;
  For how shall I deal with the daughter
    of My people?
8 Their tongue *is* an arrow shot out;
  It speaks deceit;
  One speaks peaceably to his neighbor
    with his mouth,
  But in his heart he lies in wait.
9 Shall I not punish them for these
    things?" says the LORD.

"Shall I not avenge Myself
    on such a nation as this?"

10 I will take up a weeping and wailing
    for the mountains,
  And for the habitations of the
    wilderness a lamentation,
  Because they are burned up,
  So that no one can pass through *them*;
  Nor can *men* hear the voice of the
    cattle.
  Both the birds of the heavens
    and the beasts have fled;
  They are gone.

11 "I will make Jerusalem a heap of ruins
    and a den of jackals.
  I will make the cities of Judah desolate,
    without an inhabitant."

12 Who *is* the wise man who may understand this? And *who is he* to whom the
mouth of the LORD has spoken, that he
may declare it? Why does the land perish
and burn up like a wilderness, so that no
one can pass through?
13 And the LORD said, "Because they
have forsaken My law which I set before
them, and have not obeyed My voice, nor
walked according to it,
14 "but they have walked according to
the imagination of their own heart and
after the Baals, which their fathers taught
them,"
15 therefore thus says the LORD of hosts,
the God of Israel: "Behold, I will feed
them, this people, with wormwood, and
give them water of gall to drink.
16 "I will scatter them also among the
Gentiles, whom neither they nor their fathers have known. And I will send a
sword after them until I have consumed
them."

The People Mourn in Judgment

17 Thus says the LORD of hosts:

  "Consider and call for the mourning
    women,
  That they may come;
  And send for skillful wailing women,
  That they may come.
18 Let them make haste
  And take up a wailing for us,
  That our eyes may run with tears,
  And our eyelids gush with water.
19 For a voice of wailing is heard
    from Zion:

'How we are plundered!
We are greatly ashamed,
Because we have forsaken the land,
Because we have been cast out of our
dwellings.' "

20 Yet hear the word of the LORD,
O women,
And let your ear receive the word of
His mouth;
Teach your daughters wailing,
And everyone her neighbor a
lamentation.

21 For death has come through our
windows,
Has entered our palaces,
To kill off the children—
no longer to be outside!
And the young men—
no longer on the streets!

22 Speak, "Thus says the LORD:

'Even the carcasses of men shall fall as
refuse on the open field,
Like cuttings after the harvester,
And no one shall gather *them*.' "

23 Thus says the LORD:

"Let not the wise *man*
glory in his wisdom,
Let not the mighty *man*
glory in his might,
Nor let the rich *man*
glory in his riches;

24 But let him who glories glory in this,
That he understands and knows Me,
That I *am* the LORD, exercising
lovingkindness, judgment, and
righteousness in the earth.
For in these I delight," says the LORD.

25 "Behold, the days are coming," says
the LORD, "that I will punish all *those
who are* circumcised with the uncircumcised—

26 "Egypt, Judah, Edom, the people of
Ammon, Moab, and all *who are* in the
farthest corners, who dwell in the wilderness. For all *these* nations *are* uncircumcised, and all the house of Israel *are*
uncircumcised in the heart."

Idols and the True God

10 Hear the word which the LORD
speaks to you, O house of Israel.

2 Thus says the LORD:

"Do not learn the way of the Gentiles;
Do not be dismayed at the signs of
heaven,
For the Gentiles are dismayed at them.

3 For the customs of the peoples *are*
futile;
For *one* cuts a tree from the forest,
The work of the hands of the
workman, with the ax.

4 They decorate it with silver and gold;
They fasten it with nails and hammers
So that it will not topple.

5 They *are* upright, like a palm tree,
And they cannot speak;
They must be carried,
Because they cannot go *by themselves*.
Do not be afraid of them,
For they cannot do evil,
Nor can they do any good."

6 Inasmuch as *there is* none like You,
O LORD
(You *are* great,
and Your name *is* great in might),

7 who would not fear You,
O King of the nations?
For this is Your rightful due,
For among all the wise *men*
of the nations,
And in all their kingdoms,
There is none like You.

8 But they are altogether dull-hearted
and foolish;
A wooden idol *is* a worthless doctrine.

9 Silver is beaten into plates;
It is brought from Tarshish,
And gold from Uphaz,
The work of the craftsman
And of the hands of the metalsmith;
Blue and purple *are* their clothing;
They *are* all the work of skillful *men*.

10 But the LORD *is* the true God;
He *is* the living God
and the everlasting King.
At His wrath the earth will tremble,
And the nations will not be able to
abide His indignation.

11 Thus you shall say to them: "The
gods that have not made the heavens and
the earth shall perish from the earth and
from under these heavens."

12 He has made the earth by His power,
He has established the world
by His wisdom,
And has stretched out the heavens
at His discretion.

13 When He utters His voice,

There is a multitude of waters
   in the heavens:
"And He causes the vapors to ascend
   from the ends of the earth.
He makes lightning for the rain,
He brings the wind
   out of His treasures."[5]

14 Everyone is dull-hearted,
   without knowledge;
Every metalsmith is put to shame by
   the graven image;
For his molded image *is* falsehood,
And *there is* no breath in them.
15 They *are* futile, a work of errors;
   In the time of their punishment they
   shall perish.
16 The Portion of Jacob *is* not like them,
   For He *is* the Maker of all *things*,
And Israel *is* the tribe of His
   inheritance;
The LORD of hosts *is* His name.

The Coming Captivity of Judah

17 Gather up your wares from the land,
   O inhabitant of the fortress!

18 For thus says the LORD:

"Behold, I will throw out at this time
   The inhabitants of the land,
And will distress them,
   That they may find *it so.*"

19 Woe is me for my hurt!
   My wound is severe.
But I say, "Truly this *is* an infirmity,
   And I must bear it."
20 My tent is plundered,
   And all my cords are broken;
My children have gone from me,
   And they *are* no more.
There is no one to pitch my tent
   anymore,
Or set up my curtains.

21 For the shepherds have become
   dull-hearted,
And have not sought the LORD;
Therefore they shall not prosper,
   And all their flocks shall be scattered.
22 Behold, the noise of the report has
   come,
And a great commotion out of the
   north country,
To make the cities of Judah desolate,
   a den of jackals.

23 O LORD, I know the way of man *is* not
   in himself;

It is not in man who walks to direct his
   own steps.
24 O LORD, correct me, but with justice;
   Not in Your anger,
   lest You bring me to nothing.
25 Pour out Your fury on the Gentiles,
   who do not know You,
And on the families who do not call on
   Your name;
For they have eaten up Jacob,
Devoured him and consumed him,
And made his habitation desolate.

The Broken Covenant

11 The word that came to Jeremiah
from the LORD, saying,
2 "Hear the words of this covenant, and
speak to the men of Judah and to the inhabitants of Jerusalem;
3 "and say to them, 'Thus says the
LORD God of Israel: "Cursed *is* the man
who does not obey the words of this covenant
4 "which I commanded your fathers in
the day *that* I brought them out of the
land of Egypt, from the iron furnace, saying, 'Obey My voice, and do according to
all that I command you; so shall you be
My people, and I will be your God,'
5 "that I may establish the oath which I
have sworn to your fathers, to give them a
land flowing with milk and honey, as *it is*
this day." ' " Then I answered and said,
"So be it, LORD."
6 Then the LORD said to me, "Proclaim
all these words in the cities of Judah and
in the streets of Jerusalem, saying: 'Hear
the words of this covenant and do them.
7 'For I earnestly exhorted your fathers
in the day *that* I brought them up out of
the land of Egypt, until this day, rising
early and exhorting, saying, "Obey My
voice."
8 'Yet they did not obey or incline their
ear, but everyone walked in the imagination of his evil heart; therefore I will
bring upon them all the words of this
covenant, which I commanded *them* to
do, but *which* they have not done.' "
9 And the LORD said to me, "A conspiracy has been found among the men of
Judah and among the inhabitants of Jerusalem.
10 "They have turned back to the iniquities of their forefathers who refused to
hear My words, and they have gone after
other gods to serve them; the house of

5 Compare Psalm 135:7

Israel and the house of Judah have broken My covenant which I made with their fathers."

11 Therefore thus says the LORD: "Behold, I will surely bring calamity on them which they will not be able to escape; and though they cry out to Me, I will not listen to them.

12 "Then the cities of Judah and the inhabitants of Jerusalem will go and cry out to the gods to whom they offer incense, but they will not save them at all in the time of their trouble.

13 "For *according to* the number of your cities were your gods, O Judah; and *according to* the number of the streets of Jerusalem you have set up altars to *that* shameful thing, altars to burn incense to Baal.

14 "Therefore do not pray for this people, or lift up a cry or prayer for them; for I will not hear *them* in the time that they cry out to Me because of their trouble.

15 "What has My beloved to do in My house,
Having done lewd deeds with many?
And the holy flesh has passed from you.
When you do evil, then you rejoice.
16 The LORD called your name,
Green Olive Tree,
Lovely *and* of Good Fruit.
With the noise of a great tumult
He has kindled fire on it,
And its branches are broken.

17 "For the LORD of hosts, who planted you, has pronounced doom against you for the evil of the house of Israel and of the house of Judah, which they have done against themselves to provoke Me to anger in offering incense to Baal."

Jeremiah's Life Threatened

18 Now the LORD gave me knowledge *of it*, and I know *it*; for You showed me their doings.

19 But I *was* like a docile lamb brought to the slaughter; and I did not know that they had devised schemes against me, *saying*, "Let us destroy the tree with its fruit, and let us cut him off from the land of the living, that his name may be remembered no more."

20 But, O LORD of hosts,
You who judge righteously,

Testing the mind and the heart,
Let me see Your vengeance on them,
For to You I have revealed my cause.

21 "Therefore thus says the LORD concerning the men of Anathoth who seek your life, saying, 'Do not prophesy in the name of the LORD, lest you die by our hand'—

22 "therefore thus says the LORD of hosts: 'Behold, I will punish them. The young men shall die by the sword, their sons and their daughters shall die by famine;

23 'and there shall be no remnant of them, for I will bring catastrophe on the men of Anathoth, *even* the year of their punishment.' "

Jeremiah's Question

12 Righteous *are* You, O LORD,
when I plead with You;
Yet let me talk with You about *Your* judgments.
Why does the way of the wicked prosper?
Why are those happy who deal so treacherously?
2 You have planted them,
yes, they have taken root;
They grow, yes, they bear fruit.
You *are* near in their mouth
But far from their mind.

3 But You, O LORD, know me;
You have seen me,
And You have tested my heart toward You.
Pull them out like sheep for the slaughter,
And prepare them for the day of slaughter.
4 How long will the land mourn,
And the herbs of every field wither?
The beasts and birds are consumed,
For the wickedness of those who dwell there,
Because they said,
"He will not see our final end."

The LORD Answers Jeremiah

5 "If you have run with the footmen,
and they have wearied you,
Then how can you contend with horses?
And *if* in the land of peace,
In which you trusted, *they wearied you*,
Then how will you do in the flooding of the Jordan?

6   For even your brothers,
    the house of your father,
    Even they have dealt treacherously
    with you;
    Yes, they have called a multitude after
    you.
    Do not believe them,
    Even though they speak smooth words
    to you.

7   "I have forsaken My house,
    I have left My heritage;
    I have given the dearly beloved of My
    soul into the hand of her enemies.
8   My heritage is to Me like a lion in the
    forest;
    It cries out against Me;
    Therefore I have hated it.
9   My heritage is to Me like a speckled
    vulture;
    The vultures all around are against her.
    Come, assemble all the beasts of the
    field,
    Bring them to devour!

10 "Many rulers[6] have destroyed My
    vineyard,
    They have trodden My portion under
    foot;
    They have made My pleasant portion
    a desolate wilderness.
11 They have made it desolate;
    Desolate, it mourns to Me;
    The whole land is made desolate,
    Because no one takes it to heart.
12 The plunderers have come
    On all the desolate heights in the
    wilderness,
    For the sword of the LORD shall
    devour
    From one end of the land to the other
    end of the land;
    No flesh shall have peace.
13 They have sown wheat
    but reaped thorns;
    They have put themselves to pain
    but do not profit.
    But be ashamed of your harvest
    Because of the fierce anger of the
    LORD."

14 Thus says the LORD: "Against all My
evil neighbors who touch the inheritance
which I have caused My people Israel to
inherit—behold, I will pluck them out of
their land and pluck out the house of Ju-
dah from among them. 15 "Then it shall be, after I have plucked
them out, that I will return and have

compassion on them and bring them
back, everyone to his heritage and every-
one to his land. 16 "And it shall be, if they will diligently
learn the ways of My people, to swear by
My name, 'As the LORD lives,' as they
taught My people to swear by Baal, then
they shall be established in the midst of
My people. 17 "But if they do not obey, I will utterly
pluck up and destroy that nation," says
the LORD.

Symbol of the Linen Sash

13 Thus the LORD said to me: "Go
and get yourself a linen sash, and
put it around your waist, but do not put
it in water." 2   So I got a sash according to the word
of the LORD, and put it around my waist. 3   And the word of the LORD came to
me the second time, saying, 4   "Take the sash that you acquired,
which is around your waist, and arise, go
to the Euphrates,[7] and hide it there in a
hole in the rock." 5   So I went and hid it by the Euphrates,
as the LORD commanded me. 6   And it came to pass after many days
that the LORD said to me, "Arise, go to
the Euphrates, and take from there the
sash which I commanded you to hide
there." 7   Then I went to the Euphrates and
dug, and I took the sash from the place
where I had hidden it; and there was the
sash, ruined. It was profitable for nothing. 8   "Then the word of the LORD came to
me, saying, 9   "Thus says the LORD: 'In this manner
I will ruin the pride of Judah and the
great pride of Jerusalem. 10 'This evil people, who refuse to hear
My words, who walk in the imagination
of their heart, and walk after other gods
to serve them and worship them, shall be
just like this sash which is profitable for
nothing. 11 'For as the sash clings to the waist of a
man, so I have caused the whole house of
Israel and the whole house of Judah to
cling to Me,' says the LORD, 'that they
may become My people, for renown, for
praise, and for glory; but they would not
hear.'

6 Literally *shepherds* or *pastors*   7 Hebrew *Perath*

Symbol of the Wine Bottles

12 "Therefore you shall speak to them this word: 'Thus says the LORD God of Israel: "Every bottle shall be filled with wine." ' And they will say to you, 'Do we not certainly know that every bottle will be filled with wine?'
13 "Then you shall say to them, 'Thus says the LORD: "Behold, I will fill all the inhabitants of this land—even the kings who sit on David's throne, the priests, the prophets, and all the inhabitants of Jerusalem—with drunkenness!
14 "And I will dash them one against another, even the fathers and the sons together," says the LORD. "I will not pity nor spare nor have mercy, but will destroy them." ' "

Pride Precedes Captivity

15 Hear and give ear:
   Do not be proud,
   For the LORD has spoken.
16 Give glory to the LORD your God
   Before He causes darkness,
   And before your feet stumble
   On the dark mountains,
   And while you are looking for light,
   He turns it into the shadow of death
   And makes *it* dense darkness.
17 But if you will not hear it,
   My soul will weep in secret for *your*
      pride;
   My eyes will weep bitterly
   And run down with tears,
   Because the LORD's flock has been
      taken captive.

18 Say to the king and to the queen
      mother,
   "Humble yourselves;
   Sit down,
   For your rule shall collapse,
      the crown of your glory."
19 The cities of the South shall be
      shut up,
   And no one shall open *them*;
   Judah shall be carried away captive,
      all of it;
   It shall be wholly carried away captive.

20 Lift up your eyes and see
   Those who come from the north.
   Where *is* the flock *that* was given
      to you,
   Your beautiful sheep?
21 What will you say when He punishes
      you?
   For you have taught them

To be chieftains, to be head over you.
   Will not pangs seize you,
   Like a woman in labor?
22 And if you say in your heart,
   "Why have these things come upon
      me?"
   For the greatness of your iniquity
   Your skirts have been uncovered,
   Your heels made bare.
23 Can the Ethiopian change his skin
      or the leopard its spots?
   Then may you also do good
      who are accustomed to do evil.

24 "Therefore I will scatter them like
      stubble
   That passes away by the wind of the
      wilderness.
25 This is your lot,
   The portion of your measures from
      Me," says the LORD,
   "Because you have forgotten Me
   And trusted in falsehood.
26 Therefore I will uncover your skirts
      over your face,
   That your shame may appear.
27 I have seen your adulteries
   And your *lustful* neighings,
   The lewdness of your harlotry,
   Your abominations on the hills in the
      fields.
   Woe to you, O Jerusalem!
   Will you still not be made clean?"

Sword, Famine, and Pestilence

14 The word of the LORD that came to Jeremiah concerning the droughts.

2 "Judah mourns,
   And her gates languish;
   They mourn for the land,
   And the cry of Jerusalem has gone up.
3 Their nobles have sent their lads for
      water;
   They went to the cisterns
   and found no water.
   They returned with their vessels empty;
   They were ashamed and confounded
   And covered their heads.
4 Because the ground is parched,
   For there was no rain in the land,
   The plowmen were ashamed;
   They covered their heads.
5 Yes, the deer also gave birth in the
      field,
   But left because there was no grass.
6 And the wild donkeys stood in the
      desolate heights;
   They sniffed at the wind like jackals;

Their eyes failed because *there was* no grass.'"

7 O LORD, though our iniquities testify against us,
Do it for Your name's sake;
For our backslidings are many,
We have sinned against You.
8 O the Hope of Israel,
his Savior in time of trouble,
Why should You be like a stranger in the land,
And like a wayfaring man *who* turns aside to tarry for a night?
9 Why should You be like a man astonished,
Like a mighty one *who* cannot save?
Yet You, O LORD, *are* in our midst,
And we are called by Your name;
Do not leave us!

10 Thus says the LORD to this people:

"Thus they have loved to wander;
They have not restrained their feet.
Therefore the LORD does not accept them;
He will remember their iniquity now,
And punish their sins."

11 Then the LORD said to me, "Do not pray for this people, for *their* good.
12 "When they fast, I will not hear their cry; and when they offer burnt offering and grain offering, I will not accept them. But I will consume them by the sword, by the famine, and by the pestilence."
13 Then I said, "Ah, Lord GOD! Behold, the prophets say to them, 'You shall not see the sword, nor shall you have famine, but I will give you assured peace in this place.'"
14 And the LORD said to me, "The prophets prophesy lies in My name. I have not sent them, commanded them, nor spoken to them; they prophesy to you a false vision, divination, a worthless thing, and the deceit of their heart.
15 "Therefore thus says the LORD concerning the prophets who prophesy in My name, whom I did not send, and who say, 'Sword and famine shall not be in this land'—'By sword and famine those prophets shall be consumed!
16 'And the people to whom they prophesy shall be cast out in the streets of Jerusalem because of the famine and the sword; they will have no one to bury

them—them nor their wives, their sons nor their daughters—for I will pour their wickedness on them.'
17 "Therefore you shall say this word to them:

'Let my eyes flow with tears night and day,
And let them not cease;
For the virgin daughter of my people
Has been broken with a mighty stroke,
with a very severe blow.
18 If I go out to the field,
Then behold, those slain with the sword!
And if I enter the city,
Then behold, those sick from famine!
Yes, both prophet and priest go about in a land they do not know.'"

The People Plead for Mercy

19 Have You utterly rejected Judah?
Has Your soul loathed Zion?
Why have You stricken us
so that *there is* no healing for us?
We looked for peace,
but *there was* no good;
And for the time of healing,
and there was trouble.
20 We acknowledge, O LORD,
our wickedness
And the iniquity of our fathers,
For we have sinned against You.
21 Do not abhor *us*,
for Your name's sake;
Do not disgrace the throne of Your glory.
Remember, do not break Your covenant with us.
22 Are there any among the idols of the nations that can cause rain?
Or can the heavens give showers?
Are You not He, O LORD our God?
Therefore we will wait for You,
Since You have made all these.

The LORD Will Not Relent

15 Then the LORD said to me, "Though Moses and Samuel stood before Me, *yet* My mind *could* not *be* favorable toward this people. Cast *them* out of My sight, and let them go forth.
2 "And it shall be, if they say to you, 'Where should we go?' then you shall tell them, 'Thus says the LORD:

"Such as *are* for death, to death;
And such as *are* for the sword,
to the sword;

And such as *are* for the famine,
to the famine;
And such as *are* for the captivity,
to the captivity." '

3 "And I will appoint over them four forms *of destruction*," says the LORD: "the sword to slay, the dogs to drag, the birds of the heavens and the beasts of the earth to devour and destroy.
4 "I will hand them over to trouble, to all kingdoms of the earth, because of Manasseh the son of Hezekiah, king of Judah, for what he did in Jerusalem.

5 "For who will have pity on you,
O Jerusalem?
Or who will bemoan you?
Or who will turn aside to ask
how you are doing?
6 You have forsaken Me," says the LORD,
"You have gone backward.
Therefore I will stretch out My hand
against you and destroy you;
I am weary of relenting!
7 And I will winnow them with a
winnowing fan in the gates of the
land;
I will bereave *them* of children;
I will destroy My people,
Since they do not return from their
ways.
8 Their widows will be increased to Me
more than the sand of the seas;
I will bring against them,
Against the mother of the young men,
A plunderer at noonday;
I will cause anguish and terror to fall
on them suddenly.

9 "She languishes who has borne seven;
She has breathed her last;
Her sun has gone down
While *it was* yet day;
She has been ashamed
and confounded.
And the remnant of them
I will deliver to the sword
Before their enemies," says the LORD.

Jeremiah's Dejection

10 Woe is me, my mother,
That you have borne me,
A man of strife and a man of
contention to the whole earth!
I have neither lent for interest,
Nor have men lent to me for interest.
Every one of them curses me.

11 The LORD said:

"Surely it will be well with your
remnant;
Surely I will cause the enemy to
intercede with you
In the time of adversity
and in the time of affliction.
12 Can anyone break iron,
The northern iron and the bronze?
13 Your wealth and your treasures
I will give as plunder without price,
Because of all your sins,
Throughout your territories.
14 And I will make *you* cross over with
your enemies
Into a land *which* you do not know;
For a fire is kindled in My anger,
Which shall burn upon you."

15 O LORD, You know;
Remember me and visit me,
And take vengeance for me on my
persecutors.
Do not take me away in Your
longsuffering.
Know that for Your sake
I have suffered rebuke.
16 Your words were found,
and I ate them,
And Your word was to me
the joy and rejoicing of my heart;
For I am called by Your name,
O LORD God of hosts.
17 I did not sit in the assembly of the
mockers,
Nor did I rejoice;
I sat alone because of Your hand,
For You have filled me with
indignation.
18 Why is my pain perpetual
And my wound incurable,
Which refuses to be healed?
Will You surely be to me like an
unreliable stream,
As waters *that* fail?

The LORD Reassures Jeremiah

19 Therefore thus says the LORD:

"If you return,
Then I will bring you back;
You shall stand before Me;
If you take out the precious from the
vile,
You shall be as My mouth.
Let them return to you,
But you must not return to them.

20 And I will make you to this people
    a fortified bronze wall;
    And they will fight against you,
    But they shall not prevail against you;
    For I *am* with you to save you
    And deliver you," says the LORD.
21 "I will deliver you from the hand
    of the wicked,
    And I will redeem you from the grip
    of the terrible."

Jeremiah's Life-Style and Message

16 The word of the LORD also came to me, saying,
2 "You shall not take a wife, nor shall you have sons or daughters in this place."
3 For thus says the LORD concerning the sons and daughters who are born in this place, and concerning their mothers who bore them and their fathers who begot them in this land:
4 "They shall die gruesome deaths; they shall not be lamented nor shall they be buried, *but* they shall be like refuse on the face of the earth. They shall be consumed by the sword and by famine, and their corpses shall be meat for the birds of heaven and for the beasts of the earth."
5 For thus says the LORD: "Do not enter the house of mourning, nor go to lament or bemoan them; for I have taken away My peace from this people," says the LORD, "lovingkindness and mercies.
6 "Both the great and the small shall die in this land. They shall not be buried; neither shall men lament for them, cut themselves, nor make themselves bald for them.
7 "Nor shall *men* break *bread* in mourning for them, to comfort them for the dead; nor shall *men* give them the cup of consolation to drink for their father or their mother.
8 "Also you shall not go into the house of feasting to sit with them, to eat and drink."
9 For thus says the LORD of hosts, the God of Israel: "Behold, I will cause to cease from this place, before your eyes and in your days, the voice of mirth and the voice of gladness, the voice of the bridegroom and the voice of the bride.
10 "And it shall be, when you show this people all these words, and they say to you, 'Why has the LORD pronounced all this great disaster against us? Or what *is* our iniquity? Or what *is* our sin that we

have committed against the LORD our God?'
11 "then you shall say to them, 'Because your fathers have forsaken Me,' says the LORD; 'they have walked after other gods and have served them and worshiped them, and have forsaken Me and not kept My law.
12 'And you have done worse than your fathers, for behold, each one walks according to the imagination of his own evil heart, so that no one listens to Me.
13 'Therefore I will cast you out of this land into a land that you do not know, neither you nor your fathers; and there you shall serve other gods day and night, where I will not show you favor.'

God Will Restore Israel

14 "Therefore behold, the days are coming," says the LORD, "that it shall no more be said, 'The LORD lives who brought up the children of Israel from the land of Egypt,'
15 "but, 'The LORD lives who brought up the children of Israel from the land of the north and from all the lands where He had driven them.' For I will bring them back into their land which I gave to their fathers.
16 "Behold, I will send for many fishermen," says the LORD, "and they shall fish them; and afterward I will send for many hunters, and they shall hunt them from every mountain and every hill, and out of the holes of the rocks.
17 "For My eyes *are* on all their ways; they are not hidden from My face, nor is their iniquity hidden from My eyes.
18 "And first I will repay double for their iniquity and their sin, because they have defiled My land; they have filled My inheritance with the carcasses of their detestable and abominable idols."

19 O LORD, my strength and my fortress,
    My refuge in the day of affliction,
    The Gentiles shall come to You
    From the ends of the earth and say,
    "Surely our fathers have inherited lies,
    Worthlessness and unprofitable *things.*"
20 Will a man make gods for himself,
    Which *are* not gods?

21 "Therefore behold, I will this once
    cause them to know,
    I will cause them to know
    My hand and My might;

And they shall know that My name
is the LORD.

Judah's Sin and Punishment

17 "The sin of Judah *is* written
　　　with a pen of iron;
With the point of a diamond
　　it is engraved
On the tablet of their heart,
And on the horns of your altars,
2　While their children remember
　　Their altars and their wooden images[8]
　　By the green trees on the high hills.
3　O My mountain in the field,
　　I will give as plunder your wealth,
　　all your treasures,
　　And your high places of sin
　　within all your borders.
4　And you, even yourself,
　　Shall let go of your heritage which I
　　　gave you;
　　And I will cause you to serve your
　　　enemies
　　In the land which you do not know;
　　For you have kindled a fire in My
　　　anger *which* shall burn forever."

5　Thus says the LORD:

"Cursed *is* the man who trusts in man
And makes flesh his strength,
Whose heart departs from the LORD.
6　For he shall be like a shrub in the
　　　desert,
　　And shall not see when good comes,
　　But shall inhabit the parched places in
　　　the wilderness,
　　In a salt land *which is* not inhabited.

7　"Blessed *is* the man who trusts
　　　in the LORD,
　　And whose hope is the LORD.
8　For he shall be like a tree
　　　planted by the waters,
　　Which spreads out its roots by the
　　　river,
　　And will not fear[9] when heat comes;
　　But her leaf will be green,
　　And will not be anxious in the year
　　　of drought,
　　Nor will cease from yielding fruit.

9　"The heart *is* deceitful above all *things*,
　　And desperately wicked;
　　Who can know it?
10　I, the LORD, search the heart,
　　I test the mind,
　　Even to give every man according to
　　　his ways,
　　And according to the fruit of his
　　　doings.

11　"*As* a partridge that broods
　　　but does not hatch,
　　So is he who gets riches,
　　　but not by right;
　　It will leave him in the midst
　　　of his days,
　　And at his end he will be a fool."

12　A glorious high throne from the
　　　beginning
　　Is the place of our sanctuary.
13　O LORD, the hope of Israel,
　　All who forsake You shall be ashamed.

"Those who depart from Me
Shall be written in the earth,
Because they have forsaken the LORD,
The fountain of living waters."

Jeremiah Prays for Deliverance

14　Heal me, O LORD,
　　　and I shall be healed;
　　Save me, and I shall be saved,
　　For You *are* my praise.
15　Indeed they say to me,
　　"Where *is* the word of the LORD?
　　Let it come now!"
16　As for me, I have not hurried away
　　　from *being* a shepherd *who* follows
　　　You,
　　Nor have I desired the woeful day;
　　You know what came out of my lips;
　　It was right there before You.
17　Do not be a terror to me;
　　You *are* my hope in the day of doom.
18　Let them be ashamed who
　　　persecute me,
　　But do not let me be put to shame;
　　Let them be dismayed,
　　But do not let me be dismayed.
　　Bring on them the day of doom,
　　And destroy them with double
　　　destruction!

Hallow the Sabbath Day

19　Thus the LORD said to me: "Go and
stand in the gate of the children of the
people, by which the kings of Judah come
in and by which they go out, and in all
the gates of Jerusalem;
20　"and say to them, 'Hear the word of
the LORD, you kings of Judah, and all Judah, and all the inhabitants of Jerusalem,
who enter by these gates.
21　'Thus says the LORD: "Take heed to
yourselves, and bear no burden on the
Sabbath day, nor bring *it* in by the gates
of Jerusalem;

8 Hebrew *Asherim*, Canaanite deities　　9 Qere and Targum read *see*.

22 "nor carry a burden out of your houses on the Sabbath day, nor do any work, but hallow the Sabbath day, as I commanded your fathers.
23 "But they did not obey nor incline their ear, but made their neck stiff, that they might not hear nor receive instruction.
24 "And it shall be, if you diligently heed Me," says the LORD, "to bring no burden through the gates of this city on the Sabbath day, but hallow the Sabbath day, to do no work in it,
25 "then shall enter the gates of this city kings and princes sitting on the throne of David, riding in chariots and on horses, they and their princes, accompanied by the men of Judah and the inhabitants of Jerusalem; and this city shall remain forever.
26 "And they shall come from the cities of Judah and from the places around Jerusalem, from the land of Benjamin and from the lowland, from the mountains and from the South, bringing burnt offerings and sacrifices, grain offerings and incense, bringing sacrifices of praise to the house of the LORD.
27 "But if you will not heed Me to hallow the Sabbath day, such as not carrying a burden when entering the gates of Jerusalem on the Sabbath day, then I will kindle a fire in its gates, and it shall devour the palaces of Jerusalem, and it shall not be quenched." ' "

The Potter and the Clay

18 The word which came to Jeremiah from the LORD, saying:
2 "Arise and go down to the potter's house, and there I will cause you to hear My words."
3 Then I went down to the potter's house, and there he was, making something at the wheel.
4 And the vessel that he made of clay was marred in the hand of the potter; so he made it again into another vessel, as it seemed good to the potter to make.
5 Then the word of the LORD came to me, saying:
6 "O house of Israel, can I not do with you as this potter?" says the LORD. "Look, as the clay is in the potter's hand, so are you in My hand, O house of Israel!
7 "The instant I speak concerning a na-

tion and concerning a kingdom, to pluck up, to pull down, and to destroy it,
8 "if that nation against whom I have spoken turns from its evil, I will relent of the disaster that I thought to bring upon it.
9 "And the instant I speak concerning a nation and concerning a kingdom, to build and to plant it,
10 "if it does evil in My sight so that it does not obey My voice, then I will relent concerning the good with which I said I would benefit it.
11 "Now therefore, speak to the men of Judah and to the inhabitants of Jerusalem, saying, 'Thus says the LORD: "Behold, I am fashioning a disaster and devising a plan against you. Return now every one from his evil way, and make your ways and your doings good." ' "

God's Warning Rejected

12 And they said, "That is hopeless! So we will walk according to our own plans, and we will every one do the imagination of his evil heart."
13 Therefore thus says the LORD:

"Ask now among the Gentiles,
Who has heard such things?
The virgin of Israel has done a very
    horrible thing.
14 Will a man leave the snow-water of
    Lebanon,
Which comes from the rock of the field?
Will the cold flowing waters be
    forsaken for strange waters?

15 "Because My people have forgotten Me,
They have burned incense to worthless
    idols.
And they have caused themselves to
    stumble in their ways,
From the ancient paths,
To walk in pathways
    and not on a highway,
16 To make their land desolate
    and a perpetual hissing;
Everyone who passes by it will be
    astonished
And shake his head.
17 I will scatter them as with an east wind
    before the enemy;
I will show them the back
    and not the face
In the day of their calamity."

Jeremiah Persecuted

18 Then they said, "Come and let us devise plans against Jeremiah; for the law shall not perish from the priest, nor counsel from the wise, nor the word from the prophet. Come and let us attack him with the tongue, and let us not give heed to any of his words."

19 Give heed to me, O LORD,
  And listen to the voice of those who
    contend with me!
20 Shall evil be repaid for good?
  For they have dug a pit for my life.
  Remember that I stood before You
  To speak good for them,
  And to turn away Your wrath from
    them.
21 Therefore deliver up their children to
    the famine,
  And pour out their *blood*
  By the force of the sword;
  Let their wives *become* widows
  And bereaved of their children.
  Let their men be put to death,
  Their young men *be* slain
  By the sword in battle.
22 Let a cry be heard from their houses,
  When You bring a troop suddenly
    upon them;
  For they have dug a pit to take me,
  And hidden snares for my feet.
23 Yet, LORD, You know all their counsel
  Which is against me, to slay *me*.
  Provide no atonement for their
    iniquity,
  Nor blot out their sin from Your sight;
  But let them be overthrown before
    You.
  Deal *thus* with them
  In the time of Your anger.

The Sign of the Broken Flask

19 Thus says the LORD: "Go and get a potter's earthen flask, and *take* some of the elders of the people and some of the elders of the priests.
2 "And go out to the Valley of the Son of Hinnom, which *is* by the entry of the Potsherd Gate; and proclaim there the words that I will tell you,
3 "and say, 'Hear the word of the LORD, O kings of Judah and inhabitants of Jerusalem. Thus says the LORD of hosts, the God of Israel: "Behold, I will bring such a catastrophe on this place, that whoever hears of it, his ears will tingle.
4 "Because they have forsaken Me and made this an alien place, because they

have burned incense in it to other gods whom neither they, their fathers, nor the kings of Judah have known, and have filled this place with the blood of the innocents
5 "(they have also built the high places of Baal, to burn their sons with fire *for* burnt offerings to Baal, which I did not command or speak, nor did it come into My mind),
6 "therefore behold, the days are coming," says the LORD, "that this place shall no more be called Tophet or the Valley of the Son of Hinnom, but the Valley of Slaughter.
7 "And I will make void the counsel of Judah and Jerusalem in this place, and I will cause them to fall by the sword before their enemies and by the hands of those who seek their lives; their corpses I will give as meat for the birds of the heaven and for the beasts of the earth.
8 "I will make this city desolate and a hissing; everyone who passes by it will be astonished and hiss because of all its plagues.
9 "And I will cause them to eat the flesh of their sons and the flesh of their daughters, and everyone shall eat the flesh of his friend in the siege and in the desperation with which their enemies and those who seek their lives shall drive them to despair." '
10 "Then you shall break the flask in the sight of the men who go with you,
11 "and say to them, 'Thus says the LORD of hosts: "Even so I will break this people and this city, as *one* breaks a potter's vessel, which cannot be made whole again; and they shall bury *them* in Tophet till *there is* no place to bury.
12 "Thus I will do to this place," says the LORD, "and to its inhabitants, and make this city like Tophet.
13 "And the houses of Jerusalem and the houses of the kings of Judah shall be defiled like the place of Tophet, because of all the houses on whose roofs they have burned incense to all the host of heaven, and poured out drink offerings to other gods." ' "
14 Then Jeremiah came from Tophet, where the LORD had sent him to prophesy; and he stood in the court of the Lord's house and said to all the people,
15 "Thus says the LORD of hosts, the God of Israel: 'Behold, I will bring on

this city and on all her towns all the doom that I have pronounced against it, because they have stiffened their necks that they might not hear My words.' "

The Word of God to Pashhur

20 Now Pashhur the son of Immer, the priest who *was* also chief governor in the house of the LORD, heard that Jeremiah prophesied these things.
2 Then Pashhur struck Jeremiah the prophet, and put him in the stocks that *were* in the high gate of Benjamin, which *was* by the house of the LORD.
3 And it happened on the next day that Pashhur brought Jeremiah out of the stocks. Then Jeremiah said to him, "The LORD has not called your name Pashhur, but Magor-Missabib.[10]
4 "For thus says the LORD: 'Behold, I will make you a terror to yourself and to all your friends; and they shall fall by the sword of their enemies, and your eyes shall see *it*. I will give all Judah into the hand of the king of Babylon, and he shall carry them captive to Babylon and slay them with the sword.
5 'Moreover I will deliver all the wealth of this city, all its produce, and all its precious things; all the treasures of the kings of Judah I will give into the hand of their enemies, who will plunder them, seize them, and carry them to Babylon.
6 'And you, Pashhur, and all who dwell in your house, shall go into captivity. You shall go to Babylon, and there you shall die, and be buried there, you and all your friends, to whom you have prophesied lies.' "

Jeremiah's Unpopular Ministry

7   O LORD, You induced me,
        and I was persuaded;
    You are stronger than I,
        and have prevailed.
    I am in derision daily;
    Everyone mocks me.
8   For when I spoke, I cried out;
    I shouted, "Violence and plunder!"
    Because the word of the LORD was
        made to me
    A reproach and a derision daily.
9   Then I said, "I will not make mention
        of Him,
    Nor speak anymore in His name."
    But *His word* was in my heart
        like a burning fire
    Shut up in my bones;

    I was weary of holding *it* back,
        And I could not.
10   For I heard many mocking:
    "Fear on every side!"
    "Report," *they say,*
        "and we will report it!"
    All my acquaintances watched for my
        stumbling, *saying,*
    "Perhaps he can be induced;
    Then we will prevail against him,
    And we will take our revenge on him."

11   But the LORD *is* with me as a mighty,
        awesome one.
    Therefore my persecutors will stumble,
        and will not prevail.
    They will be greatly ashamed,
        for they will not prosper.
    Their everlasting confusion will never
        be forgotten.
12   But, O LORD of hosts,
    You who test the righteous,
    And see the mind and heart,
    Let me see Your vengeance on them;
    For I have pleaded my cause before
        You.

13   Sing to the LORD! Praise the LORD!
    For He has delivered the life of the
        poor
    From the hand of evildoers.

14   Cursed *be* the day in which I was born!
    Let the day not be blessed
        in which my mother bore me!
15   Let the man *be* cursed
    Who brought news to my father,
        saying,
    "A male child has been born to you!"
    Making him very glad.
16   And let that man be like the cities
    Which the LORD overthrew,
        and did not relent;
    Let him hear the cry in the morning
    And the shouting at noon,
17   Because he did not kill me from
        the womb,
    That my mother might have been
        my grave,
    And her womb always enlarged
        with me.
18   Why did I come forth from the womb
        to see labor and sorrow,
    That my days should be consumed
        with shame?

Jerusalem's Doom Is Sealed

21 The word which came to Jeremiah from the LORD when King Zedekiah sent to him Pashhur the son of

10 Literally *Fear On Every Side*

Melchiah, and Zephaniah the son of Maaseiah, the priest, saying,

2 "Please inquire of the LORD for us, for Nebuchadnezzar[11] king of Babylon makes war against us. Perhaps the LORD will deal with us according to all His wonderful works, that *the king* may go away from us."

3 Then Jeremiah said to them, "Thus you shall say to Zedekiah,

4 'Thus says the LORD God of Israel: "Behold, I will turn back the weapons of war that *are* in your hands, with which you fight against the king of Babylon and the Chaldeans[12] who besiege you outside the walls; and I will assemble them in the midst of this city.

5 "I Myself will fight against you with an outstretched hand and with a strong arm, even in anger and fury and great wrath.

6 "I will strike the inhabitants of this city, both man and beast; they shall die of a great pestilence.

7 "And afterward," says the LORD, "I will deliver Zedekiah king of Judah, his servants and the people, and such as are left in this city from the pestilence and the sword and the famine, into the hand of Nebuchadnezzar king of Babylon, into the hand of their enemies, and into the hand of those who seek their life; and he shall strike them with the edge of the sword. He shall not spare them, or have pity or mercy." '

8 "Now you shall say to this people, 'Thus says the LORD: "Behold, I set before you the way of life and the way of death.

9 "He who remains in this city shall die by the sword, by famine, and by pestilence; but he who goes out and defects to the Chaldeans who besiege you, he shall live, and his life shall be as a prize to him.

10 "For I have set My face against this city for adversity and not for good," says the LORD. "It shall be given into the hand of the king of Babylon, and he shall burn it with fire." ' "

Message to the House of David

11 "And concerning the house of the king of Judah, *say,* 'Hear the word of the LORD,

12 'O house of David! Thus says the LORD:

"Execute judgment in the morning;
And deliver *him who is* plundered
Out of the hand of the oppressor,
Lest My fury go out like fire
And burn so that no one can quench *it,*
Because of the evil of your doings.

13 "Behold, I *am* against you,
O inhabitant of the valley,
And rock of the plain," says the LORD,
"Who say, 'Who shall come down
against us?
Or who shall enter our habitations?'
14 But I will punish you according to the
fruit of your doings," says the LORD;
"I will kindle a fire in its forest,
And it shall devour all things
around it." ' "

22 Thus says the LORD: "Go down to the house of the king of Judah, and there speak this word,

2 "and say, 'Hear the word of the LORD, O king of Judah, you who sit on the throne of David, you and your servants and your people who enter these gates!

3 'Thus says the LORD: "Execute judgment and righteousness, and deliver the plundered out of the hand of the oppressor. Do no wrong and do no violence to the stranger, the fatherless, or the widow, nor shed innocent blood in this place.

4 "For if you indeed do this thing, then shall enter the gates of this house, riding on horses and in chariots, accompanied by servants and people, kings who sit on the throne of David.

5 "But if you will not hear these words, I swear by Myself," says the LORD, "that this house shall become a desolation." ' "

6 For thus says the LORD to the house of the king of Judah:

"You *are* Gilead to Me,
The head of Lebanon;
Yet I surely will make you
a wilderness,
And cities *which* are not inhabited.
7 I will prepare destroyers against you,
Everyone with his weapons;
They shall cut down your choice cedars
And cast *them* into the fire.

8 "And many nations will pass by this city; and everyone will say to his neighbor, 'Why has the LORD done so to this great city?'

9 "Then they will answer, 'Because they have forsaken the covenant of the LORD

11 Hebrew *Nebuchadrezzar,* and so elsewhere   12 Or *Babylonians*

their God, and worshiped other gods and served them.' "

10 Weep not for the dead,
    nor bemoan him;
But weep bitterly for him who goes
    away,
For he shall return no more,
Nor see his native country.

Message to the Sons of Josiah

11 For thus says the LORD concerning Shallum[13] the son of Josiah, king of Judah, who reigned instead of Josiah his father, who went from this place: "He shall not return here anymore,
12 "but he shall die in the place where they have led him captive, and shall see this land no more.

13 "Woe to him who builds his house by
    unrighteousness
And his chambers by injustice,
Who uses his neighbor's service without
    wages
And gives him nothing for his work,
14 Who says, 'I will build myself a wide
    house with spacious chambers,
And cut out windows for it,
Paneling *it* with cedar
And painting *it* with vermilion.'

15 "Shall you reign because you enclose
    yourself in cedar?
Did not your father eat and drink,
And do justice and righteousness?
Then *it was* well with him.
16 He judged the cause of the poor and
    needy;
Then *it was* well.
Was not this knowing Me?"
    says the LORD.
17 "Yet your eyes and your heart *are* for
    nothing but your covetousness,
For shedding innocent blood,
And practicing oppression and
    violence."

18 Therefore thus says the LORD concerning Jehoiakim the son of Josiah, king of Judah:

"They shall not lament for him,
    Saying, 'Alas, my brother!'
    or 'Alas, my sister!'
They shall not lament for him,
    Saying, 'Alas, master!'
    or 'Alas, his glory!'

19 He shall be buried with the burial
    of a donkey,
Dragged and cast out beyond the gates
    of Jerusalem.

20 "Go up to Lebanon, and cry out,
And lift up your voice in Bashan;
Cry from Abarim,
For all your lovers are destroyed.
21 I spoke to you in your prosperity,
But you said, 'I will not hear.'
This *has been* your manner from your
    youth,
That you did not obey My voice.
22 The wind shall eat up all your rulers,
And your lovers shall go into captivity;
Surely then you will be ashamed and
    humiliated
For all your wickedness.
23 O inhabitant of Lebanon,
Making your nest in the cedars,
How gracious will you be when pangs
    come upon you,
Like the pain of a woman in labor?

Message to Coniah

24 "*As* I live," says the LORD, "though Coniah[14] the son of Jehoiakim, king of Judah, were the signet on My right hand, yet I would pluck you off;
25 "and I will give you into the hand of those who seek your life, and into the hand *of those* whose face you fear—the hand of Nebuchadnezzar king of Babylon and the hand of the Chaldeans.
26 "So I will cast you out, and your mother who bore you, into another country where you were not born; and there you shall die.
27 "But to the land to which they desire to return, there they shall not return.

28 "Is this man Coniah a despised,
    broken idol?
Is he a vessel in which *is* no pleasure?
Why are they cast out,
    he and his descendants,
And cast into a land which they
    do not know?
29 O earth, earth, earth,
Hear the word of the LORD!
30 Thus says the LORD:
'Write this man down as childless,
A man *who* shall not prosper in his
    days;
For none of his descendants shall
    prosper,
Sitting on the throne of David,
And ruling anymore in Judah.' "

---

13 Also called *Jehoahaz*   14 Also called *Jeconiah* and *Jehoiachin*

The Branch of Righteousness

23 "Woe to the shepherds who destroy and scatter the sheep of My pasture!" says the LORD.
2 Therefore thus says the LORD God of Israel against the shepherds who feed My people: "You have scattered My flock, driven them away, and not attended to them. Behold, I will attend to you for the evil of your doings," says the LORD.
3 "But I will gather the remnant of My flock out of all countries where I have driven them, and bring them back to their folds; and they shall be fruitful and increase.
4 "I will set up shepherds over them who will feed them; and they shall fear no more, nor be dismayed, nor shall they be lacking," says the LORD.

5 "Behold, *the* days are coming,"
    says the LORD,
"That I will raise to David
    a Branch of righteousness;
A King shall reign and prosper,
And execute judgment and
    righteousness in the earth.
6 In His days Judah will be saved,
And Israel will dwell safely;
Now this *is* His name by which He will
    be called:

THE LORD
OUR RIGHTEOUSNESS.[15]

7 "Therefore, behold, *the* days are coming," says the LORD, "that they shall no longer say, 'As the LORD lives who brought up the children of Israel from the land of Egypt,'
8 but, 'As the LORD lives who brought up and led the descendants of the house of Israel from the north country and from all the countries where I had driven them.' And they shall dwell in their own land."

False Prophets and Empty Oracles

9 My heart within me is broken
Because of the prophets;
All my bones shake.
I am like a drunken man,
And like a man whom wine has
    overcome,
Because of the LORD,
And because of His holy words.
10 For the land is full of adulterers;

For because of a curse the land
    mourns.
The pleasant places of the wilderness
    are dried up.
Their course of life is evil,
And their might *is* not right.

11 "For both prophet and priest are
    profane;
Yes, in My house I have found their
    wickedness," says the LORD.
12 "Therefore their way shall be to them
Like slippery *ways*;
In the darkness they shall be driven on
And fall in them;
For I will bring disaster on them,
The year of their punishment,"
    says the LORD.
13 "And I have seen folly in the prophets
    of Samaria:
They prophesied by Baal
And caused My people Israel to err.
14 Also I have seen a horrible thing in the
    prophets of Jerusalem:
They commit adultery and walk in lies;
They also strengthen the hands of
    evildoers,
So that no one turns back from his
    wickedness.
All of them are like Sodom to Me,
And her inhabitants like Gomorrah.
15 Therefore thus says the LORD of hosts
    concerning the prophets:
'Behold, I will feed them with
    wormwood,
And make them drink the water
    of gall;
For from the prophets of Jerusalem
Profaneness has gone out into all the
    land.' "

16 Thus says the LORD of hosts:

"Do not listen to the words of the
    prophets who prophesy to you.
They make you worthless;
They speak a vision of their own heart,
Not from the mouth of the LORD.
17 They continually say to those who
    despise Me,
'The LORD has said,
    "You shall have peace" ';
And to everyone who walks according
    to the imagination of his own heart,
'No evil shall come upon you.' "

18 For who has stood in the counsel of
    the LORD,
And has perceived and heard His
    word?

15 Hebrew *YHWH Tsidkenu*

Who has marked His word
and heard *it*?
19 Behold, a whirlwind of the LORD has
gone forth in fury—
A violent whirlwind!
It will fall violently on the head of the
wicked.
20 The anger of the LORD will not turn
back
Until He has executed and performed
the thoughts of His heart.
In the latter days you will understand
it perfectly.

21 "I have not sent these prophets,
yet they ran.
I have not spoken to them,
yet they prophesied.
22 But if they had stood in My counsel,
And had caused My people to hear My
words,
Then they would have turned them
from their evil way
And from the evil of their doings.

23 "*Am* I a God near at hand,"
says the LORD,
"And not a God afar off?
24 Can anyone hide himself in secret
places,
So I shall not see him?"
says the LORD;
"Do I not fill heaven and earth?"
says the LORD.

25 "I have heard what the prophets have
said who prophesy lies in My name, saying, 'I have dreamed, I have dreamed!'
26 "How long will *this* be in the heart of
the prophets who prophesy lies? Indeed
they are prophets of the deceit of their
own heart,
27 "who try to make My people forget
My name by their dreams which everyone
tells his neighbor, as their fathers forgot
My name for Baal.

28 "The prophet who has a dream,
let him tell a dream;
And he who has My word,
let him speak My word faithfully.
What *is* the chaff to the wheat?"
says the LORD.
29 "*Is* not My word like a fire?"
says the LORD,
"And like a hammer *that* breaks the
rock in pieces?

30 "Therefore behold, I *am* against the
prophets," says the LORD, "who steal My
words every one from his neighbor.
31 "Behold, I *am* against the prophets,"
says the LORD, "who use their tongues
and say, 'He says.'
32 "Behold, I *am* against those who
prophesy false dreams," says the LORD,
"and tell them, and cause My people to
err by their lies and by their recklessness.
Yet I did not send them or command
them; therefore they shall not profit this
people at all," says the LORD.
33 "So when these people or the prophet
or the priest ask you, saying, 'What is the
oracle of the LORD?' you shall then say
to them, 'What oracle?' I will even forsake you," says the LORD.
34 "And *as for* the prophet and the priest
and the people who say, 'The oracle of
the LORD!' I will even punish that man
and his house.
35 "Thus every one of you shall say to
his neighbor, and every one to his
brother, 'What has the LORD answered?'
and, 'What has the LORD spoken?'
36 "And the oracle of the LORD you shall
mention no more. For every man's word
will be his oracle, for you have perverted
the words of the living God, the LORD of
hosts, our God.
37 "Thus you shall say to the prophet,
'What has the LORD answered you?' and,
'What has the LORD spoken?'
38 "But since you say, 'The oracle of the
LORD!' therefore thus says the LORD:
'Because you say this word, "The oracle
of the LORD!" and I have sent to you,
saying, 'Do not say, "The oracle of the
LORD!" '
39 'therefore behold, I, even I, will utterly forget you and forsake you, and the
city that I gave you and your fathers, and
will cast you out of My presence.
40 'And I will bring an everlasting reproach upon you, and a perpetual shame,
which shall not be forgotten.' "

The Sign of Two Baskets of Figs

24 The LORD showed me, and there
were two baskets of figs set before
the temple of the LORD, after Nebuchadnezzar king of Babylon had carried away
captive Jeconiah the son of Jehoiakim,
king of Judah, and the princes of Judah
with the craftsmen and smiths, from Jerusalem, and had brought them to Babylon.

2 One basket *had* very good figs, like the figs *that are* first ripe; and the other basket *had* very bad figs which could not be eaten, they were so bad."
3 Then the LORD said to me, "What do you see, Jeremiah?" And I said, "Figs, the good figs, very good; and the bad, very bad, which cannot be eaten, they are so bad."
4 Again the word of the LORD came to me, saying,
5 "Thus says the LORD, the God of Israel: 'Like these good figs, so will I acknowledge those who are carried away captive from Judah, whom I have sent out of this place for *their own* good, into the land of the Chaldeans.
6 'For I will set My eyes on them for good, and I will bring them back to this land; I will build them and not pull *them* down, and I will plant them and not pluck *them* up.
7 'Then I will give them a heart to know Me, that I *am* the LORD; and they shall be My people, and I will be their God, for they shall return to Me with their whole heart.
8 'And as the bad figs which cannot be eaten, they are so bad'—surely thus says the LORD—'so will I give up Zedekiah the king of Judah, his princes, the residue of Jerusalem who remain in this land, and those who dwell in the land of Egypt.
9 'I will deliver them to trouble into all the kingdoms of the earth, for *their* harm, *to be* a reproach and a byword, a taunt and a curse, in all places where I shall drive them.
10 'And I will send the sword, the famine, and the pestilence among them, till they are consumed from the land that I gave to them and their fathers.'"

Seventy Years of Desolation

25 The word that came to Jeremiah concerning all the people of Judah, in the fourth year of Jehoiakim the son of Josiah, king of Judah (which *was* the first year of Nebuchadnezzar king of Babylon),
2 which Jeremiah the prophet spoke to all the people of Judah and to all the inhabitants of Jerusalem, saying:
3 "From the thirteenth year of Josiah the son of Amon, king of Judah, even to this day, this *is* the twenty-third year in which the word of the LORD has come to

me; and I have spoken to you, rising early and speaking, but you have not listened.
4 "And the LORD has sent to you all His servants the prophets, rising early and sending *them*, but you have not listened nor inclined your ear to hear.
5 "They said, 'Repent now everyone of his evil way and his evil doings, and dwell in the land that the LORD has given to you and your fathers forever and ever.
6 'Do not go after other gods to serve them and worship them, and do not provoke Me to anger with the works of your hands; and I will not harm you.'
7 "Yet you have not listened to Me," says the LORD, "that you might provoke Me to anger with the works of your hands to your own hurt.
8 "Therefore thus says the LORD of hosts: 'Because you have not heard My words,
9 'behold, I will send and take all the families of the north,' says the LORD, 'and Nebuchadnezzar the king of Babylon, My servant, and will bring them against this land, against its inhabitants, and against these nations all around, and will utterly destroy them, and make them an astonishment, a hissing, and perpetual desolations.
10 'Moreover I will take from them the voice of mirth and the voice of gladness, the voice of the bridegroom and the voice of the bride, the sound of the millstones and the light of the lamp.
11 'And this whole land shall be a desolation *and* an astonishment, and these nations shall serve the king of Babylon seventy years.
12 'Then it will come to pass, when seventy years are completed, *that* I will punish the king of Babylon and that nation, the land of the Chaldeans, for their iniquity,' says the LORD; 'and I will make it a perpetual desolation.
13 'So I will bring on that land all My words which I have pronounced against it, all that is written in this book, which Jeremiah has prophesied concerning all the nations.
14 '(For many nations and great kings shall be served by them also; and I will repay them according to their deeds and according to the works of their own hands.)'"

Judgment on the Nations

15 For thus says the LORD God of Israel to me: "Take this wine cup of fury from My hand, and cause all the nations, to whom I send you, to drink it. 16 "And they will drink and stagger and go mad because of the sword that I will send among them."

17 Then I took the cup from the LORD's hand, and made all the nations drink, to whom the LORD had sent me: 18 Jerusalem and the cities of Judah, its kings and its princes, to make them a desolation, an astonishment, a hissing, and a curse, as *it is* this day; 19 Pharaoh king of Egypt, his servants, his princes, and all his people; 20 all the mixed multitude, all the kings of the land of Uz, all the kings of the land of the Philistines (namely, Ashkelon, Gaza, Ekron, and the remnant of Ashdod); 21 Edom, Moab, and the people of Ammon; 22 all the kings of Tyre, all the kings of Sidon, and the kings of the coastlands which *are* across the sea; 23 Dedan, Tema, Buz, and all *who are* in the farthest corners; 24 all the kings of Arabia and all the kings of the mixed multitude who dwell in the desert; 25 all the kings of Zimri, all the kings of Elam, and all the kings of the Medes; 26 all the kings of the north, far and near, one with another; and all the kingdoms of the world which *are* on the face of the earth. Also the king of Sheshach[16] shall drink after them.

27 "Therefore you shall say to them, 'Thus says the LORD of hosts, the God of Israel: "Drink, be drunk, and vomit! Fall and rise no more, because of the sword which I will send among you." ' 28 "And it shall be, if they refuse to take the cup from your hand to drink, then you shall say to them, 'Thus says the LORD of hosts: "You shall certainly drink! 29 "For behold, I begin to bring calamity on the city which is called by My name, and should you be utterly unpunished? You shall not be unpunished, for I will call for a sword on all the inhabitants of the earth," says the LORD of hosts.' 30 "Therefore prophesy against them all these words, and say to them:

16 Code word for *Babylon* (compare 51:41)

'The LORD will roar from on high,
And utter His voice from His holy
    habitation;
He will roar mightily against His fold.
He will give a shout,
    as those who tread *the grapes*,
Against all the inhabitants of the earth.
31 A noise will come to the ends of the
    earth—
For the LORD has a controversy with
    the nations;
He will plead His case with all flesh.
He will give those *who are* wicked
    to the sword,' says the LORD."

32 Thus says the LORD of hosts:

"Behold, disaster shall go forth
From nation to nation,
And a great whirlwind
    shall be raised up
From the farthest parts of the earth.

33 "And at that day the slain of the LORD shall be from *one* end of the earth even to the *other* end of the earth. They shall not be lamented, or gathered, or buried; they shall become refuse on the ground.

34"Wail, shepherds, and cry!
Roll about *in the ashes*,
You leaders of the flock!
For the days of your slaughter and
    your dispersions are fulfilled;
You shall fall like a precious vessel.
35 And the shepherds will have no way
    to flee,
Nor the leaders of the flock to escape.
36 A voice of the cry of the shepherds,
And a wailing of the leaders to the
    flock *will be heard*.
For the LORD has plundered their
    pasture,
37 And the peaceful habitations
    are cut down
Because of the fierce anger of the
    LORD.
38 He has left his lair like the lion;
For their land is desolate
Because of the fierceness of the
    Oppressor,
And because of His fierce anger."

Jeremiah Saved from Death

26 In the beginning of the reign of Jehoiakim the son of Josiah, king of Judah, this word came from the LORD, saying,

2 "Thus says the LORD: 'Stand in the court of the LORD's house, and speak to all the cities of Judah, which come to worship *in* the LORD's house, all the words that I command you to speak to them. Do not diminish a word.
3 'Perhaps everyone will listen and turn from his evil way, that I may relent concerning the calamity which I purpose to bring on them because of the evil of their doings.'
4 "And you shall say to them, 'Thus says the LORD: "If you will not listen to Me, to walk in My law which I have set before you,
5 "to heed the words of My servants the prophets whom I sent to you, both rising up early and sending *them* (but you have not heeded),
6 "then I will make this house like Shiloh, and will make this city a curse to all the nations of the earth." ' "
7 So the priests and the prophets and all the people heard Jeremiah speaking these words in the house of the LORD.
8 Now it happened, when Jeremiah had made an end of speaking all that the LORD had commanded *him* to speak to all the people, that the priests and the prophets and all the people seized him, saying, "You will surely die!
9 "Why have you prophesied in the name of the LORD, saying, 'This house shall be like Shiloh, and this city shall be desolate, without an inhabitant'?" And all the people were gathered against Jeremiah in the house of the LORD.
10 When the princes of Judah heard these things, they came up from the king's house to the house of the LORD and sat down in the entry of the new gate of the LORD's *house.*
11 And the priests and the prophets spoke to the princes and all the people, saying, "This man deserves to die! For he has prophesied against this city, as you have heard with your ears."
12 Then Jeremiah spoke to all the princes and all the people, saying: "The LORD sent me to prophesy against this house and against this city with all the words that you have heard.
13 "Now therefore, amend your ways and your doings, and obey the voice of the LORD your God; then the LORD will relent concerning the doom that He has pronounced against you.

14 "As for me, here I am, in your hand; do with me as seems good and proper to you.
15 "But know for certain that if you put me to death, you will surely bring innocent blood on yourselves, on this city, and on its inhabitants; for truly the LORD has sent me to you to speak all these words in your hearing."
16 So the princes and all the people said to the priests and the prophets, "This man does not deserve to die. For he has spoken to us in the name of the LORD our God."
17 Then certain of the elders of the land rose up and spoke to all the assembly of the people, saying:
18 "Micah of Moresheth prophesied in the days of Hezekiah king of Judah, and spoke to all the people of Judah, saying, 'Thus says the LORD of hosts:

"Zion shall be plowed *like* a field,
    Jerusalem shall become heaps of ruins,
And the mountain of the temple[17]
    Like the bare hills of the forest." '[18]

19 "Did Hezekiah king of Judah and all Judah ever put him to death? Did he not fear the LORD and seek the LORD's favor? And the Lord relented concerning the doom which He had pronounced against them. But we are doing great evil against ourselves."
20 Now there was also a man who prophesied in the name of the LORD, Urijah the son of Shemaiah of Kirjath Jearim, who prophesied against this city and against this land according to all the words of Jeremiah.
21 And when Jehoiakim the king, with all his mighty men and all the princes, heard his words, the king sought to put him to death; but when Urijah heard *it,* he was afraid and fled, and went to Egypt.
22 Then Jehoiakim the king sent men to Egypt: Elnathan the son of Achbor, and *other* men *who went* with him to Egypt.
23 And they brought Urijah from Egypt and brought him to Jehoiakim the king, who killed him with the sword and cast his dead body into the graves of the common people.
24 Nevertheless the hand of Ahikam the son of Shaphan was with Jeremiah, so that they should not give him into the hand of the people to put him to death.

17 Literally *house*   18 Compare Micah 3:12

Symbol of the Bonds and Yokes

27 In the beginning of the reign of Jehoiakim[19] the son of Josiah, king of Judah, this word came to Jeremiah from the LORD, saying,

2 "Thus says the LORD to me: 'Make for yourselves bonds and yokes, and put them on your neck,

3 'and send them to the king of Edom, the king of Moab, the king of the Ammonites, the king of Tyre, and the king of Sidon, by the hand of the messengers who come to Jerusalem to Zedekiah king of Judah.

4 'And command them to say to their masters, "Thus says the LORD of hosts, the God of Israel—thus you shall say to your masters:

5 'I have made the earth, the man and the beast that *are* on the ground, by My great power and by My outstretched arm, and have given it to whom it seemed proper to Me.

6 'And now I have given all these lands into the hand of Nebuchadnezzar the king of Babylon, My servant; and the beasts of the field I have also given him to serve him.

7 'So all nations shall serve him and his son and his son's son, until the time of his land comes; and then many nations and great kings shall make him serve them.

8 'And it shall be, *that* the nation and kingdom which will not serve Nebuchadnezzar the king of Babylon, and which will not put its neck under the yoke of the king of Babylon, that nation I will punish,' says the LORD, 'with the sword, the famine, and the pestilence, until I have consumed them by his hand.

9 'Therefore do not listen to your prophets, your diviners, your dreamers, your soothsayers, or your sorcerers, who speak to you, saying, "You shall not serve the king of Babylon."

10 'For they prophesy a lie to you, to remove you far from your land; and I will drive you out, and you will perish.

11 'But the nations that bring their necks under the yoke of the king of Babylon and serve him, I will let them remain in their own land,' says the LORD, 'and they shall till it and dwell in it.' "

12 I also spoke to Zedekiah king of Judah according to all these words, saying, "Bring your necks under the yoke of the king of Babylon, and serve him and his people, and live!

13 "Why will you die, you and your people, by the sword, by the famine, and by the pestilence, as the LORD has spoken against the nation that will not serve the king of Babylon?

14 "Therefore do not listen to the words of the prophets who speak to you, saying, 'You shall not serve the king of Babylon,' for they prophesy a lie to you;

15 "for I have not sent them," says the LORD, "yet they prophesy a lie in My name, that I may drive you out, and that you may perish, you and the prophets who prophesy to you."

16 Also I spoke to the priests and to all this people, saying, "Thus says the LORD: 'Do not listen to the words of your prophets who prophesy to you, saying, "Behold, the vessels of the LORD's house will now shortly be brought back from Babylon"; for they prophesy a lie to you.

17 'Do not listen to them; serve the king of Babylon, and live! Why should this city be laid waste?

18 'But if they *are* prophets, and if the word of the LORD is with them, let them now make intercession to the LORD of hosts, that the vessels which are left in the house of the LORD, *in* the house of the king of Judah, and at Jerusalem, do not go to Babylon.'

19 "For thus says the LORD of hosts concerning the pillars, concerning the Sea, concerning the carts, and concerning the remainder of the vessels that remain in this city,

20 "which Nebuchadnezzar king of Babylon did not take, when he carried away captive Jeconiah the son of Jehoiakim, king of Judah, from Jerusalem to Babylon, and all the nobles of Judah and Jerusalem—

21 "yes, thus says the LORD of hosts, the God of Israel, concerning the vessels that remain in the house of the LORD, and in the house of the king of Judah and of Jerusalem:

22 'They shall be carried to Babylon, and there they shall be until the day that I visit them,' says the LORD. 'Then I will bring them up and restore them to this place.' "

Hananiah's Falsehood and Doom

28 And it happened in the same year, at the beginning of the reign of

19 A few manuscripts read *Zedekiah* (compare 27:3, 12; 28:1).

Zedekiah king of Judah, in the fourth year *and* in the fifth month, *that* Hananiah the son of Azur the prophet, who *was* from Gibeon, spoke to me in the house of the LORD in the presence of the priests and of all the people, saying,

2 "Thus speaks the LORD of hosts, the God of Israel, saying: 'I have broken the yoke of the king of Babylon.

3 'Within two full years I will bring back to this place all the vessels of the LORD's house, that Nebuchadnezzar king of Babylon took away from this place and carried to Babylon.

4 'And I will bring back to this place Jeconiah the son of Jehoiakim, king of Judah, with all the captives of Judah who went to Babylon,' says the LORD, 'for I will break the yoke of the king of Babylon.' "

5 Then the prophet Jeremiah spoke to the prophet Hananiah in the presence of the priests and in the presence of all the people who stood in the house of the LORD,

6 and the prophet Jeremiah said, "Amen! The LORD do so; the LORD perform your words which you have prophesied, to bring back the vessels of the LORD's house and all who were carried away captive, from Babylon to this place.

7 "Nevertheless hear now this word that I speak in your hearing and in the hearing of all the people:

8 "The prophets who have been before me and before you of old prophesied against many countries and great kingdoms—of war and disaster and pestilence.

9 "As for the prophet who prophesies of peace, when the word of the prophet comes to pass, the prophet will be known *as* one whom the LORD has truly sent."

10 Then Hananiah the prophet took the yoke off the prophet Jeremiah's neck and broke it.

11 And Hananiah spoke in the presence of all the people, saying, "Thus says the LORD: 'Even so I will break the yoke of Nebuchadnezzar king of Babylon from the neck of all nations within the space of two full years.' " And the prophet Jeremiah went his way.

12 Then the word of the LORD came to Jeremiah, after Hananiah the prophet had broken the yoke from the neck of the prophet Jeremiah, saying,

13 "Go and tell Hananiah, saying, 'Thus says the LORD: "You have broken the yokes of wood, but you have made in their place yokes of iron."

14 'For thus says the LORD of hosts, the God of Israel: "I have put a yoke of iron on the neck of all these nations, that they may serve Nebuchadnezzar king of Babylon; and they shall serve him. I have given him the beasts of the field also." ' "

15 Then the prophet Jeremiah said to Hananiah the prophet, "Hear now, Hananiah, the LORD has not sent you, but you make this people trust in a lie.

16 "Therefore thus says the LORD: 'Behold, I will cast you from the face of the earth. This year you shall die, because you have taught rebellion against the LORD.' "

17 So Hananiah the prophet died the same year in the seventh month.

Jeremiah's Letter to the Captives

29 Now these *are* the words of the letter that Jeremiah the prophet sent from Jerusalem to the remainder of the elders who were carried away captive—to the priests, the prophets, and all the people whom Nebuchadnezzar had carried away captive from Jerusalem to Babylon.

2 (This happened after Jeconiah the king, the queen mother, the eunuchs, the princes of Judah and Jerusalem, the craftsmen, and the smiths had departed from Jerusalem.)

3 *The letter was sent* by the hand of Elasah the son of Shaphan, and Gemariah the son of Hilkiah, whom Zedekiah king of Judah sent to Babylon, to Nebuchadnezzar king of Babylon, saying,

4 Thus says the LORD of hosts, the God of Israel, to all who were carried away captive, whom I have caused to be carried away from Jerusalem to Babylon:

5 Build houses and dwell *in them*; plant gardens and eat their fruit.

6 Take wives and beget sons and daughters; and take wives for your sons and give your daughters to husbands, so that they may bear sons and daughters—that you may be increased there, and not diminished.

7 And seek the peace of the city where I have caused you to be carried away captive, and pray to the LORD for it; for in its peace you will have peace.

8 For thus says the LORD of hosts, the God of Israel: Do not let your prophets and your diviners who are in your midst deceive you, nor listen to your dreams which you cause to be dreamed.

9 For they prophesy falsely to you in My name; I have not sent them, says the LORD.

10 For thus says the LORD: After seventy years are completed at Babylon, I will visit you and perform My good word toward you, and cause you to return to this place.

11 For I know the thoughts that I think toward you, says the LORD, thoughts of peace and not of evil, to give you a future and a hope.

12 Then you will call upon Me and go and pray to Me, and I will listen to you.

13 And you will seek Me and find *Me*, when you search for Me with all your heart.

14 I will be found by you, says the LORD, and I will bring you back from your captivity; I will gather you from all the nations and from all the places where I have driven you, says the LORD, and I will bring you to the place from which I cause you to be carried away captive.

15 Because you have said, "The LORD has raised up prophets for us in Babylon"—

16 therefore thus says the LORD concerning the king who sits on the throne of David, concerning all the people who dwell in this city, and concerning your brethren who have not gone out with you into captivity—

17 thus says the LORD of hosts: Behold, I will send on them the sword, the famine, and the pestilence, and will make them like rotten figs that cannot be eaten, they are so bad.

18 And I will pursue them with the sword, with famine, and with pestilence; and I will deliver them to trouble among all the kingdoms of the earth—to be a curse, an astonishment, a hissing, and a reproach among all the nations where I have driven them,

19 because they have not heeded My words, says the LORD, which I sent to them by My servants the prophets, rising up early and sending *them*; neither would you heed, says the LORD.

20 Therefore hear the word of the LORD, all you of the captivity, whom I have sent from Jerusalem to Babylon.

21 Thus says the LORD of hosts, the God of Israel, concerning Ahab the son of Kolaiah, and Zedekiah the son of Maaseiah, who prophesy a lie to you in My name: Behold, I will deliver them into the hand of Nebuchadnezzar king of Babylon, and he shall slay them before your eyes.

22 And because of them a curse shall be taken up by all the captivity of Judah who *are* in Babylon, saying, "The LORD make you like Zedekiah and Ahab, whom the king of Babylon roasted in the fire";

23 because they have done disgraceful things in Israel, have committed adultery with their neighbors' wives, and have spoken lying words in My name, which I have not commanded them. Indeed I know, and *am* a witness, says the LORD.

24 You shall also speak to Shemaiah the Nehelamite, saying,

25 Thus speaks the LORD of hosts, the God of Israel, saying: You have sent letters in your name to all the people who *are* at Jerusalem, to Zephaniah the son of Maaseiah the priest, and to all the priests, saying,

26 "The LORD has made you priest instead of Jehoiada the priest, so that there should be officers *in* the house of the LORD over every man *who* is demented and considers himself a prophet, that you should put him in prison and in the stocks.

27 Now therefore, why have you not reproved Jeremiah of Anathoth who makes himself a prophet to you?

28 For he has sent to us *in* Babylon, saying, 'This *captivity is* long; build houses and dwell *in them*, and plant gardens and eat their fruit.' "

29 Now Zephaniah the priest read this letter in the hearing of Jeremiah the prophet. **30** Then the word of the LORD came to Jeremiah, saying: **31** "Send to all those in captivity, saying, 'Thus says the LORD concerning Shemaiah the Nehelamite: "Because Shemaiah has prophesied to you, and I have not sent him, and he has caused you to trust in a lie," **32** 'therefore thus says the LORD: "Behold, I will punish Shemaiah the Nehelamite and his family: he shall not have anyone to dwell among this people, nor shall he see the good that I will do for My people," says the LORD, "because he has taught rebellion against the LORD." ' "

Restoration of Israel and Judah

30 The word that came to Jeremiah from the LORD, saying, **2** "Thus speaks the LORD God of Israel, saying: 'Write in a book for yourself all the words that I have spoken to you. **3** 'For behold, the days are coming,' says the LORD, 'that I will bring back from captivity My people Israel and Judah,' says the LORD. 'And I will cause them to return to the land that I gave to their fathers, and they shall possess it.' " **4** Now these *are* the words that the LORD spoke concerning Israel and Judah. **5** "For thus says the LORD:

'We have heard a voice of trembling,
Of fear, and not of peace.
6 Ask now, and see,
Whether a man is ever in labor with child?
So why do I see every man
with his hands on his loins
Like a woman in labor,
And all faces turned pale?
7 Alas! For that day *is* great,
So that none *is* like it;
And it *is* the time of Jacob's trouble,
But he shall be saved out of it.

8 'For it shall come to pass in that day,'
Says the LORD of hosts,
'*That* I will break his yoke
from your neck,
And will burst your bonds;
Foreigners shall no more enslave them.
9 But they shall serve the LORD
their God,

And David their king,
Whom I will raise up for them.

10 'Therefore do not fear, O My servant
Jacob,' says the LORD,
'Nor be dismayed, O Israel;
For behold, I will save you from afar,
And your seed from the land of their captivity.
Jacob shall return,
have rest and be quiet,
And no one shall make *him* afraid.
11 For I *am* with you,' says the LORD,
'to save you;
Though I make a full end of all nations
where I have scattered you,
Yet I will not make a complete end of you.
But I will correct you in justice,
And will not let you go altogether unpunished.'

12 "For thus says the LORD:

'Your affliction *is* incurable,
Your wound *is* severe.
13 *There is* no one to plead your cause,
That you may be bound up;
You have no healing medicines.
14 All your lovers have forgotten you;
They do not seek you;
For I have wounded you with the wound of an enemy,
With the chastisement of a cruel one,
For the multitude of your iniquities,
Because your sins have increased.
15 Why do you cry about your affliction?
Your sorrow *is* incurable.
Because of the multitude of your iniquities,
Because your sins have increased,
I have done these things to you.

16 'Therefore all those who devour
you shall be devoured;
And all your adversaries, every one of them, shall go into captivity;
Those who plunder you
shall become plunder,
And all who prey upon you
I will make a prey.
17 For I will restore health to you
And heal you of your wounds,'
says the LORD,
'Because they called you an outcast
saying:
"This *is* Zion;
No one seeks her." '

18 "Thus says the LORD:

'Behold, I will bring back the captivity
of Jacob's tents,
And have mercy on his dwelling
places;
The city shall be built upon its own
mound,
And the palace shall remain according
to its own plan.
19 Then out of them shall proceed
thanksgiving
And the voice of those who make
merry;
I will multiply them,
and they shall not diminish;
I will also glorify them,
and they shall not be small.
20 Their children also shall be as before,
And their congregation shall be
established before Me;
And I will punish all who oppress
them.
21 Their nobles shall be from among
them,
And their governor shall come from
their midst;
Then I will cause him to draw near,
And he shall approach Me;
For who *is* this who pledged his heart
to approach Me?' says the LORD.
22 'You shall be My people,
And I will be your God.' "

23 Behold, the whirlwind of the LORD
Goes forth with fury,
A continuing whirlwind;
It will fall violently on the head
of the wicked.
24 The fierce anger of the LORD
will not return until He has done it,
And until He has performed
the intents of His heart.

In the latter days you will consider it.

The Remnant of Israel Saved

31 "At the same time," says the
LORD, "I will be the God of all the
families of Israel, and they shall be My
people."
2 Thus says the LORD:

"The people who survived the sword
Found grace in the wilderness—
Israel, when I went to give him rest."

3 The LORD has appeared of old to me,
saying:
"Yes, I have loved you
with an everlasting love;

Therefore with lovingkindness
I have drawn you.
4 Again I will build you,
and you shall be rebuilt,
O virgin of Israel!
You shall again be adorned
with your tambourines,
And shall go forth in the dances
of those who rejoice.
5 You shall yet plant vines
on the mountains of Samaria;
The planters shall plant
and eat *them* as ordinary food.
6 For there shall be a day
When the watchmen will cry on Mount
Ephraim,
'Arise, and let us go up *to* Zion,
To the LORD our God.' "

7 For thus says the LORD:

"Sing with gladness for Jacob,
And shout among the chief of the
nations;
Proclaim, give praise, and say,
'O LORD, save Your people,
The remnant of Israel!'
8 Behold, I will bring them from the
north country,
And gather them from the ends of the
earth,
Among them the blind and the lame,
The woman with child
And the one who labors with child,
together;
A great throng shall return there.
9 They shall come with weeping,
And with supplications I will lead
them.
I will cause them to walk by the rivers
of waters,
In a straight way in which they shall
not stumble;
For I am a Father to Israel,
And Ephraim *is* My firstborn.

10 "Hear the word of the LORD, O nations,
And declare *it* in the isles afar off,
and say,
'He who scattered Israel will gather
him,
And keep him as a shepherd *does* his
flock.'
11 For the LORD has redeemed Jacob,
And ransomed him from the hand of
one stronger than he.
12 Therefore they shall come
and sing in the height of Zion,
Streaming to the goodness of the
LORD—

For wheat and new wine and oil,
For the young of the flock
    and the herd;
Their souls shall be like a well-watered
    garden,
And they shall sorrow no more at all.
13 "Then shall the virgin rejoice in the
    dance,
And the young men and the old,
    together;
For I will turn their mourning to joy,
Will comfort them,
And make them rejoice
    rather than sorrow.
14 I will satiate the soul of the priests
    with abundance,
And My people shall be satisfied with
    My goodness," says the LORD.

Mercy on Ephraim

15 Thus says the LORD:

"A voice was heard in Ramah,
Lamentation *and* bitter weeping,
Rachel weeping for her children,
Refusing to be comforted for her
    children,
Because they *are* no more."

16 Thus says the LORD:

"Refrain your voice from weeping,
And your eyes from tears;
For your work shall be rewarded,"
    says the LORD,
"And they shall come back
    from the land of the enemy.
17 There is hope in your future,"
    says the LORD,
"That *your* children shall come back
    to their own border.

18 "I have surely heard Ephraim
    bemoaning himself:
'You have chastised me,
    and I was chastised,
Like an untrained bull;
Restore me, and I will return,
For You *are* the LORD my God.
19 Surely, after my turning, I repented;
And after I was instructed,
    I struck myself on the thigh;
I was ashamed, yes, even humiliated,
Because I bore the reproach of my
    youth.'
20 *Is* Ephraim My dear son?
Is he a pleasant child?
For though I spoke against him,

I earnestly remember him still;
Therefore My heart yearns for him;
I will surely have mercy on him,"
    says the LORD.

21 "Set up signposts,
    Make landmarks;
Set your heart toward the highway,
The way in *which* you went.
Turn back, O virgin of Israel,
Turn back to these your cities.
22 How long will you gad about,
O you backsliding daughter?
For the LORD has created a new thing
    in the earth—
A woman shall encompass a man."

Future Prosperity of Judah

23 Thus says the LORD of hosts, the God
of Israel: "They shall again use this
speech in the land of Judah and in its
cities, when I bring back their captivity:
'The LORD bless you, O habitation of justice, *and* mountain of holiness!'
24 "And there shall dwell in Judah itself,
and in all its cities together, farmers and
those going out with flocks.
25 "For I have satiated the weary soul,
and I have replenished every sorrowful
soul."
26 After this I awoke and looked around,
and my sleep was sweet to me.
27 "Behold, the days are coming," says
the LORD, "that I will sow the house of
Israel and the house of Judah with the
seed of man and the seed of beast.
28 "And it shall come to pass, *that* as I
have watched over them to pluck up, to
break down, to throw down, to destroy,
and to afflict, so I will watch over them to
build and to plant," says the LORD.
29 "In those days they shall say no more:

'The fathers have eaten sour grapes,
And the children's teeth are set on
    edge.'

30 "But every one shall die for his own
iniquity; every man who eats the sour
grapes, his teeth shall be set on edge.

A New Covenant

31 "Behold, the days are coming," says
the LORD, "when I will make a new covenant with the house of Israel and with
the house of Judah—
32 "not according to the covenant that I
made with their fathers in the day *that* I

took them by the hand to bring them out of the land of Egypt, My covenant which they broke, though I was a husband to them," says the LORD.
33 "But this *is* the covenant that I will make with the house of Israel: After those days, says the LORD, I will put My law in their minds, and write it on their hearts; and I will be their God, and they shall be My people.
34 "No more shall every man teach his neighbor, and every man his brother, saying, 'Know the LORD,' for they all shall know Me, from the least of them to the greatest of them," says the LORD. "For I will forgive their iniquity, and their sin I will remember no more."

35 Thus says the LORD,
Who gives the sun for a light by day,
And the ordinances of the moon and
    the stars for a light by night,
Who disturbs the sea,
And its waves roar
(The LORD of hosts *is* His name):

36 "If those ordinances depart
From before Me," says the LORD,
"*Then* the seed of Israel shall also cease
From being a nation before Me
    forever."

37 Thus says the LORD:

"If heaven above can be measured,
And the foundations of the earth
    searched out beneath,
I will also cast off all the seed of Israel
For all that they have done,"
says the LORD.

38 "Behold, the days are coming," says the LORD, "that the city shall be built for the LORD from the Tower of Hananeel to the Corner Gate.
39 "The surveyor's line shall again extend straight forward over the hill Gareb; then it shall turn toward Goath.
40 "And the whole valley of the dead bodies and of the ashes, and all the fields as far as the Brook Kidron, to the corner of the Horse Gate toward the east, *shall be* holy to the LORD. It shall not be plucked up or thrown down anymore forever."

Jeremiah Buys a Field

32 The word that came to Jeremiah from the LORD in the tenth year of Zedekiah king of Judah, which was the eighteenth year of Nebuchadnezzar.
2 For then the king of Babylon's army besieged Jerusalem, and Jeremiah the prophet was shut up in the court of the prison, which *was in* the king of Judah's house.
3 For Zedekiah king of Judah had shut him up, saying, "Why do you prophesy and say, 'Thus says the LORD: "Behold, I will give this city into the hand of the king of Babylon, and he shall take it;
4 "and Zedekiah king of Judah shall not escape from the hand of the Chaldeans, but shall surely be delivered into the hand of the king of Babylon, and shall speak with him face to face,[20] and see him eye to eye;
5 "then he shall lead Zedekiah to Babylon, and there he shall be until I visit him," says the LORD; "though you fight with the Chaldeans, you shall not succeed" '?"
6 And Jeremiah said, "The word of the LORD came to me, saying,
7 'Behold, Hanameel the son of Shallum your uncle will come to you, saying, "Buy my field which *is* in Anathoth, for the right of redemption *is* yours to buy *it*." '
8 "Then Hanameel my uncle's son came to me in the court of the prison according to the word of the LORD, and said to me, 'Please buy my field that *is* in Anathoth, which *is* in the country of Benjamin; for the right of inheritance *is* yours, and the redemption yours; buy *it* for yourself.' Then I knew that this was the word of the LORD.
9 "So I bought the field from Hanameel, the son of my uncle who *was* in Anathoth, and weighed *out to* him the money—seventeen shekels of silver.
10 "And I signed the deed and sealed *it*, took witnesses, and weighed the money in the balances.
11 "So I took the purchase deed, *both* that which was sealed *according* to the law and custom, and that which was open;
12 "and I gave the purchase deed to Baruch the son of Neriah, son of Mahseiah, in the presence of Hanameel my uncle's *son,* and in the presence of the witnesses who signed the purchase deed, before all the Jews who sat in the court of the prison.

20 Literally *mouth to mouth*

13 "Then I charged Baruch before them, saying,

14 'Thus says the LORD of hosts, the God of Israel: "Take these deeds, both this purchase deed which is sealed and this deed which is open, and put them in an earthen vessel, that they may last many days."

15 'For thus says the LORD of hosts, the God of Israel: "Houses and fields and vineyards shall be possessed again in this land."'

Jeremiah Prays for Understanding

16 "Now when I had delivered the purchase deed to Baruch the son of Neriah, I prayed to the LORD, saying:

17 'Ah, Lord GOD! Behold, You have made the heavens and the earth by Your great power and outstretched arm. There is nothing too hard for You.

18 'You show lovingkindness to thousands, and repay the iniquity of the fathers into the bosom of their children after them—the Great, the Mighty God, whose name is the LORD of hosts.

19 'You are great in counsel and mighty in work, for your eyes are open to all the ways of the sons of men, to give everyone according to his ways and according to the fruit of his doings.

20 'You have set signs and wonders in the land of Egypt, to this day, and in Israel and among other men; and You have made Yourself a name, as it is this day.

21 'You have brought Your people Israel out of the land of Egypt with signs and wonders, with a strong hand and an outstretched arm, and with great terror;

22 'You have given them this land, of which You swore to their fathers to give them— "a land flowing with milk and honey."[21]

23 'And they came in and took possession of it, but they have not obeyed Your voice or walked in Your law. They have done nothing of all that You commanded them to do; therefore You have caused all this calamity to come upon them.

24 'Look, the siege mounds! They have come to the city to take it; and the city has been given into the hand of the Chaldeans who fight against it, because of the sword and famine and pestilence. What You have spoken has happened; there You see it!

25 'And You have said to me, O Lord GOD, "Buy the field for money, and take witnesses"!—yet the city has been given into the hand of the Chaldeans.' "

God's Assurance of the People's Return

26 Then the word of the LORD came to Jeremiah, saying,

27 "Behold, I am the LORD, the God of all flesh. Is there anything too hard for Me?"

28 Therefore thus says the LORD: "Behold, I will give this city into the hand of the Chaldeans, into the hand of Nebuchadnezzar king of Babylon, and he shall take it.

29 "And the Chaldeans who fight against this city shall come and set fire to this city and burn it, with the houses on whose roofs they have offered incense to Baal and poured out drink offerings to other gods, to provoke Me to anger;

30 "because the children of Israel and the children of Judah have done only evil before Me from their youth. For the children of Israel have provoked Me only to anger with the work of their hands," says the LORD.

31 "For this city has been to Me a provocation of My anger and My fury from the day that they built it, even to this day; so I will remove it from before My face

32 "because of all the evil of the children of Israel and the children of Judah, which they have done to provoke Me to anger—they, their kings, their princes, their priests, their prophets, the men of Judah, and the inhabitants of Jerusalem.

33 "And they have turned to Me the back, and not the face; though I taught them, rising up early and teaching them, yet they have not listened to receive instruction.

34 "But they set their abominations in the house which is called by My name, to defile it.

35 "And they built the high places of Baal which are in the Valley of the Son of Hinnom, to cause their sons and their daughters to pass through the fire to Molech, which I did not command them, nor did it come into My mind that they should do this abomination, to cause Judah to sin.

36 "Now therefore, thus says the LORD, the God of Israel, concerning this city of which you say, 'It shall be delivered into the hand of the king of Babylon by the

21 Exodus 3:8

sword, by the famine, and by the pestilence':

37 'Behold, I will gather them out of all countries where I have driven them in My anger, in My fury, and in great wrath; I will bring them back to this place, and I will cause them to dwell safely.

38 'They shall be My people, and I will be their God;

39 'then I will give them one heart and one way, that they may fear Me forever, for the good of them and their children after them.

40 'And I will make an everlasting covenant with them, that I will not turn away from doing them good; but I will put My fear in their hearts so that they will not depart from Me.

41 'Yes, I will rejoice over them to do them good, and I will assuredly plant them in this land, with all My heart and with all My soul.'

42 "For thus says the LORD: 'Just as I have brought all this great calamity on this people, so I will bring on them all the good that I have promised them.

43 'And fields will be bought in this land of which you say, "It is desolate, without man or beast; it has been given into the hand of the Chaldeans."

44 'Men will buy fields for money, sign deeds and seal them, and take witnesses, in the land of Benjamin, in the places around Jerusalem, in the cities of Judah, in the cities of the mountains, in the cities of the lowland, and in the cities of the South; for I will cause their captives to return,' says the LORD."

Excellence of the Restored Nation

33 Moreover the word of the LORD came to Jeremiah a second time, while he was still shut up in the court of the prison, saying,

2 "Thus says the LORD who made it, the LORD who formed it to establish it (the LORD is His name):

3 'Call to Me, and I will answer you, and show you great and mighty things, which you do not know.'

4 "For thus says the LORD, the God of Israel, concerning the houses of this city and the houses of the kings of Judah, which have been pulled down to *fortify*[22] against the siege mounds and the sword:

5 'They come to fight with the Chaldeans, but *only* to fill their places[23] with the

dead bodies of men whom I will slay in My anger and My fury, all for whose wickedness I have hidden My face from this city.

6 'Behold, I will bring it health and healing; I will heal them and reveal to them the abundance of peace and truth.

7 'And I will cause the captives of Judah and the captives of Israel to return, and will rebuild those places as at the first.

8 'I will cleanse them from all their iniquity by which they have sinned against Me, and I will pardon all their iniquities by which they have sinned and by which they have transgressed against Me.

9 'Then it shall be to Me a name of joy, a praise, and an honor before all nations of the earth, who shall hear all the good that I do to them; they shall fear and tremble for all the goodness and all the prosperity that I provide for it.'

10 "Thus says the LORD: 'Again there shall be heard in this place—of which you say, "It *is* desolate, without man and without beast" —in the cities of Judah, in the streets of Jerusalem that are desolate, without man and without inhabitant and without beast,

11 'the voice of joy and the voice of gladness, the voice of the bridegroom and the voice of the bride, the voice of those who will say:

"Praise the LORD of hosts,
   For the LORD *is* good,
   For His mercy *endures* forever"—

and of those *who will* bring the sacrifice of praise into the house of the LORD. For I will cause the captives of the land to return as at the first,' says the LORD.

12 "Thus says the LORD of hosts: In this place which is desolate, without man and without beast, and in all its cities, there shall again be a habitation of shepherds causing *their* flocks to lie down.

13 'In the cities of the mountains, in the cities of the lowland, in the cities of the South, in the land of Benjamin, in the places around Jerusalem, and in the cities of Judah, the flocks shall again pass under the hands of him who counts *them*,' says the LORD.

14 'Behold, the days are coming,' says the LORD, 'that I will perform that good

22 Compare Isaiah 22:10   23 Compare 2 Kings 23:14

thing which I have promised to the house
of Israel and to the house of Judah:

15 'In those days and at that time
I will cause to grow up to David
A Branch of righteousness;
He shall execute judgment and
righteousness in the earth.
16 In those days Judah will be saved,
And Jerusalem will dwell safely.
And this *is the name* by which she will
be called:

THE LORD
OUR RIGHTEOUSNESS.[24]

17 "For thus says the LORD: 'David shall
never lack a man to sit on the throne of
the house of Israel;
18 'nor shall the priests, the Levites, lack
a man to offer burnt offerings before Me,
to kindle grain offerings, and to sacrifice
continually.' "

The Permanence of God's Covenant

19 And the word of the LORD came to
Jeremiah, saying,
20 "Thus says the LORD: 'If you can
break My covenant with the day and My
covenant with the night, so that there will
not be day and night in their season,
21 'then My covenant may also be broken with David My servant, so that he
shall not have a son to reign on his
throne, and with the Levites, the priests,
My ministers.
22 'As the host of heaven cannot be numbered, nor the sand of the sea measured,
so will I multiply the descendants of David My servant and the Levites who minister to Me.' "
23 Moreover the word of the LORD came
to Jeremiah, saying,
24 "Have you not considered what these
people have spoken, saying, 'The two
families which the LORD has chosen, He
has also cast them off'? Thus they have
despised My people, as if they should no
more be a nation before them.
25 "Thus says the LORD: 'If My covenant *is* not with day and night, *and if* I
have not appointed the ordinances of
heaven and earth,
26 'then I will cast away the descendants
of Jacob and David My servant, *so* that I
will not take *any* of his descendants *to be*
rulers over the descendants of Abraham,
Isaac, and Jacob. For I will cause their

captives to return, and will have mercy on
them.' "

Zedekiah Warned by God

34 The word which came to Jeremiah
from the LORD, when Nebuchadnezzar king of Babylon and all his army,
all the kingdoms of the earth under his
dominion, and all the people, fought
against Jerusalem and all its cities, saying,
2 "Thus says the LORD, the God of Israel: 'Go and speak to Zedekiah king of
Judah and tell him, "Thus says the LORD:
'Behold, I will give this city into the hand
of the king of Babylon, and he shall burn
it with fire.
3 'And you shall not escape from his
hand, but shall surely be taken and delivered into his hand; your eyes shall see the
eyes of the king of Babylon, he shall
speak with you face to face,[25] and you
shall go to Babylon.' " '
4 "Yet hear the word of the LORD, O
Zedekiah king of Judah! Thus says the
LORD concerning you: 'You shall not die
by the sword.
5 '*But* you shall die in peace; as in the
ceremonies of your fathers, the former
kings who were before you, so they shall
burn incense for you and lament for you,
saying, "Alas, lord!" ' For I have pronounced the word," says the LORD.
6 Then Jeremiah the prophet spoke all
these words to Zedekiah king of Judah in
Jerusalem,
7 when the king of Babylon's army
fought against Jerusalem and all the cities
of Judah that were left, against Lachish
and Azekah; for *only* these fortified cities
remained of the cities of Judah.

Treacherous Treatment of Slaves

8 This is the word that came to Jeremiah from the LORD, after King Zedekiah had made a covenant with all the
people who *were* at Jerusalem to proclaim
liberty to them:
9 that every man should set free his
male and female slave—a Hebrew man or
woman—that no one should keep a Jewish brother in bondage.
10 Now when all the princes and all the
people, who had entered into the covenant, heard that everyone should set free
his male and female slaves, that no one

24 Compare 23:5, 6   25 Literally *mouth to mouth*

should keep them in bondage anymore, they obeyed and let *them* go.

11 But afterward they changed their minds and made the male and female slaves return, whom they had set free, and brought them into subjection as male and female slaves.

12 Therefore the word of the LORD came to Jeremiah from the LORD, saying,

13 "Thus says the LORD, the God of Israel: 'I made a covenant with your fathers in the day that I brought them out of the land of Egypt, out of the house of bondage, saying,

14 "At the end of seven years let every man set free his Hebrew brother, who has been sold to him; and when he has served you six years, you shall let him go free from you." But your fathers did not obey Me nor incline their ear.

15 'Then you recently turned and did what was right in My sight—every man proclaiming liberty to his neighbor; and you made a covenant before Me in the house which is called by My name.

16 'Then you turned around and profaned My name, and every one of you brought back his male and female slaves, whom he had set at liberty, at their pleasure, and brought them back into subjection, to be your male and female slaves.'

17 "Therefore thus says the LORD: 'You have not obeyed Me in proclaiming liberty, every one to his brother and every one to his neighbor. Behold, I proclaim liberty to you,' says the LORD—'to the sword, to pestilence, and to famine! And I will deliver you to trouble among all the kingdoms of the earth.

18 'And I will give the men who have transgressed My covenant, who have not performed the words of the covenant which they made before Me, when they cut the calf in two and passed between the parts of it—

19 'the princes of Judah, the princes of Jerusalem, the eunuchs, the priests, and all the people of the land who passed between the parts of the calf—

20 'I will give them into the hand of their enemies and into the hand of those who seek their life. Their dead bodies shall be for meat for the birds of the heaven and the beasts of the earth.

21 'And I will give Zedekiah king of Judah and his princes into the hand of their enemies, into the hand of those who seek

their life, and into the hand of the king of Babylon's army which has gone back from you.

22 'Behold, I will command,' says the LORD, 'and cause them to return to this city. They will fight against it and take it and burn it with fire; and I will make the cities of Judah a desolation without inhabitant.' "

The Obedient Rechabites

35 The word which came to Jeremiah from the LORD in the days of Jehoiakim the son of Josiah, king of Judah, saying,

2 "Go to the house of the Rechabites, speak to them, and bring them into the house of the LORD, into one of the chambers, and give them wine to drink."

3 Then I took Jaazaniah the son of Jeremiah, the son of Habazziniah, his brothers and all his sons, and the whole house of the Rechabites,

4 and I brought them into the house of the LORD, into the chamber of the sons of Hanan the son of Igdaliah, a man of God, which *was* by the chamber of the princes, above the chamber of Maaseiah the son of Shallum, the keeper of the door.

5 Then I set before the sons of the house of the Rechabites bowls full of wine, and cups; and I said to them, "Drink wine."

6 But they said, "We will drink no wine, for Jonadab the son of Rechab, our father, commanded us, saying, 'You shall drink no wine, you nor your sons, forever.

7 'You shall not build a house, sow seed, plant a vineyard, nor have *any of these*; but all your days you shall dwell in tents, that you may live many days in the land where you are sojourners.'

8 "Thus we have obeyed the voice of Jonadab the son of Rechab, our father, in all that he charged us, to drink no wine all our days, we, our wives, our sons, or our daughters,

9 "nor to build ourselves houses to dwell in; nor do we have vineyard, field, or seed.

10 "But we have dwelt in tents, and have obeyed and done according to all that Jonadab our father commanded us.

11 "But it came to pass, when Nebuchadnezzar king of Babylon came up into the land, that we said, 'Come, let us go to

Jerusalem for fear of the army of the Chaldeans and for fear of the army of the Syrians.' So we dwell at Jerusalem."

12 Then came the word of the LORD to Jeremiah, saying,

13 "Thus says the LORD of hosts, the God of Israel: 'Go and tell the men of Judah and the inhabitants of Jerusalem, "Will you not receive instruction to obey My words?" says the LORD.

14 "The words of Jonadab the son of Rechab, which he commanded his sons, not to drink wine, are performed; for to this day they drink none, and obey their father's commandment. But although I have spoken to you, rising early and speaking, you did not obey Me.

15 "I have also sent to you all My servants the prophets, rising up early and sending them, saying, 'Turn now everyone from his evil way, amend your doings, and do not go after other gods to serve them; then you will dwell in the land which I have given you and your fathers.' But you have not inclined your ear, nor obeyed Me.

16 "Surely the sons of Jonadab the son of Rechab have performed the commandment of their father, which he commanded them, but this people has not obeyed Me."

17 "Therefore thus says the LORD God of hosts, the God of Israel: 'Behold, I will bring on Judah and on all the inhabitants of Jerusalem all the doom that I have pronounced against them; because I have spoken to them but they have not heard, and I have called to them but they have not answered.' "

18 And Jeremiah said to the house of the Rechabites, "Thus says the LORD of hosts, the God of Israel: 'Because you have obeyed the commandment of Jonadab your father, and kept all his precepts and done according to all that he commanded you,

19 'therefore thus says the LORD of hosts, the God of Israel: "Jonadab the son of Rechab shall not lack a man to stand before Me forever." ' "

The Scroll Read in the Temple

36 Now it came to pass in the fourth year of Jehoiakim the son of Josiah, king of Judah, that this word came to Jeremiah from the LORD, saying:

2 "Take a scroll of a book and write on it all the words that I have spoken to you against Israel, against Judah, and against all the nations, from the day I spoke to you, from the days of Josiah even to this day.

3 "It may be that the house of Judah will hear all the adversities which I purpose to bring upon them, that everyone may turn from his evil way, that I may forgive their iniquity and their sin."

4 Then Jeremiah called Baruch the son of Neriah; and Baruch wrote on a scroll of a book, at the instruction of Jeremiah,[26] all the words of the LORD which He had spoken to him.

5 And Jeremiah commanded Baruch, saying, "I am confined, I cannot go into the house of the LORD.

6 "You go, therefore, and read from the scroll which you have written at my instruction,[27] the words of the LORD, in the hearing of the people in the LORD's house on the day of fasting. And you shall also read them in the hearing of all Judah who come from their cities.

7 "It may be that they will present their supplication before the LORD, and everyone will turn from his evil way. For great is the anger and the fury that the LORD has pronounced against this people.

8 And Baruch the son of Neriah did according to all that Jeremiah the prophet commanded him, reading from the book the words of the LORD in the LORD's house.

9 Now it came to pass in the fifth year of Jehoiakim the son of Josiah, king of Judah, in the ninth month, that they proclaimed a fast before the LORD to all the people in Jerusalem, and to all the people who came from the cities of Judah to Jerusalem.

10 Then Baruch read from the book the words of Jeremiah in the house of the LORD, in the chamber of Gemariah the son of Shaphan the scribe, in the upper court at the entry of the New Gate of the LORD's house, in the hearing of all the people.

The Scroll Read in the Palace

11 When Michaiah the son of Gemariah, the son of Shaphan, heard all the words of the LORD from the book,

12 he then went down to the king's house, into the scribe's chamber; and there all the princes were sitting—Elish-

---

26 Literally from Jeremiah's mouth	27 Literally from my mouth

ama the scribe, Delaiah the son of Shemaiah, Elnathan the son of Achbor, Gemariah the son of Shaphan, Zedekiah the son of Hananiah, and all the princes. 13 Then Michaiah declared to them all the words that he had heard when Baruch read the book in the hearing of the people. 14 Therefore all the princes sent Jehudi the son of Nethaniah, the son of Shelemiah, the son of Cushi, to Baruch, saying, "Take in your hand the scroll from which you have read in the hearing of the people, and come." So Baruch the son of Neriah took the scroll in his hand and came to them. 15 And they said to him, "Sit down now, and read it in our hearing." So Baruch read it in their hearing. 16 Now it happened, when they had heard all the words, that they looked in fear from one to another, and said to Baruch, "We will surely tell the king of all these words." 17 And they asked Baruch, saying, "Tell us now, how did you write all these words—at his instruction?"28 18 So Baruch answered them, "He proclaimed with his mouth all these words to me, and I wrote them with ink in the book." 19 Then the princes said to Baruch, "Go and hide, you and Jeremiah; and let no one know where you are."

The King Destroys Jeremiah's Scroll

20 And they went to the king, into the court; but they stored the scroll in the chamber of Elishama the scribe, and told all the words in the hearing of the king. 21 So the king sent Jehudi to bring the scroll, and he took it from Elishama the scribe's chamber. And Jehudi read it in the hearing of the king and in the hearing of all the princes who stood beside the king. 22 Now the king was sitting in the winter house in the ninth month, with a fire burning on the hearth before him. 23 And it happened, when Jehudi had read three or four columns, that the king cut it with the scribe's knife and cast it into the fire that was on the hearth, until all the scroll was consumed in the fire that was on the hearth. 24 Yet they were not afraid, nor did they

tear their garments, the king nor any of his servants who heard all these words. 25 Nevertheless Elnathan, Delaiah, and Gemariah implored the king not to burn the scroll; but he would not listen to them. 26 And the king commanded Jerahmeel the king's29 son, Seraiah the son of Azriel, and Shelemiah the son of Abdeel, to seize Baruch the scribe and Jeremiah the prophet, but the LORD hid them.

Jeremiah Rewrites the Scroll

27 Now after the king had burned the scroll with the words which Baruch had written at the instruction of Jeremiah,30 the word of the LORD came to Jeremiah, saying: 28 "Take yet another scroll, and write on it all the former words that were in the first scroll which Jehoiakim the king of Judah has burned. 29 "And you shall say to Jehoiakim king of Judah, 'Thus says the LORD: "You have burned this scroll, saying, 'Why have you written in it that the king of Babylon will certainly come and destroy this land, and cause man and beast to cease from here?' " 30 'Therefore thus says the LORD concerning Jehoiakim king of Judah: "He shall have no one to sit on the throne of David, and his dead body shall be cast out to the heat of the day and the frost of the night. 31 "I will punish him, his family, and his servants for their iniquity; and I will bring on them, on the inhabitants of Jerusalem, and on the men of Judah all the doom that I have pronounced against them; but they did not heed." ' " 32 Then Jeremiah took another scroll and gave it to Baruch the scribe, the son of Neriah, who wrote on it at the instruction of Jeremiah31 all the words of the book which Jehoiakim king of Judah had burned in the fire. And besides, there were added to them many similar words.

Zedekiah's Vain Hope

37 Then King Zedekiah the son of Josiah reigned instead of Coniah the son of Jehoiakim, whom Nebuchadnezzar king of Babylon made king in the land of Judah. 2 But neither he nor his servants nor the

---

28 Literally with his mouth   29 Hebrew Hammelech   30 Literally from Jeremiah's mouth
31 Literally from Jeremiah's mouth

people of the land gave heed to the words of the LORD which He spoke by the prophet Jeremiah.

3 And Zedekiah the king sent Jehucal the son of Shelemiah, and Zephaniah the son of Maaseiah, the priest, to the prophet Jeremiah, saying, "Pray now to the LORD our God for us."

4 Now Jeremiah was coming and going among the people, for they had not *yet* put him in prison.

5 Then Pharaoh's army came up from Egypt; and when the Chaldeans who were besieging Jerusalem heard news of them, they departed from Jerusalem.

6 And the word of the LORD came to the prophet Jeremiah, saying,

7 "Thus says the LORD, the God of Israel, 'Thus you shall say to the king of Judah, who sent you to Me to inquire of Me: "Behold, Pharaoh's army which has come up to help you will return to Egypt, to their own land.

8 "And the Chaldeans shall come back and fight against this city, and take it and burn it with fire." '

9 "Thus says the LORD: 'Do not deceive yourselves, saying, "The Chaldeans will surely depart from us," for they will not depart.

10 'For though you had defeated the whole army of the Chaldeans who fight against you, and there remained *only* wounded men among them, they would rise up, every man in his tent, and burn the city with fire.' "

Jeremiah Imprisoned

11 And it happened, when the army of the Chaldeans left *the siege* of Jerusalem for fear of Pharaoh's army,

12 that Jeremiah went out of Jerusalem to go into the land of Benjamin to claim his property there among the people.

13 And when he was in the gate of Benjamin, a captain of the guard *was* there whose name *was* Irijah the son of Shelemiah, the son of Hananiah; and he seized Jeremiah the prophet, saying, "You are defecting to the Chaldeans!"

14 Then Jeremiah said, "*It is* false! I am not defecting to the Chaldeans." But he did not listen to him. So Irijah seized Jeremiah and brought him to the princes.

15 Therefore the princes were angry with Jeremiah, and they struck him and put him in prison in the house of Jonathan the scribe. For they had made that the prison.

16 When Jeremiah entered the dungeon and the cells, and Jeremiah had remained there many days,

17 then Zedekiah the king sent and took him *out*. The king asked him secretly in his house, and said, "Is there *any* word from the LORD?" And Jeremiah said, "There is." Then he said, "You shall be delivered into the hand of the king of Babylon!"

18 Moreover Jeremiah said to King Zedekiah, "What offense have I committed against you, against your servants, or against this people, that you have put me in prison?

19 "Where now *are* your prophets who prophesied to you, saying, 'The king of Babylon will not come against you or against this land?'

20 "Therefore please hear now, O my lord the king. Please, let my petition be accepted before you, and do not make me return to the house of Jonathan the scribe, lest I die there."

21 Then Zedekiah the king commanded that they should commit Jeremiah to the court of the prison, and that they should give him daily a piece of bread from the bakers' street, until all the bread in the city was gone. Thus Jeremiah remained in the court of the prison.

Jeremiah in the Dungeon

38 Now Shephatiah the son of Mattan, Gedaliah the son of Pashhur, Jucal[32] the son of Shelemiah, and Pashhur the son of Malchiah heard the words that Jeremiah had spoken to all the people, saying,

2 "Thus says the LORD: 'He who remains in this city shall die by the sword, by famine, and by pestilence; but he who goes over to the Chaldeans shall live; his life shall be as a prize to him, and he shall live.'[33]

3 "Thus says the LORD: 'This city shall surely be given into the hand of the king of Babylon's army, which shall take it.' "

4 Therefore the princes said to the king, "Please, let this man be put to death, for thus he weakens the hands of the men of war who remain in this city, and the hands of all the people, by speaking such words to them. For this man does not

---

32 Same as *Jehucal* (compare 37:3)   33 Compare 21:9

seek the welfare of this people, but their harm."

5 Then Zedekiah the king said, "Look, he *is* in your hand. For the king can *do* nothing against you."

6 So they took Jeremiah and cast him into the dungeon of Malchiah the king's[34] son, which *was* in the court of the prison, and they let Jeremiah down with ropes. And in the dungeon *there was* no water, but mire. So Jeremiah sank in the mire.

7 Now Ebed-Melech the Ethiopian, one of the eunuchs, who was in the king's house, heard that they had put Jeremiah in the dungeon. When the king was sitting at the Gate of Benjamin,

8 Ebed-Melech went out of the king's house and spoke to the king, saying:

9 "My lord the king, these men have done evil in all that they have done to Jeremiah the prophet, whom they have cast into the dungeon, and he is likely to die from hunger in the place where he is. For *there is* no more bread in the city."

10 Then the king commanded Ebed-Melech the Ethiopian, saying, "Take from here thirty men with you, and lift Jeremiah the prophet out of the dungeon before he dies."

11 So Ebed-Melech took the men with him and went into the house of the king under the treasury, and took from there old clothes and old rags, and let them down by ropes into the dungeon to Jeremiah.

12 Then Ebed-Melech the Ethiopian said to Jeremiah, "Please put these old clothes and rags under your armpits, under the ropes." And Jeremiah did so.

13 So they pulled Jeremiah up with ropes and lifted him out of the dungeon. And Jeremiah remained in the court of the prison.

Zedekiah's Fears and Jeremiah's Advice

14 Then Zedekiah the king sent and had Jeremiah the prophet brought to him at the third entrance of the house of the LORD. And the king said to Jeremiah, "I will ask you something. Hide nothing from me."

15 Then Jeremiah said to Zedekiah, "If I declare *it* to you, will you not surely put me to death? And if I give you counsel, you will not listen to me."

16 So Zedekiah the king swore secretly to Jeremiah, saying, "*As* the LORD lives, who made our very souls, I will not put you to death, nor will I give you into the hand of these men who seek your life."

17 Then Jeremiah said to Zedekiah, "Thus says the LORD, the God of hosts, the God of Israel: 'If you surely surrender to the king of Babylon's princes, then your soul shall live; this city shall not be burned with fire, and you and your house shall live.

18 'But if you do not surrender to the king of Babylon's princes, then this city shall be given into the hand of the Chaldeans; they shall burn it with fire, and you shall not escape from their hand.' "

19 And Zedekiah the king said to Jeremiah, "I am afraid of the Jews who have defected to the Chaldeans, lest they deliver me into their hand, and they abuse me."

20 But Jeremiah said, "They shall not deliver *you*. Please, obey the voice of the LORD which I speak to you. So it shall be well with you, and your soul shall live.

21 "But if you refuse to surrender, this *is* the word that the LORD has shown me:

22 'Now behold, all the women who are left in the king of Judah's house *shall be* surrendered to the king of Babylon's princes, and those *women* shall say:

"Your close friends have set upon you
    And prevailed against you;
Your feet have sunk in the mire,
    And they have turned away again."

23 'So they shall surrender all your wives and children to the Chaldeans. You shall not escape from their hand, but shall be taken by the hand of the king of Babylon. And you shall cause this city to be burned with fire.' "

24 Then Zedekiah said to Jeremiah, "Let no one know of these words, and you shall not die.

25 "But if the princes hear that I have talked with you, and they come to you and say to you, 'Declare to us now what you have said to the king, and also what the king said to you; do not hide *it* from us, and we will not put you to death,'

26 "then you shall say to them, 'I presented my request before the king, that he would not make me return to Jonathan's house to die there.' "

27 Then all the princes came to Jeremiah

34 Hebrew *Hammelech*

and asked him. And he told them according to all these words that the king had commanded. So they stopped speaking with him, for the conversation had not been heard.

28 Now Jeremiah remained in the court of the prison until the day that Jerusalem was taken. And he was *there* when Jerusalem was taken.

The Fall of Jerusalem

39 In the ninth year of Zedekiah king of Judah, in the tenth month, Nebuchadnezzar king of Babylon and all his army came against Jerusalem, and besieged it.

2 In the eleventh year of Zedekiah, in the fourth month, on the ninth *day* of the month, the city was penetrated.

3 Then all the princes of the king of Babylon came in and sat in the Middle Gate: Nergal-Sharezer, Samgar-Nebo, Sarsechim, Rabsaris,[35] Nergal-Sarezer, Rabmag,[36] with the rest of the princes of the king of Babylon.

4 So it was, when Zedekiah the king of Judah and all the men of war saw them, that they fled and went out of the city by night, by way of the king's garden, by the gate between the two walls. And he went out by way of the plain.[37]

5 But the Chaldean army pursued them and overtook Zedekiah in the plains of Jericho. And when they had captured him, they brought him up to Nebuchadnezzar king of Babylon, to Riblah in the land of Hamath, where he pronounced judgment on him.

6 Then the king of Babylon killed the sons of Zedekiah before his eyes in Riblah; the king of Babylon also killed all the nobles of Judah.

7 Moreover he put out Zedekiah's eyes, and bound him with bronze fetters to carry him off to Babylon.

8 And the Chaldeans burned the king's house and the houses of the people with fire, and broke down the walls of Jerusalem.

9 Then Nebuzaradan the captain of the guard carried away captive to Babylon the remnant of the people who remained in the city and those who defected to him, with the rest of the people who remained.

10 But Nebuzaradan the captain of the guard left in the land of Judah the poor people, who had nothing, and gave them vineyards and fields at the same time.

Jeremiah Goes Free

11 Now Nebuchadnezzar king of Babylon gave charge concerning Jeremiah to Nebuzaradan the captain of the guard, saying,

12 "Take him and look after him, and do him no harm; but do to him just as he says to you."

13 So Nebuzaradan the captain of the guard sent Nebushasban, Rabsaris, Nergal-Sharezer, Rabmag, and all the king of Babylon's chief officers;

14 then they sent *someone* to take Jeremiah from the court of the prison, and committed him to Gedaliah the son of Ahikam, the son of Shaphan, that he should take him home. So he dwelt among the people.

15 Now the word of the LORD had come to Jeremiah while he was shut up in the court of the prison, saying,

16 "Go and speak to Ebed-Melech the Ethiopian, saying, 'Thus says the LORD of hosts, the God of Israel: "Behold, I will bring My words upon this city for adversity and not for good, and they shall be *performed* in that day before you.

17 "But I will deliver you in that day," says the LORD, "and you shall not be given into the hand of the men of whom you *are* afraid.

18 "For I will surely deliver you, and you shall not fall by the sword; but your life shall be as a prize to you, because you have put your trust in Me," says the LORD.' "

Jeremiah with Gedaliah the Governor

40 The word that came to Jeremiah from the LORD after Nebuzaradan the captain of the guard had let him go from Ramah, when he had taken him bound in chains among all who were carried away captive from Jerusalem and Judah, who were carried away captive to Babylon.

2 And the captain of the guard took Jeremiah and said to him: "The LORD your God has pronounced this doom on this place.

3 "Now the LORD has brought *it*, and has done just as He said. Because you *people* have sinned against the LORD, and

---

35 A title, probably *Chief Officer;* also verse 13   36 A title, probably *Troop Commander;* also verse 13
37 Or *the arabah,* that is, the Jordan Valley

not obeyed His voice, therefore this thing has come upon you.

4 "And now look, I free you this day from the chains that *were* on your hand. If it seems good to you to come with me to Babylon, come, and I will look after you. But if it seems wrong for you to come with me to Babylon, remain here. See, all the land *is* before you; wherever it seems good and convenient for you to go, go there."

5 Now while Jeremiah had not yet gone back, *Nebuzaradan said*, "Go back to Gedaliah the son of Ahikam, the son of Shaphan, whom the king of Babylon has made governor over the cities of Judah, and dwell with him among the people. Or go wherever it seems convenient for you to go." So the captain of the guard gave him rations and a gift and let him go.

6 Then Jeremiah went to Gedaliah the son of Ahikam, to Mizpah, and dwelt with him among the people who were left in the land.

7 Now when all the captains of the armies who *were* in the fields, they and their men, heard that the king of Babylon had made Gedaliah the son of Ahikam governor in the land, and had committed to him men, women, children, and the poorest of the land who had not been carried away captive to Babylon,

8 then they came to Gedaliah at Mizpah—Ishmael the son of Nethaniah, Johanan and Jonathan the sons of Kareah, Seraiah the son of Tanhumeth, the sons of Ephai the Netophathite, and Jezaniah[38] the son of a Maachathite, they and their men.

9 And Gedaliah the son of Ahikam, the son of Shaphan, took an oath before them and their men, saying, "Do not be afraid to serve the Chaldeans. Dwell in the land and serve the king of Babylon, and it shall be well with you.

10 "As for me, I will indeed dwell at Mizpah and serve the Chaldeans who come to us. But you, gather wine and summer fruit and oil, put *them* in your vessels, and dwell in your cities that you have taken."

11 Likewise, when all the Jews who *were* in Moab, among the Ammonites, in Edom, and who *were* in all the countries, heard that the king of Babylon had left a remnant of Judah, and that he had set over them Gedaliah the son of Ahikam, the son of Shaphan,

12 then all the Jews returned out of all places where they had been driven, and came to the land of Judah, to Gedaliah at Mizpah, and gathered wine and summer fruit in abundance.

13 Moreover Johanan the son of Kareah and all the captains of the forces that *were* in the fields came to Gedaliah at Mizpah,

14 and said to him, "Do you certainly know that Baalis the king of the Ammonites has sent Ishmael the son of Nethaniah to murder you?" But Gedaliah the son of Ahikam did not believe them.

15 Then Johanan the son of Kareah spoke secretly to Gedaliah in Mizpah, saying, "Let me go, please, and I will kill Ishmael the son of Nethaniah, and no one will know *it*. Why should he murder you, so that all the Jews who are gathered to you would be scattered, and the remnant in Judah perish?"

16 But Gedaliah the son of Ahikam said to Johanan the son of Kareah, "You shall not do this thing, for you speak falsely concerning Ishmael."

Insurrection Against Gedaliah

41 Now it came to pass in the seventh month *that* Ishmael the son of Nethaniah, the son of Elishama, of the royal family and of the officers of the king, came with ten men to Gedaliah the son of Ahikam, at Mizpah. And there they ate bread together in Mizpah.

2 Then Ishmael the son of Nethaniah, and the ten men who were with him, arose and struck Gedaliah the son of Ahikam, the son of Shaphan, with the sword, and killed him whom the king of Babylon had made governor over the land.

3 Ishmael also struck down all the Jews who were with him, *that is*, with Gedaliah at Mizpah, and the Chaldeans who were found there, the men of war.

4 And it happened, on the second day after he had killed Gedaliah, when as yet no one knew *it*,

5 that certain men came from Shechem, from Shiloh, and from Samaria, eighty men with their beards shaved and their clothes torn, having cut themselves, with offerings and incense in their hand, to bring *them* to the house of the LORD.

6 Now Ishmael the son of Nethaniah

38 Spelled *Jaazaniah* in 2 Kings 25:23

went out from Mizpah to meet them, weeping as he went along; and it happened as he met them that he said to them, "Come to Gedaliah the son of Ahikam!"

7 So it was, when they came into the midst of the city, that Ishmael the son of Nethaniah killed them *and cast them* into the midst of a pit, he and the men who were with him.

8 But ten men were found among them who said to Ishmael, "Do not kill us, for we have treasures of wheat, barley, oil, and honey in the field." So he desisted and did not kill them among their brethren.

9 Now the pit into which Ishmael had cast all the dead bodies of the men whom he had slain, because of Gedaliah, *was* the same one Asa the king had made for fear of Baasha king of Israel. Ishmael the son of Nethaniah filled it with *the* slain.

10 Then Ishmael carried away captive all the rest of the people who *were* in Mizpah, the king's daughters and all the people who remained in Mizpah, whom Nebuzaradan the captain of the guard had committed to Gedaliah the son of Ahikam. And Ishmael the son of Nethaniah carried them away captive and departed to go over to the Ammonites.

11 But when Johanan the son of Kareah and all the captains of the forces that *were* with him heard of all the evil that Ishmael the son of Nethaniah had done,

12 they took all the men and went to fight with Ishmael the son of Nethaniah; and they found him by the great pool that *is* in Gibeon.

13 So it was, when all the people who *were* with Ishmael saw Johanan the son of Kareah, and all the captains of the forces who *were* with him, that they were glad.

14 Then all the people whom Ishmael had carried away captive from Mizpah turned around and came back, and went to Johanan the son of Kareah.

15 But Ishmael the son of Nethaniah escaped from Johanan with eight men and went to the Ammonites.

16 Then Johanan the son of Kareah, and all the captains of the forces that were with him, took from Mizpah all tne rest of the people whom he had recovered from Ishmael the son of Nethaniah after he had murdered Gedaliah the son of Ahikam—the mighty men of war and the

women and the children and the eunuchs, whom he had brought back from Gibeon.

17 And they departed and dwelt in the habitation of Chimham, which is near Bethlehem, as they went on their way to Egypt,

18 because of the Chaldeans; for they were afraid of them, because Ishmael the son of Nethaniah had murdered Gedaliah the son of Ahikam, whom the king of Babylon had made governor in the land.

The Flight to Egypt Forbidden

42 Then all the captains of the forces, Johanan the son of Kareah, Jezaniah the son of Hoshaiah, and all the people, from the least to the greatest, came near

2 and said to Jeremiah the prophet, "Please, let our petition be acceptable to you, and pray for us to the LORD your God, for all this remnant (since we are left *but* a few of many, as you can see),

3 "that the LORD your God may show us the way in which we should walk and the thing we should do."

4 Then Jeremiah the prophet said to them, "I have heard. Indeed, I will pray to the LORD your God according to your words, and it shall be, *that* whatever the LORD answers you, I will declare *it* to you. I will keep nothing back from you."

5 Then they said to Jeremiah, "Let the LORD be a true and faithful witness between us, if we do not do according to everything which the LORD your God sends us by you.

6 "Whether *it is* pleasing or displeasing, we will obey the voice of the LORD our God to whom we send you, that it may be well with us when we obey the voice of the LORD our God."

7 And it happened after ten days that the word of the LORD came to Jeremiah.

8 Then he called Johanan the son of Kareah, all the captains of the forces which *were* with him, and all the people from the least even to the greatest,

9 and said to them, "Thus says the LORD, the God of Israel, to whom you sent me to present your petition before Him:

10 'If you will still abide in this land, then I will build you and not pull *you* down, and I will plant you and not pluck *you* up. For I relent concerning the disaster that I have brought upon you.

11 'Do not be afraid of the king of Babylon, of whom you are afraid; do not be afraid of him,' says the LORD, 'for I *am* with you, to save you and deliver you from his hand.
12 'And I will show you mercy, that he may have mercy on you and cause you to return to your own land.'
13 "But if you say, 'We will not dwell in this land,' disobeying the voice of the LORD your God,
14 "saying, 'No, but we will go to the land of Egypt where we shall see no war, nor hear the sound of the trumpet, nor be hungry for bread, and there we will dwell'—
15 "Then hear now the word of the LORD, O remnant of Judah! Thus says the LORD of hosts, the God of Israel: 'If you wholly set your faces to enter Egypt, and go to sojourn there,
16 'then it shall be *that* the sword which you feared shall overtake you there in the land of Egypt; the famine of which you were afraid shall follow close after you there *in* Egypt; and there you shall die.
17 'So shall it be with all the men who set their faces to go to Egypt to sojourn there. They shall die by the sword, by famine, and by pestilence. And none of them shall remain or escape from the disaster that I will bring upon them.'
18 "For thus says the LORD of hosts, the God of Israel: 'As My anger and My fury have been poured out on the inhabitants of Jerusalem, so will My fury be poured out on you when you enter Egypt. And you shall be an oath, an astonishment, a curse, and a reproach; and you shall see this place no more.'
19 "The LORD has said concerning you, O remnant of Judah, 'Do not go to Egypt!' Know certainly that I have admonished you this day.
20 "For you were hypocrites in your hearts when you sent me to the LORD your God, saying, 'Pray for us to the LORD our God, and according to all that the LORD your God says, so declare to us and we will do *it*.'
21 "And I have this day declared *it* to you, but you have not obeyed the voice of the LORD your God, or anything which He has sent you by me.
22 "Now therefore, know certainly that you shall die by the sword, by famine,

and by pestilence in the place where you desire to go to sojourn."

Jeremiah Taken to Egypt

43 Now it happened, when Jeremiah had stopped speaking to all the people all the words of the LORD their God, for which the LORD their God had sent him to them, all these words,
2 that Azariah the son of Hoshaiah, Johanan the son of Kareah, and all the proud men spoke, saying to Jeremiah, "You speak falsely! The LORD our God has not sent you to say, 'Do not go to Egypt to sojourn there.'
3 "But Baruch the son of Neriah has set you against us, to deliver us into the hand of the Chaldeans, that they may put us to death or carry us away captive to Babylon."
4 So Johanan the son of Kareah, all the captains of the forces, and all the people would not obey the voice of the LORD, to remain in the land of Judah.
5 But Johanan the son of Kareah and all the captains of the forces took all the remnant of Judah who had returned to dwell in the land of Judah, from all nations where they had been driven—
6 men, women, children, the king's daughters, and every person whom Nebuzaradan the captain of the guard had left with Gedaliah the son of Ahikam, the son of Shaphan, and Jeremiah the prophet and Baruch the son of Neriah.
7 So they went to the land of Egypt, for they did not obey the voice of the LORD. And they went as far as Tahpanhes.
8 Then the word of the LORD came to Jeremiah in Tahpanhes, saying,
9 "Take large stones in your hand, and hide them in the sight of the men of Judah, in the clay in the brick courtyard which *is* at the entrance to Pharaoh's house in Tahpanhes;
10 "and say to them, 'Thus says the LORD of hosts, the God of Israel: "Behold, I will send and bring Nebuchadnezzar the king of Babylon, My servant, and will set his throne above these stones that I have hidden. And he will spread his royal pavilion over them.
11 "When he comes, he shall strike the land of Egypt *and deliver* to death *those appointed* for death, and to captivity *those appointed* for captivity, and to the sword *those appointed* for the sword.

12 "I will kindle a fire in the houses of the gods of Egypt, and he shall burn them and carry them away captive. And he shall array himself with the land of Egypt, as a shepherd puts on his garment, and he shall go out from there in peace. 13 "He shall also break the sacred pillars of Beth Shemesh[39] that *are* in the land of Egypt; and the houses of the gods of the Egyptians he shall burn with fire." ' "

Israelites Will Be Punished in Egypt

44 The word that came to Jeremiah concerning all the Jews who dwell in the land of Egypt, who dwell at Migdol, at Tahpanhes, at Noph,[40] and in the country of Pathros, saying, 2 "Thus says the LORD of hosts, the God of Israel: 'You have seen all the calamity that I have brought on Jerusalem and on all the cities of Judah; and behold, this day they *are* a desolation, and no one dwells in them, 3 'because of their wickedness which they have committed to provoke Me to anger, in that they went to burn incense *and* to serve other gods whom they did not know, they nor you nor your fathers. 4 'However I have sent to you all My servants the prophets, rising early and sending *them,* saying, "Oh, do not do this abominable thing that I hate!" 5 'But they did not listen or incline their ear to turn from their wickedness, to burn no incense to other gods. 6 'So My fury and My anger were poured out and kindled in the cities of Judah and in the streets of Jerusalem; and they are wasted *and* desolate, as it is this day.' 7 "Now therefore, thus says the LORD, the God of hosts, the God of Israel: 'Why do you commit *this* great evil against yourselves, to cut off from you man and woman, child and infant, out of Judah, leaving none to remain, 8 'in that you provoke Me to wrath with the works of your hands, burning incense to other gods in the land of Egypt where you have gone to dwell, that you may cut yourselves off and be a curse and a reproach among all the nations of the earth? 9 'Have you forgotten the wickedness of your fathers, the wickedness of the kings of Judah, the wickedness of their wives, your own wickedness, and the wickedness

of your wives, which they committed in the land of Judah and in the streets of Jerusalem? 10 'They have not been humbled, to this day, nor have they feared; they have not walked in My law or in My statutes that I set before you and your fathers.' 11 "Therefore thus says the LORD of hosts, the God of Israel: 'Behold, I will set My face against you for catastrophe and for cutting off all Judah. 12 'And I will take the remnant of Judah who have set their faces to go into the land of Egypt to sojourn there, and they shall all be consumed *and* fall in the land of Egypt. They shall be consumed by the sword *and* by famine. They shall die, from the least to the greatest, by the sword and by famine; and they shall be an oath *and* an astonishment and a curse and a reproach! 13 'For I will punish those who dwell in the land of Egypt, as I have punished Jerusalem, by the sword, by famine, and by pestilence, 14 'so that none of the remnant of Judah who have gone into the land of Egypt to sojourn there shall escape or survive, lest they return to the land of Judah, to which they desire to return and dwell. For none shall return except those who escape.' " 15 Then all the men who knew that their wives had burned incense to other gods, with all the women who stood by, a great multitude, and all the people who dwelt in the land of Egypt, in Pathros, answered Jeremiah, saying: 16 "*As for* the word that you have spoken to us in the name of the LORD, we will not listen to you! 17 "But we will certainly do whatever has gone out of our own mouth, to burn incense to the queen of heaven and pour out drink offerings to her, as we have done, we and our fathers, our kings and our princes, in the cities of Judah and in the streets of Jerusalem. For *then* we had plenty of food, were well-off, and saw no trouble. 18 "But since we stopped burning incense to the queen of heaven and pouring out drink offerings to her, we have lacked everything and have been consumed by the sword and by famine." 19 *The women also said,* "And when we burned incense to the queen of heaven and poured out drink offerings to her, did

---

39 Literally *House Of The Sun,* ancient On; later called *Heliopolis*   40 That is, ancient Memphis

we make cakes for her, to worship her, and pour out drink offerings to her without our husbands' *permission*?"
20 Then Jeremiah spoke to all the people—the men, the women, and all the people who had given him *that* answer—saying:
21 "The incense that you burned in the cities of Judah and in the streets of Jerusalem, you and your fathers, your kings and your princes, and the people of the land, did not the LORD remember them, and did it *not* come into His mind?
22 "So the LORD could no longer bear *it*, because of the evil of your doings *and* because of the abominations which you committed. Therefore your land is a desolation, an astonishment, a curse, and without an inhabitant, as *it is* this day.
23 "Because you have burned incense and because you have sinned against the LORD, and have not obeyed the voice of the LORD or walked in His law, in His statutes or in His testimonies, therefore this calamity has happened to you, as *at* this day."
24 Moreover Jeremiah said to all the people and to all the women, "Hear the word of the LORD, all Judah who *are* in the land of Egypt!
25 "Thus says the LORD of hosts, the God of Israel, saying: 'You and your wives have spoken with your mouths and fulfilled with your hands, saying, "We will surely perform our vows that we have made, to burn incense to the queen of heaven and pour out drink offerings to her." You will surely fulfill your vows and perform your vows!'
26 "Therefore hear the word of the LORD, all Judah who dwell in the land of Egypt: 'Behold, I have sworn by My great name,' says the LORD, 'that My name shall no more be named in the mouth of any man of Judah in all the land of Egypt, saying, "The Lord GOD lives."
27 'Behold, I will watch over them for adversity and not for good. And all the men of Judah who *are* in the land of Egypt shall be consumed by the sword and by famine, until there is an end to them.
28 'Yet a small number who escape the sword shall return from the land of Egypt to the land of Judah; and all the remnant of Judah, who have gone to the land of

Egypt to sojourn there, shall know whose words will stand, Mine or theirs.
29 'And this *shall be* a sign to you,' says the LORD, 'that I will punish you in this place, that you may know that My words will surely stand against you for adversity.'
30 "Thus says the LORD: 'Behold, I will give Pharaoh Hophra king of Egypt into the hand of his enemies and into the hand of those who seek his life, as I gave Zedekiah king of Judah into the hand of Nebuchadnezzar king of Babylon, his enemy who sought his life.' "

Assurance to Baruch

45 The word that Jeremiah the prophet spoke to Baruch the son of Neriah, when he had written these words in a book at the instruction of Jeremiah,[41] in the fourth year of Jehoiakim the son of Josiah, king of Judah, saying,
2 "Thus says the LORD, the God of Israel, to you, O Baruch:
3 'You said, "Woe is me now! For the LORD has added grief to my sorrow. I fainted in my sighing, and I find no rest." '
4 "Thus you shall say to him, 'Thus says the LORD: "Behold, what I have built I will break down, and what I have planted I will pluck up, that is, this whole land.
5 "And do you seek great things for yourself? Do not seek *them*; for behold, I will bring adversity on all flesh," says the LORD. "But I will give your life to you as a prize in all places, wherever you go." ' "

Judgment on Egypt

46 The word of the LORD which came to Jeremiah the prophet against the nations.
2 Against Egypt.
Concerning the army of Pharaoh Necho, king of Egypt, which was by the River Euphrates in Carchemish, and which Nebuchadnezzar king of Babylon defeated in the fourth year of Jehoiakim the son of Josiah, king of Judah:

3 "Order the buckler and shield,
      And draw near to battle!
4 Harness the horses,
      And mount up, you horsemen!
      Stand forth with *your* helmets,
      Polish the spears,
      Put on the armor!

---

41 Literally *from Jeremiah's mouth*

5 Why have I seen them dismayed *and*
    turned back?
Their mighty ones are beaten down;
They have speedily fled,
And did not look back,
For fear *was* all around,"
    says the LORD.
6 "Do not let the swift flee away,
    Nor the mighty man escape;
They will stumble and fall
Toward the north,
    by the River Euphrates.

7 "Who *is* this coming up like a flood,
    Whose waters move like the rivers?
8 Egypt rises up like a flood,
    And *its* waters move like the rivers;
And he says, 'I will go up
    and cover the earth,
I will destroy the city and its
    inhabitants.'
9 Come up, O horses,
    and rage, O chariots!
And let the mighty men come forth:
The Ethiopians and the Libyans
    who handle the shield,
And the Lydians who handle
    and bend the bow.
10 For this *is* the day of the Lord GOD of
    hosts,
A day of vengeance,
That He may avenge Himself on His
    adversaries.
The sword shall devour;
It shall be satiated
    and made drunk with their blood;
For the Lord GOD of hosts
    has a sacrifice
In the north country
    by the River Euphrates.

11 "Go up to Gilead and take balm,
    O virgin, the daughter of Egypt;
In vain you will use many medicines;
    You shall not be cured.
12 The nations have heard of your shame,
    And your cry has filled the land;
For the mighty man has stumbled
    against the mighty;
They both have fallen together."

Babylonia Will Strike Egypt

13 The word that the LORD spoke to Jeremiah the prophet, how Nebuchadnezzar
king of Babylon would come *and* strike
the land of Egypt.

14 "Declare in Egypt,
    and proclaim in Migdol;

Proclaim in Noph[42]
    and in Tahpanhes;
Say, 'Stand fast and prepare yourselves,
For the sword devours all around you.'
15 Why are your valiant *men* swept away?
    They did not stand
Because the LORD drove them away.
16 He made many fall;
    Yes, one fell upon another.
And they said, 'Arise!
Let us go back to our own people
And to the land of our nativity
From the oppressing sword.'
17 They cried there,
    'Pharaoh, king of Egypt,
    is but a noise.
He has passed by the appointed time!'

18 "*As* I live," says the King,
    Whose name *is* the LORD of hosts,
"Surely as Tabor *is* among the
    mountains
And as Carmel by the sea,
    so he shall come.
19 O you daughter dwelling in Egypt,
    Prepare yourself to go into captivity!
For Noph[43] shall be waste
    and be desolate, without inhabitant.

20 "Egypt *is like* a very pretty heifer,
    But destruction comes,
    it comes from the north.
21 Also her mercenaries are in her midst
    like fat bulls,
For they also are turned back,
They have fled away together.
They did not stand,
For the day of their calamity
    had come upon them,
The time of their punishment.
22 Her noise shall go like a serpent,
    For they shall march with an army
And come against her with axes,
    Like those who chop wood.

23 "They shall cut down her forest,"
    says the LORD,
"Though it cannot be searched,
Because they *are* innumerable,
And more numerous than
    grasshoppers.
24 The daughter of Egypt shall be
    ashamed;
She shall be delivered into the hand
Of the people of the north."

25 The LORD of hosts, the God of Israel,
says: "Behold, I will bring punishment
on Amon[44] of No, [45] and Pharaoh and

42 That is, ancient Memphis   43 That is, ancient Memphis   44 A sun god   45 That is, ancient Thebes

Egypt, with their gods and their kings—
Pharaoh and those who trust in him.
26 "And I will deliver them into the hand
of those who seek their lives, into the
hand of Nebuchadnezzar king of Babylon
and the hand of his servants. Afterward
it shall be inhabited as in the days of
old," says the LORD.

God Will Preserve Israel

27"But do not fear, O My servant Jacob,
    And do not be dismayed, O Israel!
    For behold, I will save you from afar,
    And your offspring from the land of
        their captivity;
    Jacob shall return,
        have rest and be at ease;
    No one shall make *him* afraid.
28 Do not fear, O Jacob My servant,"
        says the LORD,
    "For I *am* with you;
    For I will make a complete end
        of all the nations
    To which I have driven you,
    But I will not make a complete end
        of you.
    I will rightly correct you,
    For I will not leave you wholly
        unpunished."

Judgment on Philistia

47 The word of the LORD that came
to Jeremiah the prophet against
the Philistines, before Pharaoh attacked
Gaza.
2   Thus says the LORD:

    "Behold, waters rise out of the north,
    And shall be an overflowing flood;
    They shall overflow the land and all
        that is in it,
    The city and those who dwell within;
    Then the men shall cry,
    And all the inhabitants of the land
        shall wail.
3   At the noise of the stamping hooves
        of his strong horses,
    At the rushing of his chariots,
    At the rumbling of his wheels,
    The fathers will not look back
        for *their* children,
    Lacking courage,
4   Because of the day that comes
        to plunder all the Philistines,
    To cut off from Tyre and Sidon
        every helper who remains;
    For the LORD shall plunder the
        Philistines,
    The remnant of the country of
        Caphtor.

5   Baldness has come upon Gaza,
    Ashkelon is cut off
    With the remnant of their valley.
    How long will you cut yourself?

6   "O you sword of the LORD,
    How long until you are quiet?
    Put yourself up into your scabbard,
    Rest and be still!
7   How can it be quiet,
    Seeing the LORD has given it a charge
    Against Ashkelon
        and against the seashore?
    There He has appointed it."

Judgment on Moab

48 Against Moab.
    Thus says the LORD of hosts, the
God of Israel:

    "Woe to Nebo!
    For it is plundered,
    Kirjathaim is shamed *and* taken;
    The high stronghold[46] is shamed
        and dismayed—
2   No more praise of Moab.
    In Heshbon they have devised evil
        against her:
    'Come, and let us cut her off
        as a nation.'
    You also shall be cut down,
        O Madmen![47]
    The sword shall pursue you;
3   A voice of crying *shall be* from
        Horonaim:
    'Plundering and great destruction!'

4   "Moab is destroyed;
    Her little ones have caused a cry
        to be heard;
5   For in the ascent of Luhith
        they ascend with continual weeping;
    For in the descent of Horonaim
        the enemies have heard a cry of
        destruction.

6   "Flee, save your lives!
    And be like the juniper[48] in the
        wilderness.
7   For because you have trusted in your
        works and your treasures,
    You also shall be taken.
    And Chemosh shall go forth into
        captivity,
    His priests and his princes together.
8   And the plunderer shall come against
        every city;
    No one shall escape.
    The valley also shall perish,

46 Hebrew *Misgab*   47 A city of Moab   48 Or *Aroer,* a city of Moab

And the plain shall be destroyed,
As the LORD has spoken.

9 "Give wings to Moab,
That she may flee and get away;
For her cities shall be desolate,
Without any to dwell in them.
10 Cursed *is* he who does
the work of the LORD deceitfully,
And cursed *is* he who keeps back
his sword from blood.

11 "Moab has been at ease from his youth;
He has settled on his dregs,
And has not been emptied from vessel
to vessel,
Nor has he gone into captivity.
Therefore his taste remained in him,
And his scent has not changed.

12 "Therefore behold, the days are
coming," says the LORD,
"That I shall send him wine-workers
Who will tip him over
And empty his vessels
And break the bottles.
13 Moab shall be ashamed of Chemosh,
As the house of Israel was ashamed
of Bethel, their confidence.

14 "How can you say, 'We *are* mighty
And strong men for the war'?
15 Moab is plundered and gone up *from*
her cities;
Her chosen young men have gone
down to the slaughter,"
says the King,
Whose name *is* the LORD of hosts.

16 "The calamity of Moab *is* near at hand,
And his affliction comes quickly.
17 Bemoan him,
all you who are around him;
And all you who know his name,
Say, 'How the strong staff is broken,
The beautiful rod!'

18 "O daughter inhabiting Dibon,
Come down from *your* glory,
And sit in thirst;
For the plunderer of Moab has come
against you,
He has destroyed your strongholds.
19 O inhabitant of Aroer,
Stand by the way and watch;
Ask him who flees
And her who escapes;
Say, 'What has happened?'
20 Moab is shamed,
for he is broken down.

Wail and cry!
Tell it in Arnon,
that Moab is plundered.

21 "And judgment has come
on the plain country:
On Holon and Jahzah and Mephaath,
22 On Dibon and Nebo
and Beth Diblathaim,
23 On Kirjathaim and Beth Gamul
and Beth Meon,
24 On Kerioth and Bozrah,
On all the cities of the land of Moab,
Far or near.
25 The horn of Moab is cut off,
And his arm is broken,"
says the LORD.

26 "Make him drunk,
For he magnified *himself* against the
LORD.
Moab shall wallow in his vomit,
And he shall also be in derision.
27 For was not Israel a derision to you?
Was he found among thieves?
For whenever you speak of him,
You shake *your head in scorn.*
28 You who dwell in Moab,
Leave the cities and dwell in the rock,
And be like the dove *which* makes
her nest
In the sides of the cave's mouth.

29 "We have heard the pride of Moab
(He *is* exceedingly proud),
Of his loftiness and arrogance
and pride,
And of the haughtiness of his heart."

30 "I know his wrath," says the LORD,
"But it *is* not right;
His lies have made nothing right.
31 Therefore I will wail for Moab,
And I will cry out for all Moab;
I will mourn for the men of Kir Heres.
32 O vine of Sibmah! I will weep for you
with the weeping of Jazer.
Your plants have gone over the sea,
They reach to the sea of Jazer.
The plunderer has fallen on your
summer fruit and your vintage.
33 Joy and gladness are taken
From the plentiful field
And from the land of Moab;
I have caused wine to fail from the
winepresses;
No one will tread with joyous
shouting—
Not joyous shouting!

34 "From the cry of Heshbon
     to Elealeh and to Jahaz
They have uttered their voice,
From Zoar to Horonaim,
Like a three-year-old heifer;[49]
For the waters of Nimrim
     also shall be desolate.

35 "Moreover," says the LORD,
"I will cause to cease in Moab
The one who offers *sacrifices* in the
     high places
And burns incense to his gods.
36 Therefore My heart shall wail
     like flutes for Moab,
And like flutes My heart shall wail
For the men of Kir Heres.
Therefore the riches they have acquired
     have perished.

37 "For every head *shall be* bald,
     and every beard clipped;
On all the hands *shall be* cuts,
     and on the loins sackcloth—
38 A general lamentation
On all the housetops of Moab,
And in its streets;
For I have broken Moab like a vessel
     in which *is* no pleasure,"
     says the LORD.
39 "They shall wail:
'How she is broken down!
How Moab has turned her back
     with shame!
So Moab shall be a derision
And a dismay to all those about her.' "

40 For thus says the LORD:

"Behold, one shall fly like an eagle,
And spread his wings over Moab.
41 Kerioth is taken,
And the strongholds are surprised;
The mighty men's hearts in Moab
     on that day shall be
Like the heart of a woman in birth
     pangs.
42 And Moab shall be destroyed as a
     people,
Because he has magnified *himself*
     against the LORD.
43 Fear and the pit and the snare *shall be*
     upon you,
O inhabitant of Moab," says the LORD.
44 "He who flees from the fear
     shall fall into the pit,
And he who gets out of the pit
     shall be caught in the snare.
For upon Moab, upon it I will bring

The year of their punishment,"
     says the LORD.

45 "Those who fled stood under the
     shadow of Heshbon
Because of exhaustion.
But a fire shall come out of Heshbon,
A flame from the midst of Sihon,
And shall devour the brow of Moab,
The crown of the head of the sons
     of tumult.
46 Woe to you, O Moab!
The people of Chemosh perish;
For your sons have been taken captive,
And your daughters captive.

47 "Yet I will bring back the captives
     of Moab
In the latter days," says the LORD.

Thus far *is* the judgment of Moab.

Judgment on Ammon

49 Against the Ammonites.
     Thus says the LORD:

"Has Israel no sons?
Has he no heir?
Why *then* does Milcham[50] inherit Gad,
And his people dwell in its cities?
2 Therefore behold, the days are
     coming," says the LORD,
"That I will cause to be heard
     an alarm of war
In Rabbah of the Ammonites;
It shall be a desolate mound,
And her villages shall be burned
     with fire.
Then Israel shall take possession of his
     inheritance," says the LORD.

3 "Wail, O Heshbon, for Ai is plundered!
Cry, you daughters of Rabbah,
Gird yourselves with sackcloth!
Lament and run to and fro
     by the walls;
For Milcham shall go into captivity
With his priests and his princes
     together.
4 Why do you glory in the valleys,
Your flowing valley,
     O backsliding daughter?
Who trusted in her treasures, *saying*,
'Who will come against me?'
5 Behold, I will bring fear upon you,"
Says the Lord GOD of hosts,
"From all those who are around you;
You shall be driven out,
     everyone headlong,

49 Or *The Third Eglath,* an unknown city (compare Isaiah 15:5)
50 Hebrew *Malcham,* literally *their king,* a god of the Ammonites; also called *Molech* (compare verse 3)

And no one will gather those who
wander off.
6 But afterward I will bring back
The captives of the people of Ammon,"
says the LORD.

Judgment on Edom

7 Against Edom.
Thus says the LORD of hosts:

"*Is* wisdom no more in Teman?
Has counsel perished from the
prudent?
Has their wisdom vanished?
8 Flee, turn back, dwell in the depths,
O inhabitants of Dedan!
For I will bring the calamity of Esau
upon him,
The time *that* I will punish him.
9 If grape-gatherers came to you,
Would they not leave *some* gleaning
grapes?
If thieves by night,
Would they not destroy
until they have enough?
10 But I have made Esau bare;
I have uncovered his secret places,[51]
And he shall not be able to hide
himself.
His descendants are plundered,
His brethren and his neighbors,
And he *is* no more.
11 Leave your fatherless children,
I will preserve *them* alive;
And let your widows trust in Me."

12 For thus says the LORD: "Behold,
those whose judgment *was* not to drink of
the cup have assuredly drunk. And *are*
you the one who will altogether go unpunished? You shall not go unpunished,
but you shall surely drink *of it.*
13 "For I have sworn by Myself," says
the LORD, "that Bozrah shall become a
desolation, a reproach, a waste, and a
curse. And all its cities shall be perpetual
wastes."

14 I have heard a message from the LORD,
And an ambassador has been sent
to the nations:
"Gather together, come against her,
And rise up to battle!

15 "For indeed, I will make you small
among nations,
Despised among men.
16 Your fierceness has deceived you,
The pride of your heart,

O you who dwell in the clefts
of the rock,
Who hold the height of the hill!
Though you make your nest
as high as the eagle,
I will bring you down from there,"
says the LORD.[52]

17 "Edom also shall be an astonishment;
Everyone who goes by it
will be astonished
And will hiss at all its plagues.
18 As in the overthrow of Sodom
and Gomorrah
And their neighboring *cities,*"
says the LORD,
"No one shall abide there,
Nor shall a son of man dwell in it.

19 "Behold, he shall come up like a lion
from the flooding of the Jordan
Against the habitation of the strong;
But I will suddenly make him run
away from her.
And who *is* a chosen *man*
that I may appoint over her?
For who *is* like Me?
Who will arraign Me?
And who *is* that shepherd
Who will withstand Me?"

20 Therefore hear the counsel of the LORD
that He has taken against Edom,
And His purposes that He has
proposed against the inhabitants
of Teman:
Surely the least of the flock shall draw
them out;
Surely He shall make their habitations
desolate with them.
21 The earth shakes at the noise of their
fall;
At the cry its noise is heard at
the Red Sea.
22 Behold, He shall come up
and fly like the eagle,
And spread His wings over Bozrah;
The heart of the mighty men of Edom
in that day shall be
Like the heart of a woman in birth
pangs.

Judgment on Damascus

23 Against Damascus.

"Hamath and Arpad are shamed,
For they have heard bad news.
They are fainthearted;
There is trouble on the sea;
It cannot be quiet.

---

51 Compare Obadiah 5, 6   52 Compare Obadiah 3, 4

24 Damascus has grown feeble
   And turns to flee,
   And fear has seized *her.*
   Anguish and sorrows have taken her
      like a woman in labor.
25 Why is the city of praise not deserted,
      the city of My joy?
26 Therefore her young men shall fall in
      her streets,
   And all the men of war shall be cut off
      in that day," says the LORD of hosts.
27 "I will kindle a fire in the wall of
      Damascus,
   And it shall consume the palaces of
      Ben-Hadad."[53]

Judgment on Kedar and Hazor

28 Against Kedar and against the kingdoms of Hazor, which Nebuchadnezzar
king of Babylon shall strike.
   Thus says the LORD:

   "Arise, go up to Kedar,
   And devastate the men of the East!
29 Their tents and their flocks
      they shall take away.
   They shall take for themselves their
      curtains,
   All their vessels and their camels;
   And they shall cry out to them,
   'Fear *is* on every side!'

30 "Flee, get far away!
   Dwell in the depths,
   O inhabitants of Hazor!"
      says the LORD.
   "For Nebuchadnezzar king of Babylon
      has taken counsel against you,
   And has conceived a plan against you.

31 "Arise, go up to the wealthy nation
      that dwells securely," says the LORD,
   "Which has neither gates nor bars,
   Dwelling alone.
32 Their camels shall be for booty,
   And the multitude of their cattle for
      plunder.
   I will scatter to all winds those in the
      farthest corners,
   And I will bring their calamity from all
      its sides," says the LORD.
33 "Hazor shall be a dwelling for jackals,
      a desolation forever;
   No one shall reside there,
   Nor son of man dwell in it."

Judgment on Elam

34 The word of the LORD that came to
Jeremiah the prophet against Elam, in the

beginning of the reign of Zedekiah king
of Judah, saying,
35 "Thus says the LORD of hosts:

   'Behold, I will break the bow of Elam,
   The foremost of their might.
36 Against Elam I will bring the four
      winds
   From the four quarters of heaven,
   And scatter them toward all those
      winds;
   There shall be no nations where the
      outcasts of Elam will not go.
37 For I will cause Elam to be dismayed
      before their enemies
   And before those who seek their life.
   I will bring disaster upon them,
   My fierce anger,' says the LORD;
   'And I will send the sword after them
   Until I have consumed them.
38 I will set My throne in Elam,
   And will destroy from there the king
      and the princes,' says the LORD.

39 'But it shall come to pass in the latter
      days:
   I will bring back the captives of Elam,'
      says the LORD."

Judgment on Babylon and Babylonia

50 The word that the LORD spoke
against Babylon *and* against the
land of the Chaldeans by Jeremiah the
prophet.
2 "Declare among the nations,
   Proclaim, and set up a standard;
   Proclaim, *and* do not conceal *it—*
   Say, 'Babylon is taken, Bel is shamed.
   Merodach[54] is broken in pieces;
   Her idols are humiliated,
   Her images are broken in pieces.'
3 For out of the north a nation comes up
      against her,
   Which shall make her land desolate,
   And no one shall dwell therein.
   They shall move, they shall depart,
   Both man and beast.

4 "In those days and in that time,"
      says the LORD,
   "The children of Israel shall come,
   They and the children of Judah
      together;
   With continual weeping they shall
      come,
   And seek the LORD their God.
5 They shall ask the way to Zion,
   With their faces toward it, *saying,*
   'Come and let us join ourselves
      to the LORD

53 Compare Amos 1:4   54 A Babylonian god; sometimes spelled *Marduk*

In a perpetual covenant
That will not be forgotten.'

6 "My people have been lost sheep.
Their shepherds have led them astray;
They have turned them away *on the*
mountains.
They have gone from mountain to hill;
They have forgotten their resting place.
7 All who found them have devoured
them;
And their adversaries said,
'We have not offended,
Because they have sinned against the
LORD, the habitation of justice,
The LORD, the hope of their fathers.'

8 "Move from the midst of Babylon,
Go out of the land of the Chaldeans;
And be like the rams before the flocks.
9 For behold, I will raise and cause to
come up against Babylon
An assembly of great nations
from the north country,
And they shall array themselves
against her;
From there she shall be captured.
Their arrows *shall be* like *those* of an
expert warrior;
None shall return in vain.
10 And Chaldea shall become plunder;
All who plunder her shall be satisfied,"
says the LORD.

11 "Because you were glad,
because you rejoiced,
You destroyers of My heritage,
Because you have grown fat
like a heifer threshing grain,
And you bellow like bulls,
12 Your mother shall be deeply ashamed;
She who bore you shall be ashamed.
Behold, the least of the nations
shall be a wilderness,
A dry land and a desert.
13 Because of the wrath of the LORD
She shall not be inhabited,
But she shall be wholly desolate.
Everyone who goes by Babylon
shall be horrified
And hiss at all her plagues.

14 "Put yourselves in array
against Babylon all around,
All you who bend the bow;
Shoot at her, spare no arrows,
For she has sinned against the LORD.
15 Shout against her all around;
She has given her hand,
Her foundations have fallen,

Her walls are thrown down;
For it *is* the vengeance of the LORD.
Take vengeance on her.
As she has done, so do to her.
16 Cut off the sower from Babylon,
And him who handles the sickle at
harvest time.
For fear of the oppressing sword
Everyone shall turn to his own people,
And everyone shall flee to his own
land.

17 "Israel *is* like scattered sheep;
The lions have driven *him* away.
First the king of Assyria devoured him;
Now at last this Nebuchadnezzar king
of Babylon has broken his bones."

18 Therefore thus says the LORD of
hosts, the God of Israel:

"Behold, I will punish the king of
Babylon and his land,
As I have punished the king of Assyria.
19 But I will bring back Israel to his
habitation,
And he shall feed on Carmel and
Bashan;
His soul shall be satisfied on Mount
Ephraim and Gilead.
20 In those days and in that time,"
says the LORD,
"The iniquity of Israel shall be sought,
but *there shall be* none;
And the sins of Judah,
but they shall not be found;
For I will pardon those whom I
preserve.

21 "Go up against the land of Merathaim,
against it,
And against the inhabitants of Pekod.
Waste and utterly destroy them,"
says the LORD,
"And do according to all that I have
commanded you.
22 A sound of battle *is* in the land,
And of great destruction.
23 How the hammer of the whole earth
has been cut apart and broken!
How Babylon has become
a desolation among the nations!
I have laid a snare for you;
24 You have indeed been trapped,
O Babylon,
And you were not aware;
You have been found and also caught,
Because you have contended against
the Lord.

25 The LORD has opened His armory,
And has brought out the weapons of
His indignation;
For this *is* the work of the Lord God
of hosts
In the land of the Chaldeans.
26 Come against her from the farthest
border;
Open her storehouses;
Cast her up as heaps of ruins,
And destroy her utterly;
Let nothing of her be left.
27 Slay all her bulls,
Let them go down to the slaughter.
Woe to them!
For their day has come,
the time of their punishment.
28 The voice of those who flee
and escape from the land of Babylon
Declares in Zion the vengeance of the
LORD our God,
The vengeance of His temple.

29"Call together the archers against
Babylon.
All you who bend the bow,
encamp against it all around;
Let none of them escape.
Repay her according to her work;
According to all she has done,
do to her;
For she has been proud against the
LORD,
Against the Holy One of Israel.
30 Therefore her young men shall fall in
the streets,
And all her men of war shall be cut off
in that day," says the LORD.
31 "Behold, I *am* against you,
O you most proud!"
says the Lord GOD of hosts;
"For your day has come,
The time *that* I will punish you.
32 The most proud shall stumble and fall,
And no one will raise him up;
I will kindle a fire in his cities,
And it will devour all around him."

33 Thus says the LORD of hosts:

"The children of Israel *were* oppressed,
Along with the children of Judah;
All who took them captive have held
them fast;
They have refused to let them go.
34 Their Redeemer *is* strong;
The LORD of hosts *is* His name.
He will thoroughly plead their case,
That He may give rest to the land,
And disquiet the inhabitants of
Babylon.

35"A sword *is* against the Chaldeans,"
says the LORD,
"Against the inhabitants of Babylon,
And against her princes
and her wise men.
36 A sword *is* against the soothsayers,
and they will be fools.
A sword *is* against her mighty men,
and they will be dismayed.
37 A sword *is* against their horses,
Against their chariots,
And against all the mixed peoples who
are in her midst;
And they will become like women.
A sword *is* against her treasures,
and they will be robbed.
38 A drought *is* against her waters,
and they will be dried up.
For it *is* the land of carved images,
And they are insane with *their* idols.

39 "Therefore the wild desert beasts
shall dwell *there* with the jackals,
And the ostriches shall dwell in it.
It shall be inhabited no more forever,
Nor shall it be dwelt in from
generation to generation.
40 As God overthrew Sodom
and Gomorrah
And their neighboring *cities*,"
says the LORD,
"*So* no one shall reside there,
Nor son of man dwell in it.

41"Behold, a people shall come from
the north,
And a great nation and many kings
Shall be raised up from the ends
of the earth.
42 They shall hold the bow and the lance;
They *are* cruel
and shall not show mercy.
Their voice shall roar like the sea;
They shall ride on horses,
Set in array, like a man for the battle,
Against you, O daughter of Babylon.

43 "The king of Babylon has heard
the report about them,
And his hands grow feeble;
Anguish has taken hold of him,
Pangs as of a woman in childbirth.

44 "Behold, he shall come up like a lion
from the flooding of the Jordan
Against the habitation of the strong;
But I will make them suddenly run
away from her.
And who *is* a chosen *man*
that I may appoint over her?

For who *is* like Me?
Who will arraign Me?
And who *is* that shepherd
Who will withstand Me?"

45 Therefore hear the counsel of the LORD
that He has taken against Babylon,
And His purposes that He has
proposed against the land
of the Chaldeans:
Surely the least of the flock shall draw
them out;
Surely He will make their habitation
desolate with them.
46 At the noise of the taking of Babylon
The earth trembles,
And the cry is heard among the
nations.

The Utter Destruction of Babylon

51

Thus says the LORD:

"Behold, I will raise up against Babylon,
Against those who dwell in Leb
Kamai,[55]
A destroying wind.
2 And I will send winnowers to Babylon,
Who shall winnow her
and empty her land.
For in the day of doom
They shall be against her all around.
3 Against *her* let the archer bend his
bow,
And lift himself up against *her* in his
armor.
Do not spare her young men;
Utterly destroy all her army.
4 Thus the slain shall fall
in the land of the Chaldeans,
And *those* thrust through in her streets.
5 For Israel is not forsaken, nor Judah,
By his God, the LORD of hosts,
Though their land was filled with sin
against the Holy One of Israel."

6 Flee from the midst of Babylon,
And every one save his life!
Do not be cut off in her iniquity,
For this *is* the time of the LORD's
vengeance;
He shall recompense her.
7 Babylon *was* a golden cup in the
LORD's hand,
That made all the earth drunk.
The nations drank her wine;
Therefore the nations are deranged.
8 Babylon has suddenly fallen
and been destroyed.
Wail for her!

Take balm for her pain;
Perhaps she may be healed.
9 We would have healed Babylon,
But she is not healed.
Forsake her, and let us go
everyone to his own country;
For her judgment reaches to heaven
and is lifted up to the skies.
10 The LORD has revealed our
righteousness.
Come and let us declare in Zion
the work of the LORD our God.

11 Make the arrows bright!
Gather the shields!
The LORD has raised up the spirit
of the kings of the Medes.
For His plan *is* against Babylon to
destroy it,
Because it *is* the vengeance of the
LORD,
The vengeance for His temple.
12 Set up the standard on the walls
of Babylon;
Make the guard strong,
Set up the watchmen,
Prepare the ambushes.
For the LORD has both devised
and done
What He spoke against the inhabitants
of Babylon.
13 O you who dwell by many waters,
Abundant in treasures,
Your end has come,
The measure of your covetousness.
14 The LORD of hosts has sworn by
Himself:
"Surely I will fill you with men,
as with locusts,
And they shall lift up a shout
against you."

15 He has made the earth by His power;
He has established the world
by His wisdom,
And stretched out the heaven
by His understanding.
16 When He utters *His* voice—
There is a multitude of waters in the
heavens:
"He causes the vapors to ascend from
the ends of the earth;
He makes lightnings for the rain;
He brings the wind out of His
treasuries."[56]

17 Everyone is dull-hearted,
without knowledge;

---

55 Code word for *Chaldea* (Babylonia); may be translated *The Midst of Those Who Rise Up Against Me*
56 Compare Psalm 135:7

Every metalsmith is put to shame by
   the carved image;
For his molded image *is* falsehood,
   And *there is* no breath in them.
18 They *are* futile, a work of errors;
   In the time of their punishment
   they shall perish.
19 The Portion of Jacob *is* not like them,
   For He *is* the Maker of all things;
   And *Israel is* the tribe of His
   inheritance.
The LORD of hosts *is* His name.

20"You *are* My battle-ax
   and weapons of war:
For with you I will break the nation in
   pieces;
With you I will destroy kingdoms;
21 With you I will break in pieces
   the horse and its rider;
With you I will break in pieces
   the chariot and its rider;
22 With you also I will break in pieces
   man and woman;
With you I will break in pieces
   old and young;
With you I will break in pieces
   the young man and the maiden;
23 With you also I will break in pieces
   the shepherd and his flock;
With you I will break in pieces
   the farmer and his yoke of oxen;
And with you I will break in pieces
   governors and rulers.

24"And I will repay Babylon
And all the inhabitants of Chaldea
For all the evil they have done
In Zion in your sight," says the LORD.

25 "Behold, I *am* against you,
   O destroying mountain,
Who destroys all the earth,"
   says the LORD.
"And I will stretch out My hand
   against you,
Roll you down from the rocks,
And make you a burnt mountain.
26 They shall not take from you a stone
   for a corner
Nor a stone for a foundation,
But you shall be desolate forever,"
   says the LORD.

27 Set up a banner in the land,
Blow the trumpet among the nations!
Prepare the nations against her,
Call the kingdoms together against her:
   Ararat, Minni, and Ashchenaz.
Appoint a marshal against her;

Cause the horses to come up like the
   bristling locusts.
28 Prepare against her the nations,
   With the kings of the Medes,
Its governors and all its rulers,
All the land of his dominion.
29 And the land will tremble and sorrow;
For every purpose of the LORD
   shall be performed against Babylon,
To make the land of Babylon
   a desolation without inhabitant.
30 The mighty men of Babylon have
   ceased fighting,
They have remained in their
   strongholds;
Their might has failed,
They became *like* women;
They have burned her dwelling places,
The bars of her *gate* are broken.
31 One runner will run to meet another,
And one messenger to meet another,
To show the king of Babylon
   that his city is taken on *all* sides;
32 The passages are blocked,
The reeds they have burned with fire,
And the men of war are terrified.

33 For thus says the LORD of hosts, the
God of Israel:

"The daughter of Babylon
   is like a threshing floor
When it is time to thresh her;
Yet a little while
And the time of her harvest
   will come."

34"Nebuchadnezzar the king of Babylon
Has devoured me, he has crushed me;
He has made me an empty vessel,
He has swallowed me up like a
   monster;
He has filled his stomach with my
   delicacies,
He has spit me out.
35 Let the violence *done* to me and my
   flesh *be* upon Babylon,"
The inhabitant of Zion will say;
"And my blood be upon the inhabitants
   of Chaldea!"
Jerusalem will say.

36 Therefore thus says the LORD:

"Behold, I will plead your case
   and take vengeance for you.
I will dry up her sea
   and make her springs dry.
37 Babylon shall become a heap,
A dwelling place for jackals,

An astonishment and a hissing,
Without an inhabitant.
38 They shall roar together like lions,
They shall growl like lions' whelps.
39 In their excitement
I will prepare their feasts;
I will make them drunk,
That they may rejoice,
And sleep a perpetual sleep
And not awake," says the LORD.
40 I will bring them down
Like lambs to the slaughter,
Like rams with male goats.

41 "Oh, how Sheshach[57] is taken!
Oh, how the praise of the whole earth
is seized!
How Babylon has become
desolate among the nations!
42 The sea has come up over Babylon;
She is covered with the multitude
of its waves.
43 Her cities are a desolation,
A dry land and a wilderness,
A land where no one dwells,
Through which no son of man passes.
44 I will punish Bel in Babylon,
And I will bring out of his mouth
what he has swallowed;
And the nations shall not stream
to him anymore.
Yes, the wall of Babylon shall fall.

45 "My people, go out of the midst of her!
And let everyone deliver himself
from the fierce anger of the LORD.
46 And lest your heart faint,
And you fear for the rumor
that will be heard in the land
(A rumor will come one year,
And after that, in another year
A rumor will come,
And violence in the land,
Ruler against ruler),
47 Therefore behold, the days are coming
That I will bring judgment on the
carved images of Babylon;
Her whole land shall be ashamed,
And all her slain shall fall in her midst.
48 Then the heavens and the earth
and all that is in them
Shall sing joyously over Babylon;
For the plunderers shall come to her
from the north," says the LORD.

49 As Babylon has caused the slain of
Israel to fall,
So at Babylon the slain of all the earth
shall fall.

50 You who have escaped the sword,
Get away! Do not stand still!
Remember the LORD afar off,
And let Jerusalem come to your mind.

51 We are ashamed because we have
heard reproach.
Shame has covered our faces,
For strangers have come into the
sanctuaries of the LORD's house.

52 "Therefore behold, the days are
coming," says the LORD,
"That I will bring judgment on her
carved images,
And throughout all her land the
wounded shall groan.
53 Though Babylon were to mount up to
heaven,
And though she were to fortify the
height of her strength,
Yet from Me plunderers would come
to her," says the LORD.

54 The sound of a cry
comes from Babylon,
And great destruction
from the land of the Chaldeans,
55 Because the LORD is plundering
Babylon
And silencing her loud voice,
Though her waves roar like great
waters,
And the noise of their voice is uttered,
56 Because the plunderer comes against
her, against Babylon,
And her mighty men are taken.
Every one of their bows is broken;
For the LORD is the God of
recompense,
He will surely repay.

57 "And I will make drunk
Her princes and wise men,
Her governors, her deputies,
and her mighty men.
And they shall sleep a perpetual sleep
And not awake," says the King,
Whose name is the LORD of hosts.

58 Thus says the LORD of hosts:

"The broad walls of Babylon
shall be utterly broken,
And her high gates
shall be burned with fire;
The people will labor in vain,
And the nations, because of the fire;
And they shall be weary."

57 A code word for Babylon (compare Jeremiah 25:26)

Jeremiah's Command to Seraiah

59 The word which Jeremiah the prophet commanded Seraiah the son of Neriah, the son of Mahseiah, when he went with Zedekiah the king of Judah to Babylon in the fourth year of his reign. And Seraiah *was* the quartermaster.
60 So Jeremiah wrote in a book all the evil that would come upon Babylon, all these words that are written against Babylon.
61 And Jeremiah said to Seraiah, "When you arrive in Babylon and see it, and read all these words,
62 "then you shall say, 'O LORD, You have spoken against this place to cut it off, so that none shall remain in it, neither man nor beast, but it shall be desolate forever.'
63 "Now it shall be, when you have finished reading this book, *that* you shall tie a stone to it and throw it out into the Euphrates.
64 "Then you shall say, 'Thus Babylon shall sink and not rise from the catastrophe that I will bring upon her. And they shall be weary.'" Thus far *are* the words of Jeremiah.

The Fall of Jerusalem Reviewed

52 Zedekiah *was* twenty-one years old when he became king, and he reigned eleven years in Jerusalem. His mother's name *was* Hamutal the daughter of Jeremiah of Libnah.
2 He also did evil in the sight of the LORD, according to all that Jehoiakim had done.
3 For because of the anger of the LORD *this* happened in Jerusalem and Judah, till He finally cast them out from His presence. Then Zedekiah rebelled against the king of Babylon.
4 Now it came to pass in the ninth year of his reign, in the tenth month, on the tenth *day* of the month, *that* Nebuchadnezzar king of Babylon and all his army came against Jerusalem and encamped against it; and *they* built a siege wall against it all around.
5 So the city was besieged until the eleventh year of King Zedekiah.
6 By the fourth month, on the ninth day of the month, the famine had become so severe in the city that there was no food for the people of the land.
7 Then the city wall was broken through, and all the men of war fled and went out of the city at night by way of the gate between the two walls, which *was* by the king's garden, even though the Chaldeans *were* near the city all around. And they went by way of the plain.[58]
8 But the army of the Chaldeans pursued the king, and they overtook Zedekiah in the plains of Jericho. All his army was scattered from him.
9 So they took the king and brought him up to the king of Babylon at Riblah in the land of Hamath, and he pronounced judgment on him.
10 Then the king of Babylon killed the sons of Zedekiah before his eyes. And he killed all the princes of Judah in Riblah.
11 He also put out the eyes of Zedekiah; and the king of Babylon bound him in bronze fetters, took him to Babylon, and put him in prison till the day of his death.

The Temple and City Plundered and Burned

12 Now in the fifth month, on the tenth *day* of the month (which *was* the nineteenth year of King Nebuchadnezzar king of Babylon), Nebuzaradan, the captain of the guard, *who* served the king of Babylon, came to Jerusalem.
13 He burned the house of the LORD and the king's house; all the houses of Jerusalem, that is, all the houses of the great *men*, he burned with fire.
14 And all the army of the Chaldeans who *were* with the captain of the guard broke down all the walls of Jerusalem all around.
15 Then Nebuzaradan the captain of the guard carried away captive *some* of the poor people, the rest of the people who remained in the city, the defectors who had deserted to the king of Babylon, and the rest of the craftsmen.
16 But Nebuzaradan the captain of the guard left *some* of the poor of the land as vinedressers and farmers.
17 The bronze pillars that *were* in the house of the LORD, and the carts and the bronze Sea that *were* in the house of the LORD, the Chaldeans broke in pieces, and carried all their bronze to Babylon.
18 They also took away the pots, the shovels, the trimmers, the bowls, the spoons, and all the bronze utensils with which the priests ministered.
19 The basins, the firepans, the bowls, the pots, the lampstands, the spoons, and

58 Or *the arabah,* that is, the Jordan Valley

the cups, whatever *was* of solid gold and whatever *was* of solid silver, the captain of the guard took away.

20 The two pillars, one Sea, the twelve bronze bulls which *were* under *it, and* the carts, which King Solomon had made for the house of the LORD—the bronze of all these articles was beyond measure.

21 Now *concerning* the pillars: the height of one pillar *was* eighteen cubits, a measuring line of twelve cubits could measure its circumference, and its thickness *was* four fingers; *it was* hollow.

22 A capital of bronze *was* on it; and the height of one capital *was* five cubits, with a network and pomegranates all around the capital, all of bronze. The second pillar, with pomegranates, was the same.

23 There were ninety-six pomegranates on the sides; all the pomegranates, all around on the network, *were* one hundred.

The People Exiled to Babylonia

24 The captain of the guard took Seraiah the chief priest, Zephaniah the second priest, and the three doorkeepers.

25 He also took out of the city an officer who had charge of the men of war, seven men of the king's close associates who were found in the city, the principal scribe of the army who mustered the people of the land, and sixty men of the people of the land who were found in the midst of the city.

26 And Nebuzaradan the captain of the guard took these and brought them to the king of Babylon at Riblah.

27 Then the king of Babylon struck them and put them to death at Riblah in the land of Hamath. Thus Judah was carried away captive from its own land.

28 These *are* the people whom Nebuchadnezzar carried away captive: in the seventh year, three thousand and twenty-three Jews;

29 in the eighteenth year of Nebuchadnezzar he carried away captive from Jerusalem eight hundred and thirty-two persons;

30 in the twenty-third year of Nebuchadnezzar, Nebuzaradan the captain of the guard carried away captive of the Jews seven hundred and forty-five persons. All the persons *were* four thousand six hundred.

Jehoiachin Released from Prison

31 Now it came to pass in the thirty-seventh year of the captivity of Jehoiachin king of Judah, in the twelfth month, on the twenty-fifth *day* of the month, *that* Evil-Merodach[59] king of Babylon, in the first *year* of his reign, lifted up the head of Jehoiachin king of Judah and brought him out of prison.

32 And he spoke kindly to him and gave him a more prominent seat than those of the kings who *were* with him in Babylon.

33 So Jehoiachin changed from his prison garments, and he ate bread regularly before the king all the days of his life.

34 And as for his provisions, there was a regular ration given him by the king of Babylon, a portion for each day until the day of his death, all the days of his life.

59 Or *Awil-Marduk*

Introduction to Lamentations

What happens when after a lifetime of work, a project falls through and failure is the final result? Lamentations deals with this profound question.

The prophet Jeremiah, had spent his entire life mourning, praying, and encouraging his people to turn to God. Jeremiah admonished the nation of Judah not to align with and depend upon the mighty nations of Egypt and Babylon. He implored them to put aside pagan practices which they had adopted from these foreign nations, and return to pure worship of the true God.

The nation, however, failed to heed Jeremiah's call to repentance. Now, with Jerusalem destroyed by Nebuchadnezzar in 586 B.C., Jeremiah sat among the ashes bemoaning his cherished city. His people had been carried off to captivity, Judah's finest soldiers lay slain on the heights surrounding the city, and the buildings had been burned and reduced to a heap of rubble.

Amidst the outpouring of his poetic lamentations, Jeremiah was able to look to the all-powerful, loving, merciful God.

> *Through* the LORD'S mercies we are not consumed,
> Because His compassions fail not.
> *They are* new every morning;
> Great *is* Your faithfulness.
> "The LORD *is* my portion," says my soul,
> "Therefore I hope in Him!"

> (Lam. 3:22–24)

In the toughest times Jeremiah ever faced, he turned to God with praise, trust, and hope. Trying times are times to triumph! Regardless of the situation, Jeremiah could still praise God. Amidst the affliction, Jeremiah worshiped God.

> For the Lord will not cast off forever.
> Though He causes grief,
> Yet He will show compassion
> According to the multitude of His mercies.

> (Lam. 3:31, 32)

The Book of

Lamentations

Jerusalem in Affliction

HOW lonely sits the city
 That was full of people!
 How like a widow is she,
Who *was* great among the nations!
The princess among the provinces
Has become a slave!

2 She weeps bitterly in the night,
 Her tears *are* on her cheeks;
 Among all her lovers
 She has none to comfort *her*.
 All her friends have dealt treacherously
 with her;
 They have become her enemies.

3 Judah has gone into captivity,
 Under affliction and hard servitude;
 She dwells among the nations,
 She finds no rest;
 All her persecutors overtake her
 in dire straits.

4 The roads to Zion mourn
 Because no one comes to the set feasts.
 All her gates are desolate;
 Her priests sigh,
 Her virgins are afflicted,
 And she *is* in bitterness.

5 Her adversaries have become
 the master,
 Her enemies prosper;
 For the LORD has afflicted her
 Because of the multitude of her
 transgressions.
 Her children have gone into captivity
 before the enemy.

6 And from the daughter of Zion
 All her splendor has departed.
 Her princes have become like deer
 That find no pasture,
 That flee without strength
 Before the pursuer.

7 In the days of her affliction and
 roaming,
 Jerusalem remembers all her pleasant
 things
 That she had in the days of old.

When her people fell into the hand
 of the enemy,
With no one to help her,
The adversaries saw her
 And mocked at her downfall.[1]

8 Jerusalem has sinned grievously,
 Therefore she has become vile.[2]
 All who honored her despise her
 Because they have seen her nakedness;
 Yes, she sighs and turns away.

9 Her uncleanness *is* in her skirts;
 She did not consider her destiny;
 Therefore her collapse was awesome;
 She had no comforter.
 "O LORD, behold my affliction,
 For *the* enemy has magnified *himself!*"

10 The adversary has spread his hand
 Over all her pleasant things;
 For she has seen the nations enter
 her sanctuary,
 Those whom You commanded
 Not to enter Your congregation.

11 All her people sigh,
 They seek bread;
 They have given their valuables for
 food to restore life.
 "See, O LORD, and consider,
 For I am scorned."

12 "Is it nothing to you,
 all you who pass by?
 Behold and see
 If there is any sorrow like my sorrow,
 Which has been brought on me,
 Which the LORD has inflicted *on me*
 In the day of His fierce anger.

13 "From above He has sent fire
 into my bones,
 And it overpowered them;
 He has spread a net for my feet
 And turned me back;
 He has made me desolate
 And faint all the day.

14 "The yoke of my transgressions
 was bound;
 They were woven together
 by His hands,

1 Vulgate reads *her Sabbaths*.   2 Septuagint and Vulgate read *moved* or *removed*.

And thrust upon my neck.
He made my strength fail;
The Lord delivered me into the hands
 of *those whom* I am not able to
 withstand.

15 "The Lord has trampled underfoot
 all my mighty *men* in my midst;
He has called an assembly against me
To crush my young men;
The Lord trampled *as* in a winepress
The virgin daughter of Judah.

16 "For these *things* I weep;
My eye, my eye overflows with water;
Because the comforter, who should
 restore my life,
Is far from me.
My children are desolate
Because the enemy prevailed."

17 Zion spreads out her hands,
But there is no one to comfort her;
The LORD has commanded
 concerning Jacob
That those around him *become* his
 adversaries;
Jerusalem has become an unclean thing
 among them.

18 "The LORD is righteous,
For I rebelled against His
 commandment.
Hear now, all peoples,
And behold my sorrow;
My virgins and my young men
Have gone into captivity.

19 "I called for my lovers,
But they deceived me;
My priests and my elders
Breathed their last in the city,
While they sought food
To restore their life.

20 "See, O LORD, that I *am* in distress;
My soul is troubled;
My heart is overturned within me,
For I have been very rebellious.
Outside the sword bereaves,
At home *it is* like death.

21 "They have heard that I sigh,
With no one to comfort me.
All my enemies have heard of my
 trouble;
They are glad that You have done *it*.
Bring on the day *that* You have
 announced,
That they may become like me.

22 "Let all their wickedness come
 before You,
And do to them as You have done to
 me
For all my transgressions;
For my sighs *are* many,
And my heart *is* faint."

God's Anger with Jerusalem

2 How the Lord has covered the
 daughter of Zion
With a cloud in His anger!
He cast down from heaven to the earth
The beauty of Israel,
And did not remember His footstool
In the day of His anger.

2 The Lord has swallowed up
 and has not pitied
All the habitations of Jacob.
He has thrown down in His wrath
The strongholds of the daughter of
 Judah;
He has brought *them* down to the
 ground;
He has profaned the kingdom
 and its princes.

3 He has cut off in fierce anger
Every horn of Israel;
He has drawn back His right hand
From before the enemy.
He has blazed against Jacob
 like a flaming fire
Which devours all around.

4 Standing like an enemy,
 He has bent His bow;
With His right hand, like an adversary,
He has slain all *who were* pleasing
 to His eye;
On the tent of the daughter of Zion,
He has poured out His fury like fire.

5 The Lord was like an enemy.
He has swallowed up Israel,
He has swallowed up all her palaces;
He has destroyed her strongholds,
And has increased mourning and
 lamentation
In the daughter of Judah.

6 He has done violence
 to His tabernacle,
As if it were a garden;
He has destroyed His place
 of assembly;
The LORD has caused
The appointed feasts and Sabbaths
 to be forgotten in Zion.

In His burning indignation He has
spurned the king and the priest.

7 The Lord has spurned His altar,
He has abandoned His sanctuary;
He has given up the walls of her
palaces
Into the hand of the enemy.
They have made a noise in the house
of the LORD
As on the day of a set feast.

8 The LORD has purposed to destroy
The wall of the daughter of Zion.
He has stretched out a line;
He has not withdrawn His hand
from destroying;
Therefore He has caused the rampart
and wall to lament;
They languished together.

9 Her gates have sunk into the ground;
He has destroyed and broken her bars.
Her king and her princes are among
the nations;
The Law is no more,
And her prophets find no vision
from the LORD.

10 The elders of the daughter of Zion
Sit on the ground and keep silence;
They throw dust on their heads
And gird themselves with sackcloth.
The virgins of Jerusalem
Bow their heads to the ground.

11 My eyes fail with tears,
My heart is troubled;
My bile is poured on the ground
Because of the destruction of the
daughter of my people,
Because the children and the infants
Faint in the streets of the city.

12 They say to their mothers,
"Where is grain and wine?"
As they swoon like the wounded
In the streets of the city,
As their life is poured out
In their mothers' bosom.

13 How shall I console you?
To what shall I liken you,
O daughter of Jerusalem?
What shall I compare with you,
that I may comfort you,
O virgin daughter of Zion?
For your ruin is spread wide
as the sea;
Who can heal you?

14 Your prophets have seen for you
False and deceptive visions;
They have not uncovered your iniquity,
To bring back your captives,
But have envisioned for you
false prophecies and delusions.

15 All who pass by clap their hands at
you;
They hiss and shake their heads
At the daughter of Jerusalem:
"Is this the city that is called
'The perfection of beauty,
The joy of the whole earth'?"

16 All your enemies have opened their
mouth against you;
They hiss and gnash their teeth.
They say, "We have swallowed her up!
Surely this is the day we have
waited for;
We have found it, we have seen it."

17 The LORD has done what He
purposed;
He has fulfilled His word
Which He commanded in days of old.
He has thrown down
and has not pitied,
And He has caused your enemy to
rejoice over you;
He has exalted the horn of your
adversaries.

18 Their heart cried out to the Lord,
"O wall of the daughter of Zion,
Let tears run down like a river
day and night;
Give yourself no relief;
Give your eyes no rest.

19 "Arise, cry out in the night,
At the beginning of the watches;
Pour out your heart like water
before the face of the Lord.
Lift your hands toward Him
For the life of your young children,
Who faint from hunger
at the head of every street."

20 "See, O LORD, and consider!
To whom have You done this?
Should the women eat their offspring,
The children they have cuddled?³
Should the priest and prophet be slain
In the sanctuary of the Lord?

21 "Young and old lie
On the ground in the streets;
My virgins and my young men

3 Vulgate reads a span long.

Have fallen by the sword;
You have slain *them* in the day of
  Your anger,
You have slaughtered *and* not pitied.

22 "You have invited as to a feast day
The terrors that surround me.
In the day of the LORD's anger
There was no refugee or survivor.
Those whom I have borne
  and brought up
My enemies have destroyed."

The Prophet's Anguish and Hope

3 I *am* the man *who* has seen affliction
  by the rod of His wrath.
2 He has led me and made *me* walk
In darkness and not *in* light.
3 Surely He has turned His hand
  against me
Time and time again
  throughout the day.

4 He has aged my flesh and my skin,
And broken my bones.
5 He has besieged me
And surrounded *me* with bitterness
  and woe.
6 He has set me in dark places
Like the dead of long ago.

7 He has hedged me in so that
  I cannot get out;
He has made my chain heavy.
8 Even when I cry and shout,
He shuts out my prayer.
9 He has blocked my ways
  with hewn stone;
He has made my paths crooked.

10 He *has been* to me *like* a bear
  lying in wait,
Like a lion in ambush.
11 He has turned aside my ways
  and torn me in pieces;
He has made me desolate.
12 He has bent His bow
And set me up as a target
  for the arrow.

13 He has caused the arrows of His quiver
To pierce my loins.[4]
14 I have become the ridicule of all
  my people,
And their taunting song all the day.
15 He has filled me with bitterness,
He has made me drink wormwood.
16 He has also broken my teeth with
  gravel,
And covered me with ashes.

17 You have moved my soul far from
  peace;
I have forgotten prosperity.
18 And I said, "My strength and my hope
Have perished from the LORD."

19 Remember my affliction and roaming,
The wormwood and the gall.
20 My soul still remembers ·
And sinks within me.
21 This I recall to my mind,
Therefore I have hope.

22 *Through* the LORD's mercies
    we are not consumed,
  Because His compassions fail not.
23 *They are* new every morning;
  Great *is* Your faithfulness.
24 "The LORD *is* my portion,"
    says my soul,
  "Therefore I hope in Him!"

25 The LORD *is* good to those
    who wait for Him,
  To the soul *who* seeks Him.
26 *It is* good that *one* should hope
    and wait quietly
  For the salvation of the LORD.
27 *It is* good for a man to bear
  The yoke in his youth.

28 Let him sit alone and keep silent,
Because God[5] has laid *it* on him;
29 Let him put his mouth in the dust—
There may yet be hope.
30 Let him give *his* cheek to the one
  who strikes him,
And be full of reproach.

31 For the Lord will not cast off forever.
32 Though He causes grief,
Yet He will show compassion
According to the multitude of His
  mercies.
33 For He does not afflict willingly,
Nor grieve the children of men.

34 To crush under His feet
All the prisoners of the earth,
35 To turn aside the justice *due* a man
Before the face of the Most High,
36 Or subvert a man in his cause—
The Lord does not approve.

37 Who *is* he *who* speaks
    and it comes to pass,
  When the Lord has not commanded *it*?
38 *Is* it not from the mouth of the
    Most High
  That woe and well-being proceed?

4 Literally *kidneys*   5 Literally *He*

39 Why should a living man complain,
   A man for the punishment of his sins?

40 Let us search out and examine our
   ways,
   And turn back to the LORD;
41 Let us lift our hearts and hands
   To God in heaven.
42 We have transgressed and rebelled;
   You have not pardoned.

43 You have covered *Yourself* with anger
   And pursued us;
   You have slain *and* not pitied.
44 You have covered Yourself with
   a cloud,
   That prayer should not pass through.
45 You have made us an offscouring
   and refuse
   In the midst of the peoples.

46 All our enemies
   Have opened their mouths against us.
47 Fear and a snare have come upon us,
   Desolation and destruction.
48 My eyes overflow with rivers of water
   For the destruction of the daughter of
   my people.

49 My eyes flow and do not cease,
   Without interruption,
50 Till the LORD from heaven
   Looks down and sees.
51 My eyes bring suffering to my soul
   Because of all the daughters of my city.

52 My enemies without cause
   Hunted me down like a bird.
53 They silenced[6] my life in the pit
   And threw stones at me.
54 The waters flowed over my head;
   I said, "I am cut off!"

55 I called on Your name, O LORD,
   From the lowest pit.
56 You have heard my voice:
   "Do not hide Your ear
   From my sighing,
   from my cry for help."
57 You drew near on the day
   I called on You,
   And said, "Do not fear!"

58 O Lord, You have pleaded
   the case for my soul;
   You have redeemed my life.
59 O LORD, You have seen *how*
   I am wronged;
   Judge my case.

60 You have seen all their vengeance,
   All their schemes against me.
61 You have heard their reproach,
   O LORD,
   All their schemes against me,
62 The lips of my enemies
   And their whispering against me
   all the day.
63 Look at their sitting down
   and their rising up;
   I *am* their taunting song.

64 Repay them, O LORD,
   According to the work of their hands.
65 Give them a veiled[7] heart;
   Your curse *be* upon them!
66 In Your anger,
   Pursue and destroy them
   From under the heavens of the LORD.

The Degradation of Zion

4 How the gold has become dim!
   How changed the fine gold!
   The stones of the sanctuary
   are scattered
   At the head of every street.

2 The precious sons of Zion,
   Valuable as fine gold,
   How they are regarded as clay pots,
   The work of the hands of the potter!

3 Even the jackals present their breasts
   To nurse their young;
   But the daughter of my people *has
   become* cruel,
   Like ostriches in the wilderness.

4 The tongue of the infant clings
   To the roof of its mouth for thirst;
   The young children ask for bread,
   But no one breaks *it* for them.

5 Those who ate delicacies
   Are desolate in the streets;
   Those who were brought up in scarlet
   Embrace ash heaps.

6 The punishment of the iniquity
   of the daughter of my people
   Is greater than the punishment
   of the sin of Sodom,
   Which was overthrown in a moment,
   With no hand to help her!

7 Her Nazirites[8] were brighter than snow
   And whiter than milk;

---

6 Septuagint reads *put to death.*   7 A Jewish tradition reads *sorrow of.*   8 Or *nobles*

They were more ruddy in body
    than rubies,
Like sapphire in their appearance.

8   *Now* their appearance is blacker than
    soot;
They go unrecognized in the streets;
Their skin clings to their bones,
It has become as dry as wood.

9   *Those* slain by the sword are better off
Than *those* who die of hunger;
For these pine away,
Stricken *for lack* of the fruits
    of the field.

10 The hands of the compassionate
    women
Have cooked their own children;
They became food for them
In the destruction of the daughter
    of my people.

11 The LORD has fulfilled His fury,
He has poured out His fierce anger.
He kindled a fire in Zion,
And it has devoured its foundations.

12 The kings of the earth,
And all inhabitants of the world,
Would not have believed
That the adversary and the enemy
Could enter the gates of Jerusalem—

13 Because of the sins of her prophets
And the iniquities of her priests,
Who shed in her midst
The blood of the just.

14 They wandered blind in the streets;
They have defiled themselves
    with blood,
So that no one would touch their
    garments.

15 They cried out to them,
"Go away, unclean!
Go away, go away,
Do not touch us!"
When they fled and wandered,
Those among the nations said,
"They shall no longer dwell *here*."

16 The face[9] of the LORD scattered them;
He no longer regards them.
The people[10] do not respect the priests
Nor show favor to the elders.

17 Still our eyes failed us,
Watching vainly for our help;

In our watching we watched
For a nation *that* could not save *us*.

18 They tracked our steps
So that we could not walk
    in our streets.
Our end was near;
Our days were over,
For our end had come.

19 Our pursuers were swifter
Than the eagles of the heavens.
They pursued us on the mountains
And lay in wait for us in the
    wilderness.

20 The breath of our nostrils,
    the anointed of the LORD,
Was caught in their pits,
Of whom we said, "Under his shadow
We shall live among the nations."

21 Rejoice and be glad,
    O daughter of Edom,
You who dwell in the land of Uz!
The cup shall also pass over to you
And you shall become drunk
    and make yourself naked.

22 *The punishment of* your iniquity
    is accomplished,
O daughter of Zion;
He will no longer send you into
    captivity.
He will punish your iniquity,
O daughter of Edom;
He will uncover your sins!

A Prayer for Restoration

5 Remember, O LORD,
    what has come upon us;
Look, and behold our reproach!
2 Our inheritance has been turned over
    to aliens,
And our houses to foreigners.
3 We have become orphans and waifs,
Our mothers *are* like widows.

4 We pay for the water we drink,
And our wood comes at a price.
5 *They* pursue at our heels;[11]
We labor *and* have no rest.
6 We have given our hand *to* the
    Egyptians
And the Assyrians,
    to be satisfied with bread.

7 Our fathers sinned *and are* no more,
But we bear their iniquities.

9 Targum reads *anger.*   10 Literally *they*   11 Literally *necks*

8 Servants rule over us;
There is none to deliver us
from their hand.
9 We get our bread at the risk
of our lives,
Because of the sword in the wilderness.

10 Our skin is hot as an oven,
Because of the fever of famine.
11 They ravished the women in Zion,
The maidens in the cities of Judah.
12 Princes were hung up by their hands,
And elders were not respected.
13 Young men ground at the millstones;
Boys staggered under loads of wood.
14 The elders have ceased gathering at
the gate,
And the young men from their music.

15 The joy of our heart has ceased;
Our dance has turned into mourning.

16 The crown has fallen from our head.
Woe to us, for we have sinned!
17 Because of this our heart is faint;
Because of these things
our eyes grow dim;
18 Because of Mount Zion which is
desolate,
With foxes walking about on it.

19 You, O LORD, remain forever;
Your throne from generation to
generation.
20 Why do You forget us forever,
And forsake us for so long a time?
21 Turn us back to You, O LORD,
and we will be restored;
Renew our days as of old,
22 Unless You have utterly rejected us,
And are very angry with us!

Introduction to Ezekiel

A star is best seen at night. This clearly exemplifies Ezekiel's life and presence among his people in an age of war and uncertainty. During stormy times, he stood alone as a beacon to guide and direct those who were failing.

Ezekiel was not only a prophet who had many God-given visions, but he had personal vision, fortitude, and the ability to look beyond his present-day circumstances.

Known as "the watchman," Ezekiel probably completed this book by 565 B.C. In a series of prophetic messages, Ezekiel devoted his life to warning of the impending judgment coming upon the nation of Judah. Ezekiel's time was an era of desperation. When surrounding nations were rising in conflict with each other, only those with a strong faith in God would be certain to endure. Ezekiel, whose name means "Strengthened by God," continually and confidently served as a shining light in the nation's darkest hour—the destruction of the temple by Nebuchadnezzar in 586 B.C. and the subsequent Babylonian captivity. During their captivity, Ezekiel reminded the people that as certain as judgment had come upon them, so would God's comfort and blessings. The prophet believed that failure is never final, but God's love is!

During the captivity, surrounded by negative influences, Ezekiel built up the hopes of the people of returning to their land and rebuilding the temple of God. In the midst of affliction, Ezekiel gave the people God's vision for victory!

"I will give you a new heart and put a new spirit within you" (Ezek. 36:26).

The Book of
Ezekiel

Ezekiel's Vision of God

NOW it came to pass in the thirtieth year, in the fourth *month*, on the fifth *day* of the month, as I *was* among the captives by the River Chebar, *that* the heavens were opened and I saw visions of God.

2 On the fifth *day* of the month, which *was* in the fifth year of King Jehoiachin's captivity,

3 the word of the LORD came expressly to Ezekiel the priest, the son of Buzi, in the land of the Chaldeans[1] by the River Chebar; and the hand of the LORD was upon him there.

4 Then I looked, and behold, a whirlwind was coming out of the north, a great cloud with raging fire engulfing itself; and brightness *was* all around it and radiating out of its midst like the color of amber, out of the midst of the fire.

5 Also from within it *came* the likeness of four living creatures. And this *was* their appearance: they had the likeness of a man.

6 Each one had four faces, and each one had four wings.

7 Their legs *were* straight, and the soles of their feet *were* like the soles of calves' feet. They sparkled like the color of burnished bronze.

8 *They had* the hands of a man under their wings on their four sides; and each of the four had faces and wings.

9 Their wings touched one another. *The creatures* did not turn when they went, but each one went straight forward.

10 As for the likeness of their faces, *each* had the face of a man, each of the four had the face of a lion on the right side, each of the four had the face of an ox on the left side, and each of the four had the face of an eagle.

11 Thus *were* their faces. Their wings *were* stretched upward; two *wings* of each one touched one another, and two covered their bodies.

12 And each one went straight forward; they went wherever the spirit wanted to go, and they did not turn when they went.

13 As for the likeness of the living creatures, their appearance *was* like burning coals of fire, *and* like the appearance of torches. *Fire* was going back and forth among the living creatures; the fire was bright, and out of the fire went lightning.

14 And the living creatures ran back and forth, in appearance like a flash of lightning.

15 Now as I looked at the living creatures, behold, a wheel *was* on the earth beside each living creature with its four faces.

16 The appearance of the wheels and their works *was* like the color of beryl, and all four had the same likeness. The appearance of their works *was*, as it were, a wheel in the middle of a wheel.

17 When they went, they went toward any one of four directions; they did not turn aside when they went.

18 As for their rims, they were so high they were awesome; and their rims *were* full of eyes, all around the four of them.

19 When the living creatures went, the wheels went beside them; and when the living creatures were lifted up from the earth, the wheels were lifted up.

20 Wherever the spirit wanted to go, they went, *because* there the spirit went; and the wheels were lifted together with them, for the spirit of the living creatures *was* in the wheels.

21 When those went, *these* went; when those stood, *these* stood; and when those were lifted up from the earth, the wheels were lifted up together with them, for the spirit of the living creatures *was* in the wheels.

22 The likeness of the firmament above the heads of the living creatures *was* like the color of an awesome crystal, stretched out over their heads.

23 And under the firmament their wings *spread out* straight, one toward another. Each one had two which covered one side, and each one had two which covered the other side of the body.

1 Or *Babylonians,* and so elsewhere in this book

24 When they went, I heard the noise of their wings, like the noise of many waters, like the voice of the Almighty, a tumult like the noise of an army; and when they stood still, they let down their wings.
25 A voice came from above the firmament that *was* over their heads; whenever they stood, they let down their wings.
26 And above the firmament over their heads *was* the likeness of a throne, in appearance like a sapphire stone; on the likeness of the throne *was* a likeness with the appearance of a man high above it.
27 Also from the appearance of His waist and upward I saw, as it were, the color of amber with the appearance of fire all around within it; and from the appearance of His waist and downward I saw, as it were, the appearance of fire with brightness all around.
28 Like the appearance of a rainbow in a cloud on a rainy day, so *was* the appearance of the brightness all around it. This *was* the appearance of the likeness of the glory of the LORD.

Ezekiel Sent to Rebellious Israel

So when I saw *it*, I fell on my face, and I heard a voice of One speaking.

2 And He said to me, "Son of man, stand on your feet, and I will speak to you."
2 Then the Spirit entered me when He spoke to me, and set me on my feet; and I heard Him who spoke to me.
3 And He said to me: "Son of man, I am sending you to the children of Israel, to a rebellious nation that has rebelled against Me; they and their fathers have transgressed against Me to this very day.
4 "For *they are* impudent and stubborn children. I am sending you to them, and you shall say to them, 'Thus says the Lord GOD.'
5 "As for them, whether they hear or whether they refuse—for they *are* a rebellious house—yet they will know that a prophet has been among them.
6 "And you, son of man, do not be afraid of them nor be afraid of their words, though briers and thorns *are* with you and you dwell among scorpions; do not be afraid of their words or dismayed by their looks, though they *are* a rebellious house.
7 "You shall speak My words to them,

whether they hear or whether they refuse, for they *are* rebellious.
8 "But you, son of man, hear what I say to you. Do not be rebellious like that rebellious house; open your mouth and eat what I give you."
9 Now when I looked, there was a hand stretched out to me; and behold, a scroll of a book *was* in it.
10 Then He spread it before me; and *there was* writing on the inside and on the outside, and written on it *were* lamentations and mourning and woe.

3 Moreover He said to me, "Son of man, eat what you find; eat this scroll, and go, speak to the house of Israel."
2 So I opened my mouth, and He caused me to eat that scroll.
3 And He said to me, "Son of man, feed your belly, and fill your stomach with this scroll that I give you." So I ate *it*, and it was in my mouth like honey in sweetness.
4 And He said to me: "Son of man, go to the house of Israel and speak with My words to them.
5 "For you *are* not sent to a people of unfamiliar speech and of hard language, *but* to the house of Israel,
6 "not to many people of unfamiliar speech and of hard language, whose words you cannot understand. Surely, had I sent you to them, they would have listened to you.
7 "But the house of Israel will not listen to you, because they will not listen to Me; for all the house of Israel *are* impudent and hard-hearted.
8 "Behold, I have made your face strong against their faces, and your forehead strong against their foreheads.
9 "Like adamant stone, harder than flint, I have made your forehead; do not be afraid of them, nor be dismayed at their looks, though they *are* a rebellious house."
10 Moreover He said to me: "Son of man, receive into your heart all My words that I speak to you, and hear with your ears.
11 "And go, get to the captives, to the children of your people, and speak to them and tell them, 'Thus says the Lord GOD,' whether they hear, or whether they refuse."
12 Then the Spirit lifted me up, and I heard behind me a great thunderous

voice: "Blessed *is* the glory of the LORD from His place!"

13 *I* also *heard* the noise of the wings of the living creatures that touched one another, and the noise of the wheels beside them, and a great thunderous noise.

14 So the Spirit lifted me up and took me away, and I went in bitterness, in the heat of my spirit; but the hand of the LORD was strong upon me.

15 Then I came to the captives at Tel Abib, who dwelt by the River Chebar; and I sat where they sat, and remained there astonished among them seven days.

Ezekiel Is a Watchman

16 Now it came to pass at the end of seven days that the word of the LORD came to me, saying,

17 "Son of man, I have made you a watchman for the house of Israel; therefore hear a word from My mouth, and give them warning from Me:

18 "When I say to the wicked, 'You shall surely die,' and you give him no warning, nor speak to warn the wicked from his wicked way, to save his life, that same wicked *man* shall die in his iniquity; but his blood I will require at your hand.

19 "Yet, if you warn the wicked, and he does not turn from his wickedness, nor from his wicked way, he shall die in his iniquity; but you have delivered your soul.

20 "Again, when a righteous *man* turns from his righteousness and commits iniquity, and I lay a stumbling block before him, he shall die; because you did not give him warning, he shall die in his sin, and his righteousness which he has done shall not be remembered; but his blood I will require at your hand.

21 "Nevertheless if you warn the righteous *man* that the righteous should not sin, and he does not sin, he shall surely live because he took warning; also you will have delivered your soul."

22 Then the hand of the LORD was upon me there, and He said to me, "Arise, go out into the plain, and there I shall talk with you."

23 So I arose and went out into the plain, and behold, the glory of the LORD stood there, like the glory which I saw by the River Chebar; and I fell on my face.

24 Then the Spirit entered me and set me on my feet, and spoke with me and said

to me: "Go, shut yourself inside your house.

25 "And you, O son of man, surely they will put ropes on you and bind you with them, so that you cannot go out among them.

26 "I will make your tongue cling to the roof of your mouth, so that you shall be mute and not be a reprover to them, for they *are* a rebellious house.

27 "But when I speak with you, I will open your mouth, and you shall say to them, 'Thus says the Lord GOD.' He who hears, let him hear; and he who refuses, let him refuse; for they *are* a rebellious house.

The Siege of Jerusalem Portrayed

4 "You also, son of man, take a clay tablet and lay it before you, and portray on it a city, Jerusalem.

2 "Lay siege against it, build a siege wall against it, and heap up a mound against it; set camps against it also, and place battering rams against it all around.

3 "Moreover take for yourself an iron plate, and set it *as* an iron wall between you and the city. Set your face against it, and it shall be besieged, and you shall lay siege against it. This *will be* a sign to the house of Israel.

4 "Lie also on your left side, and lay the iniquity of the house of Israel upon it. *According* to the number of the days that you lie on it, you shall bear their iniquity.

5 "For I have laid on you the years of their iniquity, according to the number of the days, three hundred and ninety days; so you shall bear the iniquity of the house of Israel.

6 "And when you have completed them, lie again on your right side; then you shall bear the iniquity of the house of Judah forty days. I have laid on you a day for each year.

7 "Therefore you shall set your face toward the siege of Jerusalem; your arm *shall be* uncovered, and you shall prophesy against it.

8 "And surely I will constrain you so that you cannot turn from one side to another till you have ended the days of your siege.

9 "Also take for yourself wheat, barley, beans, lentils, millet, and spelt; put them into one vessel, and make bread of them for yourself. *During* the number of days

that you lie on your side, three hundred and ninety days, you shall eat it.

10 "And your food which you eat *shall be* by weight, twenty shekels a day; from time to time you shall eat it.

11 "You shall also drink water by measure, one-sixth of a hin; from time to time you shall drink.

12 "And you shall eat it *as* barley cakes; and bake it using fuel of human waste in their sight."

13 Then the LORD said, "So shall the children of Israel eat their defiled bread among the Gentiles, where I will drive them."

14 So I said, "Ah, Lord GOD! Indeed I have never defiled myself from my youth till now; I have never eaten what died of itself or was torn by beasts, nor has abominable flesh ever come into my mouth."

15 Then He said to me, "See, I am giving you cow dung instead of human waste, and you shall prepare your bread over it."

16 Moreover He said to me, "Son of man, surely I will cut off the supply of bread in Jerusalem; they shall eat bread by weight and with anxiety, and shall drink water by measure and with dread,

17 "that they may lack bread and water, and be dismayed with one another, and waste away because of their iniquity.

A Sword Against Jerusalem

5 "And you, son of man, take a sharp sword, take it as a barber's razor, and pass *it* over your head and your beard; then take balances to weigh and divide the hair.

2 "You shall burn with fire one-third in the midst of the city, when the days of the siege are finished; then you shall take one-third and strike around *it* with the sword, and one-third you shall scatter in the wind: I will draw out a sword after them.

3 "You shall also take a small number of them and bind them in the edge of your *garment*.

4 "Then take some of them again and throw them into the midst of the fire, and burn them in the fire; *for* from there a fire will go out into all the house of Israel.

5 "Thus says the Lord GOD: 'This *is* Jerusalem; I have set her in the midst of the nations and the countries all around her.

6 'She has rebelled against My judgments by doing wickedness more than the nations, and against My statutes more than the countries that *are* all around her; for they have refused My judgments, and they have not walked in My statutes.'

7 "Therefore thus says the Lord GOD: 'Because you have multiplied *disobedience* more than the nations that *are* all around you, *and* have not walked in My statutes, nor kept My judgments, nor even done according to the judgments of the nations that *are* all around you,'

8 "therefore thus says the Lord GOD: 'Indeed I, even I, *am* against you and will execute judgments in your midst in the sight of the nations.

9 'And I will do among you what I have never done, and the like of which I will never do again, because of all your abominations.

10 'Therefore fathers shall eat *their* sons in your midst, and sons shall eat their fathers; and I will execute judgments among you, and all of you who remain I will scatter to all the winds.

11 'Therefore, *as* I live,' says the Lord GOD, 'surely, because you have defiled My sanctuary with all your detestable things and with all your abominations, therefore I will also diminish *you*; My eye will not spare, nor will I have any pity.

12 'One-third of you shall die of the pestilence, and be consumed with famine in your midst; and one-third shall fall by the sword all around you; and I will scatter another third to all the winds, and I will draw out a sword after them.

13 'Thus shall My anger be spent, and I will cause My fury to rest upon them, and I will be avenged; and they shall know that I, the LORD, have spoken *it* in My zeal, when I have spent My fury upon them.

14 'Moreover I will make you a waste and a reproach among the nations that *are* all around you, in the sight of all who pass by.

15 'So it shall be a reproach, a taunt, a lesson, and an astonishment to the nations that *are* all around you, when I execute judgments among you in anger and in fury and in furious rebukes. I, the LORD, have spoken.

16 'When I send against them the terrible arrows of famine which shall be for *their*

destruction, *and* which I will send to destroy you, I will increase the famine upon you and cut off your supply of bread.

17 'So I will send against you famine and wild beasts, and they will bereave you. Pestilence and blood shall pass through you, and I will bring the sword against you. I, the LORD, have spoken.' "

Judgment on Idolatrous Israel

6 Now the word of the LORD came to me, saying:

2 "Son of man, set your face toward the mountains of Israel, and prophesy against them,

3 "and say, 'O mountains of Israel, hear the word of the Lord GOD!' Thus says the Lord GOD to the mountains, to the hills, to the ravines, and to the valleys: "Indeed I, *even* I, will bring a sword against you, and I will destroy your high places.

4 "Then your altars shall be desolate, your incense altars shall be broken, and I will cast down your slain *men* before your idols.

5 "And I will lay the corpses of the children of Israel before their idols, and I will scatter your bones all around your altars.

6 "In all your dwelling places the cities shall be laid waste, and the high places shall be desolate, so that your altars may be laid waste and made desolate, your idols may be broken and made to cease, your incense altars may be cut down, and your works may be abolished.

7 "The slain shall fall in your midst, and you shall know that I *am* the LORD.

8 "Yet I will leave a remnant, so that you may have *some* who escape the sword among the nations, when you are scattered through the countries.

9 "Then those of you who escape will remember Me among the nations where they are carried captive, because I was crushed by their adulterous heart which has departed from Me, and by their eyes which play the harlot after their idols; they will loathe themselves for the evils which they committed in all their abominations.

10 "And they shall know that I *am* the LORD, *and that* I have not said in vain that I would bring this calamity upon them."

11 'Thus says the Lord GOD: "Pound your fists and stamp your feet, and say, 'Alas, for all the evil abominations of the house of Israel! For they shall fall by the sword, by famine, and by pestilence.

12 'He who is far off shall die by the pestilence, he who is near shall fall by the sword, and he who remains and is besieged shall die by the famine. Thus will I spend My fury upon them.

13 'Then you shall know that I *am* the LORD, when their slain *men* are among their idols all around their altars, on every high hill, on all the mountaintops, under every green tree, and under every thick oak, wherever they offered sweet incense to all their idols.

14 'So I will stretch out My hand against them and make the land desolate, yes, more desolate than the wilderness toward Diblah, in all their habitations. Then they shall know that I *am* the LORD.' " '."

Judgment on Israel Is Near

7 Moreover the word of the LORD came to me, saying,

2 "And you, son of man, thus says the Lord GOD to the land of Israel:

'An end! The end has come
   upon the four corners of the land.
3 Now the end *has come* upon you,
   And I will send My anger against you;
I will judge you
   according to your ways,
And I will repay you
   for all your abominations.
4 My eye will not spare you,
   Nor will I have pity;
But I will repay your ways,
And your abominations
   shall be in your midst;
Then you shall know
   that I *am* the LORD!'

5 "Thus says the Lord GOD:

'A disaster, a singular disaster;
Behold, it has come!
6 An end has come,
The end has come;
It has dawned for you;
Behold, it has come!
7 Doom has come to you,
   you who dwell in the land;
The time has come,
A day of trouble *is* near,
And not of rejoicing in the mountains.
8 Now upon you I will soon pour out
   My fury,
And spend My anger upon you;

I will judge you
    according to your ways,
And I will repay you
    for all your abominations.

9 'My eye will not spare,
    Nor will I have pity;
I will repay you
    according to your ways,
And your abominations
    will be in your midst.
Then you will know
    that I *am* the LORD who strikes.

10 'Behold, the day!
    Behold, it has come!
Doom has gone out;
The rod has blossomed,
    Pride has budded.
11 Violence has risen up
    into a rod of wickedness;
None of them *shall remain*,
None of their multitude,
None of them;
Nor *shall there be* wailing for them.
12 The time has come,
    The day draws near.

'Let not the buyer rejoice,
    Nor the seller mourn,
For wrath *is* on their whole multitude.
13 For the seller shall not return
    to what has been sold,
Though he may still be alive;
For the vision concerns the whole
    multitude,
And it shall not turn back;
No one will strengthen himself
Who lives in iniquity.

14 'They have blown the trumpet
    and made everyone ready,
But no one goes to battle;
For My wrath *is* on all their multitude.
15 The sword *is* outside,
And the pestilence and famine within.
Whoever *is* in the field
Will die by the sword;
And whoever *is* in the city,
Famine and pestilence will devour him.

16 'Those who survive will escape
    and be on the mountains
Like doves of the valleys,
All of them mourning,
    Each for his iniquity.
17 Every hand will be feeble,
    And every knee will be *as* weak *as*
water.

18 They will also be girded with
    sackcloth;
Horror will cover them;
Shame *will be* on every face,
Baldness on all their heads.

19 'They will throw their silver
    into the streets,
And their gold will be like refuse;
Their silver and their gold
    will not be able to deliver them
In the day of the wrath of the LORD;
They will not satisfy their souls,
Nor fill their stomachs,
Because it became their stumbling
    block of iniquity.

20 'As for the beauty of his ornaments,
    He set it in majesty;
But they made from it
The images of their abominations
And their detestable things;
Therefore I have made it
Like refuse to them.
21 I will give it as plunder
Into the hands of strangers,
And to the wicked of the earth as
    spoil;
And they shall defile it.
22 I will turn My face from them,
And they will defile My secret place;
For robbers shall enter it
    and defile it.

23 'Make a chain,
For the land is filled with crimes
    of blood,
And the city is full of violence.
24 Therefore I will bring the worst of the
    Gentiles,
And they will possess their houses;
I will cause the pomp of the strong
    to cease,
And their holy places shall be defiled.
25 Destruction comes;
They will seek peace,
    but *there shall be* none.
26 Disaster will come upon disaster,
And rumor will be upon rumor.
Then they will seek a vision
    from a prophet;
But the law will perish
    from the priest,
And counsel from the elders.

27 'The king will mourn,
The prince will be clothed with
    desolation,
And the hands of the common people
    will tremble.

I will do to them
according to their way,
And according to what they deserve
I will judge them;
Then they shall know
that I *am* the LORD!' "

Abominations in the Temple

8 And it came to pass in the sixth year, in the sixth *month*, on the fifth *day* of the month, as I sat in my house with the elders of Judah sitting before me, that the hand of the Lord GOD fell upon me there.
2 Then I looked, and there was a likeness, like the appearance of fire—from the appearance of His waist and downward, fire; and from His waist and upward, like the appearance of brightness, like the color of amber.
3 He stretched out the form of a hand, and took me by a lock of my hair; and the Spirit lifted me up between earth and heaven, and brought me in visions of God to Jerusalem, to the door of the north gate of the inner *court*, where the seat of the image of jealousy *was*, which provokes to jealousy.
4 And behold, the glory of the God of Israel *was* there, like the vision that I saw in the plain.
5 Then He said to me, "Son of man, lift your eyes now toward the north." So I lifted my eyes toward the north, and there, north of the altar gate, was this image of jealousy in the entrance.
6 Furthermore He said to me, "Son of man, do you see what they are doing, the great abominations that the house of Israel commits here, to make Me go far away from My sanctuary? Now turn again, you will see greater abominations."
7 So He brought me to the door of the court; and when I looked, there was a hole in the wall.
8 Then He said to me, "Son of man, dig into the wall"; and when I dug into the wall, there was a door.
9 And He said to me, "Go in, and see the wicked abominations which they are doing there."
10 So I went in and saw, and there—every sort of creeping thing, abominable beasts, and all the idols of the house of Israel, portrayed all around on the walls.
11 And there stood before them seventy men of the elders of the house of Israel, and in their midst stood Jaazaniah the

son of Shaphan. Each man had a censer in his hand, and a thick cloud of incense went up.
12 Then He said to me, "Son of man, have you seen what the elders of the house of Israel do in the dark, every man in the room of his idols? For they say, 'The LORD does not see us, the LORD has forsaken the land.' "
13 And He said to me, "Turn again, *and* you will see greater abominations that they are doing."
14 So He brought me to the door of the north gate of the LORD's house; and to my dismay, women were sitting there weeping for Tammuz.
15 Then He said to me, "Have you seen *this*, O son of man? Turn again, you will see greater abominations than these."
16 So He brought me into the inner court of the LORD's house; and there, at the door of the temple of the LORD, between the porch and the altar, *were* about twenty-five men with their backs toward the temple of the LORD and their faces toward the east, and they were worshiping the sun toward the east.
17 Then He said to me, "Have you seen *this*, O son of man? Is it a trivial thing to the house of Judah to commit the abominations which they commit here? For they have filled the land with violence; then they have returned to provoke Me to anger. Indeed they put the branch to their nose.
18 "Therefore I also will act in fury. My eye will not spare nor will I have pity; and though they cry in My ears with a loud voice, I will not hear them."

The Wicked Are Slain

9 Then He called out in my hearing with a loud voice, saying, "Let those who have charge over the city draw near, each *with* a deadly weapon in his hand."
2 And suddenly six men came from the direction of the upper gate, which faces north, each with his battle-ax in his hand. One man among them *was* clothed with linen and had a writer's inkhorn at his side. They went in and stood beside the bronze altar.
3 Now the glory of the God of Israel had gone up from the cherub, where it had been, to the threshold of the temple.[2] And He called to the man clothed with

2 Literally *house*

linen, who *had* the writer's inkhorn at his side;

4 and the LORD said to him, "Go through the midst of the city, through the midst of Jerusalem, and put a mark on the foreheads of the men who sigh and cry over all the abominations that are done within it."

5 To the others He said in my hearing, "Go after him through the city and kill; do not let your eye spare, nor have any pity.

6 "Utterly slay old *and* young men, maidens and little children and women; but do not come near anyone on whom *is* the mark; and begin at My sanctuary." So they began with the elders who *were* before the temple.

7 Then He said to them, "Defile the temple, and fill the courts with the slain. Go out!" And they went out and killed in the city.

8 So it was, that while they were killing them, I was left *alone*; and I fell on my face and cried out, and said, "Ah, Lord GOD! Will You destroy all the remnant of Israel in pouring out Your fury on Jerusalem?"

9 Then He said to me, "The iniquity of the house of Israel and Judah *is* exceedingly great, and the land is full of bloodshed, and the city full of perversity; for they say, 'The LORD has forsaken the land, and the LORD does not see!'

10 "And as for Me also, My eye will neither spare, nor will I have pity, *but* I will recompense their deeds on their own head."

11 Just then, the man clothed with linen, who *had* the inkhorn at his side, reported back and said, "I have done as You commanded me."

The Glory Departs from the Temple

10 And I looked, and there in the firmament that was above the head of the cherubim, there appeared something like a sapphire stone, having the appearance of the likeness of a throne.

2 And He spoke to the man clothed with linen, and said, "Go in among the wheels, under the cherub, fill your hands with coals of fire from among the cherubim, and scatter *them* over the city." And he went in as I watched.

3 Now the cherubim were standing on the south side of the temple[3] when the man went in, and the cloud filled the inner court.

4 Then the glory of the LORD went up from the cherub, *and paused* over the threshold of the temple; and the house was filled with the cloud, and the court was full of the brightness of the LORD's glory.

5 And the sound of the wings of the cherubim was heard *even* in the outer court, like the voice of Almighty God when He speaks.

6 Now it happened, when He commanded the man clothed in linen, saying, "Take fire from among the wheels, from among the cherubim," that he went in and stood beside the wheels.

7 And the cherub stretched out his hand from among the cherubim to the fire that *was* among the cherubim, and took *some of it* and put *it* into the hands of the *man* clothed with linen, who took *it* and went out.

8 The cherubim appeared to have the form of a man's hand under their wings.

9 And when I looked, there were four wheels by the cherubim, one wheel by one cherub and another wheel by each other cherub; the wheels appeared *to have* the color of a beryl stone.

10 *As for* their appearance, all four looked alike—as it were, a wheel in the middle of a wheel.

11 When they went, they went toward *any of* their four directions; they did not turn aside when they went, but followed in the direction the head was facing. They did not turn aside when they went.

12 And their whole body, with their back, their hands, their wings, and the wheels that the four had, *were* full of eyes all around.

13 As for the wheels, they were called in my hearing, "Wheel."

14 Each one had four faces: the first face *was* the face of a cherub, the second face the face of a man, the third the face of a lion, and the fourth the face of an eagle.

15 And the cherubim were lifted up. This *was* the living creature I saw by the River Chebar.

16 When the cherubim went, the wheels went beside them; and when the cherubim lifted their wings to mount up from the earth, the same wheels also did not turn from beside them.

---

3 Literally *house,* also in verses 4 and 18

17 When *the cherubim* stood still, *the wheels* stood still, and when *one* was lifted up, *the other* lifted itself up, for the spirit of the living creature *was* in them.
18 Then the glory of the LORD departed from the threshold of the temple and stood over the cherubim.
19 And the cherubim lifted their wings and mounted up from the earth in my sight. When they went out, the wheels *were* beside them; and they stood at the door of the east gate of the LORD's house, and the glory of the God of Israel *was* above them.
20 This *is* the living creature I saw under the God of Israel by the River Chebar, and I knew they *were* cherubim.
21 Each one had four faces and each one four wings, and the likeness of the hands of a man *was* under their wings.
22 And the likeness of their faces *was* the same *as* the faces which I had seen by the River Chebar, their appearance and their persons. They each went straight forward.

Judgment on Wicked Counselors

11 Then the Spirit lifted me up and brought me to the east gate of the LORD's house, which faces eastward; and there at the door of the gate were twenty-five men, among whom I saw Jaazaniah the son of Azzur, and Pelatiah the son of Benaiah, princes of the people.
2 And He said to me: "Son of man, these *are* the men who devise iniquity and give wicked counsel in this city,
3 "who say, 'The time is not near to build houses; this *city is* the caldron, and we *are* the meat.'
4 "Therefore prophesy against them, prophesy, O son of man!"
5 Then the Spirit of the LORD fell upon me, and said to me, "Speak! 'Thus says the LORD: "Thus you have said, O house of Israel; for I know the things that come into your mind.
6 "You have multiplied your slain in this city, and you have filled its streets with the slain."
7 'Therefore thus says the Lord GOD: "Your slain whom you have laid in its midst, they *are* the meat, and this *city is* the caldron; but I shall bring you out of the midst of it.
8 "You have feared the sword; and I

will bring a sword upon you," says the Lord GOD.
9 "And I will bring you out of its midst, and deliver you into the hands of strangers, and execute judgments on you.
10 "You shall fall by the sword. I will judge you at the border of Israel. Then you shall know that I *am* the LORD.
11 "This *city* shall not be your caldron, nor shall you be the meat in its midst. I will judge you at the border of Israel.
12 "And you shall know that I *am* the LORD; for you have not walked in My statutes nor executed My judgments, but have done according to the customs of the Gentiles which *are* all around you." ' "
13 Now it happened, while I was prophesying, that Pelatiah the son of Benaiah died. Then I fell on my face and cried with a loud voice, and said, "Ah, Lord GOD! Will You make a complete end of the remnant of Israel?"

God Will Restore Israel

14 Again the word of the LORD came to me, saying,
15 "Son of man, your brethren, your relatives, your kinsmen, and all the house of Israel in its entirety, *are* those about whom the inhabitants of Jerusalem have said, 'Get far away from the LORD; this land has been given to us as a possession.'
16 "Therefore say, 'Thus says the Lord GOD: "Although I have cast them far off among the Gentiles, and although I have scattered them among the countries, yet I shall be a little sanctuary for them in the countries where they have gone." '
17 "Therefore say, 'Thus says the Lord GOD: "I will gather you from the peoples, assemble you from the countries where you have been scattered, and I will give you the land of Israel." '
18 "And they will go there, and they will take away all its detestable things and all its abominations from there.
19 "Then I will give them one heart, and I will put a new spirit within them,[4] and take the stony heart out of their flesh, and give them a heart of flesh,
20 "that they may walk in My statutes and keep My judgments and do them; and they shall be My people, and I will be their God.
21 "But *as for those* whose hearts walk after the heart of their detestable things

4 Literally *you*

and their abominations, I will recompense their deeds on their own heads," says the Lord GOD.

22 Then the cherubim lifted up their wings, with the wheels beside them, and the glory of the God of Israel *was* high above them.

23 And the glory of the LORD went up from the midst of the city and stood on the mountain, which *is* on the east side of the city.

24 Then the Spirit took me up and brought me in a vision by the Spirit of God into Chaldea,[5] to those in captivity. And the vision that I had seen went up from me.

25 So I spoke to those in captivity of all the things the LORD had shown me.

Judah's Captivity Portrayed

12 Now the word of the LORD came to me, saying:

2 "Son of man, you dwell in the midst of a rebellious house, which has eyes to see but does not see, and ears to hear but does not hear; for they *are* a rebellious house.

3 "Therefore, son of man, prepare your belongings for captivity, and go into captivity by day in their sight. You shall go from your place into captivity to another place in their sight. It may be that they will consider, though they *are* a rebellious house.

4 "By day you shall bring out your belongings in their sight, as though going into captivity; and at evening you shall go in their sight, like those who go into captivity.

5 "Dig through the wall in their sight, and carry your belongings out through it.

6 "In their sight you shall bear *them* on *your* shoulders *and* carry *them* out at twilight; you shall cover your face, so that you cannot see the ground, for I have made you a sign to the house of Israel."

7 So I did as I was commanded. I brought out my belongings by day, as though going into captivity, and at evening I dug through the wall with my hand. I brought *them* out at twilight, *and* I bore *them* on *my* shoulder in their sight.

8 And in the morning the word of the LORD came to me, saying,

9 "Son of man, has not the house of Israel, the rebellious house, said to you, 'What are you doing?'

10 "Say to them, 'Thus says the Lord GOD: "This burden *concerns* the prince in Jerusalem and all the house of Israel who are among them." '

11 "Say, 'I *am* a sign to you. As I have done, so shall it be done to them; they shall be carried away into captivity.'

12 "And the prince who *is* among them shall bear *his belongings* on *his* shoulder at twilight and go out. They shall dig through the wall to carry *them* out through it. He shall cover his face, so that he cannot see the ground with *his* eyes.

13 "I will also spread My net over him, and he shall be caught in My snare. I will bring him to Babylon, *to* the land of the Chaldeans; yet he shall not see it, though he shall die there.

14 "I will scatter to every wind all who *are* around him to help him, and all his troops; and I will draw out the sword after them.

15 "Then they shall know that I *am* the LORD, when I scatter them among the nations and disperse them throughout the countries.

16 "But I will spare a few of their men from the sword, from famine, and from pestilence, that they may declare all their abominations among the Gentiles wherever they go. Then they shall know that I *am* the LORD."

Judgment Not Postponed

17 Moreover the word of the LORD came to me, saying,

18 "Son of man, eat your bread with quaking, and drink your water with trembling and anxiety.

19 "And say to the people of the land, 'Thus says the Lord GOD to the inhabitants of Jerusalem *and* to the land of Israel: "They shall eat their bread with anxiety, and drink their water with dread, so that her land may be emptied of all who are in it, because of the violence of all those who dwell in it.

20 "Then the cities that are inhabited shall be laid waste, and the land shall become desolate; and you shall know that I *am* the LORD." ' "

21 And the word of the LORD came to me, saying,

22 "Son of man, what *is* this proverb *that* you *people* have about the land of Israel, which says, 'The days are prolonged, and every vision fails'?

---

5 Or *Babylon,* and so elsewhere in this book

23 "Tell them therefore, 'Thus says the Lord GOD: "I will lay this proverb to rest, and they shall no more use it as a proverb in Israel." But say to them, "The days are at hand, and the fulfillment of every vision.

24 "For no more shall there be any false vision or flattering divination within the house of Israel.

25 "For I am the LORD. I speak, and the word which I speak will come to pass; it will no more be postponed; for in your days, O rebellious house, I will say the word and perform it," says the Lord GOD.' "

26 Again the word of the LORD came to me, saying,

27 "Son of man, look, the house of Israel is saying, 'The vision that he sees is for many days from now, and he prophesies of times far off.'

28 "Therefore say to them, 'Thus says the Lord GOD: "None of My words will be postponed any more, but the word which I speak will be done," says the Lord GOD.' "

Woe to Foolish Prophets

13 And the word of the LORD came to me, saying,

2 "Son of man, prophesy against the prophets of Israel who prophesy, and say to those who prophesy out of their own heart, 'Hear the word of the LORD!' "

3 Thus says the Lord GOD: "Woe to the foolish prophets, who follow their own spirit and have seen nothing!

4 "O Israel, your prophets are like foxes in the deserts.

5 "You have not gone up into the gaps to build a wall for the house of Israel to stand in battle on the day of the LORD.

6 "They have envisioned futility and false divination, saying, 'Thus says the LORD!' But the LORD has not sent them; yet they hope that the word may be confirmed.

7 "Have you not seen a futile vision, and have you not spoken false divination? You say, 'The LORD says,' but I have not spoken."

8 Therefore thus says the Lord GOD: "Because you have spoken nonsense and envisioned lies, therefore I am indeed against you," says the Lord GOD.

9 "My hand will be against the prophets who envision futility and who divine lies;

they shall not be in the assembly of My people, nor be written in the record of the house of Israel, nor shall they enter into the land of Israel. Then you shall know that I am the Lord GOD.

10 "Because, indeed, because they have seduced My people, saying, 'Peace!' when there is no peace—and one builds a boundary wall, and they plaster it with untempered mortar—

11 "say to those who plaster it with untempered mortar, that it will fall. There will be flooding rain, and you, O great hailstones, shall fall; and a stormy wind shall tear it down.

12 "Surely, when the wall has fallen, will it not be said to you, 'Where is the mortar with which you plastered it?' "

13 Therefore thus says the Lord GOD: "I will cause a stormy wind to break forth in My fury; and there shall be a flooding rain in My anger, and great hailstones in fury to consume it.

14 "So I will break down the wall you have plastered with untempered mortar, and bring it down to the ground, so that its foundation will be uncovered; it will fall, and you shall be consumed in the midst of it. Then you shall know that I am the LORD.

15 "Thus will I accomplish My wrath on the wall and on those who have plastered it with untempered mortar; and I will say to you, 'The wall is no more, nor those who plastered it,

16 'that is, the prophets of Israel who prophesy concerning Jerusalem, and who see visions of peace for her when there is no peace,' " says the Lord GOD.

17 "Likewise, son of man, set your face against the daughters of your people, who prophesy out of their own heart; prophesy against them,

18 "and say, 'Thus says the Lord GOD: "Woe to the women who sew magic charms on their sleeves and make veils for the heads of people of every height to hunt souls! Will you hunt the souls of My people, and keep yourselves alive?

19 "And will you profane Me among My people for handfuls of barley and for pieces of bread, killing people who should not die, and keeping people alive who should not live, by your lying to My people who listen to lies?"

20 'Therefore thus says the Lord GOD: "Behold, I am against your magic charms

by which you hunt souls there like birds. I will tear them from your arms, and let the souls go, the souls you hunt like birds. 21 "I will also tear off your veils and deliver My people out of your hand, and they shall no longer be as prey in your hand. Then you shall know that I *am* the LORD." ' "

22 "Because with lies you have made the heart of the righteous sad, whom I have not made sad; and you have strengthened the hands of the wicked, so that he does not turn from his wicked way to save his life.

23 "Therefore you shall no longer envision futility nor practice divination; for I will deliver My people out of your hand, and you shall know that I *am* the LORD." ' "

Idolatry Will Be Punished

14 Now some of the elders of Israel came to me and sat before me.

2 And the word of the LORD came to me, saying,

3 "Son of man, these men have set up their idols in their hearts, and put before them that which causes them to stumble into iniquity. Should I let Myself be inquired of at all by them?

4 "Therefore speak to them, and say to them, 'Thus says the Lord GOD: "Everyone of the house of Israel who sets up his idols in his heart, and puts before him what causes him to stumble into iniquity, and then comes to the prophet, I the LORD will answer him who comes, according to the multitude of his idols,

5 "that I may seize the house of Israel by their heart, because they are all estranged from Me by their idols." '

6 "Therefore say to the house of Israel, 'Thus says the Lord GOD: "Repent, turn away from your idols, and turn your faces away from all your abominations.

7 "For anyone of the house of Israel, or of the strangers who sojourn in Israel, who separates himself from Me and sets up his idols in his heart and puts before him what causes him to stumble into iniquity, then comes to a prophet to inquire of him concerning Me, I the LORD will answer him by Myself.

8 "I will set My face against that man and make him a sign and a proverb, and I will cut him off from the midst of My people. Then you shall know that I *am* the LORD.

9 "And if the prophet is induced to speak anything, I the LORD have induced that prophet, and I will stretch out My hand against him and destroy him from among My people Israel.

10 "And they shall bear their iniquity; the punishment of the prophet shall be the same as the punishment of the one who inquired,

11 "that the house of Israel may no longer stray from Me, nor be profaned anymore with all their transgressions, but that they may be My people and I may be their God," says the Lord GOD.' "

Judgment on Persistent Unfaithfulness

12 The word of the LORD came again to me, saying:

13 "Son of man, when a land sins against Me by persistent unfaithfulness, I will stretch out My hand against it; I will cut off its supply of bread, send famine on it, and cut off man and beast from it.

14 "*Though* these three men, Noah, Daniel, and Job, *were* in it, they would deliver *only* themselves by their righteousness," says the Lord GOD.

15 "If I cause wild beasts to pass through the land, and they empty it, and make it so desolate that no man may pass through because of the beasts,

16 "even *though* these three men *were* in it, *as* I live," says the Lord GOD, "they would deliver neither sons nor daughters; only they would be delivered, and the land would be desolate.

17 "Or *if* I bring a sword on that land, and say, 'Sword, go through the land,' and I cut off man and beast from it,

18 "even *though* these three men *were* in it, *as* I live," says the Lord GOD, "they would deliver neither sons nor daughters, but only they themselves would be delivered.

19 "Or *if* I send a pestilence into that land and pour out My fury on it in blood, and cut off from it man and beast,

20 "even though Noah, Daniel, and Job *were* in it, *as* I live," says the Lord GOD, "they would deliver neither son nor daughter; they would deliver *only* themselves by their righteousness."

21 For thus says the Lord GOD: "How much more it shall be when I send My four severe judgments on Jerusalem—the

sword and famine and wild beasts and pestilence—to cut off man and beast from it?

22 "Yet behold, there shall be left in it a remnant who will be brought out, *both* sons and daughters; surely they will come out to you, and you will see their ways and their doings. Then you will be comforted concerning the disaster that I have brought upon Jerusalem, *indeed* all that I have brought upon it.

23 "And they will comfort you, when you see their ways and their doings; and you shall know that I have done nothing without cause that I have done in it," says the Lord GOD.

The Outcast Vine

15 Then the word of the LORD came to me, saying:

2 "Son of man, how is the wood of the vine *better* than any other wood, the vine branch which is among the trees of the forest?

3 "Is wood taken from it to make any object? Or can *men* make a peg from it to hang any vessel on?

4 "Instead, it is thrown into the fire for fuel; the fire devours both ends of it, and its middle is burned. Is it useful for *any* work?

5 "Indeed, when it was whole, no object could be made from it. How much less will it be useful for *any* work when the fire has devoured it, and it is burned?

6 "Therefore thus says the Lord GOD: 'Like the wood of the vine among the trees of the forest, which I have given to the fire for fuel, so I will give up the inhabitants of Jerusalem;

7 'and I will set My face against them. They will go out from *one* fire, but *another* fire shall devour them. Then you shall know that I *am* the LORD, when I set My face against them.

8 'Thus I will make the land desolate, because they have persisted in unfaithfulness,' says the Lord GOD."

God's Love for Jerusalem

16 Again the word of the LORD came to me, saying,

2 "Son of man, cause Jerusalem to know her abominations,

3 "and say, 'Thus says the Lord GOD to Jerusalem: "Your birth and your nativity *are* from the land of Canaan; your father

was an Amorite and your mother a Hittite.

4 "*As for* your nativity, on the day you were born your navel cord was not cut, nor were you washed in water to cleanse *you*; you were not rubbed with salt nor swathed in swaddling cloths.

5 "No eye pitied you, to do any of these things for you, to have compassion on you; but you were thrown out into the open field, when you yourself were loathed on the day you were born.

6 "And when I passed by you and saw you struggling in your own blood, I said to you in your blood, 'Live!' Yes, I said to you in your blood, 'Live!'

7 "I made you thrive like a plant in the field; and you grew, matured, and became very beautiful. *Your* breasts were formed, your hair grew, but you *were* naked and bare.

8 "When I passed by you again and looked upon you, indeed your time *was* the time of love; so I spread My wing over you and covered your nakedness. Yes, I swore an oath to you and entered into a covenant with you, and you became Mine," says the Lord GOD.

9 "Then I washed you in water; yes, I thoroughly washed off your blood, and I anointed you with oil.

10 "I clothed you in embroidered cloth and gave you sandals of badger skin; I clothed you with fine linen and covered you with silk.

11 "I adorned you with ornaments, put bracelets on your wrists, and a chain on your neck.

12 "And I put a jewel in your nose, earrings in your ears, and a beautiful crown on your head.

13 "Thus you were adorned with gold and silver, and your clothing *was of* fine linen, silk, and embroidered cloth. You ate *pastry of* fine flour, honey, and oil. You were exceedingly beautiful, and succeeded to royalty.

14 "Your fame went out among the nations because of your beauty, for it *was* perfect through My splendor which I had bestowed on you," says the Lord GOD.

Jerusalem's Harlotry

15 "But you trusted in your own beauty, played the harlot because of your fame, and poured out your harlotry on everyone passing by who *would have* it.

Many Logs
Burn Brightly Together

In the Sinai wilderness and southland of Palestine, the Bedouin and his tribe roam the desert land in a nomadic life-style. The Bedouin depends completely on the resources of the land to provide for his needs.

A scarce and precious commodity in the desert is wood. The Bedouin gathers kindling and branches whenever he has the chance. He will never let the smallest twig pass by, for he never knows when he will find more fuel for his fire. The most valuable of all is when he finds a log from an old acacia tree or he trades with another tribe for one.

In the winter months, the desert can be extremely cold. This is when the Bedouin unloads his camels and brings out the largest logs and kindling he has gathered. In careful arrangement, he stacks the kindling together and starts his fire, then when the flames are hot, he adds the logs. He never allows one log to burn alone, for he knows that the fire will not last. Many logs will burn brightly together, but take one aside and it will no longer burn.

Like scarce large pieces of wood in the desert, dreams that come into our minds must be gathered. No dream can be passed by, for you never know when another will come along. When God gives you a dream, grab it, save it and use it! Throw it on the kindling of your time, talents, energies, and education so that they will burn brightly together. We must always hold in our imagination new objectives, greater goals, and loftier dreams. Then when the time is right, throw them on the fire!

16 "You took some of your garments and adorned multicolored high places for yourself, and played the harlot on them. *Such* things should not happen, nor be.
17 "You have also taken your beautiful jewelry from My gold and My silver, which I had given you, and made for yourself male images and played the harlot with them.
18 "You took your embroidered garments and covered them, and you set My oil and My incense before them.
19 "Also My food which I gave you—the pastry of fine flour, oil, and honey *which* I fed you—you set it before them as sweet incense; and *so* it was," says the Lord GOD.
20 "Moreover you took your sons and your daughters, whom you bore to Me, and these you sacrificed to them to be devoured. *Were* your *acts* of harlotry a small matter,
21 "that you have slain My children and offered them up to them by causing them to pass through *the fire*?
22 "And in all your abominations and acts of harlotry you did not remember the days of your youth, when you were naked and bare, struggling in your blood.
23 "Then it was so, after all your wickedness—'Woe, woe to you!' says the Lord GOD—
24 "*that* you also built for yourself a shrine, and made a high place for yourself in every street.
25 "You built your high places at the head of every road, and made your beauty to be abhorred. You offered yourself to everyone who passed by, and multiplied your acts of harlotry.
26 "You also committed harlotry with the Egyptians, your very fleshly neighbors, and increased your acts of harlotry to provoke Me to anger.
27 "Behold, therefore, I stretched out My hand against you, diminished your allotment, and gave you up to the will of those who hate you, the daughters of the Philistines, who were ashamed of your lewd behavior.
28 "You also played the harlot with the Assyrians, because you were insatiable; indeed you played the harlot with them and still were not satisfied.
29 "Moreover you multiplied your acts of harlotry as far as the land of the trader, Chaldea; and even then you were not satisfied.
30 "How degenerate is your heart!" says the Lord GOD, "seeing you do all these *things*, the deeds of a brazen harlot.

Jerusalem's Adultery

31 "You erected your shrine at the head of every road, and built your high place in every street. Yet you were not like a harlot, because you scorned payment.
32 "*You are* an adulterous wife, *who* takes strangers instead of her husband.
33 "Men make payment to all harlots, but you made your payments to all your lovers, and hired them to come to you from all around for your harlotry.
34 "You are the opposite of *other* women in your harlotry, because no one solicited you to be a harlot. In that you gave payment but no payment was given you, therefore you are the opposite."

Jerusalem's Lovers Will Abuse Her

35 'Now then, O harlot, hear the word of the LORD!
36 'Thus says the Lord GOD: "Because your filthiness was poured out and your nakedness uncovered in your harlotry with your lovers, and with all your abominable idols, and because of the blood of your children which you gave to them,
37 "surely, therefore, I will gather all your lovers with whom you took pleasure, all those you loved, *and* all those you hated; I will gather them from all around against you and will uncover your nakedness to them, that they may see all your nakedness.
38 "And I will judge you as women who break wedlock or shed blood are judged; I will bring blood upon you in fury and jealousy.
39 "I will also give you into their hand, and they shall throw down your shrines and break down your high places. They shall also strip you of your clothes, take your beautiful jewelry, and leave you naked and bare.
40 "They shall also bring up an assembly against you, and they shall stone you with stones and thrust you through with their swords.
41 "They shall burn your houses with fire, and execute judgments on you in the sight of many women; and I will make

you cease playing the harlot, and you shall no longer hire lovers.
42 "So I will lay to rest My fury toward you, and My jealousy shall depart from you. I will be quiet, and be angry no more.
43 "Because you did not remember the days of your youth, but agitated Me with all these *things*, surely I will also recompense your deeds on *your own* head," says the Lord GOD. "And you shall not commit lewdness in addition to all your abominations.

More Wicked than Samaria and Sodom

44 "Indeed everyone who quotes proverbs will use *this* proverb against you: 'Like mother, like daughter!'
45 "You *are* your mother's daughter, loathing husband and children; and you *are* the sister of your sisters, who loathed their husbands and children; your mother *was* a Hittite and your father an Amorite.
46 "Your elder sister *is* Samaria, who dwells with her daughters to the north of you; and your younger sister, who dwells to the south of you, *is* Sodom and her daughters.
47 "You did not walk in their ways nor act according to their abominations; but, as *if that were* too little, you became more corrupt than they in all your ways.
48 "*As* I live," says the Lord GOD, "neither your sister Sodom nor her daughters have done as you and your daughters have done.
49 "Look, this was the iniquity of your sister Sodom: She and her daughter had pride, fullness of food, and abundance of idleness; neither did she strengthen the hand of the poor and needy.
50 "And they were haughty and committed abomination before Me; therefore I took them away as I saw *fit*.
51 "Samaria did not commit half of your sins; but you have multiplied your abominations more than they, and have justified your sisters by all the abominations which you have done.
52 "You who judged your sisters, bear your own shame also, because the sins which you committed were more abominable than theirs; they are more righteous than you. Yes, be disgraced also, and bear your own shame, because you justified your sisters.
53 "When I bring back their captives, the captives of Sodom and her daughters, and the captives of Samaria and her daughters, then *I will also bring back* the captives of your captivity among them,
54 "that you may bear your own shame and be disgraced by all that you did when you comforted them.
55 "When your sisters, Sodom and her daughters, return to their former state, and Samaria and her daughters return to their former state, then you and your daughters will return to your former state.
56 "For your sister Sodom was not a byword in your mouth in the days of your pride,
57 "before your wickedness was uncovered. It was like the time of the reproach of the daughters of Syria and all *who were* around her, and of the daughters of the Philistines, who despise you everywhere.
58 "You have paid for your lewdness and your abominations," says the LORD.
59 'For thus says the Lord GOD: "I will deal with you as you have done, who despised the oath by breaking the covenant.

An Everlasting Covenant

60 "Nevertheless I will remember My covenant with you in the days of your youth, and I will establish an everlasting covenant with you.
61 "Then you will remember your ways and be ashamed, when you receive your older and your younger sisters; for I will give them to you for daughters, but not because of My covenant with you.
62 "And I will establish My covenant with you. Then you shall know that I *am* the LORD,
63 "that you may remember and be ashamed, and never open your mouth anymore because of your shame, when I provide you an atonement for all you have done," says the Lord GOD.' "

The Eagles and the Vine

17 And the word of the LORD came to me, saying,
2 "Son of man, pose a riddle, and speak a parable to the house of Israel,
3 "and say, 'Thus says the Lord GOD:

"A great eagle with large wings
    and long pinions,
Full of feathers of various colors,
Came to Lebanon

And took from the cedar the highest
branch.
4 He cropped off its topmost young twig
And carried it to a land of trade;
He set it in a city of merchants.
5 Then he took some of the seed of the
land
And planted it in a fertile field;
He placed *it* by abundant waters
And set it like a willow tree.
6 And it grew and became a spreading
vine of low stature;
Its branches turned toward him,
But its roots were under it.
So it became a vine,
Brought forth branches,
And put forth shoots.

7 "But there was another great eagle
with large wings and many feathers;
And behold, this vine bent its roots
toward him,
And stretched its branches toward him,
From the garden terrace where it had
been planted,
That he might water it.
8 It was planted in good soil by many
waters,
To bring forth branches, bear fruit,
And become a majestic vine." '

9 "Say, 'Thus says the Lord GOD:

"Will it thrive?
Will he not pull up its roots,
Cut off its fruit,
And leave it to wither?
All of its spring leaves will wither,
And no great power or many people
Will be needed to pluck it up
by its roots.
10 Behold, *it is* planted,
Will it thrive?
Will it not utterly wither
when the east wind touches it?
It will wither in the garden terrace
where it grew." ' "

11 Moreover the word of the LORD came
to me, saying,
12 "Say now to the rebellious house: 'Do
you not know what these *things mean*?'
Tell *them*, 'Indeed the king of Babylon
went to Jerusalem and took its king and
princes, and led them with him to Babylon.

13 'And he took the king's offspring,
made a covenant with him, and put him
under oath. He also took away the
mighty of the land,
14 'that the kingdom might be abased
and not lift itself up, *but* that by keeping
his covenant it might stand.
15 'But he rebelled against him by sending his ambassadors to Egypt, that they
might give him horses and many people.
Will he prosper? Will he who does such
things escape? Can he break a covenant
and still be delivered?
16 '*As* I live,' says the Lord GOD, 'surely
in the place *where* the king *dwells* who
made him king, whose oath he despised
and whose covenant he broke—with him
in the midst of Babylon he shall die.
17 'Nor will Pharaoh with *his* mighty
army and great company do anything in
the war, when they heap up a siege
mound and build a wall to cut off many
persons.
18 'Since he despised the oath by breaking the covenant, and in fact gave his
hand and still did all these *things*, he shall
not escape.' "
19 Therefore thus says the Lord GOD:
"*As* I live, surely My oath which he despised, and My covenant which he broke,
I will recompense on his own head.
20 "I will spread My net over him, and
he shall be taken in My snare. I will
bring him to Babylon and try him there
for the treason which he committed
against Me.
21 "All his fugitives with all his troops
shall fall by the sword, and those who remain shall be scattered to every wind;
and you shall know that I, the LORD,
have spoken."

Israel Exalted at Last

22 Thus says the Lord GOD: "I will take
also *one* of the highest branches of the
high cedar and set *it* out. I will crop off
from the topmost of its young twigs a
tender one, and will plant *it* on a high
and prominent mountain.
23 "On the mountain height of Israel I
will plant it; and it will bring forth
boughs, and bear fruit, and be a majestic
cedar. Under it will dwell birds of every
sort; in the shadow of its branches they
will dwell.
24 "And all the trees of the field shall
know that I, the LORD, have brought

down the high tree and exalted the low tree, dried up the green tree and made the dry tree flourish; I, the LORD, have spoken and have done *it*."

A False Proverb Refuted

18 The word of the LORD came to me again, saying, 2 "What do you mean when you use this proverb concerning the land of Israel, saying:

'The fathers have eaten sour grapes,
And the children's teeth
    are set on edge'?

3 "*As* I live," says the Lord GOD, "you shall no longer use this proverb in Israel.

4 "Behold, all souls are Mine;
The soul of the father
As well as the soul of the son is Mine;
The soul who sins shall die.
5 But if a man is just
And does what is lawful and right;
6 If he has not eaten on the mountains,
Nor lifted up his eyes
    to the idols of the house of Israel,
Nor defiled his neighbor's wife,
Nor approached a woman during her
    impurity;
7 If he has not oppressed anyone,
But has restored to the debtor
    his pledge;
Has robbed no one by violence,
But has given his bread to the hungry
And covered the naked with clothing;
8 If he has not exacted usury
Nor taken any increase,
But has withdrawn his hand from
    iniquity
And executed true judgment
    between man and man;
9 *If* he has walked in My statutes
And kept My judgments faithfully—
He *is* just;
He shall surely live!"
Says the Lord GOD.

10 "If he begets a son *who is* a robber
Or a shedder of blood,
Who does any of these *things*
11 And does none of those *duties*,
But has eaten on the mountains
Or defiled his neighbor's wife;
12 If he has oppressed the poor
    and needy,
Robbed by violence,
Not restored the pledge,

Lifted his eyes to the idols,
Or committed abomination;
13 If he has exacted usury
Or taken increase—
Shall he then live—
He shall not live!
If he has done any of these
    abominations,
He shall surely die;
His blood shall be upon him.

14 "*If*, however, he begets a son
Who sees all the sins which his father
    has done,
And considers but does not do
    likewise;
15 *Who* has not eaten on the mountains,
Nor lifted his eyes
    to the idols of the house of Israel,
Nor defiled his neighbor's wife;
16 Has not oppressed anyone,
Nor withheld a pledge,
Nor robbed by violence,
But has given his bread to the hungry
And covered the naked with clothing;
17 *Who* has withdrawn his hand from the
    poor
And not received usury or increase,
But has executed My judgments
And walked in My statutes—
He shall not die for the iniquity of his
    father;
He shall surely live!

18 "*As for* his father,
Because he cruelly oppressed,
Robbed his brother by violence,
And did what *is* not good among his
    people,
Behold, he shall die for his iniquity.

Turn and Live

19 "Yet you say, 'Why should the son not bear the guilt of the father?' Because the son has done what is lawful and right, and has kept all My statutes and done them, he shall surely live.
20 "The soul who sins shall die. The son shall not bear the guilt of the father, nor the father bear the guilt of the son. The righteousness of the righteous shall be upon himself, and the wickedness of the wicked shall be upon himself.
21 "But if a wicked man turns from all his sins which he has committed, keeps all My statutes, and does what is lawful and right, he shall surely live; he shall not die.
22 "None of the transgressions which he

has committed shall be remembered against him; because of the righteousness which he has done, he shall live.
23 "Do I have any pleasure at all that the wicked should die?" says the Lord GOD, "*and* not that he should turn from his ways and live?
24 "But when a righteous man turns away from his righteousness and commits iniquity, and does according to all the abominations that the wicked *man* does, shall he live? All the righteousness which he has done shall not be remembered; because of the unfaithfulness of which he is guilty and the sin which he has committed, because of them he shall die.
25 "Yet you say, 'The way of the Lord is not fair.' Hear now, O house of Israel, is it not My way which is fair, and your ways which are not fair?
26 "When a righteous *man* turns away from his righteousness, commits iniquity, and dies in it, it is because of the iniquity which he has done that he dies.
27 "Again, when a wicked *man* turns away from the wickedness which he committed, and does what is lawful and right, he preserves himself alive.
28 "Because he considers and turns away from all the transgressions which he committed, he shall surely live; he shall not die.
29 "Yet the house of Israel says, 'The way of the Lord is not fair.' O house of Israel, is it not My ways which are fair, and your ways which are not fair?
30 "Therefore I will judge you, O house of Israel, every one according to his ways," says the Lord GOD. "Repent, and turn from all your transgressions, so that iniquity will not be your ruin.
31 "Cast away from you all the transgressions which you have committed, and get yourselves a new heart and a new spirit. For why should you die, O house of Israel?
32 "For I have no pleasure in the death of one who dies," says the Lord GOD. "Therefore turn and live!"

Israel Degraded

19 "Moreover take up a lamentation for the princes of Israel,
2 "and say:

'What *is* your mother? A lioness:
    She lay down among the lions;

Among the young lions
    she nourished her cubs.
3 She brought up one of her cubs,
    And he became a young lion;
He learned to catch prey,
    And he devoured men.
4 The nations also heard of him;
    He was trapped in their pit,
And they brought him with chains
    to the land of Egypt.

5 'When she saw that she waited,
    that her hope was lost,
She took another of her cubs
    and made him a young lion.
6 He roved among the lions,
    And became a young lion;
He learned to catch prey;
    He devoured men.
7 He knew their desolate places,
    And laid waste their cities;
The land with its fullness was
    desolated
By the noise of his roaring.
8 Then the nations set against him
    from the provinces on every side,
And spread their net over him;
    He was trapped in their pit.
9 They put him in a cage with chains,
    And brought him to the king of
        Babylon;
They brought him in nets,
    That his voice should no longer be
        heard on the mountains of Israel.

10 'Your mother *was* like a vine
    in your bloodline,
Planted by the waters,
Fruitful and full of branches
Because of many waters.
11 She had strong branches for scepters of
        rulers.
She towered in stature above the thick
        branches,
And was seen in her height amid the
        dense foliage.
12 But she was plucked up in fury,
    She was cast down to the ground,
And the east wind dried her fruit.
Her strong branches were broken
        and withered;
The fire consumed them.
13 And now she *is* planted
    in the wilderness,
In a dry and thirsty land.
14 Fire has come out from a rod of her
        branches
And devoured her fruit,
So that she has no strong branch—
    a scepter for ruling.' "

This *is* a lamentation, and has become a lamentation.

The Rebellions of Israel

20 It came to pass in the seventh year, in the fifth *month*, on the tenth *day* of the month, *that* certain of the elders of Israel came to inquire of the LORD, and sat before me.
2 Then the word of the LORD came to me, saying,
3 "Son of man, speak to the elders of Israel, and say to them, 'Thus says the Lord GOD: "Have you come to inquire of Me? *As* I live," says the Lord GOD, "I will not be inquired of by you." '
4 "Will you judge them, son of man, will you judge *them*? Then make known to them the abominations of their fathers.
5 "Say to them, 'Thus says the Lord GOD: "On the day when I chose Israel and lifted My hand in an oath to the descendants of the house of Jacob, and made Myself known to them in the land of Egypt, I lifted My hand in an oath to them, saying, 'I *am* the LORD your God.'
6 "On that day I lifted My hand in an oath to them, to bring them out of the land of Egypt into a land that I had searched out for them, flowing with milk and honey, the glory of all lands.
7 "Then I said to them, 'Each of you, throw away the abominations which are before his eyes, and do not defile yourselves with the idols of Egypt. I *am* the LORD your God.'
8 "But they rebelled against Me and would not obey Me. They did not all cast away the abominations which were before their eyes, nor did they forsake the idols of Egypt. Then I said, 'I will pour out My fury on them and fulfill My anger against them in the midst of the land of Egypt.'
9 "But I acted for My name's sake, that it should not be profaned before the Gentiles among whom they *were*, in whose sight I had made Myself known to them, to bring them out of the land of Egypt.
10 "Therefore I made them go out of the land of Egypt and brought them into the wilderness.
11 "And I gave them My statutes and showed them My judgments, 'which, *if* a man does, he shall live by them.'⁶
12 "Moreover I also gave them My Sabbaths, to be a sign between them and Me,

that they might know that I *am* the LORD who sanctifies them.
13 "Yet the house of Israel rebelled against Me in the wilderness; they did not walk in My statutes; they despised My judgments, which, if a man does, he shall live by them; and they greatly defiled My Sabbaths. Then I said I would pour out My fury on them in the wilderness, to consume them.
14 "But I acted for My name's sake, that it should not be profaned before the Gentiles, in whose sight I had brought them out.
15 "So I also lifted My hand in an oath to them in the wilderness, that I would not bring them into the land which I had given *them*, flowing with milk and honey, the glory of all lands,
16 "because they despised My judgments and did not walk in My statutes, but profaned My Sabbaths; for their heart went after their idols.
17 "Nevertheless My eye spared them from destruction. I did not make an end of them in the wilderness.
18 "But I said to their children in the wilderness, 'Do not walk in the statutes of your fathers, nor observe their judgments, nor defile yourselves with their idols.
19 'I *am* the LORD your God: Walk in My statutes, keep My judgments, and do them;
20 'hallow My Sabbaths, and they will be a sign between Me and you, that you may know that I *am* the LORD your God.'
21 "Notwithstanding, the children rebelled against Me; they did not walk in My statutes, and were not careful to observe My judgments, 'which, *if* a man does, he shall live by them';⁷ but they profaned My Sabbaths. Then I said I would pour out My fury on them and fulfill My anger against them in the wilderness.
22 "Nevertheless I withdrew My hand and acted for My name's sake, that it should not be profaned in the sight of the Gentiles, in whose sight I had brought them out.
23 "Also I lifted My hand in an oath to those in the wilderness, that I would scatter them among the Gentiles and disperse them throughout the countries,
24 "because they had not executed My judgments, but had despised My statutes,

6 Leviticus 18:5   7 Leviticus 18:5

profaned My Sabbaths, and their eyes were fixed on their fathers' idols. 25 "Therefore I also gave them up to statutes *that were* not good, and judgments by which they could not live; 26 "and I pronounced them unclean because of their ritual gifts, in that they caused all their firstborn to pass through *the fire*, that I might make them desolate and that they might know that I am the LORD." '

27 "Therefore, son of man, speak to the house of Israel, and say to them, 'Thus says the Lord GOD: "In this too your fathers have blasphemed Me, by being unfaithful to Me.

28 "*For* when I brought them into the land *for* which I had lifted My hand in an oath to give them, and they saw all the high hills and all the thick trees, there they offered their sacrifices and provoked Me with their offerings. There they also sent up their sweet aroma and poured out their drink offerings.

29 "Then I said to them, 'What *is* this high place to which you go?' So its name is called Bamah⁸ to this day." '

30 "Therefore say to the house of Israel, 'Thus says the Lord GOD: "Are you defiling yourselves in the manner of your fathers, and committing harlotry according to their abominations?

31 "For when you offer your gifts and make your sons pass through the fire, you defile yourselves with all your idols, even to this day. So shall I be inquired of by you, O house of Israel? *As* I live," says the Lord GOD, "I will not be inquired of by you.

32 "What you have in your mind shall never be, when you say, 'We will be like the Gentiles, like the families in other countries, serving wood and stone.'

God Will Restore Israel

33 "*As* I live," says the Lord GOD, "surely with a mighty hand, with an outstretched arm, and with fury poured out, I will rule over you.

34 "I will bring you out from the peoples and gather you out of the countries where you are scattered, with a mighty hand, with an outstretched arm, and with fury poured out.

35 "And I will bring you into the wilderness of the peoples, and there I will plead My case with you face to face.

36 "Just as I pleaded My case with your fathers in the wilderness of the land of Egypt, so I will plead My case with you," says the Lord GOD.

37 "I will make you pass under the rod, and I will bring you into the bond of the covenant;

38 "I will purge the rebels from among you, and those who transgress against Me; I will bring them out of the country where they sojourn, but they shall not enter the land of Israel. Then you will know that I *am* the LORD.

39 "As for you, O house of Israel," thus says the Lord GOD: "Go, serve every one of you his idols—and hereafter—if you will not obey me; but profane My holy name no more with your gifts and your idols.

40 "For on My holy mountain, on the mountain height of Israel," says the Lord GOD, "there all the house of Israel, all of them in the land, shall serve Me; there I will accept them, and there I will require your offerings and the firstfruits of your sacrifices, together with all your holy things.

41 "I will accept you as a sweet aroma when I bring you out from the peoples and gather you out of the countries where you have been scattered; and I will be hallowed in you before the Gentiles.

42 "Then you shall know that I *am* the LORD, when I bring you into the land of Israel, into the country *for* which I lifted My hand in an oath to give to your fathers.

43 "And there you shall remember your ways and all your doings with which you were defiled; and you shall loathe yourselves in your own sight because of all the evils that you have committed.

44 "Then you shall know that I *am* the LORD, when I have dealt with you for My name's sake, not according to your wicked ways nor according to your corrupt doings, O house of Israel," says the Lord GOD.' "

Fire in the Forest

45 Furthermore the word of the LORD came to me, saying,

46 "Son of man, set your face toward the south; preach against the south and prophesy against the forest land, the South,⁹

8 Literally *High Place*   9 Hebrew *Negev*

⁴⁷ "and say to the forest of the South,
'Hear the word of the LORD! Thus says
the Lord GOD: "Behold, I will kindle a
fire in you, and it shall devour every
green tree and every dry tree in you; the
blazing flame shall not be quenched, and
all faces from the south to the north shall
be scorched by it.
⁴⁸ "All flesh shall see that I, the LORD,
have kindled it; it shall not be
quenched." ' "
⁴⁹ Then I said, "Ah, Lord GOD! They
say of me, 'Does he not speak parables?' "

Babylon, the Sword of God

21 And the word of the LORD came
to me, saying,
² "Son of man, set your face toward Jerusalem, preach against the holy places,
and prophesy against the land of Israel;
³ "and say to the land of Israel, 'Thus
says the LORD: "Behold, I *am* against
you, and I will draw My sword out of its
sheath and cut off both righteous and
wicked from you.
⁴ "Because I will cut off both righteous
and wicked from you, therefore My
sword shall go out of its sheath against all
flesh from south *to* north,
⁵ "that all flesh may know that I, the
LORD, have drawn My sword out of its
sheath; it shall not return anymore." '
⁶ "Sigh therefore, son of man, with a
breaking heart, and sigh with bitterness
before their eyes.
⁷ "And it shall be when they say to you,
'Why are you sighing?' that you shall answer, 'Because of the news; when it
comes, every heart will melt, all hands
will be feeble, every spirit will faint, and
all knees will be weak *as* water. Behold,
it is coming and shall be brought to pass,'
says the Lord GOD."
⁸ Again the word of the LORD came to
me, saying,
⁹ "Son of man, prophesy and say, 'Thus
says the LORD!

"Say:

'A sword, a sword is sharpened
And also polished!
¹⁰ Sharpened to make a dreadful
    slaughter,
Polished to flash like lightning!
Should we then make mirth?

It despises the scepter of My son,
As it does all wood.
¹¹ And He has given it to be polished,
That it may be handled;
This sword is sharpened,
    and it is polished
To be given into the hand of the
    slayer.'

¹² "Cry and wail, son of man;
For it will be against My people,
Against all the princes of Israel.
Terrors including the sword
    will be against My people;
Therefore strike *your* thigh.

¹³ "Because *it is* a testing,
And what if *the sword* despises
    even the scepter?
The scepter shall be no *more*,"

says the Lord GOD.

¹⁴"You therefore, son of man, prophesy,
And strike *your* hands together.
The third time let the sword
    do double *damage*.
It is the sword *that* slays,
The sword that slays the great *men*,
That enters their private chambers.
¹⁵ I have set the point of the sword
    against all their gates,
That the heart may melt
    and many may stumble.
Ah! *It is* made bright;
It is grasped for slaughter:

¹⁶ "Swords at the ready!
Thrust right!
Set your blade!
Thrust left—
Wherever your edge is ordered!

¹⁷ "I also will beat My fists together,
And I will cause My fury to rest;
I, the LORD, have spoken."

¹⁸ The word of the LORD came to me
again, saying:
¹⁹ "And son of man, appoint for yourself
two ways for the sword of the king of
Babylon to go; both of them shall go
from the same land. Make a sign; put *it*
at the head of the road to the city.
²⁰ "Appoint a road for the sword to go
to Rabbah of the Ammonites, and to Judah, into fortified Jerusalem.
²¹ "For the king of Babylon stands at
the parting of the road, at the fork of the

two roads, to use divination: he shakes the arrows, he consults the images, he looks at the liver.

22 "In his right hand is the divination for Jerusalem: to set up battering rams, to call for a slaughter, to lift the voice with shouting, to set battering rams against the gates, to heap up a *siege* mound, and to build a wall.

23 "And it will be to them like a false divination in the eyes of those who have sworn oaths with them; but he will bring their iniquity to remembrance, that they may be taken.

24 "Therefore thus says the Lord GOD: 'Because you have made your iniquity to be remembered, in that your transgressions are uncovered, so that in all your doings your sins appear—because you have come to remembrance, you shall be taken in hand.

25 'Now to you, O profane, wicked prince of Israel, whose day has come, whose iniquity *shall* end,

26 "thus says the Lord GOD:

'Remove the turban,
   and take off the crown;
Nothing *shall remain* the same.
Exalt the lowly,
   and abase the exalted.
27 Overthrown, overthrown,
   I will make it overthrown!
It shall be no *longer*,
Until He comes whose right it is,
And I will give it *to Him*.'

A Sword Against the Ammonites

28 "And you, son of man, prophesy and say, 'Thus says the Lord GOD concerning the Ammonites and concerning their reproach,' and say:

'A sword, a sword *is* drawn,
Polished for slaughter,
For consuming, for flashing—
29 While they see vain visions for you,
While they divine a lie to you,
To bring you on the necks of the
   wicked, the slain
Whose day has come,
Whose iniquity *shall* end.

30 'Return *it* to its sheath.
I will judge you
In the place where you were created,
In the land of your nativity.
31 I will pour out My indignation on you;

I will blow against you with the fire of
   My wrath,
And deliver you into the hands
   of brutal men *who are* skillful to
   destroy.
32 You shall be fuel for the fire;
Your blood shall be in the midst
   of the land.
You shall not be remembered,
For I the LORD have spoken.' "

Sins of Jerusalem

22 Moreover the word of the LORD came to me, saying,

2 "Now, son of man, will you judge, will you judge the bloody city? Yes, show her all her abominations!

3 "Then say, 'Thus says the Lord GOD: "The city sheds blood in her own midst, that her time may come; and she makes idols within herself to defile herself.

4 "You have become guilty by the blood which you have shed, and have defiled yourself with the idols which you have made. You have caused your days to draw near, and have come to *the end of* your years; therefore I have made you a reproach to the nations, and a mockery to all countries.

5 "*Those* near and *those* far from you will mock you as infamous and full of tumult.

6 "Look, the princes of Israel: each one has used his power to shed blood in you.

7 "In you they have made light of father and mother; in your midst they have oppressed the stranger; in you they have mistreated the fatherless and the widow.

8 "You have despised My holy things and profaned My Sabbaths.

9 "In you are men who slander to cause bloodshed; in you are those who eat on the mountains; in your midst they commit lewdness.

10 "In you men uncover their fathers' nakedness; in you they violate women who are set apart during their impurity.

11 "One commits abomination with his neighbor's wife; another lewdly defiles his daughter-in-law; and another in you violates his sister, his father's daughter.

12 "In you they take bribes to shed blood; you take usury and increase; you have made profit from your neighbors by extortion, and have forgotten Me," says the Lord GOD.

13 "Behold, therefore, I beat My fists at the dishonest profit which you have

made, and at the bloodshed which has been in your midst.

14 "Can your heart endure, or can your hands remain strong, in the days when I shall deal with you? I, the LORD, have spoken, and will do *it*.

15 "I will scatter you among the nations, disperse you throughout the countries, and remove your filthiness completely from you.

16 "You shall defile yourself in the sight of the nations; then you shall know that I *am* the LORD." ' "

Israel in the Furnace

17 The word of the LORD came to me, saying,

18 "Son of man, the house of Israel has become dross to Me; they *are* all bronze, tin, iron, and lead, in the midst of a furnace; they have become dross from silver.

19 "Therefore thus says the Lord GOD: 'Because you have all become dross, therefore behold, I will gather you into the midst of Jerusalem.

20 '*As men* gather silver, bronze, iron, lead, and tin into the midst of a furnace, to blow fire on it, to melt *it*; so I will gather *you* in My anger and in My fury, and I will leave *you there* and melt you.

21 'Yes, I will gather you and blow on you with the fire of My wrath, and you shall be melted in its midst.

22 'As silver is melted in the midst of a furnace, so shall you be melted in its midst; then you shall know that I, the LORD, have poured out My fury on you.' "

Israel's Wicked Leaders

23 And the word of the LORD came to me, saying,

24 "Son of man, say to her: 'You *are* a land that is not cleansed or rained on in the day of indignation.'

25 "The conspiracy of her prophets in her midst is like a roaring lion tearing the prey; they have devoured people; they have taken treasure and precious things; they have made many widows in her midst.

26 "Her priests have violated My law and profaned My holy things; they have not distinguished between the holy and unholy, nor have they made known *the difference* between the unclean and the clean; and they have hidden their eyes

from My Sabbaths, so that I am profaned among them.

27 "Her princes in her midst *are* like wolves tearing the prey, to shed blood, to destroy people, and to get dishonest gain.

28 "Her prophets plastered them with untempered *mortar*, seeing false visions, and divining lies for them, saying, 'Thus says the Lord GOD,' when the LORD had not spoken.

29 "The people of the land have used oppressions, committed robbery, and mistreated the poor and needy; and they wrongfully oppress the stranger.

30 "So I sought for a man among them who would make a wall, and stand in the gap before Me on behalf of the land, that I should not destroy it; but I found no one.

31 "Therefore I have poured out My indignation on them; I have consumed them with the fire of My wrath; and I have recompensed their deeds on their own heads," says the Lord GOD.

Two Harlot Sisters

23 The word of the LORD came again to me, saying:

2 "Son of man, there were two women,
The daughters of one mother.
3 They committed harlotry in Egypt,
They committed harlotry
in their youth;
Their breasts were there embraced,
Their virgin bosom was there pressed.
4 Their names: Oholah[10] the elder
and Oholibah[11] her sister;
They were Mine,
And they bore sons and daughters.
As for their names,
Samaria *is* Oholah,
and Jerusalem *is* Oholibah.

The Older Sister, Samaria

5 "Oholah played the harlot
even though she was Mine;
And she lusted for her lovers,
the neighboring Assyrians,
6 *Who were* clothed in purple,
Captains and rulers,
All of them desirable young men,
Horsemen riding on horses.
7 Thus she committed her harlotry
with them,
All of them choice men of Assyria;
And with all for whom she lusted,
With all their idols, she defiled herself.

10 Literally *Her Own Tabernacle*   11 Literally *My Tabernacle Is In Her*

8 She has never given up her harlotry
   brought from Egypt,
   For in her youth
      they had lain with her,
   Pressed her virgin bosom,
   And poured out their immorality
      upon her.

9 "Therefore I have delivered her
      Into the hand of her lovers,
   Into the hand of the Assyrians,
      For whom she lusted.
10 They uncovered her nakedness,
   Took away her sons and daughters,
   And slew her with the sword;
   She became a byword among women,
   For they had executed judgment on
      her.

The Younger Sister, Jerusalem

11 "Now although her sister Oholibah
saw *this*, she became more corrupt in her
inordinate love than she, and in her harlotry more corrupt than her sister's
harlotry.

12 "She lusted for the neighboring
      Assyrians,
   Captains and rulers,
   Clothed most gorgeously,
   Horsemen riding on horses,
   All of them desirable young men.
13 Then I saw that she was defiled;
   Both *took* the same way.
14 But she increased her harlotry;
   She looked at men
      portrayed on the wall,
   Images of Chaldeans
      portrayed in vermilion,
15 Girded with belts around their waists,
   Flowing turbans on their heads,
   All of them looking like captains,
   In the manner of the Babylonians of
      Chaldea,
   The land of their nativity.
16 As soon as her eyes saw them,
   She lusted for them
   And sent messengers to them in
      Chaldea.

17 "Then the Babylonians came to her,
      into the bed of love,
   And they defiled her with their
      immorality;
   So she was defiled by them,
      and alienated herself from them.
18 She revealed her harlotry
      and uncovered her nakedness.
   Then I alienated Myself from her,

   As I had alienated Myself from her
      sister.

19 "Yet she multiplied her harlotry
   In calling to remembrance the days of
      her youth,
   When she had played the harlot
      in the land of Egypt.
20 For she lusted for her paramours,
   Whose flesh *is like* the flesh of donkeys,
   And whose issue *is like*
      the issue of horses.
21 Thus you called to remembrance
      the lewdness of your youth,
   When the Egyptians pressed your
      bosom
   Because of your youthful breasts.

Judgment on Jerusalem

22 "Therefore, Oholibah, thus says the
Lord GOD:

   'Behold, I will stir up your lovers
      against you,
   From whom you have alienated
      yourself,
   And I will bring them against you
      from every side:
23 The Babylonians,
   All the Chaldeans,
   Pekod, Shoa, Koa,
   All the Assyrians with them,
   All of them desirable young men,
   Governors and rulers,
   Captains and men of renown,
   All of them riding on horses.
24 And they shall come against you
   With chariots, wagons, and war-horses,
   With a horde of people.
   They shall array against you
   Buckler, shield, and helmet all around.

   'I will delegate judgment to them,
   And they shall judge you
      according to their judgments.
25 I will set My jealousy against you,
   And they shall deal furiously with you;
   They shall remove your nose
      and your ears,
   And your remnant shall fall by the
      sword;
   They shall take your sons
      and your daughters,
   And your remnant shall be devoured
      by fire.
26 They shall also strip you of your
      clothes
   And take away your beautiful jewelry.

27 'Thus I will make you cease
    your lewdness and your harlotry
    Brought from the land of Egypt,
    So that you will not lift your eyes to
        them,
    Nor remember Egypt anymore.'

28 "For thus says the Lord GOD: 'Surely
I will deliver you into the hand *of those*
whom you hate, into the hand *of those*
from whom you alienated yourself.
29 'They will deal hatefully with you,
take away all you have worked for, and
leave you naked and bare. The nakedness of your harlotry shall be uncovered,
both your lewdness and your harlotry.
30 'I will do these *things* to you because
you have gone as a harlot after the Gentiles, because you have become defiled by
their idols.
31 'You have walked in the way of your
sister; therefore I will put her cup in your
hand.'
32 "Thus says the Lord GOD:

'You shall drink of your sister's cup,
    The deep and wide one;
    You shall be laughed to scorn
    And held in derision;
    It contains much.
33 You will be filled with drunkenness
        and sorrow,
    The cup of horror and desolation,
    The cup of your sister Samaria.
34 You shall drink and drain it,
    You shall break its shards,
    And tear at your own breasts;
    For I have spoken,'
    Says the Lord GOD.

35 "Therefore thus says the Lord GOD:

'Because you have forgotten Me
    and cast Me behind your back,
Therefore you shall bear the *penalty*
Of your lewdness and your harlotry.' "

Both Sisters Judged

36 The LORD also said to me: "Son of
man, will you judge Oholah and Oholibah? Then declare to them their abominations.
37 "For they have committed adultery,
and blood *is* on their hands. They have
committed adultery with their idols, and
even sacrificed their sons whom they bore
to Me, passing them through *the fire*, to
devour *them*.

38 "Moreover they have done this to Me:
They have defiled My sanctuary on the
same day and profaned My Sabbaths.
39 "For after they had slain their children for their idols, on the same day they
came into My sanctuary to profane it;
and indeed thus they have done in the
midst of My house.
40 "Furthermore you sent for men to
come from afar, to whom a messenger
was sent; and there they came. And you
washed yourself for them, painted your
eyes, and adorned yourself with ornaments.
41 "You sat on a stately couch, with a
table prepared before it, on which you
had set My incense and My oil.
42 "The sound of a carefree multitude
was with her, and Sabeans *were* brought
from the wilderness with men of the common sort, who put bracelets on their
wrists and beautiful crowns on their
heads.
43 "Then I said concerning *her who had
grown* old in adulteries, 'Will they commit
harlotry with her now, and she *with
them*?'
44 "Yet they went in to her, as men go in
to a woman who plays the harlot; thus
they went in to Oholah and Oholibah, the
lewd women.
45 "But righteous men will judge them
after the manner of adulteresses, and after the manner of women who shed
blood, because they *are* adulteresses, and
blood *is* on their hands.
46 "For thus says the Lord GOD: 'Bring
up an assembly against them, give them
up to trouble and plunder.
47 'The assembly shall stone them with
stones and execute them with their
swords; they shall slay their sons and
their daughters, and burn their houses
with fire.
48 'Thus I will cause lewdness to cease
from the land, that all women may be
taught not to practice your lewdness.
49 'They shall repay you for your lewdness, and you shall pay for your idolatrous sins. Then you shall know that I
am the Lord GOD.' "

Symbol of the Cooking Pot

24 Again, in the ninth year, in the
tenth month, on the tenth *day* of
the month, the word of the LORD came to
me, saying,

2 "Son of man, write down the name of the day, this very day—the king of Babylon started his siege against Jerusalem this very day.
3 "And utter a parable to the rebellious house, and say to them, 'Thus says the Lord GOD:

"Put on a pot, set it on,
And also pour water into it.
4 Gather pieces of meat in it,
Every good piece,
The thigh and the shoulder.
Fill it with choice cuts;
5 Take the choice of the flock.
Also pile fuel bones under it,
Make it boil well,
And let the cuts simmer in it."

6 'Therefore thus says the Lord GOD:

"Woe to the bloody city,
To the pot whose scum is in it,
And whose scum is not gone from it!
Bring it out piece by piece,
On which no lot has fallen.
7 For her blood is in her midst;
She set it on top of a rock;
She did not pour it on the ground,
To cover it with dust.
8 That it may raise up fury
and take vengeance,
I have set her blood on top of a rock,
That it may not be covered."

9 'Therefore thus says the Lord GOD:

"Woe to the bloody city!
I too will make the pyre great.
10 Heap on the wood,
Kindle the fire;
Cook the meat well,
Mix in the spices,
And let the cuts be burned up.

11 "Then set the pot empty on the coals,
That it may become hot
and its bronze may burn,
That its filthiness may be melted in it,
That its scum may be consumed.
12 She has wearied herself with lies,
And her great scum
has not gone from her.
Let her scum be in the fire!
13 In your filthiness is lewdness.
Because I have purged you,
and you were not purged,
You will not be purged of your
filthiness anymore,

Till I have caused My fury
to rest upon you.
14 I, the LORD, have spoken it;
It shall come to pass,
and I will do it;
I will not hold back,
Nor will I spare,
Nor will I relent;
According to your ways
And according to your deeds
They will judge you,"
Says the Lord GOD.' "

The Prophet's Wife Dies

15 Also the word of the LORD came to me, saying,
16 "Son of man, behold, I take away from you the desire of your eyes with one stroke; yet you shall neither mourn nor weep, nor shall your tears run down.
17 "Sigh in silence, make no mourning for the dead; bind your turban on your head, and put your sandals on your feet; do not cover your lips, and do not eat man's bread of sorrow."
18 So I spoke to the people in the morning, and at evening my wife died; and the next morning I did as I was commanded.
19 And the people said to me, "Will you not tell us what these things signify to us, that you behave so?"
20 Then I answered them, "The word of the LORD came to me, saying,
21 'Speak to the house of Israel, "Thus says the Lord GOD: 'Behold, I will profane My sanctuary, your arrogant boast, the desire of your eyes, the delight of your soul; and your sons and daughters whom you left behind shall fall by the sword.
22 'And you shall do as I have done; you shall not cover your lips nor eat man's bread of sorrow.
23 'Your turbans shall be on your heads and your sandals on your feet; you shall neither mourn nor weep, but you shall pine away in your iniquities and mourn with one another.
24 'Thus Ezekiel is a sign to you; according to all that he has done you shall do; and when this comes, you shall know that I am the Lord GOD.' "
25 'And you, son of man—will it not be in the day when I take from them their stronghold, their joy and their glory, the desire of their eyes, and that on which they set their minds, their sons and their daughters:

26 'on that day one who escapes will come to you to let *you* hear *it* with *your* ears;
27 'on that day your mouth will be opened to him who has escaped; you shall speak and no longer be mute. Thus you will be a sign to them, and they shall know that I *am* the LORD.' "

Proclamation Against Ammon

25 The word of the LORD came to me, saying,
2 "Son of man, set your face against the Ammonites, and prophesy against them.
3 "Say to the Ammonites, 'Hear the word of the Lord GOD! Thus says the Lord GOD: "Because you said, 'Aha!' against My sanctuary when it was profaned, and against the land of Israel when it was desolate, and against the house of Judah when they went into captivity,
4 "indeed, therefore, I will deliver you as a possession to the men of the East, and they shall set their encampments among you and make their dwellings among you; they shall eat your fruit, and they shall drink your milk.
5 "And I will make Rabbah a stable for camels and Ammon a resting place for flocks. Then you shall know that I *am* the LORD."
6 'For thus says the Lord GOD: "Because you clapped *your* hands, stamped your feet, and rejoiced in heart with all your disdain for the land of Israel,
7 "indeed, therefore, I will stretch out My hand against you, and give you as plunder to the nations; I will cut you off from the peoples, and I will cause you to perish from the countries; I will destroy you, and you shall know that I *am* the LORD."

Proclamation Against Moab

8 'Thus says the Lord GOD: "Because Moab and Seir say, 'Look! The house of Judah *is* like all the nations,'
9 "therefore, behold, I will clear the territory of Moab of cities, of the cities on its frontier, the glory of the country, Beth Jeshimoth, Baal Meon, and Kirjathaim.
10 "To the men of the East I will give it as a possession, together with the Ammonites, that the Ammonites may not be remembered among the nations.
11 "And I will execute judgments upon

Moab, and they shall know that I *am* the LORD."

Proclamation Against Edom

12 'Thus says the Lord GOD: "Because of what Edom did against the house of Judah by taking vengeance, and has greatly offended by avenging itself on them,"
13 'therefore thus says the Lord GOD: "I will also stretch out My hand against Edom, cut off man and beast from it, and make it desolate from Teman; Dedan shall fall by the sword.
14 "I will lay My vengeance on Edom by the hand of My people Israel, that they may do in Edom according to My anger and according to My fury; and they shall know My vengeance," says the Lord GOD.

Proclamation Against Philistia

15 'Thus says the Lord GOD: "Because the Philistines dealt vengefully and took vengeance with a spiteful heart, to destroy because of the old hatred,"
16 'therefore thus says the Lord GOD: "I will stretch out My hand against the Philistines, and I will cut off the Cherethites and destroy the remnant of the seacoast.
17 "I will execute great vengeance on them with furious rebukes; and they shall know that I *am* the LORD, when I lay My vengeance upon them." ' "

Proclamation Against Tyre

26 And it came to pass in the eleventh year, on the first *day* of the month, *that* the word of the LORD came to me, saying,
2 "Son of man, because Tyre has said against Jerusalem, 'Aha! She is broken who *was* the gateway of the peoples; now she is turned over to me; I shall be filled; she is laid waste.'
3 "Therefore thus says the Lord GOD: 'Behold, I *am* against you, O Tyre, and will cause many nations to come up against you, as the sea causes its waves to come up.
4 'And they shall destroy the walls of Tyre and break down her towers; I will also scrape her dust from her, and make her like the top of a rock.
5 'It shall be *a place for* spreading nets in the midst of the sea, for I have spoken,' says the Lord GOD; 'it shall become plunder for the nations.

6 'Also her daughter *villages* which *are* in the fields shall be slain by the sword. Then they shall know that I am the LORD.'

7 "For thus says the Lord GOD: 'Behold, I will bring against Tyre from the north Nebuchadnezzar[12] king of Babylon, king of kings, with horses, with chariots, and with horsemen, and an army with many people.

8 'He will slay with the sword your daughter *villages* in the fields; he will heap up a siege mound against you, build a wall against you, and raise a defense against you.

9 'He will direct his battering rams against your walls, and with his axes he will break down your towers.

10 'Because of the abundance of his horses, their dust will cover you; your walls will shake at the noise of the horsemen, the wagons, and the chariots, when he enters your gates, as men enter a city that has been breached.

11 'With the hooves of his horses he will trample all your streets; he will slay your people by the sword, and your strong pillars will fall to the ground.

12 'They will plunder your riches and pillage your merchandise; they will break down your walls and destroy your pleasant houses; they will lay your stones, your timber, and your soil in the midst of the water.

13 'I will put an end to the sound of your songs, and the sound of your harps shall be heard no more.

14 'I will make you like the top of a rock; you shall be *a place for* spreading nets, and you shall never be rebuilt, for I the LORD have spoken,' says the Lord GOD.

15 "Thus says the Lord GOD to Tyre: 'Will the coastlands not shake at the sound of your fall, when the wounded cry, when slaughter is made in the midst of you?

16 'Then all the princes of the sea will come down from their thrones, lay aside their robes, and take off their embroidered garments; they will clothe themselves with trembling; they will sit on the ground, tremble *every* moment, and be astonished at you.

17 'And they will take up a lamentation for you, and say to you:

"How you have perished,
O one inhabited by seafaring men,
O renowned city,
Who was strong at sea,
She and her inhabitants,
Who caused their terror
to be on all her inhabitants!
18 Now the coastlands tremble
on the day of your fall;
Yes, the coastlands by the sea
are troubled at your departure." '

19 "For thus says the Lord GOD: 'When I make you a desolate city, like cities that are not inhabited, when I bring the deep upon you, and great waters cover you,
20 'then I will bring you down with those who descend into the Pit, to the people of old, and I will make you dwell in the lowest part of the earth, in places desolate from antiquity, with those who go down to the Pit, so that you may never be inhabited; and I shall establish glory in the land of the living.
21 'I will make you a terror, and you *shall be* no *more*; though you are sought for, you will never be found again,' says the Lord GOD."

Lamentation for Tyre

27 The word of the LORD came again to me, saying,
2 "Now, son of man, take up a lamentation for Tyre,
3 "and say to Tyre, 'You who are situated at the entrance of the sea, merchant of the peoples on many coastlands, thus says the Lord GOD:

"O Tyre, you have said,
'I *am* perfect in beauty.'
4   Your borders *are* in the midst
of the seas.
Your builders have perfected your
beauty.
5   They made all *your* planks
of fir trees from Senir;
They took a cedar from Lebanon
to make you a mast.
6   *Of* oaks from Bashan
they made your oars;
The company of Ashurites
have inlaid your planks
With ivory from the coasts of Cyprus.[13]
7   Fine embroidered linen from Egypt
was what you spread for your sail;
Blue and purple from the coasts of
Elishah was what covered you.

---

12 Hebrew *Nebuchadrezzar*, and so elsewhere in this book   13 Hebrew *Kittim*, western lands, especially Cyprus

EZEKIEL 27

8 "Inhabitants of Sidon and Arvad
   were your oarsmen;
   Your *own* wise men, O Tyre,
   were in you;
   They became your pilots.
9 Elders of Gebal and its wise men
   Were in you to caulk your seams;
   All the ships of the sea
   And their oarsmen were in you
   To market your merchandise.

10 "Those from Persia, Lydia,[14]
   and Libya[15]
   Were in your army as men of war;
   They hung shield and helmet in you;
   They gave splendor to you.
11 Men of Arvad with your army
   were on your walls *all* around,
   And the men of Gammad
   were in your towers;
   They hung their shields
   on your walls *all* around;
   They made your beauty perfect.

12 "Tarshish *was* your merchant because of your many luxury goods. They gave you silver, iron, tin, and lead for your goods.
13 "Javan, Tubal, and Meshech *were* your traders. They bartered human lives and vessels of bronze for your merchandise.
14 "Those from the house of Togarmah traded for your wares with horses, steeds, and mules.
15 "The men of Dedan *were* your traders; many isles *were* the market of your hand. They brought you ivory tusks and ebony as payment.
16 "Syria *was* your merchant because of the abundance of goods you made. They gave you for your wares emeralds, purple, embroidery, fine linen, corals, and rubies.
17 "Judah and the land of Israel *were* your traders. They traded for your merchandise wheat of Minnith, millet, honey, oil, and balm.
18 "Damascus *was* your merchant because of the abundance of goods you made, because of your many luxury items, with the wine of Helbon and with white wool.
19 "Dan and Javan paid for your wares, traversing back and forth. Wrought iron, cassia, and cane were among your merchandise.
20 "Dedan *was* your merchant in saddlecloths for riding.

21 "Arabia and all the princes of Kedar *were* your regular merchants. They traded with you in lambs, rams, and goats.
22 "The merchants of Sheba and Raamah *were* your merchants. They traded for your wares the choicest spices, all kinds of precious stones, and gold.
23 "Haran, Canneh, Eden, the merchants of Sheba, Assyria, *and* Chilmad *were* your merchants.
24 "These *were* your merchants in choice items—in purple clothes, in embroidered garments, in chests of multicolored apparel, in strong twined cords, which were in your marketplace.

25 "The ships of Tarshish were carriers
   of your merchandise.
   You were filled and very glorious
   in the midst of the seas.
26 Your oarsmen brought you
   into many waters,
   But the east wind broke you
   in the midst of the seas.

27 "Your riches, wares, and merchandise,
   Your mariners and pilots,
   Your caulkers and merchandisers,
   All your men of war who *are* in you,
   And the entire company which *is* in
   your midst,
   Will fall into the midst of the seas
   on the day of your ruin.
28 The common-land will shake at the
   sound of the cry of your pilots.

29 "All who handle the oar,
   The mariners,
   All the pilots of the sea
   Will come down from their ships
   and stand on the shore.
30 They will make their voice heard
   because of you;
   They will cry bitterly
   and cast dust on their heads;
   They will roll about in ashes;
31 They will shave themselves completely
   bald because of you,
   Gird themselves with sackcloth,
   And weep for you
   With bitterness of heart
   and bitter wailing.
32 In their wailing for you
   They will take up a lamentation,
   And lament for you,
   'What *city is* like Tyre,
   Destroyed in the midst of the sea?

14 Hebrew *Lud*   15 Hebrew *Put*

33 'When your wares went out by sea,
    You satisfied many people;
    You enriched the kings of the earth
    With your many luxury goods
        and your merchandise.
34 But *when* you are broken by the seas
        in the depths of the waters,
    Your merchandise and the entire
        company will fall in your midst.
35 All the inhabitants of the isles
        will be astonished at you;
    Their kings will be greatly afraid,
    And *their* countenance will be troubled.
36 The merchants among the peoples
        will hiss at you;
    You will become a horror,
        and *be* no more forever." ' "

Proclamation Against the King of Tyre

28 The word of the LORD came to me
    again, saying,
2 "Son of man, say to the prince of
Tyre, 'Thus says the Lord GOD:

"Because your heart *is* lifted up,
    And you say, 'I *am* a god,
    I sit *in* the seat of gods,
    In the midst of the seas,'
    Yet you *are* a man, and not a god,
    Though you set your heart
        as the heart of a god
3 (Behold, you *are* wiser than Daniel!
    There is no secret that can be hidden
        from you!
4 With your wisdom
        and your understanding
    You have gained riches for yourself,
    And gathered gold and silver
        into your treasuries;
5 By your great wisdom in trade
        you have increased your riches,
    And your heart is lifted up
        because of your riches),"

6 'Therefore thus says the Lord GOD:

"Because you have set your heart
    as the heart of a god,
7 Behold, therefore, I will bring strangers
        against you,
    The most terrible of the nations;
    And they shall draw their swords
        against the beauty of your wisdom,
    And defile your splendor.
8 They shall throw you down
        into the Pit,
    And you shall die the death
        of the slain
    In the midst of the seas.

9 "Will you still say before him
        who slays you,
    'I *am* a god'?
    But you *shall be* a man, and not a god,
    In the hand of him who slays you.
10 You shall die the death of the
        uncircumcised
    By the hand of aliens;
    For I have spoken,"
    says the Lord GOD.' "

Lamentation for the King of Tyre

11 Moreover the word of the LORD came
to me, saying,
12 "Son of man, take up a lamentation
for the king of Tyre, and say to him,
'Thus says the Lord GOD:

"You *were* the seal of perfection,
    Full of wisdom and perfect in beauty.
13 You were in Eden, the garden of God;
    Every precious stone *was* your
        covering:
    The sardius, topaz, and diamond,
    Beryl, onyx, and jasper,
    Sapphire, turquoise,
        and emerald with gold.
    The workmanship of your timbrels
        and pipes
    Was prepared for you
        on the day you were created.

14 "You *were* the anointed cherub who
        covers;
    I established you;
    You were on the holy mountain of
        God;
    You walked back and forth
        in the midst of fiery stones.
15 You *were* perfect in your ways
        from the day you were created,
    Till iniquity was found in you.

16 "By the abundance of your trading
    You became filled with violence within,
        And you sinned;
    Therefore I cast you as a profane thing
        Out of the mountain of God;
    And I destroyed you,
        O covering cherub,
    From the midst of the fiery stones.

17 "Your heart was lifted up
        because of your beauty;
    You corrupted your wisdom
        for the sake of your splendor;
    I cast you to the ground,
    I laid you before kings,
    That they might gaze at you.

18 "You defiled your sanctuaries
  By the multitude of your iniquities,
  By the iniquity of your trading;
  Therefore I brought fire from your
      midst;
  It devoured you,
  And I turned you to ashes
      upon the earth
  In the sight of all who saw you.
19 All who knew you among the peoples
      are astonished at you;
  You have become a horror,
  And *shall be* no more forever." ' "

Proclamation Against Sidon

20 Then the word of the LORD came to
me, saying,
21 "Son of man, set your face toward Sidon, and prophesy against her,
22 "and say, 'Thus says the Lord GOD:

  "Behold, I *am* against you, O Sidon;
  I will be glorified in your midst;
  And they shall know that I *am* the
      LORD,
  When I execute judgments in her
      and am hallowed in her.
23 For I will send pestilence upon her,
  And blood in her streets;
  The wounded shall be judged in her
      midst
  By the sword against her on every side;
  Then they shall know
      that I *am* the LORD.

24 "And there shall no longer be a pricking brier or a painful thorn for the house
of Israel from among all *who are* around
them, who despise them. Then they shall
know that I *am* the Lord GOD."

Israel's Future Blessing

25 'Thus says the Lord GOD: "When I
have gathered the house of Israel from
the peoples among whom they are scattered, and am hallowed in them in the
sight of the Gentiles, then they will dwell
in their own land which I gave to My servant Jacob. 26 "And they will dwell safely there,
build houses, and plant vineyards; yes,
they will dwell securely, when I execute
judgments on all those around them who
despise them. Then they shall know that
I *am* the LORD their God." ' "

Proclamation Against Egypt

29 In the tenth year, in the tenth
month, on the twelfth *day* of the

month, the word of the LORD came to
me, saying,
2 "Son of man, set your face against
Pharaoh king of Egypt, and prophesy
against him, and against all Egypt.
3 "Speak, and say, 'Thus says the Lord
GOD:

  "Behold, I *am* against you,
  O Pharaoh king of Egypt,
  O great monster who lies in the midst
      of his rivers,
  Who has said, 'My River[16] *is* my own;
  I have made *it* for myself.'
4 But I will put hooks in your jaws,
  And cause the fish of your rivers
      to stick to your scales;
  I will bring you up out of the midst
      of your rivers,
  And all the fish in your rivers
      will stick to your scales.
5 I will leave you in the wilderness,
  You and all the fish of your rivers;
  You shall fall on the open field;
  You shall not be picked up
      or gathered.
  I have given you as food
  To the beasts of the field
  And to the birds of the heavens.

6 "Then all the inhabitants of Egypt
  Shall know that I *am* the LORD,
  Because they have been a staff of reed
      to the house of Israel.
7 When they took hold of you with the
      hand,
  You broke
      and tore all their shoulders;
  When they leaned on you,
  You broke
      and made all their loins shake."

8 'Therefore thus says the Lord GOD:
"Surely I will bring a sword upon you
and cut off from you man and beast.
9 "And the land of Egypt shall become
desolate and waste; then they will know
that I *am* the LORD, because he said, 'The
River *is* mine, and I have made *it*.'
10 "Indeed, therefore, I *am* against you
and against your rivers, and I will make
the land of Egypt utterly waste and desolate, from Migdol [17] *to* Syene, as far as the
border of Ethiopia.
11 "Neither foot of man shall pass
through it nor foot of beast pass through
it, and it shall be uninhabited forty years.
12 "I will make the land of Egypt desolate in the midst of the countries *that are*

16 That is, the Nile   17 Or *tower*

desolate; and among the cities *that are* laid waste, her cities shall be desolate forty years; and I will scatter the Egyptians among the nations and disperse them throughout the countries."

13 'Yet, thus says the Lord GOD: "At the end of forty years I will gather the Egyptians from the peoples among whom they were scattered.

14 "I will bring back the captives of Egypt and cause them to return to the land of Pathros, to the land of their origin, and there they shall be a lowly kingdom.

15 "It shall be the lowliest of kingdoms; it shall never again exalt itself above the nations, for I will diminish them so that they will not rule over the nations anymore.

16 "No longer shall it be the confidence of the house of Israel, but will remind them of *their* iniquity when they turned to follow them. Then they shall know that I *am* the Lord GOD." ' "

Babylonia Will Plunder Egypt

17 And it came to pass in the twenty-seventh year, in the first *month*, on the first *day* of the month, that the word of the LORD came to me, saying,

18 "Son of man, Nebuchadnezzar king of Babylon caused his army to labor strenuously against Tyre; every head *was* made bald, and every shoulder rubbed raw; yet neither he nor his army received wages from Tyre, for the labor which they expended on it.

19 "Therefore thus says the Lord GOD: 'Surely I will give the land of Egypt to Nebuchadnezzar king of Babylon; he shall take away her wealth, carry off her spoil, and remove her pillage; and that will be the wages for his army.

20 'I have given him the land of Egypt *for* his labor, because they worked for Me,' says the Lord GOD.

21 'In that day I will cause the horn of the house of Israel to spring forth, and I will open your mouth to speak in their midst. Then they shall know that I *am* the LORD.' "

Egypt and Her Allies Will Fall

30 The word of the LORD came to me again, saying,

2 "Son of man, prophesy and say, 'Thus says the Lord GOD:

"Wail, 'Woe to the day!'
3 For the day *is* near,
  Even the day of the LORD *is* near;
  It will be a day of clouds,
    the time of the Gentiles.
4 The sword shall come upon Egypt,
  And great anguish shall be in Ethiopia,
  When the slain fall in Egypt,
  And they take away her wealth,
  And her foundations are broken down.

5 "Ethiopia, Libya,[18] Lydia,[19] all the mingled people, Chub, and the men of the lands who are allied, shall fall with them by the sword."
6 'Thus says the LORD:

"Those who uphold Egypt shall fall,
  And the pride of her power shall come
    down.
  From Migdol *to* Syene
  Those within her shall fall by the
    sword,"
Says the Lord GOD.

7 "They shall be desolate in the midst
    of the desolate countries,
  And her cities shall be in the midst
    of the cities *that are* laid waste.
8 Then they will know
    that I *am* the LORD,
  When I have set a fire in Egypt
  And all her helpers are destroyed.
9 On that day messengers shall go forth
    from Me in ships
  To make the careless Ethiopians afraid,
  And great anguish shall come upon
    them,
  As on the day of Egypt;
  For indeed it is coming!"

10 'Thus says the Lord GOD:

"I will also make a multitude of Egypt
    to cease
  By the hand of Nebuchadnezzar
    king of Babylon.
11 He and his people with him,
    the most terrible of the nations,
  Shall be brought to destroy the land;
  They shall draw their swords against
    Egypt,
  And fill the land with the slain.
12 I will make the rivers dry,
  And sell the land into the hand of the
    wicked;
  I will make the land waste,
    and all that is in it,
  By the hand of aliens.
  I, the LORD, have spoken."

18 Hebrew *Put*　　19 Hebrew *Lud*

13 'Thus says the Lord God:

"I will also destroy the idols,
And cause the images to cease
   from Noph;[20]
There shall no longer be princes
   from the land of Egypt;
I will put fear in the land of Egypt.
14 I will make Pathros desolate,
Set fire to Zoan,
And execute judgments in No.[21]
15 I will pour My fury on Sin,[22]
   the strength of Egypt;
I will cut off the multitude of No,
16 And set a fire in Egypt;
Sin shall have great pain,
No shall be split open,
And Noph *shall be in* distress daily.
17 The young men of Aven[23]
   and Pi Beseth shall fall by the sword,
And these *cities* shall go into captivity.
18 At Tehaphnehes[24] the day shall also be
   darkened,
When I break the yokes of Egypt there.
And her arrogant strength
   shall cease in her;
As for her, a cloud shall cover her,
And her daughters
   shall go into captivity.
19 Thus I will execute judgments on
   Egypt,
Then they shall know
   that I *am* the Lord." ' "

Proclamation Against Pharaoh

20 And it came to pass in the eleventh
year, in the first *month*, on the seventh
day of the month, *that* the word of the
Lord came to me, saying,
21 "Son of man, I have broken the arm
of Pharaoh king of Egypt; and see, it has
not been bandaged for healing, nor a
splint put on to bind it, to make it strong
enough to hold a sword.
22 "Therefore thus says the Lord God:
'Surely I *am* against Pharaoh king of
Egypt, and will break his arms, both the
strong one and the one that was broken;
and I will make the sword fall out of his
hand.
23 'I will scatter the Egyptians among
the nations, and disperse them throughout the countries.
24 'I will strengthen the arms of the king
of Babylon and put My sword in his
hand; but I will break Pharaoh's arms,
and he will groan before him with the
groanings of a mortally wounded *man.*

25 'Thus I will strengthen the arms of the
king of Babylon, but the arms of Pharaoh
shall fall down; they shall know that I *am*
the Lord, when I put My sword into the
hand of the king of Babylon and he
stretches it out against the land of Egypt.
26 'I will scatter the Egyptians among
the nations and disperse them throughout
the countries. Then they shall know that
I *am* the Lord.' "

Egypt Cut Down Like a Great Tree

31 Now it came to pass in the eleventh year, in the third *month*, on
the first *day* of the month, *that* the word
of the Lord came to me, saying,
2 "Son of man, say to Pharaoh king of
Egypt and to his multitude:

'Whom are you like in your greatness?
3 Indeed Assyria *was* a cedar in
   Lebanon,
With fine branches that shaded the
   forest,
And of high stature;
And its top was among the thick
   boughs.
4 The waters made it grow;
Underground waters gave it height,
With their rivers running around
   the place where it was planted,
And sent out rivulets
   to all the trees of the field.

5 'Therefore its height was exalted
   above all the trees of the field;
Its boughs were multiplied,
And its branches became long
   because of the abundance of water,
As it sent them out.
6 All the birds of the heavens
   made their nests in its boughs;
Under its branches all the beasts of the
   field brought forth their young;
And in its shadow all great nations
   made their home.

7 'Thus it was beautiful in greatness
   and in the length of its branches,
Because its roots reached to abundant
   waters.
8 The cedars in the garden of God
   could not hide it;
The fir trees were not like its boughs,
And the chestnut[25] trees were not like
   its branches;
No tree in the garden of God
   was like it in beauty.

20 That is, ancient Memphis   21 That is, ancient Thebes   22 That is, ancient Pelusium
23 That is, ancient On (Heliopolis)   24 Spelled *Tahpanhes* in Jeremiah 43:7 and elsewhere   ·25 Hebrew *armon*

9 I made it beautiful with a multitude of
    branches,
    So that all the trees of Eden envied it,
    That *were* in the garden of God.'

10 "Therefore thus says the Lord GOD:
'Because you have increased in height,
and it set its top among the thick boughs,
and its heart was lifted up in its height,
11 'therefore I will deliver it into the
hand of the mighty one of the nations,
and he shall surely deal with it; I have
driven it out for its wickedness.
12 'And aliens, the most terrible of the
nations, have cut it down and left it; its
branches have fallen on the mountains
and in all the valleys; its boughs lie broken by all the rivers of the land; and all
the peoples of the earth have gone from
under its shadow and left it.

13 'On its ruin will remain
    all the birds of the heavens,
    And all the beasts of the field
    will come to its branches—

14 'So that no trees by the waters may
ever again exalt themselves for their
height, nor set their tops among the thick
boughs, that no tree which drinks water
may ever be high enough to reach up to
them.

'For they have all been delivered
    to death,
To the depths of the earth,
Among the children of men who go
    down to the Pit.'

15 "Thus says the Lord GOD: 'In the day
when it went down to hell, I caused
mourning. I covered the deep because of
it. I restrained its rivers, and the great
waters were held back. I caused Lebanon
to mourn for it, and all the trees of the
field wilted because of it.
16 'I made the nations shake at the
sound of its fall, when I cast it down to
hell together with those who descend into
the Pit; and all the trees of Eden, the
choice and best of Lebanon, all that drink
water, were comforted in the depths of
the earth.
17 'They also went down to hell with it,
with those *slain* by the sword; and *those
who were* its *strong* arm dwelt in its shadows among the nations.
18 'To which of the trees in Eden will

you then be likened in glory and greatness? Yet you shall be brought down
with the trees of Eden to the depths of the
earth; you shall lie in the midst of the
uncircumcised, with *those* slain by the
sword. This *is* Pharaoh and all his multitude,' says the Lord GOD."

Lamentation for Pharaoh and Egypt

32 And it came to pass in the twelfth
    year, in the twelfth *month*, on the
first *day* of the month, *that* the word of
the LORD came to me, saying,
2 "Son of man, take up a lamentation
for Pharaoh king of Egypt, and say to
him:

'You are like a young lion among the
    nations,
And you *are* like a monster in the seas,
Bursting forth in your rivers,
Troubling the waters with your feet,
And fouling their rivers.'

3 "Thus says the Lord GOD:

'I will therefore spread My net over you
    with a company of many people,
And they will draw you up in My net.
4 Then I will leave you on the land;
I will cast you out on the open fields,
And cause to settle on you all the birds
    of the heavens.
And with you I will fill the beasts of
    the whole earth.
5 I will lay your flesh on the mountains,
And fill the valleys with your carcass.

6 'I will also water the land
    with the flow of your blood,
Even to the mountains;
And the riverbeds will be full of you.
7 When *I* put out your light,
I will cover the heavens,
    and make its stars dark;
I will cover the sun with a cloud,
And the moon shall not give her light.
8 All the bright lights of the heavens
    I will make dark over you,
And bring darkness upon your land,'
Says the Lord GOD.

9 'I will also trouble the hearts of many
peoples, when I bring your destruction
among the nations, into the countries
which you have not known.
10 'Yes, I will make many peoples astonished at you, and their kings shall be horribly afraid of you when I brandish My

sword before them; and they shall tremble *every* moment, every man for his own life, in the day of your fall.'

11 "For thus says the Lord GOD: 'The sword of the king of Babylon shall come upon you.

12 'By the swords of the mighty warriors, all of them the most terrible of the nations, I will cause your multitude to fall.

'They shall plunder the pomp of Egypt,
    And all its multitude shall be destroyed.
13 Also I will destroy all its beasts
    From beside its great waters;
The foot of man shall muddy them
    no more,
Nor shall the hooves of beasts muddy
    them.
14 Then I will make their waters clear,
    And make their rivers run like oil,'
Says the Lord GOD.

15 'When I make the land of Egypt
    desolate,
And the country is destitute of all that
    once filled it,
When I strike all who dwell in it,
Then they shall know that I *am* the
    LORD.

16 'This *is* the lamentation
    With which they shall lament her;
The daughters of the nations shall
    lament her;
They shall lament for her, for Egypt,
And for all her multitude,'
Says the Lord GOD."

Egypt and Others Consigned to the Pit

17 It came to pass also in the twelfth year, on the fifteenth *day* of the month, *that* the word of the LORD came to me, saying:

18 "Son of man,
    wail over the multitude of Egypt,
And cast them down to the depths of
    the earth,
Her and the daughters of the famous
    nations,
With those who go down to the Pit:
19 'Whom do you surpass in beauty?
Go down,
    be placed with the uncircumcised.'

20 "They shall fall in the midst
    of *those* slain by the sword;
She is delivered to the sword,
Drawing her and all her multitudes.

21 The strong among the mighty
    Shall speak to him out of the midst of
    hell
With those who help him:
'They have gone down,
They lie with the uncircumcised,
    slain by the sword.'

22 "Assyria *is* there, and all her company,
    With their graves all around her,
All of them slain, fallen by the sword.
23 Her graves are set in the recesses of the
    Pit,
And her company is all around her
    grave,
All of them slain, fallen by the sword,
Who caused terror in the land of the
    living.

24 "There *is* Elam and all her multitude,
    All around her grave,
All of them slain, fallen by the sword,
Who have gone down uncircumcised
    to the lower parts of the earth,
Who caused their terror in the land of
    the living;
Now they bear their shame with those
    who go down to the Pit.
25 They have set her bed
    in the midst of the slain,
With all her multitude,
With her graves all around it,
All of them uncircumcised,
    slain by the sword;
Though their terror was caused
In the land of the living,
Yet they bear their shame
With those who go down to the Pit;
It was put in the midst of the slain.

26 "There *are* Meshech and Tubal
    and all their multitudes,
With all their graves around it,
All of them uncircumcised,
    slain by the sword,
Though they caused their terror in the
    land of the living.
27 They do not lie with the mighty
    Who are fallen of the uncircumcised,
Who have gone down to hell
    with their weapons of war;
They have laid their swords
    under their heads,
But their iniquities will be
    on their bones,
Because of the terror of the mighty
    in the land of the living.
28 Yes, you shall be broken in the midst
    of the uncircumcised,
And lie with *those* slain by the sword.

29"There *is* Edom,
Her kings and all her princes,
Who despite their might
Are laid beside *those who were* slain
by the sword;
They shall lie with the uncircumcised,
And with those who go down to the
Pit.
30 There *are* the princes of the north,
All of them, and all the Sidonians,
Who have gone down with the slain
In shame at the terror which they
caused by their might;
They lie uncircumcised
with *those* slain by the sword,
And bear their shame
with those who go down to the Pit.

31"Pharaoh will see them
And be comforted over all his
multitude,
Pharaoh and all his army,
Slain by the sword,"
Says the Lord GOD.

32 "For I have caused My terror
in the land of the living;
And he shall be placed in the midst of
the uncircumcised
With *those* slain by the sword,
Pharaoh and all his multitude,"
Says the Lord GOD.

The Watchman and His Message

33 Again the word of the LORD came
to me, saying,
2 "Son of man, speak to the children of
your people, and say to them: 'When I
bring the sword upon a land, and the
people of the land take a man from their
territory and make him their watchman,
3 'when he sees the sword coming upon
the land, if he blows the trumpet and
warns the people,
4 'then whoever hears the sound of the
trumpet and does not take warning, if the
sword comes and takes him away, his
blood shall be on his *own* head.
5 'He heard the sound of the trumpet,
but did not take warning; his blood shall
be upon himself. But he who takes warning will save his life.
6 'But if the watchman sees the sword
coming and does not blow the trumpet,
and the people are not warned, and the
sword comes and takes *any* person from
among them, he is taken away in his iniquity; but his blood I will require at the
watchman's hand.'

7 "So you, son of man: I have made you
a watchman for the house of Israel; therefore you shall hear a word from My
mouth and warn them for Me.
8 "When I say to the wicked, 'O wicked
man, you shall surely die!' and you do
not speak to warn the wicked from his
way, that wicked *man* shall die in his iniquity; but his blood I will require at your
hand.
9 "Nevertheless if you warn the wicked
to turn from his way, and he does not
turn from his way, he shall die in his iniquity; but you have delivered your soul.
10 "Therefore you, O son of man, say to
the house of Israel: 'Thus you say, "If our
transgressions and our sins *lie* upon us,
and we pine away in them, how can we
then live?" '
11 "Say to them: '*As* I live,' says the
Lord GOD, 'I have no pleasure in the
death of the wicked, but that the wicked
turn from his way and live. Turn, turn
from your evil ways! For why should you
die, O house of Israel?'

The Fairness of God's Judgment

12 "Therefore you, O son of man, say to
the children of your people: 'The righteousness of the righteous man shall not
deliver him in the day of his transgression; as for the wickedness of the wicked,
he shall not fall because of it in the day
that he turns from his wickedness; nor
shall the righteous be able to live because
of *his righteousness* in the day that he
sins.'
13 "When I say to the righteous *that* he
shall surely live, but he trusts in his own
righteousness and commits iniquity, none
of his righteous works shall be remembered; but because of the iniquity that he
has committed, he shall die.
14 "Again, when I say to the wicked,
'You shall surely die,' if he turns from his
sin and does what is lawful and right,
15 "*if* the wicked restores the pledge,
gives back what he has stolen, and walks
in the statutes of life without committing
iniquity, he shall surely live; he shall
not die.
16 "None of his sins which he has committed shall be remembered against him;
he has done what is lawful and right; he
shall surely live.
17 "Yet the children of your people say,

'The way of the LORD is not fair.' But it is their way which is not fair!

18 "When the righteous turns from his righteousness and commits iniquity, he shall die because of it.

19 "But when the wicked turns from his wickedness and does what is lawful and right, he shall live because of it.

20 "Yet you say, 'The way of the LORD is not fair.' O house of Israel, I will judge every one of you according to his own ways."

The Fall of Jerusalem

21 And it came to pass in the twelfth year of our captivity, in the tenth *month*, on the fifth *day* of the month, *that* one who had escaped from Jerusalem came to me and said, "The city has been captured!"

22 Now the hand of the LORD had been upon me the evening before the man came who had escaped. And He had opened my mouth; so when he came to me in the morning, my mouth was opened, and I was no longer mute.

The Cause of Judah's Ruin

23 Then the word of the LORD came to me, saying:

24 "Son of man, they who inhabit those ruins in the land of Israel are saying, 'Abraham was only one, and he inherited the land. But we *are* many; the land has been given to us as a possession.'

25 "Therefore say to them, 'Thus says the Lord GOD: "You eat *meat* with blood, you lift up your eyes toward your idols, and shed blood. Should you then possess the land?

26 "You rely on your sword, you commit abominations, and you defile one another's wives. Should you then possess the land?"'

27 "Say thus to them, 'Thus says the Lord GOD: "*As* I live, surely those who *are* in the ruins shall fall by the sword, and the one who *is* in the open field I will give to the beasts to be devoured, and those who *are* in the strongholds and caves shall die of the pestilence.

28 "For I will make the land most desolate, her arrogant strength shall cease, and the mountains of Israel shall be so desolate that no one will pass through.

29 "Then they shall know that I *am* the LORD, when I have made the land most desolate because of all their abominations which they have committed."'

Hearing and Not Doing

30 "As for you, son of man, the children of your people are talking about you beside the walls and in the doors of the houses; and they speak to one another, everyone saying to his brother, 'Please come and hear what the word is that comes from the LORD.'

31 "So they come to you as people do, they sit before you *as* My people, and they hear your words, but they do not do them; for with their mouth they show much love, *but* their hearts pursue their own gain.

32 "Indeed you *are* to them as a very lovely song of one who has a pleasant voice and can play well on an instrument; for they hear your words, but they do not do them.

33 "And when this comes to pass— surely it will come—then they will know that a prophet has been among them."

Irresponsible Shepherds

34 And the word of the LORD came to me, saying,

2 "Son of man, prophesy against the shepherds of Israel, prophesy and say to them, 'Thus says the Lord GOD to the shepherds: "Woe to the shepherds of Israel who feed themselves! Should not the shepherds feed the flocks?

3 "You eat the fat and clothe yourselves with the wool; you slaughter the fatlings, *but* you do not feed the flock.

4 "The weak you have not strengthened, nor have you healed those who were sick, nor bound up the broken, nor brought back what was driven away, nor sought what was lost; but with force and cruelty you have ruled them.

5 "So they were scattered because *there was* no shepherd; and they became food for all the beasts of the field when they were scattered.

6 "My sheep wandered through all the mountains, and on every high hill; yes, My flock was scattered over the whole face of the earth, and no one was seeking or searching *for them*."

7 'Therefore, you shepherds, hear the word of the LORD:

8 "*as* I live," says the Lord GOD,

"surely because My flock became a prey, and My flock became food for every beast of the field, because *there was* no shepherd, nor did My shepherds search for My flock, but the shepherds fed themselves and did not feed My flock"—
9 'therefore, O shepherds, hear the word of the LORD!
10 'Thus says the Lord GOD: "Behold, I *am* against the shepherds, and I will require My flock at their hand; I will cause them to cease feeding the sheep, and the shepherds shall feed themselves no more; for I will deliver My flock from their mouths, that they may no longer be food for them."

God, the True Shepherd

11 'For thus says the Lord GOD: "Indeed I Myself will search for My sheep and seek them out.
12 "As a shepherd seeks out his flock on the day he is among his scattered sheep, so will I seek out My sheep and deliver them from all the places where they were scattered on a cloudy and dark day.
13 "And I will bring them out from the peoples and gather them from the countries, and will bring them to their own land; I will feed them on the mountains of Israel, in the valleys and in all the inhabited places of the country.
14 "I will feed them in good pasture, and their fold shall be on the high mountains of Israel. There they shall lie down in a good fold and feed in rich pasture on the mountains of Israel.
15 "I will feed My flock, and I will make them lie down," says the Lord GOD.
16 "I will seek what was lost and bring back what was driven away, bind up the broken and strengthen what was sick; but I will destroy the fat and the strong, and feed them in judgment."
17 'And *as for* you, O My flock, thus says the Lord GOD: "Behold, I shall judge between sheep and sheep, between rams and goats.
18 "*Is it* too little for you to have eaten up the good pasture, that you must tread down with your feet the residue of your pasture—and to have drunk of the clear waters, that you must foul the residue with your feet?
19 "And *as for* My flock, they eat what you have trampled with your feet, and

they drink what you have fouled with your feet."
20 'Therefore thus says the Lord GOD to them: "Behold, I Myself will judge between the fat and the lean sheep.
21 "Because you have pushed with side and shoulder, butted all the weak ones with your horns, and scattered them abroad,
22 "therefore I will save My flock, and they shall no longer be a prey; and I will judge between sheep and sheep.
23 "I will establish one shepherd over them, and he shall feed them—My servant David. He shall feed them and be their shepherd.
24 "And I, the LORD, will be their God, and My servant David a prince among them; I, the LORD, have spoken.
25 "I will make a covenant of peace with them, and cause wild beasts to cease from the land; and they will dwell safely in the wilderness and sleep in the woods.
26 "I will make them and the places all around My hill a blessing; and I will cause showers to come down in their season; there shall be showers of blessing.
27 "Then the trees of the field shall yield their fruit, and the earth shall yield her increase. They shall be safe in their land; and they shall know that I *am* the LORD, when I have broken the bands of their yoke and delivered them from the hand of those who enslaved them.
28 "And they shall no longer be a prey for the nations, nor shall beasts of the land devour them; but they shall dwell safely, and no one shall make *them* afraid.
29 "I will raise up for them a garden of renown, and they shall no longer be consumed with hunger in the land, nor bear the shame of the Gentiles anymore.
30 "Thus they shall know that I, the LORD their God, *am* with them, and *that* they, the house of Israel, *are* My people," says the Lord GOD.' "
31 "You are My flock, the flock of My pasture; you *are* men, *and* I *am* your God," says the Lord GOD.' "

Judgment on Mount Seir

35 Moreover the word of the LORD came to me, saying,
2 "Son of man, set your face against Mount Seir and prophesy against it,
3 "and say to it, 'Thus says the Lord GOD:

"Behold, O Mount Seir,
   I *am* against you;
   I will stretch out My hand against you,
   And make you most desolate;
4 I shall lay your cities waste,
   And you shall be desolate.
   Then you shall know
     that I *am* the LORD.

5 "Because you have had an ancient hatred, and have shed *the blood of* the children of Israel by the power of the sword at the time of their calamity, *when* their iniquity *came to an* end,
6 "therefore, *as* I live," says the Lord GOD, "I will prepare you for blood, and blood shall pursue you; since you have not hated blood, therefore blood shall pursue you.
7 "Thus I will make Mount Seir most desolate, and cut off from it the one who leaves and the one who returns.
8 "And I will fill its mountains with the slain; on your hills and in your valleys and in all your ravines those who are slain by the sword shall fall.
9 "I will make you perpetually desolate, and your cities shall be uninhabited; then you shall know that I *am* the LORD.
10 "Because you have said, 'These two nations and these two countries shall be mine, and we will possess them,' although the LORD was there,
11 "therefore, *as* I live," says the Lord GOD, "I will do according to your anger and according to the envy which you showed in your hatred against them; and I will make Myself known among them when I judge you.
12 "Then you shall know that I *am* the LORD. I have heard all your blasphemies which you have spoken against the mountains of Israel, saying, 'They are desolate; they are given to us to consume.'
13 "Thus with your mouth you have boasted against Me and multiplied your words against Me; I have heard *them*."
14 'Thus says the Lord GOD: "The whole earth will rejoice when I make you desolate.
15 "As you rejoiced because the inheritance of the house of Israel was desolate, so I will do to you; you shall be desolate, O Mount Seir, as well as all of Edom—all of it! Then they shall know that I *am* the LORD." '

Blessing on Israel

36 "And you, son of man, prophesy to the mountains of Israel, and say, 'O mountains of Israel, hear the word of the LORD!
2 'Thus says the Lord GOD: "Because the enemy has said of you, 'Aha! The ancient heights have become our possession,' " '
3 "therefore prophesy, and say, 'Thus says the Lord GOD: "Because they made *you* desolate and swallowed you up on every side, so that you became the possession of the rest of the nations, and you are taken up by the lips of talkers and slandered by the people"—
4 'therefore, O mountains of Israel, hear the word of the Lord GOD! Thus says the Lord GOD to the mountains, the hills, the rivers, the valleys, the desolate wastes, and the cities that have been forsaken, which became plunder and mockery to the rest of the nations all around—
5 'therefore thus says the Lord GOD: "Surely I have spoken in My burning jealousy against the rest of the nations and against all Edom, who gave My land to themselves as a possession, with whole-hearted joy *and* spiteful minds, in order to plunder its open country." '
6 "Therefore prophesy concerning the land of Israel, and say to the mountains, the hills, the rivers, and the valleys, 'Thus says the Lord GOD: "Behold, I have spoken in My jealousy and My fury, because you have borne the shame of the nations."
7 'Therefore thus says the Lord GOD: "I have lifted My hand in an oath that surely the nations that *are* around you shall bear their own shame.
8 "But you, O mountains of Israel, you shall shoot forth your branches and yield your fruit to My people Israel, for they are about to come.
9 "For indeed I *am* for you, and I will turn to you, and you shall be tilled and sown.
10 "I will multiply men upon you, all the house of Israel, all of it; and the cities shall be inhabited and the ruins rebuilt.
11 "I will multiply upon you man and beast; and they shall increase and bear young; I will make you inhabited as in former times, and do better *for you* than at your beginnings. Then you shall know that I *am* the LORD.

12 "Yes, I will cause men to walk on you, My people Israel; they shall take possession of you, and you shall be their inheritance; no more shall you bereave them *of their children.*"
13 'Thus says the Lord GOD: "Because they say to you, 'You devour men and bereave your nation *of children,*'
14 "therefore you shall devour men no more, nor bereave your nation anymore," says the Lord GOD.
15 "Nor will I let you hear the taunts of the nations anymore, nor bear the reproach of the peoples anymore, nor shall you cause your nation to stumble anymore," says the Lord GOD.'"

The Renewal of Israel

16 Moreover the word of the LORD came to me, saying:
17 "Son of man, when the house of Israel dwelt in their own land, they defiled it by their own ways and deeds; to Me their way was like the uncleanness of a woman in her customary impurity.
18 "Therefore I poured out My fury on them for the blood they had shed on the land, and for their idols *with which* they had defiled it.
19 "So I scattered them among the nations, and they were dispersed throughout the countries; I judged them according to their ways and their deeds.
20 "When they came to the nations, wherever they went, they profaned My holy name—when they said of them, 'These *are* the people of the LORD, *and* yet they have gone out of His land.'
21 "But I had concern for My holy name, which the house of Israel had profaned among the nations wherever they went.
22 "Therefore say to the house of Israel, 'Thus says the Lord GOD: "I do not do *this* for your sake, O house of Israel, but for My holy name's sake, which you have profaned among the nations wherever you went.
23 "And I will sanctify My great name, which has been profaned among the nations, which you have profaned in their midst; and the nations shall know that I *am* the LORD," says the Lord GOD, "when I am hallowed in you before their eyes.
24 "For I will take you from among the nations, gather you out of all countries, and bring you into your own land.

25 "Then I will sprinkle clean water on you, and you shall be clean; I will cleanse you from all your filthiness and from all your idols.
26 "I will give you a new heart and put a new spirit within you; I will take the heart of stone out of your flesh and give you a heart of flesh.
27 "I will put My Spirit within you and cause you to walk in My statutes, and you will keep My judgments and do *them.*
28 "Then you shall dwell in the land that I gave to your fathers; you shall be My people, and I will be your God.
29 "I will deliver you from all your uncleannesses. I will call for the grain and multiply it, and bring no famine upon you.
30 "And I will multiply the fruit of your trees and the increase of your fields, so that you need never again bear the reproach of famine among the nations.
31 "Then you will remember your evil ways and your deeds that *were* not good; and you will loathe yourselves in your own sight, for your iniquities and your abominations.
32 "Not for your sake do I do *this,*" says the Lord GOD, "let it be known to you. Be ashamed and confounded for your own ways, O house of Israel!"
33 'Thus says the Lord GOD: "On the day that I cleanse you from all your iniquities, I will also enable *you* to dwell in the cities, and the ruins shall be rebuilt.
34 "The desolate land shall be tilled instead of lying desolate in the sight of all who pass by.
35 "So they will say, 'This land that was desolate has become like the garden of Eden; and the wasted, desolate, and ruined cities *are now* fortified *and* inhabited.'
36 "Then the nations which are left all around you shall know that I, the LORD, have rebuilt the ruined places *and* planted what was desolate. I, the LORD, have spoken *it,* and I will do *it.*"
37 'Thus says the Lord GOD: "I will also let the house of Israel inquire of Me to do this for them: I will increase their men like a flock.
38 "Like a flock offered as holy sacrifices, like the flock at Jerusalem on its feast days, so shall the ruined cities be filled with flocks of men. Then they shall know that I *am* the LORD."' "

The Dry Bones Live

37 The hand of the LORD came upon me and brought me out in the Spirit of the LORD, and set me down in the midst of the valley; and it *was* full of bones.

2 Then He caused me to pass by them all around, and behold, *there were* very many in the open valley; and indeed *they were* very dry.

3 And He said to me, "Son of man, can these bones live?" So I answered, "O Lord GOD, You know."

4 Again He said to me, "Prophesy to these bones, and say to them, 'O dry bones, hear the word of the LORD!

5 'Thus says the Lord GOD to these bones: "Surely I will cause breath to enter into you, and you shall live.

6 "I will put sinews on you and bring flesh upon you, cover you with skin and put breath in you; and you shall live. Then you shall know that I *am* the LORD." ' "

7 So I prophesied as I was commanded; and as I prophesied, there was a noise, and suddenly a rattling; and the bones came together, bone to bone.

8 Indeed, as I looked, the sinews and the flesh came upon them, and the skin covered them over; but *there was* no breath in them.

9 Then He said to me, "Prophesy to the breath, prophesy, son of man, and say to the breath, 'Thus says the Lord GOD: "Come from the four winds, O breath, and breathe on these slain, that they may live." ' "

10 So I prophesied as He commanded me, and breath came into them, and they lived, and stood upon their feet, an exceedingly great army.

11 Then He said to me, "Son of man, these bones are the whole house of Israel. They indeed say, 'Our bones are dry, our hope is lost, and we ourselves are cut off!'

12 "Therefore prophesy and say to them, 'Thus says the Lord GOD: "Behold, O My people, I will open your graves and cause you to come up from your graves, and bring you into the land of Israel.

13 "Then you shall know that I *am* the LORD, when I have opened your graves, O My people, and brought you up from your graves.

14 "I will put My Spirit in you, and you shall live, and I will place you in your own land. Then you shall know that I, the LORD, have spoken *it* and performed *it*," says the LORD.' "

One Kingdom, One King

15 Again the word of the LORD came to me, saying,

16 "As for you, son of man, take a stick for yourself and write on it: 'For Judah and for the children of Israel, his companions.' Then take another stick and write on it, 'For Joseph, the stick of Ephraim, and *for* all the house of Israel, his companions.'

17 "Then join them one to another for yourself into one stick, and they will become one in your hand.

18 "And when the children of your people speak to you, saying, 'Will you not show us what you *mean* by these?'—

19 "say to them, 'Thus says the Lord GOD: "Surely I will take the stick of Joseph, which *is* in the hand of Ephraim, and the tribes of Israel, his companions; and I will join them with it, with the stick of Judah, and make them one stick, and they will be one in My hand." '

20 "And the sticks on which you write will be in your hand before their eyes.

21 "Then say to them, 'Thus says the Lord GOD: "Surely I will take the children of Israel from among the nations, wherever they have gone, and will gather them from every side and bring them into their own land;

22 "and I will make them one nation in the land, on the mountains of Israel; and one king shall be king over them all; they shall no longer be two nations, nor shall they ever be divided into two kingdoms again.

23 "They shall not defile themselves anymore with their idols, nor with their detestable things, nor with any of their transgressions; but I will deliver them from all their dwelling places in which they have sinned, and will cleanse them. Then they shall be My people, and I will be their God.

24 "David My servant *shall be* king over them, and they shall all have one shepherd; they shall also walk in My judgments and observe My statutes, and do them.

25 "Then they shall dwell in the land that I have given to Jacob My servant, where your fathers dwelt; and they shall dwell

there, they, their children, and their children's children, forever; and My servant David *shall be* their prince forever.

26 "Moreover I will make a covenant of peace with them, and it shall be an everlasting covenant with them; I will establish them and multiply them, and I will set My sanctuary in their midst forevermore.

27 "My tabernacle also shall be with them; indeed I will be their God, and they shall be My people.

28 "The nations also will know that I, the LORD, sanctify Israel, when My sanctuary is in their midst forevermore." ' "

Gog and Allies Attack Israel

38 Now the word of the LORD came to me, saying,

2 "Son of man, set your face against Gog, of the land of Magog, the prince of Rosh,[26] Meshech, and Tubal, and prophesy against him,

3 "and say, 'Thus says the Lord GOD: "Behold, I *am* against you, O Gog, the prince of Rosh, Meshech, and Tubal.

4 "I will turn you around, put hooks into your jaws, and lead you out, with all your army, horses, and horsemen, all splendidly clothed, a great company *with* bucklers and shields, all of them handling swords.

5 "Persia, Ethiopia,[27] and Libya[28] are with them, all of them *with* shield and helmet;

6 "Gomer and all its troops; the house of Togarmah *from* the far north and all its troops—many people *are* with you.

7 "Prepare yourself and be ready, you and all your companies that are gathered about you; and be a guard for them.

8 "After many days you will be visited. In the latter years you will come into the land of those brought back from the sword *and* gathered from many people on the mountains of Israel, which had long been desolate; they were brought out of the nations, and now all of them dwell safely.

9 "You will ascend, coming like a storm, covering the land like a cloud, you and all your troops and many peoples with you."

10 'Thus says the Lord GOD: "On that day it shall come to pass *that* thoughts will arise in your mind, and you will make an evil plan:

11 "You will say, 'I will go up against a land of unwalled villages; I will go to a peaceful people, who dwell safely, all of them dwelling without walls, and having neither bars nor gates'—

12 "to take plunder and to take booty, to stretch out your hand against the waste places *that are again* inhabited, and against a people gathered from the nations, who have acquired livestock and goods, who dwell in the midst of the land.

13 "Sheba, Dedan, the merchants of Tarshish, and all their young lions will say to you, 'Have you come to take plunder? Have you gathered your army to take booty, to carry away silver and gold, to take away livestock and goods, to take great plunder?' ' '

14 "Therefore, son of man, prophesy and say to Gog, 'Thus says the Lord GOD: "On that day when My people Israel dwell safely, will you not know *it*?

15 "Then you will come from your place out of the far north, you and many peoples with you, all of them riding on horses, a great company and a mighty army.

16 "You will come up against My people Israel like a cloud, to cover the land. It will be in the latter days that I will bring you against My land, so that the nations may know Me, when I am hallowed in you, O Gog, before their eyes."

17 'Thus says the Lord GOD: "Are *you* he of whom I have spoken in former days by My servants the prophets of Israel, who prophesied for years in those days that I would bring you against them?

Judgment on Gog

18 "And it will come to pass at the same time, when Gog comes against the land of Israel," says the Lord GOD, "*that* My fury will show in My face.

19 "For in My jealousy *and* in the fire of My wrath I have spoken: 'Surely in that day there shall be a great earthquake in the land of Israel,

20 'so that the fish of the sea, the birds of the heavens, the beasts of the field, all creeping things that creep on the earth, and all men who *are* on the face of the earth shall shake at My presence. The mountains shall be thrown down, the steep places shall fall, and every wall shall fall to the ground.'

21 "I will call for a sword against Gog

---

26 Targum, Vulgate, and Aquila read *chief prince of* (also verse 3).   27 Hebrew *Cush*   28 Hebrew *Put*

throughout all My mountains," says the
Lord GOD. "Every man's sword will be
against his brother.
22 "And I will bring him to judgment
with pestilence and bloodshed; I will rain
down on him, on his troops, and on the
many peoples who *are* with him, flooding
rain, great hailstones, fire, and brimstone.
23 "Thus I will magnify Myself and sanctify Myself, and I will be known in the
eyes of many nations. Then they shall
know that I *am* the LORD." '

Gog's Armies Destroyed

39 "And you, son of man, prophesy
against Gog, and say, 'Thus says
the Lord GOD: "Behold, I *am* against
you, O Gog, prince of Rosh,[29] Meshech,
and Tubal;
2 "and I will turn you around and lead
you on, bringing you up from the far
north, and bring you against the mountains of Israel.
3 "Then I will knock the bow out of
your left hand, and cause the arrows to
fall out of your right hand.
4 "You shall fall upon the mountains of
Israel, you and all your troops and the
peoples who *are* with you; I will give you
to birds of prey of every sort and *to* the
beasts of the field to be devoured.
5 "You shall fall on the open field; for I
have spoken," says the Lord GOD.
6 "And I will send fire on Magog and
on those who live in security in the coastlands. Then they shall know that I *am*
the LORD.
7 "So I will make My holy name known
in the midst of My people Israel, and I
will not *let them* profane My holy name
anymore. Then the nations shall know
that *I am* the LORD, the Holy One in Israel.
8 "Surely it is coming, and it shall be
done," says the Lord GOD. "This *is* the
day of which I have spoken.
9 "Then those who dwell in the cities of
Israel will go out and set on fire and burn
the weapons, both the shields and bucklers, the bows and arrows, the javelins
and spears; and they will make fires with
them for seven years.
10 "They will not take wood from the
field nor cut down *any* from the forests,
because they will make fires with the
weapons; and they will plunder those

who plundered them, and pillage those
who pillaged them," says the Lord GOD.

The Burial of Gog

11 "It will come to pass in that day *that* I
will give Gog a burial place there in Israel, the valley of those who pass by east
of the sea; and it will obstruct travelers,
because there they will bury Gog and all
his multitude. Therefore they will call *it*
the Valley of Hamon Gog.[30]
12 "For seven months the house of Israel
will be burying them, in order to cleanse
the land.
13 "Indeed all the people of the land will
be burying *them*, and they will gain renown for it on the day that I am glorified," says the Lord GOD.
14 "They will set apart men regularly
employed, with the help of a search party,
to pass through the land and bury those
bodies remaining on the ground, in order
to cleanse it. At the end of seven months
they will make a search.
15 "The search party will pass through
the land; and *whenever anyone* sees a
man's bone, he shall set up a marker by
it, till the buriers have buried it in the
Valley of Hamon Gog.
16 "*The* name of *the* city *will* also *be* Ha-
monah. Thus they shall cleanse the
land." '

A Triumphant Festival

17 "And as for you, son of man, thus
says the Lord GOD, 'Speak to every sort
of bird and to every beast of the field:

> "Assemble yourselves and come;
> Gather together from all sides
>   to My sacrificial meal
> Which I am sacrificing for you,
> A great sacrificial meal
>   on the mountains of Israel,
> That you may eat flesh
>   and drink blood.
18 You shall eat the flesh of the mighty,
> Drink the blood of the princes of the
>   earth,
> Of rams and lambs,
> Of goats and bulls,
> All of them fatlings of Bashan.
19 You shall eat fat till you are full,
> And drink blood till you are drunk,
> At My sacrificial meal
> Which I am sacrificing for you.
20 You shall be filled at My table
> With horses and riders,

---

29 See note at 38:2.   30 Literally *The Multitude of Gog*

With mighty men
And with all the men of war,"
says the Lord GOD.

Israel Restored to the Land

21 "I will set My glory among the nations; all the nations shall see My judgment which I have executed, and My hand which I have laid on them.
22 "So the house of Israel shall know that I *am* the LORD their God from that day forward.
23 "The Gentiles shall know that the house of Israel went into captivity for their iniquity; because they were unfaithful to Me, therefore I hid My face from them. I gave them into the hand of their enemies, and they all fell by the sword.
24 "According to their uncleanness and according to their transgressions I have dealt with them, and hidden My face from them." '
25 "Therefore thus says the Lord GOD: 'Now I will bring back the captives of Jacob, and have mercy on the whole house of Israel; and I will be jealous for My holy name—
26 'after they have borne their shame, and all their unfaithfulness in which they were unfaithful to Me, when they dwelt safely in their *own* land and no one made *them* afraid.
27 'When I have brought them back from the peoples and gathered them out of their enemies' lands, and I am hallowed in them in the sight of many nations,
28 'then they shall know that I *am* the LORD their God, who sent them into captivity among the nations, but also brought them back to their *own* land, and left none of them captive any longer.
29 'And I will not hide My face from them anymore; for I shall have poured out My Spirit on the house of Israel,' says the Lord GOD."

A New City, a New Temple

40 In the twenty-fifth year of our captivity, at the beginning of the year, on the tenth *day* of the month, in the fourteenth year after the city was captured, on the very same day the hand of the LORD was upon me; and He took me there.
2 In the visions of God He took me into the land of Israel and set me on a very high mountain; on it toward the south *was* something like the structure of a city.
3 He took me there, and behold, *there was* a man whose appearance *was* like the appearance of bronze. He had a line of flax and a measuring rod in his hand, and he stood in the gateway.
4 And the man said to me, "Son of man, look with your eyes and hear with your ears, and fix your mind on everything I show you; for you *were* brought here so that I might show *them* to you. Declare to the house of Israel everything you see."
5 Now there was a wall all around the outside of the temple.[31] In the man's hand was a measuring rod six cubits *long, each being a* cubit and a handbreadth; and he measured the width of the wall structure, one rod; and the height, one rod.

The Eastern Gateway of the Temple

6 Then he went to the gateway which faced east; and he went up its stairs and measured the threshold of the gateway, *which was* one rod wide, and the other threshold *was* one rod wide.
7 Each gate chamber *was* one rod long and one rod wide; between the gate chambers *was a space of* five cubits; and the threshold of the gateway by the vestibule of the inside gate *was* one rod.
8 He also measured the vestibule of the inside gate, one rod.
9 Then he measured the vestibule of the gateway, eight cubits; and the gateposts, two cubits. The vestibule of the gate *was* on the inside.
10 In the eastern gateway *were* three gate chambers on one side and three on the other; the three *were* all the same size; also the gateposts were of the same size on this side and that side.
11 He measured the width of the entrance to the gateway, ten cubits; *and* the length of the gate, thirteen cubits.
12 *There was* a space in front of the gate chambers, one cubit *on this side* and one cubit on that side; the gate chambers *were* six cubits on this side and six cubits on that side.
13 Then he measured the gateway from the roof of *one* gate chamber to the roof of the other; the width *was* twenty-five cubits, as door faces door.
14 He measured the gateposts, sixty cubits high, and the court all around the gateway *extended* to the gatepost.

31 Literally *house,* and so elsewhere in this book

15 *From* the front of the entrance gate to the front of the vestibule of the inner gate *was* fifty cubits.

16 *There were* beveled window *frames* in the gate chambers and in their intervening archways on the inside of the gateway all around, and likewise in the vestibules. *There were* windows all around on the inside. And on each gatepost *were* palm trees.

The Outer Court

17 Then he brought me into the outer court; and *there were* chambers and a pavement made all around the court; thirty chambers faced the pavement.

18 The pavement was by the side of the gateways, corresponding to the length of the gateways; *this was* the lower pavement.

19 Then he measured the width from the front of the lower gateway to the front of the inner court exterior, one hundred cubits toward the east and the north.

The Northern Gateway

20 On the outer court was also a gateway facing north, and he measured its length and its width.

21 Its gate chambers, three on this side and three on that side, its gateposts and its archways, had the same measurements as the first gate; its length *was* fifty cubits and its width twenty-five cubits.

22 Its windows and those of its archways, and also its palm trees, *had* the same measurements as the gateway facing east; it was ascended by seven steps, and its archway *was* in front of it.

23 A gate of the inner court was opposite the northern gateway, just as the eastern *gateway*; and he measured from gateway to gateway, one hundred cubits.

The Southern Gateway

24 After that he brought me toward the south, and there a gateway was facing south; and he measured its gateposts and archways according to these same measurements.

25 *There were* windows in it and in its archways all around like those windows; its length *was* fifty cubits and its width twenty-five cubits.

26 Seven steps led up to it, and its archway *was* in front of them; and it had palm trees on its gateposts, one on this side and one on that side.

27 *There was* also a gateway on the inner court, facing south; and he measured from gateway to gateway toward the south, one hundred cubits.

Gateways of the Inner Court

28 Then he brought me to the inner court through the southern gateway; he measured the southern gateway according to these same measurements.

29 Also its gate chambers, its gateposts, and its archways *were* according to these same measurements; *there were* windows in it and in its archways all around; *it was* fifty cubits long and twenty-five cubits wide.

30 *There were* archways all around, twenty-five cubits long and five cubits wide.

31 Its archways faced the outer court, palm trees *were* on its gateposts, and going up to it *were* eight steps.

32 Then he brought me into the inner court facing east; he measured the gateway according to these same measurements.

33 Also its gate chambers, its gateposts, and its archways *were* according to these same measurements; and *there were* windows in it and in its archways all around; *it was* fifty cubits long and twenty-five cubits wide.

34 Its archways faced the outer court, and palm trees *were* on its gateposts on this side and on that side; and going up to it *were* eight steps.

35 Then he brought me to the north gateway and measured *it* according to these same measurements—

36 also its gate chambers, its gateposts, and its archways. It had windows all around; its length *was* fifty cubits and its width twenty-five cubits.

37 Its gateposts faced the outer court, palm trees *were* on its gateposts on this side and on that side, and going up to it *were* eight steps.

Where Sacrifices Were Prepared

38 *There was* a chamber and its entrance by the gateposts of the gateway, where they washed the burnt offering.

39 In the vestibule of the gateway *were* two tables on this side and two tables on that side, on which to slay the burnt offering, the sin offering, and the trespass offering.

40 At the outer side of the vestibule, as one goes up to the entrance of the northern gateway, *were* two tables; and on the other side of the vestibule of the gateway *were* two tables.
41 Four tables *were* on this side and four tables on that side, by the side of the gateway, eight tables on which they slaughtered *the sacrifices.*
42 *There were* also four tables of hewn stone for the burnt offering, one cubit and a half long, one cubit and a half wide, and one cubit high; on these they laid the instruments with which they slaughtered the burnt offering and the sacrifice.
43 Inside *were* hooks, a handbreadth wide, fastened all around; and the flesh of the sacrifices *was* on the tables.

Chambers for Singers and Priests

44 Outside the inner gate *were* the chambers for the singers in the inner court, one facing south at the side of the northern gateway, and the other facing north at the side of the southern gateway.
45 Then he said to me, "This chamber which faces south *is* for the priests who have charge of the temple.
46 "The chamber which faces north *is* for the priests who have charge of the altar; these *are* the sons of Zadok, from the sons of Levi, who come near the LORD to minister to Him."

Dimensions of the Inner Court and Vestibule

47 And he measured the court, one hundred cubits long and one hundred cubits wide, foursquare. The altar *was* in front of the temple.
48 Then he brought me to the vestibule of the temple and measured the doorposts of the vestibule, five cubits on this side and five cubits on that side; and the width of the gateway was three cubits on this side and three cubits on that side.
49 The length of the vestibule *was* twenty cubits, and the width eleven cubits; and by the steps which led up to it *there were* pillars by the doorposts, one on this side and another on that side.

Dimensions of the Sanctuary

41 Then he brought me into the sanctuary[32] and measured the doorposts, six cubits wide on one side and six

cubits wide on the other side—the width of the tabernacle.
2 The width of the entryway *was* ten cubits, and the side walls of the entrance *were* five cubits on this side and five cubits on the other side; and he measured its length, forty cubits, and its width, twenty cubits.
3 Then he went inside and measured the doorposts, two cubits; and the entrance, six cubits *high*; and the width of the entrance, seven cubits.
4 He measured the length, twenty cubits; and the width, twenty cubits, beyond the sanctuary; and he said to me, "This *is* the Most Holy *Place.*"

The Side Chambers on the Wall

5 Next, he measured the wall of the temple, six cubits. The width of each side chamber all around the temple *was* four cubits on every side.
6 The side chambers *were* in three stories, one above the other, thirty chambers in each story; they rested on ledges which *were* for the side chambers all around, that they might be supported, but not fastened to the wall of the temple.
7 As one went up from story to story, the side chambers became wider all around, because their supporting ledges in the wall of the temple ascended like steps; therefore the width of the structure increased as one went up *from* the lowest story to the highest by way of the middle one.
8 I also saw an elevation all around the temple; it was the foundation of the side chambers, a full rod, *that is*, six cubits *high.*
9 The thickness of the outer wall of the side chambers *was* five cubits, and so also the remaining terrace by the place of the side chambers of the temple.
10 And between *it and* the *wall* chambers was a width of twenty cubits all around the temple on every side.
11 The doors of the side chambers opened on the terrace, one door toward the north and another toward the south; and the width of the terrace *was* five cubits all around.

The Building at the Western End

12 The building that fronted the separating courtyard at its western end *was* seventy cubits wide; the wall of the building

32 Hebrew *heykal,* here the main room of the temple, sometimes called the *holy place* (compare Exodus 26:33)

was five cubits thick all around, and its length ninety cubits.

Dimensions and Design of the Temple Area

13 So he measured the temple, one hundred cubits long; and the separating courtyard with the building and its walls *was* one hundred cubits long;
14 also the width of the eastern face of the temple, including the separating courtyard, *was* one hundred cubits.
15 He measured the length of the building behind it, facing the separating courtyard, with its galleries on the one side and on the other side, one hundred cubits, as well as the inner temple and the porches of the court,
16 their doorposts and the beveled window frames. And the galleries all around their three stories opposite the threshold were paneled with wood from the ground to the windows—the windows were covered—
17 from the space above the door, even to the inner room,[33] as well as outside, and on every wall all around, inside and outside, by measure.
18 And *it was* made with cherubim and palm trees, a palm tree between cherub and cherub. *Each* cherub had two faces,
19 so that the face of a man *was* toward a palm tree on one side, and the face of a young lion toward a palm tree on the other side; thus *it was* made throughout the temple all around.
20 From the floor to the space above the door, and on the wall of the sanctuary, cherubim and palm trees *were* carved.
21 The doorposts of the temple *were* square, *and so also* the front of the sanctuary; the appearance *of the one* was like the appearance *of the other.*
22 The altar *was* of wood, three cubits high, and its length two cubits. Its corners, its length, and its sides *were* of wood; and he said to me, "This *is* the table that *is* before the LORD."
23 The temple and the sanctuary had two doors.
24 The doors had two panels *apiece,* two folding panels: two *panels* for one door and two panels for the other *door.*
25 Cherubim and palm trees *were* carved on the doors of the temple just as they *were* carved on the walls. A wooden canopy *was* on the front of the vestibule outside.

26 *There were* beveled window *frames* and palm trees on one side and on the other, on the sides of the vestibule—also on the side chambers of the temple and on the canopies.

The Chambers for the Priests

42 Then he brought me out into the outer court, by the way toward the north; and he brought me into the chamber which *was* opposite the separating courtyard, and which *was* opposite the building toward the north.
2 Facing the length, *which was* one hundred cubits (the width was fifty cubits), was the north door.
3 Opposite the inner court of twenty *cubits,* and opposite the pavement of the outer court, *was* gallery against gallery in three *stories.*
4 In front of the chambers, toward the inside, *was* a walk ten cubits wide, at a distance of one cubit; and their doors faced north.
5 Now the upper chambers *were* shorter, because the galleries took away *space* from them more than from the lower and middle stories of the building.
6 For they *were* in three *stories* and did not have pillars like the pillars of the courts; therefore *the upper level* was shortened more than the lower and middle levels from the ground up.
7 And a wall which *was* outside ran parallel to the chambers, at the front of the chambers, toward the outer court; its length *was* fifty cubits.
8 The length of the chambers toward the outer court *was* fifty cubits, whereas that facing the temple *was* one hundred cubits.
9 At the lower chambers *was* the entrance on the east side, as one goes into them from the outer court.
10 *There were* also chambers in the thickness of the wall of the court toward the east, opposite the separating courtyard and opposite the building.
11 *There was* a walk in front of them also, and their appearance *was* like the chambers which *were* toward the north; they *were* as long and as wide as the others, and all their exits and entrances *were* according to plan.
12 And corresponding to the doors of the chambers that *were* facing south, as one enters them, *there was* a door in front of

---

33 Literally *house,* here *the Most Holy Place*

the walk, the way directly in front of the wall toward the east.

13 Then he said to me, "The north chambers *and* the south chambers, which *are* opposite the separating courtyard, *are* the holy chambers where the priests who approach the LORD shall eat the most holy offerings. There they shall lay the most holy offerings—the grain offering, the sin offering, and the trespass offering—for the place *is* holy.

14 "When the priests enter them, they shall not go out of the holy *chamber* into the outer court; but there they shall leave their garments in which they minister, for they *are* holy. They shall put on other garments; then they may approach *that* which *is* for the people."

Outer Dimensions of the Temple

15 Now when he had finished measuring the inner temple, he brought me out through the gateway that faces toward the east, and measured it all around.

16 He measured the east side with the measuring rod,[34] five hundred rods by the measuring rod all around.

17 He measured the north side, five hundred rods by the measuring rod all around.

18 He measured the south side, five hundred rods by the measuring rod.

19 He came around to the west side *and* measured five hundred rods by the measuring rod.

20 He measured it on the four sides; it had a wall all around, five hundred *cubits* long and five hundred wide, to separate the holy areas from the common.

The Temple, the LORD'S Dwelling Place

43 Afterward he brought me to the gate, the gate that faces toward the east.

2 And behold, the glory of the God of Israel came from the way of the east. His voice *was* like the sound of many waters; and the earth shone with His glory.

3 *It was* like the appearance of the vision which I saw—like the vision which I saw when I[35] came to destroy the city. The visions *were* like the vision which I saw by the River Chebar; and I fell on my face.

4 And the glory of the LORD came into the temple by way of the gate which faces toward the east.

5 The Spirit lifted me up and brought me into the inner court; and behold, the glory of the LORD filled the temple.

6 Then I heard *Him* speaking to me from the temple, while a man stood beside me.

7 And He said to me, "Son of man, *this* is the place of My throne and the place of the soles of My feet, where I will dwell in the midst of the children of Israel forever. No more shall the house of Israel defile My holy name, they nor their kings, by their harlotry or with the carcasses of their kings on their high places.

8 "When they set their threshold by My threshold, and their doorpost by My doorpost, with a wall between them and Me, they defiled My holy name by the abominations which they committed; therefore I have consumed them in My anger.

9 "Now let them put their harlotry and the carcasses of their kings far away from Me, and I will dwell in their midst forever.

10 "Son of man, describe the temple to the house of Israel, that they may be ashamed of their iniquities; and let them measure the pattern.

11 "And if they are ashamed of all that they have done, make known to them the design of the temple and its arrangement, its exits and its entrances, its entire design and all its ordinances, all its forms and all its laws. Write *it* down in their sight, so that they may keep its whole design and all its ordinances, and perform them.

12 "This *is* the law of the temple: The whole area surrounding the mountaintop *shall be* most holy. Behold, this *is* the law of the temple.

Dimensions of the Altar

13 "These are the measurements of the altar in cubits (the *cubit is* one cubit and a handbreadth): the base one cubit high and one cubit wide, with a rim all around its edge of one span. This *is* the height of the altar:

14 "from the base on the ground to the lower ledge, two cubits; the width of the ledge, one cubit; from the smaller ledge to the larger ledge, four cubits; and the width of the ledge, *one* cubit.

15 "The altar hearth *is* four cubits high,

---

34 Compare 40:5 35 Some Hebrew manuscripts and Vulgate read *He.*

with four horns extending upward from the hearth.

16 "The altar hearth *is* twelve cubits long, twelve wide, square at its four corners;

17 "the ledge, fourteen *cubits* long and fourteen wide on its four sides, with a rim of half a cubit around it; its base, one cubit all around; and its steps face toward the east."

Consecrating the Altar

18 And He said to me, "Son of man, thus says the Lord GOD: 'These *are* the ordinances for the altar on the day when it is made, for sacrificing burnt offerings on it, and for sprinkling blood on it.

19 'You shall give a young bull for a sin offering to the priests, the Levites, who are of the seed of Zadok, who approach Me to minister to Me,' says the Lord GOD.

20 'You shall take some of its blood and put *it* on the four horns of the altar, on the four corners of the ledge, and on the rim around it; thus you shall cleanse it and make atonement for it.

21 'Then you shall also take the bull of the sin offering, and burn it in the appointed place of the temple, outside the sanctuary.

22 'On the second day you shall offer a kid of the goats without blemish for a sin offering; and they shall cleanse the altar, as they cleansed *it* with the bull.

23 'When you have finished cleansing *it,* you shall offer a young bull without blemish, and a ram from the flock without blemish.

24 'When you offer them before the LORD, the priests shall throw salt on them, and they will offer them up *as* a burnt offering to the LORD.

25 'Every day for seven days you shall prepare a goat *for* a sin offering; they shall also prepare a young bull and a ram from the flock, both without blemish.

26 'Seven days they shall make atonement for the altar and purify it, and so consecrate *it.*

27 'When these days are over it shall be, on the eighth day and thereafter, that the priests shall offer your burnt offerings and your peace offerings on the altar; and I will accept you,' says the Lord GOD."

The East Gate and the Prince

44 Then He brought me back to the outer gate of the sanctuary which faces toward the east, but it *was* shut.

2 And the LORD said to me, "This gate shall be shut; it shall not be opened, and no man shall enter by it, because the LORD God of Israel has entered by it; therefore it shall be shut.

3 "*As for* the prince, *because* he *is* the prince, he may sit in it to eat bread before the LORD; he shall enter by way of the vestibule of the gateway, and go out the same way."

Those Admitted to the Temple

4 Then He brought me by way of the north gate to the front of the temple; so I looked, and behold, the glory of the LORD filled the house of the LORD; and I fell on my face.

5 And the LORD said to me, "Son of man, mark well, see with your eyes and hear with your ears, all that I say to you concerning all the ordinances of the house of the LORD and all its laws. Mark well who may enter the house and all who go out from the sanctuary.

6 "Now say to the rebellious, to the house of Israel, 'Thus says the Lord GOD: "O house of Israel, let us have no more of all your abominations.

7 "When you brought in foreigners, uncircumcised in heart and uncircumcised in flesh, to be in My sanctuary to defile it—My house—and when you offered My food, the fat and the blood, then they broke My covenant because of all your abominations.

8 "And you have not kept charge of My holy things, but you have set *others* to keep charge of My sanctuary for you."

9 'Thus says the Lord GOD: "No foreigner, uncircumcised in heart or uncircumcised in flesh, shall enter My sanctuary, including any foreigner who *is* among the children of Israel.

Laws Governing Priests

10 "And the Levites who went far from Me, when Israel went astray, who strayed away from Me after their idols, they shall bear their iniquity.

11 "Yet they shall be ministers in My sanctuary, *as* gatekeepers of the house and ministers of the house; they shall slay

the burnt offering and the sacrifice for the people, and they shall stand before them to minister to them.

12 "Because they ministered to them before their idols and caused the house of Israel to fall into iniquity, therefore I have lifted My hand in an oath against them," says the Lord GOD, "that they shall bear their iniquity.

13 "And they shall not come near Me to minister to Me as priest, nor come near any of My holy things, nor into the Most Holy *Place*; but they shall bear their shame and their abominations which they have committed.

14 "Nevertheless I will make them keep charge of the temple, for all its work, and for all that has to be done in it.

15 "But the priests, the Levites, the sons of Zadok, who kept charge of My sanctuary when the children of Israel went astray from Me, they shall come near Me to minister to Me; and they shall stand before Me to offer to Me the fat and the blood," says the Lord GOD.

16 "They shall enter My sanctuary, and they shall come near My table to minister to Me, and they shall keep My charge.

17 "And it shall be, whenever they enter the gates of the inner court, that they shall put on linen garments; no wool shall come upon them while they minister within the gates of the inner court or within the house.

18 "They shall have linen turbans on their heads and linen trousers on their bodies; they shall not clothe themselves with *anything that causes* sweat.

19 "When they go out to the outer court, to the *outer* court to the people, they shall take off their garments in which they have ministered, leave them in the holy chambers, and put on other garments; and in their holy garments they shall not sanctify the people.

20 "Nor shall they shave their heads, nor let their hair grow long; but they shall keep their hair well trimmed.

21 "No priest shall drink wine when he enters the inner court.

22 "They shall not take as wife a widow or a divorced woman, but take virgins of the descendants of the house of Israel, or widows of priests.

23 "And they shall teach My people *the difference* between the holy and the un-

holy, and cause them to discern between the unclean and the clean.

24 "In controversy they shall stand as judges, *and* judge it according to My judgments. They shall keep My laws and My statutes in all My appointed meetings, and they shall hallow My Sabbaths.

25 "They shall not defile *themselves* by coming near a dead person. Only for father or mother, for son or daughter, for brother or unmarried sister may they defile themselves.

26 "After he is cleansed, they shall count seven days for him.

27 "And on the day that he goes to the sanctuary to minister in the sanctuary, he must offer his sin offering in the inner court," says the Lord GOD.

28 "It shall be, in regard to their inheritance, *that* I *am* their inheritance. You shall give them no possession in Israel, for I *am* their possession.

29 "They shall eat the grain offering, the sin offering, and the trespass offering; every dedicated thing in Israel shall be theirs.

30 "The best of all firstfruits of any kind, and every sacrifice of any kind from all your sacrifices, shall be the priest's; also you shall give to the priest the first of your ground meal, to cause a blessing to rest on your house.

31 "The priests shall not eat anything, bird or beast, that died naturally or was torn *by wild animals*.

The Holy District

45 "Moreover, when you divide the land by lot into inheritance, you shall set apart a district for the LORD, a holy portion of the land; its length *shall be* twenty-five thousand *cubits*, and the width ten thousand. It *shall be* holy throughout its territory all around.

2 "Of this there shall be a square plot for the sanctuary, five hundred by five hundred *rods*, with fifty cubits around it for an open space.

3 "So this is the district you shall measure: twenty-five thousand *cubits* long and ten thousand wide; in it shall be the sanctuary, the Most Holy *Place*.

4 "It shall be a holy *portion* of the land, belonging to the priests, the ministers of the sanctuary, who come near to minister to the LORD; it shall be a place for their houses and a holy place for the sanctuary.

5 *"An area* twenty-five thousand *cubits* long and ten thousand wide shall belong to the Levites, the ministers of the temple; they shall have twenty chambers as a possession.

Properties of the City and the Prince

6 "You shall appoint as the property of the city *an area* five thousand *cubits* wide and twenty-five thousand long, adjacent to the district of the holy *portion*; it shall belong to the whole house of Israel.
7 "The prince shall have *a portion* on one side and the other of the holy district and the city's property; and bordering on the holy district and the city's property, extending westward on the west side and eastward on the east side, the length *shall be* side by side with one of the *tribal* portions, from the west border to the east border.
8 "The land shall be his possession in Israel; and My princes shall no more oppress My people, but they shall give *the rest of* the land to the house of Israel, according to their tribes."

Laws Governing the Prince

9 'Thus says the Lord GOD: "Enough, O princes of Israel! Remove violence and plundering, execute justice and righteousness, and stop dispossessing My people," says the Lord GOD.
10 "You shall have just balances, a just ephah, and a just bath.
11 "The ephah and the bath shall be of the same measure, so that the bath contains one-tenth of a homer, and the ephah one-tenth of a homer; their measure shall be according to the homer.
12 "The shekel *shall be* twenty gerahs; twenty shekels, twenty-five shekels, *and* fifteen shekels shall be your mina.
13 "This *is* the offering which you shall offer: you shall give one-sixth of an ephah from a homer of wheat, and one-sixth of an ephah from a homer of barley.
14 "The ordinance concerning oil, the bath of oil, *is* one-tenth of a bath from a kor. A kor *is* a homer or ten baths, for ten baths *are* a homer.
15 "And one lamb shall be given from a flock of two hundred, from the rich pastures of Israel. These shall be for grain offerings, burnt offerings, and peace offerings, to make atonement for them," says the Lord GOD.

16 "All the people of the land shall give this offering for the prince in Israel.
17 "Then it shall be the prince's part *to give* burnt offerings, grain offerings, and drink offerings, at the feasts, the New Moons, the Sabbaths, and at all the appointed seasons of the house of Israel. He shall prepare the sin offering, the grain offering, the burnt offering, and the peace offerings to make atonement for the house of Israel."

Keeping the Feasts

18 'Thus says the Lord GOD: "In the first *month*, on the first *day* of the month, you shall take a young bull without blemish and cleanse the sanctuary.
19 "The priest shall take some of the blood of the sin offering and put *it* on the doorposts of the temple, on the four corners of the ledge of the altar, and on the gateposts of the gate of the inner court.
20 "And so you shall do on the seventh *day* of the month for everyone who has sinned unintentionally or in ignorance. Thus you shall make atonement for the temple.
21 "In the first *month*, on the fourteenth day of the month, you shall observe the Passover, a feast of seven days; unleavened bread shall be eaten.
22 "And on that day the prince shall prepare for himself and for all the people of the land a bull *for* a sin offering.
23 "On the seven days of the feast he shall prepare a burnt offering to the LORD, seven bulls and seven rams without blemish, daily for seven days, and a kid of the goats daily *for* a sin offering.
24 "And he shall prepare a grain offering of one ephah for each bull and one ephah for each ram, together with a hin of oil for each ephah.
25 "In the seventh *month*, on the fifteenth day of the month, at the feast, he shall do likewise for seven days, according to the sin offering, the burnt offering, the grain offering, and the oil."

The Manner of Worship

46 'Thus says the Lord GOD: "The gateway of the inner court that faces toward the east shall be shut the six working days; but on the Sabbath it shall be opened, and on the day of the New Moon it shall be opened.
2 "The prince shall enter by way of the

vestibule of *that* gateway from the outside, and stand by the gatepost. The priests shall prepare his burnt offering and his peace offerings. He shall worship at the threshold of the gate. Then he shall go out, but the gate shall not be shut until evening.

3 "Likewise the people of the land shall worship at the entrance to this gateway before the Lord on the Sabbaths and the New Moons.

4 "The burnt offering that the prince offers to the Lord on the Sabbath day *shall be* six lambs without blemish, and a ram without blemish;

5 "and the grain offering *shall be* one ephah for a ram, and the grain offering for the lambs, as much as he wants to give, as well as a hin of oil with every ephah.

6 "On the day of the New Moon *it shall be* a young bull without blemish, six lambs, and a ram; they shall be without blemish.

7 "He shall prepare a grain offering of an ephah for a bull, an ephah for a ram, as much as he wants to give for the lambs, and a hin of oil with every ephah.

8 "When the prince enters, he shall go in by way of the vestibule of *that* gateway, and go out the same way.

9 "But when the people of the land come before the Lord on the appointed feast days, whoever enters by way of the north gate to worship shall go out by way of the south gate; and whoever enters by way of the south gate shall go out by way of the north gate. He shall not return by way of the gate through which he came, but shall go out through the opposite gate.

10 "The prince shall then be in their midst. When they go in, he shall go in; and when they go out, he shall go out.

11 "At the festivals and the appointed feast days the grain offering shall be an ephah for a bull, an ephah for a ram, as much as he wants to give for the lambs, and a hin of oil with every ephah.

12 "Now when the prince makes a voluntary burnt offering or voluntary peace offering to the Lord, the gate that faces toward the east shall then be opened for him; and he shall prepare his burnt offering and his peace offerings as he did on the Sabbath day. Then he shall go out,

and after he goes out the gate shall be shut.

13 "You shall daily make a burnt offering to the Lord *of* a lamb of the first year without blemish; you shall prepare it every morning.

14 "And you shall prepare a grain offering with it every morning, a sixth of an ephah, and a third of a hin of oil to moisten the fine flour. This grain offering is a perpetual ordinance, to be made regularly to the Lord.

15 "Thus they shall prepare the lamb, the grain offering, and the oil, *as* a regular burnt offering every morning."

The Prince and Inheritance Laws

16 'Thus says the Lord God: "If the prince gives a gift *of some* of his inheritance to any of his sons, it shall belong to his sons; it is their possession by inheritance.

17 "But if he gives a gift of some of his inheritance to one of his servants, it shall be his until the year of liberty, after which it shall return to the prince. But his inheritance shall belong to his sons; it shall become theirs.

18 "Moreover the prince shall not take any of the people's inheritance by evicting them from their property; he shall provide an inheritance for his sons from his own property, so that none of My people may be scattered from his property." ' "

How the Offerings Were Prepared

19 Then he brought me through the entrance, which *was* at the side of the gate, into the holy chambers of the priests which face toward the north; and there, a place *was* situated at their extreme western end.

20 And he said to me, "This *is* the place where the priests shall boil the trespass offering and the sin offering, *and* where they shall bake the grain offering, so that they do not bring *them* out into the outer court to sanctify the people."

21 Then he brought me out into the outer court and caused me to pass by the four corners of the court; and in fact, in every corner of the court *there was another* court.

22 In the four corners of the court *were* enclosed courts, forty *cubits* long and

thirty wide; all four corners *were* the same size.

23 *There was* a row *of building stones* all around in them, all around the four of them; and cooking hearths were made under the rows of stones all around.

24 And he said to me, "These *are* the kitchens where the ministers of the temple shall boil the sacrifices of the people."

The Healing Waters and Trees

47 Then he brought me back to the door of the temple; and there was water, flowing from under the threshold of the temple toward the east, for the front of the temple faced east; the water was flowing from under the right side of the temple, south of the altar.

2 He brought me out by way of the north gate, and led me around on the outside to the outer gateway that faces east; and there was water, running out on the right side.

3 Then, when the man went out to the east with the line in his hand, he measured one thousand cubits, and he brought me through the waters; the water *came up to my* ankles.

4 Again he measured one thousand and brought me through the waters; the water *came up to my* knees. Again he measured one thousand and brought me through; the water *came up to my* waist.

5 Again he measured one thousand, *and it was* a river that I could not cross; for the water was too deep, water in which one must swim, a river that could not be crossed.

6 He said to me, "Son of man, have you seen *this?*" Then he brought me and returned me to the bank of the river.

7 When I returned, there, along the bank of the river, *were* very many trees on one side and the other.

8 Then he said to me: "This water flows toward the eastern region, goes down into the valley, and enters the sea. When it reaches the sea, *its* waters are healed.

9 "And it shall be *that* every living thing that moves, wherever the rivers go, will live. There will be a very great multitude of fish, because these waters go there; for they will be healed, and everything will live wherever the river goes.

10 "It shall be *that* fishermen will stand by it from En Gedi to En Eglaim; they

will be *places* for spreading their nets. Their fish will be of the same kinds as the fish of the Great Sea, exceedingly many.

11 "But its swamps and marshes will not be healed; they will be given over to salt.

12 "Along the bank of the river, on this side and that, will grow all *kinds of* trees used for food; their leaves will not wither, and their fruit will not fail. They will bear fruit every month, because their water flows from the sanctuary. Their fruit will be for food, and their leaves for medicine."

Borders of the Land

13 Thus says the Lord GOD: "These *are* the borders by which you shall divide the land as an inheritance among the twelve tribes of Israel. Joseph *shall have two* portions.

14 "You shall inherit it equally with one another; for I lifted My hand in an oath to give it to your fathers, and this land shall fall to you as your inheritance.

15 "This *shall be* the border of the land on the north: from the Great Sea, *by* the road to Hethlon, as one goes to Zedad,

16 "Hamath, Berothah, Sibraim (which *is* between the border of Damascus and the border of Hamath), to Hazar Hatticon (which *is* on the border of Hauran).

17 "Thus the boundary shall be from the Sea to Hazar Enan, the border of Damascus; and as for the north, northward, it is the border of Hamath. *This is* the north side.

18 "On the east side you shall mark out the border from between Hauran and Damascus, and between Gilead and the land of Israel, along the Jordan, and along the eastern side of the sea. *This is* the east side.

19 "The south side, toward the South,[36] *shall be* from Tamar to the waters of Meribah by Kadesh, along the brook to the Great Sea. *This is* the south side, toward the South.

20 "The west side *shall be* the Great Sea, from the *southern* boundary until one comes to a point opposite Hamath. This *is* the west side.

21 "Thus you shall divide this land among yourselves according to the tribes of Israel.

22 "It shall be that you will divide it by lot as an inheritance for yourselves, and for the strangers who sojourn among you

36 Hebrew *Negev*

and who bear children among you. They shall be to you as native-born among the children of Israel; they shall have an inheritance with you among the tribes of Israel.

23 "And it shall be *that* in whatever tribe the stranger sojourns, there you shall give *him* his inheritance," says the Lord GOD.

Division of the Land

48 "Now these *are* the names of the tribes: From the northern border along the road to Hethlon at the entrance of Hamath, to Hazar Enan, the border of Damascus northward, in the direction of Hamath, *there shall be* one *portion for* Dan from its east to its west side;

2 "by the border of Dan, from the east side to the west, one *portion for* Asher;

3 "by the border of Asher, from the east side to the west, one *portion for* Naphtali;

4 "by the border of Naphtali, from the east side to the west, one *portion for* Manasseh;

5 "by the border of Manasseh, from the east side to the west, one *portion for* Ephraim;

6 "by the border of Ephraim, from the east side to the west, one *portion for* Reuben;

7 "by the border of Reuben, from the east side to the west, one *portion for* Judah;

8 "by the border of Judah, from the east side to the west, shall be the district which you shall set apart, twenty-five thousand *cubits* in width, and *in* length the same as one of the *other* portions, from the east side to the west, with the sanctuary in the center.

9 "The district that you shall set apart for the LORD *shall be* twenty-five thousand *cubits* in length and ten thousand in width.

10 "To these, *namely*, to the priests, shall *this* holy district belong: on the north twenty-five thousand *cubits in length*, on the west ten thousand in width, on the east ten thousand in width, and on the south twenty-five thousand in length. The sanctuary of the LORD shall be in the center.

11 "*It shall be* for the priests of the sons of Zadok, who are sanctified, who have kept My charge, who did not go astray when the children of Israel went astray, as the Levites went astray.

12 "And *this* district of land that is set apart shall be to them a thing most holy by the border of the Levites.

13 "Opposite the border of the priests, the Levites *shall have an area* twenty-five thousand *cubits* in length and ten thousand in width; its entire length *shall be* twenty-five thousand and its width ten thousand.

14 "And they shall not sell or exchange any of it; they may not alienate this best *part* of the land, for *it is* holy to the LORD.

15 "The five thousand *cubits* in width that remain, along the edge of the twenty-five thousand, shall be for general use by the city, for dwellings and common-land; and the city shall be in the center.

16 "These *shall be* its measurements: the north side four thousand five hundred *cubits*, the south side four thousand five hundred, the east side four thousand five hundred, and the west side four thousand five hundred.

17 "The common-land of the city shall be: to the north two hundred and fifty *cubits*, to the south two hundred and fifty, to the east two hundred and fifty, and to the west two hundred and fifty.

18 "The rest of the length, alongside the district of the holy *portion, shall be* ten thousand *cubits* to the east and ten thousand to the west. It shall be adjacent to the district of the holy *portion*, and its produce shall be food for the workers of the city.

19 "The workers of the city, from all the tribes of Israel, shall cultivate it.

20 "The entire district *shall be* twenty-five thousand *cubits* by twenty-five thousand *cubits*, foursquare. You shall set apart the holy district with the property of the city.

21 "The rest *shall belong* to the prince, on one side and on the other of the holy district and of the city's property, next to the twenty-five thousand *cubits* of the *holy* district as far as the eastern border, and westward next to the twenty-five thousand as far as the western border, adjacent to the *tribal* portions; *it shall belong* to the prince. It shall be the holy district, and the sanctuary of the temple *shall be* in the center.

22 "Moreover, apart from the possession of the Levites and the possession of the city *which are* in the midst of what *belongs* to the prince, *the area* between the

border of Judah and the border of Benjamin shall belong to the prince.

23 "As for the rest of the tribes, from the east side to the west, Benjamin *shall have* one *portion*;

24 "by the border of Benjamin, from the east side to the west, Simeon *shall have* one *portion*;

25 "by the border of Simeon, from the east side to the west, Issachar *shall have* one *portion*;

26 "by the border of Issachar, from the east side to the west, Zebulun *shall have* one *portion*;

27 "by the border of Zebulun, from the east side to the west, Gad *shall have* one *portion*;

28 "by the border of Gad, on the south side, toward the South,[37] the border shall be from Tamar *to* the waters of Meribah *by* Kadesh, along the brook to the Great Sea.

29 "This *is* the land which you shall divide by lot as an inheritance among the tribes of Israel, and these *are* their portions," says the Lord GOD.

The Gates of the City and Its Name

30 "These *are* the exits of the city. On the north side, measuring four thousand five hundred *cubits*

31 "(the gates of the city *shall be* named after the tribes of Israel), the three gates northward: one gate for Reuben, one gate for Judah, and one gate for Levi;

32 "on the east side, four thousand five hundred *cubits*, three gates: one gate for Joseph, one gate for Benjamin, and one gate for Dan;

33 "on the south side, measuring four thousand five hundred *cubits*, three gates: one gate for Simeon, one gate for Issachar, and one gate for Zebulun;

34 "on the west side, four thousand five hundred *cubits* with their three gates: one gate for Gad, one gate for Asher, and one gate for Naphtali.

35 "All the way around *shall be* eighteen thousand cubits; and the name of the city from *that* day *shall be*: THE LORD *IS* THERE."[38]

37 Hebrew *Negev*   38 Hebrew *YHWH Shammah*

Introduction to Daniel

Perhaps one of the greatest possibility thinkers in the Bible is Daniel. Reared in Babylon during the Israelite exile there, Daniel was a godly and wise young man who did not surrender leadership of his life to the forces and people around him.

Written by Daniel about 605–536 B.C., the book records the Jewish plight under King Nebuchadnezzar and Cyrus of Persia. It is truly an uplifting example of: no matter who you are, where you are, and under what circumstances you are, you can overcome any problem.

Three great examples of this thinking stand out in this book. The first is that of Daniel and three young men, Shadrach, Meshach and Abed-Nego. When taken into the household of the king, they were told to forsake their Jewish diets, ordained by God, and to eat only what was served in the king's court. Courageously, the boys challenged the reasoning of this demand. If they could keep to their diets for two weeks, they would prove to be healthier than their peers. Granted permission, the boys remained on their diets and after the testing period, they excelled in strength and stature over all the rest. God honored their faith!

A second incident and an even more marvelous account of these same young men, minus Daniel, is when they were thrown into a fiery furnace as the death penalty for not bowing down to the false gods. They were willing to die for their faith and God exalted them. They were unscorched and eventually released!

Finally, in the last pages of this book we learn of Daniel in the lion's den. When cast into the den, he was left untouched. God protected him and honored him for his strength and courage.

Daniel and his friends would not surrender leadership of their lives to the forces of society—the images of kings or the false gods of foreign nations. The only one they would surrender leadership to was God. That was possibility thinking in action!

The Book of
Daniel

Daniel and His Friends Obey God

IN the third year of the reign of Jehoiakim king of Judah, Nebuchadnezzar king of Babylon came to Jerusalem and besieged it.
2 And the Lord gave Jehoiakim king of Judah into his hand, with some of the articles of the house of God, which he carried into the land of Shinar to the house of his god; and he brought the articles into the treasure house of his god.
3 Then the king instructed Ashpenaz, the master of his eunuchs, to bring some of the children of Israel and some of the king's descendants and some of the nobles,
4 young men in whom *there was* no blemish, but good-looking, gifted in all wisdom, possessing knowledge and quick to understand, who *had* ability to serve in the king's palace, and whom they might teach the language and literature of the Chaldeans.
5 And the king appointed for them a daily provision of the king's delicacies and of the wine which he drank, and three years of training for them, so that at the end of *that time* they might serve before the king.
6 Now from among those of the sons of Judah were Daniel, Hananiah, Mishael, and Azariah.
7 To them the chief of the eunuchs gave names: he gave Daniel *the name* Belteshazzar; to Hananiah, Shadrach; to Mishael, Meshach; and to Azariah, Abed-Nego.
8 But Daniel purposed in his heart that he would not defile himself with the portion of the king's delicacies, nor with the wine which he drank; therefore he requested of the chief of the eunuchs that he might not defile himself.
9 Now God had brought Daniel into the favor and good will of the chief of the eunuchs.
10 And the chief of the eunuchs said to Daniel, "I fear my lord the king, who has appointed your food and drink. For why should he see your faces looking worse than the young men who *are* your age? Then you would endanger my head before the king."
11 So Daniel said to the steward[1] whom the chief of the eunuchs had set over Daniel, Hananiah, Mishael, and Azariah,
12 "Please test your servants for ten days, and let them give us vegetables to eat and water to drink.
13 "Then let our countenances be examined before you, and the countenances of the young men who eat the portion of the king's delicacies; and as you see fit, *so* deal with your servants."
14 So he consented with them in this matter, and tested them ten days.
15 And at the end of ten days their countenance appeared better and fatter in flesh than all the young men who ate the portion of the king's delicacies.
16 Thus the steward took away their portion of delicacies and the wine that they were to drink, and gave them vegetables.
17 As for these four young men, God gave them knowledge and skill in all literature and wisdom; and Daniel had understanding in all visions and dreams.
18 Now at the end of the days, when the king had said that they should be brought in, the chief of the eunuchs brought them in before Nebuchadnezzar.
19 Then the king interviewed[2] them, and among them all none was found like Daniel, Hananiah, Mishael, and Azariah; therefore they served before the king.
20 And in all matters of wisdom *and* understanding about which the king examined them, he found them ten times better than all the magicians *and* astrologers who *were* in all his realm.
21 Thus Daniel continued until the first year of King Cyrus.

Nebuchadnezzar's Dream

2 Now in the second year of Nebuchadnezzar's reign, Nebuchadnezzar had dreams; and his spirit was *so* troubled that his sleep left him.
2 Then the king gave the command to

---

1 Hebrew *Melzar*, also in verse 16   2 Literally *talked with them*

call the magicians, the astrologers, the sorcerers, and the Chaldeans to tell the king his dreams. So they came and stood before the king.

3 And the king said to them, "I have had a dream, and my spirit is anxious to know the dream."

4 Then the Chaldeans spoke to the king in Aramaic,[3] "O king, live forever! Tell your servants the dream, and we will give the interpretation."

5 But the king answered and said to the Chaldeans, "My decision is firm: if you do not make known the dream to me, and its interpretation, you shall be cut in pieces, and your houses shall be made an ash heap.

6 "However, if you tell the dream and its interpretation, you shall receive from me gifts, rewards, and great honor. Therefore tell me the dream and its interpretation."

7 They answered again and said, "Let the king tell his servants the dream, and we will give its interpretation."

8 The king answered and said, "I know for certain that you would gain time, because you see that my decision is firm:

9 "if you do not make known the dream to me, there is only one decree for you! For you have agreed to speak lying and corrupt words before me till the time has changed. Therefore tell me the dream, and I shall know that you can give me its interpretation."

10 The Chaldeans answered the king, and said, "There is not a man on earth who can tell the king's matter; therefore no king, lord, or ruler has ever asked such things of any magician, astrologer, or Chaldean.

11 "It is a difficult thing that the king requires, and there is no other who can tell it to the king except the gods, whose dwelling is not with flesh."

12 For this reason the king was angry and very furious, and gave a command to destroy all the wise men of Babylon.

13 So the decree went out, and they began killing the wise men; and they sought Daniel and his companions, to kill them.

God Reveals Nebuchadnezzar's Dream

14 Then with counsel and wisdom Daniel answered Arioch, the captain of the king's guard, who had gone out to kill the wise men of Babylon;

15 he answered and said to Arioch the king's captain, "Why is the decree from the king so urgent?" Then Arioch made the decision known to Daniel.

16 So Daniel went in and asked the king to give him time, that he might tell the king the interpretation.

17 Then Daniel went to his house, and made the decision known to Hananiah, Mishael, and Azariah, his companions,

18 that they might seek mercies from the God of heaven concerning this secret, so that Daniel and his companions might not perish with the rest of the wise men of Babylon.

19 Then the secret was revealed to Daniel in a night vision. So Daniel blessed the God of heaven.

20 Daniel answered and said:

"Blessed be the name of God
    forever and ever,
    For wisdom and might are His.
21 And He changes the times
    and the seasons;
He removes kings and raises up kings;
He gives wisdom to the wise
And knowledge to those who have
    understanding.
22 He reveals deep and secret things;
He knows what is in the darkness,
And light dwells with Him.

23 "I thank You and praise You,
    O God of my fathers;
You have given me wisdom and might,
And have now made known to me
    what we asked of You,
For You have made known to us
    the king's demand."

Daniel Explains the Dream

24 Therefore Daniel went to Arioch, whom the king had appointed to destroy the wise men of Babylon. He went and said thus to him: "Do not destroy the wise men of Babylon; take me before the king, and I will tell the king the interpretation."

25 Then Arioch quickly brought Daniel before the king, and said thus to him, "I have found a man of the captives[4] of Judah, who will make known to the king the interpretation."

26 The king answered and said to Daniel, whose name was Belteshazzar, "Are you able to make known to me the dream

---

3 The original language of Daniel 2:4b through 7:28 is Aramaic. 4 Literally of the sons of the captivity

which I have seen, and its interpretation?"

27 Daniel answered in the presence of the king, and said, "The secret which the king has demanded, the wise *men*, the astrologers, the magicians, and the soothsayers cannot declare to the king.

28 "But there is a God in heaven who reveals secrets, and He has made known to King Nebuchadnezzar what will be in the latter days. Your dream, and the visions of your head upon your bed, were these:

29 "As for you, O king, thoughts came *to* your *mind while* on your bed, *about* what would come to pass after this; and He who reveals secrets has made known to you what will be.

30 "But as for me, this secret has not been revealed to me because I have more wisdom than anyone living, but for *our* sakes who make known the interpretation to the king, and that you may know the thoughts of your heart.

31 "You, O king, were watching; and behold, a great image! This great image, whose splendor *was* excellent, stood before you; and its form *was* awesome.

32 "This image's head *was* of fine gold, its chest and arms of silver, its belly and thighs[5] of bronze,

33 "its legs of iron, its feet partly of iron and partly of clay.[6]

34 "You watched while a stone was cut out without hands, which struck the image on its feet of iron and clay, and broke them in pieces.

35 "Then the iron, the clay, the bronze, the silver, and the gold were crushed together, and became like chaff from the summer threshing floors; the wind carried them away so that no trace of them was found. And the stone that struck the image became a great mountain and filled the whole earth.

36 "This *is* the dream. Now we will tell the interpretation of it before the king.

37 "You, O king, *are* a king of kings. For the God of heaven has given you a kingdom, power, strength, and glory;

38 "and wherever the children of men dwell, or the beasts of the field and the birds of the heaven, He has given *them* into your hand, and has made you ruler over them all—you *are* this head of gold.

39 "But after you shall arise another kingdom inferior to yours; then another,

a third kingdom of bronze, which shall rule over all the earth.

40 "And the fourth kingdom shall be as strong as iron, inasmuch as iron breaks in pieces and shatters all *things*; and like iron that crushes, *that kingdom* will break in pieces and crush all the others.

41 "Whereas you saw the feet and toes, partly of potter's clay and partly of iron, the kingdom shall be divided; yet the strength of the iron shall be in it, just as you saw the iron mixed with ceramic clay.

42 "And *as* the toes of the feet *were* partly of iron and partly of clay, *so* the kingdom shall be partly strong and partly fragile.

43 "As you saw iron mixed with ceramic clay, they will mingle with the seed of men; but they will not adhere to one another, just as iron does not mix with clay.

44 "And in the days of these kings the God of heaven will set up a kingdom which shall never be destroyed; and the kingdom shall not be left to other people; it shall break in pieces and consume all these kingdoms, and it shall stand forever.

45 "Inasmuch as you saw that the stone was cut out of the mountain without hands, and that it broke in pieces the iron, the bronze, the clay, the silver, and the gold—the great God has made known to the king what will come to pass after this. The dream is certain, and its interpretation is sure."

Daniel and His Friends Promoted

46 Then King Nebuchadnezzar fell on his face, prostrate before Daniel, and commanded that they should present an offering and incense to him.

47 The king answered Daniel, and said, "Truly your God *is* the God of gods, the Lord of kings, and a revealer of secrets, since you could reveal this secret."

48 Then the king promoted Daniel and gave him many great gifts; and he made him ruler over the whole province of Babylon, and chief administrator over all the wise *men* of Babylon.

49 Also Daniel petitioned the king, and he set Shadrach, Meshach, and Abed-Nego over the affairs of the province of Babylon; but Daniel *sat* in the gate[7] of the king.

5 Or *sides*   6 Or *baked clay,* also verses 34, 35, and 42   7 That is, the king's court

The Image of Gold

3 Nebuchadnezzar the king made an image of gold, whose height *was* sixty cubits *and* its width six cubits. He set it up in the plain of Dura, in the province of Babylon. ² And King Nebuchadnezzar sent *word* to gather together the satraps, the administrators, the governors, the counselors, the treasurers, the judges, the magistrates, and all the officials of the provinces, to come to the dedication of the image which King Nebuchadnezzar had set up. ³ So the satraps, the administrators, the governors, the counselors, the treasurers, the judges, the magistrates, and all the officials of the provinces gathered together for the dedication of the image that King Nebuchadnezzar had set up; and they stood before the image that Nebuchadnezzar had set up.

⁴ Then a herald cried aloud: "To you it is commanded, O peoples, nations, and languages, ⁵ *that* at the time you hear the sound of the horn, flute, harp, lyre, *and* psaltery, in symphony with all kinds of music, you shall fall down and worship the gold image that King Nebuchadnezzar has set up; ⁶ "and whoever does not fall down and worship shall be cast immediately into the midst of a burning fiery furnace."

⁷ So at that time, when all the people heard the sound of the horn, flute, harp, *and* lyre, in symphony with all kinds of music, all the people, nations, and languages fell down *and* worshiped the gold image which King Nebuchadnezzar had set up.

Daniel's Friends Disobey the King

⁸ Therefore at that time certain Chaldeans came forward and accused the Jews. ⁹ They spoke and said to King Nebuchadnezzar, "O king, live forever! ¹⁰ "You, O king, have made a decree that everyone who hears the sound of the horn, flute, harp, lyre, *and* psaltery, in symphony with all kinds of music, shall fall down and worship the gold image; ¹¹ "and whoever does not fall down and worship shall be cast into the midst of a burning fiery furnace. ¹² "There are certain Jews whom you have set over the affairs of the province of Babylon: Shadrach, Meshach, and Abed-

Nego; these men, O king, have not paid due regard to you. They do not serve your gods or worship the gold image which you have set up."

¹³ Then Nebuchadnezzar, in rage and fury, gave the command to bring Shadrach, Meshach, and Abed-Nego. So they brought these men before the king. ¹⁴ Nebuchadnezzar spoke, saying to them, "*Is it* true, Shadrach, Meshach, and Abed-Nego, *that* you do not serve my gods or worship the gold image which I have set up? ¹⁵ "Now if you are ready at the time you hear the sound of the horn, flute, harp, lyre, *and* psaltery, in symphony with all kinds of music, and you fall down and worship the image which I have made, *good!* But if you do not worship, you shall be cast immediately into the midst of a burning fiery furnace. And who *is* the god who will deliver you from my hands?"

¹⁶ Shadrach, Meshach, and Abed-Nego answered and said to the king, "O Nebuchadnezzar, we have no need to answer you in this matter. ¹⁷ "If that *is the case,* our God whom we serve is able to deliver us from the burning fiery furnace, and He will deliver *us* from your hand, O king. ¹⁸ "But if not, let it be known to you, O king, that we do not serve your gods, nor will we worship the gold image which you have set up."

Saved in Fiery Trial

¹⁹ Then Nebuchadnezzar was full of fury, and the expression on his face changed toward Shadrach, Meshach, and Abed-Nego. *Therefore* he spoke and commanded that they heat the furnace seven times more than it was usually heated. ²⁰ And he commanded certain mighty men of valor who *were* in his army to bind Shadrach, Meshach, and Abed-Nego, *and* cast *them* into the burning fiery furnace. ²¹ Then these men were bound in their coats, their trousers, their turbans, and their *other* garments, and were cast into the midst of the burning fiery furnace. ²² Therefore, because the king's command was urgent, and the furnace exceedingly hot, the flame of the fire killed

those men who took up Shadrach, Meshach, and Abed-Nego.
23 And these three men, Shadrach, Meshach, and Abed-Nego, fell down bound into the midst of the burning fiery furnace.
24 Then King Nebuchadnezzar was astonished; and he rose in haste *and* spoke, saying to his counselors, "Did we not cast three men bound into the midst of the fire?" They answered and said to the king, "True, O king."
25 "Look!" he answered, "I see four men loose, walking in the midst of the fire; and they are not hurt, and the form of the fourth is like the Son of God."[8]

Nebuchadnezzar Praises God

26 Then Nebuchadnezzar went near the mouth of the burning fiery furnace *and* spoke, saying, "Shadrach, Meshach, and Abed-Nego, servants of the Most High God, come out, and come *here.*" Then Shadrach, Meshach, and Abed-Nego came from the midst of the fire.
27 And the satraps, administrators, governors, and the king's counselors gathered together, and they saw these men on whose bodies the fire had no power; the hair of their head was not singed nor were their garments affected, and the smell of fire was not on them.
28 Nebuchadnezzar spoke, saying, "Blessed be the God of Shadrach, Meshach, and Abed-Nego, who sent His Angel[9] and delivered His servants who trusted in Him, and they have frustrated the king's word, and yielded their bodies, that they should not serve nor worship any god except their own God!
29 "Therefore I make a decree that any people, nation, or language which speaks anything amiss against the God of Shadrach, Meshach, and Abed-Nego shall be cut in pieces, and their houses shall be made an ash heap; because there is no other God who can deliver like this."
30 Then the king promoted Shadrach, Meshach, and Abed-Nego in the province of Babylon.

Nebuchadnezzar's Second Dream

4 Nebuchadnezzar the king,
To all peoples, nations and
languages that dwell in all the earth:
Peace be multiplied to you.

2 I thought it good to declare the signs and wonders that the Most High God has worked for me.

3 How great *are* His signs,
And how mighty His wonders!
His kingdom *is* an everlasting kingdom,
And His dominion *is* from generation
to generation.

4 I, Nebuchadnezzar, was at rest in my house, and flourishing in my palace.
5 I saw a dream which made me afraid, and the thoughts on my bed and the visions of my head troubled me.
6 Therefore I issued a decree to bring in all the wise *men* of Babylon before me, that they might make known to me the interpretation of the dream.
7 Then the magicians, the astrologers, the Chaldeans, and the soothsayers came in, and I told them the dream; but they did not make known to me its interpretation.
8 But at last Daniel came before me (his name *is* Belteshazzar, according to the name of my god; in him *is* the Spirit of the Holy God), and I told the dream before him, *saying:*
9 "Belteshazzar, chief of the magicians, because I know that the Spirit of the Holy God *is* in you, and no secret troubles you, explain to me the visions of my dream that I have seen, and its interpretation.
10 "These *were* the visions of my head *while* on my bed:

I was looking, and behold,
A tree in the midst of the earth,
And its height was great.
11 The tree grew and became strong;
Its height reached to the heavens,
And it could be seen to the ends
of all the earth.
12 Its leaves *were* lovely,
Its fruit abundant,
And in it *was* food for all.
The beasts of the field found shade
under it,
The birds of the heavens dwelt
in its branches,
And all flesh was fed from it.

13 "I saw in the visions of my head *while* on my bed, and there was a watcher,

8 Or *a son of the gods*   9 Or *angel*

a holy one, coming down from heaven.
14 He cried aloud and said thus:

'Chop down the tree
    and cut off its branches,
Strip off its leaves and scatter its fruit.
Let the beasts get out from under it,
And the birds from its branches.
15 Nevertheless leave the stump and roots
        in the earth,
Bound with a band of iron and bronze,
In the tender grass of the field.
Let it be wet with the dew of heaven,
And *let* him graze with the beasts
On the grass of the earth.
16 Let his heart be changed from
        that of a man,
Let him be given the heart of an
        animal,
And let seven times[10] pass over him.

17 'This decision *is* by the decree
        of the watchers,
And the sentence by the word
        of the holy ones,
In order that the living may know
That the Most High rules in the
        kingdom of men,
Gives it to whomever He will,
And sets over it the lowest of men.'

18 "This dream I, King Nebuchadnezzar, have seen. Now you, Belteshazzar, declare its interpretation, since all the wise *men* of my kingdom are not able to make known to me the interpretation; but you *are* able, for the Spirit of the Holy God *is* in you."

Daniel Explains the Second Dream

19 Then Daniel, whose name was Belteshazzar, was astonished for a time, and his thoughts troubled him. *So* the king spoke, and said, "Belteshazzar, do not let the dream or its interpretation trouble you." Belteshazzar answered and said, "My lord, *may* the dream concern those who hate you, and its interpretation concern your enemies!
20 The tree that you saw, which grew and became strong, whose height reached to the heavens and which *could be seen* by all the earth,
21 whose leaves *were* lovely and its fruit abundant, in which *was* food for all, under which the beasts of the field

dwelt, and on whose branches the birds of the heaven had their habitation—
22 it *is* you, O king, who have grown and become strong; for your greatness has grown and reaches to the heavens, and your dominion to the end of the earth.
23 And inasmuch as the king saw a watcher, a holy one, coming down from heaven and saying, 'Chop down the tree and destroy it, but leave its stump and roots in the earth, *bound* with a band of iron and bronze in the tender grass of the field; let it be wet with the dew of heaven, and let him graze with the beasts of the field, till seven times pass over him';
24 this is the interpretation, O king, and this is the decree of the Most High, which has come upon my lord the king:
25 They shall drive you from men, your dwelling shall be with the beasts of the field, and they shall make you eat grass like oxen. They shall wet you with the dew of heaven, and seven times shall pass over you, till you know that the Most High rules in the kingdom of men, and gives it to whomever He chooses.
26 And inasmuch as they gave the command to leave the stump *and* roots of the tree, your kingdom shall be assured to you, after you come to know that Heaven rules.
27 Therefore, O king, let my counsel be acceptable to you; break off your sins by *being* righteous, and your iniquities by showing mercy to *the* poor. Perhaps there may be a lengthening of your prosperity."

Nebuchadnezzar's Humiliation

28 All *this* came upon King Nebuchadnezzar.
29 At the end of the twelve months he was walking about the royal palace of Babylon.
30 The king spoke, saying, "Is not this great Babylon, that I have built for a royal dwelling by my mighty power and for the honor of my majesty?"
31 While the word *was still* in the king's mouth, a voice fell from heaven: "King Nebuchadnezzar, to you it is

10 Possibly *seven years,* also in verses 23, 25, and 32

spoken: the kingdom has departed from you!

32 And they shall drive you from men, and your dwelling *shall be* with the beasts of the field. They shall make you eat grass like oxen; and seven times shall pass over you, until you know that the Most High rules in the kingdom of men, and gives it to whomever He chooses."

33 That very hour the word was fulfilled concerning Nebuchadnezzar; he was driven from men and ate grass like oxen; his body was wet with the dew of heaven till his hair had grown like eagles' *feathers* and his nails like birds' *claws*.

Nebuchadnezzar Praises God

34 And at the end of the time[11] I, Nebuchadnezzar, lifted my eyes to heaven, and my understanding returned to me; and I blessed the Most High and praised and honored Him who lives forever:

For His dominion *is* an everlasting dominion,
And His kingdom *is* from generation to generation.

35 All the inhabitants of the earth *are* reputed as nothing;
He does according to His will in the army of heaven
And *among* the inhabitants of the earth.
No one can restrain His hand
Or say to Him,
"What have You done?"

36 At the same time my reason returned to me, and for the glory of my kingdom, my honor and splendor returned to me. My counselors and nobles resorted to me, I was restored to my kingdom, and excellent majesty was added to me.

37 Now I, Nebuchadnezzar, praise and extol and honor the King of heaven, all of whose works *are* truth, and His ways justice. And those who walk in pride He is able to abase.

Belshazzar's Feast

5 Belshazzar the king made a great feast for a thousand of his lords, and drank wine in the presence of the thousand.

2 While he tasted the wine, Belshazzar gave the command to bring the gold and silver vessels which his father Nebuchadnezzar had taken from the temple which *had been* in Jerusalem, that the king and his lords, his wives, and his concubines might drink from them.

3 Then they brought the gold vessels that had been taken from the temple of the house of God which *had been* in Jerusalem; and the king and his lords, his wives, and his concubines drank from them.

4 They drank wine, and praised the gods of gold and silver, bronze and iron, wood and stone.

5 In the same hour the fingers of a man's hand appeared and wrote opposite the lampstand on the plaster of the wall of the king's palace; and the king saw the part of the hand that wrote.

6 Then the king's countenance changed, and his thoughts troubled him, so that the joints of his hips were loosened and his knees knocked against each other.

7 The king cried aloud to bring in the astrologers, the Chaldeans, and the soothsayers. *And* the king spoke, saying to the wise *men* of Babylon, "Whoever reads this writing, and tells me its interpretation, shall be clothed with purple and *have* a chain of gold around his neck; and he shall be the third ruler in the kingdom."

8 Now all the king's wise *men* came, but they could not read the writing, or make known to the king its interpretation.

9 Then King Belshazzar was greatly troubled, his countenance was changed, and his lords were astonished.

10 The queen, because of the words of the king and his lords, came to the banquet hall. *And* the queen spoke, saying, "O king, live forever! Do not let your thoughts trouble you, nor let your countenance change.

11 "There is a man in your kingdom in whom *is* the Spirit of the Holy God. And in the days of your father, light and understanding and wisdom, like the wisdom of the gods, were found in him; and King Nebuchadnezzar your father—your father the king—made him chief of the magicians, astrologers, Chaldeans, *and* soothsayers.

12 "Inasmuch as an excellent spirit, knowledge, understanding, interpreting

11 Literally *days*

dreams, solving riddles, and explaining enigmas[12] were found in this Daniel, whom the king named Belteshazzar, now let Daniel be called, and he will give the interpretation."

The Writing on the Wall Explained

13 Then Daniel was brought in before the king. *And* the king spoke, and said to Daniel, "*Are* you that Daniel who is one of the captives[13] from Judah, whom my father the king brought from Judah?
14 "I have heard of you, that the Spirit of God *is* in you, and *that* light and understanding and excellent wisdom are found in you.
15 Now the wise *men*, the astrologers, have been brought in before me, that they should read this writing and make known to me its interpretation, but they could not give the interpretation of the thing.
16 "And I have heard of you, that you can give interpretations and explain enigmas. Now if you can read the writing and make known to me its interpretation, you shall be clothed with purple and *have* a chain of gold around your neck, and shall be the third ruler in the kingdom."
17 Then Daniel answered, and said before the king, "Let your gifts be for yourself, and give your rewards to another; yet I will read the writing to the king, and make known to him the interpretation.
18 "O king, the Most High God gave Nebuchadnezzar your father a kingdom and majesty, glory and honor.
19 "And because of the majesty that He gave him, all peoples, nations, and languages trembled and feared before him. Whomever he wished, he executed; whomever he wished, he kept alive; whomever he wished, he set up; and whomever he wished, he put down.
20 "But when his heart was lifted up, and his spirit was hardened in pride, he was deposed from his kingly throne, and they took his glory from him.
21 "Then he was driven from the sons of men, his heart was made like the beasts, and his dwelling *was* with the wild donkeys. They fed him with grass like oxen, and his body was wet with the dew of heaven, till he knew that the Most High God rules in the kingdom of men, and appoints over it whomever He chooses.

22 "But you his son, Belshazzar, have not humbled your heart, although you knew all this.
23 "And you have lifted yourself up against the Lord of heaven. They have brought the vessels of His house before you, and you and your lords, your wives and your concubines, have drunk wine from them. And you have praised the gods of silver and gold, bronze and iron, wood and stone, which do not see or hear or know; and the God who *holds* your breath in His hand and owns all your ways, you have not glorified.
24 "Then the fingers[14] of the hand were sent from Him, and this writing was written.
25 "And this is the inscription that was written:

MENE,[15] MENE, TEKEL,[16] UPHARSIN.[17]

26 "This *is* the interpretation of *each* word. MENE: God has numbered your kingdom, and finished it;
27 "TEKEL: You have been weighed in the balances, and found wanting;
28 "PERES: Your kingdom has been divided, and given to the Medes and Persians."[18]
29 Then Belshazzar gave the command, and they clothed Daniel with purple and *put* a chain of gold around his neck, and made a proclamation concerning him that he should be the third ruler in the kingdom.

Belshazzar's Fall

30 That very night Belshazzar, king of the Chaldeans, was slain.
31 And Darius the Mede received the kingdom, *being* about sixty-two years old.

The Plot Against Daniel

6 It pleased Darius to set over the kingdom one hundred and twenty satraps, to be over the whole kingdom;
2 and over these, three governors, of whom Daniel *was* one, that the satraps might give account to them, so that the king would suffer no loss.
3 Then this Daniel distinguished himself above the governors and satraps, because an excellent spirit *was* in him; and

---

12 Literally *untie knots,* also in verse 16   13 Literally *of the sons of the captivity*   14 Literally *palm*
15 Literally *a mina (50 shekels)* from the verb "to number"   16 Literally *a shekel* from the verb "to weigh"
17 Literally *and half-shekels* from the verb "to divide"   18 Aramaic *Paras,* consonant with *Peres*

the king gave thought to setting him over the whole realm.

4 So the governors and satraps sought to find *some* charge against Daniel concerning the kingdom; but they could find no charge or fault, because he *was* faithful; nor was there any error or fault found in him.

5 Then these men said, "We shall not find any charge against this Daniel unless we find *it* against him concerning the law of his God."

6 So these governors and satraps thronged before the king, and said thus to him: "King Darius, live forever!

7 "All the governors of the kingdom, the administrators and satraps, the counselors and advisors, have consulted together to establish a royal statute and to make a firm decree, that whoever petitions any god or man for thirty days, except you, O king, shall be cast into the den of lions.

8 "Now, O king, establish the decree and sign the writing, so that it cannot be changed, according to the law of the Medes and Persians, which does not alter."

9 Therefore King Darius signed the written decree.

Daniel in the Lions' Den

10 Now when Daniel knew that the writing was signed, he went home. And in his upper room, with his windows open toward Jerusalem, he knelt down on his knees three times that day, and prayed and gave thanks before his God, as was his custom since early days.

11 Then these men assembled and found Daniel praying and making supplication before his God.

12 And they went before the king, and spoke concerning the king's decree: "Have you not signed a decree that every man who *petitions* any god or man within thirty days, except you, O king, shall be cast into the den of lions?" The king answered and said, "The thing *is* true, according to the law of the Medes and Persians, which does not alter."

13 So they answered and said before the king, "That Daniel, who is one of the captives[19] from Judah, does not show due regard for you, O king, or for the decree that you have signed, but makes his petition three times a day."

14 And the king, when he heard *these* words, was greatly displeased with himself, and set *his* heart on Daniel to deliver him; and he labored till the going down of the sun to deliver him.

15 Then these men approached the king, and said to the king, "Know, O king, that *it is* the law of the Medes and Persians that no decree or statute which the king establishes may be changed."

16 So the king gave the command, and they brought Daniel and cast *him* into the den of lions. *But* the king spoke, saying to Daniel, "Your God, whom you serve continually, He will deliver you."

17 Then a stone was brought and laid on the mouth of the den, and the king sealed it with his own signet ring and with the signets of his lords, that the purpose concerning Daniel might not be changed.

Daniel Saved from the Lions

18 Now the king went to his palace and spent the night fasting; and no musicians[20] were brought before him. Also his sleep went from him.

19 Then the king arose very early in the morning and went in haste to the den of lions.

20 And when he came to the den, he cried out with a lamenting voice to Daniel. The king spoke, saying to Daniel, "Daniel, servant of the living God, has your God, whom you serve continually, been able to deliver you from the lions?"

21 Then Daniel said to the king, "O king, live forever!

22 "My God sent His angel and shut the lions' mouths, so that they have not hurt me, because I was found innocent before Him; and also, O king, I have done no wrong before you."

23 Then the king was exceedingly glad for him, and commanded that they should take Daniel up out of the den. So Daniel was taken up out of the den, and no injury whatever was found on him, because he believed in his God.

Darius Honors God

24 And the king gave the command, and they brought those men who had accused Daniel, and they cast *them* into the den of lions—them, their children, and their wives; and the lions overpowered them, and broke all their bones in pieces before they ever came to the bottom of the den.

19 Literally *of the sons of the captivity*   20 Exact meaning unknown

25 Then King Darius wrote:

To all peoples, nations, and
languages that dwell in all the earth:
Peace be multiplied to you.
26 I make a decree that in every
dominion of my kingdom men must
tremble and fear before the God of
Daniel.

For He is the living God,
And steadfast forever;
His kingdom is the one which
    shall not be destroyed,
And His dominion shall endure
    to the end.
27 He delivers and rescues,
And He works signs and wonders
In heaven and on earth,
Who has delivered Daniel from the
    power of the lions.

28 So this Daniel prospered in the reign
of Darius and in the reign of Cyrus the
Persian.

Vision of the Four Beasts

7 In the first year of Belshazzar king of
Babylon, Daniel had a dream and visions of his head while on his bed. Then
he wrote down the dream, telling the
main facts.[21]
2 Daniel spoke, saying, "I saw in my vision by night, and behold, the four winds
of heaven were stirring up the Great Sea.
3 "And four great beasts came up from
the sea, each different from the other.
4 "The first was like a lion, and had eagle's wings. I watched till its wings were
plucked off; and it was lifted up from the
earth and made to stand on two feet like
a man, and a man's heart was given to it.
5 "And suddenly another beast, a second, like a bear. It was raised up on one
side, and had three ribs in its mouth between its teeth. And they said thus to it:
'Arise, devour much flesh!'
6 "After this I looked, and there was another, like a leopard, which had on its
back four wings of a bird. The beast also
had four heads, and dominion was given
to it.
7 "After this I saw in the night visions,
and behold, a fourth beast, dreadful and
terrible, exceedingly strong. It had huge
iron teeth; it was devouring, breaking in
pieces, and trampling the residue with its
feet. It was different from all the beasts

that were before it, and it had ten horns.
8 "I was considering the horns, and
there was another horn, a little one, coming up among them, before whom three
of the first horns were plucked out by the
roots. And there, in this horn, were eyes
like the eyes of a man, and a mouth
speaking pompous words.

Vision of the Ancient of Days

9 "I watched till thrones were put in
    place,
And the Ancient of Days was seated;
His garment was white as snow,
And the hair of His head was like
    pure wool.
His throne was a fiery flame,
Its wheels a burning fire;
10 A fiery stream issued
And came forth from before Him.
A thousand thousands ministered
    to Him;
Ten thousand times ten thousand
    stood before Him.
The court[22] was seated,
And the books were opened.

11 "I watched then because of the sound
of the pompous words which the horn
was speaking; I watched till the beast was
slain, and its body destroyed and given to
the burning flame.
12 "As for the rest of the beasts, they had
their dominion taken away, yet their lives
were prolonged for a season and a time.

13 "I was watching in the night visions,
And behold, One like the Son of Man,
Coming with the clouds of heaven!
He came to the Ancient of Days,
And they brought Him near before
    Him.
14 Then to Him was given dominion
    and glory and a kingdom,
That all peoples, nations, and
    languages should serve Him.
His dominion is an everlasting
    dominion,
Which shall not pass away,
And His kingdom the one
Which shall not be destroyed.

Daniel's Visions Interpreted

15 "I, Daniel, was grieved in my spirit
within my body, and the visions of my
head troubled me.
16 "I came near to one of those who
stood by, and asked him the truth of all

21 Literally the head (or chief) of the words   22 Or judgment

this. So he told me and made known to me the interpretation of these things:

17 'Those great beasts, which are four, *are* four kings[23] *which* arise out of the earth.

18 'But the saints of the Most High shall receive the kingdom, and possess the kingdom forever, even forever and ever.'

19 "Then I wished to know the truth about the fourth beast, which was different from all the others, exceedingly dreadful, *with* its teeth of iron and its nails of bronze, *which* devoured, broke in pieces, and trampled the residue with its feet;

20 "and about the ten horns that *were* on its head, and *about* the other *horn* which came up, before which three fell, namely, that horn which had eyes and a mouth which spoke pompous words, whose appearance *was* greater than his fellows.

21 "I was watching; and the same horn was making war against the saints, and prevailing against them,

22 "until the Ancient of Days came, and a judgment was made *in favor* of the saints of the Most High, and the time came for the saints to possess the kingdom.

23 "Thus he said:

'The fourth beast shall be
A fourth kingdom on earth,
Which shall be different from all *other* kingdoms,
And shall devour the whole earth,
Trample it and break it in pieces.

24 The ten horns *are* ten kings
Who shall arise from this kingdom.
And another shall rise after them;
He shall be different from the first *ones,*
And shall subdue three kings.

25 He shall speak *pompous* words
against the Most High,
Shall persecute[24] the saints of
the Most High,
And shall intend to change times
and law.
Then the saints[25] shall be given
into his hand
For a time and times and half a time.

26 'But the court shall be seated,
And they shall take away his
dominion,
To consume and destroy *it* forever.

27 Then the kingdom and dominion,
And the greatness of the kingdoms
under the whole heaven,
Shall be given to the people,
the saints of the Most High.
His kingdom *is* an everlasting kingdom,
And all dominions shall serve
and obey Him.'

28 "This *is* the end of the account.[26] As for me, Daniel, my thoughts greatly troubled me, and my countenance changed; but I kept the matter in my heart."

Vision of a Ram and a Goat

8 In the third year of the reign of King Belshazzar a vision appeared *to* me—to me, Daniel—after the one that appeared to me the first time.

2 I saw in the vision, and it so happened while I was looking, that I *was* in Shushan, the citadel, which *is* in the province of Elam; and I saw in the vision that I was by the River Ulai.

3 Then I lifted my eyes and saw, and there, standing beside the river, was a ram which had two horns, and the two horns *were* high; but one *was* higher than the other, and the higher *one* came up last.

4 I saw the ram pushing westward, northward, and southward, so that no beast could withstand him; nor *was there any* that could deliver from his hand, but he did according to his will and became great.

5 And as I was considering, suddenly a male goat came from the west, across the surface of the whole earth, without touching the ground; and the goat *had* a notable horn between his eyes.

6 Then he came to the ram that had two horns, which I had seen standing beside the river, and ran at him with furious power.

7 And I saw him confronting the ram; he was moved with rage against him, attacked the ram, and broke his two horns. There was no power in the ram to withstand him, but he cast him down to the ground and trampled him; and there was no one that could deliver the ram from his hand.

8 Therefore the male goat grew very great; but when he became strong, the large horn was broken, and in place of it

---

23 Representing their kingdoms (compare verse 23)   24 Literally *wear out*   25 Literally *they*
26 Literally *the word*

four notable ones came up toward the four winds of heaven.

9 And out of one of them came a little horn which grew exceedingly great toward the south, toward the east, and toward the Glorious *Land.*

10 And it grew up to the host of heaven; and it cast down *some* of the host and *some* of the stars to the ground, and trampled them.

11 He even exalted *himself* as high as the Prince of the host; and by him the daily *sacrifices* were taken away, and the place of His sanctuary was cast down.

12 Because of transgression, an army was given over *to the horn* to oppose the daily *sacrifices*; and he cast truth down to the ground. He did *all this* and prospered.

13 Then I heard a holy one speaking; and *another* holy one said to that certain *one* who was speaking, "How long *will* the vision *be, concerning* the daily *sacrifices* and the transgression of desolation, the giving of both the sanctuary and the host to be trampled under foot?"

14 And he said to me, "For two thousand three hundred days;[27] then the sanctuary shall be cleansed."

Gabriel Interprets the Vision

15 Now it happened, when I, Daniel, had seen the vision and was seeking the meaning, that suddenly there stood before me one having the appearance of a man.

16 And I heard a man's voice between the banks *of* the Ulai, who called, and said, "Gabriel, make this *man* understand the vision."

17 So he came near where I stood, and when he came I was afraid and fell on my face; but he said to me, "Understand, son of man, that the vision *refers* to the time of the end."

18 Now, as he was speaking with me, I was in a deep sleep with my face to the ground; but he touched me, and stood me upright.

19 And he said, "Look, I am making known to you what shall happen in the latter time of the indignation; for at the appointed time the end *shall be.*

20 "The ram which you saw, having the two horns—*they are* the kings of Media and Persia.

21 "And the male goat *is* the kingdom[28]

of Greece. The large horn that *is* between its eyes *is* the first king.

22 "As for the broken *horn* and the four that stood up in its place, four kingdoms shall arise out of that nation, but not with its power.

23 "And in the latter time of their kingdom,
When the transgressors have reached their fullness,
A king shall arise,
Having fierce features,
Who understands sinister schemes.

24 His power shall be mighty,
but not by his own power;
He shall destroy fearfully,
And shall prosper and thrive;
He shall destroy the mighty,
and *also* the holy people.

25 "Through his cunning
He shall cause deceit to prosper under his hand;
And he shall magnify *himself* in his heart.
He shall destroy many in *their* prosperity.
He shall even rise against the Prince of princes;
But he shall be broken without *human* hand.

26 "And the vision of the evenings and mornings
Which was told is true;
Therefore seal up the vision,
For *it refers* to many days *in the future.*"

27 And I, Daniel, fainted and was sick for days; afterward I arose and went about the king's business. I was astonished by the vision, but no one understood it.

Daniel's Prayer for the People

9 In the first year of Darius the son of Ahasuerus, of the lineage of the Medes, who was made king over the realm of the Chaldeans—

2 in the first year of his reign I, Daniel, understood by the books the number of the years *specified* by the word of the LORD, *given* through Jeremiah the prophet, that He would accomplish seventy years in the desolations of Jerusalem.

27 Literally *evening-mornings*   28 Literally *king*, representing his kingdom (compare 7:17, 23)

3 Then I set my face toward the Lord God to make request by prayer and supplications, with fasting, sackcloth, and ashes.
4 And I prayed to the LORD my God, and made confession, and said, "O Lord, great and awesome God, who keeps His covenant and mercy with those who love Him, and with those who keep His commandments,
5 "we have sinned and committed iniquity, we have done wickedly and rebelled, even by departing from Your precepts and Your judgments.
6 "Neither have we heeded Your servants the prophets, who spoke in Your name to our kings and our princes, to our fathers and all the people of the land.
7 "O Lord, righteousness *belongs* to You, but to us shame of face, as *it is* this day—to the men of Judah, to the inhabitants of Jerusalem and all Israel, those near and those far off in all the countries to which You have driven them, because of the unfaithfulness which they have committed against You.
8 "O Lord, to us *belongs* shame of face, to our kings, our princes, and our fathers, because we have sinned against You.
9 "To the Lord our God *belong* mercy and forgiveness, though we have rebelled against Him.
10 "We have not obeyed the voice of the LORD our God, to walk in His laws, which He set before us by His servants the prophets.
11 "Yes, all Israel has transgressed Your law, and has departed so as not to obey Your voice; therefore the curse and the oath written in the Law of Moses the servant of God have been poured out on us, because we have sinned against Him.
12 "And He has confirmed His words, which He spoke against us and against our judges who judged us, by bringing upon us a great disaster; for under the whole heaven such never has been done as what has been done to Jerusalem.
13 "As *it is* written in the Law of Moses, all this disaster has come upon us; yet we have not made our prayer before the LORD our God, that we might turn from our iniquities and understand Your truth.
14 "Therefore the LORD has kept the disaster in mind, and brought it upon us; for the LORD our God *is* righteous in all the works which He does, though we have not obeyed His voice.
15 "And now, O Lord our God, who brought Your people out of the land of Egypt with a mighty hand, and made Yourself a name, as *it is* this day—we have sinned, we have done wickedly!
16 "O Lord, according to all Your righteousness, I pray, let Your anger and Your fury be turned away from Your city Jerusalem, Your holy mountain; because for our sins, and for the iniquities of our fathers, Jerusalem and Your people *have become* a reproach to all *who are* around us.
17 "Now therefore, our God, hear the prayer of Your servant, and his supplications, and for the Lord's sake cause Your face to shine on Your sanctuary, which is desolate.
18 "O my God, incline Your ear and hear; open Your eyes and see our desolations, and the city which is called by Your name; for we do not present our supplications before You because of our righteous deeds, but because of Your great mercies.
19 "O Lord, hear! O Lord, forgive! O Lord, listen and act! Do not delay for Your own sake, my God, for Your city and Your people are called by Your name."

The Seventy-Weeks Prophecy

20 Now while I *was* speaking, praying, and confessing my sin and the sin of my people Israel, and presenting my supplication before the LORD my God for the holy mountain of my God,
21 yes, while I *was* speaking in prayer, the man Gabriel, whom I had seen in the vision at the beginning, being caused to fly swiftly, reached me about the time of the evening offering.
22 And he informed *me*, and talked with me, and said, "O Daniel, I have now come forth to give you skill to understand.
23 "At the beginning of your supplications the command went out, and I have come to tell *you*, for you *are* greatly beloved; therefore consider the matter, and understand the vision:

24 "Seventy weeks[29] are determined
     For your people and for your holy city,
     To finish the transgression,

29 Literally *sevens*, and so throughout the chapter

To make an end of sins,
To make reconciliation for iniquity,
To bring in everlasting righteousness,
To seal up vision and prophecy,
And to anoint the Most Holy.

25 "Know therefore and understand,
That from the going forth of the
command
To restore and build Jerusalem
Until Messiah the Prince,
There shall be seven weeks
and sixty-two weeks;
The street[30] shall be built again,
and the wall,[31]
Even in troublesome times.

26 "And after the sixty-two weeks
Messiah shall be cut off,
but not for Himself;
And the people of the prince
who is to come
Shall destroy the city and the
sanctuary.
The end of it *shall be* with a flood,
And till the end of the war
desolations are determined.
27 Then he shall confirm a covenant with
many for one week;
But in the middle of the week
He shall bring an end to sacrifice
and offering.
And on the wing of abominations
shall be one who makes desolate,
Even until the consummation,
which is determined,
Is poured out on the desolate."

Vision of the Glorious Man

10 In the third year of Cyrus king of
Persia a message was revealed to
Daniel, whose name was called Belteshazzar. The message *was* true, but the
appointed time *was* long;[32] and he understood the message, and had understanding of the vision.
2 In those days I, Daniel, was mourning
three full weeks.
3 I ate no pleasant food, no meat or
wine came into my mouth, nor did I
anoint myself at all, till three whole
weeks were fulfilled.
4 Now on the twenty-fourth day of the
first month, as I was by the side of the
great river, that *is*, the Tigris,[33]
5 I lifted my eyes and looked, and behold, a certain man clothed in linen,
whose waist *was* girded with gold of
Uphaz!

6 His body *was* like beryl, his face like
the appearance of lightning, his eyes like
torches of fire, his arms and feet like burnished bronze in color, and the sound of
his words like the voice of a multitude.
7 And I, Daniel, alone saw the vision,
for the men who were with me did not see
the vision; but a great terror fell upon
them, so that they fled to hide themselves.
8 Therefore I was left alone when I saw
this great vision, and no strength remained in me; for my vigor was turned to
frailty in me, and I retained no strength.
9 Yet I heard the sound of his words;
and while I heard the sound of his words
I was in a deep sleep on my face, with my
face to the ground.

Prophecies Concerning Persia and Greece

10 Then, suddenly, a hand touched me,
which made me tremble on my knees and
on the palms of my hands.
11 And he said to me, "O Daniel, man
greatly beloved, understand the words
that I speak to you, and stand upright,
for I have now been sent to you." While
he was speaking this word to me, I stood
trembling.
12 Then he said to me, "Do not fear,
Daniel, for from the first day that you set
your heart to understand, and to humble
yourself before your God, your words
were heard; and I have come because of
your words.
13 "But the prince of the kingdom of
Persia withstood me twenty-one days;
and behold, Michael, one of the chief
princes, came to help me, for I had been
left alone there with the kings of Persia.
14 "Now I have come to make you understand what will happen to your people
in the latter days, for the vision *refers* to
many days yet *to come*."
15 When he had spoken such words to
me, I turned my face toward the ground
and became speechless.
16 And suddenly, *one* having the likeness
of the sons of men touched my lips; then
I opened my mouth and spoke, saying to
him who stood before me, "My lord, because of the vision my sorrows have overwhelmed me, and I have retained no
strength.
17 "For how can this servant of my lord
talk with you, my lord? As for me, no
strength remains in me now, nor is any
breath left in me."

30 Or *open square*   31 Or *moat*   32 Or *and of great conflict*   33 Hebrew *Hiddekel*

18 Then again, *the one* having the likeness of a man touched me and strengthened me.
19 And he said, "O man greatly beloved, fear not! Peace *be* to you; be strong, yes, be strong!" So when he spoke to me I was strengthened, and said, "Let my lord speak, for you have strengthened me."
20 Then he said, "Do you know why I have come to you? And now I must return to fight with the prince of Persia; and when I have gone forth, indeed the prince of Greece will come.
21 "But I will tell you what is noted in the Scripture of Truth. (No one upholds me against these, except Michael your prince.

11 "Also in the first year of Darius the Mede, I, *even* I, stood up to confirm and strengthen him.)
2 "And now I will tell you the truth: Behold, three more kings will arise in Persia, and the fourth shall be far richer than *them* all; by his strength, through his riches, he shall stir up all against the realm of Greece.
3 "Then a mighty king shall arise, who shall rule with great dominion, and do according to his will.
4 "And when he has arisen, his kingdom shall be broken up and divided toward the four winds of heaven, but not among his posterity nor according to his dominion with which he ruled; for his kingdom shall be uprooted, even for others besides these.

Warring Kings of North and South

5 "Then the king of the South shall become strong, as well as *one* of his princes; and he shall gain power over him and have dominion. His dominion *shall be* a great dominion.
6 "And at the end of *some* years they shall join forces, for the daughter of the king of the South shall go to the king of the North to make an agreement; but she shall not retain the power of her authority, and neither he nor his authority[34] shall stand; but she shall be given up, with those who brought her, and with him who begot her, and with him who strengthened her in *those* times.
7 "But from a branch of her roots *one* shall arise in his place, who shall come with an army, enter the fortress of the

king of the North, and deal with them and prevail.
8 "And he shall also carry their gods captive to Egypt, with their princes[35] *and* their precious articles of silver and gold; and he shall continue *more* years than the king of the North.
9 "Then the king of the North[36] shall come to the kingdom of the king of the South, but shall return to his own land.
10 "However his sons shall stir up strife, and assemble a multitude of great forces; and *one* shall certainly come and overwhelm and pass through; then he shall return to his fortress and stir up strife.
11 "And the king of the South shall be moved with rage, and go out and fight with him, with the king of the North, who shall muster a great multitude; but the multitude shall be given into the hand of his *enemy*.
12 "When he has taken away the multitude, his heart will be lifted up; and he will cast down tens of thousands, but he will not prevail.
13 "For the king of the North will return and muster a multitude greater than the former, and shall certainly come at the end of some years with a great army and much equipment.
14 "And in those times many shall rise up against the king of the South; also *certain* violent men[37] of your people shall exalt themselves in fulfillment of the vision, but they shall fall.
15 "So the king of the North shall come and build a siege mound, and take a fortified city; and the forces[38] of the South shall not withstand *him*. Even his choice troops *shall have* no strength to resist.
16 "But he who comes against him shall do according to his own will, and no one shall stand against him. He shall stand in the Glorious Land with destruction in his power.[39]
17 "He shall also set his face to enter with the strength of his whole kingdom, and upright ones[40] with him; thus shall he do. And he shall give him the daughter of women to destroy it; but she shall not stand *with him*, or be for him.
18 "After this he shall turn his face to the coastlands, and shall take many. But a ruler shall bring the reproach against them to an end; and with the reproach removed, he shall turn back on him.

---

34 Literally *arm*   35 Or *molded images*   36 Literally *he*   37 Or *robbers,* literally *sons of breakage*
38 Literally *arms*   39 Literally *hand*   40 Or *bring equitable terms*

19 "Then he shall turn his face toward the fortress of his own land; but he shall stumble and fall, and not be found.

20 "There shall arise in his place one who imposes taxes *on* the glorious kingdom; but within a few days he shall be destroyed, but not in anger or in battle.

21 "And in his place shall arise a vile person, to whom they will not give the honor of royalty; but he shall come in peaceably, and seize the kingdom by intrigue.

22 "With the force[41] of a flood they shall be swept away from before him and be broken, and also the prince of the covenant.

23 "And after the league *is made* with him he shall act deceitfully, for he shall come up and become strong with a small *number of* people.

24 "He shall enter peaceably, even into the richest places of the province; and he shall do *what* his fathers have not done, nor his forefathers: he shall disperse among them the plunder, spoil, and riches; and he shall devise his plans against the strongholds, but *only* for a time.

25 "He shall stir up his power and his courage against the king of the South with a great army. And the king of the South shall be stirred up to battle with a very great and mighty army; but he shall not stand, for they shall devise plans against him.

26 "Yes, those who eat of the portion of his delicacies shall destroy him; his army shall be swept away, and many shall fall down slain.

27 "Both these kings' hearts *shall be* bent on evil, and they shall speak lies at the same table; but it shall not prosper, for the end *will* still *be* at the appointed time.

28 "While returning to his land with great riches, his heart shall be *moved* against the holy covenant; so he shall do *damage* and return to his own land.

The Northern King's Blasphemies

29 "At the appointed time he shall return and go toward the south; but it shall not be like the former or the latter.

30 "For ships from Cyprus[42] shall come against him; therefore he shall be grieved, and return in rage against the holy covenant, and do *damage*. So he shall return

and show regard for those who forsake the holy covenant.

31 "And forces[43] shall be mustered by him, and they shall defile the sanctuary fortress; then they shall take away the daily *sacrifices*, and place *there* the abomination of desolation.

32 "Those who do wickedly against the covenant he shall corrupt with flattery; but the people who know their God shall be strong, and carry out *great exploits*.

33 "And those of the people who understand shall instruct many; yet *for many* days they shall fall by sword and flame, by captivity and plundering.

34 "Now when they fall, they shall be aided with a little help; but many shall join with them by intrigue.

35 "And *some* of those of understanding shall fall, to refine them, purge *them*, and make *them* white, *until* the time of the end; because *it is* still for the appointed time.

36 "Then the king shall do according to his own will: he shall exalt and magnify himself above every god, shall speak blasphemies against the God of gods, and shall prosper till the wrath has been accomplished; for what has been determined shall be done.

37 "He shall regard neither the God[44] of his fathers nor the desire of women, nor regard any god; for he shall magnify himself above *them* all.

38 "But in their place he shall honor a god of fortresses; and a god which his fathers did not know he shall honor with gold and silver, with precious stones and pleasant things.

39 "Thus he shall act against the strongest fortresses with a foreign god, which he shall acknowledge, *and* advance *its* glory; and he shall cause them to rule over many, and divide the land for gain.

The Northern King's Conquests

40 "At the time of the end the king of the South shall attack him; and the king of the North shall come against him like a whirlwind, with chariots, horsemen, and with many ships; and he shall enter the countries, overwhelm *them*, and pass through.

41 "He shall also enter the Glorious Land, and many *countries* shall be overthrown; but these shall escape from his

41 Literally *arms*   42 Hebrew *Kittim,* western lands, especially Cyprus   43 Literally *arms*   44 Or *gods*

hand: Edom, Moab, and the prominent people of Ammon.
42 "He shall stretch out his hand against the countries, and the land of Egypt shall not escape.
43 "He shall have power over the treasures of gold and silver, and over all the precious things of Egypt; also the Libyans and Ethiopians *shall follow* at his heels.
44 "But news from the east and the north shall trouble him; therefore he shall go out with great fury to destroy and annihilate many.
45 "And he shall plant the tents of his palace between the seas and the glorious holy mountain; yet he shall come to his end, and no one will help him.

Prophecy of the End Time

12 "At that time Michael shall stand up,
The great prince who stands *watch* over the sons of your people;
And there shall be a time of trouble,
Such as never was since there was a nation,
Even to that time.
And at that time your people shall be delivered,
Every one who is found written in the book.
2 And many of those who sleep in the dust of the earth shall awake,
Some to everlasting life,
Some to shame *and* everlasting contempt.
3 Those who are wise shall shine
Like the brightness of the firmament,
And those who turn many to righteousness
Like the stars forever and ever.

4 "But you, Daniel, shut up the words, and seal the book until the time of the end; many shall run to and fro, and knowledge shall increase."
5 Then I, Daniel, looked; and there stood two others, one on this riverbank and the other on that riverbank.
6 And *one* said to the man clothed in linen, who *was* above the waters of the river, "How long shall the fulfillment of these wonders *be?*"
7 Then I heard the man clothed in linen, who *was* above the waters of the river, when he held up his right hand and his left hand to heaven, and swore by Him who lives forever, that *it shall be* for a time, times, and half *a time*; and when the power of the holy people has been completely shattered, all these *things* shall be finished.
8 Although I heard, I did not understand. Then I said, "My lord, what *shall be* the end of these *things?*"
9 And he said, "Go *your way*, Daniel, for the words *are* closed up and sealed till the time of the end.
10 "Many shall be purified, made white, and refined, but the wicked shall do wickedly; and none of the wicked shall understand, but the wise shall understand.
11 "And from the time *that* the daily *sacrifice* is taken away, and the abomination of desolation is set up, *there shall be* one thousand two hundred and ninety days.
12 "Blessed *is* he who waits, and comes to the one thousand three hundred and thirty-five days.
13 "But you, go *your way* till the end; for you shall rest, and will arise to your inheritance at the end of the days."

Introduction to Hosea

God used a shocking and dramatic illustration of His love for the people of Israel through the life and marriage of Hosea the prophet to Gomer the prostitute.

Written by the prophet himself sometime between 790 and 710 B.C., the theme of the Book of Hosea is God's unending love despite Israel's unfaithfulness to Him. God used Hosea's marriage and family life to illustrate Israel's relationship with God.

Hosea married Gomer, bringing her into a forgiving, loving relationship with him. But when she returned to her former lovers Hosea showed his true love for Gomer by seeking her out, forgiving her, and marrying her again.

Hosea's forgiveness of Gomer is especially significant considering that prostitutes in Israel were unclean and not worthy of God's love. Furthermore, such an act of adultery was punishable by death. Yet, Israel, like Gomer, was to be the recipient of God's love and forgiveness. God would seek Israel out and marry her again.

O Israel, return to the LORD your God,
For you have stumbled because of your iniquity;
Take words with you,
And return to the LORD.
Say to Him,
"Take away all iniquity;
Receive *us* graciously,
For we will offer the sacrifices of our lips."
Who *is* wise?
Let him understand these things.
Who is prudent?
Let him know them.
For the ways of the LORD *are* right;
The righteous walk in them,
But transgressors stumble in them.

(Hos. 14:1, 2, 9)

Hosea emphasizes God's forgiveness and redeeming love for all people. Even when they failed, God welcomed them back. Failure is never final—but God's love is!

The Book of

Hosea

THE word of the LORD that came to Hosea the son of Beeri, in the days of Uzziah, Jotham, Ahaz, *and* Hezekiah, kings of Judah, and in the days of Jeroboam the son of Joash, king of Israel.

The Family of Hosea

2 When the LORD began to speak by Hosea, the LORD said to Hosea:

"Go, take yourself a wife of harlotry
And children of harlotry,
For the land has committed
great harlotry
By departing from the LORD."

3 So he went and took Gomer the daughter of Diblaim, and she conceived and bore him a son.
4 Then the LORD said to him:

"Call his name Jezreel,
For in a little *while*
I will avenge the bloodshed of Jezreel
on the house of Jehu,
And bring an end to the kingdom of
the house of Israel.
5 It shall come to pass in that day
That I will break the bow of Israel
in the Valley of Jezreel."

6 And she conceived again and bore a daughter. Then *God* said to him:

"Call her name Lo-Ruhamah,[1]
For I will no longer have mercy
on the house of Israel,
But I will utterly take them away.[2]
7 Yet I will have mercy
on the house of Judah,
Will save them by the LORD their God,
And will not save them by bow,
Nor by sword or battle,
By horses or horsemen."

8 Now when she had weaned Lo-Ruhamah, she conceived and bore a son.
9 Then *God* said:

"Call his name Lo-Ammi,[3]

For you *are* not My people,
And I will not be your *God.*

The Restoration of Israel

10 "Yet the number of the children of Israel
Shall be as the sand of the sea,
Which cannot be measured
or numbered.
And it shall come to pass
In the place where it was said to them,
'You *are* not My people,'[4]
There it shall be said to them,
'You *are* the sons of the living God.'
11 Then the children of Judah
and the children of Israel
Shall be gathered together,
And appoint for themselves one head;
And they shall come up out of the
land,
For great *will be* the day of Jezreel!

2 Say to your brethren, 'My people,'[5]
And to your sisters, 'Mercy[6] *is shown.*'

God's Unfaithful People

2 "Bring charges against your mother,
bring charges;
For she *is* not My wife,
nor *am* I her Husband!
Let her put away her harlotries
from her sight,
And her adulteries
from between her breasts;
3 Lest I strip her naked
And expose her,
as in the day she was born,
And make her like a wilderness,
And set her like a dry land,
And slay her with thirst.

4 "I will not have mercy on her children,
For they *are* the children of harlotry.
5 For their mother has played the harlot;
She who conceived them has done
shamefully.
For she said, 'I will go after my lovers,
Who give *me* my bread and my water,
My wool and my linen,
My oil and my drink.'

---

1 Literally *No-Mercy*   2 Or *That I may forgive them at all*   3 Literally *Not-My-People*
4 Hebrew *Lo-Ammi* (compare verse 9)   5 Hebrew *Ammi* (compare verses 9 and 10)
6 Hebrew *Ruhamah* (compare verse 6)

6 "Therefore, behold,
  I will hedge up your way with thorns,
  And wall her in,
  So that she cannot find her paths.
7 She will chase her lovers,
  But not overtake them;
  Yes, she will seek them,
    but not find *them.*
  Then she will say,
  'I will go and return to my first
    husband,
  For then *it was* better for me
    than now.'
8 For she did not know
  That I gave her grain, new wine, and
    oil,
  And multiplied her silver and gold—
  Which they prepared for Baal.

9 "Therefore I will return and take away
  My grain in its time
  And My new wine in its season,
  And will take back My wool
    and My linen,
  Given to cover her nakedness.
10 Now I will uncover her lewdness
    in the sight of her lovers,
  And no one shall deliver her from My
    hand.
11 I will also cause all her mirth to cease,
  Her feast days,
  Her New Moons,
  Her Sabbaths—
  All her appointed feasts.

12 "And I will destroy her vines
    and her fig trees,
  Of which she has said,
  'These *are* my rewards that my lovers
    have given me.'
  So I will make them a forest,
  And the beasts of the field shall eat
    them.
13 I will punish her
  For the days of the Baals to which she
    burned incense.
  She decked herself with her earrings
    and jewelry,
  And went after her lovers.
  Then she forgot Me," says the LORD.

God's Mercy on His People

14 "Therefore, behold, I will allure her,
  Will bring her into the wilderness,
  And speak comfort to her.
15 I will give her
  her vineyards from there,

And the Valley of Achor
  as a door of hope;
She shall sing there,
As in the days of her youth,
As in the day when she came up
  from the land of Egypt.

16 "And it shall be, in that day,"
  Says the LORD,
  "*That* you will call Me 'My Husband,'[7]
  And no longer call Me 'My Master,'[8]
17 For I will take from her mouth the
    names of the Baals,
  And they shall be remembered by their
    name no more.
18 In that day I will make a covenant
    for them
  With the beasts of the field,
  With the birds of the air,
  And *with* the creeping things of the
    ground.
  Bow and sword of battle
  I will shatter from the earth,
  To make them lie down safely.

19 "I will betroth you to Me forever;
  Yes, I will betroth you to Me
  In righteousness and justice,
  In lovingkindness and mercy;
20 I will betroth you to Me
    in faithfulness,
  And you shall know the LORD.

21 "It shall come to pass in that day
  That I will answer," says the LORD;
  "I will answer the heavens,
  And they shall answer the earth.
22 The earth shall answer
  With grain,
  With new wine,
  And with oil;
  They shall answer Jezreel.[9]
23 Then I will sow her for Myself in the
    earth,
  And I will have mercy on *her who had*
    not obtained mercy;[10]
  Then I will say to *those who were* not
    My people,[11]
  'You *are* My people!'
  And they shall say,
  '*You are* my God!' "

Israel Will Return to God

3 Then the LORD said to me, "Go
  again, love a woman *who is* loved by
a lover[12] and is committing adultery, just
like the love of the LORD for the children
of Israel, who look to other gods and love
the raisin cakes *of the pagans.*"

---

7 Hebrew *Ishi*   8 Hebrew *Baali*   9 Literally *God Will Sow*   10 Hebrew *Lo-Ruhamah*   11 Hebrew *Lo-Ammi*
12 Literally *friend* or *husband*

2 So I bought her for myself for fifteen *shekels* of silver, and one and one-half homers of barley. 3 And I said to her, "You shall stay with me many days; you shall not play the harlot, nor shall you have a man; thus I *will* also *be* toward you." 4 For the children of Israel shall abide many days without king or prince, without sacrifice or sacred pillar, without ephod or teraphim. 5 Afterward the children of Israel shall return, seek the LORD their God and David their king, and fear the LORD and His goodness in the latter days.

God's Charge Against Israel

4 Hear the word of the LORD,
You children of Israel,
For the LORD *brings* a charge
against the inhabitants of the land:

"There is no truth or mercy
Or knowledge of God in the land.
2 *By* swearing and lying,
Killing and stealing and committing adultery,
They break all restraint,
With bloodshed after bloodshed.
3 Therefore the land will mourn;
And everyone who dwells there will waste away
With the beasts of the field
And the birds of the air;
Even the fish of the sea will be taken away.

4 "Now let no man contend,
or reprove another,
For your people *are* like those who contend with the priest.
5 Therefore you shall stumble in the day;
The prophet also shall stumble with you in the night;
And I will destroy your mother.
6 My people are destroyed for lack of knowledge.
Because you have rejected knowledge,
I also will reject you from being priest for Me;
Because you have forgotten the law of your God,
I also will forget your children.

7 "The more they increased,
The more they sinned against Me;
I will change their glory into shame.
8 They eat up the sin of My people;
They set their heart on their iniquity.

9 And it shall be: like people, like priest.
So I will punish them for their ways,
And reward them for their deeds.
10 For they shall eat,
but not have enough;
They shall commit harlotry,
but not increase;
Because they have ceased obeying the LORD.

The Idolatry of Israel

11 "Harlotry, wine, and new wine
enslave the heart.
12 My people ask counsel from their wooden *idols*,
And their staff informs them.
For the spirit of harlotry has caused *them* to stray,
And they have played the harlot against their God.
13 They offer sacrifices
on the mountaintops,
And burn incense on the hills,
Under oaks, poplars, and terebinths,
Because their shade *is* good.
Therefore your daughters commit harlotry,
And your brides commit adultery.

14 "I will not punish your daughters when they commit harlotry,
Nor your brides when they commit adultery;
For *the men* themselves go apart with harlots,
And offer sacrifices with a ritual harlot.[13]
Therefore people *who* do not understand will be trampled.

15 "Though you, Israel, play the harlot,
Let not Judah offend.
Do not come up to Gilgal,
Nor go up to Beth Aven,
Nor swear an oath, *saying*,
'As the LORD lives'—

16 "For Israel is stubborn
Like a stubborn calf;
Now the LORD will let them forage
Like a lamb in open country.

17 "Ephraim *is* joined to idols,
Let him alone.
18 Their drink is rebellion,
They commit harlotry continually.
Her rulers dearly[14] love dishonor.
19 The wind has wrapped her up
in its wings,

13 Compare Deuteronomy 23:18   14 Hebrew is difficult; a Jewish tradition reads *Her rulers shamefully love, 'Give!'*

And they shall be ashamed
 because of their sacrifices.

Impending Judgment on Israel and Judah

5 "Hear this, O priests!
   Take heed, O house of Israel!
 Give ear, O house of the king!
 For yours *is* the judgment,
 Because you have been a snare to
   Mizpah
 And a net spread on Tabor.
2 The revolters are deeply involved in
   slaughter,
 Though I rebuke them all.
3 I know Ephraim,
 And Israel is not hidden from Me;
 For now, O Ephraim,
   you commit harlotry;
 Israel is defiled.

4 "They do not direct their deeds
 Toward turning to their God,
 For the spirit of harlotry is in their
   midst,
 And they do not know the LORD.
5 The pride of Israel testifies to his face;
 Therefore Israel and Ephraim stumble
   in their iniquity;
 Judah also stumbles with them.

6 "With their flocks and herds
 They shall go to seek the LORD,
 But they will not find *Him;*
 He has withdrawn Himself from them.
7 They have dealt treacherously with the
   LORD,
 For they have begotten pagan children.
 Now a New Moon shall devour them
   and their heritage.

8 "Blow the ram's horn in Gibeah,
 The trumpet in Ramah!
 Cry aloud *at* Beth Aven,
 '*Look* behind you, O Benjamin!'
9 Ephraim shall be desolate
   in the day of rebuke;
 Among the tribes of Israel
 I make known what is sure.

10 "The princes of Judah are like those
   who remove a landmark;
 I will pour out my wrath on them like
   water.
11 Ephraim is oppressed
   and broken in judgment,
 Because he willingly walked by *human*
   precept.
12 Therefore I *will be* to Ephraim
 like a moth,

And to the house of Judah
 like rottenness.

13 "When Ephraim saw his sickness,
 And Judah *saw* his wound,
 Then Ephraim went to Assyria
 And sent to King Jareb;
 Yet he cannot cure you,
 Nor heal you of your wound.
14 For I *will be* like a lion to Ephraim,
 And like a young lion to the house of
   Judah.
 I, *even* I, will tear *them* and go away;
 I will take *them* away,
   and no one shall rescue.
15 I will return again to My place
 Till they acknowledge their offense.
 Then they will seek My face;
 In their affliction
   they will diligently seek Me."

A Call to Repentance

6 Come, and let us return to the LORD;
   For He has torn, but He will heal us;
 He has stricken, but He will bind
   us up.
2 After two days He will revive us;
 On the third day He will raise us up,
 That we may live in His sight.
3 Let us know,
 Let us pursue the knowledge of the
   LORD.
 His going forth is established as the
   morning;
 He will come to us like the rain,
 Like the latter *and* former rain to the
   earth.

Impenitence of Israel and Judah

4 "O Ephraim, what shall I do to you?
 O Judah, what shall I do to you?
 For your faithfulness is like
   a morning cloud,
 And like the early dew it goes away.
5 Therefore I have hewn *them* by the
   prophets,
 I have slain them by the words
   of My mouth;
 And your judgments *are like* light
   that goes forth.
6 For I desire mercy and not sacrifice,
 And the knowledge of God
   more than burnt offerings.

7 "But like men[15] they transgressed the
   covenant;
 There they dealt treacherously
   with Me.

15 Or *like Adam*

8 Gilead *is* a city of evildoers,
   And is defiled with blood.
9 As bands of robbers lie in wait
       for a man,
   So the company of priests murder
       on the way to Shechem;
   Surely they commit lewdness.
10 I have seen a horrible thing in the
       house of Israel:
   There *is* the harlotry of Ephraim;
   Israel is defiled.
11 Also, O Judah, a harvest is appointed
       for you,
   When I return the captives of My
       people.

7 "When I would have healed Israel,
   Then the iniquity of Ephraim was
       uncovered,
   And the wickedness of Samaria.
   For they have committed fraud;
   The thief comes in;
   A band of robbers takes spoil outside.
2 They do not consider in their hearts
   That I remember all their wickedness;
   Now their own deeds have surrounded
       them;
   They are before My face.
3 They make a king glad with their
       wickedness,
   And princes with their lies.

4 "They *are* all adulterers.
   Like an oven heated by a baker—
   He ceases stirring *the fire*
       after kneading the dough,
   Until it is leavened.
5 In the day of our king
   Princes have made *him* sick,
       inflamed with wine;
   He stretched out his hand with scoffers.
6 They prepare their heart like an oven,
   While they lie in wait;
   Their baker sleeps all night;
   In the morning it burns like
       a flaming fire.
7 They are all hot, like an oven,
   And have devoured their judges;
   All their kings have fallen.
   There is none among them
       who calls upon Me.

8 "Ephraim has mixed himself
       among the peoples;
   Ephraim is a cake unturned.
9 Aliens have devoured his strength,
   But he does not know *it;*
   Yes, gray hairs are here and there
       on him,
   Yet he does not know *it.*

10 And the pride of Israel testifies
       to his face,
   But they do not return to the LORD
       their God,
   Nor seek Him for all this.

Futile Reliance on the Nations

11 "Ephraim also is like a silly dove,
       without sense—
   They call to Egypt,
   They go to Assyria.
12 Wherever they go,
   I will spread My net on them;
   I will bring them down like birds of
       the air;
   I will chastise them
   According to what their congregation
       has heard.

13 "Woe to them, for they have fled
       from Me!
   Destruction to them,
   Because they have transgressed
       against Me!
   Though I redeemed them,
   Yet they have spoken lies against Me.
14 They did not cry out to Me with their
       heart
   When they wailed upon their beds.

   "They assemble together for grain
       and new wine,
   They rebel against Me;
15 Though I disciplined *and* strengthened
       their arms,
   Yet they devise evil against Me;
16 They return,
   but not to the Most High;[16]
   They are like a deceitful bow.
   Their princes shall fall by the sword
   For the cursings of their tongue.
   This *shall be* their derision in the land
       of Egypt.

The Apostasy of Israel

8 "*Set* the trumpet[17] to your mouth!
   He shall come like an eagle against the
       house of the LORD,
   Because they have transgressed My
       covenant
   And rebelled against My law.
2 Israel will cry to Me,
   'My God, we know You!'
3 Israel has cast off the good;
   The enemy will pursue him.

4 "They set up kings, but not by Me;
   They made princes,
       and I did not acknowledge *it.*

16 Or *upward*   17 Hebrew *shophar,* ram's horn

From their silver and gold
They made idols for themselves—
That they might be cut off.
5 Your calf is rejected, O Samaria!
My anger is aroused against them.
How long *will it be* until they attain to
   innocence?
6 For from Israel *is* even this:
A workman made it, and it *is* not God;
But the calf of Samaria shall be broken
   to pieces.

7 "They sow the wind,
And reap the whirlwind.
The stalk has no bud;
It shall never produce meal.
If it should produce,
Aliens would swallow it up.
8 Israel is swallowed up;
Now they are among the Gentiles
Like a vessel in which *there is* no
   pleasure.
9 For they have gone up to Assyria,
Like a wild donkey alone by itself;
Ephraim has hired lovers.
10 Yes, though they have hired among the
   nations,
Now I will gather them;
And they shall sorrow a little,[18]
Because of the burden[19] of the king of
   princes.

11 "Because Ephraim has made
   many altars for sin,
They have become for him
   altars for sinning.
12 I have written for him
   the great things of My law,
But they were considered
   a strange thing.
13 *For* the sacrifices of My offerings
   they sacrifice flesh and eat *it*,
But the LORD does not accept them.
Now He will remember their iniquity
   and punish their sins.
They shall return to Egypt.

14 "For Israel has forgotten his Maker,
And has built temples;[20]
Judah also has multiplied fortified
   cities;
But I will send fire upon his cities,
And it shall devour his palaces."

Judgment of Israel's Sin

9 Do not rejoice, O Israel, with joy like
      other peoples,
For you have played the harlot against
   your God.

You have loved *for* reward on every
   threshing floor.
2 The threshing floor and the winepress
Shall not feed them,
And the new wine shall fail in her.

3 They shall not dwell in the LORD's
   land,
But Ephraim shall return to Egypt,
And shall eat unclean *things* in Assyria.
4 They shall not offer wine *offerings*
   to the LORD,
Nor shall their sacrifices be pleasing
   to Him.
It shall be like bread of mourners
   to them;
All who eat it shall be defiled.
For their bread *shall be* for their life;
It shall not come into the house of the
   LORD.

5 What will you do in the appointed day,
And in the day of the feast of the
   LORD?
6 For indeed they are gone because
   of destruction.
Egypt shall gather them up;
Memphis shall bury them.
Nettles shall possess their valuables
   of silver;
Thorns *shall be* in their tents.

7 The days of punishment have come;
The days of recompense have come.
Israel knows!
The prophet *is* a fool,
The spiritual man *is* insane,
Because of the greatness of your
   iniquity and great enmity.
8 The watchman of Ephraim *is* with my
   God;
But the prophet *is* a fowler's snare in
   all his ways,
And enmity in the house of his God.
9 They are deeply corrupted,
As in the days of Gibeah.
He will remember their iniquity;
He will punish their sins.

10 "I found Israel
Like grapes in the wilderness;
I saw your fathers
As the firstfruits on the fig tree
   in its first season.
But they went to Baal Peor,
And separated themselves
   to that shame;
They became an abomination
   like the thing they loved.

18 Or *begin to diminish*   19 Or *oracle*   20 Or *palaces*

11 *As for* Ephraim, their glory shall fly
     away like a bird—
   No birth, no pregnancy,
     and no conception!
12 Though they bring up their children,
   Yet I will bereave them to the last
     man.
   Yes, woe to them when I depart from
     them!
13 Just as I saw Ephraim like Tyre,
     planted in a pleasant place,
   So Ephraim will bring out his children
     to the murderer."

14 Give them, O LORD—
   What will You give?
   Give them a miscarrying womb
   And dry breasts.

15 "All their wickedness *is* in Gilgal,
   For there I hated them.
   Because of the evil of their deeds
   I will drive them from My house;
   I will love them no more.
   All their princes *are* rebellious.
16 Ephraim is stricken,
   Their root is dried up;
   They shall bear no fruit.
   Yes, were they to bear children,
   I would kill the beloved *fruit* of their
     womb."

17 My God will cast them away,
   Because they did not obey Him;
   And they shall be wanderers among
     the nations.

Israel's Sin and Captivity

10 Israel empties *his* vine;
       He brings forth fruit for himself.
   According to the multitude of his fruit
   He has increased the altars;
   According to the bounty of his land
   They have embellished *his* sacred
     pillars.
2 Their heart is divided;
   Now they are held guilty.
   He will break down their altars;
   He will ruin their sacred pillars.

3 For now they say,
   "We have no king,
   Because we did not fear the LORD.
   And as for a king,
     what would he do for us?"
4 They have spoken words,
   Swearing falsely in making a covenant.
   Thus judgment springs up like hemlock
     in the furrows of the field.

5 The inhabitants of Samaria fear
   Because of the calf[21] of Beth Aven.
   For its people mourn for it,
   And its priests shriek for it—
   Because its glory has departed from it.
6 *The idol* also shall be carried to Assyria
   As a present for King Jareb.
   Ephraim shall receive shame,
   And Israel shall be ashamed of his own
     counsel.

7 *As for* Samaria, her king is cut off
   Like a twig on the water.
8 Also the high places of Aven,
     the sin of Israel,
   Shall be destroyed.
   The thorn and thistle shall grow on
     their altars;
   They shall say to the mountains,
     "Cover us!"
   And to the hills, "Fall on us!"

9 "O Israel, you have sinned from the
     days of Gibeah;
   There they stood.
   The battle in Gibeah against the
     children of iniquity[22]
   Did not overtake them.
10 When *it is* My desire,
     I will chasten them.
   Peoples shall be gathered against them
   When I bind them for their two
     transgressions.[23]
11 Ephraim *is* a trained heifer
   That loves to thresh *grain;*
   But I harnessed her fair neck,
   I will make Ephraim pull *a plow.*
   Judah shall plow;
   Jacob shall break his clods."

12 Sow for yourselves righteousness;
   Reap in mercy;
   Break up your fallow ground,
   For *it is* time to seek the LORD,
   Till He comes and rains righteousness
     on you.

13 You have plowed wickedness;
   You have reaped iniquity.
   You have eaten the fruit of lies,
   Because you trusted in your own way,
   In the multitude of your mighty men.
14 Therefore tumult shall arise among
     your people,
   And all your fortresses shall be
     plundered
   As Shalman plundered Beth Arbel in
     the day of battle—
   A mother dashed in pieces upon *her*
     children.

---

21 Literally *calves*
22 So read many Hebrew manuscripts, Septuagint, and Vulgate; Masoretic Text reads *unruliness.*
23 Or *in their two habitations*

15 Thus it shall be done to you, O Bethel,
Because of your great wickedness.
In a morning the king of Israel
Shall be cut off utterly.

God's Continuing Love for Israel

11 "When Israel *was* a child,
    I loved him,
And out of Egypt I called My son.
2 *As* they called them,
So they went from them;
They sacrificed to the Baals,
And burned incense to carved images.

3 "I taught Ephraim to walk,
Taking them by their arms;
But they did not know that I healed
them.
4 I drew them with gentle cords,[24]
With bands of love,
And I was to them as those who take
the yoke from their neck.[25]
I stooped *and* fed them.

5 "He shall not return to the land
of Egypt;
But the Assyrian shall be his king,
Because they refused to repent.
6 And the sword shall slash in his cities,
Devour his districts,
And consume *them*,
Because of their own counsels.
7 My people are bent on backsliding
from Me.
Though they call to the Most High,[26]
None at all exalt *Him*.

8 "How can I give you up, Ephraim?
How can I hand you over, Israel?
How can I make you like Admah?
How can I set you like Zeboiim?
My heart churns within Me;
My sympathy is stirred.
9 I will not execute the fierceness
of My anger;
I will not again destroy Ephraim.
For I *am* God, and not man,
The Holy One in your midst;
And I will not come with terror.[27]

10 "They shall walk after the LORD.
He will roar like a lion.
When He roars,
Then *His* sons shall come trembling
from the west;
11 They shall come trembling like a bird
from Egypt,
Like a dove from the land of Assyria.

And I will let them dwell in their
houses,"
Says the LORD.

God's Anger with Judah's Sin

12 "Ephraim has encompassed Me with
lies,
And the house of Israel with deceit;
But Judah still walks with God,
Even with the Holy One[28] *who is*
faithful.

12 Ephraim feeds on the wind,
    And pursues the east wind;
He daily increases lies and desolation.
Also they make a covenant with the
Assyrians,
And oil is carried to Egypt.

2 The LORD also *brings* a charge against
Judah,
And will punish Jacob
according to his ways;
According to his deeds
He will recompense him.
3 He took his brother by the heel in the
womb,
And in his strength he struggled with
God.[29]
4 Yes, he struggled with the Angel
and prevailed;
He wept, and sought favor from Him.
He found Him *in* Bethel,
And there He spoke to us—
5 That is, the LORD God of hosts.
The LORD *is* His memorial.
6 So you, by *the help of* your God,
return;
Observe mercy and justice,
And wait on your God continually.

7 A cunning Canaanite!
Deceitful scales *are* in his hand;
He loves to oppress.
8 And Ephraim said,
"Surely I have become rich,
I have found wealth for myself;
In all my labors
They shall find in me no iniquity that
is sin."

9 "But I *am* the LORD your God,
Ever since the land of Egypt;
I will again make you dwell in tents,
As in the days of the appointed feast.
10 I have also spoken by the prophets,
And have multiplied visions;
I have given symbols through the
witness of the prophets."

24 Literally *of a man* 25 Literally *jaws* 26 Or *upward* 27 Or *I will not enter a city* 28 Or *holy ones*
29 Compare Genesis 32:28

11 Though Gilead *has* idols—
   Surely they are vanity—
   Though they sacrifice bulls in Gilgal,
   Indeed their altars *shall be* heaps
      in the furrows of the field.

12 Jacob fled to the country of Syria;
   Israel served for a spouse,
   And for a wife he tended *sheep.*
13 By a prophet the LORD brought Israel
      out of Egypt,
   And by a prophet he was preserved.
14 Ephraim provoked *Him* to anger most
      bitterly;
   Therefore his Lord will leave on him
      his bloodguilt,
   And return his reproach upon him.

Relentless Judgment on Israel

13 When Ephraim spoke, trembling,
   He exalted *himself* in Israel;
   But when he offended in Baal, he died.
2 Now they sin more and more,
   And have made for themselves
      molded images,
   Idols of their silver,
      according to their skill;
   All of it *is* the work of craftsmen.
   They say of them,
   "Let the men who sacrifice[30] kiss the
      calves!"
3 Therefore they shall be like the
      morning cloud
   And like the early dew that passes
      away,
   Like chaff blown off from a threshing
      floor
   And like smoke from a chimney.

4 "Yet I *am* the LORD your God
   Ever since the land of Egypt,
   And you shall know no God but Me;
   For *there is* no savior besides Me.
5 I knew you in the wilderness,
   In the land of great drought.
6 When they had pasture,
      they were filled;
   They were filled
      and their heart was exalted;
   Therefore they forgot Me.

7 "So I will be to them like a lion;
   Like a leopard by the road
      I will observe *them;*
8 I will meet them
      like a bear deprived *of her cubs;*
   I will tear open their rib cage,

And there I will devour them
      like a lion.
   The wild beast shall tear them.

9 "O Israel, you are destroyed,[31]
   But your help[32] *is* from Me.
10 I will be your King;[33]
   Where *is any other,*
   That he may save you in all your
      cities?
   And your judges to whom you said,
   'Give me a king and princes'?
11 I gave you a king in My anger,
   And took *him* away in My wrath.

12 "The iniquity of Ephraim *is* bound up;
   His sin *is* stored up.
13 The sorrows of a woman in childbirth
      shall come upon him.
   He *is* an unwise son,
   For he should not stay long
      where children are born.

14 "I will ransom them from the power
      of the grave;[34]
   I will redeem them from death.
   O Death, I will be your plagues![35]
   O Grave, I will be your destruction![36]
   Pity is hidden from My eyes.

15 Though he is fruitful among *his*
      brethren,
   An east wind shall come;
   The wind of the LORD shall come up
      from the wilderness.
   Then his spring shall become dry,
   And his fountain shall be dried up.
   He shall plunder the treasury of every
      desirable prize.
16 Samaria is held guilty,[37]
   For she has rebelled against her God.
   They shall fall by the sword,
   Their infants shall be dashed in pieces,
   And their women with child ripped
      open.

Israel Restored at Last

14 O Israel, return to the LORD your
      God,
   For you have stumbled because of your
      iniquity;
2 Take words with you,
   And return to the LORD.
   Say to Him,
   "Take away all iniquity;
   Receive *us* graciously,
   For we will offer the sacrifices[38] of our
      lips.

---

30 Or *those who offer human sacrifice*   31 Literally *it* or *he destroyed you*   32 Literally *in your help*
33 Septuagint, Syriac, Targum, and Vulgate read, *Where is your king?*   34 Hebrew *Sheol*
35 Septuagint reads *where is your punishment?*   36 Septuagint reads *where is your sting?*
37 Septuagint reads *shall be disfigured*   38 Literally *bull calves;* Septuagint reads *fruit.*

The Olive Tree

The ancient olive tree holds an intrinsic beauty to the biblical writer. Its knotted, twisted trunk has dominated the landscape of Israel for thousands of years.

Unlike the country's tall cedars, straight cypress, and fragrant fruit trees, the beauty of the olive tree is expressed more through function than in outward appearance. To the western mind-set, one might look at the tree's form and pronounce it unattractive. Yet in Hebrew thought, the very nature of the olive tree is lovely.

Throughout the ages, prophets focused on the olive tree to illustrate inner beauty. The tree's value is measured in service. The delicate olive oil held a prize role in anointing the many kings of the land. For the common person, the oil was needed to fuel their lamps and light their way. Even today, olives and olive oil are a main staple to the Middle Eastern diet.

The olive branch has long been a symbol of peace and goodwill. Following the great flood, Noah's dove carried an olive twig back to the ark as a sign of God's peace and promise that the waters had receded.

For strength and endurance the olive tree is unsurpassed. Even in the most inhospitable chalky soil of the Judean wilderness, the olive tree is found. Cut back to the roots, the tree will grow back and live to a span of thousands of years.

Should we not look at ourselves as the people of Israel look at the olive tree? Like the olive tree, our self-worth is also expressed in service.

Be like an olive tree. Anoint those around you with love. Help light the way. Be a symbol of God's peace. And when people cut you down—grow back. Bloom where you are planted!

3 Assyria shall not save us,
We will not ride on horses,
Nor will we say anymore to the work
of our hands,
'*You are* our gods.'
For in You the fatherless finds mercy."

4 "I will heal their backsliding,
I will love them freely,
For My anger has turned away from
him.

5 I will be like the dew to Israel;
He shall grow like the lily,
And lengthen his roots like Lebanon.

6 His branches shall spread;
His beauty shall be like an olive tree,
And his fragrance like Lebanon.

7 Those who dwell under his shadow
shall return;

They shall be revived *like* grain,
And grow like the vine.
Their scent[39] *shall be* like the wine of
Lebanon.

8 "Ephraim *shall say*,
'What have I to do anymore with
idols?'
I have heard and observed him.
I *am* like a green cypress tree;
Your fruit is found in Me."

9 Who *is* wise?
Let him understand these things.
Who is prudent?
Let him know them.
For the ways of the LORD *are* right;
The righteous walk in them,
But transgressors stumble in them.

39 Literally *remembrance*

Introduction to Joel

The Book of Joel makes a national appeal to the people of Israel about 835 B.C., for repentance based on God's judgment and the promise of deliverance and blessing in the day of the Lord.

Israel was faced with severe plagues and a drought due to their rebellion against God. Joel urges them to see God in the times of calamity and to turn to Him. In the day of distress, God will also bring forth a day of deliverance. He gives them the promise that whoever calls upon the name of the Lord will be saved.

> So rend your heart, and not your garments;
> Return to the LORD your God,
> For He *is* gracious and merciful,
> Slow to anger, and of great kindness;
> And He relents from doing harm.

> (Joel 2:13)

The day of the Lord is mentioned six times by Joel. Perhaps this points to the future and the second coming of Christ. Jesus Himself alludes to this reference in Matthew 24 when He speaks of His final return and victory.

Joel encourages the people to change their hearts, which will be visible in their outward actions. God calls them to return to Him, for even in times of great distress, He is gracious and compassionate, slow to anger, and overflowing with loving-kindness. Joel urges them to call on God, to repent, to "turn around." Repentance means to change direction, to set new goals and to establish new standards.

Joel wanted the people to seek God's plan for their lives and to commit themselves to it. For whoever turns to God will not be disappointed!

> Lord, forgive me for not having the faith to live the life I should have lived. I am ready to dream your dreams. I am going to live right, think right, pray right, and do right! I am trusting you to give me the power. Together, we shall succeed!

> Amen.

The Book of
Joel

THE word of the LORD that came to Joel the son of Pethuel.

The Land Laid Waste

2 Hear this, you elders,
And give ear, all you inhabitants of the land!
Has *anything like* this happened in your days,
Or even in the days of your fathers?
3 Tell your children about it,
Let your children *tell* their children,
And their children another generation.

4 What the chewing locust[1] left,
the swarming locust has eaten;
What the swarming locust left,
the crawling locust has eaten;
And what the crawling locust left,
the consuming locust has eaten.

5 Awake, you drunkards, and weep;
And wail, all you drinkers of wine,
Because of the new wine,
For it has been cut off from your mouth.
6 For a nation has come up against My land,
Strong, and without number;
His teeth *are* the teeth of a lion,
And he has the fangs of a fierce lion.
7 He has laid waste My vine,
And ruined My fig tree;
He has stripped it bare
and thrown *it* away;
Its branches are made white.

8 Lament like a virgin girded with sackcloth
For the husband of her youth.
9 The grain offering
and the drink offering
Have been cut off from the house of the LORD;
The priests mourn,
who minister to the LORD.
10 The field is wasted,
The land mourns;
For the grain is ruined,
The new wine is dried up,
The oil fails.

11 Be ashamed, you farmers,
Wail, you vinedressers,
For the wheat and the barley;
Because the harvest of the field has perished.
12 The vine has dried up,
And the fig tree has withered;
The pomegranate tree,
The palm tree also,
And the apple tree—
All the trees of the field are withered;
Surely joy has withered away from the sons of men.

Mourning for the Land

13 Gird yourselves and lament,
you priests;
Wail, you who minister before the altar;
Come, lie all night in sackcloth,
You who minister to my God;
For the grain offering
and the drink offering
Are withheld from the house
of your God.
14 Consecrate a fast,
Call a sacred assembly;
Gather the elders
And all the inhabitants of the land
Into the house of the LORD your God,
And cry out to the LORD.

15 Alas for the day!
For the day of the LORD *is* at hand;
It shall come as destruction from the Almighty.
16 Is not the food cut off before our eyes,
Joy and gladness from the house of our God?
17 The seed *grain* shrivels under the clods,
Storehouses are in shambles;
Barns are broken down,
For the grain has withered.
18 How the beasts groan!
The herds of cattle are restless,
Because they have no pasture;
Even the flocks of sheep suffer *your* punishment.[2]

19 O LORD, to You I cry out;
For fire has devoured the open pastures,

1 Exact identity of these locusts is unknown.   2 Septuagint and Vulgate read *are made desolate.*

And a flame has burned all the trees
    of the field.
20 The beasts of the field also cry out
    to You,
For the water brooks are dried up,
And fire has devoured the open
    pastures.

The Day of the LORD

2 Blow the trumpet in Zion,
    And sound an alarm in My holy
      mountain!
Let all the inhabitants of the land
    tremble;
For the day of the LORD is coming,
For it is at hand:
2 A day of darkness and gloominess,
A day of clouds and thick darkness,
Like the morning *clouds* spread over
    the mountains.
A people *come*, great and strong,
The like of whom has never been;
Nor will there ever be any *such* after
    them,
Even for many successive generations.

3 A fire devours before them,
And behind them a flame burns;
The land *is* like the Garden of Eden
    before them,
And behind them a desolate
    wilderness;
Surely nothing shall escape them.
4 Their appearance is like the appearance
    of horses;
And like swift steeds, so they run.
5 With a noise like chariots
Over mountaintops they leap,
Like the noise of a flaming fire
    that devours the stubble,
Like a strong people set in battle array.

6 Before them the people writhe in pain;
All faces are drained of color.[3]
7 They run like mighty men,
They climb the wall like men of war;
Every one marches in formation,
And they do not break ranks.
8 They do not push one another;
Every one marches in his own column.[4]
And *when* they lunge between the
    weapons,
They are not cut down.[5]
9 They run to and fro in the city,
They run on the wall;
They climb into the houses,
They enter at the windows like a thief.

10 The earth quakes before them,
The heavens tremble;

The sun and moon grow dark,
And the stars diminish their brightness.
11 The LORD gives voice before His army,
For His camp is very great;
For strong *is the One* who executes His
    word.
For the day of the LORD *is* great
    and very terrible;
Who can endure it?

A Call to Repentance

12 "Now, therefore," says the LORD,
"Turn to me with all your heart,
With fasting, with weeping,
    and with mourning."
13 So rend your heart,
    and not your garments;
Return to the LORD your God,
For He *is* gracious and merciful,
Slow to anger, and of great kindness;
And He relents from doing harm.
14 Who knows *if* He will turn and relent,
And leave a blessing behind Him—
A grain offering and a drink offering
For the LORD your God?

15 Blow the trumpet in Zion,
Consecrate a fast,
Call a sacred assembly;
16 Gather the people,
Sanctify the congregation,
Assemble the elders,
Gather the children
    and nursing babes;
Let the bridegroom go out from his
    chamber,
And the bride from her dressing room.
17 Let the priests, who minister to the
    LORD,
Weep between the porch and the altar;
Let them say, "Spare Your people,
    O LORD,
And do not give Your heritage to
    reproach,
That the nations should rule over them.
Why should they say among the
    peoples,
'Where *is* their God?' "

The Land Refreshed

18 Then the LORD will be zealous for His
    land,
And pity His people.
19 The LORD will answer
    and say to His people,
"Behold, I will send you grain and
    new wine and oil,
And you will be satisfied by them;

---

3 Septuagint, Targum, and Vulgate read *gather blackness.*   4 Literally *his own highway*
5 That is, they are not halted by losses

I will no longer make you a reproach
among the nations.

20 "But I will remove far from you the
northern *army*,
And will drive him away into a barren
and desolate land,
With his face toward the eastern sea
And his back toward the western sea;
His stench will come up,
And his foul odor will rise,
Because he has done monstrous
things."

21 Fear not, O land;
Be glad and rejoice,
For the LORD has done marvelous
things!
22 Do not be afraid,
you beasts of the field;
For the open pastures are springing up,
And the tree bears its fruit;
The fig tree and the vine yield their
strength.
23 Be glad then, you children of Zion,
And rejoice in the LORD your God;
For He has given you the former rain
faithfully,[6]
And He will cause the rain to come
down for you—
The former rain,
And the latter rain in the first *month*.
24 The threshing floors shall be full of
wheat,
And the vats shall overflow with
new wine and oil.

25 "So I will restore to you the years that
the swarming locust has eaten,
The crawling locust,
The consuming locust,
And the chewing locust,[7]
My great army which I sent among
you.
26 You shall eat in plenty and be satisfied,
And praise the name of the LORD your
God,
Who has dealt wondrously with you;
And My people shall never be put to
shame.
27 Then you shall know that I *am* in the
midst of Israel,
And *that* I *am* the LORD your God
And there is no other.
My people shall never be put to shame.

God's Spirit Poured Out

28 "And it shall come to pass afterward
That I will pour out My Spirit on all
flesh;

Your sons and your daughters shall
prophesy,
Your old men shall dream dreams,
Your young men shall see visions;
29 And also on *My* menservants
and on *My* maidservants
I will pour out My Spirit in those days.

30 "And I will show wonders
in the heavens and in the earth:
Blood and fire and pillars of smoke.
31 The sun shall be turned into darkness,
And the moon into blood,
Before the coming of the great and
terrible day of the LORD.
32 And it shall come to pass
That whoever calls on the name of the
LORD
Shall be saved.
For in Mount Zion and in Jerusalem
there shall be deliverance,
As the LORD has said,
Among the remnant whom the LORD
calls.

God Judges the Nations

3 "For behold, in those days
and at that time,
When I bring back the captives of
Judah and Jerusalem,
2 I will also gather all nations,
And bring them down to the Valley of
Jehoshaphat;
And I will enter into judgment with
them there
On account of My people,
My heritage Israel,
Whom they have scattered among the
nations;
They have also divided up My land.
3 They have cast lots for My people,
Have given a boy *in exchange* for a
harlot,
And sold a girl for wine,
that they may drink.

4 "Indeed, what have you to do with Me,
O Tyre and Sidon,
and all the coasts of Philistia?
Will you retaliate against Me?
But if you retaliate against Me,
Swiftly and speedily I will return your
retaliation upon your own head;
5 Because you have taken My silver
and My gold,
And have carried into your temples
My prized possessions.
6 Also the people of Judah
and the people of Jerusalem
You have sold to the Greeks,

6 Or *the teacher of righteousness*   7 Compare 1:4

That you may remove them far from
their borders.

7 "Behold, I will raise them
Out of the place to which you have
sold them,
And will return your retaliation upon
your own head.
8 I will sell your sons and your daughters
Into the hand of the people of Judah,
And they will sell them to the
Sabeans,[8]
To a people far off;
For the LORD has spoken."

9 Proclaim this among the nations:
"Prepare for war!
Wake up the mighty men,
Let all the men of war draw near,
Let them come up.
10 Beat your plowshares into swords
And your pruninghooks into spears;
Let the weak say, 'I am strong.' "
11 Assemble and come, all you nations,
And gather together all around.
Cause Your mighty ones to go down
there, O LORD.

12 "Let the nations be wakened,
and come up to the Valley of
Jehoshaphat;
For there I will sit to judge
all the surrounding nations.
13 Put in the sickle, for the harvest is ripe.
Come, go down;
For the winepress is full,
The vats overflow—
For their wickedness is great."

14 Multitudes, multitudes in the valley of
decision!
For the day of the LORD is near in the
valley of decision.

15 The sun and moon will grow dark,
And the stars will diminish their
brightness.
16 The LORD also will roar from Zion,
And utter His voice from Jerusalem;
The heavens and earth will shake;
But the LORD will be a shelter for His
people,
And the strength of the children of
Israel.

17 "So you shall know that I am the LORD
your God,
Dwelling in Zion My holy mountain.
Then Jerusalem shall be holy,
And no aliens shall ever pass through
her again."

God Blesses His People

18 And it will come to pass in that day
That the mountains shall drip with new
wine,
The hills shall flow with milk,
And all the brooks of Judah shall be
flooded with water;
A fountain shall flow from the house of
the LORD
And water the Valley of Acacias.

19 "Egypt shall be a desolation,
And Edom a desolate wilderness,
Because of violence against the people
of Judah,
For they have shed innocent blood in
their land.
20 But Judah shall abide forever,
And Jerusalem from generation to
generation.
21 "For I will acquit them of bloodguilt,
whom I had not acquitted;
For the LORD dwells in Zion."

8 Literally *Shebaites* (compare Isaiah 60:6 and Ezekiel 27:22)

Introduction to Amos

Failure is never final, but God's love and forgiveness is.

The Book of Amos is a prime example of God's relationship with the nation of Israel. There was a direct correlation between their obedience to God and His blessings upon them and their rebellion against God and the resulting circumstances. As a just and perfect God, He sent prophets, including Amos, to help enable His people to return to Him in times of disobedience.

Amos, a shepherd from the village of Tekoa, five miles south of Bethlehem, was living in Israel and prophesied between 760 and 753 B.C. He was called by God to appeal to the people to return to a pure worship of God. The Israelites had taken on the pagan worship and practices of the surrounding nations. Amos pronounced the downfall of these nations and appealed to the Israelites to seek God.

God gave the nation many chances to return to Him, warning them that the worship of these false gods could only produce negative results in their lives. The ancient nation refused to give up their cultic worship and to receive the natural consequences for their rebellion. They were carried off in captivity by the Assyrians.

Amos reveals the forgiving nature of God when He promises restoration and the assurance of God's presence despite their captivity:

I will bring back the captives of My people Israel;
They shall build the waste cities and inhabit *them*;
They shall plant vineyards and drink wine from them;
They shall also make gardens and eat fruit from them.

(Amos 9:14)

The Book of

Amos

T HE words of Amos, who was among the herdsmen of Tekoa, which he saw concerning Israel in the days of Uzziah king of Judah, and in the days of Jeroboam the son of Joash, king of Israel, two years before the earthquake.

2 And he said:

"The LORD roars from Zion,
And utters His voice from Jerusalem;
The pastures of the shepherds mourn,
And the top of Carmel withers."

Judgment on the Nations

3 Thus says the LORD:

"For three transgressions of Damascus,
and for four,
I will not turn away its *punishment,*
Because they have threshed Gilead
with implements of iron.
4 But I will send a fire into the house of
Hazael,
Which shall devour the palaces
of Ben-Hadad.
5 I will also break the *gate* bar of
Damascus,
And cut off the inhabitant from the
Valley of Aven,
And the one who holds the scepter
from Beth Eden.
The people of Syria shall go captive
to Kir,"
Says the LORD.

6 Thus says the LORD:

"For three transgressions of Gaza,
and for four,
I will not turn away its *punishment,*
Because they took captive the whole
captivity
To deliver *them* up to Edom.
7 But I will send a fire upon the wall of
Gaza,
Which shall devour its palaces.
8 I will cut off the inhabitant from
Ashdod,

And the one who holds the scepter
from Ashkelon;
I will turn My hand against Ekron,
And the remnant of the Philistines
shall perish,"
Says the Lord GOD.

9 Thus says the LORD:

"For three transgressions of Tyre,
and for four,
I will not turn away its *punishment,*
Because they delivered up the whole
captivity to Edom,
And did not remember the covenant of
brotherhood.
10 But I will send a fire upon the wall of
Tyre,
Which shall devour its palaces."

11 Thus says the LORD:

"For three transgressions of Edom,
and for four,
I will not turn away its *punishment,*
Because he pursued his brother with
the sword,
And cast off all pity;
His anger tore perpetually,
And he kept his wrath forever.
12 But I will send a fire upon Teman,
Which shall devour the palaces of
Bozrah."

13 Thus says the LORD:

"For three transgressions of the people
of Ammon, and for four,
I will not turn away its *punishment,*
Because they ripped open the women
with child in Gilead,
That they might enlarge their territory.
14 But I will kindle a fire in the wall of
Rabbah,
And it shall devour its palaces,
Amid shouting in the day of battle,
And a tempest in the day of the
whirlwind.
15 Their king shall go into captivity,
He and his princes together,"
Says the LORD.

2 Thus says the LORD:

"For three transgressions of Moab,
and for four,
I will not turn away its *punishment,*
Because he burned the bones of the
king of Edom to lime.
2 But I will send a fire upon Moab,
And it shall devour the palaces of
Kerioth;
Moab shall die with tumult,
With shouting *and* trumpet sound.
3 And I will cut off the judge from its
midst,
And slay all its princes with him,"
Says the LORD.

Judgment on Judah

4 Thus says the LORD:

"For three transgressions of Judah,
and for four,
I will not turn away its *punishment,*
Because they have despised
the law of the LORD,
And have not kept
His commandments.
Their lies lead them astray,
Lies after which their fathers walked.
5 But I will send a fire upon Judah,
And it shall devour the palaces of
Jerusalem."

Judgment on Israel

6 Thus says the LORD:

"For three transgressions of Israel,
and for four,
I will not turn away its *punishment,*
Because they sell the righteous for
silver,
And the poor for a pair of sandals.
7 They pant after[1] the dust of the earth
which is on the head of the poor,
And pervert the way of the humble.
A man and his father go in to the *same*
girl,
To defile My holy name.
8 They lie down by every altar on clothes
taken in pledge,
And drink the wine of the condemned
in the house of their god.

9 "Yet *it was* I *who* destroyed the Amorite
before them,
Whose height *was* like the height of the
cedars,
And he *was as* strong as the oaks;
Yet I destroyed his fruit above
And his roots beneath.

10 Also *it was* I *who* brought you up from
the land of Egypt,
And led you forty years through the
wilderness,
To possess the land of the Amorite.
11 I raised up some of your sons
as prophets,
And some of your young men
as Nazirites.
Is it not so, O you children of Israel?"
Says the LORD.
12 "But you gave the Nazirites wine to
drink,
And commanded the prophets saying,
'Do not prophesy!'

13 "Behold, I am weighed down by you,
As a cart is weighed down *that is* full
of sheaves.
14 Therefore flight shall perish from the
swift,
The strong shall not strengthen his
power,
Nor shall the mighty deliver himself;
15 He shall not stand who handles the
bow,
The swift of foot shall not deliver
himself,
Nor shall he who rides a horse deliver
himself.
16 The most courageous men of might
Shall flee naked in that day,"
Says the LORD.

Authority of the Prophet's Message

3 Hear this word that the LORD has
spoken against you, O children of Israel, against the whole family which I
brought up from the land of Egypt, saying:

2 "You only have I known of all the
families of the earth;
Therefore I will punish you for all your
iniquities."

3   Can two walk together,
unless they are agreed?
4   Will a lion roar in the forest,
when he has no prey?
Will a young lion cry out of his den,
if he has caught nothing?
5   Will a bird fall into a snare on the
earth, where there is no trap for it?
Will a snare spring up from the earth,
if it has caught nothing at all?
6   If a trumpet is blown in a city,
will not the people be afraid?
If there is calamity in a city,
will not the LORD have done *it?*

1 Or *trample on*

7 Surely the Lord GOD does nothing,
  Unless He reveals His secret
    to His servants the prophets.
8 A lion has roared!
  Who will not fear?
  The Lord GOD has spoken!
  Who can but prophesy?

Punishment of Israel's Sins

9 "Proclaim in the palaces at Ashdod,
  And in the palaces in the land of
    Egypt, and say:
  'Assemble on the mountains of
    Samaria;
  See great tumults in her midst,
  And the oppressed within her.
10 For they do not know to do right,'
  Says the LORD,
  'Who store up violence and robbery in
    their palaces.' "

11 Therefore thus says the Lord GOD:

  "An adversary *shall be* all around the
    land;
  He shall sap your strength from you,
  And your palaces shall be plundered."

12 Thus says the LORD:

  "As a shepherd takes from the mouth of
    a lion
  Two legs or a piece of an ear,
  So shall the children of Israel be
    taken out
  Who dwell in Samaria—
  In the corner of a bed
    and on the edge[2] of a couch!
13 Hear and testify against the house of
    Jacob,"
  Says the Lord GOD, the God of hosts,
14 "That in the day I punish Israel for
    their transgressions,
  I will also visit *destruction* on the altars
    of Bethel;
  And the horns of the altar shall be
    cut off
  And fall to the ground.
15 I will destroy the winter house along
    with the summer house;
  The houses of ivory shall perish,
  And the great houses shall have an
    end,"
  Says the LORD.

4 Hear this word, you cows of Bashan,
    who *are* on the mountain of
    Samaria,
  Who oppress the poor,

Who crush the needy,
  Who say to your husbands,[3]
    "Bring *wine,* let us drink!"
2 The Lord GOD has sworn by His
    holiness:
  "Behold, the days shall come upon you
  When He will take you away with
    fishhooks,
  And your posterity with fishhooks.
3 You will go out *through* broken *walls,*
  Each one straight ahead of her,
  And you will be cast into Harmon,"
  Says the LORD.

4 "Come to Bethel and transgress,
  At Gilgal multiply transgression;
  Bring your sacrifices every morning,
  Your tithes every three days.[4]
5 Offer a sacrifice of thanksgiving with
    leaven,
  Proclaim *and* announce the freewill
    offerings;
  For this you love,
  You children of Israel!"
  Says the Lord GOD.

Israel Did Not Accept Correction

6 "Also I gave you cleanness of teeth in
    all your cities,
  And lack of bread in all your places;
  Yet you have not returned to Me,"
  Says the LORD.

7 "I also withheld rain from you,
  When *there were* still three months
    to the harvest.
  I made it rain on one city,
  I withheld rain from another city.
  One part was rained upon,
  And where it did not rain the part
    withered.
8 So two *or* three cities wandered to
    another city to drink water,
  But they were not satisfied;
  Yet you have not returned to Me,"
  Says the LORD.

9 "I blasted you with blight and mildew.
  When your gardens increased,
  Your vineyards,
  Your fig trees,
  And your olive trees,
  The locust devoured *them;*
  Yet you have not returned to Me,"
  Says the LORD.

10 "I sent among you a plague after the
    manner of Egypt;
  Your young men I killed with a sword,

2 Hebrew is uncertain.   3 Literally *their lords* or *their masters*   4 Or *years* (compare Deuteronomy 14:28)

Along with your captive horses;
I made the stench of your camps come
up into your nostrils;
Yet you have not returned to Me,"
Says the LORD.

11 "I overthrew *some* of you,
As God overthrew Sodom and
Gomorrah,
And you were like a firebrand plucked
from the burning;
Yet you have not returned to Me,"
Says the LORD.

12 "Therefore thus will I do to you,
O Israel;
And because I will do this to you,
Prepare to meet your God, O Israel!"

13 For behold,
He who forms mountains,
And creates the wind,
Who declares to man what his[5]
thought *is,*
And makes the morning darkness,
Who treads the high places of the
earth—
The LORD God of hosts *is* His name.

A Lament for Israel

5 Hear this word which I take up
against you, *this* lamentation, O
house of Israel:

2 The virgin of Israel has fallen;
She will rise no more.
She lies forsaken on her land;
There is no one to raise her up.

3 For thus says the Lord GOD:

"The city that goes out by a thousand
Shall have a hundred left,
And that which goes out by a hundred
Shall have ten left to the house of
Israel."

A Call to Repentance

4 For thus says the LORD to the house
of Israel:

"Seek Me and live;
5 But do not seek Bethel,
Nor enter Gilgal,
Nor pass over to Beersheba;
For Gilgal shall surely go into
captivity,
And Bethel shall come to nothing.
6 Seek the LORD and live,

Lest He break out like fire *in* the house
of Joseph,
And devour *it,*
With no one to quench *it* in Bethel—
7 You who turn justice to wormwood,
And lay righteousness to rest in the
earth!"

8 He made the Pleiades and Orion;
He turns the shadow of death into
morning
And makes the day dark as night;
He calls for the waters of the sea
And pours them out on the face of the
earth;
The LORD *is* His name.
9 He rains ruin upon the strong,
So that fury comes upon the fortress.

10 They hate the one who rebukes in the
gate,
And they abhor the one who speaks
uprightly.
11 Therefore, because you tread down the
poor
And take grain taxes from him,
Though you have built houses of hewn
stone,
Yet you shall not dwell in them;
You have planted pleasant vineyards,
But you shall not drink wine from
them.
12 For I know your manifold
transgressions
And your mighty sins.
You afflict the just *and* take bribes;
You divert the poor *from justice* at the
gate.
13 Therefore the prudent keep silent at
that time,
For it *is* an evil time.

14 Seek good and not evil,
That you may live;
So the LORD God of hosts
will be with you,
As you have spoken.
15 Hate evil, love good;
Establish justice in the gate.
It may be that the LORD God of hosts
Will be gracious to the remnant of
Joseph.

The Day of the LORD

16 Therefore the LORD God of hosts, the
Lord, says this:

"*There shall be* wailing in all streets,
And they shall say in all the highways,

5 Or *His*

'Alas! Alas!'
They shall call the farmer to mourning,
And skillful lamenters to wailing.
17 In all vineyards *there shall be* wailing,
For I will pass through you,"
Says the LORD.

18 Woe to you who desire the day of the
   LORD!
For what good *is* the day of the LORD
to you?
It *will be* darkness, and not light.
19 It *will be* as though a man fled from a
   lion,
And a bear met him;
Or *as though* he went into the house,
Leaned his hand on the wall,
And a serpent bit him.
20 *Is* not the day of the LORD darkness,
and not light?
Is it not very dark,
with no brightness in it?

21 "I hate, I despise your feast days,
And I do not savor your sacred
assemblies.
22 Though you offer Me burnt offerings
and your grain offerings,
I will not accept *them,*
Nor will I regard your fattened peace
offerings.
23 Take away from Me the noise of your
songs,
For I will not hear the melody of your
stringed instruments.
24 But let justice run down like water,
And righteousness like a mighty
stream.

25 "Did you offer Me sacrifices and
offerings
In the wilderness forty years,
O house of Israel?
26 You also carried Sikkuth[6] your king[7]
And Chiun,[8] your idols,
The star of your gods,
Which you made for yourselves.
27 Therefore I will send you into captivity
beyond Damascus,"
Says the LORD,
whose name *is* the God of hosts.

Warnings to Zion and Samaria

6 Woe to you *who are* at ease in Zion,
And trust in Mount Samaria,
Notable persons in the chief nation,
To whom the house of Israel comes!
2 Go over to Calneh and see;

And from there go to Hamath the
great;
Then go down to Gath of the
Philistines.
Are you better than these kingdoms?
Or is their territory greater than your
territory?

3 *Woe to* you who put far off the day of
doom,
Who cause the seat of violence to come
near;
4 Who lie on beds of ivory,
Stretch out on your couches,
Eat lambs from the flock
And calves from the midst of the stall;
5 Who chant to the sound of stringed
instruments,
And invent for yourselves musical
instruments like David;
6 Who drink wine from bowls,
And anoint yourselves with the best
ointments,
But are not grieved for the affliction of
Joseph.
7 Therefore they shall now go captive as
the first of the captives,
And those who recline at banquets
shall be removed.

8 The Lord GOD has sworn by Himself,
The LORD God of hosts says:
"I abhor the pride of Jacob,
And hate his palaces;
Therefore I will deliver up *the* city
And all that is in it."

9 Then it shall come to pass, that if ten
men remain in one house, they shall die.
10 And when a kinsman *of the dead*, with
one who will burn *the bodies*, picks up the
bodies[9] to take them out of the house, he
will say to one inside the house, *"Are
there* any more with you?" Then someone will say, "None." And he will say,
"Hold your tongue! For we dare not
mention the name of the LORD."

11 For behold, the LORD gives a
command:
He will break the great house into bits,
And the little house into pieces.

12 Do horses run on rocks?
Does *one* plow *there* with oxen?
Yet you have turned justice into gall,
And the fruit of righteousness into
wormwood,
13 You who rejoice over Lo Debar,[10]

---

6 A pagan deity   7 Septuagint and Vulgate read *tabernacle of Moloch.*   8 A pagan deity   9 Literally *bones*
10 Literally *Nothing*

Who say, "Have we not taken
Karnaim[11] for ourselves
By our own strength?"

14 "But, behold, I will raise up a nation
against you,
O house of Israel,"
Says the LORD God of hosts;
"And they will afflict you from the
entrance of Hamath
To the Valley of the Arabah."

Vision of the Locusts

7 Thus the Lord GOD showed me: Behold, He formed locust swarms at the beginning of the late crop; indeed *it was* the late crop after the king's mowings.
2 And so it was, when they had finished eating the grass of the land, that I said:

"O Lord GOD, forgive, I pray!
Oh, that Jacob may stand,
For he *is* small!"
3 So the LORD relented concerning this.
"It shall not be," said the LORD.

Vision of the Fire

4 Thus the Lord GOD showed me: Behold, the Lord GOD called for conflict by fire, and it consumed the great deep and devoured the territory.
5 Then I said:

"O Lord GOD, cease, I pray!
Oh, that Jacob may stand,
For he *is* small!"
6 So the LORD relented concerning this.
"This also shall not be,"
said the Lord GOD.

Vision of the Plumb Line

7 Thus He showed me: Behold, the Lord stood on a wall *made* with a plumb line, with a plumb line in His hand.
8 And the LORD said to me, "Amos, what do you see?" And I said, "A plumb line." Then the Lord said:

"Behold, I am setting a plumb line
In the midst of My people Israel;
I will not pass by them anymore.
9 The high places of Isaac shall be
desolate,
And the sanctuaries of Israel shall be
laid waste.
I will rise with the sword against the
house of Jeroboam."

Amaziah's Complaint

10 Then Amaziah the priest of Bethel sent to Jeroboam king of Israel, saying, "Amos has conspired against you in the midst of the house of Israel. The land is not able to bear all his words.
11 "For thus Amos has said:

'Jeroboam shall die by the sword,
And Israel shall surely be led away
captive
From their own land.' "

12 Then Amaziah said to Amos:

"Go, you seer!
Flee to the land of Judah.
There eat bread,
And there prophesy.
13 But never again prophesy at Bethel,
For it *is* the king's sanctuary,
And it *is* the royal residence."

14 Then Amos answered, and said to Amaziah:

"I *was* no prophet,
Nor *was* I a son of a prophet,
But I *was* a herdsman
And a tender of sycamore fruit.
15 Then the LORD took me as I followed
the flock,
And the LORD said to me,
'Go, prophesy to My people Israel.'
16 Now therefore,
hear the word of the LORD:
You say, 'Do not prophesy against
Israel,
And do not spout against the house of
Isaac.'

17 "Therefore thus says the LORD:

'Your wife shall be a harlot in the city;
Your sons and daughters shall fall by
the sword;
Your land shall be divided by *survey*
line;
You shall die in a defiled land;
And Israel shall surely be led away
captive
From his own land.' "

Vision of the Summer Fruit

8 Thus the Lord GOD showed me: Behold, a basket of summer fruit.
2 And He said, "Amos, what do you see?" So I said, "A basket of summer fruit." Then the LORD said to me:

11 Literally *Horns,* symbol of strength

"The end has come upon my people
 Israel;
I will not pass by them anymore.
3 And the songs of the temple
 Shall be wailing in that day,"
 Says the Lord GOD—
"Many dead bodies everywhere,
 They shall throw *them* out in silence."

4 Hear this, you who swallow up[12] the
 needy,
 And make the poor of the land fail,

5 Saying:

"When will the New Moon be past,
 That we may sell grain?
And the Sabbath,
 That we may trade *our* wheat?
Making the ephah small
 and the shekel large,
Falsifying the balances by deceit,
6 That we may buy the poor for silver,
And the needy for a pair of sandals—
Even sell the bad wheat?"

7 The LORD has sworn by the pride of
 Jacob:
"Surely I will never forget any of their
 works.
8 Shall the land not tremble for this,
And everyone mourn who dwells in it?
All of it shall swell like the River,[13]
Heave and subside
Like the River of Egypt.

9 "And it shall come to pass in that day,"
 says the Lord GOD,
"That I will make the sun go down at
 noon,
And I will darken the earth in broad
 daylight;
10 I will turn your feasts into mourning,
And all your songs into lamentation;
I will bring sackcloth on every waist,
And baldness on every head;
I will make it like mourning for an
 only *son*,
And its end like a bitter day.

11 "Behold, the days are coming,"
 says the Lord GOD,
"That I will send a famine on the land,
Not a famine of bread,
Nor a thirst for water,
But of hearing the words of the LORD.
12 They shall wander from sea to sea,
And from north to east;
They shall run to and fro,
 seeking the word of the LORD,
But shall not find *it*.

13 "In that day the fair virgins
And strong young men
Shall faint from thirst.
14 Those who swear by the sin[14] of
 Samaria,
Who say,
'As your god lives, O Dan!'
And, 'As the way of Beersheba lives!'
They shall fall and never rise again."

The Destruction of Israel

9 I saw the Lord standing by the altar,
and He said:

"Strike the doorposts,
 that the thresholds may shake,
And break them on the heads
 of them all.
I will slay the last of them with the
 sword.
He who flees from them shall not get
 away,
And he who escapes from them shall
 not be delivered.

2 "Though they dig into hell,[15]
From there my hand shall take them;
Though they climb up to heaven,
From there I will bring them down;
3 And though they hide themselves on
 top of Carmel,
From there I will search
 and take them;
Though they hide from My sight at the
 bottom of the sea,
From there I will command the
 serpent, and it shall bite them;
4 Though they go into captivity before
 their enemies,
From there I will command the sword,
And it shall slay them.
I will set My eyes on them for harm
 and not for good."

5 The Lord GOD of hosts,
He who touches the earth and it melts,
And all who dwell there mourn;
All of it shall swell like the River,
And subside like the River of Egypt.[16]
6 He who builds His layers in the sky,
And has founded His strata in the
 earth;
Who calls for the waters of the sea,
And pours them out on the face of the
 earth—
The LORD *is* His name.

12 Or *trample on* (compare 2:7)
13 That is, the Nile; some Hebrew manuscripts, Septuagint, Syriac, Targum, Vulgate, and 9:5 read *River;* Masoretic
Text reads *the light.*   14 Or *Ashima,* a Syrian goddess   15 Hebrew *Sheol*   16 That is, *the Nile*

7 *"Are* you not like the people of Ethiopia
    to Me,
O children of Israel?" says the LORD.
"Did I not bring up Israel from the land
    of Egypt,
The Philistines from Caphtor,
And the Syrians from Kir?

8 "Behold, the eyes of the Lord GOD *are*
    on the sinful kingdom,
And I will destroy it from the face of
    the earth;
Yet I will not utterly destroy the house
    of Jacob,"
Says the LORD.

9 "For surely I will command,
And will sift the house of Israel among
    all nations,
As *grain* is sifted in a sieve;
Yet not the smallest grain shall fall to
    the ground.
10 All the sinners of My people shall die
    by the sword,
Who say, 'The calamity shall not
    overtake *us*
Nor confront us.'

Israel Will Be Restored

11 "On that day I will raise up

The tabernacle[17] of David,
    which has fallen down,
And repair its damages;
I will raise up its ruins,
And rebuild it as in the days of old;
12 That they may possess the remnant of
    Edom,[18]
And all the Gentiles who are called by
    My name,"
Says the LORD who does this thing.

13 "Behold, the days are coming,"
    says the LORD,
"When the plowman shall overtake the
    reaper,
And the treader of grapes him who
    sows seed;
The mountains shall drip with sweet
    wine,
And all the hills shall flow *with it.*
14 I will bring back the captives of My
    people Israel;
They shall build the waste cities
    and inhabit *them;*
They shall plant vineyards
    and drink wine from them;
They shall also make gardens
    and eat fruit from them.
15 I will plant them in their land,
And no longer shall they be pulled up
From the land I have given them,"
Says the LORD your God.

17 Literally *booth,* figure of a deposed dynasty   18 Septuagint reads *mankind.*

Introduction to Obadiah

Obadiah is a prophetic announcement of the destruction of the ancient kingdom of Edom. According to this book, we learn that the Edomites were heartless scavengers who looked with joy upon the destruction of God's people. They cowardly assisted the warring armies, possibly the ancient Babylonians, in defeating the Israelites.

> Indeed, you should not have gazed on their affliction
> In the day of their calamity,
> Nor laid *hands* on their substance
> In the day of their calamity.
> You should not have stood at the crossroads
> To cut off those among them who escaped;
> Nor should you have delivered up those among them who remained
> In the day of distress.
>
> (Obad. 13, 14)

Scholars differ as to the date of this book. Some place it during the ninth century B.C., corresponding to the destruction of Jerusalem by Jehoram, while others believe it was written in 586 B.C. during the onslaught by Nebuchadnezzar. The book contains only twenty-one verses, making it difficult to determine the time, situation, and the attacking enemy from the text itself.

Obadiah, whose name means "Servant of Yahweh," assures the people of Israel that God will overcome their enemy. He foretells them that God will deal justly with those who have wronged them.

Although Obadiah is the shortest book in the Old Testament, its message is one of the strongest. God will defeat all evil and negative forces in our lives and provide the ultimate victory over our enemies and problems. He will raise up positive leaders to establish His kingdom. God is greater than our greatest problems and stronger than our strongest foe!

The Book of
Obadiah

The Coming Judgment on Edom

THE vision of Obadiah.

Thus says the Lord GOD concerning Edom
(We have heard a report from the LORD,
And a messenger has been sent among the nations, *saying,*
"Arise, and let us rise up against her for battle"):

2 "Behold, I will make you small among the nations;
You shall be greatly despised.
3 The pride of your heart has deceived you,
You who dwell in the clefts of the rock,
Whose habitation is high;
You who say in your heart,
'Who will bring me down to the ground?'
4 Though you exalt *yourself as* high as the eagle,
And though you set your nest among the stars,
From there I will bring you down,"
says the LORD.

5 "If thieves had come to you,
If robbers by night—
Oh, how you will be cut off!—
Would they not have stolen till they had enough?
If grape-gatherers had come to you,
Would they not have left *some* gleanings?

6 "Oh, how Esau shall be searched out!
How his hidden treasures shall be sought after!
7 All the men in your confederacy
Shall force you to the border;
The men at peace with you
Shall deceive you
and prevail against you.
Those who eat your bread shall lay a trap[1] for you.
No one is aware of it.

8 "Will I not in that day," says the LORD,
"Even destroy the wise *men* from Edom,

And understanding from the mountains of Esau?
9 Then your mighty men, O Teman,
shall be dismayed,
To the end that everyone from the mountains of Esau
May be cut off by slaughter.

Edom Mistreated His Brother

10 "For *your* violence against your brother Jacob,
Shame shall cover you,
And you shall be cut off forever.
11 In the day that you stood on the other side—
In the day that strangers carried captive his forces,
When foreigners entered his gates
And cast lots for Jerusalem—
Even you *were* as one of them.

12 But you should not have gazed on the day of your brother
In the day of his captivity;[2]
Nor should you have rejoiced over the children of Judah
In the day of their destruction;
Nor should you have spoken proudly
In the day of distress.
13 You should not have entered the gate of My people
In the day of their calamity.
Indeed, you should not have gazed on their affliction
In the day of their calamity,
Nor laid *hands* on their substance
In the day of their calamity.
14 You should not have stood at the crossroads
To cut off those among them who escaped;
Nor should you have delivered up those among them who remained
In the day of distress.

15 "For the day of the LORD upon all the nations *is* near;
As you have done,
it shall be done to you;

1 Or *wound,* or *plot*   2 Literally *on the day he became a foreigner*

Your reprisal shall return upon your
own head.
16 For as you drank on my holy
mountain,
So shall all the nations drink
continually;
Yes, they shall drink, and swallow,
And they shall be as though they had
never been.

Israel's Final Triumph

17 "But on Mount Zion there shall be
deliverance,
And there shall be holiness;
The house of Jacob shall possess their
possessions.
18 The house of Jacob shall be a fire,
And the house of Joseph a flame;
But the house of Esau *shall be* stubble;
They shall kindle them
and devour them,

And no survivor shall *remain* of the
house of Esau,"
For the LORD has spoken.

19 *The inhabitants of* the South[3]
Shall possess the mountains of Esau,
And *the inhabitants of* the Philistine
lowland.
They shall possess the fields of
Ephraim
And the fields of Samaria.
Benjamin *shall possess* Gilead.
20 And the captives of this host of the
children of Israel
Shall possess the land of the Canaanites
As far as Zarephath.
The captives of Jerusalem who are in
Sepharad
Shall possess the cities of the South.[4]
21 Then saviors[5] shall come to Mount
Zion
To judge the mountains of Esau,
And the kingdom shall be the LORD's.

3 Hebrew *Negev*   4 Hebrew *Negev*   5 Or *deliverers*

Introduction to Jonah

The Book of Jonah is best known for the story of the prophet's three days in the belly of a fish. But the main message of this book is a powerful affirmation of God's love and forgiveness for all people.

Written sometime between 782 and 753 B.C., probably by Jonah himself, the book records Jonah's experience in learning of God's mercy. The only Old Testament prophet from the region of Galilee, a gentile area known as "the circle" (of the nations), Jonah lived in the town of Gath Hepher, located three miles from Nazareth. Jonah, a Jew, was given a mission by God to go to the gentile nation and its capital Nineveh.

During Jonah's time, there was much hatred from the Israelites toward the Gentiles. God called Jonah to travel to Nineveh so that he could encourage the people, his natural enemies, to turn to God. Jonah failed to recognize God's love for all persons and fled in the opposite direction toward Tarshish.

Jonah writes a lively, spirited autobiography of his travel by sea, where he was thrown overboard, swallowed by a great fish, and finally spit up on the shores. God's message finally got through to him. Jonah went to the city of Nineveh where the people listened to his words and turned to God.

Jonah argued with God that he was not needed by God to begin with. He fled because he was embarrassed, afraid, and did not want to feel awkward. God could have made the city repent without Jonah's presence. Yet God made it clear that He does His greatest works through His smallest people. He used Jonah as a vessel of His truth, to proclaim that His lovingkindness is for all people.

The greatest power in the world is a positive idea. And the most powerful, positive idea is one that comes from God. Faith is opening your mind to God's thoughts. God will do great things through people dedicated to Him.

The Book of

Jonah

Jonah's Disobedience

NOW the word of the LORD came to Jonah the son of Amittai, saying,
2 "Arise, go to Nineveh, that great city, and cry out against it; for their wickedness has come up before Me."
3 But Jonah arose to flee to Tarshish from the presence of the LORD. He went down to Joppa, and found a ship going to Tarshish; so he paid the fare, and went down into it, to go with them to Tarshish from the presence of the LORD.

The Storm at Sea

4 But the LORD sent out a great wind on the sea, and there was a mighty tempest on the sea, so that the ship was about to be broken up.
5 Then the mariners were afraid; and every man cried out to his god, and threw the cargo that *was* in the ship into the sea, to lighten the load.[1] But Jonah had gone down into the lowest parts of the ship, had lain down, and was fast asleep.
6 So the captain came to him, and said to him, "What do you mean, sleeper? Arise, call on your God; perhaps your God will consider us, so that we may not perish."
7 And they said to one another, "Come, let us cast lots, that we may know for whose cause this trouble *has come* upon us." So they cast lots, and the lot fell on Jonah.
8 Then they said to him, "Please tell us! For whose cause *is* this trouble upon us? What is your occupation? And where do you come from? What is your country? And of what people are you?"
9 And he said to them, "I *am* a Hebrew; and I fear the LORD, the God of heaven, who made the sea and the dry *land*."

Jonah Thrown into the Sea

10 Then the men were exceedingly afraid, and said to him, "Why have you done this?" For the men knew that he fled from the presence of the LORD, because he had told them.

11 Then they said to him, "What shall we do to you that the sea may be calm for us?"—for the sea was growing more tempestuous.
12 And he said to them, "Pick me up and throw me into the sea; then the sea will become calm for you. For I know that this great tempest *is* because of me."
13 Nevertheless the men rowed hard to bring *the ship* to land, but they could not, for the sea continued to grow more tempestuous against them.
14 Therefore they cried out to the LORD and said, "We pray, O LORD, please do not let us perish for this man's life, and do not charge us with innocent blood; for You, O LORD, have done as it pleased You."
15 So they picked up Jonah and threw him into the sea, and the sea ceased from its raging.
16 Then the men feared the LORD exceedingly, and offered a sacrifice to the LORD and made vows.

Jonah's Prayer and Deliverance

17 Now the LORD had prepared a great fish to swallow Jonah. And Jonah was in the belly of the fish three days and three nights.

2 Then Jonah prayed to the LORD his God from the fish's belly.
2 And he said:

"I cried out to the LORD because of my affliction,
And He answered me.

"Out of the belly of Sheol I cried,
And You heard my voice.
3 For You cast me into the deep,
Into the heart of the seas,
And the floods surrounded me;
All Your billows and Your waves passed over me.
4 Then I said, 'I have been cast out of Your sight;
Yet I will look again toward Your holy temple.'
5 The waters encompassed me,
even to my soul;

1 Literally *from upon them*

The deep closed around me;
Weeds were wrapped around my head.
6 I went down to the moorings of the
  mountains;
The earth with its bars *closed* behind
  me forever;
Yet You have brought up my life from
  the pit,
O LORD, my God.

7 "When my soul fainted within me,
I remembered the LORD;
And my prayer went *up* to You,
Into Your holy temple.

8 "Those who regard worthless idols
Forsake their own Mercy.
9 But I will sacrifice to You
With the voice of thanksgiving;
I will pay what I have vowed.
Salvation *is* of the LORD."

10 So the LORD spoke to the fish, and it
vomited Jonah onto dry *land.*

Jonah Preaches at Nineveh

3 Now the word of the LORD came to
  Jonah the second time, saying,
2 "Arise, go to Nineveh, that great city,
and preach to it the message that I tell
you."
3 So Jonah arose and went to Nineveh,
according to the word of the LORD. Now
Nineveh was an exceedingly great city, a
three-day journey[2] *in extent.*
4 And Jonah began to enter the city on
the first day's walk. Then he cried out
and said, "Yet forty days, and Nineveh
shall be overthrown!"

The People of Nineveh Believe

5 So the people of Nineveh believed
God, proclaimed a fast, and put on sackcloth, from the greatest to the least of
them.
6 Then word came to the king of Nineveh; and he arose from his throne and
laid aside his robe, covered *himself* with
sackcloth and sat in ashes.
7 And he caused *it* to be proclaimed
and published throughout Nineveh by
the decree of the king and his nobles, saying, "Let neither man nor beast, herd nor
flock, taste anything; do not let them eat,
or drink water.
8 "But let man and beast be covered
with sackcloth, and cry mightily to God;
yes, let every one turn from his evil way
and from the violence that is in his hands.

9 "Who can tell *if* God will turn and
relent, and turn away from His fierce anger, so that we may not perish?"
10 Then God saw their works, that they
turned from their evil way; and God relented from the disaster that He had said
He would bring upon them, and He did
not do it.

Jonah's Anger and God's Kindness

4 But it displeased Jonah exceedingly,
  and he became angry.
2 So he prayed to the LORD, and said,
"Ah, LORD, was not this what I said
when I was still in my country? Therefore I fled previously to Tarshish; for I
know that You *are* a gracious and merciful God, slow to anger and abundant in
lovingkindness, One who relents from doing harm.
3 "Therefore now, O LORD, please take
my life from me, for *it is* better for me to
die than to live!"
4 Then the LORD said, "*Is it* right for
you to be angry?"
5 So Jonah went out of the city and sat
on the east side of the city. There he
made himself a shelter and sat under it in
the shade, till he might see what would
become of the city.
6 And the LORD God prepared a plant[3]
and made it come up over Jonah, that it
might be shade for his head to deliver
him from his misery. So Jonah was very
grateful for the plant.
7 But as morning dawned the next day
God prepared a worm, and it *so* damaged
the plant that it withered.
8 And it happened, when the sun arose,
that God prepared a vehement east wind;
and the sun beat on Jonah's head, so that
he grew faint. Then he wished death for
himself, and said, "*It is* better for me to
die than to live."
9 Then God said to Jonah, "*Is it* right
for you to be angry about the plant?"
And he said, "*It is* right for me to be angry, even to death!"
10 But the LORD said, "You have had
pity on the plant for which you have not
labored, nor made it grow, which came
up in a night and perished in a night.
11 "And should I not pity Nineveh, that
great city, in which are more than one
hundred and twenty thousand persons
who cannot discern between their right
hand and their left, and *also* much livestock?"

2 Exact meaning unknown   3 Hebrew *Kikayon,* exact identity unknown

Introduction to Micah

Micah was one of the many prophets God raised up to keep His light shining in a difficult and sorrowful time in the history of Judah and Israel. He was from the prominent city of Moresheth in Judah, overlooking the fertile coastal plain of the Mediterranean Sea. The book was written between 735 and 710 B.C.

A beautiful account of hope in the face of hardship, mercy in time of distress, and promise in the moment of confusion, Micah recounts how God will restore His people after captivity. In the midst of pending destruction, Micah foretells the coming birth of the Messiah. The birthplace, Bethlehem, was a tiny insignificant village, but from there God would raise up the Deliverer.

> But you, Bethlehem Ephrathah,
> *Though* you are little among the thousands of Judah,
> *Yet* out of you shall come forth to Me
> The One to be ruler in Israel,
> Whose goings forth *have been* from of old,
> From everlasting.
>
> (Mic. 5:2)

Almost every chapter of Micah includes a positive inspirational promise for the people of Israel to hold on to in their times of despair. He assures them of the restoration of Israel and their future mercy before God:

> Therefore I will look to the LORD;
> I will wait for the God of my salvation;
> My God will hear me.
>
> (Mic. 7:7)

Micah's name means "Who Is Like Yahweh." In reminding his readers of God's gracious love and mercy, Micah assures them that God is able to forgive their sins completely:

> Who *is* a God like You,
> Pardoning iniquity
> And passing over the transgression of the remnant of His heritage?
> He does not retain His anger forever,
> Because He delights *in* mercy.
>
> (Mic. 7:18)

The Book of

Micah

THE word of the LORD that came to Micah of Moresheth in the days of Jotham, Ahaz, *and* Hezekiah, kings of Judah, which he saw concerning Samaria and Jerusalem.

The Coming Judgment on Israel

2 Hear, all you peoples!
Listen, O earth, and all that is in it!
Let the Lord GOD be a witness against you,
The Lord from His holy temple.

3 For behold, the LORD is coming out of His place;
He will come down
And tread on the high places of the earth.
4 The mountains will melt under him,
And the valleys will split
Like wax before the fire,
Like waters poured down a steep place.
5 All this is for the transgression of Jacob
And for the sins of the house of Israel.
What *is* the transgression of Jacob?
Is it not Samaria?
And what *are* the high places of Judah?
Are they not Jerusalem?

6 "Therefore I will make Samaria a heap of ruins in the field,
Places for planting a vineyard;
I will pour down her stones into the valley,
And I will uncover her foundations.
7 All her carved images shall be beaten to pieces,
And all her pay as a harlot shall be burned with the fire;
All her idols I will lay desolate,
For she gathered *it* from the pay of a harlot,
And they shall return to the pay of a harlot."

Mourning for Israel and Judah

8 Therefore I will wail and howl,
I will go stripped and naked;
I will make a wailing like the jackals
And a mourning like the ostriches,
9 For her wounds *are* incurable.
For it has come to Judah;
It has come to the gate of My people,
Even to Jerusalem.

10 Tell *it* not in Gath,
Weep not at all in Beth Aphrah,[1]
Roll yourself in the dust.
11 Pass by in naked shame,
you inhabitant of Shaphir;
The inhabitant of Zaanan[2]
does not go out.
Beth Ezel mourns;
Its place to stand is taken away from you.

12 For the inhabitant of Maroth
pined[3] for good,
But disaster came down from the LORD
To the gate of Jerusalem.
13 O inhabitant of Lachish,
Harness the chariot to the swift steeds
(She *was* the beginning of sin to the daughter of Zion),
For the transgressions of Israel were found in you.

14 Therefore you shall give presents to Moresheth Gath;[4]
The houses of Achzib[5] *shall be* a lie to the kings of Israel.
15 I will yet bring an heir to you,
O inhabitant of Mareshah;[6]
The glory of Israel
shall come to Adullam.
16 Make yourself bald
and cut off your hair,
Because of your precious children;
Enlarge your baldness like an eagle,
For they shall go from you into captivity.

Woe to Evildoers

2 Woe to those who devise iniquity,
And work out evil on their beds!
At morning light they practice it,
Because it is in the power of their hand.

---

1 Literally *House of Dust*   2 Literally *Going Out*   3 Literally *was sick*   4 Literally *Possession of Gath*
5 Literally *Lie*   6 Literally *Inheritance*

2   They covet fields
        and take *them* by violence,
    Also houses, and seize *them*.
    So they oppress a man and his house,
    A man and his inheritance.

3   Therefore thus says the LORD:

    "Behold, against this family I am
        devising disaster,
    From which you cannot remove your
        necks;
    Nor shall you walk haughtily,
    For this *is* an evil time.
4   In that day *one* shall take up a proverb
        against you,
    And lament with a bitter lamentation,
        and say:
    'We are utterly destroyed!
    He has changed the heritage of my
        people;
    How He has removed *it* from me!
    To a turncoat He has divided our
        fields.' "

5   Therefore you will have no one to
        determine boundaries[7] by lot
    In the congregation of the LORD.

Lying Prophets

6   "Do not prattle," *you say to those* who
        prophesy.
    So they shall not prophesy to you;[8]
    They shall not return insult for insult.[9]
7   *You who are* named the house of
        Jacob:
    "Is the Spirit of the LORD restricted?
    Are these His doings?
    Do not My words do good
    To him who walks uprightly?

8   "Lately My people have risen up as an
        enemy—
    You pull off the robe with the garment
    From those who trust *you,*
        as they pass by,
    Like men returned from war.
9   The women of My people you cast out
    From their pleasant houses;
    From their children
    You have taken away My glory forever.

10 "Arise and depart,
    For this *is* not *your* rest;
    Because it is defiled,
        it shall destroy *you,*
    Even with utter destruction.
11 If a man should walk in a false spirit
    And speak a lie, *saying,*

'I will prophesy to you of wine and
        drink,'
Even he would be the prattler of this
        people.

Israel Restored

12 "I will surely assemble all of you,
        O Jacob,
    I will surely gather the remnant of
        Israel;
    I will put them together like sheep of
        the fold,[10]
    Like a flock in the midst of their
        pasture;
    They shall make a loud noise because
        of *so many* men.
13 The one who breaks open will come up
        before them;
    They will break out,
    Pass through the gate,
    And go out by it;
    Their king will pass before them,
    With the LORD at their head."

Wicked Rulers and Prophets

3   And I said:

    "Hear now, O heads of Jacob,
    And you rulers of the house of Israel:
    Is it not for you to know justice?
2   You who hate good and love evil;
    Who strip the skin from *My* people,[11]
    And the flesh from their bones;
3   Who also eat the flesh of My people,
    Flay their skin from them,
    Break their bones,
    And chop *them* in pieces
    Like *meat* for the pot,
    Like flesh in the caldron."

4   Then they will cry to the LORD,
    But He will not hear them;
    He will even hide His face from them
        at that time,
    Because they have been evil in their
        deeds.

5   Thus says the LORD concerning the
        prophets
    Who make my people stray;
    Who chant "Peace"
    While they chew with their teeth,
    But who prepare war against him
    Who puts nothing into their mouths:
6   "Therefore you shall have night
        without vision,
    And you shall have darkness
        without divination;

---

7 Literally *one casting a surveyor's line*   8 Literally *to these*   9 Vulgate reads *he shall not take shame.*
10 Hebrew *bozrah*   11 Literally *them*

The sun shall go down on the prophets,
And the day shall be dark for them.
7   So the seers shall be ashamed,
And the diviners abashed;
Indeed they shall all cover their lips;
For *there is* no answer from God."

8   But truly I am full of power
by the Spirit of the LORD,
And of justice and might,
To declare to Jacob his transgression
And to Israel his sin.
9   Now hear this,
You heads of the house of Jacob
And rulers of the house of Israel,
Who abhor justice
And pervert all equity,
10 Who build up Zion with bloodshed
And Jerusalem with iniquity:
11 Her heads judge for a bribe,
Her priests teach for pay,
And her prophets divine for money.
Yet they lean on the LORD, and say,
"Is not the LORD among us?
No harm can come upon us."
12 Therefore because of you
Zion shall be plowed *like* a field,
Jerusalem shall become heaps of ruins,
And the mountain of the temple[12]
Like the bare hills of the forest.

The LORD'S Reign in Zion

4   Now it shall come to pass in the latter
days
That the mountain of the LORD's house
Shall be established on the top of the
mountains,
And shall be exalted above the hills;
And peoples shall flow to it.
2   Many nations shall come and say,
"Come, and let us go up to the
mountain of the LORD,
To the house of the God of Jacob;
He will teach us His ways,
And we shall walk in His paths."
For out of Zion the law shall go forth,
And the word of the LORD from
Jerusalem.
3   He shall judge between many peoples,
And rebuke strong nations afar off;
They shall beat their swords
into plowshares,
And their spears into pruning hooks;
Nation shall not lift up sword against
nation,
Neither shall they learn war any
more.[13]

4   But everyone shall sit under his vine
and under his fig tree,

And no one shall make *them* afraid;
For the mouth of the LORD of hosts
has spoken.
5   For all people walk
each in the name of his god,
But we will walk
in the name of the LORD our God
Forever and ever.

Zion's Future Triumph

6   "In that day," says the LORD,
"I will assemble the lame,
I will gather the outcast
And those whom I have afflicted;
7   I will make the lame a remnant,
And the outcast a strong nation;
So the LORD will reign over them in
Mount Zion
From now on, even forever.
8   And you, O tower of the flock,
The stronghold of the daughter of
Zion,
To you shall it come,
Even the former dominion shall come,
The kingdom of the daughter of
Jerusalem."

9   Now why do you cry aloud?
Is there no king in your midst?
Has your counselor perished?
For pangs have seized you like a
woman in labor.
10 Be in pain, and labor to bring forth,
O daughter of Zion,
Like a woman in birth pangs.
For now you shall go forth from the
city,
You shall dwell in the field,
And you shall go *even* to Babylon.
There you shall be delivered;
There the LORD will redeem you
From the hand of your enemies.

11 Now also many nations have gathered
against you,
Who say, "Let her be defiled,
And let our eye look upon Zion."
12 But they do not know the thoughts of
the LORD,
Nor do they understand His counsel;
For He will gather them like sheaves to
the threshing floor.

13 "Arise and thresh, O daughter of Zion;
For I will make your horn iron,
And I will make your hooves bronze;
You shall beat in pieces many peoples;
I will consecrate their gain to the
LORD,

12 Literally *house*   13 Compare Isaiah 2:2–4

And their substance to the Lord of the
whole earth."

5 Now gather yourself in troops,
O daughter of troops;
He has laid siege against us;
They will strike the judge of Israel with
a rod on the cheek.

The Coming Messiah

2 "But you, Bethlehem Ephrathah,
Though you are little among the
thousands of Judah,
Yet out of you shall come forth to Me
The One to be ruler in Israel,
Whose goings forth *have been* from
of old,
From everlasting."

3 Therefore He shall give them up,
Until the time *that* she who is in labor
has given birth;
Then the remnant of His brethren
Shall return to the children of Israel.
4 And He shall stand and feed *His flock*
In the strength of the LORD,
In the majesty of the name of the
LORD His God;
And they shall abide,
For now He shall be great
To the ends of the earth;
5 And this *One* shall be peace.

Judgment on Israel's Enemies

When the Assyrian comes into our
land,
And when he treads in our palaces,
Then we will raise against him
Seven shepherds and eight princely
men.
6 They shall waste with the sword the
land of Assyria,
And the land of Nimrod at its
entrances;
Thus He shall deliver *us* from the
Assyrian,
When he comes into our land
And when he treads within our
borders.

7 Then the remnant of Jacob
Shall be in the midst of many peoples,
Like dew from the LORD,
Like showers on the grass,
That tarry for no man
Nor wait for the sons of men.
8 And the remnant of Jacob
Shall be among the Gentiles,

In the midst of many peoples,
Like a lion among the beasts of the
forest,
Like a young lion among flocks of
sheep,
Who, if he passes through,
Both treads down and tears in pieces,
And none can deliver.
9 Your hand shall be lifted against your
adversaries,
And all your enemies shall be cut off.

10 "And it shall be in that day,"
says the LORD,
"That I will cut off your horses from your
midst
And destroy your chariots.
11 I will cut off the cities of your land
And throw down all your strongholds.
12 I will cut off sorceries from your hand,
And you shall have no soothsayers.
13 Your carved images I will also cut off,
And your sacred pillars from your
midst;
You shall no more worship
the work of your hands;
14 I will pluck your wooden images[14] from
your midst;
Thus I will destroy your cities.
15 And I will execute vengeance in anger
and fury
On the nations that have not heard."[15]

God Pleads with Israel

6 Hear now what the LORD says:

"Arise, plead your case before the
mountains,
And let the hills hear your voice.
2 Hear, O you mountains, the LORD's
complaint,
And you strong foundations of the
earth;
For the LORD has a complaint against
His people,
And He will contend with Israel.

3 "O My people,
what have I done to you?
And how have I wearied you?
Testify against Me.
4 For I brought you up from the land of
Egypt,
I redeemed you from the house of
bondage;
And I sent before you Moses, Aaron,
and Miriam.
5 O My people, remember now
What Balak king of Moab counseled,

14 Hebrew *Asherim*, Canaanite deities   15 Or *obeyed*

And what Balaam the son of Beor
    answered him,
From Acacia Grove[16] to Gilgal,
That you may know the righteousness
    of the LORD."

6 With what shall I come before the
    LORD,
And bow myself before the High God?
Shall I come before Him with burnt
    offerings,
With calves a year old?
7 Will the LORD be pleased with
    thousands of rams
Or ten thousand rivers of oil?
Shall I give my firstborn *for* my
    transgression,
The fruit of my body *for* the sin of my
    soul?

8 He has shown you, O man, what *is*
    good;
And what does the LORD require of
    you
But to do justly,
To love mercy,
And to walk humbly with your God?

Punishment of Israel's Injustice

9 The LORD'S voice cries to the city—
Wisdom shall see Your name:

"Hear the Rod!
Who has appointed it?
10 Are there yet the treasures of
    wickedness
In the house of the wicked,
And the short measure *that is* an
    abomination?
11 Shall I count pure
    those with the wicked balances,
And with the bag of deceitful weights?
12 For her rich men are full of violence,
Her inhabitants have spoken lies,
And their tongue is deceitful in their
    mouth.

13 "Therefore I will also make *you* sick by
    striking you,
By making *you* desolate because of
    your sins.
14 You shall eat, but not be satisfied;
Hunger[17] *shall be* in your midst.
You may carry *some* away,[18]
    but shall not save *them;*
And what you do rescue I will give
    over to the sword.

15 "You shall sow, but not reap;
You shall tread the olives,
    but not anoint yourselves with oil;
And *make* sweet wine,
    but not drink wine.
16 For the statutes of Omri are kept;
All the works of Ahab's house *are
    done;*
And you walk in their counsels,
That I may make you a desolation,
And your inhabitants a hissing.
Therefore you shall bear the reproach
    of My people."

Sorrow for Israel's Sins

7 Woe is me!
    For I am like those who gather
        summer fruits,
Like those who glean vintage grapes;
There is no cluster to eat
Of the first-ripe fruit *which* my soul
    desires.
2 The faithful *man* has perished from the
    earth,
And *there is* no one upright among
    men.
They all lie in wait for blood;
Every man hunts his brother with a
    net.

3 That they may successfully do evil with
    both hands—
The prince asks *for gifts,*
The judge *seeks* a bribe,
And the great *man* utters his evil
    desire;
So they scheme together.
4 The best of them *is* like a brier;
The most upright *is sharper* than a
    thorn hedge;
The day of your watchman and your
    punishment comes;
Now shall be their perplexity.

5 Do not trust in a friend;
Do not put your confidence in a
    companion;
Guard the doors of your mouth
From her who lies in your bosom.
6 For son dishonors father,
Daughter rises against her mother,
Daughter-in-law against
    her mother-in-law;
A man's enemies *are* the men of his
    own house.
7 Therefore I will look to the LORD;
I will wait for the God of my
    salvation;
My God will hear me.

16 Hebrew *Shittim* (compare Joshua 2:1, 3:1; Numbers 25:1)   17 Or *emptiness,* or *humiliation*
18 Targum and Vulgate read *you shall take hold.*

Israel's Confession and Comfort

8 Do not rejoice over me, my enemy;
When I fall, I will arise;
When I sit in darkness,
The LORD *will be* a light to me.
9 I will bear the indignation of the
LORD,
Because I have sinned against Him,
Until He pleads my case
And executes justice for me;
He will bring me forth to the light,
And I will see His righteousness.
10 Then *she who is* my enemy will see,
And shame will cover her who said to
me,
"Where is the LORD your God?"
My eyes will see her;
Now she will be trampled down
Like mire in the streets.

11 *In* the day when your walls are to be
built,
In that day the decree shall go far and
wide.[19]
12 *In* that day they[20] shall come to you
From Assyria and the fortified cities,[21]
From the fortress[22] to the River,[23]
From sea to sea,
And mountain *to* mountain.
13 Yet the land shall be desolate
Because of those who dwell in it,
And for the fruit of their deeds.

God Will Forgive Israel

14 Shepherd Your people with Your staff,
The flock of Your heritage,
Who dwell solitarily *in* a woodland,
In the midst of Carmel;
Let them feed *in* Bashan and Gilead,
As in days of old.

15 "As in the days when you came out of
the land of Egypt,
I will show them[24] marvelous *things*."

16 The nations shall see and be ashamed
of all their might;
They shall put *their* hand over *their*
mouth;
Their ears shall be deaf.
17 They shall lick the dust like a serpent;
They shall crawl from their holes like
snakes of the earth.
They shall be afraid of the LORD our
God,
And shall fear because of You.

18 Who *is* a God like You,
Pardoning iniquity
And passing over the transgression of
the remnant of His heritage?

He does not retain His anger forever,
Because He delights *in* mercy.
19 He will again have compassion on us,
And will subdue our iniquities.

You will cast all our[25] sins
Into the depths of the sea.
20 You will give truth to Jacob
And mercy to Abraham,
Which You have sworn to our fathers
From days of old.

---

19 Or *the boundary shall be extended*   20 Literally *he*, collective of the captives
21 Hebrew *arey mazor*, possibly *cities of Egypt*   22 Hebrew *mazor*, possibly *Egypt*   23 That is, the Euphrates
24 Literally *him*, collective for the captives   25 Literally *their*

Introduction to Nahum

Nahum had courage! Courage is always an option. You never lose it, because you can always choose it.

The Book of Nahum was written sometime between 663 and 612 B.C., during the height of the Assyrian empire, centered in the city of Nineveh. Nahum, called by God, announces the destruction of the Assyrian kingdom due to their barbarous acts and cruel, violent ways.

The prophet Nahum was a courageous individual willing to stand up for the oppressed before an Assyria who prided herself on her wickedness. He was not afraid to face the Assyrian army. Though he was only one man, he stood up to his problem.

Nahum, whose name means "Comfort," expresses the comfort of God to his people in the face of cruel opposition. Nahum proves that God is stronger than their problem:

> The LORD has His way
> In the whirlwind and in the storm,
> And the clouds *are* the dust of His feet.
> He rebukes the sea and makes it dry,
> And dries up all the rivers.
> Bashan and Carmel wither,
> And the flower of Lebanon wilts.
> The mountains quake before Him,
> The hills melt,
> And the earth heaves at His presence,
> Yes, the world and all who dwell in it.

(Nah. 1:3-5)

Nahum and the people of Judah depended on God's ability, not their own ability. They knew that God was stronger and bigger than any problem. With God, they could not fail!

The Book of

Nahum

THE burden[1] against Nineveh. The book of the vision of Nahum the Elkoshite.

God's Wrath on His Enemies

2 God is jealous, and the LORD avenges;
The LORD avenges and is furious.
The LORD will take vengeance on His adversaries,
And He reserves wrath for His enemies;
3 The LORD is slow to anger and great in power,
And will not at all acquit the wicked.

The LORD has His way
In the whirlwind and in the storm,
And the clouds are the dust of His feet.
4 He rebukes the sea and makes it dry,
And dries up all the rivers.
Bashan and Carmel wither,
And the flower of Lebanon wilts.
5 The mountains quake before Him,
The hills melt,
And the earth heaves[2] at His presence,
Yes, the world and all who dwell in it.

6 Who can stand before His indignation?
And who can endure the fierceness of His anger?
His fury is poured out like fire,
And the rocks are thrown down by Him.

7 The LORD is good,
A stronghold in the day of trouble;
And He knows those who trust in Him.
8 But with an overflowing flood
He will make an utter end of its place,
And darkness will pursue His enemies.

9 What do you conspire against the LORD?
He will make an utter end of it.
Affliction will not rise up a second time.
10 For while tangled like thorns,
And while drunken like drunkards,
They shall be devoured like stubble fully dried.

11 From you comes forth one
Who plots evil against the LORD,
A wicked counselor.

12 Thus says the LORD:

"Though they are safe,
and likewise many,
Yet in this manner they will be cut down
When he passes through.
Though I have afflicted you,
I will afflict you no more;
13 For now I will break off his yoke from you,
And burst your bonds apart."

14 The LORD has given a command concerning you:
"Your name shall be perpetuated no longer.
Out of the house of your gods
I will cut off the carved image
and the molded image.
I will dig your grave,
For you are vile."

15 Behold, on the mountains
The feet of him who brings good tidings,
Who proclaims peace!
O Judah, keep your appointed feasts,
Perform your vows.
For the wicked one shall no more pass through you;
He is utterly cut off.

The Destruction of Nineveh

2 He who scatters[3] has come up before your face.
Man the fort!
Watch the road!
Strengthen your flanks!
Fortify your power mightily.

2 For the LORD will restore the excellence of Jacob
Like the excellence of Israel,
For the emptiers have emptied them out
And ruined their vine branches.

1 Or oracle 2 Targum reads burns. 3 Vulgate reads he who destroys.

3 The shields of his mighty men *are*
        made red,
The valiant men *are* in scarlet.
The chariots *come* with flaming torches
In the day of his preparation,
And the spears are brandished.[4]
4 The chariots rage in the streets,
They jostle one another in the broad
        roads;
They seem like torches,
They run like lightning.

5 He remembers his worthies;
They stumble in their walk;
They make haste to her walls,
And the defense is prepared.
6 The gates of the rivers are opened,
And the palace is dissolved.
7 It is decreed:[5]
She shall be led away captive,
She shall be brought up;
And her maidservants shall lead *her*
        as with the voice of doves,
Beating their breasts.

8 Though Nineveh of old *was* like a pool
        of water,
Now they flee away.
"Halt! Halt!" *they cry*;
But no one turns back.
9 Take spoil of silver!
Take spoil of gold!
There is no end of treasure,
Or wealth of every desirable prize.
10 She is empty, desolate, and waste!
The heart melts, and the knees shake;
Much pain *is* in every side,
And all their faces are drained of
        color.[6]

11 Where *is* the dwelling of the lions,
And the feeding place of the young
        lions,
Where the lion walked,
        the lioness *and* lion's cub,
And no one made *them* afraid?
12 The lion tore in pieces enough for his
        cubs,
Killed for his lionesses,
Filled his caves with prey,
And his dens with flesh.

13"Behold, I *am* against you," says the
LORD of hosts, "I will burn your[7] chariots
in smoke, and the sword shall devour
your young lions; I will cut off your prey
from the earth, and the voice of your
messengers shall be heard no more."

The Woe of Nineveh

3 Woe to the bloody city!
    It *is* all full of lies *and* robbery.
Its victim never departs.
2 The noise of a whip
And the noise of rattling wheels,
Of galloping horses,
Of clattering chariots!
3 Horsemen charge with bright sword
        and glittering spear.
There is a multitude of slain,
A great number of bodies,
Countless corpses—
They stumble over the corpses—
4 Because of the multitude of harlotries
        of the seductive harlot,
The mistress of sorceries,
Who sells nations through her
        harlotries,
And families through her sorceries.

5 "Behold, I *am* against you,"
        says the LORD of hosts;
"I will lift up your skirts over your face,
I will show the nations your nakedness,
And the kingdoms your shame.
6 I will cast abominable filth upon you,
Make you vile,
And make you a spectacle.
7 It shall come to pass *that* all who look
        upon you
Will flee from you, and say,
'Nineveh is laid waste!
Who will bemoan her?'
Where shall I seek comforters for
        you?"

8 Are you better than No Amon[8]
That was situated by the River,[9]
That had the waters around her,
Whose rampart *was like* the sea,
Whose wall *was like* the sea?
9 Ethiopia and Egypt *were* her strength,
And *it was* boundless;
Put and Lubim were your[10] helpers.
10 Yet she *was* carried away,
She went into captivity;
Her young children also were dashed
        to pieces
At the head of every street;
They cast lots for her honorable men,
And all her great men were bound in
        chains.
11 You also will be drunk;
You will be hidden;
You also will seek refuge from the
        enemy.

---

4 Literally *the cypresses are shaken*   5 Hebrew *Huzzab*   6 Compare Joel 2:6   7 Literally *her*
8 That is, ancient Thebes; Targum and Vulgate read *populous Alexandria.*
9 Literally *rivers,* that is, the Nile and the surrounding canals   10 Septuagint reads *her.*

12 All your strongholds *are* fig trees with
ripened figs:
If they are shaken,
They fall into the mouth of the eater.
13 Surely, your people in your midst *are*
women!
The gates of your land are wide open
for your enemies;
Fire shall devour the bars of your
gates.

14 Draw your water for the siege!
Fortify your strongholds!
Go into the clay and tread the mortar!
Make strong the brick kiln!
15 There the fire will devour you,
The sword will cut you off;
It will eat you up like a locust.

Make yourself many—
like the locust!
Make yourself many—
like the *swarming* locusts!

16 You have multiplied your merchants
more than the stars of heaven.
The locust plunders and flies away.
17 Your commanders *are* like *swarming*
locusts,
And your captains like great
grasshoppers,
Which camp in the hedges on a cold
day;
But when the sun rises they flee away,
And the place where they *are* is not
known.
18 Your shepherds slumber,
O king of Assyria;
Your nobles rest *in the dust.*
Your people are scattered on the
mountains,
And no one gathers them.
19 Your injury *has* no healing,
Your wound is severe.
All who hear news of you
Will clap *their* hands over you,
For upon whom has not your
wickedness passed continually?

Introduction to Habakkuk

Tough times never last but tough people do! Habakkuk continually trusted God in the face of all adversity!

The Book of Habakkuk concerns the message of the prophet by the same name to the people of Judah between 609 to 597 B.C. A contemporary of Zephaniah and Jeremiah, Habakkuk was called by God to forewarn the people of coming destruction by the Chaldeans.

Although he was the bearer of bad news, Habakkuk presented the promise, "the just shall live by his faith" (Hab. 2:4). The positively oriented personality derives its strength from faith and can stand in confidence and can trust in God while facing tough times. This particular verse is quoted three times in the New Testament as one of the great promises of God.

Habakkuk also placed his trust in God, despite not totally understanding the reasons for and outcome of the situation.

Yet I will rejoice in the LORD,
I will joy in the God of my salvation.
The LORD God is my strength;
He will make my feet like deer's *feet*,
And He will make me walk on my high hills.

(Hab. 3:18, 19)

Though not understanding all, Habakkuk had faith. Though times might have been tough, he trusted God. Though he did not know the final outcome of the circumstances, he was able to rejoice! For he knew that "the just will live by his faith"!

Thank You Father,
For dangers that teach me to be brave; for suffering from which I learn patience; for pain which teaches me tenderness. Thank You for leading me through tough times. Help me to remember in this trying time that there is no progress without pain, no conversion without crisis, no service without suffering. Trying times are times to try more faith! I'm trying! You're helping. Thank You Lord.

Amen.

The Book of

Habakkuk

THE burden[1] which the prophet Habakkuk saw.

The Prophet's Question

2 O LORD, how long shall I cry,
And You will not hear?
Even cry out to You, "Violence!"
And You will not save.
3 Why do You show me iniquity,
And cause *me* to see trouble?
For plundering and violence
are before me;
There is strife, and contention arises.
4 Therefore the law is powerless,
And justice never goes forth.
For the wicked surround the righteous;
Therefore perverse judgment proceeds.

The LORD'S Reply

5 "Look among the nations and watch—
Be utterly astounded!
For *I will* work a work in your days
Which you would not believe,
though it were told *you.*
6 For indeed I am raising up the
Chaldeans,
A bitter and hasty nation
Which marches through the breadth of
the earth,
To possess dwelling places *that are* not
theirs.
7 They are terrible and dreadful;
Their judgment and their dignity
proceed from themselves.
8 Their horses also are swifter than
leopards,
And more fierce than evening wolves.
Their chargers charge ahead;
Their cavalry comes from afar;
They fly as the eagle *that* hastens to
eat.

9 "They all come for violence;
Their faces are set *like* the east wind.
They gather captives like sand.
10 They scoff at kings,
And princes are scorned by them.
They deride every stronghold,
For they heap up *mounds of* earth
and seize it.

11 Then *his* mind[2] changes,
and he transgresses;
He commits offense,
Imputing this power to his god."

The Prophet's Second Question

12 Are You not from everlasting,
O LORD my God, my Holy One?
We shall not die.
O LORD, You have appointed them
for judgment;
O Rock, You have marked them
for correction.
13 *You are* of purer eyes than to behold
evil,
And cannot look on wickedness.
Why do You look on those who deal
treacherously,
And hold Your tongue when the
wicked devours
One more rightous than he?
14 *Why* do You make men like fish of the
sea,
Like creeping things *that have* no ruler
over them?

15 They take up all of them with a hook,
They catch them in their net,
And gather them in their dragnet.
Therefore they rejoice and are glad.
16 Therefore they sacrifice to their net,
And burn incense to their dragnet;
Because by them their share *is*
sumptuous
And their food plenteous.
17 Shall they therefore empty their net,
And continue to slay nations without
pity?

2 I will stand my watch
And set myself on the rampart,
And watch to see what He will say to
me,
And what I will answer when I am
reproved.

The Just Live by Faith

2 Then the LORD answered me and
said:

1 Or *oracle*   2 Literally *spirit* or *wind*

"Write the vision
And make *it* plain on tablets,
That he may run who reads it.
3 For the vision *is* yet for an appointed time;
But at the end it will speak,
and it will not lie.
Though it tarries, wait for it;
Because it will surely come,
It will not tarry.

4 "Behold the proud,
His soul is not upright in him;
But the just shall live by his faith.

Woe to the Wicked

5 "Indeed, because he transgresses by wine,
He is a proud man,
And he does not stay at home.
Because he enlarges his desire as hell,[3]
And he *is* like death,
and cannot be satisfied,
He gathers to himself all nations
And heaps up for himself all peoples.

6 "Shall not all these take up a proverb against him,
And a taunting riddle against him,
and say,
'Woe to him who increases
What is not his—how long?
And to him who loads himself with many pledges'?[4]
7 Will not your creditors[5] rise up suddenly?
Will they not awaken who oppress you?
And you will become their booty.
8 Because you have plundered many nations,
All the remnant of the people shall plunder you,
Because of men's blood
And the violence of the land
and the city,
And of all who dwell in it.

9 "Woe to him who covets evil gain for his house,
That he may set his nest on high,
That he may be delivered from the power of disaster!
10 You gave shameful counsel to your house,
Cutting off many peoples,
And sinned *against* your soul.

11 For the stone will cry out from the wall,
And the beam from the timbers will answer it.

12 "Woe to him who builds a town with bloodshed,
Who establishes a city by iniquity!
13 Behold, *is it* not of the LORD of hosts
That the peoples labor to feed the fire,[6]
And nations weary themselves in vain?
14 For the earth will be filled
With the knowledge of the glory of the LORD,
As the waters cover the sea.

15 "Woe to him who gives drink to his neighbor,
Pressing[7] *him to* your bottle,
Even to make *him* drunk,
That you may look on his nakedness!
16 You are filled with shame instead of glory.
You also—drink!
And be exposed as uncircumcised!
The cup of the LORD's right hand *will be* turned against you,
And utter shame *will be* on your glory.
17 For the violence *done to* Lebanon will cover you,
And the plunder of beasts *which* made them afraid,
Because of men's blood
And the violence of the land *and* the city,
And of all who dwell in it.

18 "What profit is the image,
that its maker should carve it,
The molded image, a teacher of lies,
That the maker of its mold should trust in it,
To make mute idols?
19 Woe to him who says to wood, 'Awake!'
To silent stone, 'Arise! It shall teach!'
Behold, it is overlaid with gold and silver,
And in it there is no breath at all.
20 But the LORD is in His holy temple.
Let all the earth keep silence before Him."

The Prophet's Prayer

3 A prayer of Habakkuk the prophet, on Shigionoth.[8]

2 O LORD, I have heard your speech *and* was afraid;

---

3 Hebrew *Sheol* 4 Syriac and Vulgate read *thick clay.* 5 Literally *those who bite you*
6 Literally *for what satisfies fire,* that is, for what is of no lasting value 7 Literally *attaching* or *joining*
8 Exact meaning unknown

O LORD, revive Your work
in the midst of the years!
In the midst of the years
make *it* known;
In wrath remember mercy.

3 God came from Teman,
The Holy One from
Mount Paran.   Selah

His glory covered the heavens,
And the earth was full of His praise.
4 *His* brightness was like the light;
He had rays *flashing* from His hand,
And there His power *was* hidden.
5 Before Him went pestilence,
And fever followed at His feet.

6 He stood and measured the earth;
He looked and startled the nations.
And the everlasting mountains were
scattered,
The perpetual hills bowed.
His ways *are* everlasting.
7 I saw the tents of Cushan in affliction;
The curtains of the land of Midian
trembled.

8 O LORD, were *You* displeased with the
rivers,
Was Your anger against the rivers,
Was Your wrath against the sea,
That You rode on Your horses,
Your chariots of salvation?
9 Your bow was made quite ready;
Oaths were sworn over *Your*
arrows.[9]   Selah

You divided the earth with rivers.
10 The mountains saw You *and* trembled;
The overflowing of the water
passed by.
The deep uttered its voice,
And lifted its hands on high.
11 The sun and moon stood still in their
habitation;
At the light of Your arrows they went,
At the shining of Your glittering spear.

12 You marched through the land in
indignation;
You trampled the nations in anger.
13 You went forth for the salvation of
Your people,
For salvation with Your Anointed.
You struck the head from the house of
the wicked,
By laying bare from foundation to
neck.   Selah

14 You thrust through with his own
arrows
The head of his villages.
They came out like a whirlwind to
scatter me;
Their rejoicing was like feasting on the
poor in secret.
15 You walked through the sea with Your
horses,
Through the heap of great waters.

16 When I heard, my body trembled;
My lips quivered at *the* voice;
Rottenness entered my bones;
And I trembled in myself,
That I might rest in the day of trouble.
When he comes up to the people,
He will invade them with his troops.

A Hymn of Faith

17 Though the fig tree may not blossom,
Nor fruit be on the vines;
Though the labor of the olive may fail,
And the fields yield no food;
Though the flock be cut off from the
fold,
And there be no herd in the stalls—
18 Yet I will rejoice in the LORD,
I will joy in the God of my salvation.

19 The LORD God[10] is my strength;
He will make my feet like deer's *feet*,
And He will make me walk on my high
hills.

To the Chief Musician. With my
stringed instruments.

9 Literally *rods* or *tribes* (compare verse 14)   10 Hebrew *YHWH Adonai*

Introduction to Zephaniah

There is always a bright future, if you will build with God on your hopes and not your hurts.

Although the Book of Zephaniah describes the destruction of Judah, Philistia, Moab, Ammon, Ethiopia, and Assyria by the mighty nation of Babylon, the underlying theme is God's gracious ability and power to turn these nations' scars into stars.

It was written by the prophet Zephaniah (whose name means "Hidden by Yahweh") between 640 and 612 B.C. Only three chapters long, Zephaniah points to the positive future of all nations who turn to God. Zephaniah was confident that through the coming disaster, those who would remain true to God would stand firm and receive God's goodness. In asking them to seek God, Zephaniah assured the nations that no one was too far from God's love, no nation was too small for His power!

Powerful promises dominate the close of the book, telling the people to respond positively to God's unending love:

The LORD your God in your midst,
The Mighty One, will save;
He will rejoice over you with gladness,
He will quiet *you* in His love,
He will rejoice over you with singing.

At that time I will bring you back,
Even at the time I gather you;
For I will give you fame and praise
Among all the peoples of the earth,
When I return your captives before your eyes,
Says the LORD.

(Zeph. 3:17, 20)

God has the power to save and restore the nations to Himself. Zephaniah encourages them to focus on their prospects, not their problems! Their opportunities, not their obstacles! Their future, not their failures!

The Book of
Zephaniah

THE word of the LORD which came to Zephaniah the son of Cushi, the son of Gedaliah, the son of Amariah, the son of Hezekiah, in the days of Josiah the son of Amon, king of Judah.

The Great Day of the LORD

2 "I will utterly consume all *things*
   From the face of the land,"
   Says the LORD;
3 "I will consume man and beast;
   I will consume the birds of the heavens,
   The fish of the sea,
   And the stumbling blocks[1] along with the wicked.
   I will cut off man from the face of the land,"
   Says the LORD.

4 "I will stretch out My hand against Judah,
   And against all the inhabitants of Jerusalem.
   I will cut off every trace of Baal from this place,
   The names of the idolatrous priests[2] with the *pagan* priests—
5 Those who worship the host of heaven on the housetops;
   Those who worship and swear *oaths* by the LORD,
   But who *also* swear by Milcom;[3]
6 Those who have turned back from *following* the LORD,
   And have not sought the LORD, nor inquired of Him."

7 Be silent in the presence
   of the Lord GOD;
   For the day of the LORD *is* at hand,
   For the LORD has prepared a sacrifice;
   He has invited[4] His guests.

8 "And it shall be,
   In the day of the LORD's sacrifice,
   That I will punish the princes
   and the king's children,
   And all such as are clothed with foreign apparel.

9 In the same day I will punish
   All those who leap over the threshold,[5]
   Who fill their masters' houses with violence and deceit.

10 "And there shall be on that day,"
   says the LORD,
   "The sound of a mournful cry from the Fish Gate,
   A wailing from the Second Quarter,
   And a loud crashing from the hills.
11 Wail, you inhabitants of Maktesh![6]
   For all the merchant people
   are cut down;
   All those who handle money
   are cut off.

12 "And it shall come to pass at that time
   That I will search Jerusalem with lamps,
   And punish the men
   Who are settled in complacency,[7]
   Who say in their heart,
   'The LORD will not do good,
   Nor will He do evil.'
13 Therefore their goods shall become booty,
   And their houses a desolation;
   They shall build houses,
   but not inhabit *them;*
   They shall plant vineyards,
   but not drink their wine."

14 The great day of the LORD *is* near;
   It is near and hastens quickly.
   The noise of the day of the LORD is bitter;
   There the mighty men shall cry out.
15 That day *is* a day of wrath,
   A day of trouble and distress,
   A day of devastation and desolation,
   A day of darkness and gloominess,
   A day of clouds and thick darkness,
16 A day of trumpet and alarm
   Against the fortified cities
   And against the high towers.

17 "I will bring distress upon men,
   And they shall walk like blind men,
   Because they have sinned against the LORD;

---

1 Figurative of idols   2 Hebrew *chemarim*
3 Or *Malcham,* an Ammonite god, also called *Molech* (compare Leviticus 18:21)
4 Literally *set apart, consecrated*   5 Compare 1 Samuel 5:5   6 Literally *Mortar,* a market district of Jerusalem
7 Literally *on their lees,* that is, settled like the dregs of wine

Their blood shall be poured out
    like dust,
And their flesh like refuse."

18 Neither their silver nor their gold
Shall be able to deliver them
In the day of the LORD's wrath;
But the whole land shall be devoured
By the fire of His jealousy,
For He will make speedy riddance
Of all those who dwell in the land.

A Call to Repentance

2 Gather yourselves together,
    yes, gather together,
O undesirable[8] nation,
2 Before the decree is issued,
Before the day passes like chaff,
Before the LORD's fierce anger comes
    upon you,
Before the day of the LORD's anger
    comes upon you!
3 Seek the LORD,
    all you meek of the earth,
Who have upheld His justice.
Seek righteousness, seek humility.
It may be that you will be hidden
In the day of the LORD's anger.

Judgment on Nations

4 For Gaza shall be forsaken,
And Ashkelon desolate;
They shall drive out Ashdod at
    noonday,
And Ekron shall be uprooted.
5 Woe to the inhabitants of the seacoast,
The nation of the Cherethites!
The word of the LORD *is* against you,
O Canaan, land of the Philistines:
"I will destroy you;
So there shall be no inhabitant."

6 The seacoast shall be pastures,
With shelters[9] for shepherds
    and folds for flocks.
7 The coast shall be for the remnant of
    the house of Judah;
They shall feed *their* flocks there;
In the houses of Ashkelon they shall lie
    down at evening.
For the LORD their God will intervene
    for them,
And return their captives.

8 "I have heard the reproach of Moab,
And the revilings of the people of
    Ammon,
With which they have reproached My
    people,

And made arrogant threats against
    their borders.
9 Therefore, as I live,"
Says the LORD of hosts,
    the God of Israel,
"Surely Moab shall be like Sodom,
And the people of Ammon like
    Gomorrah—
Overrun with weeds and saltpits,
And a perpetual desolation;
The residue of My people shall plunder
    them,
And the remnant of My people shall
    possess them."

10 This they shall have for their pride,
Because they have *reproached*
    and made arrogant threats
Against the people of the LORD of
    hosts.
11 The LORD *will be* awesome to them,
For He will reduce to nothing all the
    gods of the earth;
People shall worship Him,
Each one from his place,
Indeed all the shores of the nations.

12 "You Ethiopians also,
You shall be slain by My sword."

13 And He will stretch out His hand
    against the north,
Destroy Assyria,
And make Nineveh a desolation,
As dry as the wilderness.
14 The herds shall lie down in her midst,
Every beast of the nation.
Both the pelican and the bittern
Shall lodge on the capitals *of* her
    pillars;
Their voice shall sing in the windows;
Desolation *shall be* at the threshold;
For He will lay bare the cedar work.
15 This is the rejoicing city
That dwelt securely,
That said in her heart,
"I *am it,* and *there is* none besides me."
How has she become a desolation,
A place for beasts to lie down!
Everyone who passes by her
Shall hiss and shake his fist.

The Wickedness of Jerusalem

3 Woe to her who is rebellious
    and polluted,
To the oppressing city!
2 She has not obeyed *His* voice,
She has not received correction;
She has not trusted in the LORD,
She has not drawn near to her God.

8 Or *shameless*   9 Literally *excavations,* either *underground huts* or *cisterns*

3 Her princes in her midst *are* roaring
  lions;
  Her judges *are* evening wolves
  That leave not a bone till morning.
4 Her prophets are insolent,
  treacherous people;
  Her priests have polluted the
  sanctuary,
  They have done violence to the law.
5 The LORD *is* righteous,
  He is in her midst,
  He will do no unrighteousness.
  Every morning He brings His justice
  to light;
  He never fails,
  But the unjust knows no shame.

6 "I have cut off nations,
  Their fortresses are devastated;
  I have made their streets desolate,
  With none passing by.
  Their cities are destroyed;
  There is no one, no inhabitant.
7 I said, 'Surely you will fear Me,
  You will receive instruction'—
  So that her dwelling would not be
  cut off,
  Despite everything for which
  I punished her.
  But they rose early
  and corrupted all their deeds.

A Faithful Remnant

8 "Therefore wait for Me," says the LORD,
  "Until the day I rise up for plunder;
  My determination *is* to gather the
  nations
  To My assembly of kingdoms,
  To pour on them My indignation,
  All my fierce anger;
  All the earth shall be devoured
  With the fire of My jealousy.

9 "For then I will restore to the peoples
  a pure language,
  That they all may call on the name of
  the LORD,
  To serve Him with one accord.
10 From beyond the rivers of Ethiopia
  My worshipers,
  The daughter of My dispersed ones,
  Shall bring My offering.
11 In that day you shall not be shamed
  for any of your deeds
  In which you transgress against Me;
  For then I will take away from your
  midst

Those who rejoice in your pride,
And you shall no longer be haughty
In My holy mountain.
12 I will leave in your midst
  A meek and humble people,
  And they shall trust in the name of the
  LORD.
13 The remnant of Israel shall do no
  unrighteousness
  And speak no lies,
  Nor shall a deceitful tongue be found
  in their mouth;
  For they shall feed *their* flocks
  and lie down,
  And no one shall make *them* afraid."

Joy in God's Faithfulness

14 Sing, O daughter of Zion!
  Shout, O Israel!
  Be glad and rejoice with all *your* heart,
  O daughter of Jerusalem!
15 The LORD has taken away your
  judgments,
  He has cast out your enemy.
  The King of Israel, the LORD,
  is in your midst;
  You shall see[10] disaster no more.

16 In that day it shall be said to
  Jerusalem:
  "Do not fear;
  Zion, let not your hands be weak.
17 The LORD your God in your midst,
  The Mighty One, will save;
  He will rejoice over you with gladness,
  He will quiet *you* in His love,
  He will rejoice over you with singing."

18 "I will gather those who sorrow over the
  appointed assembly,
  Who are among you,
  To whom its reproach *is* a burden.
19 Behold, at that time
  I will deal with all who afflict you;
  I will save the lame,
  And gather those who were driven out;
  I will appoint them for praise and fame
  In every land where they were put to
  shame.
20 At that time I will bring you back,
  Even at the time I gather you;
  For I will give you fame and praise
  Among all the peoples of the earth,
  When I return your captives before
  your eyes,"
  Says the LORD.

10 Some Hebrew manuscripts, Septuagint, and Bomberg read *see;* Masoretic Text and Vulgate read *fear.*

Introduction to Haggai

Haggai is a poignant, hard-hitting, straight-to-the-point, no-questions-asked book to encourage people to get started and never quit!

Written after Israel's return from exile in Babylon in 520 B.C., Haggai motivated the people to believe in themselves and to undertake the task of rebuilding the temple in Jerusalem. Although Haggai was very old, about eighty, he was strong enough to rally the people behind him.

Haggai was faced with innumerable negative thinkers who imagined every excuse possible not to build the temple. They said they must wait for "the right time" to begin, for the necessary funds, and for the large amount of people and material needed for the tasks. Haggai, being elderly, may have seen Solomon's temple in all its glory before its destruction. This motivated him to encourage the people because he had a vision of what they could do with their time, talents, and ability if they only applied themselves.

Haggai told the people that they did not have a materiel problem, they had a motivational problem. They did not have a money problem, they had an idea problem! They only needed to do two things to be successful. Get started. And never quit!

Postponing tough decisions is, more often than not, the result of a lack of faith. God promises to bless us when we make a commitment to live and walk by faith. We expect God to bless our lives and professions when we stop doing nothing and start doing something. In deciding to begin, our biggest problem is solved. We will succeed for beginning is half done!

The Book of

Haggai

The Command to Build God's House

IN the second year of King Darius, in the sixth month, on the first day of the month, the word of the LORD came by Haggai the prophet to Zerubbabel the son of Shealtiel, governor of Judah, and to Joshua the son of Jehozadak, the high priest, saying,
2 "Thus speaks the LORD of hosts, saying: 'This people says, "The time has not come, the time that the LORD's house should be built." ' "
3 Then the word of the LORD came by Haggai the prophet, saying,
4 "Is it time for you yourselves to dwell in your paneled houses, and this temple¹ to lie in ruins?"
5 Now therefore, thus says the LORD of hosts: "Consider your ways!

6 "You have sown much,
    and bring in little;
You eat, but do not have enough;
You drink, but you are not filled with
    drink;
You clothe yourselves,
    but no one is warm;
And he who earns wages,
Earns wages to put into a bag with
    holes."

7 Thus says the LORD of hosts: "Consider your ways!
8 "Go up to the mountains and bring wood and build the temple, that I may take pleasure in it and be glorified," says the LORD.
9 "You looked for much, but indeed it came to little; and when you brought it home, I blew it away. Why?" says the LORD of hosts. "Because of My house that is in ruins, while every one of you runs to his own house.
10 "Therefore the heavens above you withhold the dew, and the earth withholds its fruit.
11 "For I called for a drought on the land and the mountains, on the grain and the new wine and the oil, on whatever the ground brings forth, on men and live-stock, and on all the labor of your hands."

The People's Obedience

12 Then Zerubbabel the son of Shealtiel, and Joshua the son of Jehozadak, the high priest, with all the remnant of the people, obeyed the voice of the LORD their God, and the words of Haggai the prophet, as the LORD their God had sent him; and the people feared the presence of the LORD.
13 Then Haggai, the LORD's messenger, spoke the LORD's message to the people, saying, "I am with you, says the LORD."
14 So the LORD stirred up the spirit of Zerubbabel the son of Shealtiel, governor of Judah, and the spirit of Joshua the son of Jehozadak, the high priest, and the spirit of all the remnant of the people; and they came and worked on the house of the LORD of hosts, their God,
15 on the twenty-fourth day of the sixth month, in the second year of King Darius.

The Coming Glory of God's House

2 In the seventh month, on the twenty-first day of the month, the word of the LORD came by Haggai the prophet, saying:
2 "Speak now to Zerubbabel the son of Shealtiel, governor of Judah, and to Joshua the son of Jehozadak, the high priest, and to the remnant of the people, saying:
3 'Who is left among you who saw this temple² in its former glory? And how do you see it now? In comparison with it, is this not in your eyes as nothing?
4 'Yet now be strong, Zerubbabel,' says the LORD; 'and be strong, Joshua, son of Jehozadak, the high priest; and be strong, all you people of the land,' says the LORD, 'and work; for I am with you,' says the LORD of hosts.
5 'According to the word that I covenanted with you when you came out of Egypt, so My Spirit remains among you; do not fear!'

1 Literally house (also verse 8)   2 Literally house (also verses 7 and 9)

6 "For thus says the LORD of hosts: "Once more (it *is* a little while) I will shake heaven and earth, the sea and dry land;
7 'and I will shake all nations, and they shall come to the Desire of All Nations,[3] and I will fill this temple with glory,' says the LORD of hosts.
8 'The silver *is* Mine, and the gold *is* Mine,' says the LORD of hosts.
9 'The glory of this latter temple shall be greater than the former,' says the LORD of hosts. 'And in this place I will give peace,' says the LORD of hosts."

The People Are Defiled

10 On the twenty-fourth *day* of the ninth *month*, in the second year of Darius, the word of the LORD came by Haggai the prophet, saying,
11 "Thus says the LORD of hosts: 'Now, ask the priests concerning the law, saying,
12 "If one carries holy meat in the fold of his garment, and with the edge he touches bread or stew, wine or oil, or any food, will it become holy?" ' " Then the priests answered and said, "No."
13 And Haggai said, "If *one who is* unclean *because* of a dead body touches any of these, will it be unclean?" So the priests answered and said, "It shall be unclean."
14 Then Haggai answered and said, " 'So is this people, and so is this nation before Me,' says the LORD, 'and so is every work of their hands; and what they offer there is unclean.

Promised Blessing

15 'And now, carefully consider from this day forward: from before stone was laid upon stone in the temple of the LORD—

3 Or *the desire of all nations*

16 'since those *days,* when *one* came to a heap of twenty ephahs, there were *but* ten; when *one* came to the wine vat to draw out fifty baths from the press, there were *but* twenty.
17 'I struck you with blight and mildew and hail in all the labors of your hands; yet you did not *turn* to Me,' says the LORD.
18 'Consider now from this day forward, from the twenty-fourth day of the ninth month, from the day that the foundation of the LORD's temple was laid—consider it:
19 'Is the seed still in the barn? As yet the vine, the fig tree, the pomegranate, and the olive tree have not yielded *fruit.* But from this day *forward* I will bless *you.* ' "

Zerubbabel Chosen as a Signet

20 And again the word of the LORD came to Haggai on the twenty-fourth day of the month, saying,
21 "Speak to Zerubbabel, governor of Judah, saying:

'I will shake heaven and earth.
22 I will overthrow the throne
    of kingdoms;
I will destroy the strength
    of the Gentile kingdoms.
I will overthrow the chariots
And those who ride in them;
The horses and their riders shall come
    down,
Every one by the sword of his brother.

23 'In that day,' says the LORD of hosts, 'I will take you, Zerubbabel My servant, the son of Shealtiel,' says the LORD, 'and will make you as a signet *ring*; for I have chosen you,' says the LORD of hosts."

Introduction to Zechariah

Zechariah has been relevant to people during every age. The prophet wrote the book, at least the first eight chapters, as a very young man in the years 520 to 518 B.C. Zechariah continued the message of the earlier prophet Haggai. He encouraged the people of Israel to complete the temple of God. His message supplemented Haggai's by urging the people to build up the spiritual quality in their lives. Zechariah also inspired a proper attitude in worship.

Through a series of God-given visions, Zechariah extends the people's perspective to look beyond their present circumstances to the future. Zechariah reminded them that God had a plan for their future in the coming of the Messiah. God promised to work miraculous events for His people.

Having just returned from years of Babylonian captivity, it was difficult for the Israelites to feel secure in establishing long-term goals. Zechariah gave the people hope and the vision to see and to trust in the future as they planned ahead. This enabled them to complete the temple and to develop a positive, worshipful attitude toward God.

> For the seed *shall be* prosperous,
> The vine shall give its fruit,
> The ground shall give her increase,
> And the heavens shall give their dew.
> I will cause the remnant of this people
> To possess all these *things*.
> And it shall come to pass
> *That* just as you were a curse among the nations,
> O house of Judah and house of Israel,
> So I will save you, and you shall be a blessing.
> Do not fear,
> Let your hands be strong.

(Zech. 8:12, 13)

Zechariah taught the people that though they did not know what the future held, they knew the God who held the future.

The Book of
Zechariah

A Call to Repentance

IN the eighth month of the second year of Darius, the word of the LORD came to Zechariah the son of Berechiah, the son of Iddo the prophet, saying,
2 "The LORD has been very angry with your fathers.
3 "Therefore say to them, 'Thus says the LORD of hosts: "Return to Me," says the LORD of hosts, "and I will return to you," says the LORD of hosts.
4 "Do not be like your fathers, to whom the former prophets preached, saying, 'Thus says the LORD of hosts: "Turn now from your evil ways and your evil deeds." ' But they did not hear nor heed Me," says the LORD.

5 "Your fathers, where are they?
And the prophets, do they live forever?
6 Yet surely My words and My statutes,
Which I commanded My servants the
prophets,
Did they not overtake your fathers?"

"So they returned and said:

'Just as the LORD of hosts determined
to do to us,
According to our ways
and according to our deeds,
So He has dealt with us.' " ' "

Vision of the Horses

7 On the twenty-fourth day of the eleventh month, which is the month Shebat, in the second year of Darius, the word of the LORD came to Zechariah the son of Berechiah, the son of Iddo the prophet:
8 I saw by night, and behold, a man riding on a red horse, and it stood among the myrtle trees in the hollow; and behind him were horses: red, sorrel, and white.
9 Then I said, "My lord, what are these?" So the angel who talked with me said to me, "I will show you what they are."

10 And the man who stood among the myrtle trees answered and said, "These are the ones whom the LORD has sent to walk to and fro throughout the earth."
11 So they answered the Angel of the LORD, who stood among the myrtle trees, and said, "We have walked to and fro throughout the earth, and behold, all the earth is resting quietly."

The LORD Will Comfort Zion

12 Then the Angel of the LORD answered and said, "O LORD of hosts, how long will You not have mercy on Jerusalem and on the cities of Judah, against which You were angry these seventy years?"
13 And the LORD answered the angel who talked to me, with good and comforting words.
14 So the angel who spoke with me said to me, "Proclaim, saying, 'Thus says the LORD of hosts:

"I am zealous for Jerusalem
And for Zion with great zeal.
15 I am exceedingly angry with the
nations at ease;
For I was a little angry,
And they helped—but with evil intent."

16 'Therefore thus says the LORD:

"I am returning to Jerusalem with
mercy;
My house shall be built in it,"
says the LORD of hosts,
"And a surveyor's line shall be stretched
out over Jerusalem." '

17 "Again proclaim, saying, 'Thus says the LORD of hosts:

"My cities shall again spread out
through prosperity;
The LORD will again comfort Zion,
And will again choose Jerusalem." ' "

Vision of the Horns

18 Then I raised my eyes and looked, and there were four horns.
19 And I said to the angel who talked

with me, "What *are* these?" So he answered me, "These *are* the horns that have scattered Judah, Israel, and Jerusalem."

20 Then the LORD showed me four craftsmen.

21 And I said, "What are these coming to do?" So he said, "These *are* the horns that scattered Judah, so that no one could lift up his head; but the craftsmen[1] are coming to terrify them, to cast out the horns of the nations that lifted up *their* horn against the land of Judah to scatter it."

Vision of the Measuring Line

2 Then I raised my eyes and looked, and behold, a man with a measuring line in his hand.

2 So I said, "Where are you going?" And he said to me, "To measure Jerusalem, to see what *is* its width and what *is* its length."

3 And there *was* the angel who talked with me, going out; and another angel was coming out to meet him,

4 who said to him, "Run, speak to this young man, saying: 'Jerusalem shall be inhabited *as* towns without walls, because of the multitude of men and livestock in it.

5 'For I,' says the LORD, 'will be a wall of fire all around her, and I will be the glory in her midst.' "

Future Joy of Zion and Many Nations

6 "Up, up! Flee from the land of the north," says the LORD; "for I have spread you abroad like the four winds of heaven," says the LORD.

7 "Up, Zion! Escape, you who dwell with the daughter of Babylon."

8 For thus says the LORD of hosts: "He sent Me after glory, to the nations which plunder you; for he who touches you touches the apple of His eye.

9 "For surely I will shake My hand against them, and they shall become spoil for their servants. Then you will know that the LORD of hosts has sent Me.

10 "Sing and rejoice, O daughter of Zion! For behold, I am coming and I will dwell in your midst," says the LORD.

11 "Many nations shall be joined to the LORD in that day, and they shall become My people. And I will dwell in your

midst. Then you will know that the LORD of hosts has sent Me to you.

12 "And the LORD will take possession of Judah as His inheritance in the Holy Land, and will again choose Jerusalem.

13 "Be silent, all flesh, before the LORD, for He is aroused from His holy habitation!"

Vision of the High Priest

3 Then he showed me Joshua the high priest standing before the Angel of the LORD, and Satan standing at his right hand to oppose him.

2 And the LORD said to Satan, "The LORD rebuke you, Satan! The LORD who has chosen Jerusalem rebuke you! *Is* this not a brand plucked from the fire?"

3 Now Joshua was clothed with filthy garments, and was standing before the Angel.

4 Then He answered and spoke to those who stood before Him, saying, "Take away the filthy garments from him." And to him He said, "See, I have removed your iniquity from you, and I will clothe you with rich robes."

5 And I said, "Let them put a clean turban on his head." So they put a clean turban on his head, and they put the clothes on him. And the Angel of the LORD stood by.

The Coming Branch

6 Then the Angel of the LORD admonished Joshua, saying,

7 "Thus says the LORD of hosts:

'If you will walk in My ways,
And if you will keep My command,
Then you shall also judge My house,
And likewise have charge of My
    courts;
I will give you places to walk
Among these who stand here.

8 'Hear, O Joshua, the high priest,
You and your companions who sit
    before you,
For they are a wondrous sign;
For behold, I am bringing forth My
    Servant the BRANCH.

9 For behold, the stone
That I have laid before Joshua:
Upon the stone *are* seven eyes.
Behold, I will engrave its inscription,'
Says the LORD of hosts,
'And I will remove the iniquity of that
    land in one day.

---

1 Literally *these*

10 In that day,' says the LORD of hosts,
'Everyone will invite his neighbor
Under his vine and under his fig
tree.' "

Vision of the Lampstand and Olive Trees

4 Now the angel who talked with me
came back and wakened me, as a
man who is wakened out of his sleep.
2 And he said to me, "What do you
see?" So I said, "I am looking, and there
is a lampstand of solid gold with a bowl
on top of it, and on the stand seven lamps
with seven pipes to the seven lamps.
3 "Two olive trees are by it, one at the
right of the bowl and the other at its left."
4 So I answered and spoke to the angel
who talked with me, saying, "What are
these, my lord?"
5 Then the angel who talked with me
answered and said to me, "Do you not
know what these are?" And I said, "No,
my lord."
6 So he answered and said to me:

"This is the word of the LORD to
Zerubbabel:
'Not by might nor by power,
but by My Spirit,'
Says the LORD of hosts.
7 'Who are you, O great mountain?
Before Zerubbabel you shall become a
plain!
And he shall bring forth the capstone
With shouts of "Grace, grace to it!" ' "

8 Moreover the word of the LORD came
to me, saying:

9 "The hands of Zerubbabel
Have laid the foundation of this
temple;[2]
His hands shall also finish it.
Then you will know
That the LORD of hosts has sent Me
to you.
10 For who has despised the day of small
things?
For these seven rejoice to see
The plumb line in the hand of
Zerubbabel.
They are the eyes of the LORD,
Which scan to and fro throughout the
whole earth."

11 Then I answered and said to him,
"What are these two olive trees, one at the

right of the lampstand and the other at its
left?"
12 And I further answered and said to
him, "What are these two olive branches
that drip into the receptacles[3] of the two
gold pipes from which the golden oil
drains?"
13 Then he answered me and said, "Do
you not know what these are?" And I
said, "No, my lord."
14 So he said, "These are the two
anointed ones, who stand beside the Lord
of the whole earth."

Vision of the Flying Scroll

5 Then I turned and raised my eyes,
and saw there a flying scroll.
2 And he said to me, "What do you
see?" So I answered, "I see a flying
scroll. Its length is twenty cubits and its
width ten cubits."
3 Then he said to me, "This is the curse
that goes out over the face of the whole
earth: 'Every thief shall be expelled,' according to what is on this side of the scroll;
and, 'Every perjurer shall be expelled,'
according to what is on that side of it."

4 "I will send out the curse,"
says the LORD of hosts;
"It shall enter the house of the thief
And the house of the one who swears
falsely by My name.
It shall remain in the midst of his
house
And consume it,
with its timber and stones."

Vision of the Woman in a Basket

5 Then the angel who talked with me
came out and said to me, "Lift your eyes
now, and see what this is that goes forth."
6 So I asked, "What is it?" And he said,
"It is a basket[4] that is going forth." He
also said, "This is their resemblance
throughout the earth:
7 "Here is a lead disc lifted up, and this
is a woman sitting inside the basket";
8 then he said, "This is Wickedness!"
And he thrust her down into the basket,
and threw the lead cover[5] over its mouth.
9 Then I raised my eyes and looked,
and there were two women, coming with
the wind in their wings; for they had
wings like the wings of a stork, and they
lifted up the basket between earth and
heaven.

2 Literally house 3 Literally into the hands of 4 Hebrew ephah, a measuring container, and so elsewhere
5 Literally stone

10 So I said to the angel who talked with me, "Where are they carrying the basket?"

11 And he said to me, "To build a house for it in the land of Shinar;[6] when it is ready, *the basket* will be set there on its base."

Vision of the Four Chariots

6 Then I turned and raised my eyes and looked, and behold, four chariots *were* coming from between two mountains, and the mountains *were* mountains of bronze.

2 With the first chariot *were* red horses, with the second chariot black horses,

3 with the third chariot white horses, and with the fourth chariot dappled horses—strong *steeds*.

4 Then I answered and said to the angel who talked with me, "What *are* these, my lord?"

5 And the angel answered and said to me, "These *are* four spirits of heaven, who go out from *their* station before the Lord of all the earth.

6 "The one with the black horses is going to the north country, the white are going after them, and the dappled are going toward the south country."

7 Then the strong *steeds* went out, eager to go, that they might walk to and fro throughout the earth. And He said, "Go, walk to and fro throughout the earth." So they walked to and fro throughout the earth.

8 And He called to me, and spoke to me, saying, "See, those who go toward the north country have given rest to My Spirit in the north country."

The Command to Crown Joshua

9 Then the word of the Lord came to me, saying:

10 "Receive *the gift* from the captives— from Heldai, Tobijah, and Jedaiah, who have come from Babylon—and go the same day and enter the house of Josiah the son of Zephaniah.

11 "Take the silver and gold, make an elaborate crown, and set *it* on the head of Joshua the son of Jehozadak, the high priest.

12 "Then speak to him, saying, 'Thus says the Lord of hosts, saying:

"Behold, the Man whose name *is* the BRANCH!

From His place He shall branch out, And He shall build the temple of the Lord;

13 Yes, He shall build the temple of the Lord.

He shall bear the glory, And shall sit and rule on His throne; So He shall be a priest on His throne, And the counsel of peace shall be between them both." '

14 "Now the elaborate crown shall be for a memorial in the temple of the Lord for Helem, Tobijah, Jedaiah, and Hen the son of Zephaniah.

15 "Even *those who* are far away shall come and build the temple of the Lord. Then you shall know that the Lord of hosts has sent Me to you. And *this* shall come to pass if you diligently obey the voice of the Lord your God."

Obedience Better than Fasting

7 Now in the fourth year of King Darius it came to pass *that* the word of the Lord came to Zechariah, on the fourth day of the ninth month, *which is* Chislev,

2 when the people[7] sent Sherezer,[8] with Regem-Melech and his men, *to* the house of God,[9] to pray before the Lord,

3 *and* to ask the priests who *were* in the house of the Lord of hosts, and the prophets, saying, "Should I weep in the fifth month and fast as I have done for so many years?"

4 Then the word of the Lord of hosts came to me, saying,

5 "Say to all the people of the land, and to the priests: 'When you fasted and mourned in the fifth and seventh *months* during those seventy years, did you really fast for Me—for Me?

6 'When you eat and when you drink, do you not eat and drink *for yourselves?*

7 '*Should you* not *have obeyed* the words which the Lord proclaimed through the former prophets when Jerusalem and the cities around it were inhabited and prosperous, and the South[10] and the Lowland were inhabited?' "

Disobedience Resulted in Exile

8 Then the word of the Lord came to Zechariah, saying,

9 "Thus says the Lord of hosts:

---

6 That is, Babylon   7 Literally *they* (compare verse 5)   8 Or *Sar-Ezer*   9 Hebrew *Bethel*   10 Hebrew *Negev*

'Execute true justice,
Show mercy and compassion
Everyone to his brother.
10 Do not oppress the widow or the
   fatherless,
The alien or the poor.
Let none of you plan evil in his heart
Against his brother.'

11 "But they refused to heed, shrugged
their shoulders, and stopped their ears so
that they could not hear.
12 "Yes, they made their hearts like flint,
refusing to hear the law and the words
which the LORD of hosts had sent by His
Spirit through the former prophets. Thus
great wrath came from the LORD of hosts.
13 "Therefore it happened, *that* just as
He proclaimed and they would not hear,
so they called out and I would not listen,"
says the LORD of hosts.
14 "But I scattered them with a whirlwind among all the nations which they
had not known. Thus the land became
desolate after them, so that no one passed
through or returned; for they made the
pleasant land desolate."

Jerusalem, Holy City of the Future

8 Again the word of the LORD of hosts
came, saying,
2 "Thus says the LORD of hosts:

'I am zealous for Zion with great zeal;
With great fervor I am zealous for her.'

3 "Thus says the LORD:

'I will return to Zion,
And dwell in the midst of Jerusalem.
Jerusalem shall be called
   the City of Truth,
The Mountain of the LORD of hosts,
The Holy Mountain.'

4 "Thus says the LORD of hosts:

'Old men and old women shall again sit
In the streets of Jerusalem,
Each one with his staff in his hand
Because of great age.
5 The streets of the city
Shall be full of boys and girls
Playing in its streets.'

6 "Thus says the LORD of hosts:

'If it is marvelous in the eyes of the
   remnant of this people in these days,

Will it also be marvelous in My eyes?'
Says the LORD of hosts.

7 "Thus says the LORD of hosts:

'Behold, I will save My people
   from the land of the east
And from the land of the west;
8 I will bring them *back*,
And they shall dwell in the midst of
   Jerusalem.
They shall be My people
And I will be their God,
In truth and righteousness.'

9 "Thus says the LORD of hosts:

'Let your hands be strong,
You who have been hearing in these
   days
These words by the mouth of the
   prophets,
Who were in the day
That the foundation was laid
For the house of the LORD of hosts,
That the temple might be built.
10 For before these days
There were no wages for man
   nor any hire for beast;
There was no peace from the enemy for
   whoever went out or came in;
For I set all men, everyone, against his
   neighbor.

11 'But now I *will* not *treat* the remnant
of this people as in the former days,' says
the LORD of hosts.

12 'For the seed *shall be* prosperous,
The vine shall give its fruit,
The ground shall give her increase,
And the heavens shall give their dew.
I will cause the remnant of this people
To possess all these *things.*
13 And it shall come to pass
That just as you were a curse among
   the nations,
O house of Judah and house of Israel,
So I will save you,
   and you shall be a blessing.
Do not fear,
Let your hands be strong.'

14 "For thus says the LORD of hosts:

'Just as I determined to punish you
When your fathers provoked Me to
   wrath,'
Says the LORD of hosts,
'And I would not relent,

15 So again in these days
I am determined to do good
To Jerusalem
 and to the house of Judah.
Do not fear.
16 These *are* the things you shall do:
Speak each man the truth to his
 neighbor;
Give judgment in your gates for truth,
 justice, and peace;
17 Let none of you think evil in your[11]
 heart against your neighbor;
And do not love a false oath.
For all these *are things* that I hate,'
Says the LORD."

18 Then the word of the LORD of hosts
came to me, saying,
19 "Thus says the LORD of hosts:

'The fast of the fourth *month,*
The fast of the fifth,
The fast of the seventh,
And the fast of the tenth,
Shall be joy and gladness
 and cheerful feasts
For the house of Judah.
Therefore love truth and peace.'

20 "Thus says the LORD of hosts:

'Peoples shall yet come,
Inhabitants of many cities;
21 The inhabitants of one *city* shall go to
 another, saying,
"Let us continue to go
 and pray before the LORD,
And seek the LORD of hosts.
I myself will go also."
22 Yes, many peoples and strong nations
Shall come to seek the LORD of hosts
 in Jerusalem,
And to pray before the LORD.'

23 "Thus says the LORD of hosts: 'In
those days ten men from every language
of the nations shall grasp the sleeve of a
Jewish man, saying, "Let us go with you,
for we have heard *that* God *is* with
you." ' "

Israel Defended Against Enemies

9 The burden[12] of the word of the LORD
 Against the land of Hadrach,
And Damascus its resting place
(For the eyes of men
And all the tribes of Israel
Are on the LORD);
2 Also *against* Hamath,
 which borders on it,

And *against* Tyre and Sidon,
 though they are very wise.
3 For Tyre built herself a tower,
Heaped up silver like the dust,
And gold like the mire of the streets.
4 Behold, the LORD will cast her out;
He will destroy her power in the sea,
And she will be devoured by fire.

5 Ashkelon shall see it and fear;
Gaza also shall be very sorrowful;
And Ekron,
 for He dried up her expectation.
The king shall perish from Gaza,
And Ashkelon shall not be inhabited.

6 "A mixed race shall settle in Ashdod,
And I will cut off the pride of the
 Philistines.
7 I will take away the blood
 from his mouth,
And the abominations
 from between his teeth.
But he who remains,
 even he *shall be* for our God,
And shall be like a leader in Judah,
And Ekron like a Jebusite.
8 I will camp around My house
Because of the army,
Because of him who passes by
 and him who returns.
No more shall an oppressor pass
 through them,
For now I have seen with My eyes.

The Coming King

9 "Rejoice greatly, O daughter of Zion!
Shout, O daughter of Jerusalem!
Behold, your King is coming to you;
He *is* just and having salvation,
Lowly and riding on a donkey,
 A colt, the foal of a donkey.
10 I will cut off the chariot from Ephraim
And the horse from Jerusalem;
The battle bow shall be cut off.
He shall speak peace to the nations;
His dominion *shall be* 'from sea to sea,
And from the River
 to the ends of the earth.'[13]

God Will Save His People

11 "As for you also,
Because of the blood of your covenant,
I will set your prisoners free from the
 waterless pit.
12 Return to the stronghold,
You prisoners of hope.

11 Literally *his* 12 Or *oracle* 13 Compare Psalm 72:8

Allow God to Do the Unexpected

When Jesus rode into Jerusalem on a donkey during Passover week, His reception was overwhelming. Multitudes rushed out to greet Him shouting, "Hosanna! Blessed *is* He who comes in the name of the LORD!" (Mark 11:9). They threw palm branches and garments down in Jesus' path as they welcomed Him into the city.

The people had been yearning for a messiah. They longed for a political leader to lead them in a revolt against Rome. Their actions confirm that they expected Jesus to assume this role. "Hosanna" meaning "save now," in the Jewish religion was often a salute to kings. Their shouts of "Blessed *is* He who comes in the name of the Lord," referred to a kingly political leader who would deliver the Jews from the oppression of the Romans. As they threw palm branches in front of Jesus they performed an act which represented freedom. Many coins used in the temple during the New Testament period bear inscriptions of palm branches. This was a symbol of Jewish nationalism. The Romans had reason to be concerned.

But God did not send Jesus to simply establish a political kingdom. Christ's kingdom was much, much more. Not until after His death and resurrection did the disciples and the other followers realize what Jesus' kingdom was all about. It did not consist of swords, arms, and a political dictatorship. Rather, His was a kingdom of hope, love, and forgiveness.

The people all expected a king, a political messiah. But God did the unexpected. He did the impossible. When God raised Jesus Christ from the dead, He freed them of their oppression of sin, death, and despair. Unlock your thinking and lock in your faith. Allow God to do the unexpected. Let Him accomplish the impossible in your life!

Even today I declare
That I will restore double to you.
13 For I have bent Judah, My *bow,*
Fitted the bow with Ephraim,
And raised up your sons, O Zion,
Against your sons, O Greece,
And made you like the sword of a
   mighty man."

14 Then the LORD will be seen over them,
And His arrow will go forth like
   lightning.
The Lord GOD will blow the trumpet,
And go with whirlwinds from the
   south.
15 The LORD of hosts will defend them;
They shall devour and subdue with
   sling stones.
They shall drink *and* roar as if with
   wine;
They shall be filled *with blood* like
   basins,
Like the corners of the altar.
16 The LORD their God will save them in
   that day,
As the flock of His people.
For they *shall be like* the jewels of a
   crown,
Lifted like a banner over His land—
17 For how great is their[14] goodness
And how great their beauty!
Grain shall make the young men
   thrive,
And new wine the young women.

Restoration of Judah and Israel

10 Ask the LORD for rain
In the time of the latter rain.[15]
The LORD will make flashing clouds;
He will give them showers of rain,
Grass in the field for everyone.

2 For the idols[16] speak delusion;
The diviners envision lies,
And tell false dreams;
They comfort in vain.
Therefore the people[17] wend their way
   like sheep;
They are in trouble because *there is* no
   shepherd.

3 "My anger is kindled against the
   shepherds,
And I will punish the goatherds.
For the LORD of hosts will visit His
   flock,
The house of Judah,
And will make them as His royal horse
   in the battle.

4 From him comes the cornerstone,
From him the tent peg,
From him the battle bow,
From him every ruler[18] together.
5 They shall be like mighty *men,*
Who tread down *their enemies*
In the mire of the streets in the battle.
They shall fight because the LORD is
   with them,
And the riders on horses shall be put
   to shame.

6 "I will strengthen the house of Judah,
And I will save the house of Joseph.
I will bring them back,
Because I have mercy on them.
They shall be as though I had not cast
   them aside;
For I *am* the LORD their God,
And I will hear them.
7 *Those of* Ephraim shall be
   like a mighty man,
And their heart shall rejoice
   as if with wine.
Yes, their children shall see *it*
   and be glad;
Their heart shall rejoice in the LORD.
8 I will whistle for them
   and gather them,
For I will redeem them;
And they shall increase as they once
   increased.

9 "I will sow them among the peoples,
And they shall remember Me in far
   countries;
They shall live,
   together with their children,
And they shall return.
10 I will also bring them back from the
   land of Egypt,
And gather them from Assyria.
I will bring them into the land of
   Gilead and Lebanon,
Until no *more room* is found for them.
11 He shall pass through the sea with
   affliction,
And strike the waves of the sea:
All the depths of the River[19]
   shall dry up.
Then the pride of Assyria shall be
   brought down,
And the scepter of Egypt shall depart.

12 "So I will strengthen them in the LORD,
And they shall walk up and down in
   His name,"
Says the LORD.

---

14 Literally *his*   15 That is, spring rain   16 Hebrew *teraphim*   17 Literally *they*   18 Or *despot*
19 That is, the Nile

Desolation of Israel

11 Open your doors, O Lebanon,
That fire may devour your cedars.
2 Wail, O cypress,
for the cedar has fallen,
Because the mighty *trees* are ruined.
Wail, O oaks of Bashan,
For the thick forest has come down.
3 *There is* the sound of wailing
shepherds!
For their glory is in ruins.
There is the sound of roaring lions!
For the pride[20] of the Jordan is in
ruins.

Prophecy of the Shepherds

4 Thus says the LORD my God, "Feed
the flock for slaughter,
5 "whose owners slaughter them and
feel no guilt; those who sell them say,
'Blessed be the LORD, for I am rich'; and
their shepherds do not pity them.
6 "For I will no longer pity the inhabitants of the land," says the LORD. "But
indeed I will give everyone into his neighbor's hand and into the hand of his king.
They shall attack the land, and I will not
deliver *them* from their hand."
7 So I fed the flock for slaughter, in particular the poor of the flock. I took for
myself two staffs: the one I called
Beauty,[21] and the other I called Bonds;[22]
and I fed the flock.
8 I dismissed the three shepherds in one
month. My soul loathed them, and their
soul also abhorred me.
9 Then I said, "I will not feed you. Let
what is dying die, and what is perishing
perish. Let those that are left eat each
other's flesh."
10 And I took my staff, Beauty, and cut
it in two, that I might break the covenant
which I had made with all the peoples.
11 So it was broken on that day. Thus
the poor of the flock, who were watching
me, knew that it *was* the word of the
LORD.
12 Then I said to them, "If it is agreeable
to you, give *me* my wages; and if not, refrain." So they weighed out for my wages
thirty *pieces* of silver.
13 And the LORD said to me, "Throw it
to the potter"—that princely price they
set on me. So I took the thirty *pieces* of
silver and threw them into the house of
the LORD for the potter.

14 Then I cut in two my other staff,
Bonds, that I might break the brotherhood between Judah and Israel.
15 And the LORD said to me, "Next, take
for yourself the implements of a foolish
shepherd.
16 "For indeed I will raise up a shepherd
in the land *who* will not care for those
who are cut off, nor seek the young, nor
heal those that are broken, nor feed those
that still stand. But he will eat the flesh
of the fat and tear their hooves in pieces.

17 Woe to the worthless shepherd,
Who leaves the flock!
A sword *shall be* against his arm
And against his right eye;
His arm shall completely wither,
And his right eye shall be totally
blinded.

The Coming Deliverance of Judah

12 The burden[23] of the word of the
LORD against Israel. Thus says
the LORD, who stretches out the heavens,
lays the foundation of the earth, and
forms the spirit of man within him:
2 "Behold, I will make Jerusalem a cup
of drunkenness to all the surrounding
peoples, when they lay siege against Judah and Jerusalem.
3 "And it shall happen in that day that
I will make Jerusalem a very heavy stone
for all peoples; all who would heave it
away will surely be cut in pieces, though
all nations of the earth are gathered
against it.
4 "In that day," says the LORD, "I will
strike every horse with confusion, and its
rider with madness; I will open My eyes
on the house of Judah, and will strike every horse of the peoples with blindness.
5 "And the governors of Judah shall say
in their heart, 'The inhabitants of Jerusalem *are* my strength in the LORD of hosts,
their God.'
6 "In that day I will make the governors
of Judah like a firepan in the woodpile,
and like a fiery torch in the sheaves; they
shall devour all the surrounding peoples
on the right hand and on the left, but Jerusalem shall be inhabited again in her
own place—Jerusalem.
7 "The LORD will save the tents of Judah first, so that the glory of the house of
David and the glory of the inhabitants of
Jerusalem shall not become greater than
that of Judah.

20 Or *thicket, flood plain*   21 Or *Grace* (also at verse 10)   22 Or *Unity* (also at verse 14)   23 Or *oracle*

8 "In that day the LORD will defend the inhabitants of Jerusalem; the one who is feeble among them in that day shall be like David, and the house of David *shall be* like God, like the Angel of the LORD before them. 9 "It shall be in that day *that* I will seek to destroy all the nations that come against Jerusalem.

Mourning for the Pierced One

10 "And I will pour on the house of David and on the inhabitants of Jerusalem the Spirit of grace and supplication; then they will look on Me whom they have pierced; they will mourn for Him as one mourns for *his* only *son*, and grieve for Him as one grieves for a firstborn. 11 "In that day there shall be a great mourning in Jerusalem, like the mourning at Hadad Rimmon in the plain of Megiddo.[24] 12 "And the land shall mourn, every family by itself: the family of the house of David by itself, and their wives by themselves; the family of the house of Nathan by itself, and their wives by themselves; 13 "the family of the house of Levi by itself, and their wives by themselves; the family of Shimei by itself, and their wives by themselves; 14 "all the families that remain, every family by itself, and their wives by themselves.

Idolatry Cut Off

13 "In that day a fountain shall be opened for the house of David and for the inhabitants of Jerusalem, for sin and for uncleanness. 2 "It shall be in that day," says the LORD of hosts, "*that* I will cut off the names of the idols from the land, and they shall no longer be remembered. I will also cause the prophets and the unclean spirit to depart from the land. 3 "It shall come to pass *that* if anyone still prophesies, then his father and mother who begot him will say to him, 'You shall not live, because you have spoken lies in the name of the LORD.' And his father and mother who begot him shall thrust him through when he prophesies. 4 "And it shall be in that day *that* every prophet will be ashamed of his vision

when he prophesies; they will not wear a robe of coarse hair to deceive. 5 "But he will say, 'I *am* no prophet, I *am* a farmer; for a man taught me to keep cattle from my youth.' 6 "And *someone* will say to him, 'What are these wounds in your hands?' Then he will answer, '*Those* with which I was wounded in the house of my friends.'

The Shepherd Savior

7 "Awake, O sword, against My Shepherd,
 Against the Man who is My
  Companion,"
 Says the LORD of hosts.
 "Strike the Shepherd,
 And the sheep will be scattered;
 Then I will turn My hand against the
  little ones.
8 And it shall come to pass in all the
  land,"
 Says the LORD,
 "*That* two thirds in it shall be cut off
  and die,
 But *one* third shall be left in it:
9 I will bring the *one* third through the
  fire,
 Will refine them as silver is refined,
 And test them as gold is tested.
 They will call on My name,
 And I will answer them.
 I will say, 'This *is* My people';
 And each one will say,
 'The LORD *is* my God.' "

The Day of the LORD

14 Behold, the day of the LORD is
  coming,
 And your spoil will be divided in your
  midst.
2 For I will gather all the nations to
  battle against Jerusalem;
 The city shall be taken,
 The houses rifled,
 And the women ravished.
 Half of the city shall go into captivity,
 But the remnant of the people shall not
  be cut off from the city.
3 Then the LORD will go forth
 And fight against those nations,
 As He fights in the day of battle.
4 And in that day His feet will stand on
  the Mount of Olives,
 Which faces Jerusalem on the east.
 And the Mount of Olives shall be split
  in two,
 From east to west,
 Making a very large valley;

24 Hebrew *Megiddon*

Half of the mountain shall move
toward the north
And half of it toward the south.
5 Then you shall flee *through* My
mountain valley,
For the mountain valley shall reach to
Azal.
Yes, you shall flee
As you fled from the earthquake
In the days of Uzziah king of Judah.
Thus the LORD my God will come,
And all the saints with You.[25]

6 It shall come to pass in that day
That there will be no light;
The lights will diminish.
7 It shall be one day
Which is known to the LORD—
Neither day nor night.
But at evening time it shall happen
That it will be light.

8 And in that day it shall be
That living waters shall flow from
Jerusalem,
Half of them toward the eastern sea
And half of them toward the western
sea;
In both summer and winter it shall
occur.
9 And the LORD shall be King over all
the earth.
In that day it shall be—
"The LORD *is* one,"[26]
And His name one.

10 All the land shall be turned into a
plain from Geba to Rimmon south of
Jerusalem. Jerusalem[27] shall be raised up
and inhabited in her place from Benjamin's Gate to the place of the First Gate
and the Corner Gate, and *from* the Tower
of Hananeel to the king's winepresses.

11 *The people* shall dwell in it;
And no longer shall there be utter
destruction,
But Jerusalem shall be safely inhabited.

12 And this shall be the plague with
which the LORD will strike all the people
who fought against Jerusalem:

Their flesh shall dissolve
while they stand on their feet,
Their eyes shall dissolve
in their sockets,

And their tongues shall dissolve
in their mouths.

13 It shall come to pass in that day
That a great panic from the LORD
will be among them.
Everyone will seize the hand of his
neighbor,
And raise his hand against his
neighbor's hand;
14 Judah also will fight at Jerusalem.
And the wealth of all the surrounding
nations
Shall be gathered together:
Gold, silver, and apparel in great
abundance.

15 Such also shall be the plague
On the horse *and* the mule,
On the camel and the donkey,
And on all the cattle that will be in
those camps.
So *shall* this plague *be.*

The Nations Worship the King

16 And it shall come to pass *that* everyone who is left of all the nations which
came against Jerusalem shall go up from
year to year to worship the King, the
LORD of hosts, and to keep the Feast of
Tabernacles.
17 And it shall be *that* whichever of the
families of the earth do not come up to
Jerusalem to worship the King, the LORD
of hosts, on them there will be no rain.
18 If the family of Egypt will not come
up and enter in, they *shall have* no *rain*;
they shall receive the plague with which
the LORD strikes the nations who do not
come up to keep the Feast of Tabernacles.
19 This shall be the punishment of Egypt
and the punishment of all the nations
that do not come up to keep the Feast of
Tabernacles.
20 In that day "HOLINESS TO THE
LORD" shall be *engraved* on the bells of
the horses. The pots in the LORD's house
shall be like the bowls before the altar.
21 Yes, every pot in Jerusalem and Judah
shall be holiness to the LORD of hosts.[28]
Everyone who sacrifices shall come and
take them and cook in them. In that day
there shall no longer be a Canaanite in
the house of the LORD of hosts.

25 The ancient versions and some Hebrew manuscripts read *Him.*   26 Compare Deuteronomy 6:4   27 Literally *she*
28 Or *on every pot . . . shall be (engraved)* "HOLINESS TO THE LORD OF HOSTS"

Introduction to Malachi

The Book of Malachi was written sometime between 450 and 400 B.C. following Israel's return from captivity in Babylon. Malachi sought to bring the people back to a pure worship of God, encouraging them to shed the cultural and pagan practices they had adopted while in exile.

The temple in Jerusalem had been rebuilt, but the people were ignorant as to how they were to worship God. General lack of belief in God's providential care led the people to steal from the temple by not tithing. Their life-styles revealed a lack of trust in God's ability to provide for their needs.

Malachi presented twenty-three probing questions between God and the people in a self-examining essay. He allowed the nation to see for itself that they had turned from God. Malachi then assured them that God loved them and had promised to make them "My jewels" (Mal. 3:17). By affirming God's love toward them, Malachi was able to prepare their hearts for a relationship with God.

Malachi was one in a long series of prophets that God raised up to keep His light of love, hope, and forgiveness shining. Malachi was the last prophet in the Old Testament. His words to the people prepared them for the "four hundred silent years," during which they would have no other prophets to lead them. Generations were to cling to the hope of the coming Messiah for over four centuries, during which they would suffer greatly under Alexander the Great, the Seleucids, the Ptolemies, and the Romans.

Malachi not only taught them to await the Savior of the world, but to live a positive life of faith. He urged them to give freely, promising that by doing so God would return their gifts sevenfold. The words of Malachi enabled the people to trust God and to take Him at His word. Then they were able to live positively and hold on to hope!

The Book of
Malachi

THE burden[1] of the word of the LORD to Israel by Malachi.

Israel Beloved of God

2 "I have loved you," says the LORD.
"Yet you say,
'In what way have You loved us?'
"*Was* not Esau Jacob's brother?"
Says the LORD.
"Yet Jacob I have loved;
3 But Esau I have hated,
And laid waste his mountains
and his heritage
For the jackals of the wilderness."

4 Even though Edom has said,
"We have been impoverished,
But we will return
and build the desolate places,"

Thus says the LORD of hosts:

"They may build,
but I will throw down;
They shall be called the Territory of
Wickedness,
And the people against whom the
LORD will have indignation forever.
5 Your eyes shall see,
And you shall say,
'The LORD is magnified beyond the
border of Israel.'

Polluted Offerings

6 "A son honors *his* father,
And a servant *his* master.
If then I am the Father,
Where *is* My honor?
And if I *am* a Master,
Where *is* My reverence?
Says the LORD of hosts
To you priests who despise My name.
Yet you say, 'In what way have we
despised Your name?'

7 "*You* offer defiled food on My altar.
But you say,
'In what way have we defiled You?'
By saying,
'The table of the LORD is contemptible.'
8 And when you offer the blind as a
sacrifice,
Is it not evil?

And when you offer the lame and sick,
Is it not evil?
Offer it then to your governor!
Would he be pleased with you?
Would he accept you favorably?"
Says the LORD of hosts.

9 "But now entreat God's favor,
That He may be gracious to us.
While this is being *done* by your hands,
Will He accept you favorably?"
Says the LORD of hosts.
10 "Who *is there* even among you who
would shut the doors,
So that you would not kindle fire *on*
My altar in vain?
I have no pleasure in you,"
Says the LORD of hosts,
"Nor will I accept an offering from your
hands.
11 For from the rising of the sun,
even to its going down,
My name *shall be* great among the
Gentiles;
In every place incense *shall be* offered
to My name,
And a pure offering;
For My name shall be great among the
nations,"
Says the LORD of hosts.

12 "But you profane it,
In that you say,
'The table of the LORD[2] is defiled;
And its fruit, its food,
is contemptible.'
13 You also say,
'Oh, what a weariness!'
And you sneer at it,"
Says the LORD of hosts.
"And you bring the stolen,
the lame, and the sick;
Thus you bring an offering!
Should I accept this from your hand?"
Says the LORD.
14 "But cursed *be* the deceiver
Who has in his flock a male,
And makes a vow,
But sacrifices to the Lord what is
blemished—
For I *am* a great King,"
Says the LORD of hosts,

1 Or *oracle*   2 Masoretic Text reads *Lord.*

"And My name *is to be* feared among
the nations.

Corrupt Priests

2 "And now, O priests,
this commandment is for you.
² If you will not hear,
And if you will not take *it* to heart,
To give glory to My name,"
Says the LORD of hosts,
"I will send a curse upon you,
And I will curse your blessings.
Yes, I have cursed them already,
Because you do not take *it* to heart.

³ "Behold, I will rebuke your descendants
And spread refuse on your faces,
The refuse of your solemn feasts;
And *one* will take you away with it.
⁴ Then you shall know that I have sent
this commandment to you,
That My covenant with Levi may
continue,"
Says the LORD of hosts.
⁵ "My covenant was with him,
one of life and peace,
And I gave them to him *that he
might* fear *Me;*
So he feared Me
And was reverent before My name.
⁶ The law of truth³ was in his mouth,
And injustice was not found on his
lips.
He walked with Me in peace and
equity,
And turned many away from iniquity.

⁷ "For the lips of a priest should keep
knowledge,
And *people* should seek the law from
his mouth;
For he is the messenger of the LORD of
hosts.
⁸ But you have departed from the way;
You have caused many to stumble at
the law.
You have corrupted the covenant of
Levi,"
Says the LORD of hosts.
⁹ "Therefore I also have made you
contemptible and base
Before all the people,
Because you have not kept My ways
But have shown partiality in the law."

Treachery of Infidelity

10 Have we not all one Father?
Has not one God created us?

Why do we deal treacherously with one
another
By profaning the covenant of the
fathers?
¹¹ Judah has dealt treacherously,
And an abomination has been
committed in Israel and in
Jerusalem,
For Judah has profaned
The LORD's holy *institution* which He
loves:
He has married the daughter of a
foreign god.
¹² May the LORD cut off from the tents of
Jacob
The man who does this,
being awake and aware,⁴
And who brings an offering to the
LORD of hosts.

13 And this is the second thing you do:
You cover the altar of the LORD with
tears,
With weeping and crying;
So He does not regard the offering
anymore,
Nor receive *it* with good will from your
hands.
¹⁴ Yet you say, "For what reason?"
Because the LORD has been witness
Between you and the wife of your
youth,
With whom you have dealt
treacherously;
Yet she is your companion
And your wife by covenant.
¹⁵ But did He not make *them* one,
Having a remnant of the Spirit?
And why one?
He seeks godly offspring.
Therefore take heed to your spirit,
And let none deal treacherously with
the wife of his youth.

¹⁶ "For the LORD God of Israel says
That He hates divorce,
For it covers one's garment with
violence,"
Says the LORD of hosts.
"Therefore take heed to your spirit,
That you do not deal treacherously."

17 You have wearied the LORD with your
words;
Yet you say,
"In what way have we wearied *Him?*"
In that you say,
"Everyone who does evil
Is good in the sight of the LORD,

---

3 Or *true instruction*   4 Talmud and Vulgate read *teacher and student.*

And He delights in them,"
Or, "Where *is* the God of justice?"

The Coming Messenger

3 "Behold, I send My messenger,
And he will prepare the way
    before Me.
And the Lord, whom you seek,
Will suddenly come to His temple,
Even the Messenger of the covenant,
In whom you delight.
Behold, He is coming,"
Says the LORD of hosts.

2 "But who can endure the day of His
    coming?
And who can stand when He appears?
For He *is* like a refiner's fire
And like fuller's soap.
3   He will sit as a refiner
    and a purifier of silver;
He will purify the sons of Levi,
And purge them as gold and silver,
That they may offer to the LORD
An offering in righteousness.

4 "Then the offering of Judah
    and Jerusalem
Will be pleasant to the LORD,
As in the days of old,
As in former years.
5   And I will come near you for
    judgment;
I will be a swift witness
Against sorcerers,
Against adulterers,
Against perjurers,
Against those who exploit wage earners
    and widows and the fatherless,
And against those who turn away an
    alien—
Because they do not fear Me,"
Says the LORD of hosts.

6 "For I *am* the LORD, I do not change;
Therefore you are not consumed,
O sons of Jacob.
7   Yet from the days of your fathers
You have gone away from My
    ordinances
And have not kept *them.*
Return to Me,
    and I will return to you,"
Says the LORD of hosts.
"But you said,
'In what way shall we return?'

Do Not Rob God

8 "Will a man rob God?
Yet you have robbed Me!

But you say,
'In what way have we robbed You?'
In tithes and offerings.
9   You are cursed with a curse,
For you have robbed Me,
Even this whole nation.
10 Bring all the tithes into the storehouse,
That there may be food in My house,
And prove Me now in this,"
Says the LORD of hosts,
"If I will not open for you the windows
    of heaven
And pour out for you *such* blessing
That *there will* not *be room* enough *to*
    receive it.

11 "And I will rebuke the devourer for
    your sakes,
So that he will not destroy the fruit of
    your ground,
Nor shall the vine fail to bear fruit for
    you in the field,"
Says the LORD of hosts;
12 "And all nations will call you blessed,
For you will be a delightful land,"
Says the LORD of hosts.

The People Complain Harshly

13 "Your words have been harsh
    against Me,"
Says the LORD,
"Yet you say,
'What have we spoken against You?'
14 You have said,
'It is vain to serve God;
What profit *is it* that we have kept His
    ordinance,
And that we have walked as mourners
Before the LORD of hosts?
15 So now we call the proud blessed,
For those who do wickedness are
    raised up;
Yes, *those who* tempt God go free.' "

A Book of Remembrance

16 Then those who feared the LORD
    spoke to one another,
And the LORD listened
    and heard *them;*
So a book of remembrance was written
    before Him
For those who fear the LORD
And who meditate on His name.

17 "They shall be Mine,"
    says the LORD of hosts,
"On the day that I make them My
    jewels.[5]

5 Literally *special treasure*

And I will spare them
As a man spares his own son who
    serves him."
18 Then you shall again discern
Between the righteous and the wicked,
Between one who serves God
And one who does not serve Him.

The Great Day of God

4 "For behold, the day is coming,
    Burning like an oven,
And all the proud,
    yes, all who do wickedly will be
    stubble.
And the day which is coming shall
    burn them up,"
Says the LORD of hosts,
"That will leave them neither root
    nor branch.
2 But to you who fear My name
The Sun of Righteousness shall arise
With healing in His wings;
And you shall go out

And grow fat like stall-fed calves.
3 You shall trample the wicked,
For they shall be ashes under the soles
    of your feet
On the day that I do *this*,"
Says the LORD of hosts.

4 "Remember the Law of Moses,
    My servant,
Which I commanded him in Horeb for
    all Israel,
With the statutes and judgments.
5 Behold, I will send you Elijah the
    prophet
Before the coming of the great and
    dreadful day of the LORD.
6 And he will turn
The hearts of the fathers
    to the children,
And the hearts of the children
    to their fathers,
Lest I come and strike the earth with a
    curse."

Called to Prepare the Way

John the Baptist was unique to modern man. He was called by God to prepare the way for the earthly ministry of Jesus Christ.

The son of Elizabeth and Zacharias, a priest who carried out important temple functions, John the Baptist grew up in Jerusalem surrounded with a comfortable, cosmopolitan life-style. In society's terms, he had everything he wanted—prestige and religious stature. Yet when it came time for him to carry out his calling, he left his family and went to live in the wilderness of Judea. Here he lived a nomadic life-style. The Bible records that he ate locust and honey, perhaps a way of describing yogurt, the sweet milk of goats and the locust plant which grows wild in the wilderness.

John the Baptist carried on the majority of his ministry within earshot of the New Testament village of Jericho. Soon throngs of people from the mountains of Judea, Samaria, and beyond the Jordan came to hear John the Baptist. John encouraged them to believe in God. Romans, Jews, Samaritans, women—he accepted them all into a symbolic act of baptism and preparation for the coming of the Messiah, Jesus Christ.

A common practice among kings in ancient times was to send forth a scout to insure the road was safe, clear, and prepared before their journey. This was John the Baptist's task, only the road he made ready was the hearts and minds of men and women. He was "the voice of one crying in the wilderness: Prepare the way of the LORD, make His paths straight" (Matt. 3:3).

Those familiar with Jewish prophecies expected Elijah to come before the Messiah. When John the Baptist's disciples asked Jesus whether or not he was the Messiah, Jesus told them to inform John that "*the* blind see, *the* lame walk, *the* lepers are cleansed, *the* deaf hear, *the* dead are raised, *the* poor have the gospel preached to them" (Luke 7:22). Jesus then explained to His listeners, "What did you go out into the wilderness to see? . . . A prophet? [Elijah] . . . there is not a greater prophet than John the Baptist" (Luke 7:24–28).

In the Old Testament, Elijah was taken up into heaven just outside of Jericho. The fact that John the Baptist practiced most of his ministry in the very same district, must have stirred his listeners to remember the prophetic call, "Behold, I will send you Elijah the prophet" (Mal. 4:5).

John the Baptist prepared the way for Jesus Christ. Now that Christ has come, our responsibility continues to be the same: to prepare the hearts of men and women for the Good News of Jesus Christ. We are messengers called to prepare the way where we are, with whom we meet, and with what we have. Like John the Baptist, we can encourage others to believe in God. Our lives can be a living message of God's positive love and joy. Let us be bold enough to get out of our comfortable existence and share the exciting news—Jesus Christ has come!

The

NEW TESTAMENT

Introduction to Matthew

When one opens his life to Jesus Christ the positive possibilities are endless! Matthew writes to let his readers know that with God scars are turned into stars, obstacles into opportunities, hurts into hopes, sin into salvation, and shame into a positive self-esteem.

Matthew is the most orderly account of the Good News of Jesus Christ. Perhaps Matthew's training as a tax collector added to his organized presentation. The Gospel of Matthew was written primarily to Jews, containing more Old Testament quotations than any of the other Gospels. Almost exclusively, Matthew incorporates the phrase "that it might be fulfilled which was spoken by the prophets."

Matthew's knowledge of the Old Testament was unsurpassed. He was among many Jewish youth who memorized the Law and the Prophets by rote memory. They utilized songs and hand movements to assist in the memorization process. Four New Testament synagogues have been discovered in Palestine. Three of these have rooms known as the "midrash" room, a phrase referring to the compilation of Old Testament verses from various portions of Scripture and arranged to present evidence from the Law. Matthew uses a similar technique to present Jesus Christ as the Jewish Messiah who has fulfilled all the Old Testament prophecies concerning the Messiah.

Although Matthew is Jewish in his orientation, he writes with a gentile slant. This is most likely due to his association with the Romans and Greeks when he served as a tax collector on the famous *Via Maris*. He flavors his presentation with a universal outlook, especially when he records Jesus' last words:

Go therefore and make disciples of all the nations, baptizing them in the name of the Father and of the Son and of the Holy Spirit, teaching them to observe all things that I have commanded you; and lo, I am with you always, *even* to the end of the age.

(Matt. 28:19, 20)

The Gospel According to
Matthew

The Genealogy of Jesus Christ

THE book of the genealogy of Jesus Christ, the Son of David, the Son of Abraham:

2 Abraham begot Isaac, Isaac begot Jacob, and Jacob begot Judah and his brothers.

3 Judah begot Perez and Zerah by Tamar, Perez begot Hezron, and Hezron begot Ram.

4 Ram begot Amminadab, Amminadab begot Nahshon, and Nahshon begot Salmon.

5 Salmon begot Boaz by Rahab, Boaz begot Obed by Ruth, Obed begot Jesse,

6 and Jesse begot David the king.

David the king begot Solomon by her *who had been the wife* of Uriah.

7 Solomon begot Rehoboam, Rehoboam begot Abijah, and Abijah begot Asa.[1]

8 Asa begot Jehoshaphat, Jehoshaphat begot Joram, and Joram begot Uzziah.

9 Uzziah begot Jotham, Jotham begot Ahaz, and Ahaz begot Hezekiah.

10 Hezekiah begot Manasseh, Manasseh begot Amon,[2] and Amon begot Josiah.

11 Josiah begot Jeconiah and his brothers about the time they were carried away to Babylon.

12 And after they were brought to Babylon, Jeconiah begot Shealtiel, and Shealtiel begot Zerubbabel.

13 Zerubbabel begot Abiud, Abiud begot Eliakim, and Eliakim begot Azor.

14 Azor begot Zadok, Zadok begot Achim, and Achim begot Eliud.

15 Eliud begot Eleazar, Eleazar begot Matthan, and Matthan begot Jacob.

16 And Jacob begot Joseph the husband of Mary, of whom was born Jesus who is called Christ.

17 So all the generations from Abraham to David *are* fourteen generations, from David until the captivity in Babylon *are* fourteen generations, and from the captivity in Babylon until the Christ *are* fourteen generations.

Christ Born of Mary

18 Now the birth of Jesus Christ was as follows: After His mother Mary was betrothed to Joseph, before they came together, she was found with child of the Holy Spirit.

19 Then Joseph her husband, being a just *man*, and not wanting to make her a public example, was minded to put her away secretly.

20 But while he thought about these things, behold, an angel of the Lord appeared to him in a dream, saying, "Joseph, son of David, do not be afraid to take to you Mary your wife, for that which is conceived in her is of the Holy Spirit.

21 "And she will bring forth a Son, and you shall call His name JESUS, for He will save His people from their sins."

22 Now all this was done that it might be fulfilled which was spoken by the Lord through the prophet, saying:

23 *"Behold, a virgin shall be with child, and bear a Son, and they shall call His name Immanuel,"*[3] which is translated, "God with us."

24 Then Joseph, being aroused from sleep, did as the angel of the Lord commanded him and took to him his wife,

25 and did not know her till she had brought forth her firstborn Son.[4] And he called His name JESUS.

Wise Men from the East

2 Now after Jesus was born in Bethlehem of Judea in the days of Herod the king, behold, wise men from the East came to Jerusalem,

2 saying, "Where is He who has been born King of the Jews? For we have seen His star in the East and have come to worship Him."

3 When Herod the king heard *these things,* he was troubled, and all Jerusalem with him.

4 And when he had gathered all the

---

1 NU-Text reads *Asaph.*   2 NU-Text reads *Amos.*   3 Isaiah 7:14   4 NU-Text reads *a Son.*

The King by Might—
the King by Right

The obscure village of Bethlehem is located in the southland of Judah, a remote corner of the world where Abraham, Isaac, Jacob, and David the shepherd king, roamed the arid hillsides. The town's name literally means "house of bread." It was into this house of bread that Jesus, the Bread of Life, was born.

At the Child's birth, His newlywed parents, Joseph and Mary, named him Joshua, meaning "God Saves." But the world would know Him by His Greek name, Jesus. Following the thirty-three-day waiting period for new mothers, the young family journeyed to Jerusalem to offer their sacrifice at the temple. Theirs was a poor person's sacrifice: two small birds. It was at the temple that two Jerusalemites, Simeon and Anna, told Jesus' parents that they foresaw great things in the Child's future.

Jesus was immediately accepted as a king by wise men and humble working-class shepherds alike. But there was one man in the vicinity who was not happy about a baby born ruler of his people—that was the ruthless King Herod. Things began to turn sour in Herod's mind when he was visited in his plush Jerusalem palace by three trained specialists in the fields of natural sciences, astrology, and medicine. They reported their knowledge of an ancient prophecy by Micah that a ruler of Israel would come from Bethlehem.

For one who had acquired possession of his kingdom by political ingenuity, daring military campaign, and murderous persecution, this birth of a king was not easy to accept. Before, when his throne was threatened, Herod put to death anyone he remotely suspected, including many of his in-laws, one of his wives, and four of his sons. Now, he attempted trickery to enlist the help of the palace visitors, saying he also wanted to worship the Child, while hiding in his heart his intention of killing the infant.

Herod's plan was exposed to Joseph and Mary and the wise men by messengers sent from God. The wise men returned home a different route, while Mary and Joseph found safety in Egypt. Herod attempted to solve the "infant king" problem by slaying every male in the region two years and under.

Herod probably sent his soldiers from the magnificent fortress palace Herodian to carry out his orders. The close proximity of Bethlehem to the Herodian vividly accents the contrast between Herod's cruel, material kingdom and the spiritual, life-giving kingdom of Jesus. Herod was a king by might. Jesus was a king by right. Born the Son of God, His divine birthright gave Him the authority and the power to establish God's kingdom forever!

chief priests and scribes of the people together, he inquired of them where the Christ was to be born.

5 So they said to him, "In Bethlehem of Judea, for thus it is written by the prophet:

6 'But you, Bethlehem, in the land
   of Judah,
   Are not the least among the rulers
   of Judah;
   For out of you shall come a Ruler
   Who will shepherd My people
   Israel.'" 5

7 Then Herod, when he had secretly called the wise men, determined from them what time the star appeared.

8 And he sent them to Bethlehem and said, "Go and search diligently for the young Child, and when you have found Him, bring back word to me, that I may come and worship Him also."

9 When they heard the king, they departed; and behold, the star which they had seen in the East went before them, till it came and stood over where the young Child was.

10 When they saw the star, they rejoiced with exceedingly great joy.

11 And when they had come into the house, they saw the young Child with Mary His mother, and fell down and worshiped Him. And when they had opened their treasures, they presented gifts to Him: gold, frankincense, and myrrh.

12 Then, being divinely warned in a dream that they should not return to Herod, they departed for their own country another way.

The Flight into Egypt

13 Now when they had departed, behold, an angel of the Lord appeared to Joseph in a dream, saying, "Arise, take the young Child and His mother, flee to Egypt, and stay there until I bring you word; for Herod will seek the young Child to destroy Him."

14 When he arose, he took the young Child and His mother by night and departed for Egypt,

15 and was there until the death of Herod, that it might be fulfilled which was spoken by the Lord through the prophet, saying, "Out of Egypt I called My Son." 6

Massacre of the Innocents

16 Then Herod, when he saw that he was deceived by the wise men, was exceedingly angry; and he sent forth and put to death all the male children who were in Bethlehem and in all its districts, from two years old and under, according to the time which he had determined from the wise men.

17 Then was fulfilled what was spoken by Jeremiah the prophet, saying:

18 "A voice was heard in Ramah,
    Lamentation, weeping,
      and great mourning,
    Rachel weeping for her children,
    Refusing to be comforted,
      because they were no more." 7

The Home in Nazareth

19 But when Herod was dead, behold, an angel of the Lord appeared in a dream to Joseph in Egypt,

20 saying, "Arise, take the young Child and His mother, and go to the land of Israel, for those who sought the young Child's life are dead."

21 Then he arose, took the young Child and His mother, and came into the land of Israel.

22 But when he heard that Archelaus was reigning over Judea instead of his father Herod, he was afraid to go there. And being warned by God in a dream, he turned aside into the region of Galilee.

23 And he came and dwelt in a city called Nazareth, that it might be fulfilled which was spoken by the prophets, "He shall be called a Nazarene."

John the Baptist Prepares the Way

3 In those days John the Baptist came preaching in the wilderness of Judea,

2 and saying, "Repent, for the kingdom of heaven is at hand!"

3 For this is he who was spoken of by the prophet Isaiah, saying:

"The voice of one crying
    in the wilderness:
'Prepare the way of the LORD,
   Make His paths straight.'" 8

4 And John himself was clothed in camel's hair, with a leather belt around his waist; and his food was locusts and wild honey.

5 Micah 5:2   6 Hosea 11:1   7 Jeremiah 31:15   8 Isaiah 40:3

5 Then Jerusalem, all Judea, and all the region around the Jordan went out to him 6 and were baptized by him in the Jordan, confessing their sins.
7 But when he saw many of the Pharisees and Sadducees coming to his baptism, he said to them, "Brood of vipers! Who has warned you to flee from the wrath to come?
8 "Therefore bear fruits worthy of repentance,
9 "and do not think to say to yourselves, 'We have Abraham as *our* father.' For I say to you that God is able to raise up children to Abraham from these stones.
10 "And even now the ax is laid to the root of the trees. Therefore every tree which does not bear good fruit is cut down and thrown into the fire.
11 "I indeed baptize you with water unto repentance, but He who is coming after me is mightier than I, whose sandals I am not worthy to carry. He will baptize you with the Holy Spirit and fire.[9]
12 "His winnowing fan *is* in His hand, and He will thoroughly purge His threshing floor, and gather His wheat into the barn; but He will burn up the chaff with unquenchable fire."

John Baptizes Jesus

13 Then Jesus came from Galilee to John at the Jordan to be baptized by him.
14 And John *tried to* prevent Him, saying, "I have need to be baptized by You, and are You coming to me?"
15 But Jesus answered and said to him, "Permit *it to be so* now, for thus it is fitting for us to fulfill all righteousness." Then he allowed Him.
16 Then Jesus, when He had been baptized, came up immediately from the water; and behold, the heavens were opened to Him, and He saw the Spirit of God descending like a dove and alighting upon Him.
17 And suddenly a voice *came* from heaven, saying, "This is My beloved Son, in whom I am well pleased."

Satan Tempts Jesus

4 Then Jesus was led up by the Spirit into the wilderness to be tempted by the devil.

2 And when He had fasted forty days and forty nights, afterward He was hungry.
3 Now when the tempter came to Him, he said, "If You are the Son of God, command that these stones become bread."
4 But He answered and said, "It is written, '*Man shall not live by bread alone, but by every word that proceeds from the mouth of God.*'"[10]
5 Then the devil took Him up into the holy city, set Him on the pinnacle of the temple,
6 and said to Him, "If You are the Son of God, throw Yourself down. For it is written:

'*He shall give His angels charge
    concerning you,*'

and,

'*In their hands they shall bear you up,
    Lest you dash your foot against a
    stone.*'"[11]

7 Jesus said to him, "It is written again, '*You shall not tempt the LORD your God.*'"[12]
8 Again, the devil took Him up on an exceedingly high mountain, and showed Him all the kingdoms of the world and their glory.
9 And he said to Him, "All these things I will give You if You will fall down and worship me."
10 Then Jesus said to him, "Away with you,[13] Satan! For it is written, '*You shall worship the LORD your God, and Him only you shall serve.*'"[14]
11 Then the devil left Him, and behold, angels came and ministered to Him.

Jesus Begins His Galilean Ministry

12 Now when Jesus heard that John had been put in prison, He departed to Galilee.
13 And leaving Nazareth, He came and dwelt in Capernaum, which is by the sea, in the regions of Zebulun and Naphtali,
14 that it might be fulfilled which was spoken by Isaiah the prophet, saying:

15 "*The land of Zebulun and the land
        of Naphtali,
    The way of the sea, beyond the Jordan,
        Galilee of the Gentiles:*
16 *The people who sat in darkness saw
        a great light,*

---

9 M-Text omits *and fire.*   10 Deuteronomy 8:3   11 Psalm 91:11, 12   12 Deuteronomy 6:16
13 M-Text reads *Get behind Me.*   14 Deuteronomy 6:13

And upon those who sat in the region
and shadow of death
Light has dawned."[15]

17 From that time Jesus began to preach and to say, "Repent, for the kingdom of heaven is at hand."

Four Fishermen Called as Disciples

18 Now Jesus, walking by the Sea of Galilee, saw two brothers, Simon called Peter, and Andrew his brother, casting a net into the sea; for they were fishermen. 19 And He said to them, "Follow Me, and I will make you fishers of men." 20 Then they immediately left *their* nets and followed Him. 21 And going on from there, He saw two other brothers, James *the son* of Zebedee, and John his brother, in the boat with Zebedee their father, mending their nets. And He called them, 22 and immediately they left the boat and their father, and followed Him.

Jesus Heals a Great Multitude

23 Now Jesus went about all Galilee, teaching in their synagogues, preaching the gospel of the kingdom, and healing all kinds of sickness and all kinds of disease among the people. 24 Then His fame went throughout all Syria; and they brought to Him all sick people who were afflicted with various diseases and torments, and those who were demon-possessed, epileptics, and paralytics; and He healed them. 25 And great multitudes followed Him—from Galilee, and *from* Decapolis, Jerusalem, Judea, and beyond the Jordan.

The Beatitudes

5 And seeing the multitudes, He went up on a mountain, and when He was seated His disciples came to Him. 2 Then He opened His mouth and taught them, saying:

3 "Blessed *are* the poor in spirit,
    For theirs is the kingdom of heaven.
4 Blessed *are* those who mourn,
    For they shall be comforted.
5 Blessed *are* the meek,
    For they shall inherit the earth.
6 Blessed *are* those who hunger and
        thirst for righteousness,
    For they shall be filled.

7 Blessed *are* the merciful,
    For they shall obtain mercy.
8 Blessed *are* the pure in heart,
    For they shall see God.
9 Blessed *are* the peacemakers,
    For they shall be called sons of God.
10 Blessed are those who are persecuted
        for righteousness' sake,
    For theirs is the kingdom of heaven.

11 "Blessed are you when they revile and persecute you, and say all kinds of evil against you falsely for My sake. 12 "Rejoice and be exceedingly glad, for great *is* your reward in heaven, for so they persecuted the prophets who were before you.

Believers Are Salt and Light

13 "You are the salt of the earth; but if the salt loses its flavor, how shall it be seasoned? It is then good for nothing but to be thrown out and trampled under foot by men. 14 "You are the light of the world. A city that is set on a hill cannot be hidden. 15 "Nor do they light a lamp and put it under a basket, but on a lampstand, and it gives light to all *who are* in the house. 16 "Let your light so shine before men, that they may see your good works and glorify your Father in heaven.

Christ Fulfills the Law

17 "Do not think that I came to destroy the Law or the Prophets. I did not come to destroy but to fulfill. 18 "For assuredly, I say to you, till heaven and earth pass away, one jot or one tittle will by no means pass from the law till all is fulfilled. 19 "Whoever therefore breaks one of the least of these commandments, and teaches men so, shall be called least in the kingdom of heaven; but whoever does and teaches *them*, he shall be called great in the kingdom of heaven. 20 "For I say to you, that unless your righteousness exceeds *the righteousness* of the scribes and Pharisees, you will by no means enter the kingdom of heaven.

Murder Begins in the Heart

21 "You have heard that it was said to those of old, 'You shall not murder,'[16] and whoever murders will be in danger of the judgment.

15 Isaiah 9:1, 2   16 Exodus 20:13; Deuteronomy 5:17

You Are the Light of the World

You are the light of the world. A city that is set on a hill cannot be hidden.

(Matt. 5:14)

Jesus spoke this promise to His followers overlooking the beautiful Sea of Galilee. Surrounded on all sides by high mountains, the lake is twelve miles long and seven miles wide. Nestled between these hills and the lake were many Jewish towns from which villagers came to hear Jesus.

Every evening the Jewish populace had a constant reminder of the oppression of their Roman overlords. At sundown, the mighty Roman legions lit bonfires at their hilltop command post as they guarded and maintained the famous thoroughfares, the *Via Maris*, and the King's Highway. In the first century as many as twelve to fourteen legions, each consisting of six thousand men were stationed in Galilee. Their fires were a spectacular sight from anywhere on the lake.

Jesus' illustration dramatically punctuated His teaching on the kingdom of God. His call to be a "light—a city that is set on a hill" was a challenge to His listeners. Archaeologists have discovered that as many as ninety Greco-Roman towns were set on the eastern hills. The lights from the town lamps burned brightly above the sea below. The faith of Jesus' listeners was to be as visible and bright to the people around them as were the lights from the towns and camps that lit up the evening sky.

Jesus' call is as alive today as it was when the bonfires encircled the Sea of Galilee. Your life will burn with enthusiasm and joy when you announce and advance the kingdom of God. It may begin with lighting one candle by touching one person in your world today. But soon the fire will spread. Your life will be a mighty roaring bonfire encircling your world with the warmth of God's love!

22 "But I say to you that whoever is angry with his brother without a cause[17] shall be in danger of the judgment. And whoever says to his brother, 'Raca!' shall be in danger of the council. But whoever says, 'You fool!' shall be in danger of hell fire.

23 "Therefore if you bring your gift to the altar, and there remember that your brother has something against you,

24 "leave your gift there before the altar, and go your way. First be reconciled to your brother, and then come and offer your gift.

25 "Agree with your adversary quickly, while you are on the way with him, lest your adversary deliver you to the judge, the judge hand you over to the officer, and you are thrown into prison.

26 "Assuredly, I say to you, you will by no means get out of there till you have paid the last penny.

Adultery in the Heart

27 "You have heard that it was said to those of old,[18] 'You shall not commit adultery.'[19]

28 "But I say to you that whoever looks at a woman to lust for her has already committed adultery with her in his heart.

29 "And if your right eye causes you to sin, pluck it out and cast it from you; for it is more profitable for you that one of your members perish, than for your whole body to be cast into hell.

30 "And if your right hand causes you to sin, cut it off and cast it from you; for it is more profitable for you that one of your members perish, than for your whole body to be cast into hell.

Marriage Is Sacred and Binding

31 "Furthermore it has been said, 'Whoever divorces his wife, let him give her a certificate of divorce.'[20]

32 "But I say to you that whoever divorces his wife for any reason except sexual immorality causes her to commit adultery; and whoever marries a woman who is divorced commits adultery.

Jesus Forbids Oaths

33 "Again you have heard that it was said to those of old, 'You shall not swear falsely, but shall perform your oaths to the Lord.'

34 "But I say to you, do not swear at all: neither by heaven, for it is God's throne;

35 "nor by the earth, for it is His footstool; nor by Jerusalem, for it is the city of the great King.

36 "Nor shall you swear by your head, because you cannot make one hair white or black.

37 "But let your 'Yes' be 'Yes,' and your 'No,' 'No.' For whatever is more than these is from the evil one.

Go the Second Mile

38 "You have heard that it was said, 'An eye for an eye and a tooth for a tooth.'[21]

39 "But I tell you not to resist an evil person. But whoever slaps you on your right cheek, turn the other to him also.

40 "If anyone wants to sue you and take away your tunic, let him have your cloak also.

41 "And whoever compels you to go one mile, go with him two.

42 "Give to him who asks you, and from him who wants to borrow from you do not turn away.

Love Your Enemies

43 "You have heard that it was said, 'You shall love your neighbor[22] and hate your enemy.'

44 "But I say to you, love your enemies, bless those who curse you, do good to those who hate you, and pray for those who spitefully use you and persecute you,[23]

45 "that you may be sons of your Father in heaven; for He makes His sun rise on the evil and on the good, and sends rain on the just and on the unjust.

46 "For if you love those who love you, what reward have you? Do not even the tax collectors do the same?

47 "And if you greet your brethren[24] only, what do you do more than others? Do not even the tax collectors[25] do so?

48 "Therefore you shall be perfect, just as your Father in heaven is perfect.

Do Good to Please God

6 "Take heed that you do not do your charitable deeds before men, to be

---

17 NU-Text omits without a cause.   18 NU-Text and M-Text omit to those of old.
19 Exodus 20:14; Deuteronomy 5:18   20 Deuteronomy 24:1
21 Exodus 21:24; Leviticus 24:20; Deuteronomy 19:21   22 Leviticus 19:18
23 NU-Text omits three clauses from this verse, leaving, "But I say to you, love your enemies and pray for those who persecute you."   24 M-Text reads friends.   25 NU-Text reads Gentiles.

seen by them. Otherwise you have no reward from your Father in heaven.

2 "Therefore, when you do a charitable deed, do not sound a trumpet before you as the hypocrites do in the synagogues and in the streets, that they may have glory from men. Assuredly, I say to you, they have their reward.

3 "But when you do a charitable deed, do not let your left hand know what your right hand is doing,

4 "that your charitable deed may be in secret; and your Father who sees in secret will Himself reward you openly.

The Model Prayer

5 "And when you pray, you shall not be like the hypocrites. For they love to pray standing in the synagogues and on the corners of the streets, that they may be seen by men. Assuredly, I say to you, they have their reward.

6 "But you, when you pray, go into your room, and when you have shut your door, pray to your Father who *is* in the secret *place*; and your Father who sees in secret will reward you openly.

7 "But when you pray, do not use vain repetitions as the heathen *do*. For they think that they will be heard for their many words.

8 "Therefore do not be like them. For your Father knows the things you have need of before you ask Him.

9 "In this manner, therefore, pray:

Our Father in heaven,
Hallowed be Your name.
10 Your kingdom come.
Your will be done
On earth as *it is* in heaven.
11 Give us this day our daily bread.
12 And forgive us our debts,
As we forgive our debtors.
13 And do not lead us into temptation,
But deliver us from the evil one.
For Yours is the kingdom and the
power and the glory forever.
Amen.[26]

14 "For if you forgive men their trespasses, your heavenly Father will also forgive you.

15 "But if you do not forgive men their trespasses, neither will your Father forgive your trespasses.

Fasting to Be Seen Only by God

16 "Moreover, when you fast, do not be like the hypocrites, with a sad countenance. For they disfigure their faces that they may appear to men to be fasting. Assuredly, I say to you, they have their reward.

17 "But you, when you fast, anoint your head and wash your face,

18 "so that you do not appear to men to be fasting, but to your Father who *is* in the secret *place*; and your Father who sees in secret will reward you openly.[27]

Lay Up Treasures in Heaven

19 "Do not lay up for yourselves treasures on earth, where moth and rust destroy and where thieves break in and steal;

20 "but lay up for yourselves treasures in heaven, where neither moth nor rust destroys and where thieves do not break in and steal.

21 "For where your treasure is, there your heart will be also.

The Lamp of the Body

22 "The lamp of the body is the eye. If therefore your eye is good, your whole body will be full of light.

23 "But if your eye is bad, your whole body will be full of darkness. If therefore the light that is in you is darkness, how great *is* that darkness!

You Cannot Serve God and Riches

24 "No one can serve two masters; for either he will hate the one and love the other, or else he will be loyal to the one and despise the other. You cannot serve God and mammon.

Do Not Worry

25 "Therefore I say to you, do not worry about your life, what you will eat or what you will drink; nor about your body, what you will put on. Is not life more than food and the body more than clothing?

26 "Look at the birds of the air, for they neither sow nor reap nor gather into barns; yet your heavenly Father feeds them. Are you not of more value than they?

27 "Which of you by worrying can add one cubit to his stature?

26 NU-Text omits *For Yours* through *Amen.*   27 NU-Text and M-Text omit *openly.*

28 "So why do you worry about clothing? Consider the lilies of the field, how they grow: they neither toil nor spin;

29 "and yet I say to you that even Solomon in all his glory was not arrayed like one of these.

30 "Now if God so clothes the grass of the field, which today is, and tomorrow is thrown into the oven, *will He* not much more *clothe* you, O you of little faith?

31 "Therefore do not worry, saying, 'What shall we eat?' or 'What shall we drink?' or 'What shall we wear?'

32 "For after all these things the Gentiles seek. For your heavenly Father knows that you need all these things.

33 "But seek first the kingdom of God and His righteousness, and all these things shall be added to you.

34 "Therefore do not worry about tomorrow, for tomorrow will worry about its own things. Sufficient for the day *is* its own trouble.

Do Not Judge

7 "Judge not, that you be not judged. 2 "For with what judgment you judge, you will be judged; and with the *same* measure you use, it will be measured back to you.

3 "And why do you look at the speck in your brother's eye, but do not consider the plank in your own eye?

4 "Or how can you say to your brother, 'Let me remove the speck out of your eye'; and look, a plank *is* in your own eye?

5 "Hypocrite! First remove the plank from your own eye, and then you will see clearly to remove the speck out of your brother's eye.

6 "Do not give what is holy to the dogs; nor cast your pearls before swine, lest they trample them under their feet, and turn and tear you in pieces.

Keep Asking, Seeking, Knocking

7 "Ask, and it will be given to you; seek, and you will find; knock, and it will be opened to you.

8 "For everyone who asks receives, and he who seeks finds, and to him who knocks it will be opened.

9 "Or what man is there among you who, if his son asks for bread, will give him a stone?

10 "Or if he asks for a fish, will he give him a serpent?

11 "If you then, being evil, know how to give good gifts to your children, how much more will your Father who is in heaven give good things to those who ask Him!

12 "Therefore, whatever you want men to do to you, do also to them, for this is the Law and the Prophets.

The Narrow Way

13 "Enter by the narrow gate; for wide *is* the gate and broad *is* the way that leads to destruction, and there are many who go in by it.

14 "Because[28] narrow *is* the gate and difficult *is* the way which leads to life, and there are few who find it.

You Will Know Them by Their Fruits

15 "Beware of false prophets, who come to you in sheep's clothing, but inwardly they are ravenous wolves.

16 "You will know them by their fruits. Do men gather grapes from thornbushes or figs from thistles?

17 "Even so, every good tree bears good fruit, but a bad tree bears bad fruit.

18 "A good tree cannot bear bad fruit, nor *can* a bad tree bear good fruit.

19 "Every tree that does not bear good fruit is cut down and thrown into the fire.

20 "Therefore by their fruits you will know them.

I Never Knew You

21 "Not everyone who says to Me, 'Lord, Lord,' shall enter the kingdom of heaven, but he who does the will of My Father in heaven.

22 "Many will say to Me in that day, 'Lord, Lord, have we not prophesied in Your name, cast out demons in Your name, and done many wonders in Your name?'

23 "And then I will declare to them, 'I never knew you; depart from Me, you who practice lawlessness!'

Build on the Rock

24 "Therefore whoever hears these sayings of Mine, and does them, I will liken him to a wise man who built his house on the rock:

25 "and the rain descended, the floods came, and the winds blew and beat on

28 NU-Text and M-Text read *How* . . . !

A House Built On Rock

On the slopes above the northwest shores of the Sea of Galilee, sits the ancient Jewish village of Chorazin. Matthew records that in this town many of Jesus' miracles took place. This village was also the origin for one of Jesus' most familiar teachings. Archaeologists have discovered first- and second-century remnants of the town which indicate that the village was built on the rocky slopes of the hill and in the adjacent waterbed below.

In this region a major mountain range running east to west caught most of the country's rainfall. The majority of the rain comes in the winter months, January and February. As much as thirty-seven inches of rain falls in the two-month span. The high density of water causes flash floods in the several watershed systems, including the Wadi Ammud where Chorazin is located. These wadis naturally drained water from the high mountain regions to the lake below.

Even today, it is not uncommon to see a ten-foot wall of water burst suddenly upon the plains surrounding the lake. Jesus vividly described the sudden floods that often roared without warning through the water systems. "Whoever hears these sayings of Mine, and does them, I will liken him to a wise man who built his house on the rock: and the rain descended, the floods came, and the winds blew and beat on that house; and it did not fall, for it was founded on the rock. Now everyone who hears these sayings of Mine, and does not do them, will be like a foolish man who built his house on the sand: and the rain descended, the floods came, and the winds blew and beat on that house; and it fell. And great was its fall" (Matt. 7:24-27).

Many structures of ancient houses from Jesus' day still stand—on the high rocks above. But in the sandy wadi below, only rubble remains bearing witness to the homes that were crushed by storms.

What is the foundation of your life? Set it high and firm on the rock of Jesus. Build your life on Him. When the winds and rains of life's problems descend on you—you will not fall—for you are founded on rock!

that house; and it did not fall, for it was founded on the rock.

26 "Now everyone who hears these sayings of Mine, and does not do them, will be like a foolish man who built his house on the sand:

27 "and the rain descended, the floods came, and the winds blew and beat on that house; and it fell. And great was its fall."

28 And so it was, when Jesus had ended these sayings, that the people were astonished at His teaching,

29 for He taught them as one having authority, and not as the scribes.

Jesus Cleanses a Leper

8 When He had come down from the mountain, great multitudes followed Him.

2 And behold, a leper came and worshiped Him, saying, "Lord, if You are willing, You can make me clean."

3 Then Jesus put out *His* hand and touched him, saying, "I am willing; be cleansed." And immediately his leprosy was cleansed.

4 And Jesus said to him, "See that you tell no one; but go your way, show yourself to the priest, and offer the gift that Moses commanded, as a testimony to them."

Jesus Heals a Centurion's Servant

5 Now when Jesus had entered Capernaum, a centurion came to Him, pleading with Him,

6 saying, "Lord, my servant is lying at home paralyzed, dreadfully tormented."

7 And Jesus said to him, "I will come and heal him."

8 The centurion answered and said, "Lord, I am not worthy that You should come under my roof. But only speak a word, and my servant will be healed.

9 "For I also am a man under authority, having soldiers under me. And I say to this *one,* 'Go,' and he goes; and to another, 'Come,' and he comes; and to my servant, 'Do this,' and he does *it.*"

10 When Jesus heard *it,* He marveled, and said to those who followed, "Assuredly, I say to you, I have not found such great faith, not even in Israel!

11 "And I say to you that many will come from east and west, and sit down with Abraham, Isaac, and Jacob in the kingdom of heaven.

12 "But the sons of the kingdom will be cast out into outer darkness. There will be weeping and gnashing of teeth."

13 Then Jesus said to the centurion, "Go your way; and as you have believed, *so* let it be done for you." And his servant was healed that same hour.

Peter's Mother-in-Law Healed

14 Now when Jesus had come into Peter's house, He saw his wife's mother lying sick with a fever.

15 And He touched her hand, and the fever left her. Then she arose and served them.[29]

Many Healed after Sabbath Sunset

16 When evening had come, they brought to Him many who were demon-possessed. And He cast out the spirits with a word, and healed all who were sick,

17 that it might be fulfilled which was spoken by Isaiah the prophet, saying:

*"He Himself took our infirmities
And bore our sicknesses."*[30]

The Cost of Discipleship

18 Now when Jesus saw great multitudes about Him, He gave a command to depart to the other side.

19 Then a certain scribe came and said to Him, "Teacher, I will follow You wherever You go."

20 And Jesus said to him, "Foxes have holes and birds of the air *have* nests, but the Son of Man has nowhere to lay *His* head."

21 Then another of His disciples said to Him, "Lord, let me first go and bury my father."

22 But Jesus said to him, "Follow Me, and let the dead bury their own dead."

Wind and Wave Obey Jesus

23 Now when He got into a boat, His disciples followed Him.

24 And suddenly a great tempest arose on the sea, so that the boat was covered with the waves. But He was asleep.

25 Then His disciples came to *Him* and awoke Him, saying, "Lord, save us! We are perishing!"

26 But He said to them, "Why are you

29 NU-Text and M-Text read *Him.*   30 Isaiah 53:4

Stilling the Storm

The Sea of Galilee is only twelve miles long, seven miles wide and seven hundred feet deep. Yet over her waters come some of the most ferocious, vicious storms in the Middle East. Why?

The Sea of Galilee is located scarcely fifty miles from the coast of the Mediterranean Sea. To the northeast of her rise the Syro-Phoenician mountains of Lebanon. When a low pressure system comes off the Mediterranean and clashes with a high pressure system from these mountains, the calm surface of the Sea of Galilee can be suddenly transformed into a raging storm with waves fifteen to twenty feet high.

It is a constant danger for fishermen to be out on the lake in the springtime and early fall, when the storms occur most frequently. During these seasons it is not uncommon for the weather to be perfect when the fishermen leave the seashore without a cloud in the sky. But within minutes the sky can become overcast and large swells can mount to toss their boats about.

During one of these storms Jesus and His disciples were at sea. As the storm raged more violently around them, Jesus stood up in the middle of the boat and yelled out into the face of the storm, "Peace, be still!" Immediately the storm subsided. The disciples wondered among themselves "Who can this be, that even the wind and the sea obey Him" (Mark 4:41).

There are times in our lives when everything seems to be calm. But like one of the sudden storms on the Sea of Galilee, problems can suddenly arise and begin to overwhelm us. They transform our lives into a raging storm of stress and difficulty. Without someone to turn to, these problems can be overwhelming. Yet with our faith in God, we are assured that the voice of Jesus and the presence of God will still the storm of problems that suddenly come upon us. We have the calming peace and assurance that Jesus will stand up and say to our problems, "Peace, be still!"

fearful, O you of little faith?" Then He arose and rebuked the winds and the sea. And there was a great calm.

27 And the men marveled, saying, "Who can this be, that even the winds and the sea obey Him?"

Two Demon-Possessed Men Healed

28 When He had come to the other side, to the country of the Gergesenes,[31] there met Him two demon-possessed *men*, coming out of the tombs, exceedingly fierce, so that no one could pass that way.

29 And suddenly they cried out, saying, "What have we to do with You, Jesus, You Son of God? Have You come here to torment us before the time?"

30 Now a good way off from them there was a herd of many swine feeding.

31 So the demons begged Him, saying, "If You cast us out, permit us to go away[32] into the herd of swine."

32 And He said to them, "Go." So when they had come out, they went into the herd of swine. And suddenly the whole herd of swine ran violently down the steep place into the sea, and perished in the water.

33 Then those who kept *them* fled; and they went away into the city and told everything, including what *had happened* to the demon-possessed *men*.

34 And behold, the whole city came out to meet Jesus. And when they saw Him, they begged *Him* to depart from their region.

Jesus Forgives and Heals a Paralytic

9 So He got into a boat, crossed over, and came to His own city.

2 And behold, they brought to Him a paralytic lying on a bed. And Jesus, seeing their faith, said to the paralytic, "Son, be of good cheer; your sins are forgiven you."

3 And at once some of the scribes said within themselves, "This *Man* blasphemes!"

4 But Jesus, knowing their thoughts, said, "Why do you think evil in your hearts?

5 "For which is easier, to say, 'Your sins are forgiven you,' or to say, 'Arise and walk'?

6 "But that you may know that the Son of Man has power on earth to forgive

sins"—then He said to the paralytic, "Arise, take up your bed, and go to your house."

7 And he arose and departed to his house.

8 Now when the multitudes saw *it,* they marveled[33] and glorified God who had given such power to men.

Matthew the Tax Collector

9 Then as Jesus passed on from there, He saw a man named Matthew sitting at the tax office. And He said to him, "Follow Me." And he arose and followed Him.

10 And so it was, as Jesus sat at the table in the house, *that* behold, many tax collectors and sinners came and sat down with Him and His disciples.

11 And when the Pharisees saw *it,* they said to His disciples, "Why does your Teacher eat with tax collectors and sinners?"

12 But when Jesus heard *that,* He said to them, "Those who are well have no need of a physician, but those who are sick.

13 "But go and learn what *this* means: '*I desire mercy and not sacrifice.*'[34] For I did not come to call the righteous, but sinners, to repentance."[35]

Jesus Is Questioned about Fasting

14 Then the disciples of John came to Him, saying, "Why do we and the Pharisees fast often,[36] but Your disciples do not fast?"

15 And Jesus said to them, "Can the friends of the bridegroom mourn as long as the bridegroom is with them? But the days will come when the bridegroom will be taken away from them, and then they will fast.

16 "No one puts a piece of unshrunk cloth on an old garment; for the patch pulls away from the garment, and the tear is made worse.

17 "Nor do *people* put new wine into old wineskins, or else the wineskins break, the wine is spilled, and the wineskins are ruined. But they put new wine into new wineskins, and both are preserved."

A Girl Restored to Life and a Woman Healed

18 While He spoke these things to them, behold, a ruler came and worshiped Him, saying, "My daughter has just died, but

31 NU-Text reads *Gadarenes.*   32 NU-Text reads *send us.*   33 NU-Text reads *were afraid.*   34 Hosea 6:6
35 NU-Text omits *to repentance.*   36 NU-Text brackets *often.*

come and lay Your hand on her and she will live."

19 So Jesus arose and followed him, and so *did* His disciples.

20 And suddenly, a woman who had a flow of blood for twelve years came from behind and touched the hem of His garment;

21 for she said to herself, "If only I may touch His garment, I shall be made well."

22 But Jesus turned around, and when He saw her He said, "Be of good cheer, daughter; your faith has made you well." And the woman was made well from that hour.

23 And when Jesus came into the ruler's house, and saw the flute players and the noisy crowd wailing,

24 He said to them, "Make room, for the girl is not dead, but sleeping." And they laughed Him to scorn.

25 But when the crowd was put outside, He went in and took her by the hand, and the girl arose.

26 And the report of this went out into all that land.

Two Blind Men Healed

27 When Jesus departed from there, two blind men followed Him, crying out and saying, "Son of David, have mercy on us!"

28 And when He had come into the house, the blind men came to Him. And Jesus said to them, "Do you believe that I am able to do this?" They said to Him, "Yes, Lord."

29 Then He touched their eyes, saying, "According to your faith let it be to you."

30 And their eyes were opened. And Jesus sternly warned them, saying, "See *that* no one knows *it.*"

31 But when they had departed, they spread the news about Him in all that country.

A Mute Man Speaks

32 As they went out, behold, they brought to Him a man, mute and demon-possessed.

33 And when the demon was cast out, the mute spoke. And the multitudes marveled, saying, "It was never seen like this in Israel!"

34 But the Pharisees said, "He casts out demons by the ruler of the demons."

The Compassion of Jesus

35 And Jesus went about all the cities and villages, teaching in their synagogues, preaching the gospel of the kingdom, and healing every sickness and every disease among the people.[37]

36 But when He saw the multitudes, He was moved with compassion for them, because they were weary[38] and scattered, like sheep having no shepherd.

37 Then He said to His disciples, "The harvest truly *is* plentiful, but the laborers *are* few.

38 "Therefore pray the Lord of the harvest to send out laborers into His harvest."

The Twelve Apostles

10 And when He had called His twelve disciples to *Him,* He gave them power *over* unclean spirits, to cast them out, and to heal all kinds of sickness and all kinds of disease.

2 Now the names of the twelve apostles are these: first, Simon, who is called Peter, and Andrew his brother; James the *son* of Zebedee, and John his brother;

3 Philip and Bartholomew; Thomas and Matthew the tax collector; James the *son* of Alphaeus, and Lebbaeus, whose surname was[39] Thaddaeus;

4 Simon the Canaanite,[40] and Judas Iscariot, who also betrayed Him.

Sending Out the Twelve

5 These twelve Jesus sent out and commanded them, saying: "Do not go into the way of the Gentiles, and do not enter a city of the Samaritans.

6 "But go rather to the lost sheep of the house of Israel.

7 "And as you go, preach, saying, 'The kingdom of heaven is at hand.'

8 "Heal the sick, cleanse the lepers, raise the dead,[41] cast out demons. Freely you have received, freely give.

9 "Provide neither gold nor silver nor copper in your moneybelts,

10 "nor bag for *your* journey, nor two tunics, nor sandals, nor staffs; for a worker is worthy of his food.

11 "Now whatever city or town you enter, inquire who in it is worthy, and stay there till you go out.

12 "And when you go into a household, greet it.

---

37 NU-Text omits *among the people.*   38 NU-Text and M-Text read *harassed.*
39 NU-Text omits *Lebbaeus, whose surname was.*   40 NU-Text reads *Canaanaean.*
41 NU-Text reads *raise the dead, cleanse the lepers;* M-Text omits *raise the dead.*

Reach Out in Faith

There was a widely-held belief in the ancient Middle East that certain prophets, places, and objects had specific healing powers. The hot springs of Galilee brought people from all corners of the Roman empire to sit in their healing baths. The pools of Bethesda in Jerusalem were reputed to have miraculous healing properties. Even in some of the remote areas of the Middle East today, villagers look to "holy men" to provide healing from their diseases and infirmities.

During Jesus' ministry, it was not uncommon for people to fall down at the feet of various prophets, grabbing their garments in hope of a transmission of power. Jesus never condoned this action, but He did applaud the faith it exemplified.

On one such occasion, Jesus was passing through a crowd enroute to the house of an important Capernaum ruler whose daughter had died. Suddenly, He turned and asked who touched Him. He recognized that someone had called out for help. He took the time to acknowledge the touch. A woman stepped forward and admitted that she believed that if she could simply touch the hem of Jesus' garment, she would be healed. Jesus told her to rejoice; her faith had made her well.

When we reach out in faith to touch God, He always acknowledges us. Our Lord is never too busy. He is always ready to be an unending source of strength and healing power. When we approach God with positive faith, He says to us, "Be of good cheer . . . your faith has made you well" (Matt. 9:22).

13 "If the household is worthy, let your peace come upon it. But if it is not worthy, let your peace return to you.
14 "And whoever will not receive you nor hear your words, when you depart from that house or city, shake off the dust from your feet.
15 "Assuredly, I say to you, it will be more tolerable for the land of Sodom and Gomorrah in the day of judgment than for that city!

Persecutions Are Coming

16 "Behold, I send you out as sheep in the midst of wolves. Therefore be wise as serpents and harmless as doves.
17 "But beware of men, for they will deliver you up to councils and scourge you in their synagogues.
18 "And you will be brought before governors and kings for My sake, as a testimony to them and to the Gentiles.
19 "But when they deliver you up, do not worry about how or what you should speak. For it will be given to you in that hour what you should speak;
20 "for it is not you who speak, but the Spirit of your Father who speaks in you.
21 "Now brother will deliver up brother to death, and a father *his* child; and children will rise up against parents and cause them to be put to death.
22 "And you will be hated by all for My name's sake. But he who endures to the end will be saved.
23 "But when they persecute you in this city, flee to another. For assuredly, I say to you, you will not have gone through the cities of Israel before the Son of Man comes.
24 "A disciple is not above *his* teacher, nor a servant above his master.
25 "It is enough for a disciple that he be like his teacher, and a servant like his master. If they have called the master of the house Beelzebub,[42] how much more *will they call* those of his household!
26 "Therefore do not fear them. For there is nothing covered that will not be revealed, and hidden that will not be known.

Jesus Teaches the Fear of God

27 "Whatever I tell you in the dark, speak in the light; and what you hear in the ear, preach on the housetops.

28 "And do not fear those who kill the body but cannot kill the soul. But rather fear Him who is able to destroy both soul and body in hell.
29 "Are not two sparrows sold for a copper coin? And not one of them falls to the ground apart from your Father's will.
30 "But the very hairs of your head are all numbered.
31 "Do not fear therefore; you are of more value than many sparrows.

Confess Christ Before Men

32 "Therefore whoever confesses Me before men, him I will also confess before My Father who is in heaven.
33 "But whoever denies Me before men, him I will also deny before My Father who is in heaven.

Christ Brings Division

34 "Do not think that I came to bring peace on earth. I did not come to bring peace but a sword.
35 "For I have come to 'set a man *against his father, a daughter against her mother, and a daughter-in-law against her mother-in-law.*'
36 "And '*a man's foes will be those of his own household.*'[43]
37 "He who loves father or mother more than Me is not worthy of Me. And he who loves son or daughter more than Me is not worthy of Me.
38 "And he who does not take his cross and follow after Me is not worthy of Me.
39 "He who finds his life will lose it, and he who loses his life for My sake will find it.

A Cup of Cold Water

40 "He who receives you receives Me, and he who receives Me receives Him who sent Me.
41 "He who receives a prophet in the name of a prophet shall receive a prophet's reward. And he who receives a righteous man in the name of a righteous man shall receive a righteous man's reward.
42 "And whoever gives one of these little ones only a cup of cold *water* in the name of a disciple, assuredly, I say to you, he shall by no means lose his reward."

John the Baptist Sends Messengers to Jesus

11 Now it came to pass, when Jesus finished commanding His twelve

---

42 NU-Text and M-Text read *Beelzebul*   43 Micah 7:6

disciples, that He departed from there to teach and to preach in their cities.

2 And when John had heard in prison about the works of Christ, he sent two of[44] his disciples

3 and said to Him, "Are You the Coming One, or do we look for another?"

4 Jesus answered and said to them, "Go and tell John the things which you hear and see:

5 "*The* blind receive their sight and *the* lame walk; *the* lepers are cleansed and *the* deaf hear; *the* dead are raised up and *the* poor have the gospel preached to them.

6 "And blessed is he who is not offended because of Me."

7 As they departed, Jesus began to say to the multitudes concerning John: "What did you go out into the wilderness to see? A reed shaken by the wind?

8 "But what did you go out to see? A man clothed in soft garments? Indeed, those who wear soft *clothing* are in kings' houses.

9 "But what did you go out to see? A prophet? Yes, I say to you, and more than a prophet.

10 "For this is *he* of whom it is written:

'Behold, I send My messenger
    before Your face,
Who will prepare Your way
    before You.'[45]

11 "Assuredly, I say to you, among those born of women there has not risen one greater than John the Baptist; but he who is least in the kingdom of heaven is greater than he.

12 "And from the days of John the Baptist until now the kingdom of heaven suffers violence, and the violent take it by force.

13 "For all the prophets and the law prophesied until John.

14 "And if you are willing to receive *it,* he is Elijah who is to come.

15 "He who has ears to hear, let him hear!

16 "But to what shall I liken this generation? It is like children sitting in the marketplaces and calling to their companions,

17 "and saying:

'We played the flute for you,
    And you did not dance;
We mourned to you,
    And you did not lament.'

18 "For John came neither eating nor drinking, and they say, 'He has a demon.'

19 "The Son of Man came eating and drinking, and they say, 'Look, a gluttonous man and a winebibber, a friend of tax collectors and sinners!' But wisdom is justified by her children."[46]

Woe to the Impenitent Cities

20 Then He began to upbraid the cities in which most of His mighty works had been done, because they did not repent:

21 "Woe to you, Chorazin! Woe to you, Bethsaida! For if the mighty works which were done in you had been done in Tyre and Sidon, they would have repented long ago in sackcloth and ashes.

22 "But I say to you, it will be more tolerable for Tyre and Sidon in the day of judgment than for you.

23 "And you, Capernaum, who are exalted to heaven, will be[47] brought down to Hades; for if the mighty works which were done in you had been done in Sodom, it would have remained until this day.

24 "But I say to you that it shall be more tolerable for the land of Sodom in the day of judgment than for you."

Jesus Gives True Rest

25 At that time Jesus answered and said, "I thank You, Father, Lord of heaven and earth, because You have hidden these things from the wise and prudent and have revealed them to babes.

26 "Even so, Father, for so it seemed good in Your sight.

27 "All things have been delivered to Me by My Father, and no one knows the Son except the Father. Nor does anyone know the Father except the Son, and *he* to whom the Son wills to reveal *Him.*

28 "Come to Me, all *you* who labor and are heavy laden, and I will give you rest.

29 "Take My yoke upon you and learn from Me, for I am gentle and lowly in heart, and you will find rest for your souls.

30 "For My yoke *is* easy and My burden is light."

---

44 NU-Text reads *by* for *two of.*   45 Malachi 3:1   46 NU-Text reads *works.*
47 NU-Text reads *will you be exalted to heaven? No, you will be.*

Jesus Is Lord of the Sabbath

12 At that time Jesus went through the grainfields on the Sabbath. And His disciples were hungry, and began to pluck heads of grain and to eat.
2 But when the Pharisees saw *it*, they said to Him, "Look, Your disciples are doing what is not lawful to do on the Sabbath!"
3 Then He said to them, "Have you not read what David did when he was hungry, he and those who were with him:
4 "how he entered the house of God and ate the showbread which was not lawful for him to eat, nor for those who were with him, but only for the priests?
5 "Or have you not read in the law that on the Sabbath the priests in the temple profane the Sabbath, and are blameless?
6 "But I say to you that in this place there is *One* greater than the temple.
7 "But if you had known what *this* means, 'I *desire mercy and not sacrifice*,'[48] you would not have condemned the guiltless.
8 "For the Son of Man is Lord even[49] of the Sabbath."

Healing on the Sabbath

9 Now when He had departed from there, He went into their synagogue.
10 And behold, there was a man who had a withered hand. And they asked Him, saying, "Is it lawful to heal on the Sabbath?"—that they might accuse Him.
11 Then He said to them, "What man is there among you who has one sheep, and if it falls into a pit on the Sabbath, will not lay hold of it and lift *it* out?
12 "Of how much more value then is a man than a sheep? Therefore it is lawful to do good on the Sabbath."
13 Then He said to the man, "Stretch out your hand." And he stretched *it* out, and it was restored as whole as the other.
14 Then the Pharisees went out and took counsel against Him, how they might destroy Him.

Behold, My Servant

15 But when Jesus knew *it*, He withdrew from there; and great multitudes[50] followed Him, and He healed them all.
16 And He warned them not to make Him known,
17 that it might be fulfilled which was spoken by Isaiah the prophet, saying:

18 "Behold, My Servant whom I have chosen,
   My Beloved in whom My soul is well pleased;
   I will put My Spirit upon Him,
   And He will declare justice to the Gentiles.
19 He will not quarrel nor cry out,
   Nor will anyone hear His voice in the streets.
20 A bruised reed He will not break,
   And smoking flax He will not quench,
   Till He sends forth justice to victory.
21 And in His name Gentiles will trust."[51]

A House Divided Cannot Stand

22 Then one was brought to Him who was demon-possessed, blind and mute; and He healed him, so that the blind and[52] mute man both spoke and saw.
23 And all the multitudes were amazed and said, "Could this be the Son of David?"
24 But when the Pharisees heard *it* they said, "This *fellow* does not cast out demons except by Beelzebub,[53] the ruler of the demons."
25 But Jesus knew their thoughts, and said to them: "Every kingdom divided against itself is brought to desolation, and every city or house divided against itself will not stand.
26 "And if Satan casts out Satan, he is divided against himself. How then will his kingdom stand?
27 "And if I cast out demons by Beelzebub, by whom do your sons cast *them* out? Therefore they shall be your judges.
28 "But if I cast out demons by the Spirit of God, surely the kingdom of God has come upon you.
29 "Or *else* how can one enter a strong man's house and plunder his goods, unless he first binds the strong man? And then he will plunder his house.
30 "He who is not with Me is against Me, and he who does not gather with Me scatters abroad.

The Unpardonable Sin

31 "Therefore I say to you, every sin and blasphemy will be forgiven men, but the

48 Hosea 6:6   49 NU-Text and M-Text omit *even.*   50 NU-Text brackets *multitudes.*
51 Isaiah 42:1-4   52 NU-Text omits *blind and.*   53 NU-Text and M-Text read *Beelzebul*

blasphemy *against* the Spirit will not be forgiven men.

32 "Anyone who speaks a word against the Son of Man, it will be forgiven him; but whoever speaks against the Holy Spirit, it will not be forgiven him, either in this age or in the *age* to come.

A Tree Known by Its Fruit

33 "Either make the tree good and its fruit good, or else make the tree bad and its fruit bad; for a tree is known by *its* fruit.

34 "Brood of vipers! How can you, being evil, speak good things? For out of the abundance of the heart the mouth speaks.

35 "A good man out of the good treasure of his heart[54] brings forth good things, and an evil man out of the evil treasure brings forth evil things.

36 "But I say to you that for every idle word men may speak, they will give account of it in the day of judgment.

37 "For by your words you will be justified, and by your words you will be condemned."

The Scribes and Pharisees Ask for a Sign

38 Then some of the scribes and Pharisees answered, saying, "Teacher, we want to see a sign from You."

39 But He answered and said to them, "An evil and adulterous generation seeks after a sign, and no sign will be given to it except the sign of the prophet Jonah.

40 "For as Jonah was three days and three nights in the belly of the great fish, so will the Son of Man be three days and three nights in the heart of the earth.

41 "The men of Nineveh will rise in the judgment with this generation and condemn it, because they repented at the preaching of Jonah; and indeed a greater than Jonah *is* here.

42 "The queen of the South will rise up in the judgment with this generation and condemn it, for she came from the ends of the earth to hear the wisdom of Solomon; and indeed a greater than Solomon *is* here.

An Unclean Spirit Returns

43 "When an unclean spirit goes out of a man, he goes through dry places, seeking rest, and finds none.

44 "Then he says, 'I will return to my house from which I came.' And when he comes, he finds it empty, swept, and put in order.

45 "Then he goes and takes with him seven other spirits more wicked than himself, and they enter and dwell there; and the last *state* of that man is worse than the first. So shall it also be with this wicked generation."

Jesus' Mother and Brothers Send for Him

46 While He was still talking to the multitudes, behold, His mother and brothers stood outside, seeking to speak with Him.

47 Then one said to Him, "Look, Your mother and Your brothers are standing outside, seeking to speak with You."

48 But He answered and said to the one who told Him, "Who is My mother and who are My brothers?"

49 And He stretched out His hand toward His disciples and said, "Here are My mother and My brothers!

50 "For whoever does the will of My Father in heaven is My brother and sister and mother."

The Parable of the Sower

13 On the same day Jesus went out of the house and sat by the sea.

2 And great multitudes were gathered together to Him, so that He got into a boat and sat; and the whole multitude stood on the shore.

3 Then He spoke many things to them in parables, saying: "Behold, a sower went out to sow.

4 "And as he sowed, some *seed* fell by the wayside; and the birds came and devoured them.

5 "Some fell on stony places, where they did not have much earth; and they immediately sprang up because they had no depth of earth.

6 "But when the sun was up they were scorched, and because they had no root they withered away.

7 "And some fell among thorns, and the thorns sprang up and choked them.

8 "But others fell on good ground and yielded a crop: some a hundredfold, some sixty, some thirty.

9 "He who has ears to hear, let him hear!"

---

54 NU-Text and M-Text omit *of his heart*.

The Purpose of Parables

10 And the disciples came and said to Him, "Why do You speak to them in parables?"

11 He answered and said to them, "Because it has been given to you to know the mysteries of the kingdom of heaven, but to them it has not been given.

12 "For whoever has, to him more will be given, and he will have abundance; but whoever does not have, even what he has will be taken away from him.

13 "Therefore I speak to them in parables, because seeing they do not see, and hearing they do not hear, nor do they understand.

14 "And in them the prophecy of Isaiah is fulfilled, which says:

'Hearing you will hear
  and shall not understand,
And seeing you will see
  and not perceive;
15 For the heart of this people
  has grown dull.
Their ears are hard of hearing,
And their eyes they have closed,
Lest they should see with their eyes
  and hear with their ears,
Lest they should understand
  with their heart and turn,
So that I should[55] heal them.'[56]

16 "But blessed *are* your eyes for they see, and your ears for they hear;

17 "for assuredly, I say to you that many prophets and righteous *men* desired to see what you see, and did not see *it,* and to hear what you hear, and did not hear *it.*

The Parable of the Sower Explained

18 "Therefore hear the parable of the sower:

19 "When anyone hears the word of the kingdom, and does not understand *it,* then the wicked *one* comes and snatches away what was sown in his heart. This is he who received seed by the wayside.

20 "But he who received the seed on stony places, this is he who hears the word and immediately receives it with joy;

21 "yet he has no root in himself, but endures only for a while. For when tribulation or persecution arises because of the word, immediately he stumbles.

22 "Now he who received seed among the thorns is he who hears the word, and the cares of this world and the deceitfulness of riches choke the word, and he becomes unfruitful.

23 "But he who received seed on the good ground is he who hears the word and understands *it,* who indeed bears fruit and produces: some a hundredfold, some sixty, some thirty."

The Parable of the Wheat and the Tares

24 Another parable He put forth to them, saying: "The kingdom of heaven is like a man who sowed good seed in his field;

25 "but while men slept, his enemy came and sowed tares among the wheat and went his way.

26 "But when the grain had sprouted and produced a crop, then the tares also appeared.

27 "So the servants of the owner came and said to him, 'Sir, did you not sow good seed in your field? How then does it have tares?'

28 "He said to them, 'An enemy has done this.' The servants said to him, 'Do you want us then to go and gather them up?'

29 "But he said, 'No, lest while you gather up the tares you also uproot the wheat with them.

30 'Let both grow together until the harvest, and at the time of harvest I will say to the reapers, "First gather together the tares and bind them in bundles to burn them, but gather the wheat into my barn." ' "

The Parable of the Mustard Seed

31 Another parable He put forth to them, saying: "The kingdom of heaven is like a mustard seed, which a man took and sowed in his field,

32 "which indeed is the least of all the seeds; but when it is grown it is greater than the herbs and becomes a tree, so that the birds of the air come and nest in its branches."

The Parable of the Leaven

33 Another parable He spoke to them: "The kingdom of heaven is like leaven, which a woman took and hid in three measures[57] of meal till it was all leavened."

55 NU-Text and M-Text read *would.*   56 Isaiah 6:9, 10   57 Greek *three sata,* approximately two pecks

The Mustard Seed

There are infinite possibilities in little beginnings if God is in them! God's kingdom, as recorded in the Gospels, is compared to the smallest item in the biblical farmer's experience—the mustard seed.

Throughout the land of Jesus, mustard trees grew in abundance by the Sea of Galilee and in the southern hill country of Judea on the Mount of Olives. These trees were not individually planted by local farmers, but by birds and the wind carrying their seeds and scattering them about. Once rooted, the trees grew to a height of eight to twelve feet. In the springtime, these colorful yellow plants are found with birds nesting among their branches.

Jesus taught that the kingdom of God is like both the seed and the full-grown mustard tree. Small or large, God's providential care is there for its growth. To Jesus' listeners, the mustard seed symbolized something small and apparently dead. Yet they knew that when it was sown, it was resurrected into a full, living tree. Jesus spelled this out when He said, "Unless a grain of wheat falls into the ground and dies, it remains alone; but if it dies, it produces much grain" (John 12:24). Paul also drew from this teaching when he said about our bodies, "this mortal has put on immortality" (1 Cor. 15:53, 54).

We can be confident that out of the tiniest of possibilities, God will raise and establish His kingdom. Out of our little beginnings He will reap a full harvest. Whether you have a great task or a small responsibility, do it joyfully, for out of your endeavors God will raise bountiful blessings. Anyone can count the seeds in an apple, but only God can count the apples in a seed!

Prophecy and the Parables

34 All these things Jesus spoke to the multitude in parables; and without a parable He did not speak to them, *35* that it might be fulfilled which was spoken by the prophet, saying:

"I will open My mouth in parables;
I will utter things which have been
kept secret from the foundation
of the world."[58]

The Parable of the Tares Explained

36 Then Jesus sent the multitude away and went into the house. And His disciples came to Him, saying, "Explain to us the parable of the tares of the field." *37* He answered and said to them: "He who sows the good seed is the Son of Man. *38* "The field is the world, the good seeds are the sons of the kingdom, but the tares are the sons of the wicked *one.* *39* "The enemy who sowed them is the devil, the harvest is the end of the age, and the reapers are the angels. *40* "Therefore as the tares are gathered and burned in the fire, so it will be at the end of this age. *41* "The Son of Man will send out His angels, and they will gather out of His kingdom all things that offend, and those who practice lawlessness, *42* "and will cast them into the furnace of fire. There will be wailing and gnashing of teeth. *43* "Then the righteous will shine forth as the sun in the kingdom of their Father. He who has ears to hear, let him hear!

The Parable of the Hidden Treasure

44 "Again, the kingdom of heaven is like treasure hidden in a field, which a man found and hid; and for joy over it he goes and sells all that he has and buys that field.

The Parable of the Pearl of Great Price

45 "Again, the kingdom of heaven is like a merchant seeking beautiful pearls, *46* "who, when he had found one pearl of great price, went and sold all that he had and bought it.

The Parable of the Dragnet

47 "Again, the kingdom of heaven is like a dragnet that was cast into the sea and gathered some of every kind, *48* "which, when it was full, they drew to shore; and they sat down and gathered the good into vessels, but threw the bad away. *49* "So it will be at the end of the age. The angels will come forth, separate the wicked from among the just, *50* "and cast them into the furnace of fire. There will be wailing and gnashing of teeth." *51* Jesus said to them,[59] "Have you understood all these things?" They said to Him, "Yes, Lord."[60] *52* Then He said to them, "Therefore every scribe instructed concerning[61] the kingdom of heaven is like a householder who brings out of his treasure *things* new and old."

Jesus Rejected at Nazareth

53 Now it came to pass, when Jesus had finished these parables, that He departed from there. *54* And when He had come to His own country, He taught them in their synagogue, so that they were astonished and said, "Where did this *Man* get this wisdom and *these* mighty works? *55* "Is this not the carpenter's son? Is not His mother called Mary? And His brothers James, Joses,[62] Simon, and Judas? *56* "And His sisters, are they not all with us? Where then did this *Man* get all these things?" *57* So they were offended at Him. But Jesus said to them, "A prophet is not without honor except in his own country and in his own house." *58* And He did not do many mighty works there because of their unbelief.

John the Baptist Beheaded

14 At that time Herod the tetrarch heard the report about Jesus *2* and said to his servants, "This is John the Baptist; he is risen from the dead, and therefore these powers are at work in him."

58 Psalm 78:2   59 NU-Text omits *Jesus said to them.*   60 NU-Text omits *Lord.*
61 Or *for.*   62 NU-Text reads *Joseph.*

3 For Herod had laid hold of John and bound him, and put *him* in prison for the sake of Herodias, his brother Philip's wife.
4 For John had said to him, "It is not lawful for you to have her."
5 And although he wanted to put him to death, he feared the multitude, because they counted him as a prophet.
6 But when Herod's birthday was celebrated, the daughter of Herodias danced before them and pleased Herod.
7 Therefore he promised with an oath to give her whatever she might ask.
8 So she, having been prompted by her mother, said, "Give me John the Baptist's head here on a platter."
9 And the king was sorry; nevertheless, because of the oaths and because of those who sat with him at the table, he commanded *it* to be given *to her.*
10 So he sent and had John beheaded in prison.
11 And his head was brought on a platter and given to the girl, and she brought *it* to her mother.
12 Then his disciples came and took away the body and buried it, and went and told Jesus.

Feeding the Five Thousand

13 When Jesus heard *it,* He departed from there by boat to a deserted place by Himself. But when the multitudes heard it, they followed Him on foot from the cities.
14 And when Jesus went out He saw a great multitude; and He was moved with compassion for them, and healed their sick.
15 When it was evening, His disciples came to Him, saying, "This is a deserted place, and the hour is already late. Send the multitudes away, that they may go into the villages and buy themselves food."
16 But Jesus said to them, "They do not need to go away. You give them something to eat."
17 And they said to Him, "We have here only five loaves and two fish."
18 He said, "Bring them here to Me."
19 Then He commanded the multitudes to sit down on the grass. And He took the five loaves and the two fish, and looking up to heaven, He blessed and broke and gave the loaves to the disciples; and the disciples gave to the multitudes.
20 So they all ate and were filled, and they took up twelve baskets full of the fragments that remained.
21 Now those who had eaten were about five thousand men, besides women and children.

Jesus Walks on the Sea

22 Immediately Jesus made His disciples get into the boat and go before Him to the other side, while He sent the multitudes away.
23 And when He had sent the multitudes away, He went up on a mountain by Himself to pray. And when evening had come, He was alone there.
24 But the boat was now in the middle of the sea,[63] tossed by the waves, for the wind was contrary.
25 Now in the fourth watch of the night Jesus went to them, walking on the sea.
26 And when the disciples saw Him walking on the sea, they were troubled, saying, "It is a ghost!" And they cried out for fear.
27 But immediately Jesus spoke to them, saying, "Be of good cheer! It is I; do not be afraid."
28 And Peter answered Him and said, "Lord, if it is You, command me to come to You on the water."
29 So He said, "Come." And when Peter had come down out of the boat, he walked on the water to go to Jesus.
30 But when he saw that the wind was boisterous,[64] he was afraid; and beginning to sink he cried out, saying, "Lord, save me!"
31 And immediately Jesus stretched out *His* hand and caught him, and said to him, "O you of little faith, why did you doubt?"
32 And when they got into the boat, the wind ceased.
33 Then those who were in the boat came and[65] worshiped Him, saying, "Truly You are the Son of God."

Many Touch Him and Are Made Well

34 When they had crossed over, they came to the land of[66] Gennesaret.
35 And when the men of that place recognized Him, they sent out into all that surrounding region, brought to Him all who were sick,

---

63 NU-Text reads *many furlongs away from the land.*   64 NU-Text brackets *that* and *boisterous.*
65 NU-Text omits *came and.*   66 NU-Text reads *came to land at.*

36 and begged Him that they might only touch the hem of His garment. And as many as touched it were made perfectly well.

Defilement Comes from Within

15 Then the scribes and Pharisees who were from Jerusalem came to Jesus, saying,
2 "Why do Your disciples transgress the tradition of the elders? For they do not wash their hands when they eat bread."
3 But He answered and said to them, "Why do you also transgress the commandment of God because of your tradition?
4 "For God commanded, saying, 'Honor your father and your mother';[67] and, 'He who curses father or mother, let him be put to death.'[68]
5 "But you say, 'Whoever says to his father or mother, "Whatever profit you might have received from me has been dedicated to the temple"—
6 'is released from honoring[69] his father or mother.' "Thus you have made the commandment[70] of God of no effect by your tradition.
7 "Hypocrites! Well did Isaiah prophesy about you, saying:

8 'These people draw near to Me
    with their mouth,
   And[71] honor Me with their lips,
   But their heart is far from Me.
9 And in vain they worship Me,
   Teaching as doctrines the
    commandments of men.' "[72]

10 Then He called the multitude and said to them, "Hear and understand:
11 "Not what goes into the mouth defiles a man; but what comes out of the mouth, this defiles a man."
12 Then His disciples came and said to Him, "Do You know that the Pharisees were offended when they heard this saying?"
13 But He answered and said, "Every plant which My heavenly Father has not planted will be uprooted.
14 "Let them alone. They are blind leaders of the blind. And if the blind leads the blind, both will fall into a ditch."

15 Then Peter answered and said to Him, "Explain this parable to us."
16 So Jesus said, "Are you also still without understanding?
17 "Do you not yet understand that whatever enters the mouth goes into the stomach and is eliminated?
18 "But those things which proceed out of the mouth come from the heart, and they defile a man.
19 "For out of the heart proceed evil thoughts, murders, adulteries, fornications, thefts, false witness, blasphemies.
20 "These are the things which defile a man, but to eat with unwashed hands does not defile a man."

A Gentile Shows Her Faith

21 Then Jesus went out from there and departed to the region of Tyre and Sidon.
22 And behold, a woman of Canaan came from that region and cried out to Him, saying, "Have mercy on me, O Lord, Son of David! My daughter is severely demon-possessed."
23 But He answered her not a word. And His disciples came and urged Him, saying, "Send her away, for she cries out after us."
24 But He answered and said, "I was not sent except to the lost sheep of the house of Israel."
25 Then she came and worshiped Him, saying, "Lord, help me!"
26 But He answered and said, "It is not good to take the children's bread and throw it to the little dogs."
27 And she said, "True, Lord, yet even the little dogs eat the crumbs which fall from their masters' table."
28 Then Jesus answered and said to her, "O woman, great is your faith! Let it be to you as you desire." And her daughter was healed from that very hour.

Jesus Heals Great Multitudes

29 And Jesus departed from there, skirted the Sea of Galilee, and went up on the mountain and sat down there.
30 Then great multitudes came to Him, having with them those who were lame, blind, mute, maimed, and many others; and they laid them down at Jesus' feet, and He healed them.

67 Exodus 20:12; Deuteronomy 5:16   68 Exodus 21:17   69 NU-Text omits or mother.
70 NU-Text reads word.   71 NU-Text omits draw near to Me with their mouth, And.   72 Isaiah 29:13

31 So the multitude marveled when they saw *the* mute speaking, *the* maimed made whole, *the* lame walking, and *the* blind seeing; and they glorified the God of Israel.

Feeding the Four Thousand

32 Then Jesus called His disciples *to Him* and said, "I have compassion on the multitude, because they have now continued with Me three days and have nothing to eat. And I do not want to send them away hungry, lest they faint on the way." 33 Then His disciples said to Him, "Where could we get enough bread in the wilderness to fill such a great multitude?" 34 Jesus said to them, "How many loaves do you have?" And they said, "Seven, and a few little fish." 35 And He commanded the multitude to sit down on the ground. 36 And He took the seven loaves and the fish and gave thanks, broke *them* and gave *them* to His disciples; and the disciples *gave* to the multitude. 37 So they all ate and were filled, and they took up seven large baskets full of the fragments that were left. 38 Now those who ate were four thousand men, besides women and children. 39 And He sent away the multitude, got into the boat, and came to the region of Magdala.[73]

The Pharisees and Sadducees Seek a Sign

16 Then the Pharisees and Sadducees came, and testing Him asked that He would show them a sign from heaven. 2 He answered and said to them, "When it is evening you say, '*It will be* fair weather, for the sky is red'; 3 "and in the morning, '*It will be* foul weather today, for the sky is red and threatening.' Hypocrites![74] You know how to discern the face of the sky, but you cannot *discern* the signs of the times. 4 "A wicked and adulterous generation seeks after a sign, and no sign shall be given to it except the sign of the prophet[75] Jonah." And He left them and departed.

The Leaven of the Pharisees and Sadducees

5 And when His disciples had come to the other side, they had forgotten to take bread.

6 Then Jesus said to them, "Take heed and beware of the leaven of the Pharisees and the Sadducees." 7 And they reasoned among themselves, saying, "*It is* because we have taken no bread." 8 But when Jesus perceived it, He said to them, "O you of little faith, why do you reason among yourselves because you have brought no bread?[76] 9 "Do you not yet understand, or remember the five loaves of the five thousand and how many baskets you took up? 10 "Nor the seven loaves of the four thousand and how many large baskets you took up? 11 "How is it you do not understand that I did not speak to you concerning bread?—*but* you should beware of the leaven of the Pharisees and Sadducees." 12 Then they understood that He did not tell *them* to beware of the leaven of bread, but of the doctrine of the Pharisees and Sadducees.

Peter Confesses Jesus as the Christ

13 When Jesus came into the region of Caesarea Philippi, He asked His disciples, saying, "Who do men say that I, the Son of Man, am?" 14 So they said, "Some *say* John the Baptist, some Elijah, and others Jeremiah or one of the prophets." 15 He said to them, "But who do you say that I am?" 16 And Simon Peter answered and said, "You are the Christ, the Son of the living God." 17 Jesus answered and said to him, "Blessed are you, Simon Bar-Jonah, for flesh and blood has not revealed *this* to you, but My Father who is in heaven. 18 "And I also say to you that you are Peter, and on this rock I will build My church, and the gates of Hades shall not prevail against it. 19 "And I will give you the keys of the kingdom of heaven, and whatever you bind on earth will be bound in heaven, and whatever you loose on earth will be loosed in heaven." 20 Then He commanded His disciples that they should tell no one that He was Jesus the Christ.

73 NU-Text reads *Magadan*.   74 NU-Text omits *Hypocrites*.
75 NU-Text omits *the prophet*.   76 NU-Text reads *you have no bread*.

Jesus Predicts His Death and Resurrection

21 From that time Jesus began to show to His disciples that He must go to Jerusalem, and suffer many things from the elders and chief priests and scribes, and be killed, and be raised again the third day. **22** Then Peter took Him aside and began to rebuke Him, saying, "Far be it from You, Lord; this shall not happen to You!" **23** But He turned and said to Peter, "Get behind Me, Satan! You are an offense to Me, for you are not mindful of the things of God, but the things of men."

Take Up the Cross and Follow Him

24 Then Jesus said to His disciples, "If anyone desires to come after Me, let him deny himself, and take up his cross, and follow Me. **25** "For whoever desires to save his life will lose it, and whoever loses his life for My sake will find it. **26** "For what is a man profited if he gains the whole world, and loses his own soul? Or what will a man give in exchange for his soul? **27** "For the Son of Man will come in the glory of His Father with His angels, and then He will reward each according to his works. **28** "Assuredly, I say to you, there are some standing here who shall not taste death till they see the Son of Man coming in His kingdom."

Jesus Transfigured on the Mount

17 Now after six days Jesus took Peter, James, and John his brother, brought them up on a high mountain by themselves, **2** and was transfigured before them. His face shone like the sun, and His clothes became as white as the light. **3** And behold, Moses and Elijah appeared to them, talking with Him. **4** Then Peter answered and said to Jesus, "Lord, it is good for us to be here; if You wish, let us[77] make here three tabernacles: one for You, one for Moses, and one for Elijah." **5** While he was still speaking, behold, a bright cloud overshadowed them; and suddenly a voice came out of the cloud,

saying, "This is My beloved Son, in whom I am well pleased. Hear Him!" **6** And when the disciples heard it, they fell on their faces and were greatly afraid. **7** But Jesus came and touched them and said, "Arise, and do not be afraid." **8** And when they had lifted up their eyes, they saw no one but Jesus only. **9** Now as they came down from the mountain, Jesus commanded them, saying, "Tell the vision to no one until the Son of Man is risen from the dead." **10** And His disciples asked Him, saying, "Why then do the scribes say that Elijah must come first?" **11** Then Jesus answered and said to them, "Elijah truly is coming first[78] and will restore all things. **12** "But I say to you that Elijah has come already, and they did not know him but did to him whatever they wished. Likewise the Son of Man is also about to suffer at their hands." **13** Then the disciples understood that He spoke to them of John the Baptist.

A Boy Is Healed

14 And when they had come to the multitude, a man came to Him, kneeling down to Him and saying, **15** "Lord, have mercy on my son, for he is an epileptic[79] and suffers severely; for he often falls into the fire and often into the water. **16** "So I brought him to Your disciples, but they could not cure him." **17** Then Jesus answered and said, "O faithless and perverse generation, how long shall I be with you? How long shall I bear with you? Bring him here to Me." **18** And Jesus rebuked the demon, and he came out of him; and the child was cured from that very hour. **19** Then the disciples came to Jesus privately and said, "Why could we not cast him out?" **20** So Jesus said to them, "Because of your unbelief;[80] for assuredly, I say to you, if you have faith as a mustard seed, you will say to this mountain, 'Move from here to there,' and it will move; and nothing will be impossible for you. **21** "However, this kind does not go out except by prayer and fasting."[81]

---

77 NU-Text reads *I will.*   78 NU-Text omits *first.*   79 Literally *moon-struck.*
80 NU-Text reads *little faith.*   81 NU-Text omits this verse.

Jesus Again Predicts His Death and Resurrection

22 Now while they were staying[82] in Galilee, Jesus said to them, "The Son of Man is about to be betrayed into the hands of men,
23 "and they will kill Him, and the third day He will be raised up." And they were exceedingly sorrowful.

Peter and His Master Pay Their Taxes

24 And when they had come to Capernaum,[83] those who received the *temple* tax came to Peter and said, "Does your Teacher not pay the *temple* tax?"
25 He said, "Yes." And when he had come into the house, Jesus anticipated him, saying, "What do you think, Simon? From whom do the kings of the earth take customs or taxes, from their *own* sons or from strangers?"
26 Peter said to Him, "From strangers." Jesus said to him, "Then the sons are free.
27 "Nevertheless, lest we offend them, go to the sea, cast in a hook, and take the fish that comes up first. And when you have opened its mouth, you will find a piece of money;[84] take that and give it to them for Me and you."

Who Is the Greatest?

18 At that time the disciples came to Jesus, saying, "Who then is greatest in the kingdom of heaven?"
2 And Jesus called a little child to Him, set him in the midst of them,
3 and said, "Assuredly, I say to you, unless you are converted and become as little children, you will by no means enter the kingdom of heaven.
4 "Therefore whoever humbles himself as this little child is the greatest in the kingdom of heaven.
5 "And whoever receives one little child like this in My name receives Me.

Jesus Warns of Offenses

6 "But whoever causes one of these little ones who believe in Me to sin, it would be better for him if a millstone were hung around his neck, and he were drowned in the depth of the sea.
7 "Woe to the world because of offenses! For offenses must come, but woe to that man by whom the offense comes!

8 "And if your hand or foot causes you to sin, cut it off and cast *it* from you. It is better for you to enter into life lame or maimed, rather than having two hands or two feet, to be cast into the everlasting fire.
9 "And if your eye causes you to sin, pluck it out and cast *it* from you. It is better for you to enter into life with one eye, rather than having two eyes, to be cast into hell fire.

The Parable of the Lost Sheep

10 "Take heed that you do not despise one of these little ones, for I say to you that in heaven their angels always see the face of My Father who is in heaven.
11 "For the Son of Man has come to save that which was lost.[85]
12 "What do you think? If a man has a hundred sheep, and one of them goes astray, does he not leave the ninety-nine and go to the mountains to seek the one that is straying?
13 "And if he should find it, assuredly, I say to you, he rejoices more over that *sheep* than over the ninety-nine that did not go astray.
14 "Even so it is not the will of your Father who is in heaven that one of these little ones should perish.

Dealing with a Sinning Brother

15 "Moreover if your brother sins against you, go and tell him his fault between you and him alone. If he hears you, you have gained your brother.
16 "But if he will not hear *you*, take with you one or two more, that '*by the mouth of two or three witnesses every word may be established.*'[86]
17 "And if he refuses to hear them, tell *it* to the church. But if he refuses even to hear the church, let him be to you like a heathen and a tax collector.
18 "Assuredly, I say to you, whatever you bind on earth will be bound in heaven, and whatever you loose on earth will be loosed in heaven.
19 "Again I say[87] to you that if two of you agree on earth concerning anything that they ask, it will be done for them by My Father in heaven.
20 "For where two or three are gathered together in My name, I am there in the midst of them."

---

82 NU-Text reads *gathering together*.   83 NU-Text reads *Capharnaum* (here and elsewhere).
84 Greek *stater*, the exact amount to pay the temple tax (didrachma) for two.   85 NU-Text omits this verse.
86 Deuteronomy 19:15   87 NU-Text and M-Text read *Again, assuredly, I say*.

The Lost Sheep

The Gospel of Luke records that the Pharisees were adamantly opposed to Jesus eating with tax gatherers and other "immoral" people, and they questioned Him on His association with unrighteous men and women. Jesus replied in a parable. A man had one hundred sheep, but upon counting them discovered there were only ninety-nine. One was missing. Immediately he went in search of the lost sheep. It was an almost daily occurrence in a shepherd's life to look for a sheep which had strayed from the flock. Jesus drew from this task to illustrate God's love for everyone.

Today, in the Judean wilderness, a shepherd will appoint other shepherds to watch his flock while he goes to find a lost sheep. In the twisted folds and narrow canyon gullies of the wilderness, it is easy for a sheep to stray into the open mouth of a cave or wander aimlessly down an adjacent riverbed. The shepherd will search and call out for the lost sheep, sometimes throwing stones at the mouths of caves to scare a sheep out of hiding. On one such occasion, in 1948, while searching for his lost sheep, a young shepherd boy threw a stone into a cave. He heard the sound of pottery breaking. It turned out to be the containers of the famous Dead Sea Scrolls, containing the earliest manuscripts of the Old Testament.

Once a shepherd has found his sheep, he will place the lamb on his shoulder, grabbing its feet with one hand, while keeping his other hand free to hold his staff and defend himself against attacking animals. The shepherd can often be heard singing, rejoicing that the sheep that was lost now is found.

Jesus' answer to the Pharisees reveals that God is constantly guarding and caring for His sheep. He particularly goes to much effort to find those who have gone astray from His flock. God specifically sent Jesus Christ into the world to seek and save that which was lost.

In our lives, let us look to Jesus, the Good Shepherd, keeping our eyes on Him and heeding His call. If we go astray, we can be confident that He will come and search for us. He will find us, lift us up on His shoulders and bring us safely home. Then there will be much rejoicing—for the sheep that was lost is now found!

The Parable of the Unforgiving Servant

21 Then Peter came to Him and said, "Lord, how often shall my brother sin against me, and I forgive him? Up to seven times?"

22 Jesus said to him, "I do not say to you, up to seven times, but up to seventy times seven.

23 "Therefore the kingdom of heaven is like a certain king who wanted to settle accounts with his servants.

24 "And when he had begun to settle accounts, one was brought to him who owed him ten thousand talents.

25 "But as he was not able to pay, his master commanded that he be sold, with his wife and children and all that he had, and that payment be made.

26 "The servant therefore fell down before him, saying, 'Master, have patience with me, and I will pay you all.'

27 "Then the master of that servant was moved with compassion, released him, and forgave him the debt.

28 "But that servant went out and found one of his fellow servants who owed him a hundred denarii; and he laid hands on him and took *him* by the throat, saying, 'Pay me what you owe!'

29 "So his fellow servant fell down at his feet[88] and begged him, saying, 'Have patience with me, and I will pay you all.'[89]

30 "And he would not, but went and threw him into prison till he should pay the debt.

31 "So when his fellow servants saw what had been done, they were very grieved, and came and told their master all that had been done.

32 "Then his master, after he had called him, said to him, 'You wicked servant! I forgave you all that debt because you begged me.

33 'Should you not also have had compassion on your fellow servant, just as I had pity on you?'

34 "And his master was angry, and delivered him to the torturers until he should pay all that was due to him.

35 "So My heavenly Father also will do to you if each of you, from his heart, does not forgive his brother his trespasses."[90]

Marriage and Divorce

19 Now it came to pass, when Jesus had finished these sayings, *that* He departed from Galilee and came to the region of Judea beyond the Jordan.

2 And great multitudes followed Him, and He healed them there.

3 The Pharisees also came to Him, testing Him, and saying to Him, "Is it lawful for a man to divorce his wife for *just* any reason?"

4 And He answered and said to them, "Have you not read that He who made[91] *them* at the beginning 'made them male and female,'[92]

5 "and said, 'For this reason a man shall leave his father and mother and be joined to his wife, and the two shall become one flesh'?[93]

6 "So then, they are no longer two but one flesh. Therefore what God has joined together, let not man separate."

7 They said to Him, "Why then did Moses command to give a certificate of divorce, and to put her away?"

8 He said to them, "Moses, because of the hardness of your hearts, permitted you to divorce your wives, but from the beginning it was not so.

9 "And I say to you, whoever divorces his wife, except for sexual immorality, and marries another, commits adultery; and whoever marries her who is divorced commits adultery."

10 His disciples said to Him, "If such is the case of the man with *his* wife, it is better not to marry."

Jesus Teaches on Celibacy

11 But He said to them, "All cannot accept this saying, but only *those* to whom it has been given:

12 "For there are eunuchs who were born thus from *their* mother's womb, and there are eunuchs who were made eunuchs by men, and there are eunuchs who have made themselves eunuchs for the kingdom of heaven's sake. He who is able to accept *it,* let him accept *it.*"

Jesus Blesses Little Children

13 Then little children were brought to Him that He might put *His* hands on them and pray, but the disciples rebuked them.

14 But Jesus said, "Let the little children come to Me, and do not forbid them; for of such is the kingdom of heaven."

88 NU-Text omits *at his feet.* 89 NU-Text and M-Text omit *all.* 90 NU-Text omits *his trespasses.*
91 NU-Text reads *created.* 92 Genesis 1:27; 5:2 93 Genesis 2:24

15 And He laid *His* hands on them and departed from there.

Jesus Counsels the Rich Young Ruler

16 Now behold, one came and said to Him, "Good[94] Teacher, what good thing shall I do that I may have eternal life?" 17 So He said to him, "Why do you call Me good?[95] No one *is* good but One, *that is*, God.[96] But if you want to enter into life, keep the commandments." 18 He said to Him, "Which ones?" Jesus said, "'*You shall not murder,*' '*You shall not commit adultery,*' '*You shall not steal,*' '*You shall not bear false witness,*' 19 '*Honor your father and your mother,*'[97] and, '*You shall love your neighbor as yourself.*'"[98] 20 The young man said to Him, "All these things I have kept from my youth.[99] What do I still lack?" 21 Jesus said to him, "If you want to be perfect, go, sell what you have and give to the poor, and you will have treasure in heaven; and come, follow Me." 22 But when the young man heard that saying, he went away sorrowful, for he had great possessions.

With God All Things Are Possible

23 Then Jesus said to His disciples, "Assuredly, I say to you that it is hard for a rich man to enter the kingdom of heaven. 24 "And again I say to you, it is easier for a camel to go through the eye of a needle than for a rich man to enter the kingdom of God." 25 When His disciples heard *it*, they were exceedingly amazed, saying, "Who then can be saved?" 26 But Jesus looked at *them* and said to them, "With men this is impossible, but with God all things are possible." 27 Then Peter answered and said to Him, "See, we have left all and followed You. Therefore what shall we have?" 28 So Jesus said to them, "Assuredly I say to you, that in the regeneration, when the Son of Man sits on the throne of His glory, you who have followed Me will also sit on twelve thrones, judging the twelve tribes of Israel. 29 "And everyone who has left houses or brothers or sisters or father or mother or wife[100] or children or lands, for My name's sake, shall receive a hundredfold, and inherit everlasting life. 30 "But many *who are* first will be last, and the last first.

The Parable of the Workers in the Vineyard

20 "For the kingdom of heaven is like a landowner who went out early in the morning to hire laborers for his vineyard. 2 "Now when he had agreed with the laborers for a denarius a day, he sent them into his vineyard. 3 "And he went out about the third hour and saw others standing idle in the marketplace, 4 "and said to them, 'You also go into the vineyard, and whatever is right I will give you.' And they went. 5 "Again he went out about the sixth and the ninth hour, and did likewise. 6 "And about the eleventh hour he went out and found others standing idle,[101] and said to them, 'Why have you been standing here idle all day?' 7 "They said to him 'Because no one hired us.' He said to them, 'You also go into the vineyard, and whatever is right you will receive.'[102] 8 "So when evening had come, the owner of the vineyard said to his steward, 'Call the laborers and give them *their* wages, beginning with the last to the first.' 9 "And when those came who *were* hired about the eleventh hour, they each received a denarius. 10 "But when the first came, they supposed that they would receive more; and they likewise received each a denarius. 11 "And when they had received *it*, they murmured against the landowner, 12 "saying, 'These last *men* have worked *only* one hour, and you made them equal to us who have borne the burden and the heat of the day.' 13 "But he answered one of them and said, 'Friend, I am doing you no wrong. Did you not agree with me for a denarius? 14 'Take *what is* yours and go your way. I wish to give to this last man *the same* as to you. 15 'Is it not lawful for me to do what I

---

94 NU-Text omits *Good.*   95 NU-Text reads *Why do you ask Me about what is good?*
96 NU-Text reads *There is One who is good.*   97 Exodus 20:12–16; Deuteronomy 5:16–20   98 Leviticus 19:18
99 NU-Text omits *from my youth.*   100 NU-Text omits *or wife.*   101 NU-Text omits *idle.*
102 NU-Text omits the last clause of this verse.

wish with my own things? Or is your eye evil because I am good?" 16 "So the last will be first, and the first last. For many are called, but few chosen."[103]

Jesus a Third Time Predicts His Death and Resurrection

17 Then Jesus, going up to Jerusalem, took the twelve disciples aside on the road and said to them, 18 "Behold, we are going up to Jerusalem, and the Son of Man will be betrayed to the chief priests and to the scribes; and they will condemn Him to death, 19 "and deliver Him to the Gentiles to mock and to scourge and to crucify. And the third day He will rise again."

Salome Asks a Favor

20 Then the mother of Zebedee's sons came to Him with her sons, kneeling down and asking something from Him. 21 And He said to her, "What do you wish?" She said to Him, "Grant that these two sons of mine may sit, one on Your right hand and the other on the left, in Your kingdom." 22 But Jesus answered and said, "You do not know what you ask. Are you able to drink the cup that I am about to drink, and be baptized with the baptism that I am baptized with?"[104] They said to Him, "We are able." 23 So He said to them, "You will indeed drink My cup, and be baptized with the baptism that I am baptized with;[105] but to sit on My right hand and on My left is not Mine to give, but it is for those for whom it is prepared by My Father." 24 And when the ten heard it, they were moved with indignation against the two brothers. 25 But Jesus called them to Himself and said, "You know that the rulers of the Gentiles lord it over them, and those who are great exercise authority over them. 26 "Yet it shall not be so among you; but whoever desires to become great among you, let him be your servant. 27 "And whoever desires to be first among you, let him be your slave— 28 "just as the Son of Man did not come to be served, but to serve, and to give His life a ransom for many."

Two Blind Men Receive Their Sight

29 Now as they departed from Jericho, a great multitude followed Him. 30 And behold, two blind men sitting by the road, when they heard that Jesus was passing by, cried out, saying, "Have mercy on us, O Lord, Son of David!" 31 Then the multitude warned them that they should be quiet; but they cried out all the more, saying, "Have mercy on us, O Lord, Son of David!" 32 So Jesus stood still and called them, and said, "What do you want Me to do for you?" 33 They said to Him, "Lord, that our eyes may be opened." 34 So Jesus had compassion and touched their eyes. And immediately their eyes received sight, and they followed Him.

The Triumphal Entry

21 Now when they drew near to Jerusalem, and came to Bethphage,[106] at the Mount of Olives, then Jesus sent two disciples, 2 saying to them, "Go into the village opposite you, and immediately you will find a donkey tied, and a colt with her. Loose them and bring them to Me. 3 "And if anyone says anything to you, you shall say, 'The Lord has need of them,' and immediately he will send them." 4 All[107] this was done that it might be fulfilled which was spoken by the prophet, saying:

5 "Tell the daughter of Zion,
'Behold, your King is coming to you,
Lowly, and sitting on a donkey,
A colt, the foal of a donkey.' "[108]

6 So the disciples went and did as Jesus commanded them. 7 They brought the donkey and the colt, laid their clothes on them, and set Him[109] on them. 8 And a very great multitude spread their garments on the road; others cut down branches from the trees and spread them on the road. 9 Then the multitudes who went before and those who followed cried out, saying:

---

103 NU-Text omits the last sentence of this verse.
104 NU-Text omits and be baptized with the baptism that I am baptized with.
105 NU-Text omits and be baptized with the baptism that I am baptized with.   106 M-Text reads Bethsphage.
107 NU-Text omits All.   108 Zechariah 9:9   109 NU-Text reads and He sat.

"Hosanna to the Son of David!
'Blessed is He who comes
in the name of the LORD!'[110]
Hosanna in the highest!"

10 And when He had come into Jerusalem, all the city was moved, saying, "Who is this?"
11 So the multitudes said, "This is Jesus, the prophet from Nazareth of Galilee."

Jesus Cleanses the Temple

12 Then Jesus went into the temple of God[111] and drove out all those who bought and sold in the temple, and overturned the tables of the moneychangers and the seats of those who sold doves.
13 And He said to them, "It is written, *'My house shall be called a house of prayer,'*[112] but you have made it a *'den of thieves.'*"[113]
14 Then *the* blind and *the* lame came to Him in the temple, and He healed them.
15 But when the chief priests and scribes saw the wonderful things that He did, and the children crying out in the temple and saying, "Hosanna to the Son of David!" they were indignant
16 and said to Him, "Do You hear what these are saying?" And Jesus said to them, "Yes. Have you never read, *'Out of the mouth of babes and nursing infants You have perfected praise'?*"[114]
17 Then He left them and went out of the city to Bethany, and He lodged there.

The Fig Tree Withered

18 Now in the morning, as He returned to the city, He was hungry.
19 And seeing a fig tree by the road, He came to it and found nothing on it but leaves, and said to it, "Let no fruit grow on you ever again." And immediately the fig tree withered away.

The Lesson of the Withered Fig Tree

20 Now when the disciples saw *it,* they marveled, saying, "How did the fig tree wither away so soon?"
21 So Jesus answered and said to them, "Assuredly, I say to you, if you have faith and do not doubt, you will not only do what was done to the fig tree, but also if you say to this mountain, 'Be removed and be cast into the sea,' it will be done.
22 "And all things, whatever you ask in prayer, believing, you will receive."

Jesus' Authority Questioned

23 Now when He came into the temple, the chief priests and the elders of the people confronted Him as He was teaching, and said, "By what authority are You doing these things? And who gave You this authority?"
24 But Jesus answered and said to them, "I also will ask you one thing, which if you tell Me, I likewise will tell you by what authority I do these things:
25 "The baptism of John, where was it from? From heaven or from men?" And they reasoned among themselves, saying, "If we say, 'From heaven,' He will say to us, 'Why then did you not believe him?'
26 "But if we say, 'From men,' we fear the multitude, for all count John as a prophet."
27 So they answered Jesus and said, "We do not know." And He said to them, "Neither will I tell you by what authority I do these things.

The Parable of the Two Sons

28 "But what do you think? A man had two sons, and he came to the first and said, 'Son, go, work today in my vineyard.'
29 "He answered and said, 'I will not,' but afterward he regretted it and went.
30 "Then he came to the second and said likewise. And he answered and said, 'I go, sir,' but he did not go.
31 "Which of the two did the will of *his* father?" They said to Him, "The first." Jesus said to them, "Assuredly, I say to you that tax collectors and harlots enter the kingdom of God before you.
32 "For John came to you in the way of righteousness, and you did not believe him; but tax collectors and harlots believed him; and when you saw *it,* you did not afterward relent and believe him.

The Parable of the Wicked Vinedressers

33 "Hear another parable: There was a certain landowner who planted a vineyard and set a hedge around it, dug a winepress in it and built a tower. And he leased it to vinedressers and went into a far country.
34 "Now when vintage-time drew near, he sent his servants to the vinedressers, that they might receive its fruit.

110 Psalm 118:26   111 NU-Text omits *of God.*   112 Isaiah 56:7   113 Jeremiah 7:11   114 Psalm 8:2

Faith to Move Mountains

Two thousand years ago, Jesus Christ and His disciples stood on the Mount of Olives. They had just completed a twenty-six-mile journey from Jericho to Jerusalem. Before them was the Golden City with its magnificent temple set like a jewel among the beautiful Judean hills. Beyond lay an unforgettable view of the glistening blue Mediterranean Sea, nearly always visible on the clear spring days of Passover. Behind them to the east was the vast desert stretching down to the salt-filled sea.

Here on the Mount of Olives, Christ's words about faith were vividly illustrated. Perhaps He stooped down, grabbed a handful of the chalky mountain soil and let it sift through His fingers as He pointed to the seas within view, and declared, "If you have faith and do not doubt, you will not only do what was done to the fig tree, but also if you say to this mountain, 'Be removed and be cast into the sea,' it will be done" (Matt. 21:21).

During this season, the Mount of Olives is colorfully alive with a patchwork of red anemones, poppies, and bright yellow mustard flowers. The disciples had only to look at the golden mustard plant surrounding them to remember the tiny seed from which it was sown.

A faith that small can move mountains. It can move the mountains in your life today! How do you get this mountain-moving faith? Christ told us Himself, "And all things, whatever you ask in prayer, believing, you will receive" (Matt. 21:22).

35 "And the vinedressers took his servants, beat one, killed one, and stoned another.
36 "Again he sent other servants, more than the first, and they did likewise to them.
37 "Then last of all he sent his son to them, saying, 'They will respect my son.'
38 "But when the vinedressers saw the son, they said among themselves, 'This is the heir. Come, let us kill him and seize his inheritance.'
39 "And they caught him, and cast *him* out of the vineyard, and killed *him*.
40 "Therefore, when the owner of the vineyard comes, what will he do to those vinedressers?"
41 They said to Him, "He will destroy those wicked men miserably, and lease *his* vineyard to other vinedressers who will render to him the fruits in their seasons."
42 Jesus said to them, "Did you never read in the Scriptures:

'The stone which the builders rejected
Has become the chief cornerstone.
This was the LORD's doing,
And it is marvelous in our eyes'?[115]

43 "Therefore I say to you, the kingdom of God will be taken from you and given to a nation bearing the fruits of it.
44 "And whoever falls on this stone will be broken; but on whomever it falls, it will grind him to powder."
45 Now when the chief priests and Pharisees heard His parables, they perceived that He was speaking of them.
46 But when they sought to lay hands on Him, they feared the multitudes, because they took Him for a prophet.

The Parable of the Wedding Feast

22 And Jesus answered and spoke to them again by parables and said:
2 "The kingdom of heaven is like a certain king who arranged a marriage for his son,
3 "and sent out his servants to call those who were invited to the wedding; and they were not willing to come.
4 "Again, he sent out other servants, saying, 'Tell those who are invited, "See, I have prepared my dinner; my oxen and fatted cattle *are* killed, and all things *are* ready. Come to the wedding."'

5 "But they made light of it and went their ways, one to his own farm, another to his business.
6 "And the rest seized his servants, treated *them* spitefully, and killed *them*.
7 "But when the king heard *about it*, he was furious. And he sent out his armies, destroyed those murderers, and burned up their city.
8 "Then he said to his servants, 'The wedding is ready, but those who were invited were not worthy.
9 'Therefore go into the highways, and as many as you find, invite to the wedding.'
10 "So those servants went out into the highways and gathered together all whom they found, both bad and good. And the wedding *hall* was filled with guests.
11 "But when the king came in to see the guests, he saw a man there who did not have on a wedding garment.
12 "So he said to him, 'Friend, how did you come in here without a wedding garment?' And he was speechless.
13 "Then the king said to the servants, 'Bind him hand and foot, take him away, and[116] cast *him* into outer darkness; there will be weeping and gnashing of teeth.'
14 "For many are called, but few *are* chosen."

The Pharisees: Is It Lawful to Pay Taxes to Caesar?

15 Then the Pharisees went and plotted how they might entangle Him in *His* talk.
16 And they sent to Him their disciples with the Herodians, saying, "Teacher, we know that You are true, and teach the way of God in truth; nor do You care about anyone, for You do not regard the person of men.
17 "Tell us, therefore, what do You think? Is it lawful to pay taxes to Caesar, or not?"
18 But Jesus perceived their wickedness, and said, "Why do you test Me, *you* hypocrites?
19 "Show Me the tax money." So they brought Him a denarius.
20 And He said to them, "Whose image and inscription *is* this?"
21 They said to Him, "Caesar's." And He said to them, "Render therefore to Caesar the things that are Caesar's, and to God the things that are God's."

115 Psalm 118:22, 23   116 NU-Text omits *take him away and.*

22 When they had heard *these words,* they marveled, and left Him and went their way.

The Sadducees: What about the Resurrection?

23 The same day the Sadducees, who say there is no resurrection, came to Him and asked Him,

24 saying: "Teacher, Moses said that if a man dies, having no children, his brother shall marry his wife and raise up offspring for his brother.

25 "Now there were with us seven brothers. The first died after he had married, and having no offspring, left his wife to his brother.

26 "Likewise the second also, and the third, even to the seventh.

27 "And last of all the woman died also.

28 "Therefore, in the resurrection, whose wife of the seven will she be? For they all had her."

29 Jesus answered and said to them, "You are mistaken, not knowing the Scriptures nor the power of God.

30 "For in the resurrection they neither marry nor are given in marriage, but are like angels of God[117] in heaven.

31 "But concerning the resurrection of the dead, have you not read what was spoken to you by God, saying,

32 *'I am the God of Abraham, the God of Isaac, and the God of Jacob'?*[118] God is not the God of the dead, but of the living."

33 And when the multitudes heard *this,* they were astonished at His teaching.

The Scribes: Which Is the First Commandment of All?

34 But when the Pharisees heard that He had silenced the Sadducees, they gathered together.

35 Then one of them, a lawyer, asked *Him a question,* testing Him, and saying,

36 "Teacher, which *is* the great commandment in the law?"

37 Jesus said to him, *"'You shall love the LORD your God with all your heart, with all your soul, and with all your mind.'*[119]

38 "This is *the* first and great commandment.

39 "And *the* second *is* like it: *'You shall love your neighbor as yourself.'*[120]

40 "On these two commandments hang all the Law and the Prophets."

Jesus: How Can David Call His Descendant Lord?

41 While the Pharisees were gathered together, Jesus asked them,

42 saying, "What do you think about the Christ? Whose Son is He?" They said to Him, *"The Son* of David."

43 He said to them, "How then does David in the Spirit call Him *'Lord,'* saying:

44 *'The LORD said to my Lord,*
  "Sit at My right hand,
    Till I make Your enemies
      Your footstool"'?[121]

45 "If David then calls Him *'Lord,'* how is He his Son?"

46 And no one was able to answer Him a word, nor from that day on did anyone dare question Him anymore.

Woe to the Scribes and Pharisees

23 Then Jesus spoke to the multitudes and to His disciples,

2 saying: "The scribes and the Pharisees sit in Moses' seat.

3 "Therefore whatever they tell you to observe,[122] *that* observe and do, but do not do according to their works; for they say, and do not do.

4 "For they bind heavy burdens, hard to bear, and lay *them* on men's shoulders; but they *themselves* will not move them with one of their fingers.

5 "But all their works they do to be seen by men. They make their phylacteries broad and enlarge the borders of their garments.

6 "They love the best places at feasts, the best seats in the synagogues,

7 "greetings in the marketplaces, and to be called by men, 'Rabbi, Rabbi.'

8 "But you, do not be called 'Rabbi'; for One is your Teacher, the Christ,[123] and you are all brethren.

9 "Do not call anyone on earth your father; for One is your Father, He who is in heaven.

10 "And do not be called teachers; for One is your Teacher, the Christ.

11 "But he who is greatest among you shall be your servant.

12 "And whoever exalts himself will be abased, and he who humbles himself will be exalted.

---

117 NU-Text omits *of God.* 118 Exodus 3:6, 15 119 Deuteronomy 6:5 120 Leviticus 19:18
121 Psalm 110:1 122 NU-Text omits *to observe.* 123 NU-Text omits *the Christ.*

13 "But woe to you, scribes and Pharisees, hypocrites! For you shut up the kingdom of heaven against men; for you neither go in *yourselves*, nor do you allow those who are entering to go in.

14 "Woe to you, scribes and Pharisees, hypocrites! For you devour widows' houses, and for a pretense make long prayers. Therefore you will receive greater condemnation.[124]

15 "Woe to you, scribes and Pharisees, hypocrites! For you travel land and sea to win one proselyte, and when he is won, you make him twice as much a son of hell as yourselves.

16 "Woe to you, blind guides, who say, 'Whoever swears by the temple, it is nothing; but whoever swears by the gold of the temple, he is obliged *to perform it*.'

17 "Fools and blind! For which is greater, the gold or the temple that sanctifies[125] the gold?

18 "And, 'Whoever swears by the altar, it is nothing; but whoever swears by the gift that is on it, he is obliged *to perform it*.'

19 "Fools and blind! For which is greater, the gift or the altar that sanctifies the gift?

20 "Therefore he who swears by the altar, swears by it and by all things on it.

21 "He who swears by the temple, swears by it and by Him who dwells[126] in it.

22 "And he who swears by heaven, swears by the throne of God and by Him who sits on it.

23 "Woe to you, scribes and Pharisees, hypocrites! For you pay tithe of mint and anise and cumin, and have neglected the weightier *matters* of the law: justice and mercy and faith. These you ought to have done, without leaving the others undone.

24 "Blind guides, who strain out a gnat and swallow a camel!

25 "Woe to you, scribes and Pharisees, hypocrites! For you cleanse the outside of the cup and dish, but inside they are full of extortion and self-indulgence.[127]

26 "Blind Pharisee, first cleanse the inside of the cup and dish, that the outside of them may be clean also.

27 "Woe to you, scribes and Pharisees, hypocrites! For you are like whitewashed tombs which indeed appear beautiful outwardly, but inside are full of dead *men's* bones and all uncleanness.

28 "Even so you also outwardly appear righteous to men, but inside you are full of hypocrisy and lawlessness.

29 "Woe to you, scribes and Pharisees, hypocrites! Because you build the tombs of the prophets and adorn the monuments of the righteous,

30 "and say, 'If we had lived in the days of our fathers, we would not have been partakers with them in the blood of the prophets.'

31 "Therefore you are witnesses against yourselves that you are sons of those who murdered the prophets.

32 "Fill up, then, the measure of your fathers' *guilt*.

33 "Serpents, brood of vipers! How can you escape the condemnation of hell?

34 "Therefore, indeed, I send you prophets, wise men, and scribes: *some* of them you will kill and crucify, and *some* of them you will scourge in your synagogues and persecute from city to city,

35 "that on you may come all the righteous blood shed on the earth, from the blood of righteous Abel to the blood of Zechariah, son of Berechiah, whom you murdered between the temple and the altar.

36 "Assuredly, I say to you, all these things will come upon this generation.

Jesus Laments over Jerusalem

37 "O Jerusalem, Jerusalem, the one who kills the prophets and stones those who are sent to her! How often I wanted to gather your children together, as a hen gathers her chicks under *her* wings, but you were not willing!

38 "See! Your house is left to you desolate;

39 "for I say to you, you shall see Me no more till you say, '*Blessed is He who comes in the name of the Lord!*'"[128]

Jesus Predicts the Destruction of the Temple

24 Then Jesus went out and departed from the temple, and His disciples came to *Him* to show Him the buildings of the temple.

2 And Jesus said to them, "Do you not see all these things? Assuredly, I say to you, not one stone shall be left here upon another, that shall not be thrown down."

---

124 NU-Text omits this verse.   125 NU-Text reads *sanctified.*   126 M-Text reads *dwelt.*
127 M-Text reads *unrighteousness.*   128 Psalm 118:26

The Signs of the Times and the End of the Age

3 Now as He sat on the Mount of Olives, the disciples came to Him privately, saying, "Tell us, when will these things be? And what *will be* the sign of Your coming, and of the end of the age?"
4 And Jesus answered and said to them: "Take heed that no one deceives you.
5 "For many will come in My name, saying, 'I am the Christ,' and will deceive many.
6 "And you will hear of wars and rumors of wars. See that you are not troubled; for all[129] *these things* must come to pass, but the end is not yet.
7 "For nation will rise against nation, and kingdom against kingdom. And there will be famines, pestilences,[130] and earthquakes in various places.
8 "All these *are* the beginning of sorrows.
9 "Then they will deliver you up to tribulation and kill you, and you will be hated by all nations for My name's sake.
10 "And then many will be offended, will betray one another, and will hate one another.
11 "Then many false prophets will rise up and deceive many.
12 "And because lawlessness will abound, the love of many will grow cold.
13 "But he who endures to the end shall be saved.
14 "And this gospel of the kingdom will be preached in all the world as a witness to all the nations, and then the end will come.

The Great Tribulation

15 "Therefore when you see the 'abomination of desolation,'[131] spoken of by Daniel the prophet, standing in the holy place" (whoever reads, let him understand),
16 "then let those who are in Judea flee to the mountains.
17 "Let him who is on the housetop not come down to take anything out of his house.
18 "And let him who is in the field not go back to get his clothes.
19 "But woe to those who are pregnant and to those with nursing babies in those days!
20 "And pray that your flight may not be in winter or on the Sabbath.

21 "For then there will be great tribulation, such as has not been since the beginning of the world until this time, no, nor ever shall be.
22 "And unless those days were shortened, no flesh would be saved; but for the elect's sake those days will be shortened.
23 "Then if anyone says to you, 'Look, here *is* the Christ!' or 'There!' do not believe *it*.
24 "For false christs and false prophets will arise and show great signs and wonders, so as to deceive, if possible, even the elect.
25 "See, I have told you beforehand.
26 "Therefore if they say to you, 'Look, He is in the desert!' do not go out; *or* 'Look, *He is* in the inner rooms!' do not believe *it*.
27 "For as the lightning comes from the east and flashes to the west, so also will the coming of the Son of Man be.
28 "For wherever the carcass is, there the eagles will be gathered together.

The Coming of the Son of Man

29 "Immediately after the tribulation of those days the sun will be darkened, and the moon will not give its light; the stars will fall from heaven, and the powers of the heavens will be shaken.
30 "Then the sign of the Son of Man will appear in heaven, and then all the tribes of the earth will mourn, and they will see the Son of Man coming on the clouds of heaven with power and great glory.
31 "And He will send His angels with a great sound of a trumpet, and they will gather together His elect from the four winds, from one end of heaven to the other.

The Parable of the Fig Tree

32 "Now learn this parable from the fig tree: When its branch has already become tender and puts forth leaves, you know that summer *is* near.
33 "So you also, when you see all these things, know that it[132] is near, at the *very* doors.
34 "Assuredly, I say to you, this generation will by no means pass away till all these things are fulfilled.
35 "Heaven and earth will pass away, but My words will by no means pass away.

129 NU-Text omits *all*.   130 NU-Text omits *pestilences*.   131 Daniel 11:31; 12:11   132 Or *He*

No One Knows the Day or Hour

36 "But of that day and hour no one knows, no, not even the angels of heaven,[133] but My Father only.
37 "But as the days of Noah were, so also will the coming of the Son of Man be.
38 "For as in the days before the flood, they were eating and drinking, marrying and giving in marriage, until the day that Noah entered the ark,
39 "and did not know until the flood came and took them all away, so also will the coming of the Son of Man be.
40 "Then two men will be in the field: one will be taken and the other left.
41 "Two women will be grinding at the mill: one will be taken and the other left.
42 "Watch therefore, for you do not know what hour[134] your Lord is coming.
43 "But know this, that if the master of the house had known what hour the thief would come, he would have watched and not allowed his house to be broken into.
44 "Therefore you also be ready, for the Son of Man is coming at an hour when you do not expect Him.

The Faithful Servant and the Evil Servant

45 "Who then is a faithful and wise servant, whom his master made ruler over his household, to give them food in due season?
46 "Blessed is that servant whom his master, when he comes, will find so doing.
47 "Assuredly, I say to you that he will make him ruler over all his goods.
48 "But if that evil servant says in his heart, 'My master is delaying his coming,' [135]
49 "and begins to beat his fellow servants, and to eat and drink with the drunkards,
50 "the master of that servant will come on a day when he is not looking for him and at an hour that he is not aware of,
51 "and will cut him in two and appoint him his portion with the hypocrites. There shall be weeping and gnashing of teeth.

The Parable of the Wise and Foolish Virgins

25 "Then the kingdom of heaven shall be likened to ten virgins who took their lamps and went out to meet the bridegroom.
2 "Now five of them were wise, and five were foolish.
3 "Those who were foolish took their lamps and took no oil with them,
4 "but the wise took oil in their vessels with their lamps.
5 "But while the bridegroom was delayed, they all slumbered and slept.
6 "And at midnight a cry was heard: 'Behold, the bridegroom is coming;[136] go out to meet him!'
7 "Then all those virgins arose and trimmed their lamps.
8 "And the foolish said to the wise, 'Give us some of your oil, for our lamps are going out.'
9 "But the wise answered, saying, 'No, lest there should not be enough for us and you; but go rather to those who sell, and buy for yourselves.'
10 "And while they went to buy, the bridegroom came, and those who were ready went in with him to the wedding; and the door was shut.
11 "Afterward the other virgins came also, saying, 'Lord, Lord, open to us!'
12 "But he answered and said, 'Assuredly, I say to you, I do not know you.'
13 "Watch therefore, for you know neither the day nor the hour[137] in which the Son of Man is coming.

The Parable of the Talents

14 "For the kingdom of heaven is like a man traveling to a far country, who called his own servants and delivered his goods to them.
15 "And to one he gave five talents, to another two, and to another one, to each according to his own ability; and immediately he went on a journey.
16 "Then he who had received the five talents went and traded with them, and made another five talents.
17 "And likewise he who had received two gained two more also.
18 "But he who had received one went and dug in the ground, and hid his lord's money.
19 "After a long time the lord of those servants came and settled accounts with them.
20 "So he who had received five talents came and brought five other talents, saying, 'Lord, you delivered to me five tal-

133 NU-Text adds nor the Son.   134 NU-Text reads day.   135 NU-Text omits his coming.
136 NU-Text omits is coming.   137 NU-Text omits the rest of this verse.

ents; look, I have gained five more talents besides them.'

21 "His lord said to him, 'Well *done*, good and faithful servant; you were faithful over a few things, I will make you ruler over many things. Enter into the joy of your lord.'

22 "He also who had received two talents came and said, 'Lord, you delivered to me two talents; look, I have gained two more talents besides them.'

23 "His lord said to him, 'Well *done*, good and faithful servant; you have been faithful over a few things, I will make you ruler over many things. Enter into the joy of your lord.'

24 "Then he who had received the one talent came and said, 'Lord, I knew you to be a hard man, reaping where you have not sown, and gathering where you have not scattered seed.

25 'And I was afraid, and went and hid your talent in the ground. Look, *there* you have *what is* yours.'

26 "But his lord answered and said to him, 'You wicked and lazy servant, you knew that I reap where I have not sown, and gather where I have not scattered seed.

27 'Therefore you ought to have deposited my money with the bankers, and at my coming I would have received back my own with interest.

28 'Therefore take the talent from him, and give *it* to him who has ten talents.

29 'For to everyone who has, more will be given, and he will have abundance; but from him who does not have, even what he has will be taken away.

30 'And cast the unprofitable servant into the outer darkness. There will be weeping and gnashing of teeth.'

The Son of Man Will Judge the Nations

31 "When the Son of Man comes in His glory, and all the holy[138] angels with Him, then He will sit on the throne of His glory.

32 "All the nations will be gathered before Him, and He will separate them one from another, as a shepherd divides *his* sheep from the goats.

33 "And He will set the sheep on His right hand, but the goats on the left.

34 "Then the King will say to those on His right hand, 'Come, you blessed of My Father, inherit the kingdom prepared for you from the foundation of the world:

35 'for I was hungry and you gave Me food; I was thirsty and you gave Me drink; I was a stranger and you took Me in;

36 'I *was* naked and you clothed Me; I was sick and you visited Me; I was in prison and you came to Me.'

37 "Then the righteous will answer Him, saying, 'Lord, when did we see You hungry and feed *You*, or thirsty and give *You* drink?

38 'When did we see You a stranger and take *You* in, or naked and clothe *You?*

39 'Or when did we see You sick, or in prison, and come to You?'

40 "And the King will answer and say to them, 'Assuredly, I say to you, inasmuch as you did *it* to one of the least of these My brethren, you did *it* to Me.'

41 "Then He will also say to those on the left hand, 'Depart from Me, you cursed, into the everlasting fire prepared for the devil and his angels:

42 'for I was hungry and you gave Me no food; I was thirsty and you gave Me no drink;

43 'I was a stranger and you did not take Me in, naked and you did not clothe Me, sick and in prison and you did not visit Me.'

44 "Then they also will answer Him,[139] saying, 'Lord, when did we see You hungry or thirsty or a stranger or naked or sick or in prison, and did not minister to You?'

45 "Then He will answer them, saying, 'Assuredly, I say to you, inasmuch as you did not do *it* to one of the least of these, you did not do *it* to Me.'

46 "And these will go away into everlasting punishment, but the righteous into eternal life."

The Plot to Kill Jesus

26 Now it came to pass, when Jesus had finished all these sayings, *that* He said to His disciples,

2 "You know that after two days is the Passover, and the Son of Man will be delivered up to be crucified."

3 Then the chief priests, the scribes,[140] and the elders of the people assembled at the palace of the high priest, who was called Caiaphas,

---

138 NU-Text omits *holy*. 139 NU-Text and M-Text omit *Him.* 140 NU-Text omits *the scribes.*

4 and plotted to take Jesus by trickery and kill *Him.*
5 But they said, "Not during the feast, lest there be an uproar among the people."

The Anointing at Bethany

6 And when Jesus was in Bethany at the house of Simon the leper,
7 a woman came to Him having an alabaster flask of very costly fragrant oil, and she poured it on His head as He sat *at the table.*
8 But when His disciples saw *it,* they were indignant, saying, "To what purpose *is* this waste?
9 "For this fragrant oil might have been sold for much and given to *the* poor."
10 But when Jesus was aware of *it,* He said to them, "Why do you trouble the woman? For she has done a good work for Me.
11 "For you have the poor with you always, but Me you do not have always.
12 "For in pouring this fragrant oil on My body, she did *it* for My burial.
13 "Assuredly, I say to you, wherever this gospel is preached in the whole world, what this woman has done will also be told as a memorial to her."

Judas Agrees to Betray Jesus

14 Then one of the twelve, called Judas Iscariot, went to the chief priests
15 and said, "What are you willing to give me if I deliver Him to you?" And they counted out to him thirty pieces of silver.
16 So from that time he sought opportunity to betray Him.

Jesus Celebrates Passover with His Disciples

17 Now on the first *day* of the *Feast of the Unleavened Bread* the disciples came to Jesus, saying to Him, "Where do You want us to prepare for You to eat the Passover?"
18 And He said, "Go into the city to a certain man, and say to him, 'The Teacher says, "My time is at hand; I will keep the Passover at your house with My disciples." ' "
19 So the disciples did as Jesus had directed them; and they prepared the Passover.
20 Now when evening had come, He sat down with the twelve.

21 Now as they were eating, He said, "Assuredly, I say to you, one of you will betray Me."
22 And they were exceedingly sorrowful, and each of them began to say to Him, "Lord, is it I?"
23 Then He answered and said, "He who dipped *his* hand with Me in the dish will betray Me.
24 "The Son of Man goes as it is written of Him, but woe to that man by whom the Son of Man is betrayed! It would have been good for that man if he had not been born."
25 Then Judas, who was betraying Him, answered and said, "Rabbi, is it I?" He said to him, "You have said it."

Jesus Institutes the Lord's Supper

26 And as they were eating, Jesus took bread, blessed[141] *it* and broke *it,* and gave *it* to the disciples and said, "Take, eat; this is My body."
27 Then He took the cup, and gave thanks, and gave *it* to them, saying, "Drink from it, all of you.
28 "For this is My blood of the new[142] covenant, which is shed for many for the remission of sins.
29 "But I say to you, I will not drink of this fruit of the vine from now on until that day when I drink it new with you in My Father's kingdom."
30 And when they had sung a hymn, they went out to the Mount of Olives.

Jesus Predicts Peter's Denial

31 Then Jesus said to them, "All of you will be made to stumble because of Me this night, for it is written:

'I will strike the Shepherd,
And the sheep of the flock
will be scattered.'[143]

32 "But after I have been raised, I will go before you to Galilee."
33 Peter answered and said to Him, "Even if all are made to stumble because of You, I will never be made to stumble."
34 Jesus said to him, "Assuredly, I say to you that this night, before the rooster crows, you will deny Me three times."
35 Peter said to Him, "Even if I have to die with You, I will not deny You!" And so said all the disciples.

141 M-Text reads *gave thanks for.*   142 NU-Text omits *new.*   143 Zechariah 13:7

The Prayer in the Garden

36 Then Jesus came with them to a place called Gethsemane, and said to the disciples, "Sit here while I go and pray over there."
37 And He took with Him Peter and the two sons of Zebedee, and He began to be sorrowful and deeply distressed.
38 Then He said to them, "My soul is exceedingly sorrowful, even to death. Stay here and watch with Me."
39 He went a little farther and fell on His face, and prayed, saying, "O My Father, if it is possible, let this cup pass from Me; nevertheless, not as I will, but as You will."
40 Then He came to the disciples and found them asleep, and said to Peter, "What, could you not watch with Me one hour?
41 "Watch and pray, lest you enter into temptation. The spirit indeed is willing, but the flesh is weak."
42 He went away again a second time and prayed, saying, "O My Father, if this cup cannot pass away from Me unless[144] I drink it, Your will be done."
43 And He came and found them asleep again, for their eyes were heavy.
44 So He left them, went away again, and prayed the third time, saying the same words.
45 Then He came to His disciples and said to them, "Are you still sleeping and resting? Behold, the hour is at hand, and the Son of Man is being betrayed into the hands of sinners.
46 "Rise, let us be going. See, he who betrays Me is at hand."

Betrayal and Arrest in Gethsemane

47 And while He was still speaking, behold, Judas, one of the twelve, with a great multitude with swords and clubs, came from the chief priests and elders of the people.
48 Now His betrayer had given them a sign, saying, "Whomever I kiss, He is the One; seize Him."
49 Then immediately he went up to Jesus and said, "Greetings, Rabbi!" and kissed Him.
50 And Jesus said to him, "Friend, why have you come?" Then they came and laid hands on Jesus and took Him.

51 And suddenly, one of those who were with Jesus stretched out his hand and drew his sword, struck the servant of the high priest, and cut off his ear.
52 Then Jesus said to him, "Put your sword in its place, for all who take the sword will perish[145] by the sword.
53 "Or do you think that I cannot now pray to My Father, and He will provide Me with more than twelve legions of angels?
54 "How then could the Scriptures be fulfilled, that it must happen thus?"
55 In that hour Jesus said to the multitudes, "Have you come out, as against a robber, with swords and clubs to take Me? I sat daily with you, teaching in the temple, and you did not seize Me.
56 "But all this was done that the Scriptures of the prophets might be fulfilled." Then all the disciples forsook Him and fled.

Jesus Faces the Sanhedrin

57 And those who had laid hold of Jesus led Him away to Caiaphas the high priest, where the scribes and the elders were assembled.
58 But Peter followed Him at a distance to the high priest's courtyard. And he went in and sat with the servants to see the end.
59 Now the chief priests, the elders,[146] and all the council sought false testimony against Jesus to put Him to death,
60 but found none. Even though many false witnesses came forward, they found none.[147] But at last two false witnesses[148] came forward
61 and said, "This fellow said, 'I am able to destroy the temple of God and to build it in three days.' "
62 And the high priest arose and said to Him, "Do You answer nothing? What is it that these men testify against You?"
63 But Jesus kept silent. And the high priest answered and said to Him, "I adjure You by the living God that You tell us if You are the Christ, the Son of God."
64 Jesus said to him, "It is as you said. Nevertheless, I say to you, hereafter you will see the Son of Man sitting at the right hand of the Power, and coming on the clouds of heaven."

---

144 NU-Text reads if this may not pass away unless.   145 M-Text reads die.   146 NU-Text omits the elders.
147 NU-Text puts a comma after but found none, does not capitalize Even, and omits they found none.
148 NU-Text omits false witnesses.

65 Then the high priest tore his clothes, saying, "He has spoken blasphemy! What further need do we have of witnesses? Look, now you have heard His blasphemy!
66 "What do you think?" They answered and said, "He is deserving of death."
67 Then they spat in His face and beat Him; and others struck *Him* with the palms of their hands,
68 saying, "Prophesy to us, Christ! Who is the one who struck You?"

Peter Denies Jesus, and Weeps Bitterly

69 Now Peter sat outside in the courtyard. And a servant girl came to him, saying, "You also were with Jesus of Galilee."
70 But he denied it before *them* all, saying, "I do not know what you are saying."
71 And when he had gone out to the gateway, another *girl* saw him and said to those *who were* there, "This *fellow* also was with Jesus of Nazareth."
72 But again he denied with an oath, "I do not know the Man!"
73 And after a while those who stood by came to *him* and said to Peter, "Surely you also are *one* of them, because your speech betrays you."
74 Then he began to curse and swear, *saying,* "I do not know the Man!" And immediately a rooster crowed.
75 And Peter remembered the word of Jesus who had said to him, "Before the rooster crows, you will deny Me three times." Then he went out and wept bitterly.

Jesus Handed Over to Pontius Pilate

27 When morning came, all the chief priests and elders of the people took counsel against Jesus to put Him to death.
2 And when they had bound Him, they led Him away and delivered Him to Pontius[149] Pilate the governor.

Judas Hangs Himself

3 Then Judas, His betrayer, seeing that He had been condemned, was remorseful and brought back the thirty pieces of silver to the chief priests and elders,
4 saying, "I have sinned by betraying innocent blood." And they said, "What *is that* to us? You see *to it!*"

5 Then he threw down the pieces of silver in the temple and departed, and went and hanged himself.
6 But the chief priests took the silver pieces and said, "It is not lawful to put them into the treasury, because they are the price of blood."
7 And they took counsel and bought with them the potter's field, to bury strangers in.
8 Therefore that field has been called the Field of Blood to this day.
9 Then was fulfilled what was spoken by Jeremiah the prophet, saying, *"And they took the thirty pieces of silver, the value of Him who was priced, whom they of the children of Israel priced,*
10 *"and gave them for the potter's field, as the LORD directed me."*[150]

Jesus Faces Pilate

11 Now Jesus stood before the governor. And the governor asked Him, saying, "Are You the King of the Jews?" So Jesus said to him, *"It is as* you say."
12 And while He was being accused by the chief priests and elders, He answered nothing.
13 Then Pilate said to Him, "Do You not hear how many things they testify against You?"
14 And He answered him not one word, so that the governor marveled greatly.

Taking the Place of Barabbas

15 Now at the feast the governor was accustomed to releasing to the multitude one prisoner whom they wished.
16 And they had then a notorious prisoner called Barabbas.[151]
17 Therefore, when they had gathered together, Pilate said to them, "Whom do you want me to release to you? Barabbas, or Jesus who is called Christ?"
18 For he knew that because of envy they had delivered Him.
19 While he was sitting on the judgment seat, his wife sent to him, saying, "Have nothing to do with that just Man, for I have suffered many things today in a dream because of Him."
20 But the chief priests and elders persuaded the multitudes that they should ask for Barabbas and destroy Jesus.
21 The governor answered and said to them, "Which of the two do you want me

---

149 NU-Text omits *Pontius.*   150 Jeremiah 32:6–9   151 NU-Text reads *Jesus Barabbas.*

to release to you?" They said, "Barabbas!"
22 Pilate said to them, "What then shall I do with Jesus who is called Christ?" *They* all said to him, "Let Him be crucified!"
23 Then the governor said, "Why, what evil has He done?" But they cried out all the more, saying, "Let Him be crucified!"
24 When Pilate saw that he could not prevail at all, but rather *that* a tumult was rising, he took water and washed *his* hands before the multitude, saying, "I am innocent of the blood of this just Person.[152] You see *to it*."
25 And all the people answered and said, "His blood *be* on us and on our children."
26 Then he released Barabbas to them; and when he had scourged Jesus, he delivered *Him* to be crucified.

The Soldiers Mock Jesus

27 Then the soldiers of the governor took Jesus into the Praetorium and gathered the whole garrison around Him.
28 And they stripped Him and put a scarlet robe on Him.
29 When they had twisted a crown of thorns, they put *it* on His head, and a reed in His right hand. And they bowed the knee before Him and mocked Him, saying, "Hail, King of the Jews!"
30 Then they spat on Him, and took the reed and struck Him on the head.
31 Then when they had mocked Him, they took the robe off Him, put His *own* clothes on Him, and led Him away to be crucified.

The King on a Cross

32 Now as they came out, they found a man of Cyrene, Simon by name. Him they compelled to bear His cross.
33 And when they had come to a place called Golgotha, that is to say, Place of a Skull,
34 they gave Him sour[153] wine mingled with gall to drink. But when He had tasted *it*, He would not drink.
35 Then they crucified Him, and divided His garments, casting lots,[154] that it might be fulfilled which was spoken by the prophet:

*"They divided My garments among them,
And for My clothing they cast lots."*[155]

36 Sitting down, they kept watch over Him there.
37 And they put up over His head the accusation written against Him:

THIS IS JESUS
THE KING OF THE JEWS.

38 Then two robbers were crucified with Him, one on the right and another on the left.
39 And those who passed by blasphemed Him, wagging their heads
40 and saying, "You who destroy the temple and build *it* in three days, save Yourself! If You are the Son of God, come down from the cross."
41 Likewise the chief priests, also mocking with the scribes and elders,[156] said,
42 "He saved others; Himself He cannot save. If He is the King of Israel,[157] let Him now come down from the cross, and we will believe Him.[158]
43 "He trusted in God; let Him deliver Him now if He will have Him; for He said, 'I am the Son of God.'"
44 Even the robbers who were crucified with Him reviled Him with the same thing.

Jesus Dies on the Cross

45 Now from the sixth hour until the ninth hour there was darkness over all the land.
46 And about the ninth hour Jesus cried out with a loud voice, saying, "Eli, Eli, lama sabachthani?" that is, *"My God, My God, why have You forsaken Me?"*[159]
47 Some of those who stood there, when they heard *that*, said, "This *Man* is calling for Elijah!"
48 Immediately one of them ran and took a sponge, filled *it* with sour wine and put *it* on a reed, and gave it to Him to drink.
49 The rest said, "Let Him alone; let us see if Elijah will come to save Him."
50 Jesus, when He had cried out again with a loud voice, yielded up His spirit.
51 And behold, the veil of the temple was torn in two from top to bottom; and the earth quaked, and the rocks were split,

152 NU-Text omits *just*.   153 NU-Text omits *sour*.   154 NU-Text and M-Text omit the rest of this verse.
155 Psalm 22:18   156 M-Text reads *with the scribes, the Pharisees, and the elders.*
157 NU-Text reads *He is the King of Israel!*   158 NU-Text and M-Text read *we will believe in Him.*
159 Psalm 22:1

The King Forever

Jesus Christ was tried before Pontius Pilate in the Roman praetorium inside the Antonia fortress. Here, Rome's legions were garrisoned overlooking the temple of Jerusalem. This large pavement area has been unearthed, consisting of hugh limestone blocks, each weighing several tons.

Archaeologists have discovered an interesting game dating back to the New Testament period. Etched into the stone pavement of the praetorium is a playing board for a game known among the Roman soldiers as "king for a day." Various shapes of squares, pie-like slices, and rectangles were cut into the surface of the stone. Dice made from sheep's knucklebones were cast onto these marks. The soldier who threw his dice on just the right shape won the game. His reward was to be "king for a day."

As king, the soldier was dressed in a beautiful purple robe imported from the city of Colossae, where the special purple dye was extracted from seashells. This particular style of robe was reserved for royalty, and the color was often reserved by emperors for their use only. In addition to the robe, the "king" received a crown, scepter, and anything else he wished, including wine, women, and song, but there was one catch. At the end of the day, the "king" was put to death.

This game sheds new light on the Romans' mocking and scourging of Jesus. They beat Him, dressed Him in a purple robe, gave Him a crown of thorns and told Him He could make demands to save Himself. By mocking Jesus, the Roman and Herodian soldiers saw an opportunity to play the "king for a day" game in a perverse and twisted manner.

Unknown to them, the "king" they mocked was not just another man. In fact, He was and is the true King. His love was evident for those who crucified Him when He cried out from the cross, "Father, forgive them, for they do not know what they do" (Luke 23:34).

Jesus, the Son of God, was not simply to be king for the day, for the cords of death could not hold Him. By His resurrection He revealed that He was and is King forever!

52 and the graves were opened; and many bodies of the saints who had fallen asleep were raised;
53 and coming out of the graves after His resurrection, they went into the holy city and appeared to many.
54 Now when the centurion and those with him, who were guarding Jesus, saw the earthquake and the things that had happened, they feared greatly, saying, "Truly this was the Son of God!"
55 And many women who followed Jesus from Galilee, ministering to Him, were there looking on from afar,
56 among whom were Mary Magdalene, Mary the mother of James and Joses,[160] and the mother of Zebedee's sons.

Jesus Buried in Joseph's Tomb

57 Now when evening had come, there came a rich man from Arimathea, named Joseph, who himself had also become a disciple of Jesus.
58 This man went to Pilate and asked for the body of Jesus. Then Pilate commanded.the body to be given to him.
59 And when Joseph had taken the body, he wrapped it in a clean linen cloth,
60 and laid it in his new tomb which he had hewn out of the rock; and he rolled a large stone against the door of the tomb, and departed.
61 And Mary Magdalene was there, and the other Mary, sitting opposite the tomb.

Pilate Sets a Guard

62 On the next day, which followed the Day of Preparation, the chief priests and Pharisees gathered together to Pilate,
63 saying, "Sir, we remember, while He was still alive, how that deceiver said, 'After three days I will rise.'
64 "Therefore command that the tomb be made secure until the third day, lest His disciples come by night[161] and steal Him *away*, and say to the people, 'He has risen from the dead.' So the last deception will be worse than the first."
65 Pilate said to them, "You have a guard; go your way, make *it* as secure as you know how."
66 So they went and made the tomb secure, sealing the stone and setting the guard.

He Is Risen

28 Now after the Sabbath, as the first *day* of the week began to dawn, Mary Magdalene and the other Mary came to see the tomb.
2 And behold, there was a great earthquake; for an angel of the Lord descended from heaven, and came and rolled back the stone from the door,[162] and sat on it.
3 His countenance was like lightning, and his clothing as white as snow.
4 And the guards shook for fear of him, and became like dead *men.*
5 But the angel answered and said to the women, "Do not be afraid, for I know that you seek Jesus who was crucified.
6 "He is not here; for He is risen, as He said. Come, see the place where the Lord lay.
7 "And go quickly and tell His disciples that He is risen from the dead, and indeed He is going before you into Galilee; there you will see Him. Behold, I have told you."
8 So they departed quickly from the tomb with fear and great joy, and ran to bring His disciples word.

The Women Worship the Risen Lord

9 And as they went to tell His disciples,[163] behold, Jesus met them, saying, "Rejoice!" And they came and held Him by the feet and worshiped Him.
10 Then Jesus said to them, "Do not be afraid. Go *and* tell My brethren to go to Galilee, and there they will see Me."

The Soldiers Are Bribed

11 Now while they were going, behold, some of the guard came into the city and reported to the chief priests all the things that had happened.
12 When they had assembled with the elders and taken counsel, they gave a large sum of money to the soldiers,
13 saying, "Tell them, 'His disciples came at night and stole Him *away* while we slept.'
14 "And if this comes to the governor's ears, we will appease him and make you secure."
15 So they took the money and did as they were instructed; and this saying is

160 NU-Text reads *Joseph.*   161 NU-Text omits *by night.*
162 NU-Text omits *from the door.*   163 NU-Text omits the first clause of this verse.

The Centurion

Among the Roman ranks stationed in Judea during the time of Christ were the crack tenth and twelfth legions. From these superior troops came the soldiers and their centurion commander who crucified Christ. The Roman centurion was a highly-trained officer having command over one hundred men. Under his authority the soldiers beat, mocked and eventually nailed Jesus to the cross. They were well experienced in crucifying criminals. The centurion was himself a veteran who had witnessed and carried out numerous crucifixions. Yet the commander realized that there was something mysteriously different about *this* crucifixion! From his understanding, Jesus had done nothing worthy of death. Although he was responsible for carrying out his orders, the centurion stood out among the soldiers in his legion. Having observed the entire scene of Jesus' death, the centurion declared, "Truly this was the Son of God!" (Matt. 27:54).

Against the background of the Roman pagan worship of many gods, the centurion's assertion had unique significance. Roman emperors often requested that divine homage be paid only to themselves. Any other worship or admiration of other gods was considered treason and was punishable by death. Well aware of these consequences, the centurion boldly declared his faith. Even though he was personally responsible for the crucifixion of Jesus Christ, the centurion could accept God's love and forgiveness.

We must also be bold and courageous enough to stand out against the crowd and worship God when others mock Him. We must accept God's love and forgiveness and make a positive affirmation of our faith. In doing so, we have the assurance of Christ's promise. If we affirm Him before men, He will affirm us before God.

commonly reported among the Jews until this day.

The Great Commission

16 Then the eleven disciples went away into Galilee, to the mountain which Jesus had appointed for them. **17** And when they saw Him, they worshiped Him; but some doubted. **18** Then Jesus came and spoke to them, saying, "All authority has been given to Me in heaven and on earth. **19** "Go therefore[164] and make disciples of all the nations, baptizing them in the name of the Father and of the Son and of the Holy Spirit, **20** "teaching them to observe all things that I have commanded you; and lo, I am with you always, *even* to the end of the age." Amen.[165]

164 M-Text omits *therefore*. 165 Nu-Text omits *Amen*.

Introduction to Mark

Mark is the shortest and is thought to be the earliest Gospel, written about A.D. 45–65. John Mark was the apostle Peter's amanuensis—a Greek word meaning scribe or secretary. It is most probable that Mark recorded the eyewitness accounts of Peter. This Gospel may have been written while Peter and Mark were in prison in Rome. Mark pays careful attention to translate Aramaic expressions to Latin and Greek for his gentile readers.

Mark is the second in the arrangement of the so-called synoptic Gospels (meaning "to see together"). A major theme throughout the Gospel of Mark is the urgency of belief in Jesus Christ and the kingdom of God. The word "immediately" occurs repeatedly: at Jesus' baptism "immediately . . . He saw the heavens parting and the Spirit descending upon Him like a dove" (Mark 1:10); Jesus called them and "immediately they [disciples] left their nets" (Mark 1:18); "immediately His fame spread throughout all the region around Galilee" (Mark 1:28); "immediately the leprosy left him, and he was cleansed" (Mark 1:42). Mark wants to convince his readers of the urgency to evangelize the Jewish people and the gentile nations. After spending time with Jesus, the disciples must now do what Jesus had prepared them for—to carry on His ministry.

Mark was a "do it now" person! He knew that the biggest obstacle was to get started. Yet after spending three years with Jesus, he witnessed how his Lord acted—immediately, to heal human hurts and sufferings.

The Gospel of Mark not only gives us a greater understanding of our Lord, but an attitude and life-style which we can follow. Do it now!

The Gospel According to

Mark

John the Baptist Prepares the Way

THE beginning of the gospel of Jesus Christ, the Son of God. 2 As it is written in the Prophets:[1]

"Behold, I send My messenger
before Your face,
Who will prepare Your way
before You." [2]
3 "The voice of one crying in the
wilderness:
'Prepare the way of the LORD,
Make His paths straight.' "[3]

4 John came baptizing in the wilderness and preaching a baptism of repentance for the remission of sins. 5 And all the land of Judea, and those from Jerusalem, went out to him and were all baptized by him in the Jordan River, confessing their sins. 6 Now John was clothed with camel's hair and with a leather belt around his waist, and he ate locusts and wild honey. 7 And he preached, saying, "There comes One after me who is mightier than I, whose sandal strap I am not worthy to stoop down and loose. 8 "I indeed baptized you with water, but He will baptize you with the Holy Spirit."

John Baptizes Jesus

9 It came to pass in those days that Jesus came from Nazareth of Galilee, and was baptized by John in the Jordan. 10 And immediately, coming up from[4] the water, He saw the heavens parting and the Spirit descending upon Him like a dove. 11 Then a voice came from heaven, "You are My beloved Son, in whom I am well pleased."

Satan Tempts Jesus

12 And immediately the Spirit drove Him into the wilderness. 13 And He was there in the wilderness forty days, tempted by Satan, and was with the wild beasts; and the angels ministered to Him.

Jesus Begins His Galilean Ministry

14 Now after John was put in prison, Jesus came to Galilee, preaching the gospel of the kingdom[5] of God, 15 and saying, "The time is fulfilled, and the kingdom of God is at hand. Repent, and believe in the gospel."

Four Fishermen Called as Disciples

16 And as He walked by the Sea of Galilee, He saw Simon and Andrew his brother casting a net into the sea; for they were fishermen. 17 Then Jesus said to them, "Come after Me, and I will make you become fishers of men." 18 And immediately they left their nets and followed Him. 19 When He had gone a little farther from there, He saw James the son of Zebedee, and John his brother, who also were in the boat mending their nets. 20 And immediately He called them, and they left their father Zebedee in the boat with the hired servants, and went after Him.

Jesus Casts Out an Unclean Spirit

21 Then they went into Capernaum, and immediately on the Sabbath He entered the synagogue and taught. 22 And they were astonished at His teaching, for He taught them as one having authority, and not as the scribes. 23 Now there was a man in their synagogue with an unclean spirit. And he cried out, 24 saying, "Let us alone! What have we to do with You, Jesus of Nazareth? Did You come to destroy us? I know who You are—the Holy One of God!" 25 But Jesus rebuked him, saying, "Be quiet, and come out of him!" 26 And when the unclean spirit had convulsed him and cried out with a loud voice, he came out of him.

---

1 NU-Text reads Isaiah the prophet. 2 Malachi 3:1 3 Isaiah 40:3
4 NU-Text reads out of. 5 NU-Text omits of the kingdom.

Peter's House in Capernaum

Archaeologists believe they have unearthed the house of the disciple Peter in Capernaum. Numerous fishhooks and coins from the time of Christ have been found in the house indicating that it was a fisherman's dwelling. First-century inscriptions showing early Christian veneration of the site as Peter's house provide written and pictorial evidence to support this claim.

In the course of Jesus' ministry, Christ spent many days in the town of Capernaum. On one such occasion, Jesus taught in the house of Peter and his mother-in-law. While there, a group of men attempted to bring a paralyzed man to Jesus to be healed. However, the crowd pressing in on all sides of the house presented an impossible situation for this small band of believers. But they were not to be discouraged.

Determined to conquer their problem, the men climbed to the roof of the house and raised the paralytic on a stretcher. The tile roof was quickly disassembled, and the man was then lowered on the stretcher to Jesus in the room below. Jesus recognized their display of faith and determination. Even though many obstacles barred them from getting to Jesus, the men moved forward, for they knew that Jesus was the answer. In response to their faith, Jesus healed the paralytic.

Throughout the Gospels we read of other incidents where people did everything they could to get to Jesus. They traveled hundreds of miles in adverse conditions, payed toll taxes, and suffered persecution and rejection. Why? They knew that Jesus had the healing power and the teaching that they needed. Through faith, God turned their problems into possibilities and their obstacles into opportunities!

What obstacle prevents you from getting close to Jesus? You know He is the answer. Make Him your goal. Be determined and persistent. When faced with a mountain of a problem—find a way through!

27 Then they were all amazed, so that they questioned among themselves, saying, "What is this? What new doctrine *is* this? For with authority[6] He commands even the unclean spirits, and they obey Him."
28 And immediately His fame spread throughout all the region around Galilee.

Peter's Mother-in-Law Healed

29 Now as soon as they had come out of the synagogue, they entered the house of Simon and Andrew, with James and John.
30 But Simon's wife's mother lay sick with a fever, and they told Him about her at once.
31 So He came and took her by the hand and lifted her up, and immediately the fever left her. And she served them.

Many Healed after Sabbath Sunset

32 Now at evening, when the sun had set, they brought to Him all who were sick and those who were demon-possessed.
33 And the whole city was gathered together at the door.
34 Then He healed many who were sick with various diseases, and cast out many demons; and He did not allow the demons to speak, because they knew Him.

Preaching in Galilee

35 Now in the morning, having risen a long while before daylight, He went out and departed to a solitary place; and there He prayed.
36 And Simon and those *who were* with Him searched for Him.
37 When they found Him, they said to Him, "Everyone is looking for You."
38 But He said to them, "Let us go into the next towns, that I may preach there also, because for this purpose I have come forth."
39 And He was preaching in their synagogues throughout all Galilee, and casting out demons.

Jesus Cleanses a Leper

40 Then a leper came to Him, imploring Him, kneeling down to Him and saying to Him, "If You are willing, You can make me clean."
41 And Jesus, moved with compassion, put out *His* hand and touched him, and

said to him, "I am willing; be cleansed."
42 As soon as He had spoken, immediately the leprosy left him, and he was cleansed.
43 And He strictly warned him and sent him away at once.
44 And He said to him, "See that you say nothing to anyone; but go your way, show yourself to the priest, and offer for your cleansing those things which Moses commanded, as a testimony to them."
45 But he went out and began to proclaim *it* freely, and to spread the matter, so that Jesus could no longer openly enter the city, but was outside in deserted places; and they came to Him from every quarter.

Jesus Forgives and Heals a Paralytic

2 And again He entered Capernaum after *some* days, and it was heard that He was in the house.
2 Immediately[7] many gathered together, so that there was no longer room to receive *them,* not even near the door. And He preached the word to them.
3 Then they came to Him, bringing a paralytic who was carried by four *men.*
4 And when they could not come near Him because of the crowd, they uncovered the roof where He was. And when they had broken through, they let down the bed on which the paralytic was lying.
5 When Jesus saw their faith, He said to the paralytic, "Son, your sins are forgiven you."
6 But some of the scribes were sitting there and reasoning in their hearts,
7 "Why does this *Man* speak blasphemies like this? Who can forgive sins but God alone?"
8 And immediately, when Jesus perceived in His spirit that they reasoned thus within themselves, He said to them, "Why do you reason about these things in your hearts?
9 "Which is easier, to say to the paralytic, '*Your* sins are forgiven you,' or to say, 'Arise, take up your bed and walk'?
10 "But that you may know that the Son of Man has power on earth to forgive sins"—He said to the paralytic,
11 "I say to you, arise, take up your bed, and go your way to your house."
12 And immediately he arose, took up the bed, and went out in the presence of

6 NU-Text reads *What is this? A new doctrine with authority.*   7 NU-Text omits *immediately.*

them all, so that all were amazed and glorified God, saying, "We never saw *anything* like this!"

Matthew the Tax Collector

13 Then He went out again by the sea; and all the multitude came to Him, and He taught them.
14 And as He passed by, He saw Levi the *son* of Alphaeus sitting at the tax office, and said to him, "Follow Me." And he arose and followed Him.
15 Now it happened, as He was dining in *Levi's* house, that many tax collectors and sinners also sat together with Jesus and His disciples; for there were many, and they followed Him.
16 And when the scribes and[8] Pharisees saw Him eating with the tax collectors and sinners, they said to His disciples, "How *is it* that He eats and drinks with tax collectors and sinners?"
17 When Jesus heard *it*, He said to them, "Those who are well have no need of a physician, but those who are sick. I did not come to call *the* righteous, but sinners, to repentance."[9]

Jesus Is Questioned about Fasting

18 And the disciples of John and of the Pharisees were fasting. And they came and said to Him, "Why do the disciples of John and of the Pharisees fast, but Your disciples do not fast?"
19 So Jesus said to them, "Can the friends of the bridegroom fast while the bridegroom is with them? As long as they have the bridegroom with them they cannot fast.
20 "But the days will come when the bridegroom will be taken away from them, and then they will fast in those days.
21 "No one sews a piece of unshrunk cloth on an old garment; or else the new piece pulls away from the old, and the tear is made worse.
22 "And no one puts new wine into old wineskins; or else the new wine bursts the wineskins, the wine is spilled, and the wineskins are ruined. But new wine must be put into new wineskins."

Jesus Is Lord of the Sabbath

23 Now it happened that He went through the grainfields on the Sabbath;

and as they went His disciples began to pluck the heads of grain.
24 And the Pharisees said to Him, "Look, why do they do what is not lawful on the Sabbath?"
25 But He said to them, "Have you never read what David did when he was in need and hungry, he and those with him:
26 "how he went into the house of God *in the days* of Abiathar the high priest, and ate the showbread, which is not lawful to eat, except for the priests, and also gave some to those who were with him?"
27 And He said to them, "The Sabbath was made for man, and not man for the Sabbath.
28 "Therefore the Son of Man is also Lord of the Sabbath."

Healing on the Sabbath

3 And He entered the synagogue again, and a man was there who had a withered hand.
2 And they watched Him closely, whether He would heal him on the Sabbath, so that they might accuse Him.
3 Then He said to the man who had the withered hand, "Step forward."
4 And He said to them, "Is it lawful on the Sabbath to do good or to do evil, to save life or to kill?" But they kept silent.
5 So when He had looked around at them with anger, being grieved by the hardness of their hearts, He said to the man, "Stretch out your hand." And he stretched *it* out, and his hand was restored as whole as the other.[10]
6 Then the Pharisees went out and immediately plotted with the Herodians against Him, how they might destroy Him.

A Great Multitude Follows Jesus

7 But Jesus withdrew with His disciples to the sea. And a great multitude from Galilee followed Him, and from Judea
8 and Jerusalem and Idumea and beyond the Jordan; and those from Tyre and Sidon, a great multitude, when they heard how many things He was doing, came to Him.
9 And He told His disciples that a small boat should be kept ready for Him because of the multitude, lest they should crush Him.
10 For He healed many, so that as many

8 NU-Text reads *of the.*   9 NU-Text omits *to repentance.*   10 NU-Text omits *as whole as the other.*

as had afflictions pressed about Him to touch Him.

11 And the unclean spirits, whenever they saw Him, fell down before Him and cried out, saying, "You are the Son of God."

12 But He sternly warned them that they should not make Him known.

The Twelve Apostles

13 And He went up on the mountain and called *to Him* those He Himself wanted. And they came to Him.

14 Then He appointed twelve,[11] that they might be with Him and that He might send them out to preach,

15 and to have power to heal sicknesses and[12] to cast out demons:

16 Simon,[13] to whom He gave the name Peter;

17 James the *son* of Zebedee and John the brother of James, to whom He gave the name Boanerges, that is, "Sons of Thunder";

18 Andrew, Philip, Bartholomew, Matthew, Thomas, James the *son* of Alphaeus, Thaddaeus, Simon the Canaanite;

19 and Judas Iscariot, who also betrayed Him. And they went into a house.

A House Divided Cannot Stand

20 And the multitude came together again, so that they could not so much as eat bread.

21 But when His own people heard *about this*, they went out to lay hold of Him, for they said, "He is out of His mind."

22 And the scribes who came down from Jerusalem said, "He has Beelzebub," and, "By the ruler of the demons He casts out demons."

23 So He called them *to Him* and said to them in parables: "How can Satan cast out Satan?

24 "If a kingdom is divided against itself, that kingdom cannot stand.

25 "And if a house is divided against itself, that house cannot stand.

26 "And if Satan has risen up against himself, and is divided, he cannot stand, but has an end.

27 "No one can enter a strong man's house and plunder his goods, unless he first binds the strong man, and then he will plunder his house.

The Unpardonable Sin

28 "Assuredly, I say to you, all sins will be forgiven the sons of men, and whatever blasphemies they may utter;

29 "but he who blasphemes against the Holy Spirit never has forgiveness, but is subject to eternal condemnation"—

30 because they said, "He has an unclean spirit."

Jesus' Mother and Brothers Send for Him

31 Then His brothers and His mother came, and standing outside they sent to Him, calling Him.

32 And a multitude was sitting around Him; and they said to Him, "Look, Your mother and Your brothers[14] are outside seeking You."

33 But He answered them, saying, "Who is My mother, or My brothers?"

34 And He looked around in a circle at those who sat about Him, and said, "Here are My mother and My brothers!

35 "For whoever does the will of God is My brother and My sister and mother."

The Parable of the Sower

4 And again He began to teach by the sea. And a great multitude was gathered to Him, so that He got into a boat and sat *in it* on the sea; and the whole multitude was on the land facing the sea.

2 Then He taught them many things by parables, and said to them in His teaching:

3 "Listen! Behold, a sower went out to sow.

4 "And it happened, as he sowed, *that* some *seed* fell by the wayside; and the birds of the air[15] came and devoured it.

5 "Some fell on stony ground, where it did not have much earth; and immediately it sprang up because it had no depth of earth.

6 "But when the sun was up it was scorched, and because it had no root it withered away.

7 "And some *seed* fell among thorns; and the thorns grew up and choked it, and it yielded no crop.

8 "But other *seed* fell on good ground and yielded a crop that sprang up, increased and produced: some thirtyfold, some sixty, and some a hundred."

---

11 NU-Text adds *whom He also named apostles.*　　12 NU-Text omits *to heal sicknesses and.*
13 NU-Text reads *and He appointed the twelve: Simon . . . .*　　14 NU-Text and M-Text add *and your sisters.*
15 NU-Text and M-Text omit *of the air.*

9 And He said to them,[16] "He who has ears to hear, let him hear!"

The Purpose of Parables

10 But when He was alone, those around Him with the twelve asked Him about the parable.
11 And He said to them, "To you it has been given to know the mystery of the kingdom of God; but to those who are outside, all things come in parables,
12 "so that

'Seeing they may see and not perceive,
And hearing they may hear and not
understand;
Lest they should turn,
And their sins be forgiven them.' "[17]

The Parable of the Sower Explained

13 And He said to them, "Do you not understand this parable? How then will you understand all the parables?
14 "The sower sows the word.
15 "And these are the ones by the wayside where the word is sown. And when they hear, Satan comes immediately and takes away the word that was sown in their hearts.
16 "These likewise are the ones sown on stony ground who, when they hear the word, immediately receive it with gladness;
17 "and they have no root in themselves, and so endure only for a time. Afterward, when tribulation or persecution arises for the word's sake, immediately they stumble.
18 "Now these are the ones sown among thorns; *they are* the ones who hear the word,
19 "and the cares of this world, the deceitfulness of riches, and the desires for other things entering in choke the word, and it becomes unfruitful.
20 "But these are the ones sown on good ground, those who hear the word, accept *it,* and bear fruit: some thirtyfold, some sixty, and some a hundred."

Light Under a Basket

21 And He said to them, "Is a lamp brought to be put under a basket or under a bed? Is it not to be set on a lampstand?
22 "For there is nothing hidden which will not be revealed, nor has anything been kept secret but that it should come to light.
23 "If anyone has ears to hear, let him hear."
24 And He said to them, "Take heed what you hear. With the same measure you use, it will be measured to you; and to you who hear, more will be given.
25 "For whoever has, to him more will be given; but whoever does not have, even what he has will be taken away from him."

The Parable of the Growing Seed

26 And He said, "The kingdom of God is as if a man should scatter seed on the ground,
27 "and should sleep by night and rise by day, and the seed should sprout and grow, he himself does not know how.
28 "For the earth yields crops by itself: first the blade, then the head, after that the full grain in the head.
29 "But when the grain ripens, immediately he puts in the sickle, because the harvest has come."

The Parable of the Mustard Seed

30 And He said, "To what shall we liken the kingdom of God? Or with what parable shall we picture it?
31 *"It is* like a mustard seed which, when it is sown on the ground, is smaller than all the seeds on earth;
32 "but when it is sown, it grows up and becomes greater than all herbs, and shoots out large branches, so that the birds of the air may nest under its shade."

Jesus' Use of Parables

33 And with many such parables He spoke the word to them as they were able to hear *it.*
34 But without a parable He did not speak to them. And when they were alone, He explained all things to His disciples.

Wind and Wave Obey Jesus

35 On the same day, when evening had come, He said to them, "Let us cross over to the other side."
36 Now when they had left the multitude, they took Him along in the boat as He was. And other little boats were also with Him.

16 NU-Text and M-Text omit *to them.*   17 Isaiah 6:9, 10

The Gadarene Demoniac

On the southeastern shores of the Sea of Galilee, towering salted cliffs stretch down to the lake. In the face of these cliffs are many honeycombed caves. In one such cave lived a demon-possessed man who for many years prevented travelers from passing along the road. The Bible tells us he harassed them and frightened them. Each time the demoniac was put in chains, he broke the bonds. He was one of the most feared men of the region.

During one of Jesus' trips to the eastern shore of the lake He came to the area of Gadara, a gentile region known for pig farming. It was here that the demoniac haunted the villagers. Upon seeing Jesus, the Gadarene demoniac bowed down and worshiped Him. The demons within this man asked Jesus to leave him alone. Seeing the man's great need, Jesus commanded the demons to leave him. The demons answered, "My name *is* Legion; for we are many" (Mark 5:9). This response reflects the culture and influence of the Romans upon the countryside. Immediately, Jesus commanded the demons to leave the man and to go into the pigs. The demons entered the swine who ran down the steep cliff and into the sea. Normally pigs swim well, but in this case the swine drowned.

The people from the region of Gadara had two choices for response to Jesus' miracle: to be excited that Jesus healed the man; or to be deeply disturbed that Jesus destroyed their main source of income. Witnesses ran into the city and told the townspeople what had happened. When the entire city of Gadara went out and saw the healed man and that the pigs were no longer grazing on the hillside, they asked Jesus to leave because He had destroyed their major industry.

The people chose to look at what they had lost, not what Jesus had given them. They did not see the valuable healing of a human being, but the loss of some pigs. They focused on the negative not the positive. They did not understand that the God who healed the demon-possessed man could have provided all of their needs if they only asked.

The healed man wanted to travel with Jesus, but Jesus had other plans for him. Jesus said, "Go home to your friends, and tell them what great things the Lord has done for you, and how He has had compassion on you" (Mark 5:19). So the healed man departed, proclaimed throughout Decapolis what Jesus had done, and all marveled.

In every situation in our lives we have the opportunity to look at the negative or the positive. We must always learn to accentuate the positive. Look at what Jesus has given you. In all aspects of life, look at what you have left—never at what you have lost!

37 And a great windstorm arose, and the waves beat into the boat, so that it was already filling.
38 But He was in the stern, asleep on a pillow. And they awoke Him and said to Him, "Teacher, do You not care that we are perishing?"
39 Then He arose and rebuked the wind, and said to the sea, "Peace, be still!" And the wind ceased and there was a great calm.
40 But He said to them, "Why are you so fearful? How *is it* that you have no faith?" 18
41 And they feared exceedingly, and said to one another, "Who can this be, that even the wind and the sea obey Him!"

A Demon-Possessed Man Healed

5 Then they came to the other side of the sea, to the country of the Gadarenes.19
2 And when He had come out of the boat, immediately there met Him out of the tombs a man with an unclean spirit,
3 who had *his* dwelling among the tombs; and no one could bind him,20 not even with chains,
4 because he had often been bound with shackles and chains. And the chains had been pulled apart by him, and the shackles broken in pieces; neither could anyone tame him.
5 And always, night and day, he was in the mountains and in the tombs, crying out and cutting himself with stones.
6 But when he saw Jesus from afar, he ran and worshiped Him.
7 And he cried out with a loud voice and said, "What have I to do with You, Jesus, Son of the Most High God? I implore You by God that You do not torment me."
8 For He said to him, "Come out of the man, unclean spirit!"
9 Then He asked him, "What *is* your name?" And he answered, saying, "My name *is* Legion; for we are many."
10 And he begged Him earnestly that He would not send them out of the country.
11 Now a large herd of swine was feeding there near the mountains.
12 And all the demons begged Him, saying, "Send us to the swine, that we may enter them."
13 And at once Jesus21 gave them permis-

sion. Then the unclean spirits went out and entered the swine (there were about two thousand); and the herd ran violently down the steep place into the sea, and drowned in the sea.
14 Now those who fed the swine fled, and they told *it* in the city and in the country. And they went out to see what it was that had happened.
15 Then they came to Jesus, and saw the one *who had been* demon-possessed and had the legion, sitting and clothed and in his right mind. And they were afraid.
16 And those who saw it told them how it happened to him *who had been* demon-possessed, and about the swine.
17 Then they began to plead with Him to depart from their region.
18 And when He got into the boat, he who had been demon-possessed begged Him that he might be with Him.
19 However, Jesus did not permit him, but said to him, "Go home to your friends, and tell them what great things the Lord has done for you, and how He has had compassion on you."
20 And he departed and began to proclaim in Decapolis all that Jesus had done for him; and all marveled.

A Girl Restored to Life and a Woman Healed

21 Now when Jesus had crossed over again by boat to the other side, a great multitude gathered to Him; and He was by the sea.
22 And behold, one of the rulers of the synagogue came, Jairus by name. And when he saw Him, he fell at His feet
23 and begged Him earnestly, saying, "My little daughter lies at the point of death. Come and lay Your hands on her, that she may be healed, and she will live."
24 So *Jesus* went with him, and a great multitude followed Him and thronged Him.
25 Now a certain woman had a flow of blood for twelve years,
26 and had suffered many things from many physicians. She had spent all that she had and was no better, but rather grew worse.
27 When she heard about Jesus, she came behind *Him* in the crowd and touched His garment;
28 for she said, "If only I may touch His clothes, I shall be made well."

18 NU-Text reads *Have you still no faith?*　19 NU-Text reads *Gerasenes.*
20 NU-Text adds *anymore.*　21 NU-Text reads *And He gave.*

Let Go and Let God

In the Bible, the vinedresser is the keeper of the vineyard or watchman over the field. At first glance, his responsibilities seem to fall only during spring and harvest when he can be seen planting the seeds or reaping the crops. The remaining part of the year, the vinedresser will busy himself helping clear a neighbor's rocky field or aiding in the building of a new house in the village. The vinedresser could worry about pestilence, droughts, famine, or the scorching hot east winds, but he knows that God controls these events.

Does this mean that the vinedresser does not care for the field? No. He has learned the secret of patience. He has done his task, now the power of God, through nature, will bring the crops to fruition. The vinedresser realizes the invaluable secret "to let go and let God." Jesus taught that we should be like the patient vinedresser. We should not be negative, worrying about events and circumstances beyond our control. Jesus encouraged us not to be of little faith but to have patience, not to be anxious but to understand that God sees the end from the beginning. Despite the vinedresser's apparent lack of concern—his faith was rewarded. Jesus described a similar reward in the parable of the soils "some a hundredfold, some sixty, some thirty" (Matt. 13:8).

May God grant us the wisdom to know when to plant and when to sow; when to hold on and when to let go; when to undertake new tasks and when to let God bring them to completion; and the knowledge to make the right decisions with dignity!

29 Immediately the fountain of her blood was dried up, and she felt in *her* body that she was healed of the affliction. 30 And Jesus, immediately knowing in Himself that power had gone out of Him, turned around in the crowd and said, "Who touched My clothes?" 31 But His disciples said to Him, "You see the multitude thronging You, and You say, 'Who touched Me?' " 32 And He looked around to see her who had done this thing. 33 But the woman, fearing and trembling, knowing what had happened to her, came and fell down before Him and told Him the whole truth. 34 And He said to her, "Daughter, your faith has made you well. Go in peace, and be healed of your affliction."

35 While He was still speaking, *some* came from the ruler of the synagogue's *house* who said, "Your daughter is dead. Why trouble the Teacher any further?" 36 As soon as Jesus heard the word that was spoken, He said to the ruler of the synagogue, "Do not be afraid; only believe." 37 And He permitted no one to follow Him except Peter, James, and John the brother of James. 38 Then He came to the house of the ruler of the synagogue, and saw a tumult and those who wept and wailed loudly. 39 When He came in, He said to them, "Why make this commotion and weep? The child is not dead, but sleeping." 40 And they laughed Him to scorn. But when He had put them all out, He took the father and the mother of the child, and those *who were* with Him, and entered where the child was lying. 41 Then He took the child by the hand, and said to her, "Talitha, cumi," which is translated, "Little girl, I say to you, arise." 42 Immediately the girl arose and walked, for she was twelve years *of age.* And they were overcome with great amazement. 43 But He commanded them strictly that no one should know it, and said that *something* should be given her to eat.

Jesus Rejected at Nazareth

6 Then He went out from there and came to His own country, and His disciples followed Him. 2 And when the Sabbath had come, He began to teach in the synagogue. And many hearing *Him* were astonished, saying, "Where *did* this *Man get* these things? And what wisdom *is* this which is given to Him, that such mighty works are performed by His hands! 3 "Is this not the carpenter, the Son of Mary, and brother of James, Joses, Judas, and Simon? And are not His sisters here with us?" And they were offended at Him.

4 But Jesus said to them, "A prophet is not without honor except in his own country, among his own relatives, and in his own house." 5 Now He could do no mighty work there, except that He laid His hands on a few sick people and healed *them.* 6 And He marveled because of their unbelief. Then He went about the villages in a circuit, teaching.

Sending Out the Twelve

7 And He called the twelve *to Him,* and began to send them out two *by* two, and gave them power over unclean spirits. 8 He commanded them to take nothing for the journey except a staff—no bag, no bread, no copper in *their* money belts— 9 but to wear sandals, and not to put on two tunics. 10 Also He said to them, "In whatever place you enter a house, stay there till you depart from that place. 11 "And whoever[22] will not receive you nor hear you, when you depart from there, shake off the dust under your feet as a testimony against them.[23] Assuredly, I say to you, it will be more tolerable for Sodom and Gomorrah in the day of judgment than for that city!" 12 So they went out and preached that *people* should repent. 13 And they cast out many demons, and anointed with oil many who were sick, and healed *them.*

John the Baptist Beheaded

14 Now King Herod heard *of Him,* for His name had become well-known. And he said, "John the Baptist is risen from the dead, and therefore these powers are at work in him." 15 Others said, "It is Elijah." And others said, "It is the Prophet, or[24] like one of the prophets."

22 NU-Text reads *whatever place.*   23 NU-Text omits the rest of this verse.   24 NU-Text and M-Text omit *or.*

16 But when Herod heard, he said, "This is John, whom I beheaded; he has been raised from the dead!"
17 For Herod himself had sent and laid hold of John, and bound him in prison for the sake of Herodias, his brother Philip's wife; for he had married her.
18 For John had said to Herod, "It is not lawful for you to have your brother's wife."
19 Therefore Herodias held it against him and wanted to kill him, but she could not;
20 for Herod feared John, knowing that he *was* a just and holy man, and he protected him. And when he heard him, he did many things, and heard him gladly.
21 Then an opportune day came when Herod on his birthday gave a feast for his nobles, the high officers, and the chief *men* of Galilee.
22 And when Herodias' daughter herself came in and danced, and pleased Herod and those who sat with him, the king said to the girl, "Ask me whatever you want, and I will give *it* to you."
23 He also swore to her, "Whatever you ask me, I will give you, up to half of my kingdom."
24 So she went out and said to her mother, "What shall I ask?" And she said, "The head of John the Baptist!"
25 Immediately she came in with haste to the king and asked, saying, "I want you to give me at once the head of John the Baptist on a platter."
26 And the king was exceedingly sorry; *yet*, because of the oaths and because of those who sat with him, he did not want to refuse her.
27 And immediately the king sent an executioner and commanded his head to be brought. And he went and beheaded him in prison,
28 brought his head on a platter, and gave it to the girl; and the girl gave it to her mother.
29 And when his disciples heard *of it*, they came and took away his corpse and laid it in a tomb.

Feeding the Five Thousand

30 Then the apostles gathered to Jesus and told Him all things, both what they had done and what they had taught.
31 And He said to them, "Come aside by yourselves to a deserted place and rest a while." For there were many coming and going, and they did not even have time to eat.
32 So they departed to a deserted place in the boat by themselves.
33 But the multitudes[25] saw them departing, and many knew Him and ran there on foot from all the cities. They arrived before them and came together to Him.
34 And Jesus, when He came out, saw a great multitude and was moved with compassion for them, because they were like sheep not having a shepherd. So He began to teach them many things.
35 And when the day was now far spent, His disciples came to Him and said, "This is a deserted place, and already the hour *is* late.
36 "Send them away, that they may go into the surrounding country and villages and buy themselves bread;[26] for they have nothing to eat."
37 But He answered and said to them, "You give them something to eat." And they said to Him, "Shall we go and buy two hundred denarii worth of bread and give them *something* to eat?"
38 But He said to them, "How many loaves do you have? Go and see." And when they found out they said, "Five, and two fish."
39 Then He commanded them to make them all sit down in groups on the green grass.
40 So they sat down in ranks, in hundreds and in fifties.
41 And when He had taken the five loaves and the two fish, He looked up to heaven, blessed and broke the loaves, and gave *them* to His disciples to set before them; and the two fish He divided among *them* all.
42 So they all ate and were filled.
43 And they took up twelve baskets full of fragments and of the fish.
44 Now those who had eaten the loaves were about[27] five thousand men.

Jesus Walks on the Sea

45 Immediately He made His disciples get into the boat and go before Him to the other side, to Bethsaida, while He sent the multitude away.
46 And when He had sent them away, He departed to the mountain to pray.

25 NU-Text and M-Text read *they*.   26 NU-Text reads *something to eat* and omits the rest of verse.
27 NU-Text and M-Text omit *about*.

The Other Side

A major portion of Jesus' ministry took place around the shores of the Sea of Galilee. The area was widely influenced by the Roman and Greek civilizations. This influence was primarily felt on the eastern shores of the sea where the cities were separated both culturally, religiously and geographically from the Jewish cities of Capernaum, Chorazin, and Bethsaida, located on the lake's western shores. According to Matthew, Jesus concentrated His teachings and miracles in these Jewish towns. This area was known by the Jewish population as "our side."

On occasion Jesus traveled to "the other side" to teach the people. This phrase refers not only to the eastern side of the Sea of Galilee, but more culturally and religiously to the gentile region. "The other side" was a specific reference given by the Jewish villagers to the Greek and Roman centers located on the other side of the lake. These included the cities of Hippus, Gergesa, and Gadara.

According to the Gospels, thousands of people followed Jesus to the other side. This was no easy task for the Jews. Whether they journeyed by boat or land, Rome levied a heavy sea and land tax to finance their wars in Europe. Travel to the predominantly gentile region was greatly discouraged by the religious community. Once there, the food of the Gentiles was unacceptable to the Jewish dietary laws. Those who traveled with young families found the ten-to-twenty mile journey even more difficult.

Despite the physical, cultural, and religious obstacles of travel to "the other side," the Bible records that on two occasions there were crowds of four thousand and five thousand people to hear Jesus. We know that these were mostly Jewish villagers who had traveled a long distance to hear Jesus. Since there were many gentile towns nearby, their complaints about nothing to eat can be interpreted that there was no food available for the Jewish diet.

Sometimes people may ridicule us, often it will take time out of our busy schedules, and it will certainly run contrary to the status quo for us to follow Jesus. Yet the reward for doing so remains the same: "He received them and spoke to them about the kingdom of God, and healed those who had need of healing . . . so they all ate and were filled" (Luke 9:11, 17).

47 Now when evening came, the boat was in the middle of the sea; and He *was* alone on the land.
48 Then He saw them straining at rowing, for the wind was against them. And about the fourth watch of the night He came to them, walking on the sea, and would have passed them by.
49 But when they saw Him walking on the sea, they supposed it was a ghost, and cried out;
50 for they all saw Him and were troubled. And immediately He talked with them and said to them, "Be of good cheer! It is I; do not be afraid."
51 Then He went up into the boat to them, and the wind ceased. And they were greatly amazed in themselves beyond measure, and marveled.
52 For they had not understood about the loaves, because their heart was hardened.

Many Touch Him and Are Made Well

53 When they had crossed over, they came to the land of Gennesaret and anchored there.
54 And when they came out of the boat, immediately the people recognized Him,
55 ran through that whole surrounding region, and began to carry about on beds those who were sick to wherever they heard He was.
56 Wherever He entered, into villages, cities, or the country, they laid the sick in the marketplaces, and begged Him that they might just touch the border of His garment. And as many as touched Him were made well.

Defilement Comes from Within

7 Then the Pharisees and some of the scribes came together to Him, having come from Jerusalem.
2 Now when[28] they saw some of His disciples eat bread with defiled, that is, with unwashed hands, they found fault.
3 For the Pharisees and all the Jews do not eat unless they wash *their* hands in a special way, holding the tradition of the elders.
4 *When they come* from the marketplace, they do not eat unless they wash. And there are many other things which they have received and hold, *like* the washing of cups, pitchers, copper vessels, and couches.
5 Then the Pharisees and scribes asked Him, "Why do Your disciples not walk according to the tradition of the elders, but eat bread with unwashed hands?"
6 He answered and said to them, "Well did Isaiah prophesy of you hypocrites, as it is written:

'This people honors Me with their lips,
    But their heart is far from Me.
7 And in vain they worship Me,
    Teaching as doctrines the
        commandments of men.'[29]

8 "For laying aside the commandment of God, you hold the tradition of men[30]— the washing of pitchers and cups, and many other such things you do."
9 And He said to them, "*All too* well you reject the commandment of God, that you may keep your tradition.
10 "For Moses said, '*Honor your father and your mother*';[31] and, '*He who curses father or mother, let him be put to death.*'[32]
11 "But you say, 'If a man says to his father or mother, "Whatever profit you might have received from me *is* Corban (that is, dedicated *to the temple*)";
12 "and you no longer let him do anything for his father or his mother,
13 "making the word of God of no effect through your tradition which you have handed down. And many such things you do."
14 And when He had called all the multitude *to Him*, He said to them, "Hear Me, everyone, and understand:
15 "There is nothing that enters a man from outside which can defile him; but the things which come out of him, those are the things that defile a man.
16 "If anyone has ears to hear, let him hear!"[33]
17 And when He had entered a house away from the crowd, His disciples asked Him concerning the parable.
18 So He said to them, "Are you thus without understanding also? Do you not perceive that whatever enters a man from outside cannot defile him,
19 "because it does not enter his heart

28 NU-Text omits *when* and *they found fault.*   29 Isaiah 29:13   30 NU-Text omits the rest of this verse.
31 Exodus 20:12; Deuteronomy 5:16   32 Exodus 21:17   33 NU-Text omits this verse.

but his stomach, and is eliminated, *thus* purifying all foods?"[34]
20 And He said, "What comes out of a man, that defiles a man.
21 "For from within, out of the heart of men, proceed evil thoughts, adulteries, fornications, murders,
22 "thefts, covetousness, wickedness, deceit, licentiousness, an evil eye, blasphemy, pride, foolishness.
23 "All these evil things come from within and defile a man."

A Gentile Shows Her Faith

24 And from there He arose and went to the region of Tyre and Sidon.[35] And He entered a house and wanted no one to know *it*, but He could not be hidden.
25 For a woman whose young daughter had an unclean spirit heard about Him, and she came and fell at His feet.
26 The woman was a Greek, a Syro-Phoenician by birth, and she kept asking Him to cast the demon out of her daughter.
27 But Jesus said to her, "Let the children be filled first, for it is not good to take the children's bread and throw *it* to the little dogs."
28 And she answered and said to Him, "Yes, Lord, yet even the little dogs under the table eat from the children's crumbs."
29 Then He said to her, "For this saying go your way; the demon has gone out of your daughter."
30 And when she had come to her house, she found the demon gone out, and her daughter lying on the bed.

Jesus Heals a Deaf Mute

31 And again, departing from the region of Tyre and Sidon, He came through the midst of the region of Decapolis to the Sea of Galilee.
32 Then they brought to Him one who was deaf and had an impediment in his speech, and they begged Him to put His hand on him.
33 And He took him aside from the multitude, and put His fingers in his ears, and He spat and touched his tongue.
34 Then, looking up to heaven, He sighed, and said to him, "Ephphatha," that is, "Be opened."
35 Immediately his ears were opened,

and the impediment of his tongue was loosed, and he spoke plainly.
36 Then He commanded them that they should tell no one; but the more He commanded them, the more widely they proclaimed *it*.
37 And they were astonished beyond measure, saying, "He has done all things well. He makes both the deaf to hear and the mute to speak."

Feeding the Four Thousand

8 In those days, the multitude being very great and having nothing to eat, Jesus called His disciples *to Him* and said to them,
2 "I have compassion on the multitude, because they have now been with Me three days and have nothing to eat.
3 "And if I send them away hungry to their own houses, they will faint on the way; for some of them have come from afar."
4 Then His disciples answered Him, "How can one satisfy these people with bread here in the wilderness?"
5 He asked them, "How many loaves do you have?" And they said, "Seven."
6 And He commanded the multitude to sit down on the ground. And He took the seven loaves and gave thanks, broke *them* and gave *them* to His disciples to set before *them*; and they set *them* before the multitude.
7 And they had a few small fish; and having blessed them, He said to set them also before *them*.
8 So they ate and were filled, and they took up seven large baskets of leftover fragments.
9 Now those who had eaten were about four thousand. And He sent them away.
10 And immediately He got into the boat with His disciples and came to the region of Dalmanutha.

The Pharisees Seek a Sign

11 And the Pharisees came out and began to dispute with Him, seeking from Him a sign from heaven, testing Him.
12 But He sighed deeply in His spirit, and said, "Why does this generation seek a sign? Assuredly, I say to you, no sign shall be given to this generation."

34 NU-Text ends quotation with *eliminated* by setting off the final clause as Mark's comment that Jesus has declared all foods clean.   35 NU-Text omits *and Sidon.*

Beware of the Leaven of the Pharisees and Herod

13 And He left them, and getting into the boat again, departed to the other side. *14* Now the disciples[36] had forgotten to take bread, and they did not have more than one loaf with them in the boat. *15* Then He charged them, saying, "Take heed, beware of the leaven of the Pharisees and the leaven of Herod." *16* So they reasoned among themselves, saying, "*It is* because we have no bread." *17* And Jesus, being aware of *it*, said to them, "Why do you reason because you have no bread? Do you not yet perceive nor understand? Is your heart still[37] hardened? *18* "Having eyes, do you not see? And having ears, do you not hear? And do you not remember? *19* "When I broke the five loaves for the five thousand, how many baskets full of fragments did you take up?" They said to Him, "Twelve." *20* "And when I broke the seven for the four thousand, how many large baskets full of fragments did you take up?" And they said, "Seven." *21* So He said to them, "How *is it* you do not understand?"

A Blind Paralytic Healed at Bethsaida

22 Then He came to Bethsaida; and they brought a blind man to Him, and begged Him to touch him. *23* So He took the blind man by the hand and led him out of the town. And when He had spit on his eyes and put His hands on him, He asked him if he saw anything. *24* And he looked up and said, "I see men like trees, walking." *25* Then He put *His* hands on his eyes again and made him look up. And he was restored and saw everyone clearly. *26* And He sent him away to his house, saying, "Neither go into the town, nor tell anyone in the town." [38]

Peter Confesses Jesus as the Christ

27 Now Jesus and His disciples went out to the towns of Caesarea Philippi; and on the road He asked His disciples, saying to them, "Who do men say that I am?" *28* And they answered, "John the Baptist; but some *say*, Elijah; and others, one of the prophets."

29 He said to them, "But who do you say that I am?" And Peter answered and said to Him, "You are the Christ." *30* Then He charged them that they should tell no one about Him.

Jesus Predicts His Death and Resurrection

31 And He began to teach them that the Son of Man must suffer many things, and be rejected by the elders and chief priests and scribes, and be killed, and after three days rise again. *32* He spoke this word openly. And Peter took Him aside and began to rebuke Him. *33* But when He had turned around and looked at His disciples, He rebuked Peter, saying, "Get behind Me, Satan! For you are not mindful of the things of God, but the things of men."

Take Up the Cross and Follow Him

34 And when He had called the people *to Him*, with His disciples also, He said to them, "Whoever desires to come after Me, let him deny himself, and take up his cross, and follow Me. *35* "For whoever desires to save his life will lose it, but whoever loses his life for My sake and the gospel's will save it. *36* "For what will it profit a man if he gains the whole world, and loses his own soul? *37* "Or what will a man give in exchange for his soul? *38* "For whoever is ashamed of Me and My words in this adulterous and sinful generation, of him the Son of Man also will be ashamed when He comes in the glory of His Father with the holy angels."

9 And He said to them, "Assuredly, I say to you that there are some standing here who will not taste death till they see the kingdom of God present with power."

Jesus Transfigured on the Mount

2 Now after six days Jesus took Peter, James, and John, and led them up on a high mountain apart by themselves; and He was transfigured before them. *3* His clothes became shining, exceedingly white, like snow, such as no launderer on earth can whiten them. *4* And Elijah appeared to them with Moses, and they were talking with Jesus. *5* Then Peter answered and said to

Jesus, "Rabbi, it is good for us to be here; and let us make three tabernacles: one for You, one for Moses, and one for Elijah"—
6 because he did not know what to say, for they were greatly afraid.
7 And a cloud came and overshadowed them; and a voice came out of the cloud, saying, "This is My beloved Son. Hear Him!"
8 Suddenly, when they had looked around, they saw no one anymore, but only Jesus with themselves.
9 Now as they came down from the mountain, He commanded them that they should tell no one the things they had seen, till the Son of Man had risen from the dead.
10 So they kept this word to themselves, questioning what the rising from the dead meant.
11 And they asked Him, saying, "Why do the scribes say that Elijah must come first?"
12 Then He answered and told them, "Elijah does come first, and restores all things. And how is it written concerning the Son of Man, that He must suffer many things and be treated with contempt?
13 "But I say to you that Elijah has also come, and they did to him whatever they wished, as it is written of him."

A Boy Is Healed

14 And when He came to the disciples, He saw a great multitude around them, and scribes disputing with them.
15 Immediately, when they saw Him, all the people were greatly amazed, and running to *Him*, greeted Him.
16 And He asked the scribes, "What are you discussing with them?"
17 Then one from the multitude answered and said, "Teacher, I brought You my son, who has a mute spirit.
18 "And wherever he seizes him, he throws him down; he foams at the mouth, gnashes his teeth, and becomes rigid. So I spoke to Your disciples, that they should cast him out, but they could not."
19 He answered him and said, "O faithless generation, how long shall I be with you? How long shall I bear with you? Bring him to Me."
20 Then they brought him to Him. And when he saw Him, immediately the spirit

convulsed him, and he fell on the ground and wallowed, foaming at the mouth.
21 So He asked his father, "How long has this been happening to him?" And he said, "From childhood.
22 "And often he has thrown him both into the fire and into the water to destroy him. But if You can do anything, have compassion on us and help us."
23 Jesus said to him, "If you can believe,[39] all things *are* possible to him who believes."
24 Immediately the father of the child cried out and said with tears, "Lord, I believe; help my unbelief!"
25 When Jesus saw that the people came running together, He rebuked the unclean spirit, saying to him, "*You* deaf and dumb spirit, I command you, come out of him, and enter him no more!"
26 Then *the spirit* cried out, convulsed him greatly, and came out of him. And he became as one dead, so that many said, "He is dead."
27 But Jesus took him by the hand and lifted him up, and he arose.
28 And when He had come into the house, His disciples asked Him privately, "Why could we not cast him out?"
29 So He said to them, "This kind can come out by nothing but prayer and fasting."[40]

Jesus Again Predicts His Death and Resurrection

30 Then they departed from there and passed through Galilee, and He did not want anyone to know *it*.
31 For He taught His disciples and said to them, "The Son of Man is being delivered into the hands of men, and they will kill Him. And after He is killed, He will rise the third day."
32 But they did not understand this saying, and were afraid to ask Him.

Who Is the Greatest?

33 Then He came to Capernaum. And when He was in the house He asked them, "What was it you disputed among yourselves on the road?"
34 But they kept silent, for on the road they had disputed among themselves who *would be the* greatest.
35 And He sat down, called the twelve, and said to them, "If anyone desires to be

39 NU-Text reads "*If You can! All things. . . .*" 40 NU-Text omits *and fasting.*

first, he shall be last of all and servant of all."

36 Then He took a little child and set him in the midst of them. And when He had taken him in His arms, He said to them,

37 "Whoever receives one of these little children in My name receives Me; and whoever receives Me, receives not Me but Him who sent Me."

Jesus Forbids Sectarianism

38 Now John answered Him, saying, "Teacher, we saw someone who does not follow us casting out demons in Your name, and we forbade him because he does not follow us."

39 But Jesus said, "Do not forbid him, for no one who works a miracle in My name can soon afterward speak evil of Me.

40 "For he who is not against us is on our⁴¹ side.

41 "For whoever gives you a cup of water to drink in My name, because you belong to Christ, assuredly, I say to you, he will by no means lose his reward.

Jesus Warns of Offenses

42 "And whoever causes one of these little ones who believe in Me to stumble, it would be better for him if a millstone were hung around his neck, and he were thrown into the sea.

43 "And if your hand makes you sin, cut it off. It is better for you to enter into life maimed, than having two hands, to go to hell, into the fire that shall never be quenched—

44 "where *their worm does not die and the fire is not quenched.'*⁴²

45 "And if your foot makes you sin, cut it off. It is better for you to enter life lame, than having two feet, to be cast into hell, into the fire that shall never be quenched—

46 "where *their worm does not die and the fire is not quenched.'*⁴³

47 "And if your eye makes you sin, pluck it out. It is better for you to enter the kingdom of God with one eye, than having two eyes, to be cast into hell fire—

48 "where *their worm does not die and the fire is not quenched.'*⁴⁴

Tasteless Salt Is Worthless

49 "For everyone will be seasoned with fire,⁴⁵ and every sacrifice will be seasoned with salt.

50 "Salt *is* good, but if the salt loses its flavor, how will you season it? Have salt in yourselves, and have peace with one another."

Marriage and Divorce

10 Then He arose from there and came to the region of Judea by the other side of the Jordan. And the people gathered to Him again, and as He was accustomed, He taught them again.

2 The Pharisees came and asked Him, "Is it lawful for a man to divorce *his* wife?" testing Him.

3 And He answered and said to them, "What did Moses command you?"

4 They said, "Moses permitted *a man* to write a certificate of divorce, and to dismiss *her."*

5 And Jesus answered and said to them, "Because of the hardness of your heart he wrote you this precept.

6 "But from the beginning of the creation, God *'made them male and female.'*⁴⁶

7 *'For this reason a man shall leave his father and mother and be joined to his wife,*

8 *and the two shall become one flesh';*⁴⁷ so then they are no longer two, but one flesh.

9 "Therefore what God has joined together, let not man separate."

10 And in the house His disciples asked Him again about the same *matter.*

11 So He said to them, "Whoever divorces his wife and marries another commits adultery against her.

12 "And if a woman divorces her husband and marries another, she commits adultery."

Jesus Blesses Little Children

13 Then they brought young children to Him, that He might touch them; but the disciples rebuked those who brought *them.*

14 But when Jesus saw *it,* He was greatly displeased and said to them, "Let the little children come to Me, and do not for-

---

41 M-Text reads *against you is on your side.* **42** NU-Text omits this verse.
43 NU-Text omits the last clause of verse 45 and all of verse 46. **44** Isaiah 66:24
45 NU-Text omits the rest of this verse. **46** Genesis 1:27; 5:2 **47** Genesis 2:24

You Are the Salt of the Earth

Jesus often used everyday life experiences when teaching about the kingdom of God. He turned common subjects into a tool to inspire Christian faith. On one such occasion, Jesus used the illustration of salt, saying, "You are the salt of the earth" (Matt. 5:13). This commodity held special functions in the biblical life-style.

Salt symbolized many things to the biblical person. Of course, it flavored food as it does today. Yet it was also considered to be a pure, acceptable sacrificial offering to God (Ezek. 43:24).

Perhaps Jesus was bringing to His listeners' minds the village of Tarachia, which was in view from where He spoke. This small town's main industry was curing and salting fish. In fact, the town's name means "salted fish." The fish, salted and cured there, was well-known and shipped throughout the Roman empire.

Salt was an important element in preserving fish and all kinds of foods. Due to the low elevation of Tarachia in Galilee, 700 feet below sea level, temperatures often exceeded 100 degrees with 80 to 90 percent humidity in the summer. This caused food to spoil quickly. The fish had to be cured and salted immediately.

Jesus may have recalled the famous salt covenant spoken of in the Old Testament. The Book of Numbers records that God sealed many of His promises with the Israelites through a salt covenant (Num. 18:19). Even today, salt symbolizes a covenant of peace in the Middle East.

"You are the salt of the earth." To Jesus' listeners, this was an important challenge. Like the salt of the biblical world, we should have preserving qualities when we share the love of Jesus Christ. The apostle Paul reminds us in Colossians 4:6, to season our speech to bless the lives of other people with a positive flavor and spirit. We should share God's covenant of peace and forgiveness with the world. Like salt, may our lives be a pure and acceptable offering of service to our God.

bid them; for of such is the kingdom of God. 15 "Assuredly, I say to you, whoever does not receive the kingdom of God as a little child will by no means enter it." 16 And He took them up in His arms, put *His* hands on them, and blessed them.

Jesus Counsels the Rich Young Ruler

17 Now as He was going out on the road, one came running, knelt before Him, and asked Him, "Good Teacher, what shall I do that I may inherit eternal life?" 18 So Jesus said to him, "Why do you call Me good? No one *is* good but One, *that is,* God. 19 "You know the commandments: '*Do not commit adultery,*' '*Do not murder,*' '*Do not steal,*' '*Do not bear false witness,*' '*Do not defraud,*' '*Honor your father and your mother.*'" 48 20 And he answered and said to Him, "Teacher, all these I have observed from my youth." 21 Then Jesus, looking at him, loved him, and said to him, "One thing you lack: Go your way, sell whatever you have and give to the poor, and you will have treasure in heaven; and come, take up the cross, and follow Me." 22 But he was sad at this word, and went away grieved, for he had great possessions.

With God All Things Are Possible

23 Then Jesus looked around and said to His disciples, "How hard it is for those who have riches to enter the kingdom of God!" 24 And the disciples were astonished at His words. But Jesus answered again and said to them, "Children, how hard it is for those who trust in riches49 to enter the kingdom of God! 25 "It is easier for a camel to go through the eye of a needle than for a rich man to enter the kingdom of God." 26 And they were astonished beyond measure, saying among themselves, "Who then can be saved?" 27 But looking at them, Jesus said, "With men *it is* impossible, but not with God; for with God all things are possible." 28 Then Peter began to say to Him, "See, we have left all and followed You."

29 So Jesus answered and said, "Assuredly, I say to you, there is no one who has left house or brothers or sisters or father or mother or wife50 or children or lands, for My sake and the gospel's, 30 "who shall not receive a hundredfold now in this time—houses and brothers and sisters and mothers and children and lands, with persecutions—and in the age to come, eternal life. 31 "But many *who are* first will be last, and the last first."

Jesus a Third Time Predicts His Death and Resurrection

32 Now they were on the road, going up to Jerusalem, and Jesus was going before them; and they were amazed. And as they followed they were afraid. Then He took the twelve aside again and began to tell them the things that would happen to Him: 33 "Behold, we are going up to Jerusalem, and the Son of Man will be delivered to the chief priests and to the scribes, and they will condemn Him to death and deliver Him to the Gentiles; 34 "and they will mock Him, and scourge Him, and spit on Him, and kill Him. And the third day He will rise again."

Greatness Is Serving

35 Then James and John, the sons of Zebedee, came to Him, saying, "Teacher, we want You to do for us whatever we ask." 36 And He said to them, "What do you want Me to do for you?" 37 They said to Him, "Grant us that we may sit, one on Your right hand and the other on Your left, in Your glory." 38 But Jesus said to them, "You do not know what you ask. Can you drink the cup that I drink, and be baptized with the baptism that I am baptized with?" 39 And they said to Him, "We can." And Jesus said to them, "You will indeed drink the cup that I drink, and with the baptism I am baptized with you will be baptized; 40 "but to sit on My right hand and on My left is not Mine to give, but *it is for those* for whom it is prepared." 41 And when the ten heard *it,* they began to be greatly displeased with James and John.

---

48 Exodus 20:12–16; Deuteronomy 5:16–20   49 NU-Text omits *for those who trust in riches.*
50 NU-Text omits *or wife.*

42 But Jesus called them to *Himself* and said to them, "You know that those who are considered rulers over the Gentiles lord it over them, and their great ones exercise authority over them. 43 "Yet it shall not be so among you; but whoever desires to become great among you shall be your servant. 44 "And whoever of you desires to be first shall be slave of all. 45 "For even the Son of Man did not come to be served, but to serve, and to give His life a ransom for many."

Jesus Heals Blind Bartimaeus

46 Then they came to Jericho. And as He went out of Jericho with His disciples and a great multitude, blind Bartimaeus, the son of Timaeus, sat by the road begging. 47 And when he heard that it was Jesus of Nazareth, he began to cry out and say, "Jesus, Son of David, have mercy on me!" 48 Then many warned him to be quiet; but he cried out all the more, "Son of David, have mercy on me!" 49 So Jesus stood still and commanded him to be called. Then they called the blind man, saying to him, "Be of good cheer. Rise, He is calling you." 50 And throwing aside his garment, he rose and came to Jesus. 51 And Jesus answered and said to him, "What do you want Me to do for you?" The blind man said to Him, "Rabboni, that I may receive my sight." 52 Then Jesus said to him, "Go your way; your faith has made you well." And immediately he received his sight and followed Jesus on the road.

The Triumphal Entry

11 Now when they came near Jerusalem, to Bethphage[51] and Bethany, at the Mount of Olives, He sent out two of His disciples; 2 and He said to them, "Go into the village opposite you; and as soon as you have entered it you will find a colt tied, on which no one has sat. Loose it and bring *it*. 3 "And if anyone says to you, 'Why are you doing this?' say, 'The Lord has need of it,' and immediately he will send it here."

4 So they went their way, and found the[52] colt tied by the door outside on the street, and they loosed it. 5 And some of those who stood there said to them, "What are you doing, loosing the colt?" 6 So they spoke to them just as Jesus had commanded. And they let them go. 7 Then they brought the colt to Jesus and threw their garments on it, and He sat on it. 8 And many spread their garments on the road, and others cut down leafy branches from the trees and spread *them* on the road. 9 Then those who went before and those who followed cried out, saying:

"Hosanna!
'Blessed is He who comes in the name of the LORD!'[53]
10 Blessed *is* the kingdom of our father David
That comes in the name of the Lord![54]
Hosanna in the highest!"

11 And Jesus went into Jerusalem and into the temple. So when He had looked around at all things, as the hour was already late, He went out to Bethany with the twelve.

The Fig Tree Withered

12 Now the next day, when they had come out from Bethany, He was hungry. 13 And seeing from afar a fig tree having leaves, He went to see if perhaps He would find something on it. And when He came to it, He found nothing but leaves, for it was not the season for figs. 14 In response Jesus said to it, "Let no one eat fruit from you ever again." And His disciples heard *it*.

Jesus Cleanses the Temple

15 So they came to Jerusalem. And Jesus went into the temple and began to drive out those who bought and sold in the temple, and overturned the tables of the moneychangers and the seats of those who sold doves. 16 And He would not allow anyone to carry wares through the temple. 17 Then He taught, saying to them, "Is it not written, 'My house shall be called a house of prayer for all nations'?[55] But you have made it a 'den of thieves.'"[56]

51 M-Text reads *Bethsphage.*   52 NU-Text and M-Text read *a.*   53 Psalm 118:26
54 NU-Text omits *in the name of the Lord.*   55 Isaiah 56:7   56 Jeremiah 7:11

18 And the scribes and chief priests heard it and sought how they might destroy Him; for they feared Him, because all the people were astonished at His teaching.
19 And when evening had come, He went out of the city.

The Lesson of the Withered Fig Tree

20 Now in the morning, as they passed by, they saw the fig tree dried up from the roots.
21 And Peter, remembering, said to Him, "Rabbi, look! The fig tree which You cursed has withered away."
22 So Jesus answered and said to them, "Have faith in God.
23 "For assuredly, I say to you, whoever says to this mountain, 'Be removed and be cast into the sea,' and does not doubt in his heart, but believes that those things he says will come to pass, he will have whatever he says.
24 "Therefore I say to you, whatever things you ask when you pray, believe that you receive *them*, and you will have *them*.

Forgiveness and Prayer

25 "And whenever you stand praying, if you have anything against anyone, forgive him, that your Father in heaven may also forgive you your trespasses.
26 "But if you do not forgive, neither will your Father in heaven forgive your trespasses."57

Jesus' Authority Questioned

27 Then they came again to Jerusalem. And as He was walking in the temple, the chief priests, the scribes, and the elders came to Him.
28 And they said to Him, "By what authority are You doing these things? And who gave You this authority to do these things?"
29 But Jesus answered and said to them, "I will also ask you one question; then answer Me, and I will tell you by what authority I do these things:
30 "The baptism of John—was it from heaven or from men? Answer Me."
31 And they reasoned among themselves, saying, "If we say, 'From heaven,' He will say, 'Why then did you not believe him?'
32 "But if we say, 'From men' "—they

feared the people, for all counted John to have been a prophet indeed.
33 So they answered and said to Jesus, "We do not know." And Jesus answered and said to them, "Neither will I tell you by what authority I do these things."

The Parable of the Wicked Vinedressers

12 Then He began to speak to them in parables: "A man planted a vineyard and set a hedge around *it*, dug *a place for* the wine vat and built a tower. And he leased it to vinedressers and went into a far country.
2 "Now at vintage-time he sent a servant to the vinedressers, that he might receive some of the fruit of the vineyard from the vinedressers.
3 "And they took *him* and beat him and sent *him* away empty-handed.
4 "Again he sent them another servant, and at him they threw stones,58 wounded *him* in the head, and sent *him* away shamefully treated.
5 "And again he sent another, and him they killed; and many others, beating some and killing some.
6 "Therefore still having one son, his beloved, he also sent him to them last, saying, 'They will respect my son.'
7 "But those vinedressers said among themselves, 'This is the heir. Come, let us kill him, and the inheritance will be ours.'
8 "And they took him and killed *him* and cast *him* out of the vineyard.
9 "Therefore what will the owner of the vineyard do? He will come and destroy the vinedressers, and give the vineyard to others.
10 "Have you not read this Scripture:

'The stone which the builders rejected
Has become the chief cornerstone.
11 This was the LORD's doing,
And it is marvelous in our eyes'?"59

12 And they sought to lay hold of Him, but feared the multitude, for they knew He had spoken the parable against them. So they left Him and went away.

The Pharisees: Is It Lawful to Pay Taxes to Caesar?

13 Then they sent to Him some of the Pharisees and the Herodians, to catch Him in *His* words.

57 NU-Text omits this verse. 58 NU-Text omits *and at him they threw stones*. 59 Psalm 118:22, 23

14 When they had come, they said to Him, "Teacher, we know that You are true, and care about no one; for You do not regard the person of men, but teach the way of God in truth. Is it lawful to pay taxes to Caesar, or not?
15 "Shall we pay, or shall we not pay?" But He, knowing their hypocrisy, said to them, "Why do you test Me? Bring Me a denarius that I may see it."
16 So they brought it. And He said to them, "Whose image and inscription is this?" And they said to Him, "Caesar's."
17 Then Jesus answered and said to them, "Render to Caesar the things that are Caesar's, and to God the things that are God's." And they marveled at Him.

The Sadducees: What about the Resurrection?

18 Then some Sadducees, who say there is no resurrection, came to Him; and they asked Him, saying:
19 "Teacher, Moses wrote to us that if a man's brother dies, and leaves his wife behind, and leaves no children, his brother should take his wife and raise up offspring for his brother.
20 "Now there were seven brothers. The first took a wife; and dying, he left no offspring.
21 "And the second took her, and he died; nor did he leave any offspring. And the third likewise.
22 "So the seven had her and left no offspring. Last of all the woman died also.
23 "Therefore, in the resurrection, when they rise, whose wife will she be? For all seven had her as wife."
24 Jesus answered and said to them, "Are you not therefore mistaken, because you do not know the Scriptures nor the power of God?
25 "For when they rise from the dead, they neither marry nor are given in marriage, but are like angels in heaven.
26 "But concerning the dead, that they rise, have you not read in the book of Moses, in the burning bush passage, how God spoke to him, saying, 'I am the God of Abraham, the God of Isaac, and the God of Jacob'?[60]
27 "He is not the God of the dead, but the God of the living. You are therefore greatly mistaken."

The Scribes: Which Is the First Commandment of All?

28 Then one of the scribes came, and having heard them reasoning together, perceiving[61] that He had answered them well, asked Him, "Which is the first commandment of all?"
29 Jesus answered him, "The first of all the commandments is: 'Hear, O Israel, the LORD our God, the LORD is one.
30 'And you shall love the LORD your God with all your heart, with all your soul, with all your mind, and with all your strength.'[62] This is the first commandment.[63]
31 "And the second, like it, is this: 'You shall love your neighbor as yourself.'[64] There is no other commandment greater than these."
32 So the scribe said to Him, "Well said, Teacher. You have spoken the truth, for there is one God, and there is no other but He.
33 "And to love Him with all the heart, with all the understanding, with all the soul,[65] and with all the strength, and to love one's neighbor as oneself, is more than all the whole burnt offerings and sacrifices."
34 So when Jesus saw that he answered wisely, He said to him, "You are not far from the kingdom of God." And after that no one dared question Him.

Jesus: How Can David Call His Descendant Lord?

35 Then Jesus answered and said, while He taught in the temple, "How is it that the scribes say that the Christ is the Son of David?
36 "For David himself said by the Holy Spirit:

'The LORD said to my Lord,
"Sit at My right hand,
Till I make Your enemies
    Your footstool."'[66]

37 "Therefore David himself calls Him 'Lord'; how is He then his Son?" And the common people heard Him gladly.

Beware of the Scribes

38 Then He said to them in His teaching, "Beware of the scribes, who desire to go

60 Exodus 3:6, 15 61 NU-Text reads seeing. 62 Deuteronomy 6:4, 5 63 NU-Text omits this sentence.
64 Leviticus 19:18 65 NU-Text omits with all the soul. 66 Psalm 110:1

around in long robes, *love* greetings in the marketplaces,

39 "the best seats in the synagogues, and the best places at feasts,

40 "who devour widows' houses, and for a pretense make long prayers. These will receive greater condemnation."

The Widow's Two Mites

41 Now Jesus sat opposite the treasury and saw how the people put money into the treasury. And many *who were* rich put in much.

42 Then one poor widow came and threw in two mites,[67] which make a quadrans.

43 So He called His disciples *to Him* and said to them, "Assuredly, I say to you that this poor widow has put in more than all those who have given to the treasury;

44 "for they all put in out of their abundance, but she out of her poverty put in all that she had, her whole livelihood."

Jesus Predicts the Destruction of the Temple

13 Then as He went out of the temple, one of His disciples said to Him, "Teacher, see what manner of stones and what buildings *are here!*"

2 And Jesus answered and said to him, "Do you see these great buildings? Not *one* stone shall be left upon another, that shall not be thrown down."

The Signs of the Times and the End of the Age

3 Now as He sat on the Mount of Olives opposite the temple, Peter, James, John, and Andrew asked Him privately,

4 "Tell us, when will these things be? And what *will be* the sign when all these things will be fulfilled?"

5 And Jesus, answering them, began to say: "Take heed that no one deceives you.

6 "For many will come in My name, saying, 'I am *He*,' and will deceive many.

7 "And when you hear of wars and rumors of wars, do not be troubled; for *such things* must happen, but the end *is* not yet.

8 "For nation will rise against nation, and kingdom against kingdom. And there will be earthquakes in various places, and there will be famines and troubles.[68] These *are* the beginnings of sorrows.

9 "But watch out for yourselves, for they will deliver you up to councils, and you will be beaten in the synagogues. And you will be brought[69] before rulers and kings for My sake, for a testimony to them.

10 "And the gospel must first be preached to all the nations.

11 "But when they arrest *you* and deliver you up, do not worry beforehand, or premeditate[70] what you will speak. But whatever is given you in that hour, speak that; for it is not you who speak, but the Holy Spirit.

12 "Now brother will betray brother to death, and a father *his* child; and children will rise up against parents and cause them to be put to death.

13 "And you will be hated by all *men* for My name's sake. But he who endures to the end shall be saved.

The Great Tribulation

14 "But when you see the *'abomination of desolation,'*[71] spoken of by Daniel the prophet,[72] standing where it ought not" (let the reader understand), "then let those who are in Judea flee to the mountains.

15 "And let him who is on the housetop not go down into the house, nor enter to take anything out of his house.

16 "And let him who is in the field not go back to get his garment.

17 "But woe to those who are pregnant and to those with nursing babies in those days!

18 "And pray that your flight may not be in winter.

19 "For *in* those days there will be tribulation, such as has not been from the beginning of creation which God created until this time, nor ever shall be.

20 "And unless the Lord had shortened those days, no flesh would be saved; but for the elect's sake, whom He chose, He shortened the days.

21 "Then if anyone says to you, 'Look, here *is* the Christ!' or, 'Look, *He is* there!' do not believe it.

22 "For false christs and false prophets will rise and show signs and wonders to deceive, if possible, even the elect.

---

67 Greek *two lepta;* very small copper coins worth a fraction of a penny   68 NU-Text omits *and troubles.*
69 NU-Text and M-Text read *will stand.*   70 NU-Text omits *or premeditate.*
71 Daniel 11:31; 12:11   72 NU-Text omits *spoken of by Daniel the prophet.*

The Widow's Mite

The temple area was crowded and noisy as usual. The Pharisees and Sadducees were observing the activities from their power center in the inner courtyard. Richly robed merchants deposited large amounts of money in the temple treasury box on the grand staircase. One woman, clothed in black, with a small child clinging to her side dropped two mites for her offering, pausing for a quiet prayer.

Jesus observed the scene and turned to the crowd around Him and said, "This poor widow has put in more than all those who have given to the treasury; for they all put in out of their abundance, but she out of her poverty put in all that she had, her whole livelihood" (Mark 12:43, 44).

The Bible records the above scene, labeling the woman a widow. In ancient times, widows had little or no means of income. They were dependent on the gifts of relatives or friends. In this case, Jesus reveals that she gave all she had to live on.

The widow gave two "mites"—the smallest denomination in circulation. A Greek copper coin, the mite is worth a mere fraction of a penny. Two mites would not even equal one cent. Yet, Jesus commended this woman for the large amount she gave.

The widow's mites is a beautiful illustration of the attitude of giving. While other merchants gave large amounts of their wealth, their offering was most likely for recognition and praise from man. The widow, however, displayed a heart of gratitude to God, despite the loss of her husband and lack of financial security. She could still trust God for her basic needs, thereby enabling her to give out of her need.

We can learn much from the poor widow who gave all she had to live on. Let us, with equal gratitude, give to God the talents, time, energy, and financial resources we have to live on. And then with trust and confidence watch as God turns our offerings into opportunities! For we have the promise of Jesus: "Give, and it will be given to you: good measure, pressed down, shaken together, and running over" (Luke 6:38).

23 "But take heed; see, I have told you all things beforehand.

The Coming of the Son of Man

24 "But in those days, after that tribulation, the sun will be darkened, and the moon will not give its light;
25 "the stars of heaven will fall, and the powers in heaven will be shaken.
26 "Then they will see the Son of Man coming in the clouds with great power and glory.
27 "And then He will send His angels, and gather together His elect from the four winds, from the farthest part of earth to the farthest part of heaven.

The Parable of the Fig Tree

28 "Now learn this parable from the fig tree: When its branch has already become tender, and puts forth leaves, you know that summer is near.
29 "So you also, when you see these things happening, know that it[73] is near, at the very doors.
30 "Assuredly, I say to you, this generation will by no means pass away till all these things take place.
31 "Heaven and earth will pass away, but My words will by no means pass away.

No One Knows the Day or Hour

32 "But of that day and hour no one knows, neither the angels in heaven, nor the Son, but only the Father.
33 "Take heed, watch and pray; for you do not know when the time is.
34 "It is like a man going to a far country, who left his house and gave authority to his servants, and to each his work, and commanded the doorkeeper to watch.
35 "Watch therefore, for you do not know when the master of the house is coming—in the evening, at midnight, at the crowing of the rooster, or in the morning—
36 "lest, coming suddenly, he find you sleeping.
37 "And what I say to you, I say to all: Watch!"

The Plot to Kill Jesus

14 After two days it was the Passover and the Feast of Unleavened Bread. And the chief priests and the scribes sought how they might take Him by trickery and put Him to death.
2 But they said, "Not during the feast, lest there be an uproar of the people."

The Anointing at Bethany

3 And being in Bethany at the house of Simon the leper, as He sat at the table, a woman came having an alabaster flask of very costly oil of spikenard. And she broke the flask and poured it on His head.
4 But there were some who were indignant among themselves, and said, "Why was this fragrant oil wasted?
5 "For it might have been sold for more than three hundred denarii and given to the poor." And they criticized her sharply.
6 But Jesus said, "Let her alone. Why do you trouble her? She has done a good work for Me.
7 "For you have the poor with you always, and whenever you wish you may do them good; but Me you do not have always.
8 "She has done what she could. She has come beforehand to anoint My body for burial.
9 "Assuredly, I say to you, wherever this gospel is preached throughout the whole world, what this woman did will also be spoken of as a memorial to her."

Judas Agrees to Betray Jesus

10 Then Judas Iscariot, one of the twelve, went to the chief priests to betray Him to them.
11 So when they heard it, they were glad, and promised to give him money. So he sought how he might conveniently betray Him.

Jesus Celebrates the Passover with His Disciples

12 Now on the first day of Unleavened Bread, when they killed the Passover lamb, His disciples said to Him, "Where do You want us to go and prepare, that You may eat the Passover?"
13 So He sent out two of His disciples and said to them, "Go into the city, and a man will meet you carrying a pitcher of water; follow him.
14 "And wherever he goes in, say to the master of the house, 'The Teacher says,

73 Or He

A Man with a Pitcher

Be prepared to do the uncommon when God calls you. One individual in the New Testament who was so willing is simply referred to as "a man . . . carrying a pitcher."

During the final week before our Lord's crucifixion, Jesus called Peter and John and asked them to go into the city of Jerusalem to prepare the Passover meal. There they would see a man carrying a pitcher. They were to follow him as he led them to the room where Jesus would eat the Last Supper with His disciples.

In the cultural society of the New Testament, it was most common to see a woman, not a man, carrying a jar or a pitcher of water. We know nothing more about the man whom God instructed to carry the pitcher of water. But from the culture and time we do know that he was called to do something out of the ordinary. Yet his call from God was clear, and he carried out his task. By doing so, he actually entertained and served the Son of God and His disciples by leading them to the room where they would share their last meal together during Jesus' earthly ministry.

At this meal, Jesus instituted the Lord's Supper of the New Covenant, which to this day serves as a holy communion of new life and forgiveness to people everywhere.

By faithfully following God's call, the man with the pitcher served God and Jesus Christ in a unique way. He was the "man behind the scenes," in one of the greatest events of the world.

When God calls you with certainty to perform a task that is uncommon or unusual, do it with total commitment. For you never know when you will be serving God's children in a special way. God takes the ordinary out of life. He makes it extraordinary!

"Where is the guest room in which I may eat the Passover with My disciples?" '
15 "Then he will show you a large upper room, furnished *and* prepared; there make ready for us."
16 And His disciples went out, and came into the city, and found it just as He had said to them; and they prepared the Passover.
17 In the evening He came with the twelve.
18 Now as they sat and ate, Jesus said, "Assuredly, I say to you, one of you who eats with Me will betray Me."
19 And they began to be sorrowful, and to say to Him one by one, "*Is* it I?" And another *said,* "*Is* it I?"[74]
20 Then He answered and said to them, "*It is* one of the twelve, who dips with Me in the dish.
21 "The Son of Man indeed goes just as it is written of Him, but woe to that man by whom the Son of Man is betrayed! It would have been good for that man if he had never been born."

Jesus Institutes the Lord's Supper

22 And as they were eating, Jesus took bread, blessed *it* and broke *it,* and gave *it* to them and said, "Take, eat;[75] this is My body."
23 Then He took the cup, and when He had given thanks He gave *it* to them, and they all drank from it.
24 And He said to them, "This is My blood of the new[76] covenant, which is shed for many.
25 "Assuredly, I say to you, I will no longer drink of the fruit of the vine until that day when I drink it new in the kingdom of God."
26 And when they had sung a hymn, they went out to the Mount of Olives.

Jesus Predicts Peter's Denial

27 Then Jesus said to them, "All of you will be made to stumble because of Me this night,[77] for it is written:

'I will strike the Shepherd,
And the sheep will be scattered.'[78]

28 "But after I have been raised, I will go before you to Galilee."

29 But Peter said to Him, "Even if all are made to stumble, yet I *will* not *be.*"
30 And Jesus said to him, "Assuredly, I say to you that today, *even* this night, before the rooster crows twice, you will deny Me three times."
31 But he spoke more vehemently, "If I have to die with You, I will not deny You!" And they all said likewise.

The Prayer in the Garden

32 Then they came to a place which was named Gethsemane; and He said to His disciples, "Sit here while I pray."
33 And He took Peter, James, and John with Him, and He began to be troubled and deeply distressed.
34 Then He said to them, "My soul is exceedingly sorrowful, *even* to death. Stay here and watch."
35 He went a little farther, and fell on the ground, and prayed that if it were possible, the hour might pass from Him.
36 And He said, "Abba, Father, all things *are* possible for You. Take this cup away from Me; nevertheless, not what I will, but what You *will.*"
37 Then He came and found them sleeping, and said to Peter, "Simon, are you sleeping? Could you not watch one hour?
38 "Watch and pray, lest you enter into temptation. The spirit truly *is* ready, but the flesh *is* weak."
39 Again He went away and prayed, and spoke the same words.
40 And when He returned, He found them asleep again, for their eyes were heavy; and they did not know what to answer Him.
41 Then He came the third time and said to them, "Are you still sleeping and resting? It is enough! The hour has come; behold, the Son of Man is being betrayed into the hands of sinners.
42 "Rise up, let us go. See, My betrayer is at hand."

Betrayal and Arrest in Gethsemane

43 And immediately, while He was still speaking, Judas, one of the twelve, with a great multitude with swords and clubs, came from the chief priests and the scribes and the elders.
44 Now His betrayer had given them a signal, saying, "Whomever I kiss, He is

74 NU-Text omits this sentence.   75 NU-Text omits *eat.*   76 NU-Text omits *new.*
77 NU-Text omits *because of Me this night.*   78 Zechariah 13:7

the One; take Him and lead *Him* away safely."

45 And as soon as He had come, immediately he went up to Him and said to Him, "Rabbi, Rabbi!" and kissed Him.

46 Then they laid their hands on Him and took Him.

47 And one of those who stood by drew his sword and struck the servant of the high priest, and cut off his ear.

48 Then Jesus answered and said to them, "Have you come out, as against a robber, with swords and clubs to take Me?

49 "I was daily with you in the temple teaching, and you did not take Me. But the Scriptures must be fulfilled."

50 Then they all forsook Him and fled.

A Young Man Flees Naked

51 Now a certain young man followed Him, having a linen cloth thrown around *his* naked *body*. And the young men laid hold of him,

52 and he left the linen cloth and fled from them naked.

Jesus Faces the Sanhedrin

53 And they led Jesus away to the high priest; and with him were assembled all the chief priests, the elders, and the scribes.

54 But Peter followed Him at a distance, right into the courtyard of the high priest. And he sat with the servants and warmed himself at the fire.

55 And the chief priests and all the council sought testimony against Jesus to put Him to death, and found none.

56 For many bore false witness against Him, but their testimonies did not agree.

57 And some rose up and bore false witness against Him, saying,

58 "We heard Him say, 'I will destroy this temple that *is* made with hands, and within three days I will build another made without hands.' "

59 But not even then did their testimony agree.

60 And the high priest stood up in the midst and asked Jesus, saying, "Do You answer nothing? What *is it* these men testify against You?"

61 But He kept silent and answered nothing. Again the high priest asked Him, saying to Him, "Are You the Christ, the Son of the Blessed?"

62 And Jesus said, "I am. And you will see the Son of Man sitting at the right hand of the Power, and coming with the clouds of heaven."

63 Then the high priest tore his clothes and said, "What further need do we have of witnesses?

64 "You have heard the blasphemy! What do you think?" And they all condemned Him to be worthy of death.

65 Then some began to spit on Him, and to blindfold Him, and to beat Him, and to say to Him, "Prophesy!" And the officers struck Him with the palms of their hands.[79]

Peter Denies Jesus, and Weeps

66 Now as Peter was below in the courtyard, one of the servant girls of the high priest came.

67 And when she saw Peter warming himself, she looked at him and said, "You also were with Jesus of Nazareth."

68 But he denied it, saying, "I neither know nor understand what you are saying." And he went out on the porch, and a rooster crowed.

69 And the servant girl saw him again, and began to say to those who stood by, "This is one of them."

70 But he denied it again. And a little later those who stood by said to Peter again, "Surely you are *one* of them; for you are a Galilean, and your speech shows *it*."[80]

71 But he began to curse and swear, "I do not know this Man of whom you speak!"

72 And a second time *the* rooster crowed. And Peter called to mind the word that Jesus had said to him, "Before the rooster crows twice, you will deny Me three times." And when he thought about it, he wept.

Jesus Faces Pilate

15 Immediately, in the morning, the chief priests held a consultation with the elders and scribes and the whole council; and they bound Jesus, led *Him* away, and delivered *Him* to Pilate.

2 Then Pilate asked Him, "Are You the King of the Jews?" And He answered and said to him, "*It is as* you say."

3 And the chief priests accused Him of many things, but He answered nothing.

---

79 NU-Text reads *received Him with slaps.*   80 NU-Text omits *and your speech shows it.*

4 Then Pilate asked Him again, saying, "Do You answer nothing? See how many things they testify against You!"[81]
5 But Jesus still answered nothing, so that Pilate marveled.

Taking the Place of Barabbas

6 Now at the feast he was accustomed to releasing one prisoner to them, whomever they requested.
7 And there was one named Barabbas, *who was* chained with his fellow insurrectionists; they had committed murder in the insurrection.
8 Then the multitude, crying aloud,[82] began to ask *him to do* just as he had always done for them.
9 But Pilate answered them, saying, "Do you want me to release to you the King of the Jews?"
10 For he knew that the chief priests had handed Him over because of envy.
11 But the chief priests stirred up the crowd, so that he should rather release Barabbas to them.
12 And Pilate answered and said to them again, "What then do you want me to do *with Him* whom you call the King of the Jews?"
13 So they cried out again, "Crucify Him!"
14 Then Pilate said to them, "Why, what evil has He done?" And they cried out more exceedingly, "Crucify Him!"
15 So Pilate, wanting to gratify the crowd, released Barabbas to them; and he delivered Jesus, after he had scourged *Him*, to be crucified.

The Soldiers Mock Jesus

16 Then the soldiers led Him away into the hall called Praetorium, and they called together the whole garrison.
17 And they clothed Him with purple; and they twisted a crown of thorns, put it on His *head*,
18 and began to salute Him, "Hail, King of the Jews!"
19 Then they struck Him on the head with a reed and spat on Him; and bowing the knee, they worshiped Him.
20 And when they had mocked Him, they took the purple off Him, put His own clothes on Him, and led Him out to crucify Him.

The King on a Cross

21 Now they compelled a certain man, Simon a Cyrenian, the father of Alexander and Rufus, as he was coming out of the country and passing by, to bear His cross.
22 And they brought Him to the place Golgotha, which is translated, Place of a Skull.
23 Then they gave Him wine mingled with myrrh to drink, but He did not take *it.*
24 And when they crucified Him, they divided His garments, casting lots for them to determine what every man should take.
25 Now it was the third hour, and they crucified Him.
26 And the inscription of His accusation was written above:

THE KING OF THE JEWS.

27 With Him they also crucified two robbers, one on His right and the other on His left.
28 So the Scripture was fulfilled[83] which says, *"And He was numbered with the transgressors."*[84]
29 And those who passed by blasphemed Him, wagging their heads and saying, "Aha! *You* who destroy the temple and build *it* in three days,
30 "save Yourself, and come down from the cross!"
31 Likewise the chief priests also, together with the scribes, mocked and said among themselves, "He saved others; Himself He cannot save.
32 "Let the Christ, the King of Israel, descend now from the cross, that we may see and believe."[85] And those who were crucified with Him reviled Him.

Jesus Dies on the Cross

33 Now when the sixth hour had come, there was darkness over the whole land until the ninth hour.
34 And at the ninth hour Jesus cried out with a loud voice, saying, "Eloi, Eloi, lama sabachthani?" which is translated, *"My God, My God, why have You forsaken Me?"*[86]
35 Some of those who stood by, when they heard *it,* said, "Look, He is calling for Elijah!"

81 NU-Text reads *of which they accuse You.* 82 NU-Text reads *going up.* 83 Isaiah 53:12
84 NU-Text omits this verse. 85 M-Text adds *Him.* 86 Psalm 22:1

36 Then someone ran and filled a sponge full of sour wine, put *it* on a reed, and offered *it* to Him to drink, saying, "Let Him alone; let us see if Elijah will come to take Him down."
37 And Jesus cried out with a loud voice, and breathed His last.
38 Then the veil of the temple was torn in two from top to bottom.
39 Now when the centurion, who stood opposite Him, saw that He cried out like this and breathed His last,[87] he said, "Truly this Man was the Son of God!"
40 There were also women looking on from afar, among whom were Mary Magdalene, Mary the mother of James the Less and of Joses, and Salome,
41 who also followed Him and ministered to Him when He was in Galilee; and many other women who came up with Him to Jerusalem.

Jesus Buried in Joseph's Tomb

42 Now when evening had come, because it was the Preparation Day, that is, the day before the Sabbath,
43 Joseph of Arimathea, a prominent council member, who was himself waiting for the kingdom of God, coming and taking courage, went in to Pilate and asked for the body of Jesus.
44 Pilate marveled that He was already dead; and summoning the centurion, he asked him if He had been dead for some time.
45 And when he found out from the centurion, he granted the body to Joseph.
46 Then he bought fine linen, took Him down, and wrapped Him in the linen. And he laid Him in a tomb which had been hewn out of the rock, and rolled a stone against the door of the tomb.
47 And Mary Magdalene and Mary *the mother* of Joses observed where He was laid.

He Is Risen

16 Now when the Sabbath was past, Mary Magdalene, Mary *the mother* of James, and Salome bought spices, that they might come and anoint Him.
2 Very early in the morning, on the first *day* of the week, they came to the tomb when the sun had risen.
3 And they said among themselves, "Who will roll away the stone from the door of the tomb for us?"
4 But when they looked up, they saw that the stone had been rolled away—for it was very large.
5 And entering the tomb, they saw a young man clothed in a long white robe sitting on the right side; and they were alarmed.
6 But he said to them, "Do not be alarmed. You seek Jesus of Nazareth, who was crucified. He is risen! He is not here. See the place where they laid Him.
7 "But go *and* tell His disciples—and Peter—that He is going before you into Galilee; there you will see Him, as He said to you."
8 And they went out quickly[88] and fled from the tomb, for they trembled and were amazed. And they said nothing to anyone, for they were afraid.

Mary Magdalene Sees the Risen Lord

9 Now when *He* rose early on the first *day* of the week, He appeared first to Mary Magdalene, out of whom He had cast seven demons.
10 She went and told those who had been with Him, as they mourned and wept.
11 And when they heard that He was alive and had been seen by her, they did not believe.

Jesus Appears to Two Disciples

12 After that, He appeared in another form to two of them as they walked and went into the country.
13 And they went and told *it* to the rest, *but* they did not believe them either.

The Great Commission

14 Afterward He appeared to the eleven as they sat at the table; and He rebuked their unbelief and hardness of heart, because they did not believe those who had seen Him after He had risen.
15 And He said to them, "Go into all the world and preach the gospel to every creature.
16 "He who believes and is baptized will be saved; but he who does not believe will be condemned.
17 "And these signs will follow those who believe: In My name they will cast out demons; they will speak with new tongues;

87 NU-Text reads *that He thus breathed His last.*   88 NU-Text and M-Text omit *quickly.*

Mary Magdalene—
Equal Before God

Throughout Jesus' ministry, He sought to bring people into a proper relationship with God. He ignored religious, social, cultural, and ethnic status quo. Instead, He elevated all persons to an equal position. This is perhaps most evident in His treatment of women. One woman, Mary Magdalene, is a beautiful illustration of Christ's redemptive love.

Mary Magdalene was from the town of Magdala, located three miles northwest of Tiberias. With a population of 15,000, it was a town known for its sensuality and pleasure-oriented life-style. Greco-Roman baths from the first century are still visible just outside of Magdala. Ancient historians tell that it was a seat of prostitution. Simply being from the town where prostitution was extensively practiced would throw suspicion on her in the New Testament period.

During Jesus' day, women were often relegated to the position of a possession or degraded to the role of a sex object. It was unthinkable for a man to travel with any woman besides his wife. In fact, a man was not allowed to speak with a woman other than his wife. Jesus' ministry revolutionized all of this. Numerous times Jesus spoke openly with women. Mary Magdalene was among the women who followed Jesus and became His disciples. In society's standing, this could have ruined the impact of Jesus' ministry; yet Jesus felt a need to elevate women to their proper place.

Once, while dining at a Pharisee's house, Jesus allowed a woman to wash His feet with expensive perfume and dry them with her hair. This act was unheard of in the society of the time; yet Jesus acknowledged her faith as a beautiful act of worship. In Samaria, Jesus spoke openly with the woman at the well who had five husbands. When the disciples saw this they were alarmed, for Jesus was speaking with a woman, and a Samaritan, with whom the Jews had no contact. When teaching on adultery, Jesus was traveling with His disciples and several women. His attitude did not condemn, but rather gave hope and dignity to the women who were with Him.

Mary Magdalene was bestowed great honors among women, for she was present at Christ's death, His burial, and was the first to see the resurrected Jesus. Although she was from one of the most notorious towns of the entire nation, Mary Magdalene was given this great honor.

Jesus continues to elevate all women and persons to an honorable position. He never condemns us. Rather, He forgives us and gives us hope! We are God's children. He is our Father. We can stand with dignity and forgiveness, equal before God.

18 "they[89] will take up serpents; and if they drink anything deadly, it will by no means hurt them; they will lay hands on the sick, and they will recover."

Christ Ascends to God's Right Hand

19 So then, after the Lord had spoken to them, He was received up into heaven, and sat down at the right hand of God. 20 And they went out and preached everywhere, the Lord working with *them* and confirming the word through the accompanying signs. Amen.[90]

89 NU-Text reads *and in their hands they will.*
90 Verses 9–20 are bracketed in NU-Texts as not original. They are lacking in Codex Sinaiticus and Codex Vaticanus, although nearly all other manuscripts of Mark contain them.

Introduction to Luke

The Gospel of Luke presents a detailed, historical account of the life of Jesus Christ. With great accuracy and clarity, Luke portrays the Son of God as a compassionate, unprejudiced, accepting, and forgiving person.

Written about A.D. 60, Luke is the third of the synoptic Gospels (meaning "to see together"). From his writing, we gain a better understanding of the chronological events and happenings in the life of Christ.

Luke presents Jesus as one who broke down religious, cultural, social, and economic barriers. He constantly put His reputation on the line by associating with people of poor repute. A friend of outcasts and sinners, Jesus challenged the status quo.

Jesus confounded traditional messianic expectations of a king. Luke's account of the Savior's birth in a manger presents a vivid picture of the seemingly unsuitable birthplace of our Lord. His ministry and life did not meet all the expectations the people had of the Messiah.

And just as you want men to do to you, you also do to them likewise. But if you love those who love you, what credit is that to you? For even sinners love those who love them. But love your enemies, do good, and lend, hoping for nothing in return; and your reward will be great, and you will be sons of the Highest. For He is kind to the unthankful and evil.

(Luke 6:31, 32, 35)

Through His death and resurrection, Jesus faced and conquered His greatest enemy. His victory over death far exceeded the beliefs of even His most faithful followers. As Luke discloses, Jesus constantly preached, taught, and lived the unexpected. Jesus Christ truly was and is today the greatest possibility thinker that ever lived!

The Gospel According to
Luke

Dedication to Theophilus

INASMUCH as many have taken in hand to set in order a narrative of those things which are most surely believed among us,
2 just as those who from the beginning were eyewitnesses and ministers of the word delivered them to us,
3 it seemed good to me also, having had perfect understanding of all things from the very first, to write to you an orderly account, most excellent Theophilus,
4 that you may know the certainty of those things in which you were instructed.

John's Birth Announced to Zacharias

5 There was in the days of Herod, the king of Judea, a certain priest named Zacharias, of the division of Abijah. His wife *was* of the daughters of Aaron, and her name *was* Elizabeth.
6 And they were both righteous before God, walking in all the commandments and ordinances of the Lord blameless.
7 But they had no child, because Elizabeth was barren, and they were both well advanced in years.
8 So it was, that while he was serving as priest before God in the order of his division,
9 according to the custom of the priesthood, his lot fell to burn incense when he went into the temple of the Lord.
10 And the whole multitude of the people was praying outside at the hour of incense.
11 Then an angel of the Lord appeared to him, standing on the right side of the altar of incense.
12 And when Zacharias saw *him*, he was troubled, and fear fell upon him.
13 But the angel said to him, "Do not be afraid, Zacharias, for your prayer is heard; and your wife Elizabeth will bear you a son, and you shall call his name John.
14 "And you will have joy and gladness, and many will rejoice at his birth.

15 "For he will be great in the sight of the Lord, and shall drink neither wine nor strong drink. He will also be filled with the Holy Spirit, even from his mother's womb.
16 "And he will turn many of the children of Israel to the Lord their God.
17 "He will also go before Him in the spirit and power of Elijah, *'to turn the hearts of the fathers to the children,'*[1] and the disobedient to the wisdom of the just, to make ready a people prepared for the Lord."
18 And Zacharias said to the angel, "How shall I know this? For I am an old man, and my wife is well advanced in years."
19 And the angel answered and said to him, "I am Gabriel, who stands in the presence of God, and was sent to speak to you and bring you these glad tidings.
20 "But behold, you will be mute and not able to speak until the day these things take place, because you did not believe my words which will be fulfilled in their own time."
21 And the people waited for Zacharias, and marveled that he lingered so long in the temple.
22 But when he came out, he could not speak to them; and they perceived that he had seen a vision in the temple, for he beckoned to them and remained speechless.
23 And so it was, as soon as the days of his service were completed, that he departed to his own house.
24 Now after those days his wife Elizabeth conceived; and she hid herself five months, saying,
25 "Thus the Lord has dealt with me, in the days when He looked on *me*, to take away my reproach among men."

Christ's Birth Announced to Mary

26 Now in the sixth month the angel Gabriel was sent by God to a city of Galilee named Nazareth,
27 to a virgin betrothed to a man whose

1 Malachi 4:5, 6

name was Joseph, of the house of David. The virgin's name *was* Mary.

28 And having come in, the angel said to her, "Rejoice, highly favored *one*, the Lord *is* with you; blessed *are* you among women!"[2]

29 But when she saw *him*,[3] she was troubled at his saying, and considered what manner of greeting this was.

30 Then the angel said to her, "Do not be afraid, Mary, for you have found favor with God.

31 "And behold, you will conceive in your womb and bring forth a Son, and shall call His name JESUS.

32 "He will be great, and will be called the Son of the Highest; and the Lord God will give Him the throne of His father David.

33 "And He will reign over the house of Jacob forever, and of His kingdom there will be no end."

34 Then Mary said to the angel, "How can this be, since I do not know a man?"

35 And the angel answered and said to her, "*The* Holy Spirit will come upon you, and the power of the Highest will overshadow you; therefore, also, that Holy One who is to be born will be called the Son of God.

36 "Now indeed, Elizabeth your relative has also conceived a son in her old age; and this is now the sixth month for her who was called barren.

37 "For with God nothing will be impossible."

38 Then Mary said, "Behold the maidservant of the Lord! Let it be to me according to your word." And the angel departed from her.

Mary Visits Elizabeth

39 Now Mary arose in those days and went into the hill country with haste, to a city of Judah,

40 and entered the house of Zacharias and greeted Elizabeth.

41 And it happened, when Elizabeth heard the greeting of Mary, that the babe leaped in her womb; and Elizabeth was filled with the Holy Spirit.

42 Then she spoke out with a loud voice and said, "Blessed *are* you among women, and blessed *is* the fruit of your womb!

43 "But why *is* this *granted* to me, that the mother of my Lord should come to me?

44 "For indeed, as soon as the voice of your greeting sounded in my ears, the babe leaped in my womb for joy.

45 "Blessed *is* she who believed, for there will be a fulfillment of those things which were told her from the Lord."

The Song of Mary

46 And Mary said:

"My soul magnifies the Lord,
47 And my spirit has rejoiced
in God my Savior.
48 For He has regarded the lowly state
of His maidservant;
For behold, henceforth all generations
will call me blessed.
49 For He who is mighty has done
great things for me,
And holy *is* His name.
50 And His mercy *is* on those
who fear Him
From generation to generation.
51 He has shown strength with His arm;
He has scattered *the* proud in the
imagination of their hearts.
52 He has put down the mighty
from *their* thrones,
And exalted *the* lowly.
53 He has filled *the* hungry
with good things,
And *the* rich He has sent away empty.
54 He has helped His servant Israel,
In remembrance of *His* mercy,
55 As He spoke to our fathers,
To Abraham and to his seed forever."

56 And Mary remained with her about three months, and returned to her house.

Birth of John the Baptist

57 Now Elizabeth's full time came for her to be delivered, and she brought forth a son.

58 When her neighbors and relatives heard how the Lord had shown great mercy to her, they rejoiced with her.

Circumcision of John the Baptist

59 Now so it was, on the eighth day, that they came to circumcise the child; and they would have called him by the name of his father, Zacharias.

60 And his mother answered and said, "No; he shall be called John."

61 But they said to her, "There is no one

2 NU-Text omits *blessed are you among women.*   3 NU-Text omits *when she saw him.*

among your relatives who is called by this name."

62 So they made signs to his father—what he would have him called.

63 And he asked for a writing tablet, and wrote, saying, "His name is John." And they all marveled.

64 Immediately his mouth was opened and his tongue *loosed*, and he spoke, praising God.

65 Then fear came on all who dwelt around them; and all these sayings were discussed throughout all the hill country of Judea.

66 And all those who heard *them* kept *them* in their hearts, saying, "What kind of child will this be?" And the hand of the Lord was with him.

Zacharias' Prophecy

67 Now his father Zacharias was filled with the Holy Spirit, and prophesied, saying:

68 "Blessed *is* the Lord God of Israel,
For He has visited and redeemed His people,
69 And has raised up a horn of salvation for us
In the house of His servant David,
70 As He spoke by the mouth of His holy prophets,
Who *have been* since the world began,
71 That we should be saved from our enemies
And from the hand of all who hate us,
72 To perform the mercy *promised* to our fathers
And to remember His holy covenant,
73 The oath which He swore to our father Abraham:
74 To grant us that we,
Being delivered from the hand of our enemies,
Might serve Him without fear,
75 In holiness and righteousness before Him all the days of our life.
76 And you, child, will be called the prophet of the Highest;
For you will go before the face of the Lord to prepare His ways,
77 To give knowledge of salvation to His people
By the remission of their sins,
78 Through the tender mercy of our God,
With which the Dayspring from on high has visited[4] us;
79 To give light to those who sit in darkness and the shadow of death,

To guide our feet into the way of peace."

80 So the child grew and became strong in spirit, and was in the deserts till the day of his manifestation to Israel.

Christ Born of Mary

2 And it came to pass in those days *that* a decree went out from Caesar Augustus that all the world should be registered.

2 This census first took place while Quirinius was governing Syria.

3 So all went to be registered, everyone to his own city.

4 And Joseph also went up from Galilee, out of the city of Nazareth, into Judea, to the city of David, which is called Bethlehem, because he was of the house and lineage of David,

5 to be registered with Mary, his betrothed wife,[5] who was with child.

6 So it was, that while they were there, the days were completed for her to be delivered.

7 And she brought forth her firstborn Son, and wrapped Him in swaddling cloths, and laid Him in a manger, because there was no room for them in the inn.

Glory in the Highest

8 Now there were in the same country shepherds living out in the fields, keeping watch over their flock by night.

9 And behold,[6] an angel of the Lord stood before them, and the glory of the Lord shone around them, and they were greatly afraid.

10 Then the angel said to them, "Do not be afraid, for behold, I bring you good tidings of great joy which will be to all people.

11 "For there is born to you this day in the city of David a Savior, who is Christ the Lord.

12 "And this *will be* the sign to you: You will find a Babe wrapped in swaddling cloths, lying in a manger."

13 And suddenly there was with the angel a multitude of the heavenly host praising God and saying:

14 "Glory to God in the highest,
And on earth peace,
good will toward men!"[7]

4 NU-Text reads *shall visit.*   5 NU-Text omits *wife.*
6 NU-Text omits *behold.*   7 NU-Text reads *toward men of good will.*

15 So it was, when the angels had gone away from them into heaven, that the shepherds said to one another, "Let us now go to Bethlehem and see this thing that has come to pass, which the Lord has made known to us."
16 And they came with haste and found Mary and Joseph, and the Babe lying in a manger.   •
17 Now when they had seen *Him*, they made widely[8] known the saying which was told them concerning this Child.
18 And all those who heard *it* marveled at those things which were told them by the shepherds.
19 But Mary kept all these things and pondered *them* in her heart.
20 Then the shepherds returned, glorifying and praising God for all the things that they had heard and seen, as it was told them.

Circumcision of Jesus

21 And when eight days were completed for the circumcision of the Child,[9] His name was called JESUS, the name given by the angel before He was conceived in the womb.

Jesus Presented in the Temple

22 Now when the days of her purification according to the law of Moses were completed, they brought Him to Jerusalem to present *Him* to the Lord
23 (as it is written in the law of the Lord, *"Every male who opens the womb shall be called holy to the LORD"*),[10]
24 and to offer a sacrifice according to what is said in the law of the Lord, *"A pair of turtledoves or two young pigeons."*[11]

Simeon Sees God's Salvation

25 And behold, there was a man in Jerusalem whose name was Simeon, and this man was just and devout, waiting for the Consolation of Israel, and the Holy Spirit was upon him.
26 And it had been revealed to him by the Holy Spirit that he would not see death before he had seen the Lord's Christ.
27 So he came by the Spirit into the temple. And when the parents brought in the Child Jesus, to do for Him according to the custom of the law,

28 he took Him up in his arms and blessed God and said:

29 "Lord, now You are letting Your
    servant depart in peace,
    According to Your word;
30 For my eyes have seen Your salvation
31 Which You have prepared before the
    face of all peoples,
32 A light to *bring* revelation to the
    Gentiles,
    And the glory of Your people Israel."

33 And Joseph and His mother[12] marveled at those things which were spoken of Him.
34 Then Simeon blessed them, and said to Mary His mother, "Behold, this *Child* is destined for the fall and rising of many in Israel, and for a sign which will be spoken against
35 (yes, a sword will pierce through your own soul also), that the thoughts of many hearts may be revealed."

Anna Bears Witness to the Redeemer

36 Now there was one, Anna, a prophetess, the daughter of Phanuel, of the tribe of Asher. She was of a great age, and had lived with a husband seven years from her virginity;
37 and this woman *was* a widow of about eighty-four years,[13] who did not depart from the temple, but served *God* with fastings and prayers night and day.
38 And coming in that instant she gave thanks to the Lord,[14] and spoke of Him to all those who looked for redemption in Jerusalem.

The Family Returns to Nazareth

39 So when they had performed all things according to the law of the Lord, they returned to Galilee, to their *own* city, Nazareth.
40 And the Child grew and became strong in spirit,[15] filled with wisdom; and the grace of God was upon Him.

The Boy Jesus Amazes the Scholars

41 His parents went to Jerusalem every year at the Feast of the Passover.
42 And when He was twelve years old, they went up to Jerusalem according to the custom of the feast.
43 When they had finished the days, as they returned, the Boy Jesus lingered be-

---

8 NU-Text omits *widely.*   9 NU-Text reads *for His circumcision.*   10 Exodus 13:2, 12, 15   11 Leviticus 12:8
12 NU-Text reads *And His father and mother.*   13 NU-Text reads *a widow until she was eighty-four.*
14 NU-Text reads *to God.*   15 NU-Text omits *in spirit.*

Too Insignificant—
Except for God!

In the flow of human history, God often chooses the insignificant to accomplish the impossible.

Little is known of Nazareth, the small town where Jesus was reared. The Old Testament and other ancient manuscripts are silent about the city's existence. The town's name never appears among the city lists in the annals of any conquests of the world's great conquerors. Archaeologists have unearthed evidence that probably no more than twelve families lived in this village during New Testament times—among them Mary and Joseph.

Nazareth is located in the sparsely wooded low-lying hill country of Galilee. Jesus grew up practicing the trade of his earthly father. Throughout the ages, Jesus has been called a carpenter. Yet the carpentry of His town actually included stonemasonry. The original Greek word for carpenter can also be understood as stonemason. This was the town's main industry. It was a hard laborer's job in the quarries, cutting large blocks of limestone to fashion into walls for houses. There was very little wood nearby. Archaeology has shown that all of the buildings of Nazareth were built of stone.

The Bible tells that "Jesus increased in wisdom and stature" (Luke 2:52). Except for His visit to Jerusalem at the age of twelve, little more is known of His childhood. Nazareth is situated on a ridge overlooking the stage of His country's history. As any young boy would, Jesus probably climbed the nearby mountain peaks and looked out onto the scenes where Jonah fled from God, Elijah founded his ministry, Gideon defeated the Midianites, and King Thutmose III, Sennacherib, Nebuchadnezzar, Alexander the Great, and Caesar Augustus mounted their invasions.

Less than two miles away were two of the great military centers for Roman legions stationed in Galilee. Any journey outside of His town would have brought the young Jesus in contact with the troops at the nearby cities of Jotapata and Sepphoris.

Below Nazareth, large trading caravans from Egypt, Assyria, Babylon, Persia, Greece, and Rome traveled the highways. The western road traversed the Jezreel Valley reaching the Greco-Roman seaport of Caesarea and the harlot city of Phoenicia. To the east was the King's Highway that ran to the Greek cities of the Decapolis. To the north and south was the famous *Via Maris*—"the way of the sea," where warring armies had marched in their quest for wealth and power.

For the majority of His life, Jesus lived in this tiny village which held picturesque views of the rise and fall of men's mighty kingdoms. Here He grew to manhood, facing all the impressions and temptations of His world. For this insignificant village, Jesus set out to do the seemingly impossible—to establish the kingdom of God.

hind in Jerusalem. And Joseph and His mother[16] did not know *it;*
44 but supposing Him to have been in the company, they went a day's journey, and sought Him among *their* relatives and acquaintances.
45 So when they did not find Him, they returned to Jerusalem, seeking Him.
46 Now so it was that after three days they found Him in the temple, sitting in the midst of the teachers, both listening to them and asking them questions.
47 And all who heard Him were astonished at His understanding and answers.
48 So when they saw Him, they were amazed; and His mother said to Him, "Son, why have You done this to us? Look, Your father and I have sought You anxiously."
49 And He said to them, "Why *is it* that you sought Me? Did you not know that I must be about My Father's business?"
50 But they did not understand the statement which He spoke to them.

Jesus Advances in Wisdom and Favor

51 Then He went down with them and came to Nazareth, and was subject to them, but His mother kept all these things in her heart.
52 And Jesus increased in wisdom and stature, and in favor with God and men.

John the Baptist Prepares the Way

3 Now in the fifteenth year of the reign of Tiberius Caesar, Pontius Pilate being governor of Judea, Herod being tetrarch of Galilee, his brother Philip tetrarch of Iturea and the region of Trachonitis, and Lysanias tetrarch of Abilene,
2 Annas and Caiaphas being high priests,[17] the word of God came to John the son of Zacharias in the wilderness.
3 And he went into all the region around the Jordan, preaching a baptism of repentance for the remission of sins,
4 as it is written in the book of the words of Isaiah the prophet, saying:

"The voice of one crying in the wilderness:
'Prepare the way of the LORD,
Make His paths straight.
5 Every valley shall be filled

And every mountain and hill
brought low;
And the crooked places
shall be made straight
And the rough ways made smooth;
6 And all flesh shall see the salvation
of God.' "[18]

John Preaches to the People

7 Then he said to the multitudes that came out to be baptized by him, "Brood of vipers! Who warned you to flee from the wrath to come?
8 "Therefore bear fruits worthy of repentance, and do not begin to say to yourselves, 'We have Abraham as *our* father.' For I say to you that God is able to raise up children to Abraham from these stones.
9 "And even now the ax is laid to the root of the trees. Therefore every tree which does not bear good fruit is cut down and thrown into the fire."
10 So the people asked him, saying, "What shall we do then?"
11 He answered and said to them, "He who has two tunics, let him give to him who has none; and he who has food, let him do likewise."
12 Then tax collectors also came to be baptized, and said to him, "Teacher, what shall we do?"
13 And he said to them, "Collect no more than what is appointed for you."
14 Likewise the soldiers asked him, saying, "And what shall we do?" So he said to them, "Do not intimidate anyone or accuse falsely, and be content with your wages."
15 Now as the people were in expectation, and all reasoned in their hearts about John, whether he was the Christ *or* not,
16 John answered, saying to *them* all, "I indeed baptize you with water; but One mightier than I is coming, whose sandal strap I am not worthy to loose. He will baptize you with the Holy Spirit and with fire.
17 "His winnowing fan *is* in His hand, and He will thoroughly purge His threshing floor, and gather the wheat into His barn; but the chaff He will burn with unquenchable fire."
18 And with many other exhortations he preached to the people.

---

16 NU-Text reads *And His parents.*   17 NU-Text and M-Text read *in the high priesthood of Annas and Caiaphas.*
18 Isaiah 40:3–5

19 But Herod the tetrarch, being rebuked by him concerning Herodias, his brother Philip's wife,[19] and for all the evils which Herod had done, 20 also added this, above all, that he shut John up in prison.

John Baptizes Jesus

21 Now when all the people were baptized, it came to pass that Jesus also was baptized; and while He prayed, the heaven was opened. 22 And the Holy Spirit descended in bodily form like a dove upon Him, and a voice came from heaven which said, "You are My beloved Son; in You I am well pleased."

The Genealogy of Jesus Christ

23 Now Jesus Himself began *His ministry* at about thirty years of age, being (as was supposed) *the* son of Joseph, *the son* of Heli, 24 *the son* of Matthat,[20] *the son* of Levi, *the son* of Melchi, *the son* of Janna, *the son* of Joseph, 25 *the son* of Mattathiah, *the son* of Amos, *the son* of Nahum, *the son* of Esli, *the son* of Naggai, 26 *the son* of Maath, *the son* of Mattathiah, *the son* of Semei, *the son* of Joseph, *the son* of Judah, 27 *the son* of Joannas, *the son* of Rhesa, *the son* of Zerubbabel, *the son* of Shealtiel, *the son* of Neri, 28 *the son* of Melchi, *the son* of Addi, *the son* of Cosam, *the son* of Elmodam, *the son* of Er, 29 *the son* of Jose, *the son* of Eliezer, *the son* of Jorim, *the son* of Matthat, *the son* of Levi, 30 *the son* of Simeon, *the son* of Judah, *the son* of Joseph, *the son* of Jonan, *the son* of Eliakim, 31 *the son* of Melea, *the son* of Menan, *the son* of Mattathah, *the son* of Nathan, *the son* of David, 32 *the son* of Jesse, *the son* of Obed, *the son* of Boaz, *the son* of Salmon, *the son* of Nahshon, 33 *the son* of Amminadab, *the son* of Ram, *the son* of Hezron, *the son* of Perez, *the son* of Judah,

34 *the son* of Jacob, *the son* of Isaac, *the son* of Abraham, *the son* of Terah, *the son* of Nahor, 35 *the son* of Serug, *the son* of Reu, *the son* of Peleg, *the son* of Eber, *the son* of Shelah, 36 *the son* of Cainan, *the son* of Arphaxad, *the son* of Shem, *the son* of Noah, *the son* of Lamech, 37 *the son* of Methuselah, *the son* of Enoch, *the son* of Jared, *the son* of Mahalalel, *the son* of Cainan, 38 *the son* of Enos, *the son* of Seth, *the son* of Adam, *the son* of God.

Satan Tempts Jesus

4 Then Jesus, being filled with the Holy Spirit, returned from the Jordan and was led by the Spirit into[21] the wilderness, 2 being tempted for forty days by the devil. And in those days He ate nothing, and afterward, when they had ended, He was hungry. 3 And the devil said to Him, "If You are the Son of God, command this stone to become bread." 4 But Jesus answered him, saying,[22] "It is written, *'Man shall not live by bread alone, but by every word of God.'"*[23] 5 Then the devil, taking Him up on a high mountain, showed Him[24] all the kingdoms of the world in a moment of time. 6 And the devil said to Him, "All this authority I will give You, and their glory; for *this* has been delivered to me, and I give it to whomever I wish. 7 "Therefore, if You will worship before me, all will be Yours." 8 And Jesus answered and said to him, "Get behind Me, Satan![25] For[26] it is written, *'You shall worship the LORD your God, and Him only you shall serve.'"*[27] 9 Then he brought Him to Jerusalem, set Him on the pinnacle of the temple, and said to Him, "If You are the Son of God, throw Yourself down from here. 10 "For it is written:

'He shall give His angels charge over You,
To keep You,'

---

19 NU-Text reads *his brother's wife.*
20 This and several other names in the genealogy are spelled somewhat differently in the NU-Text. Since the New King James Version uses the Old Testament spelling for persons mentioned in the New Testament, these variations, which come from the Greek, have not been footnoted.　21 NU-Text reads *in.*　22 Deuteronomy 8:3
23 NU-Text omits *but by every word of God.*　24 NU-Text reads *And taking Him up, he showed Him.*
25 NU-Text omits *Get behind Me, Satan.*　26 NU-Text and M-Text omit *For.*　27 Deuteronomy 6:13

11 "and,

'In their hands they shall bear You up,
Lest You dash Your foot against
a stone.'" 28

12 And Jesus answered and said to him, "It has been said, *'You shall not tempt the LORD your God.'"* 29
13 Now when the devil had ended every temptation, he departed from Him until an opportune time.

Jesus Begins His Galilean Ministry

14 Then Jesus returned in the power of the Spirit to Galilee, and news of Him went out through all the surrounding region.
15 And He taught in their synagogues, being glorified by all.

Jesus Rejected at Nazareth

16 So He came to Nazareth, where He had been brought up. And as His custom was, He went into the synagogue on the Sabbath day, and stood up to read.
17 And He was handed the book of the prophet Isaiah. And when He had opened the book, He found the place where it was written:

18 *"The Spirit of the LORD is upon Me,*
Because He has anointed Me to preach
the gospel to the poor.
He has sent Me to heal the
*brokenhearted,*30
To preach deliverance to the captives
And recovery of sight to the blind,
To set at liberty those who are
oppressed,
19 *To preach the acceptable year of the*
*LORD."*31

20 Then He closed the book, and gave *it* back to the attendant and sat down. And the eyes of all who were in the synagogue were fixed on Him.
21 And He began to say to them, "Today this Scripture is fulfilled in your hearing."
22 So all bore witness to Him, and marveled at the gracious words which proceeded out of His mouth. And they said, "Is this not Joseph's son?"
23 And He said to them, "You will surely say this proverb to Me, 'Physician, heal yourself! Whatever we have heard done

in Capernaum,32 do also here in Your country.'"
24 Then He said, "Assuredly, I say to you, no prophet is accepted in his own country.
25 "But I tell you truly, many widows were in Israel in the days of Elijah, when the heaven was shut up three years and six months, and there was a great famine throughout all the land;
26 "but to none of them was Elijah sent except to Zarephath,33 *in the region* of Sidon, to a woman *who was* a widow.
27 "And many lepers were in Israel in the time of Elisha the prophet, and none of them was cleansed except Naaman the Syrian."
28 Then all those in the synagogue, when they heard these things, were filled with wrath,
29 and rose up and thrust Him out of the city; and they led Him to the brow of the hill on which their city was built, that they might throw Him down over the cliff.
30 Then passing through the midst of them, He went His way.

Jesus Casts Out an Unclean Spirit

31 Then He went down to Capernaum, a city of Galilee, and was teaching them on the Sabbaths.
32 And they were astonished at His teaching, for His word was with authority.
33 Now in the synagogue there was a man who had a spirit of an unclean demon. And he cried out with a loud voice,
34 saying, "Let *us* alone! What have we to do with You, Jesus of Nazareth? Did You come to destroy us? I know You, who You are—the Holy One of God!"
35 But Jesus rebuked him, saying, "Be quiet, and come out of him!" And when the demon had thrown him in *their* midst, it came out of him and did not hurt him.
36 So they were all amazed and spoke among themselves, saying, "What a word this *is*! For with authority and power He commands the unclean spirits, and they come out."
37 And the report about Him went out into every place in the surrounding region.

28 Psalm 91:11, 12   29 Deuteronomy 6:16   30 NU-Text omits *to heal the brokenhearted.*   31 Isaiah 61:1, 2
32 Here and elsewhere the NU-Text spelling is *Capharnaum.*   33 Greek *Sarepta*

Peter's Mother-in-Law Healed

38 Now He arose from the synagogue and entered Simon's house. But Simon's wife's mother was sick with a high fever, and they made request of Him concerning her.

39 So He stood over her and rebuked the fever, and it left her. And immediately she arose and served them.

Many Healed after Sabbath Sunset

40 Now when the sun was setting, all those who had anyone sick with various diseases brought them to Him; and He laid His hands on every one of them and healed them.

41 And demons also came out of many, crying out and saying, "You are the Christ,³⁴ the Son of God!" And He, rebuking *them*, did not allow them to speak, for they knew that He was the Christ.

Jesus Preaches in Galilee

42 Now when it was day, He departed and went into a deserted place. And the crowd sought Him and came to Him, and tried to keep Him from leaving them;

43 but He said to them, "I must preach the kingdom of God to the other cities also, because for this purpose I have been sent."

44 And He was preaching in the synagogues of Galilee.³⁵

Four Fishermen Called as Disciples

5 Now so it was, as the multitude pressed about Him to hear the word of God, that He stood by the Lake of Gennesaret,

2 and saw two boats standing by the lake; but the fishermen had gone from them and were washing *their* nets.

3 Then He got into one of the boats, which was Simon's, and asked him to put out a little from the land. And He sat down and taught the multitudes from the boat.

4 Now when He had stopped speaking, He said to Simon, "Launch out into the ·deep and let down your nets for a catch."

5 But Simon answered and said to Him, "Master, we have toiled all night and caught nothing; nevertheless at Your word I will let down the net."

6 And when they had done this, they caught a great number of fish, and their net was breaking.

7 So they signaled to *their* partners in the other boat to come and help them. And they came and filled both the boats, so that they began to sink.

8 When Simon Peter saw *it*, he fell down at Jesus' knees, saying, "Depart from me, for I am a sinful man, O Lord!"

9 For he and all who were with him were astonished at the catch of fish which they had taken;

10 and so also *were* James and John, the sons of Zebedee, who were partners with Simon. And Jesus said to Simon, "Do not be afraid. From now on you will catch men."

11 So when they had brought their boats to land, they forsook all and followed Him.

Jesus Cleanses a Leper

12 And it happened when He was in a certain city, that behold, a man who was full of leprosy saw Jesus; and he fell on *his* face and implored Him, saying, "Lord, if You are willing, You can make me clean."

13 Then He put out *His* hand and touched him, saying, "I am willing; be cleansed." And immediately the leprosy left him.

14 And He charged him to tell no one, "But go and show yourself to the priest, and make an offering for your cleansing, as a testimony to them, just as Moses commanded."

15 Then the report went around concerning Him all the more; and great multitudes came together to hear, and to be healed by Him of their infirmities.

16 So He Himself *often* withdrew into the wilderness and prayed.

Jesus Forgives and Heals a Paralytic

17 Now it happened on a certain day, as He was teaching, that there were Pharisees and teachers of the law sitting by, who had come out of every town of Galilee, Judea, and Jerusalem. And the power of the Lord was *present* to heal them.³⁶

18 Then behold, men brought on a bed a man who was paralyzed. And they sought to bring him in and lay *him* before Him.

---

34 NU-Text omits *the Christ.*   35 NU-Text reads *Judea.*   36 NU-Text reads *present with Him to heal.*

Let Down Your Nets

The occupation of fisherman in Jesus' day was hard, toilsome work. Most of the fishing was done at night near the shores. The method was usually to drag a net between two boats in hopes of catching fish. Fishing was done close to shore where the fish hid under the many rocks and boulders near the water's surface. It was not uncommon to fish throughout the night, only to return home with nothing.

One morning, Peter and his brother, Andrew, and their partners, James and John, were mending their nets by the shores of the Sea of Galilee. Jesus asked Peter to launch out into the deep water and let down his nets for a catch. Peter responded, "Master, we have toiled all night and caught nothing; nevertheless at Your word I will let down the net" (Luke 5:5).

Jesus asked Peter to do the uncommon and the unexpected. Peter and Andrew must have looked foolish as they went out into the deep water in one boat, dragging a net over the side in the middle of the day. But Peter's faith was rewarded. "When they had done this, they caught a great number of fish, and their net was breaking. So they signaled to *their* partners in the other boat to come help them. And they came and filled both the boats, so that they began to sink" (Luke 5:6, 7).

Jesus wanted to unlock Peter's thinking to understand what faith in God could do. Jesus wants us, like Peter, to realize that when we think we have exhausted all possibilities, remember, we haven't!

We may have toiled in the usual manner for days, months, and even years. But God calls us to cast our nets one more time, to try again when we have run out of hope, to believe in His ability, not our ability. Then when we have done the uncommon, the unexpected, and even the impossible for God, He will reward us. Our nets will overflow!

19 And when they could not find how they might bring him in, because of the crowd, they went up on the housetop and let him down with *his* bed through the tiling into the midst before Jesus.
20 So when He saw their faith, He said to him, "Man, your sins are forgiven you."
21 And the scribes and the Pharisees began to reason, saying, "Who is this who speaks blasphemies? Who can forgive sins but God alone?"
22 But when Jesus perceived their thoughts, He answered and said to them, "Why are you reasoning in your hearts?
23 "Which is easier, to say, 'Your sins are forgiven you,' or to say, 'Rise up and walk'?
24 "But that you may know that the Son of Man has power on earth to forgive sins"—He said to the man who was paralyzed, "I say to you, arise, take up your bed, and go to your house."
25 Immediately he rose up before them, took up what he had been lying on, and departed to his own house, glorifying God.
26 And they were all amazed, and they glorified God and were filled with fear, saying, "We have seen strange things today!"

Matthew the Tax Collector

27 After these things He went out and saw a tax collector named Levi, sitting at the tax office. And He said to him, "Follow Me."
28 And he left all, rose up, and followed Him.
29 Then Levi gave Him a great feast in his own house. And there were a great number of tax collectors and others who sat down with them.
30 But their scribes and the Pharisees[37] murmured against His disciples, saying, "Why do You eat and drink with tax collectors and sinners?"
31 And Jesus answered and said to them, "Those who are well do not need a physician, but those who are sick.
32 "I have not come to call *the* righteous, but sinners, to repentance."

Jesus Is Questioned about Fasting

33 Then they said to Him, "Why do[38] the disciples of John fast often and make prayers, and likewise those of the Pharisees, but Yours eat and drink?"
34 And He said to them, "Can you make the friends of the bridegroom fast while the bridegroom is with them?
35 "But the days will come when the bridegroom will be taken away from them; then they will fast in those days."
36 Then He spoke a parable to them: "No one puts a piece from a new garment on an old one;[39] otherwise the new makes a tear, and also the piece that was *taken* out of the new does not match the old.
37 "And no one puts new wine into old wineskins; or else the new wine will burst the wineskins and be spilled, and the wineskins will be ruined.
38 "But new wine must be put into new wineskins, and both are preserved.[40]
39 "And no one, having drunk old *wine*, immediately[41] desires new; for he says, 'The old is better.'"[42]

Jesus Is Lord of the Sabbath

6 Now it happened on the second Sabbath after the first[43] that He went through the grainfields. And His disciples plucked the heads of grain and ate *them*, rubbing *them* in *their* hands.
2 And some of the Pharisees said to them, "Why are you doing what is not lawful to do on the Sabbath?"
3 But Jesus answering them said, "Have you not even read this, what David did when he was hungry, he and those who were with him:
4 "how he went into the house of God, took and ate the showbread, and also gave some to those *who were* with him, which is not lawful for any but the priests to eat?"
5 And He said to them, "The Son of Man is also Lord of the Sabbath."

Healing on the Sabbath

6 Now it happened on another Sabbath, also, that He entered the synagogue and taught. And a man was there whose right hand was withered.
7 And the scribes and Pharisees watched Him closely, whether He would heal on the Sabbath, that they might find an accusation against Him.
8 But He knew their thoughts, and said to the man who had the withered hand,

---

37 NU-Text reads *But the Pharisees and their scribes.*   38 NU-Text omits *Why do,* making the verse a statement.
39 NU-Text reads *No one tears a piece from a new garment and puts it on an old one.*
40 NU-Text omits *and both are preserved.*   41 NU-Text omits *immediately.*
42 NU-Text reads *good.*   43 NU-Text reads *on a Sabbath.*

"Arise and stand here." And he arose and stood.
9 Then Jesus said to them, "I will ask you one thing: Is it lawful on the Sabbath to do good or to do evil, to save life or to destroy it?"[44]
10 And looking around at them all, He said to the man,[45] "Stretch out your hand." And he did so, and his hand was restored as whole as the other.[46]
11 But they were filled with rage, and discussed with one another what they might do to Jesus.

The Twelve Apostles

12 Now it came to pass in those days that He went out to the mountain to pray, and continued all night in prayer to God.
13 And when it was day, He called His disciples to Him; and from them He chose twelve whom He also named apostles:
14 Simon, whom He also named Peter, and Andrew his brother; James and John; Philip and Bartholomew;
15 Matthew and Thomas; James the son of Alphaeus, and Simon called the Zealot;
16 Judas the son of James, and Judas Iscariot who also became a traitor.

Jesus Heals a Great Multitude

17 And He came down with them and stood on a level place with a crowd of His disciples and a great multitude of people from all Judea and Jerusalem, and from the seacoast of Tyre and Sidon, who came to hear Him and be healed of their diseases,
18 as well as those who were tormented with unclean spirits. And they were healed.
19 And the whole multitude sought to touch Him, for power went out from Him and healed them all.

The Beatitudes

20 Then He lifted up His eyes toward His disciples, and said:

"Blessed are you poor,
  For yours is the kingdom of God.
21 Blessed are you who hunger now,
  For you shall be filled.
Blessed are you who weep now,
  For you shall laugh.

22 Blessed are you when men hate you,
  And when they exclude you,
  And revile you, and cast out your
    name as evil,
  For the Son of Man's sake.
23 Rejoice in that day and leap for joy!
  For indeed your reward is great
    in heaven,
  For in like manner their fathers did
    to the prophets.

Jesus Pronounces Woes

24 "But woe to you who are rich,
  For you have received your
    consolation.
25 Woe to you who are full,
  For you shall hunger.
Woe to you who laugh now,
  For you shall mourn and weep.
26 Woe to you[47] when all[48] men speak
    well of you,
  For so did their fathers
    to the false prophets.

Love Your Enemies

27 "But I say to you who hear: Love your enemies, do good to those who hate you,
28 "bless those who curse you, and pray for those who spitefully use you.
29 "To him who strikes you on the one cheek, offer the other also. And from him who takes away your cloak, do not withhold your tunic either.
30 "Give to everyone who asks of you. And from him who takes away your goods do not ask them back.
31 "And just as you want men to do to you, you also do to them likewise.
32 "But if you love those who love you, what credit is that to you? For even sinners love those who love them.
33 "And if you do good to those who do good to you, what credit is that to you? For even sinners do the same.
34 "And if you lend to those from whom you hope to receive back, what credit is that to you? For even sinners lend to sinners to receive as much back.
35 "But love your enemies, do good, and lend, hoping for nothing in return; and your reward will be great, and you will be sons of the Highest. For He is kind to the unthankful and evil.
36 "Therefore be merciful, just as your Father also is merciful.

44 M-Text reads to kill.   45 NU-Text and M-Text read to him.   46 NU-Text omits as whole as the other.
47 NU-Text and M-Text omit to you.   48 M-Text omits all.

Do Not Judge

37 "Judge not, and you shall not be judged. Condemn not, and you shall not be condemned. Forgive, and you will be forgiven.
38 "Give, and it will be given to you: good measure, pressed down, shaken together, and running over will be put into your bosom. For with the same measure that you use, it will be measured back to you."
39 And He spoke a parable to them: "Can the blind lead the blind? Will they not both fall into the ditch?
40 "A disciple is not above his teacher, but everyone who is perfectly trained will be like his teacher.
41 "And why do you look at the speck in your brother's eye, but do not perceive the plank in your own eye?
42 "Or how can you say to your brother, 'Brother, let me remove the speck that is in your eye,' when you yourself do not see the plank that is in your own eye? Hypocrite! First remove the plank from your own eye, and then you will see clearly to remove the speck that is in your brother's eye.

A Tree Is Known by Its Fruit

43 "For a good tree does not bear bad fruit, nor does a bad tree bear good fruit.
44 "For every tree is known by its own fruit. For men do not gather figs from thorns, nor do they gather grapes from a bramble bush.
45 "A good man out of the good treasure of his heart brings forth good; and an evil man out of the evil treasure of his heart[49] brings forth evil. For out of the abundance of the heart his mouth speaks.

Build on the Rock

46 "But why do you call Me 'Lord, Lord,' and do not do the things which I say?
47 "Whoever comes to Me, and hears My sayings and does them, I will show you whom he is like:
48 "He is like a man building a house, who dug deep and laid the foundation on the rock. And when the flood arose, the stream beat vehemently against that house, and could not shake it, for it was founded on the rock.[50]

49 "But he who heard and did nothing is like a man who built a house on the earth without a foundation, against which the stream beat vehemently; and immediately it fell.[51] And the ruin of that house was great."

Jesus Heals a Centurion's Servant

7 Now when He concluded all His sayings in the hearing of the people, He entered Capernaum.
2 And a certain centurion's servant, who was dear to him, was sick and ready to die.
3 So when he heard about Jesus, he sent elders of the Jews to Him, pleading with Him to come and heal his servant.
4 And when they came to Jesus, they begged Him earnestly, saying that the one for whom He should do this was worthy,
5 "for he loves our nation, and has built us a synagogue."
6 Then Jesus went with them. And when He was already not far from the house, the centurion sent friends to Him, saying to Him, "Lord, do not trouble Yourself, for I am not worthy that You should enter under my roof.
7 "Therefore I did not even think myself worthy to come to You. But say the word, and my servant will be healed.
8 "For I also am a man placed under authority, having soldiers under me. And I say to one, 'Go,' and he goes; and to another, 'Come,' and he comes; and to my servant, 'Do this,' and he does it."
9 When Jesus heard these things, He marveled at him, and turned around and said to the crowd that followed Him, "I say to you, I have not found such great faith, not even in Israel!"
10 And those who were sent, returning to the house, found the servant well who had been sick.[52]

Jesus Raises the Son of the Widow of Nain

11 Now it happened, the day after, that He went into a city called Nain; and many of His disciples went with Him, and a large crowd.
12 And when He came near the gate of the city, behold, a dead man was being carried out, the only son of his mother; and she was a widow. And a large crowd from the city was with her.

---

49 NU-Text omits treasure of his heart.   50 NU-Text reads for it was well built.
51 NU-Text reads collapsed.   52 NU-Text omits who had been sick.

13 When the Lord saw her, He had compassion on her and said to her, "Do not weep."
14 Then He came and touched the open coffin, and those who carried *him* stood still. And He said, "Young man, I say to you, arise."
15 And he who was dead sat up and began to speak. And He presented him to his mother.
16 Then fear came upon all, and they glorified God, saying, "A great prophet has risen up among us"; and, "God has visited His people."
17 And this report about Him went throughout all Judea and all the surrounding region.

John the Baptist Sends Messengers to Jesus

18 Then the disciples of John reported to him concerning all these things.
19 And John, calling two of his disciples to *him*, sent *them* to Jesus,[53] saying, "Are You the Coming One, or do we look for another?"
20 When the men had come to Him, they said, "John the Baptist has sent us to You, saying, 'Are You the Coming One, or do we look for another?' "
21 And that very hour He cured many *people* of *their* infirmities, afflictions, and evil spirits; and to many *who were* blind He gave sight.
22 Then Jesus answered and said to them, "Go and tell John the things you have seen and heard: that *the* blind see, *the* lame walk, *the* lepers are cleansed, *the* deaf hear, *the* dead are raised, *the* poor have the gospel preached to them.
23 "And blessed is *he* who is not offended because of Me."
24 When the messengers of John had departed, He began to speak to the multitudes concerning John: "What did you go out into the wilderness to see? A reed shaken by the wind?
25 "But what did you go out to see? A man clothed in soft garments? Indeed those who are gorgeously appareled and live in luxury are in kings' courts.
26 "But what did you go out to see? A prophet? Yes, I say to you, and more than a prophet.
27 "This is *he* of whom it is written:

'Behold, I send My messenger
before Your face,

Who will prepare Your way
before You.'[54]

28 "For I say to you, among those born of women there is not a greater prophet than John the Baptist;[55] but he who is least in the kingdom of God is greater than he."
29 And when all the people heard *Him*, even the tax collectors justified God, having been baptized with the baptism of John.
30 But the Pharisees and lawyers rejected the counsel of God for themselves, not having been baptized by him.
31 And the Lord said,[56] "To what then shall I liken the men of this generation, and what are they like?
32 "They are like children sitting in the marketplace and calling to one another, saying:

'We played the flute for you,
And you did not dance;
We mourned to you,
And you did not weep.'

33 "For John the Baptist came neither eating bread nor drinking wine, and you say, 'He has a demon.'
34 "The Son of Man has come eating and drinking, and you say, 'Look, a glutton and a winebibber, a friend of tax collectors and sinners!'
35 "But wisdom is justified by all her children."

A Sinful Woman Forgiven

36 Then one of the Pharisees asked Him to eat with him. And He went to the Pharisee's house, and sat down to eat.
37 And behold, a woman in the city who was a sinner, when she knew that *Jesus* sat at the table in the Pharisee's house, brought an alabaster flask of fragrant oil,
38 and stood at His feet behind *Him* weeping; and she began to wash His feet with her tears, and wiped *them* with the hair of her head; and she kissed His feet and anointed *them* with the fragrant oil.
39 Now when the Pharisee who had invited Him saw *this*, he spoke to himself, saying, "This man, if He were a prophet, would know who and what manner of woman *this is* who is touching Him, for she is a sinner."

53 NU-Text reads *the Lord.*   54 Malachi 3:1
55 NU-Text reads *there is none greater than John.*   56 NU-Text and M-Text omit *and the Lord said.*

Forgiven More

He was called a friend of sinners. And so He was, for Jesus disgraced no one, but openly offered forgiveness and love to the lowest of society. Unimpressed with status, He ignored prestige but honored praise.

While dining at Simon the Pharisee's house, Jesus encountered an unusual situation. Upon entering the house He was not extended the expected greeting of a kiss. Nor did a servant offer to wash His feet, which were dirty and dusty from the crude roads. An obvious offense, Jesus ignored the insult of the host without question and reclined to take part in the feast.

The banquet, open to the public, was suddenly interrupted by the outburst of a woman. Falling at Jesus' feet, the woman, known in the city as a prostitute, took upon herself the role of the host. She revealed an alabaster flask filled with expensive fragrant oil. The woman poured the oil over Jesus' feet, anointing Him as an honored guest. Her tears of joy fell to wash His feet, as she kissed them in a supreme act of devotion. Upon realizing that she had no towel to dry Jesus' feet, the woman let down her hair to wipe them off. No woman in the ancient Middle East would let down her hair before a man other than her husband. To do so was considered an immoral act and possibly was punishable by death. Yet in desperation to express her love and gratitude for a new life, she put aside the cultural norms to serve Jesus.

The snubbed Pharisee kept to himself his outrage at this display of devotion. Unimpressed with her gratitude, Simon could only see an immoral woman letting down her hair to the disgrace and defilement of them all. If Jesus were "righteous," He would not let her touch Him.

Jesus turned to Simon and said, "Simon . . . there was a certain creditor who had two debtors. One owed five hundred denarii, and the other fifty. And when they had nothing with which to repay he freely forgave them both. Tell Me, therefore, which of them will love him more?" Simon answered, "I suppose the *one* whom he forgave more." Jesus said, "You have rightly judged" (Luke 7:41-43). The Aramaic word "debt" which Jesus probably used also means "sin." This play on words by Jesus contrasted the woman's sin with the debt in the parable. Simon was unable to escape the logic and had to make the reasonable conclusion: "the one who was forgiven more."

Love is a response to grace, a reaction to a gift freely given. The woman loved Jesus more because she had been forgiven more. Unconcerned with the standards of society, she poured forth her praise and joy in gratitude to Jesus.

We, who have been forgiven more, can also love more. Like the woman, express your thankfulness to God in a display of service and praise. Do not be concerned with what others might think. Any criticism they give should also be ignored. Rather, exude positive praise to God through your actions to Him and those around you. Like the woman, take on the role of a host, anointing those around you with love. Be a servant, washing the lives of others with joy. And be daring, willing to risk shame and rejection as you share your faith in devotion to God.

40 And Jesus answered and said to him, "Simon, I have something to say to you." And he said, "Teacher, say it."
41 "There was a certain creditor who had two debtors. One owed five hundred denarii, and the other fifty.
42 "And when they had nothing with which to repay, he freely forgave them both. Tell Me, therefore, which of them will love him more?"
43 Simon answered and said, "I suppose the *one* whom he forgave more." And He said to him, "You have rightly judged."
44 Then He turned to the woman and said to Simon, "Do you see this woman? I entered your house; you gave Me no water for My feet, but she has washed My feet with her tears and wiped *them* with the hair of her head.
45 "You gave Me no kiss, but this woman has not ceased to kiss My feet since the time I came in.
46 "You did not anoint My head with oil, but this woman has anointed My feet with fragrant oil.
47 "Therefore I say to you, her sins, *which are* many, are forgiven, for she loved much. But to whom little is forgiven, *the same* loves little."
48 And He said to her, "Your sins are forgiven."
49 And those who sat at the table with Him began to say to themselves, "Who is this who even forgives sins?"
50 Then He said to the woman, "Your faith has saved you. Go in peace."

Many Women Minister to Jesus

8 Now it came to pass, afterward, that He went through every city and village, preaching and bringing the glad tidings of the kingdom of God. And the twelve *were* with Him,
2 and certain women who had been healed of evil spirits and infirmities— Mary called Magdalene, out of whom had come seven demons,
3 and Joanna the wife of Chuza, Herod's steward, and Susanna, and many others who provided for Him[57] from their substance.

The Parable of the Sower

4 And when a great multitude had gathered, and *others* had come to Him from every city, He spoke by a parable:
5 "A sower went out to sow his seed. And as he sowed, some fell by the wayside; and it was trampled down, and the birds of the air devoured it.
6 "Some fell on rock; and as soon as it sprang up, it withered away because it lacked moisture.
7 "And some fell among thorns, and the thorns sprang up with it and choked it.
8 "But others fell on good ground, sprang up, and yielded a crop a hundredfold." When He had said these things He cried, "He who has ears to hear, let him hear!"

The Purpose of Parables

9 Then His disciples asked Him, saying, "What does this parable mean?"
10 And He said, "To you it has been given to know the mysteries of the kingdom of God, but to the rest *it is given* in parables, that

'Seeing they may not see,
And hearing they may not
understand.'[58]

The Parable of the Sower Explained

11 "Now the parable is this: The seed is the word of God.
12 "Those by the wayside are the ones who hear; then the devil comes and takes away the word out of their hearts, lest they should believe and be saved.
13 "But the ones on the rock *are those* who, when they hear, receive the word with joy; and these have no root, who believe for a while and in time of temptation fall away.
14 "And the ones *that* fell among thorns are those who, when they have heard, go out and are choked with cares, riches, and pleasures of life, and bring no fruit to maturity.
15 "But the ones *that* fell on the good ground are those who, having heard the word with a noble and good heart, keep *it* and bear fruit with patience.

The Parable of the Revealed Light

16 "No one, when he has lit a lamp, covers it with a vessel or puts *it* under a bed, but sets *it* on a lampstand, that those who enter may see the light.
17 "For nothing is secret that will not be revealed, nor *anything* hidden that will not be known and come to light.

---

57 NU-Text and M-Text read *them.*   58 Isaiah 6:9

18 "Therefore take heed how you hear. For whoever has, to him *more* will be given; and whoever does not have, even what he seems to have will be taken from him."

Jesus' Mother and Brothers Come to Him

19 Then His mother and brothers came to Him, and could not approach Him because of the crowd. 20 And it was told Him *by some*, who said, "Your mother and Your brothers are standing outside, desiring to see You." 21 But He answered and said to them, "My mother and My brothers are these who hear the word of God and do it."

Wind and Wave Obey Jesus

22 Now it happened, on a certain day, that He got into a boat with His disciples. And He said to them, "Let us go over to the other side of the lake." And they launched out. 23 But as they sailed He fell asleep. And a windstorm came down on the lake, and they were filling *with water*, and were in jeopardy. 24 And they came to Him and awoke Him, saying, "Master, Master, we are perishing!" Then He arose and rebuked the wind and the raging of the water. And they ceased, and there was a calm. 25 But He said to them, "Where is your faith?" And they were afraid, and marveled, saying to one another, "Who can this be? For He commands even the winds and water, and they obey Him!"

A Demon-Possessed Man Healed

26 Then they sailed to the country of the Gadarenes,[59] which is opposite Galilee. 27 And when He stepped out on the land, there met Him a certain man from the city who had demons for a long time. And he wore no clothes,[60] nor did he live in a house but in the tombs. 28 When he saw Jesus, he cried out, fell down before Him, and with a loud voice said, "What have I to do with You, Jesus, Son of the Most High God? I beg You, do not torment me!" 29 For He had commanded the unclean spirit to come out of the man. For it had often seized him, and he was kept under guard, bound with chains and shackles;

and he broke the bonds and was driven by the demon into the wilderness. 30 Jesus asked him, saying, "What is your name?" And he said, "Legion," because many demons had entered him. 31 And they begged Him that He would not command them to go out into the abyss. 32 Now a herd of many swine was feeding there on the mountain. And they begged Him that He would permit them to enter them. And He permitted them. 33 Then the demons went out of the man and entered the swine, and the herd ran violently down the steep place into the lake and drowned. 34 When those who fed *them* saw what had happened, they fled and told *it* in the city and in the country. 35 Then they went out to see what had happened, and came to Jesus, and found the man from whom the demons had departed, sitting at the feet of Jesus, clothed and in his right mind. And they were afraid. 36 They also who had seen *it* told them by what means he who had been demon-possessed was healed. 37 Then the whole multitude of the surrounding region of the Gadarenes[61] asked Him to depart from them, for they were seized with great fear. And He got into the boat and returned. 38 Now the man from whom the demons had departed begged Him that he might be with Him. But Jesus sent him away, saying, 39 "Return to your own house, and tell what great things God has done for you." And he went his way and proclaimed throughout the whole city what great things Jesus had done for him.

A Girl Restored to Life and a Woman Healed

40 So it was, when Jesus returned, that the multitude welcomed Him, for they were all waiting for Him. 41 And behold, there came a man named Jairus, and he was a ruler of the synagogue. And he fell down at Jesus' feet and begged Him to come to his house, 42 for he had an only daughter about twelve years of age, and she was dying. But as He went, the multitudes thronged Him. 43 Now a woman, having a flow of blood

59 NU-Text reads *Gerasenes*.   60 NU-Text reads *who had demons and for a long time wore no clothes*.
61 NU-Text reads *Gerasenes*.

for twelve years, who had spent all her livelihood on physicians and could not be healed by any,
44 came from behind and touched the border of His garment. And immediately her flow of blood stopped.
45 And Jesus said, "Who touched Me?" When all denied it, Peter and those with him[62] said, "Master, the multitudes throng You and press *You*, and You say, 'Who touched Me?' "[63]
46 But Jesus said, "Somebody touched Me, for I perceived power going out from Me."
47 Now when the woman saw that she was not hidden, she came trembling; and falling down before Him, she declared to Him in the presence of all the people the reason she had touched Him and how she was healed immediately.
48 And He said to her, "Daughter, be of good cheer;[64] your faith has made you well. Go in peace."
49 While He was still speaking, someone came from the ruler of the synagogue's *house*, saying to him, "Your daughter is dead. Do not trouble the Teacher."[65]
50 But when Jesus heard *it*, He answered him, saying, "Do not be afraid; only believe, and she will be made well."
51 When He came into the house, He permitted no one to go in[66] except Peter, James, and John,[67] and the father and mother of the girl.
52 Now all wept and mourned for her; but He said, "Do not weep; she is not dead, but sleeping."
53 And they laughed Him to scorn, knowing that she was dead.
54 But He put them all out,[68] took her by the hand and called, saying, "Little girl, arise."
55 Then her spirit returned, and she arose immediately. And He commanded that she be given *something* to eat.
56 And her parents were astonished, but He charged them to tell no one what had happened.

Sending Out the Twelve

9 Then He called His twelve disciples together and gave them power and authority over all demons, and to cure diseases.
2 He sent them to preach the kingdom of God and to heal the sick.
3 And He said to them, "Take nothing for the journey, neither staffs nor bag nor bread nor money; and do not have two tunics apiece.
4 "Whatever house you enter, stay there, and from there depart.
5 "And whoever will not receive you, when you go out of that city, shake off the very dust from your feet as a testimony against them."
6 So they departed and went through the towns, preaching the gospel and healing everywhere.

John the Baptist Beheaded

7 Now Herod the tetrarch heard of all that was done by Him; and he was perplexed, because it was said by some that John had risen from the dead,
8 and by some that Elijah had appeared, and by others that one of the old prophets had risen again.
9 And Herod said, "John I have beheaded, but who is this of whom I hear such things?" And he sought to see Him.

Feeding the Five Thousand

10 And the apostles, when they had returned, told Him all that they had done. And He took them and went aside privately into a deserted place belonging to the city called Bethsaida.
11 But when the multitudes knew *it*, they followed Him; and He received them and spoke to them about the kingdom of God, and healed those who had need of healing.
12 When the day began to wear away, the twelve came and said to Him, "Send the multitude away, that they may go into the surrounding towns and country, and lodge and get provisions; for we are in a deserted place here."
13 But He said to them, "You give them something to eat." And they said, "We have no more than five loaves and two fish, unless we go and buy food for all these people."
14 For there were about five thousand men. And He said to His disciples, "Make them sit down in groups of fifty."
15 And they did so, and made them all sit down.

---

62 NU-Text omits *and those with him.*   63 NU-Text omits *and you say, 'Who touched Me?'*
64 NU-Text omits *be of good cheer.*   65 NU-Text adds *anymore.*   66 NU-Text adds *with Him.*
67 NU-Text and M-Text read *Peter, John, and James.*   68 NU-Text omits *put them all out.*

16 Then He took the five loaves and the two fish, and looking up to heaven, He blessed and broke *them*, and gave *them* to the disciples to set before the multitude. 17 So they all ate and were filled, and twelve baskets of the leftover fragments were taken up by them.

Peter Confesses Jesus as the Christ

18 And it happened, as He was alone praying, *that* His disciples joined Him, and He asked them, saying, "Who do the crowds say that I am?"
19 So they answered and said, "John the Baptist, but some *say* Elijah; and others *say* that one of the old prophets has risen again."
20 He said to them, "But who do you say that I am?" Peter answered and said, "The Christ of God."

Jesus Predicts His Death and Resurrection

21 And He strictly warned and commanded them to tell this to no one, 22 saying, "The Son of Man must suffer many things, and be rejected by the elders and chief priests and scribes, and be killed, and be raised the third day."

Take Up the Cross and Follow Him

23 Then He said to *them* all, "If anyone desires to come after Me, let him deny himself, and take up his cross daily,[69] and follow Me.
24 "For whoever desires to save his life will lose it, but whoever loses his life for My sake will save it.
25 "For what advantage is it to a man if he gains the whole world, and is himself destroyed or lost?
26 "For whoever is ashamed of Me and My words, of him the Son of Man will be ashamed when He comes in His *own* glory, and *in His* Father's, and of the holy angels.
27 "But I tell you truly, there are some standing here who shall not taste death till they see the kingdom of God."

Jesus Transfigured on the Mount

28 And it came to pass, about eight days after these sayings, that He took Peter, John, and James and went up on the mountain to pray.
29 And as He prayed, the appearance of His face was altered, and His robe *became* white *and* glistening.

30 Then behold, two men talked with Him, who were Moses and Elijah,
31 who appeared in glory and spoke of His decease which He was about to accomplish at Jerusalem.
32 But Peter and those with him were heavy with sleep; and when they were fully awake, they saw His glory and the two men who stood with Him.
33 And it happened, as they were parting from Him, *that* Peter said to Jesus, "Master, it is good for us to be here; and let us make three tabernacles: one for You, one for Moses, and one for Elijah"— not knowing what he said.
34 While he was saying this, a cloud came and overshadowed them; and they were fearful as they entered the cloud.
35 Then a voice came out of the cloud, saying, "This is My beloved Son.[70] Hear Him!"
36 And when the voice had ceased, Jesus was found alone. But they kept quiet, and told no one in those days any of the things they had seen.

A Boy Is Healed

37 Now it happened on the next day, when they had come down from the mountain, that a great multitude met Him.
38 Suddenly a man from the multitude cried out, saying, "Teacher, I implore You, look on my son, for he is my only child.
39 "And behold, a spirit seizes him, and he suddenly cries out; it convulses him so that he foams *at the mouth*, and bruising him, it departs from him with great difficulty.
40 "So I implored Your disciples to cast it out, but they could not."
41 Then Jesus answered and said, "O faithless and perverse generation, how long shall I be with you and bear with you? Bring your son here."
42 And as he was still coming, the demon threw him down and convulsed *him.* Then Jesus rebuked the unclean spirit, healed the child, and gave him back to his father.

Jesus Again Predicts His Death

43 And they were all amazed at the majesty of God. But while everyone marveled at all the things which Jesus did, He said to His disciples,

---

69 M-Text omits *daily.*   70 NU-Text reads *This is My Son, the Chosen One.*

44 "Let these words sink down into your ears, for the Son of Man is about to be delivered into the hands of men."
45 But they did not understand this saying, and it was hidden from them so that they did not perceive it; and they were afraid to ask Him about this saying.

Who Is the Greatest?

46 Then a dispute arose among them as to which of them would be greatest.
47 And Jesus, perceiving the thought of their heart, took a little child and set him by Him,
48 and said to them, "Whoever receives this little child in My name receives Me; and whoever receives Me receives Him who sent Me. For he who is least among you all will be great."

Jesus Forbids Sectarianism

49 Then John answered and said, "Master, we saw someone casting out demons in Your name, and we forbade him because he does not follow with us."
50 But Jesus said to him, "Do not forbid him, for he who is not against us[71] is for us."[71]

A Samaritan Village Rejects the Savior

51 Now it came to pass, when the time had come for Him to be received up, that He steadfastly set His face to go to Jerusalem,
52 and sent messengers before His face. And as they went, they entered a village of the Samaritans, to prepare for Him.
53 But they did not receive Him, because His face was set for the journey to Jerusalem.
54 And when His disciples James and John saw this, they said, "Lord, do You want us to command fire to come down from heaven and consume them, just as Elijah did?"[72]
55 But He turned and rebuked them,[73] and said, "You do not know what manner of spirit you are of.
56 "For the Son of Man did not come to destroy men's lives but to save them."[74] And they went to another village.

The Cost of Discipleship

57 Now it happened as they journeyed on the road, that someone said to Him, "Lord, I will follow You wherever You go."
58 And Jesus said to him, "Foxes have holes and birds of the air have nests, but the Son of Man has nowhere to lay His head."
59 Then He said to another, "Follow Me." But he said, "Lord, let me first go and bury my father."
60 Jesus said to him, "Let the dead bury their own dead, but you go and preach the kingdom of God."
61 And another also said, "Lord, I will follow You, but let me first go and bid them farewell who are at my house."
62 But Jesus said to him, "No one, having put his hand to the plow, and looking back, is fit for the kingdom of God."

The Seventy Sent Out

10 After these things the Lord appointed seventy others also,[75] and sent them two by two before His face into every city and place where He Himself was about to go.
2 Then He said to them, "The harvest truly is great, but the laborers are few; therefore pray the Lord of the harvest to send out laborers into His harvest.
3 "Go your way; behold, I send you out as lambs among wolves.
4 "Carry neither money bag, sack, nor sandals; and greet no one along the road.
5 "But whatever house you enter, first say, 'Peace to this house.'
6 "And if a son of peace is there, your peace will rest on it; if not, it will return to you.
7 "And remain in the same house, eating and drinking such things as they give, for the laborer is worthy of his wages. Do not go from house to house.
8 "Whatever city you enter, and they receive you, eat such things as are set before you.
9 "And heal the sick who are there, and say to them, 'The kingdom of God has come near to you.'
10 "But whatever city you enter, and they do not receive you, go out into its streets and say,
11 'The very dust of your city which clings to us[76] we wipe off against you. Nevertheless know this, that the kingdom of God has come near you.'

---

71 NU-Text reads you.   72 NU-Text omits just as Elijah did.   73 NU-Text omits the rest of this verse.
74 NU-Text omits the first sentence of this verse.   75 NU-Text reads seventy-two others.
76 NU-Text reads our feet.

Never Look Back

In teaching total commitment, Jesus used an illustration familiar to all His listeners. "No one, having put his hand to the plow, and looking back, is fit for the kingdom of God" (Luke 9:62).

During the planting season in the Middle East, farmers can be seen plowing their fields throughout the land. Plowing in biblical Palestine took a tremendous amount of effort. The light, wooden plow pulled by oxen or donkeys, required the worker to direct all his strength and attention to the task of plowing straight furrows. Among the laborers, it was totally unacceptable to look back after "putting his hand to the plow." In fact, in many parts of the Middle East while traveling or working, to look back is thought to bring the ultimate misfortune upon oneself.

If the farmer plows unevenly and looks back, it only results in an even more crooked furrow. If he looks back at all, his weight is taken off the plow, prohibiting him from making an even furrow in the earth.

Jesus calls us to focus all of our attention and strength on serving God and His kingdom. Jesus encourages us to look ahead, not back. Look at what lies before us, not at our past mistakes.

The apostle Paul also exemplifies this attitude when he says, "Forgetting those things which are behind . . . I press toward the goal for the prize of the upward call of God in Christ Jesus" (Phil. 3:13, 14).

Put your hand to the plow today and never look back. Then you will truly be fit for the kingdom of God. You can say with certainty, I have locked the door on yesterday and have thrown the key away, tomorrow has no fears for me since I have found today!

12 "But[77] I say to you that it will be more tolerable in that Day for Sodom than for that city.

Woe to the Impenitent Cities

13 "Woe to you, Chorazin! Woe to you, Bethsaida! For if the mighty works which were done in you had been done in Tyre and Sidon, they would have repented a great while ago, sitting in sackcloth and ashes.
14 "But it will be more tolerable for Tyre and Sidon at the judgment than for you.
15 "And you, Capernaum, who are exalted to heaven, will be thrust down to Hades.[78]
16 "He who hears you hears Me, he who rejects you rejects Me, and he who rejects Me rejects Him who sent Me."

The Seventy Return with Joy

17 Then the seventy[79] returned with joy, saying, "Lord, even the demons are subject to us in Your name."
18 And He said to them, "I saw Satan fall like lightning from heaven.
19 "Behold, I give you the authority to trample on serpents and scorpions, and over all the power of the enemy, and nothing shall by any means hurt you.
20 "Nevertheless do not rejoice in this, that the spirits are subject to you, but rather[80] rejoice because your names are written in heaven."

Jesus Rejoices in Spirit

21 In that hour Jesus rejoiced in the Spirit and said, "I praise You, Father, Lord of heaven and earth, that You have hidden these things from the wise and prudent and revealed them to babes. Even so, Father, for so it seemed good in Your sight.
22 "All[81] things have been delivered to Me by My Father, and no one knows who the Son is but the Father, and who the Father is but the Son, and the one to whom the Son wills to reveal Him."
23 And He turned to His disciples and said privately, "Blessed are the eyes which see the things you see;
24 "for I tell you that many prophets and kings have desired to see what you see, and have not seen it, and to hear what you hear, and have not heard it."

The Parable of the Good Samaritan

25 And behold, a certain lawyer stood up and tested Him, saying, "Teacher, what shall I do to inherit eternal life?"
26 He said to him, "What is written in the law? What is your reading of it?"
27 So he answered and said, " 'You shall love the LORD your God with all your heart, with all your soul, with all your strength, and with all your mind,'[82] and 'your neighbor as yourself.' "[83]
28 And He said to him, "You have answered rightly; do this and you will live."
29 But he, wanting to justify himself, said to Jesus, "And who is my neighbor?"
30 Then Jesus answered and said: "A certain man went down from Jerusalem to Jericho, and fell among thieves, who stripped him of his clothing, wounded him, and departed, leaving him half dead.
31 "Now by chance a certain priest came down that road. And when he saw him, he passed by on the other side.
32 "Likewise a Levite, when he arrived at the place, came and looked, and passed by on the other side.
33 "But a certain Samaritan, as he journeyed, came where he was. And when he saw him, he had compassion on him,
34 "and went to him and bandaged his wounds, pouring on oil and wine; and he set him on his own animal, brought him to an inn, and took care of him.
35 "On the next day, when he departed,[84] he took out two denarii, gave them to the innkeeper, and said to him, 'Take care of him; and whatever more you spend, when I come again, I will repay you.'
36 "So which of these three do you think was neighbor to him who fell among the thieves?"
37 And he said, "He who showed mercy on him." Then Jesus said to him, "Go and do likewise."

Mary and Martha Worship and Serve

38 Now it happened as they went that He entered a certain village; and a certain woman named Martha welcomed Him into her house.
39 And she had a sister called Mary, who also sat at Jesus'[85] feet and heard His word.

---

77 NU-Text and M-Text omit But.
78 NU-Text reads will you be exalted to heaven? You will be thrust down to Hades!   79 NU-Text reads seventy-two.
80 NU-Text and M-Text omit rather.   81 M-Text reads And turning to the disciples He said, "All . . . .
82 Deuteronomy 6:5   83 Leviticus 19:18   84 NU-Text omits when he departed.   85 NU-Text reads the Lord's.

The Good Samaritan

The story of the Good Samaritan is a powerful illustration of how we should meet the needs of other people. Against the historical background, this parable is even more challenging.

During New Testament times, there was a great division between the Jewish populace and their neighbors, the Samaritans. Their disagreements centered around a religious point. The Samaritans believed the true place of worship was in Samaria on Mount Gerizim; the Jews held that the temple at Jerusalem was the rightful place.

The Jews disliked the Samaritans so much that they chose not to go near their towns. Even when they traveled to Galilee, they avoided the direct route through Samaria and took the longer, more arduous trip through the wilderness, through Jericho, and up the desert Rift Valley.

This road, from Jerusalem to Jericho, was known as *Maale Addumin*, meaning, "the ascent of blood." For here thieves and robbers often attacked the travelers.

It was along this road that Jesus told the story of the Good Samaritan. A Jewish man was traveling this route when thieves jumped him, beat him, and left him for dead. Shortly thereafter, a Levitical priest traveled by, but upon seeing the man, crossed the road and left him. Soon after, another Jewish man passed by and also offered no assistance. Finally, a Samaritan, who normally did not journey on this road, came upon the beaten man. Not only did he stop, but he carried the Jew to an inn where he paid two days' wages to insure the man's recovery.

Jesus commended the Samaritan for truly having love for his neighbor. Despite his religious, cultural, and ethnic differences, the Samaritan reached out to meet the needs of the Jew.

In the same manner, we must look out for the needs of those around us. We can put away our prejudices and sacrifice our time, money, and energy to help heal the spiritual, emotional, and physical needs of both our neighbors and strangers.

Find a need and fill it. Find a hurt and heal it!

40 But Martha was distracted with much serving, and she approached Him and said, "Lord, do You not care that my sister has left me to serve alone? Therefore tell her to help me." 41 And Jesus[86] answered and said to her, "Martha, Martha, you are worried and troubled about many things. 42 But one thing is needed, and Mary has chosen that good part, which will not be taken away from her."

The Model Prayer

11 And it came to pass, as He was praying in a certain place, when He ceased, *that* one of His disciples said to Him, "Lord, teach us to pray, as John also taught his disciples."
2 So He said to them, "When you pray, say:

Our Father in heaven,[87]
Hallowed be Your name.
Your kingdom come.[88]
Your will be done
On earth as *it is* in heaven.
3 Give us day by day our daily bread.
4 And forgive us our sins,
For we also forgive everyone who is indebted to us.
And do not lead us into temptation,
But deliver us from the evil one."[89]

A Friend Comes at Midnight

5 And He said to them, "Which of you shall have a friend, and go to him at midnight and say to him, 'Friend, lend me three loaves; 6 'for a friend of mine has come to me on his journey, and I have nothing to set before him'; 7 "and he will answer from within and say, 'Do not trouble me; the door is now shut, and my children are with me in bed; I cannot rise and give to you'? 8 "I say to you, though he will not rise and give to him because he is his friend, yet because of his persistence he will rise and give him as many as he needs.

Keep Asking, Seeking, Knocking

9 "And I say to you, ask, and it will be given to you; seek, and you will find; knock, and it will be opened to you. 10 "For everyone who asks receives, and he who seeks finds, and to him who knocks it will be opened. 11 "If a son asks for bread[90] from any father among you, will he give him a stone? Or if *he asks* for a fish, will he give him a serpent instead of a fish? 12 "Or if he asks for an egg, will he offer him a scorpion? 13 "If you then, being evil, know how to give good gifts to your children, how much more will *your* heavenly Father give the Holy Spirit to those who ask Him!"

A House Divided Cannot Stand

14 And He was casting out a demon, and it was mute. So it was, when the demon had gone out, that the mute spoke; and the multitudes marveled. 15 But some of them said, "He casts out demons by Beelzebub,[91] the ruler of the demons." 16 And others, testing *Him*, sought from Him a sign from heaven. 17 But He, knowing their thoughts, said to them: "Every kingdom divided against itself is brought to desolation, and a house *divided* against a house falls. 18 "If Satan also is divided against himself, how will his kingdom stand? Because you say I cast out demons by Beelzebub. 19 "And if I cast out demons by Beelzebub, by whom do your sons cast *them* out? Therefore they will be your judges. 20 "But if I cast out demons with the finger of God, surely the kingdom of God has come upon you. 21 "When a strong man, fully armed, guards his own palace, his goods are in peace. 22 "But when a stronger than he comes upon him and overcomes him, he takes from him all his armor in which he trusted, and divides his spoils. 23 "He who is not with Me is against Me, and he who does not gather with Me scatters.

An Unclean Spirit Returns

24 "When an unclean spirit goes out of a man, he goes through dry places, seeking rest; and finding none, he says, 'I will return to my house from which I came.' 25 "And when he comes, he finds *it* swept and put in order.

86 NU-Text reads the Lord.   87 NU-Text omits Our and in heaven.   88 NU-Text omits the rest of this verse.
89 NU-Text omits But deliver us from the evil one.
90 NU-Text omits the words from bread through for in the next sentence.
91 NU-Text and M-Text read Beelzebul

Teach Us to Pray

The disciples often observed Jesus retreating alone to the mountains to pray. It seemed as if He gained some unseen strength from this act. Wanting to learn more of this divine communication, the disciples asked Jesus, "Lord, teach us to pray" (Luke 11:1).

In first-century Judaism, prayer was most often done by priests and high holy men openly in the temple. They stood on the temple stairs, bowing and praying dramatically. The older the priest and the longer his shawl, the holier the individual.

Every day at noon, the Sanhedrin, consisting of the Pharisees and Sadducees, met for afternoon prayer. Their prayer rituals were intense. Each member held a phylactery, a three-inch square black wooden box. Inscribed on the surface of the box was the name of God. Inside were the four sacred passages from the Torah. Attached to the phylactery were long leather straps. During the prayers, the priests wrapped these straps around their arms. Their chants in Hebrew could be heard throughout the temple area.

Jesus demonstrated a different attitude toward prayer when He said:

And when you pray, you shall not be like the hypocrites. For they love to pray standing in the synagogues and on the corners of the streets, that they may be seen by men. Assuredly, I say to you, they have their reward. But you, when you pray, go into your room, and when you have shut your door, pray to your Father who *is* in the secret *place*; and your Father who sees in secret will reward you openly. But when you pray, do not use vain repetitions as the heathen *do*. For they think that they will be heard for their many words. Therefore do not be like them. For your Father knows the things you have need of before you ask Him.

(Matt. 6:5–8).

The supreme example of true prayer is the Lord's Prayer. It is interesting that Jesus chose the reverent term "Our Father," or *Avinu* in Hebrew. Later, Jesus makes it clear to us of our privilege to call God *Abba* meaning "Daddy," an obviously intimate term of affection.

It is evident that in our prayers we should come to God with an attitude of reverence and worship, yet also with a feeling of a close, intimate relationship with our Father. He knows our needs, even before we ask. And He will meet them.

26 "Then he goes and takes with *him* seven other spirits more wicked than himself, and they enter and dwell there; and the last *state* of that man is worse than the first."

Keeping the Word

27 And it happened, as He spoke these things, that a certain woman from the crowd raised her voice and said to Him, "Blessed *is* the womb that bore You, and *the* breasts which nursed You!"

28 But He said, "More than that, blessed *are* those who hear the word of God and keep it!"

Seeking a Sign

29 And while the crowds were thickly gathered together, He began to say, "This is an evil generation. It seeks a sign, and no sign will be given to it except the sign of Jonah the prophet.[92]

30 "For as Jonah became a sign to the Ninevites, so also the Son of Man will be to this generation.

31 "The queen of the South will rise up in the judgment with the men of this generation and condemn them, for she came from the ends of the earth to hear the wisdom of Solomon; and indeed a greater than Solomon *is* here.

32 "The men of Nineveh will rise up in the judgment with this generation and condemn it, for they repented at the preaching of Jonah; and indeed a greater than Jonah *is* here.

The Lamp of the Body

33 "No one, when he has lit a lamp, puts *it* in a secret place or under a basket, but on a lampstand, that those who come in may see the light.

34 "The lamp of the body is the eye. Therefore, when your eye is good, your whole body also is full of light. But when *your eye* is bad, your body also *is* full of darkness.

35 "Therefore take heed that the light which is in you is not darkness.

36 "If then your whole body *is* full of light, having no part dark, *the* whole *body* will be full of light, as when the bright shining of a lamp gives you light."

Woe to the Pharisees and Lawyers

37 And as He spoke, a certain Pharisee asked Him to dine with him. So He went in and sat down to eat.

38 And when the Pharisee saw *it*, he marveled that He had not first washed before dinner.

39 But the Lord said to him, "Now you Pharisees make the outside of the cup and dish clean, but your inward part is full of greed and wickedness.

40 "Foolish ones! Did not He who made the outside make the inside also?

41 "But rather give alms of such things as you have; then indeed all things are clean to you.

42 "But woe to you Pharisees! For you tithe mint and rue and all manner of herbs, and pass by justice and the love of God. These you ought to have done, without leaving the others undone.

43 "Woe to you Pharisees! For you love the best seats in the synagogues and greetings in the marketplaces.

44 "Woe to you, scribes and Pharisees, hypocrites![93] For you are like graves which are not seen, and the men who walk over *them* are not aware *of them*."

45 Then one of the lawyers answered and said to Him, "Teacher, by saying these things You reproach us also."

46 And He said, "Woe to you also, *you* lawyers! For you load men with burdens hard to bear, and you yourselves do not touch the burdens with one of your fingers.

47 "Woe to you! For you build the tombs of the prophets, and your fathers killed them.

48 "In fact, you bear witness that you approve the deeds of your fathers; for they indeed killed them, and you build their tombs.

49 "Therefore the wisdom of God also said, 'I will send them prophets and apostles, and *some* of them they will kill and persecute,'

50 "that the blood of all the prophets which was shed from the foundation of the world may be required of this generation,

51 "from the blood of Abel to the blood of Zechariah who perished between the altar and the temple. Yes, I say to you, it shall be required of this generation.

52 "Woe to you lawyers! For you have taken away the key of knowledge. You did not enter in yourselves, and those who were entering in you hindered."

92 NU-Text omits *the prophet.* 93 NU-Text omits *scribes and Pharisees, hypocrites.*

53 And as He said these things to them,[94] the scribes and the Pharisees began to assail *Him* vehemently, and to cross-examine Him about many things,
54 lying in wait for Him, and seeking to catch Him in something He might say, that they might accuse Him.[95]

Beware of Hypocrisy

12 In the meantime, when an innumerable multitude of people had gathered together, so that they trampled one another, He began to say to His disciples first *of all*, "Beware of the leaven of the Pharisees, which is hypocrisy.
2 "For there is nothing covered that will not be revealed, nor hidden that will not be known.
3 "Therefore whatever you have spoken in the dark will be heard in the light, and what you have spoken in the ear in inner rooms will be proclaimed on the housetops.

Jesus Teaches the Fear of God

4 "And I say to you, My friends, do not be afraid of those who kill the body, and after that have no more that they can do.
5 "But I will show you whom you should fear: Fear Him who, after He has killed, has power to cast into hell; yes, I say to you, fear Him!
6 "Are not five sparrows sold for two copper coins?[96] And not one of them is forgotten before God.
7 "But the very hairs of your head are all numbered. Do not fear therefore; you are of more value than many sparrows.

Confess Christ before Men

8 "Also I say to you, whoever confesses Me before men, him the Son of Man also will confess before the angels of God.
9 "But he who denies Me before men will be denied before the angels of God.
10 "And anyone who speaks a word against the Son of Man, it will be forgiven him; but to him who blasphemes against the Holy Spirit, it will not be forgiven.
11 "Now when they bring you to the synagogues and magistrates and authorities, do not worry about how or what you should answer, or what you should say.
12 "For the Holy Spirit will teach you in that very hour what you ought to say."

The Parable of the Rich Fool

13 Then one from the crowd said to Him, "Teacher, tell my brother to divide the inheritance with me."
14 But He said to him, "Man, who made Me a judge or an arbitrator over you?"
15 And He said to them, "Take heed and beware of covetousness,[97] for one's life does not consist in the abundance of the things he possesses."
16 Then He spoke a parable to them, saying: "The ground of a certain rich man yielded plentifully.
17 "And he thought within himself, saying, 'What shall I do, since I have no room to store my crops?'
18 "So he said, 'I will do this: I will pull down my barns and build greater, and there I will store all my crops and my goods.
19 'And I will say to my soul, "Soul, you have many goods laid up for many years; take your ease; eat, drink, *and* be merry." '
20 "But God said to him, '*You* fool! This night your soul will be required of you; then whose will those things be which you have provided?'
21 "So *is* he who lays up treasure for himself, and is not rich toward God."

Do Not Worry

22 And He said to His disciples, "Therefore I say to you, do not worry about your life, what you will eat; nor about the body, what you will put on.
23 "Life is more than food, and the body *is more* than clothing.
24 "Consider the ravens, for they neither sow nor reap, which have neither storehouse nor barn; and God feeds them. Of how much more value are you than the birds?
25 "And which of you by worrying can add one cubit to his stature?
26 "If you then are not able to do *the* least, why are you anxious for the rest?
27 "Consider the lilies, how they grow: they neither toil nor spin; and yet I say to you, even Solomon in all his glory was not arrayed like one of these.
28 "If then God so clothes the grass, which today is in the field and tomorrow is thrown into the oven, how much more *will He clothe* you, O *you* of little faith?

94 NU-Text reads *And when He left there.*   95 NU-Text omits *and seeking* and *that they might accuse Him.*
96 Greek *assarion,* a coin of very small value   97 NU-Text reads *all covetousness.*

29 "And do not seek what you should eat or what you should drink, nor have an anxious mind.
30 "For all these things the nations of the world seek after, and your Father knows that you need these things.
31 "But seek the kingdom of God, and all these things⁹⁸ shall be added to you.
32 "Do not fear, little flock, for it is your Father's good pleasure to give you the kingdom.
33 "Sell what you have and give alms; provide yourselves money bags which do not grow old, a treasure in the heavens that does not fail, where no thief approaches nor moth destroys.
34 "For where your treasure is, there your heart will be also.

The Faithful Servant and the Evil Servant

35 "Let your waist be girded and *your* lamps burning;
36 "and you yourselves be like men who wait for their master, when he will return from the wedding, that when he comes and knocks they may open to him immediately.
37 "Blessed *are* those servants whom the master, when he comes, will find watching. Assuredly, I say to you that he will gird himself and have them sit down *to eat,* and will come and serve them.
38 "And if he should come in the second watch, or come in the third watch, and find *them* so, blessed are those servants.
39 "But know this, that if the master of the house had known what hour the thief would come, he would have watched and⁹⁹ not allowed his house to be broken into.
40 "Therefore you also be ready, for the Son of Man is coming at an hour you do not expect."
41 Then Peter said to Him, "Lord, do You speak this parable *only* to us, or to all *people?*"
42 And the Lord said, "Who then is that faithful and wise steward, whom *his* master will make ruler over his household, to give *them their* portion of food in due season?
43 "Blessed *is* that servant whom his master will find so doing when he comes.
44 "Truly, I say to you that he will make him ruler over all that he has.
45 "But if that servant says in his heart, 'My master is delaying his coming,' and

begins to beat the menservants and maidservants, and to eat and drink and be drunk,
46 "the master of that servant will come on a day when he is not looking for *him,* and at an hour when he is not aware, and will cut him in two and appoint *him* his portion with the unbelievers.
47 "And that servant who knew his master's will, and did not prepare *himself* or do according to his will, shall be beaten with many *stripes.*
48 "But he who did not know, yet committed things worthy of stripes, shall be beaten with few. For everyone to whom much is given, from him much will be required; and to whom much has been committed, of him they will ask the more.

Christ Brings Division

49 "I came to send fire on the earth, and how I wish it were already kindled!
50 "But I have a baptism to be baptized with, and how distressed I am till it is accomplished!
51 "Do *you* suppose that I came to give peace on earth? I tell you, not at all, but rather division.
52 "For from now on five in one house will be divided: three against two, and two against three.
53 "Father will be divided against son and son against father, mother against daughter and daughter against mother, mother-in-law against her daughter-in-law and daughter-in-law against her mother-in-law."

Discern the Time

54 Then He also said to the multitudes, "When *you see* a cloud rising out of the west, immediately you say, 'A shower is coming'; and so it is.
55 "And when you see the south wind blow, you say, 'There will be hot weather'; and there is.
56 "Hypocrites! You can discern the face of the sky and of the earth, but how *is it* you do not discern this time?

Make Peace with Your Adversary

57 "Yes, and why, even of yourselves, do you not judge what is right?
58 "When you go with your adversary to the magistrate, make every effort along the way to settle with him, lest he drag you to the judge, the judge deliver you to

98 NU-Text reads *His kingdom, and these things.*   99 NU-Text reads *he would not have allowed.*

the officer, and the officer throw you into prison.
59 "I tell you, you shall not depart from there till you have paid the very last mite."

Repent or Perish

13 There were present at that season some who told Him about the Galileans whose blood Pilate had mingled with their sacrifices.
2 And Jesus answered and said to them, "Do you suppose that these Galileans were worse sinners than all *other* Galileans, because they suffered such things?
3 "I tell you, no; but unless you repent you will all likewise perish.
4 "Or those eighteen on whom the tower in Siloam fell and killed them, do you think that they were worse sinners than all *other* men who dwelt in Jerusalem?
5 "I tell you, no; but unless you repent you will all likewise perish."

The Parable of the Barren Fig Tree

6 He also spoke this parable: "A certain *man* had a fig tree planted in his vineyard, and he came seeking fruit on it and found none.
7 "Then he said to the keeper of his vineyard, 'Look, for three years I have come seeking fruit on this fig tree and find none. Cut it down; why does it use up the ground?'
8 "But he answered and said to him, 'Sir, let it alone this year also, until I dig around it and fertilize *it*.
9 'And if it bears fruit, *well*. But if not, after that[100] you can cut it down.' "

A Spirit of Infirmity

10 Now He was teaching in one of the synagogues on the Sabbath.
11 And behold, there was a woman who had a spirit of infirmity eighteen years, and was bent over and could in no way raise *herself* up.
12 But when Jesus saw her, He called *her* to *Him* and said to her, "Woman, you are loosed from your infirmity."
13 And He laid *His* hands on her, and immediately she was made straight, and glorified God.
14 But the ruler of the synagogue answered with indignation, because Jesus had healed on the Sabbath; and he said

to the crowd, "There are six days on which men ought to work; therefore come and be healed on them, and not on the Sabbath day."
15 The Lord then answered him and said, "Hypocrite![101] Does not each one of you on the Sabbath loose his ox or *his* donkey from the stall, and lead *it* away to water it?
16 "So ought not this woman, being a daughter of Abraham, whom Satan has bound—think of it—for eighteen years, be loosed from this bond on the Sabbath?"
17 And when He said these things, all His adversaries were put to shame; and all the multitude rejoiced for all the glorious things that were done by Him.

The Parable of the Mustard Seed

18 Then He said, "What is the kingdom of God like? And to what shall I compare it?
19 "It is like a mustard seed, which a man took and put in his garden; and it grew and became a large[102] tree, and the birds of the air nested in its branches."

The Parable of the Leaven

20 And again He said, "To what shall I liken the kingdom of God?
21 "It is like leaven, which a woman took and hid in three measures[103] of meal till it was all leavened."

The Narrow Way

22 And He went through the cities and villages, teaching, and journeying toward Jerusalem.
23 Then one said to Him, "Lord, are there few who are saved?" And He said to them,
24 "Strive to enter through the narrow gate, for many, I say to you, will seek to enter and will not be able.
25 "When once the Master of the house has risen up and shut the door, and you begin to stand outside and knock at the door, saying, 'Lord, Lord, open for us,' and He will answer and say to you, 'I do not know you, where you are from,'
26 "then you will begin to say, 'We ate and drank in Your presence, and You taught in our streets.'
27 "But He will say, 'I tell you I do not

---

100 NU-Text reads *And if it bears fruit after that, well. But if not, you can cut it down.*
101 NU-Text and M-Text read *Hypocrites.*   102 NU-Text omits *large.*
103 Greek *sata,* approximately two pecks

know you, where you are from. Depart from Me, all you workers of iniquity.'
28 "There will be weeping and gnashing of teeth, when you see Abraham and Isaac and Jacob and all the prophets in the kingdom of God, and yourselves thrust out.
29 "They will come from the east and the west, from the north and the south, and sit down in the kingdom of God.
30 "And indeed there are last who will be first, and there are first who will be last."
31 On that very day[104] some Pharisees came, saying to Him, "Get out and depart from here, for Herod wants to kill You."
32 And He said to them, "Go, tell that fox, 'Behold, I cast out demons and perform cures today and tomorrow, and the third *day* I shall be perfected.'
33 "Nevertheless I must journey today, tomorrow, and the *day* following; for it cannot be that a prophet should perish outside of Jerusalem.

Jesus Laments over Jerusalem

34 "O Jerusalem, Jerusalem, the one who kills the prophets and stones those who are sent to her! How often I wanted to gather your children together, as a hen *gathers* her brood under *her* wings, but you were not willing!
35 "See! Your house is left to you desolate; and assuredly,[105] I say to you, you shall not see Me until *the time* comes when you say, '*Blessed is He who comes in the name of the LORD!*'"[106]

A Man with Dropsy Healed on the Sabbath

14 Now it happened, as He went into the house of one of the rulers of the Pharisees to eat bread on the Sabbath, that they watched Him closely.
2 And behold, there was a certain man before Him who had dropsy.
3 And Jesus, answering, spoke to the lawyers and Pharisees, saying, "Is it lawful to heal on the Sabbath?"[107]
4 But they kept silent. And He took *him* and healed him, and let him go.
5 Then He answered them, saying, "Which of you, having a donkey[108] or an ox that has fallen into a pit, will not immediately pull him out on the Sabbath day?"

6 And they could not answer Him regarding these things.

Take the Lowly Place

7 So He told a parable to those who were invited, when He noted how they chose the best places, saying to them:
8 "When you are invited by anyone to a wedding feast, do not sit down in the best place, lest one more honorable than you be invited by him;
9 "and he who invited you and him come and say to you, 'Give place to this man,' and then you begin with shame to take the lowest place.
10 "But when you are invited, go and sit down in the lowest place, so that when he who invited you comes he may say to you, 'Friend, go up higher.' Then you will have glory in the presence of those who sit at the table with you.
11 "For whoever exalts himself will be abased, and he who humbles himself will be exalted."
12 Then He also said to him who invited Him, "When you give a dinner or a supper, do not ask your friends, your brothers, your relatives, nor *your* rich neighbors, lest they also invite you back, and you be repaid.
13 "But when you give a feast, invite *the* poor, *the* maimed, *the* lame, *the* blind.
14 "And you will be blessed, because they cannot repay you; for you shall be repaid at the resurrection of the just."

The Parable of the Great Supper

15 Now when one of those who sat at the table with Him heard these things, he said to Him, "Blessed *is* he who shall eat bread[109] in the kingdom of God!"
16 Then He said to him, "A certain man gave a great supper and invited many,
17 "and sent his servant at supper time to say to those who were invited, 'Come, for all things are now ready.'
18 "But they all with one *accord* began to make excuses. The first said to him, 'I have bought a piece of ground, and I must go and see it. I ask you to have me excused.'
19 "And another said, 'I have bought five yoke of oxen, and I am going to test them. I ask you to have me excused.'
20 "Still another said, 'I have married a wife, and therefore I cannot come.'

---

104 NU-Text reads *in that very hour.*   105 NU-Text and M-Text omit *assuredly.*   106 Psalm 118:26
107 NU-Text adds *or not.*   108 NU-Text and M-Text read *son.*   109 M-Text reads *the best.*

Compel Them to Come In

In the course of Jesus' ministry, He taught His disciples through a parable to extend an invitation for everyone to come and sit at a banquet feast in the kingdom of God. "Go out into the highways and hedges, and compel *them* to come in, that my house may be filled" (Luke 14:23).

The highways referred to in Jesus' parable were the famous *Via Maris* and King's Highway which ran through gentile regions. The hedges, byways, indicated the smaller connecting travel routes between the major highways. These passed through the remote Jewish villages. In teaching His disciples to go into the highways and byways, Jesus extended His invitation to enter God's kingdom to both the Gentile and the Jew. God's forgiveness and love are offered to all mankind.

Jesus implored an attitude still evident today when inviting someone to dine. Jesus said, "**compel** them to come in." A common practice in the Middle East is to invite someone for dinner, knowing full well that the person will turn down the invitation the first time. As a matter of fact, it is not courteous to accept at first. It is expected that the host will invite you again and insist that you come.

A common dinner invitation dialogue might go like this:

"Oh, please come and dine at our house."

"Oh, no, we couldn't. Thank you very much anyway."

"No, we insist that you come."

"Oh, we really couldn't."

"Oh, but you must come. We have so much to give you. We have prepared everything for you. We have you in our minds, thoughts, and prayers. Please come and honor us with your presence."

Then the invited guest will say, "Well, if you've done all that, we can do nothing but come. Of course, we'll be there."

This is the attitude that Jesus wishes His disciples to convey to people about God's love and forgiveness in inviting them to share in the kingdom of God. It is an invitation that is constantly available to all. Though many will turn it down upon the first, second, and third request, the call is to continually insist and invite them to share in Jesus' love and forgiveness.

Who can you share a positive experience of joy and forgiveness with in your world? What highways and byways can you travel to meet and share with them the love of Jesus Christ? Remember, God's kingdom is for all people. Compel them to come in!

21 "So that servant came and reported these things to his master. Then the master of the house, being angry, said to his servant, 'Go out quickly into the streets and lanes of the city, and bring in here *the* poor and *the* maimed and *the* lame and *the* blind.'

22 "And the servant said, 'Master, it is done as you commanded, and still there is room.'

23 "Then the master said to the servant, 'Go out into the highways and hedges, and compel *them* to come in, that my house may be filled.

24 'For I say to you that none of those men who were invited shall taste my supper.'"

Leaving All to Follow Christ

25 And great multitudes went with Him. And He turned and said to them,

26 "If anyone comes to Me and does not hate his father and mother, wife and children, brothers and sisters, yes, and his own life also, he cannot be My disciple.

27 "And whoever does not bear his cross and come after Me cannot be My disciple.

28 "For which of you, intending to build a tower, does not sit down first and count the cost, whether he has *enough* to finish *it*—

29 "lest, after he has laid the foundation, and is not able to finish *it*, all who see *it* begin to mock him,

30 "saying, 'This man began to build and was not able to finish.'

31 "Or what king, going to make war against another king, does not sit down first and consider whether he is able with ten thousand to meet him who comes against him with twenty thousand?

32 "Or else, while the other is still a great way off, he sends a delegation and asks conditions of peace.

33 "So likewise, whoever of you does not forsake all that he has cannot be My disciple.

Tasteless Salt Is Worthless

34 "Salt *is* good; but if the salt has lost its flavor, how shall it be seasoned?

35 "It is neither fit for the land nor for the dunghill, *but* men throw it out. He who has ears to hear, let him hear!"

The Parable of the Lost Sheep

15 Then all the tax collectors and the sinners drew near to Him to hear Him.

2 And the Pharisees and scribes murmured, saying, "This man receives sinners and eats with them."

3 So He spoke this parable to them, saying:

4 "What man of you, having a hundred sheep, if he loses one of them, does not leave the ninety-nine in the wilderness, and go after the one which is lost until he finds it?

5 "And when he has found *it*, he lays *it* on his shoulders, rejoicing.

6 "And when he comes home, he calls together *his* friends and neighbors, saying to them, 'Rejoice with me, for I have found my sheep which was lost!'

7 "I say to you that likewise there will be more joy in heaven over one sinner who repents than over ninety-nine just persons who need no repentance.

The Parable of the Lost Coin

8 "Or what woman, having ten silver coins,[110] if she loses one coin, does not light a lamp, sweep the house, and seek diligently until she finds *it*?

9 "And when she has found *it*, she calls *her* friends and neighbors together, saying, 'Rejoice with me, for I have found the piece which I lost!'

10 "Likewise, I say to you, there is joy in the presence of the angels of God over one sinner who repents."

The Parable of the Lost Son

11 Then He said: "A certain man had two sons.

12 "And the younger of them said to *his* father, 'Father, give me the portion of goods that falls *to me*.' So he divided to them *his* livelihood.

13 "And not many days after, the younger son gathered all together, journeyed to a far country, and there wasted his possessions with prodigal living.

14 "But when he had spent all, there arose a severe famine in that land, and he began to be in want.

15 "Then he went and joined himself to a citizen of that country, and he sent him into his fields to feed swine.

110 Greek *drachma,* a valuable coin often worn in a ten-piece garland by married women

The Lost Coin

"What woman, having ten silver coins, if she loses one coin, does not light a lamp, sweep the house, and seek diligently until she finds *it*? And when she has found *it*, she calls *her* friends and neighbors together, saying, 'Rejoice with me, for I have found the piece which I lost!' Likewise, I say to you, there is joy in the presence of the angels of God over one sinner who repents" (Luke 15:8–10).

The ancient dress of Palestinian women helps illuminate this parable of Jesus. The coin which the woman searches for so diligently holds immense value to her. Not simply in its monetary wealth, but because it is most probable that it was the type of coin attached to the headdress of the woman's dowry. Even today Bedouin women in Palestine wear ten, fifty, even one hundred coins attached to the scarfs which cover their heads. The coin this woman lost had special sentimental value to her.

By lighting a lamp and sweeping her floor, the woman did everything she could to help locate the lost coin. Perhaps a shimmer of light bouncing off the coin would help her detect it. Maybe the tinkling sound made by the coin as the broom strands reached down between the basaltic stone cracks, loosening it from its lodging place would reveal its location.

Like the woman who searched for her coin, we can be assured that we are special to God. Like the one sentimental coin, we hold unique value and worth to our Father. For we are His valued possession, giving glory to Him. We can have the confidence that He will light our way, look for us, and when He finds us, pick us up and rejoice.

16 "And he would gladly have filled his stomach with the pods that the swine ate, and no one gave him *anything*.

17 "But when he came to himself, he said, 'How many of my father's hired servants have bread enough and to spare, and I perish with hunger!

18 'I will arise and go to my father, and will say to him, "Father, I have sinned against heaven and before you,

19 and I am no longer worthy to be called your son. Make me like one of your hired servants." '

20 "And he arose and came to his father. But when he was still a great way off, his father saw him and had compassion, and ran and fell on his neck and kissed him.

21 "And the son said to him, 'Father, I have sinned against heaven and in your sight, and am no longer worthy to be called your son.'

22 "But the father said to his servants, 'Bring[111] out the best robe and put *it* on him, and put a ring on his hand and sandals on *his* feet.

23 'And bring the fatted calf here and kill *it*, and let us eat and be merry;

24 'for this my son was dead and is alive again; he was lost and is found.' And they began to be merry.

25 "Now his older son was in the field. And as he came and drew near to the house, he heard music and dancing.

26 "So he called one of the servants and asked what these things meant.

27 "And he said to him, 'Your brother has come, and because he has received him safe and sound, your father has killed the fatted calf.'

28 "But he was angry and would not go in. Therefore his father came out and pleaded with him.

29 "So he answered and said to *his* father, 'Lo, these many years I have been serving you; I never transgressed your commandment at any time; and yet you never gave me a young goat, that I might make merry with my friends.

30 'But as soon as this son of yours came, who has devoured your livelihood with harlots, you killed the fatted calf for him.'

31 "And he said to him, 'Son, you are always with me, and all that I have is yours.

32 'It was right that we should make merry and be glad, for your brother was

dead and is alive again, and was lost and is found.' "

The Parable of the Unjust Steward

16 And He also said to His disciples: "There was a certain rich man who had a steward, and an accusation was brought to him that this man was wasting his goods.

2 "So he called him and said to him, 'What is this I hear about you? Give an account of your stewardship, for you can no longer be steward.'

3 "Then the steward said within himself, 'What shall I do? For my master is taking the stewardship away from me. I cannot dig; I am ashamed to beg.

4 'I have resolved what to do, that when I am put out of the stewardship, they may receive me into their houses.'

5 "So he called every one of his master's debtors to *him*, and said to the first, 'How much do you owe my master?'

6 "And he said, 'A hundred measures[112] of oil.' So he said to him, 'Take your bill, and sit down quickly and write fifty.'

7 "Then he said to another, 'And how much do you owe?' So he said, 'A hundred measures[113] of wheat.' And he said to him, 'Take your bill, and write eighty.'

8 "So the master commended the unjust steward because he had dealt shrewdly. For the sons of this world are more shrewd in their generation than the sons of light.

9 "And I say to you, make friends for yourselves by unrighteous mammon, that when you fail,[114] they may receive you into everlasting habitations.

10 "He who *is* faithful in *what is* least is faithful also in much; and he who is unjust in *what is* least is unjust also in much.

11 "Therefore if you have not been faithful in the unrighteous mammon, who will commit to your trust the true *riches?*

12 "And if you have not been faithful in what is another man's, who will give you what is your own?

13 "No servant can serve two masters; for either he will hate the one and love the other, or else he will be loyal to the one and despise the other. You cannot serve God and mammon."

The Law, the Prophets, and the Kingdom

14 Now the Pharisees, who were lovers of

---

111 NU-Text reads *Quickly bring.*   112 Greek *batos,* eight or nine gallons each (Old Testament *bath*)
113 Greek *koros,* ten or twelve bushels each (Old Testament *kor*)   114 NU-Text reads *it fails.*

The Prodigal Son

Throughout Jesus' ministry, He occasionally drew from Jewish culture to illustrate His truths. Perhaps one of His most familiar stories is that of the Prodigal Son. Similar parables were also used by the rabbis of His day, but Jesus gave them fresh new meanings.

The story of the Prodigal Son focuses on an average young man from a small village in the Jordan River valley. This town is in Perea, a sparsely populated Jewish area south of Galilee on the road to Jerusalem. His father is a wealthy landowner, whose many servants care for the fields and flocks of his land.

Like any other boy his age, the son possibly looks up at the high mountain range surrounding his village and wonders about the lights of the towns sitting on the ridge. This is the gentile Decapolis, known for its Greek temples, art, games, and literature. It is considered the "far-off land," reflecting not its geographical distance, but its cultural distance from the religious beliefs of the Jewish population.

One day, consumed by his curiosity, the young boy leaves behind his family and makes haste for this pagan country. Here the story tells that he "wasted his possessions with prodigal living" (Luke 15:13). At this time, a great famine sweeps over the land, bringing severe hardship to the mountainous Decapolis region. The Perean area is not affected, however, for it is located seven hundred feet below sea level. Its several underground springs keep the land fertile and alive. The young boy, now moneyless and hungry, persuades a local farmer to let him care for his hogs. Upon realizing that the hogs he feeds have a better life than he does, the boy decides to return home with hopes of being hired as a servant on his father's farm.

Here the rabbinical teaching explains that once someone leaves his faith and indulges in the culture and religion of the Greek cities, he is considered dead. The father cannot forgive his son for his wanderings and sins in the gentile land. The boy is cut off from his family, friends, and religion forever.

Jesus, however, gives this story a new ending. Now, the boy receives forgiveness from his father, who celebrates his homecoming by killing a fatted calf and throwing a feast. No longer is man cut off from God. Instead, there is much rejoicing. Man is forgiven.

money, also heard all these things, and they derided Him.

15 And He said to them, "You are those who justify yourselves before men, but God knows your hearts. For what is highly esteemed among men is an abomination in the sight of God.

16 "The law and the prophets *were* until John. Since that time the kingdom of God has been preached, and everyone is pressing into it.

17 "And it is easier for heaven and earth to pass away than for one tittle of the law to fail.

18 "Whoever divorces his wife and marries another commits adultery; and whoever marries her who is divorced from *her* husband commits adultery.

The Rich Man and Lazarus

19 "There was a certain rich man who was clothed in purple and fine linen and fared sumptuously every day.

20 "But there was a certain beggar named Lazarus, full of sores, who was laid at his gate,

21 "desiring to be fed with the crumbs which fell[115] from the rich man's table. Moreover the dogs came and licked his sores.

22 "So it was that the beggar died, and was carried by the angels to Abraham's bosom. The rich man also died and was buried.

23 "And being in torments in Hades, he lifted up his eyes and saw Abraham afar off, and Lazarus in his bosom.

24 "Then he cried and said, 'Father Abraham, have mercy on me, and send Lazarus that he may dip the tip of his finger in water and cool my tongue; for I am tormented in this flame.'

25 "But Abraham said, 'Son, remember that in your lifetime you received your good things, and likewise Lazarus evil things; but now he is comforted and you are tormented.

26 'And besides all this, between us and you there is a great gulf fixed, so that those who want to pass from here to you cannot, nor can those from there pass to us.'

27 "Then he said, 'I beg you therefore, father, that you would send him to my father's house,

28 'for I have five brothers, that he may

testify to them, lest they also come to this place of torment.'

29 "Abraham said to him, 'They have Moses and the prophets; let them hear them.'

30 "And he said, 'No, father Abraham; but if one goes to them from the dead, they will repent.'

31 "But he said to him, 'If they do not hear Moses and the prophets, neither will they be persuaded though one rise from the dead.' "

Jesus Warns of Offenses

17 Then He said to the disciples, "It is impossible that no offenses should come, but woe *to him* through whom they do come!

2 "It would be better for him if a millstone were hung around his neck, and he were thrown into the sea, than that he should offend one of these little ones.

3 "Take heed to yourselves. If your brother sins against you,[116] rebuke him; and if he repents, forgive him.

4 "And if he sins against you seven times in a day, and seven times in a day returns to you,[117] saying, 'I repent,' you shall forgive him."

Faith and Duty

5 And the apostles said to the Lord, "Increase our faith."

6 So the Lord said, "If you have faith as a mustard seed, you can say to this mulberry tree, 'Be pulled up by the roots and be planted in the sea,' and it would obey you.

7 "And which of you, having a servant plowing or tending sheep, will say to him when he has come in from the field, 'Come at once and sit down to eat'?

8 "But will he not rather say to him, 'Prepare something for my supper, and gird yourself and serve me till I have eaten and drunk, and afterward you will eat and drink'?

9 "Does he thank that servant because he did the things that were commanded him? I think not.[118]

10 "So likewise you, when you have done all those things which you are commanded, say, 'We are unprofitable servants. We have done what was our duty to do.' "

115 NU-Text reads *with what fell.*   116 NU-Text omits *against you.*   117 M-Text omits *to you.*
118 NU-Text ends verse with *commanded;* M-Text omits *him.*

Ten Lepers Cleansed

11 Now it happened as He went to Jerusalem that He passed through the midst of Samaria and Galilee.
12 Then as He entered a certain village, there met Him ten men who were lepers, who stood afar off.
13 And they lifted up *their* voices and said, "Jesus, Master, have mercy on us!"
14 So when He saw *them*, He said to them, "Go, show yourselves to the priests." And so it was that as they went, they were cleansed.
15 Now one of them, when he saw that he was healed, returned, and with a loud voice glorified God,
16 and fell down on *his* face at His feet, giving Him thanks. And he was a Samaritan.
17 So Jesus answered and said, "Were there not ten cleansed? But where *are* the nine?
18 "Were there not any found who returned to give glory to God except this foreigner?"
19 And He said to him, "Arise, go your way. Your faith has made you well."

The Coming of the Kingdom

20 Now when He was asked by the Pharisees when the kingdom of God would come, He answered them and said, "The kingdom of God does not come with observation;
21 "nor will they say, 'See here!' or 'See there!'[119] For indeed, the kingdom of God is within you."
22 Then He said to the disciples, "The days will come when you will desire to see one of the days of the Son of Man, and you will not see *it*.
23 "And they will say to you, 'Look here!' or 'Look there!'[119] Do not go after *them* or follow *them*.
24 "For as the lightning that flashes out of one *part* under heaven shines to the other *part* under heaven, so also the Son of Man will be in His day.
25 "But first He must suffer many things and be rejected by this generation.
26 "And as it was in the days of Noah, so it will be also in the days of the Son of Man:
27 "They ate, they drank, they married wives, they were given in marriage, until

the day that Noah entered the ark, and the flood came and destroyed them all.
28 "Likewise as it was also in the days of Lot: They ate, they drank, they bought, they sold, they planted, they built;
29 "but on the day that Lot went out of Sodom it rained fire and brimstone from heaven and destroyed *them* all.
30 "Even so will it be in the day when the Son of Man is revealed.
31 "In that day, he who is on the housetop, and his goods *are* in the house, let him not come down to take them away. And likewise the one who is in the field, let him not turn back.
32 "Remember Lot's wife.
33 "Whoever seeks to save his life will lose it, and whoever loses his life will preserve it.
34 "I tell you, in that night there will be two *men* in one bed: the one will be taken and the other will be left.
35 "Two *women* will be grinding together: the one will be taken and the other left.
36 "Two *men* will be in the field: the one will be taken and the other left."[120]
37 And they answered and said to Him, "Where, Lord?" So He said to them, "Wherever the body is, there the eagles will be gathered together."

The Parable of the Persistent Widow

18 Then He spoke a parable to them, that men always ought to pray and not lose heart,
2 saying: "There was in a certain city a judge who did not fear God nor regard man.
3 "Now there was a widow in that city; and she came to him, saying, 'Avenge me of my adversary.'
4 "And he would not for a while; but afterward he said within himself, 'Though I do not fear God nor regard man,
5 'yet because this widow troubles me I will avenge her, lest by her continual coming she weary me.' "
6 Then the Lord said, "Hear what the unjust judge said.
7 "And shall God not avenge His own elect who cry out day and night to Him, though He bears long with them?
8 "I tell you that He will avenge them speedily. Nevertheless, when the Son of Man comes, will He really find faith on the earth?"

---

119 NU-Text reverses *here* and *there*.   120 NU-Text and M-Text omit verse 36.

Return to Give Thanks

Leprosy was a dreaded and deadly disease in the Middle East during the time of Christ. According to Jewish Levitical law, lepers were to live alone outside the city. They were not to come in contact with any other person. Theirs was a life of isolation, only having contact with each other. Oftentimes they congregated in small groups, living meagerly on scraps people would spare.

It was one such group that Jesus came upon when traveling through the area of Perea on His way to Jerusalem. Their cries for help did not go unheard. Having compassion on them, Jesus healed the lepers of their disease. He told them to go before the Levitical priests to show themselves as clean. This practice of the Levitical law was the leper's one hope to live a normal life in society.

In faith, the lepers journeyed to the priests. As they began their travel, the disease left them. They went before the priests who confirmed they were well. Of the ten lepers that Jesus healed, only one took the time and energy to return to find and thank Jesus for what He had done.

In the same manner, Jesus heals us of our emotional, spiritual, and physical diseases. Yet how often do we return to thank Him? We must, like the one leper, return to give thanks. It is easy to cry out to God when we are in pain. But when we are surrounded with prosperity, may we also acknowledge Him for His gifts. The one leper who returned was a Samaritan—the least likely to come back to Jesus. But despite the cultural barriers between the Jews and Samaritans, the leper did return to give thanks.

Let us not be held back by barriers, but let us always make the effort to have a thankful and grateful heart before our Lord.

The Parable of the Pharisee and the Tax Collector

9 Also He spoke this parable to some who trusted in themselves that they were righteous, and despised others:
10 "Two men went up to the temple to pray, one a Pharisee and the other a tax collector.
11 "The Pharisee stood and prayed thus with himself, 'God, I thank You that I am not like other men—extortioners, unjust, adulterers, or even as this tax collector.
12 'I fast twice a week; I give tithes of all that I possess.'
13 "And the tax collector, standing afar off, would not so much as raise *his* eyes to heaven, but beat his breast, saying, 'God be merciful to me a sinner!'
14 "I tell you, this man went down to his house justified *rather* than the other; for everyone who exalts himself will be abased, and he who humbles himself will be exalted."

Jesus Blesses Little Children

15 Then they also brought infants to Him that He might touch them; but when *His* disciples saw *it*, they rebuked them.
16 But Jesus called them to *Him* and said, "Let the little children come to Me, and do not forbid them; for of such is the kingdom of God.
17 "Assuredly, I say to you, whoever does not receive the kingdom of God as a little child will by no means enter it."

Jesus Counsels the Rich Young Ruler

18 Now a certain ruler asked Him, saying, "Good Teacher, what shall I do to inherit eternal life?"
19 So Jesus said to him, "Why do you call Me good? No one *is* good but One, *that is*, God.
20 "You know the commandments: '*Do not commit adultery,*' '*Do not murder,*' '*Do not steal,*' '*Do not bear false witness,*' '*Honor your father and your mother.*' " [121]
21 And he said, "All these I have kept from my youth."
22 So when Jesus heard these things, He said to him, "You still lack one thing. Sell all that you have and distribute to the poor, and you will have treasure in heaven; and come, follow Me."
23 But when he heard this, he became very sorrowful, for he was very rich.

With God All Things Are Possible

24 And when Jesus saw that he became very sorrowful, He said, "How hard it is for those who have riches to enter the kingdom of God!
25 "For it is easier for a camel to go through a needle's eye than for a rich man to enter the kingdom of God."
26 And those who heard it said, "Who then can be saved?"
27 But He said, "The things which are impossible with men are possible with God."
28 Then Peter said, "See, we have left all [122] and followed You."
29 So He said to them, "Assuredly, I say to you, there is no one who has left house or parents or brothers or wife or children, for the sake of the kingdom of God,
30 "who shall not receive many times more in this present time, and in the age to come everlasting life."

Jesus a Third Time Predicts His Death and Resurrection

31 Then He took the twelve aside and said to them, "Behold, we are going up to Jerusalem, and all things that are written by the prophets concerning the Son of Man will be accomplished.
32 "For He will be delivered to the Gentiles and will be mocked and insulted and spit upon.
33 "And they will scourge *Him* and put Him to death. And the third day He will rise again."
34 But they understood none of these things; this saying was hidden from them, and they did not know the things which were spoken.

A Blind Man Receives His Sight

35 Then it happened, that as He was coming near Jericho, that a certain blind man sat by the road begging.
36 And hearing a multitude passing by, he asked what it meant.
37 So they told him that Jesus of Nazareth was passing by.
38 And he cried out, saying, "Jesus, Son of David, have mercy on me!"
39 Then those who went before warned him that he should be quiet; but he cried out all the more, "Son of David, have mercy on me!"

121 Exodus 20:12-16; Deuteronomy 5:16-20   122 NU-Text reads *our own.*

40 So Jesus stood still and commanded him to be brought to Him. And when he had come near, He asked him,
41 saying, "What do you want Me to do for you?" And he said, "Lord, that I may receive my sight."
42 Then Jesus said to him, "Receive your sight; your faith has saved you."
43 And immediately he received his sight, and followed Him, glorifying God. And all the people, when they saw *it*, gave praise to God.

Jesus Comes to Zacchaeus' House

19 Then *Jesus* entered and passed through Jericho.
2 Now behold, *there was* a man named Zacchaeus who was a chief tax collector, and he was rich.
3 And he sought to see who Jesus was, but could not because of the crowd, for he was of short stature.
4 So he ran ahead and climbed up into a sycamore tree to see Him, for He was going to pass that *way*.
5 And when Jesus came to the place, He looked up and saw him,[123] and said to him, "Zacchaeus, make haste and come down, for today I must stay at your house."
6 So he made haste and came down, and received Him joyfully.
7 But when they saw *it*, they all murmured, saying, "He has gone to be a guest with a man who is a sinner."
8 Then Zacchaeus stood and said to the Lord, "Look, Lord, I give half of my goods to the poor; and if I have taken anything from anyone by false accusation, I restore fourfold."
9 And Jesus said to him, "Today salvation has come to this house, because he also is a son of Abraham;
10 "for the Son of Man has come to seek and to save that which was lost."

The Parable of the Minas[124]

11 Now as they heard these things, He spoke another parable, because He was near Jerusalem and because they thought the kingdom of God would appear immediately.
12 Therefore He said: "A certain nobleman went into a far country to receive for himself a kingdom and to return.
13 "So he called ten of his servants, delivered to them ten minas, and said to them, 'Do business till I come.'
14 "But his citizens hated him, and sent a delegation after him, saying, 'We will not have this *man* to reign over us.'
15 "And so it was that when he returned, having received the kingdom, he then commanded these servants, to whom he had given the money, to be called to him, that he might know how much every man had gained by trading.
16 "Then came the first, saying, 'Master, your mina has earned ten minas.'
17 "And he said to him, 'Well *done*, good servant; because you were faithful in a very little, have authority over ten cities.'
18 "And the second came, saying, 'Master, your mina has earned five minas.'
19 "Likewise he said to him, 'You also be over five cities.'
20 "And another came, saying, 'Master, here is your mina, which I have kept put away in a handkerchief.
21 'For I feared you, because you are an austere man. You collect what you did not deposit, and reap what you did not sow.'
22 "And he said to him, 'Out of your own mouth I will judge you, *you* wicked servant. You knew that I was an austere man, collecting what I did not deposit and reaping what I did not sow.
23 'Why then did you not put my money in the bank, that at my coming I might have collected it with interest?'
24 "And he said to those who stood by, 'Take the mina from him, and give *it* to him who has ten minas.'
25 ("But they said to him, 'Master, he has ten minas.')
26 'For I say to you, that to everyone who has will be given; and from him who does not have, even what he has will be taken away from him.
27 'But bring here those enemies of mine, who did not want me to reign over them, and slay *them* before me.' "

The Triumphal Entry

28 When He had said this, He went on ahead, going up to Jerusalem.
29 And it came to pass, when He came near to Bethphage[125] and Bethany, at the mountain called Olivet, *that* He sent two of His disciples,
30 saying, "Go into the village opposite

123 NU-Text omits *and saw him.*
124 The *mina* (Greek *mna*, Hebrew *minah*) was worth about three months' salary.   125 M-Text reads *Bethsphage.*

you, where as you enter you will find a colt tied, on which no one has ever sat. Loose him and bring *him here.*

31 "And if anyone asks you, 'Why are you loosing *him?*' thus you shall say to him, 'Because the Lord has need of him.' "

32 So those who were sent departed and found *it* just as He had said to them.

33 But as they were loosing the colt, the owners of it said to them, "Why are you loosing the colt?"

34 And they said, "The Lord has need of him."

35 Then they brought him to Jesus. And they threw their own garments on the colt, and they set Jesus on him.

36 And as He went, they spread their clothes on the road.

37 Then, as He was now drawing near the descent of the Mount of Olives, the whole multitude of the disciples began to rejoice and praise God with a loud voice for all the mighty works they had seen,

38 saying:

" *'Blessed is the King who comes in the name of the LORD!'*[126]
Peace in heaven and glory in the highest!"

39 And some of the Pharisees called to Him from the crowd, "Teacher, rebuke Your disciples."

40 But He answered and said to them, "I tell you that if these should keep silent, the stones would immediately cry out."

Jesus Weeps over Jerusalem

41 Now as He drew near, He saw the city and wept over it,

42 saying, "If you had known, even you, especially in this your day, the things *that* make for your peace! But now they are hidden from your eyes.

43 "For *the* days will come upon you when your enemies will build an embankment around you, surround you and close you in on every side,

44 "and level you, and your children within you, to the ground; and they will not leave in you one stone upon another, because you did not know the time of your visitation."

Jesus Cleanses the Temple

45 Then He went into the temple and began to drive out those who bought and sold in it,[127]

46 saying to them, "It is written, '*My house is*[128] *a house of prayer,*'[129] but you have made it a '*den of thieves.*' "[130]

47 And He was teaching daily in the temple. But the chief priests, the scribes, and the leaders of the people sought to destroy Him,

48 and were unable to do anything; for all the people were very attentive to hear Him.

Jesus' Authority Questioned

20 Now it happened on one of those days, as He taught the people in the temple and preached the gospel, *that* the chief priests and the scribes, together with the elders, confronted *Him*

2 and spoke to Him, saying, "Tell us, by what authority are You doing these things? Or who is he who gave You this authority?"

3 But He answered and said to them, "I will also ask you one thing, and answer Me:

4 "The baptism of John—was it from heaven or from men?"

5 And they reasoned among themselves, saying, "If we say, 'From heaven,' He will say, 'Why then[131] did you not believe him?'

6 "But if we say, 'From men,' all the people will stone us, for they are persuaded that John was a prophet."

7 So they answered that they did not know where *it was* from.

8 And Jesus said to them, "Neither will I tell you by what authority I do these things."

The Parable of the Wicked Vinedressers

9 Then He began to tell the people this parable: "A certain man planted a vineyard, leased it to vinedressers, and went into a far country for a long time.

10 "Now at vintage-time he sent a servant to the vinedressers, that they might give him some of the fruit of the vineyard. But the vinedressers beat him and sent *him* away empty-handed.

126 Psalm 118:26   127 NU-Text reads *those who were selling.*   128 NU-Text reads *shall be.*
129 Isaiah 56:7   130 Jeremiah 7:11   131 NU-Text and M-Text omit *then.*

11 "Again he sent another servant; and they beat him also, treated *him* shamefully, and sent *him* away empty-handed.
12 "And again he sent a third; and they wounded him also and cast *him* out.
13 "Then the owner of the vineyard said, 'What shall I do? I will send my beloved son. Probably they will respect *him* when they see him.'
14 "But when the vinedressers saw him, they reasoned among themselves, saying, 'This is the heir. Come, let us kill him, that the inheritance may be ours.'
15 "So they cast him out of the vineyard and killed *him*. Therefore what will the owner of the vineyard do to them?
16 "He will come and destroy those vinedressers and give the vineyard to others." And when they heard *it* they said, "Certainly not!"
17 And He looked at them and said, "What then is this that is written:

'The stone which the builders rejected
Has become the chief cornerstone'?[132]

18 "Whoever falls on that stone will be broken; but on whomever it falls, it will grind him to powder."
19 And the chief priests and the scribes that very hour sought to lay hands on Him, but they feared the people[133]—for they knew that He had spoken this parable against them.

The Pharisees: Is It Lawful to Pay Taxes to Caesar?

20 So they watched *Him*, and sent spies who pretended to be righteous, that they might seize on His words, in order to deliver Him to the power and the authority of the governor.
21 And they asked Him, saying, "Teacher, we know that You say and teach rightly, and You do not show personal favoritism, but teach the way of God truly:
22 "Is it lawful for us to pay taxes to Caesar or not?"
23 But He perceived their craftiness, and said to them, "Why do you test Me?[134]
24 "Show Me a denarius. Whose image and inscription does it have?" They answered and said, "Caesar's."
25 And He said to them, "Render therefore to Caesar the things that are Cae-

sar's, and to God the things that are God's."
26 But they could not catch Him in His words in the presence of the people. And they marveled at His answer and kept silent.

The Sadducees: What about the Resurrection?

27 Then some of the Sadducees, who deny that there is a resurrection, came to *Him* and asked Him,
28 saying: "Teacher, Moses wrote to us *that* if a man's brother dies, having a wife, and he dies without children, his brother should take his wife and raise up offspring for his brother.
29 "Now there were seven brothers. And the first took a wife, and died without children.
30 "And the second[135] took her as wife, and he died childless.
31 "Then the third took her, and in like manner the seven also; and they left no children,[136] and died.
32 "Last of all the woman died also.
33 "Therefore, in the resurrection, whose wife does she become? For all seven had her as wife."
34 And Jesus answered and said to them, "The sons of this age marry and are given in marriage.
35 "But those who are counted worthy to attain that age, and the resurrection from the dead, neither marry nor are given in marriage;
36 "nor can they die anymore, for they are equal to the angels and are sons of God, being sons of the resurrection.
37 "Now even Moses showed in the *burning* bush *passage* that the dead are raised, when he called the Lord 'the God of Abraham, the God of Isaac, and the God of Jacob.'[137]
38 "For He is not the God of the dead but of the living, for all live to Him."
39 Then some of the scribes answered and said, "Teacher, You have spoken well."
40 But after that they dared not question Him anymore.

Jesus: How Can David Call His Descendant Lord?

41 And He said to them, "How can they say that the Christ is David's Son?

132 Psalm 118:22   133 M-Text reads *but they were afraid*.   134 NU-Text omits *Why do you test Me?*
135 NU-Text ends verse 30 here.   136 NU-Text and M-Text read *the seven also left no children*.
137 Exodus 3:6, 15

Render to God What Is God's

In New Testament Palestine, the Jews suffered under heavy taxation from their Roman oppressors. The emperor demanded a tribute tax paid as divine homage to himself. He ordered the agriculture to be taxed. The travel roads, buildings, fishing licenses, and even animals were taxed.

More than two-thirds of a person's earned income was taxed and payable to the Roman authorities. The Jewish people carried the burden of taxes to pay for the Roman wars at the other end of the empire. In addition, the Jewish people were obligated to pay temple and religious taxes. The question of taxation was a hotly contested issue during the time of Jesus. Much blood had been shed in revolts prior to and following Jesus' ministry.

One day while Jesus taught at the temple, some Pharisees and Herodians, trying to trick Jesus, asked him whether it was lawful to pay taxes to Caesar or not. While doing so they held up a denarius. Undoubtedly this event took place outside the main temple enclosure, for coins with images of man or beast were forbidden in the temple area.

Jesus raised His voice above the crowd and declared, "Render therefore to Caesar the things that are Caesar's, and to God the things that are God's" (Matt. 22:21). His answer satisfied the Herodian authorities and the Pharisees. It also pointed out to His followers that although they were taxed unjustly in many cases, they should not become so preoccupied with hatred and rebellion that they will be unable to spread the message of God's love and forgiveness. The Jewish people were burdened with taxes beyond reason, but Jesus taught them not to focus on the negative situation. Instead, He encouraged them to dwell on the positive by yielding their God-given talents to spread the message of God's love and forgiveness.

We cannot always change a situation, but we can change our attitude. We cannot always change other people's actions, but we can control and change our reactions. Caesar's image was indelibly minted on the coin, whereas Jews were forbidden to make any image of God. This was to recognize that God is above His creation as well as in His creation. Everything in creation is a gift from God. Jesus prompted people to emphasize a positive response to God rather than the negative response to mankind.

Jesus taught not against Caesar but against the worries induced by paying tribute to Caesar. In times of injustice, do not become overly concerned or robbed of the joy of serving God with your time, talents, and abilities. Render to God what is God's. What you are is God's gift to you. What you become is your gift to God!

42 "Now David himself said in the Book of Psalms,

'The LORD said to my Lord,
"Sit at My right hand,
43 Till I make Your enemies
Your footstool."'[138]

44 "David therefore calls Him '*Lord*'; how is He then his Son?"

Beware of the Scribes

45 Then, in the hearing of all the people, He said to His disciples,
46 "Beware of the scribes, who desire to walk in long robes, love greetings in the marketplaces, the best seats in the synagogues, and the best places at feasts,
47 "who devour widows' houses, and for a pretense make long prayers. These will receive greater condemnation."

The Widow's Two Mites

21 Then He looked up and saw the rich putting their gifts into the treasury,
2 and He saw also a certain poor widow putting in two mites.
3 So He said, "Truly I say to you that this poor widow has put in more than all;
4 "for all these out of their abundance have put in offerings for God,[139] but she out of her poverty has put in all the livelihood that she had."

Jesus Predicts the Destruction of the Temple

5 Then, as some spoke of the temple, how it was adorned with beautiful stones and donations, He said,
6 "*As for* these things which you see, the days will come in which not one stone shall be left upon another that shall not be thrown down."

The Signs of the Times and the End of the Age

7 And they asked Him, saying, "Teacher, but when will these things be? And what sign *will there be* when these things are about to take place?"
8 And He said: "Take heed that you not be deceived. For many, will come in My name, saying, 'I am *He*,' and, 'The time has drawn near.' Therefore[140] do not go after them.
9 "But when you hear of wars and commotions, do not be terrified; for these

things must come to pass first, but the end *will not come* immediately."
10 Then He said to them, "Nation will rise against nation, and kingdom against kingdom.
11 "And there will be great earthquakes in various places, and famines and pestilences; and there will be fearful sights and great signs from heaven.
12 "But before all these things, they will lay their hands on you and persecute *you*, delivering *you* up to the synagogues and prisons, and you will be brought before kings and rulers for My name's sake.
13 "But it will turn out for you as an occasion for testimony.
14 "Therefore settle *it* in your hearts not to meditate beforehand on what you will answer;
15 "for I will give you a mouth and wisdom which all your adversaries will not be able to contradict or resist.
16 "You will be betrayed even by parents and brothers, relatives and friends; and they will send *some* of you to *your* death.
17 "And you will be hated by all for My name's sake.
18 "But not a hair of your head shall be lost.
19 "In your patience possess your souls.

The Destruction of Jerusalem

20 "But when you see Jerusalem surrounded by armies, then know that its desolation is near.
21 "Then let those in Judea flee to the mountains, let those who are in the midst of her depart, and let not those who are in the country enter her.
22 "For these are the days of vengeance, that all things which are written may be fulfilled.
23 "But woe to those who are pregnant and to those who are nursing babies in those days! For there will be great distress in the land and wrath upon this people.
24 "And they will fall by the edge of the sword, and be led away captive into all nations. And Jerusalem will be trampled by Gentiles until the times of the Gentiles are fulfilled.

The Coming of the Son of Man

25 "And there will be signs in the sun, in the moon, and in the stars; and on the

---

138 Psalm 110:1   139 NU-Text omits *for God.*   140 NU-Text omits *Therefore.*

earth distress of nations, with perplexity, the sea and the waves roaring;
26 "men's hearts failing them from fear and the expectation of those things which are coming on the earth, for the powers of heaven will be shaken.
27 "Then they will see the Son of Man coming in a cloud with power and great glory.
28 "Now when these things begin to happen, look up and lift up your heads, because your redemption draws near."

The Parable of the Fig Tree

29 And He spoke to them a parable: "Look at the fig tree, and all the trees.
30 "When they are already budding, you see and know for yourselves that summer is now near.
31 "So you, likewise, when you see these things happening, know that the kingdom of God is near.
32 "Assuredly, I say to you, this generation will by no means pass away till all things are fulfilled.
33 "Heaven and earth will pass away, but My words will by no means pass away.

The Importance of Watching

34 "But take heed to yourselves, lest your hearts be weighed down with carousing, drunkenness, and cares of this life, and that Day come on you unexpectedly.
35 "For it will come as a snare on all those who dwell on the face of the whole earth.
36 "Watch therefore, and pray always that you may be counted worthy[141] to escape all these things that will come to pass, and to stand before the Son of Man."
37 And in the daytime He was teaching in the temple, but at night He went out and stayed on the mountain called Olivet.
38 Then early in the morning all the people came to Him in the temple to hear Him.

The Plot to Kill Jesus

22 Now the Feast of Unleavened Bread drew near, which is called Passover.
2 And the chief priests and the scribes sought how they might kill Him, for they feared the people.

3 Then Satan entered Judas, surnamed Iscariot, who was numbered among the twelve.
4 So he went his way and conferred with the chief priests and captains, how he might betray Him to them.
5 And they were glad, and agreed to give him money.
6 Then he promised and sought opportunity to betray Him to them in the absence of the multitude.

Jesus and His Disciples Prepare the Passover

7 Then came the Day of Unleavened Bread, when the Passover must be killed.
8 And He sent Peter and John, saying, "Go and prepare the Passover for us, that we may eat."
9 So they said to Him, "Where do You want us to prepare?"
10 And He said to them, "Behold, when you have entered the city, a man will meet you carrying a pitcher of water; follow him into the house which he enters.
11 "Then you shall say to the master of the house, 'The Teacher says to you, "Where is the guest room in which I may eat the Passover with My disciples?"'
12 "Then he will show you a large, furnished upper room; there make ready."
13 So they went and found it as He had said to them, and they prepared the Passover.

Jesus Institutes the Lord's Supper

14 And when the hour had come, He sat down, and the twelve[142] apostles with Him.
15 Then He said to them, "With *fervent* desire I have desired to eat this Passover with you before I suffer;
16 "for I say to you, I will no longer eat of it until it is fulfilled in the kingdom of God."
17 Then He took the cup, and gave thanks, and said, "Take this and divide *it* among yourselves;
18 "for I say to you,[143] I will not drink of the fruit of the vine until the kingdom of God comes."
19 And He took bread, gave thanks and broke *it*, and gave *it* to them, saying, "This is My body which is given for you; do this in remembrance of Me."
20 Likewise He also *took* the cup after supper, saying, "This cup *is* the new covenant in My blood, which is shed for you.

141 NU-Text reads *may have strength.*   142 NU-Text omits *twelve.*   143 NU-Text adds *from now on.*

21 "But behold, the hand of My betrayer *is* with Me on the table.
22 "And truly the Son of Man goes as it has been determined, but woe to that man by whom He is betrayed!"
23 Then they began to question among themselves, which of them it was who would do this thing.

The Disciples Argue about Greatness

24 But there was also rivalry among them, as to which of them should be considered the greatest.
25 And He said to them, "The kings of the Gentiles exercise lordship over them, and those who exercise authority over them are called 'benefactors.'
26 "But not so *among* you; on the contrary, he who is greatest among you, let him be as the younger, and he who governs as he who serves.
27 "For who *is* greater, he who sits at the table, or he who serves? *Is* it not he who sits at the table? Yet I am among you as the One who serves.
28 "But you are those who have continued with Me in My trials.
29 "And I bestow upon you a kingdom, just as My Father bestowed *one* upon Me,
30 "that you may eat and drink at My table in My kingdom,[144] and sit on thrones judging the twelve tribes of Israel."

Jesus Predicts Peter's Denial

31 And the Lord said,[145] "Simon, Simon! Indeed, Satan has asked for you, that he may sift *you* as wheat.
32 "But I have prayed for you, that your faith should not fail; and when you have returned to *Me*, strengthen your brethren."
33 But he said to Him, "Lord, I am ready to go with You, both to prison and to death."
34 Then He said, "I tell you, Peter, the rooster will not crow this day before you will deny three times that you know Me."

Wallet, Bag, and Sword

35 And He said to them, "When I sent you without money bag, sack, and sandals, did you lack anything?" So they said, "Nothing."
36 Then He said to them, "But now, he who has a money bag, let him take *it*, and likewise a sack; and he who has no sword, let him sell his garment and buy one.
37 "For I say to you that this which is written must still be accomplished in Me: 'And He was numbered with the transgressors.'[146] For the things concerning Me have an end."
38 Then they said, "Lord, look, here *are* two swords." And He said to them, "It is enough."

The Prayer in the Garden

39 And coming out, He went to the Mount of Olives, as He was accustomed, and His disciples also followed Him.
40 When He came to the place, He said to them, "Pray that you may not enter into temptation."
41 And He was withdrawn from them about a stone's throw, and He knelt down and prayed,
42 saying, "Father, if it is Your will, remove this cup from Me; nevertheless not My will, but Yours, be done."
43 Then an angel appeared to Him from heaven, strengthening Him.
44 And being in agony, He prayed more earnestly. And His sweat became like great drops of blood falling down to the ground.[147]
45 When He rose up from prayer, and had come to His disciples, He found them sleeping from sorrow.
46 Then He said to them, "Why do you sleep? Rise and pray, lest you enter into temptation."

Betrayal and Arrest in Gethsemane

47 And while He was still speaking, behold, a multitude; and he who was called Judas, one of the twelve, went before them and drew near to Jesus to kiss Him.
48 But Jesus said to him, "Judas, are you betraying the Son of Man with a kiss?"
49 When those around Him saw what was going to happen, they said to Him, "Lord, shall we strike with the sword?"
50 And one of them struck the servant of the high priest and cut off his right ear.
51 But Jesus answered and said, "Permit even this." And He touched his ear and healed him.
52 Then Jesus said to the chief priests, captains of the temple, and the elders who had come to Him, "Have you come

144 M-Text omits *in My kingdom.*   145 NU-Text omits *And the Lord said.*   146 Isaiah 53:12
147 NU-Text brackets verses 43 and 44.

Gethsemane

The Garden of Gethsemane is located outside of Jerusalem across the Kidron Valley on the slopes of the Mount of Olives. Filled with beautiful, old, twisted olive trees, Gethsemane means "Garden of the Olive Press."

As Jesus and His disciples went to the garden, they passed through Jerusalem late at night, sometime between eleven and twelve o'clock. The last flickering lights of families sharing the Passover meal, celebrating God's deliverance from Egypt, glowed from inside the houses along the city streets. When the small band arrived in Gethsemane, the disciples, tired and full from the feast, retired under the many trees.

Jesus, however, knowing what was before Him, prayed in anguish to God for help and strength. He knew that all things were possible with God, and even asked God to take away the "cup" he was called upon to drink. Yet our Lord added the phrase, "Nevertheless not My will, but Yours, be done" (Luke 22:42). How dejected and saddened Jesus must have been as He knelt in the olive grove. Even His closest friends slept during His greatest time of need. Yet Jesus knew God would stand by and strengthen Him to carry out His purpose to demonstrate God's love for the lost and hurting world.

In the darkness of the night, the sound of horses on the limestone block streets were heard. Light from the torches carried by the Roman cohort also revealed the faces of the temple officers, chief priests, elders, scribes, and Judas Iscariot. When Judas gave Jesus the betrayal kiss, he probably used the common Passover greeting to kiss a friend or relative on both cheeks.

Jesus asked the Roman soldiers, "Whom are you seeking?" They answered Him, "Jesus of Nazareth." Jesus replied, "I am *He*" (John 18:4, 5). Immediately, the Romans drew back. It is possible that they grouped into a defensive phalanx position, owing to their vulnerable location on the lower slopes of the Mount of Olives. The Romans probably expected Jesus to be a revolutionary with a band of followers like so many others who had revolted against Rome in Jerusalem. The fact that a cohort, consisting of six hundred men, came to arrest Jesus indicates this is what they anticipated.

The disciples quickly fled, leaving Jesus alone to be taken to trial for crimes He never committed. His disciples and friends had deserted Him, but Jesus had confidence and the knowledge that God would never desert Him. Jesus' demonstration of faith in God allows us the confidence that even when trials come and our friends and companions desert us, God will offer us the same protection and love He gave to His Son. Faith is believing in God even when you do not feel Him near you.

> I believe in the sun
> Even when it is not shining.
> I believe in love
> Even when I do not feel it.
> I believe in God
> Even when He is silent.

out, as against a robber, with swords and clubs? 53 "When I was with you daily in the temple, you did not try to seize Me. But this is your hour, and the power of darkness."

Peter Denies Jesus, and Weeps Bitterly

54 Then, having arrested Him, they led *Him* and brought Him into the high priest's house. And Peter followed at a distance. 55 Now when they had kindled a fire in the midst of the courtyard and sat down together, Peter sat among them. 56 And a certain servant girl, seeing him as he sat by the fire, looked intently at him and said, "This man was also with Him." 57 But he denied Him,[148] saying, "Woman, I do not know Him." 58 And after a little while another saw him and said, "You also are of them." But Peter said, "Man, I am not!" 59 Then after about an hour had passed, another confidently affirmed, saying, "Surely this *fellow* also was with Him, for he is a Galilean." 60 But Peter said, "Man, I do not know what you are saying!" And immediately, while he was still speaking, the rooster[149] crowed. 61 And the Lord turned and looked at Peter. And Peter remembered the word of the Lord, how He had said to him, "Before the rooster crows,[150] you will deny Me three times." 62 Then Peter went out and wept bitterly.

Jesus Mocked and Beaten

63 Now the men who held Jesus mocked Him and beat Him. 64 And having blindfolded Him, they struck Him on the face and asked Him,[151] saying, "Prophesy! Who is it that struck You?" 65 And many other things they blasphemously spoke against Him.

Jesus Faces the Sanhedrin

66 As soon as it was day, the elders of the people, both chief priests and scribes, came together and led Him into their council, saying, 67 "If You are the Christ, tell us." But

He said to them, "If I tell you, you will by no means believe. 68 "And if I also ask *you*, you will by no means answer Me or let *Me* go.[152] 69 "Hereafter the Son of Man will sit on the right hand of the power of God." 70 Then they all said, "Are You then the Son of God?" And He said to them, "You *rightly* say that I am." 71 And they said, "What further testimony do we need? For we have heard it ourselves from His own mouth."

Jesus Handed Over to Pontius Pilate

23 Then the whole multitude of them arose and led Him to Pilate. 2 And they began to accuse Him, saying, "We found this *fellow* perverting the[153] nation, and forbidding to pay taxes to Caesar, saying that He Himself is Christ, a King." 3 So Pilate asked Him, saying, "Are You the King of the Jews?" And He answered him and said, "*It is as* you say." 4 Then Pilate said to the chief priests and the crowd, "I find no fault in this Man." 5 But they were the more fierce, saying, "He stirs up the people, teaching throughout all Judea, beginning from Galilee to this place."

Jesus Faces Herod

6 When Pilate heard of Galilee,[154] he asked if the Man were a Galilean. 7 And as soon as he knew that He belonged to Herod's jurisdiction, he sent Him to Herod, who was also in Jerusalem at that time. 8 Now when Herod saw Jesus, he was exceedingly glad; for he had desired for a long *time* to see Him, because he had heard many things about Him, and he hoped to see some miracle done by Him. 9 Then he questioned Him with many words, but He answered him nothing. 10 And the chief priests and scribes stood and vehemently accused Him. 11 Then Herod, with his men of war, treated Him with contempt and mocked *Him*, arrayed Him in a gorgeous robe, and sent Him back to Pilate. 12 That very day Pilate and Herod became friends with each other, for before *that* they had been at enmity with each other.

---

148 NU-Text reads *denied it*.   149 NU-Text and M-Text read *a rooster*.   150 NU-Text adds *today*.
151 NU-Text reads *And having blindfolded Him, they asked Him*.   152 NU-Text omits *also* and *Me or let Me go*.
153 NU-Text reads *our*.   154 NU-Text omits *of Galilee*.

Taking the Place of Barabbas

13 Then Pilate, when he had called together the chief priests, the rulers, and the people,
14 said to them, "You have brought this Man to me, as one who misleads the people. And indeed, having examined *Him* in your presence, I have found no fault in this Man concerning those things of which you accuse Him;
15 "no, neither did Herod, for I sent you back to him;[155] and indeed nothing worthy of death has been done by Him.
16 "I will therefore chastise Him and release *Him*"
17 (for it was necessary for him to release one to them at the feast).[156]
18 And they all cried out at once, saying, "Away with this *Man*, and release to us Barabbas"—
19 who had been thrown into prison for a certain insurrection made in the city, and for murder.
20 Pilate, therefore, wishing to release Jesus, again called out to them.
21 But they shouted, saying, "Crucify *Him*, crucify Him!"
22 And he said to them the third time, "Why, what evil has He done? I have found no reason for death in Him. I will therefore chastise Him and let *Him* go."
23 But they were insistent, demanding with loud voices that He be crucified. And the voices of these men and of the chief priests prevailed.[157]
24 So Pilate gave sentence that it should be as they requested.
25 And he released to them[158] the one they requested, who for insurrection and murder had been thrown into prison; but he delivered Jesus to their will.

The King on a Cross

26 Now as they led Him away, they laid hold of a certain man, Simon a Cyrenian, who was coming from the country, and on him they laid the cross that he might bear *it* after Jesus.
27 And a great multitude of the people followed Him, and women who also mourned and lamented Him.
28 But Jesus, turning to them, said,

"Daughters of Jerusalem, do not weep for Me, but weep for yourselves and for your children.
29 "For indeed the days are coming in which they will say, 'Blessed *are* the barren, *the* wombs that never bore, and *the* breasts which never nursed!'
30 "Then they will begin 'to say to the mountains, "Fall on us!" and to the hills, "Cover us!" '[159]
31 "For if they do these things in the green wood, what will be done in the dry?"
32 There were also two others, criminals, led with Him to be put to death.
33 And when they had come to the place called Calvary, there they crucified Him, and the criminals, one on the right hand and the other on the left.
34 Then Jesus said, "Father, forgive them, for they do not know what they do."[160] And they divided His garments and cast lots.
35 And the people stood looking on. But even the rulers with them sneered, saying, "He saved others; let Him save Himself if He is the Christ, the chosen of God."
36 And the soldiers also mocked Him, coming and offering Him sour wine,
37 and saying, "If You are the King of the Jews, save Yourself."
38 And an inscription also was written over Him in letters of Greek, Latin, and Hebrew:[161]

THIS IS THE KING OF THE JEWS.

39 Then one of the criminals who were hanged blasphemed Him, saying, "If You are the Christ,[162] save Yourself and us."
40 But the other, answering, rebuked him, saying, "Do you not even fear God, seeing you are under the same condemnation?
41 "And we indeed justly, for we receive the due reward of our deeds; but this Man has done nothing wrong."
42 Then he said to Jesus, "Lord,[163] remember me when You come into Your kingdom."
43 And Jesus said to him, "Assuredly, I say to you, today you will be with Me in Paradise."

---

155 NU-Text reads *for he sent Him back to us.*   156 NU-Text omits verse 17.
157 NU-Text omits *and of the chief priests.*   158 NU-Text and M-Text omit *to them.*   159 Hosea 10:8
160 NU-Text brackets the first sentence of verse 34.
161 NU-Text omits *written* and *in letters of Greek, Latin, and Hebrew.*   162 NU-Text reads *Are You not the Christ?*
163 NU-Text reads *And he said, "Jesus, remember me.*

The Empty Tomb—
a Silent Witness

Through the centuries various theories have been advanced to explain away the resurrection of Jesus Christ. Yet in light of the facts concerning Jesus' death and burial, these theories remain unconvincing.

After Jesus Christ was crucified under Roman authority, His body was taken down from the cross to be buried. As was the custom of the day, His body was wrapped in one hundred pounds of preserving burial ointment. He was then placed in the tomb of a Jerusalem Sanhedrin member, Joseph of Arimathea.

A Roman guard, consisting of twelve men from the empire's crack legion, was stationed in front of Jesus' tomb. The soldiers were under orders that no one was to come near the tomb. Should they leave their post for any reason, the punishment was death. The Roman and Jewish leaders secured the burial place of Jesus by ordering a two-ton stone to be placed in front of the tomb's opening. Finally, the emperor's seal of authority was fixed to the stone covering the tomb. Anyone who broke the seal was punished by death.

Yet, somehow, three days later the tomb of Christ was empty. The followers of Jesus claimed that He had risen from the dead. Did He? If not, what are the alternatives? Could the Jewish leaders have stolen the body? No, for they had no motive and certainly could not have overpowered the Roman soldiers. Also, they would have produced the body to disprove the resurrection claims of the Christians.

Could the disciples have stolen the body? These men, who abandoned Jesus at His arrest and crucifixion, did not possess the military power nor any other means to overthrow twelve of the emperor's top guards, who were within shouting distance of the entire Roman garrison. On the contrary, the disciples were frightened and secretly hid in the city. Could the women have stolen the body? Are we to believe that three women moved a two-ton stone after overpowering twelve Roman soldiers?

It has been suggested that Jesus Christ was not completely dead; somehow He regained consciousness in the cold tomb; rid himself of one hundred pounds of gooey ointment; pushed a two-ton stone away; overpowered twelve Roman soldiers; then walked into the city on feet which had been pierced by nails and appeared to His disciples and followers as the Lord of Life. All of these theories are preposterous. The only possible explanation is that Jesus Christ was resurrected from the dead by the power of God the Father on Easter morning. The empty tomb still stands as a silent witness inviting even the most critical skeptic to examine the evidence concerning Jesus Christ's resurrection.

You may ask, "Then where does faith come in?" Christian faith is based on historical reality, not blind subjectivity. There is much evidence supporting the resurrection of Jesus which can be examined by anyone who wishes to approach Scripture from a historical method.

Yet there remains another very important aspect of our faith. That is commitment to the resurrected Jesus Christ. The level of commitment always goes beyond the knowledge of the facts. When you put yourself in an airplane, you do not know with complete certainty that the plane will not crash. Yet you put your complete body into it. That does not mean that you do not trust that the mechanics have done their work, the pilot knows how to fly, and the plane is structurally sound.

The level of commitment always goes beyond the knowledge of the facts. You cannot prove the resurrection of Jesus with complete certainty. But there is sufficient evidence to warrant belief in the Christian faith.

Be encouraged by the evidence of Jesus' resurrection. The apostle Peter urges us to become familiar with the facts concerning Christ's resurrection so we can give intelligent, reasonable answers of the hope within us to anyone who should ask.

Jesus Dies on the Cross

44 And it was[164] about the sixth hour, and there was darkness over all the earth until the ninth hour.
45 Then the sun was darkened,[165] and the veil of the temple was torn in two.
46 And when Jesus had cried out with a loud voice, He said, "Father, *'into Your hands I commend My spirit.'* "[166] And having said this, He breathed His last.
47 Now when the centurion saw what had happened, he glorified God, saying, "Certainly this was a righteous Man!"
48 And the whole crowd who came together to that sight, seeing what had been done, beat their breasts and returned.
49 But all His acquaintances, and the women who followed Him from Galilee, stood at a distance, watching these things.

Jesus Buried in Joseph's Tomb

50 And behold, *there was* a man named Joseph, a council member, a good and just man.
51 He had not consented to their counsel and deed. *He was* from Arimathea, a city of the Jews, who himself was also waiting[167] for the kingdom of God.
52 This *man* went to Pilate and asked for the body of Jesus.
53 Then he took it down, wrapped it in linen, and laid it in a tomb *that was* hewn out of the rock, where no one had ever lain before.
54 That day was the Preparation, and the Sabbath drew near.
55 And the women who had come with Him from Galilee followed after, and they observed the tomb and how His body was laid.
56 Then they returned and prepared spices and fragrant oils. And they rested on the Sabbath according to the commandment.

He Is Risen

24 Now on the first *day* of the week, very early in the morning, they, and certain *other women* with them,[168] came to the tomb bringing the spices which they had prepared.
2 But they found the stone rolled away from the tomb.

3 Then they went in and did not find the body of the Lord Jesus.
4 And it happened, as they were greatly[169] perplexed about this, that behold, two men stood by them in shining garments.
5 Then, as they were afraid and bowed *their* faces to the earth, they said to them, "Why do you seek the living among the dead?
6 "He is not here, but is risen! Remember how He spoke to you when He was still in Galilee,
7 "saying, 'The Son of Man must be delivered into the hands of sinful men, and be crucified, and the third day rise again.' "
8 And they remembered His words.
9 Then they returned from the tomb and told all these things to the eleven and to all the rest.
10 It was Mary Magdalene, Joanna, Mary *the mother* of James, and the other *women* with them, who told these things to the apostles.
11 And their words seemed to them like idle tales, and they did not believe them.
12 But Peter arose and ran to the tomb; and stooping down, he saw the linen cloths lying[170] by themselves; and he departed, marveling to himself at what had happened.

The Road to Emmaus

13 Now behold, two of them were traveling that same day to a village called Emmaus, which was *about* seven miles[171] from Jerusalem.
14 And they talked together of all these things which had happened.
15 So it was, while they conversed and reasoned, that Jesus Himself drew near and went with them.
16 But their eyes were restrained, so that they did not know Him.
17 And He said to them, "What kind of conversation *is* this that you have with one another as you walk and are sad?"[172]
18 Then the one whose name was Cleopas answered and said to Him, "Are You the only stranger in Jerusalem, and have You not known the things which happened there in these days?"
19 And He said to them, "What things?"

164 NU-Text adds *now.* 165 NU-Text reads *obscured.* 166 Psalm 31:5 167 NU-Text reads *who was waiting.*
168 NU-Text omits *and certain other women with them.* 169 NU-Text omits *greatly.* 170 NU-Text omits *lying.*
171 Greek *sixty stadia* 172 NU-Text reads *as you walk? And they stood still, looking sad.*

And they said to Him, "The things concerning Jesus of Nazareth, who was a Prophet mighty in deed and word before God and all the people,
20 "and how the chief priests and our rulers delivered Him to be condemned to death, and crucified Him.
21 "But we were hoping that it was He who was going to redeem Israel. Indeed, besides all this, today is the third day since these things happened.
22 "Yes, and certain women of our company, who arrived at the tomb early, astonished us.
23 "When they did not find His body, they came saying that they had also seen a vision of angels who said He was alive.
24 "And certain of those *who were* with us went to the tomb and found *it* just as the women had said; but Him they did not see."
25 Then He said to them, "O foolish ones, and slow of heart to believe in all that the prophets have spoken!
26 "Ought not the Christ to have suffered these things and to enter into His glory?"
27 And beginning at Moses and all the Prophets, He expounded to them in all the Scriptures the things concerning Himself.

The Disciples' Eyes Opened

28 Then they drew near to the village where they were going, and He indicated that He would have gone farther.
29 But they constrained Him, saying, "Abide with us, for it is toward evening, and the day is far spent." And He went in to stay with them.
30 Now it came to pass, as He sat at the table with them, that He took bread, blessed and broke *it*, and gave it to them.
31 Then their eyes were opened and they knew Him; and He vanished from their sight.
32 And they said to one another, "Did not our heart burn within us while He talked with us on the road, and while He opened the Scriptures to us?"
33 So they rose up that very hour and returned to Jerusalem, and found the eleven and those *who were* with them gathered together,

34 saying, "The Lord is risen indeed, and has appeared to Simon!"
35 And they told about the things *that had happened* on the road, and how He was known to them in the breaking of bread.

Jesus Appears to His Disciples

36 Now as they said these things, Jesus Himself stood in the midst of them, and said to them, "Peace to you."
37 But they were terrified and frightened, and supposed they had seen a spirit.
38 And He said to them, "Why are you troubled? And why do doubts arise in your hearts?
39 "Behold My hands and My feet, that it is I Myself. Handle Me and see, for a spirit does not have flesh and bones as you see I have."
40 When He had said this, He showed them His hands and His feet.[173]
41 But while they still did not believe for joy, and marveled, He said to them, "Have you any food here?"
42 So they gave Him a piece of a broiled fish and some honeycomb.[174]
43 And He took *it* and ate in their presence.

The Scriptures Opened

44 Then He said to them, "These *are* the words which I spoke to you while I was still with you, that all things must be fulfilled which were written in the Law of Moses and *the* Prophets and *the* Psalms concerning Me."
45 And He opened their understanding, that they might comprehend the Scriptures.
46 Then He said to them, "Thus it is written, and thus it was necessary for the Christ to suffer and to rise[175] from the dead the third day,
47 "and that repentance and remission of sins should be preached in His name to all nations, beginning at Jerusalem.
48 "And you are witnesses of these things.
49 "Behold, I send the Promise of My Father upon you; but tarry in the city of Jerusalem[176] until you are endued with power from on high."

---

173 Some printed New Testaments omit this verse. It is found in nearly all Greek manuscripts.
174 NU-Text omits *and some honeycomb*.   175 NU-Text reads *written, that the Christ should suffer and rise*.
176 NU-Text omits *of Jerusalem*.

The Ascension

50 And He led them out as far as Bethany, and He lifted up His hands and blessed them.
51 Now it came to pass, while He blessed them, that He was parted from them and carried up into heaven.
52 And they worshiped Him, and returned to Jerusalem with great joy,
53 and were continually in the temple praising and[177] blessing God. Amen.[178]

177 NU-Text omits *praising and.*   178 NU-Text omits *Amen.*

Introduction to John

The apostle John in an artistic theological masterpiece presents the love of God as demonstrated in the person and work of Jesus Christ. Written probably between A.D. 80 and 90, John's aim is to reveal Jesus as the Incarnate Word of God, who came to establish the proper relationship between God and man.

John's Gospel is theological in its treatment of the events in the life of Jesus Christ. More than the synoptic Gospels, John gives his readers a personal look into the love God has for the world. "For God so loved the world that He gave His only begotten Son, that whoever believes in Him should not perish but have everlasting life" (John 3:16).

John records some of the prayers and teachings of Jesus that are not mentioned in the other Gospels. He includes the "I am" passages in which Jesus reveals the relationship between God and man.

I am the bread of life (John 6:48).
I am the light of the world (John 8:12).
I am the door of the sheep (John 10:7).
I am the good shepherd (John 10:11).
I am the resurrection and the life (John 11:25).
I am the way, the truth, and the life (John 14:6).
I am the true vine (John 15:1).

In chapters 15—17, John interweaves the dependency of a right relationship with God to experience the fullness of loving relationships with others. Jesus, Himself, is the great vehicle of God's love for us, presenting us as His friends before God. "Greater love has no one than this, than to lay down one's life for his friends" (John 15:13).

John truly is the "Gospel of Love" as Jesus brings us into a loving relationship with God and others. Then we can go out and proclaim, "God loves you and so do I."

The Gospel According to

John

The Eternal Word

IN the beginning was the Word, and the Word was with God, and the Word was God.
2 He was in the beginning with God.
3 All things were made through Him, and without Him nothing was made that was made.
4 In Him was life, and the life was the light of men.
5 And the light shines in the darkness, and the darkness did not comprehend it.

John's Witness: The True Light

6 There was a man sent from God, whose name *was* John.
7 This man came for a witness, to bear witness of the Light, that all through him might believe.
8 He was not that Light, but *was sent* to bear witness of that Light.
9 *That was* the true Light which gives light to every man who comes into the world.
10 He was in the world, and the world was made through Him, and the world did not know Him.
11 He came to His own, and His own did not receive Him.
12 But as many as received Him, to them He gave the right to become children of God, *even* to those who believe in His name:
13 who were born, not of blood, nor of the will of the flesh, nor of the will of man, but of God.

The Word Becomes Flesh

14 And the Word became flesh and dwelt among us, and we beheld His glory, the glory as of the only begotten of the Father, full of grace and truth.
15 John bore witness of Him and cried out, saying, "This was He of whom I said, 'He who comes after me is preferred before me, for He was before me.' "
16 And[1] of His fullness we have all received, and grace for grace.

17 For the law was given through Moses, *but* grace and truth came through Jesus Christ.
18 No one has seen God at any time. The only begotten Son,[2] who is in the bosom of the Father, He has declared *Him.*

A Voice in the Wilderness

19 Now this is the testimony of John, when the Jews sent priests and Levites from Jerusalem to ask him, "Who are you?"
20 He confessed, and did not deny, but confessed, "I am not the Christ."
21 And they asked him, "What then? Are you Elijah?" He said, "I am not." "Are you the Prophet?" And he answered, "No."
22 Then they said to him, "Who are you, that we may give an answer to those who sent us? What do you say about yourself?"
23 He said: "I *am*

'The voice of one crying in the wilderness:
"Make straight the way of the LORD," '[3]

as the prophet Isaiah said."
24 Now those who were sent were from the Pharisees.
25 And they asked him, saying, "Why then do you baptize if you are not the Christ, nor Elijah, nor the Prophet?"
26 John answered them, saying, "I baptize with water, but there stands One among you whom you do not know.
27 "It is He who, coming after me, is preferred before me, whose sandal strap I am not worthy to loose."
28 These things were done in Bethabara[4] beyond the Jordan, where John was baptizing.

The Lamb of God

29 The next day John saw Jesus coming toward him, and said, "Behold! The

---

1 NU-Text reads *For.*   2 NU-Text reads *only begotten God.*   3 Isaiah 40:3
4 NU-Text and M-Text read *Bethany.*

Lamb of God who takes away the sin of the world!

30 "This is He of whom I said, 'After me comes a Man who is preferred before me, for He was before me.'

31 "I did not know Him; but that He should be revealed to Israel, therefore I came baptizing with water."

32 And John bore witness, saying, "I saw the Spirit descending from heaven like a dove, and He remained upon Him.

33 "I did not know Him, but He who sent me to baptize with water said to me, 'Upon whom you see the Spirit descending, and remaining on Him, this is He who baptizes with the Holy Spirit.'

34 "And I have seen and testified that this is the Son of God."

The First Disciples

35 Again, the next day, John stood with two of his disciples.

36 And looking at Jesus as He walked, he said, "Behold the Lamb of God!"

37 The two disciples heard him speak, and they followed Jesus.

38 Then Jesus turned, and seeing them following, said to them, "What do you seek?" They said to Him, "Rabbi" (which is to say, when translated, Teacher), "where are You staying?"

39 He said to them, "Come and see." They came and saw where He was staying, and remained with Him that day (now it was about the tenth hour).

40 One of the two who heard John speak, and followed Him, was Andrew, Simon Peter's brother.

41 He first found his own brother Simon, and said to him, "We have found the Messiah" (which is translated, the Christ).

42 And he brought him to Jesus. Now when Jesus looked at him, He said, "You are Simon the son of Jonah.[5] You shall be called Cephas" (which is translated, A Stone).

Philip and Nathanael

43 The following day Jesus wanted to go to Galilee, and He found Philip and said to him, "Follow Me."

44 Now Philip was from Bethsaida, the city of Andrew and Peter.

45 Philip found Nathanael and said to him, "We have found Him of whom Moses in the law, and also the prophets, wrote—Jesus of Nazareth, the son of Joseph."

46 And Nathanael said to him, "Can anything good come out of Nazareth?" Philip said to him, "Come and see."

47 Jesus saw Nathanael coming toward Him, and said of him, "Behold, an Israelite indeed, in whom is no guile!"

48 Nathanael said to Him, "How do You know me?" Jesus answered and said to him, "Before Philip called you, when you were under the fig tree, I saw you."

49 Nathanael answered and said to Him, "Rabbi, You are the Son of God! You are the King of Israel!"

50 Jesus answered and said to him, "Because I said to you, 'I saw you under the fig tree,' do you believe? You will see greater things than these."

51 And He said to him, "Most assuredly, I say to you, hereafter[6] you shall see heaven open, and the angels of God ascending and descending upon the Son of Man."

Water Turned to Wine

2 On the third day there was a wedding in Cana of Galilee, and the mother of Jesus was there.

2 Now both Jesus and His disciples were invited to the wedding.

3 And when they ran out of wine, the mother of Jesus said to Him, "They have no wine."

4 Jesus said to her, "Woman, what does your concern have to do with Me? My hour has not yet come."

5 His mother said to the servants, "Whatever He says to you, do it."

6 Now there were set there six waterpots of stone, according to the manner of purification of the Jews, containing twenty or thirty gallons apiece.

7 Jesus said to them, "Fill the waterpots with water." And they filled them up to the brim.

8 And He said to them, "Draw some out now, and take it to the master of the feast." And they took it.

9 When the master of the feast had tasted the water that was made wine, and did not know where it came from (but the servants who had drawn the water knew), the master of the feast called the bridegroom.

5 NU-Text reads John.   6 NU-Text omits hereafter.

10 And he said to him, "Every man at the beginning sets out the good wine, and when the *guests* have well drunk, then that *which is* inferior; *but* you have kept the good wine until now."
11 This beginning of signs Jesus did in Cana of Galilee, and manifested His glory; and His disciples believed in Him.
12 After this He went down to Capernaum, He, His mother, His brothers, and His disciples; and they did not stay there many days.

Jesus Cleanses the Temple

13 Now the Passover of the Jews was at hand, and Jesus went up to Jerusalem.
14 And He found in the temple those who sold oxen and sheep and doves, and the moneychangers doing business.
15 When He had made a whip of cords, He drove them all out of the temple, with the sheep and the oxen, and poured out the changers' money and overturned the tables.
16 And He said to those who sold doves, "Take these things away! Do not make My Father's house a house of merchandise!"
17 Then His disciples remembered that it was written, *"Zeal for Your house has eaten[7] Me up."*[8]
18 So the Jews answered and said to Him, "What sign do You show to us, since You do these things?"
19 Jesus answered and said to them, "Destroy this temple, and in three days I will raise it up."
20 Then the Jews said, "It has taken forty-six years to build this temple, and will You raise it up in three days?"
21 But He was speaking of the temple of His body.
22 Therefore, when He had risen from the dead, His disciples remembered that He had said this to them;[9] and they believed the Scripture and the word which Jesus had said.

The Discerner of Hearts

23 Now when He was in Jerusalem at the Passover, during the feast, many believed in His name when they saw the signs which He did.
24 But Jesus did not commit Himself to them, because He knew all *men,*
25 and had no need that anyone should testify of man, for He knew what was in man.

The New Birth

3 There was a man of the Pharisees named Nicodemus, a ruler of the Jews.
2 This man came to Jesus by night and said to Him, "Rabbi, we know that You are a teacher come from God; for no one can do these signs that You do unless God is with him."
3 Jesus answered and said to him, "Most assuredly, I say to you, unless one is born again, he cannot see the kingdom of God."
4 Nicodemus said to Him, "How can a man be born when he is old? Can he enter a second time into his mother's womb and be born?"
5 Jesus answered, "Most assuredly, I say to you, unless one is born of water and the Spirit, he cannot enter the kingdom of God.
6 "That which is born of the flesh is flesh, and that which is born of the Spirit is spirit.
7 "Do not marvel that I said to you, 'You must be born again.'
8 "The wind blows where it wishes, and you hear the sound of it, but cannot tell where it comes from and where it goes. So is everyone who is born of the Spirit."
9 Nicodemus answered and said to Him, "How can these things be?"
10 Jesus answered and said to him, "Are you the teacher of Israel, and do not know these things?
11 "Most assuredly, I say to you, We speak what We know and testify what We have seen, and you do not receive Our witness.
12 "If I have told you earthly things and you do not believe, how will you believe if I tell you heavenly things?
13 "No one has ascended to heaven but He who came down from heaven, *that is,* the Son of Man who is in heaven.[10]
14 "And as Moses lifted up the serpent in the wilderness, even so must the Son of Man be lifted up,
15 "that whoever believes in Him should not perish but[11] have eternal life.
16 "For God so loved the world that He gave His only begotten Son, that whoever

---

7 NU-Text and M-Text read *will eat.*   8 Psalm 69:9   9 NU-Text and M-Text omit *to them.*
10 NU-Text omits *who is in heaven.*   11 NU-Text omits *not perish but.*

The Spirit of God

Jesus drew from God's creation to describe the nature of God. To illustrate the Spirit of God, Jesus likened it to the wind. In the well-known dialogue with Nicodemus, Jesus said, "The wind blows where it wishes, and you hear the sound of it, but cannot tell where it comes from and where it goes. So is everyone who is born of the Spirit" (John 3:8).

The winds of Jerusalem shift constantly. Exposed on the top of a ridge, the city has winds coming from every direction of the compass. The nature of the winds also varies from a hot east desert wind to a cool Mediterranean breeze. In the course of a day, the winds can shift four or five times.

We cannot physically see the Spirit of God. But just as we "see" the wind blowing through the trees, so we see the *effects* of the Spirit of God in our lives. We hear the rush and rustle of the wind in nature. Likewise, we hear the Spirit of God in the words of His people and in His word and work.

As a Jew, Jesus sometimes spoke in the Hebrew language. The same word for wind, "ruah" also means spirit. In this play on words, Jesus gave a beautiful description of the Spirit of God.

When the first Christians received the Spirit, as recorded in the second chapter of Acts, He came with the rushing sound of a wind. As Jesus said, we do not always know when and how the Spirit of God comes into our lives anymore than we can see the wind. God's presence may come to us suddenly like the rushing of a wind. Sometimes, God's Spirit comes to us quietly like a cool, soft breeze.

Throughout our lives, we must be aware of God's Spirit and always welcome Him. For then we will let other people "see" and "hear" God's Spirit as they watch His effects in our lives. Like the winds of Jerusalem, the Spirit of God can come to people in many ways, yet the effect is the same—a new birth!

believes in Him should not perish but have everlasting life.

17 "For God did not send His Son into the world to condemn the world, but that the world through Him might be saved.

18 "He who believes in Him is not condemned; but he who does not believe is condemned already, because he has not believed in the name of the only begotten Son of God.

19 "And this is the condemnation, that the light has come into the world, and men loved darkness rather than light, because their deeds were evil.

20 "For everyone practicing evil hates the light and does not come to the light, lest his deeds should be exposed.

21 "But he who does the truth comes to the light, that his deeds may be clearly seen, that they have been done in God."

John the Baptist Exalts Christ

22 After these things Jesus and His disciples came into the land of Judea, and there He remained with them and baptized.

23 Now John also was baptizing in Aenon near Salim, because there was much water there. And they came and were baptized.

24 For John had not yet been thrown into prison.

25 Then there arose a dispute between some of John's disciples and the Jews about purification.

26 And they came to John and said to him, "Rabbi, He who was with you beyond the Jordan, to whom you have testified—behold, He is baptizing, and all are coming to Him!"

27 John answered and said, "A man can receive nothing unless it has been given to him from heaven.

28 "You yourselves bear me witness, that I said, 'I am not the Christ,' but, 'I have been sent before Him.'

29 "He who has the bride is the bridegroom; but the friend of the bridegroom, who stands and hears him, rejoices greatly because of the bridegroom's voice. Therefore this joy of mine is fulfilled.

30 "He must increase, but I must decrease.

31 "He who comes from above is above all; he who is of the earth is earthly and speaks of the earth. He who comes from heaven is above all.

32 "And what He has seen and heard, that He testifies; and no one receives His testimony.

33 "He who has received His testimony has certified that God is true.

34 "For He whom God has sent speaks the words of God, for God does not give the Spirit by measure.

35 "The Father loves the Son, and has given all things into His hand.

36 "He who believes in the Son has everlasting life; and he who does not believe the Son shall not see life, but the wrath of God abides on him."

A Samaritan Woman Meets Her Messiah

4 Therefore, when the Lord knew that the Pharisees had heard that Jesus made and baptized more disciples than John

2 (though Jesus Himself did not baptize, but His disciples),

3 He left Judea and departed again to Galilee.

4 But He needed to go through Samaria.

5 So He came to a city of Samaria which is called Sychar, near the plot of ground that Jacob gave to his son Joseph.

6 Now Jacob's well was there. Jesus therefore, being wearied from His journey, sat thus by the well. It was about the sixth hour.

7 A woman of Samaria came to draw water. Jesus said to her, "Give Me a drink."

8 For His disciples had gone away into the city to buy food.

9 Then the woman of Samaria said to Him, "How is it that You, being a Jew, ask a drink from me, a Samaritan woman?" For Jews have no dealings with Samaritans.

10 Jesus answered and said to her, "If you knew the gift of God, and who it is who says to you, 'Give Me a drink,' you would have asked Him, and He would have given you living water."

11 The woman said to Him, "Sir, You have nothing to draw with, and the well is deep. Where then do You get that living water?

12 "Are You greater than our father Jacob, who gave us the well, and drank from it himself, as well as his sons and his livestock?"

13 Jesus answered and said to her, "Whoever drinks of this water will thirst again,
14 "but whoever drinks of the water that I shall give him will never thirst. But the water that I shall give him will become in him a fountain of water springing up into everlasting life."
15 The woman said to Him, "Sir, give me this water, that I may not thirst, nor come here to draw."
16 Jesus said to her, "Go, call your husband, and come here."
17 The woman answered and said, "I have no husband." Jesus said to her, "You have well said, 'I have no husband,'
18 "for you have had five husbands, and the one whom you now have is not your husband; in that you spoke truly."
19 The woman said to Him, "Sir, I perceive that You are a prophet.
20 "Our fathers worshiped on this mountain, and you *Jews* say that in Jerusalem is the place where one ought to worship."
21 Jesus said to her, "Woman, believe Me, the hour is coming when you will neither on this mountain, nor in Jerusalem, worship the Father.
22 "You worship what you do not know; we know what we worship, for salvation is of the Jews.
23 "But the hour is coming, and now is, when the true worshipers will worship the Father in spirit and truth; for the Father is seeking such to worship Him.
24 "God *is* Spirit, and those who worship Him must worship in spirit and truth."
25 The woman said to Him, "I know that Messiah is coming" (who is called Christ). "When He comes, He will tell us all things."
26 Jesus said to her, "I who speak to you am *He*."

The Whitened Harvest

27 And at this *point* His disciples came, and they marveled that He talked with a woman; yet no one said, "What do You seek?" or, "Why are You talking with her?"
28 The woman then left her waterpot, went her way into the city, and said to the men,
29 "Come, see a Man who told me all things that I ever did. Could this be the Christ?"

30 Then they went out of the city and came to Him.
31 In the meantime His disciples urged Him, saying, "Rabbi, eat."
32 But He said to them, "I have food to eat of which you do not know."
33 Therefore the disciples said to one another, "Has anyone brought Him *anything* to eat?"
34 Jesus said to them, "My food is to do the will of Him who sent Me, and to finish His work.
35 "Do you not say, 'There are still four months and *then* comes the harvest'? Behold, I say to you, lift up your eyes and look at the fields, for they are already white for harvest!
36 "And he who reaps receives wages, and gathers fruit for eternal life, that both he who sows and he who reaps may rejoice together.
37 "For in this the saying is true: 'One sows and another reaps.'
38 "I sent you to reap that for which you have not labored; others have labored, and you have entered into their labors."

The Savior of the World

39 And many of the Samaritans of that city believed in Him because of the word of the woman who testified, "He told me all that I *ever* did."
40 So when the Samaritans had come to Him, they urged Him to stay with them; and He stayed there two days.
41 And many more believed because of His own word.
42 Then they said to the woman, "Now we believe, not because of what you said, for we have heard for ourselves and know that this is indeed the Christ,[12] the Savior of the world."

Welcome at Galilee

43 Now after the two days He departed from there and went to Galilee.
44 For Jesus Himself testified that a prophet has no honor in his own country.
45 So when He came to Galilee, the Galileans received Him, having seen all the things He did in Jerusalem at the feast; for they also had gone to the feast.

A Nobleman's Son Healed

46 So Jesus came again to Cana of Galilee where He had made the water wine.

12 NU-Text omits *the Christ.*

And there was a certain nobleman whose son was sick at Capernaum.

47 When he heard that Jesus had come out of Judea into Galilee, he went to Him and implored Him to come down and heal his son, for he was at the point of death.

48 Then Jesus said to him, "Unless you *people* see signs and wonders, you will by no means believe."

49 The nobleman said to Him, "Sir, come down before my child dies!"

50 Jesus said to him, "Go your way; your son lives." So the man believed the word that Jesus spoke to him, and he went his way.

51 And as he was now going down, his servants met him and told *him*, saying, "Your son lives!"

52 Then he inquired of them the hour when he got better. And they said to him, "Yesterday at the seventh hour the fever left him."

53 So the father knew that *it was* at the same hour in which Jesus said to him, "Your son lives." And he himself believed, and his whole household.

54 This again *is* the second sign *that* Jesus did when He had come out of Judea into Galilee.

A Man Healed at the Pool of Bethesda

5 After this there was a feast of the Jews, and Jesus went up to Jerusalem.

2 Now there is in Jerusalem by the Sheep *Gate* a pool, which is called in Hebrew, Bethesda,[13] having five porches.

3 In these lay a great multitude of sick people, blind, lame, paralyzed, waiting for the moving of the water.

4 For an angel went down at a certain time into the pool and stirred up the water; then whoever stepped in first, after the stirring of the water, was made well of whatever disease he had.[14]

5 Now a certain man was there who had an infirmity thirty-eight years.

6 When Jesus saw him lying there, and knew that he already had been *in that condition* a long time, He said to him, "Do you want to be made well?"

7 The sick man answered Him, "Sir, I have no man to put me into the pool when the water is stirred up; but while I am coming, another steps down before me."

8 Jesus said to him, "Rise, take up your bed and walk."

9 And immediately the man was made well, took up his bed, and walked. And that day was the Sabbath.

10 The Jews therefore said to him who was cured, "It is the Sabbath; it is not lawful for you to carry *your* bed."

11 He answered them, "He who made me well said to me, 'Take up your bed and walk.'"

12 Then they asked him, "Who is the Man who said to you, 'Take up your bed and walk'?"

13 But the one who was healed did not know who it was, for Jesus had withdrawn, a multitude being in *that* place.

14 Afterward Jesus found him in the temple, and said to him, "See, you have been made well. Sin no more, lest a worse thing come upon you."

15 The man departed and told the Jews that it was Jesus who had made him well.

Honor the Father and the Son

16 For this reason the Jews persecuted Jesus, and sought to kill Him,[15] because He had done these things on the Sabbath.

17 But Jesus answered them, "My Father has been working until now, and I have been working."

18 Therefore the Jews sought all the more to kill Him, because He not only broke the Sabbath, but also said that God was His Father, making Himself equal with God.

19 Then Jesus answered and said to them, "Most assuredly, I say to you, the Son can do nothing of Himself, but what He sees the Father do; for whatever He does, the Son also does in like manner.

20 "For the Father loves the Son, and shows Him all things that He Himself does; and He will show Him greater works than these, that you may marvel.

21 "For as the Father raises the dead and gives life to *them*, even so the Son gives life to whom He will.

22 "For the Father judges no one, but has committed all judgment to the Son,

23 "that all should honor the Son just as they honor the Father. He who does not

13 NU-Text reads *Bethzatha.*
14 NU-Text omits *waiting for the moving of the water* at the end of verse 3, and all of verse 4.
15 NU-Text omits *and sought to kill Him.*

A Nobleman's Journey to Cana

A beautiful illustration of one man's faith took place in the small village of Cana in Galilee. An important official of Herod's court in Tiberias heard that Jesus was in the area. A few days earlier this nobleman's son had contracted a severe illness and was at the point of death.

Jesus' reputation preceded Him. The nobleman believed Jesus was sent by God and could heal his ill son. So the next morning, at sunrise, the nobleman set out on the twenty-mile journey from Capernaum to Cana. When he arrived in Cana, the nobleman implored Jesus to return to Capernaum and heal his son. Jesus, realizing the time and distance involved in the official's journey, knew the man had great faith in God. Recognizing this faith, Jesus told the official to return home—his son was alive and well. The nobleman believed Jesus and immediately began the descent back to Capernaum.

The nobleman believed it before he saw it. He believed Jesus' promise that his son was healed before he actually saw the boy. The nobleman's faith was further demonstrated by the fact that he stayed overnight in a small village on his way back to Capernaum. In light of the fact that his son was dying, the nobleman had tremendous faith in Jesus' words to rest overnight, rather than journey all night to see his son.

The next morning, while the official completed his journey to Capernaum, his servants ran to him, explaining the good news. His son was alive and well. The official asked what time the fever had left the boy. The servants replied, "Yesterday at the seventh hour the fever left him" (John 4:52). The official noted the time (one o'clock—the seventh hour) and knew it was Jesus' words that healed the boy.

Our faith, like the nobleman's, must first believe God can help us. Second, we must make the effort to go to God and ask Him to meet our needs. Then we must take God at His word, letting the peace and confidence of His faithfulness fill our hearts and minds. And when we find our problem solved, our hurts healed, and our lives renewed—note the time. Give credit to God where it is due.

honor the Son does not honor the Father who sent Him.

Life and Judgment Are Through the Son

24 "Most assuredly, I say to you, he who hears My word and believes in Him who sent Me has everlasting life, and shall not come into judgment, but has passed from death into life.

25 "Most assuredly, I say to you, the hour is coming, and now is, when the dead will hear the voice of the Son of God; and those who hear will live.

26 "For as the Father has life in Himself, so He has granted the Son to have life in Himself,

27 "and has given Him authority to execute judgment also, because He is the Son of Man.

28 "Do not marvel at this; for the hour is coming in which all who are in the graves will hear His voice

29 "and come forth—those who have done good, to the resurrection of life, and those who have done evil, to the resurrection of condemnation.

30 "I can of Myself do nothing. As I hear, I judge; and My judgment is righteous, because I do not seek My own will but the will of the Father who sent Me.

The Fourfold Witness

31 "If I bear witness of Myself, My witness is not true.

32 "There is another who bears witness of Me, and I know that the witness which He witnesses of Me is true.

33 "You have sent to John, and he has bore witness to the truth.

34 "Yet I do not receive testimony from man, but I say these things that you may be saved.

35 "He was the burning and shining lamp, and you were willing for a time to rejoice in his light.

36 "But I have a greater witness than John's; for the works which the Father has given Me to finish—the very works that I do—bear witness of Me, that the Father has sent Me.

37 "And the Father Himself, who sent Me, has testified of Me. You have neither heard His voice at any time, nor seen His form.

38 "But you do not have His word abiding in you, because whom He sent, Him you do not believe.

39 "You search the Scriptures, for in them you think you have eternal life; and these are they which testify of Me.

40 "But you are not willing to come to Me that you may have life.

41 "I do not receive honor from men.

42 "But I know you, that you do not have the love of God in you.

43 "I have come in My Father's name, and you do not receive Me; if another comes in his own name, him you will receive.

44 "How can you believe, who receive honor from one another, and do not seek the honor that comes from the only God?

45 "Do not think that I shall accuse you to the Father; there is one who accuses you—Moses, in whom you trust.

46 "For if you believed Moses, you would believe Me; for he wrote about Me.

47 "But if you do not believe his writings, how will you believe My words?"

Feeding the Five Thousand

6 After these things Jesus went over the Sea of Galilee, which is the Sea of Tiberias.

2 Then a great multitude followed Him, because they saw His signs which He performed on those who were diseased.

3 And Jesus went up on a mountain, and there He sat with His disciples.

4 Now the Passover, a feast of the Jews, was near.

5 Then Jesus lifted up His eyes, and seeing a great multitude coming toward Him, He said to Philip, "Where shall we buy bread, that these may eat?"

6 But this He said to test him, for He Himself knew what He would do.

7 Philip answered Him, "Two hundred denarii worth of bread is not sufficient for them, that every one of them may have a little."

8 One of His disciples, Andrew, Simon Peter's brother, said to Him,

9 "There is a lad here who has five barley loaves and two small fish, but what are they among so many?"

10 Then Jesus said, "Make the people sit down." Now there was much grass in the place. So the men sat down, in number about five thousand.

11 And Jesus took the loaves, and when He had given thanks He distributed them to the disciples, and the disciples[16] to

16 NU-Text omits to the disciples, and the disciples.

those sitting down; and likewise of the fish, as much as they wanted.

12 So when they were filled, He said to His disciples, "Gather up the fragments that remain, so that nothing is lost."

13 Therefore they gathered *them* up, and filled twelve baskets with the fragments of the five barley loaves which were left over by those who had eaten.

14 Then those men, when they had seen the sign that Jesus did, said, "This is truly the Prophet who is to come into the world."

Jesus Walks on the Sea

15 Therefore when Jesus perceived that they were about to come and take Him by force to make Him king, He departed again to a mountain by Himself alone.

16 And when evening came, His disciples went down to the sea,

17 got into the boat, and went over the sea toward Capernaum. And it was now dark, and Jesus had not come to them.

18 Then the sea arose because a great wind was blowing.

19 So when they had rowed about three or four miles,[17] they saw Jesus walking on the sea and drawing near the boat; and they were afraid.

20 But He said to them, "It is I; do not be afraid."

21 Then they willingly received Him into the boat, and immediately the boat was at the land where they were going.

The Bread from Heaven

22 On the following day, when the people who were standing on the other side of the sea saw that there was no other boat there, except that one which His disciples had entered,[18] and that Jesus had not entered the boat with His disciples, but His disciples had gone away alone—

23 however, other boats came from Tiberias, near the place where they ate bread after the Lord had given thanks—

24 when the people therefore saw that Jesus was not there, nor His disciples, they also got into boats and came to Capernaum, seeking Jesus.

25 And when they found Him on the other side of the sea, they said to Him, "Rabbi, when did You come here?"

26 Jesus answered them and said, "Most assuredly, I say to you, you seek Me, not because you saw the signs, but because you ate of the loaves and were filled.

27 "Do not labor for the food which perishes, but for the food which endures to everlasting life, which the Son of Man will give you, because God the Father has set His seal on Him."

28 Then they said to Him, "What shall we do, that we may work the works of God?"

29 Jesus answered and said to them, "This is the work of God, that you believe in Him whom He sent."

30 Therefore they said to Him, "What sign will You perform then, that we may see it and believe You? What work will You do?

31 "Our fathers ate the manna in the desert; as it is written, *'He gave them bread from heaven to eat.'* "[19]

32 Then Jesus said to them, "Most assuredly, I say to you, Moses did not give you the bread from heaven, but My Father gives you the true bread from heaven.

33 "For the bread of God is He who comes down from heaven and gives life to the world."

34 Then they said to Him, "Lord, give us this bread always."

35 And Jesus said to them, "I am the bread of life. He who comes to Me shall never hunger, and he who believes in Me shall never thirst.

36 "But I said to you that you have seen Me and yet do not believe.

37 "All that the Father gives Me will come to Me, and the one who comes to Me I will by no means cast out.

38 "For I have come down from heaven, not to do My own will, but the will of Him who sent Me.

39 "This is the will of the Father who sent Me, that of all He has given Me I should lose nothing, but should raise it up at the last day.

40 "And this is the will of Him who sent Me, that everyone who sees the Son and believes in Him may have everlasting life; and I will raise him up at the last day."

Rejected by His Own

41 The Jews then murmured against Him, because He said, "I am the bread which came down from heaven."

---

17 Greek *twenty-five or thirty stadia*   18 NU-Text omits *that* and *which his disciples had entered.*
19 Exodus 16:4; Nehemiah 9:15; Psalm 78:24

42 And they said, "Is not this Jesus, the son of Joseph, whose father and mother we know? How is it then that He says, 'I have come down from heaven'?"

43 Jesus therefore answered and said to them, "Do not murmur among yourselves.

44 "No one can come to Me unless the Father who sent Me draws him; and I will raise him up at the last day.

45 "It is written in the prophets, *'And they shall all be taught by God.'*[20] Therefore everyone who has heard and learned[21] from the Father comes to Me.

46 "Not that anyone has seen the Father, except He who is from God; He has seen the Father.

47 "Most assuredly, I say to you, he who believes in Me[22] has everlasting life.

48 "I am the bread of life.

49 "Your fathers ate the manna in the wilderness, and are dead.

50 "This is the bread which comes down from heaven, that one may eat of it and not die.

51 "I am the living bread which came down from heaven. If anyone eats of this bread, he will live forever; and the bread that I shall give is My flesh, which I shall give for the life of the world."

52 The Jews therefore quarreled among themselves, saying, "How can this *Man* give us *His* flesh to eat?"

53 Then Jesus said to them, "Most assuredly, I say to you, unless you eat the flesh of the Son of Man and drink His blood, you have no life in you.

54 "Whoever eats My flesh and drinks My blood has eternal life, and I will raise him up at the last day.

55 "For My flesh is food indeed,[23] and My blood is drink indeed.

56 "He who eats My flesh and drinks My blood abides in Me, and I in him.

57 "As the living Father sent Me, and I live because of the Father, so he who feeds on Me will live because of Me.

58 "This is the bread which came down from heaven—not as your fathers ate the manna, and are dead. He who eats this bread will live forever."

59 These things He said in the synagogue as He taught in Capernaum.

Many Disciples Turn Away

60 Therefore many of His disciples, when they heard *this*, said, "This is a hard saying; who can understand it?"

61 When Jesus knew in Himself that His disciples murmured about this, He said to them, "Does this offend you?

62 "*What* then if you should see the Son of Man ascend where He was before?

63 "It is the Spirit who gives life; the flesh profits nothing. The words that I speak to you are spirit, and *they* are life.

64 "But there are some of you who do not believe." For Jesus knew from the beginning who they were who did not believe, and who would betray Him.

65 And He said, "Therefore I have said to you that no one can come to Me unless it has been granted to him by My Father."

66 From that *time* many of His disciples went back and walked with Him no more.

67 Then Jesus said to the twelve, "Do you also want to go away?"

68 Then Simon Peter answered Him, "Lord, to whom shall we go? You have the words of eternal life.

69 "Also we have come to believe and know that You are the Christ, the Son of the living God."[24]

70 Jesus answered them, "Did I not choose you, the twelve, and one of you is a devil?"

71 He spoke of Judas Iscariot, *the son* of Simon, for it was he who would betray Him, being one of the twelve.

Jesus' Brothers Disbelieve

7 After these things Jesus walked in Galilee; for He did not want to walk in Judea, because the Jews sought to kill Him.

2 Now the Jews' Feast of Tabernacles was at hand.

3 His brothers therefore said to Him, "Depart from here and go into Judea, that Your disciples also may see the works that You are doing.

4 "For no one does anything in secret while he himself seeks to be known openly. If You do these things, show Yourself to the world."

5 For even His brothers did not believe in Him.

6 Then Jesus said to them, "My time has not yet come, but your time is always ready.

20 Isaiah 54:13   21 M-Text reads *hears and has learned.*   22 NU-Text omits *in Me.*
23 NU-Text reads *true food* and *true drink.*   24 NU-Text reads *You are the Holy One of God.*

7 "The world cannot hate you, but it hates Me because I testify of it that its works are evil.
8 "You go up to this feast. I am not yet[25] going up to this feast, for My time has not yet fully come."
9 When He had said these things to them, He remained in Galilee.

The Heavenly Scholar

10 But when His brothers had gone up, then He also went up to the feast, not openly, but as it were in secret.
11 Then the Jews sought Him at the feast, and said, "Where is He?"
12 And there was much murmuring among the people concerning Him. Some said, "He is good"; others said, "No, on the contrary, He deceives the people."
13 However, no one spoke openly of Him for fear of the Jews.
14 Now about the middle of the feast Jesus went up into the temple and taught.
15 And the Jews marveled, saying, "How does this Man know letters, having never studied?"
16 Jesus[26] answered them and said, "My doctrine is not Mine, but His who sent Me.
17 "If anyone wants to do His will, he shall know concerning the doctrine, whether it is from God or whether I speak on My own authority.
18 "He who speaks from himself seeks his own glory; but He who seeks the glory of the One who sent Him is true, and no unrighteousness is in Him.
19 "Did not Moses give you the law, and yet none of you keeps the law? Why do you seek to kill Me?"
20 The people answered and said, "You have a demon. Who is seeking to kill You?"
21 Jesus answered and said to them, "I did one work, and you all marvel.
22 "Moses therefore gave you circumcision (not that it is from Moses, but from the fathers), and you circumcise a man on the Sabbath.
23 "If a man receives circumcision on the Sabbath, so that the law of Moses should not be broken, are you angry with Me because I made a man completely well on the Sabbath?
24 "Do not judge according to appear-

ance, but judge with righteous judgment."

Could This Be the Christ?

25 Then some of them from Jerusalem said, "Is this not He whom they seek to kill?
26 "But look! He speaks boldly, and they say nothing to Him. Do the rulers know indeed that this is truly[27] the Christ?
27 "However, we know where this Man is from; but when the Christ comes, no one knows where He is from."
28 Then Jesus cried out, as He taught in the temple, saying, "You both know Me, and you know where I am from; and I have not come of Myself, but He who sent Me is true, whom you do not know.
29 "But[28] I know Him, for I am from Him, and He sent Me."
30 Then they sought to take Him; but no one laid a hand on Him, because His hour had not yet come.
31 And many of the people believed in Him, and said, "When the Christ comes, will He do more signs than these which this Man has done?"

Jesus and the Religious Leaders

32 The Pharisees heard the crowd murmuring these things concerning Him, and the Pharisees and the chief priests sent officers to take Him.
33 Then Jesus said to them,[29] "I shall be with you a little while longer, and then I go to Him who sent Me.
34 "You will seek Me and not find Me, and where I am you cannot come."
35 Then the Jews said among themselves, "Where does He intend to go that we shall not find Him? Does He intend to go to the Dispersion among the Greeks and teach the Greeks?
36 "What is this thing that He said, 'You will seek Me and not find Me, and where I am you cannot come'?"

The Promise of the Holy Spirit

37 On the last day, that great day of the feast, Jesus stood and cried out, saying, "If anyone thirsts, let him come to Me and drink.
38 "He who believes in Me, as the Scripture has said, out of his heart will flow rivers of living water."

25 NU-Text omits yet.   26 NU-Text and M-Text read So Jesus.   27 NU-Text omits truly.
28 NU-Text and M-Text omit But.   29 NU-Text and M-Text omit to them.

39 But this He spoke concerning the Spirit, whom those believing[30] in Him would receive; for the Holy[31] Spirit was not yet *given*, because Jesus was not yet glorified.

Who Is He?

40 Therefore many[32] from the crowd, when they heard this saying, said, "Truly this is the Prophet."
41 Others said, "This is the Christ," but some said, "Will the Christ come out of Galilee?
42 "Has not the Scripture said that the Christ comes from the seed of David and from the town of Bethlehem, where David was?"
43 So there was a division among the people because of Him.
44 Now some of them wanted to take Him, but no one laid hands on Him.

Rejected by the Authorities

45 Then the officers came to the chief priests and Pharisees, who said to them, "Why have you not brought Him?"
46 The officers answered, "No man ever spoke like this Man!"
47 Then the Pharisees answered them, "Are you also deceived?
48 "Have any of the rulers or the Pharisees believed in Him?
49 "But this crowd that does not know the law is accursed."
50 Nicodemus (he who came to Jesus by night,[33] being one of them) said to them,
51 "Does our law judge a man before it hears him and knows what he is doing?"
52 They answered and said to him, "Are you also from Galilee? Search and look, for no prophet has arisen[34] out of Galilee."

An Adulteress Faces the Light of the World

53 And everyone went to his *own* house.[35]
8 But Jesus went to the Mount of Olives.
2 But early[36] in the morning He came again into the temple, and all the people came to Him; and He sat down and taught them.

3 Then the scribes and Pharisees brought to Him a woman caught in adultery. And when they had set her in the midst,
4 they said to Him, "Teacher, this woman was caught[37] in adultery, in the very act.
5 "Now Moses, in the law, commanded[38] us that such should be stoned.[39] But what do You say?"[40]
6 This they said, testing Him, that they might have *something* of which to accuse Him. But Jesus stooped down and wrote on the ground with *His* finger, as though He did not hear.[41]
7 So when they continued asking Him, He raised Himself up[42] and said to them, "He who is without sin among you, let him throw a stone at her first."
8 And again He stooped down and wrote on the ground.
9 Then those who heard *it*, being convicted by *their* conscience,[43] went out one by one, beginning with the oldest *even* to the last. And Jesus was left alone, and the woman standing in the midst.
10 When Jesus had raised Himself up and saw no one but the woman, He said to her,[44] "Woman, where are those accusers of yours?[45] Has no one condemned you?"
11 She said, "No one, Lord." And Jesus said to her, "Neither do I condemn you; go and[46] sin no more."
12 Then Jesus spoke to them again, saying, "I am the light of the world. He who follows Me shall not walk in darkness, but have the light of life."

Jesus Defends His Self-Witness

13 The Pharisees therefore said to Him, "You bear witness of Yourself; Your witness is not true."
14 Jesus answered and said to them, "Even if I bear witness of Myself, My witness is true, for I know where I came from and where I am going; but you do not know where I come from and where I am going.
15 "You judge according to the flesh; I judge no one.

---

30 NU-Text reads *who believed.*   31 NU-Text omits *Holy.*   32 NU-Text reads *some.*   33 NU-Text reads *before.*
34 NU-Text reads *is to rise.*
35 The words *But Jesus* through *sin no more* (8:11) are bracketed by NU-Text as not original. They are present in over 900 manuscripts.   36 M-Text reads *very early.*   37 M-Text reads *we found this woman.*
38 M-Text reads *in our law Moses commanded.*   39 NU-Text and M-Text read *to stone such.*
40 M-Text adds *about her.*   41 NU-Text and M-Text omit *as though He did not hear.*
42 M-Text reads *He looked up.*   43 NU-Text and M-Text omit *being convicted by their own conscience.*
44 NU-Text omits *and saw no one but the woman;* M-Text reads *He saw her and said.*
45 NU-Text and M-Text omit *of yours.*   46 NU-Text and M-text add *from now on.*

Expect the Unexpected

Learn to expect the unexpected. During the New Testament period, the Jewish people had rigid expectations. They yearned for a messiah. Their literature shows they specifically expected the Messiah to come from Bethlehem in Judea. They were right. Jesus was born in Bethlehem. However, when He was a baby His parents fled with Him to Egypt to escape cruel Herod. When they returned to the land, they settled in the town of Nazareth.

Nazareth probably comes from the Hebrew word for "branch." The prophet Isaiah foretold that the Messiah would grow up like a young branch for the Lord. Nazareth was an insignificant village in New Testament times. Nathanael suggests that nothing good could come out of Nazareth (John 1:46). For it was a simple fact that all the great leaders of Israel came from Jerusalem or another major city in Judea.

The only other prophet from the region was Jonah whose village, Gath Hepher was located one-and-a-half miles from Nazareth. The village where Jesus was reared is never mentioned in the Old Testament and had little status in the New Testament. It was never mentioned in any of the annals of cities conquered in the region, nor in any other extra-biblical literature. Yet here the Savior of the world "increased in wisdom and stature" (Luke 2:52).

By expecting the Messiah to come from Bethlehem, the Jewish leaders completely fought Jesus' claim as the Son of God. Set in their ways, they failed to recognize the One they waited for. One day, while Jesus taught in the temple, the leaders asked Him, "Has not the Scripture said that the Christ comes from the seed of David and from the town of Bethlehem?" (John 7:42). They did not think Jesus of Nazareth could possibly be the Messiah. Their expectations limited God. When Jesus, the true Messiah finally came to them, they could not accept Him because of their presuppositions.

You must learn to allow God to do the unexpected in your lives. Do not limit God with your locked-in thinking. Unlock your faith. Allow God to touch you, reach you, and come to you in unexpected ways through people, places, and events in life you never dreamed of before. By expecting the unexpected, God can use the insignificant to accomplish the impossible. Expect a miracle!

16 "And yet if I do judge, My judgment is true; for I am not alone, but I *am* with the Father who sent Me.

17 "It is also written in your law that the testimony of two men is true.

18 "I am One who bears witness of Myself, and the Father who sent Me bears witness of Me."

19 Then they said to Him, "Where is Your Father?" Jesus answered, "You know neither Me nor My Father. If you had known Me, you would have known My Father also."

20 These words Jesus spoke in the treasury, as He taught in the temple; and no one laid hands on Him, for His hour had not yet come.

Jesus Predicts His Departure

21 Then Jesus said to them again, "I am going away, and you will seek Me, and will die in your sin. Where I go you cannot come."

22 So the Jews said, "Will He kill Himself, because He says, 'Where I go you cannot come'?"

23 And He said to them, "You are from beneath; I am from above. You are of this world; I am not of this world.

24 "Therefore I said to you that you will die in your sins; for if you do not believe that I am *He*, you will die in your sins."

25 Then they said to Him, "Who are You?" And Jesus said to them, "Just what I have been saying to you from the beginning.

26 "I have many things to say and to judge concerning you, but He who sent Me is true; and I speak to the world those things which I heard from Him."

27 They did not understand that He spoke to them of the Father.

28 Then Jesus said to them, "When you lift up the Son of Man, then you will know that I am *He*, and *that* I do nothing of Myself; but as My Father taught Me, I speak these things.

29 "And He who sent Me is with Me. The Father has not left Me alone, for I always do those things that please Him."

The Truth Shall Make You Free

30 As He spoke these words, many believed in Him.

31 Then Jesus said to those Jews who believed Him, "If you abide in My word, you are My disciples indeed.

32 "And you shall know the truth, and the truth shall make you free."

33 They answered Him, "We are Abraham's descendants, and have never been in bondage to anyone. How *can* you say, 'You will be made free'?"

34 Jesus answered them, "Most assuredly, I say to you, whoever commits sin is a slave of sin.

35 "And a slave does not abide in the house forever, *but* a son abides forever.

36 "Therefore if the Son makes you free, you shall be free indeed.

Abraham's Seed and Satan's

37 "I know that you are Abraham's descendants, but you seek to kill Me, because My word has no place in you.

38 "I speak what I have seen with My Father, and you do what you have seen with[47] your father."

39 They answered and said to Him, "Abraham is our father." Jesus said to them, "If you were Abraham's children, you would do the works of Abraham.

40 "But now you seek to kill Me, a Man who has told you the truth which I heard from God. Abraham did not do this.

41 "You do the deeds of your father." Then they said to Him, "We were not born of fornication; we have one Father—God."

42 Jesus said to them, "If God were your Father, you would love Me, for I proceeded forth and came from God; nor have I come of Myself, but He sent Me.

43 "Why do you not understand My speech? Because you are not able to listen to My word.

44 "You are of *your* father the devil, and the desires of your father you want to do. He was a murderer from the beginning, and *does not* stand in the truth, because there is no truth in him. When he speaks a lie, he speaks from his own *resources*, for he is a liar and the father of it.

45 "But because I tell the truth, you do not believe Me.

46 "Which of you convicts Me of sin? And if I tell the truth, why do you not believe Me?

47 "He who is of God hears God's words; therefore you do not hear, because you are not of God."

47 NU-Text reads *heard from*.

Find a Hurt and Heal It!

When the time came for Jesus to begin His public ministry, He left Nazareth and settled in Capernaum by the Sea of Galilee. Of all the places in Palestine—why did Jesus go there?

The Gospels and other sources from the New Testament period tell us that multitudes of sick, crippled, paralytics, lepers, lame, blind, and deaf people already lived by the Sea of Galilee before Jesus settled in the region. Why did they go there?

The Sea of Galilee is located in a volcanic region seven hundred feet below sea level. Molten lava deep within the earth steams from the natural rock fissures and heats the many springs around the lake. People in the Greco-Roman world of the New Testament believed these hot springs had healing powers. They built cities near these pools and erected beautiful marble bathhouses with inlaid mosaic floors. One of the hot springs was named after the emperor Tiberius. Businessmen and physicians charged high fees for the ill to sit in these baths.

Here in the region where people were suffering and hurting, Jesus came to heal them and demonstrate the kingdom of God. He found out where they were and went to them. He knew of their hurts and He healed them. Today, Jesus finds us and comes to us where we are. He knows our hurts. Whether it is a lack of joy, low self-worth, guilt from an unhealthy life-style, or a physical affliction—Jesus heals us.

We can also go out and meet the needs of others. Because many people are afraid to come for help, we must first go to them with an attitude of concern. Then, when they know that we will not turn away, they can freely accept our help. Let us be like our Lord Jesus Christ as we exude joy, build others up, and aid in their physical needs. We, like our Lord, will "find a need and fill it. Find a hurt and heal it!"

Before Abraham Was, I AM

48 Then the Jews answered and said to Him, "Do we not say rightly that You are a Samaritan and have a demon?"

49 Jesus answered, "I do not have a demon; but I honor My Father, and you dishonor Me.

50 "And I do not seek My *own* glory; there is One who seeks and judges.

51 "Most assuredly, I say to you, if anyone keeps My word he shall never see death."

52 Then the Jews said to Him, "Now we know that You have a demon! Abraham is dead, and the prophets; and You say, 'If anyone keeps My word he shall never taste death.'

53 "Are You greater than our father Abraham, who is dead? And the prophets are dead. Whom do You make Yourself out to be?"

54 Jesus answered, "If I honor Myself, My honor is nothing. It is My Father who honors Me, of whom you say that He is your[48] God.

55 "Yet you have not known Him, but I know Him. And if I say, 'I do not know Him,' I shall be a liar like you; but I do know Him and keep His word.

56 "Your father Abraham rejoiced to see My day, and he saw *it* and was glad."

57 Then the Jews said to Him, "You are not yet fifty years old, and have You seen Abraham?"

58 Jesus said to them, "Most assuredly, I say to you, before Abraham was, I AM."

59 Then they took up stones to throw at Him; but Jesus hid Himself and went out of the temple,[49] going through the midst of them, and so passed by.

A Man Born Blind Receives Sight

9 Now as *Jesus* passed by, He saw a man who was blind from birth.

2 And His disciples asked Him, saying, "Rabbi, who sinned, this man or his parents, that he was born blind?"

3 Jesus answered, "Neither this man nor his parents sinned, but that the works of God should be revealed in him.

4 "I[50] must work the works of Him who sent Me while it is day; *the* night is coming when no one can work.

5 "As long as I am in the world, I am the light of the world."

6 When He had said these things, He spat on the ground and made clay with the saliva; and He anointed the eyes of the blind man with the clay.

7 And He said to him, "Go, wash in the pool of Siloam" (which is translated, Sent). So he went and washed, and came back seeing.

8 Therefore the neighbors and those who previously had seen that he was blind[51] said, "Is not this he who sat and begged?"

9 Some said, "This is he." Others *said*, "He is like him."[52] He said, "I am *he*."

10 Therefore they said to him, "How were your eyes opened?"

11 He answered and said, "A Man called Jesus made clay and anointed my eyes and said to me, 'Go to the pool of[53] Siloam and wash.' So I went and washed, and I received sight."

12 Then they said to him, "Where is He?" He said, "I do not know."

The Pharisees Excommunicate the Healed Man

13 They brought him who formerly was blind to the Pharisees.

14 Now it was a Sabbath when Jesus made the clay and opened his eyes.

15 Then the Pharisees also asked him again how he had received his sight. He said to them, "He put clay on my eyes, and I washed, and I see."

16 Therefore some of the Pharisees said, "This Man is not from God, because He does not keep the Sabbath." Others said, "How can a man who is a sinner do such miracles?" And there was a division among them.

17 They said to the blind man again, "What do you say about Him because He opened your eyes?" He said, "He is a prophet."

18 But the Jews did not believe concerning him, that he had been blind and received his sight, until they called the parents of him who had received his sight.

19 And they asked them, saying, "Is this your son, who you say was born blind? How then does he now see?"

20 His parents answered them and said, "We know that this is our son, and that he was born blind;

Sent by God

Throughout Jesus' ministry on earth, a major truth He communicated was that He was uniquely sent from God. A common phrase spoken by Jesus was "the very works that I do—bear witness of Me, that the Father has **sent** Me" (John 5:36).

Such emphasis was placed on this truth that the Gospel of John records the word **sent** twenty-five times in the first nine chapters. John 8 and 9 tell of a heated discussion on this subject between some of the religious leaders and Jesus. Jesus claimed that He was **sent** from God and was equal with God. Some of the Pharisees and Sadducees adamantly denied His claim.

This dispute came to a climax as Jesus and His disciples left the temple area. Again, Jesus asserted this fact. "I must work the works of Him who sent Me while it is day; *the night is coming when no one can work. As long as I am in the world, I am the light of the world"* (John 9:4, 5). Having said this, Jesus approached a blind man outside the temple. He made mud and placed it on the man's eyes and said, "Go, wash in the pool of Siloam (which is translated, **Sent**)" (John 9:7). The fact that Siloam means **sent** is a clear challenge by Jesus for everyone to examine His works and ultimately His claims. The pool of Siloam has an interesting history. Seven centuries earlier God had miraculously delivered the inhabitants of Jerusalem from the siege of the Assyrian general, Sennacherib. For this reason, it may have held a religious significance to many witnesses of this miracle.

After the blind man washed in the pool, he came back seeing—his sight fully restored. He and his parents were immediately questioned on the issue of where Jesus was **sent** from. His parents refused to answer for fear of being put out of the synagogue. But the blind man confidently answered, "Why, this is a marvelous thing, that you do not know where He is from . . . Since the world began it has been unheard of that anyone opened the eyes of one who was born blind. If this Man were not from God, He could do nothing" (John 9:30, 32, 33).

Later in His ministry, after His resurrection, Jesus disclosed this incredible truth: "As the Father has **sent** Me, I also **send** you" (John 20:21).

The healed blind man believed Jesus' words and experienced His works. By believing Christ's claim, we can confidently answer the question, "Where was this Man **sent** from?"

21 "but by what means he now sees we do not know, or who opened his eyes we do not know. He is of age; ask him. He will speak for himself."
22 His parents said these *things* because they feared the Jews, for the Jews had agreed already that if anyone confessed *that* He *was* Christ, he would be put out of the synagogue.
23 Therefore his parents said, "He is of age; ask him."
24 So they again called the man who was blind, and said to him, "Give God the glory! We know that this Man is a sinner."
25 He answered and said, "Whether He is a sinner *or not* I do not know. One thing I know: that though I was blind, now I see."
26 Then they said to him again, "What did He do to you? How did He open your eyes?"
27 He answered them, "I told you already, and you did not listen. Why do you want to hear *it* again? Do you also want to become His disciples?"
28 Then they reviled him and said, "You are His disciple, but we are Moses' disciples.
29 "We know that God spoke to Moses; *as for* this *fellow*, we do not know where He is from."
30 The man answered and said to them, "Why, this is a marvelous thing, that you do not know where He is from, and *yet* He has opened my eyes!
31 "Now we know that God does not hear sinners; but if anyone is a worshiper of God and does His will, He hears him.
32 "Since the world began it has been unheard of that anyone opened the eyes of one who was born blind.
33 "If this Man were not from God, He could do nothing."
34 They answered and said to him, "You were completely born in sins, and are you teaching us?" And they cast him out.

True Vision and True Blindness

35 Jesus heard that they had cast him out; and when He had found him, He said to him, "Do you believe in the Son of God?"[54]
36 He answered and said, "Who is He, Lord, that I may believe in Him?"
37 And Jesus said to him, "You have both seen Him and it is He who is talking with you."
38 Then he said, "Lord, I believe!" And he worshiped Him.
39 And Jesus said, "For judgment I have come into this world, that those who do not see may see, and that those who see may be made blind."
40 Then *some* of the Pharisees who were with Him heard these words, and said to Him, "Are we blind also?"
41 Jesus said to them, "If you were blind, you would have no sin; but now you say, 'We see.' Therefore your sin remains.

Jesus the True Shepherd

10 "Most assuredly, I say to you, he who does not enter the sheepfold by the door, but climbs up some other way, the same is a thief and a robber.
2 "But he who enters by the door is the shepherd of the sheep.
3 "To him the doorkeeper opens, and the sheep hear his voice; and he calls his own sheep by name and leads them out.
4 "And when he brings out his own sheep, he goes before them; and the sheep follow him, for they know his voice.
5 "Yet they will by no means follow a stranger, but will flee from him, for they do not know the voice of strangers."
6 Jesus used this illustration, but they did not understand the things which He spoke to them.

Jesus the Good Shepherd

7 Then Jesus said to them again, "Most assuredly, I say to you, I am the door of the sheep.
8 "All who *ever* came before Me[55] are thieves and robbers, but the sheep did not hear them.
9 "I am the door. If anyone enters by Me, he will be saved, and will go in and out and find pasture.
10 "The thief does not come except to steal, and to kill, and to destroy. I have come that they may have life, and that they may have *it* more abundantly.
11 "I am the good shepherd. The good shepherd gives His life for the sheep.
12 "But *he who is* a hireling and not the shepherd, one who does not own the sheep, sees the wolf coming and leaves the sheep and flees; and the wolf catches the sheep and scatters them.

54 NU-Text reads *Son of Man*.   55 M-Text omits *before Me*.

Jesus the Good Shepherd

Jesus' parable of the Good Shepherd is deeply rooted in the everyday responsibilities of a shepherd. His listeners could easily visualize each aspect of His teaching as He detailed how He cares for His flock.

Even today, the duties of a shepherd are much the same as when Jesus first taught this parable. The shepherd's daily routine begins by leading his flock out to the wilderness to pasture. There in the hot, dry countryside he must find food and water for his sheep and guard against wild animals and thieves.

Jesus presents the unique relationship held between a sheepherder and his flock. "I am the good shepherd; and I know My *sheep*, and am known by My own. My sheep hear My voice, and I know them, and they follow Me" (John 10:14, 27).

Each shepherd has a specific call he voices which readily identifies him and summons his flock. This can be a clicking sound made with the tongue flicking against the teeth or a high-pitched shrill. Often several shepherds and their flocks intermingle while refreshing at small streams in the wilderness. Once the sheep have been watered, a shepherd will call his flock from a group of hundreds of sheep and his small flock will emerge to follow him.

As dusk approaches, shepherds voice their own identifiable calls to lead their flocks through the narrow canyon gullies. A common practice of the shepherd is to make use of the natural sheepfolds formed by the twisted geological structure of the land. Here they are fed, watered, and kept for the night. The security of the flock is ensured on three sides by the steep canyon walls. The wider outlet is narrowed by building a wall of stones and thorn branches. The shepherd leaves a small entranceway at the intersection of the walls where he takes his watch post and actually serves as the door to guard his flock. No animal or thief is able to enter the fold without passing by the shepherd. When the safety of the morning dawn arrives, the shepherd calls his sheep and leads them out and finds pasture.

Jesus drew directly from this practice. "I am the door. If anyone enters by Me, he will be saved, and will go in and out and find pasture. The thief does not come except to steal, and to kill, and to destroy. I have come that they may have life, and that they may have *it* more abundantly" (John 10:9, 10).

13 "The hireling flees because he is a hireling and does not care about the sheep.

14 "I am the good shepherd; and I know My *sheep*, and am known by My own.

15 "As the Father knows Me, even so I know the Father; and I lay down My life for the sheep.

16 "And other sheep I have which are not of this fold; them also I must bring, and they will hear My voice; and there will be one flock *and* one shepherd.

17 "Therefore My Father loves Me, because I lay down My life that I may take it again.

18 "No one takes it from Me, but I lay it down of Myself. I have power to lay it down, and I have power to take it again. This command I have received from My Father."

19 Therefore there was a division again among the Jews because of these sayings.

20 And many of them said, "He has a demon and is mad. Why do you listen to Him?"

21 Others said, "These are not the words of one who has a demon. Can a demon open the eyes of the blind?"

The Shepherd Knows His Sheep

22 Now it was the Feast of Dedication in Jerusalem, and it was winter.

23 And Jesus walked in the temple, in Solomon's porch.

24 Then the Jews surrounded Him and said to Him, "How long do You keep us in doubt? If You are the Christ, tell us plainly."

25 Jesus answered them, "I told you, and you do not believe. The works that I do in My Father's name, they bear witness of Me.

26 "But you do not believe, because you are not of My sheep, as I said to you.56

27 "My sheep hear My voice, and I know them, and they follow Me.

28 "And I give them eternal life, and they shall never perish; neither shall anyone snatch them out of My hand.

29 "My Father, who has given *them* to Me, is greater than all; and no one is able to snatch *them* out of My Father's hand.

30 "I and My Father are one."

Renewed Efforts to Stone Jesus

31 Then the Jews took up stones again to stone Him.

32 Jesus answered them, "Many good works I have shown you from My Father. For which of those works do you stone Me?"

33 The Jews answered Him, saying, "For a good work we do not stone You, but for blasphemy, and because You, being a Man, make Yourself God."

34 Jesus answered them, "Is it not written in your law, 'I said, "You are gods" '?57

35 "If He called them gods, to whom the word of God came (and the Scripture cannot be broken),

36 "do you say of Him whom the Father sanctified and sent into the world, 'You are blaspheming,' because I said, 'I am the Son of God'?

37 "If I do not do the works of My Father, do not believe Me;

38 "but if I do, though you do not believe Me, believe the works, that you may know and believe58 that the Father *is* in Me, and I in Him."

39 Therefore they sought again to seize Him, but He escaped out of their hand.

The Believers Beyond Jordan

40 And He went away again beyond the Jordan to the place where John was baptizing at first, and there He stayed.

41 Then many came to Him and said, "John performed no sign, but all the things that John spoke about this Man were true."

42 And many believed in Him there.

The Death of Lazarus

11 Now a certain *man* was sick, Lazarus of Bethany, the town of Mary and her sister Martha.

2 It was *that* Mary who anointed the Lord with fragrant oil and wiped His feet with her hair, whose brother Lazarus was sick.

3 Therefore the sisters sent to Him, saying, "Lord, behold, he whom You love is sick."

4 When Jesus heard *that*, He said, "This sickness is not unto death, but for the glory of God, that the Son of God may be glorified through it."

5 Now Jesus loved Martha and her sister and Lazarus.

6 So, when He heard that he was sick, He stayed two more days in the place where He was.

56 NU-Text omits *as I said to you.* 57 Psalm 82:6 58 NU-Text reads *understand.*

7 Then after this He said to *the* disciples, "Let us go to Judea again."
8 *The* disciples said to Him, "Rabbi, lately the Jews sought to stone You, and are You going there again?"
9 Jesus answered, "Are there not twelve hours in the day? If anyone walks in the day, he does not stumble, because he sees the light of this world.
10 "But if one walks in the night, he stumbles, because the light is not in him."
11 These things He said, and after that He said to them, "Our friend Lazarus sleeps, but I go that I may wake him up."
12 Then His disciples said, "Lord, if he sleeps he will get well."
13 However, Jesus spoke of his death, but they thought that He was speaking about taking rest in sleep.
14 Then Jesus said to them plainly, "Lazarus is dead.
15 "And I am glad for your sakes that I was not there, that you may believe. Nevertheless let us go to him."
16 Then Thomas, who is called Didymus, said to his fellow disciples, "Let us also go, that we may die with Him."

I Am the Resurrection and the Life

17 So when Jesus came, He found that he had already been in the tomb four days.
18 Now Bethany was near Jerusalem, about two miles[59] away.
19 And many of the Jews had joined the women around Martha and Mary, to comfort them concerning their brother.
20 Then Martha, as soon as she heard that Jesus was coming, went and met Him, but Mary was sitting in the house.
21 Then Martha said to Jesus, "Lord, if You had been here, my brother would not have died.
22 "But even now I know that whatever You ask of God, God will give You."
23 Jesus said to her, "Your brother will rise again."
24 Martha said to Him, "I know that he will rise again in the resurrection at the last day."
25 Jesus said to her, "I am the resurrection and the life. He who believes in Me, though he may die, he shall live.
26 "And whoever lives and believes in Me shall never die. Do you believe this?"
27 She said to Him, "Yes, Lord, I believe that You are the Christ, the Son of God, who is to come into the world."

Jesus and Death, the Last Enemy

28 And when she had said these things, she went her way and secretly called Mary her sister, saying, "The Teacher has come and is calling for you."
29 As soon as she heard *that*, she arose quickly and came to Him.
30 Now Jesus had not yet come into the town, but was[60] in the place where Martha met Him.
31 Then the Jews who were with her in the house, and comforting her, when they saw that Mary rose up quickly and went out, followed her, saying, "She is going to the tomb to weep there."[61]
32 Then, when Mary came where Jesus was, and saw Him, she fell down at His feet, saying to Him, "Lord, if You had been here, my brother would not have died."
33 Therefore, when Jesus saw her weeping, and the Jews who came with her weeping, He groaned in the spirit and was troubled.
34 And He said, "Where have you laid him?" They said to Him, "Lord, come and see."
35 Jesus wept.
36 Then the Jews said, "See how He loved him!"
37 And some of them said, "Could not this Man, who opened the eyes of the blind, also have kept this man from dying?"

Lazarus Raised from the Dead

38 Then Jesus, again groaning in Himself, came to the tomb. It was a cave, and a stone lay against it.
39 Jesus said, "Take away the stone." Martha, the sister of him who was dead, said to Him, "Lord, by this time there is a stench, for he has been *dead* four days."
40 Jesus said to her, "Did I not say to you that if you would believe you would see the glory of God?"
41 Then they took away the stone *from the place* where the dead man was lying.[62] And Jesus lifted up *His* eyes and said, "Father, I thank You that You have heard Me.

---

59 Greek *fifteen stadia*   60 NU-Text adds *still*.
61 NU-Text reads *supposing that she was going to the tomb to weep there.*
62 NU-Text omits *from the place where the dead man was lying.*

42 "And I know that You always hear Me, but because of the people who are standing by I said *this*, that they may believe that You sent Me."
43 Now when He had said these things, He cried with a loud voice, "Lazarus, come forth!"
44 And he who had died came out bound hand and foot with graveclothes, and his face was wrapped with a cloth. Jesus said to them, "Loose him, and let him go."

The Plot to Kill Jesus

45 Then many of the Jews who had come to Mary, and had seen the things Jesus did, believed in Him.
46 But some of them went away to the Pharisees and told them the things Jesus did.
47 Then the chief priests and the Pharisees gathered a council and said, "What shall we do? For this Man works many signs.
48 "If we let Him alone like this, everyone will believe in Him, and the Romans will come and take away both our place and nation."
49 And one of them, Caiaphas, being high priest that year, said to them, "You know nothing at all,
50 "nor do you consider that it is expedient for us[63] that one man should die for the people, and not that the whole nation should perish."
51 Now this he did not say on his own *authority*; but being high priest that year he prophesied that Jesus would die for the nation,
52 and not for that nation only, but also that He would gather together in one the children of God who were scattered abroad.
53 Then from that day on they plotted to put Him to death.
54 Therefore Jesus no longer walked openly among the Jews, but went from there into the country near the wilderness, to a city called Ephraim, and there remained with His disciples.
55 And the Passover of the Jews was near, and many went from the country up to Jerusalem before the Passover, to purify themselves.
56 Then they sought Jesus, and spoke among themselves as they stood in the temple, "What do you think—that He will not come to the feast?"
57 Now both the chief priests and the Pharisees had given a command, that if anyone knew where He was, he should report *it*, that they might seize Him.

The Anointing at Bethany

12 Then, six days before the Passover, Jesus came to Bethany, where Lazarus was who had been dead,[64] whom He had raised from the dead.
2 There they made Him a supper; and Martha served, but Lazarus was one of those who sat at the table with Him.
3 Then Mary took a pound of very costly oil of spikenard, anointed the feet of Jesus, and wiped His feet with her hair. And the house was filled with the fragrance of the oil.
4 Then one of His disciples, Judas Iscariot, Simon's *son*, who would betray Him, said,
5 "Why was this fragrant oil not sold for three hundred denarii[65] and given to the poor?"
6 This he said, not that he cared for the poor, but because he was a thief, and had the money box; and he used to take what was put in it.
7 Then Jesus said, "Let her alone; she has kept[66] this for the day of My burial.
8 "For the poor you have with you always, but Me you do not have always."

The Plot to Kill Lazarus

9 Then a great many of the Jews knew that He was there; and they came, not for Jesus' sake only, but that they might also see Lazarus, whom He had raised from the dead.
10 But the chief priests took counsel that they might also put Lazarus to death,
11 because on account of him many of the Jews went away and believed in Jesus.

The Triumphal Entry

12 The next day a great multitude that had come to the feast, when they heard that Jesus was coming to Jerusalem,
13 took branches of palm trees and went out to meet Him, and cried out:

"Hosanna!
'Blessed is He who comes
    in the name of the LORD!'[67]
The King of Israel!"

63 NU-Text reads *you.*   64 NU-Text omits *who had been dead.*   65 About one year's wages for a worker.
66 NU-Text reads *that she may keep.*   67 Psalm 118:26

14 Then Jesus, when He had found a young donkey, sat on it; as it is written:

15 *"Fear not, daughter of Zion;*
Behold, your King is coming,
Sitting on a donkey's colt."[68]

16 His disciples did not understand these things at first; but when Jesus was glorified, then they remembered that these things were written about Him and *that* they had done these things to Him.
17 Therefore the people, who were with Him when He called Lazarus out of his tomb and raised him from the dead, bore witness.
18 For this reason the people also met Him, because they heard that He had done this sign.
19 The Pharisees therefore said among themselves, "You see that you are accomplishing nothing. Look, the world has gone after Him!"

The Fruitful Grain of Wheat

20 Now there were certain Greeks among those who came up to worship at the feast.
21 Then they came to Philip, who was from Bethsaida of Galilee, and asked him, saying, "Sir, we wish to see Jesus."
22 Philip came and told Andrew, and in turn Andrew and Philip told Jesus.
23 But Jesus answered them, saying, "The hour has come that the Son of Man should be glorified.
24 "Most assuredly, I say to you, unless a grain of wheat falls into the ground and dies, it remains alone; but if it dies, it produces much grain.
25 "He who loves his life will lose it, and he who hates his life in this world will keep it for eternal life.
26 "If anyone serves Me, let him follow Me; and where I am, there My servant will be also. If anyone serves Me, him *My* Father will honor.

Jesus Predicts His Death on the Cross

27 "Now My soul is troubled, and what shall I say? 'Father, save Me from this hour'? But for this purpose I came to this hour.
28 "Father, glorify Your name." Then a voice came from heaven, *saying,* "I have both glorified *it* and will glorify *it* again."
29 Therefore the people who stood by

and heard *it* said that it had thundered. Others said, "An angel has spoken to Him."
30 Jesus answered and said, "This voice did not come because of Me, but for your sake.
31 "Now is the judgment of this world; now the ruler of this world will be cast out.
32 "And I, if I am lifted up from the earth, will draw all *peoples* to Myself."
33 This He said, signifying by what death He would die.
34 The people answered Him, "We have heard from the law that the Christ remains forever; and how *can* You say, 'The Son of Man must be lifted up'? Who is this Son of Man?"
35 Then Jesus said to them, "A little while longer the light is with you. Walk while you have the light, lest darkness overtake you; he who walks in darkness does not know where he is going.
36 "While you have the light, believe in the light, that you may become sons of light." These things Jesus spoke, and departed, and was hidden from them.

Who Has Believed Our Report?

37 But although He had done so many signs before them, they did not believe in Him,
38 that the word of Isaiah the prophet might be fulfilled, which he spoke:

"Lord, who has believed our report?
And to whom has the arm
of the LORD been revealed?"[69]

39 Therefore they could not believe, because Isaiah said again:

40 *"He has blinded their eyes and*
hardened their heart,
Lest they should see with their eyes
And understand with their heart,
Lest they should turn,
so that I should heal them."[70]

41 These things Isaiah said when[71] he saw His glory and spoke of Him.

Walk in the Light

42 Nevertheless even among the rulers many believed in Him, but because of the Pharisees they did not confess *Him,* lest they should be put out of the synagogue;

⁴³ for they loved the praise of men more than the praise of God.
⁴⁴ Then Jesus cried out and said, "He who believes in Me, believes not in Me but in Him who sent Me.
⁴⁵ "And he who sees Me sees Him who sent Me.
⁴⁶ "I have come *as* a light into the world, that whoever believes in Me should not abide in darkness.
⁴⁷ "And if anyone hears My words and does not believe,⁷² I do not judge him; for I did not come to judge the world but to save the world.
⁴⁸ "He who rejects Me, and does not receive My words, has that which judges him—the word that I have spoken will judge him in the last day.
⁴⁹ "For I have not spoken on My own *authority*; but the Father who sent Me gave Me a command, what I should say and what I should speak.
⁵⁰ "And I know that His command is everlasting life. Therefore, whatever I speak, just as the Father has told Me, so I speak."

The Master Becomes a Servant

13 Now before the feast of the Passover, when Jesus knew that His hour had come that He should depart from this world to the Father, having loved His own who were in the world, He loved them to the end.
2 And supper being ended,⁷³ the devil having already put it into the heart of Judas Iscariot, Simon's *son*, to betray Him,
3 Jesus, knowing that the Father had given all things into His hands, and that He had come from God and was going to God,
4 rose from supper and laid aside His garments, took a towel and girded Himself.
5 After that, He poured water into a basin and began to wash the disciples' feet, and to wipe *them* with the towel with which He was girded.
6 Then He came to Simon Peter. And *Peter* said to Him, "Lord, are You washing my feet?"
7 Jesus answered and said to him, "What I am doing you do not understand now, but you will know after this."
8 Peter said to Him, "You shall never wash my feet!" Jesus answered him, "If I

do not wash you, you have no part with Me."
9 Simon Peter said to Him, "Lord, not my feet only, but also *my* hands and *my* head!"
10 Jesus said to him, "He who is bathed needs only to wash *his* feet, but is completely clean; and you are clean, but not all of you."
11 For He knew who would betray Him; therefore He said, "You are not all clean."

We Also Must Serve

12 So when He had washed their feet, taken His garments, and sat down again, He said to them, "Do you know what I have done to you?
13 "You call me Teacher and Lord, and you say well, for *so* I am.
14 "If I then, *your* Lord and Teacher, have washed your feet, you also ought to wash one another's feet.
15 "For I have given you an example, that you should do as I have done to you.
16 "Most assuredly, I say to you, a servant is not greater than his master; nor is he who is sent greater than he who sent him.
17 "If you know these things, happy are you if you do them.
18 "I do not speak concerning all of you. I know whom I have chosen; but that the Scripture may be fulfilled, 'He who eats bread with Me⁷⁴ has lifted up his heel against Me.'⁷⁵
19 "Now I tell you before it comes, that when it does come to pass, you may believe that I am *He*.
20 "Most assuredly, I say to you, he who receives whomever I send receives Me; and he who receives Me receives Him who sent Me."
21 When Jesus had said these things, He was troubled in spirit, and testified and said, "Most assuredly, I say to you, one of you will betray Me."
22 Then the disciples looked at one another, perplexed about whom He spoke.
23 Now there was leaning on Jesus' bosom one of His disciples, whom Jesus loved.
24 Simon Peter therefore motioned to him to ask who it was of whom He spoke.
25 Then, leaning back⁷⁶ on Jesus' breast, he said to Him, "Lord, who is it?"

72 NU-Text reads *keep them.*   73 NU-Text reads *And during supper.*   74 NU-Text reads *My bread.*
75 Psalm 41:9   76 NU-Text and M-Text add *thus.*

Servant of All

Jesus Christ is the greatest servant the world has ever known. At the Last Supper, Jesus exemplified the real meaning of love and service when, as Lord and Teacher, He willingly washed the feet of His disciples. In doing so, Jesus demonstrated the humble role of service to others, which we must be willing to take upon ourselves during our lives.

In both the ancient and modern Middle East the feet are considered the dirtiest part of the body. Usually covered only by open sandals, the feet were constantly trodding in the dust and dirt during the summer months. In the winter, the rain turned the red terra rosa and rendzina soils and the black basaltic earth into thick, wet mud, making it impassable in many parts of the land. One step in the mire leaves large clods of mud stuck to the feet.

In biblical times it was customary to remove your sandals before entering a house or holy place. A harsh insult was to kick another person with your feet. The ultimate triumph over an enemy was to make him your footstool.

The Gospels record that Jesus began to wash each of the disciples' feet, taking upon Himself the lowliest of all tasks. When Jesus began to wash Peter's feet, the fisherman objected vehemently. His Lord was too far above this degrading act. Yet, Jesus replied clearly, "Do you know what I have done to you? You call me Teacher and Lord, and you say well, for *so* I am. If I then, *your* Lord and Teacher, have washed your feet, you also ought to wash one another's feet. For I have given you an example, that you should do as I have done to you" (John 13:12-15).

Jesus served the disciples in an unusual, traditionally unacceptable, and unexpected way. By His actions, He taught us that true greatness is accompanied by loving service and success comes from serving others.

Whom can you serve today in an unusual and unexpected way? When God brings a seemingly humbling, degrading responsibility into your life, accept it with positive joy. "If anyone desires to be first, he shall be last of all and servant of all" (Mark 9:35).

26 Jesus answered, "It is he to whom I shall give a piece of bread when I have dipped *it*." And having dipped the bread, He gave *it* to Judas Iscariot, *the son* of Simon.
27 Now after the piece of bread, Satan entered him. Then Jesus said to him, "What you do, do quickly."
28 But no one at the table knew for what reason He said this to him.
29 For some thought, because Judas had the money box, that Jesus had said to him, "Buy *those things* we need for the feast," or that he should give something to the poor.
30 Having received the piece of bread, he then went out immediately. And it was night.

The New Commandment

31 So, when he had gone out, Jesus said, "Now the Son of Man is glorified, and God is glorified in Him.
32 "If God is glorified in Him, God will also glorify Him in Himself, and glorify Him immediately.
33 "Little children, I shall be with you a little while longer. You will seek Me; and as I said to the Jews, 'Where I am going, you cannot come,' so now I say to you.
34 "A new commandment I give to you, that you love one another; as I have loved you, that you also love one another.
35 "By this all will know that you are My disciples, if you have love for one another."

Jesus Predicts Peter's Denial

36 Simon Peter said to Him, "Lord, where are You going?" Jesus answered him, "Where I am going you cannot follow Me now, but you shall follow Me afterward."
37 Peter said to Him, "Lord, why can I not follow You now? I will lay down my life for Your sake."
38 Jesus answered him, "Will you lay down your life for My sake? Most assuredly, I say to you, the rooster shall not crow till you have denied Me three times.

The Way, the Truth, and the Life

14 "Let not your heart be troubled; you believe in God, believe also in Me.

2 "In My Father's house are many mansions;[77] if *it were* not *so,* I would have told you. I go to prepare a place for you.[78]
3 "And if I go and prepare a place for you, I will come again and receive you to Myself; that where I am, *there* you may be also.
4 "And where I go you know, and the way you know."
5 Thomas said to Him, "Lord, we do not know where You are going, and how can we know the way?"
6 Jesus said to him, "I am the way, the truth, and the life. No one comes to the Father except through Me.

The Father Revealed

7 "If you had known Me, you would have known My Father also; and from now on you know Him and have seen Him."
8 Philip said to Him, "Lord, show us the Father, and it is sufficient for us."
9 Jesus said to him, "Have I been with you so long, and yet you have not known Me, Philip? He who has seen Me has seen the Father; so how can you say, 'Show us the Father'?
10 "Do you not believe that I am in the Father, and the Father in Me? The words that I speak to you I do not speak on My own *authority*; but the Father who dwells in Me does the works.
11 "Believe Me that I *am* in the Father and the Father in Me, or else believe Me for the sake of the works themselves.

The Answered Prayer

12 "Most assuredly, I say to you, he who believes in Me, the works that I do he will do also; and greater *works* than these he will do, because I go to My Father.
13 "And whatever you ask in My name, that I will do, that the Father may be glorified in the Son.
14 "If you ask[79] anything in My name, I will do *it.*

Jesus Promises Another Helper

15 "If you love Me, keep[80] My commandments.
16 "And I will pray the Father, and He will give you another Helper, that He may abide with you forever,

---

77 Literally *dwellings*
78 NU-Text adds a word which would cause the text to read either *if it were not so, would I have told you that I go to prepare a place for you?* or *if it were not so I would have told you; for I go to prepare a place for you.*
79 NU-Text adds *Me.*   80 NU-Text reads *you will keep.*

In My Father's House

There were many kinds of dwellings in the biblical world. Some people lived in tents, others in caves, but most lived in houses built of stone, commonly referred to as the house or *beit (beth)*. The meaning of the Hebrew word *beth* goes far beyond a mere shelter or protection from the elements. The house is a place for love and sharing, for meals and making peace with enemies, for hosting guests while deepening love and friendship among family members.

Whenever a new house is built or a family moves, it is a festive occasion, full of feasting and rejoicing. But before the actual move into the new house takes place, it is customary for the owner or head of the family to go to the house first to prepare everything. All the rooms for each member of the family must be perfectly in order. Then the head family member brings everyone together into the new house.

Jesus refers to this custom when He speaks of our future with Him in heaven. "In My Father's house are many mansions; if *it were* not *so,* I would have told you. I go to prepare a place for you . . . I will come again and receive you to Myself; that where I am, *there* you may be also" (John 14:2, 3).

The disciples traveling with Jesus undoubtedly were exposed to the itinerant life-style of their teacher. How refreshing it must have been for them to hear that Jesus was providing a true place of rest and care for them!

This promise is directed to us as well, for Jesus confirmed that our future with Him is secure. Our coming home will be much celebrated with rejoicing when we meet our Lord and heavenly Father in our new home. Jesus Himself will come to receive us. Until then, let us live joyously and confidently, expectant of the time when Jesus will bring us to our eternal home.

17 *"even* the Spirit of truth, whom the world cannot receive, because it neither sees Him nor knows Him; but you know Him, for He dwells with you and will be in you.
18 "I will not leave you orphans; I will come to you.

Indwelling of the Father and the Son

19 "A little while longer and the world will see Me no more, but you will see Me. Because I live, you will live also.
20 "At that day you will know that I *am* in My Father, and you in Me, and I in you.
21 "He who has My commandments and keeps them, it is he who loves Me. And he who loves Me will be loved by My Father, and I will love him and manifest Myself to him."
22 Judas (not Iscariot) said to Him, "Lord, how is it that You will manifest Yourself to us, and not to the world?"
23 Jesus answered and said to him, "If anyone loves Me, he will keep My word; and My Father will love him, and We will come to him and make Our home with him.
24 "He who does not love Me does not keep My words; and the word which you hear is not Mine but the Father's who sent Me.

The Gift of His Peace

25 "These things I have spoken to you while being present with you.
26 "But the Helper, the Holy Spirit, whom the Father will send in My name, He will teach you all things, and bring to your remembrance all things that I said to you.
27 "Peace I leave with you, My peace I give to you; not as the world gives do I give to you. Let not your heart be troubled, neither let it be afraid.
28 "You have heard Me say to you, 'I am going away and coming *back* to you.' If you loved Me, you would rejoice because I said,[81] 'I am going to the Father,' for My Father is greater than I.
29 "And now I have told you before it comes, that when it does come to pass, you may believe.
30 "I will no longer talk much with you, for the ruler of this world is coming, and he has nothing in Me.

31 "But that the world may know that I love the Father, and as the Father gave Me commandment, so I do. Arise, let us go from here.

The True Vine

15 "I am the true vine, and My Father is the vinedresser.
2 "Every branch in Me that does not bear fruit He takes away; and every *branch* that bears fruit He prunes, that it may bear more fruit.
3 "You are already clean because of the word which I have spoken to you.
4 "Abide in Me, and I in you. As the branch cannot bear fruit of itself, unless it abides in the vine, neither can you, unless you abide in Me.
5 "I am the vine, you *are* the branches. He who abides in Me, and I in him, bears much fruit; for without Me you can do nothing.
6 "If anyone does not abide in Me, he is cast out as a branch and is withered; and they gather them and throw *them* into the fire, and they are burned.
7 "If you abide in Me, and My words abide in you, you will[82] ask what you desire, and it shall be done for you.
8 "By this My Father is glorified, that you bear much fruit; so you will be My disciples.

Love and Joy Perfected

9 "As the Father loved Me, I also have loved you; abide in My love.
10 "If you keep My commandments, you will abide in My love, just as I have kept My Father's commandments and abide in His love.
11 "These things I have spoken to you, that My joy may remain in you, and *that* your joy may be full.
12 "This is My commandment, that you love one another as I have loved you.
13 "Greater love has no one than this, than to lay down one's life for his friends.
14 "You are My friends if you do whatever I command you.
15 "No longer do I call you servants, for a servant does not know what his master is doing; but I have called you friends, for all things that I heard from My Father I have made known to you.
16 "You did not choose Me, but I chose you and appointed you that you should go and bear fruit, and *that* your fruit

---

81 NU-Text omits *I said.*   82 NU-Text omits *you will.*

The Vineyard
and the Vinedresser

When the biblical vinedresser prepared to plant his field, he found a use for everything. First he cleared the rocky Judean soil of stones and thistles. These stones were built into a watchtower and protective wall enclosing the field. The thorns were then placed on top of the wall, serving as a natural barbed wire to keep wild animals out.

The vineyards in Palestine are unlike those often seen today growing on trellises above the ground. Instead, the vines grow along the surface of the earth. In the warm spring and early summer months, the vine cannot depend on rainfall for its water. Only in the early morning hours is there enough moisture available from the night's dew to water the plants. However, once the sun rises high overhead, the ground quickly cracks and dries before the water has soaked in.

To ensure that the vine has sufficient water, the vinedresser will lift up the vine and support it with a rock. In doing so, the vinedresser allows the morning moisture to seep into the ground under the vine. The plant then shades the earth from the sun to enable the water to completely soak in. Some of the branches are naturally arched and curved to allow this process without the support of rocks. Others are heavy and must be cut back to prevent the branches from crushing the fruit. Jesus illustrates this process in John 15. "I am the true vine, and My Father is the vinedresser. Every branch in Me that does not bear fruit He takes away; and every *branch* that bears fruit He prunes, that it may bear more fruit" (John 15:1, 2).

The Greek word is translated "takes away" which would then refer to the death of an unfruitful believer or the eventual judgment of his labors (v. 6). This Greek word can also be translated "lifts up" which would then indicate the vinedresser's activities. This correlates perfectly with the ministry that Jesus has as He builds us up until we are able to bear fruit as vital Christians.

Jesus is the vine, and we are the branches. When we, for whatever reason, do not have the strength, knowledge, or maturity to bear fruit, He lifts us up. He supports us so we can bear fruit. And when we are heavy with this fruit, He prunes us of the negative influences in life so we can bear more fruit. What is this fruit? Jesus explains at the end of His parable. "Go and bear fruit, and *that* your fruit should remain . . . These things I command you, that you love one another" (John 15:16, 17).

should remain, that whatever you ask the Father in My name He may give you.
17 "These things I command you, that you love one another.

The World's Hatred

18 "If the world hates you, you know that it hated Me before *it hated* you.
19 "If you were of the world, the world would love its own. Yet because you are not of the world, but I chose you out of the world, therefore the world hates you.
20 "Remember the word that I said to you, 'A servant is not greater than his master.' If they persecuted Me, they will also persecute you. If they kept My word, they will keep yours also.
21 "But all these things they will do to you for My name's sake, because they do not know Him who sent Me.
22 "If I had not come and spoken to them, they would have no sin, but now they have no excuse for their sin.
23 "He who hates Me hates My Father also.
24 "If I had not done among them the works which no one else did, they would have no sin; but now they have seen and also hated both Me and My Father.
25 "But *this happened* that the word might be fulfilled which is written in their law, 'They hated Me without a cause.'[83]

The Coming Rejection

26 "But when the Helper comes, whom I shall send to you from the Father, the Spirit of truth who proceeds from the Father, He will testify of Me.
27 "And you also will bear witness, because you have been with Me from the beginning.

16 "These things I have spoken to you, that you should not be made to stumble.
2 "They will put you out of the synagogues; yes, the time is coming that whoever kills you will think that he offers God service.
3 "And these things they will do to you[84] because they have not known the Father nor Me.
4 "But these things I have told you, that when the[85] time comes, you may remember that I told you of them. And these things I did not say to you at the beginning, because I was with you.

The Work of the Holy Spirit

5 "But now I go away to Him who sent Me, and none of you asks Me, 'Where are You going?'
6 "But because I have said these things to you, sorrow has filled your heart.
7 "Nevertheless I tell you the truth. It is to your advantage that I go away; for if I do not go away, the Helper will not come to you; but if I depart, I will send Him to you.
8 "And when He has come, He will convict the world of sin, and of righteousness, and of judgment:
9 "of sin, because they do not believe in Me;
10 "of righteousness, because I go to My Father and you see Me no more;
11 "of judgment, because the ruler of this world is judged.
12 "I still have many things to say to you, but you cannot bear *them* now.
13 "However, when He, the Spirit of truth, has come, He will guide you into all truth; for He will not speak on His own *authority*, but whatever He hears He will speak; and He will tell you things to come.
14 "He will glorify Me, for He will take of what is Mine and declare *it* to you.
15 "All things that the Father has are Mine. Therefore I said that He will take of Mine and declare *it* to you.[86]

Sorrow Will Turn to Joy

16 "A little while, and you will not see Me; and again a little while, and you will see Me, because I go to the Father."
17 Then *some* of His disciples said among themselves, "What is this that He says to us, 'A little while, and you will not see Me'; and again a little while, and you will see Me'; and, 'because I go to the Father'?"
18 They said therefore, "What is this that He says, 'A little while'? We do not know what He is saying."
19 Now Jesus knew that they desired to ask Him, and He said to them, "Are you inquiring among yourselves about what I said, 'A little while, and you will not see Me; and again a little while, and you will see Me'?
20 "Most assuredly, I say to you that you will weep and lament, but the world will

---

83 Psalm 69:4   84 NU-Text and M-Text omit *to you.*   85 NU-Text reads *their.*
86 NU-Text and M-Text read *He takes of mine and will declare it to you.*

rejoice; and you will be sorrowful, but your sorrow will be turned into joy.
21 "A woman, when she is in labor, has sorrow because her hour has come; but as soon as she has given birth to the child, she no longer remembers the anguish, for joy that a human being has been born into the world.
22 "Therefore you now have sorrow; but I will see you again and your heart will rejoice, and your joy no one will take from you.
23 "And in that day you will ask Me nothing. Most assuredly, I say to you, whatever you ask the Father in My name He will give you.
24 "Until now you have asked nothing in My name. Ask, and you will receive, that your joy may be full.

Jesus Christ Has Overcome the World

25 "These things I have spoken to you in figurative language; but the time is coming when I will no longer speak to you in figurative language, but I will tell you plainly about the Father.
26 "In that day you will ask in My name, and I do not say to you that I shall pray the Father for you;
27 "for the Father Himself loves you, because you have loved Me, and have believed that I came forth from God.
28 "I came forth from the Father and have come into the world. Again, I leave the world and go to the Father."
29 His disciples said to Him, "See, now You are speaking plainly, and using no figure of speech!
30 "Now we are sure that You know all things, and have no need that anyone should question You. By this we believe that You came forth from God."
31 Jesus answered them, "Do you now believe?
32 "Indeed the hour is coming, yes, has now come, that you will be scattered, each to his own, and will leave Me alone. And yet I am not alone, because the Father is with Me.
33 "These things I have spoken to you, that in Me you may have peace. In the world you will[87] have tribulation; but be of good cheer, I have overcome the world."

Jesus Prays for Himself

17 Jesus spoke these words, lifted up His eyes to heaven, and said: "Father, the hour has come. Glorify Your Son, that Your Son also may glorify You,
2 "as You have given Him authority over all flesh, that He should[88] give eternal life to as many as You have given Him.
3 "And this is eternal life, that they may know You, the only true God, and Jesus Christ whom You have sent.
4 "I have glorified You on the earth. I have finished the work which You have given Me to do.
5 "And now, O Father, glorify Me together with Yourself, with the glory which I had with You before the world was.

Jesus Prays for His Disciples

6 "I have manifested Your name to the men whom You have given Me out of the world. They were Yours, You gave them to Me, and they have kept Your word.
7 "Now they have known that all things which You have given Me are from You.
8 "For I have given to them the words which You have given Me; and they have received *them*, and have known surely that I came forth from You; and they have believed that You sent Me.
9 "I pray for them. I do not pray for the world but for those whom You have given Me, for they are Yours.
10 "And all Mine are Yours, and Yours are Mine, and I am glorified in them.
11 "Now I am no longer in the world, but these are in the world, and I come to You. Holy Father, keep through Your name those whom You have given Me,[89] that they may be one as We *are*.
12 "While I was with them in the world,[90] I kept them in Your name. Those whom You gave Me I have kept;[91] and none of them is lost except the son of perdition, that the Scripture might be fulfilled.
13 "But now I come to You, and these things I speak in the world, that they may have My joy fulfilled in themselves.
14 "I have given them Your word; and the world has hated them because they are not of the world, just as I am not of the world.

---

87 NU-Text and M-Text omit *will.*   88 M-Text reads *shall.*
89 NU-Text and M-Text read *keep them through Your name which You have given Me.*
90 NU-Text omits *in the world.*   91 NU-Text reads *in Your name which You gave me. And I guarded them* (or *it*).

15 "I do not pray that You should take them out of the world, but that You should keep them from the evil *one*.
16 "They are not of the world, just as I am not of the world.
17 "Sanctify them by Your truth. Your word is truth.
18 "As You sent Me into the world, I also have sent them into the world.
19 "And for their sakes I sanctify Myself, that they also may be sanctified by the truth.

Jesus Prays for All Believers

20 "I do not pray for these alone, but also for those who will[92] believe in Me through their word;
21 "that they all may be one, as You, Father, *are* in Me, and I in You; that they also may be one in Us, that the world may believe that You sent Me.
22 "And the glory which You gave Me I have given them, that they may be one just as We are one:
23 "I in them, and You in Me; that they may be made perfect in one, and that the world may know that You have sent Me, and have loved them as You have loved Me.
24 "Father, I desire that they also whom You gave Me may be with Me where I am, that they may behold My glory which You have given Me; for You loved Me before the foundation of the world.
25 "O righteous Father! The world has not known You, but I have known You; and these have known that You sent Me.
26 "And I have declared to them Your name, and will declare *it*, that the love with which You loved Me may be in them, and I in them."

Betrayal and Arrest in Gethsemane

18 When Jesus had spoken these words, He went out with His disciples over the Brook Kidron, where there was a garden, which He and His disciples entered.
2 And Judas, who betrayed Him, also knew the place; for Jesus often met there with His disciples.
3 Then Judas, having received a detachment *of troops*, and officers from the chief priests and Pharisees, came there with lanterns, torches, and weapons.
4 Jesus therefore, knowing all things that would come upon Him, went for-

ward and said to them, "Whom are you seeking?"
5 They answered Him, "Jesus of Nazareth." Jesus said to them, "I am *He*." And Judas, who betrayed Him, also stood with them.
6 Then—when He said to them, "I am *He*,"—they drew back and fell to the ground.
7 Then He asked them again, "Whom are you seeking?" And they said, "Jesus of Nazareth."
8 Jesus answered, "I have told you that I am *He*. Therefore, if you seek Me, let these go their way,"
9 that the saying might be fulfilled which He spoke, "Of those whom You gave Me I have lost none."
10 Then Simon Peter, having a sword, drew it and struck the high priest's servant, and cut off his right ear. The servant's name was Malchus.
11 Then Jesus said to Peter, "Put your sword into the sheath. Shall I not drink the cup which My Father has given Me?"

Before the High Priest

12 Then the detachment *of troops* and the captain and the officers of the Jews arrested Jesus and bound Him.
13 And they led Him away to Annas first, for he was the father-in-law of Caiaphas who was high priest that year.
14 Now it was Caiaphas who gave counsel to the Jews that it was expedient that one man should die for the people.

Peter Denies Jesus

15 And Simon Peter followed Jesus, and so *did* another[93] disciple. Now that disciple was known to the high priest, and went with Jesus into the courtyard of the high priest.
16 But Peter stood at the door outside. Then the other disciple, who was known to the high priest, went out and spoke to her who kept the door, and brought Peter in.
17 Then the servant girl who kept the door said to Peter, "You are not also *one* of this Man's disciples, are you?" He said, "I am not."
18 And the servants and officers who had made a fire of coals stood there, for it was cold, and they warmed themselves. And Peter stood with them and warmed himself.

92 NU-Text and M-Text omit *will*.   93 M-Text reads *the other*.

Peter—Denial to Declaration

On the evening of Jesus Christ's trial and crucifixion, the apostle Peter was in a severe state of depression. Hours earlier, Peter had boldly asserted that he would never deny his Master. Yet later, during Christ's trial, Peter sat crouching in fear, warming himself by a fire. A servant of the high priest's court approached Peter and for the third time asked if he knew Jesus. Peter flatly denied his Lord. Upon his denial, Jesus looked at Peter. Their eyes met, and Peter ran out weeping bitterly.

The house of Caiaphas, the High Priest, the scene of Jesus' trial before the Sanhedrin, has been unearthed in Jerusalem. The find included many coins, including both Roman and those used exclusively in the temple. A major thoroughfare ran through the courtyard where Jesus was tried. Hebrew inscriptions including the word *corban* meaning "sacrificial gift" were found etched above the lintel of the door. It was in this courtyard that Peter denied Jesus.

For many years Peter had stood by Jesus. He left his fishing nets to follow his Lord wholeheartedly. He stood up for Christ many times in many places before many people. Even hours earlier in the Garden of Gethsemane, Peter boldly was ready to fight for Him. Yet when Jesus was in His most desperate hour of need, Peter abandoned Him.

The emotional scars left on Peter's life must have been devastating. Yet within forty days Peter stood in the Jerusalem temple proclaiming Jesus before three thousand people. This speech took place only one hundred yards from where he had flatly denied Christ as his Lord and Savior. What happened? Why the change in Peter? Three days after Peter's denial, the young fisherman witnessed the risen Christ. Jesus' love and forgiveness freed Peter from the emotional scars seared upon his heart. God's love demonstrated through the cross enabled Peter to turn his scar into a star!

Many times we may deny Jesus, unintentionally or willfully, choosing not to include Him in our lives. But we are assured with confidence that Jesus Christ has given us His kingdom. There is no sin too great, too severe, or too scary to separate us from the love of God.

Let Jesus Christ's love turn your scar into a star. Turn your denials into declarations of His love and forgiveness for all mankind. Then like Peter, go and proclaim boldly what your Lord has done!

Jesus Questioned by the High Priest

19 The high priest then asked Jesus about His disciples and His doctrine.
20 Jesus answered him, "I spoke openly to the world. I always taught in synagogues and in the temple, where the Jews always meet,94 and in secret I have said nothing.
21 "Why do you ask Me? Ask those who have heard Me what I said to them. Indeed they know what I said."
22 And when He had said these things, one of the officers who stood by struck Jesus with the palm of his hand, saying, "Do You answer the high priest like that?"
23 Jesus answered him, "If I have spoken evil, bear witness of the evil; but if well, why do you strike Me?"
24 Then Annas sent Him bound to Caiaphas the high priest.

Peter Denies Twice More

25 Now Simon Peter stood and warmed himself. Therefore they said to him, "You are not also *one* of His disciples, are you?" He denied *it* and said, "I am not!"
26 One of the servants of the high priest, a relative *of him* whose ear Peter cut off, said, "Did I not see you in the garden with Him?"
27 Peter then denied again; and immediately a rooster crowed.

In Pilate's Court

28 Then they led Jesus from Caiaphas to the Praetorium, and it was early morning. But they themselves did not go into the Praetorium, lest they should be defiled, but that they might eat the Passover.
29 Pilate then went out to them and said, "What accusation do you bring against this Man?"
30 They answered and said to him, "If He were not an evildoer, we would not have delivered Him up to you."
31 Then Pilate said to them, "You take Him and judge Him according to your law." Therefore the Jews said to him, "It is not lawful for us to put anyone to death,"
32 that the saying of Jesus might be fulfilled which He spoke, signifying by what death He would die.
33 Then Pilate entered the Praetorium again, called Jesus, and said to Him, "Are You the King of the Jews?"

34 Jesus answered him, "Are you speaking for yourself on this, or did others tell you this about Me?"
35 Pilate answered, "Am I a Jew? Your own nation and the chief priests have delivered You to me. What have You done?"
36 Jesus answered, "My kingdom is not of this world. If My kingdom were of this world, My servants would fight, so that I should not be delivered to the Jews; but now My kingdom is not from here."
37 Pilate therefore said to Him, "Are You a king then?" Jesus answered, "You say *rightly* that I am a king. For this cause I was born, and for this cause I have come into the world, that I should bear witness to the truth. Everyone who is of the truth hears My voice."
38 Pilate said to Him, "What is truth?" And when he had said this, he went out again to the Jews, and said to them, "I find no fault in Him *at all*.

Taking the Place of Barabbas

39 "But you have a custom that I should release someone to you at the Passover. Do you therefore want me to release to you the King of the Jews?"
40 Then they all cried again, saying, "Not this Man, but Barabbas!" Now Barabbas was a robber.

The Soldiers Mock Jesus

19 So then Pilate took Jesus and scourged *Him.*
2 And the soldiers twisted a crown of thorns and put *it* on His head, and they put on Him a purple robe.
3 Then they said,95 "Hail, King of the Jews!" And they struck Him with their hands.
4 Pilate then went out again, and said to them, "Behold, I am bringing Him out to you, that you may know that I find no fault in Him."

Pilate's Decision

5 Then Jesus came out, wearing the crown of thorns and the purple robe. And *Pilate* said to them, "Behold the Man!"
6 Therefore, when the chief priests and officers saw Him, they cried out, saying, "Crucify *Him*, crucify *Him!*" Pilate said to them, "You take Him and crucify *Him*, for I find no fault in Him."

94 NU-Text reads *where all the Jews meet.*   95 NU-Text reads *And they came up to Him and said.*

7 The Jews answered him, "We have a law, and according to our[96] law He ought to die, because He made Himself the Son of God."

8 Therefore, when Pilate heard that saying, he was the more afraid,

9 and went again into the Praetorium, and said to Jesus, "Where are You from?" But Jesus gave him no answer.

10 Then Pilate said to Him, "Are You not speaking to me? Do You not know that I have power to crucify You, and power to release You?"

11 Jesus answered, "You could have no power at all against Me unless it had been given you from above. Therefore the one who delivered Me to you has the greater sin."

12 From then on Pilate sought to release Him, but the Jews cried out, saying, "If you let this Man go, you are not Caesar's friend. Whoever makes himself a king speaks against Caesar."

13 When Pilate therefore heard that saying, he brought Jesus out and sat down in the judgment seat in a place that is called The Pavement, but in Hebrew, Gabbatha.

14 Now it was the Preparation Day of the Passover, and about the sixth hour. And he said to the Jews, "Behold your King!"

15 But they cried out, "Away with Him, away with Him! Crucify Him!" Pilate said to them, "Shall I crucify your King?" The chief priests answered, "We have no king but Caesar!"

16 So he delivered Him to them to be crucified. So they took Jesus and led Him away.[97]

The King on a Cross

17 And He, bearing His cross, went out to a place called the Place of a Skull, which is called in Hebrew, Golgotha,

18 where they crucified Him, and two others with Him, one on either side, and Jesus in the center.

19 Now Pilate wrote a title and put it on the cross. And the writing was:

JESUS OF NAZARETH, THE KING OF THE JEWS.

20 Then many of the Jews read this title, for the place where Jesus was crucified was near the city; and it was written in Hebrew, Greek, and Latin.

21 Then the chief priests of the Jews said to Pilate, "Do not write, 'The King of the Jews,' but, 'He said, "I am the King of the Jews."'"

22 Pilate answered, "What I have written, I have written."

23 Then the soldiers, when they had crucified Jesus, took His garments and made four parts, to each soldier a part, and also the tunic. Now the tunic was without seam, woven from the top in one piece.

24 They said therefore among themselves, "Let us not tear it, but cast lots for it, whose it shall be," that the Scripture might be fulfilled which says:

"They divided My garments among them,
And for My clothing they cast lots."[98]

Therefore the soldiers did these things.

Behold Your Mother

25 Now there stood by the cross of Jesus His mother, and His mother's sister, Mary the wife of Clopas, and Mary Magdalene.

26 When Jesus therefore saw His mother, and the disciple whom He loved standing by, He said to His mother, "Woman, behold your son!"

27 Then He said to the disciple, "Behold your mother!" And from that hour that disciple took her to his own home.

It Is Finished

28 After this, Jesus, knowing[99] that all things were now accomplished, that the Scripture might be fulfilled, said, "I thirst!"

29 Now a vessel full of sour wine was sitting there; and they filled a sponge with sour wine, put it on hyssop, and put it to His mouth.

30 So when Jesus had received the sour wine, He said, "It is finished!" And bowing His head, He gave up His spirit.

Jesus' Side Is Pierced

31 Therefore, because it was the Preparation Day, that the bodies should not remain on the cross on the Sabbath (for that Sabbath was a high day), the Jews asked Pilate that their legs might be broken, and that they might be taken away.

32 Then the soldiers came and broke the legs of the first and of the other who was crucified with Him.

---

96 NU-Text reads the law.   97 NU-Text omits and led Him away.   98 Psalm 22:18   99 M-Text reads seeing.

33 But when they came to Jesus and saw that He was already dead, they did not break His legs.
34 But one of the soldiers pierced His side with a spear, and immediately blood and water came out.
35 And he who has seen has testified, and his testimony is true; and he knows that he is telling the truth, so that you may believe.
36 For these things were done that the Scripture should be fulfilled, *"Not one of His bones shall be broken."*[100]
37 And again another Scripture says, *"They shall look on Him whom they pierced."*[101]

Jesus Buried in Joseph's Tomb

38 After this, Joseph of Arimathea, being a disciple of Jesus, but secretly, for fear of the Jews, asked Pilate that he might take away the body of Jesus; and Pilate gave *him* permission. So he came and took the body of Jesus.
39 And Nicodemus, who at first came to Jesus by night, also came, bringing a mixture of myrrh and aloes, about a hundred pounds.
40 Then they took the body of Jesus, and bound it in strips of linen with the spices, as the custom of the Jews is to bury.
41 Now in the place where He was crucified there was a garden, and in the garden a new tomb in which no one had yet been laid.
42 So there they laid Jesus, because of the Jews' Preparation *Day,* for the tomb was nearby.

The Empty Tomb

20 On the first *day* of the week Mary Magdalene came to the tomb early, while it was still dark, and saw *that* the stone had been taken away from the tomb.
2 Then she ran and came to Simon Peter, and to the other disciple, whom Jesus loved, and said to them, "They have taken away the Lord out of the tomb, and we do not know where they have laid Him."
3 Peter therefore went out, and the other disciple, and were going to the tomb.
4 So they both ran together, and the other disciple outran Peter and came to the tomb first.
5 And he, stooping down and looking in, saw the linen cloths lying *there*; yet he did not go in.
6 Then Simon Peter came, following him, and went into the tomb; and he saw the linen cloths lying *there*,
7 and the handkerchief that had been around His head, not lying with the linen cloths, but folded together in a place by itself.
8 Then the other disciple, who came to the tomb first, went in also; and he saw and believed.
9 For as yet they did not know the Scripture, that He must rise again from the dead.
10 Then the disciples went away again to their own homes.

Mary Magdalene Sees the Risen Lord

11 But Mary stood outside by the tomb weeping, and as she wept she stooped down *and looked* into the tomb.
12 And she saw two angels in white sitting, one at the head and the other at the feet, where the body of Jesus had lain.
13 Then they said to her, "Woman, why are you weeping?" She said to them, "Because they have taken away my Lord, and I do not know where they have laid Him."
14 Now when she had said this, she turned around and saw Jesus standing *there*, and did not know that it was Jesus.
15 Jesus said to her, "Woman, why are you weeping? Whom are you seeking?" She, supposing Him to be the gardener, said to Him, "Sir, if You have carried Him away, tell me where You have laid Him, and I will take Him away."
16 Jesus said to her, "Mary!" She turned and said to Him,[102] "Rabboni!" (which is to say, Teacher).
17 Jesus said to her, "Do not cling to Me, for I have not yet ascended to My Father; but go to My brethren and say to them, 'I am ascending to My Father and your Father, and *to* My God and your God.' "
18 Mary Magdalene came and told the disciples that she had seen the Lord,[103] and *that* He had spoken these things to her.

100 Exodus 12:46; Numbers 9:12; Psalm 34:20   101 Zechariah 12:10   102 NU-Text adds *in Hebrew.*
103 NU-Text reads *disciples, "I have seen the Lord."*...

Where Jesus Lay

North of the city of Jerusalem are the famous Sanhedrin tombs, hewn out of the chalky mountainside. Over seventy of these tombs, traditionally thought to be the burial place of the Jewish Sanhedrin, have been unearthed. Each dates to the era of Christ. The unique style of these tombs represents the burial architecture of the Jewish people in the first century. This style lasted only a short time. The design fits exactly the description of the tomb of Jesus Christ as recorded in the Scriptures.

The Gospels report that on the first Easter morning, John and Peter went to the tomb. John stooped to look into the tomb, while Peter impetuously ran inside. Entrance into the Sanhedrin tombs also requires one to stoop down to enter the two-to-three-foot opening. Tombs before and after Jesus' time were constructed differently, with larger openings. Sealed with a two-ton stone, this entryway leads to a ten-foot-square chamber, where waist-high slabs surround each side of the walls. Here the bodies were placed to be anointed. On each side of the tomb were individual mausoleums where the bodies were permanently placed after the anointing process.

The literally accurate description of Jesus' tomb is strong,contemporary,eyewitness evidence of the empty tomb. The resurrection account continues, reporting that Mary Magdalene saw angels sitting one at the head and the other at the feet of where Jesus had lain (John 20:11–13). Since the women had not finished anointing the body, most likely the angels were located at the foot and head of the slabs of the inner chamber. Jesus' grave clothes were neatly rolled and folded, separate from the head cloth on these slabs.

It is a recorded fact that Jesus was buried in the tomb of Joseph of Arimathea, a member of the Sanhedrin. Another Sanhedrin member, Nicodemus, also helped in the burial process. Not all Jews, including the religious leaders, wanted to see Jesus crucified. From this account, we understand that some actually served the Lord in a most unusual way. By burying Jesus, Nicodemus and Joseph of Arimathea risked ridicule, slander, and excommunication. Their courage and belief were great.

The cords of death could not hold the power of God. On the third day, Jesus rose again. The empty tomb is the greatest witness of the deity and victory of Jesus Christ. With faith we can go and proclaim what the angel told the women that first Easter morning, "He is not here; for He is risen, as He said" (Matt. 28:6). Like Nicodemus and Joseph of Arimathea, let us have courage to serve our Lord in unique and unusual ways.

The Apostles Commissioned

19 Then, the same day at evening, being the first *day* of the week, when the doors were shut where the disciples were assembled,[104] for fear of the Jews, Jesus came and stood in the midst, and said to them, "Peace *be* with you." **20** Now when He had said this, He showed them *His* hands and His side. Then the disciples were glad when they saw the Lord. **21** Then Jesus said to them again, "Peace to you! As the Father has sent Me, I also send you." **22** And when He had said this, He breathed on *them*, and said to them, "Receive the Holy Spirit. **23** "If you forgive the sins of any, they are forgiven them; if you retain the *sins* of any, they are retained."

Seeing and Believing

24 But Thomas, called Didymus, one of the twelve, was not with them when Jesus came. **25** The other disciples therefore said to him, "We have seen the Lord." But he said to them, "Unless I see in His hands the print of the nails, and put my finger into the print of the nails, and put my hand into His side, I will not believe." **26** And after eight days His disciples were again inside, and Thomas with them. Jesus came, the doors being shut, and stood in the midst, and said, "Peace to you!" **27** Then He said to Thomas, "Reach your finger here, and look at My hands; and reach your hand *here*, and put *it* into My side. Do not be unbelieving, but believing." **28** And Thomas answered and said to Him, "My Lord and my God!" **29** Jesus said to him, "Thomas,[105] because you have seen Me, you have believed. Blessed *are* those who have not seen and *yet* have believed."

That You May Believe

30 And truly Jesus did many other signs in the presence of His disciples, which are not written in this book; **31** but these are written that you may believe that Jesus is the Christ, the Son of God, and that believing you may have life in His name.

Breakfast by the Sea

21 After these things Jesus showed Himself again to the disciples at the Sea of Tiberias, and in this way He showed *Himself*: **2** Simon Peter, Thomas called Didymus, Nathanael of Cana in Galilee, the *sons* of Zebedee, and two others of His disciples were together. **3** Simon Peter said to them, "I am going fishing." They said to him, "We are going with you also." They went out and immediately[106] got into the boat, and that night they caught nothing. **4** But when the morning had now come, Jesus stood on the shore; yet the disciples did not know that it was Jesus. **5** Then Jesus said to them, "Children, have you any food?" They answered Him, "No." **6** And He said to them, "Cast the net on the right side of the boat, and you will find *some*." So they cast, and now they were not able to draw it in because of the multitude of fish. **7** Therefore that disciple whom Jesus loved said to Peter, "It is the Lord!" Now when Simon Peter heard that it was the Lord, he put on *his* outer garment (for he had removed it), and plunged into the sea. **8** But the other disciples came in the little boat (for they were not far from land, but about two hundred cubits), dragging the net with fish. **9** Then, as soon as they had come to land, they saw a fire of coals there, and fish laid on it, and bread. **10** Jesus said to them, "Bring some of the fish which you have just caught." **11** Simon Peter went up and dragged the net to land, full of large fish, one hundred and fifty-three; and although there were so many, the net was not broken. **12** Jesus said to them, "Come *and* eat breakfast." Yet none of the disciples dared ask Him, "Who are You?"—knowing that it was the Lord. **13** Jesus then came and took the bread and gave it to them, and likewise the fish. **14** This *is* now the third time Jesus showed Himself to His disciples after He was raised from the dead.

Jesus Restores Peter

15 So when they had eaten breakfast, Jesus said to Simon Peter, "Simon, *son of*

---

104 NU-Text omits *assembled*.   105 NU-Text and M-Text omit *Thomas*.   106 NU-Text omits *immediately*.

Believe It Before You See It

The apostle Thomas has often been criticized for his lack of faith concerning the resurrection of Jesus Christ. During one of Jesus' resurrection appearances, He came to the disciples when they were hiding together in a room in Jerusalem. Thomas was not present. Later the disciples told Thomas of what they had seen. Thomas boldly declared, "Unless I see in His hands the print of the nails, and put my finger into the print of the nails, and put my hand into His side, I will not believe" (John 20:25). Thomas was a man of conviction.

Eight days later, Jesus again appeared to the disciples still in hiding. Only this time Thomas was present. Jesus said to Thomas, " 'Reach your finger here, and look at My hands; and reach your hand *here*, and put *it* into My side. Do not be unbelieving, but believing.' And Thomas answered and said to Him, 'My Lord and my God!' Jesus said to him, 'Thomas, because you have seen Me, you have believed. Blessed *are* those who have not seen and *yet* have believed' " (John 20:27–29).

A characteristic of Thomas has often been overlooked. Earlier in Jesus' ministry, when He faced mounting resistance from Jewish leaders in Jerusalem, all of the disciples tried to persuade Him not to return to Judea. Thomas was the only disciple who boldly proclaimed, "Let us also go, that we may die with Him" (John 11:16).

Thomas was willing to make a commitment and stick with it. The difficulty for Thomas was not his lack of faith in Jesus, but in his concrete thinking. When Jesus was alive and there was hope for a political messianic kingdom led by Jesus, Thomas was willing to die for His cause. But once Jesus was dead, Thomas's dream of freedom from the Roman overlords was finished. His locked-in thinking kept him from invisioning and believing an even greater kingdom.

Thomas teaches us not to pour our plans in concrete. Allow God to do the impossible in your life. Expect a miracle. Commit yourself completely as Thomas did. But do not allow locked-in thinking to keep you from anticipating the impossible. You have to believe it before you see it!

Jonah,[107] do you love Me more than these?" He said to Him, "Yes, Lord; You know that I love You." He said to him, "Feed My lambs."

16 He said to him again a second time, "Simon, *son* of Jonah,[107] do you love Me?" He said to Him, "Yes, Lord; You know that I love You." He said to him, "Tend My sheep."

17 He said to him the third time, "Simon, *son* of Jonah,[107] do you love Me?" Peter was grieved because He said to him the third time, "Do you love Me?" And he said to Him, "Lord, You know all things; You know that I love You." Jesus said to him, "Feed My sheep.

18 "Most assuredly, I say to you, when you were younger, you girded yourself and walked where you wished; but when you are old, you will stretch out your hands, and another will gird you and carry *you* where you do not wish."

19 This He spoke, signifying by what death he would glorify God. And when He had spoken this, He said to him, "Follow Me."

107 NU-Text reads *John.*

The Beloved Disciple and His Book

20 Then Peter, turning around, saw the disciple whom Jesus loved following, who also had leaned on His breast at the supper, and said, "Lord, who is the one who betrays You?"

21 Peter, seeing him, said to Jesus, "But Lord, what *about* this man?"

22 Jesus said to him, "If I will that he remain till I come, what *is that* to you? You follow Me."

23 Then this saying went out among the brethren that this disciple would not die. Yet Jesus did not say to him that he would not die, but, "If I will that he remain till I come, what *is that* to you?"

24 This is the disciple who testifies of these things, and wrote these things; and we know that his testimony is true.

25 And there are also many other things that Jesus did, which if they were written one by one, I suppose that even the world itself could not contain the books that would be written. Amen.

Introduction to Acts

The Book of Acts is one of the most fascinating accounts of the power of possibility thinking. When Jesus Christ instilled His spirit into the lives of twelve men, they went out to literally change the world!

Written in the early 60s A.D., Acts is the account of the initial spread of Christianity. It was written by Luke, the same author whose Gospel also bears his name. Luke gives a first-hand account of the events surrounding the early church. He personally accompanied Paul during several evangelistic trips through Syria, Asia Minor, Greece, and Rome where they planted and nourished many new churches. (This is indicated by the pronouns "we" or "us" found in Acts 16:10-17; 20:5—21:18; and 27:1—28:16.)

Luke writes this book to Christian Gentiles who were interested in this newly found faith. The book is addressed to Theophilus (Acts 1:1). This name (meaning "lover of God") could refer to an individual who wanted to know more about Christianity or to a people who truly loved God.

Acts presents the origin of our faith with extreme accuracy. Archaeologists confirm that Luke was among the most reliable historians of antiquity. A master of the Greek language, Luke gives the most detailed account of the early church of all the Gospels and Epistles.

Acts portrays the success of the gospel as it spread like wildfire from Jerusalem to Rome in only thirty years. In the face of persecution, the early church's growth and development is inspiring. Without Luke's account, our knowledge of the spread of Christianity would be much less. Numerous lists of cities, dates, events, persons, and their beliefs throughout the Roman empire are recorded here as nowhere else in the entire New Testament.

This is the epitomy of possibility thinking. It all began with twelve men and a few women who lived and walked with our Lord. Once afraid of their Roman overloads, these possibility thinkers caught the vision and spirit of God. Like a small spring that bursts forth into a mighty river, the message and love of Jesus Christ trickled down from the heights of Jerusalem and roared out to change the world forever!

The Acts
of the Apostles

Prologue

THE former account I made, O Theophilus, of all that Jesus began both to do and teach, 2 until the day in which He was taken up, after He through the Holy Spirit had given commandments to the apostles whom He had chosen, 3 to whom He also presented Himself alive after His suffering by many infallible proofs, being seen by them during forty days and speaking of the things pertaining to the kingdom of God.

The Holy Spirit Promised

4 And being assembled together with *them*, He commanded them not to depart from Jerusalem, but to wait for the Promise of the Father, "which," *He said*, "you have heard from Me; 5 "for John truly baptized with water, but you shall be baptized with the Holy Spirit not many days from now." 6 Therefore, when they had come together, they asked Him, saying, "Lord, will You at this time restore the kingdom to Israel?" 7 And He said to them, "It is not for you to know times or seasons which the Father has put in His own authority. 8 "But you shall receive power when the Holy Spirit has come upon you; and you shall be witnesses to Me[1] in Jerusalem, and in all Judea and Samaria, and to the end of the earth."

Jesus Ascends to Heaven

9 Now when He had spoken these things, while they watched, He was taken up, and a cloud received Him out of their sight. 10 And while they looked steadfastly toward heaven as He went up, behold, two men stood by them in white apparel, 11 who also said, "Men of Galilee, why do you stand gazing up into heaven? This *same* Jesus, who was taken up from you into heaven, will so come in like manner as you saw Him go into heaven."

The Upper Room Prayer Meeting

12 Then they returned to Jerusalem from the Mount called Olivet, which is near Jerusalem, a Sabbath day's journey. 13 And when they had entered, they went up into the upper room where they were staying: Peter, James, John, and Andrew; Philip and Thomas; Bartholomew and Matthew; James *the son* of Alphaeus and Simon the Zealot; and Judas *the son* of James. 14 These all continued with one accord in prayer and supplication,[2] with the women and Mary the mother of Jesus, and with His brothers.

Matthias Chosen

15 And in those days Peter stood up in the midst of the disciples[3] (altogether the number of names was about a hundred and twenty), and said, 16 "Men *and* brethren, this Scripture had to be fulfilled, which the Holy Spirit spoke before by the mouth of David concerning Judas, who became a guide to those who arrested Jesus; 17 "for he was numbered with us and obtained a part in this ministry." 18 (Now this man purchased a field with the wages of iniquity; and falling headlong, he burst open in the middle and all his entrails gushed out. 19 And it became known to all those dwelling in Jerusalem; so that field is called in their own language, Akel Dama, that is, Field of Blood.) 20 "For it is written in the book of Psalms:

'Let his habitation be desolate,
And let no one live in it';[4]

and,

'Let[5] another take his office.'[6]

21 "Therefore, of these men who have accompanied us all the time that the Lord Jesus went in and out among us, 22 "beginning from the baptism of John to that day when He was taken up from

1 NU-Text reads *My witnesses.*   2 NU-Text omits *and supplication.*   3 NU-Text reads *brethren.*   4 Psalm 69:25
5 Psalm 109:8   6 Greek *episkopen*

Go into All the World

During Jesus' ministry, He specifically told His disciples that, following His death and resurrection, they would see Him in Galilee. This was the place where Jesus spent a great deal of His early ministry. Galilee means "Circle" (of the nations). Here, the ancient world's highways crisscrossed to find outlets at the coastal cities of Phoenicia and the desert capitals of Ammon and Damascus. Galilee was the first place where Jesus began His ministry, healing the lame, making the blind to see, and curing all who were brought to Him.

Following Jesus' resurrection, the angel at the tomb told the disciples and the women to go into Galilee. There they would see Jesus. As these followers made their journey to Galilee, Jesus appeared to them on a high mountain. Through this resurrection appearance, Jesus completed the final victory over death in an area so known for its death-ridden history.

In the "Circle" (of the nations) Jesus commissioned His disciples to carry the good news of His resurrection and God's love and forgiveness to all lands, cultures, and peoples. That commission continues for us today. Like the first disciples, we can share our faith with all people. We have the same comforting promise that Jesus gave to His disciples before His ascension, "And lo, I am with you always" (Matt. 28:20).

us, one of these must become a witness with us of His resurrection."

23 And they proposed two: Joseph called Barsabas, who was surnamed Justus, and Matthias.

24 And they prayed and said, "You, O Lord, who know the hearts of all, show which of these two You have chosen

25 "to take part in this ministry and apostleship from which Judas by transgression fell, that he might go to his own place."

26 And they cast their lots, and the lot fell on Matthias. And he was numbered with the eleven apostles.

Coming of the Holy Spirit

2 Now when the Day of Pentecost had fully come, they were all with one accord[7] in one place.

2 And suddenly there came a sound from heaven, as of a rushing mighty wind, and it filled the whole house where they were sitting.

3 Then there appeared to them divided tongues, as of fire, and one sat upon each of them.

4 And they were all filled with the Holy Spirit and began to speak with other tongues, as the Spirit gave them utterance.

The Crowd's Response

5 Now there were dwelling in Jerusalem Jews, devout men, from every nation under heaven.

6 And when this sound occurred, the multitude came together, and were confused, because everyone heard them speak in his own language.

7 Then they were all amazed and marveled, saying to one another, "Look, are not all these who speak Galileans?

8 "And how is it that we hear, each in our own language in which we were born?

9 "Parthians and Medes and Elamites, those dwelling in Mesopotamia, Judea and Cappadocia, Pontus and Asia,

10 "Phrygia and Pamphylia, Egypt and the parts of Libya adjoining Cyrene, visitors from Rome, both Jews and proselytes,

11 "Cretans and Arabs—we hear them speaking in our own tongues the wonderful works of God."

12 So they were all amazed and perplexed, saying to one another, "Whatever could this mean?"

13 Others mocking said, "They are full of new wine."

Peter's Sermon

14 But Peter, standing up with the eleven, raised his voice and said to them, "Men of Judea and all who dwell in Jerusalem, let this be known to you, and heed my words.

15 "For these are not drunk, as you suppose, since it is only the third hour of the day.

16 "But this is what was spoken by the prophet Joel:

17 'And it shall come to pass in the last
     days, says God,
   That I will pour out of My Spirit
     on all flesh;
   Your sons and your daughters
     shall prophesy,
   Your young men shall see visions,
   Your old men shall dream dreams.
18 And on My menservants and on My
     maidservants
   I will pour out My Spirit in those days;
   And they shall prophesy.
19 I will show wonders in heaven above
   And signs in the earth beneath:
   Blood and fire and vapor of smoke.
20 The sun shall be turned into darkness,
   And the moon into blood,
   Before the coming of the great and
     notable day of the LORD.
21 And it shall come to pass that whoever
   calls on the name of the LORD shall
   be saved.'[8]

22 "Men of Israel, hear these words: Jesus of Nazareth, a Man attested by God to you by miracles, wonders, and signs which God did through Him in your midst, as you yourselves also know—

23 "Him, being delivered by the determined counsel and foreknowledge of God, you have taken[9] by lawless hands, have crucified, and put to death;

24 "whom God raised up, having loosed the pains of death, because it was not possible that He should be held by it.

25 "For David says concerning Him:

'I foresaw the LORD always
   before my face,
   For He is at my right hand,
     that I may not be shaken;

---

7 NU-Text reads together.   8 Joel 2:28–32   9 NU-Text omits have taken.

26 Therefore my heart rejoiced,
   and my tongue was glad;
   Moreover my flesh will also rest
   in hope,
27 Because You will not leave
   my soul in Hades,
   Nor will You allow Your Holy One
   to see corruption.
28 You have made known to me
   the ways of life;
   You will make me full of joy
   in Your presence.'¹⁰

29 "Men *and* brethren, let *me* speak freely to you of the patriarch David, that he is both dead and buried, and his tomb is with us to this day.
30 "Therefore, being a prophet, and knowing that God had sworn with an oath to him that of the fruit of his body, according to the flesh, He would raise up the Christ to sit on his throne,¹¹
31 "he, foreseeing this, spoke concerning the resurrection of the Christ, that His soul was not left in Hades, nor did His flesh see corruption.
32 "This Jesus God has raised up, of which we are all witnesses.
33 "Therefore being exalted to the right hand of God, and having received from the Father the promise of the Holy Spirit, He poured out this which you now see and hear.
34 "For David did not ascend into the heavens, but he says himself:

'The LORD said to my Lord,
"Sit at My right hand,
35 Till I make Your enemies Your
   footstool." '¹²

36 "Therefore let all the house of Israel know assuredly that God has made this Jesus, whom you crucified, both Lord and Christ."
37 Now when they heard *this*, they were cut to the heart, and said to Peter and the rest of the apostles, "Men *and* brethren, what shall we do?"
38 Then Peter said to them, "Repent, and let every one of you be baptized in the name of Jesus Christ for the remission of sins; and you shall receive the gift of the Holy Spirit.
39 "For the promise is to you and to your children, and to all who are afar off, as many as the Lord our God will call."

A Vital Church Grows

40 And with many other words he testified and exhorted them, saying, "Be saved from this perverse generation."
41 Then those who gladly¹³ received his word were baptized; and that day about three thousand souls were added *to them.*
42 And they continued steadfastly in the apostles' doctrine and fellowship, in the breaking of bread, and in prayers.
43 Then fear came upon every soul, and many wonders and signs were done through the apostles.
44 Now all who believed were together, and had all things in common,
45 and sold their possessions and goods, and divided them among all, as anyone had need.
46 So continuing daily with one accord in the temple, and breaking bread from house to house, they ate their food with gladness and simplicity of heart,
47 praising God and having favor with all the people. And the Lord added to the church¹⁴ daily those who were being saved.

A Lame Man Healed

3 Now Peter and John went up together to the temple at the hour of prayer, the ninth *hour.*
2 And a certain man lame from his mother's womb was carried, whom they laid daily at the gate of the temple which is called Beautiful, to ask alms from those who entered the temple;
3 who, seeing Peter and John about to go into the temple, asked for alms.
4 And fixing his eyes on him, with John, Peter said, "Look at us."
5 So he gave them his attention, expecting to receive something from them.
6 Then Peter said, "Silver and gold I do not have, but what I do have I give you: In the name of Jesus Christ of Nazareth, rise up and walk."
7 And he took him by the right hand and lifted *him* up, and immediately his feet and ankle bones received strength.
8 So he, leaping up, stood and walked and entered the temple with them—walking, leaping, and praising God.
9 And all the people saw him walking and praising God.

10 Psalm 16:8–11
11 NU-Text omits *according to the flesh, He would raise up the Christ* and completes the verse with *He would seat one on his throne.*   12 Psalm 110:1   13 NU-Text omits *gladly.*   14 NU-Text omits *to the church.*

10 Then they knew that it was he who sat begging alms at the Beautiful Gate of the temple; and they were filled with wonder and amazement at what had happened to him.

Preaching in Solomon's Portico

11 Now as the lame man who was healed held on to Peter and John, all the people ran together to them in the porch which is called Solomon's, greatly amazed.
12 So when Peter saw it, he responded to the people: "Men of Israel, why do you marvel at this? Or why look so intently at us, as though by our own power or godliness we had made this man walk?
13 "The God of Abraham, Isaac, and Jacob, the God of our fathers, glorified His Servant Jesus, whom you delivered up and denied in the presence of Pilate, when he was determined to let *Him* go.
14 "But you denied the Holy One and the Just, and asked for a murderer to be granted to you,
15 "and killed the Prince of life, whom God raised from the dead, of which we are witnesses.
16 "And His name, through faith in His name, has made this man strong, whom you see and know. Yes, the faith which *comes* through Him has given him this perfect soundness in the presence of you all.
17 "Yet now, brethren, I know that you did it in ignorance, as *did* also your rulers.
18 "But those things which God foretold by the mouth of all His prophets, that the Christ would suffer, He has thus fulfilled.
19 "Repent therefore and be converted, that your sins may be blotted out, so that times of refreshing may come from the presence of the Lord,
20 "and that He may send Jesus Christ, who was preached to you before,[15]
21 "whom heaven must receive until the times of restoration of all things, which God has spoken by the mouth of all His holy prophets since the world began.
22 "For Moses truly said to the fathers, 'The LORD your God will raise up for you a Prophet like me from your brethren. Him you shall hear in all things, whatever He says to you.
23 'And it shall come to pass that every soul who will not hear that Prophet shall be utterly destroyed from among the people.'[16]
24 "Yes, and all the prophets, from Samuel and those who follow, as many as have spoken, have also foretold[17] these days.
25 "You are sons of the prophets, and of the covenant which God made with our fathers, saying to Abraham, 'And in your seed all the families of the earth shall be blessed.'[18]
26 "To you first, God, having raised up His Servant Jesus, sent Him to bless you, in turning away every one *of you* from your iniquities."

Peter and John Arrested

4 Now as they spoke to the people, the priests, the captain of the temple, and the Sadducees came upon them,
2 being greatly disturbed that they taught the people and preached in Jesus the resurrection from the dead.
3 And they laid hands on them, and put *them* in custody until the next day, for it was already evening.
4 However, many of those who heard the word believed; and the number of the men came to be about five thousand.

Addressing the Sanhedrin

5 And it came to pass, on the next day, that their rulers, elders, and scribes,
6 as well as Annas the high priest, Caiaphas, John, and Alexander, and as many as were of the family of the high priest, were gathered together at Jerusalem.
7 And when they had set them in the midst, they asked, "By what power or by what name have you done this?"
8 Then Peter, filled with the Holy Spirit, said to them, "Rulers of the people and elders of Israel:
9 "If we this day are judged for a good deed *done* to *the* helpless man, by what means he has been made well,
10 "let it be known to you all, and to all the people of Israel, that by the name of Jesus Christ of Nazareth, whom you crucified, whom God raised from the dead, by Him this man stands here before you whole.
11 "This is the 'stone which was rejected by you builders, which has become the chief cornerstone.'[19]

---

15 NU-Text and M-Text read *Christ Jesus, who was ordained for you before.*   16 Deuteronomy 18:15, 18, 19
17 NU-Text and M-Text read *proclaimed.*   18 Genesis 22:18; 26:4; 28:14   19 Psalm 118:22

12 "Nor is there salvation in any other, for there is no other name under heaven given among men by which we must be saved."

The Name of Jesus Forbidden

13 Now when they saw the boldness of Peter and John, and perceived that they were uneducated and untrained men, they marveled. And they realized that they had been with Jesus. 14 And seeing the man who had been healed standing with them, they could say nothing against it. 15 But when they had commanded them to go aside out of the council, they conferred among themselves, 16 saying, "What shall we do to these men? For, indeed, that a notable miracle has been done through them is evident to all who dwell in Jerusalem, and we cannot deny it. 17 "But so that it spreads no further among the people, let us severely threaten them, that from now on they speak to no man in this name." 18 And they called them and commanded them not to speak at all nor teach in the name of Jesus. 19 But Peter and John answered and said to them, "Whether it is right in the sight of God to listen to you more than to God, you judge. 20 "For we cannot but speak the things which we have seen and heard." 21 So when they had further threatened them, they let them go, finding no way of punishing them, because of the people, since they all glorified God for what had been done. 22 For the man was over forty years old on whom this miracle of healing had been performed.

Prayer for Boldness

23 And being let go, they went to their own companions and reported all that the chief priests and elders had said to them. 24 So when they heard that, they raised their voice to God with one accord and said: "Lord, You are God, who made heaven and earth and the sea, and all that is in them, 25 "who by the mouth of Your servant David[20] have said:

'Why did the nations rage,
And the people plot vain things?
26 The kings of the earth took their stand,
And the rulers were gathered together
Against the LORD and against His
Christ.'[21]

27 "For truly against Your holy Servant Jesus, whom You anointed, both Herod and Pontius Pilate, with the Gentiles and the people of Israel, were gathered together 28 "to do whatever Your hand and Your purpose determined before to be done. 29 "Now, Lord, look on their threats, and grant to Your servants that with all boldness they may speak Your word, 30 "by stretching out Your hand to heal, and that signs and wonders may be done through the name of Your holy Servant Jesus." 31 And when they had prayed, the place where they were assembled together was shaken; and they were all filled with the Holy Spirit, and they spoke the word of God with boldness.

Sharing in All Things

32 Now the multitude of those who believed were of one heart and one soul; neither did anyone say that any of the things he possessed was his own, but they had all things in common. 33 And with great power the apostles gave witness to the resurrection of the Lord Jesus. And great grace was upon them all. 34 Nor was there anyone among them who lacked; for all who were possessors of lands or houses sold them, and brought the proceeds of the things that were sold, 35 and laid them at the apostles' feet; and they distributed to each as anyone had need. 36 And Joses,[22] who was also named Barnabas by the apostles (which is translated Son of Encouragement), a Levite of the country of Cyprus, 37 having land, sold it, and brought the money and laid it at the apostles' feet.

Lying to the Holy Spirit

5 But a certain man named Ananias, with Sapphira his wife, sold a possession.

20 NU-Text reads who through the Holy Spirit, by the mouth of our father, your servant David.
21 Psalm 2:1, 2   22 NU-Text reads Joseph.

2 And he kept back *part* of the proceeds, his wife also being aware *of it*, and brought a certain part and laid *it* at the apostles' feet.
3 But Peter said, "Ananias, why has Satan filled your heart to lie to the Holy Spirit and keep back *part* of the price of the land for yourself?
4 "While it remained, was it not your own? And after it was sold, was it not in your own control? Why have you conceived this thing in your heart? You have not lied to men but to God."
5 Then Ananias, hearing these words, fell down and breathed his last. So great fear came upon all those who heard these things.
6 And the young men arose and wrapped him up, carried *him* out, and buried *him*.
7 Now it was about three hours later when his wife came in, not knowing what had happened.
8 And Peter answered her, "Tell me whether you sold the land for so much?" And she said, "Yes, for so much."
9 Then Peter said to her, "How is it that you have agreed together to test the Spirit of the Lord? Look, the feet of those who have buried your husband *are* at the door, and they will carry you out."
10 Then immediately she fell down at his feet and breathed her last. And the young men came in and found her dead, and carrying *her* out, buried *her* by her husband.
11 So great fear came upon all the church and upon all who heard these things.

Continuing Power in the Church

12 And through the hands of the apostles many signs and wonders were done among the people. And they were all with one accord in Solomon's Porch.
13 Yet none of the rest dared join them, but the people esteemed them highly.
14 And believers were increasingly added to the Lord, multitudes of both men and women,
15 so that they brought the sick out into the streets and laid *them* on beds and couches, that at least the shadow of Peter passing by might fall on some of them.
16 Also a multitude gathered from the surrounding cities to Jerusalem, bringing sick people and those who were tor-

mented by unclean spirits, and they were all healed.

Imprisoned Apostles Freed

17 Then the high priest rose up, and all those who *were* with him (which is the sect of the Sadducees), and they were filled with indignation,
18 and laid their hands on the apostles and put them in the common prison.
19 But at night an angel of the Lord opened the prison doors and brought them out, and said,
20 "Go, stand in the temple and speak to the people all the words of this life."
21 And when they heard *that*, they entered the temple early in the morning and taught. But the high priest and those with him came and called the council together, with all the elders of the children of Israel, and sent to the prison to have them brought.

Apostles on Trial Again

22 But when the officers came and did not find them in the prison, they returned and reported,
23 saying, "Indeed we found the prison shut securely, and the guards standing outside[23] before the doors; but when we opened them, we found no one inside!"
24 Now when the high priest,[24] the captain of the temple, and the chief priests heard these things, they wondered what the outcome would be.
25 Then one came and told them, saying,[25] "Look, the men whom you put in prison are standing in the temple and teaching the people!"
26 Then the captain went with the officers and brought them without violence, for they feared the people, lest they should be stoned.
27 And when they had brought them, they set *them* before the council. And the high priest asked them,
28 saying, "Did we not strictly command you not to teach in this name? And look, you have filled Jerusalem with your doctrine, and intend to bring this Man's blood on us!"
29 Then Peter and the *other* apostles answered and said: "We ought to obey God rather than men.
30 "The God of our fathers raised up Jesus whom you murdered by hanging on a tree.

23 NU-Text and M-Text omit *outside*.　　24 NU-Text omits *the high priest*.　　25 NU-Text and M-Text omit *saying*.

31 "Him God has exalted to His right hand *to be* Prince and Savior, to give repentance to Israel and forgiveness of sins. 32 "And we are His witnesses to these things, and *so* also *is* the Holy Spirit whom God has given to those who obey Him."

Gamaliel's Advice

33 When they heard *this*, they were furious and took counsel to kill them. 34 Then one in the council stood up, a Pharisee named Gamaliel, a teacher of the law held in respect by all the people, and commanded them to put the apostles outside for a little while. 35 And he said to them: "Men of Israel, take heed to yourselves what you intend to do regarding these men. 36 "For some time ago Theudas rose up, claiming to be somebody. A number of men, about four hundred, joined him. He was slain, and all who obeyed him were scattered and came to nothing. 37 "After this man, Judas of Galilee rose up in the days of the census, and drew away many people after him. He also perished, and all who obeyed him were dispersed. 38 "And now I say to you, keep away from these men and let them alone; for if this plan or this work is of men, it will come to nothing; 39 "but if it is of God, you cannot overthrow it—lest you even be found to fight against God."

40 And they agreed with him, and when they had called for the apostles and beaten *them*, they commanded that they should not speak in the name of Jesus, and let them go. 41 So they departed from the presence of the council, rejoicing that they were counted worthy to suffer shame for His[26] name. 42 And daily in the temple, and in every house, they did not cease teaching and preaching Jesus *as* the Christ.

Seven Chosen to Serve

6 Now in those days, when *the number of* the disciples was multiplying, there arose a murmuring against the Hebrews by the Hellenists, because their widows were neglected in the daily distribution. 2 Then the twelve summoned the multitude of the disciples and said, "It is not desirable that we should leave the word of God and serve tables. 3 "Therefore, brethren, seek out from among you seven men of *good* reputation, full of the Holy Spirit and wisdom, whom we may appoint over this business; 4 "but we will give ourselves continually to prayer and to the ministry of the word." 5 And the saying pleased the whole multitude. And they chose Stephen, a man full of faith and the Holy Spirit, and Philip, Prochorus, Nicanor, Timon, Parmenas, and Nicolas, a proselyte from Antioch, 6 whom they set before the apostles; and when they had prayed, they laid hands on them. 7 And the word of God spread, and the number of the disciples multiplied greatly in Jerusalem, and a great many of the priests were obedient to the faith.

Stephen Accused of Blasphemy

8 And Stephen, full of faith[27] and power, did great wonders and signs among the people. 9 Then there arose some from what is called the Synagogue of the Freedmen (Cyrenians, Alexandrians, and those from Cilicia and Asia), disputing with Stephen. 10 And they were not able to resist the wisdom and the Spirit by which he spoke. 11 Then they secretly induced men to say, "We have heard him speak blasphemous words against Moses and God." 12 And they stirred up the people, the elders, and the scribes; and they came upon *him*, seized him, and brought *him* to the council. 13 They also set up false witnesses who said, "This man does not cease to speak blasphemous[28] words against this holy place and the law; 14 "for we have heard him say that this Jesus of Nazareth will destroy this place and change the customs which Moses delivered to us." 15 And all who sat in the council, looking steadfastly at him, saw his face as the face of an angel.

26 NU-Text reads *the name;* M-Text reads *the name of Jesus.*   27 NU-Text reads *grace.*
28 NU-Text omits *blasphemous.*

Stephen's Address: The Call of Abraham

7 Then the high priest said, "Are these things so?"
2 And he said, "Men and brethren and fathers, listen: The God of glory appeared to our father Abraham when he was in Mesopotamia, before he dwelt in Haran,
3 "and said to him, *'Get out of your country and from your relatives, and come to a land that I will show you.'*[29]
4 "Then he came out of the land of the Chaldeans and dwelt in Haran. And from there, when his father was dead, He moved him to this land in which you now dwell.
5 "And *God* gave him no inheritance in it, not even *enough* to set his foot on. But even when *Abraham* had no child, He promised to give it to him for a possession, and to his descendants after him.
6 "But God spoke in this way: that his descendants would sojourn in a foreign land, and that they would bring them into bondage and oppress *them* four hundred years.
7 *'And the nation to whom they will be in bondage I will judge,'*[30] said God, *'and after that they shall come out and serve Me in this place.'*[31]
8 "Then He gave him the covenant of circumcision; and so *Abraham* begot Isaac and circumcised him on the eighth day; and Isaac *begot* Jacob, and Jacob *begot* the twelve patriarchs.

The Patriarchs in Egypt

9 "And the patriarchs, becoming envious, sold Joseph into Egypt. But God was with him
10 "and delivered him out of all his troubles, and gave him favor and wisdom in the presence of Pharaoh, king of Egypt; and he made him governor over Egypt and all his house.
11 "Now a famine and great trouble came over all the land of Egypt and Canaan, and our fathers found no sustenance.
12 "But when Jacob heard that there was grain in Egypt, he sent out our fathers first.
13 "And the second *time* Joseph was made known to his brothers, and Joseph's family became known to the Pharaoh.
14 "Then Joseph sent and called his fa-

ther Jacob and all his relatives to *him*, seventy-five people.
15 "So Jacob went down to Egypt; and he died, he and our fathers.
16 "And they were carried back to Shechem and laid in the tomb that Abraham bought for a sum of money from the sons of Hamor, *the father* of Shechem.

God Delivers Israel by Moses

17 "But when the time of the promise drew near which God had sworn to Abraham, the people grew and multiplied in Egypt
18 "till another king arose who did not know Joseph.
19 "This man dealt treacherously with our people, and oppressed our forefathers, making them expose their babies, so that they might not live.
20 "At this time Moses was born, and was well pleasing to God; and he was brought up in his father's house for three months.
21 "But when he was set out, Pharaoh's daughter took him away and brought him up as her own son.
22 "And Moses was learned in all the wisdom of the Egyptians, and was mighty in words and deeds.
23 "But when he was forty years old, it came into his heart to visit his brethren, the children of Israel.
24 "And seeing one of *them* suffer wrong, he defended and avenged him who was oppressed, and struck down the Egyptian.
25 "For he supposed that his brethren would have understood that God would deliver them by his hand, but they did not understand.
26 "And the next day he appeared to two of them as they were fighting, and *tried to* reconcile them, saying, 'Men, you are brethren; why do you wrong one another?'
27 "But he who did his neighbor wrong pushed him away, saying, *'Who made you a ruler and a judge over us?*
28 *'Do you want to kill me as you did the Egyptian yesterday?'*[32]
29 "Then, at this saying, Moses fled and became a sojourner in the land of Midian, where he had two sons.
30 "And when forty years had passed, an Angel of the Lord[33] appeared to him in a

29 Genesis 12:1   30 Genesis 15:14   31 Exodus 3:12   32 Exodus 2:14   33 NU-Text omits *of the Lord.*

flame of fire in a bush, in the wilderness of Mount Sinai.
31 "When Moses saw *it*, he marveled at the sight; and as he drew near to observe, the voice of the Lord came to him,
32 *"saying, 'I am the God of your fathers—the God of Abraham, the God of Isaac, and the God of Jacob.'*[34] And Moses trembled and dared not look.
33 *'Then the LORD said to him, "Take your sandals off your feet, for the place where you stand is holy ground.*
34 *"I have certainly seen the oppression of my people who are in Egypt; I have heard their groaning and have come down to deliver them. And now come, I will send you to Egypt."* [35]
35 "This Moses whom they rejected, saying, *'Who made you a ruler and a judge?'*[36] is the one God sent *to be* a ruler and a deliverer by the hand of the Angel who appeared to him in the bush.
36 "He brought them out, after he had shown wonders and signs in the land of Egypt, and in the Red Sea, and in the wilderness forty years.

Israel Rebels Against God

37 "This is that Moses who said to the children of Israel,[37] *'The LORD your God will raise up for you a Prophet like me from your brethren. Him you shall hear.'*[38]
38 "This is he who was in the congregation in the wilderness with the Angel who spoke to him on Mount Sinai, and *with* our fathers, the one who received the living oracles to give to us,
39 "whom our fathers would not obey, but rejected. And in their hearts they turned back to Egypt,
40 "saying to Aaron, *'Make us gods to go before us; as for this Moses who brought us out of the land of Egypt, we do not know what has become of him.'*[39]
41 "And they made a calf in those days, offered sacrifices to the idol, and rejoiced in the works of their own hands.
42 "Then God turned and gave them up to worship the host of heaven, as it is written in the book of the Prophets:

'Did you offer Me slaughtered animals and sacrifices during forty years in the wilderness, O house of Israel?

43 *Yes, you took up the tabernacle of Moloch, And the star of your god Remphan, Images which you made to worship; And I will carry you away beyond Babylon.'*[40]

God's True Tabernacle

44 "Our fathers had the tabernacle of witness in the wilderness, as He appointed, instructing Moses to make it according to the pattern that he had seen,
45 "which our fathers, having received it in turn, also brought with Joshua into the land possessed by the Gentiles, whom God drove out before the face of our fathers until the days of David,
46 "who found favor before God and asked to find a dwelling for the God of Jacob.
47 "But Solomon built Him a house.
48 "However, the Most High does not dwell in temples made with hands, as the prophet says:

49 *'Heaven is My throne, And earth is My footstool. What house will you build for Me? says the LORD, Or what is the place of My rest?*
50 *Has My hand not made all these things?'*[41]

Israel Resists the Holy Spirit

51 *"You* stiffnecked and uncircumcised in heart and ears! You always resist the Holy Spirit; as your fathers *did,* so *do* you.
52 "Which of the prophets did your fathers not persecute? And they killed those who foretold the coming of the Just One, of whom you now have become the betrayers and murderers,
53 "who have received the law by the direction of angels and have not kept *it.*"

Stephen the Martyr

54 When they heard these things they were cut to the heart, and they gnashed at him with *their* teeth.
55 But he, being full of the Holy Spirit, gazed into heaven and saw the glory of God, and Jesus standing at the right hand of God,
56 and said, "Look! I see the heavens opened and the Son of Man standing at the right hand of God!"

34 Exodus 3:6, 15   35 Exodus 3:5, 7, 8, 10   36 Exodus 2:14   37 Deuteronomy 18:15
38 NU-Text and M-Text omit *Him you shall hear.*   39 Exodus 32:1, 23   40 Amos 5:25–27   41 Isaiah 66:1, 2

57 Then they cried out with a loud voice, stopped their ears, and ran at him with one accord;
58 and they cast *him* out of the city and stoned *him*. And the witnesses laid down their clothes at the feet of a young man named Saul.
59 And they stoned Stephen as he was calling on *God* and saying, "Lord Jesus, receive my spirit."
60 Then he knelt down and cried out with a loud voice, "Lord, do not charge them with this sin." And when he had said this, he fell asleep.

Saul Persecutes the Church

8 Now Saul was consenting to his death. At that time a great persecution arose against the church which was at Jerusalem; and they were all scattered throughout the regions of Judea and Samaria, except the apostles.
2 And devout men carried Stephen *to his burial*, and made great lamentation over him.
3 As for Saul, he made havoc of the church, entering every house, and dragging off men and women, committing *them* to prison.

Christ Is Preached in Samaria

4 Therefore those who were scattered went everywhere preaching the word.
5 Then Philip went down to the [42] city of Samaria and preached Christ to them.
6 And the multitudes with one accord heeded the things spoken by Philip, hearing and seeing the miracles which he did.
7 For unclean spirits, crying with a loud voice, came out of many who were possessed; and many who were paralyzed and lame were healed.
8 And there was great joy in that city.

The Sorcerer's Profession of Faith

9 But there was a certain man called Simon, who previously practiced sorcery in the city and astonished the people of Samaria, claiming that he was someone great,
10 to whom they all gave heed, from the least to the greatest, saying, "This man is the great power of God."
11 And they heeded him because he had astonished them with his sorceries for a long time.
12 But when they believed Philip as he preached the things concerning the kingdom of God and the name of Jesus Christ, both men and women were baptized.
13 Then Simon himself also believed; and when he was baptized he continued with Philip, and was amazed, seeing the miracles and signs which were done.

The Sorcerer's Sin

14 Now when the apostles who were at Jerusalem heard that Samaria had received the word of God, they sent Peter and John to them,
15 who, when they had come down, prayed for them that they might receive the Holy Spirit.
16 For as yet He had fallen upon none of them. They had only been baptized in the name of the Lord Jesus.
17 Then they laid hands on them, and they received the Holy Spirit.
18 Now when Simon saw that through the laying on of the apostles' hands the Holy Spirit was given, he offered them money,
19 saying, "Give me this power also, that anyone on whom I lay hands may receive the Holy Spirit."
20 But Peter said to him, "Your money perish with you, because you thought that the gift of God could be purchased with money!
21 "You have neither part nor portion in this matter, for your heart is not right in the sight of God.
22 "Repent therefore of this your wickedness, and pray God if perhaps the thought of your heart may be forgiven you.
23 "For I see that you are poisoned by bitterness and bound by iniquity."
24 Then Simon answered and said, "Pray to the Lord for me, that none of the things which you have spoken may come upon me."
25 So when they had testified and preached the word of the Lord, they returned to Jerusalem, preaching the gospel in many villages of the Samaritans.

Christ Is Preached to an Ethiopian

26 Now an angel of the Lord spoke to Philip, saying, "Arise and go toward the south along the road which goes down from Jerusalem to Gaza." This is desert.

42 Or *a*

The Unnamed Men and Women

The early Christians in Jerusalem enjoyed a tremendous amount of freedom sharing their new-found faith. They taught openly in the temple and in the "Freed Man's Synagogue," which was recently discovered in Jerusalem.

Between A.D. 40-60, however, resistance mounted from the Jewish leaders in the Jerusalem temple. One church leader, Stephen, was stoned to death outside the city walls. The Jerusalem congregation was forced to flee to the coast of North Africa and the Mediterranean islands. Here, in exile, they met and enjoyed the freedom they initially had shared in Jerusalem.

But their freedom was not enough. They realized the objective God gave them was not to simply meet in seclusion, but to share His message of love and forgiveness to all mankind. They believed in management by objectives. So they developed a strategy to carry out the directive of Christ. They split up into groups of twos and traveled to as many cities as possible along the coast of Africa, Palestine, Greece, and Rome.

The Book of Acts does not mention these men and women other than to say they shared the Good News with those who lived along the coast of Palestine. The unnamed people in the Book of Acts did not care who got the credit. They simply wanted to make sure God's work was done. For they believed God's love was not love unless they gave it away.

What can you do in your world today to share God's love, regardless of who gets the credit? Remember God does His greatest works and His greatest projects through His smallest people!

27 So he arose and went. And behold, a man of Ethiopia, a eunuch of great authority under Candace the queen of the Ethiopians, who had charge of all her treasury, and had come to Jerusalem to worship,
28 was returning. And sitting in his chariot, he was reading Isaiah the prophet.
29 Then the Spirit said to Philip, "Go near and overtake this chariot."
30 So Philip ran to him, and heard him reading the prophet Isaiah, and said, "Do you understand what you are reading?"
31 And he said, "How can I, unless someone guides me?" And he asked Philip to come up and sit with him.
32 The place in the Scripture which he read was this:

"He was led as a sheep to the slaughter;
And like a lamb silent before its shearer,
So He opened not His mouth.
33 In His humiliation His justice was taken away.
And who will declare His generation?
For His life is taken from the earth."[43]

34 So the eunuch answered Philip and said, "I ask you, of whom does the prophet say this, of himself or of some other man?"
35 Then Philip opened his mouth, and beginning at this Scripture, preached Jesus to him.
36 Now as they went down the road, they came to some water. And the eunuch said, "See, here is water. What hinders me from being baptized?"
37 Then Philip said, "If you believe with all your heart, you may." And he answered and said, "I believe that Jesus Christ is the Son of God."[44]
38 So he commanded the chariot to stand still. And both Philip and the eunuch went down into the water, and he baptized him.
39 Now when they came up out of the water, the Spirit of the Lord caught Philip away, so that the eunuch saw him no more; and he went on his way rejoicing.
40 But Philip was found at Azotus. And passing through, he preached in all the cities till he came to Caesarea.

The Damascus Road: Saul Converted

9 Then Saul, still breathing threats and murder against the disciples of the Lord, went to the high priest
2 and asked letters from him to the synagogues of Damascus, so that if he found any who were of the Way, whether men or women, he might bring them bound to Jerusalem.
3 And as he journeyed he came near Damascus, and suddenly a light shone around him from heaven.
4 Then he fell to the ground, and heard a voice saying to him, "Saul, Saul, why are you persecuting Me?"
5 And he said, "Who are You, Lord?" And the Lord said, "I am Jesus, whom you are persecuting.[45] It is hard for you to kick against the goads."
6 So he, trembling and astonished, said, "Lord, what do You want me to do?" And the Lord said to him, "Arise and go into the city, and you will be told what you must do."
7 And the men who journeyed with him stood speechless, hearing a voice but seeing no one.
8 Then Saul arose from the ground, and when his eyes were opened he saw no one. But they led him by the hand and brought him into Damascus.
9 And he was three days without sight, and neither ate nor drank.

Ananias Baptizes Saul

10 Now there was a certain disciple at Damascus named Ananias; and to him the Lord said in a vision, "Ananias." And he said, "Here I am, Lord."
11 So the Lord said to him, "Arise and go to the street called Straight, and inquire at the house of Judas for one called Saul of Tarsus, for behold, he is praying.
12 "And in a vision he has seen a man named Ananias coming in and putting his hand on him, so that he might receive his sight."
13 Then Ananias answered, "Lord, I have heard from many about this man, how much harm he has done to Your saints in Jerusalem.
14 "And here he has authority from the chief priests to bind all who call on Your name."

43 Isaiah 53:7, 8
44 NU-Text and M-Text omit this verse. It is found in Western texts, including the Latin tradition.
45 NU-Text and M-Text omit the last sentence of verse 5 and begin verse 6 with *But arise and go.*

Great People—Ordinary People

Great people are just ordinary people with an extraordinary amount of determination. One such man among the first disciples was the evangelist, Philip. God gave Philip a dream to share the Good News of Jesus Christ with as many people as he could during his lifetime. It was Philip's call to break down as many cultural, religious, and ethnic barriers as possible.

Philip began his ministry in Samaria, a region where no upstanding Jew from the Jerusalem area was ever seen. He preached in the synagogues and established churches in the region.

A beautiful example of Philip's determination and ministry was on the road from Jerusalem to Gaza where he met an Ethiopian eunuch. The eunuch was reading a famous passage from the Book of Isaiah, concerning the Messiah. Philip seized the opportunity, approached the eunuch, and shared with him the fulfillment of the messianic prophecy in the person and work of Jesus Christ. The Ethiopian eunuch believed and was baptized. The new convert continued his journey to North Africa, where, tradition tells us, he founded the first Christian church in Ethiopia.

Philip continued his work in the coastal cities of Palestine. He preached in Gaza, Jaffa, and finally settled in Caesarea. Here he shared the gospel with many people of diverse cultural, religious, and ethnic backgrounds. In the New Testament period, Caesarea was the largest Greco-Roman city on the coast of Palestine. Through its gates walked people from all corners of the empire to trade their wares and share news of events elsewhere in the empire.

Philip saw Caesarea as an opportunity to multiply his resources by sharing with as many sources as possible. He built a dream in Caesarea and the dream built him up. Who knows how many people he was responsible for converting? Only God can count the apples in one seed.

Where can you plant a seed in your world today? What dream has God instilled in you? Multiply your resources—share your faith. Remember: great people are just ordinary people with an extraordinary amount of determination!

¹⁵ But the Lord said to him, "Go, for he is a chosen vessel of Mine to bear My name before Gentiles, kings, and the children of Israel.
¹⁶ "For I will show him how many things he must suffer for My name's sake."
¹⁷ And Ananias went his way and entered the house; and laying his hands on him he said, "Brother Saul, the Lord Jesus,⁴⁶ who appeared to you on the road as you came, has sent me that you may receive your sight and be filled with the Holy Spirit."
¹⁸ Immediately there fell from his eyes something like scales, and he received his sight at once; and he arose and was baptized.
¹⁹ And when he had received food, he was strengthened. Then Saul spent some days with the disciples at Damascus.

Saul Preaches Christ

²⁰ Immediately he preached the Christ⁴⁷ in the synagogues, that He is the Son of God.
²¹ Then all who heard were amazed, and said, "Is this not he who destroyed those who called on this name in Jerusalem, and has come here for that purpose, so that he might bring them bound to the chief priests?"
²² But Saul increased all the more in strength, and confounded the Jews who dwelt in Damascus, proving that this Jesus is the Christ.

Saul Escapes Death

²³ Now after many days were past, the Jews plotted to kill him.
²⁴ But their plot became known to Saul. And they watched the gates day and night, to kill him.
²⁵ Then the disciples took him by night and let him down through the wall in a large basket.

Saul at Jerusalem

²⁶ And when Saul had come to Jerusalem, he tried to join the disciples; but they were all afraid of him, and did not believe that he was a disciple.
²⁷ But Barnabas took him and brought him to the apostles. And he declared to them how he had seen the Lord on the road, and that He had spoken to him,

and how he had preached boldly at Damascus in the name of Jesus.
²⁸ So he was with them at Jerusalem, coming in and going out.
²⁹ And he spoke boldly in the name of the Lord Jesus and disputed against the Hellenists, but they attempted to kill him.
³⁰ When the brethren found out, they brought him down to Caesarea and sent him out to Tarsus.

The Church Prospers

³¹ Then the churches⁴⁸ throughout all Judea, Galilee, and Samaria had peace and were edified. And walking in the fear of the Lord and in the comfort of the Holy Spirit, they were multiplied.

Aeneas Healed

³² Now it came to pass, as Peter went through all parts of the country, that he also came down to the saints who dwelt in Lydda.
³³ There he found a certain man named Aeneas, who had been bedridden eight years and was paralyzed.
³⁴ And Peter said to him, "Aeneas, Jesus the Christ heals you. Arise and make your bed." Then he arose immediately.
³⁵ So all who dwelt at Lydda and Sharon saw him and turned to the Lord.

Dorcas Restored to Life

³⁶ At Joppa there was a certain disciple named Tabitha, which is translated Dorcas. This woman was full of good works and charitable deeds which she did.
³⁷ But it happened in those days that she became sick and died. When they had washed her, they laid her in an upper room.
³⁸ And since Lydda was near Joppa, and the disciples had heard that Peter was there, they sent two men to him, imploring him not to delay in coming to them.
³⁹ Then Peter arose and went with them. When he had come, they brought him to the upper room. And all the widows stood by him weeping, showing the tunics and garments which Dorcas had made while she was with them.
⁴⁰ But Peter put them all out, and knelt down and prayed. And turning to the body he said, "Tabitha, arise." And she opened her eyes, and when she saw Peter she sat up.

46 M-Text omits Jesus.   47 NU-Text reads Jesus.   48 NU-Text reads church . . . was edified.

41 Then he gave her *his* hand and lifted her up; and when he had called the saints and widows, he presented her alive.
42 And it became known throughout all Joppa, and many believed on the Lord.
43 So it was that he stayed many days in Joppa with Simon, a tanner.

Cornelius Sends a Delegation

10 There was a certain man in Caesarea called Cornelius, a centurion of what was called the Italian Regiment,
2 a devout *man* and one who feared God with all his household, who gave alms generously to the people, and prayed to God always.
3 About the ninth hour of the day he saw clearly in a vision an angel of God coming in and saying to him, "Cornelius!"
4 And when he observed him, he was afraid, and said, "What is it, lord?" So he said to him, "Your prayers and your alms have come up for a memorial before God.
5 "Now send men to Joppa, and send for Simon whose surname is Peter.
6 "He is lodging with Simon, a tanner, whose house is by the sea.⁴⁹ He will tell you what you must do."
7 And when the angel who spoke to him had departed, Cornelius called two of his household servants and a devout soldier from among those who waited on him continually.
8 So when he had explained all *these* things to them, he sent them to Joppa.

Peter's Vision

9 The next day, as they went on their journey and drew near the city, Peter went up on the housetop to pray, about the sixth hour.
10 Then he became very hungry and wanted to eat; but while they made ready, he fell into a trance
11 and saw heaven opened and an object like a great sheet bound at the four corners, descending to him and let down to the earth.
12 In it were all kinds of four-footed animals of the earth, wild beasts, creeping things, and birds of the air.
13 And a voice came to him, "Rise, Peter; kill and eat."
14 But Peter said, "Not so, Lord! For I have never eaten anything common or unclean."
15 And a voice *spoke* to him again the second time, "What God has cleansed you must not call common."
16 This was done three times. And the object was taken up into heaven again.

Summoned to Caesarea

17 Now while Peter wondered within himself what this vision which he had seen meant, behold, the men who had been sent from Cornelius had made inquiry for Simon's house, and stood before the gate.
18 And they called and asked whether Simon, whose surname was Peter, was lodging there.
19 While Peter thought about the vision, the Spirit said to him, "Behold, three men are seeking you.
20 "Arise therefore, go down and go with them, doubting nothing; for I have sent them."
21 Then Peter went down to the men who had been sent to him from Cornelius,⁵⁰ and said, "Yes, I am he whom you seek. For what reason have you come?"
22 And they said, "Cornelius *the* centurion, a just man, one who fears God and has a good reputation among all the nation of the Jews, was divinely instructed by a holy angel to summon you to his house, and to hear words from you."
23 Then he invited them in and lodged *them.* On the next day Peter went away with them, and some brethren from Joppa accompanied him.

Peter Meets Cornelius

24 And the following day they entered Caesarea. Now Cornelius was waiting for them, and had called together his relatives and close friends.
25 As Peter was coming in, Cornelius met him and fell down at his feet and worshiped *him.*
26 But Peter lifted him up, saying, "Stand up; I myself am also a man."
27 And as he talked with him, he went in and found many who had come together.
28 Then he said to them, "You know how unlawful it is for a Jewish man to keep company with or go to one of another nation. But God has shown me

---

49 NU-Text and M-Text omit the last sentence of this verse.
50 NU-Text and M-Text omit *who had been sent to him from Cornelius.*

that I should not call any man common or unclean.

29 "Therefore I came without objection as soon as I was sent for. I ask, then, for what reason have you sent for me?"

30 And Cornelius said, "Four days ago I was fasting until this hour; and[51] at the ninth hour I prayed in my house, and behold, a man stood before me in bright clothing,

31 "and said, 'Cornelius, your prayer has been heard, and your alms are remembered in the sight of God.

32 'Send therefore to Joppa and call Simon here, whose surname is Peter. He is lodging in the house of Simon, a tanner, by the sea.[52] When he comes, he will speak to you.'

33 "So I sent to you immediately, and you have done well to come. Now therefore, we are all present before God, to hear all the things commanded you by God."

Preaching to Cornelius' Household

34 Then Peter opened his mouth and said: "In truth I perceive that God shows no partiality.

35 "But in every nation whoever fears Him and works righteousness is accepted by Him.

36 "The word which God sent to the children of Israel, preaching peace through Jesus Christ—He is Lord of all—

37 "that word you know, which was proclaimed throughout all Judea, and began from Galilee after the baptism which John preached:

38 "how God anointed Jesus of Nazareth with the Holy Spirit and with power, who went about doing good and healing all who were oppressed by the devil, for God was with Him.

39 "And we are witnesses of all things which He did both in the land of the Jews and in Jerusalem, whom they[53] killed by hanging on a tree.

40 "Him God raised up on the third day, and showed Him openly,

41 "not to all the people, but to witnesses chosen before by God, even to us who ate and drank with Him after He arose from the dead.

42 "And He commanded us to preach to the people, and to testify that it is He who was ordained by God to be Judge of the living and the dead.

43 "To Him all the prophets witness that, through His name, whoever believes in Him will receive remission of sins."

The Holy Spirit Falls on the Gentiles

44 While Peter was still speaking these words, the Holy Spirit fell upon all those who heard the word.

45 And those of the circumcision who believed were astonished, as many as came with Peter, because the gift of the Holy Spirit had been poured out on the Gentiles also.

46 For they heard them speak with tongues and magnify God. Then Peter answered,

47 "Can anyone forbid water, that these should not be baptized who have received the Holy Spirit just as we have?"

48 And he commanded them to be baptized in the name of the Lord. Then they asked him to stay a few days.

Peter Defends God's Grace

11 Now the apostles and brethren who were in Judea heard that the Gentiles had also received the word of God.

2 And when Peter came up to Jerusalem, those of the circumcision contended with him,

3 saying, "You went in to uncircumcised men and ate with them!"

4 But Peter explained it to them in order from the beginning, saying:

5 "I was in the city of Joppa praying; and in a trance I saw a vision, an object descending like a great sheet, let down from heaven by four corners; and it came to me.

6 "When I observed it intently and considered, I saw four-footed animals of the earth, wild beasts, creeping things, and birds of the air.

7 "And I heard a voice saying to me, 'Rise, Peter; kill and eat.'

8 "But I said, 'Not so, Lord! For nothing common or unclean has at any time entered my mouth.'

9 "But the voice answered me again from heaven, 'What God has cleansed you must not call common.'

10 "Now this was done three times, and all were drawn up again into heaven.

51 NU-Text reads Four days ago to this hour, I was praying.   52 NU-Text omits the last sentence of this verse.
53 NU-Text and M-Text add also.

11 "At that very moment, three men stood before the house where I was, having been sent to me from Caesarea.
12 "Then the Spirit told me to go with them, doubting nothing. Moreover these six brethren accompanied me, and we entered the man's house.
13 "And he told us how he had seen an angel standing in his house, who said to him, 'Send men to Joppa, and call for Simon whose surname is Peter,
14 'who will tell you words by which you and all your household will be saved.'
15 "And as I began to speak, the Holy Spirit fell upon them, as upon us at the beginning.
16 "Then I remembered the word of the Lord, how He said, 'John indeed baptized with water, but you shall be baptized with the Holy Spirit.'
17 "If therefore God gave them the same gift as *He gave* us when we believed on the Lord Jesus Christ, who was I that I could withstand God?"
18 When they heard these things they became silent; and they glorified God, saying, "Then God has also granted to the Gentiles repentance to life."

Barnabas and Saul at Antioch

19 Now those who were scattered after the persecution that arose over Stephen traveled as far as Phoenicia, Cyprus, and Antioch, preaching the word to no one but the Jews only.
20 But some of them were men from Cyprus and Cyrene, who, when they had come to Antioch, spoke to the Hellenists, preaching the Lord Jesus.
21 And the hand of the Lord was with them, and a great number believed and turned to the Lord.
22 Then news of these things came to the ears of the church in Jerusalem, and they sent out Barnabas to go as far as Antioch.
23 When he came and had seen the grace of God, he was glad, and encouraged them all that with purpose of heart they should continue with the Lord.
24 For he was a good man, full of the Holy Spirit and of faith. And a great many people were added to the Lord.
25 Then Barnabas departed for Tarsus to seek Saul.
26 And when he had found him, he brought him to Antioch. So it was that for a whole year they assembled with the church and taught a great many people. And the disciples were first called Christians in Antioch.

Relief to Judea

27 And in these days prophets came from Jerusalem to Antioch.
28 Then one of them, named Agabus, stood up and showed by the Spirit that there was going to be a great famine throughout all the world, which also happened in the days of Claudius Caesar.
29 Then the disciples, each according to his ability, determined to send relief to the brethren dwelling in Judea.
30 This they also did, and sent it to the elders by the hands of Barnabas and Saul.

Herod's Violence to the Church

12 Now about that time Herod the king stretched out *his* hand to harass some from the church.
2 Then he killed James the brother of John with the sword.
3 And because he saw that it pleased the Jews, he proceeded further to seize Peter also. Now it was *during* the Days of Unleavened Bread.
4 So when he had apprehended him, he put *him* in prison, and delivered *him* to four squads of soldiers to keep him, intending to bring him before the people after Passover.

Peter Freed from Prison

5 Peter was therefore kept in prison, but constant[54] prayer was offered to God for him by the church.
6 And when Herod was about to bring him out, that night Peter was sleeping, bound with two chains between two soldiers; and the guards before the door were keeping the prison.
7 Now behold, an angel of the Lord stood by *him*, and a light shone in the prison; and he struck Peter on the side and raised him up, saying, "Arise quickly!" And his chains fell off *his* hands.
8 Then the angel said to him, "Gird yourself and tie on your sandals"; and so he did. And he said to him, "Put on your garment and follow me."
9 So he went out and followed him, and did not know that what was done by the

---

54 NU-Text reads *constantly* (or *earnestly*).

angel was real, but thought he was seeing a vision.

10 When they were past the first and the second guard posts, they came to the iron gate that leads to the city, which opened to them of its own accord; and they went out and went down one street, and immediately the angel departed from him.

11 And when Peter had come to himself, he said, "Now I know for certain that the Lord has sent His angel, and has delivered me from the hand of Herod and *from* all the expectation of the Jewish people."

12 So, when he had considered *this*, he came to the house of Mary, the mother of John whose surname was Mark, where many were gathered together praying.

13 And as Peter knocked at the door of the gate, a girl named Rhoda came to answer.

14 When she recognized Peter's voice, because of *her* gladness she did not open the gate, but ran in and announced that Peter stood before the gate.

15 But they said to her, "You are beside yourself!" Yet she kept insisting that it was so. So they said, "It is his angel."

16 Now Peter continued knocking; and when they opened *the door* and saw him, they were astonished.

17 But motioning to them with his hand to keep silent, he declared to them how the Lord had brought him out of the prison. And he said, "Go, tell these things to James and to the brethren." And he departed and went to another place.

18 Then, as soon as it was day, there was no small stir among the soldiers about what had become of Peter.

19 But when Herod had searched for him and not found him, he examined the guards and commanded that *they* should be put to death. And he went down from Judea to Caesarea, and stayed *there*.

Herod's Violent Death

20 Now Herod had been very angry with the people of Tyre and Sidon; but they came to him with one accord, and having made Blastus the king's chamberlain their friend, they asked for peace, because their country was supplied with food by the king's *country*.

21 So on a set day Herod, arrayed in royal apparel, sat on his throne and gave an oration to them.

22 And the people kept shouting, "The voice of a god and not of a man!"

23 Then immediately an angel of the Lord struck him, because he did not give glory to God. And he was eaten by worms and died.

24 But the word of God grew and multiplied.

Barnabas and Saul Appointed

25 And Barnabas and Saul returned from[55] Jerusalem when they had fulfilled *their* ministry, and they also took with them John whose surname was Mark.

13 Now in the church that was at Antioch there were certain prophets and teachers: Barnabas, Simeon who was called Niger, Lucius of Cyrene, Manaen who had been brought up with Herod the tetrarch, and Saul.

2 As they ministered to the Lord and fasted, the Holy Spirit said, "Now separate to Me Barnabas and Saul for the work to which I have called them."

3 Then, having fasted and prayed, and laid hands on them, they sent *them* away.

Preaching in Cyprus

4 So, being sent out by the Holy Spirit, they went down to Seleucia, and from there they sailed to Cyprus.

5 And when they arrived in Salamis, they preached the word of God in the synagogues of the Jews. They also had John as *their* assistant.

6 Now when they had gone through the island[56] to Paphos, they found a certain sorcerer, a false prophet, a Jew whose name *was* Bar-Jesus,

7 who was with the proconsul, Sergius Paulus, an intelligent man. This man called for Barnabas and Saul and sought to hear the word of God.

8 But Elymas the sorcerer (for so his name is translated) withstood them, seeking to turn the proconsul away from the faith.

9 Then Saul, who also *is called* Paul, filled with the Holy Spirit, looked intently at him

10 and said, "O full of all deceit and all fraud, *you* son of the devil, *you* enemy of all righteousness, will you not cease perverting the straight ways of the Lord?

55 NU-Text and M-Text read *to.*   56 NU-Text reads *the whole island.*

Son of Encouragement

Often we read the Bible and come across names like Priscilla, Aquila, and Onesimus. We see their names once and never hear from them again. One of these names is Barnabas.

Barnabas means, "son of encouragement." He is introduced to us in the Book of Acts. What little we can gather is that Barnabas trained the apostle Paul after Paul's conversion on the road to Damascus. When Barnabas was finished with this task, the Jerusalem church desperately needed someone to take control of the young church in Antioch, Syria. They were looking for someone strong, steady, and firm, who could be an encouragement to build up the people in their newfound faith. The church in Antioch, Syria was surrounded with all sorts of mystery religions. It was easy for the new Christians to be persuaded to let false doctrines infiltrate the church. So the Jerusalem church turned to someone they could count on. Barnabas was active in the leadership of the church in Antioch.

Barnabas spent many years there, during which time he may have discipled John Mark, the apostle who wrote the Gospel of Mark. The Bible does not directly record any of this information. We have to rely on indirect references in the Bible, as well as extra biblical literature to surmise what Barnabas's life was like.

Barnabas was one of those people who did not care who got all the credit, as long as he was serving God with his talents, gifts, and abilities.

Remember, God can do wonderful things through someone who does not really care who gets the credit. Be that special person of encouragement to someone in your life. Perhaps God has given you the gift of encouragement. You may not be centrally recognized by everyone, but remember, God sees your good works and He rewards you!

11 "And now, indeed, the hand of the Lord *is* upon you, and you shall be blind, not seeing the sun for a time." And immediately a dark mist fell on him, and he went around seeking someone to lead him by the hand.
12 Then the proconsul believed, when he saw what had been done, being astonished at the teaching of the Lord.

At Antioch in Pisidia

13 Now when Paul and his party set sail from Paphos, they came to Perga in Pamphylia; and John, departing from them, returned to Jerusalem.
14 But when they departed from Perga, they came to Antioch in Pisidia, and went into the synagogue on the Sabbath day and sat down.
15 And after the reading of the Law and the Prophets, the rulers of the synagogue sent to them, saying, "Men *and* brethren, if you have any word of exhortation for the people, say on."
16 Then Paul stood up, and motioning with *his* hand said, "Men of Israel, and you who fear God, listen:
17 "The God of this people Israel[57] chose our fathers, and exalted the people when they dwelt as strangers in the land of Egypt, and with an uplifted arm He brought them out of it.
18 "Now for a time of about forty years He put up with their ways in the wilderness.
19 "And when He had destroyed seven nations in the land of Canaan, He distributed their land to them by allotment.
20 "After that He gave *them* judges for about four hundred and fifty years, until Samuel the prophet.
21 "And afterward they asked for a king; so God gave them Saul the son of Kish, a man of the tribe of Benjamin, for forty years.
22 "And when He had removed him, He raised up for them David as king, to whom also He gave testimony and said, '*I have found David*[58] the *son* of Jesse, a man after My own heart, who will do all My will.'[59]
23 "From this man's seed, according to *the* promise, God raised up for Israel a Savior—Jesus—[60]
24 "after John had first preached, before His coming, the baptism of repentance to all the people of Israel.
25 "And as John was finishing his course, he said, 'Who do you think I am? I am not *He*. But behold, there comes One after me, the sandals of whose feet I am not worthy to loose.'
26 "Men *and* brethren, sons of the family of Abraham, and those among you who fear God, to you the word of this salvation has been sent.
27 "For those who dwell in Jerusalem, and their rulers, because they did not know Him, nor even the voices of the Prophets which are read every Sabbath, have fulfilled *them* in condemning *Him*.
28 "And though they found no cause for death *in Him*, they asked Pilate that He should be put to death.
29 "Now when they had fulfilled all that was written concerning Him, they took *Him* down from the tree and laid *Him* in a tomb.
30 "But God raised Him from the dead.
31 "He was seen for many days by those who came up with Him from Galilee to Jerusalem, who are His witnesses to the people.
32 "And we declare to you glad tidings—that promise which was made to the fathers.
33 "God has fulfilled this for us their children, in that He has raised up Jesus. As it is also written in the second Psalm:

'You are My Son,
Today I have begotten You.'[61]

34 "And that He raised Him from the dead, no more to return to corruption, He has spoken thus:

'I will give you the sure mercies of David.'[62]

35 "Therefore He also says in another *Psalm*:

'You will not allow Your Holy One to see corruption.'[63]

36 "For David, after he had served his own generation by the will of God, fell asleep, was buried with his fathers, and saw corruption;

---

57 M-Text omits *Israel.*   58 Psalm 89:20   59 1 Samuel 13:14   60 M-Text reads *for Israel salvation.*
61 Psalm 2:7   62 Isaiah 55:3   63 Psalm 16:10

37 "but He whom God raised up saw no corruption.
38 "Therefore let it be known to you, brethren, that through this Man is preached to you the forgiveness of sins;
39 "and by Him everyone who believes is justified from all things from which you could not be justified by the law of Moses.
40 "Beware therefore, lest what has been spoken in the prophets come upon you:

41 'Behold, you despisers,
   Marvel and perish;
   For I work a work in your days,
   A work which you will by no means
      believe,
   Though one were to declare it to
      you.' " 64

Blessing and Conflict at Antioch

42 And when the Jews went out of the synagogue,65 the Gentiles begged that these words might be preached to them the next Sabbath.
43 Now when the congregation had broken up, many of the Jews and devout proselytes followed Paul and Barnabas, who, speaking to them, persuaded them to continue in the grace of God.
44 And the next Sabbath almost the whole city came together to hear the word of God.
45 But when the Jews saw the multitudes, they were filled with envy; and contradicting and blaspheming, they opposed the things spoken by Paul.
46 Then Paul and Barnabas grew bold and said, "It was necessary that the word of God should be spoken to you first; but since you reject it, and judge yourselves unworthy of everlasting life, behold, we turn to the Gentiles.
47 "For so the Lord has commanded us:

'I have set you to be a light
   to the Gentiles,
That you should be for salvation
   to the ends of the earth.' " 66

48 Now when the Gentiles heard this, they were glad and glorified the word of the Lord. And as many as had been appointed to eternal life believed.
49 And the word of the Lord was being spread throughout all the region.

50 But the Jews stirred up the devout and prominent women and the chief men of the city, raised up persecution against Paul and Barnabas, and expelled them from their region.
51 But they shook off the dust from their feet against them, and came to Iconium.
52 And the disciples were filled with joy and with the Holy Spirit.

At Iconium

14 Now it happened in Iconium that they went together to the synagogue of the Jews, and so spoke that a great multitude both of the Jews and of the Greeks believed.
2 But the unbelieving Jews stirred up the Gentiles and poisoned their minds against the brethren.
3 Therefore they stayed there a long time, speaking boldly in the Lord, who was bearing witness to the word of His grace, granting signs and wonders to be done by their hands.
4 But the multitude of the city was divided: part sided with the Jews, and part with the apostles.
5 And when a violent attempt was made by both the Gentiles and Jews, with their rulers, to abuse and stone them,
6 they became aware of it and fled to Lystra and Derbe, cities of Lycaonia, and to the surrounding region.
7 And they were preaching the gospel there.

Idolatry at Lystra

8 And in Lystra a certain man without strength in his feet was sitting, a cripple from his mother's womb, who had never walked.
9 This man heard Paul speaking. Paul, observing him intently and seeing that he had faith to be healed,
10 said with a loud voice, "Stand up straight on your feet!" And he leaped and walked.
11 Now when the people saw what Paul had done, they raised their voices, saying in the Lycaonian language, "The gods have come down to us in the likeness of men!"
12 And Barnabas they called Zeus, and Paul, Hermes, because he was the chief speaker.

64 Habakkuk 1:5
65 Or And when they went out of the synagogue of the Jews; NU-Text reads And when they went out of the synagogue, they begged. 66 Isaiah 49:6

13 Then the priest of Zeus, whose temple was in front of their city, brought oxen and garlands to the gates, intending to sacrifice with the multitudes.
14 But when the apostles Barnabas and Paul heard this, they tore their clothes and ran in among the multitude, crying out
15 and saying, "Men, why are you doing these things? We also are men with the same nature as you, and preach to you that you should turn from these vain things to the living God, who made the heaven, the earth, the sea, and all things that are in them,
16 "who in bygone generations allowed all nations to walk in their own ways.
17 "Nevertheless He did not leave Himself without witness, in that He did good, gave us rain from heaven and fruitful seasons, filling our hearts with food and gladness."
18 And with these sayings they could scarcely restrain the multitudes from sacrificing to them.

Stoning, Escape to Derbe

19 Then Jews from Antioch and Iconium came there; and having persuaded the multitudes, they stoned Paul and dragged him out of the city, supposing him to be dead.
20 However, when the disciples gathered around him, he rose up and went into the city. And the next day he departed with Barnabas to Derbe.

Strengthening the Converts

21 And when they had preached the gospel to that city and made many disciples, they returned to Lystra, Iconium, and Antioch,
22 strengthening the souls of the disciples, exhorting them to continue in the faith, and saying, "We must through many tribulations enter the kingdom of God."
23 So when they had appointed elders in every church, and prayed with fasting, they commended them to the Lord in whom they had believed.
24 And after they had passed through Pisidia, they came to Pamphylia.
25 Now when they had preached the word in Perga, they went down to Attalia.
26 From there they sailed to Antioch,

where they had been commended to the grace of God for the work which they had completed.
27 And when they had come and gathered the church together, they reported all that God had done with them, and that He had opened the door of faith to the Gentiles.
28 So they stayed there a long time with the disciples.

Conflict over Circumcision

15 And certain men came down from Judea and taught the brethren, "Unless you are circumcised according to the custom of Moses, you cannot be saved."
2 Therefore, when Paul and Barnabas had no small dissension and dispute with them, they determined that Paul and Barnabas and certain others of them should go up to Jerusalem, to the apostles and elders, about this question.
3 So, being sent on their way by the church, they passed through Phoenicia and Samaria, describing the conversion of the Gentiles; and they caused great joy to all the brethren.
4 And when they had come to Jerusalem, they were received by the church and the apostles and the elders; and they reported all things that God had done with them.
5 But some of the sect of the Pharisees who believed rose up, saying, "It is necessary to circumcise them, and to command them to keep the law of Moses."

The Jerusalem Council

6 So the apostles and elders came together to consider this matter.
7 And when there had been much dispute, Peter rose up and said to them: "Men and brethren, you know that a good while ago God chose among us, that by my mouth the Gentiles should hear the word of the gospel and believe.
8 "So God, who knows the heart, acknowledged them, by giving them the Holy Spirit just as He did to us,
9 "and made no distinction between us and them, purifying their hearts by faith.
10 "Now therefore, why do you test God by putting a yoke on the neck of the disciples which neither our fathers nor we were able to bear?

Followers of the Way

In biblical times, names had specific meanings. They often reflected the city or village from which a person came, such as Joseph of Arimathea, Jesus of Nazareth, or Mary Magdalene (of Magdala). Another motive for names referred to a certain characteristic about the person. For instance, Nathanael means "God has given."

The early Christians, primarily of Jewish heritage, converted to Christianity either through personal contact with Jesus or by the message of the disciples. At that time, they were known as "followers of the Way." This name was derived from Jesus' statement, "I am the way, the truth, and the life. No one comes to the Father except through Me" (John 14:6). Paul directly referred to this name when he made his defense before the Roman authorities and the Jewish council as recorded in the Book of Acts. Speaking of his fight against Christianity before his conversion, Paul said, "I persecuted this Way to the death" (Acts 22:4).

In the latter part of the first century A.D., the followers of the Way became known as "Nazarenes." Eventually they took on the name "Christian" meaning "Christ one." This is in keeping with the promise that God would give true believers a new name, the name of God, written upon their heart and engraved upon their soul.

Ancient Middle East names were carefully chosen, for they were an honor, considered to be a gift of God. Strong evidence in the New Testament and first-century inscriptions support the practice that when people became Christians, they often changed their names. We know, for instance, that Saul changed his name to Paul.

Our new life in Christ is also a new beginning. We also take on a new name—the name of Christ. As a Christian, it may not always be easy to live up to the meaning of our name, yet the reward for living by faith is immeasurable. During the early centuries, many Christians came under persecution. They were asked, "Are you a Christian?" If they answered in the affirmative, they were often thrown to the lions or other means of being put to death.

We may not be personally persecuted for our faith, yet we can learn a vital lesson from these early believers. They understood that their spiritual lives through Christ far surpassed physical and personal success without Christ. For as Paul wrote, "To live is Christ, and to die is gain" (Phil. 1:21).

As Christians we take on the power and life of Jesus Christ. We put an end to our old selfish, negative life. We take on a positive, fulfilling life for God. In faith, like the early Christians, we believe that every end is a new beginning!

11 "But we believe that through the grace of the Lord Jesus Christ[67] we shall be saved in the same manner as they."
12 Then all the multitude kept silent and listened to Barnabas and Paul declaring how many miracles and wonders God had worked through them among the Gentiles.
13 And after they had become silent, James answered, saying, "Men *and* brethren, listen to me:
14 "Simon has declared how God at the first visited the Gentiles to take out of them a people for His name.
15 "And with this the words of the prophets agree, just as it is written:

16 'After this I will return
And will rebuild the tabernacle of
    David which has fallen down.
I will rebuild its ruins,
And I will set it up,
17 So that the rest of mankind may seek
    the LORD,
Even all the Gentiles who are called by
    My name,
Says the LORD who does all these
    things.'[68]

18 "Known to God from eternity are all His works.[69]
19 "Therefore I judge that we should not trouble those from among the Gentiles who are turning to God,
20 "but that we write to them to abstain from things polluted by idols, *from* sexual immorality, *from* things strangled, and *from* blood.
21 "For Moses has had throughout many generations those who preach him in every city, being read in the synagogues every Sabbath."

The Jerusalem Decree

22 Then it pleased the apostles and elders, with the whole church, to send chosen men of their own company to Antioch with Paul and Barnabas, *namely*, Judas who was also named Barsabas,[70] and Silas, leading men among the brethren.
23 They wrote this *letter* by them:

The apostles, the elders, and the brethren,
To the brethren who are of the Gentiles in Antioch, Syria, and Cilicia: Greetings.
24 Since we have heard that some who went out from us have troubled you with words, unsettling your souls, saying, '*You must* be circumcised and keep the law'[71]—to whom we gave no *such* commandment—
25 it seemed good to us, being assembled with one accord, to send chosen men to you with our beloved Barnabas and Paul,
26 men who have risked their lives for the name of our Lord Jesus Christ.
27 We have therefore sent Judas and Silas, who will also report the same things by word of mouth.
28 For it seemed good to the Holy Spirit, and to us, to lay upon you no greater burden than these necessary things:
29 that you abstain from things offered to idols, from blood, from things strangled, and from sexual immorality. If you keep yourselves from these, you will do well.
Farewell.

Continuing Ministry in Syria

30 So when they were sent off, they came to Antioch; and when they had gathered the multitude together, they delivered the letter.
31 When they had read it, they rejoiced over its encouragement.
32 Now Judas and Silas, themselves being prophets also, exhorted the brethren with many words and strengthened *them*.
33 And after they had stayed *there* for a time, they were sent back with greetings from the brethren to the apostles.[72]
34 However, it seemed good to Silas to remain there.[73]
35 Paul and Barnabas also remained in Antioch, teaching and preaching the word of the Lord, with many others also.

Division over John Mark

36 Then after some days Paul said to Barnabas, "Let us now go back and visit our brethren in every city where we have preached the word of the Lord, *and see* how they are doing."
37 Now Barnabas was determined to take with them John called Mark.
38 But Paul insisted that they should not take with them the one who had departed

---

67 NU-Text and M-Text omit *Christ*.   68 Amos 9:11, 12
69 NU-Text reads *Says the Lord, who makes these things known from eternity (of old)*.
70 NU-Text and M-Text read *Barsabbas*.   71 NU-Text omits *saying, 'You must be circumcised and keep the law'*.
72 NU-Text reads *to those who had sent them*.   73 NU-Text and M-Text omit this verse.

from them in Pamphylia, and had not gone with them to the work.
39 Then the contention became so sharp that they parted from one another. And so Barnabas took Mark and sailed to Cyprus;
40 but Paul chose Silas and departed, being commended by the brethren to the grace of God.
41 And he went through Syria and Cilicia, strengthening the churches.

Timothy Joins Paul and Silas

16 Then he came to Derbe and Lystra. And behold, a certain disciple was there, named Timothy, *the* son of a certain Jewish woman who believed, but his father *was* Greek.
2 He was well spoken of by the brethren who were at Lystra and Iconium.
3 Paul wanted to have him go on with him. And he took *him* and circumcised him because of the Jews who were in that region, for they all knew that his father was Greek.
4 And as they went through the cities, they delivered to them the decrees to keep, which were determined by the apostles and elders at Jerusalem.
5 So the churches were strengthened in the faith, and increased in number daily.

The Macedonian Call

6 Now when they had gone through Phrygia and the region of Galatia, they were forbidden by the Holy Spirit to preach the word in Asia.
7 After they had come to Mysia, they tried to go into Bithynia, but the Spirit[74] did not permit them.
8 So passing by Mysia, they came down to Troas.
9 And a vision appeared to Paul in the night. A man of Macedonia stood and pleaded with him, saying, "Come over to Macedonia and help us."
10 Now after he had seen the vision, immediately we sought to go to Macedonia, concluding that the Lord had called us to preach the gospel to them.

Lydia Baptized at Philippi

11 Therefore, sailing from Troas, we ran a straight course to Samothrace, and the next *day* came to Neapolis,

12 and from there to Philippi, which is the foremost city of that part of Macedonia, a colony. And we were staying in that city for some days.
13 And on the Sabbath day we went out of the city to the riverside, where prayer was customarily made; and we sat down and spoke to the women who met *there*.
14 Now a certain woman named Lydia heard *us*. She was a seller of purple from the city of Thyatira, who worshiped God. The Lord opened her heart to heed the things spoken by Paul.
15 And when she and her household were baptized, she begged *us*, saying, "If you have judged me to be faithful to the Lord, come to my house and stay." And she constrained us.

Paul and Silas Imprisoned

16 Now it happened, as we went to prayer, that a certain slave girl possessed with a spirit of divination met us, who brought her masters much profit by fortune-telling.
17 This girl followed Paul and us, and cried out, saying, "These men are the servants of the Most High God, who proclaim to us the way of salvation."
18 And this she did for many days. But Paul, greatly annoyed, turned and said to the spirit, "I command you in the name of Jesus Christ to come out of her." And he came out that very hour.
19 But when her masters saw that their hope of profit was gone, they seized Paul and Silas and dragged *them* into the marketplace to the authorities.
20 And they brought them to the magistrates, and said, "These men, being Jews, exceedingly trouble our city;
21 "and they teach customs which are not lawful for us, being Romans, to receive or observe."
22 Then the multitude rose up together against them; and the magistrates tore off their clothes and commanded *them* to be beaten with rods.
23 And when they had laid many stripes on them, they threw *them* into prison, commanding the jailer to keep them securely.
24 Having received such a charge, he put them into the inner prison and fastened their feet in the stocks.

74 NU-Text adds *of Jesus.*

The Philippian Jailer Saved

25 But at midnight Paul and Silas were praying and singing hymns to God, and the prisoners were listening to them.
26 Suddenly there was a great earthquake, so that the foundations of the prison were shaken; and immediately all the doors were opened and everyone's chains were loosed.
27 And the keeper of the prison, awaking from sleep and seeing the prison doors open, supposing the prisoners had fled, drew his sword and was about to kill himself.
28 But Paul called with a loud voice, saying, "Do yourself no harm, for we are all here."
29 Then he called for a light, ran in, and fell down trembling before Paul and Silas.
30 And he brought them out and said, "Sirs, what must I do to be saved?"
31 So they said, "Believe on the Lord Jesus Christ, and you will be saved, you and your household."
32 Then they spoke the word of the Lord to him and to all who were in his house.
33 And he took them the same hour of the night and washed *their* stripes. And immediately he and all his family were baptized.
34 Now when he had brought them into his house, he set food before them; and he rejoiced, having believed in God with all his household.

Paul Refuses to Depart Secretly

35 And when it was day, the magistrates sent the officers, saying, "Let those men go."
36 So the keeper of the prison reported these words to Paul, saying, "The magistrates have sent to let you go. Now therefore depart, and go in peace."
37 But Paul said to them, "They have beaten us openly, uncondemned Romans, *and* have thrown *us* into prison. And now do they put us out secretly? No indeed! Let them come themselves and get us out."
38 And the officers told these words to the magistrates, and they were afraid when they heard that they were Romans.
39 Then they came and pleaded with them and brought *them* out, and asked *them* to depart from the city.

40 So they went out of the prison and entered *the house of* Lydia; and when they had seen the brethren, they encouraged them and departed.

Preaching Christ at Thessalonica

17 Now when they had passed through Amphipolis and Apollonia, they came to Thessalonica, where there was a synagogue of the Jews.
2 Then Paul, as his custom was, went in to them, and for three Sabbaths reasoned with them from the Scriptures,
3 explaining and demonstrating that the Christ had to suffer and rise again from the dead, and *saying,* "This Jesus whom I preach to you is the Christ."
4 And some of them were persuaded; and a great multitude of the devout Greeks, and not a few of the leading women, joined Paul and Silas.

Assault on Jason's House

5 But the Jews who were not persuaded, becoming envious,[75] took some of the evil men from the marketplace, and gathering a mob, set all the city in an uproar and attacked the house of Jason, and sought to bring them out to the people.
6 But when they did not find them, they dragged Jason and some brethren to the rulers of the city, crying out, "These who have turned the world upside down have come here too.
7 "Jason has harbored them, and these are all acting contrary to the decrees of Caesar, saying there is another king— Jesus."
8 And they troubled the crowd and the rulers of the city when they heard these things.
9 So when they had taken security from Jason and the rest, they let them go.

Ministering at Berea

10 Then the brethren immediately sent Paul and Silas away by night to Berea. When they arrived, they went into the synagogue of the Jews.
11 These were more fair-minded than those in Thessalonica, in that they received the word with all readiness, and searched the Scriptures daily *to find out* whether these things were so.
12 Therefore many of them believed, and also not a few of the Greeks, prominent women as well as men.

75 NU-Text omits *who were not persuaded;* M-Text omits *becoming envious.*

13 But when the Jews from Thessalonica learned that the word of God was preached by Paul at Berea, they came there also and stirred up the crowds.
14 Then immediately the brethren sent Paul away, to go to the sea; but both Silas and Timothy remained there.
15 So those who conducted Paul brought him to Athens; and receiving a command for Silas and Timothy to come to him with all speed, they departed.

The Philosophers at Athens

16 Now while Paul waited for them at Athens, his spirit was provoked within him when he saw that the city was given over to idols.
17 Therefore he reasoned in the synagogue with the Jews and with the *Gentile* worshipers, and in the marketplace daily with those who happened to be there.
18 Then[76] certain Epicurean and Stoic philosophers encountered him. And some said, "What does this babbler want to say?" Others said, "He seems to be a proclaimer of foreign gods," because he preached to them Jesus and the resurrection.
19 And they took him and brought him to the Areopagus, saying, "May we know what this new doctrine *is* of which you speak?
20 "For you are bringing some strange things to our ears. Therefore we want to know what these things mean."
21 For all the Athenians and the foreigners who were there spent their time in nothing else but either to tell or to hear some new thing.

Addressing the Areopagus

22 Then Paul stood in the midst of the Areopagus and said, "Men of Athens, I perceive that in all things you are very religious;
23 "for as I was passing through and considering the objects of your worship, I even found an altar with this inscription:

TO THE UNKNOWN GOD.

Therefore, the One whom you worship without knowing, Him I proclaim to you:
24 "God, who made the world and everything in it, since He is Lord of heaven and earth, does not dwell in temples made with hands.
25 "Nor is He worshiped with men's hands, as though He needed anything, since He gives to all life, breath, and all things.
26 "And He has made from one blood[77] every nation of men to dwell on all the face of the earth, and has determined their preappointed times and the boundaries of their habitation,
27 "so that they should seek the Lord, in the hope that they might grope for Him and find Him, though He is not far from each one of us;
28 "for in Him we live and move and have our being, as also some of your own poets have said, 'For we are also His offspring.'
29 "Therefore, since we are the offspring of God, we ought not to think that the Divine Nature is like gold or silver or stone, something shaped by art and man's devising.
30 "Truly, these times of ignorance God overlooked, but now commands all men everywhere to repent,
31 "because He has appointed a day on which He will judge the world in righteousness by the Man whom He has ordained. He has given assurance of this to all by raising Him from the dead."
32 And when they heard of the resurrection of the dead, some mocked, while others said, "We will hear you again on this *matter.*"
33 So Paul departed from among them.
34 However, some men joined him and believed, among them Dionysius the Areopagite, a woman named Damaris, and others with them.

Ministering at Corinth

18 After these things Paul departed from Athens and went to Corinth.
2 And he found a certain Jew named Aquila, born in Pontus, who had recently come from Italy with his wife Priscilla (because Claudius had commanded all the Jews to depart from Rome); and he came to them.
3 So, because he was of the same trade, he stayed with them and worked; for by occupation they were tentmakers.
4 And he reasoned in the synagogue every Sabbath, and persuaded both Jews and Greeks.
5 When Silas and Timothy had come from Macedonia, Paul was constrained

76 NU-Text and M-Text add *also.*   77 NU-Text omits *blood.*

by the Spirit, and testified to the Jews *that* Jesus *is* the Christ.

6 But when they opposed him and blasphemed, he shook *his* garments and said to them, "Your blood *be* upon your *own* heads; I *am* clean. From now on I will go to the Gentiles."

7 And he departed from there and entered the house of a certain *man* named Justus,[78] *one* who worshiped God, whose house was next door to the synagogue.

8 Then Crispus, the ruler of the synagogue, believed on the Lord with all his household. And many of the Corinthians, hearing, believed and were baptized.

9 Now the Lord spoke to Paul in the night by a vision, "Do not be afraid, but speak, and do not keep silent;

10 "for I am with you, and no one will attack you to hurt you; for I have many people in this city."

11 And he continued *there* a year and six months, teaching the word of God among them.

12 Now when Gallio was proconsul of Achaia, the Jews with one accord rose up against Paul and brought him to the judgment seat,

13 saying, "This *fellow* persuades men to worship God contrary to the law."

14 And when Paul was about to open *his* mouth, Gallio said to the Jews, "If it were a matter of wrongdoing or wicked crimes, O Jews, there would be reason why I should bear with you.

15 "But if it is a question of words and names and your own law, look *to it* yourselves; for I do not want to be a judge of such *matters*."

16 And he drove them from the judgment seat.

17 Then all the Greeks[79] took Sosthenes, the ruler of the synagogue, and beat *him* before the judgment seat. But Gallio took no notice of these things.

Paul Returns to Antioch

18 So Paul still remained a good while. Then he took leave of the brethren and sailed for Syria, and Priscilla and Aquila *were* with him. He had *his* hair cut off at Cenchrea, for he had taken a vow.

19 And he came to Ephesus, and left them there; but he himself entered the synagogue and reasoned with the Jews.

20 When they asked *him* to stay a longer time with them, he did not consent,

21 but took leave of them, saying, "I must by all means keep this coming feast in Jerusalem;[80] but I will return again to you, God willing." And he sailed from Ephesus.

22 And when he had landed at Caesarea, and gone up and greeted the church, he went down to Antioch.

23 After he had spent some time *there*, he departed and went over *all* the region of Galatia and Phrygia in order, strengthening all the disciples.

Ministry of Apollos

24 Now a certain Jew named Apollos, born at Alexandria, an eloquent man *and* mighty in the Scriptures, came to Ephesus.

25 This man had been instructed in the way of the Lord; and being fervent in spirit, he spoke and taught accurately the things of the Lord, though he knew only the baptism of John.

26 So he began to speak boldly in the synagogue. When Aquila and Priscilla heard him, they took him aside and explained to him the way of God more accurately.

27 And when he desired to cross to Achaia, the brethren wrote, exhorting the disciples to receive him; and when he arrived, he greatly helped those who had believed through grace;

28 for he vigorously refuted the Jews publicly, showing from the Scriptures that Jesus is the Christ.

Paul at Ephesus

19 And it happened, while Apollos was at Corinth, that Paul, having passed through the upper regions, came to Ephesus. And finding some disciples

2 he said to them, "Did you receive the Holy Spirit when you believed?" And they said to him, "We have not so much as heard whether there is a Holy Spirit."

3 And he said to them, "Into what then were you baptized?" So they said, "Into John's baptism."

4 Then Paul said, "John indeed baptized with a baptism of repentance, saying to the people that they should believe on Him who would come after him, that is, on Christ Jesus."

5 When they heard *this*, they were baptized in the name of the Lord Jesus.

---

78 NU-Text reads *Titius Justus*.   79 NU-Text reads *they all*.   80 NU-Text omits *I must* through *Jerusalem*.

6 And when Paul had laid hands on them, the Holy Spirit came upon them, and they spoke with tongues and prophesied.
7 Now the men were about twelve in all.
8 And he went into the synagogue and spoke boldly for three months, reasoning and persuading concerning the things of the kingdom of God.
9 But when some were hardened and did not believe, but spoke evil of the Way before the multitude, he departed from them and withdrew the disciples, reasoning daily in the school of Tyrannus.
10 And this continued for two years, so that all who dwelt in Asia heard the word of the Lord Jesus, both Jews and Greeks.

Miracles Glorify Christ

11 Now God worked unusual miracles by the hands of Paul,
12 so that even handkerchiefs or aprons were brought from his body to the sick, and the diseases left them and the evil spirits went out of them.
13 Then some of the itinerant Jewish exorcists took it upon themselves to call the name of the Lord Jesus over those who had evil spirits, saying, "We 81 adjure you by the Jesus whom Paul preaches."
14 Also there were seven sons of Sceva, a Jewish chief priest, who did so.
15 And the evil spirit answered and said, "Jesus I know, and Paul I know; but who are you?"
16 Then the man in whom the evil spirit was leaped on them, overpowered 82 them, and prevailed against them, 83 so that they fled out of that house naked and wounded.
17 This became known both to all Jews and Greeks dwelling in Ephesus; and fear fell on them all, and the name of the Lord Jesus was magnified.
18 And many who had believed came confessing and telling their deeds.
19 Also, many of those who had practiced magic brought their books together and burned *them* in the sight of all. And they counted up the value of them, and *it* totaled fifty thousand *pieces* of silver.
20 So the word of the Lord grew mightily and prevailed.

The Riot at Ephesus

21 When these things were accomplished, Paul purposed in the Spirit, when he had passed through Macedonia and Achaia, to go to Jerusalem, saying, "After I have been there, I must also see Rome."
22 So he sent into Macedonia two of those who ministered to him, Timothy and Erastus, but he himself stayed in Asia for a time.
23 And about that time there arose a great commotion about the Way.
24 For a certain man named Demetrius, a silversmith, who made silver shrines of Diana, 84 brought no small profit to the craftsmen.
25 He called them together with the workers of similar occupation, and said: "Men, you know that we have our prosperity by this trade.
26 "Moreover you see and hear that not only at Ephesus, but throughout almost all Asia, this Paul has persuaded and turned away many people, saying that they are not gods which are made with hands.
27 "So not only is this trade of ours in danger of falling into disrepute, but also the temple of the great goddess Diana may be despised and her magnificence destroyed, 85 whom all Asia and the world worship."
28 And when they heard *this*, they were full of wrath and cried out, saying, "Great *is* Diana of the Ephesians!"
29 So the whole city was filled with confusion, and rushed into the theater with one accord, having seized Gaius and Aristarchus, Macedonians, Paul's travel companions.
30 And when Paul wanted to go in to the people, the disciples would not allow him.
31 Then some of the officials of Asia, who were his friends, sent to him pleading that he would not venture into the theater.
32 Some therefore cried one thing and some another, for the assembly was confused, and most of them did not know why they had come together.
33 And they drew Alexander out of the multitude, the Jews putting him forward. And Alexander motioned with his hand, and wanted to make his defense to the people.

---

81 NU-Text reads *I*.   82 M-Text reads *and they overpowered*.   83 NU-Text reads *both of them*.
84 Greek *Artemis*   85 NU-Text reads *she be deposed from her magnificence*.

34 But when they found out that he was a Jew, all with one voice cried out for about two hours, "Great *is* Diana of the Ephesians!"

35 And when the city clerk had quieted the crowd, he said: "Men of Ephesus, what man is there who does not know that the city of the Ephesians is temple guardian of the great goddess Diana, and of the *image* which fell down from Zeus?

36 "Therefore, since these things cannot be denied, you ought to be quiet and do nothing rashly.

37 "For you have brought these men here who are neither robbers of temples nor blasphemers of your[86] goddess.

38 "Therefore, if Demetrius and his fellow craftsmen have a case against anyone, the courts are open and there are proconsuls. Let them bring charges against one another.

39 "But if you have any other inquiry to make, it shall be determined in the lawful assembly.

40 "For we are in danger of being called in question for today's uproar, there being no reason which we may give to account for this disorderly gathering."

41 And when he had said these things, he dismissed the assembly.

Journeys in Greece

20 After the uproar had ceased, Paul called the disciples to *him*, embraced *them*, and departed to go to Macedonia.

2 Now when he had gone over that region and encouraged them with many words, he came to Greece

3 and stayed three months. And when the Jews plotted against him as he was about to sail to Syria, he decided to return through Macedonia.

4 And Sopater of Berea accompanied him to Asia—also Aristarchus and Secundus of the Thessalonians, and Gaius of Derbe, and Timothy, and Tychicus and Trophimus of Asia.

5 These men, going ahead, waited for us at Troas.

6 But we sailed away from Philippi after the Days of Unleavened Bread, and in five days joined them at Troas, where we stayed seven days.

Ministering at Troas

7 Now on the first *day* of the week, when the disciples came together to break bread, Paul, ready to depart the next day, spoke to them and continued his message until midnight.

8 There were many lamps in the upper room where they[87] were gathered together.

9 And in a window sat a certain young man named Eutychus, who was sinking into a deep sleep. He was overcome by sleep; and as Paul continued speaking, he fell down from the third story and was taken up dead.

10 But Paul went down, fell on him, and embracing *him* said, "Do not trouble yourselves, for his life is in him."

11 Now when he had come up, had broken bread and eaten, and talked a long while, even till daybreak, he departed.

12 And they brought the young man in alive, and they were not a little comforted.

From Troas to Miletus

13 Then we went ahead to the ship and sailed to Assos, there intending to take Paul on board; for so he had given orders, intending himself to go on foot.

14 And when he met us at Assos, we took him on board and came to Mitylene.

15 We sailed from there, and the next *day* came opposite Chios; the following *day* we arrived at Samos and stayed at Trogyllium; the next *day* we came to Miletus.

16 For Paul had decided to sail past Ephesus, so that he would not have to spend time in Asia; for he was hurrying to be at Jerusalem, if possible, on the Day of Pentecost.

The Ephesian Elders Exhorted

17 From Miletus he sent to Ephesus and called for the elders of the church.

18 And when they had come to him, he said to them: "You know, from the first day that I came to Asia, in what manner I always lived among you,

19 "serving the Lord with all humility, with many tears and trials which happened to me by the plotting of the Jews;

20 "*and* how I kept back nothing that was helpful, but proclaimed it to you, and

taught you publicly and from house to house,

21 "testifying to Jews, and also to Greeks, repentance toward God and faith toward our Lord Jesus Christ.

22 "And see, now I go bound in the spirit to Jerusalem, not knowing the things that will happen to me there,

23 "except that the Holy Spirit testifies in every city, saying that chains and tribulations await me.

24 "But none of these things move me; nor do I count my life dear to myself,[88] so that I may finish my race with joy, and the ministry which I received from the Lord Jesus, to testify to the gospel of the grace of God.

25 "And indeed, now I know that you all, among whom I have gone preaching the kingdom of God, will see my face no more.

26 "Therefore I testify to you this day that I am innocent of the blood of all men.

27 "For I have not shunned to declare to you the whole counsel of God.

28 "Therefore take heed to yourselves and to all the flock, among which the Holy Spirit has made you overseers, to shepherd the church of God[89] which He purchased with His own blood.

29 "For I know this, that after my departure savage wolves will come in among you, not sparing the flock.

30 "Also from among yourselves men will rise up, speaking perverse things, to draw away the disciples after themselves.

31 "Therefore watch, and remember that for three years I did not cease to warn everyone night and day with tears.

32 "And now, brethren, I commend you to God and to the word of His grace, which is able to build you up and give you an inheritance among all those who are sanctified.

33 "I have coveted no one's silver or gold or apparel.

34 "Yes,[90] you yourselves know that these hands have provided for my necessities, and for those who were with me.

35 "I have shown you in every way, by laboring like this, that you must support the weak. And remember the words of the Lord Jesus, that He said, 'It is more blessed to give than to receive.' "

36 And when he had said these things, he knelt down and prayed with them all.

37 Then they all wept freely, and fell on Paul's neck and kissed him,

38 sorrowing most of all for the words which he spoke, that they would see his face no more. And they accompanied him to the ship.

Warnings on the Journey to Jerusalem

21 Now it came to pass, that when we had departed from them and set sail, running a straight course we came to Cos, the following day to Rhodes, and from there to Patara.

2 And finding a ship sailing over to Phoenicia, we went aboard and set sail.

3 When we had sighted Cyprus, we passed it on the left, sailed to Syria, and landed at Tyre; for there the ship was to unload her cargo.

4 And finding disciples,[91] we stayed there seven days. They told Paul through the Spirit not to go up to Jerusalem.

5 When we had come to the end of those days, we departed and went on our way; and they all accompanied us, with wives and children, till we were out of the city. And we knelt down on the shore and prayed.

6 When we had taken our leave of one another, we boarded the ship, and they returned home.

7 And when we had finished our voyage from Tyre, we came to Ptolemais, greeted the brethren, and stayed with them one day.

8 On the next day we who were Paul's companions[92] departed and came to Caesarea, and entered the house of Philip the evangelist, who was one of the seven, and stayed with him.

9 Now this man had four virgin daughters who prophesied.

10 And as we stayed many days, a certain prophet named Agabus came down from Judea.

11 When he had come to us, he took Paul's belt, bound his own hands and feet, and said, "Thus says the Holy Spirit, 'So shall the Jews at Jerusalem bind the man who owns this belt, and deliver him into the hands of the Gentiles.' "

12 And when we heard these things, both we and those from that place pleaded with him not to go up to Jerusalem.

---

88 NU-Text reads But I do not count my life of any value or dear to myself.   89 M-Text reads of the Lord and God.
90 NU-Text and M-Text omit Yes.   91 NU-Text reads the disciples.
92 NU-Text omits who were Paul's companions.

13 Then Paul answered, "What do you mean by weeping and breaking my heart? For I am ready not only to be bound, but also to die at Jerusalem for the name of the Lord Jesus."
14 So when he would not be persuaded, we ceased, saying, "The will of the Lord be done."

Paul Urged to Make Peace

15 And after those days we packed and went up to Jerusalem.
16 Also some of the disciples from Caesarea went with us and brought with them one, Mnason of Cyprus, an early disciple, with whom we were to lodge.
17 And when we had come to Jerusalem, the brethren received us gladly.
18 On the following *day* Paul went in with us to James, and all the elders were present.
19 When he had greeted them, he told in detail those things which God had done among the Gentiles through his ministry.
20 And when they heard *it*, they glorified the Lord. And they said to him, "You see, brother, how many myriads of Jews there are who have believed, and they are all zealous for the law;
21 "but they have been informed about you that you teach all the Jews who are among the Gentiles to forsake Moses, saying that they ought not to circumcise *their* children nor to walk according to the customs.
22 "What then? The assembly must certainly meet, for they will hear that you have come.[93]
23 "Therefore do what we tell you: We have four men who have taken a vow.
24 "Take them and be purified with them, and pay their expenses so that they may shave *their* heads, and that all may know that those things of which they were informed concerning you are nothing, but *that* you yourself also walk orderly and keep the law.
25 "But concerning the Gentiles who believe, we have written *and* decided that they should observe no such thing,[94] except that they should keep themselves from *things* offered to idols, from blood, from things strangled, and from sexual immorality."

Arrested in the Temple

26 Then Paul took the men, and the next day, having been purified with them, entered the temple to announce the expiration of the days of purification, at which time an offering should be made for each one of them.
27 And when the seven days were almost ended, the Jews from Asia, seeing him in the temple, stirred up the whole crowd and laid hands on him,
28 crying out, "Men of Israel, help! This is the man who teaches all *men* everywhere against the people, the law, and this place; and furthermore he also brought Greeks into the temple and has defiled this holy place."
29 (For they had previously[95] seen Trophimus the Ephesian with him in the city, whom they supposed that Paul had brought into the temple.)
30 And all the city was disturbed; and the people ran together, seized Paul, and dragged him out of the temple; and immediately the doors were shut.
31 Now as they were seeking to kill him, news came to the commander of the garrison that all Jerusalem was in an uproar.
32 He immediately took soldiers and centurions, and ran down to them. And when they saw the commander and the soldiers, they stopped beating Paul.
33 Then the commander came near and took him, and commanded *him* to be bound with two chains; and he asked who he was and what he had done.
34 And some among the multitude cried one thing and some another. And when he could not ascertain the truth because of the tumult, he commanded him to be taken into the barracks.
35 And when he reached the stairs, he had to be carried by the soldiers because of the violence of the mob.
36 For the multitude of the people followed after, crying out, "Away with him!"

Addressing the Jerusalem Mob

37 And as Paul was about to be led into the barracks, he said to the commander, "May I speak to you?" He replied, "Can you speak Greek?
38 "Are you not the Egyptian who some time ago raised an insurrection and led

93 NU-Text reads *What then is to be done? They will certainly.*
94 NU-Text omits *that they should observe no such thing except.*   95 M-Text omits *previously.*

the four thousand assassins out into the wilderness?"

39 But Paul said, "I am a Jew from Tarsus, in Cilicia, a citizen of no mean city; and I implore you, permit me to speak to the people."

40 So when he had given him permission, Paul stood on the stairs and motioned with his hand to the people. And when there was a great silence, he spoke to *them* in the Hebrew language, saying,

22 "Men, brethren, and fathers, hear my defense before you now."

2 And when they heard that he spoke to them in the Hebrew language, they kept all the more silent. Then he said:

3 "I am indeed a Jew, born in Tarsus of Cilicia, but brought up in this city at the feet of Gamaliel, taught according to the strictness of our fathers' law, and was zealous toward God as you all are today.

4 "I persecuted this Way to the death, binding and delivering into prisons both men and women,

5 "as also the high priest bears me witness, and all the council of the elders, from whom I also received letters to the brethren, and went to Damascus to bring in chains even those who were there to Jerusalem to be punished.

6 "Now it happened, as I journeyed and came near Damascus at about noon, suddenly a great light from heaven shone around me.

7 "And I fell to the ground and heard a voice saying to me, 'Saul, Saul, why are you persecuting Me?'

8 "So I answered, 'Who are You, Lord?' And He said to me, 'I am Jesus of Nazareth, whom you are persecuting.'

9 "Now those who were with me indeed saw the light and were afraid,96 but they did not hear the voice of Him who spoke to me.

10 "So I said, 'What shall I do, Lord?' And the Lord said to me, 'Arise and go into Damascus, and there you will be told all things which are appointed for you to do.'

11 "And since I could not see for the glory of that light, being led by the hand of those who were with me, I came into Damascus.

12 "Then one, Ananias, a devout man according to the law, having a good testimony with all the Jews who dwelt *there*,

13 "came to me; and he stood and said

to me, 'Brother Saul, receive your sight.' And at that same hour I looked up at him.

14 "Then he said, 'The God of our fathers has chosen you that you should know His will, and see the Just One, and hear the voice of His mouth.

15 'For you will be His witness to all men of what you have seen and heard.

16 'And now why are you waiting? Arise and be baptized, and wash away your sins, calling on the name of the Lord.'

17 "Then it happened, when I returned to Jerusalem and was praying in the temple, that I was in a trance

18 "and saw Him saying to me, 'Make haste and get out of Jerusalem quickly, for they will not receive your testimony concerning Me.'

19 "So I said, 'Lord, they know that in every synagogue I imprisoned and beat those who believe on You.

20 'And when the blood of Your martyr Stephen was shed, I also was standing by consenting to his death,97 and guarding the clothes of those who were killing him.'

21 "Then He said to me, 'Depart, for I will send you far from here to the Gentiles.' "

Paul's Roman Citizenship

22 And they listened to him until this word, and *then* they raised their voices and said, "Away with such a *fellow* from the earth, for he is not fit to live!"

23 Then, as they cried out and tore off *their* clothes and threw dust into the air,

24 the commander ordered him to be brought into the barracks, and said that he should be examined under scourging, so that he might know why they shouted so against him.

25 And as they bound him with thongs, Paul said to the centurion who stood by, "Is it lawful for you to scourge a man who is a Roman, and uncondemned?"

26 When the centurion heard *that*, he went and told the commander, saying, "Take care what you do, for this man is a Roman."

27 Then the commander came and said to him, "Tell me, are you a Roman?" He said, "Yes."

28 And the commander answered, "With a large sum I obtained this citizenship." And Paul said, "But I was born *a citizen*."

96 NU-Text omits *and were afraid.* 97 NU-Text omits *to his death.*

29 Then immediately those who were about to examine him withdrew from him; and the commander was also afraid after he found out that he was a Roman, and because he had bound him.

The Sanhedrin Divided

30 The next day, because he wanted to know for certain why he was accused by the Jews, he released him from *his* bonds, and commanded the chief priests and all their council to appear, and brought Paul down and set him before them.

23 Then Paul, looking earnestly at the council, said, "Men *and* brethren, I have lived in all good conscience before God until this day."
2 And the high priest Ananias commanded those who stood by him to strike him on the mouth.
3 Then Paul said to him, "God will strike you, *you* whitewashed wall! For you sit to judge me according to the law, and do you command me to be struck contrary to the law?"
4 And those who stood by said, "Do you revile God's high priest?"
5 Then Paul said, "I did not know, brethren, that he was the high priest; for it is written, 'You shall not speak evil of the ruler of your people.' "[98]
6 But when Paul perceived that one part were Sadducees and the other Pharisees, he cried out in the council, "Men *and* brethren, I am a Pharisee, the son of a Pharisee; concerning the hope and resurrection of the dead I am being judged!"
7 And when he had said this, a dissension arose between the Pharisees and the Sadducees; and the assembly was divided.
8 For *the* Sadducees say that there is no resurrection—and no angel or spirit; but the Pharisees confess both.
9 Then there arose a loud outcry. And the scribes *who were* of the Pharisees' party arose and protested, saying, "We find no evil in this man; but if a spirit or an angel has spoken to him, let us not fight against God."[99]
10 And when there arose a great dissension, the commander, fearing lest Paul might be pulled to pieces by them, commanded the soldiers to go down and take him by force from among them, and bring *him* into the barracks.

The Plot Against Paul

11 But the following night the Lord stood by him and said, "Be of good cheer, Paul; for as you have testified for Me in Jerusalem, so you must also bear witness at Rome."
12 And when it was day, some of the Jews banded together and bound themselves under an oath, saying that they would neither eat nor drink till they had killed Paul.
13 Now there were more than forty who had formed this conspiracy.
14 They came to the chief priests and elders, and said, "We have bound ourselves under a great oath that we will eat nothing until we have killed Paul.
15 "Now you, therefore, together with the council, suggest to the commander that he be brought down to you tomorrow,[100] as though you were going to make further inquiries concerning him; but we are ready to kill him before he comes near."
16 And when Paul's sister's son heard of their ambush, he went and entered the barracks and told Paul.
17 Then Paul called one of the centurions to *him* and said, "Take this young man to the commander, for he has something to tell him."
18 So he took him and brought *him* to the commander and said, "Paul the prisoner called me to *him* and asked *me* to bring this young man to you. He has something to say to you."
19 Then the commander took him by the hand, went aside and asked *him* privately, "What is it that you have to tell me?"
20 And he said, "The Jews have agreed to ask that you bring Paul down to the council tomorrow, as though they were going to inquire more fully about him.
21 "But do not yield to them, for more than forty of them lie in wait for him, men who have bound themselves by an oath that they will neither eat nor drink till they have killed him; and now they are ready, waiting for the promise from you."
22 So the commander let the young man depart, and commanded *him*, "Tell no one that you have revealed these things to me."

98 Exodus 22:28   99 NU-Text omits last clause and reads *what if a spirit or an angel has spoken to him?*
100 NU-Text omits *tomorrow.*

Sent to Felix

23 And he called for two centurions, saying, "Prepare two hundred soldiers, seventy horsemen, and two hundred spearmen to go to Caesarea at the third hour of the night; 24 "and provide mounts to set Paul on, and bring *him* safely to Felix the governor."

25 He wrote a letter in the following manner:

26 Claudius Lysias,

To the most excellent governor Felix:

Greetings.

27 This man was seized by the Jews and was about to be killed by them. Coming with the troops I rescued him, having learned that he was a Roman. 28 And when I wanted to know the reason they accused him, I brought him before their council. 29 I found out that he was accused concerning questions of their law, but had nothing charged against him worthy of death or chains. 30 And when it was told me that the Jews lay in wait for the man,[101] I sent him immediately to you, and also commanded his accusers to state before you the charges against him. Farewell.

31 Then the soldiers, as they were commanded, took Paul and brought *him* by night to Antipatris. 32 The next day they left the horsemen to go on with him, and returned to the barracks. 33 When they came to Caesarea and had delivered the letter to the governor, they also presented Paul to him. 34 And when the governor had read *it*, he asked what province he was from. And when he understood that *he was* from Cilicia, 35 he said, "I will hear you when your accusers also have come." And he commanded him to be kept in Herod's Praetorium.

Accused of Sedition

24 Now after five days Ananias the high priest came down with the elders and a certain orator *named* Tertullus. These gave evidence to the governor against Paul. 2 And when he was called upon, Tertullus began his accusation, saying: "Seeing that through you we enjoy great peace, and prosperity is being brought to this nation by your foresight, 3 "we accept *it* always and in all places, most noble Felix, with all thankfulness. 4 "Nevertheless, not to be tedious to you any further, I beg you to hear, by your courtesy, a few words from us. 5 "For we have found this man *a* plague, a creator of dissension among all the Jews throughout the world, and a ringleader of the sect of the Nazarenes. 6 "He even tried to profane the temple, and we seized him,[102] and wanted to judge him according to our law. 7 "But the commander Lysias came by and with great violence took *him* out of our hands, 8 "commanding his accusers to come to you. By examining him yourself you may ascertain all these things of which we accuse him." 9 And the Jews also assented, maintaining that these things were so.

The Defense Before Felix

10 Then Paul, after the governor had nodded to him to speak, answered: "Inasmuch as I know that you have been for many years a judge of this nation, I do the more cheerfully answer for myself, 11 "because you may ascertain that it is no more than twelve days since I went up to Jerusalem to worship. 12 "And they neither found me in the temple disputing with anyone nor inciting the crowd, either in the synagogues or in the city. 13 "Nor can they prove the things of which they now accuse me. 14 "But this I confess to you, that according to the Way which they call a sect, so I worship the God of my fathers, believing all things which are written in the Law and in the Prophets. 15 "I have hope in God, which they themselves also accept, that there will be a resurrection of *the* dead,[103] both of *the* just and *the* unjust. 16 "This *being* so, I myself always strive to have a conscience without offense toward God and men. 17 "Now after many years I came to bring alms and offerings to my nation,

---

101 NU-Text reads *there would be a plot against the man.*
102 NU-Text ends the sentence here and omits the rest of verse 6, all of verse 7, and the first clause of verse 8.
103 NU-Text omits *of the dead.*

18 "in the midst of which some Jews
from Asia found me purified in the temple, neither with a multitude nor with tumult.
19 "They ought to have been here before
you to object if they had anything against
me.
20 "Or else let those who are *here* themselves say if they found any wrongdoing[104] in me while I stood before the
council,
21 "unless *it is* for this one statement
which I cried out, standing among them,
'Concerning the resurrection of the dead
I am being judged by you this day.' "

Felix Procrastinates

22 But when Felix heard these things,
having more accurate knowledge of *the*
Way, he adjourned the proceedings and
said, "When Lysias the commander
comes down, I will make a decision on
your case."
23 So he commanded the centurion to
keep Paul and to let *him* have liberty, and
told him not to forbid any of his friends
to provide for or visit him.
24 And after some days, when Felix
came with his wife Drusilla, who was
Jewish, he sent for Paul and heard him
concerning the faith in Christ.
25 Now as he reasoned about righteousness, self-control, and the judgment to
come, Felix was afraid and answered,
"Go away for now; when I have a convenient time I will call for you."
26 Meanwhile he also hoped that money
would be given him by Paul, that he
might release him.[105] Therefore he sent
for him more often and conversed with
him.
27 But after two years Porcius Festus
succeeded Felix; and Felix, wanting to do
the Jews a favor, left Paul bound.

Paul Appeals to Caesar

25 Now when Festus had come to the
province, after three days he went
up from Caesarea to Jerusalem.
2 Then the high priest[106] and the chief
men of the Jews informed him against
Paul; and they petitioned him,
3 asking a favor against him, that he
would summon him to Jerusalem—while
they lay in ambush along the road to kill
him.

4 But Festus answered that Paul should
be kept at Caesarea, and that he himself
was going *there* shortly.
5 "Therefore," he said, "let those who
have authority among you go down with
me and accuse this man, to see if there is
any fault in him."
6 And when he had remained among
them more than ten days, he went down
to Caesarea. And the next day, sitting on
the judgment seat, he commanded Paul
to be brought.
7 When he had come, the Jews who had
come down from Jerusalem stood about
and laid many serious complaints against
Paul, which they could not prove,
8 while he answered for himself, "Neither against the law of the Jews, nor
against the temple, nor against Caesar
have I offended in anything at all."
9 But Festus, wanting to do the Jews a
favor, answered Paul and said, "Are you
willing to go up to Jerusalem and there be
judged before me concerning these
things?"
10 Then Paul said, "I stand at Caesar's
judgment seat, where I ought to be
judged. To the Jews I have done no
wrong, as you very well know.
11 "For if I am an offender, or have committed anything worthy of death, I do not
object to dying; but if there is nothing in
these things of which these men accuse
me, no one can deliver me to them. I appeal to Caesar."
12 Then Festus, when he had conferred
with the council, answered, "You have
appealed to Caesar? To Caesar you shall
go!"

Paul Before Agrippa

13 And after some days King Agrippa
and Bernice came to Caesarea to greet
Festus.
14 When they had been there many days,
Festus laid Paul's case before the king,
saying: "There is a certain man left a
prisoner by Felix,
15 "about whom the chief priests and the
elders of the Jews informed *me*, when I
was in Jerusalem, asking for a judgment
against him.
16 "To them I answered, 'It is not the
custom of the Romans to deliver any man
to destruction[107] before the accused meets
the accusers face to face, and has oppor-

---

104 NU-Text and M-Text read *what wrongdoing they have found.*   105 NU-Text omits *that he might release him.*
106 NU-Text reads *chief priests.*   107 NU-Text omits *to destruction,* although it is implied.

tunity to answer for himself concerning the charge against him.'

17 "Therefore when they had come together, without any delay, the next day I sat on the judgment seat and commanded the man to be brought in.

18 "When the accusers stood up, they brought no accusation against him of such things as I supposed,

19 "but had some questions against him about their own religion and about one, Jesus, who had died, whom Paul affirmed to be alive.

20 "And because I was uncertain of such questions, I asked whether he was willing to go to Jerusalem and there be judged concerning these matters.

21 "But when Paul appealed to be reserved for the decision of Augustus, I commanded him to be kept till I could send him to Caesar."

22 Then Agrippa said to Festus, "I also would like to hear the man myself." "Tomorrow," he said, "you shall hear him."

23 So the next day, when Agrippa and Bernice had come with great pomp, and had entered the auditorium with the commanders and the prominent men of the city, at Festus' command Paul was brought in.

24 And Festus said: "King Agrippa and all the men who are here present with us, you see this man about whom the whole assembly of the Jews petitioned me, both at Jerusalem and here, crying out that he was not fit to live any longer.

25 "But when I found that he had committed nothing worthy of death, and that he himself had appealed to Augustus, I decided to send him.

26 "I have nothing certain to write to my lord concerning him. Therefore I have brought him out before you, and especially before you, King Agrippa, so that after the examination has taken place I may have something to write.

27 "For it seems to me unreasonable to send a prisoner and not to specify the charges against him."

Paul's Early Life

26 Then Agrippa said to Paul, "You are permitted to speak for yourself." So Paul stretched out his hand and answered for himself:

2 "I think myself happy, King Agrippa, because today I shall answer for myself

before you concerning all the things of which I am accused by the Jews,

3 "especially because you are expert in all customs and questions which have to do with the Jews. Therefore I beg you to hear me patiently.

4 "My manner of life from my youth, which was spent from the beginning among my own nation at Jerusalem, all the Jews know.

5 "They knew me from the first, if they were willing to testify, that according to the strictest sect of our religion I lived a Pharisee.

6 "And now I stand and am judged for the hope of the promise made by God to our fathers.

7 "To this *promise* our twelve tribes, earnestly serving *God* night and day, hope to attain. For this hope's sake, King Agrippa, I am accused by the Jews.

8 "Why should it be thought incredible by you that God raises the dead?

9 "Indeed, I myself thought I must do many things contrary to the name of Jesus of Nazareth.

10 "This I also did in Jerusalem, and many of the saints I shut up in prison, having received authority from the chief priests; and when they were put to death, I cast my vote against *them*.

11 "And I punished them often in every synagogue and compelled *them* to blaspheme; and being exceedingly enraged against them, I persecuted *them* even to foreign cities.

Paul Recounts His Conversion

12 "While thus occupied, as I journeyed to Damascus with authority and commission from the chief priests,

13 "at midday, O king, along the road I saw a light from heaven, brighter than the sun, shining around me and those who journeyed with me.

14 "And when we all had fallen to the ground, I heard a voice speaking to me and saying in the Hebrew language, 'Saul, Saul, why are you persecuting Me? *It is* hard for you to kick against the goads.'

15 "So I said, 'Who are You, Lord?' And He said, 'I am Jesus, whom you are persecuting.

16 'But rise and stand on your feet; for I have appeared to you for this purpose, to make you a minister and a witness both

of the things which you have seen and of the things which I will yet reveal to you. 17 'I will deliver you from the *Jewish* people, as well as *from* the Gentiles, to whom I now[108] send you, 18 'to open their eyes *and*[109] to turn *them* from darkness to light, and *from* the power of Satan to God, that they may receive forgiveness of sins and an inheritance among those who are sanctified by faith in Me.'

Paul's Post-Conversion Life

19 "Therefore, King Agrippa, I was not disobedient to the heavenly vision, 20 "but declared first to those in Damascus and in Jerusalem, and throughout all the region of Judea, and *then* to the Gentiles, that they should repent, turn to God, and do works befitting repentance. 21 "For these reasons the Jews seized me in the temple and tried to kill *me*. 22 "Therefore, having obtained help from God, to this day I stand, witnessing both to small and great, saying no other things than those which the prophets and Moses said would come— 23 "that the Christ would suffer, that He would be the first to rise from the dead, and would proclaim light to the *Jewish* people and to the Gentiles."

Agrippa Parries Paul's Challenge

24 Now as he thus made his defense, Festus said with a loud voice, "Paul, you are beside yourself! Much learning is driving you mad!" 25 But he said, "I am not mad, most noble Festus, but speak the words of truth and reason. 26 "For the king, before whom I also speak freely, knows these things; for I am convinced that none of these things escapes his attention, since this thing was not done in a corner. 27 "King Agrippa, do you believe the prophets? I know that you do believe." 28 Then Agrippa said to Paul, "You almost persuade me to become a Christian." 29 And Paul said, "I would to God that not only you, but also all who hear me today, might become both almost and altogether such as I am, except for these chains." 30 When he had said these things, the king stood up, as well as the governor

and Bernice and those who sat with them; 31 and when they had gone aside, they talked among themselves, saying, "This man is doing nothing worthy of death or chains." 32 Then Agrippa said to Festus, "This man might have been set free if he had not appealed to Caesar."

The Voyage to Rome Begins

27 And when it was decided that we should sail to Italy, they delivered Paul and some other prisoners to *one* named Julius, a centurion of the Augustan Regiment. 2 So, entering a ship of Adramyttium, we put to sea, meaning to sail along the coasts of Asia. Aristarchus, a Macedonian of Thessalonica, was with us. 3 And the next *day* we landed at Sidon. And Julius treated Paul kindly and gave *him* liberty to go to his friends and receive care. 4 When we had put to sea from there, we sailed under *the shelter of* Cyprus, because the winds were contrary. 5 And when we had sailed over the sea which is off Cilicia and Pamphylia, we came to Myra, *a city* of Lycia. 6 There the centurion found an Alexandrian ship sailing to Italy, and he put us on board. 7 And when we had sailed slowly many days, and arrived with difficulty off Cnidus, the wind not permitting us to proceed, we sailed under *the shelter of* Crete off Salmone. 8 Passing it with difficulty, we came to a place called Fair Havens, near the city *of* Lasea.

Paul's Warning Ignored

9 Now when much time had been spent, and sailing was now dangerous because the Fast was already over, Paul advised them, 10 saying, "Men, I perceive that this voyage will end with disaster and much loss, not only of the cargo and ship, but also our lives." 11 Nevertheless the centurion was more persuaded by the helmsman and the owner of the ship than by the things spoken by Paul. 12 And because the harbor was not suitable to winter in, the majority advised to

108 NU-Text and M-Text omit *now*.   109 NU-Text and M-Text read *in order.*

set sail from there also, if by any means they could reach Phoenix, a harbor of Crete opening toward the southwest and northwest, *and* winter *there.*

In the Tempest

13 When the south wind blew softly, supposing that they had obtained *their* purpose, putting out to sea, they sailed close by Crete.
14 But not long after, a tempestuous head wind arose, called Euroclydon.[110]
15 So when the ship was caught, and could not head into the wind, we let *her* drive.
16 And running under *the shelter of* an island called Clauda,[111] we secured the skiff with difficulty.
17 When they had taken it on board, they used cables to undergird the ship; and fearing lest they should run aground on the Syrtis[112] *Sands*, they struck sail and so were driven.
18 And because we were exceedingly tempest-tossed, the next *day* they lightened the ship.
19 On the third *day* we threw the ship's tackle overboard with our own hands.
20 Now when neither sun nor stars appeared for many days, and no small tempest beat on *us,* all hope that we would be saved was finally given up.
21 But after long abstinence from food, then Paul stood in the midst of them and said, "Men, you should have listened to me, and not have sailed from Crete and incurred this disaster and loss.
22 "And now I urge you to take heart, for there will be no loss of life among you, but only of the ship.
23 "For there stood by me this night an angel of the God to whom I belong and whom I serve,
24 "saying, 'Do not be afraid, Paul; you must be brought before Caesar; and indeed God has granted you all those who sail with you.'
25 "Therefore take heart, men, for I believe God that it will be just as it was told me.
26 "However, we must run aground on a certain island."
27 But when the fourteenth night had come, as we were driven up and down in the Adriatic *Sea,* about midnight the sailors sensed that they were drawing near some land.

28 And they took soundings and found *it* to be twenty fathoms; and when they had gone a little farther, they took soundings again and found *it* to be fifteen fathoms.
29 Then, fearing lest we should run aground on the rocks, they dropped four anchors from the stern, and prayed for day to come.
30 And as the sailors were seeking to escape from the ship, when they had let down the skiff into the sea, under pretense of putting out anchors from the prow,
31 Paul said to the centurion and the soldiers, "Unless these men stay in the ship, you cannot be saved."
32 Then the soldiers cut away the ropes of the skiff and let it fall off.
33 And as day was about to dawn, Paul implored *them* all to take food, saying, "Today is the fourteenth day you have waited and continued without food, and eaten nothing.
34 "Therefore I urge you to take nourishment, for this is for your survival, since not a hair will fall from the head of any of you."
35 And when he had said these things, he took bread and gave thanks to God in the presence of them all; and when he had broken *it* he began to eat.
36 Then they were all encouraged, and also took food themselves.
37 And in all we were two hundred and seventy-six persons on the ship.
38 So when they had eaten enough, they lightened the ship and threw out the wheat into the sea.

Shipwrecked on Malta

39 Now when it was day, they did not recognize the land; but they observed a bay with a beach, onto which they planned to run the ship if possible.
40 And they let go the anchors and left *them* in the sea, meanwhile loosing the rudder ropes; and they hoisted the mainsail to the wind and made for shore.
41 But striking a place where two seas met, they ran the ship aground; and the prow stuck fast and remained immovable, but the stern was being broken up by the violence of the waves.
42 Now the soldiers' plan was to kill the prisoners, lest any of them should swim away and escape.

110 NU-Text reads *Euraquilon.*   111 NU-Text reads *Cauda.*   112 M-Text reads *Syrtes.*

43 But the centurion, wanting to save Paul, kept them from *their* purpose, and commanded that those who could swim should jump *overboard* first and get to land,
44 and the rest, some on boards and some on *broken pieces* of the ship. And so it was that they all escaped safely to land.

Paul's Ministry on Malta

28 Now when they had escaped, they then found out that the island was called Malta.
2 And the natives showed us unusual kindness; for they kindled a fire and made us all welcome, because of the rain that was falling and because of the cold.
3 But when Paul had gathered a bundle of sticks and laid *them* on the fire, a viper came out because of the heat, and fastened on his hand.
4 So when the natives saw the creature hanging from his hand, they said to one another, "No doubt this man is a murderer, whom, though he has escaped the sea, yet justice does not allow to live."
5 But he shook off the creature into the fire and suffered no harm.
6 However, they were expecting that he would swell up or suddenly fall down dead; but after they had looked for a long time and saw no harm come to him, they changed their minds and said that he was a god.
7 Now in that region there was an estate of the leading citizen of the island, whose name was Publius, who received us and entertained us courteously for three days.
8 And it happened that the father of Publius lay sick of a fever and dysentery. Paul went in to him and prayed, and he laid his hands on him and healed him.
9 So when this was done, the rest of those on the island who had diseases also came and were healed.
10 They also honored us in many ways; and when we departed, they provided such things as were necessary.

Arrival at Rome

11 After three months we sailed in an Alexandrian ship whose figurehead was the Twin Brothers, which had wintered at the island.
12 And landing at Syracuse, we stayed three days.

13 From there we circled round and reached Rhegium. And after one day the south wind blew; and the next day we came to Puteoli,
14 where we found brethren, and were invited to stay with them seven days. And so we went toward Rome.
15 And from there, when the brethren heard about us, they came to meet us as far as Appii Forum and Three Inns. When Paul saw them, he thanked God and took courage.
16 Now when we came to Rome, the centurion delivered the prisoners to the captain of the guard; but Paul was permitted to dwell by himself with the soldier who guarded him.

Paul's Ministry at Rome

17 And it came to pass after three days that Paul called the leaders of the Jews together. So when they had come together, he said to them: "Men *and* brethren, though I have done nothing against our people or the customs of our fathers, yet I was delivered as a prisoner from Jerusalem into the hands of the Romans,
18 "who, when they had examined me, wanted to let *me* go, because there was no cause for putting me to death.
19 "But when the Jews spoke against *it*, I was compelled to appeal to Caesar, not that I had anything of which to accuse my nation.
20 "For this reason therefore I have called for you, to see *you* and speak with *you*, because for the hope of Israel I am bound with this chain."
21 And they said to him, "We neither received letters from Judea concerning you, nor have any of the brethren who came reported or spoken any evil of you.
22 "But we desire to hear from you what you think; for concerning this sect, we know that it is spoken against everywhere."
23 So when they had appointed him a day, many came to him at *his* lodging, to whom he explained and solemnly testified of the kingdom of God, persuading them concerning Jesus from both the Law of Moses and the Prophets, from morning till evening.
24 And some were persuaded by the things which were spoken, and some disbelieved.

25 So when they did not agree among themselves, they departed after Paul had said one word: "The Holy Spirit spoke rightly through Isaiah the prophet to our[113] fathers,

26 "saying,

'Go to this people and say:
"Hearing you will hear,
   and shall not understand;
And seeing you will see,
   and not perceive;
27 For the heart of this people
   has grown dull.
Their ears are hard of hearing,
And their eyes they have closed,
Lest they should see with their eyes
   and hear with their ears,

Lest they should understand with their
   heart and turn,
So that I should heal them." '[114]

28 "Therefore let it be known to you that the salvation of God has been sent to the Gentiles, and they will hear it!"

29 And when he had said these words, the Jews departed and had a great dispute among themselves.[115]

30 Then Paul dwelt two whole years in his own rented house, and received all who came to him,

31 preaching the kingdom of God and teaching the things which concern the Lord Jesus Christ with all confidence, no one forbidding him.

113 NU-Text reads *your.* 114 Isaiah 6:9, 10 115 NU-Text omits this verse.

Introduction to Romans

Rome A.D. 56, was the seat of one of the greatest empires the world has ever known. Its mighty Emperors Caligula, Claudius, and then Nero, ruled in lavish dominion over the cosmopolitan center of one million inhabitants. Roman law and forms of worship ruled supreme, demanding the attention and respect in the hearts of men and women. Here, a tiny sect known as "Christians" flourished.

To these believers, Paul wrote the longest of his thirteen New Testament letters, introducing himself in advance of his upcoming visit. Sometimes called "Paul's testament," Romans presents a beautifully detailed doctrinal statement of Christianity.

Paul presents the need for all people to realize their position before God—one which falls short of God's glorious design and plan for their lives. But by an act of God's grace and faith, they are restored to their rightful relationship with God. Because of the confidence of forgiveness, all believers can present their talents, gifts, and abilities—whatever they are—as an act of worship to God.

Paul also encourages his readers to realize that God is in control when he says, "All things work together for good to those who love God" (Rom. 8:28). He also comforts them with the knowledge that nothing can separate them from the love of God. This was especially appropriate for the Roman church, for they were to face much persecution from both their Roman overlords and the Jews who lived in the capital. Yet nothing could separate them from the love of God. The church in Rome grew to be a great center of faith that today echoes around the world.

Paul, who later died a martyr's death in Rome, gave great words of faith which are as alive and vital to us today as they were to the first Christians who read them nearly two thousand years ago. The knowledge of God's grace and forgiveness frees us not only from sin, but from anxiety, guilt, depression, and a negative self-image. The stress flows out and salvation flows in!

The Epistle of Paul the Apostle to the

Romans

Greeting

PAUL, a servant of Jesus Christ, called *to be* an apostle, separated to the gospel of God
2 which He promised before through His prophets in the Holy Scriptures,
3 concerning His Son Jesus Christ our Lord, who was born of the seed of David according to the flesh,
4 and declared *to be* the Son of God with power, according to the Spirit of holiness, by the resurrection from the dead,
5 through whom we have received grace and apostleship for obedience to the faith among all nations for His name,
6 among whom you also are the called of Jesus Christ;

7 To all who are in Rome, beloved of God, called *to be* saints:

Grace to you and peace from God our Father and the Lord Jesus Christ.

Desire to Visit Rome

8 First, I thank my God through Jesus Christ for you all, that your faith is spoken of throughout the whole world.
9 For God is my witness, whom I serve with my spirit in the gospel of His Son, that without ceasing I make mention of you always in my prayers,
10 making request if, by some means, now at last I may find a way in the will of God to come to you.
11 For I long to see you, that I may impart to you some spiritual gift, so that you may be established—
12 that is, that I may be encouraged together with you by the mutual faith both of you and me.
13 Now I do not want you to be unaware, brethren, that I often planned to come to you (but was hindered until now), that I might have some fruit among you also, just as among the other Gentiles.
14 I am a debtor both to Greeks and to barbarians, both to wise and to unwise.

15 So, as much as is in me, *I am* ready to preach the gospel to you who are in Rome also.

The Just Live by Faith

16 For I am not ashamed of the gospel of Christ,[1] for it is the power of God to salvation for everyone who believes, for the Jew first and also for the Greek.
17 For in it the righteousness of God is revealed from faith to faith; as it is written, *"The just shall live by faith."*[2]

God's Wrath on Unrighteousness

18 For the wrath of God is revealed from heaven against all ungodliness and unrighteousness of men, who suppress the truth in unrighteousness,
19 because what may be known of God is manifest in them, for God has shown *it* to them.
20 For since the creation of the world His invisible *attributes* are clearly seen, being understood by the things that are made, *even* His eternal power and Godhead, so that they are without excuse,
21 because, although they knew God, they did not glorify *Him* as God, nor were thankful, but became futile in their thoughts, and their foolish hearts were darkened.
22 Professing to be wise, they became fools,
23 and changed the glory of the incorruptible God into an image made like corruptible man—and birds and four-footed beasts and creeping things.
24 Therefore God also gave them up to uncleanness, in the lusts of their hearts, to dishonor their bodies among themselves,
25 who exchanged the truth of God for the lie, and worshiped and served the creature rather than the Creator, who is blessed forever. Amen.
26 For this reason God gave them up to vile passions. For even their women exchanged the natural use for what is against nature.

1 NU-Text omits *of Christ.* 2 Habakkuk 2:4

27 Likewise also the men, leaving the natural use of the woman, burned in their lust for one another, men with men committing what is shameful, and receiving in themselves the penalty of their error which was due.
28 And even as they did not like to retain God in *their* knowledge, God gave them over to a debased mind, to do those things which are not fitting;
29 being filled with all unrighteousness, sexual immorality,[3] wickedness, covetousness, maliciousness; full of envy, murder, strife, deceit, evil-mindedness; *they are* whisperers,
30 backbiters, haters of God, violent, proud, boasters, inventors of evil things, disobedient to parents,
31 undiscerning, untrustworthy, unloving, unforgiving,[4] unmerciful;
32 who, knowing the righteous judgment of God, that those who practice such things are worthy of death, not only do the same but also approve of those who practice them.

God's Righteous Judgment

2 Therefore you are inexcusable, O man, whoever you are who judge, for in whatever you judge another you condemn yourself; for you who judge practice the same things.
2 But we know that the judgment of God is according to truth against those who practice such things.
3 And do you think this, O man, you who judge those practicing such things, and doing the same, that you will escape the judgment of God?
4 Or do you despise the riches of His goodness, forbearance, and longsuffering, not knowing that the goodness of God leads you to repentance?
5 But in accordance with your hardness and your impenitent heart you are treasuring up for yourself wrath in the day of wrath and revelation of the righteous judgment of God,
6 who *"will render to each one according to his deeds"*:[5]
7 eternal life to those who by patient continuance in doing good seek for glory, honor, and immortality;
8 but to those who are self-seeking and do not obey the truth, but obey unrighteousness—indignation and wrath,

9 tribulation and anguish, on every soul of man who does evil, of the Jew first and also of the Greek;
10 but glory, honor, and peace to everyone who works what is good, to the Jew first and also to the Greek.
11 For there is no partiality with God.
12 For as many as have sinned without law will also perish without law, and as many as have sinned in the law will be judged by the law
13 (for not the hearers of the law *are* just in the sight of God, but the doers of the law will be justified;
14 for when Gentiles, who do not have the law, by nature do the things *contained* in the law, these, although not having the law, are a law to themselves,
15 who show the work of the law written in their hearts, their conscience also bearing witness, and between themselves *their* thoughts accusing or else excusing *them*)
16 in the day when God will judge the secrets of men by Jesus Christ, according to my gospel.

The Jews Guilty as the Gentiles

17 Indeed[6] you are called a Jew, and rest on the law, and make your boast in God,
18 and know *His* will, and approve the things that are excellent, being instructed out of the law,
19 and are confident that you yourself are a guide to the blind, a light to those who are in darkness,
20 an instructor of the foolish, a teacher of babes, having the form of knowledge and truth in the law.
21 You, therefore, who teach another, do you not teach yourself? You who preach that a man should not steal, do you steal?
22 You who say, "Do not commit adultery," do you commit adultery? You who abhor idols, do you rob temples?
23 You who make your boast in the law, do you dishonor God through breaking the law?
24 For *"The name of God is blasphemed among the Gentiles because of you,"*[7] as it is written.

Circumcision of No Avail

25 For circumcision is indeed profitable if you keep the law; but if you are a breaker of the law, your circumcision has become uncircumcision.

---

3 NU-Text omits *sexual immorality.*   4 NU-Text omits *unforgiving.*   5 Psalm 62:12; Proverbs 24:12
6 NU-Text reads *But if.*   7 Isaiah 52:5; Ezekiel 36:22

26 Therefore, if an uncircumcised man keeps the righteous requirements of the law, will not his uncircumcision be counted as circumcision? 27 And will not the physically uncircumcised, if he fulfills the law, judge you who, *even* with *your* written *code* and circumcision, *are* a transgressor of the law? 28 For he is not a Jew who *is one* outwardly, nor *is* that circumcision *which is* outward in the flesh; 29 but *he is* a Jew who *is one* inwardly, and circumcision *is that* of the heart, in the Spirit, *and* not in the letter; whose praise *is* not from men but from God.

God's Judgment Defended

3 What advantage then has the Jew, or what *is* the profit of circumcision? 2 Much in every way! Chiefly because to them were committed the oracles of God. 3 For what if some did not believe? Will their unbelief make the faithfulness of God without effect? 4 Certainly not! Indeed, let God be true but every man a liar. As it is written:

"That You may be justified
    in Your words,
And may overcome when
    You are judged."[8]

5 But if our unrighteousness demonstrates the righteousness of God, what shall we say? *Is* God unjust who inflicts wrath? (I speak as a man.) 6 Certainly not! For then how will God judge the world? 7 For if the truth of God has increased through my lie to His glory, why am I also still judged as a sinner? 8 And *why* not *say,* "Let us do evil that good may come"?—as we are slanderously reported and as some affirm that we say. Their condemnation is just.

All Have Sinned

9 What then? Are we better *than they?* Not at all. For we have previously charged both Jews and Greeks that they are all under sin. 10 As it is written:

"There is none righteous, no, not one;

11 There is none who understands;
    There is none who seeks after God.
12 They have all gone out of the way;
    They have together become
        unprofitable;
    There is none who does good,
        no, not one."[9]
13 "Their throat is an open tomb;
    With their tongues they have practiced
        deceit";[10]
    "The poison of asps is under their
        lips";[11]
14 "Whose mouth is full of cursing and
        bitterness."[12]
15 "Their feet are swift to shed blood;
16 Destruction and misery are in their
        ways;
17 And the way of peace they have not
        known."[13]
18 "There is no fear of God before their
        eyes."[14]

19 Now we know that whatever the law says, it says to those who are under the law, that every mouth may be stopped, and all the world may become guilty before God. 20 Therefore by the deeds of the law no flesh will be justified in His sight, for by the law *is* the knowledge of sin.

God's Righteousness through Faith

21 But now the righteousness of God apart from the law is revealed, being witnessed by the Law and the Prophets, 22 even the righteousness of God *which is* through faith in Jesus Christ to all and on all[15] who believe. For there is no difference; 23 for all have sinned and fall short of the glory of God, 24 being justified freely by His grace through the redemption that is in Christ Jesus, 25 whom God set forth *to be* a propitiation by His blood, through faith, to demonstrate His righteousness, because in His forbearance God had passed over the sins that were previously committed, 26 to demonstrate at the present time His righteousness, that He might be just and the justifier of the one who has faith in Jesus.

Boasting Excluded

27 Where *is* boasting then? It is excluded. By what law? Of works? No, but by the law of faith.

8 Psalm 51:4   9 Psalms 14:1–3; 53:1–3; Ecclesiastes 7:20   10 Psalm 5:9   11 Psalm 140:3   12 Psalm 10:7
13 Isaiah 59:7, 8   14 Psalm 36:1   15 NU-Text omits *and on all.*

Forgiveness for Everyone

During the Passover meal, Jesus demonstrated an attitude of forgiveness unparalleled in the history of man.

It was the custom for the host to dip the sop (bread) in the lamb stew and give it to the most honored guest at the banquet table. Jesus told His disciples that whoever dipped the sop with Him was the one who would betray Him. Knowing what Judas was going to do, Jesus still bestowed upon him the greatest honor available. Not only was this an honor, but an offering of forgiveness. For the partaking of a meal was a traditional covenant of peace and forgiveness. By giving Judas the sop, Jesus offered him peace and forgiveness if he would accept it. Judas must have recognized this symbolism, yet chose to rebel and turn away.

If Jesus can forgive a follower who betrayed Him, how much more can He forgive us? Jesus' love is sufficient to forgive even the greatest sin. We can be confident of His love and forgiveness no matter who we are, what we have done, or what we will ever do in the future.

What wonderful confidence we can have in the assurance that Jesus Christ can forgive all our sins—past, present, and future—if we only accept it!

28 Therefore we conclude that a man is justified by faith apart from the deeds of the law.

29 Or *is* He the God of the Jews only? *Is* He not also the God of the Gentiles? Yes, of the Gentiles also,

30 since *there is* one God who will justify the circumcised by faith and the uncircumcised through faith.

31 Do we then make void the law through faith? Certainly not! On the contrary, we establish the law.

Abraham Justified by Faith

4 What then shall we say that Abraham our father has found according to the flesh?[16]

2 For if Abraham was justified by works, he has *something of which* to boast, but not before God.

3 For what does the Scripture say? *"Abraham believed God, and it was accounted to him for righteousness."*[17]

4 Now to him who works, the wages are not counted as grace but as debt.

David Celebrates the Same Truth

5 But to him who does not work but believes on Him who justifies the ungodly, his faith is accounted for righteousness,

6 just as David also describes the blessedness of the man to whom God imputes righteousness apart from works:

7 *"Blessed are those whose lawless deeds are forgiven,
And whose sins are covered;*

8 *Blessed is the man to whom the Lord shall not impute sin."*[18]

Abraham Justified Before Circumcision

9 *Does* this blessedness then *come* upon the circumcised *only*, or upon the uncircumcised also? For we say that faith was accounted to Abraham for righteousness.

10 How then was it accounted? While he was circumcised, or uncircumcised? Not while circumcised, but while uncircumcised.

11 And he received the sign of circumcision, a seal of the righteousness of the faith which *he had while still* uncircumcised, that he might be the father of all those who believe, though they are uncir-

cumcised, that righteousness might be imputed to them also,

12 and the father of circumcision to those who not only *are* of the circumcision, but who also walk in the steps of the faith which our father Abraham *had while still* uncircumcised.

The Promise Granted Through Faith

13 For the promise that he would be the heir of the world *was* not to Abraham or to his seed through the law, but through the righteousness of faith.

14 For if those who are of the law *are* heirs, faith is made void and the promise made of no effect,

15 because the law brings about wrath; for where there is no law *there is* no transgression.

16 Therefore *it is* of faith that *it might be* according to grace, so that the promise might be sure to all the seed, not only to those who are of the law, but also to those who are of the faith of Abraham, who is the father of us all

17 (as it is written, *"I have made you a father of many nations"*[19]) in the presence of Him whom he believed, *even* God, who gives life to the dead and calls those things which do not exist as though they did;

18 who, contrary to hope, in hope believed, so that he became the father of many nations, according to what was spoken, *"So shall your descendants be."*[20]

19 And not being weak in faith, he did not consider his own body, already dead (since he was about a hundred years old), and the deadness of Sarah's womb.

20 He did not waver at the promise of God through unbelief, but was strengthened in faith, giving glory to God,

21 and being fully convinced that what He had promised He was also able to perform.

22 And therefore *"it was accounted to him for righteousness."*[21]

23 Now it was not written for his sake alone that it was imputed to him,

24 but also for us. It shall be imputed to us who believe in Him who raised up Jesus our Lord from the dead,

25 who was delivered up because of our offenses, and was raised because of our justification.

---

16 Or *Abraham our (fore)father according to the flesh has found?*   17 Genesis 15:6   18 Psalm 32:1, 2
19 Genesis 17:5   20 Genesis 15:5   21 Genesis 15:6

Faith Triumphs in Trouble

5 Therefore, having been justified by faith, we have[22] peace with God through our Lord Jesus Christ,
2 through whom also we have access by faith into this grace in which we stand, and rejoice in hope of the glory of God.
3 And not only *that*, but we also glory in tribulations, knowing that tribulation produces perseverance;
4 and perseverance, character; and character, hope.
5 Now hope does not disappoint, because the love of God has been poured out in our hearts by the Holy Spirit who was given to us.

Christ in Our Place

6 For when we were still without strength, in due time Christ died for the ungodly.
7 For scarcely for a righteous man will one die; yet perhaps for a good man someone would even dare to die.
8 But God demonstrates His own love toward us, in that while we were still sinners, Christ died for us.
9 Much more then, having now been justified by His blood, we shall be saved from wrath through Him.
10 For if when we were enemies we were reconciled to God through the death of His Son, much more, having been reconciled, we shall be saved by His life.
11 And not only *that*, but we also rejoice in God through our Lord Jesus Christ, through whom we have now received the reconciliation.

Death in Adam, Life in Christ

12 Therefore, just as through one man sin entered the world, and death through sin, and thus death spread to all men, because all sinned—
13 (For until the law sin was in the world, but sin is not imputed when there is no law.
14 Nevertheless death reigned from Adam to Moses, even over those who had not sinned according to the likeness of the transgression of Adam, who is a type of Him who was to come.
15 But the free gift *is* not like the offense. For if by the one man's offense many died, much more the grace of God and the gift by the grace of the one Man, Jesus Christ, abounded to many.

16 And the gift *is* not like *that which* came through the one who sinned. For the judgment *which came* from one *offense resulted* in condemnation, but the free gift *which came* from many offenses *resulted* in justification.
17 For if by the one man's offense death reigned through the one, much more those who receive abundance of grace and of the gift of righteousness will reign in life through the One, Jesus Christ.)
18 Therefore, as through one man's offense *judgment* came to all men, resulting in condemnation, even so through one Man's righteous act *the free gift came* to all men, resulting in justification of life.
19 For as by one man's disobedience many were made sinners, so also by one Man's obedience many will be made righteous.
20 Moreover the law entered that the offense might abound. But where sin abounded, grace abounded much more,
21 so that as sin reigned in death, even so grace might reign through righteousness to eternal life through Jesus Christ our Lord.

Dead to Sin, Alive to God

6 What shall we say then? Shall we continue in sin that grace may abound?
2 Certainly not! How shall we who died to sin live any longer in it?
3 Or do you not know that as many of us as were baptized into Christ Jesus were baptized into His death?
4 Therefore we were buried with Him through baptism into death, that just as Christ was raised from the dead by the glory of the Father, even so we also should walk in newness of life.
5 For if we have been united together in the likeness of His death, certainly we also shall be *in the likeness* of *His* resurrection,
6 knowing this, that our old man was crucified with *Him*, that the body of sin might be done away with, that we should no longer be slaves of sin.
7 For he who has died has been freed from sin.
8 Now if we died with Christ, we believe that we shall also live with Him,
9 knowing that Christ, having been raised from the dead, dies no more. Death no longer has dominion over Him.

22 Another ancient reading is, *let us have peace.*

10 For *the death* that He died, He died to sin once for all; but *the life* that He lives, He lives to God.
11 Likewise you also, reckon yourselves to be dead indeed to sin, but alive to God in Christ Jesus our Lord.
12 Therefore do not let sin reign in your mortal body, that you should obey it in its lusts.
13 And do not present your members *as* instruments of unrighteousness to sin, but present yourselves to God as being alive from the dead, and your members *as* instruments of righteousness to God.
14 For sin shall not have dominion over you, for you are not under law but under grace.

From Slaves of Sin to Slaves of God

15 What then? Shall we sin because we are not under law but under grace? Certainly not!
16 Do you not know that to whom you present yourselves slaves to obey, you are that one's slaves whom you obey, whether of sin to death, or of obedience to righteousness?
17 But God be thanked that *though* you were slaves of sin, yet you obeyed from the heart that form of doctrine to which you were delivered.
18 And having been set free from sin, you became slaves of righteousness.
19 I speak in human *terms* because of the weakness of your flesh. For just as you presented your members *as* slaves of uncleanness, and of lawlessness *leading* to *more* lawlessness, so now present your members *as* slaves *of* righteousness for holiness.
20 For when you were slaves of sin, you were free in regard to righteousness.
21 What fruit did you have then in the things of which you are now ashamed? For the end of those things *is* death.
22 But now having been set free from sin, and having become slaves of God, you have your fruit to holiness, and the end, everlasting life.
23 For the wages of sin *is* death, but the gift of God *is* eternal life in Christ Jesus our Lord.

Freed from the Law

7 Or do you not know, brethren (for I speak to those who know the law), that the law has dominion over a man as long as he lives?
2 For the woman who has a husband is bound by the law to *her* husband as long as he lives. But if the husband dies, she is released from the law of *her* husband.
3 So then if, while *her* husband lives, she marries another man, she will be called an adulteress; but if her husband dies, she is free from that law, so that she is no adulteress, though she has married another man.
4 Therefore, my brethren, you also have become dead to the law through the body of Christ, that you may be married to another, *even* to Him who was raised from the dead, that we should bear fruit to God.
5 For when we were in the flesh, the passions of sins which were aroused by the law were at work in our members to bear fruit to death.
6 But now we have been delivered from the law, having died to what we were held by, so that we should serve in the newness of the Spirit and not *in* the oldness of the letter.

Sin's Advantage in the Law

7 What shall we say then? *Is* the law sin? Certainly not! On the contrary, I would not have known sin except through the law. For I would not have known covetousness unless the law had said, *"You shall not covet."*[23]
8 But sin, taking opportunity by the commandment, produced in me all *manner of evil* desire. For apart from the law sin *was* dead.
9 I was alive once without the law, but when the commandment came, sin revived and I died.
10 And the commandment, which *was* to *bring* life, I found to *bring* death.
11 For sin, taking occasion by the commandment, deceived me, and by it killed *me.*
12 Therefore the law *is* holy, and the commandment holy and just and good.

Law Cannot Save from Sin

13 Has then what is good become death to me? Certainly not! But sin, that it might appear sin, was producing death in me through what is good, so that sin through the commandment might become exceedingly sinful.

23 Exodus 20:17; Deuteronomy 5:21

14 For we know that the law is spiritual, but I am carnal, sold under sin.
15 For what I am doing, I do not understand. For what I will to do, that I do not practice; but what I hate, that I do.
16 If, then, I do what I will not to do, I agree with the law that *it is* good.
17 But now, *it is* no longer I who do it, but sin that dwells in me.
18 For I know that in me (that is, in my flesh) nothing good dwells; for to will is present with me, but *how* to perform what is good I do not find.
19 For the good that I will *to do,* I do not do; but the evil I will not *to do,* that I practice.
20 Now if I do what I will not *to do,* it is no longer I who do it, but sin that dwells in me.
21 I find then a law, that evil is present with me, the one who wills to do good.
22 For I delight in the law of God according to the inward man.
23 But I see another law in my members, warring against the law of my mind, and bringing me into captivity to the law of sin which is in my members.
24 O wretched man that I am! Who will deliver me from this body of death?
25 I thank God—through Jesus Christ our Lord! So then, with the mind I myself serve the law of God, but with the flesh the law of sin.

Free from Indwelling Sin

8 *There is* therefore now no condemnation to those who are in Christ Jesus,[24] who do not walk according to the flesh, but according to the Spirit.
2 For the law of the Spirit of life in Christ Jesus has made me free from the law of sin and death.
3 For what the law could not do in that it was weak through the flesh, God *did* by sending His own Son in the likeness of sinful flesh, on account of sin: He condemned sin in the flesh,
4 that the righteous requirement of the law might be fulfilled in us who do not walk according to the flesh but according to the Spirit.
5 For those who live according to the flesh set their minds on the things of the flesh, but those *who live* according to the Spirit, the things of the Spirit.
6 For to be carnally minded *is* death,

but to be spiritually minded *is* life and peace.
7 Because the carnal mind *is* enmity against God; for it is not subject to the law of God, nor indeed can be.
8 So then, those who are in the flesh cannot please God.
9 But you are not in the flesh but in the Spirit, if indeed the Spirit of God dwells in you. Now if anyone does not have the Spirit of Christ, he is not His.
10 And if Christ *is* in you, the body *is* dead because of sin, but the Spirit *is* life because of righteousness.
11 But if the Spirit of Him who raised Jesus from the dead dwells in you, He who raised Christ from the dead will also give life to your mortal bodies through His Spirit who dwells in you.

Sonship Through the Spirit

12 Therefore, brethren, we are debtors—not to the flesh, to live according to the flesh.
13 For if you live according to the flesh you will die; but if by the Spirit you put to death the deeds of the body, you will live.
14 For as many as are led by the Spirit of God, these are sons of God.
15 For you did not receive the spirit of bondage again to fear, but you received the Spirit of adoption by whom we cry out, "Abba, Father."
16 The Spirit Himself bears witness with our spirit that we are children of God,
17 and if children, then heirs—heirs of God and joint heirs with Christ, if indeed we suffer with *Him,* that we may also be glorified together.

From Suffering to Glory

18 For I consider that the sufferings of this present time are not worthy *to be compared* with the glory which shall be revealed in us.
19 For the earnest expectation of the creation eagerly waits for the revealing of the sons of God.
20 For the creation was subjected to futility, not willingly, but because of Him who subjected *it* in hope;
21 because the creation itself also will be delivered from the bondage of corruption into the glorious liberty of the children of God.

24 NU-Text omits the rest of this verse.

Family of God

Jesus placed us in the most intimate relationship with God—calling us sons and daughters. In the ancient world, the firstborn son of a household possessed great authority and power. He was the first in line of succession to his father's household. Everything under his father's jurisdiction and authority was granted by birthright to the oldest son.

Of particular interest was the son's power to grant freedom to slaves and to adopt other people as members of his family. These adopted sons and daughters were then granted the same privileges as the son. This cultural background forms the basis for Jesus' statement, "Therefore if the Son makes you free, you shall be free indeed" (John 8:36).

As the Son of God, Jesus has the sole right to free us of our sin, guilt, low self-esteem, and negative self-image. He grants us to share in an intimate relationship similar to the one He possesses with God His Father. We are given the right to address God as *Abba*, meaning "Daddy," instead of the more traditional, reverent *Avinu*, meaning "Our Father." In Jesus' day it was unthinkable to address God the Creator of the universe in such intimate terms. Throughout the New Testament this privilege was extolled by all of the early Christians and teachers. Paul assures us that we have received the spirit of adoption as sons and daughters of God and have the right to address him as *Abba*.

We have been granted a birthright by the firstborn Son of God, Jesus Christ, who has adopted us into the family of God. We have been granted the greatest honor available. As God's children, we are special!

22 For we know that the whole creation groans and labors with birth pangs together until now.
23 And not only *they*, but we also who have the firstfruits of the Spirit, even we ourselves groan within ourselves, eagerly waiting for the adoption, the redemption of our body.
24 For we were saved in this hope, but hope that is seen is not hope; for why does one still hope for what he sees?
25 But if we hope for what we do not see, *then* we eagerly wait for *it* with perseverance.
26 Likewise the Spirit also helps in our weaknesses. For we do not know what we should pray for as we ought, but the Spirit Himself makes intercession for us[25] with groanings which cannot be uttered.
27 Now He who searches the hearts knows what the mind of the Spirit *is*, because He makes intercession for the saints according to *the will of* God.
28 And we know that all things work together for good to those who love God, to those who are the called according to *His* purpose.
29 For whom He foreknew, He also predestined *to be* conformed to the image of His Son, that He might be the firstborn among many brethren.
30 Moreover whom He predestined, these He also called; whom He called, these He also justified; and whom He justified, these He also glorified.

God's Everlasting Love

31 What then shall we say to these things? If God *is* for us, who *can be* against us?
32 He who did not spare His own Son, but delivered Him up for us all, how shall He not with Him also freely give us all things?
33 Who shall bring a charge against God's elect? *It is* God who justifies.
34 Who *is* he who condemns? *It is* Christ who died, and furthermore is also risen, who is even at the right hand of God, who also makes intercession for us.
35 Who shall separate us from the love of Christ? *Shall* tribulation, or distress, or persecution, or famine, or nakedness, or peril, or sword?
36 As it is written:

"For Your sake we are killed
  all day long;
We are accounted as sheep
  for the slaughter."[26]

37 Yet in all these things we are more than conquerors through Him who loved us.
38 For I am persuaded that neither death nor life, nor angels nor principalities nor powers, nor things present nor things to come,
39 nor height nor depth, nor any other created thing, shall be able to separate us from the love of God which is in Christ Jesus our Lord.

Israel's Rejection of Christ

9 I tell the truth in Christ, I am not lying, my conscience also bearing me witness in the Holy Spirit,
2 that I have great sorrow and continual grief in my heart.
3 For I could wish that I myself were accursed from Christ for my brethren, my kinsmen according to the flesh,
4 who are Israelites, to whom *pertain* the adoption, the glory, the covenants, the giving of the law, the service *of God*, and the promises;
5 of whom *are* the fathers and from whom, according to the flesh, Christ *came*, who is over all, *the* eternally blessed God. Amen.

Israel's Rejection and God's Purpose

6 But it is not that the word of God has taken no effect. For they *are* not all Israel who *are* of Israel,
7 nor *are they* all children because they are the seed of Abraham; but, *"In Isaac your seed shall be called."*[27]
8 That is, those who *are* the children of the flesh, these *are* not the children of God; but the children of the promise are counted as the seed.
9 For this *is* the word of promise: *"At this time I will come and Sarah shall have a son."*[28]
10 And not only *this*, but when Rebecca also had conceived by one man, *even* by our father Isaac
11 (for *the children* not yet being born, nor having done any good or evil, that the purpose of God according to election might stand, not of works but of Him who calls),

---

25 NU-Text omits *for us.*   26 Psalm 44:22   27 Genesis 21:12   28 Genesis 18:10, 14

12 it was said to her, *"The older shall serve the younger."*²⁹
13 As it is written, *"Jacob I have loved, but Esau I have hated."*³⁰

Israel's Rejection and God's Justice

14 What shall we say then? *Is there* unrighteousness with God? Certainly not!
15 For He says to Moses, *"I will have mercy on whomever I will have mercy, and I will have compassion on whomever I will have compassion."*³¹
16 So then *it is* not of him who wills, nor of him who runs, but of God who shows mercy.
17 For the Scripture says to Pharaoh, *"Even for this same purpose I have raised you up, that I might show My power in you, and that My name might be declared in all the earth."*³²
18 Therefore He has mercy on whom He wills, and whom He wills He hardens.
19 You will say to me then, "Why does He still find fault? For who has resisted His will?"
20 But indeed, O man, who are you to reply against God? Will the thing formed say to him who formed *it,* "Why have you made me like this?"
21 Does not the potter have power over the clay, from the same lump to make one vessel for honor and another for dishonor?
22 *What* if God, wanting to show *His* wrath and to make His power known, endured with much longsuffering the vessels of wrath prepared for destruction,
23 and that He might make known the riches of His glory on the vessels of mercy, which He had prepared beforehand for glory,
24 *even* us whom He called, not of the Jews only, but also of the Gentiles?
25 As He says also in Hosea:

*"I will call them My people,
who were not My people,
And her beloved,
who was not beloved."*³³
26 *"And it shall come to pass in the place
where it was said to them,
'You are not My people,'
There they will be called sons
of the living God."*³⁴

27 Isaiah also cries out concerning Israel:³⁵

*"Though the number of the children of
Israel be as the sand of the sea,
The remnant will be saved.*
28 *For He will finish the work
and cut it short in righteousness,
Because the LORD will make a short
work upon the earth."*³⁶

29 And as Isaiah said before:

*"Unless the LORD of Sabaoth
had left us a seed,
We would have become like Sodom,
And we would have been made like
Gomorrah."*³⁷

Present Condition of Israel

30 What shall we say then? That Gentiles, who did not pursue righteousness, have attained to righteousness, even the righteousness of faith;
31 but Israel, pursuing the law of righteousness, has not attained to the law of righteousness.³⁸
32 Why? Because *they did* not *seek it* by faith, but as it were, by the works of the law.³⁹ For they stumbled at that stumbling stone.
33 As it is written:

*"Behold, I lay in Zion a stumbling stone
and rock of offense,
And whoever believes on Him will not
be put to shame."*⁴⁰

Israel Needs the Gospel

10 Brethren, my heart's desire and prayer to God for Israel⁴¹ is that they may be saved.
2 For I bear them witness that they have a zeal for God, but not according to knowledge.
3 For they being ignorant of God's righteousness, and seeking to establish their own righteousness, have not submitted to the righteousness of God.
4 For Christ *is* the end of the law for righteousness to everyone who believes.
5 For Moses writes about the righteousness which is of the law, *"The man who does those things shall live by them."*⁴²

29 Genesis 25:23   30 Malachi 1:2, 3   31 Exodus 33:19   32 Exodus 9:16   33 Hosea 2:23   34 Hosea 1:10
35 Isaiah 10:22, 23   36 NU-Text reads *For the Lord will finish the work and cut it short upon the earth.*
37 Isaiah 1:9   38 NU-Text omits *of righteousness.*   39 NU-Text reads *by works.*   40 Isaiah 8:14; 28:16
41 NU-Text reads *them.*   42 Leviticus 18:5

6 But the righteousness of faith speaks in this way, *"Do not say in your heart, 'Who will ascend into heaven?' "*[43] (that is, to bring Christ down *from above*) 7 or, *" 'Who will descend into the abyss?' "*[44] (that is, to bring Christ up from the dead). 8 But what does it say? *"The word is near you, even in your mouth and in your heart"*[45] (that is, the word of faith which we preach): 9 that if you confess with your mouth the Lord Jesus and believe in your heart that God has raised Him from the dead, you will be saved. 10 For with the heart one believes to righteousness, and with the mouth confession is made to salvation. 11 For the Scripture says, *"Whoever believes on Him will not be put to shame."*[46] 12 For there is no distinction between Jew and Greek, for the same Lord over all is rich to all who call upon Him. 13 For *"whoever calls upon the name of the LORD shall be saved."*[47]

Israel Rejects the Gospel

14 How then shall they call on Him in whom they have not believed? And how shall they believe in Him of whom they have not heard? And how shall they hear without a preacher? 15 And how shall they preach unless they are sent? As it is written:

*"How beautiful are the feet of those
who preach the gospel of peace,*[48]
*Who bring glad tidings of good
things!"*[49]

16 But they have not all obeyed the gospel. For Isaiah says, *"Lord, who has believed our report?"*[50] 17 So then faith *comes* by hearing, and hearing by the word of God. 18 But I say, have they not heard? Yes indeed:

*"Their sound has gone out
to all the earth,
And their words to the ends
of the world."*[51]

19 But I say, did Israel not know? First Moses says:

*"I will provoke you to jealousy
by those who are not a nation,
I will anger you
by a foolish nation."*[52]

20 But Isaiah is very bold and says:

*"I was found by those
who did not seek Me;
I was made manifest to those
who did not ask for Me."*[53]

21 But to Israel he says:

*"All day long I have stretched
out My hands
To a disobedient and contrary
people."*[54]

Israel's Rejection Not Total

11 I say then, has God cast away His people? Certainly not! For I also am an Israelite, of the seed of Abraham, *of* the tribe of Benjamin. 2 God has not cast away His people whom He foreknew. Or do you not know what the Scripture says of Elijah, how he pleads with God against Israel, saying, 3 *"LORD, they have killed Your prophets and torn down Your altars, and I alone am left, and they seek my life"?*[55] 4 But what does the divine response say to him? *"I have reserved for Myself seven thousand men who have not bowed the knee to Baal."*[56] 5 Even so then, at this present time there is a remnant according to the election of grace. 6 And if by grace, then *it is* no longer of works; otherwise grace is no longer grace.[57] But if *it is* of works, it is no longer grace; otherwise work is no longer work. 7 What then? Israel has not obtained what it seeks; but the elect have obtained it, and the rest were hardened. 8 Just as it is written:

*"God has given them a spirit of stupor,
Eyes that they should not see
And ears that they should not hear,
To this very day."*[58]

9 And David says:

*"Let their table become a snare
and a trap,*

---

43 Deuteronomy 30:12   44 Deuteronomy 30:13   45 Deuteronomy 30:14   46 Isaiah 28:16   47 Joel 2:32
48 NU-Text omits *preach the gospel of peace, Who.*   49 Isaiah 52:7; Nahum 1:15   50 Isaiah 53:1
51 Psalm 19:4   52 Deuteronomy 32:21   53 Isaiah 65:1   54 Isaiah 65:2   55 1 Kings 19:10, 14
56 1 Kings 19:18   57 NU-Text omits the rest of this verse.   58 Deuteronomy 29:4; Isaiah 29:10

A stumbling block and
a recompense to them;
10 Let their eyes be darkened,
that they may not see,
And bow down their back always."[59]

Israel's Rejection Not Final

11 I say then, have they stumbled that they should fall? Certainly not! But through their fall, to provoke them to jealousy, salvation *has come* to the Gentiles.
12 Now if their fall *is* riches for the world, and their failure riches for the Gentiles, how much more their fullness!
13 For I speak to you Gentiles; inasmuch as I am an apostle to the Gentiles, I magnify my ministry,
14 if by any means I may provoke to jealousy *those who are* my flesh and save some of them.
15 For if their being cast away *is* the reconciling of the world, what *will* their acceptance *be* but life from the dead?
16 For if the firstfruit *is* holy, the lump *is* also *holy*; and if the root *is* holy, so *are* the branches.
17 And if some of the branches were broken off, and you, being a wild olive tree, were grafted in among them, and with them became a partaker of the root and fatness of the olive tree,
18 do not boast against the branches. But if you boast, *remember that* you do not support the root, but the root supports you.
19 You will say then, "Branches were broken off that I might be grafted in."
20 Well *said*. Because of unbelief they were broken off, and you stand by faith. Do not be haughty, but fear.
21 For if God did not spare the natural branches, He may not spare you either.
22 Therefore consider the goodness and severity of God: on those who fell, severity; but toward you, goodness,[60] if you continue in *His* goodness. Otherwise you also will be cut off.
23 And they also, if they do not continue in unbelief, will be grafted in, for God is able to graft them in again.
24 For if you were cut out of the olive tree which is wild by nature, and were grafted contrary to nature into a good olive tree, how much more will these, who

are the natural *branches,* be grafted into their own olive tree?
25 For I do not desire, brethren, that you should be ignorant of this mystery, lest you should be wise in your own opinion, that hardening in part has happened to Israel until the fullness of the Gentiles has come in.
26 And so all Israel will be saved, as it is written:

"The Deliverer will come out of Zion,
And He will turn away ungodliness
from Jacob;
27 For this is My covenant with them,
When I take away their sins."[61]

28 Concerning the gospel *they are* enemies for your sake, but concerning the election *they are* beloved for the sake of the fathers.
29 For the gifts and the calling of God *are* irrevocable.
30 For as you were once disobedient to God, yet have now obtained mercy through their disobedience,
31 even so these also have now been disobedient, that through the mercy shown you they also may obtain mercy.
32 For God has committed them all to disobedience, that He might have mercy on all.
33 Oh, the depth of the riches both of the wisdom and knowledge of God! How unsearchable *are* His judgments and His ways past finding out!

34 "For who has known the mind
of the LORD?
Or who has become His counselor?"[62]
35 "Or who has first given to Him
And it shall be repaid to him?"[63]

36 For of Him and through Him and to Him *are* all things, to whom *be* glory forever. Amen.

Living Sacrifices to God

12 I beseech you therefore, brethren, by the mercies of God, that you present your bodies a living sacrifice, holy, acceptable to God, *which is* your reasonable service.
2 And do not be conformed to this world, but be transformed by the renewing of your mind, that you may prove what *is* that good and acceptable and perfect will of God.

59 Psalm 69:22, 23   60 NU-Text adds *of God.*   61 Isaiah 59:20, 21
62 Isaiah 40:13; Jeremiah 23:18   63 Job 41:11

Serve God with Spiritual Gifts

3 For I say, through the grace given to me, to everyone who is among you, not to think *of himself* more highly than he ought to think, but to think soberly, as God has dealt to each one a measure of faith.
4 For as we have many members in one body, but all the members do not have the same function,
5 so we, *being* many, are one body in Christ, and individually members of one another.
6 Having then gifts differing according to the grace that is given to us, *let us use them*: if prophecy, *let us prophesy* in proportion to our faith;
7 or ministry, *let us use it* in *our* ministering; he who teaches, in teaching;
8 he who exhorts, in exhortation; he who gives, with liberality; he who leads, with diligence; he who shows mercy, with cheerfulness.

Behave Like a Christian

9 *Let* love *be* without hypocrisy. Abhor what is evil. Cling to what is good.
10 *Be* kindly affectionate to one another with brotherly love, in honor giving preference to one another;
11 not lagging in diligence, fervent in spirit, serving the Lord;
12 rejoicing in hope, patient in tribulation, continuing steadfastly in prayer;
13 distributing to the needs of the saints, given to hospitality.
14 Bless those who persecute you; bless and do not curse.
15 Rejoice with those who rejoice, and weep with those who weep.
16 Be of the same mind toward one another. Do not set your mind on high things, but associate with the humble. Do not be wise in your own opinion.
17 Repay no one evil for evil. Have regard for good things in the sight of all men.
18 If it is possible, as much as depends on you, live peaceably with all men.
19 Beloved, do not avenge yourselves, but *rather* give place to wrath; for it is written, *"Vengeance is Mine, I will repay,"*[64] says the Lord.

20 *"Therefore if your enemy hungers, feed him;*

If he thirsts, give him a drink; For in so doing you will heap coals of fire on his head."[65]

21 Do not be overcome by evil, but overcome evil with good.

Submit to Government

13 Let every soul be subject to the governing authorities. For there is no authority except from God, and the authorities that exist are appointed by God.
2 Therefore whoever resists the authority resists the ordinance of God, and those who resist will bring judgment on themselves.
3 For rulers are not a terror to good works, but to evil. Do you want to be unafraid of the authority? Do what is good, and you will have praise from the same.
4 For he is God's minister to you for good. But if you do evil, be afraid; for he does not bear the sword in vain; for he is God's minister, an avenger to *execute* wrath on him who practices evil.
5 Therefore *you* must be subject, not only because of wrath but also for conscience' sake.
6 For because of this you also pay taxes, for they are God's ministers attending continually to this very thing.
7 Render therefore to all their due: taxes to whom taxes *are due*, customs to whom customs, fear to whom fear, honor to whom honor.

Love Your Neighbor

8 Owe no one anything except to love one another, for he who loves another has fulfilled the law.
9 For the commandments, *"You shall not commit adultery," "You shall not murder," "You shall not steal," "You shall not bear false witness,"*[66] *"You shall not covet,"*[67] and if *there is* any other commandment, are *all* summed up in this saying, namely, *"You shall love your neighbor as yourself."*[68]
10 Love does no harm to a neighbor; therefore love *is* the fulfillment of the law.

Put on Christ

11 And *do* this, knowing the time, that now *it is* high time to awake out of sleep;

---

64 Deuteronomy 32:35   65 Proverbs 25:21, 22   66 NU-Text omits *"You shall not bear false witness."*
67 Exodus 20:13–15, 17; Deuteronomy 5:17–19, 21   68 Leviticus 19:18

for now our salvation *is* nearer than when we *first* believed.
12 The night is far spent, the day is at hand. Therefore let us cast off the works of darkness, and let us put on the armor of light.
13 Let us walk properly, as in the day, not in revelry and drunkenness, not in licentiousness and lewdness, not in strife and envy.
14 But put on the Lord Jesus Christ, and make no provision for the flesh, to *fulfill its* lusts.

The Law of Liberty

14 Receive one who is weak in the faith, *but* not to disputes over doubtful things.
2 For one believes he may eat all things, but he who is weak eats *only* vegetables.
3 Let not him who eats despise him who does not eat, and let not him who does not eat judge him who eats; for God has received him.
4 Who are you to judge another's servant? To his own master he stands or falls. Indeed, he will be made to stand, for God is able to make him stand.
5 One person esteems *one* day above another; another esteems every day *alike.* Let each be fully convinced in his own mind.
6 He who observes the day, observes *it* to the Lord;[69] and he who does not observe the day, to the Lord he does not observe *it.* He who eats, eats to the Lord, for he gives God thanks; and he who does not eat, to the Lord he does not eat, and gives God thanks.
7 For none of us lives to himself, and no one dies to himself.
8 For if we live, we live to the Lord; and if we die, we die to the Lord. Therefore, whether we live or die, we are the Lord's.
9 For to this end Christ died and rose[70] and lived again, that He might be Lord of both the dead and the living.
10 But why do you judge your brother? Or why do you show contempt for your brother? For we shall all stand before the judgment seat of Christ.[71]
11 For it is written:

"As I live, says the LORD,
Every knee shall bow to Me,

And every tongue shall confess to God."[72]

12 So then each of us shall give account of himself to God.
13 Therefore let us not judge one another anymore, but rather resolve this, not to put a stumbling block or a cause to fall in *our* brother's way.

The Law of Love

14 I know and am convinced by the Lord Jesus that *there is* nothing unclean of itself; but to him who considers anything to be unclean, to him *it is* unclean.
15 Yet if your brother is grieved because of *your* food, you are no longer walking in love. Do not destroy with your food the one for whom Christ died.
16 Therefore do not let your good be spoken of as evil;
17 for the kingdom of God is not food and drink, but righteousness and peace and joy in the Holy Spirit.
18 For he who serves Christ in these things[73] *is* acceptable to God and approved by men.
19 Therefore let us pursue the things *which make* for peace and the things by which one may edify another.
20 Do not destroy the work of God for the sake of food. All things indeed *are* pure, but *it is* evil for the man who eats with offense.
21 *It is* good neither to eat meat nor drink wine nor *do anything* by which your brother stumbles or is offended or is made weak.[74]
22 Do you have faith?[75] Have *it* to yourself before God. Happy *is* he who does not condemn himself in what he approves.
23 But he who doubts is condemned if he eats, because *he does* not *eat* from faith; for whatever *is* not from faith is sin.[76]

Bearing Others' Burdens

15 We then who are strong ought to bear with the scruples of the weak, and not to please ourselves.
2 Let each of us please *his* neighbor for *his* good, leading to edification.
3 For even Christ did not please Himself; but as it is written, *"The reproaches*

---

69 NU-Text omits the rest of this sentence.   70 NU-Text omits *and rose.*   71 NU-Text reads *of God.*
72 Isaiah 45:23   73 NU-Text reads *this.*   74 NU-Text omits *or is offended or is made weak.*
75 NU-Text reads *The faith which you have—have.*   76 M-Text puts Romans 16:25–27 here.

of those who reproached You fell on Me."[77]

4 For whatever things were written before were written for our learning, that we through the patience and comfort of the Scriptures might have hope.
5 Now may the God of patience and comfort grant you to be like-minded toward one another, according to Christ Jesus,
6 that you may with one mind *and* one mouth glorify the God and Father of our Lord Jesus Christ.

Glorify God Together

7 Therefore receive one another, just as Christ also received us,[78] to the glory of God.
8 Now I say that Jesus Christ has become a servant to the circumcision for the truth of God, to confirm the promises *made* to the fathers,
9 and that the Gentiles might glorify God for *His* mercy, as it is written:

"For this reason I will confess
    to You among the Gentiles,
And sing to Your name."[79]

10 And again he says:

"Rejoice, O Gentiles, with His
    people!"[80]

11 And again:

"Praise the LORD, all you Gentiles!
Laud Him, all you peoples!"[81]

12 And again, Isaiah says:

"There shall be a root of Jesse;
And He who shall rise to reign
    over the Gentiles,
In Him the Gentiles shall hope."[82]

13 Now may the God of hope fill you with all joy and peace in believing, that you may abound in hope by the power of the Holy Spirit.

From Jerusalem to Illyricum

14 Now I myself am confident concerning you, my brethren, that you also are full of goodness, filled with all knowledge, able also to admonish one another.[83]

15 Nevertheless, brethren, I have written more boldly to you on *some* points, as reminding you, because of the grace given to me by God,
16 that I might be a minister of Jesus Christ to the Gentiles, ministering the gospel of God, that the offering of the Gentiles might be acceptable, sanctified by the Holy Spirit.
17 Therefore I have reason to glory in Christ Jesus in the things *which pertain* to God.
18 For I will not dare to speak of any of those things which Christ has not accomplished through me, in word and deed, to make the Gentiles obedient—
19 in mighty signs and wonders, by the power of the Spirit of God, so that from Jerusalem and round about to Illyricum I have fully preached the gospel of Christ.
20 And so I have made it my aim to preach the gospel, not where Christ was named, lest I should build on another man's foundation,
21 but as it is written:

"To whom He was not announced,
    they shall see;
And those who have not heard
    shall understand."[84]

Plan to Visit Rome

22 For this reason I also have been much hindered from coming to you.
23 But now no longer having a place in these parts, and having a great desire these many years to come to you,
24 whenever I journey to Spain, I shall come to you.[85] For I hope to see you on my journey, and to be helped on my way there by you, if first I may enjoy your *company* for a while.
25 But now I am going to Jerusalem to minister to the saints.
26 For it pleased those from Macedonia and Achaia to make a certain contribution for the poor among the saints who are in Jerusalem.
27 It pleased them indeed, and they are their debtors. For if the Gentiles have been partakers of their spiritual things, their duty is also to minister to them in material things.
28 Therefore, when I have performed this and have sealed to them this fruit, I shall go by way of you to Spain.

77 Psalm 69:9   78 NU-Text and M-Text read *you.*   79 2 Samuel 22:50; Psalm 18:49   80 Deuteronomy 32:43
81 Psalm 117:1   82 Isaiah 11:10   83 M-Text reads *others.*   84 Isaiah 52:15
85 NU-Text omits *I shall come to you* (and joins *Spain* with the next sentence).

29 But I know that when I come to you, I shall come in the fullness of the blessing of the gospel[86] of Christ.
30 Now I beg you, brethren, through the Lord Jesus Christ, and through the love of the Spirit, that you strive together with me in *your* prayers to God for me,
31 that I may be delivered from those in Judea who do not believe, and that my service for Jerusalem may be acceptable to the saints,
32 that I may come to you with joy by the will of God, and may be refreshed together with you.
33 Now the God of peace *be* with you all. Amen.

Sister Phoebe Commended

16 I commend to you Phoebe our sister, who is a servant of the church in Cenchrea,
2 that you may receive her in the Lord in a manner worthy of the saints, and assist her in whatever business she has need of you; for indeed she has been a helper of many and of myself also.

Greeting Roman Saints

3 Greet Priscilla and Aquila, my fellow workers in Christ Jesus,
4 who risked their own necks for my life, to whom not only I give thanks, but also all the churches of the Gentiles.
5 Likewise *greet* the church that is in their house. Greet my beloved Epaenetus, who is the firstfruits of Achaia[87] to Christ.
6 Greet Mary, who labored much for us.
7 Greet Andronicus and Junia, my kinsmen and my fellow prisoners, who are of note among the apostles, who also were in Christ before me.
8 Greet Amplias, my beloved in the Lord.
9 Greet Urbanus, our fellow worker in Christ, and Stachys, my beloved.
10 Greet Apelles, approved in Christ. Greet those who are of the *household* of Aristobulus.
11 Greet Herodion, my kinsman. Greet those who are of the *household* of Narcissus who are in the Lord.
12 Greet Tryphena and Tryphosa, who have labored in the Lord. Greet the be-

loved Persis, who labored much in the Lord.
13 Greet Rufus, chosen in the Lord, and his mother and mine.
14 Greet Asyncritus, Phlegon, Hermas, Patrobas, Hermes, and the brethren who are with them.
15 Greet Philologus and Julia, Nereus and his sister, and Olympas, and all the saints who are with them.
16 Greet one another with a holy kiss. The[88] churches of Christ greet you.

Avoid Divisive Persons

17 Now I urge you, brethren, note those who cause divisions and offenses, contrary to the doctrine which you learned, and avoid them.
18 For those who are such do not serve our Lord Jesus[89] Christ, but their own belly, and by smooth words and flattering speech deceive the hearts of the simple.
19 For your obedience has become known to all. Therefore I am glad on your behalf; but I want you to be wise in what is good, and simple concerning evil.
20 And the God of peace will crush Satan under your feet shortly. The grace of our Lord Jesus Christ *be* with you. Amen.

Greetings from Paul's Friends

21 Timothy, my fellow worker, and Lucius, Jason, and Sosipater, my kinsmen, greet you.
22 I, Tertius, who wrote *this* epistle, greet you in the Lord.
23 Gaius, my host and *the host* of the whole church, greets you. Erastus, the treasurer of the city, greets you, and Quartus, a brother.
24 The grace of our Lord Jesus Christ *be* with you all. Amen.[90]

Benediction

25 Now to Him who is able to establish you according to my gospel and the preaching of Jesus Christ, according to the revelation of the mystery *which was* kept secret since the world began
26 but now has been made manifest, and by the prophetic Scriptures has been made known to all nations, according to the commandment of the everlasting God, for obedience to the faith—
27 to God, alone wise, *be* glory through Jesus Christ forever. Amen.[91]

---

86 NU-Text omits *of the gospel.*   87 NU-Text reads *Asia.*   88 NU-Text reads *All the churches.*
89 NU-Text and M-Text omit *Jesus.*   90 NU-Text omits this verse.
91 M-Text puts Romans 16:25–27 after Romans 14:23.

Introduction to
First Corinthians

It is a constant challenge for Christians to bloom where they are planted! This is what the apostle Paul encouraged the Corinthians to do.

The First Epistle to the Corinthians was written by the apostle Paul while in Ephesus to the young and struggling church in the city of Corinth, Greece. Throughout this letter, Paul encourages the church to live up to its calling from God.

The city of Corinth was a wealthy economic center with international trade because of its established seaport. Its strong fortress, built on solid rock hundreds of feet above the Corinthian plain, provided great military advantages to the Roman empire. A cosmopolitan center, Corinth was known for its immoral behavior. One ancient writer explained that to be called a "Corinthian" was to be called a fornicator. The city's great temple for Aphrodite was popular for its one thousand prostitutes who performed their rituals in the worship of the "goddess of love." It was in this negative environment that the young church which Paul helped to establish, floundered.

Paul spent over a year-and-a-half in Corinth during A.D. 50 and 51. He later returned on another journey to the church sometime between A.D. 53 and 54. Paul corresponded more with this body of believers than any other church in the New Testament period. This was most likely due to the serious problems facing the Christians there.

Throughout First Corinthians we learn that the young believers were led off track by their surroundings. Drunken parties, cheating, untruthfulness, immorality, adultery, and other immoral acts were infiltrating the church. Paul's apostleship was questioned and even the resurrection of Jesus Christ was denied. Paul treats these problems from both a theological and a practical viewpoint. He encourages the church to become unified and demonstrate their oneness through love. Paul reminds them that even though they may be talented, devoted, generous, and faithful enough to move mountains, if love is absent, there can be no profit. He implores them to make love their aim. For love isn't love until you give it away.

Paul's patience in confirming and encouraging the Corinthian church indicates that his love was more than just words. He was committed to their health and well-being as a growing, positive church. Paul's vision was to build up the Corinthian church. By doing so, he also was built up. Paul demonstrates in this letter that love truly is deciding to make *your* problem *my* problem.

The First Epistle of Paul the Apostle to the
Corinthians

Greeting

PAUL, called *to be* an apostle of Jesus Christ through the will of God, and Sosthenes *our* brother,

2 To the church of God which is at Corinth, to those who are sanctified in Christ Jesus, called *to be* saints, with all who in every place call on the name of Jesus Christ our Lord, both theirs and ours:

3 Grace to you and peace from God our Father and the Lord Jesus Christ.

Spiritual Gifts at Corinth

4 I thank my God always concerning you for the grace of God which was given to you by Christ Jesus,

5 that you were enriched in everything by Him in all utterance and all knowledge,

6 even as the testimony of Christ was confirmed in you,

7 so that you come short in no gift, eagerly waiting for the revelation of our Lord Jesus Christ,

8 who will also confirm you to the end, *that you may be* blameless in the day of our Lord Jesus Christ.

9 God *is* faithful, by whom you were called into the fellowship of His Son, Jesus Christ our Lord.

Sectarianism Is Sin

10 Now I plead with you, brethren, by the name of our Lord Jesus Christ, that you all speak the same thing, and *that* there be no divisions among you, but *that* you be perfectly joined together in the same mind and in the same judgment.

11 For it has been declared to me concerning you, my brethren, by those of Chloe's *household*, that there are contentions among you.

12 Now I say this, that each of you says, "I am of Paul," or "I am of Apollos," or "I am of Cephas," or "I am of Christ."

13 Is Christ divided? Was Paul crucified for you? Or were you baptized in the name of Paul?

14 I thank God that I baptized none of you except Crispus and Gaius,

15 lest anyone should say that I had baptized in my own name.

16 Yes, I also baptized the household of Stephanas. Besides, I do not know whether I baptized any other.

17 For Christ did not send me to baptize, but to preach the gospel, not with wisdom of words, lest the cross of Christ should be made of no effect.

Christ the Power and Wisdom of God

18 For the message of the cross is foolishness to those who are perishing, but to us who are being saved it is the power of God.

19 For it is written:

"I will destroy the wisdom of the wise,
And bring to nothing the
understanding of the prudent."[1]

20 Where *is* the wise? Where *is* the scribe? Where *is* the disputer of this age? Has not God made foolish the wisdom of this world?

21 For since, in the wisdom of God, the world through wisdom did not know God, it pleased God through the foolishness of the message preached to save those who believe.

22 For Jews request a sign, and Greeks seek after wisdom;

23 but we preach Christ crucified, to the Jews a stumbling block and to the Greeks[2] foolishness,

24 but to those who are called, both Jews and Greeks, Christ the power of God and the wisdom of God.

25 Because the foolishness of God is wiser than men, and the weakness of God is stronger than men.

Glory Only in the Lord

26 For you see your calling, brethren, that not many wise according to the flesh, not many mighty, not many noble, *are* called.

1 Isaiah 29:14   2 NU-Text reads *Gentiles*.

27 But God has chosen the foolish things of the world to put to shame the wise, and God has chosen the weak things of the world to put to shame the things which are mighty;
28 and the base things of the world and the things which are despised God has chosen, and the things which are not, to bring to nothing the things that are,
29 that no flesh should glory in His presence.
30 But of Him you are in Christ Jesus, who became for us wisdom from God—and righteousness and sanctification and redemption—
31 that, as it is written, *"He who glories, let him glory in the LORD."*[3]

Christ Crucified

2 And I, brethren, when I came to you, did not come with excellence of speech or of wisdom declaring to you the testimony[4] of God.
2 For I determined not to know anything among you except Jesus Christ and Him crucified.
3 I was with you in weakness, in fear, and in much trembling.
4 And my speech and my preaching *were* not with persuasive words of human[5] wisdom, but in demonstration of the Spirit and of power,
5 that your faith should not be in the wisdom of men but in the power of God.

Spiritual Wisdom

6 However, we speak wisdom among those who are mature, yet not the wisdom of this age, nor of the rulers of this age, who are coming to nothing.
7 But we speak the wisdom of God in a mystery, the hidden *wisdom* which God ordained before the ages for our glory,
8 which none of the rulers of this age knew; for had they known, they would not have crucified the Lord of glory.
9 But as it is written:

"Eye has not seen, nor ear heard,
Nor have entered into the heart of man
The things which God has prepared for
those who love Him."[6]

10 But God has revealed *them* to us through His Spirit. For the Spirit searches all things, yes, the deep things of God.

11 For what man knows the things of a man except the spirit of the man which is in him? Even so no one knows the things of God except the Spirit of God.
12 Now we have received, not the spirit of the world, but the Spirit who is from God, that we might know the things that have been freely given to us by God.
13 These things we also speak, not in words which man's wisdom teaches but which the Holy[7] Spirit teaches, comparing spiritual things with spiritual.
14 But the natural man does not receive the things of the Spirit of God, for they are foolishness to him; nor can he know *them*, because they are spiritually discerned.
15 But he who is spiritual judges all things, yet he himself is *rightly* judged by no one.
16 For *"Who has known the mind of the LORD that he may instruct Him?"*[8] But we have the mind of Christ.

Sectarianism Is Carnal

3 And I, brethren, could not speak to you as to spiritual *people* but as to carnal, as to babes in Christ.
2 I fed you with milk and not with solid food; for until now you were not able *to receive it*, and even now you are still not able;
3 for you are still carnal. For where *there are* envy, strife, and divisions among you, are you not carnal and behaving like *mere* men?
4 For when one says, "I am of Paul," and another, "I *am* of Apollos," are you not carnal?

Watering, Working, Warning

5 Who then is Paul, and who *is* Apollos, but ministers through whom you believed, as the Lord gave to each one?
6 I planted, Apollos watered, but God gave the increase.
7 So then neither he who plants is anything, nor he who waters, but God who gives the increase.
8 Now he who plants and he who waters are one, and each one will receive his own reward according to his own labor.
9 For we are God's fellow workers; you are God's field, *you are* God's building.
10 According to the grace of God which was given to me, as a wise master builder

3 Jeremiah 9:24   4 NU-Text reads *mystery.*   5 NU-Text omits *human.*   6 Isaiah 64:4
7 NU-Text omits *Holy.*   8 Isaiah 40:13

You Are Living Stones

The architecture of the temple in the New Testament period is a fascinating work of art. Started by Herod the Great, approximately 20 B.C., the temple was completed somewhere around A.D. 27, forty-six years later.

Made from solid limestone, quarried from the hills around Jerusalem, the temple stood as one of the great buildings of the ancient world. The ancient historian, Josephus, lauded the structure. "He who has not seen the Jerusalem temple has not seen a beautiful building."

Recent archaeological excavations have focused on exposing remains of the temple mount, the enclosure upon which the New Testament temple was built. Already archaeological teams have unearthed temple stones ranging in size from forty tons to seven hundred tons. The builders of the temple quarried large blocks of limestone, with which they employed an ancient architectural design known as "headers and stretchers." Stones of equal length were placed in an alternate pattern. The first block was lined up with the end of the stone facing outside—the length of it going into the building. The second stone was situated so the side or length faced outside. The subsequent stone was like the first. This pattern continued around the base of the structure. In addition, the builders left two inches of space between each stone. This was done so that when the heat of the summer came and the temple stones expanded, they would have room to push outward. In the coolness of winter, the limestone contracted. The remarkable strength of the temple was that it could expand and contract during severe winters or intense heat. The temple had room to breathe. Each stone was placed one upon the other with a half-inch tilt inward, until it reached hundreds of feet in height.

The apostle Peter reminds us of the beauty of the temple when he asks us to be built together, dependent upon one another into a living temple of God. We are choice stones built upon the foundation of Jesus Christ. Like the stones from the temple two thousand years ago, we must be dependent upon each other. We expand and contract when the heat of problems and cold of negative influences come our way. Then others will say about us, "Those who have not seen their lives have not seen the love of Christ."

I have laid the foundation, and another builds on it. But let each one take heed how he builds on it.
11 For no other foundation can anyone lay than that which is laid, which is Jesus Christ.
12 Now if anyone builds on this foundation *with* gold, silver, precious stones, wood, hay, straw,
13 each one's work will become manifest; for the Day will declare it, because it will be revealed by fire; and the fire will test each one's work, of what sort it is.
14 If anyone's work which he has built on *it* endures, he will receive a reward.
15 If anyone's work is burned, he will suffer loss; but he himself will be saved, yet so as through fire.
16 Do you not know that you are the temple of God and *that* the Spirit of God dwells in you?
17 If anyone defiles the temple of God, God will destroy him. For the temple of God is holy, which *temple* you are.

Avoid Worldly Wisdom

18 Let no one deceive himself. If anyone among you seems to be wise in this age, let him become a fool that he may become wise.
19 For the wisdom of this world is foolishness with God. For it is written, *"He catches the wise in their own craftiness";* 9
20 and again, *"The LORD knows the thoughts of the wise, that they are futile."* 10
21 Therefore let no one glory in men. For all things are yours:
22 whether Paul or Apollos or Cephas, or the world or life or death, or things present or things to come—all are yours.
23 And you *are* Christ's, and Christ *is* God's.

Stewards of the Mysteries of God

4 Let a man so consider us, as servants of Christ and stewards of the mysteries of God.
2 Moreover it is required in stewards that one be found faithful.
3 But with me it is a very small thing that I should be judged by you or by a human court.11 In fact, I do not even judge myself.
4 For I know nothing against myself, yet I am not justified by this; but He who judges me is the Lord.

5 Therefore judge nothing before the time, until the Lord comes, who will both bring to light the hidden things of darkness and reveal the counsels of the hearts; and then each one's praise will come from God.

Fools for Christ's Sake

6 Now these things, brethren, I have figuratively transferred to myself and Apollos for your sakes, that you may learn in us not to think beyond what is written, that none of you may be puffed up on behalf of one against the other.
7 For who makes you differ *from another?* And what do you have that you did not receive? Now if you did indeed receive *it*, why do you glory as if you had not received *it?*
8 You are already full! You are already rich! You have reigned as kings without us—and indeed I could wish you did reign, that we also might reign with you!
9 For I think that God has displayed us, the apostles, last, as men condemned to death; for we have been made a spectacle to the world, both to angels and to men.
10 We *are* fools for Christ's sake, but you *are* wise in Christ! We *are* weak, but you *are* strong! You *are* distinguished, but we *are* dishonored!
11 *Even* to the present hour we both hunger and thirst, and we are poorly clothed, and beaten, and homeless.
12 And we labor, working with our own hands. Being reviled, we bless; being persecuted, we endure *it*;
13 being defamed, we entreat. We have been made as the filth of the world, the offscouring of all things until now.

Paul's Paternal Care

14 I do not write these things to shame you, but as my beloved children I warn *you.*
15 For though you might have ten thousand instructors in Christ, yet *you do* not *have* many fathers; for in Christ Jesus I have begotten you through the gospel.
16 Therefore I urge you, imitate me.
17 For this reason I have sent Timothy to you, who is my beloved and faithful son in the Lord, who will remind you of my ways in Christ, as I teach everywhere in every church.
18 Now some are puffed up, as though I were not coming to you.

9 Job 5:13   10 Psalm 94:11   11 Literally *day*

19 But I will come to you shortly, if the Lord wills, and I will know, not the word of those who are puffed up, but the power. 20 For the kingdom of God *is* not in word but in power. 21 What do you want? Shall I come to you with a rod, or in love and a spirit of gentleness?

Immorality Defiles the Church

5 It is actually reported *that there is* sexual immorality among you, and such sexual immorality as is not even named[12] among the Gentiles—that a man has his father's wife! 2 And you are puffed up, and have not rather mourned, that he who has done this deed might be taken away from among you. 3 For I indeed, as absent in body but present in spirit, have already judged, as though I were present, *concerning* him who has so done this deed. 4 In the name of our Lord Jesus Christ, when you are gathered together, along with my spirit, with the power of our Lord Jesus Christ, 5 deliver such a one to Satan for the destruction of the flesh, that his spirit may be saved in the day of the Lord Jesus.[13] 6 Your glorying *is* not good. Do you not know that a little leaven leavens the whole lump? 7 Therefore purge out the old leaven, that you may be a new lump, since you truly are unleavened. For indeed Christ, our Passover, was sacrificed for us.[14] 8 Therefore let us keep the feast, not with old leaven, nor with the leaven of malice and wickedness, but with the unleavened *bread* of sincerity and truth.

Immorality Must Be Judged

9 I wrote to you in my epistle not to keep company with sexually immoral people. 10 Yet *I* certainly *did* not *mean* with the sexually immoral people of this world, or with the covetous, or extortioners, or idolaters, since then you would need to go out of the world. 11 But now I have written to you not to keep company with anyone named a brother, who is a fornicator, or covetous, or an idolater, or a reviler, or a drunkard, or an extortioner—not even to eat with such a person. 12 For what *have* I *to do* with judging those also who are outside? Do you not judge those who are inside? 13 But those who are outside God judges. Therefore *"put away from yourselves that wicked person."*[15]

Do Not Sue the Brethren

6 Dare any of you, having a matter against another, go to law before the unrighteous, and not before the saints? 2 Do you not know that the saints will judge the world? And if the world will be judged by you, are you unworthy to judge the smallest matters? 3 Do you not know that we shall judge angels? How much more, things that pertain to this life? 4 If then you have judgments concerning things pertaining to this life, do you appoint those who are least esteemed by the church to judge? 5 I say this to your shame. Is it so, that there is not a wise man among you, not even one, who will be able to judge between his brethren? 6 But brother goes to law against brother, and that before unbelievers! 7 Now therefore, it is already an utter failure for you that you go to law against one another. Why do you not rather accept wrong? Why do you not rather *let yourselves* be defrauded? 8 No, you yourselves do wrong and defraud, and *you do* these things *to your* brethren! 9 Do you not know that the unrighteous will not inherit the kingdom of God? Do not be deceived. Neither fornicators, nor idolaters, nor adulterers, nor homosexuals,[16] nor sodomites, 10 nor thieves, nor covetous, nor drunkards, nor revilers, nor extortioners will inherit the kingdom of God. 11 And such were some of you. But you were washed, but you were sanctified, but you were justified in the name of the Lord Jesus and by the Spirit of our God.

Glorify God in Body and Spirit

12 All things are lawful for me, but all things are not helpful. All things are lawful for me, but I will not be brought under the power of any.

---

12 NU-Text omits *named.*   13 NU-Text omits *Jesus.*   14 NU-Text omits *for us.*
15 Deuteronomy 17:7; 19:19; 22:21, 24; 24:7   16 That is, catamites

13 Foods for the stomach and the stomach for foods, but God will destroy both it and them. Now the body *is* not for sexual immorality but for the Lord, and the Lord for the body. 14 And God both raised up the Lord and will also raise us up by His power. 15 Do you not know that your bodies are members of Christ? Shall I then take the members of Christ and make *them* members of a harlot? Certainly not! 16 Or do you not know that he who is joined to a harlot is one body *with her?* For "The two," He says, "shall become one flesh."[17] 17 But he who is joined to the Lord is one spirit *with Him.* 18 Flee sexual immorality. Every sin that a man does is outside the body, but he who commits sexual immorality sins against his own body. 19 Or do you not know that your body is the temple of the Holy Spirit *who is* in you, whom you have from God, and you are not your own? 20 For you were bought at a price; therefore glorify God in your body[18] and in your spirit, which are God's.

Principles of Marriage

7 Now concerning the things of which you wrote to me: *It is* good for a man not to touch a woman. 2 Nevertheless, because of sexual immorality, let each man have his own wife, and let each woman have her own husband. 3 Let the husband render to his wife the affection due her, and likewise also the wife to her husband. 4 The wife does not have authority over her own body, but the husband *does.* And likewise the husband does not have authority over his own body, but the wife *does.* 5 Do not deprive one another except with consent for a time, that you may give yourselves to fasting and prayer; and come together again so that Satan does not tempt you because of your lack of self-control. 6 But I say this as a concession, not as a commandment. 7 For I wish that all men were even as I myself. But each one has his own gift from God, one in this manner and another in that.

8 But I say to the unmarried and to the widows: It is good for them if they remain even as I am; 9 but if they cannot exercise self-control, let them marry. For it is better to marry than to burn *with passion.*

Keep Your Marriage Vows

10 Now to the married I command, *yet* not I but the Lord: A wife is not to depart from *her* husband. 11 But even if she does depart, let her remain unmarried or be reconciled to *her* husband. And a husband is not to divorce *his* wife. 12 But to the rest I, not the Lord, say: If any brother has a wife who does not believe, and she is willing to live with him, let him not divorce her. 13 And a woman who has a husband who does not believe, if he is willing to live with her, let her not divorce him. 14 For the unbelieving husband is sanctified by the wife, and the unbelieving wife is sanctified by the husband; otherwise your children would be unclean, but now they are holy. 15 But if the unbeliever departs, let him depart; a brother or a sister is not under bondage in such *cases.* But God has called us to peace. 16 For how do you know, O wife, whether you will save *your* husband? Or how do you know, O husband, whether you will save *your* wife?

Live as You Are Called

17 But as God has distributed to each one, as the Lord has called each one, so let him walk. And so I ordain in all the churches. 18 Was anyone called while circumcised? Let him not become uncircumcised. Was anyone called while uncircumcised? Let him not be circumcised. 19 Circumcision is nothing and uncircumcision is nothing, but keeping the commandments of God *is what matters.* 20 Let each one remain in the same calling in which he was called. 21 Were you called *while* a slave? Do not be concerned about it; but if you can be made free, rather use *it.* 22 For he who is called in the Lord *while* a slave is the Lord's freedman. Likewise he who is called *while* free is Christ's slave.

17 Genesis 2:24   18 NU-Text ends the verse at *body.*

23 You were bought at a price; do not become slaves of men.

24 Brethren, let each one remain with God in that *calling* in which he was called.

To the Unmarried and Widows

25 Now concerning virgins: I have no commandment from the Lord; yet I give judgment as one whom the Lord in His mercy *has made* trustworthy.

26 I suppose therefore that this is good because of the present distress—that *it is* good for a man to remain as he is:

27 Are you bound to a wife? Do not seek to be loosed. Are you loosed from a wife? Do not seek a wife.

28 But even if you do marry, you have not sinned; and if a virgin marries, she has not sinned. Nevertheless such will have trouble in the flesh, but I would spare you.

29 But this I say, brethren, the time *is* short, so that from now on even those who have wives should be as though they had none,

30 those who weep as though they did not weep, those who rejoice as though they did not rejoice, those who buy as though they did not possess,

31 and those who use this world as not misusing *it*. For the form of this world is passing away.

32 But I want you to be without care. He who is unmarried cares for the things *that* *belong* to the Lord—how he may please the Lord.

33 But he who is married cares about the things of the world—how he may please *his* wife.

34 There is[19] a difference between a wife and a virgin. The unmarried woman cares about the things of the Lord, that she may be holy both in body and in spirit. But she who is married cares about the things of the world—how she may please *her* husband.

35 And this I say for your own profit, not that I may put a leash on you, but for what is proper, and that you may serve the Lord without distraction.

36 But if any man thinks he is behaving improperly toward his virgin, if she is past the flower of *her* youth, and thus it must be, let him do what he wishes; he does not sin; let them marry.

37 Nevertheless he who stands steadfast in his heart, having no necessity, but has power over his own will, and has so determined in his heart that he will keep his virgin,[20] does well.

38 So then he who gives *her*[21] in marriage does well, but he who does not give *her* in marriage does better.

39 A wife is bound by law as long as her husband lives; but if her husband dies, she is at liberty to be married to whom she wishes, only in the Lord.

40 But she is happier if she remains as she is, according to my judgment—and I think I also have the Spirit of God.

Be Sensitive to Conscience

8 Now concerning things offered to idols: We know that we all have knowledge. Knowledge puffs up, but love edifies.

2 And if anyone thinks that he knows anything, he knows nothing yet as he ought to know.

3 But if anyone loves God, this one is known by Him.

4 Therefore concerning the eating of things offered to idols, we know that an idol *is* nothing in the world, and that *there is* no other God but one.

5 For even if there are so-called gods, whether in heaven or on earth (as there are many gods and many lords),

6 yet for us *there is only* one God, the Father, of whom *are* all things, and we for Him; and one Lord Jesus Christ, through whom *are* all things, and through whom we *live*.

7 However, *there is* not in everyone that knowledge; for some, with consciousness of the idol, until now eat *it* as a thing offered to an idol; and their conscience, being weak, is defiled.

8 But food does not commend us to God; for neither if we eat are we the better, nor if we do not eat are we the worse.

9 But beware lest somehow this liberty of yours become a stumbling block to those who are weak.

10 For if anyone sees you who have knowledge eating in an idol's temple, will not the conscience of him who is weak be emboldened to eat those things offered to idols?

11 And because of your knowledge shall the weak brother perish, for whom Christ died?

---

19 M-Text adds *also.*   20 Or *virgin daughter*   21 NU-Text reads *his own virgin.*

12 But when you thus sin against the brethren, and wound their weak conscience, you sin against Christ.
13 Therefore, if food makes my brother stumble, I will never again eat meat, lest I make my brother stumble.

A Pattern of Self-Denial

9 Am I not an apostle? Am I not free? Have I not seen Jesus Christ our Lord? Are you not my work in the Lord?
2 If I am not an apostle to others, yet doubtless I am to you. For you are the seal of my apostleship in the Lord.
3 My defense to those who examine me is this:
4 Do we have no right to eat and drink?
5 Do we have no right to take along a believing wife, as do also the other apostles, the brothers of the Lord, and Cephas?
6 Or is it only Barnabas and I who have no right to refrain from working?
7 Who ever goes to war at his own expense? Who plants a vineyard and does not eat of its fruit? Or who tends a flock and does not drink of the milk of the flock?
8 Do I say these things as a mere man? Or does not the law say the same also?
9 For it is written in the law of Moses, *"You shall not muzzle an ox while it treads out the grain."*[22] Is it oxen God is concerned about?
10 Or does He say it altogether for our sakes? For our sakes, no doubt, this is written, that he who plows should plow in hope, and he who threshes in hope should be partaker of his hope.
11 If we have sown spiritual things for you, is it a great thing if we reap your material things?
12 If others are partakers of this right over you, are we not even more? Nevertheless we have not used this right, but endure all things lest we hinder the gospel of Christ.
13 Do you not know that those who minister the holy things eat of the things of the temple, and those who serve at the altar partake of the offerings of the altar?
14 Even so the Lord has commanded that those who preach the gospel should live from the gospel.
15 But I have used none of these things, nor have I written these things that it should be done so to me; for it would be better for me to die than that anyone should make my boasting void.
16 For if I preach the gospel, I have nothing to boast of, for necessity is laid upon me; yes, woe is me if I do not preach the gospel!
17 For if I do this willingly, I have a reward; but if against my will, I have been entrusted with a stewardship.
18 What is my reward then? That when I preach the gospel, I may present the gospel of Christ[23] without charge, that I may not abuse my authority in the gospel.

Serving All Men

19 For though I am free from all *men*, I have made myself a servant to all, that I might win the more;
20 and to the Jews I became as a Jew, that I might win Jews; to those who are under the law, as under the law,[24] that I might win those who are under the law;
21 to those who are without law, as without law (not being without law toward God,[25] but under law toward Christ[26]), that I might win those who are without law;
22 to the weak I became as[27] weak, that I might win the weak. I have become all things to all men, that I might by all means save some.
23 Now this I do for the gospel's sake, that I may be partaker of it with you.

Striving for a Crown

24 Do you not know that those who run in a race all run, but one receives the prize? Run in such a way that you may obtain it.
25 And everyone who competes for the prize is temperate in all things. Now they do it to obtain a perishable crown, but we for an imperishable crown.
26 Therefore I run thus: not with uncertainty. Thus I fight: not as one who beats the air.
27 But I discipline my body and bring it into subjection, lest, when I have preached to others, I myself should become disqualified.

Old Testament Examples

10 Moreover, brethren, I do not want you to be unaware that all our fathers were under the cloud, all passed through the sea,

22 Deuteronomy 25:4   23 NU-Text omits of Christ.   24 NU-Text adds though not being myself under the law.
25 NU-Text reads God's law.   26 NU-Text reads Christ's law.   27 NU-Text omits as.

The Games

"Run in such a way that you obtain *it*" (1 Cor. 9:24).

Everywhere in the New Testament world, Greek society left its mark on the culture and religion of the people. Perhaps one of the greatest contributions was that of the Olympic Games.

Held every four years in Greece since its inception, the Olympic Games quickly became world renowned. There was scarcely a city in the Roman empire where mention of the games did not bring excited discussion. Many cities were anxious to host the games. Two cities in Palestine were granted this honor: Dor and Samaria.

During the reign of King Herod in Palestine, he built magnificent accommodations for the games. In Assyria he constructed a hippodrome larger than the one in Rome, as well as gladiator stadiums and other facilities. In Samaria, Herod built horse racing stadiums and theaters to host plays for visitors attending the games. The ancient historian, Josephus, records that over one-hundred-foot-high marble pillars visible from the seashore were also built at Samaria.

The writers of the New Testament were also influenced by the Greeks and the Olympic Games. The apostle Paul encourages his readers to press on to the prize of the upward goal of God in Christ Jesus. He urges believers to run in such a way that they may win. Paul compares the Christian life-style to the continuous training and preparation for the games.

As Christians, we must bring our thoughts and abilities to their fullest potential by training, exercising, and demonstrating them before God and others. God's gift to you is who you are. Your gift to God or the prize you give to God is what you do with the talents and abilities He has given you.

2 all were baptized into Moses in the cloud and in the sea,
3 all ate the same spiritual food,
4 and all drank the same spiritual drink. For they drank of that spiritual Rock that followed them, and that Rock was Christ.
5 But with most of them God was not well pleased, for *their bodies* were scattered in the wilderness.
6 Now these things became our examples, to the intent that we should not lust after evil things as they also lusted.
7 And do not become idolaters as *were* some of them. As it is written, *"The people sat down to eat and drink, and rose up to play."*[28]
8 Nor let us commit sexual immorality, as some of them did, and in one day twenty-three thousand fell;
9 nor let us tempt Christ, as some of them also tempted, and were destroyed by serpents;
10 nor murmur, as some of them also murmured, and were destroyed by the destroyer.
11 Now all[29] these things happened to them as examples, and they were written for our admonition, on whom the ends of the ages have come.
12 Therefore let him who thinks he stands take heed lest he fall.
13 No temptation has overtaken you except such as is common to man; but God *is* faithful, who will not allow you to be tempted beyond what you are able, but with the temptation will also make the way of escape, that you may be able to bear *it.*

Flee from Idolatry

14 Therefore, my beloved, flee from idolatry.
15 I speak as to wise men; judge for yourselves what I say.
16 The cup of blessing which we bless, is it not the communion of the blood of Christ? The bread which we break, is it not the communion of the body of Christ?
17 For we, *being* many, are one bread *and* one body; for we all partake of that one bread.
18 Observe Israel after the flesh: Are not those who eat of the sacrifices partakers of the altar?

19 What am I saying then? That an idol is anything, or what is offered to idols is anything?
20 But *I* say that the things which the Gentiles sacrifice they sacrifice to demons and not to God, and I do not want you to have fellowship with demons.
21 You cannot drink the cup of the Lord and the cup of demons; you cannot partake of the Lord's table and of the table of demons.
22 Or do we provoke the Lord to jealousy? Are we stronger than He?

All to the Glory of God

23 All things are lawful for me,[30] but all things are not helpful; all things are lawful for me,[30] but all things do not edify.
24 Let no one seek his own, but each one the other's *well-being.*
25 Eat whatever is sold in the meat market, asking no questions for conscience' sake;
26 for *"The earth is the LORD's, and all its fullness."*[31]
27 If any of those who do not believe invites you *to dinner,* and you desire to go, eat whatever is set before you, asking no question for conscience' sake.
28 But if anyone says to you, "This was offered to idols," do not eat it for the sake of the one who told you, and for conscience' sake;[32] for *"The earth is the LORD's, and all its fullness."*[33]
29 Conscience, I say, not your own, but that of the other. For why is my liberty judged by another *man's* conscience?
30 But if I partake with thanks, why am I evil spoken of for *the food* over which I give thanks?
31 Therefore, whether you eat or drink, or whatever you do, do all to the glory of God.
32 Give no offense, either to the Jews or to the Greeks or to the church of God,
33 just as I also please all *men* in all *things,* not seeking my own profit, but the *profit* of many, that they may be saved.

11 Imitate me, just as I also *imitate* Christ.

Head Coverings

2 Now I praise you, brethren, that you remember me in all things and keep the traditions as I delivered *them* to you.

---

28 Exodus 32:6   29 NU-Text omits *all.*   30 NU-Text omits *for me.*   31 Psalm 24:1
32 NU-Text omits the rest of this verse.   33 Psalm 24:1

3 But I want you to know that the head of every man is Christ, the head of woman *is* man, and the head of Christ *is* God.

4 Every man praying or prophesying, having *his* head covered, dishonors his head.

5 But every woman who prays or prophesies with *her* head uncovered dishonors her head, for that is one and the same as if her head were shaved.

6 For if a woman is not covered, let her also be shorn. But if it is shameful for a woman to be shorn or shaved, let her be covered.

7 For a man indeed ought not to cover *his* head, since he is the image and glory of God; but woman is the glory of man.

8 For man is not from woman, but woman from man.

9 Nor was man created for the woman, but woman for the man.

10 For this reason the woman ought to have *a symbol of* authority on *her* head, because of the angels.

11 Nevertheless, neither *is* man independent of woman, nor woman independent of man, in the Lord.

12 For as the woman *was* from the man, even so the man also *is* through the woman; but all things are from God.

13 Judge among yourselves. Is it proper for a woman to pray to God with her head uncovered?

14 Does not even nature itself teach you that if a man has long hair, it is a dishonor to him?

15 But if a woman has long hair, it is a glory to her; for *her* hair is given to her[34] for a covering.

16 But if anyone seems to be contentious, we have no such custom, nor *do* the churches of God.

Conduct at the Lord's Supper

17 Now in giving these instructions I do not praise *you,* since you come together not for the better but for the worse.

18 For first of all, when you come together as a church, I hear that there are divisions among you, and in part I believe it.

19 For there must also be factions among you, that those who are approved may be recognized among you.

20 Therefore when you come together in one place, it is not to eat the Lord's Supper.

21 For in eating, each one takes his own supper ahead of *others*; and one is hungry and another is drunk.

22 What! Do you not have houses to eat and drink in? Or do you despise the church of God and shame those who have nothing? What shall I say to you? Shall I praise you in this? I do not praise *you.*

Institution of the Lord's Supper

23 For I received from the Lord that which I also delivered to you: that the Lord Jesus on the *same* night in which He was betrayed took bread;

24 and when He had given thanks, He broke *it* and said, "Take, eat;[35] this is My body which is broken[36] for you; do this in remembrance of Me."

25 In the same manner *He* also *took* the cup after supper, saying, "This cup is the new covenant in My blood. This do, as often as you drink *it*, in remembrance of Me."

26 For as often as you eat this bread and drink this cup, you proclaim the Lord's death till He comes.

Examine Yourself

27 Therefore whoever eats this bread or drinks *this* cup of the Lord in an unworthy manner will be guilty of the body and blood[37] of the Lord.

28 But let a man examine himself, and so let him eat of *that* bread and drink of *that* cup.

29 For he who eats and drinks in an unworthy manner[38] eats and drinks judgment to himself, not discerning the Lord's[39] body.

30 For this reason many *are* weak and sick among you, and many sleep.

31 For if we would judge ourselves, we would not be judged.

32 But when we are judged, we are chastened by the Lord, that we may not be condemned with the world.

33 Therefore, my brethren, when you come together to eat, wait for one another.

34 But if anyone is hungry, let him eat at home, lest you come together for judgment. And the rest I will set in order when I come.

---

34 M-Text omits *to her.*   35 NU-Text omits *Take, eat.*   36 NU-Text omits *broken.*
37 NU-Text and M-Text read *the blood.*   38 NU-Text omits *in an unworthy manner.*   39 NU-Text omits *Lord's.*

Spiritual Gifts: Unity in Diversity

12 Now concerning spiritual *gifts*, brethren, I do not want you to be ignorant:

2 You know that[40] you were Gentiles, carried away to these dumb idols, however you were led.

3 Therefore I make known to you that no one speaking by the Spirit of God calls Jesus accursed, and no one can say that Jesus is Lord except by the Holy Spirit.

4 Now there are diversities of gifts, but the same Spirit.

5 There are differences of ministries, but the same Lord.

6 And there are diversities of activities, but it is the same God who works all in all.

7 But the manifestation of the Spirit is given to each one for the profit *of all*:

8 for to one is given the word of wisdom through the Spirit, to another the word of knowledge through the same Spirit,

9 to another faith by the same Spirit, to another gifts of healings by the same[41] Spirit,

10 to another the working of miracles, to another prophecy, to another discerning of spirits, to another *different* kinds of tongues, to another the interpretation of tongues.

11 But one and the same Spirit works all these things, distributing to each one individually as He wills.

Unity and Diversity in One Body

12 For as the body is one and has many members, but all the members of that one body, being many, are one body, so also *is* Christ.

13 For by one Spirit we were all baptized into one body—whether Jews or Greeks, whether slaves or free—and have all been made to drink into[42] one Spirit.

14 For in fact the body is not one member but many.

15 If the foot should say, "Because I am not a hand, I am not of the body," is it therefore not of the body?

16 And if the ear should say, "Because I am not an eye, I am not of the body," is it therefore not of the body?

17 If the whole body *were* an eye, where *would be* the hearing? If the whole *were* hearing, where *would be* the smelling?

18 But now God has set the members, each one of them, in the body just as He pleased.

19 And if they *were* all one member, where *would* the body *be?*

20 But now indeed *there are* many members, yet one body.

21 And the eye cannot say to the hand, "I have no need of you"; nor again the head to the feet, "I have no need of you."

22 No, much rather, those members of the body which seem to be weaker are necessary.

23 And those *members* of the body which we think to be less honorable, on these we bestow greater honor; and our unpresentable *parts* have greater modesty,

24 but our presentable *parts* have no need. But God composed the body, having given greater honor to that *part* which lacks it,

25 that there should be no schism in the body, but *that* the members should have the same care for one another.

26 And if one member suffers, all the members suffer with *it;* or if one member is honored, all the members rejoice with *it.*

27 Now you are the body of Christ, and members individually.

28 And God has appointed these in the church: first apostles, second prophets, third teachers, after that miracles, then gifts of healings, helps, administrations, varieties of tongues.

29 *Are* all apostles? *Are* all prophets? *Are* all teachers? *Are* all workers of miracles?

30 Do all have gifts of healings? Do all speak with tongues? Do all interpret?

31 But earnestly desire the best[43] gifts. And yet I show you a more excellent way.

The Greatest Gift

13 Though I speak with the tongues of men and of angels, but have not love, I have become *as* sounding brass or a clanging cymbal.

2 And though I have *the gift of* prophecy, and understand all mysteries and all knowledge, and though I have all faith, so that I could remove mountains, but have not love, I am nothing.

3 And though I bestow all my goods to feed *the poor*, and though I give my body

---

40 NU-Text and M-Text add *when.*   41 NU-Text reads *one.*   42 NU-Text omits *into.*
43 NU-Text reads *greater.*

to be burned,[44] but have not love, it profits me nothing.

4 Love suffers long *and* is kind; love does not envy; love does not parade itself, is not puffed up;

5 does not behave rudely, does not seek its own, is not provoked, thinks no evil;

6 does not rejoice in iniquity, but rejoices in the truth;

7 bears all things, believes all things, hopes all things, endures all things.

8 Love never fails. But whether *there are* prophecies, they will fail; whether *there are* tongues, they will cease; whether *there is* knowledge, it will vanish away.

9 For we know in part and we prophesy in part.

10 But when that which is perfect has come, then that which is in part will be done away.

11 When I was a child, I spoke as a child, I understood as a child, I thought as a child; but when I became a man, I put away childish things.

12 For now we see in a mirror, dimly, but then face to face. Now I know in part, but then I shall know just as I also am known.

13 And now abide faith, hope, love, these three; but the greatest of these *is* love.

Prophecy and Tongues

14 Pursue love, and desire spiritual *gifts*, but especially that you may prophesy.

2 For he who speaks in a tongue does not speak to men but to God, for no one understands *him*; however, in the spirit he speaks mysteries.

3 But he who prophesies speaks edification and exhortation and comfort to men.

4 He who speaks in a tongue edifies himself, but he who prophesies edifies the church.

5 I wish you all spoke with tongues, but even more that you prophesied; for[45] he who prophesies *is* greater than he who speaks with tongues, unless indeed he interprets, that the church may receive edification.

Tongues Must Be Interpreted

6 But now, brethren, if I come to you speaking with tongues, what shall I profit you unless I speak to you either by revelation, by knowledge, by prophesying, or by teaching?

7 Even things without life, whether flute or harp, when they make a sound, unless they make a distinction in the sounds, how will it be known what is piped or played?

8 For if the trumpet makes an uncertain sound, who will prepare himself for battle?

9 So likewise you, unless you utter by the tongue words easy to understand, how will it be known what is spoken? For you will be speaking into the air.

10 There are, it may be, so many kinds of languages in the world, and none of them *is* without significance.

11 Therefore, if I do not know the meaning of the language, I shall be a foreigner to him who speaks, and he who speaks *will be* a foreigner to me.

12 Even so you, since you are zealous for spiritual *gifts, let it be* for the edification of the church *that* you seek to excel.

13 Therefore let him who speaks in a tongue pray that he may interpret.

14 For if I pray in a tongue, my spirit prays, but my understanding is unfruitful.

15 What is *the result* then? I will pray with the spirit, and I will also pray with the understanding. I will sing with the spirit, and I will also sing with the understanding.

16 Otherwise, if you bless with the spirit, how will he who occupies the place of the uninformed say "Amen" at your giving of thanks, since he does not understand what you say?

17 For you indeed give thanks well, but the other is not edified.

18 I thank my God I speak with tongues more than you all;

19 yet in the church I would rather speak five words with my understanding, that I may teach others also, than ten thousand words in a tongue.

Tongues a Sign to Unbelievers

20 Brethren, do not be children in understanding; however, in malice be babes, but in understanding be mature.

21 In the law it is written:

> "With men of other tongues
> and other lips

44 NU-Text reads *so I may boast.*   45 NU-Text reads *and.*

I will speak to this people;
And yet, for all that,
    they will not hear Me,"[46]

says the Lord.
22 Therefore tongues are for a sign, not to those who believe but to unbelievers; but prophesying is not for unbelievers but for those who believe.
23 Therefore if the whole church comes together in one place, and all speak with tongues, and there come in *those who are* uninformed or unbelievers, will they not say that you are out of your mind?
24 But if all prophesy, and an unbeliever or an uninformed person comes in, he is convinced by all, he is judged by all.
25 And thus[47] the secrets of his heart are revealed; and so, falling down on *his* face, he will worship God and report that God is truly among you.

Order in Church Meetings

26 How is it then, brethren? Whenever you come together, each of you has a psalm, has a teaching, has a tongue, has a revelation, has an interpretation. Let all things be done for edification.
27 If anyone speaks in a tongue, *let there be* two or at the most three, *each* in turn, and let one interpret.
28 But if there is no interpreter, let him keep silent in church, and let him speak to himself and to God.
29 Let two or three prophets speak, and let the others judge.
30 But if *anything* is revealed to another who sits by, let the first keep silent.
31 For you can all prophesy one by one, that all may learn and all may be encouraged.
32 And the spirits of the prophets are subject to the prophets.
33 For God is not *the author* of confusion but of peace, as in all the churches of the saints.
34 Let your[48] women keep silent in the churches, for they are not permitted to speak; but *they are* to be submissive, as the law also says.
35 And if they want to learn something, let them ask their own husbands at home; for it is shameful for women to speak in church.
36 Or did the word of God come *origi-*

nally from you? Or *was it* you only that it reached?
37 If anyone thinks himself to be a prophet or spiritual, let him acknowledge that the things which I write to you are the commandments of the Lord.
38 But if anyone is ignorant, let him be ignorant.[49]
39 Therefore, brethren, desire earnestly to prophesy, and do not forbid to speak with tongues.
40 Let all things be done decently and in order.

The Risen Christ, Faith's Reality

15 Moreover, brethren, I declare to you the gospel which I preached to you, which also you received and in which you stand,
2 by which also you are saved, if you hold fast that word which I preached to you—unless you believed in vain.
3 For I delivered to you first of all that which I also received: that Christ died for our sins according to the Scriptures,
4 and that He was buried, and that He rose again the third day according to the Scriptures,
5 and that He was seen by Cephas, then by the twelve.
6 After that He was seen by over five hundred brethren at once, of whom the greater part remain to the present, but some have fallen asleep.
7 After that He was seen by James, then by all the apostles.
8 Then last of all He was seen by me also, as by one born out of due time.
9 For I am the least of the apostles, who am not worthy to be called an apostle, because I persecuted the church of God.
10 But by the grace of God I am what I am, and His grace toward me was not in vain; but I labored more abundantly than they all, yet not I, but the grace of God *which was* with me.
11 Therefore, whether *it was* I or they, so we preach and so you believed.

The Risen Christ, Our Hope

12 Now if Christ is preached that He has been raised from the dead, how do some among you say that there is no resurrection of the dead?
13 But if there is no resurrection of the dead, then Christ is not risen.

---

46 Isaiah 28:11, 12   47 NU-Text omits *And thus.*   48 NU-Text omits *your.*
49 NU-Text reads *If anyone does not recognize this, he is not recognized.*

14 And if Christ is not risen, then our preaching *is* vain and your faith *is* also vain.

15 Yes, and we are found false witnesses of God, because we have testified of God that He raised up Christ, whom He did not raise up—if in fact the dead do not rise.

16 For if *the* dead do not rise, then Christ is not risen.

17 And if Christ is not risen, your faith *is* futile; you are still in your sins!

18 Then also those who have fallen asleep in Christ have perished.

19 If in this life only we have hope in Christ, we are of all men the most pitiable.

The Last Enemy Destroyed

20 But now Christ is risen from the dead, *and* has become the firstfruits of those who have fallen asleep.

21 For since by man *came* death, by Man also *came* the resurrection of the dead.

22 For as in Adam all die, even so in Christ all shall be made alive.

23 But each one in his own order: Christ the firstfruits, afterward those *who are* Christ's at His coming.

24 Then *comes* the end, when He delivers the kingdom to God the Father, when He puts an end to all rule and all authority and power.

25 For He must reign till He has put all enemies under His feet.

26 The last enemy *that* will be destroyed *is* death.

27 For "*He has put all things under His feet.*"⁵⁰ But when He says "all things are put under *Him,*" *it is* evident that He who put all things under Him is excepted.

28 Now when all things are made subject to Him, then the Son Himself will also be subject to Him who put all things under Him, that God may be all in all.

Effects of Denying the Resurrection

29 Otherwise, what will they do who are baptized for the dead, if the dead do not rise at all? Why then are they baptized for the dead?

30 And why do we stand in jeopardy every hour?

31 I affirm, by the boasting in you which I have in Christ Jesus our Lord, I die daily.

32 If, in the manner of men, I have fought with beasts at Ephesus, what advantage *is it* to me? If *the* dead do not rise, "*Let us eat and drink, for tomorrow we die.*"⁵¹

33 Do not be deceived: "Evil company corrupts good habits."

34 Awake to righteousness, and do not sin; for some do not have the knowledge of God. I speak *this* to your shame.

A Glorious Body

35 But someone will say, "How are the dead raised up? And with what body do they come?"

36 Foolish one, what you sow is not made alive unless it dies.

37 And what you sow, you do not sow that body that shall be, but mere grain—perhaps wheat or some other *grain.*

38 But God gives it a body as He pleases, and to each seed its own body.

39 All flesh *is* not the same flesh, but *there is* one *kind of* flesh⁵² of men, another flesh of beasts, another of fish, *and* another of birds.

40 *There are* also celestial bodies and terrestrial bodies; but the glory of the celestial *is* one, and the *glory* of the terrestrial *is* another.

41 *There is* one glory of the sun, another glory of the moon, and another glory of the stars; for *one* star differs from *another* star in glory.

42 So also *is* the resurrection of the dead. *The body* is sown in corruption, it is raised in incorruption.

43 It is sown in dishonor, it is raised in glory. It is sown in weakness, it is raised in power.

44 It is sown a natural body, it is raised a spiritual body. There is a natural body, and there is a spiritual body.

45 And so it is written, "*The first man Adam became a living being.*"⁵³ The last Adam *became* a life-giving spirit.

46 However, the spiritual is not first, but the natural, and afterward the spiritual.

47 The first man *was* of the earth, made of dust; the second Man *is* the Lord⁵⁴ from heaven.

48 As *was* the *man* of dust, so also *are* those *who are made* of dust; and as *is* the heavenly *Man,* so also *are* those *who are* heavenly.

49 And as we have borne the image of

---

50 Psalm 8:6   51 Isaiah 22:13   52 NU-Text and M-Text omit *of flesh.*   53 Genesis 2:7
54 NU-Text deletes *the Lord.*

the *man* of dust, we shall also bear[55] the image of the heavenly *Man.*

Our Final Victory

50 Now this I say, brethren, that flesh and blood cannot inherit the kingdom of God; nor does corruption inherit incorruption.

51 Behold, I tell you a mystery: We shall not all sleep, but we shall all be changed—

52 in a moment, in the twinkling of an eye, at the last trumpet. For the trumpet will sound, and the dead will be raised incorruptible, and we shall be changed.

53 For this corruptible must put on incorruption, and this mortal *must* put on immortality.

54 So when this corruptible has put on incorruption, and this mortal has put on immortality, then shall be brought to pass the saying that is written: *"Death is swallowed up in victory."*[56]

55 *"O Death, where is your sting?"[57]*
O Hades, where is your victory?"[58]

56 The sting of death *is* sin, and the strength of sin *is* the law.

57 But thanks *be* to God, who gives us the victory through our Lord Jesus Christ.

58 Therefore, my beloved brethren, be steadfast, immovable, always abounding in the work of the Lord, knowing that your labor is not in vain in the Lord.

Collection for the Saints

16 Now concerning the collection for the saints, as I have given orders to the churches of Galatia, so you must do also:

2 On the first *day* of the week let each one of you lay something aside, storing up as he may prosper, that there be no collections when I come.

3 And when I come, whomever you approve by *your* letters I will send to bear your gift to Jerusalem.

4 But if it is fitting that I go also, they will go with me.

Personal Plans

5 Now I will come to you when I pass through Macedonia (for I am passing through Macedonia).

6 But it may be that I will remain, or even spend the winter with you, that you

may send me on my journey, wherever I go.

7 For I do not wish to see you now on the way; but I hope to stay a while with you, if the Lord permits.

8 But I will tarry in Ephesus until Pentecost.

9 For a great and effective door has opened to me, and *there are* many adversaries.

10 Now if Timothy comes, see that he may be with you without fear; for he does the work of the Lord, as I also *do.*

11 Therefore let no one despise him. But send him on his journey in peace, that he may come to me; for I am waiting for him with the brethren.

12 Now concerning *our* brother Apollos, I strongly urged him to come to you with the brethren, but he was quite unwilling to come at this time; however, he will come when he has a convenient time.

Final Exhortations

13 Watch, stand fast in the faith, be brave, be strong.

14 Let all *that* you *do* be done with love.

15 I urge you, brethren—you know the household of Stephanas, that it is the firstfruits of Achaia, and *that* they have devoted themselves to the ministry of the saints—

16 that you also submit to such, and to everyone who works and labors with *us.*

17 I am glad about the coming of Stephanas, Fortunatus, and Achaicus, for what was lacking on your part they supplied.

18 For they refreshed my spirit and yours; therefore acknowledge such men.

Greetings and a Solemn Farewell

19 The churches of Asia greet you. Aquila and Priscilla greet you heartily in the Lord, with the church that is in their house.

20 All the brethren greet you. Greet one another with a holy kiss.

21 The salutation with my own hand—Paul.

22 If anyone does not love the Lord Jesus Christ, let him be accursed.[59] O Lord, come![60]

23 The grace of our Lord Jesus Christ *be* with you.

24 My love *be* with you all in Christ Jesus. Amen.

---

55 M-Text reads *let us also bear.*   56 Isaiah 25:8   57 Hosea 13:14
58 NU-Text reads *O death, where is your victory? O death, where is your sting?*   59 Greek *anathema*
60 Aramaic *Maranatha*

Introduction to Second Corinthians

The second letter from Paul to the Corinthians is a great example of expecting the best in other people. This Epistle is the most emotional of all Paul's letters to a church. Writing in A.D. 55, Paul corresponds with a church which he cared for greatly, but which had a history of serious problems.

Paul is joyful to learn that they have returned to a positive and productive Christian life-style. The book overflows with promises and affirmations as he continues to build up the believers. "If anyone *is* in Christ, *he is* a new creation; old things have passed away; behold, all things have become new" (2 Cor. 5:17).

The Corinthian church was exposed to persecution and cultural separation. The city of Corinth was filled with pagan, negative influences. (See Introduction to First Corinthians.) Paul encourages them to be possibility thinkers despite their circumstances. "*We are* hard pressed on every side, yet not crushed; *we are* perplexed, but not in despair; persecuted, but not forsaken; struck down, but not destroyed" (2 Cor. 4:8, 9). Paul reminds them that they are winners!

The Corinthians were to expect the best in their lives and in other people. To do so, they needed to connect with God's power—now! "Not that we are sufficient of ourselves to think of anything as *being* from ourselves, but our sufficiency *is* from God" (2 Cor. 3:5).

Faith calls us to believe in the best. If you believe the best will happen and it does not, you lose nothing! For you have the joy of anticipating something wonderful. The happiness that comes through positive anticipation pays dividends instantaneously. Each smile, every happy heartbeat, every elegant thought is an immediate reward. Paul had the skill and sensitivity to motivate, inspire, and remain devoted to the Corinthians in their time of need.

The Second Epistle of Paul the Apostle to the

Corinthians

Greeting

PAUL, an apostle of Jesus Christ by the will of God, and Timothy *our* brother,

To the church of God which is at Corinth, with all the saints who are in all Achaia:

2 Grace to you and peace from God our Father and the Lord Jesus Christ.

Comfort in Suffering

3 Blessed *be* the God and Father of our Lord Jesus Christ, the Father of mercies and God of all comfort,

4 who comforts us in all our tribulation, that we may be able to comfort those who are in any trouble, with the comfort with which we ourselves are comforted by God.

5 For as the sufferings of Christ abound in us, so our consolation also abounds through Christ.

6 Now if we are afflicted, *it is* for your consolation and salvation, which is effective for enduring the same sufferings which we also suffer. Or if we are comforted, *it is* for your consolation and salvation.

7 And our hope for you *is* steadfast, because we know that as you are partakers of the sufferings, so also *you will partake* of the consolation.

Delivered from Suffering

8 For we do not want you to be ignorant, brethren, of our trouble which came to us in Asia: that we were burdened beyond measure, above strength, so that we despaired even of life.

9 Yes, we had the sentence of death in ourselves, that we should not trust in ourselves but in God who raises the dead,

10 who delivered us from so great a death, and does[1] deliver us; in whom we trust that He will still deliver *us*,

11 you also helping together in prayer for us, that thanks may be given by many

persons on our[2] behalf for the gift *granted* to us through many.

Paul's Sincerity

12 For our boasting is this: the testimony of our conscience that we conducted ourselves in the world in simplicity and godly sincerity, not with fleshly wisdom but by the grace of God, and more abundantly toward you.

13 For we are not writing any other things to you than what you read or understand. Now I trust you will understand, even to the end

14 (as also you have understood us in part), that we are your boast as you also *are* ours, in the day of the Lord Jesus.

Sparing the Church

15 And in this confidence I intended to come to you before, that you might have a second benefit—

16 to pass by way of you to Macedonia, to come again from Macedonia to you, and be helped by you on my way to Judea.

17 Therefore, when I was planning this, did I do it lightly? Or the things I plan, do I plan according to the flesh, that with me there should be Yes, Yes, and No, No?

18 But *as* God *is* faithful, our word to you was not Yes and No.

19 For the Son of God, Jesus Christ, who was preached among you by us—by me, Silvanus, and Timothy—was not Yes and No, but in Him was Yes.

20 For all the promises of God in Him *are* Yes, and in Him Amen, to the glory of God through us.

21 Now He who establishes us with you in Christ and has anointed us *is* God,

22 who also has sealed us and given us the Spirit in our hearts as a deposit.

23 Moreover I call God as witness against my soul, that to spare you I came no more to Corinth.

24 Not that we have dominion over your

1 NU-Text reads *shall.* 2 M-Text reads *your behalf.*

Speak of God's Presence

The spoken word in biblical times served as a constant reminder of God's presence among men and women. Not one day passed when the name of God was not used as a greeting or blessing, given in hope or encouragement.

This practice has continued for thousands of years. Examples of this are heard in the everyday language of the Middle East today. Many common phrases containing the name of God and sharing His presence include:

Good morning, may God's light be upon you.
Hurry up, let's go. O God, help.
Hello, may the peace of God come upon you.
May the peace of God be with you also.
How is it going? How is God with you?
Take care, go under the protection and hand of God.
Get well soon. May God give you health and strength.

This style of language is also reflected throughout the New Testament. Many of the Epistles include greetings and benedictions similar to those heard in the Middle East today.

But may the God of all grace . . . perfect, establish, strengthen, and settle *you* (1 Pet. 5:10).
Grace to you and peace from God our Father and the Lord Jesus Christ (2 Cor. 1:2).
And *whatever* you do in word or deed, *do* all in the name of the Lord Jesus, giving thanks to God the Father through Him (Col. 3:17).

By keeping the name of God in everyday language, the biblical personality as well as modern men and women in the Middle East are constantly reminded of God's presence and power at work in their lives. It is recognition of God's involvement in even the most common events.

In today's society, it may seem awkward to speak of God's existence and presence so openly to strangers. However, we can demonstrate God's love in *action* to those with whom we come in contact.

It is not enough to simply love in word, but we must love in deed. By uplifting, encouraging, planting God's positive thoughts, meeting needs, healing hurts, and speaking of our faith, we truly make the presence of God known and loved in others' lives.

faith, but are fellow workers for your joy; for by faith you stand.

2 But I determined this within myself, that I would not come again to you in sorrow.
2 For if I make you sorrowful, then who is he who makes me glad but the one who is made sorrowful by me?

Forgive the Offender

3 And I wrote this very thing to you, lest, when I came, I should have sorrow over those from whom I ought to have joy, having confidence in you all that my joy is *the joy* of you all.
4 For out of much affliction and anguish of heart I wrote to you, with many tears, not that you should be grieved, but that you might know the love which I have so abundantly for you.
5 But if anyone has caused grief, he has not grieved me, but all of you to some extent—not to be too severe.
6 This punishment which *was inflicted* by the majority *is* sufficient for such a man,
7 so that, on the contrary, you *ought* rather to forgive and comfort *him*, lest perhaps such a one be swallowed up with too much sorrow.
8 Therefore I urge you to reaffirm *your* love to him.
9 For to this end I also wrote, that I might put you to the test, whether you are obedient in all things.
10 Now whom you forgive anything, I also *forgive*. For if indeed I have forgiven anything, I have forgiven[3] that one for your sakes in the presence of Christ,
11 lest Satan should take advantage of us; for we are not ignorant of his devices.

Triumph in Christ

12 Furthermore, when I came to Troas to *preach* Christ's gospel, and a door was opened to me by the Lord,
13 I had no rest in my spirit, because I did not find Titus my brother; but taking my leave of them, I departed for Macedonia.
14 Now thanks *be* to God who always leads us in triumph in Christ, and through us diffuses the fragrance of His knowledge in every place.
15 For we are to God the fragrance of Christ among those who are being saved and among those who are perishing.
16 To the one *we are* the aroma of death

to death, and to the other the aroma of life to life. And who *is* sufficient for these things?
17 For we are not, as so many,[4] peddling the word of God; but as of sincerity, but as from God, we speak in the sight of God in Christ.

Christ's Epistle

3 Do we begin again to commend ourselves? Or do we need, as some *others*, epistles of commendation to you or *letters* of commendation from you?
2 You are our epistle written in our hearts, known and read by all men;
3 *you are* manifestly an epistle of Christ, ministered by us, written not with ink but by the Spirit of the living God, not on tablets of stone but on tablets of flesh, *that is*, of the heart.

The Spirit, Not the Letter

4 And we have such trust through Christ toward God.
5 Not that we are sufficient of ourselves to think of anything as *being* from ourselves, but our sufficiency *is* from God,
6 who also made us sufficient as ministers of the new covenant, not of the letter but of the Spirit;[5] for the letter kills, but the Spirit gives life.

Glory of the New Covenant

7 But if the ministry of death, written *and* engraved on stones, was glorious, so that the children of Israel could not look steadily at the face of Moses because of the glory of his countenance, which *glory* was passing away,
8 how will the ministry of the Spirit not be more glorious?
9 For if the ministry of condemnation *had* glory, the ministry of righteousness exceeds much more in glory.
10 For even what was made glorious had no glory in this respect, because of the glory that excels.
11 For if what is passing away *was* glorious, what remains *is* much more glorious.
12 Therefore, since we have such hope, we use great boldness of speech—
13 unlike Moses, *who* put a veil over his face so that the children of Israel could not look steadily at the end of what was passing away.
14 But their minds were hardened. For until this day the same veil remains unlifted in the reading of the Old Testa-

---

3 NU-Text reads *what I have forgiven, if I have forgiven anything.*   4 M-Text reads *the rest.*   5 Or *spirit*

ment, because the *veil* is taken away in Christ.
15 But even to this day, when Moses is read, a veil lies on their heart.
16 Nevertheless when one turns to the Lord, the veil is taken away.
17 Now the Lord is the Spirit; and where the Spirit of the Lord *is*, there *is* liberty.
18 But we all, with unveiled face, beholding as in a mirror the glory of the Lord, are being transformed into the same image from glory to glory, just as by the Spirit of the Lord.

The Light of Christ's Gospel

4 Therefore, since we have this ministry, as we have received mercy, we do not lose heart.
2 But we have renounced the hidden things of shame, not walking in craftiness nor handling the word of God deceitfully, but by manifestation of the truth commending ourselves to every man's conscience in the sight of God.
3 But even if our gospel is veiled, it is veiled to those who are perishing,
4 whose minds the god of this age has blinded, who do not believe, lest the light of the gospel of the glory of Christ, who is the image of God, should shine on them.
5 For we do not preach ourselves, but Christ Jesus the Lord, and ourselves your servants for Jesus' sake.
6 For it is the God who commanded light to shine out of darkness who has shone in our hearts to *give* the light of the knowledge of the glory of God in the face of Jesus Christ.

Cast Down but Unconquered

7 But we have this treasure in earthen vessels, that the excellence of the power may be of God and not of us.
8 *We are* hard pressed on every side, yet not crushed; *we are* perplexed, but not in despair;
9 persecuted, but not forsaken; struck down, but not destroyed—
10 always carrying about in the body the dying of the Lord Jesus, that the life of Jesus also may be manifested in our body.
11 For we who live are always delivered to death for Jesus' sake, that the life of Jesus also may be manifested in our mortal flesh.
12 So then death is working in us, but life in you.

13 But since we have the same spirit of faith, according to what is written, *"I believed and therefore I spoke,"*[6] we also believe and therefore speak,
14 knowing that He who raised up the Lord Jesus will also raise us up with Jesus, and will present *us* with you.
15 For all things *are* for your sakes, that grace, having spread through the many, may cause thanksgiving to abound to the glory of God.

Seeing the Invisible

16 Therefore we do not lose heart. Even though our outward man is perishing, yet the inward *man* is being renewed day by day.
17 For our light affliction, which is but for a moment, is working for us a far more exceeding *and* eternal weight of glory,
18 while we do not look at the things which are seen, but at the things which are not seen. For the things which are seen *are* temporary, but the things which are not seen *are* eternal.

Assurance of the Resurrection

5 For we know that if our earthly house, *this* tent, is destroyed, we have a building from God, a house not made with hands, eternal in the heavens.
2 For in this we groan, earnestly desiring to be clothed with our habitation which is from heaven,
3 if indeed, having been clothed, we shall not be found naked.
4 For we who are in *this* tent groan, being burdened, not because we want to be unclothed, but further clothed, that mortality may be swallowed up by life.
5 Now He who has prepared us for this very thing *is* God, who also has given us the Spirit as a guarantee.
6 Therefore *we are* always confident, knowing that while we are at home in the body we are absent from the Lord.
7 For we walk by faith, not by sight.
8 We are confident, yes, well pleased rather to be absent from the body and to be present with the Lord.

The Judgment Seat of Christ

9 Therefore we make it our aim, whether present or absent, to be well pleasing to Him.

6 Psalm 116:10

10 For we must all appear before the judgment seat of Christ, that each one may receive the things *done* in the body, according to what he has done, whether good or bad.

11 Knowing, therefore, the terror of the Lord, we persuade men; but we are well-known to God, and I also trust are well-known in your consciences.

Be Reconciled to God

12 For we do not commend ourselves again to you, but give you opportunity to glory on our behalf, that you may have *something to answer* those who glory in appearance and not in heart.

13 For if we are beside ourselves, *it is* for God; or if we are of sound mind, *it is* for you.

14 For the love of Christ constrains us, because we judge thus: that if One died for all, then all died;

15 and He died for all, that those who live should live no longer for themselves, but for Him who died for them and rose again.

16 Therefore, from now on, we regard no one according to the flesh. Even though we have known Christ according to the flesh, yet now we know *Him thus* no longer.

17 Therefore, if anyone *is* in Christ, *he is* a new creation; old things have passed away; behold, all things have become new.

18 Now all things *are* of God, who has reconciled us to Himself through Jesus Christ, and has given us the ministry of reconciliation,

19 that is, that God was in Christ reconciling the world to Himself, not imputing their trespasses to them, and has committed to us the word of reconciliation.

20 Therefore we are ambassadors for Christ, as though God were pleading through us: we implore *you* on Christ's behalf, be reconciled to God.

21 For He made Him who knew no sin *to be* sin for us, that we might become the righteousness of God in Him.

Marks of the Ministry

6 We then, *as* workers together *with* Him also plead with *you* not to receive the grace of God in vain.

2 For He says:

"*In an acceptable time I have heard you,
And in the day of salvation I have helped you.*"[7]

Behold, now *is* the accepted time; behold, now *is* the day of salvation.

3 We give no offense in anything, that our ministry may not be blamed.

4 But in all *things* we commend ourselves as ministers of God: in much patience, in tribulations, in needs, in distresses,

5 in stripes, in imprisonments, in tumults, in labors, in sleeplessness, in fastings;

6 by purity, by knowledge, by long-suffering, by kindness, by the Holy Spirit, by sincere love,

7 by the word of truth, by the power of God, by the armor of righteousness on the right hand and on the left,

8 by honor and dishonor, by evil report and good report; as deceivers, and *yet* true;

9 as unknown, and *yet* well-known; as dying, and behold we live; as chastened, and *yet* not killed;

10 as sorrowful, yet always rejoicing; as poor, yet making many rich; as having nothing, and *yet* possessing all things.

Be Holy

11 O Corinthians! We have spoken openly to you, our heart is wide open.

12 You are not restricted by us, but you are restricted by your *own* affections.

13 Now in return for the same (I speak as to children), you also be open.

14 Do not be unequally yoked together with unbelievers. For what fellowship has righteousness with lawlessness? And what communion has light with darkness?

15 And what accord has Christ with Belial? Or what part has a believer with an unbeliever?

16 And what agreement has the temple of God with idols? For you[8] are the temple of the living God. As God has said:

"*I will dwell in them
And walk among them.
I will be their God,
And they shall be My people.*"[9]

17 Therefore

---

7 Isaiah 49:8   8 NU-Text reads *we*.   9 Leviticus 26:12; Jeremiah 32:38; Ezekiel 37:27

*"Come out from among them
And be separate, says the Lord.
Do not touch what is unclean,
And I will receive you."*[10]
18 *"I will be a Father to you,
And you shall be My sons
and daughters,
Says the LORD Almighty."*[11]

7 Therefore, having these promises, beloved, let us cleanse ourselves from all filthiness of the flesh and spirit, perfecting holiness in the fear of God.

The Corinthians' Repentance

2 Open *your hearts* to us. We have wronged no one, we have corrupted no one, we have defrauded no one.
3 I do not say *this* to condemn; for I have said before that you are in our hearts, to die together and to live together.
4 Great *is* my boldness of speech toward you, great *is* my boasting on your behalf. I am filled with comfort. I am exceedingly joyful in all our tribulation.
5 For indeed, when we came to Macedonia, our flesh had no rest, but we were troubled on every side. Outside *were* conflicts, inside *were* fears.
6 Nevertheless God, who comforts the downcast, comforted us by the coming of Titus,
7 and not only by his coming, but also by the consolation with which he was comforted in you, when he told us of your earnest desire, your mourning, your zeal for me, so that I rejoiced even more.
8 For even if I made you sorry with my letter, I do not regret it; though I did regret it. For I perceive that the same epistle made you sorry, though only for a while.
9 Now I rejoice, not that you were made sorry, but that your sorrow led to repentance. For you were made sorry in a godly manner, that you might suffer loss from us in nothing.
10 For godly sorrow produces repentance to salvation, not to be regretted; but the sorrow of the world produces death.
11 For observe this very thing, that you sorrowed in a godly manner: What diligence it produced in you, *what* clearing *of yourselves*, *what* indignation, *what* fear, *what* vehement desire, *what* zeal, *what*

vindication! In all *things* you proved yourselves to be clear in this matter.
12 Therefore, although I wrote to you, *I did* not *do it* for the sake of him who had done the wrong, nor for the sake of him who suffered wrong, but that our care for you in the sight of God might appear to you.

The Joy of Titus

13 Therefore we have been comforted in your comfort. And we rejoiced exceedingly more for the joy of Titus, because his spirit has been refreshed by you all.
14 For if in anything I have boasted to him about you, I am not ashamed. But as we spoke all things to you in truth, even so our boasting to Titus was found true.
15 And his affections are greater for you as he remembers the obedience of you all, how with fear and trembling you received him.
16 Therefore I rejoice that I have confidence in you in everything.

Excel in Giving

8 Moreover, brethren, we make known to you the grace of God bestowed on the churches of Macedonia:
2 that in a great trial of affliction the abundance of their joy and their deep poverty abounded in the riches of their liberality.
3 For I bear witness that according to *their* ability, yes, and beyond *their* ability, *they were* freely willing,
4 imploring us with much urgency that we would receive[12] the gift and the fellowship of the ministering to the saints.
5 And *this they did*, not as we had hoped, but first gave themselves to the Lord, and *then* to us by the will of God.
6 So we urged Titus, that as he had begun, so he would also complete this grace in you as well.
7 But as you abound in everything—in faith, in speech, in knowledge, in all diligence, and in your love for us—*see* that you abound in this grace also.

Christ Our Pattern

8 I speak not by commandment, but I am testing the sincerity of your love by the diligence of others.
9 For you know the grace of our Lord Jesus Christ, that though He was rich, yet

---

10 Isaiah 52:11; Ezekiel 20:34, 41   11 2 Samuel 7:14
12 NU-Text and M-Text omit *that we would receive,* thus changing text to *urgency for the favor and fellowship . . . .*

for your sakes He became poor, that you through His poverty might become rich.
10 And in this I give *my* advice: It is to your advantage not only to be doing what you began and were desiring to do a year ago;
11 but now you also must complete the doing *of it*; that as *there was* a readiness to desire *it*, so *there* also *may be* a completion out of what *you* have.
12 For if there is first a willing mind, *it is* accepted according to what one has, *and* not according to what he does not have.
13 For *I do* not *mean* that others should be eased and you burdened;
14 but by an equality, *that* now at this time your abundance may *supply* their lack, that their abundance also may *supply* your lack—that there may be equality.
15 As it is written, *"He who gathered much had nothing left over, and he who gathered little had no lack."*[13]

Collection for the Judean Saints

16 But thanks *be* to God who puts[14] the same earnest care for you into the heart of Titus.
17 For he not only accepted the exhortation, but being more diligent, he went to you of his own accord.
18 And we have sent with him the brother whose praise *is* in the gospel throughout all the churches,
19 and not only *that*, but who was also chosen by the churches to travel with us with this gift, which is administered by us to the glory of the Lord Himself and *to show* your ready mind,
20 avoiding this: that anyone should blame us in this lavish gift which is administered by us—
21 providing honorable things, not only in the sight of the Lord, but also in the sight of men.
22 And we have sent with them our brother whom we have often proved diligent in many things, but now much more diligent, because of the great confidence which *we have* in you.
23 If *anyone inquires* about Titus, *he is* my partner and fellow worker concerning you. Or if our brethren *are inquired about, they are* messengers of the churches, the glory of Christ.
24 Therefore show to them, and[15] before

the churches, the proof of your love and of our boasting on your behalf.

Administering the Gift

9 Now concerning the ministering to the saints, it is superfluous for me to write to you;
2 for I know your willingness, about which I boast of you to the Macedonians, that Achaia was ready a year ago; and your zeal has stirred up the majority.
3 Yet I have sent the brethren, lest our boasting of you should be in vain in this respect, that, as I said, you may be ready;
4 lest if *some* Macedonians come with me and find you unprepared, we (not to mention you!) should be ashamed of this confident boasting.[16]
5 Therefore I thought it necessary to exhort the brethren to go to you ahead of time, and prepare your bountiful gift beforehand, which *you had* previously promised, that it may be ready as *a matter of* generosity and not as a grudging obligation.

The Cheerful Giver

6 But this *I say*: He who sows sparingly will also reap sparingly, and he who sows bountifully will also reap bountifully.
7 *So let* each one *give* as he purposes in his heart, not grudgingly or of necessity; for God loves a cheerful giver.
8 And God *is* able to make all grace abound toward you, that you, always having all sufficiency in all *things*, have an abundance for every good work.
9 As it is written:

*"He has dispersed abroad,
He has given to the poor;
His righteousness remains forever."*[17]

10 Now may[18] He who supplies seed to the sower, and bread for food, supply and multiply the seed you have *sown* and increase the fruits of your righteousness,
11 while *you are* enriched in everything for all liberality, which causes thanksgiving through us to God.
12 For the administration of this service not only supplies the needs of the saints, but also is abounding through many thanksgivings to God,
13 while, through the proof of this ministry, they glorify God for the obedience of your confession to the gospel of Christ,

---

13 Exodus 16:18   14 NU-Text reads *has put.*   15 NU-Text and M-Text omit *and.*
16 NU-Text reads *this confidence.*   17 Psalm 112:9   18 NU-Text reads *Now He who supplies . . . will supply . . . .*

and for *your* liberal sharing with them and all *men*,

14 and by their prayer for you, who long for you because of the exceeding grace of God in you.

15 Thanks *be* to God for His indescribable gift!

The Spiritual War

10 Now I, Paul, myself am pleading with you by the meekness and gentleness of Christ—who in presence *am* lowly among you, but being absent am bold toward you.

2 But I beg *you* that when I am present I may not be bold with that confidence by which I intend to be bold against some, who think of us as if we walked according to the flesh.

3 For though we walk in the flesh, we do not war according to the flesh.

4 For the weapons of our warfare *are* not carnal but mighty in God for pulling down strongholds,

5 casting down arguments and every high thing that exalts itself against the knowledge of God, bringing every thought into captivity to the obedience of Christ,

6 and being ready to punish all disobedience when your obedience is fulfilled.

Reality of Paul's Authority

7 Do you look at things according to the outward appearance? If anyone is convinced in himself that he is Christ's, let him again consider this in himself, that just as he *is* Christ's, even so we *are* Christ's.[19]

8 For even if I should boast somewhat more about our authority, which the Lord gave us[20] for edification and not for your destruction, I shall not be ashamed—

9 lest I seem to terrify you by letters.

10 "For *his* letters," they say, "*are* weighty and powerful, but *his* bodily presence *is* weak, and *his* speech contemptible."

11 Let such a person consider this, that what we are in word by letters when we are absent, such *we will* also *be* in deed when we are present.

Limits of Paul's Authority

12 For we dare not class ourselves or compare ourselves with those who commend themselves. But they, measuring themselves by themselves, and comparing themselves among themselves, are not wise.

13 We, however, will not boast beyond measure, but within the limits of the sphere which God appointed us—a sphere which especially includes you.

14 For we are not extending ourselves beyond *our sphere* (thus not reaching you), for it was to you that we came with the gospel of Christ;

15 not boasting of things beyond measure, *that is,* in other men's labors, but having hope, *that* as your faith is increased, we shall be greatly enlarged by you in our sphere,

16 to preach the gospel in the *regions* beyond you, *and* not to boast in another man's sphere of accomplishment.

17 But *"He who glories, let him glory in the LORD."*[21]

18 For not he who commends himself is approved, but whom the Lord commends.

Concern for Their Faithfulness

11 Oh, that you would bear with me in a little folly—and indeed you do bear with me.

2 For I am jealous for you with godly jealousy. For I have betrothed you to one husband, that I may present *you as* a chaste virgin to Christ.

3 But I fear, lest somehow, as the serpent deceived Eve by his craftiness, so your minds may be corrupted from the simplicity[22] that is in Christ.

4 For if he who comes preaches another Jesus whom we have not preached, or *if* you receive a different spirit which you have not received, or a different gospel which you have not accepted, you may well put up with it.

Paul and False Apostles

5 For I consider that I am not at all inferior to the most eminent apostles.

6 Even though *I am* untrained in speech, yet *I am* not in knowledge. But we have been thoroughly made manifest[23] among you in all things.

7 Did I commit sin in abasing myself that you might be exalted, because I preached the gospel of God to you free of charge?

---

19 NU-Text reads *even as we are.*   20 NU-Text omits *us.*
22 NU-Text adds *and purity.*   23 NU-Text omits *been.*   21 Jeremiah 9:24

8 I robbed other churches, taking wages *from them* to minister to you.

9 And when I was present with you, and in need, I was a burden to no one, for what was lacking to me the brethren who came from Macedonia supplied. And in everything I kept myself from being burdensome to you, and so I will keep *myself.*

10 As the truth of Christ is in me, no one shall stop me from this boasting in the regions of Achaia.

11 Why? Because I do not love you? God knows!

12 But what I do, I will also continue to do, that I may cut off the opportunity from those who desire an opportunity to be regarded just as we are in the things of which they boast.

13 For such *are* false apostles, deceitful workers, transforming themselves into apostles of Christ.

14 And no wonder! For Satan himself transforms himself into an angel of light.

15 Therefore *it is* no great thing if his ministers also transform themselves into ministers of righteousness, whose end will be according to their works.

Reluctant Boasting

16 I say again, let no one think me a fool. If otherwise, at least receive me as a fool, that I also may boast a little.

17 What I speak, I speak not according to the Lord, but as it were, foolishly, in this confidence of boasting.

18 Seeing that many boast according to the flesh, I also will boast.

19 For you put up with fools gladly, since you *yourselves* are wise!

20 For you put up with it if one brings you into bondage, if one devours *you,* if one takes *from you,* if one exalts himself, if one strikes you on the face.

21 To *our* shame, I say that we were too weak for that! But in whatever anyone is bold—I speak foolishly—I am bold also.

Suffering for Christ

22 Are they Hebrews? So *am* I. Are they Israelites? So *am* I. Are they the seed of Abraham? So *am* I.

23 Are they ministers of Christ?—I speak as a fool—I *am* more: in labors more abundant, in stripes above measure, in prisons more frequently, in deaths often.

24 From the Jews five times I received forty *stripes* minus one.

25 Three times I was beaten with rods; once I was stoned; three times I was shipwrecked; a night and a day I have been in the deep;

26 *in* journeys often, *in* perils of waters, *in* perils of robbers, *in* perils of *my own* countrymen, *in* perils of the Gentiles, *in* perils in the city, *in* perils in the wilderness, *in* perils in the sea, *in* perils among false brethren;

27 in weariness and toil, in sleeplessness often, in hunger and thirst, in fastings often, in cold and nakedness—

28 besides the other things, what comes upon me daily: my deep concern for all the churches.

29 Who is weak, and I am not weak? Who is made to stumble, and I do not burn with indignation?

30 If I must boast, I will boast in the things which concern my infirmity.

31 The God and Father of our Lord Jesus Christ, who is blessed forever, knows that I am not lying.

32 In Damascus the governor, under Aretas the king, was guarding the city of the Damascenes with a garrison, desiring to apprehend me;

33 but I was let down in a basket through a window in the wall, and escaped from his hands.

The Vision of Paradise

12 It is doubtless[24] not profitable for me to boast. I will come to visions and revelations of the Lord:

2 I know a man in Christ who fourteen years ago—whether in the body I do not know, or whether out of the body I do not know, God knows—such a one was caught up to the third heaven.

3 And I know such a man—whether in the body or out of the body I do not know, God knows—

4 how he was caught up into Paradise and heard inexpressible words, which it is not lawful for a man to utter.

5 Of such a one I will boast; yet of myself I will not boast, except in my infirmities.

6 For though I might desire to boast, I will not be a fool; for I will speak the truth. But I forbear, lest anyone should think of me above what he sees me *to be* or hears from me.

24 NU-Text reads *necessary, though not profitable to boast.*

The Thorn in the Flesh

7 And lest I should be exalted above measure by the abundance of the revelations, a thorn in the flesh was given to me, a messenger of Satan to buffet me, lest I be exalted above measure. 8 Concerning this thing I pleaded with the Lord three times that it might depart from me. 9 And He said to me, "My grace is sufficient for you, for My strength is made perfect in weakness." Therefore most gladly I will rather boast in my infirmities, that the power of Christ may rest upon me. 10 Therefore I take pleasure in infirmities, in reproaches, in needs, in persecutions, in distresses, for Christ's sake. For when I am weak, then I am strong.

Signs of an Apostle

11 I have become a fool in boasting;[25] you have compelled me. For I ought to have been commended by you; for in nothing was I behind the most eminent apostles, though I am nothing. 12 Truly the signs of an apostle were accomplished among you with all perseverance, in signs and wonders and mighty deeds. 13 For what is it in which you were inferior to other churches, except that I myself was not burdensome to you? Forgive me this wrong!

Love for the Church

14 Now for the third time I am ready to come to you. And I will not be burdensome to you; for I do not seek yours, but you. For the children ought not to lay up for the parents, but the parents for the children. 15 And I will very gladly spend and be spent for your souls; though the more abundantly I love you, the less I am loved. 16 But be that as it may, I did not burden you. Nevertheless, being crafty, I caught you with guile! 17 Did I take advantage of you by any of those whom I sent to you? 18 I urged Titus, and sent our brother with him. Did Titus take advantage of you? Did we not walk in the same spirit? Did we not walk in the same steps? 19 Again, do you think[26] that we excuse

ourselves to you? We speak before God in Christ. But we do all things, beloved, for your edification. 20 For I fear lest, when I come, I shall not find you such as I wish, and that I shall be found by you such as you do not wish; lest there be contentions, jealousies, outbursts of wrath, selfish ambitions, backbitings, whisperings, conceits, tumults; 21 and lest, when I come again, my God will humble me among you, and I shall mourn for many who have sinned before and have not repented of the uncleanness, fornication, and licentiousness which they have practiced.

Coming with Authority

13 This will be the third time I am coming to you. "By the mouth of two or three witnesses every word shall be established."[27] 2 I have told you before, and foretell as if I were present the second time, and now being absent I write[28] to those who have sinned before, and to all the rest, that if I come again I will not spare— 3 since you seek a proof of Christ speaking in me, who is not weak toward you, but mighty in you. 4 For though He was crucified in weakness, yet He lives by the power of God. For we also are weak in Him, but we shall live with Him by the power of God toward you. 5 Examine yourselves as to whether you are in the faith. Prove yourselves. Do you not know yourselves, that Jesus Christ is in you?—unless indeed you are disqualified. 6 But I trust that you will know that we are not disqualified.

Paul Prefers Gentleness

7 Now I[29] pray to God that you do no evil, not that we should appear approved, but that you should do what is honorable, though we may seem disqualified. 8 For we can do nothing against the truth, but for the truth. 9 For we are glad when we are weak and you are strong. And this also we pray, that you may be made complete. 10 Therefore I write these things being absent, lest being present I should use

25 NU-Text omits in boasting.   26 NU-Text reads You have been thinking for a long time. . . .
27 Deuteronomy 19:15   28 NU-Text omits I write.   29 NU-Text reads we.

sharpness, according to the authority which the Lord has given me for edification and not for destruction.

Greetings and Benediction

11 Finally, brethren, farewell. Become complete. Be of good comfort, be of one mind, live in peace; and the God of love and peace will be with you.

12 Greet one another with a holy kiss.

13 All the saints greet you.

14 The grace of the Lord Jesus Christ, and the love of God, and the communion of the Holy Spirit *be* with you all. Amen.

Introduction to Galatians

The apostle Paul wrote this letter to the Christians in the region of Galatia sometime between A.D. 49 and 55, from either Antioch in Syria or Ephesus.

What we are is God's gift to us and what we become is our gift to God!

Paul writes to remind all Christians that our relationship with God is a gift of grace, not earned by the works of the law. As Christians, we are freed from rules and regulations such as those dictated by Jewish legalism. Our perfection before God is not earned, but is freely given, when we place our faith in Jesus Christ. In Him, we can find our self-worth because of His death on the cross. Since God has made us alive in the Spirit, our lives should reflect the love and positive attitudes that come from knowing Jesus Christ in a very real and personal way.

Paul encourages Christians to continue doing good to one another, reminding us that we are heirs to an inheritance given freely to us by God through Jesus Christ. That is an inheritance to become sons and daughters of God. As God's children, we have the right to address God in the most intimate terms, as *Abba* or "Daddy."

Freed from the law, we can now fulfill the law in one action—love God and love others.

For you, brethren, have been called to liberty; only do not *use* liberty as an opportunity for the flesh, but through love serve one another. And let us not grow weary while doing good, for in due season we shall reap if we do not lose heart.

(Gal. 5:13; 6:9)

The cross of Christ was the premier demonstration of the sacrificial love God has for us. We can reenact this when we live out the greeting, "God loves you and so do I!"

The Epistle of Paul the Apostle to the
Galatians

Greeting

PAUL, an apostle (not from men nor through man, but through Jesus Christ and God the Father who raised Him from the dead),
2 and all the brethren who are with me,

To the churches of Galatia:

3 Grace to you and peace from God the Father and our Lord Jesus Christ,
4 who gave Himself for our sins, that He might deliver us from this present evil age, according to the will of our God and Father,
5 to whom *be* glory forever and ever. Amen.

Only One Gospel

6 I marvel that you are turning away so soon from Him who called you in the grace of Christ, to a different gospel,
7 which is not another; but there are some who trouble you and want to pervert the gospel of Christ.
8 But even if we, or an angel from heaven, preach any other gospel to you than what we have preached to you, let him be accursed.
9 As we have said before, so now I say again, if anyone preaches any other gospel to you than what you have received, let him be accursed.
10 For do I now persuade men, or God? Or do I seek to please men? For if I still pleased men, I would not be a servant of Christ.

Call to Apostleship

11 But I make known to you, brethren, that the gospel which was preached by me is not according to man.
12 For I neither received it from man, nor was I taught *it*, but *it came* through the revelation of Jesus Christ.
13 For you have heard of my former conduct in Judaism, how I persecuted the church of God beyond measure and *tried to* destroy it.

14 And I advanced in Judaism beyond many of my contemporaries in my own nation, being more exceedingly zealous for the traditions of my fathers.
15 But when it pleased God, who separated me from my mother's womb and called *me* through His grace,
16 to reveal His Son in me, that I might preach Him among the Gentiles, I did not immediately confer with flesh and blood,
17 nor did I go up to Jerusalem to those *who were* apostles before me; but I went to Arabia, and returned again to Damascus.

Contacts at Jerusalem

18 Then after three years I went up to Jerusalem to see Peter,[1] and remained with him fifteen days.
19 But I saw none of the other apostles except James, the Lord's brother.
20 (Now *concerning* the things which I write to you, indeed, before God, I do not lie.)
21 Afterward I went into the regions of Syria and Cilicia;
22 and I was unknown by face to the churches of Judea which *were* in Christ.
23 But they were hearing only, "He who formerly persecuted us now preaches the faith which he once *tried to* destroy."
24 And they glorified God in me.

Defending the Gospel

2 Then after fourteen years I went up again to Jerusalem with Barnabas, and also took Titus with *me*.
2 And I went up by revelation, and communicated to them that gospel which I preach among the Gentiles, but privately to those who were of reputation, lest by any means I might run, or had run, in vain.
3 Yet not even Titus who *was* with me, being a Greek, was compelled to be circumcised.
4 But *this occurred* because of false brethren secretly brought in (who came in

---

1 NU-Text reads *Cephas.*

by stealth to spy out our liberty which we have in Christ Jesus, that they might bring us into bondage),
5 to whom we did not yield submission even for an hour, that the truth of the gospel might continue with you.
6 But from those who seemed to be something—whatever they were, it makes no difference to me; God shows personal favoritism to no man—for those who seemed *to be something* added nothing to me.
7 But on the contrary, when they saw that the gospel for the uncircumcised had been committed to me, as *the gospel* for the circumcised *was* to Peter
8 (for He who worked effectively in Peter for the apostleship to the circumcised also worked effectively in me toward the Gentiles),
9 and when James, Cephas, and John, who seemed to be pillars, perceived the grace that had been given to me, they gave me and Barnabas the right hand of fellowship, that we *should go* to the Gentiles and they to the circumcised.
10 *They desired* only that we should remember the poor, the very thing which I also was eager to do.

No Return to the Law

11 But when Peter[2] had come to Antioch, I withstood him to his face, because he was to be blamed;
12 for before certain men came from James, he would eat with the Gentiles; but when they came, he withdrew and separated himself, fearing those who were of the circumcision.
13 And the rest of the Jews also played the hypocrite with him, so that even Barnabas was carried away with their hypocrisy.
14 But when I saw that they were not straightforward about the truth of the gospel, I said to Peter before *them* all, "If you, being a Jew, live in the manner of Gentiles and not as the Jews, why do you[3] compel Gentiles to live as Jews?[4]
15 "We *who are* Jews by nature, and not sinners of the Gentiles,
16 "knowing that a man is not justified by the works of the law but by faith in Jesus Christ, even we have believed in Christ Jesus, that we might be justified by

faith in Christ and not by the works of the law; for by the works of the law no flesh shall be justified.
17 "But if, while we seek to be justified by Christ, we ourselves also are found sinners, *is* Christ therefore a minister of sin? Certainly not!
18 "For if I build again those things which I destroyed, I make myself a transgressor.
19 "For I through the law died to the law that I might live to God.
20 "I have been crucified with Christ; it is no longer I who live, but Christ lives in me; and the *life* which I now live in the flesh I live by faith in the Son of God, who loved me and gave Himself for me.
21 "I do not set aside the grace of God; for if righteousness *comes* through the law, then Christ died in vain."

Justification by Faith

3 O foolish Galatians! Who has bewitched you that you should not obey the truth,[5] before whose eyes Jesus Christ was clearly portrayed among you[6] as crucified?
2 This only I want to learn from you: Did you receive the Spirit by the works of the law, or by the hearing of faith?
3 Are you so foolish? Having begun in the Spirit, are you now being made perfect by the flesh?
4 Have you suffered so many things in vain—if indeed *it was* in vain?
5 Therefore He who supplies the Spirit to you and works miracles among you, *does He do it* by the works of the law, or by the hearing of faith?—
6 just as Abraham *"believed God, and it was accounted to him for righteousness."*[7]
7 Therefore know that *only* those who are of faith are sons of Abraham.
8 And the Scripture, foreseeing that God would justify the nations by faith, preached the gospel to Abraham beforehand, *saying, "In you all the nations shall be blessed."*[8]
9 So then those who *are* of faith are blessed with believing Abraham.

The Law Brings a Curse

10 For as many as are of the works of the law are under the curse; for it is written,

2 NU-Text reads *Cephas*.   3 NU-Text reads *How can you.*   4 Some interpreters stop the quotation here.
5 NU-Text omits *that you should not obey the truth.*   6 NU-Text omits *among you.*   7 Genesis 15:6
8 Genesis 12:3; 18:18; 22:18; 26:4; 28:14

"Cursed is everyone who does not continue in all things which are written in the book of the law, to do them."[9]
[11] But that no one is justified by the law in the sight of God is evident, for "The just shall live by faith."[10]
[12] Yet the law is not of faith, but "The man who does them shall live by them."[11]
[13] Christ has redeemed us from the curse of the law, having become a curse for us (for it is written, "Cursed is everyone who hangs on a tree"[12]),
[14] that the blessing of Abraham might come upon the Gentiles in Christ Jesus, that we might receive the promise of the Spirit through faith.

The Changeless Promise

[15] Brethren, I speak in the manner of men: Though it is only a man's covenant, yet if it is confirmed, no one annuls or adds to it.
[16] Now to Abraham and his Seed were the promises made. He does not say, "And to seeds," as of many, but as of one, "And to your Seed,"[13] who is Christ.
[17] And this I say, that the law, which was four hundred and thirty years later, cannot annul the covenant that was confirmed before by God in Christ,[14] that it should make the promise of no effect.
[18] For if the inheritance is of the law, it is no longer of promise; but God gave it to Abraham by promise.

Purpose of the Law

[19] What purpose then does the law serve? It was added because of transgressions, till the Seed should come to whom the promise was made; and it was appointed through angels by the hand of a mediator.
[20] Now a mediator does not mediate for one only, but God is one.
[21] Is the law then against the promises of God? Certainly not! For if there had been a law given which could have given life, truly righteousness would have been by the law.
[22] But the Scripture has confined all under sin, that the promise by faith in Jesus Christ might be given to those who believe.
[23] But before faith came, we were kept under guard by the law, kept for the faith which would afterward be revealed.

[24] Therefore the law was our tutor to bring us to Christ, that we might be justified by faith.
[25] But after faith has come, we are no longer under a tutor.

Sons and Heirs

[26] For you are all sons of God through faith in Christ Jesus.
[27] For as many of you as were baptized into Christ have put on Christ.
[28] There is neither Jew nor Greek, there is neither slave nor free, there is neither male nor female; for you are all one in Christ Jesus.
[29] And if you are Christ's, then you are Abraham's seed, and heirs according to the promise.

4 Now I say that the heir, as long as he is a child, does not differ at all from a slave, though he is master of all,
[2] but is under guardians and stewards until the time appointed by the father.
[3] Even so we, when we were children, were in bondage under the elements of the world.
[4] But when the fullness of the time had come, God sent forth His Son, born[15] of a woman, born under the law,
[5] to redeem those who were under the law, that we might receive the adoption as sons.
[6] And because you are sons, God has sent forth the Spirit of His Son into your hearts, crying out, "Abba, Father!"
[7] Therefore you are no longer a slave but a son, and if a son, then an heir of[16] God through Christ.

Fears for the Church

[8] But then, indeed, when you did not know God, you served those which by nature are not gods.
[9] But now after you have known God, or rather are known by God, how is it that you turn again to the weak and beggarly elements, to which you desire again to be in bondage?
[10] You observe days and months and seasons and years.
[11] I am afraid for you, lest I have labored for you in vain.
[12] Brethren, I urge you to become as I am, for I am as you are. You have not injured me at all.

---

9 Deuteronomy 27:26   10 Habakkuk 2:4   11 Leviticus 18:5   12 Deuteronomy 21:23
13 Genesis 12:7; 13:15; 24:7   14 NU-Text omits in Christ.   15 Or made
16 NU-Text reads through God and omits through Christ.

13 You know that because of physical infirmity I preached the gospel to you at the first.
14 And my trial which was in my flesh you did not despise or reject, but you received me as an angel of God, *even* as Christ Jesus.
15 What[17] then was the blessing you enjoyed? For I bear you witness that, if possible, you would have plucked out your own eyes and given them to me.
16 Have I therefore become your enemy because I tell you the truth?
17 They zealously court you, *but* for no good; yes, they want to exclude you, that you may be zealous for them.
18 But it is good to be zealous in a good thing always, and not only when I am present with you.
19 My little children, for whom I labor in birth again until Christ is formed in you,
20 I would like to be present with you now and to change my tone; for I have doubts about you.

Two Covenants

21 Tell me, you who desire to be under the law, do you not hear the law?
22 For it is written that Abraham had two sons: the one by a bondwoman, the other by a freewoman.
23 But he *who was* of the bondwoman was born according to the flesh, and he of the freewoman through promise,
24 which things are symbolic. For these are the[18] two covenants: the one from Mount Sinai which gives birth to bondage, which is Hagar—
25 for this Hagar is Mount Sinai in Arabia, and corresponds to Jerusalem which now is, and is in bondage with her children—
26 but the Jerusalem above is free, which is the mother of us all.
27 For it is written:

"Rejoice, O barren,
   You who do not bear!
Break forth and shout,
   You who do not travail!
For the desolate has
   many more children
Than she who has a husband."[19]

28 Now we, brethren, as Isaac *was,* are children of promise.

29 But, as he who was born according to the flesh then persecuted him *who was born* according to the Spirit, even so *it is* now.
30 Nevertheless what does the Scripture say? "Cast out the bondwoman and her son, for the son of the bondwoman shall not be heir with the son of the freewoman."[20]
31 So then, brethren, we are not children of the bondwoman but of the free.

Christian Liberty

5 Stand fast therefore in the liberty by which Christ has made us free,[21] and do not be entangled again with a yoke of bondage.
2 Indeed I, Paul, say to you that if you become circumcised, Christ will profit you nothing.
3 And I testify again to every man who becomes circumcised that he is a debtor to keep the whole law.
4 You have become estranged from Christ, you who *attempt to* be justified by law; you have fallen from grace.
5 For we through the Spirit eagerly wait for the hope of righteousness by faith.
6 For in Christ Jesus neither circumcision nor uncircumcision avails anything, but faith working through love.

Love Fulfills the Law

7 You ran well. Who hindered you from obeying the truth?
8 This persuasion does not *come* from Him who calls you.
9 A little leaven leavens the whole lump.
10 I have confidence in you, in the Lord, that you will have no other mind; but he who troubles you shall bear his judgment, whoever he is.
11 And I, brethren, if I still preach circumcision, why do I still suffer persecution? Then the offense of the cross has ceased.
12 I could wish that those who trouble you would even cut themselves off!
13 For you, brethren, have been called to liberty; only do not *use* liberty as an opportunity for the flesh, but through love serve one another.
14 For all the law is fulfilled in one word, *even* in this: "You shall love your neighbor as yourself."[22]

17 NU-Text reads *Where.*   18 NU-Text and M-Text omit *the.*   19 Isaiah 54:1   20 Genesis 21:10
21 NU-Text reads *For freedom Christ has made us free; stand fast therefore.*   22 Leviticus 19:18

15 But if you bite and devour one another, beware lest you be consumed by one another!

Walking in the Spirit

16 I say then: Walk in the Spirit, and you shall not fulfill the lust of the flesh.
17 For the flesh lusts against the Spirit, and the Spirit against the flesh; and these are contrary to one another, so that you do not do the things that you wish.
18 But if you are led by the Spirit, you are not under the law.
19 Now the works of the flesh are evident, which are: adultery,23 fornication, uncleanness, licentiousness,
20 idolatry, sorcery, hatred, contentions, jealousies, outbursts of wrath, selfish ambitions, dissensions, heresies,
21 envy, murders,24 drunkenness, revelries, and the like; of which I tell you beforehand, just as I also told *you* in time past, that those who practice such things will not inherit the kingdom of God.
22 But the fruit of the Spirit is love, joy, peace, longsuffering, kindness, goodness, faithfulness,
23 gentleness, self-control. Against such there is no law.
24 And those *who are* Christ's have crucified the flesh with its passions and desires.
25 If we live in the Spirit, let us also walk in the Spirit.
26 Let us not become conceited, provoking one another, envying one another.

Bear and Share the Burdens

6 Brethren, if a man is overtaken in any trespass, you who *are* spiritual restore such a one in a spirit of gentleness, considering yourself lest you also be tempted.
2 Bear one another's burdens, and so fulfill the law of Christ.
3 For if anyone thinks himself to be something, when he is nothing, he deceives himself.
4 But let each one examine his own work, and then he will have rejoicing in himself alone, and not in another.
5 For each one shall bear his own load.

Be Generous and Do Good

6 Let him who is taught the word share in all good things with him who teaches.
7 Do not be deceived, God is not mocked; for whatever a man sows, that he will also reap.
8 For he who sows to his flesh will of the flesh reap corruption, but he who sows to the Spirit will of the Spirit reap everlasting life.
9 And let us not grow weary while doing good, for in due season we shall reap if we do not lose heart.
10 Therefore, as we have opportunity, let us do good to all, especially to those who are of the household of faith.

Glory Only in the Cross

11 See with what large letters I have written to you with my own hand!
12 As many as desire to make a good showing in the flesh, these *try to* compel you to be circumcised, only that they may not suffer persecution for the cross of Christ.
13 For not even those who are circumcised keep the law, but they desire to have you circumcised that they may glory in your flesh.
14 But God forbid that I should glory except in the cross of our Lord Jesus Christ, by whom25 the world has been crucified to me, and I to the world.
15 For in Christ Jesus neither circumcision nor uncircumcision avails anything, but a new creation.

Blessing and a Plea

16 And as many as walk according to this rule, peace and mercy *be* upon them, and upon the Israel of God.
17 From now on let no one trouble me, for I bear in my body the marks of the Lord Jesus.
18 Brethren, the grace of our Lord Jesus Christ *be* with your spirit. Amen.

23 NU-Text omits *adultery.*   24 NU-Text omits *murders.*   25 Or *by which* (the cross)

Introduction to Ephesians

The apostle Paul wrote this letter to the Christians in Ephesus around A.D. 60, while imprisoned in Rome. This Epistle presents the doctrine of God who is all-powerful and wise in His loving design for the world.

Ephesians teaches us how to share in the life of the risen Christ. Most relevant to church doctrine, this letter discusses the nature of the church and how it should be demonstrated to the world.

Rich in promises, Ephesians presents confident passages which Christians can draw upon today. God "is able to do exceedingly abundantly above all that we ask or think, according to the power that works in us" (Eph. 3:20). We are assured that "the love of Christ which passes knowledge" (Eph. 3:19). Our talents and gifts can be used to build up the church and to help us more fully understand Jesus Christ and share Him with others (Eph. 4:7–16).

The pagan culture of the city of Ephesus was filled with immoral and negative influences. Worship of the goddess Diana with its ceremonial prostitution was an Ephesus trademark. It was known as a city of refuge where murderers, thieves, and robbers, could live freely.

Against this negative, emotional, and physical environment, the church was encouraged to live a positive Christian life-style. Negative influences can be battled successfully by relying on the positive power of God. As Christians we can put on the armor of God to defeat the negative forces which would destroy us.

Stand therefore, having girded your waist with truth, having put on the breastplate of righteousness, and having shod your feet with the preparation of the gospel of peace; above all, taking the shield of faith with which you will be able to quench all the fiery darts of the wicked one. And take the helmet of salvation, and the sword of the Spirit, which is the word of God;

(Eph. 6:14–17)

The Epistle of Paul the Apostle to the

Ephesians

Greeting

PAUL, an apostle of Jesus Christ by the will of God,

To the saints who are in Ephesus, and faithful in Christ Jesus:

2 Grace to you and peace from God our Father and the Lord Jesus Christ.

Redemption in Christ

3 Blessed *be* the God and Father of our Lord Jesus Christ, who has blessed us with every spiritual blessing in the heavenly *places* in Christ,

4 just as He chose us in Him before the foundation of the world, that we should be holy and without blame before Him in love,

5 having predestined us to adoption as sons by Jesus Christ to Himself, according to the good pleasure of His will,

6 to the praise of the glory of His grace, by which He has made us accepted in the Beloved.

7 In Him we have redemption through His blood, the forgiveness of sins, according to the riches of His grace

8 which He made to abound toward us in all wisdom and prudence,

9 having made known to us the mystery of His will, according to His good pleasure which He purposed in Himself,

10 that in the dispensation of the fullness of the times He might gather together in one all things in Christ, both[1] which are in heaven and which are on earth—in Him,

11 in whom also we have obtained an inheritance, being predestined according to the purpose of Him who works all things according to the counsel of His will,

12 that we who first trusted in Christ should be to the praise of His glory.

13 In Him you also *trusted*, after you heard the word of truth, the gospel of your salvation; in whom also, having believed, you were sealed with the Holy Spirit of promise,

14 who[2] is the guarantee of our inheritance until the redemption of the purchased possession, to the praise of His glory.

Prayer for Spiritual Wisdom

15 Therefore I also, after I heard of your faith in the Lord Jesus and your love for all the saints,

16 do not cease to give thanks for you, making mention of you in my prayers:

17 that the God of our Lord Jesus Christ, the Father of glory, may give to you the spirit of wisdom and revelation in the knowledge of Him,

18 the eyes of your understanding[3] being enlightened; that you may know what is the hope of His calling, what are the riches of the glory of His inheritance in the saints,

19 and what *is* the exceeding greatness of His power toward us who believe, according to the working of His mighty power

20 which He worked in Christ when He raised Him from the dead and seated *Him* at His right hand in the heavenly *places*,

21 far above all principality and power and might and dominion, and every name that is named, not only in this age but also in that which is to come.

22 And He put all *things* under His feet, and gave Him *to be* head over all *things* to the church,

23 which is His body, the fullness of Him who fills all in all.

By Grace Through Faith

2 And you *He made alive*, who were dead in trespasses and sins,

2 in which you once walked according to the course of this world, according to the prince of the power of the air, the spirit who now works in the sons of disobedience,

3 among whom also we all once conducted ourselves in the lusts of our flesh, fulfilling the desires of the flesh and of the mind, and were by nature children of wrath, just as the others.

---

1 NU-Text and M-Text omit *both*.   2 NU-Text reads *which*.   3 NU-Text and M-Text read *hearts*.

4 But God, who is rich in mercy, because of His great love with which He loved us,

5 even when we were dead in trespasses, made us alive together with Christ (by grace you have been saved),

6 and raised *us* up together, and made *us* sit together in the heavenly *places* in Christ Jesus,

7 that in the ages to come He might show the exceeding riches of His grace in *His* kindness toward us in Christ Jesus.

8 For by grace you have been saved through faith, and that not of yourselves; *it is* the gift of God,

9 not of works, lest anyone should boast.

10 For we are His workmanship, created in Christ Jesus for good works, which God prepared beforehand that we should walk in them.

Brought Near by His Blood

11 Therefore remember that you, once Gentiles in the flesh—who are called Uncircumcision by what is called the Circumcision made in the flesh by hands—

12 that at that time you were without Christ, being aliens from the commonwealth of Israel and strangers from the covenants of promise, having no hope and without God in the world.

13 But now in Christ Jesus you who once were far off have been made near by the blood of Christ.

Christ Our Peace

14 For He Himself is our peace, who has made both one, and has broken down the middle wall of division *between us,*

15 having abolished in His flesh the enmity, *that is,* the law of commandments *contained* in ordinances, so as to create in Himself one new man *from* the two, *thus* making peace,

16 and that He might reconcile them both to God in one body through the cross, thereby putting to death the enmity.

17 And He came and preached peace to you who were afar off and to those who were near.

18 For through Him we both have access by one Spirit to the Father.

Christ Our Cornerstone

19 Now, therefore, you are no longer strangers and foreigners, but fellow citizens with the saints and members of the household of God,

20 having been built on the foundation of the apostles and prophets, Jesus Christ Himself being the chief corner*stone,*

21 in whom the whole building, being joined together, grows into a holy temple in the Lord,

22 in whom you also are being built together for a habitation of God in the Spirit.

The Mystery Revealed

3 For this reason I, Paul, the prisoner of Jesus Christ for you Gentiles—

2 if indeed you have heard of the dispensation of the grace of God which was given to me for you,

3 how that by revelation He made known to me the mystery (as I wrote before in a few words,

4 by which, when you read, you may understand my knowledge in the mystery of Christ),

5 which in other ages was not made known to the sons of men, as it has now been revealed by the Spirit to His holy apostles and prophets:

6 that the Gentiles should be fellow heirs, of the same body, and partakers of His promise in Christ through the gospel,

7 of which I became a minister according to the gift of the grace of God given to me by the effective working of His power.

Purpose of the Mystery

8 To me, who am less than the least of all the saints, this grace was given, that I should preach among the Gentiles the unsearchable riches of Christ,

9 and to make all *people* see what *is* the fellowship[4] of the mystery, which from the beginning of the ages has been hidden in God who created all things through Jesus Christ;[5]

10 to the intent that now the manifold wisdom of God might be made known by the church to the principalities and powers in the heavenly *places,*

11 according to the eternal purpose which He accomplished in Christ Jesus our Lord,

12 in whom we have boldness and access with confidence through faith in Him.

13 Therefore I ask that you do not lose

4 NU-Text and M-Text read *stewardship (dispensation).*   5 NU-Text omits *through Jesus Christ.*

heart at my tribulations for you, which is your glory.

Appreciation of the Mystery

14 For this reason I bow my knees to the Father of our Lord Jesus Christ,[6]

15 from whom the whole family in heaven and earth is named,

16 that He would grant you, according to the riches of His glory, to be strengthened with might through His Spirit in the inner man,

17 that Christ may dwell in your hearts through faith; that you, being rooted and grounded in love,

18 may be able to comprehend with all the saints what *is* the width and length and depth and height—

19 to know the love of Christ which passes knowledge; that you may be filled with all the fullness of God.

20 Now to Him who is able to do exceedingly abundantly above all that we ask or think, according to the power that works in us,

21 to Him *be* glory in the church by Christ Jesus throughout all ages, world without end. Amen.

Walk in Unity

4 I, therefore, the prisoner of the Lord, beseech you to have a walk worthy of the calling with which you were called,

2 with all lowliness and gentleness, with longsuffering, bearing with one another in love,

3 endeavoring to keep the unity of the Spirit in the bond of peace.

4 *There is* one body and one Spirit, just as you were called in one hope of your calling;

5 one Lord, one faith, one baptism;

6 one God and Father of all, who *is* above all, and through all, and in you[7] all.

Spiritual Gifts

7 But to each one of us grace was given according to the measure of Christ's gift.

8 Therefore He says:

"When He ascended on high,
He led captivity captive,
And gave gifts to men."[8]

9 (Now this, *"He ascended"*—what does it mean but that He also first[9] descended into the lower parts of the earth?

10 He who descended is also the One

who ascended far above all the heavens, that He might fill all things.)

11 And He Himself gave some *to be* apostles, some prophets, some evangelists, and some pastors and teachers,

12 for the equipping of the saints for the work of ministry, for the edifying of the body of Christ,

13 till we all come to the unity of the faith and the knowledge of the Son of God, to a perfect man, to the measure of the stature of the fullness of Christ;

14 that we should no longer be children, tossed to and fro and carried about with every wind of doctrine, by the trickery of men, in the cunning craftiness by which they lie in wait to deceive,

15 but, speaking the truth in love, may grow up in all things into Him who is the head—Christ—

16 from whom the whole body, joined and knit together by what every joint supplies, according to the effective working by which every part does its share, causes growth of the body for the edifying of itself in love.

The New Man

17 This I say, therefore, and testify in the Lord, that you should no longer walk as the rest of the[10] Gentiles walk, in the futility of their mind,

18 having their understanding darkened, being alienated from the life of God, because of the ignorance that is in them, because of the hardening of their heart;

19 who, being past feeling, have given themselves over to licentiousness, to work all uncleanness with greediness.

20 But you have not so learned Christ,

21 if indeed you have heard Him and have been taught by Him, as the truth is in Jesus:

22 that you put off, concerning your former conduct, the old man which grows corrupt according to the deceitful lusts,

23 and be renewed in the spirit of your mind, ·

24 and that you put on the new man which was created according to God, in righteousness and true holiness.

Do Not Grieve the Spirit

25 Therefore, putting away lying, each one speak truth with his neighbor, for we are members of one another.

6 NU-Text omits *of our Lord Jesus Christ.*   7 NU-Text omits *you;* M-Text reads *us.*   8 Psalm 68:18
9 NU-Text omits *first.*   10 NU-Text omits *rest of the.*

26 *"Be angry, and do not sin"*:[11] do not let the sun go down on your wrath, 27 nor give place to the devil.
28 Let him who stole steal no longer, but rather let him labor, working with *his* hands what is good, that he may have something to give him who has need.
29 Let no corrupt communication proceed out of your mouth, but what is good for necessary edification, that it may impart grace to the hearers.
30 And do not grieve the Holy Spirit of God, by whom you were sealed for the day of redemption.
31 Let all bitterness, wrath, anger, clamor, and evil speaking be put away from you, with all malice.
32 And be kind to one another, tenderhearted, forgiving one another, just as God in Christ also forgave you.

Walk in Love

5 Therefore be followers of God as dear children.
2 And walk in love, as Christ also has loved us and given Himself for us, an offering and a sacrifice to God for a sweet-smelling aroma.
3 But fornication and all uncleanness or covetousness, let it not even be named among you, as is fitting for saints;
4 neither filthiness, nor foolish talking, nor coarse jesting, which are not fitting, but rather giving of thanks.
5 For this you know,[12] that no fornicator, unclean person, nor covetous man, who is an idolater, has any inheritance in the kingdom of Christ and God.
6 Let no one deceive you with empty words, for because of these things the wrath of God comes upon the sons of disobedience.
7 Therefore do not be partakers with them.

Walk in Light

8 For you were once darkness, but now *you are* light in the Lord. Walk as children of light
9 (for the fruit of the Spirit[13] *is* in all goodness, righteousness, and truth),
10 proving what is acceptable to the Lord.
11 And have no fellowship with the unfruitful works of darkness, but rather expose *them*.

12 For it is shameful even to speak of those things which are done by them in secret.
13 But all things that are exposed are made manifest by the light, for whatever makes manifest is light.
14 Therefore He says:

"Awake, you who sleep,
Arise from the dead,
And Christ will give you light."

Walk in Wisdom

15 See then that you walk circumspectly, not as fools but as wise,
16 redeeming the time, because the days are evil.
17 Therefore do not be unwise, but understand what the will of the Lord *is*.
18 And do not be drunk with wine, in which is dissipation; but be filled with the Spirit,
19 speaking to one another in psalms and hymns and spiritual songs, singing and making melody in your heart to the Lord,
20 giving thanks always for all things to God the Father in the name of our Lord Jesus Christ,
21 submitting to one another in the fear of God.[14]

Marriage—Christ and the Church

22 Wives, submit to your own husbands, as to the Lord.
23 For the husband is head of the wife, as also Christ is head of the church; and He is the Savior of the body.
24 Therefore, just as the church is subject to Christ, so *let* the wives *be* to their own husbands in everything.
25 Husbands, love your wives, just as Christ also loved the church and gave Himself for it,
26 that He might sanctify and cleanse it with the washing of water by the word,
27 that He might present it to Himself a glorious church, not having spot or wrinkle or any such thing, but that it should be holy and without blemish.
28 So husbands ought to love their own wives as their own bodies; he who loves his wife loves himself.
29 For no one ever hated his own flesh, but nourishes and cherishes it, just as the Lord *does* the church.
30 For we are members of His body,[15] of His flesh and of His bones.

---

11 Psalm 4:4   12 NU-Text reads *For know this.*   13 NU-Text reads *light.*   14 NU-Text reads *Christ.*
15 NU-Text omits the rest of this verse.

31 *"For this reason a man shall leave his father and mother and be joined to his wife, and the two shall become one flesh."*[16]
32 This is a great mystery, but I speak concerning Christ and the church.
33 Nevertheless let each one of you in particular so love his own wife as himself, and let the wife *see* that she respects *her* husband.

Children and Parents

6 Children, obey your parents in the Lord, for this is right.
2 *"Honor your father and mother,"*[17] which is the first commandment with promise:
3 *"that it may be well with you and you may live long on the earth."*[17]
4 And you, fathers, do not provoke your children to wrath, but bring them up in the training and admonition of the Lord.

Servants and Masters

5 Servants, be obedient to those who are your masters according to the flesh, with fear and trembling, in sincerity of heart, as to Christ;
6 not with eyeservice, as men-pleasers, but as servants of Christ, doing the will of God from the heart,
7 with good will doing service, as to the Lord, and not to men,
8 knowing that whatever good anyone does, he will receive the same from the Lord, whether *he is* a slave or free.
9 And you, masters, do the same things to them, giving up threatening, knowing that your own Master also[18] is in heaven, and there is no partiality with Him.

The Whole Armor of God

10 Finally, my brethren, be strong in the Lord and in the power of His might.
11 Put on the whole armor of God, that you may be able to stand against the wiles of the devil.

12 For we do not wrestle against flesh and blood, but against principalities, against powers, against the rulers of the darkness of this age,[19] against spiritual *hosts* of wickedness in the heavenly *places.*
13 Therefore take up the whole armor of God, that you may be able to withstand in the evil day, and having done all, to stand.
14 Stand therefore, having girded your waist with truth, having put on the breastplate of righteousness,
15 and having shod your feet with the preparation of the gospel of peace;
16 above all, taking the shield of faith with which you will be able to quench all the fiery darts of the wicked one.
17 And take the helmet of salvation, and the sword of the Spirit, which is the word of God;
18 praying always with all prayer and supplication in the Spirit, being watchful to this end with all perseverance and supplication for all the saints—
19 and for me, that utterance may be given to me, that I may open my mouth boldly to make known the mystery of the gospel,
20 for which I am an ambassador in chains; that in it I may speak boldly, as I ought to speak.

A Gracious Greeting

21 But that you also may know my affairs *and* how I am doing, Tychicus, a beloved brother and faithful minister in the Lord, will make all things known to you;
22 whom I have sent to you for this very purpose, that you may know our affairs, and *that* he may comfort your hearts.
23 Peace to the brethren, and love with faith, from God the Father and the Lord Jesus Christ.
24 Grace *be* with all those who love our Lord Jesus Christ in sincerity. Amen.

16 Genesis 2:24   17 Deuteronomy 5:16   18 NU-Text reads *He who is both their Master and yours.*
19 NU-Text reads *rulers of this darkness.*

Introduction to Philippians

The Book of Philippians is a motivational, goal-oriented letter, inspiring the Christians in Philippi and those throughout the world today, to believe that they can do great things for God!

Paul wrote this Epistle while imprisoned in Rome about A.D. 61. His words of faith, though he was captive, are filled with determination and confidence to serve God no matter what the cost. Paul confirms that there is no gain without pain: "For to me, to live *is* Christ, and to die *is* gain" (Phil. 1:21).

The people of Philippi are presented with specific goals to strive toward in this letter: to become like-minded; to love one another; and to focus their thoughts on what is true, honest, just, pure, lovely, of good report, virtuous, and praiseworthy. Paul encourages them to filter out negative thoughts and to be controlled by positive thoughts. Then they can let worry drain out and let God's peace flow in.

Paul reminds them that what they do and what they become will be determined by the thoughts and goals they pursue. Their greatest asset is that God is working in and through them. "Being confident of this very thing, that He who has begun a good work in you will complete *it* until the day of Jesus Christ" (Phil. 1:6). And "it is God who works in you both to will and to do for *His* good pleasure" (Phil. 2:13).

Throughout this exciting and challenging letter, Paul affirms that they are God's project—and God never fails! Great people are common people committed to uncommon goals! "I can do all things through Christ who strengthens me" (Phil. 4:13).

In Philippians we discover that a true Christian is a mind through which Christ thinks, a heart through which Christ loves, a tongue through which Christ speaks, a face through which Christ glows, and a hand through which Christ lifts!

The Epistle of Paul the Apostle to the

Philippians

Greeting

PAUL and Timothy, servants of Jesus Christ,

To all the saints in Christ Jesus who are in Philippi, with the bishops[1] and deacons:

2 Grace to you and peace from God our Father and the Lord Jesus Christ.

Thankfulness and Prayer

3 I thank my God upon every remembrance of you,
4 always in every prayer of mine making request for you all with joy,
5 for your fellowship in the gospel from the first day until now,
6 being confident of this very thing, that He who has begun a good work in you will complete *it* until the day of Jesus Christ;
7 just as it is right for me to think this of you all, because I have you in my heart, inasmuch as both in my chains and in the defense and confirmation of the gospel, you all are partakers with me of grace.
8 For God is my witness, how greatly I long for you all with the affection of Jesus Christ.
9 And this I pray, that your love may abound still more and more in knowledge and all discernment,
10 that you may approve the things that are excellent, that you may be sincere and without offense till the day of Christ,
11 being filled with the fruits of righteousness which *are* by Jesus Christ, to the glory and praise of God.

Christ Is Preached

12 But I want you to know, brethren, that the things *which happened* to me have actually turned out for the furtherance of the gospel,
13 so that it has become evident to the whole palace guard, and to all the rest, that my chains are in Christ;
14 and most of the brethren in the Lord, having become confident by my chains,

are much more bold to speak the word without fear.
15 Some indeed preach Christ even from envy and strife, and some also from good will:
16 The former[2] preach Christ from selfish ambition, not sincerely, supposing to add affliction to my chains;
17 but the latter out of love, knowing that I am appointed for the defense of the gospel.
18 What then? Only *that* in every way, whether in pretense or in truth, Christ is preached; and in this I rejoice, yes, and will rejoice.

To Live Is Christ

19 For I know that this will turn out for my salvation through your prayer and the supply of the Spirit of Jesus Christ,
20 according to my earnest expectation and hope that in nothing I shall be ashamed, but *that* with all boldness, as always, so now also Christ will be magnified in my body, whether by life or by death.
21 For to me, to live *is* Christ, and to die *is* gain.
22 But if *I* live on in the flesh, this *will mean* fruit from *my* labor; yet what I shall choose I cannot tell.
23 For[3] I am hard pressed between the two, having a desire to depart and be with Christ, *which is* far better.
24 Nevertheless to remain in the flesh *is* more needful for you.
25 And being confident of this, I know that I shall remain and continue with you all for your progress and joy of faith,
26 that your rejoicing for me may be more abundant in Jesus Christ by my coming to you again.

Striving and Suffering for Christ

27 Only let your conduct be worthy of the gospel of Christ, so that whether I come and see you or am absent, I may hear of your affairs, that you stand fast in one spirit, with one mind striving together for the faith of the gospel,

1 Literally *overseers*   2 NU-Text reverses the contents of verses 16 and 17.   3 NU-Text and M-Text read *But.*

28 and not in any way terrified by your adversaries, which is to them a proof of perdition, but to you of salvation,[4] and that from God.

29 For to you it has been granted on behalf of Christ, not only to believe in Him, but also to suffer for His sake.

30 having the same conflict which you saw in me and now hear *is* in me.

Unity Through Humility

2 Therefore if *there is* any consolation in Christ, if any comfort of love, if any fellowship of the Spirit, if any affection and mercy,

2 fulfill my joy by being like-minded, having the same love, *being* of one accord, of one mind.

3 *Let* nothing *be done* through selfish ambition or conceit, but in lowliness of mind let each esteem others better than himself.

4 Let each of you look out not only for his own interests, but also for the interests of others.

The Humbled and Exalted Christ

5 Let this mind be in you which was also in Christ Jesus,

6 who, being in the form of God, did not consider it robbery to be equal with God,

7 but made Himself of no reputation, taking the form of a servant, *and* coming in the likeness of men.

8 And being found in appearance as a man, He humbled Himself and became obedient to *the point of* death, even the death of the cross.

9 Therefore God also has highly exalted Him and given Him the name which is above every name,

10 that at the name of Jesus every knee should bow, of those in heaven, and of those on earth, and of those under the earth,

11 and *that* every tongue should confess that Jesus Christ *is* Lord, to the glory of God the Father.

Light Bearers

12 Therefore, my beloved, as you have always obeyed, not as in my presence only, but now much more in my absence, work out your own salvation with fear and trembling;

13 for it is God who works in you both to will and to do for *His* good pleasure.

14 Do all things without murmuring and disputing,

15 that you may become blameless and harmless, children of God without fault in the midst of a crooked and perverse generation, among whom you shine as lights in the world,

16 holding fast the word of life, so that I may rejoice in the day of Christ that I have not run in vain or labored in vain.

17 Yes, and if I am being poured out *as a drink offering* on the sacrifice and service of your faith, I am glad and rejoice with you all.

18 For the same reason you also be glad and rejoice with me.

Timothy Commended

19 But I trust in the Lord Jesus to send Timothy to you shortly, that I also may be encouraged when I know your state.

20 For I have no one like-minded, who will sincerely care for your state.

21 For all seek their own, not the things which are of Christ Jesus.

22 But you know his proven character, that as a son with *his* father he served with me in the gospel.

23 Therefore I hope to send him at once, as soon as I see how it goes with me.

24 But I trust in the Lord that I myself shall also come shortly.

Epaphroditus Praised

25 Yet I considered it necessary to send to you Epaphroditus, my brother, fellow worker, and fellow soldier, but your messenger and the one who ministered to my need;

26 since he was longing for you all, and was distressed because you had heard that he was sick.

27 For indeed he was sick almost unto death; but God had mercy on him, and not only on him but on me also, lest I should have sorrow upon sorrow.

28 Therefore I sent him the more eagerly, that when you see him again you may rejoice, and I may be less sorrowful.

29 Receive him therefore in the Lord with all gladness, and hold such men in esteem;

30 because for the work of Christ he came close to death, not regarding his

---

4 NU-Text reads *of your salvation.*

life, to supply what was lacking in your service toward me.

All for Christ

3 Finally, my brethren, rejoice in the Lord. For me to write the same things to you *is* not tedious, but for you *it is* safe.
2 Beware of dogs, beware of evil workers, beware of the mutilation!
3 For we are the circumcision, who worship God in the Spirit,[5] rejoice in Christ Jesus, and have no confidence in the flesh,
4 though I also might have confidence in the flesh. If anyone else thinks he may have confidence in the flesh, I more so:
5 circumcised the eighth day, of the stock of Israel, *of* the tribe of Benjamin, a Hebrew of the Hebrews; concerning the law, a Pharisee;
6 concerning zeal, persecuting the church; concerning the righteousness which is in the law, blameless.
7 But what things were gain to me, these I have counted loss for Christ.
8 But indeed I also count all things loss for the excellence of the knowledge of Christ Jesus my Lord, for whom I have suffered the loss of all things, and count them as rubbish, that I may gain Christ
9 and be found in Him, not having my own righteousness, which *is* from the law, but that which *is* through faith in Christ, the righteousness which is from God by faith;
10 that I may know Him and the power of His resurrection, and the fellowship of His sufferings, being conformed to His death,
11 if, by any means, I may attain to the resurrection from the dead.

Pressing Toward the Goal

12 Not that I have already attained, or am already perfected; but I press on, that I may lay hold of that for which Christ Jesus has also laid hold of me.
13 Brethren, I do not count myself to have apprehended; but one thing *I do*, forgetting those things which are behind and reaching forward to those things which are ahead,
14 I press toward the goal for the prize of the upward call of God in Christ Jesus.
15 Therefore let us, as many as are ma-

ture, have this mind; and if in anything you think otherwise, God will reveal even this to you.
16 Nevertheless, to *the degree* that we have already attained, let us walk by the same rule,[6] let us be of the same mind.

Our Citizenship in Heaven

17 Brethren, join in following my example, and note those who so walk, as you have us for a pattern.
18 For many walk, of whom I have told you often, and now tell you even weeping, *that they are* the enemies of the cross of Christ:
19 whose end *is* destruction, whose god *is their* belly, and *whose* glory *is* in their shame—who set their mind on earthly things.
20 For our citizenship is in heaven, from which we also eagerly wait for the Savior, the Lord Jesus Christ,
21 who will transform our lowly body that it may be conformed to His glorious body, according to the working by which He is able even to subdue all things to Himself.

4 Therefore, my beloved and longed-for brethren, my joy and crown, so stand fast in the Lord, beloved.

Be United, Joyful, and in Prayer

2 I implore Euodia and I implore Syntyche to be of the same mind in the Lord.
3 And[7] I urge you also, true companion, help these women who labored with me in the gospel, with Clement also, and the rest of my fellow workers, whose names *are* in the Book of Life.
4 Rejoice in the Lord always. Again I will say, rejoice!
5 Let your gentleness be known to all men. The Lord *is* at hand.
6 Be anxious for nothing, but in everything by prayer and supplication, with thanksgiving, let your requests be made known to God;
7 and the peace of God, which surpasses all understanding, will guard your hearts and minds through Christ Jesus.

Meditate on These Things

8 Finally, brethren, whatever things are true, whatever things are noble, whatever things *are* just, whatever things *are* pure, whatever things *are* lovely, whatever things *are* of good report, if *there is* any

---

5 NU-Text and M-Text read *who worship in the Spirit of God.*   6 NU-Text omits *rule* and the rest of verse.
7 NU-Text and M-Text read *Yes.*

Change Your Thoughts and Change Your World

The apostle Paul was a Jewish Roman citizen from the bustling cosmopolitan city of Tarsus in the province of Cilicia. As a young boy, he spent much time in the small Jewish village of Gishalav in northern Galilee. His relatives probably fought in the major revolts against Rome in A.D. 66. About the age of twelve, Paul, then known as Saul, began his studies in Jerusalem under the famous Rabbi Gamaliel. Saul excelled in his knowledge of the Jewish law and customs. He was at the top of his class. Eventually he rose to a prominent position in the synagogue at Jerusalem. Here he met Stephen and other early Christians. Zealously protecting his Jewish forefathers' laws and traditions, Saul joined in the fight against these "heretics."

Saul persecuted many early church members even to the point of death. During one such pursuit, as Saul journeyed from Jerusalem to Damascus, the resurrected Christ appeared to him. Through this experience, Saul was converted and eventually his name was changed to Paul.

Paul was one of the most zealous, enthusiastic, outspoken leaders of the early Christian movement. But it did not happen overnight. Following Paul's conversion, he spent fourteen years in training. Paul realized that Christ was the goal of the law he had been taught. He had to unlearn all of the non-positive influences of his upbringing. He filtered out the negative doctrines which taught judgment and legalism, and replaced them with the gospel of hope, love, peace, patience, kindness, forgiveness, and gentleness—against which there is no law. Paul renewed his energy by renewing his mind. Jesus was the fulfillment of the law, the freedom to which the law pointed.

If you change your thoughts, you can change your world. Paul taught us: "Finally, brethren, whatever things are true, whatever things are noble, whatever things *are* just, whatever things *are* pure, whatever things *are* lovely, whatever things *are* of good report, if *there is* any virtue and if *there is* anything praiseworthy—meditate on these things . . . and the God of peace will be with you" (Phil. 4:8, 9).

virtue and if *there is* anything praiseworthy—meditate on these things.
9 The things which you learned and received and heard and saw in me, these do, and the God of peace will be with you.

Philippian Generosity

10 But I rejoiced in the Lord greatly that now at last your care for me has flourished again; though you surely did care, but you lacked opportunity.
11 Not that I speak in regard to need, for I have learned in whatever state I am, to be content:
12 I know how to be abased, and I know how to abound. Everywhere and in all things I have learned both to be full and to be hungry, both to abound and to suffer need.
13 I can do all things through Christ[8] who strengthens me.
14 Nevertheless you have done well that you shared in my distress.
15 Now you Philippians know also that in the beginning of the gospel, when I departed from Macedonia, no church shared with me concerning giving and receiving but you only.
16 For even in Thessalonica you sent *aid* once and again for my necessities.
17 Not that I seek the gift, but I seek the fruit that abounds to your account.
18 Indeed I have all and abound. I am full, having received from Epaphroditus the things *which were sent* from you, a sweet-smelling aroma, an acceptable sacrifice, well pleasing to God.
19 And my God shall supply all your need according to His riches in glory by Christ Jesus.
20 Now to our God and Father *be* glory forever and ever. Amen.

Greeting and Blessing

21 Greet every saint in Christ Jesus. The brethren who are with me greet you.
22 All the saints greet you, but especially those who are of Caesar's household.
23 The grace of our Lord Jesus Christ be with you all.[9] Amen.

8 NU-Text reads *Him who.*   9 NU-Text reads *your spirit.*

Appeal to Caesar

Perhaps one of Paul's greatest assets was that he was an uncommon person committed to uncommon goals. He was willing to attempt to do great things for God and expect great things from God.

Paul suffered many imprisonments. One was at Caesarea by the Sea, the great coastal city of Palestine. Here Paul spent two years in prison and appeared before two governors who tried his case: Festus and Felix.

Festus decided Paul was to be granted freedom; but Paul declined in favor of a greater goal. He wished to stay in prison to have his case heard before Caesar. As a Roman citizen, Paul had the right to appeal his case to the emperor. Festus told Paul he would have been set free had it not been for this request. Paul had appealed to Caesar, so to Caesar he would go.

Paul was willing to attempt to do great things for God, even if he failed, rather than accept his freedom. This meant further imprisonment for Paul, but the cost was worth the opportunity to speak to one of the world's great leaders about the greatest event in history. The Book of Philippians reveals the outcome of Paul's plan. "All the saints greet you, but especially those who are of Caesar's household" (Phil. 4:22). Paul's message of Jesus Christ infiltrated the mighty kingdom of Caesar. All it took was one man's commitment to an uncommon goal.

What goal would you set for yourself if you knew you would not fail? Who is the Caesar—the greater authority, the powerful overlord in your life? Appeal to Caesar; face your fear confidently. Set your goal then pay the toll. Paul payed the cost of imprisonment to succeed. You may pay the price of time, energy, criticism, financial security, or reputation. But remember the words of Paul and be encouraged. "Being confident of this very thing, that He who has begun a good work in you will complete *it* until the day of Jesus Christ" (Phil. 1:6).

Introduction to Colossians

Paul wrote this letter to the Christians at Colosse from Rome about A.D. 60. The Colossians were mostly converted Gentiles who lived in the cosmopolitan city known for its fine wools and dyes, located on the major trade route between east and west in Asia Minor (modern Turkey).

To Christians in a city greatly influenced by its neighbors, Paul writes to encourage them in their newfound faith from adopting any foreign doctrines or untruths into their belief and worship. It would have been easy for the Colossians to incorporate Jewish legalism, Greek philosophical speculative religion, and other pagan ideas, due to their constant contact with the east and its mysticism.

Paul encourages his readers with the truth that Jesus Christ is the image of the invisible God and that through Him all things were created and are held together. He speaks of the mystery of God "which is Christ in you, the hope of glory" (Col. 1:27). Paul holds up high ideals for the Colossians, and by sharing these goals with them he is confident his readers will live up to them.

Colossians is a prime example of the belief that "I'm not what *I* think I am; I'm not what *you* think I am; I am what *I* think *you think* I am." The Colossians were able to believe in themselves because they believed that Paul believed in them. He made it quite clear, " When Christ *who is* our life appears, then you also will appear with Him in glory" (Col. 3:4).

If Paul believed the best about the Christians in Colosse who were faced with numerous negative obstacle to their faith, should we not also believe the best about ourselves and others? For with God as our strength we will succeed!

The Epistle of Paul the Apostle to the
Colossians

Greeting

PAUL, an apostle of Jesus Christ by the will of God, and Timothy our brother,

2 To the saints and faithful brethren in Christ *who are* in Colosse:

Grace to you and peace from God our Father and the Lord Jesus Christ.[1]

Their Faith in Christ

3 We give thanks to the God and Father of our Lord Jesus Christ, praying always for you,
4 since we heard of your faith in Christ Jesus and of your love for all the saints;
5 because of the hope which is laid up for you in heaven, of which you heard before in the word of the truth of the gospel,
6 which has come to you, as *it has* also in all the world, and is bringing forth fruit,[2] as *it is* also among you since the day you heard and knew the grace of God in truth;
7 as you also learned from Epaphras, our dear fellow servant, who is a faithful minister of Christ on your behalf,
8 who also declared to us your love in the Spirit.

Preeminence of Christ

9 For this reason we also, since the day we heard it, do not cease to pray for you, and to ask that you may be filled with the knowledge of His will in all wisdom and spiritual understanding;
10 that you may have a walk worthy of the Lord, fully pleasing *Him*, being fruitful in every good work and increasing in the knowledge of God;
11 strengthened with all might, according to His glorious power, for all patience and longsuffering with joy;
12 giving thanks to the Father who has qualified us to be partakers of the inheritance of the saints in the light.
13 He has delivered us from the power of darkness and translated *us* into the kingdom of the Son of His love, .
14 in whom we have redemption through His blood,[3] the forgiveness of sins.
15 He is the image of the invisible God, the firstborn over all creation.
16 For by Him all things were created that are in heaven and that are on earth, visible and invisible, whether thrones or dominions or principalities or powers. All things were created through Him and for Him.
17 And He is before all things, and in Him all things consist.
18 And He is the head of the body, the church, who is the beginning, the firstborn from the dead, that in all things He may have the preeminence.

Reconciled in Christ

19 For it pleased *the Father that* in Him all the fullness should dwell,
20 and by Him to reconcile all things to Himself, by Him, whether things on earth or things in heaven, having made peace through the blood of His cross.
21 And you, who once were alienated and enemies in your mind by wicked works, yet now He has reconciled
22 in the body of His flesh through death, to present you holy, and blameless, and irreproachable in His sight—
23 if indeed you continue in the faith, grounded and steadfast, and are not moved away from the hope of the gospel which you heard, which was preached to every creature under heaven, of which I, Paul, became a minister.

Sacrificial Service for Christ

24 I now rejoice in my sufferings for you, and fill up in my flesh what is lacking in the afflictions of Christ, for the sake of His body, which is the church,
25 of which I became a minister according to the stewardship from God which was given to me for you, to fulfill the word of God,
26 the mystery which has been hidden

---

1 NU-Text omits *and the Lord Jesus Christ.*   2 NU-Text and M-Text add *and growing.*
3 NU-Text and M-Text omit *through His blood.*

from ages and from generations, but now has been revealed to His saints.

27 To them God willed to make known what are the riches of the glory of this mystery among the Gentiles: which[4] is Christ in you, the hope of glory.

28 Him we preach, warning every man and teaching every man in all wisdom, that we may present every man perfect in Christ Jesus.

29 To this *end* I also labor, striving according to His working which works in me mightily.

Not Philosophy but Christ

2 For I want you to know what a great conflict I have for you and those in Laodicea, and *for* as many as have not seen my face in the flesh,

2 that their hearts may be encouraged, being knit together in love, and *attaining* to all riches of the full assurance of understanding, to the knowledge of the mystery of God, both of the Father and[5] of Christ,

3 in whom are hidden all the treasures of wisdom and knowledge.

4 Now this I say lest anyone should deceive you with persuasive words.

5 For though I am absent in the flesh, yet I am with you in spirit, rejoicing to see your *good* order and the steadfastness of your faith in Christ.

6 As you have therefore received Christ Jesus the Lord, so walk in Him,

7 rooted and built up in Him and established in the faith, as you have been taught, abounding in it[6] with thanksgiving.

8 Beware lest anyone cheat you through philosophy and empty deceit, according to the tradition of men, according to the basic principles of the world, and not according to Christ.

9 For in Him dwells all the fullness of the Godhead bodily;

10 and you are complete in Him, who is the head of all principality and power.

Not Legalism but Christ

11 In Him you were also circumcised with the circumcision made without hands, by putting off the body of the sins[7] of the flesh, by the circumcision of Christ,

12 buried with Him in baptism, in which you also were raised with *Him* through

faith in the working of God, who raised Him from the dead.

13 And you, being dead in your trespasses and the uncircumcision of your flesh, He has made alive together with Him, having forgiven you all trespasses,

14 having wiped out the handwriting of requirements that was against us, which was contrary to us. And He has taken it out of the way, having nailed it to the cross.

15 Having disarmed principalities and powers, He made a public spectacle of them, triumphing over them in it.

16 Therefore let no one judge you in food or in drink, or regarding a festival or a new moon or sabbaths,

17 which are a shadow of things to come, but the substance is of Christ.

18 Let no one defraud you of your reward, taking delight in *false* humility and worship of angels, intruding into those things which he has not[8] seen, vainly puffed up by his fleshly mind,

19 and not holding fast to the Head, from whom all the body, nourished and knit together by joints and ligaments, grows with the increase *which is* from God.

20 Therefore,[9] if you died with Christ from the basic principles of the world, why, as *though* living in the world, do you subject yourselves to regulations—

21 "Do not touch, do not taste, do not handle,"

22 which all concern things which perish with the using—according to the commandments and doctrines of men?

23 These things indeed have an appearance of wisdom in self-imposed religion, *false* humility, and neglect of the body, *but are* of no value against the indulgence of the flesh.

Not Carnality but Christ

3 If then you were raised with Christ, seek those things which are above, where Christ is, sitting at the right hand of God.

2 Set your mind on things above, not on things on the earth.

3 For you died, and your life is hidden with Christ in God.

4 When Christ *who is* our life appears, then you also will appear with Him in glory.

---

4 M-Text reads *who.*   5 NU-Text omits *both of the Father and.*   6 NU-Text omits *in it.*
7 NU-Text omits *of the sins.*   8 NU-Text omits *not.*   9 NU-Text and M-Text omit *Therefore.*

Hidden Treasure

People of the biblical world often stored great amounts of wealth in the ground for safekeeping. The earth itself was the central bank of the ancient world. If a warring army or band of thieves plundered or robbed a village, they would not find the town's treasure, for it was hidden secretly in the field. In Jesus' parable of the talents, one servant buried his money. Solomon said, "Search for [wisdom] as *for* hidden treasures" (Prov. 2:4).

On several occasions in modern times, archaeologists or farmers plowing their fields have unearthed thousands of coins, jewelry, gold, silver, or pearls hidden in the countryside. The famous Dead Sea Scrolls contain a document known as "The Copper Scroll" that describes sixty-four hiding places of buried treasure. Many scholars of biblical studies and archaeology believe that the Qumran community, who lived near the Dead Sea, hid these scrolls from the invading Roman army in A.D. 68.

There are three ways of locating hidden treasure. The first is to find an ancient map describing the treasure's location. The second is to stumble across the treasure while traveling or plowing a field. And the third is to simply have someone tell you where it is. Regardless of how it was found, in biblical times, hidden treasure belonged to the owner of the field in which it was buried. Jesus said, "Again, the kingdom of heaven is like treasure hidden in a field, which a man found and hid; and for joy over it he goes and sells all that he has and buys that field" (Matt. 13:44).

The hidden treasure Jesus spoke of is the kingdom of God. When you enter into a relationship with God and discover the riches of knowing Him, you will put all your efforts into getting to know Him better, through reading His Word, prayer, and service. Then you will discover as the apostle Paul, "In [Christ] are hidden all the treasures of wisdom and knowledge" (Col. 2:3).

5 Therefore put to death your members which are on the earth: fornication, uncleanness, passion, evil desire, and covetousness, which is idolatry.

6 Because of these things the wrath of God is coming upon the sons of disobedience,

7 in which you also once walked when you lived in them.

8 But now you must also put off all these: anger, wrath, malice, blasphemy, filthy language out of your mouth.

9 Do not lie to one another, since you have put off the old man with his deeds,

10 and have put on the new *man* who is renewed in knowledge according to the image of Him who created him,

11 where there is neither Greek nor Jew, circumcised nor uncircumcised, barbarian, Scythian, slave *nor* free, but Christ *is* all and in all.

Character of the New Man

12 Therefore, as *the* elect of God, holy and beloved, put on tender mercies, kindness, humbleness of mind, meekness, longsuffering;

13 bearing with one another, and forgiving one another, if anyone has a complaint against another; even as Christ forgave you, so you also *must do.*

14 But above all these things put on love, which is the bond of perfection.

15 And let the peace of God rule in your hearts, to which also you were called in one body; and be thankful.

16 Let the word of Christ dwell in you richly in all wisdom, teaching and admonishing one another in psalms and hymns and spiritual songs, singing with grace in your hearts to the Lord.

17 And *whatever* you do in word or deed, *do* all in the name of the Lord Jesus, giving thanks to God the Father through Him.

The Christian Home

18 Wives, submit to your own husbands, as is fitting in the Lord.

19 Husbands, love your wives and do not be bitter toward them.

20 Children, obey your parents in all things, for this is well pleasing to the Lord.

21 Fathers, do not provoke your children, lest they become discouraged.

22 Servants, obey in all things your masters according to the flesh, not with eyeservice, as men-pleasers, but in sincerity of heart, fearing God.

23 And whatever you do, do it heartily, as to the Lord and not to men,

24 knowing that from the Lord you will receive the reward of the inheritance; for[10] you serve the Lord Christ.

25 But he who does wrong will be repaid for *the wrong* which he has done, and there is no partiality.

4 Masters, give your servants what is just and fair, knowing that you also have a Master in heaven.

Christian Graces

2 Continue earnestly in prayer, being vigilant in it with thanksgiving;

3 meanwhile praying also for us, that God would open to us a door for the word, to speak the mystery of Christ, for which I am also in chains,

4 that I may make it manifest, as I ought to speak.

5 Walk in wisdom toward those *who are* outside, redeeming the time.

6 *Let* your speech always *be* with grace, seasoned with salt, that you may know how you ought to answer each one.

Final Greetings

7 Tychicus, *who is* a beloved brother, a faithful minister, and a fellow servant in the Lord, will tell you all the news about me.

8 I am sending him to you for this very purpose, that he[11] may know your circumstances and comfort your hearts,

9 with Onesimus, a faithful and beloved brother, who is *one* of you. They will make known to you all things which *are* happening here.

10 Aristarchus my fellow prisoner greets you, with Mark the cousin of Barnabas (about whom you received instructions: if he comes to you, welcome him),

11 and Jesus who is called Justus. These *are my* only fellow workers for the kingdom of God who are of the circumcision; they have proved to be a comfort to me.

12 Epaphras, who is *one* of you, a servant of Christ, greets you, always laboring fer-

---

10 NU-Text omits *for.*   11 NU-Text reads *you may know our circumstances and he may.*

Co-Workers with God

Whatever you do in word or deed, *do* all in the name of the Lord Jesus.

(Col. 3:17)

Work held a religious significance to the people of the biblical world. To them the term *work* was synonymous with people and God working together. God was considered at the center of both work and play. Without His help, man's endeavors could not be successful. When asked the question, "How is the harvest?" the sowers in the fields replied, "God is working bountifully." Even today, stonemasons sing songs to implore God's help in their tasks. Asking God's assistance in daily functions is an essential aspect of everyday life.

Jesus expressed an intimate relationship between His work and God's work. "My Father has been working until now, and I have been working" (John 5:17). The miracles Jesus performed in the presence of many people bear witness that God worked in and through Him. Jesus declared, "This is the work of God, that you believe in Him whom He sent" (John 6:29).

The early apostles also realized the need of God's power in their work of evangelizing the nations. Paul said, "*Whatever* you do in word or deed, *do* all in the name of the Lord Jesus . . ." (Col. 3:17). Having God as our co-worker and co-helper insures us that whatever work we undertake will be successful and have God's blessings. Jesus Himself promised us that the works He did we also would do. After a long life of sharing in God's work, Paul assures his readers in Philippians that God is at work in Christians to accomplish His good pleasure.

Whatever we do, we can be confident that God will work with us. Keep God in your thoughts throughout the day as you undertake daily tasks. Remember, it only takes two to make a miracle—God and you!

vently for you in prayers, that you may stand perfect and complete[12] in all the will of God.

13 For I bear him witness that he has a great zeal[13] for you, and those who are in Laodicea, and those in Hierapolis.

14 Luke the beloved physician and Demas greet you.

15 Greet the brethren who are in Laodicea, and Nymphas and the church that is in his[14] house.

Closing Exhortations and Blessing

16 Now when this epistle is read among you, see that it is read also in the church of the Laodiceans, and that you likewise read the epistle from Laodicea.

17 And say to Archippus, "Take heed to the ministry which you have received in the Lord, that you may fulfill it."

18 This salutation by my own hand— Paul. Remember my chains. Grace be with you. Amen.

12 NU-Text reads *fully assured.*   13 NU-Text reads *concern.*   14 NU-Text reads *Nympha . . . her house.*

Introduction to First Thessalonians

God is stronger and bigger than any problem! With Him you can overcome any obstacle!

First Thessalonians was written between A.D. 50 and 51 by Paul from Corinth to the Christians in Thessalonica, Greece. These new believers were facing tough persecution from both the Jews and the Gentiles.

Paul had personally evangelized the Thessalonians with several people making commitments to Jesus Christ. But the outraged Jewish population forced Paul to escape by night to the city of Berea, sixty miles away. When a group of Jews followed Paul, he had to flee a second time to the city of Athens.

Since Paul's absence, the new church was the focus of persecution. Paul writes to encourage them and to rejoice with his friends as they grow in their faith. They have remained steadfast, despite the troubles, and have even grown stronger during their trials. Paul commends them for turning their thoughts to God, not to their problems.

We give thanks to God always for you all, making mention of you in our prayers, remembering without ceasing your work of faith, labor of love, and patience of hope in our Lord Jesus Christ in the sight of our God and Father.

(1 Thess. 1:2, 3)

Paul was not unfamiliar with persecution because of a faithful testimony. He had experienced trouble throughout the Roman empire. Even so, he had learned to focus his efforts on the present in light of the second coming of Jesus Christ. This is what he urges the Thessalonians to do. The present life, despite its problems, is a precious gift from God which should be enjoyed. Paul assures them that God's faithful ability could accomplish anything in their lives "He who calls you *is* faithful, who also will do *it*" (1 Thess. 5:24). God is stronger and bigger than any problem!

The First Epistle of Paul the Apostle to the

Thessalonians

Greeting

PAUL, Silvanus, and Timothy,

To the church of the Thessalonians in God the Father and the Lord Jesus Christ:

Grace to you and peace from God our Father and the Lord Jesus Christ.[1]

Their Good Example

2 We give thanks to God always for you all, making mention of you in our prayers,
3 remembering without ceasing your work of faith, labor of love, and patience of hope in our Lord Jesus Christ in the sight of our God and Father,
4 knowing, beloved brethren, your election by God.
5 For our gospel did not come to you in word only, but also in power, and in the Holy Spirit and in much assurance, as you know what kind of men we were among you for your sake.
6 And you became followers of us and of the Lord, having received the word in much affliction, with joy of the Holy Spirit,
7 so that you became examples to all in Macedonia and Achaia who believe.
8 For from you the word of the Lord has sounded forth, not only in Macedonia and Achaia, but also in every place. Your faith toward God has gone out, so that we do not need to say anything.
9 For they themselves declare concerning us what manner of entry we had to you, and how you turned to God from idols to serve the living and true God,
10 and to wait for His Son from heaven, whom He raised from the dead, *even* Jesus who delivers us from the wrath to come.

Paul's Conduct

2 For you yourselves know, brethren, that our coming to you was not in vain.

2 But even[2] after we had suffered before and were spitefully treated at Philippi, as you know, we were bold in our God to speak to you the gospel of God in much conflict.
3 For our exhortation *did* not *come* from deceit or uncleanness, nor *was it* in guile.
4 But as we have been approved by God to be entrusted with the gospel, even so we speak, not as pleasing men, but God who tests our hearts.
5 For neither at any time did we use flattering words, as you know, nor a cloak for covetousness—God *is* witness.
6 Nor did we seek glory from men, either from you or from others, when we might have made demands as apostles of Christ.
7 But we were gentle among you, just as a nursing *mother* cherishes her own children.
8 So, affectionately longing for you, we were well pleased to impart to you not only the gospel of God, but also our own lives, because you had become dear to us.
9 For you remember, brethren, our labor and toil; for laboring night and day, that we might not be a burden to any of you, we preached to you the gospel of God.
10 You *are* witnesses, and God *also*, how devoutly and justly and blamelessly we behaved ourselves among you who believe;
11 as you know how we exhorted, and comforted, and charged every one of you, as a father *does* his own children,
12 that you would have a walk worthy of God who calls you into His own kingdom and glory.

Their Conversion

13 For this reason we also thank God without ceasing, because when you received the word of God which you heard from us, you welcomed *it* not *as* the word of men, but as it is in truth, the word of

---

1 NU-Text omits *from God our Father and the Lord Jesus Christ.*   2 NU-Text and M-Text omit *even.*

In the Name of God

Some trust in chariots, and some in horses;
But we will remember the name of the LORD our God.
(Ps. 20:7)

In ancient times, it was customary to invoke the name of a ruler or king to validate authority. Letters were sent between pharaohs, princes, and emperors bearing the scarab seal or signet ring imprint of the name of the monarch. Messengers presenting themselves before kings were introduced as coming in the name of the ruler who sent them.

Archaeologists have unearthed much evidence that names played a dominant role in the ancient Middle East society. Various forms of communication have been found containing the name of Thutmose III, Sennacherib, Alexander the Great, Cleopatra, and the Roman caesars. Greetings were exchanged, victories declared, cities built, peace made, and worship invoked in the name of rulers and gods.

This belief that the name had special power was so important that people put their trust in the name they considered to have supreme authority. To ridicule or curse the name of a ruler or god was to make an assault on the individual.

The concept of going in the name of a ruler carried over into the New Testament period and is often reflected in the words of Jesus. In teaching His disciples how to pray, Jesus asked them to respect or "hallow" the name of God. Jesus told His followers that belief in His name would grant them eternal life.

The New Testament apostles declared that at the name of Jesus every knee shall bow. Many of the Epistles open with an invocation mentioning the name of Jesus. The early Christians were encouraged to come to one another in the name of Jesus. Spiritual victories and great power and authority were associated with His name.

In our lives, this power of the name of Jesus is as real as it was in the early church. If we place our trust in Him and in our God, then we have access to the greatest authority and power. In our daily existence, we may hear people talk about how they work for a large, important company, how they take pride in their family name, or how they act under the auspices of a specific title. This is all fine. But as Christians, we come in the name of the supreme authority. We come in the name of the Lord. And we have the promise that He gave to us, "Whatever you ask in prayer, believing, you will receive" (Matt. 21:22). "And nothing will be impossible for you" (Matt. 17:20).

God, which also effectively works in you who believe.

14 For you, brethren, became imitators of the churches of God which are in Judea in Christ Jesus. For you also suffered the same things from your own countrymen, just as they *did* from the Jews, 15 who killed both the Lord Jesus and their own prophets, and have persecuted us; and they do not please God and are contrary to all men, 16 forbidding us to speak to the Gentiles that they may be saved, so as always to fill up *the measure of* their sins; but wrath has come upon them to the uttermost.

Longing to See Them

17 But we, brethren, having been taken away from you for a short time in presence, not in heart, endeavored more eagerly to see your face with great desire. 18 Therefore we wanted to come to you—even I, Paul, time and again—but Satan hindered us. 19 For what *is* our hope, or joy, or crown of rejoicing? *Is it* not even you in the presence of our Lord Jesus Christ at His coming? 20 For you are our glory and joy.

Concern for Their Faith

3 Therefore, when we could no longer endure it, we thought it good to be left in Athens alone, 2 and sent Timothy, our brother and minister of God, and our fellow laborer in the gospel of Christ, to establish you and encourage you concerning your faith, 3 that no one should be shaken by these afflictions; for you yourselves know that we are appointed to this. 4 For, in fact, we told you before when we were with you that we would suffer tribulation, just as it happened, and you know. 5 For this reason, when I could no longer endure it, I sent to know your faith, lest by some means the tempter had tempted you, and our labor might be in vain.

Encouraged by Timothy

6 But now that Timothy has come to us from you, and brought us good news of your faith and love, and that you always have good remembrance of us, greatly desiring to see us, as we also *to see* you— 7 therefore, brethren, in all our afflic-

tion and distress we were comforted concerning you by your faith. 8 For now we live, if you stand fast in the Lord. 9 For what thanks can we render to God for you, for all the joy with which we rejoice for your sake before our God, 10 night and day praying exceedingly that we may see your face and perfect what is lacking in your faith?

Prayer for the Church

11 Now may our God and Father Himself, and our Lord Jesus Christ, direct our way to you. 12 And may the Lord make you increase and abound in love to one another and to all, just as we *do* to you, 13 so that He may establish your hearts blameless in holiness before our God and Father at the coming of our Lord Jesus Christ with all His saints.

Plea for Purity

4 Finally then, brethren, we urge and exhort in the Lord Jesus that you should abound more and more, just as you received from us how you ought to walk and to please God; 2 for you know what commandments we gave you through the Lord Jesus. 3 For this is the will of God, your sanctification: that you should abstain from sexual immorality; 4 that each of you should know how to possess his own vessel in sanctification and honor, 5 not in passion of lust, like the Gentiles who do not know God; 6 that no one should take advantage of and defraud his brother in this matter, because the Lord *is* the avenger of all such, as we also forewarned you and testified. 7 For God did not call us to uncleanness, but in holiness. 8 Therefore he who rejects *this* does not reject man, but God, who has also given[3] us His Holy Spirit.

A Brotherly and Orderly Life

9 But concerning brotherly love you have no need that I should write to you, for you yourselves are taught by God to love one another; 10 and indeed you do so toward all the brethren who are in all Macedonia. But

3 NU-Text reads *who also gives.*

we urge you, brethren, that you increase more and more;

11 that you also aspire to lead a quiet life, to mind your own business, and to work with your own hands, as we commanded you,

12 that you may walk properly toward those who are outside, and *that* you may lack nothing.

The Comfort of Christ's Coming

13 But I do not want you to be ignorant, brethren, concerning those who have fallen asleep, lest you sorrow as others who have no hope.

14 For if we believe that Jesus died and rose again, even so God will bring with Him those who sleep in Jesus.[4]

15 For this we say to you by the word of the Lord, that we who are alive *and* remain until the coming of the Lord will by no means precede those who are asleep.

16 For the Lord Himself will descend from heaven with a shout, with the voice of an archangel, and with the trumpet of God. And the dead in Christ will rise first.

17 Then we who are alive *and* remain shall be caught up together with them in the clouds to meet the Lord in the air. And thus we shall always be with the Lord.

18 Therefore comfort one another with these words.

The Day of the Lord

5 But concerning the times and the seasons, brethren, you have no need that I should write to you.

2 For you yourselves know perfectly that the day of the Lord so comes as a thief in the night.

3 For when they say, "Peace and safety!" then sudden destruction comes upon them, as labor pains upon a pregnant woman. And they shall not escape.

4 But you, brethren, are not in darkness, so that this Day should overtake you as a thief.

5 You are all sons of light and sons of the day. We are not of the night nor of darkness.

6 Therefore let us not sleep, as others *do*, but let us watch and be sober.

7 For those who sleep, sleep at night, and those who get drunk are drunk at night.

8 But let us who are of the day be sober, putting on the breastplate of faith and love, and *as* a helmet the hope of salvation.

9 For God did not appoint us to wrath, but to obtain salvation through our Lord Jesus Christ,

10 who died for us, that whether we wake or sleep, we should live together with Him.

11 Therefore comfort each other and edify one another, just as you also are doing.

Various Exhortations

12 And we urge you, brethren, to recognize those who labor among you, and are over you in the Lord and admonish you,

13 and to esteem them very highly in love for their work's sake. Be at peace among yourselves.

14 Now we exhort you, brethren, warn those who are unruly, comfort the fainthearted, uphold the weak, be patient with all.

15 See that no one renders evil for evil to anyone, but always pursue what is good both for yourselves and for all.

16 Rejoice always,

17 pray without ceasing,

18 in everything give thanks; for this is the will of God in Christ Jesus for you.

19 Do not quench the Spirit.

20 Do not despise prophecies.

21 Test all things; hold fast what is good.

22 Abstain from every form of evil.

Blessing and Admonition

23 Now may the God of peace Himself sanctify you completely; and may your whole spirit, soul, and body be preserved blameless at the coming of our Lord Jesus Christ.

24 He who calls you *is* faithful, who also will do *it.*

25 Brethren, pray for us.

26 Greet all the brethren with a holy kiss.

27 I charge you by the Lord that this epistle be read to all the holy[5] brethren.

28 The grace of our Lord Jesus Christ *be* with you. Amen.

4 Or *those who through Jesus sleep*   5 NU-Text omits *holy.*

Introduction to Second Thessalonians

The Thessalonians are outstanding examples of Christian believers who stood firm in their faith and showed love and charity toward each other. Second Thessalonians is the second of Paul's letters from Corinth to these believers, written only a few months following his first correspondence in A.D. 51.

Possibly due to their location on the *Via Egnatia*—the famous highway from Rome to the east, the Thessalonians were exposed to itinerant false teachers claiming that the second coming of Christ was about to take place. In response, the people had left their jobs and businesses to await the Lord's return.

Paul exhorts them to return to work and to be patient regarding God's timing for Jesus' return. He urges them not to be so heavenly minded that they were no earthly good.

Paul encourages the Thessalonians to continue living the positive Christian life-style which they were committed to. They should also plan for their future—because they would have to live there! And as they plan, Paul prays that God may give them peace in every circumstance, knowing God was with them. God's presence is not to be just in the future, but is in the present also!

Therefore, brethren, stand fast and hold the traditions which you were taught, whether by word or our epistle. Now may our Lord Jesus Christ Himself, and our God and Father, who has loved us and given *us* everlasting consolation and good hope by grace, comfort your hearts and establish you in every good word and work.

(2 Thess. 2:15–17)

The Second Epistle of Paul the Apostle to the

Thessalonians

Greeting

PAUL, Silvanus, and Timothy,

To the church of the Thessalonians in God our Father and the Lord Jesus Christ:

2 Grace to you and peace from God our Father and the Lord Jesus Christ.

God's Final Judgment and Glory

3 We are bound to thank God always for you, brethren, as it is fitting, because your faith grows exceedingly, and the love of every one of you all abounds toward each other,

4 so that we ourselves boast of you among the churches of God for your patience and faith in all your persecutions and tribulations that you endure,

5 *which is* manifest evidence of the righteous judgment of God, that you may be counted worthy of the kingdom of God, for which you also suffer;

6 since *it is* a righteous thing with God to repay with tribulation those who trouble you,

7 and to *give* you who are troubled rest with us when the Lord Jesus is revealed from heaven with His mighty angels,

8 in flaming fire taking vengeance on those who do not know God, and on those who do not obey the gospel of our Lord Jesus Christ.

9 These shall be punished with everlasting destruction from the presence of the Lord and from the glory of His power,

10 when He comes, in that Day, to be glorified in His saints and to be admired among all those who believe,[1] because our testimony among you was believed.

11 Therefore we also pray always for you that our God would count you worthy of *this* calling, and fulfill all the good pleasure of *His* goodness and the work of faith with power,

12 that the name of our Lord Jesus Christ may be glorified in you, and you in Him, according to the grace of our God and the Lord Jesus Christ.

The Great Apostasy

2 Now, brethren, concerning the coming of our Lord Jesus Christ and our gathering together to Him, we ask you,

2 not to be soon shaken in mind or troubled, either by spirit or by word or by letter, as if from us, as though the day of Christ[2] had come.

3 Let no one deceive you by any means; for *that Day will not come* unless the falling away comes first, and the man of sin[3] is revealed, the son of perdition,

4 who opposes and exalts himself above all that is called God or that is worshiped, so that he sits as God[4] in the temple of God, showing himself that he is God.

5 Do you not remember that when I was still with you I told you these things?

6 And now you know what is restraining, that he may be revealed in his own time.

7 For the mystery of lawlessness is already at work; only He[5] who now restrains *will do so* until He is taken out of the way.

8 And then the lawless one will be revealed, whom the Lord will consume with the breath of His mouth and destroy with the brightness of His coming.

9 The coming of the *lawless one* is according to the working of Satan, with all power, signs, and lying wonders,

10 and with all unrighteous deception among those who perish, because they did not receive the love of the truth, that they might be saved.

11 And for this reason God will send them strong delusion, that they should believe the lie,

12 that they all may be condemned who did not believe the truth but had pleasure in unrighteousness.

---

1 NU-Text and M-Text read *have believed.*   2 NU-Text reads *Lord.*   3 NU-Text reads *lawlessness.*
4 NU-Text omits *as God.*   5 Or *he*

Stand Fast

13 But we are bound to give thanks to God always for you, brethren beloved by the Lord, because God from the beginning chose you for salvation through sanctification by the Spirit and belief in the truth,

14 to which He called you by our gospel, for the obtaining of the glory of our Lord Jesus Christ.

15 Therefore, brethren, stand fast and hold the traditions which you were taught, whether by word or our epistle.

16 Now may our Lord Jesus Christ Himself, and our God and Father, who has loved us and given *us* everlasting consolation and good hope by grace,

17 comfort your hearts and establish you in every good word and work.

Pray for Us

3 Finally, brethren, pray for us, that the word of the Lord may have *free* course and be glorified, just as *it is* with you,

2 and that we may be delivered from unreasonable and wicked men; for not all have faith.

3 But the Lord is faithful, who will establish you and guard *you* from the evil one.

4 And we have confidence in the Lord concerning you, both that you do and will do the things we command you.

5 Now may the Lord direct your hearts into the love of God and into the patience of Christ.

Warning Against Idleness

6 But we command you, brethren, in the name of our Lord Jesus Christ, that

6 NU-Text and M-Text read *they.*

you withdraw from every brother who walks disorderly and not according to the tradition which he[6] received from us.

7 For you yourselves know how you ought to follow us, for we were not disorderly among you;

8 nor did we eat anyone's bread free of charge, but worked with labor and toil night and day, that we might not be a burden to any of you,

9 not because we do not have authority, but to make ourselves an example of how you should follow us.

10 For even when we were with you, we commanded you this: If anyone will not work, neither shall he eat.

11 For we hear that there are some who walk among you in a disorderly manner, not working at all, but are busybodies.

12 Now those who are such we command and exhort through our Lord Jesus Christ that they work in quietness and eat their own bread.

13 But *as for* you, brethren, do not grow weary *in* doing good.

14 And if anyone does not obey our word in this epistle, note that person and do not keep company with him, that he may be ashamed.

15 Yet do not count *him* as an enemy, but admonish *him* as a brother.

Benediction

16 Now may the Lord of peace Himself give you peace always in every way. The Lord *be* with you all.

17 The salutation of Paul with my own hand, which is a sign in every epistle; so I write.

18 The grace of our Lord Jesus Christ *be* with you all. Amen.

Introduction to
First Timothy

Encouragement can be one of the greatest gifts you will ever give or receive. Never be afraid to accept or offer encouragement when it is in your power to do so.

First Timothy, Second Timothy, and Titus are known as the Pastoral Epistles. Written around A.D. 62, from Macedonia, these letters contain advice to a young pastor, Timothy, regarding the church in Ephesus.

Paul encourages Timothy in his work, urging him not to be ashamed of his youth. Even though he is young, God will use him. The goal of Timothy's instruction should be love from a pure heart, a good conscience, and sincere faith. "Let no one despise your youth, but be an example to the believers in word, in conduct, in love, in spirit, in faith, in purity" (1 Tim. 4:12).

Although this book deals primarily with church matters, it also offers possibility thinking attitudes. Paul encourages Timothy to help his congregation establish wisdom and right values. He points out that contentment does not come from possessions, but from a positive attitude toward life.

Finally, Paul urges Timothy not to neglect the gift that God has given him. He should train his faith with self-discipline as does an athlete. "Meditate on these things; give yourself entirely to them, that your progress may be evident to all" (1 Tim. 4:15).

This great letter of inspiration points out a dynamic lesson to Timothy and to all people hoping to do the work of God: What you are is God's gift to you. What you become is your gift to God!

Lord, make my life a window for Your light to shine through and a mirror to reflect Your love to all I meet! Amen.

The First Epistle of Paul the Apostle to
Timothy

Greeting

PAUL, an apostle of Jesus Christ, by the commandment of God our Savior and the Lord Jesus Christ, our hope,

2 To Timothy, *my* true son in the faith:

Grace, mercy, *and* peace from God our Father and Jesus Christ our Lord.

No Other Doctrine

3 As I urged you when I went into Macedonia—remain in Ephesus that you may charge some that they teach no other doctrine,

4 nor give heed to fables and endless genealogies, which cause disputes rather than godly edification which is in faith.

5 Now the purpose of the commandment is love from a pure heart, *from* a good conscience, and *from* sincere faith,

6 from which some, having strayed, have turned aside to idle talk,

7 desiring to be teachers of the law, understanding neither what they say nor the things which they affirm.

8 But we know that the law *is* good if one uses it lawfully,

9 knowing this: that the law is not made for a righteous person, but for *the* lawless and insubordinate, for *the* ungodly and for sinners, for *the* unholy and profane, for murderers of fathers and murderers of mothers, for manslayers,

10 for fornicators, for sodomites, for kidnappers, for liars, for perjurers, and if there is any other thing that is contrary to sound doctrine,

11 according to the glorious gospel of the blessed God which was committed to my trust.

Glory to God for His Grace

12 And I thank Christ Jesus our Lord who has enabled me, because He counted me faithful, putting *me* into the ministry,

13 although I was formerly a blasphemer, a persecutor, and an insolent man; but I obtained mercy because I did *it* ignorantly in unbelief.

14 And the grace of our Lord was exceedingly abundant, with faith and love which are in Christ Jesus.

15 This *is* a faithful saying and worthy of all acceptance, that Christ Jesus came into the world to save sinners, of whom I am chief.

16 However, for this reason I obtained mercy, that in me first Jesus Christ might show all longsuffering, as a pattern to those who are going to believe on Him for everlasting life.

17 Now to the King eternal, immortal, invisible, to God who alone is wise,[1] *be* honor and glory forever and ever. Amen.

Fight the Good Fight

18 This charge I commit to you, son Timothy, according to the prophecies previously made concerning you, that by them you may wage the good warfare,

19 having faith and a good conscience, which some having rejected, concerning the faith have suffered shipwreck,

20 of whom are Hymenaeus and Alexander, whom I delivered to Satan that they may learn not to blaspheme.

Pray for All Men

2 Therefore I exhort first of all that supplications, prayers, intercessions, *and* giving of thanks be made for all men,

2 for kings and all who are in authority, that we may lead a quiet and peaceable life in all godliness and reverence.

3 For this *is* good and acceptable in the sight of God our Savior,

4 who desires all men to be saved and to come to the knowledge of the truth.

5 For *there is* one God and one Mediator between God and men, *the* Man Christ Jesus,

6 who gave Himself a ransom for all, to be testified in due time,

7 for which I was appointed a preacher and an apostle—I am speaking the truth in Christ[2] *and* not lying—a teacher of the Gentiles in faith and truth.

1 NU-Text reads *to the only God.*   2 NU-Text omits *in Christ.*

Men and Women in the Church

8 Therefore I desire that the men pray everywhere, lifting up holy hands, without wrath and doubting;
9 in like manner also, that the women adorn themselves in modest apparel, with propriety and moderation, not with braided hair or gold or pearls or costly clothing,
10 but, which is proper for women professing godliness, with good works.
11 Let a woman learn in silence with all submission.
12 And I do not permit a woman to teach or to have authority over a man, but to be in silence.
13 For Adam was formed first, then Eve.
14 And Adam was not deceived, but the woman being deceived, fell into transgression.
15 Nevertheless she will be saved in childbearing if they continue in faith, love, and holiness, with self-control.

Qualifications of Overseers

3 This *is* a faithful saying: If a man desires the position of a bishop,[3] he desires a good work.
2 A bishop then must be blameless, the husband of one wife, temperate, sober-minded, of good behavior, hospitable, able to teach;
3 not given to wine, not violent, not greedy for money,[4] but gentle, not quarrelsome, not covetous;
4 one who rules his own house well, having *his* children in submission with all reverence
5 (for if a man does not know how to rule his own house, how will he take care of the church of God?);
6 not a novice, lest being puffed up with pride he fall into the *same* condemnation as the devil.
7 Moreover he must have a good testimony among those who are outside, lest he fall into reproach and the snare of the devil.

Qualifications of Deacons

8 Likewise deacons *must be* reverent, not double-tongued, not given to much wine, not greedy for money,
9 holding the mystery of the faith with a pure conscience.
10 But let these also first be proved; then

let them serve as deacons, being *found* blameless.
11 Likewise *their* wives *must be* reverent, not slanderers, temperate, faithful in all things.
12 Let deacons be the husbands of one wife, ruling *their* children and their own houses well.
13 For those who have served well as deacons obtain for themselves a good standing and great boldness in the faith which is in Christ Jesus.

The Great Mystery

14 These things I write to you, though I hope to come to you shortly;
15 but if I am delayed, *I write* so that you may know how you ought to conduct yourself in the house of God, which is the church of the living God, the pillar and ground of the truth.
16 And without controversy great is the mystery of godliness:

God[5] was manifested in the flesh,
Justified in the Spirit,
Seen by angels,
Preached among the Gentiles,
Believed on in the world,
Received up in glory.

The Great Apostasy

4 Now the Spirit expressly says that in latter times some will depart from the faith, giving heed to deceiving spirits and doctrines of demons,
2 speaking lies in hypocrisy, having their own conscience seared with a hot iron,
3 forbidding to marry, *and commanding* to abstain from foods which God created to be received with thanksgiving by those who believe and know the truth.
4 For every creature of God *is* good, and nothing is to be refused if it is received with thanksgiving;
5 for it is sanctified by the word of God and prayer.

A Good Servant of Jesus Christ

6 If you instruct the brethren in these things, you will be a good minister of Jesus Christ, nourished in the words of faith and of the good doctrine which you have carefully followed.
7 But reject profane and old wives' fables, and exercise yourself *rather* to godliness.

3 Literally *overseer*   4 NU-Text omits *not greedy for money.*   5 NU-Text reads *who.*

8 For bodily exercise profits a little, but godliness is profitable for all things, having promise of the life that now is and of that which is to come.

9 This *is* a faithful saying and worthy of all acceptance.

10 For to this *end* we both labor and suffer reproach,[6] because we trust in the living God, who is *the* Savior of all men, especially of those who believe.

Take Heed to Your Ministry

11 These things command and teach.

12 Let no one despise your youth, but be an example to the believers in word, in conduct, in love, in spirit,[7] in faith, in purity.

13 Till I come, give attention to reading, to exhortation, to doctrine.

14 Do not neglect the gift that is in you, which was given to you by prophecy with the laying on of the hands of the presbytery.

15 Meditate on these things; give yourself entirely to them, that your progress may be evident to all.

16 Take heed to yourself and to the doctrine. Continue in them, for in doing this you will save both yourself and those who hear you.

Treatment of Church Members

5 Do not rebuke an older man, but exhort *him* as a father, *the* younger men as brothers,

2 *the* older women as mothers, *the* younger as sisters, with all purity.

Honor True Widows

3 Honor widows who are really widows.

4 But if any widow has children or grandchildren, let them first learn to show piety at home and to repay their parents; for this is good and[8] acceptable before God.

5 Now she who is really a widow, and left alone, trusts in God and continues in supplications and prayers night and day.

6 But she who lives in pleasure is dead while she lives.

7 And these things command, that they may be blameless.

8 But if anyone does not provide for his own, and especially for those of his household, he has denied the faith and is worse than an unbeliever.

9 Do not let a widow under sixty years old be taken into the number, *and not unless* she has been the wife of one man,

10 well reported for good works: if she has brought up children, if she has lodged strangers, if she has washed the saints' feet, if she has relieved the afflicted, if she has diligently followed every good work.

11 But refuse *the* younger widows; for when they have begun to grow wanton against Christ, they desire to marry,

12 having condemnation because they have cast off their first faith.

13 And besides they learn *to be* idle, wandering about from house to house, and not only idle but also gossips and busybodies, saying things which they ought not.

14 Therefore I desire that *the* younger widows marry, bear children, manage the house, give no opportunity to the adversary to speak reproachfully.

15 For some have already turned aside after Satan.

16 If any believing man or[9] woman has widows, let them relieve them, and do not let the church be burdened, that it may relieve those who are really widows.

Honor the Elders

17 Let the elders who rule well be counted worthy of double honor, especially those who labor in the word and doctrine.

18 For the Scripture says, *"You shall not muzzle an ox while it treads out the grain,"*[10] and, "The laborer *is* worthy of his wages."[11]

19 Do not receive an accusation against an elder except from two or three witnesses.

20 Those who are sinning rebuke in the presence of all, that the rest also may fear.

21 I charge *you* before God and the Lord Jesus Christ and the elect angels that you observe these things without prejudice, doing nothing with partiality.

22 Do not lay hands on anyone hastily, nor share in other people's sins; keep yourself pure.

23 No longer drink only water, but use a little wine for your stomach's sake and your frequent infirmities.

24 Some men's sins are clearly evident,

---

6 NU-Text reads *We labor and strive.*   7 NU-Text omits *in spirit.*   8 NU-Text and M-Text omit *good and.*
9 NU-Text omits *man or.*   10 Deuteronomy 25:4   11 Luke 10:7

preceding *them* to judgment, but those of some *men* follow later.

25 Likewise, the good works *of some* are clearly evident, and those that are otherwise cannot be hidden.

Honor Masters

6 Let as many servants as are under the yoke count their own masters worthy of all honor, so that the name of God and *His* doctrine may not be blasphemed.

2 And those who have believing masters, let them not despise *them* because they are brethren, but rather serve *them* because those who are benefited are believers and beloved. Teach and exhort these things.

Error and Greed

3 If anyone teaches otherwise and does not consent to wholesome words, *even* the words of our Lord Jesus Christ, and to the doctrine which is according to godliness,

4 he is proud, knowing nothing, but is obsessed with disputes and arguments over words, from which come envy, strife, reviling, evil suspicions,

5 useless wranglings of men of corrupt minds and destitute of the truth, who suppose that godliness is a *means of* gain. From such withdraw yourself.[12]

6 But godliness with contentment is great gain.

7 For we brought nothing into *this* world, *and it is* certain[13] we can carry nothing out.

8 And having food and clothing, with these we shall be content.

9 But those who desire to be rich fall into temptation and a snare, and *into* many foolish and harmful lusts which drown men in destruction and perdition.

10 For the love of money is a root of all *kinds of* evil, for which some have strayed from the faith in their greediness, and pierced themselves through with many sorrows.

The Good Confession

11 But you, O man of God, flee these things and pursue righteousness, godliness, faith, love, patience, gentleness.

12 Fight the good fight of faith, lay hold on eternal life, to which you were also called and have confessed the good confession in the presence of many witnesses.

13 I urge you in the sight of God who gives life to all things, and *before* Christ Jesus who witnessed the good confession before Pontius Pilate,

14 that you keep *this* commandment without spot, blameless until our Lord Jesus Christ's appearing,

15 which He will manifest in His own time, *He who is* the blessed and only Potentate, the King of kings and Lord of lords,

16 who alone has immortality, dwelling in unapproachable light, whom no man has seen or can see, to whom *be* honor and everlasting power. Amen.

Instructions to the Rich

17 Command those who are rich in this present age not to be haughty, nor to trust in uncertain riches but in the living God, who gives us richly all things to enjoy.

18 *Let them* do good, that they be rich in good works, ready to give, willing to share,

19 storing up for themselves a good foundation for the time to come, that they may lay hold on eternal life.

Guard the Faith

20 O Timothy! Guard what was committed to your trust, avoiding the profane *and* vain babblings and contradictions of what is falsely called knowledge—

21 by professing it, some have strayed concerning the faith. Grace *be* with you. Amen.

12 NU-Text omits this sentence.   13 NU-Text omits *and it is certain.*

Introduction to
Second Timothy

Second Timothy is a work of great inspiration by the apostle Paul. Written probably in A.D. 67 while he was imprisoned in Rome, this letter demonstrates Paul's positive attitude despite the negative circumstances of his life.

Paul writes the young pastor, Timothy, to encourage him and to continue his training. Now sixty years old, Paul hopes to share his insights of over thirty years in the ministry. As he writes to Timothy, we learn that the apostle is facing a death sentence and the Christians who once supported him have now deserted him.

> For this reason I also suffer these things; nevertheless I am not ashamed, for I know whom I have believed and am persuaded that He is able to keep what I have committed to Him until that Day.
>
> (2 Tim. 1:12)

Nonetheless, Paul's letter exudes positive faith-building news. He never expresses bitterness to those who have forsaken him. In spite of being abandoned, he neither condemns nor criticizes anyone. He only seeks to build up others and to continue the ministry which God has given him.

> I have fought the good fight, I have finished the race, I have kept the faith. Finally, there is laid up for me the crown of righteousness, which the Lord, the righteous Judge, will give to me on that Day, and not to me only but also to all who have loved His appearing.
>
> (2 Tim. 4:7, 8)

While awaiting final trial, Paul helps to convert members of Caesar's household. During the greatest test of his faith, Paul overcomes with possibility thinking! He knows that a star is best seen at night. And even though his friends have left him, God will never leave him. Paul is confident that God will help him to keep on keeping on. He knows that tough times never last, but tough people do!

The Second Epistle of Paul the Apostle to

Timothy

Greeting

PAUL, an apostle of Jesus Christ[1] by the will of God, according to the promise of life which is in Christ Jesus,

2 To Timothy, *my* beloved son:

Grace, mercy, *and* peace from God the Father and Christ Jesus our Lord.

Timothy's Faith and Heritage

3 I thank God, whom I serve with a pure conscience, as *my* forefathers *did*, as without ceasing I remember you in my prayers night and day,

4 greatly desiring to see you, being mindful of your tears, that I may be filled with joy,

5 when I call to remembrance the genuine faith that is in you, which dwelt first in your grandmother Lois and your mother Eunice, and I am persuaded is in you also.

6 Therefore I remind you to stir up the gift of God which is in you through the laying on of my hands.

7 For God has not given us a spirit of fear, but of power and of love and of a sound mind.

Not Ashamed of the Gospel

8 Therefore do not be ashamed of the testimony of our Lord, nor of me His prisoner, but share with me in the sufferings for the gospel according to the power of God,

9 who has saved us and called *us* with a holy calling, not according to our works, but according to His own purpose and grace which was given to us in Christ Jesus before time began,

10 but has now been revealed by the appearing of our Savior Jesus Christ, *who* has abolished death and brought life and immortality to light through the gospel,

11 to which I was appointed a preacher, an apostle, and a teacher of the Gentiles.[2]

12 For this reason I also suffer these things; nevertheless I am not ashamed, for I know whom I have believed and am persuaded that He is able to keep what I have committed to Him until that Day.

Be Loyal to the Faith

13 Hold fast the pattern of sound words which you have heard from me, in faith and love which are in Christ Jesus.

14 That good thing which was committed to you, keep by the Holy Spirit who dwells in us.

15 This you know, that all those in Asia have turned away from me, among whom are Phygellus and Hermogenes.

16 The Lord grant mercy to the household of Onesiphorus, for he often refreshed me, and was not ashamed of my chain;

17 but when he arrived in Rome, he sought me out very diligently and found *me*.

18 The Lord grant to him that he may find mercy from the Lord in that Day— and you know very well how many ways he ministered to me at Ephesus.

Be Strong in Grace

2 You therefore, my son, be strong in the grace that is in Christ Jesus.

2 And the things that you have heard from me among many witnesses, commit these to faithful men who will be able to teach others also.

3 You therefore must endure[3] hardship as a good soldier of Jesus Christ.

4 No one engaged in warfare entangles himself with the affairs of *this* life, that he may please him who enlisted him as a soldier.

5 And also if anyone competes in athletics, he is not crowned unless he competes according to the rules.

6 The hard-working farmer must be first to partake of the crops.

7 Consider what I say, and may[4] the Lord give you understanding in all things.

8 Remember that Jesus Christ, of the

---

1 NU-Text and M-Text read *Christ Jesus*. 2 NU-Text omits *of the Gentiles*. 3 NU-Text reads *share*.
4 NU-Text reads *the Lord will give you*.

Lord, Send Us

Deep in the stone chambers beneath the Church of the Holy Sepulchre in Jerusalem is an inscription bearing silent witness to the early church. Etched upon the walls are the words, "Lord, we went . . ." Next to the inscription is a picture of a fishing boat rowing away from Palestine toward other lands of the Roman empire.

Jesus gave His disciples the commission, "As the Father has sent Me, I also send you" (John 20:21). It took great faith on the part of the disciples and the early Christians to realize that they were entrusted with the task of carrying the Good News of Jesus Christ's death, burial, and resurrection to a lost and dying world.

Most of the early Jewish Christians had never left the hill country of Judea. The Jews of that period had a tremendous fear of the sea. That was where Leviathan and other sea creatures lived. Through the centuries Israel had warred with people from the coastal areas.

Jesus instituted a revolutionary-type outlook of the world in the disciples. He enabled them to release their negative fears and to trust Him fully. We have the same comfort and assurance that Jesus gave to the early Christians. "But the Helper, the Holy Spirit, whom the Father will send in My name, He will teach you all things, and bring to your remembrance all things that I said to you" (John 14:26).

The disciples of the early church went forth in the knowledge that they were given Christ's peace and assurance. They could accomplish anything that they attempted to do—even convert the mighty Roman empire.

Etched in the wall opposite the inscription, "Lord, we went . . ." is the symbol of the mighty tenth and twelfth Roman legions from whose ranks came the soldiers who crucified Christ. The early Christians knew and understood the totality of Jesus' message of forgiveness. They put aside their prejudices against the Roman overlords and took the Good News of Jesus' love and forgiveness to lands and peoples whom they had suffered under.

May we be like the early disciples sent forth by God and leave an inscription of love, peace, joy, and forgiveness on the hearts and minds of those around us for coming generations to read—"Lord, we went."

seed of David, was raised from the dead according to my gospel,
9 for which I suffer trouble as an evildoer, *even* to the point of chains; but the word of God is not chained.
10 Therefore I endure all things for the sake of the elect, that they also may obtain the salvation which is in Christ Jesus with eternal glory.
11 *This is* a faithful saying:

For if we died with *Him,*
We shall also live with *Him.*
12 If we endure,
We shall also reign with *Him.*
If we deny *Him,*
He also will deny us.
13 If we are faithless,
He remains faithful;
He cannot deny Himself.

Approved and Disapproved Workers

14 Remind *them* of these things, charging *them* before the Lord not to strive about words to no profit, to the ruin of the hearers.
15 Be diligent to present yourself approved to God, a worker who does not need to be ashamed, rightly dividing the word of truth.
16 But shun profane *and* vain babblings, for they will increase to more ungodliness.
17 And their message will spread like cancer. Hymenaeus and Philetus are of this sort,
18 who have strayed concerning the truth, saying that the resurrection is already past; and they overthrow the faith of some.
19 Nevertheless the solid foundation of God stands, having this seal: "The Lord knows those who are His," and, "Let everyone who names the name of Christ[5] depart from iniquity."
20 But in a great house there are not only vessels of gold and silver, but also of wood and clay, some for honor and some for dishonor.
21 Therefore if anyone cleanses himself from the latter, he will be a vessel for honor, sanctified and useful for the Master, prepared for every good work.
22 Flee also youthful lusts; but pursue righteousness, faith, love, peace with those who call on the Lord out of a pure heart.

23 But avoid foolish and ignorant disputes, knowing that they generate strife.
24 And a servant of the Lord must not quarrel but be gentle to all, able to teach, patient,
25 in humility correcting those who are in opposition, if God perhaps will grant them repentance, so that they may know the truth,
26 and *that* they may come to their senses *and escape* the snare of the devil, having been taken captive by him to *do* his will.

Perilous Times and Perilous Men

3 But know this, that in the last days perilous times will come:
2 For men will be lovers of themselves, lovers of money, boasters, proud, blasphemers, disobedient to parents, unthankful, unholy,
3 unloving, unforgiving, slanderers, without self-control, brutal, despisers of good,
4 traitors, headstrong, haughty, lovers of pleasure rather than lovers of God,
5 having a form of godliness but denying its power. And from such people turn away!
6 For of this sort are those who creep into households and make captives of gullible women loaded down with sins, led away by various lusts,
7 always learning and never able to come to the knowledge of the truth.
8 Now as Jannes and Jambres resisted Moses, so do these also resist the truth: men of corrupt minds, disapproved concerning the faith;
9 but they will progress no further, for their folly will be manifest to all, as theirs also was.

The Man of God and the Word of God

10 But you have carefully followed my doctrine, manner of life, purpose, faith, longsuffering, love, perseverance,
11 persecutions, afflictions, which happened to me at Antioch, at Iconium, at Lystra—what persecutions I endured. And out of *them* all the Lord delivered me.
12 Yes, and all who desire to live godly in Christ Jesus will suffer persecution.
13 But evil men and impostors will grow worse and worse, deceiving and being deceived.

5 NU-Text and M-Text read *the Lord.*

14 But *as for* you, continue in the things which you have learned and been assured of, knowing from whom you have learned *them,*
15 and that from childhood you have known the Holy Scriptures, which are able to make you wise for salvation through faith which is in Christ Jesus.
16 All Scripture *is* given by inspiration of God, and *is* profitable for doctrine, for reproof, for correction, for instruction in righteousness,
17 that the man of God may be complete, thoroughly equipped for every good work.

Preach the Word

4 I charge *you* therefore before God and the Lord Jesus Christ, who will judge the living and the dead at[6] His appearing and His kingdom:
2 Preach the word! Be ready in season *and* out of season. Convince, rebuke, exhort, with all longsuffering and teaching.
3 For the time will come when they will not endure sound doctrine, but according to their own desires, *because* they have itching ears, they will heap up for themselves teachers;
4 and they will turn *their* ears away from the truth, and be turned aside to fables.
5 But you be watchful in all things, endure afflictions, do the work of an evangelist, fulfill your ministry.

Paul's Valedictory

6 For I am already being poured out *as a drink offering,* and the time of my departure is at hand.
7 I have fought the good fight, I have finished the race, I have kept the faith.
8 Finally, there is laid up for me the crown of righteousness, which the Lord, the righteous Judge, will give to me on that Day, and not to me only but also to all who have loved His appearing.

The Abandoned Apostle

9 Be diligent to come to me quickly;
10 for Demas has forsaken me, having loved this present world, and has departed for Thessalonica—Crescens for Galatia, Titus for Dalmatia.
11 Only Luke is with me. Get Mark and bring him with you, for he is useful to me for ministry.
12 And Tychicus I have sent to Ephesus.
13 Bring the cloak that I left with Carpus at Troas when you come—and the books, especially the parchments.
14 Alexander the coppersmith did me much harm. May the Lord repay him according to his works.
15 You also must beware of him, for he has greatly resisted our words.
16 At my first defense no one stood with me, but all forsook me. May it not be charged against them.

The Lord Is Faithful

17 But the Lord stood with me and strengthened me, so that the message might be preached fully through me, and *that* all the Gentiles might hear. And I was delivered out of the mouth of the lion.
18 And the Lord will deliver me from every evil work and preserve *me* for His heavenly kingdom. To Him *be* glory forever and ever. Amen!

Come before Winter

19 Greet Prisca and Aquila, and the household of Onesiphorus.
20 Erastus stayed in Corinth, but Trophimus I have left in Miletus sick.
21 Do your utmost to come before winter. Eubulus greets you, as well as Pudens, Linus, Claudia, and all the brethren.

Farewell

22 The Lord Jesus Christ[7] be with your spirit. Grace be with you. Amen.

6 NU-Text omits *therefore* and reads *by* for *at.*   7 NU-Text omits *Jesus Christ.*

Introduction to Titus

Paul taught Titus to believe that his church had real possibilities. In any environment the church can grow and prosper.

The apostle Paul wrote this letter from Greece between A.D. 62 and 65 to Titus, a Christian pastor residing on the island of Crete. The major thrust of the book concerns the administration of the churches at Crete.

Paul commends Titus, encouraging him to be a great pastor. Titus' earnestness as a successful church leader is mentioned as a challenging example to the Corinthians. Titus must meet some challenges of his own in guiding the churches. He must continue to avoid legalistic or mythical influences which would creep into the church. Paul exhorts Titus to speak things which adorn the doctrine of God, those words which are positive, inspirational, and uplifting. Titus is to be a positive leader and is not to surrender leadership to his problems; Titus is to take control of the situation to reshape, reorganize, and rejuvinate the church so that it will share the positive, life-giving message of Jesus Christ with a dying world.

Titus is encouraged to focus his thoughts on God and the blessed hope of Jesus Christ's return. Paul urges him to focus on God and not on his problems. For we are saved through faith in Jesus Christ, the demonstration of God's love for us.

For the grace of God that brings salvation has appeared to all men, teaching us that, denying ungodliness and worldly lusts, we should live soberly, righteously, and godly in the present age, looking for the blessed hope and glorious appearing of our great God and Savior Jesus Christ.

(Titus 2:11-13)

The Epistle of Paul the Apostle to

Titus

Greeting

PAUL, a servant of God and an apostle of Jesus Christ, according to the faith of God's elect and the acknowledgment of the truth which is according to godliness,

2 in hope of eternal life which God, who cannot lie, promised before time began,

3 but has in due time manifested His word through preaching, which was committed to me according to the commandment of God our Savior;

4 To Titus, *my* true son in *our* common faith:

Grace, mercy, *and* peace from God the Father and the Lord Jesus Christ[1] our Savior.

Qualified Elders

5 For this reason I left you in Crete, that you should set in order the things that are lacking, and appoint elders in every city as I commanded you—

6 if a man is blameless, the husband of one wife, having faithful children not accused of dissipation or insubordination.

7 For a bishop[2] must be blameless, as a steward of God, not self-willed, not quick-tempered, not given to wine, not violent, not greedy for money,

8 but hospitable, a lover of what is good, sober-minded, just, holy, self-controlled,

9 holding fast the faithful word as he has been taught, that he may be able, by sound doctrine, both to exhort and convict those who contradict.

The Elders' Task

10 For there are many insubordinate, both idle talkers and deceivers, especially those of the circumcision,

11 whose mouths must be stopped, who subvert whole households, teaching things which they ought not, for the sake of dishonest gain.

12 One of them, a prophet of their own, said, "Cretans *are* always liars, evil beasts, lazy gluttons."

13 This testimony is true. Therefore rebuke them sharply, that they may be sound in the faith,

14 not giving heed to Jewish fables and commandments of men who turn from the truth.

15 To the pure all things are pure, but to those who are defiled and unbelieving nothing is pure; but even their mind and conscience are defiled.

16 They profess to know God, but in works they deny Him, being abominable, disobedient, and disqualified for every good work.

Qualities of a Sound Church

2 But as for you, speak the things which are proper for sound doctrine:

2 that the older men be sober, reverent, temperate, sound in faith, in love, in patience;

3 the older women likewise, that they be reverent in behavior, not slanderers, not given to much wine, teachers of good things—

4 that they admonish the young women to love their husbands, to love their children,

5 to be discreet, chaste, homemakers, good, obedient to their own husbands, that the word of God may not be blasphemed.

6 Likewise exhort the young men to be sober-minded,

7 in all things showing yourself *to be* a pattern of good works; in doctrine *showing* integrity, reverence, incorruptibility,[3]

8 sound speech that cannot be condemned, that one who is an opponent may be ashamed, having nothing evil to say of you.[4]

9 *Exhort* servants to be obedient to their own masters, to be well pleasing in all *things*, not answering back,

10 not pilfering, but showing all good fidelity, that they may adorn the doctrine of God our Savior in all things.

1 NU-Text reads and Christ Jesus.   2 Literally *overseer*   3 NU-Text omits *incorruptibility*.
4 NU-Text and M-Text read *us*.

Trained by Saving Grace

11 For the grace of God that brings salvation has appeared to all men,

12 teaching us that, denying ungodliness and worldly lusts, we should live soberly, righteously, and godly in the present age,

13 looking for the blessed hope and glorious appearing of our great God and Savior Jesus Christ,

14 who gave Himself for us, that He might redeem us from every lawless deed and purify for Himself *His* own special people, zealous for good works.

15 Speak these things, exhort, and rebuke with all authority. Let no one despise you.

Graces of the Heirs of Grace

3 Remind them to be subject to rulers and authorities, to obey, to be ready for every good work,

2 to speak evil of no one, to be peaceable, gentle, showing all humility to all men.

3 For we ourselves were also once foolish, disobedient, deceived, serving various lusts and pleasures, living in malice and envy, hateful and hating one another.

4 But when the kindness and the love of God our Savior toward man appeared,

5 not by works of righteousness which we have done, but according to His mercy He saved us, through the washing of regeneration and renewing of the Holy Spirit,

6 whom He poured out on us abundantly through Jesus Christ our Savior,

7 that having been justified by His grace we should become heirs according to the hope of eternal life.

8 This is a faithful saying, and these things I want you to affirm constantly, that those who have believed in God should be careful to maintain good works. These things are good and profitable to men.

Avoid Dissension

9 But avoid foolish disputes, genealogies, contentions, and strivings about the law; for they are unprofitable and useless.

10 Reject a divisive man after the first and second admonition,

11 knowing that such a person is warped and sinning, being self-condemned.

Final Messages

12 When I send Artemas to you, or Tychicus, be diligent to come to me at Nicopolis, for I have decided to spend the winter there.

13 Send Zenas the lawyer and Apollos on their journey with haste, that they may lack nothing.

14 And let our *people* also learn to maintain good works, to *meet* urgent needs, that they may not be unfruitful.

Farewell

15 All who *are* with me greet you. Greet those who love us in the faith. Grace *be* with you all. Amen.

Introduction to Philemon

Forgiveness is the language of love! This is the theme of the Epistle to Philemon. This book was written between A.D. 58 and 63, during Paul's first Roman imprisonment. It is the shortest of all of Paul's letters.

During Paul's imprisonment, he met an ex-slave named Onesimus who had been caught stealing from his master, Philemon. Now Paul writes to Philemon pleading for him to accept Onesimus as a brother and to forgive him for his former actions. Paul reminds Philemon that because of Onesimus's newfound faith in Christ, he would be a benefit to his brothers and sisters in the church at Colosse.

The apostle Paul encourages Philemon to forgive Onesimus so that he can live up to the true meaning of his name, "useful." In a play on words, Paul reminds Philemon that if the useful one, Onesimus, is accepted back, he can truly become useful for Philemon and the church.

Onesimus was accepted back into the church and a later tradition tells us that Onesimus rose to the rank of bishop in the church at Ephesus.

Because of Philemon's forgiveness and the forgiveness of others, Onesimus truly was able to become "the useful one."

The Book of Philemon is a beautiful illustration of what can be accomplished in a person's life when complete forgiveness is given and accepted. Forgiveness means change. People who never change are either perfect to begin with or stubborn forever after.

Whether you need to change and forgive someone else, or change and forgive yourself, this book positively illustrates the rewards for doing so. A beautiful prayer is the right start:

I am willing, wanting, and waiting to change into the person You want me to be, Lord. Amen.

The Epistle of Paul the Apostle to

Philemon

Greeting

PAUL, a prisoner of Christ Jesus, and Timothy *our* brother,

To Philemon our beloved *friend* and fellow laborer,
2 to the beloved[1] Apphia, Archippus our fellow soldier, and to the church in your house:

3 Grace to you and peace from God our Father and the Lord Jesus Christ.

Philemon's Love and Faith

4 I thank my God, making mention of you always in my prayers,
5 hearing of your love and faith which you have toward the Lord Jesus and toward all the saints,
6 that the sharing of your faith may become effective by the acknowledgment of every good thing which is in you[2] in Christ Jesus.
7 For we have[3] great joy[4] and consolation in your love, because the hearts of the saints have been refreshed by you, brother.

The Plea for Onesimus

8 Therefore, though I might be very bold in Christ to command you what is fitting,
9 *yet* for love's sake I rather appeal *to you*—being such a one as Paul, the aged, and now also a prisoner of Jesus Christ—
10 I appeal to you for my son Onesimus, whom I have begotten *while* in my chains,
11 who once was unprofitable to you, but now is profitable to you and to me.
12 I am sending him back.[5] You there-fore receive him, that is, my own heart,
13 whom I wished to keep with me, that on your behalf he might minister to me in my chains for the gospel.
14 But without your consent I wanted to do nothing, that your good deed might not be by compulsion, as it were, but vol-untary.
15 For perhaps he departed for a while for this *purpose*, that you might receive him forever,
16 no longer as a slave but more than a slave, *as* a beloved brother, especially to me but how much more to you, both in the flesh and in the Lord.

Philemon's Obedience Encouraged

17 If then you count me as a partner, re-ceive him as *you would* me.
18 But if he has wronged you or owes *you* anything, put that on my account.
19 I, Paul, am writing with my own hand. I will repay—not to mention to you that you owe me even your own self besides.
20 Yes, brother, let me have joy from you in the Lord; refresh my heart in the Lord.
21 Having confidence in your obedience, I write to you, knowing that you will do even more than I say.
22 But, meanwhile, also prepare a guest room for me, for I trust that through your prayers I shall be granted to you.

Farewell

23 Epaphras, my fellow prisoner in Christ Jesus, greets you,
24 *as do* Mark, Aristarchus, Demas, Luke, my fellow laborers.
25 The grace of our Lord Jesus Christ *be* with your spirit. Amen.

---

1 NU-Text reads *to our sister Apphia.* 2 NU-Text and M-Text read *us.* 3 NU-Text reads *had.*
4 M-Text reads *thanksgiving.* 5 NU-Text reads *back to you in person, that is, my own heart.*

Introduction to Hebrews

Now faith is the substance of things hoped for, the evidence of things not seen.

(Heb. 11:1)

Although the author of the Book of Hebrews is unknown, scholars have placed the date of writing in the 60s A.D. prior to the destruction of the Jerusalem temple in A.D. 70. Some feel this Epistle may have been written either by Paul, Barnabas, Luke, or Apollos.

A work of highly polished Greek literature, this book is rivaled in the New Testament with its mastery of the language only by Luke and Acts. Its intended audience was Jewish Christians, possibly those living in Rome.

The theme of Hebrews points out the superiority of Jesus Christ over Judaism. In a step-by-step outline, the author reveals how Jesus is the Great High Priest according to the order of Melchizedek. The author knew his readers had a great understanding of and familiarity with the Old Testament, having been trained as upright Jews. Therefore, he draws from over twenty-nine passages and fifty-three symbolic illustrations of the Old Testament, to show how Christianity embodies the New Covenant between God and His people.

Faith is also a dominant thread which runs throughout the book. The famous "faith chapter" (Heb. 11) recounts the lives of great possibility thinkers of the Bible as an inspiration for us to have a similar enduring faith, looking to the same eternal God to supply our needs.

With great encouragement and exhortation, this book builds up the faith of all believers, hoping to bring them into a more vital relationship with Jesus Christ.

The Epistle to the

Hebrews

God's Supreme Revelation

GOD, who at various times and in different ways spoke in time past to the fathers by the prophets,
2 has in these last days spoken to us by *His* Son, whom He has appointed heir of all things, through whom also He made the worlds;
3 who being the brightness of *His* glory and the express image of His person, and upholding all things by the word of His power, when He had by Himself[1] purged our[2] sins, sat down at the right hand of the Majesty on high,
4 having become so much better than the angels, as He has by inheritance obtained a more excellent name than they.

The Son Exalted above Angels

5 For to which of the angels did He ever say:

"You are My Son,
Today I have begotten You"?[3]

And again:

"I will be to Him a Father,
And He shall be to Me a Son"?[4]

6 But when He again brings the firstborn into the world, He says:

"Let all the angels of God
worship Him."[5]

7 And of the angels He says:

"Who makes His angels spirits
And His ministers a flame of fire."[6]

8 But to the Son *He says*:

"Your throne, O God,
is forever and ever;
A scepter of righteousness is the
scepter of Your Kingdom.

9 You have loved righteousness and
hated lawlessness;
Therefore God, Your God,
has anointed You
With the oil of gladness more than
Your companions."[7]

10 And:

"You, LORD, in the beginning laid
the foundation of the earth,
And the heavens are the work
of Your hands;
11 They will perish, but You remain;
And they will all grow old
like a garment;
12 Like a cloak You will fold
them up,
And they will be changed.
But You are the same,
And Your years will not fail."[8]

13 But to which of the angels has He ever said:

"Sit at My right hand,
Till I make Your enemies
Your footstool"?[9]

14 Are they not all ministering spirits sent forth to minister for those who will inherit salvation?

Do Not Neglect Salvation

2 Therefore we must give the more earnest heed to the things we have heard, lest we drift away.
2 For if the word spoken through angels proved steadfast, and every transgression and disobedience received a just reward,
3 how shall we escape if we neglect so great a salvation, which at the first began to be spoken by the Lord, and was confirmed to us by those who heard *Him,*
4 God also bearing witness both with signs and wonders, with various miracles, and gifts of the Holy Spirit, according to His own will?

1 NU-Text omits *by Himself.* 2 NU-Text omits *our.* 3 Psalm 2:7 4 2 Samuel 7:14
5 Deuteronomy 32:43 (Septuagint, Dead Sea Scrolls); Psalm 97:7 6 Psalm 104:4 7 Psalm 45:6, 7
8 Psalm 102:25–27 9 Psalm 110:1

The Son Made Lower than Angels

5 For He has not put the world to come, of which we speak, in subjection to angels.

6 But one testified in a certain place, saying:

"What is man that You
   are mindful of him,
Or the son of man that You
   take care of him?
7 You made him a little lower
   than the angels;
You crowned him with glory and
   honor,[10]
And set him over the works
   of Your hands.
8 You have put all things
   in subjection under his feet."[11]

For in that He put all in subjection under him, He left nothing that is not put under him. But now we do not yet see all things put under him.

9 But we see Jesus, who was made a little lower than the angels, for the suffering of death crowned with glory and honor, that He, by the grace of God, might taste death for everyone.

Bringing Many Sons to Glory

10 For it was fitting for Him, for whom are all things and by whom are all things, in bringing many sons to glory, to make the author of their salvation perfect through sufferings.

11 For both He who sanctifies and those who are being sanctified are all of one, for which reason He is not ashamed to call them brethren,

12 saying:

"I will declare Your name to My
   brethren;
In the midst of the congregation
   I will sing praise to You."[12]

13 And again:

"I will put My trust in Him."[13]

And again:

"Here am I and the children
   whom God has given Me."[14]

14 Inasmuch then as the children have partaken of flesh and blood, He Himself likewise shared in the same, that through death He might destroy him who had the power of death, that is, the devil,

15 and release those who through fear of death were all their lifetime subject to bondage.

16 For indeed He does not give aid to angels, but He does give aid to the seed of Abraham.

17 Therefore, in all things He had to be made like His brethren, that He might be a merciful and faithful High Priest in things pertaining to God, to make propitiation for the sins of the people.

18 For in that He Himself has suffered, being tempted, He is able to aid those who are tempted.

The Son Was Faithful

3 Therefore, holy brethren, partakers of the heavenly calling, consider the Apostle and High Priest of our confession, Christ Jesus,

2 who was faithful to Him who appointed Him, as Moses also was faithful in all His house.

3 For this One has been counted worthy of more glory than Moses, inasmuch as He who built the house has more honor than the house.

4 For every house is built by someone, but He who built all things is God.

5 And Moses indeed was faithful in all His house as a servant, for a testimony of those things which would be spoken afterward,

6 but Christ as a Son over His own house, whose house we are if we hold fast the confidence and the rejoicing of the hope firm to the end.[15]

Be Faithful

7 Therefore, as the Holy Spirit says:

"Today, if you will hear His voice,
8   Do not harden your hearts
      as in the rebellion,
   In the day of trial in the wilderness,
9   Where your fathers tested Me,
      proved Me,
   And saw My works forty years.
10   Therefore I was angry with that
      generation,

---

10 NU-Text and M-Text omit the rest of verse 7.   11 Psalm 8:4–6   12 Psalm 22:22
13 2 Samuel 22:3; Isaiah 8:17   14 Isaiah 8:18   15 NU-Text omits firm to the end.

And said, 'They always go astray
  in their heart,
And they have not known My ways.'
11 So I swore in My wrath,
'They shall not enter My rest.' "[16]

12 Beware, brethren, lest there be in any of you an evil heart of unbelief in departing from the living God; 13 but exhort one another daily, while it is called "Today," lest any of you be hardened through the deceitfulness of sin. 14 For we have become partakers of Christ if we hold the beginning of our confidence steadfast to the end, 15 while it is said:

"Today, if you will hear His voice,
Do not harden your hearts as in the
  rebellion."[17]

Failure of the Wilderness Wanderers

16 For who, having heard, rebelled? Indeed, was it not all who came out of Egypt, led by Moses? 17 Now with whom was He angry forty years? Was it not with those who sinned, whose corpses fell in the wilderness? 18 And to whom did He swear that they would not enter His rest, but to those who did not obey? 19 So we see that they could not enter in because of unbelief.

The Promise of Rest

4 Therefore, since a promise remains of entering His rest, let us fear lest any of you seem to have come short of it. 2 For indeed the gospel was preached to us as well as to them; but the word which they heard did not profit them,[18] not being mixed with faith in those who heard it. 3 For we who have believed do enter that rest, as He has said:

"So I swore in My wrath,
They shall not enter My rest,"[19]

although the works were finished from the foundation of the world. 4 For He has spoken in a certain place of the seventh day in this way: "And God rested on the seventh day from all His works";[20]

5 and again in this place: "They shall not enter My rest."[21] 6 Since therefore it remains that some must enter it, and those to whom it was first preached did not enter because of disobedience, 7 again He designates a certain day, saying in David, "Today," after such a long time, as it has been said:

"Today, if you will hear His voice,
Do not harden your hearts."[22]

8 For if Joshua had given them rest, then He would not afterward have spoken of another day. 9 There remains therefore a rest for the people of God. 10 For he who has entered His rest has himself also ceased from his works as God did from His.

The Word Discovers Our Condition

11 Let us therefore be diligent to enter that rest, lest anyone fall after the same example of disobedience. 12 For the word of God is living and powerful, and sharper than any two-edged sword, piercing even to the division of soul and spirit, and of joints and marrow, and is a discerner of the thoughts and intents of the heart. 13 And there is no creature hidden from His sight, but all things are naked and open to the eyes of Him to whom we must give account.

Our Compassionate High Priest

14 Seeing then that we have a great High Priest who has passed through the heavens, Jesus the Son of God, let us hold fast our confession. 15 For we do not have a High Priest who cannot sympathize with our weaknesses, but was in all points tempted as we are, yet without sin. 16 Let us therefore come boldly to the throne of grace, that we may obtain mercy and find grace to help in time of need.

Qualifications for High Priesthood

5 For every high priest taken from among men is appointed for men in

16 Psalm 95:7-11   17 Psalm 95:7, 8
18 NU-Text and M-Text finish verse as follows: since they were not united by faith with those who heard.
19 Psalm 95:11   20 Genesis 2:2   21 Psalm 95:11   22 Psalm 95:7, 8

things *pertaining* to God, that he may offer both gifts and sacrifices for sins.
2 He can have compassion on those who are ignorant and going astray, since he himself is also beset by weakness.
3 Because of this he is required as for the people, so also for himself, to offer for sins.
4 And no man takes this honor to himself, but he who is called by God, just as Aaron *was.*

A Priest Forever

5 So also Christ did not glorify Himself to become High Priest, *but it* was He who said to Him:

"You are My Son,
Today I have begotten You."[23]

6 As *He* also *says* in another *place:*

"You are a priest forever
According to the order of
Melchizedek";[24]

7 who, in the days of His flesh, when He had offered up prayers and supplications, with vehement cries and tears to Him who was able to save Him from death, and was heard because of His godly fear,
8 though He was a Son, *yet* He learned obedience by the things which He suffered.
9 And having been perfected, He became the author of eternal salvation to all who obey Him,
10 called by God as High Priest *"according to the order of Melchizedek,"*
11 of whom we have much to say, and hard to explain, since you have become dull of hearing.

Spiritual Immaturity

12 For though by this time you ought to be teachers, you need *someone* to teach you again the first principles of the oracles of God; and you have come to need milk and not solid food.
13 For everyone who partakes *only* of milk *is* unskilled in the word of righteousness, for he is a babe.
14 But solid food belongs to those who are of full age, *that is,* those who by reason of use have their senses exercised to discern both good and evil.

The Peril of Not Progressing

6 Therefore, leaving the discussion of the elementary *principles* of Christ, let us go on to perfection, not laying again the foundation of repentance from dead works and of faith toward God,
2 of the doctrine of baptisms, of laying on of hands, of resurrection of the dead, and of eternal judgment.
3 And this we will[25] do if God permits.
4 For *it is* impossible for those who were once enlightened, and have tasted the heavenly gift, and have become partakers of the Holy Spirit,
5 and have tasted the good word of God and the powers of the age to come,
6 if they fall away, to renew them again to repentance, since they crucify again for themselves the Son of God, and put *Him* to an open shame.
7 For the earth which drinks in the rain that often comes upon it, and bears herbs useful for those by whom it is cultivated, receives blessing from God;
8 but if it bears thorns and briars, *it is* rejected and near to being cursed, whose end *is* to be burned.

A Better Estimate

9 But, beloved, we are confident of better things concerning you, yes, things that accompany salvation, though we speak in this manner.
10 For God *is* not unjust to forget your work and labor of[26] love which you have shown toward His name, *in that* you have ministered to the saints, and do minister.
11 And we desire that each one of you show the same diligence to the full assurance of hope until the end,
12 that you do not become sluggish, but imitate those who through faith and patience inherit the promises.

God's Infallible Purpose in Christ

13 For when God made a promise to Abraham, because He could swear by no one greater, He swore by Himself,
14 saying, *"Surely blessing I will bless you, and multiplying I will multiply you."*[27]
15 And so, after he had patiently endured, he obtained the promise.
16 For men indeed swear by the greater, and an oath for confirmation *is* for them an end of all dispute.

23 Psalm 2:7   24 Psalm 110:4   25 M-Text reads *let us do.*   26 NU-Text omits *labor of.*   27 Genesis 22:17

17 Thus God, determining to show more abundantly to the heirs of promise the immutability of His counsel, confirmed *it* by an oath,
18 that by two immutable things, in which it *is* impossible for God to lie, we might[28] have strong consolation, who have fled for refuge to lay hold of the hope set before *us.*
19 This *hope* we have as an anchor of the soul, both sure and steadfast, and which enters the Presence *behind* the veil,
20 where the forerunner has entered for us, *even* Jesus, having become High Priest forever according to the order of Melchizedek.

The King of Righteousness

7 For this Melchizedek, king of Salem, priest of the Most High God, who met Abraham returning from the slaughter of the kings and blessed him,
2 to whom also Abraham gave a tenth part of all, first being translated "king of righteousness," and then also king of Salem, meaning "king of peace,"
3 without father, without mother, without genealogy, having neither beginning of days nor end of life, but made like the Son of God, remains a priest continually.
4 Now consider how great this man *was,* to whom even the patriarch Abraham gave a tenth of the spoils.
5 And indeed those who are of the sons of Levi, who receive the priesthood, have a commandment to receive tithes from the people according to the law, that is, from their brethren, though they have come from the loins of Abraham;
6 but he whose genealogy is not derived from them received tithes from Abraham and blessed him who had the promises.
7 Now beyond all contradiction the lesser is blessed by the better.
8 Here mortal men receive tithes, but there he *receives them,* of whom it is witnessed that he lives.
9 Even Levi, who receives tithes, paid tithes through Abraham, so to speak,
10 for he was still in the loins of his father when Melchizedek met him.

Need for a New Priesthood

11 Therefore, if perfection were through the Levitical priesthood (for under it the people received the law), what further need *was there* that another priest should rise according to the order of Melchizedek, and not be called according to the order of Aaron?
12 For the priesthood being changed, of necessity there is also a change of the law.
13 For He of whom these things are spoken belongs to another tribe, from which no man has officiated at the altar.
14 For *it is* evident that our Lord arose from Judah, of which tribe Moses spoke nothing concerning priesthood.[29]
15 And it is yet far more evident if, in the likeness of Melchizedek, there arises another priest
16 who has come, not according to the law of a fleshly commandment, but according to the power of an endless life.
17 For He testifies:[30]

> *"You are a priest forever*
> *According to the order of*
> *Melchizedek."*[31]

18 For on the one hand there is an annulling of the former commandment because of its weakness and unprofitableness,
19 for the law made nothing perfect; on the other hand, *there is the* bringing in of a better hope, through which we draw near to God.

Greatness of the New Priest

20 And inasmuch as *He was* not *made priest* without an oath
21 (for they have become priests without an oath, but He with an oath by Him who said to Him:

> *"The LORD has sworn*
> *And will not relent,*
> *'You are a priest forever*[32]
> *According to the order of*
> *Melchizedek' "*),[33]

22 by so much more Jesus has become a surety of a better covenant.
23 And there were many priests, because they were prevented by death from continuing.
24 But He, because He continues forever, has an unchangeable priesthood.
25 Therefore He is also able to save to the uttermost those who come to God through Him, since He ever lives to make intercession for them.

---

28 M-Text omits *might.*   29 NU-Text reads *priests.*   30 NU-Text reads *it is testified.*   31 Psalm 110:4
32 NU-Text ends the quotation here.   33 Psalm 110:4

26 For such a High Priest was fitting for us, *who is* holy, harmless, undefiled, separate from sinners, and has become higher than the heavens;
27 who does not need daily, as those high priests, to offer up sacrifices, first for His own sins and then for the people's, for this He did once for all when He offered up Himself.
28 For the law appoints as high priests men who have weakness, but the word of the oath, which came after the law, *appoints* the Son who has been perfected forever.

The New Priestly Service

8 Now *this is* the main point of the things we are saying: We have such a High Priest, who is seated at the right hand of the throne of the Majesty in the heavens,
2 a Minister of the sanctuary and of the true tabernacle which the Lord erected, and not man.
3 For every high priest is appointed to offer both gifts and sacrifices. Therefore *it is* necessary that this One also have something to offer.
4 For if He were on earth, He would not be a priest, since there are priests who offer the gifts according to the law;
5 who serve the copy and shadow of the heavenly things, as Moses was divinely instructed when he was about to make the tabernacle. For He said, *"See that you make all things according to the pattern shown you on the mountain."*[34]
6 But now He has obtained a more excellent ministry, inasmuch as He is also Mediator of a better covenant, which was established on better promises.

A New Covenant

7 For if that first *covenant* had been faultless, then no place would have been sought for a second.
8 Because finding fault with them, He says: *"Behold, the days are coming,"* says the LORD, *"when I will make a new covenant with the house of Israel and with the house of Judah—*
9 *"not according to the covenant that I made with their fathers in the day when I took them by the hand to lead them out of the land of Egypt; because they did not continue in My covenant, and I disregarded them,"* says the LORD.

10 *"For this is the covenant that I will make with the house of Israel: After those days,"* says the LORD, *"I will put My laws in their mind and write them on their hearts; and I will be their God, and they shall be My people.*
11 *"None of them shall teach his neighbor, and none his brother, saying, 'Know the LORD,' for all shall know Me, from the least of them to the greatest of them.*
12 *"For I will be merciful to their unrighteousness, and their sins and their lawless deeds*[35] *I will remember no more."*[36]
13 In that He says, *"A new covenant,"* He has made the first obsolete. Now what is becoming obsolete and growing old is ready to vanish away.

The Earthly Sanctuary

9 Then indeed, even the first *covenant* had ordinances of divine service and the earthly sanctuary.
2 For a tabernacle was prepared: the first *part,* in which *was* the lampstand, the table, and the showbread, which is called the sanctuary;
3 and behind the second veil, the part of the tabernacle which is called the Holiest of All,
4 which had the golden altar of incense and the ark of the covenant overlaid on all sides with gold, in which *were* the golden pot that had the manna, Aaron's rod that budded, and the tablets of the covenant;
5 and above it were the cherubim of glory overshadowing the mercy seat. Of these things we cannot now speak in detail.

Limitations of the Earthly Service

6 Now when these things had been thus prepared, the priests always went into the first part of the tabernacle, performing the services.
7 But into the second part the high priest *went* alone once a year, not without blood, which he offered for himself and *for* the people's sins *committed* in ignorance;
8 the Holy Spirit indicating this, that the way into the Holiest of All was not yet made manifest while the first tabernacle was still standing.
9 It *was* symbolic for the present time in which both gifts and sacrifices are offered

34 Exodus 25:40   35 NU-Text omits *and their lawless deeds.*   36 Jeremiah 31:31–34

which cannot make him who performed the service perfect in regard to the conscience—
10 *concerned* only with foods and drinks, various washings, and fleshly ordinances imposed until the time of reformation.

The Heavenly Sanctuary

11 But Christ came *as* High Priest of the good things to come,[37] with the greater and more perfect tabernacle not made with hands, that is, not of this creation.
12 Not with the blood of goats and calves, but with His own blood He entered the Most Holy Place once for all, having obtained eternal redemption.
13 For if the blood of bulls and goats . and the ashes of a heifer, sprinkling the unclean, sanctifies for the purifying of the flesh,
14 how much more shall the blood of Christ, who through the eternal Spirit offered Himself without spot to God, purge your conscience from dead works to serve the living God?
15 And for this reason He is the Mediator of the new covenant, by means of death, for the redemption of the transgressions under the first covenant, that those who are called may receive the promise of the eternal inheritance.

The Mediator's Death Necessary

16 For where there *is* a testament, there must also of necessity be the death of the testator.
17 For a testament *is* in force after men are dead, since it has no power at all while the testator lives.
18 Therefore not even the first *covenant* was dedicated without blood.
19 For when Moses had spoken every precept to all the people according to the law, he took the blood of calves and goats, with water, scarlet wool, and hyssop, and sprinkled both the book itself and all the people,
20 saying, *"This is the blood of the covenant which God has commanded you."*[38]
21 Then likewise he sprinkled with blood both the tabernacle and all the vessels of the ministry.
22 And according to the law almost all things are purged with blood, and without shedding of blood there is no remission.

Greatness of Christ's Sacrifice

23 Therefore *it was* necessary that the copies of the things in the heavens should be purified with these, but the heavenly things themselves with better sacrifices than these.
24 For Christ has not entered the holy places made with hands, *which are* copies of the true, but into heaven itself, now to appear in the presence of God for us;
25 not that He should offer Himself often, as the high priest enters the Most Holy Place every year with blood of another—
26 He then would have had to suffer often since the foundation of the world; but now, once at the end of the ages, He has appeared to put away sin by the sacrifice of Himself.
27 And as it is appointed for men to die once, but after this the judgment,
28 so Christ was offered once to bear the sins of many. To those who eagerly wait for Him He will appear a second time, apart from sin, for salvation.

Animal Sacrifices Insufficient

10 For the law, having a shadow of the good things to come, *and* not the very image of the things, can never with these same sacrifices, which they offer continually year by year, make those who approach perfect.
2 For then would they not have ceased to be offered? For the worshipers, once purged, would have had no more consciousness of sins.
3 But in those *sacrifices there is* a reminder of sins every year.
4 For *it is* not possible that the blood of bulls and goats could take away sins.

Christ's Death Fulfills God's Will

5 Therefore, when He came into the world, He said:

> "Sacrifice and offering You did not
>   desire,
> But a body You have prepared for Me.
> 6 In burnt offerings and *sacrifices for sin*
>   You had no pleasure.
> 7 Then I said, 'Behold, I have come—
> In the volume of the book
>   it is written of Me—
> To do Your will, O God.' "[39]

8 Previously saying, *"Sacrifice and offering, burnt offerings, and offerings for*

---

37 NU-Text reads *that have come.*   38 Exodus 24:8   39 Psalm 40:6-8

sin You did not desire, nor had pleasure in them" (which are offered according to the law),
9 then He said, *"Behold, I have come to do Your will, O God."*[40] He takes away the first that He may establish the second.
10 By that will we have been sanctified through the offering of the body of Jesus Christ once *for all.*

Christ's Death Perfects the Sanctified

11 And every priest stands ministering daily and offering repeatedly the same sacrifices, which can never take away sins.
12 But this Man, after He had offered one sacrifice for sins forever, sat down at the right hand of God,
13 from that time waiting till His enemies are made His footstool.
14 For by one offering He has perfected forever those who are being sanctified.
15 And the Holy Spirit also witnesses to us; for after He had said before,
16 *"This is the covenant that I will make with them after those days, says the* LORD: *I will put My laws into their hearts, and in their minds I will write them,"*[41]
17 then He adds, *"Their sins and their lawless deeds I will remember no more."*[42]
18 Now where there is remission of these, *there is* no longer an offering for sin.

Hold Fast Your Confession

19 Therefore, brethren, having boldness to enter the Holiest by the blood of Jesus,
20 by a new and living way which He consecrated for us, through the veil, that is, His flesh,
21 and *having* a High Priest over the house of God,
22 let us draw near with a true heart in full assurance of faith, having our hearts sprinkled from an evil conscience and our bodies washed with pure water.
23 Let us hold fast the confession of *our* hope without wavering, for He who promised *is* faithful.
24 And let us consider one another in order to stir up love and good works,
25 not forsaking the assembling of ourselves together, as *is* the manner of some, but exhorting *one another*, and so much the more as you see the Day approaching.

The Just Live by Faith

26 For if we sin willfully after we have received the knowledge of the truth, there no longer remains a sacrifice for sins,
27 but a certain fearful expectation of judgment, and fiery indignation which will devour the adversaries.
28 Anyone who has rejected Moses' law dies without mercy on the testimony of two or three witnesses.
29 Of how much worse punishment, do you suppose, will he be thought worthy who has trampled the Son of God underfoot, counted the blood of the covenant by which he was sanctified a common thing, and insulted the Spirit of grace?
30 For we know Him who said, *"Vengeance is Mine; I will repay,"*[43] says the Lord."[44] And again, *"The* LORD *will judge His people."*[45]
31 It is a fearful thing to fall into the hands of the living God.
32 But recall the former days in which, after you were illuminated, you endured a great struggle with sufferings:
33 partly while you were made a spectacle both by reproaches and tribulations, and partly while you became companions of those who were so treated;
34 for you had compassion on me[46] in my chains, and joyfully accepted the plundering of your goods, knowing that you have a better and an enduring possession for yourselves in heaven.[47]
35 Therefore do not cast away your confidence, which has great reward.
36 For you have need of endurance, so that after you have done the will of God, you may receive the promise:

37 *"For yet a little while,*
    And He[48] *who is coming will come*
        and will not tarry.
38 *Now the*[49] *just shall live by faith;*
    But if anyone draws back,
    My soul has no pleasure in him."[50]

39 But we are not of those who draw back to perdition, but of those who believe to the saving of the soul.

---

40 NU-Text and M-Text omit *O God.*   41 Jeremiah 31:33   42 Jeremiah 31:34   43 Deuteronomy 32:35
44 NU-Text omits *says the Lord.*   45 Deuteronomy 32:36
46 NU-Text reads *the prisoners* instead of *me in my chains.*   47 NU-Text omits *in heaven.*   48 Or *that which*
49 NU-Text reads *my just one.*   50 Habakkuk 2:3, 4

By Faith We Understand

11 Now faith is the substance of things hoped for, the evidence of things not seen.
2 For by it the elders obtained a *good* testimony.
3 By faith we understand that the worlds were framed by the word of God, so that the things which are seen were not made of things which are visible.

Faith at the Dawn of History

4 By faith Abel offered to God a more excellent sacrifice than Cain, through which he obtained witness that he was righteous, God testifying of his gifts; and through it he being dead still speaks.
5 By faith Enoch was translated so that he did not see death, *"and was not found because God had translated him";*[51] for before his translation he had this testimony, that he pleased God.
6 But without faith *it is* impossible to please *Him,* for he who comes to God must believe that He is, and *that* He is a rewarder of those who diligently seek Him.
7 By faith Noah, being divinely warned of things not yet seen, moved with godly fear, prepared an ark for the saving of his household, by which he condemned the world and became heir of the righteousness which is according to faith.

Faithful Abraham

8 By faith Abraham obeyed when he was called to go out to the place which he would *afterward* receive as an inheritance. And he went out, not knowing where he was going.
9 By faith he sojourned in the land of promise as *in* a foreign country, dwelling in tents with Isaac and Jacob, the heirs with him of the same promise;
10 for he waited for the city which has foundations, whose builder and maker *is* God.
11 By faith Sarah herself also received strength to conceive seed, and she bore a child[52] when she was past the age, because she judged Him faithful who had promised.
12 Therefore from one man, and him as good as dead, were born *as many* as the stars of the sky in multitude—innumerable as the sand which is by the seashore.

The Heavenly Hope

13 These all died in faith, not having received the promises, but having seen them afar off were assured of *them,*[53] embraced *them,* and confessed that they were strangers and pilgrims on the earth.
14 For those who say such things declare plainly that they seek a homeland.
15 And truly if they had called to mind that *country* from which they had come out, they would have had opportunity to return.
16 But now they desire a better, that is, a heavenly *country.* Therefore God is not ashamed to be called their God, for He has prepared a city for them.

The Faith of the Patriarchs

17 By faith Abraham, when he was tested, offered up Isaac, and he who had received the promises offered up his only begotten *son,*
18 of whom it was said, *"In Isaac your seed shall be called,"*[54]
19 accounting that God *was* able to raise *him* up, even from the dead, from which he also received him in a figurative sense.
20 By faith Isaac blessed Jacob and Esau concerning things to come.
21 By faith Jacob, when he was dying, blessed each of the sons of Joseph, and worshiped, *leaning* on the top of his staff.
22 By faith Joseph, when he was dying, made mention of the departure of the children of Israel, and gave instructions concerning his bones.

The Faith of Moses

23 By faith Moses, when he was born, was hidden three months by his parents, because they saw *he was* a beautiful child; and they were not afraid of the king's command.
24 By faith Moses, when he became of age, refused to be called the son of Pharaoh's daughter,
25 choosing rather to suffer affliction with the people of God than to enjoy the passing pleasures of sin,
26 esteeming the reproach of Christ greater riches than the treasures in[55] Egypt; for he looked to the reward.
27 By faith he forsook Egypt, not fearing the wrath of the king; for he endured as seeing Him who is invisible.

---

51 Genesis 5:24   52 NU-Text omits *she bore a child.*   53 NU-Text and M-Text omit *were assured of them.*
54 Genesis 21:12   55 NU-Text and M-Text read *of.*

28 By faith he kept the Passover and the sprinkling of blood, lest he who destroyed the firstborn should touch them.
29 By faith they passed through the Red Sea as by dry *land,* *whereas* the Egyptians, attempting *to do* so, were drowned.

By Faith They Overcame

30 By faith the walls of Jericho fell down after they were encircled for seven days.
31 By faith the harlot Rahab did not perish with those who did not believe, when she had received the spies with peace.
32 And what more shall I say? For the time would fail me to tell of Gideon and Barak and Samson and Jephthah, also *of* David and Samuel and the prophets:
33 who through faith subdued kingdoms, worked righteousness, obtained promises, stopped the mouths of lions,
34 quenched the violence of fire, escaped the edge of the sword, out of weakness were made strong, became valiant in battle, turned to flight the armies of the aliens.
35 Women received their dead raised to life again. And others were tortured, not accepting deliverance, that they might obtain a better resurrection.
36 Still others had trial of mockings and scourgings, yes, and of chains and imprisonment.
37 They were stoned, they were sawn in two, were tempted,[56] were slain with the sword. They wandered about in sheepskins and goatskins, being destitute, afflicted, tormented—
38 of whom the world was not worthy. They wandered in deserts and mountains, *in* dens and caves of the earth.
39 And all these, having obtained a good testimony through faith, did not receive the promise,
40 God having provided something better for us, that they should not be made perfect apart from us.

The Race of Faith

12 Therefore we also, since we are surrounded by so great a cloud of witnesses, let us lay aside every weight, and the sin which so easily ensnares *us,* and let us run with endurance the race that is set before us,
2 looking unto Jesus, the author and finisher of *our* faith, who for the joy that was set before Him endured the cross, despising the shame, and has sat down at the right hand of the throne of God.

The Discipline of God

3 For consider Him who endured such hostility from sinners against Himself, lest you become weary and discouraged in your souls.
4 You have not yet resisted to bloodshed, striving against sin.
5 And you have forgotten the exhortation which speaks to you as to sons:

> "My son, do not despise the chastening
>   of the LORD,
> Nor be discouraged when you are
>   rebuked by Him;
> **6** For whom the LORD loves He chastens,
> And scourges every son whom He
>   receives."[57]

7 If[58] you endure chastening, God deals with you as with sons; for what son is there whom a father does not chasten?
8 But if you are without chastening, of which all have become partakers, then you are illegitimate and not sons.
9 Furthermore, we have had human fathers who corrected *us,* and we paid *them* respect. Shall we not much more readily be in subjection to the Father of spirits and live?
10 For they indeed for a few days chastened *us* as seemed *best* to them, but He for *our* profit, that *we* may be partakers of His holiness.
11 Now no chastening seems to be joyful for the present, but grievous; nevertheless, afterward it yields the peaceable fruit of righteousness to those who have been trained by it.

Renew Your Spiritual Vitality

12 Therefore strengthen the hands which hang down, and the feeble knees,
13 and make straight paths for your feet, so that what is lame may not be *dislocated,* but rather be healed.
14 Pursue peace with all *men,* and holiness, without which no one will see the Lord:
15 looking diligently lest anyone fall short of the grace of God; lest any root of bitterness springing up cause trouble, and by this many become defiled;

56 NU-Text omits *were tempted.*   57 Proverbs 3:11, 12
58 NU-Text and M-Text read *It is for discipline that you endure.*

16 lest there *be* any fornicator or profane person like Esau, who for one morsel of food sold his birthright.

17 For you know that afterward, when he wanted to inherit the blessing, he was rejected, for he found no place for repentance, though he sought it diligently with tears.

The Glorious Company

18 For you have not come to the mountain that[59] may be touched and that burned with fire, and to blackness and darkness[60] and tempest,

19 and the sound of a trumpet and the voice of words, so that those who heard *it* begged that the word should not be spoken to them anymore.

20 (For they could not endure what was commanded: *"And if so much as a beast touches the mountain, it shall be stoned*[61] *or thrust through with an arrow."*[62]

21 And so terrifying was the sight *that* Moses said, *"I am exceedingly afraid and trembling."*[63])

22 But you have come to Mount Zion and to the city of the living God, the heavenly Jerusalem, to an innumerable company of angels,

23 to the general assembly and church of the firstborn *who are* registered in heaven, to God the Judge of all, to the spirits of just men made perfect,

24 to Jesus the Mediator of the new covenant, and to the blood of sprinkling that speaks better things than *that of* Abel.

Hear the Heavenly Voice

25 See that you do not refuse Him who speaks. For if they did not escape who refused Him who spoke on earth, much more *shall we not escape* if we turn away from Him who *speaks* from heaven,

26 whose voice then shook the earth; but now He has promised, saying, *"Yet once more I shake*[64] *not only the earth, but also heaven."*[65]

27 Now this, *"Yet once more,"* indicates the removal of those things that are being shaken, as of things that are made, that the things which cannot be shaken may remain.

28 Therefore, since we are receiving a kingdom which cannot be shaken, let us have grace, by which we may[66] serve God acceptably with reverence and godly fear.

29 For our God *is* a consuming fire.

Concluding Moral Directions

13 Let brotherly love continue.

2 Do not forget to entertain strangers, for by so *doing* some have unwittingly entertained angels.

3 Remember the prisoners as if chained with them, *and* those who are mistreated, since you yourselves are in the body also.

4 Marriage *is* honorable among all, and the bed undefiled; but fornicators and adulterers God will judge.

5 *Let your* conduct *be* without covetousness, *and be* content with such things as you have. For He Himself has said, *"I will never leave you nor forsake you."*[67]

6 So we may boldly say:

"The LORD is my helper;
I will not fear.
What can man do to me?"[68]

Concluding Religious Directions

7 Remember those who rule over you, who have spoken the word of God to you, whose faith follow, considering the outcome of *their* conduct.

8 Jesus Christ *is* the same yesterday, today, and forever.

9 Do not be carried about[69] with various and strange doctrines. For *it is* good that the heart be established by grace, not with foods which have not profited those who have been occupied with them.

10 We have an altar from which those who serve the tabernacle have no right to eat.

11 For the bodies of those beasts, whose blood is brought into the sanctuary by the high priest for sin, are burned outside the camp.

12 Therefore Jesus also, that He might sanctify the people with His own blood, suffered outside the gate.

13 Therefore let us go forth to Him, outside the camp, bearing His reproach.

14 For here we have no continuing city, but we seek the one to come.

15 Therefore by Him let us continually

---

59 NU-Text reads *to that which.*   60 NU-Text reads *gloom.*   61 NU-Text and M-Text omit the rest of this verse.
62 Exodus 19:12, 13   63 Deuteronomy 9:19   64 NU-Text reads *will shake.*   65 Haggai 2:6
66 M-Text omits *may.*   67 Deuteronomy 31:6, 8; Joshua 1:5   68 Psalm 118:6
69 NU-Text and M-Text read *away.*

offer the sacrifice of praise to God, that is, the fruit of our lips, giving thanks to His name.

16 But do not forget to do good and to share, for with such sacrifices God is well pleased.

17 Obey those who rule over you, and be submissive, for they watch out for your souls, as those who must give account. Let them do so with joy and not with grief, for that would be unprofitable for you.

Prayer Requested

18 Pray for us; for we are confident that we have a good conscience, in all things desiring to live honorably.

19 But I especially urge you to do this, that I may be restored to you the sooner.

70 NU-Text and M-Text read us.

Benediction, Final Exhortation, Farewell

20 Now may the God of peace who brought up our Lord Jesus from the dead, that great Shepherd of the sheep, through the blood of the everlasting covenant,

21 make you complete in every good work to do His will, working in you[70] what is well pleasing in His sight, through Jesus Christ, to whom be glory forever and ever. Amen.

22 And I appeal to you, brethren, bear with the word of exhortation, for I have written to you in few words.

23 Know that our brother Timothy has been set free, with whom I shall see you if he comes shortly.

24 Greet all those who rule over you, and all the saints. Those from Italy greet you.

25 Grace be with you all. Amen.

Introduction to James

Written by James, the half-brother of Jesus, between A.D. 45 and 50, James is a letter to all Jewish Christians or "the twelve tribes which are scattered abroad" (James 1:1).

James is the most practical of all the Epistles, demonstrating that love and Christian faith must be shared through works and deeds. It encourages faith to be lived out by sharing and helping one another. James also encourages his readers to stand fast in the face of trials:

> My brethren, count it all joy when you fall into various trials, knowing that the testing of your faith produces patience. But let patience have *its* perfect work, that you may be perfect and complete, lacking nothing. If any of you lacks wisdom, let him ask of God, who gives to all liberally and without reproach, and it will be given to him.
>
> (James 1:2–5)

James must have witnessed his brother Jesus' attitude of concern for those who were in need. Perhaps this is why he appeals to us not to be simply hearers of the Word, but doers of the Word by caring for the poor, visiting the sick and depressed, and helping widows. We should be a light of hope when others are going through tough times.

An attitude of acceptance is also needed toward those who have not lived up to their faith. James encourages us not to judge but to welcome them back with loving-kindness. Much like his brother who touched the lives of all people, James tells us to be like Jesus. To find a need and fill it, find a hurt and heal it!

The Epistle of

James

Greeting to the Twelve Tribes

J AMES, a servant of God and of the Lord Jesus Christ,

To the twelve tribes which are scattered abroad:

Greetings.

Profiting from Trials

2 My brethren, count it all joy when you fall into various trials,
3 knowing that the testing of your faith produces patience.
4 But let patience have *its* perfect work, that you may be perfect and complete, lacking nothing.
5 If any of you lacks wisdom, let him ask of God, who gives to all liberally and without reproach, and it will be given to him.
6 But let him ask in faith, with no doubting, for he who doubts is like a wave of the sea driven and tossed by the wind.
7 For let not that man suppose that he will receive anything from the Lord;
8 *he is* a double-minded man, unstable in all his ways.

The Perspective of Rich and Poor

9 Let the lowly brother glory in his exaltation,
10 but the rich in his humiliation, because as a flower of the field he will pass away.
11 For no sooner has the sun risen with a burning heat than it withers the grass; its flower falls, and its beautiful appearance perishes. So the rich man also will fade away in his pursuits.

Loving God under Trials

12 Blessed *is* the man who endures temptation; for when he has been proved, he will receive the crown of life which the Lord has promised to those who love Him.
13 Let no one say when he is tempted, "I am tempted by God"; for God cannot be tempted by evil, nor does He Himself tempt anyone.
14 But each one is tempted when he is drawn away by his own desires and enticed.
15 Then, when desire has conceived, it gives birth to sin; and sin, when it is full-grown, brings forth death.
16 Do not be deceived, my beloved brethren.
17 Every good gift and every perfect gift is from above, and comes down from the Father of lights, with whom there is no variation or shadow of turning.
18 Of His own will He brought us forth by the word of truth, that we might be a kind of firstfruits of His creatures.

Qualities Needed in Trials

19 Therefore,[1] my beloved brethren, let every man be swift to hear, slow to speak, slow to wrath;
20 for the wrath of man does not produce the righteousness of God.

Doers—Not Hearers

21 Therefore lay aside all filthiness and overflow of wickedness, and receive with meekness the implanted word, which is able to save your souls.
22 But be doers of the word, and not hearers only, deceiving yourselves.
23 For if anyone is a hearer of the word and not a doer, he is like a man observing his natural face in a mirror;
24 for he observes himself, goes away, and immediately forgets what kind of man he was.
25 But he who looks into the perfect law of liberty and continues *in it*, and is not a forgetful hearer but a doer of the work, this one will be blessed in what he does.
26 If anyone among you[2] thinks he is religious, and does not bridle his tongue but deceives his own heart, this one's religion *is* useless.
27 Pure and undefiled religion before God and the Father is this: to visit orphans and widows in their trouble, *and* to keep oneself unspotted from the world.

1 NU-Text reads *Know (this)* or *(This) you know.*   2 NU-Text omits *among you.*

Beware of Personal Favoritism

2 My brethren, do not hold the faith of our Lord Jesus Christ, *the Lord* of glory, with partiality.
2 For if there should come into your assembly a man with gold rings, in fine apparel, and there should also come in a poor man in filthy clothes,
3 and you pay attention to the one wearing the fine clothes and say to him, "You sit here in a good place," and say to the poor man, "You stand there," or, "Sit here at my footstool,"
4 have you not shown partiality among yourselves, and become judges with evil thoughts?
5 Listen, my beloved brethren: Has God not chosen the poor of this world *to be* rich in faith and heirs of the kingdom which He promised to those who love Him?
6 But you have dishonored the poor man. Do not the rich oppress you and drag you into the courts?
7 Do they not blaspheme that noble name by which you are called?
8 If you really fulfill *the* royal law according to the Scripture, *"You shall love your neighbor as yourself,"*[3] you do well;
9 but if you show partiality, you commit sin, and are convicted by the law as transgressors.
10 For whoever shall keep the whole law, and yet stumble in one *point*, he is guilty of all.
11 For He who said, *"Do not commit adultery,"*[4] also said, *"Do not murder."*[5] Now if you do not commit adultery, but you do murder, you have become a transgressor of the law.
12 So speak and so do as those who will be judged by the law of liberty.
13 For judgment is without mercy to the one who has shown no mercy. Mercy triumphs over judgment.

Faith Without Works Is Dead

14 What *does it* profit, my brethren, if someone says he has faith but does not have works? Can faith save him?
15 If a brother or sister is naked and destitute of daily food,
16 and one of you says to them, "Depart in peace, be warmed and filled," but you do not give them the things which are needed for the body, what *does it* profit?
17 Thus also faith by itself, if it does not have works, is dead.
18 But someone will say, "You have faith, and I have works." Show me your faith without your[6] works, and I will show you my faith by my[6] works.
19 You believe that there is one God. You do well. Even the demons believe—and tremble!
20 But do you want to know, O foolish man, that faith without works is dead?[7]
21 Was not Abraham our father justified by works when he offered Isaac his son on the altar?
22 Do you see that faith was working together with his works, and by works faith was made perfect?
23 And the Scripture was fulfilled which says, *"Abraham believed God, and it was accounted to him for righteousness."*[8] And he was called the friend of God.
24 You see then that a man is justified by works, and not by faith only.
25 Likewise, was not Rahab the harlot also justified by works when she received the messengers and sent *them* out another way?
26 For as the body without the spirit is dead, so faith without works is dead also.

The Untamable Tongue

3 My brethren, let not many of you become teachers, knowing that we shall receive a stricter judgment.
2 For we all stumble in many things. If anyone does not stumble in word, he *is* a perfect man, able also to bridle the whole body.
3 Indeed,[9] we put bits in horses' mouths that they may obey us, and we turn their whole body.
4 Look also at ships: although they are so large and are driven by fierce winds, they are turned by a very small rudder wherever the pilot desires.
5 Even so the tongue is a little member and boasts great things. See how great a forest a little fire kindles!
6 And the tongue *is* a fire, a world of iniquity. The tongue is so set among our members that it defiles the whole body, and sets on fire the course of nature; and it is set on fire by hell.

3 Leviticus 19:18   4 Exodus 20:14; Deuteronomy 5:18   5 Exodus 20:13; Deuteronomy 5:17
6 NU-Text omits *your* and *my.*   7 NU-Text reads *useless.*   8 Genesis 15:6   9 NU-Text reads *Now if.*

7 For every kind of beast and bird, of reptile and creature of the sea, is tamed and has been tamed by mankind.
8 But no man can tame the tongue. *It is* an unruly evil, full of deadly poison.
9 With it we bless our God and Father, and with it we curse men, who have been made in the similitude of God.
10 Out of the same mouth proceed blessing and cursing. My brethren, these things ought not to be so.
11 Does a spring send forth fresh *water* and bitter from the same opening?
12 Can a fig tree, my brethren, bear olives, or a grapevine bear figs? Thus no spring *can* yield both salt water and fresh. 10

Heavenly Versus Demonic Wisdom

13 Who *is* wise and understanding among you? Let him show by good conduct *that* his works *are done* in the meekness of wisdom.
14 But if you have bitter envy and self-seeking in your hearts, do not boast and lie against the truth.
15 This wisdom does not descend from above, but *is* earthly, sensual, demonic.
16 For where envy and self-seeking *exist*, confusion and every evil thing *will be* there.
17 But the wisdom that is from above is first pure, then peaceable, gentle, willing to yield, full of mercy and good fruits, without partiality and without hypocrisy.
18 Now the fruit of righteousness is sown in peace by those who make peace.

Pride Promotes Strife

4 Where do wars and fights *come* from among you? Do *they* not *come* from your *desires for* pleasure that war in your members?
2 You lust and do not have. You murder and covet and cannot obtain. You fight and war. Yet11 you do not have because you do not ask.
3 You ask and do not receive, because you ask amiss, that you may spend *it* on your pleasures.
4 Adulterers and12 adulteresses! Do you not know that friendship with the world is enmity with God? Whoever therefore wants to be a friend of the world makes himself an enemy of God.

5 Or do you think that the Scripture says in vain, "The Spirit who dwells in us yearns jealously"?
6 But He gives more grace. Therefore He says:

"God resists the proud,
But gives grace to the humble." 13

Humility Cures Worldliness

7 Therefore submit to God. Resist the devil and he will flee from you.
8 Draw near to God and He will draw near to you. Cleanse *your* hands, *you* sinners; and purify *your* hearts, *you* doubleminded.
9 Lament and mourn and weep! Let your laughter be turned to mourning and *your* joy to gloom.
10 Humble yourselves in the sight of the Lord, and He will lift you up.

Do Not Judge a Brother

11 Do not speak evil of one another, brethren. He who speaks evil of a brother and judges his brother, speaks evil of the law and judges the law. But if you judge the law, you are not a doer of the law but a judge.
12 There is one Lawgiver,14 who is able to save and to destroy. Who15 are you to judge another? 16

Do Not Boast about Tomorrow

13 Come now, you who say, "Today or tomorrow we will17 go to such and such a city, spend a year there, buy and sell, and make a profit";
14 whereas you do not know what *will happen* tomorrow. For what *is* your life? It is even a vapor that appears for a little time and then vanishes away.
15 Instead you *ought* to say, "If the Lord wills, we shall live and do this or that."
16 But now you boast in your arrogance. All such boasting is evil.
17 Therefore, to him who knows to do good and does not do *it*, to him it is sin.

Rich Oppressors Will Be Judged

5 Come now, *you* rich, weep and howl for your miseries that are coming upon *you!*
2 Your riches are corrupted, and your garments are moth-eaten.

---

10 NU-Text reads *Neither can a salty spring produce fresh water.*   11 NU-Text and M-Text omit *Yet.*
12 NU-Text omits *Adulterers and.*   13 Proverbs 3:34   14 NU-Text adds *and Judge.*
15 NU-Text and M-Text read *But who.*   16 NU-Text reads *a neighbor.*   17 M-Text reads *let us.*

3 Your gold and silver are corroded, and their corrosion will be a witness against you and will eat your flesh like fire. You have heaped up treasure in the last days.
4 Indeed the wages of the laborers who mowed your fields, which you kept back by fraud, cry out; and the cries of the reapers have reached the ears of the Lord of Sabaoth.
5 You have lived on the earth in pleasure and luxury; you have fattened your hearts as[18] in a day of slaughter.
6 You have condemned, you have murdered the just; he does not resist you.

Be Patient and Persevering

7 Therefore be patient, brethren, until the coming of the Lord. See *how* the farmer waits for the precious fruit of the earth, waiting patiently for it until it receives the early and latter rain.
8 You also be patient. Establish your hearts, for the coming of the Lord is at hand.
9 Do not grumble against one another, brethren, lest you be condemned.[19] Behold, the Judge is standing at the door!
10 My brethren, take the prophets, who spoke in the name of the Lord, as an example of suffering and patience.
11 Indeed we count them blessed who endure. You have heard of the perseverance of Job and seen the end *intended by* the Lord— that the Lord is very compassionate and merciful.
12 But above all, my brethren, do not swear, either by heaven or by earth or with any other oath. But let your "Yes," be "Yes," and *your* "No," "No," lest you fall into judgment.[20]

Meeting Specific Needs

13 Is anyone among you suffering? Let him pray. Is anyone cheerful? Let him sing psalms.
14 Is anyone among you sick? Let him call for the elders of the church, and let them pray over him, anointing him with oil in the name of the Lord.
15 And the prayer of faith will save the sick, and the Lord will raise him up. And if he has committed sins, he will be forgiven.
16 Confess *your* trespasses[21] to one another, and pray for one another, that you may be healed. The effective, fervent prayer of a righteous man avails much.
17 Elijah was a man with a nature like ours, and he prayed earnestly that it would not rain; and it did not rain on the land for three years and six months.
18 And he prayed again, and the heaven gave rain, and the earth produced its fruit.

Bring Back the Erring One

19 Brethren, if anyone among you wanders from the truth, and someone turns him back,
20 let him know that he who turns a sinner from the error of his way will save a soul[22] from death and cover a multitude of sins.

18 NU-Text omits *as*.   19 NU-Text and M-Text read *judged.*   20 M-Text reads *hypocrisy.*
21 NU-Text reads *Therefore confess your sins.*   22 NU-Text reads *his soul.*

Introduction to First Peter

The apostle Peter was a bold individual who accompanied Jesus throughout His ministry. Peter's life had been transformed by the risen Lord Jesus Christ—from the depths of despair to the heights of hope! Peter wanted his readers to know that the resurrection of Jesus Christ was not done behind a curtain of obscurity but was open to the scrutiny and examination of the entire world!

The apostle wrote this letter to Christians in Asia Minor who were suffering great persecution. Written between A.D. 63 and 64, most likely from Rome, First Peter has often been called the "Epistle of Hope."

The Christian life, as Peter reveals, is to be centered around hope. This may seem inconceivable to those suffering for their faith. Yet Peter encourages them to stay true to their calling by God. Their faith is being tested through fire like gold. Peter promises that with hope, they will stand true.

Peter also discusses the effect their positive Christian life-styles can have on the unbelieving society around them. He urges them to fervently love one another and strangers as well.

Peter realized that encouragement was the key to keeping the faith and the dream of these early Christians alive. He offered them the vital ingredient to their success—hope!

Blessed be the God and Father of our Lord Jesus Christ, who according to His abundant mercy has begotten us again to a living hope through the resurrection of Jesus Christ from the dead, to an inheritance incorruptible and undefiled and that does not fade away, reserved in heaven for you.

(1 Pet. 1:3, 4)

The First Epistle of

Peter

Greeting to the Elect Pilgrims

PETER, an apostle of Jesus Christ,

To the pilgrims of the Dispersion in Pontus, Galatia, Cappadocia, Asia, and Bithynia,
2 elect according to the foreknowledge of God the Father, in sanctification of the Spirit, for obedience and sprinkling of the blood of Jesus Christ:

Grace to you and peace be multiplied.

A Heavenly Inheritance

3 Blessed *be* the God and Father of our Lord Jesus Christ, who according to His abundant mercy has begotten us again to a living hope through the resurrection of Jesus Christ from the dead,
4 to an inheritance incorruptible and undefiled and that does not fade away, reserved in heaven for you,
5 who are kept by the power of God through faith for salvation ready to be revealed in the last time.
6 In this you greatly rejoice, though now for a little while, if need be, you have been grieved by various trials,
7 that the genuineness of your faith, *being* much more precious than gold that perishes, though it is tested by fire, may be found to praise, honor, and glory at the revelation of Jesus Christ,
8 whom having not seen[1] you love. Though now you do not see *Him,* yet believing, you rejoice with joy inexpressible and full of glory,
9 receiving the end of your faith—the salvation of *your* souls.
10 Of this salvation the prophets have inquired and searched diligently, who prophesied of the grace *that would come* to you,
11 searching what, or what manner of time, the Spirit of Christ who was in them was indicating when He testified beforehand the sufferings of Christ and the glories that would follow.
12 To them it was revealed that, not to

themselves, but to us[2] they were ministering the things which now have been reported to you through those who have preached the gospel to you by the Holy Spirit sent from heaven—things which angels desire to look into.

Living Before God Our Father

13 Therefore gird up the loins of your mind, be sober, and rest *your* hope fully upon the grace that is to be brought to you at the revelation of Jesus Christ;
14 as obedient children, not conforming yourselves to the former lusts, *as* in your ignorance;
15 but as He who called you *is* holy, you also be holy in all *your* conduct,
16 because it is written, *"Be holy, for I am holy."*[3]
17 And if you call on the Father, who without partiality judges according to each one's work, conduct yourselves throughout the time of your sojourning *here* in fear;
18 knowing that you were not redeemed with corruptible things, *like* silver or gold, from your aimless conduct *received* by tradition from your fathers,
19 but with the precious blood of Christ, as of a lamb without blemish and without spot.
20 He indeed was foreordained before the foundation of the world, but was manifest in these last times for you
21 who through Him believe in God, who raised Him from the dead and gave Him glory, so that your faith and hope are in God.

The Enduring Word

22 Since you have purified your souls in obeying the truth through the Spirit[4] in sincere love of the brethren, love one another fervently with a pure heart,
23 having been born again, not of corruptible seed but incorruptible, through the word of God which lives and abides forever,[5]
24 because

---

1 M-Text reads *known.*   2 NU-Text and M-Text read *you.*   3 Leviticus 11:44, 45; 19:2; 20:7
4 NU-Text omits *through the Spirit.*   5 NU-Text omits *forever.*

"All flesh is as grass,
And all the glory of man[6]
as the flower of the grass.
The grass withers,
And its flower falls away,
25 *But the word of the LORD*
endures forever."[7]

Now this is the word which by the gospel was preached to you.

2 Therefore, laying aside all malice, all guile, hypocrisy, envy, and all evil speaking,

2 as newborn babes, desire the pure milk of the word, that you may grow thereby,[8]

3 if indeed you have tasted that the Lord *is* gracious.

The Chosen Stone and His Chosen People

4 Coming to Him *as to* a living stone, rejected indeed by men, but chosen by God *and* precious,

5 you also, as living stones, are being built up a spiritual house, a holy priesthood, to offer up spiritual sacrifices acceptable to God through Jesus Christ.

6 Therefore it is also contained in the Scripture,

"Behold, I lay in Zion
A chief cornerstone, elect, precious,
And he who believes on Him will by
no means be put to shame."[9]

7 Therefore, to you who believe, *He is* precious; but to those who are disobedient,[10]

"The stone which the builders rejected
Has become the chief cornerstone,"[11]

8 and

"A stone of stumbling
And a rock of offense."[12]

They stumble, being disobedient to the word, to which they also were appointed.

9 But you *are* a chosen generation, a royal priesthood, a holy nation, His own special people, that you may proclaim the praises of Him who called you out of darkness into His marvelous light;

10 who once *were* not a people but *are* now the people of God, who had not obtained mercy but now have obtained mercy.

Living Before the World

11 Beloved, I beg *you* as sojourners and pilgrims, abstain from fleshly lusts which war against the soul,

12 having your conduct honorable among the Gentiles, that when they speak against you as evildoers, they may, by *your* good works which they observe, glorify God in the day of visitation.

Submission to Government

13 Therefore submit yourselves to every ordinance of man for the Lord's sake, whether to the king as supreme,

14 or to governors, as to those who are sent by him for the punishment of evildoers and *for the* praise of those who do good.

15 For this is the will of God, that by doing good you may put to silence the ignorance of foolish men—

16 as free, yet not using *your* liberty as a cloak for vice, but as servants of God.

17 Honor all *people.* Love the brotherhood. Fear God. Honor the king.

Submission to Masters

18 Servants, *be* submissive to *your* masters with all fear, not only to the good and gentle, but also to the harsh.

19 For this *is* commendable, if because of conscience toward God one endures grief, suffering wrongfully.

20 For what credit *is it* if, when you are beaten for your faults, you take it patiently? But when you do good and suffer *for it,* if you take it patiently, this *is* commendable before God.

21 For to this you were called, because Christ also suffered for us,[13] leaving us[14] an example, that you should follow His steps:

22 *"Who committed no sin,*
Nor was guile found in His mouth";[15]

23 who, when He was reviled, did not revile in return; when He suffered, He did not threaten, but committed *Himself* to Him who judges righteously;

24 who Himself bore our sins in His own body on the tree, that we, having died to

---

6 NU-Text reads *all its glory.*   7 Isaiah 40:6–8   8 NU-Text adds *up to salvation.*   9 Isaiah 28:16
10 NU-Text reads *to those who disbelieve.*   11 Psalm 118:22   12 Isaiah 8:14   13 NU-Text reads *you.*
14 NU-Text and M-Text read *you.*   15 Isaiah 53:9

sins, might live for righteousness—by whose stripes you were healed.

25 For you were like sheep going astray, but have now returned to the Shepherd and Overseer[16] of your souls.

Submission to Husbands

3 Likewise *you* wives, *be* submissive to your own husbands, that even if some do not obey the word, they, without a word, may be won by the conduct of their wives,

2 when they observe your chaste conduct *accompanied* by fear.

3 Do not let your beauty be that outward *adorning* of arranging the hair, of wearing gold, or of putting on *fine* apparel;

4 but *let it be* the hidden person of the heart, with the incorruptible *ornament* of a gentle and quiet spirit, which is very precious in the sight of God.

5 For in this manner, in former times, the holy women who trusted in God also adorned themselves, being submissive to their own husbands,

6 as Sarah obeyed Abraham, calling him lord, whose daughters you are if you do good and are not afraid with any terror.

A Word to Husbands

7 Likewise *you* husbands, dwell with *them* with understanding, giving honor to the wife, as to the weaker vessel, and as *being* heirs together of the grace of life, that your prayers may not be hindered.

Called to Blessing

8 Finally, all of *you be* of one mind, having compassion for one another; love as brothers, *be* tenderhearted, *be* courteous;[17]

9 not returning evil for evil or reviling for reviling, but on the contrary blessing, knowing that you were called to this, that you may inherit a blessing.

10 For

> "He who would love life
>   And see good days,
>   Let him refrain his tongue from evil,
>   And his lips from speaking guile;
> 11 Let him turn away from evil
>   and do good;
>   Let him seek peace and pursue it.

12 For the eyes of the LORD
    are on the righteous,
  And his ears *are* open to their prayers;
  But the face of the LORD is against
    those who do evil."[18]

Suffering for Right and Wrong

13 And who *is* he who will harm you if you become followers of what is good?

14 But even if you should suffer for righteousness' sake, *you are* blessed. "And do not be afraid of their threats, nor be troubled."[19]

15 But sanctify the Lord God[20] in your hearts, and always *be* ready to *give* a defense to everyone who asks you a reason for the hope that is in you, with meekness and fear;

16 having a good conscience, that when they defame you as evildoers, those who revile your good conduct in Christ may be ashamed.

17 For *it is* better, if it is the will of God, to suffer for doing good than for doing evil.

Christ's Suffering and Ours

18 For Christ also suffered once for sins, the just for the unjust, that He might bring us[21] to God, being put to death in the flesh but made alive by the Spirit,

19 by whom also He went and preached to the spirits in prison,

20 who formerly were disobedient, when once the longsuffering of God waited[22] in the days of Noah, while the ark was being prepared, in which a few, that is, eight souls, were saved through water.

21 There is also an antitype which now saves us, *namely* baptism (not the removal of the filth of the flesh, but the answer of a good conscience toward God), through the resurrection of Jesus Christ,

22 who has gone into heaven and is at the right hand of God, angels and authorities and powers having been made subject to Him.

4 Therefore, since Christ suffered for us[23] in the flesh, arm yourselves also with the same mind, for he who has suffered in the flesh has ceased from sin,

2 that he no longer should live the rest of *his* time in the flesh for the lusts of men, but for the will of God.

3 For we *have spent* enough of our past lifetime[24] in doing the will of the Gen-

---

16 Greek *episkopon*   17 NU-Text reads *humble.*   18 Psalm 34:12-16   19 Isaiah 8:12
20 NU-Text reads *Christ as Lord.*   21 NU-Text and M-Text read *you.*
22 NU-Text and M-Text read *waited patiently.*   23 NU-Text omits *for us.*   24 NU-Text reads *time.*

tiles—when we walked in licentiousness, lusts, drunkenness, revelries, drinking parties, and abominable idolatries.
4 In regard to these, they think it strange that you do not run with *them* in the same flood of dissipation, speaking evil of *you*.
5 They will give an account to Him who is ready to judge the living and the dead.
6 For this reason the gospel was preached also to those who are dead, that they might be judged according to men in the flesh, but live according to God in the spirit.

Serving for God's Glory

7 But the end of all things is at hand; therefore be serious and watchful in your prayers.
8 And above all things have fervent love for one another, for *"love will cover a multitude of sins."*25
9 *Be* hospitable to one another without grumbling.
10 As each one has received a gift, minister it to one another, as good stewards of the manifold grace of God.
11 If anyone speaks, *let him speak* as the oracles of God. If anyone ministers, *let him do it* as with the ability which God supplies, that in all things God may be glorified through Jesus Christ, to whom belong the glory and the dominion forever and ever. Amen.

Suffering for God's Glory

12 Beloved, do not think it strange concerning the fiery trial which is to try you, as though some strange thing happened to you;
13 but rejoice to the extent that you partake of Christ's sufferings, that when His glory is revealed, you may also be glad with exceeding joy.
14 If you are reproached for the name of Christ, blessed *are you*, for the Spirit of glory and of God rests upon you.26 On their part He is blasphemed, but on your part He is glorified.
15 But let none of you suffer as a murderer, a thief, an evildoer, or as a busybody in other people's matters.
16 Yet if *anyone suffers* as a Christian, let him not be ashamed, but let him glorify God in this matter.27

17 For the time *has come* for judgment to begin at the house of God; and if *it begins* with us first, what will *be* the end of those who do not obey the gospel of God?
18 Now

*"If the righteous one is scarcely saved,
Where will the ungodly and the sinner
appear?"*28

19 Therefore let those who suffer according to the will of God commit their souls *to Him* in doing good, as to a faithful Creator.

Shepherd the Flock

5 The elders who are among you I exhort, I who am a fellow elder and a witness of the sufferings of Christ, and also a partaker of the glory that will be revealed:
2 Shepherd the flock of God which is among you, serving as overseers, not by constraint but willingly,29 not for dishonest gain but eagerly;
3 nor as being lords over those entrusted to you, but being examples to the flock;
4 and when the Chief Shepherd appears, you will receive the crown of glory that does not fade away.

Submit to God, Resist the Devil

5 Likewise you younger people, submit yourselves to *your* elders. Yes, all of *you* be submissive to one another, and be clothed with humility, for

*"God resists the proud,
But gives grace to the humble."*30

6 Therefore humble yourselves under the mighty hand of God, that He may exalt you in due time,
7 casting all your care upon Him, for He cares for you.
8 Be sober, be vigilant; because31 your adversary the devil walks about like a roaring lion, seeking whom he may devour.
9 Resist him, steadfast in the faith, knowing that the same sufferings are experienced by your brotherhood in the world.
10 But may32 the God of all grace, who

25 Proverbs 10:12   26 NU-Text omits the rest of this verse.   27 NU-Text reads *name.*   28 Proverbs 11:31
29 NU-Text adds *according to God.*   30 Proverbs 3:34   31 NU-Text and M-Text omit *because.*
32 NU-Text reads *But the God of all grace will . . . perfect, establish, strengthen, and settle you.*

called us[33] to His eternal glory by Christ Jesus, after you have suffered a while, perfect, establish, strengthen, and settle *you*.

11 To Him *be* the glory and the dominion forever and ever. Amen.

Farewell and Peace

12 By Silvanus, our faithful brother as I consider him, I have written to you briefly, exhorting and testifying that this is the true grace of God in which you stand.

13 She who is in Babylon, elect together with *you*, greets you; and *so does* Mark my son.

14 Greet one another with a kiss of love. Peace to you all who are in Christ Jesus. Amen.

33 NU-Text and M-Text read *you.*

Introduction to Second Peter

The second letter of Peter to Christians in Asia Minor was written shortly before Peter's martyrdom probably in A.D. 64. Peter knew his death was imminent, yet he displays strong positive characteristics by encouraging other Christians also suffering persecution to focus their thoughts on God's exceeding great and precious promises.

Peter reminds his readers that their faith is based on the historical centainty of Jesus Christ's resurrection, "For we did not follow cunningly devised fables when we made known to you the power and coming of our Lord Jesus Christ, but were eyewitnesses of His majesty" (2 Pet. 1:16). This personal conviction carried Peter from the small fishing village of Bethsaida, on the shores of the Sea of Galilee, to the mighty pagan center of Rome. And this same faith would carry them through any difficult and trying time.

Because they lived on the famous travel route connecting the east with Rome, Christians in Asia Minor were exposed to many strange ideas and false religions. Peter warns them not to mix the negative doctrines of these false religions with their positive Christian faith.

It would have been easy for these Christians to have given in to the persecution and false doctrines, yet Peter encouraged them to fix their hope on the power of God and Christ's second coming. They had the strength to do this because God had given them everything that pertained to life and godliness. They were not to be intimidated by the impossibilities of their surroundings, but they were to be motivated by the greater possibility—life in Jesus Christ!

The Second Epistle of

Peter

Greeting the Faithful

SIMON PETER, a servant and apostle of Jesus Christ,

To those who have obtained like precious faith with us by the righteousness of our God and Savior Jesus Christ:

2 Grace and peace be multiplied to you in the knowledge of God and of Jesus our Lord,
3 as His divine power has given to us all things that *pertain* to life and godliness, through the knowledge of Him who called us by glory and virtue,
4 by which have been given to us exceedingly great and precious promises, that through these you may be partakers of the divine nature, having escaped the corruption *that is* in the world through lust.

Fruitful Growth in the Faith

5 But also for this very reason, giving all diligence, add to your faith virtue, to virtue knowledge,   .
6 to knowledge self-control, to self-control perseverance, to perseverance godliness,
7 to godliness brotherly kindness, and to brotherly kindness love.
8 For if these things are yours and abound, *you will be* neither barren nor unfruitful in the knowledge of our Lord Jesus Christ.
9 For he who lacks these things is short-sighted, even to blindness, and has forgotten that he was purged from his old sins.
10 Therefore, brethren, be even more diligent to make your calling and election sure, for if you do these things you will never stumble;
11 for so an entrance will be supplied to you abundantly into the everlasting kingdom of our Lord and Savior Jesus Christ.

Peter's Approaching Death

12 Therefore I will not be negligent to remind you always of these things, though you know *them*, and *are* established in the present truth.
13 Yes, I think it is right, as long as I am in this tent, to stir you up by reminding *you*,
14 knowing that shortly I *must* put off my tent, just as our Lord Jesus Christ showed me.
15 Moreover I will be careful to ensure that you always have a reminder of these things after my decease.

The Trustworthy Prophetic Word

16 For we did not follow cunningly devised fables when we made known to you the power and coming of our Lord Jesus Christ, but were eyewitnesses of His majesty.
17 For He received from God the Father honor and glory when such a voice came to Him from the Excellent Glory: "This is My beloved Son, in whom I am well pleased."
18 And we heard this voice which came from heaven when we were with Him on the holy mountain.
19 We also have the prophetic word made more sure, which you do well to heed as a light that shines in a dark place, until the day dawns and the morning star rises in your hearts;
20 knowing this first, that no prophecy of Scripture is of any private interpretation,[1]
21 for prophecy never came by the will of man, but holy men of God[2] spoke *as they were* moved by the Holy Spirit.

Destructive Doctrines

2 But there were also false prophets among the people, even as there will be false teachers among you, who will secretly bring in destructive heresies, even denying the Lord who bought them, *and* bring on themselves swift destruction.
2 And many will follow their destructive ways, because of whom the way of truth will be blasphemed.
3 By covetousness they will exploit you with deceptive words; for a long time

1 Or *origin*   2 NU-Text reads *but men spoke from God.*

I Will Build My Church

One of the most remarkable elements of our faith is that Jesus Christ has called us to fulfill His ministry—to help build His church. If He trusts us—how can we do less?

Near the end of His earthly ministry, Jesus took his closest disciples to a high mountain in northern Galilee. Here in the region of Caesarea Philippi was a major seat of political and religious power.

The area was known for its pagan worship and divine homage to political rulers. The Canaanite god, Baal, and the Greek gods, Pan and Aphrodite, inspired devotion from their followers. Caesar Augustus, Mark Anthony, Nero, and Claudius elevated themselves to the rank of deity to demand political flattery from their subjects.

Among the Jews, the gentile cities of Caesarea Philippi, Jaffa, Ptolemais, Caesarea, Rome, Tyre, and Sidon were all feared and branded the "gates of hell." No upright Jew would go near these pagan centers.

Against this background, Jesus summoned His disciples to make a decision. " 'But who do you say that I am?' Peter answered and said, 'You are the Christ, the Son of the living God.' Jesus answered and said to him, 'Blessed are you, Simon Bar-Jonah, for flesh and blood has not revealed *this* to you, but My Father who is in heaven . . . you are Peter, and on this rock I will build My church, and the gates of Hades shall not prevail against it' " (Matt. 16:15–18). This was a spiritual reference to "the rulers of the darkness of this age" (Eph. 6:12) with cultural and historical relevance.

Not until after Jesus' death and resurrection did Peter understand the full meaning of his Lord's commission. Inspired by Christ's promise, Peter fulfilled his call. He was the first disciple to bring the Good News of Jesus Christ to the cities of Jaffa, Caesarea, and Rome. He put aside his prejudice, hatred, and contempt for the cities known as the "gates of hell." God gave him the message of love, hope, and forgiveness for all mankind.

One simple fisherman from the shores of Galilee walked straight into the gates of hell to build the foundation of the church of God, and nothing prevailed against him.

their judgment has not been idle, and their destruction does[3] not slumber.

Doom of False Teachers

4 For if God did not spare the angels who sinned, but cast *them* down to hell and delivered *them* into chains of darkness, to be reserved for judgment;
5 and did not spare the ancient world, but saved Noah, *one of* eight *people*, a preacher of righteousness, bringing in the flood on the world of the ungodly;
6 and turning the cities of Sodom and Gomorrah into ashes, condemned *them* to destruction, making *them* an example to those who afterward would live ungodly;
7 and delivered righteous Lot, *who was* oppressed with the filthy conduct of the wicked
8 (for that righteous man, dwelling among them, tormented *his* righteous soul from day to day by seeing and hearing *their* lawless deeds)—
9 *then* the Lord knows how to deliver the godly out of temptations and to reserve the unjust under punishment for the day of judgment,
10 and especially those who walk according to the flesh in the lust of uncleanness and despise authority. *They are* presumptuous, self-willed; they are not afraid to speak evil of dignitaries,
11 whereas angels, who are greater in power and might, do not bring a reviling accusation against them before the Lord.

Depravity of False Teachers

12 But these, like natural brute beasts made to be caught and destroyed, speak evil of the things they do not understand, and will utterly perish in their own corruption,
13 *and* will receive the wages of unrighteousness, *as* those who count it pleasure to carouse in the daytime. *They are* spots and blemishes, carousing in their own deceptions while they feast with you,
14 having eyes full of adultery and that cannot cease from sin, beguiling unstable souls. *They have* a heart trained in covetous practices, *and are* accursed children.
15 They have forsaken the right way and gone astray, following the way of Balaam the *son* of Beor, who loved the wages of unrighteousness;

16 but he was rebuked for his iniquity: a dumb donkey speaking with a man's voice restrained the madness of the prophet.
17 These are wells without water, clouds[4] carried by a tempest, to whom the gloom of darkness is reserved forever.[5]

Deceptions of False Teachers

18 For when they speak great swelling *words* of emptiness, they allure through the lusts of the flesh, through licentiousness, the ones who have actually escaped[6] from those who live in error.
19 While they promise them liberty, they themselves are slaves of corruption; for by whom a person is overcome, by him also he is brought into bondage.
20 For if, after they have escaped the pollutions of the world through the knowledge of the Lord and Savior Jesus Christ, they are again entangled in them and overcome, the latter end is worse for them than the beginning.
21 For it would have been better for them not to have known the way of righteousness, than having known *it*, to turn from the holy commandment delivered to them.
22 But it has happened to them according to the true proverb: "A dog *returns to his own vomit*,"[7] and, "a sow, having washed, to her wallowing in the mire."

God's Promise Is Not Slack

3 Beloved, I now write to you this second epistle (in *both of* which I stir up your pure minds by way of reminder),
2 that you may be mindful of the words which were spoken before by the holy prophets, and of the commandment of us[8] the apostles of the Lord and Savior,
3 knowing this first: that scoffers will come in the last days, walking according to their own lusts,
4 and saying, "Where is the promise of His coming? For since the fathers fell asleep, all things continue as *they were* from the beginning of creation."
5 For this they willfully forget: that by the word of God the heavens were of old, and the earth standing out of water and in the water,
6 by which the world *that* then existed perished, being flooded with water.

---

3 M-Text reads *will*.   4 NU-Text reads *and mists*.   5 NU-Text omits *forever*.
6 NU-Text reads *are barely escaping*.   7 Proverbs 26:11   8 NU-Text and M-Text read *commandment of the apostles of your Lord and Savior* or *commandment of your apostles of the Lord and Savior*.

7 But the heavens and the earth *which* now *exist* are kept in store by the same word, reserved for fire until the day of judgment and perdition of ungodly men.
8 But, beloved, do not forget this one thing, that with the Lord one day *is* as a thousand years, and a thousand years as one day.
9 The Lord is not slack concerning *His* promise, as some count slackness, but is longsuffering toward us,⁹ not willing that any should perish but that all should come to repentance.

The Day of the Lord

10 But the day of the Lord will come as a thief in the night, in which the heavens will pass away with a great noise, and the elements will melt with fervent heat; both the earth and the works that are in it will be burned up.¹⁰
11 Therefore, since all these things will be dissolved, what manner *of persons* ought you to be in holy conduct and godliness,
12 looking for and hastening the coming of the day of God, because of which the heavens will be dissolved being on fire, and the elements will melt with fervent heat?

13 Nevertheless we, according to His promise, look for new heavens and a new earth in which righteousness dwells.

Be Steadfast

14 Therefore, beloved, looking forward to these things, be diligent to be found by Him in peace, without spot and blameless;
15 and account *that* the longsuffering of our Lord *is* salvation—as also our beloved brother Paul, according to the wisdom given to him, has written to you,
16 as also in all his epistles, speaking in them of these things, in which are some things hard to understand, which those *who are* untaught and unstable twist to their own destruction, as *they do* also the rest of the Scriptures.
17 You therefore, beloved, since you know *these things* beforehand, beware lest you also fall from your own steadfastness, being led away with the error of the wicked;
18 but grow in the grace and knowledge of our Lord and Savior Jesus Christ. To Him *be* the glory both now and forever. Amen.

9 NU-Text reads *you.*   10 NU-Text reads *laid bare* (literally *found*).

Introduction to First John

The First Epistle of John was written by the apostle John sometime in the 80s or 90s of the first century. John, the son of Zebedee, most likely wrote this letter prior to being banished to the island of Patmos by the Roman Emperor Domitian.

John's aim was to strengthen his readers (Christians in Asia Minor), to give them knowledge, joy, and assurance in their faith. He also hoped to build their confidence and self-esteem as they realized God was faithful to forgive their sins and wipe any guilt from their lives. Then they could truly be free to carry out God's command to love one another.

John reminds us that love is not just by word, but by deed and truth. The life of a believer is more than just saying "I love you." It is living it out! John writes about a reaction concerning the humanity of Jesus Christ. In today's society, we often face the opposite position—that Jesus was not really God. John assures his readers from a first-hand experience that Jesus is fully God and fully man, whose unique purpose is to restore fellowship between men and women and their Creator Father.

John encourages his readers to be practical and action-oriented in living out their faith. In demonstrating love, he makes it clear that love is not love until you give it away!

Beloved, let us love one another, for love is of God; and everyone who loves is born of God and knows God. He who does not love does not know God, for God is love. In this the love of God was manifested toward us, that God has sent His only begotten Son into the world, that we might live through Him. Beloved, if God so loved us, we also ought to love one another.

(1 John 4:7–9, 11)

The First Epistle of

John

What Was Heard, Seen, and Touched

THAT which was from the beginning, which we have heard, which we have seen with our eyes, which we have looked upon, and our hands have handled, concerning the Word of life—
2 the life was manifested, and we have seen, and bear witness, and declare to you that eternal life which was with the Father and was manifested to us—
3 that which we have seen and heard we declare to you, that you also may have fellowship with us; and truly our fellowship is with the Father and with His Son Jesus Christ.
4 And these things we write to you that your[1] joy may be full.

The Basis of Fellowship with Him

5 This is the message which we have heard from Him and declare to you, that God is light and in Him is no darkness at all.
6 If we say that we have fellowship with Him, and walk in darkness, we lie and do not practice the truth.
7 But if we walk in the light as He is in the light, we have fellowship with one another, and the blood of Jesus Christ His Son cleanses us from all sin.
8 If we say that we have no sin, we deceive ourselves, and the truth is not in us.
9 If we confess our sins, He is faithful and just to forgive us our sins and to cleanse us from all unrighteousness.
10 If we say that we have not sinned, we make Him a liar, and His word is not in us.

2 My little children, these things I write to you, that you may not sin. And if anyone sins, we have an Advocate with the Father, Jesus Christ the righteous.
2 And He Himself is the propitiation for our sins, and not for ours only but also for the whole world.

The Test of Knowing Him

3 Now by this we know that we know Him, if we keep His commandments.
4 He who says, "I know Him," and does not keep His commandments, is a liar, and the truth is not in him.
5 But whoever keeps His word, truly the love of God is perfected in him. By this we know that we are in Him.
6 He who says he abides in Him ought himself also to walk just as He walked.
7 Brethren,[2] I write no new commandment to you, but an old commandment which you have had from the beginning. The old commandment is the word which you heard from the beginning.[3]
8 Again, a new commandment I write to you, which thing is true in Him and in you, because the darkness is passing away, and the true light is already shining.
9 He who says he is in the light, and hates his brother, is in darkness until now.
10 He who loves his brother abides in the light, and there is no cause for stumbling in him.
11 But he who hates his brother is in darkness and walks in darkness, and does not know where he is going, because the darkness has blinded his eyes.

Their Spiritual State

12 I write to you, little children,
　Because your sins are forgiven you
　　for His name's sake.
13 I write to you, fathers,
　Because you have known Him
　　who is from the beginning.
I write to you, young men,
　Because you have overcome
　　the wicked one.
I write to you, little children,
　Because you have known the Father.
14 I have written to you, fathers,
　Because you have known Him
　　who is from the beginning.
I have written to you, young men,
　Because you are strong, and the word
　　of God abides in you,

---

1 NU-Text and part of M-Text read our.　2 NU-Text reads Beloved.　3 NU-Text omits from the beginning.

And you have overcome the wicked one.

Do Not Love the World

15 Do not love the world or the things in the world. If anyone loves the world, the love of the Father is not in him. 16 For all that *is* in the world—the lust of the flesh, the lust of the eyes, and the pride of life—is not of the Father but is of the world. 17 And the world is passing away, and the lust of it; but he who does the will of God abides forever.

Deceptions of the Last Hour

18 Little children, it is the last hour; and as you have heard that the[4] Antichrist is coming, even now many antichrists have come, by which we know that it is the last hour. 19 They went out from us, but they were not of us; for if they had been of us, they would have continued with us; but *they went out* that they might be made manifest, that none of them were of us. 20 But you have an anointing from the Holy One, and you know all things.[5] 21 I have not written to you because you do not know the truth, but because you know it, and that no lie is of the truth. 22 Who is a liar but he who denies that Jesus is the Christ? He is antichrist who denies the Father and the Son. 23 Whoever denies the Son does not have the Father either; he who acknowledges the Son has the Father also.

Let Truth Abide in You

24 Therefore let that abide in you which you heard from the beginning. If what you heard from the beginning abides in you, you also will abide in the Son and in the Father. 25 And this is the promise that He has promised us—eternal life. 26 These *things* I have written to you concerning those who *try to* deceive you. 27 But the anointing which you have received from Him abides in you, and you do not need that anyone teach you; but as the same anointing teaches you concerning all things, and is true, and is not a lie, and just as it has taught you, you will[6] abide in Him.

The Children of God

28 And now, little children, abide in Him, that when[7] He appears, we may have confidence and not be ashamed before Him at His coming. 29 If you know that He is righteous, you know that everyone who practices righteousness is born of Him.

3 Behold what manner of love the Father has bestowed on us, that we should be called children of God![8] Therefore the world does not know us,[9] because it did not know Him. 2 Beloved, now we are children of God; and it has not yet been revealed what we shall be, but we know that when He is revealed, we shall be like Him, for we shall see Him as He is. 3 And everyone who has this hope in Him purifies himself, just as He is pure.

Sin and the Child of God

4 Whoever commits sin also commits lawlessness, and sin is lawlessness. 5 And you know that He was manifested to take away our sins, and in Him there is no sin. 6 Whoever abides in Him does not sin. Whoever sins has neither seen Him nor known Him. 7 Little children, let no one deceive you. He who practices righteousness is righteous, just as He is righteous. 8 He who sins is of the devil, for the devil has sinned from the beginning. For this purpose the Son of God was manifested, that He might destroy the works of the devil. 9 Whoever has been born of God does not sin, for His seed remains in him; and he cannot sin, because he has been born of God.

The Imperative of Love

10 In this the children of God and the children of the devil are manifest: Whoever does not practice righteousness is not of God, nor *is* he who does not love his brother. 11 For this is the message that you heard from the beginning, that we should love one another, 12 not as Cain *who* was of the wicked one and murdered his brother. And why did

---

4 NU-Text omits *the.*   5 NU-Text reads *you all know.*   6 NU-Text reads *you abide.*   7 NU-Text reads *if.*
8 NU-Text adds *And we are.*   9 M-Text reads *you.*

he murder him? Because his works were evil and his brother's righteous.
13 Do not marvel, my brethren, if the world hates you.
14 We know that we have passed from death to life, because we love the brethren. He who does not love *his* brother[10] abides in death.
15 Whoever hates his brother is a murderer, and you know that no murderer has eternal life abiding in him.

The Outworking of Love

16 By this we know love, because He laid down His life for us. And we also ought to lay down *our* lives for the brethren.
17 But whoever has this world's goods, and sees his brother in need, and shuts up his heart from him, how does the love of God abide in him?
18 My little children, let us not love in word or in tongue, but in deed and in truth.
19 And by this we know[11] that we are of the truth, and shall assure our hearts before Him.
20 For if our heart condemns us, God is greater than our heart, and knows all things.
21 Beloved, if our heart does not condemn us, we have confidence toward God.
22 And whatever we ask we receive from Him, because we keep His commandments and do those things that are pleasing in His sight.
23 And this is His commandment: that we should believe on the name of His Son Jesus Christ and love one another, as He gave us[12] commandment.

The Spirit of Truth and the Spirit of Error

24 Now he who keeps His commandments abides in Him, and He in him. And by this we know that He abides in us, by the Spirit whom He has given us.

4 Beloved, do not believe every spirit, but test the spirits, whether they are of God; because many false prophets have gone out into the world.
2 By this you know the Spirit of God: Every spirit that confesses that Jesus Christ has come in the flesh is of God,
3 and every spirit that does not confess that Jesus Christ has come in the flesh[13] is not of God. And this is the *spirit* of the Antichrist, which you have heard was coming, and is now already in the world.
4 You are of God, little children, and have overcome them, because He who is in you is greater than he who is in the world.
5 They are of the world. Therefore they speak *as* of the world, and the world hears them.
6 We are of God. He who knows God hears us; he who is not of God does not hear us. By this we know the spirit of truth and the spirit of error.

Knowing God Through Love

7 Beloved, let us love one another, for love is of God; and everyone who loves is born of God and knows God.
8 He who does not love does not know God, for God is love.
9 In this the love of God was manifested toward us, that God has sent His only begotten Son into the world, that we might live through Him.
10 In this is love, not that we loved God, but that He loved us and sent His Son *to be* the propitiation for our sins.
11 Beloved, if God so loved us, we also ought to love one another.

Seeing God Through Love

12 No one has seen God at any time. If we love one another, God abides in us, and His love has been perfected in us.
13 By this we know that we abide in Him, and He in us, because He has given us of His Spirit.
14 And we have seen and testify that the Father has sent the Son *as* Savior of the world.
15 Whoever confesses that Jesus is the Son of God, God abides in him, and he in God.
16 And we have known and believed the love that God has for us. God is love, and he who abides in love abides in God, and God in him.

The Consummation of Love

17 Love has been perfected among us in this: that we may have boldness in the day of judgment; because as He is, so are we in this world.
18 There is no fear in love; but perfect love casts out fear, because fear involves

---

10 NU-Text omits *his brother.*   11 NU-Text reads *we shall know.*   12 M-Text omits *us.*
13 NU-Text omits *that* and *Christ has come in the flesh.*

God Loves You and So Do I!

One day, while teaching in the temple, Jesus was asked by a Pharisee, "Teacher, which *is* the great commandment in the law?" Jesus replied, "You shall love the LORD your God with all your heart, with all your soul, and with all your mind" (Matt. 22:36, 37).

Then he added, "And *the* second *is* like it: You shall love your neighbor as yourself" (Matt. 22:39). This term "like" can be understood as equal. The two commandments are contingent, each dependent upon the other.

Jesus lived a life that was worthy of this teaching, for throughout His ministry His goal was to reveal the love of God through His love for all people. He taught His disciples, "As the Father loved Me, I also have loved you" (John 15:9). "A new commandment I give to you, that you love one another" (John 13:34).

The supreme act of love came when Jesus willingly died on the cross to bring us into an intimate relationship with God. Through the cross, Jesus declared His love for all people. Because of His love in our lives, we now can love each other.

The cross itself symbolizes this relationship of love. Like the vertical post of the cross, our lives must receive the love of God from above. Then like outstretched arms in a horizontal position, we can extend this love to others. As God loves us so we should love each other.

Our lives can reflect this relationship, because from the love of God we receive the feeling of self-worth that enables us to love other people without the fear of rejection. Then we can live a life which truly says, "God loves you and so do I!"

torment. But he who fears has not been made perfect in love.
19 We love Him[14] because He first loved us.

Obedience by Faith

20 If someone says, "I love God," and hates his brother, he is a liar; for he who does not love his brother whom he has seen, how can[15] he love God whom he has not seen?
21 And this commandment we have from Him: that he who loves God *must* love his brother also.

5 Whoever believes that Jesus is the Christ is born of God, and everyone who loves Him who begot also loves him who is begotten of Him.
2 By this we know that we love the children of God, when we love God and keep His commandments.
3 For this is the love of God, that we keep His commandments. And His commandments are not burdensome.
4 For whatever is born of God overcomes the world. And this is the victory that has overcome the world—our[16] faith.
5 Who is he who overcomes the world, but he who believes that Jesus is the Son of God?

The Certainty of God's Witness

6 This is He who came by water and blood—Jesus Christ; not only by water, but by water and blood. And it is the Spirit who bears witness, because the Spirit is truth.
7 For there are three who bear witness in heaven: the Father, the Word, and the Holy Spirit; and these three are one.
8 And there are three that bear witness on earth:[17] the Spirit, the water, and the blood; and these three agree as one.
9 If we receive the witness of men, the witness of God is greater; for this is the witness of God which[18] He has testified of His Son.
10 He who believes in the Son of God has the witness in himself; he who does not believe God has made Him a liar, because he has not believed the testimony that God has given of His Son.
11 And this is the testimony: that God has given us eternal life, and this life is in His Son.
12 He who has the Son has life; he who does not have the Son of God does not have life.
13 These things I have written to you who believe in the name of the Son of God, that you may know that you have eternal life,[19] and that you may *continue to* believe in the name of the Son of God.

Confidence and Compassion in Prayer

14 Now this is the confidence that we have in Him, that if we ask anything according to His will, He hears us.
15 And if we know that He hears us, whatever we ask, we know that we have the petitions that we have asked of Him.
16 If anyone sees his brother sinning a sin *which does* not *lead* to death, he will ask, and He will give him life for those who commit sin not *leading* to death. There is sin *leading* to death. I do not say that he should pray about that.
17 All unrighteousness is sin, and there is sin not *leading* to death.

Knowing the True—Rejecting the False

18 We know that whoever is born of God does not sin; but he who has been born of God keeps himself,[20] and the wicked one does not touch him.
19 We know that we are of God, and the whole world lies *under the sway of* the wicked one.
20 And we know that the Son of God has come and has given us an understanding, that we may know Him who is true; and we are in Him who is true, in His Son Jesus Christ. This is the true God and eternal life.
21 Little children, keep yourselves from idols. Amen.

---

14 NU-Text omits *Him.*   15 NU-Text reads *he cannot.*   16 M-Text reads *your.*
17 NU-Text and M-Text omit the words from *in heaven* (verse 7) through *on earth* (verse 8). Only four or five very late *Greek* manuscripts contain these words.   18 NU-Text reads *God, that.*
19 NU-Text omits the rest of this verse.   20 NU-Text reads *him.*

Introduction to Second John

The Second Epistle of John is a powerful illustration that love is staying involved. Written in the late 80s to early 90s A.D., probably from Ephesus and possibly to a nearby church, this letter shows John's continual concern and involvement for this congregation.

The phrase "to the elect lady and her children" (v.1) is probably a literary device which refers to the church as a whole rather than a specific person. John encourages the Christians to beware of the many false teachers in the region of Ephesus who did not teach the truth of Jesus Christ. John also commends them for their walk in faith. He urges them to continue living with the greatest positive influence they can demonstrate—love.

What is perfect love? There are three levels of love: "I love you because I need you"; "I love you because I want you"; and "I love you because you need me." John demonstrates that truly the latter is the definition of perfect love. This is what Christian love is all about. John points his readers to the source of perfect love—Jesus Christ!

John's commitment to his fellow Christians affirms his message. Love is staying involved!

The Second Epistle of

John

Greeting the Elect Lady

THE ELDER,

To the elect lady and her children, whom I love in truth, and not only I, but also all those who have known the truth, 2 because of the truth which abides in us and will be with us forever:

3 Grace, mercy, *and* peace will be with you[1] from God the Father and from the Lord Jesus Christ, the Son of the Father, in truth and love.

Walk in Christ's Commandments

4 I rejoiced greatly that I have found *some* of your children walking in truth, as we received commandment from the Father.

5 And now I plead with you, lady, not as though I wrote a new commandment to you, but that which we have had from the beginning: that we love one another.

6 This is love, that we walk according to His commandments. This is the commandment, that as you have heard from the beginning, you should walk in it.

Beware of Antichrist Deceivers

7 For many deceivers have gone out into the world who do not confess Jesus Christ *as* coming in the flesh. This is a deceiver and an antichrist.

8 Look to yourselves, that we[2] do not lose those things we worked for, but *that* we[2] may receive a full reward.

9 Whoever transgresses[3] and does not abide in the doctrine of Christ does not have God. He who abides in the doctrine of Christ has both the Father and the Son.

10 If anyone comes to you and does not bring this doctrine, do not receive him into your house nor greet him;

11 for he who greets him shares in his evil deeds.

John's Farewell Greeting

12 Having many things to write to you, I did not wish *to do so* with paper and ink; but I hope to come to you and speak face to face, that our joy may be full.

13 The children of your elect sister greet you. Amen.

---

1 NU-Text and M-Text read *us.*   2 NU-Text reads *you.*   3 NU-Text reads *goes ahead.*

Introduction to Third John

This letter is the third of John's short messages of encouragement written most likely from Ephesus in the late 80s or early 90s A.D.

This brief Epistle was written to Gaius, a close friend, and to other Christians living probably in the province Asia. John's greatest joy was to hear that these believers with whom he had been in continual contact were still walking in the truth. They kept on keeping on in the faith.

At this point in John's life, he was elderly and was the sole survivor of those who had personally walked with Jesus when He was on earth. Perhaps because John had lived an itinerant life-style with Jesus, he understood the need for hospitality to Christians and traveling ministers. He urges believers to go out of their way to take in and provide for the men and women traveling and spreading the gospel of Christ throughout Asia Minor. John asks them to continue living in love. As believers in Jesus Christ, they had the opportunity to help spread the message of faith by their support and encouragement of the evangelists. From their small seeds of love, enormous harvests of goodness would abound. We, too, can sow seeds of love in our world today. Love is going out of our way!

The Third Epistle of

John

Greeting to Gaius

THE ELDER,

To the beloved Gaius, whom I love in truth:

2 Beloved, I pray that you may prosper in all things and be in health, just as your soul prospers.

3 For I rejoiced greatly when brethren came and testified of the truth *that is* in you, just as you walk in the truth.

4 I have no greater joy than to hear that my children walk in truth.[1]

Gaius Commended for Generosity

5 Beloved, you do faithfully whatever you do for the brethren and[2] for strangers,

6 who have borne witness of your love before the church. If you send them forward on their journey in a manner worthy of God, you will do well,

7 because they went forth for His name's sake, taking nothing from the Gentiles.

8 We therefore ought to receive[3] such, that we may become fellow workers for the truth.

Diotrephes and Demetrius

9 I wrote to the church, but Diotrephes, who loves to have the preeminence among them, does not receive us.

10 Therefore, if I come, I will call to mind his deeds which he does, prating against us with malicious words. And not content with that, he himself does not receive the brethren, and forbids those who wish to, putting *them* out of the church.

11 Beloved, do not imitate what is evil, but what is good. He who does good is of God, but[4] he who does evil has not seen God.

12 Demetrius has a *good* testimony from all, and from the truth itself. And we also bear witness, and you know that our testimony is true.

Farewell Greeting

13 I had many things to write, but I do not wish to write to you with pen and ink;

14 but I hope to see you shortly, and we shall speak face to face. Peace to you. Our friends greet you. Greet the friends by name.

1 NU-Text reads *the truth.*   2 NU-Text adds *especially.*   3 NU-Text reads *support.*
4 NU-Text and M-Text omit *but.*

Introduction to Jude

Unveil yourself to the love of God and involve yourself in the lives of others.

Jude was written by the half-brother of Jesus Christ, Jude, to Christians everywhere, encouraging them to be built up in their faith. Jude warns against the negative influences that could bring them down. He calls their attention to false teachers and heretics who are immoral, covetous, proud, and divisive. By building up their faith, they can remain positive and strong.

Jude knew the importance of trusting his life to the most powerful person in the universe—Jesus Christ.

But you, beloved, building yourselves up on your most holy faith, praying in the Holy Spirit, keep yourselves in the love of God, looking for the mercy of our Lord Jesus Christ unto eternal life.

(Jude 20, 21)

Jude has one of the most beautiful benedictions in the entire New Testament. Expressing confidence in God's ability to lift up, to strengthen, and to help us live positively, these words of faith are as meaningful today, with the many negative forces of people and circumstances, as they were to the first Christians.

Now to Him who is able to keep you from stumbling,
And to present *you* faultless
Before the presence of His glory with exceeding joy,
To God our Savior,
Who alone is wise,
Be glory and majesty,
Dominion and power,
Both now and forever.
Amen.

(Jude 24, 25)

The Epistle of
Jude

Greeting to the Called

JUDE, a servant of Jesus Christ, and brother of James,

To those who are called, sanctified[1] by God the Father, and preserved in Jesus Christ:

2 Mercy, peace, and love be multiplied to you.

Contend for the Faith

3 Beloved, while I was very diligent to write to you concerning our common salvation, I found it necessary to write to you exhorting you to contend earnestly for the faith which was once for all delivered to the saints.
4 For certain men have crept in unnoticed, who long ago were marked out for this condemnation, ungodly men, who turn the grace of our God into licentiousness and deny the only Lord God[2] and our Lord Jesus Christ.

Old and New Apostates

5 But I want to remind you, though you once knew this, that the Lord, having saved the people out of the land of Egypt, afterward destroyed those who did not believe.
6 And the angels who did not keep their proper domain, but left their own habitation, He has reserved in everlasting chains under darkness for the judgment of the great day;
7 as Sodom and Gomorrah, and the cities around them in a similar manner to these, having given themselves over to sexual immorality and gone after strange flesh, are set forth as an example, suffering the vengeance of eternal fire.
8 Likewise also these dreamers defile the flesh, reject authority, and speak evil of dignitaries.
9 Yet Michael the archangel, in contending with the devil, when he disputed about the body of Moses, dared not bring against him a reviling accusation, but said, "The Lord rebuke you!"

10 But these speak evil of whatever they do not know; and whatever they know naturally, like brute beasts, in these things they corrupt themselves.
11 Woe to them! For they have gone in the way of Cain, have run greedily in the error of Balaam for profit, and perished in the rebellion of Korah.

Apostates Depraved and Doomed

12 These are spots in your love feasts, while they feast with you without fear, serving *only* themselves; *they are* clouds without water, carried about[3] by the winds; late autumn trees without fruit, twice dead, pulled up by the roots;
13 raging waves of the sea, foaming up their own shame; wandering stars for whom is reserved the blackness of darkness forever.
14 Now Enoch, the seventh from Adam, prophesied about these men also, saying, "Behold, the Lord comes with ten thousands of His saints,
15 "to execute judgment on all, to convict all who are ungodly among them of all their ungodly deeds which they have committed in an ungodly way, and of all the harsh things which ungodly sinners have spoken against Him."

Apostates Predicted

16 These are murmurers, complainers, walking according to their own lusts; and they mouth great swelling *words*, flattering people to gain advantage.
17 But you, beloved, remember the words which were spoken before by the apostles of our Lord Jesus Christ:
18 how they told you that there would be mockers in the last time who would walk according to their own ungodly lusts.
19 These are sensual persons, who cause divisions, not having the Spirit.

Maintain Your Life with God

20 But you, beloved, building yourselves up on your most holy faith, praying in the Holy Spirit,

---

1 NU-Text reads *beloved.*   2 NU-Text omits *God.*   3 NU-Text and M-Text read *along.*

21 keep yourselves in the love of God, looking for the mercy of our Lord Jesus Christ unto eternal life.
22 And on some have compassion, making a distinction;[4]
23 but others save with fear, pulling *them* out of the fire,[5] hating even the garment defiled by the flesh.

Glory to God

24 Now to Him who is able to keep you[6] from stumbling, And to present *you* faultless Before the presence of His glory with exceeding joy,
25 To God our Savior,[7] Who alone is wise,[8] *Be* glory and majesty, Dominion and power,[9] Both now and forever. Amen.

4 NU-Text reads *who are doubting* (or *making distinctions*).
5 NU-Text reads *and on some have mercy with fear* and omits *with fear* in first clause.   6 M-Text reads *them.*
7 NU-Text reads *To the only God, our Savior* and omits *wise.*   8 NU-Text adds *through Jesus Christ our Lord.*
9 NU-Text adds *Before all time.*

Introduction to Revelation

Every end is a new beginning.

The Book of Revelation was written in the 90s A.D. by the apostle John during his exile on the island of Patmos. It was addressed to seven churches in Asia Minor.

Revelation has been called the treatise for hard times, because its audience was suffering severe persecution. Christianity was growing in numbers but was constantly coming in direct conflict with the morals and religions of the time. Unbelieving Jews and Gentiles alike despised this new religion, and the political powers opposed any lordship other than Caesar's. The church was in a life-and-death struggle.

John assures the believers that the ultimate future and outcome of the world is in God's hands. In a series of visions, God reveals to John in prophetic symbolism the second coming of Jesus Christ and the creation of a new world. John also forewarns the church that tough times are coming, but they must hold on to hope. God will gain victory over the negative forces and evil powers in the world.

> And God will wipe away every tear from their eyes; there shall be no more death, nor sorrow, nor crying; and there shall be no more pain, for the former things have passed away . . . Behold, I make all things new.

> (Rev. 21:4, 5)

Tough times never last, but tough people do! Who are tough people? Tough people are those who believe in God and His ability to overcome negative, evil powers and establish a positive, life-giving world!

Through John's Revelation we are assured that the end of the world will be a new beginning. God will restore believers to their rightful position with God in the new creation.

> And he showed me a pure river of water of life, clear as crystal, proceeding from the throne of God and of the Lamb. In the middle of its street, and on either side of the river, *was* the tree of life, which bore twelve fruits, each *tree* yielding its fruit every month. And the leaves of the tree *were* for the healing of the nations.

> (Rev. 22:1, 2)

The curse of death will be removed and all believers will have access to the Tree of Life from which man was banished in the Garden of Eden. Jesus offers everyone the chance to eat of the Tree of Life and drink freely of the Water of Life.

Let us look to Jesus, the *Alpha* and *Omega*, the Beginning and the End, the First and the Last. Every end truly is a new beginning!

The Revelation
of Jesus Christ

Introduction and Benediction

THE Revelation of Jesus Christ, which God gave Him to show His servants—things which must shortly take place. And He sent and signified *it* by His angel to His servant John, 2 who bore witness to the word of God, and to the testimony of Jesus Christ, and to all things that he saw. 3 Blessed *is* he who reads and those who hear the words of this prophecy, and keep those things which are written in it; for the time *is* near.

Greeting the Seven Churches

4 John, to the seven churches which are in Asia:

Grace to you and peace from Him who is and who was and who is to come, and from the seven Spirits who are before His throne, 5 and from Jesus Christ, the faithful witness, the firstborn from the dead, and the ruler over the kings of the earth. To Him who loved us and washed[1] us from our sins in His own blood, 6 and has made us kings[2] and priests to His God and Father, to Him *be* glory and dominion forever and ever. Amen. 7 Behold, He is coming with clouds, and every eye will see Him, and they *also* who pierced Him. And all the tribes of the earth will mourn because of Him. Even so, Amen. 8 "I am the Alpha and the Omega, *the* Beginning and *the* End,"[3] says the Lord,[4] "who is and who was and who is to come, the Almighty."

Vision of the Son of Man

9 I, John, both your brother and companion in tribulation, and in the kingdom and patience of Jesus Christ, was on the island that is called Patmos for the word of God and for the testimony of Jesus Christ.

10 I was in the Spirit on the Lord's Day, and I heard behind me a loud voice, as of a trumpet, 11 saying, "I am the Alpha and the Omega, the First and the Last," and,[5] "What you see, write in a book and send *it* to the seven churches which are in Asia:[6] to Ephesus, to Smyrna, to Pergamos, to Thyatira, to Sardis, to Philadelphia, and to Laodicea."

12 Then I turned to see the voice that spoke with me. And having turned I saw seven golden lampstands, 13 and in the midst of the seven lampstands *One* like the Son of Man, clothed with a garment down to the feet and girded about the chest with a golden band. 14 His head and *His* hair *were* white like wool, as white as snow, and His eyes like a flame of fire; 15 His feet *were* like fine brass, as if refined in a furnace, and His voice as the sound of many waters; 16 He had in His right hand seven stars, out of His mouth went a sharp two-edged sword, and His countenance *was* like the sun shining in its strength.

17 And when I saw Him, I fell at His feet as dead. But He laid His right hand on me, saying to me,[7] "Do not be afraid; I am the First and the Last. 18 "I *am* He who lives, and was dead, and behold, I am alive forevermore. Amen. And I have the keys of Hades and of Death. 19 "Write[8] the things which you have seen, and the things which are, and the things which will take place after this. 20 "The mystery of the seven stars which you saw in My right hand, and the seven golden lampstands: The seven stars are the angels of the seven churches, and the seven lampstands which you saw[9] are the seven churches.

---

1 NU-Text and M-Text read *loves us and freed.*   2 NU-Text and M-Text read *a kingdom.*
3 NU-Text and M-Text omit *the Beginning and the End.*   4 NU-Text and M-Text add *God.*
5 NU-Text and M-Text omit *I am* through third *and.*   6 NU-Text and M-Text omit *which are in Asia.*
7 NU-Text and M-Text omit *to me.*   8 NU-Text and M-Text read *Therefore, write.*
9 NU-Text and M-Text omit *which you saw.*

The Loveless Church

2 "To the angel of the church of Ephesus write,

'These things says He who holds the seven stars in His right hand who walks in the midst of the seven golden lampstands:
2 "I know your works, your labor, your patience, and that you cannot bear those who are evil. And you have tested those who say they are apostles and are not, and have found them liars;
3 "and you have persevered and have patience, and have labored for My name's sake and have not become weary.
4 "Nevertheless I have *this* against you, that you have left your first love.
5 "Remember therefore from where you have fallen; repent and do the first works, or else I will come to you quickly and remove your lampstand from its place—unless you repent.
6 "But this you have, that you hate the deeds of the Nicolaitans, which I also hate.
7 "He who has an ear, let him hear what the Spirit says to the churches. To him who overcomes I will give to eat from the tree of life, which is in the midst of the Paradise of God." '

The Persecuted Church

8 "And to the angel of the church in Smyrna write,

'These things says the First and the Last, who was dead, and came to life:
9 "I know your works, tribulation, and poverty (but you are rich); and *I know* the blasphemy of those who say they are Jews and are not, but *are* a synagogue of Satan.
10 "Do not fear any of those things which you are about to suffer. Indeed, the devil is about to throw *some* of you into prison, that you may be tested, and you will have tribulation ten days. Be faithful until death, and I will give you the crown of life.
11 "He who has an ear, let him hear what the Spirit says to the churches. He who overcomes shall not be hurt by the second death." '

The Compromising Church

12 "And to the angel of the church in Pergamos write,

'These things says He who has the sharp two-edged sword:
13 "I know your works, and where you dwell, where Satan's throne *is*. And you hold fast to My name, and did not deny My faith even in the days in which Antipas *was* My faithful martyr, who was killed among you, where Satan dwells.
14 "But I have a few things against you, because you have there those who hold the doctrine of Balaam, who taught Balak to put a stumbling block before the children of Israel, to eat things sacrificed to idols, and to commit sexual immorality.
15 "Thus you also have those who hold the doctrine of the Nicolaitans, which thing I hate.[10]
16 'Repent, or else I will come to you quickly and will fight against them with the sword of My mouth.
17 "He who has an ear, let him hear what the Spirit says to the churches. To him who overcomes I will give some of the hidden manna to eat. And I will give him a white stone, and on the stone a new name written which no one knows except him who receives *it*." '

The Corrupt Church

18 "And to the angel of the church in Thyatira write,

'These things says the Son of God, who has eyes like a flame of fire, and His feet like fine brass:
19 "I know your works, love, service, faith, and your patience; and *as* for your works, the last *are* more than the first.
20 "Nevertheless I have a few things against you, because you allow[11] that woman[12] Jezebel, who calls herself a prophetess, to teach and beguile[13] My servants to commit sexual immorality and to eat things sacrificed to idols.
21 "And I gave her time to repent of her sexual immorality, and she did not repent.[14]
22 "Indeed I will cast her into a sickbed, and those who commit adultery with her into great tribulation, unless they repent of their[15] deeds.

---

10 NU-Text and M-Text read *likewise* for *which thing I hate.*
11 NU-Text and M-Text read *I have against you that you put up with.*   12 M-Text reads *your wife Jezebel.*
13 NU-Text and M-Text read *and teaches and beguiles.*
14 NU-Text and M-Text read *time to repent, and she does not want to repent of her sexual immorality.*
15 NU-Text and M-Text read *her.*

23 "And I will kill her children with death. And all the churches shall know that I am He who searches the minds and hearts. And I will give to each one of you according to your works.
24 "But to you I say, and to the rest in Thyatira, as many as do not have this doctrine, and who have not known the depths of Satan, as they call *them,* I will put on you no other burden.
25 "But hold fast what you have till I come.
26 "And he who overcomes, and keeps My works until the end, to him I will give power over the nations—

27 'He shall rule them
     with a rod of iron;
     As the potter's vessels
     shall be broken to pieces'[16]—

as I also have received from My Father;
28 "and I will give him the morning star.
29 "He who has an ear, let him hear what the Spirit says to the churches." '

The Dead Church

3 "And to the angel of the church in Sardis write,
'These things says He who has the seven Spirits of God and the seven stars: "I know your works, that you have a name that you are alive, but you are dead.
2 "Be watchful, and strengthen the things which remain, that are ready to die, for I have not found your works perfect before God.[17]
3 "Remember therefore how you have received and heard; hold fast and repent. Therefore if you will not watch, I will come upon you as a thief, and you will not know what hour I will come upon you.
4 "You[18] have a few names even in Sardis who have not defiled their garments; and they shall walk with Me in white, for they are worthy.
5 "He who overcomes shall be clothed in white garments, and I will not blot out his name from the Book of Life; but I will confess his name before My Father and before His angels.
6 "He who has an ear, let him hear what the Spirit says to the churches." '

The Faithful Church

7 "And to the angel of the church in Philadelphia write,
'These things says He who is holy, He who is true, "He who has the key of David, He who opens and no one shuts, and shuts and no one opens":[19]
8 "I know your works. See, I have set before you an open door, and no one can shut it; for you have a little strength, have kept My word, and have not denied My name.
9 "Indeed I will make *those* of the synagogue of Satan, who say they are Jews and are not, but lie—indeed I will make them come and worship before your feet, and to know that I have loved you.
10 "Because you have kept My command to persevere, I also will keep you from the hour of trial which shall come upon the whole world, to test those who dwell on the earth.
11 "Behold,[20] I come quickly! Hold fast what you have, that no one may take your crown.
12 "He who overcomes, I will make him a pillar in the temple of My God, and he shall go out no more. And I will write on him the name of My God and the name of the city of My God, the New Jerusalem, which comes down out of heaven from My God. And *I will write on him* My new name.
13 "He who has an ear, let him hear what the Spirit says to the churches." '

The Lukewarm Church

14 "And to the angel of the church of the Laodiceans[21] write,
'These things says the Amen, the Faithful and True Witness, the Beginning of the creation of God:
15 "I know your works, that you are neither cold nor hot. I could wish you were cold or hot.
16 "So then, because you are lukewarm, and neither cold nor hot, I will spew you out of My mouth.
17 "Because you say, 'I am rich, have become wealthy, and have need of nothing'—and do not know that you are wretched, miserable, poor, blind, and naked—
18 "I counsel you to buy from Me gold refined in the fire, that you may be rich;

16 Psalm 2:9   17 NU-Text and M-Text read *my God.*
18 NU-Text and M-Text read *Nevertheless you have a few names in Sardis.*   19 Isaiah 22:22
20 NU-Text and M-Text omit *Behold.*   21 NU-Text and M-Text read *in Laodicea.*

and white garments, that you may be clothed, *that* the shame of your nakedness may not be revealed; and anoint your eyes with eye salve, that you may see.
19 "As many as I love, I rebuke and chasten. Therefore be zealous and repent.
20 "Behold, I stand at the door and knock. If anyone hears My voice and opens the door, I will come in to him and dine with him, and he with Me.
21 "To him who overcomes I will grant to sit with Me on My throne, as I also overcame and sat down with My Father on His throne.
22 "He who has an ear, let him hear what the Spirit says to the churches." ' "

The Throne Room of Heaven

4 After these things I looked, and behold, a door *standing* open in heaven. And the first voice which I heard *was* like a trumpet speaking with me, saying, "Come up here, and I will show you things which must take place after this."
2 Immediately I was in the Spirit; and behold, a throne set in heaven, and *One* sat on the throne.
3 And He who sat there was 22 like a jasper and a sardius stone in appearance; and *there was* a rainbow around the throne, in appearance like an emerald.
4 Around the throne *were* twenty-four thrones, and on the thrones I saw twenty-four elders sitting, clothed in white robes; and they had crowns of gold on their heads.
5 And from the throne proceeded lightnings, thunderings, and voices. And *there were* seven lamps of fire burning before the throne, which are the 23 seven Spirits of God.
6 Before the throne *there was* 24 a sea of glass, like crystal. And in the midst of the throne, and around the throne, *were* four living creatures full of eyes in front and in back.
7 The first living creature *was* like a lion, the second living creature like a calf, the third living creature had a face like a man, and the fourth living creature *was* like a flying eagle.
8 And *the* four living creatures, each having six wings, were full of eyes around

and within. And they do not rest day or night, saying:

"Holy, holy, holy,25
Lord God Almighty,
Who was and is and is to come!"

9 Whenever the living creatures give glory and honor and thanks to Him who sits on the throne, who lives forever and ever,
10 the twenty-four elders fall down before Him who sits on the throne and worship Him who lives forever and ever, and cast their crowns before the throne, saying:

11 "You are worthy, O Lord,26
To receive glory and honor
    and power;
For You created all things,
And by Your will they exist27
    and were created."

The Lamb Takes the Scroll

5 And I saw in the right *hand* of Him who sat on the throne a scroll written inside and on the back, sealed with seven seals.
2 Then I saw a strong angel proclaiming with a loud voice, "Who is worthy to open the scroll and to loose its seals?"
3 And no one in heaven or on the earth or under the earth was able to open the scroll, or to look at it.
4 So I wept much, because no one was found worthy to open and read28 the scroll, or to look at it.
5 But one of the elders said to me, "Do not weep. Behold, the Lion of the tribe of Judah, the Root of David, has prevailed to open the scroll and to loose29 its seven seals."
6 And I looked, and behold,30 in the midst of the throne and of the four living creatures, and in the midst of the elders, stood a Lamb as though it had been slain, having seven horns and seven eyes, which are the seven Spirits of God sent out into all the earth.
7 Then He came and took the scroll out of the right hand of Him who sat on the throne.

---

22 M-Text deletes *and He who sat there was* (which makes the description in verse 3 modify the throne rather than God).   23 M-Text omits *the.*   24 NU-Text and M-Text add *something like.*   25 M-Text has *holy* nine times.
26 NU-Text and M-Text read *Our Lord and God.*   27 NU-Text and M-Text read *existed.*
28 NU-Text and M-Text omit *and read.*   29 NU-Text and M-Text omit *to loose.*
30 NU-Text and M-Text omit *and behold.*

Reason to Believe

The total dedication and commitment of the early disciples to their newfound faith is strong evidence for the truth of the New Testament and the resurrection of Jesus Christ.

A look at the disciples' lives gives added insight into the power of God's Son. Twelve men from various walks of life left everything to follow Jesus. They traveled with Him for approximately three years, but upon Jesus' arrest and crucifixion each one fled and hid in fear. Yet something incredible happened shortly thereafter, for within a few days after Jesus' death and burial, the disciples proclaimed God's love and forgiveness through the death and resurrection of Jesus Christ openly and bravely.

Their commitment to this belief cannot be explained in any psychological terms other than they believed what they claimed actually happened. Several of the disciples had a strong dislike, and in some cases, hatred for the gentile nations. Yet, remarkably, their attitudes changed to love. They insisted on traveling to obscure places to share God's love and forgiveness to people of all races. They claimed that Jesus Christ, the Son of God, was crucified and rose from the dead, thereby giving all people hope over their greatest foe—death. They insisted on sharing this news, even to the point of death. According to tradition eleven of the twelve disciples suffered a martyr's death for what they believed, preached, and taught.

Herod had James killed by the sword in Palestine (Acts 12:2). What we know of the deaths of the other disciples is shrouded in tradition. Philip was said to have been hanged in Hierapolis in Asia Minor. Matthew was killed by the sword in Parthia. Andrew was crucified on an X-shaped cross in Patrae in Achaia. Mark was dragged to pieces by the people in Alexandria in front of the great idol, Serapis. Peter was crucified upside down in Rome. Paul had his head cut off in Rome. Jude was crucified in Edessa. Thomas was killed by a spear thrust through his side in India. Bartholomew was beaten and crucified in Asia Minor. Luke was nailed to an olive tree by a pagan priest in Greece. John was the only disciple who did not die for his faith. But even he was said to have been boiled in a cauldron of scalding oil, but he survived and was banished to the island of Patmos by the Emperor Domitian.

If the disciples knew the resurrection of Jesus Christ was a hoax, or could be explained in any other way, they would not have been willing to die for their faith. Throughout history, many martyrs have died for something that was true. But few have died for what they knew to be a lie. It is virtually impossible to gather twelve men or women together and have them propagate a lie, spread it everywhere so that people believe it, and die for it, knowing it to be a lie. It is a psychological impossibility. The disciples and hundreds of other first-century martyrs knew the resurrection of Jesus Christ was the truth, and they sealed their testimony in their own blood.

Because of their faith, commitment, and dedication, we have the confidence that what they recorded, taught, and preached was true. We can believe wholeheartedly with them the statement of Jesus, "I am the resurrection and the life. He who believes in Me, though he may die, he shall live" (John 11:25).

Worthy Is the Lamb

8 Now when He had taken the scroll, the four living creatures and the twenty-four elders fell down before the Lamb, each having a harp, and golden bowls full of incense, which are the prayers of the saints.
9 And they sang a new song, saying:

"You are worthy to take the scroll,
And to open its seals;
For You were slain,
And have redeemed us to God
    by Your blood
Out of every tribe and tongue
    and people and nation,
10 And have made us[31] kings[32] and priests
    to our God;
And we[33] shall reign on the earth."

11 Then I looked, and I heard the voice of many angels around the throne, the living creatures, and the elders; and the number of them was ten thousand times ten thousand, and thousands of thousands,
12 saying with a loud voice:

"Worthy is the Lamb who was slain
To receive power and riches and
    wisdom,
And strength and honor and glory
    and blessing!"

13 And every creature which is in heaven and on the earth and under the earth and such as are in the sea, and all that are in them, I heard saying:

"Blessing and honor and glory
    and power
Be to Him who sits on the throne,
And to the Lamb, forever and ever!"[34]

14 Then the four living creatures said, "Amen!" And the twenty-four[35] elders fell down and worshiped Him who lives forever and ever.[36]

First Seal: The Conqueror

6 Now I saw when the Lamb opened one of the seals;[37] and I heard one of the four living creatures saying with a voice like thunder, "Come and see."

2 And I looked, and behold, a white horse. And he who sat on it had a bow; and a crown was given to him, and he went out conquering and to conquer.

Second Seal: Conflict on Earth

3 When He opened the second seal, I heard the second living creature saying, "Come and see."[38]
4 And another horse, fiery red, went out. And it was granted to the one who sat on it to take peace from the earth, and that *people* should kill one another; and there was given to him a great sword.

Third Seal: Scarcity on Earth

5 When He opened the third seal, I heard the third living creature say, "Come and see." And I looked, and behold, a black horse, and he who sat on it had a pair of scales in his hand.
6 And I heard a voice in the midst of the four living creatures saying, "A quart[39] of wheat for a denarius,[40] and three quarts of barley for a denarius; and do not harm the oil and the wine."

Fourth Seal: Widespread Death on Earth

7 When He opened the fourth seal, I heard the voice of the fourth living creature saying, "Come and see."
8 And I looked, and behold, a pale horse. And the name of him who sat on it was Death, and Hades followed with him. And power was given to them over a fourth of the earth, to kill with sword, with hunger, with death, and by the beasts of the earth.

Fifth Seal: The Cry of the Martyrs

9 When He opened the fifth seal, I saw under the altar the souls of those who had been slain for the word of God and for the testimony which they held.
10 And they cried with a loud voice, saying, "How long, O Lord, holy and true, until You judge and avenge our blood on those who dwell on the earth?"
11 And a white robe was given to each of them; and it was said to them that they should rest a little while longer, until both *the number of* their fellow servants and their brethren, who would be killed as they *were*, was completed.

---

31 NU-Text and M-Text read *them*.   32 NU-Text reads *kingdom*.   33 NU-Text and M-Text read *they*.
34 M-Text adds *Amen*.   35 NU-Text and M-Text omit *twenty-four*.
36 NU-Text and M-Text omit *Him who lives forever and ever*.   37 NU-Text and M-Text read *seven seals*.
38 NU-Text and M-Text omit *and see*.   39 Greek *choinix;* that is, approximately one quart
40 This was approximately one day's wage for a worker.

Sixth Seal: Cosmic Disturbances

12 I looked when He opened the sixth seal, and behold,⁴¹ there was a great earthquake; and the sun became black as sackcloth of hair, and the moon⁴² became like blood.

13 And the stars of heaven fell to the earth, as a fig tree drops its late figs when it is shaken by a mighty wind.

14 Then the sky receded as a scroll when it is rolled up, and every mountain and island was moved out of its place.

15 And the kings of the earth, the great men, the rich men, the commanders, the mighty men, every slave and every free man, hid themselves in the caves and in the rocks of the mountains,

16 and said to the mountains and rocks, "Fall on us and hide us from the face of Him who sits on the throne and from the wrath of the Lamb!

17 "For the great day of His wrath has come, and who is able to stand?"

The Sealed of Israel

7 After these things I saw four angels standing at the four corners of the earth, holding the four winds of the earth, that the wind should not blow on the earth, on the sea, or on any tree.

2 Then I saw another angel ascending from the east, having the seal of the living God. And he cried with a loud voice to the four angels to whom it was granted to harm the earth and the sea,

3 saying, "Do not harm the earth, the sea, or the trees till we have sealed the servants of our God on their foreheads."

4 And I heard the number of those who were sealed. One hundred *and* forty-four thousand of all the tribes of the children of Israel *were* sealed:

5 of the tribe of Judah
    twelve thousand *were* sealed;⁴³
of the tribe of Reuben
    twelve thousand *were* sealed;
of the tribe of Gad
    twelve thousand *were* sealed;
6 of the tribe of Asher
    twelve thousand *were* sealed;
of the tribe of Naphtali
    twelve thousand *were* sealed;
of the tribe of Manasseh
    twelve thousand *were* sealed;

7 of the tribe of Simeon
    twelve thousand *were* sealed;
of the tribe of Levi
    twelve thousand *were* sealed;
of the tribe of Issachar
    twelve thousand *were* sealed;
8 of the tribe of Zebulun
    twelve thousand *were* sealed;
of the tribe of Joseph
    twelve thousand *were* sealed;
of the tribe of Benjamin
    twelve thousand *were* sealed.

A Multitude from the Great Tribulation

9 After these things I looked, and behold, a great multitude which no one could number, of all nations, tribes, peoples, and tongues, standing before the throne and before the Lamb, clothed with white robes, with palm branches in their hands,

10 and crying out with a loud voice, saying, "Salvation *belongs* to our God who sits on the throne, and to the Lamb!"

11 And all the angels stood around the throne and the elders and the four living creatures, and fell on their faces before the throne and worshiped God,

12 saying:

"Amen! Blessing and glory
    and wisdom,
Thanksgiving and honor and power
    and might,
Be to our God forever and ever.
Amen."

13 Then one of the elders answered, saying to me, "Who are these arrayed in white robes, and where did they come from?"

14 And I said to him, "Sir, you know." So he said to me, "These are the ones who come out of the great tribulation, and washed their robes and made them white in the blood of the Lamb.

15 "Therefore they are before the throne of God, and serve Him day and night in His temple. And He who sits on the throne will dwell among them.

16 "They shall neither hunger anymore nor thirst anymore; the sun shall not strike them, nor any heat;

17 "for the Lamb who is in the midst of the throne will shepherd them and lead them to living fountains of waters.⁴⁴ And

---

41 NU-Text and M-Text omit *behold.*   42 NU-Text and M-Text read *the whole moon.*
43 In NU-Text and M-Text *were sealed* is stated only in verses 5a and 8c; the words are understood in the remainder of the passage.   44 NU-Text and M-Text read *fountains of the waters of life.*

God will wipe away every tear from their eyes."

Seventh Seal: Prelude to the Seven Trumpets

8 When He opened the seventh seal, there was silence in heaven for about half an hour.
2 And I saw the seven angels who stand before God, and to them were given seven trumpets.
3 Then another angel, having a golden censer, came and stood at the altar. And he was given much incense, that he should offer it with the prayers of all the saints upon the golden altar which was before the throne.
4 And the smoke of the incense, with the prayers of the saints, ascended before God from the angel's hand.
5 Then the angel took the censer, filled it with fire from the altar, and threw it to the earth. And there were noises, thunderings, lightnings, and an earthquake.
6 So the seven angels who had the seven trumpets prepared themselves to sound.

First Trumpet: Vegetation Struck

7 The first angel sounded: And hail and fire followed, mingled with blood, and they were thrown to the earth;[45] and a third of the trees were burned up, and all green grass was burned up.

Second Trumpet: The Seas Struck

8 Then the second angel sounded: And something like a great mountain burning with fire was thrown into the sea, and a third of the sea became blood;
9 and a third of the living creatures in the sea died, and a third of the ships were destroyed.

Third Trumpet: The Waters Struck

10 Then the third angel sounded: And a great star fell from heaven, burning like a torch, and it fell on a third of the rivers and on the springs of water;
11 and the name of the star is Wormwood; and a third of the waters became wormwood; and many men died from the water, because it was made bitter.

Fourth Trumpet: The Heavens Struck

12 Then the fourth angel sounded: And a third of the sun was struck, a third of the moon, and a third of the stars, so that a third of them were darkened; and a third of the day did not shine, and likewise the night.
13 And I looked, and I heard an angel[46] flying through the midst of heaven, saying with a loud voice, "Woe, woe, woe to the inhabitants of the earth, because of the remaining blasts of the trumpet of the three angels who are about to sound!"

Fifth Trumpet: The Locusts from the Bottomless Pit

9 Then the fifth angel sounded: And I saw a star fallen from heaven to the earth. And to him was given the key to the bottomless pit.
2 And he opened the bottomless pit, and smoke arose out of the pit like the smoke of a great furnace. And the sun and the air were darkened because of the smoke of the pit.
3 Then out of the smoke locusts came upon the earth. And to them was given power, as the scorpions of the earth have power.
4 They were commanded not to harm the grass of the earth, or any green thing, or any tree, but only those men who do not have the seal of God on their foreheads.
5 And they were not given authority to kill them, but to torment them for five months. And their torment was like the torment of a scorpion when it strikes a man.
6 In those days men will seek death and will not find it; they will desire to die, and death will flee from them.
7 And the shape of the locusts was like horses prepared for battle; and on their heads were crowns of something like gold, and their faces were like the faces of men.
8 They had hair like women's hair, and their teeth were like lions' teeth.
9 And they had breastplates like breastplates of iron, and the sound of their wings was like the sound of chariots with many horses running into battle.
10 They had tails like scorpions, and there were stings in their tails. And their power was to hurt men five months.
11 And they had as king over them the angel of the bottomless pit, whose name in Hebrew is Abaddon, but in Greek he has the name Apollyon.
12 One woe is past. Behold, still two more woes are coming after these things.

45 NU-Text and M-Text add and a third of the earth was burned up.   46 NU-Text and M-Text read eagle.

Sixth Trumpet: The Angels from the Euphrates

13 Then the sixth angel sounded: And I heard a voice from the four horns of the golden altar which is before God, 14 saying to the sixth angel who had the trumpet, "Release the four angels who are bound at the great river Euphrates." 15 So the four angels, who had been prepared for the hour and day and month and year, were released to kill a third of mankind. 16 Now the number of the army of the horsemen *was* two hundred million, and I heard the number of them.

17 And thus I saw the horses in the vision: those who sat on them had breastplates of fiery red, hyacinth blue, and sulfur yellow; and the heads of the horses *were* like the heads of lions; and out of their mouths came fire, smoke, and brimstone. 18 By these three *plagues* a third of mankind was killed—by the fire and the smoke and the brimstone which came out of their mouths. 19 For their power[47] is in their mouth and in their tails; for their tails *are* like serpents, having heads; and with them they do harm.

20 But the rest of mankind, who were not killed by these plagues, did not repent of the works of their hands, that they should not worship demons, and idols of gold, silver, brass, stone, and wood, which can neither see nor hear nor walk; 21 and they did not repent of their murders or their sorceries[48] or their sexual immorality or their thefts.

The Mighty Angel with the Scroll

10 And I saw still another mighty angel coming down from heaven, clothed with a cloud. And a rainbow *was* on his head, his face *was* like the sun, and his feet like pillars of fire. 2 And he had a little book open in his hand. And he set his right foot on the sea and *his* left *foot* on the land, 3 and cried with a loud voice, as *when* a lion roars. And when he cried out, seven thunders uttered their voices. 4 Now when the seven thunders uttered their voices, I was about to write; but I heard a voice from heaven saying to me,[49]

"Seal up the things which the seven thunders uttered, and do not write them." 5 And the angel whom I saw standing on the sea and on the land lifted up his hand[50] to heaven 6 and swore by Him who lives forever and ever, who created heaven and the things that are in it, the earth and the things that are in it, and the sea and the things that are in it, that there should be delay no longer, 7 but in the days of the sounding of the seventh angel, when he is about to sound, the mystery of God would be finished, as He declared to His servants the prophets.

John Eats the Little Book

8 Then the voice which I heard from heaven spoke to me again and said, "Go, take the little book which is open in the hand of the angel who stands on the sea and on the earth." 9 And I went to the angel and said to him, "Give me the little book." And he said to me, "Take and eat it; and it will make your stomach bitter, but it will be as sweet as honey in your mouth." 10 And I took the little book out of the angel's hand and ate it, and it was as sweet as honey in my mouth. But when I had eaten it, my stomach became bitter. 11 And he[51] said to me, "You must prophesy again about many peoples, nations, tongues, and kings."

The Two Witnesses

11 Then I was given a reed like a measuring rod. And the angel stood,[52] saying, "Rise and measure the temple of God, the altar, and those who worship there. 2 "But leave out the court which is outside the temple, and do not measure it, for it has been given to the Gentiles. And they will tread the holy city under foot *for* forty-two months. 3 "And I will give *power* to my two witnesses, and they will prophesy one thousand two hundred and sixty days, clothed in sackcloth." 4 These are the two olive trees and the two lampstands standing before the God[53] of the earth. 5 And if anyone wants to harm them, fire proceeds from their mouth and de-

vours their enemies. And if anyone wants to harm them, he must be killed in this manner.
6 These have power to shut heaven, so that no rain falls in the days of their prophecy; aℏd they have power over waters to turn them to blood, and to strike the earth with all plagues, as often as they desire.

The Witnesses Killed

7 Now when they finish their testimony, the beast that ascends out of the bottomless pit will make war against them, overcome them, and kill them.
8 And their dead bodies *will lie* in the street of the great city which spiritually is called Sodom and Egypt, where also our⁵⁴ Lord was crucified.
9 Then *those* from the peoples, tribes, tongues, and nations will see their dead bodies three and a half days, and not allow their dead bodies to be put into graves.
10 And those who dwell on the earth will rejoice over them, make merry, and send gifts to one another, because these two prophets tormented those who dwell on the earth.

The Witnesses Resurrected

11 Now after the three and a half days the breath of life from God entered them, and they stood on their feet, and great fear fell on those who saw them.
12 And they⁵⁵ heard a loud voice from heaven saying to them, "Come up here." And they ascended to heaven in a cloud, and their enemies saw them.
13 In the same hour there was a great earthquake, and a tenth of the city fell. In the earthquake seven thousand men were killed, and the rest were afraid and gave glory to the God of heaven.
14 The second woe is past. Behold, the third woe is coming quickly.

Seventh Trumpet: The Kingdom Proclaimed

15 Then the seventh angel sounded: And there were loud voices in heaven, saying, "The kingdoms⁵⁶ of this world have become *the kingdoms* of our Lord and of His Christ, and He shall reign forever and ever!"
16 And the twenty-four elders who sat

before God on their thrones fell on their faces and worshiped God,
17 saying:

"We give You thanks,
 O Lord God Almighty,
The One who is and who was
 and who is to come,⁵⁷
Because You have taken Your great
 power and reigned.
18 The nations were angry,
 and Your wrath has come,
And the time of the dead,
 that they should be judged,
And that You should reward Your
 servants the prophets and the saints,
And those who fear Your name,
 small and great,
And should destroy those
 who destroy the earth."

19 Then the temple of God was opened in heaven, and the ark of His covenant⁵⁸ was seen in His temple. And there were lightnings, noises, thunderings, an earthquake, and great hail.

The Woman, the Child, and the Dragon

12 Now a great sign appeared in heaven: a woman clothed with the sun, with the moon under her feet, and on her head a garland of twelve stars.
2 Then being with child, she cried out in labor and in pain to give birth.
3 And another sign appeared in heaven: behold, a great, fiery red dragon having seven heads and ten horns, and seven diadems on his heads.
4 His tail drew a third of the stars of heaven and threw them to the earth. And the dragon stood before the woman who was ready to give birth, to devour her Child as soon as it was born.
5 And she bore a male Child who was to rule all nations with a rod of iron. And her Child was caught up to God and *to* His throne.
6 Then the woman fled into the wilderness, where she has a place prepared by God, that they should feed her there one thousand two hundred and sixty days.

Satan Thrown Out of Heaven

7 And war broke out in heaven: Michael and his angels fought against the dragon; and the dragon and his angels fought,

---

54 NU-Text and M-Text read *their.*   55 M-Text reads *I.*   56 NU-Text and M-Text read *kingdom . . . has.*
57 NU-Text and M-Text omit *and who is to come.*   58 M-Text reads *the covenant of the Lord.*

8 but they did not prevail, nor was a place found for them[59] in heaven any longer.
9 So the great dragon was cast out, that serpent of old, called the Devil and Satan, who deceives the whole world; he was cast to the earth, and his angels were cast out with him.
10 Then I heard a loud voice saying in heaven, "Now salvation, and strength, and the kingdom of our God, and the power of His Christ have come, for the accuser of our brethren, who accused them before our God day and night, has been cast down.
11 "And they overcame him by the blood of the Lamb and by the word of their testimony, and they did not love their lives to the death.
12 "Therefore rejoice, O heavens, and you who dwell in them! Woe to the inhabitants of the earth and the sea! For the devil has come down to you, having great wrath, because he knows that he has a short time."

The Woman Persecuted

13 Now when the dragon saw that he had been cast to the earth, he persecuted the woman who gave birth to the male *Child*.
14 But the woman was given two wings of a great eagle, that she might fly into the wilderness to her place, where she is nourished for a time and times and half a time, from the presence of the serpent.
15 So the serpent spewed water out of his mouth like a flood after the woman, that he might cause her to be carried away by the flood.
16 But the earth helped the woman, and the earth opened its mouth and swallowed up the flood which the dragon had spewed out of his mouth.
17 And the dragon was enraged with the woman, and he went to make war with the rest of her offspring, who keep the commandments of God and have the testimony of Jesus Christ.[60]

The Beast from the Sea

13 Then I[61] stood on the sand of the sea. And I saw a beast rising up out of the sea, having seven heads and ten horns, and on his horns ten crowns, and on his heads a blasphemous name.
2 Now the beast which I saw was like a leopard, his feet were like *the feet of* a bear, and his mouth like the mouth of a lion. And the dragon gave him his power, his throne, and great authority.
3 I saw one of his heads as if it had been mortally wounded, and his deadly wound was healed. And all the world marveled and followed the beast.
4 So they worshiped the dragon who gave authority to the beast; and they worshiped the beast, saying, "Who *is* like the beast? Who is able to make war with him?"
5 And he was given a mouth speaking great things and blasphemies, and he was given authority to continue[62] for forty-two months.
6 Then he opened his mouth in blasphemy against God, to blaspheme His name, His tabernacle, and those who dwell in heaven.
7 And it was granted to him to make war with the saints and to overcome them. And authority was given him over every tribe,[63] tongue, and nation.
8 And all who dwell on the earth will worship him, whose names have not been written in the Book of Life of the Lamb slain from the foundation of the world.
9 If anyone has an ear, let him hear.
10 He who leads into captivity shall go into captivity; he who kills with the sword must be killed with the sword. Here is the patience and the faith of the saints.

The Beast from the Land

11 Then I saw another beast coming up out of the earth, and he had two horns like a lamb and spoke like a dragon.
12 And he exercises all the authority of the first beast in his presence, and causes the earth and those who dwell in it to worship the first beast, whose deadly wound was healed.
13 He performs great signs, so that he even makes fire come down from heaven on the earth in the sight of men.
14 And he deceives those[64] who dwell on the earth by those signs which he was granted to do in the sight of the beast, telling those who dwell on the earth to make an image to the beast who was wounded by the sword and lived.

59 M-Text reads *him.*   60 NU-Text and M-Text omit *Christ.*   61 NU-Text reads *he.*
62 M-Text reads *make war.*   63 NU-Text and M-Text add *and people.*   64 M-Text reads *my own people.*

15 He was granted *power* to give breath to the image of the beast, that the image of the beast should both speak and cause as many as would not worship the image of the beast to be killed.
16 And he causes all, both small and great, rich and poor, free and slave, to receive a mark on their right hand or on their foreheads,
17 and that no one may buy or sell except one who has the mark or the name of the beast, or the number of his name.
18 Here is wisdom. Let him who has understanding calculate the number of the beast, for it is the number of a man: His number *is* 666.

The Lamb and the 144,000

14 Then I looked, and behold, a[65] Lamb standing on Mount Zion, and with Him one hundred *and* forty-four thousand, having[66] His Father's name written on their foreheads.
2 And I heard a voice from heaven, like the voice of many waters, and like the voice of loud thunder. And I heard the sound of harpists playing their harps.
3 And they sang as it were a new song before the throne, before the four living creatures, and the elders; and no one could learn that song except the hundred *and* forty-four thousand who were redeemed from the earth.
4 These are the ones who were not defiled with women, for they are virgins. These are the ones who follow the Lamb wherever He goes. These were redeemed[67] from *among* men, *being* firstfruits to God and to the Lamb.
5 And in their mouth was found no guile,[68] for they are without fault before the throne of God.[69]

The Proclamations of Three Angels

6 Then I saw another angel flying in the midst of heaven, having the everlasting gospel to preach to those who dwell on the earth—to every nation, tribe, tongue, and people—
7 saying with a loud voice, "Fear God and give glory to Him, for the hour of His judgment has come; and worship Him who made heaven and earth, the sea and springs of water."

8 And another angel followed, saying, "Babylon[70] is fallen, is fallen, that great city, because she has made all nations drink of the wine of the wrath of her fornication."
9 Then a third angel followed them, saying with a loud voice, "If anyone worships the beast and his image, and receives *his* mark on his forehead or on his hand,
10 "he himself shall also drink of the wine of the wrath of God, which is poured out full strength into the cup of His indignation. And he shall be tormented with fire and brimstone in the presence of the holy angels and in the presence of the Lamb.
11 "And the smoke of their torment ascends forever and ever; and they have no rest day or night, who worship the beast and his image, and whoever receives the mark of his name."
12 Here is the patience of the saints; here *are* those[71] who keep the commandments of God and the faith of Jesus.
13 Then I heard a voice from heaven saying to me,[72] "Write: 'Blessed *are* the dead who die in the Lord from now on.' " "Yes," says the Spirit, "that they may rest from their labors, and their works follow them."

Reaping the Earth's Harvest

14 And I looked, and behold, a white cloud, and on the cloud sat *One* like the Son of Man, having on His head a golden crown, and in His hand a sharp sickle.
15 And another angel came out of the temple, crying with a loud voice to Him who sat on the cloud, "Thrust in Your sickle and reap, for the time has come for You[73] to reap, for the harvest of the earth is ripe."
16 So He who sat on the cloud thrust in His sickle on the earth, and the earth was reaped.

Reaping the Grapes of Wrath

17 Then another angel came out of the temple which is in heaven, he also having a sharp sickle.
18 And another angel came out from the altar, who had power over fire, and he cried with a loud cry to him who had the

---

65 NU-Text and M-Text read *the*.   66 NU-Text and M-Text add *His name and.*   67 M-Text adds *by Jesus.*
68 NU-Text and M-Text read *falsehood.*   69 NU-Text and M-Text omit *before the throne of God.*
70 NU-Text and M-Text read *Babylon the great is fallen* and omit *is fallen, that great city, because.*
71 NU-Text and M-Text omit *here are those.*   72 NU-Text and M-Text omit *to me.*
73 NU-Text and M-Text omit *for you.*

sharp sickle, saying, "Thrust in your sharp sickle and gather the clusters of the vine of the earth, for her grapes are fully ripe."
19 So the angel thrust his sickle into the earth and gathered the vine of the earth, and threw *it* into the great winepress of the wrath of God.
20 And the winepress was trampled outside the city, and blood came out of the winepress, up to the horses' bridles, for one thousand six hundred furlongs.

Prelude to the Bowl Judgments

15 Then I saw another sign in heaven, great and marvelous: seven angels having the seven last plagues, for in them the wrath of God is complete.
2 And I saw *something* like a sea of glass mingled with fire, and those who have the victory over the beast, over his image and over his mark[74] *and* over the number of his name, standing on the sea of glass, having harps of God.
3 And they sing the song of Moses, the servant of God, and the song of the Lamb, saying:

"Great and marvelous *are* Your works,
    Lord God Almighty!
Just and true *are* Your ways,
    O King of the saints![75]
4 Who shall not fear You, O Lord,
    and glorify Your name?
For *You* alone *are* holy.
For all nations shall come and worship
    before You,
For Your judgments have been
    manifested."

5 After these things I looked, and behold,[76] the temple of the tabernacle of the testimony in heaven was opened.
6 And out of the temple came the seven angels having the seven plagues, clothed in pure bright linen, and having their chests girded with golden bands.
7 Then one of the four living creatures gave to the seven angels seven golden bowls full of the wrath of God who lives forever and ever.
8 The temple was filled with smoke from the glory of God and from His power, and no one was able to enter the temple till the seven plagues of the seven angels were completed.

16 Then I heard a loud voice from the temple saying to the seven angels, "Go and pour out the bowls[77] of the wrath of God on the earth."

First Bowl: Malignant Sores

2 So the first went and poured out his bowl upon the earth, and a foul and loathsome sore came upon the men who had the mark of the beast and those who worshiped his image.

Second Bowl: The Sea Turns to Blood

3 Then the second angel poured out his bowl on the sea, and it became blood as of a dead *man*; and every living creature in the sea died.

Third Bowl: The Waters Turn to Blood

4 Then the third angel poured out his bowl on the rivers and springs of water, and they became blood.
5 And I heard the angel of the waters saying:

"You are righteous, O Lord,[78]
    The One who is and who was
        and who is to be,
    Because You have judged these
        things.
6 For they have shed the blood
        of saints and prophets,
    And You have given them blood
        to drink.
    For it is their just due."

7 And I heard another from[79] the altar saying, "Even so, Lord God Almighty, true and righteous *are* Your judgments."

Fourth Bowl: Men Are Scorched

8 Then the fourth angel poured out his bowl on the sun, and power was given to him to scorch men with fire.
9 And men were scorched with great heat, and they blasphemed the name of God who has power over these plagues; and they did not repent and give Him glory.

Fifth Bowl: Darkness and Pain

10 Then the fifth angel poured out his bowl on the throne of the beast, and his kingdom became full of darkness; and

---

74 NU-Text and M-Text omit *over his mark.*   75 NU-Text and M-Text read *nations.*
76 NU-Text and M-Text omit *behold.*   77 NU-Text and M-Text read *seven bowls.*
78 NU-Text and M-Text omit *O Lord.*   79 NU-Text and M-Text omit *another from.*

they gnawed their tongues because of the pain.
11 And they blasphemed the God of heaven because of their pains and their sores, and did not repent of their deeds.

Sixth Bowl: Euphrates Dried Up

12 Then the sixth angel poured out his bowl on the great river Euphrates, and its water was dried up, so that the way of the kings from the east might be prepared.
13 And I saw three unclean spirits like frogs *coming* out of the mouth of the dragon, out of the mouth of the beast, and out of the mouth of the false prophet.
14 For they are spirits of demons, performing signs, *which* go out to the kings of the earth and[80] of the whole world, to gather them to the battle of that great day of God Almighty.
15 "Behold, I am coming as a thief. Blessed *is* he who watches, and keeps his garments, lest he walk naked and they see his shame."
16 And they gathered them together to the place called in Hebrew, Armageddon.[81]

Seventh Bowl: The Earth Utterly Shaken

17 Then the seventh angel poured out his bowl into the air, and a loud voice came out of the temple of heaven, from the throne, saying, "It is done!"
18 And there were noises and thunderings and lightnings; and there was a great earthquake, such a mighty and great earthquake as had not occurred since men were on the earth.
19 Now the great city was divided into three parts, and the cities of the nations fell. And great Babylon was remembered before God, to give her the cup of the wine of the fierceness of His wrath.
20 Then every island fled away, and the mountains were not found.
21 And great hail from heaven fell upon men, *every hailstone* about the weight of a talent. And men blasphemed God because of the plague of the hail, since that plague was exceedingly great.

The Scarlet Woman and the Scarlet Beast

17 Then one of the seven angels who had the seven bowls came and talked with me, saying to me,[82] "Come, I will show you the judgment of the great harlot who sits on many waters,
2 "with whom the kings of the earth committed fornication, and the inhabitants of the earth were made drunk with the wine of her fornication."
3 So he carried me away in the Spirit into the wilderness. And I saw a woman sitting on a scarlet beast *which was* full of names of blasphemy, having seven heads and ten horns.
4 The woman was arrayed in purple and scarlet, and adorned with gold and precious stones and pearls, having in her hand a golden cup full of abominations and the filthiness of her fornication.[83]
5 And on her forehead a name *was* written:

MYSTERY,
BABYLON THE GREAT,
THE MOTHER OF HARLOTS
AND OF THE ABOMINATIONS
OF THE EARTH.

6 And I saw the woman, drunk with the blood of the saints and with the blood of the martyrs of Jesus. And when I saw her, I marveled with great amazement.

The Meaning of the Woman and the Beast

7 But the angel said to me, "Why did you marvel? I will tell you the mystery of the woman and of the beast that carries her, which has the seven heads and the ten horns.
8 "The beast that you saw was, and is not, and will ascend out of the bottomless pit and go to perdition. And those who dwell on the earth will marvel, whose names are not written in the Book of Life from the foundation of the world, when they see the beast that was, and is not, and yet is.[84]
9 "Here *is* the mind which has wisdom: The seven heads are seven mountains on which the woman sits.
10 There are also seven kings. Five have fallen, one is, *and* the other has not yet come. And when he comes, he must continue a short time.
11 "And the beast that was, and is not, is himself also the eighth, and is of the seven, and is going to perdition.
12 "And the ten horns which you saw are ten kings who have received no kingdom

---

80 NU-Text and M-Text omit *of the earth and.*   81 M-Text reads *Megiddo.*   82 NU-Text and M-Text omit *to me.*
83 M-Text reads *the filthiness of the fornication of the earth.*   84 NU-Text and M-Text read *and shall be present.*

as yet, but they receive authority for one hour as kings with the beast.

13 "These are of one mind, and they will give their power and authority to the beast.

14 "These will make war with the Lamb, and the Lamb will overcome them, for He is Lord of lords and King of kings; and those *who are* with Him *are* called, chosen, and faithful."

15 And he said to me, "The waters which you saw, where the harlot sits, are peoples, multitudes, nations, and tongues.

16 "And the ten horns which you saw on the beast, these will hate the harlot, make her desolate and naked, eat her flesh and burn her with fire.

17 "For God has put it into their hearts to fulfill His purpose, to be of one mind, and to give their kingdom to the beast, until the words of God are fulfilled.

18 "And the woman whom you saw is that great city which reigns over the kings of the earth."

The Fall of Babylon the Great

18 After these things I saw another angel coming down from heaven, having great authority, and the earth was illuminated with his glory.

2 And he cried mightily[85] with a loud voice, saying, "Babylon the great is fallen, is fallen, and has become a habitation of demons, a prison for every foul spirit, and a cage for every unclean and hated bird!

3 "For all the nations have drunk of the wine of the wrath of her fornication, the kings of the earth have committed fornication with her, and the merchants of the earth have become rich through the abundance of her luxury."

4 And I heard another voice from heaven saying, "Come out of her, my people, lest you share in her sins, and lest you receive of her plagues.

5 "For her sins have reached[86] to heaven, and God has remembered her iniquities.

6 "Render to her just as she rendered to you,[87] and repay her double according to her works; in the cup which she has mixed, mix for her double.

7 "In the measure that she glorified herself and lived luxuriously, in the same measure give her torment and sorrow; for she says in her heart, 'I sit *as* queen, and am no widow, and will not see sorrow.'

8 "Therefore her plagues will come in one day—death and mourning and famine. And she will be utterly burned with fire, for strong *is* the Lord God who judges[88] her.

The World Mourns Babylon's Fall

9 "And the kings of the earth who committed fornication and lived luxuriously with her will weep and lament for her, when they see the smoke of her burning,

10 "standing at a distance for fear of her torment, saying, 'Alas, alas, that great city Babylon, that mighty city! For in one hour your judgment has come.'

11 "And the merchants of the earth will weep and mourn over her, for no one buys their merchandise anymore:

12 "merchandise of gold and silver, precious stones and pearls, fine linen and purple, silk and scarlet, every kind of citron wood, every kind of object of ivory, every kind of object of most precious wood, bronze, iron, and marble;

13 "and cinnamon and incense, fragrant oil and frankincense, wine and oil, fine flour and wheat, cattle and sheep, horses and chariots, and bodies and souls of men.

14 "And the fruit that your soul longed for has gone from you, and all the things which are rich and splendid have gone from you,[89] and you shall find them no more at all.

15 "The merchants of these things, who became rich by her, will stand at a distance for fear of her torment, weeping and wailing,

16 "and saying, 'Alas, alas, that great city that was clothed in fine linen, purple, and scarlet, and adorned with gold and precious stones and pearls!

17 'For in one hour such great riches came to nothing.' And every shipmaster, all who travel by ship, sailors, and as many as trade on the sea, stood at a distance

18 "and cried out when they saw the smoke of her burning, saying, 'What *is* like this great city?'

19 "And they threw dust on their heads and cried out, weeping and wailing, and

---

85 NU-Text and M-Text omit *mightily.*   86 NU-Text and M-Text read *have been heaped up.*
87 NU-Text and M-Text omit *to you.*   88 NU-Text and M-Text read *has judged.*
89 NU-Text and M-Text read *been lost to you.*

saying, 'Alas, alas, that great city, in which all who had ships on the sea became rich by her wealth! For in one hour she is made desolate.'
20 "Rejoice over her, O heaven, and *you* holy apostles[90] and prophets, for God has avenged you on her!'"

Finality of Babylon's Fall

21 Then a mighty angel took up a stone like a great millstone and threw *it* into the sea, saying, "Thus with violence the great city Babylon shall be thrown down, and shall not be found anymore.
22 "The sound of harpists, musicians, flutists, and trumpeters shall not be heard in you anymore. And no craftsman of any craft shall be found in you anymore. And the sound of a millstone shall not be heard in you anymore.
23 "And the light of a lamp shall not shine in you anymore. And the voice of bridegroom and bride shall not be heard in you anymore. For your merchants were the great men of the earth, for by your sorcery all the nations were deceived.
24 "And in her was found the blood of prophets and saints, and of all who were slain on the earth."

Heaven Exults over Babylon

19 After these things I heard a loud voice of a great multitude in heaven, saying, "Alleluia! Salvation and glory and honor and power to the Lord[91] our God!
2 "For true and righteous *are* His judgments, because He has judged the great harlot who corrupted the earth with her fornication; and He has avenged on her the blood of His servants *shed* by her."
3 Again they said, "Alleluia! And her smoke rises up forever and ever!"
4 And the twenty-four elders and the four living creatures fell down and worshiped God who sat on the throne, saying, "Amen! Alleluia!"
5 Then a voice came from the throne, saying, "Praise our God, all you His servants and those who fear Him, both small and great!"
6 And I heard, as it were, the voice of a great multitude, as the sound of many waters and as the sound of mighty thun-

derings, saying, "Alleluia! For the Lord God Omnipotent reigns!
7 "Let us be glad and rejoice and give Him glory, for the marriage of the Lamb has come, and His wife has made herself ready."
8 And to her it was granted to be arrayed in fine linen, clean and bright, for the fine linen is the righteous acts of the saints.
9 Then he said to me, "Write: 'Blessed *are* those who are called to the marriage supper of the Lamb!' " And he said to me, "These are the true sayings of God."
10 And I fell at his feet to worship him. But he said to me, "See *that you do* not *do that!* I am your fellow servant, and of your brethren who have the testimony of Jesus. Worship God! For the testimony of Jesus is the spirit of prophecy."

Christ on a White Horse

11 Then I saw heaven opened, and behold, a white horse. And He who sat on him *was* called Faithful and True, and in righteousness He judges and makes war.
12 His eyes *were* like a flame of fire, and on His head *were* many crowns. He had[92] a name written that no one knew except Himself.
13 He *was* clothed with a robe dipped in blood, and His name is called The Word of God.
14 And the armies in heaven, clothed in fine linen, white and clean, followed Him on white horses.
15 Now out of His mouth goes a sharp[93] sword, that with it He should strike the nations. And He Himself will rule them with a rod of iron. He Himself treads the winepress of the fierceness and wrath of Almighty God.
16 And He has on *His* robe and on His thigh a name written:

KING OF KINGS
AND LORD OF LORDS.

The Beast and His Armies Defeated

17 Then I saw an angel standing in the sun; and he cried with a loud voice, saying to all the birds that fly in the midst of heaven, "Come and gather together for the supper of the great God,[94]

---

90 NU-Text and M-Text read *saints and apostles.*   91 NU-Text and M-Text omit *the Lord.*
92 M-Text adds *names written, and.*   93 M-Text adds *two-edged.*   94 NU-Text and M-Text read *the great supper of G*

18 "that you may eat the flesh of kings, the flesh of captains, the flesh of mighty men, the flesh of horses and of those who sit on them, and the flesh of all *people*, free and slave, both small and great."
19 And I saw the beast, the kings of the earth, and their armies, gathered together to make war against Him who sat on the horse and against His army.
20 Then the beast was captured, and with him the false prophet who worked signs in his presence, by which he deceived those who received the mark of the beast and those who worshiped his image. These two were cast alive into the lake of fire burning with brimstone.
21 And the rest were killed with the sword which proceeded from the mouth of Him who sat on the horse. And all the birds were filled with their flesh.

Satan Bound 1000 Years

20 Then I saw an angel coming down from heaven, having the key to the bottomless pit and a great chain in his hand.
2 He laid hold of the dragon, that serpent of old, who is *the* Devil and Satan, and bound him for a thousand years;
3 and he cast him into the bottomless pit, and shut him up, and set a seal on him, so that he should deceive the nations no more till the thousand years were finished. But after these things he must be released for a little while.

The Saints Reign with Christ 1000 Years

4 And I saw thrones, and they sat on them, and judgment was committed to them. And *I saw* the souls of those who had been beheaded for their witness to Jesus and for the word of God, who had not worshiped the beast or his image, and had not received *his* mark on their foreheads or on their hands. And they lived and reigned with Christ for a[95] thousand years.
5 But the rest of the dead did not live again until the thousand years were finished. This *is* the first resurrection.
6 Blessed and holy *is* he who has part in the first resurrection. Over such the second death has no power, but they shall be priests of God and of Christ, and shall reign with Him a thousand years.

Satanic Rebellion Crushed

7 Now when the thousand years have expired, Satan will be released from his prison
8 and will go out to deceive the nations which are in the four corners of the earth, Gog and Magog, to gather them together to battle, whose number *is* as the sand of the sea.
9 They went up on the breadth of the earth and surrounded the camp of the saints and the beloved city. And fire came down from God out of heaven and devoured them.
10 And the devil, who deceived them, was cast into the lake of fire and brimstone where the beast and the false prophet *are*. And they will be tormented day and night forever and ever.

The Great White Throne Judgment

11 Then I saw a great white throne and Him who sat on it, from whose face the earth and the heaven fled away. And there was found no place for them.
12 And I saw the dead, small and great, standing before God,[96] and books were opened. And another book was opened, which is *the Book* of Life. And the dead were judged according to their works, by the things which were written in the books.
13 The sea gave up the dead who were in it, and Death and Hades delivered up the dead who were in them. And they were judged, each one according to his works.
14 Then Death and Hades were cast into the lake of fire. This is the second death.[97]
15 And anyone not found written in the Book of Life was cast into the lake of fire.

All Things Made New

21 And I saw a new heaven and a new earth, for the first heaven and the first earth had passed away. Also there was no more sea.
2 Then I, John,[98] saw the holy city, New Jerusalem, coming down out of heaven from God, prepared as a bride adorned for her husband.
3 And I heard a loud voice from heaven saying, "Behold, the tabernacle of God *is* with men, and He will dwell with them, and they shall be His people, and God

---

95 M-Text reads *the*.　96 NU-Text and M-Text read *the throne*.　97 NU-Text and M-Text add *the lake of fire*.
98 NU-Text and M-Text omit *John*.

Himself will be with them *and be* their God.

4 "And God will wipe away every tear from their eyes; there shall be no more death, nor sorrow, nor crying; and there shall be no more pain, for the former things have passed away." ⋅

5 Then He who sat on the throne said, "Behold, I make all things new." And He said to me,[99] "Write, for these words are true and faithful."

6 And He said to me, "It is done![100] I am the Alpha and the Omega, the Beginning and the End. I will give of the fountain of the water of life freely to him who thirsts.

7 "He who overcomes shall inherit all things,[101] and I will be his God and he shall be My son.

8 "But the cowardly, unbelieving,[102] abominable, murderers, sexually immoral, sorcerers, idolaters, and all liars shall have their part in the lake which burns with fire and brimstone, which is the second death."

The New Jerusalem

9 Then one of the seven angels who had the seven bowls filled with the seven last plagues came to me[103] and talked with me, saying, "Come, I will show you the bride, the Lamb's wife."[104]

10 And he carried me away in the Spirit to a great and high mountain, and showed me the great city, the holy[105] Jerusalem, descending out of heaven from God,

11 having the glory of God. And her light *was* like a most precious stone, like a jasper stone, clear as crystal.

12 Also she had a great and high wall with twelve gates, and twelve angels at the gates, and names written on them, which are *the names* of the twelve tribes of the children of Israel:

13 three gates on the east, three gates on the north, three gates on the south, and three gates on the west.

14 Now the wall of the city had twelve foundations, and on them were the names[106] of the twelve apostles of the Lamb.

15 And he who talked with me had a gold reed to measure the city, its gates, and its wall.

16 And the city is laid out as a square, and its length is as great as its breadth. And he measured the city with the reed: twelve thousand furlongs. Its length, breadth, and height are equal.

17 Then he measured its wall: one hundred *and* forty-four cubits, *according* to the measure of a man, that is, of an angel.

18 And the construction of its wall was *of* jasper; and the city *was* pure gold, like clear glass.

19 And the foundations of the wall of the city *were* adorned with all kinds of precious stones: the first foundation *was* jasper, the second sapphire, the third chalcedony, the fourth emerald,

20 the fifth sardonyx, the sixth sardius, the seventh chrysolite, the eighth beryl, the ninth topaz, the tenth chrysoprase, the eleventh jacinth, and the twelfth amethyst.

21 And the twelve gates *were* twelve pearls: each individual gate was of one pearl. And the street of the city *was* pure gold, like transparent glass.

The Glory of the New Jerusalem

22 But I saw no temple in it, for the Lord God Almighty and the Lamb are its temple.

23 And the city had no need of the sun or of the moon to shine in it,[107] for the glory[108] of God illuminated it, and the Lamb *is* its light.

24 And the nations of those who are saved[109] shall walk in its light, and the kings of the earth bring their glory and honor into it.[110]

25 Its gates shall not be shut at all by day (there shall be no night there).

26 And they shall bring the glory and the honor of the nations into it.[111]

27 But there shall by no means enter it anything that defiles, or causes[112] an abomination or a lie, but only those who are written in the Lamb's Book of Life.

---

99 NU-Text and M-Text omit *to me.*   100 M-Text omits *it is done.*   101 M-Text reads *I shall give him these things.*
102 M-Text adds *and sinners.*   103 NU-Text and M-Text omit *to me.*
104 M-Text reads *I will show you the woman, the Lamb's bride.*
105 NU-Text and M-Text omit *the great* and read *the holy city, Jerusalem.*
106 NU-Text and M-Text read *twelve names.*   107 NU-Text and M-Text omit *in it.*
108 M-Text reads *the very glory.*   109 NU-Text and M-Text omit *of those who are saved.*
110 M-Text reads *the glory and honor of the nations to Him.*   111 M-Text adds *that they may enter in.*
112 NU-Text and M-Text read *anything profane nor one who causes.*

The River of Life

22 And he showed me a pure[113] river of water of life, clear as crystal, proceeding from the throne of God and of the Lamb.

2 In the middle of its street, and on either side of the river, *was* the tree of life, which bore twelve fruits, each *tree* yielding its fruit every month. And the leaves of the tree *were* for the healing of the nations.

3 And there shall be no more curse, but the throne of God and of the Lamb, shall be in it, and His servants shall serve Him.

4 They shall see His face, and His name *shall be* on their foreheads.

5 And there shall be no night there: They need no lamp nor light of the sun, for the Lord God gives them light. And they shall reign forever and ever.

The Time Is Near

6 Then he said to me, "These words *are* faithful and true." And the Lord God of the holy[114] prophets sent His angel to show His servants the things which must shortly take place.

7 "Behold, I am coming quickly! Blessed *is* he who keeps the words of the prophecy of this book."

8 Now I, John, saw and heard[115] these things. And when I heard and saw, I fell down to worship before the feet of the angel who showed me these things.

9 Then he said to me, "See *that you do not do that.* For I am your fellow servant, and of your brethren the prophets, and of those who keep the words of this book. Worship God."

10 And he said to me, "Do not seal the words of the prophecy of this book, for the time is at hand.

11 "He who is unjust, let him be unjust still; he who is filthy, let him be filthy still; he who is righteous, let him be righteous[116] still; he who is holy, let him be holy still."

Jesus Testifies to the Churches

12 "And behold, I am coming quickly, and My reward *is* with Me, to give to every one according to his work.

13 "I am the Alpha and the Omega, *the* Beginning and *the* End, the First and the Last."[117]

14 Blessed *are* those who do His commandments,[118] that they may have the right to the tree of life, and may enter through the gates into the city.

15 But outside *are* dogs and sorcerers and sexually immoral and murderers and idolaters, and whoever loves and practices a lie.

16 "I, Jesus, have sent My angel to testify to you these things in the churches. I am the Root and the Offspring of David, the Bright and Morning Star."

17 And the Spirit and the bride say, "Come!" And let him who hears say, "Come!" And let him who thirsts come. And whoever desires, let him take the water of life freely.

A Warning

18 For I testify to everyone who hears the words of the prophecy of this book: If anyone adds to these things, God will add[119] to him the plagues that are written in this book;

19 and if anyone takes away from the words of the book of this prophecy, God shall take away[120] his part from the Book[121] of Life, from the holy city, and *from* the things which are written in this book.

I Am Coming Quickly

20 He who testifies to these things says, "Surely I am coming quickly." Amen. Even so, come, Lord Jesus!

21 The grace of our Lord Jesus Christ *be* with you all.[122] Amen.

---

113 NU-Text and M-Text omit *pure.*   114 NU-Text and M-Text read *spirits of the prophets.*
115 NU-Text and M-Text read *am the one who heard and saw.*   116 NU-Text and M-Text read *do righteousness.*
117 NU-Text and M-Text read *the First and the Last, the Beginning and the End.*
118 NU-Text reads *wash their robes.*   119 M-Text reads *may God add.*   120 M-Text reads *may God take away.*
121 NU-Text and M-Text read *tree.*   122 NU-Text reads *with all;* M-Text reads *with all the saints.*

The Greatest Possibility Thinker That Ever Lived

The Greatest Possibility Thinker
That Ever Lived

Impossibility Thinking

You know what that is?
It's the kind of thinking that says:
"It's impossible!"
"It won't work."
"It'll never happen."
"I haven't got what it takes."
"Why bother to try?"
So
JESUS should have been
the world's greatest impossibility
thinker
For He had *nothing* going for Him.

JESUS was

a member of a despised minority,
a citizen of an occupied country,
a nobody as far as the Romans were
concerned,
a joke to the occupying power,
a nuisance to His fellow Jews.

JESUS lived among an oppressed,
cynical, and
embittered people!

Taxes were oppressive.
Freedom was unknown.
Survival was uncertain.
Religion was restrictive, negative,
and joyless.

Yet Jesus never made an inflammatory
speech, never organized a guerilla
force, and never led a march on
Jerusalem or Rome.

JESUS inherited no illustrious name.

His father was a common laborer.
His mother was a simple, homespun
type.
His uncles and aunts; who were they?
His grandparents? Nobodies!

He could never point with pride to a
prestigious address. Rather
He came from a city reputed to be
culturally deprived and morally
corrupt.
"Can anything good come out of
Nazareth?"
was a common expression.

JESUS was uneducated.
Whatever His schooling was, it was
simple. The only account of His writing
was a note He scribbled in the sand.
He had
No academic degrees,
No certificates of special merit,
award or achievement:
No trophies or medals;
And He never received an honorary
doctorate of divinity degree!

JESUS lived and died untraveled. He
never visited the exciting, glamorous
world outside His own country. He saw
none of the sights so important to the
secular world of His day. Like

The glistening temples of Athens:
with the Parthenon on the acropolis
holding the golden statue of Athena;

or
Rome—with its impressive forum,
colosseum, and theatres: or
The marble, pillar-lined streets of
Alexandria.
Or the spectacular city of Ephesus!

All He saw was people: lonely, hurting,
sick, depressed, fearful, troubled hearts!
It made Him cry!

JESUS never became an intimate friend
of men of power and influence.

He had no "big connections"—V.I.P.'s
did not seek Him out. Had He ever
been asked for letters of character
reference—who could He list? No
peer professors; famous authors;
powerful politicians; ranking
generals; or lordly churchmen.

He couldn't have been a
name-dropper if He wanted to!
(Except to say—as He did—that He
and God were very close.)

JESUS had no organization.

His followers were men with

broken speech,
rough hands, and
cracked fingernails.

They were
unpolished, uncultured,
unlettered, and ignorant failures,

In many ways, and in critical times,
they proved to be
unstable,
uncertain,
undependable, and
disappointing.

Yes,
JESUS knew

ingratitude,
rejection,
misunderstanding, and
betrayal!

JESUS—by all the psychological laws of
human development, should have lived
and died a

judgmental,
frustrated,
critical,
angry,
unbelieving,
cynical,
rebellious,
violence-prone,
emotionally-deprived,
radically militant revolutionary!

JESUS lived and died in poverty. He had:

No home of His own,
No insurance policy,
No Social Security card,
No retirement plan:
He performed a miracle to raise the
money to pay His taxes!

His estate? He left behind only one
simple robe, a cheap prize to entice
the gambling soldiers at the cross.

So He died empty-handed—except
for fresh wounds—leaving no fortune
and no heirs.

JESUS remained unmarried,
a single adult
all His life.

So He spent His years without the
encouragement,

comfort, or
companionship
of a wife or children.

In a society where children were a
man's greatest treasure, He died
never having fathered a single son or
daughter.

So He died.
Childless.

JESUS

Think of it: At His death

He was only thirty-three years
old!
He was so young.
He died before His mother!
He was not given a half-century,
or more, to make His mark,
write His books, build His
empire, and conquer the world.

This—at least and at last—should
have made Him a
cynical impossibility thinker, crying
out through tight
lips, and bitter tears:

"It isn't fair!"
"I'm too young to die!"
"Others live long and
longer—why can't I?"
"O God—give me more time!"

JESUS—

Where was His Heavenly Father
when Jesus needed Him most?

JESUS—

All His life He was good, kind, and
loving, and very religious.
Every Sabbath—He was in the
synagogue.
The Holy Scriptures—how He loved
to read them.

Prayer? His life was a prayer for all
seasons!

JESUS—

How He loved His Heavenly Father.
How He trusted His Heavenly Father.
How He served His Heavenly Father.

JESUS—

Now on His cross—when He needs
His God most—
God seems to have abandoned Him.

This man, Jesus, turned out to be

**THE WORLD'S GREATEST
POSSIBILITY THINKER!**

No founder of any religion ever used the
word *possible* more than Jesus did!

"For with God all things are possible"
(Mark 10:27).

"The things which are impossible with
men are possible with God" (Luke
18:27).

"All things *are* possible to him who
believes" (Mark 9:23).

"Father, all things *are* possible" (Mark
14:36).

"If you have faith as a mustard seed, you
will say to this mountain, 'Move . . .' and
nothing will be impossible" (Matt.
17:20).

"With God nothing will be impossible"
(Luke 1:37).

"With men *it is* impossible, but not with
God" (Mark 10:27).

"With God all things are possible" (Matt.
19:26).

THE GREATEST POSSIBILITY THINKER

To **JESUS**

Every problem was a possibility in disguise.

Sickness—was an opportunity for healing.
Sin—was an opportunity for forgiveness.
Sorrow—was an opportunity for compassion.

Personal abuse was an opportunity to leave a good impression and show the world how possibility thinkers react!

To **JESUS**

Every person was a gold mine of undiscovered hidden possibilities!

Peter? A tough-talking fisherman:
    But—he could make a great
    leader of a great new church.
Mary Magdalene? A common
prostitute:
    But—she could become a
    sensitive, sweet soul. She could
    one day anoint His body for
    burial.
Matthew? A vulgar materialist:
    But—he had possibilities to
    become a great writer! Even the
    gospel!

No wonder Jesus rushed to meet the outcast, riff-raff of humanity!

To **JESUS**

The important fact about you and me
    is not that
WE ARE SINNERS
But that
WE CAN BE SAINTS.

So Jesus never called any person a sinner! He became angry only with

religious people who made people feel they were miserable, guilty sinners.

Instead Jesus rushed to build—in the worst of sinners—a belief that they, too, could be saved for inspiring service!

So
JESUS proclaimed the greatest possibility:

The immeasurable

MERCY
OF
GOD

To **JESUS**

the whole world was
    jammed,
    pregnant,
    loaded,
    bulging, with
        untapped,
        undiscovered,
        undetected

POSSIBILITIES!

JESUS really believed in the supreme possibilities!

Jesus preached these grand possibilities:

Man *can* be born again!
Character *can* be changed!
You *can* become a new person!
Life *can* be beautiful!
There *is* a solution to every problem!
There *is* a light behind every shadow!

Yes,
JESUS had an unshakeable faith in these ultimate possibilities:

God exists!
Life goes on beyond death!
Heaven is for real!

He was prepared to prove it:
by dying—and rising again!

He saw the possibility of
ultimate justice!
So
He had as much to say about hell as
He did about heaven.

JESUS

Saw the possibility of heaven and hell
in eternity.
He also saw the possibility of a transformed world—
here on planet earth.
He was impressed by what the world
could become—
never depressed by what the world
was.
He truly believed in the possibility of
transformed lives.
He truly believed that common people can become
uncommonly powerful.
He knew without a shadow of doubt
that ordinary persons
could become extraordinary persons
if they could
become possibility thinkers.

So He would give self-confidence to
inferiority-complexed people.
He would make it possible for guilt-
infected, failure-plagued, problem-
swamped persons to start loving
themselves and stop hating themselves!

What enormous self-confidence this great
Possibility Thinker had! Listen to what
Christ said:

"I am the good shepherd" (John
10:11).

"I am the door. If anyone enters by
Me, he will be saved" (John 10:9).

"I am the bread of life" (John 6:35).

"I am the vine, you *are* the branches.
He who abides in Me, and I in him,
bears much fruit" (John 15:5).

"I am the way, the truth, and the life.
No one comes to the Father, except
through Me" (John 14:6).

"I am the resurrection and the life.
He who believes in Me, though he
may die, he shall live" (John 11:25).

Then came the end. He was accused of
stirring up the people. He was placed on
trial. He was charged with blasphemy.
Did He not claim to be the promised
Messiah? At least, did He not allow
people to get the impression that He was
the Son of God? In His public trial He was
challenged to deny His deity, to withdraw
His blasphemous statements, and clear up
the confused minds of the simple people
who believed Him to be God visiting
earth in human form.

But He could not tell a lie, so He
remained silent. The verdict was
predictable: death by crucifixion! A
crowd gathered to see how a possibility
thinker dies. How did He die? He died
seeing and seizing the possibilities of the
moment! He practiced what He had
preached all His life! He turned the hell
into a heaven.

For here was His chance to save the soul
of a lost thief who was being crucified
beside Him.

This was a spectacular opportunity to
dramatically teach all men of all ages to
come that death can be a grand reunion
with God!

So His last spoken words were loaded with great expectations. "Father, into Your hands I commend My spirit" (Luke 23:46).

There was a final gasp—and He was gone. The Roman commander in charge of the execution turned away—converted on the spot, he was overheard saying, "Certainly this was a righteous Man!" (Luke 23:47).

The body was taken down and sealed in a tomb. Then it happened! Easter! He was resurrected. He came back to life again.

Why do we believe this fantastic tale? Because of the incredible change in His followers. They saw Him alive again. Where they were cowards, they became fearless proclaimers in the city streets—in daylight! Where they were impossibility thinkers—they became possibility thinkers!

Think Now About Your Personal Possibilities

Today, twenty centuries later, Christ literally lives in millions of human beings all around the world! By His death He solved His greatest problem. What was that? He could only be in one place at a time. Now, through the power of His Holy Spirit, He is able to live in millions of lives all around this world! Think of the possibilities:

Christ can infiltrate
any race,
any religion,
any community,
any country!

THE GOOD NEWS IS— CHRIST CAN LIVE IN— EVEN YOU

That is what it is all about!

BEING A CHRISTIAN IS offering yourself to Him

Your mind—for Christ to think through,
Your heart—for Christ to love through,
Your lips—for Christ to speak through,
Your hands—for Christ to touch through!

Just imagine what possibilities for exciting living this opens up to you!

If Christ can live within you then it is possible for you, too,

To—Turn your problems into opportunities!
To—Tackle your opportunities and succeed!
To—Dream great dreams and make them come true!
To—Switch from jealousy and self-pity to really caring about others who are much worse off than you are.
To—Pick up the broken hopes and start over again!
To—See great possibilities in those unattractive people!
To—Become a truly beautiful person—like Jesus!

Your Prayer for a New and Exciting Life

Jesus Christ—I've come to see that many things are possible that I never before believed were possible.

I believe it's possible—that You were sent by God into the world to be my Savior. I accept You now.

I believe it's possible—eternal life!

I believe it's possible—that Christ is alive this moment and trying to penetrate my life through my brain as I read these words!

I believe it's possible—for His Holy Spirit to live within me! I confess my sin. I ask Christ to save me. I invite Him to come into my life. I believe it's possible!

Amen.

Now pray this Possibility-Thinking Prayer every day:

**Lord, show me the person
You want to speak to
through my life today.**

Amen.

Prayers for Positive Faith

Prayers for Positive Faith

Morning Affirmation

The sky is bright, my Father, with the morning light. Always after night there is a new day. Always after winter there is a springtime. Always after the seed is dropped in the soil to die, new life springs forth. Always after the tough times, there comes the recovery. Always, my Father, when a penitent, contrite heart bows in repentance before you, there comes the joy of fresh pardon. And so now, my Father, I come, expecting good things to happen, for I have stepped into the circle of Your love, and I find mercy and Your peace here. Strength is coming like a warm rain driven by warm winds. Healing is coming through the living Christ. Thank You, Father. Amen.

Thank You, Lord, that You have come to give us affirmation as persons, salvation as sinners, to turn us into the potential people of being a part of this world's solution, messengers of real love. Thank You, Jesus Christ, I accept You as my Savior. I accept You for all the forgiveness that I need. I embrace Your holy cross, and by the sacrifice of Your precious life, I have been made clean. What can wash away my sin? Nothing but the blood of Jesus. Amen.

Morning Meditation

Thank You, Father, that the dawning has come. The sun is shining. The birds are singing and the flowers are blooming. Clouds are sliding silently through the soundless sea of space, and there is a Spirit that is moving in my mind and heart now. You are here and I am waiting. Bless me, O Father, in the name of Christ. Amen.

A Prayer for Inner Peace

You will keep him in perfect peace whose mind is stayed on You, O Lord. My face changes when I focus on Christ. My heart changes when I focus on Christ. My mind changes when I focus on His cross. Jesus Christ, I really remember You, I really love You, and now I want to show it by saying, Jesus Christ come into my life, save me from my sin, cleanse me from my negative thinking, fill me with Your positive thoughts, fill me with Your Holy Spirit, and may we walk together through the best years of my life. Amen.

A Prayer for Support

O Lord my God, my rock upon whom I build my dreams.
I come to You today to feel again Your mighty strength.

As the foundation of a great building silently supports its beautiful burden.

So may I feel You carry me and my dreams along
in Your supportive arms of love.

And as the fortress gallantly protects a vulnerable city from deadly assaults, so
wrap me in Your protective arms of love, so that I may feel Your
protection.

As the granite landmarks remain immovable in the midst of the shifting sands,
so I fix my eyes on You, my unchanging point of reference—when I
become confused and lost in the maze of today's values.

And so, Lord, I build my dreams on Your love—my solid Rock.

And I ask for Your protection on my dream from the negative assaults
that come my way.

I look to You for guidance, lest my dreams lose their true direction which is
toward You and Your glory.

Thank You for hearing my prayer, for sending me Jesus, my Friend,
my Lord, and my Rock.

A Perfect Friend

Thank You, Jesus, when I am lonely, You give me love.
When I am guilty, You grant me forgiveness.
When I doubt, You give faith.
When I have a searching mind and hear, You give direction.
When I feel empty, You fill me with joy.
God, You never fail me. You are here now. You are born within me now.
You are saving me by Your grace. It will be a joyous day. Amen.

A New Dawn

O Lord, it is good to sing praises to You in the morning.
To consider Your guidance during the day, and to remember
    Your faithfulness at sunset.

As each day dawns with new opportunities and unexpected surprises,
    I am grateful for the gift of fresh beginnings.
And as I pursue the dreams You send my way, I am conscious
    of Your ever-present guiding hand.

When I become confused, I can feel You gently lead.
When I tire, You carry me along.
When I stumble and fall, You pick me up.

And so as I journey to the end of my day, I rejoice and am eternally grateful
    to You for the difference You have made.
Without You my life would be empty, dark, and broken.
But instead You have come bringing life, light, and healing.
And so I thank You and praise You! Amen.

The Lord's Prayer

I sense an inner strength surging within me now.
I sense an inner joy breaking forth all around me.
I feel Your loving presence as I focus my prayers
    for _____ before You,
    the loving and eternal God of us all.
Teach us to pray, as Your Son taught, saying . . .

"Our Father in heaven,
Hallowed be Your name.
Your kingdom come.
Your will be done
On earth as *it is* in heaven.
Give us this day our daily bread.
And forgive us our debts,
As we forgive our debtors.
And do not lead us into temptation,
But deliver us from the evil one.
For Yours is the kingdom and the power
    and the glory forever. Amen."

Mountains to Climb

Our Father, I come to You today to bless Your Holy Name.
You are great and You are loving.
Send me Your peace, Your presence, and Your courage.

For I find myself with tall mountains to climb, rough roads to trod, deep valleys
    to forge, and vast oceans to bridge.

As people in days of old knelt to be knighted before their king, so I bend my
    knee before You, O King of Kings and Lord of Lords.

May I feel Your tap on my shoulder, Your healing touch in my life. And when I
    arise may I stand taller and stronger than ever before.

For I know that there is no mountain too tall to climb, no ocean too vast to
    bridge, no race too long to run, and no world too large to overcome
    with the help of Your powerful and mighty hand.

I thank You, O Lord, for making all these things possible through Jesus Christ,
    Your Son. Amen.

A Prayer of Dependence

Dear Lord, I come to You in much the same way that sheep return to their
    shepherd.
I have been stubborn in the past and have wandered from Your care.
I have become confused and lost my way.
And I have run into thorns that have cut deep.
But now, I run with my arms open wide to You.
For as a shepherd protects his sheep, so You lift me, O Lord, in Your protective
    arms above the overwhelming times of life.
And as a shepherd guides his sheep, so You sustain me with the words of life
    in Your book, the Bible.
And as a shepherd loves his sheep, so I feel Your forgiving hand of love heal the
    hurts within my heart today.

Thank You, gentle Shepherd.
I will love and praise You forevermore.

New Possibilities

O Lord, I praise You this morning and sing songs of joy because of the peace,
    the love, and the hope that You have given me.

I look expectantly to the new dreams You want me to dream, the new goals
    You want me to reach, and the new mountains You want me to climb.

As I scale the mountain trail, I pray that You will refresh me with unexpected
    meadows along the way, that You will shelter me when I am beset
    by storms. And that You will give me the grace to look for the gold mines
    in the detours.

I have within me the capacity to be a gem, a jewel, and a light
    to those who are struggling around me.
So help me, Lord, to discover the possibilities that You have put
    in each new day.
Help me to see the face that needs Your smile, open my ears to the cries
    of our hurting world, and give me the courage to touch the lives
    that so desperately need You.

I praise You, I love You, and I trust You, O Lord,
    my strength and my Redeemer. Amen.

Choose Life

O Lord, my God, whose power and might is stronger than anything
    I might ever face.
I know that You are watching me in every step I take, leading me toward
    the abundant life You have planned for me.

Today, as every day, I am faced with decisions.

I must chose. Will I respond negatively or positively to the ideas
    You will bring my way?

Will I align myself with loneliness or brighten someone's day?

Will I look anxiously toward tomorrow with fear, or will I place my life
    in Your care and face my future with hope?

PRAYERS FOR POSITIVE FAITH

O Lord, I am so grateful for the gift of choice. I have the ability to choose.

And with Your help and guidance,
I can choose happiness,
I can choose joy,
I can choose love,
I can choose life.

And so I praise You and thank You through whose mercy
   and grace my life is full.

Because of You I can live and love abundantly.

Thank You, Lord.

A Prayer for a New Day

Dear Heavenly Father:
Thank You for the new day that awaits me today,
And for the new possibilities that
You have put into my tomorrows.

I rejoice this morning in the knowledge that with the nights come new days,
With the winter comes the spring, and
With the Cross comes the Resurrection.

Just as the buds of green leaves appear on dry, barren trees,
As the tender sprouts push their way through the stubborn soil, so, O Lord,
   may I feel the creativity You have planted within me push its way
   through my barren times,
To bloom into a beautiful, new idea, a fresh concept, and an unexpected
   opportunity.

Just as the shafts of sunshine send their bright, warm rays across the empty
   black night, so, O Lord, this morning send positive thoughts into my
   mind to erase the negative influences that have blinded me.
Thank You, Lord, for new days and for new life.

The Presence of God

Thank You, Father, for the light that surrounds me, for
    the hope that surges into me, for
    the love that controls my mood.
I am experiencing Your presence. Praise be to You, O God.
I worship You, the Eternal Source of all Life.

I thank You for the joy I have in knowing You as my personal Lord and Savior.
I thank You that I know what it is like to have You in the center of my being.
I pray that You will fill my heart right now with a warmth that will spread
    throughout my body and that I will feel Your Holy Spirit penetrating
    and moving throughout me, giving me a direction and an aim and a goal
    in life.
O Lord, I pray that in this hour You will inspire me and motivate me and give
    me the drive to be Your voice in my world.

This I pray in Your Son's name. Amen.

A Prayer for New Hope

O Father, I look around me to see the beautiful world
    which You have given me.

The majestic mountains, the restful blue skies, and the towering trees
    are all the handiwork of Your greatness.

As the wistful breezes stir the air, so, O Lord, stir my heart and fill my life
    with Your loving Spirit.

Reach down and touch my life with Yours.
For with Your special touch, O Lord, I am changed.

I gain new hope, when all around I see despair.
I receive new faith, when struggles and hurts are great.
I am bathed in Your peace, when tensions and worries abound.
And bright ideas come, when all possibilities seem lost.

So it is no wonder that I am glad that I come with praise and thankfulness.
For I know that Your goodness will never end.

I rejoice in the assurance that even now You are leading me into new
  and challenging possibilities.

Hear me now as I pray. Amen.

A Prayer for the Church

Thank You, Father, that You have created a church,
a collection of human beings,
ecclesia, the called-out people,
those people who have accepted Christ
as Savior and Lord
and now offer themselves—bodies,
minds, and souls.

Through the Holy Spirit,
these, Your family,
carry out Christ's love and caring
in an alienated lonely world.
Thank You, Father.

May Your blessings rest upon each minister
and each lay person in their duties.

Strengthen the work of the church
that the world may discover
that there is another life they never tasted.
The life and the love of Jesus
who can save us from our shame,
our sins,
our unbelief,
our scepticism,
our cynicism,
and can fill us with emotional power
of health and wholeness.

Thank You, God, for the church,
a place where we offer ourselves as volunteers
in this the work of God,
an opportunity and a challenge
to find our place
to be minds through
which Christ can think,
hands through which Christ can lift,
faces through which He can smile,
voices through which He can talk and sing,
examples through which others can be led in the Way.

Grace, mercy, and God's peace
be with you, my fellow ministers
of Christ's church.

May the doors of Your church always be open wide
to all who wish to come—from the mountains,
from the seashore, from the roadside,
from homes and hotels.

May they be open to all—
the lovely and unlovely,
the deserted, the lonely,
the doubting, and the believing.

May the doors of Your church, O God,
be always a gateway to joyful
and abundant living.

The door by which all—young and old,
rich and poor, may enter into
a relationship with Jesus Christ
as Lord and Savior.

An Intimate Prayer

Dear God, as I reach out to grasp the hand of a friend, or a stranger,
Even so now, O God, I reach out to You.

You are there, reaching out to me, You reach out—out of the sky, out of the
    heavens, out of the Scriptures, You reach out from the cross—
Because You want to give me new life.

O God, thank You for what You can do, for what You are doing, and for what
    You are waiting anxiously to do in me.
Move in and show me the treasures that are waiting to be discovered in me—
Treasures of health and physical fitness,
Prosperity instead of poverty, joy instead of despair, love instead of loneliness.

I thank You, Lord, that my impossibilities are Your opportunities.

O God, hear me as I reach out with my struggling, faltering, stumbling,
    clumsy faith.
Help me to trust these moments of faith and to doubt my doubts in Your name,
    my Lord.

God's Goodness

O Lord, my God, my Guide and Friend, it is good to sing praises to You
    and to remember Your faithfulness and steadfast love.

I am reminded that as the sun rises every morning and as the waves roll in
    unceasingly, so Your love is just as unending.

Friendships come and go,
opportunities ebb and flow,
but Your love and care for me is as constant as the seasons
    and as endless as the heavens.
For that, O Lord, I am forever grateful.

No matter how confused I may become,
no matter how lost I may seem to be,
I can run to Your loving arms, there to regain my bearings and set out again,
for I want to feel Your love, so I can in turn love.
I want to be upheld by Your strength, and in turn strengthen.
I want to be renewed by Your grace and then go and glow for You.

Hear my prayer this morning, O Lord, and grant unto me Your peace. Amen.

Tune into God's Thoughts

Thank You, Father, that my mind is designed to pick up Your thoughts and that my heart has been created to welcome the feeling of love, Your Spirit within.

Thank You, Father, that I can in this time of prayer, have the freedom to reach out and let the thoughts that are in me come out. Touch them, bless them, and ordain them to become the seeds of better living. Grace, mercy, and God's peace is with You now. Amen.

Thank You, Lord, that You have called me to develop the potential and the possibility that is built into every one of Your children and that includes me. Release, O God, within me the attitude, "I can do it, with the help of God." Let it begin with me now.

Jesus Christ, I want to thank You, that You have come to be my Savior, my Lord, my Best Friend. Thank You for walking with me and talking with me.

Thank You for the joy we share as we walk in prayer. Father, whisper in my ear to give me a dream for today, a dream that makes life wonderful and eternity exciting. Amen.

Renewal

Thank You, Father, for bringing me to a path that leads to light, for causing me to see the spark and to follow it, for tuning my ear to hear the still, small voice of the Spirit and to listen.

Thank You, God, for the good things that are happening deep within my spirit at this moment. Thank You, Jesus Christ, that You have not forgotten me, even when I have forgotten You. And now we are together.

Father, thank You for Jesus Christ, my beautiful Lord and Savior, who came to forgive me of my sins. By His incarnation He has honored me, by His crucifixion, He has placed a value on my soul, by His resurrection, He has taken early retirement and given me His good job, spreading love around.

Jesus Christ, You are the Great Repairer of the breach; You are the restorer of paths to dwell in, and You have called me to carry on in Your good name. Give me this day the strength to do it well. Amen.

A Prayer for Healing

Jesus Christ, You are alive. You have given me the Good News. Life is abundant, and now life is eternal to those who know You and that includes me. "God so loved the world that He gave His only begotten Son, that whoever believes in Him should not perish but have everlasting life."

You have promised it, Lord. "I am the resurrection and the life. He who believes in Me, though he may die, he shall live." You have promised that if I have faith as the grain of a mustard seed, I can say to my mountain, "move" and nothing will be impossible. Jesus Christ, look at me. You know who I am. You know where I come from. You know what problems I carry in my heart, and my mind, and in my physical, organic body.

O Lord, you know a lot more about me than I do. A lot more about me than any doctor, any psychiatrist, or any counselor knows.

O God, give me the gift of faith. I receive this gift, and I feel a warm glow. Your faith is flowing from my mind, across my face, across my lips, down my neck, and through my body. I am feeling the healing presence of the God of all eternity. In the name of my Lord, I praise You, and I thank You, Jesus Christ. Amen.

For Others in Need

I thank You, Father, for the blessings that are being poured into my life with
every passing moment in this time of prayer.

I sense that my mind is being cleansed of negative thoughts, my soul is being
purged and washed clean, and my heart is being filled with love, peace,
joy, hope, and faith.

O God, many around me today and this past week have traveled over rough
roads; others have traveled through low valleys of pain and trouble; still
others are climbing steep mountains. Through laughter and tears we work
and live together in Your world. For each of these, my brothers and
sisters—Your children, I pray today.

Some have had exciting awards and others crushing blows, and so I pray the
prayer with the psalmist,

Every morning I shall praise Him for His kindness, every evening I shall
rejoice in all His faithfulness.

I remember especially . . .

_____

_____

_____

(Use for names of others to pray for today).

To Give Something Back

Lord, thank You for what You have given to me, and Lord, help me to give
something back. Let me go out today and try to lift up those who are really
hurting. Dear Jesus, I thank You that You have taught me that God loves me.
Do something wonderful in my life, Lord, not for my sake, but for the sake of
people who are hungry and lost. Amen.

A Prayer for Tough Times

Thank You, Father, that I am surrounded by light. There are no gloomy corners in Your presence. The sun filters through the clouds and no shadow can ever turn the starlight off.

Thank You, Father, that after winter comes spring, after death comes a new resurrection, and so I wait for the rock to crack and for the flower to open into blossom today through my faith in You.

I experience Your grace, mercy, and peace now. I do not understand it, so I rejoice in experiencing it. Amen.

A Prayer of Thanksgiving

I come to You now with so much to thank You for.
As your child I want to shout for joy and sing Your praises for all You have done for me.

Thank You for these moments when I withdraw from the world's pressures and anxieties into a quiet place where the sun is shining and the green trees are bending against blue skies, the flowers are blooming, the grass is green, and the water is clean.

There is a fresh fragrance in the air and I sense it is the presence of my God whose love and peace is filling my life now.

Father, give me now the courage to step into life with new drive and motivation. Help me to channel the creative ideas You give me into beautiful life-changing goals.
Give me the strength to hold on to hope as I meet the many challenges throughout the day.

And Lord, give me love as I share with others all the things You have done in my life.
So I may say with integrity to those I meet,
"God loves you and so do I." Amen.

The Blessings of Christmas

O loving Father, as the joy of morning bursts through the sky,
So I come before You bringing songs of joy and praise.
I rejoice in the Good News of the birth of Your Son, knowing that my heart
    will take wings as it is filled with the love of Christmas.

With the birth of Christ in my life, I receive the gift of love in my heart.
And as the star of hope brought light to a dark world that night,
So illuminate all negative thoughts within me with the bright light of faith.

For as Christmas captured God's dream of bringing me back to Him, so now
    crystalize my courage so I can dream new dreams and sight new stars.
And with the Christ child as my north star, I look expectantly to a New Year,
Knowing that Your Spirit will shine in splendor in my life.

Christmas Prayer

O Father, as the burst of an infant's cry penetrated a dark, silent night,

So may Your love fill my life this morning with the joy of Christmastime.

For that Child, Your Son, has brought a star of hope and a prism of peace
    into a world needing a guiding light.

Now I come to thank You and join the angels in singing,
"Glory to God in the highest."

For with the birth of Your Son, my own life is reborn, giving me

Peace, even in the midst of turbulence,
Hope, despite despair,
Joy, in place of sorrow, and
Love, to overcome all strife and tensions.

So now, I gratefully receive Your gift of Your Son, the Christmas Child,
    and I celebrate with carols of song and praise. Amen.

A Prayer of Commitment

What a beautiful thing You can do, O God, in a human being. You are able to take a manger and turn it into a cradle of a king. And You can come and live inside a man, a woman, or a child sometimes cracked, chipped, splintered, battered, and as rough as a manger and transform them into beautiful creations.

Thank You for what You will do in my life now, for I kneel before You and welcome You in, Lord Jesus. When I rise from my kneeling prayer, may I stand taller than I ever have before and face the sun knowing that God is my Friend, into all eternity. I ask this prayer in the name of my Savior who taught us to pray together saying, Our Father . . . .

O God, I feel that this is a moment of great decision for many people. I am so thankful, Father, that we have the opportunities to change our minds. O God, the innkeeper did not have a second chance, we do. I want to thank You now, O Lord, that You want to live within us, You want to build us up, You want to save our immortal souls for heaven. O God, thank You. Amen.

A Prayer of Blessing

And now may the Lord bless you and keep you.
May the Lord make His face to shine upon you
and be gracious unto you,
and may God give to you His peace
in your going out
and in your coming in,
in your lying down
and in your rising up,
in your labor and in your leisure,
in your laughter and in your tears,
until you come to stand before Jesus
in that day in which there is no
sunset and no dawning. Amen.

Positive Faith
for
Power-Filled Living

FAITH IS . . .

Dreaming God's dream

Be renewed in the spirit of your mind (Eph. 4:23).

What's the purpose of life anyway?
Only to eat, drink, work, play, make love?
Or do you have a brain designed to dream dreams?
Is your mind created to be an architect, drawing plans?
Can you imagine beautiful accomplishments?

Think of this:
The human being
is the only creature in the universe
that has the capacity for exercising creative imagination!

This divine quality of *dreaming*
what you want to be,
where you want to go,
what you'd love to do,
projects you hope to achieve,
goals you'd like to reach—
all of this makes you human
and the most unique creature in all of creation!

You really are "made in the image" of the Creator—God!
So you are fulfilling your destiny
as a child of God in human flesh
when you start dreaming the beautiful
dreams God Himself is inspiring in your mind.

A radio is designed to pick up the sounds that are here in this room now!
A television is engineered to pick up the moving pictures that are in the air-waves around you now.
Your mind was invented and created by God to pick up the messages and mental pictures He is sending your way.

That's exciting!
Faith is dreaming God's dreams!

FAITH IS . . .

Breathing your native air

I have come that they may have life, and that they
may have *it* more abundantly (John 10:10).

It's terribly important to understand that a believer is a normal person. Faith is
the mark of normality. A persistently negative and cynical attitude is a mark of
emotional illness.

Birds were designed to fly. The air under the wings of a bird is a natural habitat
of the flying fowl.

Water is the natural habitat of the fish.

Faith is the native air to be breathed in and out by human beings.

It is normal to have faith. It is abnormal to be cynical. Therefore you welcome
all stimuli that would encourage you to have faith. Reject all negative forces that
would destroy faith and replace it with unbelief.

When you practice positive belief, you are more controlled by positive
emotions—love, joy, courage, faith, enthusiasm.

These are the qualities of an emotionally healthy person. Persons who are not
breathing the natural air of faith, but are breathing the polluted air of doubt and
unbelief, are quickly susceptible to a lower morality. They are quickly consumed
by negative emotions—all of which are measured and marked as symptoms of
something less than true wholeness and health as a human being.

You were created to be a believer!

Faith is finding your native air.

That's why you feel so great when you're optimistic!

Thank You, Father, for causing me to be a normal, healthy human being by
motivating me to walk the walk of faith. Amen.

FAITH IS . . .
Wanting more out of life

Delight yourself also in the LORD,
And He shall give you the desires of your heart (Ps. 37:4).

Faith is a choice, not an argument.
It is a decision, not a debate.
It is a commitment, not a controversy.
Faith fulfills some need in your heart.
It can be defined as wanting more out of life.
Even the super affluent are attracted to faith; they soon realize that all of their wealth, social standing, and personal power leave a void in their lives. When you have more money than you can enjoy, what is left?

Saint Augustine said: "Our souls are restless till they rest in Thee." We suspect that out there, somewhere, there is always something more. From where does this intuition for "something more" come? It is built into our nature.

The human being has been called an incurably religious animal by instinct and nature.

Be careful what you want—you'll get it! Wanting is believing, and believing produces results.

Strong faith is often the expression of deep desire.

Likewise doubt is the lack of desire. A host of conscious or subconscious forces can keep you from wanting to believe. Fears of what God might do *to* your life or *in* your life can keep you from wanting to believe. Internalized guilt can make the possibility of God a threatening concept. Deep-seated, negative emotions can kill the desire to believe leaving you with a negative inclination to doubt. Having trouble believing? Why don't you want to believe?

Our Bible verse contains God's promise of blessings upon faith. God promises to bless the person who has strong desires. This is because in God's eyes desire and faith are one and the same: "He shall give you the desires of your heart."

FAITH IS . . .

Doubting your doubts

God is not the God of the dead, but of the living (Matt. 22:32).

"There lives more faith in honest doubt, than in half the creeds," Alfred Lord Tennyson wrote in *In Memoriam.*

I find that some people who have serious questions about the existence of God want desperately to believe. Their probing inquiry reflects thoughtful doubt.

Actually, they are far more responsible and serious in their pursuit of a commitment to God than those who blindly recite cold creeds without really daring to explore the tough questions.

Doubt can be a positive force when we learn to doubt our doubts and have faith in our faith!

It is quite apparent that the believer in God and the Bible has as strong a foundation for a rational system of belief as any doubter has for the philosophy of irreligion he has fabricated.

Faith in God will
   increase your moral strength,
      increase your days of joy,
         reduce your days of despair.

I've never seen a person who has been more respected as a leader in the philosophy and faith of religion than Jesus Christ.

Jesus believed in God. He believed in prayer.

He believed in heaven and hell and eternal life.

He believed in salvation.

He believed in every single human being!

He believed in possibility thinking and He believed in faith.

If your doubts collide and clash with the viewpoint of Jesus Christ, it is the better part of wisdom to believe the believer and doubt the doubter. Then you are on your way to a great life.

FAITH IS . . .

Becoming normal

And when Jesus went out He saw a great multitude; and He was moved
with compassion for them, and healed their sick (Matt. 14:14).

In the Broadway play, *The Man of La Mancha,* Don Quixote is near death. He
has been mocked and scorned because he is such a positive thinker! Finally, in a
splendid self-defense, he asks the ultimate question. "Who is crazy? Am I crazy
because I see the world as it could become? Or is the world crazy because it only
sees itself as it is?"

Who is normal, the cynic or the believer? The positive thinker or the negative
thinker? The believer in God—or the atheist? The despairing pessimist or the
hopeful optimist?

By now we all know the answer! We must affirm that health is normal, and
sickness is abnormal. That basic value judgment is beyond controversy.

Unbelief is a sickness, and skepticism is damnably dangerous. It gives birth to
a multitude of spiritual demons that can malignantly destroy your mental health
and spread an epidemic of despair wherever you go. As soon as you surrender
yourself to negative thoughts, you become host to an infectious spiritual disease
and become the carrier of another epidemic of gloom and doom.

It is normal for a child to dance and laugh and play. It is not normal for a child
to be downcast, morbid, withdrawn, and sulking in isolation. It is normal to be a
happy believer.

Who is crazy? The realist or the idealist?

The answer is obvious. The Beautiful Dreamer, with His exalted visions of
glorious possibilities, is the Uplifting Force in society! He comes bringing solutions. He then becomes the Great Physician, the Healing Source, the Hopeful
Friend. We can follow Him.

His name? Jesus, the Lord. My Savior. My Friend.

FAITH IS . . .

Thinking God's thoughts

For I know the thoughts that I think toward you, says the LORD, thoughts of peace and not of evil, to give you a future and a hope (Jer. 29:11).

Each new year is an appointment to become an authentic optimist.

Each new day is justification for being enthusiastic about life again.

Each dawning is God's invitation to start over and build a new life, beginning with the present moment.

Every new week is an opportunity to make new and noble resolutions! Every Monday morning you have a standing appointment to meet new opportunities! What does it mean to have faith?

Faith is opening your mind for God's thoughts to flow in. And when His thoughts flow in, life will change, for you will have a dream. You will see possibilities in the day—the week—the month—the year that is waiting to unfold.

Faith moves mountains.

The greatest power in the world is a positive idea.

And the most powerful positive idea is one that comes directly from the God who created the world and broke sunshine through the black of night.

Today I will think God's thoughts. This very moment, I will open my mind to let God's thoughts enter my brain. I will listen to the idea that comes from God, and it will turn me into a new and different person. I feel a freshness and a newness coming over me now as God's thoughts begin to take control over my consciousness.

I am set free, liberated, by new thoughts that come from God. Now I know what possibility thinking is—it is the mental activity that happens when I let faith take over.

Thank You, God, that I am being born again. Your Holy Spirit is filling my mind with your thoughts. I am excited about today, and I'm excited about my future. Amen.

FAITH IS . . .
Praying for guidance

Show me Your ways, O LORD;
Teach me Your paths.
Lead me in Your truth and teach me,
For You *are* the God of my salvation (Ps. 25:4).

The walk of faith is an adventure in a holy partnership. You are a human being with a mortal starting point at birth and a mortal terminal point at death. The span between your birth and death is your earthly life. Your purpose is to fit into a holy scheme, and become a participant with God. He created the world and all of us human beings for the purpose of creatively achieving His holy and happy purposes.

You are walking the walk of faith when you dream God's dreams and seek God's guidance.

Therefore, faith is not merely a super-aggressive activity into which you plunge with a gung-ho attitude, to achieve the first impulse that explodes in your mind. Rather, faith is a steady, stable, and steadfast process of opening your conscious and subconscious mind through prayer to the Holy Spirit. The eternal God will shape your will and direct your way!

God promised He will give you guidance.

In the depth of your heart, you know with an unflinching certainty, and with an invincible awareness, the course of action your life must take. This is God Himself, answering your prayers for guidance. He gives you a strong and powerful will to proceed along the determined pathway. Consider these prayers of affirmation:

I am driven by a divine destiny.

I am praying for guidance now.

I am opening my mind consistently and constantly to God, the way the tip of a branch is unceasingly alert and responsive to the wind!

FAITH IS . . .

Setting a goal

One thing *I do,* forgetting those things which are behind and reaching forward to those things which are ahead, I press toward the goal for the prize of the upward call of God (Phil. 3:13, 14).

Faith is not merely thinking holy and happy thoughts.

God's thoughts must take the form of good and godly goals.

No act of faith is more dynamic, more constructive, than setting incredible goals!

Have you noticed how negative thinkers avoid setting goals?

"Goals—who needs them? I'll just wing it, thank you. I prefer to roll with the punches."

"I don't want to get trapped by a commitment. Isn't that what happens when you set a goal?"

"I've had enough disappointments. I don't want to be set up only to be let down. Goals? No more failures, thank you."

Failure is not a matter of failing to meet your goal. Failure is not making the most of the possibilities seen and unseen, known and unknown, in your present and in your future!

Use faith to set positive goals, and you'll be sure to rise to the higher plateau. I guarantee that . . .

• when you set a challenging goal, you'll be farther ahead tomorrow than you are today. Even a little can turn out to be a lot!

• you'll be a happier person. Someone stopped me recently and asked, "Why do you always seem to be in such a happy mood?" My answer: "Because I've always got unfulfilled goals, and my goals distract me from my worries!"

• you will feel that your life has value!

If you have goals, you are bound to inspire somebody who is hurting. You will discover your own worth.

Goals—what are they anyway? They are impossible problems awaiting to be solved by someone with this incredible power called faith! So get set to set goals, and move upward!

FAITH IS . . .

Committing to action

> Go your way; and as you have believed, *so* let
> it be done for you (Matt. 8:13).

Miracles never happen just through meditation—but with mighty action! Read carefully in the Gospels the words of Jesus and notice the verbs. *Follow, go, seek, ask, knock.* The walk of faith is not merely the serene, silent, spiritual, unspeaking stroll of a holy man in the stillness of the sunrise or the secret silence of the sunset.

Faith is the mental activity that draws God into our mind and imagination until a passion begins to inflame our wills, motivating us to action!

It is then that the commitment is made. And what is a commitment? It is entering into an honorable contract, pledging oneself before the problems are solved. Every commitment generates a new set of problems. And if we waited until we saw solutions to problems before we made the commitment, we would obviously not be walking the walk of faith! It is for that reason that commitment—
 in marriage,
  in religion,
   in interpersonal relationships,
    in devotion and dedication to your career goal
   or the fulfillment of a project
becomes self-inspiring.

Walk the walk of faith today. Make a fresh commitment to God, saying prayerfully and sincerely:

"God, I'm ready to take the plunge. Give me the push that I need, and I'm trusting that with Your help we'll tackle every problem at every turn of the road with a positive mental attitude! And together we'll succeed joyously!"

FAITH IS . . .

Merging to make miracles

Whoever desires to become great among you shall be your servant. And whoever of you desires to be first shall be slave of all (Mark 10:43, 44).

It takes two to make a miracle. When a believing human being merges his will with God's powers, miracles happen. Miracles require faith—and faith is often spelled *w-o-r-k*.

There is a great misconception today that faith is simply a matter of asking God to perform a miracle, sitting back, and waiting for it to happen. Don't be misled! Prosperous, wealthy Christian people don't become great by manipulating, perhaps dishonestly, to get to the top of the ladder. They work for it after they've prayed through their plans!

Jesus Himself encourages the pursuit of greatness. But our Lord makes it clear that the pathway to success is the path of service.

If you want to be great—be prepared to be a servant.

This works in the business world, too. In a free economy, people buy only the products and services that meet their needs. The professional person who becomes ego-involved instead of human-service-oriented, soon finds himself in trouble.

Great things happen when we follow our prayer with hard work. Work means serving; and serving involves thinking about others' needs and meeting them at their level.

Today, ask yourself: Have I been sitting back just waiting for God to pour out blessings in my life without making an effort myself? Am I willing to merge with God to make a miracle? I believe it will happen as I become a servant.

FAITH IS . . .

Knowing it can be done

I can do all things through Christ who strengthens me (Phil. 4:13).

Faith is an inner conviction.
It is an unshakeable assurance.
It is the profound "knowing" that comes before reality confirms it.
Faith is a sense of destiny: "It's possible." "It's going to happen."
Faith is knowing that you can do it.

The person who walks the walk of faith knows he can solve his problem!

He *knows* that he can detach himself from that awful habit.
He *knows* he can extricate himself from his negative enslavements.
The person who walks the walk of faith faces his projects, affirming:
I *know* I can do it—*if* God will help me. And I'm sure God wants to help me!
I know I can do it *when* I'm totally dedicated to Him, which I really am!

I know I can do it *after* everything is in readiness. And I am trusting God to help me get my act together!

I know I can do it *only* with the help of my Lord. He is my Best Friend. He wants me to succeed.

I can do all things *through* Christ who strengthens me! I know it's possible after all.

Deep down in your heart, you know it will work out. An unquenchable confidence keeps fueling your feelings that you're going to make it.

Again and again the person who succeeds did so because he or she didn't know it was impossible!

FAITH IS . . .

Leaping into the unknown

> So he, leaping up, stood and walked and entered the temple with them—
> walking, leaping, and praising God (Acts 3:8).

Faith is often called a "leap." How appropriate! How else could you possibly move from one point to another when there is no direct link?

How do you cross over a crevice when there is no bridge?

Faith is leaping across gaps that exist between

the known and the unknown

the proven and the unproven

the actual and the possible

the grasp and the reach

the "I've got it" and the "I want it"

the knowledge and the mystery

the material reality and the spiritual reality

the truth exposed and the truth undiscovered

the goals achieved and the goals still pursued

youth and maturity

sickness and health

sin and forgiveness

life and death

time and eternity.

Yes, there is always a chasm between today and tomorrow. I cannot be sure I can cope with tomorrow. But by a running leap I will jump into tomorrow with expectancy! There is always a chasm between my present achievements and my unfulfilled hopes and dreams. By faith I make the leap—and grow!

There is always a chasm between where I'm at and where I'm going—by faith I make the leap forward!

What lies ahead? Tomorrow? Next week? Next month? Next year? Beyond this life?

I believe in faith! I believe in believers! I believe in God! I believe in Jesus Christ! I believe in tomorrow! I'm going to take the leap of faith!

Positive Verses for Possibility Thinking

Positive Verses for Possibility Thinking

Positive Verses for Possibility Thinking

The Bible is filled with positive motivational verses to enable you to live a happy and fulfilled life. This unique key to these verses will help you to unlock the power of God's truth. It includes modern words that describe your world. Whether you are feeling anxious or ambitious, concerned or confident, stressful or successful, this possibility thinker's index will lead you to the verse that meets your needs.

Acceptance—John 5:24; 6:51; 2 Cor. 6:2
Accomplishment—Matt. 7:17; Gal. 6:9; Col. 3:17
Action—Deut. 1:21; Matt. 25:36, 40; John 14:12
Affection—John 13:34; Rom. 12:10; 1 Thess. 2:8
Analyzation—Josh. 24:15; John 7:17
Anxiety—Matt. 6:25, 34; Rom. 8:28; Phil. 4:6; 1 Pet. 5:6, 7
Application—Prov. 2:2; John 15:14
Aspiration—Matt. 5:6; 6:21; Phil. 3:12; 1 Thess. 4:11
Attainment—John 14:14; 3 John 2
Attitude—Matt. 5:16, 44; John 14:15; Rom. 12:16; Phil. 2:5
Beauty—Ps. 149:4; Zech. 9:16, 17; Rom. 10:15
Beginning—John 1:1-3; Col. 3:10
Belief—Matt. 8:2, 13; 16:13, 16; 21:22; Rom. 10:10, 11; 2 Cor. 4:13
Beneficial—Ps. 1:1-3; John 15:7; 1 Thess. 5:15
Celebration—Neh. 8:10-12; Esth. 9:19
Challenge—Deut. 1:21
Change—Matt. 18:3; 1 Cor. 15:51; 2 Cor. 5:17
Cleansing—2 Cor. 7:1; Eph. 5:25-27; 1 John 1:7, 9
Comfort—Matt. 5:4; 2 Cor. 1:4; 2 Thess. 2:16, 17
Commission—Matt. 10:16; John 20:21; Acts 1:8
Commitment—Matt. 10:22; 1 Cor. 9:24; Luke 9:23
Completion—Job 5:26; 2 Tim. 4:6-8

Concentration—Matt. 7:7, 8; John 9:4; Rom. 15:20; 1 Cor. 9:24; Phil. 3:14
Confidence—Matt. 10:32; 16:18; Eph. 6:14-18; Phil. 1:6; 4:13
Courage—Deut. 31:6; 1 Cor. 16:13
Creation—Gen. 5:1; Matt. 12:35; 2 Cor. 5:17
Death—Matt. 4:16; 16:28; John 11:25; 1 Cor. 15:22, 26; 2 Tim. 1:10
Decision—Deut. 30:19; Prov. 16:33
Delight—Job 33:26; 1 Cor. 1:31
Dependence—Ex. 13:21; Deut. 7:9; 2 Cor. 3:5; 1 Thess. 5:24
Depression—Prov. 12:25
Design—Ps. 8:1; Eph. 4:16
Desire—Matt. 6:20, 33; 13:44-46; Luke 9:23; Rom. 14:19; Phil. 4:6
Development—Ps. 1:1-3; Mark 4:8; 1 Cor. 13:11, 12
Dignity—Phil. 1:27; Col. 1:10
Discipline—1 Thess. 5:14; 2 Tim. 2:3-5
Doubt—Matt. 14:31; 2 Cor. 5:7
Education—Deut. 6:6, 7; Matt. 5:19; 28:20; Col. 1:28
Encouragement—1 Sam. 23:16, 17; 1 Cor. 1:4-7; Col. 3:16
Endurance—Matt. 24:13; 1 Cor. 4:12; 2 Cor. 4:8, 9; 2 Tim. 2:12
Enjoyment—Ps. 4:7; 16:9
Enthusiasm—Ex. 15:2; 1 Thess. 2:13; 3:9
Esteem—Rom. 13:9; Phil. 2:3; 1 Tim. 4:4
Examination—Ps. 26:2; 2 Cor. 13:5
Example—Matt. 20:26-28; Rom. 10:17; 2 Cor. 3:18; 1 Tim. 4:12
Excellence—Ps. 8:1; 2 Cor. 4:7

POSITIVE VERSES

Experience—Rom. 15:13; Eph. 1:18, 19
Failure—Job 10:12; 42:10
Faith—Matt. 9:29; 17:20; Rom. 10:17;
12:3; 2 Cor. 5:7; Gal. 3:11
Fear—Matt. 10:28; 17:7;
Mark 5:36; 6:50
Focus—Phil. 4:8
Follower—Matt. 4:19; 16:24;
Mark 1:17; 8:34
Forgiveness—Matt. 6:12, 14; Mark 2:5;
Rom. 12:14; Eph. 1:7; Col. 3:13
Foundation—Ps. 1:3; 2 Cor. 1:21, 22;
Col. 2:7; 1 Thess. 3:13; 1 Pet. 5:10
Fulfillment—Matt. 5:17, 18
Future—Matt. 6:30, 34; Rom. 8:28
Gain—Deut. 28:11; Mark 8:36;
Phil. 3:7; 1 Tim. 6:6
Gift—Luke 11:11–13; 1 Tim. 4:14;
James 1:17
Glory—2 Cor. 4:17; 1 Thess. 2:12
Good Deeds—Prov. 3:27; Gal. 6:9;
Phil. 2:4
Grace—Deut. 7:6–9; John 1:14, 17;
Rom. 3:24
Gratitude—Ps. 7:17; 1 Thess. 2:13
Greatness—Matt. 5:19; 20:26; 23:11;
Eph. 1:19
Grief—Job 9:27; Ps. 3:4; 4:1; 6:2;
John 16:20, 22
Growth—Deut. 32:11; Mark 4:32
Heart—1 Sam. 16:7; Matt. 5:8; 6:21;
Luke 6:45
Honesty—Lev. 19:35; Prov. 12:22
Honor—Ex. 20:12; Deut. 5:16; John
12:26; Eph. 6:2, 3; Col. 3:24
Hope—Rom. 5:5; 8:25; 12:12;
1 Cor. 9:10
Humility—2 Chr. 7:14; Matt. 18:4;
23:12; James 4:10
Hunger—Matt. 5:6; 6:11, 25, 26;
John 6:35
Ideal—Gen. 1:27; Matt. 26:39;
1 Tim. 1:17; 3:16
Identity—Phil. 3:21; Col. 2:10;
1 John 3:1
Imagination—Ps. 2:8; John 14:12–14
Implementation—Matt. 7:24, 25;
Luke 11:28
Impossibility—Matt. 19:26; Mark 10:27;
Luke 18:27
Improvement—1 Chr. 28:9; Eph. 3:19

Increase—1 Cor. 3:6, 7; 1 Thess. 3:12,
13; 4:10
Influence—1 Tim. 4:12; 2 Tim. 2:2
Intercession—Rom. 8:26, 27, 34; 1 Tim.
2:5; Heb. 9:15; James 5:16
Investment—Matt. 13:12, 23; 25:29;
2 Cor. 9:6
Involvement—Gen. 14:14–16;
Luke 10:33–35
Joy—Ps. 9:1, 2; Luke 2:10, 11;
John 15:11; Col. 1:11
Judgment—Ps. 7:8; 9:4, 8; Rom. 14:13
Justification—Rom. 3:30; Gal. 3:8
Keep (on)—2 Cor. 4:8, 9; Phil. 1:6
Keep (up)—Gal. 6:9
Kindness—Ps. 117:2; Gal. 6:9, 10;
Col. 3:12
Knowledge—Rom. 11:33; 1 Cor. 12:8;
Col. 1:9
Labor—John 4:36; 5:17; 1 Cor. 15:58;
1 Thess. 1:3; 2:9
Laughter—Gen. 21:6; Eccl. 3:1, 4
Leadership—John 4:42; 8:12;
Rom. 14:9; Col. 1:16, 17
Learning—Prov. 1:7–9; Matt. 11:29
Liberty—John 5:24; 8:32, 36;
2 Cor. 3:17; Gal. 5:13
Limitless—Matt. 21:21; Mark 9:23;
11:23; Eph. 3:20
Loss—Mark 8:36; Luke 15:8, 9
Love—1 Cor. 13:4–8, 13; Col. 3:14;
1 Thess. 3:12; 1 Tim. 1:5; 1 John
3:18, 23; 4:7, 8
Maintenance—Gal. 6:9; 1 Thess. 1:3;
Titus 3:8
Maturity—Matt. 20:26; 1 Cor. 13:11,
12; Phil. 1:27; Col. 2:6, 7
Measurement—Deut. 25:15; Rom. 12:3
Meditation—Ps. 19:14; 119:97;
Jer. 32:17
Mercy—Eph. 1:7; 2:8; Jude 2
Might—2 Cor. 4:7; Eph. 1:19
Motivation—Col. 1:10; 2 Pet. 3:14;
1 John 4:19
Need—Nah. 1:7; Heb. 4:16; 1 Pet. 5:7
Negative—Job 2:10; Hab. 3:17, 18;
1 Pet. 3:10, 11
Nurturing—1 Thess. 2:7, 8; Col. 2:6, 7
Obedience—Col. 3:20; 1 John 5:3
Oneness—Matt. 19:6; Rom. 14:8; 1 Cor.
6:15, 19, 20; 12:12; John 17:21–23

Opinion—2 Tim. 2:25
Opportunity—2 Cor. 6:2; Gal. 6:10
Pardon—Rom. 12:14; Eph. 1:7;
 1 John 1:9
Patience—Rom. 12:12; James 1:3, 4; 5:8
Peace—Rom. 12:18; 14:19; Eph. 2:14;
 Phil. 4:7
Perception—Rom. 10:17
Perfection—Phil. 3:12; Col. 1:28
Perseverance—2 Cor. 4:8; Gal. 6:9;
 Phil. 4:13
Persistence—Luke 18:1; 1 Tim. 6:12
Plan—Prov. 16:9; 21:5
Positive—1 Thess. 2:12; 5:15
Preparation—Eph. 6:14–18; 2 Tim. 2:21
Promise—Eph. 3:20; 1 Pet. 1:3, 4;
 2 Pet. 1:4
Purity—1 Thess. 4:7; 2 Tim. 2:22
Purpose—Rom. 14:7, 8; 15:20;
 2 Cor. 5:9; Col. 3:23
Pursuit—1 Cor. 14:1; Phil. 3:12–14;
 1 Thess. 5:15; 1 Tim. 6:11
Put Aside—1 Cor. 13:11; Phil. 3:13
Qualification—Col. 1:12
Quality—2 Tim. 2:15; 1 Pet. 5:10
Quest—Col. 3:2; 1 Pet. 3:11
Question—Jer. 33:3; Phil. 4:6;
 1 John 5:14, 15
Quiet—Is. 30:15; 1 Thess. 4:11;
 1 Tim. 2:1, 2
Quitting—Phil. 4:13
Race—1 Cor. 9:24, 26; Phil. 2:16
Radiance—Matt. 5:16; 2 Cor. 4:6;
 Phil. 2:15
Reaching Out—Phil. 3:12–14
Reality—Eccl. 1:10; John 14:2
Receive—1 Cor. 15:3; 1 Thess. 2:13
Rejoice—Ps. 118:24; Rom. 12:15;
 1 Thess. 5:16–18; 1 Pet. 1:8
Reliance—2 Chr. 13:18; Is. 50:10;
 1 Thess. 5:24
Renewal—Rom. 12:2; 2 Cor. 4:16;
 Eph. 4:23, 24
Representative—2 Cor. 2:14; 3:18
Request—Phil. 4:6; Col. 4:2
Results—Rom. 5:3, 4; Gal. 6:8–10
Revival—Ps. 85:6; 119:25; Is. 57:15
Reward—1 Cor. 9:25; Phil. 3:14;
 Col. 3:10; James 1:12
Salvation—John 3:16; 1 Tim. 2:4; 1 John
 1:9; 5:13

Satisfaction—Ps. 17:15; 91:16; 105:40;
 John 4:14
See—John 1:50; 9:25
Self-esteem—1 Cor. 6:20; Eph. 2:10;
 Phil. 3:21; Col. 2:10; 1 Tim. 4:4
Skepticism—Luke 1:18, 19;
 John 20:27–29
Speech—2 Cor. 4:13; Col. 4:6
Starting Point—2 Cor. 5:7
Strength—Jer. 1:18; 2 Cor. 12:9, 10;
 Col. 1:10, 11; 2 Tim. 2:1
Stress—2 Cor. 4:8, 9, 17
Success—2 Cor. 3:5; Phil. 1:6; 3:14
Support—Rom. 12:10, 13–15;
 1 John 3:16
Sureness—2 Tim. 1:12; Heb. 3:6;
 1 John 2:28
Steadfastness—1 Cor. 15:58; Phil. 2:16;
 1 Tim. 6:12; Rev. 3:11
Talent—Rom. 14:12; 1 Tim. 4:14
Test—Ps. 17:3; James 1:2–4; 1 Pet. 1:6, 7
Thanksgiving—Ps. 100:4; 2 Cor. 9:15;
 Heb. 13:15
Tough Times—Phil. 4:6; 2 Thess. 3:3;
 2 Tim. 1:7; 2:3
Transformation—2 Cor. 3:18; Col. 3:4
Transition—Ps. 103:26; Is. 40:31
Trial—James 1:2–4; 1 Pet. 1:6, 7
Triumph—1 Cor. 10:13; 15:57
Trust—Ps. 40:4; Eph. 1:13
Truth—1 Cor. 13:6; Eph. 4:21; 1 John
 3:18
Try—Phil. 2:16; 3:12–14
Uncertainty—Job 19:25, 26;
 John 14:1–3; 1 John 2:26, 27
Understanding—Prov. 8:9; Phil. 4:7;
 Col. 2:2; 1 John 5:20
Unemployed—Ps. 37:5; Prov. 16:9;
 Jer. 29:11, 12; Rom. 8:28
Unfolding—Col. 2:3
Unity—Gen. 2:24; Mark 10:9;
 1 Cor. 12:4–7, 12
Unknown—Jer. 29:11; 33:3
Uplift—Is. 40:31; Jer. 29:12
Useful—Rom. 12:1; 2 Tim. 2:21
Validity—1 Cor. 15:3–8; 1 John 5:6, 7
Value—Luke 12:7, 24; Phil. 3:21
Venture—Num. 13:30; Matt. 25:16, 17,
 20–23
Victory—Eph. 3:20; 1 John 2:14; 4:4;
 5:4, 5

POSITIVE VERSES

Vision—Jer. 33:3; Eph. 1:18
Watchfulness—1 Cor. 16:13; Eph. 6:18;
  2 Tim. 4:5
Weakness—Rom. 8:26; 2 Cor. 12:9, 10;
  13:4; Heb. 4:15
Weary—Is. 40:31; Gal. 6:9;
  2 Thess. 3:13
Winning—1 Cor. 9:24; 2 Tim. 4:7
Wisdom—Prov. 2:6, 7; Eph. 3:19;

Col. 1:9; James 3:17
Witness—Matt. 24:14; Acts 1:8; 22:15
Work—1 Cor. 9:10; Phil. 2:13;
  Col. 1:10; 1 Tim. 5:18
Yearning—Song 5:4; Is. 63:15
Yielding—1 John 2:6
Youth—Eccl. 11:9; Jer. 1:7, 8;
  1 Tim. 4:12
Zeal—1 Cor. 9:16-21; 2 Cor. 9:2

Concordance

— A —

ABASE
and *a* the exalted............ Ezek 21:26
pride He is able to *a*....... Dan 4:37

ABASED
himself will be *a*............. Matt 23:12
I know how to be *a*........Phil 4:12

ABBA
And He said, "*A*............ Mark 14:36
whom we cry out, "*A*..... Rom 8:15
crying out, "*A*...............Gal 4:6

ABHOR
My soul shall not *a*......... Lev 26:11
Therefore I *a* myself........Job 42:6
nations will *a* him........... Prov 24:24
a the pride of Jacob........ Amos 6:8
A what is evil...............Rom 12:9

ABHORRED
a His own inheritance...... Ps 106:40
he who is *a* of the..........Prov 22:14
and their soul also *a*........Zech 11:8

ABHORRENT
you have made us *a*........ Ex 5:21

ABHORS
So that his life *a*............. Job 33:20

ABIDE
nor *a* in its paths............ Job 24:13
Lord, who may *a*...........Ps 15:1
He shall *a* before God..... Ps 61:7
the Most High Shall *a*......Ps 91:1
Him, "If you *a*.............. John 8:31
And a slave does not *a*.... John 8:35
Helper, that He may *a*....John 14:16
"*A* in Me................. John 15:4
"If you *a* in Me.............John 15:7
a in My love............... John 15:9
And now *a* faith............. 1 Co 13:13
does the love of God *a*.... 1 Jn 3:17
this we know that we *a*.... 1 Jn 4:13

ABIDES
them, Even He who *a*..... Ps 55:19
He who *a* in Me............John 15:5
lives and *a* forever......... 1 Pe 1:23
will of God *a* forever.......1 Jn 2:17

ABIDING
do not have His word *a*... John 5:38
has eternal life *a*............. 1 Jn 3:15

ABILITY
understand, who had *a*.....Dan 1:4
according to his own *a*.....Matt 25:15
and beyond their *a*.........2 Co 8:3
a which God supplies.......1 Pe 4:11

ABLE
you are *a* to number........Gen 15:5
shall give as he is *a*........Deut 16:17
For who is *a* to judge...... 1 Ki 3:9
"The LORD is *a*............. 2 Ch 25:9
Who then is *a* to stand.... Job 41:10

God whom we serve is *a*..Dan 3:17
God is *a* to raise up....... Matt 3:9
believe that I am *a*.........Matt 9:28
fear Him who is *a*...........Matt 10:28
Are you *a* to drink the.... Matt 20:22
beyond what you are *a*.... 1 Co 10:13
And God is *a* to make.....2 Co 9:8
may be *a* to comprehend..Eph 3:18
persuaded that He is *a*....2 Ti 1:12
learning and never *a*.......2 Ti 3:7
being tempted, He is *a*.... Heb 2:18
that God was *a* to.......... Heb 11:19
to Him who is *a*............. Jude 24
has come, and who is *a*....Rev 6:17

ABOLISHED
your works may be *a*......Ezek 6:6
having *a* in His flesh.......Eph 2:15
Christ, who has *a*...........2 Ti 1:10

ABOMINABLE
not make yourselves *a*..... Lev 11:43
They have done *a*.......... Ps 14:1
your grave like an *a*........ Is 14:19
Oh, do not do this *a*...... Jer 44:4
they deny Him, being *a*... Tit 1:16
and *a* idolatries.............1 Pe 4:3
unbelieving, *a*................Rev 21:8

ABOMINATION
every shepherd is an *a*..... Gen 46:34
If we sacrifice the *a*........Ex 8:26
You have made me an *a*.. Ps 88:8
yes, seven are an *a*........Prov 6:16
wickedness is an *a*..........Prov 8:7
false balance is an *a*....... Prov 11:1
the scoffer is an *a*......... Prov 24:9
prayer shall be an *a*.......Prov 28:9
An unjust man is an *a*..... Prov 29:27
incense is an *a*...............Is 1:13
and place there the *a*.......Dan 11:31
the *a* of desolation.......... Dan 12:11
when you see the '*a*........ Matt 24:15
among men is an *a*......... Luke 16:15

ABOMINATIONS
to follow the *a*................Deut 18:9
delights in their *a*............Is 66:3
will put away your *a*.......Jer 4:1
your harlotry, your........ Jer 13:27
you will see greater *a*....... Ezek 8:6
a which they commit....... Ezek 8:17
you, throw away the *a*..... Ezek 20:7
show her all her *a*.......... Ezek 22:2
a golden cup full of *a*...... Rev 17:4
harlots and of the *a*........Rev 17:5

ABOUND
lawlessness will *a*........... Matt 24:12
the offense might *a*........ Rom 5:20
sin that grace may *a*........ Rom 6:1
thanksgiving to *a*............2 Co 4:15
to make all grace *a*.........2 Co 9:8
and I know how to *a*.......Phil 4:12
that you should *a*........... 1 Th 4:1
things are yours and *a*..... 2 Pe 1:8

ABOUNDED
But where sin *a*.............. Rom 5:20

ABOUNDING
and *a* in mercy.............. Ps 103:8
immovable, always *a*........1 Co 15:58

ABOVE
that is in heaven *a*......... Ex 20:4
"He sent from *a*............ 2 Sa 22:17
A it stood seraphim.........Is 6:2
nor a servant *a*............... Matt 10:24
"He who comes from *a*....John 3:31
I am from *a*................... John 8:23
been given you from *a*..... John 19:11
of all, who is *a*............... Eph 4:6
the name which is *a*........ Phil 2:9
things which are *a*..........Col 3:1
perfect gift is from *a*........Jas 1:17

ABSENT
For I indeed, as *a*..........1 Co 5:3
in the body we are *a*....... 2 Co 5:6

ABSTAIN
we write to them to *a*...... Acts 15:20
A from every form.......... 1 Th 5:22
and commanding to *a*......1 Ti 4:3
and pilgrims, *a*.............. 1 Pe 2:11

ABUNDANCE
is the sound of *a*............. 1 Ki 18:41
workmen with you in *a*... 1 Ch 22:15
shall flourish, And *a*.......Ps 72:7
eyes bulge with *a*........... Ps 73:7
nor he who loves *a*.........Eccl 5:10
delight itself in *a*............. Is 55:2
For out of the *a*..............Matt 12:34
put in out of their *a*....... Mark 12:44
not consist in the *a*..........Luke 12:15
of affliction the *a*............ 2 Co 8:2
above measure by the *a*... 2 Co 12:7
rich through the *a*........... Rev 18:3

ABUNDANT
Longsuffering and *a*........Ps 86:15
slow to anger and *a*........Jon 4:2
in labors more *a*............. 2 Co 11:23
Lord was exceedingly *a*....1 Ti 1:14
a mercy has begotten.......1 Pe 1:3

ABUNDANTLY
a satisfied with the.......... Ps 36:8
may have it more *a*......... John 10:10
to do exceedingly *a*........ Eph 3:20
to show more *a* to the..... Heb 6:17

ACCEPT
For I will *a* him............... Job 42:8
a your burnt..................Ps 20:3
offering, I will not *a*........ Jer 14:12
Should I *a* this from....... Mal 1:13

ACCEPTABLE
sought to find *a*.............. Eccl 12:10
a time I have heard.......... Is 49:8
proclaim the *a* year......... Is 61:2
preach the a year.......... Luke 4:19
is that good and *a*..........Rom 12:2
proving what is *a*............ Eph 5:10
For this is good and *a*......1 Ti 2:3
spiritual sacrifices *a*........ 1 Pe 2:5

ACCEPTED
"Behold, now is the *a*......2 Co 6:2
which He has made us *a*.. Eph 1:6

ACCESS
whom also we have *a*...... Rom 5:2
we have boldness and *a*... Eph 3:12

ACCOMPLISHED
today the LORD has *a*.....1 Sa 11:13
A desire *a* is sweet to.....Prov 13:19
must still be *a*............ Luke 22:37
all things were now *a*......John 19:28

ACCORD
and Israel with one *a*......Josh 9:2
serve Him with one *a*...... Zeph 3:9
continued with one *a*....... Acts 1:14
daily with one *a*............Acts 2:46
a has Christ with............2 Co 6:15
love, being of one *a*....... Phil 2:2

ACCOUNT
they will give *a*.............. Matt 12:36
The former *a* I made....... Acts 1:1
of us shall give *a*............Rom 14:12
put that on my *a*.............Phm 18
those who must give *a*..... Heb 13:17

ACCOUNTED
in the LORD, and He *a*... Gen 15:6
And that was *a* to him.....Ps 106:31
his faith is *a*................... Rom 4:5
a as sheep for the.......... Rom 8:36
God, and it was *a*........... Gal 3:6
God, and it was *a*........... Jas 2:23

ACCURSED
he who is hanged is *a*..... Deut 21:23
regarding the *a*.............. Josh 7:1
years old shall be *a*......... Is 65:20
not know the law is *a*......John 7:49
that I myself were *a*....... Rom 9:3
of God calls Jesus *a*....... 1 Co 12:3
to you, let him be *a*........ Gal 1:8

ACCUSATION
reign, they wrote an *a*..... Ezra 4:6
over His head the *a*........Matt 27:37
they might find an *a*.......Luke 6:7
Do not receive an *a*....... 1 Ti 5:19
not bring a reviling *a*......2 Pe 2:11

ACCUSE
anyone or a falsely..........Luke 3:14
they began to *a* Him...... Luke 23:2
think that I shall *a*......... John 5:45

ACCUSED
forward and *a* the Jews....Dan 3:8
while He was being *a*..... Matt 27:12

ACCUSER
have come, for the *a*....... Rev 12:10

ACCUSING
their thoughts *a*.............. Rom 2:15

ACKNOWLEDGE
did he *a* his brothers...... Deut 33:9
a my transgressions......... Ps 51:3
in all your ways *a*.......... Prov 3:6
and Israel does not *a*......Is 63:16
a your iniquity............ ...Jer 3:13
spiritual, let him *a*..........1 Co 14:37

ACKNOWLEDGED
of Israel, and God *a*........Ex 2:25
a my sin to You............. Ps 32:5

ACKNOWLEDGES
there is no one who *a*......Ps 142:4
a the Son has the............1 Jn 2:23

ACQUAINTANCES
You have put away my *a*. Ps 88:8
All my *a* watched for......Jer 20:10
But all His *a*.................Luke 23:49

ACQUAINTED
lying down, And are *a*.....Ps 139:3
a man of sorrows and *a*... Is 53:3

ACQUIT
at all *a* the wicked.......... Nah 1:3

ACT
seen every great *a*..........Deut 11:7
is time for You to *a*....... Ps 119:126
His *a*, His unusual *a*........Is 28:21
in the very *a*................. John 8:4

ACTS
LORD, the righteous *a*.....Judg 5:11
to Moses, His *a*.............. Ps 103:7
declare Your mighty *a*..... Ps 145:4
of Your awesome *a*......... Ps 145:6

ADD
"You shall not *a*............Deut 4:2
Do not *a* to His words.....Prov 30:6

ADDED
things shall be *a*..............Matt 6:33
And the Lord *a* to the.....Acts 2:47
many people were *a*........Acts 11:24
It was *a* because of........ Gal 3:19

ADMONISH
also to *a* one another......Rom 15:14
a him as a brother.......... 2 Th 3:15

ADMONISHED
further, my son, be *a*......Eccl 12:12
Angel of the LORD *a*......Zech 3:6

ADMONISHING
a one another in............. Col 3:16

ADMONITION
were written for our *a*..... 1 Co 10:11
in the training and *a*........Eph 6:4

ADOPTION
the Spirit of *a*.................Rom 8:15
waiting for the *a*........... Rom 8:23
to whom pertain the *a*.... Rom 9:4
we might receive the *a*....Gal 4:5
a as sons by Jesus...........Eph 1:5

ADORN
a the monuments............ Matt 23:29
also, that the women *a*.... 1 Ti 2:9

ADORNED
By His Spirit He *a*..........Job 26:13
You shall again be *a*........Jer 31:4
temple, how it was *a*....... Luke 21:5
God also *a* themselves..... 1 Pe 3:5
prepared as a bride *a*......Rev 21:2

ADULTERER
neighbor's wife, the *a*...... Lev 20:10
The eye of the *a*.............Job 24:15

ADULTERERS
the land is full of *a*........ Jer 23:10
nor idolaters, nor *a*......... 1 Co 6:9
a God will judge............Heb 13:4
A and adulteresses..........Jas 4:4

ADULTERIES
I have seen your *a*.........Jer 13:27
her sight, and her *a*.........Hos 2:2
evil thoughts, *a*.............Mark 7:21

ADULTEROUS
a generation...................Matt 12:39

ADULTERY
You shall not commit *a*....Ex 20:14
Whoever commits *a*........Prov 6:32
Israel had committed *a*.... Jer 3:8
already committed *a*....... Matt 5:28
is divorced commits *a*..... Matt 5:32
another commits *a*..........Mark 10:11
a woman caught in *a*...... John 8:3
and those who commit *a*.. Rev 2:22

ADVANTAGE
a will it be to You.......... Job 35:3
man has no *a* over.......... Eccl 3:19
"For what *a* is it to........ Luke 9:25
a that I go away............John 16:7
What *a* then has the.......Rom 3:1
Satan should take *a*......... 2 Co 2:11
no one should take *a*...... 1 Th 4:6
people to gain *a*..............Jude 16

ADVERSARIES
The *a* of the LORD.........1 Sa 2:10
rid Myself of My *a*.........Is 1:24
a will not be able...........Luke 21:15
and there are many *a*...... 1 Co 16:9
terrified by your *a*..........Phil 1:28
will devour the *a*............Heb 10:27

ADVERSARY
in the way as an *a*..........Num 22:22
battle he become our *a*... 1 Sa 29:4
how long will the *a*........ Ps 74:10
a has spread his hand...... Lam 1:10
"Agree with your *a*........ Matt 5:25
'Avenge me of my *a*........Luke 18:3
opportunity to the *a*....... 1 Ti 5:14
a the devil walks............1 Pe 5:8

ADVERSITIES
you out of all your *a*....... 1 Sa 10:19
known my soul in *a*........Ps 31:7

ADVERSITY
them with every *a*.......... 2 Ch 15:6
I shall never be in *a*........ Ps 10:6
from the days of *a*.........Ps 94:13
brother is born for *a*.......Prov 17:17
faint in the day of *a*....... Prov 24:10
the day of *a* consider.......Eccl 7:14
you the bread of *a*..........Is 30:20

ADVICE
And blessed is your *a*......1 Sa 25:33
in this I give my *a*..........2 Co 8:10

ADVOCATE
sins, we have an A..........1 Jn 2:1

AFAR

and worship from *a*........ Ex 24:1
sons shall come from *a*.... Is 60:4
And not a God *a*............Jer 23:23
and saw Abraham *a*....... Luke 16:23
to all who are *a*.............Acts 2:39
to you who were *a*........ Eph 2:17
but having seen them *a*....Heb 11:13

AFFAIRS

He will guide his *a*..........Ps 112:5
I may hear of your *a*....... Phil 1:27
himself with the *a*........... 2 Ti 2:4

AFFECTION

to his wife the *a*............. 1 Co 7:3
for you all with the *a*.......Phil 1:8
the Spirit, if any *a*..........Phil 2:1

AFFECTIONATE

Be kindly *a* to one......... Rom 12:10

AFFLICT

a them with their............Ex 1:11
oath to *a* her soul........... Num 30:13
may be bound to *a* you....Judg 16:6
a the descendants............1 Ki 11:39
will hear, and *a* them...... Ps 55:19
a Your heritage........... Ps 94:5
a man to *a* his soul........ Is 58:5
to destroy, and to *a*........Jer 31:28
For He does not *a*......... Lam 3:33
a the just and take......... Amos 5:12
deal with all who *a*.........Zeph 3:19

AFFLICTED

"Why have You *a*..........Num 11:11
and the Almighty has *a*....Ruth 1:21
To him who is *a*............. Job 6:14
hears the cry of the *a*...... Job 34:28
How You *a* the peoples... Ps 44:2
a I went astray............... Ps 119:67
I am *a* very much.......... Ps 119:107
a time they have *a*.......... Ps 129:1
The cause of the *a*.......... Ps 140:12
days of the *a* are evil...... Prov 15:15
smitten by God, and *a*.....Is 53:4
oppressed and He was *a*...Is 53:7
"O you *a* one.................Is 54:11
Why have we *a* our........ Is 58:3
and satisfy the *a*............. Is 58:10
her virgins are *a*............. Lam 1:4
she has relieved the *a*...... 1 Ti 5:10
being destitute, *a*............ Heb 11:37

AFFLICTION

in the land of my *a*........ Gen 41:52
is, the bread of *a*............ Deut 16:3
indeed look on the *a*....... 1 Sa 1:11
LORD saw that the *a*......2 Ki 14:26
a take hold of me........... Job 30:16
days of *a* confront me......Job 30:27
held in the cords of *a*......Job 36:8
of death, Bound in *a*....... Ps 107:10
is my comfort in my *a*..... Ps 119:50
and it is an evil *a*............Eccl 6:2
a He was afflicted.......... Is 63:9
refuge in the day of *a*..... Jer 16:19
"O LORD, behold my *a*...Lam 1:9
not grieved for the *a*....... Amos 6:6
For our light *a*................2 Co 4:17
supposing to add *a*......... Phil 1:16
the word in much *a*........1 Th 1:6

AFRAID

garden, and I was *a*........Gen 3:10
saying, "Do not be *a*......Gen 15:1
his face, for he was *a*..... Ex 3:6
none will make you *a*..... Lev 26:6
of whom you are *a*.........Deut 7:19
I will not be *a*................ Ps 3:6
ungodliness made me *a*....Ps 18:4
Do not be *a* when one....Ps 49:16
Whenever I am *a*............ Ps 56:3
farthest parts are *a*....... Ps 65:8
a conspiracy, nor be *a*.... Is 8:12
one will make them *a*..... Is 17:2
that you should be *a*.......Is 51:12
dream which made me *a*.. Dan 4:5
do not be *a*...................Matt 14:27
if you do evil, be *a*........ Rom 13:4
do good and are not *a*....1 Pe 3:6

AFTERWARD

A he will let you go........ Ex 11:1
a we will speak...............Job 38:1
a receive me to glory.......Ps 73:24
you shall follow Me *a*.....John 13:36
the firstfruits, *a*..............1 Co 15:23

AGAIN

day He will rise *a*.......... Matt 20:19
'You must be born *a*...... John 3:7
to renew them *a*............. Heb 6:6
having been born *a*......... 1 Pe 1:23

AGAINST

his hand shall be *a*...... Gen 16:12
'I will set My face *a*........ Lev 20:3
come to 'set *a* man *a*...... Matt 10:35
or house divided *a*......... Matt 12:25
Me is *a* Me..................Matt 12:30
a the Spirit will not........ Matt 12:31
For nation will rise *a*..... Matt 24:7
out, as *a* a robber........... Matt 26:55
I have sinned *a*..............Luke 15:18
lifted up his heel *a*.......... John 13:18
LORD and *a* His Christ...Acts 4:26
to kick *a* the goads..........Acts 9:5
all men everywhere *a*......Acts 21:28
let us not fight *a*............ Acts 23:9
a the promises of God.....Gal 3:21
we do not wrestle *a*........Eph 6:12
I have a few things *a*...... Rev 2:20

AGE

well-advanced in *a*..........Gen 18:11
Israel were dim with *a*..... Gen 48:10
the flower of their *a*........ 1 Sa 2:33
the grave at a full *a*........Job 5:26
a is as nothing................Ps 39:5
and in the *a* to come...... Mark 10:30
"The sons of this *a*.........Luke 20:34
He is of *a*......................John 9:21
who are of full *a*............Heb 5:14
the powers of the *a*........ Heb 6:5

AGED

Wisdom is with *a* men..... Job 12:12
a one as Paul, the......... Phm 9

AGES

ordained before the *a*...... 1 Co 2:7
a was not made known.... Eph 3:5
at the end of the *a*.........Heb 9:26

AGONY

And being in *a*............... Luke 22:44

AGREE

A with your adversary..... Matt 5:25
that if two of you *a*.........Matt 18:19
testimonies did not *a*....... Mark 14:56
and these three *a*...........1 Jn 5:8

AGREED

unless they are *a*.............Amos 3:3
they were glad, and *a*...... Luke 22:5

AGREEMENT

with Sheol we are in *a*.....Is 28:15
the North to make an *a*... Dan 11:6
what *a* has the temple.....2 Co 6:16

AIR

the birds of the *a*........... Gen 1:26
of the *a* have nests.......... Luke 9:58
as one who beats the *a*.... 1 Co 9:26
be speaking into the *a*..... 1 Co 14:9
of the power of the *a*..... Eph 2:2
meet the Lord in the *a*.... 1 Th 4:17
his bowl into the *a*.......... Rev 16:17

ALARM

to sound the *a* against......2 Ch 13:12
and *a* against the fortified.Zeph 1:16

ALIEN

because you were an *a*.....Deut 23:7
I am an *a* in their........... Job 19:15
who turn away an *a*........Mal 3:5

ALIENATED

a herself from them........Ezek 23:17
darkened, being *a*.......... Eph 4:18
you, who once were *a*......Col 1:21

ALIENS

For we are *a* and.............1 Ch 29:15
For I have loved *a*.......... Jer 2:25
A have devoured his........Hos 7:9
Christ, being *a*................Eph 2:12
the armies of the *a*.........Heb 11:34

ALIKE

Everything occurs *a*.........Eccl 9:2
esteems every day *a*........ Rom 14:5

ALIVE

in the ark remained *a*...... Gen 7:23
with them went down *a*...Num 16:33
LORD your God are *a*.....Deut 4:4
I kill and I make *a*.........Deut 32:39
Let them go down *a*.......Ps 55:15
he preserves himself *a*......Ezek 18:27
heard that He was *a*........Mark 16:11
son was dead and is *a*..... Luke 15:24
presented Himself *a*.........Acts 1:3
indeed to sin, but *a*.........Rom 6:11
I was *a* once without...... Rom 7:9
all shall be made *a*...........1 Co 15:22
trespasses, made us *a*.......Eph 2:5
flesh, He has made *a*....... Col 2:13
that we who are *a*........... 1 Th 4:15
the flesh but made *a*........1 Pe 3:18
and behold, I am *a*.........Rev 1:18
a name that you are *a*..... Rev 3:1
These two were cast *a*..... Rev 19:20

ALLELUIA

Again they said, "*A*........ Rev 19:3

ALLOW

a Your Holy One............Ps 16:10
a My faithfulness............ Ps 89:33
a those who are..............Matt 23:13

ALLURE (cont.)

a Your Holy One............ Acts 2:27
who will not a................ 1 Co 10:13

ALLURE

behold, I will a................ Hos 2:14
of emptiness, they a........ 2 Pe 2:18

ALMOND

a blossoms on one........... Ex 25:33
a tree blossoms............... Eccl 12:5

ALMOST

for me, my feet had a.....Ps 73:2
a persuade me to............ Acts 26:28
a all things are............... Heb 9:22

ALMS

But rather give a............ Luke 11:41
you have and give a........ Luke 12:33
I came to bring a............ Acts 24:17

ALOES

with myrrh and a............ Ps 45:8
my bed with myrrh, a....Prov 7:17
mixture of myrrh and a....John 19:39

ALPHA

"I am the A and the....... Rev 1:8
"I am the A and the....... Rev 22:13

ALTAR

Then Noah built an a...... Gen 8:20
'An a of earth you......... Ex 20:24
a shall be kept................Lev 6:9
it to you upon the a....... Lev 17:11
offering for the a........... Num 7:84
of Gad called the a........ Josh 22:34
and tear down the a....... Judg 6:25
"Go up, erect an a.........2 Sa 24:18
out against the a............ 1 Ki 13:2
I will go to the a............ Ps 43:4
day there will be an a.....Is 19:19
Lord has spurned His a....Lam 2:7
you cover the a.............. Mal 2:13
your gift to the a............ Matt 5:23
swears by the a...............Matt 23:18
I even found an a........... Acts 17:23
the offerings of the a.......1 Co 9:13
partakers of the a........ 1 Co 10:18
which had the golden a....Heb 9:4
We have an a from.......... Heb 13:10
Isaac his son on the a....Jas 2:21
and stood at the a.......... Rev 8:3

ALTARS

a Hezekiah has taken...... 2 Ki 18:22
Even Your a, O LORD....Ps 84:3
on the horns of your a....Jer 17:1
a shall be broken............ Ezek 6:4
has made many a............ Hos 8:11
a shall be heaps............. Hos 12:11
destruction on the a....... Amos 3:14
and torn down Your a.....Rom 11:3

ALWAYS

delight, rejoicing a......... Prov 8:30
the poor with you a.......Matt 26:11
Me you do not have a...... Matt 26:11
lo, I am with you a........ Matt 28:20
'Son, you are a.............. Luke 15:31
to them, that men a........ Luke 18:1
immovable, a.............. 1 Co 15:58
Rejoice in the Lord a......Phil 4:4
thus we shall a.............. 1 Th 4:17
a be ready to give a........ 1 Pe 3:15

AM

to Moses, "I A WHO I... Ex 3:14
First and I a the Last...... Is 44:6
in My name, I a............ Matt 18:20
a the bread of life.........John 6:35
a the light of the............John 8:12
I a from above............... John 8:23
Abraham was, I A.......... John 8:58
"I a the door................ John 10:9
a the good shepherd....... John 10:11
a the resurrection............John 11:25
to him, "I a the way...... John 14:6
of God I a what I a....... 1 Co 15:10
a, for I a as you are....... Gal 4:12

AMAZED

trembled and were a.......Mark 16:8

AMBASSADOR

but a faithful a.............. Prov 13:17
for which I am an a........ Eph 6:20

AMBASSADORS

which sends a by sea....... Is 18:2
cry outside, the a........... Is 33:7
Therefore we are a.........2 Co 5:20

AMBITION

Christ from selfish a....... Phil 1:16
through selfish a............. Phil 2:3

AMEN

uninformed say "A.......... 1 Co 14:16
are Yes, and in Him A....2 Co 1:20
creatures said, "A.......... Rev 5:14

AMEND

A your ways and your..... Jer 7:3
from his evil way, a........Jer 35:15

ANCHOR

hope we have as an a...... Heb 6:19

ANCIENT

Do not remove the a.......Prov 23:10
a times that I................ Is 37:26
"until the A of Days...... Dan 7:22

ANGEL

Now the A of the LORD..Gen 16:7
A who has redeemed me..Gen 48:16
"Behold, I send an A...... Ex 23:20
the donkey saw the a......Num 22:23
For I have seen the A..... Judg 6:22
Manoah said to the A.....Judg 13:17
in my sight as an a.......... 1 Sa 29:9
a who was destroying......2 Sa 24:16
night that the a.............. 2 Ki 19:35
the A of His Presence.....Is 63:9
struggled with the A...... Hos 12:4
standing before the A...... Zech 3:3
like God, like the A........Zech 12:8
things, behold, an a........Matt 1:20
for an a of the Lord.......Matt 28:2
Then an a of the Lord.....Luke 1:11
And behold, an a............Luke 2:9
a appeared to Him from.. Luke 22:43
For an a went down at.... John 5:4
a has spoken to Him....... John 12:29
But at night an a........... Acts 5:19
A who appeared to him... Acts 7:35
Then immediately an a.... Acts 12:23
and no a or spirit............Acts 23:8
a has spoken to him........ Acts 23:9
by me this night an a......Acts 27:23
himself into an a.............2 Co 11:14

ANGELS

even if we, or an a.........Gal 1:8
Then I saw a strong a......Rev 5:2
over them the a.............. Rev 9:11
Then I saw an a.............. Rev 19:17
Jesus, have sent My a......Rev 22:16

ANGELS

if He charges His a......... Job 4:18
lower than the a............. Ps 8:5
He shall give His a.........Ps 91:11
Praise Him, all His a......Ps 148:2
He shall give His a......... Matt 4:6
a will come forth............ Matt 13:49
a always see the face...... Matt 18:10
but are like a................ Matt 22:30
no, not even the a.......... Matt 24:36
and all the holy a........... Matt 25:31
twelve legions of a......... Matt 26:53
the presence of the a...... Luke 15:10
was carried by the a....... Luke 16:22
are equal to the a.......... Luke 20:36
And she saw two a.........John 20:12
that we shall judge a...... 1 Co 6:3
head, because of the a..... 1 Co 11:10
and worship of a.............Col 2:18
with His mighty a.......... 2 Th 1:7
the Spirit, seen by a....... 1 Ti 3:16
much better than the a.... Heb 1:4
does not give aid to a..... Heb 2:16
company of a................ Heb 12:22
entertained a................. Heb 13:2
things which a desire....... 1 Pe 1:12
did not spare the a.........2 Pe 2:4
a who did not keep........Jude 6
Michael and his a........... Rev 12:7

ANGER

Cursed be their a........... Gen 49:7
sun, that the fierce a...... Num 25:4
fierceness of His a.......... Deut 13:17
of this great a................ Deut 29:24
So the a of the LORD.... Judg 10:7
to provoke Me to a......... 1 Ki 16:2
For His a is but for a..... Ps 30:5
let Your wrathful a........ Ps 69:24
a time He turned His a....Ps 78:38
made a path for His a..... Ps 78:50
You prolong Your a....... Ps 85:5
the power of Your a....... Ps 90:11
gracious, Slow to a........ Ps 103:8
Nor will He keep His a....Ps 103:9
harsh word stirs up a...... Prov 15:1
a sins against his own...... Prov 20:2
a rests in the bosom....... Eccl 7:9
a the Holy One of.......... Is 1:4
a is not turned away....... Is 5:25
a is turned away............. Is 12:1
I will not cause My a......Jer 3:12
For great is the a........... Jer 36:7
and I will send My a....... Ezek 7:3
does not retain His a....... Mic 7:18
fierceness of His a.......... Nah 1:6
a is kindled against........ Zech 10:3
around at them with a.... Mark 3:5
bitterness, wrath, a.........Eph 4:31

ANGRY

Cain, "Why are you a..... Gen 4:6
Let not the Lord be a.....Gen 18:30
the Son, lest He be a...... Ps 2:12
judge, And God is a........ Ps 7:11
When once You are a......Ps 76:7
Will You be a forever.....Ps 79:5
friendship with an a........Prov 22:24
backbiting tongue an a.....Prov 25:23
a man stirs up strife........ Prov 29:22

ANGUISH

in your spirit to be *a*....... Eccl 7:9
I was *a* with My people... Is 47:6
nor will I always be *a*...... Is 57:16
covetousness I was *a*.......Is 57:17
right for you to be *a*.......Jon 4:4
LORD has been very *a*.... Zech 1:2
I am exceedingly *a*......... Zech 1:15
you that whoever is *a*...... Matt 5:22
"*Be a, and do not*......... Eph 4:26
Therefore I was a............Heb 3:10
with whom was He *a*...... Heb 3:17
The nations were *a*.........Rev 11:18

ANGUISH

a has come upon me....... 2 Sa 1:9
a make him afraid.........Job 15:24
I will be in *a* over my...... Ps 38:18
a have overtaken............ Ps 119:143
longer remembers the *a*... John 16:21
tribulation and *a*............ Rom 2:9
much affliction and *a*.......2 Co 2:4

ANIMAL

of every clean *a*............Gen 7:2
'Whoever kills an *a*......... Lev 24:18
the life of his *a*..............Prov 12:10
set him on his own *a*...... Luke 10:34

ANIMALS

of *a* after their kind.........Gen 6:20
The *a* enter dens.............Job 37:8
sacrifices of fat *a*.............Ps 66:15
of four-footed *a*.............. Acts 10:12

ANISE

tithe of mint and *a*.......... Matt 23:23

ANNUL

and who will *a*.................Is 14:27
years later, cannot *a*........Gal 3:17

ANNULLING

one hand there is an *a*..... Heb 7:18

ANOINT

You shall *a* them............. Ex 28:41
but you shall not *a*...........Deut 28:40
you shall *a* for Me the..... 1 Sa 16:3
a yourself with oil........... 2 Sa 14:2
a my head with oil......... Ps 23:5
Arise, you princes, *a*....... Is 21:5
a the Most Holy............. Dan 9:24
when you fast, *a*............. Matt 6:17
a My body for burial....... Mark 14:8
they might come and *a*... Mark 16:1
a your eyes with eye........Rev 3:18

ANOINTED

the priest, who is *a*........ Lev 16:32
"Surely the LORD's *a*......1 Sa 16:6
destroy the LORD's *a*......2 Sa 1:14
he cursed the LORD's *a*...2 Sa 19:21
shows mercy to His *a*...... 2 Sa 22:51
"Do not touch My *a*........1 Ch 16:22
the LORD saves His *a*... Ps 20:6
because the LORD has *a*..Is 61:1
"These are the two *a*......Zech 4:14
because He has a............ Luke 4:18
but this woman has *a*.......Luke 7:46
a the eyes of the............John 9:6
It was that Mary who *a*...John 11:2
Jesus, whom You *a*.........Acts 4:27
and has *a* us is God........ 2 Co 1:21

ANOINTING

also made the holy *a*...... Ex 37:29
them pray over him, *a*.....Jas 5:14
But you have an *a*........... 1 Jn 2:20
but as the same *a*............1 Jn 2:27

ANOTHER

that you love one *a*......... John 13:34
and He will give you *a*.....John 14:16
'*Let a take his*................ Acts 1:20

ANSWER

will give Pharaoh an *a*..... Gen 41:16
a I should take back........2 Sa 24:13
Him, he could not *a*........Job 9:3
call, and I will *a*.............Job 13:22
how shall I *a* Him...........Job 31:14
and you shall *a*...............Job 40:7
the day that I call, *a*.......Ps 102:2
In Your faithfulness *a*......Ps 143:1
a turns away wrath..........Prov 15:1
A man has joy by the *a*...Prov 15:23
He who gives a right *a*....Prov 24:26
a a fool according........... Prov 26:4
was there none to *a*.........Is 50:2
for there is no *a*.............Mic 3:7
or what you should *a*......Luke 12:11
ought to *a* each one........ Col 4:6

ANSWERS

a a matter before he........Prov 18:13
but the rich *a*................. Prov 18:23
money *a* every thing........Eccl 10:19

ANT

Go to the *a*....................Prov 6:6

ANTICHRIST

have heard that the *A*......1 Jn 2:18
a who denies the.............1 Jn 2:22
is the spirit of the *A*........1 Jn 4:3
is a deceiver and an *a*......2 Jn 7

ANTITYPE

a which now saves us.......1 Pe 3:21

ANXIETIES

the multitude of my *a*......Ps 94:19
Try me, and know my *a*...Ps 139:23

ANXIETY

A in the heart of man......Prov 12:25
eat their bread with *a*......Ezek 12:19

ANXIOUS

drink, nor have an *a*.......Luke 12:29
Be *a* for nothing............. Phil 4:6

APART

that you shall set *a*.........Ex 13:12
she shall be set *a*............ Lev 15:19
the LORD has set *a*.........Ps 4:3
justified by faith *a*..........Rom 3:28

APOSTLE

called to be an *a*............ Rom 1:1
inasmuch as I am an *a*....Rom 11:13
Am I not an *a*................. 1 Co 9:1
the signs of an *a* were......2 Co 12:12
a preacher and an *a*........ 1 Ti 2:7
consider the *A*................Heb 3:1

APOSTLES

of the twelve *a*............... Matt 10:2
whom He also named *a*... Luke 6:13
displayed us, the *a*.......... 1 Co 4:9

APPETITE

am the least of the *a*...... 1 Co 15:9
to the most eminent *a*......2 Co 11:5
themselves into *a*............. 2 Co 11:13
none of the other *a*......... Gal 1:19
gave some to be *a*...........Eph 4:11
who say they are *a*.......... Rev 2:2
heaven, and you holy *a*....Rev 18:20

APOSTLESHIP

in this ministry and *a*.......Acts 1:25
received grace and *a*........Rom 1:5
are the seal of my *a*........ 1 Co 9:2
in Peter for the *a*............ Gal 2:8

APPAREL

is glorious in His *a*..........Is 63:1
clothed with foreign *a*......Zeph 1:8
by them in white *a*..........Acts 1:10
themselves in modest *a*....1 Ti 2:9
gold rings, in fine *a*.........Jas 2:2
of putting on fine *a*.........1 Pe 3:3

APPEAL

I *a* to Caesar..................Acts 25:11
love's sake I rather *a*.......Phm 9

APPEAR

and let the dry land *a*......Gen 1:9
all your males shall *a*.......Ex 23:17
all Israel comes to *a*........Deut 31:11
shall I come and *a*........... Ps 42:2
Let Your work *a*............. Ps 90:16
He shall *a* in His............ Ps 102:16
doings your sins *a*........... Ezek 21:24
faces that they may *a*......Matt 6:16
also outwardly *a*............. Matt 23:28
kingdom of God would *a*. Luke 19:11
For we must all *a*............ 2 Co 5:10
for Him He will *a*........... Heb 9:28
and the sinner a.............. 1 Pe 4:18

APPEARANCE

Do not look at his *a*........1 Sa 16:7
a is blacker than soot...... Lam 4:8
as He prayed, the *a*.........Luke 9:29
judge according to *a*........John 7:24
those who glory in *a*........2 Co 5:12
to the outward *a*............. 2 Co 10:7
found in *a* as a man....... Phil 2:8
indeed have an *a*............ Col 2:23

APPEARED

an angel of the Lord *a*.....Luke 1:11
who *a* in glory and......... Luke 9:31
brings salvation has *a*.......Tit 2:11
of the ages, He has *a*...... Heb 9:26

APPEARING

Lord Jesus Christ's *a*....... 1 Ti 6:14
been revealed by the *a*....2 Ti 1:10
and the dead at His *a*......2 Ti 4:1
who have loved His *a*......2 Ti 4:8
hope and glorious *a*.........Tit 2:13

APPEARS

can stand when He *a*.......Mal 3:2
who is our life *a*..............Col 3:4
the Chief Shepherd *a*.......1 Pe 5:4
in Him, that when He *a*...1 Jn 2:28

APPETITE

or satisfy the *a*................Job 38:39
are a man given to *a*.......Prov 23:2

APPLE

He kept him as the *a*......Deut 32:10
and my law as the *a*........ Prov 7:2
Like an *a* tree among...... Song 2:3
you touches the *a*...........Zech 2:8

APPLES

fitly spoken is like *a*........ Prov 25:11
refresh me with *a*...........Song 2:5

APPLIED

a my heart to know........Eccl 7:25

APPOINT

I will even *a* terror.........Lev 26:16
a each of them to his......Num 4:19
a me ruler over the.........2 Sa 6:21
a salvation for walls.........Is 26:1
For God did not *a*........ 1 Th 5:9
a elders in every city....... Tit 1:5

APPOINTED

You have *a* his limits......Job 14:5
To loose those *a*............ Ps 102:20
And as it is *a* for men..... Heb 9:27

APPROACH

a anyone who is near.......Lev 18:6
And cause to *a* You........ Ps 65:4
year, make those who *a*.. Heb 10:1

APPROACHING

take delight in *a* God...... Is 58:2
as you see the Day *a*.......Heb 10:25

APPROVE

their posterity who *a*....... Ps 49:13
do the same but also *a*.....Rom 1:32
a the things that............ Rom 2:18
a the things that are........Phil 1:10

APPROVED

to God and *a* by men...... Rom 14:18
to present yourself *a*........2 Ti 2:15

ARBITRATOR

Me a judge or an *a*........ Luke 12:14

ARCHANGEL

with the voice of an *a*......1 Th 4:16
Yet Michael the *a*..........Jude 9

ARGUMENTS

fill my mouth with *a*........Job 23:4
casting down *a* and.........2 Co 10:5

ARISE

needy, Now I will *a*.........Ps 12:5
A for our help..............Ps 44:26
Let God *a*..................Ps 68:1
A, shine....................Is 60:1
but the LORD will *a*........Is 60:2
Righteousness shall *a*......Mal 4:2
false prophets will *a*....... Matt 24:24
'I will *a* and go to..........Luke 15:18
you who sleep, *a*...........Eph 5:14

"Make yourself an *a*.......Gen 6:14
him, she took an *a*........Ex 2:3
Bezaleel made the *a*....... Ex 37:1
seat which is on the *a*......Lev 16:2
Let us bring the *a*...........1 Sa 4:3
of incense and the *a*.......Heb 9:4
of Noah, while the *a*....... 1 Pe 3:20
in heaven, and the *a*.......Rev 11:19

ARM

with an outstretched *a*..... Ex 6:6
"Has the LORD's *a*........Num 11:23
With him is an *a*.............2 Ch 32:8
a that has no strength......Job 26:2
Have you an *a* like God...Job 40:9
Break the *a* of the.......... Ps 10:15
You have a mighty *a*.......Ps 89:13
a have gained Him the.....Ps 98:1
a shall rule for Him.........Is 40:10
therefore His own *a*........ Is 59:16
strength with His *a*.........Luke 1:51
with an uplifted *a*...........Acts 13:17
a yourselves also with...... 1 Pe 4:1

ARMED

For You have *a* me with..2 Sa 22:40
a strong man, fully *a*...... Luke 11:21

ARMIES

make captains of the *a*.....Deut 20:9
"I defy the *a*...................1 Sa 17:10
any number to His *a*...... Job 25:3
not go out with our *a*...... Ps 60:10
And he sent out his *a*......Matt 22:7
surrounded by *a*.............Luke 21:20
And the *a* in heaven.......Rev 19:14
the earth, and their *a*...... Rev 19:19

ARMOR

but he put his *a*..............1 Sa 17:54
spears, put on the *a*........ Jer 46:4
let us put on the *a*...........Rom 13:12
Put on the whole *a*.........Eph 6:11

ARMS

are the everlasting *a*.......Deut 33:27
into the clash of *a*...........Job 39:21
It is God who *a*.............Ps 18:32
a will judge the.............. Is 51:5
took them up in His *a*.....Mark 10:16
took Him up in his *a*......Luke 2:28

ARMY

the multitude of an *a*.......Ps 33:16
an exceedingly great *a*..... Ezek 37:10
the number of the *a*........Rev 9:16

AROMA

smelled a soothing *a*.......Gen 8:21
the one we are the *a*.......2 Co 2:16
for a sweet-smelling *a*..... Eph 5:2
a sweet-smelling *a*..........Phil 4:18

AROUSED

the LORD was greatly *a*...Num 11:10
his wrath was *a*.............Job 32:2
Then Joseph, being *a*......Matt 1:24

ARRAYED

his glory was not *a*.........Matt 6:29
"Who are these *a*...........Rev 7:13
The woman was *a*..........Rev 17:4

ARROGANCE

pride and *a* and the........Prov 8:13
I will halt the *a*.............. Is 13:11

ARROGANT

the fruit of the *a*.............Is 10:12
My sanctuary, your *a*.......Ezek 24:21

ARROW

deliverance and the *a*.......2 Ki 13:17
a cannot make him flee....Job 41:28
make ready their *a*..........Ps 11:2

ARROWS

a that flies by day...........Ps 91:5
a sword, and a sharp *a*.... Prov 25:18
Their tongue is an *a*........Jer 9:8
as a target for the *a*........ Lam 3:12

ARROWS

He sent out *a* and...........2 Sa 22:15
a pierce me deeply..........Ps 38:2
There He broke the *a*......Ps 76:3
Like *a* in the hand of...... Ps 127:4
He has caused the *a*.......Lam 3:13
were sworn over Your *a*...Hab 3:9

ASCEND

Who may *a* into the........ Ps 24:3
If I *a* into heaven...........Ps 139:8
'I will *a* into heaven........Is 14:13
see the Son of Man *a*......John 6:62

ASCENDED

You have *a* on high.........Ps 68:18
Who has *a* into heaven.... Prov 30:4
"No one has *a*...............John 3:13
"*When He a on high*........Eph 4:8
also the One who *a*.........Eph 4:10
And they *a* to heaven......Rev 11:12

ASCENDING

angels of God were *a*...... Gen 28:12
the angels of God *a*........John 1:51

ASCRIBE

a greatness to our God.... Deut 32:3
a righteousness...............Job 36:3
A strength to God...........Ps 68:34

ASHAMED

I am too *a* and..............Ezra 9:6
all my enemies be *a*........ Ps 6:10
Let me not be *a*............. Ps 25:2
who waits on You be *a*..... Ps 25:3
The wise men are *a*........Jer 8:9
forsake You shall be *a*.....Jer 17:13
and Israel shall be *a*........ Hos 10:6
For whoever is *a*............Mark 8:38
am not *a* of the gospel.....Rom 1:16
nothing I shall be *a*.........Phil 1:20
Therefore God is not *a*.... Heb 11:16
in Christ may be *a*.......... 1 Pe 3:16
let him not be *a*.............1 Pe 4:16
and not be *a* before........1 Jn 2:28

ASHES

are proverbs of *a*............Job 13:12
become like dust and *a*.... Job 30:19
For I have eaten *a*.......... Ps 102:9
He feeds on *a*............... Is 44:20
sackcloth and sat in *a*......Jon 3:6
in sackcloth and *a*..........Luke 10:13
and goats and the *a*........Heb 9:13

ASIDE

of you lay something *a*.....1 Co 16:2
lay *a* all filthiness...........Jas 1:21
Therefore, laying *a*......... 1 Pe 2:1

ASK

Why is it that you *a*........ Gen 32:29
when your children *a*.......Josh 4:6
A a sign for yourself........Is 7:11
They shall *a* the way....... Jer 50:5
the young children *a*........Lam 4:4
A the LORD for rain in....Zech 10:1
things, whatever you *a*.....Matt 21:22
a, and it will be..............Luke 11:9
that whatever You *a*........John 11:22

ASKS

a anything in My name.... John 14:14
in that day you will *a*...... John 16:23
something, let them *a*...... 1 Co 14:35
above all that we *a*......... Eph 3:20
wisdom, let him *a*.......... Jas 1:5
But let him *a* in faith....Jas 1:6
because you do not *a*......Jas 4:2
us, whatever we *a*........... 1 Jn 5:15

ASKS

For everyone who *a*........ Matt 7:8
you who, if his son *a*...... Matt 7:9
Or if he *a* for a fish........ Luke 11:11

ASLEEP

down, and was fast *a*......Jon 1:5
But He was *a*.............Matt 8:24
but some have fallen *a*....1 Co 15:6
those who are *a*..............1 Th 4:15
the fathers fell *a*.............. 2 Pe 3:4

ASSEMBLING

not forsaking the *a*......... Heb 10:25

ASSEMBLY

to kill this whole *a*......... Ex 16:3
It is a sacred *a*............... Lev 23:36
The *a* of the wicked........ Ps 22:16
to be feared in the *a*....... Ps 89:7
praise Him in the *a*........ Ps 107:32
fast, call a sacred *a*........ Joel 1:14
to the general *a*.............. Heb 12:23
come into your *a*............. Jas 2:2

ASSURANCE

night, and have no *a*...... Deut 28:66
riches of the full *a*.........Col 2:2
Spirit and in much *a*.......1 Th 1:5
to the full *a* of hope........Heb 6:11
a true heart in full *a*........Heb 10:22

ASTONISHED

Just as many were *a*........ Is 52:14
that the people were *a*..... Matt 7:28
who heard Him were *a*.... Luke 2:47

ASTONISHMENT

you shall become an *a*..... Deut 28:37
a has taken hold............. Jer 8:21

ASTRAY

is a people who go *a*....... Ps 95:10
a fool, shall not go *a*...... Is 35:8
their lies leave them *a*.......Amos 2:4
and one of them goes *a*... Matt 18:12
'They always go *a*........... Heb 3:10
like sheep going *a*...........1 Pe 2:25

ATONEMENT

a year he shall make *a*.....Ex 30:10
priest shall make *a*.......... Lev 16:30
the blood that makes *a*.... Lev 17:11
for it is the Day of *A*...... Lev 23:28
what shall I make *a*......... 2 Sa 21:3
offerings to make *a*......... Neh 10:33
a is provided for............ Prov 16:6
there will be no *a*............ Is 22:14
I provide you an *a*......... Ezek 16:63

ATTAIN

It is high, I cannot *a*....... Ps 139:6
understanding will *a*........ Prov 1:5
it be until they *a*............. Hos 8:5
worthy to *a* that age....... Luke 20:35
by any means, I may *a*.... Phil 3:11

ATTEND

just cause, O LORD, *A*... Ps 17:1
And *a* to the voice of...... Ps 86:6
Behold, I will *a*.............Jer 23:2

ATTENTION

My son, give *a* to my...... Prov 4:20
Till I come, give *a*.......... 1 Ti 4:13
and you pay *a* to the...... Jas 2:3

ATTENTIVE

Let Your ears be *a*..........Ps 130:2
the people were very *a*.... Luke 19:48

ATTESTED

a Man *a* by God to you... Acts 2:22

AUTHOR

For God is not the *a*....... 1 Co 14:33
He became the *a*........... Heb 5:9
unto Jesus, the *a*.............Heb 12:2

AUTHORITIES

a that exist are............... Rom 13:1
of God, angels and *a*.......1 Pe 3:22

AUTHORITY

Jew, wrote with full *a*......Esth 9:29
the righteous are in *a*...... Prov 29:2
them as one having *a*......Matt 7:29
are great exercise *a*........ Matt 20:25
All *a* has been given........Matt 28:18
a I will give You.............Luke 4:6
and has given Him *a*....... John 5:27
You have given Him *a*.....John 17:2
has put in His own *a*....... Acts 1:7
For there is no *a*.............Rom 13:1
to have a symbol of *a*......1 Co 11:10
and all who are in *a*........ 1 Ti 2:2
and rebuke with all *a*......Tit 2:15
the flesh, reject *a*............Jude 8

AUTUMN

a trees without fruit.........Jude 12

AVAILS

nor uncircumcision *a*........Gal 5:6
of a righteous man *a*....... Jas 5:16

AVENGE

for He will *a* the.............Deut 32:43
A me of my adversary..... Luke 18:3
you that He will *a*...........Luke 18:8
Beloved, do not *a*........... Rom 12:19
a our blood on those....... Rev 6:10

AVENGER

'The *a* of blood............. Num 35:19
the enemy and the *a*.......Ps 8:2
God's minister, an *a*....... Rom 13:4
the Lord is the *a*.............1 Th 4:6

AVENGES

It is God who *a*............2 Sa 22:48
When He *a* blood.......... Ps 9:12

AWAKE

be satisfied when I *a*...... Ps 17:15
I lie *a*........................... Ps 102:7
A, lute and harp............. Ps 108:2
My eyes are *a* through..... Ps 119:148
A, O north wind............Song 4:16
but my heart is *a*........... Song 5:2
of the earth shall *a*.........Dan 12:2
it is high time to *a*.......... Rom 13:11

A to righteousness........1 Co 15:34
"*A*, you who sleep.......... Eph 5:14

AWAY

the wind drives *a*........... Ps 1:4
Do not cast me *a*.......... Ps 51:11
a time to cast *a*.............. Eccl 3:5
fair one, and come *a*...... Song 2:10
and the shadows flee *a*....Song 2:17
minded to put her *a*....... Matt 1:19
and earth will pass *a*.......Matt 24:35
and steal Him *a*............. Matt 27:64
the rich He has sent *a*..... Luke 1:53
of God who takes *a*........John 1:29
"I am going *a*................John 8:21
they cried out, "*A*..........John 19:15
"They have taken *a*.........John 20:2
crying out, "*A*................Acts 21:36
the veil is taken *a*.......... 2 Co 3:14
Barnabas was carried *a*... Gal 2:13
unless the falling *a*........ 2 Th 2:3
in Asia have turned *a*..... 2 Ti 1:15
heard, lest we drift *a*...... Heb 2:1
if they fall *a*................. Heb 6:6
which can never take *a*.... Heb 10:11
that does not fade *a*....... 1 Pe 5:4
the world is passing *a*......1 Jn 2:17
and the heaven fled *a*..... Rev 20:11
if anyone takes *a*........... Rev 22:19
God shall take *a*............ Rev 22:19

AWE

the world stand in *a*....... Ps 33:8
my heart stands in *a*........Ps 119:161

AWESOME

a is this place............... Gen 28:17
a thing that I will do...... Ex 34:10
God, the great and *a*......Deut 7:21
God, mighty and *a*.........Deut 10:17
Angel of God, very *a*......Judg 13:6
a deeds for Your land......2 Sa 7:23
heaven, O great and *a*.....Neh 1:5
hand shall teach You *a*.... Ps 45:4
By *a* deeds in.................Ps 65:5
a are Your works...........Ps 66:3
He is *a* in His doing........ Ps 66:5
O God, You are more *a*... Ps 68:35
He is *a* to the kings........Ps 76:12
Your great and *a* name... Ps 99:3
of the might of Your *a*.... Ps 145:6
When You did *a* things... Is 64:3
with me as a mighty, *a*... Jer 20:11
her collapse was *a*......... Lam 1:9
"O Lord, great and *a*...... Dan 9:4

AWL

his ear with an *a*............Ex 21:6
you shall take an *a*......... Deut 15:17

AX

a stroke with the *a*......... Deut 19:5
Abimelech took an *a*....... Judg 9:48
a tree, the iron *a*............ 2 Ki 6:5
If the *a* is dull................ Eccl 10:10
a boast itself against........ Is 10:15
And even now the *a*........Matt 3:10

— B —

BABBLER

b is no different............. Eccl 10:11
"What does this *b*.......... Acts 17:18

BABBLINGS

the profane and vain *b*.....1 Ti 6:20

BABE
the *b* leaped in my.........Luke 1:44
You will find a *B*...........Luke 2:12
for he is a *b*...................Heb 5:13

BABES
Out of the mouth of *b*.....Ps 8:2
b shall rule over them......Is 3:4
revealed them to *b*..........Matt 11:25
Out of the mouth of *b*.....Matt 21:16
a teacher of *b*.................Rom 2:20
as to carnal, as to *b*........ 1 Co 3:1
as newborn *b*..................1 Pe 2:2

BACK
Jordan turned *b*..............Ps 114:3
but a rod is for the *b*...... Prov 10:13
for the fool's *b*...............Prov 26:3
I gave My *b* to those.......Is 50:6
cast Me behind your *b*.....Ezek 23:35
found Him, bring *b*.........Matt 2:8
plow, and looking *b*.........Luke 9:62
they drew *b* and fell.........John 18:6
I am sending him *b*..........Phm 12
of those who draw *b*........Heb 10:39
someone turns him *b*.......Jas 5:19
inside and on the *b*..........Rev 5:1

BACKBITERS
b, haters of God..............Rom 1:30

BACKBITING
b tongue an angry...........Prov 25:23

BACKSLIDER
The *b* in heart will be......Prov 14:14

BACKSLIDINGS
b will reprove you...........Jer 2:19
and I will heal your *b*......Jer 3:22
b have increased.............Jer 5:6
for our *b* are many.........Jer 14:7

BACKWARD
fell off the seat *b*............1 Sa 4:18
shadow ten degrees *b*...... 2 Ki 20:11

BAD
speak to you either *b*.......Gen 24:50
it, good for *b* or *b*.......... Lev 27:10
b tree bears *b* fruit.........Matt 7:17

BAG
is sealed up in a *b*...........Job 14:17
wages to put into a *b*.......Hag 1:6
"nor *b* for your..............Matt 10:10

BAKER
the butler and the *b*........ Gen 40:1

BAKERS
of bread from the *b*.........Jer 37:21

BAKES
kindles it and *b* bread......Is 44:15

BALANCE
be weighed in a just *b*..... Job 31:6
b is an abomination.........Prov 11:1
small dust on the *b*..........Is 40:15

BALANCES
You shall have just *b*.......Lev 19:36
falsifying the *b*...............Amos 8:5

BALD
shall not make any *b*.......Lev 21:5
every head shall be *b*.......Jer 48:37
completely *b* because.......Ezek 27:31

BALDHEAD
Go up, you *b*..................2 Ki 2:23

BALM
a little *b* and a...............Gen 43:11
Is there no *b* in..............Jer 8:22

BAND
A *b* of robbers takes.......Hos 7:1
with a golden *b*..............Rev 1:13

BANDAGED
him and *b* his wounds......Luke 10:34

BANKERS
my money with the *b*.......Matt 25:27

BANNERS
we will set up our *b*........Ps 20:5
They set up their *b*.........Ps 74:4
as an army with *b*...........Song 6:4

BANQUET
b that I have prepared.....Esth 5:4
companions make a *b*......Job 41:6
lords, came to the *b*........Dan 5:10

BANQUETING
He brought me to the *b*...Song 2:4

BANQUETS
b shall be removed..........Amos 6:7

BAPTISM
coming to his *b*..............Matt 3:7
b that I am baptized........Matt 20:22
"The *b* of John...............Matt 21:25
"But I have a *b*..............Luke 12:50
said, "Into John's *b*........Acts 19:3
with Him through *b*........Rom 6:4
Lord, one faith, one *b*.....Eph 4:5
buried with Him in *b*......Col 2:12
now saves us, namely *b*....1 Pe 3:21

BAPTISMS
of the doctrine of *b*.........Heb 6:2

BAPTIZE
"I indeed *b* you with....... Matt 3:11
"Why then do you *b*....... John 1:25
Himself did not *b*............John 4:2
did not send me to *b*.......1 Co 1:17

BAPTIZED
"I have need to be *b*.......Matt 3:14
b will be saved...............Mark 16:16
b more disciples..............John 4:1
every one of you be *b*..... Acts 2:38
all his family were *b*........Acts 16:33
believed and were *b*........Acts 18:8
Arise and be *b*...............Acts 22:16
were *b* into Christ...........Rom 6:3
I thank God that I *b*.......1 Co 1:14
b the household..............1 Co 1:16
all were *b* into Moses......1 Co 10:2
Spirit we were all *b*.........1 Co 12:13
who are *b* for the dead....1 Co 15:29
of you as were *b*............Gal 3:27

BAPTIZING
b them in the name of.....Matt 28:19
therefore I came *b*..........John 1:31

BARBARIAN
nor uncircumcised, *b*....... Col 3:11

BARE
make yourselves *b*..........Is 32:11
The LORD has made *b*....Is 52:10

BARLEY
a land of wheat and *b*.....Deut 8:8
b bread tumbled.............Judg 7:13
beginning of *b* harvest.... Ruth 1:22
here who has five *b*.........John 6:9
and three quarts of *b*......Rev 6:6

BARN
seed still in the *b*............Hag 2:19
the wheat into my *b*........Matt 13:30
storehouse nor *b*............Luke 12:24

BARNS
b will be filled................Prov 3:10
b are broken down..........Joel 1:17
reap nor gather into *b*..... Matt 6:26
I will pull down my *b*......Luke 12:18

BARREN
But Sarai was *b*..............Gen 11:30
b has borne seven...........1 Sa 2:5
He grants the *b*..............Ps 113:9
"Sing, O *b*.....................Is 54:1
'Blessed are the *b*...........Luke 23:29
"Rejoice, O *b*................Gal 4:27
you will be neither *b*.......2 Pe 1:8

BARRENNESS
A fruitful land into *b*.......Ps 107:34

BARS
has strengthened the *b*.....Ps 147:13
bronze and cut the *b*.......Is 45:2
the earth with its *b*.........Jon 2:6

BASE
the elder, and the *b*........ Is 3:5
and the *b* things of..........1 Co 1:28

BASIN
poured water into a *b*......John 13:5

BASKET
Cursed shall be your *b*.....Deut 28:17
b had very good figs........Jer 24:2
and put it under a *b*........Matt 5:15
I was let down in a *b*...... 2 Co 11:33

BASKETS
I had three white *b*.........Gen 40:16
and there were two *b*......Jer 24:1
they took up twelve *b*......Matt 14:20
up seven large *b*.............Matt 15:37

BATHED
My sword shall be *b*........Is 34:5
to him, "He who is *b*......John 13:10

BATS
to the moles and *b*..........Is 2:20

BATTLE
b is the LORD's...............1 Sa 17:47
out to God in the *b*........1 Ch 5:20
strength for the *b*...........Ps 18:39

BEAR

for the day of *b*..............Prov 21:31
the *b* to the strong.........Eccl 9:11
who turn back the *b*.........Is 28:6
A sound of *b* is in the....Jer 50:22
prepare himself for *b*.......1 Co 14:8
became valiant in *b*.........Heb 11:34
gather them to the *b*.......Rev 16:14

BEAR

greater than I can *b*........Gen 4:13
whom Sarah shall *b*.........Gen 17:21
"You shall not *b*..............Ex 20:16
from the paw of the *b*.....1 Sa 17:37
They shall *b* you up in.....Ps 91:12
b a broken spirit..............Prov 18:14
be clean, you who *b*........Is 52:11
b their iniquities.............Is 53:11
LORD could no longer *b*..Jer 44:22
b deprived of her cubs...Hos 13:8
lion, and a *b* met him......Amos 5:19
He shall *b* the glory........Zech 6:13
child, and *b* a Son..........Matt 1:23
A good tree cannot *b*.....Matt 7:18
How long shall I *b*..........Matt 17:17
by, to *b* His cross..........Mark 15:21
wife Elizabeth will *b*.......Luke 1:13
And whoever does not *b*..Luke 14:27
in Me that does not *b*.....John 15:2
for he does not *b*............Rom 13:4
are strong ought to *b*......Rom 15:1
you may be able to *b*......1 Co 10:13
B one another's..............Gal 6:2
I *b* in my body the..........Gal 6:17
b the sins of many.........Heb 9:28
like the feet of a *b*.........Rev 13:2

BEARD

the edges of your *b*........Lev 19:27
I caught it by its *b*.........1 Sa 17:35
took Amasa by the *b*......2 Sa 20:9
Running down on the *b*...Ps 133:2

BEARING

goes forth weeping, *B*......Ps 126:6
And He, *b* His cross.......John 19:17
b with one another.........Col 3:13
the camp, *b* His reproach.Heb 13:13

BEARS

every branch that *b*........John 15:2
b all things....................1 Co 13:7
it is the Spirit who *b*......1 Jn 5:6

BEAST

b has devoured him.........Gen 37:20
You preserve man and *b*..Ps 36:6
I was like a *b* before.......Ps 73:22
to the *b* its food.............Ps 147:9
b touches the mountain...Heb 12:20
And I saw a *b* rising.......Rev 13:1
Then I saw another *b*......Rev 13:11
the mark of the *b*...........Rev 19:20

BEASTS

are we counted as *b*........Job 18:3
like the *b* that perish.......Ps 49:12
and four-footed *b*...........Rom 1:23
I have fought with *b*........1 Co 15:32
like brute *b*...................Jude 10

BEAT

I will *b* down his foes......Ps 89:23
You shall *b* him with a....Prov 23:14
b their swords into..........Is 2:4
you shall *b* in pieces........Mic 4:13

spat in His face and *b*......Matt 26:67
but *b* his breast..............Luke 18:13

BEATEN

and you will be *b*............Mark 13:9
his will, shall be *b*..........Luke 12:47
Three times I was *b*........2 Co 11:25
it if, when you are *b*.......1 Pe 2:20

BEAUTIFUL

but Rachel was *b*............Gen 29:17
B in elevation.................Ps 48:2
has made everything *b*....Eccl 3:11
my love, you are as *b*.....Song 6:4
of the LORD shall be *b*...Is 4:2
How *b* upon the.............Is 52:7
indeed appear *b*.............Matt 23:27
begging alms at the *B*......Acts 3:10
they saw he was a *b*........Heb 11:23

BEAUTIFY

b the humble with..........Ps 149:4
b the place of My..........Is 60:13

BEAUTY

for glory and for *b*..........Ex 28:2
"The *b* of Israel is..........2 Sa 1:19
To behold the *b*..............Ps 27:4
and *b* is vain.................Prov 31:30
see the King in His *b*......Is 33:17
no *b* that we should........Is 53:2
the one I called *B*...........Zech 11:7
Do not let your *b*..........1 Pe 3:3

BECAME

b a living being..............Gen 2:7
to the Jews I *b*..............1 Co 9:20

BED

house, if I make my *b*.....Job 17:13
remember You on my *b*...Ps 63:6
If I make my *b* in hell....Ps 139:8
Also our *b* is green........Song 1:16
b is too short for a.........Is 28:20
you have set your *b*........Is 57:7
Arise, take up your *b*......Matt 9:6
be two men in one *b*.......Luke 17:34
and the *b* undefiled.........Heb 13:4

BEDS

sing aloud on their *b*......Ps 149:5
shall rest in their *b*.........Is 57:2
who lie on *b* of ivory......Amos 6:4

BEE

Egypt, and for the *b*........Is 7:18

BEFOREHAND

up, do not worry *b*.........Mark 13:11
told you all things *b*.......Mark 13:23
not to meditate *b*...........Luke 21:14
when He testified *b*........1 Pe 1:11

BEG

I would *b* mercy of my....Job 9:15
I am ashamed to *b*.........Luke 16:3
b you as sojourners.........1 Pe 2:11

BEGAN

Then men *b* to call on.....Gen 4:26
since the world *b*............Luke 1:70

BEGETS

b a scoffer does.............Prov 17:21
b a wise child will.........Prov 23:24
b a hundred children.......Eccl 6:3

BEGGAR

and lifts the *b*................1 Sa 2:8
there was a certain *b*.......Luke 16:20

BEGGARLY

weak and *b* elements.......Gal 4:9

BEGINNING

b God created the..........Gen 1:1
Though your *b* was.........Job 8:7
of the LORD is the *b*......Ps 111:10
that God does from *b*......Eccl 3:11
who made them at the *b*..Matt 19:4
In the *b* was the Word....John 1:1
This *b* of signs Jesus......John 2:11
a murderer from the *b*....John 8:44
with Me from the *b*........John 15:27
the *b*, the firstborn.........Col 1:18
having neither *b*.............Heb 7:3
True Witness, the *B*........Rev 3:14
and the Omega, the *B*.....Rev 21:6

BEGOTTEN

I have *b* You................Ps 2:7
heart, 'Who has *b*..........Is 49:21
glory as of the only *b*.....John 1:14
Christ Jesus I have *b*......1 Co 4:15
abundant mercy has *b*.....1 Pe 1:3
loves him who is *b*.........1 Jn 5:1

BEGUILING

b unstable souls.............2 Pe 2:14

BEGUN

Having *b* in the Spirit......Gal 3:3
that He who has *b*..........Phil 1:6

BEHALF

to speak on God's *b*........Job 36:2
you on Christ's *b*............2 Co 5:20
has been granted on *b*.....Phil 1:29

BEHAVE

I will *b* wisely in a.........Ps 101:2
does not *b* rudely...........1 Co 13:5

BEHAVED

sent him, and *b* wisely.....1 Sa 18:5
and blamelessly we *b*.......1 Th 2:10

BEHAVIOR

of good *b*, hospitable.......1 Ti 3:2
they be reverent in *b*.......Tit 2:3

BEHEADED

he sent and had John *b*...Matt 14:10
those who had been *b*......Rev 20:4

BEHOLD

the eyes to *b* the sun......Eccl 11:7
B, you are fair..............Song 1:15
B, the virgin shall..........Is 7:14
Judah, "*B* your God.......Is 40:9
B the Lamb of God.........John 1:36
I am, that they may *b*.....John 17:24
to them, "*B* the Man......John 19:5
B what manner of love....1 Jn 3:1

BEHOLDING

with unveiled face, *b*.......2 Co 3:18

BEING

man became a living *b*.....Gen 2:7
God while I have my *b*....Ps 104:33
move and have our *b*......Acts 17:28
who, *b* in the form of.....Phil 2:6

BELIEF

by the Spirit and *b*..........2 Th 2:13

BELIEVE

B in the LORD your...... 2 Ch 20:20
tears, "Lord, I *b*.............Mark 9:24
b that you receive...........Mark 11:24
because they did not *b*....Mark 16:14
have no root, who *b*.......Luke 8:13
and slow of heart to *b*..... Luke 24:25
even to those who *b*.......John 1:12
how will you *b*.............John 3:12
sent, Him you do not *b*... John 5:38
we may see it and *b*.......John 6:30
to him, "Do you *b*.......John 9:35
this, that they may *b*...... John 11:42
you *b* in God.............. John 14:1
written that you may *b*.... John 20:31
King Agrippa, do you *b*... Acts 26:27
the Lord Jesus and *b*...... Rom 10:9
And how shall they *b*..... Rom 10:14
a wife who does not *b*..... 1 Co 7:12
I spoke," we also *b*..... 2 Co 4:13
given to those who *b*...... Gal 3:22
Christ, not only to *b*.......Phil 1:29
comes to God must *b*..... Heb 11:6
b that there is one.......... Jas 2:19
Even the demons *b*........Jas 2:19
Beloved, do not *b*..........1 Jn 4:1

BELIEVED

And he *b* in the LORD....Gen 15:6
b That I would see the.... Ps 27:13
Who has *b* our report...... Is 53:1
of that city *b* in Him....... John 4:39
seen Me, you have *b*..... John 20:29
who heard the word *b*..... Acts 4:4
of those who *b* were of.... Acts 4:32
Holy Spirit when you *b*....Acts 19:2
"*Abraham b God*........... Rom 4:3
I know whom I have *b*... 2 Ti 1:12

BELIEVERS

be an example to the *b*...1 Ti 4:12
are benefited are *b*..........1 Ti 6:2

BELIEVES

The simple *b* every..........Prov 14:15
"He who *b* and is........... Mark 16:16
that whoever *b* in Him.....John 3:16
"He who *b* in the Son..... John 3:36
with the heart one *b*........Rom 10:10
b all things..............1 Co 13:7

BELIEVING

you ask in prayer, *b*........ Matt 21:22
blessed with *b* Abraham...Gal 3:9

BELLY

on your *b* you shall go.....Gen 3:14
And Jonah was in the *b*...Jon 1:17
three nights in the *b*...... Matt 12:40
whose god is their *b*........ Phil 3:19

BELONG

To the Lord our God *b*... Dan 9:9
My name, because you *b*..Mark 9:41

BELOVED

"The *b* of the LORD...... Deut 33:12
so He gives His *b*........... Ps 127:2
of myrrh is my *b*............Song 1:13
My *b* is mine..................Song 2:16
b more than another.......Song 5:9
Where has your *b*...........Song 6:1
leaning upon her *b*.........Song 8:5

a song of my *B*...............Is 5:1
for you are greatly *b*...... Dan 9:23
"This is My *b*.................Matt 3:17
election they are *b*......... Rom 11:28
us accepted in the *B*.......Eph 1:6
b physician and Demas.... Col 4:14
than a slave, as a *b*........ Phm 16
"This is My *b*..................2 Pe 1:17
our *b* brother Paul.......... 2 Pe 3:15
the saints and the *b*........Rev 20:9

BELT

with a leather *b*.............. Matt 3:4
us, he took Paul's *b*........ Acts 21:11

BEND

The wicked *b* their bow... Ps 11:2

BENEATH

and on the earth *b*......... Deut 4:39
"You are from *b*.............John 8:23

BENEFACTORS

them are called '*b*...........Luke 22:25

BENEFIT

That I may see the *b*.......Ps 106:5
people who could not *b*... Is 30:5
might have a second *b*.... 2 Co 1:15

BEREAVE

I will *b* them of..............Jer 15:7
no more shall you *b*........ Ezek 36:12
children, yet I will *b*........Hos 9:12

BESEECH

Return, we *b* You...........Ps 80:14
b you therefore...............Rom 12:1
of the Lord, *b* you to...... Eph 4:1

BESIDE

He leads me *b* the.......... Ps 23:2
"Paul, you are *b*............. Acts 26:24
For if we are *b*................2 Co 5:13

BEST

with the *b* ointments........Amos 6:6
'Bring out the *b*..............Luke 15:22
earnestly desire the *b*.......1 Co 12:31

BESTOW

LORD, that He may *b*....Ex 32:29
b greater honor............. 1 Co 12:23

BESTOWED

love the Father has *b*.......1 Jn 3:1

BETRAY

the outcasts, do not *b*......Is 16:3
you, one of you will *b*.... Matt 26:21
"Now brother will *b*........ Mark 13:12

BETRAYED

Man is about to be *b*.......Matt 17:22
in which He was *b*.......... 1 Co 11:23

BETRAYING

"Judas, are you *b*........... Luke 22:48

BETRAYS

See, he who *b* Me is at....Matt 26:46
who is the one who *b*......John 21:20

BETROTH

"You shall *b* a wife.........Deut 28:30
"I will *b* you to Me.........Hos 2:19

BETROTHED

to a virgin *b* to a man..... Luke 1:27
For I have *b* you to.........2 Co 11:2

BETTER

b than sacrifice...............1 Sa 15:22
It is *b* to trust in.............Ps 118:8
B is a little with the........Prov 15:16
B is a dry morsel............Prov 17:1
B is the poor who...........Prov 19:1
It is *b* to dwell in............Prov 21:19
b is a neighbor............... Prov 27:10
B is a handful with.........Eccl 4:6
Two are *b* than one........Eccl 4:9
B is a poor and wise....... Eccl 4:13
were the former days *b*...Eccl 7:10
countenance appeared *b*...Dan 1:15
For it is *b* to marry......... 1 Co 7:9
Christ, which is far *b*.......Phil 1:23
b than the angels............Heb 1:4
b things concerning......... Heb 6:9
b things than that........... Heb 12:24

BEWARE

"*B* of false prophets........ Matt 7:15
b of evil workers.............Phil 3:2
B lest anyone cheat.........Col 2:8

BEWITCHED

b you that you should......Gal 3:1

BEYOND

b what is written.............1 Co 4:6
b their ability................. 2 Co 8:3
advanced in Judaism *b*.....Gal 1:14

BILLOWS

b have gone over me.......Ps 42:7
all Your *b* and Your........Jon 2:3

BIND

b the cluster of the..........Job 38:31
b the wild ox in the.........Job 39:10
b them around your........ Prov 3:3
B them on your fingers.... Prov 7:3
B up the testimony......... Is 8:16
but He will *b* us up......... Hos 6:1
and whatever you *b*........Matt 16:19
B him hand and foot....... Matt 22:13
b heavy burdens........... Matt 23:4

BIRD

the blood of the *b*...........Lev 14:52
with him as with a *b*.......Job 41:5
soul, "Flee as a *b*........... Ps 11:1
has escaped as a *b*.......... Ps 124:7
b hastens to the snare......Prov 7:23
for a *b* of the air may......Eccl 10:20
fly away like a *b*.............Hos 9:11
unclean and hated *b*........Rev 18:2

BIRDS

b will eat your flesh........ Gen 40:19
b make their nests...........Ps 104:17
b caught in a snare..........Eccl 9:12
"Look at the *b*................ Matt 6:26
Foxes have holes and *b*....Matt 8:20

BIRTH

heaven, who gives it *b*.....Job 38:29
makes the deer give *b*......Ps 29:9
the day of one's *b*...........Eccl 7:1
bring to the time of *b*...... Is 66:9
the deer also gave *b*........Jer 14:5
Now the *b* of Jesus......... Matt 1:18
will rejoice at his *b*.........Luke 1:14

BIRTHDAY

who was blind from *b*......John 9:1
conceived, it gives *b*........Jas 1:15

BIRTHDAY

which was Pharaoh's *b*.....Gen 40:20
b gave a feast for his......Mark 6:21

BIRTHRIGHT

"Sell me your *b*..............Gen 25:31
Esau despised his *b*........Gen 25:34
according to his *b*............Gen 43:33
of food sold his *b*............Heb 12:16

BISHOP

the position of a *b*.......... 1 Ti 3:1
b must be blameless........ Tit 1:7

BIT

and they *b* the people......Num 21:6
be harnessed with *b*.........Ps 32:9

BITE

A serpent may *b*..............Eccl 10:11
But if you *b* and.............Gal 5:15

BITS

the great house into *b*......Amos 6:11
Indeed, we put *b*............Jas 3:3

BITTER

made their lives *b*........... Ex 1:14
b herbs they..................Ex 12:8
to those who are *b*.........Prov 31:6
who put *b* for sweet........ Is 5:20
and do not be *b*.............Col 3:19
But if you have *b*............Jas 3:14
make your stomach *b*...... Rev 10:9

BITTERLY

has dealt very *b*..............Ruth 1:20
And Hezekiah wept *b*......2 Ki 20:3
he went out and wept *b*...Matt 26:75

BITTERNESS

man dies in the *b*............Job 21:25
heart knows its own *b*......Prov 14:10
all my years in the *b*...... Is 38:15
you are poisoned by *b*..... Acts 8:23
b springing up cause........Heb 12:15

BLACK

My skin grows *b*............Job 30:30
wavy, and *b* as a raven....Song 5:11
one hair white or *b*......... Matt 5:36
a *b* horse......................Rev 6:5
and the sun became *b*......Rev 6:12

BLACKNESS

the heavens with *b*..........Is 50:3
whom is reserved the *b*....Jude 13

BLACKSMITH

The *b* with the tongs....... Is 44:12
I have created the *b*........Is 54:16

BLADE

went in after the *b*..........Judg 3:22
first the *b*......................Mark 4:28

BLAME

that anyone should *b*.......2 Co 8:20
be holy and without *b*......Eph 1:4

BLAMELESS

"You shall be *b*..............Deut 18:13
and that man was *b*.........Job 1:1

when You speak, And *b*.. Ps 51:4
Let my heart be *b*...........Ps 119:80
end, that you may be *b*....1 Co 1:8
which is in the law, *b*..... Phil 3:6
you holy, and *b*..............Col 1:22
your hearts *b* in.............1 Th 3:13
body be preserved *b*.......1 Th 5:23
bishop then must be *b*..... 1 Ti 3:2
deacons, being found *b*....1 Ti 3:10
without spot and *b*..........2 Pe 3:14

BLAMELESSLY

b we behaved.................1 Th 2:10

BLASPHEME

b Your name forever.......Ps 74:10
compelled them to *b*.......Acts 26:11
may learn not to *b*..........1 Ti 1:20
b that noble name..........Jas 2:7
God, to *b* His name........ Rev 13:6

BLASPHEMED

a foolish people has *b*......Ps 74:18
b continually every.........Is 52:5
who passed by *b* Him......Matt 27:39
who were hanged *b*.........Luke 23:39
The name of God is b..... Rom 2:24
doctrine may not be *b*..... 1 Ti 6:1
On their part He is *b*..... 1 Pe 4:14
great heat, and they *b*..... Rev 16:9

BLASPHEMER

I was formerly a *b*........... 1 Ti 1:13

BLASPHEMERS

boasters, proud, *b*...........2 Ti 3:2

BLASPHEMES

b the name of the LORD. Lev 24:16
"This Man *b*.................. Matt 9:3

BLASPHEMIES

false witness, *b*...............Matt 15:19
is this who speaks *b*........ Luke 5:21
great things and *b*.......... Rev 13:5

BLASPHEMY

men, but the *b* against.....Matt 12:31
"He has spoken *b*...........Matt 26:65
was full of names of *b*..... Rev 17:3

BLEATING

"What then is this *b*........1 Sa 15:14

BLEMISH

shall be without *b*...........Ex 12:5
LORD, a ram without *b*...Lev 6:6
be holy and without *b*.....Eph 5:27
as of a lamb without *b*.....1 Pe 1:19

BLEMISHED

to the Lord what is *b*...... Mal 1:14

BLESS

b those who *b* you.........Gen 12:3
You go unless You *b*......Gen 32:26
"The LORD *b* you and.... Num 6:24
b the LORD at all...........Ps 34:1
b You while I live...........Ps 63:4
b His holy name............Ps 103:1
b the house of Israel....... Ps 115:12
b those who fear the...... Ps 115:13
b you in the name of.......Ps 129:8
I will abundantly *b*..........Ps 132:15
b those who curse........... Luke 6:28
B those who persecute.....Rom 12:14

Being reviled, we *b*.........1 Co 4:12
With it we *b* our God......Jas 3:9

BLESSED

And God *b* them............ Gen 1:22
the earth shall be *b*.........Gen 12:3
b be those who...............Gen 27:29
indeed he shall be *b*........Gen 27:33
B is he who...................Num 24:9
B shall be the.................Deut 28:4
You have *b* the work of...Job 1:10
B is the man Who walks.. Ps 1:1
B is the man to whom..... Ps 32:2
B is the nation whose...... Ps 33:12
B is he who considers......Ps 41:1
B are those who keep......Ps 106:3
B is he who comes..........Ps 118:26
b Who fears the LORD....Ps 128:4
rise up and call her *b*..... Prov 31:28
will call you *b*................ Mal 3:12
B are the poor in............Matt 5:3
B are those who mourn... Matt 5:4
B are the meek.............. Matt 5:5
B are those who hunger...Matt 5:6
B are the merciful...........Matt 5:7
B are the pure in............Matt 5:8
B are the peacemakers.....Matt 5:9
B are those who are........Matt 5:10
B are you when they.......Matt 5:11
b is he who is.................Matt 11:6
b are your eyes..............Matt 13:16
b is He who comes......... Matt 21:9
hand, 'Come, you *b*........ Matt 25:34
Jesus took bread, *b*........ Matt 26:26
b are you among women..Luke 1:28
B are those who have......John 20:29
It is more *b* to give......... Acts 20:35
the Creator, who is *b*..... Rom 1:25
all, the eternally *b*..........Rom 9:5
B be the God and..........Eph 1:3
b God which was.............1 Ti 1:11
the lesser is *b*.................Heb 7:7
this one will be *b*.............Jas 1:25
B is he who reads........... Rev 1:3
B are the dead who.........Rev 14:13
B is he who watches....... Rev 16:15
B are those who are........ Rev 19:9
B and holy is he who.......Rev 20:6
B is he who keeps the..... Rev 22:7
B are those who do His... Rev 22:14

BLESSING

and you shall be a *b*........Gen 12:2
I will command My *b*......Lev 25:21
before you today a *b*.......Deut 11:26
The *b* of a perishing........Job 29:13
Your *b* is upon Your.......Ps 3:8
The *b* of the LORD.........Prov 10:22
shall be showers of *b*.......Ezek 34:26
relent, and leave a *b*....... Joel 2:14
and you shall be a *b*........Zech 8:13
the fullness of the *b*........ Rom 15:29
b which we bless.............1 Co 10:16
that the *b* of Abraham.....Gal 3:14
with every spiritual *b*.......Eph 1:3
cultivated, receives *b*.......Heb 6:7
to inherit the *b*...............Heb 12:17
honor and glory and *b*..... Rev 5:12

BLESSINGS

of the law, the *b*.............Josh 8:34
B are on the head of.......Prov 10:6

BLIGHT

I blasted you with *b*........ Amos 4:9
'I struck you with *b*.........Hag 2:17

BLIND

I was eyes to the b.........Job 29:15
B yourselves and be........ Is 29:9
To open b eyes................Is 42:7
I will bring the b............ Is 42:16
b people who have eyes... Is 43:8
His watchmen are b........ Is 56:10
They wandered b............Lam 4:14
when you offer the b......Mal 1:8
b receive their sight........Matt 11:5
b leads the b..................Matt 15:14
of sight to the b.............Luke 4:18
to Him, "Are we b........ John 9:40
miserable, poor, b..........Rev 3:17

BLINDED

b their eyes and..............John 12:40
of this age has b............2 Co 4:4
the darkness has b.......... 1 Jn 2:11

BLINDS

a bribe, for a bribe b.......Deut 16:19

BLOOD

of your brother's b..........Gen 4:10
b shall be shed.............. Gen 9:6
you are a husband of b.... Ex 4:25
b that makes atonement... Lev 17:11
b sustains its life............Lev 17:14
do not cover my b......... Job 16:18
is there in my b.............. Ps 30:9
And condemn innocent b. Ps 94:21
hands are full of b.......... Is 1:15
also disclose her b..........Is 26:21
and the moon into b.......Joel 2:31
For this is My b.............Matt 26:28
called the Field of B......Matt 27:8
His b be on us and........ Matt 27:25
new covenant in My b.... Luke 22:20
were born, not of b........John 1:13
b has eternal life............John 6:54
b every nation of men..... Acts 17:26
with His own b..............Acts 20:28
propitiation by His b....... Rom 3:25
justified by His b............Rom 5:9
through His b................Eph 1:7
made water by the b........Eph 2:13
against flesh and b..........Eph 6:12
peace through the b....... Col 1:20
"This is the b................Heb 9:20
are purged with b........... Heb 9:22
of b there is no.............. Heb 9:22
the Holiest by the b....... Heb 10:19
sprinkling of the b..........1 Pe 1:2
with the precious b........1 Pe 1:19
b of Jesus Christ His....... 1 Jn 1:7
our sins in His own b..... Rev 1:5
us to God by Your b.......Rev 5:9
them white in the b........Rev 7:14
overcame him by the b.... Rev 12:11
a robe dipped in b..........Rev 19:13

BLOODGUILTINESS

Deliver me from b.......... Ps 51:14

BLOODSHED

the land is full of b........ Ezek 9:9
build up Zion with b....... Mic 3:10

BLOODTHIRSTY

The LORD abhors the b.. Ps 5:6
B and deceitful men........ Ps 55:23

BLOSSOM

Israel shall b and bud...... Is 27:6
and b as the rose............ Is 35:1
the fig tree may not b......Hab 3:17

BLOT

say that He would b........2 Ki 14:27
from my sins, And b...... Ps 51:9
and I will not b.............. Rev 3:5

BLOTTED

Let them be b out of......Ps 69:28
I have b out...................Is 44:22
your sins may be b..........Acts 3:19

BLOWS

B that hurt cleanse.........Prov 20:30
breath of the LORD b..... Is 40:7
"The wind b where it..... John 3:8

BOAST

puts on his armor b.........1 Ki 20:11
soul shall make its b........Ps 34:2
God we b all day long..... Ps 44:8
and make your b............Rom 2:17
that we are your b.......... 2 Co 1:14
you, and not to b............2 Co 10:16
that I also may b............ 2 Co 11:16
lest anyone should b........Eph 2:9
your hearts, do not b......Jas 3:14

BOASTERS

God, violent, proud, b.....Rom 1:30
lovers of money, b..........2 Ti 3:2

BOASTFUL

b shall not stand............. Ps 5:5
I was envious of the b..... Ps 73:3

BOASTING

Where is b then...............Rom 3:27
should make my b..........1 Co 9:15
you, great is my b..........2 Co 7:4
All such b is evil............Jas 4:16

BOASTS

Whoever falsely b.......... Prov 25:14

BODIES

valley of the dead b........ Jer 31:40
b a living sacrifice...........Rom 12:1
not know that your b......1 Co 6:15
also celestial b................1 Co 15:40
wives as their own b.......Eph 5:28
and chariots, and b......... Rev 18:13

BODILY

b form like a dove.......... Luke 3:22
b presence is weak.......... 2 Co 10:10
of the Godhead b........... Col 2:9
b exercise...................... 1 Ti 4:8

BODY

b clings to the ground......Ps 44:25
b is carved ivory............Song 5:14
b was wet with the dew... Dan 4:33
of the b is the eye...........Matt 6:22
those who kill the b........ Matt 10:28
this is My b................... Matt 26:26
and asked for the b........Matt 27:58
around his naked b..........Mark 14:51
of the temple of His b.....John 2:21
deliver me from this b..... Rom 7:24
redemption of our b........Rom 8:23
many members in one b....Rom 12:4
and the Lord for the b....1 Co 6:13
against his own b............1 Co 6:18
not know that your b......1 Co 6:19
glorify God in your b......1 Co 6:20
But I discipline my b.......1 Co 9:27
one bread and one b.......1 Co 10:17

BONES

b which is broken........... 1 Co 11:24
be guilty of the b............1 Co 11:27
For as the b is one..........1 Co 12:12
baptized into one b......... 1 Co 12:13
b is not one member....... 1 Co 12:14
are the b of Christ.......... 1 Co 12:27
though I give my b.........1 Co 13:3
It is sown a natural b...... 1 Co 15:44
both to God in one b...... Eph 2:16
be magnified in my b......Phil 1:20
in the b of His flesh........ Col 1:22
by putting off the b........ Col 2:11
and neglect of the b........ Col 2:23
were called in one b....... Col 3:15
b You have prepared.......Heb 10:5
the offering of the b........Heb 10:10
For as the b without.......Jas 2:26
our sins in His own b......1 Pe 2:24

BOILS

Job with painful b...........Job 2:7

BOLD

the righteous are b..........Prov 28:1
whatever anyone is b.......2 Co 11:21
are much more b............ Phil 1:14

BOLDLY

I may open my mouth b.. Eph 6:19
therefore come b............ Heb 4:16
So we may b say.............Heb 13:6

BOLDNESS

Great is my b of.............2 Co 7:4
in whom we have b........Eph 3:12
but that with all b..........Phil 1:20
standing and great b.......1 Ti 3:13
brethren, having b..........Heb 10:19
that we may have b........1 Jn 4:17

BOND

bring you into the b........Ezek 20:37
of the Spirit in the b....... Eph 4:3
love, which is the b.........Col 3:14

BONDAGE

because of the b.............. Ex 2:23
out of the house of b......Ex 13:14
the spirit of b................. Rom 8:15
might bring us into b....... Gal 2:4
which gives birth to b......Gal 4:24
again with a yoke of b..... Gal 5:1
lifetime subject to b........ Heb 2:15
he is brought into b.........2 Pe 2:19

BONDS

Let us break Their b...... Ps 2:3

BONDWOMAN

"Cast out this b..............Gen 21:10
the one by a b................Gal 4:22

BONE

"This is now b................Gen 2:23
b clings to my skin..........Job 19:20
bones came together, b....Ezek 37:7

BONES

shall carry up my b..........Gen 50:25
which made all my b........ Job 4:14
His b are like beams....... Job 40:18
I can count all My b........Ps 22:17
And my b waste away...... Ps 31:10
I kept silent, my b.......... Ps 32:3
the wind, or how the b.... Eccl 11:5
say to them, 'O dry b.....: Ezek 37:4

b are the whole house..... Ezek 37:11
of dead men's *b*.............. Matt 23:27
b shall be broken............ John 19:36
concerning his *b*.............. Heb 11:22

BOOK
you will find in the *b*....... Ezra 4:15
distinctly from the *b*........ Neh 8:8
were inscribed in a *b*....... Job 19:23
"Search from the *b*......... Is 34:16
'Write in a *b* for............. Jer 30:2
found written in the *b*..... Dan 12:1
so a *b* of remembrance.... Mal 3:16
are written in the *b*........ Gal 3:10
sprinkled both the *b*........ Heb 9:19
in the Lamb's *B*............. Rev 21:27
the prophecy of this *b*..... Rev 22:18
the words of the *b*......... Rev 22:19

BOOKS
b there is no end............ Eccl 12:12
not contain the *b*........... John 21:25
magic brought their *b*..... Acts 19:19
God, and *b* were opened.. Rev 20:12

BOOTH
b which a watchman........ Job 27:18
of Zion is left as a *b*...... Is 1:8

BORDERS
and enlarge your *b*......... Ex 34:24
makes peace in your *b*..... Ps 147:14
and enlarge the *b*.......... Matt 23:5

BORE
conceived and *b* Cain...... Gen 4:1
and to Sarah who *b*....... Is 51:2
b the sin of many........... Is 53:12
and He *b* them and........ Is 63:9
b our sicknesses............ Matt 8:17
who Himself *b* our sins.... 1 Pe 2:24
b a male Child who was... Rev 12:5

BORN
"Every son who is *b*....... Ex 1:22
yet man is *b* to............. Job 5:7
"Man who is *b*............. Job 14:1
'This one was *b*........... Ps 87:4
A time to be *b*............ Eccl 3:2
unto us a Child is *b*...... Is 9:6
Or shall a nation be *b*..... Is 66:8
b Jesus who is called...... Matt 1:16
"For there is *b*............ Luke 2:11
unless one is *b* again...... John 3:3
"That which is *b*.......... John 3:6
For this cause I was *b*..... John 18:37
me also, as by one *b*...... 1 Co 15:8
of the bondwoman was *b*. Gal 4:23
having been *b* again........ 1 Pe 1:23
who loves is *b* of God..... 1 Jn 4:7
is the Christ is *b*........... 1 Jn 5:1
know that whoever is *b*.... 1 Jn 5:18

BORNE
And as we have *b*.......... 1 Co 15:49

BORROWER
b is servant to the.......... Prov 22:7
lender, so with the *b*...... Is 24:2

BORROWS
The wicked *b* and does.... Ps 37:21

BOSOM
man take fire to his *b*..... Prov 6:27
consolation of her *b*....... Is 66:11

angels to Abraham's *b*..... Luke 16:22
Son, who is in the *b*....... John 1:18
leaning on Jesus' *b*......... John 13:23

BOTTOMLESS
given the key to the *b*..... Rev 9:1
ascend out of the *b*........ Rev 17:8
the key to the *b*........... Rev 20:1

BOUGHS
cedars with its *b*............ Ps 80:10
She sent out her *b*......... Ps 80:11

BOUGHT
the hand of him who *b*.... Lev 25:28
not your Father, who *b*.... Deut 32:6
b the threshing floor........ 2 Sa 24:24
b the field from............. Jer 32:9
all that he had and *b*...... Matt 13:46
For you were *b* at a....... 1 Co 6:20
denying the Lord who *b*... 2 Pe 2:1

BOUND
of the wicked have *b*...... Ps 119:61
b the waters in a........... Prov 30:4
not been closed or *b*....... Is 1:6
on earth will be *b*......... Matt 16:19
b hand and foot with...... John 11:44
And see, now I go *b*...... Acts 20:22
of Israel I am *b*............ Acts 28:20
who has a husband is *b*... Rom 7:2
Are you *b* to a wife........ 1 Co 7:27
Devil and Satan, and *b*.... Rev 20:2

BOUNDARY
b that they may not......... Ps 104:9

BOUNTIFUL
b eye will be blessed....... Prov 22:9
the miser said to be *b*..... Is 32:5
you into a *b* country........ Jer 2:7

BOUNTIFULLY
Because He has dealt *b*.... Ps 13:6
and he who sows *b*......... 2 Co 9:6

BOW
b remained in strength..... Gen 49:24
"You shall not *b*........... Ex 23:24
to serve them and *b*....... Judg 2:19
b is renewed in my......... Job 29:20
will not trust in my *b*...... Ps 44:6
He breaks the *b*............ Ps 46:9
like a deceitful *b*.......... Ps 78:57
let us worship and *b*...... Ps 95:6
B down Your heavens..... Ps 144:5
not save them by *b*........ Hos 1:7
who sat on it had a *b*...... Rev 6:2

BOWED
stood all around and *b*..... Gen 37:7
b the heavens also.......... 2 Sa 22:10
whose knees have not *b*... 1 Ki 19:18
They have *b* down and.... Ps 38:6
And they *b* the knee....... Matt 27:29
men who have not *b*....... Rom 11:4

BOWL
his hand in the *b*.......... Prov 19:24
or the golden *b*........... Eccl 12:6
and poured out his *b*...... Rev 16:2

BOWLS
who drink wine from *b*.... Amos 6:6
a harp, and golden *b*...... Rev 5:8
Go and pour out the *b*.... Rev 16:1
who had the seven *b*...... Rev 21:9

BOWS
"The *b* of the mighty....... 1 Sa 2:4

BOX
Judas had the money *b*.... John 13:29

BOYS
shall be full of *b*........... Zech 8:5

BRAIDED
not with *b* hair or.......... 1 Ti 2:9

BRAMBLE
gather grapes from a *b*..... Luke 6:44

BRANCH
blossoms on one *b*......... Ex 25:33
b will not be green......... Job 15:32
from Israel, palm *b*........ Is 9:14
B shall grow out of........ Is 11:1
raise to David a *B*......... Jer 23:5
grow up to David a *B*..... Jer 33:15
forth My Servant the *B*.... Zech 3:8
whose name is the *B*...... Zech 6:12
b has already become...... Matt 24:32
b that bears fruit He...... John 15:2
b cannot bear fruit......... John 15:4
he is cast out as a *b*....... John 15:6

BRANCHES
in the sun, and his *b*...... Job 8:16
and bring forth *b*.......... Job 14:9
and cut down the *b*........ Is 18:5
and its *b* are broken....... Jer 11:16
His *b* shall spread.......... Hos 14:6
vine, you are the *b*........ John 15:5
b were broken off.......... Rom 11:17

BRASS
become as sounding *b*..... 1 Co 13:1
feet were like fine *b*....... Rev 1:15

BRAVE
in the faith, be *b*.......... 1 Co 16:13

BREACHES
Heal its *b*.................. Ps 60:2

BREAD
face you shall eat *b*........ Gen 3:19
of Salem brought out *b*.... Gen 14:18
Behold, I will rain *b*...... Ex 16:4
shall eat unleavened *b*..... Ex 23:15
not live by *b* alone......... Deut 8:3
lives, but of half have *b*... 1 Ki 17:12
new wine, a land of *b*..... 2 Ki 18:32
that his life abhors *b*...... Job 33:20
people as they eat *b*....... Ps 14:4
Can He give *b* also........ Ps 78:20
up late, To eat the *b*...... Ps 127:2
her poor with *b*........... Ps 132:15
For they eat the *b*......... Prov 4:17
b eaten in secret is........ Prov 9:17
B gained by deceit is...... Prov 20:17
Go, eat your *b* with....... Eccl 9:7
Cast your *b* upon the..... Eccl 11:1
b will be given him........ Is 33:16
for what is not *b*.......... Is 55:2
to share your *b*............ Is 58:7
We get our *b* at the...... Lam 5:9
who give me my *b*........ Hos 2:5
For their *b* shall be....... Hos 9:4
and lack of *b* in all........ Amos 4:6
these stones become *b*.... Matt 4:3
not live by *b* alone......... Matt 4:4
this day our daily *b*....... Matt 6:11

BREADTH

eating, Jesus took *b*.........Matt 26:26
no bag, no *b*.................. Mark 6:8
is he who shall eat *b*...... Luke 14:15
gives you the true *b*........ John 6:32
"I am the *b* of life......... John 6:48
having dipped the *b*........John 13:26
b which we break............1 Co 10:16
He was betrayed took *b*...1 Co 11:23
as you eat this *b*............ 1 Co 11:26
did we eat anyone's *b*......2 Th 3:8
and eat their own *b*........2 Th 3:12

BREADTH

is as great as its *b*........... Rev 21:16

BREAK

b their bones and............Num 24:8
torment my soul, and *b*...Job 19:2
They *b* up my path.......... Job 30:13
B their teeth in their....... Ps 58:6
And now they *b* down..... Ps 74:6
b My statutes And do......Ps 89:31
covenant I will not *b*...... Ps 89:34
Remember, do not *b*.......Jer 14:21
together to *b* bread........ Acts 20:7

BREAKING

in the *b* of bread............ Acts 2:42
b bread from house to..... Acts 2:46
weeping and *b* my heart...Acts 21:13
dishonor God through *b*...Rom 2:23

BREAKS

He *b* in pieces mighty......Job 34:24
My soul *b* with longing.... Ps 119:20
Until the day *b*.............Song 2:17
"Whoever therefore *b*......Matt 5:19

BREAST

back on Jesus' *b*............. John 13:25

BREASTPLATE

a *b*, an ephod.................Ex 28:4
righteousness as a *b*.........Is 59:17
having put on the *b*.........Eph 6:14

BREASTS

blessings of the *b*........... Gen 49:25
on My mother's *b*........... Ps 22:9
doe, let her *b* satisfy.......Prov 5:19
Your two *b* are like........Song 4:5
b which nursed You........ Luke 11:27
done, beat their *b*.......... Luke 23:48

BREATH

nostrils the *b* of life........Gen 2:7
at the blast of the *b*...... 2 Sa 22:16
that there was no *b*....... 1 Ki 17:17
perish, and by the *b*......Job 4:9
as long as my *b*............. Job 27:3
has made me, and the *b*...Job 33:4
You take away their *b*..... Ps 104:29
Man is like a *b*............. Ps 144:4
everything that has *b*...... Ps 150:6
they all have one *b*........ Eccl 3:19
from it, Who gives *b*...... Is 42:5
Surely I will cause *b*.......Ezek 37:5
God who holds your *b*....Dan 5:23
gives to all life, *b*..........Acts 17:25
consume with the *b*........ 2 Th 2:8
power to give *b*.............. Rev 13:15

BREATHE

me, And such as *b*.........Ps 27:12
winds, O breath, and *b*....Ezek 37:9

BREATHES

indeed he *b* his last........Job 14:10

BRETHREN

presence of all his *b*........ Gen 16:12
be lifted above his *b*.......Deut 17:20
and you are all *b*............ Matt 23:8
least of these My *b*........ Matt 25:40
Go and tell My *b*..........Matt 28:10
firstborn among many *b*... Rom 8:29
to judge between his *b*....1 Co 6:5
thus sin against the *b*.......1 Co 8:12
over five hundred *b*.......1 Co 15:6
perils among false *b*........ 2 Co 11:26
b secretly brought...........Gal 2:4
to be made like His *b*.....Heb 2:17
sincere love of the *b*.......1 Pe 1:22
because we love the *b*.....1 Jn 3:14
our lives for the *b*...........1 Jn 3:16
does not receive the *b*..... 3 Jn 10
of your *b* the prophets.....Rev 22:9

BRIBE

you shall take no *b*......... Ex 23:8
b blinds the eyes.............Deut 16:19
b debases the heart........ Eccl 7:7

BRIBERY

consume the tents of *b*....Job 15:34

BRIBES

hand is full of *b*..............Ps 26:10
but he who hates *b*........ Prov 15:27
but he who receives *b*.....Prov 29:4
Everyone loves *b*............ Is 1:23
the just and take *b*......... Amos 5:12

BRICK

people straw to make *b*...Ex 5:7
incense on altars of *b*..... Is 65:3
Make strong the *b*..........Nah 3:14

BRICKS

"Come, let us make *b*..... Gen 11:3
b which they made......... Ex 5:8
deliver the quota of *b*......Ex 5:18
b have fallen down..........Is 9:10

BRIDE

them on you as a *b*........ Is 49:18
"He who has the *b*..........John 3:29
I will show you the *b*.......Rev 21:9
the Spirit and the *b*........Rev 22:17

BRIDEGROOM

righteousness, as a *b*........Is 61:10
and as the *b* rejoices....... Is 62:5
mourn as long as the *b*... Matt 9:15
b will be taken away....... Matt 9:15
went out to meet the *b*.. Matt 25:1
b fast while the.............Mark 2:19
the friend of the *b*......... John 3:29

BRIDLE

with bit and *b*............... Ps 32:9
b the whole body............Jas 3:2

BRIER

b shall come up the........Is 55:13
longer be a pricking *b*.....Ezek 28:24
of them is like a *b*......... Mic 7:4

BRIERS

there shall come up *b*...... Is 5:6
their words, though *b*...... Ezek 2:6

BRIGHTNESS

From the *b* before Him....2 Sa 22:13
and kings to the *b*...........Is 60:3
goes forth as *b*............... Is 62:1
very dark, with no *b*........Amos 5:20
who being the *b*..............Heb 1:3

BRIMSTONE

Then the LORD rained *b*. Gen 19:24
B is scattered on his.......Job 18:15
fire, smoke, and *b*...........Rev 9:17
the lake of fire and *b*..... Rev 20:10

BRING

LORD your God will *b*.... Deut 30:3
b back his soul.............. Job 33:30
For they *b* down.............Ps 55:3
Lord said, "I will *b*......... Ps 68:22
B forth your...................Is 41:21
b forth justice.................Is 42:3
b My righteousness..........Is 46:13
Though they *b* up their....Hos 9:12
"And she will *b*.............Matt 1:21
b no fruit to maturity...... Luke 8:14
b this Man's blood.......... Acts 5:28
Who shall *b* a charge......Rom 8:33
b Christ down from.........Rom 10:6
b Christ up from the.......Rom 10:7
even so God will *b*..........1 Th 4:14

BROAD

set me in a *b* place..........Ps 118:5
b is the way that.............Matt 7:13
their phylacteries *b*..........Matt 23:5

BROKE

b them at the foot of......Ex 32:19
b open the fountain.........Ps 74:15
covenant which they *b*.....Jer 31:32
He blessed and *b*........... Matt 14:19
b the flask and poured.....Mark 14:3
b the legs of the............. John 19:32

BROKEN

he has *b* My covenant......Gen 17:14
I am like a *b* vessel.........Ps 31:12
their bows shall be *b*...... Ps 37:15
He has *b* his covenant.... Ps 55:20
heart the spirit is *b*..........Prov 15:13
b spirit dries the.............Prov 17:22
but who can bear a *b*...... Prov 18:14
in the staff of this *b*........Is 36:6
heart within me is *b*........Jer 23:9
is oppressed and *b*.......... Hos 5:11
this stone shall be *b*........Matt 21:44
Scripture cannot be *b*......John 10:35
is My body which is *b*......1 Co 11:24
vessels shall be b.............Rev 2:27

BROKEN-HEARTED

He heals the *b* And.........Ps 147:3

BRONZE

So Moses made a *b*.........Num 21:9
your head shall be *b*.......Deut 28:23
b serpent that Moses....... 2 Ki 18:4
Or is my flesh *b*............. Job 6:12
b as rotten wood.............Job 41:27
broken the gates of *b*...... Ps 107:16
b I will bring.................Is 60:13
b walls against the..........Jer 1:18
people a fortified *b*......... Jer 15:20
a third kingdom of *b*...... Dan 2:39
make your hooves *b*........Mic 4:13
were mountains of *b*.......Zech 6:1

BROOD

The *b* of evildoers...........Is 14:20
"*B* of vipers..................Matt 12:34
as a hen gathers her *b*.....Luke 13:34

BROOK

stones from the *b*...........1 Sa 17:40
shall drink of the *b*.........Ps 110:7
disciples over the *B*.........John 18:1

BROOKS

good land, a land of *b*.....Deut 8:7
b that pass away.............Job 6:15
for the water *b*...............Ps 42:1

BROTHER

Where is Abel your *b*.....Gen 4:9
he were my friend or *b*....Ps 35:14
speak against your *b*.......Ps 50:20
and a *b* is born for.........Prov 17:17
b offended is harder........Prov 18:19
has neither son nor *b*.....Eccl 4:8
and do not trust any *b*....Jer 9:4
he pursued his *b*............Amos 1:11
Was not Esau Jacob's *b*... Mal 1:2
b will deliver up............Matt 10:21
how often shall my *b*......Matt 18:21
"Teacher, tell my *b*........Luke 12:13
b will rise again............John 11:23
do you judge your *b*.......Rom 14:10
b goes to law against.......1 Co 6:6
shall the weak *b*............1 Co 8:11
slave, as a beloved *b*.......Phm 16
He who loves his *b*.........1 Jn 2:10
and murdered his *b*.........1 Jn 3:12
Whoever hates his *b*.......1 Jn 3:15
b sinning a sin which........1 Jn 5:16
I, John, both your *b*........Rev 1:9

BROTHER'S

Am I my *b* keeper..........Gen 4:9
at the speck in your *b*.....Matt 7:3

BROTHERHOOD

the covenant of *b*...........Amos 1:9
I might break the *b*.........Zech 11:14
Love the *b*....................1 Pe 2:17
experienced by your *b*.....1 Pe 5:9

BROTHERLY

to one another with *b*......Rom 12:10
b love continue...............Heb 13:1

BROTHERS

My *b* have dealt..............Job 6:15
a stranger to my *b*..........Ps 69:8
is My mother, or My *b*....Mark 3:33
b are these who hear.......Luke 8:21
b did not believe.............John 7:5
love as *b*.......................1 Pe 3:8

BROUGHT

He *b* out His people.......Ps 105:43
The king has *b* me into....Song 1:4

BRUISE

He shall *b* your head......Gen 3:15
LORD binds up the *b*......Is 30:26
the LORD to *b* Him........Is 53:10

BRUISED

b reed He will not..........Is 42:3
He was *b* for our..........Is 53:5
b reed He will not.........Matt 12:20

BRUTAL

b men who are...............Ezek 21:31

BUCKLER

be your shield and *b*........Ps 91:4

BUD

it bring forth and *b*.........Is 55:10

BUFFET

of Satan to *b* me.............2 Co 12:7

BUILD

b ourselves a city............Gen 11:4
"Would you *b* a house.....2 Sa 7:5
b a house for the name....1 Ki 8:17
that the LORD will *b*......1 Ch 17:10
Solomon who shall *b*...... 1 Ch 28:6
able to *b* Him a temple...2 Ch 2:6
labor in vain who *b*........Ps 127:1
down, and a time to *b*....Eccl 3:3
house that you will *b*......Is 66:1
I will *b* them and not......Jer 24:6
Who *b* up Zion with........Mic 3:10
b the desolate.................Mal 1:4
'This man began to *b*......Luke 14:30
What house will you *b*....Acts 7:49
b you up and give you.....Acts 20:32
named, lest I should *b*.....Rom 15:20
"For if I *b* again............Gal 2:18

BUILDER

me, as a wise master *b*.... 1 Co 3:10
foundations, whose *b*.......Heb 11:10

BUILDING

field, you are God's *b*......1 Co 3:9
destroyed, we have a *b*....2 Co 5:1
in whom the whole *b*......Eph 2:21
But you, beloved, *b*........ Jude 20

BUILDS

The LORD *b* up............ Ps 147:2
Every wise woman *b*.......Prov 14:1
one take heed how he *b*...1 Co 3:10

BUILT

Wisdom has *b* her house.. Prov 9:1
my works great, I *b*.......Eccl 2:4
Babylon, that I have *b*.....Dan 4:30
to a wise man who *b*.......Matt 7:24
a foolish man who *b*........Matt 7:26
work which he has *b*.......1 Co 3:14
having been *b* on the.......Eph 2:20
rooted and *b* up in Him...Col 2:7
For every house is *b*........Heb 3:4
stones, are being *b*..........1 Pe 2:5

BULL

I will not take a *b*..........Ps 50:9
like an untrained *b*.........Jer 31:18

BULLS

in the blood of *b*............ Is 1:11
For if the blood of *b*.......Heb 9:13

BULWARKS

Mark well her *b*.............Ps 48:13
for walls and *b*...............Is 26:1

BURDEN

You have laid the *b*........Num 11:11
one knows his own *b*......2 Ch 6:29
so that I am a *b*.............Job 7:20
Cast your *b* on the.........Ps 55:22
the grasshopper is a *b*......Eccl 12:5
in that day that his *b*......Is 10:27
its reproach is a *b*..........Zeph 3:18

BURY

easy and My *b* is light..... Matt 11:30
as it may, I did not *b*......2 Co 12:16
we might not be a *b*........1 Th 2:9
on you no other *b*...........Rev 2:24

BURDENED

but you have *b* Me with...Is 43:24

BURDENS

and looked at their *b*.......Ex 2:11
For they bind heavy *b*..... Matt 23:4
Bear one another's *b*.......Gal 6:2

BURDENSOME

his life will be *b*.............Is 15:4
I myself was not *b*..........2 Co 12:13
commandments are not *b*. 1 Jn 5:3

BURIAL

indeed he has no *b*.........Eccl 6:3
she did it for My *b*.........Matt 26:12
for the day of My *b*........John 12:7
Stephen to his *b*............. Acts 8:2

BURIED

and there will I be *b*....... Ruth 1:17
I saw the wicked *b*.........Eccl 8:10
away the body and *b*......Matt 14:12
also died and was *b*........Luke 16:22
Therefore we were *b*.......Rom 6:4
and that He was *b*.......... 1 Co 15:4
b with Him in baptism.....Col 2:12

BURN

the bush does not *b*.........Ex 3:3
that My wrath may *b*.......Ex 32:10
b their chariots...............Josh 11:6
both will *b* together.........Is 1:31
"Did not our heart *b*.......Luke 24:32
eat her flesh and *b*..........Rev 17:16

BURNED

If anyone's work is *b*.......1 Co 3:15
I give my body to be *b*....1 Co 13:3
whose end is to be *b*.......Heb 6:8
be touched and that *b*......Heb 12:18
are *b* outside the camp....Heb 13:11
in it will be *b*.................2 Pe 3:10
all green grass was *b*....... Rev 8:7

BURNING

b torch that passed..........Gen 15:17
with severe *b* fever..........Deut 28:22
on his lips like a *b*..........Prov 16:27
b fire shut up in my........Jer 20:9
b jealousy against the......Ezek 36:5
plucked from the *b*..........Amos 4:11
a great mountain *b*..........Rev 8:8
fell from heaven, *b*..........Rev 8:10

BURNT

lamb for a *b* offering.......Gen 22:7
delight in *b* offering.........Ps 51:16
b offerings are not..........Jer 6:20
Though you offer Me *b*....Amos 5:22

BURST

it is ready to *b*...............Job 32:19
with doors, when it *b*......Job 38:8
the new wine will *b*........Luke 5:37
falling headlong, he *b*.......Acts 1:18

BURY

b your dead in the..........Gen 23:6
was no one to *b* them......Ps 79:3
go and *b* my father.........Matt 8:21
and let the dead *b*..........Matt 8:22

BUSH

from the midst of a *b*...... Ex 3:2
Him who dwelt in the *b*... Deut 33:16
to him in the *b*.............. Acts 7:35

BUSINESS

in ships, Who do *b*..........Ps 107:23
farm, another to his *b*......Matt 22:5
about My Father's *b*........Luke 2:49

BUSYBODIES

at all, but are *b*.............. 2 Th 3:11
but also gossips and *b*...... 1 Ti 5:13

BUTLER

b did not remember........ Gen 40:23

BUTTER

So he took *b* and milk..... Gen 18:8
were smoother than *b*...... Ps 55:21
of milk produces *b*.......... Prov 30:33

BUY

in Egypt to *b* grain..........Gen 41:57
B the truth.................... Prov 23:23
Yes, come, *b* wine and... Is 55:1
that we may *b* the poor... Amos 8:6
b food for all these.......... Luke 9:13
B those things we.......... John 13:29
rejoice, those who *b*..........1 Co 7:30
spend a year there, *b*........Jas 4:13
"I counsel you to *b*........ Rev 3:18
and that no one may *b*.... Rev 13:17

BUYER

nothing," cries the *b*.......Prov 20:14
as with the *b*.................. Is 24:2
'Let not the *b*..................Ezek 7:12

BUYS

a field and *b* it.............. Prov 31:16
has and *b* that field........ Matt 13:44
b their merchandise........ Rev 18:11

BYWORD

But He has made me a *b*.Job 17:6
You make us a *b*............ Ps 44:14

— C —

CAGE

c is full of birds.............. Jer 5:27
foul spirit, and a *c*......... Rev 18:2

CAKE

Ephraim is a *c*.................Hos 7:8

CAKES

Sustain me with *c*..........Song 2:5
and love the raisin *c*........Hos 3:1

CALAMITIES

refuge, Until these *c*........Ps 57:1

CALAMITY

for the day of their *c*.......Deut 32:35
will laugh at your *c*......... Prov 1:26
c shall come suddenly...... Prov 6:15
If there is *c* in a............ Amos 3:6

CALCULATED

c the dust of the............. Is 40:12

CALDRON

this city is the *c*.............. Ezek 11:3

CALF

and made a molded *c*...... Ex 32:4
They made a *c* in Horeb.. Ps 106:19
is, than a fatted *c*...........Prov 15:17
like a stubborn *c*.............Hos 4:16
Your *c* is rejected........... Hos 8:5
And bring the fatted *c*..... Luke 15:23
creature like a *c*..............Rev 4:7

CALL

I will *c* to the LORD....... 1 Sa 12:17
c their lands after............Ps 49:11
To you, O men, I *c*.........Prov 8:4
c upon Him while He...... Is 55:6
'C to Me........................ Jer 33:3
Arise, *c* on your God....... Jon 1:6
They will *c* on My name.. Zech 13:9
c His name JESUS......... Matt 1:21
c the righteous................Matt 9:13
Lord our God will *c*.........Acts 2:39
c them My people............Rom 9:25
then shall they *c*............. Rom 10:14
For God did not *c*...........1 Th 4:7

CALLED

c the light Day............... Gen 1:5
c his wife's name Eve......Gen 3:20
"I, the LORD, have *c*......Is 42:6
I have *c* you by your....... Is 43:1
The LORD has *c* Me ......Is 49:1
and out of Egypt I *c*........Hos 11:1
"Out of Egypt I *c*......... Matt 2:15
and dwelt in a city *c*.......Matt 2:23
For many are *c*...............Matt 20:16
to those who are the *c*.... Rom 8:28
these He also *c*...............Rom 8:30
But God has *c* us to........ 1 Co 7:15
praises of Him who *c*.......1 Pe 2:9
knowledge of Him who *c*. 2 Pe 1:3
that we should be *c*.........1 Jn 3:1

CALLING

the gifts and the *c*.......... Rom 11:29
For you see your *c*.......... 1 Co 1:26
remain in the same *c*.......1 Co 7:20
a walk worthy of the *c*....Eph 4:1
in one hope of your *c*......Eph 4:4
us with a holy *c*.............. 2 Ti 1:9
of the heavenly *c*............ Heb 3:1
to make your *c* and........2 Pe 1:10

CALLS

c them all by name......... Ps 147:4
there is no one who *c*...... Is 64:7
David himself *c*.............. Mark 12:37
c his own sheep.............. John 10:3
For "whoever *c*...............Rom 10:13

CALM

the sea will become *c*...... Jon 1:12
there was a great *c*......... Matt 8:26

CALMED

Surely I have *c*............... Ps 131:2

CALVES

counsel and made two *c*... 1 Ki 12:28
their cow *c* without......... Job 21:10
like stall-fed *c*.................Mal 4:2
blood of goats and *c*........Heb 9:12
he took the blood of *c*..... Heb 9:19

CAMEL

it is easier for a *c*...........Matt 19:24
and swallow a *c*.............. Matt 23:24

CAMP

"This is God's *c*.............Gen 32:2
who went before the *c*..... Ex 14:19
to Him, outside the *c*...... Heb 13:13

CAN

I *c* do all things.............. Phil 4:13

CANCER

will spread like *c*.............2 Ti 2:17

CANE

bought Me no sweet *c*..... Is 43:24
Sheba, and sweet *c*..........Jer 6:20

CANOPIES

He made darkness *c*........ 2 Sa 22:12

CANOPY

His *c* around Him was..... Ps 18:11

CAPSTONE

bring forth the *c*............. Zech 4:7

CAPTAIN

which, having no *c*..........Prov 6:7

CAPTIVE

have led captivity *c*........ Ps 68:18
of your neck, O *c*........... Is 52:2
they shall now go *c*........ Amos 6:7
and be led away *c*...........Luke 21:24
He led captivity *c*...........Eph 4:8

CAPTIVES

will bring back the *c*.......Amos 9:14
and return their *c*...........Zeph 2:7
households and make *c*.... 2 Ti 3:6

CAPTIVITY

bring you back from *c*..... Deut 30:3
high, You have led......Ps 68:18
Judah has gone into *c*...... Lam 1:3
from David until the *c*..... Matt 1:17
and bringing me into *c*.....Rom 7:23
every thought into *c*........ 2 Co 10:5
on high, He led *c*............Eph 4:8
shall go into *c*................ Rev 13:10

CARCASS

honey were in the *c*........Judg 14:8
For wherever the *c*..........Matt 24:28

CARE

"Lord, do You not *c*.......Luke 10:40
you to be without *c*........1 Co 7:32
who will sincerely *c*........ Phil 2:20
how will he take *c*.......... 1 Ti 3:5
casting all your *c*............1 Pe 5:7

CARED

he said, not that he *c*...... John 12:6

CARELESS

but he who is *c*...............Prov 19:16

CARES

No one *c* for my soul...... Ps 142:4
and are choked with *c*.... Luke 8:14
He who is unmarried *c*.... 1 Co 7:32
for He *c* for you............. 1 Pe 5:7

CARNAL

spiritual, but I am *c*........ Rom 7:14
c mind is enmity............. Rom 8:7
for you are still *c*............ 1 Co 3:3
our warfare are not *c*.......2 Co 10:4

CARNALLY
we may know them c.......Gen 19:5
that we may know him c..Judg 19:22
c minded is death............Rom 8:6

CAROUSE
count it pleasure to c.......2 Pe 2:13

CAROUSING
be weighed down with c...Luke 21:34

CARPENTER
"Is this not the c............ Mark 6:3

CARRIED
the LORD your God c.....Deut 1:31
and c our sorrows........... Is 53:4
parted from them and c...Luke 24:51
c me away in the............ Rev 17:3

CARRY
their hands cannot c........Job 5:12
c them away like a.........Ps 90:5
I am not worthy to c........Matt 3:11
for you to c your bed.....John 5:10
it is certain we can c....... 1 Ti 6:7

CARRYING
a man will meet you c.... Mark 14:13
always c about in the.......2 Co 4:10

CASE
c that is too hard............ Deut 1:17
I have prepared my c...... Job 13:18
I would present my c.......Job 23:4
"Present your c.............. Is 41:21
Festus laid Paul's c.........Acts 25:14

CASSIA
myrrh and aloes and c..... Ps 45:8

CAST
When they c you down.... Job 22:29
c away Their.................. Ps 2:3
Why are you c down........ Ps 42:5
But You have c us off...... Ps 44:9
c me away from Your......Ps 51:11
He c on them the........... Ps 78:49
the LORD will not c........Ps 94:14
me up and c me away......Ps 102:10
and the earth shall c........Is 26:19
My sight, as I have c.......Jer 7:15
C away from you all........Ezek 18:31
brought Daniel and c.......Dan 6:16
Israel has c off the.........Hos 8:3
c all our sins into............Mic 7:19
whole body to be c........ Matt 5:29
the kingdom will be c..... Matt 8:12
spirits, to c them out.......Matt 10:1
In My name they will c....Mark 16:17
I will by no means c.......John 6:37
c away His people...........Rom 11:1
c away your confidence.... Heb 10:35
c their crowns before.......Rev 4:10
the great dragon was c....Rev 12:9

CASTING
nation which I am c........ Lev 20:23
Andrew his brother, c......Matt 4:18
c down arguments........... 2 Co 10:5
c all your care............... 1 Pe 5:7

CASTS
"And if Satan c.............. Matt 12:26
but perfect love c............1 Jn 4:18

CATCH
in wait to c the poor....... Ps 10:9
c Him in His words........Mark 12:13
down your nets for a c.....Luke 5:4
From now on you will c...Luke 5:10

CATCHES
and the wolf c the...........John 10:12
c the wise in their.......... 1 Co 3:19

CATERPILLAR
their crops to the c..........Ps 78:46

CATTLE
c you shall take as.......... Josh 8:2
does not let their c..........Ps 107:38

CAUGHT
behind him was a ram c...Gen 22:13
and that night they c.......John 21:3
Spirit of the Lord c.........Acts 8:39
And her Child was c.......Rev 12:5

CAUSE
I would commit my c.......Job 5:8
my enemy without c.........Ps 7:4
hate me without a c........Ps 35:19
c His face to shine......... Ps 67:1
C me to know the way.... Ps 143:8
one to plead his c........... Prov 18:17
God, Who pleads the c....Is 51:22
He judged the c.............Jer 22:16
brother without a c.........Matt 5:22
hated Me without a c......John 15:25
For this c I was born.......John 18:37

CAVES
the people hid in c..........1 Sa 13:6
rocks, and into the........ Is 2:19
in dens and c of the........ Heb 11:38

CEASE
and night shall not c........Gen 8:22
Why should the work c....Neh 6:3
There the wicked c.........Job 3:17
He makes wars c............ Ps 46:9
C listening to................. Prov 19:27
C to do evil.................. Is 1:16
tongues, they will c......... 1 Co 13:8
do not c to give.............Eph 1:16
do not c to pray for........ Col 1:9

CEASED
c building the city........... Gen 11:8
the sea, and the sea c......Jon 1:15

CEASES
for the godly man c.........Ps 12:1

CEASING
c your work of faith........ 1 Th 1:3
thank God without c....... 1 Th 2:13
pray without c................ 1 Th 5:17

CEDAR
dwell in a house of c.......2 Sa 7:2
He shall grow like a c......Ps 92:12
of our houses are c.........Song 1:17
it, paneling it with c........Jer 22:14
Indeed Assyria was a c....Ezek 31:3

CEDARS
the LORD breaks the c....Ps 29:5
c of Lebanon which He....Ps 104:16

CELESTIAL
but the glory of the c...... 1 Co 15:40

CENSER
Aaron, each took his c.... Lev 10:1
Each man had a c...........Ezek 8:11
the angel took the c........ Rev 8:5

CERTIFICATE
a man to write a c.......... Mark 10:4

CERTIFIED
His testimony has c.........John 3:33

CHAFF
c that a storm.................Job 21:18
c which the wind.............Ps 1:4
Let them be like c.........Ps 35:5
be chased like the c.........Is 17:13
You shall conceive c.......Is 33:11
the day passes like c.......Zeph 2:2
He will burn up the c......Matt 3:12

CHAIN
he has made my c...........Lam 3:7
pit and a great c.............Rev 20:1

CHAINED
of God is not c................2 Ti 2:9
the prisoners as if c.........Heb 13:3

CHAINS
their kings with c............Ps 149:8
your neck with c.............Song 1:10
And his c fell off...........Acts 12:7
am, except for these c.....Acts 26:29
Remember my c..............Col 4:18
minister to me in my c....Phm 13
delivered them into c.......2 Pe 2:4

CHAMBERLAIN
Blastus the king's c.........Acts 12:20

CHAMBERS
and the c of the south..... Job 9:9
brought me into his c...... Song 1:4
and his c by injustice.......Jer 22:13

CHAMPION
And a c went out from.... 1 Sa 17:4

CHANGE
c his countenance............Job 14:20
c the night into day........Job 17:12
and who can make Him c.Job 23:13
Because they do not c..... Ps 102:26
a cloak You will c.........Ps 102:26
with those given to c....... Prov 24:21
Can the Ethiopian c........Jer 13:23
c times and law.............. Dan 7:25
c their glory into............Hos 4:7
the LORD, I do not c.....Mal 3:6
now and to c my tone......Gal 4:20
there is also a c.............. Heb 7:12

CHANGED
But My people have c..... Jer 2:11
c the glory of the........... Rom 1:23
but we shall all be c........ 1 Co 15:51
the priesthood being c..... Heb 7:12

CHANGERS
and poured out the c.......John 2:15

CHANNELS
c of waters were seen...... Ps 18:15

CHARACTER
and c, hope...................Rom 5:4

CHARIOT
He took off their *c*..........Ex 14:25
that suddenly a *c*........... 2 Ki 2:11
makes the clouds His *c*... Ps 104:3
and overtake this *c*..........Acts 8:29

CHARIOTS
the clatter of his *c*...........Judg 5:28
Some trust in *c*...............Ps 20:7
The *c* of God are............Ps 68:17

CHARITABLE
you do not do your *c*.......Matt 6:1
"that your *c* deed............Matt 6:4
c deeds which she.......... Acts 9:36

CHARM
C is deceitful and............Prov 31:30

CHARMERS
heed the voice of *c*..........Ps 58:5

CHARMS
women who sew magic *c*.. Ezek 13:18

CHASE
Five of you shall *c*.......... Lev 26:8
How could one *c*............ Deut 32:30
angel of the LORD *c*....... Ps 35:5

CHASTE
may present you as a *c*... 2 Co 11:2
to be discreet, *c*..............Tit 2:5
c conduct accompanied.... 1 Pe 3:2

CHASTEN
C your son while there.... Prov 19:18
is My desire, I will *c*........Hos 10:10
a father does not *c*..........Heb 12:7
I love, I rebuke and *c*......Rev 3:19

CHASTENED
c my soul with fasting.....Ps 69:10
c every morning..............Ps 73:14
The LORD has *c* me....... Ps 118:18
In vain I have *c*...............Jer 2:30
c us as seemed best.........Heb 12:10

CHASTENING
have not seen the *c*........Deut 11:2
do not despise the *c*........Job 5:17
'I have borne *c*...............Job 34:31
a prayer when Your *c*...... Is 26:16
if you are without *c*........Heb 12:8
Now no *c* seems to be...... Heb 12:11

CHASTENS
the LORD loves He *c*.......Heb 12:6

CHASTISE
and I, even I, will *c*........ Lev 26:28
c them according.............Hos 7:12
I will therefore *c*............Luke 23:22

CHASTISEMENT
the *c* for our peace..........Is 53:5

CHATTER
c leads only to...............Prov 14:23

CHEAT
Beware lest anyone *c*.......Col 2:8

CHEEK
Let him give his *c*..........Lam 3:30
with a rod on the *c*........ Mic 5:1
on your right *c*.............. Matt 5:39

CHEEKBONE
my enemies on the *c*....... Ps 3:7

CHEEKS
c are lovely with............Song 1:10
His *c* are like a bed........Song 5:13
struck Me, and My *c*...... Is 50:6

CHEER
and let your heart *c*........Eccl 11:9
"Son, be of good *c*.........Matt 9:2

CHEERFUL
for God loves a *c*............2 Co 9:7
Is anyone *c*....................Jas 5:13

CHEERFULNESS
shows mercy, with *c*........ Rom 12:8

CHEESE
and curdle me like *c*.......Job 10:10

CHERISHES
but nourishes and *c*........ Eph 5:29
as a nursing mother *c*...... 1 Th 2:7

CHERUB
He rode upon a *c*........... 2 Sa 22:11

CHERUBIM
and He placed *c*............. Gen 3:24
dwell between the *c*........Ps 80:1
fire from among the *c*.....Ezek 10:2
above it were the *c*......... Heb 9:5

CHIEF
is white and ruddy, *c*.......Song 5:10
of whom I am *c*...............1 Ti 1:15
Zion a *c* cornerstone.......1 Pe 2:6
has become the *c*............1 Pe 2:7
C Shepherd appears........... 1 Pe 5:4

CHILD
Like a weaned *c*.............. Ps 131:2
c is known by his............Prov 20:11
Train up a *c* in the.........Prov 22:6
For unto us a *C*...............Is 9:6
c shall lead them.............Is 11:6
When Israel was a *c*.........Hos 11:1
virgin shall be with *c*....... Matt 1:23
He took a little *c*............Mark 9:36
of God as a little *c*..........Mark 10:15
kind of *c* will this be...... Luke 1:66
So the *c* grew and..........Luke 1:80
When I was a *c*............... 1 Co 13:11
And she bore a male *C*....Rev 12:5

CHILDBEARING
she will be saved in *c*...... 1 Ti 2:15

CHILDBIRTH
pain as a woman in *c*.......Is 13:8

CHILDHOOD
from your flesh, for *c*...... Eccl 11:10
And he said, "From *c*......Mark 9:21
c you have known...........2 Ti 3:15

CHILDLESS
give me, seeing I go *c*......Gen 15:2
this man down as *c*.........Jer 22:30

CHILDREN
she bore Jacob no *c*........ Gen 30:1
And all of you are *c*........Ps 82:6
c are a heritage.............. Ps 127:3

He has blessed your *c*......Ps 147:13
Let the *c* of Zion be........Ps 149:2
c are blessed after..........Prov 20:7
c rise up and call her......Prov 31:28
c are their oppressors...... Is 3:12
c whom the LORD has.... Is 8:18
be the peace of your *c*.....Is 54:13
they are My people, *c*......Is 63:8
the hearts of the *c*..........Mal 4:6
c will rise up against......Matt 10:21
and become as little *c*......Matt 18:3
c were brought to Him.... Matt 19:13
"Let the little *c*...............Matt 19:14
the right to become *c*...... John 1:12
you were Abraham's *c*.....John 8:39
spirit that we are *c*..........Rom 8:16
but as my beloved *c*........1 Co 4:14
Brethren, do not be *c*......1 Co 14:20
c ought not to lay up.......2 Co 12:14
and were by nature *c*.......Eph 2:3
should no longer be *c*...... Eph 4:14
Walk as *c* of light........... Eph 5:8
and harmless, *c*..............Phil 2:15
now we are *c* of God.......1 Jn 3:2
that we love the *c*...........1 Jn 5:2
to hear that my *c*............3 Jn 4

CHOOSE
therefore *c* life................Deut 30:19
c none of his ways......... Prov 3:31
evil and *c* the good.......... Is 7:15
will still *c* Israel.............. Is 14:1
will again *c* Jerusalem......Zech 1:17
"You did not *c*................John 15:16
yet what I shall *c*............Phil 1:22

CHOOSES
in the way He *c*..............Ps 25:12

CHOSE
a good while ago God *c*.. Acts 15:7
just as He *c* us in Him.... Eph 1:4
from the beginning *c*...... 2 Th 2:13

CHOSEN
of Jacob, His *c*...............1 Ch 16:13
people whom He has *c*... Ps 33:12
a covenant with My *c*...... Ps 89:3
c the way of truth........... Ps 119:30
servant whom I have *c*....Is 43:10
c that good part.............Luke 10:42
I know whom I have *c*.....John 13:18
c you that you should...... Acts 22:14
c the foolish things..........1 Co 1:27
Has God not *c* the poor...Jas 2:5
But you are a *c*.............. 1 Pe 2:9

CHRIST
genealogy of Jesus *C*....... Matt 1:1
Jesus who is called *C*.......Matt 1:16
"You are the *C*................ Matt 16:16
if You are the *C*..............Matt 26:63
a Savior, who is *C*.......... Luke 2:11
that He Himself is *C*........Luke 23:2
the law that the *C*...........John 12:34
he preached the *C*...........Acts 9:20
have the Spirit of *C*..........Rom 8:9
It is *C* who died.............. Rom 8:34
C did not please.............. Rom 15:3
Is *C* divided................... 1 Co 1:13
Him you are in *C* Jesus... 1 Co 1:30
to be justified by *C*..........Gal 2:17
been crucified with *C*......Gal 2:20
but *C* lives in me.............Gal 2:20
your Seed," who is *C*... Gal 3:16
before by God in *C*........Gal 3:17

CHRISTIAN (continued)

C may dwell in your........Eph 3:17
C will give you...............Eph 5:14
C is head of the..............Eph 5:23
to me, to live is C..........Phil 1:21
confess that Jesus C........Phil 2:11
through C who...............Phil 4:13
which is C in you............Col 1:27
C who is our..................Col 3:4
C is all and in all............Col 3:11
and men, the Man C...... 1 Ti 2:5
Jesus C is the same........Heb 13:8
C His Son cleanses us......1 Jn 1:7
that Jesus is the C..........1 Jn 5:1
of His C have come...... Rev 12:10
and reigned with C.........Rev 20:4

CHRISTIAN

me to become a C......... Acts 26:28
anyone suffers as a C...... 1 Pe 4:16

CHRISTIANS

were first called C...........Acts 11:26

CHRISTS

"For false c and..............Matt 24:24

CHURCH

rock I will build My c......Matt 16:18
them, tell it to the c........Matt 18:17
c daily those who were.... Acts 2:47
elders in every c.............. Acts 14:23
do you despise the c........1 Co 11:22
be made known by the c.. Eph 3:10
also loved the c.............. Eph 5:25
Himself a glorious c........ Eph 5:27
as the Lord does the c.... Eph 5:29
body, which is the c........ Col 1:24
and do not let the c........ 1 Ti 5:16
general assembly and c.... Heb 12:23
To the angel of the c......Rev 2:1

CHURCHES

strengthening the c.........Acts 15:41
The c of Christ greet...... Rom 16:16
imitators of the c............ 1 Th 2:14
John, to the seven c........ Rev 1:4
angels of the seven c...... Rev 1:20
these things in the c........ Rev 22:16

CHURNING

For as the c of milk........ Prov 30:33

CHURNS

My heart c within Me......Hos 11:8

CIRCLE

He walks above the c......Job 22:14
when He drew a c..........Prov 8:27
who sits above the c........Is 40:22

CIRCUIT

of heaven, And its c........Ps 19:6
comes again on its c........Eccl 1:6

CIRCUMCISE

c the foreskin of your...... Deut 10:16
LORD your God will c.... Deut 30:6
C yourselves to the.........Jer 4:4
is necessary to c them......Acts 15:5

CIRCUMCISED

among you shall be c.......Gen 17:10
who will justify the c....... Rom 3:30
While he was c................Rom 4:10
the gospel for the c......... Gal 2:7
if you become c..............Gal 5:2

c the eighth day..............Phil 3:5
In Him you were also c... Col 2:11

CIRCUMCISION

him the covenant of c...... Acts 7:8
c which is outward.......... Rom 2:28
c is that of the heart........Rom 2:29
a servant to the c............Rom 15:8
C is nothing and............1 Co 7:19
Christ Jesus neither c......Gal 5:6
For we are the c............. Phil 3:3
circumcised with the c......Col 2:11
those of the c................Tit 1:10

CIRCUMSPECTLY

then that you walk c........Eph 5:15

CISTERN

waters of his own c......... 2 Ki 18:31
from your own c............Prov 5:15

CITIES

He overthrew those c...... Gen 19:25
repair the ruined c.......... Is 61:4
c are a wilderness........... Is 64:10
c will be laid waste..........Jer 4:7
three parts, and the c...... Rev 16:19

CITIZEN

But I was born a c..........Acts 22:28

CITIZENS

"But his c hated him...... Luke 19:14
but fellow c with the....... Eph 2:19

CITIZENSHIP

sum I obtained this c.......Acts 22:28
For our c is in heaven..... Phil 3:20

CITY

And he built a c............. Gen 4:17
shall make glad the c.......Ps 46:4
c shall flourish...............Ps 72:16
They found no c............Ps 107:4
c that is compact............Ps 122:3
the LORD guards the c....Ps 127:1
at the entry of the c........Prov 8:3
c has become a harlot......Is 1:21
upon Zion, the c.............Is 33:20
after the holy c...............Is 48:2
How lonely sits the c......Lam 1:1
Nineveh, that great c......Jon 4:11
c that dwelt securely.......Zeph 2:15
to the oppressing c.........Zeph 3:1
c called Nazareth...........Matt 2:23
c that is set on a............Matt 5:14
He has prepared a c........Heb 11:16
Zion and to the c...........Heb 12:22
have no continuing c...... Heb 13:14
will tread the holy c....... Rev 11:2
fallen, that great c...........Rev 14:8
and the beloved c........... Rev 20:9
John, saw the holy c.......Rev 21:2
c was pure gold..............Rev 21:18
c had no need of the........Rev 21:23
the gates into the c......... Rev 22:14

CLAP

c their hands at him........Job 27:23
Oh, c your hands............Ps 47:1
Let the rivers c..............Ps 98:8
of the field shall c..........Is 55:12

CLAY

dwell in houses of c........Job 4:19
have made me like c....... Job 10:9

are defenses of c.............Job 13:12
been formed out of c.......Job 33:6
takes on form like c........ Job 38:14
pit, Out of the miry c......Ps 40:2
be esteemed as the c....... Is 29:16
Shall the c say to him...... Is 45:9
we are the c..................Is 64:8
"Look, as the c..............Jer 18:6
iron and partly of c.........Dan 2:33
blind man with the c....... John 9:6
have power over the c..... Rom 9:21

CLEAN

seven each of every c...... Gen 7:2
between unclean and c.....Lev 10:10
wash in them and be c.....2 Ki 5:12
Who can bring a c.......... Job 14:4
He who has c hands and.. Ps 24:4
make yourselves c........... Is 1:16
Then I will sprinkle c...... Ezek 36:25
You can make me c........ Matt 8:2
all things are c..............Luke 11:41
but is completely c.........John 13:10
"You are not all c..........John 13:11
"You are already c.........John 15:3
in fine linen, c...............Rev 19:8

CLEANSE

You shall c the altar........Ex 29:36
C me from secret............Ps 19:12
And c me from my sin.....Ps 51:2
How can a young man c.. Ps 119:9
I will c you from all........ Ezek 36:25
c the lepers, raise...........Matt 10:8
might sanctify and c........ Eph 5:26
C your hands.................Jas 4:8
us our sins and to c.........1 Jn 1:9

CLEANSED

Surely I have c...............Ps 73:13
the lepers are c...............Matt 11:5
Were there not ten c.......Luke 17:17

CLEANSES

Therefore if anyone c...... 2 Ti 2:21
Jesus Christ His Son c..... 1 Jn 1:7

CLEAR

c shining after rain..........2 Sa 23:4
fair as the moon, c.........Song 6:10
yourselves to be c........... 2 Co 7:11
like a jasper stone, c....... Rev 21:11
of life, c as crystal..........Rev 22:1

CLEFTS

to go into the c..............Is 2:21
valleys and in the c.........Is 7:19
you who dwell in the c.... Jer 49:16

CLERK

c had quieted the............Acts 19:35

CLIFF

secret places of the c.......Song 2:14

CLIMB

go into thickets and c......Jer 4:29
mighty men, they c.........Joel 2:7
though they c up to........Amos 9:2

CLIMBS

c up some other way.......John 10:1

CLING

and that you may c......... Deut 30:20
to her, "Do not c...........John 20:17
C to what is good...........Rom 12:9

CLOAK

c You will change them... Ps 102:26
let him have your c......... Matt 5:40
c You will fold them ...... Heb 1:12
your liberty as a c........... 1 Pe 2:16

CLOSE

c friends abhor me......... Job 19:19
of Christ he came c........ Phil 2:30

CLOSED

and has c your eyes......... Is 29:10
for the words are c......... Dan 12:9
the deep c around me...... Jon 2:5

CLOTH

a piece of unshrunk c...... Matt 9:16
in a clean linen c........... Matt 27:59

CLOTHE

c them with tunics........... Ex 40:14
c me with skin and......... Job 10:11
c her priests with........... Ps 132:16
His enemies I will c......... Ps 132:18
Though you c yourself..... Jer 4:30
He not much more c....... Matt 6:30

CLOTHED

of skin, and c them......... Gen 3:21
Have you c his neck........ Job 39:19
off my sackcloth and c..... Ps 30:11
The pastures are c........... Ps 65:13
The LORD is c............. Ps 93:1
You are c with honor...... Ps 104:1
c himself with cursing...... Ps 109:18
Let Your priests be c....... Ps 132:9
all her household is c....... Prov 31:21
c you with fine linen....... Ezek 16:10
A man c in soft............. Matt 11:8
I was naked and you c.... Matt 25:36
legion, sitting and c........ Mark 5:15
And they c Him with....... Mark 15:17
rich man who was c....... Luke 16:19
desiring to be c............. 2 Co 5:2
that you may be c.......... Rev 3:18
a woman c with the sun... Rev 12:1
He was c with a robe...... Rev 19:13

CLOTHES

c will abhor me............. Job 9:31
c became shining........... Mark 9:3
they spread their c......... Luke 19:36
laid down their c........... Acts 7:58
and tore off their c......... Acts 22:23
a poor man in filthy c...... Jas 2:2

CLOTHING

c they cast lots............. Ps 22:18
c is woven with gold........ Ps 45:13
will provide your c......... Prov 27:26
and honor are her c........ Prov 31:25
of vengeance for c......... Is 59:17
the body more than c...... Matt 6:25
do you worry about c...... Matt 6:28
to you in sheep's c......... Matt 7:15
those who wear soft c...... Matt 11:8
c as white as snow......... Matt 28:3
c they cast lots............. John 19:24
before me in bright c....... Acts 10:30

CLOTHS

wrapped in swaddling c.... Luke 2:12
in, saw the linen c........... John 20:5

CLOUD

My rainbow in the c........ Gen 9:13
day in a pillar of c.......... Ex 13:21
c covered the mountain.... Ex 24:15
c descended and stood..... Ex 33:9
c did not depart............. Neh 9:19
He led them with the c.... Ps 78:14
his favor is like a c......... Prov 16:15
these who fly like a c...... Is 60:8
like a morning c............. Hos 6:4
behold, a bright c.......... Matt 17:5
of Man coming in a c...... Luke 21:27
c received Him out of...... Acts 1:9
were under the c............ 1 Co 10:1
by so great a c.............. Heb 12:1

CLOUDS

a morning without c........ 2 Sa 23:4
c poured out water.......... Ps 77:17
and hail, snow and c....... Ps 148:8
c drop down the dew....... Prov 3:20
he who regards the c....... Eccl 11:4
of Man coming on the c... Matt 24:30
with them in the c.......... 1 Th 4:17
they are c without......... Jude 12
He is coming with c........ Rev 1:7

CLOUDY

them by day with a c...... Neh 9:12
spoke to them in the c..... Ps 99:7

CLOVEN

the hoof, having c.......... Lev 11:3
chew the cud or have c.... Deut 14:7

CLUSTER

beloved is to me a c........ Song 1:14
wine is found in the c...... Is 65:8

COAL

in his hand a live c......... Is 6:6
it shall not be a c.......... Is 47:14

COALS

wicked He will rain c....... Ps 11:6
C were kindled by it........ Ps 18:8
Let burning c fall............ Ps 140:10
Can one walk on hot c..... Prov 6:28
so you will heap c.......... Prov 25:22
doing you will heap c....... Rom 12:20

COBRA

it becomes c venom......... Job 20:14
c that stops its ear.......... Ps 58:4
the lion and the c........... Ps 91:13

COBRA'S

shall play by the c........... Is 11:8

COFFIN

and he was put in a c...... Gen 50:26
David followed the c........ 2 Sa 3:31
and touched the open c.... Luke 7:14

COIN

sold for a copper c......... Matt 10:29
if she loses one c........... Luke 15:8

COLD

and harvest, and c.......... Gen 8:22
can stand before His c...... Ps 147:17
Like the c of snow in...... Prov 25:13
c water to a weary......... Prov 25:25
c water in the name of.... Matt 10:42
of many will grow c........ Matt 24:12
that you are neither c...... Rev 3:15

COLLECTED

coming I might have c..... Luke 19:23

COLLECTION

from Jerusalem the c....... 2 Ch 24:6
concerning the c............ 1 Co 16:1

COLT

and his donkey's c.......... Gen 49:11
on a donkey, a c............ Zech 9:9
on a donkey, a c............ Matt 21:5
own garments on the c.... Luke 19:35

COME

then does wisdom c........ Job 28:20
of glory shall c.............. Ps 24:7
Our God shall c............. Ps 50:3
You all flesh will c......... Ps 65:2
C with me from Lebanon. Song 4:8
He will c and save you.... Is 35:4
who have no money, c..... Is 55:1
Your kingdom c............ Matt 6:10
"C to Me................... Matt 11:28
For many will c............ Matt 24:5
Israel, let Him now c....... Matt 27:42
If anyone desires to c...... Luke 9:23
kingdom of God has c..... Luke 10:9
"I have c in My............ John 5:43
and I have not c............ John 7:28
thirsts, let him c............ John 7:37
c that they may have....... John 10:10
c as a light into the........ John 12:46
I will c to you............... John 14:18
"If I had not c.............. John 15:22
savage wolves will c........ Acts 20:29
O Lord, c................... 1 Co 16:22
"Behold, I c quickly........ Rev 3:11
the door, I will c........... Rev 3:20
the bride says, "C........... Rev 22:17

COMELINESS

He has no form or c........ Is 53:2

COMES

Who is this who c.......... Is 63:1
'Come,' and he c........... Matt 8:9
Lord's death till He c...... 1 Co 11:26
Then c the end.............. 1 Co 15:24

COMFORT

with him, and to c him.... Job 2:11
and Your staff, they c...... Ps 23:4
When will You c............ Ps 119:82
yes, c My people........... Is 40:1
For the LORD will c....... Is 51:3
c all who mourn............ Is 61:2
she has none to c her...... Lam 1:2
the LORD will again c..... Zech 1:17
and God of all c........... 2 Co 1:3
trouble, with the c......... 2 Co 1:4
in Christ, if any c.......... Phil 2:1
c each other and edify..... 1 Th 5:11

COMFORTED

So Isaac was c after........ Gen 24:67
soul refused to be c........ Ps 77:2
For the LORD has c....... Is 49:13
refusing to be c............. Jer 31:15
but now he is c............. Luke 16:25

COMFORTER

she had no c................ Lam 1:9

COMFORTS

the army, as one who c.... Job 29:25
I, even I, am He who c.... Is 51:12

him, and restore c...........Is 57:18
one whom his mother c....Is 66:13
who c us in all our..........2 Co 1:4
who c the downcast.........2 Co 7:6

COMING

your salvation is c............Is 62:11
behold, the day is c.........Mal 4:1
but He who is c.............Matt 3:11
"Are You the C............. Matt 11:3
be the sign of Your c...... Matt 24:3
is delaying his c.............Matt 24:48
see the Son of Man c.... Mark 13:26
mightier than I is c.........Luke 3:16
are Christ's at His c....... 1 Co 15:23
to you the power and c...2 Pe 1:16
the promise of His c........2 Pe 3:4
"Behold, I am c............. Rev 22:7
"Surely I am c.............Rev 22:20

COMMAND

in order that he may c.....Gen 18:19
"The LORD will c..........Deut 28:8
"in that I c you............. Deut 30:16
c His lovingkindness........Ps 42:8
C victories for Jacob........Ps 44:4
to all that I c................Jer 11:4
if it is You, c................ Matt 14:28
c fire to come down....... Luke 9:54
c I have received....... John 10:18
And I know that His c....John 12:50
if you do whatever I c..... John 15:14
do the things we c..........2 Th 3:4

COMMANDED

"Have you c the.............Job 38:12
c His covenant forever......Ps 111:9
For there the LORD c..... Ps 133:3
it is the God who c.........2 Co 4:6
not endure what was c.....Heb 12:20

COMMANDMENT

The c of the LORD is......Ps 19:8
c is exceedingly broad......Ps 119:96
For the c is a lamp..........Prov 6:23
Me is taught by the c...... Is 29:13
which is the great c........ Matt 22:36
"A new c I give to..........John 13:34
the Father gave Me c...... John 14:31
law, but when the c........Rom 7:9
the c might become.........Rom 7:13
which is the first c..........Eph 6:2
c is the word which........ 1 Jn 2:7
And this is His c.............1 Jn 3:23
as we received c............. 2 Jn 4
This is the c.................2 Jn 6

COMMANDMENTS

covenant, the Ten C........Ex 34:28
to observe all these c......Deut 6:25
who remember His c....... Ps 103:18
Do not hide Your c........Ps 119:19
myself in Your c............Ps 119:47
For I believe Your c........Ps 119:66
Your c are faithful.......... Ps 119:86
c More than gold............ Ps 119:127
as doctrines the c............Matt 15:9
c hang all the Law.......... Matt 22:40
"He who has My c.........John 14:21
according to the c............Col 2:22
Now he who keeps His c..1 Jn 3:24

COMMANDS

with authority He c.........Mark 1:27

COMMEND

into Your hands I c.........Luke 23:46
But food does not c........ 1 Co 8:8

COMMENDABLE

For this is c.................... 1 Pe 2:19
patiently, this is c............1 Pe 2:20

COMMENDED

A man will be c.............Prov 12:8
c the unjust steward........ Luke 16:8
where they had been c.....Acts 14:26

COMMENDING

of the truth c................. 2 Co 4:2

COMMENDS

but whom the Lord c.......2 Co 10:18

COMMIT

"You shall not c............. Ex 20:14
C your works to the........ Prov 16:3
mammon, who will c......Luke 16:11
c sexual immorality.......... 1 Co 10:8
c these to faithful............2 Ti 2:2
c their souls to Him........ 1 Pe 4:19
c sin not leading............ 1 Jn 5:16

COMMITS

to you, whoever c...........John 8:34
sin also c lawlessness....... 1 Jn 3:4

COMMITTED

For My people have c......Jer 2:13
c things worthy...............Luke 12:48
Guard what was c...........1 Ti 6:20
"Who c no sin................ 1 Pe 2:22
c Himself to Him who..... 1 Pe 2:23

COMMON

of the c people sins......... Lev 4:27
poor have this in c..........Prov 22:2
c people heard Him.........Mark 12:37
had all things in c...........Acts 2:44
never eaten anything c.....Acts 10:14
not call any man c..........Acts 10:28
my true son in our c........Tit 1:4
concerning our c............Jude 3

COMMOTION

there arose a great c........Acts 19:23

COMMUNED

I c with my heart............Eccl 1:16

COMMUNION

bless, is it not the c.........1 Co 10:16
c has light with...............2 Co 6:14
c of the Holy Spirit.........2 Co 13:14

COMPANION

a man my equal, My c.....Ps 55:13
I am a c of all those........Ps 119:63
the Man who is My C......Zech 13:7
urge you also, true c....... Phil 4:3
your brother and c.......... Rev 1:9

COMPANIONS

are rebellious, and c........Is 1:23
and calling to their c.......Matt 11:16
more than Your c...........Heb 1:9
while you became c.........Heb 10:33

COMPANY

Great was the c.............. Ps 68:11
epistle not to keep c........1 Co 5:9

c corrupts good habits......1 Co 15:33
and do not keep c...........2 Th 3:14
to an innumerable c........ Heb 12:22

COMPARED

the heavens can be c....... Ps 89:6
may desire cannot be c.... Prov 8:11
are not worthy to be c..... Rom 8:18

COMPASSION

show you mercy, have c...Deut 13:17
His people and have c..... Deut 32:36
He, being full of c.......... Ps 78:38
are a God full of c..........Ps 86:15
will return and have c......Jer 12:15
yet He will show c.......... Lam 3:32
c everyone to his............. Zech 7:9
He was moved with c...... Matt 9:36
also have had c..............Matt 18:33
"I have c on the............. Mark 8:2
whomever I will have c.... Rom 9:15
He can have c on those... Heb 5:2
of one mind, having c......1 Pe 3:8
And on some have c....... Jude 22

COMPASSIONATE

c women have cooked......Lam 4:10
the Lord is very c........... Jas 5:11

COMPEL

c them to come in...........Luke 14:23

COMPELS

the spirit within me c.......Job 32:18
"And whoever c............. Matt 5:41

COMPLACENCY

slay them, and the c........Prov 1:32
who are settled in c.........Zeph 1:12

COMPLAIN

should a living man c.......Lam 3:39

COMPLAINERS

These are murmurers, c... Jude 16

COMPLAINT

"Even today my c...........Job 23:2
I pour out my c..............Ps 142:2
for the LORD has a c....... Mic 6:2
if anyone has a c............ Col 3:13

COMPLAINTS

Who has c.....................Prov 23:29
laid many serious c.........Acts 25:7

COMPLETE

that you may be made c...2 Co 13:9
work in you will c...........Phil 1:6
and you are c in Him......Col 2:10
of God may be c............ 2 Ti 3:17
make you c in every........Heb 13:21
the wrath of God is c...... Rev 15:1

COMPLETELY

because I made a man c...John 7:23
Himself sanctify you c......1 Th 5:23

COMPOSED

But God c the body........ 1 Co 12:24

COMPREHEND

which we cannot c..........Job 37:5
c my path and my lying... Ps 139:3
the darkness did not c..... John 1:5
may be able to c.............Eph 3:18

CONCEAL
Almighty I will not c....... Job 27:11
c pride from man............ Job 33:17
of God to c a matter....... Prov 25:2

CONCEALED
c Your lovingkindness...... Ps 40:10
than love carefully c........ Prov 27:5

CONCEIT
selfish ambition or c........ Phil 2:3

CONCEITED
Let us not become c........ Gal 5:26

CONCEIVE
the virgin shall c............. Is 7:14
And behold, you will c.... Luke 1:31

CONCEIVED
in sin my mother c.......... Ps 51:5
when desire has c........... Jas 1:15

CONCERN
Neither do I c myself....... Ps 131:1
the things which c........... Acts 28:31
my deep c for all the....... 2 Co 11:28

CONCILIATION
c pacifies great............... Eccl 10:4

CONCLUSION
Let us hear the c............ Eccl 12:13

CONDEMN
say to God, 'Do not c..... Job 10:2
world to c the world....... John 3:17
her, "Neither do I c........ John 8:11
judge another you c........ Rom 2:1
our heart does not c........ 1 Jn 3:21

CONDEMNATION
will receive greater c....... Matt 23:14
can you escape the c....... Matt 23:33
subject to eternal c......... Mark 3:29
And this is the c............ John 3:19
the resurrection of c....... John 5:29
Their c is just................ Rom 3:8
therefore now no c.......... Rom 8:1
of c had glory................ 2 Co 3:9
having c because they...... 1 Ti 5:12
marked out for this c....... Jude 4

CONDEMNED
words you will be c........ Matt 12:37
does not believe is c....... John 3:18
c sin in the flesh............ Rom 8:3

CONDEMNS
Who is he who c............ Rom 8:34
For if our heart c............ 1 Jn 3:20

CONDUCT
c yourselves like men....... 1 Sa 4:9
who are of upright c........ Ps 37:14
c yourself in the............. 1 Ti 3:15
c that his works are......... Jas 3:13
to each one's work, c...... 1 Pe 1:17
from your aimless c......... 1 Pe 1:18
may be won by the c....... 1 Pe 3:1

CONFESS
c my transgressions......... Ps 32:5
that if you c with........... Rom 10:9
every tongue shall c......... Rom 14:11
C your trespasses........... Jas 5:16

If we c our sins............. 1 Jn 1:9
but I will c his name....... Rev 3:5

CONFESSED
c that He was Christ....... John 9:22
c the good confession...... 1 Ti 6:12

CONFESSES
prosper, but whoever c.... Prov 28:13
c that Jesus is the........... 1 Jn 4:15

CONFESSION
of Israel, and make c....... Josh 7:19
with the mouth c............ Rom 10:10
confessed the good c....... 1 Ti 6:12
witnessed the good c....... 1 Ti 6:13
High Priest of our c........ Heb 3:1
let us hold fast our c....... Heb 4:14

CONFIDENCE
You who are the c.......... Ps 65:5
the LORD Than to put c.. Ps 118:8
c shall be your............... Is 30:15
Jesus, and have no c....... Phil 3:3
if we hold fast the c....... Heb 3:6
appears, we may have c... 1 Jn 2:28

CONFIRM
c the promises................ Rom 15:8
who will also c............... 1 Co 1:8

CONFIRMED
covenant that was c......... Gal 3:17
by the Lord, and was c.... Heb 2:3
c it by an oath............... Heb 6:17

CONFIRMING
c the word through the.... Mark 16:20

CONFLICT
having the same c.......... Phil 1:30
to know what a great c.... Col 2:1

CONFLICTS
Outside were c............... 2 Co 7:5

CONFORMED
predestined to be c......... Rom 8:29
And do not be c............. Rom 12:2
sufferings, being c.......... Phil 3:10
body that it may be c...... Phil 3:21

CONFOUNDED
who seek You be c......... Ps 69:6

CONFUSE
c their language.............. Gen 11:7

CONFUSED
there the LORD c............ Gen 11:9
for the assembly was c..... Acts 19:32

CONFUSION
c Who plot my hurt......... Ps 35:4
us drink the wine of c...... Ps 60:3

CONGREGATION
Nor sinners in the c......... Ps 1:5
c I will praise You.......... Ps 22:22
I have hated the c.......... Ps 26:5
God stands in the c......... Ps 82:1
also in the c of the......... Ps 89:5
will rest in the c............ Prov 21:16
people, sanctify the c...... Joel 2:16
c I will sing praise.......... Heb 2:12

CONQUER
conquering and to c........ Rev 6:2

CONQUERORS
we are more than c......... Rom 8:37

CONSCIENCE
convicted by their c......... John 8:9
strive to have a c.......... Acts 24:16
I am not lying, my c........ Rom 9:1
wrath but also for c........ Rom 13:5
no questions for c.......... 1 Co 10:25
faith with a pure c......... 1 Ti 3:9
having their own c.......... 1 Ti 4:2
to God, purge your c....... Heb 9:14
from an evil c and our..... Heb 10:22
having a good c............. 1 Pe 3:16

CONSECRATE
c himself this day............ 1 Ch 29:5
the trumpet in Zion, c..... Joel 2:15
c their gain to the.......... Mic 4:13

CONSENT
entice you, do not c........ Prov 1:10
and does not c to........... 1 Ti 6:3

CONSENTED
you saw a thief, you c..... Ps 50:18
He had not c to their...... Luke 23:51

CONSENTING
Now Saul was c to his..... Acts 8:1

CONSIDER
When I c Your heavens... Ps 8:3
C her palaces................ Ps 48:13
C carefully what is.......... Prov 23:1
C the work of God......... Eccl 7:13
My people do not c......... Is 1:3
c the operation.............. Is 5:12
your God will c.............. Jon 1:6
"C your ways................ Hag 1:5
C the lilies of the.......... Matt 6:28
"C the ravens............... Luke 12:24
Let a man so c us........... 1 Co 4:1
c how great this man...... Heb 7:4
c one another in order..... Heb 10:24
c Him who endured........ Heb 12:3

CONSIDERS
c all their works............. Ps 33:15

CONSIST
in Him all things c.......... Col 1:17

CONSOLATION
waiting for the C............ Luke 2:25
have received your c........ Luke 6:24
abound in us, so our c..... 2 Co 1:5
if there is any c............. Phil 2:1
given us everlasting c....... 2 Th 2:16
we might have strong c.... Heb 6:18

CONSOLATIONS
Are the c of God too...... Job 15:11

CONSOLE
c those who mourn.......... Is 61:3

CONSPIRE
What do you c against..... Nah 1:9

CONSTANT
c prayer was.................. Acts 12:5

CONSTRAINED
Macedonia, Paul was c.....Acts 18:5

CONSTRAINS
the love of Christ c......... 2 Co 5:14

CONSULT
They only c to cast..........Ps 62:4

CONSULTED
c together against............Ps 83:3

CONSUME
your midst, lest I c..........Ex 33:3
this great fire will c......... Deut 5:25
C them in wrath............. Ps 59:13
whom the Lord will c...... 2 Th 2:8

CONSUMED
but the bush was not c.....Ex 3:2
c the burnt.....................1 Ki 18:38
For we have been c.........Ps 90:7
mercies we are not c....... Lam 3:22
beware lest you be c........Gal 5:15

CONSUMING
the LORD was like a c.... Ex 24:17
before you as a c............ Deut 9:3
For our God is a c......... Heb 12:29

CONSUMMATION
I have seen the c............ Ps 119:96

CONSUMPTION
will strike you with c...... Deut 28:22

CONTAIN
of heavens cannot c.........2 Ch 2:6
c the books that would.... John 21:25

CONTEMPT
He pours c on princes......Job 12:21
wicked comes, c comes.... Prov 18:3
and everlasting c............Dan 12:2
and be treated with c.......Mark 9:12

CONTEMPTIBLE
of the LORD is c............ Mal 1:7
also have made you c...... Mal 2:9
and his speech c............. 2 Co 10:10

CONTEND
show me why You c........Job 10:2
Will you c for God.........Job 13:8
let us c together.............Is 43:26
for I will c with him........Is 49:25
then how can you c.........Jer 12:5
c earnestly for the..........Jude 3

CONTENDED
Therefore the people c.....Ex 17:2

CONTENT
state I am, to be c.......... Phil 4:11
these we shall be c..........1 Ti 6:8
covetousness, and be c.....Heb 13:5

CONTENTION
By pride comes only c..... Prov 13:10
lips enter into c.............. Prov 18:6
and c will leave............. Prov 22:10
strife and a man of c.......Jer 15:10

CONTENTIONS
Casting lots causes c........Prov 18:18

sorcery, hatred, c............Gal 5:20
genealogies, c.................Tit 3:9

CONTENTIOUS
than with a c and...........Prov 21:19
house shared with a c......Prov 25:24
anyone seems to be c......1 Co 11:16

CONTENTMENT
c is great gain.................1 Ti 6:6

CONTINUAL
a merry heart has a c...... Prov 15:15
in wrath with a c............ Is 14:6
c coming she weary me....Luke 18:5
c grief in my heart.......... Rom 9:2

CONTINUALLY
heart was only evil c........Gen 6:5
His praise shall c............ Ps 34:1
and Your truth c.............Ps 40:11
of God endures c.............Ps 52:1
I keep Your law c..........Ps 119:44
Before Me c are grief......Jer 6:7
and wait on your God c...Hos 12:6
will give ourselves c.........Acts 6:4
remains a priest c............Heb 7:3
c offer the sacrifice..........Heb 13:15

CONTINUE
tells lies shall not c..........Ps 101:7
persuaded them to c........Acts 13:43
Shall we c in sin that.......Rom 6:1
who does not c in all ..... Gal 3:10
C earnestly in prayer.......Col 4:2
because they did not c.....Heb 8:9
Let brotherly love c.........Heb 13:1
asleep, all things c...........2 Pe 3:4

CONTINUED
c steadfastly in the.......... Acts 2:42
us, they would have c......1 Jn 2:19

CONTRADICTIONS
vain babblings and c........1 Ti 6:20

CONTRARY
to worship God c............Acts 18:13
and these are c...............Gal 5:17
please God and are c.......1 Th 2:15
other thing that is c.........1 Ti 1:10

CONTRIBUTION
to make a certain c......... Rom 15:26

CONTRITE
saves such as have a c..... Ps 34:18
A broken and a c............ Ps 51:17
with him who has a c....... Is 57:15
poor and of a c spirit.......Is 66:2

CONTROVERSY
for the LORD has a c.......Jer 25:31
c great is...................... 1 Ti 3:16

CONVERSION
describing the c.............. Acts 15:3

CONVERTED
unless you are c.............Matt 18:3

CONVICT
He has come, He will c... John 16:8
c those who................... Tit 1:9
c all who are.................Jude 15

CONVICTS
"Which of you c............. John 8:46

CONVINCED
Let each be fully c.......... Rom 14:5

COOKED
c their own children........ Lam 4:10

COOL
in the garden in the c...... Gen 3:8
water and c my tongue.... Luke 16:24

COPIES
necessary that the c........ Heb 9:23
hands, which are c.......... Heb 9:24

COPPER
hills you can dig c........... Deut 8:9
of cups, pitchers, c..........Mark 7:4
sold for two c coins........ Luke 12:6

COPPERSMITH
c did me much harm....... 2 Ti 4:14

COPY
who serve the c.............. Heb 8:5

CORD
this line of scarlet c........Josh 2:18
and a threefold c........... Eccl 4:12
before the silver c........... Eccl 12:6

CORDS
in pieces the c................ Ps 129:4
he is caught in the c........Prov 5:22
draw iniquity with c.........Is 5:18
them with gentle c.......... Hos 11:4
had made a whip of c......John 2:15

CORNER
was not done in a c.........Acts 26:26

CORNERSTONE
Or who laid its c.............Job 38:6
Has become the chief c....Ps 118:22
stone, a precious c.......... Is 28:16
become the chief c.......... Matt 21:42
in Zion a chief c............. 1 Pe 2:6

CORPSE
c was thrown on the........1 Ki 13:24
c trodden under foot....... Is 14:19

CORRECT
with rebukes You c......... Ps 39:11
C your son.....................Prov 29:17
But I will c you in.......... Jer 30:11

CORRECTED
human fathers who c....... Heb 12:9

CORRECTION
nor detest His c.............. Prov 3:11
Harsh c is for him who.... Prov 15:10
c will drive it.................Prov 22:15
Do not withhold c...........Prov 23:13
they received no c...........Jer 2:30
for reproof, for c............ 2 Ti 3:16

CORRECTS
is the man whom God c...Job 5:17
the LORD loves He c...... Prov 3:12

CORROD
and silver are c...............Jas 5:3

CORRUPT

have together become *c*... Ps 14:3
have together become *c*... Ps 53:3
old man which grows *c*... Eph 4:22
men of *c* minds.................2 Ti 3:8
in these things they *c*.......Jude 10

CORRUPTED

for all flesh had *c*............Gen 6:12
no one, we have *c*............2 Co 7:2
so your minds may be *c*...2 Co 11:3
Your riches are *c*............Jas 5:2
the great harlot who *c*..... Rev 19:2

CORRUPTIBLE

For this *c* must put on......1 Co 15:53
redeemed with *c* things.... 1 Pe 1:18

CORRUPTION

Your Holy One to see *c*...Ps 16:10
God raised up saw no *c*... Acts 13:37
from the bondage of *c*..... Rom 8:21
The body is sown in *c*......1 Co 15:42
c inherit incorruption....... 1 Co 15:50
of the flesh reap *c*............Gal 6:8
having escaped the *c*........2 Pe 1:4
perish in their own *c*....... 2 Pe 2:12

COST

and count the *c*.............. Luke 14:28

COULD

has done what she *c*....... Mark 14:8
c remove mountains........ 1 Co 13:2
which no one *c* number....Rev 7:9

COUNCILS

deliver you up to *c*..........Mark 13:9

COUNSEL

and strength, He has *c*......Job 12:13
the *c* of the wicked is...... Job 21:16
when the friendly *c*......... Job 29:4
is this who darkens *c*......Job 38:2
Who walks not in the *c*...Ps 1:1
We took sweet *c*............Ps 55:14
guide me with Your *c*......Ps 73:24
have none of my *c*.......... Prov 1:30
Where there is no *c*........Prov 11:14
C in the heart of man......Prov 20:5
by wise *c* wage war....... Prov 20:18
whom did He take *c*.......Is 40:14
'You are great in *c*..........Jer 32:19
chief priests took *c*..........John 12:10
by the determined *c*........ Acts 2:23
according to the *c*.......... Eph 1:11
immutability of His *c*......Heb 6:17
"I *c* you to buy from....... Rev 3:18

COUNSELOR

be called wonderful, *C*.....Is 9:6
but there was no *c*.......... Is 41:28
Has your *c* perished........ Mic 4:9
who has become His *c*..... Rom 11:34

COUNSELORS

c there is safety.............. Prov 11:14

COUNT

c the people of Israel.......2 Sa 24:4
c my life dear to............Acts 20:24
c me as a partner........... Phm 17
His promise, as some *c*....2 Pe 3:9

COUNTED

Even a fool is *c*............. Prov 17:28
c as the small dust.......... Is 40:15

the wages are not *c*........ Rom 4:4
He *c* me faithful............. 1 Ti 1:12
who rule well be *c*.......... 1 Ti 5:17

COUNTENANCE

the LORD lift up His *c*.... Num 6:26
c they did not cast.......... Job 29:24
up the light of Your *c*......Ps 4:6
His *c* is like Lebanon.......Song 5:15
with a sad *c*................... Matt 6:16
His *c* was like................Matt 28:3
of the glory of his *c*.........2 Co 3:7
sword, and His *c*............Rev 1:16

COUNTRY

"Get out of your *c*.........Gen 12:1
good news from a far *c*.... Prov 25:25
and went into a far *c*......Matt 21:33
as in a foreign *c*..............Heb 11:9
that is, a heavenly *c*........ Heb 11:16

COURAGE

strong and of good *c*...... Deut 31:6
thanked God and took *c*.. Acts 28:15

COURT

appoint my day in *c*........ Job 9:19
by you or by a human *c*...1 Co 4:3
They zealously *c*............ Gal 4:17

COURTEOUS

be tenderhearted, be *c*.....1 Pe 3:8

COURTS

he may dwell in Your *c*... Ps 65:4
even faints For the *c*....... Ps 84:2
flourish in the *c*............. Ps 92:13
And into His *c*.............. Ps 100:4
drink it in My holy *c*......Is 62:9

COVENANT

I will establish My *c*........Gen 6:18
day the LORD made a *c*.. Gen 15:18
for Me, behold, My *c*......Gen 17:4
as a perpetual *c*.............. Ex 31:16
it is a *c* of salt...............Num 18:19
Remember His *c* always...1 Ch 16:15
"I have made a *c*............Job 31:1
will show them His *c*......Ps 25:14
c shall stand firm........... Ps 89:28
sons will keep My *c*........Ps 132:12
and give You as a *c*........ Is 42:6
the words of this *c*......... Jer 11:2
'I made a *c* with your......Jer 34:13
I might break the *c*......... Zech 11:10
the Messenger of the *c*.....Mal 3:1
This cup is the new *c*......Luke 22:20
c that was confirmed....... Gal 3:17
Mediator of a better *c*.... Heb 8:6
c had been faultless........ Heb 8:7
He says, "A new *c*.......... Heb 8:13
Mediator of the new *c*..... Heb 12:24
of the everlasting *c*.........Heb 13:20

COVENANTED

your kingdom, as I *c*.......2 Ch 7:18
to the word that I *c*........Hag 2:5

COVENANTS

the glory, the *c*...............Rom 9:4
these are the two *c*.........Gal 4:24

COVER

the rock, and will *c*........Ex 33:22
He shall *c* you with........ Ps 91:4
c Yourself with light........Ps 104:2

LORD as the waters *c*......Is 11:9
and will no more *c*.......... Is 26:21
from the wind, and a *c*... Is 32:2
not to *c* his head..............1 Co 11:7
c a multitude of sins........Jas 5:20

COVERED

The depths have *c*..........Ex 15:5
c my transgressions as......Job 31:33
Whose sin is *c*................ Ps 32:1
the wings of a dove *c*..... Ps 68:13
c all their sin.................Ps 85:2
You have *c* me in my......Ps 139:13
with two he *c* his face.....Is 6:2
of Jacob will be *c*.......... Is 27:9
You have *c* Yourself.......Lam 3:44
For there is nothing *c*......Matt 10:26

COVERING

spread a cloud for a *c*......Ps 105:39
make sackcloth their *c*..... Is 50:3
given to her for a *c*......... 1 Co 11:15

COVERINGS

and made themselves *c*.... Gen 3:7

COVET

"You shall not *c*............. Ex 20:17
c fields and take them..... Mic 2:2
You murder and *c*...........Jas 4:2

COVETED

c no one's silver..............Acts 20:33

COVETOUS

nor thieves, nor *c*............1 Co 6:10
trained in *c* practices....... 2 Pe 2:14

COVETOUSNESS

but he who hates *c*..........Prov 28:16
for nothing but your *c*.....Jer 22:17
heed and beware of *c*......Luke 12:15
would not have known *c*.. Rom 7:7
all uncleanness or *c*........ Eph 5:3
conduct be without *c*...... Heb 13:5

COWARDLY

the *c*, unbelieving............Rev 21:8

CRAFTILY

His people, To deal *c*......Ps 105:25

CRAFTINESS

wise in their own *c*..........Job 5:13
not walking in *c*..............2 Co 4:2
deceived Eve by his *c*......2 Co 11:3
in the cunning *c*.............Eph 4:14

CRAFTSMAN

instructor of every *c*........Gen 4:22
c encouraged the.............Is 41:7
c stretches out his........... Is 44:13

CRAFTY

Jonadab was a very *c*.......2 Sa 13:3
the devices of the *c*.........Job 5:12
They have taken *c*..........Ps 83:3
of a harlot, and a *c*.........Prov 7:10
Nevertheless, being *c*......2 Co 12:16

CRANE

Like a *c* or a swallow...... Is 38:14

CRAVES

and his soul still *c*...........Is 29:8

CREAM

she brought out *c*...........Judg 5:25
were bathed with *c*.........Job 29:6

CREATE

peace and *c* calamity....... Is 45:7
For behold, I *c*...............Is 65:17

CREATED

So God *c* man in His.......Gen 1:27
Spirit, they are *c*.............Ps 104:30
and they were *c*.............Ps 148:5
and see who has *c*..........Is 40:26
of Israel has *c*...............Is 41:20
For the LORD has *c*........Jer 31:22
Has not one God *c*..........Mal 2:10
Nor was man *c* for the.....1 Co 11:9
c in Christ Jesus............Eph 2:10
hidden in God who *c*......Eph 3:9
new man which was *c*.....Eph 4:24
Him all things were *c*......Col 1:16
from foods which God *c*...1 Ti 4:3
for You *c* all things.........Rev 4:11

CREATION

c which God................Mark 13:19
c was subjected..............Rom 8:20
know that the whole *c*.....Rom 8:22
Christ, he is a new *c*......2 Co 5:17
anything, but a new *c*......Gal 6:15
firstborn over all *c*.........Col 1:15

CREATOR

Remember now your *C*....Eccl 12:1
God, the LORD, the *C*....Is 40:28
rather than the *C*...........Rom 1:25
to a faithful *C*................ 1 Pe 4:19

CREATURE

the gospel to every *c*....... Mark 16:15
For every *c* of God is......1 Ti 4:4
And there is no *c*...........Heb 4:13
And every *c* which is.......Rev 5:13
and every living *c*...........Rev 16:3

CREATURES

created great sea *c*......... Gen 1:21
firstfruits of His *c*..........Jas 1:18
were four living *c*...........Rev 4:6

CREDIT

who love you, what *c*...... Luke 6:32
For what *c* is it if............1 Pe 2:20

CREDITOR

Every *c* who has lent......Deut 15:2
c is coming to take my.....2 Ki 4:1
c seize all that he............Ps 109:11
There was a certain *c*...... Luke 7:41

CREEP

of the forest *c*................ Ps 104:20
sort are those who *c*........2 Ti 3:6

CREEPING

c thing and beast of........Gen 1:24
every sort of *c* thing........Ezek 8:10

CREPT

For certain men have *c*....Jude 4

CRIB

donkey its master's *c*.......Is 1:3

CRIED

the poor who *c* out......... Job 29:12
They *c* to You................Ps 22:5
of the depths I have *c*......Ps 130:1

CRIES

your brother's blood *c*..... Gen 4:10
with vehement *c*............. Heb 5:7

CRIMES

land is filled with *c*.........Ezek 7:23

CRIMINALS

also two others, *c*...........Luke 23:32

CROOKED

turn aside to their *c*........Ps 125:5
whose ways are *c*............ Prov 2:15
c places shall be made.... Is 40:4
c places straight.............. Is 45:2
c places shall be made.... Luke 3:5
in the midst of a *c*.......... Phil 2:15

CROSS

does not take his *c*.........Matt 10:38
to bear His *c*.................Matt 27:32
come down from the *c*.....Matt 27:40
lest the *c* of Christ......... 1 Co 1:17
persecution for the *c*........Gal 6:12
glory except in the *c*.......Gal 6:14
one body through the *c*.....Eph 2:16
the enemies of the *c*.....Phil 3:18
Him endured the *c*.........Heb 12:2

CROWD

shall not follow a *c*.........Ex 23:2

CROWN

You set a *c* of pure.........Ps 21:3
c the year with Your....... Ps 65:11
have profaned his *c*......... Ps 89:39
upon Himself His *c*......... Ps 132:18
The *c* of the wise is.........Prov 14:24
head is a *c* of glory.........Prov 16:31
Woe to the *c* of pride.....Is 28:1
hosts will be for a *c*.........Is 28:5
c has fallen from our......Lam 5:16
they had twisted a *c*....... Matt 27:29
obtain a perishable *c*....... 1 Co 9:25
brethren, my joy and *c*.... Phil 4:1
laid up for me the *c*........ 2 Ti 4:8
he will receive the *c*........Jas 1:12
no one may take your *c*... Rev 3:11
on His head a golden *c*...Rev 14:14

CROWNED

angels, And You have *c*...Ps 8:5
but the prudent are *c*......Prov 14:18
athletics, he is not *c*........ 2 Ti 2:5
You *c* him with glory.......Heb 2:7

CROWNS

and they had *c* of gold.....Rev 4:4
on his horns ten *c*...........Rev 13:1
His head were many *c*.....Rev 19:12

CRUCIFIED

"Let Him be *c*..............Matt 27:22
Calvary, there they *c*.......Luke 23:33
lawless hands, have *c*.......Acts 2:23
that our old man was *c*....Rom 6:6
Was Paul *c* for you........ 1 Co 1:13
Jesus Christ and Him *c*....1 Co 2:2
they would have *c*.....1 Co 2:8
though He was *c*.............2 Co 13:4
"I have been *c*............... Gal 2:20

CRUCIFY

out again, "*C* Him..........Mark 15:13
I have power to *c* You......John 19:10
since they *c* again............Heb 6:6

CRUEL

wrath, for it is *c*............. Gen 49:7
spirit and *c* bondage........Ex 6:9
hate me with *c* hatred.....Ps 25:19
of the wicked are *c*........ Prov 12:10

CRUELTY

of *c* are in their.............Gen 49:5
the habitations of *c*.........Ps 74:20
c you have ruled.............Ezek 34:4

CRUSH

that a foot may *c*...........Job 39:15
That your foot may *c*......Ps 68:23
the poor, who *c*..............Amos 4:1
of peace will *c*...............Rom 16:20

CRUSHED

in the dust, who are *c*......Job 4:19
c my life to the...............Ps 143:3
every side, yet not *c*........2 Co 4:8

CRUST

man is reduced to a *c*...... Prov 6:26

CRY

and their *c* came up to.....Ex 2:23
of oppressions they *c*......Job 35:9
heart and my flesh *c*........Ps 84:2
I *c* out with my whole..... Ps 119:145
Does not wisdom *c*..........Prov 8:1
"What shall I *c*................Is 40:6
nor lift up a *c*..................Jer 7:16
c mightily to God............Jon 3:8
at midnight a *c*................Matt 25:6
His own elect who *c*........Luke 18:7

CRYING

"The voice of one *c*.........Matt 3:3
nor sorrow, nor *c*............Rev 21:4

CRYSTAL

nor *c* can equal it...........Job 28:17
your gates of *c*................ Is 54:12
of an awesome *c*.............Ezek 1:22
a sea of glass, like *c*........Rev 4:6

CUBIT

shall finish it to a *c*......... Gen 6:16
worrying can add one *c*....Matt 6:27

CUCUMBERS

in Egypt, the *c*...............Num 11:5
a hut in a garden of *c*......Is 1:8

CUNNING

the serpent was more *c*.... Gen 3:1
c comes quickly..............Job 5:13
c craftiness by which........Eph 4:14

CUP

My *c* runs over...............Ps 23:5
c are drained by them......Ps 73:10
the LORD there is a *c*..... Ps 75:8
I will take up the *c*......... Ps 116:13
the dregs of the *c*............Is 51:17
men give them the *c*........Jer 16:7
"Take this wine *c*............Jer 25:15
The *c* of the LORD's.......Hab 2:16
make Jerusalem a *c*.........Zech 12:2
little ones only a *c*..........Matt 10:42
Then He took the *c*.........Matt 26:27
possible, let this *c*...........Matt 26:39
c is the new covenant......Luke 22:20
You cannot drink the *c*.....1 Co 10:21
c is the new covenant......1 Co 11:25
to give her the *c*.............Rev 16:19

CURE
but they could not c........ Matt 17:16
and to c diseases...........Luke 9:1

CURES
demons and perform c..... Luke 13:32

CURSE
c the ground for man's.....Gen 8:21
c a ruler of your............. Ex 22:28
'You shall not c..............Lev 19:14
c this people for me........ Num 22:6
Balaam, "Neither c......... Num 23:25
your God turned the c..... Deut 23:5
said to him, 'C David....... 2 Sa 16:10
C God and die............... Job 2:9
mouth, But they c...........Ps 62:4
The c of the LORD is.... Prov 3:33
Do not c the king........... Eccl 10:20
do not c the rich.............Eccl 10:20
"I will send a c..............Mal 2:2
are cursed with a c.........Mal 3:9
law are under the c......... Gal 3:10

CURSED
c more than all cattle......Gen 3:14
C is the man who.......... Jer 17:5
c is he who keeps.......... Jer 48:10
Depart from Me, you c....Matt 25:41
and near to being c........Heb 6:8

CURSES
I will curse him who c..... Gen 12:3
For everyone who c........Lev 20:9
c his father or his...........Prov 20:20

CURSINGS
by the sword for the c..... Hos 7:16

CURTAIN
of each c shall be..........Ex 26:2
the heavens like a c.......Ps 104:2

CUSTOM
to me, As Your c.......... Ps 119:132
according to the c........... Acts 15:1
we have no such c...........1 Co 11:16

CUT
confidence shall be c....... Job 8:14
evildoers shall be c.........Ps 37:9
the wicked will be c........ Prov 2:22
causes you to sin, c......... Matt 5:30
"and will c him in..........Matt 24:51
him whose ear Peter c.....John 18:26
He had his hair c............Acts 18:18

CYMBAL
or a clanging c.................1 Co 13:1

— D —

DAILY
much as they gather d..... Ex 16:5
d He shall be................. Ps 72:15
to me, watching d.......... Prov 8:34
Yet they seek Me d.........Is 58:2
Give us this day our d..... Matt 6:11
I sat d with you..............Matt 26:55
take up his cross d........ Luke 9:23
the Scriptures d............. Acts 17:11
our Lord, I die d............1 Co 15:31
stands ministering d........Heb 10:11

DANCE
and their children d.........Job 21:11
His name with the d........Ps 149:3

mourn, and a time to d....Eccl 3:4
d has turned into............ Lam 5:15
And you did not d.......... Matt 11:17

DANCED
Then David d before.......2 Sa 6:14
daughter of Herodias d.... Matt 14:6

DANCING
saw the calf and the d..... Ex 32:19
me my mourning into d... Ps 30:11
he heard music and d...... Luke 15:25

DARE
someone would even d.....Rom 5:7
D any of you.................. 1 Co 6:1

DARK
dwell in the d cloud........ 1 Ki 8:12
I am d.......................... Song 1:5
d place of the earth.........Is 45:19
d places like the dead.....Lam 3:6
and makes the day d...... Amos 5:8
and the day shall be d..... Mic 3:6
I tell you in the d........... Matt 10:27
while it was still d...........John 20:1
shines in a d place......... 2 Pe 1:19

DARKENED
so that the land was d..... Ex 10:15
Let their eyes be d.........Ps 69:23
their understanding d......Eph 4:18

DARKNESS
d He called Night......... Gen 1:5
shall enlighten my d....... 2 Sa 22:29
through the deep d.........Job 22:13
Those who sat in d.........Ps 107:10
d shall not hide.............. Ps 139:12
d have seen a.................Is 9:2
I will make d light......... Is 42:16
and deep d the people..... Is 60:2
Israel, Or a land of d..... Jer 2:31
body will be full of d......Matt 6:23
cast out into outer d.......Matt 8:12
and the power of d.........Luke 22:53
d rather than light..........John 3:19
d does not know.............John 12:35
For you were once d.......Eph 5:8
the rulers of the d..........Eph 6:12
us from the power of d....Col 1:13
of the night nor of d.......1 Th 5:5
and to blackness and d....Heb 12:18
called you out of d.........1 Pe 2:9
d is reserved................. 2 Pe 2:17
and in Him is no d.........1 Jn 1:5
Him, and walk in d.........1 Jn 1:6
d is passing away........... 1 Jn 2:8
blackness of d forever......Jude 13

DARTS
quench all the fiery d...... Eph 6:16

DASH
You shall d them in........ Ps 2:9
lest you d your foot........ Matt 4:6

DASHED
hand, O LORD, has d......Ex 15:6
also will be d to.............Is 13:16
infants shall be d...........Hos 13:16

DAUGHTER
had neither son nor d......Judg 11:34
Rejoice greatly, O d........Zech 9:9
"Fear not, d of Zion.......John 12:15
the son of Pharaoh's d....Heb 11:24

DAUGHTERS
he begot sons and d........ Gen 5:4
of God saw the d...........Gen 6:2
a bird, and all the d........ Eccl 12:4
d shall prophesy..............Acts 2:17
man had four virgin d..... Acts 21:9
shall be My sons and d.... 2 Co 6:18

DAY
God called the light D..... Gen 1:5
and d and night.............. Gen 8:22
shall observe this d..........Ex 12:17
Remember the Sabbath d. Ex 20:8
and cursed the d.............Job 3:1
d utters speech............... Ps 19:2
For a d in Your courts.....Ps 84:10
d which the LORD has.... Ps 118:24
not strike you by d..........Ps 121:6
night shines as the d.......Ps 139:12
do not know what a d..... Prov 27:1
For the d of the LORD....Joel 2:11
who put far off the d......Amos 6:3
for the d of the LORD.....Zeph 1:7
who has despised the d.....Zech 4:10
who can endure the d......Mal 3:2
d our daily bread............Matt 6:11
and Gomorrah in the d....Matt 10:15
sent Me while it is d........John 9:4
great and notable d......... Acts 2:20
person esteems one d...... Rom 14:5
D will declare it.............1 Co 3:13
again the third d.............1 Co 15:4
perfectly that the d..........1 Th 5:2
and sons of the d............1 Th 5:5
with the Lord one d........2 Pe 3:8

DAYS
d are swifter than a.........Job 7:6
Let me alone, for my d....Job 7:16
of woman is of few d.......Job 14:1
blessed the latter d.........Job 42:12
The d of our lives are......Ps 90:10
for length of d................Prov 3:2
Why were the former d....Eccl 7:10
before the difficult d.......Eccl 12:1
and tested them ten d......Dan 1:14
had shortened those d......Mark 13:20
raise it up in three d....... John 2:20
You observe d and.........Gal 4:10
life and see good d..........1 Pe 3:10

DAYSPRING
with which the D............ Luke 1:78

DEACONS
with the bishops and d.....Phil 1:1
d must be reverent..........1 Ti 3:8
d be the husbands...........1 Ti 3:12

DEAD
"We shall all be d...........Ex 12:33
he stood between the d....Num 16:48
work wonders for the d....Ps 88:10
who have long been d......Ps 143:3
but the d know nothing....Eccl 9:5
shall cast out the d.........Is 26:19
d bury their own d..........Matt 8:22
d are raised up and........ Matt 11:5
not the God of the d......Matt 22:32
for this my son was d......Luke 15:24
d will hear the voice.......John 5:25
was raised from the d......Rom 6:4
yourselves to be d...........Rom 6:11
from the law sin was d.....Rom 7:8
be Lord of both the d......Rom 14:9
resurrection of the d........1 Co 15:12

DEADLY
baptized for the *d*.......... 1 Co 15:29
made alive, who were *d*... Eph 2:1
And the *d* in Christ.........1 Th 4:16
d while she lives............. 1 Ti 5:6
without works is *d*...........Jas 2:26
d did not live again......... Rev 20:5
And the *d* were judged.... Rev 20:12

DEADLY
they drink anything *d*..... Mark 16:18
evil, full of *d* poison........Jas 3:8
d wound was healed........ Rev 13:3

DEADNESS
the *d* of Sarah's womb..... Rom 4:19

DEAF
makes the mute, the *d*..... Ex 4:11
d shall hear the words..... Is 29:18
d shall be unstopped........Is 35:5
d as My messenger..........Is 42:19
d who have ears............. Is 43:8
their ears shall be *d*........Mic 7:16
are cleansed and the *d*..... Matt 11:5

DEAL
Do you thus *d* with the....Deut 32:6
My Servant shall *d*.......... Is 52:13

DEATH
Let me die the *d*............Num 23:10
d parts you and me......... Ruth 1:17
and the shadow of *d*........Job 10:21
You will bring me to *d*.... Job 30:23
For in *d* there is no.........Ps 6:5
I sleep the sleep of *d*...... Ps 13:3
of the shadow of *d*.......... Ps 23:4
my soul from *d*.............. Ps 56:13
can live and not see *d*..... Ps 89:48
house leads down to *d*..... Prov 2:18
who hate me love *d*........Prov 8:36
D and life are in the...... Prov 18:21
swallow up *d* forever....... Is 25:8
no pleasure in the *d*....... Ezek 18:32
redeem them from *d*.......Hos 13:14
turns the shadow of *d*.....Amos 5:8
who shall not taste *d*...... Matt 16:28
but has passed from *d*......John 5:24
he shall never see *d*........John 8:51
Nevertheless *d* reigned.....Rom 5:14
as sin reigned in *d*..........Rom 5:21
D no longer has..............Rom 6:9
the wages of sin is *d*.......Rom 6:23
to bear fruit to *d*........... Rom 7:5
proclaim the Lord's *d*.... 1 Co 11:26
since by man came *d*...... 1 Co 15:21
D is swallowed up in...... 1 Co 15:54
The sting of *d* is sin..... 1 Co 15:56
we are the aroma of *d*.....2 Co 2:16
d is working in us...........2 Co 4:12
the world produces *d*......2 Co 7:10
to the point of *d*............Phil 2:8
d crowned with glory.......Heb 2:9
who had the power of *d*...Heb 2:14
that he did not see *d*......Heb 11:5
brings forth *d*................Jas 1:15
to God, being put to *d*.... 1 Pe 3:18
is sin leading to *d*...........1 Jn 5:16
Be faithful until *d*.......... Rev 2:10
Over such the second *d*...Rev 20:6
shall be no more *d*......... Rev 21:4
which is the second *d*..... Rev 21:8

DEBTOR
I am a *d* both to............Rom 1:14
that he is a *d* to keep......Gal 5:3

DEBTORS
As we forgive our *d*....... Matt 6:12
of his master's *d*............ Luke 16:5
brethren, we are *d*.......... Rom 8:12
and they are their *d*........ Rom 15:27

DECEIT
d shall not dwell............. Ps 101:7
D is in the heart of......... Prov 12:20
nor was any *d* in His.......Is 53:9
They hold fast to *d*......... Jer 8:5
"O full of all *d*............... Acts 13:10
philosophy and empty *d*... Col 2:8

DECEITFUL
deliver me from the *d*......Ps 43:1
d men shall not............. Ps 55:23
of the wicked are *d*........ Prov 12:5
of an enemy are *d*..........Prov 27:6
"The heart is *d*................Jer 17:9
are false apostles, *d*.........2 Co 11:13

DECEITFULLY
an idol, Nor sworn *d*....... Ps 24:4
the word of God *d*.......... 2 Co 4:2

DECEITFULNESS
this world and the *d*........ Matt 13:22
hardened through the *d*....Heb 3:13

DECEIVE
'Do not *d* yourselves....... Jer 37:9
rise up and *d* many.......... Matt 24:11
wonders, so as to *d*......... Matt 24:24
Let no one *d* himself....... 1 Co 3:18
they lie in wait to *d*........Eph 4:14
Let no one *d* you with.....Eph 5:6
we have no sin, we *d*.......1 Jn 1:8

DECEIVED
"The serpent *d*............... Gen 3:13
d heart has turned him.... Is 44:20
by the commandment, *d*...Rom 7:11
as the serpent *d*............. 2 Co 11:3
but the woman being *d*... 1 Ti 2:14
deceiving and being *d*.....2 Ti 3:13

DECEIVER
But cursed be the *d*........Mal 1:14
how that *d* said.............Matt 27:63
This is a *d* and an...........2 Jn 7

DECEIVES
heed that no one *d*......... Matt 24:4
d his own heart.............. Jas 1:26

DECENTLY
all things be done *d*.........1 Co 14:40

DECEPTION
d all the day long............Ps 38:12

DECEPTIVE
you with *d* words............2 Pe 2:3

DECISION
but its every *d*................ Prov 16:33
in the valley of *d*............Joel 3:14 .

DECLARE
The heavens *d* the...........Ps 19:1
d Your name to My.......... Ps 22:22
d what He has done........ Ps 66:16
d that the LORD is......... Ps 92:15
d His generation............. Is 53:8
"I will *d* Your name....... Heb 2:12
seen and heard we *d*....... 1 Jn 1:3

DECLARED
the Father, He has *d*.......John 1:18
and *d* to be the Son of.... Rom 1:4

DECREE
I will declare the *d*..........Ps 2:7
d which shall not pass......Ps 148:6
in those days that a *d*..... Luke 2:1

DEDICATED
house and has not *d*........ Deut 20:5
every *d* thing in.............. Ezek 44:29
is Corban (that is, *d*........ Mark 7:11
first covenant was *d*........Heb 9:18

DEDICATION
sacrifices at the *d*............Ezra 6:17
it was the Feast of *D*.......John 10:22

DEED
d has been done.............. Judg 19:30
you do a charitable *d*.......Matt 6:2
you do in word or *d*........Col 3:17

DEEDS
Declare His *d* among.......Ps 9:11
vengeance on their *d*....... Ps 99:8
harlot by their own *d*.......Ps 106:39
declare His *d* among........Is 12:4
they surpass the *d*..........Jer 5:28
because their *d*...............John 3:19
"You do the *d*................John 8:41
one according to his *d*.....Rom 2:6
you put to death the *d*.... Rom 8:13
shares in his evil *d*......... 2 Jn 11

DEEP
LORD God caused a *d*.... Gen 2:21
He lays up the *d*.............Ps 33:7
D calls unto *d*............... Ps 42:7
In His hand are the *d*......Ps 95:4
His wonders in the *d*...... Ps 107:24
put out in *d* darkness.......Prov 20:20
led them through the *d*... Is 63:13
d closed around me.........Jon 2:5
d uttered its voice........... Hab 3:10
Launch out into the *d*.....Luke 5:4
I have been in the *d*........2 Co 11:25

DEEPER
D than Sheol.................Job 11:8

DEEPLY
Drink, yes, drink *d*.......... Song 5:1
But He sighed *d*............. Mark 8:12

DEER
"Naphtali is a *d*.............. Gen 49:21
As the *d* pants for the..... Ps 42:1
shall leap like a *d*........... Is 35:6

DEFEATED
and Israel was *d*............. 1 Sa 4:10

DEFECT
who has any *d*................Lev 21:17

DEFEND
'For I will *d* this............. 2 Ki 19:34
d my own ways before.....Job 13:15
D the poor and.............. Ps 82:3
d the fatherless..............Is 1:17
of hosts *d* Jerusalem........Is 31:5

DEFENDER
a *d* of widows................Ps 68:5

DEFENSE
For wisdom is a *d*...........Eccl 7:12
d will be the..................Is 33:16
am appointed for the *d*....Phil 1:17
d no one stood with me...2 Ti 4:16
be ready to give a *d*........1 Pe 3:15

DEFILE
the heart, and they *d*......Matt 15:18
also these dreamers *d*......Jude 8

DEFILED
d the dwelling place.......Ps 74:7
For your hands are *d*.......Is 59:3
lest they should be *d*.......John 18:28
to those who are *d*.........Tit 1:15
and conscience are *d*.......Tit 1:15
even the garment *d*.........Jude 23

DEFILES
mouth, this *d* a man........Matt 15:11
d the temple of God.......1 Co 3:17
it anything that *d*............Rev 21:27

DEFRAUD
'You shall not *d*.............Lev 19:13
d his brother in this.........1 Th 4:6

DEFRAUDED
let yourselves be *d*.......... 1 Co 6:7
no one, we have *d*..........2 Co 7:2

DEGENERATE
before Me into the *d*.......Jer 2:21
d is your heart................Ezek 16:30

DELICACIES
let me eat of their *d*........Ps 141:4
Do not desire his *d*........Prov 23:3
of the king's *d*................Dan 1:5

DELICATE
be called tender and *d*.....Is 47:1
a lovely and *d* woman......Jer 6:2

DELIGHT
the LORD as great *d*.......1 Sa 15:22
And his heart took *d*.......2 Ch 17:6
Will he *d* himself in.........Job 27:10
But his *d* is in the...........Ps 1:2
D yourself also in the.......Ps 37:4
I *d* to do Your will..........Ps 40:8
Your law had been my *d*..Ps 119:92
d ourselves with love.......Prov 7:18
and I was daily His *d*......Prov 8:30
truthfully are His *d*.........Prov 12:22
and let your soul *d*.........Is 55:2
call the Sabbath a *d*........Is 58:13
For I *d* in the law of......Rom 7:22

DELIGHTED
"The LORD *d* only in......Deut 10:15

DELIGHTS
O love, with your *d*........Song 7:6
for the LORD *d* in you....Is 62:4
forever, because He *d*......Mic 7:18

DELIVER
d them out of the hand....Ex 3:8
He shall *d* you in six......Job 5:19
is no one who can *d*......Job 10:7
D him from going down...Job 33:24
Let Him *d* Him.............Ps 22:8
d their soul from...........Ps 33:19
I will *d* him and honor....Ps 91:15

d you from the immoral...Prov 2:16
wickedness will not *d*......Eccl 8:8
have I no power to *d*......Is 50:2
we serve is able to *d*......Dan 3:17
into temptation, but *d*.....Matt 6:13
let Him *d* Him now if.....Matt 27:43
d such a one to Satan.....1 Co 5:5
And the Lord will *d*......2 Ti 4:18
d the godly out of..........2 Pe 2:9

DELIVERANCE
d He gives to His king.....Ps 18:50
but *d* is of the LORD.....Prov 21:31
to preach *d* to the.........Luke 4:18
not accepting *d*..............Heb 11:35

DELIVERED
d the poor who cried......Job 29:12
For You have *d* my soul..Ps 56:13
For He has *d* the life......Jer 20:13
All things have been *d*.....Matt 11:27
who was *d* up because.....Rom 4:25
But now we have been *d*.Rom 7:6
who *d* us from so great....2 Co 1:10
was once for all *d*..........Jude 3

DELIVERER
the LORD raised up a *d*...Judg 3:9
LORD gave Israel a *d*......2 Ki 13:5
D will come out of.........Rom 11:26

DELIVERERS
d who saved them...........Neh 9:27

DELIVERS
d the kingdom to God.....1 Co 15:24
dead, even Jesus who *d*...1 Th 1:10

DELUSION
send them strong *d*.........2 Th 2:11

DEMON
Jesus rebuked the *d*........Matt 17:18
you say, 'He has a *d*......Luke 7:33
Samaritan and have a *d*...John 8:48

DEMONIC
is earthly, sensual, *d*.......Jas 3:15

DEMONS
They sacrificed to *d*........Deut 32:17
their daughters to *d*........Ps 106:37
authority over all *d*........Luke 9:1
even the *d* are subject......Luke 10:17
Lord and the cup of *d*....1 Co 10:21
Even the *d* believe.........Jas 2:19
a habitation of *d*............Rev 18:2

DEMONSTRATE
faith, to *d* His...............Rom 3:25

DEMONSTRATES
d His own love toward.....Rom 5:8

DEN
in the viper's *d*..............Is 11:8
by My name, become a *d*.Jer 7:11
cast him into the *d*.........Dan 6:16
it a '*d of thieves*............Matt 21:13

DENARIUS
the laborers for a *d*........Matt 20:2
they brought Him a *d*......Matt 22:19
quart of wheat for a *d*.....Rev 6:6

DENIED
before men will be *d*.......Luke 12:9
Peter then *d* again..........John 18:27
d the Holy One and the...Acts 3:14
things cannot be *d*..........Acts 19:36
household, he has *d*........1 Ti 5:8
word, and have not *d*......Rev 3:8

DENIES
"But whoever *d*..............Matt 10:33
d that Jesus is the..........1 Jn 2:22

DENS
lie down in their *d*.........Ps 104:22
and mountains, in *d*........Heb 11:38

DENY
Lest I be full and *d*........Prov 30:9
let him *d* himself...........Matt 16:24
He cannot *d* Himself.......2 Ti 2:13
in works they *d*.............Tit 1:16
d the only Lord.............Jude 4
d My faith even.............Rev 2:13

DENYING
but *d* its power..............2 Ti 3:5
d ungodliness and..........Tit 2:12
d the Lord who bought....2 Pe 2:1

DEPART
scepter shall not *d*..........Gen 49:10
they say to God, 'D........Job 21:14
D from evil..................Ps 34:14
fear the LORD and *d*......Prov 3:7
the mountains shall *d*......Is 54:10
on the left hand, 'D........Matt 25:41
times some will *d*...........1 Ti 4:1

DEPARTED
the day that you *d*.........Deut 9:7

DEPARTING
heart of unbelief in *d*......Heb 3:12

DEPARTURE
d savage wolves will........Acts 20:29
and the time of my *d*......2 Ti 4:6

DEPOSIT
in our hearts as a *d*........2 Co 1:22

DEPRESSION
of man causes *d*.............Prov 12:25

DEPRIVE
d myself of good............Eccl 4:8
d one another except.......1 Co 7:5

DEPTH
because they had no *d*.....Matt 13:5
nor height nor *d*............Rom 8:39
Oh, the *d* of the............Rom 11:33
width and length and *d*....Eph 3:18

DEPTHS
d have covered them.......Ex 15:5
The *d* also trembled........Ps 77:16
my soul from the *d*........Ps 86:13
led them through the *d*....Ps 106:9
go down again to the *d*....Ps 107:26
d I was brought forth......Prov 8:24
our sins into the *d*.........Mic 7:19
have not known the *d*......Rev 2:24

DERANGED
the nations are *d*............Jer 51:7

DERISION
shall hold them in *d*........ Ps 2:4
I am in *d* daily............... Jer 20:7

DESCEND
His glory shall not *d*.......Ps 49:17
d now from the cross......Mark 15:32
Lord Himself will *d*..........1 Th 4:16
This wisdom does not *d*...Jas 3:15

DESCENDANTS
All you *d* of Jacob.......... Ps 22:23
d shall inherit the............Ps 25:13
In the LORD all the *d*.... Is 45:25
"We are Abraham's *d*.....John 8:33

DESCENDED
because the LORD *d*....... Ex 19:18
that He also first *d*.........Eph 4:9
He who *d* is also the...... Eph 4:10

DESCENDING
were ascending and *d*...... Gen 28:12
"I saw the Spirit *d*.......... John 1:32
of God ascending and *d*... John 1:51
the holy Jerusalem, *d*...... Rev 21:10

DESERT
d shall rejoice.................Is 35:1
and rivers in the *d*.......... Is 43:19
'Look, He is in the *d*......Matt 24:26

DESERTED
d place by Himself......... Matt 14:13

DESERTS
led them through the *d*.... Is 48:21
They wandered in *d*........ Heb 11:38

DESERVE
to them what they *d*........Ps 28:4
d I will judge them......... Ezek 7:27

DESIRABLE
the eyes, and a tree *d*......Gen 3:6
d that we should leave..... Acts 6:2

DESIRE
d shall be for your......... Gen 3:16
for we do not *d*.............Job 21:14
him his heart's *d*............Ps 21:2
Behold, You *d* truth in.... Ps 51:6
upon earth that I *d*......... Ps 73:25
The *d* of the wicked........ Ps 112:10
And satisfy the *d*........... Ps 145:16
The *d* of the slothful...... Prov 21:25
a burden, and *d* fails....... Eccl 12:5
the *d* of our soul is......... Is 26:8
d I have desired.............Luke 22:15
"Father, I *d* that............John 17:24
all manner of evil *d*........Rom 7:8
Brethren, my heart's *d*....Rom 10:1
d the best gifts............. 1 Co 12:31
d spiritual gifts.............. 1 Co 14:1
the two, having a *d*........ Phil 1:23
passion, evil *d*................ Col 3:5
d has conceived............. Jas 1:15

DESIRED
d are they than gold........Ps 19:10
One thing I have *d*.........Ps 27:4
guides them to their *d*..... Ps 107:30
What is *d* in a man is...... Prov 19:22
Whatever my eyes *d*....... Eccl 2:10
desire I have *d*.............. Luke 22:15

DESIRES
Who is the man who *d*.... Ps 34:12
shall give you the *d*........Ps 37:4
the devil, and the *d*........John 8:44
fulfilling the *d*............... Eph 2:3
not come from your *d*.....Jas 4:1

DESOLATE
on me, For I am *d*...........Ps 25:16
the wilderness in a *d*....... Ps 107:4
my children and am *d*......Is 49:21
any more be termed *D*.... Is 62:4
to make your land *d*........Jer 4:7
house is left to you *d*......Matt 23:38
one hour she is made *d*...Rev 18:19

DESOLATION
the '*abomination of d*......Matt 24:15
then know that its *d*....... Luke 21:20

DESOLATIONS
LORD, Who has made *d*..Ps 46:8

DESPAIRED
turned my heart and *d*.....Eccl 2:20
strength, so that we *d*......2 Co 1:8

DESPERATELY
he flees *d* from its...........Job 27:22

DESPISE
if you *d* My statutes........ Lev 26:15
d Me shall be lightly........1 Sa 2:30
d your mother when she.. Prov 23:22
d your feast days............ Amos 5:21
to you priests who *d*.......Mal 1:6
one and *d* the other........ Matt 6:24
d the riches of His......... Rom 2:4
d the church of God........1 Co 11:22
and *d* authority............... 2 Pe 2:10

DESPISED
poor man's wisdom is *d*... Eccl 9:16
d the word of the Holy.... Is 5:24
He is *d* and rejected.......Is 53:3
the things which are *d*..... 1 Co 1:28

DESPISES
wisdom *d* his neighbor..... Prov 11:12
d the word will be........... Prov 13:13
d his neighbor sins......... Prov 14:21
but a foolish man *d*.........Prov 15:20
d the scepter of My........Ezek 21:10

DESPISING
the cross, *d* the shame..... Heb 12:2

DESTINY
did not consider her *d*..... Lam 1:9

DESTITUTE
the prayer of the *d*.........Ps 102:17
of corrupt minds and *d*.... 1 Ti 6:5
sister is naked and *d*.......Jas 2:15

DESTROY
d the righteous............... Gen 18:23
d all the wicked.............. Ps 101:8
of the LORD I will *d*......Ps 118:10
the wicked He will *d*....... Ps 145:20
why should you *d*...........Eccl 7:16
shall not hurt nor *d*........ Is 11:9
have mercy, but will *d*..... Jer 13:14
d them with double......... Jer 17:18
I did not come to *d*........Matt 5:17
Him who is able to *d*......Matt 10:28

DESIRES
Barabbas and *d* Jesus...... Matt 27:20
d this temple that is........ Mark 14:58
to save life or to *d*......... Luke 6:9
d men's lives but to........Luke 9:56
d the work of God for..... Rom 14:20
d the wisdom of the....... 1 Co 1:19
foods, but God will *d*...... 1 Co 6:13
able to save and to *d*......Jas 4:12

DESTROYED
d all living things............ Gen 7:23
d those who hated me..... 2 Sa 22:41
My people are *d*............. Hos 4:6
"O Israel, you are *d*........Hos 13:9
house, this tent, is *d*........2 Co 5:1

DESTROYER
the paths of the *d*........... Ps 17:4
him who is a great *d*....... Prov 18:9
destroyed by the *d*..........1 Co 10:10

DESTRUCTION
not be afraid of *d*........... Job 5:21
D has no covering...........Job 26:6
d come upon him............Ps 35:8
cast them down to *d*....... Ps 73:18
You turn man to *d*.........Ps 90:3
d that lays waste............ Ps 91:6
your life from *d*.............. Ps 103:4
d will come to the...........Prov 10:29
Pride goes before *d*........ Prov 16:18
d the heart of a man....... Prov 18:12
called the City of *D*....... Is 19:18
neither wasting nor *d*......Is 60:18
heifer, But *d* comes.........Jer 46:20
wrath prepared for *d*...... Rom 9:22
one to Satan for the *d*.... 1 Co 5:5
whose end is *d*............... Phil 3:19
then sudden *d*................ 1 Th 5:3
with everlasting *d*...........2 Th 1:9
which drown men in *d*..... 1 Ti 6:9
twist to their own *d*......... 2 Pe 3:16

DESTRUCTIVE
bring in *d* heresies...........2 Pe 2:1

DETERMINED
Since his days are *d*........Job 14:5
of hosts will make a *d*.... Is 10:23
"Seventy weeks are *d*..... Dan 9:24
d their preappointed....... Acts 17:26
For I *d* not to know........ 1 Co 2:2

DETESTABLE
shall not eat any *d*.......... Deut 14:3

DEVICE
there is no work or *d*...... Eccl 9:10

DEVICES
not ignorant of his *d*........2 Co 2:11

DEVIL
to be tempted by the *d*... Matt 4:1
prepared for the *d*..........Matt 25:41
forty days by the *d*..........Luke 4:2
then the *d* comes and...... Luke 8:12
and one of you is a *d*...... John 6:70
of your father the *d*........John 8:44
d having already put........John 13:2
give place to the *d*.......... Eph 4:27
the wiles of the *d*............ Eph 6:11
the snare of the *d*........... 2 Ti 2:26
Resist the *d* and he......... Jas 4:7
the works of the *d*.......... 1 Jn 3:8
contending with the *d*......Jude 9
Indeed, the *d* is about..... Rev 2:10

DEVIOUS
crooked, and who are d...Prov 2:15

DEVISE
Do not d evil against......Prov 3:29
Woe to those who d........Mic 2:1

DEVISES
d wickedness on his........Ps 36:4
he d evil continually........Prov 6:14
d wicked plans to............Is 32:7
But a generous man d..... Is 32:8

DEVOID
He who is d of wisdom....Prov 11:12

DEVOTED
d offering is most...........Lev 27:28
"Every d thing in............Num 18:14
Your servant, Who is d....Ps 119:38

DEVOUR
A fire shall d before........Ps 50:3
For you d widows'.......... Matt 23:14
bite and d one another.... Gal 5:15
seeking whom he may d...1 Pe 5:8
d her Child as................ Rev 12:4

DEVOURED
Some wild beast has d..... Gen 37:20
rebel, you shall be d........Is 1:20
the curse has d..............Is 24:6
Your sword has d........... Jer 2:30
For shame has d............Jer 3:24
have d their judges........Hos 7:7
trees, The locust d......... Amos 4:9
birds came and d them.... Matt 13:4
of heaven and d them......Rev 20:9

DEVOURER
I will rebuke the d.........Mal 3:11

DEVOURING
You love all d words....... Ps 52:4
the flame of d fire...........Is 29:6

DEVOUT
man was just and d.........Luke 2:25
d men carried................Acts 8:2
d soldier from among...... Acts 10:7
d proselytes...................Acts 13:43

DEW
God give you of the d..... Gen 27:28
shall also drop d............Deut 33:28
his favor is like d...........Prov 19:12
your d is like the d......... Is 26:19
like the early d..............Hos 6:4
many peoples, like d....... Mic 5:7

DIADEM
LORD, and a royal d.......Is 62:3

DIADEMS
ten horns, and seven d.....Rev 12:3

DIAMOND
d it is engraved...............Jer 17:1

DIE
it you shall surely d.........Gen 2:17
but a person shall d.........2 Ch 25:4
sees that wise men d....... Ps 49:10
I shall not d..................Ps 118:17
who are appointed to d....Prov 31:8
how does a wise man d....Eccl 2:16

born, and a time to d...... Eccl 3:2
why should you d............Eccl 7:17
wicked way, he shall d....Ezek 3:19
"Even if I have to d.......Matt 26:35
"nor can they d..............Luke 20:36
eat of it and not d.......... John 6:50
to you that you will d.....John 8:24
though he may d............John 11:25
that one man should d....John 11:50
that Jesus would d......... John 11:51
our law He ought to d.....John 19:7
the flesh you will d......... Rom 8:13
For as in Adam all d.......1 Co 15:22
and to d is gain.............. Phil 1:21
for men to d once........... Heb 9:27
are the dead who d......... Rev 14:13

DIED
And all flesh d............... Gen 7:21
"Oh, that we had d.........Ex 16:3
was that the beggar d....... Luke 16:22
in due time Christ d........ Rom 5:6
Christ d for us................Rom 5:8
For he who has d............Rom 6:7
Now if we d with........... Rom 6:8
sin revived and I d.......... Rom 7:9
that if One d for all....... 2 Co 5:14
and He d for all............. 2 Co 5:15
through the law d........... Gal 2:19
who d for us...................1 Th 5:10
For if we d with Him...... 2 Ti 2:11
These all d in faith.........Heb 11:13
having d to sins.............. 1 Pe 2:24

DIES
made alive unless it d......1 Co 15:36

DIFFERS
for one star d from......... 1 Co 15:41

DILIGENCE
d is man's......................Prov 12:27
d it produced in you.......2 Co 7:11
of your love by the d.......2 Co 8:8

DILIGENT
And my spirit makes d.... Ps 77:6
d makes one rich............ Prov 10:4
of the d will rule............Prov 12:24
d shall be made rich........Prov 13:4
Let us therefore be d.......Heb 4:11

DILIGENTLY
if you d obey My...........Deut 11:13
d followed every good..... 1 Ti 5:10
d lest anyone fall............ Heb 12:15

DIM
His eyes were not d........ Deut 34:7
the windows grow d........Eccl 12:3
the gold has become d.....Lam 4:1

DIMLY
we see in a mirror, d.......1 Co 13:12

DINE
asked Him to d with.......Luke 11:37
come in to him and d...... Rev 3:20

DINNER
I have prepared my d...... Matt 22:4
invites you to d.............. 1 Co 10:27

DIP
d your piece of bread...... Ruth 2:14

DIPPED
d his finger in the........... Lev 9:9
of bread when I have d....John 13:26
clothed with a robe d...... Rev 19:13

DIRECT
the morning I will d........ Ps 5:3
d their work in truth....... Is 61:8
Now may the Lord d.......2 Th 3:5

DIRT
I cast them out like d..... Ps 18:42
cast up mire and d.......... Is 57:20

DISAPPEARS
As water d from the........Job 14:11

DISARMS
and d the mighty............ Job 12:21

DISASTER
D will come upon........... Ezek 7:26
you shall see d............... Zeph 3:15
voyage will end with d..... Acts 27:10

DISCERN
Can I d between the........2 Sa 19:35
Then you shall again d....Mal 3:18
d the face of the sky....... Matt 16:3
senses exercised to d....... Heb 5:14

DISCERNED
they are spiritually d........1 Co 2:14

DISCERNER
d of the thoughts............ Heb 4:12

DISCERNMENT
and takes away the d.......Job 12:20

DISCERNS
a wise man's heart d........Eccl 8:5

DISCIPLE
d is not above his........... Matt 10:24
in the name of a d...........Matt 10:42
he cannot be My d..........Luke 14:26
d whom Jesus loved........ John 21:7

DISCIPLES
but Your d do not fast.....Matt 9:14
d transgress the.............. Matt 15:2
took the twelve d............Matt 20:17
My word, you are My d...John 8:31
to become His d.............John 9:27
but we are Moses' d........John 9:28
so you will be My d........John 15:8

DISCIPLINES
but he who loves him d... Prov 13:24

DISCORD
and one who sows d........Prov 6:19

DISCOURAGED
will not fail nor be d....... Is 42:4
lest they become d.......... Col 3:21
you become weary and d..Heb 12:3

DISCRETION
d will preserve you.......... Prov 2:11
out knowledge and d....... Prov 8:12
woman who lacks d......... Prov 11:22
The d of a man makes.....Prov 19:11
the heavens at His d........ Jer 10:12

DISFIGURE
d their faces that............Matt 6:16

DISGUISES
and he *d* his face...........Job 24:15
He who hates, *d*............Prov 26:24

DISHONOR
d Who wish me evil........Ps 40:14
d the pride of all............Is 23:9
Father, and you *d* Me.....John 8:49
d their bodies among.......Rom 1:24
and another for *d*............Rom 9:21
It is sown in *d*..............1 Co 15:43
honor and some for *d*......2 Ti 2:20

DISHONORED
But you have *d* the.........Jas 2:6

DISHONORS
For son *d* father.............Mic 7:6
covered, *d* his head.........1 Co 11:4

DISOBEDIENCE
d many were made..........Rom 5:19
works in the sons of *d*.....Eph 2:2
d received a just.............Heb 2:2

DISOBEDIENT
out My hands to a *d*.......Rom 10:21
d, deceived, serving.........Tit 3:3
They stumble, being *d*.....1 Pe 2:8
who formerly were *d*.......1 Pe 3:20

DISORDERLY
for this *d* gathering..........Acts 19:40
brother who walks *d*........2 Th 3:6

DISPENSATION
d of the fullness of..........Eph 1:10
d of the grace of God......Eph 3:2

DISPERSE
d them throughout the.....Ezek 20:23

DISPERSION
intend to go to the *D*......John 7:35
the pilgrims of the *D*.......1 Pe 1:1

DISPLEASE
LORD see it, and it *d*.....Prov 24:18

DISPLEASED
that David had done *d*.....2 Sa 11:27
You have been *d*............Ps 60:1
it, He was greatly *d*........Mark 10:14

DISPUTER
Where is the *d* of this......1 Co 1:20

DISPUTES
d rather than godly.........1 Ti 1:4
but is obsessed with *d*.....1 Ti 6:4
foolish and ignorant *d*......2 Ti 2:23
But avoid foolish *d*.........Tit 3:9

DISQUALIFIED
myself should become *d*...1 Co 9:27
indeed you are *d*............2 Co 13:5
though we may seem *d*....2 Co 13:7

DISSENSION
had no small *d* and.........Acts 15:2

DISSENSIONS
selfish ambitions, *d*..........Gal 5:20

DISSIPATION
not accused of *d*............Tit 1:6
in the same flood of *d*.....1 Pe 4:4

DISSOLVED
of heaven shall be *d*........Is 34:4
the heavens will be *d*......2 Pe 3:12

DISTINCTION
"and made no *d*.............Acts 15:9
For there is no *d*............Rom 10:12
compassion, making a *d*...Jude 22

DISTRESS
me in the day of my *d*.....Gen 35:3
"When you are in *d*........Deut 4:30
my life from every *d*........1 Ki 1:29
you out of dire *d*............Job 36:16
keep you from *d*............Job 36:19
d them in His deep.........Ps 2:5
on the LORD in *d*..........Ps 118:5
a whirlwind, when *d*.......Prov 1:27
and on the earth *d*.........Luke 21:25
tribulation, or *d*.............Rom 8:35
of the present *d*.............1 Co 7:26

DISTRESSED
heart within me is *d*........Ps 143:4
troubled and deeply *d*.....Mark 14:33

DISTRESSES
bring me out of my *d*......Ps 25:17

DISTRIBUTE
that you have and *d*........Luke 18:22

DISTRIBUTED
and they *d* to each as......Acts 4:35
But as God has *d*............1 Co 7:17

DISTRIBUTING
d to the needs of the.......Rom 12:13

DITCH
will fall into a *d*.............Matt 15:14

DIVERSITIES
Now there are *d*............1 Co 12:4

DIVIDE
D the living child............1 Ki 3:25
d their tongues...............Ps 55:9
d the spoil with the........Prov 16:19
d the inheritance............Luke 12:13
"Take this and *d*............Luke 22:17

DIVIDED
and the waters were *d*.....Ex 14:21
death they were not *d*......2 Sa 1:23
And You *d* the sea..........Neh 9:11
"Who has *d* a channel.....Job 38:25
shall they ever be *d*........Ezek 37:22
kingdom has been *d*........Dan 5:28
your land shall be *d*........Amos 7:17
"Every kingdom *d*..........Matt 12:25
and a house *d* against......Luke 11:17
in one house will be *d*.....Luke 12:52
So he *d* to them his.........Luke 15:12
appeared to them *d*.........Acts 2:3
d them among all...........Acts 2:45
Is Christ *d*....................1 Co 1:13
the great city was *d*.........Rev 16:19

DIVIDES
at home *d* the spoil.........Ps 68:12

DIVIDING
rightly *d* the word of.......2 Ti 2:15

DIVINATION
shall you practice *d*.........Lev 19:26
Even though *d* is on........Prov 16:10
darkness without *d*..........Mic 3:6
a spirit of *d* met us.........Acts 16:16

DIVINE
futility and who *d*...........Ezek 13:9
and her prophets *d*.........Mic 3:11
d service and the............Heb 9:1
d power has given..........2 Pe 1:3

DIVINERS
your prophets, your *d*......Jer 27:9

DIVISION
So there was a *d*............John 7:43
the middle wall of *d*........Eph 2:14
piercing even to the *d*.....Heb 4:12

DIVISIONS
note those who cause *d*....Rom 16:17
and that there be no *d*.....1 Co 1:10
envy, strife, and *d*..........1 Co 3:3
hear that there are *d*.......1 Co 11:18
persons, who cause *d*......Jude 19

DIVISIVE
Reject a *d* man after.......Tit 3:10

DIVORCE
her a certificate of *d*.......Deut 24:1
of your mother's *d*..........Is 50:1
a certificate of *d*............Mark 10:4

DO
set in them to *d* evil........Eccl 8:11
I will also *d* it................Is 46:11
men to *d* to you, *d*.......Matt 7:12
d this and you will..........Luke 10:28
He sees the Father *d*.......John 5:19
without Me you can *d*......John 15:5
"Sirs, what must I *d*.......Acts 16:30
d evil that good may.......Rom 3:8
For what I will to *d*........Rom 7:15
good that I will to *d*........Rom 7:19
or whatever you *d*, *d*....1 Co 10:31
d all things through.........Phil 4:13
d in word or deed, *d*.....Col 3:17
d good and to share........Heb 13:16
and *d* this or that............Jas 4:15

DOCTRINE
said, 'my *d* is pure..........Job 11:4
for I give you good *d*.......Prov 4:2
idol is a worthless *d*........Jer 10:8
of bread, but of the *d*......Matt 16:12
What new *d* is this..........Mark 1:27
"My *d* is not Mine..........John 7:16
Jerusalem with your *d*.....Acts 5:28
heart that form of *d*........Rom 6:17
with every wind of *d*.......Eph 4:14
is contrary to sound *d*.....1 Ti 1:10
followed my *d*...............2 Ti 3:10
is profitable for *d*............2 Ti 3:16
not endure sound *d*........2 Ti 4:3
in *d* showing.................Tit 2:7
they may adorn the *d*......Tit 2:10
not abide in the *d*...........2 Jn 9

DOCTRINES
the commandments and *d*.Col 2:22
spirits and *d* of..............1 Ti 4:1
various and strange *d*.......Heb 13:9

DOERS

of God, but the *d*........... Rom 2:13
But be *d* of the word.......Jas 1:22

DOG

to David, "Am I a *d*....... 1 Sa 17:43
They growl like a *d*........ Ps 59:6
d returns to his own........ Prov 26:11
d is better than a............ Eccl 9:4
d returns to his own........ 2 Pe 2:22

DOGS

Yes, they are greedy *d*.....Is 56:11
what is holy to the *d*....... Matt 7:6
d eat the crumbs which....Matt 15:27
Moreover the *d* came...... Luke 16:21
But outside are *d*........... Rev 22:15

DOMINION

let them have *d*............. Gen 1:26
"*D* and fear belong.........Job 25:2
made him to have *d*....... Ps 8:6
Let them not have *d*.......Ps 19:13
besides You have had *d*... Is 26:13
d is an everlasting.........Dan 4:34
sin shall not have *d*......... Rom 6:14
Not that we have *d*......... 2 Co 1:24
glory and majesty, *d*.......Jude 25

DONKEY

d saw the Angel.............. Num 22:23
Does the wild *d*.............Job 6:5
d its master's crib............Is 1:3
and riding on a *d*............Zech 9:9
colt, the foal of a *d*........ Matt 21:5
He had found a young *d*..John 12:14
d speaking with a............2 Pe 2:16

DONKEY'S

d colt is born a man........Job 11:12

DONKEYS

d quench their thirst........Ps 104:11
a chariot of *d*................. Is 21:7
And the wild *d* stood.......Jer 14:6

DOOM

for the day of *d*............Prov 16:4

DOOR

sin lies at the *d*..............Gen 4:7
Keep watch over the *d*.....Ps 141:3
d turns on its hinges........Prov 26:14
stone against the *d*.......... Matt 27:60
to you, I am the *d*..........John 10:7
and effective *d*..............1 Co 16:9
d was opened to me by....2 Co 2:12
would open to us a *d*.......Col 4:3
is standing at the *d*........Jas 5:9
before you an open *d*..... Rev 3:8
I stand at the *d*.............. Rev 3:20
and behold, a *d*.............. Rev 4:1

DOORKEEPER

I would rather be a *d*...... Ps 84:10
"To him the *d*...............John 10:3

DOORPOSTS

write them on the *d*........ Deut 6:9
"Strike the *d*.................Amos 9:1

DOORS

up, you everlasting *d*.......Ps 24:7
the entrance of the *d*.......Prov 8:3
when the *d* are shut in....Eccl 12:4
who would shut the *d*...... Mal 1:10

DOUBLE

from the LORD's hand *d*..Is 40:2
first I will repay *d*...........Jer 16:18
worthy of *d* honor..........1 Ti 5:17
and repay her *d*.............. Rev 18:6

DOUBLE-MINDED

I hate the *d*................... Ps 119:113
he is a *d* man.................Jas 1:8
your hearts, you *d*...........Jas 4:8

DOUBT

life shall hang in *d*......... Deut 28:66
faith, why did you *d*........Matt 14:31

DOUBTING

without wrath and *d*........1 Ti 2:8
in faith, with no *d*...........Jas 1:6

DOUBTS

And why do *d* arise in.....Luke 24:38
for I have *d* about you.....Gal 4:20
doubting, for he who *d*....Jas 1:6

DOVE

d found no resting...........Gen 8:9
I had wings like a *d*........ Ps 55:6
I mourned like a *d*..........Is 38:14
also is like a silly *d*.........Hos 7:11
descending like a *d*.........Matt 3:16

DOVES

and moan sadly like a *d*.....Is 59:11
and harmless as *d*........... Matt 10:16
of those who sold *d*........Matt 21:12

DOWNCAST

who comforts the *d*......... 2 Co 7:6

DRAGNET

gather them in their *d*.....Hab 1:15
d that was cast.............. Matt 13:47

DRAGON

a great, fiery red *d*..........Rev 12:3
fought against the *d*........Rev 12:7
they worshiped the *d*...... Rev 13:4
He laid hold of the *d*.......Rev 20:2

DRAIN

wicked of the earth *D*......Ps 75:8

DRAINED

all faces are *d*.................Joel 2:6

DRANK

them, and they all *d*........Mark 14:23
d the same spiritual.........1 Co 10:4

DRAW

d honey from the rock.....Deut 32:13
me to *d* near to God.......Ps 73:28
and the years *d*..............Eccl 12:1
Woe to those who *d*........Is 5:18
with joy you will *d*..........Is 12:3
"*D* some out now...........John 2:8
You have nothing to *d*.....John 4:11
will *d* all peoples.............John 12:32
let us *d* near with a........Heb 10:22
D near to God and He....Jas 4:8

DRAWN

The wicked have *d*.........Ps 37:14
tempted when he is *d*...... Jas 1:14

DRAWS

And my life *d* near to......Ps 88:3
your redemption *d*.......... Luke 21:28

DREAD

fear of you and the *d*...... Gen 9:2
begin to put the *d*...........Deut 2:25

DREADFUL

of the great and *d*...........Mal 4:5

DREAM

Now Joseph dreamed a *d*. Gen 37:5
I speak to him in a *d*...... Num 12:6
will fly away like a *d*.......Job 20:8
As a *d* when one awakes..Ps 73:20
like those who *d*............Ps 126:1
For a *d* comes through.....Eccl 5:3
her, shall be as a *d*......... Is 29:7
prophet who has a *d*.......Jer 23:28
do not let the *d*..............Dan 4:19
your old men shall *d*...... Joel 2:28
to Joseph in a *d*.............Matt 2:13
things today in a *d*..........Matt 27:19
your old men shall *d*........Acts 2:17

DREAMERS

d defile the flesh.............Jude 8

DREAMS

in the multitude of *d*.......Eccl 5:7
when a hungry man *d*......Is 29:8
Nebuchadnezzar had *d*.....Dan 2:1

DREGS

d shall all the wicked.......Ps 75:8
has settled on his *d*.........Jer 48:11

DRIED

My strength is *d*............. Ps 22:15
of her blood was *d*..........Mark 5:29
saw the fig tree *d*...........Mark 11:20
and its water was *d*......... Rev 16:12

DRIFT

have heard, lest we *d*...... Heb 2:1

DRINK

"What shall we *d*............Ex 15:24
"Do not *d* wine or..........Lev 10:9
and let him *d* of the........Job 21:20
gave me vinegar to *d*.......Ps 69:21
D water from your own... Prov 5:15
mocker, intoxicating *d*.... Prov 20:1
lest they *d* and forget..... Prov 31:5
Give strong *d* to him....... Prov 31:6
Let him *d* and forget...... Prov 31:7
d your wine with a..........Eccl 9:7
follow intoxicating *d*....... Is 5:11
mixing intoxicating *d*......Is 5:22
d dry the milk of the......Is 60:16
My servants shall *d*......... Is 65:13
bosom, that you may *d*....Is 66:11
d water by measure........Ezek 4:11
Bring wine, let us *d*........Amos 2:1
to you of wine and *d*......Mic 2:11
and you gave Me no *d*.....Matt 25:42
that day when I *d*...........Matt 26:29
mingled with gall to *d*.....Matt 27:34
with myrrh to *d*..............Mark 15:23
to her, "Give Me a *d*...... John 4:7
him come to Me and *d*....John 7:37
d wine nor do anything....Rom 14:21
do, as often as you *d*.......1 Co 11:25
all been made to *d*..........1 Co 12:13
No longer *d* only water....1 Ti 5:23
has made all nations *d*.....Rev 14:8

DRINKS

to her, "Whoever *d*........John 4:13
d My blood has...............John 6:54
For he who eats and *d*....1 Co 11:29
For the earth which *d*......Heb 6:7

DRIPPING

wife are a continual *d*......Prov 19:13
His lips are lilies, *d*.........Song 5:13

DRIVE

of the wicked *d*............. Ps 36:11
They shall *d* you from..... Dan 4:25
temple and began to *d*..... Mark 11:15

DRIVEN

They were *d* out from......Job 30:5
Let them be *d* backward.. Ps 40:14
sail and so were *d*.......... Acts 27:17
a wave of the sea *d*.........Jas 1:6

DROP

They *d* on the pastures.... Ps 65:12
the nations are as a *d*...... Is 40:15

DROSS

of the earth like *d*...........Ps 119:119
Take away the *d*............Prov 25:4
purge away your *d*...........Is 1:25
of Israel has become *d*.....Ezek 22:18

DROUGHT

through a land of *d*.........Jer 2:6
in the year of *d*............. Jer 17:8
For I called for a *d*......... Hag 1:11

DROVE

So He *d* out the man.......Gen 3:24
temple of God and *d*......Matt 21:12
a whip of cords, He *d*.....John 2:15

DROWN

nor can the floods *d*........ Song 8:7
harmful lusts which *d*.......1 Ti 6:9

DROWSINESS

d will clothe a................ Prov 23:21

DRUNK

of the wine and was *d*..... Gen 9:21
d my wine with my milk.. Song 5:1
you afflicted, and *d*.......... Is 51:21
My anger, made them *d*...Is 63:6
be satiated and made *d*....Jer 46:10
the guests have well *d*......John 2:10
For these are not *d*.......... Acts 2:15
and another is *d*............. 1 Co 11:21
And do not be *d*.............Eph 5:18
and those who get *d*.........1 Th 5:7
the earth were made *d*.....Rev 17:2
And I saw the woman, *d*..Rev 17:6

DRUNKARD

d could be included.........Deut 29:19
d is a proverb in the.......Prov 26:9
to and fro like a *d*........... Is 24:20
or a reviler, or a *d*..........1 Co 5:11

DRUNKEN

I am like a *d* man...........Jer 23:9

DRUNKENNESS

will be filled with *d*........Ezek 23:33
Jerusalem a cup of *d*....... Zech 12:2
with carousing, *d*............ Luke 21:34
not in revelry and *d*........ Rom 13:13

envy, murders, *d*......,.....Gal 5:21
lusts, *d*...........................1 Pe 4:3

DRY

place, and let the *d*......... Gen 1:9
made the sea into *d*.........Ex 14:21
It was *d* on the fleece......Judg 6:40
I will *d* up her sea.......... Jer 51:36
d tree flourish................ Ezek 17:24
will make the rivers *d*.....Ezek 30:12
will be done in the *d*....... Luke 23:31

DUE

because it is your *d*......... Lev 10:13
their food in *d* season......Ps 104:27
pay all that was *d*........... Matt 18:34
d time Christ died.......... Rom 5:6
to whom taxes are *d*.......Rom 13:7
d season we shall........... Gal 6:9
exalt you in *d* time.......... 1 Pe 5:6

DULL

heart of this people *d*...... Is 6:10
people has grown d......... Matt 13:15
you have become *d*......... Heb 5:11

DUMB

the tongue of the *d*......... Is 35:6
You deaf and *d* spirit...... Mark 9:25

DUNGHILL

the land nor for the *d*......Luke 14:35

DUST

formed man of the *d*...... Gen 2:7
d you shall return........... Gen 3:19
descendants as the *d*.......Gen 13:16
now, I who am but *d*......Gen 18:27
"Who can count the *d*..... Num 23:10
lay your gold in the *d*......Job 22:24
and repent in *d*...............Job 42:6
Will the *d* praise You......Ps 30:9
like the whirling *d*...........Ps 83:13
show favor to her *d*........Ps 102:14
that we are *d*................. Ps 103:14
or the primeval *d*............Prov 8:26
all are from the *d*...........Eccl 3:20
counted as the small *d*..... Is 40:15
They shall lick the *d*........Mic 7:17
city, shake off the *d*........ Matt 10:14
image of the man of *d*.....1 Co 15:49

DUTY

this is the whole *d*...........Eccl 12:13
done what was our *d*.......Luke 17:10

DWELL

O LORD, make me *d*......Ps 4:8
Who may *d* in Your holy. Ps 15:1
He himself shall *d*...........Ps 25:13
D in the land................. Ps 37:3
the LORD God might *d*...Ps 68:18
of my God Than *d*.........Ps 84:10
Him, That glory may *d*....Ps 85:9
he will *d* on high............ Is 33:16
"I *d* in the high and.........Is 57:15
They shall no longer *d*.....Lam 4:15
they enter and *d* there..... Matt 12:45
of Judea and all who *d*....Acts 2:14
"*I will d* in them*...........2 Co 6:16
that Christ may *d*...........Eph 3:17
the fullness should *d*.......Col 1:19
the word of Christ *d*.......Col 3:16
men, and He will *d*......... Rev 21:3

DWELLING

A people *d* alone............Num 23:9
is the way to the *d*..........Job 38:19
a foreign country, *d*........Heb 11:9

DWELLS

He who *d* in the secret.... Ps 91:1
but the Father who *d*......John 14:10
do it, but sin that *d*........Rom 7:17
the Spirit of God *d*........ Rom 8:9
from the dead *d*.............Rom 8:11
the Spirit of God *d*........ 1 Co 3:16
d all the fullness............. Col 2:9
which righteousness *d*......2 Pe 3:13
you, where Satan *d*.........Rev 2:13

DWELT

became flesh and *d*......... John 1:14

DYING

I do not object to *d*........ Acts 25:11
in the body the *d*............2 Co 4:10
Jacob, when he was *d*.....Heb 11:21

— E —

EAGLE

As an *e* stirs up its..........Deut 32:11
e swooping on its prey.....Job 9:26
fly away like an *e*............Prov 23:5
the way of an *e*.............. Prov 30:19
nest as high as the *e*.......Jer 49:16
had the face of an *e*........ Ezek 1:10
like a flying *e*................. Rev 4:7
two wings of a great *e*..... Rev 12:14

EAGLES

how I bore you on *e*........Ex 19:4
up with wings like *e*........ Is 40:31
are swifter than *e*............Jer 4:13
e will be gathered........... Matt 24:28

EAR

shall pierce his *e*.............Ex 21:6
Does not the *e* test..........Job 12:11
Bow down Your *e*..........Ps 31:2
and the *e* of the wise......Prov 18:15
he awakens My *e*............ Is 50:4
e is uncircumcised..........Jer 6:10
what you hear in the *e*.....Matt 10:27
off his right *e*................. John 18:10
not seen, nor e heard......1 Co 2:9
if the *e* should say...........1 Co 12:16
"He who has an *e*........... Rev 2:7

EARLY

Very *e* in the morning..... Mark 16:2
arrived at the tomb *e*.......Luke 24:22

EARNEST

must give the more *e*.......Heb 2:1

EARNESTLY

He prayed more *e*...........Luke 22:44
in this we groan, *e*..........2 Co 5:2
e that it would not..........Jas 5:17
you to contend *e*............Jude 3

EARS

both his *e* will tingle........2 Ki 21:12
Whoever shuts his *e*........ Prov 21:13
and hear with their *e*....... Is 6:10
"He who has *e*............... Matt 11:15
e are hard of hearing*...... Matt 13:15
they have itching *e*..........2 Ti 4:3
e are open to their*..........1 Pe 3:12

EARTH

e which is under you....... Deut 28:23
e are the LORD's............1 Sa 2:8
coming to judge the *e*......1 Ch 16:33
service for man on *e*.......Job 7:1
he hangs the *e* on.......... Job 26:7
foundations of the *e*....... Job 38:4
e is the LORD's...............Ps 24:1
the shields of the *e*.........Ps 47:9
You visit the *e*...............Ps 65:9
You had formed the *e*..... Ps 90:2
Let the *e* be moved.........Ps 99:1
glory is above the *e*.........Ps 148:13
wisdom founded the *e*.....Prov 3:19
there was ever an *e*........ Prov 8:23
For three things the *e*..... Prov 30:21
e abides forever............. Eccl 1:4
for the meek of the *e*...... Is 11:4
e is My footstool.............Is 66:1
and the *e* shone with....... Ezek 43:2
I will darken the *e*.......... Amos 8:9
e will be filled................ Hab 2:14
shall inherit the *e*............Matt 5:5
heaven and *e* pass away... Matt 5:18
e as it is in heaven......... Matt 6:10
treasures on *e*...................Matt 6:19
then shook the *e*............Heb 12:26
"Do not harm the *e*........ Rev 7:3
from whose face the *e*.....Rev 20:11
new heaven and a new *e*.. Rev 21:1

EARTHLY

If I have told you *e*........John 3:12
we know that if our *e*......2 Co 5:1
their mind on *e* things.....Phil 3:19
from above, but is *e*........Jas 3:15

EARTHQUAKE

after the wind an *e*.........1 Ki 19:11
as you fled from the *e*..... Zech 14:5
there was a great *e*.........Matt 28:2
there was a great *e*.........Rev 6:12

EARTHQUAKES

And there will be *e*.........Mark 13:8

EASE

I was at *e*...................... Job 16:12
you women who are at *e*..Is 32:9
to you who are at *e*.........Amos 6:1
take your *e*................... Luke 12:19

EASIER

"Which is *e*...................Mark 2:9
"It is *e* for a camel..........Mark 10:25

EAST

goes toward the *e*...........Gen 2:14
the LORD brought an *e*... Ex 10:13
e wind scattered.............Job 38:24
As far as the *e*.............. Ps 103:12
descendants from the *e*.... Is 43:5
wise men from the *E*.......Matt 2:1
many will come from *e*.... Matt 8:11
will come from the *e*...... Luke 13:29
e might be prepared........ Rev 16:12

EAT

you may freely *e*............Gen 2:16
'You shall not *e*.............Gen 3:17
up my people as they *e*...Ps 53:4
good to *e* much honey..... Prov 25:27
e this scroll................... Ezek 3:1
on your couches, *e*......... Amos 6:4
e the flesh of My...........Mic 3:3
life, what you will *e*........Matt 6:25

You to *e* the Passover......Matt 26:17
give us His flesh to *e*......John 6:52
one believes he may *e*.....Rom 14:2
e meat nor drink wine..... Rom 14:21
I will never again *e*......... 1 Co 8:13
neither shall he *e*............ 2 Th 3:10
e your flesh like fire........Jas 5:3

EATEN

Have you *e* from the....... Gen 3:11
e my honeycomb with my.Song 5:1
e the fruit of lies.............Hos 10:13
And he was *e* by worms...Acts 12:23

EATS

The righteous *e*..............Prov 13:25
receives sinners and *e*..... Luke 15:2
"Whoever *e* My flesh......John 6:54
e this bread will live.......John 6:58
e despise him who does....Rom 14:3
He who *e*, *e* to the.........Rom 14:6
an unworthy manner *e*.....1 Co 11:29

EDIFICATION

his good, leading to *e*.....Rom 15:2
prophesies speaks *e*........1 Co 14:3
things be done for *e*........1 Co 14:26
the Lord gave us for *e*....2 Co 10:8
has given me for *e*..........2 Co 13:10
rather than godly *e*..........1 Ti 1:4

EDIFIES

puffs up, but love *e*.........1 Co 8:1
he who prophesies *e*........1 Co 14:4

EDIFY

all things do not *e*..........1 Co 10:23
and *e* one another...........1 Th 5:11

EDIFYING

of the body for the *e*.......Eph 4:16

EFFECTIVELY

for He who worked *e*...... Gal 2:8
e works in you who.........1 Th 2:13

EGG

in the white of an *e*.........Job 6:6
Or if he asks for an *e*..... Luke 11:12

EIGHT

a few, that is, *e*.............. 1 Pe 3:20

ELDER

The *e* and honorable....... Is 9:15
against an *e* except..........1 Ti 5:19
I who am a fellow *e*........ 1 Pe 5:1

ELDERS

and seventy of the *e*.......Ex 24:1
And teach his *e*.............. Ps 105:22
and counsel from the *e*.... Ezek 7:26
the tradition of the *e*...... Matt 15:2
be rejected by the *e*....... Luke 9:22
they had appointed *e*...... Acts 14:23
and called for the *e*......... Acts 20:17
e who rule well be..........1 Ti 5:17
lacking, and appoint *e*.....Tit 1:5
e obtained a good........... Heb 11:2
Let him call for the *e*...... Jas 5:14
e who are among you I....1 Pe 5:1
I saw twenty-four *e*......... Rev 4:4

ELECT

whom I uphold, My *E*..... Is 42:1
and Israel My *e*.............. Is 45:4

e shall long enjoy the...... Is 65:22
gather together His *e*.......Matt 24:31
e have obtained it.......... Rom 11:7
e according to the.......... 1 Pe 1:2
a *chief cornerstone, e*.....1 Pe 2:6
e sister greet you............ 2 Jn 13

ELECTION

e they are beloved..........Rom 11:28
calling and *e* sure............2 Pe 1:10

ELEMENTS

weak and beggarly *e*.......Gal 4:9
e will melt with...............2 Pe 3:10

ELEVEN

and his *e* sons.................Gen 32:22
e disciples went away......Matt 28:16
numbered with the *e*........Acts 1:26

ELOQUENT

O my Lord, I am not *e*....Ex 4:10
an *e* man and mighty in... Acts 18:24

EMBALM

to *e* his father................Gen 50:2

EMBANKMENT

will build an *e*................ Luke 19:43

EMERALDS

for your wares *e*............. Ezek 27:16

EMPTY

appear before Me *e*........ Ex 23:15
e things which................ 1 Sa 12:21
not listen to *e* talk..........Job 35:13
LORD makes the earth *e*..Is 24:1
comes, he finds it *e*........Matt 12:44
He has sent away *e*........ Luke 1:53
you with *e* words........... Eph 5:6

EMPTY-HEADED

e man will be wise.......... Job 11:12

ENABLED

our Lord who has *e*........1 Ti 1:12

ENCHANTER

and the expert *e*............. Is 3:3

ENCOMPASSED

the waves of death *e*.......2 Sa 22:5
The pangs of death *e*.......Ps 18:4
The pains of death *e*.......Ps 116:3

ENCOURAGED

is, that I may be *e*.......... Rom 1:12
and all may be *e*.............1 Co 14:31
their hearts may be *e*.....Col 2:2

END

yet your latter *e*.............Job 8:7
make me to know my *e*... Ps 39:4
shall keep it to the *e*...... Ps 119:33
e is the way of death.......Prov 14:12
There was no *e* of all......Eccl 4:16
Declaring the *e*............... Is 46:10
Our *e* was near..............Lam 4:18
whose iniquity shall *e*.....Ezek 21:25
what shall be the *e*.........Dan 12:8
e has come upon my.......Amos 8:2
the harvest is the *e*......... Matt 13:39
to pass, but the *e*...........Matt 24:6
always, even to the *e*...... Matt 28:20
He loved them to the *e*....John 13:1

ENDEAVORING

For Christ is the *e*..........Rom 10:4
ages, world without *e*......Eph 3:21
the hope firm to the *e*..... Heb 3:6
but now, once at the *e*.....Heb 9:26
of Job and seen the *e*..... Jas 5:11
But the *e* of all.............1 Pe 4:7
what will be the *e*............ 1 Pe 4:17
the latter *e* is worse........2 Pe 2:20
My works until the *e*...... Rev 2:26
Beginning and the *E*........Rev 22:13

ENDEAVORING

e to keep the unity..........Eph 4:3

ENDLESS

and *e* genealogies.............1 Ti 1:4
to the power of an *e*........Heb 7:16

ENDS

All the *e* of the world......Ps 22:27
established all the *e*........Prov 30:4
she came from the *e*........Matt 12:42
to the e of the................Acts 13:47
their words to the e........ Rom 10:18

ENDURANCE

For you have need of *e*....Heb 10:36
e the race that...............Heb 12:1

ENDURE

But the LORD shall *e*......Ps 9:7
as the sun and moon *e*.....Ps 72:5
His name shall *e*.............Ps 72:17
nor does a crown *e*..........Prov 27:24
"Can your heart *e*...........Ezek 22:14
being persecuted, we *e*....1 Co 4:12
Therefore I *e* all............. 2 Ti 2:10
them blessed who *e*........Jas 5:11

ENDURED

what persecutions I *e*.......2 Ti 3:11
he had patiently *e*.......... Heb 6:15
e as seeing Him who is.... Heb 11:27
For consider Him who *e*...Heb 12:3

ENDURES

And His truth *e*..............Ps 100:5
For His mercy *e*..............Ps 136:1
But he who *e* to the........ Matt 10:22
e only for a while...........Matt 13:21
for the food which *e*........John 6:27
he has built on it *e*..........1 Co 3:14
hopes all things, *e*...........1 Co 13:7
is the man who *e*............Jas 1:12
the word of the LORD e.. 1 Pe 1:25

ENDURING

the LORD is clean, *e*........Ps 19:9
e possession for.............. Heb 10:34

ENEMIES

Your *e* be scattered........Num 10:35
delivers me from my *e*.... Ps 18:48
the presence of my *e*....... Ps 23:5
Let not my *e* triumph...... Ps 25:2
But my *e* are vigorous.... Ps 38:19
e will lick the dust...........Ps 72:9
me wiser than my *e*........Ps 119:98
I count them my *e*..........Ps 139:22
e are the men of his........ Mic 7:6
to you, love your *e*..........Matt 5:44
be saved from our *e*........ Luke 1:71
e we were reconciled....... Rom 5:10
the gospel they are *e*...... Rom 11:28
till He has put all *e*......... 1 Co 15:25
were alienated and *e*........Col 1:21

His *e* are made His......... Heb 10:13
and devours their *e*......... Rev 11:5

ENEMY

then I will be an *e*.......... Ex 23:22
regard me as Your *e*........Job 13:24
He counts me as His *e*....Job 33:10
Or have plundered my *e*.. Ps 7:4
You may silence the *e*..... Ps 8:2
e does not triumph..........Ps 41:11
e who reproaches me.......Ps 55:12
e has persecuted my........ Ps 143:3
If your *e* is hungry.......... Prov 25:21
e are deceitful................ Prov 27:6
with the wound of an *e*....Jer 30:14
rejoice over me, my *e*.....Mic 7:8
and hate your *e*.............. Matt 5:43
last *e* that will be........... 1 Co 15:26
become your *e* because.... Gal 4:16
not count him as an *e*......2 Th 3:15
makes himself an *e*..........Jas 4:4

ENGRAVE

two onyx stones and *e*..... Ex 28:9
e its inscription............... Zech 3:9

ENJOY

e its sabbaths as long....... Lev 26:34
therefore *e* pleasure".......Eccl 2:1
richly all things to *e*.........1 Ti 6:17
than to *e* the passing....... Heb 11:25

ENJOYMENT

So I commended *e*.......... Eccl 8:15

ENLARGES

He *e* nations.................. Job 12:23
e his desire as hell..........Hab 2:5

ENLIGHTEN

E my eyes.................... Ps 13:3
LORD my God will *e*...... Ps 18:28

ENLIGHTENED

those who were once *e*.....Heb 6:4

ENMITY

And I will put *e*..............Gen 3:15
the carnal mind is *e*........Rom 8:7
in His flesh the *e*........... Eph 2:15
putting to death the *e*...... Eph 2:16
with the world is *e*.......... Jas 4:4

ENOUGH

never say, "It is *e*........... Prov 30:15
It is *e*..........................Mark 14:41
servants have bread *e*...... Luke 15:17

ENRAGED

being exceedingly *e*......... Acts 26:11
And the dragon was *e*......Rev 12:17

ENRICHED

that you were *e*.............. 1 Co 1:5
while you are *e*...............2 Co 9:11

ENSNARED

The wicked is *e*.............. Prov 12:13

ENSNARES

sin which so easily *e*........ Heb 12:1

ENTANGLE

how they might *e*............ Matt 22:15

ENTANGLES

engaged in warfare *e*....... 2 Ti 2:4

ENTER

E into His gates..............Ps 100:4
Do not *e* into judgment... Ps 143:2
E into the rock...............Is 2:10
He shall *e* into peace.......Is 57:2
you will by no means *e*....Matt 5:20
"*E* by the narrow...........Matt 7:13
e the kingdom of God..... Matt 19:24
E into the joy of your..... Matt 25:21
and pray, lest you *e*........Matt 26:41
"Strive to *e* through........ Luke 13:24
you, he who does not *e*...John 10:1
who have believed do *e*...Heb 4:3
e the Holiest by the.........Heb 10:19
e the temple till the........Rev 15:8
e through the gates..........Rev 22:14

ENTERED

Then Satan *e* Judas........ Luke 22:3
through one man sin *e*..... Rom 5:12
ear heard, nor have *e*...... 1 Co 2:9
the forerunner has *e*........ Heb 6:20
e the Most Holy Place..... Heb 9:12

ENTERS

If anyone *e* by Me.......... John 10:9
e the Presence behind...... Heb 6:19

ENTICED

his own desires and *e*.......Jas 1:14

ENTICING

e speech she caused.........Prov 7:21

ENTIRELY

give yourself *e*................ 1 Ti 4:15

ENTRANCE

The *e* of Your words....... Ps 119:130
e will be supplied............2 Pe 1:11

ENTREAT

E me not to leave you..... Ruth 1:16
But now *e* God's favor.....Mal 1:9
being defamed, we *e*........1 Co 4:13

ENTREATED

man of God *e* the LORD. 1 Ki 13:6
e our God for this...........Ezra 8:23

ENVIOUS

For I was *e* of the...........Ps 73:3
Do not be *e* of evil......... Prov 24:1
patriarchs, becoming *e*..... Acts 7:9

ENVY

e slays a simple...............Job 5:2
e the oppressor...............Prov 3:31
e is rottenness................ Prov 14:30
not let your heart *e*........ Prov 23:17
e have now perished........Eccl 9:6
full of *e*....................... Rom 1:29
not in strife and *e*.......... Rom 13:13
love does not *e*.............. 1 Co 13:4
e, murders.................... Gal 5:21
living in malice and *e*.......Tit 3:3
For where *e* and............. Jas 3:16
guile, hypocrisy, *e*...........1 Pe 2:1

EPISTLE

You are our *e* written......2 Co 3:2
are manifestly an *e*..........2 Co 3:3
by word or our *e*............ 2 Th 2:15

our word in this *e*...........2 Th 3:14
is a sign in every *e*..........2 Th 3:17

EPISTLES
e of commendation to......2 Co 3:1
as also in all his *e*...........2 Pe 3:16

EQUAL
it was you, a man my *e*... Ps 55:13
and you made them *e*...... Matt 20:12
making Himself *e*..........John 5:18
it robbery to be *e*...........Phil 2:6

EQUALITY
that there may be *e*.........2 Co 8:14

EQUITY
You have established *e*... Ps 99:4
judgment, and *e*..............Prov 1:3
and *e* cannot enter.......... Is 59:14
and pervert all *e*..............Mic 3:9
with Me in peace and *e*...Mal 2:6

ERR
you cause you to *e*........... Is 3:12
My people Israel to *e*...... Jer 23:13

ERROR
God that it was an *e*........Eccl 5:6
e which was due............. Rom 1:27
a sinner from the *e*.........Jas 5:20
led away with the *e*........ 2 Pe 3:17
and the spirit of *e*........... 1 Jn 4:6
run greedily in the *e*.......Jude 11

ERRORS
can understand his *e*........Ps 19:12

ESCAPE
E to the mountains......... Gen 19:17
and they shall not *e*........Job 11:20
Shall they *e* by............. Ps 56:7
speaks lies will not *e*.......Prov 19:5
and how shall we *e*..........Is 20:6
e all these things............Luke 21:36
same, that you will *e*...... Rom 2:3
also make the way of *e*... 1 Co 10:13
how shall we *e* if we.......Heb 2:3
e who refused Him who... Heb 12:25

ESCAPED
my flesh, and I have *e*.....Job 19:20
Our soul has *e* as a......... Ps 124:7
after they have *e*.............2 Pe 2:20

ESTABLISH
to *e* them forever............2 Ch 9:8
'Your seed I will *e*.......... Ps 89:4
e the work of our.............Ps 90:17
E Your word to Your......Ps 119:38
e an everlasting...............Ezek 16:60
e justice in the gate......Amos 5:15
seeking to *e* their own..... Rom 10:3
faithful, who will *e*.......... 2 Th 3:3
E your hearts..................Jas 5:8
a while, perfect, *e*...........1 Pe 5:10

ESTABLISHED
also is firmly *e*................1 Ch 16:30
David my father be *e*.......2 Ch 1:9
a rock, And *e* my steps....Ps 40:2
e a testimony in Jacob..... Ps 78:5
Your throne is *e*............. Ps 93:2
let all your ways be *e*..... Prov 4:26
e the clouds above.......... Prov 8:28
lip shall be *e* forever........Prov 12:19

house shall be *e*.............. Is 2:2
by His power, He has *e*... Jer 10:12
built up in Him and *e*......Col 2:7
covenant, which was *e*..... Heb 8:6
that the heart be *e*.......... Heb 13:9

ESTABLISHES
The king *e* the land by.....Prov 29:4
Now He who *e* us with.... 2 Co 1:21

ESTEEM
high wall in his own *e*......Prov 18:11
and we did not *e*.............Is 53:3
e others better than.........Phil 2:3
and hold such men in *e*....Phil 2:29
e them very highly.......... 1 Th 5:13

ESTEEMED
For what is highly *e*.........Luke 16:15
those who are least *e*.......1 Co 6:4

ESTEEMS
One person *e* one day......Rom 14:5

ESTRANGED
The wicked are *e*............. Ps 58:3
because they are all *e*...... Ezek 14:5
You have become *e*.........Gal 5:4

ETERNAL
e God is your refuge....... Deut 33:27
For man goes to his *e*.......Eccl 12:5
I do that I may have *e*......Matt 19:16
in the age to come, *e*.......Mark 10:30
not perish but have *e*.......John 3:15
you think you have *e*.......John 5:39
And I give them *e* life......John 10:28
that He should give *e*...... John 17:2
"And this is *e* life............John 17:3
e life to those who by......Rom 2:7
the gift of God is *e*........ Rom 6:23
e weight of glory.............2 Co 4:17
are not seen as *e*............. 2 Co 4:18
not made with hands, *e*....2 Co 5:1
lay hold on *e* life............. 1 Ti 6:12
e life which God.............Tit 1:2
and of *e* judgment...........Heb 6:2
e life which was.............. 1 Jn 1:2
that no murderer has *e*.... 1 Jn 3:15
God has given us *e*..........1 Jn 5:11
that you have *e* life.......... 1 Jn 5:13
Jesus Christ unto *e*..........Jude 21

ETERNITY
Also He has put *e*...........Eccl 3:11
One Who inhabits *e*........ Is 57:15

EUNUCH
of Ethiopia, a *e*............. Acts 8:27

EUNUCHS
have made themselves *e*... Matt 19:12

EVANGELIST
of Philip the *e*................ Acts 21:8
do the work of an *e*........ 2 Ti 4:5

EVANGELISTS
some prophets, some *e*.....Eph 4:11

EVEN
E in laughter the........... Prov 14:13
E a child is known.......... Prov 20:11
e nature itself teach.........1 Co 11:14
e denying the Lord who...2 Pe 2:1

EVENING
At *e* they return............. Ps 59:6
e it is cut down and........Ps 90:6
of my hands as the *e*...... Ps 141:2
e do not withhold your.... Eccl 11:6
and more fierce than *e*.....Hab 1:8

EVERLASTING
God of Israel from *e*....... 1 Ch 16:36
of the LORD is from *e*.....Ps 103:17
righteousness is an *e*........Ps 119:142
Your kingdom is an *e*...... Ps 145:13
in YAH, the LORD, is *e*...Is 26:4
will be to you an *e*...........Is 60:19
from *E* is Your name....... Is 63:16
awake, some to *e* life.......Dan 12:2
and inherit *e* life.............Matt 19:29
not perish but have *e*.......John 3:16
Him who sent Me has *e*....John 5:24
endures to *e* life.............John 6:27
in Him may have *e*.........John 6:40
believes has *e* life...........John 6:47
unworthy of *e* life........... Acts 13:46
of the Spirit reap *e*..........Gal 6:8
e destruction from the......2 Th 1:9

EVERYONE
said, 'Repent now *e*.........Jer 25:5
e who is born of the........John 3:8
E who is of the truth.......John 18:37

EVIDENCE
e of things not seen..........Heb 11:1

EVIDENT
the sight of God is *e*........Gal 3:11
of some are clearly *e*....... 1 Ti 5:25
e that our Lord arose...... Heb 7:14

EVIL
of good and *e*.................Gen 2:9
knowing good and *e*....... Gen 3:5
his heart was only *e*........Gen 6:5
e have been the..............Gen 47:9
rebellious and *e* city....... Ezra 4:12
e shall touch you............Job 5:19
I looked for good, *e*........Job 30:26
Nor shall *e* dwell............Ps 5:4
I will fear no *e*............... Ps 23:4
E shall slay the...............Ps 34:21
He does not abhor *e*........Ps 36:4
e more than good...........Ps 52:3
e shall befall you............Ps 91:10
To do *e* is like sport........ Prov 10:23
shall be filled with *e*........ Prov 12:21
e will bow before the....... Prov 14:19
keeping watch on the *e*.... Prov 15:3
Whoever rewards *e*..........Prov 17:13
e will not depart.............Prov 17:13
e all the days of her........ Prov 31:12
There is a severe *e*.......... Eccl 5:13
of men are full of *e*......... Eccl 9:3
to those who call *e*.......... Is 5:20
is taken away from *e*....... Is 57:1
of peace and not of *e*......Jer 29:11
commit this great *e*..........Jer 44:7
Seek good and not *e*........Amos 5:14
deliver us from the *e*....... Matt 6:13
If you then, being *e*.........Matt 7:11
Why do you think *e*......... Matt 9:4
e treasure brings............. Matt 12:35
everyone practicing *e*.......John 3:20
bear witness of the *e*....... John 18:23
e I will not to do............ Rom 7:19
then a law, that *e*............Rom 7:21
done any good or *e*.........Rom 9:11

EVIL-MINDEDNESS
Abhor what is *e*..............Rom 12:9
Repay no one *e* for.........Rom 12:17
not be overcome by *e*......Rom 12:21
simple concerning *e*.......Rom 16:19
provoked, thinks no *e*......1 Co 13:5
from every form of *e*.......1 Th 5:22

EVIL-MINDEDNESS
strife, deceit, *e*................ Rom 1:29

EVILDOER
If He were not an *e*........ John 18:30
suffer trouble as an *e*.......2 Ti 2:9
a thief, an *e*....................1 Pe 4:15

EVILDOERS
e shall be cut off.............Ps 37:9
Depart from me, you *e*....Ps 119:115
iniquity, a brood of *e*.......Is 1:4
e shall never be..............Is 14:20
against you as *e*..............1 Pe 2:12

EVILS
e have surrounded me......Ps 40:12
have committed two *e*......Jer 2:13

EXALT
God, and I will *e*.............Ex 15:2
e the horn of His............1 Sa 2:10
e His name together........Ps 34:3
E the LORD our God.....Ps 99:5
are my God, I will *e*........Ps 118:28
If I do not *e*...................Ps 137:6
into heaven, I will *e*........Is 14:13
E the lowly....................Ezek 21:26
e yourself as high as........Obad 4

EXALTATION
e comes neither from.......Ps 75:6
who rejoice in My *e*........Is 13:3
brother glory in his *e*.......Jas 1:9

EXALTED
Let God be *e*................. 2 Sa 22:47
I have built You an *e*......2 Ch 6:2
name, which is *e*............Neh 9:5
When vileness is *e*..........Ps 12:8
I will be *e* among the......Ps 46:10
righteous shall be *e*.........Ps 75:10
favor our horn is *e*..........Ps 89:17
You are *e* far above........Ps 97:9
His name alone is *e*.........Ps 148:13
upright the city is *e*.........Prov 11:11
LORD alone shall be *e*.....Is 2:11
valley shall be *e*..............Is 40:4
"Him God has *e*..............Acts 5:31
And lest I should be *e*.....2 Co 12:7
also has highly *e*.............Phil 2:9

EXALTS
Righteousness *e*..............Prov 14:34
high thing that *e*..............2 Co 10:5
e himself above all..........2 Th 2:4

EXAMINE
E me, O LORD...............Ps 26:2
But let a man *e*...............1 Co 11:28
But let each one *e*..........Gal 6:4

EXAMPLE
to make her a public *e*....Matt 1:19
I have given you an *e*......John 13:15
in following my *e*...........Phil 3:17
to make ourselves an *e*....2 Th 3:9
youth, but be an *e*..........1 Ti 4:12
us, leaving us an *e*..........1 Pe 2:21

making them an *e*..........2 Pe 2:6
are set forth as an *e*........Jude 7

EXAMPLES
happened to them as *e*.....1 Co 10:11
so that you became *e*.......1 Th 1:7
to you, but being *e*..........1 Pe 5:3

EXCEEDING
He might show the *e*.......Eph 2:7

EXCEEDINGLY
for the LORD must be *e*..1 Ch 22:5
You have made him *e*......Ps 21:6
is far off and *e* deep.......Eccl 7:24
e high mountain.............Matt 4:8
"Rejoice and be *e*...........Matt 5:12

EXCEEDS
your righteousness *e*........Matt 5:20

EXCEL
you His angels, Who *e*.....Ps 103:20
but you *e* them all...........Prov 31:29
that you seek to *e*...........1 Co 14:12

EXCELLENCE
e You have overthrown....Ex 15:7
did not come with *e*........1 Co 2:1

EXCELLENT
He is *e* in power............Job 37:23
It shall be as *e*...............Ps 141:5
will speak of *e* things......Prov 8:6
like Lebanon, *e*..............Song 5:15
For He has done *e*..........Is 12:5
in counsel and *e*.............Is 28:29
"Inasmuch as an *e*..........Dan 5:12
the things that are *e*........Rom 2:18
the things that are *e*........Phil 1:10
e sacrifice than Cain.......Heb 11:4
came to Him from the *E*..2 Pe 1:17

EXCELS
Do you see a man who *e*. Prov 22:29
I saw that wisdom *e*........Eccl 2:13
of the glory that *e*..........2 Co 3:10

EXCHANGE
will a man give in *e*.........Matt 16:26

EXCHANGED
nor can it be *e*...............Job 28:17
e the truth of God for.....Rom 1:25
For even their women *e*...Rom 1:26

EXCUSE
God be angry at your *e*....Eccl 5:6
but now they have no *e*...John 15:22
they are without *e*..........Rom 1:20
do you think that we *e*....2 Co 12:19

EXCUSES
accord began to make *e*...Luke 14:18

EXECUTE
e vengeance on the.........Ps 149:7
if you thoroughly *e*........Jer 7:5
e the fierceness..............Hos 11:9
e judgment also.............John 5:27
e wrath on him who.......Rom 13:4

EXECUTES
by the judgment He *e*.....Ps 9:16
e righteousness..............Ps 103:6
e justice for the.............Ps 146:7
e justice for me.............Mic 7:9

EXERCISE
those who are great *e*......Matt 20:25
e yourself rather............1 Ti 4:7
e profits a little..............1 Ti 4:8

EXERCISED
have their senses *e*.........Heb 5:14

EXHORT
such we command and *e*.. 2 Th 3:12
e him as a father.............1 Ti 5:1
and *e* these things...........1 Ti 6:2
doctrine, both to *e*.........Tit 1:9
Speak these things, *e*......Tit 2:15
e one another.................Heb 3:13

EXHORTATION
you have any word of *e*...Acts 13:15
he who exhorts, in *e*.......Rom 12:8
to reading, to *e*..............1 Ti 4:13
with the word of *e*.........Heb 13:22

EXHORTED
For I earnestly *e*.............Jer 11:7
e the brethren with.........Acts 15:32
as you know how we *e*....1 Th 2:11

EXILE
and also an *e* from..........2 Sa 15:19
The captive *e* hastens......Is 51:14

EXIST
things which do not *e*......Rom 4:17
by Your will they *e*.........Rev 4:11

EXPECT
an hour you do not *e*......Luke 12:40

EXPECTATION
The *e* of the poor..........Ps 9:18
God alone, For my *e*.......Ps 62:5
the people were in *e*.......Luke 3:15
a certain fearful *e*..........Heb 10:27

EXPERT
and the *e* enchanter.........Is 3:3
those of an *e* warrior.......Jer 50:9
because you are *e*............Acts 26:3

EXPLAIN
was no one who could *e*..Gen 41:24
days they could not *e*......Judg·14:14
E this parable to us.........Matt 15:15
to say, and hard to *e*.......Heb 5:11

EXPLAINED
He *e* all things to His......Mark 4:34

EXPLOIT
e all your......................Is 58:3
against those who *e*.........Mal 3:5
they will *e* you with........2 Pe 2:3

EXPOSED
his deeds should be *e*......John 3:20
all things that are *e*........Eph 5:13

EXPOUNDED
He *e* to them in all.........Luke 24:27

EXPRESS
man cannot *e* it..............Eccl 1:8
of His glory and the *e*.....Heb 1:3

EXPRESSLY
of the LORD came *e*.......Ezek 1:3
Now the Spirit *e*.............1 Ti 4:1

EXTEND

none to *e* mercy to him....Ps 109:12
"Behold, I will *e*.............Is 66:12

EXTINGUISHED

broken, my days are *e*..... Job 17:1
they are *e*......................Is 43:17

EXTOL

I will *e* You...................Ps 30:1
E Him who rides............ Ps 68:4

EXTOLLED

shall be exalted and *e*......Is 52:13

EXTORTION

e gathers it for him......... Prov 28:8
your neighbors by *e*.........Ezek 22:12
they are full of *e*.............Matt 23:25

EXTORTIONERS

e will inherit...................1 Co 6:10

EXULT

in anguish, I would *e*.......Job 6:10

EYE

"*e* for *e*......................Ex 21:24
the ear, but now my *e*.....Job 42:5
guide you with My *e*.......Ps 32:8
Behold, the *e* of the........Ps 33:18
He who formed the *e*...... Ps 94:9
and the seeing *e*.............Prov 20:12
who has a bountiful *e*..... Prov 22:9
A man with an evil *e*......Prov 28:22
e that mocks his.............Prov 30:17
e is not satisfied.............Eccl 1:8
labors, nor is his *e*.......... Eccl 4:8
for they shall see *e*......... Is 52:8
e seen any God besides...Is 64:4
the apple of His *e*..........Zech 2:8
if your right *e*.................Matt 5:29
it was said, '*An e*...........Matt 5:38
plank in your own *e*........ Matt 7:3
e causes you to sin.......... Matt 18:9
Or is your *e* evil............Matt 20:15
e makes you sin.............. Mark 9:47
through a needle's *e*........Luke 18:25
Because I am not an *e*.....1 Co 12:16
whole body were an *e*......1 Co 12:17
the twinkling of an *e*....... 1 Co 15:52
every *e* will see Him......Rev 1:7
your eyes with *e* salve......Rev 3:18

EYELIDS

His eyes behold, His *e*.....Ps 11:4
e look right before.......... Prov 4:25

EYES

e will be opened.............Gen 3:5
and you can be our *e*......Num 10:31
she put paint on her *e*.....2 Ki 9:30
"For the *e* of the............ 2 Ch 16:9
Do You have *e* of flesh...Job 10:4
and my *e* shall behold......Job 19:27
I was *e* to the blind.........Job 29:15
e observe from afar.........Job 39:29
e are secretly fixed..........Ps 10:8
e are ever toward me......Ps 25:15
The *e* of the LORD are....Ps 34:15
e fail while I wait............Ps 69:3
e shall you look..............Ps 91:8
I will lift up my *e*............Ps 121:1
not give sleep to my *e*..... Ps 132:4
e saw my substance.........Ps 139:16
e look straight ahead.......Prov 4:25

but the *e* of a fool...........Prov 17:24
Will you set your *e*.........Prov 23:5
Who has redness of *e*..... Prov 23:29
be wise in his own *e*.......Prov 26:5
so the *e* of man are........Prov 27:20
The wise man's *e*............ Eccl 2:14
e than the wandering.......Eccl 6:9
You have dove's *e*...........Song 1:15
e have seen the King...... Is 6:5
of the book, and the *e*..... Is 29:18
e fail from looking.......... Is 38:14
LORD, are not Your *e*....Jer 5:3
who have *e* and see........Jer 5:21
e will weep bitterly..........Jer 13:17
For I will set My *e*..........Jer 24:6
rims were full of *e*..........Ezek 1:18
full of *e* all around.........Ezek 10:12
that horn which had *e*.....Dan 7:20
horn between his *e*.........Dan 8:5
You are of purer *e*.........Hab 1:13
But blessed are your *e*.....Matt 13:16
"He put clay on my *e*.....John 9:15
e they have closed.......... Acts 28:27
e that they should not....Rom 11:8
plucked out your own *e*.. Gal 4:15
have seen with our *e*...... 1 Jn 1:1
the lust of the *e*............. 1 Jn 2:16
as snow, and His *e*........Rev 1:14
and anoint your *e*...........Rev 3:18
creatures full of *e*...........Rev 4:6
horns and seven *e*..........Rev 5:6
tear from their *e*............Rev 21:4

EYESERVICE

not with *e*......................Eph 6:6
the flesh, not with *e*....... Col 3:22

EYEWITNESSES

the beginning were *e*....... Luke 1:2
e of His majesty............. 2 Pe 1:16

— F —

FABLES

nor give heed to *f*........... 1 Ti 1:4
be turned aside to *f*.........2 Ti 4:4
cunningly devised *f*.........2 Pe 1:16

FACE

For I have seen God *f*..... Gen 32:30
f shone while he............. Ex 34:29
he put a veil on his *f*.....Ex 34:33
the LORD make His *f*..... Num 6:25
Then he turned his *f*.......2 Ki 20:2
curse You to Your *f*........Job 1:11
me, I will see Your *f*.......Ps 17:15
Why do You hide Your *f*.Ps 44:24
And cause His *f*.............Ps 67:1
of his *f* is changed..........Eccl 8:1
sins have hidden His *f*..... Is 59:2
I have made your *f*........ Ezek 3:8
but to us shame of *f*........Dan 9:7
before Your *f*, who.........Matt 11:10
f shone like the sun........Matt 17:2
always before my f..........Acts 2:25
dimly, but then *f*.............1 Co 13:12
look steadily at the *f*...... 2 Co 3:7
with unveiled *f*............... 2 Co 3:18
withstood him to his *f*.....Gal 2:11
his natural *f* in a............Jas 1:23
but the f of the LORD.... 1 Pe 3:12
They shall see His *f*........Rev 22:4

FACES

f were not ashamed.........Ps 34:5
hid, as it were, our *f*...... Is 53:3

be afraid of their *f*......... Jer 1:8
and all *f* turned pale.......Jer 30:6
they disfigure their *f*.......Matt 6:16

FACTIONS

there must also be *f*........ 1 Co 11:19

FADE

we all *f* as a leaf.............Is 64:6
and the leaf shall *f*..........Jer 8:13
rich man also will *f*.........Jas 1:11
and that does not *f*..........1 Pe 1:4

FADES

withers, the flower *f*........Is 40:7

FAIL

eyes shall look and *f*.......Deut 28:32
flesh and my heart *f*........Ps 73:26
of the thirsty to *f*............Is 32:6
and their tongues *f*.........Is 41:17
whose waters do not *f*.....Is 58:11
have caused wine to *f*.....Jer 48:33
of the olive may *f*..........Hab 3:17
nor shall the vine *f*.........Mal 3:11
that when you *f*.............Luke 16:9
tittle of the law to *f*........Luke 16:17
faith should not *f*...........Luke 22:32
they will *f*......................1 Co 13:8
Your years will not f...... Heb 1:12
For the time would *f*...... Heb 11:32

FAILED

Not a word *f* of any........Josh 21:45
my relatives have *f*..........Job 19:14
Refuge has *f* me.............Ps 142:4

FAILING

"men's hearts *f*...............Luke 21:26

FAILS

My strength *f* because......Ps 31:10
My spirit *f*.....................Ps 143:7
and every vision *f*...........Ezek 12:22
Love never *f*..................1 Co 13:8

FAINT

the youths shall *f*............Is 40:30
shall walk and not *f*........Is 40:31
my heart is *f* in me.........Jer 8:18
and the infants *f*.............Lam 2:11

FAINTED

thirsty, Their soul *f*........Ps 107:5

FAINTHEARTED

unruly, comfort the *f*.......1 Th 5:14

FAINTS

longs, yes, even *f*............Ps 84:2
My soul *f* for Your.........Ps 119:81
and the whole heart *f*...... Is 1:5
the earth, neither *f*..........Is 40:28

FAIR

Behold, you are *f*............Song 1:15
of the Lord is not *f*.........Ezek 18:25
to a place called *F*...........Acts 27:8
what is just and *f*............Col 4:1

FAIR-MINDED

These were more *f*.........Acts 17:11

FAIRER

f than the sons...............Ps 45:2

FAIREST

another beloved, O f...... Song 5:9
your beloved gone, O f.... Song 6:1

FAITH

in whom is no f............ Deut 32:20
shall live by his f............ Hab 2:4
you, O you of little f..... Matt 6:30
not found such great f..... Matt 8:10
f as a mustard seed........ Matt 17:20
it that you have no f....... Mark 4:40
to them, "Have f........ Mark 11:22
"Increase our f.............. Luke 17:5
will He really find f........ Luke 18:8
a man full of f............... Acts 6:5
are sanctified by f.......... Acts 26:18
for obedience to the f..... Rom 1:5
God is revealed from f..... Rom 1:17
God which is through f.... Rom 3:22
f apart from the deeds..... Rom 3:28
his f is accounted for...... Rom 4:5
f is made void and the.... Rom 4:14
those who are of the f..... Rom 4:16
f which we preach).......... Rom 10:8
f comes by hearing.......... Rom 10:17
and you stand by f.......... Rom 11:20
in proportion to our f..... Rom 12:6
Do you have f............... Rom 14:22
he does not eat from f..... Rom 14:23
though I have all f......... 1 Co 13:2
And now abide f............. 1 Co 13:13
For we walk by f............ 2 Co 5:7
the flesh I live by f........ Gal 2:20
or by the hearing of f..... Gal 3:2
f are sons of Abraham..... Gal 3:7
the law is not of f.......... Gal 3:12
But after f has come....... Gal 3:25
f working through love..... Gal 5:6
of the household of f....... Gal 6:10
been saved through f...... Eph 2:8
one Lord, one f.............. Eph 4:5
to the unity of the f....... Eph 4:13
taking the shield of f...... Eph 6:16
ceasing your work of f..... 1 Th 1:3
for not all have f........... 1 Th 3:2
having f and a good....... 1 Ti 1:19
the mystery of the f........ 1 Ti 3:9
he has denied the f........ 1 Ti 5:8
I have kept the f............ 2 Ti 4:7
in our common f............. Tit 1:4
not being mixed with f..... Heb 4:2
f is the substance........... Heb 11:1
without f it is................ Heb 11:6
someone says he has f..... Jas 2:14
Show me your f.............. Jas 2:18
and not by f only........... Jas 2:24
f will save the sick......... Jas 5:15
add to your f virtue......... 2 Pe 1:5
on your most holy f......... Jude 20
the patience and the f..... Rev 13:10
of God and the f............ Rev 14:12

FAITHFUL

God, He is God, the f...... Deut 7:9
f disappear from among... Ps 12:1
LORD preserves the f....... Ps 31:23
whose spirit was not f..... Ps 78:8
eyes shall be on the f...... Ps 101:6
f spirit conceals a........... Prov 11:13
but who can find a f........ Prov 20:6
f witness between us........ Jer 42:5
the Holy One who is f..... Hos 11:12
"Who then is a f.............. Matt 24:45
good and f servant......... Matt 25:23
"He who is f in what....... Luke 16:10
if you have not been f..... Luke 16:12

have judged me to be f.... Acts 16:15
God is f........................ 1 Co 1:9
is my beloved and f......... 1 Co 4:17
But as God is f............... 2 Co 1:18
f brethren in Christ........ Col 1:2
He who calls you is f....... 1 Th 5:24
This is a f saying and...... 1 Ti 1:15
f High Priest in.............. Heb 2:17
as Moses also was f........ Heb 3:2
He who promised is f...... Heb 10:23
He is f and just to.......... 1 Jn 1:9
Be f until death.............. Rev 2:10
words are true and f....... Rev 21:5

FAITHFULNESS

I have declared Your f..... Ps 40:10
f You shall establish........ Ps 89:2
Your f also surrounds...... Ps 89:8
And Your f every night... Ps 92:2
f endures to all.............. Ps 119:90
In Your f answer me....... Ps 143:1
counsels of old are f........ Is 25:1
great is Your f............... Lam 3:23
unbelief make the f......... Rom 3:3

FAITHLESS

"O f generation.............. Mark 9:19
If we are f.................... 2 Ti 2:13

FALL

a deep sleep to f............. Gen 2:21
but do not let me f......... 2 Sa 24:14
Let them f by their........ Ps 5:10
For I am ready to f......... Ps 38:17
Yes, all kings shall f....... Ps 72:11
a righteous man may f.... Prov 24:16
but the wicked shall f..... Prov 24:16
digs a pit will f.............. Prov 26:27
all their host shall f........ Is 34:4
men shall utterly f.......... Is 40:30
of music, you shall f....... Dan 3:5
And great was its f......... Matt 7:27
the blind, both will f...... Matt 15:14
the stars will f............... Matt 24:29
"I saw Satan f............... Luke 10:18
that they should f........... Rom 11:11
take heed lest he f.......... 1 Co 10:12
with pride he f............... 1 Ti 3:6
if they f away............... Heb 6:6
lest anyone f short of...... Heb 12:15
it all joy when you f....... Jas 1:2
and rocks, "F................. Rev 6:16

FALLEN

"Babylon is f................. Is 21:9
you have f from grace..... Gal 5:4
And I saw a star f.......... Rev 9:1
"Babylon is f................. Rev 14:8

FALLING

great drops of blood f..... Luke 22:44
f away comes first.......... 2 Th 2:3

FALLS

who is alone when he f.... Eccl 4:10
"And whoever f.............. Matt 21:44
master he stands or f...... Rom 14:4
its flower f.................... Jas 1:11
so that no rain f............. Rev 11:6

FALSE

You shall not bear f........ Ex 20:16
I hate every f way.......... Ps 119:104
gives heed to f lips......... Prov 17:4
f witness shall perish....... Prov 21:28
and do not love a f......... Zech 8:17

Beware of f prophets....... Matt 7:15
f christs and f................ Matt 24:24
and we are found f.......... 1 Co 15:15
among f brethren............ 2 Co 11:26
of f brethren.................. Gal 2:4
f prophets have gone...... 1 Jn 4:1
mouth of the f prophet.... Rev 16:13

FALSEHOOD

those who speak f........... Ps 5:6
and brings forth f........... Ps 7:14
For their deceit is f........ Ps 119:118
remove f and lies far...... Prov 30:8
f we have..................... Is 28:15
offspring of f................. Is 57:4

FALSELY

it, and swears f.............. Lev 6:3
Nor have we dealt f........ Ps 44:17
surely they swear f......... Jer 5:2
words, swearing f........... Hos 10:4
of evil against you f........ Matt 5:11
f called knowledge.......... 1 Ti 6:20

FAME

Sheba heard of the f....... 1 Ki 10:1
"Your f went out........... Ezek 16:14
them for praise and f...... Zeph 3:19
Then His f went............ Matt 4:24

FAMILIES

in you all the f.............. Gen 12:3
And makes their f........... Ps 107:41
the God of all the f........ Jer 31:1
f which the LORD has..... Jer 33:24
in your seed all the f...... Acts 3:25

FAMILY

shall mourn, every f....... Zech 12:12
f were baptized.............. Acts 16:33
from whom the whole f.... Eph 3:15

FAMINE

Now there was a f.......... Gen 12:10
keep them alive in f........ Ps 33:19
He called for a f............ Ps 105:16
send the sword, the f...... Jer 24:10
of the fever of f............. Lam 5:10
I will increase the f........ Ezek 5:16
there arose a severe f..... Luke 15:14

FAMINES

And there will be f......... Matt 24:7

FAMISH

righteous soul to f.......... Prov 10:3

FAMISHED

honorable men are f........ Is 5:13

FAMOUS

and may his name be f.... Ruth 4:14

FAN

not to f or to cleanse...... Jer 4:11
"His winnowing f........... Matt 3:12

FAR

removed my brothers f.... Job 19:13
Your judgments are f...... Ps 10:5
Be not f from Me........... Ps 22:11
those who are f.............. Ps 73:27
The LORD is f from the.. Prov 15:29
but it was f from me....... Eccl 7:23
removed their hearts f.... Is 29:13
Those near and those f.... Ezek 22:5

going to a *f* country.........Mark 13:34
though He is not *f*.......... Acts 17:27
you who once were *f*.......Eph 2:13

FARMER
The hard-working *f*......... 2 Ti 2:6
See how the *f* waits.........Jas 5:7

FASHIONED
have made me and *f*.......Job 10:8

FAST
f as you do this day.........Is 58:4
f that I have chosen......... Is 58:5
Moreover, when you *f*..... Matt 6:16
disciples do not *f*............ Matt 9:14
'I *f* twice a week............Luke 18:12

FASTED
'Why have we *f*.............. Is 58:3
'When you *f* and............Zech 7:5
And when He had *f*........ Matt 4:2

FASTENED
were its foundations *f*...... Job 38:6
'the peg that is *f*............ Is 22:25

FASTING
humbled myself with *f*.... Ps 35:13
are weak through *f*..........Ps 109:24
house on the day of *f*..... Jer 36:6
except by prayer and *f*.....Matt 17:21
give yourselves to *f*......... 1 Co 7:5

FASTINGS
in sleeplessness, in *f*......... 2 Co 6:5

FAT
and you will eat the *f*...... Gen 45:18
f is the LORD's.............. Lev 3:16
Now Eglon was a very *f*...Judg 3:17
have closed up their *f*...... Ps 17:10

FATHER
man shall leave his *f*........Gen 2:24
and you shall be a *f*........ Gen 17:4
'You are my *f*................ Job 17:14
I was a *f* to the poor.......Job 29:16
A *f* of the fatherless....... Ps 68:5
f pities his children..........Ps 103:13
the instruction of a *f*.......Prov 4:1
God, everlasting *F*.......... Is 9:6
O LORD, are our *F*........ Is 63:16
time cry to Me, 'My *f*......Jer 3:4
for I am a *F* to Israel...... Jer 31:9
"A son honors his *f*.........Mal 1:6
Have we not all one *F*..... Mal 2:10
Our *F* in heaven............Matt 6:9
"He who loves *f*............ Matt 10:37
does anyone know the *F*.. Matt 11:27
'*He who curses f*............. Matt 15:4
for One is your *F*...........Matt 23:9
F will be divided...........Luke 12:53
F loves the Son.............. John 3:35
F has been working.........John 5:17
F raises the dead............ John 5:21
F judges no one.............John 5:22
He has seen the *F*............John 6:46
F who sent Me bears.......John 8:18
we have one *F*................John 8:41
of your *f* the devil..........John 8:44
"I and My *F* are one........John 10:30
and believe that the *F*......John 10:38
'I am going to the *F*.......John 14:28
F is the vinedresser.........John 15:1
came forth from the *F*..... John 16:28

that he might be the *f*......Rom 4:11
"*I have made you a f*...... Rom 4:17
"*I will be a F*................2 Co 6:18
one God and *F* of all.......Eph 4:6
but exhort him as a *f*......1 Ti 5:1
I will be to Him a F........Heb 1:5
without *f*.....................Heb 7:3
comes down from the *F*...Jas 1:17
if you call on the *F*......... 1 Pe 1:17
and testify that the *F*.......1 Jn 4:14

FATHER'S
you in My *F* kingdom..... Matt 26:29
I must be about My *F*..... Luke 2:49
F house are many............John 14:2
that a man has his *f*........ 1 Co 5:1

FATHERLESS
my hand against the *f*......Job 31:21
the helper of the *f*..........Ps 10:14
To do justice to the *f*...... Ps 10:18
He relieves the *f*............Ps 146:9
the fields of the *f*...........Prov 23:10
do not defend the *f*......... Is 1:23
they may rob the *f*......... Is 10:2
You the *f* finds mercy.....Hos 14:3

FATHERS
the LORD God of our *f*...Ezra 7:27
f trusted in You.............Ps 22:4
our ears, O God, Our *f*... Ps 44:1
have sinned with our *f*..... Ps 106:6
f ate the manna.............John 6:31
of whom are the *f*..........Rom 9:5
you do not have many *f*...1 Co 4:15
unaware that all our *f*......1 Co 10:1

FATLING
and the *f* together...........Is 11:6

FATNESS
as with marrow and *f*......Ps 63:5
of the root and *f*............Rom 11:17

FATTED
f cattle are....................Matt 22:4
has killed the *f*.............. Luke 15:27

FATTENED
f your hearts as.............. Jas 5:5

FAULT
find no charge or *f*......... Dan 6:4
I have found no *f*...........Luke 23:14
does He still find *f*.........Rom 9:19
of God without *f*............Phil 2:15
for they are without *f*...... Rev 14:5

FAULTLESS
covenant had been *f*........Heb 8:7
to present you *f*.............Jude 24

FAULTS
"I remember my *f*...........Gen 41:9
me from secret *f*............Ps 19:12
are beaten for your *f*.......1 Pe 2:20

FAVOR
granted me life and *f*......Job 10:12
f You will.....................Ps 5:12
His *f* is for life..............Ps 30:5
A good man obtains *f*......Prov 12:2
but his *f* is like dew.........Prov 19:12
and seek the LORD's *f*....Jer 26:19
and stature, and in *f*........Luke 2:52

God and having *f*...........Acts 2:47
to do the Jews a *f*.......... Acts 24:27

FAVORABLE
And will He be *f*............ Ps 77:7
Lord, You have been *f*.... Ps 85:1

FAVORED
Because You *f* them........Ps 44:3
"Rejoice, highly *f*.......... Luke 1:28

FAVORITISM
do not show personal *f*.... Luke 20:21
God shows personal *f*..... Gal 2:6

FEAR
this and live, for I *f*........Gen 42:18
f the people of the.......... Num 14:9
to put the dread and *f*.... Deut 2:25
f Me all the days........... Deut 4:10
f the LORD your God..... Deut 6:2
book, that you may *f*......Deut 28:58
said, "Does Job *f*..........Job 1:9
Yes, you cast off *f*......... Job 15:4
Surely no *f* of me will.....Job 33:7
He mocks at *f*............... Job 39:22
they are in great *f*.......... Ps 14:5
The *f* of the LORD is...... Ps 19:9
of death, I will *f*............ Ps 23:4
Whom shall I *f*.............. Ps 27:1
Let all the earth *f*.......... Ps 33:8
Oh, *f* the LORD.............. Ps 34:9
There is no *f* of God....... Ps 36:1
they are in great *f*..........Ps 53:5
hear, all you who *f*.........Ps 66:16
f You As long as the.......Ps 72:5
heart to *f* Your name...... Ps 86:11
The *f* of the LORD is...... Ps 111:10
f You will be glad........... Ps 119:74
f the LORD and depart....Prov 3:7
The *f* of man brings a......Prov 29:25
it, that men should *f*.......Eccl 3:14
F God and keep His.......Eccl 12:13
Let Him that *f*.............. Is 8:13
"Be strong, do not *f*.......Is 35:4
do you not *f* Me............Jer 5:22
who would not *f*............Jer 10:7
but I will put My *f*.........Jer 32:40
f My name the Sun......... Mal 4:2
f Him who is able........... Matt 10:28
"Do not *f*....................Luke 12:32
a judge who did not *f*......Luke 18:2
"Do you not even *f*........Luke 23:40
And walking in the *f*.......Acts 9:31
the rest also may *f*......... 1 Ti 5:20
given us a spirit of *f*....... 2 Ti 1:7
those who through *f*........ Heb 2:15
His rest, let us *f*............. Heb 4:1
because of His godly *f*..... Heb 5:7
F God........................1 Pe 2:17
love casts out *f*.............. 1 Jn 4:18
"Do not *f* any of........... Rev 2:10

FEARED
But the midwives *f*.........Ex 1:17
He is also to be *f*............1 Ch 16:25
f God more than............Neh 7:2
Yourself, are to be *f*.......Ps 76:7
Then those who *f*...........Mal 3:16

FEARFUL
f in praises, doing........... Ex 15:11
them, "Why are you *f*..... Matt 8:26
It is a *f* thing to.............Heb 10:31

FEARFUL-HEARTED
to those who are *f*...........Is 35:4

FEARFULLY
praise You, for I am *f*..... Ps 139:14

FEARFULNESS
F and trembling have.......Ps 55:5
f has seized the................Is 33:14

FEARING
is devoted to *f* You......... Ps 119:38
sincerity of heart, *f*.........Col 3:22
forsook Egypt, not *f*........ Heb 11:27

FEARS
upright man, one who *f*... Job 1:8
Who is the man that *f*..... Ps 25:12
me from all my *f*............ Ps 34:4
an oath as he who *f*....... Eccl 9:2
every nation whoever *f*.... Acts 10:35
f has not been made........1 Jn 4:18

FEAST
Then he made them a *f*... Gen 19:3
and you shall keep a *f*..... Num 29:12
f is made for laughter...... Eccl 10:19
f day the terrors that...... Lam 2:22
hate, I despise your *f*.......Amos 5:21
every year at the *F*.........Luke 2:41
when you give a *f*...........Luke 14:13
Now the Passover, a *f*.......John 6:4
great day of the *f*...........John 7:37
let us keep the *f*............. 1 Co 5:8

FEASTING
go to the house of *f*....... Eccl 7:2

FEASTS
I will turn your *f*............Amos 8:10
the best places at *f*.........Luke 20:46
spots in your love *f*........ Jude 12

FED
f me all my life long.......Gen 48:15
and *f* you with manna......Deut 8:3
but the shepherds *f*........ Ezek 34:8
f you with milk and.........1 Co 3:2

FEEBLE
strengthened the *f*...........Job 4:4
And there was none *f*......Ps 105:37
And my flesh is *f*............Ps 109:24
Every hand will be *f*.......Ezek 7:17
hang down, and the *f*...... Heb 12:12

FEED
ravens to *f* you there.......1 Ki 17:4
Death shall *f* on them......Ps 49:14
of the righteous *f*............Prov 10:21
and *f* your flocks.............Is 61:5
to him, "*F* My lambs......John 21:15
to him, "*F* My sheep.......John 21:17
your enemy hungers, f..... Rom 12:20
my goods to *f* the poor.... 1 Co 13:3

FEEDS
Ephraim *f* on the wind.....Hos 12:1
your heavenly Father *f*....Matt 6:26

FEET
So she lay at his *f*.......... Ruth 3:14
so my *f* did not slip.........2 Sa 22:37
f they hang far............... Job 28:4
I was *f* to the lame..........Job 29:15
all things under his *f*........Ps 8:6

He makes my *f* like the... Ps 18:33
You have set my *f*...........Ps 31:8
does not allow our *f*....... Ps 66:9
f had almost stumbled......Ps 73:2
f have been standing........Ps 122:2
for their *f* run to.............Prov 1:16
Her *f* go down to death... Prov 5:5
sandals off your *f*............Is 20:2
called him to His *f*...........Is 41:2
up the dust of your *f*....... Is 49:23
mountains are the *f*........ Is 52:7
place of My *f* glorious......Is 60:13
are the dust of His *f*........Nah 1:3
in that day His *f*............. Zech 14:4
two hands or two *f*..........Matt 18:8
began to wash His *f*....... Luke 7:38
also sat at Jesus' *f*..........Luke 10:39
wash the disciples' *f*........John 13:5
at the apostles' *f*............ Acts 4:35
f are swift to shed..........Rom 3:15
beautiful are the f..........Rom 10:15
all things under His f.......1 Co 15:27
and having shod your *f*.... Eph 6:15
fell at His *f* as dead........Rev 1:17
And I fell at his *f*...........Rev 19:10

FEIGNED
before them, *f* madness....1 Sa 21:13

FELLOW
f servants who owed........Matt 18:28
begins to beat his *f*.........Matt 24:49
f worker concerning.........2 Co 8:23
f citizens with the...........Eph 2:19
Gentiles should be *f*........Eph 3:6
rest of my *f* workers........Phil 4:3
These are my only *f*........Col 4:11
that we may become *f*..... 3 Jn 8
I am your *f* servant......... Rev 19:10

FELLOWSHIP
doctrine and *f*.................Acts 2:42
were called into the *f*.......1 Co 1:9
not want you to have *f*.... 1 Co 10:20
f has righteousness.......... 2 Co 6:14
the right hand of *f*......... Gal 2:9
And have no *f* with the....Eph 5:11
for your *f* in the..............Phil 1:5
of love, if any *f*.............. Phil 2:1
and the *f* of His.............Phil 3:10
also may have *f*.............. 1 Jn 1:3
we say that we have *f*......1 Jn 1:6
the light, we have *f*......... 1 Jn 1:7

FENCE
and a tottering *f*............. Ps 62:3

FENCED
He has *f* up my way........Job 19:8

FERTILIZE
I dig around it and *f*........Luke 13:8

FERVENT
and being *f* in spirit.........Acts 18:25
f prayer of a.................. Jas 5:16
all things have *f*.............1 Pe 4:8
will melt with *f*...............2 Pe 3:10

FERVENTLY
you, always laboring *f*......Col 4:12
love one another *f*...........1 Pe 1:22

FESTIVAL
night when a holy *f*.........Is 30:29
or regarding a *f*.............. Col 2:16

FETTERS
hurt his feet with *f*..........Ps 105:18
their nobles with *f*...........Ps 149:8

FEVER
f which shall...................Lev 26:16
my bones burn with *f*..... Job 30:30
and rebuked the *f*.......... Luke 4:39

FEW
f and evil have been........Gen 47:9
f days and full of............Job 14:1
Let his days be *f*............Ps 109:8
let your words be *f*..........Eccl 5:2
and there are *f*...............Matt 7:14
but the laborers are *f*.......Matt 9:37
called, but *f* chosen.........Matt 20:16
"Lord, are there *f*...........Luke 13:23
prepared, in which a *f*..... 1 Pe 3:20
I have a *f* things............. Rev 2:20

FIDELITY
but showing all good *f*..... Tit 2:10

FIELD
Let the *f* be joyful.......... Ps 96:12
to house, who add *f*........ Is 5:8
becomes a fruitful *f*........ Is 32:15
"The *f* is the world........ Matt 13:38
and buys that *f*.............. Matt 13:44
f has been called the....... Matt 27:8
you are God's *f*.............. 1 Co 3:9

FIELDS
f yield no food.............. Hab 3:17
living out in the *f*...........Luke 2:8
eyes and look at the *f*.....John 4:35

FIERCENESS
f has deceived you...........Jer 49:16
the winepress of the *f*......Rev 19:15

FIERY
So the LORD sent *f*........ Num 21:6
right hand came a *f*........Deut 33:2
shall make them as a *f*.....Ps 21:9
offspring will be a *f*........Is 14:29
midst of a burning *f*....... Dan 3:6
concerning the *f*..............1 Pe 4:12
f red dragon having........Rev 12:3

FIG
f leaves together.............Gen 3:7
his vine and his *f*........... 1 Ki 4:25
fruit falling from a *f*........ Is 34:4
f tree may not blossom.... Hab 3:17
fruit on this *f*..................Luke 13:7
"Look at the *f*................Luke 21:29
I saw you under the *f*......John 1:50
Can a *f* tree...................Jas 3:12
f tree drops its late..........Rev 6:13

FIGHT
"The LORD will *f*...........Ex 14:14
you go with me to *f*....... 1 Ki 22:4
Our God will *f* for us...... Neh 4:20
My servants would *f*........John 18:36
to him, let us not *f*.........Acts 23:9
F the good *f*...................1 Ti 6:12
have fought the good *f*.....2 Ti 4:7
You *f* and war...............Jas 4:2

FIGHTS
your God is He who *f*..... Josh 23:10
because my lord *f*........... 1 Sa 25:28
f come from among you...Jas 4:1

FIGS

puts forth her green *f*...... Song 2:13
f set before the................Jer 24:1
from thornbushes or *f*.....Matt 7:16
men do not gather *f*....... Luke 6:44
or a grapevine bear *f*......Jas 3:12

FIGURATIVELY

brethren, I have *f*.......... 1 Co 4:6

FIGURE

and using no *f*...............John 16:29

FILL

f the earth and subdue.....Gen 1:28
wealth, that I may *f*........ Prov 8:21
"do I not *f* heaven..........Jer 23:24
f this temple with............Hag 2:7
F the waterpots.............. John 2:7
that He might *f*............. Eph 4:10
so as always to *f*............. 1 Th 2:16

FILLED

the whole earth be *f*........Ps 72:19
Then our mouth was *f*..... Ps 126:2
for they shall be *f*.......... Matt 5:6
Let the children be *f*...... Mark 7:27
he would gladly have *f*....Luke 15:16
being *f* with all............... Rom 1:29
full of goodness, *f*.......... Rom 15:14
that you may be *f*.......... Eph 3:19
but be *f* with the............Eph 5:18
being *f* with the............. Phil 1:11
peace, be warmed and *f*..Jas 2:16

FILTH

has washed away the *f*..... Is 4:4
been made as the *f*..........1 Co 4:13
the removal of the *f*....... 1 Pe 3:21

FILTHINESS

from all your *f*...............Ezek 36:25
ourselves from all *f*......... 2 Co 7:1
lay aside all *f*................ Jas 1:21
abominations and the *f*.... Rev 17:4

FILTHY

is abominable and *f*.........Job 15:16
with *f* garments..............Zech 3:3
malice, blasphemy, *f*.......Col 3:8
poor man in *f* clothes...... Jas 2:2
oppressed with the *f*........ 2 Pe 2:7
let him be *f*...................Rev 22:11

FIND

sure your sin will *f*......... Num 32:23
Almighty, we cannot *f*...... Job 37:23
life to those who *f*...........Prov 4:22
that no one can *f*...........Eccl 3:11
waters, for you will *f*...... Eccl 11:1
seek, and you will *f*........Matt 7:7
for My sake will *f*...... Matt 10:39
when he comes, will *f*..... Matt 24:46
f a Babe wrapped........... Luke 2:12
f no fault in this Man...... Luke 23:4
I *f* then a law................. Rom 7:21
f grace to help in........... Heb 4:16

FINDING

great things past *f*..........Job 9:10
and *f* none....................Luke 11:24
and His ways past *f*........ Rom 11:33

FINDS

f me *f* life.....................Prov 8:35
f a wife *f* a good............Prov 18:22

Whatever your hand *f*......Eccl 9:10
and he who seeks *f*........ Matt 7:8
f his life will lose............ Matt 10:39
and he who seeks *f*........ Luke 11:10

FINE

Then I beat them as *f*.....2 Sa 22:43
gold, Yea, than much *f*....Ps 19:10
f gold is a wise.............. Prov 25:12
set on bases of *f* gold...... Song 5:15
more rare than *f*............Is 13:12
and for *f* clothing...........Is 23:18
how changed the *f*..........Lam 4:1
rings, in *f* apparel........... Jas 2:2
for the *f* linen is the....... Rev 19:8

FINGER

written with the *f*............Ex 31:18
f shall be thicker............1 Ki 12:10
the pointing of the *f*........Is 58:9
dip the tip of his *f*..........Luke 16:24
the ground with His *f*...... John 8:6
"Reach your *f*...............John 20:27

FINGERS

the work of Your *f*.........Ps 8:3
he points with his *f*........ Prov 6:13
that which their own *f*.... Is 2:8
with one of their *f*..........Matt 23:4

FINISH

city, to *f* the...................Dan 9:24
he has enough to *f*..........Luke 14:28
has given Me to *f*...........John 5:36
so that I may *f*............... Acts 20:24

FINISHED

f the work which You......John 17:4
He said, "It is *f*.............John 19:30
I have *f* the race............2 Ti 4:7
thousand years were *f*..... Rev 20:3

FIRE

rained brimstone and *f*....Gen 19:24
to him in a flame of *f*.....Ex 3:2
by day, and *f* was over.... Ex 40:38
God who answers by *f*.... 1 Ki 18:24
LORD was not in the *f*.... 1 Ki 19:12
I was musing, the *f*........ Ps 39:3
We went through *f*..........Ps 66:12
They have set *f*.............Ps 74:7
f goes before Him............Ps 97:3
F and hail......................Ps 148:8
burns as the *f*.................Is 9:18
says the LORD, whose *f*...Is 31:9
you walk through the *f*... Is 43:2
f that burns all the..........Is 65:5
on whose bodies the *f*.....Dan 3:27
He break out like *f*......... Amos 5:6
for conflict by *f*.............Amos 7:4
like a refiner's *f*.............Mal 3:2
the Holy Spirit and *f*...... Matt 3:11
f is not quenched...........Mark 9:44
"I came to send *f*...........Luke 12:49
tongues, as of *f*..............Acts 2:3
f taking vengeance.......... 2 Th 1:8
and that burned with *f*.....Heb 12:18
And the tongue is a *f*.....Jas 3:6
vengeance of eternal *f*.....Jude 7
f came down from God....Rev 20:9
into the lake of *f*............ Rev 20:14

FIREBRAND

f plucked from the.......... Amos 4:11

FIREBRANDS

a madman who throws *f*...Prov 26:18
two stubs of smoking *f*.....Is 7:4

FIRM

their strength is *f*............ Ps 73:4
f the feeble knees...........Is 35:3
of the hope *f* to the........Heb 3:6

FIRMAMENT

Thus God made the *f*......Gen 1:7
f shows His handiwork.....Ps 19:1
in His mighty *f*.............. Ps 150:1
brightness of the *f*..........Dan 12:3

FIRST

The *f* one to plead his..... Prov 18:17
f father sinned................Is 43:27
desires to be *f*................ Matt 20:27
f shall be slave.............. Mark 10:44
And the gospel must *f*.... Mark 13:10
evil, of the Jew *f*........... Rom 2:9
"Or who has *f*................Rom 11:35
f man Adam became a....1 Co 15:45
f a willing mind............. 2 Co 8:12
that we who *f* trusted..... Eph 1:12
For Adam was formed *f*...1 Ti 2:13
f covenant had been........Heb 8:7
love Him because He *f*.... 1 Jn 4:19
I am the *F* and the.........Rev 1:17
you have left your *f*........Rev 2:4
is the *f* resurrection........ Rev 20:5

FIRST-RIPE

f fruit which my soul....... Mic 7:1

FIRSTBORN

LORD struck all the *f*......Ex 12:29
I will make him My *f*......Ps 89:27
Shall I give my *f*............Mic 6:7
brought forth her *f*..........Matt 1:25
that He might be the *f*....Rom 8:29
invisible God, the *f*.........Col 1:15
the beginning, the *f*.........Col 1:18
witness, the *f* from..........Rev 1:5

FIRSTFRUIT

For if the *f* is holy.......... Rom 11:16

FIRSTFRUITS

and with the *f*................ Prov 3:9
also who have the *f*........Rom 8:23
and has become the *f*...... 1 Co 15:20
Christ the *f*.................... 1 Co 15:23
might be a kind of *f*........Jas 1:18
among men, being *f*........ Rev 14:4

FISH

f taken in a cruel net.......Eccl 9:12
had prepared a great *f*.....Jon 1:17
do You make men like *f*. Hab 1:14
Or if he asks for a *f*........Matt 7:10
belly of the great *f*......... Matt 12:40
five loaves and two *f*...... Matt 14:17
and likewise the *f*...........John 21:13

FISHERMEN

The *f* also will mourn..... Is 19:8
I will send for many *f*......Jer 16:16

FISHERS

and I will make you *f*..... Matt 4:19

FIT

and looking back, is *f*......Luke 9:62

FITTING

Is it *f* to say to a............ Job 34:18
Luxury is not *f*.............. Prov 19:10
so honor is not *f*............Prov 26:1
things which are not *f*.....Rom 1:28
a High Priest was *f*.........Heb 7:26

FIVE

f smooth stones............... 1 Sa 17:40
about *f* thousand men......Matt 14:21
and *f* were foolish.......... Matt 25:2

FIXED

f My limit for it..............Job 38:10
is a great gulf *f*..............Luke 16:26

FLAME

appeared to him in a *f*.... Ex 3:2
f will dry out his..............Job 15:30
f consumes the chaff........Is 5:24
and tempest And the *f*....Is 29:6
nor shall the *f*............... Is 43:2
behind them a *f*..............Joel 2:3
am tormented in this *f*.... Luke 16:24
and His ministers a f....... Heb 1:7
and His eyes like a *f*....... Rev 1:14

FLAMES

the LORD divides the *f*....Ps 29:7

FLAMING

f sword which turned...... Gen 3:24
f fire in their land.......... Ps 105:32
in *f* fire taking................2 Th 1:8

FLATTER

I do not know how to *f*... Job 32:22
They *f* with their.............Ps 5:9

FLATTERED

Nevertheless they *f*..........Ps 78:36

FLATTERING

f mouth works ruin........ Prov 26:28
f speech deceive.............Rom 16:18
any time did we use *f*..... 1 Th 2:5
swelling words, *f*............Jude 16

FLATTERS

with one who *f* with........ Prov 20:19
f his neighbor spreads...... Prov 29:5

FLATTERY

shall corrupt with *f*.........Dan 11:32

FLAVOR

the salt loses its *f*............ Matt 5:13

FLAX

f He will not quench....... Is 42:3
f He will not quench.......Matt 12:20

FLED

The sea saw it and *f*.....Ps 114:3
who have *f* for refuge...... Heb 6:18

FLEE

f away secretly................Gen 31:27
those who hate You *f*...... Num 10:35
such a man as I *f*............Neh 6:11
who see me outside *f*.......Ps 31:11
Or where can I *f*.........Ps 139:7
and the shadows *f*..........Song 2:17
who are in Judea *f*.........Matt 24:16
F sexual immorality.........1 Co 6:18

f these things and............1 Ti 6:11
devil and he will *f*..........Jas 4:7

FLESH

bone of my bones and *f*... Gen 2:23
shall become one *f*.......... Gen 2:24
f had corrupted their....... Gen 6:12
f I shall see God.............Job 19:26
My *f* also will rest in..... Ps 16:9
that they were but *f*....... Ps 78:39
My heart and my *f*.......... Ps 84:2
f shall bless His holy....... Ps 145:21
is wearisome to the *f*.....Eccl 12:12
and all *f* shall see it........Is 40:5
"All *f* is grass.................Is 40:6
out My Spirit on all *f*..... Joel 2:28
Simon Bar-Jonah, for *f*... Matt 16:17
two shall become one f... Matt 19:5
were shortened, no *f*....... Matt 24:22
two shall become one f... Mark 10:8
f shall see the................Luke 3:6
And the Word became *f*.. John 1:14
I shall give is My *f*.........John 6:51
unless you eat the *f*........John 6:53
f profits nothing...........John 6:63
according to the *f*...........John 8:15
when we were in the *f*.... Rom 7:5
of God, but with the *f*.... Rom 7:25
on the things of the *f*......Rom 8:5
you are not in the *f*........Rom 8:9
to the *f* you will die........ Rom 8:13
f should glory in His........1 Co 1:29
"shall become one f.........1 Co 6:16
there is one kind of *f*......1 Co 15:39
For the *f* lusts................ Gal 5:17
have crucified the *f*........ Gal 5:24
good showing in the *f*.....Gal 6:12
may glory in your *f*........Gal 6:13
f has ceased from sin.......1 Pe 4:1
of his time in the *f*..........1 Pe 4:2
the lust from the *f*.......... 1 Jn 2:16
has come in the *f*............1 Jn 4:2
dreamers defile the *f*....... Jude 8

FLESHLY

f wisdom but by the........ 2 Co 1:12
law of a *f* commandment..Heb 7:16
f lusts which..................1 Pe 2:11

FLIES

will send swarms of *f*.......Ex 8:21
He sent swarms of *f*........ Ps 78:45
Dead *f* putrefy the..........Eccl 10:1

FLIGHT

f shall perish from...........Amos 2:14
And pray that your *f*....... Matt 24:20

FLINT

out of the rock of *f*........ Deut 8:15
will seem like *f*..............Is 5:28
set My face like a *f*.........Is 50:7

FLOAT

and he made the iron *f*.... 2 Ki 6:6

FLOCK

Your people like a *f*........Ps 77:20
wilderness like a *f*.......... Ps 78:52
lead Joseph like a *f*........ Ps 80:1
the footsteps of the *f*...... Song 1:8
He will feed His *f*........... Is 40:11
you do not feed the *f*...... Ezek 34:3
are My *f*, the *f*............ Ezek 34:31
though the *f* be cut........ Hab 3:17
my God, "Feed the *f*.....Zech 11:4

sheep of the f.................Matt 26:31
Do not fear, little *f*......... Luke 12:32
there will be one *f*........... John 10:16
of the milk of the *f*........ 1 Co 9:7
Shepherd the *f* of God.....1 Pe 5:2
examples to the *f*............ 1 Pe 5:3

FLOCKS

are clothed with *f*...........Ps 65:13

FLOOD

the waters of the *f*......... Gen 7:10
sat enthroned at the *F*..... Ps 29:10
them away like a *f*.......... Ps 90:5
the days before the *f*....... Matt 24:38
bringing in the *f*.............2 Pe 2:5
of his mouth like a *f*.......Rev 12:15

FLOODING

will you do in the *f*.........Jer 12:5

FLOODS

me, And the *f* of........... Ps 18:4
f on the dry ground.........Is 44:3
rain descended, the *f*....... Matt 7:25

FLOURISH

the righteous shall *f*........Ps 72:7

FLOURISHED

your care for me has *f*.....Phil 4:10

FLOURISHES

In the morning it *f*......... Ps 90:6

FLOW

f away as waters which.... Ps 58:7
and the waters *f*.............Ps 147:18
that its spices may *f*........Song 4:16
all nations shall *f*........... Is 2:2
of his heart will *f*...........John 7:38

FLOWER

comes forth like a *f*........Job 14:2
As a *f* of the field........Ps 103:15
beauty is a fading *f*......... Is 28:4
is like the *f* of the..........Is 40:6
grass withers, the *f*.........Is 40:7
if she is past the *f*.......... 1 Co 7:36
of man as the f...............1 Pe 1:24

FLOWERS

f appear on the earth.......Song 2:12

FLOWING

'a land *f* with milk.......... Deut 6:3
of wisdom is a *f*.............Prov 18:4
the Gentiles like a *f*....... Is 66:12

FLUTE

play the harp and *f*........ Gen 4:21
sound of the horn, *f*........ Dan 3:5

FLUTES

instruments and *f*............ Ps 150:4

FLUTISTS

harpists, musicians, *f*....... Rev 18:22

FLY

For then I would *f*......... Ps 55:6
soon cut off, and we *f*.....Ps 90:10
they *f* away like an..........Prov 23:5

FOE

and scattered the *f*......... Ps 18:14

FOES

My enemies and *f* .... Ps 27:2
I will beat down his *f* ..... Ps 89:23
f will be those............... Matt 10:36

FOLD

are not of this *f*.............. John 10:16
a cloak You will *f*.......... Heb 1:12

FOLDING

slumber, a little *f*........... Prov 6:10

FOLLOW

f what is altogether........ Deut 16:20
to Me, you who *f*..........Is 51:1
f You wherever You go... Matt 8:19
He said to him, "*F*........Matt 9:9
up his cross, and *f*..........Mark 8:34
someone who does not *f*.. Mark 9:38
will by no means *f*.......... John 10:5
serves Me, let him *f*....... John 12:26
those of some men *f*........1 Ti 5:24
that you should *f*............ 1 Pe 2:21
f the Lamb wherever He.. Rev 14:4
and their works *f*........... Rev 14:13

FOLLOWED

f the LORD my God...... Josh 14:8
LORD took me as I *f*..... Amos 7:15
we have left all and *f*......Mark 10:28

FOLLOWS

My soul *f* close behind.....Ps 63:8
f Me shall not walk......... John 8:12

FOLLY

taken much notice of *f*.....Job 35:15
not turn back to *f*........... Ps 85:8
F is joy to him who is.... Prov 15:21
of fools is *f*.................... Prov 16:22
f is set in great.............. Eccl 10:6

FOOD

you it shall be for *f*......... Gen 1:29
that lives shall be *f*.........Gen 9:3
stranger, giving him *f*......Deut 10:18
He gives *f* in.................. Job 36:31
he may bring forth *f*........ Ps 104:14
Who gives *f* to all........... Ps 136:25
Much *f* is in the.............. Prov 13:23
night, and provides *f*....... Prov 31:15
f which you eat shall...... Ezek 4:10
the fields yield no *f*......... Hab 3:17
that there may be *f*......... Mal 3:10
to give them *f*................ Matt 24:45
and you gave Me *f*......... Matt 25:35
and he who has *f*............ Luke 3:11
have you any *f*............... John 21:5
they ate their *f*............... Acts 2:46
our hearts with *f*............. Acts 14:17
destroy with your *f*.........Rom 14:15
f makes my brother.........1 Co 8:13
the same spiritual *f*.........1 Co 10:3
sower, and bread for *f*..... 2 Co 9:10
And having *f* and............1 Ti 6:8
and not solid *f*................Heb 5:12
But solid *f* belongs to..... Heb 5:14
of *f* sold his................... Heb 12:16
destitute of daily *f*..........Jas 2:15

FOODS

F for the stomach........... 1 Co 6:13
f which God................... 1 Ti 4:3

FOOL

f has said in his.............. Ps 14:1
is like sport to a *f*.......... Prov 10:23
f will be servant.............Prov 11:29
f is right in his own........Prov 12:15
f lays open his folly........ Prov 13:16
is too lofty for a *f*.......... Prov 24:7
whoever says, 'You *f*...... Matt 5:22
I speak as a *f*.................2 Co 11:23
I have become a *f*...........2 Co 12:11

FOOLISH

of the *f* women speaks.....Job 2:10
I was so *f* and................ Ps 73:22
f pulls it down with........ Prov 14:1
f man squanders it......... Prov 21:20
For My people are *f*........Jer 4:22
Has not God made *f*....... 1 Co 1:20
O *f* Galatians.................. Gal 3:1
were also once *f*............. Tit 3:3
But avoid *f* disputes........ Tit 3:9

FOOLISHLY

I speak *f*........................2 Co 11:21

FOOLISHNESS

O God, You know my *f*..Ps 69:5
Forsake *f* and live........... Prov 9:6
of fools proclaims *f*........ Prov 12:23
The *f* of a man twists..... Prov 19:3
F is bound up in the........Prov 22:15
devising of *f* is sin.......... Prov 24:9
person will speak *f*.......... Is 32:6
of the cross is *f*...............1 Co 1:18
Because the *f* of God...... 1 Co 1:25

FOOLS

f despise wisdom.............Prov 1:7
folly of *f* is deceit...........Prov 14:8
F mock at sin................. Prov 14:9
has no pleasure in *f*.........Eccl 5:4
We are *f* for Christ's....... 1 Co 4:10

FOOT

will not allow your *f*........ Ps 121:3
f will not stumble............ Prov 3:23
From the sole of the *f*..... Is 1:6
you turn away your *f*....... Is 58:13
f causes you to sin......... Matt 18:8
You dash Your f............Luke 4:11
If the *f* should say.......... 1 Co 12:15

FOOTMEN

have run with the *f*........ Jer 12:5

FOOTSTEPS

f. were not known............Ps 77:19
And shall make His *f*...... Ps 85:13

FOOTSTOOL

Your enemies Your *f*.....Ps 110:1
Your enemies Your f....... Matt 22:44
"Sit here at my *f*............. Jas 2:3

FORBID

said, "Do not *f*...............Mark 9:39
"Can anyone *f*................Acts 10:47
prophesy, and do not *f*.... 1 Co 14:39
f that I should glory........ Gal 6:14

FORBIDDING

confidence, no one *f*.......Acts 28:31
f us to speak to the.........1 Th 2:16
f to marry.....................1 Ti 4:3

FORCE

violent take it by *f*......... Matt 11:12
come and take Him by *f*.. John 6:15
a testament is in *f*.......... Heb 9:17

FORCEFUL

f are right words.............Job 6:25

FORCES

Though they join *f*.......... Prov 11:21

FOREFATHERS

f who refused to hear...... Jer 11:10
and oppressed our *f*........Acts 7:19
conscience, as my *f*......... 2 Ti 1:3

FOREHEADS

against their *f*................. Ezek 3:8
put a mark on the *f*........Ezek 9:4
seal of God on their *f*.....Rev 9:4
his mark on their *f*......... Rev 20:4

FOREIGNER

"I am a *f* and a.............. Gen 23:4
of me, since I am a *f*......Ruth 2:10
to God except this *f*....... Luke 17:18
who speaks will be a *f*.... 1 Co 14:11

FOREIGNERS

with the children of *f*......Is 2:6
f shall build up your........ Is 60:10
f who were there spent.... Acts 17:21
longer strangers and *f*.... Eph 2:19

FOREKNEW

For whom He *f*.............. Rom 8:29
His people whom He *f*....Rom 11:2

FOREKNOWLEDGE

counsel and *f* of God......Acts 2:23
according to the *f*............1 Pe 1:2

FOREORDAINED

He indeed was *f*.............. 1 Pe 1:20

FORERUNNER

f has entered for us.........Heb 6:20

FORESAW

'I *f* the LORD................ Acts 2:25

FORESEEING

f that God would............ Gal 3:8

FORESEES

A prudent man *f*.............Prov 22:3

FOREST

beast of the *f* is Mine...... Ps 50:10
See how great a *f*...........Jas 3:5

FORESTS

And strips the *f*.............. Ps 29:9

FORETOLD

have also *f* these days...... Acts 3:24
killed those who *f*........... Acts 7:52

FOREVER

and eat, and live *f*..........Gen 3:22
to our children *f*............. Deut 29:29
has loved Israel *f*............ 1 Ki 10:9
I would not live *f*............Job 7:16
from this generation *f*...... Ps 12:7
LORD sits as King *f*........ Ps 29:10
Do not cast us off *f*.........Ps 44:23

throne, O God, is *f*.........Ps 45:6
"You are a priest *f*.....Ps 110:4
His mercy endures *f*........Ps 136:1
will bless Your name *f*.....Ps 145:1
Who keeps truth *f*...........Ps 146:6
The LORD shall reign *f*... Ps 146:10
for riches are not *f*.........Prov 27:24
Trust in the LORD *f*........Is 26:4
of our God stands *f*........Is 40:8
My salvation will be *f*......Is 51:6
will not cast off *f*........... Lam 3:31
be the name of God *f*.....Dan 2:20
like the stars *f*..............Dan 12:3
of the LORD our God *f*... Mic 4:5
and the glory *f*.............. Matt 6:13
the Christ remains *f*........John 12:34
who is blessed *f*..............2 Co 11:31
to whom be glory *f*......... Gal 1:5
and Father be glory *f*.......Phil 4:20
throne, O God, is *f*......... Heb 1:8
has been perfected *f*........ Heb 7:28
lives and abides *f*............1 Pe 1:23
of darkness *f*..................Jude 13
power, both now and *f*... Jude 25
And they shall reign *f*.....Rev 22:5

FOREVERMORE

Blessed be the LORD *f*....Ps 89:52
this time forth and *f*........Ps 113:2
behold, I am alive *f*........Rev 1:18

FOREWARNED

all such, as we also *f*.......1 Th 4:6

FORGAVE

f the iniquity of my.........Ps 32:5
to repay, he freely *f*........Luke 7:42
God in Christ also *f*........Eph 4:32
even as Christ *f*..............Col 3:13

FORGED

The proud have *f*............Ps 119:69

FORGERS

But you *f* of lies.............Job 13:4

FORGET

For God has made me *f*...Gen 41:51
yourselves, lest you *f*......Deut 4:23
f the covenant of your..... Deut 4:31
f the LORD who brought. Deut 6:12
the paths of all who *f*......Job 8:13
all the nations that *f*........Ps 9:17
this, you who *f*..............Ps 50:22
f the works of God......... Ps 78:7
I will not *f* Your word.....Ps 119:16
If I *f* you.....................Ps 137:5
My son, do not *f*............Prov 3:1
f her nursing child...........Is 49:15
f the LORD your Maker.. Is 51:13
f her ornaments...............Jer 2:32
f your work and labor......Heb 6:10

FORGETFULNESS

in the land of *f*..............Ps 88:12

FORGETS

f the covenant of her.......Prov 2:17
and immediately *f*...........Jas 1:24

FORGETTING

f those things which.........Phil 3:13

FORGIVE

dwelling place, and *f*.......1 Ki 8:39
f their sin and heal..........2 Ch 7:14

good, and ready to *f*.......Ps 86:5
And *f* us our debts..........Matt 6:12
Father will also *f*...........Matt 6:14
f men their trespasses..... Matt 6:15
his heart, does not *f*........Matt 18:35
Who can *f* sins but God... Mark 2:7
f the sins of any..............John 20:23
you ought rather to *f*.......2 Co 2:7
anything, I also *f*............ 2 Co 2:10
F me this wrong............. 2 Co 12:13
f us our sins and to.........1 Jn 1:9

FORGIVEN

transgression is *f*............ Ps 32:1
sins be *f* them................ Mark 4:12
to whom little is *f*.......... Luke 7:47
indeed I have *f*...............2 Co 2:10
f you all trespasses......... Col 2:13
sins, he will be *f*............Jas 5:15
your sins are *f*................1 Jn 2:12

FORGIVENESS

But there is *f* with..........Ps 130:4
God belong mercy and *f*.. Dan 9:9
preached to you the *f*...... Acts 13:38
they may receive *f*..........Acts 26:18
His blood, the *f*..............Eph 1:7

FORGIVES

f all your iniquities..........Ps 103:3
Who is this who even *f*.... Luke 7:49

FORGIVING

tenderhearted, *f*..............Eph 4:32
and *f* one another........... Col 3:13

FORGOT

remember Joseph, but *f*... Gen 40:23
f the LORD their God..... Judg 3:7
f His works And His....... Ps 78:11
They soon *f* His works....Ps 106:13

FORGOTTEN

f the God who fathered... Deut 32:18
"Why have You *f*........... Ps 42:9
If we had *f* the name.......Ps 44:20
memory of them is *f*........Eccl 9:5
you will not be *f*............Is 44:21
and my Lord has *f*.......... Is 49:14
I have *f* prosperity..........Lam 3:17
not one of them is *f*........Luke 12:6
f the exhortation.............Heb 12:5
f that he was purged........2 Pe 1:9

FORM

earth was without *f*........ Gen 1:2
Who would *f* a god or..... Is 44:10
f the light and create...... Is 45:7
descended in bodily *f*......Luke 3:22
time, nor seen His *f*........John 5:37
For the *f* of this..............1 Co 7:31
who, being in the *f*.........Phil 2:6
Abstain from every *f*....... 1 Th 5:22
having a *f* of..................2 Ti 3:5

FORMED

And the LORD God *f*..... Gen 2:7
And His hands *f*............. Ps 95:5
f my inward parts...........Ps 139:13
f all things gives the....... Prov 26:10
say of him who *f*............Is 29:16
Me there was no God *f*....Is 43:10
This people I have *f*........ Is 43:21
"Before I *f* you in..........Jer 1:5
Will the thing *f*..............Rom 9:20
say to him who *f*............Rom 9:20

until Christ is *f*...............Gal 4:19
For Adam was *f* first....... 1 Ti 2:13

FORMER

f lovingkindnesses.......... Ps 89:49
f days better than...........Eccl 7:10
f rain to the earth........... Hos 6:3
f prophets preached.........Zech 1:4
f conduct in Judaism........Gal 1:13
your *f* conduct................Eph 4:22
f things have passed........ Rev 21:4

FORMS

clay say to him who *f*...... Is 45:9
f the spirit of man...........Zech 12:1

FORNICATION

We were not born of *f*.....John 8:41
of the wrath of her *f*...... Rev 14:8

FORNICATOR

a brother, who is a *f*....... 1 Co 5:11
you know, that no *f*........ Eph 5:5
lest there be any *f*...........Heb 12:16

FORNICATORS

but *f* and adulterers.........Heb 13:4

FORSAKE

but if you *f* Him..............2 Ch 15:2
"If his sons *f*..................Ps 89:30
f His inheritance............. Ps 94:14
But I did not *f*................ Ps 119:87
father, and do not *f*........Prov 1:8
worthless idols *f*..............Jon 2:8
of you does not *f*........... Luke 14:33
never leave you nor f......Heb 13:5

FORSAKEN

God, why have You *f*......Ps 22:1
seen the righteous *f*........Ps 37:25
you dread will be *f*..........Is 7:16
cities will be as a *f*..........Is 17:9
a mere moment I have *f*.. Is 54:7
no longer be termed *F*.....Is 62:4
they have *f* Me...............Jer 2:13
God, why have You *f*..... Matt 27:46
persecuted, but not *f*....... 2 Co 4:9
for Demas has *f*..............2 Ti 4:10
f the right way................2 Pe 2:15

FORSAKING

f the assembling.............Heb 10:25

FORSOOK

f God who made him...... Deut 32:15
all the disciples *f*............Matt 26:56
with me, but all *f*...........2 Ti 4:16
By faith he *f* Egypt........ Heb 11:27

FORTRESS

LORD is my rock, my *f*...2 Sa 22:2
my rock of refuge, A *f*.... Ps 31:2

FOUL

My wounds are *f*............Ps 38:5
f weather today............. Matt 16:3
a prison for every *f*......... Rev 18:2

FOUND

f a helper comparable...... Gen 2:20
where can wisdom be *f*.... Job 28:12
when You may be *f*.........Ps 32:6
f My servant David......... Ps 89:20
a thousand I have *f*......... Eccl 7:28

this only I have *f*............ Eccl 7:29
f the one I love.............. Song 3:4
while He may be *f*.......... Is 55:6
Your fruit is *f*.................Hos 14:8
fruit on it and *f* none......Luke 13:6
he was lost and is *f*........ Luke 15:24
f the Messiah" (which......John 1:41
I *f* to bring death............. Rom 7:10
and be *f* in Him...............Phil 3:9
be diligent to be *f*........... 2 Pe 3:14

FOUNDATION

he shall lay its *f*................Josh 6:26
His *f* is in the holy...........Ps 87:1
and justice are the *f*....... Ps 89:14
Of old You laid the *f*..... Ps 102:25
has an everlasting *f*....... Prov 10:25
deep and laid the *f*.........Luke 6:48
the earth without a *f*...... Luke 6:49
loved Me before the *f*.....John 17:24
I have laid the *f*..............1 Co 3:10
f can anyone lay than...... 1 Co 3:11
us in Him before the *f*.....Eph 1:4
the solid *f* of God............2 Ti 2:19
not laying again the *f*......Heb 6:1
Lamb slain from the *f*.....Rev 13:8
the first *f* was jasper........Rev 21:19

FOUNDATIONS

when I laid the *f*..............Job 38:4
f are destroyed................Ps 11:3
You who laid the *f*..........Ps 104:5
shall raise up the *f*.......... Is 58:12
And the *f* of the wall.......Rev 21:19

FOUNDED

For He has *f* it upon..... Ps 24:2
shake it, for it was *f*.......Luke 6:48

FOUNTAIN

will become in him a *f*.....John 4:14

FOUNTAINS

on that day all the *f*....... Gen 7:11
f be dispersed abroad...... Prov 5:16
when there were no *f*..... Prov 8:24
lead them to living *f*........ Rev 7:17

FOX

build, if even a *f*..............Neh 4:3
"Go, tell that *f*...............Luke 13:32

FOXES

caught three hundred *f*....Judg 15:4
f that spoil the vines........Song 2:15
F have holes and birds.....Luke 9:58

FRAGMENTS

f that remained...............Matt 14:20
of the leftover *f*...............Luke 9:17
baskets with the *f*............John 6:13

FRAGRANCE

garments is like the *f*.....Song 4:11
was filled with the *f*........John 12:3
we are to God the *f*........ 2 Co 2:15

FRAIL

That I may know how *f*... Ps 39:4

FRAME

For He knows our *f*........ Ps 103:14
f was not hidden.............Ps 139:15

FRAMED

that the worlds were *f*......Heb 11:3

FREE

and the servant is *f*........ Job 3:19
let the oppressed go *f*...... Is 58:6
'You will be made *f*........John 8:33
if the Son makes you *f*....John 8:36
And having been set *f*.... Rom 6:18
now having been set *f*..... Rom 6:22
Jesus has made me *f*.......Rom 8:2
Am I not *f*.....................1 Co 9:1
is neither slave nor *f*........Gal 3:28
Jerusalem above is *f*........Gal 4:26
Christ has made us *f*........Gal 5:1
he is a slave or *f*.............Eph 6:8
poor, *f* and slave............Rev 13:16

FREED

has died has been *f*......... Rom 6:7

FREEDMAN

slave is the Lord's *f*.......1 Co 7:22

FREELY

the garden you may *f*...... Gen 2:16
I will love them *f*............Hos 14:4
F you have received........ Matt 10:8
f give us all...................Rom 8:32
that have been *f*.............. 1 Co 2:12
the water of life *f*...........Rev 22:17

FREEWOMAN

the other by a *f*.............. Gal 4:22
with the son of the *f*........ Gal 4:30

FRESH

My glory is *f* within........Job 29:20
They shall be *f*................Ps 92:14
both salt water and *f*.......Jas 3:12

FRIEND

a man speaks to his *f*......Ex 33:11
of Abraham Your *f*.........2 Ch 20:7
though he were my *f*....... Ps 35:14
f You have put................Ps 88:18
f loves at all times...........Prov 17:17
f who sticks closer...........Prov 18:24
not forsake your own *f*.... Prov 27:10
a *f* of tax collectors........ Matt 11:19
of you shall have a *f*.......Luke 11:5
f Lazarus sleeps..............John 11:11
you are not Caesar's *f*....John 19:12
Philemon our beloved *f*....Phm 1
he was called the *f*..........Jas 2:23
wants to be a *f*...............Jas 4:4

FRIENDS

and hate your *f*...............2 Sa 19:6
My *f* scorn me................Job 16:20
f have forgotten me.........Job 19:14
the rich has many *f*........ Prov 14:20
one's life for his *f*.......... John 15:13
"You are My *f*................John 15:14
I have called you *f*.......... John 15:15
to forbid any of his *f*......Acts 24:23

FROGS

your territory with *f*........ Ex 8:2
f coming out of the........ Rev 16:13

FRONTLETS

on your hand and as *f*..... Ex 13:16
and they shall be as *f*...... Deut 6:8

FROZEN

the broad waters are *f*..... Job 37:10

FRUIT

and showed them the *f*.... Num 13:26
Blessed shall be the *f*......Deut 28:4
brings forth its *f*.............Ps 1:3
f is better than gold........Prov 8:19
The *f* of the righteous......Prov 11:30
with good by the *f*.......... Prov 12:14
f was sweet to my.......... Song 2:3
they shall eat the *f*.......... Is 3:10
like the first *f*.................Is 28:4
"I create the *f*................Is 57:19
f is found in Me..............Hos 14:8
does not bear good *f*...... Matt 3:10
good tree bears good *f*.....Matt 7:17
not drink of this *f*...........Matt 26:29
and blessed is the *f*........ Luke 1:42
life, and bring no *f*.........Luke 8:14
and he came seeking *f*.... Luke 13:6
'And if it bears *f*............Luke 13:9
branch that bears *f*.........John 15:2
that you bear much *f*......John 15:8
should go and bear *f*......John 15:16
f did you have then in.... Rom 6:21
God, you have your *f*...... Rom 6:22
that we should bear *f*......Rom 7:4
But the *f* of the.............Gal 5:22
but I seek the *f*.............Phil 4:17
yields the peaceable *f*...... Heb 12:11
Now the *f* of..................Jas 3:18
autumn trees without *f*....Jude 12
tree yielding its *f*............Rev 22:2

FRUITFUL

them, saying, "Be *f*........Gen 1:22
a *f* bough, a *f*...............Gen 49:22
wife shall be like a *f*.......Ps 128:3
heaven and *f* seasons.......Acts 14:17
pleasing Him, being *f*...... Col 1:10

FRUITS

Therefore bear *f*............. Matt 3:8
know them by their *f*......Matt 7:16
and increase the *f*.......... 2 Co 9:10
of mercy and good *f*.......Jas 3:17
which bore twelve *f*........Rev 22:2

FUEL

people shall be as *f*......... Is 9:19
into the fire for *f*........... Ezek 15:4

FULFILL

the LORD, to *f* his vow... Lev 22:21
And you shall *f*.............. 1 Ki 5:9
f all your petitions...........Ps 20:5
f the desire of those........Ps 145:19
for us to *f* all................ Matt 3:15
f the law of Christ..........Gal 6:2
f my joy by being........... Phil 2:2
and *f* all the good...........2 Th 1:11
If you really *f*................Jas 2:8

FULFILLED

the law till all is *f*.......... Matt 5:18
of the Gentiles are *f*........Luke 21:24
all things must be *f*......... Luke 24:44
of the law might be *f*......Rom 8:4
loves another has *f*......... Rom 13:8
For all the law is *f*..........Gal 5:14

FULFILLMENT

for there will be a *f*.........Luke 1:45
love is the *f* of the.......... Rom 13:10

FULL

"I went out *f*..................Ruth 1:21
For I am *f* of words........ Job 32:18

FULL-GROWN

of the LORD is f............ Ps 29:4
who has his quiver f........ Ps 127:5
Lest I be f and deny.......Prov 30:9
yet the sea is not f......... Eccl 1:7
the whole earth is f........ Is 6:3
and it was f of bones...... Ezek 37:1
But truly I am f............Mic 3:8
whole body will be f.......Matt 6:22
of the Father, f............John 1:14
that your joy may be f.....John 15:11
chose Stephen, a man f....Acts 6:5
You are already f...........1 Co 4:8
learned both to be f........ Phil 4:12
I am f....................... Phil 4:18

FULL-GROWN

and sin, when it is f....... Jas 1:15

FULLNESS

satisfied with the f...........Ps 36:8
f we have all received......John 1:16
to Israel until the f.........Rom 11:25
But when the f of the......Gal 4:4
dispensation of the f........Eph 1:10
filled with all the f........Eph 3:19
Him dwells all the f........Col 2:9

FUNCTION

do not have the same f.... Rom 12:4

FURIOUS

You have been f............Ps 89:38
f man do not go............ Prov 22:24
fury and in f rebukes......Ezek 5:15
LORD avenges and is f....Nah 1:2
this, they were f............ Acts 5:33

FURIOUSLY

for he drives f.............. 2 Ki 9:20

FURNACE

you out of the iron f...... Deut 4:20
tested you in the f..........Is 48:10
of a burning fiery f........Dan 3:6
cast them into the f........Matt 13:42
the smoke of a great f..... Rev 9:2

FURNISHED

also f her table.............. Prov 9:2
a large upper room, f...... Mark 14:15

FURY

F is not in Me..............Is 27:4
they are full of the f........Is 51:20
f to His adversaries......... Is 59:18
and My own f...............Is 63:5
even in anger and f.......Jer 21:5
and I will cause My f......Ezek 5:13
Thus will I spend My f.... Ezek 6:12
in anger and f on the......Mic 5:15

FUTILE

For it is not a f.............. Deut 32:47
of the peoples are f.........Jer 10:3
wise, that they are f........ 1 Co 3:20
risen, your faith is f.........1 Co 15:17

FUTILITY

allotted months of f........Job 7:3
f have You created all..... Ps 89:47
was subjected to f.......... Rom 8:20

FUTURE

For the f of that man..... Ps 37:37
The f of the wicked........Ps 37:38
to give you a f..............Jer 29:11

— G —

GAIN

g than fine gold.............. Prov 3:14
will have no lack of g...... Prov 31:11
a time to g.....................Eccl 3:6
to get dishonest g............Ezek 22:27
him who covets evil g..... Hab 2:9
and to die is g.............Phil 1:21
rubbish, that I may g......Phil 3:8
is a means of g...............1 Ti 6:5
contentment is great g..... 1 Ti 6:6
for dishonest g................1 Pe 5:2

GAINED

g more wisdom than all....Eccl 1:16
g five more talents.......... Matt 25:20

GAINS

g the whole world.......... Matt 16:26

GALL

They also gave me g.......Ps 69:21
the wormwood and the g..Lam 3:19
turned justice into g........ Amos 6:12
wine mingled with g....... Matt 27:34

GAP

and stand in the g.......... Ezek 22:30

GARDEN

LORD God planted a g....Gen 2:8
g enclosed is my............. Song 4:12
like a watered g..............Is 58:11
Eden, the garden of God......Ezek 28:13
raise up for them a g......Ezek 34:29
where there was a g...... John 18:1
g a new tomb in which.... John 19:41

GARDENER

Him to be the g..............John 20:15

GARDENS

I made myself g............Eccl 2:5
plant g and eat their........Jer 29:5

GARLANDS

brought oxen and g......... Acts 14:13

GARMENT

beautiful Babylonian g.....Josh 7:21
g that is moth-eaten........ Job 13:28
made sackcloth my g....... Ps 69:11
with light as with a g.......Ps 104:2
one who takes away a g...Prov 25:20
the hem of His g............ Matt 9:20
have on a wedding g....... Matt 22:11
cloth on an old g........... Mark 2:21
all grow old like a g....... Heb 1:11
hating even the g............Jude 23

GARMENTS

g did not wear out on......Deut 8:4
Why are your g hot........Job 37:17
They divide My g............Ps 22:18
g always be white...........Eccl 9:5
g rolled in blood............Is 9:5
from Edom, with dyed g..Is 63:1
Take away the filthy g.....Zech 3:4
man clothed in soft g......Matt 11:8
spread their g on the....... Matt 21:8
and divided His g...........Matt 27:35
by them in shining g........Luke 24:4
g are moth-eaten............Jas 5:2
be clothed in white g.......Rev 3:5

GARRISON

gathered the whole g...... Matt 27:27
Damascenes with a g.......2 Co 11:32

GATE

This is the g of the.........Ps 118:20
by the narrow g............. Matt 7:13
by the Sheep G a pool....John 5:2
laid daily at the g...........Acts 3:2
suffered outside the g..... Heb 13:12
each individual g............ Rev 21:21

GATES

possess the g of those...... Gen 24:60
g are burned with fire......Neh 1:3
they go down to the g..... Job 17:16
up your heads, O you g...Ps 24:7
The LORD loves the g.....Ps 87:2
Open to me the g........... Ps 118:19
is known in the g........... Prov 31:23
go through the g............Is 62:10
and the g of Hades........ Matt 16:18
wall with twelve g.......... Rev 21:12
g were twelve pearls.......Rev 21:21
g shall not be shut......... Rev 21:25

GATHER

g my soul together.......... Ps 26:9
G My saints..................Ps 50:5
and a time to g stones..... Eccl 3:5
g the lambs with His....... Is 40:11
g His wheat into the........Matt 3:12
sow nor reap nor g.........Matt 6:26
Do men g grapes from....Matt 7:16
g where I have not..........Matt 25:26
g together His............... Mark 13:27

GATHERED

g little had no lack..........Ex 16:18
And g out of the lands.... Ps 107:3
g some of every kind.......Matt 13:47
the nations will be g........Matt 25:32

GATHERING

g together of the.............Gen 1:10
g together to Him...........2 Th 2:1

GATHERS

g the waters of the..........Ps 33:7
His heart g iniquity.........Ps 41:6
g her food in the............ Prov 6:8
The Lord GOD, who g....Is 56:8
together, as a hen g........ Matt 23:37

GAVE

to be with me, she g....... Gen 3:12
g You this authority.......Matt 21:23
that He g His only..........John 3:16
Those whom You g.........John 17:12
but God g the increase.... 1 Co 3:6
g Himself for our sins......Gal 1:4
g Himself for me............Gal 2:20
g Himself for it..............Eph 5:25
The sea g up the dead..... Rev 20:13

GAZED

g into heaven and saw..... Acts 7:55

GAZING

why do you stand g........Acts 1:11

GENEALOGIES

fables and endless g.........1 Ti 1:4

GENEALOGY

The book of the g..........Matt 1:1
mother, without g........... Heb 7:3

GENERATION

perverse and crooked g....Deut 32:5
The g of the upright........Ps 112:2
g shall praise Your..........Ps 145:4
g that curses its............. Prov 30:11
g that is pure in its.........Prov 30:12
One g passes away..........Eccl 1:4
g it shall lie.....................Is 34:10
who will declare His g..... Is 53:8
and adulterous g............Matt 12:39
this g will by no.............Matt 24:34
from this perverse g........ Acts 2:40
But you are a chosen g....1 Pe 2:9

GENERATIONS

be remembered in all g....Ps 45:17
Your praise to all g.........Ps 79:13
for a thousand g............. Ps 105:8
g will call me blessed......Luke 1:48

GENEROUS

g soul will be made........ Prov 11:25
no longer be called g....... Is 32:5
g man devises g.............. Is 32:8

GENTILES

G were separated...........Gen 10:5
as a light to the G.......... Is 42:6
G shall come to your.......Is 60:3
the riches of the G.........Is 61:6
all these things the G..... Matt 6:32
into the way of the G..... Matt 10:5
revelation to the G.........Luke 2:32
G are fulfilled................ Luke 21:24
bear My name before G...Acts 9:15
poured out on the G...... Acts 10:45
a light to the G.............. Acts 13:47
blasphemed among the G. Rom 2:24
also the God of the G..... Rom 3:29
named among the G........1 Co 5:1
mystery among the G...... Col 1:27
a teacher of the G.......... 1 Ti 2:7
nothing from the G.........3 Jn 7

GENTLE

g tongue breaks a bone....Prov 25:15
from Me, for I am g.......Matt 11:29
But we were g among.....1 Th 2:7
to be peaceable, g..........Tit 3:2
only to the good and g.... 1 Pe 2:18
ornament of a g..............1 Pe 3:4

GENTLENESS

g has made me great...... Ps 18:35
love and a spirit of g....... 1 Co 4:21
g, self-control................ Gal 5:23
all lowliness and g..........Eph 4:2
Let your g be known to.. Phil 4:5
love, patience, g.............. 1 Ti 6:11

GHOST

supposed it was a g........ Mark 6:49

GIFT

g makes room for him.... Prov 18:16
A g in secret pacifies...... Prov 21:14
is the g of God................Eccl 3:13
If you knew the g.......... John 4:10
But the free g is not........Rom 5:15
but the g of God is......... Rom 6:23
each one has his own g.... 1 Co 7:7
though I have the g........1 Co 13:2
it is the g of God............Eph 2:8
Not that I seek the g.......Phil 4:17
Do not neglect the g....... 1 Ti 4:14
you to stir up the g........ 2 Ti 1:6

tasted the heavenly g......Heb 6:4
Every good g and every...Jas 1:17
one has received a g........1 Pe 4:10

GIFTED

the women who were g....Ex 35:25
but good-looking, g.........Dan 1:4

GIFTS

g you shall offer............ Num 18:29
You have received g.......Ps 68:18
and Seba Will offer g...... Ps 72:10
though you give many g... Prov 6:35
to one who gives g.........Prov 19:6
how to give good g........ Matt 7:11
rich putting their g..........Luke 21:1
g differing.....................Rom 12:6
are diversities of g...........1 Co 12:4
and desire spiritual g...... 1 Co 14:1
captive, and gave g.........Eph 4:8

GIRD

G Your sword upon........ Ps 45:3
of wrath You shall g.......Ps 76:10
I will g you.....................Is 45:5
and another will g..........John 21:18
Therefore g up the..........1 Pe 1:13

GIRDED

a towel and g Himself.....John 13:4
down to the feet and g.... Rev 1:13

GIVE

g thanks to the LORD..... 1 Ch 16:8
g me wisdom and...........2 Ch 1:10
G ear to my prayer........Ps 17:1
G to them according.......Ps 28:4
g you the desires.............Ps 37:4
Yes, the LORD will g......Ps 85:12
G me understanding....... Ps 119:34
g me your heart..............Prov 23:26
You will g truth to..........Mic 7:20
"G to him who asks....... Matt 5:42
G us this day our...........Matt 6:11
what you have and g...... Matt 19:21
authority I will g............Luke 4:6
g them eternal life..........John 10:28
A new commandment I g.John 13:34
but what I do have I g.... Acts 3:6
g us all things.................Rom 8:32
G no offense.................1 Co 10:32
So let each one g............2 Co 9:7
g him who has need........ Eph 4:28
g thanks to God always...2 Th 2:13
g yourself entirely.......... 1 Ti 4:15
good works, ready to g.... 1 Ti 6:18

GIVEN

to him more will be g......Matt 13:12
has, more will be g......... Matt 25:29
to whom much is g.........Luke 12:48
g Me I should lose.........John 6:39
Spirit was not yet g.........John 7:39
have been freely g...........1 Co 2:12
not g to wine................. 1 Ti 3:3

GIVES

He who g to the poor......Prov 28:27
For God g wisdom and....Eccl 2:26
g life to the world...........John 6:33
All that the Father g........John 6:37
The good shepherd g......John 10:11
not as the world g...........John 14:27
g us richly all things........ 1 Ti 6:17
who g to all liberally....... Jas 1:5

But He g more grace.......Jas 4:6
g grace to the humble.....Jas 4:6

GLAD

I will be g and.................Ps 9:2
my heart is g..................Ps 16:9
Be g in the LORD and.... Ps 32:11
streams shall make g....... Ps 46:4
And wine that makes g.... Ps 104:15
I was g when they said.... Ps 122:1
make merry and be g..... Luke 15:32
he saw it and was g........John 8:56

GLADNESS

in the day of your g........ Num 10:10
day of feasting and g....... Esth 9:17
You have put g in my......Ps 4:7
me to hear joy and g.......Ps 51:8
Serve the LORD with g....Ps 100:2
shall obtain joy and g...... Is 35:10
over you with g.............. Zeph 3:17
receive it with g............. Mark 4:16

GLASS

there was a sea of g........ Rev 4:6
like transparent g............Rev 21:21

GLORIFIED

the people I must be g....Lev 10:3
and they g the God of..... Matt 15:31
Jesus was not yet g......... John 7:39
when Jesus was g............John 12:16
By this My Father is g.....John 15:8
"I have g You on the...... John 17:4
g His Servant Jesus........ Acts 3:13
these He also g...............Rom 8:30
things God may be g........1 Pe 4:11

GLORIFY

My altar, and I will g...... Is 60:7
g your Father in.............. Matt 5:16
"Father, g Your name...John 12:28
"He will g Me................John 16:14
And now, O Father, g.....John 17:5
what death he would g....John 21:19
God, they did not g........ Rom 1:21
therefore g God in.......... 1 Co 6:20
also Christ did not g.......Heb 5:5
ashamed, but let him g.... 1 Pe 4:16

GLORIOUS

daughter is all g............. Ps 45:13
And blessed be His g...... Ps 72:19
G things are spoken........ Ps 87:3
is honorable and g.......... Ps 111:3
g splendor of Your.........Ps 145:5
habitation, holy and g..... Is 63:15
it to Himself a g.............Eph 5:27
be conformed to His g.... Phil 3:21
g appearing of our.......... Tit 2:13

GLORY

Please, show me Your g...Ex 33:18
g has departed from........ 1 Sa 4:21
G in His holy name.........1 Ch 16:10
a shield for me, My g...... Ps 3:3
You who set Your g........ Ps 8:1
Who is this King of g...... Ps 24:8
the place where Your g....Ps 26:8
Your power and Your g...Ps 63:2
shall speak of the g......... Ps 145:11
wise shall inherit g......... Prov 3:35
The g of young men is.....Prov 20:29
It is the g of God to........ Prov 25:2
"G to the righteous.........Is 24:16
g I will not give.............. Is 42:8

GLORYING

g will be seen upon......... Is 60:2
then be likened in g....... Ezek 31:18
I will change their g........ Hos 4:7
and I will be the g......... Zech 2:5
He shall bear the g....... Zech 6:13
that they may have g..... Matt 6:2
the power and the g....... Matt 6:13
g was not arrayed........... Matt 6:29
Man will come in the g... Matt 16:27
with power and great g.... Matt 24:30
"G to God in the............Luke 2:14
and we beheld His g....John 1:14
and manifested His g......John 2:11
I do not seek My own g.. John 8:50
"Give God the g............John 9:24
g which I had with You... John 17:5
g which You gave Me I... John 17:22
he did not give g....... Acts 12:23
doing good seek for g...... Rom 2:7
fall short of the g........... Rom 3:23
in faith, giving g........... Rom 4:20
the adoption, the g.........Rom 9:4
the riches of His g....... Rom 9:23
God, alone wise, be g......Rom 16:27
who glories, let him g...... 1 Co 1:31
Therefore let no one g.... 1 Co 3:21
but woman is the g......... 1 Co 11:7
of the g that excels..........2 Co 3:10
of the gospel of the g..... 2 Co 4:4
eternal weight of g........... 2 Co 4:17
who glories, let him g..... 2 Co 10:17
that they may g............. Gal 6:13
forbid that I should g...... Gal 6:14
to His riches in g.........Phil 4:19
appear with Him in g...... Col 3:4
For you are our g........... 1 Th 2:20
many sons to g............. Heb 2:10
grass, and all the g.......1 Pe 1:24
to whom belong the g.....1 Pe 4:11
for the Spirit of g.............1 Pe 4:14
the presence of His g......Jude 24
O Lord, to receive g....... Rev 4:11
g of God illuminated....... Rev 21:23

GLORYING

Your g is not good...........1 Co 5:6

GLUTTON

g will come to poverty..... Prov 23:21
you say, 'Look, a g........Luke 7:34

GLUTTONS

g shames his...................Prov 28:7
evil beasts, lazy g............Tit 1:12

GNASHING

will be weeping and g......Matt 8:12

GO

He said, "Let Me g........Gen 32:26
'Let My people go.......Ex 5:1
Presence does not g........Ex 33:15
for wherever you g.........Ruth 1:16
"Look, I g forward........ Job 23:8
For I used to g............Ps 42:4
g astray as soon as.......... Ps 58:3
I will g in the................. Ps 71:16
Those who g down to....Ps 107:23
Where can I g from........Ps 139:7
G to the ant.............Prov 6:6
All g to one place..........Eccl 3:20
of mourning than to g......Eccl 7:2
of Zion shall g.................Is 2:3
You wherever You g....... Matt 8:19
do not g out...................Matt 24:26
He said to them, "G....... Mark 16:15

And I say to one, 'G......Luke 7:8
also want to g away........John 6:67
to whom shall we g........John 6:68
g you cannot come..........John 8:21
I g to prepare a place......John 14:2
will do, because I g........John 14:12
seek Me, let these g.......John 18:8
My God, and he shall g... Rev 3:12

GOADS

of the wise are like g.......Eccl 12:11
to kick against the g........Acts 9:5

GOAL

I press toward the g........ Phil 3:14

GOATS

drink the blood of g........ Ps 50:13
his sheep from the g........Matt 25:32
with the blood of g......... Heb 9:12
g could take away.......... Heb 10:4

GOD

G created the heavens..... Gen 1:1
Abram of G Most High... Gen 14:19
and I will be their G....... Gen 17:8
of the Mighty G............ Gen 49:24
the G of Abraham.......... Ex 3:6
He is my G....................Ex 15:2
Stand before G for the.... Ex 18:19
I am the LORD your G... Ex 20:2
"This is your g............... Ex 32:4
"G is not a man.......... Num 23:19
G is a consuming fire..... Deut 4:24
great and awesome G..... Deut 7:21
my people, and your G....Ruth 1:16
know that there is a G.....1 Sa 17:46
a rock, except our G......2 Sa 22:32
If the LORD is G........... 1 Ki 18:21
G is greater than all.......2 Co 4:2
G is greater than........... Job 33:12
"Behold, G is mighty...... Job 36:5
"Behold, G is great........Job 36:26
You have been My G......Ps 22:10
Where is your G.............Ps 42:3
G is our refuge...............Ps 46:1
G is in the midst of.........Ps 46:5
G is the King of all.........Ps 47:7
The Mighty One, G........ Ps 50:1
I am G.........................Ps 50:7
me a clean heart, O G....Ps 51:10
Our G is the G............... Ps 68:20
Who is so great a G........Ps 77:13
Restore us, O G............ Ps 80:7
You alone are G.............Ps 86:10
Exalt the LORD our G....Ps 99:9
Yes, our G is merciful......Ps 116:5
give thanks to the G........Ps 136:26
For G is in heaven..........Eccl 5:2
Counselor, Mighty G.......Is 9:6
G is my salvation............Is 12:2
Behold, this is our G.......Is 25:9
"Behold your G.............Is 40:9
Is there a G besides........Is 44:8
to Zion, "Your G...........Is 52:7
stricken, smitten by G..... Is 53:4
and I will be their G........Jer 31:33
and I saw visions of G.....Ezek 1:1
Who is a G like You......Mic 7:18
"G with us....................Matt 1:23
in G my Savior...............Luke 1:47
the Word was with G...... John 1:1
enter the kingdom of G... John 3:3
"For G so loved the........John 3:16
has certified that G.........John 3:33
"G is Spirit...................John 4:24

"My Lord and my G.......John 20:28
Christ is the Son of G..... Acts 8:37
to the unknown G...........Acts 17:23
Indeed, let G be true...... Rom 3:4
If G is for us...................Rom 8:31
G is faithful.................. 1 Co 1:9
us there is only one G..... 1 Co 8:6
G shall supply all...........Phil 4:19
and I will be their G....... Heb 8:10
G is a consuming fire...... Heb 12:29
G is greater than our.......1 Jn 3:20
for G is love................. 1 Jn 4:8
No one has seen G......... 1 Jn 4:12
in the temple of My G....Rev 3:12
gave glory to the G.........Rev 11:13
G Himself will be...........Rev 21:3
and I will be his G..........Rev 21:7

GODDESS

after Ashtoreth the g.......1 Ki 11:5
of the great g Diana........Acts 19:35

GODHEAD

eternal power and G....... Rom 1:20
the fullness of the G........Col 2:9

GODLINESS

is the mystery of g.......... 1 Ti 3:16
g is profitable.................. 1 Ti 4:8
But g with contentment....1 Ti 6:6
having a form of g........... 2 Ti 3:5
pertain to life and g........ 2 Pe 1:3
to perseverance g............2 Pe 1:6

GODLY

Himself him who is g......Ps 4:3
everyone who is g...........Ps 32:6
who desire to live g.........2 Ti 3:12
righteously, and g........... Tit 2:12
reverence and g fear........Heb 12:28
to deliver the g...............2 Pe 2:9

GODS

your God is God of g......Deut 10:17
the household g..............2 Ki 23:24
He judges among the g....Ps 82:1
I said, "You are g..........Ps 82:6
yourselves with g............Is 57:5
If He called them g.........John 10:35
g have come down to us., Acts 14:11

GOLD

And the g of that land.....Gen 2:12
a mercy seat of pure g....Ex 25:17
multiply silver and g........Deut 17:17
If I have made g.............Job 31:24
are they than g..............Ps 19:10
Yea, than much fine g..... Ps 19:10
is like apples of g...........Prov 25:11
is Mine, and the g...........Hag 2:8
g I do not have.............. Acts 3:6
with braided hair or g......1 Ti 2:9
a man with g rings......... Jas 2:2
Your g and silver are......Jas 5:3
more precious than g.......1 Pe 1:7
like silver or g................1 Pe 1:18
of the city was pure g......Rev 21:21

GONE

I am g like a shadow.......Ps 109:23
I have g astray like a.......Ps 119:176
the word has g out of.....Is 45:23
like sheep have g............Is 53:6

GOOD

God saw that it was g......Gen 1:10
but God meant it for g.... Gen 50:20
LORD has promised g..... Num 10:29
you have spoken is g....... 2 Ki 20:19
seeking the g of his......... Esth 10:3
indeed accept g..............Job 2:10
Who will show us any g... Ps 4:6
is none who does g......... Ps 14:1
G and upright is the........ Ps 25:8
that he may see g........... Ps 34:12
Truly God is g to............Ps 73:1
g man deals graciously..... Ps 112:5
Your Spirit is g............Ps 143:10
g man obtains favor........Prov 12:2
g word makes it glad...... Prov 12:25
on the evil and the g...... Prov 15:3
A merry heart does g..... Prov 17:22
who knows what is g...... Eccl 6:12
learn to do g.................Is 1:17
Zion, you may bring g..... Is 40:9
tidings of g things........... Is 52:7
talked to me, with g....... Zech 1:13
they may see your g........ Matt 5:16
said, "Be of g cheer....... Matt 9:22
"A g man out of the...... Matt 12:35
G Teacher, what g......... Matt 19:16
No one is g but One....... Matt 19:17
For she has done a g......Matt 26:10
behold, I bring you g......Luke 2:10
on earth peace, g.......... Luke 2:14
"Can anything g........... John 1:46
Some said, "He is g........ John 7:12
g works I have shown.....John 10:32
who went about doing g...Acts 10:38
For he was a g man....... Acts 11:24
in that He did g.............Acts 14:17
g man someone would..... Rom 5:7
in my flesh) nothing g.....Rom 7:18
overcome evil with g...... Rom 12:21
Jesus for g works........... Eph 2:10
fruitful in every g...........Col 1:10
know that the law is g..... 1 Ti 1:8
For this is g and............ 1 Ti 2:3
bishop, he desires a g..... 1 Ti 3:1
for this is g and.............. 1 Ti 5:4
be rich in g works.......... 1 Ti 6:18
prepared for every g........2 Ti 2:21
and have tasted the g..... Heb 6:5
Every g gift and every..... Jas 1:17
g works which they....... 1 Pe 2:12
to suffer for doing g........ 1 Pe 3:17

GOODNESS

I will make all My g.......Ex 33:19
and abounding in g......... Ex 34:6
You are my Lord, My g...Ps 16:2
Surely g and mercy........ Ps 23:6
That I would see the g....Ps 27:13
how great is Your g....... Ps 31:19
The g of God endures..... Ps 52:1
how great is their g....... Zech 9:17
the riches of His g.......... Rom 2:4
consider the g and........Rom 11:22
kindness, g.....................Gal 5:22

GOODS

When g increase.............. Eccl 5:11
and plunder his g........... Matt 12:29
ruler over all his g......... Matt 24:47
Soul, you have many g.... Luke 12:19
man was wasting his g..... Luke 16:1
I give half of my g......... Luke 19:8
has this world's g............ 1 Jn 3:17

GOSPEL

The beginning of the g.....Mark 1:1
and believe in the g........Mark 1:15
g must first be................ Mark 13:10
to testify to the g.......... Acts 20:24
separated to the g........... Rom 1:1
not ashamed of the g.......Rom 1:16
should live from the g.....1 Co 9:14
if our g is veiled............. 2 Co 4:3
to a different g............... Gal 1:6
of truth, the g............... Eph 1:13
the mystery of the g....... Eph 6:19
g which you heard...........Col 1:23
the everlasting g............. Rev 14:6

GOSSIPS

only idle but also g......... 1 Ti 5:13

GOVERNMENT

and the g will be upon.....Is 9:6

GRACE

But Noah found g..........Gen 6:8
G is poured upon Your...Ps 45:2
The LORD will give g.....Ps 84:11
the Spirit of g................Zech 12:10
and the g of God was......Luke 2:40
g and truth came........... John 1:17
And great g was upon..... Acts 4:33
G to you and peace........Rom 1:7
receive abundance of g.... Rom 5:17
g is no longer g............. Rom 11:6
The g of our Lord...........Rom 16:20
For you know the g.........2 Co 8:9
g is sufficient.................2 Co 12:9
The g of the Lord........... 2 Co 13:14
you have fallen from g.....Gal 5:4
to the riches of His g......Eph 1:7
g you have been............. Eph 2:8
dispensation of the g...... Eph 3:2
g was given according...... Eph 4:7
G be with all those......... Eph 6:24
shaken, let us have g.......Heb 12:28
But He gives more g......Jas 4:6
this is the true g............. 1 Pe 5:12
but grow in the g...........2 Pe 3:18

GRACIOUS

he said, "God be g.......... Gen 43:29
I will be g to whom I...... Ex 33:19
then He is g to him.........Job 33:24
wise man's mouth are g.... Eccl 10:12
of hosts will be g........... Amos 5:15
know that You are a g.....Jon 4:2
that He may be g............Mal 1:9
at the gracious words which...... Luke 4:22
that the Lord is g............1 Pe 2:3

GRAFTED

in unbelief, will be g....... Rom 11:23

GRAIN

Israel went to buy g....... Gen 42:5
it treads out the g.......... Deut 25:4
You provide their g........Ps 65:9
be an abundance of g..... Ps 72:16
him who withholds g...... Prov 11:26
be revived like g............. Hos 14:7
G shall make the young... Zech 9:17
to pluck heads of g........ Matt 12:1
unless a g of wheat........ John 12:24
it treads out the g........... 1 Co 9:9

GRANT

And g us Your............... Ps 85:7
G that these two...........Matt 20:21
who overcomes I will g.... Rev 3:21

GRAPES

in the blood of g.............Gen 49:11
their g are g................... Deut 32:32
g give a good smell........ Song 2:13
vines have tender g......... Song 2:15
brought forth wild g....... Is 5:2
Yet gleaning g will be..... Is 17:6
"There shall be no g...... Jer 8:13
have eaten sour g...........Ezek 18:2
Do men gather g........... Matt 7:16
g are fully ripe.............. Rev 14:18

GRASPING

all is vanity and g........... Eccl 1:14

GRASS

they were as the g...........2 Ki 19:26
offspring like the g........Job 5:25
g which grows up............Ps 90:5
his days are like g.......... Ps 103:15
The g withers................. Is 40:7
to sit down on the g........ Matt 14:19
"All flesh is as g............. 1 Pe 1:24

GRASSHOPPERS

inhabitants are like g....... Is 40:22
captains like great g........ Nah 3:17

GRAVE

g does not come............. Job 7:9
for the g as my house...... Job 17:13
my soul up from the g..... Ps 30:3
the power of the g.......... Ps 49:15
or wisdom in the g..........Eccl 9:10
And they made His g..... Is 53:9
the power of the g.......... Hos 13:14

GRAVES

there were no g.............. Ex 14:11
and the g were opened.... Matt 27:52
g which are not.............. Luke 11:44
g will hear His voice.......John 5:28

GRAY

would bring down my g... Gen 42:38
the man of g hairs...........Deut 32:25
of old men is their g.......Prov 20:29

GREAT

and make your name g.... Gen 12:2
He has done us this g...... 1 Sa 5:9
For the LORD is g.......... 1 Ch 16:25
I build will be g..............2 Ch 2:5
"The work is g................Neh 4:19
Who does g things......... Job 5:9
G men are not always......Job 32:9
in the g congregation...... Ps 22:25
g are Your works............ Ps 92:5
my God, You are very g..Ps 104:1
"The LORD has done g...Ps 126:2
g is the sum of them....... Ps 139:17
in the place of g men...... Prov 25:6
g is the Holy One........... Is 12:6
And do you seek g......... Jer 45:5
g is Your faithfulness...... Lam 3:23
The g day of the LORD...Zeph 1:14
he shall be called g........ Matt 5:19
one pearl of g price........Matt 13:46
desires to become g........Matt 20:26
g drops of blood............. Luke 22:44
that he was someone g....Acts 8:9
G is Diana of the............Acts 19:28
that I have g sorrow.......Rom 9:2
without controversy g...... 1 Ti 3:16
with contentment is g...... 1 Ti 6:6
But in a g house.............2 Ti 2:20

appearing of our g......... Tit 2:13
See how g a forest.......... Jas 3:5
g men, the rich men....... Rev 6:15
mystery, Babylon the g.... Rev 17:5
Then I saw a g white...... Rev 20:11
the dead, small and g..... Rev 20:12

GREATER
the throne will I be g...... Gen 41:40
g than all the gods.......... Ex 18:11
whose appearance was g...Dan 7:20
kingdom of heaven is g...Matt 11:11
place there is One g........ Matt 12:6
g than Jonah is here....... Matt 12:41
g than Solomon is here.... Matt 12:42
g things than these.......... John 1:50
g than our father............ John 4:12
a servant is not g........... John 13:16
g than he who sent him... John 13:16
G love has no one.......... John 15:13
'A servant is not g.......... John 15:20
parts have g modesty....... 1 Co 12:23
he who prophesies is g.... 1 Co 14:5
swear by no one g..........Heb 6:13
condemns us, God is g.....1 Jn 3:20
witness of God is g.......... 1 Jn 5:9

GREATEST
little child is the g.......... Matt 18:4
be considered the g........ Luke 22:24
but the g of these is....... 1 Co 13:13

GREATNESS
And in the g of Your...... Ex 15:7
According to the g.......... Ps 79:11
g is unsearchable.............Ps 145:3
I will declare Your g....... Ps 145:6
I have attained g............Eccl 1:16
traveling in the g........... Is 63:1
is the exceeding g.......... Eph 1:19

GREED
part is full of g.............. Luke 11:39

GREEDINESS
all uncleanness with g...... Eph 4:19
the faith in their g..........1 Ti 6:10

GREEDY
of everyone who is g....... Prov 1:19
not violent, not g............1 Ti 3:3
not violent, not g............Tit 1:7

GREEK
written in Hebrew, G...... John 19:20
and also for the G......... Rom 1:16
with me, being a G........ Gal 2:3
is neither Jew nor G........Gal 3:28

GREEN
lie down in g pastures......Ps 23:2

GREET
g your brethren only........Matt 5:47
G one another with a...... 1 Co 16:20
into your house nor g...... 2 Jn 10
G the friends by name.....3 Jn 14

GREETED
and g Elizabeth.............. Luke 1:40

GREW
And the Child g............. Luke 2:40
But the word of God g.... Acts 12:24
the word of the Lord g.... Acts 19:20

GRIEF
burden and his own g......2 Ch 6:29
g were fully weighed........Job 6:2
Though I speak, my g......Job 16:6
observe trouble and g......Ps 10:14
of mirth may be g...........Prov 14:13
much wisdom is much g...Eccl 1:18
and acquainted with g......Is 53:3
joy and not with g.......... Heb 13:17

GRIEVE
g the children of men...... Lam 3:33
g the Holy Spirit.............Eph 4:30

GRIEVED
earth, and He was g........Gen 6:6
Has not my soul g..........Job 30:25
forty years I was g.......... Ps 95:10
a woman forsaken and g.. Is 54:6
g His Holy Spirit............ Is 63:10
with anger, being g......... Mark 3:5
and went away g............Mark 10:22
Peter was g because........ John 21:17

GRIEVOUS
g task God has given.......Eccl 1:13
for the present, but g...... Heb 12:11

GRINDERS
when the g cease............ Eccl 12:3

GRINDING
the sound of g is low.......Eccl 12:4
g the faces of the............Is 3:15
"Two women will be g.....Matt 24:41

GROAN
The dying g in the.........Job 24:12
even we ourselves g........Rom 8:23
who are in this tent g...... 2 Co 5:4

GROANING
So God heard their g.......Ex 2:24
I am weary with my g......Ps 6:6
Then Jesus, again g........John 11:38

GROANINGS
g which cannot............... Rom 8:26

GROPE
And you shall g............. Deut 28:29
They g in the dark........Job 12:25
We g for the wall like......Is 59:10
hope that they might g.....Acts 17:27

GROUND
"Cursed is the g............. Gen 3:17
you stand is holy g......... Ex 3:5
up your fallow g............ Jer 4:3
give its fruit, the g........ Zech 8:12
others fell on good g....... Matt 13:8
bought a piece of g........ Luke 14:18
God, the pillar and g.......1 Ti 3:15

GROUNDED
being rooted and g..........Eph 3:17

GROW
all of them will g........... Ps 102:26
the horn of David g........ Ps 132:17
the earth will g...............Is 51:6
you shall go out and g.... Mal 4:2
truth in love, may g........ Eph 4:15
and they will all g..........Heb 1:11
but g in the grace and..... 2 Pe 3:18

GRUDGINGLY
in his heart, not g...........2 Co 9:7

GUARANTEE
us the Spirit as a g.........2 Co 5:5
who is the g of our........ Eph 1:14

GUARD
g the way to the tree......Gen 3:24
will be your rear g.......... Is 52:12
G the doors of your........ Mic 7:5
we were kept under g.......Gal 3:23
G what was committed.... 1 Ti 6:20

GUARDIANS
but is under g and..........Gal 4:2

GUARDS
Unless the LORD g.........Ps 127:1
And the g shook for........Matt 28:4

GUIDANCE
and excellent in g............Is 28:29

GUIDE
He will be our g............. Ps 48:14
father, You are the g.......Jer 3:4
g our feet into the..........Luke 1:79
has come, He will g........ John 16:13
Judas, who became a g.... Acts 1:16
you yourself are a g........ Rom 2:19

GUIDES
to you, blind g............... Matt 23:16
unless someone g........... Acts 8:31

GUILE
spirit there is no g..........Ps 32:2
from speaking g..............Ps 34:13
in whom is no g..............John 1:47
no sin, nor was g............ 1 Pe 2:22
mouth was found no g..... Rev 14:5

GUILT
they accept their g.......... Lev 26:41
g has grown up to the.....Ezra 9:6
of your fathers' g............ Matt 23:32

GUILTLESS
g who takes His name..... Ex 20:7
have condemned the g..... Matt 12:7

GUILTY
"We are truly g.............. Gen 42:21
we have been very g........Ezra 9:7
the world may become g.. Rom 3:19
in one point, he is g........Jas 2:10

GULF
you there is a great g...... Luke 16:26

— H —

HABITATION
to Your holy h............... Ex 15:13
your rightful h...............Job 8:6
Is God in His holy h.......Ps 68:5
their h be desolate.......... Ps 69:25
the Most High, your h....Ps 91:9
go to a city for h............Ps 107:7
establish a city for h........Ps 107:36
but He blesses the h........Prov 3:33
in a peaceful h...............Is 32:18
Jerusalem, a quiet h........Is 33:20
from His holy h..............Zech 2:13
'Let his h be.................. Acts 1:20

be clothed with our *h*...... 2 Co 5:2
built together for a *h*....... Eph 2:22
but left their own *h*......... Jude 6

HABITATIONS
are full of the *h*............. Ps 74:20
into everlasting *h*........... Luke 16:9

HADES
be brought down to *H*..... Matt 11:23
H shall not.................... Matt 16:18
being in torments in *H*....Luke 16:23
not leave my soul in *H*.... Acts 2:27
I have the keys of *H*....... Rev 1:18
H were cast into the........Rev 20:14

HAIL
cause very heavy *h*......... Ex 9:18
seen the treasury of *h*......Job 38:22
He casts out His *h*.......... Ps 147:17
h will sweep away the......Is 28:17
of the plague of the *h*......Rev 16:21

HAILSTONES
clouds passed with *h*........Ps 18:12

HAIR
bring down my gray *h*......Gen 42:38
the *h* on my body stood...Job 4:15
Your *h* is like a flock...... Song 4:1
you cannot make one *h*....Matt 5:36
"But not a *h* of your....... Luke 21:18
if a woman has long *h*..... 1 Co 11:15
not with braided *h*......... 1 Ti 2:9
h like women's *h*........... Rev 9:8

HAIRS
are more than the *h*........ Ps 40:12
h I will carry you............ Is 46:4
yes, gray *h* are here........ Hos 7:9
"But the very *h*.............. Matt 10:30

HAIRY
h garment all over..........Gen 25:25
him, "He was a *h*........... 2 Ki 1:8

HALLOW
hosts, Him you shall *h*.....Is 8:13
h the Holy One of.......... Is 29:23
h the Sabbath day...........Jer 17:24

HALLOWED
the Sabbath day and *h*.....Ex 20:11
but I will be *h*................ Lev 22:32
who is holy shall be *h*......Is 5:16
heaven, *h* be Your name..Matt 6:9

HAMMER
h that breaks the rock..... Jer 23:29
How the *h* of the whole...Jer 50:23

HAND
h shall be against............ Gen 16:12
tooth for tooth, *h*...........Ex 21:24
the *h* of God was very.....1 Sa 5:11
and strengthened his *h*.....1 Sa 23:16
Uzzah put out his *h*........2 Sa 6:6
let us fall into the *h*........ 2 Sa 24:14
Then, by the good *h*.......Ezra 8:18
He would loose his *h*.......Job 6:9
he stretches out his *h*......Job 15:25
that your own right *h*......Job 40:14
h has held me up............Ps 18:35
My times are in Your *h*...Ps 31:15
and night Your *h*............ Ps 32:4
Your right *h* is full.........Ps 48:10

Let Your *h* be upon the...Ps 80:17
h shall be established.......Ps 89:21
"Sit at My right *h*........... Ps 110:1
days is in her right *h*.......Prov 3:16
heart is in the *h*.............Prov 21:1
Whatever your *h*............Eccl 9:10
is at his right *h*.............. Eccl 10:2
do not withhold your *h*.... Eccl 11:6
His left *h* is under my.....Song 8:3
My *h* has laid the............Is 48:13
Behold, the LORD's *h*..... Is 59:1
are the work of Your *h*....Is 64:8
Am I a God near at *h*......Jer 23:23
of heaven is at *h*............Matt 3:2
if your right *h*............... Matt 5:30
do not let your left *h*......Matt 6:3
h makes you sin.............Mark 9:43
sitting at the right *h*........ Mark 14:62
delivered from the *h*........Luke 1:74
at the right *h* of God......Acts 7:55
is even at the right *h*...... Rom 8:34
with my own *h*............... 1 Co 16:21
to you with my own *h*......Gal 6:11
The Lord is at *h*............. Phil 4:5
"Sit at My right *h*.......... Heb 1:13
down at the right *h*......... Heb 10:12
stars in His right *h*......... Rev 2:1

HANDIWORK
firmament shows His *h*.... Ps 19:1

HANDLE
h the law did not know....Jer 2:8
H Me and see................ Luke 24:39
do not taste, do not *h*......Col 2:21

HANDLED
and our hands have *h*...... 1 Jn 1:1

HANDS
the *h* are the *h*..............Gen 27:22
here we are, in your *h*.....Josh 9:25
took his life in his *h*........1 Sa 19:5
put my life in my *h*.........1 Sa 28:21
but His *h* make whole......Job 5:18
and cleanse my *h*............Job 9:30
h have made me and......Job 10:8
They pierced My *h*..........Ps 22:16
h formed the dry land......Ps 95:5
stretches out her *h*..........Prov 31:19
say, 'He has no *h*............Is 45:9
these wounds in your *h*....Zech 13:6
than having two *h*........... Matt 18:8
"Behold My *h* and My....Luke 24:39
only, but also my *h*.........John 13:9
h the print of the...........John 20:25
know that these *h*...........Acts 20:34
his *h* what is good...........Eph 4:28
lifting up holy *h*............. 1 Ti 2:8
the laying on of the *h*......1 Ti 4:14
to fall into the *h*............ Heb 10:31

HANDWRITING
having wiped out the *h*.... Col 2:14

HANGED
for he who is *h*...............Deut 21:23
and went and *h* himself....Matt 27:5

HANGS
h the earth on nothing.....Job 26:7
is everyone who *h*...........Gal 3:13

HAPPEN
show us what will *h*.........Is 41:22
understand what will *h*.....Dan 10:14
not know what will *h*.......Jas 4:14

HAPPINESS
one year, and bring *h*...... Deut 24:5

HAPPY
H is the man who has......Ps 127:5
H are the people who......Ps 144:15
H is the man who finds....Prov 3:13
mercy on the poor, *h*...... Prov 14:21
trusts in the LORD, *h*......Prov 16:20
h is he who keeps.......... Prov 29:18
know these things, *h*.......John 13:17
H is he who does not...... Rom 14:22

HARASS
and Judah shall not *h*...... Is 11:13
h some from the church... Acts 12:1

HARD
"Is anything too *h*...........Gen 18:14
His heart is as *h*............Job 41:24
shown Your people *h*...... Ps 60:3
I knew you to be a *h*...... Matt 25:24
This is a *h* saying...........John 6:60
are some things *h*...........2 Pe 3:16

HARDEN
But I will *h* his heart.......Ex 4:21
Do not *h* your hearts......Ps 95:8
h your hearts as.............Heb 3:8

HARDENED
But Pharaoh *h* his...........Ex 8:32
Who has *h* himself.......... Job 9:4
their heart was *h*............Mark 6:52
eyes and *h* their heart..... John 12:40
and the rest were *h*.........Rom 11:7
lest any of you be *h*........ Heb 3:13

HARDENS
A wicked man *h* his........ Prov 21:29
h his heart will fall.......... Prov 28:14
and whom He wills He *h*. Rom 9:18

HARDSHIP
h that has befallen us...... Num 20:14
h as a good soldier..........2 Ti 2:3

HARLOT
of a *h* named Rahab........Josh 2:1
h is a deep pit................Prov 23:27
h is one body with her.....1 Co 6:16
h Rahab did not perish.... Heb 11:31
of the great *h* who......... Rev 17:1

HARLOTRIES
the land with your *h*........Jer 3:2
Let her put away her *h*....Hos 2:2

HARLOTRY
through her casual *h*........Jer 3:9
the lewdness of your *h*.....Jer 13:27
let them put their *h*........Ezek 43:9
are the children of *h*........Hos 2:4
Ephraim, you commit *h*... Hos 5:3
for the spirit of *h*............Hos 5:4

HARLOTS
his blood while the *h*.......1 Ki 22:38
h enter the.....................Matt 21:31
great, the mother of *h*..... Rev 17:5

HARM
do My prophets no *h*.......1 Ch 16:22
and I will not *h*.............. Jer 25:6
and do not *h* the oil........ Rev 6:6

HARMLESS

become blameless and *h*...Phil 2:15
for us, who is holy, *h*...... Heb 7:26

HARP

those who play the *h*... Gen 4:21
with the lute and *h*...........Ps 150:3
Lamb, each having a *h*.... Rev 5:8

HARPS

We hung our *h* Upon the.Ps 137:2
playing their *h*................ Rev 14:2

HARSH

Your words have been *h*.. Mal 3:13
but also to the *h*.............1 Pe 2:18

HARVEST

seedtime and *h*............ Gen 8:22
to the joy of *h*................Is 9:3
shall eat up your *h*..........Jer 5:17
"The *h* is past................ Jer 8:20
of her *h* will come.........Jer 51:33
h truly is plentiful........... Matt 9:37
pray the Lord of the *h*.....Matt 9:38
sickle, because the *h*........Mark 4:29
already white for *h*..........John 4:35
the *h* of the earth is...... Rev 14:15

HASTE

you shall eat it in *h*.......Ex 12:11
For I said in my *h*...........Ps 31:22
And they came with *h*..... Luke 2:16
"Zacchaeus, make *h*........Luke 19:5

HASTEN

be multiplied who *h*........ Ps 16:4
Do not *h* in your............ Eccl 7:9
I, the LORD, will ....Is 60:22

HASTENING

h the coming of the.........2 Pe 3:12

HASTENS

and he sins who *h*...........Prov 19:2
with an evil eye *h*........... Prov 28:22
is near and *h* quickly....... Zeph 1:14

HASTILY

heart utter anything *h*...... Eccl 5:2
lay hands on anyone *h*.....1 Ti 5:22

HATE

'You shall not *h*..............Lev 19:17
h all workers of............. Ps 5:5
h the righteous shall........Ps 34:21
love the LORD, *h* evil..... Ps 97:10
h every false way........... Ps 119:104
h the double-minded........Ps 119:113
I *h* and abhor lying........ Ps 119:163
love, and a time to *h*.......Eccl 3:8
h robbery for burnt........ Is 61:8
You who *h* good and.......Mic 3:2
either he will *h*............Matt 6:24

HATED

Therefore I *h* life............Eccl 2:17
h all my labor in............Eccl 2:18
but Esau I have *h*...........Mal 1:3
And you will be *h*...........Matt 10:22
have seen and also *h*...... John 15:24
but Esau I have h...........Rom 9:13
For no one ever *h*..........Eph 5:29
and h lawlessness............Heb 1:9

HATEFUL

h woman when she is...... Prov 30:23
in malice and envy, *h*...... Tit 3:3

HATERS

The *h* of the LORD.........Ps 81:15
backbiters, *h* of God....... Rom 1:30

HATES

six things the LORD *h*..... Prov 6:16
lose it, and he who *h*.......John 12:25
"If the world *h*.............John 15:18
h his brother is...............1 Jn 2:11

HAUGHTY

Your eyes are on the *h*....2 Sa 22:28
bring down *h* looks......... Ps 18:27
my heart is not *h*............Ps 131:1
h spirit before a fall........ Prov 16:18
A proud and *h* man........ Prov 21:24
Do not be *h*....................Rom 11:20
age not to be *h*..............1 Ti 6:17

HAVEN

shall dwell by the *h*.........Gen 49:13
to their desired *h*............ Ps 107:30

HAVOC

for Saul, he made *h*........ Acts 8:3

HEAD

He shall bruise your *h*..... Gen 3:15
my skin, and laid my *h*....Job 16:15
return upon his own *h*..... Ps 7:16
h is covered with dew......Song 5:2
The whole *h* is sick......... Is 1:5
it to bow down his *h*....... Is 58:5
could lift up his *h*.......... Zech 1:21
you swear by your *h*........Matt 5:36
having his *h* covered........1 Co 11:4
and gave Him to be *h*.....Eph 1:22
For the husband is *h*....... Eph 5:23
His *h* and His hair.......... Rev 1:14

HEADS

men to ride over our *h*.... Ps 66:12
Him, wagging their *h*.......Matt 27:39
dragon having seven *h*..... Rev 12:3

HEAL

I wound and I *h*............. Deut 32:39
O LORD, *h* me.............. Ps 6:2
sent Me to *h* the............Is 61:1
h your backslidings..........Jer 3:22
who can *h* you................Lam 2:13
torn, but He will *h*..........Hos 6:1
"*H* the sick....................Matt 10:8
so that I should h............Matt 13:15
sent Me to h the............Luke 4:18
Physician, *h* yourself........Luke 4:23

HEALED

His word and *h* them.......Ps 107:20
and return and be *h*........ Is 6:10
His stripes we are *h*........ Is 53:5
h the hurt of My............Jer 6:14
When I would have *h*...... Hos 7:1
and He *h* them.............. Matt 4:24
he had faith to be *h*........ Acts 14:9
that you may be *h*.......... Jas 5:16
his deadly wound was *h*... Rev 13:3

HEALING

h shall spring forth.......... Is 58:8
so that there is no *h*........Jer 14:19
Your injury has no *h*....... Nah 3:19

shall arise with *h*............Mal 4:2
and *h* all kinds of...........Matt 4:23
tree were for the *h*..........Rev 22:2

HEALINGS

to another gifts of *h*........ 1 Co 12:9
Do all have gifts of *h*...... 1 Co 12:30

HEALS

h all your diseases..........Ps 103:3
h the stroke of their........Is 30:26
Jesus the Christ *h*.......... Acts 9:34

HEALTH

to the soul and *h*........... Prov 16:24
and for a time of *h*......... Jer 8:15
no recovery for the *h*.......Jer 8:22
all things and be in *h*.......3 Jn 2

HEAP

I could *h* up words..........Job 16:4
sea together as a *h*......... Ps 33:7
ears, they will *h*..............2 Ti 4:3

HEAPS

Though he *h* up silver......Job 27:16

HEAR

"*H*, O Israel.................. Deut 6:4
Him you shall *h*..............Deut 18:15
H me when I call............Ps 4:1
O You who *h* prayer........Ps 65:2
h what God the LORD.... Ps 85:8
ear, shall He not *h*..........Ps 94:9
h the words of the.......... Prov 22:17
h rather than to give....... Eccl 5:1
H, O heavens.................Is 1:2
H, you who are afar........Is 33:13
Let the earth *h*...............Is 34:1
I spoke, you did not *h*..... Is 65:12
hearing you will h..........Matt 13:14
if he will not *h*...............Matt 18:16
Take heed what you *h*......Mark 4:24
ears, do you not *h*.......... Mark 8:18
h the sound of it.............John 3:8
that God does not *h*.......John 9:31
And how shall they *h*.......Rom 10:14
man be swift to *h*............Jas 1:19
h what the Spirit says...... Rev 2:7

HEARD

h the sound of the.......... Gen 3:8
h their cry because of...... Ex 3:7
you only *h* a voice.......... Deut 4:12
certainly God has *h*......... Ps 66:19
quietly, should be *h*.........Eccl 9:17
Have you not *h*............... Is 40:21
world men have not *h*......Is 64:4
Who has *h* such a thing... Is 66:8
h Ephraim bemoaning......Jer 31:18
that they will be *h*...........Matt 6:7
h the word believed.........Acts 4:4
I say, have they not *h*...... Rom 10:18
not seen, nor ear h..........1 Co 2:9
h inexpressible................2 Co 12:4
things that you have *h*...... 2 Ti 2:2
the things we have *h*........Heb 2:1
the word which they *h*.....Heb 4:2
from death, and was *h*.....Heb 5:7
which we have *h*..............1 Jn 1:1
Lord's Day, and I *h*........ Rev 1:10

HEARER

if anyone is a *h*.............. Jas 1:23
is not a forgetful *h*..........Jas 1:25

HEARERS
for not the *h* of the........Rom 2:13
impart grace to the *h*......Eph 4:29
of the word, and not *h*.... Jas 1:22

HEARING
and read in the *h*...........Ex 24:7
Book of Moses in the *h*... Neh 13:1
Do not speak in the *h*..... Prov 23:9
'Keep on *h*....................Is 6:9
h they do not...............Matt 13:13
h they may hear............. Mark 4:12
If the whole were *h*........1 Co 12:17
or by the *h* of faith........ Gal 3:2
have become dull of *h*..... Heb 5:11

HEARS
for Your servant *h*.......... 1 Sa 3:9
out, and the LORD *h*...... Ps 34:17
He who *h* you *h* Me.......Luke 10:16
of God *h* God's words..... John 8:47
"And if anyone *h*...........John 12:47
who is of the truth *h*....... John 18:37
He who knows God *h*......1 Jn 4:6
And let him who *h*.........Rev 22:17

HEART
h was only evil.............. Gen 6:5
for you know the *h*......... Ex 23:9
great searchings of *h*........Judg 5:16
h rejoices in the LORD....1 Sa 2:1
God gave him another *h*.. 1 Sa 10:9
LORD looks at the *h*....... 1 Sa 16:7
his wives turned his *h*...... 1 Ki 11:4
He pierces my *h*............. Job 16:13
How my *h* yearns within.. Job 19:27
For God made my *h*........Job 23:16
My *h* is in turmoil and.....Job 30:27
My *h* also instructs me.....Ps 16:7
your *h* live forever......... Ps 22:26
h is overflowing............. Ps 45:1
My *h* is steadfast...........Ps 57:7
Thus my *h* was grieved.... Ps 73:21
My *h* and my flesh cry.... Ps 84:2
h shall depart from me.... Ps 101:4
look and a proud *h*......... Ps 101:5
with my whole *h*............Ps 111:1
h is not haughty.............Ps 131:1
h makes a cheerful.........Prov 15:13
The king's *h* is in the.......Prov 21:1
as he thinks in his *h*....... Prov 23:7
with a wicked *h*.............. Prov 26:23
h reveals the man.......... Prov 27:19
trusts in his own *h*.......... Prov 28:26
The *h* of the wise is....... Eccl 7:4
and a wise man's *h*.........Eccl 8:5
h yearned for him...........Song 5:4
and the whole *h*..............Is 1:5
h shall resound.............. Is 16:11
the yearning of Your *h*.... Is 63:15
the mind and the *h*........ Jer 11:20
h is deceitful above........ Jer 17:9
I will give them a *h*........Jer 24:7
therefore My *h* yearns..... Jer 31:20
and take the stony *h*.......Ezek 11:19
get yourselves a new *h*.....Ezek 18:31
uncircumcised in *h*......... Ezek 44:7
are the pure in *h*............ Matt 5:8
is, there your *h*.............Matt 6:21
of the *h* proceed evil...... Matt 15:19
h will flow rivers............John 7:38
"Let not your *h*............John 14:1
believed were of one *h*.... Acts 4:32
Satan filled your *h*......... Acts 5:3
h is not right in the........ Acts 8:21
h that God has raised...... Rom 10:9

in sincerity of *h*.............. Eph 6:5
refresh my *h* in the........ Phm 20
and shuts up his *h*...........1 Jn 3:17
if our *h* condemns us....... 1 Jn 3:20

HEARTILY
you do, do it *h*.............. Col 3:23

HEARTS
God tests the *h*...............Ps 7:9
who seek God, your *h*.... Ps 69:32
Let the *h* of those............Ps 105:3
And he will turn the *h*.....Mal 4:6
h failing them from........ Luke 21:26
purifying their *h*..............Acts 15:9
will guard your *h*............Phil 4:7
of God rule in your *h*...... Col 3:15

HEATHEN
repetitions as the *h*.........Matt 6:7
him be to you like a *h*.....Matt 18:17

HEAVEN
called the firmament *H*.... Gen 1:8
precious things of *h*........Deut 33:13
looks down from *h*..........Ps 14:2
word is settled in *h*.........Ps 119:89
For God is in *h*.............. Eccl 5:2
"*H* is My throne............Is 66:1
"If *h* above can be..........Jer 31:37
and the birds of the *h*......Dan 2:38
come to know that *H*...... Dan 4:26
for the kingdom of *h*.......Matt 3:2
your Father in *h*............. Matt 5:16
on earth as it is in *h*........Matt 6:10
"*H* and earth will............Matt 24:35
from Him a sign from *h*... Mark 8:11
have sinned against *h*......Luke 15:18
you shall see *h*................ John 1:51
one has ascended to *h*..... John 3:13
the true bread from *h*......John 6:32
a voice came from *h*........John 12:28
sheet, let down from *h*......Acts 11:5
the whole family in *h*......Eph 3:15
laid up for you in *h*........Col 1:5
and the *h* gave rain........Jas 5:18
there was silence in *h*...... Rev 8:1
sign appeared in *h*..........Rev 12:1
And I saw a new *h*......... Rev 21:1

HEAVENLY
your *h* Father will...........Matt 6:14
h host praising God.........Luke 2:13
if I tell you *h* things.........John 3:12
are those who are *h*........ 1 Co 15:48
blessing in the *h*............. Eph 1:3
and have tasted the *h*......Heb 6:4
h things themselves........ Heb 9:23
a better, that is, a *h*........ Heb 11:16
the living God, the *h*.......Heb 12:22

HEAVENS
I will make your *h*.......... Lev 26:19
and the highest *h*...........Deut 10:14
h cannot contain............. 1 Ki 8:27
the LORD made the *h*..... 1 Ch 16:26
Till the *h* are no more.....Job 14:12
in the *h* shall laugh........ Ps 2:4
h declare the glory........ Ps 19:1
Let the *h* declare His.......Ps 50:6
h can be compared.........Ps 89:6
The *h* are Yours............. Ps 89:11
For as the *h* are high.......Ps 103:11
When He prepared the *h*.. Prov 8:27
h are higher than the.......Is 55:9
behold, I create new *h*.....Is 65:17

and behold, the *h*........... Matt 3:16
h will be shaken............Matt 24:29
h are the work of Your...Heb 1:10
h will pass away.............2 Pe 3:10

HEAVINESS
And I am full of *h*.......... Ps 69:20
My soul melts from *h*...... Ps 119:28

HEAVY
the bondage was *h*.......... Neh 5:18

HEDGE
behold, I will *h*...............Hos 2:6
sharper than a thorn *h*..... Mic 7:4
a vineyard and set a *h*..... Mark 12:1

HEDGED
and whom God has *h*......Job 3:23
You have *h* me behind.... Ps 139:5
He has *h* me in so that.... Lam 3:7

HEED
By taking *h* according......Ps 119:9
if you diligently *h*...........Jer 17:24
and let us not give *h*....... Jer 18:18
nor give *h* to fables......... 1 Ti 1:4
the more earnest *h*.........Heb 2:1

HEEDS
h counsel is wise.............Prov 12:15

HEEL
you shall bruise His *h*......Gen 3:15
took hold of Esau's *h*...... Gen 25:26
Has lifted up his *h*.......... Ps 41:9
has lifted up his *h*...........John 13:18

HEIGHT
"Is not God in the *h*....... Job 22:12
looked down from the *h*..Ps 102:19
nor *h* nor depth.............Rom 8:39
length and depth and *h*....Eph 3:18

HEIR
Has he no *h*...................Jer 49:1
Now I say that the *h*....... Gal 4:1
if a son, then an *h*.......... Gal 4:7
He has appointed *h*.........Heb 1:2
the world and became *h*...Heb 11:7

HEIRS
if children, then *h*........... Rom 8:17
of God and joint *h*..........Rom 8:17
should be fellow *h*..........Eph 3:6
be rich in faith and *h*......Jas 2:5
vessel, and as being *h*......1 Pe 3:7

HELL
shall be turned into *h*...... Ps 9:17
go down alive into *h*........Ps 55:15
house is the way to *h*.......Prov 7:27
his soul from *h*...............Prov 23:14
H and Destruction are..... Prov 27:20
"*H* from beneath is.........Is 14:9
be in danger of *h* fire...... Matt 5:22
to be cast into *h*.............Matt 18:9
the condemnation of *h*....Matt 23:33
power to cast into *h*........ Luke 12:5
it is set on fire by *h*........Jas 3:6

HELMET
a breastplate, and a *h*.....Is 59:17
And take the *h* of..........Eph 6:17
and love, and as a *h*........1 Th 5:8

HELP

the shield of your *h*.........Deut 33:29
Is my *h* not within me.....Job 6:13
"There is no *h*.................Ps 3:2
May He send you *h*.........Ps 20:2
He is our *h* and our........Ps 33:20
yet praise Him, The *h*.....Ps 42:11
A very present *h*.............Ps 46:1
Give us *h* from trouble....Ps 60:11
God, make haste to *h*......Ps 71:12
"I have given *h*..............Ps 89:19
LORD had been my *h*.....Ps 94:17
there was none to *h*........Ps 107:12
He is their *h* and............Ps 115:9
Our *h* is in the name.......Ps 124:8
let no one *h* him.............Prov 28:17
h my unbelief.................Mark 9:24
tell her to *h* me..............Luke 10:40
and find grace to *h*.........Heb 4:16

HELPED

far the LORD has *h*........1 Sa 7:12
fall, But the LORD *h*......Ps 118:13
of salvation I have *h*.......Is 49:8
h His servant Israel........Luke 1:54

HELPER

I will make him a *h*.........Gen 2:18
Behold, God is my *h*.......Ps 54:4
give you another *h*.........John 14:16
"But when the *H*...........John 15:26
she has been a *h*............Rom 16:2
"The LORD is my *h*........Heb 13:6

HELPFUL

all things are not *h*.........1 Co 6:12

HELPS

the Spirit also *h*.............Rom 8:26
gifts of healings, *h*.........1 Co 12:28

HEM

and touched the *h*..........Matt 9:20
might only touch the *h*....Matt 14:36

HERE

Then I said, "*H* am I......Is 6:8

HERESIES

dissensions, *h*................Gal 5:20
in destructive *h*.............2 Pe 2:1

HERITAGE

give it to you as a *h*.......Ex 6:8
have given me the *h*.......Ps 61:5
for that is his *h*..............Eccl 3:22
for it is his *h*.................Eccl 5:18
This is the *h* of the........Is 54:17
of My people, My *h*.......Joel 3:2
the flock of Your *h*.........Mic 7:14

HID

and I *h* myself................Gen 3:10

HIDDEN

and the LORD has *h*.......2 Ki 4:27
It is *h* from the eyes........Job 28:21
h Your righteousness.......Ps 40:10
And my sins are not *h*.....Ps 69:5
Your word I have *h*........Ps 119:11
h riches of secret...........Is 45:3
there His power was *h*.....Hab 3:4
h that will not................Matt 10:26
the *h* wisdom which God..1 Co 2:7
bring to light the *h*.........1 Co 4:5
have renounced the *h*......2 Co 4:2

but let it be the *h*...........1 Pe 3:4
give some of the *h*..........Rev 2:17

HIDE

H me under the shadow...Ps 17:8
You shall *h* them in........Ps 31:20
O God, And do not *h*.....Ps 55:1
You *h* Your face............Ps 104:29
darkness shall not *h*........Ps 139:12
You are God, who *h*.......Is 45:15
h yourself from your........Is 58:7
"Fall on us and *h*...........Rev 6:16

HIDES

He *h* His face.................Ps 10:11

HIDING

You are my *h* place.........Ps 32:7
A man will be as a *h*.......Is 32:2

HIGH

priest of God Most *H*......Gen 14:18
For the LORD Most *H*....Ps 47:2
h is Your right...............Ps 89:13
are on *h* forevermore......Ps 92:8
the LORD is on *h*...........Ps 138:6
"I dwell in the *h*............Is 57:15
know that the Most *H*.....Dan 4:17
whose habitation is *h*......Obad 3
up on a *h* mountain by....Matt 17:1
your mind on *h* things.....Rom 12:16
h thing that exalts..........2 Co 10:5
and faithful *H* Priest.......Heb 2:17

HIGHER

They are *h* than heaven...Job 11:8
you, 'Friend, go up *h*.....Luke 14:10
h than the heavens.........Heb 7:26

HIGHWAY

of the upright is a *h*.......Prov 15:19
in the desert a *h*............Is 40:3
up, build up the *h*..........Is 62:10

HIGHWAYS

h shall be elevated..........Is 49:11
go into the *h*.................Matt 22:9

HILL

My King On My holy *h*...Ps 2:6
h cannot be hidden.........Matt 5:14
and *h* brought low..........Luke 3:5
to the brow of the *h*.......Luke 4:29

HILLS

of the everlasting *h*.........Gen 49:26
possess is a land of *h*......Deut 11:11
of the *h* are His also.......Ps 95:4
up my eyes to the *h*........Ps 121:1
settled, before the *h*........Prov 8:25

HINDERED

come to you (but was *h*...Rom 1:13
Who *h* you from obeying. Gal 5:7
prayers may not be *h*.......1 Pe 3:7

HIP

socket of Jacob's *h*.........Gen 32:25

HIRE

h laborers for his............Matt 20:1

HIRED

h man who eagerly..........Job 7:2
h servants have bread......Luke 15:17

HIRELING

"The *h* flees because.......John 10:13

HOLD

h my eyelids open...........Ps 77:4
right hand shall *h*...........Ps 139:10
LORD your God, will *h*...Is 41:13
I cannot *h* my peace.......Jer 4:19
h fast that word which.....1 Co 15:2
h fast our confession.......Heb 4:14
h fast and repent............Rev 3:3

HOLES

"Foxes have *h*................Matt 8:20

HOLIER

near me, for I am *h*........Is 65:5

HOLIEST

the way into the *H*.........Heb 9:8
to enter the *H* by the......Heb 10:19

HOLINESS

You, glorious in *h*...........Ex 15:11
has spoken in His *h*........Ps 60:6
I have sworn by My *h*.....Ps 89:35
H adorns Your house......Ps 93:5
the Highway of *H*...........Is 35:8
to the Spirit of *h*...........Rom 1:4
spirit, perfecting *h*..........2 Co 7:1
uncleanness, but in *h*......1 Th 4:7
be partakers of His *h*......Heb 12:10

HOLY

where you stand is *h*.......Ex 3:5
priests and a *h* nation......Ex 19:6
day, to keep it *h*............Ex 20:8
distinguish between *h*......Lev 10:10
LORD your God am *h*.....Lev 19:2
"There is none *h*............1 Sa 2:2
h seed is intermingled......Ezra 9:2
h ones will you turn........Job 5:1
God sits on His *h*...........Ps 47:8
God, In His *h* mountain...Ps 48:1
my life, for I am *h*..........Ps 86:2
"*H*, *h*, *h*...................Is 6:3
child of the *H* Spirit........Matt 1:18
baptize you with the *H*....Mark 1:8
who speak, but the *H*......Mark 13:11
H Spirit will come..........Luke 1:35
H Spirit descended.........Luke 3:22
Father give the *H*...........Luke 11:13
H Spirit will teach..........Luke 12:12
H Spirit was not............John 7:39
H Spirit has come..........Acts 1:8
all filled with the *H*........Acts 2:4
apostles' hands the *H*......Acts 8:18
to speak, the *H* Spirit.....Acts 11:15
good to the *H* Spirit.......Acts 15:28
receive the *H* Spirit........Acts 19:2
if the firstfruit is *h*.........Rom 11:16
peace and joy in the *H*....Rom 14:17
one another with a *h*.......Rom 16:16
H Spirit teaches.............1 Co 2:13
that we should be *h*........Eph 1:4
were sealed with the *H*....Eph 1:13
partakers of the *H*..........Heb 6:4
has not entered the *h*......Heb 9:24
H Spirit sent from..........1 Pe 1:12
He who called you is *h*....1 Pe 1:15
it is written, "*Be h*.........1 Pe 1:16
moved by the *H* Spirit.....2 Pe 1:21
anointing from the *H*......1 Jn 2:20
says He who is *h*............Rev 3:7
For You alone are *h*........Rev 15:4
is *h*, let him be *h*.........Rev 22:11

HOME

LORD has brought me *h*..Ruth 1:21
sparrow has found a *h*..... Ps 84:3
The stork has her *h*.........Ps 104:17
to his eternal *h*...............Eccl 12:5
said to him, "Go *h*.........Mark 5:19
to him and make Our *h*...John 14:23
took her to his own *h*.....John 19:27
let him eat at *h*............. 1 Co 11:34
own husbands at *h*.......... 1 Co 14:35
that while we are at *h*......2 Co 5:6
to show piety at *h*...........1 Ti 5:4

HOMELESS

and beaten, and *h*...........1 Co 4:11

HOMEMAKERS

be discreet, chaste, *h*.......Tit 2:5

HONEST

we are *h* men.................Gen 42:11

HONEY

What is sweeter than *h*.... Judg 14:18
And with *h* from the.......Ps 81:16
My son, eat *h* because.....Prov 24:13
not good to eat much *h*... Prov 25:27
h and milk are under.......Song 4:11
was locusts and wild *h*..... Matt 3:4

HONEYCOMB

than honey and the *h*...... Ps 19:10
words are like a *h*.........Prov 16:24
fish and some *h*..............Luke 24:42

HONOR

H your father and your....Ex 20:12
both riches and *h*............1 Ki 3:13
the king delights to *h*.......Esth 6:6
earth, And lay my *h*.......Ps 7:5
Man who is in *h*............. Ps 49:20
Sing out the *h* of His.......Ps 66:2
will deliver him and *h*......Ps 91:15
H and majesty are......... Ps 96:6
h have all His saints........ Ps 149:9
H the LORD with your....Prov 3:9
before *h* is humility........Prov 15:33
h is not fitting...............Prov 26:1
spirit will retain *h*...........Prov 29:23
Father, where is My *h*.....Mal 1:6
is not without *h*..............Matt 13:57
H your father and your....Matt 15:4
h the Son just as they.....John 5:23
"I do not receive *h*.........John 5:41
but I *h* My Father..........John 8:49
"If I *h* Myself..............John 8:54
him My Father will *h*......John 12:26
make one vessel for *h*......Rom 9:21
to whom fear, *h*...........Rom 13:7
we bestow greater *h*....... 1 Co 12:23
sanctification and *h*......... 1 Th 4:4
alone is wise, be *h*..........1 Ti 1:17
worthy of double *h*.........1 Ti 5:17
and clay, some for *h*........2 Ti 2:20
no man takes this *h*.......Heb 5:4
H the king.....................1 Pe 2:17
from God the Father *h*.... 2 Pe 1:17
give glory and *h*.............Rev 4:9

HONORABLE

of God, and he is an *h*.... 1 Sa 9:6
His work is *h* and.........Ps 111:3
It is *h* for a man to.......Prov 20:3
traders are the *h*.............Is 23:8
holy day of the LORD *h*.. Is 58:13
providing *h* things...........2 Co 8:21

Marriage is *h* among........Heb 13:4
having your conduct *h*..... 1 Pe 2:12

HONORABLY

desiring to live *h*............Heb 13:18

HONORS

h those who fear the...... Ps 15:4
'This people *h* Me...........Mark 7:6
It is My Father who *h*..... John 8:54

HOOKS

will lament who cast *h*.....Is 19:8
spears into pruning *h*.......Mic 4:3

HOPE

I should say I have *h*.......Ruth 1:12
are spent without *h*.........Job 7:6
so You destroy the *h*.......Job 14:19
where then is my *h*........ Job 17:15
h He has uprooted..........Job 19:10
also will rest in *h*............Ps 16:9
heart, All you who *h*......Ps 31:24
My *h* is in You...............Ps 39:7
For You are my *h*...........Ps 71:5
I *h* in Your word............Ps 119:147
O Israel, *h* in the...........Ps 130:7
h will not be cut............. Prov 23:18
There is more *h*.............Prov 26:12
the living there is *h*........Eccl 9:4
O the *H* of Israel...........Jer 14:8
good that one should *h*....Lam 3:26
Achor as a door of *h*......Hos 2:15
you prisoners of *h*.........Zech 9:12
"I have *h* in God...........Acts 24:15
to *h*, in *h* believed..........Rom 4:18
and rejoice in *h*..............Rom 5:2
h does not disappoint......Rom 5:5
were saved in this *h*........Rom 8:24
h that is seen is............Rom 8:24
But if we *h* for what........Rom 8:25
And now abide faith, *h*.....1 Co 13:13
life only we have *h*..........1 Co 15:19
may know what is the *h*...Eph 1:18
were called in one *h*........Eph 4:4
h which is laid.................Col 1:5
Christ in you, the *h*.........Col 1:27
For what is our *h*.............1 Th 2:19
others who have no *h*...... 1 Th 4:13
and as a helmet our *h*..... 1 Th 5:8
Jesus Christ, our *h*..........1 Ti 1:1
in *h* of eternal life...........Tit 1:2
for the blessed *h*..............Tit 2:13
to lay hold of the *h*........Heb 6:18
in of a better *h*...............Heb 7:19
us again to a living *h*....... 1 Pe 1:3
you a reason for the *h*..... 1 Pe 3:15
who has this *h* in Him..... 1 Jn 3:3

HOPED

substance of things *h*.......Heb 11:1

HORN

My shield and the *h*........Ps 18:2
h will be exalted.............Ps 112:9
goat had a notable *h*.......Dan 8:5
and has raised up a *h*..... Luke 1:69

HORRIBLE

h thing has been.............Jer 5:30
I have seen a *h*...............Hos 6:10

HORROR

and behold, *h* and...........Gen 15:12
sorrow, the cup of *h*........Ezek 23:33
you will become a *h*........Ezek 27:36

HORSE

The *h* and its rider He.....Ex 15:1
Have you given the *h*...... Job 39:19
h is a vain hope..............Ps 33:17
the strength of the *h*........Ps 147:10
h is prepared for the....... Prov 21:31
and behold, a white *h*......Rev 6:2
and behold, a black *h*...... Rev 6:5
and behold, a pale *h*...... Rev 6:8
and behold, a white *h*......Rev 19:11

HORSES

seen servants on *h*..........Eccl 10:7
h are swifter than............Jer 4:13
Do *h* run on rocks......... Amos 6:12
we put bits in *h*..............Jas 3:3

HOSANNA

H in the highest.............Matt 21:9

HOSPITABLE

of good behavior, *h*.........1 Ti 3:2
Be *h* to one another........1 Pe 4:9

HOST

Who brings out their *h*.... Is 40:26
of the heavenly *h*...........Luke 2:13

HOSTILITY

Him who endured such *h*. Heb 12:3

HOSTS

name of the LORD of *h*...1 Sa 17:45
As the LORD of *h* lives... 1 Ki 18:15
The LORD of *h* is with....Ps 46:7
LORD, all you His *h*....... Ps 103:21
Praise Him, all His *h*...... Ps 148:2
word of the LORD of *h*... Is 39:5
LORD of *h* is His name... Is 47:4
against spiritual *h*...........Eph 6:12

HOT

of the LORD was *h*.........Judg 2:14
My heart was *h* within.... Ps 39:3
are neither cold nor *h*......Rev 3:15

HOUND

My enemies would *h*....... Ps 56:2

HOUR

h what you should..........Matt 10:19
day and *h* no one knows.. Matt 24:36
Man is coming at an *h*.....Matt 24:44
Behold, the *h* is at......... Matt 26:45
But this is your *h*...........Luke 22:53
h has not yet come.........John 2:4
"But the *h* is coming......John 4:23
h has come that the........John 12:23
save Me from this *h*....... John 12:27
"Father, the *h*...............John 17:1
will not know what *h*......Rev 3:3
keep you from the *h*........Rev 3:10

HOURS

Are there not twelve *h*.... John 11:9

HOUSE

from your father's *h*........ Gen 12:1
But as for me and my *h*...Josh 24:15
h appointed for all..........Job 30:23
with them to the *h*..........Ps 42:4
the goodness of Your *h*...Ps 65:4
for her *h* leads down....... Prov 2:18
Through wisdom a *h*........Prov 24:3
better to go to the *h*........Eccl 7:2
of the *h* tremble.............Eccl 12:3

HOUSEHOLD

to the *h* of the God of.....Is 2:3
to those who join *h*.........Is 5:8
h was filled with............. Is 6:4
'Set your *h* in order........Is 38:1
h shall be called a...........Is 56:7
and beat on that *h*......... Matt 7:25
h divided against.............Matt 12:25
h shall be called a......... Matt 21:13
h may be filled................ Luke 14:23
not make My Father's *h*...John 2:16
h are many mansions......John 14:2
publicly and from *h*......... Acts 20:20
in his own rented *h*........ Acts 28:30
who rules his own *h*........ 1 Ti 3:4
the church in your *h*.......Phm 2
For every *h* is built......... Heb 3:4
His own *h*, whose *h*....... Heb 3:6
him into your *h*.............. 2 Jn 10

HOUSEHOLD

over the ways of her *h*.....Prov 31:27
"If the *h* is worthy.......... Matt 10:13
be those of his own *h*...... Matt 10:36
h were baptized.............. Acts 16:15
saved, you and your *h*..... Acts 16:31
also baptized the *h*......... 1 Co 1:16
those who are of the *h*....Gal 6:10
who are of Caesar's *h*....Phil 4:22

HOUSEHOLDER

h who brings out of.........Matt 13:52

HOUSES

h are safe from fear........ Job 21:9
Yet He filled their *h*.......Job 22:18
is that their *h*................ Ps 49:11
H and riches are an........Prov 19:14
who has left *h* or.......... Matt 19:29
you devour widows' *h*....Matt 23:14
Do you not have *h*.........1 Co 11:22

HOVERING

Spirit of God was *h*.........Gen 1:2

HOW

"*H* can this be................Luke 1:34
H long do You keep....... John 10:24
h you turned to God....... 1 Th 1:9

HUMAN

we have had *h* fathers......Heb 12:9

HUMBLE

man Moses was very *h*.....Num 12:3
h you and test you......... Deut 8:2
who is proud, and *h*........Job 40:11
the cry of the *h*.............. Ps 9:12
Do not forget the *h*.........Ps 10:12
the desire of the *h*......... Ps 10:17
h He guides in justice......Ps 25:9
h shall hear of it and......Ps 34:2
LORD lifts up the *h*........ Ps 147:6
h spirit with the.............. Prov 16:19
contrite and *h* spirit.........Is 57:15
a meek and *h* people.......Zeph 3:12
associate with the *h*........Rom 12:16
gives grace to the *h*........Jas 4:6
H yourselves in the......... Jas 4:10
gives grace to the *h*.........1 Pe 5:5
h yourselves under the..... 1 Pe 5:6

HUMBLED

h himself greatly............. 2 Ch 33:12
as a man, He *h* Himself... Phil 2:8

HUMBLENESS

mercies, kindness, *h*........ Col 3:12

HUMBLES

h Himself to behold........ Ps 113:6

HUMILIATION

to plunder, and to *h*.......Ezra 9:7
h His justice was............Acts 8:33
but the rich in his *h*........ Jas 1:10

HUMILITY

By *h* and the fear of........Prov 22:4
righteousness, seek *h*...... Zeph 2:3
the Lord with all *h*..........Acts 20:19
delight in false *h*............. Col 2:18
h correcting those........... 2 Ti 2:25
gentle, showing all *h*.......Tit 3:2
and be clothed with *h*......1 Pe 5:5

HUNGER

you, allowed you to *h*......Deut 8:3
lack and suffer *h*.............Ps 34:10
They shall neither *h*........ Is 49:10
likely to die from *h*........ Jer 38:9
are those who *h*.............. Matt 5:6
For you shall *h*..............Luke 6:25
to Me shall never *h*........John 6:35
present hour we both *h*...1 Co 4:11
They shall neither *h*........ Rev 7:16

HUNGRY

bread from the *h*............ Job 22:7
And fills the *h*................Ps 107:9
gives food to the *h*......... Ps 146:7
h soul every bitter...........Prov 27:7
your soul to the *h*........... Is 58:10
'for I was *h* and you.......Matt 25:35
when did we see You *h*... Matt 25:37
and one is *h* and............1 Co 11:21
But if anyone is *h*...........1 Co 11:34
to be full and to be *h*...... Phil 4:12

HUNT

Yet you *h* my life to........1 Sa 24:11
h the violent man............Ps 140:11
h the souls of My............Ezek 13:18

HUNTER

Nimrod the mighty *h*...... Gen 10:9
Esau was a skillful *h*........Gen 25:27

HURT

h a woman with child...... Ex 21:22
Who plot my *h*................Ps 35:4
but I was not *h*...............Prov 23:35
another to his own *h*........Eccl 8:9
They shall not *h*.............. Is 11:9
of my people I am *h*........ Jer 8:21
Woe is me for my *h*.........Jer 10:19
it will by no means *h*.......Mark 16:18
shall not be *h* by the...... Rev 2:11

HUSBAND

She also gave to her *h*..... Gen 3:6
"Surely you are a *h*.........Ex 4:25
h safely trusts her..........Prov 31:11
your Maker is your *h*.......Is 54:5
though I was a *h*.............Jer 31:32
now have is not your *h*....John 4:18
woman have her own *h*....1 Co 7:2
For the unbelieving *h*...... 1 Co 7:14
you will save your *h*........1 Co 7:16
betrothed you to one *h*....2 Co 11:2
For the *h* is head of........ Eph 5:23
the *h* of one wife............1 Ti 3:2

HUSBANDS

them ask their own *h*.......1 Co 14:35
H, love your wives..........Eph 5:25
Let deacons be the *h*.......1 Ti 3:12

HYMN

when they had sung a *h*... Matt 26:30

HYMNS

praying and singing *h*......Acts 16:25
in psalms and *h*.............. Eph 5:19

HYPOCRISY

you are full of *h*............. Matt 23:28
Pharisees, which is *h*....... Luke 12:1
Let love be without *h*...... Rom 12:9
away with their *h*............Gal 2:13
and without *h*..................Jas 3:17
malice, all guile, *h*.......... 1 Pe 2:1

HYPOCRITE

of the *h* shall perish....... Job 8:13
and the joy of the *h*.......Job 20:5
is the hope of the *h*........Job 27:8
for everyone is a *h*..........Is 9:17
also played the *h*............ Gal 2:13

HYPOCRITES

"But the *h* in heart........Job 36:13
will I go in with *h*...........Ps 26:4
"For you were *h*..............Jer 42:20
not be like the *h*.............Matt 6:5
do you test Me, you *h*....Matt 22:18
and Pharisees, *h*............. Matt 23:13

HYSSOP

Purge me with *h*............. Ps 51:7
sour wine, put it on *h*.....John 19:29

— I —

ICE

dark because of the *i*.......Job 6:16

IDLE

For they are *i*.................Ex 5:8
i person will suffer.......... Prov 19:15
i word men may speak.....Matt 12:36
saw others standing *i*....... Matt 20:3
they learn to be *i*............1 Ti 5:13
both *i* talkers and...........Tit 1:10

IDOL

if he blesses an *i*............. Is 66:3
thing offered to an *i*.......1 Co 8:7
That an *i* is anything....... 1 Co 10:19

IDOLATER

or covetous, or an *i*........1 Co 5:11
man, who is an *i*............. Eph 5:5

IDOLATERS

fornicators, nor *i*............1 Co 6:9
immoral, sorcerers, *i*.......Rev 21:8
and murderers and *i*........ Rev 22:15

IDOLATRIES

and abominable *i*............ 1 Pe 4:3

IDOLATRY

beloved, flee from *i*.........1 Co 10:14
i, sorcery...................... Gal 5:20

IDOLS

stolen the household *i*......Gen 31:19
of the peoples are *i*........ Ps 96:5

IGNORANCE

i are silver and gold....... Ps 115:4
land is also full of *i*........ Is 2:8
insane with their *i*......... Jer 50:38
in the room of his *i*........ Ezek 8:12
from their wooden *i*....... Hos 4:12
who regard worthless *i*..... Jon 2:8
i speak delusion............. Zech 10:2
things polluted by *i*....... Acts 15:20
You who abhor *i*........... Rom 2:22
This was offered to *i*....... 1 Co 10:28
keep yourselves from *i*..... 1 Jn 5:21
worship demons, and *i*..... Rev 9:20

IGNORANCE

that you did it in *i*........ Acts 3:17
i God overlooked........... Acts 17:30
sins committed in *i*........ Heb 9:7
to silence the *i*............. 1 Pe 2:15

IGNORANT

I was so foolish and *i*..... Ps 73:22
though Abraham was *i*..... Is 63:16
not want you to be *i*....... 1 Co 12:1
But if anyone is *i*.......... 1 Co 14:38
on those who are *i*........ Heb 5:2

IGNORANTLY

because I did it *i*........... 1 Ti 1:13

ILLEGITIMATE

then you are *i*.............. Heb 12:8

ILLUMINATED

after you were *i*............ Heb 10:32
and the earth was *i*........ Rev 18:1
for the glory of God *i*..... Rev 21:23

IMAGE

Us make man in Our *i*..... Gen 1:26
yourselves a carved *i*...... Deut 4:16
shall despise their *i*........ Ps 73:20
the king made an *i*........ Dan 3:1
to them, "Whose *i*....... Matt 22:20
since he is the *i*............ 1 Co 11:7
He is the *i* of the........... Col 1:15
and not the very *i*......... Heb 10:1
the beast and his *i*........ Rev 14:9
who worshiped his *i*....... Rev 19:20

IMAGINATION

according to the *i*.......... Jer 23:17
the proud in the *i*......... Luke 1:51

IMITATE

I urge you, *i* me............ 1 Co 4:16
as I also *i* Christ............ 1 Co 11:1
i those who through....... Heb 6:12

IMMANUEL

shall call His name *I*...... Is 7:14
shall call His name I....... Matt 1:23

IMMEDIATELY

i the Spirit.................. Mark 1:12
hear, Satan comes *i*....... Mark 4:15
i forgets what.............. Jas 1:24
I I was in the Spirit........ Rev 4:2

IMMORAL

i woman is a deep pit..... Prov 22:14
murderers, sexually *i*...... Rev 21:8

IMMORALITY

except sexual *i*............. Matt 5:32
i as is not even named..... 1 Co 5:1
abstain from sexual *i*...... 1 Th 4:3

IMMORTAL

to the King eternal, *i*...... 1 Ti 1:17

IMMORTALITY

glory, honor, and *i*........ Rom 2:7
mortal must put on *i*...... 1 Co 15:53
who alone has *i*............ 1 Ti 6:16
and brought life and *i*..... 2 Ti 1:10

IMMOVABLE

be steadfast, *i*.............. 1 Co 15:58

IMMUTABLE

that by two *i* things........ Heb 6:18

IMPART

see you, that I may *i*...... Rom 1:11
that it may *i* grace.......... Eph 4:29

IMPENITENT

i heart you are.............. Rom 2:5

IMPLANTED

with meekness the *i*........ Jas 1:21

IMPOSSIBLE

and nothing will be *i*....... Matt 17:20
With men this is *i*.......... Matt 19:26
God nothing will be *i*..... Luke 1:37
without faith it is *i*......... Heb 11:6

IMPOSTORS

i will grow worse........... 2 Ti 3:13

IMPRISONMENT

and of chains and *i*........ Heb 11:36

IMPRISONMENTS

in stripes, in *i*.............. 2 Co 6:5

IMPURITY

a woman during her *i*..... Ezek 18:6

IMPUTE

Do not let my lord *i*....... 2 Sa 19:19
the LORD does not *i*...... Ps 32:2
the LORD shall not i....... Rom 4:8

IMPUTED

bloodguilt shall be *i*....... Lev 17:4
might be *i* to them.......... Rom 4:11
alone that it was *i*......... Rom 4:23
but sin is not *i*............. Rom 5:13

IMPUTES

i righteousness apart....... Rom 4:6

INCENSE

the golden altar of *i*....... Heb 9:4
golden bowls full of *i*...... Rev 5:8

INCLINE

i your heart to the......... Josh 24:23
i my heart to any evil...... Ps 141:4

INCORRUPTIBLE

the glory of the *i*.......... Rom 1:23
dead will be raised *i*....... 1 Co 15:52
to an inheritance *i*......... 1 Pe 1:4
corruptible seed but *i*...... 1 Pe 1:23

INCORRUPTION

it is raised in *i*............. 1 Co 15:42
corruption inherit *i*........ 1 Co 15:50
must put on *i*.............. 1 Co 15:53

INCREASE

If riches *i*.................... Ps 62:10
the LORD give you *i*...... Ps 115:14
hear and *i* learning......... Prov 1:5
When goods *i*............... Eccl 5:11
Of the *i* of His.............. Is 9:7
and knowledge shall *i*..... Dan 12:4
Lord, "*I* our faith.......... Luke 17:5
"He must *i*................. John 3:30
but God gave the *i*......... 1 Co 3:6
grows with the *i*........... Col 2:19
for they will *i*.............. 2 Ti 2:16

INCREASED

The waters *i* and........... Gen 7:17
i your mercy which you.... Gen 19:19
nation and *i* its joy......... Is 9:3
And Jesus *i* in wisdom..... Luke 2:52

INCREASES

i knowledge *i*.............. Eccl 1:18
who have no might He *i*.. Is 40:29

INCURABLE

My wound is *i*.............. Job 34:6
'Your affliction is *i*......... Jer 30:12
Your sorrow is *i*........... Jer 30:15

INDICATING

the Holy Spirit *i*........... Heb 9:8
who was in them was *i*.... 1 Pe 1:11

INDIGNANT

saw it, they were *i*......... Matt 26:8

INDIGNATION

of His anger, Wrath, *i*.... Ps 78:49
I has taken hold............ Ps 119:53
in whose hand is My *i*..... Is 10:5
For the *i* of the LORD..... Is 34:2
have filled me with *i*....... Jer 15:17
can stand before His *i*..... Nah 1:6
they were moved with *i*... Matt 20:24
i which will devour......... Heb 10:27
into the cup of His *i*....... Rev 14:10

INDUCED

O LORD, You *i* me....... Jer 20:7
if the prophet is *i*.......... Ezek 14:9
I the LORD have *i*......... Ezek 14:9

INDULGENCE

no value against the *i*..... Col 2:23

INEXCUSABLE

Therefore you are *i*........ Rom 2:1

INEXPRESSIBLE

Paradise and heard *i*....... 2 Co 12:4
you rejoice with joy *i*...... 1 Pe 1:8

INFALLIBLE

suffering by many *i*........ Acts 1:3

INFANTS

i who never saw............ Job 3:16
they also brought *i*........ Luke 18:15

INFERIOR

another kingdom *i*......... Dan 2:39
that I am not at all *i*...... 2 Co 11:5

INFIRMITIES

He Himself took our i..... Matt 8:17
boast, except in my *i*...... 2 Co 12:5
and your frequent *i*........ 1 Ti 5:23

INFLAMING
i yourselves with gods...... Is 57:5

INHABIT
You are holy, Who *i*...... Ps 22:3
the wicked will not *i*........Prov 10:30
cities and *i* them............. Amos 9:14

INHABITANT
Cry out and shout, O *i*.... Is 12:6
And the *i* will not say...... Is 33:24

INHABITANTS
He looks On all the *i*...... Ps 33:14
Give ear, all you *i*...........Ps 49:1
Let the *i* of Sela sing.......Is 42:11
Woe to the *i* of the......... Rev 12:12

INHABITED
rejoicing in His *i*............Prov 8:31
'You shall be *i*................Is 44:26
Who formed it to be *i*.... Is 45:18

INHERIT
i the iniquities................ Job 13:26
descendants shall *i*..........Ps 25:13
The righteous shall *i*........Ps 37:29
The wise shall *i*.............. Prov 3:35
love me to *i* wealth........ Prov 8:21
The simple *i* folly...........Prov 14:18
the blameless will *i*.........Prov 28:10
i the kingdom prepared....Matt 25:34
I do that I may *i*...........Mark 10:17
unrighteous will not *i*.....1 Co 6:9
you may *i* a blessing.......1 Pe 3:9
who overcomes shall *i*.....Rev 21:7

INHERITANCE
"You shall have no *i*...... Num 18:20
is the place of His *i*........Deut 32:9
the portion of my *i*..........Ps 16:5
Yes, I have a good *i*.......Ps 16:6
i shall be forever............Ps 37:18
He will choose our *i*....... Ps 47:4
You confirmed Your *i*...... Ps 68:9
The tribe of Your *i*......... Ps 74:2
i gained hastily.............. Prov 20:21
right of *i* is yours............Jer 32:8
i has been turned...........Lam 5:2
will arise to your *i*..........Dan 12:13
And God gave him no *i*...Acts 7:5
and give you an *i*.......... Acts 20:32
For if the *i* is of the....... Gal 3:18
we have obtained an *i*.....Eph 1:11
be partakers of the *i*.......Col 1:12
receive as an *i*.............. Heb 11:8
i incorruptible.................1 Pe 1:4

INIQUITIES
How many are my *i*........ Job 13:23
i have overtaken me.......Ps 40:12
I prevail against me........Ps 65:3
forgives all your *i*...........Ps 103:3
LORD, should mark *i*......Ps 130:3
was bruised for our *i*...... Is 53:5
He shall bear their *i*........Is 53:11
i have separated you........Is 59:2

INIQUITY
God, visiting the *i*...........Ex 20:5
He has not observed *i*.....Num 23:21
O LORD, Pardon my *i*... Ps 25:11
i I have not hidden......... Ps 32:5
was brought forth in *i*.....Ps 51:5
If I regard *i* in my...........Ps 66:18
Add *i* to their.................Ps 69:27

---

workers of *i* flourish........ Ps 92:7
i boast in themselves....... Ps 94:4
Shall the throne of *i*........ Ps 94:20
i have dominion..............Ps 119:133
i will reap sorrow...........Prov 22:8
a people laden with *i*.......Is 1:4
i is taken away................ Is 6:7
has laid on Him the *i*...... Is 53:6
will remember their *i*......Hos 9:9
to those who devise *i*......Mic 2:1
like You, pardoning *i*...... Mic 7:18
all you workers of *i*.........Luke 13:27
a fire, a world of *i*.......... Jas 3:6

INJUSTICE
of truth and without *i*.....Deut 32:4
i shuts her mouth............Job 5:16
i have your fathers..........Jer 2:5

INK
us, written not with *i*......2 Co 3:3
do so with paper and *i*....2 Jn 12

INN
room for them in the *i*....Luke 2:7
brought him to an *i*........Luke 10:34

INNOCENCE
of my heart and *i*...........Gen 20:5
washed my hands in *i*...... Ps 73:13

INNOCENT
do not kill the *i*.............. Ex 23:7
a bribe to slay an *i*.........Deut 27:25
i will divide the............. Job 27:17
a bribe against the *i*........ Ps 15:5
because I was found *i*......Dan 6:22
saying, "I am *i*............... Matt 27:24
this day that I am *i*........ Acts 20:26

INNUMERABLE
i as the sand which is...... Heb 11:12
i company of angels.........Heb 12:22

INQUIRED
children of Israel *i*...........Judg 20:27
Therefore David *i*............ 1 Sa 23:2
the LORD, nor *i* of Him.. Zeph 1:6
the prophets have *i*......... 1 Pe 1:10

INQUIRY
shall make diligent *i*........ Deut 19:18

INSANE
images, and they are *i*..... Jer 50:38
the spiritual man is *i*........Hos 9:7

INSCRIBED
Oh, that they were *i*........Job 19:23
See, I have *i* you on........Is 49:16

INSPIRATION
is given by *i* of God........ 2 Ti 3:16

INSTRUCT
good Spirit to *i* them.......Neh 9:20
I will *i* you and teach...... Ps 32:8
the LORD that he may *i*.. 1 Co 2:16

INSTRUCTED
Surely you have *i*............Job 4:3
counsel, and who *i*..........Is 40:14
This man had been *i*........Acts 18:25
are excellent, being *i*.......Rom 2:18
Moses was divinely *i*.......Heb 8:5

INSTRUCTION
Seeing you hate *i*............Ps 50:17
despise wisdom and *i*.......Prov 1:7
Take firm hold of *i*......... Prov 4:13
Hear *i* and be wise.........Prov 8:33
Give *i* to a wise man...... Prov 9:9
i loves knowledge...........Prov 12:1
Cease listening to *i*.........Prov 19:27
Apply your heart to *i*...... Prov 23:12
for correction, for *i*......... 2 Ti 3:16

INSTRUCTORS
have ten thousand *i*.........1 Co 4:15

INSTRUCTS
My heart also *i*...............Ps 16:7
He who *i* the nations.......Ps 94:10

INSTRUMENT
to Him with an *i*.............Ps 33:2
On an *i* of ten strings...... Ps 92:3

INSTRUMENTS
i of cruelty are in............Gen 49:5
with stringed *i*................ Ps 150:4
your members as *i*..........Rom 6:13
and your members as *i*.....Rom 6:13

INSUBORDINATE
for the lawless and *i*........1 Ti 1:9
For there are many *i*....... Tit 1:10

INSUBORDINATION
of dissipation or *i*............Tit 1:6

INSULTED
will be mocked and *i*.......Luke 18:32
i the Spirit of grace.........Heb 10:29

INTEGRITY
In the *i* of my heart........ Gen 20:5
he holds fast to his *i*........Job 2:3
that God may know my *i*. Job 31:6
I have walked in my *i*......Ps 26:1
You uphold me in my *i*....Ps 41:12
The *i* of the upright........Prov 11:3
in doctrine showing *i*....... Tit 2:7

INTELLIGENT
Sergius Paulus, an *i*.........Acts 13:7

INTERCEDE
the LORD, who will *i*......1 Sa 2:25

INTERCESSION
of many, and made *i*....... Is 53:12
Spirit Himself makes *i*..... Rom 8:26
ever lives to make *i*.........Heb 7:25

INTERCESSOR
that there was no *i*..........Is 59:16

INTEREST
shall not charge him *i*......Ex 22:25
men lent to me for *i*........Jer 15:10
collected it with *i*............Luke 19:23

INTERPRET
Do all *i*?......................1 Co 12:30
pray that he may *i*.......... 1 Co 14:13
in turn, and let one *i*.......1 Co 14:27

INTERPRETATION
"This is the *i*..................Gen 40:12
to another the *i*...............1 Co 12:10
a revelation, has an *i*.......1 Co 14:26
of any private *i*...............2 Pe 1:20

INTERPRETATIONS

Do not *i* belong to God... Gen 40:8
that you can give *i*.......... Dan 5:16

INTRIGUE

seize the kingdom by *i*.....Dan 11:21
join with them by *i*........ Dan 11:34

INVISIBLE

of the world His *i*.......... Rom 1:20
is the image of the *i*........ Col 1:15
eternal, immortal, *i*........ 1 Ti 1:17
as seeing Him who is *i*.....Heb 11:27

INWARD

i part is destruction......... Ps 5:9
Both the *i* thought.......... Ps 64:6
You have formed my *i*.....Ps 139:13
God according to the *i*....Rom 7:22
i man is being renewed....2 Co 4:16

INWARDLY

i they are.....................Matt 7:15
is a Jew who is one ...... Rom 2:29

IRON

He regards *i* as straw.......Job 41:27
i sharpens *i*.............Prov 27:17
and your neck was an *i*....Is 48:4
its feet partly of *i*............Dan 2:33

ISRAEL

be called Jacob, but *I*...... Gen 32:28
"Hear, O *I*.................... Deut 6:4
shepherd My people *I*......2 Sa 7:7
Truly God is good to *I*.... Ps 73:1
helped His servant *I*....... Luke 1:54
For they are not all *I*......Rom 9:6
and upon the *I* of God.... Gal 6:16

ITCHING

they have *i* ears.............. 2 Ti 4:3

ITINERANT

i Jewish exorcists............ Acts 19:13

— J —

JEALOUS

God, am a *j* G.............. Ex 20:5
LORD, whose name is *J*...Ex 34:14
a consuming fire, a *j*.......Deut 4:24
For I am *j* for you.......... 2 Co 11:2

JEALOUSY

They provoked Him to *j*.. Deut 32:16
Will Your *j* burn like.......Ps 79:5
j is a husband's..............Prov 6:34
as strong as death, *j*...... Song 8:6
will provoke you to j...... Rom 10:19
for you with godly *j*........2 Co 11:2

JEOPARDY

stand in *j* every hour....... 1 Co 15:30

JESTING

talking, nor coarse *j*........ Eph 5:4

JESUS

J Christ was as.............. Matt 1:18
shall call His name *J*...... Matt 1:21
J was led up by the........ Matt 4:1
These twelve *J* sent........ Matt 10:5
and laid hands on *J*........ Matt 26:50
Barabbas and destroy *J*...Matt 27:20
we to do with You, *J*...... Mark 1:24

J withdrew with His....... Mark 3:7
J went into Jerusalem...... Mark 11:11
as they were eating, *J*.....Mark 14:22
and he delivered *J*..........Mark 15:15
J rebuked the................Luke 9:42
truth came through *J*.......John 1:17
J lifted up His eyes........John 6:5
J wept............................John 11:35
J was crucified................John 19:20
This *J* God has raised...... Acts 2:32
of Your holy Servant *J*... Acts 4:30
believed on the Lord *J*...Acts 11:17
baptized into Christ *J*...... Rom 6:3
your mouth the Lord *J*.... Rom 10:9
among you except *J*.........1 Co 2:2
the day of the Lord *J*...... 1 Co 5:5
perfect in Christ *J*........... Col 1:28
J who is called................Col 4:11
exhort in the Lord *J*........ 1 Th 4:1
But we see *J*................. Heb 2:9
looking unto *J*................ Heb 12:2
J Christ the righteous...... 1 Jn 2:1
Revelation of *J* Christ.....Rev 1:1
so, come, Lord *J*............. Rev 22:20

JEWELS

your thighs are like *j*....... Song 7:1
that I make them My *j*.... Mal 3:17

JOIN

Woe to those who *j*.........Is 5:8
'come and let us *j*........... Jer 50:5
of the rest dared *j*.......... Acts 5:13

JOINED

and mother and be *j*........Gen 2:24
for him who is *j*.............Eccl 9:4
"Ephraim is *j*................. Hos 4:17
what God has *j*.............Matt 19:6
you be perfectly *j*.........1 Co 1:10
But he who is *j*.............1 Co 6:17
whom the whole body, *j*...Eph 4:16

JOINT

j as He wrestled..............Gen 32:25
My bones are out of *j*.....Ps 22:14
j heirs with Christ........... Rom 8:17
by what every *j*..............Eph 4:16

JOINTS

and knit together by *j*......Col 2:19
and spirit, and of *j*.........Heb 4:12

JOT

one *j* or one tittle.......... Matt 5:18

JOURNEY

us go three days' *j*..........Ex 3:18
busy, or he is on a *j*........1 Ki 18:27
Nevertheless I must *j*.......Luke 13:33
wearied from His *j*.........John 4:6

JOY

LORD your God with *j*.... Deut 28:47
heart to sing for *j*...........Job 29:13
is fullness of *j*................Ps 16:11
j comes in the morning....Ps 30:5
To God my exceeding *j*...Ps 43:4
You According to the *j*...Is 9:3
j you will draw..............Is 12:3
ashes, the oil of *j*...........Is 61:3
j shall be theirs...............Is 61:7
shall sing for *j*...............Is 65:14
word was to me the *j*.....Jer 15:16
receives it with *j*.......... Matt 13:20
Enter into the *j*............. Matt 25:21

in my womb for *j*...........Luke 1:44
there will be more *j*........Luke 15:7
did not believe for *j*........ Luke 24:41
My *j* may remain in you...John 15:11
they may have My *j*........John 17:13
fill you with all *j*............Rom 15:13
that my *j* is the *j*.............2 Co 2:3
the Spirit is love, *j*.......... Gal 5:22
brethren, my *j* and..........Phil 4:1
longsuffering with *j*........Col 1:11
are our glory and *j*..........1 Th 2:20
j that was set before........Heb 12:2
count it all *j*....................Jas 1:2
j inexpressible.................1 Pe 1:8
with exceeding *j*..............1 Pe 4:13
I have no greater *j*..........3 Jn 4

JOYFUL

And my soul shall be *j*.....Ps 35:9
Make a *j* shout to the.....Ps 100:1
of prosperity be *j*........... Eccl 7:14
and make them *j*............Is 56:7
I am exceedingly *j*..........2 Co 7:4

JUDAISM

And I advanced in *J*........Gal 1:14

JUDGE

LORD *j* between you......Gen 16:5
For the LORD will *j*........Deut 32:36
coming to *j* the earth......1 Ch 16:33
Rise up, O *J* of the........Ps 94:2
sword the LORD will *j*....Is 66:16
deliver you to the *j*........ Matt 5:25
"*J* not......................... Matt 7:1
Man, who made Me a *j*...Luke 12:14
j who did not fear God....Luke 18:2
As I hear, I *j*.................John 5:30
"Do not *j* according.......John 7:24
I *j* no one.....................John 8:15
j the world but to.......... John 12:47
this, O man, you who *j*....Rom 2:3
then how will God *j*........Rom 3:6
Therefore let us not *j*...... Rom 14:13
Christ, who will *j*............2 Ti 4:1
Lord, the righteous *J*......2 Ti 4:8
heaven, to God the *J*.......Heb 12:23
But if you *j* the law........Jas 4:11
are you to *j* another........Jas 4:12

JUDGES

j who delivered...............Judg 2:16
in the days when the *j*..... Ruth 1:1
Surely He is God who *j*...Ps 58:11
He *j* among the gods......Ps 82:1
He makes the *j* of the.....Is 40:23
j are evening wolves........Zeph 3:3
For the Father *j*..............John 5:22
he who is spiritual *j*........1 Co 2:15
j me is the Lord.............. 1 Co 4:4
Him who *j* righteously..... 1 Pe 2:23

JUDGMENT

show partiality in *j*......... Deut 1:17
Teach me good *j*.............Ps 119:66
him in right *j*..................Is 28:26
from prison and from *j*.... Is 53:8
I will also speak *j*...........Jer 4:12
j was made in favor of....Dan 7:22
be in danger of the *j*...... Matt 5:21
will rise up in the *j*.........Matt 12:42
shall not come into *j*.......John 5:24
and My *j* is righteous......John 5:30
if I do judge, My *j*.........John 8:16
"Now is the *j*..................John 12:31
the righteous *j*................Rom 1:32

JUDGMENTS (continued)

j which came from one.... Rom 5:16
all stand before the *j*...... Rom 14:10
eats and drinks *j*............ 1 Co 11:29
appear before the *j*..........2 Co 5:10
after this the *j*................ Heb 9:27
For *j* is without mercy..... Jas 2:13
receive a stricter *j*.......... Jas 3:1
time has come for *j*.........1 Pe 4:17
a long time their *j*...........2 Pe 2:3
darkness for the *j*...........Jude 6

JUDGMENTS

The *j* of the LORD are.... Ps 19:9
j are a great deep.......... Ps 36:6
I dread, For Your *j*.........Ps 119:39
unsearchable are His *j*..... Rom 11:33
righteous are His *j*.......... Rev 19:2

JUST

Noah was a *j* man.......... Gen 6:9
Hear a *j* cause................ Ps 17:1
It is a joy for the *j*.......... Prov 21:15
j man who perishes........ Eccl 7:15
For there is not a *j*......... Eccl 7:20
j is uprightness............... Is 26:7
the blood of the *j*............Lam 4:13
j shall live by his............Hab 2:4
He is *j* and having...........Zech 9:9
her husband, being a *j*...... Matt 1:19
resurrection of the *j*........Luke 14:14
j persons who need no..... Luke 15:7
the Holy One and the *J*... Acts 3:14
dead, both of the *j*.......... Acts 24:15
j shall live by faith......... Rom 1:17
that He might be *j*......... Rom 3:26
whatever things are *j*...... Phil 4:8
j men made perfect....... Heb 12:23
have murdered the *j*........ Jas 5:6
He is faithful and *j*..........1 Jn 1:9
J and true are Your....... Rev 15:3

JUSTICE

for all His ways are *j*...... Deut 32:4
the Almighty pervert *j*..... Job 8:3
j as the noonday............. Ps 37:6
And Your poor with *j*....Ps 72:2
He will bring *j*.............. Ps 72:4
Do *j* to the afflicted........ Ps 82:3
and *j* are the................. Ps 89:14
revenues without *j*........Prov 16:8
do not understand *j*........Prov 28:5
j the measuring line........ Is 28:17
the LORD is a God of *j*... Is 30:18
He will bring forth *j*........ Is 42:1
No one calls for *j*............ Is 59:4
J is turned back............. Is 59:14
I, the LORD, love *j*........... Is 61:8
you, O habitation of *j*.....Jer 31:23
plundering, execute *j*...... Ezek 45:9
truth, and His ways *j*......Dan 4:37
observe mercy and *j*...... Hos 12:6
'Execute true *j*...............Zech 7:9
Where is the God of *j*..... Mal 2:17
and He will declare j...... Matt 12:18
His humiliation His j....... Acts 8:33

JUSTIFICATION

because of our *j*..............Rom 4:25
offenses resulted in *j*........Rom 5:16
men, resulting in *j*...........Rom 5:18

JUSTIFIED

Me that you may be *j*......Job 40:8
of Israel shall be *j*.......... Is 45:25
words you will be *j*.........Matt 12:37
But wisdom is *j*............. Luke 7:35

j rather than the............ Luke 18:14
who believes is *j*............ Acts 13:39
"*That You may be j*....... Rom 3:4
law no flesh will be *j*....... Rom 3:20
j freely by His grace.......Rom 3:24
having been *j* by............. Rom 5:1
these He also *j*............... Rom 8:30
but you were *j*...............1 Co 6:11
that we might be *j*..........Gal 2:16
no flesh shall be *j*.......... Gal 2:16
who attempt to be *j*........Gal 5:4
j in the Spirit................. 1 Ti 3:16
then that a man is *j*........Jas 2:24
the harlot also *j*.............. Jas 2:25

JUSTIFIER

be just and the *j*............. Rom 3:26

JUSTIFIES

He who *j* the wicked....... Prov 17:15
It is God who *j*...............Rom 8:33

JUSTIFY

j the wicked for a........... Is 5:23
wanting to *j* himself........Luke 10:29
"You are those who *j*..... Luke 16:15
is one God who will *j*...... Rom 3:30
that God would *j*............ Gal 3:8

JUSTLY

of you but to do *j*.......... Mic 6:8
"And we indeed *j*........... Luke 23:41
how devoutly and *j*.........1 Th 2:10

— K —

KEEP

k you wherever you go.... Gen 28:15
day, to *k* it holy............. Ex 20:8
and *k* My judgments.......Lev 25:18
k all My commandments.. 1 Ki 6:12
and that You would *k*......1 Ch 4:10
Even he who cannot *k*.....Ps 22:29
Oh, *k* my soul................ Ps 25:20
Do not *k* silence............. Ps 35:22
k Your righteous............Ps 119:106
k them in the midst of..... Prov 4:21
K your heart with all....... Prov 4:23
a time to *k* silence.......... Eccl 3:7
Let all the earth *k*...........Hab 2:20
k the commandments......Matt 19:17
If you love Me, *k*........... John 14:15
k through Your name....... John 17:11
orderly and *k* the law...... Acts 21:24
Let your women *k*........... 1 Co 14:34
k the unity of the............Eph 4:3
k yourself pure............... 1 Ti 5:22
k His commandments...... 1 Jn 2:3
k yourselves in the..........Jude 21
k you from stumbling......Jude 24
k those things................Rev 1:3

KEEPER

Am I my brother's *k*....... Gen 4:9
The LORD is your *k*....... Ps 121:5

KEEPERS

in the day when the *k*......Eccl 12:3

KEEPS

the faithful God who *k*.... Deut 7:9
k truth forever................Ps 146:6
k his way preserves........ Prov 16:17
k the commandment........Prov 19:16
Whoever *k* the law is a....Prov 28:7
none of you *k* the law..... John 7:19

born of God *k* himself..... 1 Jn 5:18
and *k* his garments.......... Rev 16:15

KEPT

For I have *k* the ways......2 Sa 22:22
vineyard I have not *k*...... Song 1:6
these things I have *k*....... Matt 19:20
k all these things.............Luke 2:19
love, just as I have *k*......John 15:10
k back part of the........... Acts 5:2
I have *k* the faith............2 Ti 4:7
who are *k* by the power...1 Pe 1:5
which now exist are *k*......2 Pe 3:7

KEY

The *k* of the house of......Is 22:22
have taken away the *k*.....Luke 11:52
"*He who has the k*.......... Rev 3:7
heaven, having the *k*....... Rev 20:1

KEYS

I will give you the *k*........ Matt 16:19
And I have the *k*............ Rev 1:18

KICK

is hard for you to *k*......... Acts 9:5

KIDNAPPERS

for sodomites, for *k*.........1 Ti 1:10

KIDNAPS

"He who *k* a man and..... Ex 21:16

KILL

who finds me will *k*........ Gen 4:14
k the Passover................ Ex 12:21
I *k* and I make alive........Deut 32:39
"Am I God, to *k*............ 2 Ki 5:7
a time to *k*.................... Eccl 3:3
to save life or to *k*.......... Mark 3:4
of them they will *k*..........Luke 11:49
afraid of those who *k*..... Luke 12:4
Why do you seek to *k*..... John 7:19
k and eat...................... Acts 10:13

KILLED

Abel his brother and *k*.... Gen 4:8
For I have *k* a man for....Gen 4:23
LORD *k* all the.............. Ex 13:15
"Your servant has *k*........1 Sa 17:36
for Your sake we are *k*....Ps 44:22
and scribes, and be *k*......Matt 16:21
Siloam fell and *k* them....Luke 13:4
k the Prince of life.......... Acts 3:15
me, and by it *k*.............. Rom 7:11
For Your sake we are k... Rom 8:36
who *k* both the Lord....... 1 Th 2:15
martyr, who was *k*......... Rev 2:13

KILLS

"The LORD *k* and..........1 Sa 2:6
the one who *k* the..........Matt 23:37
for the letter *k*............... 2 Co 3:6

KIND

animals after their *k*........ Gen 6:20
k can come out by..........Mark 9:29
For He is *k* to the...........Luke 6:35
suffers long and is *k*........ 1 Co 13:4
And be *k* to one............Eph 4:32

KINDLED

When His wrath is *k*....... Ps 2:12
I, the LORD, have *k*........Ezek 20:48
wish it were already *k*......Luke 12:49

KINDLY

The LORD deal k........... Ruth 1:8
Julius treated Paul k........Acts 27:3
k affectionate to one....... Rom 12:10

KINDNESS

may the LORD show k.... 2 Sa 2:6
anger, abundant in k....... Neh 9:17
me His marvelous k........ Ps 31:21
For His merciful k.......... Ps 117:2
tongue is the law of k.....Prov 31:26
k shall not depart............Is 54:10
I remember you, the k....Jer 2:2
by longsuffering, by k......2 Co 6:6
longsuffering, k...............Gal 5:22
But when the k and the... Tit 3:4
and to brotherly k...........2 Pe 1:7

KING

Then Melchizedek k........ Gen 14:18
days there was no k....... Judg 17:6
said, "Give us a k...........1 Sa 8:6
"Long live the k.............1 Sa 10:24
they anointed David k.... 2 Sa 2:4
Yet I have set My K...... Ps 2:6
The LORD is K forever... Ps 10:16
K answer us when we..... Ps 20:9
And the K of glory......... Ps 24:7
k is saved by the............Ps 33:16
k Your judgments........... Ps 72:1
For God is my K........... Ps 74:12
do who succeeds the k..... Eccl 2:12
out of prison to be k....... Eccl 4:14
when your k is a child..... Eccl 10:16
In the year that K..........Is 6:1
k will reign in................Is 32:1
the LORD is our K.......... Is 33:22
Is not her K in her.........Jer 8:19
and the everlasting K......Jer 10:10
k of Babylon, k............. Ezek 26:7
I gave you a k in My..... Hos 13:11
the LORD shall be K......Zech 14:9
He who has been born K. Matt 2:2
This Is Jesus the K.........Matt 27:37
by force to make Him k...John 6:15
"Behold your K............John 19:14
there is another k........... Acts 17:7
Now to the K eternal...... 1 Ti 1:17
only Potentate, the K...... 1 Ti 6:15
this Melchizedek, k......... Heb 7:1
Honor the k................1 Pe 2:17
k of kings and lord of......Rev 19:16

KINGDOM

you shall be to Me a k.... Ex 19:6
LORD has torn the k.......1 Sa 15:28
Yours is the k.............. 1 Ch 29:11
k is the LORD's.............Ps 22:28
the scepter of Your k...... Ps 45:6
in heaven, And His k....... Ps 103:19
is an everlasting k.......... Ps 145:13
k which shall never be..... Dan 2:44
High rules in the k..........Dan 4:17
k shall be the LORD's..... Obad 21
"Repent, for the k.......... Matt 3:2
for Yours is the k........... Matt 6:13
But seek first the k........ Matt 6:33
the mysteries of the k...... Matt 13:11
are the sons of the k...... Matt 13:38
of such is the k............Matt 19:14
up to half of my k.......... Mark 6:23
are not far from the k..... Mark 12:34
back, is fit for the k....... Luke 9:62
against nation, and k...... Luke 21:10
he cannot see the k........John 3:3
he cannot enter the k..... John 3:5

If My k were of this.......John 18:36
for the k of God is.........Rom 14:17
when He delivers the k....1 Co 15:24
will not inherit the k...... Gal 5:21
the scepter of Your K.....Heb 1:8
we are receiving a k....... Heb 12:28
into the everlasting k.......2 Pe 1:11

KINGDOMS

the k were moved.......... Ps 46:6
tremble, who shook k.....Is 14:16
showed Him all the k..... Matt 4:8
have become the k......... Rev 11:15

KINGS

The k of the earth set.....Ps 2:2
k shall fall down............. Ps 72:11
He is awesome to the k... Ps 76:12
By me k reign................ Prov 8:15
He will stand before k.....Prov 22:29
k is unsearchable............ Prov 25:3
that which destroys k......Prov 31:3
it is not for k................. Prov 31:4
K shall be your foster......Is 49:23
"They set up k............... Hos 8:4
before governors and k.... Matt 10:18
k have desired to see.......Luke 10:24
You have reigned as k.... 1 Co 4:8
and has made us k......... Rev 1:6
that the way of the k......Rev 16:12
may eat the flesh of k.....Rev 19:18

KINSMEN

k stand afar off.............Ps 38:11
for my brethren, my k..... Rom 9:3

KISS

K the Son.....................Ps 2:12
Let him k me with the....Song 1:2
"You gave Me no k......... Luke 7:45
another with a holy k...... Rom 16:16
one another with a k....... 1 Pe 5:14

KISSED

And they k one another...1 Sa 20:41
and k Him.....................Matt 26:49
and she k His feet and....Luke 7:38

KNEE

that to Me every k...........Is 45:23
And they bowed the k......Matt 27:29
have not bowed the k...... Rom 11:4
every k shall bow to....... Rom 14:11
of Jesus every k.............Phil 2:10

KNEES

make firm the feeble k.... Is 35:3
be dandled on her k....... Is 66:12
this reason I bow my k....Eph 3:14
and the feeble k............. Heb 12:12

KNEW

Adam k Eve his wife...... Gen 4:1
in the womb I k............. Jer 1:5
to them, 'I never k.........Matt 7:23
k what was in man.........John 2:25
For He made Him who k.2 Co 5:21

KNIT

of Jonathan was k...........1 Sa 18:1
k me together with...........Job 10:11
be encouraged, being k....Col 2:2

KNOCK

k, and it will be.............Matt 7:7
at the door and k............Rev 3:20

KNOW

k good and evil.............. Gen 3:22
and I did not k..............Gen 28:16
k that I am the LORD.....Ex 6:7
k that there is no God.....2 Ki 5:15
you, my son Solomon, k.. 1 Ch 28:9
Hear it, and k for.......... Job 5:27
and k nothing.................Job 8:9
k that my Redeemer.......Job 19:25
'What does God k...........Job 22:13
k Your name will put...... Ps 9:10
k that I am God............. Ps 46:10
make me to k wisdom..... Ps 51:6
Who can k it.................Jer 17:9
saying, 'K the LORD.......Jer 31:34
for you to k justice........ Mic 3:1
k what hour your Lord.... Matt 24:42
an oath, "I do not k.......Matt 26:72
the world did not k........John 1:10
We speak what We k...... John 3:11
k what we worship.......... John 4:22
k that You are...............John 6:69
hear My voice, and I k.... John 10:27
If you k these things.......John 13:17
k whom I have chosen.....John 13:18
we are sure that You k....John 16:30
k that I love You...........John 21:15
k times or seasons..........Acts 1:7
and said, "Jesus I k........Acts 19:15
wisdom did not k............1 Co 1:21
nor can he k them.......... 1 Co 2:14
For we k in part and...... 1 Co 13:9
k a man in Christ who....2 Co 12:2
k the love of Christ.........Eph 3:19
k whom I have believed...2 Ti 1:12
so that they may k......... 2 Ti 2:25
this we k that we k........ 1 Jn 2:3
He who says, "I k.......... 1 Jn 2:4
and you k all things........1 Jn 2:20
By this we k love........... 1 Jn 3:16
k that we are of the....... 1 Jn 3:19
k that He abides............ 1 Jn 3:24
k that we are of God......1 Jn 5:19
"I k your works.............Rev 2:2

KNOWLEDGE

and the tree of the k....... Gen 2:9
LORD is the God of k.....1 Sa 2:3
Can anyone teach God k..Job 21:22
who is perfect in k..........Job 36:4
unto night reveals k.........Ps 19:2
k is too wonderful..........Ps 139:6
k the depths were.......... Prov 3:20
k rather than................. Prov 8:10
Wise people store up k.... Prov 10:14
k is easy to him who...... Prov 14:6
k spares his words.......... Prov 17:27
a soul to be without k..... Prov 19:2
and he who increases k.... Eccl 1:18
k is that wisdom............Eccl 7:12
no work or device or k.... Eccl 9:10
Whom will he teach k...... Is 28:9
k shall increase..............Dan 12:4
you have rejected k.........Hos 4:6
having more accurate k.... Acts 24:22
having the form of k....... Rom 2:20
by the law is the k......... Rom 3:20
K puffs up.................... 1 Co 8:1
whether there is k...........1 Co 13:8
Christ which passes k......Eph 3:19
is falsely called k........... 1 Ti 6:20
in the grace and k..........2 Pe 3:18

KNOWN

In Judah God is k...........Ps 76:1
my mouth will I make k...Ps 89:1

KNOWS

If you had *k* Me............John 8:19
My sheep, and am *k*........John 10:14
The world has not *k*.......John 17:25
peace they have not *k*.....Rom 3:17
I would not have *k*.........Rom 7:7
"For who has *k*..............Rom 11:34
after you have *k*............Gal 4:9
requests be made *k*........Phil 4:6
k the Holy Scriptures.......2 Ti 3:15

KNOWS

"For God *k* that in......... Gen 3:5
k the secrets of the.......... Ps 44:21
he understands and *k*.......Jer 9:24
k what is in the.............. Dan 2:22
k those who trust............Nah 1:7
k the things you have..... Matt 6:8
and hour no one *k*.......... Matt 24:36
k who the Son is.............Luke 10:22
but God *k* your hearts..... Luke 16:15
searches the hearts *k*...... Rom 8:27
k the things of God.........1 Co 2:11
k those who are His........ 2 Ti 2:19
to him who *k* to do.........Jas 4:17
and *k* all things...............1 Jn 3:20
written which no one *k*.... Rev 2:17

— L —

LABOR

Six days you shall *l*........ Ex 20:9
why then do I *l*.............. Job 9:29
their boast is only *l*......... Ps 90:10
The *l* of the righteous...... Prov 10:16
l will increase................. Prov 13:11
l there is profit............... Prov 14:23
things are full of *l*........... Eccl 1:8
has man for all his *l*....... Eccl 2:22
from the womb to see *l*...Jer 20:18
to Me, all you who *l*...... Matt 11:28
"Do not *l* for the...........John 6:27
knowing that your *l*........1 Co 15:58
but rather let him *l*........ Eph 4:28
mean fruit from my *l*....... Phil 1:22
your work of faith, *l*.......1 Th 1:3
forget your work and *l*.....Heb 6:10
your works, your *l*.......... Rev 2:2

LABORED

l more abundantly than.... 1 Co 15:10
for you, lest I have *l*....... Gal 4:11

LABORERS

but the *l* are few..............Matt 9:37

LABORING

of a *l* man is sweet..........Eccl 5:12
l night and day............... 1 Th 2:9

LABORS

The person who *l*............Prov 16:26
is no end to all his *l*....... Eccl 4:8
entered into their *l*.........John 4:38
creation groans and *l*...... Rom 8:22
l more abundant............. 2 Co 11:23
may rest from their *l*....... Rev 14:13

LACK

anyone perish for *l*..........Job 31:19
the LORD shall not *l*........Ps 34:10
to the poor will not *l*.......Prov 28:27
What do I still *l*.............Matt 19:20
"One thing you *l*........... Mark 10:21

LACKED

among them who *l*.......... Acts 4:34

LACKING

the things that are *l*.........Tit 1:5

LADDER

and behold, a *l*...............Gen 28:12

LADEN

nation, a people *l*............Is 1:4
and are heavy *l*..............Matt 11:28

LADIES

wisest *l* answered her.......Judg 5:29
very day the noble *l*........ Esth 1:18

LADY

'I shall be a *l*................. Is 47:7
ELDER, To the elect *l*....2 Jn 1

LAGGING

not *l* in diligence.............Rom 12:11

LAID

But man dies and is *l*...... Job 14:10
the place where they *l*..... Mark 16:6
Where have you *l*........... John 11:34

LAKE

cast alive into the *l*..........Rev 19:20

LAMB

but where is the *l*............Gen 22:7
took the poor man's *l*......2 Sa 12:4
shall dwell with the *l*....... Is 11:6
He was led as a *l*............Is 53:7
l shall feed together.........Is 65:25
The *L* of God who takes..John 1:29
of Christ, as of a *l*.......... 1 Pe 1:19
the elders, stood a *L*...... Rev 5:6
"Worthy is the *L*........... Rev 5:12
by the blood of the *L*.....Rev 12:11
Book of Life of the *L*.....Rev 13:8
supper of the *L*.............. Rev 19:9

LAME

l take the prey................Is 33:23
l shall leap like a........... Is 35:6
when you offer the *l*........Mal 1:8
their sight and the *l*........Matt 11:5
And a certain man *l*........Acts 3:2
so that what is *l*.............Heb 12:13

LAMENTATION

was heard in Ramah, *l*.....Jer 31:15
was heard in Ramah, *l*.....Matt 2:18
and made great *l*.............Acts 8:2

LAMP

For You are my *l*............2 Sa 22:29
"How often is the *l*.........Job 21:17
You will light my *l*..........Ps 18:28
Your word is a *l*..............Ps 119:105
the *l* of the wicked.........Prov 13:9
his *l* will be put out.........Prov 20:20
Nor do they light a *l*.......Matt 5:15
"The *l* of the body.........Matt 6:22
when he has lit a *l*..........Luke 8:16
l gives you light.............Luke 11:36
does not light a *l*............Luke 15:8
burning and shining *l*.......John 5:35
l shall not shine.............Rev 18:23
They need no *l* nor.........Rev 22:5

LAMPS

he made its seven *l*........ Ex 37:23
Jerusalem with *l*.............Zeph 1:12

LAMPSTAND

branches of the *l*.............Ex 25:32
and there is a *l*...............Zech 4:2
a basket, but on a *l*.........Matt 5:15
in which was the *l*.......... Heb 9:2
and remove your *l*..........Rev 2:5

LAND

l that I will show you...... Gen 12:1
l flowing with milk.......... Ex 3:8
l which I am giving......... Josh 1:2
is heard in our *l*............. Song 2:12
they will see the *l*........... Is 33:17
Bethlehem, in the *l*........ Matt 2:6

LANDMARK

your neighbor's *l*............Deut 19:14
remove the ancient *l*.......Prov 22:28
those who remove a *l*...... Hos 5:10

LANGUAGE

whole earth had one *l*......Gen 11:1
in the Aramaic *l*............. 2 Ki 18:26
is no speech nor *l*........... Ps 19:3
a people of strange *l*........Ps 114:1
the peoples a pure *l*........ Zeph 3:9
speak in his own *l*...........Acts 2:6
blasphemy, filthy *l*..........Col 3:8

LANGUAGES

according to their *l*..........Gen 10:20
be, so many kinds of *l*......1 Co 14:10

LAST

He shall stand at *l*...........Job 19:25
First and I am the *L*........ Is 44:6
l man the same as...........Matt 20:14
l will be first................. Matt 20:16
children, it is the *l*.......... 1 Jn 2:18
the First and the *L*..........Rev 1:11

LATTER

former rain, and the *l*......Joel 2:23
l times some will.............1 Ti 4:1

LATTICE

I looked through my *l*......Prov 7:6
gazing through the *l*........ Song 2:9

LAUGH

Why did Sarah *l*............. Gen 18:13
"God has made me *l*.......Gen 21:6
All those who see Me *l*....Ps 22:7
You, O LORD, shall *l*......Ps 59:8
Woe to you who *l*...........Luke 6:25

LAUGHS

he *l* at the threat of........Job 41:29
The Lord *l* at him...........Ps 37:13

LAUGHTER

was filled with *l*..............Ps 126:2
your *l* be turned to..........Jas 4:9

LAW

stones a copy of the *l*...... Josh 8:32
When He made a *l*..........Job 28:26
The *l* of the LORD is....... Ps 19:7
The *l* of his God is in...... Ps 37:31
I delight in Your *l*...........Ps 119:70
The *l* of Your mouth is...Ps 119:77
l is my delight............... Ps 119:77
Oh, how I love Your *l*.....Ps 119:97

LAWFUL

And Your *l* is truth........Ps 119:142
and the *l* is light............Prov 6:23
shall go forth the *l*..........Is 2:3
l will proceed from Me....Is 51:4
in whose heart is My *l*....Is 51:7
the *L* is no more.............Lam 2:9
The *l* of truth was in......Mal 2:6
to destroy the *L*............Matt 5:17
for this is the *L*............Matt 7:12
hang all the *L* and the....Matt 22:40
"The *l* and the..............Luke 16:16
l was given through........John 1:17
"Does our *l* judge a.......John 7:51
l is the knowledge..........Rom 3:20
because the *l* brings........Rom 4:15
when there is no *l*..........Rom 5:13
you are not under *l*........Rom 6:14
Is the *l* sin...................Rom 7:7
For we know that the *l*....Rom 7:14
warring against the *l*......Rom 7:23
For what the *l* could.....Rom 8:3
who are without *l*..........1 Co 9:21
l that I might live..........Gal 2:19
under guard by the *l*.......Gal 3:23
born under the *l*............Gal 4:4
l is fulfilled in one..........Gal 5:14
l is not made for a.........1 Ti 1:9
into the perfect *l*...........Jas 1:25
fulfill the royal *l*...........Jas 2:8

LAWFUL

doing what is not *l*.........Matt 12:2
Is it *l* to pay taxes..........Matt 22:17
All things are *l*..............1 Co 6:12

LAWGIVER

Judah is My *l*................Ps 60:7
the LORD is our *L*.........Is 33:22
There is one *L*...............Jas 4:12

LAWLESS

l one will be revealed......2 Th 2:8
and hearing their *l*..........2 Pe 2:8

LAWLESSNESS

Me, you who practice *l*....Matt 7:23
l is already at work.........2 Th 2:7
and hated l....................Heb 1:9
and sin is *l*....................1 Jn 3:4

LAWYERS

l rejected the................Luke 7:30
Woe to you also, you *l*....Luke 11:46

LAY

nowhere to *l* His head.....Matt 8:20
l hands may receive........Acts 8:19
Do not *l* hands on..........1 Ti 5:22
l aside all.....................Jas 1:21

LAZINESS

l the building.................Eccl 10:18

LAZY

wicked and *l* servant........Matt 25:26
liars, evil beasts, *l*..........Tit 1:12

LEAD

they sank like *l*..............Ex 15:10
L me in Your truth and...Ps 25:5
L me and guide me.........Ps 31:3
Your hand shall *l*...........Ps 139:10
L me away....................Song 1:4
And do not *l* us into.......Matt 6:13
"Can the blind *l*............Luke 6:39

LEADS

He *l* me beside the..........Ps 23:2
He *l* me in the paths.......Ps 23:3
And if the blind *l*...........Matt 15:14
by name and *l* them out...John 10:3
the goodness of God *l*.....Rom 2:4

LEAF

plucked olive *l*...............Gen 8:11
Will You frighten a *l*......Job 13:25
l will be green................Jer 17:8

LEAN

all your heart, and *l*........Prov 3:5
yet they *l* on the LORD...Mic 3:11

LEANING

Then, *l* back on Jesus'.....John 13:25
l on the top of his..........Heb 11:21

LEANNESS

request, But sent *l*..........Ps 106:15
of hosts, will send *l*........Is 10:16

LEAP

by my God I can *l*..........Ps 18:29
Then the lame shall *l*......Is 35:6

LEARN

it, may hear and *l*..........Deut 31:13
l Your statutes...............Ps 119:71
lest you *l* his ways..........Prov 22:25
l to do good..................Is 1:17
neither shall they *l*.........Is 2:4
My yoke upon you and *l*..Matt 11:29
Let a woman *l* in...........1 Ti 2:11
let our people also *l*........Tit 3:14

LEARNED

Me the tongue of the *l*.....Is 50:4
who has heard and *l*........John 6:45
have not so *l* Christ.........Eph 4:20
in all things I have *l*.......Phil 4:12
l obedience by the..........Heb 5:8

LEARNING

hear and increase *l*.........Prov 1:5
l is driving you mad........Acts 26:24
were written for our *l*......Rom 15:4

LEAST

Judah, are not the l........Matt 2:6
so, shall be called *l*.........Matt 5:19
For I am the *l* of the.......1 Co 15:9

LEAVE

a man shall *l* his.............Gen 2:24
He will not *l* you nor......Deut 31:6
For You will not *l*..........Ps 16:10
Do not *l* me nor............Ps 27:9
"*I will never l*...............Heb 13:5

LEAVEN

day you shall remove *l*....Ex 12:15
of heaven is like *l*..........Matt 13:33
and beware of the *l*........Matt 16:6
know that a little *l*.........1 Co 5:6
l leavens the whole.........Gal 5:9

LEAVES

and they sewed fig *l*........Gen 3:7
nothing in it but *l*..........Matt 21:19
l the sheep and flees.......John 10:12
And the *l* of the tree......Rev 22:2

LED

l the people around by.....Ex 13:18
so the LORD alone *l*.......Deut 32:12
l them forth by the.........Ps 107:7
l them by the right.........Is 63:12
For as many as are *l*.......Rom 8:14
l captivity captive...........Eph 4:8
l away by various...........2 Ti 3:6

LEFT

l hand know what your....Matt 6:3
"See, we have *l*..............Matt 19:27
And everyone who has *l*..Matt 19:29

LEGS

Like the *l* of the lame......Prov 26:7
l are pillars of...............Song 5:15
did not break His *l*.........John 19:33

LEND

"If you *l* money to.........Ex 22:25
l him sufficient...............Deut 15:8
"And if you *l*................Luke 6:34
l me three loaves...........Luke 11:5

LENDER

is servant to the *l*..........Prov 22:7
as with the *l*.................Is 24:2

LENDING

and my servants, am *l*......Neh 5:10

LENDS

ever merciful, and *l*........Ps 37:26
deals graciously and *l*......Ps 112:5
has pity on the poor *l*.....Prov 19:17

LENGTH

The *l* of the ark shall......Gen 6:15
is your life and the *l*.......Deut 30:20
L of days is in her.........Prov 3:16
l is as great as its..........Rev 21:16

LENGTHENS

a shadow when it *l*.........Ps 109:23

LEOPARD

the *l* shall lie down.........Is 11:6
or the *l* its spots............Jer 13:23

LEPERS

And when these *l*...........2 Ki 7:8
"And many *l* were in......Luke 4:27

LET

L there be light"...........Gen 1:3
L the little children.........Matt 19:14

LETTER

the oldness of the *l*........Rom 7:6
for the *l* kills................2 Co 3:6
you sorry with my *l*........2 Co 7:8
or by word or by *l*.........2 Th 2:2

LETTERS

does this Man know *l*......John 7:15
to you or *l* of................2 Co 3:1
"For his *l*.....................2 Co 10:10
with what large *l*...........Gal 6:11

LEVIATHAN

"Can you draw out *L*......Job 41:1
L Which You have made. Ps 104:26

LEVITE

"Is not Aaron the *L*........Ex 4:14
"Likewise a *L*................Luke 10:32
a *L* of the country of......Acts 4:36

LEVITICAL

were through the L.........Heb 7:11

LIAR

for he is a *l* and the........John 8:44
but every man a *l*............ Rom 3:4
we make Him a *l*............1 Jn 1:10
Who is a *l* but he who....1 Jn 2:22
his brother, he is a *l*........1 Jn 4:20
God has made Him a *l*... 1 Jn 5:10

LIARS

"All men are *l*................Ps 116:11
Cretans are always *l*........ Tit 1:12
and have found them *l*.....Rev 2:2
l shall have their............. Rev 21:8

LIBERALITY

he who gives, with *l*........ Rom 12:8
the riches of their *l*......... 2 Co 8:2

LIBERALLY

who gives to all *l*............ Jas 1:5

LIBERTY

year, and proclaim *l*........ Lev 25:10
And I will walk at *l*........Ps 119:45
to proclaim *l* to the........Is 61:1
into the glorious *l*........... Rom 8:21
For why is my *l*.............. 1 Co 10:29
Lord is, there is *l*............2 Co 3:17
therefore in the *l*............ Gal 5:1
l as an opportunity..........Gal 5:13
the perfect law of *l*..........Jas 1:25
yet not using your *l*.........1 Pe 2:16

LICENTIOUSNESS

wickedness, deceit, *l*........Mark 7:22
drunkenness, not in *l*.......Rom 13:13
themselves over to *l*........ Eph 4:19
when we walked in *l*........1 Pe 4:3

LIE

man, that He should *l*.....Num 23:19
For now I will *l*..............Job 7:21
I will not *l* to David........ Ps 89:35
Do not *l* to one..............Col 3:9
God, who cannot *l*...........Tit 1:2
do not boast and *l*...........Jas 3:14
know it, and that no *l*......1 Jn 2:21
an abomination or a *l*......Rev 21:27

LIED

They have *l* about the......Jer 5:12
You have not *l* to men.... Acts 5:4

LIES

sin *l* at the door..............Gen 4:7
and he who speaks *l*........Prov 19:5
speaking *l* in.................. 1 Ti 4:2
and the whole world *l*......1 Jn 5:19

LIFE

the breath of *l*................Gen 2:7
l was also in the............. Gen 2:9
then you shall give *l*.......Ex 21:23
'For the *l* of the.............Lev 17:11
before you today *l*...........Deut 30:15
You have granted me *l*.... Job 10:12
In whose hand is the *l*..... Job 12:10
God takes away his *l*........Job 27:8
with the light of *l*............Job 33:30
He will redeem their *l*..... Ps 72:14
word has given me *l*........ Ps 119:50
regain the paths of *l*........Prov 2:19
She is a tree of *l*............Prov 3:18

so they will be *l*..............Prov 3:22
finds me finds *l*...............Prov 8:35
l winds upward for the.....Prov 15:24
thief hates his own *l*........Prov 29:24
is that wisdom gives *l*...... Eccl 7:12
I have cut off my *l*...........Is 38:12
you the way of *l*..............Jer 21:8
l shall be as a prize........Jer 39:18
not worry about your *l*.....Matt 6:25
l does not consist............Luke 12:15
L is more than...............Luke 12:23
l was the light................John 1:4
so the Son gives *l*............John 5:21
as the Father has *l*...........John 5:26
spirit, and they are *l*........John 6:63
have the light of *l*............John 8:12
and I lay down My *l*........John 10:15
resurrection and the *l*...... John 11:25
you lay down your *l*.........John 13:38
even God, who gives *l*.....Rom 4:17
that pertain to this *l*........1 Co 6:3
Lord Jesus, that the *l*...... 2 Co 4:10
l which I now live...........Gal 2:20
l is hidden with..............Col 3:3
of God who gives *l*..........1 Ti 6:13
For what is your *l*...........Jas 4:14
that pertain to *l*..............2 Pe 1:3
l was manifested..............1 Jn 1:2
and the pride of *l*............1 Jn 2:16
has given us eternal *l*.......1 Jn 5:11
who has the Son has *l*......1 Jn 5:12
the Lamb's Book of *L*..... Rev 21:27
right to the tree of *l*........ Rev 22:14
the water of *l* freely........ Rev 22:17
from the Book of *L*......... Rev 22:19

LIFT

I will *l* up my hands........Ps 63:4
I will *l* up my eyes to...... Ps 121:1
l up your voice like a....... Is 58:1
l our hearts and hands..... Lam 3:41
Lord, and He will *l*.........Jas 4:10

LIFTED

O LORD, for You have *l*. Ps 30:1
your heart is *l*................ Ezek 28:2
in Hades, he *l* up his.......Luke 16:23
the Son of Man be *l*.........John 3:14
"And I, if I am *l*.............John 12:32
of Man must be *l*............John 12:34

LIGHT

"Let there be *l*................Gen 1:3
"The *l* of the wicked........Job 18:5
l will shine on your.........Job 22:28
the wicked their *l*...........Job 38:15
to the dwelling of *l*..........Job 38:19
LORD, lift up the *l*..........Ps 4:6
The LORD is my *l*............Ps 27:1
Oh, send out Your *l*........Ps 43:3
L is sown for the.............Ps 97:11
And He has given us *l*...... Ps 118:27
And a *l* to my path.........Ps 119:105
The *l* of the righteous......Prov 13:9
The *l* of the eyes............Prov 15:30
the LORD gives *l*............Prov 29:13
Truly the *l* is sweet.........Eccl 11:7
let us walk in the *l*..........Is 2:5
l is darkened by the........Is 5:30
because there is no *l*........Is 8:20
moon will be as the *l*.......Is 30:26
l shall break forth..........Is 58:8
For your *l* has come........Is 60:1
be your everlasting *l*........Is 60:20
gives the sun for a *l*........ Jer 31:35
l that goes.....................Hos 6:5

"You are the *l*.................Matt 5:14
"Let your *l* so shine........Matt 5:16
body will be full of *l*........Matt 6:22
than the sons of *l*............Luke 16:8
and the life was the *l*.......John 1:4
That was the true *L*.........John 1:9
darkness rather than *l*......John 3:19
evil hates the *l*................John 3:20
truth comes to the *l*.........John 3:21
saying, "I am the *l*...........John 8:12
believe in the *l*...............John 12:36
"I have come as a *l*.........John 12:46
l the hidden....................1 Co 4:5
God who commanded *l*...2 Co 4:6
Walk as children of *l*.......Eph 5:8
You are all sons of *l*........1 Th 5:5
and immortality to *l*........ 2 Ti 1:10
into His marvelous *l*........1 Pe 2:9
do well to heed as a *l*......2 Pe 1:19
to you, that God is *l*........ 1 Jn 1:5
l as He is in the..............1 Jn 1:7
says he is in the *l*............1 Jn 2:9
and the Lamb is its *l*....... Rev 21:23
Lord God gives them *l*.....Rev 22:5

LIGHTEN

L the yoke which............1 Ki 12:9
the sea, to *l* the load.......Jon 1:5

LIGHTNING

"For as the *l*..................Matt 24:27
countenance was like *l*..... Matt 28:3
saw Satan fall like *l*.........Luke 10:18

LIGHTNINGS

were thunderings and *l*.....Ex 19:16
The *l* lit up the world......Ps 77:18
l light the world.............Ps 97:4
the throne proceeded *l*.....Rev 4:5

LIGHTS

"Let there be *l*...............Gen 1:14
Him who made great *l*.....Ps 136:7
whom you shine as *l*........Phil 2:15
from the Father of *l*........Jas 1:17

LIKE

"Who is *l* You................Ex 15:11
L a lily among thorns......Song 2:2
be made *l* His brethren....Heb 2:17

LIKE-MINDED

grant you to be *l*............Rom 15:5
For I have no one *l*.........Phil 2:20

LIKENESS

according to Our *l*...........Gen 1:26
carved image, or any *l*.....Ex 20:4
when I awake in Your *l*...Ps 17:15
His own Son in the *l*....... Rom 8:3
and coming in the *l*.........Phil 2:7

LILY

the *l* of the valleys..........Song 2:1
Like a *l* among thorns..... Song 2:2
shall grow like the *l*........Hos 14:5

LIMIT

Do you *l* wisdom to........ Job 15:8
to the sea its *l*................Prov 8:29

LIMITED

l the Holy One of...........Ps 78:41

LINE

l has gone out through.....Ps 19:4
upon precept, *l* upon.......Is 28:10
I am setting a plumb *l*.....Amos 7:8

LINEAGE

was of the house and *l*.....Luke 2:4

LINEN

her clothing is fine *l*........Prov 31:22
wrapped Him in the *l*......Mark 15:46
l is the righteous............Rev 19:8

LION

he lies down as a *l*.........Gen 49:9
like a fierce *l*..................Job 10:16
l shall eat straw.............Is 11:7
For I will be like a *l*........Hos 5:14

LIONS

My soul is among *l*.........Ps 57:4
the mouths of *l*..............Heb 11:33

LIPS

of uncircumcised *l*...........Ex 6:12
off all flattering *l*............Ps 12:3
Let the lying *l*................Ps 31:18
The *l* of the righteous.....Prov 10:21
but the *l* of knowledge....Prov 20:15
am a man of unclean *l*....Is 6:5
asps is under their *l*........Rom 3:13
I *l* will speak to this........1 Co 14:21
from evil, and his *l*.........1 Pe 3:10

LISTEN

L diligently to Me...........Is 55:2
O Lord, *l* and act.........Dan 9:19
you are not able to *l*.......John 8:43
Why do you *l* to Him....John 10:20
you who fear God, *l*.......Acts 13:16

LISTENS

but whoever *l* to me........Prov 1:33

LITTLE

l foxes that spoil the.......Song 2:15
We have a *l* sister...........Song 8:8
upon line, here a *l*..........Is 28:10
though you are *l*.............Mic 5:2
indeed it came to *l*.........Hag 1:9
for I was a *l* angry..........Zech 1:15
l ones only a cup...........Matt 10:42
"O you of *l* faith...........Matt 14:31
whoever receives one *l*....Matt 18:5
to whom *l* is forgiven....Luke 7:47
faithful in a very *l*.........Luke 19:17
exercise profits a *l*.........1 Ti 4:8

LIVE

eat, and *l* forever".........Gen 3:22
a man does, he shall *l*.....Lev 18:5
I would not *l* forever......Job 7:16
L joyfully with the.........Eccl 9:9
by these things men *l*......Is 38:16
sin, he shall surely *l*.......Ezek 3:21
"Seek Me and *l*.............Amos 5:4
but the just shall *l*.........Hab 2:4
'Man shall not *l*..........Matt 4:4
who feeds on Me will *l*...John 6:57
"for in Him we *l*..........Acts 17:28
l peaceably with all........Rom 12:18
the life which I now *l*......Gal 2:20
If we *l* in the Spirit.........Gal 5:25
to me, to *l* is Christ........Phil 1:21
l godly in Christ............2 Ti 3:12
to *l* honorably..............Heb 13:18
l according to God in......1 Pe 4:6

LIVED

died and rose and *l*........Rom 14:9
And they *l* and reigned....Rev 20:4

LIVES

but man *l* by every.........Deut 8:3
have risked their *l*..........Acts 15:26
He *l* to God..................Rom 6:10
For none of us *l*............Rom 14:7
but Christ *l* in me..........Gal 2:20
to lay down our *l*...........1 Jn 3:16
"I am He who *l*............Rev 1:18

LIVING

and man became a *l*.......Gen 2:7
In the light of the *l*.........Ps 56:13
l will take it to..............Eccl 7:2
l know that they will.......Eccl 9:5
Why should a *l* man.......Lam 3:39
the dead, but of the *l*......Matt 22:32
Why do you seek the *l*....Luke 24:5
to be Judge of the *l*........Acts 10:42
who will judge the *l*........2 Ti 4:1
the word of God is *l*........Heb 4:12
ready to judge the *l*........1 Pe 4:5
l creature was like a........Rev 4:7

LOAD

shall bear his own *l*.........Gal 6:5

LOATHE

I *l* my life......................Job 7:16
l themselves for the.........Ezek 6:9

LOATHSOME

but a wicked man is *l*......Prov 13:5

LOAVES

have here only five *l*.......Matt 14:17
He took the seven *l*........Matt 15:36
lend me three *l*..............Luke 11:5
you ate of the *l*.............John 6:26

LOCUST

What the chewing *l*........Joel 1:4
left, the swarming *l*........Joel 1:4

LOCUSTS

as numerous as *l*............Judg 7:12
He spoke, and *l* came......Ps 105:34
the *l* have no king..........Prov 30:27
and his food was *l*.........Matt 3:4
waist, and he ate *l*.........Mark 1:6
out of the smoke *l*.........Rev 9:3

LODGED

them in and *l* them........Acts 10:23
children, if she has *l*.......1 Ti 5:10

LOFTY

haughty, Nor my eyes *l*...Ps 131:1
Wisdom is too *l*.............Prov 24:7
l are their eyes..............Prov 30:13
and *L* One Who............Is 57:15

LOINS

gird up the *l* of your.......1 Pe 1:13

LONG

your days may be *l*.........Deut 5:16
who *l* for death..............Job 3:21
me the thing that I *l*.......Job 6:8
I *l* for Your salvation......Ps 119:174
go around in *l* robes.......Mark 12:38
how greatly I *l*..............Phil 1:8

LONGSUFFERING

and gracious, *L*..............Ps 86:15
is love, joy, peace, *l*.......Gal 5:22
and gentleness, with *l*.....Eph 4:2
for all patience and *l*.......Col 1:11
might show all *l*.............1 Ti 1:16
when once the *l*.............1 Pe 3:20
and account that the *l*.....2 Pe 3:15

LOOK

Do not *l* behind you........Gen 19:17
who has a haughty *l*........Ps 101:5
A proud *l*.....................Prov 6:17
that day a man will *l*........Is 17:7
L upon Zion..................Is 33:20
"*L* to Me....................Is 45:22
we *l* for light.................Is 59:9
we *l* for justice..............Is 59:11
then they will *l*..............Zech 12:10
say to you, '*L* here..........Luke 17:23
of Israel could not *l*........2 Co 3:7
while we do not *l*...........2 Co 4:18
Let each of you *l*............Phil 2:4
L to yourselves..............2 Jn 8

LOOKED

But when I *l* for good......Job 30:26
They *l* to Him and were....Ps 34:5
For He *l* down from the...Ps 102:19
He *l* for justice..............Is 5:7
"We *l* for peace............Jer 8:15
"You *l* for much............Hag 1:9
the Lord turned and *l*......Luke 22:61
for he *l* to the reward......Heb 11:26

LOOKING

the plow, and *l* back.......Luke 9:62
l for the blessed hope......Tit 2:13
l unto Jesus..................Heb 12:2
l diligently lest..............Heb 12:15
l for the mercy of..........Jude 21

LOOKS

Absalom for his good *l*....2 Sa 14:25
And he *l* at men and.......Job 33:27
God *l* down from heaven. Ps 53:2
The lofty *l* of man..........Is 2:11
to you that whoever *l*......Matt 5:28

LOOM

and the web from the *l*....Judg 16:14
cuts me off from the *l*......Is 38:12

LOOSE

l the armor of kings........Is 45:1
and whatever you *l*.........Matt 16:19
said to them, "*L* him.......John 11:44

LOOSED

You have *l* my bonds......Ps 116:16
the silver cord is *l*..........Eccl 12:6

LORD

L is my strength.............Ex 15:2
L is a man of war...........Ex 15:3
L our God, the *L*..........Deut 6:4
L your God a bull..........Deut 17:1
may know that the *L*.......1 Ki 8:60
If the *L* is God..............1 Ki 18:21
You alone are the *L*........Neh 9:6
The *L* of hosts...............Ps 24:10
belongs to the *L*.............Ps 89:18
let us sing to the *L*..........Ps 95:1
L is the great God...........Ps 95:3
Gracious is the *L*............Ps 116:5
L surrounds His people....Ps 125:2

LORDS

The *L* is righteous...........Ps 129:4
L is near to all who........ Ps 145:18
L is a God of justice....... Is 30:18
L our Righteousness........Jer 23:6
L has done marvelous......Joel 2:21
L God is my strength...... Hab 3:19
"the *L* is one.................. Zech 14:9
shall not tempt the *L*......Matt 4:7
shall worship the *L*..........Matt 4:10
Son of Man is also *L*.....Mark 2:28
who is Christ the *L*........ Luke 2:11
why do you call Me '*L*.... Luke 6:46
L is risen indeed............Luke 24:34
call me Teacher and *L*.....John 13:13
He is *L* of all................Acts 10:36
'Who are You, *L*............ Acts 26:15
with your mouth the *L*.... Rom 10:9
Greek, for the same *L*.....Rom 10:12
say that Jesus is *L*...........1 Co 12:3
second Man is the *L*.......1 Co 15:47
the Spirit of the *L*.........2 Co 3:17
that Jesus Christ is *L*......Phil 2:11
and deny the only *L*.......Jude 4
L God Omnipotent......... Rev 19:6

LORDS

many gods and many *l*.....1 Co 8:5
nor as being *l* over..........1 Pe 5:3
for He is Lord of *l*.........Rev 17:14

LORDSHIP

Gentiles exercise *l*...........Luke 22:25

LOSE

gain, and a time to *l*........Eccl 3:6
save his life will *l*...........Matt 16:25
reap if we do not *l*.........Gal 6:9
that we do not *l*..............2 Jn 8

LOSES

but if the salt *l*............... Matt 5:13
and *l* his own soul..........Matt 16:26
if she *l* one coin..............Luke 15:8
l his life will..................Luke 17:33

LOSS

he will suffer *l*................1 Co 3:15
count all things *l*............Phil 3:8

LOST

are dry, our hope is *l*...... Ezek 37:11
save that which was *l*.......Matt 18:11
the one which is *l*.......... Luke 15:4
my sheep which was *l*......Luke 15:6
the piece which I *l*..........Luke 15:9
and none of them is *l*...... John 17:12
You gave Me I have *l*......John 18:9

LOT

shall be divided by *l*........Num 26:55
You maintain my *l*..........Ps 16:5
cast in your *l* among.......Prov 1:14
l is cast into the lap........Prov 16:33
delivered righteous *L*.......2 Pe 2:7

LOTS

l causes contentions.........Prov 18:18
garments, casting *l*..........Mark 15:24
And they cast their *l*....... Acts 1:26

LOUD

I cried out with a *l*..........Gen 39:14
Him with *l* cymbals......... Ps 150:5
cried out with a *l*............Matt 27:46
I heard behind me a *l*......Rev 1:10

LOVE

l your neighbor as...........Lev 19:18
l the LORD your God..... Deut 6:5
Your *l* to me was............2 Sa 1:26
How long will you *l*.........Ps 4:2
Oh, *l* the LORD.............. Ps 31:23
l righteousness................Ps 45:7
he has set his *l*............... Ps 91:14
Oh, how I *l* Your law......Ps 119:97
peace have those who *l*...Ps 119:165
preserves all who *l*......... Ps 145:20
us take our fill of *l*.........Prov 7:18
l covers all sins...............Prov 10:12
a time to *l*...................... Eccl 3:8
People know neither *l*......Eccl 9:1
l is better than wine........ Song 1:2
banner over me was *l*...... Song 2:4
stir up nor awaken *l*........Song 3:5
I will give you my *l*........Song 7:12
l is as strong as...............Song 8:6
waters cannot quench *l*.....Song 8:7
time was the time of *l*.....Ezek 16:8
backsliding, I will *l*..........Hos 14:4
do justly, to *l* mercy........Mic 6:8
to you, *l* your enemies.....Matt 5:44
l those who *l* you..........Matt 5:46
which of them will *l*........ Luke 7:42
you do not have the *l*......John 5:42
if you have *l* for one....... John 13:35
"If you *l* Me.................. John 14:15
and My Father will *l*........John 14:23
l one another as I........... John 15:12
l has no one than this......John 15:13
l Me more than these......John 21:15
of Jonah, do you *l*...........John 21:16
You know that I *l*...........John 21:16
because the *l* of God...... Rom 5:5
Let *l* be without..............Rom 12:9
to *l* one another...............Rom 13:8
L does no harm to a....... Rom 13:10
up, but *l* edifies...............1 Co 8:1
L suffers long and is........1 Co 13:4
l does not envy...............1 Co 13:4
l does not parade.............1 Co 13:4
L never fails...................1 Co 13:8
greatest of these is *l*........ 1 Co 13:13
For the *l* of Christ..........2 Co 5:14
and the God of *l*.............2 Co 13:11
of the Spirit is *l*.............Gal 5:22
Husbands, *l* your wives.... Eph 5:25
of the Son of His *l*.........Col 1:13
l your wives and do.........Col 3:19
the commandment is *l*......1 Ti 1:5
continue in faith, *l*.......... 1 Ti 2:15
word, in conduct, in *l*......1 Ti 4:12
For the *l* of money is.......1 Ti 6:10
l their husbands..............Tit 2:4
Let brotherly *l*................Heb 13:1
having not seen you *l*...... 1 Pe 1:8
L the brotherhood......... 1 Pe 2:17
for "*l* will cover a...........1 Pe 4:8
with a kiss of *l*...............1 Pe 5:14
brotherly kindness *l*.........2 Pe 1:7
loves the world, the *l*.......1 Jn 2:15
we *l* the brethren............1 Jn 3:14
By this we know *l*............1 Jn 3:16
him, how does the *l*........ 1 Jn 3:17
Beloved, let us *l*.............. 1 Jn 4:7
know God, for God is *l*... 1 Jn 4:8
In this is *l*....................... 1 Jn 4:10
If we *l* one another.........1 Jn 4:12
L has been perfected........1 Jn 4:17
There is no fear in *l*........1 Jn 4:18
l Him because He first.....1 Jn 4:19
who loves God must *l*......1 Jn 4:21
For this is the *l*................1 Jn 5:3

LOVED

Because the LORD has *l*.. 1 Ki 10:9
L one and friend You......Ps 88:18
"I have *l* you................. Mal 1:2
Yet Jacob I have *l*.......... Mal 1:2
forgiven, for she *l*........... Luke 7:47
l the world that............... John 3:16
"See how He *l*................ John 11:36
whom Jesus *l*..................John 13:23
"As the Father *l*..............John 15:9
l them as You have........John 17:23
"*Jacob I have l*...............Rom 9:13
the Son of God, who *l*.....Gal 2:20
l the church and gave...... Eph 5:25
l righteousness................Heb 1:9
God, but that He *l*..........1 Jn 4:10
Beloved, if God so *l*........1 Jn 4:11
To Him who *l* us and..... Rev 1:5

LOVELY

l is Your tabernacle.........Ps 84:1
l woman who lacks..........Prov 11:22
he is altogether *l*.............Song 5:16
whatever things are *l*....... Phil 4:8

LOVER

a *l* of what is good..........Tit 1:8

LOVERS

For men will be *l*............2 Ti 3:2

LOVES

l righteousness................Ps 33:5
life, And *l* many days......Ps 34:12
A friend *l* at all.............. Prov 17:17
"He who *l* father or........ Matt 10:37
l his life will lose............John 12:25
l Me will be loved..........John 14:21
l a cheerful giver............2 Co 9:7
l his wife *l*.................Eph 5:28
who *l* his wife *l*.............Eph 5:28
If anyone *l* the world.......1 Jn 2:15
l God must love his.........1 Jn 4:21
l him who is...................1 Jn 5:1

LOVESICK

apples, for I am *l*............Song 2:5
you tell him I am *l*..........Song 5:8

LOVINGKINDNESS

not concealed Your *l*.......Ps 40:10
l is better than life.......... Ps 63:3
To declare Your *l*........... Ps 92:2
l I have drawn................Jer 31:3

LOW

He brings *l* and lifts........ 1 Sa 2:7
Both *l* and high..............Ps 49:2
it *l*, He lays it *l*............Is 26:5
and hill brought *l*............Luke 3:5

LOWER

made him a little *l*.......... Ps 8:5
Shall go into the *l*...........Ps 63:9
made him a little *l*...........Heb 2:7

LOWEST

and sets over it the *l*....... Dan 4:17

LOWLINESS

with all *l* and..................Eph 4:2
or conceit, but in *l*..........Phil 2:3

LOWLY

Yet He regards the *l*....... Ps 138:6
for I am gentle and *l*....... Matt 11:29
He has regarded the *l*..... Luke 1:48
and exalted the *l*............. Luke 1:52
in presence am *l*............. 2 Co 10:1
l body that it may be....... Phil 3:21
l brother glory............... Jas 1:9

LOYAL

or else he will be *l*.......... Matt 6:24

LUKEWARM

because you are *l*............ Rev 3:16

LUMP

from the same *l*.............. Rom 9:21
you may be a new *l*......... 1 Co 5:7

LUST

Do not *l* after her.......... Prov 6:25
taken by their own *l*........ Prov 11:6
looks at a woman to *l*..... Matt 5:28
not fulfill the *l*............... Gal 5:16
not in passion of *l*........... 1 Th 4:5
You *l* and do not have.... Jas 4:2
the *l* of the flesh............. 1 Jn 2:16

LUSTS

to fulfill its *l*................... Rom 13:14
l which drown men......... 1 Ti 6:9
also youthful *l*................ 2 Ti 2:22
and worldly *l*................. Tit 2:12
to the former *l*............... 1 Pe 1:14
abstain from fleshly *l*....... 1 Pe 2:11
to their own ungodly *l*..... Jude 18

LUTE

Awake, *l* and harp.......... Ps 57:8
l I will praise you............ Ps 71:22
harp with the *l*............... Ps 81:2
ten strings, On the *l*........ Ps 92:3
Awake, *l* and harp.......... Ps 108:2
Praise Him with the *l*...... Ps 150:3

LUXURY

L is not fitting................ Prov 19:10
l are in kings' courts........ Luke 7:25
in pleasure and *l*............. Jas 5:5
the abundance of her *l*..... Rev 18:3

LYING

I hate and abhor *l*........... Ps 119:163
righteous man hates *l*....... Prov 13:5
not trust in these *l*.......... Jer 7:4
in swaddling cloths, *l*....... Luke 2:12
saw the linen cloths *l*....... John 20:5
putting away *l*................ Eph 4:25
signs, and *l* wonders........ 2 Th 2:9

— M —

MAD

has a demon and is *m*...John 10:20
he said, "I am not *m*....... Acts 26:25

MADE

m the stars also.............. Gen 1:16
wife the LORD God *m*.... Gen 3:21
hear long ago how I *m*... Is 37:26
things My hand has *m*..... Is 66:2
All things were *m*........... John 1:3

MADNESS

before them, feigned *m*... 1 Sa 21:13
wisdom and to know *m*... Eccl 1:17
m is in their hearts.......... Eccl 9:3

MAGIC

to the women who sew *m*.Ezek 13:18
m brought their books..... Acts 19:19

MAGNIFICENCE

m I could not endure....... Job 31:23

MAGNIFIED

So let Your name be *m*... 2 Sa 7:26
"Let the LORD be *m*...... Ps 35:27
For You have *m* Your..... Ps 138:2
the Lord Jesus was *m*..... Acts 19:17
also Christ will be *m*....... Phil 1:20

MAGNIFIES

"My soul *m* the Lord...... Luke 1:46

MAGNIFY

m the LORD with me...... Ps 34:3
and he shall *m* himself..... Dan 8:25
m himself above every..... Dan 11:36

MAIDENS

Both young men and *m*... Ps 148:12
She has sent out her *m*... Prov 9:3

MAIDSERVANT

"I am Ruth, your *m*........ Ruth 3:9
save the son of Your *m*... Ps 86:16
"Behold the *m*.............. Luke 1:38
lowly state of His *m*........ Luke 1:48

MAIDSERVANTS

m shall lead her as.......... Nah 2:7
m I will pour out My....... Acts 2:18

MAIMED

to enter into life *m*.......... Mark 9:43
the poor and the *m*......... Luke 14:21

MAINTAIN

and *m* their cause........... 1 Ki 8:45

MAINTAINED

For You have *m* my........ Ps 9:4

MAJESTY

with God is awesome *m*...Job 37:22
splendor of Your *m*......... Ps 145:5
right hand of the *m*........ Heb 1:3
eyewitnesses of His *m*..... 2 Pe 1:16
wise, be glory and *m*....... Jude 25

MAKE

Let Us *m* man in Our..... Gen 1:26
let us *m* a name for........ Gen 11:4
m you a great nation....... Gen 12:2
"You shall not *m*........... Ex 20:4
m Our home with him..... John 14:23

MAKER

Where is God my *M*....... Job 35:10
man will look to his *M*.... Is 17:7
who strives with his *M*.... Is 45:9
M is your husband.......... Is 54:5
has forgotten his *M*........ Hos 8:14
builder and *m* is God...... Heb 11:10

MALICE

however, in *m* be babes... 1 Co 14:20
pleasures, living in *m*....... Tit 3:3
laying aside all *m*............ 1 Pe 2:1

MALICIOUSNESS

covetousness, *m*.............. Rom 1:29

MAN

"Let Us make *m*............. Gen 1:26
"You are the *m*.............. 2 Sa 12:7
"What is *m*.................... Job 7:17
For an empty-headed *m*... Job 11:12
"Are you the first *m*....... Job 15:7
m that You are mindful... Ps 8:4
What can *m* do to me...... Ps 118:6
coming of the Son of *M*... Matt 24:27
"Behold the *M*.............. John 19:5
m is not from woman...... 1 Co 11:8
since by *m* came death..... 1 Co 15:21
though our outward *m*..... 2 Co 4:16
in Himself one new *m*..... Eph 2:15
that the *m* of God may... 2 Ti 3:17
is the number of a *m*...... Rev 13:18

MANGER

Will he bed by your *m*....Job 39:9
and laid Him in a *m*........ Luke 2:7
the Babe lying in a *m*...... Luke 2:16

MANIFEST

m Myself to him............. John 14:21
is it that You will *m*........ John 14:22

MANIFESTATION

But the *m* of the............. 1 Co 12:7
deceitfully, but by *m*....... 2 Co 4:2

MANIFESTED

"I have *m* Your name..... John 17:6
God was *m* in the flesh.... 1 Ti 3:16
the life was *m*................ 1 Jn 1:2
the love of God was *m*.... 1 Jn 4:9

MANIFOLD

m are Your works........... Ps 104:24
the *m* wisdom of God...... Eph 3:10
good stewards of the *m*... 1 Pe 4:10

MANNA

of Israel ate *m*................ Ex 16:35
Had rained down *m*......... Ps 78:24
Our fathers ate the *m*...... John 6:31
of the hidden *m*.............. Rev 2:17

MANNER

Is this the *m* of man........ 2 Sa 7:19
in an unworthy *m*........... 1 Co 11:27
sorrowed in a godly *m*..... 2 Co 7:11
as is the *m* of some......... Heb 10:25
what *m* of persons........... 2 Pe 3:11
Behold what *m* of love... 1 Jn 3:1
m worthy of God............ 3 Jn 6

MANSIONS

house are many *m*........... John 14:2

MANTLE

Then he took the *m*......... 2 Ki 2:14

MARK

And the LORD set a *m*... Gen 4:15
M the blameless man....... Ps 37:37
slave, to receive a *m*....... Rev 13:16
whoever receives the *m*.... Rev 14:11

MARKET

is sold in the meat *m*....... 1 Co 10:25

MARRED

so His visage was *m*........ Is 52:14
he made of clay was *m*... Jer 18:4

MARRIAGE
nor are given in *m*.......... Matt 22:30
her in *m* does well.......... 1 Co 7:38
M is honorable among..... Heb 13:4
the *m* of the Lamb has.... Rev 19:7

MARRIED
"for I am *m* to you......... Jer 3:14
But he who is *m*.............. 1 Co 7:33
But she who is *m*............. 1 Co 7:34

MARROW
and of joints and *m*......... Heb 4:12

MARRY
it is better not to *m*.........Matt 19:10
they neither *m* nor are.....Matt 22:30
let them *m*.................... 1 Co 7:9
forbidding to *m*.............. 1 Ti 4:3
the younger widows *m*..... 1 Ti 5:14

MARRYING
and drinking, *m*.............. Matt 24:38

MARTYR
m Stephen was shed........ Acts 22:20
was My faithful *m*.......... Rev 2:13

MARTYRS
the blood of the *m*.......... Rev 17:6

MARVEL
"Do not *m* at this........... John 5:28

MARVELED
Jesus heard it, He *m*....... Matt 8:10
And the multitudes *m*......Matt 9:33
so that Pilate *m*.............. Mark 15:5
And all the world *m*........Rev 13:3
when I saw her, I *m*........Rev 17:6

MARVELOUS
M things He did............. Ps 78:12
It is *m* in our eyes.......... Ps 118:23
M are Your works.......... Ps 139:14
of darkness into His *m*.....1 Pe 2:9

MARVELS
people I will do *m*.......... Ex 34:10

MASTER
of Abraham his *m*...........Gen 24:9
a servant like his *m*........Matt 10:25
not greater than his *m*.....John 15:20
m builder I have laid....... 1 Co 3:10
and useful for the *M*....... 2 Ti 2:21

MASTERS
m besides You have........ Is 26:13
can serve two *m*............. Luke 16:13
M, give your servants...... Col 4:1
who have believing *m*..... 1 Ti 6:2

MATTER
m is found in me............ Job 19:28
He who answers a *m*....... Prov 18:13

MATTERS
the weightier *m*.............. Matt 23:23
judge the smallest *m*........1 Co 6:2

MATURE
among those who are *m*...1 Co 2:6
in understanding be *m*..... 1 Co 14:20
us, as many as are *m*.......Phil 3:15

MEANING
'What is the *m*................ Deut 6:20
if I do not know the *m*.... 1 Co 14:11

MEANT
but God *m* it for good..... Gen 50:20

MEASURE
a perfect and just *m*........ Deut 25:15
out the waters by *m*........ Job 28:25
and the short *m*.............. Mic 6:10
give the Spirit by *m*........John 3:34
to each one a *m*.............. Rom 12:3
m the temple of God......Rev 11:1

MEASURED
m the waters in the......... Is 40:12
you use, it will be *m*....... Matt 7:2
Then he *m* its wall.......... Rev 21:17

MEASURES
your house differing *m*.....Deut 25:14
weights and diverse *m*......Prov 20:10

MEASURING
the man's hand was a *m*...Ezek 40:5
behold, a man with a *m*...Zech 2:1
m themselves by............. 2 Co 10:12
given a reed like a *m*.......Rev 11:1

MEAT
Can He provide *m*.......... Ps 78:20
He also rained *m*............. Ps 78:27
good neither to eat *m*......Rom 14:21
will never again eat *m*..... 1 Co 8:13
is sold in the *m*.............. 1 Co 10:25

MEDIATE
a mediator does not *m*.....Gal 3:20

MEDIATOR
Nor is there any *m*..........Job 9:33
by the hand of a *m*......... Gal 3:19
is one God and one *M*.....1 Ti 2:5
as He is also *M*.............. Heb 8:6
to Jesus the *M* of the...... Heb 12:24

MEDICINE
does good, like *m*........... Prov 17:22

MEDICINES
you will use many *m*....... Jer 46:11

MEDITATE
Isaac went out to *m*........ Gen 24:63
but you shall *m*.............. Josh 1:8
M within your heart on....Ps 4:4
I *m* within my heart........ Ps 77:6
I will *m* on Your............ Ps 119:15
Your heart will *m*........... Is 33:18
m beforehand on what.....Luke 21:14
m on these things...........Phil 4:8

MEDITATES
in His law he *m*.............. Ps 1:2

MEDITATION
of my mouth and the *m*... Ps 19:14
m be sweet to Him.......... Ps 104:34
It is my *m* all the day...... Ps 119:97

MEDIUM
or a woman who is a *m*...Lev 20:27
me a woman who is a *m*.. 1 Sa 28:7

MEDIUM'S
shall be like a *m*............. Is 29:4

MEDIUMS
Seek those who are *m*..... Is 8:19

MEEK
with equity for the *m*.......Is 11:4
Blessed are the *m*.......... Matt 5:5

MEEKNESS
with you by the *m*...........2 Co 10:1
are done in the *m*...........Jas 3:13

MEET
For You in him with the.. Ps 21:3
prepare to *m* your God....Amos 4:12
go out to *m* him............. Matt 25:6
m the Lord in the air...... 1 Th 4:17

MEETING
In the tabernacle of *m*..... Ex 27:21
burned up all the *m*........ Ps 74:8

MELODY
make sweet *m*................. Is 23:16
singing and making *m*......Eph 5:19

MELT
You make his beauty *m*...Ps 39:11
man's heart will *m*.......... Is 13:7
the elements will *m*......... 2 Pe 3:10

MEMBER
the body is not one *m*..... 1 Co 12:14
tongue is a little *m*..........Jas 3:5

MEMBERS
you that one of your *m*....Matt 5:29
do not present your *m*......Rom 6:13
that your bodies are *m*..... 1 Co 6:15
neighbor, for we are *m*.....Eph 4:25

MEMORIAL
and this is My *m*............. Ex 3:15
also be told as a *m*..........Matt 26:13
be spoken of as a *m*........ Mark 14:9

MEMORY
The *m* of him perishes.....Job 18:17
He may cut off the *m*...... Ps 109:15
The *m* of the righteous.... Prov 10:7

MEN
m began to call on the.....Gen 4:26
saw the daughters of *m*....Gen 6:2
you shall die like *m*.........Ps 82:7
the Egyptians are *m*........ Is 31:3
make you fishers of *m*..... Matt 4:19
good will toward *m*......... Luke 2:14
from heaven or from *m*....Luke 20:4
Likewise also the *m*.........Rom 1:27
let no one glory in *m*.......1 Co 3:21
the Lord, and not to *m*....Eph 6:7
between God and *m*.........1 Ti 2:5

MENSERVANTS
And also on My *m*..........Joel 2:29
and on My *m* and on My. Acts 2:18

MENTION
I will make *m* of Your.....Ps 71:16
by You only we make *m*.. Is 26:13
You who make *m* of the.. Is 62:6
he was dying, made *m*..... Heb 11:22

MERCHANDISE
perceives that her *m*........Prov 31:18
house a house of *m*......... John 2:16

MERCHANTS

set it in a city of *m* .... Ezek 17:4
have multiplied your *m*.... Nah 3:16
m were the great men...... Rev 18:23

MERCIES

for His *m* are great......... 2 Sa 24:14
And His tender *m*..........Ps 145:9
give you the sure m........ Acts 13:34
the Father of *m*.............. 2 Co 1:3

MERCIFUL

the LORD God, *m*.......... Ex 34:6
He is ever *m*...................Ps 37:26
God be *m* to us and........Ps 67:1
Blessed are the *m*.......... Matt 5:7
saying, 'God be *m*..........Luke 18:13
For I will be m..............Heb 8:12
compassionate and *m*.......Jas 5:11

MERCY

but showing *m* to........ Ex 20:6
and abundant in *m*..........Num 14:18
m endures forever...........1 Ch 16:34
to Your *m* remember me. Ps 25:7
I trust in the *m*..............Ps 52:8
shall send forth His *m*..... Ps 57:3
You, O Lord, belongs *m*..Ps 62:12
m ceased forever.............Ps 77:8
M and truth have met......Ps 85:10
M shall be built.............. Ps 89:2
M and truth go before..... Ps 89:14
m is everlasting.............. Ps 100:5
I will sing of *m*.............Ps 101:1
For Your *m* is great........ Ps 108:4
is full of Your *m*...........Ps 119:64
the LORD there is *m*........Ps 130:7
let not *m* and truth......... Prov 3:3
who honors Him has *m*....Prov 14:31
cruel and have no *m*........Jer 6:23
Lord our God belong *m*..Dan 9:9
For I desire *m* and not.... Hos 6:6
do justly, to love *m*........Mic 6:8
'*I desire m* and not.........Matt 9:13
And His *m* is on those.....Luke 1:50
"*I will have m*................ Rom 9:15
of God who shows *m*......Rom 9:16
that He might have *m*.....Rom 11:32
m has made trustworthy...1 Co 7:25
as we have received *m*....2 Co 4:1
God, who is rich in *m*..... Eph 2:4
but I obtained *m*.............1 Ti 1:13
him that he may find *m*.. 2 Ti 1:18
to His *m* He saved us..... Tit 3:5
that we may obtain *m*......Heb 4:16
judgment is without *m*.... Jas 2:13
God, looking for the *m*....Jude 21

MERRY

m heart makes a............Prov 15:13
eat, drink, and be *m*...... Eccl 8:15
that we should make *m*....Luke 15:32

MESSAGE

I have heard a *m*............Jer 49:14
For the *m* of the cross....1 Co 1:18

MESSENGER

is a faithful *m*.................Prov 25:13
"Behold, I send My *m*.....Mal 3:1
'*Behold, I send My m*....Matt 11:10

MESSIAH

until *M* the Prince...........Dan 9:25
"We have found the *M*...John 1:41

MIDST

God is in the *m*..............Ps 46:5
that I am in the *m*..........Joel 2:27
I am there in the *m*........Matt 18:20

MIGHT

'My power and the *m*...... Deut 8:17
shall speak of the *m*....... Ps 145:6
the greatness of His *m*....Is 40:26
man glory in his *m*..........Jer 9:23
their *m* has failed............Jer 51:30
'Not by *m* nor by...........Zech 4:6
in the power of His *m*..... Eph 6:10
greater in power and *m*...2 Pe 2:11
honor and power and *m*...Rev 7:12

MIGHTIER

coming after me is *m*.......Matt 3:11

MIGHTILY

to shake the earth *m*....... Is 2:19
which works in me *m*...... Col 1:29

MIGHTY

He was a *m* hunter......... Gen 10:9
for they are too *m*...... Num 22:6
How the *m* have fallen.... 2 Sa 1:19
is wise in heart and *m*.... Job 9:4
The LORD *m* in battle.....Ps 24:8
their Redeemer is *m*........Prov 23:11
Woe to men *m* at........... Is 5:22
great in counsel and *m*...Jer 32:19
m men are made red.......Nah 2:3
m has done great...........Luke 1:49
He has put down the *m*... Luke 1:52
the flesh, not many *m*......1 Co 1:26
the working of His *m*...... Eph 1:19
from heaven with His *m*...2 Th 1:7

MILK

for water, she gave *m*......Judg 5:25
honey and *m* are under....Song 4:11
come, buy wine and *m*.....Is 55:1
and whiter than *m*...........Lam 4:7
shall flow with *m*...........Joel 3:18
have come to need *m*...... Heb 5:12
m is unskilled in the........Heb 5:13
desire the pure *m*............1 Pe 2:2

MILL

be grinding at the *m*.......Matt 24:41

MILLSTONE

m were hung around his...Matt 18:6
a stone like a great *m*...... Rev 18:21

MIND

put wisdom in the *m*....... Job 38:36
perfect peace, whose *m*....Is 26:3
nor have an anxious *m*....Luke 12:29
m I myself serve the.......Rom 7:25
who has known the m......Rom 11:34
Be of the same *m*.......... Rom 12:16
convinced in his own *m*....Rom 14:5
"*Who has known the m*....1 Co 2:16
you are out of your *m*..... 1 Co 14:23
Let this *m* be in you........Phil 2:5
to *m* your own............. 1 Th 4:11
love and of a sound *m*.....2 Ti 1:7

MINDFUL

is man that You are *m*.....Ps 8:4
The LORD has been *m*....Ps 115:12
for you are not *m*..........Matt 16:23
is man that You are m.....Heb 2:6

MINDS

people change their *m*..... Ex 13:17
put My law in their *m*.... Jer 31:33
I stir up your pure *m*.......2 Pe 3:1
He who searches the *m*....Rev 2:23

MINISTER

to make you a *m*............ Acts 26:16
for he is God's *m*...........Rom 13:4
you will be a good *m*.......1 Ti 4:6
a *M* of the sanctuary....... Heb 8:2

MINISTERED

But the child *m*..............1 Sa 2:11
a thousand thousands *m*...Dan 7:10
As they *m* to the Lord.....Acts 13:2

MINISTERS

angels spirits, His *m*........Ps 104:4
for they are God's *m*.......Rom 13:6
commend ourselves as *m*..2 Co 6:4
Are they *m* of Christ.......2 Co 11:23
If anyone *m*...................1 Pe 4:11

MINISTRIES

are differences of *m*........ 1 Co 12:5

MINISTRY

I magnify my *m*............Rom 11:13
But if the *m* of death...... 2 Co 3:7
since we have this *m*....... 2 Co 4:1
and has given us the *m*...2 Co 5:18
for the work of *m*..........Eph 4:12
m which you have...........Col 4:17
fulfill your *m*..................2 Ti 4:5
a more excellent *m*..........Heb 8:6

MINT

For you pay tithe of *m*.... Matt 23:23

MIRACLE

saying, 'Show a *m*..........Ex 7:9
no one who works a *m*.... Mark 9:39
that a notable *m*............. Acts 4:16

MIRACLES

is a sinner do such *m*.......John 9:16
God worked unusual *m*....Acts 19:11
the working of *m*............ 1 Co 12:10
Are all workers of *m*.......1 Co 12:29
with various *m*................Heb 2:4

MIRTH

I will test you with *m*...... Eccl 2:1
is in the house of *m*........ Eccl 7:4
joy is darkened, the *m*.....Is 24:11

MISER

eat the bread of a *m*....... Prov 23:6

MISERIES

m that are coming...........Jas 5:1

MISERY

would forget your *m*........Job 11:16
and remember his *m*........Prov 31:7

MISTREATED

But the Egyptians *m*........Deut 26:6
and those who are *m*.......Heb 13:3

MITES

widow putting in two *m*... Luke 21:2

MOAN

m sadly like doves...........Is 59:11

MOCK

I will *m* when your..........Prov 1:26
Fools *m* at sin................ Prov 14:9
to the Gentiles to *m*........Matt 20:19

MOCKED

at noon, that Elijah *m*..... 1 Ki 18:27
"I am one *m* by his.........Job 12:4
knee before Him and *m*...Matt 27:29
deceived, God is not *m*....Gal 6:7

MOCKER

Wine is a *m*................... Prov 20:1

MOCKERS

that there would be *m*..... Jude 18

MOCKINGS

others had trial of *m*...... Heb 11:36

MOCKS

He who *m* the poor........Prov 17:5

MODERATION

with propriety and *m*.......1 Ti 2:9

MOMENT

consume them in a *m*...... Num 16:21
In a *m* they die.............. Job 34:20
face from you for a *m*..... Is 54:8
in a *m*, in the.................1 Co 15:52
which is but for a *m*........2 Co 4:17

MONEY

does not put out his *m*.....Ps 15:5
m answers every............. Eccl 10:19
be redeemed without *m*... Is 52:3
and you who have no *m*...Is 55:1
and hid his lord's *m*........ Matt 25:18
promised to give him *m*... Mark 14:11
"Carry neither *m*........... Luke 10:4
I sent you without *m*...... Luke 22:35
be purchased with *m*....... Acts 8:20
not greedy for *m*...........1 Ti 3:3
m is a root of all............ 1 Ti 6:10
not greedy for *m*.............Tit 1:7

MONEYCHANGERS

the tables of the *m*.........Matt 21:12
m doing business............John 2:14

MONSTER

me up like a *m*.............Jer 51:34
of Egypt, o great *m*........Ezek 29:3

MOON

Until the *m* is no more.... Ps 72:7
morning, fair as the *m*..... Song 6:10
sun and *m* grow dark.......Joel 2:10
m will not give its.......... Mark 13:24

MORNING

the eyelids of the *m*........ Job 41:18
Evening and *m* and at..... Ps 55:17
the wings of the *m*.......... Ps 139:9
looks forth as the *m*........ Song 6:10
Lucifer, son of the *m*....... Is 14:12
established as the *m*........ Hos 6:3
very early in the *m*..........Luke 24:1
the Bright and *M* Star..... Rev 22:16

MORSEL

or eaten my *m* by........... Job 31:17
Better is a dry *m*............ Prov 17:1
Esau, who for one *m*....... Heb 12:16

MORTAL

sin reign in your *m*.........Rom 6:12
and this *m* must put........ 1 Co 15:53

MORTALITY

m may be swallowed....... 2 Co 5:4

MORTALS

with idolatrous *m*............ Ps 26:4

MOST

His mouth is *m* sweet...... Song 5:16
on your *m* holy faith....... Jude 20

MOTH

m will eat them.............. Is 50:9
where *m* and rust............Matt 6:19

MOTHER

because she was the *m*..... Gen 3:20
Like a joyful *m*.............. Ps 113:9
the only one of her *m*......Song 6:9
m might have been my.... Jer 20:17
leave *his father and m*..... Matt 19:5
"Behold your *m*............John 19:27
free, which is the *m*......... Gal 4:26
the *m* of harlots.............Rev 17:5

MOUNT

come up to *M* Sinai.........Ex 19:23
you like *M* Carmel..........Song 7:5
they shall *m* up with.......Is 40:31
for this Hagar is *M*.......... Gal 4:25

MOUNTAIN

to Horeb, the *m*............. Ex 3:1
"But as a *m* falls............ Job 14:18
You have made my *m*..... Ps 30:7
of many peaks is the *m*...Ps 68:15
let us go up to the *m*...... Is 2:3
image became a great *m*.. Dan 2:35
Who are you, O great *m*..Zech 4:7
you will say to this *m*...... Matt 17:20
with Him on the holy *m*...2 Pe 1:18

MOUNTAINS

He removes the *m*.......... Job 9:5
Surely the *m* yield...........Job 40:20
m will bring peace..........Ps 72:3
excellent Than the *m*.......Ps 76:4
m were brought forth...... Ps 90:2
m melt like wax at the..... Ps 97:5
m skipped like rams........ Ps 114:4
m surround Jerusalem..... Ps 125:2
m shall depart and the...... Is 54:10
in Judea flee to the *m*..... Matt 24:16
that I could remove *m*..... 1 Co 13:2
m were not found........... Rev 16:20

MOURN

and you *m* at last........... Prov 5:11
a time to *m*.....................Eccl 3:4
are those who *m*............Matt 5:4
Lament and *m* and weep..Jas 4:9
of the earth will *m*.......... Rev 1:7

MOURNED

we *m* to you.................. Matt 11:17
and have not rather *m*..... 1 Co 5:2

MOURNING

This is a grievous *m*........ Gen 50:11
m all the day long..........Ps 38:6
m shall be ended............ Is 60:20
men break bread in *m*..... Jer 16:7
I will turn their *m*...........Jer 31:13

MORTAL

shall be a great *m*.......... Zech 12:11
be turned to *m* and........ Jas 4:9

MOURNS

heavily, as one who *m*..... Ps 35:14
The earth *m* and fades.....Is 24:4
for Him as one *m*........... Zech 12:10

MOUTH

Who has made man's *m*...Ex 4:11
Out of the *m* of babes..... Ps 8:2
The *m* of the righteous.... Ps 37:30
m shall speak wisdom..... Ps 49:3
iniquity stops its *m*.........Ps 107:42
knowledge, but the *m*...... Prov 10:14
m preserves his life......... Prov 13:3
The *m* of an immoral...... Prov 22:14
and a flattering *m*........... Prov 26:28
m speaking pompous...... Dan 7:8
the doors of your *m*....... Mic 7:5
m defiles a man.............. Matt 15:11
m I will judge you......... Luke 19:22
I will give you a *m*.........Luke 21:15
m confession is made......Rom 10:10
m great swelling words.....Jude 16
spew you out of My *m*.....Rev 3:16

MOVE

and the earth will *m*........Is 13:13
the mountain shall *m*....... Zech 14:4
in Him we live and *m*......Acts 17:28

MOVED

shall never be *m*............. Ps 15:5
she shall not be *m*.......... Ps 46:5
spoke as they were *m*...... 2 Pe 1:21

MUCH

m study is.....................Eccl 12:12
m better than wine is.......Song 4:10
to whom *m* is given.........Luke 12:48
M more then.................. Rom 5:9

MULTIPLIED

sorrows shall be *m*.......... Ps 16:4
of the disciples *m*............Acts 6:7
word of God grew and *m*. Acts 12:24

MULTIPLY

"Be fruitful and *m*.......... Gen 1:22
m your descendants........Gen 16:10
m my days as the........... Job 29:18
m the descendants..........Jer 33:22

MULTITUDE

stars of heaven in *m*........Deut 1:10
Your house in the *m*........ Ps 5:7
m that kept a pilgrim......Ps 42:4
In the *m* of words sin...... Prov 10:19
In a *m* of people is a.......Prov 14:28
compassion on the *m*......Matt 15:32
with the angel a *m*..........Luke 2:13
"*love will cover a m*........ 1 Pe 4:8
and behold, a great *m*..... Rev 7:9

MURDER

"You shall not *m*............Ex 20:13
'You shall not *m*............Matt 5:21
threats and *m* against.......Acts 9:1
You *m* and covet and......Jas 4:2

MURDERED

sons of those who *m*........Matt 23:31
up Jesus whom you *m*..... Acts 5:30
one and *m* his brother..... 1 Jn 3:12

MURDERER
He was a *m* from the...... John 8:44
and asked for a *m*...........Acts 3:14
of you suffer as a *m*........ 1 Pe 4:15
his brother is a *m*........... 1 Jn 3:15

MURDERERS
in it, but now *m*............ Is 1:21
and profane, for *m*..........1 Ti 1:9
abominable, *m*................Rev 21:8

MURDERS
evil thoughts, *m*..............Matt 15:19
envy, *m*.......................Gal 5:21

MURMURED
"and you *m* in your........Deut 1:27
But *m* in their tents.........Ps 106:25
as some of them also *m*... 1 Co 10:10

MURMURERS
These are *m*...................Jude 16

MURMURING
all things without *m*.........Phil 2:14

MUSIC
So David played *m*...........1 Sa 18:10
m are brought low.......... Eccl 12:4
the house, he heard *m*.....Luke 15:25

MUSING
While I was *m*................Ps 39:3

MUTE
Or who makes the *m*.......Ex 4:11
m who does not open...... Ps 38:13
I was *m* with silence........Ps 39:2
I was *m*......................Ps 39:9

MUTILATION
beware of the *m*............ Phil 3:2

MUZZLE
"You shall not *m*........ Deut 25:4
" *You shall not m*............1 Ti 5:18

MYSTERIES
to you to know the *m*......Matt 13:11
and understand all *m*.......1 Co 13:2
the spirit he speaks *m*......1 Co 14:2

MYSTERIOUS
today, it is not too *m*...... Deut 30:11

MYSTERY
given to know the *m*....... Mark 4:11
wisdom of God in a *m*....1 Co 2:7
Behold, I tell you a *m*....1 Co 15:51
made known to us the *m*..Eph 1:9
This is a great *m*...........Eph 5:32
m which has been.......... Col 1:26
the *m* of godliness...........1 Ti 3:16

— N —

NAILED
n it to the cross..............Col 2:14

NAKED
And they were both *n*..... Gen 2:25
knew that they were *n*...... Gen 3:7
N I came from my.........Job 1:21
Isaiah has walked *n*.........Is 20:3
'I was *n* and you............Matt 25:36
and fled from them *n*..... Mark 14:52

shall not be found *n*....... 2 Co 5:3
but all things are *n*.........Heb 4:13
brother or sister is *n*........Jas 2:15
poor, blind, and *n*...........Rev 3:17

NAKEDNESS
of Canaan, saw the *n*.......Gen 9:22
or famine, or *n*...............Rom 8:35
often, in cold and *n*.........2 Co 11:27
n may not be revealed..... Rev 3:18

NAME
Abram called on the *n*.....Gen 13:4
Israel shall be your *n*.......Gen 35:10
This is My *n* forever........Ex 3:15
shall not take the *n*......... Ex 20:7
are called by the *n*..........Deut 28:10
glorious and awesome *n*...Deut 28:58
by My *n* will humble.......2 Ch 7:14
and he has no *n*.............Job 18:17
excellent is Your *n*..........Ps 8:1
n will put their trust........Ps 9:10
be His glorious *n*............Ps 72:19
n is great in Israel...........Ps 76:1
do not call on Your *n*......Ps 79:6
to Your *n* give glory........Ps 115:1
above all Your *n*............Ps 138:2
He calls them all by *n*...... Ps 147:4
The *n* of the LORD is a...Prov 18:10
A good *n* is to be...........Prov 22:1
what is His Son's *n*......... Prov 30:4
make mention of Your *n*..Is 26:13
the LORD, that is My *n*..Is 42:8
be to the LORD for a *n*...Is 55:13
be called by a new *n*...... Is 62:2
Everlasting is Your *n*.......Is 63:16
who calls on Your *n*........Is 64:7
it shall be to Me a *n*...... Jer 33:9
and made Yourself a *n*.... Dan 9:15
we will walk in the *n*.......Mic 4:5
They will call on My *n*.....Zech 13:9
n shall be great..............Mal 1:11
to you who fear My *n*......Mal 4:2
you shall call His *n*......... Matt 1:21
hallowed be Your *n*.........Matt 6:9
prophesied in Your *n*.......Matt 7:22
righteous man in the *n*.....Matt 10:41
n Gentiles will trust........Matt 12:21
together in My *n*............Matt 18:20
many will come in My *n*.. Matt 24:5
"My *n* is Legion.............Mark 5:9
The virgin's *n* was...........Luke 1:27
"His *n* is John.................Luke 1:63
and cast out your *n*........Luke 6:22
who believe in His *n*....... John 1:12
comes in his own *n*.........John 5:43
his own sheep by *n*........ John 10:3
through faith in His *n*......Acts 3:16
there is no other *n*..........Acts 4:12
suffer shame for His *n*.....Acts 5:41
which is above every *n*.....Phil 2:9
deed, do all in the *n*........Col 3:17
a more excellent *n*.......... Heb 1:4
blaspheme that noble *n*....Jas 2:7
reproached for the *n*........1 Pe 4:14
you hold fast to My *n*......Rev 2:13
n that you are alive..........Rev 3:1
having His Father's *n*......Rev 14:1
and glorify Your *n*......... Rev 15:4
n written that no one.......Rev 19:12

NAME'S
saved them for His *n*...... Ps 106:8
forgiven you for His *n*..... 1 Jn 2:12

NAMED
let my name be *n*...........Gen 48:16
I have *n* you.................. Is 45:4

NARROW
"Enter by the *n* gate....... Matt 7:13
n is the gate and............Matt 7:14

NATION
make you a great *n*........ Gen 12:2
You slay a righteous *n*.....Gen 20:4
priests and a holy *n*.........Ex 19:6
dealt thus with any *n*.......Ps 147:20
exalts a *n*.....................Prov 14:34
up sword against *n*..........Is 2:4
that the righteous *n*.........Is 26:2
a small one a strong *n*..... Is 60:22
n that was not called....... Is 65:1
n changed its gods..........Jer 2:11
I will make them one *n*....Ezek 37:22
since there was a *n*..........Dan 12:1
n will rise against............Matt 24:7
for he loves our *n*...........Luke 7:5
those who are not a n......Rom 10:19
tribe, tongue, and *n*........ Rev 13:7

NATIONS
itself among the *n*...........Num 23:9
Why do the *n* rage.........Ps 2:1
I will give You The *n*.......Ps 2:8
n shall serve Him............Ps 72:11
n shall call Him..............Ps 72:17
n shall fear the name.......Ps 102:15
is high above all *n*...........Ps 113:4
All *n* before Him are........Is 40:17
n who do not know......... Is 55:5
the wise men of the *n*......Jer 10:7
n shall be joined.............Zech 2:11
disciples of all the *n*........ Matt 28:19
who was to rule all *n*.......Rev 12:5
the healing of the *n*.........Rev 22:2

NATURAL
women exchanged the *n*...Rom 1:26
the men, leaving the *n*..... Rom 1:27
did not spare the *n*..........Rom 11:21
n man does not receive....1 Co 2:14
It is sown a *n* body.........1 Co 15:44
not first, but the *n*..........1 Co 15:46

NATURE
for what is against *n*........Rom 1:26
n itself teach you............ 1 Co 11:14
We who are Jews by *n*.....Gal 2:15
n children of wrath..........Eph 2:3
of the divine *n*................2 Pe 1:4

NEAR
that has God so *n*...........Deut 4:7
But the word is very *n*.....Deut 30:14
The LORD is *n* to all...... Ps 145:18
upon Him while He is *n*...Is 55:6
know that it is *n*.............Matt 24:33
kingdom of God is *n*.......Luke 21:31
"*The word is n*...............Rom 10:8
to those who were *n*........Eph 2:17
for the time is *n*............. Rev 1:3

NEARER
now our salvation is *n*......Rom 13:11

NECESSARY
mouth more than my *n*....Job 23:12
and thus it was *n*............Luke 24:46
burden than these *n*........ Acts 15:28
I found it *n* to write........Jude 3

NECESSITIES

have provided for my *n*....Acts 20:34
and again for my *n*.........Phil 4:16

NECESSITY

n is laid upon me............1 Co 9:16
not grudgingly or of *n*......2 Co 9:7

NECK

smooth part of his *n*........Gen 27:16
and grace to your *n*......Prov 3:22
n was an iron sinew.........Is 48:4
were hung around his *n*... Matt 18:6
ran and fell on his *n*........Luke 15:20

NECKS

stiffened their *n*.............Neh 9:29
with outstretched *n*......Is 3:16
who risked their own *n*.... Rom 16:4

NEED

in nakedness, and in *n*.....Deut 28:48
the things you have *n*..... Matt 6:8
'The Lord has *n*.............Matt 21:3
each as anyone had *n*..... Acts 4:35
hand, "I have no *n*........ 1 Co 12:21
who ministered to my *n*.. Phil 2:25
supply all your *n*.............Phil 4:19
to help in time of *n*........Heb 4:16
sees his brother in *n*........1 Jn 3:17
And the city had no *n*.... Rev 21:23

NEEDY

your poor and your *n*...... Deut 15:11
They push the *n*............Job 24:4
n shall not always be....... Ps 9:18
He will deliver the *n*...... Ps 72:12
And lifts the *n*...........Ps 113:7
to rob the *n* of.............. Is 10:2
n will lie down in............Is 14:30
a strength to the *n*......... Is 25:4

NEGLECT

n the gift that is..............1 Ti 4:14
if we *n* so great a...........Heb 2:3

NEGLECTED

n the weightier............ Matt 23:23
their widows were *n*........ Acts 6:1

NEIGHBOR

you shall love your *n*.......Lev 19:18
For better is a *n*............ Prov 27:10
every man teach his *n*......Jer 31:34
gives drink to his *n*...... Hab 2:15
You shall love your *n*...... Matt 5:43
And who is my *n*...........Luke 10:29
You shall love your *n*...... Rom 13:9

NEST

and make its *n*............. Job 39:27
n is a man who wanders...Prov 27:8
though you set your *n*.....Obad 4
that he may set his *n*.......Hab 2:9

NET

me with His *n*.............Job 19:6
have hidden their *n*........Ps 35:7
They have prepared a *n*..Ps 57:6
an antelope in a *n*...........Is 51:20
catch them in their *n*...... Hab 1:15
I will let down the *n*........Luke 5:5
to them, "Cast the *n*....... John 21:6

NEVER

in Me shall *n* thirst.........John 6:35
in Me shall *n* die............ John 11:26

Love *n* fails....................1 Co 13:8
n take away sins............ Heb 10:11
"*I* will *n* leave you......... Heb 13:5
for prophecy *n* came by... 2 Pe 1:21

NEW

Now there arose a *n*........Ex 1:8
the LORD creates a *n*.....Num 16:30
They chose *n* gods.......... Judg 5:8
and there is nothing *n*......Eccl 1:9
Behold, I will do a *n*......Is 43:19
For behold, I create *n*.... Is 65:17
when I will make a *n*......Jer 31:31
n every morning............. Lam 3:23
wine into *n* wineskins...... Matt 9:17
of the *n* covenant...........Matt 26:28
n commandment I give.... John 13:34
tell or to hear some *n*......Acts 17:21
he is a *n* creation............2 Co 5:17
n man who is renewed.....Col 3:10
when *I* will make a *n*......Heb 8:8
n heavens and a *n*..........2 Pe 3:13
n name written which...... Rev 2:17
And they sang a *n*.......... Rev 5:9
And I saw a *n* heaven..... Rev 21:1
I make all things *n*..........Rev 21:5

NEWNESS

also should walk in *n*.......Rom 6:4
should serve in the *n*....... Rom 7:6

NEWS

soul, so is good *n*............Prov 25:25
him who brings good *n*.... Is 52:7

NIGHT

darkness He called *N*......Gen 1:5
It is a *n* of solemn.......... Ex 12:42
pillar of fire by *n*........... Ex 13:22
and the *n* be ended........Job 7:4
gives songs in the *n*........Job 35:10
n reveals.......................Ps 19:2
awake through the *n*.......Ps 119:148
and stars to rule by *n*...... Ps 136:9
desired You in the *n*........ Is 26:9
and perished in a *n*......... Jon 4:10
and continued all *n*......... Luke 6:12
man came to Jesus by *n*...John 3:2
n is coming when no....... John 9:4
came to Jesus by *n*.........John 19:39
The *n* is far spent........... Rom 13:12
as a thief in the *n*...........1 Th 5:2
We are not of the *n*........1 Th 5:5
there shall be no *n*..........Rev 21:25
there shall be no *n*.........Rev 22:5

NINE

where are the *n*..............Luke 17:17

NINETY-NINE

he not leave the *n*...........Matt 18:12
n just persons................Luke 15:7

NOBLE

whatever things are *n*...... Phil 4:8
not blaspheme that *n*......Jas 2:7

NOBLES

voice of *n* was hushed......Job 29:10
king is the son of *n*.........Eccl 10:17
n have sent their lads...... Jer 14:3
your *n* rest in the............Nah 3:18

NOISE

The *n* of a multitude....... Is 13:4
people who make a *n*...... Is 17:12

of Egypt, is but a *n*........Jer 46:17
They have made a *n*........Lam 2:7
away with a great *n*........2 Pe 3:10

NOSTRILS

n the breath of life..........Gen 2:7
breath of God in my *n*.....Job 27:3
breath is in his *n*.............Is 2:22

NOTHING

For now you are *n*..........Job 6:21
rich, yet has *n*................ Prov 13:7
"It is good for *n*.............Prov 20:14
before Him are as *n*........Is 40:17
their works are *n*............ Is 41:29
I can of Myself do *n*.......John 5:30
Me you can do *n*............John 15:5
men, it will come to *n*..... Acts 5:38
n the things that............1 Co 1:28
For I know *n* against.......1 Co 4:4
have not love, I am *n*......1 Co 13:2
love, it profits me *n*........ 1 Co 13:3
Be anxious for *n*............Phil 4:6
For we brought *n*............1 Ti 6:7
complete, lacking *n*......... Jas 1:4
name's sake, taking *n*...... 3 Jn 7

NOTORIOUS

n prisoner called............ Matt 27:16

NOURISHED

"I have *n* and................Is 1:2
n and knit together........ Col 2:19
n in the words of...........1 Ti 4:6

NOURISHES

n and cherishes it...........Eph 5:29

NUMBER

if a man could *n*............ Gen 13:16
that I may know the *n*....2 Sa 24:2
things without *n*.............Job 5:9
For now You *n* my steps..Job 14:16
n the clouds by wisdom....Job 38:37
teach us to *n* our days..... Ps 90:12
He counts the *n*.............Ps 147:4
which no one could *n*...... Rev 7:9
His *n* is 666................. Rev 13:18

NUMBERED

are more than can be *n*....Ps 40:5
God has *n* your kingdom..Dan 5:26
'And He was *n* with....... Luke 22:37

— O —

OAKS

Wail, O *o* of Bashan....... Zech 11:2

OARSMEN

o brought you into.......... Ezek 27:26

OATH

people feared the *o*.........1 Sa 14:26
for the sake of your *o*......Eccl 8:2
I may establish the *o*...... Jer 11:5
And you shall be an *o*.....Jer 42:18
he denied with an *o*........ Matt 26:72
o which He swore.......... Luke 1:73
themselves under an *o*..... Acts 23:12

OATHS

shall perform your o........Matt 5:33
because of the o............. Matt 14:9

OBEDIENCE

and apostleship for o....... Rom 1:5
o many will be made....... Rom 5:19
captivity to the o............ 2 Co 10:5
confidence in your o........Phm 21
yet He learned o............Heb 5:8
for o and sprinkling.........1 Pe 1:2

OBEDIENT

you are willing and o.......Is 1:19
of the priests were o........Acts 6:7
to make the Gentiles o.... Rom 15:18
Servants, be o to............ Eph 6:5
Himself and became o..... Phil 2:8
homemakers, good, o...... Tit 2:5
as o children.................. 1 Pe 1:14

OBEY

LORD, that I should o.....Ex 5:2
God and o His voice....... Deut 4:30
o the commandments.......Deut 11:27
His voice we will o..........Josh 24:24
o is better than...............1 Sa 15:22
they hear of me they o.... Ps 18:44
if you diligently o...........Zech 6:15
o God rather than...........Acts 5:29
and do not o the truth..... Rom 2:8
yourselves slaves to o.... Rom 6:16
o your parents in all.......Col 3:20
Servants, o in all...........Col 3:22
on those who do not o.....2 Th 1:8
O those who rule...........Heb 13:17
if some do not o.............1 Pe 3:1

OBEYED

of sin, yet you o............. Rom 6:17
they have not all o.......... Rom 10:16
By faith Abraham o........ Heb 11:8
as Sarah o Abraham........1 Pe 3:6

OBEYING

o the truth through......... 1 Pe 1:22

OBSERVANCE

the LORD, a solemn o.....Ex 12:42

OBSERVATION

does not come with o...... Luke 17:20

OBSERVE

man, and o the upright.... Ps 37:37
and let your eyes o......... Prov 23:26
o mercy and justice......... Hos 12:6
o all things that.............. Matt 28:20
o days and months and.... Gal 4:10
o your chaste conduct...... 1 Pe 3:2

OBSERVED

all these I have o............Mark 10:20

OBSERVES

o the wind will not..........Eccl 11:4
He who o the day..........Rom 14:6

OBSERVING

o his natural face............Jas 1:23

OBSOLETE

Now what is becoming o.. Heb 8:13

OBSTINATE

and made his heart o.......Deut 2:30
I knew that you were o....Is 48:4

OBTAIN

They shall o joy and........Is 35:10
you they also may o........ Rom 11:31
o salvation through.........1 Th 5:9
and covet and cannot o....Jas 4:2

OBTAINED

o a part in this................ Acts 1:17
to God, yet have now o... Rom 11:30
endured, he o the........... Heb 6:15
To those who have o.......2 Pe 1:1

OBTAINS

o favor from the LORD... Prov 8:35

OFFEND

I will o no more............. Job 34:31
that devour him will o..... Jer 2:3
lest we o them.................Matt 17:27
than that he should o...... Luke 17:2
them, "Does this o..........John 6:61

OFFENDED

So they were o at Him.... Matt 13:57
stumbles or is o.............. Rom 14:21

OFFENDER

who make a man an o..... Is 29:21
"For if I am an o............Acts 25:11

OFFENSE

and a rock of o.............. Is 8:14
You are an o to Me........ Matt 16:23
by the one man's o.......... Rom 5:17
Give no o......................1 Co 10:32
the o of the cross............Gal 5:11
sincere and without o...... Phil 1:10
and a rock of o...............1 Pe 2:8

OFFENSES

For o must come............ Matt 18:7
impossible that no o........ Luke 17:1
up because of our o........ Rom 4:25

OFFER

o the blind as a.............. Mal 1:8
come and o your gift....... Matt 5:24
let us continually o..........Heb 13:15

OFFERED

to eat those things o........1 Co 8:10
the eternal Spirit o..........Heb 9:14
so Christ was o..............Heb 9:28
o one sacrifice............... Heb 10:12
By faith Abel o.............. Heb 11:4

OFFERING

you shall bring your o......Lev 1:2
o You did not require......Ps 40:6
You make His soul an o.. Is 53:10
to the LORD an o............Mal 3:3
Himself for us, an o........Eph 5:2
out as a drink o..............Phil 2:17
o You did not............... Heb 10:5
o He has perfected.......... Heb 10:14
is no longer an o............ Heb 10:18

OFFERINGS

and offered burnt o.........Gen 8:20
He remember all your o...Ps 20:3
In burnt o and...............Heb 10:6

OFFICE

let another take his o...... Ps 109:8
sitting at the tax o...........Matt 9:9

OFFICERS

also make your o............ Is 60:17

OFFSCOURING

You have made us an o... Lam 3:45
the o of all things........... 1 Co 4:13

OFFSPRING

My blessing on your o..... Is 44:3
He seeks godly o............ Mal 2:15
wife and raise up o......... Matt 22:24
For we are also His o...... Acts 17:28
am the Root and the O... Rev 22:16

OFTEN

o I wanted to gather........Luke 13:34
as o as you eat this........ 1 Co 11:26
in sleeplessness............. 2 Co 11:27
should offer Himself o..... Heb 9:25

OIL

for the anointing o.......... Ex 25:6
I cease giving my o......... Judg 9:9
a bin, and a little o......... 1 Ki 17:12
poured out rivers of o......Job 29:6
anointed with fresh o...... Ps 92:10
the heart of man, O........Ps 104:15
like the precious o.......... Ps 133:2
be as excellent o.............Ps 141:5
thousand rivers of o........ Mic 6:7
very costly fragrant o.......Matt 26:7
o might have been sold....Matt 26:9
anointing him with o....... Jas 5:14
and do not harm the o.....Rev 6:6

OINTMENT

O and perfume delight.....Prov 27:9
your name is o...............Song 1:3

OLD

young, and now am o......Ps 37:25
all manner, new and o.....Song 7:13
was said to those of o......Matt 5:21
yet fifty years o..............John 8:57
but when you are o......... John 21:18
your o men shall dream.. Acts 2:17
o man was crucified........Rom 6:6
of the O Testament........2 Co 3:14
o things have passed........2 Co 5:17
have put off the o man....Col 3:9
obsolete and growing o.... Heb 8:13
that serpent of o............. Rev 20:2

OLDER

o shall serve the............. Gen 25:23
o than your father..........Job 15:10
"Now his o son was........ Luke 15:25
not rebuke an o man........1 Ti 5:1
o women as mothers........1 Ti 5:2

OLDEST

beginning with the o........John 8:9

OLIVE

a freshly plucked o.........Gen 8:11
I am like a green o......... Ps 52:8
of the o may fail............Hab 3:17
o tree which is wild........Rom 11:24

OMNIPOTENT

For the Lord God O....... Rev 19:6

ONCE

died, He died to sin *o*..... Rom 6:10
for men to die *o*............ Heb 9:27
also suffered *o*............... 1 Pe 3:18

ONE

God may speak in *o* way..Job 33:14
Two are better than *o*......Eccl 4:9
you will be gathered *o*..... Is 27:12
O thing you lack............Mark 10:21
o thing is needed........... Luke 10:42
and My Father are *o*...... John 10:30
Me, that they may be *o*... John 17:11
o accord in the temple..... Acts 2:46
for you are all *o*.............. Gal 3:28
to create in Himself *o*...... Eph 2:15
There is *o* body and........ Eph 4:4
o body and *o* Spirit......... Eph 4:4
o hope of your calling.....Eph 4:4
o Lord........................... Eph 4:5
o faith.......................... Eph 4:5
o baptism...................... Eph 4:5
o God and Father of...... Eph 4:6
For there is *o* God and.... 1 Ti 2:5
o Mediator between God. 1 Ti 2:5
the husband of *o* wife.... 1 Ti 3:2
a thousand years as *o*...... 2 Pe 3:8
and these three are *o*....... 1 Jn 5:7

OPEN

o His lips against you...... Job 11:5
You *o* Your hand............ Ps 104:28
O your mouth for the...... Prov 31:8
and no one shall *o*.......... Is 22:22
a lamb in *o* country......... Hos 4:16
Can a demon *o* the eyes.. John 10:21
our heart is wide *o*.......... 2 Co 6:11
things are naked and *o*.... Heb 4:13
o the scroll and to.......... Rev 5:2

OPENED

o not His mouth............ Is 53:7
Then their eyes were *o*.... Luke 24:31
o the Scriptures.............. Luke 24:32
o their understanding....... Luke 24:45
effective door has *o*........ 1 Co 16:9
when the Lamb *o*........... Rev 6:1
Then I saw heaven *o*....... Rev 19:11

OPENS

o the ears of men........... Job 33:16
The LORD *o* the eyes of.. Ps 146:8
him the doorkeeper *o*...... John 10:3
and shuts and no one o.... Rev 3:7

OPINION

dared not declare my *o*.... Job 32:6
be wise in your own *o*..... Rom 11:25

OPINIONS

falter between two *o*........ 1 Ki 18:21

OPPORTUNITY

But sin, taking *o*............ Rom 7:8
as we have *o*.................. Gal 6:10
but you lacked *o*............ Phil 4:10
they would have had *o*..... Heb 11:15

OPPOSES

who *o* and exalts............. 2 Th 2:4

OPPRESS

you shall not *o*.............. Lev 25:17
You that You should *o*.... Job 10:3
He does not *o*................ Job 37:23
he loves to *o*................. Hos 12:7

o the widow or the.......... Zech 7:10
Do not the rich *o*............ Jas 2:6

OPPRESSED

Whom have I *o*.............. 1 Sa 12:3
For he has *o* and........... Job 20:19
fatherless and the *o*......... Ps 10:18
for all who are *o*............ Ps 103:6
The tears of the *o*........... Eccl 4:1
He was *o* and He was...... Is 53:7
her midst, and the *o*........ Amos 3:9
healing all who were *o*..... Acts 10:38
Lot, who was *o* with........ 2 Pe 2:7

OPPRESSES

o the poor reproaches...... Prov 14:31
o the poor to increase...... Prov 22:16
A poor man who *o*......... Prov 28:3

OPPRESSION

have surely seen the *o*..... Ex 3:7
"For the *o* of the............ Ps 12:5
Do not trust in *o*............ Ps 62:10
their life from *o*............. Ps 72:14
brought low Through *o*.... Ps 107:39
Redeem me from the *o*.... Ps 119:134
considered all the *o*......... Eccl 4:1
o destroys a wise............ Eccl 7:7
justice, but behold, *o*....... Is 5:7
certainly seen the o......... Acts 7:34

OPPRESSIONS

of *o* they cry out............ Job 35:9

OPPRESSOR

the voice of the *o*........... Job 3:18
Do not envy the *o*.......... Prov 3:31
is a great *o*.................... Prov 28:16
of the fury of the *o*......... Is 51:13
No more shall an *o*......... Zech 9:8

OPPRESSORS

not leave me to my *o*...... Ps 119:121
o there was power........... Eccl 4:1

ORACLES

received the living *o*........ Acts 7:38
were committed the *o*...... Rom 3:2
principles of the *o*.......... Heb 5:12
let him speak as the *o*..... 1 Pe 4:11

ORDAINED

and infants You have *o*.... Ps 8:2
o you a prophet.............. Jer 1:5
the Man whom He has *o*..Acts 17:31

ORDER

'Set your house in *o*........ 2 Ki 20:1
set your words in *o*......... Job 33:5
you, And set them in *o*....Ps 50:21
swept, and put in *o*......... Matt 12:44
done decently and in *o*.... 1 Co 14:40
each one in his own *o*...... 1 Co 15:23
to see your good *o*.......... Col 2:5
according to the o........... Heb 5:6

ORDERS

o his conduct aright......... Ps 50:23

ORDINANCE

resists the *o* of God........ Rom 13:2
yourselves to every *o*....... 1 Pe 2:13

ORDINANCES

Do you know the *o*......... Job 38:33
"If those *o* depart........... Jer 31:36

not appointed the *o*......... Jer 33:25
gone away from My *o*...... Mal 3:7
and fleshly *o* imposed...... Heb 9:10

ORNAMENT

of gold and an *o*............. Prov 25:12
with them all as an *o*....... Is 49:18
the incorruptible *o*.......... 1 Pe 3:4

ORNAMENTS

will be graceful *o*........... Prov 1:9
a virgin forget her *o*........ Jer 2:32

ORPHANS

We have become *o*.......... Lam 5:3
I will not leave you *o*...... John 14:18
to visit *o* and widows....... Jas 1:27

OSTRICHES

o will dwell there........... Is 13:21
become cruel, like *o*........ Lam 4:3
a mourning like the *o*...... Mic 1:8

OUGHT

what Israel *o* to do.......... 1 Ch 12:32
These you *o* to have........ Matt 23:23
pray for as we *o*............. Rom 8:26
how you *o* to conduct...... 1 Ti 3:15
which they *o* not............. 1 Ti 5:13
persons *o* you to be......... 2 Pe 3:11

OUTCAST

they called you an *o*........ Jer 30:17

OUTCASTS

gathers together the *o*...... Ps 147:2
will assemble the *o*.......... Is 11:12
hide the *o*..................... Is 16:3
Let My *o* dwell with........ Is 16:4

OUTRAN

the other disciple *o*......... John 20:4

OUTSIDE

and dish, that the *o*......... Matt 23:26
Pharisees make the *o*....... Luke 11:39
toward those who are *o*... Col 4:5
to Him, *o* the camp........ Heb 13:13
But *o* are dogs and........ Rev 22:15

OUTSTRETCHED

and with an *o* arm.......... Deut 26:8
against you with an *o*...... Jer 21:5

OUTWARD

at the *o* appearance........ 1 Sa 16:7
your beauty be that *o*...... 1 Pe 3:3

OUTWARDLY

appear beautiful *o*........... Matt 23:27
not a Jew who is one *o*.... Rom 2:28

OUTWIT

The enemy shall not *o*..... Ps 89:22

OVEN

make them as a fiery *o*.... Ps 21:9
burning like an *o*............ Mal 4:1
is thrown into the *o*......... Matt 6:30

OVERCAME

My throne, as I also *o*..... Rev 3:21
"And they *o* him by........ Rev 12:11

OVERCOME
good cheer, I have *o*....... John 16:33
o evil with good..............Rom 12:21
because you have *o*......... 1 Jn 2:13
and the Lamb will *o*........ Rev 17:14

OVERCOMES
of God *o* the world......... 1 Jn 5:4
o I will give to eat.......... Rev 2:7
o shall not be hurt.......... Rev 2:11
o shall inherit all.............Rev 21:7

OVERFLOWING
My heart is *o* with a........Ps 45:1

OVERSEER
Then he made him *o*....... Gen 39:4
having no captain, *o*........Prov 6:7
to the Shepherd and *O*.... 1 Pe 2:25

OVERSEERS
Spirit has made you *o*......Acts 20:28
you, serving as *o*.............1 Pe 5:2

OVERSHADOW
of the Highest will *o*.....Luke 1:35

OVERTAKE
does righteousness *o*........ Is 59:9
you feared shall *o*........... Jer 42:16
and *o* this chariot............Acts 8:29
that this Day should *o*..... 1 Th 5:4

OVERTAKEN
No temptation has *o*........1 Co 10:13
if a man is *o* in any.........Gal 6:1

OVERTHREW
So He *o* those cities........ Gen 19:25
will be as when God *o*.....Is 13:19
As God *o* Sodom and......Jer 50:40
"I *o* some of you........... Amos 4:11

OVERTHROW
you shall utterly *o*...........Ex 23:24
o the righteous in............Prov 18:5
o the throne of............. Hag 2:22
o the faith of some........2 Ti 2:18

OVERTHROWN
Their judges are *o*...........Ps 141:6
of Sodom, which was *o*....Lam 4:6
I will make it *o*.............. Ezek 21:27
and Nineveh shall be *o*.... Jon 3:4

OVERTHROWS
and *o* the mighty............Job 12:19
o them in the night........ Job 34:25
o the words of the.......... Prov 22:12

OVERTURNED
my heart is *o* within........ Lam 1:20
o the tables of the...........Matt 21:12
money and *o* the tables....John 2:15

OVERWHELM
o the fatherless...............Job 6:27
sends them out, they *o*.... Job 12:15

OVERWHELMED
When my heart is *o*.....Ps 61:2
and my spirit was *o*......... Ps 77:3
o their enemies................Ps 78:53
waters would have *o*........Ps 124:4
my spirit is *o* within........ Ps 143:4

OVERWORK
Do not *o* to be rich.........Prov 23:4

OWE
'How much do you *o*.......Luke 16:5
O no one anything.......... Rom 13:8
o me even your own........Phm 19

OWED
o him ten thousand........ Matt 18:24
fellow servants who *o*...... Matt 18:28
o five hundred denarii..... Luke 7:41

OWN
He came to His *o*........... John 1:11
having loved His *o*.........John 13:1
world would love its *o*..... John 15:19
and you are not your *o*.... 1 Co 6:19
But each one has his *o*.... 1 Co 7:7
For all seek their *o*......... Phil 2:21
from our sins in His *o*..... Rev 1:5

OX
shall not muzzle an *o*.......Deut 25:4
"Will the wild *o*.............Job 39:9
you bind the wild *o*.........Job 39:10
like a young wild *o*......... Ps 29:6
exalted like a wild *o*........Ps 92:10
o knows its owner............Is 1:3
had the face of an *o*........Ezek 1:10
Sabbath loose his *o*......... Luke 13:15
shall not muzzle an o.......1 Co 9:9

— P —

PACE
are majestic in *p*.............Prov 30:29

PAILS
p are full of milk............ Job 21:24

PAIN
p you shall bring.............Gen 3:16
p as a woman in.............. Is 13:8
are filled with *p*.............. Is 21:3
before her *p* came...........Is 66:7
Why is my *p* perpetual.....Jer 15:18
shall be no more *p*.......... Rev 21:4

PAINED
My heart is severely *p*..... Ps 55:4
I am *p* in my very..........Jer 4:19

PAINFUL
this, It was too *p*........... Ps 73:16

PAINS
The *p* of death................ Ps 116:3
having loosed the *p*........ Acts 2:24
upon them, as labor *p*..... 1 Th 5:3

PAINT
· and she put *p* on her.......2 Ki 9:30
your eyes with *p*............. Jer 4:30

PAINTING
it with cedar and *p*..........Jer 22:14

PALACE
enter the King's *p*...........Ps 45:15
a *p* of foreigners............. Is 25:2
guards his own *p*............Luke 11:21
evident to the whole *p*.....Phil 1:13

PALACES
Out of the ivory *p*...........Ps 45:8
God is in her *p*...............Ps 48:3
has entered our *p*............Jer 9:21

PALE
his face now grow *p*........ Is 29:22
and all faces turned *p*......Jer 30:6
behold, a *p* horse............Rev 6:8

PALM
of water and seventy *p*.....Ex 15:27
p trees and went out....... John 12:13
p branches in their.......... Rev 7:9

PALMS
struck Him with the *p*......Matt 26:67

PANGS
The *p* of death............... Ps 18:4
P and sorrows will.......... Is 13:8
labors with birth *p*.......... Rom 8:22

PANICKED
the men of Benjamin *p*....Judg 20:41

PANT
They *p* after the dust.......Amos 2:7

PANTS
As the deer *p* for the...... Ps 42:1

PAPYRUS
"Can the *p* grow up........ Job 8:11

PARABLE
open my mouth in a *p*.....Ps 78:2
p He did not speak......... Matt 13:34
do You speak this *p*........ Luke 12:41

PARABLES
'Does he not speak *p*.......Ezek 20:49
understand all the *p*........ Mark 4:13
rest it is given in *p*.........Luke 8:10

PARADE
love does not *p*...............1 Co 13:4

PARADISE
will be with Me in *P*...... Luke 23:43
was caught up into *P*.......2 Co 12:4
in the midst of the *P*....... Rev 2:7

PARCHMENTS
especially the *p*...............2 Ti 4:13

PARDON
p your transgressions....... Ex 23:21
O LORD, *P* my iniquity...Ps 25:11
He will abundantly *p*...... Is 55:7
p all their iniquities........Jer 33:8

PARDONING
is a God like You, *p*....... Mic 7:18

PARENTS
will rise up against *p*....... Matt 10:21
has left house or *p*.......... Luke 18:29
disobedient to *p*.............Rom 1:30
to lay up for the *p*..........2 Co 12:14

PART
You have no *p* in the...... Josh 22:25
has chosen that good *p*.... Luke 10:42
you, you have no *p*......... John 13:8
For we know in *p*........... 1 Co 13:9

p has a believer..............2 Co 6:15
shall take away his *p*.......Rev 22:19

PARTAKE
for we all *p* of that..........1 Co 10:17
you cannot *p* of the.........1 Co 10:21

PARTAKER
And have been a *p*.........Ps 50:18
in hope should be *p*........1 Co 9:10
Christ, and also a *p*.........1 Pe 5:1

PARTAKERS
Gentiles have been *p*.......Rom 15:27
of the sacrifices *p*............1 Co 10:18
know that as you are *p*....2 Co 1:7
gospel, you all are *p*.......Phil 1:7
qualified us to be *p*.........Col 1:12
For we have become *p*....Heb 3:14

PARTED
them, that He was *p*.....Luke 24:51
so sharp that they *p*........Acts 15:39

PARTIAL
You shall not be *p*.........Lev 19:15

PARTIALITY
'You shall not show *p*......Deut 1:17
unjustly, And show *p*......Ps 82:2
is not good to show *p*......Prov 18:5
but have shown *p*............Mal 2:9
that God shows no *p*.......Acts 10:34
For there is no *p*............Rom 2:11
doing nothing with *p*.......1 Ti 5:21
but if you show *p*............Jas 2:9
good fruits, without *p*......Jas 3:17

PARTIES
revelries, drinking *p*........1 Pe 4:3

PARTITION
the Testimony, and *p*.......Ex 40:3

PARTNER
Whoever is a *p* with a.....Prov 29:24
you count me as a *p*........Phm 17

PARTRIDGE
when one hunts a *p*.........1 Sa 26:20

PARTS
anything but death *p*.......Ruth 1:17
in the inward *p*................Ps 51:6
Shout, you lower *p*.........Is 44:23
but our presentable *p*......1 Co 12:24
into the lower *p*..............Eph 4:9

PASS
I will *p* over you.............Ex 12:13
of the sea That *p*...........Ps 8:8
When you *p* through the..Is 43:2
"I will make you *p*.........Ezek 20:37
I will not *p* by them........Amos 7:8
and earth will *p*..............Matt 24:35

PASSED
And behold, the LORD *p*.1 Ki 19:11
forbearance God had *p*....Rom 3:25
High Priest who has *p*.....Heb 4:14
We know that we have *p*. 1 Jn 3:14

PASSES
For the wind *p* over it.....Ps 103:16
of Christ which *p*............Eph 3:19

PASSION
than to burn with *p*.........1 Co 7:9
uncleanness, *p*................Col 3:5

PASSIONS
gave them up to vile *p*.....Rom 1:26

PASSOVER
It is the LORD's *P*..........Ex 12:11
of King Josiah this *P*.......2 Ki 23:23
I will keep the *P*............Matt 26:18
indeed Christ, our *P*.......1 Co 5:7
By faith he kept the *P*.....Heb 11:28

PAST
My days are *p*................Job 17:11
lo, the winter is *p*...........Song 2:11
and His ways *p* finding....Rom 11:33
ways spoke in time *p*.......Heb 1:1
p lifetime in doing...........1 Pe 4:3

PASTORS
and some *p* and..............Eph 4:11

PASTURE
the sheep of Your *p*........Ps 74:1
the people of His *p*.........Ps 95:7
feed them in good *p*........Ezek 34:14
in and out and find *p*......John 10:9

PASTURES
to lie down in green *p*..... Ps 23:2

PATH
p no bird knows.............Job 28:7
You will show me the *p*...Ps 16:11
lead me in a smooth *p*....Ps 27:11
But the *p* of the just.......Prov 4:18
way in the sea and a *p*...Is 43:16

PATHS
He leads me in the *p*.......Ps 23:3
Teach me Your *p*............Ps 25:4
and all her *p* are.............Prov 3:17
p they have not...............Is 42:16
themselves crooked *p*......Is 59:8
make His p straight........Matt 3:3
and make straight *p*.........Heb 12:13

PATIENCE
'Master, have *p*..............Matt 18:26
and bear fruit with *p*.......Luke 8:15
Now may the God of *p*....Rom 15:5
labor of love, and *p*........1 Th 1:3
faith, love, *p*...................1 Ti 6:11
your faith produces *p*......Jas 1:3
p have its perfect............Jas 1:4
in the kingdom and *p*......Rev 1:9
Here is the *p* and the.....Rev 13:10

PATIENT
rejoicing in hope, *p*.........Rom 12:12
uphold the weak, be *p*.....1 Th 5:14

PATIENTLY
the LORD, and wait *p*.....Ps 37:7
if you take it *p*...............1 Pe 2:20

PATRIARCHS
begot the twelve *p*..........Acts 7:8

PATTERN
p which you were shown.. Ex 26:30
as you have us for a *p*.....Phil 3:17
Hold fast the *p*...............2 Ti 1:13
p shown you on the........Heb 8:5

PAVILION
shall hide me in His *p*.....Ps 27:5
them secretly in a *p*........Ps 31:20

PAWS
He *p* in the valley..........Job 39:21

PAY
with which to *p*..............Prov 22:27
priests teach for *p*..........Mic 3:11
with me, and I will *p*......Matt 18:26
p taxes to Caesar..........Matt 22:17
For you *p* tithe of..........Matt 23:23

PEACE
"These men are at *p*.......Gen 34:21
I will give *p* in the.........Lev 26:6
you, and give you *p*........Num 6:26
'Make *p* with me by a.... 2 Ki 18:31
field shall be at *p*...........Job 5:23
both lie down in *p*..........Ps 4:8
Seek *p*..........................Ps 34:14
For He will speak *p*.......Ps 85:8
p have those who love.....Ps 119:165
I am for *p*......................Ps 120:7
Pray for the *p* of...........Ps 122:6
P be within your walls.....Ps 122:7
P be upon Israel............Ps 125:5
war, and a time of *p*......Eccl 3:8
Father, Prince of *P*........Is 9:6
keep him in perfect *p*.....Is 26:3
p they have not..............Is 59:8
slightly, saying, '*P*..........Jer 6:14
"We looked for *p*...........Jer 8:15
give you assured *p*.........Jer 14:13
they will seek *p*..............Ezek 7:25
P be multiplied..............Dan 4:1
this One shall be *p*........Mic 5:5
place I will give *p*..........Hag 2:9
is worthy, let your *p*.......Matt 10:13
that I came to bring *p*.....Matt 10:34
and on earth *p*...............Luke 2:14
if a son of *p* is there.......Luke 10:6
that make for your *p*......Luke 19:42
I leave with you, My *p*....John 14:27
in Me you may have *p*....John 16:33
Grace to you and *p*........Rom 1:7
by faith, we have *p*.........Rom 5:1
God has called us to *p*....1 Co 7:15
p will be with you...........2 Co 13:11
Spirit is love, joy, *p*........Gal 5:22
He Himself is our *p*........Eph 2:14
and the *p* of God...........Phil 4:7
heaven, having made *p*.... Col 1:20
And let the *p* of God......Col 3:15
Be at *p* among...............1 Th 5:13
faith, love, *p*.................2 Ti 2:22
meaning "king of *p*,".......Heb 7:2
is sown in *p* by those......Jas 3:18
p be multiplied..............2 Pe 1:2

PEACEABLE
and *p* life in all..............1 Ti 2:2
is first pure, then *p*........Jas 3:17

PEACEABLY
depends on you, live *p*.....Rom 12:18

PEACEMAKERS
Blessed are the *p*...........Matt 5:9

PEARL
he had found one *p*.........Matt 13:46
gate was of one *p*...........Rev 21:21

PEARLS

nor cast your *p*...............Matt 7:6
hair or gold or *p*.............1 Ti 2:9
gates were twelve *p*.........Rev 21:21

PEG

wife, took a tent *p*..........Judg 4:21
will fasten him as a *p*........Is 22:23

PEN

My tongue is the *p*...........Ps 45:1
on it with a man's *p*.........Is 8:1
to write to you with *p*......3 Jn 13

PENNY

have paid the last *p*.........Matt 5:26

PENTECOST

P had fully come............Acts 2:1

PEOPLE

will take you as My *p*......Ex 6:7
Who is like you, a *p*........Deut 33:29
p shall be my *p*..............Ruth 1:16
p who know the joyful....Ps 89:15
We are His *p* and the.....Ps 100:3
Happy are the *p*..............Ps 144:15
Blessed is Egypt My *p*...Is 19:25
this is a rebellious *p*.......Is 30:9
p who provoke Me.........Is 65:3
and they shall be My *p*...Jer 24:7
for you are not My *p*......Hos 1:9
like *p*, like priest...........Hos 4:9
to make ready a *p*..........Luke 1:17
take out of them a *p*.....Acts 15:14
who were not My p.........Rom 9:25
and they shall be My p...2 Co 6:16
His own special *p*..........Tit 2:14
LORD will judge His *p*....Heb 10:30
but are now the *p*.........1 Pe 2:10
tribe and tongue and *p*....Rev 5:9
they shall be His *p*.........Rev 21:3

PERCEIVE

given you a heart to *p*.....Deut 29:4
but I cannot *p*...............Job 23:8
seeing, but do not *p*.......Is 6:9
they may see and not p...Mark 4:12

PERDITION

except the son of *p*.........John 17:12
to them a proof of *p*......Phil 1:28
revealed, the son of *p*......2 Th 2:3
who draw back to *p*.......Heb 10:39
day of judgment and *p*....2 Pe 3:7

PERFECT

Noah was a just man, *p*...Gen 6:9
one who is *p* in............Job 36:4
for God, His way is *p*....Ps 18:30
You were *p* in your........Ezek 28:15
Father in heaven is *p*.....Matt 5:48
"If you want to be *p*......Matt 19:21
they may be made *p*.......John 17:23
and *p* will of God..........Rom 12:2
when that which is *p*......1 Co 13:10
present every man *p*.......Col 1:28
the law made nothing *p*...Heb 7:19
of just men made *p*.......Heb 12:23
good gift and every *p*.....Jas 1:17
in word, he is a *p*.........Jas 3:2
p love casts out fear........1 Jn 4:18

PERFECTED

third day I shall be *p*......Luke 13:32
or am already *p*..............Phil 3:12

the Son who has been *p*...Heb 7:28
the love of God is *p*........1 Jn 2:5

PERFECTION

the *p* of beauty..............Ps 50:2
consummation of all *p*.....Ps 119:96
let us go on to *p*............Heb 6:1

PERFORM

p Your statutes...............Ps 119:112
am ready to *p* My word...Jer 1:12
p what is good I............Rom 7:18

PERIL

or nakedness, or *p*.........Rom 8:35

PERILOUS

from the *p* pestilence.......Ps 91:3
in the last days *p*...........2 Ti 3:1

PERILS

journeys often, in *p*.........2 Co 11:26

PERISH

"Surely we die, we *p*......Num 17:12
All flesh would *p*...........Job 34:15
They *p* at the rebuke.......Ps 80:16
very day his plans *p*.......Ps 146:4
so that we may not *p*......Jon 1:6
little ones should *p*........Matt 18:14
will all likewise *p*...........Luke 13:3
in Him should not *p*.......John 3:16
and they shall never *p*.....John 10:28
concern things which *p*....Col 2:22
among those who *p*........2 Th 2:10
that any should *p*...........2 Pe 3:9

PERISHABLE

do it to obtain a *p*..........1 Co 9:25

PERISHED

p being innocent.............Job 4:7
Truth has *p* and has........Jer 7:28
The faithful man has *p*.....Mic 7:2

PERISHING

We are *p*......................Matt 8:25
to those who are *p*..........2 Co 4:3

PERJURER

p shall be expelled..........Zech 5:3

PERMIT

the Spirit did not *p*.........Acts 16:7
And I do not *p* a woman. 1 Ti 2:12

PERMITS

you, if the Lord *p*...........1 Co 16:7
we will do if God *p*........Heb 6:3

PERMITTED

p no one to do them.......Ps 105:14

PERPETUATED

Your name shall be *p*......Nah 1:14

PERPLEXED

at one another, *p*...........John 13:22
we are *p*......................2 Co 4:8

PERSECUTE

p me as God does...........Job 19:22
p me wrongfully.............Ps 119:86
when they revile and *p*....Matt 5:11
Bless those who *p*..........Rom 12:14

PERSECUTED

p the poor and needy......Ps 109:16
p the prophets who.........Matt 5:12
If they *p* Me.................John 15:20
p the church of God........1 Co 15:9
p, but not forsaken.........2 Co 4:9
p us now preaches the.....Gal 1:23

PERSECUTES

wicked in his pride *p*.......Ps 10:2

PERSECUTION

p arises because of.........Matt 13:21
At that time a great *p*.....Acts 8:1
do I still suffer *p*...........Gal 5:11

PERSECUTOR

a blasphemer, a *p*...........1 Ti 1:13

PERSEVERANCE

tribulation produces *p*......Rom 5:3
to this end with all *p*.......Eph 6:18
longsuffering, love, *p*.......2 Ti 3:10
to self-control *p*.............2 Pe 1:6

PERSEVERE

kept My command to *p*....Rev 3:10

PERSON

In whose eyes a vile *p*.....Ps 15:4
p will suffer hunger........Prov 19:15
do not regard the *p*.........Matt 22:16
express image of His *p*.....Heb 1:3
let it be the hidden *p*.......1 Pe 3:4

PERSUADE

"You almost *p* me..........Acts 26:28
the Lord, we *p* men.........2 Co 5:11
For do I now *p* men........Gal 1:10

PERSUADED

a ruler is *p*..................Prov 25:15
neither will they be *p*......Luke 16:31
p that He is able.............2 Ti 1:12

PERSUASIVE

p words of human...........1 Co 2:4
you with *p* words............Col 2:4

PERTAINING

Priest in things *p*............Heb 2:17
for men in things *p*.........Heb 5:1

PERVERSE

because your way is *p*.....Num 22:32
for the *p* person is an......Prov 3:32
p lips far from you..........Prov 4:24
p heart will be...............Prov 12:8
p man sows strife..........Prov 16:28
but he who is *p*.............Prov 28:18
from this *p* generation.....Acts 2:40

PERVERT

"You shall not *p* justice... Deut 16:19
and *p* all equity.............Mic 3:9
p the gospel of Christ......Gal 1:7

PERVERTING

We found this fellow *p*....Luke 23:2
will you not cease *p*........Acts 13:10

PERVERTS

p the words of the..........Ex 23:8
p his ways will become.... Prov 10:9

PESTILENCE
from the perilous *p*......... Ps 91:3
p that walks in............... Ps 91:6
Before Him went *p*......... Hab 3:5

PESTILENCES
will be famines, *p*........... Matt 24:7

PETITION
of Israel grant your *p*...... 1 Sa 1:17

PETITIONS
fulfill all your *p*.............. Ps 20:5
p that we have asked.......1 Jn 5:15

PHARISEE
to pray, one a *P*............. Luke 18:10
and brethren, I am a *P*....Acts 23:6

PHILOSOPHERS
p encountered him.......... Acts 17:18

PHILOSOPHY
cheat you through *p*........ Col 2:8

PHYLACTERIES
They make their *p*.......... Matt 23:5

PHYSICIAN
Gilead, is there no *p*....... Jer 8:22
have no need of a *p*........ Matt 9:12
Luke the beloved *p*......... Col 4:14

PHYSICIANS
are all worthless *p*...........Job 13:4
her livelihood on *p*..........Luke 8:43

PIECES
for my wages thirty *p*...... Zech 11:12
they took the thirty p...... Matt 27:9
shall be broken to p....... Rev 2:27

PIERCE
and his master shall *p*......Ex 21:6
a sword will *p*............... Luke 2:35

PIERCED
p My hands and My feet..Ps 22:16
on Me whom they have *p*.Zech 12:10
of the soldiers *p*.............John 19:34
p themselves through.......1 Ti 6:10
and they also who *p*........ Rev 1:7

PIERCING
p even to the division...... Heb 4:12

PIETY
first learn to show *p*........1 Ti 5:4

PILGRIMAGE
heart is set on *p*.............. Ps 84:5
In the house of my *p*.......Ps 119:54

PILGRIMS
we are aliens and *p*.........1 Ch 29:15
were strangers and *p*....... Heb 11:13

PILLAR
and she became a *p*.........Gen 19:26
and by night in a *p*......... Ex 13:21
the living God, the *p*.......1 Ti 3:15

PILLARS
break their sacred *p*........ Ex 34:13
I set up its *p* firmly......... Ps 75:3

out her seven *p*.............. Prov 9:1
blood and fire and *p*.......Joel 2:30
and his feet like *p*........... Rev 10:1

PILOT
rudder wherever the *p*.... Jas 3:4

PINE
cypress tree and the *p*......Is 41:19
for these *p* away............. Lam 4:9

PINNACLE
set Him on the *p*............ Luke 4:9

PIT
cast him into some *p*....... Gen 37:20
soul draws near the *P*......Job 33:22
who go down to the *p*..... Ps 28:1
woman is a deep *p*.......... Prov 22:14
a harlot is a deep *p*........Prov 23:27
fall into his own *p*..........Prov 28:10
my life in the *p*.............. Lam 3:53
who descend into the *P*...Ezek 31:16
up my life from the *p*......Jon 2:6
from the waterless *p*.......Zech 9:11
if it falls into a *p*............ Matt 12:11
into the bottomless *p*....... Rev 20:3

PITCHERS
hand, with empty *p*.........Judg 7:16
the washing of cups, *p*....Mark 7:4

PITIABLE
of all men the most *p*...... 1 Co 15:19

PITS
The proud have dug *p*.... Ps 119:85

PITY
eye shall have no *p*........ Deut 7:16
"Have *p* on me.............. Job 19:21
for someone to take *p*..... Ps 69:20
He who has *p* on the.......Prov 19:17
p He redeemed them.......Is 63:9
land, and *p* His people.... Joel 2:18
And should I not *p*......... Jon 4:11
just as I had *p*................Matt 18:33

PLACE
p know him anymore.......Job 7:10
All go to one *p*............... Eccl 3:20
return again to My *p*....... Hos 5:15
Come, see the *p*............. Matt 28:6
My word has no *p*..........John 8:37
I go to prepare a *p*......... John 14:2
might go to his own *p*......Acts 1:25

PLACES
set them in slippery *p*...... Ps 73:18
dark *p* of the earth.........Ps 74:20
and the rough *p*............. Is 40:4
They love the best *p*.......Matt 23:6
in the heavenly *p*........... Eph 1:3

PLAGUE
bring yet one more *p*.......Ex 11:1
p come near your............Ps 91:10
so the *p* was stopped....... Ps 106:30

PLAGUES
I will send all My *p*........Ex 9:14
I will be your *p*.............. Hos 13:14
p that are written...........Rev 22:18

PLAINLY
the Christ, tell us *p*.........John 10:24
now You are speaking *p*.. John 16:29
such things declare *p*....... Heb 11:14

PLAN
p evil things in their........Ps 140:2
Let none of you *p*...........Zech 7:10

PLANK
First remove the *p*.......... Matt 7:5

PLANS
He makes the *p* of the.....Ps 33:10
In that very day his *p*......Ps 146:4
that devises wicked *p*.......Prov 6:18
A man's heart *p*............. Prov 16:9

PLANT
a time to *p*.................... Eccl 3:2
Him as a tender *p*...........Is 53:2
they shall *p* vineyards......Is 65:21
into the degenerate *p*......Jer 2:21
p which My heavenly.......Matt 15:13

PLANTED
shall be like a tree *P*....... Ps 1:3
Your right hand has *p*......Ps 80:15
shall they be *p*................Is 40:24
by the roots and be *p*......Luke 17:6
I *p*, Apollos watered....... 1 Co 3:6

PLANTS
our sons may be as *p*.......Ps 144:12
down its choice *p*............Is 16:8
neither he who *p*............. 1 Co 3:7

PLATTER
head here on a *p*............ Matt 14:8

PLAY
and rose up to *p*............. Ex 32:6
P skillfully with a............Ps 33:3
nursing child shall *p*........ Is 11:8
and rose up to p............. 1 Co 10:7

PLEAD
the one who would *p*.......Judg 6:31
Oh, that one might *p*.......Job 16:21
p my cause against an......Ps 43:1
p with your friend...........Prov 6:3
Behold, I will *p*..............Jer 2:35
p His case with all.......... Jer 25:31

PLEADED
Then Moses *p* with the....Ex 32:11
this thing I *p* with...........2 Co 12:8

PLEADING
though God were *p*.........2 Co 5:20

PLEASANT
food, that it was *p*.........Gen 3:6
they despised the *p*......... Ps 106:24
how good and how *p*......Ps 133:1
and knowledge is *p*......... Prov 2:10
P words are like a...........Prov 16:24
p places of the...............Jer 23:10
Is he a *p* child................Jer 31:20
I ate no *p* food...............Dan 10:3

PLEASANTNESS
Her ways are ways of *p*... Prov 3:17

PLEASE
When a man's ways *p*......Prov 16:7
do those things that *p*......John 8:29

PLEASED

in the flesh cannot *p*........Rom 8:8
p his neighbor for his...... Rom 15:2
how he may *p* the Lord... 1 Co 7:32
Or do I seek to *p* men.... Gal 1:10
is impossible to *p* Him.....Heb 11:6

PLEASED

Then You shall be *p*........Ps 51:19
The LORD is well *p*........ Is 42:21
Would he be *p* with you.. Mal 1:8
in whom I am well *p*....... Matt 3:17
God was not well *p*.........1 Co 10:5
testimony, that he *p*........ Heb 11:5
in whom I am well *p*....... 2 Pe 1:17

PLEASES

He does whatever He *p*... Ps 115:3
Whatever the LORD *p*.....Ps 135:6

PLEASING

sacrifice, well *p*...............Phil 4:18
for this is well *p*............. Col 3:20
in you what is well *p*....... Heb 13:21

PLEASURE

not a God who takes *p*.... Ps 5:4
Do good in Your good *p*..Ps 51:18
Your servants take *p*...... Ps 102:14
p will be a poor man......Prov 21:17
for He has no *p*..............Eccl 5:4
shall perform all My *p*..... Is 44:28
your fast you find *p*.........Is 58:3
nor finding your own *p*..... Is 58:13
"Do I have any *p*........... Ezek 18:23
I have no *p* in you......... Mal 1:10
your Father's good *p*....... Luke 12:32
to the good *p* of His.......Eph 1:5
fulfill all the good *p*........ 2 Th 1:11
p is dead while................1 Ti 5:6
for sin you had no *p*........Heb 10:6
back, my soul has no *p*.... Heb 10:38
p that war in your...........Jas 4:1
on the earth in *p*.......... Jas 5:5

PLEASURES

Your right hand are *p*......Ps 16:11
cares, riches, and *p*......... Luke 8:14
to enjoy the passing *p*......Heb 11:25

PLEIADES

Bear, Orion, and the *P*....Job 9:9

PLENTIFUL

You, O God, sent a *p*..... Ps 68:9
The harvest truly is *p*...... Matt 9:37

PLENTIFULLY

rich man yielded *p*.......... Luke 12:16

PLENTY

p which were in the........Gen 41:53
LORD will grant you *p*.... Deut 28:11
his land will have *p*......... Prov 28:19

PLOT

And the people *p*............Ps 2:1
p became known to Saul.. Acts 9:24

PLOTS

The wicked *p* against....... Ps 37:12

PLOTTED

and *p* to take Jesus by..... Matt 26:4

PLOW

sluggard will not *p*......... Prov 20:4
Does one *p* there with..... Amos 6:12
put his hand to the *p*.......Luke 9:62
he who plows should *p*.... 1 Co 9:10

PLOWED

"Zion shall be *p*.............. Jer 26:18
You have *p* wickedness.... Hos 10:13
of you Zion shall be *p*..... Mic 3:12

PLOWMAN

p shall overtake the.........Amos 9:13

PLUCK

grain, you may *p*............ Deut 23:25
who pass by the way *p*.....Ps 80:12
obey, I will utterly *p*....... Jer 12:17
p the heads of grain........ Mark 2:23

PLUCKED

p the victim from his....... Job 29:17
cheeks to those who *p*..... Is 50:6
And His disciples *p*......... Luke 6:1
you would have *p*.......... Gal 4:15

PLUMB

a *p* line, with a *p*............Amos 7:7
rejoice to see the *p*......... Zech 4:10

PLUNDER

p the Egyptians.............. Ex 3:22
who pass by the way *p*.....Ps 89:41
the *p* of the poor is........Is 3:14
p you shall become......... Jer 30:16
house and *p* his goods..... Matt 12:29

PLUNDERED

stouthearted were *p*.........Ps 76:5
a people robbed and *p*.....Is 42:22
"And when you are *p*......Jer 4:30
Because you have *p*........Hab 2:8

PLUNDERING

me because of the *p*........ Is 22:4
accepted the *p* of your..... Heb 10:34

POETS

some of your own *p*........ Acts 17:28

POISON

The *p* of asps is under..... Ps 140:3
"The *p* of asps is........... Rom 3:13
evil, full of deadly *p*........Jas 3:8

POISONED

I see that you are *p*........Acts 8:23
p their minds against....... Acts 14:2

POLLUTIONS

have escaped the *p*.........2 Pe 2:20

POMP

multitude and their *p*.......Is 5:14
p is brought down to....... Is 14:11
had come with great *p*..... Acts 25:23

POMPOUS

and a mouth speaking *p*...Dan 7:8

PONDER

P the path of your......... Prov 4:26

PONDERED

p them in her heart........ Luke 2:19

PONDERS

p all his paths................Prov 5:21

POOL

the wilderness a *p*.......... Is 41:18
by the Sheep Gate a *p*.....John 5:2

POOLS

also covers it with *p*........ Ps 84:6
a wilderness into *p*.......... Ps 107:35
your eyes like the *p*........Song 7:4

POOR

p shall not give less........ Ex 30:15
be partial to the *p*...........Lev 19:15
p will never cease........... Deut 15:11
So the *p* have hope......... Job 5:16
and forsaken the *p*..........Job 20:19
I delivered the *p*............Job 29:12
soul grieved for the *p*...... Job 30:25
p shall eat and be........... Ps 22:26
p man cried out............. Ps 34:6
But I am *p* and needy..... Ps 40:17
goodness for the *p*.......... Ps 68:10
Let the *p* and needy.......Ps 74:21
Yet He sets the *p*........... Ps 107:41
He raises the *p*...............Ps 113:7
a slack hand becomes *p*... Prov 10:4
p man is hated even........ Prov 14:20
who has mercy on the *p*...Prov 14:21
He who oppresses the *p*...Prov 14:31
p reproaches his Maker....Prov 17:5
p man is better than a..... Prov 19:22
p have this in common....Prov 22:2
Do not rob the *p*........... Prov 22:22
p man who oppresses......Prov 28:3
remembered that same *p*.. Eccl 9:15
for silver, and the *p*....... Amos 2:6
the alien or the *p*...........Zech 7:10
in particular the *p*.......... Zech 11:7
"Blessed are the *p*.......... Matt 5:3
p have the gospel...........Matt 11:5
For you have the *p*........ Matt 26:11
your sakes He became *p*.. 2 Co 8:9
should remember the *p*... Gal 2:10
God not chosen the *p*.....Jas 2:5
have dishonored the *p*.... Jas 2:6
wretched, miserable, *p*....Rev 3:17

PORTION

For the LORD's *p*...........Deut 32:9
This is the *p* from God....Job 20:29
You, O LORD, are the *p*.Ps 16:5
heart and my *p* forever....Ps 73:26
You are my *p*................Ps 119:57
I will divide Him a *p*.......Is 53:12
rejoice in their *p*............. Is 61:7
The *P* of Jacob is not.....Jer 10:16
they have trodden My *p*...Jer 12:10
"The LORD is my *p*........Lam 3:24
and appoint him his *p*.....Matt 24:51
to give them their *p*....... Luke 12:42
Father, give me the *p*...... Luke 15:12

PORTRAYED

Christ was clearly *p*.........Gal 3:1

POSITION

If a man desires the *p*......1 Ti 3:1

POSSESS

descendants shall *p*..........Gen 22:17
p the land which............Josh 1:11
In your patience *p*..........Luke 21:19
p his own vessel..............1 Th 4:4

POSSESSED

much land yet to be *p*..... Josh 13:1
"The LORD *p* me at....... Prov 8:22
of the things he *p*.......... Acts 4:32

POSSESSING

and yet *p* all things......... 2 Co 6:10

POSSESSION

as an everlasting *p*......... Gen 17:8
they did not gain *p*..........Ps 44:3
of the purchased *p*.......... Eph 1:14
and an enduring *p*...........Heb 10:34

POSSESSIONS

is full of Your *p*............. Ps 104:24
kinds of precious *p*.........Prov 1:13
Yes, I had greater *p*........Eccl 2:7
for he had great *p*........Mark 10:22
and there wasted his *p*.....Luke 15:13
and sold their *p*.............. Acts 2:45

POSSIBLE

God all things are *p*....... Matt 19:26
p that the blood..............Heb 10:4

POSTERITY

to preserve a *p*.............. Gen 45:7
p shall serve Him............Ps 22:30
p who approve their........ Ps 49:13

POT

to Aaron, "Take a *p*....... Ex 16:33
from a boiling *p*..............Job 41:20
The refining *p* is for........ Prov 17:3
p that had the manna...... Heb 9:4

POTENTATE

the blessed and only *P*.....1 Ti 6:15

POTS

when we sat by the *p*...... Ex 16:3
also took away the *p*....... Jer 52:18
are regarded as clay *p*.....Lam 4:2

POTSHERD

for himself a *p*................Job 2:8
is dried up like a *p*..........Ps 22:15
Let the *p* strive with........Is 45:9

POUR

P out your heart.............Ps 62:8
P out Your wrath........... Ps 79:6
p My Spirit on your........ Is 44:3
and let the skies *p*...........Is 45:8
P out Your fury.............Jer 10:25
that I will *p* out My....... Joel 2:28
"And I will *p*.................. Zech 12:10
angels, "Go and *p*..........Rev 16:1

POURED

And now my soul is *p*..... Job 30:16
I am *p* out like water...... Ps 22:14
Grace is *p* upon Your......Ps 45:2
name is ointment *p*......... Song 1:3
visited You, they *p*..........Is 26:16
strong, because He *p*.......Is 53:12
and My fury will be *p*......Jer 7:20
His fury is *p* out like......Nah 1:6
broke the flask and *p*...... Mark 14:3
of God has been *p*......... Rom 5:5
if I am being *p*.............. Phil 2:17
I am already being *p*....... 2 Ti 4:6
whom He *p* out on us......Tit 3:6

POVERTY

of the poor is their *p*.......Prov 10:15
but it leads to *p*..............Prov 11:24
P and shame will come.... Prov 13:18
leads only to *p*............... Prov 14:23
lest you come to *p*.......... Prov 20:13
who can understand.....Prov 30:8
p has put in all the..........Luke 21:4
and their deep *p*............. 2 Co 8:2
p might become rich........2 Co 8:9
tribulation, and *p*............ Rev 2:9

POWER

that I may show My *p*..... Ex 9:16
become glorious in *p*...... Ex 15:6
for God has *p* to help......2 Ch 25:8
him who is without *p*......Job 26:2
p who can understand......Job 26:14
p belongs to God...........Ps 62:11
p Your enemies shall.......Ps 66:3
gives strength and *p*........ Ps 68:35
a king, there is *p*...........Eccl 8:4
No one has *p* over the.....Eccl 8:8
the strength of His *p*........Is 40:26
truly I am full of *p*..........Mic 3:8
anger and great in *p*........Nah 1:3
Not by might nor by *p*....Zech 4:6
the kingdom and the *p*.....Matt 6:13
the Son of Man has *p*.....Matt 9:6
who had given such *p*.....Matt 9:8
Scriptures nor the *p*........Matt 22:29
And the *p* of the Lord....Luke 5:17
p went out from Him...... Luke 6:19
you are endued with *p*....Luke 24:49
I have *p* to lay it............John 10:18
it down, and I have *p*......John 10:18
not know that I have *p*.... John 19:10
"You could have no *p*..... John 19:11
you shall receive *p*.......... Acts 1:8
as though by our own *p*... Acts 3:12
man is the great *p*..........Acts 8:10
"Give me this *p*.............. Acts 8:19
for it is the *p*................. Rom 1:16
even His eternal *p*..........Rom 1:20
saved it is the *p*.............1 Co 1:18
Greeks, Christ the *p*.......1 Co 1:24
be brought under the *p*....1 Co 6:12
that the *p* of Christ........2 Co 12:9
greatness of His *p*.......... Eph 1:19
working of His *p*............Eph 3:7
the Lord and in the *p*.....Eph 6:10
to His glorious *p*............Col 1:11
the glory of His *p*.......... 2 Th 1:9
of fear, but of *p*............. 2 Ti 1:7
by the word of His *p*......Heb 1:3
him who had the *p*.........Heb 2:14
but according to the *p*.... Heb 7:16
as His divine *p*...............2 Pe 1:3
dominion and *p*..............Jude 25
to him I will give *p*........ Rev 2:26
glory and honor and *p*.....Rev 4:11
honor and glory and *p*..... Rev 5:13

POWERFUL

of the LORD is *p*............Ps 29:4
of God is living and *p*......Heb 4:12

POWERS

principalities and *p*.......... Col 2:15
word of God and the *p*.... Heb 6:5

PRAISE

your brothers shall *p*....... Gen 49:8
"He is your *p*.................Deut 10:21
I will sing *p* to the......... Judg 5:3
p shall be of You in........ Ps 22:25

For *p* from the upright.....Ps 33:1
p shall continually be.......Ps 34:1
the people shall *p*........... Ps 45:17
Whoever offers *p*............ Ps 50:23
P is awaiting You........... Ps 65:1
Make His *p* glorious.......Ps 66:2
Let all the peoples *p*....... Ps 67:3
Let heaven and earth *p*....Ps 69:34
p shall be continually.......Ps 71:6
And the heavens will *p*.... Ps 89:5
silent, O God of my *p*...... Ps 109:1
Seven times a day I *p*......Ps 119:164
All Your works shall *p*.... Ps 145:10
shall speak the *p*.............Ps 145:21
P the LORD.................. Ps 148:1
that has breath *p*............ Ps 150:6
Let another man *p*.......... Prov 27:2
let her own works *p*........ Prov 31:31
and your gates *P*............Is 60:18
He makes Jerusalem a *p*.. Is 62:7
for You are my *p*............Jer 17:14
Me a name of joy, a *p*.... Jer 33:9
give you fame and *p*.......Zeph 3:20
You have perfected p..... Matt 21:16
of men more than the *p*...John 12:43
p is not from men but..... Rom 2:29
then each one's *p*............1 Co 4:5
the brother whose *p*....... 2 Co 8:18
should be to the *p*...........Eph 1:12
to the glory and *p*..........Phil 1:11
I will sing p to You........Heb 2:12
the sacrifice of *p*............Heb 13:15
and for the *p* of those......1 Pe 2:14
saying, "*P* our God........Rev 19:5

PRAISED

who is worthy to be *p*......2 Sa 22:4
daily He shall be *p*..........Ps 72:15
LORD's name is to be *p*..Ps 113:3
and greatly to be *p*..........Ps 145:3
where our fathers *p*.........Is 64:11
the Most High and *p*.......Dan 4:34

PRAISES

Who inhabit the *p*...........Ps 22:3
it is good to sing *p*..........Ps 147:1
husband also, and he *p*.... Prov 31:28
shall proclaim the *p*........Is 60:6
you may proclaim the *p*... 1 Pe 2:9

PRAISEWORTHY

if there is anything *p*....... Phil 4:8

PRAISING

They will still be *p*..........Ps 84:4
of the heavenly host *p*..... Luke 2:13
in the temple *p*...............Luke 24:53

PRATING

p fool will fall................ Prov 10:8

PRAY

LORD in ceasing to *p*......1 Sa 12:23
at noon I will *p*...............Ps 55:17
who hate you, and *p*....... Matt 5:44
"And when you *p*...........Matt 6:5
"But you, when you *p*.... Matt 6:6
manner, therefore, *p*....... Matt 6:9
"Watch and *p*................Matt 26:41
to the mountain to *p*....... Mark 6:46
"Lord, teach us to *p*.......Luke 11:1
men always ought to *p*.....Luke 18:1
"And I will *p*................. John 14:16
I do not *p* for the........... John 17:9
"I do not *p* for.............. John 17:20
know what we should *p*... Rom 8:26

PRAYED

I will *p* with the..............1 Co 14:15
p without ceasing........... 1 Th 5:17
Brethren, *p* for us........... 1 Th 5:25
desire that the men *p*...... 1 Ti 2:8
Let him *p*......................Jas 5:13
to one another, and *p*....Jas 5:16
say that he should *p*........1 Jn 5:16
p that you may prosper....3 Jn 2

PRAYED

Pharisee stood and *p*...... Luke 18:11
p more earnestly.............Luke 22:44
p earnestly that it...........Jas 5:17

PRAYER

in heaven their *p*............ 1 Ki 8:45
p made in this place........2 Ch 7:15
fear, and restrain *p*........ Job 15:4
and my *p* is pure............ Job 16:17
p would return to my..... Ps 35:13
A *p* to the God of my..... Ps 42:8
P also will be made........Ps 72:15
Let my *p* come before..... Ps 88:2
He shall regard the *p*.....Ps 102:17
But I give myself to *p*.....Ps 109:4
to the LORD, but the *p*... Prov 15:8
not go out except by *p*....Matt 17:21
all night in *p* to God...... Luke 6:12
continually to *p*............. Acts 6:4
where *p* was..................Acts 16:13
steadfastly in *p*............. Rom 12:12
to fasting and *p*............. 1 Co 7:5
always with all *p*.......... Eph 6:18
but in everything by *p*..... Phil 4:6
the word of God and *p*...1 Ti 4:5
And the *p* of faith..........Jas 5:15

PRAYERS

though you make many *p*.Is 1:15
a pretense make long *p*....Matt 23:14
fervently for you in *p*...... Col 4:12
that supplications, *p*........ 1 Ti 2:1
p may not be hindered....1 Pe 3:7
are open to their p..........1 Pe 3:12
and watchful in your *p*....1 Pe 4:7
which are the *p*............. Rev 5:8

PREACH

that great city, and *p*......Jon 3:2
time Jesus began to *p*......Matt 4:17
you hear in the ear, *p*.....Matt 10:27
p deliverance to the........Luke 4:18
p the kingdom of God.....Luke 9:60
And how shall they *p*...... Rom 10:15
p Christ crucified............ 1 Co 1:23
is me if I do not *p*........... 1 Co 9:16
was I or they, so we *p*....1 Co 15:11
For we do not *p*.............. 2 Co 4:5
p Christ even from.......... Phil 1:15
P the word.................... 2 Ti 4:2

PREACHED

p that people..................Mark 6:12
out and *p* everywhere......Mark 16:20
of sins should be *p*.........Luke 24:47
p Christ to them..............Acts 8:5
through this Man is *p*...... Acts 13:38
lest, when I have *p*......... 1 Co 9:27
whom we have not *p*......2 Co 11:4
than what we have *p*...... Gal 1:8
in truth, Christ is *p*........ Phil 1:18
the gospel was *p*........... Heb 4:2
also He went and *p*.........1 Pe 3:19

PREACHER

The words of the *P*........ Eccl 1:1
they hear without a *p*...... Rom 10:14

I was appointed a *p*........1 Ti 2:7
of eight people, a *p*.........2 Pe 2:5

PREACHES

the Jesus whom Paul *p*.... Acts 19:13
p another Jesus whom..... 2 Co 11:4
p any other gospel.......... Gal 1:9
p the faith which he........ Gal 1:23

PREACHING

p Jesus as the................Acts 5:42
to my gospel and the *p*.... Rom 16:25
not risen, then our *p*....... 1 Co 15:14

PRECEDE

p those who are asleep.... 1 Th 4:15

PRECEPT

p must be upon *p*........... Is 28:10

PRECEPTS

and commanded them *p*...Neh 9:14
All His *p* are sure...........Ps 111:7
us To keep Your *p*..........Ps 119:4
how I love Your *p*..........Ps 119:159
and kept all his *p*...........Jer 35:18

PRECIOUS

because my life was *p*.....1 Sa 26:21
P in the sight of the........Ps 116:15
How *p* also are Your......Ps 139:17
She is more *p* than..........Prov 3:15
Since you were *p*............ Is 43:4
p things shall not............ Is 44:9
If you take out the *p*.......Jer 15:19
The *p* sons of Zion......... Lam 4:2
farmer waits for the *p*......Jas 5:7
being much more *p*.........1 Pe 1:7
who believe, He is *p*....... 1 Pe 2:7
which is very *p*...............1 Pe 3:4

PREDESTINED

He foreknew, He also *p*...Rom 8:29
having *p* us to................. Eph 1:5
inheritance, being *p*........Eph 1:11

PREEMINENCE

He may have the *p*......... Col 1:18
loves to have the *p*.........3 Jn 9

PREFERENCE

in honor giving *p*............ Rom 12:10

PREFERRED

comes after me is *p*.........John 1:15

PREJUDICE

these things without *p*......1 Ti 5:21

PREMEDITATE

p what you will...............Mark 13:11

PREPARATION

Now it was the *P*...........John 19:14
your feet with the *p*........ Eph 6:15

PREPARE

p your hearts for the........ 1 Sa 7:3
p a table before me in..... Ps 23:5
p mercy and truth........... Ps 61:7
P the way of the LORD... Is 40:3
P the way for the............ Is 62:10
P the way of the LORD.. Mark 1:3
will, and did not *p*.......... Luke 12:47
p a place for you............. John 14:2

PREPARED

place which I have *p*....... Ex 23:20
You *p* room for it........... Ps 80:9
When He *p* the heavens...Prov 8:27
for the LORD has *p*........ Zeph 1:7
for whom it is *p*..............Matt 20:23
which You have *p*........... Luke 2:31
mercy, which He had *p*....Rom 9:23
things which God has p....1 Co 2:9
Now He who has *p*......... 2 Co 5:5
p beforehand that we.......Eph 2:10
God, for He has *p*........... Heb 11:16

PRESBYTERY

of the hands of the *p*.......1 Ti 4:14

PRESENCE

themselves from the *p*......Gen 3:8
went out from the *p*........ Gen 4:16
we die in your *p*............. Gen 47:15
P will go with you...........Ex 33:14
and honor the *p*..............Lev 19:32
afraid in any man's *p*......Deut 1:17
am terrified at His *p*.......Job 23:15
p is fullness of joy...........Ps 16:11
shall dwell in Your *p*......Ps 140:13
not tremble at My *p*........Jer 5:22
shall shake at My *p*.........Ezek 38:20
Be silent in the *p*...........Zeph 1:7
and drank in Your *p*....... Luke 13:26
full of joy in Your p.......Acts 2:28
but his bodily *p*.............. 2 Co 10:10
obeyed, not as in my *p*.... Phil 2:12

PRESENT

we are all *p* before.........Acts 10:33
a law, that evil is *p*......... Rom 7:21
p your bodies a living..... Rom 12:1
or death, or things *p*....... 1 Co 3:22
absent in body but *p*....... 1 Co 5:3
not only when I am *p*......Gal 4:18
that He might *p*..............Eph 5:27
to *p* yourself.................. 2 Ti 2:15
p you faultless................ Jude 24

PRESENTED

treasures, they *p*.............Matt 2:11
For just as you *p*............ Rom 6:19

PRESENTS

Kings will bring *p*........... Ps 68:29

PRESERVE

before you to *p* life......... Gen 45:5
You shall *p* me from........Ps 32:7
O LORD, You *p* man...... Ps 36:6
He shall *p* your soul........Ps 121:7
The LORD shall *p*...........Ps 121:8
children, I will *p*.............Jer 49:11
pardon those whom I *p*....Jer 50:20
loses his life will *p*.......... Luke 17:33
every evil work and *p*......2 Ti 4:18

PRESERVED

and my life is *p*.............. Gen 32:30
soul, and body be *p*........ 1 Th 5:23

PRESERVES

For the LORD *p* the........Ps 31:23
p the souls of His............ Ps 97:10
The LORD *p* the simple...Ps 116:6
who guards his mouth *p*...Prov 13:3
he who keeps his way *p*...Prov 16:17

PRESS

I *p* toward the goal.........Phil 3:14

PRESSED

p her virgin bosom..........Ezek 23:8
We are hard *p* on every...2 Co 4:8
For I am hard *p*............. Phil 1:23

PRESUMPTUOUS

servant also from *p*......... Ps 19:13

PRETENSE

whole heart, but in *p*.......Jer 3:10
p make long prayers........Matt 23:14

PREVAIL

no man shall *p*............... 1 Sa 2:9
our tongue we will *p*....... Ps 12:4
but they shall not *p*........Jer 1:19
of Hades shall not *p*.......Matt 16:18

PREVAILED

hand, that Israel *p*......... Ex 17:11
with the Angel and *p*......Hos 12:4
grew mightily and *p*.........Acts 19:20

PREY

the mountains of *p*..........Ps 76:4
has not given us as *p*.......Ps 124:6
Shall the *p* be taken........Is 49:24
evil makes himself a *p*.....Is 59:15
shall no longer be a *p*.....Ezek 34:22
when he has no *p*.......... Amos 3:4

PRICE

be weighed for its *p*.......Job 28:15
a fool the purchase *p*.......Prov 17:16
one pearl of great *p*........ Matt 13:46
back part of the *p*..........Acts 5:3
you were bought at a *p*....1 Co 6:20

PRIDE

p come against me.......... Ps 36:11
p serves as.................Ps 73:6
p and arrogance and........Prov 8:13
By *p* comes only.............Prov 13:10
P goes before................Prov 16:18
p will bring him low.......Prov 29:23
and her daughter had *p*...Ezek 16:49
p He is able to abase........Dan 4:37
was hardened in *p*..........Dan 5:20
has sworn by the *p*.........Amos 8:7
For the *p* of the.............Zech 11:3
evil eye, blasphemy, *p*.....Mark 7:22
p he fall into the............1 Ti 3:6
of the eyes, and the *p*.....1 Jn 2:16

PRIEST

he was the *p* of God....... Gen 14:18
Myself a faithful *p*.........1 Sa 2:35
p forever According........ Ps 110:4
the *p* and the prophet......Is 28:7
so He shall be a *p*..........Zech 6:13
of a *p* should keep.........Mal 2:7
and faithful High *P*........ Heb 2:17
we have a great High *P*.... Heb 4:14
p forever according........Heb 5:6
Christ came as High *P*.....Heb 9:11

PRIESTHOOD

be an everlasting *p*......... Ex 40:15
have defiled the *p*..........Neh 13:29
p being changed............Heb 7:12
has an unchangeable *p*.....Heb 7:24
house, a holy *p*.............1 Pe 2:5
generation, a royal *p*.....1 Pe 2:9

PRIESTS

to Me a kingdom of *p*..... Ex 19:6
her *p* teach for pay........ Mic 3:11

made us kings and *p*.......Rev 1:6
but they shall be *p*..........Rev 20:6

PRINCE

"Who made you a *p*.....Ex 2:14
is the house of the *p*.......Job 21:28
is the downfall of a *p*.....Prov 14:28
everlasting Father, *P*.......Is 9:6
until Messiah the *P*.........Dan 9:25
except Michael your *p*......Dan 10:21
days without king or *p*.....Hos 3:4
p asks for gifts................Mic 7:3
and killed the *P*.............Acts 3:15
His right hand to be *P*.....Acts 5:31
according to the *p*...........Eph 2:2

PRINCES

He is not partial to *p*......Job 34:19
To bind his *p* at his.........Ps 105:22
He may seat him with *p*...Ps 113:8
to put confidence in *p*......Ps 118:9
P also sit and speak.......Ps 119:23
P and all judges of..........Ps 148:11
good, nor to strike *p*.......Prov 17:26
is a child, and your *p*......Eccl 10:16
of nobles, and your *p*......Eccl 10:17
children to be their *p*......Is 3:4
p will rule with...............Is 32:1
He brings the *p*..............Is 40:23

PRINCIPAL

Wisdom is the *p*............. Prov 4:7

PRINCIPALITY

far above all *p*...............Eph 1:21
is the head of all *p*..........Col 2:10

PRINCIPLES

from the basic *p*............. Col 2:20
again the first *p*............. Heb 5:12

PRISON

and put him into the *p*.....Gen 39:20
Bring my soul out of *p*.... Ps 142:7
in darkness from the *p*.....Is 42:7
the opening of the *p*........Is 61:1
should put him in *p*........Jer 29:26
John had heard in *p*........Matt 11:2
I was in *p* and you..........Matt 25:36
to the spirits in *p*............1 Pe 3:19

PRISONER

the groaning of the *p*.......Ps 79:11
reason I, Paul, the *p*.......Eph 3:1
Lord, nor of me His *p*.....2 Ti 1:8

PRISONERS

p rest together................Job 3:18
does not despise His *p*.....Ps 69:33
gives freedom to the *p*.....Ps 146:7
the stronghold, you *p*......Zech 9:12
Remember the *p* as if......Heb 13:3

PRISONS

the synagogues and *p*.......Luke 21:12
p more frequently.......... 2 Co 11:23

PRIZE

life shall be as a *p*..........Jer 21:9
but one receives the *p*..... 1 Co 9:24
the goal for the *p*...........Phil 3:14

PROCEED

For they *p* from evil........Jer 9:3
of the same mouth *p*.......Jas 3:10

PROCEEDED

for I *p* forth...................John 8:42

PROCEEDS

by every word that *p*.......Deut 8:3
by every word that *p*.......Matt 4:4
Spirit of truth who *p*......John 15:26
back part of the *p*...........Acts 5:2

PROCLAIM

you, and I will *p*.............Ex 33:19
p the name of the LORD. Deut 32:3
p it not in the................2 Sa 1:20
and they shall *p*.............Is 60:6
began to *p* it freely.........Mark 1:45
knowing, Him I *p*............ Acts 17:23
drink this cup, you *p*.......1 Co 11:26

PROCLAIMED

p the good news............. Ps 40:9
company of those who *p*.. Ps 68:11
he went his way and *p*.....Luke 8:39
inner rooms will be *p*...... Luke 12:3

PROCLAIMER

"He seems to be a *p*....... Acts 17:18

PROCLAIMS

good news, who *p*...........Is 52:7

PROCONSUL

seeking to turn the *p*.......Acts 13:8
when Gallio was *p*.......... Acts 18:12

PRODIGAL

with *p* living...................Luke 15:13

PRODUCE

land shall yield its *p*........ Lev 26:4
all kinds of *p*..................Ps 144:13

PROFANE

and offered *p* fire............Lev 10:1
and priest are *p*..............Jer 23:11
"But you *p* it................Mal 1:12
tried to *p* the temple....... Acts 24:6
But reject *p* and old........1 Ti 4:7
p person like Esau.......... Heb 12:16

PROFANED

p his crown by casting..... Ps 89:39
and *p* My Sabbaths........ Ezek 22:8
p the LORD's holy..........Mal 2:11

PROFANENESS

of Jerusalem *p* has.......... Jer 23:15

PROFANING

p the covenant of the...... Mal 2:10

PROFESS

They *p* to know God.......Tit 1:16

PROFESSING

P to be wise...................Rom 1:22
is proper for women *p*.....1 Ti 2:10

PROFIT

p is there in my blood..... Ps 30:9
p has a man from all.......Eccl 1:3
there was no *p* under.......Eccl 2:11
for they will not *p*..........Is 57:12
words that cannot *p*.........Jer 7:8
p which you have made... Ezek 22:13
p is it that we have........ Mal 3:14
For what will it *p*...........Mark 8:36

PROFITABLE

her masters much *p*........Acts 16:16
hope of *p* was gone........Acts 16:19
brought no small *p*........Acts 19:24
not seeking my own *p*......1 Co 10:33
Christ will *p* you............Gal 5:2
about words to no *p*........2 Ti 2:14
them, but He for our *p*....Heb 12:10
What does it *p*............Jas 2:14
and sell, and make a *p*....Jas 4:13

PROFITABLE

"Can a man be *p*............Job 22:2
It is doubtless not *p*........2 Co 12:1
of God, and is *p*............2 Ti 3:16
things are good and *p*......Tit 3:8
to you, but now is *p*........Phm 11

PROFITED

For what is a man *p*........Matt 16:26

PROFITS

p a man nothing that.......Job 34:9
have not love, it *p*..........1 Co 13:3
exercise *p* a little............1 Ti 4:8

PROFOUND

with things too *p*.............Ps 131:1

PROLONG

you will not *p* your........Deut 4:26
p Your anger to all.........Ps 85:5
nor will he *p* his days......Eccl 8:13

PROLONGED

and his days are *p*...........Eccl 8:12

PROLONGS

The fear of the LORD *p*.. Prov 10:27

PROMISE

of all His good *p*............1 Ki 8:56
Behold, I send the *P*.......Luke 24:49
but to wait for the *P*.......Acts 1:4
"For the *p* is to you........Acts 2:39
p drew near which God... Acts 7:17
for the hope of the *p*......Acts 26:6
is made void and the *p*... Rom 4:14
p might be sure..............Rom 4:16
it is no longer of *p*.........Gal 3:18
Therefore, since a *p*.......Heb 4:1
p the immutability...........Heb 6:17
did not receive the *p*.......Heb 11:39
they *p* them liberty.........2 Pe 2:19
p that He has promised....1 Jn 2:25

PROMISED

bless you as He has *p*....Deut 1:11
Him faithful who had *p*....Heb 11:11

PROMISES

For all the *p* of God........2 Co 1:20
his Seed were the *p*........Gal 3:16
patience inherit the *p*......Heb 6:12
having received the *p*......Heb 11:13
great and precious *p*.......2 Pe 1:4

PROMPTLY

disciplines him *p*.............Prov 13:24

PROOF

which is to them a *p*.......Phil 1:28

PROOFS

by many infallible *p*........Acts 1:3

PROPER

you, but for what is *p*......1 Co 7:35
Is it *p* for a woman to..... 1 Co 11:13
but, which is *p*...............1 Ti 2:10

PROPERLY

Let us walk *p*.................Rom 13:13

PROPHECY

miracles, to another *p*......1 Co 12:10
for *p* never came by the...2 Pe 1:21
is the spirit of *p*.............Rev 19:10
of the book of this *p*......Rev 22:19

PROPHESIED

upon them, that they *p*.... Num 11:25
to them, yet they *p*.........Jer 23:21
Lord, have we not *p*.......Matt 7:22
prophets and the law *p*.... Matt 11:13
virgin daughters who *p*....Acts 21:9
even more that you *p*...... 1 Co 14:5

PROPHESIES

for the prophet who *p*..... Jer 28:9
woman who prays or *p*.... 1 Co 11:5
p edifies the church...........1 Co 14:4

PROPHESY

prophets, "Do not *p*......Is 30:10
the prophets *p* falsely...... Jer 5:31
your daughters shall *p*.....Joel 2:28
Who can but *p*...............Amos 3:8
saying, "*P* to us.............Matt 26:68
your daughters shall p......Acts 2:17
if prophecy, let us *p*........Rom 12:6
know in part and we *p*.....1 Co 13:9
desire earnestly to *p*........1 Co 14:39

PROPHET

shall be your *p*...............Ex 7:1
raise up for you a *P*........Deut 18:15
arisen in Israel a *p*.........Deut 34:10
"I alone am left a *p*.........1 Ki 18:22
is no longer any *p*...........Ps 74:9
and I ordained you a *p*....Jer 1:5
p is induced to speak......Ezek 14:9
The *p* is a fool...............Hos 9:7
nor was I a son of a *p*.....Amos 7:14
send you Elijah the *p*..... Mal 4:5
p shall receive a.............Matt 10:41
p is not without honor..... Matt 13:57
by Daniel the *p*.............Mark 13:14
is not a greater *p*...........Luke 7:28
it cannot be that a *p*.......Luke 13:33
Nazareth, who was a *P*....Luke 24:19
"Are you the *P*..............John 1:21
"This is truly the *P*.........John 6:14
with him the false *p*........Rev 19:20

PROPHETIC

p word made more sure...2 Pe 1:19

PROPHETS

LORD's people were *p*.....Num 11:29
Saul also among the *p*.....1 Sa 10:12
the mouth of all his *p*......1 Ki 22:22
Where now are your *p*.....Jer 37:19
prophesy against the *p*.....Ezek 13:2
Her *p* are insolent...........Zeph 3:4
the Law or the *P*...........Matt 5:17
is the Law and the *P*......Matt 7:12
or one of the *p*..............Matt 16:14
the tombs of the *p*.........Matt 23:29
indeed, I send you *p*....... Matt 23:34
one who kills the *p*........Matt 23:37

PROSPEROUS

Then many false *p*.........Matt 24:11
have Moses and the *p*.....Luke 16:29
You are sons of the *p*......Acts 3:25
p did your fathers not......Acts 7:52
To Him all the *p*............Acts 10:43
do you believe the *p*......Acts 26:27
before through His *p*.......Rom 1:2
by the Law and the *P*.....Rom 3:21
have killed Your p..........Rom 11:3
p are subject to the.........1 Co 14:32
to be apostles, some *p*.....Eph 4:11
brethren, take the *p*........Jas 5:10
this salvation the *p*..........1 Pe 1:10
were also false *p*.............2 Pe 2:1
because many false *p*.......1 Jn 4:1
blood of saints and *p*......Rev 16:6
found the blood of *p*.......Rev 18:24
of your brethren the *p*..... Rev 22:9

PROPITIATION

set forth to be a *p*...........Rom 3:25
to God, to make *p*..........Heb 2:17
He Himself is the *p*.........1 Jn 2:2
His Son to be the *p*.........1 Jn 4:10

PROPORTION

let us prophesy in *p*........Rom 12:6

PROPRIETY

modest apparel, with *p*.... 1 Ti 2:9

PROSECUTOR

answer me, that my *P*......Job 31:35

PROSELYTE

and sea to win one *p*.......Matt 23:15

PROSELYTES

Rome, both Jews and *p*... Acts 2:10

PROSPER

made all he did to *p*........Gen 39:3
you shall not *p*...............Deut 28:29
LORD, God made him *p*..2 Ch 26:5
they *p* who love you........Ps 122:6
his sins will not *p*............Prov 28:13
of the LORD shall *p*........Is 53:10
against you shall *p*..........Is 54:17
please, and it shall *p*.......Is 55:11
of the wicked *p*.............Jer 12:1
King shall reign and *p*.....Jer 23:5
storing up as he may *p*.... 1 Co 16:2
I pray that you may *p*......3 Jn 2

PROSPERED

since the LORD has *p*......Gen 24:56

PROSPERING

His ways are always *p*.....Ps 10:5

PROSPERITY

p all your days...............Deut 23:6
p exceed the fame...........1 Ki 10:7
p the destroyer..............Job 15:21
spend their days in *p*.......Job 36:11
Now in my *p* I said.........Ps 30:6
has pleasure in the *p*.......Ps 35:27
When I saw the *p*..........Ps 73:3
I pray, send now *p*.........Ps 118:25
the day of *p* be joyful.....Eccl 7:14
that we have our *p*..........Acts 19:25

PROSPEROUS

had made his journey *p*... Gen 24:21
will make your way *p*...... Josh 1:8

PROSPERS
he turns, he *p*................. Prov 17:8
just as your soul *p*.......... 3 Jn 2

PROSTRATE
of the proud lie *p*........... Job 9:13

PROUD
p waves must stop...........Job 38:11
tongue that speaks *p*........Ps 12:3
And fully repays the *p*.....Ps 31:23
does not respect the *p*.....Ps 40:4
a haughty look and a *p*....Ps 101:5
p He knows from afar.....Ps 138:6
the house of the *p*.......Prov 15:25
Everyone who is *p*......... Prov 16:5
p heart stirs up................Prov 28:25
is better than the *p*.........Eccl 7:8
by wine, he is a *p*.........Hab 2:5
he has scattered the *p*.....Luke 1:51
"God resists the *p*...........1 Pe 5:5

PROVE
p yourself a man..............1 Ki 2:2
does your arguing *p*........Job 6:25
p Me now in this............Mal 3:10
mind, that you may *p*.....Rom 12:2
P yourselves...................2 Co 13:5

PROVED
p you at the waters of.....Ps 81:7
also first be *p*.................1 Ti 3:10
when he has been *p*........Jas 1:12

PROVERB
an astonishment, a *p*.....Deut 28:37
incline my ear to a *p*......Ps 49:4
that hang limp is a *p*......Prov 26:7
of a drunkard is a *p*......Prov 26:9
one shall take up a *p*......Mic 2:4
to the true *p*.................2 Pe 2:22

PROVERBS
spoke three thousand *p*....1 Ki 4:32
in order many *p*..............Eccl 12:9

PROVIDE
"My son, God will *p*...... Gen 22:8
Can He *p* meat for His....Ps 78:20
prosperity that I *p*...........Jer 33:9
"*P* neither gold nor........Matt 10:9
if anyone does not *p*........1 Ti 5:8

PROVIDED
these hands have *p*..........Acts 20:34
p something better..........Heb 11:40

PROVIDES
p food for the raven........Job 38:41
p her supplies in the........Prov 6:8

PROVISION
abundantly bless her *p*....Ps 132:15
Christ, and make no *p*....Rom 13:14

PROVOKE
do not *p* Him................Ex 23:21
p God are secure............Job 12:6
"Do they *p* Me to.........Jer 7:19
p them to jealousy......... Rom 11:11
you, fathers, do not *p*.....Eph 6:4

PROVOKED
How often they *p*...........Ps 78:40
p the Most High.............Ps 78:56
Thus they *p* Him to........Ps 106:29

his spirit was *p*...............Acts 17:16
seek its own, is not *p*.....1 Co 13:5

PRUDENCE
to give *p* to the..............Prov 1:4
wisdom, dwell with *p*.......Prov 8:12
us in all wisdom and *p*.....Eph 1:8

PRUDENT
p man covers shame.........Prov 12:16
A *p* man conceals...........Prov 12:23
The wisdom of the *p*......Prov 14:8
p man considers well........Prov 14:15
heart will be called *p*......Prov 16:21
p acquires knowledge......Prov 18:15
p wife is from the...........Prov 19:14
p man foresees evil.........Prov 22:3
perished from the *p*.........Jer 49:7
Therefore the *p*..............Amos 5:13
from the wise and *p*........Matt 11:25

PRUDENTLY
Servant shall deal *p*.........Is 52:13

PRUNES
that bears fruit He *p*.......John 15:2

PSALM
and the sound of a *p*.......Ps 98:5
in the second *P*..............Acts 13:33
each of you has a *p*.........1 Co 14:26

PSALMIST
and the sweet *p*..............2 Sa 23:1

PSALMS
Sing to Him, sing *p*.........1 Ch 16:9
to one another in *p*.........Eph 5:19
Let him sing *p*.................Jas 5:13

PSALTERY
harp, lyre, and *p*.............Dan 3:10

PUFFED
Now some are *p* up.........1 Co 4:18
itself, is not *p*................1 Co 13:4
a novice, lest being *p*.......1 Ti 3:6

PUFFS
Knowledge *p* up.............. 1 Co 8:1

PULL
P me out of the net........ Ps 31:4
I will *p* down my barns....Luke 12:18

PUNISH
take that man and *p*........Deut 22:18
p the righteous is............Prov 17:26
"I will *p* the world...........Is 13:11
Shall I not *p* them for.....Jer 5:9
p all who oppress them.....Jer 30:20
p your iniquity................Lam 4:22
So I will *p* them for........Hos 4:9

PUNISHED
You our God have *p*.......Ezra 9:13
because He has not *p*......Job 35:15
p them often in every......Acts 26:11
These shall be *p*............. 2 Th 1:9

PUNISHES
will you say when He *p*... Jer 13:21

PUNISHMENT
p is greater than I...........Gen 4:13
you do in the day of *p*....Is 10:3

p they shall be cast......... Jer 8:12
p they shall perish...........Jer 10:15
a man for the *p*..............Lam 3:39
The *p* of the iniquity.......Lam 4:6
days of *p* have come........Hos 9:7
not turn away its *p*..........Amos 1:3
into everlasting *p*............ Matt 25:46
p which was inflicted....... 2 Co 2:6
Of how much worse *p*..... Heb 10:29
sent by him for the *p*.......1 Pe 2:14
the unjust under *p*............ 2 Pe 2:9

PURCHASED
of God could be *p*...........Acts 8:20
of the *p* possession..........Eph 1:14

PURE
a mercy seat of *p* gold.....Ex 25:17
Can a man be more *p*.....Job 4:17
if you were *p* and...........Job 8:6
'my doctrine is *p*.............Job 11:4
that he could be *p*...........Job 15:14
the heavens are not *p*.....Job 15:15
the stars are not *p*..........Job 25:5
of the LORD are *p*...........Ps 12:6
will show Yourself *p*........Ps 18:26
To such as are *p*............Ps 73:1
of the *p* are pleasant.......Prov 15:26
ways of a man are *p*.......Prov 16:2
my heart clean, I am *p*.....Prov 20:9
but as for the *p*..............Prov 21:8
a generation that is *p*......Prov 30:12
Shall I count *p*...............Mic 6:11
things indeed are *p*.........Rom 14:20
whatever things are *p*...... Phil 4:8
keep yourself *p*...............1 Ti 5:22
p all things are *p*..........Tit 1:15
above is first *p*...............Jas 3:17
babes, desire the *p*..........1 Pe 2:2
just as He is *p*.................1 Jn 3:3

PURER
p eyes than to behold...... Hab 1:13

PURGE
P me with hyssop............Ps 51:7
p them as gold and.........Mal 3:3
p His threshing floor....... Matt 3:12
p your conscience...........Heb 9:14

PURGED
away, and your sin *p*....... Is 6:7
and you were not *p*.........Ezek 24:13
He had by Himself *p*.......Heb 1:3
all things are *p*...............Heb 9:22

PURIFICATION
for the water of *p*...........Num 19:9
with the water of *p*.........Num 31:23

PURIFIED
earth, *P* seven times........Ps 12:6
Since you have *p*.............1 Pe 1:22

PURIFIES
hope in Him *p* himself.....1 Jn 3:3

PURIFY
p the sons of Levi...........Mal 3:3
and *p* your hearts............Jas 4:8

PURIFYING
thus *p* all foods..............Mark 7:19
p their hearts by.............Acts 15:9
sanctifies for the *p*.........Heb 9:13

PURIM

called these days P..........Esth 9:26

PURITY

be delivered by the p.....Job 22:30
He who loves p of......... Prov 22:11
by p, by knowledge.........2 Co 6:6
spirit, in faith, in p..........1 Ti 4:12

PURPLE

who was clothed in p.......Luke 16:19
they put on Him a p...... John 19:2
She was a seller of p...... Acts 16:14

PURPOSE

And fulfill all your p....... Ps 20:4
p is established............... Prov 20:18
a time for every p...........Eccl 3:1
p that is purposed.......... Is 14:26
But for this p I came......John 12:27
them all that with p.........Acts 11:23
to the eternal p............. Eph 3:11
Now the p of the........... 1 Ti 1:5
to fulfill His p................. Rev 17:17

PURPOSED

For the LORD had p.......2 Sa 17:14
LORD of hosts has p.......Is 23:9
But Daniel p in his........Dan 1:8
pleasure which He p........Eph 1:9

PURPOSES

each one give as he p......2 Co 9:7

PURSE

let us all have one p.......Prov 1:14

PURSUE

And will You p dry.........Job 13:25
p my honor as the wind...Job 30:15
The sword shall p...........Jer 48:2
but their hearts p...........Ezek 33:31
Let us know, let us p......Hos 6:3
p righteousness............... Rom 9:30
P love............................1 Co 14:1
p righteousness............... 1 Ti 6:11
him seek peace and p...... 1 Pe 3:11

PURSUES

Evil p sinners................. Prov 13:21
flee when no one p......... Prov 28:1

PURSUING

but Israel, p the law........ Rom 9:31

PUT

Also He has p eternity.....Eccl 3:11
what you will p on.......... Matt 6:25
p my hand into His........John 20:25
But p on the Lord.......... Rom 13:14

— Q —

QUAIL

and it brought q............. Num 11:31
and He brought q........... Ps 105:40

QUAKED

the whole mountain q......Ex 19:18
and the earth q...............Matt 27:51

QUAKES

The earth q before..........Joel 2:10

QUALIFIED

the Father who has q.......Col 1:12

QUARREL

see how he seeks a q.......2 Ki 5:7
any fool can start a q...... Prov 20:3
He will not q nor cry.......Matt 12:19
of the Lord must not q.... 2 Ti 2:24

QUARRELSOME

but gentle, not q.............1 Ti 3:3

QUARTZ

be made of coral or q......Job 28:18

QUEEN

Q Vashti also made a....... Esth 1:9
hand stands the q............Ps 45:9
burn incense to the q......Jer 44:17
"The q of the South....... Matt 12:42
under Candace the q....... Acts 8:27
heart, 'I sit as q.............. Rev 18:7

QUEENS

There are sixty q........... Song 6:8
q your nursing mothers.... Is 49:23

QUENCH

Many waters cannot q.....Song 8:7
so that no one can q....... Jer 4:4
flax He will not q...........Matt 12:20
q all the fiery................. Eph 6:16
Do not q the Spirit......... 1 Th 5:19

QUENCHED

LORD, the fire was q.....Num 11:2
They were q like a..........Ps 118:12
their fire is not q............ Is 66:24
that shall never be q.......Mark 9:43
and the fire is not q........ Mark 9:44
q the violence of fire...... Heb 11:34

QUESTIONS

test him with hard q........1 Ki 10:1
and asking them q..........Luke 2:46
market, asking no q........ 1 Co 10:25

QUICK-TEMPERED

q acts foolishly............... Prov 14:17
not self-willed, not q....... Tit 1:7

QUICKLY

have turned aside q........Ex 32:8
with your adversary q..... Matt 5:25
"What you do, do q.......John 13:27
"Behold, I come q......... Rev 3:11
Surely I am coming q...... Rev 22:20

QUIET

lain still and been q.........Job 3:13
'Take heed, and be q...... Is 7:4
earth is at rest and q....... Is 14:7
gladness, He will q.........Zeph 3:17
warned him to be q........Mark 10:48
aspire to lead a q............1 Th 4:11
we may lead a q and.......1 Ti 2:2
a gentle and q spirit........ 1 Pe 3:4

QUIETED

calmed and q my soul......Ps 131:2
the city clerk had q......... Acts 19:35

QUIETNESS

will give peace and q.......1 Ch 22:9
When He gives q............Job 34:29
is a handful with q..........Eccl 4:6
in q and confidence.........Is 30:15
of righteousness, q.......... Is 32:17
that they work in q......... 2 Th 3:12

QUIETS

q the earth by the...........Job 37:17

QUIVER

q rattles against him.......Job 39:23
the man who has his q.....Ps 127:5
q He has hidden Me........Is 49:2
Their q is like an............ Jer 5:16

— R —

RABBI

be called by men, 'R....... Matt 23:7
do not be called 'R........ Matt 23:8

RACA

to his brother, 'R........... Matt 5:22

RACE

man to run its r............. Ps 19:5
r is not to the swift........ Eccl 9:11
who run in a r all run......1 Co 9:24
I have finished the r.......2 Ti 4:7
with endurance the r....... Heb 12:1

RAGE

Disperse the r of your..... Job 40:11
Why do the nations r.......Ps 2:1
Why did the nations r...... Acts 4:25

RAGES

he r against all wise.........Prov 18:1

RAGS

clothe a man with r.........Prov 23:21

RAIN

had not caused it to r......Gen 2:5
And the r was on the...... Gen 7:12
He gives r on the............Job 5:10
to the gentle r................Job 37:6
sent a plentiful r.............Ps 68:9
clouds, Who prepares r....Ps 147:8
snow in summer and r..... Prov 26:1
r which leaves no food.....Prov 28:3
not return after the r....... Eccl 12:2
the r is over and gone..... Song 2:11
our God, Who gives r.....Jer 5:24
I will r down on him....... Ezek 38:22
given you the former r.....Joel 2:23
there will be no r........... Zech 14:17
the good, and sends r...... Matt 5:45
"and the r descended......Matt 7:25
He did good, gave us r.... Acts 14:17
r that often comes...........Heb 6:7
that it would not r.......... Jas 5:17
and the heaven gave r..... Jas 5:18

RAINBOW

"I set My r in the...........Gen 9:13
and there was a r............Rev 4:3

RAINED

Had r down manna on.....Ps 78:24
r fire and brimstone...... Luke 17:29

RAINS

r righteousness................Hos 10:12

RAISE

third day He will r......... Hos 6:2
that God is able to r....... Matt 3:9
in three days I will r.......John 2:19
and I will r him up at......John 6:40
Lord and will also r........1 Co 6:14
and the Lord will r.........Jas 5:15

RAISED

this purpose I have *r*....... Ex 9:16
be killed, and be *r*......... Matt 16:21
"whom God *r* up........... Acts 2:24
just as Christ was *r*...... Rom 6:4
Spirit of Him who *r*........ Rom 8:11
And God both *r* up the... 1 Co 6:14
"How are the dead *r*...... 1 Co 15:35
and the dead will be *r*..... 1 Co 15:52
and *r* us up together........ Eph 2:6
then you were *r*.............. Col 3:1

RAISES

r the poor out of the....... Ps 113:7
r those who are bowed.... Ps 146:8
For as the Father *r*......... John 5:21
but in God who *r*............ 2 Co 1:9

RAM

r which had two horns..... Dan 8:3

RAMS

the sweet aroma of *r*....... Ps 66:15
r of Nebaioth shall.......... Is 60:7

RAN

they both *r* together....... John 20:4
You *r* well..................... Gal 5:7

RANSOM

r would not help you....... Job 36:18
Nor give to God a *r*........ Ps 49:7
The *r* of a man's life....... Prov 13:8
"I will *r* them from....... Hos 13:14
to give His life a *r*......... Mark 10:45
who gave Himself a *r*...... 1 Ti 2:6

RANSOMED

And the *r* of the LORD... Is 35:10
redeemed Jacob, and *r*.....Jer 31:11

RARE

of the LORD was *r*......... 1 Sa 3:1
make a mortal more *r*......Is 13:12

RASH

Do not be *r* with your..... Eccl 5:2

RASHLY

So that he spoke *r*.......... Ps 106:33
and do nothing *r*............ Acts 19:36

RAVEN

food for the *r*................. Job 38:41
and black as a *r*.............. Song 5:11

RAVENOUS

inwardly they are *r*......... Matt 7:15

RAVENS

And to the young *r*......... Ps 147:9
"Consider the *r*.............. Luke 12:24

RAVISHED

You have *r* my heart....... Song 4:9
r the women in Zion....... Lam 5:11

RAZOR

Like a sharp *r*................ Ps 52:2

REACHED

earth, and its top *r*.......... Gen 28:12
For her sins have *r*.......... Rev 18:5

REACHING

thus not *r* you.............. 2 Co 10:14
r forward to those........... Phil 3:13

READ

"Did you never *r*........... Matt 21:42
day, and stood up to *r*..... Luke 4:16
hearts, known and *r*........ 2 Co 3:2
when Moses is *r*............. 2 Co 3:15
when this epistle is *r*........ Col 4:16

READER

let the *r* understand........ Mark 13:14

READINESS

the word with all *r*......... Acts 17:11
that as there was a *r*........ 2 Co 8:11

READING

r the prophet Isaiah........ Acts 8:30
give attention to *r*........... 1 Ti 4:13

READS

that he may run who *r*..... Hab 2:2
Blessed is he who *r*......... Rev 1:3

READY

"The LORD was *r*........... Is 38:20
and those who were *r*...... Matt 25:10
The spirit truly is *r*......... Mark 14:38
"Lord, I am *r*................. Luke 22:33
and being *r* to punish...... 2 Co 10:6
Be *r* in season and out..... 2 Ti 4:2
and always be *r*.............. 1 Pe 3:15

REAP

in tears Shall *r*............... Ps 126:5
r the whirlwind............... Hos 8:7
they neither sow nor *r*..... Matt 6:26
you knew that I *r*............ Matt 25:26
that he will also *r*........... Gal 6:7
due season we shall *r*....... Gal 6:9

REAPED

wheat but *r* thorns.......... Jer 12:13
you have *r* iniquity......... Hos 10:13

REAPER

r does not fill his............ Ps 129:7

REAPERS

I will say to the *r*........... Matt 13:30
r are the angels.............. Matt 13:39

REAPING

r what I did not.............. Luke 19:22

REAPS

One sows and another *r*... John 4:37

REASON

out wisdom and the *r*...... Eccl 7:25
Come now, and let us *r*... Is 1:18
faith, why do you *r*......... Matt 16:8
words of truth and *r*....... Acts 26:25
who asks you a *r*............ 1 Pe 3:15

REASONED

for three Sabbaths *r*........ Acts 17:2
r about righteousness....... Acts 24:25

REBEL

"Only do not *r*............... Num 14:9
Will you *r* against the...... Neh 2:19
There are those who *r*..... Job 24:13
And they did not *r*.......... Ps 105:28
if you refuse and *r*.......... Is 1:20

REBELLING

more against Him By *r*.... Ps 78:17

REBELLION

r is as the sin................. 1 Sa 15:23
For he adds *r* to his........ Job 34:37
evil man seeks only *r*....... Prov 17:11
you have taught *r*........... Jer 28:16
hearts as in the r............ Heb 3:8
and perished in the *r*....... Jude 11

REBELLIOUS

r exalt themselves........... Ps 66:7
But the *r* dwell in a......... Ps 68:6
day long to a *r* people..... Is 65:2
a defiant and *r* heart....... Jer 5:23
their princes are *r*.......... Hos 9:15

REBELS

are all stubborn *r*........... Jer 6:28

REBUILD

God, to *r* its ruins.......... Ezra 9:9
tombs, that I may *r*......... Neh 2:5
r it as in the days of....... Amos 9:11

REBUKE

They perish at the *r*........ Ps 80:16
At Your *r* they fled........ Ps 104:7
r a wise man................. Prov 9:8
r is better than love........ Prov 27:5
better to hear the *r*........ Eccl 7:5
sake I have suffered *r*..... Jer 15:15
r strong nations............. Mic 4:3
sins against you, *r*.......... Luke 17:3
r Your disciples............. Luke 19:39
Do not *r* an older man..... 1 Ti 5:1
who are sinning *r*........... 1 Ti 5:20
r them sharply............... Tit 1:13
The Lord *r* you............. Jude 9
As many as I love, I *r*..... Rev 3:19

REBUKED

r the winds and the........ Matt 8:26
r their unbelief.............. Mark 16:14
when you are r by Him..... Heb 12:5
but he was *r* for his........ 2 Pe 2:16

REBUKES

with *r* You correct.......... Ps 39:11
r a wicked man gets........ Prov 9:7
r a man will find more..... Prov 28:23

RECALL

r the former days........... Heb 10:32

RECEIVE

He shall *r* blessing.......... Ps 24:5
r us graciously............... Hos 14:2
you are willing to *r*......... Matt 11:14
believing, you will *r*........ Matt 21:22
and His own did not *r*..... John 1:11
"I do not *r* honor........... John 5:41
will come again and *r*...... John 14:3
the world cannot *r*.......... John 14:17
Ask, and you will *r*......... John 16:24
R the Holy Spirit........... John 20:22
"Lord Jesus, *r*............... Acts 7:59
r the Holy Spirit............ Acts 19:2
R one who is weak.......... Rom 14:1
that each one may *r*........ 2 Co 5:10
r the grace of God in...... 2 Co 6:1
r the Spirit by the.......... Gal 3:2
R him therefore in the..... Phil 2:29
suppose that he will *r*..... Jas 1:7
whatever we ask we *r*...... 1 Jn 3:22

RECEIVED

r your consolation.......... Luke 6:24
in your lifetime you r...... Luke 16:25
But as many as r............ John 1:12
for God has r him...........Rom 14:3
For I r from the Lord......1 Co 11:23
r Christ...................... Col 2:6
r up in glory................. 1 Ti 3:16
For He r from God the....2 Pe 1:17

RECEIVES

r reproof is prudent........Prov 15:5
r you r Me..................Matt 10:40
r one little child............Matt 18:5
and whoever r Me..........Mark 9:37

RECEIVING

r a kingdom which......... Heb 12:28

RECOMPENSE

He will accept no r........ Prov 6:35
not say, "I will r............Prov 20:22
days of r have come....... Hos 9:7

RECOMPENSED

of my hands He has r......2 Sa 22:21
the LORD has r me.........2 Sa 22:25

RECONCILE

and that He might r........ Eph 2:16
r all things to................ Col 1:20

RECONCILED

First be r to your........... Matt 5:24
were enemies we were r...Rom 5:10
Christ's behalf, be r.........2 Co 5:20

RECONCILIATION

now received the r.......... Rom 5:11
to us the word of r..........2 Co 5:19

RECONCILING

cast away is the r........... Rom 11:15
God was in Christ r.........2 Co 5:19

RECORD

r My name I will come.... Ex 20:24

RED

the first came out r......... Gen 25:25
though they are r............Is 1:18
Why is Your apparel r.....Is 63:2
for the sky is r.............. Matt 16:2

REDEEM

man you shall surely r..... Num 18:15
in our power to r them.....Neh 5:2
In famine He shall r........Job 5:20
R me from the hand of....Job 6:23
can by any means r........Ps 49:7
But God will r my soul....Ps 49:15
r their life from............. Ps 72:14
And He shall r Israel.......Ps 130:8
all that it cannot r..........Is 50:2
I will r them from..........Hos 13:14
was going to r Israel.......Luke 24:21
r those who were............Gal 4:5
us, that He might r.......... Tit 2:14

REDEEMED

people whom You have r. Ex 15:13
r them from the hand......Ps 106:10
Let the r of the LORD.... Ps 107:2
r shall walk there...........Is 35:9
sea a road for the r.........Is 51:10
and you shall be r..........Is 52:3

and r His people............Luke 1:68
Christ has r us from........ Gal 3:13
that you were not r.........1 Pe 1:18
were slain, and have r..... Rev 5:9
These were r from.......... Rev 14:4

REDEEMER

For I know that my R..... Job 19:25
Most High God their r.....Ps 78:35
for their R is mighty.......Prov 23:11
the LORD and your R..... Is 41:14
R will come to Zion........ Is 59:20
our R from Everlasting.... Is 63:16
Their R is strong...........Jer 50:34

REDEEMING

r the time.................... Eph 5:16

REDEMPTION

For the r of their............ Ps 49:8
with Him is abundant r....Ps 130:7
r is yours to buy it..........Jer 32:7
those who looked for r.... Luke 2:38
heads, because your r......Luke 21:28
grace through the r......... Rom 3:24
the adoption, the r..........Rom 8:23
sanctification and r.........1 Co 1:30
In Him we have r........... Eph 1:7
for the day of r............. Eph 4:30
obtained eternal r........... Heb 9:12

REED

r He will not break......... Is 42:3
r shaken by the wind......Matt 11:7
on the head with a r.......Mark 15:19

REEDS

r flourish without............Job 8:11
the beasts of the r..........Ps 68:30

REFINED

where gold is r.............. Job 28:1
us as silver is r.............. Ps 66:10

REFINER

He will sit as a r............Mal 3:3

REFORMATION

until the time of r.......... Heb 9:10

REFRAIN

R from meddling with......2 Ch 35:21
who have no right to r.....1 Co 9:6
good days, let him r........1 Pe 3:10

REFRESH

bread, that you may r......Gen 18:5
r my heart in the Lord....Phm 20

REFRESHED

of God, and may be r......Rom 15:32
r my spirit and yours......1 Co 16:18
his spirit has been r.........2 Co 7:13
for he often r................2 Ti 1:16

REFRESHES

r the soul of his.............Prov 25:13

REFRESHING

r may come from the.......Acts 3:19

REFUGE

six cities of r.................Num 35:6
eternal God is your r.......Deut 33:27
you have come for r.........Ruth 2:12
But the LORD is his r..... Ps 14:6

God is our r and.............Ps 46:1
wings I will make my r....Ps 57:1
God is a r for us.............Ps 62:8
You are my strong r........Ps 71:7
who have fled for r.........Heb 6:18

REFUSE

r the evil and choose.......Is 7:15
through deceit they r.......Jer 9:6
hear or whether they r.....Ezek 2:5
See that you do not r......Heb 12:25

REFUSED

They r to obey...............Neh 9:17

REFUSES

My soul r to touch..........Job 6:7
"And if he r to hear........Matt 18:17

REGARD

r the rich more than........Job 34:19
r iniquity in my heart...... Ps 66:18
r the prayer of the..........Ps 102:17
did not fear God nor r.....Luke 18:2

REGARDED

my hand and no one r.....Prov 1:24
r the lowly state.............Luke 1:48

REGARDS

r reproof will be............. Prov 13:18
He no longer r them........Lam 4:16

REGENERATION

to you, that in the r........Matt 19:28
the washing of r..............Tit 3:5

REGISTERED

So all went to be r.........Luke 2:3
firstborn who are r..........Heb 12:23

REGRETTED

but afterward he r..........Matt 21:29

REGULATIONS

yourselves to r................Col 2:20

REIGN

but a king shall r............1 Sa 12:12
hypocrite should not r.....Job 34:30
so the LORD will r..........Mic 4:7
"And He will r..............Luke 1:33
not have this man to r.....Luke 19:14
righteousness will r.........Rom 5:17
so grace might r.............Rom 5:21
do not let sin r..............Rom 6:12
For He must r till He......1 Co 15:25
and we shall r on the......Rev 5:10
of Christ, and shall r.......Rev 20:6

REIGNED

so that as sin r...............Rom 5:21
You have r as kings........1 Co 4:8
And they lived and r.......Rev 20:4

REIGNS

God r over the nations.... Ps 47:8
The LORD r..................Ps 93:1
to Zion, "Your God r.....Is 52:7
Lord God Omnipotent r...Rev 19:6

REJECT

will these people r..........Num 14:11
r all those who stray.......Ps 119:118
"All too well you r.........Mark 7:9
R a divisive man............Tit 3:10

REJECTED

r Has become the chief.... Ps 118:22
He is despised and r........Is 53:3
r has become the chief.... Matt 21:42
many things and be r......Luke 17:25
This Moses whom they r.. Acts 7:35
to a living stone, r.......... 1 Pe 2:4
r has become the chief.... 1 Pe 2:7

REJECTION

you shall know My r...... Num 14:34

REJECTS

he who r Me r................Luke 10:16
r this does not reject....... 1 Th 4:8

REJOICE

so the LORD will r........ Deut 28:63
let the field r..................1 Ch 16:32
and let Your saints r....... 2 Ch 6:41
r who put their trust....Ps 5:11
people, Let Jacob r......... Ps 14:7
R in the LORD...............Ps 33:1
mutual confusion Who r...Ps 35:26
The righteous shall r...... Ps 58:10
of Your wings I will r......Ps 63:7
But the king shall r........ Ps 63:11
Let them r before God.... Ps 68:3
In Your name they r....... Ps 89:16
Let the heavens r...........Ps 96:11
Let the earth r............. Ps 97:1
righteous see it and r......Ps 107:42
We will r and be glad..... Ps 118:24
who r in doing evil.........Prov 2:14
be blessed, and r.......... Prov 5:18
she shall r in time to...... Prov 31:25
R, O young man.............Eccl 11:9
We will be glad and r......Song 1:4
among men shall r.......... Is 29:19
I will greatly r............... Is 61:10
My servants shall r......... Is 65:13
your heart shall r........... Is 66:14
'Yes, I will r.................. Jer 32:41
Do not r over me.......... Mic 7:8
He will r over you......... Zeph 3:17
Nevertheless do not r...... Luke 10:20
loved Me, you would r.... John 14:28
but the world will r........ John 16:20
and your heart will r...... John 16:22
R with those who.......... Rom 12:15
and in this I r...............Phil 1:18
faith, I am glad and r......Phil 2:17
R in the Lord always...... Phil 4:4
R always.....................1 Th 5:16
yet believing, you r......... 1 Pe 1:8

REJOICED

for good as He r.............Deut 30:9
for my heart r................ Eccl 2:10
and my spirit has r........Luke 1:47
In that hour Jesus r........Luke 10:21
Your father Abraham r....John 8:56
But I r in the Lord........ Phil 4:10

REJOICES

glad, and my glory r........Ps 16:9
but r in the truth............ 1 Co 13:6

REJOICING

His works with r.............Ps 107:22
The voice of r and.......... Ps 118:15
For they are the r........... Ps 119:111
come again with r.......... Ps 126:6
r in His inhabited............Prov 8:31
he went on his way r....... Acts 8:39
yet always r.................. 2 Co 6:10

or joy, or crown of r.......1 Th 2:19
confidence and the r........Heb 3:6

RELEASE

do you want me to r...... Matt 27:17
and power to r You........ John 19:10
R the four angels............ Rev 9:14

RELENT

sworn And will not r....... Ps 110:4
and will not r.................Jer 4:28
then the LORD will r....... Jer 26:13
if He will turn and r........Joel 2:14
sworn and will not r........ Heb 7:21

RELENTED

So the LORD r from the.. Ex 32:14
the LORD looked and r... 1 Ch 21:15
and God r from the........Jon 3:10

RELIEF

saw that there was r....... Ex 8:15
that I may find r.............Job 32:20

RELIEVE

of my lips would r..........Job 16:5
r those who are really......1 Ti 5:16

RELIEVED

You have r me when I.....Ps 4:1

RELIEVES

r the fatherless............... Ps 146:9

RELIGION

about their own r...........Acts 25:19
in self-imposed r............ Col 2:23
heart, this one's r...........Jas 1:26
and undefiled r..............Jas 1:27

RELIGIOUS

things you are very r...... Acts 17:22
you thinks he is r............Jas 1:26

RELY

name of the LORD and r. Is 50:10
"You r on your sword..... Ezek 33:26

REMAIN

shall let none of it r........ Ex 12:10
r angry forever............... Jer 3:5
and this city shall r.........Jer 17:25
that if ten men r............Amos 6:9
you, that My joy may r....John 15:11
your fruit should r..........John 15:16
If I will that he r...........John 21:22
the greater part r........... 1 Co 15:6
Nevertheless to r...........Phil 1:24
we who are alive and r.... 1 Th 4:15
the things which r.......... Rev 3:2

REMAINDER

With the r of wrath.........Ps 76:10
I am deprived of the r..... Is 38:10

REMAINED

Also my wisdom r............Eccl 2:9
And Mary r with her.......Luke 1:56
like a dove, and He r......John 1:32

REMAINS

"While the earth r......... Gen 8:22
Therefore your sin r........John 9:41
There r therefore a.........Heb 4:9
sin, for His seed r...........1 Jn 3:9

REMEMBER

"But r me when it is....... Gen 40:14
R the Sabbath day.......... Ex 20:8
r that you were a............Deut 15:15
R His marvelous works.... 1 Ch 16:12
But we will r the name.... Ps 20:7
r the sins of my youth..... Ps 25:7
r Your name in the......... Ps 119:55
R now your Creator........ Eccl 12:1
r your love more than......Song 1:4
r the former things.......... Is 43:18
"I r you.......................Jer 2:2
and their sin I will r........Jer 31:34
r the covenant of........... Amos 1:9
in wrath r mercy............Hab 3:2
and to r His holy............ Luke 1:72
"R Lot's wife................ Luke 17:32
r the words of the...........Acts 20:35
R my chains..................Col 4:18
R that Jesus Christ.........2 Ti 2:8
R those who rule............ Heb 13:7

REMEMBERED

Then God r Noah........... Gen 8:1
r His covenant with........Ex 2:24
I r God....................... Ps 77:3
r His covenant forever.....Ps 105:8
r Your judgments............Ps 119:52
Who r us in our lowly..... Ps 136:23
yea, we wept When we r..Ps 137:1
r that same poor man...... Eccl 9:15
r the days of old............. Is 63:11
And Peter r the word...... Matt 26:75
r the word of the Lord.... Acts 11:16

REMEMBERS

My soul still r.................Lam 3:20

REMEMBRANCE

in death there is no r.......Ps 6:5
r my song in the night..... Ps 77:6
There is no r of..............Eccl 1:11
Put Me in r.................... Is 43:26
do this in r of Me.......... Luke 22:19
do this in r of Me........... 1 Co 11:24

REMIND

r you always of these.......2 Pe 1:12
But I want to r you.........Jude 5

REMINDER

there is a r of sins..........Heb 10:3
you always have a r.........2 Pe 1:15
pure minds by way of r....2 Pe 3:1

REMISSION

repentance for the r........ Mark 1:4
Jesus Christ for the r....... Acts 2:38
where there is r..............Heb 10:18

REMNANT

to us a very small r.........Is 1:9
The r will return............. Is 10:21
be well with your r........Jer 15:11
I will gather the r........... Jer 23:3
and all the r of Judah...... Jer 44:28
Yet I will leave a r.........Ezek 6:8
r whom the LORD calls....Joel 2:32
I will not treat the r........ Zech 8:11
time there is a r..............Rom 11:5

REMORSEFUL

been condemned, was r....Matt 27:3

REMOVE

R Your plague from me... Ps 39:10
R Your gaze from me......Ps 39:13

REMOVED

r your foot from evil...... Prov 4:27
r falsehood and lies......... Prov 30:8
Therefore r sorrow.......... Eccl 11:10
r this cup from Me..........Luke 22:42
r your lampstand............Rev 2:5

REMOVED

Though the earth be r..... Ps 46:2
r our transgressions......... Ps 103:12
will never be r................Prov 10:30
and the hills be r............ Is 54:10
this mountain, 'Be r........ Matt 21:21

REMOVES

r the mountains.............. Job 9:5

REND

So r your heart...............Joel 2:13

RENDER

What shall I r to the..... Ps 116:12
who will r to him the......Matt 21:41
R therefore to Caesar..... Matt 22:21

RENEW

r a steadfast................... Ps 51:10
r the face of the............. Ps 104:30
on the LORD shall r........Is 40:31

RENEWED

that your youth is r........ Ps 103:5
inward man is being r......2 Co 4:16
and be r in the spirit....... Eph 4:23
the new man who is r...... Col 3:10

RENEWING

transformed by the r........Rom 12:2
of regeneration and r.......Tit 3:5

RENOUNCE

Why do the wicked r.......Ps 10:13

RENOUNCED

r the covenant of Your.... Ps 89:39
r the hidden things..........2 Co 4:2

RENOUNCES

greedy and r the LORD... Ps 10:3

RENOWN

were of old, men of r...... Gen 6:4

REPAID

done, so God has r.......... Judg 1:7
And he has r me evil.......1 Sa 25:21
good shall be r.............. Prov 13:21
Shall evil be r.................Jer 18:20

REPAIR

r the house of your......... 2 Ch 24:5
r the ruined cities............Is 61:4

REPAY

He will r him to his........Deut 7:10
silence, but will r.......... Is 65:6
He will surely r.............. Jer 51:56
again, I will r................Luke 10:35
because they cannot r......Luke 14:14
R no one evil for evil...... Rom 12:17
is Mine, I will r............. Rom 12:19
r their parents................. 1 Ti 5:4
I will r.........................Phm 19

REPAYS

and who r him for what... Job 21:31
r the proud person.......... Ps 31:23

shall he be who r............Ps 137:8
the LORD, Who fully r....Is 66:6

REPENT

I abhor myself, and r......Job 42:6
R, for the kingdom......... Matt 3:2
you r you will all............ Luke 13:3
said to them, "R.............Acts 2:38
men everywhere to r...... Acts 17:30
be zealous and r............. Rev 3:19

REPENTANCE

you with water unto r......Matt 3:11
a baptism of r for the..... Mark 1:4
persons who need no r.....Luke 15:7
sorrow produces r........... 2 Co 7:10
will grant them r.............2 Ti 2:25
renew them again to r..... Heb 6:6
found no place for r........ Heb 12:17
all should come to r........ 2 Pe 3:9

REPENTED

No man r of his.............Jer 8:6
after my turning, I r.......Jer 31:19
it, because they r............ Matt 12:41

REPETITIONS

r as the heathen do......... Matt 6:7

REPORT

circulate a false r............ Ex 23:1
For it is not a good r...... 1 Sa 2:24
r makes the bones..........Prov 15:30
Who has believed our r....Is 53:1
who has believed our r......Rom 10:16
things are of good r......Phil 4:8

REPRIMANDED

And they r him sharply....Judg 8:1

REPROACH

r me as long as I live...... Job 27:6
does he take up a r.........Ps 15:3
You make us a r.............Ps 44:13
sake I have borne r.........Ps 69:7
R has broken my heart.... Ps 69:20
nation, but sin is a r.......Prov 14:34
with dishonor comes r......Prov 18:3
do not fear the r............Is 51:7
not remember the r.........Is 54:4
bring an everlasting r.......Jer 23:40
because I bore the r........Jer 31:19
you shall bear the r........Mic 6:16
these things You r..........Luke 11:45
lest he fall into r.............1 Ti 3:7
esteeming the r..............Heb 11:26
and without r.................Jas 1:5

REPROACHED

If you are r for the......... 1 Pe 4:14

REPROACHES

is not an enemy who r.....Ps 55:12
oppresses the poor r.......Prov 14:31
curse, and Israel to r.......Is 43:28
in infirmities, in r...........2 Co 12:10

REPROACHFULLY

they strike me r..............Job 16:10

REPROOF

astonished at His r..........Job 26:11
Turn at my r..................Prov 1:23
but he who refuses r........Prov 10:17
but he who hates r..........Prov 12:1
ear that hears the r.........Prov 15:31

R is more effective..........Prov 17:10
for doctrine, for r........... 2 Ti 3:16

REPROOFS

r of instruction are..........Prov 6:23

REPROVE

He will surely r.............. Job 13:10
And let him r me.............Ps 141:5
Do not r a scoffer...........Prov 9:8
r the oppressor................Is 1:17

REPROVES

r a scoffer gets shame......Prov 9:7

REPUTATION

seven men of good r........Acts 6:3
to those who were of r.... Gal 2:2
made Himself of no r...... Phil 2:7

REQUEST

not withheld the r...........Ps 21:2
He gave them their r.......Ps 106:15
the Lord God to make r..Dan 9:3
For Jews r a sign............1 Co 1:22
of mine making r............Phil 1:4

REQUESTS

r be made known............Phil 4:6

REQUIRE

the LORD your God r.....Deut 10:12
a foreigner you may r......Deut 15:3
"You will not r...............Ps 10:13
offering You did not r......Ps 40:6
what does the LORD r.....Mic 6:8

REQUIRED

of the world may be r......Luke 11:50
your soul will be r..........Luke 12:20
him much will be r..........Luke 12:48
Moreover it is r..............1 Co 4:2

REQUIREMENTS

keeps the righteous r.......Rom 2:26
r that was against us........Col 2:14

RESCUE

R me from their.............. Ps 35:17
and no one shall r...........Hos 5:14

RESERVE

r the unjust under...........2 Pe 2:9

RESERVED

Which I have r for the.....Job 38:23
"I have r for Myself....... Rom 11:4
r in heaven for you..........1 Pe 1:4
of darkness, to be r.........2 Pe 2:4
habitation, He has r........Jude 6

RESIST

r an evil person.............. Matt 5:39
r the Holy Spirit............Acts 7:51
R the devil and he...........Jas 4:7

RESISTED

For who has r His will.....Rom 9:19
Jannes and Jambres r......2 Ti 3:8
for he has greatly r.........2 Ti 4:15
You have not yet r..........Heb 12:4

RESISTS

"God r the proud...........Jas 4:6
for "God r the proud......1 Pe 5:5

RESOLVED

'I have r what to do....... Luke 16:4

RESPECT

Have r to the covenant.... Ps 74:20
his eyes will have r.........Is 17:7
saying, 'They will r........Matt 21:37
of the law held in r........Acts 5:34
and we paid them r........Heb 12:9

RESPECTED

And the LORD r Abel.....Gen 4:4
little folly to one r......... Eccl 10:1

RESPONSE

in whose mouth is no r.... Ps 38:14

REST

is the Sabbath of r......... Ex 31:15
you shall find no r......... Deut 28:65
to build a house of r....... 1 Ch 28:2
I would have been at r.... Job 3:13
the weary are at r.......... Job 3:17
R in the LORD.............Ps 37:7
fly away and be at r....... Ps 55:6
of the LORD shall r........ Is 11:2
whole earth is at r..........Is 14:7
"This is the r................. Is 28:12
sake I will not r............Is 62:1
is the place of My r........Is 66:1
then you will find r........ Jer 6:16
and I will give you r.......Matt 11:28
and you will find r.......Matt 11:29
shall not enter My r........ Heb 3:11
remains therefore a r......Heb 4:9
to enter that r.............. Heb 4:11
And they do not r.......... Rev 4:8
that they should r.......... Rev 6:11
"that they may r............ Rev 14:13
But the r of the dead..... Rev 20:5

RESTED

He had done, and He r... Gen 2:2
glory of the LORD r........Ex 24:16
when the Spirit r..........Num 11:25
"And God r on the........ Heb 4:4

RESTING

do not plunder his r........ Prov 24:15
r place shall be............... Is 11:10
all the earth is r............Zech 1:11
still sleeping and r.......... Matt 26:45

RESTLESS

I am r in my complaint.... Ps 55:2

RESTORATION

until the times of r......... Acts 3:21

RESTORE

R to me the joy.............Ps 51:12
I still must r.................Ps 69:4
r your judges as.............Is 1:26
r them to this place........ Jer 27:22
For I will r health to....... Jer 30:17
"So I will r to you.......... Joel 2:25
declare that I will r........ Zech 9:12
and will r all things........ Matt 17:11
I r fourfold................. Luke 19:8
You at this time r........... Acts 1:6
who are spiritual r..........Gal 6:1

RESTORER

may he be to you a r...... Ruth 4:15

RESTORES

with joy, for He r........... Job 33:26
He r my soul.................Ps 23:3

RESTRAIN

now r Your hand............ 2 Sa 24:16
Therefore I will not r...... Job 7:11
Will You r Yourself........ Is 64:12
no one can r His hand..... Dan 4:35

RESTRAINED

r my feet from every....... Ps 119:101
Are they r..................... Is 63:15

RESTRAINS

For nothing r the LORD.. 1 Sa 14:6
r his lips is wise.............. Prov 10:19
only He who now r......... 2 Th 2:7

RESTRAINT

they have cast off r........... Job 30:11
they break all r...........Hos 4:2

RESTS

r quietly in the heart....... Prov 14:33

RESURRECTION

who say there is no r......Matt 22:23
"Therefore, in the r........ Matt 22:28
done good, to the r.........John 5:29
to her, "I am the r..........John 11:25
them Jesus and the r....... Acts 17:18
that there will be a r....... Acts 24:15
the likeness of His r....... Rom 6:5
say that there is no r....... 1 Co 15:12
and the power of His r.... Phil 3:10
that the r is already........2 Ti 2:18
obtain a better r............ Heb 11:35
This is the first r............Rev 20:5

RETAIN

happy are all who r........Prov 3:18
spirit to r the spirit.........Eccl 8:8
r the sins of any............ John 20:23
like to r God in their.......Rom 1:28

RETURN

So the LORD will r........ 1 Ki 2:32
And r to our neighbors....Ps 79:12
R, O LORD...................Ps 90:13
none who go to her r...... Prov 2:19
womb, naked shall he r....Eccl 5:15
the clouds do not r.........Eccl 12:2
let him r to the LORD.....Is 55:7
it shall not r to Me......... Is 55:11
"If you will r................Jer 4:1
for they shall r.............. Jer 24:7
me, and I will r............. Jer 31:18
say, 'I will go and r........Hos 2:7
help of your God, r........Hos 12:6
"R to Me.................... Zech 1:3
he says, 'I will r............Matt 12:44

RETURNED

And they r and sought.....Ps 78:34
yet you have not r......... Amos 4:6
astray, but have now r.....1 Pe 2:25

RETURNING

"I am r to Jerusalem...... Zech 1:16
r evil for evil or..............1 Pe 3:9

RETURNS

spirit departs, he r......... Ps 146:4
As a dog r to his own..... Prov 26:11
"A dog r to his own.......2 Pe 2:22

REVEAL

The heavens will r..........Job 20:27
I will heal them and r......Jer 33:6
the Son wills to r Him..... Matt 11:27
r His Son in me..............Gal 1:16
otherwise, God will r.......Phil 3:15

REVEALED

things which are r........... Deut 29:29
of the LORD shall be r....Is 40:5
righteousness to be r....... Is 56:1
Then the secret was r...... Dan 2:19
the Son of Man is r.........Luke 17:30
the wrath of God is r...... Rom 1:18
glory which shall be r...... Rom 8:18
But God has r them to.... 1 Co 2:10
as it has now been r.........Eph 3:5
but now has been r.........Col 1:26
the Lord Jesus is r.......... 2 Th 1:7
lawless one will be r........ 2 Th 2:8
ready to be r in the.........1 Pe 1:5
when His glory is r.........1 Pe 4:13
r what we shall be...........1 Jn 3:2

REVEALER

Lord of kings, and a r..... Dan 2:47

REVEALING

waits for the r................ Rom 8:19

REVEALS

as a talebearer r............. Prov 20:19
r deep and secret...........Dan 2:22
r secrets has made..........Dan 2:29
r His secret to His.......... Amos 3:7

REVELATION

Where there is no r........Prov 29:18
the day of wrath and r.....Rom 2:5
has a tongue, has a r......1 Co 14:26
it came through the r.......Gal 1:12
spirit of wisdom and r......Eph 1:17
r He made known to.......Eph 3:3
and glory at the r...........1 Pe 1:7

REVELATIONS

come to visions and r...... 2 Co 12:1

REVELRIES

drunkenness, r.................Gal 5:21
lusts, drunkenness, r........1 Pe 4:3

REVENGE

and we will take our r..... Jer 20:10

REVENUES

than vast r without.........Prov 16:8

REVERENCE

and r My sanctuary........ Lev 19:30
And to be held in r......... Ps 89:7
Master, where is My r..... Mal 1:6
submission with all r........1 Ti 3:4
God acceptably with r......Heb 12:28

REVERENT

man who is always r........Prov 28:14
their wives must be r.......1 Ti 3:11
older men be sober, r......Tit 2:2

REVILE

are you when they r........ Matt 5:11
r God's high priest..........Acts 23:4
evildoers, those who r......1 Pe 3:16

REVILED

crucified with Him r........Mark 15:32
who, when He was r....... 1 Pe 2:23

REVILER

or an idolater, or a r.......1 Co 5:11

REVILERS

nor drunkards, nor r.........1 Co 6:10

REVILING

come envy, strife, r.........1 Ti 6:4

REVILINGS

be afraid of their r..........Is 51:7

REVIVAL

give us a measure of r..... Ezra 9:8

REVIVE

troubles, Shall r...............Ps 71:20
Will You not r us........... Ps 85:6
R me according to Your...Ps 119:25
r the spirit of the............Is 57:15
two days He will r......... Hos 6:2
r Your work in the..........Hab 3:2

REVIVED

they shall be r................ Hos 14:7
came, sin r and I died..... Rom 7:9

REVOLT

You will r more and........Is 1:5

REVOLTED

Israel have deeply r.........Is 31:6
they have r and.............. Jer 5:23

REVOLTERS

r are deeply involved....... Hos 5:2

REWARD

exceedingly great r.......... Gen 15:1
them there is great r........Ps 19:11
r me evil for good.........Ps 35:12
"Surely there is a r......... Ps 58:11
look, And see the r........Ps 91:8
will be a sure r............... Prov 11:18
and the LORD will r...... Prov 25:22
and this was my r........... Eccl 2:10
behold, His r is with........Is 40:10
r them for their deeds...Hos 4:9
You have loved for r....... Hos 9:1
for great is your r........... Matt 5:12
you have no r from........Matt 6:1
you, they have their r..... Matt 6:2
receive a prophet's r.......Matt 10:41
by no means lose his r..... Matt 10:42
r will be great................ Luke 6:35
we receive the due r........Luke 23:41
will receive his own r.......1 Co 3:8
defraud you of your r......Col 2:18
for he looked to the r......Heb 11:26
may receive a full r.........2 Jn 8
quickly, and My r........... Rev 22:12

REWARDED

Thus they have r.............Ps 109:5

REWARDER

and that He is a r........... Heb 11:6

REWARDS

Whoever r evil for......... Prov 17:13
and follows after r...........Is 1:23
and give your r...............Dan 5:17

RICH

Abram was very r........... Gen 13:2
makes poor and makes r.. 1 Sa 2:7
r man will lie down.........Job 27:19
The r among the people...Ps 45:12
when one becomes r.........Ps 49:16
soul will be made r........ Prov 11:25
who makes himself r.......Prov 13:7
r has many friends......... Prov 14:20
The r and the poor......... Prov 22:2
r rules over the poor........Prov 22:7
r man is wise in his........ Prov 28:11
do not curse the r........... Eccl 10:20
it is hard for a r............. Matt 19:23
to you who are r.............Luke 6:24
from the r man's table.... Luke 16:21
for he was very r............ Luke 18:23
Lord over all is r............ Rom 10:12
You are already r........... 1 Co 4:8
though He was r.............2 Co 8:9
who desire to be r...........1 Ti 6:9
but the r in his............... Jas 1:10
So the r man also will......Jas 1:11
of this world to be r.......Jas 2:5
you say, 'I am r.............. Rev 3:17

RICHES

Both r and honor come....1 Ch 29:12
He swallows down r........Job 20:15
He heaps up r................. Ps 39:6
the abundance of his r.....Ps 62:10
If r increase................... Ps 62:10
r will be in his house.......Ps 112:3
in her left hand r............ Prov 3:16
R and honor are............. Prov 8:18
R do not profit.............. Prov 11:4
in his r will fall.............. Prov 11:28
yet has great r................ Prov 13:7
of the wise is their r........Prov 14:24
and r are an................... Prov 19:14
of the LORD are r......... Prov 22:4
r are not forever............Prov 27:24
r kept for their owner......Eccl 5:13
darkness and hidden r......Is 45:3
you shall eat the r...........Is 61:6
so is he who gets r...........Jer 17:11
have increased your r..... Ezek 28:5
for those who have r........ Mark 10:23
do you despise the r........Rom 2:4
might make known the r..Rom 9:23
what are the r................. Eph 1:18
show the exceeding r.......Eph 2:7
the unsearchable r...........Eph 3:8
trust in uncertain r..........1 Ti 6:17
r than the treasures........ Heb 11:26
r are corrupted.............. Jas 5:2
to receive power and r.....Rev 5:12

RICHLY

Christ dwell in you r....... Col 3:16
God, who gives us r......... 1 Ti 6:17

RIDDLE

"Let me pose a r............. Judg 14:12

RIDDLES

the wise and their r.........Prov 1:6

RIDE

wind and cause me to r....Job 30:22
in Your majesty r........... Ps 45:4
have caused men to r...... Ps 66:12

RIDER

r He has thrown............. Ex 15:1
the horse and its r...........Job 39:18

RIDES

Behold, the LORD r........Is 19:1

RIDICULE

Whom do you r..............Is 57:4

RIGHT

you shall do what is r......Deut 6:18
the r of the firstborn....... Deut 21:17
did what was r in his.......Judg 21:25
"Is your heart r..............2 Ki 10:15
them forth by the r.........Ps 107:7
Lord, "Sit at My r.........Ps 110:1
is a way which seems r.... Prov 14:12
way of a man is r............Prov 21:2
things that are r............. Is 45:19
until He comes whose r... Ezek 21:27
of the LORD are r.......... Hos 14:9
do not know to do r........ Amos 3:10
and whatever is r............ Matt 20:4
clothed and in his r.........Mark 5:15
not judge what is r..........Luke 12:57
to them He gave the r.....John 1:12
your heart is not r...........Acts 8:21
Do we have no r............. 1 Co 9:4
seven stars in His r.........Rev 2:1

RIGHTEOUS

also destroy the r............ Gen 18:23
and they justify the r.......Deut 25:1
"You are more r.............1 Sa 24:17
that he could be r............Job 15:14
r will hold to his way......Job 17:9
"The r see it and............Job 22:19
knows the way of the r.... Ps 1:6
LORD, will bless the r.....Ps 5:12
r God tests the hearts...... Ps 7:9
What can the r................Ps 11:3
The r cry out................. Ps 34:17
the LORD upholds the r.. Ps 37:17
r shows mercy and.......... Ps 37:21
I have not seen the r....... Ps 37:25
The r will be in.............. Ps 112:6
The LORD is r in all....... Ps 145:17
The LORD loves the r..... Ps 146:8
will not allow the r.........Prov 10:3
r is a well of life............ Prov 10:11
The labor of the r........... Prov 10:16
r will be gladness............Prov 10:28
r is delivered from......... Prov 11:8
r will be delivered...........Prov 11:21
r will flourish................. Prov 11:28
r will be recompensed......Prov 11:31
r man regards the life......Prov 12:10
r should choose his..........Prov 12:26
r there is much............... Prov 15:6
the prayer of the r.......... Prov 15:29
the r run to it and...........Prov 18:10
r are bold as a lion......... Prov 28:1
When the r are in...........Prov 29:2
r considers the cause....... Prov 29:7
Do not be overly r.......... Eccl 7:16
event happens to the r..... Eccl 9:2
r that it shall be.............Is 3:10
the gates, that the r........ Is 26:2
with My r right hand.......Is 41:10
by His knowledge My r....Is 53:11
The r perishes................ Is 57:1
people shall all be r........Is 60:21
R are You.....................Jer 12:1
your sins by being r........Dan 4:27
they sell the r................ Amos 2:6
not come to call the r...... Matt 9:13
r men desired to see........Matt 13:17
r will shine forth as........ Matt 13:43
And they were both r......Luke 1:6

RIGHTEOUSLY

that they were *r*..............Luke 18:9
Certainly this was a *r*......Luke 23:47
"There is none *r*........... Rom 3:10
r man will one die...........Rom 5:7
witness that he was *r*....... Heb 11:4
Jesus Christ the *r*............ 1 Jn 2:1
just as He is *r*.................. 1 Jn 3:7
r are Your..................... Rev 16:7
fine linen is the *r*............ Rev 19:8

RIGHTEOUSLY

judge the people *r*...........Ps 67:4
He who walks *r* and........ Is 33:15
should live soberly, *r*........Tit 2:12
to Him who judges *r*........ 1 Pe 2:23

RIGHTEOUSNESS

it to him for *r*................ Gen 15:6
My *r* I hold fast...............Job 27:6
I put on *r*...................... Job 29:14
I will ascribe *r*.................Job 36:3
I call, O God of my *r*........Ps 4:1
righteous, He loves *r*....... Ps 11:7
from the LORD, And *r*...Ps 24:5
shall speak of Your *r*........Ps 35:28
the good news of *r*...........Ps 40:9
You love *r* and hate........ Ps 45:7
heavens declare His *r*...... Ps 50:6
sing aloud of Your *r*........Ps 51:14
R and peace have........... Ps 85:10
R will go before Him......Ps 85:13
r they are exalted............Ps 89:16
will return to *r*.............. Ps 94:15
R and justice are the....... Ps 97:2
And he who does *r*......... Ps 106:3
r endures forever............Ps 111:3
r is an everlasting............Ps 119:142
r delivers from death....... Prov 10:2
The *r* of the blameless..... Prov 11:5
The *r* of the upright........ Prov 11:6
r leads to life................. Prov 11:19
the way of *r* is life.......... Prov 12:28
R keeps him whose way...Prov 13:6
R exalts a nation............Prov 14:34
found in the way of *r*...... Prov 16:31
He who follows *r*............ Prov 21:21
r lodged in it..................Is 1:21
r He shall judge..............Is 11:4
R shall be the belt......... Is 11:5
he will not learn ....Is 26:10
and *r* the plummet..........Is 28:17
r will be peace...............Is 32:17
in the LORD I have *r*....... Is 45:24
who are far from *r*.........Is 46:12
r will be forever.............Is 51:8
I will declare your *r*.......Is 57:12
and His own *r*...............Is 59:16
r as a breastplate........... Is 59:17
be called trees of *r*.........Is 61:3
r goes forth as...............Is 62:1
THE LORD OUR *R*.......Jer 23:6
to David a Branch of *r*....Jer 33:15
has revealed our *r*...........Jer 51:10
The *r* of the righteous......Ezek 18:20
"O Lord, *r* belongs......... Dan 9:7
in everlasting *r*.............. Dan 9:24
who turn many to *r*.......Dan 12:3
for yourselves *r*.............Hos 10:12
to fulfill all *r*............... Matt 3:15
exceeds the *r* of the........Matt 5:20
to you in the way of *r*.... Matt 21:32
in holiness and *r*...........Luke 1:75
For in it the *r*................Rom 1:17
even the *r* of God.......... Rom 3:22
a seal of the *r*................ Rom 4:11
accounted to him for r..... Rom 4:22

r will reign in life............Rom 5:17
might reign through *r*...... Rom 5:21
is life because of *r*...........Rom 8:10
who did not pursue *r*......Rom 9:30
pursuing the law of *r*...... Rom 9:31
ignorant of God's *r*......... Rom 10:3
we might become the *r*.... 2 Co 5:21
r comes through the........ Gal 2:21
the breastplate of *r*.........Eph 6:14
not having my own *r*....... Phil 3:9
things and pursue *r*........ 1 Ti 6:11
r which we have............. Tit 3:5
r which is according........Heb 11:7
does not produce the *r*....Jas 1:20
should suffer for *r*...........1 Pe 3:14
a preacher of *r*...............2 Pe 2:5
a new earth in which *r*....2 Pe 3:13
who practices *r*.............. 1 Jn 2:29
He who practices *r*..........1 Jn 3:7
does not practice *r*.......... 1 Jn 3:10

RIGHTLY

wise uses knowledge *r*.....Prov 15:2
R do they love you......... Song 1:4
"You have answered *r*..... Luke 10:28
r dividing the word..........2 Ti 2:15

RIGHTS

and her marriage *r*.......... Ex 21:10

RINGLEADER

the world, and a *r*...........Acts 24:5

RINGS

a man with gold *r*........... Jas 2:2

RIPE

figs that are first *r*...........Jer 24:2

RISE

is vain for you to *r*..........Ps 127:2
"Now I will *r*................. Is 33:10
for He makes His sun *r*... Matt 5:45
of Nineveh will *r*...........Matt 12:41
third day He will *r*........ Matt 20:19
persuaded though one *r*... Luke 16:31
third day He will *r*.........Luke 18:33
had to suffer and *r*......... Acts 17:3
be the first to *r*..............Acts 26:23
fact the dead do not *r*......1 Co 15:15
in Christ will *r*...............1 Th 4:16

RISEN

of the LORD is *r*.............Is 60:1
women there has not *r*.....Matt 11:11
disciples that He is *r*.......Matt 28:7
"The Lord is *r*...............Luke 24:34
furthermore is also *r*.......Rom 8:34
then Christ is not *r*.........1 Co 15:13
if Christ is not *r*............ 1 Co 15:17
But now Christ is *r*......... 1 Co 15:20

RISES

shall I do when God *r*.....Job 31:14
every tongue which *r*.......Is 54:17

RISING

may know from the *r*.......Is 45:6
questioning what the *r*.....Mark 9:10
for the fall and *r*............Luke 2:34

RIVALRY

But there was also *r*........ Luke 22:24

RIVER

Indeed the *r* may rage.....Job 40:23
them drink from the *r*......Ps 36:8

r whose streams shall.......Ps 46:4
The *r* of God is full.........Ps 65:9
went through the *r*.........Ps 66:6
peace to her like a *r*.......Is 66:12
in the Jordan *R*.............Mark 1:5
he showed me a pure *r*.... Rev 22:1

RIVERS

He turns *r* into a...........Ps 107:33
R of water run down.......Ps 119:136
By the *r* of Babylon....... Ps 137:1
All the *r* run into the......Eccl 1:7
us a place of broad *r*.......Is 33:21
the wilderness and *r*.......Is 43:19
the sea, I make the *r*.......Is 50:2
his heart will flow.........John 7:38

ROAD

I will even make a *r*........Is 43:19
depths of the sea a *r*....... Is 51:10
seen the Lord on the *r*.....Acts 9:27

ROAR

Let the sea *r*..................1 Ch 16:32
Though its waters *r*......... Ps 46:3
The young lions *r*...........Ps 104:21
'The LORD will *r*...........Jer 25:30
He will *r* like a lion........Hos 11:10
The LORD also will *r*......Joel 3:16
Will a lion *r* in the........Amos 3:4

ROARING

wrath is like the *r*.......... Prov 19:12
Like a *r* lion and a.........Prov 28:15
and the waves *r*.............Luke 21:25
walks about like a *r*........1 Pe 5:8

ROARS

their voice *r* like the.......Jer 6:23
"The LORD *r* from.........Amos 1:2
as when a lion *r*..............Rev 10:3

ROB

r the poor because he......Prov 22:22
r the needy of justice.......Is 10:2
"Will a man *r* God.........Mal 3:8
do you *r* temples............Rom 2:22

ROBBED

r their treasuries............. Is 10:13
But this is a people *r*......Is 42:22
Yet you have *r* Me.........Mal 3:8
r other churches.............2 Co 11:8

ROBBER

a son who is a *r*.............Ezek 18:10
is a thief and a *r*............John 10:1
Now Barabbas was a *r*.....John 18:40

ROBBERS

and Israel to the *r*..........Is 42:24
also crucified two *r*.........Mark 15:27
Me are thieves and *r*.......John 10:8
here who are neither *r*.....Acts 19:37
waters, in perils of *r*........2 Co 11:26

ROBBERY

Nor vainly hope in *r*........Ps 62:10
I hate *r* for burnt............Is 61:8
did not consider it *r*........ Phil 2:6

ROBE

justice was like a *r*..........Job 29:14
instead of a rich *r*...........Is 3:24
covered me with the *r*.....Is 61:10
'Bring out the best *r*........Luke 15:22
on Him a purple *r*..........John 19:2
And a white *r* was..........Rev 6:11

ROBES

to the King in *r*.............. Ps 45:14
have stained all My *r*.......Is 63:3
clothe you with rich *r*...... Zech 3:4
to walk in long *r*......Luke 20:46
clothed with white *r*........ Rev 7:9

ROCK

you shall strike the *r*....... Ex 17:6
and struck the *r*.............Num 20:11
R who begot you...........Deut 32:18
For their *r* is not........Deut 32:31
nor is there any *r*..........1 Sa 2:2
"The LORD is my *r*....... 2 Sa 22:2
And who is a *r*.............2 Sa 22:32
Blessed be my *R*........... 2 Sa 22:47
away, and as a *r*............Job 14:18
set me high upon a *r*.......Ps 27:5
For You are my *r*...........Ps 31:3
r that is higher than.......Ps 61:2
And my God the *r*.........Ps 94:22
Who turned the *r*...........Ps 114:8
been mindful of the *R*.... Is 17:10
shadow of a great *r*........Is 32:2
his house on the *r*..........Matt 7:24
r I will build My............Matt 16:18
"Some fell on *r*.............Luke 8:6
stumbling stone and r...... Rom 9:33
R that followed them......1 Co 10:4

ROCKS

and the *r* were split........Matt 27:51
to the mountains and *r*.... Rev 6:16

ROD

And Moses took the *r*.... Ex 4:20
chasten him with the *r*......2 Sa 7:14
Your *r* and Your staff.....Ps 23:4
The *r* and reproof give....Prov 29:15
shall come forth a *R*.......Is 11:1
you pass under the *r*.......Ezek 20:37
I come to you with a *r*.... 1 Co 4:21
rule them with a r..........Rev 2:27

ROLL

ruinous storm they *r*........Job 30:14
r away the stone............Mark 16:3

ROLLED

the heavens shall be *r*......Is 34:4
the stone had been *r*....... Mark 16:4

ROOM

You prepared *r* for it......Ps 80:9
until no more *r*..............Zech 10:10
you a large upper *r*........ Mark 14:15
no *r* for them in the........Luke 2:7
still there is *r*............. Luke 14:22
into the upper *r*.............Acts 1:13

ROOMS

make *r* in the ark...........Gen 6:14
He is in the inner *r*........Matt 24:26

ROOSTER

him, "Before the *r*.........Matt 26:75

ROOT

r bearing bitterness...........Deut 29:18
the foolish taking *r*..........Job 5:3
r may grow old in the.......Job 14:8
day there shall be a *R*.... Is 11:10
shall again take *r*...........Is 37:31
because they had no *r*.....Matt 13:6
and if the *r* is holy..........Rom 11:16
of money is a *r*..............1 Ti 6:10

lest any *r* of..................Heb 12:15
I am the *R* and the........ Rev 22:16

ROOTED

that you, being *r*............Eph 3:17
r and built up in Him...... Col 2:7

ROOTS

because its *r* reached....... Ezek 31:7
and lengthen his *r*..........Hos 14:5
dried up from the *r*........Mark 11:20
pulled up by the *r*..........Jude 12

ROSE

I am the *r* of Sharon....... Song 2:1
and blossom as the *r*......Is 35:1
end Christ died and *r*..... Rom 14:9
buried, and that He *r*...... 1 Co 15:4
that Jesus died and *r*......1 Th 4:14

RUBIES

of wisdom is above *r*...... Job 28:18
more precious than *r*...... Prov 3:15
is better than *r*............. Prov 8:11
worth is far above *r*.......Prov 31:10
your pinnacles of *r*......... Is 54:12
ruddy in body than *r*...... Lam 4:7

RUDDY

Now he was *r*...............1 Sa 16:12
beloved is white and *r*..... Song 5:10

RUIN

r those two can bring......Prov 24:22
have made a city a *r*.......Is 25:2
will not be your *r*..........Ezek 18:30
And the *r* of that...........Luke 6:49
to no profit, to the *r*....... 2 Ti 2:14

RUINED

shall be utterly *r*............ Is 60:12
the mighty trees are *r*..... Zech 11:2
wineskins will be *r*......... Luke 5:37

RUINS

rebuild the old *r*............ Is 61:4

RULE

and he shall *r*............... Gen 3:16
r the raging of the..........Ps 89:9
A wise servant will *r*....... Prov 17:2
Yet he will *r* over all.......Eccl 2:19
puts an end to all *r*......... 1 Co 15:24
us walk by the same *r*......Phil 3:16
let the peace of God *r*.....Col 3:15
Let the elders who *r*........1 Ti 5:17
Remember those who *r*....Heb 13:7

RULER

the sheep, to be *r*...........2 Sa 7:8
down to eat with a *r*........Prov 23:1
bear is a wicked *r*..........Prov 28:15
r pays attention..............Prov 29:12
to Me the One to be *r*.....Mic 5:2
by Beelzebub, the *r*........Matt 12:24
I will make you *r*...........Matt 25:21
the *r* of this world..........John 12:31
because the *r* of this........John 16:11
'Who made you a *r*.........Acts 7:27
speak evil of the r...........Acts 23:5

RULERS

And the *r* take counsel.... Ps 2:2
r decree justice..............Prov 8:15
"You know that the *r*......Matt 20:25
"Have any of the *r*.........John 7:48

r are not a.....................Rom 13:3
which none of the *r*........1 Co 2:8
powers, against the *r*....... Eph 6:12
to be subject to *r*...........Tit 3:1

RULES

'He who *r* over men........2 Sa 23:3
them know that God *r*.....Ps 59:13
He *r* by His power..........Ps 66:7
r his spirit than he......... Prov 16:32
that the Most High *r*...... Dan 4:17
that the Most High *r*.......Dan 4:32
r his own house well........1 Ti 3:4
according to the *r*...........2 Ti 2:5

RULING

r their children...............1 Ti 3:12

RUMOR

r will be upon *r*.............Ezek 7:26

RUMORS

hear of wars and *r*..........Matt 24:6
you hear of wars and *r*.... Mark 13:7

RUN

I will *r* in the way of......Ps 119:32
r and not be weary..........Is 40:31
many shall *r* to and........Dan 12:4
Therefore I *r* thus..........1 Co 9:26
I might *r*, or had *r*.........Gal 2:2
that I have not *r*.............Phil 2:16
us, and let us *r*..............Heb 12:1
that you do not *r*............1 Pe 4:4

RUNNER

are swifter than a *r*......... Job 9:25
r will run to meet........... Jer 51:31

RUNS

word *r* very swiftly..........Ps 147:15
nor of him who *r*............Rom 9:16

— S —

SABAOTH

S had left us a................Rom 9:29
ears of the Lord of *S*......Jas 5:4

SABBATH

'Tomorrow is a *S*............Ex 16:23
"Remember the *S*...........Ex 20:8
S was made for man........Mark 2:27
is also Lord of the *S*.......Mark 2:28
not only broke the *S*....... John 5:18

SABBATHS

S you shall keep............. Ex 31:13
The New Moons, the *S*....Is 1:13
also gave them My *S*....... Ezek 20:12

SACKCLOTH

You have put off my *s*.....Ps 30:11
and remove the *s*...........Is 20:2

SACRED

iniquity and the *s*...........Is 1:13

SACRIFICE

do you kick at My *s*........1 Sa 2:29
S and offering You did.... Ps 40:6
offer to You the *s*...........Ps 116:17
to the LORD than *s*........Prov 21:3
For the LORD has a *s*.... Is 34:6
who will bring the *s*........Jer 33:11
of My offerings they *s*.....Hos 8:13

SACRIFICED

But I will s to You.........Jon 2:9
LORD has prepared a s... Zeph 1:7
offer the blind as a s...... Mal 1:8
desire mercy and not s..... Matt 9:13
s will be seasoned...... Mark 9:49
an offering and a s.........Eph 5:2
aroma, an acceptable s.....Phil 4:18
put away sin by the s....Heb 9:26
He had offered one s......Heb 10:12
no longer remains a s...... Heb 10:26
God a more excellent s...Heb 11:4
offer the s of praise........Heb 13:15

SACRIFICED

s their sons And their......Ps 106:37
to eat things s................. Rev 2:14

SACRIFICES

The s of God are a......... Ps 51:17
multitude of your s.........Is 1:11
Bring no more futile s.... Is 1:13
he who s a lamb.............Is 66:3
acceptable, nor your s......Jer 6:20
by him the daily s......... Dan 8:11
burnt offerings and s........Mark 12:33
priests, to offer up s........Heb 7:27
s God is well pleased...Heb 13:16
offer up spiritual s..........1 Pe 2:5

SAD

Why is your face s......... Neh 2:2
s countenance the.......... Eccl 7:3
whom I have not made s..Ezek 13:22
as you walk and are s....Luke 24:17

SAFE

and I shall be s...............Ps 119:117
in the LORD shall be s.... Prov 29:25
he has received him s..... Luke 15:27

SAFELY

And He led them on s....Ps 78:53
make them lie down s......Hos 2:18

SAFETY

sons are far from s..........Job 5:4
take your rest in s......Job 11:18
will set him in the s.........Ps 12:5
say, "Peace and s............1 Th 5:3

SAFETY'S

by you for s sake........... Prov 3:29

SAINTS

ten thousands of s...........Deut 33:2
the feet of His s............. 1 Sa 2:9
puts no trust in His s......Job 15:15
s who are on the earth....Ps 16:3
does not forsake His s.... Ps 37:28
"Gather My s.................Ps 50:5
the souls of His s...........Ps 97:10
Is the death of His s.....Ps 116:15
the way of His s........... Prov 2:8
war against the s............Dan 7:21
shall persecute the s....... Dan 7:25
Jesus, called to be s......1 Co 1:2
the least of all the s...... Eph 3:8
Christ with all His s........ 1 Th 3:13
be glorified in His s........2 Th 1:10
all delivered to the s.......Jude 3
ways, o King of the s...... Rev 15:3
shed the blood of s......... Rev 16:6
the camp of the s...........Rev 20:9

SALT

shall season with s...........Lev 2:13
"You are the s................ Matt 5:13
s loses its flavor.............Mark 9:50

SALVATION

still, and see the s...........Ex 14:13
For this is all my s..........2 Sa 23:5
the good news of His s.... 1 Ch 16:23
S belongs to the LORD....Ps 3:8
is my light and my s.......Ps 27:1
on earth, Your s.............Ps 67:2
God is the God of s......Ps 68:20
And Your s all the day....Ps 71:15
Surely His s is near........ Ps 85:9
He has become my s....... Ps 118:14
S is far from the............Ps 119:155
God will appoint s.......... Is 26:1
with an everlasting s........Is 45:17
for My s is about to....... Is 56:1
call your walls S............. Is 60:18
s as a lamp that burns..... Is 62:1
LORD our God is the s... Jer 3:23
joy in the God of my s.... Hab 3:18
is just and having s......... Zech 9:9
raised up a horn of s...... Luke 1:69
eyes have seen Your s..... Luke 2:30
to him, "Today s............ Luke 19:9
what we worship, for s....John 4:22
"Nor is there s............... Acts 4:12
you should be for s......... Acts 13:47
the power of God to s..... Rom 1:16
s is nearer than.............Rom 13:11
now is the day of s..........2 Co 6:2
work out your own s....... Phil 2:12
wrath, but to obtain s......1 Th 5:9
chose you for s............... 2 Th 2:13
also may obtain the s.......2 Ti 2:10
of God that brings s........ Tit 2:11
neglect so great a s......... Heb 2:3
s the prophets have.........1 Pe 1:10

SAMARITAN

But a certain S................ Luke 10:33
a drink from me, a S.......John 4:9

SANCTIFICATION

righteousness and s..........1 Co 1:30
will of God, your s...........1 Th 4:3
salvation through s...........2 Th 2:13

SANCTIFIED

s this house which you..... 1 Ki 9:3
I have commanded My s... Is 13:3
you were born I s............Jer 1:5
Him whom the Father s...John 10:36
they also may be s...........John 17:19
might be acceptable, s.... Rom 15:16
to those who are s........... 1 Co 1:2
washed, but you were s....1 Co 6:11
husband is s by the......... 1 Co 7:14
for it is s by the.............1 Ti 4:5
those who are being s......Heb 2:11
will we have been s........Heb 10:10
who are called, s.............Jude 1

SANCTIFIES

or the temple that s........Matt 23:17
For both He who s..........Heb 2:11

SANCTIFY

"S to Me, all the........... Ex 13:2
therefore s yourselves...... Lev 11:44
would send and s them.... Job 1:5
s My great name.............Ezek 36:23
that I, the LORD, s........Ezek 37:28

SANCTUARY

let them make Me a s......Ex 25:8
I went into the s.............Ps 73:17
set fire to Your s.............Ps 74:7
O God, is in the s...........Ps 77:13
He will be as a s.............Is 8:14
He has abandoned His s.. Lam 2:7
I shall be a little s...........Ezek 11:16
to shine on Your s.......... Dan 9:17
and the earthly s.............Heb 9:1

SAND

descendants as the s......, Gen 32:12
be heavier than the s.......Job 6:3
in number than the s.......Ps 139:18
O Israel, be as the s........Is 10:22
innumerable as the s........Heb 11:12

SAPPHIRES

are the source of s.........Job 28:6

SAT

of Babylon, There we s...Ps 137:1
I s down in his shade......Song 2:3
s alone because of..........Jer 15:17
up into heaven, and s...... Mark 16:19
And He who s there was..Rev 4:3

SATAN

S stood up against...........1 Ch 21:1
before the LORD, and S..Job 1:6
And the LORD said to S..Zech 3:2
"Away with you, S.........Matt 4:10
"Get behind Me, S.........Matt 16:23
"How can S cast out....... Mark 3:23
to them, "I saw S........ Luke 10:18
S has asked for you........Luke 22:31
S filled your heart...........Acts 5:3
such a one to S.............. 1 Co 5:5
For S himself................. 2 Co 11:14
to the working of S.........2 Th 2:9
are a synagogue of S....... Rev 2:9
you, where S dwells....... Rev 2:13
known the depths of S.....Rev 2:24
called the Devil and S..... Rev 12:9
years have expired, S......Rev 20:7

SATIATED

s the weary soul.............Jer 31:25
It shall be s and made..... Jer 46:10

SATISFIED

I shall be s when I..........Ps 17:15
his land will be s............Prov 12:11
a good man will be s......Prov 14:14
s soul loathes the...........Prov 27:7
that are never s..............Prov 30:15
silver will not be s..........Eccl 5:10
left hand and not be s..... Is 9:20
of His soul, and be s....... Is 53:11
My people shall be s....... Jer 31:14
still were not s...............Ezek 16:28
but they were not s.........Amos 4:8
and cannot be s............. Hab 2:5

SATISFIES

s your mouth with good... Ps 103:5
s the longing soul...........Ps 107:9

SATISFY

s us early with Your........Ps 90:14
long life I will s..............Ps 91:16
s her poor with bread......Ps 132:15
for what does not s.........Is 55:2

SATISFYING

eats to the s of his..........Prov 13:25

SAVE

the LORD does not s.......1 Sa 17:47
there was none to s.........2 Sa 22:42
s the humble person........Job 22:29
Oh, s me for Your..........Ps 6:4
S Your people................Ps 28:9
send from heaven and s... Ps 57:3
s the children of the.......Ps 72:4
s the souls of the...........Ps 72:13
LORD, and He will s.......Prov 20:22
He will come and s.........Is 35:4
LORD was ready to s......Is 38:20
s your children..............Is 49:25
that it cannot s..............Is 59:1
mighty to s...................Is 63:1
one who cannot s...........Jer 14:9
s you and deliver you......Jer 15:20
s me...........................Jer 17:14
O LORD, s Your people..Jer 31:7
other, that he may s.......Hos 13:10
Assyria shall not s..........Hos 14:3
the Mighty One, will s....Zeph 3:17
Jesus, for He will s........Matt 1:21
s his life will................Matt 16:25
s that which was...........Matt 18:11
s life or to kill.............Mark 3:4
let Him s Himself if.......Luke 23:35
You are the Christ, s......Luke 23:39
'Father, s Me from.........John 12:27
but to s the world..........John 12:47
and s some of them........Rom 11:14
the world to s sinners......1 Ti 1:15
doing this you will s....... 1 Ti 4:16
able to s your souls.........Jas 1:21
Can faith s him..............Jas 2:14

SAVED

like you, a people s........Deut 33:29
But You have s us from...Ps 44:7
and we are not s.............Jer 8:20
"Who then can be s........Matt 19:25
"He s others..................Matt 27:42
that we should be s........Luke 1:71
"Your faith has s...........Luke 7:50
through Him might be s...John 3:17
them, saying, "Be s........Acts 2:40
what must I do to be s....Acts 16:30
For we were s in this......Rom 8:24
is that they may be s......Rom 10:1
all Israel will be s..........Rom 11:26
his spirit may be s.........1 Co 5:5
which also you are s.......1 Co 15:2
those who are being s......2 Co 2:15
grace you have been s.....Eph 2:8
all men to be s...............1 Ti 2:4
she will be s in..............1 Ti 2:15
to His mercy He s..........Tit 3:5
eight souls, were s..........1 Pe 3:20
of those who are s..........Rev 21:24

SAVES

s the needy from the.......Job 5:15
s such as have a.............Ps 34:18
antitype which now s.......1 Pe 3:21

SAVIOR

forgot God their S..........Ps 106:21
He will send them a S.....Is 19:20

of Israel, your S.............Is 43:3
Me, a just God and a S...Is 45:21
I, the LORD, am your S..Is 60:16
So He became their S......Is 63:8
for there is no s.............Hos 13:4
rejoiced in God my S......Luke 1:47
the city of David a S.......Luke 2:11
the Christ, the S............John 4:42
to be Prince and S.........Acts 5:31
up for Israel a S.............Acts 13:23
and He is the S..............Eph 5:23
of God our S and the......1 Ti 1:1
God, who is the S...........1 Ti 4:10
of our S Jesus Christ.......2 Ti 1:10
God and S Jesus Christ....Tit 2:13

SAVIORS

s shall come to Mount.....Obad 21

SAVOR

days, and I do not s........Amos 5:21

SAWN

stoned, they were s.........Heb 11:37

SAY

"But I s to you that.......Matt 5:22
But who do you s...........Matt 16:15
s that we have no sin......1 Jn 1:8

SAYING

disclose my dark s..........Ps 49:4
cannot accept this s........Matt 19:11
"This is a hard s............John 6:60
This is a faithful s..........1 Ti 1:15

SAYINGS

I will utter dark s..........Ps 78:2
whoever hears these s......Matt 7:24

SCALES

deceitful s are in his.......Hos 12:7
on it had a pair of s........Rev 6:5

SCARLET

s cord in the window.......Josh 2:18
are like a strand of s.......Song 4:3
your sins are like s..........Is 1:18
s beast which was full......Rev 17:3

SCATTER

I will s you among the.....Lev 26:33
S the peoples who...........Ps 68:30
s the sheep of My...........Jer 23:1
I will s to all winds.........Jer 49:32

SCATTERED

lest we be s abroad.........Gen 11:4
of iniquity shall be s........Ps 92:9
"You have s My flock.....Jer 23:2
s Israel will gather..........Jer 31:10
Israel is like a sheep........Jer 50:17
they were weary and s.....Matt 9:36
the sheep will be s..........Mark 14:27
that you will be s...........John 16:32

SCATTERS

s the frost like ashes........Ps 147:16
There is one who s.........Prov 11:24
throne of judgment s......Prov 20:8
not gather with Me s.......Matt 12:30

SCEPTER

s shall not depart...........Gen 49:10
S shall rise out of...........Num 24:17
A s of righteousness........Ps 45:6
a s of righteousness........Heb 1:8

SCHEMER

will be called a s.............Prov 24:8

SCHEMES

who brings wicked s........Ps 37:7
have sought out many s... Eccl 7:29

SCHISM

there should be no s........1 Co 12:25

SCHOOL

daily in the s of..............Acts 19:9

SCOFF

They s and speak............Ps 73:8
They s at kings..............Hab 1:10

SCOFFER

"He who reproves a s......Prov 9:7
s does not listen..............Prov 13:1
s seeks wisdom and........Prov 14:6
s is an abomination........ Prov 24:9

SCOFFERS

S ensnare a city..............Prov 29:8
s will come in the...........2 Pe 3:3

SCORCHED

sun was up they were s....Matt 13:6
And men were s with......Rev 16:9

SCORN

My friends s me..............Job 16:20
to our neighbors, A s......Ps 44:13
they laughed Him to s.....Matt 9:24

SCORNED

consider, for I am s........Lam 1:11
and princes are s............Hab 1:10

SCORNS

He s the scornful............Prov 3:34
s obedience to his...........Prov 30:17

SCORPIONS

and you dwell among s....Ezek 2:6
on serpents and s...........Luke 10:19
They had tails like s........Rev 9:10

SCOURGE

hosts will stir up a s........Is 10:26
up to councils and s........Matt 10:17
will mock Him, and s......Mark 10:34

SCOURGES

s every son whom.......... Heb 12:6

SCRIBE

"Where is the s.............. Is 33:18

SCRIBES

and not as the s..............Matt 7:29
"But woe to you, s........Matt 23:13
"Beware of the s............Mark 12:38

SCRIPTURE

what is noted in the S......Dan 10:21
S was fulfilled which.......Mark 15:28
"Today this S................Luke 4:21
S cannot be broken.........John 10:35
For what does the S.........Rom 4:3
S has confined all...........Gal 3:22
All S is given by.............2 Ti 3:16
that no prophecy of S......2 Pe 1:20

SCRIPTURES

not knowing the S...........Matt 22:29
S must be fulfilled...........Mark 14:49
and mighty in the S........Acts 18:24
have known the Holy S...2 Ti 3:15
also the rest of the S.......2 Pe 3:16

SCROLL

In the s of the Book........Ps 40:7
and note it on a s...........Is 30:8
eat this s.......................Ezek 3:1
saw there a flying s.........Zech 5:1
on the throne a s............Rev 5:1
was able to open the s.....Rev 5:3
the sky receded as a s......Rev 6:14

SEA

drowned in the Red S.....Ex 15:4
This great and wide s......Ps 104:25
who go down to the s......Ps 107:23
to the s its limit..............Prov 8:29
rebuke I dry up the s......Is 50:2
the waters cover the s......Hab 2:14
and the s obey Him........Matt 8:27
throne there was a s........Rev 4:6
standing on the s............Rev 15:2
there was no more s........Rev 21:1

SEAL

Set me as a s upon.........Song 8:6
of circumcision, a s........Rom 4:11
stands, having this s........2 Ti 2:19
He opened the second s...Rev 6:3

SEALED

My transgression is s.......Job 14:17
who also has s us and......2 Co 1:22
by whom you were s.......Eph 4:30
of those who were s........Rev 7:4

SEAM

tunic was without s.........John 19:23

SEANCE

"Please conduct a s.........1 Sa 28:8

SEARCH

"Can you s out the.........Job 11:7
Would not God s...........Ps 44:21
glory of kings is to s.......Prov 25:2
found it by secret s.........Jer 2:34
I, the LORD, s the..........Jer 17:10
s the Scriptures...............John 5:39

SEARCHED

O LORD, You have s.....Ps 139:1
s the Scriptures............Acts 17:11
and s diligently...............1 Pe 1:10

SEARCHES

for the LORD s all..........1 Ch 28:9
s the hearts knows..........Rom 8:27
For the Spirit s...............1 Co 2:10
that I am He who s.........Rev 2:23

SEASON

there is a s.....................Eccl 3:1
Be ready in s and out......2 Ti 4:2

SEASONED

how shall it be s.............Matt 5:13
For everyone will be s.....Mark 9:49

SEASONS

days and months and s.....Gal 4:10
the times and the s..........1 Th 5:1

SEAT

shall make a mercy s.......Ex 25:17
I might come to His s......Job 23:3
That He may s him with..Ps 113:8
sit in Moses' s................Matt 23:2
before the judgment s......2 Co 5:10
the mercy s.....................Heb 9:5

SEATS

at feasts, the best s.........Matt 23:6
you love the best s..........Luke 11:43

SECRET

s things belong...............Deut 29:29
The s of the LORD is......Ps 25:14
In the s place of His.......Ps 27:5
When I was made in s.....Ps 139:15
do not disclose the s........Prov 25:9
I have not spoken in s......Is 45:19
Father who is in the s......Matt 6:6
are done by them in s......Eph 5:12

SECRETLY

"Now a word was s........Job 4:12
He lies in wait s.............Ps 10:9

SECRETS

would show you the s......Job 11:6
For He knows the s.........Ps 44:21
A talebearer reveals s......Prov 11:13
heaven who reveals s.......Dan 2:28
God will judge the s.......Rom 2:16
And thus the s of his.......1 Co 14:25

SECT

him (which is the s.........Acts 5:17
to the strictest s..............Acts 26:5

SECURELY

pleasures, who dwell s.....Is 47:8
nation that dwells s.........Jer 49:31

SEDUCED

flattering lips she s.........Prov 7:21
because they have s........Ezek 13:10

SEE

for no man shall s..........Ex 33:20
the LORD does not s.......1 Sa 16:7
in my flesh I shall s........Job 19:26
s the works of God.........Ps 66:5
lest they s with their.......Is 6:10
for sin, He shall s..........Is 53:10
for they shall s God.......Matt 5:8
seeing they do not s........Matt 13:13
s greater things than.......John 1:50
rejoiced to s My day......John 8:56
we wish to s Jesus..........John 12:21
and the world will s.......John 14:19
Him, for we shall s........1 Jn 3:2
They shall s His face.......Rev 22:4

SEED

s shall be called.............Gen 21:12
s shall be its stump........Is 6:13
He shall see His s...........Is 53:10
you a noble vine, a s......Jer 2:21
s is the word of God.......Luke 8:11
had left us as a s...........Rom 9:29
to each s its own body....1 Co 15:38
S were the promises........Gal 3:16
you are Abraham's s.......Gal 3:29
Jesus Christ, of the s......2 Ti 2:8

of corruptible s...............1 Pe 1:23
not sin, for His s............1 Jn 3:9

SEEDS

the world, the good s......Matt 13:38
not say, "And to s.........Gal 3:16

SEEK

will find Him if you s......Deut 4:29
and pray and s My face...2 Ch 7:14
your heart to s God........2 Ch 19:3
s your God as you do.....Ezra 4:2
may God above not s......Job 3:4
countenance not s...........Ps 10:4
LORD, That will I s........Ps 27:4
You said, "S My face......Ps 27:8
Early will I s You...........Ps 63:1
s me diligently will.........Prov 8:17
s one's own glory...........Prov 25:27
s justice........................Is 1:17
Should they s the dead....Is 8:19
the Gentiles shall s.........Is 11:10
Jacob, 'S Me in vain'......Is 45:19
S the LORD while He.....Is 55:6
Yet they s Me daily.........Is 58:2
s great things for............Jer 45:5
s what was lost..............Ezek 34:16
"S Me and live..............Amos 5:4
and people should s........Mal 2:7
things the Gentiles s........Matt 6:32
s, and you will find.........Matt 7:7
s diligently until she.......Luke 15:8
of Man has come to s......Luke 19:10
because I do not s...........John 5:30
"You will s Me and........John 7:34
in doing good s...............Rom 2:7
Because they did not s.....Rom 9:32
Let no one s his own.......1 Co 10:24
for I do not s yours........2 Co 12:14
For all s their own..........Phil 2:21
s those things which........Col 3:1
s the one to come...........Heb 13:14

SEEKING

run to and fro, s.............Amos 8:12
and he came s fruit.........Luke 13:6
for the Father is s...........John 4:23
like a roaring lion, s.......1 Pe 5:8

SEEKS

no one s her...................Jer 30:17
receives, and he who s.....Matt 7:8
there is none who s.........Rom 3:11

SEEMS

There is a way which s....Prov 14:12
have, even what he s.......Luke 8:18
If anyone among you s....1 Co 3:18

SEEN

s God face to face..........Gen 32:30
All this I have s.............Eccl 8:9
s the one I love.............Song 3:3
Who has s such things....Is 66:8
s strange things today......Luke 5:26
No one has s God at........John 1:18
time, nor s His form........John 5:37
I speak what I have s......John 8:38
s Me has s the...............John 14:9
things which we have s....Acts 4:20
s Jesus Christ our...........1 Co 9:1
things which are not s......2 Co 4:18
whom no man has s.........1 Ti 6:16
heard, which we have s....1 Jn 1:1

SEES
here seen Him who *s*.......Gen 16:13
s all the sons of men...... Ps 33:13
s his brother in need....... 1 Jn 3:17
s his brother sinning........ 1 Jn 5:16

SELF-CONFIDENT
a fool rages and is *s*........ Prov 14:16

SELF-CONTROL
about righteousness, *s*.....Acts 24:25
they cannot exercise *s*......1 Co 7:9
gentleness, *s*...................Gal 5:23
slanderers, without *s*........2 Ti 3:3
to knowledge *s*............... 2 Pe 1:6

SELF-CONTROLLED
just, holy, *s*...................Tit 1:8

SELF-SEEKING
where envy and *s* exist.....Jas 3:16

SELL
said, "*S* me your............Gen 25:31
s Your people for.......... Ps 44:12
s the righteous...............Amos 2:6
s whatever you have.......Mark 10:21
no sword, let him *s*........ Luke 22:36
no one may buy or *s*....... Rev 13:17

SEND
He shall *s* from heaven.... Ps 57:3
"Whom shall I *s*............. Is 6:8
s them a Savior............. Is 19:20
"Behold, I *s* you out...... Matt 10:16
The Son of Man will *s*...Matt 13:41
s Lazarus that he........... Luke 16:24
whom the Father will *s*... John 14:26
has sent Me, I also *s*....... John 20:21

SENSELESS
Understand, you *s*..........Ps 94:8

SENSES
of use have their *s*.......... Heb 5:14

SENSUAL
but is earthly, *s*.............. Jas 3:15
These are *s* persons........Jude 19

SENT
and His Spirit have *s*....... Is 48:16
s these prophets...............Jer 23:21
As the Father has *s*........John 20:21
unless they are *s*............. Rom 10:15
s His Son to be the......... 1 Jn 4:10

SEPARATE
'he shall *s* himself.......... Num 6:3
s yourselves from the.......Ezra 10:11
let not man *s*................Matt 19:6
Who shall *s* us from....... Rom 8:35
harmless, undefiled, *s*...... Heb 7:26

SEPARATED
but the poor is *s*........... Prov 19:4
The LORD has utterly *s*... Is 56:3
to be an apostle, *s*........... Rom 1:1
it pleased God, who *s*.....Gal 1:15

SERAPHIM
Above it stood *s*............. Is 6:2

SERIOUS
therefore be *s* and..........1 Pe 4:7

SERPENT
s was more cunning........Gen 3:1
"The *s* deceived me.........Gen 3:13
"Make a fiery *s*.............Num 21:8
like the poison of a *s*.......Ps 58:4
s you shall trample.........Ps 91:13
their tongues like a *s*...... Ps 140:3
air, the way of a *s*.........Prov 30:19
s may bite when it is.......Eccl 10:11
be a fiery flying *s*............Is 14:29
and wounded the *s*..........Is 51:9
will he give him a *s*......... Matt 7:10
Moses lifted up the *s*.....John 3:14
was cast out, that *s*......... Rev 12:9

SERPENTS
is the poison of *s*........... Deut 32:33
Therefore be wise as *s*..... Matt 10:16
to trample on *s*...............Luke 10:19

SERVANT
a *s* of servants he...........Gen 9:25
s who earnestly.................Job 7:2
and the fool will be *s*......Prov 11:29
s will rule over a son.......Prov 17:2
A *s* will not be...............Prov 29:19
Who is blind but My *s*... Is 42:19
"Is Israel a *s*...................Jer 2:14
and a *s* his master...........Mal 1:6
you, let him be your *s*.... Matt 20:26
good and faithful *s*..........Matt 25:21
You wicked and lazy *s*....Matt 25:26
the unprofitable *s*............Matt 25:30
that *s* who knew his....... Luke 12:47
s does not know what......John 15:15
against Your holy *S*........Acts 4:27

SERVANTS
puts no trust in His *s*........Job 4:18
For all are Your *s*............Ps 119:91
on the ground like *s*........Eccl 10:7
shall call you the *S*..........Is 61:6
S rule over us..................Lam 5:8
We are unprofitable *s*...... Luke 17:10
longer do I call you *s*...... John 15:15
so consider us, as *s*.........1 Co 4:1
S, be obedient to............Eph 6:5
Masters, give your *s*........Col 4:1
for vice, but as *s*.............1 Pe 2:16
s shall serve Him............ Rev 22:3

SERVE
LORD your God and *s*.... Deut 6:13
land, so you shall *s*........ Jer 5:19
s Him with one accord.....Zeph 3:9
You cannot *s* God and....Matt 6:24
to be served, but to *s*...... Matt 20:28
the mind I myself *s*........ Rom 7:25
but through love *s*...........Gal 5:13
s the Lord Christ............Col 3:24
s the living God.............Heb 9:14
s Him day and night in.... Rev 7:15

SERVES
"If anyone *s* Me............. John 12:26

SERVICE
do you mean by this *s*..... Ex 12:26
that he offers God *s*.........John 16:2
is your reasonable *s*.......Rom 12:1
with good will doing *s*......Eph 6:7
your works, love, *s*..........Rev 2:19

SERVING
years I have been *s*......... Luke 15:29
s the Lord with all.......... Acts 20:19

SHAKES
s the earth out of its........Job 9:6
s the Wilderness............ Ps 29:8

fervent in spirit, *s*........... Rom 12:11
you, *s* as overseers.......... 1 Pe 5:2

SET
"See, I have *s*................ Deut 30:15
s the LORD always........ Ps 16:8
I will *s* him on high........Ps 91:14
s aside the grace............ Gal 2:21

SETTLE
"Therefore *s* it in............Luke 21:14

SETTLED
and my speech *s*............. Job 29:22
O LORD, Your word is *s*.Ps 119:89
the mountains were *s*......Prov 8:25
s accounts with them....... Matt 25:19

SEVEN
S times a day I praise......Ps 119:164
s other spirits more......... Luke 11:26
s times in a day...............Luke 17:4
out from among you *s*..... Acts 6:3
s churches which are.......Rev 1:4

SEVENTY
S weeks are................... Dan 9:24
up to *s* times seven......... Matt 18:22
Then the *s* returned.........Luke 10:17

SEVERE
My wound is *s*................Jer 10:19
not to be too *s*................ 2 Co 2:5

SEVERITY
the goodness and *s*.........Rom 11:22

SHADE
I sat down in his *s*..........Song 2:3
be a tabernacle for *s*.......Is 4:6
may nest under its *s*........ Mark 4:32

SHADOW
May darkness and the *s*... Job 3:5
He flees like a *s*............. Job 14:2
Hide me under the *s*....... Ps 17:8
walks about like a *s*.......Ps 39:6
like a passing *s*............... Ps 144:4
he passes like a *s*............Eccl 6:12
and to trust in the *s*....... Is 30:2
in the *s* of His hand....... Is 49:2
which are a *s* of..............Col 2:17
the law, having a *s*.........Heb 10:1
is no variation or *s*.........Jas 1:17

SHADOWS
my members are like *s*.....Job 17:7
and the *s* flee away......... Song 2:17

SHAKE
Who is he who will *s*.......Job 17:3
s the earth.................... Is 2:19
S yourself from the......... Is 52:2
s their heads at the......... Lam 2:15
and the knees *s*.............. Nah 2:10
hiss and *s* his fist........... Zeph 2:15
I will *s* all nations........... Hag 2:7
s not only the earth........ Heb 12:26

SHAKEN
he will never be *s*........... Ps 112:6
together was *s*................ Acts 4:31
not to be soon *s*............. 2 Th 2:2

SHAKES
s the earth out of its........Job 9:6
s the Wilderness............ Ps 29:8

SHAME
you turn my glory to s.....Ps 4:2
let them be put to s.......Ps 83:17
s who serve carved.........Ps 97:7
hate Zion Be put to s.....Ps 129:5
s shall be the...................Prov 3:35
is a son who causes s......Prov 10:5
hide My face from s.......Is 50:6
S has covered our..........Jer 51:51
their glory into s............Hos 4:7
never be put to s...........Joel 2:26
the unjust knows no s.....Zeph 3:5
worthy to suffer s...........Acts 5:41
will not be put to s.........Rom 9:33
to put to s the wise.........1 Co 1:27
I say this to your s..........1 Co 6:5
glory is in their s...........Phil 3:19
put Him to an open s......Heb 6:6

SHAMEFUL
committing what is s........Rom 1:27
for it is s for women.......1 Co 14:35
For it is s even to..........Eph 5:12

SHARE
a stranger does not s......Prov 14:10
s your bread with the......Is 58:7
is taught the word s.........Gal 6:6
to give, willing to s.........1 Ti 6:18
to do good and to s.........Heb 13:16

SHARING
for your liberal s.............2 Co 9:13

SHARP
s as a two-edged sword....Prov 5:4

SHARPEN
s their tongue like a........Ps 64:3
and one does not s..........Eccl 10:10

SHARPENS
my adversary s His.........Job 16:9

SHARPNESS
present I should use s......2 Co 13:10

SHATTERED
at ease, but He has s.......Job 16:12

SHEATH
'Return it to its s...........Ezek 21:30
your sword into the s......John 18:11

SHEAVES
Bringing his s.................Ps 126:6
Nor he who binds s.........Ps 129:7
gather them like s..........Mic 4:12

SHED
which is s for many.........Matt 26:28

SHEDDING
blood, and without s........Heb 9:22

SHEEP
astray like a lost s...........Ps 119:176
slaughter, and as a s.......Is 53:7
Pull them out like s......Jer 12:3
have been lost s.............Jer 50:6
will search for My s........Ezek 34:11
shall judge between s......Ezek 34:17
s will be scattered..........Zech 13:7
rather to the lost s..........Matt 10:6
I send you out as s.........Matt 10:16
And He will set the s......Matt 25:33

having a hundred s.........Luke 15:4
and he calls his own s......John 10:3
and I know My s............John 10:14
s I have which are not.....John 10:16
"He was led as a s..........Acts 8:32
like s going astray...........1 Pe 2:25

SHEEPFOLDS
lie down among the s......Ps 68:13

SHEET
object like a great s.........Acts 10:11

SHELTER
I will trust in the s..........Ps 61:4
In You I take s..............Ps 143:9
the LORD will be a s......Joel 3:16

SHELTERS
s him all the day long......Deut 33:12
be pastures, with s..........Zeph 2:6

SHEOL
down to the gates of S.....Job 17:16
not leave my soul in S.....Ps 16:10
S laid hold of me............Ps 116:3
S cannot thank..............Is 38:18
the belly of S I cried.......Jon 2:2

SHEPHERD
s is an abomination.........Gen 46:34
s My people Israel..........2 Sa 5:2
The LORD is my s..........Ps 23:1
s Jacob His people..........Ps 78:71
His flock like a s............Is 40:11
of Cyrus, 'He is My s......Is 44:28
s who follows You..........Jer 17:16
because there was no s.....Ezek 34:5
I will establish one s........Ezek 34:23
"As a s takes from..........Amos 3:12
to the worthless s...........Zech 11:17
'I will strike the S..........Matt 26:31
"I am the good s............John 10:11
s the church of God.......Acts 20:28
the dead, that great S......Heb 13:20
S the flock of God..........1 Pe 5:2
when the Chief S............1 Pe 5:4
of the throne will s..........Rev 7:17

SHEPHERDS
your sons shall be s........Num 14:33
And they are s who.........Is 56:11
And I will give you s.......Jer 3:15
s who destroy and..........Jer 23:1
s who feed My people.....Jer 23:2
s have led them astray.....Jer 50:6
s fed themselves.............Ezek 34:8
in the same country s......Luke 2:8

SHIELD
I am your s...................Gen 15:1
he is a s to all who.........2 Sa 22:31
My s and the horn of......Ps 18:2
God is a sun and s..........Ps 84:11
truth shall be your s........Ps 91:4
all, taking the s.............Eph 6:16

SHINE
LORD make His face s....Num 6:25
cause His face to s..........Ps 67:1
the cherubim, s..............Ps 80:1
Make Your face s..........Ps 119:135
who are wise shall s........Dan 12:3
the righteous will s.........Matt 13:43
among whom you s.........Phil 2:15

SHINED
them a light has s...........Is 9:2

SHINES
And the light s...............John 1:5
heed as a light that s.......2 Pe 1:19

SHINING
the earth, by clear s........2 Sa 23:4
His clothes became s.......Mark 9:3
light is already s.............1 Jn 2:8
was like the sun s...........Rev 1:16

SHIPS
pass by like swift s.........Job 9:26
down to the sea in s........Ps 107:23
like the merchant s.........Prov 31:14
Look also at s...............Jas 3:4

SHIPWRECK
faith have suffered s........1 Ti 1:19

SHOOT
They s out the lip..........Ps 22:7
But God shall s.............Ps 64:7

SHORT
have sinned and fall s......Rom 3:23
the work and cut it s.......Rom 9:28

SHORTENED
his youth You have s.......Ps 89:45
the wicked will be s........Prov 10:27
those days were s...........Matt 24:22

SHOUT
s joyfully to the Rock......Ps 95:1
S joyfully to the LORD....Ps 98:4
Make a joyful s.............Ps 100:1
from heaven with a s.......1 Th 4:16

SHOW
a land that I will s..........Gen 12:1
S me Your ways............Ps 25:4
s yourselves men............Is 46:8
s Him greater works........John 5:20
s us the Father..............John 14:8

SHOWBREAD
you shall set the s...........Ex 25:30
s which had been taken....1 Sa 21:6
s which was not lawful.....Matt 12:4

SHOWERS
make it soft with s..........Ps 65:10
s have been withheld.......Jer 3:3
can the heavens give s.....Jer 14:22
from the LORD, like s.....Mic 5:7

SHRINES
who made silver s...........Acts 19:24

SHUNNED
feared God and s evil......Job 1:1

SHUT
"Or who s in the sea.......Job 38:8
Has He in anger s..........Ps 77:9
For you s up the............Matt 23:13

SHUTS
s his ears to the cry.........Prov 21:13
s his eyes from seeing......Is 33:15
brother in need, and s......1 Jn 3:17
who opens and no one s...Rev 3:7

SICK

have made him s..............Hos 7:5
I was s and you..............Matt 25:36
he whom You love is s....John 11:3
many are weak and s.......1 Co 11:30
have left in Miletus s......2 Ti 4:20
faith will save the s.........Jas 5:15

SICKLE

Put in the s....................Joel 3:13
"Thrust in Your s...........Rev 14:15

SICKNESS

will sustain him in s........Prov 18:14
He said, "This s..............John 11:4

SICKNESSES

and bore our s...............Matt 8:17

SIDE

The LORD is on my s....Ps 118:6
the net on the right s.......John 21:6

SIFT

s the nations with the......Is 30:28
s the house of Israel........Amos 9:9
for you, that he may s....Luke 22:31

SIFTS

A wise king s out the......Prov 20:26

SIGH

our years like a s............Ps 90:9
the merry-hearted s.........Is 24:7
of the men who s............Ezek 9:4

SIGHING

For my s comes before....Job 3:24
s is not hidden................Ps 38:9

SIGHT

and see this great s.........Ex 3:3
seemed good in Your s....Matt 11:26
by faith, not by s.............2 Co 5:7

SIGN

Show me a s for good......Ps 86:17
will give you a s.............Is 7:14
for an everlasting s..........Is 55:13
we want to see a s.......Matt 12:38
seeks after a s.............Matt 12:39
And what will be the s....Matt 24:3
s which will be spoken.....Luke 2:34
again is the second s.......John 4:54
For Jews request a s.......1 Co 1:22
Now a great s appeared...Rev 12:1

SIGNS

and let them be for s.......Gen 1:14
you not know their s.......Job 21:29
They performed His s......Ps 105:27
We are for s and............Is 8:18
How great are His s.......Dan 4:3
cannot discern the s........Matt 16:3
the accompanying s......Mark 16:20
s Jesus did in Cana of......John 2:11
no one can do these s......John 3:2
you people see s............John 4:48
because you saw the s......John 6:26
this Man works many s....John 11:47
Jesus did many other s.....John 20:30
demons, performing s.....Rev 16:14

SILENCE

That You may s..............Ps 8:2
I was mute with s...........Ps 39:2

soon have settled in s......Ps 94:17
"Sit in s.........................Is 47:5
seal, there was s.............Rev 8:1

SILENT

the wicked shall be s......1 Sa 2:9
season, and am not s......Ps 22:2
Do not be s to me.........Ps 28:1
Let them be s in the.......Ps 31:17
Be s in the presence.......Zeph 1:7
Let your women keep s...1 Co 14:34

SILK

and covered you with s....Ezek 16:10

SILLY

They are s children.........Jer 4:22

SILVER

and your precious s.........Job 22:25
Though he heaps up s.....Job 27:16
s tried in a furnace.........Ps 12:6
have refined us as s........Ps 66:10
than the profits of s........Prov 3:14
chosen rather than s.......Prov 16:16
refining pot is for s.........Prov 17:3
He who loves s will........Eccl 5:10
s has become dross........Is 1:22
call them rejected s.........Jer 6:30
may buy the poor for s....Amos 8:6
him thirty pieces of s......Matt 26:15

SIMILITUDE

been made in the s.........Jas 3:9

SIMPLE

making wise the s...........Ps 19:7
LORD preserves the s.....Ps 116:6
understanding to the s.....Ps 119:130
s believes every word......Prov 14:15
the hearts of the s..........Rom 16:18

SIMPLICITY

ones, will you love s.......Prov 1:22
in the world in s.............2 Co 1:12
corrupted from the s........2 Co 11:3

SIN

he died in his own s........Num 27:3
and be sure your s..........Num 32:23
to death for his own s.....Deut 24:16
all this Job did not s.......Job 2:10
and search out my s........Job 10:6
Be angry, and do not s....Ps 4:4
my ways, Lest I s..........Ps 39:1
s is ever before me..........Ps 51:3
in s my mother................Ps 51:5
s is a reproach................Prov 14:34
good and does not s........Eccl 7:20
soul an offering for s.......Is 53:10
and He bore the s...........Is 53:12
s I will remember no.......Jer 31:34
They eat up the s...........Hos 4:8
Now they s more and......Hos 13:2
who believe in Me to s....Matt 18:6
who takes away the s......John 1:29
S no more....................John 5:14
"He who is without s......John 8:7
convict the world of s......John 16:8
they are all under s.........Rom 3:9
s entered the world.........Rom 5:12
s is not imputed.............Rom 5:13
s that grace may............Rom 6:1
died to s once for all......Rom 6:10
s shall not have..............Rom 6:14
Shall we s because we.....Rom 6:15

s that dwells in me.........Rom 7:17
Him who knew no s........2 Co 5:21
man of s is revealed........2 Th 2:3
we are, yet without s.......Heb 4:15
appeared to put away s....Heb 9:26
s willfully after we.........Heb 10:26
it gives birth to s............Jas 1:15
do it, to him it is s.........Jas 4:17
"Who committed no s......1 Pe 2:22
say that we have no s......1 Jn 1:8
that you may not s.........1 Jn 2:1
s is lawlessness...............1 Jn 3:4
in Him there is no s........1 Jn 3:5
and he cannot s.............1 Jn 3:9
for those who commit s....1 Jn 5:16
unrighteousness is s........1 Jn 5:17

SINCERE

Holy Spirit, by s love......2 Co 6:6
and from s faith.............1 Ti 1:5
s love of the brethren......1 Pe 1:22

SINCERITY

LORD, serve Him in s....Josh 24:14
unleavened bread of s......1 Co 5:8
simplicity and godly s.....2 Co 1:12
men-pleasers, but in s......Col 3:22

SINFUL

Alas, s nation................Is 1:4
and s generation............Mark 8:38
from me, for I am a s.....Luke 5:8
the hands of s men.........Luke 24:7
become exceedingly s.....Rom 7:13
likeness of s flesh...........Rom 8:3

SING

"S to the LORD............Ex 15:21
the widow's heart to s.....Job 29:13
S out the honor.............Ps 66:2
I will s of mercy and......Ps 101:1
S us one of the songs......Ps 137:3
My servants shall s.........Is 65:14
I will s with the............1 Co 14:15
congregation I will s........Heb 2:12
Let him s psalms............Jas 5:13

SINGERS

The s went before..........Ps 68:25
male and female s..........Eccl 2:8

SINGING

His presence with s.........Ps 100:2
And our tongue with s.....Ps 126:2
the time of s has come....Song 2:12
break forth into s...........Is 14:7
even with joy and s.........Is 35:2
come to Zion with s.......Is 35:10
and spiritual songs, s......Eph 5:19

SINISTER

Who understands s..........Dan 8:23

SINK

I s in deep mire.............Ps 69:2
to s he cried out............Matt 14:30

SINNED

people, "You have s.......Ex 32:30
You only, have I s..........Ps 51:4
Jerusalem has s..............Lam 1:8
Our fathers s and are......Lam 5:7
"Father, I have s...........Luke 15:18
"Rabbi, who s...............John 9:2
For as many as have s.....Rom 2:12
for all have s and...........Rom 3:23

marries, she has not s......1 Co 7:28
say that we have not s.....1 Jn 1:10
for the devil has s...........1 Jn 3:8

SINNER
s He gives the work........ Eccl 2:26
s does evil a hundred.......Eccl 8:12
s destroys much good...... Eccl 9:18
the city who was a s........Luke 7:37
s who repents than..........Luke 15:7
can a man who is a s.......John 9:16
the ungodly and the s....... 1 Pe 4:18

SINNERS
in the path of s...............Ps 1:1
Therefore He teaches s.... Ps 25:8
soul together with s........Ps 26:9
s be consumed from the...Ps 104:35
son, if s entice you.........Prov 1:10
The s in Zion are..........Is 33:14
the righteous, but s....... Matt 9:13
tax collectors and s........Matt 11:19
s love those who love...... Luke 6:32
Galileans were worse s....Luke 13:2
God does not hear s.......John 9:31
while we were still s........ Rom 5:8
many were made s...... Rom 5:19
the ungodly and for s...... 1 Ti 1:9
the world to save s..........1 Ti 1:15
separate from s...............Heb 7:26
such hostility from s....... Heb 12:3
things which ungodly s.....Jude 15

SINS
my iniquities and s.........Job 13:23
from presumptuous s...... Ps 19:13
You, Our secret s........ Ps 90:8
but he who s against........Prov 8:36
s have hidden His face....Is 59:2
the soul who s shall........Ezek 18:4
to make an end of s........Dan 9:24
if your brother s............ Matt 18:15
I take away their s...........Rom 11:27
s according to the..........1 Co 15:3
are still in your s............ 1 Co 15:17
the forgiveness of s.........Eph 1:7
s are clearly evident........ 1 Ti 5:24
once to bear the s...........Heb 9:28
If we confess our s.........1 Jn 1:9
propitiation for our s....... 1 Jn 2:2
s are forgiven you.......... 1 Jn 2:12
Whoever s has neither.....1 Jn 3:6
you share in her s...........Rev 18:4

SISTER
are my mother and my s..Job 17:14
We have a little s............Song 8:8
is My brother and s........Matt 12:50
to you Phoebe our s........Rom 16:1
s is not under bondage.....1 Co 7:15

SIT
Those who s in the..........Ps 69:12
"Come down and s..... Is 47:1
"Why do we s still..........Jer 8:14
but to s on My right........Matt 20:23
and the Pharisees s........Matt 23:2
"S at My right hand...... Heb 1:13
say to him, "You s.........Jas 2:3
I will grant to s.............. Rev 3:21
heart, 'I s as queen......... Rev 18:7

SITS
God s on His holy..........Ps 47:8
It is He who s above.......Is 40:22
so that he s as God.........2 Th 2:4
where the harlot s...........Rev 17:15

SITTING
You know my s down......Ps 139:2
see the Son of Man s.......Mark 14:62
where Christ is, s............Col 3:1

SKILL
hand forget her s............ Ps 137:5
nor favor to men of s...... Eccl 9:11
them knowledge and s..... Dan 1:17
forth to give you s.......... Dan 9:22

SKIN
God made tunics of s...... Gen 3:21
LORD and said, "S.........Job 2:4
have escaped by the s.....Job 19:20
Ethiopian change his s.....Jer 13:23
s is hot as an oven.......... Lam 5:10

SKULL
to say, Place of a S......... Matt 27:33

SKY
s receded as a scroll........ Rev 6:14

SLACK
He will not be s.............Deut 7:10
s hand becomes poor.......Prov 10:4
The Lord is not s.............2 Pe 3:9

SLAIN
s his thousands...............1 Sa 18:7
beauty of Israel is s.........2 Sa 1:19
the dead, Like the s........Ps 88:5
and all who were s..........Prov 7:26
I shall be s in the............Prov 22:13
s men are not s...............Is 22:2
no more cover her s.........Is 26:21
and the s of the LORD....Is 66:16
and night for the s..........Jer 9:1
Those s by the sword.......Lam 4:9
the prophets, I have s.......Hos 6:5
is the Lamb who was s.... Rev 5:12

SLANDER
s your own mother's........Ps 50:20
and whoever spreads s..... Prov 10:18

SLANDERERS
be reverent, not s........... 1 Ti 3:11
unforgiving, s...............2 Ti 3:3
in behavior, not s...........Tit 2:3

SLANDEROUSLY
as we are s reported........Rom 3:8

SLAUGHTER
as sheep for the s...........Ps 44:22
led as a lamb to the s......Is 53:7
but the Valley of S.........Jer 7:32
Feed the flock for s........Zech 11:4
as sheep for the s...........Rom 8:36

SLAVE
that you were a s............Deut 15:15
commits sin is a s...........John 8:34
you called while a s........1 Co 7:21
you are no longer a s...... Gal 4:7

SLAVES
should no longer be s...... Rom 6:6
though you were s.........Rom 6:17
your members as s..........Rom 6:19
do not become s............1 Co 7:23

SLAY
s the righteous...............Gen 18:25
s a righteous nation.........Gen 20:4

Evil shall s the................ Ps 34:21
Oh, that You would s......Ps 139:19
s them before me............Luke 19:27

SLEEP
God caused a deep s....... Gen 2:21
the night, when deep s.....Job 4:13
my eyes, Lest I s............. Ps 13:3
Why do You s...............Ps 44:23
have sunk into their s......Ps 76:5
They are like a s.............Ps 90:5
neither slumber nor s.......Ps 121:4
He gives His beloved s....Ps 127:2
I will not give s...............Ps 132:4
s will be sweet................Prov 3:24
For they do not s............Prov 4:16
A little s.......................Prov 6:10
Do not love s.................Prov 20:13
The s of a laboring..........Eccl 5:12
the spirit of deep s..........Is 29:10
Also his s went from....... Dan 6:18
me, I was in a deep s...... Dan 8:18
them, "Why do you s......Luke 22:46
among you, and many s...1 Co 11:30
We shall not all s............1 Co 15:51
"Awake, you who s........Eph 5:14
with Him those who s......1 Th 4:14
Therefore let us not s......1 Th 5:6

SLEEPERS
gently the lips of s..........Song 7:9

SLEEPING
is not dead, but s............Matt 9:24
"Are you still s...............Matt 26:45
that night Peter was s......Acts 12:6

SLEEPLESSNESS
in labors, in s.................2 Co 6:5
and toil, in s often.......... 2 Co 11:27

SLEEPS
wise son, but he who s....Prov 10:5
Our friend Lazarus s.......John 11:11

SLEPT
I lay down and s.............Ps 3:5
but while men s..............Matt 13:25

SLING
he had, and his s............ 1 Sa 17:40
s is he who gives.............Prov 26:8

SLIP
their foot shall s............. Deut 32:35
my footsteps may not s....Ps 17:5

SLIPPERY
way be dark and s...........Ps 35:6
set them in s places.........Ps 73:18
be to them like s............Jer 23:12

SLOTHFUL
s will be put to...............Prov 12:24
s man does not roast........Prov 12:27
s man buries his hand......Prov 19:24
by the field of the s.........Prov 24:30

SLOTHFULNESS
S casts one into a...........Prov 19:15

SLOW
but I am s of speech........Ex 4:10
He who is s to wrath.......Prov 14:29
hear, s to speak, s..........Jas 1:19

SLUGGARD

will you slumber, O s...... Prov 6:9
soul of a s desires......... Prov 13:4
s is wiser in his own........ Prov 26:16

SLUMBERED

delayed, they all s.......... Matt 25:5

SMALL

'The place is too s...........Is 49:20
I will make you s............Jer 49:15
may stand, for he is s......Amos 7:2
I will make you s............Obad 2
the day of s things......... Zech 4:10
And I saw the dead, s..... Rev 20:12

SMELL

and he smelled the s........Gen 27:27
s there will be a..............Is 3:24

SMELLS

s the battle from afar.......Job 39:25

SMITTEN

Him stricken, s................Is 53:4

SMOKE

went up like the s........... Gen 19:28
s is driven away............Ps 68:2
are consumed like s........Ps 102:3
like a wineskin in s......... Ps 119:83
like pillars of s......... Song 3:6
s shall ascend forever.......Is 34:10
vanish away like s.......... Is 51:6
fire and vapor of s.......... Acts 2:19
s arose out of the pit....... Rev 9:2
was filled with s............ Rev 15:8
And her s rises up.......... Rev 19:3

SMOOTH

speak to us s things......... Is 30:10
and the rough places s..... Is 40:4
though they speak s........Jer 12:6
the rough ways made s.....Luke 3:5

SMOOTH-SKINNED

man, and I am a s.......... Gen 27:11

SNAIL

s which melts away as......Ps 58:8

SNARE

it will surely be a s..........Ex 23:33
It became a s to............ Judg 8:27
that she may be a s........ 1 Sa 18:21
s snatches their.............Job 5:5
and he walks into a s.......Job 18:8
their table become a s..... Ps 69:22
as a bird from the s........Ps 124:7
birds caught in a s.........Eccl 9:12
and the pit and the s.......Is 24:17
I have laid a s............. Jer 50:23
s have come upon us...... Lam 3:47
is a fowler's s.............. Hos 9:8
a bird fall into a s.........Amos 3:5
it will come as a s.........Luke 21:35
temptation and a s........ 1 Ti 6:9
and escape the s............ 2 Ti 2:26

SNARED

The wicked is s..............Ps 9:16
and be broken, be s........ Is 8:15
all of them are s........... Is 42:22

SNARES

The s of death...............Ps 18:5
who seek my life lay s..... Ps 38:12

and built great s............. Eccl 9:14
wait as one who sets s..... Jer 5:26

SNATCH

s the fatherless............... Job 24:9
neither shall anyone s......John 10:28

SNATCHES

s away what was............ Matt 13:19

SNEER

and you s at it................Mal 1:13

SNORTING

s strikes terror................Job 39:20

SNOW

and heat consume the s....Job 24:19
For He says to the s........Job 37:6
the treasury of s............ Job 38:22
shall be whiter than s....... Ps 51:7
He gives s like wool........ Ps 147:16
As s in summer and....... Prov 26:1
She is not afraid of s...... Prov 31:21
shall be as white as s......Is 1:18
garment was white as s.... Dan 7:9
clothing as white as s......Matt 28:3
wool, as white as s.......... Rev 1:14

SOAP

lye, and use much s.........Jer 2:22

SOBER

of the day be s............... 1 Th 5:8
the older men be s........... Tit 2:2

SOBERLY

think, but to think s........ Rom 12:3
we should live s.............. Tit 2:12

SODA

and like vinegar on s....... Prov 25:20

SODOMITES

nor homosexuals, nor s.... 1 Co 6:9
for fornicators, for s........ 1 Ti 1:10

SOJOURN

Woe is me, that I s......... Ps 120:5
into Egypt to s there....... Is 52:4

SOJOURNED

Egypt, And Jacob s........Ps 105:23
By faith he s in the......... Heb 11:9

SOJOURNER

am a foreigner and a s.....Gen 23:4
But no s had to lodge......Job 31:32
fled and became a s........ Acts 7:29

SOJOURNERS

are strangers and s......... Lev 25:23
I beg you as s................ 1 Pe 2:11

SOJOURNING

the time of your s........... 1 Pe 1:17

SOLD

s his birthright...............Gen 25:33
the house that was s........Lev 25:33
their Rock had s.......... Deut 32:30
and He s them into the ...Judg 2:14
s themselves to do..........2 Ki 17:17
Had we been s as male....Esth 7:4
who was s as a slave.......Ps 105:17
s all that he had............ Matt 13:46

they bought, they s......... Luke 17:28
s their possessions........... Acts 2:45
but I am carnal, s........... Rom 7:14
Eat whatever is s............ 1 Co 10:25

SOLDIER

hardship as a good s........2 Ti 2:3
enlisted him as a s.......... 2 Ti 2:4

SOLDIERS

sum of money to the s.....Matt 28:12
And the s also mocked.... Luke 23:36
s twisted a crown........... John 19:2

SOLEMNLY

saying, "The man s......... Gen 43:3
s testified of the..............Acts 28:23

SOLITARY

God sets the s in............ Ps 68:6

SOMETHING

"Simon, I have s............Luke 7:40
that you may have s........2 Co 5:12
thinks himself to be s...... Gal 6:3

SON

Me, ' 'You are My S.......Ps 2:7
I was my father's s.........Prov 4:3
s makes a glad father......Prov 10:1
s is a grief to his...........Prov 17:25
And what, s of my womb.Prov 31:2
is born, unto us a S........Is 9:6
heaven, o Lucifer, s........ Is 14:12
fourth is like the S......... Dan 3:25
He is an unwise s...........Hos 13:13
prophet, nor was I a s..... Amos 7:14
s honors his father.......... Mal 1:6
will bring forth a S........Matt 1:21
This is My beloved S......Matt 3:17
Jesus, You S of God.......Matt 8:29
not the carpenter's s........Matt 13:55
You are the S of God......Matt 14:33
are the Christ, the S.......Matt 16:16
of all he sent his s...........Matt 21:37
Whose S is He..............Matt 22:42
Lord,' how is He his S.... Matt 22:45
him twice as much a s.....Matt 23:15
coming of the S of Man.. Matt 24:37
I am the S of God......... Matt 27:43
Truly this was the S....... Matt 27:54
of Jesus Christ, the S......Mark 1:1
called the S of the..........Luke 1:32
out, the only s...............Luke 7:12
"And if a s of peace........Luke 10:6
to be called your s.......... Luke 15:19
because he also is a s...... Luke 19:9
The only begotten S........John 1:18
that this is the S............John 1:34
of the only begotten S..... John 3:18
S can do nothing............John 5:19
s abides forever.............. John 8:35
you believe in the S........ John 9:35
I said, 'I am the S..........John 10:36
Woman, behold your s.....John 19:26
Jesus Christ is the S.......Acts 8:37
declared to be the S........ Rom 1:4
in the gospel of His S..... Rom 1:9
by sending His own S...... Rom 8:3
not spare His own S........ Rom 8:32
S Himself will also be..... 1 Co 15:28
live by faith in the S.......Gal 2:20
God sent forth His S....... Gal 4:4
longer a slave but a s...... Gal 4:7
the knowledge of the S.... Eph 4:13
you for my s Onesimus....Phm 10

SONG (continued)

"You are My S.............Heb 1:5
but Christ as a S...........Heb 3:6
though He was a S.........Heb 5:8
but made like the S........Heb 7:3
to be called the s.........Heb 11:24
This is My beloved S.......2 Pe 1:17
Whoever denies the S......1 Jn 2:23
God has given of His S....1 Jn 5:10
One like the S of Man.....Rev 1:13

SONG

is my strength and s........ Ex 15:2
Sing to Him a new s.........Ps 33:3
He has put a new s..........Ps 40:3
in the night His s............Ps 42:8
me, And I am the s........Ps 69:12
required of us a s...........Ps 137:3
I will sing a new s...........Ps 144:9
to my Well-beloved a s.... Is 5:1
and their taunting s.........Lam 3:14
I am their taunting s.......Lam 3:63
as a very lovely s............Ezek 33:32
And they sang a new s.... Rev 5:9
And they sing the s.........Rev 15:3

SONGS

my Maker, Who gives s...Job 35:10
surround me with s......... Ps 32:7
have been my s In the..... Ps 119:54
Sing us one of the s........ Ps 137:3
is one who sings s...........Prov 25:20
and spiritual s.................Eph 5:19

SONS

s come to honor............. Job 14:21
shall be Your s...............Ps 45:16
my beloved among the s.. Song 2:3
s shall come from afar..... Is 60:4
"Has Israel no s............. Jer 49:1
The precious s of Zion.....Lam 4:2
'You are the s................. Hos 1:10
He will purify the s.........Mal 3:3
to him, "Then the s....... Matt 17:26
and you will be s........... Luke 6:35
that you may become s....John 12:36
"You are s of the.......... Acts 3:25
of God, these are s...... Rom 8:14
who are of faith are s..... Gal 3:7
the adoption as s............ Gal 4:5
because you are s............Gal 4:6
You are all s of light....... 1 Th 5:5
in bringing many s......... Heb 2:10
speaks to you as to s....... Heb 12:5
illegitimate and not s...... Heb 12:8

SOON

For it is s cut off............ Ps 90:10
s forgot His works...........Ps 106:13

SOOTHED

or bound up, or s........... Is 1:6

SORCERER

omens, or a s................. Deut 18:10
But Elymas the s............ Acts 13:8

SORCERERS

soothsayers, or your s......Jer 27:9
outside are dogs and s..... Rev 22:15

SORCERESS

shall not permit a s......... Ex 22:18

SORCERY

For there is no s.............Num 23:23
idolatry, s.....................Gal 5:20

SORES

and putrefying s...............Is 1:6
Lazarus, full of s............Luke 16:20

SORROW

multiply your s............ Gen 3:16
s dances before him........Job 41:22
in my soul, Having s....... Ps 13:2
s is continually...............Ps 38:17
I found trouble and s.......Ps 116:3
and He adds no s............Prov 10:22
the heart may s.............. Prov 14:13
S is better than...............Eccl 7:3
Therefore remove s........ Eccl 11:10
and desperate s...............Is 17:11
you shall cry for s........... Is 65:14
to see labor and s........... Jer 20:18
Your s is incurable..........Jer 30:15
added grief to my s.........Jer 45:3
gather those who s.......... Zeph 3:18
them sleeping from s....... Luke 22:45
s has filled your.............John 16:6
s will be turned.............John 16:20
that I have great s...........Rom 9:2
s produces repentance......2 Co 7:10
lest I should have s......... Phil 2:27
s as others who have....... 1 Th 4:13
no more death, nor s.......Rev 21:4

SORROWFUL

am a woman of s spirit.... 1 Sa 1:15
But I am poor and s........Ps 69:29
For all his days are s.......Eccl 2:23
replenished every s......... Jer 31:25
were exceedingly s........ Matt 17:23
saying, he went away s.... Matt 19:22
soul is exceedingly s........ Matt 26:38
and you will be s.............John 16:20
if I make you s...............2 Co 2:2
and I may be less s.........Phil 2:28

SORROWS

the s of Sheol.................2 Sa 22:6
s God distributes.............Job 21:17
s shall be multiplied........ Ps 16:4
by men, a man of s.........Is 53:3
are the beginning of s......Matt 24:8
through with many s........1 Ti 6:10

SORRY

s that He had made man..Gen 6:6
who will be s for you.......Is 51:19
And the king was s.........Matt 14:9
For you were made s.......2 Co 7:9

SOUGHT

I s the LORD.................Ps 34:4
whole heart I have s.......Ps 119:10
s the one I love.............Song 3:1
you shall be called S........Is 62:12
"So I s for a man............Ezek 22:30
s what was lost...............Ezek 34:4
s favor from Him............Hos 12:4
LORD, and have not s....Zeph 1:6
s it diligently.................Heb 12:17

SOUL

s enter their council.........Gen 49:6
with all your s................Deut 6:5
was knit to the s.............1 Sa 18:1
your heart and your s.......1 Ch 22:19
"My s loathes life........... Job 10:1
as you do, if your s.........Job 16:4
s draws near the Pit........ Job 33:22
will not leave my s.........Ps 16:10
converting the s.............Ps 19:7

He restores my s.............Ps 23:3
s shall make its boast.......Ps 34:2
s shall be joyful..............Ps 35:9
you cast down, O my s....Ps 42:5
s silently waits................Ps 62:1
He has done for my s......Ps 66:16
Let my s live.................Ps 119:175
s knows very well...........Ps 139:14
No one cares for my s....Ps 142:4
so destroys his own s....... Prov 6:32
me wrongs his own s....... Prov 8:36
it is not good for a s....... Prov 19:2
A satisfied s loathes........ Prov 27:7
When You make His s....Is 53:10
s delight itself................Is 55:2
and your s shall live........ Is 55:3
you have heard, O my s...Jer 4:19
the s of the father as......Ezek 18:4
the proud, his s.............Hab 2:4
able to destroy both s....... Matt 10:28
and loses his own s....... Matt 16:26
with all your s...... Matt 22:37
Now My s is troubled......John 12:27
of one heart and one s....Acts 4:32
your whole spirit, s......... 1 Th 5:23
to the saving of the s.......Heb 10:39
his way will save a s....... Jas 5:20
his righteous s................ 2 Pe 2:8
health, just as your s....... 3 Jn 2

SOULS

And will save the s......... Ps 72:13
and he who wins s.......... Prov 11:30
s shall be like a.............. Jer 31:12
who made our very s.......Jer 38:16
unsettling your s............. Acts 15:24
is able to save your s.......Jas 1:21

SOUND

s heart is life.................Prov 14:30
one rises up at the s........Eccl 12:4
voice was like the s.........Ezek 43:2
s an alarm in My holy......Joel 2:1
do not s a trumpet..........Matt 6:2
s words which you..........2 Ti 1:13
that they may be s..........Tit 1:13

SOUNDNESS

There is no s in my........Ps 38:3
him this perfect s............Acts 3:16

SOUNDS

Dreadful s are in his.......Job 15:21
a distinction in the s........1 Co 14:7

SOW

s trouble reap................Job 4:8
Then let me s.................Job 31:8
s fields and plant............Ps 107:37
Those who s in tears........Ps 126:5
the wind will not s...........Eccl 11:4
Blessed are you who s....... Is 32:20
ground, and do not s........Jer 4:3
"They s the wind............Hos 8:7
S for yourselves..............Hos 10:12
s is not made alive..........1 Co 15:36

SOWER

may give seed to the s......Is 55:10
"Behold, a s went...........Matt 13:3

SOWN

shall they be s.................Is 40:24
a land that was not s.......Jer 2:2
"You have s much..........Hag 1:6
s spiritual things..............1 Co 9:11

SOWS

It is *s* in weakness............1 Co 15:43
of righteousness is *s*.........Jas 3:18

SOWS

s righteousness will.........Prov 11:18
s the good seed is the......Matt 13:37
'One *s* and another......... John 4:37
s sparingly will................2 Co 9:6
for whatever a man *s*.......Gal 6:7

SPARE

The LORD would not *s*....Deut 29:20
hand, but *s* his life..........Job 2:6
s the poor and needy.......Ps 72:13
I will not pity nor *s*.........Jer 13:14
say, "*S* Your people.........Joel 2:17
s them as a man spares....Mal 3:17
He who did not *s*...........Rom 8:32
s the natural branches......Rom 11:21
branches, He may not *s*... Rom 11:21
flesh, but I would *s*.........1 Co 7:28
if God did not *s*..............2 Pe 2:4

SPARES

s his rod hates his........... Prov 13:24

SPARKLES

it is red, when it *s*..........Prov 23:31

SPARROW

s has found a home......... Ps 84:3
awake, And am like a *s*... Ps 102:7

SPARROWS

more value than many *s*... Matt 10:31

SPAT

Then they *s* on Him........ Matt 27:30
in his ears, and He *s*....... Mark 7:33

SPEAK

only the word that I *s*......Num 22:35
s just once more............Judg 6:39
s good words to them...... 1 Ki 12:7
oh, that God would *s*...... Job 11:5
Will you *s* wickedly.........Job 13:7
For God may *s* in one..... Job 33:14
Will he *s* softly........... Job 41:3
Do not *s* in the..............Prov 23:9
and a time to *s*...............Eccl 3:7
If they do not *s*............. Is 8:20
tongue He will *s*............. Is 28:11
s anymore in his name.... Jer 20:9
at the end it will *s*..........Hab 2:3
s each man the truth....... Zech 8:16
or what you should *s*....... Matt 10:19
it is not you who *s*........ Matt 10:20
to you when all men *s*..... Luke 6:26
s what We know and.......John 3:11
s what I have seen......... John 8:38
He hears He will *s*.........John 16:13
Spirit and began to *s*....... Acts 2:4
Do all *s* with tongues.......1 Co 12:30
I would rather *s*.............1 Co 14:19
So *s* and so do as............Jas 2:12

SPEAKING

s your own words............Is 58:13
while they are still *s*...... Is 65:24
a proof of Christ *s*...... 2 Co 13:3
envy, and all evil *s*...........1 Pe 2:1

SPEAKS

to face, as a man *s*.........Ex 33:11
this day that God *s*........ Deut 5:24
day that I am He who *s*...Is 52:6

He whom God has sent *s*.John 3:34
When he *s* a lie.............John 8:44
he being dead still *s*....... Heb 11:4
of sprinkling that *s*.........Heb 12:24

SPEAR

lay hold on bow and *s*.... Jer 6:23
His side with a *s*............John 19:34

SPEARS

Whose teeth are *s*...........Ps 57:4
and their *s* into.............Is 2:4
pruninghooks into *s*........Joel 3:10

SPECK

do you look at the *s*........Matt 7:3

SPECTACLE

and make you a *s*........... Nah 3:6
we have been made a *s*...1 Co 4:9
He made a public *s*.........Col 2:15
you were made a *s*.........Heb 10:33

SPEECH

one language and one *s*....Gen 11:1
drop as the rain, my *s*..... Deut 32:2
s settled on them as........ Job 29:22
There is no *s* nor...........Ps 19:3
s is not becoming............Prov 17:7
your *s* shall be low.........Is 29:4
a people of obscure *s*......Is 33:19
not understand My *s*.......John 8:43
s deceive the hearts........Rom 16:18
and his *s* contemptible....2 Co 10:10
I am untrained in *s*........ 2 Co 11:6
s always be with grace..... Col 4:6

SPEECHLESS

your mouth for the *s*....... Prov 31:8
And he was *s*.................Matt 22:12

SPEED

they shall come with *s*..... Is 5:26

SPEEDILY

judgment be executed *s*....Ezra 7:26
to me, Deliver me *s*........ Ps 31:2
I call, answer me *s*.........Ps 102:2

SPEND

whatever more you *s*...... Luke 10:35
I will very gladly *s*.......... 2 Co 12:15
amiss, that you may *s*......Jas 4:3

SPENT

strength shall be *s*.......... Lev 26:20
For my life is *s*..............Ps 31:10
in vain, I have *s*.............Is 49:4
"But when he had *s*........ Luke 15:14

SPEW

nor hot, I will *s*..............Rev 3:16

SPIDER

s skillfully grasps.............Prov 30:28

SPIES

to them, "You are *s*.........Gen 42:9
men who had been *s*....... Josh 6:23
s who pretended.............Luke 20:20

SPIN

neither toil nor *s*.............Matt 6:28

SPINDLE

her hand holds the *s*........Prov 31:19

SPIRIT

And the *S* of God was.....Gen 1:2
S shall not strive............Gen 6:3
in whom is the *S*............Gen 41:38
and everyone whose *s*......Ex 35:21
S that is upon you and.....Num 11:17
And the *S* rested upon....Num 11:26
LORD would put His *S*....Num 11:29
he has a different *s*......... Num 14:24
in whom is the *S*............Num 27:18
portion of your *s*............2 Ki 2:9
there was no more *s*........2 Ch 9:4
s came forward and........2 Ch 18:20
also gave Your good *S*....Neh 9:20
against them by Your *S*... Neh 9:30
Then a *s* passed before.... Job 4:15
And whose *s* came from...Job 26:4
The *S* of God has made...Job 33:4
hand I commit my *s*........ Ps 31:5
s was not faithful............ Ps 78:8
You send forth Your *S*.... Ps 104:30
Your *S* is good..............Ps 143:10
The *s* of a man is the..... Prov 20:27
Who knows the *s*............Eccl 3:21
s will return to God....... Eccl 12:7
night, yes, by my *s*.........Is 26:9
out on you the *s*............. Is 29:10
are flesh, and not *s*.........Is 31:3
S has gathered them....... Is 34:16
is the life of my *S*...........Is 38:16
I have put My *S*.............Is 42:1
and His *S* have sent Me...Is 48:16
s would fail before Me....Is 57:16
"The *S* of the Lord........ Is 61:1
S entered me when He.... Ezek 2:2
the *S* lifted me up..........Ezek 3:12
who follow their own *s*.... Ezek 13:3
new heart and a new *s*....Ezek 18:31
be feeble, every *s*...........Ezek 21:7
"I will put My *S*............Ezek 36:27
in him is the *S*..............Dan 4:8
as an excellent *s*............Dan 5:12
walk in a false *s*.............Mic 2:11
and forms the *s*.............Zech 12:1
and He saw the *S*..........Matt 3:16
*I will put My *S*..............Matt 12:18
S descending upon Him... Mark 1:10
And immediately the *S*....Mark 1:12
s truly is ready..............Mark 14:38
go before Him in the *s*.... Luke 1:17
in the power of the *S*...... Luke 4:14
manner of *s* you are of.... Luke 9:55
hands I commend My *s*....Luke 23:46
they had seen a *s*...........Luke 24:37
s does not have flesh....... Luke 24:39
"God is *S*.....................John 4:24
I speak to you are *s*........ John 6:63
He was troubled in *s*....... John 13:21
"even the *S* of truth........John 14:17
when He, the *S*..............John 16:13
but if a *s* or an angel...... Acts 23:9
whom I serve with my *s*...Rom 1:9
according to the *S*...........Rom 8:5
the flesh but in the *S*......Rom 8:9
does not have the *S*........Rom 8:9
s that we are children...... Rom 8:16
what the mind of the *S*... Rom 8:27
to us through His *S*.........1 Co 2:10
also have the *S*...............1 Co 7:40
gifts, but the same *S*........1 Co 12:4
in a tongue, my *s*...........1 Co 14:14
but the *S* gives life.........2 Co 3:6
Now the Lord is the *S*.....2 Co 3:17
we have the same *s*.........2 Co 4:13
Having begun in the *S*.....Gal 3:3
has sent forth the *S*.........Gal 4:6

SPIRITS

he who sows to the *S*......Gal 6:8
with the Holy *S*..............Eph 1:13
may give to you the *s*......Eph 1:17
the unity of the *S*..........Eph 4:3
is one body and one *S*.....Eph 4:4
stand fast in one *s*.....Phil 1:27
yet I am with you in *s*....Col 2:5
and may your whole *s*......1 Th 5:23
S expressly says that........1 Ti 4:1
division of soul and *s*......Heb 4:12
through the eternal *S*......Heb 9:14
S who dwells in us..........Jas 4:5
made alive by the *S*..........1 Pe 3:18
S whom He has given us..1 Jn 3:24
do not believe every *s*.....1 Jn 4:1
By this you know the *S*....1 Jn 4:2
By this we know the *s*....1 Jn 4:6
has given us of His *S*......1 Jn 4:13
S who bears witness........1 Jn 5:6
not having the *S*..............Jude 19
I was in the *S* on the......Rev 1:10
him hear what the *S*........Rev 2:7
And the *S* and the..........Rev 22:17

SPIRITS

God, the God of the *s*.....Num 16:22
Who makes His angels *s*..Ps 104:4
the LORD weighs the *s*....Prov 16:2
power over unclean *s*......Matt 10:1
heed to deceiving *s*..........1 Ti 4:1
not all ministering *s*..........Heb 1:14
to the Father of *s*..........Heb 12:9
and preached to the *s*.....1 Pe 3:19
spirit, but test the *s*.........1 Jn 4:1

SPIRITUAL

s judges all things...........1 Co 2:15
s people but as to...........1 Co 3:1
to be a prophet or *s*........1 Co 14:37
However, the *s* is not......1 Co 15:46
s restore such a one........Gal 6:1

SPIRITUALLY

s minded is life.............Rom 8:6
because they are *s*...........1 Co 2:14

SPITEFULLY

for those who *s*..............Matt 5:44

SPITTING

face from shame and *s*.....Is 50:6

SPLENDOR

on the glorious *s*............Ps 145:5
of Zion all her *s*............Lam 1:6

SPOIL

hate us have taken *s*......Ps 44:10
when they divide the *s*....Is 9:3
He shall divide the *s*.......Is 53:12
Take *s* of silver.............Nah 2:9
s will be divided............Zech 14:1

SPOKE

s they did not hear.........Is 66:4
who feared the LORD *s*...Mal 3:16
"No man ever........John 7:46
"We know that God *s*......John 9:29
I was a child, I *s*............1 Co 13:11
in different ways *s*..........Heb 1:1
s as they were moved......2 Pe 1:21

SPOKEN

'just as you have *s*..........Num 14:28
God has *s* once..............Ps 62:11
I have not *s* in secret......Is 45:19

'What have we *s*.............Mal 3:13
why am I evil *s*...............1 Co 10:30

SPOKESMAN

So he shall be your *s*.......Ex 4:16

SPONGE

them ran and took a *s*.....Matt 27:48

SPOT

and there is no *s*............Song 4:7
church, not having *s*........Eph 5:27
commandment without *s*...1 Ti 6:14
Himself without *s*..........Heb 9:14

SPOTS

They are *s* and..............2 Pe 2:13
These are *s* in your........Jude 12

SPREAD

fell on my knees and *s*.....Ezra 9:5
They have *s* a net by......Ps 140:5
Then He *s* it before me....Eph 2:10
And the word of God *s*...Acts 6:7
the Lord was being *s*......Acts 13:49
their message will *s*.........2 Ti 2:17

SPREADS

He alone *s* out the..........Job 9:8
s them out like a tent......Is 40:22
Zion *s* out her hands......Lam 1:17

SPRING

Truth shall *s* out of........Ps 85:11
is like a murky *s*............Prov 25:26
sister, my spouse, a *s*......Song 4:12
s forth I tell you............Is 42:9
of Israel to *s* forth..........Ezek 29:21
s shall become dry..........Hos 13:15
s send forth fresh...........Jas 3:11

SPRINGING

a fountain of water *s*......John 4:14
of bitterness *s*................Heb 12:15

SPRINGS

Have you entered the *s*....Job 38:16
He sends the *s* into........Ps 104:10
and the thirsty land *s*......Is 35:7
and the dry land *s*..........Is 41:18

SPRINKLE

He *s* many nations..........Is 52:15
"Then I will *s*................Ezek 36:25

SPRINKLED

s dust on his head..........Job 2:12
and hyssop, and *s*..........Heb 9:19
having our hearts *s*.........Heb 10:22

SPRINKLING

s that speaks.................Heb 12:24
for obedience and *s*.........1 Pe 1:2

SPROUT

down, that it will *s*..........Job 14:7
and the seed should *s*......Mark 4:27

STAFF

this Jordan with my *s*......Gen 32:10
your feet, and your *s*......Ex 12:11
Your rod and Your *s*.......Ps 23:4
LORD has broken the *s*...Is 14:5
'How the strong *s*..........Jer 48:17
they have been a *s*.........Ezek 29:6
on the top of his *s*..........Heb 11:21

STAGGER

and He makes them *s*......Job 12:25
they will drink and *s*........Jer 25:16

STAGGERS

as a drunken man *s*.........Is 19:14

STAKES

s will ever be removed.....Is 33:20

STALLS

be no herd in the *s*.........Hab 3:17

STAMMERERS

s will be ready................Is 32:4

STAMMERING

For with *s* lips and..........Is 28:11
s tongue that you............Is 33:19

STAND

one shall be able to *s*......Deut 7:24
"Who is able to *s*............1 Sa 6:20
but it does not *s*............Job 8:15
lives, and He shall *s*........Job 19:25
ungodly shall not *s*.........Ps 1:5
Why do You *s* afar off.....Ps 10:1
Or who may *s* in His.......Ps 24:3
Who will *s* up for me.....Ps 94:16
And let an accuser *s*........Ps 109:6
he will not *s* before........Prov 22:29
Do not take your *s*.........Eccl 8:3
"It shall not *s*................Is 7:7
"*S* in the ways and..........Jer 6:16
not lack a man to *s*.........Jer 35:19
whose words will *s*.........Jer 44:28
and it shall *s*................Dan 2:44
but she shall not *s*.........Dan 11:17
Who can *s* before His.....Nah 1:6
And who can *s* when He..Mal 3:2
that kingdom cannot *s*.....Mark 3:24
he will be made to *s*.......Rom 14:4
Watch, *s* fast in the........1 Co 16:13
for by faith you *s*...........2 Co 1:24
having done all, to *s*........Eph 6:13
S therefore...................Eph 6:14
s fast in the Lord...........Phil 4:1
now we live, if you *s*.......1 Th 3:8
of God in which you *s*.....1 Pe 5:12
"Behold, I *s* at the..........Rev 3:20

STANDARD

LORD will lift up a *s*.......Is 59:19
Set up the *s* toward.........Jer 4:6

STANDING

the LORD, and Satan *s*....Zech 3:1
they love to pray *s*.........Matt 6:5
and the Son of Man *s*......Acts 7:56
Then I saw an angel *s*......Rev 19:11

STANDS

The LORD *s* up to plead..Is 3:13
him who thinks he *s*........1 Co 10:12

STAR

S shall come out of........Num 24:17
For we have seen His *s*....Matt 2:2
for one *s* differs from......1 Co 15:41
give him the morning *s*....Rev 2:28
And a great *s* fell...........Rev 8:10
Bright and Morning *S*......Rev 22:16

STARS

He made the *s* also.........Gen 1:16
s are not pure in His......Job 25:5

STARVED
when the morning s........Job 38:7
The moon and the s........Ps 8:3
Praise Him, all you s.......Ps 148:3
born as many as the s.....Heb 11:12
wandering s for whom..... Jude 13
a garland of twelve s....... Rev 12:1

STARVED
His strength is s..............Job 18:12

STATE
man at his best s..............Ps 39:5
us in our lowly s.......Ps 136:23
and the last s of that....... Matt 12:45
learned in whatever s.......Phil 4:11

STATURE
add one cubit to his s...... Matt 6:27
in wisdom and s..............Luke 2:52
the measure of the s........Eph 4:13

STATUTE
shall be a perpetual s.......Lev 3:17

STATUTES
The s of the LORD are...Ps 19:8
Teach me Your s.......Ps 119:12
not walked in My s.........Ezek 5:6

STAY
her feet would not s........Prov 7:11
S here and watch with..... Matt 26:38
for today I must s..........Luke 19:5

STEADFAST
yes, you could be s........Job 11:15
O God, my heart is s......Ps 57:7
their heart was not s......Ps 78:37
His heart is s.............Ps 112:7
God, and s forever.........Dan 6:26
beloved brethren, be s...1 Co 15:58
faith, grounded and s.......Col 1:23
angels proved s..........Heb 2:2
of our confidence s.........Heb 3:14
soul, both sure and s......Heb 6:19
Resist him, s in the......... 1 Pe 5:9

STEADFASTLY
s set His face to go........ Luke 9:51
And they continued s..... Acts 2:42
continuing s in..............Rom 12:12

STEADFASTNESS
good order and the s....Col 2:5
from your own s.............2 Pe 3:17

STEADILY
could not look s..............2 Co 3:13

STEADY
and his hands were s....... Ex 17:12

STEAL
"You shall not s.......... Ex 20:15
"Will you s...................Jer 7:9
s My words every one.....Jer 23:30
thieves break in and s......Matt 6:19
night and s Him away.....Matt 27:64
murder,' 'Do not s.......Mark 10:19
not come except to s.......John 10:10
a man should not s........Rom 2:21
Let him who stole s.......Eph 4:28

STEEP
s places shall fall..........Ezek 38:20
waters poured down a s... Mic 1:4
violently down the s........ Matt 8:32

STEM
forth a Rod from the s.... Is 11:1

STENCH
there will be a s..............Is 3:24
this time there is a s........John 11:39

STEP
there is but a s...............1 Sa 20:3
s has turned from the...... Job 31:7

STEPS
has held fast to His s.......Job 23:11
and count all my s........Job 31:4
and He sees all his s........Job 34:21
Uphold my s in Your...... Ps 17:5
The s of a good man....... Ps 37:23
of his s shall slide........ Ps 37:31
And established my s.......Ps 40:2
hide, they mark my s.....Ps 56:6
s had nearly slipped......Ps 73:2
Direct my s by Your....... Ps 119:133
s will not be hindered.....Prov 4:12
the LORD directs his s.....Prov 16:9
A man's s are of the...... Prov 20:24
to direct his own s..........Jer 10:23
should follow His s.........1 Pe 2:21

STEWARD
faithful and wise s..........Luke 12:42
you can no longer be s.... Luke 16:2
commended the unjust s...Luke 16:8
be blameless, as a s.........Tit 1:7

STEWARDS
of Christ and s.............. 1 Co 4:1
one another, as good s.....1 Pe 4:10

STEWARDSHIP
entrusted with a s........... 1 Co 9:17

STICK
and his bones s.............Job 33:21
For Joseph, the s...........Ezek 37:16

STICKS
a man gathering s.......... Num 15:32
"And the s on which.......Ezek 37:20

STIFF
rebellion and your s....... Deut 31:27
Do not speak with a s..... Ps 75:5

STIFFNECKED
"Now do not be s..........2 Ch 30:8
"You s and...................Acts 7:51

STILL
on your bed, and be s..... Ps 4:4
s the noise of the...........Ps 65:7
earth feared and was s.....Ps 76:8
that its waves are s.........Ps 107:29
When I awake, I am s.....Ps 139:18
time, I have been s........ Is 42:14
rest and be s.................Jer 47:6
sea, "Peace, be s..........Mark 4:39
let him be holy s............Rev 22:11

STILLBORN
I not hidden like a s........Job 3:16
as it goes, Like a s.........Ps 58:8
burial, I say that a s........Eccl 6:3

STINGS
like a serpent, and s........Prov 23:32

STIR
that he would dare s.......Job 41:10
S up Yourself..............Ps 35:23
I remind you to s.............2 Ti 1:6
another in order to s....... Heb 10:24

STIRRED
fulfilled, the LORD s.......2 Ch 36:22
And my sorrow was s......Ps 39:2
So the LORD s up the.....Hag 1:14

STIRS
and the innocent s..........Job 17:8
it s up the dead for.........Is 14:9
on Your name, who s.....Is 64:7

STOCKS
put my feet in the s........Job 13:27
s that were in the...........Jer 20:2

STOIC
and S philosophers..........Acts 17:18

STOMACH
mouth goes into the s......Matt 15:17
his heart but his s.........Mark 7:19
Foods for the s..............1 Co 6:13

STOMACH'S
little wine for your s........1 Ti 5:23

STONE
him, a pillar of s...........Gen 35:14
to the bottom like a s......Ex 15:5
s shall be a witness.........Josh 24:27
heart is as hard as s.......Job 41:24
s which the builders.........Ps 118:22
s is heavy and sand is..... Prov 27:3
I lay in Zion a s............Is 28:16
foundation, a tried s....... Is 28:16
take the heart of s.........Ezek 36:26
You watched while a s.....Dan 2:34
s will cry out from......... Hab 2:11
to silent s...................Hab 2:19
will give him a s............ Matt 7:9
s will be broken.............Matt 21:44
secure, sealing the s........Matt 27:66
s which the builders........Luke 20:17
you, let him throw a s.....John 8:7
those works do you s.......John 10:32
Jews sought to s You.......John 11:8
not on tablets of s...........2 Co 3:3
Him as to a living s........1 Pe 2:4
give him a white s..........Rev 2:17
angel took up a s............Rev 18:21
like a jasper s.................Rev 21:11

STONED
s Stephen as he was........ Acts 7:59
once I was s...................2 Co 11:25
They were s..................Heb 11:37

STONES
I will lay your s............. Is 54:11
Among the smooth s....... Is 57:6
Abraham from these s...... Matt 3:9
command that these s...... Matt 4:3
see what manner of s......Mark 13:1
also, as living s...............1 Pe 2:5
kinds of precious s........... Rev 21:19

STONY
them, and take the s....... Ezek 11:19
Some fell on s ground......Mark 4:5

STOOPED
And again He s down......John 8:8

STOPPED
speak lies shall be s.........Ps 63:11
her flow of blood s.........Luke 8:44

STORE
no room to s my crops.....Luke 12:17
exist are kept in s........... 2 Pe 3:7

STORK
s has her home in the......Ps 104:17
"Even the s in the.......... Jer 8:7

STORM
From the windy s............Ps 55:8
terror comes like a s........Prov 1:27
for a shelter from s......... Is 4:6
a refuge from the s......... Is 25:4
and a destroying s...........Is 28:2
coming like a s...... Ezek 38:9
whirlwind and in the s..... Nah 1:3

STOUTHEARTED
s were plundered........... Ps 76:5

STRAIGHT
Make Your way s........... Ps 5:8
for who can make s.........Eccl 7:13
make s in the desert a..... Is 40:3
Their legs were s........... Ezek 1:7
LORD, make is paths s.... Luke 3:4
to the street called S....... Acts 9:11
and make s paths for.......Heb 12:13

STRAIGHTFORWARD
that they were not s........ Gal 2:14

STRAIN
"Blind guides, who s....... Matt 23:24

STRAITS
and desperate s...............Deut 28:53

STRANGE
were considered a s........Hos 8:12
"We have seen s...........Luke 5:26
are bringing some s........ Acts 17:20
these, they think it s........1 Pe 4:4
s thing happened.............1 Pe 4:12

STRANGER
but he acted as a s.........Gen 42:7
"I have been a s...........Ex 2:22
neither mistreat a s........ Ex 22:21
and loves the s............... Deut 10:18
I have become a s...........Ps 69:8
s will suffer for it.........Prov 11:15
s does not share its........ Prov 14:10
should You be like a s.....Jer 14:8
I was a s and you took.... Matt 25:35
"Are You the only s...... Luke 24:18

STRANGERS
descendants will be s....... Gen 15:13
s plunder his labor.......... Ps 109:11
watches over the s...........Ps 146:9
s devour your land.......... Is 1:7
S shall stand and feed......Is 61:5
know the voice of s........John 10:5
of Israel and s............... Eph 2:12
you are no longer s......... Eph 2:19
if she has lodged s.......... 1 Ti 5:10
that they were s..........Heb 11:13
forget to entertain s........Heb 13:2
the brethren and for s......3 Jn 5

STRANGLING
that my soul chooses s.....Job 7:15

STRAP
than I, whose sandal s..... Mark 1:7

STRAW
They are like s............... Job 21:18
stones, wood, hay, s........1 Co 3:12

STRAY
the cursed, Who s...........Ps 119:21
who make my people s.... Mic 3:5

STRAYED
Yet I have not s............. Ps 119:110
for which some have s..... 1 Ti 6:10
who have s concerning.....2 Ti 2:18

STREAM
like an overflowing s....... Is 30:28
of the LORD, like a s......Is 30:33
like a flowing s............... Is 66:12

STREAMS
He dams up the s........... Job 28:11
He also brought s.......... Ps 78:16
O LORD, As the s........Ps 126:4

STREET
to be heard in the s.........Is 42:2
s called Straight............. Acts 9:11
And the s of the city...... Rev 21:21
In the middle of its s....... Rev 22:2

STREETS
the corners of the s......... Matt 6:5
You taught in our s.........Luke 13:26
out quickly into the s......Luke 14:21

STRENGTH
for by s of hand the........ Ex 13:3
just as my s was then...... Josh 14:11
my soul, march on in s.... Judg 5:21
a man is, so is his s........Judg 8:21
s no man shall................1 Sa 2:9
the God of my s............ 2 Sa 22:3
have armed me with s..... 2 Sa 22:40
the LORD glory and s..... 1 Ch 16:28
Is my s the s.................Job 6:12
Him are wisdom and s....Job 12:13
You have ordained s....... Ps 8:2
love You, O LORD, my s Ps 18:1
The LORD is their s.........Ps 27:1
The LORD is their s........Ps 28:8
The LORD will give s.....Ps 29:11
delivered by great s.........Ps 33:16
He is their s in the.........Ps 37:39
are the God of my s.......Ps 43:2
is our refuge and s...........Ps 46:1
is He who gives s...........Ps 68:35
I will go in the s.............Ps 71:16
But God is the s.............Ps 73:26
They go from s to...........Ps 84:7
the glory of their s...........Ps 89:17
S and beauty are in........Ps 96:6
made me bold with s........Ps 138:3
of the LORD is s.......... Prov 10:29
knowledge increases s...... Prov 24:5
S and honor are her...... Prov 31:25
is better than s............... Eccl 9:16
for s and not for............ Eccl 10:17
For You have been a s.... Is 25:3
him take hold of My s..... Is 27:5
of His might and the s..... Is 40:26
might He increases s.......Is 40:29

STRIKE
said, "S this people.........2 Ki 6:18
The sun shall not s..........Ps 121:6
Let the righteous s...........Ps 141:5
S a scoffer.................... Prov 19:25
s your hands.................. Ezek 21:14
s the waves of the sea......Zech 10:11
"S the Shepherd............ Zech 13:7
s the earth with a............Mal 4:6
I will s the Shepherd.......Matt 26:31
the sun shall not s...........Rev 7:16
s the earth with all.......... Rev 11:6

works it with the s.......... Is 44:12
righteousness and s...........Is 45:24
Put on your s.................. Is 52:1
O LORD, my s and my....Is 16:19
I will destroy the s........... Hag 2:22
He has shown s with....... Luke 1:51
were still without s.......... Rom 5:6
s is made perfect.............2 Co 12:9
you have a little s........... Rev 3:8

STRENGTHEN
And He shall s............... Ps 27:14
S the weak hands...........Is 35:3
"So I will s them in.........Zech 10:12
s your brethren..............Luke 22:32
s the hands.................... Heb 12:12
s the things................... Rev 3:2

STRENGTHENED
weak you have not s.......Ezek 34:4
unbelief, but was s.......... Rom 4:20
of His glory, to be s........Eph 3:16
stood with me and s........2 Ti 4:17

STRENGTHENING
s the souls of the............ Acts 14:22

STRENGTHENS
s the wise more than....... Eccl 7:19
through Christ who s....... Phil 4:13

STRETCH
will quickly s out her.......Ps 68:31
said to the man, "S.........Matt 12:13
are old, you will s...........John 21:18

STRETCHED
I have s out my hands..... Ps 88:9
His wisdom, And has s....Jer 10:12
All day long I have s.......Rom 10:21

STRETCHES
for he s out his hand.......Job 15:25

STRICKEN
My heart is s and...........Ps 102:4
yet we esteemed Him s....Is 53:4
of My people He was s....Is 53:8
You have s them............ Jer 5:3
He has s....................... Hos 6:1

STRIFE
let there be no s............. Gen 13:8
You have made us a s..... Ps 80:6
at the waters of s............Ps 106:32
Hatred stirs up s............. Prov 10:12
man stirs up s................Prov 15:18
transgression loves s........ Prov 17:19
borne me, a man of s....... Jer 15:10
and lewdness, not in s...... Rom 13:13
even from envy and s...... Phil 1:15
which come envy, s........ 1 Ti 6:4

STRINGED
of your s instruments.......Is 14:11
of your s instruments.......Amos 5:23

STRIP
s yourselves....................Is 32:11
s her naked and expose....Hos 2:3

STRIPES
their iniquity with s........Ps 89:32
s we are healed............. Is 53:5
be beaten with many s.....Luke 12:47
I received forty s............ 2 Co 11:24
s you were healed........... 1 Pe 2:24

STRIVE
My Spirit shall not s........Gen 6:3
He will not always s........Ps 103:9
Do not s with a man...... Prov 3:30
Let the potsherd s..........Is 45:9
"S to enter through........Luke 13:24
the Lord not to s............2 Ti 2:14

STRIVING
for a man to stop s........ Prov 20:3

STRONG
"Be s and conduct.......... 1 Sa 4:9
indeed He is s................Job 9:19
The LORD s and mighty..Ps 24:8
bring me into the s..........Ps 60:9
S is Your hand................Ps 89:13
A wise man is s..............Prov 24:5
s shall be as tinder..........Is 1:31
"We have a s city............ Is 26:1
the weak say, 'I am s...... Joel 3:10
"When a s man.............. Luke 11:21
We then who are s..........Rom 15:1
are weak and you are s....2 Co 13:9
my brethren, be s............ Eph 6:10
weakness were made s..... Heb 11:34
s is the Lord God.......... Rev 18:8

STRONGHOLD
of my salvation, my s...... Ps 18:2
down the trusted s......... Prov 21:22

STRUCK
s the rock twice.............. Num 20:11
the hand of God has s.....Job 19:21
s all my enemies............ Ps 3:7
Behold, He s the rock..... Ps 78:20
I was angry and s............Is 57:17
in My wrath I s.............. Is 60:10
s the head from the........Hab 3:13
'I s you with blight..........Hag 2:17
took the reed and s........Matt 27:30
Him, they s Him on the...Luke 22:64

STUBBLE
shall bring forth s...........Is 33:11
his sword, as driven s..... Is 41:2
they shall be as s............ Is 47:14
s that passes................Jer 13:24
do wickedly will be s...... Mal 4:1

STUBBORN
If a man has a s............Deut 21:18
and s children................Ezek 2:4

STUBBORN-HEARTED
"Listen to Me, you s....... Is 46:12

STUBBORNNESS
do not look on the s........Deut 9:27

STUDIED
having never s................John 7:15

STUMBLE
causes them to s............. Ps 119:165
to make my steps s......... Ps 140:4
your foot will not s....... Prov 3:23
know what makes them s. Prov 4:19
one will be weary or s..... Is 5:27
among them shall s......... Is 8:15
we s at noonday as at......Is 59:10
that they might not s....... Is 63:13
before your feet s.......... Jer 13:16
they will s and fall......... Jer 46:6
have caused many to s....Mal 2:8
you will be made to s..... Matt 26:31
if all are made to s.........Matt 26:33
immediately they s.......... Mark 4:17
who believe in Me to s.... Mark 9:42
the day, he does not s..... John 11:9
Who is made to s............2 Co 11:29
whole law, and yet s........Jas 2:10
For we all s in many.......Jas 3:2

STUMBLED
and those who s..............1 Sa 2:4
God, for you have s........Hos 14:1
s that they should.......... Rom 11:11

STUMBLES
word, immediately he s....Matt 13:21

STUMBLING
but a stone of s.............. Is 8:14
Behold, I will lay s..........Jer 6:21
watched for my s............ Jer 20:10
it became their s............Ezek 7:19
stumbled at that s.......... Rom 9:32
I lay in Zion a s............ Rom 9:33
this, not to put a s......... Rom 14:13
to the Jews a s............... 1 Co 1:23
of yours become a s........ 1 Co 8:9
and "A stone of s............ 1 Pe 2:8
is no cause for s............. 1 Jn 2:10
to keep you from s.........Jude 24

STUMBLINGBLOCK
the deaf, nor put a s....... Lev 19:14

STUPID
and regarded as s...........Job 18:3
who hates reproof is s......Prov 12:1
Surely I am more s......... Prov 30:2

SUBDUE
s the peoples under us..... Ps 47:3
shall s three kings.......... Dan 7:24
s our iniquities................Mic 7:19
s all things to................ Phil 3:21

SUBJECT
for it is not s..................Rom 8:7
Let every soul be s..........Rom 13:1
all things are made s...... 1 Co 15:28
Himself will also be s...... 1 Co 15:28
Remind them to be s........Tit 3:1
all their lifetime s..........Heb 2:15
having been made s.........1 Pe 3:22

SUBJECTED
because of Him who s..... Rom 8:20

SUBJECTION
put all things in s............Heb 2:8
more readily be in s........Heb 12:9

SUBMISSION
in silence with all s..........1 Ti 2:11
his children in s.............. 1 Ti 3:4

SUBMISSIVE
you wives, be s................1 Pe 3:1
Yes, all of you be s.........1 Pe 5:5

SUBMIT
Your enemies shall s....... Ps 66:3
Wives, s to your own......Eph 5:22
Therefore s to God......... Jas 4:7
s yourselves to every....... 1 Pe 2:13
you younger people, s......1 Pe 5:5

SUBSIDED
and the waters s............. Gen 8:1
the king's wrath s...........Esth 7:10

SUBSTANCE
Bless his s.....................Deut 33:11
the rest of their s............Ps 17:14
the LORD, and their s.....Mic 4:13

SUCCEED
For this will not s........... Num 14:41
you shall not s................Jer 32:5

SUCCESS
please give me s............. Gen 24:12
You spoil my s............... Job 30:22
but wisdom brings s......... Eccl 10:10

SUCCESSFUL
Joseph, and he was a s.... Gen 39:2

SUDDENLY
whom you seek, will s..... Mal 3:1
s there was with the........ Luke 2:13

SUE
s you and take away........Matt 5:40

SUFFER
for a stranger will s........ Prov 11:15
for the Christ to s.......... Luke 24:46
Christ, if indeed we s...... Rom 8:17
all the members s............1 Co 12:26
that they may not s........ Gal 6:12
s trouble as an................2 Ti 2:9
when you do good and s.. 1 Pe 2:20
the will of God, to s........1 Pe 3:17
s as a murderer.............. 1 Pe 4:15
you are about to s..........Rev 2:10

SUFFERED
s these things and to.......Luke 24:26
Have you s so many........ Gal 3:4
for whom I have s...........Phil 3:8
with His own blood, s.....Heb 13:12
because Christ also s........ 1 Pe 2:21
For Christ also s............. 1 Pe 3:18
since Christ s.................1 Pe 4:1
after you have s.............. 1 Pe 5:10

SUFFERING
my eyes bring s.............. Lam 3:51
Is anyone among you s.... Jas 5:13
forth as an example, s..... Jude 7

SUFFERINGS
I consider that the s........ Rom 8:18
share with me in the s.....2 Ti 1:8
perfect through s.............Heb 2:10
great struggle with s........ Heb 10:32
beforehand the s.............1 Pe 1:11

SUFFERS
Love s long and is............1 Co 13:4

SUFFICIENCY
ourselves, but our s.........2 Co 3:5
always having all s...... 2 Co 9:8

SUFFICIENT
S for the day is its......... Matt 6:34
by the majority is s......... 2 Co 2:6
Not that we are s............2 Co 3:5

SUM
How great is the s..........Ps 139:17
s I obtained this..............Acts 22:28

SUMMED
commandment, are all s... Rom 13:9

SUMMER
heat, and winter and s..... Gen 8:22
into the drought of s...... Ps 32:4
You have made s...........Ps 74:17
you know that s..............Matt 24:32

SUN
So the s stood still......... Josh 10:13
love Him be like the s..... Judg 5:31
grows green in the s........Job 8:16
a tabernacle for the s......Ps 19:4
the LORD God is a s...... Ps 84:11
s shall not strike you...... Ps 121:6
The s to rule by day.......Ps 136:8
to behold the s...............Eccl 11:7
while the s and the.........Eccl 12:2
moon, clear as the s........Song 6:10
s will be sevenfold..........Is 30:26
s returned ten degrees..... Is 38:8
s shall no longer be.........Is 60:19
s has gone down while.....Jer 15:9
LORD, Who gives the s....Jer 31:35
the s and moon grow.....Joel 2:10
s shall be turned.............Joel 2:31
s shall go down on the.....Mic 3:6
The s and moon stood.....Hab 3:11
for He makes His s.........Matt 5:45
the s was darkened..........Luke 23:45
is one glory of the s........ 1 Co 15:41
do not let the s...............Eph 4:26
s became black as........... Rev 6:12
s shall not strike............ Rev 7:16
had no need of the s....... Rev 21:23

SUPPER
man gave a great s.........Luke 14:16
to eat the Lord's S..........1 Co 11:20
took the cup after s.........1 Co 11:25
together for the s............Rev 19:17

SUPPLICATION
s that you have made...... 1 Ki 9:3
and make your s..............Job 8:5
LORD has heard my s...... Ps 6:9
to the LORD I made s.....Ps 30:8
Yourself from my s.........Ps 55:1
Let my s come before......Ps 119:170
They will make s............Is 45:14
with all prayer and s........Eph 6:18
by prayer and s..............Phil 4:6

SUPPLIES
Now may He who s.........2 Co 9:10
Therefore He who s.........Gal 3:5
by what every joint s.......Eph 4:16

SUPPLY
s what was lacking......... Phil 2:30
And my God shall s........Phil 4:19

SUPPORT
but the LORD was my s...2 Sa 22:19
this, that you must s........Acts 20:35

SUPREME
to the king as s................1 Pe 2:13

SURE
s your sin will find.......... Num 32:23
but no man is s............Job 24:22
calling and election s.......2 Pe 1:10
word made more s..........2 Pe 1:19

SURETY
Be s for Your servant......Ps 119:122
one who hates being s..... Prov 11:15
Jesus has become a s.......Heb 7:22

SURROUND
But you shall s.............. 2 Ki 11:8
LORD, mercy shall s....... Ps 32:10

SURROUNDED
All nations s me............. Ps 118:10
their own deeds have s.... Hos 7:2
and the floods s..............Jon 2:3
also, since we are s......... Heb 12:1

SURVIVOR
was no refugee or s.........Lam 2:22

SUSPICIONS
reviling, evil s..................1 Ti 6:4

SUSTAIN
You will s him on his...... Ps 41:3
of a man will s...............Prov 18:14
S me with cakes of.........Song 2:5

SWADDLING
thick darkness its s..........Job 38:9
Him in s cloths...............Luke 2:7

SWALLOW
like a flying s................. Prov 26:2
Like a crane or a s..........Is 38:14
s observe the time...........Jer 8:7
great fish to s Jonah........Jon 1:17
a gnat and s a camel....... Matt 23:24

SWEAR
shall I make you s...........1 Ki 22:16
in the earth shall s..........Is 65:16
s oaths by the LORD.......Zeph 1:5
'You shall not s...............Matt 5:33
began to curse and s.......Matt 26:74
because He could s.........Heb 6:13
my brethren, do not s......Jas 5:12

SWEARING
By s and lying................Hos 4:2

SWEARS
He who s to his own....... Ps 15:4
Everyone who s by Him...Ps 63:11
but whoever s by the.......Matt 23:18

SWEAT
In the s of your face........Gen 3:19
And His s became like.....Luke 22:44

SWEET
Though evil is s...............Job 20:12
s are Your words............Ps 119:103
His mouth is most s........ Song 5:16
but it will be as s............Rev 10:9

SWEETNESS
'Should I cease my s........Judg 9:11
called prudent, and s.......Prov 16:21
mouth like honey in s......Ezek 3:3

SWIFT
s as the eagle flies...........Deut 28:49
pass by like s ships..........Job 9:26
handles the bow, the s.....Amos 2:15
let every man be s...........Jas 1:19

SWIFTLY
His word runs very s.......Ps 147:15

SWIM
night I make my bed s.....Ps 6:6

SWOON
as they s like the............Lam 2:12

SWORD
s which turned every....... Gen 3:24
but not with your s.........Josh 24:12
the wicked with Your s....Ps 17:13
land by their own s.........Ps 44:3
my bow, Nor shall my s...Ps 44:6
their tongue a sharp s......Ps 57:4
shall not lift up s............Is 2:4
s shall be bathed.............Is 34:5
The s of the LORD is......Is 34:6
And I will send a s........ Jer 9:16
will die by the s..............Ezek 7:15
'A s................................Ezek 21:9
a s is sharpened..............Ezek 21:9
'A s, a s is......................Ezek 21:28
Bow and s of battle I..... Hos 2:18
"Awake, O s...................Zech 13:7
to bring peace but a s......Matt 10:34
for all who take the s.......Matt 26:52
s will pierce through........Luke 2:35
he does not bear the s..... Rom 13:4
the s of the Spirit............Eph 6:17
than any two-edged s.......Heb 4:12
a sharp two-edged s.........Rev 1:16
mouth goes a sharp s.......Rev 19:15

SWORDS
Yet they were drawn s.....Ps 55:21
shall beat their s.............Is 2:4
look, here are two s........Luke 22:38

SWORE
So I s in My wrath..........Ps 95:11
So I s in My wrath.........Heb 3:11
and s by Him who lives... Rev 10:6

SWORN
By Myself I have s..........Gen 22:16
The LORD has s in........Ps 132:11
I have s by Myself.........Is 45:23
"The LORD has s...........Heb 7:21

SYMBOLIC
which things are s...........Gal 4:24
It was s for the..............Heb 9:9

SYMBOLS
I have given s through.....Hos 12:10

SYMPATHIZE
Priest who cannot s.........Heb 4:15

SYMPATHY
My s is stirred...............Hos 11:8

SYNAGOGUE
He went into the s..........Luke 4:16
but are a s of Satan.........Rev 2:9

— T —

TABERNACLE
you shall make the t........Ex 26:1
t He shall hide me.......... Ps 27:5
I will abide in Your t.......Ps 61:4
In Salem also is His t...... Ps 76:2
How lovely is Your t...... Ps 84:1
quiet habitation, a t.........Is 33:20
Yes, you took up the t..... Acts 7:43
and will rebuild the t...... Acts 15:16
and more perfect t......... Heb 9:11
"Behold, the t................ Rev 21:3

TABERNACLES
us make here three t....... Matt 17:4
Feast of T was at hand.... John 7:2

TABLE
shall also make a t...... Ex 25:23
prepare a t before me......Ps 23:5
t become a snare............Ps 69:22
dogs under the t............ Mark 7:28
t become a snare............ Rom 11:9
of the Lord's t................1 Co 10:21

TABLES
t are full of vomit.......... Is 28:8
and overturned the t.......Matt 21:12
of God and serve t.........Acts 6:2

TABLET
write them on the t......... Prov 3:3
is engraved on the t.........Jer 17:1

TAIL
the head and not the t..... Deut 28:13
t drew a third of the........Rev 12:4

TAKE
T your sandal off your.....Josh 5:15
t Your Holy Spirit............Ps 51:11
t not the word of............ Ps 119:43
In You I t shelter............Ps 143:9
T words with you............Hos 14:2
T My yoke upon you and.Matt 11:29
T what is yours and........Matt 20:14
and t up his cross............Mark 8:34
T this cup away............ Mark 14:36
My life that I may t........John 10:17
I urge you to t heart........Acts 27:22

TAKEN
you are t by the words.....Prov 6:2
He was t from prison.......Is 53:8
one will be t and the....... Matt 24:40
what he has will be t...... Mark 4:25
He was t up.................. Acts 1:9
until He is t out..........2 Th 2:7

TALEBEARER
not go about as a t.........Lev 19:16
t reveals secrets............. Prov 11:13

TALENT
went and hid your t.........Matt 25:25

TALK
shall t of them when........Deut 6:7
t be vindicated............Job 11:2
with unprofitable t..........Job 15:3
My tongue also shall t......Ps 71:24
entangle Him in His t.......Matt 22:15
"I will no longer t..........John 14:30
turned aside to idle t........ 1 Ti 1:6

TALKED
within us while He t........ Luke 24:32

TALKERS
both idle t and................Tit 1:10

TALL
to a nation t and.............Is 18:2

TAMBOURINE
They sing to the t........... Job 21:12
The mirth of the t...........Is 24:8

TARES
the t also appeared.........Matt 13:26

TARGET
You set me as Your t......Job 7:20
and set me up as a t.......Lam 3:12

TARRY
who turns aside to t.........Jer 14:8
come and will not t........ Heb 10:37

TASTE
and its t was like the...... Num 11:8
Oh, t and see that the..... Ps 34:8
are Your words to my t... Ps 119:103
was sweet to my t............Song 2:3
Do not touch, do not t.... Col 2:21
might t death for.............Heb 2:9

TASTED
But when He had t........ Matt 27:34
t the heavenly gift.......... Heb 6:4
t the good word.............. Heb 6:5
t that the Lord is............ 1 Pe 2:3

TAUGHT
O God, You have t.........Ps 71:17
as His counselor has t......Is 40:13
presence, and You t...... Luke 13:26
they shall all be t............John 6:45
but as My Father t.........John 8:28
from man, nor was I t..... Gal 1:12

TAUNT
and a byword, a t........... Jer 24:9

TAX
t collectors do the.......... Matt 5:46
received the temple t........ Matt 17:24
I say to you that t...........Matt 21:31
"Show Me the t.............. Matt 22:19

TAXES
take customs or t........... Matt 17:25
Is it lawful to pay t......... Matt 22:17
forbidding to pay t......... Luke 23:2
t to whom t................... Rom 13:7

TEACH
t them diligently.............Deut 6:7
t Jacob Your judgments... Deut 33:10
t you the good and the.... 1 Sa 12:23
"Can anyone t................Job 21:22
"I will t you about.......... Job 27:11
t me what I do not see..... Job 34:32
T me Your paths............ Ps 25:4
T me Your way............. Ps 27:11
t you the fear of the........ Ps 34:11
t You awesome things......Ps 45:4
t transgressors Your.......Ps 51:13
So t us to number our..... Ps 90:12
he will t us His ways........Is 2:3
"Whom will he t............. Is 28:9
a bribe, her priests t........Mic 3:11

TEACHER
for One is your T.......... Matt 23:8
asked Him, "Good T.......Mark 10:17
know that You are a t..... John 3:2
"You call me T.............. John 13:13
named Gamaliel, a t........Acts 5:34
a t of babes, having.........Rom 2:20
a t of the Gentiles in....... 1 Ti 2:7

TEACHERS
than all my t.................. Ps 119:99
t will not be moved......... Is 30:20
prophets, third t..............1 Co 12:28
and some pastors and t.... Eph 4:11
desiring to be t................ 1 Ti 1:7
time you ought to be t.....Heb 5:12
of you become t.............Jas 3:1
there will be false t........ 2 Pe 2:1

TEACHES
Therefore He t sinners.....Ps 25:8
the Holy Spirit t............ 1 Co 2:13
If anyone t otherwise......1 Ti 6:3
the same anointing t........ 1 Jn 2:27

TEACHING
t them to observe all....... Matt 28:20
they did not cease t........Acts 5:42
he who teaches, in t........ Rom 12:7
t every man in all...........Col 1:28
t things which they.........Tit 1:11
t us that....................... Tit 2:12

TEAR
t yourself in anger..........Job 18:4
Lest they t me like a....... Ps 7:2
I, even I, will t...............Hos 5:14
feet, and turn and t.......Matt 7:6
will wipe away every t..... Rev 21:4

TEARS
I have seen your t...........2 Ki 20:5
my couch with my t.........Ps 6:6
t have been my food.......Ps 42:3
with the bread of t.......... Ps 80:5
drench you with my t.......Is 16:9
GOD will wipe away t..... Is 25:8
eyes may run with t.........Jer 9:18
My eyes fail with t.......... Lam 2:11
His feet with her t..........Luke 7:38
night and day with t........Acts 20:31
mindful of your t............ 2 Ti 1:4
vehement cries and t........Heb 5:7
it diligently with t...........Heb 12:17

TEETH
t whiter than milk.......... Gen 49:12
by the skin of my t..........Job 19:20
You have broken the t.....Ps 3:7
As vinegar to the t..........Prov 10:26
you cleanness of t........... Amos 4:6

TELL
That you may t it to........Ps 48:13
the message that I t.........Jon 3:2
"Who can t if God..........Jon 3:9
t him his fault................Matt 18:15
whatever they t..............Matt 23:3
He comes, He will t........ John 4:25

t the way of God in.........Matt 22:16
in My name, He will t..... John 14:26
even nature itself t........... 1 Co 11:14
permit a woman to t........1 Ti 2:12
things command and t.....1 Ti 4:11
T and exhort these..........1 Ti 6:2
t you again the first.........Heb 5:12

TEMPERATE
for the prize is *t*..............1 Co 9:25
husband of one wife, *t*.....1 Ti 3:2

TEMPEST
the windy storm and *t*......Ps 55:8
one, tossed with *t*...........Is 54:11
And suddenly a great *t*....Matt 8:24

TEMPLE
So Solomon built the *t*.....1 Ki 6:14
LORD is in His holy *t*......Ps 11:4
to inquire in His *t*..........Ps 27:4
suddenly come to His *t*....Mal 3:1
One greater than the *t*....Matt 12:6
murdered between the *t*...Matt 23:35
found Him in the *t*.........Luke 2:46
"Destroy this *t*................John 2:19
was speaking of the *t*......John 2:21
one accord in the *t*.........Acts 2:46
that you are the *t*...........1 Co 3:16
your body is the *t*..........1 Co 6:19
grows into a holy *t*.........Eph 2:21
sits as God in the *t*.........2 Th 2:4
Then the *t* of God was.....Rev 11:19
But I saw no *t* in it.........Rev 21:22
and the Lamb are its *t*.....Rev 21:22

TEMPLES
t made with hands...........Acts 7:48

TEMPORARY
which are seen are *t*........2 Co 4:18

TEMPT
Why do you *t* the LORD..Ex 17:2
yes, those who *t*.............Mal 3:15
t the LORD *your God*.....Matt 4:7
that Satan does not *t*.......1 Co 7:5
nor let us *t* Christ...........1 Co 10:9
nor does He Himself *t*.....Jas 1:13

TEMPTATION
do not lead us into *t*........Matt 6:13
lest you enter into *t*........Matt 26:41
in time of *t* fall away.......Luke 8:13
t has overtaken you.........1 Co 10:13
to be rich fall into *t*.........1 Ti 6:9
the man who endures *t*....Jas 1:12

TEMPTED
forty days, *t* by Satan......Mark 1:13
not allow you to be *t*.......1 Co 10:13
lest you also be *t*............Gal 6:1
has suffered, being *t*........Heb 2:18
in all points *t*...............Heb 4:15
But each one is *t*............Jas 1:14

TEMPTER
Now when the *t* came to..Matt 4:3

TENDER
your heart was *t*.............2 Ki 22:19
t shoots will not.............Job 14:7
no more be called *t*.........Is 47:1
Through the *t* mercy of....Luke 1:78
put on *t* mercies.............Col 3:12

TENDERHEARTED
to one another, *t*............Eph 4:32
love as brothers, be *t*.......1 Pe 3:8

TENDS
t a flock and does not......1 Co 9:7

TENT
shall know that your *t*......Job 5:24
like a shepherd's *t*...........Is 38:12
the place of your *t*..........Is 54:2
My *t* is plundered............Jer 10:20
earthly house, this *t*.........2 Co 5:1
long as I am in this *t*.......2 Pe 1:13
I must put off my *t*.........2 Pe 1:14

TENTMAKERS
occupation they were *t*.....Acts 18:3

TENTS
those who dwell in *t*........Gen 4:20
How lovely are your *t*......Num 24:5
The *t* of robbers.............Job 12:6
Than dwell in the *t*.........Ps 84:10
I dwell among the *t*.........Ps 120:5
LORD will save the *t*.......Zech 12:7

TERRESTRIAL
bodies and *t* bodies.........1 Co 15:40

TERRIBLE
t wilderness...................Deut 1:19
haughtiness of the *t*.........Is 13:11
is great and very *t*...........Joel 2:11

TERRIFIED
to you, 'Do not be *t*........Deut 1:29
But they were *t*.............Luke 24:37
and not in any way *t*.......Phil 1:28

TERRIFIES
and the Almighty *t*.........Job 23:16

TERRIFY
me with dreams and *t*......Job 7:14
not let dread of Him *t*.....Job 9:34
are coming to *t* them.......Zech 1:21

TERRIFYING
t was the sight................Heb 12:21

TERROR
there shall be *t*...............Deut 32:25
are nothing, you see *t*......Job 6:21
from God is a *t*..............Job 31:23
not be afraid of the *t*.......Ps 91:5
I will make you a *t*.........Jer 20:4
but a great *t* fell............Dan 10:7

TERRORS
the *t* of God are.............Job 6:4
T frighten him on...........Job 18:11
before the king of *t*.........Job 18:14
T overtake him like a......Job 27:20
consumed with *t*.............Ps 73:19

TEST
God has come to *t* you....Ex 20:20
t him with hard.............1 Ki 10:1
behold, His eyelids *t*.......Ps 11:4
t them as gold is............Zech 13:9
said, "Why do you *t*.......Matt 22:18
t the Spirit of the...........Acts 5:9
why do you *t* God by.....Acts 15:10
and the fire will *t*...........1 Co 3:13
T all things...................1 Th 5:21
but *t* the spirits..............1 Jn 4:1

TESTAMENT
where there is a *t*............Heb 9:16
For a *t* is in force...........Heb 9:17

TESTATOR
be the death of the *t*.......Heb 9:16

TESTED
things that God *t*............Gen 22:1
You have *t* my heart.......Ps 17:3
And they *t* God in..........Ps 78:18
When your fathers *t*........Ps 95:9
t them ten days..............Dan 1:14
where your fathers t........Heb 3:9
though it is *t*.................1 Pe 1:7
t those who say they........Rev 2:2

TESTIFIED
Yet the LORD *t* against...2 Ki 17:13
he who has seen has *t*......John 19:35
for as you have *t*............Acts 23:11
t beforehand the............1 Pe 1:11
of God which He has *t*....1 Jn 5:9

TESTIFIES
and heard, that He *t*.......John 3:32
that the Holy Spirit *t*.......Acts 20:23

TESTIFY
yes, your own lips *t*........Job 15:6
You, and our sins *t*.........Is 59:12
T against Me..................Mic 6:3
t what We have.............John 3:11
these are they which *t*.....John 5:39
t that the Father.............1 Jn 4:14
sent My angel to *t*..........Rev 22:16

TESTIFYING
was righteous, God *t*.......Heb 11:4
t that this is.................1 Pe 5:12

TESTIMONIES
those who keep His *t*.......Ps 119:2
For I have kept Your *t*....Ps 119:22
t are my meditation.........Ps 119:99
I love Your *t*.................Ps 119:119
t are wonderful..............Ps 119:129

TESTIMONY
two tablets of the *T*.........Ex 31:18
For He established a *t*......Ps 78:5
that I may keep the *t*.......Ps 119:88
Bind up the *t*................Is 8:16
under your feet as a *t*......Mark 6:11
Now this is the *t*............John 1:19
no one receives His *t*.......John 3:32
who has received His *t*....John 3:33
in your law that the *t*......John 8:17
and we know that his *t*....John 21:24
declaring to you the *t*......1 Co 2:1
obtained a good *t*...........Heb 11:2
he had this *t*.................Heb 11:5
has not believed the *t*.....1 Jn 5:10
And this is the *t*............1 Jn 5:11
For the *t* of Jesus is........Rev 19:10

TESTING
came to Him, *t* Him.......Matt 19:3
knowing that the *t*..........Jas 1:3

TESTS
the righteous God *t*.........Ps 7:9
gold, but the LORD *t*......Prov 17:3
men, but God who *t*........1 Th 2:4

THANK
"I *t* You and praise.........Dan 2:23
"I *t* You, Father............Matt 11:25
t that servant because......Luke 17:9
t You that I am not.........Luke 18:11
First, I *t* my God............Rom 1:8
t Christ Jesus our...........1 Ti 1:12

THANKFUL

Be *t* to Him...................Ps 100:4
Him as God, nor were *t*...Rom 1:21

THANKFULNESS

Felix, with all *t*...............Acts 24:3

THANKS

the cup, and gave *t*......... Matt 26:27
t He distributed them...... John 6:11
for he gives God *t*...........Rom 14:6
T be to God for His........2 Co 9:15
giving *t* always for..........Eph 5:20
t can we render............... 1 Th 3:9

THANKSGIVING

with the voice of *t*..........Ps 26:7
Offer to God *t*...............Ps 50:14
His presence with *t*..........Ps 95:2
into His gates with *t*........ Ps 100:4
the sacrifices of *t*...........Ps 107:22
supplication, with *t*..........Phil 4:6
vigilant in it with *t*.......... Col 4:2
to be received with *t*.........1 Ti 4:3

THEATER

and rushed into the *t*....... Acts 19:29

THIEF

When you saw a *t*........... Ps 50:18
do not despise a *t*........... Prov 6:30
t hates his own life......... Prov 29:24
t is ashamed when he...... Jer 2:26
the windows like a *t*........Joel 2:9
t shall be expelled........... Zech 5:3
known what hour the *t*....Matt 24:43
t approaches nor moth..... Luke 12:33
way, the same is a *t*........ John 10:1
because he was a *t*......... John 12:6
Lord will come as a *t*........2 Pe 3:10
upon you as a *t*.............. Rev 3:3

THIEVES

and companions of *t*........ Is 1:23
destroy and where *t*.........Matt 6:19
before Me are *t*...............John 10:8

THIGH

them hip and *t* with a.....Judg 15:8
good piece, The *t*...........Ezek 24:4

THINGS

in heaven give good *t*....... Matt 7:11
evil, speak good *t*...........Matt 12:34
kept all these *t*...............Luke 2:51
Lazarus evil *t*................Luke 16:25
the Scriptures the *t*.........Luke 24:27
share in all good *t*..........Gal 6:6

THINK

nor does his heart *t*......... Is 10:7
t that they will be........... Matt 6:7
t you have eternal...........John 5:39
not to *t* of himself...........Rom 12:3
of ourselves to *t*.............2 Co 3:5
all that we ask or *t*.........Eph 3:20

THINKS

Yet the LORD *t* upon me.Ps 40:17
for as he *t* in his............ Prov 23:7
t that he knows...............1 Co 8:2
t he stands take heed.......1 Co 10:12
For if anyone *t*.............. Gal 6:3
t he is religious...............Jas 1:26

THIRST

tongues fail for *t*............. Is 41:17
those who hunger and *t*....Matt 5:6
in Me shall never *t*..........John 6:35
said, "I *t*!"...................John 19:28
we both hunger and *t*...... 1 Co 4:11
anymore nor *t* anymore....Rev 7:16

THIRSTS

My soul *t* for God...........Ps 42:2
saying, "If anyone *t*........John 7:37
if he *t*...........................Rom 12:20
freely to him who *t*........ Rev 21:6
And let him who *t*.......... Rev 22:17

THIRSTY

and if he is *t*.................. Prov 25:21
as when a *t* man dreams...Is 29:8
the drink of the *t*.............Is 32:6
t land springs of..............Is 35:7
on him who is *t*...............Is 44:3
but you shall be *t*............Is 65:13
I was *t* and you gave...... Matt 25:35
we see You hungry or *t*... Matt 25:44

THISTLES

t grow instead of............Job 31:40
or figs from *t*..................Matt 7:16

THORN

t that goes into the..........Prov 26:9
t shall come up the..........Is 55:13
a *t* in the flesh was..........2 Co 12:7

THORNBUSHES

gather grapes from *t*........ Matt 7:16

THORNS

Both *t* and thistles it........Gen 3:18
T and snares are..............Prov 22:5
all overgrown with *t*........ Prov 24:31
the crackling of *t*............Eccl 7:6
Like a lily among *t*.......... Song 2:2
and do not sow among *t*...Jer 4:3
wheat but reaped *t*..........Jer 12:13
And some fell among *t*.... Matt 13:7
wearing the crown of *t*.....John 19:5

THOUGHT

t is that their houses........Ps 49:11
You *t* that I was.............. Ps 50:21
Both the inward *t*............Ps 64:6
I *t* about my ways...........Ps 119:59
You understand my *t*.......Ps 139:2
"Surely, as I have *t*........Is 14:24
to man what his *t*............Amos 4:13
perceiving the *t*...............Luke 9:47
"And he *t* within............Luke 12:17
I *t* as a child...................1 Co 13:11

THOUGHTS

the intent of the *t*............ 1 Ch 28:9
is in none of his *t*............Ps 10:4
t which are toward us...... Ps 40:5
t are very deep...............Ps 92:5
The LORD knows the *t*....Ps 94:11
t will be established.........Prov 16:3
unrighteous man his *t*...... Is 55:7
For My *t* are not your.....Is 55:8
long shall your evil *t*........Jer 4:14
they do not know the *t*... Mic 4:12
Jesus, knowing their *t*..... Matt 9:4
heart proceed evil *t*........ Matt 15:19
futile in their *t*................Rom 1:21
The LORD knows the *t*....1 Co 3:20

THREAT

shall flee at the *t*.............Is 30:17

THREATEN

suffered, He did not *t*......1 Pe 2:23

THREATENING

to them, giving up *t*.........Eph 6:9

THREATS

Lord, look on their *t*....... Acts 4:29
still breathing *t*............... Acts 9:1

THREE

you will deny Me *t*..........Matt 26:34
hope, love, these *t*.......... 1 Co 13:13
and these *t* are one......... 1 Jn 5:7

THRESH

he does not *t* it..............Is 28:28
t the mountains...............Is 41:15
it is time to *t* her............Jer 51:33
"Arise and *t*...................Mic 4:13

THRESHING

t shall last till the...........Lev 26:5
like the dust at *t*.............2 Ki 13:7
Oh, my *t* and the grain.... Is 21:10

THROAT

t is an open tomb............Ps 5:9
put a knife to your *t*........Prov 23:2
unshod, and your *t*..........Jer 2:25
t is an open tomb...........Rom 3:13

THRONE

LORD sitting on His *t*......1 Ki 22:19
He has prepared His *t*...... Ps 9:7
temple, The LORD's *t*...... Ps 11:4
Your *t*, O God, is...........Ps 45:6
has established His *t*........Ps 103:19
he upholds his *t*...............Prov 20:28
Lord sitting on a *t*...........Is 6:1
"Heaven is My *t*..............Is 66:1
shall be called The *T*.......Jer 3:17
do not disgrace the *t*.......Jer 14:21
A glorious high *t*............Jer 17:12
t was a fiery flame.......... Dan 7:9
sit and rule on His *t*........Zech 6:13
for it is God's *t*...............Matt 5:34
will give Him the *t*......... Luke 1:32
Your *t*, O God, is........... Heb 1:8
come boldly to the *t*........ Heb 4:16
where Satan's *t*.............. Rev 2:13
My Father on His *t*.........Rev 3:21
I saw a great white *t*.......Rev 20:11

THRONES

t are set there.................Ps 122:5
also sit on twelve *t*.......... Matt 19:28
mighty from their *t*.........Luke 1:52
invisible, whether *t*..........Col 1:16
t I saw twenty-four..........Rev 4:4

THRONG

house of God in the *t*......Ps 55:14

THROW

of your land and *t*...........Mic 5:11
t Yourself down..............Matt 4:6
children's bread and *t*...... Matt 15:26

THROWN

their slain shall be *t*.........Is 34:3
neck, and he were *t*.........Mark 9:42

THRUST

and rose up and *t*............Luke 4:29
to heaven, will be *t*.........Luke 10:15
shall be stoned or t..........Heb 12:20

THUNDER

But the *t* of His power.....Job 26:14
The voice of Your *t*.........Ps 77:18
the secret place of *t*.........Ps 81:7
t they hastened away....... Ps 104:7
that is, "Sons of *T*"........Mark 3:17
the voice of loud *t*...........Rev 14:2

THUNDERED

"The LORD *t* from......... 2 Sa 22:14
The LORD also *t*............ Ps 18:13

THUNDERINGS

people witnessed the *t*......Ex 20:18
the sound of mighty *t*...... Rev 19:6

THUNDERS

t marvelously with His..... Job 37:5
The God of glory *t*..........Ps 29:3

TIDINGS

heard these grave *t*..........Ex 33:4
be afraid of evil *t*...........Ps 112:7
I bring you good *t*...........Luke 2:10
who bring glad t..............Rom 10:15

TILL

no man to *t* the ground....Gen 2:5

TILLER

but Cain was a *t*............. Gen 4:2

TILLS

t his land will be.............Prov 12:11
t his land will have..........Prov 28:19

TIME

pray to You In a *t*.......... Ps 32:6
ashamed in the evil *t*....... Ps 37:19
how short my *t* is............Ps 89:47
A *t* to be born................Eccl 3:2
but *t* and chance............Eccl 9:11
your *t* was the *t*...........Ezek 16:8
you did not know the *t*.... Luke 19:44
t has not yet come.......... John 7:6
I have a convenient *t*......Acts 24:25
for the *t* is near............. Rev 1:3

TIMES

understanding of the *t*......1 Ch 12:32
t are not hidden..............Job 24:1
t are in Your hand...........Ps 31:15
the signs of the *t*............Matt 16:3
Gentiles until the *t*.........Luke 21:24
not for you to know *t*......Acts 1:7
their preappointed *t*........Acts 17:26
last days perilous *t*.......... 2 Ti 3:1
God, who at various *t*......Heb 1:1

TITHE

And he gave him a *t*....... Gen 14:20
LORD, a tenth of the *t*.... Num 18:26
"You shall truly *t*...........Deut 14:22
shall bring out the *t*........Deut 14:28
laying aside all the *t*........Deut 26:12
in abundantly the *t*.........2 Ch 31:5
Judah brought the *t*.........Neh 13:12
For you pay *t* of mint...... Matt 23:23

TITHES

to redeem any of his *t*..... Lev 27:31
t which you receive........ Num 18:28

and to bring the *t*...........Neh 10:37
firstfruits, and the *t*......... Neh 12:44
the articles, the *t*.............Neh 13:5
Bring all the *t*..................Mal 3:10
I give *t* of all that I........Luke 18:12
to receive *t* from the.......Heb 7:5
mortal men receive *t*........Heb 7:8
Levi, who receives *t*........ Heb 7:9

TITHING

which is the year of *t*.......Deut 26:12

TITLE

Now Pilate wrote a *t*....... John 19:19

TITTLE

away, one jot or one *t*..... Matt 5:18

TODAY

T I have begotten You.... Ps 2:7
of the field, which *t*.........Matt 6:30
the grass, which *t*...........Luke 12:28
t you will be with Me...... Luke 23:43
t I have begotten You.....Heb 1:5
"*T, if you will hear*.........Heb 3:7
the same yesterday, *t*.......Heb 13:8

TOIL

t you shall eat of.............Gen 3:17
they neither *t* nor...........Matt 6:28
our labor and *t*............... 1 Th 2:9

TOILED

"Master, we have *t*.........Luke 5:5

TOLD

Behold, I have *t*............ Matt 28:7
things which were *t*......... Luke 2:18
t me all things that I.......John 4:29
t you the truth which.......John 8:40
so, I would have *t*..........John 14:2
And now I have *t*........... John 14:29

TOLERABLE

you, it will be more *t*.......Matt 10:15

TOMB

throat is an open *t*.......... Ps 5:9
in the garden a new *t*...... John 19:41
throat is an open t...........Rom 3:13

TOMBS

like whitewashed *t*...........Matt 23:27
you build the *t*................Matt 23:29
For you build the *t*.........Luke 11:47

TOMORROW

drink, for *t* we die...........Is 22:13
t will be as today............ Is 56:12
t is thrown into the....... Matt 6:30
do not worry about *t*....... Matt 6:34
drink, for t we die..........1 Co 15:32
what will happen *t*..........Jas 4:14

TONGUE

the scourge of the *t*.........Job 5:21
hides it under his *t*..........Job 20:12
Keep your *t* from evil...... Ps 34:13
t shall speak of Your....... Ps 35:28
Lest I sin with my *t*........Ps 39:1
to you, You false *t*.........Ps 120:3
laughter, And our *t*......... Ps 126:2
remember you, Let my *t*.. Ps 137:6
is not a word on my *t*......Ps 139:4
but the perverse *t*...........Prov 10:31
forever, but a lying *t*....... Prov 12:19

A wholesome *t* is a........ Prov 15:4
t keeps his soul...............Prov 21:23
t breaks a bone...............Prov 25:15
t shall take an oath......... Is 45:23
GOD has given Me the *t*..Is 50:4
t should confess that.......Phil 2:11
does not bridle his *t*........ Jas 1:26
t is a little member.........Jas 3:5
And the *t* is a fire...........Jas 3:6
no man can tame the *t*.....Jas 3:8
love in word or in *t*.........1 Jn 3:18
every nation, tribe, *t*........Rev 14:6

TONGUES

From the strife of *t*......... Ps 31:20
will speak with new *t*......Mark 16:17
to them divided *t*............ Acts 2:3
and they spoke with *t*......Acts 19:6
I speak with the *t*............1 Co 13:1
Therefore *t* are for a....... 1 Co 14:22

TOOTH

"eye for eye, *t*................Ex 21:24
is like a bad *t*.................Prov 25:19
eye for an eye and a t......Matt 5:38

TOPHET

T was established............Is 30:33
the high places of *T*........ Jer 7:31
make this city like *T*.......Jer 19:12
like the place of *T*.......... Jer 19:13

TORCH

and like a fiery *t*.............Zech 12:6

TORCHES

When he had set the *t*..... Judg 15:5
his eyes like *t*................. Dan 10:6
come with flaming *t*........Nah 2:3

TORMENT

"How long will you *t*......Job 19:2
shall lie down in *t*........... Is 50:11
You come here to *t*.........Matt 8:29
to this place of *t*............. Luke 16:28
fear involves *t*................1 Jn 4:18
t ascends forever............Rev 14:11

TORMENTED

for I am *t* in this.............Luke 16:24
And they will be *t*..........Rev 20:10

TORMENTS

"And being in *t*.............. Luke 16:23

TORN

aside my ways and *t*........ Lam 3:11
for He has *t*................... Hos 6:1
of the temple was *t*........ Matt 27:51

TORTURED

And others were *t*..........Heb 11:35

TOSSED

t with tempest................. Is 54:11
t to and fro and.............Eph 4:14

TOTTER

drunkard, and shall *t*....... Is 24:20

TOUCH

seven no evil shall *t*.........Job 5:19
t no unclean thing...........Is 52:11
If only I may *t*................Matt 9:21
that they might only *t*......Matt 14:36
a man not to *t* a woman.. 1 Co 7:1
wicked one does not *t*......1 Jn 5:18

TOUCHED

whose hearts God had *t*... 1 Sa 10:26
t my mouth with it.......... Is 6:7
hand and *t* my mouth...... Jer 1:9
mountain that may be *t*....Heb 12:18

TOUCHES

He *t* the hills.................Ps 104:32
t you *t* the.................... Zech 2:8

TOWER

t whose top is in the........Gen 11:4
for me, And a strong *t*.....Ps 61:3
my fortress, My high *t*..... Ps 144:2
like an ivory *t*..................Song 7:4
a watchman in the *t*........Is 21:5
in it and built a *t*.......... Matt 21:33

TRADITION

transgress the *t*.............. Matt 15:2
of no effect by your *t*......Matt 15:6
according to the *t*............Col 2:8
t which he received........ 2 Th 3:6
conduct received by *t*......1 Pe 1:18

TRADITIONS

zealous for the *t*.............Gal 1:14
t which you were............ 2 Th 2:15

TRAIN

T up a child in the...Prov 22:6
t of His robe filled.......... Is 6:1

TRAINED

who is perfectly *t*........... Luke 6:40
those who have been *t*.....Heb 12:11

TRAINING

bring them up in the *t*..... Eph 6:4

TRAITOR

also became a *t*.............Luke 6:16

TRAITORS

t, headstrong.................2 Ti 3:4

TRAMPLE

Your name we will *t*.....Ps 44:5
serpent you shall *t*..........Ps 91:13
hand, to *t* My courts........Is 1:12
You shall *t* the wicked.....Mal 4:3
swine, lest they *t*............Matt 7:6
you the authority to *t*...... Luke 10:19

TRAMPLED

t them in My fury........... Is 63:3
now she will be *t*........... Mic 7:10
t the nations in anger.......Hab 3:12
Jerusalem will be *t*........Luke 21:24
worthy who has *t*........ Heb 10:29
the winepress was *t*......... Rev 14:20

TRANCE

he fell into a *t*...... Acts 10:10
t I saw a vision...............Acts 11:5

TRANSFIGURED

and was *t* before them..... Matt 17:2

TRANSFORMED

this world, but be *t*........ Rom 12:2
the Lord, are being *t*......2 Co 3:18

TRANSGRESS

t the command of the...... Num 14:41
the LORD's people *t*........1 Sa 2:24
my mouth shall not *t*....... Ps 17:3

his mouth must not *t*....... Prov 16:10
of bread a man will *t*.......Prov 28:21
do Your disciples *t*.......... Matt 15:2

TRANSGRESSED

t My covenant................ Josh 7:11
your mediators have *t*......Is 43:27
the rulers also *t*.............. Jer 2:8
their fathers have *t*.........Ezek 2:3
Yes, all Israel has *t*........ Dan 9:11
t your commandment.......Luke 15:29

TRANSGRESSES

Indeed, because he *t*........Hab 2:5
Whoever *t* and does not...2 Jn 9

TRANSGRESSION

iniquity and *t* and sin.......Ex 34:7
t is sealed up in a.......... Job 13:23
be innocent of great *t*...... Ps 19:13
because of their *t*........... Ps 107:17
He who covers a *t*..........Prov 17:9
He who loves *t* loves....... Prov 17:19
tell My people their *t*.......Is 58:1
at Gilgal multiply *t*.......... Amos 4:4
my firstborn for my *t*....... Mic 6:7
and passing over the *t*......Mic 7:18
no law there is no *t*........Rom 4:15
deceived, fell into *t*......... 1 Ti 2:14
steadfast, and every *t*......Heb 2:2

TRANSGRESSIONS

if I have covered my *t*..... Job 31:33
"I will confess my *t*........ Ps 32:5
me from all my *t*...........Ps 39:8
mercies, Blot out my *t*.....Ps 51:1
For I acknowledge my *t*... Ps 51:3
has He removed our *t*......Ps 103:12
who blots out your *t*........Is 43:25
was wounded for our *t*.....Is 53:5
for the *t* of My people..... Is 53:8
from you all the *t*............Ezek 18:31
was added because of *t*.... Gal 3:19
redemption of the *t*......... Heb 9:15

TRANSGRESSOR

and were called a *t*..........Is 48:8
I make myself a *t*............Gal 2:18

TRANSGRESSORS

Then I will teach *t*.......... Ps 51:13
to any wicked *t*................Ps 59:5
numbered with the *t*........Is 53:12
numbered with the t........ Mark 15:28

TRANSLATED

of darkness and *t*........... Col 1:13
By faith Enoch was *t*.......Heb 11:5

TRAP

of Israel, as a *t*................Is 8:14
where there is no *t*..........Amos 3:5

TRAPS

They have set *t*...............Ps 140:5
for me, And from the *t*....Ps 141:9

TRAVAIL

He shall see the *t*............Is 53:11

TRAVAILED

"Before she *t*.................. Is 66:7

TRAVAILS

Behold, the wicked *t*....... Ps 7:14

TRAVEL

For you *t* land and sea.....Matt 23:15

TREACHEROUS

the *t* dealer deals............ Is 21:2
an assembly of *t* men.......Jer 9:2
are insolent, *t*................. Zeph 3:4

TREACHEROUSLY

and you who deal *t*......... Is 33:1
happy who deal so *t*........ Jer 12:1
even they have dealt *t*.....Jer 12:6
They have dealt *t*........... Hos 5:7
Why do we deal *t*.......... Mal 2:10
that you do not deal *t*.....Mal 2:16
"This man dealt *t*...........Acts 7:19

TREAD

t down the wicked in......Job 40:12
it is He who shall *t*.........Ps 60:12
You shall *t* upon the.......Ps 91:13
shout, as those who *t*......Jer 25:30
will come down and *t*..... Mic 1:3
And they will *t*.............. Rev 11:2

TREADS

like one who *t* in the....... Is 63:2
t the high places............ Amos 4:13
an ox while it t............... 1 Ti 5:18
t the winepress.............. Rev 19:15

TREASURE

to you His good *t*...........Deut 28:12
one who finds great *t*...... Ps 119:162
for His special *t*.............. Ps 135:4
there is much *t*...............Prov 15:6
There is desirable *t*.........Prov 21:20
of the LORD is His *t*.......Is 33:6
"For where your *t*...........Matt 6:21
t brings forth evil........... Matt 12:35
t things new and old....... Matt 13:52
and you will have *t*.........Matt 19:21
So is he who lays up *t*.....Luke 12:21
But we have this *t*...........2 Co 4:7
You have heaped up *t*..... Jas 5:3

TREASURED

t the words of His..........Job 23:12

TREASURER

Erastus, the *t* of the........ Rom 16:23

TREASURES

sealed up among My *t*.....Deut 32:34
it more than hidden *t*......Job 3:21
her as for hidden *t*......... Prov 2:4
t of wickedness profit.......Prov 10:2
Getting *t* by a lying........Prov 21:6
is no end to their *t*..........Is 2:7
I will give you the *t*.........Is 45:3
Are there yet the *t*..........Mic 6:10
for yourselves *t*.............. Matt 6:19
are hidden all the *t*..........Col 2:3
riches than the *t*..............Heb 11:26

TREATY

Now Solomon made a *t*....1 Ki 3:1

TREE

"but of the *t*.................. Gen 2:17
you eaten from the *t*........Gen 3:11
there is hope for a *t*........Job 14:7
t Planted by the............. Ps 1:3
like a native green *t*........Ps 37:35
t falls to the south.......... Eccl 11:3
Like an apple *t*............... Song 2:3

TREES

for as the days of a *t*...... Is 65:22
t planted by the.............. Jer 17:8
t bears good fruit........... Matt 7:17
His own body on the *t*..... 1 Pe 2:24
give to eat from the *t*..... Rev 2:7
the river, was the *t*......... Rev 22:2

TREES

t once went forth.............. Judg 9:8
Also he spoke of *t*.......... 1 Ki 4:33
Then all the *t* of the........ Ps 96:12
The *t* of the LORD are.... Ps 104:16
all kinds of fruit *t*............ Eccl 2:5
they may be called *t*........ Is 61:3
and on beast, on the *t*..... Jer 7:20
so that all the *t*.............. Ezek 31:9
"I see men like *t*.............. Mark 8:24
late autumn *t* without...... Jude 12
the sea, or the *t*.............. Rev 7:3

TREMBLE

T before Him.............. 1 Ch 16:30
have made the earth *t*..... Ps 60:2
Let the peoples *t*............. Ps 99:1
who made the earth *t*..... Is 14:16
that the nations may *t*...... Is 64:2
'Will you not *t*................ Jer 5:22
wrath the earth will *t*...... Jer 10:10
they shall fear and *t*....... Jer 33:9
my kingdom men must *t*... Dan 6:26

TREMBLED

of Edom, the earth *t*....... Judg 5:4
for his heart *t*................ 1 Sa 4:13
Then everyone who *t*...... Ezra 9:4
the earth shook and *t*...... Ps 18:7
and indeed they *t*........... Jer 4:24

TREMBLES

The earth sees and *t*...... Ps 97:4

TREMBLING

it was a very great *t*....... 1 Sa 14:15
your water with *t*........... Ezek 12:18
in fear, and in much *t*..... 1 Co 2:3
t you received............... 2 Co 7:15
flesh, with fear and *t*...... Eph 6:5
with fear and *t*.............. Phil 2:12

TRENCH

and he made a *t*............. 1 Ki 18:32

TRESPASSES

still goes on in His *t*...... Ps 68:21
forgive men their *t*......... Matt 6:14
not imputing their *t*........ 2 Co 5:19
who were dead in *t*......... Eph 2:1
forgiven you all *t*........... Col 2:13

TRIAL

And as in the day of *t*..... Ps 95:8
in the day of *t*................ Heb 3:8
concerning the fiery *t*...... 1 Pe 4:12
t which shall come........... Rev 3:10

TRIBE

of old, The *t* of Your...... Ps 74:2
belongs to another *t*....... Heb 7:13
the Lion of the *t*............. Rev 5:5
blood out of every *t*....... Rev 5:9

TRIBES

Where the *t* go up......... Ps 122:4
to raise up the *t*............. Is 49:6
promise our twelve *t*...... Acts 26:7
t which are scattered........ Jas 1:1

TRIBULATION

there will be great *t*......... Matt 24:21
world you will have *t*....... John 16:33
in hope, patient in *t*........ Rom 12:12
joyful in all our *t*............ 2 Co 7:4
that we would suffer *t*...... 1 Th 3:4
t those who.................... 2 Th 1:6
and you will have *t*.......... Rev 2:10
with her into great *t*........ Rev 2:22
out of the great *t*............ Rev 7:14

TRIBULATIONS

t enter the kingdom......... Acts 14:22
but we also glory in *t*....... Rom 5:3
not lose heart at my *t*...... Eph 3:13
t that you endure............ 2 Th 1:4

TRIED

You have *t* me and have.. Ps 17:3
a *t* stone, a precious........ Is 28:16

TRIMMED

and *t* their lamps............. Matt 25:7

TRIUMPH

Let not my enemies *t*....... Ps 25:2
I will *t* in the works......... Ps 92:4
always leads us in *t*......... 2 Co 2:14

TRIUMPHED

the LORD, for He has *t*... Ex 15:1

TRODDEN

t the winepress alone....... Is 63:3

TROUBLE

that they were in *t*.......... Ex 5:19
no rest, for *t* comes......... Job 3:26
few days and full of *t*...... Job 14:1
for the time of *t*............. Job 38:23
have increased who *t*...... Ps 3:1
Under his tongue is *t*...... Ps 10:7
from Me, For *t* is near..... Ps 22:11
t He shall hide me.......... Ps 27:5
O LORD, for I am in *t*..... Ps 31:9
not in *t* as other men....... Ps 73:5
will be with him in *t*....... Ps 91:15
walk in the midst of *t*...... Ps 138:7
is delivered from *t*.......... Prov 11:8
of the wicked is *t*........... Prov 15:6
t they have.................... Is 26:16
also in the time of *t*........ Is 33:2
and there was *t*.............. Jer 8:15
Savior in time of *t*.......... Jer 14:8
such will have *t*.............. 1 Co 7:28
there are some who *t*....... Gal 1:7

TROUBLED

Your face, and I was *t*..... Ps 30:7
Your face, they are *t*....... Ps 104:29
wicked are like the *t*....... Is 57:20
you are worried and *t*...... Luke 10:41
to give you who are *t*...... 2 Th 1:7
shaken in mind or *t*........ 2 Th 2:2

TROUBLES

"What *t* the people........... 1 Sa 11:5
deliver you in six *t*.......... Job 5:19
The *t* of my heart have.... Ps 25:17
Out of all their *t*............. Ps 25:22
my soul is full of *t*.......... Ps 88:3
because the former *t*........ Is 65:16
will be famines and *t*...... Mark 13:8
him out of all his *t*.......... Acts 7:10

TROUBLING

spirit from God is *t*......... 1 Sa 16:15
wicked cease from *t*........ Job 3:17

TRUE

and Your words are *t*...... 2 Sa 7:28
But the LORD is the *t*...... Jer 10:10
"Let the LORD be a *t*...... Jer 42:5
we know that You are *t*... Matt 22:16
He who sent Me is *t*........ John 7:28
about this Man were *t*...... John 10:41
Indeed, let God be *t*........ Rom 3:4
whatever things are *t*....... Phil 4:8
may know Him who is *t*... 1 Jn 5:20
is holy, He who is *t*......... Rev 3:7
"These are the *t*............. Rev 19:9
for these words are *t*....... Rev 21:5

TRUMPET

Blow the *t* at the time..... Ps 81:3
"Blow the *t* in the........... Jer 4:5
deed, do not sound a *t*..... Matt 6:2
t makes an uncertain....... 1 Co 14:8
For the *t* will sound........ 1 Co 15:52
loud voice, as of a *t*........ Rev 1:10

TRUST

t is a spider's web........... Job 8:14
If God puts no *t*.............. Job 15:15
T in the LORD............... Ps 37:3
You are my *t* from my..... Ps 71:5
T in the LORD with all.... Prov 3:5
my salvation, I will *t*....... Is 12:2
Let him *t* in the name...... Is 50:10
"Do not *t* in these........... Jer 7:4
Do not *t* in a friend........ Mic 7:5
for those who *t*.............. Mark 10:24
committed to your *t*........ 1 Ti 6:20

TRUSTED

"He *t* in the LORD......... Ps 22:8
"He *t* in God................. Matt 27:43
that we who first *t*.......... Eph 1:12
the holy women who *t*..... 1 Pe 3:5

TRUSTS

But he who *t* in the........ Ps 32:10
He who *t* in his own....... Prov 28:26

TRUTH

led me in the way of *t*..... Gen 24:48
justice, a God of *t*.......... Deut 32:4
And speaks the *t*............ Ps 15:2
t continually preserve...... Ps 40:11
Behold, You desire *t*....... Ps 51:6
T shall spring out of....... Ps 85:11
t shall be your shield...... Ps 91:4
t utterly out of my.......... Ps 119:43
And Your law is *t*........... Ps 119:142
of Your word is *t*........... Ps 119:160
t is fallen in the............. Is 59:14
not valiant for the *t*........ Jer 9:3
"There is no *t*................ Hos 4:1
called the City of *T*........ Zech 8:3
speak each man the *t*....... Zech 8:16
t was in his mouth.......... Mal 2:6
you shall know the *t*........ John 8:32
"I am the way, the *t*........ John 14:6
He, the Spirit of *t*.......... John 16:13
to Him, "What is *t*.......... John 18:38
speak the words of *t*....... Acts 26:25
who suppress the *t*.......... Rom 1:18
of sincerity and *t*........... 1 Co 5:8
but, speaking the *t*.......... Eph 4:15
your waist with *t*............ Eph 6:14
in the word of the *t*........ Col 1:5

TRY

the love of the *t*...............2 Th 2:10
I am speaking the *t*.........1 Ti 2:7
they may know the *t*........2 Ti 2:25
the knowledge of the *t*....2 Ti 3:7
in the present *t*................2 Pe 1:12
way of *t* will be..............2 Pe 2:2
that we are of the *t*.........1 Jn 3:19
the Spirit is *t*...................1 Jn 5:6
t that is in you................3 Jn 3

TRY

T my mind and my heart. Ps 26:2
refine them and *t* them.... Jer 9:7
which is to *t* you..............1 Pe 4:12

TUMULT

their waves, And the *t*..... Ps 65:7
Your enemies make a *t*.... Ps 83:2

TUNIC

Also he made him a *t*...... Gen 37:3
and take away your *t*....... Matt 5:40

TUNICS

the LORD God made *t*.... Gen 3:21
not to put on two *t*......... Mark 6:9
weeping, showing the *t*....Acts 9:39

TURBAN

like a robe and a *t*.......... Job 29:14
'Remove the *t*............... Ezek 21:26

TURN

you shall not *t*................Deut 17:11
Then we will not *t*...........Ps 80:18
But let them not *t*..........Ps 85:8
Yet I do not *t*...............Ps 119:51
T at my reproof..............Prov 1:23
not let your heart *t*.........Prov 7:25
T now everyone from......Jer 35:15
"Repent, *t* away from.....Ezek 14:6
yes, let every one *t*.........Jon 3:8
T now from your evil.....Zech 1:4
on your right cheek, *t*......Matt 5:39
t the hearts of the...........Luke 1:17
you that you should *t*.......Acts 14:15
t them from darkness.......Acts 26:18
let him *t* away from........1 Pe 3:11

TURNED

kept His way and not *t*....Job 23:11
The wicked shall be *t*......Ps 9:17
Let them be *t* back and....Ps 70:2
t my feet to Your............Ps 119:59
of Israel, they have *t*.......Is 1:4
number believed and *t*.....Acts 11:21
to you, and how you *t*.....1 Th 1:9

TURNING

marvel that you are *t*......Gal 1:6
or shadow of *t*................Jas 1:17

TURNS

of the wicked He *t*..........Ps 146:9
A soft answer *t*...............Prov 15:1
but no one *t* back...........Nah 1:3
him know that he who *t*...Jas 5:20

TURTLEDOVE

the life of Your *t*...........Ps 74:19
t is heard in our land......Song 2:12

TUTOR

the law was our *t*...........Gal 3:24
no longer under a *t*.........Gal 3:25

TWIST

All day they *t* my...........Ps 56:5
and unstable *t* to............2 Pe 3:16

TWO

the ark to Noah, *t*..........Gen 7:15
t young pigeons..............Lev 12:8
T are better than one.......Eccl 4:9
t he covered his..............Is 6:2
t shall become one.........Matt 19:5
t young pigeons.............Luke 2:24
one new man from the *t*...Eph 2:15

TYPE

of Adam, who is a *t*........Rom 5:14

— U —

UNAFRAID

Do you want to be *u*.......Rom 13:3

UNBELIEF

because of their *u*..........Matt 13:58
help my *u*.....................Mark 9:24
and He rebuked their *u*... Mark 16:14
did it ignorantly in *u*......1 Ti 1:13
you an evil heart of *u*......Heb 3:12
enter in because of *u*.......Heb 3:19

UNBELIEVERS

who believe but to *u*.......1 Co 14:22
are uninformed or *u*.......1 Co 14:23
yoked together with *u*......2 Co 6:14

UNBELIEVING

Do not be *u*...................John 20:27
u Jews stirred up the.......Acts 14:2
For the *u* husband is.......1 Co 7:14
u nothing is pure............Tit 1:15
But the cowardly, *u*........Rev 21:8

UNCIRCUMCISED

You stiffnecked and *u*......Acts 7:51
not the physically *u*........Rom 2:27
by faith and the *u*..........Rom 3:30
u had been committed..... Gal 2:7

UNCLEAN

of animals that are *u*.......Gen 7:2
who touches any *u*..........Lev 7:21
I am a man of *u* lips....... Is 6:5
u shall no longer come.....Is 52:1
He commands even the *u*.Mark 1:27
He rebuked the *u*...........Mark 9:25
any man common or *u*.....Acts 10:28
there is nothing *u*...........Rom 14:14
Do not touch what is *u*....2 Co 6:17
that no fornicator, *u*........Eph 5:5

UNCLEANNESS

men's bones and all *u*......Matt 23:27
members as slaves of *u*.... Rom 6:19
did not call us to *u*..........1 Th 4:7
flesh in the lust of *u*........2 Pe 2:10

UNCLEANNESSES

from all your *u*...............Ezek 36:29

UNCLOTHED

we want to be *u*.............2 Co 5:4

UNCOVER

skirt, *u* the thigh.............Is 47:2

UNCOVERS

u deep things out of........Job 12:22

UNDEFILED

Blessed are the *u*............Ps 119:1
all, and the bed *u*...........Heb 13:4
incorruptible and *u*.........1 Pe 1:4

UNDERSTAND

u one another's speech.....Gen 11:7
if there are any who *u*.....Ps 14:2
in Egypt did not *u*..........Ps 106:7
is to *u* his way...............Prov 14:8
Evil men do not *u*..........Prov 28:5
hearing, but do not *u*...... Is 6:9
and quick to *u*...............Dan 1:4
set your heart to *u*..........Dan 10:12
u shall instruct many....... Dan 11:33
of the wicked shall *u*.......Dan 12:10
people who do not *u*.......Hos 4:14
Let him *u* these things.....Hos 14:9
Why do you not *u*..........John 8:43
u what you are reading.... Acts 8:30
lest they should *u*...........Acts 28:27
u all mysteries................1 Co 13:2
some things hard to *u*......2 Pe 3:16

UNDERSTANDING

asked for yourself *u*.........1 Ki 3:11
He has counsel and *u*......Job 12:13
is the place of *u*.............Job 28:12
depart from evil is *u*........Job 28:28
Almighty gives him *u*......Job 32:8
not endow her with *u*......Job 39:17
my heart shall bring *u*......Ps 49:3
Give me *u*.....................Ps 119:34
Your precepts I get *u*......Ps 119:104
His *u* is infinite..............Ps 147:5
apply your heart to *u*.......Prov 2:2
lean not on your own *u*... Prov 3:5
u He established.............Prov 3:19
and go in the way of *u*.... Prov 9:6
of the Holy One is *u*.......Prov 9:10
a man of *u* has wisdom....Prov 10:23
U is a wellspring.............Prov 16:22
u will find good.............Prov 19:8
and instruction and *u*......Prov 23:23
but the poor who has *u*....Prov 28:11
Spirit of wisdom and *u*.... Is 11:2
no searching of His *u*...... Is 40:28
the heaven by His *u*........Jer 51:15
also still without *u*..........Matt 15:16
And He opened their *u*....Luke 24:45
also pray with the *u*........1 Co 14:15
five words with my *u*.......1 Co 14:19
and spiritual *u*...............Col 1:9
the Lord give you *u*.........2 Ti 2:7
Who is wise and *u*..........Jas 3:13
and has given us an *u*......1 Jn 5:20

UNDERSTANDS

all plain to him who *u*..... Prov 8:9
is easy to him who *u*.......Prov 14:6
there is none who *u*.........Rom 3:11

UNDERSTOOD

Then I *u* their end..........Ps 73:17
My heart has *u* great.......Eccl 1:16
Have you not *u* from.......Is 40:21
u all these things............Matt 13:51
clearly seen, being *u*.......Rom 1:20

UNDESIRABLE

gather together, O *u*........Zeph 2:1

UNDISCERNING

u, untrustworthy.............Rom 1:31

UNDONE

Woe is me, for I am *u*.....Is 6:5
leaving the others *u*.........Matt 23:23

UNEDUCATED

that they were *u*............. Acts 4:13

UNFAITHFUL

u will be uprooted...........Prov 2:22
way of the *u* is hard........ Prov 13:15

UNFAITHFULLY

back and acted *u*............ Ps 78:57

UNFORGIVING

unloving, *u*..................... Rom 1:31

UNFORMED

substance, being yet *u*......Ps 139:16

UNFRUITFUL

and it becomes *u*............ Mark 4:19
that they may not be *u*.... Tit 3:14

UNGODLINESS

u made me afraid...........Ps 18:4
heaven against all *u*.........Rom 1:18
He will turn away u.........Rom 11:26

UNGODLY

delivered me to the *u*..... Job 16:11
u shall not stand............. Ps 1:5
of the *u* shall perish........ Ps 1:6
my cause against an *u*......Ps 43:1
u man digs up evil.......... Prov 16:27
who justifies the *u*..........Rom 4:5
Christ died for the *u*........Rom 5:6
and perdition of *u* men....2 Pe 3:7
convict all who are *u*.......Jude 15

UNHOLY

between the holy and *u*....Ezek 22:26
for sinners, for the *u*.......1 Ti 1:9

UNINFORMED

the place of the *u*........... 1 Co 14:16

UNINTENTIONALLY

kills his neighbor *u*..........Deut 4:42

UNITE

U my heart to fear..........Ps 86:11

UNITY

to dwell together in *u*......Ps 133:1
to keep the *u* of the........Eph 4:3
we all come to the *u*....... Eph 4:13

UNJUST

hope of the *u* perishes..... Prov 11:7
u knows no shame......... Zeph 3:5
master commended the *u*.. Luke 16:8
extortioners, *u*.............. Luke 18:11
of the just and the *u*....... Acts 24:15
u who inflicts wrath........Rom 3:5
For God is not *u*.......... Heb 6:10
the just for the *u*........... 1 Pe 3:18
let him be *u* still............. Rev 22:11

UNJUSTLY

long will you judge *u*.......Ps 82:2
he will deal *u*................. Is 26:10

UNKNOWN

not stand before *u*...........Prov 22:29
to the *u* God................Acts 17:23
and I was *u* by face to.....Gal 1:22

UNLEAVENED

the Feast of *U* Bread.......Ex 12:17
the Feast of *U* Bread......Mark 14:1
since you truly are *u*........1 Co 5:7

UNLOVING

untrustworthy, *u*............. Rom 1:31

UNPREPARED

with me and find you *u*....2 Co 9:4

UNPRESENTABLE

u parts have greater........ 1 Co 12:23

UNPROFITABLE

'And cast the *u*................Matt 25:30
We are *u* servants........... Luke 17:10
have together become u... Rom 3:12
who once was *u* to you.... Phm 11
for that would be *u*......... Heb 13:17

UNPROFITABLENESS

of its weakness and *u*...... Heb 7:18

UNPUNISHED

wicked will not go *u*........Prov 11:21
be rich will not go *u*........Prov 28:20

UNQUENCHABLE

up the chaff with *u*..........Matt 3:12
He will burn with *u*.........Luke 3:17

UNRIGHTEOUS

u man his thoughts..........Is 55:7
been faithful in the *u*.......Luke 16:11
u will not inherit the....... 1 Co 6:9

UNRIGHTEOUSNESS

and there is no *u*............ Ps 92:15
builds his house by *u*.......Jer 22:13
Him is true, and no *u*......John 7:18
all ungodliness and *u*....... Rom 1:18
the truth, but obey *u*.......Rom 2:8
Is there *u* with God........Rom 9:14
cleanse us from all *u*....... 1 Jn 1:9
All *u* is sin.....................1 Jn 5:17

UNRULY

warn those who are *u*...... 1 Th 5:14
It is an *u* evil................. Jas 3:8

UNSEARCHABLE

heart of kings is *u*..........Prov 25:3
u are His judgments........ Rom 11:33

UNSKILLED

only of milk is *u*............. Heb 5:13

UNSPOTTED

to keep oneself *u*............Jas 1:27

UNSTABLE

U as water..................... Gen 49:4

UNTRUSTWORTHY

undiscerning, *u*............... Rom 1:31

UNWASHED

eat bread with *u* hands.... Mark 7:5

UNWISE

He is an *u* son................Hos 13:13
Therefore do not be *u*..... Eph 5:17

UNWORTHY

and judge yourselves *u*.....Acts 13:46
u manner will be.............1 Co 11:27

UPHOLD

u the evildoers.................Job 8:20
U me according to Your.. Ps 119:116
My Servant whom I *u*......Is 42:1
there was no one to *u*......Is 63:5

UPHOLDING

u all things by the...........Heb 1:3

UPHOLDS

Your right hand *u*...........Ps 63:8
LORD *u* all who fall........Ps 145:14

UPPER

show you a large *u*..........Mark 14:15
went up into the *u*..........Acts 1:13
many lamps in the *u*........Acts 20:8

UPRIGHT

righteous and *u* is He...... Deut 32:4
where were the *u*............Job 4:7
Good and *u* is the LORD.Ps 25:8
u shall have dominion......Ps 49:14
u will be blessed............ Ps 112:2
u there arises light.......... Ps 112:4
is strength for the *u*........Prov 10:29
u will guide them........... Prov 11:3
u will deliver them......... Prov 11:6
u will flourish................Prov 14:11
u is His delight.............. Prov 15:8
of the *u* is a highway.......Prov 15:19
that God made man *u*..... Eccl 7:29
and there is no one *u*...... Mic 7:2
his soul is not *u*............. Hab 2:4

UPRIGHTNESS

to show man His *u*..........Job 33:23
me in the land of *u*.........Ps 143:10
princes for their *u*..........Prov 17:26
of the just is *u*...............Is 26:7
land of *u* he will deal...... Is 26:10

UPROOT

"then I will *u*.................2 Ch 7:20
u you from the land........ Ps 52:5
u the wheat with them.....Matt 13:29

URIM

of judgment the *U*.......... Ex 28:30
Thummim and Your *U*.... Deut 33:8

US

"*God with u*....................Matt 1:23
who is not against *u*........ Mark 9:40
If God is for *u*............... Rom 8:31
They went out from *u*......1 Jn 2:19
none of them were of *u*... 1 Jn 2:19

USE

who spitefully *u* you........Matt 5:44
leaving the natural *u*........Rom 1:27
u this world as not...........1 Co 7:31
u liberty as an............... Gal 5:13
u a little wine................1 Ti 5:23
u have their.................. Heb 5:14

USELESS

all of them are *u*............Is 44:9
are unprofitable and *u*..... Tit 3:9
one's religion is *u*............Jas 1:26

USES

if one *u* it lawfully.......... 1 Ti 1:8

USING

u no figure of speech.......John 16:29
perish with the *u*............Col 2:22
u your liberty as a...........1 Pe 2:16

USURY

'Take no u or.................Lev 25:36
put out his money at u.... Ps 15:5

UTTER

u pure knowledge.......... Job 33:3
u dark sayings of old....... Ps 78:2
let not your heart u......... Eccl 5:2
lawful for a man to u...... 2 Co 12:4

UTTERANCE

the Spirit gave them u..... Acts 2:4
u may be given to me...... Eph 6:19

UTTERED

The deep u its voice........ Hab 3:10
which cannot be u.......... Rom 8:26
the seven thunders u....... Rev 10:4

UTTERMOST

upon them to the u......... 1 Th 2:16
u those who come........... Heb 7:25

UTTERS

Day unto day u speech.... Ps 19:2
u His voice from............. Amos 1:2
and the great man u........ Mic 7:3

— V —

VAGABOND

v you shall be on the....... Gen 4:12

VAIN

the people plot a v.......... Ps 2:1
v life which he passes....... Eccl 6:12
'I have labored in v......... Is 49:4
you believed in v............ 1 Co 15:2

VALIANT

Only be v for me........... 1 Sa 18:17
They are not v for the..... Jer 9:3
v men swept away........... Jer 46:15

VALLEY

I walk through the v........ Ps 23:4
pass through the V.......... Ps 84:6
the verdure of the v....... Song 6:11
v shall be exalted............ Is 40:4
in the midst of the v........ Ezek 37:1
v shall be filled.............. Luke 3:5

VALOR

a mighty man of v.......... 1 Sa 16:18

VALUE

does not know its v......... Job 28:13
of more v than they........ Matt 6:26
they counted up the v...... Acts 19:19

VALUED

It cannot be v in the....... Job 28:16

VANISH

when it is hot, they v...... Job 6:17
For the heavens will v..... Is 51:6
knowledge, it will v........ 1 Co 13:8
old is ready to v away...... Heb 8:13

VANISHED

and He v from their........ Luke 24:31

VANITY

of vanities, all is v........... Eccl 1:2

VAPOR

best state is but v............ Ps 39:5
Surely every man is v...... Ps 39:11
It is even a v that............ Jas 4:14

VARIATION

whom there is no v......... Jas 1:17

VEGETABLES

and let them give us v..... Dan 1:12
is weak eats only v.......... Rom 14:2

VEIL

he put a v on his face...... Ex 34:33
v of the temple was........ Matt 27:51
Moses, who put a v......... 2 Co 3:13
Presence behind the v...... Heb 6:19

VENGEANCE

'You shall not take v....... Lev 19:18
V is Mine...................... Deut 32:35
spare in the day of v........ Prov 6:34
God will come with v...... Is 35:4
on the garments of v....... Is 59:17
let me see Your v........... Jer 11:20
are the days of v............ Luke 21:22
written, "V is Mine........ Rom 12:19
flaming fire taking v........ 2 Th 1:8
suffering the v................ Jude 7

VENOM

it becomes cobra v.......... Job 20:14

VESSEL

like a potter's v.............. Ps 2:9
v that he made of clay..... Jer 18:4
like a precious v............ Jer 25:34
been emptied from v....... Jer 48:11
for he is a chosen v......... Acts 9:15
lump to make one v........ Rom 9:21
to possess his own v........ 1 Th 4:4
to the weaker v.............. 1 Pe 3:7

VESSELS

longsuffering the v.......... Rom 9:22
treasure in earthen v....... 2 Co 4:7
as the potter's v.............. Rev 2:27

VEXED

grieved, And I was v....... Ps 73:21

VICE

as a cloak for v.............. 1 Pe 2:16

VICTIM

and plucked the v.......... Job 29:17

VICTORY

who gives us the v.......... 1 Co 15:57
v that has overcome........ 1 Jn 5:4

VIEW

"Go, v the land............. Josh 2:1

VIGILANT

in prayer, being v.......... Col 4:2
Be sober, be v................ 1 Pe 5:8

VIGOR

nor his natural v............ Deut 34:7

VILE

sons made themselves v.... 1 Sa 3:13
"Behold, I am v........... Job 40:4
them up to v passions...... Rom 1:26

VINDICATED

know that I shall be v..... Job 13:18

VINDICATION

Let my v come from........ Ps 17:2

VINE

to the choice v.............. Gen 49:11
their v is of the v........... Deut 32:32
You have brought a v...... Ps 80:8
planted you a noble v..... Jer 2:21
be no grapes on the v...... Jer 8:13
Israel empties his v......... Hos 10:1
shall sit under his v........ Mic 4:4
of this fruit of the v....... Matt 26:29
"I am the true v............ John 15:1

VINEDRESSER

and My Father is the v.... John 15:1

VINEGAR

As v to the teeth and...... Prov 10:26
weather, and like v......... Prov 25:20

VINES

foxes that spoil the v....... Song 2:15
nor fruit be on the v....... Hab 3:17

VINEYARD

v which Your right.......... Ps 80:15
laborers for his v........... Matt 20:1
Who plants a v and......... 1 Co 9:7

VIOLENCE

was filled with v............ Gen 6:11
You save me from v........ 2 Sa 22:3
the one who loves v........ Ps 11:5
such as breathe out v....... Ps 27:12
from oppression and v..... Ps 72:14
v covers the................... Prov 10:6
He had done no v........... Is 53:9
and v in the land........... Jer 51:46
cause the seat of v.......... Amos 6:3
way and from the v......... Jon 3:8
rich men are full of v...... Mic 6:12
For plundering and v...... Hab 1:3
one's garment with v...... Mal 2:16
of heaven suffers v......... Matt 11:12

VIOLENT

me from the v man......... Ps 18:48
Let evil hunt the v......... Ps 140:11
violence, and the v......... Matt 11:12
haters of God, v............ Rom 1:30
given to wine, not v........ 1 Ti 3:3

VIPER

and stings like a v.......... Prov 23:32
will come forth a v......... Is 14:29
which is crushed a v........ Is 59:5

VIPERS

to them, "Brood of v...... Matt 3:7

VIRGIN

v shall conceive............. Is 7:14
o you oppressed v.......... Is 23:12
v daughter of my........... Jer 14:17
The v of Israel has......... Amos 5:2
"Behold, a v shall.......... Matt 1:23
between a wife and a v..... 1 Co 7:34
you as a chaste v........... 2 Co 11:2

VIRGINS

v who took their lamps.... Matt 25:1
women, for they are v..... Rev 14:4

VIRTUE

if there is any v............. Phil 4:8
us by glory and v............ 2 Pe 1:3
to your faith v.............. 2 Pe 1:5

VISIBLE

that are on earth, v......... Col 1:16
of things which are v....... Heb 11:3

VISION

chased away like a v........ Job 20:8
Then You spoke in a v.... Ps 89:19
the Valley of V............. Is 22:1
a dream of a night v....... Is 29:7
her prophets find no v..... Lam 2:9
have night without v........ Mic 3:6
they had also seen a v..... Luke 24:23
in a trance I saw a v....... Acts 11:5
v appeared to Paul in...... Acts 16:9
to the heavenly v........... Acts 26:19

VISIONS

thoughts from the v......... Job 4:13
young men shall see v...... Joel 2:28
I will come to v............. 2 Co 12:1

VISIT

but God will surely v....... Gen 50:24
in the day when I v........ Ex 32:34
v the earth and water..... Ps 65:9
Oh, v me with Your........ Ps 106:4
v orphans and widows..... Jas 1:27

VISITATION

the time of your v.......... Luke 19:44
God in the day of v........ 1 Pe 2:12

VISITED

he will not be v............. Prov 19:23
Israel, for He has v........ Luke 1:68
how God at the first v..... Acts 15:14

VISITING

v the iniquity of............. Ex 20:5

VOICE

"I heard Your v............. Gen 3:10
v is Jacob's................... Gen 27:22
I should obey His v......... Ex 5:2
fire a still small v.......... 1 Ki 19:12
and my flute to the v...... Job 30:31
you thunder with a v...... Job 40:9
He uttered His v............ Ps 46:6
He sends out His v........ Ps 68:33
have lifted up their v...... Ps 93:3
if you will hear His v..... Ps 95:7
word, Heeding the v....... Ps 103:20
The v of rejoicing and.... Ps 118:15
and a fool's v................ Eccl 5:3
for your v is sweet.......... Song 2:14
The v of one crying in..... Is 40:3
the v of weeping shall...... Is 65:19
A v from the temple..... Is 66:6
v was heard in Ramah..... Jer 31:15
who has a pleasant v....... Ezek 33:32
v was heard in Ramah..... Matt 2:18
"The v of one crying...... Matt 3:3
And suddenly a v........... Matt 3:17
will anyone hear His v.... Matt 12:19
and suddenly a v............ Matt 17:5
for they know his v........ John 10:4
v did not come because... John 12:30
the truth hears My v....... John 18:37
the v of an archangel...... 1 Th 4:16
whose v then shook the... Heb 12:26
glory when such a v........ 2 Pe 1:17
If anyone hears My v...... Rev 3:20

VOICES

shall lift up their v......... Is 52:8
And there were loud v..... Rev 11:15

VOID

they are a nation v......... Deut 32:28
the LORD had made a v.. Judg 21:15
regarded Your law as v... Ps 119:126
Do we then make v........ Rom 3:31
heirs, faith is made v...... Rom 4:14
make my boasting v........ 1 Co 9:15

VOLUME

in the v of the book....... Heb 10:7

VOLUNTEERS

Your people shall be v..... Ps 110:3

VOMIT

'lest the land v............... Lev 18:28
man staggers in his v...... Is 19:14
returns to his own v....... 2 Pe 2:22

VOW

Then Jacob made a v...... Gen 28:20
And Jephthah made a v... Judg 11:30
he carried out his v........ Judg 11:39
v shall be performed....... Ps 65:1
When you make a v........ Eccl 5:4
not to v than to v.......... Eccl 5:5
for he had taken a v....... Acts 18:18
men who have taken a v.. Acts 21:23

VOWS

you will pay your v........ Job 22:27
I will pay My v............. Ps 22:25
V made to You are......... Ps 56:12
Make v to the LORD...... Ps 76:11
today I have paid my v.... Prov 7:14
to reconsider his v......... Prov 20:25
And what, son of my v.... Prov 31:2
to the LORD and made v. Jon 1:16

— W —

WAGE

those who exploit w........ Mal 3:5
w the good warfare......... 1 Ti 1:18

WAGES

I will give you your w...... Ex 2:9
the w of the wicked........ Prov 10:16
w will be troubled.......... Is 19:10
and he who earns w........ Hag 1:6
to you, give me my w...... Zech 11:12
and give them their w..... Matt 20:8
be content with your w... Luke 3:14
is worthy of his w......... Luke 10:7
him who works, the w..... Rom 4:4
For the w of sin is......... Rom 6:23
is worthy of his w......... 1 Ti 5:18
Indeed the w of the....... Jas 5:4

WAIL

My heart shall w........... Jer 48:36
"Son of man, w............. Ezek 32:18

WAILING

w is heard from Zion...... Jer 9:19
of heart and bitter w....... Ezek 27:31
There will be w.............. Matt 13:42

WAIT

hard service I will w....... Job 14:14
If I w for the grave........ Job 17:13
W on the LORD............. Ps 27:14

w patiently for Him........ Ps 37:7
My eyes fail while I w..... Ps 69:3
These all w for You........ Ps 104:27
And I will w on the....... Is 8:17
the LORD will w........... Is 30:18
those who w on the........ Is 40:31
not be ashamed who w.... Is 49:23
w quietly for the............ Lam 3:26
I will w for the God....... Mic 7:7
be like men who w........ Luke 12:36
then we eagerly w.......... Rom 8:25
w for one another.......... 1 Co 11:33
the Spirit eagerly w........ Gal 5:5
we also eagerly w.......... Phil 3:20
and to w for His Son....... 1 Th 1:10
To those who eagerly w... Heb 9:28

WAITED

and when I w for light..... Job 30:26
w patiently for the.......... Ps 40:1
we have w for Him........ Is 25:9
And the people w.......... Luke 1:21
day you have w and....... Acts 27:33
longsuffering of God w.... 1 Pe 3:20

WAITING

w at the posts of my....... Prov 8:34
w for the Consolation...... Luke 2:25
who himself was also w.... Luke 23:51
ourselves, eagerly w........ Rom 8:23
from that time w............ Heb 10:13

WAITS

of the adulterer w........... Job 24:15
my soul silently w.......... Ps 62:1
My soul w for the Lord... Ps 130:6
for the one who w.......... Is 64:4
the creation eagerly w..... Rom 8:19

WAKE

us, that whether we w...... 1 Th 5:10

WALK

w before Me and be........ Gen 17:1
in which they must w...... Ex 18:20
"You shall w in all......... Deut 5:33
Yea, though I w............ Ps 23:4
W about Zion................ Ps 48:12
That Israel would w....... Ps 81:13
I will w within my......... Ps 101:2
I will w before the......... Ps 116:9
Though I w in the.......... Ps 138:7
W prudently when you.... Eccl 5:1
w in the ways of your..... Eccl 11:9
come and let us w.......... Is 2:5
"This is the way, w........ Is 30:21
be weary, they shall w..... Is 40:31
w in the light of your..... Is 50:11
people, who w in a way... Is 65:2
commit adultery and w.... Jer 23:14
the righteous w.............. Hos 14:9
w humbly with your God. Mic 6:8
take up your bed and w... John 5:8
W while you have the...... John 12:35
so we also should w........ Rom 6:4
Let us w properly........... Rom 13:13
For we w by faith........... 2 Co 5:7
W in the Spirit.............. Gal 5:16
that we should w............ Eph 2:10
And w in love............... Eph 5:2
W as children of light..... Eph 5:8
attained, let us w........... Phil 3:16
note those who so w........ Phil 3:17
that you may have a w.... Col 1:10
Jesus the Lord, so w....... Col 2:6
us how you ought to w.... 1 Th 4:1

WALKED

w just as He................... 1 Jn 2:6
and they shall w............. Rev 3:4

WALKED

Methuselah, Enoch w...... Gen 5:22
by His light I w.............. Job 29:3
The people who w........... Is 9:2
He w with Me in peace....Mal 2:6
Jesus no longer w........... John 11:54
w according to the......... 2 Co 10:2
in which you once w.......Eph 2:2
to walk just as He w....... 1 Jn 2:6

WALKING

of the LORD God w....... Gen 3:8
see four men loose, w.....Dan 3:25
before God, w in all........Luke 1:6
they saw Jesus w............John 6:19
And w in the fear of....... Acts 9:31
you are no longer w....... Rom 14:15
not w in craftiness...........2 Co 4:2
of your children w..........2 Jn 4

WALKS

the LORD your God w.... Deut 23:14
is the man Who w...........Ps 1:1
He who w uprightly........Ps 15:2
He who w with............Prov 10:9
He who w with wise men. Prov 13:20
w blamelessly will be...... Prov 28:18
w wisely will be.............. Prov 28:26
Whoever w the road......Is 35:8
Who w in darkness and....Is 50:10
it is not in man who w.... Jer 10:23
do good to him who w....Mic 2:7
If anyone w in the day....John 11:9
he who w in darkness...... John 12:35
adversary the devil w......1 Pe 5:8
is in darkness and w........1 Jn 2:11

WALL

then the w of the city......Josh 6:5
his face toward the w...... 2 Ki 20:2
Like a leaning w............Ps 62:3
and like a high w............Prov 18:11
If she is a w...................Song 8:9
We grope for the w.........Is 59:10
you, you whitewashed w.. Acts 23:3
a window in the w.......... 2 Co 11:33
down the middle w.........Eph 2:14
Now the w of the city......Rev 21:14

WALLS

broken down, without w.. Prov 25:28
salvation for w.................Is 26:1
you shall call your w....... Is 60:18
By faith the w of............ Heb 11:30

WANDER

and makes them w..........Job 12:24
ones cry to God, and w... Job 38:41
Indeed, I would w...........Ps 55:7
Oh, let me not w............ Ps 119:10
they have loved to w...... Jer 14:10

WANDERED

w blind in the streets.......Lam 4:14
"My sheep w through....Ezek 34:6
They w in deserts and......Heb 11:38

WANDERERS

and they shall be w........ Hos 9:17

WANDERING

learn to be idle, w........... 1 Ti 5:13
w stars for whom is.........Jude 13

WANDERS

He w about for bread......Job 15:23
Like a bird that w...........Prov 27:8
if anyone among you w....Jas 5:19

WANT

I shall not w................... Ps 23:1
a prowler, and your w..... Prov 24:34
he began to be in w........ Luke 15:14

WANTING

balances, and found w..... Dan 5:27

WANTON

necks and w eyes............Is 3:16
have begun to grow w..... 1 Ti 5:11

WAR

There is a noise of w.......Ex 32:17
the LORD for the w........Num 32:20
my hands to make w........ 2 Sa 22:35
day of battle and w.........Job 38:23
w should rise against....... Ps 27:3
speak, they are for w.......Ps 120:7
by wise counsel wage w... Prov 20:18
will wage your own w...... Prov 24:6
shall they learn w............Is 2:4
from the distress of w......Is 21:15
we shall see no w............Jer 42:14
same horn was making w. Dan 7:21
men returned from w.......Mic 2:8
king, going to make w..... Luke 14:31
Who ever goes to w........ 1 Co 9:7
for pleasure that w.........Jas 4:1
You fight and w............. Jas 4:2
fleshly lusts which w....... 1 Pe 2:11
w broke out in heaven.....Rev 12:7
He judges and makes w... Rev 19:11

WARFARE

to her, that her w........... Is 40:2
w are not carnal.............. 2 Co 10:4
may wage the good w...... 1 Ti 1:18
w entangles....................2 Ti 2:4

WARM

they will keep w............. Eccl 4:11
but no one is w.............. Hag 1:6

WARMED

w himself at the fire........ Mark 14:54
Depart in peace, be w..... Jas 2:16

WARMING

when she saw Peter w......Mark 14:67

WARN

w the wicked from his..... Ezek 3:18
w everyone night............ Acts 20:31
beloved children I w........1 Co 4:14
w those who are unruly....1 Th 5:14

WARNED

"The man solemnly w......Gen 43:3
them Your servant is w....Ps 19:11
Then, being divinely w.....Matt 2:12
Who has w you to flee....Matt 3:7
Noah, being divinely w.... Heb 11:7

WARNING

w every man and........... Col 1:28

WARPED

such a person is w...........Tit 3:11

WARRING

w against the law of........ Rom 7:23

WARRIOR

He runs at me like a w....Job 16:14

WARS

He makes w cease to.......Ps 46:9
And you will hear of w....Matt 24:6
Where do w and fights.....Jas 4:1

WASH

w myself with snow.........Job 9:30
I will w my hands in........Ps 26:6
W me thoroughly............Ps 51:2
He shall w his feet in...... Ps 58:10
"W yourselves................ Is 1:16
O Jerusalem, w your.......Jer 4:14
head and w your face...... Matt 6:17
For they do not w...........Matt 15:2
not eat unless they w......Mark 7:3
w His feet with her......... Luke 7:38
said to him, "Go, w........John 9:7
w the disciples'...............John 13:5
"You shall never w......... John 13:8
w one another's..............John 13:14
w away your sins........... Acts 22:16

WASHED

And w my hands in.........Ps 73:13
When the Lord has w......Is 4:4
cut, nor were you w.........Ezek 16:4
w his hands before the.....Matt 27:24
My feet, but she has w.... Luke 7:44
So when He had w...........John 13:12
w their stripes................. Acts 16:33
But you were w..............1 Co 6:11
if she has w the.............. 1 Ti 5:10
Him who loved us and w. Rev 1:5
w their robes and made... Rev 7:14

WASHING

cleanse it with the w........Eph 5:26
us, through the w............Tit 3:5

WASHINGS

and drinks, various w...... Heb 9:10

WASTE

who are left shall w.........Lev 26:39
the cities are laid w.........Is 6:11
empty and makes it w......Is 24:1
w the mountains.............. Is 42:15
what purpose is this w..... Matt 26:8

WASTED

The field is w.................Joel 1:10
this fragrant oil w........... Mark 14:4
w his possessions............Luke 15:13

WASTING

w and destruction are...... Is 59:7
that this man was w......... Luke 16:1

WATCH

of them we set a w.........Neh 4:9
my steps, but do not w....Job 14:16
is past, And like a w.......Ps 90:4
Keep w over the door......Ps 141:3
and all who w for............Is 29:20
W the road.................... Nah 2:1
"W therefore.................Matt 24:42
What, could you not w.... Matt 26:40

WATCHED

"*W* and pray................. Matt 26:41
W, stand fast in the........1 Co 16:13
submissive, for they *w*..... Heb 13:17

WATCHED

in the days when God *w*.. Job 29:2
come, he would have *w*... Matt 24:43

WATCHES

w the righteous................Ps 37:32
She *w* over the ways of....Prov 31:27
Blessed is he who *w*........ Rev 16:15

WATCHFUL

But you be *w* in all.........2 Ti 4:5
be serious and *w*..............1 Pe 4:7

WATCHING

who listens to me, *w*....... Prov 8:34
the flock, who were *w*..... Zech 11:11
he comes, will find *w*......Luke 12:37

WATCHMAN

guards the city, The *w*... Ps 127:1
W, what of the night....... Is 21:11
I have made you a *w*......Ezek 3:17
the day of your *w*........... Mic 7:4

WATCHMEN

w who go about the........ Song 3:3
w shall lift up their.........Is 52:8
His *w* are blind..............Is 56:10
I have set *w* on your....... Is 62:6
Also, I set *w* over you....Jer 6:17
strong, set up the *w*...... Jer 51:12

WATER

Eden to *w* the garden......Gen 2:10
Unstable as *w*.................Gen 49:4
your bread and your *w*... Ex 23:25
of affliction and *w*..........1 Ki 22:27
w disappears from the......Job 14:11
w wears away stones.......Job 14:19
drinks iniquity like *w*......Job 15:16
not given the weary *w*.... Job 22:7
He binds up the *w*......... Job 26:8
I am poured out like *w*...Ps 22:14
Where there is no *w*........Ps 63:1
they have shed like *w*.... Ps 79:3
Drink *w* from your own...Prov 5:15
"Stolen *w* is sweet........Prov 9:17
the whole supply of *w*.....Is 3:1
and needy seek *w*........ Is 41:17
For I will pour *w*.......... Is 44:3
silence and given us *w*..... Jer 8:14
eye overflows with *w*.......Lam 1:16
will be as weak as *w*......Ezek 7:17
w the land with the........Ezek 32:6
you gave Me no *w*..........Luke 7:44
there was much *w*...........John 3:23
given you living *w*............John 4:10
rivers of living *w*.............John 7:38
blood and *w* came out..... John 19:34
"Can anyone forbid *w*..... Acts 10:47
with the washing of *w*......Eph 5:26
can yield both salt *w*....... Jas 3:12
were saved through *w*...... 1 Pe 3:20
is He who came by *w*...... 1 Jn 5:6
the Spirit, the *w*............. 1 Jn 5:8
are clouds without *w*....... Jude 12
let him take the *w*...........Rev 22:17

WATERED

w the whole face.............Gen 2:6
that it was well *w*...........Gen 13:10
I planted, Apollos *w*........1 Co 3:6

WATERS

and struck the *w*.............Ex 7:20
If He withholds the *w*.....Job 12:15
me beside the still *w*.......Ps 23:2
Though its *w* roar and.... Ps 46:3
w have come up to my.... Ps 69:1
Then the *w* would have....Ps 124:4
rich, and he who *w*......... Prov 11:25
Who has bound the *w*......Prov 30:4
your bread upon the *w*.... Eccl 11:1
a well of living *w*............Song 4:15
w cannot quench love...... Song 8:7
of the LORD as the *w*..... Is 11:9
w will fail from the......... Is 19:5
because I give *w*............. Is 43:20
have sworn that the *w*..... Is 54:9
thirsts, come to the *w*..... Is 55:1
fountain of living *w*........ Jer 2:13
w flowed over my head...Lam 3:54
the sound of many *w*.......Ezek 43:2
w encompassed me..........Jon 2:5
shall be that living *w*...... Zech 14:8
often, in perils of *w*.........2 Co 11:26
living fountains of *w*........Rev 7:17
w became wormwood...... Rev 8:11

WAVER

He did not *w* at the..... Rom 4:20

WAVERING

of our hope without *w*..... Heb 10:23

WAVES

and here your proud *w*....Job 38:11
All Your *w* and billows....Ps 42:7
The noise of their *w*........Ps 65:7
the multitude of its *w*..... Jer 51:42
was covered with the *w*....Matt 8:24
sea, tossed by the *w*........Matt 14:24
raging *w* of the sea.........Jude 13

WAX

My heart is like *w*...........Ps 22:14
w melts before the.......... Ps 68:2
mountains melt like *w*...... Ps 97:5

WAY

and show them the *w*..... Ex 18:20
day I am going the *w*...... Josh 23:14
and the right *w*...............1 Sa 12:23
As for God, His *w*..........2 Sa 22:31
to a man whose *w*...........Job 3:23
But He knows the *w*....... Job 23:10
"Where is the *w*............. Job 38:19
the LORD knows the *w*... Ps 1:6
you perish in the *w*......... Ps 2:12
Teach me Your *w*........... Ps 27:11
This is the *w* of those.....Ps 49:13
w may be known on........Ps 67:2
Your *w* was in the sea.....Ps 77:19
where there is no *w*......... Ps 107:40
I have chosen the *w*........ Ps 119:30
I hate every false *w*........Ps 119:104
in the *w* everlasting.........Ps 139:24
and preserves the.............Prov 2:8
The *w* of the wicked is....Prov 4:19
instruction are the *w*........Prov 6:23
w which seems right........Prov 14:12
not know what is the *w*...Eccl 11:5
of terrors in the *w*..........Eccl 12:5
The *w* of the just is.........Is 26:7
"This is the *w*................Is 30:21
LORD, who makes a *w*...Is 43:16
wicked forsake his *w*....... Is 55:7
O LORD, I know the *w*...Jer 10:23
one heart and one *w*...... Jer 32:39

WAYS

Israel, is it not My *w*......Ezek 18:25
w which is not fair.......... Ezek 33:17
and pervert the *w*........... Amos 2:7
the LORD has His *w*.......Nah 1:3
he will prepare the *w*.......Mal 3:1
and broad is the *w*.......... Matt 7:13
and difficult is the *w*.......Matt 7:14
will prepare Your w........ Matt 11:10
and teach the *w*..............Matt 22:16
and the *w* you know........John 14:4
to him, "I am the *w*........John 14:6
proclaim to us the *w*.......Acts 16:17
explained to him the *w*.... Acts 18:26
you a more excellent *w*....1 Co 12:31
w which He consecrated...Heb 10:20
forsaken the right *w*........ 2 Pe 2:15
to have known the *w*....... 2 Pe 2:21
have gone in the *w*..........Jude 11

WAYFARING

lie waste, the *w*.............. Is 33:8
w man who turns aside....Jer 14:8

WAYS

for all His *w* are............. Deut 32:4
they do not know its *w*....Job 24:13
is the first of the *w*......... Job 40:19
Show me Your *w*............Ps 25:4
transgressors Your *w*....... Ps 51:13
would walk in My *w*........Ps 81:13
w were directed.............. Ps 119:5
I thought about my *w*......Ps 119:59
righteous in all His *w*...... Ps 145:17
For the *w* of man are..... Prov 5:21
w please the LORD.........Prov 16:7
he will teach us His *w*.... Is 2:3
nor are your *w*............... Is 55:8
"Stand in the *w*.............Jer 6:16
"Amend your *w*..............Jer 7:3
and examine our *w*.........Lam 3:40
and owns all your *w*........Dan 5:23
w are everlasting............Hab 3:6
misery are in their w....... Rom 3:16
judgments and His *w*......Rom 11:33
unstable in all his *w*........Jas 1:8
their destructive *w*...........2 Pe 2:2
and true are Your *w*.......Rev 15:3

WEAK

then I shall become *w*......Judg 16:7
"And I am *w* today........2 Sa 3:39
O LORD, for I am *w*..... Ps 6:2
gives power to the *w*....... Is 40:29
knee will be as *w*............Ezek 7:17
let the *w* say..................Joel 3:10
not your hands be *w*........Zeph 3:16
but the flesh is *w*............Matt 26:41
And not being *w*.............Rom 4:19
Receive one who is *w*...... Rom 14:1
God has chosen the *w*..... 1 Co 1:27
We are *w*......................1 Co 4:10
w I became as *w*...........1 Co 9:22
this reason many are *w*....1 Co 11:30
For when I am *w*............ 2 Co 12:10

WEAKENED

w my strength in the........ Ps 102:23
the ground, you who *w*....Is 14:12

WEAKENS

w the hands of the men... Jer 38:4

WEAKER

house of Saul grew *w*...... 2 Sa 3:1
the wife, as to the *w*....... 1 Pe 3:7

WEAKNESS

than men, and the w....... 1 Co 1:25
I was with you in w.........1 Co 2:3
It is sown in w............... 1 Co 15:43
is also beset by w...........Heb 5:2
w were made strong........ Heb 11:34

WEAKNESSES

also helps in our w..........Rom 8:26
sympathize with our w..... Heb 4:15

WEALTH

have gained me this w..... Deut 8:17
a man of great w............ Ruth 2:1
not asked riches or w...... 2 Ch 1:11
who trust in their w.........Ps 49:6
w is his strong city.......... Prov 10:15
W gained by dishonesty...Prov 13:11
W makes many friends.....Prov 19:4
may bring to you the w....Is 60:11

WEALTHY

w nation that dwells........ Jer 49:31
am rich, have become w.. Rev 3:17

WEANED

w child shall put his........ Is 11:8
Those just w from milk....Is 28:9

WEAPON

w formed against you...... Is 54:17
with a deadly w...............Ezek 9:1

WEAPONS

is better than w.............. Eccl 9:18
the LORD and His w.......Is 13:5
For the w of our.............2 Co 10:4

WEAR

but the just will w...........Job 27:17
'What shall we w............ Matt 6:31

WEARIED

you have w Me with........Is 43:24
You are w in the............. Is 57:10
and they have w.............Jer 12:5
You have w the LORD.... Mal 2:17
therefore, being w..........John 4:6

WEARINESS

say, 'Oh, what a w..........Mal 1:13
in w and toil.................. 2 Co 11:27

WEARISOME

and much study is w........Eccl 12:12

WEARY

to Isaac, "I am w...........Gen 27:46
lest he become w............ Prov 25:17
As cold water to a w........Prov 25:25
No one will be w............ Is 5:27
you may cause the w........Is 28:12
shall run and not be w.....Is 40:31
to him who is w..............Is 50:4
I am w of holding it........Jer 6:11
w themselves to commit...Jer 9:5
I was w of holding it.......Jer 20:9
continual coming she w....Luke 18:5
And let us not grow w.....Gal 6:9
do not grow w in............ 2 Th 3:13
lest you become w.......... Heb 12:3

WEATHER

a garment in cold w........ Prov 25:20
'It will be fair w............. Matt 16:2

WEDDING

were invited to the w.......Matt 22:3
Come to the w...............Matt 22:4
find, invite to the w........ Matt 22:9
in with him to the w........Matt 25:10
day there was a w...........John 2:1

WEEKS

w are determined............Dan 9:24
w Messiah shall be cut.....Dan 9:26

WEEP

Hannah, why do you w....1 Sa 1:8
a time to w....................Eccl 3:4
you shall w no more........Is 30:19
it, my soul will w............Jer 13:17
W not for the dead..........Jer 22:10
to the LORD, w between. Joel 2:17
this commotion and w......Mark 5:39
Blessed are you who w.... Luke 6:21
to her, "Do not w...........Luke 7:13
and you did not w..........Luke 7:32
of Jerusalem, do not w.... Luke 23:28
to the tomb to w there.... John 11:31
w with those who w........ Rom 12:15
those who w as though.... 1 Co 7:30

WEEPING

of Israel, who were w......Num 25:6
w as they went up..........2 Sa 15:30
the noise of the w...........Ezra 3:13
face is flushed from w......Job 16:16
the voice of my w...........Ps 6:8
my drink with w.............Ps 102:9
of hosts called for w........Is 22:12
w shall no longer............ Is 65:19
They shall come with w.... Jer 31:9
w they shall come............Jer 50:4
were sitting there w.........Ezek 8:14
with fasting, with w.........Joel 2:12
with tears, with w........... Mal 2:13
There will be w...............Matt 8:12
outside by the tomb w.....John 20:11
Woman, why are you w...John 20:13
What do you mean by w...Acts 21:13

WEIGH

You w out the violence....Ps 58:2
O Most Upright, You w...Is 26:7

WEIGHED

nor can silver be w.........Job 28:15
W the mountains.............Is 40:12
You have been w............Dan 5:27
lest your hearts be w....... Luke 21:34

WEIGHS

eyes, but the LORD w.....Prov 16:2
Where is he who w........ Is 33:18

WEIGHT

a perfect and just w........ Deut 25:15
w is His delight.............. Prov 11:1
and eternal w of glory.... 2 Co 4:17
us lay aside every w........ Heb 12:1

WEIGHTIER

have neglected the w.......Matt 23:23

WELFARE

does not seek the w........ Jer 38:4

WELL

"If you do w..................Gen 4:7
that it may go w............ Deut 4:40
you when you do w........Ps 49:18

daughters have done w.... Prov 31:29
know that it will be w......Eccl 8:12
wheel broken at the w.....Eccl 12:6
that it shall be w.............Is 3:10
"Those who are w...........Matt 9:12
said to him, 'W done.......Matt 25:21
faith has made you w...... Mark 5:34
Now Jacob's w was......... John 4:6
the elders who rule w......1 Ti 5:17

WELL-BEING

them, And their w.......... Ps 69:22
each one the other's w.....1 Co 10:24

WELLS

draw water from the w.... Is 12:3
These are w without........2 Pe 2:17

WENT

They w out from us.........1 Jn 2:19

WEPT

and the man of God w.... 2 Ki 8:11
for the people w.............Ezra 10:1
that I sat down and w......Neh 1:4
Have I not w for him...... Job 30:25
down, yea, we w.............Ps 137:1
out and w bitterly........... Matt 26:75
He saw the city and w..... Luke 19:41
Jesus w........................ John 11:35
So I w much.................. Rev 5:4

WET

They are w with the........Job 24:8
his body was w with....... Dan 4:33

WHEAT

with the finest of w......... Ps 81:16
we may trade our w........ Amos 8:5
even sell the bad w......... Amos 8:6
but gather the w............. Matt 13:30
w falls into the...............John 12:24
perhaps w or some.......... 1 Co 15:37
oil, fine flour and w........ Rev 18:13

WHEEL

brings the threshing w......Prov 20:26
the fountain, or the w......Eccl 12:6
in the middle of a w........Ezek 1:16

WHEELS

off their chariot w...........Ex 14:25
the rumbling of his w...... Jer 47:3
appearance of the w........ Ezek 1:16
noise of rattling w...........Nah 3:2

WHIP

A w for the horse............Prov 26:3
The noise of a w.............Nah 3:2

WHIRLWIND

Elijah went up by a w..... 2 Ki 2:11
Job out of the w.............Job 38:1
them away as with a w.... Ps 58:9
w will take them away..... Is 40:24
w shall scatter them.........Is 41:16
w shall be raised.............Jer 25:32
has His way in the w.......Nah 1:3

WHISPER

my ear received a w........Job 4:12
and wizards, who w.........Is 8:19

WHISPERER

w separates the best........ Prov 16:28

WHISPERINGS
backbitings, w............... 2 Co 12:20

WHITE
My beloved is w............. Song 5:10
and make them w.......... Dan 11:35
be purified, made w...... Dan 12:10
for they are already w.... John 4:35
walk with Me in w.......... Rev 3:4
clothed in w garments..... Rev 3:5
behold, a w horse........... Rev 6:2
and made them w.......... Rev 7:14
Then I saw a great w....... Rev 20:11

WHOLE
w body were an eye........ 1 Co 12:17

WHOLESOME
w tongue is a tree.......... Prov 15:4
not consent to w words.... 1 Ti 6:3

WHOLLY
w followed the LORD...... Deut 1:36
I will not leave you w..... Jer 46:28

WICKED
w shall be silent............. 1 Sa 2:9
Should you help the w..... 2 Ch 19:2
Why do the w live and.... Job 21:7
w are reserved for the..... Job 21:30
to nobles, 'You are w.... Job 34:18
with the w every day....... Ps 7:11
w is snared in the........... Ps 9:16
w shall be turned........... Ps 9:17
do the w renounce God.... Ps 10:13
w bend their bow........... Ps 11:2
w He will rain coals........ Ps 11:6
Evil shall slay the w........ Ps 34:21
w shall be no more.......... Ps 37:10
The w watches the.......... Ps 37:32
how long will the w........ Ps 94:3
And the w be no more..... Ps 104:35
is far from the w........... Ps 119:155
if there is any w............. Ps 139:24
w will be cut off from..... Prov 2:22
w will fall by his own..... Prov 11:5
LORD is far from the w... Prov 15:29
w flee when no one........ Prov 28:1
Do not be overly w........ Eccl 7:17
not be well with the w..... Eccl 8:13
w forsake his way........... Is 55:7
But the w are like the..... Is 57:20
and desperately w.......... Jer 17:9
w shall do wickedly........ Dan 12:10
at all acquit the w........... Nah 1:3
w one does not touch..... 1 Jn 5:18
the sway of the w........... 1 Jn 5:19

WICKEDLY
Will you speak w............ Job 13:7
God will never do w....... Job 34:12
"Those who do w........... Dan 11:32
yes, all who do w........... Mal 4:1

WICKEDNESS
LORD saw that the w...... Gen 6:5
can I do this great w....... Gen 39:9
W proceeds from the...... 1 Sa 24:13
w oppress them.............. 2 Sa 7:10
Is not your w great......... Job 22:5
Oh, let the w of the........ Ps 7:9
alive into hell, For w...... Ps 55:15
in the tents of w............. Ps 84:10
I will not know w.......... Ps 101:4
eat the bread of w.......... Prov 4:17
w is an abomination........ Prov 8:7

w will not..................... Eccl 8:8
w burns as the................ Is 9:18
have trusted in your w..... Is 47:10
w will correct you........... Jer 2:19
wells up with her w......... Jer 6:7
man repented of his w..... Jer 8:6
not turn from his w......... Ezek 3:19
You have plowed w........ Hos 10:13
and cannot look on w...... Hab 1:13
for those who do w........ Mal 3:15
is full of greed and w..... Luke 11:39
sexual immorality, w....... Rom 1:29
spiritual hosts of w......... Eph 6:12
and overflow of w.......... Jas 1:21

WIDE
shall open your hand w.... Deut 15:8
opened their mouth w...... Job 29:23
w his lips shall have...... Prov 13:3
will build myself a w....... Jer 22:14
w is the gate and............ Matt 7:13
to you, our heart is w..... 2 Co 6:11

WIDOW
does no good for the w.... Job 24:21
They slay the w.............. Ps 94:6
And his wife a w............ Ps 109:9
the fatherless and w........ Ps 146:9
plead for the w.............. Is 1:17
How like a w is she........ Lam 1:1
Then one poor w........... Mark 12:42
w has children or........... 1 Ti 5:4
Do not let a w under...... 1 Ti 5:9

WIDOW'S
and I caused the w......... Job 29:13

WIDOWS
a defender of w............. Ps 68:5
and let your w trust........ Jer 49:11
w were neglected........... Acts 6:1
that the younger w......... 1 Ti 5:14
to visit orphans and w..... Jas 1:27

WIFE
and be joined to his w..... Gen 2:24
an excellent w is the........ Prov 12:4
w finds a good thing....... Prov 18:22
but a prudent w............. Prov 19:14
w whom you love all....... Eccl 9:9
like a youthful w............ Is 54:6
Go, take yourself a w...... Hos 1:2
w he tended sheep.......... Hos 12:12
with the w of his............ Mal 2:15
Whoever divorces his w... Mark 10:11
'I have married a w........ Luke 14:20
"Remember Lot's w....... Luke 17:32
all seven had her as w..... Luke 20:33
so love his own w.......... Eph 5:33
the husband of one w...... Tit 1:6
giving honor to the w...... 1 Pe 3:7
bride, the Lamb's w........ Rev 21:9

WILD
locusts and w honey........ Matt 3:4
olive tree which is w....... Rom 11:24

WILDERNESS
wasteland, a howling w.... Deut 32:10
w yields food for them.... Job 24:5
coming out of the w........ Song 3:6
made the world as a w..... Is 14:17
I will make the w.......... Is 41:18
Let the w and its............ Is 42:11
Have I been a w............ Jer 2:31
of one crying in the w..... Matt 3:3

the serpent in the w........ John 3:14
congregation in the w...... Acts 7:38

WILES
to stand against the w...... Eph 6:11

WILL
w be done on earth as..... Matt 6:10
but he who does the w.... Matt 7:21
of the two did the w........ Matt 21:31
on earth peace, good w.... Luke 2:14
nevertheless not My w..... Luke 22:42
flesh, nor of the w.......... John 1:13
I do not seek My own w.. John 5:30
not to do My own w....... John 6:38
"This is the w.............. John 6:39
wants to do His w.......... John 7:17
w is present with me....... Rom 7:18
and perfect w of God...... Rom 12:2
works in you both to..... Phil 2:13
the knowledge of His w... Col 1:9
according to His own w... Heb 2:4
come to do Your w......... Heb 10:9
good work to do His w.... Heb 13:21
but he who does the w.... 1 Jn 2:17

WILLFULLY
For if we sin w.............. Heb 10:26
For this they w.............. 2 Pe 3:5

WILLING
is of a w heart............... Ex 35:5
If you are w and............ Is 1:19
him, saying, "I am w....... Matt 8:3
The spirit indeed is w..... Matt 26:41
if there is first a w......... 2 Co 8:12
w that any should.......... 2 Pe 3:9

WILLINGLY
to futility, not w............. Rom 8:20
For if I do this w............ 1 Co 9:17
by constraint but w......... 1 Pe 5:2

WILLOWS
our harps Upon the w..... Ps 137:2

WILLS
to whom the Son w......... Matt 11:27
it is not of him who w..... Rom 9:16
say, "If the Lord w........ Jas 4:15

WIN
w one proselyte............. Matt 23:15
to all, that I might w....... 1 Co 9:19

WIND
LORD was not in the w... 1 Ki 19:11
w carries him away......... Job 27:21
the chaff which the w...... Ps 1:4
He causes His w............ Ps 147:18
will inherit the w........... Prov 11:29
He who observes the w.... Eccl 11:4
is the way of the w......... Eccl 11:5
Awake, O north........... Song 4:16
the prophets become w.... Jer 5:13
He brings the w............. Jer 51:16
Ephraim feeds on the w... Hos 12:1
and creates the w........... Amos 4:13
A reed shaken by the w... Matt 11:7
And the w ceased and..... Mark 4:39
and rebuked the w.......... Luke 8:24
"The w blows where....... John 3:8
of a rushing mighty w..... Acts 2:2
about with every w......... Eph 4:14

WINDOWS

looking through the w......Song 2:9
has come through our w...Jer 9:21
upper room, with his w....Dan 6:10
not open for you the w...Mal 3:10

WINDS

from the four w..............Ezek 37:9
be, that even the w.........Matt 8:27
holding the four w..........Rev 7:1

WINDSTORM

And a great w arose........Mark 4:37

WINE

Noah awoke from his w...Gen 9:24
w that makes glad...........Ps 104:15
W is a mocker.................Prov 20:1
Do not look on the w...Prov 23:31
love is better than w.......Song 1:2
w inflames them.............Is 5:11
Yes, come, buy w...........Is 55:1
they gave Him sour w......Matt 27:34
when they ran out of w...John 2:3
do not be drunk with w....Eph 5:18
but use a little w...........1 Ti 5:23
not given to much w........Tit 2:3
her the cup of the w...Rev 16:19

WINEBIBBERS

Do not mix with w..........Prov 23:20

WINEPRESS

I have trodden the w.......Is 63:3
for the w is full...............Joel 3:13
into the great w.............Rev 14:19
Himself treads the w.......Rev 19:15

WINESKIN

I have become like a w....Ps 119:83

WINESKINS

new wine into old w........Matt 9:17

WING

One w of the cherub.......1 Ki 6:24
so I spread My w...........Ezek 16:8

WINGS

w you have come............Ruth 2:12
He flew upon the w........Ps 18:10
the shadow of Your w.....Ps 36:7
If I take the w...............Ps 139:9
each one had six w..........Is 6:2
with healing in His w......Mal 4:2
woman was given two w...Rev 12:14

WINNOW

You shall w them............Is 41:16

WINS

w souls is wise.................Prov 11:30

WINTER

made summer and w.......Ps 74:17
For lo, the w is past........Song 2:11
w it shall occur..............Zech 14:8
flight may not be in w.....Matt 24:20

WIPE

the Lord GOD will w......Is 25:8
w them with the towel.....John 13:5
w away every tear..........Rev 21:4

WISDOM

for this is your w...........Deut 4:6
w will die with you.........Job 12:2

will make me to know w..Ps 51:6
is the man who finds w....Prov 3:13
Get w...........................Prov 4:5
W is the principal...........Prov 4:7
is the beginning of w.......Prov 9:10
is to get w than gold.......Prov 16:16
w loves his own soul........Prov 19:8
W is too lofty for a.........Prov 24:7
w is much grief...............Eccl 1:18
W is better than.............Eccl 9:16
w is justified by her........Matt 11:19
Jesus increased in w........Luke 2:52
riches both of the w........Rom 11:33
the gospel, not with w.....1 Co 1:17
Greeks seek after w.........1 Co 1:22
For the w of this............1 Co 3:19
not with fleshly w...........2 Co 1:12
now the manifold w........Eph 3:10
all the treasures of w.......Col 2:3
Walk in w toward those...Col 4:5
If any of you lacks w.......Jas 1:5
power and riches and w...Rev 5:12
and glory and w.............Rev 7:12

WISE

great nation is a w..........Deut 4:6
He catches the w............Job 5:13
God is w in heart and.....Job 9:4
men are not always w......Job 32:9
when will you be w.........Ps 94:8
w will observe these........Ps 107:43
Do not be w in your.......Prov 3:7
he who wins souls is w....Prov 11:30
The w in heart will be.....Prov 16:21
folly, lest he be w..........Prov 26:5
they are exceedingly w.....Prov 30:24
The words of the w.........Eccl 12:11
They are w to do evil......Jer 4:22
Therefore be w as...........Matt 10:16
five of them were w........Matt 25:2
barbarians, both to w......Rom 1:14
to God, alone w.............Rom 16:27
Where is the w..............1 Co 1:20
sake, but you are w.........1 Co 4:10
not as fools but as w.......Eph 5:15
are able to make you w...2 Ti 3:15

WISELY

I will behave w...............Ps 101:2
who heeds the word w.....Prov 16:20
you do not inquire w.......Eccl 7:10

WISER

he was w than all men.....1 Ki 4:31
w than the birds.............Job 35:11
w than my enemies.........Ps 119:98
of God is w than men......1 Co 1:25

WISH

for me to do what I w.....Matt 20:15
w it were already...........Luke 12:49

WISHED

Then he w death for........Jon 4:8

WITCHCRAFT

is as the sin of w............1 Sa 15:23

WITHDRAW

God will not w His.........Job 9:13
He does not w His eyes...Job 36:7
From such w yourself......1 Ti 6:5

WITHER

also shall not w.............Ps 1:3
w as the green...............Ps 37:2

leaves will not w............Ezek 47:12
How did the fig tree w.... Matt 21:20

WITHERS

The grass w...................Is 40:7
burning heat than it w.....Jas 1:11
The grass w...................1 Pe 1:24

WITHHOLD

w Your tender mercies.....Ps 40:11
good thing will He w.......Ps 84:11
Do not w good from.......Prov 3:27
your cloak, do not w.......Luke 6:29

WITHOUT

having no hope and w.....Eph 2:12
pray w ceasing..............1 Th 5:17
w controversy.................1 Ti 3:16
w works is dead.............Jas 2:26

WITHSTAND

was I that I could w........Acts 11:17
you may be able to w......Eph 6:13

WITHSTOOD

I w him to his face..........Gal 2:11

WITNESS

see, God is w between.....Gen 31:50
Surely even now my w.....Job 16:19
like the faithful w...........Ps 89:37
w does not lie................Prov 14:5
have given him as a w......Is 55:4
a true and faithful w.......Jer 42:5
I will be a swift w...........Mal 3:5
all the world as a w........Matt 24:14
This man came for a w....John 1:7
do not receive Our w......John 3:11
"If I bear w of...............John 5:31
is another who bears w....John 5:32
But I have a greater w.....John 5:36
who was bearing w..........Acts 14:3
For you will be His w......Acts 22:15
For God is my w............Phil 1:8
are three who bear w......1 Jn 5:7
If we receive the w.........1 Jn 5:9
who bore w to the word...Rev 1:2
Christ, the faithful w.......Rev 1:5
beheaded for their w.......Rev 20:4

WITNESSED

is revealed, being w.........Rom 3:21
w the good confession......1 Ti 6:13

WITNESSES

of two or three w............Deut 17:6
for Myself faithful w........Is 8:2
"You are My w..............Is 43:10
the presence of many w...1 Ti 6:12
the Holy Spirit also w......Heb 10:15
so great a cloud of w.......Heb 12:1
give power to my two w...Rev 11:3

WIVES

Husbands, love your w....Eph 5:25
w must be reverent..........1 Ti 3:11

WIZARDS

who are mediums and w...Is 8:19

WOLF

The w and the lamb........Is 65:25
the sheep, sees the w.......John 10:12

WOLVES

they are ravenous w........Matt 7:15
out as lambs among w.....Luke 10:3
my departure savage w....Acts 20:29

WOMAN
she shall be called W........Gen 2:23
w builds her house..........Prov 14:1
w who fears the LORD.... Prov 31:30
w shall encompass a........ Jer 31:22
whoever looks at a w.......Matt 5:28
"Do you see this w......... Luke 7:44
Then the w of Samaria.... John 4:9
brought to Him a w........ John 8:3
"W, behold your.............John 19:26
w was full of good.......... Acts 9:36
natural use of the w........ Rom 1:27
a man not to touch a w... 1 Co 7:1
w is the glory of man...... 1 Co 11:7
His Son, born of a w.......Gal 4:4
Let a w learn in..............1 Ti 2:11
I do not permit a w.........1 Ti 2:12
w being deceived........... 1 Ti 2:14
w clothed with the sun.....Rev 12:1
the earth helped the w.....Rev 12:16

WOMB
nations are in your w.......Gen 25:23
LORD had closed her w...1 Sa 1:5
took Me out of the w...... Ps 22:9
formed you from the w.... Is 44:2
called Me from the w....... Is 49:1
in the w I knew you.......Jer 1:5
is the fruit of your w....... Luke 1:42
"Blessed is the w........... Luke 11:27

WOMEN
blessed is she among w....Judg 5:24
among Your honorable w. Ps 45:9
O fairest among w........... Song 1:8
w rule over them............ Is 3:12
new wine the young w..... Zech 9:17
w will be grinding.......... Matt 24:41
are you among w........... Luke 1:28
w keep silent in the........1 Co 14:34
admonish the young w..... Tit 2:4
times, the holy w............. 1 Pe 3:5
not defiled with w.......... Rev 14:4

WONDER
I have become as a w......Ps 71:7
marvelous work and a w.. Is 29:14

WONDERFUL
name, seeing it is w.........Judg 13:18
Your love to me was w....2 Sa 1:26
things too w for me.........Job 42:3
Your testimonies are w.... Ps 119:129
name will be called w...... Is 9:6
of hosts, Who is the w...... Is 28:29
and scribes saw the w...... Matt 21:15
our own tongues the w.... Acts 2:11

WONDERFULLY
fearfully and w made.......Ps 139:14

WONDERS
w which I will do...........Ex 3:20
are the God who does w..Ps 77:14
Shall Your w be known... Ps 88:12
who alone does great w... Ps 136:4
Egypt with signs and w.... Jer 32:21
and how mighty His w.....Dan 4:3
He works signs and w......Dan 6:27
And I will show w.......... Joel 2:30
and done many w........... Matt 7:22
signs, and lying w........... 2 Th 2:9
both with signs and w......Heb 2:4

WONDROUS
And tell of all Your w.....Ps 26:7
w works declare that....... Ps 75:1

W works in the land of.... Ps 106:22
for they are a w..............Zech 3:8

WONDROUSLY
God, who has dealt w......Joel 2:26

WOOD
precious stones, w...........1 Co 3:12

WOODCUTTERS
but let them be w.......... Josh 9:21

WOOL
they shall be as w........... Is 1:18
head was like pure w.......Dan 7:9
hair were white like w..... Rev 1:14

WORD
w that proceeds............. Deut 8:3
w is very near you......... Deut 30:14
w I have hidden.............Ps 119:11
w has given me life......... Ps 119:50
w is a lamp to my feet.....Ps 119:105
w makes it glad.............. Prov 12:25
w spoken in due season... Prov 15:23
w fitly spoken is............. Prov 25:11
Every w of God is pure... Prov 30:5
The LORD sent a w........ Is 9:8
the w of our God...........Is 40:8
w has gone out of My..... Is 45:23
w be that goes forth........ Is 55:11
But His w was in my.......Jer 20:9
w will be his oracle........ Jer 23:36
w which I speak will.......Ezek 12:28
But only speak a w......... Matt 8:8
for every idle w.............. Matt 12:36
The seed is the w............Luke 8:11
mighty in deed and w...... Luke 24:19
beginning was the W....... John 1:1
W became flesh and........ John 1:14
if anyone keeps My w......John 8:51
w which you hear is........ John 14:24
Your w is truth.............John 17:17
and glorified the w.......... Acts 13:48
to one is given the w.......1 Co 12:8
of water by the w........... Eph 5:26
holding fast the w........... Phil 2:16
Let the w of Christ......... Col 3:16
come to you in w only.....1 Th 1:5
in every good w..............2 Th 2:17
all things by the w.......... Heb 1:3
w which they heard did....Heb 4:2
For the w of God is........ Heb 4:12
the implanted w..............Jas 1:21
does not stumble in w......Jas 3:2
through the w of God....... 1 Pe 1:23
that by the w of God......2 Pe 3:5
whoever keeps His w.......1 Jn 2:5
let us not love in w..........1 Jn 3:18
the Father, the W...........1 Jn 5:7
name is called The W...... Rev 19:13

WORDS
Give ear to my w.............Ps 5:1
Let the w of my mouth....Ps 19:14
How sweet are Your w.....Ps 119:103
pay attention to the w..... Prov 7:24
The w of the wise are......Eccl 12:11
And I have put My w.......Is 51:16
Take w with you............Hos 14:2
Do not My w do good to. Mic 2:7
pass away, but My w.......Matt 24:35
at the gracious w........... Luke 4:22
w that I speak to you...... John 6:63
You have the w of.........John 6:68
And remember the w...... Acts 20:35

not with wisdom of w......1 Co 1:17
those who hear the w...... Rev 1:3
is he who keeps the w..... Rev 22:7

WORK
day God ended His w......Gen 2:2
Moses finished the w....... Ex 40:33
people had a mind to w... Neh 4:6
You shall desire the w..... Job 14:15
for they are all the w......Job 34:19
the w of Your fingers...... Ps 8:3
I hate the w of those...... Ps 101:3
the heavens are the w......Ps 102:25
Man goes out to his w..... Ps 104:23
w is honorable and..........Ps 111:3
man does deceptive w......Prov 11:18
then I saw all the w........ Eccl 8:17
for there is no w............Eccl 9:10
God will bring every w....Eccl 12:14
that He may do His w..... Is 28:21
and all we are the w........Is 64:8
him nothing for his w...... Jer 22:13
and mighty in w.............Jer 32:19
For I will w a w............ Hab 1:5
and said, 'Son, go, w.......Matt 21:28
could do no mighty w...... Mark 6:5
we do, that we may w.....John 6:28
This is the w of God...... John 6:29
"I must w the works.......John 9:4
w which You have given..John 17:4
know that all things w..... Rom 8:28
He will finish the w........ Rom 9:28
w is no longer w............Rom 11:6
Do not destroy the w...... Rom 14:20
w will become manifest....1 Co 3:13
Are you not my w.......... 1 Co 9:1
abounding in the w......... 1 Co 15:58
without ceasing your w.... 1 Th 1:3
every good word and w....2 Th 2:17
If anyone will not..........2 Th 3:10
but a doer of the w.........Jas 1:25

WORKED
with one hand they w...... Neh 4:17
and wonders God had w.. Acts 15:12
which He w in Christ.......Eph 1:20

WORKER
w is worthy of his........... Matt 10:10
Timothy, my fellow w......Rom 16:21
w who does not need.......2 Ti 2:15

WORKERS
You hate all w of............Ps 5:5
we are God's fellow w...... 1 Co 3:9
dogs, beware of evil w.....Phil 3:2

WORKING
everywhere, the Lord w... Mark 16:20
My Father has been w...... John 5:17
according to the w.......... Eph 1:19
through faith in the w......Col 2:12
manner, not w at all........2 Th 3:11

WORKMANSHIP
For we are His w.............Eph 2:10

WORKS
the wondrous w of God... Job 37:14
are Your wonderful w...... Ps 40:5
Come and see the w........Ps 66:5
how great are Your w...... Ps 92:5
manifold are Your w....... Ps 104:24
The w of the LORD are...Ps 111:2
w shall praise You.......... Ps 145:10
and let her own w..........Prov 31:31

WORLD

For I know their w..........Is 66:18
of whose w are truth.......Dan 4:37
show Him greater w........John 5:20
w that I do in My...........John 10:25
w that I do he will do..... John 14:12
w righteousness...............Acts 10:35
might stand, not of w......Rom 9:11
let us cast off the w.......Rom 13:12
is the same God who w... 1 Co 12:6
not justified by the w...... Gal 2:16
Now the w of the flesh.... Gal 5:19
the spirit who now w........Eph 2:2
not of w, lest anyone......Eph 2:9
with the unfruitful w........Eph 5:11
for it is God who w........Phil 2:13
w they deny Him...........Tit 1:16
zealous for good w..........Tit 2:14
repentance from dead w...Heb 6:1
but does not have w.......Jas 2:14
also justified by w..........Jas 2:25
He might destroy the w... 1 Jn 3:8
"I know your w...............Rev 2:2
their w follow them........Rev 14:13
according to their w........ Rev 20:12

WORLD

He shall judge the w.......Ps 9:8
For the w is Mine...........Ps 50:12
w is established................Ps 93:1
"The field is the w.........Matt 13:38
w are more shrewd.........Luke 16:8
He was in the w...........John 1:10
For God so loved the w...John 3:16
His Son into the w.........John 3:17
the Savior of the w........John 4:42
w cannot hate you...........John 7:7
You are of this w...........John 8:23
Look, the w has gone......John 12:19
w will see Me no more.... John 14:19
"If the w hates you.......John 15:18
If you were of the w...... John 15:19
I have overcome the w.... John 16:33
do not pray for the w..... John 17:9
w has not known You.....John 17:25
w may become guilty....... Rom 3:19
be conformed to this w.... Rom 12:2
things of the w............... 1 Co 1:27
w is foolishness.............. 1 Co 3:19
w has been crucified.... Gal 6:14
without God in the w..... Eph 2:12
loved this present w........ 2 Ti 4:10
He has not put the w..... Heb 2:5
unspotted from the w..... Jas 1:27
w is enmity with God...... Jas 4:4
Do not love the w...........1 Jn 2:15
all that is in the w...........1 Jn 2:16
w is passing away............1 Jn 2:17
w does not know us........ 1 Jn 3:1
They are of the w........... 1 Jn 4:5
so are we in this w..........1 Jn 4:17
And all the w marveled... Rev 13:3

WORLDS

also He made the w........ Heb 1:2

WORM

w should feed sweetly......Job 24:20
But I am a w.................. Ps 22:6
"Fear not, you w...........Is 41:14
their w does not die........ Is 66:24
w does not die and the... Mark 9:44

WORMS

flesh is caked with w.......Job 7:5
you, and w cover you...... Is 14:11
And he was eaten by w... Acts 12:23

WORMWOOD

end she is bitter as w.......Prov 5:4
who turn justice to w.......Amos 5:7
of the star is W............. Rev 8:11

WORRY

to you, do not w.............Matt 6:25
Therefore do not w......... Matt 6:31

WORRYING

w can add one................Matt 6:27

WORSHIP

I will go yonder and w.....Gen 22:5
He is your Lord, w.......... Ps 45:11
Oh come, let us w......... Ps 95:6
and have come to w Him. Matt 2:2
will fall down and w........ Matt 4:9
And in vain they w......... Matt 15:9
w what you do not know..John 4:22
true worshipers will w.......John 4:23
the One whom you w...... Acts 17:23
w the God of my............ Acts 24:14
false humility and w......... Col 2:18
the angels of God w......... Heb 1:6
make them come and w... Rev 3:9
w Him who lives.............Rev 4:10
w Him who made.......... Rev 14:7

WORSHIPED

"Our fathers w...............John 4:20
w Him who lives.............Rev 5:14
on their faces and w........Rev 11:16
w God who sat on the..... Rev 19:4

WORSHIPER

if anyone is a w..............John 9:31

WORTHLESS

looking at w things..........Ps 119:37
A w person...................Prov 6:12
Indeed they are all w.......Is 41:29

WORTHLESSNESS

long will you love w........ Ps 4:2

WORTHY

"I am not w of the.........Gen 32:10
sandals I am not w.........Matt 3:11
inquire who in it is w...... Matt 10:11
invited were not w.......... Matt 22:8
should do this was w....... Luke 7:4
and I am no longer w......Luke 15:19
present time are not w.....Rom 8:18
apostles, who am not w... 1 Co 15:9
to have a walk w............ Eph 4:1
"The laborer is w...........1 Ti 5:18
the world was not w........Heb 11:38
white, for they are w.......Rev 3:4
"You are w...................Rev 4:11
W is the Lamb who........Rev 5:12

WOUND

I w and I heal...............Deut 32:39
My w is incurable........... Job 34:6
But God will w the.........Ps 68:21
and my w incurable.........Jer 15:18
and w their weak............ 1 Co 8:12
and his deadly w............Rev 13:3

WOUNDED

And my heart is w..........Ps 109:22
and w the serpent..........Is 51:9
But He was w for our...... Is 53:5
there remained only w..... Jer 37:10
with which I was w......... Zech 13:6
to the beast who was w....Rev 13:14

WOUNDING

killed a man for w.......... Gen 4:23

WOUNDS

And binds up their w...... Ps 147:3
Faithful are the w.......... Prov 27:6
and bandaged his w........Luke 10:34

WRANGLINGS

useless w of men of.........1 Ti 6:5

WRATH

w has gone out from....... Num 16:46
provoked the LORD to w.Deut 9:22
Had I not feared the w....Deut 32:27
w kills a foolish.............. Job 5:2
speak to them in His w....Ps 2:5
living and burning w........ Ps 58:9
Surely the w of man....... Ps 76:10
Your fierce w has gone.... Ps 88:16
Will Your w burn like..... Ps 89:46
w we are terrified........... Ps 90:7
So I swore in My w......... Ps 95:11
in the day of His w.........Ps 110:5
death is the king's w.......Prov 16:14
The king's w is like........ Prov 19:12
of great w will suffer...... Prov 19:19
w is heavier than........... Prov 27:3
W is cruel and anger a....Prov 27:4
w I will give him............Is 10:6
With a little w...............Is 54:8
in My w I struck you.......Is 60:10
I will pour out my w....... Hos 5:10
w remember mercy.........Hab 3:2
you to flee from the w.....Matt 3:7
see life, but the w..........John 3:36
For the w of God is........ Rom 1:18
up for yourself w........... Rom 2:5
the law brings about w.....Rom 4:15
wanting to show His w.....Rom 9:22
rather give place to w......Rom 12:19
not only because of w......Rom 13:5
outbursts of w................ 2 Co 12:20
nature children of w........ Eph 2:3
sun go down on your w.....Eph 4:26
Let all bitterness, and w...Eph 4:31
delivers us from the w..... 1 Th 1:10
w has come upon them.... 1 Th 2:16
holy hands, without w......1 Ti 2:8
So I swore in My w.........Heb 3:11
not fearing the w........... Heb 11:27
for the w of man does..... Jas 1:20
throne and from the w.....Rev 6:16
to you, having great w.....Rev 12:12
of the wine of the w.......Rev 14:8
winepress of the w..........Rev 14:19
for in them the w........... Rev 15:1
fierceness of His w..........Rev 16:19

WRATHFUL

w man stirs up strife........Prov 15:18

WRESTLE

For we do not w.............Eph 6:12

WRETCHED

w man that I am.............Rom 7:24
know that you are w........ Rev 3:17

WRETCHEDNESS

do not let me see my w... Num 11:15

WRINKLE

not having spot or w.......Eph 5:27

WRITE

"*W* these words.............. Ex 34:27
w bitter things................ Job 13:26
w them on the tablet....... Prov 7:3
W this man down as........ Jer 22:30
w them on their hearts.... Heb 8:10
their minds I will *w*........ Heb 10:16
I had many things to *w*....3 Jn 13

WRITING

the *w* was the *w*............. Ex 32:16

WRITINGS

do not believe his *w*........ John 5:47

WRITTEN

tablets of stone, *w*...........Ex 31:18
Have I not *w* to you........Prov 22:20
your names are *w*........ Luke 10:20
"What I have *w*.............. John 19:22
ministered by us, *w*......... 2 Co 3:3
the stone a new name *w*.. Rev 2:17
the plagues that are *w*..... Rev 22:18

WRONG

sinned, we have done *w*...2 Ch 6:37
I cry out concerning *w*.....Job 19:7
not charge them with *w*... Job 24:12
no one to do them *w*.......Ps 105:14
Do no *w* and do no........Jer 22:3
I am doing you no *w*.......Matt 20:13
Man has done nothing *w*..Luke 23:41
of them suffer *w*............. Acts 7:24
Jews I have done no *w*.... Acts 25:10
Forgive me this *w*........... 2 Co 12:13
But he who does *w*......... Col 3:25

WRONGED

then that God has *w*.......Job 19:6
We have *w* no one.......... 2 Co 7:2
But if he has *w*.............. Phm 18

WRONGS

me *w* his own soul.......... Prov 8:36

WROTE

of the hand that *w*......... Dan 5:5
stooped down and *w*.......John 8:6

WROUGHT

And skillfully *w*.............. Ps 139:15

— Y —

YEAR

first month of the *y*........ Ex 12:2
'In the *Y* of Jubilee......... Lev 27:24
the acceptable *y*.............. Is 61:2
be his until the *y*........... Ezek 46:17
to Jerusalem every *y*....... Luke 2:41
went alone once a *y*........ Heb 9:7
of sins every *y*................ Heb 10:3

YEARS

and for days and *y*......... Gen 1:14
Are Your *y* like the........ Job 10:5
y should teach................ Job 32:7
I will remember the *y*...... Ps 77:10
For a thousand *y*........... Ps 90:4
lives are seventy *y*.......... Ps 90:10
Your *y* are throughout..... Ps 102:24
y will have no end.......... Ps 102:27
when He was twelve *y*.... Luke 2:42
are not yet fifty *y*........... John 8:57
y will not fail................. Heb 1:12
for a thousand *y*............. Rev 20:2
with Him a thousand *y*.... Rev 20:6

YES

"But let your '*Y*............. Matt 5:37
No, but in Him was *Y*..... 2 Co 1:19

YESTERDAY

for we are but of *y*.........Job 8:9

YOKE

you shall break his *y*....... Gen 27:40
and He will put a *y*........ Deut 28:48
Your father made our *y*... 1 Ki 12:4
You have broken the *y*.... Is 9:4
a man to bear the *y*....... Lam 3:27
"Take My *y* upon you..... Matt 11:29
y count their own............ 1 Ti 6:1

YOKED

Do not be unequally *y*.....2 Co 6:14

YOUNG

His flesh shall be *y*.........Job 33:25
I have been *y*................. Ps 37:25
she may lay her *y*........... Ps 84:3
y ones shall lie............... Is 11:7
dream dreams, your *y*......Joel 2:28
y man followed Him........ Mark 14:51
they admonish the *y*........ Tit 2:4
I write to you, *y*............. 1 Jn 2:13

YOUNGER

they mock at me, men *y*.. Job 30:1
y son gathered all........... Luke 15:13
let him be as the *y*.......... Luke 22:26
the *y* as sisters................ 1 Ti 5:2
Likewise you *y* people..... 1 Pe 5:5

YOURS

all that I have are *y*........ 1 Ki 20:4
the battle is not *y*........... 2 Ch 20:15
I am *Y*........................... Ps 119:94
Y is the kingdom............ Matt 6:13
'Take what is *y*............... Matt 20:14
y is the kingdom............. Luke 6:20
And all Mine are *Y*......... John 17:10
For all things are *y*......... 1 Co 3:21
for I do not seek *y*.......... 2 Co 12:14

YOUTH

for he was but a *y*.......... 1 Sa 17:42
the LORD from my *y*...... 1 Ki 18:12
the sins of my *y*.............. Ps 25:7
the companion of her *y*....Prov 2:17
in the days of your *y*....... Eccl 11:9
and *y* are vanity.............. Eccl 11:10
the shame of your *y*........ Is 54:4
speak, for I am a *y*......... Jer 1:6
the kindness of your *y*..... Jer 2:2
I have kept from my *y*.....Matt 19:20
the flower of her *y*.......... 1 Co 7:36
no one despise your *y*...... 1 Ti 4:12

YOUTHFUL

Flee also *y* lusts.............. 2 Ti 2:22

YOUTHS

perceived among the *y*..... Prov 7:7
y shall faint and be......... Is 40:30

— Z —

ZEAL

The *z* of the LORD of..... 2 Ki 19:31
z has consumed me......... Ps 119:139
He shall stir up His *z*...... Is 42:13
have spoken it in My *z*.... Ezek 5:13
for Zion with great *z*....... Zech 8:2
"*Z* for Your house has.... John 2:17
that they have a *z*.......... Rom 10:2
z has stirred up the......... 2 Co 9:2

ZEALOUS

"I have been very *z*........ 1 Ki 19:10
'I am *z* for Zion with...... Zech 8:2
since you are *z*............... 1 Co 14:12
But it is good to be *z*...... Gal 4:18
z for good works........... Tit 2:14

Index to Maps

The following index is divided into two parts, one for Map 5, Jerusalem, and the other for all the other maps. Place names are given as shown on the maps. Where a place name refers to a large area, the index gives the location of the name. Where a name refers to a river, the index gives the source and mouth of the river.

In the index to Maps 1 through 4 and 6 through 9, major political divisions, such as countries and regions, are shown in capital letters (examples: EGYPT, PALESTINE). Cities are shown in upper and lower case as usual (example: Hebron). Geographical features are shown in italics (example: *Jordan River*).

INDEX TO MAPS

Map 1. The Nations of Genesis 10
Map 2. The Exodus of Israel
Map 3. The Conquest of Canaan
Map 4. The Kingdom Years
Map 6. Palestine in Christ's Time

Map 7. Paul's First and Second
    Journeys
Map 8. Paul's Third and Fourth
    Journeys
Map 9. The Holy Land in Modern Times

INDEX TO MAPS

Map 5. Jerusalem—From David to Christ

Map 1

THE NATIONS
OF GENESIS 10

JAVAN	Descendants of Japheth (Gen. 10:2–5)
PUT	Descendants of Ham (Gen. 10:6–20)
LUD	Descendants of Shem (Gen. 10:21–31)
(Lydia)	Later Biblical name

© Thomas Nelson, Inc., 1983

THE EXODUS OF ISRAEL

Map 2

The Great Sea

Gaza

Hebron

Beersheba

Arad

Wilderness of Zin

Salt Sea

MT. NEBO

Moab

Ammon

River Arnon

Brook Zered

Zoar

Punon

Edom

Ezion Geber

Arabah

Gulf of Aqaba

Kadesh Barnea

Wilderness of Paran

Way of the Philistines

Way of Shur

Route from Egypt to Arabia

Baal Zephon

Marah?

Elim?

Red Sea

MT. SINAI HOREB

Avaris

Qantir

Pithom

Succoth

Land of Goshen

Memphis

Nile

Route of the Exodus

Alternate routes of Red Sea crossing

Unsuccessful invasion of Canaan (Num. 14:39-45)

Trade routes

? Exact location questionable

Scale of Miles

0   50   100

Map 3
THE CONQUEST OF CANAAN

△ Philistine cities

▢ Cities of refuge

(1,742) Elevation, in feet

? Exact location questionable

Scale of Miles
0   10   20

The Great Sea

Galilee

Bashan

Gilead

Ammon

Philistia

Moab

MT. LEBANON (11,000)

MT. HERMON (9,200)

Sidon

Damascus

Tyre

Dan

Kedesh ▢

Hazor

Acco

Golan? ▢   Ashtaroth

Sea of Chinnereth

MT. CARMEL (1,742)

R. Kishon

Jokneam

+ MT. TABOR (1,843)
En Dor
HILL OF MOREH
Shunem

Edrei

Megiddo

R. Yarmuk

Dor

Ramoth ▢

Well of Harod
Ibleam

R. Jezreel

MT. GILBOA (1,696)

Beth Shean

Tirzah

Zaphon

R. Jabbok

MT. EBAL (3,080)
+ Shechem
MT. GERIZIM + (2,890)

Succoth

Aphek

Tappuah

Shiloh

Joppa

River Jordan

Rabbah

Jabneel

Bethel   Ai
Gezer   Gibeon
Ekron △   Kirjath
Timnah   Jearim   Gibeah
Jerusalem

Gilgal

Jericho

Ajalon

Makkedah
Ashdod △
Gath △   Jarmuth
Azekah
Beth Shemesh

Bethlehem

Heshbon   ▢ Bezer?
+ MT. NEBO (2,700)
Medeba

Adullam

Ashkelon △   Mareshah

Lachish

Hebron ▢

Gaza

Debir

En Gedi

The Salt Sea
(−1,300)

Dibon
Aroer
R. Arnon

Beersheba

4. In a northern thrust, Joshua moved from Gilgal all the way to Hazor (Josh. 11).

2. Joshua made peace with Gibeon, then moved through the Valley of Aijalon and defeated the five Amorite kings (Josh. 9–10).

1. Upon crossing the Jordan, Joshua camped awhile at Gilgal, then moved to take Jericho and Ai. Afterward he returned to Gilgal (Josh. 1–8).

3. From Makkedah, Joshua launched a southern campaign against Lachish, Hebron, Debir, and Gaza. Victorious, he returned to Gilgal (Josh. 10).

Map 4
THE KINGDOM YEARS

Probable extent of Israelite control during the Kingdom of Solomon, c. 950 B.C.

The Kingdoms of Israel and Judah, c. 860 B.C.

Boundary between Israel and Judah

? Exact location questionable

0   25   50
Scale of Miles

Riblah

Zobah

Byblos

Phoenicia MT. LEBANON MT. HERMON

Sidon
Zarephath
Damascus

Tyre
Dan
Kedesh
Syria

Hazor

The Great Sea

Acco
MT. CARMEL
Sea of Chinnereth
R. Yarmuk
Ashtaroth
Golan?

Dor
Jokneam
Megiddo
Ramoth Gilead
Taanach
Jezreel
MT. GILBOA
Dothan
Jabesh Gilead
Jordan R.
Tirzah
Zaphon
Samaria
Succoth
Shechem
R. Jabbok
Ammon
Aphek
Shiloh
Joppa
ISRAEL
Rabbah

Mizpah
Bethel
Jabneh
Gezer
Ramah
Heshbon
Philistia
Jerusalem
Beth Shemesh
Bethlehem
Medeba
Ashkelon
Tekoa
Eglon?
Adullam
Dibon
Gaza
Hebron
The Salt Sea
Aroer
R. Arnon
Ziklag?
Debir
Moab
Arad
Beersheba
Kir Hareseth

Zoar
R. Zered

JUDAH
Bozrah

River of Egypt
Kadesh Barnea
Edom

Teman

Note: Other place names significant during the time of the Kingdoms are found on Map 3.

Ezion Geber
Elath

© Thomas Nelson, Inc., 19

Map 5
JERUSALEM—
FROM DAVID TO CHRIST

Bethesda   Place names of Christ's time

Ophel   Suggested locations of place names
          from earlier kingdom period

?   Exact location questionable

Suggested extent of the City of David

Suggested extent of Solomon's expansion

Suggested extent of Hezekiah's expansion

Probable extent of Nehemiah's reconstruction

Possible location of walls during Christ's time

0   250   500 Yards
        Scale

Calvary?

Bethesda

Sheep Gate

Gate of Benjamin

Temple

Horse Gate

Gethsemane?

KIDRON VALLEY

Praetorium

Gate of Ephraim

Royal Palace

Ophel

Spring of Gihon

Hezekiah's Tunnel

City of David

Fountain Gate

Christ's Tomb?

Calvary?

Mishneh

Herod's Palace

Caiaphas' House?

Caiaphas' House?

Pool of Siloam

Dung Gate

Essene Gate

VALLEY OF HINNOM

© Thomas Nelson, Inc. 1983

Map 6
PALESTINE
IN
CHRIST'S TIME

(1,742)   Elevation, in feet

?   Exact location
    questionable

0   10   20
   Scale of Miles

34°30'   A   35°   B   Sidon   C   36°   D
                                                                  Damas

• Zarephath

MT. LEBANON
(11,000)

MT. HERMON
(9,200)

Iturea

• Tyre

Phoenicia

• Panias
(Caesarea Philippi)

33°   33°30

Trachonitis

Galilee

1

• Ptolemais

Chorazin •
Capernaum •   • Bethsaida?
Magdala •   • Gergesa
Cana •   Tiberias •

Sea
of
Galilee

MT. CARMEL
(1,742)

R. Kishon

R. Yarmuk

2   2

Nazareth •   + MT. TABOR (1,843)
Nain •   • Gerasa
Esdraelon •

32°30'   32°30

• Caesarea

MT. GILBOA
(1,696)

Scythopolis •

The Great
Sea

Samaria

Decapolis

Samaria •

Sychar •

MT. GERIZIM +
(2,890)

• Gadara?

R. Jabbok

3   3

Antipatris •

Joppa •

River Jordan

Perea

Arimathea •

Ephraim •

• Gadara?

Lydda •

Philadelphia •

32°   32

Emmaus •
Kirjath Jearim •
Beth Haccerem •

Jericho •
Jerusalem •   • Bethabara
Bethany •
Qumran •

• Azotus

Bethlehem •

4   4

• Ashkelon

Herodium •

• Medeba

Judea

Machaerus •

• Gaza

• Hebron

The Salt
Sea
(−1,300)

R. Arnon

31°   31°30

Idumea

Masada •

5   5

34°30'   Beersheba •   35°   B   35°30'   C   36°

© Thomas Nelson, Inc., 1

Map 7

PAUL'S FIRST AND SECOND JOURNEYS
(Acts 13—14; 15:39—18:22)

First missionary journey, with Barnabas and Mark (c. A.D. 46–48)

Second missionary journey, with Silas (c. A.D. 49–52)

© Thomas Nelson, Inc., 1983

Map 8

PAUL'S THIRD AND FOURTH JOURNEYS
(Acts 18:23—21:16; 27—28:16)

Third missionary journey (c. A.D. 53–57)

Fourth missionary journey (c. A.D. 59–62)

© Thomas Nelson, Inc., 1983

Map 9

THE HOLY LAND
IN MODERN TIMES

Area occupied by Israel
since June, 1967

0   25   50
Scale of Miles

Tripoli

LEBANON

Beirut

LEBANON MTS.

BEKAA VALLEY

ANTI-LEBANON MTS.

Sidon

Damascus

Tyre

Dan

U.N. Buffer Zone

1973 Line

SYRIA

Qiryat
Shemona

Quneitra
1967 Cease-Fire Line

Nahariyya

Safad

*Golan
Heights*

Akko

*Sea of
Galilee*

Haifa

Tiberias

Mediterranean Sea

Nazareth

Dera

Afula

Ramtha

Beth Shean

Hadera

Netanya

Jarash

Tulkarm

Nablus

Herzliyya

*West
Bank*

Tel Aviv

Petah

Yafo

Tiqwa

Jordan River

Rishon le Zion

Lod

Ramla

Ramalah

Amman

Ashdod

Jericho

Jerusalem

Ashqelon

Bethlehem

Madaba

Hebron

*Dead
Sea*

Dhiban

Gaza

Qiryat
Gat

En Gedi

Beersheba

Al-Arish

Karak

JORDAN

ISRAEL

EGYPT

Negev

Arabah

Sinai

Elat

Aqaba